30.00
D0437778

Hymns and Tunes — an Index

by

Katharine Smith Diehl

The Scarecrow Press, Inc.
New York and London 1966

UNIVERSITY OF VICTORIA
LIBRARY
Victoria, B. C.

Ref
BV305
D5

Copyright 1966 by

Katharine Smith Diehl

L. C. Card Number 66-13743

To

William and Annetta Kraushaar

HYMNALS ANALYZED

ARRANGED ACCORDING TO SYMBOLIC CITATION CODE

CODE

A The Hymnal 1940 (Episcopal)
B The Hymnal 1916 (Episcopal)
C The Hymnal 1916, with variant tunes, c1936 (Episcopal)
D The Church hymnal 1892 (Episcopal)
E The English hymnal (Anglican)
F Hymns ancient and modern (Anglican)
G The Methodist hymnal 1935
H The Methodist Protestant hymnal 1921
I The Methodist hymnal 1925, c1905
J Service book and Hymnal of the Lutheran Church in America
K Common service book (Lutheran)
L Book of worship (Evangelical Lutheran)
M American Lutheran hymnal
N The Hymnal and Order of service (Augustana Lutheran)
O The Lutheran hymnary (Evangelical Lutheran)
P The Concordia hymnal (Lutheran)
Q The Lutheran hymnal (Missouri Synod)
R The Hymnbook 1955 (Presbyterian)
S The Hymnal 1933 (Presbyterian U.S.A.)
T The Psalter hymnal 1927 (United Presbyterian)
U The Presbyterian hymnal 1927 (Presbyterian U.S.)
V The New Psalms and hymns 1901 (Presbyterian U.S.)
W The Church hymnary (Church of Scotland)
X Songs of praise (Anglican)
Y The American student hymnal (unaffiliated)
Z Christian worship (Baptists and Disciples)
AA Evangelical Lutheran hymnbook (Missouri Synod)
AB The Student hymnary (unaffiliated)
AC The New Hymnal for American youth (unaffiliated)
AD The New Church hymnal (unaffiliated)
AE The Hymnal (Evangelical United Brethren)
AF Pilgrim hymnal (Congregational)
AG Hymnal for Christian worship (Presbyterian U.S.)
AH The Hymnal, Army and Navy
AI The New Christian hymnal ("orthodox, evangelical faith")
AJ The Psalter (Reformed)
AK The Hymnal (Evangelical Reformed)
AL The Hymnary (United Church of Canada)
AM Trinity hymnal (Orthodox Presbyterian)
AN Hymns of the Spirit (Universalist Unitarian)
AO The Book of worship (Re-

formed)

AP The Book of praise (Presbyterian Church of Canada)

AQ Hymns for the celebration of life (Universalist Unitarian)

AR The Brethren hymnal (Church of the Brethren)

AS Hymnal 1925 (Church of the Brethren)

AT Baptist hymnal 1956 (Southern Baptist)

AU The Broadman hymnal (Baptist)

AV New Baptist hymnal c1926, 1958 printing (American Baptist)

AW The Mennonite hymnary (Mennonite General Conference)

AX Christian hymnal (Mennonite General Conference)

AY Church and Sunday School hymnal (Eastern Mennonite)

AZ The Liturgy and Offices of worship (Moravian)

BA Hymnal and Liturgies (Moravian)

BB The Church hymnal (Seventy-Day Advent)

BC Hymns (Mormon)

BD The Beacon hymnal (Universalist Unitarian)

BE Christian Science hymnal

BF Christian worship (Reformed Church in America)

BG Oxford book of carols (Anglican)

BH Union hymnal (Jewish)

BI Liturgy and hymnal (Swedenborgian: General Church)

BJ Hymns: The Yattendon hymnal (Anglican)

BK A Hymnal for Friends (Quaker)

BL Hymnal of Christian unity (Catholic-Protestant)

BM Our parish prays and sings (Catholic, especially schools)

BN The New Saint Basil hymnal

BO St. Basil's hymnal 1935 (Catholic)

BP The Monastery hymnal (Catholic)

BQ The St. Gregory hymnal (Catholic)

BR The Magnificat (New-Church)

BS Twenty four Psalms (Catholic)

BT The Handbook to the Lutheran Hymnal (Missouri Synod)

BU Ausbund (Amish Mennonite, full German text)

BV Anglican hymn book

BW Handbook to the Mennonite hymnary (Mennonite General Conference)

BX The New hymn and tune book 1914 Unitarian

BY The Baptist hymn book 1962 (British Baptist)

BZ Final report, Methodist hymnal 1966

The hymnals, arranged by date and with fuller citation, will be found in Appendix I.

QUESTIONS AND ANSWERS; or, HOW TO USE THE INDEXES

Indexes I and II

The first and second indexes are concerned with the hymns, the refrains, the variant first lines of both hymns and refrains; the authors; and the hymnals within which these hymns by these authors may be found quickly.

Here are four related quotations from Index I: First lines and variants, with citations:

O Christian, haste, thy mission high fulfilling (Thomson) AB367 X O Sion, haste 106630

O Sion, haste, thy mission high fulfilling (Thomson) A261; B474; D249; G475; [etc]; AB367 107557

O Zion, haste, thy mission (Thomson) G475 X O Sion, haste, thy mission 107387

Publish glad tidings (Thomson) R O Sion, haste, thy mission high fulfilling 108398

And here is the relevant quotation from Index II: Authors and first first lines:

Thomson, Mary Ann, 1834-1923 O Sion, haste, thy mission; X106630 O Christian, haste; X107887 O Zion, haste; R108398 Publish glad tidings

- - - - - - - -

Question: Where can I find the hymn beginning "O Zion, haste"?

Answer: Find the words alphabetically in Index I. The hymn is reported to be in Book G, as #475; the author is Thomson. Because G is the only book named, this is the first time the phrase (as you quote it) is found. You are told that other hymnals quote it differently. G475 is also mentioned at the standard entry which follows the X. (Refer to serial number for the information). Notice that all except one of the serial numbers are repeated in each index.

Question: Who wrote the hymn "O Sion, haste", and does it

begin that way?

Answer: Find the phrase alphabetically, as above. The author is Thomson. Scan the Thomsons in Index II until you find that one credited with the first line fragment. The information you wish follows the author's name and dates.

Question: Mary Ann Thomson wrote something that has "Sion" in the first line. Can you find the poem for me?

Answer: Scan the entry "Thomson, Mary Ann", at Index II. If the word appears, refer to one of the hymnals noticed. If the word had not appeared, reference to either Julian or to the Judson Concordance may be helpful. Concordances to secular poetry are useful in identifying poetry by well-known writers who usually have some religious writings to their credit.

Indexes III, IV, and V

The third, fourth, and fifth indexes are concerned with the melodies, the refrains, their variant opening melodies and refrains; the names of those melodies (these names are here called tune names); the composers; and the hymnals within which these tunes by these composers may be found quickly.

Here are six related quotations from Index III: Tune names and variants, with citations:

Carol melody, 14th c (Hohenfurth ms. 1410) X Quem pastores 1546

Dearmer (Hohenfurth ms.) X Quem pastores 2427

Quem pastores (Hohenfurth ms.) [DMSMFSLSR, MFSFM] A35; B506; C506; E543; F456; N195; O500; Q90; W349; [etc] 8754

-----. V [DMSMFSLSR, MSFMR] Q90 8754a

Quem pastores laudavere (Hohenfurth ms. 1410) X Quem pastores 8755

Shepherds left their flocks astraying (Hohenfurth ms. 1410) X Quem pastores 9966

And this is the relevant quotation from Index IV: Composers and tune names:

Hohenfurth ms. 1410 Quem pastores; X1546 Carol melody, 14c; X2427 Dearmer; X8755 Quem pastores laudavere; X9966 Shepherds left their flocks astraying

Finally this, from Index V: Melodies, a systematic index:

DMSMFSLSR, MFSFM	8754
DMSMFSLSR, MSFMR	8754a

- - - - - -

Question: In what hymnal is the melody, "Quem pastores", printed?

Answer: Find the tune name, "Quem pastores", in Index III. The information identifies seventeen hymnals, with the number of the melody in each; as, A35 means Book A, #35.

Question: "Quem pastores" is sometimes called "Quem pastores laudavere". Are there other names?

Answer: From Index III, the source of the melody is Hohenfurth ms., 1410. Look alphabetically in Index IV for this source name, and then again alphabetically for "Quem pastores". The several names are given, but not the books making use of these names.

Question: Does "Quem pastores" have a refrain?

Answer: Refer to the answer just above. There are several X serial numbers; but no R serial number. This indicates that no refrain is associated.

Question: Does "Quem pastores" always have the same notation?

Answer: The information in Index III includes one ditto entry, and the symbol V followed by a melody. Examine the melody at #8754 and at #8754a. There is a slight difference. This variant reading may be examined in Q90.

Question: How do I use Index V?

Answer: A long answer is required for this.

Index V: Melodies, a systematic index is arranged alphabetically by a special symbolic alphabet, that of the syllables of the diatonic scale which reads: Do, Re, Mi, Fa, Sol, La, Ti, Do, Re, etc. In this book the syllables are recorded as D R M F S L T D R, etc. No adjustment is made for low and high positions.

This diatonic scale has seven primary syllabic names and tones, but it has additional intermediate values which are produced by lowering or raising the basic tones by a musical half step. Lowering is indicated by use of the symbol ♭ (flat), and raising is indicated by use of the symbol # (sharp). Both lowered and raised notational values occur in hymn tunes. However Hymns and tunes: an index NEVER USES FLATS. Instead, a conversion table has been followed in translating the printed notes to the related raised, or sharped, rendering. It reads:

♭D	becomes	T	♭S	becomes	F#
♭R	"	D#	♭L	"	S#
♭M	"	R#	♭T	"	L#
♭F	"	M	♭D	"	T etc

When using Index V, the tonal value of D is low; and that of T is high. Low values precede high values; and a low tone repeated precedes any mention of the next higher tone. All tones with sharps (#) follow the simple tone, and precede any mention of the tone next above. Within Index V the readings range from DDDDDDD DDDTRD, LLL to TTTDTLTDR, DRMLTDR. If this were converted to numerals (values One to Seven) it would be the range from 1, 111, 111, 111, 721, 666 to 7, 771, 767, 121, 236, 712. No attempt or intention is made to perform the conversions. For non-musicians the example is more clear than the unfamiliar symbolic language of DoReMi.

Question: What melody is this: MFSMRDLS, DRMD, FSL when written in syllables?

Answer: Index V begins with the D entries; continues with R; then to the MD sections. Move ahead to MR ... to MM ... on to MF ... to MFM ... to MFS. Repeat this procedure until you find the proper sequence. It will be serially numbered 12058.

Refer to Index III; serial number 12058 should be identified by the tune name "Westridge" by Shaw; and the identical syllabic reading should be repeated as from the question above and from Index V. Four books contain this tune. Further information may be secured by reference to "Shaw" in Index IV.

The question just above may require more complicated identification if neither the inquirer nor the respondent can translate the musical sounds into syllables of the diatonic scale. The simplest recourse is to go to a piano with an illustration such as the one in Appendix E. Pick out the tune by using (if possible) no black keys whatsoever. If you know the names of the piano keys, there will be little trouble reporting the melody in names of the keys struck. The schedule for conversion of notes on the piano to the symbolic musical language will help you create the tune in the form reported by Index V. After the conversion, proceed as indicated just above. Trace the serial number in Index III; find a hymnal in which it is contained; have someone play it for you. Good luck!

Back to the "Quem pastores" illustration, for more questions:

Question: A melody is going around in my head. In syllables it is Do Mi Sol Mi Fa Sol La Sol Re, Mi Fa Sol Fa Mi. Can I find it in print through these indexes?

Answer: Proceed by first changing the full syllable names to initials. Continue by tracing from DDD ... to DRD ... to DMD ... Thence to DMSM ... Serial number 8754 should be indicated.

Return to Index III, to #8754. You are back at "Quem pastores". But this time the search began with melody only, and led to the discovery of books in which the melody was printed, to the source of the tune, to its tune names as here standardized, and to the cluster of variants associated with it.

Question: In this new hymnal, tune names are not used. Help me find information. The tune is in the key with neither sharps nor flats.

Answer: Refer to the illustration in Appendix D for basic tone names in all keys. Record the melody by using the syllable names reduced to the single initial letter. (That is, Do becomes D, Re becomes R, etc.)

Assume the record reads: DMSSSLSFMRDD, DMS; and the supposed source is "1st publ. Paris Processional, 1697".

The first approach will be to verify existence of this source in Index IV. There is no mention, so another method must be used.

Use Index V, and identify the tune through tracing the recorded syllables. You should reach #166. Turn, at Index III, to #166: "Adoro te devota", a Benedictine plainsong, Mode 5. Specific hymnals containing it are mentioned; and entries #167-168 give further information.

Question: Sometimes melodies are written in Key of F (one flat), and sometimes in Key of G (one sharp).. Does this make any difference in the syllables?

Answer: None. "Leoni", a Jewish traditional melody is found in many hymnals (as at AD70) written in Key of A Flat (four flats); but in others (as at AL25) written in Key of A (three sharps). This is a difference of a half tone throughout. Melodically there is no difference in the sequences. The tune is the same tune -- only the physical measurements of tonality vary. And singability! Church musicians are accepting the fact that congregations expect low-pitched songs in their church books.

In summary:

1. Citation symbols in Indexes I and III refer by letters to the hymnals, and by numbers to the specific items within these specific hymnals, to the place at which the words (or the melody, respectively) by any form of its words (or its melody, and under any tune name) are printed.

2a. Reference symbols include X, which in Index I refers from a non-standard first line and its single first identified citation to the standard form, and in Index III from a non-standard tune name without citation to the standard tune name;

2b. Reference symbols include R, which in Indexes I and III present the standard reading of the refrain of the hymn or of the melody without citations. These are the same as the citations to the standard first lines and melodies, and need not be repeated. Also;

2c. Reference symbols include V which, in Index III only, identifies a variant melody or a variant melodic refrain and cites its first appearance only. Reference to the standard readings is unnecessary because the tune name remains constant, and the variants file immediately below the standard forms.

3. Though but the first appearance of any hymn or melody in a hymnal is recorded, others within the book may be identified

by use of the hymnal's own indexes (in all but a very few instances. Cf. the Chart in Appendix G).

4. Indexes II and IV serve to gather all the primary sources (here defined as the author or composer originally responsible for the words or the music, respectively); and those intermediate sources responsible for renderings which vary considerably from the standard form and which frequently (but not always) appear under words, melody, or tune name differing from the standard form.

5. The symbols of reference -- R, V, and X -- are used correlatively within Indexes I-II and Indexes III-V. They cannot be used between these two sets of indexes.

6. Indexes I-IV are alphabeted by the roman alphabet, using all letters, in simple word-by-word order.

7. Indexes I and III use initial articles in all languages and observe these articles in alphabeting (contrary to usual library practice).

8. Indexes II and IV may use the initial articles, but they are totally disregarded (following the usual library practice).

9. Citations in Indexes I and III are to the "Hymnals analyzed".

10. References by R, V, and X in Indexes II and IV are to the relative serial numbers in Indexes I and III.

11a. Indexes I and II provide virtually identical information, but by inverted approaches. The serial numeration of Index I is used for reference purposes in Index II. Citations within specific hymnals are recorded only in Index I;

11b. Accompanying Index V (arranged by the symbolic alphabet of the syllables of the diatonic musical scale) are both Indexes III and IV, referring respectively to the tune names and to the composers. The melody is repeated in Indexes III and V. The source (composer) is repeated in Indexes III and IV, The citations are indicated but once, in Index III. The serial numbers are repeated in Indexes III and V; and are used for reference purposes only in Index IV.

12. In other words, everything within the entire sequence of five indexes can be approached in two ways except the item numbers within the individual hymnals. To have repeated these would have caused undue and unnecessary increase in the bulk of the book.

TABLE OF CONTENTS

Hymnals analyzed, arranged according to symbolic citation code — v

Questions and answers: or, How to use the indexes — vii

Hymns and tunes: an essay

- I Hymns and tunes — xvii
- II The hymnal: several of its characteristics — xxiii
- III The indexes — xxxvi
- IV Acknowledgements — liii

Part One: The hymns

- Index I First lines and variants, with citations — 1
- Index II Authors and first lines — 361

Part Two: The tunes

- Index III Tune names and variants, with citations — 551
- Index IV Composers and tune names — 909
- Index V Melodies, a systematic index — 1053

Appendixes

- A Glossary — 1149
- B Abbreviations — 1154
- C Arbitrary decisions adopted in this index — 1156
- D The scales — 1158
- E Piano keyboard — 1159
- F How this book was cumulated — 1160
- G General survey of hymnals as books of reference, with notes — 1168
- H Materials excluded from these indexes, but included in hymnals analyzed — 1174
- I Hymnals analyzed, arranged according to date of issue — 1177
- J Bibliography — 1185

I

HYMNS AND TUNES

Hymns and tunes: an index is a catalog to congregational song found in seventy-eight hymnals officially adopted for use at public worship during some part of this 20th century, chiefly in the English language, chiefly containing both words and music, and always representing United Kingdom and North American Jewish-Christian institutions.

Specifically it is an attempt to (1) identify hymns (the poems) published in these seventy-eight hymnals analyzed, to (2) associate each with its author (source), and with the variant readings or segments of the hymn, to (3) locate the printed texts within these books which were used during this 20th century through December 31, 1965. It further attempts to (4) identify melodies (the sung tune) used as hymn tunes published in these same seventy-eight hymnals analyzed (always exclusive of books symbolized by letters BT, BU, and BW which contain no music), to (5) associate each tune with its composer (source), and with the variant readings or segments of the tune, to (6) identify the names associated with these tunes, no matter the variety and number of such names, and to (7) locate the scores of these melodies within these books which were used during the 20th century through December 31, 1965.

Indirectly this catalog forms a literary first-line and author index to the poetry of these hymnals -- a segment of poetry whose analysis is incidental to secular first-line and author indexes; and a corresponding tune name, melodic, and composer index to the scores within the hymnals -- a segment of musicology whose published analysis is almost non-existent.

Further and indirectly, each of these five indexes may be helpful for identification of materials in books not here analyzed; it may clarify texts and tunes not yet properly associated; and provide a basis for further clarification of the sources here stated as standard but about which there remains irresolution.

There is no place within this introduction, and no place within the indexes, to pass judgment. Occasional comments are made after extremely close reading of these hymnals by a librarian who, for almost thirty years, has been closely associated with college and university students and who, for a bit more than one-third of that time, was organist in small parishes.

As a guide to bio-bibliography, by the simple inclusion of full personal names and dates of birth and death, dates of individual hymns and tunes (especially when source dates are not available), publication dates of anthologies from which hymns have been borrowed, this index provides a greater cumulation than any individual hymnal indexes can offer. It brings to the present time many facts cited in Julian's Dictionary of hymnology; and it blends the information presented by Baker's Biographical dictionary with that within the hymnals.

Confusion is recognized in some of the early books cited as sources. To untangle the gesang-buchs, the geistliche gesang-buchs, harps, and companions -- and then to do likewise with the publications issued by see and diocese, sometimes cited by diocesan name and other times by given form name as breviary, ritual, and sometimes by the compiler -- would have been an impossible task. The same may be said for traditional materials. Where does German traditional cease and Swiss tune begin; when does an English tune become a Devon melody; and when did a White spiritual cease being an English traditional and become an American folk hymn? It has seemed more important to do the preliminary sorting ên masse than to make tiny delineation for a tiny number of these items.

Information is more readily accessible on the literary portion of any hymnal than on its musical portion. Though they have not limited their functions to the hymns, apparently both the Hymn Society of America and the British Hymn Society are more involved in the literary studies, the hymnody, than in the music as they proceed in their Dictionary of American hymnology (under preparation) and revision of Julian's Dictionary of hymnology (under preparation).

Hopefully the search in each aspect of congregational song is now a little less tedious. It is certainly not ended.

Hymns and tunes: an index could be compiled and completed only because the hymnals analyzed were immediately in hand; and a few very hard-fact additional references close by.

All books indexed were secured rather easily except those cited as C, BI, and BJ. Book C was at the organ bench in little Saints Andrew and Stephen Mission Church (Episcopal), Douglas, Georgia, where the project was begun. On the day this editing was completed it was received as part of the collection! Book BI was on long loan from Perkins School of Theology Library, Southern Methodist University. Book BJ was also on long loan -- from the Chicago Theological Seminary Library, University of Chicago. Strangely, copies are in everybody's hands while the books are in official institutional adoption; and as suddenly they disappear from the face of the local earth. To "missions", summer camps, local less wealthy sister congregations, etc. -- but not to the book market, not to the specialized dealers, and rarely are they retained within the family more than a single generation!

Although this working collection is not available for public use, copies may be consulted in music libraries at colleges and universities which emphasize choral work, and at some of the larger theological seminaries where church music is a major study. Princeton Seminary's Benson Collection has many of these books; Yale, Chicago, Union (in New York), Catholic University of America, Washington Cathedral, and the Library of Congress may be mentioned. Smaller seminary libraries will offer some books, especially those related to the immediate denomination and its close associates. One library, Andover-Harvard, had received sometime in 1964 fifty boxes of hymnals from another of the Harvard libraries which (according to a letter under their date June 22, 1965) they doubt they can "get around to processing ... anytime soon."

Few public libraries will provide these books. Hymnals are considered -- at least by librarians -- to be too closely associated with religion to be included in the humane materials of society in community. Church and parish and temple libraries will have some books. Church organists, choir directors, ministers of music will have personal collections or will know of choir-owned copies in the neighborhood. Music librarians will be collectors, especially of the more highly liturgical and poetically sophisticated books. Denominational archives will have sample copies, occasional second and third copies for consultation, but few copies for home use.

Here, then, is a large body of literature one time plentiful as were the carrier pigeons, as quickly gone: part of the heritage of man in society -- man, perhaps at his humblest and his greatest moments, worshiping and praising his Maker.

A glance at the Symbolic Citation List of books indexed disposes one to believe they have been chosen at great random: It is hoped that this is not fact. They have come to the compiler's attention at various times, have been analyzed in denominational blôc when possible; but it was far more important to do the indexing than to be dilatory because one of the members of the Presbyterian (or other) family of churches had not yet made the book. Such delay would postpone any compilation.

Included are the full music editions of hymnals (i.e., books of congregational song) officially published by religious bodies in the Judaeo-Christian tradition, and approved for use at the chief services of worship by these bodies since 1900 and through December 31, 1965;

Also companions, or handbooks, to two of the hymnals: selected because of the wealth of additional poetry included in its original language;

Also three student hymnals, representative of the worship of the younger generation at university and college;

Also the tri-liturgical _Army and Navy hymnal_;

Also the _Oxford Book of carols_ and the _Yattendon hymnal_, both representative of books used within the Anglican Communion and of the new materials (or old materials discovered anew) which are being incorporated into more and more general hymnals within and without the Anglican Communion;

Also one book without musical notation, _Ausbund_: notation does not exist. This is said to be the "oldest hymn book officially in use by any church in America," dating from 1570 and little changed, according to The handbook to the Mennonite hymnary (p. xxx). It is commonly said in the Lancaster County (Pennsylvania) musical circles that the Amish plainchant continues the 16th century singing tradition more truly than does institutional singing that is far more sophisticated.

Usually several distinctly different hymnals have been chosen for a single denominational family. Range in date of publication has been a selection factor.

These hymnals bear Canadian, United States, and United Kingdom imprints; they are principally in the English language. Ausbund was originally prepared for the South German and Swiss Mennonites, and is today somewhat removed from the idiom commonly called "Pennsylvania Dutch." Several Catholic hymnals contain the Latin text to hymns used at the Mass in addition to many simpler hymns for lesser services and meetings.

The oldest of the truly 20th century books is the Moravian Offices of worship and Hymns (3d ed., rev. and enl.) from 1891.

The newest published hymnal is Anglican hymn book, released 30 June, 1965.

And finally, there are included the contents of an unpublished hymnal. Editor Carlton R. Young provided the Report of the Hymnal Committee of the Commission on Worship to the 1964 General Conference of the Methodist Church. By closely comparing the 1935 edition (The Methodist hymnal) with the indexes and contents of this Report, a record of the whole new book has been made. In this instance only, a book symbol (BZ) is used without hymn number. Sorry, but we could do no other.

Hopefully, and despite an apparently complicated set of indexing determinants, you can find the poem or its author, the song or its composer, the name of the tune and the very book in which it has been printed. If this be true the book will have served its purpose. Many references are given; many citations are recorded: all of them within these books which represent a generous cross section of western man's religious institutions at worship sometime during the first two-thirds of the Twentieth Century. If your question refers to the hymn or the tune used by a congregation at high worship (where books in official adoption are invariably used) it is probable you will find its answer. The denominations or faiths included are:

Amish (BU)
Anglican Communion (U.S.A., Canada, U.K., Commonwealth countries) (A, B, C, D, E, F, X, BG, BJ, BV)
Army and Navy (U.S.A.) (AH)
Baptists (U.S.A., U.K.) (Z, AT, AU, AV, BY)
Carolers (BG)
Catholic (Bl, BM, BN, BO, BP, BQ, BS)
Christian Church (Z)
Christian Reformed (AI, AJ)
Christian Science (BE)
Church of the Brethren (AR, AS)
Congregationalists (AF)
Disciples (Z)
Evangelical-United Brethren (AE)
General Church of the New Jerusalem (BI)
Jewish (Central Conference) (BH)
Lutherans (U.S.A. only) J, K, L, M, N, O, P, Q, AA, BT)
Mennonites (AW, AX, AY, BW, also BU)
Methodists (U.S.A. only) (G, H, I, BZ)
Moravians (AZ, BA)
Mormons (BC)
New Church (BR)
Presbyterians (U.S.A., Canada, U.K., Commonwealth countries) (R, S, T, U, V, W, AG, AM, AP)
Protestant Episcopal (A, B, C, D)
Quakers (BK)
Reformed (AK, AO, BF)
Seventh Day Adventists (BB)
Students (University groups) (Y, AB, AC)
Unitarian-Universalist (AN, AQ, BD, BX)
Unaffiliated (AD)
United Church of Canada (AL)

II

THE HYMNAL: SEVERAL OF ITS CHARACTERISTICS

Though it would be difficult to secure statistics, I would believe that the telephone directory is the most frequently used reference book in the western world, and the church hymnal is the second most used reference book. Falling into the natural "directory" category, the telephone book serves countless uses beyond that of indicating telephone number. Falling into the natural "anthology" category, the hymnal has uses far beyond that of presenting hymns used at worship services.

The hymnal I knew as a child, Book of worship (L), contains the liturgy and prayer book materials for public and private worship, the Augsburg Confession, and the Formula for the Government and Discipline of the Evangelical Lutheran Church, as revised in 1888. The hymnal portion in this full music edition begins on p. 267 and closes on p. 781. Its pp. 745-81 contain: Index of subjects, Index of first lines of hymns, Index of first lines of all stanzas [including the first], Alphabetical index of tunes, and Metrical index of tunes. The authors and composers were neglected.

This pattern of prayer book and hymnal bound together (either with or without distributive subtitle pages) has been fairly common in certain traditions. The Liturgy and the Offices of worship and Hymns (AZ) contains 119 pages of liturgies, thirty-two of Offices, and 479 pages of hymns on which are printed 1523 numbered hymns and additional chants.

Liturgy and hymnal for the use of the General Church of the New Jerusalem (BI) is far more complete. Its 420 pages of liturgy, 150 pages of hymns, and its twenty-seven anthems (13 in English, 11 in Hebrew with text and tune reading properly from right to left, and 2 in Greek) indicates the broadest language range of any book analyzed.

Hymns for the celebration of life (AQ) is arranged in three distinct sections, using a major title page and two subtitle pages -- each featuring a tree-of-life design. The first section has 327 hymns with tunes; the second numbered 328-558 is called "Celebrations and praise", being readings; then follow sixty pages of "Notes on hymns, tunes, and readings," and a final thirty-nine pages of various indexes.

Anglican hymn book (BV) has no liturgic material, and only eleven Amens. However, as the Hymnal for the celebration of life (AQ) is exquisite in its entire form and text, so is this in its sharp black print on bright white light-weight opaque paper, its modern layout at the "Acknowledgments" and its wealth of information displayed for easy access at the indexes. In the style long familiar to instrumental music, the metrical index gives the opening score for women's voices.

Trinity hymnal (AM) is dignified, simple, academically correct, It pursues the uses of the Orthodox Presbyterians in terminology, Biblical quotation at the head of each hymn, inclusion of a great many Psalms in meter and a large number of gospel songs. Always, however, in clear and unadorned typography, abounding in quarter notes. Guide lines are centered at the foot of the facing pages.

One pair of books (AZ and BA), both Moravian, shows a continuity of musical thinking which began in mid-18th century with the Grimm and Gregor patterns of numbering all tunes of a single meter by a single identification number, and the various tunes designated by an accompanying letter. In this index there are citations to "Gregor's 217th Metre-B" and to "Grimm's 253d Metre-A". Hymnals preceding these two had used the system, the choirs and musicians and people were accustomed to it. When Book BA was being edited, the numeration was continued, as secondary; a tabular schedule was included to show related tunes; but -- and in the fashion of the 1920s -- the tune name took precedence over the metre number.

A similar intercoding is indicated in English hymnal (E), p.xxxxi, with its parent volume which has not been indexed. However, no recent U.S. publications illustrate this kind of continuity. Rather there has seemed to be deliberate change for the sake of change. Whether the 1935 and the 1966 Methodist books (G and BZ) will be intercoded cannot be stated. The Report (BZ) which is representative of the 1966 volume does contain much related matter, but for purposes of compilation and not for purposes of exposition to the congregations. Certainly in this pair the intention to return Wesley's hymns to the literature of congregational song is illustrated.

An interesting comparison is the study of books prepared by large committees or commissions, and others prepared by a very small number of editors under guidance of their chief. The Rev. Canon Percy Dearmer edited and had published numerous hymnals. When his Songs of praise (X) came in hand the acknowledgements had a peculiar ring: hymns cited as written by persons known by initial only, and the initials sounded like the letters symbolizing names of books! A letter to Oxford University Press confirmed suspicions: Most of the initials referred to hymns by the Canon himself. There had come to be so many over the years that he hesitated to publish the fact. Now, as this Songs of praise (X) is being reprinted the Press is publishing the author's name.

The music editors of Songs of praise (X) were Ralph Vaughan and Martin Shaw. They used a joint pseudonym, also an initialism: S.M.W.V.R.

Small committees and lone editors show yet another kind of modesty: hesitation to indicate their own or their immediate superior's birth dates. This may be fine for the moment, but it creates a genuine nuisance after a quarter century or more has passed. People wonder who these folks were, when they lived, and at what point in time and place to set them.

The institutional church is somewhat in agreement that a hymnal will be viable for approximately twenty-five years. Another point of general agreement is its size: approximately 600 hymns, with sufficient tunes to serve the usual needs of the congregations. Some books are lavishly supplied with tunes; some are meager; some use a few melodies over and over again; others rarely repeat a tune. The Psalter (AJ), for example, repeated few melodies.

Influence of one book on another can be seen in several pairs of books: Yattendon hymnal (BJ) strongly influenced the American Student hymnal (Y); Oxford Book of carols (BG) seemed reflected in it. I was a student of the editor of American Student hymnal and of some of his co-editors at the time this book was being compiled and published, and the excitement about the Oxford University Press's hymnology contributions was generally known. Book BG had had more evident influence on The Hymnal 1940 (A), Service book and Hymnal (J), Book of praise (X), and Anglican hymn book (BV). Passage of an additional ten or twelve years' time caused the greater use of carols.

Among the older books, those which were prepared by and for institutional churches having headquarters in the same city were uncommonly similar. The Book of worship (L) and Book of worship (AO) were used by two major bodies whose congregations regularly used the same places of worship on alternate Sundays: the Lutheran and the Reformed congregations of Bucks, Berks, Lebanon and adjacent counties of Pennsylvania. Headquarters for both were in Philadelphia, local congregational communities were almost identical -- certainly the Sunday Schools were attended by the same people -- and historically both had similar German antecedents. The liturgies in these hymnals vary, the confessions vary, but the hymns are from one tradition and not from two. Hymnal and Liturgies (BA), also from the region but specifically from the city of Bethlehem, Pennsylvania, likewise bears almost as strong resemblance to these Lutheran and Reformed hymnals as it does to its own predecessor (AZ) -- simply because of the cross-fertilization of locale.

Contrast the texts of the Baptist hymn book (BY) and any of the Anglican books. Now contrast it with any of the Baptist books from an American press. The relationship between the British volumes will be close, though doctrinal differences be great; the relationship between the Baptist books on both sides of the Atlantic will be slight, though the doctrinal views be similar.

Another comparison may be made among all books coming from the continental reformation institutional churches (i.e., excluding the Anglican tradition). Continental tradition weighted the hymnals with stately music, with German or Scandinavian hymns -- whose translations show variously effective style; and they use little 20th century material. Until, of course, you come to Service book and hymnal (J) which profited greatly from the editorial searches made by the people who did The Hymnal 1940 (A), Hugo E. Gibson (deceased) told me one day that the "Lutherans would like to have been the creators of The Hymnal 1940", a statement he had received from one of the Evangelical Lutheran leaders (also deceased). They made of their own hymnal (J)a fine book. Its solidity and scholarship is in sharp contrast to books symbolized as K, L, M, N, O, and P. The Lutheran hymnal (Q) is from the Missouri Synod tradition, and is parallel rather than in contrast to J.

Issue of Hymnal of Christian unity (BL) in 1964 shows yet another coming together. It carries the nihil obstat of Rt. Rev. Ignatius T. Kelly, censor deputatus, and imprimatur of the Bishop of Toledo, George J. Rehring, S.T.D., dated April 24, 1964. On the list of individuals whose assistance was gratefully acknowledged are Rev. Leonard W. Ellenwood, who was chiefly responsible for the Hymnal 1940, Companion (not indexed), Rabbi Elliot D. Rosenstock, and the research staff of the British Museum! Most certainly the usual Roman Catholic congregation would, at first, be at rather a complete loss when many of the hymns were sung; and just as certainly congregations from the liturgical Protestant traditions would be quite at home.

One meets all sorts of folks in a bibliography: personal friends, teachers, community acquaintances. Within Hymns and tunes: an index there are musical giants: Wagner, Beethoven, Brahms, the folk tunes of England and Germany, Negro spirituals, and at least 131 of the melodies which Bach used in his chorales. Probably all of the melodies in the first Protestant hymnal, published in Wittenberg, 1524, are included.

Poetically there are the Brownings, Edmund Spenser, Lord Tennyson, Christina Rossetti, Jan Struther, Robert Bridges, Goethe, and Robert Frost. Translations by John Mason Neale from the classical Greek and Latin, and by Catherine Winkworth from the German are legion. Unfortunately, because the intermediate author is not recognized in the indexes, these latter are apparently neglected.

The most unexpected event occurred on the evening of 23 April 1964. It was the 400th anniversary of Shakespeare's birth, and one of his sonnets was found: "Poor soul, the centre of my sinful earth." It is the only truly Shakespearean poem discovered, though a year later the song he quotes in Act 2 of As you like it was found: "Blow, blow, thou winter wind."

It might be true that the song of the congregation at worship will be the place where true brotherhood will begin. Jew, Catholic, Protestant can sing together all of "The God of Abraham praise," except the doxology which tends to be trinitarian rather than unitarian; all can sing together, "O God, our help in ages past." Catholic and Protestant have, in the Hymnal of Christian unity, one hundred hymns mutually useful. The overtones found in Walter Chalmers Smith's "Immortal, invisible, God only wise," one of these hundred, are Vedantic. Inter-relations far beyond these suggested are frequent, and the books resulting from this hard musical and poetical thinking indicate that hymnologists and musicians pursue what is vital to their institutions' good.

In the manner of librarians critically examining books of reference, the hymnals were studied. (See Appendix G for details). Some important points may be considered in the light of these explanatory notes.

Title page, with authority symbol

"Authority" here means "auspices", either institutional or personal. Several books were sent to press without such identification, or with it stated vaguely. Most institutional approval is clearly indicated.

Table of contents

Usually complete. In several instances there was simply an outline of the hymns and no indication of preface, indexes, etc. Here and there a book showed weak editorial and press supervision through the evidence of the table of contents being printed on the verso (i. e. the left page) rather than recto page.

Sources fully acknowledged within the preface, or within its formal counterpart

Indicates a differentiation between those books which do, and do not, give specific acknowledgement for use of all new and copyright material somewhere within the formal preface or index section of the hymnal. Generally speaking, those books which contain full acknowledgements were bibliographically more regular throughout. They showed evidence of careful scholarship, and of steady editorial supervision; citations were exact, names regularly spelled, and the text of both hymn and tune had little alteration.

Birth and death dates of author and composer

Essential to either literary or musical studies are dates when the texts were created. Humanly speaking, people like to know when other folks lived. Tracing the elements of plainsong to its modern adaptations, or of folksong to its modern form, is a bit easier if dates are given to the intermediate renderings. Inclusion of this element was seen to be one of the evidences of careful editing.

Hymns (Poetry): First line index

Few poems used as hymns have names. The substitute is the opening phrase, or first line. Several of the early books contain indexes to first lines of all stanzas: a boon, but not fashionable at mid-century.

Author index

That any book of poetry should be published without a list of the men and women who wrote the poems is hard to understand! But twenty of these hymnals (exclusive of Ausbund, some of whose authors are named within the hymn, and others not yet identified) lack an author index.

Hymns of the historical faith

Intended as indication of the choice of strong theological and doctrinal orientation in the hymnal; a trait more characteristic of the 19th century books than of most of these indexed. Perhaps the best illustration of change is the Hymnal of Christian unity (BL) which bears the proper Catholic signatures and which is almost totally like the hymnals coming from the highly liturgical non-Roman Catholic institutions.

Psalter in meter

Most books contain some Psalms in meter. "The Lord is my Shepherd", "All people that on earth do dwell", and others are so well-known that their Psalter origin is forgotten. This category implies a full or certainly moderate use of the Psalms from the Scottish Psalter, 1650, etc.

19th - 20th century hymns

In most books these dominate. The 19th century was the period when the English hymn waxed important over its European counterpart and predecessor. It was the century of great evangelistic crusades; of fine translators; and of the proletarian awakening. It was the century of missionary expansion around the world.

The corresponding social awakening of religious organizations in the 20th century is evident, especially, in hymnals representative of strong liturgical traditions.

Children's hymns named

That church musicians find words and tunes for use by children at worship, fitting properly into the scheme of the church hymnal, indicates the historic thesis that the literature for life's use must be learned early, repeated often. The profound need not be esoteric. It may be as simple as Hey's "Can you count the stars?"

Tunes (Music): Tune name index, alphabetical

This is the counterpart to a first line index. At the extremes of the Roman Catholic and the very evangelistic-fundamental sects using gospel songs, this information and this index have not been traditional. A tendency towards more general use is evident in such books as The Hymnal (AE) and Hymnal of Christian unity. (BL).

Tune name index, metrical

Probably the least used index of any contained in any hymnal is this one! Congregations are musically handicapped, they are outspoken with their desire to sing the familiar words to the familiar tunes. Few in any congregation realize that the metrical index is prepared to discourage singing the familiar combinations. Fewer people realize that this index is indeed a classification of the poetry (hymn) by the number of feet in its line, and number of lines in its stanza. Still fewer do anything about it. Book AZ, the earlier Moravian hymnal index, uses the poetical/musical meter as its guide to general arrangement. The economy thus achieved permitted publication of a great anthology of hymns: there was absolutely no place for reprinting even one tune. Grimm and Gregor, mid-18th century, introduced this practice.

Anglican hymn book (BV) is the most helpful of any book musically. The metrical index (1) names and describes each meter, (2) records the tune name, (3) records the item numbers of hymns set to this tune, (4) indicates presence of a descant, faux bourdon, or special setting, (5) quotes several measures of the opening score for soprano and also voices, and (6) names item numbers where the tune is used in a different key. This innovation may encourage congregational participation, and use of variant melodies to the hymn. Surely it is far easier to sing a sample tune, than to sing a list of words called "tune names".

Composer index

Why should not mention of the musical source be just as technically and ethically essential as mention of literary source? Comparison of the record shows close association of these indexes in the books examined.

Plainsongs included

Tally is as accurate as modern settings and notation allow it to be. Many of the tunes which Luther and Walther used in their first books, issued in Wittenberg in 1524, were derived from plainsongs. Little trace remains of them in the congregational hymn, though a great deal is evident in liturgical portions of hymnals. English chant dominates the service music "at the back of the book." When Hymnal 1940 (A) introduced four settings for the Holy Communion (one of which was Gregorian from the 9th-12th centuries) tradition was broken. And when the trail-blazing Hymnal of Christian unity (BL) included Isaac Watts', "O God, our help in ages past" reverse tradition was broken. "Of the Father's love begotten" has been part of Protestant Christmas song so long that people do not associate it with plainsong!

Some of these crooked places are being made straight. Melodies from early temple and church are finding their ways back to the books.

Reformation tunes

Men active at this period in the Church's history were steeped in traditional learning and wanted the best retained. From Luther's small 1524 hymnal containing eight hymns (four by Luther, three by Paul Speratus, and one probably by Justus Jonas) and the Walther Geistliche Gesangkbuchleyn with five-part music, through the years of Bourgeois' Psalter music to about 1650 is the era implied here.

Hymnals of this 20th century with heavy liturgical and reformation heritage are the books which contain Reformation tunes in great abundance: Lutheran, Anglican, Calvinist. The Yattendon hymnal (BJ) and The Lutheran hymnal (Q) have influenced other volumes.

Folk tunes, all cultures

Folk music is quite old, somewhat weather-beaten and healed of its weaknesses; it has no known composer; and it is of the people as an act of celebration.

"Innsbruck" was a folk tune, arranged by numerous musicians -- including Bach. We are far removed from the words originally associated with it. Closer is "Harlech" and some congregations may find it difficult to use this latter melody as praise to God in song.

The prison songs, work songs, soldiers' marching songs, boating songs, and hymns of troubled people everywhere carry their own weight as part of the song of temple and church. So with the songs of the land, of the nursery, of the natural events of living: childhood, courtship, love and marriage, babies, the infant and puberty rites, old age, death. Oxford book of carols (BG) is to the fore in this literature, and the American student hymnal (Y) includes much of the same spirit.

From the U.S.A., folk contributions have come through the Appalachian mountain musicians (mostly probably almost directly from the English immigrants of many years ago), from the Southwest (none of which is apparently herein), and from the American Negro. This latter music is rushing into books headlong.

Gospel songs

Folk song and gospel song are closely associated. The primary differences are (1) age, or date of composition and (2) intention, or use of the text and tune.

The gospel song is an evangelistic teaching device, easily learned, with emotional and sometimes fearful overtones, and with very close association of words and tune; it is of recent known authorship (though frequently the writing has been done by some of the little people whose poems or tunes are purchased and published by evangelistic agents -- either anonymously or under the names of the editor); and it is intended to encourage man to praise God through his offering of honor and worship.

The intention of the folk song is celebration. This opens its way for use in the liturgical tradition. Several journalists exercised displeasure at exclusion of "Nearer my God to Thee" from Anglican Hymn book (BV). Inclusion of "The holly and the ivy" was not heralded! The latter is pure folk song, celebration of birth, one of the wonders of life; the former can boast no such wonderment.

Again, this index is passing no judgment; the examples mentioned are given as examples only.

Editorial policies, etc.: Prefatory statement on congregational song

Except as the institutional church's stated attitude towards participation by the congregation in its song, it is anomalous to find a course of lessons in "how to sing" within a hymnal. Liturgy and hymnal (BI) devotes pages 629-32 to this purpose.

Other books include general musical directions; liturgical directions for best use of the hymns presented; and several hymnals make historical statements about hymnody within the immediate denomination. This may be presented in an enlarged preface, or separately. Any of these items indicate jurisdictional interest in congregational participation.

Specialties of the book

Certain committees, while cumulating the materials for the hymnals, have studiedly or inadvertantly accumulated materials of interest to themselves. The notes, Nos. 1-30, accompanying the chart indicate some of these special features which are published and which are among the peculiarly useful specialties librarians frequently require.

Liturgical section

Institutional worship, as with all institutional activity, includes some formally organized services. The Mass is the largest and the most complex. Stage follows stage in regularly ordered steps. Variations are permitted occasionally. Some of the hymnals examined contain these elements of public worship which are regularly the responsibility of the congregation. A portion of this material is sung, a portion is spoken; some of it may be either sung or spoken.

The liturgical materials are: responsive readings (biblical and other), canticles, portions or the whole of the Mass (by any name: Holy Communion, Lord's Supper, Eucharist, Mass); responses to prayers or lessons; certain ritual acts. However, if the whole book of worship is included (and only this whole book, with its separate title page, etc.) in this category it is considered a "bound-with" book and is not tallied. An example would be the one-book edition of the Book of Common prayer and The Hymnal 1940. Only The Hymnal 1940 is considered herein.

Prayer book section (or substitute)

Reread the paragraph just above.

If, within the regulation hymnal, there are full services of worship (no matter how brief they be) this is implied within the category. The Brethren hymnal (AR) includes several brief litanies. A litany is a complete, though short, service; it is not part of traditional Church of the Brethren worship. It belongs to be counted here.

In contrast, most of the books coming from the old German or Scandinavian tradition do contain almost complete prayer books, and certain of the rituals too. Those descending from Swedenborgian origins (BI and BR), from Unitarian and Universalist origins (AN,

AQ, BD, and BX) contain the prayer books. So does Our parish prays and sings (BM) which is in the vanguard of the people's books for use in Catholic worship.

The Anglican Communion, world-wide in its use of an almost-uniform liturgy, directs -- rather than dominates -- congregational song. It will be interesting to follow the Roman Catholic hymnals during the latter third of this century. Will they be in the Lutheran pattern (as Our parish prays and sings) or the Anglican (as Hymnal of Christian unity)?

Documents of the historical faith

Surveying Notes Nos. 31-41, the range of true document relating to the faith in its early years will be noticed. The Confessions are secular documents, and are thus part of the political history of Europe in the 16th-17th centuries. The Catechisms are educational documents, essential to the initiatory lessons for the children of the church. Both sorts are binding today.

III

THE INDEXES

Several definitions, quite descriptive, must accompany these indexes. They are:

The Hymn (poem)

The Authors/Composers

The Tune name

The Melody

Following the four definitive statements are formal descriptions of each index. They are:

Index I: First lines and variants, with citations

Index II: Authors and first lines

Index III: Tune names, and variants, with citations

Index IV: Composers and tune names

Index V: Melodies, a systematic index

THE HYMN (POEM)

Hymn: a song of praise to God; specifically a metrical composition adapted to be sung in a religious service, sometimes distinct from psalm or anthem, as not being part of the text of the Bible. (O. U. D.)

Within certain limits this definition has been followed. Psalms and anthems which are printed apart from the hymns have been excluded from the Index. However a metrical version of a psalm or anthem is usually within the physical portion of the book which is called "hymnal", and is therefore indexed. The objective being identification (cataloging) of the contents of these hymnals, everything reasonably located within the section of congregational song has been included. Judgment as to whether or not they are songs of praise to God has not been passed.

Many changes are made to poems before they pass the editorial and theological scrutiny. Such simple variations as spelling cause confusion: Saviour, Savior; Sion, Zion; Alleluia, Hallelujah, Alleluja; and O, Oh. These can be arbitrarily controlled in an index (and they have been) by predetermining the spelling form.

It is impossible to control the entire text of a poem as the X references show. Which form of the first line (and only the first line as printed is here studied) was the original cannot be determined from this Index. Many variations are not here evident, because they come at second or later line.

Likewise no attempt can be made to certify that the lines are in proper order. As example, Edna St. Vincent Millay's poem, "Renascence" was used in the predecessor to AC, and began: "O God, thou canst not hide from me." In AC and in Y it was quoted; "O God, I cried, no dark disguise." And about thirty-five years later in AQ it is quoted as: "The world stands out on either side." The AQ first line stood at opening of third stanza in Y, and opening of second stanza in AC, as it had in the predecessor edition (to AC). These books were edited less than two city blocks apart -- but separated by thirty-five years in time. No wonder the careful editors to Hymns for the celebration of life remarked in a letter (dated January 11, 1965), "We wanted [the book] to be perfect. Ah, me."

A change made by John Wesley many years ago to Watts' metrical version of Psalm 90 cannot be discovered except by knowing the text. Watts wrote, "Our God, our help." Wesley changed it to read, "O God, our help." Julian says, ". . .of Watts's original it would be difficult to write too highly. It is undoubtedly one of his finest compositions, and his best paraphrase."

Refrains are frequently better known than the stanzas they accompany, perhaps because the refrain is repetitive. Sometimes it seems that the hymn is attached to the refrain, rather than the reverse. These irregularities are noticed. The regular first line is recorded with citations; but regular first line of the refrain is recorded without citations, but with a reference R to the parent text.

It is a pity that so many poems and melodies have been edited, garbles, altered, parodied, and emasculated -- and then inserted into the books used at public worship. This happens in all quarters, and without question. The originals are legally in the public domain, and theological prerogative is commonly accepted! Poet and organist did something to correct this in Yattendon hymnal (BJ), as later poet and musicians did in the Oxford Book of carols (BG). Fine scholarship has come into general acceptance, and hymnals have coincidentally become books to which both theologians and scholars can look with pride.

THE AUTHORS AND COMPOSERS

The author/composer is here defined as that person, institution, publisher, or tradition who wrote, approved, published, or transmitted to others the earliest verified text of the hymn or tune;

Editors, arrangers -- all intermediate people -- are rarely credited;

Translators are not considered, unless the work is by itself a peculiar contribution to the literature of hymnody in which event the translator is author of the version;

Compilers and hymnals are frequently cited as agents responsible for publication of the hymn or tune in some language or in some musical key;

Classical and anonymous sources (as Bible, Breviary, etc.) are accepted; the Anonymous category precedes both Index I and III normal alphabeting;

Traditional hymns and tunes are sorted by region or country of origin. "The holly and the ivy" is English traditional; whereas "Innsbruck" is associated with Heinrich Isaak's name, though he used a popular German melody as its foundation. Actually in this matter of tradition, had the decision been to become a purist there would have been added more confusion than aid. The course laid by the best hymnologists, editors, and musicians has been followed, and several fine scholars are represented by this collection of books. The part reserved for our share was that of the well-read librarian who catalogs specialist materials for the library patrons.

When the text was not a close variant -- as when the metrical rendering, the translation, or the editing caused a difference in more than a few words (but not necessarily in the quotation of the same stanzas) -- an entirely new entry was established under this second reading. Variants which became attached to this second reading were cited here only, and not with the version established as the first standard first line.

Non-English text of a hymn quoted is indexed within its alphabetic position as an independent standard first line. References follow the usual order.

No references are made from one standard reading to another standard reading, except through Index II; "Authors and first lines." Here it is hoped that these variations and versions may be collected practically -- and, hopefully, properly! Authorship and renderings of the early hymns has been especially difficult to establish consistently and accurately.

Serial numbers have little value within Index I alone. They are the means of cumulating the materials through Index II.

Reference from variants to accepted standard form of first line is given in Index I. Its converse, reference from accepted form of first line to the variants, is indicated in Index II. Similar reference pattern is established in the musical sections of this work.

In summary: First lines are always recorded, cited at first appearance within each hymnal; first line variants are always recorded, cited the first time they appear, reference (X) is made to the standard first line, citation is made at standard first line; refrains are never cited, but are always recorded and reference (R) to standard first line is made; refrain variants are cited at the time of first appearance, reference (X) is made to the standard refrain; occasionally an asterisk (*) after citation number indicates use of a variant refrain. All alphabeting is word-by-word.

THE TUNE NAME

As secular musical compositions have distinctive names, so does the music to which congregations sing their hymns. The words used to name the tune come from various sources, and are normally quite overlooked by the singer.

Placed above the score (centered, to the left, or to the right margin) will be such words as Wetterling, Deliverance, Lura, Message, Aethelwold, Second Parish, Old Hundred, St Petersburg, Olivet, Down Ampney, Pange Lingua. They form a vocabulary that is unexplored, and they offer hints of biographical worth: the biography of the melody, or of the hymn and tune together, or of the author and his assignment at the time of composition, or a friend to whom it is dedicated, or an unused middle name (as "Othello", by E.O. Excell); or pseudonymous name (as "El Nathan"). Perhaps the greatest single source of tune names has been the first lines of the hymns associated with the tunes as used at the several offices, or services, in the early and middle years of church history. Another source has been the names of saints associated with the composition of the melody, or with the hymn which it was to accompany. In Catholic circles the word Saint (usually reduced to St.) is used with tune names; in communities where the word Saint is looked on with less favor it may be omitted. This produces a variant for the indexer!

Mention has been made of the use of the first phrases of the Latin office hymns as tune names. These are the old literature. A still older musical literature is included within these indexes: that which has come from Jewish tradition. Though only one Jewish hymnal was included, Union hymnal (BH), plus a portion of another Army and Navy Hymnal (AH), thirty-three distinct Jewish traditional melodies are given. Many of these have long been associated with Jewish feasts and fasts and holy days.

Another similar literature is that which has come from the years known as the Reformation Period. A great number of these tunes are known by the first phrase of the usual hymn it accompanied, almost invariably in the German language. J.S. Bach used many of these tunes as the basis for chorales which he inserted into his many oratorios: again, the citation is normally to the first line-though much tampering has occurred to these tune names.

Traditional folk song, or other secular names are usual tune names for melodies which have long been known by "everybody", without identified composer, and usually associated with political or geographical regions or folk enclaves. "Londonderry Air" is an illustration. There are many others.

Gospel songs are known variously: by the first line, the repetitive phrase in the refrain, by the closing lines of either the first stanza or the refrain. They have, however far more frequently than have the more staid hymns, a close association of words and music. Whereas the formal hymnody is likely to interchange text and tune from service to service, and certainly from denomination to denomination, the gospel song is usually a consistent union of words and music. Consequently words from the text are logical tune name.

As these books indexed increased in number, it became more and more frequently necessary to use first lines for tune identification. Several hymnals from the less liturgic of the institutional churches had many unnamed melodies. The people using these hymnals call the tunes by the first lines of the hymn: our decision was theirs. Reference to other names was always made when necessary, but citations are given only to the standard tune name.

THE MELODY

Melody: A series of single notes arranged in musically expressive succession.

Tune: A musical setting of a hymn or psalm, usually in four-part harmony, intended for use in public worship. (O.U.D.)

The musical portion of these indexes is concerned with the melody, its source and its identification as a unique composition. The materials which were studied to secure the melodies were the tunes, the arrangements or settings of hymns for use in public worship. The names applied to these melodies are therefore called tune names, but the final index in the series is called "Melodies, a systematic index."

Music, in all its pleasing variations, is produced by many instruments animate and inanimate. The worth or meaning of music is symbolic of every intensity of every human emotion. This symbolic meaning is not considersd in Hymns and tunes. Rather, the sequence of the physical phenomena of tones within the musical octave (eight-tone scale) are the important element.

Musical traditions have developed several tonal patterns. One is prominent in the usual congregational song of the western world. The tonal scale, be it the major or its relative minor, is the combination of whole and half step intervals. The tones of the major scale have accepted syllable names: Do, Re, Mi, Fa, Sol, La, Ti and Do (which closes one sequence and opens the next).

These symbols -- Do, Re, Mi, Fa, Sol, La, Ti -- are the musical syllables used in the solmization of any diatonic scale.

These symbols -- Do, Re, Mi, Fa, Sol, La, Ti -- are not identical with the notes on a clef or the position at which a musical instrument is played. A diatonic scale has relative values only, relative to the initial tone which is to form the base of the eight-tone octave. The opening tone is always Do, according to the major scale; and La, according to the minor scale. The key in which the tune is written affects the printed notation, but does not affect the solmization.

For these reasons it is possible to write the symbols: Do Do Re Ti Do Re/Mi Mi Fa Mi Re Do/Re Do Ti Do and, however high or low it be sung, it will always sound like "My country 'tis of thee."

The stability of the tonic values of syllables make it possible to display the opening phrases of the musical literature of congregational song. The display is symbolic. There is, in fact, a chain effect of musical symbolism which begins with the five-line staff and its intervening spaces. Each line, each space has its particular and permanent name.

The diatonic scale can begin anywhere on this staff, it will close an octave higher or lower. Its initial and terminal points are determined by the key signature of the score: the number of sharps or the number of flats to be regularly observed. These sharps and flats regulate the intervals; they regulate the position for recording the melody on the five-line staff; they regulate the key tone (Do); they do not regulate the solmization of the melody.

Conversion of the notational record to sol-fa notation (Solmization) is the next symbolic act, symbolic because no music need be sounded to perform the act.

Symbolism is carried to yet another degree by reducing the syllable names of the tones from Do Re Mi Fa Sol La Ti to D R M F S L T -- possible only because there is no repetition.

A musical score may contain tones which are modified by raising or lowering them one-half step. Indication is marked by the use of sharps (#) or flats (♭). This index does not change the syllable name of the tone, but uses the sharp (#) as indicative of change. It must be carefully noticed that, in the interests of practicality, all tones affected by either flats or sharps have been written with the relative syllable followed by its sharp. This means that a flatted note is called by the syllable name next lower in the scale with a sharp. The conversion scale reads:

♭D	becomes	T	♭S	becomes	F#	
♭R	"	D#	♭L	"	S#	
♭M	"	R#	♭T	"	L#	
♭F	"	M	♭D	"	T	etc.

The musical notation is affected by the flat/sharp conversion. Melodic reproductions on instruments with determined intervals (as the piano) will not be affected. However melodic reproduction on a stringed instrument (as the violin) or a wind instrument (as a slide trombone) will be affected. Melodic reproduction by the human voice will be affected. The true tonic intervals differ slightly in color when a note is flatted or its companion is raised the half-step interval.

Because our subject is congregational song -- that is, community singing -- these niceties of tonal values do not obtain. The music is usually sung by folks whose voices are untrained; the range of tone is about one and one-third octaves. Many, many of the tunes cluster about a four or five tone range. This has not always been true. Plainsongs permitted and utilized more melodic range. The dramatic (pseudo-operatic) melodies of the 19th century have passed. The twentieth century tunes are simple, though they vary from the blithe to the solemn.

In recording melodies it was quickly apparent that a brief quotation was all that was essential for raw identification -- except in a few instances where the sounds used for singing the first line of the hymn were repeated by several composers. The record of the second line of the setting was sufficient to enforce a decision to quote sixteen successive musical syllables (terms used to name the relative tones in the diatonic scale). A very few times it has been necessary to record more than sixteen syllables; and in a mere handful of instances has it been essential to indicate the length of the poem being set to music. In this latter situation it was always the late portion of the music which varied. "Old hundred twenty fourth", by Louis Bourgeois (1551) was reduced by one ten-syllable phrase to form "Toulon". A note is given with each to indicate the metrical length: 10.10.10.10.10 for the original, and 10.10.10.10 for the reduction.

The fact that melodic quotation exceeds actual needs for identification does assist in finding the variants printed in several books. Occasionally a single hymnal will quote the melody in two different ways without indication of editor. The Bach arrangements are usually properly cited, but most variations and harmonizations are anonymous (that is, the fact of the change is neither indicated nor credited). Taking place now, however, is a real improvement in this respect. The fine companions prepared by several of the musical editorial committees have led to far greater exactitude in quoting sources (authors, composers, etc.) and in indication of editorial changes within the texts of both tunes and hymns. Greater care concerning biographical detail is being exercised.

Within this Index, the melody is quoted twice, just as are the tune names and the first lines. It was possible in cataloging the poems attributed to an author to shorten the first line, because words are a very familiar means of communication. Melodies of the tunes attributed to a composer have not been shortened beyond the length given in Index V. They are quoted in an unfamiliar language, in the musical syllables beginning with Do (written D); and they are subject to great variation from book to book. The same is true of tune names, they have been quoted in full in Indexes III and IV. Tune names are words, but unfamiliar words and coined words.

Just as concert music has several themes within a single composition, so with hymns. A hymn tune is short, offers little opportunity for variety, but distinctive airs are present. Koschat's melody known as "Poland" has a dual melody throughout. It is difficult to decide which is primary and which secondary. Normally the soprano line would be treated as primary, and the alto line as secondary; that decision is followed here.

Other melodies have preliminary phrases which are distinctive, but which may not always be quoted. Palestrina's "Victory" is illustrative. Beginning with a triple Alleluia, the body of the hymn is a sequence of five or more four-line stanzas. The tune, because it may or may not utilize the preliminary phrase, must have quotation from both vantage points.

Still another congregational song is that which uses the antiphonal statement of stanza, followed by refrain which is repetitive. Gospel songs are nearly always written in this way; so are many out-going and bright hymns as well as a large number of processional and recessional compositions.

In each of these instances involving a second theme, the record of that theme has been made just as accurately and at as great length (sixteen tones) as was the primary theme. The difference lies alone in the citations recorded. Because the name of the refrain or of the secondary melody will be that of its parent standard melody, there is no alphabetical gap between them in the index. The filing order has usually been: standard primary tune (with melodic quotation, source, and citations), followed by secondary entry bearing quotation of refrain (without citations), and this followed by variants to either standard or refrain melodies. Citations are always made to the first appearance of a variant as well as to its relative standard entry.

INDEX DESCRIPTIONS

INDEX I: First lines and variants, with citations

This is a list in simple word-by-word alphabetic order of the first lines of every first stanza, of the first lines of every refrain (chorus), and of every variation of these first lines and refrains found in all the books analyzed.

The first line is followed, in parentheses, by its source (author). Citations to the item numbers (hymn numbers) within the hymnals where it is quoted are then given, as AZ290 means Book AZ, Hymn 290. The final information is serial numeration, beginning with 100001: this being the simplest way to completely differentiate the hymn numeration from the melodic numeration which begins with One (1).

Citations are not given for refrain first lines, rather a reference (R) is made to the related standard first line.

Citations are given to the first appearance of a variant reading of the first line, or a variant reading of the refrain first line, and reference (X) is made to the related standard first line or related standard refrain first line. This citation is also recorded within the standard first line entry.

The literary problems involved in the first line identification were many. Julian's Dictionary of hymnology helped considerably. Personal knowledge helped. Many hundreds of times, however, reference to previously cited renderings of the hymn was necessary to confirm identity; other times reference to the author file was helpful.

When the text was a close variant, it was handled as above. This might be described as reference to the standard first line, for purposes of this Index.

INDEX II: Authors and first lines

This is a list in simple word-by-word alphabetic order of the accepted personal, institutional, anthology, and traditional sources of the standard first lines found within these books analyzed.

The author's name, with dates when available, is followed by a brief quotation of the first line of the first stanza of the hymn and occasionally by date associated with the text when that date is useful for identification purposes. Then follows an item number preceded by letter R or V (being refrains and variant readings) and a brief redaction of each such refrain or variant.

This index II does not identify the accepted form of the first line by serial number. That may be readily found alphabetically in Index I. Variants, refrains, etc. are numerically coded, however, to make reference both more rapid and more accurate.

The literary problems in Index II were many. Again, Julian's Dictionary and the indexes within each hymnal aided identification of dates, full personal or compilation (anthology) names, etc. The everlasting objective has been the original source: who wrote this poem (hymn) in its original form and language? Hymnal editors have frequently given the credit to the intermediate arranger, or translator. A "traditional" source has had to be used when no individual agent could be found. A kind of "Potter's Field" -- a place for the strangers: first lines of unknown origin -- was established: "Anonymous". This has been fitted into the index at the very beginning of the file (before A).

Authors of religious poetry are legion and from time immemorial. If the hymn be of biblical origin, in traditional antiphonal psalm form and text, the biblical source is used. But if the psalm be re - written to conform to western poetical practice, then either the book in which the metrical psalm was published or the human agent (author) is credited. Notice the large number of hymns with the general source, Scottish Psalters.

There is no established relation between Indexes I-II and Indexes III-IV. An accidental relation is occasionally made because a hymn tune is not given a tune name. The first line of the first stanza is substituted.

INDEX III: Tune names and variants, with citations

This is a list in simple word-by-word alphabetic order of all the tune names, or of first lines substituted for tune names not given, and of all variants of either the tune names or the first line substitutes which are associated with the particular melodies found in all the books examined.

The tune name is followed, in parentheses, by its source (composer). Then follows the quotation in syllables of the diatonic scale, approximately sixteen tones of the beginning melody. This is within brackets. Citations refer to the item numbers within each hymnal where the melody is repeated -- its first quotation only within each book. BC13 means Book BC, Hymn Tune at Hymn 13. Final information is the serial numeration, beginning with One (1): this being a separate and distinct series from that found in Index I where the numeration begins differently.

Notice carefully that a hymn tune is identified but once within a hymnal, except where variants occur. This variant would be treated either with the variant tune names, or as a absolute variant with its own associated citations. Simple repetition which occurs frequently can be discovered by reference to the Tune Name Index within the individual hymnal.

The musicological problems in Index III compilation have been legion.

This section has been two-pronged. It has involved the verbal form of the name of the melody (tune name), and it has involved the musical form that melody takes when sung (by the diatonic scale). Then there have been the many and quite variant sources which apparently belong to the song as we know it.

The tune name accepted here as standard is that name first found to be associated with the given melody, in the chronological cataloging of the hymnals. The melody is actually the pivotal item, but a systematic way of identifying it has been through its peculiar tune name.

The source accepted here as standard is the earliest cited person, institution, publication, or culture associated with the particular melody.

The melody here accepted as standard is the form in which it first appeared in the actual examination of the hymnals.

Notice carefully that no attempt is made to identify the reasons or the sources for the creation of the tune names. It is the melody which is being traced.

When tune name variants were found, references to the accepted (standard) name were prepared using X. No citations to variant names have been included. This would have added confusion to confusion, and anyone wishing to sort it out may do so from the citations which are recorded at the standard tune name entry.

When melodic variants have been close, a reference (V) with standard tune name, variant melodic reading, and single citation was prepared. Because melodic variants and refrains carry the standard tune name identification tag, it has been unnecessary to make actual references to the information anywhere. R, in this Index III, indicates refrain melody.

There is no reference from accepted tune name to the alternate tune name in Index III. Such information may be readily found through Index IV, "Composers and tune names." Virtually the only references herein are those inter-relating the unused to the used tune names. Infrequently one of the old tunes has been edited, the source is quite distinct and so is the tune name. A clear reference from each to other is made.

Serial numeration in Indexes III and V is interdependent. Index III is true sequence, from Number One. Index V is true melodic sequence, with the serial number indicating the numbered item in Index III. Thus the sung tune points to the tune name, to its composer, to verification of the melody, to citations within printed books, and to variant renderings.

Within Index III, serial numbers serve simply to display items. Through Index IV, serial numbers collect variant tune names and refrain tune names in the same way that variants and refrains are collected in Index II to the words of the hymns quoted as Index I. It is hoped that the patterns of Indexes I-II and III-IV are parallel.

In summary: Tune names are always recorded; cited at their first appearance within a hymnal; related melodies are always recorded with the standard tune names; variant tune names are always recorded but location of that variant is never cited, however a reference (X) is made to the established or standard tune name; refrains are recorded melodically, are never cited, but a reference (R) to the established standard tune name (actually, the standard melody) is made; variants to the melody are cited one time only, parallel citation at the established tune name is made, and reference V to that established tune name is prepared. The established source is quoted within the actual working file and implied within the published file at each time a tune name or its related melody is named. Variant and intermediate sources are ignored for the purposes of this Index. All alphabeting within Index III is word-by-word according to the standard tune name or its variants.

INDEX IV: Composers and tune names

This is a list in simple alphabetic word-by-word order of the accepted (established) personal, institutional, anthology, and traditional sources of the accepted (standard) melodies and associated tune names as found in the books examined.

The name of the composer of the melody, with dates when available, is followed by the tune name and associated dates when applicable, and finally by whatever variant tune names are associated with it. These variant tune names are preceded by X and the serial numbers from Index III.

Index IV does not cite serial numbers of standard tune names, nor does it repeat melodic symbolism. Both these are available alphabetically in Index III.

The literary and musicological problems of Index IV are those already named for its parallel Index III. Related to this Fourth was the very close reading of the melodic solmization each time it appeared under its (possible) seventy-five variants: Seventy-five books examined were full melody hymnals -- all except BT, BU, and BW. More complicated, and far more elusive, were melodies which bore nothing relevant to materials already indexed: tune name, source, related words, etc. A great many of these awaited the garner and sorting which came when Index V was created.

Church musicians and composers of music that has become classical are as legion as their brother hymnists (poets). Melodies from the early centuries of the Christian Era were usually handed down as plain song. So they are here, except where a more personal or exact name is associated with the melody. Some are traditional to a culture, as are many of the Jewish melodies. A few are from manuscript sources, as from the Herrnhut ms -- obviously Unitas Fratrum and here called Bohemian Brethren.

In passing: So much of practical dependence has been placed on the manuscript scores by the Moravians in our own U.S.A. that only within the recent four or five years have the choristers and trombone choir at the Lititz (Pennsylvania) Moravian Church retired their manuscripts to the vault and taken to the use of photoduplicates for the festal services of Christmas and Easter according to information from one of the Brethren (officers).

Revision of plainsong to modern setting has nearly always permitted indication of a human agent as proper source. In many instances it is a hymnal published by a diocese, a city, or an individual. A great number of the chorales which Bach arranged came from plain songs -- yet within this Index they are cited otherwise. The modern rendering is quite different enough to cite the original source with the Mode number when the plain chant is meant, and to cite the mediary when the modern rendering is indicated. With reference to Bach as composer, he is less responsible for hymn tune creation than for hymn tune arrangement. For that reason some of his better known arrangements are identified in a secondary manner only; but his own musical creations are listed under his own name at Index IV. Many of the chorales for which he did either the figured bass or the full arrangement are included in the index, and may be completely identified by comparison with the 371 chorales, named in the accompanying bibliography.

The tune name, the source, and the melody accepted as standard within Index III are the same within Index IV.

INDEX V: Melodies, a systematic index

This is a simple reproduction according to the increasing values of the syllables of the diatonic scale of every distinctive melody and each of its variants, of every distinctive refrain and each of its variants, with the proper and corresponding item number attached to its standard tune name in Index III.

For a description of the diatonic scale, see p. 1158.

The portion of melody recorded is the syllables necessary to sing approximately, and nearly always, the first sixteen vocal sounds according to the words at the beginning of hymns; the corresponding syllables to the words of the refrains; and musical invocations (which are refrains in reverse: as at Palestrina's "Victory"). Natural phrasing, that is the line endings, is indicated by commas. A very few quite brief melodies close before the end of sixteen syllables. These are punctuated by a full stop (period).

Melody which seems to be in the form of English chant is usually set to the number of syllables necessary to sing stanza one. But note well, the melodies of Father Joseph Gelineau, S.J. (found in Twenty four Psalms, book BS) are quoted as printed because the poetry retains its original antiphonal form. Only because Twenty-four Psalms is a true hymnal, and not intended as liturgy, is it included. Similar materials in many hymnals have been excluded because they are not intended for use except within the stated or liturgical portion of congregational worship.

Many uses will be found for this fifth index, but it has served the purposes of the entire Hymns and tunes; an index as definitive medium for identifying tunes which bore no relation to each other through diatonic or label similarities. It was thus that the fourteen tune names to the melody here called "Cana" by Vulpius were gathered. It was here that many tunes, usually cited as German, or English traditional, or Anonymous were identified and found to be duplicates. One tune attributed to J.S.B. Monsell (a poet, not a musician) was identified as of Slovak origin.

IV

ACKNOWLEDGMENTS

From 10 April 1957, over the signature of Richard L. Evans with indication that a copy of Hymns, the official hymnal of the Church of Jesus Christ of Latter-Day Saints, was being presented for the Index, until almost the day when these final pages of manuscript were being taken to the Scarecrow Press Editorial Office at New Brunswick, New Jersey, people and institutions have helped make this book possible. These mentioned below have been known through correspondence, personal friendship, library affiliation, the library school classrooms at both the University of Tennessee and Rutgers - The State University of New Jersey, and other sections of Rutgers jurisdiction.

It has been necessary to have the entire library of books analyzed constantly at hand. These publishers have provided gift copies of their publications: Augsburg Publishing House, Augustana Book Concern, Broadman Press, The Christian Science Board of Directors, Church of God in Christ - Mennonite, The Church of Jesus Christ of Latter-Day Saints, Concordia Publishing House, The Otterbein Press, The Presbyterian Church - U.S. through its General Assembly's Training School, The United Lutheran Publication House, and The Westminster Press.

The friends include three clergymen: Norman B. Bucher, Jr., Irving Decker, and Howard A. Merkey. Lay friends to name are: Abram Beck, Alois Braun (deceased), Rose Burges Breustedt, Georgia Moe Gibson, Luella Gish, George L. Heiges, David W. Landis, Ena B. Minchew, Bernice Schneider, and Jane Smith.

Three students in my Rutgers Library School course, "Advanced reference sources," added useful books: Sister Mary Raymund, O. S.B., Joseph H. DaRold, and Joseph N. Swab. Several others were extremely interested, and offered books which were quite outside the defined limits of the work.

Libraries and librarians (glad that someone was -- for yet another time in her life "the fool in the forest" and having a marvelous time!) were willing to assist: Mennonite Library and Archives, of Lancaster (Pennsylvania) provided Amish Ausbund sources and information, Salem College, of Salem (North Carolina) quickly sent a copy of the earlier Moravian hymnal which Lititz (Pennsylvania) friends could not provide because of legal restrictions. Elizabeth Hughey (Methodist Publishing House), Jean W. Steele (Westminster Press), and Emily M. Chandler (Wesleyan Theological Seminary, Westminster, Md) each provided necessary historical information. Theodosia Hotch (one of the Regional Librarians, Georgia) and Barbara LaMont (Douglass College Librarian) discovered books and places to secure others.

Member libraries in the American Theological Library Association quickly offered books on long loan: Bridwell Library (Perkins Theological Seminary of Southern Methodist University) and Hammond Library (Chicago Theological Seminary of the University of Chicago) could send books which were very hard to find. Andover-Harvard Theological Library and New Church Theological School (through its president, Dr. Edwin G. Capon) offered and sent hymnals which could be retained.

Credit for assistance far beyond rule by law must be fully expressed to three men: F.P. Gough, Secretary, Anglican Hymn Book Committee, for prepublication air shipment of a copy of this book which is not for sale within the U.S.A.; the Rev. R.W. Thomson, Baptist Union of Great Britain and Ireland, for air shipment of a copy of the Baptist Hymn Book just before my closing deadline for indexing; and Dr. Carlton R. Young, editor of the hymnal being published by the Methodist Church in 1966, for a copy of the Final Report of his committee. This latter gift made it possible to include the text and melodies of a not-yet-published book authorized by a major denomination in our country. To have been forced to omit this would have been unfortunate indeed.

The Knox County (Tennessee) librarians, through their chief librarian, Emma Suddath, made Julian's Dictionary of Hymnology a gift. Isabel Stouffer (Cataloger, Speer Library at Princeton Theological Seminary), Lorena Garloch and Marylouise Meder (fellow faculty at Rutgers, Graduate School of Library Service), Grace Mostue (Douglass College Reference Librarian, Rutgers), and Mary M. Andrews (briefly at Rutgers, now at the Graduate School of Library Studies, University of Hawaii) -- to each of you six librarians I am grateful for technical suggestions.

Through the offices of my dean, Neal Harlow (Graduate School of Library Service, Rutgers - The State University) a small grant from the Rutgers Research Council was secured. This made possible the assistance which Virginia High has given. If the Melodic Index (Section V) be in proper order, it is to her credit. If there be error, it is my fault. Let it never be said there is no joy in preparing exact results. The Computer will say neither "Excelsior" when the task is to be done, nor "Eureka" when it is successfully completed. The human mind and heart are still essential.

My commercial artist niece, Anne Diehl, prepared the illustrations. And Ralph Shaw gave further of his encouragement. Bless them both!

KATHARINE S. DIEHL

New Brunswick, N.J.

PART ONE: THE HYMNS

I

First Lines and Variants, With Citations

A

A babe is born all of a May (English carol, 15th c) BG 116 100001

A babe is born in Bethlehem (German carol, 14th c) M612; O194; 100002

A babe is born of high nature (English trad carol, 15th c) BG40 100003

A babe lies in the cradle (Geistliche nachtigal, 1649 German carol) A 39 100004

A boy was born in Bethlehem (German trad carol) BG85 100005

A brighter dawn is breaking (Dearmer) E126; X435 100006

A broken heart, my God, my King (Watts) I266; M75; V289 100007

A charge to keep I have (Wesley,) C D501; F328; G287; H312; I388; L527; N501; R301; U289; V472; W518; Y379; Z373; AE274; AG161; AH419; AL362; AO485; AP 593; AR312; AS328; AT358; AU157; AV203; AW214; AX 163; AY38; AZ1340; BA449; BR378; BV602; BY461; BZ 100008

A child is born in Bethlehem (Latin carol, 14th c) BG73; BL6; BM82 100009

A child this day is born (English trad carol) BG2; BR554; BV102 100010

A city awaits us we soon shall behold (Newell) AY403 100011

A debtor to mercy alone (Toplady) W703; AM99 100012

A few more years shall roll (Bonar) B443; D203; E361; H524; I578; K480; L195; M365; N592; O352; V631; AI 332; AM609; AP610; AS475; AX576; AY252; AZ1490; BA 739; BB372 100013

A fierce unrest seethes at the core (Marquis) AQ53 100014

A full surrender I have made (Oatman) AX399; AY109 100015

A gentle hand unseen by us (Warner) AX626 100016

A gladsome hymn of praise we sing (Blatchford) W28; AL593; AP715; AW403 100017

A glorious day is dawning (---) BE2 100018

A glory gilds the sacred page (Cowper) G388; H94; I198; K 170; L310; R260; U135; V75; W197; AB102; AI157; AL184; AM258; AP290; AR238; AS 176; AT186; AV74; BE334; BR235; BV310; BY252 100019

A glory in the word we find (Campbell Hymnbook.) BB656 100020

A gospel others daily see (Naylor) R The world of sinners ibid 100021

A grateful heart a garden is (Dennis) BE3 100022

A great and mighty wonder (St Germanus) A18; B82; E19; F 68; J18; K17; M363; N30; O 182; P128; Q76; X70; AW526; BB672; BV90; BY87 100023

A great and mighty wonder, Our Christmas Festal brings (St Anatolius) AA149 100024

A haze on the far horizon (Carruth) Y9; AB300; AC533 100025

A herald voice the lonely desert cheers (Pope) BR129 100026

A holy air is breathing round (Livermore) Z467; AN445; AR 501; BE4; BX480 100027

A holy stillness breathing calm (---) S38app 100028

A hymn of glory let us sing (St Bede) J110; K122; M453; Q212; AA235; AM212; AS153 100029

A King might miss the guiding Star (Benson) Y329; AC453 100030

A Lamb goes forth our griefs to share (Gerhardt) M396; O165 100031

A Lamb goes uncomplaining forth (Gerhardt) O301; AA191 100032

A late lark twitters from the quiet skies (Henley) AC537 100033

A little child, a Joy of Heart (Bates) AC458 100034

A little child on the earth has been born (Flemish trad carol) X352; BG74 100035

A little child the Saviour came (Robertson) B341; W305; AK 332; AL217; AM352; AP348; AW300; AZ290; BA284 100036

A little child there is y-born (German trad carol, 15th c) BG118; 100037

A little kingdom I possess (Alcott) BH251 100038

A little seed lay fast asleep (Writer) AL610; AW406 100039

A little that the righteous hold (U. P. Psalter, 1912) T63; AJ 97 100040

A message came to a maiden young (Dutch trad & Dearmer) A317; X226; BG100 100041

A message from the Sacred Heart (Russell) BQ68 100042

A message sweet the breezes bring (Switton) BH133 100043

A messenger of peace (Zinzendorf N. L.) AZ1193 100044

A messenger within the grave (Latin, 4th-5th c) X148 100045

A mighty fortress is our God (Luther) A551; B213; G67; H 405; I101; J150; K195; L343; M486-7; N266; O270; P239; Q 262; R91; S266; U308; V530; Y351; Z155; AA273; AB243; AC210; AD289; AE59; AF363; AG41; AH378; AI309; AK281; AM81; AN304; AO606; AQ16; AR75; AS258; AT40; AU38; AV37; AW549; BB261; BC3; BD78; BE10*; BF396; BI9; BK75; BR365; BX314; BZ *deliberate variant 100046

A mighty fortress is our Lord (Luther) M487 X A mighty fortress is our God 100047

A mighty stronghold is our God (Luther) L343 X A mighty fortress is our God 100048

A new shrine stands in beauty reared (Marshall) BH213 100049

A noble life, a simple faith (Isaacs) Z512; AN296; AQ106; BD104; BH225 100050

A parting hymn we sing (Wolfe) R443; S362; Z469; AD408; AE 335; AK343; AM363; AO445; AS468; AT397; AU292; AV 256; AZ1305; BF605 100051

A pilgrim and a stranger, I journey here below (Gerhardt) K 517; M319; O504; Q586 100052

A poor wayfaring Man of grief (Montgomery) BC153 100053

A priestly Heart the Sacred Heart Latin BQ337 100054

A ransom for all my Saviour once came (Helphingstone) AX 319 100055

A rest remaineth for the weary (Kunth) Q615 100056

A ruler once came to Jesus by night (Sleeper) AT215; AU68; AW461; AX326; AY509 100057

A safe stronghold our God is still (Luther) E362; F183; W526; X 436; AL397; AP542; AZ1028; BA679; BV402; BY 562 100058

A servant of God, the Apostle of old (Hostetter) AY299 100059

A shepherd band their flocks are keeping (---) BR546 100060

A shining city, one happy in snow and sun (Drinkwater) Y65 100061

A sinful man am I (Bonar) AZ 1312 100062

A slumber I know in Jesus' name (Landstad) AA565 100063

A solis ortus cardine (Sedulius) BT104 100064

A song of spring once more we sing (Groser) Z591 100065

A sovereign Protector I have (Toplady) W560 X Inspirer and Hearer of prayer 100066

A Star is moving through the sky (Jonae??) K542; M376 100067

A stranger and a pilgrim, I (Hammond) AZ574 100068

A stranger once did bless the earth (Clare) BY633 100069

A temple of the Lord I saw (Tarrant) X I saw the city of the Lord, Pt. II 100070

A thing of beauty is a joy forever (Keats) AC491 100071

A thousand oracles divine (Wesley, C) I75 100072

A thousand years have come and gone (Lynch) S128 100073

A time to watch, a time to pray (Neale) BV171; BY136 100074

A tower of strength, our God doth stand (Luther) D416 100075

A virgin most pure as the prophets did tell (English trad carol) BQ12 X A virgin most pure as the prophets do tell 100076

A virgin most pure, as the prophets do tell (English trad carol) BG4; BP14; BQ12 100077

A voice, a heavenly voice I hear (Wallin) J270; N238 100078

A voice by Jordan's shore (Longfellow) AN210; BX219 100079

A voice from heaven we have heard (Tomlinson) BE5 100080

A voice hath spoken from the dust (Jensen) BC291 100081

A voice upon the midnight air (Martineau) X124; AN184 100082

A way to Calvary leadeth (Liander) P176 100083

A week within the sukko green (Hess) BH189 100084

A wonderful Saviour is Jesus my Lord (Crosby) AE283; AI270; AM675; AS289; AT272; AX 510; BB651 100085

A work hath Christ for thee to do (Sedding) F430; BV35 100086

A year again is now descending (Rambach) P141 100087

A year of precious blessings (Crosby) BB480 100088

Abide among us, we implore thee (Grundtvig) O142; P95 100089

Abide among us with thy grace (Stegmann) AO140 100090

Abide in grace, Lord Jesus (Stegmann) O57; P57; AZ25; BA590 100091

Abide in me, O Lord, and I in thee (Stowe) AO703; BX283; BY775 100092

Abide in me, o'ershadow by thy love (Stowe) BX283 X Abide in me, O Lord . . . 100093

Abide in me, the true and living vine (Fillmore) AY87 100094

Abide not in the realm of dreams (Burleigh) AN297; AQ222; BE 6; BX346 100096

Abide, O dearest Jesus (Stegmann) Q53; AA9 100096

Abide with me, fast breaks the morning light (Woods) BE7 X Abide with me, fast falls the eventide (Lyte) 100097

Abide with me, fast falls the eventide (Lyte) A467; B18; D12; E363; F27; G520; H34; I50; J576; K476; L16; M289; N550; O552; P340; Q552; R64; S33; T306; U470; V42; W286; X437; Y368; Z138; AA40; AB31; AC 20; AD61; AE42; AF209; AG 23; AH169; AI49; AK51; AL 550; AM335; AN127; AO25; AP663; AQ79; AR417; AS35; AT295; AU179; AV296; AW40; AX356; AY293; AZ457; BA516; BB50; BC51; BE7, 8*; BF193; BI62; BJ20; BK72; BR326; BV500; BX163; BY686; BZ *var. by Woods 100098

Abide with me, I need thee every day (Dietrick) AX368; AY70 100099

Abide with me, my Saviour blest (Timm) M286 100100

Abide with me; 'tis eventide (Hofford) BC2 100101

Abide with us, Lord Jesus! Thy grace sustain (Stegmann) M13 X Abide with us, our Saviour, nor let . . . 100102

Abide with us, O Saviour dear (Selnecker) N268 100103

Abide with us, our Saviour, Nor let thy mercy cease (Stegmann) J192; K433; L60; N358; AK34; AW559 100104

Abide with us, the day is waning (Boye) O333; Q194 100105

Abode of peace, my Father's home forever (Rosenius) N624 100106

About the field they piped full right (English trad carol, ca 1450) BG169 100107

Above the clear blue sky (Chandler) B353; D570; W37; AP714; AZ 1191; BA811; BD195 100108

Above the heavens, eternal God! (Watts) BI68 100109

Above the hills of time the cross is gleaming (Tiplady) G145 Z236 100110

Above the trembling elements (Price) AY49 100111

Abundant fields of grain shall wave (U. P. Psalter, 1912) AJ195 X Blest be the Lord our Father's God 100112

Accept from human hands anointed (Brucker) BL48 100113

Accept, kind Father, bread and wine (Mary Francis, Sr.) BN206 100114

Accept this host, O God of Love (Brucker) BL47 100115

According to thy gracious word (Montgomery) B320; D233; E300; G410; H443; I234; J266; K191; L324; M49; N239; O151; P102: R444; S358; T363; U380; V557; W313; X259; Z456; AE 337; AF284; AG242; AI164; AK338; AL227; AM360; AO 438; AP360; AR510; AS466; AW305; AX176; AZ172; BV 367; BY306; BZ 100116

Ach bleib bei uns, Herr Jesu Christ (Selnecker) AY22d; BT292; BW557 100117

Ach bleib mit deiner Gnade (Stegmann) BT53; BW559 100118

Ach frölich will ich singen (Ausbund) BU25 100119

Ach Gott, ein manches herzeleid (Zions harfe) 1803 AY9d 100120

Ach Gott und Herr, Wie gross und schwer (Rutilius) BT317 100121

Ach Gott Vater im Höchsten Thron (H. Loch & L. Meister) BU40 100122

Ach Gott, verlass mich nicht (Franck) BT402 100123

Ach Gott! verleih mir dein Genad (Rogel) BU53 100124

Ach Gott vom Himmel, sieh darein (Luther) BT260 100125

Ach Gott vom Himmelreich (Ausbund) BU27 100126

Ach, wie gross ist deine Gnade (Olearius) BT384 100127

Across the sky the shades of night (Hamilton) D202; O206; Q110; AA164; BX181; BY710 100128

Ad Coenam Agni providi (Latin) BJ30b 100129
Ad regias Agni dapes (Latin, 4th c) BO288 100130
Ad te Rex summe (Latin) X Attende, Domine, et miserere 100131
Adam lay abounden Bounden in a bond (English trad carol, 15th c) BG180 100132
Adeste, fideles (Latin text) (Latin 18th c) Y298; AD120; AF133; AH123; AK112b; AN156; BM 64; BN10; BO150; BP12; BQ 158; BT102; BW80 100133
Adeste fideles (English text) (Latin, 18th c) X Come hither, ye faithful X O come, all ye faithful X Ye faithful, with gladness 100134
Adon olom a'sher molach (Jewish trad) AH154; BH276 100135
A'do-noy, A'do-noy, Ayl ra-chum (Jewish traditional) BH 313 100136
A-do-noy, mo o-dom va-tay-do-hu (Jewish traditional) BH334 100137
A'do-noy yim-loch l'o-lom vo-ed (Jewish traditional) BH294 100138
Adoramus te Christe, et Benedicimus tibi (Breviary) BQ190 100139
Adoramus te, panem coelitum (Latin) BQ232 100140
Adoro te devote (St Thomas Aquinas) BM30; BN88; BO32; BP48; BQ227 100141
Advent tells us Christ is near (Hankey) A235; B348; E586 100142
Afar on the mountain the Shepherd (Pratt) AX253 100143
Afar upon a foreign shore A martyr's crown (---) BQ107 100144
After thy loving kindness, Lord (Scottish Psalter, 1650) AL652; AP45; AW589 100145
Again as daylight fades and night draws near (Burgess) BD7 100146
Again, as evening's shadow falls (Longfellow) G42; I48; R62; W275; Z139; AB27; AF46; AL209; AN119; AO34; AP332; AQ271; AW280; AZ369; BA 777; BB56; BF199; BH11; BR126; BX138 100147
Again is come the new church-year (Olearius) AA140 100148
Again, O Lord and Saviour (Neumann) AK140 100149
Again, our dear redeeming Lord (Curtis) BC251 100150
Again our earthly cares we leave (Newton) BB25 X Great Shepherd of thy people, hear 100151
Again returns the day of holy rest (Mason) AO11; AW286; BB466; BR98 100152
Again the day returns of holy rest (Mason) BB466 X Again returns the day of holy rest 100153
Again the Lord's own day is here (St Thomas à Kempis??) F40; BV67 100154
Again the morn of gladness (Ellerton) B352; U440; V746; W237; AH163; AL193; AP802 100155
Again the slowly circling year (St Hilary) BN54; BO188 100156
Again thy glorious sun doth rise (Wallin) M561; N545 100157
Again we meet around the board (Snow) BC242 100158
"Against my second coming" (Wattles) Y266 100159
Ah, dearest Jesus, holy Child, make thee a bed (Luther) R173; S118; AD123; AF75; BV98 100160
Ah, dearest Jesus, holy Child (Luther) X From heaven high X Give heed, my heart 100161
Ah, dearest Jesus, how hast thou offended (Heermann) M413 X Ah holy Jesus... 100162

Ah, holy Jesus, how hast thou offended (Heermann) A71; B 155; E70; J85; K100; M413; N115; O300; P192; R191; S158; X99; AD147; AF163; AK147; AM179; AP201; AW 534; BJ42; BV151; BY137; BZ 100163

Ah, how shall fallen man (Watts) AZ1295 100164

Ah! Lord our God, let them not be confounded (Heermann) AA 280 100165

Ah! think not, the Lord delayeth (Dearmer) X59; AF112 100166

Ah, this heart is void and chill (Spitta) AZ861 100167

Ah, well it is that God should read (Aguilar) BH89 100168

Ah! what a sound! The infinite fierce chorus (Longfellow) Y251; AD360 100169

Ah! whither should I go (Wesley) H269; I283; AZ1288; BR290 100170

Aj, ten silný lev udatný (Bohemian. 1650) BT211 100171

Ajar the temple gates are swinging (Franzén) N402 100172

Al people yt on earth do dwel (Day's Psalter, 1560) Y296 100173

Al verden nu raabe for Herren med Fryd (Koren) BT44 100174

Alas! and did my Saviour bleed (Watts) G142; H170; I146; J486; K101; L242; M406; N 111; O318; P184; Q154; R199; S249; U101; V148; AA214; AE 112; AG95; AH285; AI74; AK 153; AL101; AM195; AO170; AR167; AS142; AT94, 101; AU112, 244; AV109; AW108; AX116, 311; AY249; AZ107; BA203; BB124; BZ 100175

Alas and did my Saviour bleed, with refrain: At the cross (Hudson) U97; AE289; AI74a; AS142; AT94; AU112; AX311 100176

Alas and did my Saviour bleed, with refrain: He loves me (---) AX116; AY249 100177

Alas! and did my Saviour bleed, with refrain: Help me, dear Saviour (Coffman) BB124 100178

Alas, my God! my sins are great (Rutilius) N411; O523; Q317; AA421 100179

Alas! what hourly dangers rise (Steele) V473 100180

All alone, and yet not lonely (Arnold) AZ253 100181

All are architects of fate (Longfellow) AN346; AQ175 100182

All as God wills, who wisely heeds (Whittier) G340; X438; Y132; AB209; BF405; BH88; BX279 100183

All beautiful the march of days (Wile) R96; S471; Y48; Z588; AB390; AC326; AD450; AF 456; AG56; AK429; AL580; AN131; AQ304; AR586; BB94; BD53; BF645; BK128; BX168; BZ 100184

All because we do not love them (Teasley) R Many souls today 100185

All bells in paradise (English trad carol) R Over yonder's a park X Down in yon forest 100186

All blessing, honor, thanks and praise (Speratus) N342 100187

All blessing, honor, thanks and praise (Speratus) X To us salvation now is come 100188

All creatures of our God and King (St Francis of Assisi) F172; G65; R100; W13; X439; Y307; Z157; AB47; AC45; AD 98; AE9; AF64; AG58; AH190; AK15; AL29; AN198; AQ23; AR19; AT3; BC4; BK51; BV 251; BY1; BZ 100189

All depends on our possessing (Nurnberg G-B., 1676) M280; Q425; AA363 100190

All' die ihr jetzund leidet (Ausbund) BU52 100191

All earth to Him her homage bring (U.P. Psalter, 1912) R The ends of all the earth shall hear 100192
All' Ehr' und Lob soll Gottes sein (Babst. Geistliche lieder. Leipzig, 1545) BT238 100193
All for Jesus! all for Jesus (James) AX403; AY108 100194
All glory be to God alone Babst. (Geistliche lieder 1545) M142; Q238 100195
All glory be to God most high (Decius) BX572 X All glory be to God on high 100196
All glory be to God most high, and on the earth be peace (Hay) BE9 100197
All glory be to God on high (Decius) J132; K160; M141; N300; O2; P1; Q237; AA261; AE15; AF2; AI28; AK2; AM92; AR13; AW521; AZ735; BA648; BX572 100198
All glory be to thee, most high (Decius) N300 X All glory be to God on high 100199
All glory be to thee, O Lord (---) BRp467 100200
All glory, laud, and honor (St Theodulph) A62; B143; D90; E622; F98, 597; G128; I31; J74; K86; L129; M428; P34; Q160; R187; S146; T322; U318; V157; W91; X135; Z221; AB 133; AC116; AD140; AE106; AF155; AG90; AH281; AK135; AL81; AM173; AO155; AP252; AR155; AS115; AT151; AV142; AW100; AZ849; BA206; BB15; BF309; BI102; BK134; BL25; BM47; BN32; BQ26; BR172; BV166; BY114; BZ 100201
All glory, praise and honor (St Theodulph) M428 X All glory, laud, and honor 100202
All glory to God, the Father and Son (---) Lp744 100203
All glory to the Sovereign Good (Schütz) AZ738; BA649 100204
All good gifts around us (Claudius) R We plow the fields 100205
All hail, adored Trinity (Latin, before 11th c) E633; F617; BV228 100206
All hail, all hail to the New (Lathbury) AC534 100207
All hail, dear Conqueror, all hail! (Faber) BP37 100208
All hail, our church's Elder dear (Montgomery) AZ878; BA795 100209
All hail our glorious Saviour (Seebach) R O Christians leagued together (Cassady) 100210
All hail the glorious day (Johnson) BC223 100211
All hail the glorious morn (Peacock) L266 100212
All hail the great Immanuel's name (Perronet) BI23 X All hail the power of Jesus' name 100213
All hail, the pageant of the years (Holmes) Z516; AD364; AN146; AQ205; BF491 100214
All hail the power of Jesus' name (Perronet) A355; B192; D450; E364; F217; G164; H192; I180; J426; K131; L114; M184; N153; O6; P7; Q339; R132; S192; T324; U116; V196; W139; X440; Y362; Z252; AA 93; AB87; AC135; AD180; AE 129; AF195; AG114; AH198; AK184; AL46; AM218; AN180; AO208; AP254; AR101; AS159; AT133; AU1; AV133; AW3; AX13; AY1; AZ162; BA90; BB156; BF327; BI23; BR53; BV265; BY180; BZ 100215
All hail, thou day of wondrous grace (Brueckner) M544 100216
All hail! to dear Mary (---) R 'Tis the month of our Mother 100217
All hail to the days that merit more praise (Durfey) BG5 100218
All hail to the Power who giveth men might (Dearmer) X441; Y388 100219
All hail to thee, O blessed morn (Wallin) J33; M361; N25

100220

All hail, ye little martyr flowers (Prudentius) E34 100221

All hail, ye little martyr flowers (Prudentius) X O martyrs young and fresh 100222

All hidden lie the future ways (Hosmer) AN440; AW299 100223

All his suffering ended (Havergal) R Golden harps are sounding 100224

All his work is ended (Havergal) R Golden harps are sounding 100225

All honor and praise, dominion and might (Santeuil) Y386 X Disposer Supreme and judge 100226

All is bright and cheerful round us (Neale) W609; AI378 100227

All is o'er: the pain and sorrow (Moultrie) AZ594 100228

All labor gained new dignity (Oxenham) A510; AK255 100229

All lands and peoples, all the earth (Brooke) W231 100230

All lands to God in joyful sounds [st. 3: All on the earth shall worship thee] (Scottish Psalter, 1650) AP56 100231

All lands to God, in joyful sounds [st. 3: Yea all the earth] (U. P. Psalter, 1912) T119; AJ173; AM381 100232

And let our bodies part, to different climes (Wesley) AY378 100233

All living souls shall bless thy name (Moise) BH55 100234

All mankind fell in Adam's fall (Spengler) Q369 100235

All men living are but mortal (Albinus) Q601 100236

All men on earth that live (U. P. Psalter, 1912) T454; AJ316 100237

All my heart this day rejoices (Gerhardt) M353 X All my heart this night rejoices 100238

All my heart this night rejoices (Gerhardt) A32; B545; D538; G91; J26; K22; M353; N35; O177; P130; Q77; R172; S125; W41; Y344; Z186; AA145; AB113; AC85; AD111; AF123; AG77; AH262; AI68; AK119; AL48; AM150; AN121; AR140; AW525; AZ875; BA169; BB110; BD224; BF280; BR552; BV92; BY88; BZ 100239

All my hope and consolation (St Bernard of Clairvaux) AZ910 100240

All my hope on God is founded (Neander) W448; X442; Z354; AF339; AN219; AQ35; BJ69; BY492 100241

All nations, clap your hands (U. P. Psalter, 1912) T88; AJ130 100242

All nations whom thou mad'st shall come (Scottish Psalter, 1650) AP71 100243

All nature's works His praise declare (Ware) G552; R23; S478; AD10; AE16; AK360; AN454; AR12; BX500; BZ 100244

All of seeing, all of hearing "M. J.", Father BN143 100245

All on the altar, dear Jesus (McKinney) AU83 100246

All people of the earth (McWhood) G508 100247

All people that dwell on the earth (U. P. Psalter, 1912) AJ269 100248

All people that on earth do dwell, Sing to the Lord (Kethe) A278; B249; D470; E365; F 166; G13; I16; Q14; R24; S1; T184; V3; W229; X443; Y296; AD4; AF4; AG7; AJ 268; AK24; AL669; AM1; AN496; AO10; AP86; AQ18; AR2; AS8; AT13; AU3; AW 594; AZ302; BA639; BB13; BDp. 2; BF174; BJ79; BK61; BL79; BV231; BX2; BY2; BZ 100249

All poor men and humble (Welsh trad. carol) BG34; BV94 100250
All power is given unto our Lord (Root) BE10 X A mighty fortress is our God (Luther) 100251
All praise and thanks to God (Rinkart) X406 X Now thank we all our God 100252
All praise be to God, Whom all things obey (Bridges) F566; BJ89 100253
All praise to God who reigns above (Schütz) K285 X Sing praise ... 100254
All praise to Him, who built the hills Bonar) D463 100255
All praise to Him who reigns a above (Clark) AX3; AY10 100256
All praise to Jesus' hallowed name (Latin, 11th c) AA147 100257
All praise to our redeeming Lord (Wesley) G417; I553; AL372; AW322; AX547; AY432; BZ 100258
All praise to St Patrick (Faber) AH140; BO135 100259
All praise to the Father, the Son, and Spirit (---) Lp743 100260
All praise to the Lamb! accepted I am (Wesley) AZ1422 100261
All praise to thee, eternal God (Luther) Q80 X All praise to thee, eternal Lord, clothed in a garb 100262
All praise to thee, eternal Lord, clothed in a garb (Luther) D320; J21; K18; L219; Q80; S119; AG78; AM155; BA50; BR553 100263
All praise to thee, for thou, O King divine (Tucker) A366; AF147; BV253; BY198; BZ 100264
All praise to thee, my God, this night (Ken) A165; B25; D18; E267; F23; G51; I49; J223; K471; L15; M568; N552; O560; Q558; R63; S42; U461; V45; W291; X45; Z148; AA 36; AB30; AD62; AE46; AG32; AI55; AK59; AL544; AM341; AO36; AP673; AQ270; AR49; AS31; AV19; AW33; AZ394; BA778; BB53; BF200; BJ55; BK35; BL72; BR117; BV64; BX131; BY694; BZ 100265
All praise to thee, O Lord (Beadon) O232 Glory to thee, O Lord, who by thy mighty power 100266
All praise to thee we bring (Klein) BH203 100267
All praise to thee, who safe hast kept (Ken) A152; W257; AL529b; AP653b 100268
All prophets hail thee, from of old announcing (St Rabanus Maurus) E208 100269
All-seeing Lord, whose power unknown (Bridges) BJ68 100270
All souls, O Lord, are thine (Sargent) AN431 100271
All that I am I owe to thee (U.P. Psalter, 1912) T276; AJ383; AM34 100272
All that I was, my sin, my guilt (Bonar) K304; L131; N442; O440; Q378; V376; AA308 100273
All that's good and great and true (Thring) AN481; BX 524; BY48 100274
All the bliss which we possess (Zinzendorf, N. L.) AZ1047; BA111 100275
All the gay gems of day (Denisot) BG101 100276
All the happy children, Gladly join our song (Dillingham) AL583; BD43 100277
All the past we leave behind (Whitman) X304; Y164; AB 308; AC211; AD491; AQ211 100278
All the scenes of nature quicken (Smart) X17 100279
All the toil and sorrow done (Stanley) X149; Z251 100280

All the way my Saviour leads me (Crosby) N464; R365; U211; V736; Z396; AE207; AG154; AH375; AI289; AL445; AM505; AP606; AR434; AS253; AT268; AU369; AV360; AX466; AZ965; BB259; BY537; BZ 100281

All the world give praises due (Held) AZ42; BA146 100282

All the world shall come to serve thee (Jewish) AH152; BH63 100283

All things are doubly fair (Gautier) AQ135 100284

All things are thine; no gift have we (Whittier) A227; B460; E173; G611; J244; R313; S475; U383; W254; X189; Z606; AB 328; AC310; AD413; AE349, 464; AF537; AG293; AK508; AL207; AN460; AP699; AR522; AS440; AT403; AU493; AX643; BA324; BB483; BV658; BX495; BZ 100285

All things bright and beautiful (Alexander) A311; B358; E587; F442; G447; K554; R456; W18; X444; AE429; AF478; AL582; AM636; AP725; AR93; AT8; AV400; AW410; BB421; BD39; BH252; BK10; BV233; BY733; BZ 100286

All things praise thee, Lord most high (Conder) BY3 100287

All things which live below the sky (Brailsford) X445;BY49 100288

All this night bright angels sing (Austin) BR555 X All this night shrill chanticleer 100289

All this night shrill chanticleer (Austin) BG123; BR555 100290

All those who love and obey my word (McPhail) AX585; AY 307 100291

All through the long bright days in June (Whittier) BH186 100292

All to Jesus I surrender (Van DeVenter) AT363; AU82; BB573 100293

All under the leaves, the leaves of my life (English trad carol) BG43 100294

All unseen the Master walketh (MacKellar) AP237 100295

All who with heart confiding (U. P. Psalter, 1912) T255; AJ355 100296

All-wise, All-great whose ancient plan (Dobson) BH218 100297

All ye a certain cure who seek (Latin, 18th c) S226 100298

All ye dwellers on earth, when the Shofar is sounded (Jewish traditional) BH317 100299

All ye Gentile lands, awake! (Rist) BR151 100300

All ye saints of light proclaim ("J. V. C." [Crosby?]) AX272 100301

All ye that fear God's holy name (U. P. Psalter, 1912) R35; T33; AJ48; AM6 100302

All ye that fear Jehovah's name (U. P. Psalter, 1912) T33 X All ye that fear God's holy name 100303

All ye that pass by, To Jesus draw nigh! (Wesley) L374; AZ1419; BY138 100304

All ye who grace inherit (---) Lp742 100305

All ye who like the birds can soar (Grundtvig) M636 100306

All ye who love the Lord draw near! (Tweedy) BF173 100307

All ye who on this earth do dwell (Gerhardt) Q581 100308

All ye who seek a comfort sure (Latin, 18th c) E71; F104; BJ5; BN70; BO18; BQ67; BV466 100309

All ye who seek for sure relief (Latin, 18th c) F104 X All ye who seek a comfort sure 100310

All you that are to mirth inclined (English carol, 17th c) BG51 100311

All you who seek a comfort sure (Latin, 18th c) BN70 X All ye who seek a comfort sure 100312

Alle Menschen müssen sterben (Albinus) BT601 100313

Allein Gott in der Höh' sei Ehr' (Decius) BT237; BW521 100314

Allein zu dir, Herr Jesu Christ (Schneesing) BT319 100315

Note: Alleluia has been taken as the approved spelling of this word (any language) for the purpose of the index. 100316

Alleluia! Alleluia! [etc] (Bible. Revelation) AU477 100317

Alleluia! Alleluia! Earth and heaven in sweet accord (U. P. Psalter, 1912) T456; AJ413 100318

Alleluia! Alleluia! He is coming again (Crosby) R He is coming, the "Man of Sorrows" 100319

Alleluia! Alleluia! Heart and voice to heaven raise (Wordsworth, C.) AT114 X Alleluia! Alleluia! Hearts and voices heavenward raise 100320

Alleluia! Alleluia! Hearts and voices heavenward raised (Wordsworth, C.) A92; B520; D123; E127; F137; G153; J108; K116; T345; U104; V757; W126; X150; AE126; AF180; AI87; AK174; AM204; AO186; AP219; AT114; AZ960; BA233; BV178 100321

Alleluia! Alleluia! Hearts to heaven and voices raise (Wordsworth, C.) T345 X Alleluia! Alleluia! Hearts and voices heavenward raise 100322

Alleluia! Alleluia! In His temple God be praised. (U. P. Psalter. 1912) T295; AJ409; AM9 100323

Alleluia! Alleluia! let the holy anthems rise (Caswall) AH127; BM98; BO173 100324

Alleluia, Alleluia. Praise the Lord with thanksgiving (Fyleman) R Lift your hidden faces 100325

Alleluia! alleluia! Shout aloud, ye sons of men (Greiner) M446 100326

Alleluia! Alleluia! Ye redeemed in thanks unite (Pados) BL33 100327

Alleluia! best and sweetest (Latin, 11th c) AZ1400 100328

Alleluia, Christus lebt! (Garve) BT188 100329

Alleluia! Fairest morning! Fairer than our words can Say (Krause) K439; L40; AK40 110330

Alleluia! Jesus lives! He is now the living one (Garve) O326; Q188 100331

Alleluia! Jesus lives! won the battle glorious! (Garve) J100 100332

Alleluia! Let praises ring (Darmstadt G-B., 1698) Q23 100333

Alleluia, lo He wakes (Schmolck) M449 100334

Alleluia! Lob, Preis und Ehr' (Darmstadt G-B., 1698) BT23 100335

Alleluia, praise Jehovah, From the heavens praise (U. P. Bible songs hymnal, 1927) AM 105 100336

Alleluia, praise Jehovah, O my soul, Jehovah praise (U. P. Psalter, 1912) T288; AJ400; AM53 100337

Alleluia! Praise the Savior, His the scepter (---) BI4-D 100338

Alleluia! Praise ye God (Westra) AJ430 100339

Alleluia! Raise, O raise To our God the song of praise (Conder) AM49; AP101 100340

Alleluia! sing to Jesus (Dix) A347; B193; D368; E301; F399; I176; J417; K127; W138; X260; AW124; BV383; BY168 100341

Alleluia, song of gladness

(Latin, 11th c) A54; B110; D73; E63; F82; J58; K57; AO183 100342

Alleluia, song of sweetness (Latin, 11th c) E63 X Alleluia, song of gladness 100343

Alleluia, sweetly singing (---) R Humble praises, holy Jesus 100344

Alleluia! Thine the glory; Alleluia! Amen! (Mackay) R We praise thee, O God, for the Son of thy love 100345

Alleluia 'tis done! I believe in the Son (Bliss) R 'Tis the promise 100346

Alleluia to Jesus, who died on the tree (English trad carol) R As Jacob with travel was weary 100347

Alleluia! What a Saviour! (Chapman) R Jesus! what a Friend for sinners 100348

Alleluia, what a Saviour! Who can take a poor lost sinner (Johnston) R There's a sweet and blessed story 100349

Alles ist an Gottes Segen (Nurnberg G-B., 1676) BT425 100350

Allez, mon voison, à la crèche (French trad carol) R Promptement levez-vous 100351

Alma, Alma, Alma, Redemptoris Mater (Hermannus Contractus) BO-298 X Alma Redemptoris Mater 100352

Alma Redemptoris Mater (Hermannus Contractus) BN140; BO298; BQ202 100353

Almighty Builder, bless we pray (Church) AE348; AN456; AR524; BX487 100354

Almighty Father, bless the word (Hart) D33; O56; Q52; V21; AS64; BA366 100355

Almighty Father, God of love Hear from thy throne (Hawkins) AB379 100356

Almighty Father, God of love Look down in mercy (Wiglesworth??) BH6 100357

Almighty Father, hear our cry (Bickersteth) D307 100358

Almighty Father, hear our prayer (--- American?) R542; AE462; AF502; AG331; AH 563; AR651; AT529; BF689 100359

Almighty Father, heaven and earth (Dayman) Q438; AA360; AI319; AR352; AS355 100360

Almighty Father, Lord most high (Coles) F405 100361

Almighty Father of all things that be (Dugmore) W503; BY626 100362

Almighty Father strong to save (Missionary service book 1937) A513; R522 100363

Almighty Father strong to save (Missionary service book, 1937) A513 X Eternal Father, strong to save (Whiting) 100364

Almighty Father, who dost give (Masterman) A530; F583; W 491; AK363; AL389; BY657 100365

Almighty Father, who for us thy Son didst give (Caird) BV591; BY639 100366

Almighty God, eternal Lord (Wallin) N167 100367

Almighty God, I call to thee (Luther) BR360 100368

Almighty God, I humbly ask (Kuhlmann) M258 100369

Almighty God, in humble prayer (Montgomery) AZ119; BA591; BH28; BX355 100370

Almighty God, thy lofty throne (U.P. Psalter, 1912) T89; AJ242; AM619 100371

Almighty God, thy word is cast (Cawood) J196; K432; L313; M20; N81; O261; Q49; V24; W295; AA13; AM317; AO239; AZ163; BV135 100372

Almighty God, thy word is sown (Cawood) M20 X Almighty God, thy word is cast 100373

Almighty God, who from the flood (Latin, 6th or 7th c) E61 100374

Almighty God, who hearest prayer (Lucas) BH53 100375
Almighty God, whose only Son (Baker) D499; AY456 100376
Almighty Lord, before thy throne (Steele) Q579; AA303 100377
Almighty Lord of earth and heaven (Denicke) M58 100378
Almighty Lord, whose sovereign right (Hasse) BA337 100379
Almighty Lord, with one accord (Stryker) G558; I687; U328; Y137; AE373; AI368; AK450; AO488; AR537; AS392; AW390; BF632 100380
Almighty Sovereign of the skies, to thee let songs of gladness rise (Watts or Strong??) AR593; AS427 100381
"Almost persuaded" now to believe (Bliss) P251,256; U154; AH341; AI191; AT248; AU169; AV335; AX263; AY506; BB228 100382
Aloft in yonder belfry (Brueckner) M517 100383
Alone thou goest forth, O Lord (Abelard) A68; AF159; BV169; By139; BZ 100384
Alone to God on high be praise (Decius) BR153 100385
Alone with God, the world forbidden (Oatman) R When storms of life 100386
Alone with thee, my God, in prayer (Aufranc) BB335 100387
Alone with thee, O Lord, when day is dead (Urseth) P332 100388
Along my earthly way (Edmeston) AZ1337 100389
Als Christus mit sein'r wahren Lehr (M.Sattlers) BU7 100390
Als man zählt tausend fünf hundert Jahr (H Buchel) BU29 100391
Also hat Gott die Welt geliebt (German. 1791) BT245 100392
Also redt der wahrhaftig Gott (Ausbund Psalm 50) BU128 100393
Altissimo, omnipotente, bon Signore (St Francis of Assisi) Y307 110394
Always with us, always with us (Nevin) L430; AI186; AO367; AW256 100395
Am I a soldier of the cross (Watts) A550; B488; D508; G 284; H381; I393; J554; L539; M247; N454; O490; Q445; R353; U307; V475; AA378; AE260; AH295; AI322; AM481; AO405; AR313; AS329; AT405; AU176,395*; AV213; AX425; AY122,*354*; AZ189; BA451; BB356; BZ
*with refrain 100396
Am I a soldier of the cross (Watts) refrain: In His name I'll bear the cross (---) AY354 100397
Am I a soldier of the cross (Watts) refrain: "And when the battles over" (Watts) AU395; AY122 100398
Amazing grace! how sweet the sound (Newton) G209; H288; I309; L125; R275; U143; V244; AE231; AG179; AH335; AI136; AM402; AR433; AT188; AU161; AV181; AW463; AX 322; BA423; BB295; BZ 100399
Ambrosius Klärich beschrieb (Ausbund) BU9 100400
America, America. The shouts of war shall cease (Cross) AO660; BD127; BF546 100401
America, awake! Behold the glory of the morning star (Wilson) BD178 100402
America triumphant! Brave land of pioneers (Holmes) Y280; AN372; BD176; BF547 100403
Amid the din of earthly strife (Hawkes) BX230 100404
Amid the thronging worshipers (U.P. Psalter, 1912) AJ51 100405
Amid the trials which I meet (Mund) AI288; AS311; AX488; AY88 100406
Amid the world's deceitful cares (Gothus) O391 100407

Among His people, God is known (U.P. Psalter. 1912) AJ208 100408
An alien from God and a stranger to grace (Cox) H811 100409
An angel from on high (Pratt) BC224 100410
An awe-full mystery is here (Loy) Q304; AA437 100411
An endless line of splendor (Lindsay) Z534; AD370; BF523 100412
An image of that heavenly light (Latin, 15th c) E233 100413
An Wasserflüssen Babylon (Dachstein) BT142; BW533 100414
Ancient of Days, who sittest throned in glory (Doane) A274; B519; D311; G59; I76; J137; M481; O74; R246; S58; U4; V84; Y26; Z99; AB16; AC34; AD67; AF249; AG46; AH191; AK197; AO235; AR14; AS72; AV27; BB680; BD28; BF210; BZ 100415
And am I born to die (Wesley) I590 100416
And are we yet alive (Wesley) H428 X And are we yet to live 100417
And are we yet to live (Wesley) G402; H428; I560; AX641; AY 377; BZ 100418
And art thou come with us to dwell (Greenwell) S134 100419
And art thou with us, gracious Lord (Doddridge) L514 100420
And can I yet delay (Wesley) H267; I275 100421
And can it be that I should gain (Wesley) G229; I310; W110; AL276; BV496; BY426; BZ 100422
And did those feet in ancient time (Blake) E72app.; F578; W640; X446; Y162; AC269; AL522 100423
And didst thou, Jesus, condescend ("Am-a" 1769) L403 100424
And didst thou love the race that loved not thee? (Ingelow) S330; X447; AL126; BY140 100425
And dost thou say, "Ask what thou wilt?" (Newton) AZ333 X Lord, dost thou say, "Ask" 100426
And have the bright immensities (Robbins) A354; AD171;BZ 100427
And he walks with me (Miles) R I come to the garden 100428
And I couldn't hear nobody pray (Negro spiritual) AH607 100429
And I? Is there some desert or some pathless sea (Hale) AC497 100430
And I shall see Him face to face (Crosby) R Some day the silver cord will break 100431
And is it so? "A little while," and then the life undying. (Songs of Zion, 1864) V659 100432
And is it true as I am told (Hull) AZ630 100433
And is the time approaching (Borthwick) AZ818 X Hasten the time appointed 100434
And it holds, my anchor holds (Martin) R Though the angry surges roll 100435
And let our bodies part (Wesley) G403; I227 100436
And let this feeble body frail (Wesley) I607; AA521; AY182 100437
And must I be to judgment brought (Wesley) H491; I600; AW501 100438
And must this body die (Watts) AA533 100439
And now another day is gone (Watts) F36; AX71; AY292; AZ88; BA902 100440
And now, beloved Lord, thy soul resigning (Alderson) E119; F123; W103; AZ1219 100441
And now may the courage of the early morning's dawning (---) AR677 100442
And now, my soul, another year (Browne) I570; AX629; AY246

100443

And now, O Father, mindful of the love (Bright) A189; B333; D228; E302; F397; J278; S355; W320; X261; AD402; AF292; AH222; AK340; BY307 100444

And now the sun hath sunk to rest (---) M574 100445

And now the wants are told that brought (Bright) A488; F32; W296; X41; AP335 100446

And now this holy day (Harland) AZ480 100447

And now to God the Father, God the Son (---) Lp744 100448

And now we must bid one another farewell (Clausen) O51; P63 100449

And shall we still be slaves (Doddridge & Watts) L255 100450

And take me as I am (Hamilton) R O Jesus Lord, to thee I pray 100451

And that will be glory for me (Bliss) R I know not the hour 100452

And then the Savior turned (Petursson) M410 100453

And whate'er the need may be (Ward) AHp27 100454

And when the battle's over we shall wear a crown (---) R Am I a soldier of the cross (Watts) 100455

And will the great eternal God (Doddridge) H410; I663 100456

And will the Judge descend (Doddridge) M322; Q610; AA554; AZ1289; BA737 100457

And wilt thou pardon Lord, A sinner such as I (St Joseph the Hymnographer) K323; M71; Q322; AA422 100458

Angel of peace, thou hast wandered too long (Holmes) BD184 100459

Angel, roll the rock away (Scott) M433 X Angels, roll the rock away 100460

Angel voices, ever singing (Pott) B461; D304; F246; G15; H7; I27; J240; K240; N584; R30; S455; U15; V87; W252; Y203; Z101; AC228; AD18; AE12; AG297; AH203; AI21; AK457; AL202; AM8; AO6; AP320; AR15; AV46; BA641; BB19; BF218; BV234; BY4; BZ 100461

Angel voices, sweetly singing (Bonar) BB556 100462

Angels and ministers, spirits of grace (Dearmer) A122; X238 100463

Angels at the Saviour's birth (Campbell) BE11 100464

Angels, from the realms of glory (Montgomery) A28; B80; D60; F64; G87; H140; I113; J31; K27; L221; M375; N26; O192; P127; Q136; R168; S124; T335; U49; V122; W65; X71; Z192; AA187; AC88; AD106; AE91; AF117; AG71; AH246; AI58; AK104; AL64; AM164; AO128; AP179; AR139; AS108; AT76; AU145; AV91; AW81; AX102; AY242; AZ1386; BA164; BB 113; BD228; BF285; BG119; BI534; BK147; BR159; BV93; BY89; BZ 110465

Angels, holy, high and lowly (Blackie) K280; S76; X448; AB55; AD96; AF73; BG160; BX67; BY5 100466

Angels of Jesus, angels of light (Faber) R Hark, hark my soul! angelic songs 100467

Angels of mercy, angels of light (Faber) BI74 X Hark, hark my soul! angelic songs 100468

Angels roll the rock away (Scott) B177; D116; H187; M433; AH303; AI86; AO179; BI105; BR181 100469

Angels sing his triumph as you sang his birth (Brooks) R God hath sent his angels 100470

Angels we have heard on high (French trad carol) A42; J30; R158; Z187; AD117; AE89; AF116; AH256; AK105; AN 175; AQ294; AR138; AT64;

AW82; BD227; BK143; BL9; BM65; BN12; BO154; BP16; BQ7 100471

Angels, where'er we go, attend (Wesley) AZ223 100472

Angelus ad virginem, Subintrans in conclave (Latin carol, 14th c) BG52 100473

Angularis fundamentum lapis Christus missus est (Latin, 7th c.) BT466; BW277 100474

Another day has passed away (Schuette) M565 100475

Another day is at an end (Klantendorfer) AZ400 100476

Another day is at its close (Herzog) N557 100477

Another day is dawning (Havergal) AU275 X Another year is dawning 100478

Another day is past and gone (Coffin) AZ1459 100479

Another day its course hath run (Pierpont) BX527 100480

Another six days' work is done (Stennett) H73; I70; L41; V60; BB456 100481

Another year completed (St Paulinus of Nola) E195 100482

Another year is dawning (Havergal) E285; G534; I571; U476; Z587; AE421; AG291; AH497; AI348; AK424; AN144; AO574; AR580; AS432; AT497; AU275; AV311; AW380; AX631; BD232; BF642; BK130; BX183 100483

Another year of setting suns (Chadwick) AC328; AN132; AR581; AS435; AW381; BD234 100484

Anxious heart, be rid of sadness (Brorson) P168 100485

Anywhere, dear Saviour, In thy vineyard wide (Ogden) BB344 100486

Anywhere with Jesus I can safely go (Pounds & Alexander) AI399; AM680; AS271; AX470; BB589 100487

Approach, my soul, the mercy-seat (Newton) B303; D652; F345; H48; I285; J369; K321; L410; N408; O442; Q456; R386; S10 app; U367; V461; W451; AA399; AL310; AM423; AO311; AP 490; AZ164; BA410; BV1; BY332 100488

Are thy toils and woes increasing (St Methodius II) AZ431 100489

Are ye able, asked the Master (Marlatt) Y174 X "Are ye able," said the Master 100490

"Are ye able," said the Master (Marlatt) G268; Y174; Z360; AC205; AE443; AG189; AR 311; AT351; AU396; AW392; BZ 100491

Are you adorning the doctrine (Naylor) AX158 100492

Are you formed a creature new (Zinzendorf, N. L.) AZ1062 100493

Are you ready? Are you ready? (Thompson) R There's a great day 100494

Are you tired of the life you're now living (Keegan) AU357 100495

Are you washed in the blood (Hoffman) R Have you been to Jesus 100496

Are you weary, are you heavy-hearted (Rankin) AU110; AW 476 100497

Are you weary, heavy laden (---) AX223; AY226 100498

Arglwydd, arwain trwy'r anialwch (W. Williams) BT 54; BW160 100499

Arise, all souls, arise The watch is past (Lathbury) BR186 100500

Arise and be baptized (Bickersteth) N229 100501

Arise and shine in splendor (Opitz) Q126 100502

Arise, arise and shine, On thee hath dawned (Mesechre) BE14 100503

Arise, arise, the Master calls for thee (Merrill) AT423 X Arise, O youth of Christ 100504

Arise, arise, united youth (Solberg) P371 100505

Arise, arise, ye Christians

(Rist) M329 X Arise, the kingdom is at hand 100506

Arise, my soul, arise, And with a cheerful voice (Wesley??) BR200 100507

Arise, my soul, arise, Shake off thy guilty fears (Wesley) G211; H301; I301; K138; L249; M172; N145; O357; V178; AA 240; AH365; AM223; AO344; AS205; AX112; AY263; BA91; BC227; BZ 100508

Arise, my soul, arise! Stretch forth to things eternal (Kahl) J180 100509

Arise, my soul, new light receiving (Achrenius) M309 100510

Arise my Spirit, bless the day (Rist) AZ985 100511

Arise, O Christian soldiers (---) AO474 100512

Arise, O glorious Sion (Mills) BC225 100513

Arise, O God, and shine (Hurn) O124 X Arise, O Lord, and shine 100514

Arise, O King of grace, arise (Watts) H407; V65; AO426; AZ132 100515

Arise, O Lord, and shine (Hurn) D259; N70; O124; Q642; AI169; AM386 100516

Arise, O Lord, exalt thy grace (Zinzendorf, N. L.) BA338 X In these our days exalt thy grace 100517

Arise, O Lord, our God, arise (U. P. Psalter. 1912.) R518; T264; AJ368; AM100 100518

Arise, O youth of God [with refrain] (Merrill) AT423 X Rise up, O men of God 100519

Arise, sons of the Kingdom (Rist) Q69 X Arise, the Kingdom is at hand 100520

Arise, the Kingdom is at hand (Rist) K15; L213; M329; Q69; AA142; AE75; AK93 100521

Arise to praise the Lord (Hamburg Temple hymnal) BH74 100522

Arise ye people, take your stand (Hay) BE12 100523

Arm of the Lord, awake! awake! (Shrubsole) B487; D 265; I216; R497; V591; W369; AM372; AP393 100524

Arm these thy soldiers mighty Lord (Wordsworth, C) Q332; AA410; AZ930; BX369 100525

Around my path life's mysteries (Greg) BX254 100526

Around the throne of God, a band (Neale) A120; B291; E243; F448; Q256; X239; BA 37; BV452 100527

Around the throne of God in heaven (Shepherd) K553; L583; N653; P362; S450; U326; V 653; W600; AH550; AL615; AM648; AP790; AW405; AZ169; BA818; BY608 100528

Around the throne of God, The host angelic throngs (Ware) V110 100529

Around the weary world are gently drawn (Levy) BH17 100530

Art thou weary, art thou laden [troubled; languid] (Neale) from St Stephen of Mar Saba A406; B386; D342; E366; F 348; G193; H257; I293; J517; K72; L357; Q513; R264; S221; U152; V267: W391; Z286; AB154; AC151; AD208; AE167; AG140; AK302; AL471; AM 389; AO249; AP401; AR302; AT245; AU426; AV157; AW143; AY446; AZ1140; BA477; BB 341; BF347; BR396-397; BV 467; BY409; BZ 100531

Art thou weary, heavy laden (Neale) S221 X Art thou weary, art thou laden 100532

As above the darkest storm-cloud (Howard) BR271 100533

As after the waterbrooks panteth (Grundtvig) O453; P250 100534

As birds unto the genial homeland fly (Levy) BH113 100535

As by one's sin fell all our kin (Cronenwett) M135 100536

As comes the breath of spring (Ritchie) AB96; AC65; AL151 100537
As darker, darker fall around (Longfellow, S. ??) W276; AL 564; AP669; BX141; BY687 100538
As each happy Christmas (Hey) K539; N634 100539
As every day thy mercy spares (Shrubsole) AZ675 100540
As fades the daylight splendor (Kockritz) AK52 100541
As fades the glowing orb of day (St Ambrose) BQ139 100542
As God doth lead me I will go (Gedicke) O216 100543
As gold by fire is tested (Ingemann) BE15 100544
As He heard His waiting people (McKinney) AU305 100545
As helpless as a child who clings BR526 100546
As I dream of a city I have not seen (Tuttle) R I think of a city I have not seen 100547
As I passed by a riverside (English trad carol) BG53 100548
As I sat on a sunny bank (English trad carol) BG3 100549
As it fell out one May morning (English trad carol) BG56 100550
As it fell out upon one day, Rich Dives made a feast (English trad carol) BG57 100551
As Jacob with travel was weary one day (English trad carol) BG58 100552
As Joseph was a-walking (English trad carol) BG66b X Joseph was an old man 100553
As light, O Christ, thou cam'st to earth (Russian) AL303 100554
As long as Jesus Lord remains (Zinzendorf, N. L.) AZ285; BA 272 100555
As men of old their first fruits brought (Frank v. Christierson) BZ 100556
As now the sun's declining rays (Coffin) B30; E265; F29; S 510; W274; BR534 100557
As oft with worn and weary feet (Edmeston) L234; V139; AZ669; BA75 100558
As, panting in the sultry beam (Bowdler) BR287 100559
As pants the hart for cooling streams (Tate & Brady) A450; E367; F314; G366; H332; I316; J388; K257; Q 525; R322; S317; T78; V401; X449; AD283; AE205; AF390; AG178; AJ116; AL649; AM 554; AN20; AO302; AP37; AS209; AW586; AY416; AZ 208; BA517; BH30; BR358; BT525; BV516; BX234; BY 571; BZ 100560
As pants the hart for streams of living water (U.P. Psalter, 1912) T77; AJ115 100561
As pants the wearied hart for cooling springs (Lowth) B313; D661; F314; BR102 100562
As pilgrims and strangers we journey through life (Orr) AX583 100563
As sings the mountains stream (Seymer) BE16 100564
As sinks beneath the ocean (Skavlan) P422 100565
As Sion's pilgrims in accord (Rivers) AY157 100566
As stars come with the night (Cross) AB309 100567
As swiftly my days go out on the wing (---) BC5 100568
As the angels sang, we sing (---) R Clear upon the night-air sounding 100569
As the dawn was calmly breaking (Buzzard) AY492 100570
As the dew from heaven distilling (Pratt) BC232 100571
As the disciples, when the Son had left them (Dearmer) X262 100572
As the hart when noon is burning (Collier) AI415 100573
As the hart with eager yearning

(Curtis) AK234 100574
As the rose shall blossom here (Grundtvig) M602 100575
As the storm retreating, Leaves the vales in peace (Williams) AN430; BD108; BX145 100576
As the sun doth daily rise (Latin) R42; S25; Z114; AF33; AM329; AO22; AR41; AX62; AY284; BD3 100577
As the sunflower turns in the morning (Overby) P54 100578
As the sun's enlivening eye (Newton) BX512 100579
As thirsts the hart for cooling flood (U. P. Psalter. 1912) AJ118 100580
As thirsts the hart for water-brooks (U. P. Psalter, 1912) AJ114 100581
As thou, O Lord, hast made me strong (U. P. Psalter. 1912) T27; AJ36 100582
"As thy day, thy strength shall be!" (Havergal) AZ45; BA855 100583
As torrents in summer, Half-dried in their channels (Longfellow) Y15; AB305 100584
As tranquil streams that meet and merge (Ham) AN406; AQ253 100585
As Victor in the Strife (Lee) BN45 100586
As we begin another week (Wandersleben) Q7 100587
As we leave this friendly place (Silliman) BK7 100588
As we rode down the steep hill-side (Kendon) BG146 100589
As when, in far Samaria (Hodges) A187 100590
As when the Hebrew prophet raised (Watts) AM422 AP207 100591
As when the weary traveller gains (Newton) D677; BR342 100592
As wide as the skies is thy mercy, O God! (Ingemann) M147; P292 100593
As with gladness men of old (Dix) A52; B94; D65; E39; F 79; G90; H148; J52; K38; L226; M374; N60; O219; Q127; R174; S135; T336; V 113; W63; X83; Z196; AA183; AB120; AC95; AD125; AE90; AF119; AG79; AH271; AK123; AL50; AM154; AN153; AO119; AP177; AR145; AS111; AT68; AV88; AW530; AZ1259; BA 181; BB112; BD219; BF282; BR156; BV126; BY90; BZ 100594
As you are, just as you are (Hoffman) R Shall I come 100595
Ascend, dear Lord! Thy earthly toil is done (Hoppe) N152 100596
Ascend thy throne almighty Lord (Beddome) V593 100597
Ashamed of thee, O dearest Lord (How) D598 100598
Ask the Saviour to help you (Palmer) R Yield not to temptation 100599
Ask ye what great thing I know (Schwedler) G147; R371; S312; AD149; AE288; AG180; AK 239; AO172; AR331; AT161; AV129; AZ1157; BZ 100600
Asleep in Jesus! blessed sleep (Mackay) B413; D244; H487; I583; K507; L568; M293; N 598; O593; P419; Q587; U 420; V672; AA540; AH538; AO565; AP621; AS484; AU165; AV299; AW314; AX621; AY179; AZ411; BA719; BB489 100601
Assist thy servant, Lord (---) AY37 100602
At all times praise the Lord (Howson) T298; AD271 100603
At Cana, Lord, thou didst appear (Berridge) M261 100604
At eve, when now be breathed no more (Darbyshire) X142 100605
At even, ere the sun was set (Twells) D14 X At even, when the sun was set 100606
At even when the sun was set (Twells) A168; B399; D14;

E266; F20; G48; I54; J232; K233; Q557; R55; S43; U468; W277; X42; AB132; AD135; AE99; AF55; AG24; AK57; AG 24; AK57; AL541; AM336; AP 676; AR149; AV100; AW37; BA779; BF205; BR170; BV49; BY688; BZ 100607

At evening time let there be light (Montgomery) AO39; AZ663 100608

At first I prayed for Light (Cheney) AN275; BB328 100609

At God's right hand in countless numbers (Montgomery, I.) AZ997 100610

At home and abroad on life's battlefields (Smith) AY327 100611

At Jesus' feet our infant sweet (Loy) M38 100612

At last he's blest who by the Savious's blood (Bernstein) AZ464 100613

At length there dawns the glorious day (David) G469; U335; Y256; Z511; AB269; AC286; AD343; AE405; AG251; AK400; AN356; AR371; BD124; BF497; BZ 100614

At midnight, so the sages tell (Isaacs) BH175 100615

At our life's last moment fleeting (Benedictine, "Ultima") BN191 100616

At that first Eucharist before you died (Turton) BM11 100617

At the cross, at the cross, Where I first saw the light (Hudson) U97 X Alas! and did my Saviour bleed (Watts) 100618

At the cross her station keeping (Jacopone) A76; B161; D103; E115; F118; G138; I154; J84; N104; O320; W99; AD151; AH 113; AK150; AL95; AP197; AZ643; BA211; BJ1a, 44; BL 21; BN34; BP25; BQ23 100619

At the cross her station keeping (Jacopone) X138 X In the place of sorrow, waiting (Dearmer) 100620

At the golden gate, we will come (Shacklock) R Would you know the love 100621

At the Lamb's high feast we sing (Latin, 4th c) A89; B 178; D118; E128; F139; H435; J95; AM365; AZ1061; BL28; BM2 100622

At the name of Jesus (Noel) A356; B528; D518; E368; F 225; J430; R143; T321; U121; V200; W178; X392; AF197; AI99; AL113; AM124; AP259; BA110; BV254; BY199;BZ 100623

At thy command, our dearest Lord (Isaacs) V547; AA440 100624

At thy feet, At thy pierced feet I lie (Holmes) AZ717 100625

At thy feet, O Christ, we lay (Bright) E256; F6; J203; W 265; X24; BV46; BY671 100626

At thy feet, our God and Father (Burns) G37; U473; W605; Z137; AH195; AI347; AK423; AM610; AP696; AR4; BA176; BF219; BR72; BY711; BZ 100627

At thy table, Lord of life (---) BR468 100628

At work beside his father's bench (Pullen) BK16 100629

Attend, O Saviour, to our prayer (Gambold) AZ281 100630

Attende, Domine, et miserere (Latin) BM73; BN29; BQ297 100631

Audi, benigne Conditor (St Gregory the Great) BN27; BO286 100632

Audi, Deus me vocantem (Lobwasser. Psalter, 1617) BJ 92 notes 100633

Auf, auf, ihr Reichsgenossen (Rist) BT69 100634

Auf, auf, mein Herz, mit Freuden (Gerhardt) BT192 100635

Auf Christi Himmelfahrt allein (Wegelin) BT216 100636

Auf, ihr Christen, Christi Glieder (Falckner) BT472 100637
Auf meinen lieben Gott (Weingartner) BT526 100638
Auf, Sele, auf und fäume nich! (Unparth, G.B.) AY23d 100639
Aurinko armas vallolansa (Finnish, 1836) BT545 100640
Aus dem Himmel ferne, Wo die Englein sind (W. Hey) BW433 100641
Aus Gnaden soll ich selig werden! (Scheidt) BT373 100642
Aus Gnaden wird der Mensch gerecht (Unparth, G.B.) AY43d 100643
Aus meines Herzens Grunde (Nigidius) BT548 100644
Aus tiefer Not schrei' ich zu dir (Luther) BT329; BW531 100645
Aus tiefer Noth schrey ich zu dir, Ach Gott erhör mein Rufen Dein Heil'gen Geist fend du zu mir (Ausbund. Seven Brothers) BU61 100646
Auspicious morning, hail (Smith) AZ1231 100647
Author of faith, eternal Word (Wesley) I298; AL275; BC228; BZ 100648
Author of faith, to thee I cry (Wesley) O390 100649
Author of life divine (Wesley) E303; F394; J268; W317; X263; AL226; AW309; BX484; BZ 100650
Author of the whole creation (Rist) AZ907; BA781 100651
Ave, ave verum corpus natum (Innocent VI, Pope) BQ233
X Ave verum corpus natum 100652
Ave Maria! blessed maid (Keble) E216 100653
Ave Maria gratia plena (Latin, 13th c) BP72; BQ200 100654
Ave Maria! O Virgin and Mother (St Patrick's hymnal) BQ74
X Ave Maria! Thou Virgin and Mother 100655
Ave Maria! Thou Virgin and Mother (St Patrick's hymnal) BP77; BQ74 100656
Ave, maris stella, Dei Mater (Latin, 9th c) BN127; BO263; BQ201 100657
Ave, Regina Caelorum (Latin, 12th c) BN141; BO299; BQ203 100658
Ave, Regina sacratissimi (Litany of Loreto) BN156 100659
Ave, Tu Rex Pacis Nobiscum esto (Donnelly) BP107 100660
Ave verum corpus natum (Innocent VI, Pope) BN85; BO36; BP50; BQ233 100661
Awake, and sing the song (Hammond) B261; D369; H3; L121; V193; AP257; AZ1298; BA108; BV255 100662
Awake, arise! lift up thy voice (Smart) X151 100663
Awake, awake, awake. Put on thy strength (Bible. Isaiah 52.) AU473 100664
Awake, awake good people all (English trad carol) BG47 100665
Awake, awake, O earth (Fleming) AX120; AY347 100666
Awake, awake, O Sion! Put on thy strength Divine (Gough) BR210 100667
Awake, awake to love and work (Studdert-Kennedy) A156; G455; X450; Z323; AD273; AF34; AR 369; BF392; BZ 100668
Awake, awake, ye drowsy souls (English trad carol) BG44 100669
Awake, Jerusalem, awake! (Wesley) H417; I217; BB293 100670
Awake, my heart, and marvel at nature's beauty (Gerhardt) M635 100671
Awake, my heart, and render (Gerhardt) A149 100672
Awake, my heart, with gladness (Gerhardt) Q192; AA218 100673
Awake, my soul, and with the sun (Ken) A151; B2; D2; E257; F3; G34; H26; I44; J 202; K449; L10; M552; N546;

O539; Q536; R50; V33; W256; X25; AA29; AD37; AE37; AF 32; AI45; AL529; AM331; AN 93; AP653; AQ265; AS24; AV3; AW25; AZ356; BA765; BB44; BF178; BJ9,25; BR4; BV34; 37; BX129; BY672; BZ 100674

Awake, my soul, in joyful lays (Medley) H284; I539; L163; O432; Q340; U148; V190; AA92; AI2; AM138; AO404; AP265; AS15; AT26; AV11; AX17; Ay 28; AZ293; BA478; BB667 100675

Awake, my soul, stretch every nerve (Doddridge) A577; B111; D503; G359; H385; I396; J552; K380; L535; N506; R346; S278; U291; V493; Y165; Z369; AB 241; AC195; AD302; AF362; AG197; AH436; AI321; AK285; AM480; AN298; AO401; AQ222; AR316; AS325; AT309; AU253; AV201; AZ193; BA450; BB355; BD90; BF468; BX364; BZ 100676

Awake my soul to joyful lays (Medley) Q340 X Awake my soul in joyful lays 100677

Awake, my soul, to sound His praise (Watts) V525 100678

Awake, my tongue, thy tribute bring (Needham) Z152; AT24 100679

Awake, O Church of God, the night is past (Tiplady) AR492 100680

Awake, O Lord, as in the time of old! (Twells) BY222 100681

Awake! O ye people, the Saviour is coming (Phelps) BC183 100682

Awake, our souls! Away, our fears! (Watts) I405; V480; X451; AL413; AN103; AW258; BV570; BX134; BY572 100683

Awake! The watchman crieth (Franzén) N395 100684

Awake, thou Spirit bold and daring (Bogatzky) M112 100685

Awake, thou Spirit of the watchmen (Bogatzky) A255; J255 100686

Awake, thou Spirit, who didst fire the watchmen (Bogatzky) K213; L305; N380; O116; Q 494; AA481 100687

Awake thou that sleepest, arise from death's slumber (Landstad) O159] 100688

Awake were they only those shepherds so lonely (Roberts) BG59 100689

Awake, ye saints, and raise your eyes (Doddridge) BB 175 100690

Awake, ye saints, awake (Scott) H186; L48 100691

Awake, ye saints of God, awake (Snow) BC229 100692

Awaked by Sinai's awful sound (Occum) V305 100693

Awaked from sleep we fall before (Greek) F9 100694

Away in a manger, no crib for his bed (American carol) A43; G434; K536; N637; P363; R157; S126; W657; X353; Z 199; AD116; AE435; AF137; AG76; AH265; AK109; AL598; AM641; AO630; AP729; AR 137; AS107; AT77; AU314; AV 92; AW414; AY482; BK153; BV95; BY734; BZ 100695

Away, my needless fears (Wesley) H123 100696

Away, O soul, hoist up the anchor now (Whitman) AQ78 100697

Away with gloom, away with doubt (Shillito) G158; BY181 100698

Away with our fears, Our troubles and tears (Wesley) BV213; BY223 100699

Awhile in spirit, Lord to thee (Thrupp) D80; K79 100700

Ayn Kay-lo-hay-nu (Jewish liturgical) BH275 100701

Ayn ko-mo-cho bo-e-lo-heem (Jewish Traditional) BH304 100702

Ay-yukh-nyehm (Russian trad) Y313 100703

B

Back of the loaf is the snowy flour (Babcock) AC532 100704

Back to the cross I go again (Becker) M186 100705

Backward looking o'er the past (Chadwick) BD235 100706

Backward we look, O God of all our days (Freeman) AB397; AC233; BF653 100707

Baptize us anew, with power from on high (Ogden) BB525 100708

Baptized into our Saviour's death (Doddridge) AX165 100709

Baptized into thy name most holy (Rambach) M539; N59; Q298; AA400 100710

Baptized into thy name most holy (Rambach) M539 X I am baptized into thy name 100711

Be firm and be faithful (---) BE18 100712

Be firm, ye sentinels of Truth (Sargant) BE17 100713

Be joyful in God, all ye lands of the earth (Montgomery) L74; BA368 100714

Be joyful, Mary, heavenly Queen (Latin, 17th c) BM85; BN49 100715

Be known to us in breaking bread (Montgomery) G408 X Shepherd of souls refresh and bless 100716

Be like Jesus, this my song (Rowe) R Earthly pleasures vainly call me 100717

Be, Lord, the happy guide (Dearmer) X407 100718

Be merciful, O God of grace (Conder) AY63 100719

Be merciful to me, O God (Scottish Psalter, 1650) AP47 100720

Be not dismayed, thou little flock (Altenberg) K196; N263; O85 100721

Be not dismayed whate'er betide (Martin) R124; AH381; AM696; AT274; AV366; AX480; BZ 100722

Be of good cheer, the Master said (Marlatt) Y195; AC193 100723

Be our Comfort which ne'er faileth (Gregor) AZ1109 100724

Be present at our table, Lord (Cennick) G563; W656; AR 551; AS464; AT396; AX650; AZ308; BA895; BZ 100725

Be present, Holy Trinity (Latin, ca 10th c) E159 100726

Be present with thy servants, Lord (Zinzendorf, N. L.) AZ323; BA534 100727

Be ready, Be ready, Be ready (Teasley) R Would you flee 100728

Be silent, be silent, A whisper is heard (Crosby) AR437; AS43; AU485; AX39; AY448; BB601 100729

Be still my heart, these anxious cares (Newton) AZ421; BA 706; BV497 100730

Be still, my soul, for God is near (Maclagan) J267; K181; BA292 100731

Be still, my soul: the Lord is on thy side (Schlegel) G73; Q651; R374; S281; W556; AB231; AD80; AE211; AF77; AG215; AH403; AK87; AM579; AP512; AR263; AU479; AW54; BF255; BV520; BZ 100732

Be strong! we are not here to play (Babcock) G300; I407; S488; U269; Y185; AB176; AC182; AD488; AH449; AK 293; AO395; AR304; BF400 100733

Be this henceforth my constant care (Heermann) AZ1096 100734

Be this our happy destiny (Foster) AZ1100 100735

Be thou exalted, holy Lord (Morgan) BV311 100736

Be thou exalted, O my God (Watts) BI15 100737

Be thou my Guardian and my

Guide (Williams) E369; F300; X100; BV146 100738

Be thou my helper in the strife (U.P. Psalter, 1912) T59; AJ 92 100739

Be thou my judge, O righteous Lord (U.P. Psalter, 1912) AJ69 100740

Be thou my Vision, O Lord of my heart (Irish ancient) R303; S325; W477; Z321; AC236; AD 307; AE449; AF391; AG174; AL336; AR195; AT62; BF386; BK93; BV571; BY462; BZ 100741

Be thou, O God, exalted high (Tate & Brady) AN497; AO53; AR633; BE1; BR51; BX1 100742

Be thou our Guardian and our guide (Williams) BV146 X Be thou my Guardian 100743

Be tranquil, O my soul! (Hastings) AZ478; BA857 100744

Be true and list the voice within (Colby) BE20 100745

Be with me all my journey (Crosby) U364 100746

Be with me every moment (Crosby) R Be with me all my journey 100747

Be with me, Lord, where'er I go (Cennick) U366; AZ359; BA767 100748

Be with us gracious Lord, today (Bell) BY266 100749

Be ye doers of the Word (Linthicum) R Out of James 100750

Be ye joyful, earth and sky (---) P129 100751

Be ye lamps unto yourselves (Gautama Buddha) AQ110 100752

Be ye strong in the Lord and the power of his might (Whittle) AX448; AY461 100753

Beati mortui in Domino morientes (Breviary) BQ250 100754

Beauteous are the flowers of earth (Dix) I673 100755

Beautiful day of peace and rest (Townsend) R The day dawn is breaking 100756

Beautiful Saviour Münster G-B. 1677 O576 X Fairest Lord Jesus 100757

Beautiful Sion, built above (---) BC78 100758

Beautiful Sion for me (Penrose) BC6 100759

Beautiful Star of Bethlehem, shine on (Boyce) R O, beautiful Star of Bethlehem 100760

Beautiful upon the mountain are the feet of shepherds true (French 1830-50) M93 100761

Beautiful Valley of Eden (Cushing) AU166; AV312; AX678; BB550 100762

Beautiful words, wonderful words (Bliss) R Sing them over again to me 100763

Beauty around us, Glory above (---) AK67 100764

Because I have been given much, I, too, must give (Crowell) AD314; AK259; AR340; BF500 100765

Because I knew not when my life was good (Williams) R274; AB161; BF355 100766

Because thou hast made charity the sign (Mary Francis, Sr.) BN208 100767

Because thy trust is God alone (U.P. Psalter. 1912) T170; AJ249 100768

Because you live again, O Rose (The Abatal, 1532) BN162 100769

Bedenke, Mensch, das Ende (Unparth, G.B.) AY17d 100770

Befiehl du deine Wege (Gerhardt) AW558; BT520; BW558 100771

Before Jehovah's awful throne (Watts) M503 X Before the Lord Jehovah's throne 100772

Before Jehovah's glorious throne (Watts) BA21 X Before the Lord Jehovah's throne 100773

Before my journey is complete (U.P. Psalter, 1912) T188;

AJ274 100774

Before Pilate the Jews me brought (English trad carol) X Tomorrow shall be my dancing day 100775

Before the cross of Jesus (Blanchard) AB141; AF161; AK261; BF379 100776

Before the day draws near its ending (Ellerton) R57; S509; W271; AF508 100777

Before the ending of the day (St Ambrose) B28; D21; E264; F16; BR118 100778

Before the Father's awful throne (Wesley) AZ670 100779

Before the great Three-One (Jewish Doxology) AZ1192 X The God of Abraham praise 100780

Before the heavens were stretched abroad (Watts) AZ349 100781

Before the Lord a man is small (Patton) AQ68 100782

Before the Lord Jehovah's throne (Watts) A300; B309; D473; F370; G3; H20; J161; K492; L68; M503; N290; O14; Q13; R81; S63; U444; V2; W230; AA78; AB68; AE54; AF9; AG 47; AK25; AL6; AM62; AO8; AP87; AR16; AS78; AV33; AW 272; AY413; AZ312; BA21; BB1; BV236; BW272; BX27; BY6; BZ 100783

Before the Lord we bow, The God who reigns above (Key) J339; K491; L557; N568; O520; Q575; AO23 100784

Before the throne of God above (DeChenez) BV518 100785

Before thee, God, who knowest all (Landstad) O97; Q318; AM409 100786

Before thee, Lord, a people waits (Presbyterian hymnal, 1874) T117; AJ168 100787

Before thee, Lord, I bow my head (Dean) BC231 100788

Before thee we appear, Thou wilt receive (Foster) AZ549 100789

Before thy feet I fall (Ross) X452; AB41 100790

Before thy people I confess (U.P. Psalter, 1912) AJ112; AM565 100791

Before thy throne I now appear (Hodenberg) AA35 100792

Before thy throne, O God, we kneel (Carpenter) A499; AD329; AR256; BF357 100793

Begin, my tongue, some heavenly theme (Watts) I89; P375; R86; S94; V111; Z153; AB65; AD7; AH192; AR17; AS12; AT 49; AV35 100794

Begin the day with God (Bonar) AX61; AY277 100795

Begone, unbelief; for my Saviour is near (Newton) AZ506; BV 519; BY573 100796

Begone, unbelief: my Saviour is near (Newton) BV519 X Begone unbelief; for my Saviour is near 100797

Begone! vain world, with all thy pleasures (Scheffler) O445 100798

Behold a Branch is growing (Speier Gebetbuch. 1599) K533; P138; Q645; AK113; AM153 100799

Behold a host arrayed in white (Brorson) M313 X Behold a host like mountain bright 100800

Behold a host like mountain bright (Brorson) J599; M313; N207; O492; P434; Q656 100801

Behold a humble train (Harland) D153 100802

Behold a little child (How) A237; E588; W76; BY116 100803

Behold, a Rose of Judah from tender branch (Speier Gebetbuch. 1599) BM78 100804

Behold! a royal army (Crosby) BC7 100805

Behold a simple tender babe (Southwell) BG170; BN13 100806

Behold a Sower! from afar (Gladden) A401; G391; S486; AB292; AK201; AN74; AQ122,

236; BF269; BX444 100807
Behold! a Stranger at the door (Grigg) G196; H247; I249; L 367; M193; N396; Q650; S225; U168; V258; AA51; AD202; AG143; AH326; AL489; AO247; AP405; AR255; AS194; AV155; AW141; AZ364; BA397; BB227; BV469 100808
Behold a Stranger's at the door (Grigg) V258 X Behold! a Stranger at the door 100809
Behold, all ye that serve the Lord (U.P. Book of Psalms. 1871) AP119 100810
Behold! behold He cometh (Latin) BQ3 100811
Behold, by grace, and grace alone (Olson) M124; N444 100812
Behold, by sovereign grace alone (Olson) N444 X Behold, by grace, and grace alone 100813
Behold He comes, thy King most holy (Webb) AZ701 100814
Behold, how glorious is yon sky (Ramler) O252 100815
Behold, how good a thing It is to dwell in peace (Wesley) Q405 100816
Behold, how pleasant and how good (U.P. Psalter. 1912) T266; AJ 371 100817
Behold, I stand at the door (Bible. Revelation. 2) AI273 100818
Behold, it is the spring-tide of the year (Lucas) BH129 100819
Behold Me standing at the door (Crosby) BY410 100820
Behold that star (Talley) Y323; BK164 100821
Behold the amazing gift of love (Watts) R120; W483; AL328; AP469; BV521 100822
Behold the amazing sight (Doddridge) L251 100823
Behold the Bridegroom cometh (Greek. 8th c) E3; O512 100824
Behold the Bridegroom cometh (Greek 8th c) X Behold the Bridegroom draweth nigh 100825
Behold the Bridegroom draweth nigh! (Greek. 8th c) F46 100826
Behold! the Christian warrior stand (Montgomery) I397; BE 326 100827
Behold the eternal King and Priest (Congregational Ch. hymnal. 1887) BV369; BY308 100828
Behold the glories of the Lamb (Watts) I167; AY418 100829
Behold the glories of the Lamb (Watts) X Hark how the adoring hosts above 100830
Behold the great creator makes (Pestel) E20; F69; X72 100831
Behold the great Redeemer die (Snow) BC230 100832
Behold the heavenly city stands (Howard) BR219 100833
Behold, the joyful day is nigh (Wallin) M357; N45 100834
Behold the Lamb of God, O Thou for sinners (Bridges) A338; B148; D96; F212; J83; K102; O265; Q165; S153; AK148; BB129 100835
Behold the Lamb of God, who bears (Wesley) BV468 100836
Behold the lilies of the field that bloom around (---) AY361 100837
Behold the lilies of the field They neither toil nor sow (Caddell) BV495 100838
Behold the man! how heavy lay (Muenter) M384 100839
Behold, the Master passeth by (How) D169; U86; V262; BA 396 100840
Behold the morning sun (Watts) V77 100841
Behold the mountain of the Lord (Bruce) L354; W365; AL521; AM272; BC297; BV416; BY 658 100842
Behold the Saviour at the door (Grigg) BB227 X Behold! a Stranger at the door 100843
Behold the Saviour of mankind

(Wesley, S.,Sr) G136; H170; I142; Q176; AA211; AX108; AY251; BZ 100844

Behold the shining Sabbath sun (Dennis) H86 100845

Behold the sin-atoning Lamb (Fawcett) V245 100846

Behold the stone is rolled away (Whittle) R O, day of awful story 100847

Behold the sun, that seemed but now (Wither) X43 100848

Behold the sure foundation-stone (Watts) L281; O82; Q460;AA 452 100849

Behold the temple of the Lord (Kelly) BV659 100850

Behold the throne of grace! (Newton) H54; V466; AM530; AZ 1302; BA592 100851

Behold, they stand in robes of white (Brorson) BE19 100852

Behold, thy sons and daughters, Lord (Pratt) BC24 100853

Behold us, Lord, a little space (Ellerton) B10; F13; G459; I394; J213; K429; U286; W242; X39; AF395; AK228; AL206; AN107; AO508; AP329; AZ201; BA594; BF439; BV590; BX164; BY627; BZ 100854

Behold us, Lord, before thee met (Bright) E340 100855

Behold we come, dear Lord, to thee (Austin) AL194; BV66 100856

Behold what love, that God should give (Ryden) M153; N189 100857

Behold what love the Father hath On guilty men bestowed (Boswell) AZ111; BA41 100858

Behold what love, yes, love divine (Warren) AX84 100859

Behold, what wondrous grace (Watts) U145; V316; AE72; AK81; AO93 100860

Behold, where in a mortal form (Enfield) H150; K53; AX169; AY435; AZ178; BA77 100861

Bei frühem Morgenlicht. (German c1800.) BW19 100862

Believe it, O sinner, believe it (Sayford) R Redemption! O wonderful story 100863

Believe not those who say (Brontë) X453; AB250; AC 183; AD293; AE253; AN300; AW210; BD98; BF463; BH231; BX358 100864

Believing fathers oft have told (Charteris) J540; W521 100865

Believing souls, rejoice and sing (Swertner) AX1431; BA230 100866

Bells in the high tower Ringing o'er the snow (Box) AQ303 100867

Beloved, "It is well!" God's ways are always right (Doane) L521; Q519; AA518 100868

Beloved Jesus, what law hast thou broken (Heermann) AA198 X O dearest Jesus, what law 100869

Beloved, let us love: for Love is God (Bonar) BE21 X Beloved, let us love: love is of God 100870

Beloved, let us love: love is of God (Bonar) S500; W488; AP 569; BE21; BY591 100871

Bend back the lance's point (Ruskin) AQ207 100872

Bending low in adoration (---) R Like a strong and raging fire 100873

Beneath the amazing gift of love (Watts) AM442 100874

Beneath the cross of Jesus (Clephane) A341; B150; E567; G144; J482; N451; O321; P 180; R190; S162; T344; U95; V252; W691; Y105; Z235; AB 138; AC120; AD154; AE110; AF160; AG91; AH290; AI75; AK161; AL98; AM177; AO163; AP209; AR165; AS332; AT345; AU234; AV110; AW112; BA189; BB280; BF317; BV152; BY427; BZ 100875

Beneath the forms of outward rite (Blaisdell) Y87; Z459; AB327; AE334; AR511; BF 601; BZ 100876

Beneath the shadow of the cross (Longfellow) AN187; AO481; AP567; AQ312; AR354; AS141; AZ227; BX248 100877
Beneath Thy cross I stand (Lehmann) M393 100878
Beneath thy shadow hiding (Rankin) AY93 100879
Beneath thy wing, O God, I rest (Waring) BB82 100880
Beset with snares on every hand (Doddridge) I425 100881
Beside thy manger here I stand (Gerhardt) M619 100882
Besprinkle with thy blood my heart (Hutton) AZ100 100883
Bethany, O peaceful habitation (Gregor) AZ1008; BA520 100884
Bethlehem in land of Judah (Prudentius) BR154 X Earth has many a noble city 100885
Bethlehem, of noblest cities (Prudentius) E40; X84; AW88; BN25; BO162 100886
Bethlehem, of noblest cities (Prudentius) X Earth has many a noble city 100887
Beyond, beyond that [the] boundless sea (Conder) X454; BX 158 100888
Beyond the ever-lasting hills (Ryden) J295 100889
Beyond the smiling and the weeping (Bonar) H502; I627; U 435; V696 100890
Beyond the starry skies (Turner) BB170 100891
Beyond the sunset's radiant glow (Pollard) AU88 100892
Beyond the wheeling worlds of light (Tiplady) AK73 100893
Bid the din of battle cease (Howe) AB362 100894
Birds are singing, woods are ringing (Cole) AL587; AP723; AW409 100895
Bis hieher hat mich Gott gebracht (Amilie Juliane) BT33 100896
Bless Him, ye angels (U. P. Psalter. 1912) T195 X O come, my soul, bless thou the Lord thy maker 100897
Bless me, Lord, and make me a blessing (Zelley) R I do not ask to choose 100898
Bless, O Lord, this church of thine (Mack) AR493 100899
Bless, O Lord, we pray thee (Collier) AO664 100900
Bless, O Lord, we pray, Thy congregation (Benade) AZ 1015; BA599 100901
Bless, O my soul! the living God (Watts) L82; R8; U17; V95; AY19; AZ362; BA40 100902
Bless the four corners of this house (Guiterman) G433; Z599; AC527; AD420; AR542; AW363 100903
Bless the words we here have spoken (Crosby) R Heavenly Father, we beseech thee 100904
Bless thou the gifts our hands have brought (Longfellow) G609; R553; S29app.; U495; AC340; AD505; AE465; AF538; AG326; AH568; AK507; AN508; AR673; AS493; AT533; AU490; AW611; BF693 100905
Blessed are the heirs of heaven (Klopstock) O590 100906
Blessed are the sons of God (Humphreys) Q391; V315; AA315; AM443; AR332 100907
Blessed are they that have the faith (Auerbach) BC233 100908
Blessed are they that undefiled (Scottish Psalter, 1650) AP107 100909
Blessed art thou, O Lord of all (---) BH15 100910
Blessed assurance, Jesus is mine (Crosby) G238; H298; I548; R139; V731; Z412; AE 208; AG216; AH209; AR436; AS285; AT269; AU120; AV 359; AW480; AX477; AY207; BB608; BY493; BZ 100911
Blessed be God! Blessed be His Holy Name (Latin) BO275; BP102; BQ147 100912
Blessed be the Lord God of

Israel (Psalter version) AJ p394 X Now be the God of Israel blessed (Watts) 100913

Blessed be the name, Blessed be the name (---) R O for a thousand tongues (Wesley) R All praise to Him who reigns above (Clark) 100914

Blessed be thy name Jesus Christ! -- the same (Montgomery) AZ538; BR67 100915

Blessed Bible, how I love it (Palmer) AS183; AX143; AY 194 100916

Blessed, blessed be Jehovah (Bible. Psalm 106) AP813 100917

Blessed, blessed he who knoweth (Wallin) N417 100918

Blessed book, precious book (Williams) R There's a dear and precious book 100919

Blessed city, heavenly Salem (Latin, 7th c) A383; B508; D400; E169; F474, 620; J245; X190; AZ626; BR217; BT466; BV660 100920

Blessed city, heavenly Salem (Latin 7th c) X Come thou now and be among us 100921

Blessed feasts of blessed martyrs (Latin, 12th c) A135; E184 100922

Blessed Fount of heavenly gladness (Fliedner) N386 100923

Blessed fountain, full of grace (Kelly) AY283 100924

Blessed Francis, holy father, now our hearts to thee (Franciscan manual) BN179; BQ102 100925

Blessed hour of prayer (Crosby) R 'Tis the blessed hour of prayer 100926

Blessed is the man that never (Gerhardt) O455 100927

Blessed Jesus all our hearts incline (Pfeil) AZ517 100928

Blessed Jesus, at thy word We are gathered [general] (Clausnitzer) G310; K421; M3; N302; O34; P46; Q16; AA3; AE32; AF212; AK26; AM220; AZ591; BA372; BB27; BR100; BV2 100929

Blessed Jesus, here are we [Baptism] (Schmolck) A186; E336; N225; O145; W307; AA402; AF279; AZ592; BA 282 100930

Blessed Jesu! here we stand (Schmolck) E336 X Blessed Jesus, here are we 100931

Blessed Jesus, high in glory (Macleod) W465 100932

Blessed Jesus, meek and lowly (Smith, A.R. BB268 100933

Blessed Jesus, we implore thee (Hartley) AZ1409; BA620 100934

Blessed Jesus, we will love thee (Smith) R In the early days of childhood 100935

Blessed Lord, how much I need thee (Belden) BB578 100936

Blessed Lord, in thee is refuge (Booth) AI248; AM420 100937

Blessed Lord, what shall we render (Cennick) BR75B 100938

Blessed Master, I have promised (Dickinson) G223; S244; AS 443 100939

Blessed night, when Bethlehem's plain (Bonar) BA51 X Blessed night, when first that plain 100940

Blessed night, when first that plain (Bonar) AZ1126, 1127; BA51; BI81 100941

Blessed night, when first the plain (Bonar) BI81 X Blessed night, when first that plain 100942

Blessed, O blessed moment most holy (Jastrow) BH153, 154 100943

Blessed quietness, holy quietness (Ferguson) R Joys are flowing 100944

Blessed Redeemer! precious Redeemer (Christiansen) R Up Calvary's mountain 100945

Blessed Saviour, thee I love (Duffield) AE206; AO285; AS292; AU195; AY197; AZ1282; BA452 100946

Blessed Saviour, thou hast taught me (Neale) N251 X Blessed Saviour who hast taught me 100947

Blessed Saviour, thou wilt guide us (Snow) R Truth reflects upon our senses 100948

Blessed Saviour, we adore thee (McKinney) AT138 100949

Blessed Saviour, who hast taught me (Neale) J290; K176; N251; O109; P109; Q333 100950

Blessed Saviour with love's sacred fire (Schlicht) AZ516 100951

Blessing and honour and glory and power (Bible. Revelation 5) BY305B 100952

Blessing and honor, and glory and power (Bonar) J166; K295; L146; N336; P22; R137; S196; W169; AD178; AK178; AL42; AM 219; AP253; AR103; AZ1155; BI48 100953

Blessing, honour, thanks and praise (Wesley) D241 100954

Blest are humble souls that see (Watts) AI215; AS305 100955

Blest are the moments, doubly blest (Wordsworth) B9; E263; J218; X40 100956

Blest are the pure in heart (Keble) A418; B277; D410; E370; F335; G369; I360; J394; K369; L459; N492; O469; R 226; V321; W478; X455; AF 214; AK247; AL325; AP482; AS313; AW205; AZ1370; BA 621; BR31; BV638; BY463; BZ 100957

Blest are the sons of peace (Watts) V607 100958

Blest are the undefiled in heart (Watts) L445; AM447 100959

Blest are they, supremely blest (Wolf [or Wolff]) AZ67; BA 503; 100960

Blest be that sacred covenant-love (Wesley) AZ224; BA893 100961

Blest be the day when I must roam (Moravian emigrants hymn) BA938 100962

Blest be the day when moved I was (Bunyan) X456 100963

Blest be the dear uniting love (Wesley) G404; I228; V611; Z482; AX542; BZ 100964

Blest be the everlasting God (Watts) W137; AL467; AP638; AW266; BV517 100965

Blest be the Lord! for us he cares (U.P. Psalter. 1912) T124; AJ181 100966

Blest be the Lord, by Rock, my Might (U.P. Psalter. 1912) T284; AJ392 100967

Blest be the Lord, our Father's God (U.P. Psalter. 1912) T452; AJ195, 196 100968

Blest be the tie that binds (Fawcett) A495; B489; D672; G416; H429; I556; J543; L284; M21; N356; P58; Q464; R473; S343; T380; U373; V608; W 490; Y383; Z476; AA462; AB 324; AC312; AD409; AE340; AF272; AG237; AH458; AI276; AK280; AL376; AM285; AN563; AO420; AP571; AR505; AS67; AT366; AU239; AV217; AW41; AX548; AY399; AZ1335; BA 666; BB432; BF490; BK174; BR502; BY355; BZ 100969

Blest be thy love, dear Lord (Austin) H341; AA388; BR 330 100970

Blest Christmas morn, though murky clouds (Eddy) BE23 100971

Blest Comforter Divine, whose rays of heavenly love (Sigourney) V216; BR207 100972

Blest Creator of the light (Latin) F44 100973

Blest day of God! most calm, most bright (Mason) D31; H82; L37; N309 100974

Blest Easter Day, what joy is thine (Petri) N125 100975

Blest feast of love divine (Denny) Z457; BA302; BV387; BY329

100976

Blest holder of the heavenly Keys (Breviary. Venice, 1798) R Seek ye a Patron to defend 100977

Blest hour, when mortal man retires (Raffles) BB28 100978

Blest is he that never walketh (Gerhardt) P261 100979

Blest is he who cries to heaven (Paulsen) M128 100980

Blest is he who loves God's precepts (U.P. Psalter. 1912) T1; AJ2 100981

Blest is that man who sets his soul's desire (Auslander) AQ229 100982

Blest is the bond of wedded love (Moise) BH219 100983

Blest is the Faith, divine and strong (Faber) BQ123 100984

Blest is the home when God is there (Ware) AR545 X Happy the home when God is there 100985

Blest is the man, for-ever blest (Watts) L421; Q392; AA309 100986

Blest is the man who dies in peace (Barbauld) BR431 X How blest the righteous when he dies 100987

Blest is the man who shuns the place (Watts) V442 100988

Blest is the man whose softening heart (Barbauld) V574 100989

Blest Jesus! when my soaring thoughts (Heginbothom) L437 100990

Blest Jesus, when thy cross I view (Speece) V192 100991

Blest land of Judea! thrice hallowed in song (Whittier) AC 105; AD134 100992

Blest martyr, let thy Triumph day (Prudentius) E185 100993

Blest morning, whose first dawning rays (Watts) W116; AP218 100994

Blest Spirit, one with God above (St Ambrose) K148 100995

Blest the man that fears Jehovah (U.P. Psalter. 1912) T258; AI 366; AJ360; AM626 100996

Blest the man who fears Jehovah (U.P. Book of Psalms. 1871) AP115 100997

Blest Trinity, from mortal sight (Santeuil) AZ410 100998

Bliss beyond compare which in Christ I share (---) AZ534; BA 506 100999

Bliv hos os, Mester, Dagen helder! (Boye) BT194 101000

Blow, blow, thou winter wind (Shakespeare) BG171 101001

Blow, golden trumpets, sweet and clear (Deland) AC134 101002

Blow on, thou Mighty Wind (Hopkins) BR209 101003

Blow the trumpet, trusty watchman (Gilmour) R Watchman, blow the gospel trumpet 101004

Blow winds of God, and bring us on our way (Hodge) AN 552 101005

Blow, winds of God, awake and blow (Whittier) AB74 101006

Blow ye the trumpet, blow! (Wesley) D330; G189; H229; I294; L369; V234; AM392; AO116; AP392; AT250; AV165; AZ1182; BA398; BZ 101007

Bondage and death the cup contains (Sargent) AO613 101008

Book of books, our people's strength (Dearmer) A403; G390; R248; X457; Y337; AC 69; AD196; AF253; AK203; BY241; BZ 101009

Book of grace and book of glory (MacKellar) Z439; BY242 101010

Bo-r'-chu es Adonoy (Jewish traditional) BH268 101011

Boroch atoh Adonoy (Jewish liturgy) AHp148; BH297 101012

Bo-ruch shaym k'vod mal-chuso (Jewish traditional) BH 331 101013

Bound upon th'accursed Tree

(Milman) AZ1078 101014
Boundless glory, Lord, be thine (Kelly) V389 101015
Bow down in worship now, before the Christ (Glen) BI 50D 101016
Bow down thine ear, Almighty Lord (Powell) D286; V562; AA493; BA306; BV409 101017
Bow down thine ear, Lord, hear thou my cry (Mayer) BH35 101018
Bow down thine ear, O Lord (U.P. Psalter. 1912) AM75
X Bow down thy ear. . . 101019
Bow down thy ear, O Lord, and hear (U.P. Psalter, 1912) AJ233; AM75 101020
Bow down ye followers of the Lamb (Lauterbach) AZ692 101021
Bowed down beneath a weight of woe (Kuhlman) M415 101022
Bowed low in supplication (How) W342 101023
Bowing low, then, offer homage (Avery) BM33 101024
Braving the wilds all unexplored (Freeman) S418; AB346 101025
Bread of heaven, on thee we feed (Conder) A212; B332; D224; E304; F411; K192; X264; AE330; AF281; AH505; AR512; AT395; AU232; AV253; AW311; BA293; BV370; BY309 101026
Bread of life, Christ by Whom alone we live (Zinzendorf, N. L.) AZ719 101027
Bread of the world, in mercy broken (Heber) A196; B336; D225; E305; F409; G414; H 442; I238; J279; K194; L332; R445; S353; V552; W318; X 265; Z453; AD403; AE339; AF 282; AG239; AH502; AK337; AL224; AM358; AO443; AP358; AR514; AS460; AT394; AV254; AW304; BB476; BF603; BJ19; BR472; BV371; BY310; BZ 101028
Break, day of God, O break (Burton) G504; AD355; AL 529 101029
Break forth, O beauteous heavenly light (Rist) A25; J29; AF118; AN492; AQ297; BC239; BI90; BL7; BZ 101030
Break forth, O living light of God (Frank v. Christierson) BZ 101031
Break, new-born year, on glad-eyes break! (Gill) I572; S469 101032
Break thou, O Lord, the Bread of life to me (Lathbury) BI 66 X Break thou the Bread of life 101033
Break thou the Bread of life (Lathbury) G387; H89; I325; J491; L309; M36; P87; R250; S216; T405; U381; V553; W 202; Y101; Z461; AB99; AC71; AD197; AE162; AF254; AG132; AH236; AK204; AL187; AM 256; AO243; AP291; AR236; AS182; AT178; AU192; AV81; AW288; AX144; AY439; BA 367; BB218; BF270; BI66; BR301; BV303; BY243; BZ 101034
Breaking through the clouds of darkness (Heywood) BE29 101035
Breast the wave, Christian, When it is strongest (Stammers) A565; B112; D656; H 354; BR400 101036
Breathe o'er our waiting spirits, Lord (Slemp) AU286 101037
Breathe on me, Breath of God (Hatch) A375; B380; F236; G180; I196; J470; R235; S 213; W194; X458; Y98; AB93; AC61; AD187; AE143; AF233; AG123; AK191; AL148; AN59; AO228; AP270; AR220; AT167; AV146; AW135; BB679; BF 260; BN121; BV287; BX357; BY592; BZ 101038
Breathe upon us, Holy Spirit (Hoffman) AR218; AS169 101039
Brethren, called by one vocation

(Spitta) O407 101040
Brethren, let us join to bless (Cennick) BV14 101041
Brethren, we have met to worship (Atkins) AT368; AU198; AX33 101042
Brethren, while we sojourn here (Swain) AZ1065 101043
Brich auf und werde lichte (Opitz) BT126 101044
Brief life is here our portion (St Bernard of Cluny) A596; B69; D406; E371; F275; J527; K527; L607; O612; Q448; R430; V692; W597; X459; AA557; AL 463; AO554; AP626; AZ822; BA741 101045
Brief our days, but long for singing (Patton) AQ28 101046
Bright and glorious is the sky (Grundtvig) J57 101047
Bright and joyful is the morn (Montgomery) H144; AZ61 101048
Bright the vision that delight (Mant) E372; F161; X460; BV15 101049
Bright was the guiding star that led (Auber) AZ173 101050
Brightest and best of the sons of the morning (Heber) A46; B95; D66; E41; F75; G119; H132; I114; J53; K39; L228; M377; O224; P151; Q128; R 175; S136; T337; U62; V114; W64; X85; Z202; AA181; AB 125; AD126; AF126; AG81; AH272; AI63; AK121; AL49; AM167; AO138; AP178; AR144; AS109; AT67; AV94; AW91; AX104; AY487; AZ1150; BA183; BD212; BF277; BI87; BR152; BV125; BY91; BZ 101051
Brightly beams our Father's mercy (Bliss) G254; U316; Z313; AC 253; AE290; AH438; AS351; AT 300; AU262; AW448; AX193; BB628; BC301; BZ 101052
Brightly gleams our banner (Potter & How) A559; B529; D515; G446; H445; I681; L407; S457; U306; V485, 759; W538; Z485; AC208; AD482; AH440; AO398; AP781; AV218; AZ773; BA812; BD83; BF621; BR514; BV549; BY464 101053
Bring a torch, Jeanette (French trad) Y304; AF124 101054
Bring beams of oak, and boulderstone (Johnson) AN459 101055
Bring flowers of the fairest (---) AH137; BO105 101056
Bring, heavy heart, your grief to me (Auerbach) BC349 101057
Bring, O morn, thy music (Gannett) Y17; AC5; AN8; AQ5; BD23; BF229; BX6 101058
Bring, O past, your honor (Lyttle) AQ254 101059
Bring them in, Bring them in (Thomas) R Hark 'tis the Shepherd's voice I hear 101060
Bring ye all the tithes into the storehouse (Leech) AT404; AU393 101061
Bringing in the sheaves (Shaw) R Sowing in the morning 101062
Bringing our praise, we kneel before Thy altar (Mary Francis, Sr.) BN203 101063
Broad is the road that leads to death (Watts) V447; AY394 101064
Brood o'er us with thy sheltering wing (Eddy) BE30 101065
B'ro-sh ha-sho-no yi-ko-say-vun (Jewish traditional) BH328 101066
Brother afar from the Saviour today (Berry) AX275 101067
Brother along on the highway of life (Henson) AX443 101068
Brother, hast thou wandered far (Clarke) AO251; BF341 101069
Brother, here's a message I give (Garrett) AS308 101070
Brother Man, awake! Strength withers, of tomorrow dreaming (Maurer) BF512 101071
Brother, sing your country's anthem (Bacon) AN401;

BK109 101072
Brother, thou hast left us lonely (---) AY172 101073
Brothers and sisters, we now must depart (Larsen) P69 101074
Brothers, joining hand in hand (Warner) F294 101075
Build thee more stately mansions, O my soul (Holmes) AC498 101076
Builder of mighty worlds on worlds (---) AZ215; BA322 101077
Built by Jehovah's hand (Hymns of the English Conf. 1880) BR224 101078
Built on a rock the church doth stand (Grundtvig) J151; M92; O132; P81; Q467; R432; AF 270 101079
Built on the Rock, the Church doth stand (Grundtvig) P81 X Built on a Rock 101080
Built on the Rock, without spot or wrinkle (Winsett) AX152 101081
Buried beneath the yielding wave (Beddome) BB438 101082
Bursting forth, from Pharaoh's prison (Cummins) BL26 101083
"But for a moment" -- this valley of sorrows (Pollard) AY450 101084
But for the cockerell calling the noon-hour (Fan Cheng-ta) AQ322 101085
But God hath promised strength for the day (Flint) R God hath not promised 101086
But I know whom I have believed (Whittle) R I know not why God's wondrous grace 101087
But the Lord is mindful (Bible. Psalms) AH621 101088
By all whom Thou has made (U.P. Psalter. 1912) R117; T159; AJ236 101089
By and by, when the morning comes (Tindley) R Trials dark on every hand 101090
By angels in heaven, of every degree (---) Lp742 101091
By Babel's riverside we sat in tears (U.P. Psalter. 1912) T273; AJ380 101092
By Babel's streams we sat and wept (U.P. Psalter, 1912) T272; AJ379 101093
By Christ redeemed, in Christ restored (Rawson) B335; D236; H437; I239; W322; AL 229; AO448; AP361; AS467; AW310; AZ12; BA294; BB475; BV372; BY311 101094
By cool Siloam's shady rill (Heber) A328; B351; D565; H451; I678; S349; V650; W309; AW400; AI375; AL218; AN438; AO431; AP787; AS394; AY363; AZ1448; BA838; BB340; BX517 101095
By every nation, race and tongue (George) BV32 101096
By faith I view my Saviour dying (Jukes) AX313 101097
By faith we are divinely sure (Brorson) M120 101098
By grace are ye saved through faith (Whittle) R In grace the holy God 101099
By grace I am an heir of heaven (Scheidt) M123; P274; AM584 101100
By grace I'm saved, grace free and boundless (Scheidt) Q373; AA311; AM399 101101
By help of God I fain would tell (Luther) BT259 101102
By Jesus' grave on either hand (Smith, I. G.) E121; F125; W114; AZ5 101103
By law from Sinai's clouded steep (Williams) AN129; BF190; BX16 101104
By nature deaf to things divine (Hoppe) N177 101105
By nature man cannot achieve (Denicke) M97 101106
By sin weighed down and sorely stricken (Tietze) M68 101107
By the blood that flowed from thee (Cadell) AO655; BN35; BO169; BQ20 101108

By the breadth of the blue that shines in the silence (Van Dyke) X18 101109
By the Cross her vigil keeping (Jacopone) BM80 10110
By the Cross of Jesus standing (Bonar) W104; AM185; AZ648; BR178 101111
By the first bright Easter-day (Cadell) BO172; BQ137 101112
By the gracious saving call (Pollock) A230; B142b 101113
By the holy hills surrounded (Spitta) O80 101114
By thy birth and by thy tears (Grant) G207; I280; BZ 101115
By thy birth and by thy tears (Grant) X Saviour when in dust to thee 101116
By thy blessed Word obeying (Warner) AX415 101117
By thy Cross, O Christ, and passion (Wallin) J381 101118
By weary stages, the old world ages (Masefield) X86 101119
By what means shall a young man learn (Scottish Psalter, 1650) AL678; AP107b 101120

C

Call Jehovah thy salvation (Montgomery) A448; B310; D415; R123; S292; AM566; AO360; AP76; AZ941; BA680; BB257; BE33; BX12 101121
Call the Lord thy sure salvation (Montgomery) BE33 X Call Jehovah thy salvation 101122
Call them in! The poor the wretched (Shipton) D619 101123
Called to the feast by the King are we (Landor) BB537 101124
Calling to thee, calling to thee (Crosby) R Out on the mountain 101125
Calling today, calling today (Crosby) R Jesus is tenderly calling thee home 101126
Calm me, my God, and keep me calm (Bonar) U244; AO363; AZ194; BA513; BB334 101127
Calm on the listening ear of night (Sears) A24; B84; D55; L217; N38; Z201; AI61; AK 103; AN159; AO124; AV99; AZ1463; BA53; BD209; BI98; BX189 101128
Calm soul of all things, make it mine (Arnold) AQ85 101129
Calmly, calmly lay him down (Gaskell) AN452; BX474 101130
Can a father see his child (Blake) AQ163 101131
Can a growing child like me (Dodge) AE431; AH544; AL584; AM645; AP719; AW435; BK 15 101132
Can a little child like me (Dodge) AH544 X Can a growing child like me 101133
Can a mortal flee from sorrow? (---) AZ598 101134
Can I see another's woe (Blake) X461 101135
Can men tell that you love Jesus (Sellers) R Would men know 101136
Can my soul find rest from sorrow (---) AY286 101137
Can truth divine fulfillment fail? (Stockton) H17 101138
Can you count the stars that brightly (Hey) A245; X462; BD52 101139
Canst thou count the stars (Hey) BD52 X Can you count the stars 101140
Canticle of the sun (St Francis of Assisi) X All creatures of our God and King (tr. by Draper) X Most high, omnipotent, good Lord (tr. by Robbins) 101141
Captain of Israel's host, and Guide (Wesley) AL440; AW168; BC236; BZ 101142
Captains of the saintly band (Santeüil) E177; F507 101143
Care for me, O God of grace (Ludämilia Elisabeth) P302

101144
Carried away to the realms of light (Jones) R When I have reached 101145
Carry on! carry on! Fight the good fight and true (Service) Y160 101146
Čas radosti, veselosti (Latin. 12th c) BT82 101147
Cast me not in wrath away (Albinus) M67 101148
Cast thy bread upon the waters (Hanaford) AZ260 101149
Cast thy burden on the Lord Only lean upon His word (Hill. Psalms and hymns.) H353; I468; S288; U197; V505; AI243; AM559; AO347; AR314; AT254; AV234; AZ71; BA700; BF394; 101150
Cast thy burden upon the Lord (Bible. Psalms 55,16) AU478; BB692; BC235 101151
Cast thy care on Jesus (Scott) AR196 101152
Cast upon the Lord thy care (Hymns of the English Conference, 1880) BR270 101153
Chant your songs of glad thanksgiving (Glenn) BI114 101154
Chariot rode on the mountain top (Negro spiritual) R Great Day! great day, the righteous marching 101155
Chaun dong whan lotsan mei chu (Chinese trad) Y311 101156
Cheer thy chosen witnesses, O Jesus (Batty) AZ1014 101157
"Cheer up, desponding soul" (Byrom) AZ475 101158
Cheer up, friends and neighbours (Dearmer) BG147a X Take heart, friends and neighbours 101159
Chief of sinners though I be (McComb [M'Comb]) K330; L500; M176; N421; Q342; AA 99; AI434; AZ1266; BB238 101160
Chief Shepherd of thy chosen sheep (Newton) AX635 101161
Child in the manger (MacDonald) W53; BV96; BY92 101162
Child Jesus comes from heavenly height (Anderson) BR547 101163
Child of a Virgin, Maker of thy Mother (Latin, 8th c) BN183 101164
Childhood's years are passing o'er us (Dickson) AP782 101165
Children, come, hither come (U.P. Board of Publ. 1909) R Ye children, come, give ear to me 101166
Children of God, born again of His Spirit (Brorson) M130 101167
Children of Jerusalem, Place the royal diadem (---) BI1 101168
Children of Jerusalem Sang the praise of Jesus' name (Henley) W658; AL607; AP751; AW404; AZ1285; BA822; BV 344; BY735 101169
Children of light, arise and shine! (Denny) AZ640 101170
Children of the heavenly Father (Berg) J572; N487; P368; AE256; BZ 101171
Children of the heavenly King (Cennick) A578; B517; D452; E373; F295; G326; H352; I547; K263; L457; N332; O 458; P333; R340; S347; U243; V504; W574; X463; Z267; AD 229; AG236; AH399; AI334; AM499; AO541; AP611; AR 315; AV212; AZ75; BA626; BD20; BJ95; BR434; BV550; BZ 101172
Chime, happy Christmas bells, once more (Grundtvig) N31 101173
Choose my path, O blessed Saviour (Reed) AX493; AY123 101174
Choose the right, when a choice is placed before you (Townsend) BC110 101175
Chosen not for good in me (McCheyne) V370; AZ1265 101176

Chosen seed and Zion's children (Rutström) N267 101177
Christ above all glory seated (Latin. 5th c) D371; H189; AO197; BV198 101178
Christ alone is our salvation (Latin. 7th c) O81 101179
Christ be my leader by night, as by day (Dudley-Smith) BV572 101180
Christ be with me, Christ within me (St Patrick) A268; B525; BN61; BY433b 101181
Christ, by heavenly hosts adored (Harbaugh) D188; J341; K495; Q566; V624; AA296; AI 364; AM623; AO598; AZ57; BA873; BI12 101182
Christ comes again with holy power (Campbell BE34 101183
Christ crucified, my soul, by faith (Schmidt) AZ694 101184
Christ, enthroned in highest heaven (Latin 13th c) E350 101185
Christ, everlasting Source of light (Meusslin) AA34 101186
Christ for the whole wide world (Allen) AU444 101187
Christ for the world we sing! (Wolcott) A537; B486; D580; G481; H397; I635; J311; K218; L335; P400; R489; S378; T368; U404; Y355; Z538; AB368; AD385; AE352; AF295; AG266; AH463; AK372; AL241; AM371; AO517; AP373; AR559; AS378; AT458; AU267; AV262; AW327; BA539; BB452; BF535; BY364; BZ 101188
Christ, from whom all blessings flow (Wesley) AZ1060; BV417; BY361; BZ 101189
Christ has come for our salvation (Dayman) AZ646 101190
Christ has for sin atonement made (Hoffman) AE174; AS144; AT130; AW473; BB644 101191
Christ hath a garden walled around (Watts & Bridges) X 245; AM273; AP302; BJ96; 101192
Christ hath a work for thee to do (Sedding) BV35 X A work hath Christ for thee to do 101193
Christ Himself, my Pride and Glory (Olearius) M191; Q408 101194
Christ in highest heaven enthroned (Santeüil) AZ620 101195
Christ in His heavenly garden walks all day (Palgrave) AD207; AR254 101196
Christ in His word draws near (Lynch) AI152; AM261 101197
Christ in the night He was betrayed (---) AY261 X Christ on the night He was betrayed 101198
Christ is arisen From the grave's dark prison (Latin, 11-12th c) Q187 101199
Christ is coming! let creation (MacDuff) I602; V183; W163; AL135; AM238; AS164; AW 127; AZ1388 101200
Christ is gone up; yet ere He passed (Neale) E166; F470 101201
Christ is knocking at my sad heart (Palmer) AS195; BB 565 101202
Christ is made the sure foundation (Latin, ca 7th c) A384; B457; D483; E170; F620; H406; I662; J242; K241; L293; N273; O129; P241; Q466; R433; S336; T361; U385; V572; W207; X 190; AA454; AE317; AF263; AG 232; AK324; AL163; AM268; AO415; AP293; AV248,308; AW277; AZ625; BA326; BB487; BT466; BZ 101203
Christ is now risen again (Coverdale) F601 101204
Christ is our corner-stone (Latin 7th c) B458; D294; F243; L 282; O130; Q465; S472; X464; AA453; AO462; AP303; AS437; AW9; AZ1173; BA261; BV456; BY267 101205
Christ is our Head, our strength, our life (Coffin) BN204

101206
Christ is our Master, Lord, and God (Cennick) BA446 X The doctrine of our dying Lord 101207
Christ is risen! alleluia! (Monsell) K117; AI85; BY152 101208
Christ is risen! Christ is risen! (Gurney) D113; U108; V168; X152; Z240 101209
Christ is risen from the dead (Becker) M430; N641 101210
Christ is the foundation of the house we raise (Monsell) N 279 101211
Christ is the King! O friends rejoice X242 X Christ is the King! O friends upraise 101212
Christ is the King! O friends upraise (Bell) A543; X242; BY 356 101213
Christ is the vine, we branches are (Nitschmann) AZ284 101214
Christ is the world's redeemer (St Columba) R136; W179 101215
Christ is the world's true light (Briggs) A258; R492; X60; AF198; BV418; BY659; BZ 101216
Christ ist erstanden Von der Marter alle; (Latin 11-12th c.) BT187 101217
Christ Jesus lay in death's strong bands (Luther) J98; K110; O330; Q195; AM207; BY153; BZ 101218
Christ Jesus, once to death abased (Luther) AZ912 101219
Christ lag in Todesbanden (Luther) BT195 101220
Christ leads me through no darker rooms (Baxter) A445 101221
Christ must be served indeed (Sawson) BF460 101222
Christ, my Rock, my sure Defence (Luise Henriette) AZ588 X Jesus Christ my sure Defence 101223
Christ, of all my hopes the ground (Wardlaw) B219; R314; S316; X465; AL342; AM437; AP481 101224
Christ of holiness the Fountain (Craeselius) M199 101225
Christ of the upward way (Mathams) R295; S277; AB235; AC235; AD305; AE439; AG 312; AK250; AR278; BF380; BY538 101226
Christ on the night He was betrayed (---) AX175; AY261 101227
Christ our King to heaven ascendeth (Hopkins) D127 101228
Christ our Lord will soon be coming (Hayes) AX130 101229
Christ our Redeemer died on the Cross (Foote) AU70; AX 307; AY240 101230
Christ shall have dominion (U.P. Psalter. 1912) R502; T134; AJ200; AM678 101231
Christ the fair glory of the holy holy angels (St Rabanus Maurus) A123; E242; F564 101232
Christ, the glory of the sky (Latin, 5th c) BN192 101233
Christ, the good Shepherd, God's own Son (Scheffler) AZ1424 101234
Christ, the life of all the living (Homburg) D361; J79; K98; M400; N91; Q151; AA196; AW535 101235
Christ the Lord cometh? perchance at the dawn (Wesley, E.G.) AX125; AY532 101236
Christ the Lord hath risen From his three-day prison (Weisse) BQ329 101237
Christ the Lord is my true Shepherd (Terry) BN59 101238
Christ the Lord is risen again (Weisse) D114; E129; F136; J107; K114; L268; O334; P 197; Q190; X153; AA225; AF183; AP221; AW544; AZ 1159; BA231; BV179 101239
Christ the Lord is risen! Now

the hour (Watts) R Now is the hour of darkness past 101240

Christ the Lord is risen today! Christians haste your vows (Wipo??) F131; J99; K112; M431; N130; Q191; BN40; BO175; BP38; BQ31; BV183 101241

Christ the Lord is risen today. Sons of men and angels say (Wesley) A95; B175; D111; E135; F141; G154; H181; I156; J91; K111; L261; N132; Q193; S165; U118; V159; X160; Y331; Z239; AA221; AB143; AC129; AD158; AE121; AF182; AG102; AH298; AI82; AK167; AL104; AM205; AN192; AO176; AP214; AR182; AS146; AT115; AU33; AV120; AX123; AZ46; BA232; BB134; BC10; BF318; BK135; BV180; BY154; BZ 101242

Christ the Lord, the Lord most glorious (Mueller) AZ276; BA171 101243

Christ the Lord to us is born (Tranovsky) M359; Q86; 101244

Christ the Saviour came from heaven's glory (McKinney) AU336 101245

Christ, the transforming Light (Smith, G) AU418 101246

Christ the word to earth descended (St Thomas Aquinas) BN93 101247

Christ, thou art the sure Foundation (Latin ca 7th c) N273 X Christ is made the sure Foundation 101248

Christ, thou the champion of the band we own (Loewenstern) AA279; AZ529 101249

Christ, thy all-atoning death (Zinzendorf, N. L.) BA681 X Rise, exalt our Head and King (Hehl) 101250

Christ to know is life and peace (Toplady) AZ1476 101251

Christ to us across the water (Dearmer) X302b 101252

Christ we do all adore thee (Dubois) AR634 101253

Christ we praise thee, Christ we worship thee (Latin) R O King of Kings in splendor 101254

Christ went a building to prepare (---) AX481 101255

Christ who knows all his sheep (Baxter) X288 101256

Christ who left his home in glory (Kolb) AY266 101257

Christ, who once amongst us (Bourne) F447; I683 101258

Christ who welcomed little children (Martin) BY284 101259

Christ, whose glory fills the skies (Wesley) A153; B4; D312; E258; F7; G32; J208; K450; L5; N321; O543; P150; Q359; R47; S26; U455; V30; W261; X26; AA100; AB197; AD42; AF43; AG20; AL535; AM330; AP658; AS23; AT22; AW26; AZ1271; BA46; BE35; BR12; BV36; BY673; BZ 101260

Christ will gather in His own (Zinzendorf, N. L.) AZ53 101261

Christ will me His aid afford (Oatman) AS299 101262

Christe, du Beistand deiner Kreuzgemeine (Löwenstern) BT258; BW278 101263

Christe, du Lamm Gottes, der du trägst die Sünd der Welt (Latin: Agnus Dei) BT147 101264

Christe, freundlicher Ritter (Ausbund) BU78 101265

Christe mein Herr, ich bin ganz ferr (Ausbund) BU62 101266

Christe, qui lux es et dies (Latin, before 9th c.) BT559 101267

Christe thu dich erbarmen (Ausbund) BU77 101268

Christian children must be holy (---) L460 101269

Christian, do you see him (Dearmer) X466 101270

Christian, dost thou see them (St Andrew of Crete) A556;

B126; D81; E72; F91; G275; I616; J68; K73; R360; S275; U305; V474; Y168; AB245; AC179; AD295; AF364; AG194; AI323; AK294; AM483; AO390; AR319; AV194; AZ766; BA570; BB367; BD79; BF472; BR401; BV137; BY506; BZ 101271

Christian hearts, in love united (Zinzendorf, N. L.) AZ942; BA667 101272

Christian Leaguers, rally at the Lord's command (Solberg) P373 101273

Christian, let your burning light (Coleman) AR435; AS350 101274

Christian, rise and act thy creed (Russell) Y230; Z518; AB260; AD353; AF416; AN282; AO504; BF483; BX337 101275

Christian, seek not yet repose (Elliott B128; E374; F308; I494; M240; V503; W523; X467; AB247; AL396; AM471; AP547; BA571; BB357; BE67; BR349; BV573; BY507 101276

Christian Soul, the times are calling (Edwards) AD300 101277

Christian, unflinching stand (Leachman) BV551 101278

Christian, walk carefully, danger is near (---) AX444 101279

Christian, work for Jesus (Hasloch) W343; AP585 101280

Christians awake, salute the happy morn (Byrom) A16; B 76; D56; E21; F61; G93; J19; K24; Q84; W54; X73; AF127; AK115; AL67; AP175; AR134; AW71; AZ1501; BA159; BR 148; BV97; BY93 101281

Christians, come in sweetest measures (Adam of St Victor) Q282; AA121 101282

Christians, come, new anthems raise (St Joseph the Hymnographer) AZ864 X Let us now our voices raise 101283

Christians, dismiss your fears (Hart) AZ1494; BA228 101284

Christians, keep your banners waving (Arends) M244 101285

Christians, lo, the star appeareth (Blaisdell) Y220; AB124; AC90; BD208; BF489 101286

Christians, prayer may well employ you (Arends) O165; Q444 101287

Christians, rise, put on your armor (Falckner) M248 101288

Christians, sing out with exultation (Pictet) Q100; AZ991 101289

Christians, sound the Name that saved us (Farrell) BM44 101290

Christians, to the Paschal Victim (Wipo??) A97; E130; F138 101291

Christmas brings joy to every heart (Ingemann) J46 101292

Christmas day is come; let's all prepare (Irish trad carol) BG6 101293

Christmas is here with joy untold (Ingemann) M617 101294

Christ's life our code, His cross our creed (Copeland) G331; I138 101295

Christ's love invites us To flee to Him for rest (Dober) AZ546 101296

Christ's love produces love; and, kindled thus (Zinzendorf, N. L.) AZ463 101297

Christ's loving children, for his hope abiding (St Gregory the Great) BJ49 101298

Christum wir sollen loben schon (Sedulius) BT104 101299

Christus das Lamm auf Erden kam (H. Betz) BU108 101300

Christus der Herr ist gangen (H. Betz) BU110 101301

Christus, der ist mein Leben (Vulpius. Ein schön geistliche G-B. 1609) BT597 101302

Christus factus est pro nobis

(Breviary) BQ193 101303
Christus ist erstanden Von des Todes Banden (Latin 11-12th. c.) BT190; BW544 101304
Christus vincit! Christus regnat! Christus imperat! (Latin, 8th c) BN76; BP106; BQ248 101305
Church of God, beloved and chosen (Havergal) AZ964 101306
Church of God, thou spotless virgin (Warner) AX151 101307
Church of God, whose conquering banners (Bugbee) AY518 101308
Church of Jesus, sing, Praise the Lord and King (Promnitz) AZ 533 101309
Church of the ever-living God (Bonar) BE36 101310
City not made with hands (Palgrave) A491; F259; X615; Z478; AB350; AN396; AP305 101311
City of David, Bethlehem (Rose) BI84 101312
City of God, how broad and far (Johnson) A386; B470; E375; F258; G420; I209; J330; R436; S338; W209; X468; Y66; Z426; AB320; AC267; AD386; AE319; AF261; AG229; AK330; AL171; AN410; BD191; BE37; BF589; BX451; BY255 101313
City of peace, our Mother dear (Prid) X393 101314
City strong and mighty (Pendleton) BI16-D 101315
Claro paschali gaudio. (Latin. 4th c.) BW415 101316
Cleanse my heart, O Father, cleanse it (---) BR34 101317
Clear is the call that bids us come (Bement) BF626 101318
Clear upon the night-air sounding (---) BR559 101319
Cling to the Bible, tho' all else be taken (Smith, M. J.) AX 140; AY500 101320
Close by the heedless worker's side (Studdert-Kennedy) X469 101321
Close to my Savior, there would I be (Mishler) AS219 101322
Close to Thee, close to Thee (Crosby) R Thou my everlasting portion 101323
Closer, my child, to me (Warren) R When I get weary 101324
Closer to thee, my Father, draw me (Chapman) BB632 101325
Closer with the cords of love (Chapman) R Closer to thee, my Father, draw me 101326
Come, all that heavy-laden are (Lehr) AZ1089 X My Saviour sinners doth receive 101327
Come, all ye faithful (Latin, 18th c) BI83 X O come, all ye faithful 101328
Come, all ye people, bless our God (U. P. Psalter, 1912) AJ175 101329
Come, all ye people, come away (Seltzer) J249 101330
Come all ye Saints and sing his praise (---) BC11 101331
Come, all ye saints of God (Boden) AZ1240; BA114 101332
Come, all ye Saints who dwell on earth (Phelps) BC12 101333
Come, all ye servants of the Lord (U. P. Psalter, 1912) T267 101334
Come, all ye shepherds, and be not afraid (Bohemian trad) BD221 X Come, all ye shepherds, ye children of earth 101335
Come, all ye shepherds, ye children of earth (Bohemian trad) Y308; AD108; AK111; AW79; BD221 101336
Come, all ye sons of God who have received the priesthood (Davenport) BC302 101337
Come, all ye sons of Sion (Phelps) BC303 101338
Come, all you faithful Christians (English trad carol) BG7 101339
Come all you worthy Christian men (English trad carol)

BG60 101340
Come all you worthy gentlemen (English trad carol) BG8 101341
Come along, come along, is the call that will win (Willes) BC19 101342
Come and deck the grave with flowers (Monsell) AZ241 101343
Come and hear the grand old story (Bonar) K531 101344
Come, and let us sweetly join (Wesley) AF525; AZ1056; BZ 101345
Come and rejoice with me (Charles) BY428 101346
Come, be my heart's beloved Guest (Mencken) BA295 101347
Come, blessed Saviour! Source of light (Beddome) BR22 X Come blessed Spirit! Source of light 101348
Come blessed Spirit! Source of light (Beddome) V208; BE240; BR22 101349
Come, brethren, let us hasten on (Tersteegen) O451 101350
Come, children, join to sing (Bateman) W177 X Come Christians, join to sing 101351
Come, children of tomorrow, come (Gale) AQ193 101352
Come, children, with singing, with sweet voices ringing --- BR549 101353
Come, Christian brethren, ere we part (White) V22 101354
Come, Christian children, come (Thrupp) D554 101355
Come, Christians, join to sing (Bateman) R131; S191; W177; AL597; AP755; BZ 101356
Come, come, ye Saints, no toil nor labor fear (Clayton) BC13 101357
Come, dearest Lord, descend and dwell (Watts) R531; S1 app.; V5; W297; AM250; AV36; BC 237; BY758 101358
Come down, O Love divine (Bianco da Siena) A376; B152; F235; J123; W191; X177; AF 239; BL34; BV214; BY224; BZ 101359
Come, ever blessed Spirit, come (Wordsworth) AO222; BA289; BV362 101360
Come every pious heart, that loves the Saviour's name (Stennett) V167 101361
Come, every soul by sin oppressed (Stockton) G184; I261; AE209; AH333; AI190; AM724; AR244; AS196; AT 235; AU197; AV331; AW457; AX227; AY102; BB567; BZ 101362
Come, faithful people, come away (Moultrie) E619; X 136 101363
Come, faithful Shepherd, bind me (Hutton) AZ811; BA595 101364
Come, Father, Son, and Holy Ghost (Wesley) I229; AW301; AZ98; BZ 101365
"Come, follow me," the Saviour said, Then let us (Nicholson) BC14 101366
Come, follow me, the Saviour spake (Scheffler) M232; Q 421; AA334 101367
Come for the feast is spread (Burton) H438; AI202; AM 391 101368
Come forth, my friend, the bride to meet (Alkobetz) R "Observe ye" and "remember" still 101369
Come forth, O Christian youth (Jackson) AE448 101370
Come forth, ye men of every race and nation (Smith, J.H.) Z487; AR570 101371
Come gentle peace, while shadows fall (---) BJ81 101372
Come, go with me, beyond the sea (Wheelock) BC15 101373
Come God Creator, Holy Ghost (Latin, 11th c) AA249 101374
Come, gracious Lord, descend and dwell (Watts) V5 X Come, dearest Lord, descend

and dwell 101375

Come, gracious Spirit, heavenly Dove, with light and comfort (Browne) A378; B201; D379; F232; J127; K150; L174; S209; V209; W188; AF238; AH229; AO223; AP283; AR221; AV145; AX44; AY2; AZ928; BB204; BE39; BR13a; BV215 101376

Come, hail the cause of Zion's youth (Kleinman) BC16 101377

Come, heaven-bound pilgrims, and join in God's praise (Shenk) AX56; AY323 101378

Come hither, all ye weary ones (Watts) V260 101379

Come hither, ye children, O come one and all (Schmidt) AW413 X O come, little children 101380

Come hither, ye faithful (Latin, 18th c) D50; K21; L216; M347; N33; O195; P125; AA159; AZ507; BA155; BR149 101381

Come, Holy Ghost, come, Lord our God (Hermannus Contractus) AZ1033 101382

Come, Holy Ghost, Creator blest (Latin, 9th c) A218; B375; D380; O355; P227; Q233; AH128; BM 89; BN119; BO186; BP46 101383

Come, Holy Ghost, Creator, come From thy bright heavenly (Latin, 9th c) BQ35 101384

Come, Holy Ghost, God and Lord (Luther) Q224 X Come, Holy Spirit, God and Lord X Veni creator 101385

Come, Holy Ghost, in love (Latin, 9th c) G17; H215; I184; K143; L172; O382; Q227; U129; V210; AL145; AM249; AS170; AW131; BA252; BY225 101386

Come, Holy Ghost! in us arise (Gill) AP279 101387

Come Holy Ghost, our hearts inspire, Let us Thine influence prove (Wesley) G175; H211; I181; W196; AL155; AP287; AZ148; BA132; BV288; BY244; BZ 101388

Come, Holy Ghost, our souls inspire and lighten with (Latin, 9th c) A217; B455; D289; E153; G636; J117; K 142; R237; W182; X178; AE 148; AF231; AL143; AP267; AZ373; BA133; BR481*; BV 216; BY226; BZ *composite 101389

Come Holy Ghost, our souls inspire, Let us Thine influence prove (Wesley) AZ148 X Come Holy Ghost, our hearts inspire ... 101390

Come Holy Ghost, send down those beams (Latin, 9th c) BO187 101391

Come, Holy Ghost, who ever one art (St Ambrose) B8; F11; BN120; BO183 101392

Come, Holy Ghost, with God the Son (St Ambrose) A160; E 255 101393

Come, Holy Spirit, calm my mind (Lock Chapel Collection 1803) V211; AY192 101394

Come, Holy Spirit, come! Let thy bright beams arise (Hart) D376; H219; K151; L 180; M460; Q225; T355; V214; W190; AA258; AL146; AM254; AP281; AZ1329; BA135; BB205; BV290 101395

Come, Holy Spirit come, O hear my lowly prayer (Thrupp) BV289 101396

Come, Holy Spirit, come with energy divine (Beddome) I 182 101397

Come, Holy Spirit, Dove divine, Bestow Thy glorious grace (Hickok) AR222; BF262 101398

Come, Holy Spirit, Dove divine, On these baptismal waters shine (Judson) AT385; AV 252 101399

Come, Holy Spirit from above, And from the realms (Latin, 9th c) AZ633 101400

Come, Holy Spirit, from avove and kindle in our hearts (Latin, 9th c) N159 101401

Come, Holy Spirit, from on high (---) BA283 101402

Come, Holy Spirit, God and Lord (Luther) J122; K146; L442; M471; N154; O375; Q224; AA 257; AF235; BV217 101403

Come, Holy Spirit, God-head One (St Ambrose) BM88 101404

Come, Holy Spirit, heavenly Dove, My sinful maladies remove (Browne) AP283 X Come gracious Spirit, heavenly Dove, with light and comfort from above 101405

Come, Holy Spirit, heavenly Dove, with all thy quickening powers (Watts) A369; B200; D377; G172; H209; I183; L173; M461; N161; R239; S206; T354; U130; V205; AA255; AE145; AF 240; AG128; AI123; AL156; AO 220; AP278; AS168; AT169; AU 268; AV147; AZ142; BA138; BB207; BR208; BZ 101406

Come, Holy Spirit, raise our songs (Wesley) H214 101407

Come home, come home, O why will you longer roam (Frost) R O soul, in the far-away country 101408

Come home, come home, Ye who are weary (Thompson) R Softly and tenderly 101409

Come home, poor sinner, why longer roam (Jeffrey) AX232 101410

Come, humble sinner, in whose breast (Jones) H252; I260; V293; AU454 101411

Come, humble soul, receive the good (Loy) M45 101412

Come in, O come! The door stands open now (Moule) BB336 101413

Come in, Thou blessed, honored Lord (Proud) BR83 101414

Come in, Thou blessed of the Lord (Montgomery) H416; AE341; AZ133 101415

Come Jesus, from the sapphire throne (Palmer) D297; L299; Q634; V571; AA455; BA325 101416

Come, Jesus, Redeemer, abide thou with me (Palmer) AZ 497 101417

Come, join the throng, on this glad day (Fries) BA330 101418

Come join, ye saints, with heart and voice (Medley) AZ638 101419

Come, kindred, upstand in the valour of Jesus (Clayton) X 470 101420

Come, Kingdom of our God (Johns) S404; V604; Y243; AD331; AE356; AN289; AO 525; AR571; AW269; AZ1375; BD156; BX392 101421

Come, labor on, Who dares stand idle (Borthwick) A576; B497; F339; R287; S366; X 471; AB262; AD317; AF293; BE41; BV593; BY511 101422

Come, lay his books and papers by (Greenwood) BC338 101423

Come, let our hearts and voices join (Swain) V379 101424

Come let us adore Him, Come bow at His feet (Latin, 18th c) Lp744; BR73 101425

Come let us all unite and sing (Hurditch) AP717 X Come let us all unite to sing 101426

Come let us all unite to sing, God is love (Hurditch) AE70; AP717; AS85; AW439; AX81 101427

Come, let us all with one accord (Chester) D26 101428

Come, let us anew, our journey pursue (Wesley) G536; I568; AL573; AZ22; BB369; BC17; BY712 101429

Come, let us join our cheerful songs (Watts) D447; E376; F221; H8; I24; J413; K130; L151; M414; Q343; V202; W175; X472; AA102; AL120; AO210; AR18; AS160; AV144; AW17; AY13; AZ146; BA115; BJ10; BV16; BY200 101430

Come, let us join our friends above (Wesley) F628; G422; H426; I611; K205; N210; O495

Q478; V615; AL176; AP309; AW319; AZ143; BA273; BY402; BZ 101431
Come, let us join our sacred songs (Watts) AY13 X Come, let us join our cheerful songs 101432
Come, let us join the Church above (Riley) E186 101433
Come, let us join with faithful souls (Tarrant) Y274; AB280; AC241; AF346; AK390; AN303; BD144; BF485; BX365 101434
Come, let us join with one accord (Wesley) H83; I63; U443; V66; AM323 101435
Come, let us praise our God and Lord (Montefiore) BH201 101436
Come, let us rise with Christ our Head (C. Wesley) BZ 101437
Come, let us sing a tender song (Chadwick) AB405; BF671 101438
Come, let us sing an evening hymn (Phelps) BC238 101439
Come, let us sing before the Lord (U. P. Psalter. 1912) T 180; AJ264 101440
Come let us sing in sweet accord (Stern) BH217 101441
Come, let us sing of a wonderful love (Walmsley) AL488; AM 669; AP399; BY411 101442
Come let us sing: Praise to our King (Horne) R Sing we the King who is coming to reign 101443
Come, let us sing the song of songs (Montgomery) D448; V194; AZ334; BA116; BB153; BV252 101444
Come, let us sing unto the Lord (Asso. Refd. Presby. Psalter, 1931) AM15 101445
Come, let us to the Lord our God (Morison [Morrison]) R125; W400; AD217; AI433; AL269; AM516; AP436; AW146; BV143; BY429 101446
Come, let us tune our loftiest song (West) G21; H66; I21; AT128; BZ 101447
Come, let us use the grace divine (Wesley) G540; I569 BZ 101448
Come, let us who in Christ believe (Wesley) I36; AL329; BZ 101449
Come, let us with our Lord arise (Wesley) BV69 101450
Come, let us worship and fall down before Christ (St John Chrysostom??) BL44 101451
Come, linger here with the Master (McKinney) AU453 101452
Come, listen to a prophet's voice (---) BC46 101453
Come, Lord, and tarry not (Bonar) H203; L345; R233; S188; U123; V185; AR209; AV121; AW129; AZ1334; BA 99; BB174 101454
Come, Lord, and warm each languid heart (Steele) V578 101455
Come, Lord, Thyself, in all Thy grace (Petrusson) M308 101456
Come, Lord, Thyself with Thine abounding grace (Petrusson) P424 101457
Come, lost one, your Saviour is calling (Shoemaker) AX225; AY230 101458
Come, love we God! of might is most the Father (Richard Shanne ms) BG10 101459
Come, lowly souls that mourn (Stennett) AZ1336 101460
Come, Master Workman, work with us (Hingley) Y215 101461
Come, mighty Spirit, penetrate (Bonar) AN49; BX280 101462
Come, my heart, canst thou not hear it (Knight) AB110; BF296 101463
Come, my Redeemer, come (Reed) AY264 101464
Come, my soul, thou must be waking (Canitz) A154; B3; D3; G30; J207; K445; L4; O547; R44; S487; T302; V37;

Y359; Z134; AB2; AD36; AE39; AF506; AG19; AH160; AK46; AM334; AN88; AO18; AP660; AR43; AV10; AW27; AZ595; BA769; BD1; BF177; BK39; BV38; BX150; BY674; BZ 101465

Come, my soul, thy plea prepare (Newton) BV607 X Come, my soul, thy suit prepare 101466

Come, my soul, thy suit prepare (Newton) B304; D651; E377; F 319; H60; I507; K277; L409; M74; N304; O16; Q459; R529; S17app.; U357; V467; W450; X473; AA56; AL347; AM531; AP497; AZ72; BA596; BB318; BV607; BY333 101467

Come, my way, my truth, my life (Herbert) X474; AQ123; AZ86; BL32 101468

Come now, all people, keep high mirth (Dearmer) X475 101469

Come, O come in pious lays (Wither) BX18 101470

Come, O come, thou quickening Spirit, Thou from ... (Held) J126; K149; M465; N157; O426; P231; Q226; AA246; AM247; AW548; AZ608 101471

Come, O Creator Spirit blest (Latin, before 10th c) H207; AM251; AO226; AZ375; BA 134 101472

Come, O Creator Spirit, come (Latin, before 10th c) E154; F152; X179; BJ48 101473

Come, O holy Sabbath evening (Mayer) BH105 101474

Come, O Jesus, and prepare me (Franzèn) M55; N245 101475

Come, O Lord, like morning sunlight (Littlefield) G33; AB 44; AC14; AD38; BF223; BK 42 101476

Come, O my soul, on sacred lays (Blacklock) H108; I23; AV29 101477

Come, O Sabbath day, and bring (Gottheil) AHp.150; BH118 101478

"Come, O sinner, all is ready!" (Dahl) N244 101479

Come, O Spirit, seal me thine (Warner) R Fill me with Thy Spirit, Lord 101480

Come, O thou all-victorious Lord (Wesley) I241; BV482 101481

Come, O thou God of grace (Evans) G550; I661; S483; AD415; AE347; AR523; AS 438; BF592; BZ 101482

Come, O thou King of Kings (Pratt) BC20 101483

Come, O thou Traveler unknown (Wesley) B230; E378; F343; G311; I511; J471; W416; X476; AL312; BB243; BX114; BY767; BZ 101484

Come on, my partners in distress (Wesley) I432 101485

Come! Peace of God, and dwell again on earth (Rowland) G510; Z555 101486

Come, praise your Lord and Saviour (How) D533; W70; AP748; AZ847; BA814 101487

Come, pure hearts, in sweetest measure (Latin, 12th c) A134; B288; D497; F508; AZ642; BR241 101488

Come, Rain from the heavens (Stegmann) M473 101489

Come, Redeemer, blessed Jesus (Wesley) BR160 X Come, thou long-expected Jesus 101490

Come, rejoice, the King of glory (Cannon) BC1 101491

Come rejoicing, Faithful men with rapture singing (Latin, 11th c) or earlier C22 101492

Come rejoicing, Praises voicing, Christmas day is breaking (Latin 12th c) Q82 101493

Come, ring out our joy to the Lord (Ladies of the Grail) BSp30 101494

Come, risen Lord, and deign to be our guest (Briggs) A207; X266; AF286; AW307; BV374; BY312 101495

Come, sacred Spirit, from above (Doddridge) V582 101496

Come, said Jesus' sacred voice (Barbauld) G192; H260; I257; L364; AO636; AT244; AV158; BA400; BR391 101497

Come, Saviour, come, and give thy Spirit course (Bayley) R O Jesus, Lord and Saviour, the soul's ... 101498

Come, Saviour dear, with us abide (Rutström) N298 101499

Come, Saviour Jesus, from above (Bourignon) I379 101500

Come, says Jesus' sacred voice (Barbauld) AT244 X Come said Jesus' sacred voice 101501

Come, see the place where Jesus lay (Kelly) B174; N126; AZ 632 101502

Come, sing, thou happy church of God (Zinzendorf, N. L.) AZ736 101503

Come, sing to the Lord, His name to praise (deJong) BC32 101504

Come, sing to the Lord of harvest (Monsell) BI113 X Sing to the Lord of harvest 101505

Come, sing with holy gladness (St John of Damascus) BD239 X The day of resurrection 101506

Come, sing, ye choirs exultant (Adam of St Victor) A133; E179; F509 101507

Come, sinners, to the gospel feast (Wesley) G186; H251; I256; AZ414; BZ 101508

Come, sound his praise abroad (Watts) G22; H4; I3; L81; N294; V106; Z118; AI14; AM102; AO69; AS77; BA640; BB172; BR82; BX 23; BZ 101509

Come, take by faith the Body of your Lord (Bangor Antiphoner) BA296 X Draw nigh and take the Body 101510

Come, Thou all-transforming Spirit (Evans) BE42 X Come, thou soul-transforming Spirit 101511

Come, thou almighty King (Whitfield. Hymnbook. 1757) A271; B209; D388; G2; H15; I2; J136; K164; L179; M480; N164; O73; P237; Q239; R244; S52; T296; U3; V81; Y354; Z122; AA262; AB13; AC38; AD20; AE154; AF246; AG12; AH189; AI24; AK4; AL5; AM89; AN10; AO2; AQ26; AR21; AS1; AT12; AU4; AV32; AW8; AX1; AY 27; AZ1234; BA10; BB3; BD 24; BF216; BI39; BK63; BX8; BZ 101512

Come, thou Almighty Will! Our fainting bosoms fill (Hymns of the Spirit. 1864) AN47; BX9 101513

Come, thou bright and morning-star (Rosenroth) J212; Q529; X27; AW554a 101514

Come, thou bright and morning-star (Rosenroth) X Dayspring of eternity 101515

Come, thou Desire of all thy saints (Steele) H8; V413 101516

Come, thou everlasting Spirit (Wesley) AP273; AY16; BY 227 101517

Come, thou Fount of every blessing (Robinson) G23 X Saviour, Source of every blessing 101518

Come, thou glorious day of promise (Neibaur) BC240 101519

Come, thou holy Paraclete (Latin, 13th c) E155; W186; X180; AL144;AP266 101520

Come, thou Holy Spirit, come! (Latin, 9th c) A109; B196; D378; BO189; BR205; BV225; BY228 101521

Come, thou long-expected Jesus (Wesley) A1; B55; D48; F54; G84; H133; I116; J5; K12; L404; M340; N22; O202; P120; R151; S113; T350; U64; V124; W150; AE76; AF103; AG62; AK89; AL132; AM145; AO117; AP248; AR104; AT70; AV93; AW69; AZ255; BA148; BL2; BR160; BV86; BY78; BZ 101522

Come, thou my Light, that I

may see (Kerr) AR399 101523
Come Thou now and be among us (Latin, 7th c) K242; L295; O131 101524
Come thou, O come, sweetest and kindliest (St Anselm of Canterbury) AB97; BR201 101525
Come, thou precious Ransom, come (Olearius) Q55; AA134 101526
Come thou Redeemer of the earth (St Ambrose) E14 101527
Come, thou Saviour of our race (St Ambrose) N23; O186; P 123 101528
Come, thou soul-transforming Spirit (Evans) AZ1407; BE42 101529
Come, thou universal Blessing (Wesley) AZ962 101530
Come, though with purifying fire (Scudder) Y292 101531
Come to Calvary's holy mountain (Montgomery) J82; L363; M 405; N106; O399; P253; Q149; AA212; AZ597; BA193 101532
Come to Jesus, come to Jesus (---) R Are you weary, heavy laden 101533
Come to Jesus, ye who labor (Parker) Z282; AT246; BF346 101534
Come to our dark nature's night (Rawson) BV286 X Come to our poor nature's night 101535
Come to our poor nature's night (Rawson) B203; D135; H208; V215; AB98; AI118; AK189; AL161; AM248; AO229; AP271; AZ1133; BB216; BR202; BV286; BY229 101536
Come to the church in the wildwood (Pitts) R There's a church in the valley 101537
Come to the land of peace (Hemans) BE44 101538
Come to the Light, 'tis shining for thee (Bliss) R The whole world was lost 101539
Come to the Saviour, make no delay (Root) N647; AI391; AM693; AP758; AX233 101540
Come to the Saviour now, He gently calleth thee (Wigner) G190; R261; S220; T431; U 166; V263; Z278; AG138; AK 463; AM395; AO644; AR245; AT226 101541
Come to the Saviour, On Him your burdens roll (McKinney) R O, come, all ye that labor 101542
Come tonight and do not tarry (Toews) R Come, ye weary ones 101543
Come unto Jesus; ye heavy laden (Huish) BC22 101544
"Come unto me," it is the Saviour's voice (Norton) AI 194; AS193 101545
Come unto me, when shadows darkly gather (Esling) G350; H372; I462; L358; N523; O517; V765; AO253; AR439; BB323; BX273 101546
Come unto me, ye weary (Dix) B387; D437; E379; F350; G 194; I295; L361; O514; P249; Q276; R268; S222; T432; U 165; V255; W390; Z277; AA 49; AB156; AF315; AH614; AI204; AK305; AL470; AM405; AP396; AR246; AT227; AV159; AW240; AZ844; BA401; BE43; BF343; BR353; BV470; BY412 101547
Come, we that love the Lord (Watts) G227; H12; I22; J165; K308; L455; R408; U208; V526; W447; Z119; AE282; AH199; AK30; AL288; AO72; AP444; AR441; AS287; AT308; AU8; AV343; AW443; AX29; AY138; AZ1354; BA369; BB640; BC 25; BY495; BZ 101548
Come, we who love the Lord (Watts) AK30 X Come, we that love the Lord 101549
Come with thy sins to the fountain (Crosby) AX231 101550
Come with us, O blessed Jesus (Hopkins) A211; J283 101551
Come, women, wide proclaim (Heck) AU214 101552
Come, worship at Immanuel's

feet (Watts) AZ336 101553

Come, ye children of the Lord (Wallis) BC23 101554

Come, ye disconsolate, where'er ye languish (Moore & Hastings) A483; B388; D637; G312; H441; I526; J569; K412; L366; M27; N477; O438; P266; Q531; R373; S293; U229; V428; W688; Z398; AA512; AD264; AE163; AG134; AH382; AI293; AK303; AL435; AM518; AO250; AP532; AR247; AS198; AT297; AU449; AV280; AW243; AY350; AZ1152; BA 693; BB223; BC18; BE40; BR 339; BZ 101555

Come ye faithful, raise the anthem (Hupton) E380; F222; X477; AZ627; BV257; BY201 101556

Come, ye faithful, raise the strain (St John of Damascus) A94; B170; D110; E131; F133; G151; I163; J106; K108; M445; N131; O328; P195; Q204; R205; S168; V767; X144; Z242; AD 162; AE136; AF185; AG101; AH301; AK169; AM200; AO180; AR183; AT109; AW113; AZ865; BB136; BD246; BF319; BR179; BY155; BZ 101557

Come, ye faithful servants (Levy) BH101 101558

Come, ye people, raise the anthem (Hupton) X477 X Come ye faithful, raise the anthem 101559

Come, ye people, rise and sing (Alington) R39 101560

Come, ye saints, look here and wonder (Kelly) BA235 101561

Come, ye sinners, poor and needy (Hart) G187; H255; I 259; N399; V253; W393; AI195; AL476; AM393; AP404; AT241; AU229; AV341; AW459; AX240; AY229; AZ1408; BA399; BV473; BZ 101562

Come, ye sinners, poor and wretched (Hart) V253 X Come, ye sinners, poor and needy 101563

Come, ye souls by sin afflicted (Swain) W392; AM390; AP 403; BV471; BY413 101564

Come, ye thankful people, come (Alford) A137; B421; D193; E289; F482; G545; H521; I717; J360; K484; L555; M491; N 574; O532; P243; Q574; R525; S460; T444; U483; V617; W 619; X9; Z593; AA295; AB 389; AC322; AD447; AE426; *AF461, 462; AG287; AH493; AI350; AK434; AL577; AM615; AN141; AO579; AP691; AQ 278; AR594; AT490; AU136; AV307; AW377; AZ1050; BA 861; BB496; BC29; BD198; BF650; BK136; BL55; BR490; BV648; BX177; BY724; BZ *words differ, these two poems 101565

Come, ye that fear Jehovah (U.P. Psalter. 1912) T35; AJ50; AP18 101566

Come, ye that fear the Lord, and hear (U.P. Psalter. 1912) R296; AJ174 101567

Come, ye that love the Lord (Watts) L455 X Come, we that love the lord 101568

Come, ye that love the Saviour's name (Steele) I34; V188; AM588 101569

Come, ye wanderers, all forsaken (Pollock) AX222; AY 225 101570

Come, ye weary, heavy laden (Pollock) R Come, ye wanderers 101571

Come, ye weary ones, tonight (Toews) AX234 101572

Come, ye weary sinners, come (Wesley) O515; AA58 101573

Come ye yourselves apart and rest awhile (Bickersteth) BV375 101574

Come, your hearts and voices raising (Gerhardt) Q90 101575

Comes any good from Nazareth (Sangster) Y69; AB152 101576

Cometh sunshine after rain (Gerhardt) X478 101577

Comfort, comfort ye, my people (Olearius) J12; K8; M337; N3; O170; Q61; AA130; AF104; AI440; AK90; AM148; AR333; AZ91 101578

Comfort ye, my people, saith your God (Bayly) R O joyful hope 101579

Coming home, coming home (Kirkpatrick) R I've wandered far 101580

Coming now to thee, O Christ my Lord (McKinney) AT342 101581

Command thy blessing from above (Montgomery) W241; AZ305; BA370; BY357 101582

Commit thou all that grieves thee (Gerhardt, tr. by Farlander) A446; M269; P285 101583

Commit thou all thy griefs (Gerhardt, tr. by Wesley) I435; K399; L516; N474; W546; X479; AK308; AL420; AM560; AO102; AP516; AW558a; BR316; BV525; BW558; BX309; BY574 101584

Commit thou every grievance (Gerhardt) AZ807; BA682 101585

Commit whatever grieves thee (Gerhardt, tr. by Kelly) Q520; AA525 101586

Comrades known in marches many (Halpine) Y148; AC238 101587

Concordi laetitia (Latin, 13th c) BN151; BO123; BP74; BQ197 101588

Conditor alme siderum (Latin, 9th c) BJ47b 101589

Comfirma hoc Deus (Latin) BQ 245 101590

Conquering kings their titles take (Breviary, Nevers. 1727) A324; B91; D322; E37; F191; J509; AZ69; BV552 101591

Conquering now and still to conquer (Crosby) AI330; AM665 101592

Conquering Prince and King of Glory (Tersteegen) O363; AZ 901; BV199 101593

Conquering Prince and Lord of Glory (Tersteegen) AZ901 X Conquering Prince and King of Glory 101594

Consider well your ways and lives (Torrence) AQ262 101595

Constantine! Constantine! Look above the battle scene (Henderson) Y114 101596

Content, O Lord, and free from fear (Wolcott) AE214 101597

Cor, arca legem continens (Breviary, Bologna, 1827) BN 66; BQ240 101598

Cor dulce, cor amabile Latin BN68; BO15 101599

Cor Jesu sacratissium (Litany of the Sacred Heart) BN67; BO23; BQ238 101600

Cor Jesu, salus in te sperantium (Latin) BQ237 101601

Corde natus ex Parentis (Prudentius) BT98 101602

Count your blessings (Oatman) R When upon life's billows 101603

Countless hosts before God's throne (Gregor) BA746 X O how excellent and fair 101604

Courage, brother! do not stumble (MacLeod) G298; I513; W529; AO402; AP533; BA573; BB 263; BH87; BY563 101605

Courage, my sorely tempted heart! (Boehmer) AZ512 101606

Courage my soul! While God is near (---) L512 101607

Courans à la fete, ne différons pas (French trad carol) BG154b 101608

Cover with His life, whiter than snow (Belden) R Look upon Jesus, sinless is He 191609

Create in this weak form of mine (Weitzman) BH170 101610

Creation's Lord, we give Thee thanks (Hyde) A548; Z492; AB177; AD344; AF303; AL416; AN311; AQ108, 221; BF581; BX348 101611

Creator alme siderum (Latin,

7th c) BN3; BO285; BP2; BQ 151 101612

Creator of the earth and sky (St Ambrose) E49; X44 101613

Creator of the starry height (Latin, 9th c) F45; O174; BP3 101614

Creator of the stars of night (Latin, 9th c) A6; E1; AF113; BL4; BM97; BZ 101615

Creator of the universe, we lift our minds (Hughes) BK33 101616

Creator of the world, to thee (Coffin) F83 101617

Creator of the world we pray (St Ambrose) BM96 101618

Creator Spirit, all divine (Latin, 9th c) BP45 101619

Creator Spirit, by whose aid (Latin, 9th c) A371; B198; D 381; E156; I194; J124; Q236; V219; W184; X181; AD183; AN 61; AP268; AZ376; BA140; BL 35; BX72; BY230 101620

Creator, Spirit, heavenly Dove (Latin, 9th c) M464 101621

Creator Spirit, Lord of grace (Latin, before 10th c) 101622 BP43

Cross of Christ, O sacred tree (Taylor) AS137; AX117; AY199 101623

Cross of Jesus, cross of sorrow (Simpson) R196; S155; V754; AE113; AK163; AO173; AR171; AW111; BZ 101624

Crown him! crown him! Angels crown him (Stebbins) AY267 X Look, ye saints (Kelly) 101625

Crown Him the Lord of peace (Bridges) BT341 X Crown him with many crowns 101626

Crown him upon the throne (Dearmer) X480 101627

Crown him with many crowns (Bridges) A352; B190; D374; E 381; F224; G170; H198; I179; J431; K134; L153; M452; N341; P30; Q341; R213; S190; T349; U115; V195; W136; Y333; Z250; AA104; AB88; AC136; AD170; AE132; AF199; AG100; AH328; AK176; AL115; AM216; AO198; AP227; AR105; AS157; AT152; AU18; AV141; AW118; AZ 1492; BA243; BB162; BF325; BL58; BN75; BQ43; BT341; BV209; BY182; BZ 101628

Crown His head with endless blessing (Goode) V199; AM 130; AV127 101629

Crown with thy benediction (Greenwood) O535 101630

Crushed by my sin, O Lord, to Thee (Gellert) N237; O102 101631

Cry out with joy to the Lord, all the earth! (Ladies of the Grail) BSp42 101632

D

Da Jesus an des Kreuzes Stamm (Böschenstain) BT177 101633

Daily, daily, sing the praises (Baring-Gould) E568; H515 101634

Daily, daily sing to Mary (St Bernard of Cluny) BN132 X Daily sing in praise of Mary 101635

Daily sing in praise of Mary (St Bernard of Cluny) BM52; BN132; BO59; BP79; BQ75 101636

Daisies are our silver (Struther) X354 101637

Dank sei Gott in der Höhe (Mühlmann) BT544 101638

Dankt dem Herrn! mit frohen Gaben. (G. N. Fischer) BW 376 101639

Dankt Gott in seinem hochsten Thron (Ausbund) BU43 101640

Dans cette étable (French trad carol) BG75b 101641

Dare to be a Daniel (Bliss) R Standing by a purpose true 101642

Dare to be brave, dare to be true (Rooper) AH613; AT411; AU320; AV401 101643

Dare to do right, dare to be true (Taylor) AP772 101644

Dark and thorny is the desert (---) AX449; BY388 101645
Dark hills at evening in the west (Robinson) AQ273 101646
Dark is the hour when death prevails (Smith, U.) BB492 101647
Dark the day on Calvary's cross (Watt) W112; AW538 101648
Dark the night lay, wild and dreary (Welsh trad carol) BG 9 101649
Darkening night the land doth cover (St Anatolius) AW32 BJ64 101650
Darkly rose the guilty morning (Anstice) V155 101651
Darkness o'er the earth is stealing (Landstad) O558 101652
Das alte Jahr vergangen ist (Steuerlein) BT125 101653
Das ist der Gemeinde Stärke (Preiswerk) BT461 101654
Das Wort der Wahrheit Jesu Christ (Ausbund) BU67 101655
Daughter of a mighty Father (---) BO81 101656
Daughter of God the Father (---) BO115 101657
Daughter of Zion, awake from thy sadness (Fitzgerald. Collection, 1830) L353; BB303; BE200; BI50 101658
Daughter of Zion, from the dust (Montgomery) H474 101659
Day by Day, Dear Lord, of Thee three things I pray (St Richard of Chichester) A429; R541; S 39app.; X399; AG336; AR555 101660
Day by day the manna fell (Conder) I438; AN66; AP509; AW 247; AZ44; BA27; BE46; BR 254; BX99 101661
Day by day we magnify thee (Ellerton) AP716 101662
Day is dawning in the east (Lathbury) M637 101663
Day is done, gone the sun, from the lakes (---) Y399; AC344; AG339; AH566; BB370 101664
Day is dying in the west (Lathbury) G44; I57; J234; L20; M638; N559; R65; S39; T307; U463; V54; Y96; Z144; AB23; AC17; AD47; AE43; AF45; AG31; AH168; AI53; AK481; AL562; AM343; AO27; AR50; AS25; AT29; AU87; AV12; AW31; AY440; BA782; BB51; BD13; BF202; BK44; BY689; BZ 101665
Day of judgment -- day of wonders (Newton: Dies irae) L577; N610; V684; AI98; AM 241; AZ1377; BA738 101666
Day of judgment -- day of wonders (Newton) X Day of wrath, O day of mourning (Latin, 13th c) 101667
Day of wonder, day of gladness (Hall) N129 101668
Day of wrath and doom impending (Latin, 13th c) E351 X Day of wrath! O day of mourning 101669
Day of wrath! O day of mourning (Latin, 13th c: Irons tr) A 468; D36; E351; F466; I747; K515; O601; Q607; AA555; AZ1513; BA929; BJ1b 101670
Day of wrath, O dreadful day (Latin, 13th c : Stanley tr) I599 101671
Day of wrath! that day of mourning (Latin, 13th c) O601 X Day of wrath! O day ... 101672
Days and moments quickly flying (Caswall) E382; V632; W585; AP609; AZ270; BA742 101673
Dayspring of Eternity, Brightness of the Father's glory (Rosenroth) N548 X Dayspring of Eternity, Light from endless Light 101674
Dayspring of Eternity, light from endless Light proceeding (Rosenroth) K454; M555; N 548; O548; P52; AK47 101675
Dayspring of Eternity, Light of Light, from God proceeding (Rosenroth) M555 X Dayspring of Eternity, Light from endless light 101676

Daystar on high, bright harbinger of gladness (Stainer) F604 101677

Dear angel, ever at my side (Faber) BN163; BO195; BP88; BQ112 101678

Dear Christians, let us all rejoice (Luther) M121 101679

Dear Christians, one and all rejoice (Luther) N433; O526; Q387; AA310 101680

Dear Crown of all the virgin-choir (Latin, 8th c) BQ109 101681

Dear Father, here thy children come (Rosewater) BH257 101682

Dear Father, keep me through this day (Briggs) X400 101683

Dear Father, loud the ocean rolls (Gower) Z330 101684

Dear Father-Mother, thou dost grant (Sargant) BE48 101685

Dear Father, to thy mercy-seat (Steele) AK229; AO312 101686

Dear Father, who hast made us all (Knapp) Q299 101687

Dear God, how glorious is thy name (Snelling) BE45 101688

Dear God, our Father, at Thy knee confessing (Bates) G361; Y144; Z291; AC153; AR 400; BF358 101689

Dear God, the sun whose light is sweet (Knapp) Y67; AB333; AN217 101690

Dear Guardian of Mary (Faber) AH141; BO128 101691

Dear Heart of Jesus, hear! (---) R O Sacred Heart of Christ aflame 101692

Dear Jesus, ever at my side (Faber) D564 101693

Dear Jesus, receive me (Crosby) R Loving Saviour, hear my cry 101694

Dear land, of liberty, hope of the (Richards) AO602 101695

Dear little One how sweet thou art (Faber) BO155; BQ127 101696

Dear Lord and Father of mankind (Whittier) A435; B120; E382; F184; G342; H328; I543; J467; N331; R416; S302; T406; U 242; V410; W245; X481; Y80; Z411; AB212; AC152; AD279; AE176; AF341; AG202; AH 400; AK226; AL286; AN250; AO366; AP437; AQ118; AR334; AS303; AT335; AU401; AV63; AW181; BA514; BB116; BD 112; BE49; BF421; BK83; BV608; BX285; BY50; BZ 101697

Dear Lord and Father of us all (Whittier) BE49 X Dear Lord and Father of mankind 101698

Dear Lord and Master mine (Gill) AM576 101699

Dear Lord, before we part (Psalms and hymns, 1858) BY313 101700

Dear Lord, for all in pain (Carmichael) BV396 101701

Dear Lord, I come at last (McManus) AY227 101702

Dear Lord, my soul desireth (Gambold) AZ569 101703

Dear Lord, to thy true servants give (Polack) Q482 101704

Dear Lord, today, our child (Busch) AM353 101705

Dear Lord, who sought at dawn of day (Farrington) Y108; AB276; AC112; AR279; BF 307 101706

Dear Maker of the starry skies (Latin, 7th c) BN4 101707

Dear Master, in whose life I see (Hunter) G376; S507; W460; Z318; AF208; BY465; BZ 101708

Dear Master, what can children do? (Matheson) W361 101709

Dear Redeemer, we would hallow (Warner) R By thy blessed word 101710

Dear refuge of my weary soul (Steele) H349; L511; V368; AA502 101711

Dear St Joseph, pure and gentle (---) BO132 101712

Dear Saviour, bless us ere we go (Faber) AO45 X O Saviour, bless us ere we go 101713
Dear Saviour, if these lambs should stray (Hyde) H453; V 545; AZ358; BA849 101714
Dear Saviour, stretch thy loving arms (Smyth) BR525 101715
Dear Saviour, we are thine (Doddridge) V452; AO368 101716
Dear Saviour, we bless thee that thou wast a child (Cennick) AZ490 101717
Dear Saviour, we would know thy love (---) BB147 101718
Dear Saviour, when I think of thee (Kolb) AY248 101719
Dear Shepherd of thy people hear (Newton) V569 X Great Shepherd of thy people 101720
Dear ties of mutual succor bind (Bryant) I689 101721
Dear to the heart of the Shepherd (Wingate) BC26 101722
Dearest children, God is near you (Walker) BC170 101723
Dearest Jesus, come to me (Scheffler) AZ37 101724
Dearest Jesus, draw thou near me (Kingo) O37; P39 101725
Dearest Jesu, we are here, At thy call [general hymn] (Clausnitzer) F408; G310 101726
Dearest Jesus, we are here, Gladly thy command obeying [Baptism] (Schmolck) Q300 101727
Dearest of all the names above (Watts) V128 101728
Death, death, thou hast conquered me (Sower [Sauer]) AR418 101729
Death in all this world prevaileth (Albinus) O513 101730
Death shall not destroy my comfort (---) AY191 101731
Debilis cessent elementa legis (Besnault) BT117 101732
Deceit and falsehood I abhor (U.P. Psalter. 1912) T239; AJ335 101733
Deck the hall with boughs of holly (English trad carol) BG50b 101734
Deck thyself, my soul, with gladness (Franck) A210; E306; F393; J262; K182; L48; N246; O149; P100; Q 305; W324; X267; AA432; AI426; AK334; AL221; AN 494; AW552; AZ423; BY314; BZ 101735
Deck thyself with joy and gladness (Franck) J262 X Deck thyself, my soul, with gladness 101736
Declare, O heavens, the Lord of space (Edwards) BL76 101737
Deem not that they are blest alone (Bryant) I456 X O deem not they are blest alone 101738
Deep and glorious, word victorious (Oldenburg) O251; P160 101739
Deep and precious, strong and gracious (Oldenburg) M34 101740
Deep are his wounds, and red (Johnson) J80 101741
Deep are the wounds which sin has made (Steele) H223 101742
Deep in the dust before Thy throne (Watts) L377 101743
Deep river, My home is over Jordan (Negro traditional) AR488 101744
Deeper yet, deeper yet, Into the crimson flood (Oatman) R In the blood from the cross 101745
Deeply moved and duly heeding (Zinzendorf, A. N.) AZ429 101746
Defend me, Lord, from shame (Tate & Brady) AJ82 101747
Defend me, O God, and plead my cause (Ladies of the Grail) BSp20 101748
Defend us, Lord, from every ill (Hay) I403; AV70 101749
Deign this union to approve

(Collyer) AX1268 101750
Delay not, delay not, O sinner, draw near (Hastings) L371; M24; Q278; U164; V270; AA547; AI207 101751
Deliver me from evil, Preserve me, Lord (U. P. Psalter, 1912) T277; AJ385 101752
Deliver me, my God, from all that's now enchanting (Gedicke) AZ711 101753
Den store hvide Folk vi se (Brorson) BT656 101754
Den Vater woll'n wir loben (G. Wagner) BU34 101755
Depth of mercy! can there be (Wesley) G200; H265; I267; R273; U173; V286; AG146; AI 216; AK209; AO264; AP434; AS 199; AT242; AU288; AV164; AY216; BB234; BZ 101756
Der Bräut'gam wird bald rugen (Walther) BT67 101757
Der Glaub beschutzt mich ganz und gar (Ausbund) BU60 101758
Der Heiland rufet mir und dir (Unparth. G. B.) AY34d 101759
Der herr uns segne und behüt (Unparth. G. B.) AY6d 101760
Der mange skal komme fra Ost og fra Vest (Landstad) BT415 101761
Der Tag, der ist so freudenreich (Latin 14th c) BT78 101762
Der Winter kalt, rauh ungestalt (Ausbund) BU47 101763
Descend, descend, O Sabbath Princess (Cohen) BH107 101764
Descend to thy Jerusalem, O Lord. (Taylor) BX202 X Draw night to thy Jerusalem 101765
Desire of every nation (Hoppe) N69 101766
Despair not, O heart, in thy sorrow (Prudentius) J297; O595; P418 101767
Despise not, Lord, my lowly penitence (Ha-Levi) BH162 101768
Destroy, O Lord, the carnal mind (Zinzendorf, N. L.) AZ921 101769
Deus, tuorum militum (Latin, 6th c) BN181; BO290 101770
Dha-ke-de hia-u-dha (Omaha [Indian] trad) Y314 101771
Decimus grates tibi, summe rerum (Melanchthon) BT254 101772
Did Christ o'er sinners weep (Beddome) I276; U178; V284; AY262; AZ1294 101773
Did you pray till the answer came (Poole) R Have you prayed all night 101774
Didst thou, dear Jesus, pray for me (Ryden) M404; N141 101775
Didst thou, dear Jesus, suffer shame (Maxwell) U182; V438 101776
Die Asche will nicht lassen ab (Luther) BT259 101777
Die beste Freud aus Gottes Wort (Ausbund) BU14 101778
Die ganze welt, Herr Jesu Christ (German carol, 1623) BG96b 101779
Die güldne Sonne, Voll Freud und Wonne (P. Gerhardt) BW555 101780
Die helle Sonn' leucht't herfür (Herman) BT547 101781
Die Lieb ist kalt jetzt in der Welt (L. Schornschlager) BU 57 101782
Die Nacht ist kommen (Herbert) BT556 101783
Die sach' ist dein, Herr Jesu Christ (Preiswerk) AW550b; BW550 101784
Dies est laetitia, In ortu regali (Latin, 14th c) BQ294 101785
Dies irae, dies illa (Latin, 13th c) BMp. 162; BN243; BOp. 258; BQ270D; BT607 101786
Dies ist die Nacht, da mir erschienen (Nachtenhöfer) BT88 101787
Dies sind die heil'gen Zehn Gebot (Luther) BT287 101788
Dim mine eyes with many teardrops (Rypins) BH173 101789

Dir, dir Jehova, will ich singen (Crasselius) BT21; BW569 101790

Dir, Herr, sei dieses Kind empfohlen (Neander, C.F.) BT 303 101791

Dismiss me not thy service, Lord (Lynch) E555; W354; X297; AL381; AP578; BR380; BY512 101792

Dismiss us, Lord, with blessing, we pray (Froom) BB702 101793

Dismiss us with thy blessing, Lord! (Hart) L61; U450; V20; Z639; AP342; AX80; AY 411; AZ327 101794

Disposer supreme, and Judge of the earth (Santeuil) E178; F 506; X211; Y386; BJ52; BV 459 101795

Divinity is round us (Fahs) AQ 58 101796

Do life's storms above thee roll? (Reed) AX516; AY311 101797

Do no sinful action, speak no angry word (Alexander) E589; F433; W663; AP771 101798

Do not I love thee, O my Lord (Doddridge) H329; I338; V378; AR106 101799

Do not turn the lambs away (Mitchell) R Hark! I hear my Saviour say 101800

Do ye, O men, speak righteousness (U.P. Psalter. 1912) T107; AJ 156 101801

Do you ask what most I prize (Schwedler) AZ1158; BA480 101802

Do you love the world, in its pomp and show (Warren) AX 265 101803

Do you seek for a friend who is always the same (Bills) AX 279 101804

Do what is right; the day-dawn is breaking (---) BC27 101805

Does Jesus care when my heart is pained (Graeff) AX528; AY 464 101806

Does the journey seem long (Smith, J.F.) BC245 101807

Does thy soul leap up within thee (Versteeg) AK139 101808

Dominic, our Lady's champion (Lee) BN177 101809

Dona nobis pacem, pacem (---) BK34 101810

Done is the work that saves (Bonar) AZ1179 101811

Don't forget the Sabbath, The Lord our God hath blest (Crosby) BB653 101812

Don't let your light burn low (Ussery) R O would you be a blessing 101813

Don't turn him away (Lillenas) R Patiently, tenderly pleading 101814

Don't you hear the bells now ringing (DeMarbelle) R There's a land 101815

Don't you want to go to heaven (Negro spiritual) AH597 X We are climbing Jacob's ladder 101816

Dormi, Jesu! mater ridet (Latin carol) BG175 101817

Dost thou in a manger lie (Mauburn) A29; B550; AZ1087; BR142 101818

Dost thou truly seek renown (Latin, 14th-15th c) E97 101819

Down at the cross where my Saviour died (Hoffman) AT 95; AU185; AV386; AW464; AX4 101820

Down by the river's verdant side (Bible. Psalm 137) BC 55 101821

Down from the worlds of radiant light (Proud) BR131 101822

Down in the valley where summer's laughing beam (Binyon) BG161 101823

Down in the valley with my Saviour (Cushing) AU118; AX412 101824

Down in yon forest there stands a hall (English trad carol) BG61 101825

Down the dark future, Through long generations (Longfellow) AC292 101826

Down the mines for buried treasure (Jackson) BY365 101827
Down through the ages vast (Omaha [Indian] trad) Y314 101828
Down to the sacred wave (Smith, S.F.) AS456; AU282 101829
Down with the rosemary and bays (Herrick) BG126 101830
Draw, Holy Ghost, thy sevenfold veil (Keble) D214 101831
Draw me nearer, nearer, blessed Lord (Crosby) R I am thine, O Lord 101832
Draw me, O Lord, to thee, Nearer to thee (Jacobs) N449 X Nearer my God to thee! Nearer to thee. Through word and sacrament 101833
Draw near, draw near (McKinney) AU304 101834
Draw near, O Son of God, draw near (Wesley) H465 101835
Draw nigh and take the Body of the Lord (Bangor Antiphoner, ca 690) A202; B330; D220; E 307; F386; J273; K187; L325; O150; Q307; X268; AA427; AO 442; AY433; BA296; BR475; BV373 101836
Draw night, draw nigh, Immanuel (Latin, ca 9th c) AZ677 X O come, O come, Emmanuel 101837
"Draw nigh to God, he will draw nigh to you." (Tarrant) BX 274 101838
Draw nigh to thy Jerusalem, O Lord (Taylor) S148; Y246; AC118; AD142; AF156; BF310; BV168; BX202 101839
Draw Thou my soul, O Christ (Larcom) G297; R284; U250; Y370; Z299; AB264; AC149; AE273; AF318; AG160; AK206; AR348; AS242; AT314; BZ 101840
Draw us in the Spirit's tether (Dearmer) X274b 101841
Draw us to thee, For then shall we (Funcke) M454; Q215; AA 234 101842
Draw us to thee in mind and heart (Funcke) O58; P215 101843
Draw us to thee, Lord Jesus (Funcke) AZ799; BA519 101844
Draw to the cross, which thou hast blessed (Irons) H173; Q390; AA321; BY430 101845
Dread Jehovah, God of nations (Foster) D201; I709; L560; N576; V625; AZ267 101846
Drei König wandern aus morgenland (Cornelius) BG193b 101847
Drooping souls, no longer grieve (Hastings?) AY320 101848
Drop, drop, slow tears (Fletcher) A69; E98; X125 101849
Du glaubigs Herz, so benedey (Walpurg v. Bappenheim) BU75 101850
Du Lebensbrot, Herr Jesu Christ (Rist) BT312 101851
Du unbegreislich höchstes Gut (Unparth. G. B.) AY12d 101852
Durch Gnad so will ich singen (H. Straub) BU56 101853
Dust to dust, the mortal dies (U. P. Psalter, 1912) T93; AJ136 101854
Dwell in me, O blessed Spirit (Lankton) AI124; AK464; AO 650 101855
Dying with Jesus, by death reckoned mine (Whittle) AH 401; AI313; AM708; AU58; BB583 101856

E

Each cooing dove, and sighing bough (Morris) AU437; BC 38 101857
Each little flower that opens (Alexander) R All things bright and beautiful 101858
Each morning brings us fresh out-poured (Zwick) AF498 101859
Early, my God, without delay (Watts) V8; BB72 101860
Early will I seek Thee, God, my refuge strong (Salomon

ibn Gabirol) BH18 101861
Earth arrayed in wondrous beauty (Silliman) AQ48 101862
Earth below is teeming (Monsell) Z596; AZ774 101863
Earth has many a noble city (Prudentius) A48; B93; D63; F76; J51; BR154; BV127; BZ 101864
Earth has nothing sweet or fair (Scheffler) AO304; AZ48 101865
Earth holds no treasures but perish with using (Teddlie) AX604 101866
Earth is waking, day is breaking! (---) BD150 101867
Earth thou dost visit, watering it (Scottish Psalter, 1650) AP55 101868
Earth today rejoices and celestial voices (Neale) BG141 101869
Earth was waiting, spent and restless (Smith, W.C.) BY79 101870
Earth, with all thy thousand voices (Churton) BH64 101871
Earth, with her ten thousand flowers (Taylor) BC30 101872
Earthly friends will change and falter (Neale) BG135 101873
Earthly joys no longer please us (Ford) AZ257 101874
Earthly pleasures vainly call me (Rowe) AS236 101875
Earth's mighty Maker, whose command (Latin, ca 7th c) E 59 101876
Easter eggs! Easter eggs! Give to him that begs! (Russian trad carol) BG94 101877
Easter flowers are blooming bright (Nicholson) B558; K548; AC126; AD477 101878
Easter morrow stills our sorrow (Grundtvig) P196 101879
Eastern monarch, sages three (Latin, 15th c) BL16 101880
Ecce iam noctis tenuatur umbra (St Gregory the Great) BJ75b 101881
Ecce nomen Domini Emmanuel (Latin early) BQ157 101882
Ecce panis angelorum (St Thomas Aquinas) BN86; BP53; BQ231 101883
Ecce Sacêrdos magnus (Latin) BQ246 101884
E'en in thy childhood, 'mid the desert places (Paul the Deacon) E224 101885
E'en tho' the clouds sweep fast and wild (Kuipers) R In the good ship of our Captain 101886
Ein' feste Burg ist unser Gott (Luther) AD289; BT262; BW549 101887
Ein g'fahre Zeit vor nie erhört (H. Buchel) BU46 101888
Ein grosse Freud ist ingemein (Ausbund) BU18 101889
Ein Kind geborn zu Bethlehem (German trad carol) BG85b 101890
Ein Kindlein in der Wiegen (German trad carol) BG84 101891
Ein Lämmlein geht und trägt die schuld (Gerhardt) BT142; BW533 101892
Ein Liedlein will ich singen (Ausbund) BU89 101893
Ein Mägdelein von Gleidern zart (Ausbund) BU13 101894
Eins ist not, ach Herr, dies eine (Schröder) BT366 101895
Eins Morgens früh vor Tage (Ausbund) BU66 101896
Einsmals spatziert ich hin und her (H.v. Bilach) BU48 101897
Eleazer steadfast, strong (Levinger) R In the candles' rays I see 101898
Emmanuel! we sing Thy praise (Gerhardt) K26; L140; M331; N29; O180; AA161; BA55 101899
En clára vox redarguit (Latin, 5th-6th c) BQ154 101900
En Kelohenu (Jewish) AH151 101901
En mitten in des lebens zeyt. (Munich. MSS. 15th c.) BT

590 101902
Encamped along the hills of light (Yates) AH450; AT256; AV355; AX456 101903
Ended His strife, the battle won (Latin. 1695) P198 X The strife is o'er, the battle done 101904
Enduring Soul of all our life (Oakley) X482; Y28; AB91; AD75; BF378; BX76 101905
England, arise! The long, long night is over (Carpenter) X316 101906
Engraved as in eternal brass (Watts) BV526 X My hiding-place, my refuge, tower 101907
Enhver som tror og bliver döbt (Kingo) BT301 101908
Enkindling Love, eternal Flame (Barrows) AB60; BF253 101909
Enrich, Lord, heart, mouth, hands in me (Herbert) X401; AF527 101910
Enslaved by sin and bound in chains (Steele) Q141; AA202 101911
Enter Thy courts, thou Word of life (Bridges) W250; X483; BJ98 101912
Enthrone thy God within thy heart (Penn) BV618 101913
Enthroned on high, almighty Lord! (Haweis) V204; AS167 101914
Equip me for the war (Wesley) H391; L536 101915
Ere another day shall close (---) BR104 101916
Ere I sleep, for every favor (Cennick) S511; W294; AL555; AM337; AZ877; BA783; BV48; BY690 101917
Ere mountains reared their forms sublime (Auber) BB79 101918
Ere space exists, or earth, or sky (Jewish trad; Adonoi melech) BH159 101919
Ere to the world again we go Ellis. (Psalms and hymns. 1845.) L58 101920
Ere we know our lost condition (Zinzendorf, N. L.) BA515 101921
Ere yet in darkness ends the day (St Ambrose) BJ91 101922
Ere yet the dawn hath filled the sky (Heermann) L2; M437; O335 101923
Ere you left your room this morning (Kidder) AU335; AX361; BC31 101924
Erhalt uns deine Lehre (Gryphius) BT264 101925
Erhalt uns, Herr, bei deinem Wort (Luther) BT261 101926
Ermuntert euch, ihr Frommen (Laurenti) BT72 101927
Erneure mich, o ew'ges Licht (Ruopp) BT398 101928
Erstanden, erstanden ist Jesus Christ (Walther) BT198 101929
Es b'gab sich auf ein Zeite (H. Buchel) BU45 101930
Es gibt ein wunderschönes Land (Unparth. G. B.) AY16d 101931
Es hatt' ein Mann zween knaben (M. Schneider) BU99 101932
Es ist das Heil uns kommen her (Speratus) BT377 101933
Es ist ein Reis (Ros') entsprungen (Speier Gebetbuch. 1599) BG76b; BT645 101934
Es ist ein wunder schöne Gab (Ausbund Suppl.) BU3 101935
Es ist gewisslich an der Zeit (Ringwaldt) BT611 101936
Es ist noch eine Ruh' vorhanden (Kunth) BT615 101937
Es ist noch Raum! Sein Haus ist noch nicht voll. (German) BT509 101938
Es ist vollbracht! Gott Lob, es ist vollbracht! (Gryphius) BT599 101939
Es kommt ein Schiff geladen (German trad carol) BG90b 101940
Es war die ganze Welt (Olearius) BT272 101941
Es war ein Gottesfüchtiges (Ausbund Suppl.) BU5 101942

Es waren auch zween Brüder gut (Ausbund) BU16 101943
Es woll' uns Gott genädig sein (Luther) BT500 101944
Established in the highest heavens (U.P. Psalter, 1912) T182; AJ279 101945
Eternal and immortal King (Doddridge) BX26 101946
Eternal Beam of Light divine (Wesley) AL417; BX241 101947
Eternal depth of love divine (Zinzendorf, N.L.) BB62 101948
Eternal Father, God of love (Beeden) BB31 101949
Eternal Father, strong to save (Whiting) A512; B415; D306; E540; F487; G553; J338; K503; R521; S492; T445; U363; V644; W626; X336; Z610; AB380; AD456; AE61; AF429; AH216; AL452; AM629; AO615; AP709; AR67; AT61; AV69; AW169; AZ667; BA890; BF615; BR507; BV408; BY665; BZ 101950
Eternal Father, thou hast said (Palmer) BV312 101951
Eternal Father, throned above (Raffles) Lp.473; AZ920 101952
Eternal Father, when to thee (Ganse) V85; AY414 101953
Eternal Father, who didst all create (Bridges) X484 101954
Eternal Father, whose great love (Boreham) BY288 101955
Eternal Glory of the sky (Latin, 6th c) E56 101956
Eternal God, before thy throne we bend (Ryden) J178 101957
Eternal God, Omnipotent (Rohr) M599 101958
Eternal God, our Father (Hoppe) P48 101959
Eternal God! we look to thee (Merrick) D435; BX235 101960
Eternal God, whose power upholds (Tweedy) A265; G476; J322; R485; Z535; AB369; AD358; AE357; AF294; AG276; AK367; AR560; BF530; BZ 101961
Eternal God, whose searching eye doth scan (Poteat) AR572 101962
Eternal Light, Divinity (Latin, 18th c) E632 101963
Eternal Light! eternal Light! (Binney) A478; B241; V739; W36; AL36; AP155; BB85; BV4; BY51 101964
Eternal Mind the Potter is (Dayton) BE51 101965
Eternal Monarch, King most high (Latin, 5th c) E141 101966
Eternal One, thou living God (Longfellow) AN367; AQ246; AW369; BD141; BK60; BX 441 101967
Eternal Peace, whose world of old (Brooke) BX290 101968
Eternal Power, whose high abode (Watts) E635; F621; H21; I17 101969
Eternal Ruler of the ceaseless round (Chadwick) B491; E384; J350; S406; U344; W489; X 485; Y213; Z506; AB273; AD336; AF275; AK411; AL 370; AN349; AP566; AR391; BF494; BV419; BX443; BY 358 101970
Eternal Son, eternal Love (Wesley) BZ X Spirit of grace, and health, and power 101971
Eternal Son of God, O Thou (Latin, 11th c) M514; O128; AA456 101972
Eternal Source of every joy (Doddridge) I715; AO61; AS 431; AZ935; BR81; BX171 101973
Eternal Source of joys divine (Steele) AY85 101974
Eternal Source of life and light, Supremely good (Estlin) BR37 101975
Eternal Source of light divine (Wesley) BX241 X Eternal Beam of Light divine 101976
Eternal Spirit, evermore creating (Robins) Z161 101977
Eternal Spirit, God of truth (Cotterill) AI119 101978
Eternal Spirit of the chainless

mind (Byron) AQ167 101979
Eternal Spirit, Source of life (Oakley) AB91 X Enduring Soul of all our life 101980
Eternal Spirit! we confess (Watts) L171; V206 101981
Eternal Sun of Righteousness (Wesley) AZ98 X Come, Father, Son, and Holy Ghost 101982
Eternal thanks be thine (Gersdorf) AZ781; BA122 101983
Eternity draws near, As time moves on (Warren) AX290 101984
Eternity! eternity! Where will you spend eternity? (Hoffman) R Where will you spend eternity 101985
Even me, even me, Let some drops (Codner) R Lord, I hear of showers of blessing 101986
Evening and morning, Sunset and dawning (Gerhardt) J215; K447; P291; AK49; AW555; AZ1514; BR266 101987
Evening sun descending (Hoffmann) P70 101988
Evensong is hushed in silence (Purchas) E569 101989
Ever are my longing eyes (U.P. Psalter, 1912) T43; AJ66 101990
Ever content with the ways of my Father (Kretzmann) M287 101991
Ever gracious Lord, I fly to the haven of thy breast (Wesley) BR313 101992
Ever growing, swiftly flowing (Jones) R Haste, O haste, delightful morning 101993
Ever patient, gentle, meek (Elliott) L462; AO305 101994
Everlasting arms of love (Macduff) V326; AO350; BE53 101995
Every day, every hour, Let me feel Thy cleansing power (Crosby) R Saviour, more than life to me 101996
Every day will I bless thee ("J.E. A.") R My Savior's praises will I sing 101997
Every day with Jesus Is sweeter than the day before (Loveless) AU325 101998
Every hour, every hour, Blessed Lord (Belden) R Blessed Lord, how much I need thee 101999
Every morning mercies new (Phillimore) D4; K448; Q537; T303; V31; AA28; AI46; AM328; AS20; AX57; AZ1278; BA770; BF184; BR5 102000
Every morning the red sun (Alexander) E590; W591; AZ727 102001
Every night and every morn (Blake) AQ184 102002
Every Sunday evening, To the church we go (Shumate) AU312 102003
Everything changes (Goethe) X486 102004
Every work for Jesus will be blest (Kirk) R Hear ye the Master's call 102005
Everywhere, everywhere, Christmas tonight (Brooks) AC452 102006
Ewiger Vater im Himmelreich (Ausbund) BU51 102007
Ewiger Vater vom Himmelreich (Ausbund) BU36 102008
Exalt the Lord, His praise proclaim (U.P. Psalter, 1912) T270; AJ375; AM12 102009
Exortum est in love and lysse (English trad carol, 1450) BG62 X Nowell sing we, both all and some 102010
Exsultet orbis gaudiis (Latin, 10th c) BN180; BO289 102011
Extended on a cursed tree (Gerhardt) H164 102012
Extol the love of Christ, ye saints (Coffman) AX173 102013
Exultet orbis gaudiis (Latin, 10th c) BO289 X Exsultet

orbis gaudiis 102014

F

Face to face with Christ my Saviour (Breck) AH527; AT475; AU106; AV390; AX126; BB545 102015

Facing a task unfinished (Houghton) BV313 102016

Fade, fade, each earthly joy; Jesus is mine (Bonar, J.C.) I529; N601; AS288; AU205; AX404; BB277 102017

Fading away like the stars of the morning (Bonar) AX584; AY 530 102018

Fading, still fading, the last beam is shining (---) AS32 102019

Fahre fort, fahre fort (Schmidt) BT479 102020

Fain would my soul with wonder trace (Knight) L164 102021

Fair as a beauteous tender flower (Robertson) AP206 102022

Fair beyond telling, Lord is thy dwelling (Grundtvig) M23 102023

Fair is their fame who stand in earth's high places (Housman) AN427; AQ72 102024

Fair the night in Bethlem land (Stubbs) AB117 102025

Fair waved the golden corn (Gurney) D569; E290; F338; W494; X10; AP777; BV649; BY725 102026

Fairest Bridegroom mine (Drese) M194 102027

Fairest Lord Jesus (Münster, 1677 & Leipzig, 1842) A346; B356; G111; I118; J434; K129; L111; M623; N317; O576; P6; Q657; R135; S194; U72; V751; Y58; Z261; AB84; AC137; AD 181; AE103; AF227; AG113; AH314; AI105; AK182; AM129; AN483; AO211; AR100; AT159; AU211; AV102; AW97; AX565; AZ465; BA119; BB165; BD63; BF331; BK21; BY202; BZ 102028

Faisons éclater notre joie (Pictet) BT100 102029

Faith comes by hearing God's record (Erskine) AZ342 102030

Faith grasps the blessing she desires (Martineau) BE54 102031

Faith, hope, and charity, these three (Montgomery) AZ415 102032

Faith is a living power from heaven (Herbert) I286; O337; AX455 102033

Faith is the brightest evidence (Watts) AO386 102034

Faith is the victory (Yates) R Encamped along the hills of light 102035

Faith is wisdom from on high (Cronenwett) M126 102036

Faith of our fathers, holy faith (Faber) R Faith of our fathers! living still 102037

Faith of our fathers! living still (Faber) A393; B441; G256; I415; J516; M227; N214; P370; R348; S267; T381; U210; V 743; Y109; Z348; AB168; AC 256; AD387; AE216; AF365; AG200; AH142,429; AI237; AK282; AL399; AM487; AN 546; AO607; AP545; AR320; AS322; AT252; AU201; AV249; AW154; AX434; AZ676; BA 275; BB349; BD148; BF456; BK69; BL87; BO207; BQ121; BX401; BY466; BZ 102038

Faith of our fathers! loving still (Faber: Catholic variant) AH142 X Faith of our fathers! living still 102039

Faith of our mothers, living still (Patten) AU203 102040

Faith of the larger liberty (Silliman) AQ257 102041

Faithful cross! above all other (Latin) E737 102042

Faithful Lord, my only joy and pleasure (Zinzendorf, N.L.) AZ1021 102043

Faithful Shepherd, feed me (Pollock) B357; F415 102044

Fang dein Werk mit Jesu an (Morgen- und Abend-segen. Waldenburg, 1734) BT540 102045

Far and near the fields are teeming (Thompson) AI188; AM 668; AW325; AX210; AY334; BB448 102046

Far as thy name is known (Watts) V532 102047

Far away in the depths of my spirit tonight (Cornell) BB 610 102048

Far be sorrow, tears and sighing (Latin, 13th c) AZ750 102049

Far down the ages now (Bonar) K204; BA265 102050

Far, far away on Judea's plains (McFarlane) BC33 102051

Far, far beyond the starry sky (Toews) AX607 102052

Far from all care we hail the Sabbath morning (Aufranc) BB468 102053

Far from my heavenly home (Lyte) B408; D333; V703; BJ46 102054

Far from my thoughts, vain world, begone! (Watts) H74 102055

Far from these scenes of night (Steele) H507 102056

Far in the west the sunset's golden splendour (Moore) BY691 102057

Far o'er yon horizon (Alford) AZ776 X Forward! be our watchword 102058

Far off I see the goal (Roberts) R337; S183; W572 102059

Far off, O God, and yet most near (Barber) AB37; BX508 102060

Far out on the desolate billow (Raymond) AI35 102061

Far round the world Thy children sing their song (Mathews) W373; X299; AC8; AL251; BF 622; BY366 102062

Far-shining names from age to age (Savile) F576 102063

Farewell, all earthly honors (Bone) BC35 102064

Farewell, dear friends, I bid you (Teasley) AX617 102065

Farewell, henceforth for ever (Herberger) AZ797 X Farewell I gladly bid thee 102066

Farewell I gladly bid thee (Herberger) Q407; AA532; AZ797 102067

Farewell! I say with gladness (Herberger) AA532 X Farewell I gladly bid thee 102068

Farewell, my dear brethren, the time is at hand (---) AY 407 102069

Farewell, my friends beloved (Harbottle) BY759 102070

Fast sinks the sun to rest (Latin, 18th c) F37 102071

Father, again in Jesus' name we meet (Whitmore) H6; P37; S48; U447; V15; W243; AD23; AI23; AK31; AM311; AO1; AS56; BB26; BR101; BV3 102072

Father, again to Thee our hearts we lift (Ellerton: Jewish variant) BH177 X Saviour again to thy dear name 102073

Father, again to Thy dear name we raise (Ellerton) AN126 X Saviour, again to Thy dear name 102074

Father all-holy, Lord of creation (Synnestvedt) BI24 102075

Father all-seeing, friend of all creation (Bell) X330; BY666 102076

Father Almighty, bless us with thy blessing (Berwick hymnal, 1886) Y44; Z344; AD216; AE241; AF333; AH350; AK 227; AN117; AR79; AW59; BD114; BF366; BK175; BX 160 102077

Father Almighty, darkness now is deepening (Sigmond) P61 102078

Father Almighty, grant us now thy blessing (Berwick hymnal, 1886) AE241 X Father Almighty, bless us with thy blessing 102079

Father and Friend! Thy light, Thy love (Bowring) S89; AN 79; AW63; BX90 102080

Father, as the day I greet (Hess) BH241 102081

Father, at thy footstool see (Wesley) BR503 102082

Father, be thy blessing shed (Gilman) M533; N286; O02 102083

Father bless these [this] birthday children [child] (Hess) BHp. 566 102084

Father, bless us as we part (Edworthy) AK510 102085

Father divine, the deadening power control (Tuckerman) BR427 102086

Father eternal, Ruler of creation (Housman) A532; R486; W645; X326; Y247; AB365; AC287; AD362; AF445; AK401; AW354; BZ 102087

Father, fill us with thy love (---) R538; S37app 102088

Father from thy throne on high, Far above (Pollock) BX528 X Jesus from thy throne on high 102089

Father, give thy benediction (Longfellow) G615; R557; S45app.; Y95; AD511; AF540; AK509; AR678; BK176; BZ 102090

Father, God, thy love we praise (Wesley) AZ1480; BA910 102091

Father, gracious Father! God of might and power (Faber) AH 541 X Jesus, gentlest Saviour 102092

Father, have mercy, Father, have mercy (---) R Fading, still fading. The last beam is shining 102093

Father, hear our prayer, We ask for Jesus sake (---) AU313 102094

Father, hear the prayer we offer (Willis) E385; F182; X487; AE244; AF368; AN85; BA572; BD93; BE55; BH42; BV579; BX122; BY467 102095

Father, hear thy child, In thy mercy mild (Kretzmann) M582 102096

Father, hear thy children's call (Pollock) D529; U179; AB162; AI223; AO276; AP432; AR280; AV413; BF360 102097

Father, hear us as we pray (MacAlister) S350 102098

Father, here we dedicate (Tuttiett) AZ728 X Father, let me dedicate 102099

Father, how wide thy glory shines (Watts) I79; L130 102100

Father, I come to thee (Mitchell) BI22; BR457 102101

Father, I dare believe Thee merciful and true (Wesley) H271 102102

Father, I go to Thee! (Mitchell) BR457 X Father, I come to thee 102103

Father, I know that all my life (Waring) I465; L483; O256; U209; V418; W548; AD259; AI298; AL432; AM444; AP 572; AV60; AZ732; BA697; BF451; BX291; BY468 102104

Father, I long, I faint to see (Watts) V700 102105

Father, I stretch my hands to Thee (Wesley) G202; H280; I277; AI233; AR281; AS200; AT46; AU274; AV58; AX360; AY41; BB670; BZ 102106

Father, I yield to thee my life (Aufranc) BB682 102107

Father, in heaven, hear us today (Ames) U355; Y102; AC161; AR283; AS54 102108

Father in heaven, in thy love abounding (Hibbard) BC34 102109

Father in heaven, Lo, thine angel chorus (Huffaker) AR 372 102110

Father in heaven, Thy children hear (Williams) AH617

102111

Father in heaven, we do believe (Pratt) BC41 102112

Father in heaven, we wait before Thy face (Phalen) BY344 102113

Father in heaven, who lovest all (Kipling) A506; B367; G294; U327; W647; X488; Y178, 286; AC175; AD492; AF392; AL513; AN482; AS403; AT460; AW401; BD107, 171; BF484; BV575; BX539; BY644 102114

Father, in high heaven dwelling (Rawson) L34; W283; AL549; AP683; AZ641; BV50; BY692 102115

Father! in my life's young morning (MacKellar) AX562; AY 64 102116

Father, in the morning, Unto thee I pray (Cummings) AY 69 102117

Father, in thy mysterious presence kneeling (Johnson) R384; S256; Z345; AB224; AD211; AF334; AG223; AH348; AN229; AO317; AV65; AW188; BF363; BR26; BX268 102118

Father, in thy presence kneeling (Pilcher) BY617 102119

Father, in whom we live (Wesley) L183; M478; Q241; AA270; BY38; BZ 102120

Father, lead me day by day (Hopps) G437; R458; S445; W565; AD213; AE434; AG305; AK458; AL596; AN479; AO617; AP788; AR282; AS316; BA824; BB331; BD106; BX523; BY469 102121

Father, let me dedicate (Tuttiett) B448; F72; G535; Q118; W606; AA166; AR582; AS433; AT498; AZ728; BR501; BV657; BY713 102122

Father, let thy blessing, touch us and remain (Ogden) BH102 102123

Father, let thy Kingdom come (Hopps) AN336; BX393; BY 367 102124

Father, let thy smiling face (Moore) V83 102125

Father, long before creation (Chinese, ca 1952) R107 102126

Father, loving Father, Hear thy children call (Gower) Z325 102127

Father, merciful and holy (Rist) N558; AA31 102128

Father most high, be with us (Prudentius) F112 102129

Father, most holy, merciful and loving (Latin, 10th c) BV226 X Father most holy, merciful and tender 102130

Father most holy, merciful and tender (Latin, 10th c) E160; F158; O75; P238; Q240; X 186; BV226 102131

Father, now thy sinful child (Conder) BA430 102132

Father, O hear us; Saviour, draw near us (---) AR616; AW609 102133

Father, O hear us, Seeking now to praise thee (Walmsley) BY345 102134

Father of all, from land and sea (Wordsworth) D495; I566; S426; W213; AK412; AO422; AZ9; BA669 102135

Father of all, in every age (Pope) AQ133 X What conscience dictates to be done 102136

Father of all, thy care we bless (Doddridge) I670; N532 102137

Father of all, to thee (Julian) E386; X252 102138

Father of all, we come to thee (Blaxill) BY470 102139

Father of all, we lift to thee our praise (Harvard) AN307 102140

Father of all, whose love profound (Cooper) B206; D139; E387; F164; J140; K165; L181; M477; O388; Q242; T317; W5; AA269; AK196; AL3; AM88; AP138; AZ311; BA15; BV483; BY39 102141

Father of eternal grace (Montgomery) AK246; AO380; BA 42 102142

Father of glory, to thy name (Watts) Q248; AA267 102143

Father of heaven, who hast created all (Knapp) B342; D206; K173; AA405 102144

Father of heaven, whose love profound (Cooper) Q242 X Father of all, whose love profound 102145

Father of Jesus, by whose grace (Moxley) BY268 102146

Father of Jesus Christ, My Lord (Wesley) G203; H292; I297; AA 219; AZ221 102147

Father of lights, eternal Lord (Wallin) N222 102148

Father of lights, in whom there is no shadow (Wilson & Thoburn) G592; S7app.; Y21; AC1; AD69; AR26; BF180; BK59 102149

Father of lights, we sing thy name (Doddridge) BX51 102150

Father of love and power (Rawson) Z146; BY693 102151

Father of love, our Guide and Friend (Irons) AZ1457 102152

Father of men, in whom are one (Shuttleworth) E528; G418; S489; W493; X338; AB315; AL369; AW388; BY359 102153

Father of mercies, bow thine ear (Beddome) D287; V565; AS447; AZ317; BA307; BY346 102154

Father of mercies, condescend (Morell) AZ204; BA318 102155

Father of mercies, God of love (Flowerdew) BH185 X Fountain of mercy, God of love 102156

Father of mercies! in thy word (Steele) D283; F251; G389; H92; J256; K172; L308; N218; O135; P92; Q284; R249; S218; U142; V70; Z440; AA117; AD195; AE161; AG130; AH235; AL183; AM259; AP292; AR235; AS179; AZ182; BA2; BR234; BV300; BY245; BZ 102157

Father of mercies, send thy grace (Doddridge) V573 102158

Father of mercy, Father of love (Hopps) X Hark, hark, my soul! Thy Father's voice 102159

Father of mercy, Lover of all children (Moore) A238 102160

Father of peace, and God of love (Doddridge) R328; W481; AL327; AM98; AP486; BV619; BY593 102161

Father of spirits, whose divine control (Prudentius) E352 102162

Father, our children keep (Bonar) W650; AL395 102163

Father! reveal thy son in me (Montgomery) AZ739 102164

Father, see thy children bending at thy throne (Jervois) E 308 102165

Father, see thy suppliant children (Hamburg Temple hymnal) BH150 102166

Father, Son, and Holy Ghost, Bless the young before thee (Döring) O108; P107; AP353 102167

Father, Son, and Holy Ghost In solemn power (Wesley) AZ1483 102168

Father, Son, and Holy Ghost One God whom we adore (---) Lp. 742; AZ1472 102169

Father, Son, and Holy Ghost One in Three and Three in One (Wesley) M479; AZ1277 BV628 102170

Father, Son, and Holy Ghost Three in One; from every coast (---) Lp. 743 102171

Father, Son, and Holy Spirit I'm baptized in Thy dear name (Rambach) K177; O105 102172

Father, Son, and Holy Spirit Thou One in Three (---) Lp. 743 102173

Father, Son, and Spirit, hear (Wesley) AO427 102174

Father, source of life and light (Hendrickson) P49 102175

Father, Supreme, by Whom we

live (Dewart) BA882 102176
Father, the watches of the night are o'er (Disciples' Hymn book) R530; S8app.; AN95; BX41 102177
Father, thou are calling, calling to us plainly (Blake) AN18; BX7 102178
Father, thou joy of loving hearts (St Bernard of (Clairvaux) BE56 X Jesus, thou Joy of loving hearts 102179
Father, throned on high (Montgomery) BR67 Blessed by thy name 102180
Father, throughout the coming year (Gaskell) BX179 102181
Father, thy children to thee now raise (Stephens) BC43 102182
"Father, thy will not mine, be done!" (Montgomery) AZ634 102183
Father, thy wonders do not singly stand (Very) AN41; BX45 102184
Father 'tis thine each day to yield (Osler) AO101 102185
Father, to thee we look in all our sorrow (Hosmer) E538; X347; AB207; AF467; AN227; AR86; AV221; AW249; BE57; BF407; BH96; BV401; BX272 102186
Father to thee we turn away from sorrow (Hosmer) BE57 X Father, to thee we look in all our sorrow 102187
Father, to thy dear name I lift my voice (Levy) BH85 102188
Father, to us, thy children humbly, kneeling (Clarke) AD210; AN231; BF356; BI63; BR458; BX271 102189
Father, we come in Jesus' name (Shoemaker) AX55; AY6 102190
Father, we come to thee, No other help have we (Belden) BB599 102191
Father, we come, with youth and vigor pressing (Clayton) A509 102192
Father we greet thee, God of love (Adderley) R285; X269 102193
Father, we praise thee, now the night is over (St Gregory the Great??) A157; E165; J204; R43; S24; W263; X28; Z102; AC26; AD41; AF41; AK44; AL540; AW24; BY675; BZ 102194
Father, we thank thee, Father, we thank thee (Giffin) BK9 102195
Father, we thank thee for the night (Weston) A240; R467; X355; AE438; AF479; AL585; AM659; AP720; AR554; AT 341; AU310; AW423; BK6; BY 736 102196
Father, we thank thee who has planted (Greek, from the Didache) A195; AF289; BY 315; BZ 102197
Father, we thy loving children (Adams) BE58 102198
Father, whate'er of earthly bliss (Steele) A447; B396; D670; F180; I523; K406; L473; O473; U246; V390; AH396; AM562; AN444; AO345; AS 238; AV57; AW251; AZ120; BA713; BB333; BI19; BR245; BX479 102199
Father, who art all alone, Our helper and our stay (Jones) G554; W630; Z609; AR264; BY667 102200
Father, who hast created all (Knapp) N227 102201
Father, who on man dost [doth] shower (Dearmer) B506; E 531; N195; O500; W349; X 340; AC171; AE380; BD105 102202
Father, who the light this day (Elliott) O40; Q8; AA123 102203
Father, whose hand hath led me so securely (Spitta) AZ1221; BT453 102204
Father, whose will is life and good (Rawnsley) A516; G478; R309; W353; AC169; AD316; AL254; AR387; AW326; BY

634; BZ 102205
Fear, my child, thy God and Lord (Pedersen) O110 102206
Fear not, for God the Father (Homer) AX464 102207
Fear not! God is thy shield (Taylor) BR521 102208
Fear not, my soul, alone to stand (Hunter Clare) BV576 102209
Fear not, O little flock, the foe (Altenberg) I445; L352; AA276; AM470; AP530; AZ636; BA267 102210
Fear not, thou faithful Christian flock (Altenberg) J156; W217; BJ72 102211
Fears oft affright us (Cleator) R O Father, lead us 102212
Feeble, helpless, how shall I Learn to live (Furness) K56 102213
Feed thy children, God most holy (Heermann) Q659 102214
Feet of the urgent pioneer (Patton) AQ232 102215
Felix dies, quam proprio (Besnault) BT115 102216
Fellow Christians, let us gather (Solberg) M116 102217
Fels des Meils, geöffnet mir (A.M. Toplady) BW148 102218
Fervent in spirit, serving the Lord (Kretzmann) M224 102219
Fesans raijouissance (Prost) BG 106b 102220
Fields of corn, give up your ears (Farjeon) X11; BG158 102221
Fierce and wild the storm is raging (Whittle) AU431 102222
Fierce raged the tempest o'er the deep (Thring) E541; F313; I485; O242; W83; X489; AL75; AO149; AP182; AZ1141; BA78; BR168; BV553; BY117 102223
Fierce was the billow wild (St Anatolius) N77 X Fierce was the wild billow 102224
Fierce was the storm of wind (Beadon) D71 102225
Fierce was the wild billow (St Anatolius) B416; E388; F312; K48; N77; W84; X490; Y77; AD138; AM513; AZ751; BA76; BP100; BR343 102226
Fight the good fight with all thy might (Monsell) A560; B113; D505; E389; F304; G286; I 409; J557; O258; Q447; R359; S270; T421; U299; W517; X 491; Y158; Z376; AA376; AB 240; AC207; AD291; AE257; AF367; AG201; AH453; AK298; AL400; AM484; AO392; AP 544; AR318; AT406; AU270; AV200; AZ380; BA574; BD 85; BE59; BF467; BV577; BY289; BZ 102227
Fight, then, good soldiers, Fight and be brave (Rooper) R Dare to be brave 102228
Fill me now, Fill me now (Stokes) R Hover o'er me 102229
Fill me with thy Spirit, Lord (Warner) AX137 102230
Fill thou my life, O Lord my God (Bonar) F373; U267; X492; AF396; AI277; AL346; AM495; BK68; BV621; BY 628 102231
Filled full and flushed with morning (Hooker) Y124 102232
Finita iam sunt praelia (Latin. publ Cologne 1695) BT210; BW116 102233
Firm as the mountains around us (Fox) BC42 102234
Firm this cornerstone be laid (Moise) BH212 102235
Firmly I believe and truly (Newman) E390; F186 102236
Firmly stand for the right (Whittle) R Be ye strong 102237
Fit us for thy service, Lord (Zinzendorf, N. L.) BA542 102238
Flee as a bird to your mountain (Dana) AI244; BU459; BB232 102239
Fling out the banner! let it float (Doane) A259; B482; D253;

E546; F268; G502; H473; I639; J315; L341; R506; S384; U403; W383; Y269; Z540; AB372; AC 304; AD379; AF296; AG256; AH465; AI172; AK381; AL245; AM378; AN405; AO534; AP391; AS369; AT446; AU152; AV258; AW331; BA340; BB450; BF 526 102240

Fling wide the gates of righteousness (---) BH132 102241

Fling wide thy gates, O Church (Kuhlman) M335 102242

Flower in the crannied wall (Tennyson) Y14; AC436 102243

Flung to the heedless winds (Luther) I641; M80; Q259; AZ484 102244

Föhlich pfleg ich zu singen (Ausbund) BU65 102245

Follow! follow! I would follow Jesus (Cushing) R Down in the valley 102246

Follow, I will follow thee, my Lord (Brown) R Jesus calls me 102247

"Follow me," the Master said (Voice of praise, 1887) AP766; AS333 102248

Follow the path of Jesus (Hymns and tunes, 1890) AX498; AY305 102249

Follow, we will follow Jesus (Lindsay) R Walking in the sunshine 102250

Fools in their heart have said (U.P. Psalter, 1912) T101; AJ146 102251

Footprints of Jesus that make the pathway glow (Slade) R Sweetly, Lord, have we heard 102252

For a season called to part (Newton) L64; N359 102253

For air and sunshine pure and sweet (Child songs) BY737 102254

For all the blessings of the year (Hutchinson) G546; U480; AD 444; AT495; AU301; BD202; BZ 102255

For all the love that from our earliest days (Smith) BY7 102256

For all the saints, who from their labors rest (How) A126; B295; D176; E641;F527; G527; H433; I430; J144; K 250; N629; Q463; R425; S429; T379; U309; V614; W220; X202; Y345; Z576; AB412; AC330; AD461; AE309; AF306; AG 284; AH525; AK417; AL174; AM281; AN428; AO540; AP 310; AQ75; AR419; AV283; AW317; AZ527; BA740; BB 364; BD248; BF655; BL70; BR446; BV460; BX463; BY403 BZ 102257

For all the souls who sought thy way, O Lord (Swayne) BK76 102258

For all thy care we bless thee (Doudney) U48 102259

For all thy love and goodness (How) W610 102260

For all thy saints, a noble throng (Alexander) D165; F557; BV445 102261

For all thy saints, O Lord (Mant) Q468 X For thy dear saints, O Lord 102262

For all thy saints, who from their labors rest (How) AZ527 X For all the saints, who from 102263

For all who watch tonight (Coote) BV51 102264

For Autumn's golden days (---) BD49 102265

For Christ and the Church let our voices ring (Hewitt) AR494; AS324; AX153 102266

For Christ our dear Redeemer (Hewitt) R For Christ and the Church 102267

For common gifts we bless thee, Lord (Packard) AN266; AW 176; BX321 102268

Forever at His feet I'll sit (Hoffman) R I wonder, often wonder 102269

For ever here my rest shall be (Wesley) G373; H304; I357; U180; V449; AM458; AE656; AS458; AX172; AY258; AZ187;

BA205 102270

For ever settled in the heavens, Thy word, O Lord (U.P. Psalter, 1912) T 236; AJ332; AM54 102271

For ever trusting in the Lord (U.P. Psalter, 1912) AJ100; AM569 102272

For ever we would gaze on Thee (Chatfield) BV258 102273

For-ever with the Lord, Amen so let it be (Montgomery) B516; D675; E391; F346; H517; I625; J590; K520; L604; M310; N520; O618; Q616; V656; W583; X195; AA567; AH526; AL462; AO551; AP629; AV294; AW261; AZ1303, 1304; BA721; BR430; BT616; BV428; BX311; BY609 102274

"For-ever with the Lord!" Father if 'tis thy will (Montgomery) AZ1304 X For-ever with the Lord, Amen so let it be 102275

For flowers that bloom about our feet (---) AQ30 102276

For garnered fields and meadows cropped (Leiser) BH182 102277

"For God so loved!" O wondrous theme (Whittle) AI9 102278

For God so loved this sinful world (Morris) AX476 102279

For great is the Lord, His name shall endure (Hay) R Lord, with devotion we pray 102280

For He is so precious to me (Gabriel) R So precious is Jesus, my Saviour 102281

For he loves me, yes, He loves me (Bateman) R I will early seek the Saviour 102282

For health and strength and daily food (---) AR552 102283

For help, O whither shall I flee (Neander) O499 102284

For his mercies aye endure (Milton) R Let us with a gladsome mind (Milton) R Praise, O praise our heavenly King (Trend) R Praise, O praise our God the King (Baker) 102285

For man's unceasing quest for God (Pullen) BK32; BY246 102286

For many years, O God of grace (Czamanske) Q639 102287

For me to live is Jesus (Vulpius. Ein-schön geistliche G-B. 1609) M295; Q597; AA529 102288

For mercies, countless as the sands (Newton) AQ99 102289

For mercy, courage, kindness, mirth (Binyon) X493; Y198; AC165; AQ152 102290

For mother-love and father-care (---) BH242 102291

For My sake and the Gospel's go (Bickersteth) W370; AM 377; AP384; BV335 102292

For no sect elect is the soul's wine poured (Swinburne) AQ 166 102293

For now we stand on Jordan's strand (Nelson) R My days are gliding swiftly by 102294

For our devotions, Father, we invoke Thy Spirit (Naisbitt) BC107 102295

For our transgressions thou wast wounded (LaTrobe) AZ996; BA190 102296

For peace and for plenty (Sangster) BI112 102297

For soon the reaping time will come (---) R Though in the outward Church 102298

For sun and moon and stars (---) 1929 BY738 102299

For swinging wind and treetop birds (Irwin) Y197 102300

For the beauty of the earth (Pierpoint) A296; B425; E309; F171; G18; I28; J444; K292; M588; N338; O529; P245; R2; S71; U16; W17; X494; Y357; Z167; AB313; AC46; AD94; AE14; AF66; AG59; AH206; AK12; AL15; AN32, 269; AO 65; AP140; AQ12; AR92; AT 153; AU246; AV309; AW51; AX634; AZ1257; BA642; BB22; BD40; BF257; BK126; BL78; BR68; BV18; BX13; BY8; BZ

102301
For the brave of ev'ry race (Briggs) A582; X243; AF308; AN426 102302
For the bread and for the wine (Bonar) AZ24 102303
For the bread, which Thou hast broken (Benson) G412; J282; R449; S359; Z463; AR518; BZ 102304
For the darkness shall turn to dawning (Nichol) R We've a story to tell to the nations 102305
For the deep love that kept us (Burleigh) BF181 102306
For the golden sun and the darting rain (Hess) BH184 102307
For the joy of human love (Pierpoint) AN269 X For the beauty of the earth 102308
For the mercies of the day (Missionary minstrel, 1826) L28 102309
For the might of Thine arm, we bless thee (Horne) G492; W 212; X495; Y334; BC241; BY 256; BZ 102310
For the mountains shall depart and the hills be removed (Jewish Trad: Shofar) BH316 102311
For the strength of the hills we bless thee (Horne) BC241 X For the might of thine arm 102312
For the summer's glowing pageant (Hubbell) AR595 102313
For the year that came from thee (Graham) BK31 102314
For Thee, my God, for Thee alone (Burns) W472 102315
For Thee, O dear, dear country (St Bernard of Cluny) A598; B512; D407; E392; F277; I614; J534; O608; Q614; R429; T436; V691; W598; AP627; AV278; AZ823; BO202; BR438,449 102316
For them whose ways are in the height (Roberts) AL454; AW 166 102317
For those we love within the veil (Piggott) A222; G425; J598; W218; X289; AD460; AL181; BY610 102318
For those who wrought with loving heart (Allen) AB394; BF447 102319
For thy dear saint, O Lord (Mant) X203 X For Thy dear saints 102320
For thy dear saints, O Lord (Mant) A124; B293; D181; E196; F531; J141; K249; L 298; N206; Q468; V609; X 203; AA289; AN415; AZ1364; BV461; BX461 102321
For thy mercy and thy grace (Downton) B447; D204; E286; F73; K481; L550; M367; O213; Q121; W604; X1; AA168; AK 426; AL570; AM611; AP695; AW528; BA175; BF647; BR 499; BV656; BY714 102322
For thy mercy aye pursuing (Freeman) AB70; BF254 102323
For you I am praying (Clough) R I have a Saviour, He's pleading in glory 102324

NOTE: Other compounds formed with for are filed below as compound words 102325

Forget them not, O Christ, who stand (Sangster) Y117 X O Christ, forget not them who stand 102326
Forgive, O Lord, our severing ways (Whittier) R476; S344; Y263; Z484; AD392; AF262; AN419; BD188; BF587; BX 450 102327
Forgive the things I've said in haste (Williams) AU416 102328
Forgive them, O my Father (Alexander) E112; F114 102329
Forgive us Lord, we turn to Thee (Montefiore) BH163 102330
Forsake me not, my God (Franck) K397; O521 102331
Forsake me not! O Thou, my

Lord, my Light (Hohlfeldt) BR299 102332

Forsaken once, and thrice denied (Alexander) B283; E227; F 323 102333

Fortem virili pectore (Antoniano) BN184 102334

Forth in thy name, O Lord I go (Wesley) A150; B7; D639; E259; F336; G290; H390; I400; J214; K455; N502; W651; X29; AE35; AF406; AL350; AP661; AZ402; BA537; BB47; BF441; BR381; BV604; BY629; BZ 102335

Forth in thy name, O Lord we go (Wesley) AZ402 X Forth in thy name, O Lord I go 102336

Forth to the fight he fared (Oxenham) AC508 102337

Forth to the fight, ye ransomed (Kirby) BR515 102338

Fortress-Rock, my God, my air! (Jewish hymn) BH208 102339

Forty days and forty nights (Smyttan) A55; B123; D79; E73; F92; N85; W79; X97; AF148; AK143; AO143; BV141; BY118; 102340

Forty days of Eastertide (Mason) B180 102341

Forward! be our watchword, Steps and voices joined (Alford) A561; B531; D523; E 642; H399; I384; J565; L542; S369; W579; X394; AB218; AD227; AH362; AL451; AN334; AP605; AV220; AZ775-776; BA575, 744; BD143; BF382; BR 508; BX377; BY539 102342

Forward, Christian, forward (Francis) BB353 102343

Forward, Christian Leaguers (Solberg) R Christian Leaguers, rally 102344

Forward through the ages, in unbroken line (Hosmer) A546; U374; Y113; Z498; AC263; AD 299; AE313; AF383; AN329; AQ215; AR502; AT463; AU419; AW267; BD146; BF515; BK108; BX378 102345

Founded on thee, our only Lord (Smith, S. F.) N280; Q637; S474; AF477; AR525; AS438 102346

Fountain of good, to own thy love (Doddridge) D269; L 444; W345; AL385; AM282; AP589; AW218 102347

Fountain of grace, rich, full and free (Edmeston) U241; V395; AI257; AM591 102348

Fountain of life and light (Benade) AZ1162 102349

Fountain of light and living breath (Quarles) BX115 102350

Fountain of mercy, God of love (Flowerdew) L554; W617; AP686; BA862; BH185 102351

Fountain of never-ceasing grace (Toplady) AM440 102352

Four things a man must learn to do (Van Dyke) AC485 102353

Free from the law, O happy condition (Bliss) AI129; AT 199; AU340 102354

Freedom is the finest gold that the sun strews (Thomas of Strängnäs, Bp.) AQ170 102355

Frequent the day of God returns (Browne) V68 102356

Fret not thyself, nor envious be (U.P. Psalter, 1912) T62; AJ95 102357

Freudenvoll, freudenvoll walle ich fort (Unparth. G.B.) AY 47d 102358

Freuet euch, ihr Christen alle! (Keimann) BT96 102359

Friend after friend departs (Montgomery) I587; L574; AZ1225; BA722; BH223 102360

Friend of sinners! Lord of Glory! (Hall) I130; V181; AZ266 102361

Friend of the home: as when in Galilee (Lewis) G406; AD 399; AE326; AK333; AR550; AT376; BF610; BY285 102362

Friend of the weary, O refresh us (Gotter) K347; N88 102363
Friends of Jesus in their parting (Schjörring) P66 102364
Frölich pfleg ich zu singen (Ausbund) BU65 X Fölich phleg ich 102365
Frölich so will ich singen (S.v. Bosch) BU70 102366
Fröhlich soll mein Herze springen (Gerhardt) BT77; BW525 102367
From afar, across the waters (Rohr) M634 102368
From age to age how grandly rise (Hosmer) AN423; AQ231; BX455 102369
From age to age they gather (Hosmer) Y155; AN566; AO601; BD149; BF465; BX409 102370
From all that dwell below the skies (Watts) A277; B250; D468; F630; G17; H22; J429; K293; L79; O21; P35; Q15; R33; S388; V6; W228; X408; Z104; AA79; AD6; AE5; AF11; AG4; AH182; AK386; AL16; AM3; AN498, 502; AP104; AQ 13; AR22; AS9; AY18; AZ314; BA353; BB2; BC52; BDp. 1; BE62; BI37; BJ80; BM104; BR50; BV31; BX3; BY760; BZ 102371
From all the dark places, of earth's needy races (Slade) G483; I633; AT409; AU125 102372
From all the dark places, of earth's heathen races (Slade) AU125 X From all the dark places, of earth's needy races 102373
From all the fret and fever of the day (Beardsley) AQ84 102374
From all thy saints in warfare (Nelson) B267; D174; K251; N48; O494; P240; AH457; AV 289; AZ802; BA806 102375
From all who dwell below the skies (Watts) L79 X From all that dwell 102376
From Bethany, the Master comes down Mt. Olive's slopes (Ham) Z222; AN181; AR157 102377
From city and from prairie (Hale) BX536 102378
From depths of woe I cry to thee (Luther) Q329 X Out of the depths I cry to thee 102379
From depths of woe I raise to thee (Luther) AM461 X Out of the depths I cry to thee 102380
From distant shores returning (Barth) M644 102381
From east to west, from shore to shore (Sedulius) E18; F57; J20; O291; BY94 102382
From eternity, O God (Neumann) Q411 102383
From every clime and country (Gaines) Y260 102384
From every stormy wind that blows (Stowell) A421; B32; D481; G317; H42; I495; L466; N437; R419; U365; V458; Z 394; AG210; AH353; AI231; AL426; AM528; AO319; AP 498; AR262; AS46; AT296; AU189; AV185; AX369; AZ 418; BA593; BB241; BY334; BZ 102385
From far away we come to you (Morris) BG186 102386
From foes that would the land devour (Heber) E557; AZ 1149 102387
From glory to glory advancing (Liturgy of St. James) A492; E310; F417; X496 102388
From glory unto glory (Havergal) D205; I573; S467; AE422; BD 233; BE65 102389
From God shall naught divide me (Helmbold) O349; Q393; AA509 102390
From Greenland's icy mountains (Heber) A254; B476; D254; E547; F265; G484; H479; I655; J310; K220; L338; M100; N 376; O120; P393; Q495; S385; U405; V586; W371; AA474; AG265; AH467; AI168; AL256;

AM383; AO528; AP376; AS367; AT449; AU35; AV269; AW333; AY329; AZ828; BA341; BB445; BC40; BF539; BR225 102391

From heart to heart, from creed to creed (Gannett) AN54; AQ 251; BX79 102392

From heaven above to earth I come (Luther) M356 X From heaven high I come to you 102393

From heaven high I come to you (Luther) A22; J22; M356; O181; P126; Q85; AA150; AF 121; AI418; AK114; AM166; AW 527a; BK156 102394

From heav'n the Lord with searching eye (U.P. Psalter, 1912) AM474 X The God who sits enthroned on high 102395

From heavenly Jerusalem's towers (Charles) W596 102396

From heaven's height Christ spake to call (St Peter Damiani) F540 102397

From heaven's height, Soft, vernal breezes blow (Philippson) BH 124 102398

From heaven's heights the thunder peals (Wise) BH142 102399

From homes of quiet peace (Draper) AC315 102400

From land to land the Christian goes (Zinzendorf, N.L.) AZ 903; BA724 102401

From lands beyond the waters wide (Bartholomew) AO515 102402

From lips divine like healing balm (Burleigh) H366 102403

From many ways and wide apart (Hosmer) AB318 102404

From my own works at last I cease (Wesley) AZ408 102405

From north and south and east and west (Coster) BY369 102406

From ocean unto ocean (Murray) G486; J340; K494; R509; S390; U411; Z541; AD371; AG258; AI357; AK376; AL510; AO531; AP649; AT450; BA878; BF538 102407

From out of the wood did a cuckoo fly (Czech carol) X381; BG103 102408

From out of the cloud of fiery light (Alexander) F548 102409

From out the depths, I cry, O Lord, to thee (U.P. Psalter, 1912) T260; AJ362; AM463 102410

From out the depths I cry to thee (U.P. Psalter, 1912) AJ364 102411

From out the Rock whence we were hewn (Cross) AB393 102412

From over hill and plain, There comes the signal (Cassel) AT407; AU374 102413

From peaceful slumber waking (Wallin) M558; N537 102414

From place to place the Christian goes (Zinzendorf, N.L.) O589 102415

From sense to Soul my pathway lies before me (Hay) BE64 102416

From Sinai's height a fountain gushes (Freund) AH148; BH 143 102417

From sinking sand He lifted me (Homer) R In loving-kindness Jesus came 102418

From starry heaven descending (St Alfonso de Ligouri) BN14 102419

From street and square, from hill and glen (Higginson) Y 233; AN343 102420

From the Cross the blood is falling (Bonar) AZ645 102421

From the Cross uplifted high (Haweis) H259; U157; V254 102422

From the depths do I invoke thee (U.P. Psalter, 1912) T261; AJ363 102423

From the depths my prayer ascendeth (U.P. Psalter, 1912) AJ365; AM570 102424

From the depths we cry to thee (Sr.M. Teresine) BM76 102425

From the doctrines I'll never waver (Neisser) AZ236 102426
From the eastern mountains (Thring) A49; B92; D62; E615; F595; K562; S380; U63; W66; X388; AB123; AC94; AD 127; AH270; AL257; AO139; AP382; AW89; BA186; BF293; BI91; BV128; BY95 102427
From the first man to climb the hill (---) AO64 102428
From the graves remove the dark crosses (Grundtvig) M447 102429
From the Pilgrim's rock-bound coast (Knapp) AD439 102430
From the table now retiring (Rowe) U379; V556; Z468; AH507; BF606 102431
From Thee all skill and science flow (Kingsley) A515; E525; F479; G462; J216; R315; W351; X285; AB353; AD315; AG244; AK395; AL371; AP574; AR284; BF513; BV398; BY635; BZ 102432
From thee, illustrious Teacher Paul (St Peter Damiani) BO217 102433
From these thy children gathered in thy name (Hay) BE66 102434
From thy holy habitation (Simpson) AZ1108; BA796 102435
From yon distant heaven (Hey) AW433 102436
Fryd dig, du Kristi Brud (Danish, ca 1600) BT57 102437
Full in the panting heart of Rome (Wiseman) BO205 102438
Full many shall come from the east and the west (Landstad) J333; O239; P157; Q415 102439
Full of glory, full of wonders (Faber) BL81; BQ40 102440
Full of reverence at thy word (Muenter) M44 102441
Fully surrendered, Lord divine (Morris) AX400 102442
Für Gott den Herren woll'n wir gohn (Ausbund) BU88 102443

G

Gabriel to Mary came (Latin, 14th c) F547 102444
Gabriel's message does away (Piae cantiones, 1582) BG102 102445
Galilee, bright Galilee (Sherwin) AC106; AV402 102446
Gather around the Christmas tree (---) N636 102447
Gather them in from the byways of sin (---) R In from the highways 102448
Gather us in, thou love that fillest all (Matheson) X497; Y261; AB311; AC300; AD377; AN418; AQ249; BF532; BX 449 102449
Gathering buds, gathering buds (Rowe) R Jesus has taken a beautiful bud 102450
Gathering home! Gathering home! (Slade) R Up to the bountiful Giver of life 102451
Gaudeamus igitur (Latin) Y299 102452
Gebor'n ist uns ein Kindelein (German carol, 17th c) BG 97b 102453
Geh, Seele frisch im Glauben fort (Unparth. G. B.) AY7d 102454
Gehe auf, du Trost der Heiden (Fick) BT498 102455
Gelobet sei der Herr (Olearius) BT38 102456
Gelobt sey Gott der Herre (Ausbund) BU90 102457
Gelobt sey Gott im höchsten Thron (H. Betz) BU122 102458
Gelobet seist du, Jesu Christ (Luther) BT80 102459
Gen Himmel aufgefahren ist, Alleluya (German trad carol) BG127b 102460
Gentle Jesus, meek and mild (Wesley) E591; F451; G444; K561; L464; W662; X356; AL 612; AP760; AT510; AV104; AZ38; BA820; BY739 102461
Gentle Jesus, meek and mild

(Wesley) X Lamb of God, I look to Thee (Wesley) 102462
Gentle Mary laid her child (Cook) A37; G107; R167; S453; AD115; AG68; AL57; AM640; AT73; BZ 102463
Gentle Peace, from heaven descended (---) BB511 102464
Gentle Shepherd, thou hast stilled (Meinhold) E353; V671; AA537; AI333; AO570 102465
Gently, Lord, O gently lead us (Hastings) I319; L196; U258; V345; AI300; AV54; AY351; AZ947; BA701 102466
Gently raise the sacred strain (Phelps) BC92 102467
Gethsemane, Gethsemane, I must remember thee (Norwegian) R The hour in dark Gethsemane 102468
Gird on the armor, brave soul, today (Perkins) BD80 102469
Gird on thy sword, O man, thy strength endue (Bridges) X498; AN341; AQ212 102470
Gird thy heavenly armor on (Elliott) BE67 X Christian seek not yet repose 102471
Gird us, O God, with humble might (Foulkes) AC246; BH24 102472
Give as the Lord hath prospered you (Hartsough) AX647 102473
Give ear unto me when I call (Scottish Psalter, 1650) AP4 102474
Give ear unto my words, O Lord (Scottish Psalter, 1650) AP5 102475
Give ear, ye children, to my law (Belknap) AI370; AN366; BX 402 102476
Give forth thine earnest cry (Hymns of the Spirit, 1864) BX391 102477
Give, give with a willing hand (Hartsough) R Give as the Lord 102478
Give God the Father praise, Give glory to the Son (---) AZ1376 102479
Give heed, my heart, lift up thine eyes (Luther) AD123 X Ah, dearest Jesus, holy Child 102480
Give me a foot-hold on the Rock (MacKellar) AX519; AY72 102481
Give me a new, a perfect heart (Wesley) I366 102482
"Give me, my child," the Father saith, "thy heart" (Richter) AZ705 102483
Give me, O Christ, the strength that is in Thee (Carter) BV 557; BY564 102484
Give me, O Lord, a heart of grace (Gilbert) Y196; AB 271 102485
Give me, O Lord, a spirit lowly (Loy) M257 102486
Give me, O Lord, and understanding heart (Rome) BE69 102487
Give me the Bible, Star of gladness (Owens) AX138; BB655 102488
Give me the faith which can remove (Wesley) BY347 102489
Give me the wings of faith to rise (Watts) B301; E197; F571; G424; H430; I606; J 594; V638; X204; AL179; AP312; AV279; BV462; BY404; BZ 102490
"Give me thy heart," says the Father above (Hewitt) AI196; AM723; AX260 102491
Give me to know thy will, O God (MacKellar) AY41 102492
Give me your whole heart, Love and adore me (Bhagavad-Gita) AQ134 102493
Give of your best to the Master (Grose) AS407; AT353; AU366; AV375; AW400 102494
Give peace, O God, the nations cry (Norris) A526 102495
Give praise and glory unto God (Schuetz) A287 102496
Give praise and thanks unto the Lord (Scottish Psalter, 1650) AL674; AP95 102497

Give praise to God our King (Russell) O26; P5 102498
Give thanks and praise to God above (U.P. Psalter, 1912) T222; AJ319 102499
Give thanks for the corn and the wheat (---) AQ21 102500
Give thanks to God, call on His name (Scottish Psalter, 1650) AP94 102501
Give thanks to God, for good is He (Norton) T271; AJ378 102502
Give thanks to God; He reigns above (Watts) BR78 102503
Give thanks to God, His praises sing (Bible. Psalm 136) BI21 102504
Give thanks to God most high (Watts) L103 102505
Give thanks unto the Lord, Jehovah (---) AI444; AM512 102506
Give thou thy youth to God (Bonar) AO619 102507
Give thy heart's love and labor (Gerhardt) AD232 102508
Give to our God immortal praise (Watts) J441; K307; L70; M 590; O28; P24; AA70; AL39; AM20; AP121; AW11; AZ304; BA 34; BV235; BX47; BY9 102509
Give to the winds thy fears (Gerhardt) I437; K400; L484; R364; S294; U222; V365; Z402; AB246; AD238; AE213; AF337; AG221; AL421; AN247; AP517; AS304; AW246; AZ1495; BA31; BF408; BX308; BZ 102510
"Give us each day our daily bread." (Hawkes) BX476 102511
"Give us room that we may dwell" (Kelly) BC256 102512
Give us the wings of faith to rise (Watts) F571 X Give me the wings of faith 102513
Give ye to Jehovah, O sons of the mighty (U.P. Book of Psalms, 1871) AP27 102514
Giver of concord, Prince of Peace (Wesley) I563 102515
Giving our best to the Saviour (Toews) R Loyal and true and faithful 102516
Glad day! Glad day! Is it the crowning day (Whitcomb) R Jesus may come today 102517
Glad that I live am I (Reese) X499; Y191; AC172 102518
Glad tidings to all men, Glad tidings sing (English trad) R A child this day is born 102519
Glad was my heart to hear (Montgomery) AP111 102520
Gleaning on the hillside (Thomas) R 'Tis the harvest time 102521
Gloomy night embraced the place (Crashaw) BG124 102522
Gloria, Gloria! O come let us join (Russian trad) BK13 102523
Gloria, laus et honor (St Theodulph of Orleans) BN31; BQ 168; BT160; BW100 102524
Gloriosi salvatoris Nominis praeconia (Latin, 15th c.) BT116 102525
Glorious are the lofty mountains (Warren) BB96 102526
Glorious, Glorious, Glorious is thy name (McKinney) R Blessed Saviour we adore thee 102527
Glorious majesty, before thee (Hedborn) J189; N315 102528
Glorious Mary, Queen and Giver of the Rosary (Litany of Loreto) BN156 102529
Glorious Patron! low before thee kneel thy sons (Sr. Mercedes) BQ101 102530
Glorious Saint, whose deeds immortal (Driscoll) BN178 102531
Glorious things are sung in Sion (Phelps) BC243 102532
Glorious things are sung in Sion (Phelps) BC243 X Glorious things of thee are spoken (Newton) 102533
Glorious things of thee are spoken (Newton) A385; B468; D490; E393; F257; G382; H402; I210;

J152; K197; L294; M85; N271; O88; P78; Q469; R434; S339; T358; U352; V529; W206; X 500; Z431; AA464; AB248; AD 393; AE315; AF267; AG231; AH518; AI145; AK323; AL166; AM269; AN393: AO419; AP297; AR495; AS193; AT381; AV241; AW274; AX154; AZ937; BA276; BB304; BC244; BE71; BF583; BI49; BR214; BV424; BX454; BY257; BZ 102534

Glorious Virgin, thee we sing (Breviary) BO89 102535

Glorious Yuletide, glad bells proclaim it (Olson) N43 102536

Glory and honour and laud (St Theodulph of Orleans) F598 102537

Glory and praise and dominion be thine (St Theodulph of Orleans) E621 102538

Glory and praises ever be (---) BRp. 467 102539

Glory be to God on high. Alleluia (Williams) Z100; AF65 102540

Glory be to God on high, God whose glory fills the sky (Wesley) BE72 102541

Glory be to God the Father, Glory be to God the Son Dying, risen ... (Wordsworth) AZ975 102542

Glory be to God the Father Glory be to God the Son Glory be to God the Spirit (Bonar) D617; J139; K163; Lp. 744; N666; P236; Q244; S60; W7; AA268; AC377; AK 194; AL2; AO236; AP136; AZ 1385; BA645 102543

Glory be to Jesus! Let all His children say (Ellerton) R Again the morn of gladness 102544

Glory be to Jesus, who in bitter pains (Italian, 18th c) A335; B162; D362; E99; F107; J76; K90; N639; Q158; AA208; AM 190; AZ756; BA92; BN73; BO 28; BQ72; BV154 102545

Glory be to the Father, and to the Son (Latin, 2d c) A602; G569; Hp. 9; I737; Jp. 43; Kp. 10; Lp. 45; Mp. 8; Np. 689; Op. 22; Pp. 409; Qp. 16; R545; Ssuppl. 93; T458; U488; W708; Y389; Z612; AAp. 2; AB425; AC335; AD493; AE471; AF511; AG323; AH574; AI449; AK491; AMp. xv; AO662; AR636; AS 488; AT524; AU495; AV428; AW606; AX649; BA943; BB 689; BF680; BZ 102546

Glory eternal be to thee, O God, the Father (---) BRp. 467 102547

Glory flaming in the cloud (Pendleton) BI54 102548

Glory! glory! Hallelujah (Howe) R Mine eyes have seen the glory 102549

Glory, glory! how the angels sing (Cushing) R Ring the bells of heaven 102550

Glory, Glory! Joy to my heart 'twill bring (Morris) R Jesus is coming to earth again 102551

Glory, honor, praise and pure oblations (Rutgers) BE73 102552

Glory, praise and blessing be, Lord, our Savior (---) BI 20-D; BRp. 867 102553

Glory, praise, to thee be given (Rist) AZ1083 102554

Glory to God and praise and love (Wesley) BT360 X O for a thousand tongues to sing 102555

Glory to God, Glory to God (MacFarlane) R Far, far away on Judea's plains 102556

Glory to God! Glory to God! Glory to God. (Washburne) R Softly the night is sleeping 102557

Glory to God in the highest (Warren) AX103 102558

Glory to God on high (Allen) H16; L119; M597; AX15; AZ 1237; BC44 102559

Glory to God on high (Boden)

BC44 X Glory to God on high (Allen) 102560
Glory to God the Father (Whittle) R "For God so loved!" 102561
Glory to God, whose Spirit draws (Noel) BY290 102562
Glory to God! whose witness-train (Zinzendorf, N. L.) H386; V478; AZ96; BA579 102563
Glory to His name (Hoffman) R Down at the cross 102564
Glory to the blessed Jesus (---) B347; D537; L144 102565
Glory to the Father give (Montgomery) D547; N640; AZ63; BA821 102566
Glory to the Father, Who in Christ Jesus (Gregor) AZ525 102567
Glory to the King of angels (Bonar) AC337 X Glory be to God the Father 102568
Glory to Thee, my God, this night (Ken) M568 X All praise to Thee, my God, this night 102569
Glory to Thee, O Lord, who be thy mighty power (Beadon) D 70; N74; O232; AO135; BR164 102570
Glory to thee, O Lord, who from this world of sin (Toke) D147 102571
Glory to thee, who safe hast kept (Ken) BJ25 X Awake my soul, and with the sun 102572
Glucksel' ger Tag, da ich erkor (Unparth. G. B.) AY39d 102573
Go and let my grave be made (Arndt) O588 102574
Go and seek the lost and dying (Hartzler) AE358 102575
Go and tell the sweet old story (Lyon) AY369 102576
Go as a witness for Jesus (Crosby) U314 102577
Go bury thy sorrow (Bachelor) AU293 102578
Go down, Moses (Negro spiritual) R When Israel was in Egypt's land 102579
Go, follow the Saviour (Cennick) AZ1114 102580
Go forth and stand upon the mount (Sargant) BE74 102581
Go forth in spirit, go To Calvary's holy mount (Gambold) AZ1292; BA200 102582
Go forth, my heart, and seek delight (Gerhardt) M645 102583
Go forth, strong word of God (Cross) AE159 102584
Go forth to life, O child of earth! (Longfellow) G296; W672; Z319; AN290; AW211; BD102; BF631; BX372 102585
Go forth with God! the day is now (Baron) F500 102586
Go forth, ye hearlds, in my name (Maxwell) M95; N378 102587
Go forward, Christian soldier (Tuttiett) A553; B535; D510; I387; U304; AH432; AO397; AZ855; BA577; BD81; BR 403 102588
Go, heralds of salvation, forth (Smith, S. F.) AK352; AO 536 102589
Go joyfully forth To war against sin (Barth) M541 102590
Go, labor on! spend and be spent (Bonar) A573; B490; D584; E556; G292; H378; I399; M256; N509; P409; R283; S376; T372; U285; V497; W356; Z473: AD313; AE276; AG198; AH412; AK 355; AL384; AM496; AO502; AP579; AR253; AV206; AW 231; AZ367; BA540; BF434; BV595; BY513 102591
Go labor on, spend and be spent (Bonar) X Go labor on, while it is day (Bonar) 102592
Go, labor on, while it is day (Bonar) U282; V498; AE276; AK355; BB441; BF434; BV 595 102593
Go, my soul, go every day (Worthington) AZ56 102594
Go not far from me, O my strength (Waring) AZ733 102595

Go not, my soul, in search of Him (Hosmer) AN58; AQ88; BF263; BX75 102596

Go out and gather the golden grain (Chapman) AY337 102597

"Go, preach my gospel," saith the Lord (Watts) V561; AI 180; AO455; BB440 102598

Go search it out, and bring it home (Schell) R The ninety-nine within 102599

Go tell it on the mountain (Negro Spiritual) AF488; BK 163; BZ 102600

Go, tell, Mary and Martha (Negro Spiritual) R In-a-this-a band we have sweet music 102601

Go thou, in life's fair morning (Bradbury. Oriola, 1860) AZ 846; BA815 102602

Go to dark Gethsemane (Montgomery) A70; B151; D93; E100; F110; J78; K93; L240; M416; N102; O304; P170; Q159; R193; V147; Z227; AA199; AE114; AF158; AH284; AK144; AL93; AO159; AP190; AR160; AS134; AT105; AW107; AZ1250; BA 204; BB122; BR174; BZ 102603

Go to the deeps of God's promise (Breck) AI241 102604

Go the grave in all thy glorious prime! (Montgomery) AZ458; BA725 102605

Go to the lost and dying, brother (Evilsizer) R Out in the desert 102606

Go to thy rest, fair child (Sigourney) AX627; AY177; AZ485 102607

Go when the morning shineth (Simpson) BR21 102608

Go with Jesus to thy task (Morgen- und Abendsegen. Waldenburg. 1734) M216 102609

Go, ye messengers of glory (Taylor) BC247 102610

Go, ye messengers of God (Marsden) I640 102611

God Almighty and all-seeing (Pierpont) AZ1390 102612

God Almighty, in thy temple (Baynes) D548; BA825; BY 40 102613

God and Father we adore thee (Darby & Falconer) W59 102614

God be in my head (Book of hours. 1490) A466; F332; R395; X501; AF393; AL364; AR679; BV623; BY471; BZ 102615

God be merciful to me (U.P. Psalter, 1912) R282; T97; AJ140; AM415 102616

God be with thee! Gently o'er thee (Williams) AN471; BE81; BX511 102617

God be with you now and ever (Overby) P76 102618

God be with you till we meet again (Rankin) A490; E524; F489; G557; H434; I564; L67; M650; N364; R78; U449; V26; W624; X334; Z129; AF61; AG 14; AH177; AI344; AM632; AN472; AO48; AP701; AR506; AS63; AT372; AU480; AV235; AW365; AX654; AY405; BA932; BB35; BC47; BY761; BZ 102619

God bless America, Land that I love (Berlin) AH488 102620

God bless and keep thee (DeFluiter) BB38 102621

God bless our native land, Firm may she ever stand (Mahlmann) A146; B428; G490; H530; I703; J358; K489; L559; M498; N 566; O519; P411; Q577; R514; S413; U343; W632; AA305; AB335; AC283; AD441; AE 395; AH475; AK439; AN385; AR603; AS384; AV306; AW348; AZ1232; BA871; BD173; BF 542; BI11; BR494; BX421 102622

God bless our native land, May heaven's protecting hand (Hickson) AN386; BB512; BX423; BY640 102623

God bless the master of this house (English trad carol)

BG15-16 102624

God bless the ruler of this house (English trad carol) BG44 X Awake, awake ye drowsy souls 102625

God built him a continent of glory (Silver) AC515 102626

God calling yet! Shall I not hear (Tersteegen) G185; H250; I 252; J374; K312; M76; N403; O433; P265; T434; U162; V257; AG137; AK473; AO254; AP423; AT223; AV336; AZ382; BA402; BZ 102627

God calls to man, His acres to prepare (Schroeder) AR589 102628

God comes, with succor speedy (Montgomery) BE75 X Hail to the Lord's anointed 102629

God deigning man to be (Damrosch) A131 102630

God Eternal, in thy presence, Bowed in supplication (Statler) AR392 102631

God, from all eternity (Neumann) AA343 102632

God from on high hath heard (Coffin) F63 102633

God give us Christian homes (McKinney) AT377 102634

God giveth light to all who ask (Adams) BE70 102635

God guards the good with watchful eye (U.P. Psalter, 1912) T58; AJ91 102636

God has given us a book full of stories (Penstone) BY740 102637

God hath not promised skies always blue (Flint) AX475 102638

God hath sent his angels (Brooks) B557; AO187; BD241 102639

God hath spoken -- by His prophets (Briggs) BV301; BY247; BZ 102640

God-head here in hiding, whom I do adore (St Thomas Aquinas) BL50; BN89 102641

God help me speak the helping word (Belden) R If any little word of mine 102642

God help our country to be strong (Wells) AK438 102643

God himself is present (Tersteegen) Q4 X God himself is with us 102644

God himself is with us (Tersteegen) A477; J164; K424; Q4; R13; S51; W234; Z123; AD24; AE4; AF3; AG11; AK 29; AL196; AM315; AP315; AW506; AZ1026; BA376; BV5; BZ 102645

God in heaven, hear our singing (Havergal) D578; K563; W375; AP799; BA830 102646

God in His earthly temple lays (Watts) V535 102647

God, in human flesh appearing (Hiller) M39; N226 102648

God, in the gospel of his Son (Beddome) H98; U138; V228; AM262; AO244; AR237; AV78 102649

God in whom all graces dwell (Proprium. Prague, 1720) BM74 102650

God incarnate, veil thy splendor (---) BI56 102651

God is always near me (Bliss) W664 102652

God is ascended up on high (More) BG127; BL38; BV201 102653

God is at the anvil, beating out the Sun (Sarett) Y52 102654

God is faithful, He will never (Burntvedt) P289 102655

God is forever merciful (Chinese trad) R Chaun dong whan lotsan 102656

God is gone up on high (Wesley) BV202 102657

God is good; we come before Him (Nevill) BY10 102658

God is great, God is good (---) AX653 102659

God is in His holy temple, all the earth keep silence (Montgomery) AZ1380; BA377 102660

God is in His holy temple, earthly thoughts be silent (Hymns of the Spirit, 1864) AE6; AN

23; AQ117; AR5; AW2; BC246; BD15; BH4; BX32 102661

God is in His temple, Let us fall before Him (Tersteegen) BR 14 X God is in His Temple, O let us adore 102662

God is in His temple; O let us adore him (Tersteegen) M9; BR14 102663

God is in His temple, O let us adore Him (Tersteegen) X God Himself is with us 102664

God is in His temple, The almighty Father (Matson) BY 41 102665

God is King forever: let the nations tremble (U.P. Psalter, 1912) T182; AJ266 102666

God is known among His people (U.P. Psalter, 1912) T140; AJ207; AM63 102667

God is known in loving-kindness (Heermann) BE76 102668

God is love, by him upholden (Monsell) BX327 X God is love! The heavens tell it 102669

God is love; His mercy brightens (Bowring) G75; H116; I88; K 297; L102; M156; N295; R103; S80; U24; V107; W33; Z178; AA510; AB66; AD81; AE73; AG55; AK76; AL13; AN83; AO83; AP 156; AR87; AS86; AT50; AV48; AW55; AX86; AY372; BA643; BD61; BE79; BF244; BI8; BR 74; BX121; BZ 102670

God is love: his the care (Dearmer) X502 102671

God is love: let heaven adore Him (Rees) BY52 102672

God is love! The heavens tell it (Monsell) BR61; BX327; BZ 102673

God is my Light! My soul, do not despair (Hengstenberg) AW560 102674

God is my strong salvation (Montgomery) G324; I448; R347; S92; U216; W527; AD242; AF 373; AL398; AM568; AN257; AP 25; AQ20; BD82; BE77; BF411; BH95; BR399; BX330; BY575; BZ 102675

God is near thee, therefore cheer thee (Curwen. Standard course. 1860) AP536 102676

God is not far from any one of us (Clark) AE71; AK78 102677

God is of mine inheritance (Scottish Psalter, 1650) AP11 102678

God is our refuge and defense (Montgomery) I97; BE80 102679

God is our refuge and our strength, A helper ever near us (U.P. Psalter, 1912) AJ128 12680

God is our refuge and our strength, In straits a present aid (Scottish Psalter, 1650) S91; AL651; AP41; AW588 102681

God is our refuge and our strength, Our everlasting aid (U.P. Psalter, 1912) R381; T86; AJ126; AM37 102682

God is our stronghold and our stay (Wordsworth, E) B214 102683

God is the name my soul adores (Watts) I80 102684

God is the refuge of his saints (Watts) H411; I218; L481; P290; V536; AL33; AM292; AO87; AV68; AW257; BA705; BB89; BR274 102685

God is with me, gently o'er me (Williams) BE81 X God be with thee! Gently o'er thee 102686

"God is with us, God is with us" (Mathams) BY370 102687

God is working his purpose out (Ainger) A538; B483; E548; F271; R500; W380; X300; AF 298; AP394; BE82; BV315; BY371 102688

God Jehovah reigns, His are all domains (Brondsema) AJ432 102689

God laid his rocks in courses (Gannett) AN458; AQ260;

BX491 102690
God! Let the torrents like a shout of nations (Coleridge) AC435 102691
God liveth still! Soul, despair not (Zihn) AA513 102692
God, Lord of Sabaoth, Thou who ordainest (Chorley & Ellerton) Q582 X God the Omnipotent, King who ordainest 102693
God loved our erring mortal race (Olearius) N436 102694
God loved the world of sinners lost (Stockton) AL479; AP425; AX83 102695
God loved the world so that He gave (German, 1791) Q245 102696
God loved us, so he sent his Son (Kimball) BC178 102697
God loveth the righteous, His goodness is sure (U.P. Psalter, 1912) T135; AJ201 102698
God made all His creatures free (Montgomery) BE83 102699
God made me for Himself, to serve Him here (Baker) BV 484 102700
God make my life a shining light (Betham-Edwards) BY741 X God make my life a little light 102701
God make my life a little light (Betham-Edwards) G450; BY 741 102702
God makes a path, provides a guide (Williams) AQ45 102703
God, most mighty, sovereign Lord (Harbaugh) AZ57 X Christ, by heavenly hosts adored 102704
God most truly honored thee (Currie) BN175 102705
God moves in a mysterious way (Cowper) A310; B216; D427; E394; F181; G68; H115; I96; J484; K409; L477; M148; N478; O421; P304; Q514; R112; S103; T395; U221; V92; W31; X503; Y372; Z162; AA524; AB216; AD88; AE58; AF87; AG45; AH 225; AI414; AK75; AL40; AM21; AN244; AO97; AP154; AQ34; AR78; AS81; AT53; AV55; AW60; AX85; AY84; AZ89; BA709; BB84; BC48; BD50; BE399; BF431; BH83; BK71; BR263; BV403; BX299; BY53; BZ 102706
God, my Father, hear me pray (Holme) D384 102707
God my Father loving me (Briggs) A239; X357; BY742 102708
God, my King, thy might confessing (Mant) A280; B311; D465; V521; AM2; BL98 102709
God, my supporter and my hope (Watts) L519; V339 102710
God of ages, all transcending (Neumann) M7 102711
God of all grace, thy mercy send (Greek) A180; E652 102712
God of all power, and truth, and grace (Wesley) I378; BZ 102713
God of compassion, in mercy befriend us (Moment) R122; S290 102714
God of earth and sea and heaven (Edwards) AF316 102715
God of eternal love (Seaton. Church hymn book, 1855) K265; O69 102716
God of eternity, Lord of the ages (Merrington) W642 102717
God of every land and nation (---) AZ1402 102718
God of grace and God of glory (Fosdick) A524; G279; R358; Z378; AD297; AE246; AF366; AK287; AN345; AQ27; AR321; AT465; BF464; BK77; BY372; BZ 102719
God of grace, O let thy light (Churton) BH75 102720
God of heaven, hear our singing (Havergal) K563 X God in heaven . . . 102721
God of Israel, keep us faithful (Mayer) BH52 102722
God of Israel's faithful three (Wesley) AZ1470 102723

God of love and God of power (Kennedy) BZ 102724
God of love, Our Father, Saviour (Robilliard) D298 102725
God of love, that hearest prayer (Wesley) I562; AY34 102726
God of love, who hearest prayer (Wesley) AY34 X God of love, that hearest prayer 102727
God of mercy and compassion (Vaughan) BX134 102728
God of mercy! God of grace! Hear our penitential songs (Taylor) L385 X God of mercy! God of grace! Hear our sad repentant songs 102729
God of mercy! God of grace! Hear our sad repentant songs (Taylor) K314; L385; N413 102730
God of mercy, God of grace, Show the brightness of thy face (Lyte) B312; D332; E395; F 264; K423; L96; M595; N329; Q20; S465; W379; X170; AA71; AL258; AO77; AP58; AR23; AZ1273; BA646; BV421; BY 373 102731
God of mercy, hear our prayer (Hastings) L318; BA850 102732
God of mercy, throned on high (Neele) D551; BA819 102733
God of might, God of right (Jewish) (composite) AH147; BH125 102734
God of might, we praise thy name (Franz) AK20 102735
God of my heart! Its earliest love (---) AW235 102736
God of my life, on thee I call (Cowper) AZ299 X God of my life, to thee . . . 102737
God of my life, through all my days (Doddridge) I322 102738
God of my life, thy boundless grace (Elliott) AA265; AZ14; BA12 102739
God of my life, to thee I call (Cowper) L523; Q534; V432; AA522; AZ299 102740
God of my life, whose gracious power (Wesley) H126; K405; L515; AA332; BB83 102741
God of my salvation, hear (Wesley) L397; AZ1469 102742
God of nations, throned above (Kuhlman) M500 102743
God of our boyhood, whom we yield (Forbush) Y179; Z608; BF633 102744
God of our fathers, bless this our land (Hopkins) D195 102745
God of our fathers, hear our prayer (Hopps) BX505 102746
God of our fathers, known of old (Kipling) A147; B439; E558; G497; I710; J347; U340; V745; W637; X317; Y287; Z560; AB342; AC282; AD442; AE 396; AF431; AH487; AL516; AN380; AO590; AP644; AS365; AU224; AV304; BB505; BC76; BF549; BX411 102747
God of our fathers, the strength of our people and nation (Garrison) Z158 102748
God of our fathers, unto thee (Ainger) E559 102749
God of our fathers, we come unto thee (Penrose) BC50 102750
God of our fathers, who hast safely brought us (Briggs) AQ234 102751
God of our fathers, whose almighty hand (Roberts) A143; B430; D194; G496; I704; J521; K493; M648; R515; S414; T450; U342; V744; Y283; Z551; AB 338; AC273; AD437; AE390; AF433; AG272; AH480; AI 358; AK440; AM616; AN376; AO589; AR602; AT54; AU240; AV26; AW347; BA874; BB504; BC54; BD169; BF548; BH263; BK123; BZ 102752
God of our history, our fathers worshiped thee (Lamp) AR 606 102753
God of our life, all-glorious Lord (Strodach) J209 102754

God of our life, through all the circling years (Kerr) R108; S88; Z583; AB400; AE62; AF 97; AR68; BF641; BZ 102755
God of our salvation, hear us (Kelly) L44; V25 102756
God of our saving health and peace (Milton) AP69 102757
God of our strength, enthroned above (Crosby) AV25 102758
God of our youth, be with us yet (Forbush) R God of our boyhood, whom we yield 102759
God of our youth, to whom we yield (Forbush) Z608 X God of our boyhood, whom we yield 102760
God of peace, in peace preserve us (Olson) J349 102761
God of pity, God of grace (Morris) K278; L194; S252; W240; AK223; AL204; AM466; AP327; BR33; BY431 102762
God of pity, Lord of grace (Morris) BR33 X God of pity, God of grace 102763
God of power, God of right (Bennett) BC36 102764
God of that glorious gift of grace (Monsell) AZ384 102765
God of the ages, by whose hand (Burrowes) BZ 102766
God of the changing year (Taylor) BF644; BX184 102767
God of the circling realms of light (Lee) AB360; BF569 102768
God of the earnest heart (Johnson) Y225; AN301; AQ224; BD100; BX344 102769
God of the earth, the sky, the sea (Longfellow) Y55; Z120; AB50; AC49; AD29; AF67; AK68; AN28; AQ43; AR94; AS 92; AW52; BD34; BF234; BK 127; BX49; BZ 102770
God of the fertile fields (Harkness) AE418 102771
God of the glorious sunshine (Paxton) AC42; AK69 102772
God of the living, in whose eyes (Ellerton) A225; B410; K508; W332; AF468; BX472; BY611 102773
God of the morning, at whose voice (Watts) F8; BR11; BV39; BX133; BY676 102774
God of the moving years (Morse) AR72 102775
God of the nations, hear our call (Campbell) Y276; BD 179 102776
God of the nations, near and far (Holmes) Z556; AB363; AC 296; AD354; AN399; BD185; BF564; BH226; BK107; BX 426 102777
God of the nations, who from dawn of days (Bowie) Y272; AB270; AC274; AD430; AF432; AH469; AN377; AR607; BD 164; BF545 102778
God of the nations, who hast led (Edwards) B442 102779
God of the pastures, hear our prayer (Hunter-Clare) BV645 102780
God of the prophets, bless the prophets' sons (Wortman) A220; B451; D280; Q483; R520; S481; Z472; AA486; AB329; AD414; AE321; AF470; AK349; AO450; AR520; BA310; BF 596 102781
God of the shining hosts that range on high (Rowland) AC 289 102782
God of the Spirit-wind (Marlatt) AR223 102783
God of the strong, God of the weak (Gilder) G457; Y217; Z311; AB257; AC212; AD446; BDp. 58; BF426 102784
God of the universe, to Thee ("O, Miss Mary", 1841) BB486 102785
God of truth, eternal good (Brewer) BE85 102786
God of years, thy love hath led us (Eldridge) AK362 102787
God, omnipotent Creator (Albert) AZ593 102788
God, our Father, hear us pray (Malin) BC8 102789
God, our Father, made the daylight (Compton) BK12 102790
God, our Father, we adore thee (Frazer) AT5 102791

God reigneth, He is clothed with majesty (Scottish Psalter, 1650) AP80 102792

God rest you merry, gentlemen (English carol, 18th c) A40; R166; S131; AD109; AF122; AG 67; AH259; AL66; AM160; AP 731; BG11; BV91; BY96; BZ 102793

God reveals His presence (Tersteegen) W234 X God himself is with us 102794

God righteous judgment executes (Scottish Psalter, 1650) AP 90b 102795

God save America! New world of glory (Ballantine) Z547; AH481; AN374; AO587; AU387; BF551; BK122 102796

God save our gracious King (Great Britain. National Anthem. 17th-18th c) E560; P417; AN387; BB506; BC115-a; BX545 102797

God save our gracious Queen (Great Britain. National anthem. 17th-18th c) F577; J361; W631; X318; AE392; AL508; AP639; AQ244; BV664; BY641 102798

God save our native land (Seelye) M499 102799

God saved His people from distress (U.P. Psalter, 1912) AJ180 102800

God sees the little sparrow fall (Straub) AL588; AM635; AP 721; AW408 102801

God send us men whose aim 'twill be (Gillman) Z377; AB352; AC255; AD351; AE398; AF434; AH460; AN313; AQ217; AR604; AS388; BF560; BH233; BK125; BZ 102802

God shall "wipe away all tears" (Clements) R In the land of fadeless day 102803

God so loved the world (Bible. John 3) AU476 102804

God spake, my child, God spake to thee (Hänel) K551 102805

God speaks to us in bird and song (Johnson) Z180 102806

God speed the gospel! Father in pity (Stryker) H477 102807

God supreme! to thee we pray (Moise) AH155; BH93 102808

God that doest wondrously (Moses ibn Ezra) BH176 102809

God, that madest earth and heaven (Heber & Whateley) A169; B26; D19; E268; F26; G43; J230; K468; L19; P73; R58; S41; T308; V39; W293; X46; Y306; Z143; AA44; AB 29; AC18; AD52; AF58; AG 30; AH167; AI51; AL547; AM 344; AN100; AO43; AP674; AS33; AT30; AV21; AW35; AZ 1506; BF201; BK48; BR540; BX152; BZ 102810

God the All-merciful (Chorley) AB366 X God, the Omnipotent 102811

God, the All-terrible (Chorley) B435 X God, the Omnipotent 102812

God the Almighty One (Chorley) AT42 X God the Omnipotent 102813

God the father, be our stay (German litany, 13-14th c) Q247; AA271 102814

God the Father, God the Son (Littledale) B141; D528; E 647, 655 102815

God the Father, God the Son (Pollock) A229-30-31; B142; E648, 651; F587 102816

God the Father, God the Son ([Children's litany] Thring) E654; F590 102817

God the Father, God the Word (Littledale) E653 102818

God the Father, seen of none (Littledale) E649 102819

God the Father, Son and Spirit (Polack) Q640 102820

God, the Hope of those who pray (Trask) AO657 102821

God, the Lord, a King remaineth (Keble) R90; S61; AM60; AP79 102822

God the Lord is King; before him earth with all (Rawson) AM 43; AP85 102823

God the Omnipotent, King, who ordainest (Chorley & Ellerton) A523; B435; D198; F491;

G505; I707; J354; K497; Q582; R487; S420; W641; Y264; Z565; AB366; AC284; AD368; AE404; AF446; AG281; AI356; AK405; AL517; AM617; AP650; AR608; AT42; AV72; AW351; BB78; BF567; BH265B; BZ 102824
God, though this life is but a wraith (Untermeyer) AW114 102825
God, we thank thee; not in vain (Dearmer) E353b 102826
God, who are love, the same both now and ever (Foster) AZ708 102827
God who created me, Nimble and light of limb (Beeching) W673; X504; Y140; AC170; BY11 102828
God, who hath made the daisies (Hood) W81; BY743 102829
God who made the earth, the air, the sky, the sea (Rhodes) A 248; R466; W20; X358; AC58; AL595; AM637; AP722; BV237; BY744 102830
God, who madest earth and heaven, darkness and light (Heber & Whately) AA44 X God that madest earth and heaven 102831
God who madest earth and heaven, Father, Son and Holy Ghost (Albert) J205; K446; M553; O544; Q549; AA23; AR44; AW 573a; AZ1275; BA771 102832
God, who touchest earth with beauty (Edgar) R102; Z315; AC 223; AD490; AE451; AG304; AH397; AR355; AT45; BY472; BZ 102833
God, whose city's sure foundation (Alington) F574 102834
God, whose eternal mind (Struther) X282 102835
God, whose farm is all creation (Arlott) BY726; BZ 102836
God whose name is Love, happy children we (Hoatson) A244; X359 102837
God will I bless all times; His praise (Scottish Psalter, 1650) AP32 102838
God will our strength and refuge prove (U.P. Psalter, 1912) AJ127 102839
God will take care of you (Martin) R Be not dismayed whate'er betide 102840
God with us! Oh glorious name! (Slinn) H149; V127 102841
God's boundless love and arching sky (Babcock) Y41; AO81 102842
God's dear Son without beginning (English trad carol) BG13 102843
God's eternal Word is spoken (Oldenburg) BE84 102844
God's free mercy streameth (How) BB5 X Summer suns are glowing 102845
God's glory is a wondrous thing (Faber) V477; AB237; AF 369; AN305; BE86; BX301 102846
God's law is perfect and converts the soul (Scottish Psalter, 1650) AL635; AP15; AW578 102847
God's mercies I will ever sing (Scottish Psalter, 1650) AP72 102848
God's perfect law restores (U.P. Book of Psalms, 1871) AP 14b 102849
God's trumpet wakes the slumbering world (Longfellow) G262; Y146; AB255; AC203; AD292; AN309; AQ213; AW194; BD91; BF476; BX366 102850
God's way is best; if human wisdom (Naylor) AX389 102851
God's way is the best way (Leech) AI290 102852
God's word is our great heritage (Grundtvig) J257; O137; P 91; Q283 102853
Going by, going by (Cooper) R There are lonely hearts 102854
Golden breaks the dawn (Chao) AF486 102855
Golden harps are sounding (Havergal) A359; B560; D 545; I175; J115; K549; M457; P222; S456; V750; W133;

AH307; AM213; AO199; AP736; AS152; AZ771; BA245; BR195; BY166 102856

Golden light serene and bright (Grundtvig) J210 102857

Gone are those great and good (Pierpont) AN364; BX417 102858

Gone from my heart the world and all its charms (---) AU210 102859

Gone the night! The world is filled with light (---) R Let the whole creation sing 102860

Gone! yes, but for a little while (Howard) BR450 102861

Good and pleasant 'tis to see (Müller) O397 102862

Good-bye, good-bye, We breathe a sigh (Oatman) R These scenes so bright 102863

Good-bye mourner, I'm going home (Negro spiritual) AH 598 102864

Good.bye! Our school is over (Dearmer) X386g 102865

Good cheer! good cherr! good cherr! Let all men know (Trench) Y194 X Good cheer! Let all men know That all men move 102866

Good cheer! Let all men know that all men move (Trench) X505; Y194 102867

Good cheer! Let all men know That all men move (Trench & Dearmer) X505 X Let all men know that all men love (Trench in Julian. Dictionary of hymnology) 102868

Good Christian men, rejoice and sing (Alington) F603; J109; S130; W58; X154; AF184; BK 133; BV181; BY156; BZ 102869

Good Christian men, rejoice; with heart (Latin carol, 14th c) A31; B549; G10; J39; R165; Z193; AB118; AD110; AE80; AF 125; AG70; AH258; AK116; AL61; AM159; AN177; AR129; AT74; AZ722; BD230; BF278; BK159; BV99; BY97; BZ 102870

Good day to you all (Dearmer) X386a 102871

Good Joseph had a garden (Milner-Barry) F438; BV184 102872

Good King Wenceslas (Neale) AH252; BG136 102873

Good morning to you (---) AU 308 102874

Good news from heaven the angels bring (Luther) K19; N27; AZ291; BI86 102875

Good people all, this Christmastime (English trad carol) BG14 102876

Good unto all men is the Lord (Scottish Psalter, 1650) AL 689; AP128 102877

Goodly were thy tents, O Israel (Wolcott) BX416 102878

Gospel bells, how they ring (Martin) R The gospel bells are ringing 102879

Gospel of Jesus, Gospel of light (Consterdine) R Hark, hark my soul! The voice of Jesus calling 102880

Gott, der du alles wohl bedacht (Unparth. G. B.) AY37d 102881

Gott der Vater wohn' uns bei (German litany, 13-14th c) BT247 102882

Gott des Himmels und der Erden (Albert) AW573b; BT549; BW 573 102883

Gott, du hast in deinem Sohn (Neumann) BT411 102884

Gott fähret auf gen Himmel (Sacer) BT214 102885

Got Führt ein recht Gericht (G. Blaurock) BU5 102886

Gott Heil' ger Geist, hilf uns mit Grund (Ringwaldt) BT293 102887

Gott ist die Liebe, Lässt mich erkösen (Unparth. G. B.) AY 42d 102888

Gott ist gegenwartig! (Terstee-gen) AE4; BT4; BW506 102889

Gott ist mein Licht! (Hengsten-

berg) BW560 102890
Gott mit euch, bis wir uns wiederseh'n (J.E. Rankin) AY 49d 102891
Gott segne Sachsenland (S.A. Mahlmann) BT577; BW348 102892
Gott sei Dank durch alle Welt (Held) BT91 102893
Gott sei gelobet und gebenedeiet (Luther) BT313 102894
Gott Vater, Sohn, Heiliger Geist (Ausbund) BU68 102895
Gott Zebaoth, der war, und ist (H. Betz) BU107 102896
Gottes Sohn ist kommen (Horn) BT74 102897
Grace and peace from God our blessed Saviour (Swertner) AZ1002; BA799 102898
Grace and truth shall mark the way (U.P. Psalter, 1912) R 372; T42; AJ65 102899
Grace, dear Lord, Grace, dear Lord (Minkler) AX325 102900
Grace for today, O Love divine (Robertson) BE91 102901
Grace, Grace, God's Grace (Johnston) R Marvelous grace of our loving Lord 102902
Grace, grace, Oh, that's a joyful sound (Gruenbeck) AZ1432 102903
Grace, love, and peace abide, now with you (Brown) AT539 102904
Grace! 'tis a charming sound (Doddridge) H238; I288; L126; Q374; U147; V243; AA328; AM 401; AV163; AX323; AY368; AZ1351; BA425; BY54; 102905
Gracious Father, guard thy children (---) BB663 102906
Gracious Father, hear our prayer (---) AP807 102907
Gracious God, again is ended (Neumann) Q560 102908
Gracious God, my heart review (U.P. Psalter, 1912) T98; AJ141 102909
Gracious God, we worship thee (Francis) BV19 102910
Gracious King enthroned above (Wayland) AI217; AS206 102911
Gracious Lord, our Shepherd and Salvation (Swertner) AZ 1010; BA798 102912
Gracious Lord, remember David (U.P. Psalter, 1912) T263; AJ367 102913
Gracious Saviour, gentle Shepherd, children all are dear to thee (Leeson) D555; Q627; U486; V647; W310; AA447; AI373; AL216; AM354; AP352; AW298; AZ622; BA827; BY286 102914
Gracious Saviour, gentle Shepherd, Little ones are dear to thee (Leeson) U486 X Gracioud Saviour, gentle Shepherd, children all... 102915
Gracious Saviour, gentle Shepherd, Our little ones (Leeson) AI373 X Gracious Saviour, gentle Shepherd, children all 102916
Gracious Saviour, thus before thee (Bateman) AZ272 102917
Gracious Saviour, who didst honor (Shirreff) AO563; AR547; AS417; AT503 102918
Gracious Spirit, Dove divine (Stocker) H222; K154; L175; M466; N162; O376; P230; V217; AA253; AE141; AM 245; AP286; BB215; BR204 102919
Gracious Spirit! dwell with me (Lynch) I195; R241; S214; W187; X506; Z270; AB92; AE144; AF245; AK192; AL 152; AR224; AS172; BE88; BF259; BV295; BY231 102920
Gracious Spirit, Holy Ghost (Wordsworth A379; B121; D76; E396; F233; J119; O498; W484; X507; AL367; AS346; AW174; AX541; AZ1135; BA 671; BV543; BY232 102921
Gracious Spirit - Love divine (Stocker) M466 X Gracious Spirit, Dove divine 102922

Grand Dieu! Que de merveilles (French trad carol) BG111 102923
Grant me strength when skies are azure (Weitzman) BH48 102924
Grant, most gracious Lamb of God (Scheffler) AZ40; BA453 102925
Grant that we ask, Almighty Lord (---) BRp.467 102926
Grant us, Lord, the grace of giving (---) AD507; AR674; AT537; BF695 102927
Grant us, O God, a single aim (Jones) AB283 102928
Grant us, O our heavenly Father (Thring) D574 102929
Grant us the will to fashion as we feel (Drinkwater) Y181; AC187; AK264; AR412 102930
Grant us thy light, that we may know (Tuttiett) AE375 X O grant us light 102931
Grant us Thy peace; for thou alone canst bend (Masterman) BY660 102932
Granted is the Saviour's prayer (Wesley) AO230 102933
Great and fair is she, our land (Watson) AH482; AN379; BD 177; BX414 102934
Great Arbiter of human fate (Moise) BH209 102935
Great art Thou, God! The hosts of heaven wonder (Pawels) M152 102936
Great Creator, Lord of all (Pollock) D546 102937
Great day! Great day! The righteous marching (Negro spiritual) AH605 102938
Great Giver of all good, Teach us to give like Thee (---) AE367; AR342; AS356 102939
Great God, a blessing from thy throne (Schuette) M510 102940
Great God! and wilt thou condescend (Taylor) W550 102941
Great God, as seasons disappear (Butcher) AZ313 102942
Great God, attend, while Zion sings (Watts) H415; I213; V18; BC248; BZ 102943
Great God! beneath whose piercing eye (Roscoe) H520; I708 102944
Great God, how infinite art Thou! (Watts) L97; U11; V91; AM22 102945
Great God in heaven, Who by my bed (---) BR542 102946
Great God, indulge my humble claim (Watts) H110; L439; V337; AY212 102947
Great God, let all our tuneful powers (Heginbothom) H65 102948
Great God of Abraham, hear our prayer (Cotterill) W366 102949
Great God of nations, now to thee (Woodhull) G509; I706; AH494; AK437; AO595; AR 609; AW349; AZ307; BA880; BK119 102950
Great God of wonders! all thy ways are worthy of thyself (Davies) AM71; AP161; BY 55 102951
Great God, the followers of thy Son (Ware) AN21; AW13; BX25 102952
Great God, the nations of the earth (Gibbon) I645; V600 102953
Great God! Thou dost all nations rule (Hymns of the English Conf. 1880) BR495 102954
Great God, To thee my evening song (Steele) D644; BC59 102955
Great God, to what a glorious height (Watts) L116 102956
Great God, to whom alone belong (---) H527 102957
Great God, we give Thee praise (Hymns of the English Conf. 1880) BR236 102958
Great God, we praise thy gracious care (Cennick) N541 X We thank thee, Lord, for this our food 102959
Great God, we sing that guiding hand (Doddridge) BY715 X Great God, we sing that mighty

hand 102960

Great God, we sing that mighty hand (Doddridge) G539; J533; K482; L551; M369; N49; O214; Q119; R527; S470; U475; V627; W607; Z586; AA167; AD449; AF454; AG292; AK425; AM612; AO573; AP143; AV310; AW383; AZ295; BA177; BF639; BX172; BY715; BZ 102961

Great God, what do I see and hear (Collyer) B64; D37; E4; K514; L580; N611; O604; Q604; V687; AA553; AM240; AZ748; BA734; BB195; BJ16; BV78 102962

Great God! whatever through thy church (---) BO209; BQ128 102963

Great God who hast delivered us (Extrait du Recueil. 1957) AF577 102964

Great God who knowest each man's need (Tennyson, E) AO44 102965

Great High-Priest, we view thee stooping (Hart) AZ944; BA 208 102966

Great is the Lord, and greatly He (U.P. Book of Psalms, 1871) AP42 102967

Great is the Lord our God (Watts) K243; L280; M82; Q 636; V534; AA458; AS189; AZ 1365 102968

Great is the Lord; 'tis good to praise (Snow) BC234 102969

Great is the love that brought me (Crosby) AE291 102970

Great is their joy who hide their own (Darbyshire) X241 102971

"Great is thy faithfulness," O God my Father (Chisholm) Z165; AE68; AM27; AR429; AT47; BV238; BY576 102972

Great Jehovah! we adore thee (---) Lp. 744; AZ1394; BA911 102973

Great joy and consolation I find O Christ, in Thee (Wallin) N392 102974

Great King of glory, come (Francis) I656; BB485 102975

Great King of heaven, our hearts we raise (Thomas) BC53 102976

Great King of Kings and Lord of Lords (Hacker) BQ336 102977

Great King of kings, why dost thou stay (Bonar) O605; P 427 102978

Great King of nations, hear our prayer (Gurney) Q583; V626; W643; AM621; AO584; AP643 102979

Great King of Peace, hear now Thy people's cry (Little) BL57 102980

Great King of saints, enthroned on high (---) AX638 102981

Great Lord of all thy Churches, hear (Kingsbury) V580 102982

Great Lord of Life who lives in me (Sampter) BH243 102983

Great Master, touch us with thy skillful hands! (Bonar) Z317; AC222; AR401; BK92 102984

Great mover of all hearts, whose hand (Coffin) F316 102985

Great Redeemer, we adore thee (Harris) AT154; AU362 102986

Great Refuge of the weary soul (Hymns of the English Conf. 1880) BR356 102987

Great Ruler of the land and sea (Bonar) AP711 102988

Great Saint Joseph, son of David (German hymn) BN170; BO126; BP90; BQ93 102989

Great Shepherd of the sheep, Who all thy flock (Scottish Hymnal, 1884) D571 102990

Great Shepherd of thy people, hear (Newton) F247; G313; V569; W246; AK230; AL203; AP316; AW279; AZ149; BA 332; BB25; BR16; BV6 102991

Great Shepherd of thy people, here (Newton) BB25 X Great Shepherd of thy people, hear 102992

Great Shepherd who leadest thy

people in love (U.P. Psalter, 1912) T149; AI263; AJ220 102993

Great truths are portions of the soul of man (Lowell) AB299 102994

Great Western Land, whose mighty breast (Hazard) AN375 102995

Green are the leaves, and sweet the flowers (Newman) BO110 102996

Green grow'th the holly (English trad carol) BG63 102997

Gross sind die Merck des Herren (Ausbund) BU19 102998

Gross Unbild thut mich zwingen (Ausbund) BU117 102999

Grosser Gott, wir loben dich (Franz) AW519b; BT250; BW 519 103000

Guardian of pure hearts, and Hearer (Wallin) N313 103001

Guardian of virgins and holy father, Joseph (Latin prayer, 19th c) BN169 103002

Guds Ord det er vort Arvegods (Luther) BT283 103003

Guide me, O thou great Jehovah (Williams) A434; B42; D414; E397; F296; G301; H114; I91; J520; K261; L204; M583; N452; O285; P307; Q54; R339; S104; T429; U29; V333; W564; X508; Y366; Z393; AA340; AD220; AE235; AF93; AG158; AH406; AI296; AK80; AL441; AM501; AO326; AP596; AR286; AS246; AT55; AU181; AV43; AW160; AX499; AY65; AZ1381; BA694; BB409; BC56; BE90; BI34; BR 453; BV555; BX325; BY541; BZ 103004

Guide me, O thou great Redeemer (Williams) X508 X Guide me, O thou great Jehovah 103005

Guide, O Lord, thy chariot now (Zwingli) AO605 103006

Guide of my spirit on its devious way (Cross) Y11; AB222 103007

Guide us, O thou great Jehovah (Williams) BC56 X Guide me, O thou great Jehovah 103008

Guillaume prends ton tambourin (LaMonnoye) BG82 103009

Gute Nacht, ihr meine Lieben (Unparth. G. B.) AY18d 103010

Guter Hirt, du hast gestillt (Meinhold) BT595 103011

Gwine to lay down my burden (Negro spiritual) Y322 103012

H

Hab ich das Haupt zum Freunde (P. Gerhardt) BW236 103013

Had Christ, that once was slain (Cowley Carol book) R This joyful Easter-tide 103014

Had God not come, may Israel say (Luther) O527; AA282 103015

Had I the tongues of Greeks and Jews (Watts) V381 103016

Had not the Lord been Israel's help (U.P. Psalter, 1912) AJ 352 103017

Had we naught, had we naught; Naught beyond this life to hope (Zinzendorf, N. L.) BA 749 X Had we naught, naught beyond this life 103018

Had we naught, naught beyond this life to hope (Zinzendorf, N. L.) AZ720; BA749 103019

Haec dies quam fecit Dominus (Bible. Psalm 117) BN43 103020

Hail! all hail, great Queen of heaven (Sister of Notre Dame) BQ78 103021

Hail, all hail, sweet youth angelic (A Carmelite Nun) BP97 103022

Hail, all hail, victorious Lord and Saviour (Hayn) AZ1007 103023

Hail, Alpha and Omega, hail (Cennick) AZ203; BA440 103024

Hail, angelic Bread of heaven (St Thomas Aquinas) BP54 103025

Hail Blessed Saint, hail Ursula

(---) R Afar upon a foreign shore 103026

Hail, blessed Trinity! Low here we bow (Berry) AS71 103027

Hail bright Archangel, Prince of heaven (Faber) BO196 103028

Hail! Christ, our Redeemer, God of glory and might (---) BP104 103029

Hail, Church of Christ, bought with His blood (Cennick) AZ 102 103030

Hail! festal day! to endless ages known (Fortunatus) B168 X Hail thee, festival day 103031

Hail, foamy ocean star! (Latin) R Hail, heavenly Queen! Hail, foamy ocean star! 103032

Hail full of grace and purity! (Conway) BQ86 103033

Hail, gladdening Light, of his pure glory poured (Greek, 3d c) F18; G637; W281; AB20; AD49; AL552; AP664; BF196; BR115; BV54; BY695; 103034

Hail Gladdening Light, of his pure glory poured (Greek, 3d c) X O Gladsome Light, O Grace 103035

Hail! gladdening Light, of that pure glory poured (Greek, 3d c) BR115 X Hail, gladdening Light, of His pure glory poured 103036

Hail, glorious angels, heirs of light (Austin) BJ60 X Hail glorious spirits, heirs of light 103037

Hail, glorious apostle, Saint Basil the Great (Dollard) BN174; BO1a 103038

Hail, glorious Saint Patrick! dear saint of our Isle! (Sr. Agnes) BO137; BP92; BQ96 103039

Hail, glorious spirits, heirs of light (Austin) F626; X205; BJ60 103040

Hail, Guest! We ask not what thou art (Guiterman) BK8 103041

Hail, happy day! Thou day of holy rest (Browne) BB464; BR97 103042

Hail, harbinger of morn, (St Bede, the Venerable) E225 103043

Hail, harbinger of morn (St Bede, the Venerable) X The great forerunner of the morn 103044

Hail, heavenly Queen! Hail foamy ocean star. (Latin) BO57 103045

Hail Him the King of glory (deFluiter) R Tell it to every kindred and nation 103046

Hail!holy guide of youthful days (---) BO139 103047

Hail, Holy, Holy, Holy Lord. Let powers immortal sing (Perronet) K132; M455 103048

Hail! Holy, Holy, Holy Lord, Whom One in Three we know (Wesley) K162; AZ216 103049

Hail, holy Joseph, hail! Chaste spouse of Mary (Faber) BN 171; BO131; BQ95 103050

Hail, holy Light! The world rejoices (Parker) AB8 103051

Hail, holy Queen enthroned above (Hermannus Contractus) BM 50; BN153; BO75; BP84; BQ 83 103052

Hail, Holy Spirit, bright immortal Dove (Browne) AZ442 103053

Hail, Jesus, hail, do thou, good Shepherd (St Thomas Aquinas) R Thee prostrate I adore 103054

Hail, Jesus, hail, Who for my sake (Italian, 18th c) BN74; BO27; BQ71 103055

Hail, Jesus! Israel's Hope and Light (Harbaugh) AO109 103056

Hail! Kingly Jesus, to thy feet (Thompson) AZ114; BA187 103057

Hail Mary, full of grace (Latin, 13th c) BQ149 X Hail Mary, hail Mary full of grace 103058

Hail Mary, full of grace, Hail flower of Adam's race (Camm) BN145; BO68 103059
Hail Mary, hail Mary, full of grace (Latin, 13th c) BP72; BQ149 103060
Hail! my ever blessed Jesus (Wingrove) L141; V309 103061
Hail, noble column, speak and tell (Herman) BP29 103062
Hail, O Holy Queen! Hail, O Mother all Merciful (Hermannus Contractus) BP76 103063
Hail, O Mary, full of grace (White) F499 103064
Hail, O Star that pointest (Latin, 9th c) E213 103065
Hail, Ocean's beauteous Star (Latin, 9th c) BO122 103066
Hail our monarch, son of David (Latin) Eapp3 103067
Hail, peaceful day! divinely blest (Smith) BB457 103068
Hail! princess of the host of heaven (Santeuil) F549 103069
Hail, Queen of heaven, hail our Mother compassionate (Hermannus Contractus) BL61 103070
Hail, Queen of heaven, The ocean star (Hermannus Contractus) BN133; BO102; BP81; BQ84 103071
Hail, Queen of the heavens! Hail, Mistress of earth (Hermannus Contractus) BO90 103072
Hail, Rock of ages, pierced for me (Bridges) BQ70 X This is an everlasting home 103073
Hail! sacred day of earthly rest (Thring) D25; H76; W269; AL 192; AP347; BR92; BX105 103074
Hail St Joseph; Spouse of Mary (---) R Dear St Joseph, pure and gentle 103075
Hail! sweetest dearest tie (Sutton) AY409 103076
Hail the blest morn when the great mediator (Heber) AX104 X Brightest and best 103077
Hail the day so rich in cheer (Latin, before 1422) Q78 103078
Hail the day that sees Him rise. Alleluia (Wesley) A104; D 128; E143; F147; I162; J111; L272; N148; Q213; S171; X 172; AA243; AD169; AF205; AH306; AK175; AL114; AP 222; AS154; AW117; AZ47; BA248; BB131; BR192; BV 203; BY167 103079
Hail the day when Jesus rose (Gordon) AB147 103080
Hail the glorious golden city (Adler) Y61; Z488; AB286; AC264; AD426; AF424; AN392; AQ192; BD137; BF510; BH227; BX427 103081
Hail the hero workers (Spencer) AB281; AC190; AN330; BF 436 103082
Hail the Sign, the Sign of Jesus (Baring-Gould) E592 103083
Hail thee, festival day! [Ascension sequence] (Fortunatus) A102; B184; E628; X389 103084
Hail thee, festival day! [Dedication sequence] (Fortunatus) E634; X389 103085
Hail thee, festival day! [Easter sequence] (Fortunatus) A86; B168; E624; X389 103086
Hail thee, festival day! [Whitsunday sequence] (Fortunatus) A107; B195; E630; X389 103087
Hail thee, Saviour and Atoner (Arnold of Louvain) M202 103088
Hail thee! Spirit, Lord eternal (Wallis) A110 103089
Hail, thou bright and sacred morn (Elliott) W266; BT8 103090
Hail, thou everblessed morn (Caswall) R See, amid the winter's snow 103091
Hail, thou King of saints ascending (St Bernard of Clairvaux) AZ434 103092
Hail, thou living Bread from heaven (Latin, 1815) BO54 103093

Hail, thou living Victim blest (Latin) BO46 103094

Hail, thou long-expected Jesus (Wesley) AT70 X Come, thou long-expected Jesus 103095

Hail, thou martyr host of heaven (---) AZ1080 103096

Hail, thou once despised Jesus! (Bakewell) A357; B191; D365; G166; H190; I171; J435; K60; L142; M450; N149; O303; P 221; Q367; R210; U113; V156; AA242; AE134; AH318; AI 139; AK179; AL117; AM128; AO200; AP228; AR192; AT149; AW122; AZ955, 970; BA192; BV259; BY173; BZ 103097

Hail, thou Source of every blessing (Woodd) E616; K41; M371; N64; Q129; AA182; BV124 103098

Hail thou Star of Ocean (Latin, 9th c) BM55; BO76; BQ73 103099

Hail, thou who man's Redeemer art (Latin, 7th c) BP41 103100

Hail, thou wondrous Infant Stranger (Lamb) AZ1401; BA 61 103101

Hail to the brightness of Zion's glad morning (Hastings) G488; H478; J319; M99; N381; O112; P399; R505; S391; T369; U408; V598; Z523; AC303; AD380; AG259; AH466; AK378; AM 274; AO519; AR561; AT453; AU248; AV266; AW332; AZ1151; BA343; BB302; BC182; BF524; BI16 103102

Hail to the Lord who comes (Ellerton) A115; B274; D154; E209; F544; BL18; BV441 103103

Hail to the Lord's Anointed (Montgomery) A545; B99; D 323; E45; F219; G85; H137; I650; J328; K42; L147; M325; N16; O168; Q59; R146; S111; U400; V584; W154; X87; Y 244; Z257; AA132; AB105; AC301; AD177; AE77; AF105; AH315; AK366; AL139; AM224; AN151; AO513; AP60; AQ282; AV95; AW65; AZ801; BA184; BE75; BF337; BR128; BV129; BX201; BY80; BZ 103104

Hail to the Prince of Life and Peace (Doddridge) V191 103105

Hail to the Prophet ascended to heaven (Phelps) R Praise to the man who communed with Jehovah 103106

Hail to the Sabbath day! (Bulfinch) H81; I66; AS40; AY 428 103107

Hail to thee, true Body, sprung (Innocent VI, Pope) BQ51 103108

Hail to this holy day (Bulfinch) AS40 X Hail to the Sabbath day 103109

Hail, true Body, born of Mary (Innocent VI, Pope) E311; F407 103110

Hail, true Body, truly born of the Virgin Mary mild (Innocent VI, Pope) BP50 103111

Hail, true Victim, life and light (Peckham) BN94 103112

Hail Virgin, dearest Mary, Our lovely Queen of May (---) BQ81 103113

Hail we now this happy morn (Chubb) AN147 103114

NOTE: Hallelujah, as variously spelled beginning with letter H, is herein spelled and filed as Alleluia 103115

Hands that have been handling (Liturgy of Malabar) F494 103116

Happiness, delightful name (Toplady) AZ1058; BA521 103117

Happy are they, they that love God (Coffin) E398; F261; W 440; X509; AD255; AL290; AP442; BJ34; BV532; BY496 103118

Happy day, happy day, When

Jesus washed ... (Doddridge) R O happy day, that stays [fixed] my choice 103119
Happy he that never wanders (Hamburg Temple hymnal) BH100 103120
Happy he who walketh ever (Voorsanger) AH153; BH25 103121
Happy race of witnesses (Zinzendorf, N. L.) AZ1036 103122
Happy Saint; in bliss adoring Jesus, Saviour of mankind (---) R Holy patron; thee saluting 103123
Happy soul, secure from harm (Wesley) BR319 X Shepherd, with thy tenderest love 103124
Happy soul, thy days are ended (Wesley) AZ243; BA726 103125
Happy the heart where graces reign (Watts) L454 103126
Happy the home when God is there (Ware) G428; AE388; AI366; AL394; AM627; AP708; AR545; AS415; AT374; AW361; AX556; BB413; BZ 103127
Happy the man, and happy he alone (Horace: Dryden para) AQ185 103128
Happy the man that finds the grace (Wesley) I372 103129
Happy the man who feareth God (Luther) AA446 103130
Happy the man who knows His Master of obey (Upham) BE92 103131
Happy the man whose heart can rest (McKenzie) BE93 103132
Happy the souls to Jesus joined (Wesley) BZ 103133
Happy we, who, thus united (Vaughan) BO55; BQ136 103134
Happy who in early youth (Hamburg Temple hymnal) BH253 103135
Hard is not the constant woe (Fox) AQ129 103136
Hark, a burst of heavenly music (Meigs) AO134 103137
Hark! a hearld voice is calling (Latin, 6th c) X61 X Hark! a thrilling voice 103138
Hark! a hundred notes are swelling (Briggs) X360 103139
Hark! a mystic voice is sounding (Latin, 6th c) BQ1 X Hark! a thrilling voice 103140
Hark! a thrilling voice is sounding (Latin, 6th c) A9; B63; D41; E5; F47; J1; K3; N12; O164; Q60; X61; AA133; BO 148; BQ1; BV76 103141
Hark! a voice divides the sky (Wesley) AA536; AZ1037 103142
Hark! a voice in the wilderness crying (Milligan) AD373 X There's a voice ... 103143
Hark, a voice saith all are mortal (Albinus) M305; AA 530 103144
Hark! are they not angels that gladly are bringing (Willman) AX91 103145
Hark! from the tomb a doleful sound (Watts) AY183 103146
Hark, hark my soul! Angelic songs are swelling (Faber) A472; B290; D398; E399; F 354; G532; H510; I621; J498; L587; O607; P347; R426; S 431; T430; U426; V694; W580; Y343; Z582; AB404; AC329; AD462; AG282; AH369; AK 420; AL442; AN549; AO546; AP601; AR421; AS476; AT469; AU62; AV286; AW260; AZ 1024; BA745; BB375; BD153; BF385; BI74; BO198; BQ111; BR447; BX464 103147
Hark, hark, my soul! The Saviour's voice is calling (Hopps) BR382 X Hark, hark my soul! Thy Father's voice 103148
Hark, hark, my soul! The voice of Jesus calling (Consterdine) BV316 103149
Hark, hark, my soul! Thy Father's voice is calling (Hopps) AN432; BR382; BX 465; 103150
Hark! hark! The organ loudly

peals (---) AO659 103151

Hark, hear them calling from every dark land (Warren) R Long have they waited (Schell) 103152

Hark, how all the welkin rings (Wesley) X88 X Hark, the herald angels 103153

Hark how the adoring hosts above (Watts) AP313 103154

Hark! I hear my Saviour say (Mitchell) AY343 103155

Hark, listen to the trumpeters (---) BC253 103156

Hark, my soul, how everything (Austin) E296; X19; BX94; BY719 103167

Hark, my soul! it is the Lord (Cowper) A459; B389; D599; E400; F344; I307; R263; S224; T384; U28; V373; W417; X510; AG136; AL292; AO252; AP458; AW59; AZ59; BA481; BB298; BR413; BV533; BY414 103158

Hark, ten thousand harps and voice, Sound the notes of praise (Kelly) G167; I177; K133; L154; N151; O496; P219; Q221; U112; V164; Z268; AA 238; AE139; AI91; AM225; AO 204; AR210; AS158; AT145; AU 227; AV130; AW123; AY425; AZ 600; BA93 103159

Hark, ten thousand thousand voices (Raffles) BC249 103160

Hark! tenthousand voices sounding Far and wide (Kelly) D125 103161

Hark! that shout of rapture high (Kelly) BB192 103162

Hark, the angel voices singing (Croatian trad) AK110 103163

Hark! the Church proclaims her honor (Preiswerk) M84; Q461; AA467 103164

Hark, the distant isles proclaim (Bathurst) AZ79 103165

Hark! the glad sound! The Saviour comes (Doddridge) A7; B54; D47; E6; F53; H142; I108; J6; K9; L209; M327; N19; O175; Q66; V119; W40; X62; AA139; AK97; AL54; AM162; AO108; AP164; AZ195; BA147; BJ21; BR138; BV82; BY8 103166

Hark, the heaven's sweet melody (Plumptre) AZ729 103167

Hark! the herald angels sing (Wesley) A27; B73; D51; E23, 24; F60; G86; H138; I111; J25; K25; L224; M354; N34; O198; P136; Q94; R163; S117; T333; U59; V121; W46; X74, 88; Y361; Z189; AA154; AB 111; AC77; AD105; AE81; AF 120; AG66; AH253; AI59; AK 102; AL59; AM168; AN170; AO126; AP171; AR128; AS101; AT81; AU142: AV83; AW85; AY245; AZ1074; BA163; BB 111; BC60; BD211; BF286; BI94; BJ18; BK144; BL10; BR147; BT94; BV112; BY98; BZ 103168

Hark! the herald host is singing (Latin, 11th c) BQ13 103169

Hark, the hosts of heaven are singing (Latin, 11th c) AZ 261 103170

Hark! the King of heaven is calling (Kuhlman) M380 103171

Hark! the loud celestial hymn (Walworth) D140 X Holy God we praise thy name (Franz) 103172

Hark! the skies with music sound (---) BR145 103173

Hark! the song of jubilee (Montgomery) B103; H481; I646; L348; M168; V599; W389; AL250; AM300; AO218; AP 377; AZ1051; BA344; BI31; BR194; BV317 103174

Hark! the sound of holy voices (Wordsworth) A125; B297; D 179; E198; F526; I613; J143; K248; L588; N627; Q471; V 707; X206; AA290; AI343; AL 177; AM607; AP307; AZ265; BA807; BV463 103175

Hark! the vesper hymn is stealing (Moore) Y91; AC16; AH 166 103176

Hark! the voice eternal (Julian)

A316; B518; D35 103177

Hark, the voice of children (Sonnenschein & Wolsee) BH146 103178

Hark! the voice of Jesus calling, "Follow me." (Sleight) AX255 103179

Hark, the voice of Jesus calling -- "Who will go?" (March) G288; H392; I402; J59; N80; O121; P384; Q496; U283; V501; AA476; AB348; AH421; AI189; AK383; AL387; AM691; AP586; AS379; AT440; AU407; AV268; AX205; AY332, 335; AZ954; BA345; BB447 103180

Hark, the voice of Jesus crying (March) O121 X Hark, the voice of Jesus calling 103181

Hark! the voice of love and mercy (Evans) H171; L250; V140; AI73; AM187; AO167; AZ1399; BA209; BV172 103182

Hark, the waking up of nations (Coxe) AV273 X We are living, we are dwelling 103183

Hark! through the courts of heaven (Alford) L384 103184

Hark, 'tis the Saviour's voice I hear (Dobell. Selections, 1806) M201 103185

Hark! 'Tis the Shepherd's voice I hear (Thomas) AM684; AT 429; AU266; AX213; BB625 103186

Hark, 'Tis the watchman's cry (The Revivalist, 1859) AZ1248; BA545; BV85 103187

Hark to the sound, it rings from sea to sea (Kimball) Y285; BD168 103188

Hark, what a sound, and too divine for hearing (Myers) R 150; S110; X511; AD103; AL 133; AR211 103189

Hark! what mean those holy voices (Cawood) B81; D61; H139; I109; K33; L218; M349; N28; O190; Q83; U61; V115; AA160; AH 248; AI69; AO123; AS105; AV 96; AX93; AY243; AZ274; BA 165; BI79; BR143 103190

Hark, what music fills the sky (---) AZ1132 103191

Hark! while infant voices sing (Henley) R Children of Jerusalem 103192

Har-nee-nu lay-lo-heem (Jewish traditional) BH308 103193

Hast not thy heart within thee burned (Bulfinch) AN109 103194

Hast thou heard it, O my brother (Williams) AN476; BD76; BX540 103195

Hast thou not known, hast thou not heard (Watts) X512; AF 78; AL414; AM28; AP534; BV250 103196

Hast to the plow thou put thy hand (Grundtvig) M259 103197

Haste not! haste not! do not rest! (Goethe) BH43 103198

Haste, O haste, delightful morning (Jones) BF521 103199

Haste thee away, why wilt thou stay? (Crosby) R Come with thy sins 103200

Haste, traveler, haste! The night comes on (Collyer) I251 103201

Hasten, Lord, the glorious time (Auber) H475; I637; K227; L336; M379; V592; AZ1055; BA346 103202

Hasten, O sinner, to be wise (Scott) L371 X Hasten, sinner, to be wise 103203

Hasten, sinner to be wise (Scott) H256; I248; L370; M 26; V269; AA55 103204

Hasten the time appointed (Borthwick) A257; B477; D255; M 101; AN326; AQ209; AZ818; BD186; BE196; BX430 103205

Hath not thy heart within thee burned (Bulfinch) BE94; BX 84 103206

Have faith in God, my heart (Rees) AF361; VV499; BV 577; BZ 103207

"Have faith in God," the Saviour said (Hewitt) AY359 103208

Have faith in God When your

UNIVERSITY OF VICTORIA
LIBRARY
Victoria, B. C.

pathway is lonely (McKinney) AT253; AU52 103209
Have I done any good in the world today? (Thompson) BC 58 103210
Have I need of aught, O Saviour (Davis) BB580 103211
Have mercy, Lord, on me (Tate & Brady) D351; E74; AP46; BJ65 103212
Have mercy on me, God, in your kindness (Ladies of the Grail) BSp. 22 103213
Have mercy on us, God most high (Faber) E161; BO7 103214
Have thine own way, Lord (Pollard) R302; Z324; AE270; AH 426; AI280; AM574; AR351; AS241; AT355; AU254; AV384; AW217; AX395; BB272; BZ 103215
Have thy affections been nailed to the cross? (Hoffman) AX274 103216
Have ye heard the invitation (Hoppe) N192 103217
Have ye not heard, have ye not known (Bible. Isaiah) R O thou who spreadest the heaven like a tent 103218
Have you any room for Jesus ("L. W. M.")AX259 103219
Have you been to Jesus (Hoffman) AT192; AU111; AX276 103220
Have you failed in your plan (McKinney) AT231; AU397 103221
Have you found rest and peace within (DeArmond) AX346 103222
Have you prayed all night, Till the break of day (Poole) AU121 103223
Have you read the story of the cross (Dennis) AU283 103224
Have you sought for the sheep that have wandered (Crosby) AX198; AY526 103225
Ha-yom t'-am' tsay-nu (Jewish traditional) BH333 103226
He brought me out of the miry clay (Gilmour) R My heart was distressed (Zelley) 103227
He came among us at Christmastide (German carol) R Joseph dearest, Joseph mine R Long ago and far away 103228
He comes! He comes with trumpet sound (Pratt) AX124 103230
He cometh not a King to reign (Whittier) BD70 X O Lord and Master of us all X Immortal love forever 103231
He did not die in vain (Hoppe) M192 103232
He died of a broken heart for you (Dennis) Have you read the story 103233
He died! the Great Redeemer died (Watts) BC263 X He dies! the Friend of sinners dies! 103234
He dies! the Friend of sinners dies! (Watts) I165; AO174; BC263 103235
He expecteth, He expecteth (Janvrin) BV318 103236
He has come! the Christ of God (Bonar) AZ1057 103237
He hides within the lily (Gannett) AN29; BD47; BX65 103238
He hideth my soul (Crosby) R A wonderful Saviour is Jesus my Lord 103239
He is able to deliver thee (Ogden) R 'Tis the grandest theme 103240
He is arisen! Glorious word! (Boye) M440; O329; P194; Q189 103241
He is coming again (Camp) R Lift up your heads, Pilgrims aweary 103242
He is coming, He is coming, Not as once He came before (Alexander) H204; V180; AZ 963 103243
He is coming! He is coming! We hear triumphal shouting (MacFarland) AC464 103244
He is coming, the "Man of Sorrows" (Crosby) AT121 103245

He is gone; a cloud of light (Stanley) I170; W129; AB150; BA250 103246

He is gone - beyond the skies (Stanley) W129 X He is gone; a cloud of light 103247

He is here, whom seers in old time (Prudentius) AZ898 X Of the Father's love begotten 103248

He is risen, he is risen (Alexander) A90; B179; D117; E132; F143; BC61; BR182 103249

He is waiting to receive (Latta) R Wanderer in sinful ways 103250

He is watching, He is waiting (Keegan) R Are you tired 103251

He just put Himself in my place (---) R Shall I tell you 103252

He keepeth me ever (Latta) AY 316 103253

He knoweth the way that I take (Hoffman) AX487; AY118 103254

He knoweth thy grief (Reed) AY 317 103255

He knows, He knows just what is best (Hott) R 'Tis hard to bear 103256

He knows, He knows the storms that would my way oppose (Henry) R I know my heavenly Father knows 103257

He knows the bitter, weary way (---) AU452 103258

He leadeth me! O blessed thought (Gilmore) A426; B245; D616; G242; H130; I489; J478; L544; M279; N497; P328; R338; S106; U46; V346; Z405; AD222; AE 292; AF370; AG53; AH405; AI301; AK466; AL483; AM500; AN565; AO632; AP519; AR442; AS251; AT58; AU422; AV59; AW478; AX495; BA686; BB393; BD120; BE95; BF415; BZ 103259

He leads us on through childhood's wondering years (Wiley) BY542 X He leads us on by paths we did not know 103260

He leads us on by paths we did not know (Wiley) U30; AI 295; AN240; BX264; BY542 103261

He lives again! Our risen Lord, today (Fleming) R Awake, awake O earth 103262

He lives, He lives, Christ Jesus lives today (Ackley) R I serve a risen Saviour 103263

He lives! O fainting heart, anew (Wallin) N136 103264

He lives on high (McKinney) R Christ the Saviour came 103265

He lives! the great Redeemer lives (Steele) V177; AO196; AV116; AY515 103266

He liveth long who liveth well (Bonar) W522; AL351; AN291; BF444; BX347 103267

He loves me, He loves me (---) R Alas! and did my Saviour bleed (Watts) 103268

He loves me too (Straub) R God sees the little sparrow fall 103269

He loveth me, He loveth me (Hay) AS122 103270

He must reign, Who won the right (Edwards) BA95 103271

He prayeth best who loveth best (Coleridge) BB319 X Prayer is the soul's sincere desire (Montgomery) 103272

He presses on before the race (Markham) AQ40 103273

He reigns! the Lord, the Saviour reigns (Watts) BB179 103274

He sat to watch o'er customs paid (Bright) E240; F563; X 237; BV450 103275

He seeks His wandering sheep (Newton) R The Shepherd's heart 103276

He sent His word, His holy word BE101 103277

He sleeps in Jesus -- peaceful rest (Smith) BB494 103278

He smiles within his cradle (German trad carol) BG84 103279

He stood of old, the holy Christ

(Whittier) BE96 103280

He that believes and is baptized (Kingo) J259; N230; O140; P94; Q301; AR659 103281

He that confides in his Creator (Neumark) AZ695 103282

He that dies shall not die lonely (Morris) AQ80 103283

He that goeth forth with weeping (Hastings) H466; L548; V500; AY256; AZ966; BB627; BE97 103284

He that hath God his guardian made (Tate & Brady) BE99, 100 103285

He that hath made his refuge God (Watts) V336 103286

He that is down needs fear no fall (Bunyan) F301; W557; X513 103287

He wants not friends that hath thy love (Baxter) R401; F274; W225; X514; BV430; BY360 103288

He was nailed to the cross for me (---) R What a wonderful, wonderful Saviour 103289

He was wounded for our transgressions (Oliver) R Who hath believed 103290

He waters the hills with rain from the skies (U.P. Psalter, 1912) AJ286 103291

He who dwells in the shelter of the Most High (Ladies of the Grail) BSp. 25 103292

He who has helped me hitherto (Grundtvig) M291 103293

He who himself and Lord would know (Martineau) Y56; AN106; BX87 103294

He who is upright, kind, and free from error (Horace) Y297 103295

He who made the starry skies (Chester ms. cal425) BG67 103296

He, who once in righteous vengeance (Breviary. Bologna, 1827) AZ599; BQ18 103297

He who once to die a victim (Breviary. Cluny. 1686) BM4 X Wondrous gift! The word 103298

He who suns and worlds upholdeth (Gill) BF240; BX 326 103299

He who to Jesus manfully bore witness (Latin, 8th c) F519 103300

He who would be in God confiding (Neumark) AW571a; BR 260 103301

He who would valiant be (Bunyan) A563; B117; E402; F293; G 265; J563; R345; S276; W576; X515; Y169; Z364; AB175; AC204; AD226; AF371; AG 193; AK296; AN213; AQ94; AR322; BF409; BK79; BV587; BY561; BZ 103302

He whom joyous shepherds praised (Latin, 1410) A35 103303

He, whose confession God of old accepted (Latin, 8th c) E188 103304

He will come, let us watch and be ready (Belden) R We know not the hour of the Master's appearing 103305

He will gather the wheat in His garner (MacKeever) R When Jesus shall gather the nations 103306

He will hide me, He will hide me (Servoss) R When the storms of life 103307

He will hold me fast (Habershon) R When I fear my faith will fail 103308

Head of the Church and Lord of all (Tritton) BY258 103309

Head of the Church Triumphant (Wesley) AB85; AP256; AZ 1081 103310

Head of thy Church Triumphant (Wesley) AP256 X Head of the Church Triumphant 103311

Heal me, O my Saviour, heal (Thring) B137; D356; AZ 1131; BR292 103312

Heal us, Immanuel! Hear our prayer (Cowper) BY335 103313

Healer Divine, who walkest still (Neumann) AK248 103314
Heap high the farmer's wintry hoard (Whittier) BK139 103315
Hear, hear, O ye nations, and hearing obey (Hosmer) AN398; AQ194; AT467; BD182; BF566; BX429 103316
Hear, Lord, the voice of my complaint (U.P. Psalter, 1912) T115; AJ165 103317
Hear my prayer, O hear my prayer (Hess) BH168 103318
Hear my prayer, O heavenly Father (Parr) L33 X Hear our prayer 103319
Hear my words, O gracious Lord (U.P. Psalter, 1912) R48 103320
Hear, O hear us heavenly Father (Garrett) AS53 103321
Hear, O Lord, our humble supplication (---) AK504 103322
Hear our entreaties, Lord, and show Thy mercy (---) BN29 103323
Hear our prayer, O gracious Father (Heywood) BE102 103324
Hear our prayer, O heavenly Father (Parr) D647; L33; AZ 271; BA899 103325
Hear the royal proclamation (---) AZ435 103326
Hear then, in love, O Lord, the cry (Bonar) R When the wear seeking rest 103327
Hear this, all ye people, hear (U.P. Psalter, 1912) T92; AJ135 103328
Hear thou our hymn, O Lord (Asper) BC96 103329
Hear thou our prayer, Lord (Huffman) AR658 103330
Hear thy children, gentle Jesus (Stanfield) BQ124 103331
Hear thy children, gentlest Mother (Stanfield) BQ87 103332
Hear us, Eternal King, Hear thou the praise (Davieson) BH136 103333
Hear us, O Lord, from heaven (Gill) AL338 103334
Hear us, our Father! We know thou wilt hear us (---) Z336 103335
Hear us, Thou that broodest (Thring) B524; D133 103336
Hear what God the Lord hath spoken (Cowper) I211; AZ 949; BX447 103337
Hear what the voice from heaven proclaims (Watts) E354; I588 103338
Hear ye the Master's call (Kirk) AT437; AU343 103339
Hearken, all! what holy singing (---) G108 103340
Hearken, O Lord, have mercy upon us (Latin) R To Thee, Redeemer, King of highest heaven 103341
Heart and mind, possessions, Lord (Tilak) AF394 103342
Heart of Christ my King! I greet thee (Latin, 15th c) AZ430 103343
Heart of Jesus! golden chalice (Casartelli) BQ62 103344
Heart of Jesus I adore thee (---) BQ331 103345
Heart of Mary, Heart all pure (---) BM53 103346
Heart of our Lord, O loving Heart (Latin) BN69 103347
Heart of the Holy Child, Hide me in thee ("M.B.", Sr.) BO160 103348
Hearts at Christmas time were jolly (Gerhardt) X89 103349
Heaven and earth and sea and air (Neander) K290; N330; O63; P23; R6; S27; AD99; AF75; AK45; AN34; AQ33; AW510; BX60 103350
Heaven at last, heaven at last, O, the joyful story (Bonar) R Angel voices sweetly singing 103351
Heaven holds all to me (Teddlie) R Earth holds no treasures 103352
Heaven is a holy place (Naylor) AX283 103353

Heaven is here, where hymns of gladness (Adams) G461; Y221; AC240; AN553; AO495; BF504 103354
Heavenly Father, bless me now (Clark) G304; H58; BZ 103355
Heavenly Father, God of love (Wesley) BR18 103356
Heavenly Father, I would pray (Kurzenknabe) AO325 103357
Heavenly Father, may thy blessing (Piggott) X516 103358
Heavenly Father, may thy love (Guest) BV340 103359
Heavenly Father, send thy blessing (Wordsworth) D556; E593; H446; K559; O578; U324; V646; AI372; BA829 103360
Heavenly Father, thou hast brought us (Hawkins) W603 103361
Heavenly Father, to whose eye (Conder) AZ64; BA597; BR 255 103362
Heavenly Father, we beseech Thee (Crosby) N360; AI345 103363
Heavenly Light, benignly beaming (Wallin) N325 103364
Heavenly Shepherd, Thee we pray (Woodhouse) D290; N287 103365
Heavenly Shepherd, true and holy (Thrupp. Hymns) BX529 X Saviour, like a Shepherd 103366
Heavenly Sower, Thou hast scattered (Hoppe) N79 103367
Heavenly Spirit, all others transcending (Brun) M469; O377; P229 103368
Heavenly sunlight, heavenly sunlight (Zelley) R Walking in sunlight 103369
Heavenward still our pathway tends (Schmolck) K516; O507; AK421; AZ578; BR444 103370
Heavenward stretch, my soul, thy pinions (Schmolck) BR444 X Heavenward still our pathway 103371
Heir of all the ages, I, -- (Door) AN347; AQ245 103372
Heir of all the waiting ages (Ham) AN178; AQ293 103373
Heir of the Kingdom, O why dost thou slumber? (---) BB 185 103374
Heirs of unending life (Onderdonk) D502 103375
Helft mir Gott's Güte preisen (Eber) BT112 103376
He'll never forget to keep me (Graves) R My Father has many dear children 103377
Help, Helper, help in fear and need (Moller) AA523 103378
Help, Lord Jesus, let thy blessing (Rist) O210 103379
Help, Lord, the souls which thou hast made (Newman) BN186; BO142; BQ113 103380
Help me, dear Lord, to love thee more (Buchanan) BV596 103381
Help me, dear Saviour, thee to own (Coffman) R Alas! and did my Saviour bleed (Watts) R O weary wanderer 103382
Help me, Lord, by thy great power (Hovden) M238 103383
Help me to be holy (Gordon) AE185 103384
Help us, O Lord, behold, we enter (Rist) N58; Q120; AA 171; BX182 103385
Help us, O Lord, thy yoke to wear (Cotterill) I691; AE369 103386
Help us, O Lord, to bear the cross (Sinclair) BE104 103387
Help us to help each other, Lord (Wesley) H432; I555; X517; AE275; AR374; AS349; BE105; BR285 103388
Help us to win them, help us to gather (Hott) R In from the highway 103389
Her Virgin eyes saw God incarnate born (Ken) E217; F513 103390
Heralds of Christ, who bear the King's commands (Copenhaver) G482; J320; R498; S379; U407; Z533; AB377; AC258; AD374; AE359; AG264; AK385; AR567;

AT452; BF529; BZ 103391
Here a little child I stand (Herrick) X402 103392
Here at thy table, Lord, this sacred hour (Hoyt) Z451; AO 440; AT392; BF599 103393
Here at thy table, Lord, we meet (Stennett) L322; N242; Z455; AS461 103394
Here behold me, as I cast me (Neander) K273; N352; O276 103395
Here betwixt ass and oxen mild (French, 13th c) A38 103396
Here from the world we turn (Crosby) AM345; AP330 103397
Here I can firmly rest (Gerhardt) AZ1317 103398
Here in our upper room with thee (Robinson) AE336; AR508 103399
Here in the country's heart (Gale) X518 103400
Here in the Name of Christ our Lord (Bruiningk) BA290 103401
Here in this water I do vow thee (Giles) BY291 103402
Here, in thy Name, eternal God (Montgomery) K244; L291; M 515; N277; O133; Q635; AA459 103403
Here in thy presence we appear (Clausnitzer) AZ685 103404
Here let thy people come, dear Lord (Loveman) BH5 103405
Here, Lord, assembled in Thy Name (Boaden) AO614 103406
Here, Lord of life and light, to thee (Bacon) AX637 103407
Here, Lord, we offer thee all that is fairest (Blunt) W347; AO500; AP800; BY721 103408
Here, O God, thy healing presence (Baum) BE109 103409
Here, O my Lord, I see the face to face (Bonar) A208; B334; D219; E312; F414; G415; I237; J275; K183; L329; R442; S352; T364; U382; V549; W323; X 270; Z458; AD401; AE333; AF 287; AG240; AH510; AK341; AL220; AM310; AO435; AP 354; AR519; AT391; AW303; AZ459; BA297; BE108; BF 600; BR477; BV376; BY316; BZ 103410
Here, O my Lord, I'd see thee face to face (Bonar) BE108 X Here, O my Lord, I see thee 103411
Here on the paths of everyday (Markham) AQ180 103412
Here, Saviour, we would come (Campbell. Christian hymn book) Z450 103413
Here we come awassailing (English trad carol) BG15 103414
Here we come with every burden (Slemp) R In the quiet hours of morning 103415
Here we come with gladness (Johnston) X386b; AW421; BV345 103416
Here we often are perplexed (Trabert) N142 103417
Here, where the sun shines lovingly (Auryansen) AB303 103418
Here, while the cherubim within the veil (Greek, 6th c) F391 103419
Here's love and grief beyond degree (Watts) H194 103420
Herr! Dir ist Niemand zu vergleichen! (J.A. Cramer) BW518 103421
Herr, es ist von meinem Leben (Neumann) BT560 103422
Herr, Gott, dich loben alle wir (Melanchthon) BT254 103423
Herr Gott! dich will ich loben (G. Blaurock) BU30 103424
Herr Gott, erhalt uns für und für (Helmbold) BT288 103425
Herr Gott in deinem Reiche (M. Schneider) BU96 103426
Herr Gott! streit wider meine Feind (Ausbund. Psalm 35) BU127 103427
Herr Gott! thu mich erhören (Ausbund. Psalm 86) BU129 103428
Herr Gott Vater im Himmelreich

(Ausbund) BU63 103429
Herr Gott Vater im Himmelreich (H. Betz) BU111 103430
Herr Gott Vater in deinem Thron! (M. Schneider) BU85 103431
Herr Gott Vater, von dir allein (H. Betz) BU112 103432
Herr Gott Vater, wir preisen dich (Schneegass) BT124 103433
Herr Gott Vater, zu dir ich schrey (H. Betz) BU81 103434
Herr, ich habe missgehandelt (Franck) BT326 103435
Herr Jesu Christ, dich zu uns wend (ascr to Wilhelm II, Duke) AY2d; BT3 103436
Herr Jesu Christ, du hast bereit't (Kinner) BT306 103437
Herr Jesu Christe, starker Gott, (Ausbund) BU73 103438
Herr Jesu, der du selbst (Fischer) BT485 103439
Herr Jesu, Licht der Heiden (Franck) BT138 103440
Herr, öffne mir die Herzenstür (Olearius) BT5 103441
Herr! starker Gott ins Himmels Thron (Ausbund) BU71 103442
Herr, unser Gott, lass nicht zuschanden werden (Heermann) BT269 103443
Herr, wie du willst, so schick's mit mir (Bienemann) BT406 103444
Herre Jesu Krist! Min Frelser du est (Sthen) BT353 103445
Hers the Kingdom, hers the scepter (Vere) R Holy Church now stands 103446
Herzlich lieb hab' ich dich, o Herr (Schalling) BT429 103447
Herzlich thut mich erfreuen Die liebe Sommer-Zeit (Ausbund) BU64 103448
Herzliebster Jesu, was hast du verbrochen (Heermann) BT143; BW534 103449
He's coming, coming, coming soon I know (---) R How sweet are the tidings that greet 103450
He's coming once again (Belden) BB191 103451
He's risen, He's risen, Christ Jesus, the Lord (Walther) Q198 103452
He's the Lily of the Valley (Fry) R I have found a friend in Jesus 103453
Heut' fangen wir in Gottes Nam'n (Wandersleben) BT7 103454
Heut Fänget an das neue Jahr (Unparth. G. B.) AY25d 103455
Hibernia's Patron, Saint, all hail (---) BO136 103456
Hic breve vivitur, hic breve plangitur (St. Bernard of Cluny) BT448 103457
Hide me, hide me, O blessed Saviour, hide me (Crosby) R Hide me, O my Saviour, hide 103458
Hide me, O my Saviour, hide me (Crosby) V761; AI247; AW483; AX513; AY71 103459
Hiding in thee (Cushing) R O safe to the Rock that is higher than I 103460
High in the heavens, Eternal God (Watts) G82; H112; O67; V94; AF82; AM52; AZ926; BB69; BE111; BV240; BY56 103461
High in yonder realm of light (Raffles) AY155 X High in yonder realms of light 103462
High in yonder realms of light (Raffles) L584; V714; AY155; BR442 103463
High let us swell our tuneful notes (Doddridge) F592; L 227 103464
High o'er the lonely hills, (Struther) A473; X63; AD102; AF42; AN96; AQ267 103465
High on his everlasting throne (Spangenberg) I221; AZ914; BA546 103466
High on the mountain top a banner (Johnson) BC62 103467
High-Priest before the Father's face (Zinzendorf, N. L.) AZ

231 103468
High Priest divine, from whom alone (Lewis) BY348 103469
High to heaven let song be soaring (Baum) BE112 103470
High word of God, who once didst come (Latin, 10th c) E2 103471
Highly favored congregation, founded firm on Christ (Swertner) AZ900; BA263 103472
Highly favored congregation, Loved by Jesus and esteemed (Benade) BA263 X Highly favored congregation (Swertner) 103473
Hilf Gott dass ich mög singen (Ausbund) BU123 103474
Hilf, Herr Jesu, lass gelingen (Rist) BT120 103475
Hills of the north, rejoice (Oakley) F269; J321; R478; W372; Y267; AF106; AL248; BV314; BY374 103476
Him on yonder cross I love (Rube) AZ1067 103477
Him that cometh unto me (Hewitt) R Listen to the blessed invitation 103478
Himmel, Erde, Luft und Meer. (Neander) BW510 103479
Hinunter ist der Sonnenschein (Herman) BT563 103480
Hinweg ist mir genommen (Ausbund) AU24 103481
His are the thousand sparkling rills (Alexander) A77; B156; E117; F120; W101; AM180; AP205 103482
His cheering message from the grave (Latin, 4th or 5th c) E124 103483
His face? I know not whether it be fair (Munson) AC506 103484
His flock our Shepherd feeds (---) BH111 103485
His Name for ever shall endure (Scottish Psalter, 1650) AL658; AM7; AW591 103486
His pow'r can make you what you ought to be (Nussbaum) R Would you live for Jesus 103487
His saints shall live, and to the King (U.P. Psalter, 1912) T133; AJ199 103488
His tender mercies ever sure (U.P. Psalter, 1912) R O thank the Lord, the Lord of love 103489
His trial o'er, and now, beneath His own cross (Coffin) O296 103490
His was no regal splendor (Kramer) AK127 103491
His wide dominion shall extend (U.P. Psalter, 1912) AJ194 103492
His yoke is easy, His burden is light (Warner) R I've found my Lord R The Lord is my Shepherd (Montgomery) 103493
Ho! every one that thirsts draw nigh (Wesley, J & C) H249; I258; AZ389; BA403 103494
Ho! my comrades, see the signal (Bliss) E570; AU303 103495
Ho! reapers of life's harvest (Woodbury) AO473; BB444 103496
Ho! ye that rest beneath the Rock (Sears) BR523 103497
Ho! ye that thirst approach the spring (Scottish paraphrases, 1781) AL472; AP402 103498
Ho-du la-do-noy kee tov (Jewish traditional) BH302 103499
"Hold fast till I come" (Belden) R Sweet promise is given to all who believe 103500
Hold o'er thy Church, Lord thy protecting hand (Zinzendorf, N.L.) AZ521 103501
Hold the fort, for I am coming (Bliss) R Ho! my comrades, see the signal 103502
Hold the ropes, then, hold them bravely (Jackson) R Down the mines 103503
Hold thou my hand! So weak I am, and helpless (Crosby) AP527; AU207; AX469; BY578 103504

Hold thou my hands! (Canton) E 403; W555; X519 103505
Hold to God's unchanging hand! (Wilson) R Time is filled 103506
Hold to the rod, the iron rod (Townsend) R To Nephi, seer of olden time 103507
Holiness becomes Thy house, 'Tis thou who dost dwell (Armenian liturgy) BE113 103508
Holy and infinite! viewless! eternal! (Havergal) AZ1154 103509
Holy and reverend is the name (Needham) L92; AR24; AS10 103510
Holy, and true, and righteous Lord (Wesley) I377 103511
Holy as thou, O Lord, is none (Wesley) BB80 103512
Holy Bible, book divine (Burton) H90; AI407; AK202; AM674; AS177; AT179; AU237; AV80; AX145; AY499; BB219; BE114 103513
Holy Bible, how I love it (Stratton) AX142 103514
Holy Church now stands triumphant (Vere) BL66; BM94; BN200 103515
Holy day, Jehovah's rest (Belden) BB654 103516
Holy Father, cheer our way (Robinson) A275; B16; D9; E270; F22; I56; K475; W282; X47; AL553; AP667; AW254; BR121 103517
Holy Father, great Creator (Griswold) A267; B210; D386; L188; BA657 103518
Holy Father, hear my cry (Bonar) V409; AE153; AZ1068 103519
Holy Father, in thy mercy (Stevenson) A514; E520; F488; J337; K500; N586; Q643; W629; AM630; AP713; BA891; BV406; BY668 103520
Holy Father, thou hast given (Bruce) W204; AC73; BF272 103521
Holy Father, thou hast taught me (Neale) L189; M366; V344; AA 336; BE115 103522
Holy Father, thou hast taught us (Neale) M366 X Holy Father, thou hast taught me 103523
Holy Father! We address thee (Peters) AZ619 103524
Holy Ghost, come down upon thy children (Faber) E571 103525
Holy Ghost, dispel our sadness (Gerhardt) H217; I192; N155; O381; AL147; AM246; AO233; AP275; AW134; AZ909; BZ 103526
Holy Ghost, Illuminater (Wordsworth) AZ969 X See the Conqueror mounts in triumph 103527
Holy Ghost, my conforter (Latin, 9th c) O378; AL160 103528
Holy Ghost, the Infinite (Rawson) AI118 X Come to our poor nature's night 103529
Holy Ghost, with light divine (Reed) H216; I185; K156; L184; M633; N158; Q234; U 133; V218; AA259; AG127; AH231; AI122; AN68; AO231; AS171; AT170; AU204; AV151; AX134; AY451; BA137; BB206; BE118; BX98 103530
Holy God, we praise thy name (Franz) A273; D140; J167; Q250; AF247; AH145; AW519a; AX10; BL82; BM91; BN196; BO3; BP47; BQ39; BZ 103531
Holy God, we show forth here (Dearmer) E313; X271 103532
Holy habitations, after weary flight (---) BR448 103533
Holy, Holy, holy, blessed Lord (Gerok) N337 103534
Holy, Holy, Holy, Blessed Trinity (---) R Round the throne of glory 103535
Holy, Holy, Holy is the Lord! Sing, O ye people (Crosby) Z97; AH205; AI31; AS11 103536
Holy, holy, holy Lord, Be thy glorious name adored, Be thy praise (Smith) BI26 103537

Holy, holy, holy Lord! Be thy glorious name adored Lord thy mercies (Williams) L72; BR69 103538

Holy, Holy, Holy! Lord God Almighty (Heber) A266; B205; D383; E162; F160; G1; H1; I78; J131; K158; L177; M140; N163; O72; P232; Q246; R11; S57; T316; U1; V88; W1; X187; Y18; Z107; AA263; AB 17; AC4; AD25; AE155; AF 251; AG1; AH159; AI27; AK1; AL1; AM87; AN17; AO234; AP135; AQ4; AR1; AS17; AT 1; AU6; AV1; AW1; AX12; AY 30; AZ780; BA8; BB73; BD22; BE117; BF186; BI25; BK41; BL37; BM92; BR44; BV227; BX5; BY52; BZ 103539

Holy, Holy, Holy, Lord God of Hosts, eternal King (Wordsworth) A270; B208; D385; I77; K159; L185; U2; V86; AO237; AR25; AS69; AZ1258; BA257; 103540

Holy, holy, holy, Lord God of Hosts, Heaven and earth (Lathbury) R Day is dying in the West (Lathbury) 103541

Holy, holy, holy Lord God of Hosts! When heaven and earth (Montgomery) N165; AK198; AP137; AZ1064; BA11; BI38 103542

Holy, holy, holy, Lord, Thy disciples Gather in devotion (Mackaye) Y75; AC107; AD133 103543

Holy, holy, holy, O Thou Love Eternal ("D.S.", 1920) AN503 103544

Holy, holy Lord, We with one accord (Goldsmith) BX324 103545

Holy is God! The light and darkness praise Him (Mary Francis, Sr.) BN207 103546

Holy Jesus, be my light (---) AO329 103547

Holy Jesus! Fountain streaming (Crasselius) O279 103548

Holy Jesus! God of love (Parnell) E314 103549

Holy Lamb, who thee confess (Wesley) H153; AL343 103550

Holy Lord, By thy body given to death (Swertner) AZ715 103551

Holy Lord, Holy Lord, Holy and Almighty Lord (Gregor) AK200; AW520 103552

Holy Lord, Holy Lord, Thanks and praise be ever Thine (Gregor) BA3 X Holy Lord, Thanks and praise 103553

Holy Lord, thanks and praise be ever Thine (Gregor) AZ 713; BA3 103554

Holy Love, from heaven descended (---) BR528 103555

Holy Majesty, before thee (Hedborn) N315 X Glorious Majesty, before thee 103556

Holy Mary, Mother mild (---) BO101 103557

Holy night! peaceful night! (Mohr) O178; V749; AO132; AP172; AV87; BI97 103558

Holy offerings, rich and rare (Monsell) A480; B504; D478; AO496; AZ871; BR296 103559

Holy patron! Thee saluting, Here we meet (---) BO124 103560

Holy Queen we bend before thee (St Bernard of Cluny) BO56 X Holy Queen we come before thee 103561

Holy Queen, we come before thee (St Bernard of Cluny) BN134; BO56; BP85 103562

Holy, righteous, heavenly King (Metcalfe) BB70 103563

Holy Saviour, truth Divine (Longfellow) BR43 X Holy Spirit, Truth divine 103564

Holy Saviour! we adore thee (Deck) AZ1411 103565

Holy Spirit, breathe on me (Hatch & McKinney) AT174; AU417 103566

Holy Spirit, come and shine (Latin, 9th c) AZ1124; BO

185 103567
Holy Spirit, come with light (Grundtvig) M472 103568
Holy Spirit, faithful Guide, Ever near the Christian's side (Wells) G243; H213; I193; U 132; V212; Z276; AE150; AG 126; AH227; AO232; AR443; AS252; AT165; AU245; AV152; AW137; AX135; AY196; BB211; BZ 103569
Holy Spirit, Faithful Guide, Lead us heavenward (---) BB701 103570
Holy Spirit, from on high (Bathurst) AT171 103571
Holy Spirit, gently come (Latin, 9th c) F614 103572
Holy Spirit, God of love, who our night dost brighten (Boye) Q230 103573
Holy Spirit, hear us, Help us while we sing (Parker) G438; K550; M632; W189; AL616; AM 638; AP756; BA828; BV292; BY233 103574
Holy Spirit, hear us on this Sabbath day (Mohr) AO225 X Holy Spirit, hear us on this sacred day 103575
Holy Spirit, hear us on this sacred day (Mohr) Q229; AA256; AO 225 103576
Holy Spirit, heavenly Dove (Littledale) D524 103577
Holy Spirit, in thy might (Rawson) AB98 X Come to our poor nature's night 103578
Holy Spirit, lamp of light (Rawson) BB216 X Come to our poor nature's night 103579
Holy Spirit, Light divine (Reed) AN68 X Holy Ghost, with light divine 103580
Holy Spirit, Lord of glory (Baynes) D215; N254; BA288 103581
Holy Spirit, Lord of light (Latin, 12th c) K144; L176; AZ1125; BA136; BN56; BQ34 103582
Holy Spirit, Lord of love (Maclagan) B371; D213; BA291; BF612 103583
Holy Spirit, make us strong! (Dearmer) X391 103584
Holy Spirit, Source of gladness (Gerhardt) K147; AN3; BE 119; BX119 103585
Holy Spirit, Truth divine (Longfellow) A377; B373; G173; H220; J130; R240; S 208; T356; W193; X520; Y 100; Z274; AB94; AC60; AD185; AE151; AF242; AH 232; AK188; AL154; AP284; AR219; AW136; BF267; BK 98; BM90; BR34; BV293;BY 234; BZ 103586
Holy temples on Mount Zion (Bennett) BC63 103587
Holy Trinity, thanks and praise to thee (Nyberg) BA194 X Holy Trinity, we confess with joy 103588
Holy Trinity, we confess with joy (Nyberg) AZ537; BA194 103589
Holy Week responsories (Breviary) BQ170 to 181 103590
Home, home, sweet sweet home [slight variations] R 'Mid pleasures and palaces (Payne) R 'Mid scenes of confusion (Denham) 103591
Home, sweet home! Happy home, sweet home. ("Louisa E.") R I love to think of my home above 103592
Honor and glory, power and salvation (Housman) G16; S42app.; X409 103593
Honor and glory, thanksgiving and praise (Dayman) AB51 103594
Hope of Israel, Zion's army (Townsend) BC64 103595
Hope of our hearts, O Lord, appear (Denny) AZ1444 103596
Hope of the world, Thou Christ of great compassion (Harkness) J581; R291; AE360; AF398; AT282; BZ 103597
Hora novissima, tempora pessima (St Bernard of Cluny) BT605 103598
Höret, ihr Eltern, Christus

spricht (Helmbold) BT630 103599

Hosanna! be the children's song (Montgomery) H455; I679; AR107; AS401 103600

Hosanna, Hosanna, Hosanna in the highest (---) R Gather around the Christmas tree 103601

Hosanna in the highest! Our eager hearts (Lathrop) R O bold, O foolish peasants 103602

Hosanna in the highest To our exalted Saviour (Wesley) F421 103603

Hosanna, loud hosanna (Threlfall) G127; K545; Q161; R185; S147; W93; AC117; AD478; AE107; AG89; AH279; AK136; AL82; AP749; AR156; BZ 103604

Hosanna! Music is divine (Smart) X521 103605

Hosanna! raise the pealing hymn (Havergal) D559; AZ219; BA 120 103606

Hosanna to our only Lord (---) R Jesus, to thee be endless praise 103607

Hosanna to the living Lord (Heber) A318; B53; D316; F241; J424; K425; Q70; S53; V14; AD168; AM 314; AO63; AR200; AZ392; BA 373; BF334; BY269 103608

Hosanna to the Prince of grace (Watts) AZ177 103609

Hosanna to the royal Son, Of David's ancient line (Watts) L112 103610

Hosanna we sing, like the children dear (Hodges) F453; AP753 103611

Hosanna with a cheerful sound (Watts) L14 103612

Hostis Herodes impie (Sedulius) BT131 103613

Hours and days and years and ages (Dutch) AI410 103614

Hover o'er me, Holy Spirit (Stokes) AE149; AS173; AX 136; AY204; BB212 103615

How are thy servants blest, O Lord! (Addison) E542; G71; I102; L482; X522; AW338; AZ 124; BA550; BZ 103616

How beauteous are their feet (Watts) D498; F510; H460; L303; N283; O93; Q487; V558; AA490; AO454; AP 370; AY381; BB442; BJ66; BR227 103617

How beauteous on the mountains, The feet of Him that brings (Gough) BE120; BR226 103618

How beauteous were the marks divine (Coxe) B108; G116; I127; L136; AS123; AT84; AU298; AV101; AZ340; BA 80; BE352; BZ 103619

How beautiful heaven must be (Bridgewater) R We read of a place 103620

How beautiful the sight (Montgomery) AM283; AP118 103621

How beautiful thy temples, Lord (Kooyman) BC65 103622

How beautiful to walk in the steps (Hewitt) R Trying to walk 103623

How beautiful upon the mountains (Bible. Isaiah 52) R Awake, awake 103624

How blessed are the perfect in the way (Westra) AJ428 103625

How blessed from the bonds of sin (Spitta) J60; K258; O254 103626

How blessed is the heavenly choice (Doddridge) BR462 X O happy day, that [...] my choice 103627

How blessed is the host in white (Lee) P432 103628

How blessed is the little flock (Holm) M86; O50; P268 103629

How blessed is this place, O Lord (Ryden) J241; M513; N581; BZ 103630

How blest am I, most gracious Saviour (Dessler) AZ1088 103631

How blest and lovely thy earth-

ly dwellings (Augusta) AZ544; BA334 103632
How blest are the moments that Jesus bestows (Ahnfelt. Sanger) N463 103633
How blest are thy who hear God's word (Brun) J253; M19; O46; P59; Q48 103634
How blest are thy who through the power (Hoppe) N194 103635
How blest are they whose hearts are pure (Bathurst) X523; AW206; BE121 103636
How blest is he whose trespass (U.P. Psalter, 1912) R281; T53; AJ83; AM462 103637
How blest the man that fears the Lord (U.P. Book of Psalms, 1871) AP100 103638
How blest the man who fears the Lord. And greatly loves (U.P. Psalter, 1912) T212; AJ305 103639
How blest the man, who fears to stray. (Kennedy) BH27 103640
How blest the man who thoughtfully (U.P. Psalter, 1912) T75; AJ113 103641
How blest the perfect in the way (U.P. Psalter, 1912) T225; AJ321 103642
How blest the righteous when he dies (Barbauld) H488; I582; L567; N597; V669; AO567; BR431 103643
How blest the sacred tie that binds (Barbauld) BR504 103644
How blest the tie that binds (Fawcett) BR502 X Blest be the tie that binds 103645
How blest was that life once lived upon earth (Turner) AI102 103646
How bright appears the Morning Star (Nicolai) A329; B98; J 404; X90; AB76; AW529; BA 54; BG104; BL13; BR135; BV 130 103647
How bright these glorious spirits shine (Watts, 1707, in Scottish Paraphrases, 1781) A127; B 302; E199; F528; W223; X207; AL180; AM606; AP311; AZ184; BJ40; BV464; BY405 103648
How brightly beams the Morning Star (Nicolai) X90 X How bright appears the Morning Star 103649
How brightly shines the Morning Star (Nicolai) AB76 X How bright appears the Morning Star 103650
How calm and beautiful the morn (Hastings) L265; V158; AM 209; AR184; AS147 103651
How calm and how bright is this holy day (Hoffman) AX66; AY274 103652
How calmly the evening once more is descending (Lynch) BY696 103653
How can a sinner know (Wesley) G208; H295; I303; BZ 103654
How can I cease to pray for thee? Some where ... (Dorr) X290 103655
How can I thank thee, Lord (Denicke) Q417; AA344 103656
How can she sing in the dark like this? (Havergal) BW454 103657
How charming is the place (Stennett) H420; V7 103658
How cheering is the Christian's hope? (---) BB387 103659
How condescending and how kind (Watts) L138; V150 103660
How dear to me, O Lord of Hosts (U.P. Psalter, 1912) R440; AJ225 103661
How dear to my heart is the story of old (Yates) AY355 103662
How dearly God must love us (Partridge) BY57 103663
How did my heart rejoice to hear (Watts) V610 103664
How excellent in all the earth (Scottish Psalter, 1650) AP6 103665
How fair the Church of Christ (Kingo) O406; P79 103666

How far from home? I asked (Smith) BB665 103667

How far is it to Bethlehem? (Chesterton) BG142 103668

How firm a foundation, ye saints of the Lord (Rippon's Selection of hymns, signed "K") A564; B212; D636; G315; H374; I461; J558; K344; L509; M237; N439; O340; P202; Q427; R369; S283; T397; U205; V325; Y363; Z406; AA375; AB174; AC74; AD233; AE189; AF372; AG212; AH379; AI156; AK314; AL403; AM80; AO 362; AP531; AR260; AS259; AT 262; AU199; AV228; AW151; AX146; AY33; AZ501; BA689; BB255; BC66; BD75; BE123; BF413; BR248,310; BY579; BZ 103669

How gentle God's commands (Doddridge) G69; H124; I100; R105; S279; T396; V356; Y384; Z399; AB208; AD239; AE67; AF76; AG50; AH226; AM561; AN253: AO103; AV77; AW56; AX489; AY401; BB64; BC67; BE124; BF395; BR123; BX312; BZ 103670

How glad I am each Christmas Eve (Wexelsen) P369 X I am so glad each Christmas Eve 103671

How gladly I my place have taken (Vig) M138; P280 103672

How glorious is the hour (Bulfinch) BR289 103673

How glorious is the life above (Wesley) F420 103674

How glorious is the sacred place (Watts) V540 X How glorious Zion's courts appear 103675

How glorious Zion's courts appear (Watts in Scottish Paraphrases, 1781) S340; V540; AL167; AP 298 103676

How good and pleasant is the sight (U.P. Psalter, 1912) AJ370 103677

How good is the God we adore (Hart) BV30 X This God is the God we adore 103678

How good it is for brethren (Wetzel) M643; P408 103679

How good it is, how pleasant to behold (Czerwenka)[Cervenka] AZ437; BA668 103680

How good it is to thank the Lord and praise to Thee Most High (U.P. Psalter, 1912) T171; AJ250; AM535 103681

How good it is to thank the Lord, To praise Thy name (Weisberg) BH109 103682

How goodly is thy house, O Lord! (Jacobs) BH1 103683

How great, Almighty, is thy kindness (Gellert) AW516 103684

How great at last my joy will be (Bonin) AZ905 103685

How great is your name (Ladies of the Grail) BSp.8 103686

How great the bliss to be a sheep of Jesus (Rambach) AZ709; BA499 103687

How great the goodness kept in store (U.P. Psalter, 1912) T52; AJ81; AM563 103688

How great the harvest is (Dearmer) X169; BG152 103689

How great the wisdom and the love (Snow) BC68 103690

How happy are the young who hear (Bruce) L447; N483; V233; AL291; AP446; AX503; AY367; BE215 103691

How happy are these little ones (---) AY167 103692

How happy are they who Jesus obey (Wesley) AZ1421 X O how happy are they who the Saviour obey 103693

How happy are they, who their [the] Saviour obey (Wesley) H294 X O how happy . . . 103694

How happy every child of grace (Wesley) G522; H336; I605; BZ 103695

How happy is he born and taught (Wotton) X524; AN294; AQ 99; AW208; BX351 103696

How happy is he born or taught

(Wotton) AN294 X How happy is he born and taught 103697
How happy is the man who hears (Bruce) N483 X How happy are the young who hear 103698
How happy is the pilgrim's lot (Wesley) I624 103699
How heart-affecting Christ to see (Cennick) AZ885 103700
How helpless guilty nature lies (Steele) N412; P252; V220 103701
How I love thy law, O Lord (U. P. Psalter, 1912) R253; T237; AJ333 103702
How joyful 'tis to sing (Nicholson) F493 103703
How large the promise, how divine (Watts) H456; V541 103704
How little our true majesty is shown (Wheelock) AQ69 103705
How long? How long must we wait? (Glasgow) R Long have we sought 103706
How long, O Lord, most holy and true (Widstoe) BC69 103707
How long, O Lord, our Saviour (Deck) AZ817 103708
How long wilt thou forget me (Sternhold) T17; AJ22; AM 541 103709
How lost was my condition (Newton) AZ813; BA431 103710
How lovely are thy dwellings fair (Milton) X525; AF274; AL660; AN19; AP68; AW592; BE 125; BH2,3; BR87; BX113 103711
How lovely are thy dwellings, Lord (Milton) BE125 X How lovely are thy dwellings fair! 103712
How lovely, how divinely sweet (Steele) L53 103713
How lovely is thy dwelling-place, O Lord of hosts, to me! (Scottish Psalter, 1650) G383; AL659; AP65; BZ 103714
How lovely is thy dwelling place! Within its courts we turn to thee (Brightbill) AR3 103715
How lovely, Lord of hosts, to me (U. P. Psalter, 1912) AJ229 103716
How lovely now the Morning Star (Wiesenmeyer) AA24 X How lovely shines the Morning Star 103717
How lovely shines the Morning Star, In twilight sky it gleams afar (Wiesenmeyer) Q546; AA24 103718
How lovely shines the Morning Star, The nations see and hail afar (Nicolai) Q343; AM434; AZ1097 103719

CAUTION NOTE: Two poems begin (in German) "Wie schön leuchtet." Tr. as "How lovely shines". Authors are Gerhardt and Wiesenmeyer. 103720

How many times, discouraged (Rexford) AX534; AY91 103721
How many were the silent prayers (---) AY181 103722
How marvellous God's greatness (Briem) J449 103723
How near to us, O God, thou art (Hunter. Hymns of faith and life, 1889) AD90; BF249 103724
How needful, strictly to inquire (Benade) AZ883; BA623 103725
How oft, alas! This wretched heart (Steele) V287; AX339; AY208 103726
How oft have sin and Satan strove (Watts) V335 103727
How oft, O Father, my heart is burning (Overby) P343 103728
How pleasant and how good it is (U. P. Psalter, 1912) T265; AJ369; AX546 103729
How pleasant, how divinely fair (Watts) H414; I215; V19 103730
How pleasant thus to dwell below (---) AY398 103731
How pleased and blest was I (Watts) BY270 103732
How pleasing is thy voice (Dwight)

AB384 103733

How precious is the book divine (Fawcett) H91; I201; N217; P93; Q285; U140; V74; AA111; AI153; AM265; AO242; AV79; AZ170; BA4; BR242 103734

How rich thy bounty, King of kings (Doddridge) I224 103735

How sad our state by nature is! (Watts) I268; V224; AZ108 103736

How shall come the Kingdom holy (Savage) AN358; AR573 103737

How shall I follow Him I serve (Conder) I339; K55; N94; AZ 387; BA79; BB519; BY473 103738

How shall I meet my Saviour (Gerhardt) BA149 X O how shall I receive thee 103739

How shall I sing that Majesty (Mason) E404; X526; AL32; AP150 103740

How shall the young direct their way (U.P. Psalter, 1912) R258; T226; AJ322; AM264 103741

How shall the young secure their hearts (Watts) I204; L315; N 223; O573; P379; Q286; V76; AA112; AO241; AS404 103742

How shall we celebrate thy love (Proud) BR239 103743

How shall we stand in that great day (Belden) R The judgment has set, the books have been opened 103744

How short and hasty is our life (Watts) L372 103745

How solemn are the words (Midlane) BA426 103746

How strong and sweet my Father's care (---) Z168; AC53; AO96; AR81 103747

How sweet and awful is the place (Watts) V448; AM271 103748

How sweet and silent is the place (Palmer) AB326; AH509; AN 446; BF602; BX478 103749

How sweet are the tidings that greet the pilgrim's ear (---) BB669 103750

How sweet, how heavenly is the sight (Swain) H425; I554; U372; V612; Z475; AI275; AO428; AW323; AX544; AY358; AZ 112; BA674; BB431; BE126 103751

How sweet the light of Sabbath Eve! (Edmeston) BB460 X Sweet is the light of Sabbath 103752

How sweet the name of Jesus sounds (Newton) A455; B 232; D433; E405; F192; G 347; H235; I137; J406; K343; L165; N54; O417; P278; Q 364; R130; S310; T424; U75; V374; W419; X527; Z264; AA96; AB254; AE104; AF 221; AG185; AH317; AI427; AL306; AM544; AO282; AP 457; AR108; AS286; AT160; AU455; AV135; AX14; AY21; AZ139; BA65; BB150; BJ50; BR163; BV260; BY203; BZ 103753

How sweet this bond of perfectness (Warner) AX550 103754

How sweet thy dwellings, Lord, how fair (Merrick) AZ683 103755

How sweet to leave the world awhile (Kelly) AZ391 103756

How sweet upon this sacred day (Follen) BB458 103757

How sweetly flowed the gospel sound (Bowring) H157; I290; V136; BE128 103758

How swift the torrent rolls (Doddridge) I580 103759

How tedious and tasteless the hours (Newton) G349; I538; V371; AH368; AI271; AT306; AU24; AV180; AZ1508; BB 660 103760

How to reach the masses, men of every birth (Oatman) AU 60 103761

How vain is all beneath the skies (Ford) BB490 103762

How vain the cruel Herod's fear (Sedulius) F74 103763

How vast the benefits divine (Toplady) AI127; AM95

103764
How vast the treasure we possess! (Watts) BY497 103765
How welcome was the call (Baker) AO560; AP706; AZ1371; BA846 103766
How wondrous and great Thy works, God of praise (Onderdonk) A260; B254; D467; N372; BC146 103767
How wondrous is Thy mercy, Lord (Bible. Psalm 36: Danish version) BE130 103768
How wondrous is thy world, O Lord (Lucas) BH56 103769
Humble praises, holy Jesus (---) N643; AI380 103770
Humble thyself and the Lord will draw near thee (Oatman) R If thou wouldst have 103771
Humbly I adore thee (St Thomas Aquinas) A204; BP49 103772
Humbly we adore thee, Christ, Redeemer King (St Thomas Aquinas) BM10 103773
Humility, thou secret vale (Schell) AX431 103774
Hush all ye sounds of war (Draper) Z195 103775
Hush! blessed are the dead (Bickersteth) AP618; AZ479 103776
Hush! dear child, lie still and slumber (Watts) BA851 X Hush! my dear, lie still 103777
Hush! my dear, lie still and slumber (Watts) A242; N656; X382; BA851; BG130 103778
Hushed was the evening hymn (Burns) B359; D568; G451; I674; W251; AH364; AI374; AL 211; AM655; AO626; AP806; AW416; BB428; BC252; BD196; BK23; BV361; BX518; BY474 103779

I

I aint gwine study war no more (Negro spiritual) X Gwine to lay down my burden 103780
I am a little child, you see (Zinzendorf, N.L.) BA840 X Thou, gracious Saviour, for my good 103781
I am a part of all that I have met (Tennyson) AQ65 103782
I am a poor, way-faring stranger (White spiritual) AU74 103783
I am a stranger here, within a foreign land (Cassel) AI197; AM695; AT433 103784
I am baptized into thy name (Rambach) L320; M539; P98 103785
I am bought not with riches (Kidder) AU337; AX486; AY 371; BB617 103786
I am bound for the promised land (Stennett) AH529 X On Jordan's stormy banks 103787
I am coming Lord! Coming now to thee (Hartsough) R I Hear thy welcome voice 103788
I am coming to the cross (McDonald) G246; H272; I351; R278; U177; V747; AH339; AP 430; AR257; AT243; AU260; AV173; AX306; BA903; BB600; BZ 103789
I am content! My Jesus liveth still (Möller) Q196; AA226 103790
I am dwelling on the mountain (---) AU27; AY353 103791
I am fighting in the army of the Lord (Henry) AX180 103792
I am happy today (McConnell) AT209 103793
I am in my Father's keeping (Morris) R When the early morning breaking 103794
I am Jesus' Little lamb (Hayn) K556; N650; Q648; AM643; AW430 103795
I am looking for the city built of God (Hott) AX269; AY146 103796
"I am nearing the port" (Dale) AY162 103797
I am needy, yet forgiven (Zinzendorf, C.R.) AZ425 103798
I am not skilled to understand (Greenwell) S326; W698; BV

624; BY204 103799

I am not worthy, holy Lord (Baker) B323; D234; N248; S498; W316; AD200; AI220; AL223; AP363; BA298; BV377 103800

I am redeemed but not with silver (Gray) R Nor silver nor gold 103801

I am resolved no longer to linger (Hartsough) AT216; AU105; AX298 103802

I am satisfied with Jesus (McKinney) AT436; AU375 103803

I am so glad each Christmas-Eve (Wexelsen) J45; P369 103804

I am so glad that Jesus loves me (Oakey) R I am so glad that our Father in heaven 103805

I am so glad that our Father in heaven (Oakey) G435; AH543; AL480; AM647; AP742; AT509; AU319; AX38; AY484; BB423; BY498 103806

I am so happy in Christ today (Oatman) AT194 103807

I am the Lord, O hear my voice (Scheffler) AW565 103808

I am the vine and ye are the branches (Shaw) AX414 103809

I am the way, the truth, the life (Caswall) BE131 103810

I am thine, O Lord, I have heard thy voice (Crosby) G252; H345; R320; U217; V734; Z312; AE 191; AG148; AH361; AI272; AL 490; AM713; AO648; AP483; AR444; AS232; AT349; AU56; AV368; AW475; AX411; AY473; BB594; BZ 103811

I am thinking today of that beautiful land (Hewitt) AT470; AY 508; BB626 103812

I am trusting day by day in his word (Newell) AX460; AY97 103813

I am trusting in my Saviour (Lyon) AX462; AY94 103814

I am trusting, Lord, in thee (McDonald) R I am coming to the cross 103815

I am trusting thee, Lord Jesus (Havergal) Q428; S287; U176; V353; W695; AA370; AI242; AM424; AO352; AP502; AR 265; AS265; AV202; AZ1139; BA716; BB256; BF351; BV 498; BY432 103816

I am whatever you make me, nothing more (Lane) AC516 103817

I ask not, Lord, for less to bear (Smith) BB251 103818

I ask thee for the daily strength (Waring) BX292 103819

I believe in thee, Lord Jesus (Wine) AR507 103820

I believe the Bible, it taught me how to pray (Ufford) AX139 103821

I believe the promises of God (Smith) R I was wandering 103822

I belong to Jesus (Fraser) AI 253; AM649 103823

I bind my heart this tide (Watt) R286; S243; Y143; Z302; AB 163; AC121; AE444; AG169; AK251; AR356 103824

I bind unto myself today (St Patrick) A268; B525; E212; F162; W506; X528; BV229; BY433 103825

I bless the Christ of God (Bonar) BY434 103826

I bless thee, Father, for the grace (Aguilar) BH115 103827

I bless thee, Lord, for sorrows sent (Johnson) BX257 X I praise thee, Lord for blessings sent 103828

I bow in utter need and mortal weakness (Plummer) BI65 103829

I bow my forehead in the dust (Whittier) I472; J371; N414; R109; S282; T398; U31; AB 211; AI218; AK310; AO343 103830

I bow my forehead to the dust (Whittier) J371 X I bow my forehead in the dust 103831

I bring my hymn of thankfulness (Cooke) BX317 103832

I bring my sins to Jesus (Bonar)

AY228 I lay my sins on Jesus 103833

I came defiled and guilty (Teasley) AX337 103834

I came not hither of my will (Hosmer) AN252; BX298 103835

I can hear my Saviour calling (Blandly) AH336; AR248; AS 207; AT361; AU164; AV338; AW500; AY115 103836

I cannot always trace the way (Bowring) BE133; BR341; BX 260 103837

I cannot be idle, for Jesus says, "Go." (Henry) AX190 103838

I cannot find thee! Still on restless pinion (Scudder) Y4; AB 36; AN72; BX108 103839

I cannot put the Presence by (Kemp) AC139 103840

I cannot tell thee whence it came (Brown) AS306 103841

I cannot tell why He, whom angels worship (Fullerton) BV262; BY183 103842

I cannot think of them as dead (Hosmer) AN202 X We cannot think . . . 103843

I cannot think or reason (Wattles) Y72; AC122 103844

I close my heavy eye (Bonar) BR336 103845

I come, invited by thy word (Kingo) M53 103846

I come, O Saviour, to thy table (Heyder) Q315 103847

I come to the garden alone (Miles) AH329; AU356; BB606 103848

I come to thee, O blessed Lord (Landstad) M54; O101; P104; Q330 103849

I come to thee, O Father (Moser) BB286 103850

I constant care will take (U.P. Psalter, 1912) T69; AJ105 103851

I could not do without thee (Havergal) B239; D603; E572; F353; I353; M162; O472; P276; S311; U190; V302; AI109; AZ809; BA 485; BV485 103852

I cried to God in my distress (U.P. Psalter, 1912) T247; AJ343 103853

I dared not hope that thou wouldst deisn to come (Hatch) AD 240 103854

I did thee wrong, my God (Bonar) AZ481 103855

I do not ask, O Lord, that life may be (Proctor) B385; D633; I542; S305; U43; Z340; AD266; AE204; AL431; AP 505; AR402; AW471; BA507; BF420; BR392 103856

I do not ask to choose my path (Zelley) AX416 103857

I do not come because my soul (St John) Q379; AA316 103858

I entered once a home of care (---) AY110 103859

I fell asleep in Jesus' wounds (Eber) Q585; AA545 103860

I feel the winds of God today (Adams) W528; Z301; AW 391 103861

I gave my life for thee (Havergal) M182; Q405; U163; V 748; AE171; AG145; AH287; AI138; AS244; AT399; AU222; AV378; AX312; BB230; 103862

I give my heart to thee (Latin, 9th c) BB285; BY435 103863

I give myself to thee (Symons) BV338 103864

I go to prove my soul (Browning) AC443 103865

I graciously will teach thee (U.P. Psalter, 1912) T54; AJ84 103866

I greet thee, who my sure Redeemer art (Calvin) R144; AD77; AF207; AI232; AK277; AM135; AO609 103867

I have a friend in whom I trust (Presley) AX538 103868

I have a friend so patient, kind, forbearing (Rosenius) M626; N468; P295 103869

I have a Friend so precious (Lancaster) AO611; AY326;

BB533 103870
I have a home above (Bennett) L601 103871
I have a mother yonder (Negro spiritual) AH596 103872
I have a Saviour, He's pleading in glory (Clough) G237; AE 166; AH435; AS197; AT232; AU78; AV332; AW460; AX367; BB575 103873
I have a song I love to sing (Excell) AT208; AU108; BB638 103874
I have chosen thee, my Saviour (German) M550 103875
I have decided to follow Jesus (---) AX304 103876
I have followed Truth and Justice (U.P. Psalter, 1912) T240; AJ336 103877
I have found a friend in Jesus (Fry) AT87; AU363; AW446; AX25 103878
I have head of a land on the far-away strand (Moore) AU348 103879
I have heard thy voice, Lord Jesus (Cherry) P322 103880
I have made my choice to follow (Leech) AS336; AX181 103881
I have read of a beautiful city (Atchinson) AU386 103882
I have ridden the wind (Rice) Y7 103883
I have something I would tell you (Latta) AX334; AY344 103884
I have work enough to do (Pollard) BC71 103885
I have yielded myself to thy service (Naylor) AX392 103886
I hear a sweet voice ringing clear (Hood) L502 103887
I hear a voice that comes from far (Kelly) V275 103888
I hear in the air, 'neath the canopy blue (Kuipers) AI199 103889
I hear the Saviour say (Hall) Z 284; AM690; AT225; AU258; AV337; AW462; AX320; AY235; BB527 103890
I hear the words of love (Bonar) V396; AZ1487; BV503 103891
I hear thy voice, within the silence speaking (Ham) AN232; BF 266; BX269 103892
I hear thy welcome voice (Hartsough) E573; P262; W689; AH240; AL481; AM406; AP 435; AR446; AS204; AT224; AU265; AV170; AX299; BA 908; BB224 103893
I heard a sound of voices (Thring) A593; B542; D404; I626; J597; S437; U433; AO552 103894
I heard the bells on Christmas Day (Longfellow) AB361; AD 124; AH267; AN161; AR133; AT78; AU148; BC219; BF294; BX193 103895
I heard the dear Redeemer say (Warner) AX406 103896
I heard the voice of Jesus say (Bonar) A424; B242; D673; E574; F351; G210; H297; I304; J499; K365; L161; M163; N 432; O395; Q277; R280; S236; T385; U183; V297; W410; X 529; Y83; Z288; AA46; AB199; AC147; AD204; AE170; AG 163; AH332; AI203; AK236; AL271; AM221; AO246; AP 412; AR267; AS302; AT302; AU163; AV175; AW142; AX 329; AY472; AZ1464; BA505; BB225; BF344; BJ17; BR393; BV513; BY436; BZ 103897
I hope for the salvation of the Lord (Abraham ibn Ezra) BH92 103898
I hunger and I thirst (Monsell) B325; D343; F413; L331; V 455; X272; AW308; BA299; BV378; BY317 103899
I Hus og Hjem, hvor Mand og Viv (Landstad) BT624 103900
I intend to go through (Buffum) R My heart is so happy 103901
I joyed when to the house of God (Scottish Psalter, 1650) AL682; AP110; AW599 103902
I kneel in spirit at my Saviour's cross (Cennick) AZ436 103903
I know a flower so fair and fine (Gruntvig) P380 103904

I know a kingdom without end (German, 16th c. or earlier) P117 103905

I know a lovely Angel-game (Laufenberg) BG145 notes 103906

I know a rose-tree springing (Speier Gebetbuch, 1599) A17 103907

I know a soul that is steeped in sin (---) AC467 103908

I know a way beseiged and thronging (Gjertsen) P306 103909

I know, I know, I have another building R Christ went a building 103910

I know I love thee better, Lord (Havergal) AS283; AU94; AX479 103911

I know in my heart what it means (Teasley) R When I read how my Saviour 103912

I know in whom I trust (Wallin) N434 103913

I know my faith is founded (Neumeister) Q381 103914

I know my heavenly Father knows (Henry) BB591 103915

I know no life divided (Spitta) H317; AV174; BE135 103916

I know not how that Bethlehem's babe (Farrington) A330; G112; P206; R224; S181; U204; Z206; AC143; AF149; AG118; AH321; AK241; AR270; AT276; AW99; BF330; BZ 103917

I know not the hour (Bliss) AU 341 103918

I know not what the future hath (Whittier) A441; G517; H359; J593; W558; X530; Z571; AC 332; AD465; AF360; AL427; AN78; AP520; AR422; AW241; BA707; BF665; BX469 103919

I know not where the road may lead (Cummins) A432 103920

I know not why God's wondrous grace (Whittle) AE221; AH385; AI252; AM712; AR447; AT275; AW450; AX478; AY459; BY437 103921

I know of a river whose beautiful stream (---) AX257 103922

I know of a sleep in Jesus' name (Landstad) J299; M 299; O506; P331; Q592 103923

I know that, He liveth, Redeemer and Friend (Turner) R How blest was that life 103924

I know that my Redeemer lives, and ever prays for me (Wesley) H183; I370; V175; AA 245; AH310; AI254; AM586; AO214; AS163; AV118 103925

I know that my Redeemer lives; He lives, and on the earth (Wesley) BB488 103926

I know that my Redeemer lives; He lives, who once was dead (Wesley) Z245 103927

I know that my Redeemer lives, In this my faith is fast (Gerhardt) O332 103928

I know that my Redeemer lives; O the sweet joy (Medley) BV185 X I know that my Redeemer lives; What joy the blest 103929

I know that my Redeemer lives; What comfort this sweet sentence gives (Medley) M438 X I know that my Redeemer lives! What joy the blest 103930

I know that my Redeemer lives; What joy the blest (Medley) G329; H182; I168; J387; K 136; M438; N124; P203; Q 200; AA229; AE120; AR186; AS151; AZ294, 350; BA236; BC95; BV185; BY174;BZ 103931

I know that my Redeemer liveth, and on the earth (Pounds) Z255; AR448; AT127; AU 413; AW453; AY491 103932

I know that the Lord is almighty (U.P. Psalter, 1912) T269; AJ373 103933

I know the Bible was sent from God (McKinney) AT184 103934

I know whom I believe in (Arndt) M651 103935

I lay my sins on Jesus (Bonar) D605; E575; G230; H246; I488; J492; K338; L499; M197; N418; O439; P273; Q652; T386; U191; V299; W694; AA322; AL486; AM430; AO266; AP413; AT210; AV166; AW444; AY228; AZ833; BA432; BB278 103936

I learned it in the meadow path (Larcom) X531; AB310 103937

I leave all things to God's direction (Franck) Q529; AA499 103938

I leave the burdens of my life (Navra) BH221 103939

I leave thee not, thou art my Jesus ever (Dessler) AA87 103940

I lift mine eyes unto the hills (Caddell) BH33 103941

I lift my eyes unto heaven above (Runeberg) J396 103942

I lift my heart to Thee, Saviour divine (Mudie) H337; L453; O398; W427; AI320; AS277; AZ444; BA482; BY438 103943

I lift up my eyes to the mountains; from whence shall come my help? (Ladies of the Grail) BSp. 40 103944

I little see, I little know (Hosmer) I450; BX229 103945

I live, and I know the span of my years (Ingemann) M239 103946

I live for those who love me (Banks) AS411; AV227 103947

I long for household voices gone (Whittier) BX469 X I know not what the future hath 103948

I long to behold Him arrayed (Wesley) BB200 103949

I look not back; God knows the fruitless efforts (---) N431; AI235 103950

I look to Jesus, and the face (---) L468 103951

I look to thee in every need (Longfellow) B397; E406; G 325; I473; J490; R114; S79; X532; AB200; AD237; AF92; AN258; AR83; AW244; BE134; BF402; BX284; BZ 103952

I love all beauteous things (Bridges) AQ137 103953

I love God's tiny creatures (Briggs) X361 103954

I love Him, I love Him, Because He first loved me (---) R Gone from my heart 103955

I love the Lord, because He heareth me (Collier) AI416 103956

I love the Lord, because my voice (Scottish Psalter, 1650) AL675; AP102; AW597 103957

I love the Lord for he has heard the cry of my appeal (Ladies of the Grail) BSp. 34 103958

I love the Lord, for my request and humble plea (U. P. Psalter, 1912) T217; AJ310 103959

I love the Lord: he heard my cries (Watts) H360; L452; 103960

I love the Lord; he heard my voice (Proud) BR415 103961

I love the Lord! He lent an ear (Montgomery) AZ105 103962

I love the Lord, his strength is mine (U. P. Psalter, 1912) R370; AJ34 103963

I love the Lord, the fount of grace (Kuipers) AJ426 103964

I love the Lord who died for me (Cennick) AZ335 103965

I love the Lord who heard my cry, and granted my request (U. P. Psalter, 1912) T219; AJ312 103966

I love the sacred book of God (Kelly) BB220 103967

I love the voice Divine that speaks (Proud) BR355 103968

I love Thee, I love Thee (---) AT150; BB343 103969

I love thee, O thou Lord most high (Cologne Psalteriolium, 1710) BN209 103970

I love thy Church, O God (Dwight) AN411 X I love thy kingdom, Lord 103971

I love thy Kingdom, Lord (Dwight) A388; B315; D485; G379; H418; I208; J158; K199; L292; M79; N261; O89; P83; Q462; R435; S337; T359; U353; V606; W 210; Y381; Z428; AA468; AB 323; AC311; AD398; AE316; AF269; AG233; AH516; AI146; AK329; AL172; AM280; AN411; AO419; AP300; AR490; AS191; AT382; AU196; AV247; AW275; AX149; AY380; AZ1352; BA331; BF591; BZ 103972

I love thy way of freedom, Lord (Hay) BE136 103973

I love thy Zion, Lord (Dwight) L292; X I love thy Kingdom, Lord 103974

I love to hear the story, how the Lord from heaven came (---) BR545 103975

I love to hear the story which angel voices tell (Miller) E 594; F445; N632; P364; S447; W71; AL69; AO623; AP739; AS402; BA816; BV347; BY119 103976

I love to steal awhile away (Brown) G55; H46; I498; L429; N555; U259; V44; AI226; AR51; AS49; AV18; AX72; AY291; BB317 103977

I love to tell the story (Hankey) G249; H240; I544; J324; P388; R383; S443; U312; V236; Z532; AD253; AF317; AG186; AH346; AI390; AK467; AL504; AM387; AO635; AP592; AR440; AS295; AT141; AU371; AV385; AW493; AX200; AY348; BA906; BB518; BE414; BY415; BZ 103978

I love to think of my home above ("Louisa E") AS478; AX586; AY151 103979

I love to think that Jesus saw (Skemp) AF480 103980

I may not climb the heights which saints (Tiplady) AR431 103981

I must needs go home (Pounds) AT196; AX424 103982

I must tell Jesus all of my trials (Hoffman) AT298; AV347; AX 357; AY449 103983

I name thy hallowed name (Benson) S253; AX63 103984

I near the grave, where'er I go (Brorson) N603 103985

I need no other plea (Elliott) AZ1226 103986

I need not care if days to come be dark or fair (Bradley) BR253 103987

I need thee every hour (Hawks) A438; D602; G232; H55; I506; J479; L401; M629; N462; P 319; R324; S332; T407; U303; V492; W700; Z341; AC150; AD275; AE196; AF342; AG 170; AH322; AK469; AL493; AM710; AO640; AP480; AR 306; AS218; AT334; AU193; AV346; AW187; AX354; AY68; BB258; BC79; BE137; BF364; BY475; BZ 103988

I need thee, Lord (Lear) R The way is dark 103989

I need thee, O I need thee (Lowry) R I need thee every hour (Hawks) 103990

I need thee, precious Jesus (Whitfield) D601; E576; K367; N450; O231; P155; AI221; AL 487; AM419; AO271; AP414; AS216; AT221; AV153; AX338; AY73; AZ836; BA412; BB605; BQ41 103991

I never can forget the day (Van de Venter) AU95 103992

I now have found for hope of heaven (Rothe) AK224 103993

I once was a stranger to grace and to God (McCheyne) V307 103994

I open wide the portals of my heart (Hoppe) M203 103995

I ought to love my Saviour (---) P372 103996

I owe the Lord a morning song (Herr) AX58; AY278 103997

I place myself in Jesus' hands (Spitta) O163 103998

I praise thee, Lord, for bless-

ings sent (Johnson) BE138; BX256 103999
I praise thee, O my God and Father (Mentzer) O10 104000
I praised the earth, in beauty seen (Heber) A306; F173; X 533 104001
I pray thee, dear Lord Jesus (Kingo) Q655 104002
I pray thee, Lord, to guide my ways (Watts) BI4 104003
I rejoiced when I heard them say (Ladies of the Grail) BSp.42 104004
I saw a fair maiden sitten and sing (English trad carol, 15th c) BG182 104005
I saw a mighty angel fly (---) BC255 104006
I saw a way-worn trav'ler (Matthias) AY132 104007
I saw Him in childhood with eyes brightly beaming (Birkedal) P308 104008
I saw One hanging on a tree (Newton) AU410 104009
I saw One weary, sad, and torn (Smith) BB371 104010
I saw the city of the Lord (Tarrant) Y62; AN394; AQ 204; BX428 104011
I saw the cross of Jesus (Whitfield) AT190; AU20 104012
I saw the holy city (Thring) I626 X I heard a sound a voices 104013
I saw three ships come sailing in (English trad carol) BG18 104014
I say to all men, far and near (Hardenburg) AB148; AZ95 104015
I see a Man at God's right hand (Bonar) AZ1435 104016
I see by rays surrounded (St Bernard of Clairvaux) BP71 104017
I see my Jesus crucified (---) BQ24 104018
I see my Saviour languish (Wobeser) AZ792 104019
I see the crowd in Pilate's hall (Bonar) AZ106 104020
I see the wrong that round me lies (Whittier) AN256; BX 253 104021
I see thee standing, Lamb of God (Brorson) M407; P220 104022
I serve a living Saviour (Ackley) AE287; AT279 104023
I shall approach the altar of the Lord (Burke) BL42 104024
I shall be like Him (Spencer) R When I shall reach104025
I shall go out as all men go (Pulsifer) Y130 104026
I shall know Him, I shall know Him (Crosby) R When my life work is ended 104027
I shall not want; in deserts wild (Deems) I436 104028
I shot an arrow into the air (Longfellow) AC503 104029
I sing a song of the saints of God (Scott) A243; AF481; BY259 104030
I sing of a maiden that is makèless (English trad carol, 15th c) BG183 104031
I sing the almighty power of God (Watts) H102; R84; S65; U12; V97; AE56; AF68; AG 37; AI43; AM106; AR95; AW 47; BB93; BD38; BV241; BX 64; BY58; BZ 104032
I sing the birth was born tonight (Jonson) F70; BG168 104033
I sing the mighty power of God (Watts) R84 X I sing the almighty power 104034
I sing the praise of love unbounded (Tersteegen) AK17 104035
I sing to thee with voice and heart (Gerhardt) O384; AI 294 104036
I smite upon my guilty breast (Gregor) AZ688 104037
I sought his love in sun and stars (Clark) Y8; Z385; AC142; AR89 104038
I sought the Lord, and afterward I knew (Holy songs, carols and sacred ballads,

1878) A405; B398; G316; J473; R402; S324; U193; Z403; AD 281; AF408; AG220; AI133; AK237; AM397; AR179; BR417; BY499; BZ 104039

I sought thee round about, O thou my God (Heywood) X534 104040

I stand all amazed at the love Jesus offers (Gabriel) BC80 104041

I stand amazed in the presence (Gabriel) AH304; AT139; AX 24 104042

I stood alone at the bar of God (Hussey) AU447 104043

I stood at the time-beaten portals (Teasley) AX296 104044

I surrender all (Van Deventer) R All to Jesus I surrender 104045

I thank the Lord, my Maker (MacKellar) AX632; AY302 104046

I thank thee, Lord, for life (Butcher) AC166; BY500 104047

I thank thee, Lord, for precious things (Larcom) AN271; BX 320 104048

I thank thee, Lord, for strength of arm (Davis) S397; Y211; Z499; AD320; AN279; AR375; BD135; BF505; BX334 104049

I thank thee, Savior, for the grief (Loy) M277 104050

I thank thee that how e'er we climb (Coates) Y154; AB302 104051

I thank thee, uncreated Sun (Scheffler) I367 104052

"I the good fight have fought." (Wesley) I391 104053

I think of a city I have not seen (Tuttle) AY187 104054

I think that I shall never see (Kilmer) AC437 104055

I think when I read that sweet story of old (Luke) A246; B350; D562; E595; G440; H452; I682; J497; K557; L450; N649; P359; R460; S442; U325; V645; W82; Z213; AD475; AE433; AF 483; AH553; AI384; AK460; AL603; AM650; AO622; AP 738; AR549; AS398; AT506; AU316; AV86; AW427; AY 342; AZ499; BA832; BB422; BD64; BR539; BV346; BY 120 104056

I thirst, thou wounded Lamb of God (Zinzendorf, N. L.) H339; I335; AO292 104057

I thought upon the days of old (U. P. Psalter, 1912) T143; AJ212 104058

I to the hills will lift mine eyes, From whence doth come mine aid? (Scottish Psalter, 1650) X410; AF85; AL680; AP108; BY59 104059

I to the hills will lift my eyes, O whence shall come my aid (U. P. Psalter, 1912) R377; AJ344; BZ 104060

I trusted even when I said (Ladies of the Grail) BS p. 36 104061

I vow to thee, my country, all earthly things above (Spring-Rice) Y126 X I vow to thee, my country, all other things above 104062

I vow to thee, my country, all other things above (Spring-Rice) F579; X319; Y126; AC331; BY642 104063

I wait for thy salvation, Lord (Watts) V402 104064

I waited for the Lord Most High (U. P. Psalter, 1912) AJ111; AM523 104065

I waited for the Lord my God, and patiently did bear (Scottish Psalter, 1650) AL648; AP36; AW585; BY501 104066

I waited for the Lord my God, Yea patiently drew near (U. P. Psalter, 1912) R413; T72; AJ108 104067

I walk amidst thy beauty forth (Gill) AN136; AQ327; BX 166 104068

I walk in danger all the way (Brorson) O269; P313; Q413 104069

I walk the unfrequented road (Hosmer) AQ277 104070
I walk with Love along the way (Ayers) BE139 104071
I wander through the stilly night (Curtis) BC294 104072
I wandered in the shades of night (Van Deventer) AU376 104073
Iwwant a principle within (Wesley) G299; I320; BR291; BZ 104074
I want to be a worker for the Lord (Baltzell) AX184 104075
I want to be more like Jesus (Stillman) AS226; AX376 104076
I want to love Him more (Snyder) R There is a story 104077
I was a wandering sheep (Bonar) H299; I300; L128; V382; AA 105; AI222; AM396; AV171; AZ1489; BA454 104078
I was made a Christian (Jones) K552 104079
I was once far away from the Saviour (Bobbitt) AX340 104080
I was sinking deep in sin (Rowe) AH340; AT212; AU352; AX330 104081
I was wandering and weary (Faber) AL484; AP422 104082
I was wandering in a wilderness of deep despair and sin (Smith) AX472; AY124 104083
I will a little pilgrim be (Cennick) AZ370 104084
I will arise and to my Father go (Earle) X411 104085
I will be true to Thee, Lord (Morris) R Fully surrendered, Lord divine 104086
I will bless thee, said the Saviour (Kretzmann) M532 104087
I will early seek the Saviour (Bateman) BB417 104088
I will ever sing thy praises (Gotter) AK18 104089
I will extol thee, O my God (U. P. Psalter, 1912) AJ394 104090
I will follow the upward road today (Edgar) AC502 104091
I will follow thee, my Saviour (Lawson) BB266 104092
I will guide thee, I will guide thee (Niles) R Precious promise 104093
I will hasten to Him (Hartsough) R I am resolved no longer to linger 104094
I will leave my Jesus never! (Keimann) O338 104095
I will love thee, all my treasure (Scheffler) AO293 104096
I will never, never leave thee (---) BB397 104097
I will never turn back, He's my light (Grisham) R Once I wandered 104098
I will not be afraid (Govan) AE453; AR323 104099
"I will not forget thee" (Gabriel) R Sweet is the promise 104100
I will press the battle on till the victory is won (Henry) R I am fighting 104101
I will rejoice in God, my Saviour (LaTrobe) AZ1414 104102
I will sing my Maker's praises (Gerhardt) O436; Q25; AA65 104103
I will sing of Jesus' love (Belden) BB529 104104
I will sing of my Redeemer (Bliss) AI10; AM681; AT143; AU388; AX8 104105
I will sing the wondrous story (Rowley) W683; AE293; AK 465; AM709; AO651; AT144; AU377; AV315; BV261; BY 502 104106
I will sing to my Creator (Gerhardt) AZ1082; BA28 104107
I will sing to you a song of that beautiful land (Gates) G525; AM729; AS472; AU42; AV399; AX588; AY164; BB552 104108
I will work, I will pray (Baltzell) R I want to be a worker 104109
I wonder, often wonder (Hoffman) AX30; AY346 104110
I worship thee, Lord Jesus

(Littledale) A252 104111
I worship thee, most gracious God (Faber) G328; I480; AV61; AZ209; BX302 104112
I worship thee, O Holy Ghost (Warren) G174; I186 104113
I worship thee, sweet will of God (Faber) AV61 X I worship thee, most gracious God 104114
I would be closer my Saviour (Warren) AX381 104115
I would be, dear Saviour, wholly thine (Belden) BB597 104116
I would be true for there are those who trust me (Walter) Y180; Z361; AB236; AC177; AD489; AE445; AF489; AG309; AH433; AK448; AL341; AN559; AR308; AS319; AT315; AU368; AW207; BB425; BD101; BF457; BK29; BZ 104117
I would choose to be a doorkeeper (Hinkson) X196 104118
I would gather treasures in heaven (Overby) P378 104119
I would love thee, God and Father (Guyon) AX452; AY82; AZ951 104120
I would not have my way, dear Lord, but thine (Olinger) AX 393 104121
I would not live alway; I ask not to stay (Muhlenberg) H485; I584; L565; M300; O580; Q588; V674; AA535; AZ487 104122
I would not reach the mountain's crest (Coblentz) AB304 104123
I would that I might walk, dear Lord (McManus) AY148 104124
Ich bete an die macht der liebe (Tersteegen) AW517b; BW517 104125
Ich bin bei Gott in Gnaden (Dach) BT372 104126
Ich bin ein Gast auf Erden (Gerhardt) BT586 104127
Ich bin getauft auf deinen Namen (Rambach) BT298 104128
Ich freue mich in dir (Ziegler) BT93 104129
Ich hab ein schön neu Leid gemacht (H. Landis) BU132 104130
Ich habe g'nug: mein Jesus lebet noch (Möller) BT196 104131
Ich habe nun den Grund gefunden (Rothe) BT385 104132
Ich halte Gott in allem stille (Franck) BT529 104133
Ich komm' zu deinem Abendmahle (Heyder) BT315 104134
Ich singe dir mit Herz und Mund (Gerhardt) BT569 104135
Ich trete frisch (Molanus) BT 310 104136
Ich weiss, an wen ich gläube (Neumeister) BT381 104137
Ich weiss ein lieblich Engelspiel (Laufenberg) BG145b 104138
Ich weiss einen Strom, dessen herrliche Flut (Hull. The Casket, 1865) AW232b 104139
Ich weiss, wer Gottes Wort bekennt (Ausbund) BU15 104140
Ich will dich lieben, meine Stärke (Scheffler) BT399 104141
Ich will lieben und mich üben (Unparth. G. B.) AY19d 104142
Ich will loben den Herren (Ausbund. Psalm 34) BU126 104143
Ich will von ganzem Herzen mein (Ausbund) BU116 104144
If any little word of mine (Belden and "A. N. O.") BB 629 104145
If Christ is mine, then all is mine (Beddome) AO281; AZ 138 104146
If Christ who once was slain (Cowley Carol book) BN45 X This joyful Easter-tide 104147
If God be on my side (Gerhardt) L528 104148

If God had not been on our side (Luther) Q267 104149
If God Himself be for me (Gerhardt) K335; M274; N473; O272; P275; Q528; AA526 104150
If God were not upon our side (Jonas) AA284 104151
If great wonders thou desirest (Latin) BQ100 104152
If human kindness meets return (Noel) I236; AZ1451 104153
If I can keep one spirit singing (Marlatt) AC242 X If I can stop one heart from breaking (Dickinson) 104154
If I can stop one heart from breaking (Dickinson) Y226; AC242 104155
If I come to Jesus, He will make me glad (Crosby) W669; AP 759; BV349 104156
If I walk in the pathway of duty (Oatman) AX580 104157
If I would be a child of God (Forney) AX174 104158
If Jesus Christ is a man (Gilder) AC460 104159
If, now, thou seekest miracles (Franciscan manual) BN173 104160
If, on a quiet sea, toward heaven (Toplady) G321; H355; I446; V433; AI335; AV291; BB249; BZ 104161
If on our daily course, our mind (Keble) BE140 X Now every morning is the love 104162
If only I have thee (Hardenberg) AZ1227 104163
If our all on Christ we venture (Zinzendorf, N.L.) AZ258 104164
If our God had not befriended (Churton) BH123 104165
If the Lord build not the house (Baum) BE141 104166
If the Lord does not build the house (Ladies of the Grail) BSp.48 104167
If the world from you withold of its silver and its gold (Tindley) AX468 104168
If there be that skills to reckon (St Thomas à Kempis) E250 104169
If there's sunshine in your heart (Dungan) R You can make the pathway bright 104170
If thou but suffer God to guide thee (Neumark) G272; I476; J568; K398; L485; M285; O 230; P299; Q518; R344; S105; W541; Z404; AA498; AB225; AF83; AG156; AI439; AK300; AL423; AM567; AP500; BA 718; BI46-D; BV523; BY580; BZ 104171
If thou impart thyself to me (Wesley) L423 104172
If thou wouldst have the dear Saviour from heaven (Oatman) AX430 104173
If thou wouldst life attain (Caswall) AZ1253 104174
If, through unruffled seas, toward heaven (Toplady) V433 X If, on a quiet sea, toward heaven 104175
If to Jesus for relief, My soul hath fled (Newton) AZ1478 104176
If we have forgotten the name of our God (U.P. Psalter, 1912) T83; AJ123*; AM515* *refrain unusual 104177
If ye would hear the angels sing (Greenwell) BG134 104178
If you are tired of the load of your sin (Morris) AT230; AX261 104179
If you could hie to Kolob (Phelps) BC257 104180
If you from sin are longing to be free (Jackson) AX256 104181
If you only knew my Saviour (DeArmond) AU421 104182
Igjennem Nat og Trängsel (Ingemann) Y305; BT481 104183
Ihr Christen g'mein, die ihr seyd rein (H.Betz) BU106 104184
Ihr Christen rein, allsammt gemein (M.Schneider & H. Betz) BU101 104185
Ihr jungen Helden, aufgewacht

(Unparth. G. B.) AY28d 104186
Ihr Kinder Gottes alle (Ausbund) BU124 104187
Ihr Kinderlein, kommet, o kommet doch all'! (Christian Schmidt) BW413 104188
I'll exchange my cross for a starry crown (Gabriel) R Just a few more days 104189
I'll glory in nothing but only in Jesus (Scheffler) AZ488 104190
I'll go, I'll go, A help to my Lord to be (Rowe) R My Saviour needs helpers 104191
I'll go where you want me to go, dear Lord (Brown) R It may not be on the mountain's height 104192
I'll hear what God the Lord will speak (Scottish Psalter, 1650) AP70 104193
I'll live for Him who died for me (Hudson) R My life, my love, I give to thee 104194
I'll make it my home some day (Morris) R I've heard of a beautiful city 104195
I'll of salvation take the cup (Scottish Psalter, 1650) AL676; AP103 104196
I'll praise my Maker while I've breath (Watts) G513; I534; L91; V516; AA73; AL10; BC 254; BY60; BZ 104197
I'll praise my Maker whilst I've breath (Watts) AA73 X I'll praise my Maker while I've breath 104198
I'll praise my Maker with my breath (Watts) V516 X I'll praise my Maker while I've breath 104199
I'll praise thee with my heart and tongue (Gerhardt) AZ174; BA 655 104200
I'll sing a hymn to Mary (Wyse) BN155; BO64 104201
I'll speak the honours of my King (Watts) V133 104202
I'll thee exalt, my God and King (---) BI21-D 104203
I'm a little pilgrim, and a stranger here (Curwen) AP784 104204
I'm a pilgrim, and I'm a stranger, I can tarry (Dana) N526; P348; V662; AI314; BB666; BE415 104205
I'm a pilgrim; I'm a stranger cast upon the rocky shore (Petersen) BC261 104206
I'm but a stranger here (Taylor) M312 X We are but strangers here 104207
I'm going home, I'm going home (Hunter) R My heavenly home is bright and fair 104208
I'm going there to meet (White spiritual) R I am a poor wayfaring stranger 104209
I'm kneeling at the threshold aweary, faint, and sore (Alexander) BR158 104210
I'm not ashamed to own my Lord (Watts) I441; K180; L517; R292; T422; V439; W507; AL349; AM429; AP 560; AW302; AX342; AZ129; BV501; BY292 104211
I'm pressing on the upward way (Oatman) AT319; AU269; AV374; AX382; AY462; BB631 104212
I'm the child of a King (Buell) R My Father is rich 104213
I'm trusting to the unseen hand (Sims) R There is an unseen hand 104214
Immaculate Mary! Our hearts are on fire (Parochial Hymn book) BO-62 X Immaculate Mary, your praises we sing 104215
Immaculate Mary! Thy praises we sing (Parochial Hymn book) BN144 X Immaculate Mary! Your praises we sing 104216
Immaculate Mary! Your praises we sing (Parochial Hymn book, 1897) BM54; BN144; BO62; BP80 104217
Immanuel see also Emanuel and Emmanuel 104218
Immanuel! God with us (Kretz-

man) M210 104219
Immanuel! Our God and Lord (Kretzmann) M525 104220
Immanuel, to thee we sing (Gerhardt) M331 X Emmanuel! we sing thy praise 104221
Immanuel, we sing thy praise (Gerhardt) O180 X Emmanuel! we sing thy praise 104222
Immortal babe, who this dear day (Hall) BG117 104223
Immortal by their deed and word (Hosmer) AN203; BD67; BX 228 104224
Immortal, invisible, God only wise (Smith) A301; E407; F372; G64; J172; R85; S66; W12; X535; Y23; Z159; AD 73; AF7; AL34; AM35; AN30; AQ41; AR20; AT43; BL93; BV 242; BX39; BY61; BZ 104225
Immortal Love, for ever full (Whittier) A360; B404; E408; F208; G120; H152; I128; J476; N196; P152; R229; S178; T387; U84; V135; W141; X536; Y68; Z254; AB171; AC140; AB250; AE98; AF230; AG116; AH424; AI113; AK242; AL123; AN80; 561; AO213; AP183; AQ142; AR201; AS117; AT277; AV178; AW173; BA82; BB141; BD70, 72; BE142; BF246; BK91; BR 418; BV537; BX71, 217; BY121, 125; BZ 104226
Immortal Love, within whose rightous will (Brooke) S303; U240; AB221 104227
Imposture shrinks from light (Scott) BE143 104228
Improve the shining moments (Baird) BC73 104229
In a lonely graveyard, many miles (---) AY504 104230
In a world where sorrow, Ever will be known (Smith) BC74 104231
In age and feebleness extreme (Wesley) I746 104232
In all my vast concerns with thee (Watts) V109; BR277 104233
In another land and time (Smith) X362 104234
In Asia born, from Asia hailed (Dearmer) X91 104235
In atmosphere of Love divine ("H") BE144 104236
In Bethlehem, 'neath starlit skies (Stutsman) G103; BZ 104237
In Bethlehem, that fair city (English trad carol, 15th c) BG120 104238
In boundless mercy, gracious Lord, appear (Swedenborg) BR38 104239
In calm and cool and silence (Niles, from Whittier) BK100 104240
In Christ I feel the heart of God (Larcom) Y66; AB86 104241
In Christ there is no East or West (Oxenham) A263; G 507; J342; R479; S341; U375; X537; Y273; Z480; AB357; AC299; AD378; AE403; AF 414; AG234; AI429; AK406; AL 252; AN413; AR388; AS362; AT 443; AW320; BB436; BF488; BK112; BL69; BV420; BY661; BZ 104242
In Christi Wunden schlaf' ich ein (Eber) BT585 104243
In darkness as in light (Montgomery) BT616 X For-ever with the Lord 104244
In days of old on Sinai (St Cosmas) F559 104245
In days of yore, from Britain's shore (---) (Canadian national hymn) P415 104246
In death's strong grasp the Saviour lay (Luther) M432; N134; AA224 104247
In dich hab' ich gehoffet, Herr (Reusner) BT524 104248
In doubt and temptation, I rest, Lord, in thee (U.P. Psalter, 1912) AJ202 104249
In dulci jubilo (Suso) BG86; BN15; BT92 104250
In duties and in sufferings, too (Beddome) AZ121; BA83 104251
In every condition, in sickness and health ("K" in Rippon)

BR248 X How firm a foundation 104252

In every town and village, the bells do ring (Wilson) BG162 104253

In every trouble sharp and strong (Killinghall) V327 104254

In every waking moment (---) AX344 104255

In evil long I took delight (Newton) V290; BA442 104256

In excelsis gloria (English trad. 15th c) R When Christ was born of Mary free) 104257

In exile here we wander (Cooke) D74 104258

In Flander's fields the poppies blow (McCrae) Y120 104259

In from the highway, in from the byway (Hott) AY480 104260

In from the highways and byways of sin (---) AS376; AX218; AY338 104261

In full and glad surrender (Havergal) BV632; BY439 104262

In full assurance of thy grace (U.P. Psalter, 1912) AJ185 104263

In God I find a precious gift (Seymer) BE146 104264

In God, my faithful God (Weingartner??) Q526; AA508; AZ 555 104265

In God, my Saviour I put my trust alone (Danish, 1600) O350; P 287 104266

In God rejoice! his good endures (Dearmer) X412 104267

In God the holy, wise and just (Moise) BH73 104268

In God will I trust, though my counselors say (U.P. Psalter, 1912) T15; AJ20 104269

In God's name let us on our way! (Bonn, G-B., 1561) M265 104270

In Gottes Namen heb'n wir an (Ausbund) BU121 104271

In grace the holy God did full salvation plan (Whittle) AU469 104272

In heaven above, in heaven above (Laurentii) J146; M317; N628; O263; P433 104273

In heaven is joy and gladness (Brun) O248; P344 104274

In heavenly love abiding (Waring) A431; B224; G352; H 315; I452; J574; O343; P199; R417; S284; U239; V397; W442; Y38; Z384; AB202; AC48; AD243; AE222; AF 343; AG217; AH377; AK301; AL281; AN249; AP439; AR266; AS262; AT303; AV231; AY 304; BA717; BB674; BD57; BE148; BF412; BK73; BR 421; BV524; BX466; BY581; BZ 104275

In him rejoice with heart and voice (Blatchford) R A gladsome hymn 104276

In His love abiding, Wait on the Lord (Wengel) Z391 104277

In His name I'll bear the cross (---) R Am I a soldier (Watts) 104278

In His own raiment clad (Monro) B163; D106; E656 104279

In His temple now behold Him (Pye) B273; D151; J142; K50; L229; M379; N202; Q139; AA186 104280

In holy contemplation, we sweetly now pursue (Cowper) N 179; O460 104281

In homes where pride and splendor (Radford) Z501 104282

In hope my soul, redeemed to bliss unending (Andersdatter) M292; N602; Q432 104283

In house and home where man and wife (Landstad) O229; Q624 104284

In humble, grateful lays (Foster) AZ1120; BAp.151 104285

In humility, our Savior, Grant thy Spirit (Gabbott) BC49 104286

In hymns of praise your voices raise (Blenkhorn) BC9 104287

In Jesus I find rest and peace (Danish, 1740) O418 104288

In Jesus' love abiding (Waring)

BR421 X In heavenly love abiding 104289
In Jesus' name our work must all be done (Frederiksen) O247 104290
In joyful high and holy lays (Mund) BB650 104291
In Judah's land God is well known (Scottish Psalter, 1650) AP63 104292
In life's earnest morning (Oakley) Y139; Z474; AB314; AC213; AN475; BD197; BF630; BX537 104293
In loud exalted strains (Francis) D482; Q638; AA457; AS442 104294
In love divine all earth-born fear and sorrow (Campbell) BE149 104295
In loving adoration we come to worship thee (Penfield) AH184 104296
In loving-kindness Jesus came (Homer) AI130; AM672; AT 202 104297
In manus tuas, Domini (Latin) BN193 104298
In many a stone-bound city (Sampter) BH180 104299
In memory of the Crucified (Kooyman) BC99 104300
In memory of the Saviour's love (Cotterill) G413; Z462; AE332; AI166; AL225; AR515; AS459; AT393; AX177; AY255; BF598; BZ 104301
In mercy, in goodness, how great is our King (McKenzie) BE150 104302
In mercy, Lord, incline thine ear (Wise) BH211 104303
In mercy, Lord, remember me (Watts) AX71 X And now another day is gone 104304
In mercy, Lord, this grace bestow (Zinzendorf, N. L.) AZ325; BA 538 104305
In mercy, not in wrath (Newton) D352 104306
In my quiet contemplation (Wallin) N498 104307
In numbers, and but these few (Herrick) BG176 104308
In one fraternal bond of love (Montgomery) L283 104309
In one true God we all believe (Tranovsky) Q253 104310
In our dark and doubtful strife (Brooke) BX257 104311
In our day of thanksgiving one psalm let us offer (Draper) F476 104312
In our dear Lord's garden (Armitage) AP744 104313
In our hearts celestial voices (Corelli) AL621; AP809; BB 419 104314
In our work, and in our play, Jesus be thou ever near (Dix) E596; F454 104315
In our work and in our play, Jesus be thou ever near (Piggott) X538 104316
In our work and in our play, Jesus ever with us stay (Wills) G448; AW417 104317
In Oxford town the faggots they piled (---) AC511 104318
In Paradise reposing (Littledale) E355 104319
In peace and joy I now depart (Luther) Q137; AA185 104320
In peace will I lie down to sleep (Scriver) AZ904 104321
In pleasant lands have fallen the lines (Flint) AN370; AW368; BX406 104322
In quiet hours the tranquil soul (Larned) AN267; BX318 104323
In remembrance of thy suffering (Stephens) BC258 104324
In seasons of grief to my God I'll repair (Hunter) AY328 104325
In singing till his heaven fills (Meredith) AQ8 104326
In songs of sublime adoration ("K" in Rippon's Selection, 1787) AI128 104327
In sorrow and affliction (Howard) BR404 104328
In speechless prayer and reverence (Glover) BE151 104329

In spirit I am waiting (Zinzendorf, N. L.) AZ1117 104330
In stable lowly, a little child is born (French trad) BD213 104331
In stature grows the heavenly child (Santeüil) E46; AZ210 104332
In sunny days, when all is bright (Haigh) BY476 104333
In sunshine and in storm, O God (Mayer) BH90 104334
In sweet communion, Lord, with thee (U.P. Psalter, 1912) R 126; T136; AJ203; AM557 104335
In sweet fields of autumn (Madison) AQ276 104336
In tenderness He sought me (Walton) U167; AU65 104337
In tenebris nostrae et densa caligne mentis (Camerarius) BT522 104338
In that beautiful land I'll be (Nicholson) R There's a beautiful land on high 104339
In that poor stable, how charming Jesus lies (French trad carol) BG75 104340
In that sad memorable night (Wesley) AZ653 104341
In the beginning was the word (Longfellow) AR110 104342
In the bleak mid-winter (Rossetti) A44; E25; F67; G104; J36; W 50; X75; AF128; AL56; BG187; BV100; BY99; BZ 104343
In the blood from the cross (Oatman) BB275 104344
In the candles' rays I see (Levinger) BH206 104345
In the Christian's home in glory (Harmer) AU84; AV358; AX 574 104346
In the cross, in the cross, Be my glory (Crosby) R Jesus, keep me near the cross 104347
In the cross of Christ I glory (Bowring) A336; B152; D359; E409; G149; H175; I143; J64; K62; L231; M166; N103; O262; P193; Q354; R195; S154; T343; U94; V143; W113; Y377; Z237; AA95; AB140; AC124; AD157; AE116; AF157; AG94; AH292; AI76; AK164; AL100; AN190; AO165; AP199; AR176; AS 138; AT100; AU180; AV113; AW110; AY188; AZ239; BA 197; BB125; BF316; BV556; BX213; BY141; BZ 104348
In the dark and cloudy day (Rawson) V424 104349
In the day of all days when the world (Latta) AX292; AY 152 104350
In the early days of childhood (Smith) AY486 104351
In the early morning, dark shadows stay (Leyda) S493; AL620 104352
In the field with their flocks abiding (Farrar) I117; W43 104353
In the fullness of thy grace (U.P. Psalter, 1912) AJ10 104354
In the glad time of the harvest (Santee) BB539 104355
In the good ship of our Captain (Kuipers) AI393 104356
In the harvest field there is work to do (Blackall) AU327; AX183; AY528 104357
In the heart of Jesus (Pugh) BB348 104358
In the heavens the Lord Almighty (U.P. Psalter, 1912) AJ282 104359
In the holy Father's keeping (Miller) M585; N140 104360
In the hour of my distress (Herrick) E410 104361
In the hour of trial (Montgomery) A334; B147; D340; G274; H373; I431; J561; K391; L524; M272; N257; O371; P169; Q516; R394; S255; U238; V171; W525; Y104; Z333; AA409; AB 195; AC178; AD148; AE245; AF374; AG151; AH439; AI 286; AK160; AM475; AO407; AP240; AR303; AS321; AT

317; AU467; AV187; AW195; AY477; AZ764; BA581; BB327; BF479; BR347; BZ 104362
In the land of fadeless day (Clements) AI342; AM730; AS470; BB558 104363
In the land of strangers (Bonar) AP407 104364
In the Light all light excelling (Coffin) BO6 104365
In the lonely house of mourning (Bird) AZ908 104366
In the lonely midnight (Williams) AC89; AD473; AH251; AN173; AQ292; BD215; BF287; BX 531 104367
In the Lord's atoning grief (St Bonaventura) F105 104368
In the midst of earthly life (Luther) Q590 104369
In the morning I will pray (Furness) BX126 104370
In the morning, noon, and evening (Wieand) R On the radiant threshold 104371
In the name of God, the Father (Hewett) AO418 104372
In the name of Jesus (Noel) W178 X At the name of Jesus 104373
In the Name which earth and heaven (Ellerton) D292; Q632; AA451 104374
In the old-time way (McKinney) R As He heard His waiting people 104375
In the place of sorrow, waiting (Dearmer) X138 104376
In the quiet consecration (Coote) BV379 104377
In the quiet hours of morning (Slemp) AU107 104378
In the resurrection, In the resurrection (Slovak, 1674) Q603 104379
In the rifted Rock I'm resting (James) AX512; AY453 104380
In the secret of His presence (Goreh) M211 104381
In the shadow of His wings (Atchinson) AU135 104382
In the silent midnight watches (Coxe) AX244 104383
In the still air the music lies unheard (---) U261 104384
In the sun and moon, and stars (Heber) BB178 104385
In the sweet by and by (Bennett) R There's a land that is fairer than day 104386
In the temple where our fathers (Söderberg) N349 104387
In the vineyard of our Father (MacKellar) D577; AZ1412 104388
In the warfare that is waging (Martin) AU358 104389
In thee alone, O Christ, my Lord (Schneesing) O96; Q 319 104390
In thee I love, and move and am (Erskine) AZ199 104391
In thee, Lord, have I put my trust (Reusner) Q524; AA 495 104392
In thee, my God and Saviour, forevermore the same (Baum) BE153 104393
In thee, O God, the hosts above (Palmer) BX240 104394
In thee, O Lord, I out my trust, I call upon thy name (---) T51; AJ80 104395
In thee, O Lord, I put my trust, Shamed let me never be (U.P. Psalter, 1912) T 130; AJ190 104396
In thee, O Spirit true and tender, I find my life (Fox) BE154 104397
In thee, our Father, are we all at home (Patterson) AN86 104398
In these our days exalt thy grace (Zinzendorf, N.L.) AZ1426; BA338 104399
In thine arm I rest me (Franck) AZ1075 104400
I this lone hour of deep distress (---) AY180 104401
In this our happy Christmastide (Brorson) O185 104402
In this peaceful house of prayer (Hymns of the Spirit, 1864) AN22; BR19; BX338 104403
In this Sacrament, Lord Jesus (Furniss) BN95; BO40

104404
In this Sacrament, sweet Jesus (Furniss) BO40 X In this Sacrament, Lord Jesus 104405
In this sepulchral Eden (Gregor) AZ1500; BA212 104406
In this stern hour when the spirit falters (Johnson) AQ55 104407
In this world of sin and care (Oatman) AX410; AY66 104408
In this world so full of snares (LaTrobe) AZ587 104409
In this world, the Isle of Dreams (Herrick) X348 104410
In this your month, Creation's Queen ("M.A.", Father) BN146 104411
In those twelve days let us be glad (English trad carol, 1625) R What are they that are but one? 104412
In thy cleft, O Rock of ages (Crosby) L419; AE286; AX 514 104413
In thy dear name and by thy favor (Lutheran. Ohio Synod G.B. 1870) M509 104414
In thy dear wounds I fall asleep (Eber) N596 104415
In thy glorious resurrection (Wordsworth) AZ647 104416
In thy great name, O Lord, we come (Hoskins) L57; AS60 104417
In thy heritage the heathen (U.P. Psalter, 1912) T147; AJ216 104418
In thy holy place we bow (Coffman) AY434 104419
In thy holy temple, O sacred place (McKinney) AU365 104420
In thy love and knowledge, gracious Saviour (Zinzendorf, N.L.) AZ 1004 104421
In thy name, O Lord, assembling (Kelly) K427; L205; N310; V1; AE28 104422
In thy peaceful house of prayer (Hymns of the Spirit, 1864) BR19 X In this peaceful house of prayer 104423
In thy service will I ever (Spitta) AZ945 104424
In thy wrath and hot displeasure (U.P. Psalter, 1912) T67; AJ102; AM408 104425
In time of tribulation (Montgomery) AZ793 104426
In token that thou shalt not fear (Alford) B344; D209; E337; F424; X250; BV339 104427
In triumph our Redeemer (Geijer) N137 104428
In vain we seek for peace with God (Watts) N420 104429
In vain would boasting reason find (Steele) L311; AA122 104430
In vision to His Saints God spake (U.P. Psalter, 1912) T165; AJ243 104431
In weariness and pain (Wesley) L254; AA504; AZ1311 104432
In yon blessed seats of heaven (---) AZ897 104433
In- a this-a band, we have sweet music (Negro spiritual) AH600 104434
Incline thine ear, O Lord, and show us mercy (Latin) BM 74 104435
Increase my faith, dear Lord, I pray (Van Hoose) AX457 104436
Infant holy, Infant lowly (Polish carol) G105; R164; AE430; BV103; BY100; BZ 104437
Infinite God, to thee we raise (Wesley) I10 104438
Ingrediente Domino in Sanctam (Latin) BQ169 104439
Inspirer and hearer of prayer (Toplady) B34; D643; L32; W560; AZ1512; BV53; BY 570 104440
Instantis adventum Dei (Coffin) BT68 104441
Integer vitae (Horace) Y297 104442
Into my heart, Into my heart (Clarke) AR653; AU321 104443
Into our hands the Gospel is given (Carruth) R Swiftly

we're turning 104444
Into the desert I was led (English trad carol) BG71b X Tomorrow shall be my dancing day 104445
Into the tent where the gipsy boy lay (Slade) AU378 104446
Into the tomb of ages past (Moise) BH156 104447
Into the woods my Master went (Lanier) G132; I745; U99; X126; Y84; Z225; AC119; AD 145; AH277; AR161; AT90; AU420; AV114; BB128; BD74 104448
Into thy gracious hands I fell (Dessler) I305; AZ922 104449
Involata integra et casta es Maria (Breviary) BQ208 104450
Invited, Lord, by boundless grace (Cronenwett) Q308; AA438 104451
Is God my strong Salvation! (Gerhardt) AZ798; BA683 104452
Is it nothing to you, all ye that pass by? (Faber, Antiphon) BV173 X O come and mourn 104453
Is my name written there! (Kidder) AX486 X I am bought not with riches 104454
Is not this the land of Beulah (---) R I am dwelling on the mountain 104455
Is there a god? The rising sun in answer warm (Brethren's Tune and hymnbook, 1879) AR77 104456
Is there a heart that is waiting? (James) AU93 104457
Is there any pleasure, any joy in life? (---) AX539 104458
Is this Jesus, then, the Lord (Churchman?, 1858) M336 104459
Is thy cruse of comfort failing! (Charles) AI274; AO472; BE 360; BR232 104460
Is thy heart right with God (Hoffman) R Have thy affections been nailed 104461
Is your all on the altar of sacrifice laid? (Hoffman) R You have longed for sweet peace 104462
Is your life a channel of blessing? (Smyth) AT438; AU61 104463
Isaiah, mighty seer, in days of old (Luther) Q249 104464
Israel, Israel, God is calling (Smyth) BC81 104465
Ist Gott für mich, so trete (Gerhardt) BT528 104466
Iste confessor Dómini (Latin, 8th c) BN182; BO268 104467
It came upon the midnight clear (Sears) A19; B79; D59; E26; F66; G92; H135; I110; J23; K29; L215; N39; P135; R160; S127; T338; U58; V116; W 47; X76; Y245; Z191; AB108; AC78; AD107; AE82; AF129; AG73; AH245; AK107; AL58; AM157; AN162; AO122; AP 170; AQ287; AR136; AS104; AT71; AU141; AV85; AW75; AZ1461; BA156; BB99; BC82; BD206; BE158; BF289; BK 146; BR548; BV104; BX191; BY101; BZ 104468
It fell upon a summer day (Brooke) G443; R461; S444; W80; X539; AD476; AG88; AL77; BY122 104469
It is a piteous thing to be (Hay) AQ154 104470
It is a thing most wonderful (How) E597; F435; W436; BV350; BY142 104471
"It is finished," all the pain (Brooke) AK156 104472
It is finished! Blessed Jesus (Maclagan) E120; F124 104473
It is finished! Christ hath known (Gillett) A78; E118; X139 104474
"It is finished." Man of Sorrows (Hedge) G139; AN185; BX203 104475
"It is finished," said my Saviour (Carnett) AU427 104476

"It is finished!" Shall we raise (A Collection of Psalms and hymns, 1830) AZ54 104477
It is good to sing thy praises (U. P. Psalter, 1912) R20; T172; AJ251 104478
It is my joy in life to find (Sherman) Y210 104479
It is no earthly summer's ray (Latin, 6th c) BO141 104480
It is not death to die (Malan) D419; H498; I585; K504; L561; O592; Q602; V675; AA533; AO 569; AZ1299; BA723 104481
It is so long a way that I must go (Luce) AN551 104482
It is something to have wept as we have wept (Chesterton) AQ101 104483
It is the day of all the year (Leonard) BG145 104484
It is the joyful Easter Time (Milner-Barry) AL618; BY 745 104485
It is well with my soul (Spafford) R When peace like a river 104486
It matters not what be thy lot (Eddy) BE160 104487
It may be at morn, when the day is breaking (Turner) AT120; AU49; AV389; AW455; BB536 104488
It may not be on the mountain height (Brown) BC75 X It may not be on the mountain's height 104489
It may not be on the mountain's height (Brown & Pryor) H398; EH427; AT425; AV379; AY105; BC75 104490
It may not be our lot to wield (Whittier) G291; I398 104491
It must be told (Wight) R 'Tis a sweet and tender story 104492
It passeth knowledge, that dear love of Thine (Shekleton) BY 594 104493
It pays to serve Jesus, it pays every day (Huston) R The service of Jesus 104494
It shall be well, let sinners know (Hoskins) V328 104495
It singeth low in every heart (Chadwick) G521; Z579; AB411; AN451; AO543; BF 654; BH220; BX473 104496
It sounds along the ages (Gannett) AN76; AQ247 104497
It swells upon the noonday breeze (Adams) Y250 104498
It was about the deep of night (De la Mare) BG163 104499
It was early in the morning (English trad carol) BG44 X Awake, awake ye drowsy souls 104500
It was on Christmas Day And all in the morning (English trad carol) BG17a 104501
It was on Holy Wednesday, And all in the morning (English trad carol) BG17b 104502
It was the calm and silent night! (Domett) X77 104503
It will open wide, yes, open wide (Underwood) R I've heard them sing again and again 104504
It's me, it's me, it's me, O Lord (Negro spiritual) AH 603 104505
I've anchored my soul in the "Haven of Rest" (Gilmour) R My soul in sad exile 104506
I've brought you here a bunch of May (English trad carol) BG48 104507
I've found a friend, O such a friend (Small) G241; H342; R220; U188; V763, 306; W705; Z290; AE305; AG162; AH323; AI108; AK474; AL128; AM 433; AP235; AR449; AT261; AU28; AV318; AW445; AX 527; BA483; BB531; BF459; BV626; BY440; BZ 104508
I've found a friend who is all to me (Scholefield) AT197; AU339 104509
I've found my Lord and He is mine (Warner) AX348 104510
I've found the pearl of greatest

price (Mason) L117; AI261; AM592 104511
I've got a robe, you've got a robe (Negro spiritual) Y319; AH601 104512
I've heard of a beautiful city above (Morris) AX605 104513
I've heard them sing again and again (Underwood) AY154 104514
I've reached the land of joy divine (Stites) AU114; BB554 104515
I've read of a world of beauty (Smucker) AY59 104516
I've seen the lightning flashing (---) AU400 104517
I've surrendered all, I've surrendered all (Oatman) R A full surrender I have made 104518
I've two little hands to work for Jesus (Ogden) Ay 300 104519
I've wandered far away from God (Kirkpatrick) AI213; AL474; AP431; AS203; AT237; AX302; BB560 104520
I've wandered far away o'er mountains cold (Crosby) R O hear my cry 104521

J

J'ai oui chanter le rossignol (French carol, 18th c) BG 140b 104522
Je sais, vierge Marie, Ce que je dois (French trad carol) BG162b 104523
Jeg gaar i Fare, hvor jeg gaar (Brorson) BT413 104524
Jeg kommer her, o söde Gud (Landstad) BT330 104525
Jeg staar for Gud, som alting veed (Landstad) BT318 104526
Jeg ved mig en Sovn i Jesu Navn (Landstad) BT592 104527
Jehova! Jehova! Jehova! Deinem Namen sie Ehre, Macht, und Ruhm (Pfeffel) BW507 104528
Jehovah from his throne on high (U.P. Psalter, 1912) T56; AJ87; AP30 104529
Jehovah God! Thy gracious power (Thomson) BR64 104530
Jehovah, God, who dwelt of old (Amis) I665; N281 104531
Jehovah hear thee in thy grief (U.P. Psalter, 1912) T30; AJ43 104532
Jehovah is my light (U.P. Psalter, 1912) T45; AJ71 104533
Jehovah is our strength (Barnard) L510 104534
Jehovah, Jehovah, Jehovah Thou art worthy (Pfeffel) AK494; AW507 104535
Jehovah, Jesus, Lord we own! (---) BI23-D 104536
Jehovah, let me now adore thee (Crasselius) O358; Q21; AA 67; AW569 104537
Jehovah, Lord of heaven and earth (---) BC83 104538
Jehovah, my God, on thy help I depend (U.P. Psalter, 1912) T9 104539
Jehovah reigns! He dwells in light (Watts) V102 104540
Jehovah reigns in majesty (U.P. Psalter, 1912) AJ265 104541
Jehovah reigns; let earth be glad (U.P. Psalter, 1912) T178; AJ260; AM59 104542
Jehovah reigns supreme! Let nations tremble now (---) T183; AJ267 104543
Jehovah sits enthroned in majesty most bright (U.P. Psalter, 1912) T173; AJ 252 104544
Jehovah the Lord, our Saviour and King (McNeely) AT494 104545
Jehovah, thee we glorify (Wallin) N316 104546
Jehovah to my prayer give ear (U.P. Psalter, 1912) T103; AJ148 104547
Jehovah's perfect law (U.P. Psalter, 1912) AJ38; AM448 104548
Jerusalem, arise, the heavenly glory view (Proud) BR212

104549

Jerusalem, du hochgebaute Stadt (Meyfart) BT619 104550

Jerusalem! high tower thy glorious walls (Meyfart) A594; B 543 104551

Jerusalem, Jerusalem! Die du so hoch gethront (---) AW125b 104552

Jerusalem, Jerusalem, thou city ever blest (Berg) N625 104553

Jerusalem, lift up thy voice (Wallin) M333; N5 104554

Jerusalem, my happy home ("F.B.P.", based on St. Augustine) A585; B514; D402; E638; F282 and 623; H505; I 608; J587; K524; L602; M314; N623; O609; Q618; V697; W 595; X395; AA558; AF312; AL461; AP635; AS481; AX610; AY143; AZ183; BA763; BB309; BJ56; BQ119; BR445; BT618; BV429 104555

Jerusalem on high, My song and city is (Crossman) E411; F280; L589; X197; AP633; AZ1189; BJ43; BV431 104556

Jerusalem, the glorious! The glory of the elect (St Bernard of Cluny) V710; AZ825 104557

Jerusalem the golden (St Bernard of Cluny) A597; B511; D408; E412; F278; G529; H514; I612; J584; K528; L585; M306; N622; O614; P431; Q613; R428; S435; T435; U432; V690; W599; X198; Y341; Z569; AA556; AB408; AD 466; AE307; AF309; AG283; AH523; AI338; AK422; AL463b; AM604; AN548; AO550; AP628; AR425; AS469; AT477; AU219; AV285; AW262; AZ824; BA748; BB300; BF657; BI18; BO203; BQ118; BR437; BV432; BX467; BY406; BZ 104558

Jerusalem, thou city fair and high (Meyfart) J588; K521; M315; N626; O610; Q619; AA 559; AZ1224 104559

Jesaia, dem Propheten, das geschah (Luther) BT249 104560

NOTE: Jesu and Jesus are interfiled because usage, even within a poem, varies in different anthologies (hymnals). 104561

Jesus all glorious, Christ all victorious (Boe) P208 104562

Jesus, all hail, who for our sin (Faber) AZ573 104563

Jesus, all my gladness (Franck) A453 104564

Jesus, all our ransom paid (Pollock) X Jesus, in thy dying woe (VI) 104565

Jesus, all our souls inspire (Foster) AZ50 104566

Jesus, all thy labor vast (Pollock) X Jesus, in thy dying woe (VII) 104567

Jesus and Joseph day after day (Glover) BY123 104568

Jesus, and shall it ever be (Grigg) A423; B135; D597; G258; H335; I443; J514; K71; L169; M219; N143; O360; P321; Q346; T428; U175; V436; AA91; AH367; AI318; AL353; AM425; AO 378; AP565; AR353; AS279; AU215; AV125; AW192; AZ 377; BA455; BB152; BY293 104569

Jesus, at thy invitation (Russell) AZ277 104570

Jesu, best and dearest (Franck) BJ57 104571

Jesus bids us shine with a pure clear light (Warner) W671; AH545; AL613; AM653; AP 768; AW420; BY746 104572

Jesus , bless us sensibly (Gregor) AZ590 104573

Jesus, bless is with thy Spirit (Toews) AX77 104574

Jesus, Brightness of the Father (St Rabanus Maurus??) Q257; AA287 104575

Jesus, by the Holy Spirit (Zinzendorf, N.L.) AZ263; BA600 104576

Jesus, call thou me, from the world to thee (Drese) AZ

511; BA930 104577
Jesus calls me, I must follow (Brown) AU443 104578
Jesus calls us; o'er the tumult (Alexander) A566; B268; D 143; E205; F533; G233; I545; J553; M200; N172; Q270; R 269; S223; T383; U284; V735; W500; X217; Y106; Z281; AB 159; AC144; AD201; AE164; AF 322; AG144; AH327; AI297; AK 207; AL358; AM491; AO376; AP553; AR243; AS229; AT360; AU159; AV188; AW140; AX40; AY474; AZ269; BA404; BB521; BF348; BR28; BV442; BY416; BZ 104579
Jesus came, the heavens adoring (Thring) D318; Q56; U124; V 184; AA131; AS162; AZ1410; BA150; BF335; BV84 104580
Jesus, cast a look on me (Berridge) L463 104581
Jesus Christ as King is reigning (Hiller) M628 104582
Jesus Christ from death hath risen (Lindenborn) F605 104583
Jesus Christ is made to me (Jones) AX314 104584
Jesus Christ is passing by(Smith) D592; AO638 104585
Jesus Christ is ris'n today, Alleluia! (Latin, 14th c) A85; B172; D112; E133; F134; G155; J92; K113; Lp. 742; M442; Q 199; R204; S163; T347; V756; W119; X145; AD159; AF187; AK166; AL105; AM198; AP215; AU32; AV115; AW114; AZ80, 87; BA234; BD245; BL30; BN 44; BO180; BQ27; BR190; BV 194; BY157; BZ 104586
Jesus Christ, my heart's true Captain (Cooke) BY294 104587
Jesus Christ, my Pride and Glory (Olearius) Q408 X Christ Himself my Pride and Glory104588
Jesus Christ my sure Defence (Luise Henriette) J294; K511; M444; O509; Q206; AA220; AK320; AW541; AZ588; BA238 104589
Jesus Christ, our blessed Saviour (Hus??) Q311; AA 441 104590
Jesus Christ, our Lord most holy (Grodzki) Q169; AM 196 104591
Jesus Christ the King of Ages ("A. E. E.") BM45 104592
Jesus Christ, thou Guiding-Star (Zinzendorf, N. L.) BA576 X Jesus Christ, thou Leading Star 104593
Jesus Christ, thou Leading-Star (Zinzendorf) AZ580; BA576 104594
Jesus Christus, Gottes Sohn Mit seiner leiblichen Person (J. Hus) BU38 104595
Jesus Christus, nostra salus (Hus??) BT311 104596
Jesus Christus, unser Heiland (Hus??) BT311 104597
Jesus, come and bless us (Latta) R Jesus, thou hast promised 104598
Jesus comes, His conflict over (Kelly) AZ615 104599
Jesus cometh to fulfill (Petersen) AZ789 104600
Jesu, coróna Virginum (Latin, 8th c) BO269 104601
Jesus, Creator of the world (Latin, 18th c) BP70; BQ 60 104602
Jesus, day by day Guide us on our way (Zinzendorf, N. L.) AZ535 X Jesus, lead the way 104603
Jesus dear, I come to thee (Tiffany) AY215 104604
Jesus, dear name! how sweet it sounds (Watts) AY273 104605
Jesu, deine Passion Will ich jetzt bedenken (Birken) BT 140 104606
Jesu, deine tiefen Wunden (Heermann) BT144 104607
Jesu Deus, amor meus (Latin) BQ315 104608
Jesus died for me, all to Him I owe (Hall) R I hear the Saviour say 104609

Jesu dulcis memoria (St Bernard of Clairvaux) BJ32b; BM28; BN64; BP22; BQ161; BT350; BW155, 171 104610
Jesus, ever loving Saviour (Holy Family hymns, 1860) BQ135 104611
Jesus! exalted far on high (Cotterill) K87; BA66 104612
Jesus, food of angels, monarch of the heart (St Alfonso M de Liguori) BQ54 104613
Jesus, for thee and thy blessed communion (German, 1712) P315 104614
Jesus, Fountain of my days (Matheson) AD247 104615
Jesus, Friend of little children (Mathams) W667; X363; BB 420; BV357; BY747 104616
Jesus, Friend, so kind and gentle (Gregory) R451; AF277 104617
Jesus, from thy throne on high (Pollock) B368; D526; K569; W469; AP776; BX528 104618
Jesus, from whom all blessings flow (Wesley) I561; AX156; AY62 104619
Jesus, full of all compassion (Turner) L383; V308; BB237 104620
Jesu, geh voran Auf der Lebensbahn (Zinzendorf) AW574b; BT410; BW574 104621
Jesus, gentlest Saviour (Faber) A348; B322; D576; E315; F418; AH541; BN96; BO42; BQ49 104622
Jesus, God of our Salvation (Zinzendorf, E.D.) AZ1106; BA797 104623
Jesus, good above all other (Dearmer) A322; E598; X540; BV263 104624
Jesu, grant me this I pray (Latin, 17th c) E413; F211; L412; BJ24 104625
Jesus, grant that balm and healing (St Bernard of Clairvaux) Q144 X O what precious balm and healing 104626
Jesu, great High-Priest of our profession (Zinzendorf, N.L.) AZ1001; BA89 104627
Jesus, guide our way (Zinzendorf, N.L.) BR387 X Jesus, lead the way 104628
Jesus, hail! enthroned in glory (Bakewell) AZ970 X Hail, Thou once despised Jesus 104629
Jesus' hands were kind hands, doing good to all (Cropper) BV352 104630
Jesus has taken a beautiful bud (Rowe) AX624 104631
Jesus hath procured salvation (Moravian hymn) AZ432 104632
Jesus, hear my humble pleading (Pohjala) J383 104633
Jesus, hear our fervent prayer (Foster) AZ1040 104634
Jesus, hear our humble prayer (Newton) Z640 104635
Jesus, hear our prayer, For thy children care (Zinzendorf, N.L.) AZ542; BA784 104636
Jesus, heed me, lost and dying (Offord) AZ427 104637
Jesus, high in glory (MacKeever) D550; N658; W666; AM661; AP754; BA831; BV353; BY 748 104638
Jesus, highest Heaven's completeness (St Bernard of Clairvaux) BO12 104639
Jesus Himself drew near (Habershon) BV186 104640
Jesus, holy, undefiled (Shapcote) W665; AP803 104641
Jesus, how good the thought of thee (St Bernard of Clairvaux) BN65 104642
Jesus, how sweet the thought of thee (St Bernard of Clairvaux) BJ32 104643
Jesus, I am resting, resting (Pigott) S327; AL505; AM139; AP525; BY582 104644
Jesus, I know, hath died for me (Rothe) K327 104645
Jesus, I live to thee (Harbaugh) B218; D666; G335; H314; K 374; L547; Q591; S246; T414; Z314; AA541; AE271; AK254;

AM438; AO377; AR451; AZ1327; BA529 104646

Jesus, I long for thy blessed communion (German, 1712) O461 104647

Jesus, I love thee fervently (Seebass) AZ1111 104648

Jesus, I love thy charming name (Doddridge) H330; V377; AV 140 104649

Jesus, I my cross have taken (Lyte) B378; D358; G261; H 351; I458; J512; K390; L436; M271; N446; O408; Q423; R 279; S274; U281; V446; W502; Z375; AA335; AD258; AE264; AG192; AH422; AI316; AK249; AL359; AM593; AO374, 375; AP558; AR357; AS235; AT387: AU34; AV176, 215; AX423; AY112; AZ956; BA457; BB267; BE166; BR460; BZ 104650

Jesus, I never can forget (Gerhardt) AW533 104651

Jesus, I will follow thee (Glenn) BB429 104652

Jesus, I will never leave (Kleimann) Q365; AA88 104653

Jesus, I will ponder now (Briken) Q140; AA192 104654

Jesus, I will trust thee (Walker) W696; AP511; BV505 104655

Jesus, immortal King, arise! (Seymour) I632 104656

Jesus, in my walk and living (Hjertén) N475 104657

Jesus in thee our hopes shall rest (Hymns of the English Conf. 1880) BR46 104658

Jesus, in thy dying woes [Seven words: Analytics not made] (Pollock) A82; B164; D530; J81; K84; L256; M398; Q180-186; AB136; AF166; AK 542; AP196; BF313 104659

Jesus, in thy thirst and pain (Pollock) X Jesus, in thy dying woes (V) 104660

Jesus, in thy transporting name (Steele) L157 104661

Jesus included me (Oatman) R I am so happy 104662

Jesus invites his saints (Watts) AO447; BB472; BY318 104663

Jesus is all the world to me (Thompson) AI398; AM664; AS282; AT155; AX23; BZ 104664

Jesus is coming, is coming (Gray) R The Saviour who loves me 104665

Jesus is coming to earth again (Morris) AT125 104666

Jesus is coming! We know not how soon (Wesley) R Christ the Lord cometh 104667

Jesus is God! The glorious bands (Faber) AZ1434; BO-9 104668

Jesus is God; the solid earth (Faber) BO-9 X Jesus is God! The glorious bands 104669

Jesus is my best of friends (Arrhenius) BR420 104670

Jesus is my Friend most precious (Arrhenius) N470 104671

Jesus is my joy, my all (Fritsch) N491 104672

Jesus is my Light, most fair (Richter) AZ870 104673

Jesus is now and ever will be (Oatman) R Christ will me His aid afford 104674

Jesus is our Shepherd (Stowell) W552; AP741; BR389 104675

Jesus is passing this way (James) R Is there a heart 104676

Jesus is pleading, He's interceding (Jeffrey) R Come home, poor sinner 104677

Jesus is standing at your heart's door (McKinney) AU101 104678

Jesus is standing in Pilate's hall (---) AX266 104679

Jesus is tenderly calling thee home (Crosby) R267; Z280; AE168; AH330; AI200; AM 697; AT229; AU57; AV334; AX228; BB569; BY417; BZ 104680

Jesus is the friend you need

(Reynolds) R When the sun shines bright 104681
Jesu, Jesu, Brunn des Lebens! (Unparth. G. B.) AY4d 104682
Jesus, Jesus, come to me (Scheffler) O169; P341; BP58; BQ131 104683
Jesus, Jesus, how I trust Him (Stead) R 'Tis so sweet to trust 104684
Jesus, Jesus, Jesus only(Ludämilia Elisabeth) M178; O353; P217; Q348; AA86 104685
Jesus, Jesus, Jesus, Sweetest name I know (Bridgers) R There's within my heart104686
Jesus, Jesus, nichts als Jesus (Ludämilia Elisabeth) BT348 104687
Jesus, Jesus, only Jesus (Ludämilia Elisabeth) O353 X Jesus, Jesus, Jesus only 104688
Jesus, Jesus, precious Jesus (---) R Precious Jesus, O to love thee 104689
Jesu, joy of man's desiring (Janus) AR111 104690
Jesus, keep me near the cross (Crosby) G248; N461; P182; R376; U218; V732; Z339; AE 172; AH293; AI79; AK462; AL 485; AM704; AO647; AP212; AR452; AS227; AT97; AU294; AV350; AW490; AX383; AY470; BB595; BZ 104691
Jesus, kind above all other (Adam of St Victor) F456 104692
Jesus, King of Glory (Davison) B523; D531; L127; N642 104693
Jesus, kneel beside me (Cross) G308; R225; S494; Y107; Z328; BF345 104694
Jesus knows all about our struggles (Oatman) R There's not a friend 104695
Jesu, komm doch selbst zu mir (Scheffler) BT356 104696
Jesus, Lamb of God, for me (Palmer) V145 104697
Jesus, lead the way (Zinzendorf, N. L.) A425; B449; D420; E E206; G336; J532; K260; L533; M283; N458; O505; Q410; R 334; W567; Z357; AA331; AB 226; AD228; AK284; AL447; AM504; AP613; AR305; AV 225; AW574a; AX500; AZ535, 541; BA696; BB676; BR387; BY544 104698
Jesus, lead thou on (Zinzendorf, N. L.) Q410 X Jesus, lead the way 104699
Jesus lebt, mit ihm auch ich (Gellert) BT201; BW543 104700
Jesus, let all thy lovers shine (Wesley) I321 104701
Jesus, let my final rest (Olson) N605 104702
Jesus, let my soul be fed (Pedersen) P103 104703
Jesus, let thy pitying eye (Wesley) H264; I491 104704
Jesus, let thy sufferings ease us (Wesley) AZ872 104705
Jesus, Light, serene, eternal (Berry) R Lo! a gleam from yonder heaven 104706
Jesus lives, and Jesus leads (Hood) AI101; BV264 104707
Jesus lives and so shall I (Gellert) V681; AK168; AM596 104708
Jesus lives! no longer now (Gellert) K512; L264; M435; AA 222; AO182; AZ589; BA239; BR185 104709
Jesus lives! The victory's won (Gellert) Q201 X Jesus lives! thy terrors now 104710
Jesus lives! thy terrors now (Gellert) A88; B176; D122; E134; F140; O331; Q201var; V169; W121; X155; AL116; AM203; AP229; AW543; BV 187; BY158 104711
Jesus, Lord, and precious Saviour (Arrhenius) J485; K357; M185; N482; P316 104712
Jesus Lord, be thou mine own (St Alfonso M. de Liguori) BQ44 104713
Jesus, Lord, hear our prayer

(Ellsworth) R Saviour, hear us, we pray 104714
Jesus, Lord, I ask for mercy (Vaughan) R God of mercy and compassion 104715
Jesus, Lord, most great and glorious (Zinzendorf, N. L.) AZ1101; BA489 104716
Jesus, Lord, of all creation (Wesley) BR24 X Love divine, all loves excelling 104717
Jesus, Lord of life and glory, Bend from heaven, (Cummins) B127; D350; E75; F321; K80; O25; W524; AM472; AP466; AZ1379; BA598; BR286; BV 488 104718
Jesus, Lord of life and glory, Hear thy people's (Petersen) AZ1079; BA935 104719
Jesus, Lord of our salvation (Newman) F573 104720
Jesus, Lord, our captain glorious (Feith) BA912 X Praise the Lord through every nation 104721
Jesus, Lord, Redeemer (Kirkland) W127; AM208; BV55 104722
Jesus, Lord, we look to thee (Wesley) X541; AS449; AW321; BA676; BB68; BV423; BZ 104723
Jesus' love, precious love (Littlewood) R There is no love like the love of Jesus 104724
Jesus' love unbounded (Zinzendorf, N. L.) AZ754; BA624 104725
Jesus, Lover of my soul (Wesley) A415; B223; D335; E414; F193; G338; H348; I463; J393; K371; L122; M204; N419; O244; P 154; Q345; R216; S233; T415; U262; V331; W414; X542; Y 373; Z414; AA107; AB204; AC157; AD212; AE173; AF210; AG153; AH355; AI245; AK316; AL266; AM427; AO336; AP417; AR405; AS212; AT156; AU172; AV233; AW158; AX509; AY314; AZ1044; BA523; BB401; BC84; BF370; BR313*, 323; BV506; BY441; BZ
* variant 104726
Jesus loves a little child (---) AY370 104727
Jesus loves me, Jesus loves me (Carey) K555; N659; AO620 104728
Jesus loves me! this I know (Warner) L491; R465; W660; AH546; AL623; AM633; AP 746; AT512; AU307; AW428; BA833; BV354; BY749 104729
Jesus loves the little children (Knowlton) AL604; AP743; AU311 104730
Jesus, loving to the end (Pollock) X Jesus, in thy dying woes (III) 104731
Jesus makes my heart rejoice (Hayn) AZ577; BA486 104732
Jesus, Mary, Joseph, help us (Vaughan) R Happy we, who, thus united 104733
Jesus, Master! at thy word (Liebenberg) O413; P209 104734
Jesus, Master, hear me now (Maxwell) U378; V551 104735
Jesus, Master of the feast (Wesley) L327 104736
Jesus, Master, Son of God (Seiss) K238; N390; P385 104737
Jesus, Master, whom I serve (Havergal) BA543 X Jesus, Master, whose I am 104738
Jesus, Master, whose I am (Havergal) J507; K375; O257; U317; V146; W509; AI182; AL379; AM494; AP556; AZ 1270; BA458, 543; BV627; 104739
Jesus may come today (Whitcomb) AM692 104740
Jesus, meek and gentle (Prynne) A358; B361; D567; E415; F194; I685; K567; W462; X543; AL 319; AP491; AZ768; BA637; BR305; BV554 104741
Jesu, meek and lowly (Collins) E416; F213; K74 104742
Jesu, meine Freude (Franck) BT347; BW564 104743
Jesus, meine Zuversicht (Luise

Henriette von Brandenburg) BT206; BW541 104744
Jesu, meines Lebens Leben (Homburg) BT151; BW535 104745
Jesus' mercies never fail (Scheffler) AZ39; BA896 104746
Jesus, merciful and mild (Hastings) D611; AM459 104747
Jesus merciful, Jesus pitying (Chao) R223 104748
Jesus, mighty King in Zion (Fellows) BC108 104749
Jesus, my all, to heaven is gone (Cennick) G199; I306; AW468; AZ413; BA443 104750
Jesus, my captain, to victory lead me (Schroeder) M251 104751
Jesus, my God; behold at length the time (Chadwick) BO167; BQ133 104752
Jesus, my great High Priest (Watts) Q220 X Join all the glorious names 104753
Jesus, my highest treasure (Liscovius) BA525 104754
Jesus, my King, thy kind and gracious scepter (Swertner) AZ706 104755
Jesus, my Lord! behold at length (Chadwick) BQ133 X Jesus, my God; behold at length 104756
Jesus, my Lord, how rich thy grace (Doddridge) I406; M253; N505; AZ128; BA563 104757
Jesus my Lord is real to me (Reynolds) AU346 104758
Jesus, my Lord, my God, my all, Hear me blest Saviour (Collins) A460; B228; D600; E417; F202; J504; K351; L155; T425; W430; Z383; AD246; AL295; AO297; AP454; AR358; AS129; AZ668; BA488; BF458; BV535 104759
Jesus, my Lord, my God, my all, How can I love thee (Faber) AH143; BN97; BO43; BP59; BQ53 104760
Jesus, my Lord, my God, The God supreme thou art (Wesley) AZ1353; BA49 104761
Jesus, my Lord, my Life, my All (Collins) Z383 X Jesus, my Lord, my God, my all 104762
Jesus, my Lord, thy nearness doth impart (Gregor) AZ523 104763
Jesus, my Lord, to thee I cry (Hamilton) AU86 X O Jesus, Lord, to thee I cry 104764
Jesus, my love, my chief delight (Beddome) AO288 104765
Jesus, my Saviour and my God (Stennett) L446 104766
Jesus, my Saviour, Brother, Friend (Wesley) AL322 104767
Jesus, my Saviour, let me be (Beddome) AY298 104768
Jesus, my Saviour, look on me (Elliott) A412; B390; D341; U236; V487; AM140; AO408; AZ15; BR304 104769
Jesus my Saviour, Look thou on me (Lyon) AX522; AY139 104770
Jesus, my Saviour, my Shepherd blest (Ingemann) M179 104771
Jesus, my Saviour, to Bethlehem came ("A. N.") AU14; AX31 104772
Jesus, my Savior true, guide me to thee (Huish) BC85 104773
Jesus, my Shepherd, let me share (Harbaugh) AO320 104774
Jesus, my strength, my hope (Wesley) A452; B215; D650; G343; I340; L200; O487; AL 422; AS452; BV522; BX310; BZ 104775
Jesus, my Truth, my Way (Wesley) I471; K340; Q433; AA 373 104776
Jesus, Name all names above (St Theoctistus) A342; E418; J67; K70; N52; O307; X101 104777
Jesus' name, Jesus' name, Source of life (LaTrobe)

BA64 X Jesus' name, Source of life 104778
Jesus, Name of wondrous grace (Brorson) M188 104779
Jesus! Name of wondrous love (How) A323; B90; D149; J50; K35; L159; M180; N51; O211; P144; Q114; W62; AA178; AP 176; AZ82; BA68 104780
Jesus' name shall ever be (Muhlenberg) BT114 104781
Jesus' name, Source of life and happiness (LaTrobe) AZ718; BA64 104782
Jesus nimmt die Sünder an (Neumeister) BT324; BW466 104783
"Jesus," O how sweet the name (Martin) R The name of Jesus is so sweet 104784
Jesus, O precious name (Hoppe) N55 104785
Jesus, o'er the grave victorious (Higbee) AO201 104786
Jesus of Nazareth, Saviour and King (Dougall) BC86 104787
Jesus, once of humble birth (Pratt) BC88 104788
"Jesus only!" in the shadow (Havergal) AZ610; BA70; BR 372 104789
Jesus, our best beloved Friend (Montgomery) BA541 104790
Jesus, our brother, strong and good (Davis) BK157 104791
Jesus, our Captain, Hope of our Salvation (Lowenstern) M161 104792
Jesus, our Captain, Hope of our salvation (Lowenstern) X Lord of our life, and God of our salvation 104793
Jesus, our Guardian, Guide, and Friend (Gerhardt) AZ567 104794
Jesu, our hope, our heart's desire (Latin, 7th c) F146; BV200 104795
Jesus, our Lord, how rich thy grace (Doddridge) N505 X Jesus, my Lord, how rich thy grace 104796
Jesus, our risen King (Allen) D367 104797
Jesus, our Saviour, grant us thy peace (Poppe) AW157a 104798
Jesus, our Saviour, only God and Lord (---) BRp.467 104799
Jesus, our triumphant Head (Hart) L270 104800
Jesus, our true and only Light (Heermann) BR40 X O Christ, our true and only light 104801
Jesus, pitying the sighs (Pollock) X Jesus, in thy dying woes (II) 104802
Jesus' prayer for all His brethren (Hay) BE157 104803
Jesus, priceless treasure (Franck) J575; M213; O351; P163; Q347; R414; X544; AA82; AF222; AI428; AK240; AM550; AW564; BV640; BY 768; BZ 104804
Jésu redémptor ómnium (Latin, 6th c) BP10; BQ155 104805
Jesus, Refuge of the weary (Savonarola) K92; N95; O264; Q145; AA210; AD150; AK155; AO164; AW536a 104806
Jesus reigns, He reigns victorious (---) R Hear the royal proclamation 104807
Jesu, Rex admirabilis Et Triumphator nobilis (St Bernard of Clairvaux) BT361 104808
Jesus, rule my thoughts and guide me (---) P365 104809
Jesus, save my dying soul (Hastings) L379 104810
Jesus, Saviour, come to me! (Scheffler) M165; Q356; AA 106 104811
Jesus, Saviour ever mild (Littledale) W468 104812
Jesus, Savior, hear our cry (Caddell) R By the blood that flowed from Thee 104813
Jesus, Savior, Heavenly Father (Pendleton) BI64 104814
Jesus, Saviour, I implore thee (Dober) AZ240; BA900 104815
Jesus, Saviour, infinite! With

thy blessed inward light (Rawson) BR202 X Come to our poor nature's night 104816

Jesus, Saviour, mighty Lord (---) BI10-D 104817

Jesus, Saviour, pilot me (Hopper) G269; H350; I482; J531; K270; L395; M169; N340; P161; Q 649; R336; S286; T408; U235; V340; W706; Y371; Z409; AB 227; AC160; AD225; AE254; AF213; AG155; AH309; AI302; AK468; AL444; AM497; AO328; AP607; AR288; AS248; AT337; AU158; AV238; AW161; AX501; AY308; BA704; BB398; BC121; BY543; BZ 104818

Jesus, Savior, risen Lord (---) BI22-D 104819

Jesus, Saviour, Son of God (Bonar) K78 104820

Jesus, Savior, thou art mine (Van Andel) AI438 104821

Jesus, Saviour, wondrous mild (Schmolck) M40 104822

Jesus selbst, mein Licht, mein Leben (Olearius) BT408 104823

Jesus shall lead me night and day (Martin) R Where He may lead me I will go 104824

Jesus shall reign where'er the sun (Watts) A542; B480; D261; E420; F220; G479; H195; I631; J307; K219; L344; M106; N368; O117; P164; Q511; R496; S377; T366; U392; V594; W388; X545; Y380; Z527; AA483; AB373; AC305; AD381; AE361; AF202; AG267; AH461; AI167; AK371; AL249; AM374; AO512; AP374; AR563; AS373; AT116; AU150; AV260; AW341; AY426; AZ303; BA94; BE271; BF527; BL59; BR60; BV320; BY184; BZ 104825

Jesus, Shepherd of the sheep (Cook) AA356 104826

Jesus, sinners doth receive (Neumeister) K325; N397; O411; Q324; W394; AA414; AI424; AM 394; BV478 104827

Jesus so lowly, Christ of the earth (Williams) X546 104828

Jesus, Solace of the soul (St Anselm of Lucca) AZ 104829

Jesu, sommo conforto, Tu se' tutto el mio amore (Savonarola) BW536 104830

Jesus, Son of God most high (Pollock) A232; V132; AL 606 104831

Jesus, Son of Mary, Fount of life alone (Swahili hymn) A223; E356; F469 104832

Jesus soon is coming (---) R Long for my Saviour I've been waiting 104833

Jesus, Source of my salvation (Homburg) AZ976; BA196 104834

Jesus spreads His banner o'er us (Park) G411; I235; BR469; BZ 104835

Jesus, stand among us (Pennefather) G593; R222; S13app.; W248; AE457; AK485; AL205; AP323; BV7; BY336; BZ 104836

Jesus, still lead on (Zinzendorf, N. L.) B449 X Jesus, lead the way 104837

Jesus, Sun of gladness (Knak) M198 104838

Jesus, Sun of righteousness (Rosenroth) L166; M564; O22; S30; W262; AL538; AP 659; AR414; AZ1200; BR90 104839

Jesus, tender Saviour, hast thou died for me? (Hodder. New S. S. hymn book 1863) AO618; AZ769; BA826 104840

Jesus, tender Shepherd, hear me (Duncan) A241; B360; D534; E599; G452; J235; K577; N661; S449; V649; W654; X364; AD 480; AH548; AK459; AL622; AM642; AP808; AW425; AZ 273; BB430; BR541; BV348; BY750 104841

Jesus, the all-restoring word (Wesley) I331 104842

Jesus, the calm that fills my breast (North) I549; AE223 104843

Jesus, the Christ of God (Bonar) AZ1309 104844
Jesus, the conqueror, reigns (Wesley) I172 104845
Jesus, the Father's only son (Latin, 6th c) E17 104846
Jesus the Glory of the Holy Angels (---) BO199 104847
Jesus, the loving Shepherd (Ogden) BB572 104848
Jesus, the mighty work achieved (Petursson) M386 104849
Jesus! the Name high over all (Wesley) G400; H461; I222; AL111; BV279; BZ 104850
Jesus, the Ransomer of man (Latin, 6th c) BP11 104851
Jesus, the sinner's Friend, to thee (Wesley) G201; H274; I 271; AZ403; BZ 104852
Jesus, the truth and power divine (Wesley) I220 104853
Jesu! -- the very thought is sweet (St Bernard of Clairvaux?) E238; F188; O154; W421; X548; AZ929 104854
Jesus, the very thought of thee (St Bernard of Clairvaux??) A462; B316; D434; E419; F189; G348; H326; I533; J481; K353; L113; M170; N139; Q350; R401; S309; T426; U76; V383; W422; X547; Y358; Z392; AA98; AB 81; AC158; AD251; AE230; AF 225; AG184; AH372; AI112; AK 274; AL298; AM542; AN205; AO290; AP449; AR109; AS290; AT135; AU241; AV139; AW155; AY417; AZ205; BA487; BB158; BC148; BF340; BJ7; BO13; BQ 17; BR412; BV536; BY205; BZ 104855
Jesu, the Virgin's Crown, do Thou (St Ambrose) E192 104856
Jesus, the weary wanderer's rest (Wesley) BR362 104857
Jesus, these eyes have never seen (Palmer) F347; H327; I537; J469; L167; S319; U229; V451; W418; X550; Z352; AD280; AI 116; AL300; AM545; AO283; AP451; BA518; BB166; BR414; BV534; BY206 104858
Jesus, thine all-victorious love (Wesley) G371; I375; BV 620; BZ 104859
Jesus, thine unbounded love (Hoppe) M160 104860
Jesus, thou all-redeeming Lord (Wesley) I263 104861
Jesus, thou art coming (A Sister of Notre Dame) BN98; BO51; BQ130 104862
Jesus, thou art mine forever (Loy) J518; M167; P318; Q 357; AA97 104863
Jesus, thou art my righteousness (Wesley) K328; L416 104864
Jesus, thou art my salvation (Cennick) AZ876 104865
Jesus, thou art the sinner's friend (Burnham) U189; V 295; AY45; AZ1455; BA601 104866
Jesus, thou divine Companion (Van Dyke) A511; Y85; AB277; AC191; AD318; AE415; AF 409; AG243; AK392; AL375; AO494; AR150; AW372; BA 547; BF442 104867
Jesus, thou hast bought us (Havergal) AO373 X Who is on the Lord's side? 104868
Jesus, thou hast promised That where two or three (Latta) BB602 104869
Jesus, thou Joy of loving hearts (St Bernard of Clairvaux??) A485; B328; D430; F387; G345; H439; I536; J483; K 354; L330; M171; N241; O419; R215; S354; T427; U67; V450; W420; X549; Z419; AB83; AD 404; AE227; AF290; AG206; A AH506; AI268; AK335; AL297; AM549; AO436; AP448; AR 202; AT136; AV134; AW171; BA524; BB154; BE56*; BM 29; BR375, 410; BV380; BY 207; BZ *much altered 104870
Jesus, thou my heart's delight (Flittner) AA89 104871
Jesus, thou shepherd of the

sheep (Kelly) BR482 104872
Jesus, thou Shepherd of us all (Hymns of the English Conf. 1880) BR42 104873
Jesus, thou Source of every good (Ringwaldt) AZ740 104874
Jesus, thou source of life, and light, and love (Hymns of the English Conf. 1880) BR113 104875
Jesus, thou source of life, impart (Doddridge) AZ687 104876
Jesus, thou who knowest death (Stockman) BR429 104877
Jesus, thou who once wast dead (Stockman) AZ860 104878
Jesus, thou wounded Lamb of God (Zinzendorf, N. L.) K358 104879
Jesus, thy blood and righteousness (Eber & Zinzendorf) G205; H286; I148; J376; K329; L418; M177; N426; O415; Q371; U93; V247; AA326; AL278; AM439; AO118; AP427; BV504; BY208; BZ 104880
Jesus, thy boundless love to me (Gerhardt) B229; D625; G222; H318; I333; J399; K355; L433; O347; P212; Q349; R404; S314; U234; V324; W432; Z380; AA84; AD262; AG164; AK273; AL296; AO287; AP453; AR181; AT288; AV184; AW170; AX42; AZ666; BA522; BB146; BF461; BZ 104881
Jesus, thy church with longing eyes (Bathurst) H469; K16; N9; Q64; V186; AA144 104882
Jesus, thy light again I view (Lange) BA459 104883
Jesus, thy love exceeds by far (Watts) AZ190 104884
Jesus, thy love unbounded (Bosworth's Hymns, 1865) J401; K363; N489 104885
Jesus, thy memory divine (St Bernard of Clairvaux) BP23 104886
Jesu, thy mercies are untold (Latin) F201 104887
Jesus, thy name hath power to bless (Förtsch) N50 104888
Jesus, thy name I love (Deck) K372; L118; U225; V456; AM546; AO284; AZ1245; BA63 104889
Jesus, thy word is my delight (Hammond) AZ115; BA5 104890
Jesus, thyself to us reveal (Watteville) AZ564; BA632 104891
Jesus 'till my latest breath May I ponder (Moravian) AZ 726 104892
Jesus, to thee be endless praise (---) BR54 104893
Jesus to thee I now can fly (Wesley) BB233 104894
Jesus, to thy cross I hasten (Harbaugh) AO353 104895
Jesus, to thy table led (Baynes) B327; D222; S361; W314; AL228; AP362; AZ1130; BA300; BF597; BR476; BY 319 104896
Jesus took the babes and blessed them (Loy) J260; M37; N233 104897
Jesus took the lambs and blessed them (Loy) N233 X Jesus took the babes and blessed them 104898
Jesus, transporting sound! (Wesley) AZ1177 X Let earth and heaven agree 104899
Jesus, truest Friend, unite All the consecrated band (Zinzendorf, N. L.) K209 104900
Jesus, united by thy grace (Wesley) G419; H427; I557; AL373; AX549; BZ 104901
Jesus walked this lonesome valley (White spiritual) BK168 104902
Jesus, we are far away (Pollock) S238; W399; AK212 104903
Jesus, we lift ourselves to thee (Beck) AZ134 104904
Jesus, we look to thee (Wesley) G25; V453; AZ1323; BY337 BZ 104905

Jesus, we love to meet thee (Moore) BY271 104906
Jesus, we thus obey (Wesley) AZ1326; BV381; BY320 104907
Jesus, we want to meet (Olude) BZ 104908
Jesus wept! those tears are over (MacDuff) I132; O463; AY211; AZ596 104909
Jesus! what a Friend for sinners (Chapman) AM432 104910
Jesus, what offering shall I give (Lange) AZ674; BY770 104911
Jesus, what precept is like thine (Livermore) BE163 104912
Jesus, whelmed in fears unknown (Pollock) X Jesus, in thy dying woes (IV) 104913
Jesus, when He left the sky (Rumsey??) AY396 104914
Jesus, when we go to rest (Lithuanian trad) BN194 104915
Jesus, where'er thy people meet (Cowper) B459; D296; E422; F245; G24; I37; S12app; U351; V570; W247; X551; Z115; AE 26; AF402; AL208; AM309; AP322; AZ395; BA371; BB515; BE227; BR15; BV8; BX46; BY 338; BZ 104916
Jesus, while our hearts are bleeding (Hastings) H496; L571; N599; AX622; AY171 104917
Jesus, who died a world to save (Hammond) AZ639 104918
Jesus who died, is now Seated upon His throne (Watts) AZ 1350; BA97 104919
Jesus, who calledst little ones to thee (Mudie) O572 104920
Jesus, who for my transgression (Russell) O299 104921
Jesus, who knows full well (Newton) V464; AY294; AZ1357 104922
Jesus, who on the cross did die (Whittle) R Would you lose your load of sin? 104923
Jesu, who this our Lententide (Latin) F85 104924
Jesus, who with thee can compare be? (Freylinghausen) AZ532; BA47 104925
Jesus, whom angel hosts adore (Bonar) AZ420 104926
Jesus, whom thy church doth own (Tersteegen) M89 104927
Jesus will I never leave (Keimann) AZ579; BA491 104928
Jesus, with thy church abide (Pollock) A233; B473; D525; G380; J153; K207; U350; W 208; AD397; AF301; AI148; AL168; AM278; AP299; AS 187; AZ1128; BA274; BF593; BI58; BR221; BY260; BZ 104929
Jesus, with thy death and passion (German) AZ426 104930
Jezu Kriste, Pane milý (Grodzki) BT169 104931
Join all the glorious names (Watts) J412; K44; L158; Q 220; W165; AA244; AF229; AM222; AO209; AZ1174; BT 220; BV266; BY175 104932
Join, all who love the Saviour's name (Medley) AE30 104933
Join, all ye ransomed sons of grace (Wesley) I576 104934
Join, earth and heaven, to bless the Lord our Righteousness (Wesley) AZ1165 104935
Join in the jubilee (Willes) R Thanks for the Sabbath School 104936
Join to render thanks and praises (Foster) AZ1392 104937
Jordanis oras praevia (Coffin) BT63 104938
Joseph, dearest, Joseph mine (German carol, 16th c) A45; BG77; BK155 104939
Joseph lieber, Joseph mein (German carol, 16th c) BG 77b 104940
Joseph, our certain hope below (Breviary, 1632) BO127 104941
Joseph, pure spouse of that immortal Bride (Latin, 1670)

BQ94 104942
Joseph was an old man (English trad carol) BG66 104943
Joses, the brother of Jesus, plodded from day to day (Kemps) AC457 104944
Joy and triumph everlastingly (Adam of St Victor) A129; E 200; F523; X291; BJ27 104945
Joy because the circling year (Latin) B561; Z447; AD186 104946
Joy, behold the Saviour (Whittle) R Fierce and wild the storm 104947
Joy-bells ringing, children singing (Pollard) AP774 104948
Joy cometh in the morning (Wienland) R O weary pilgrim, lift your head 104949
Joy dawned again on Easter Day (Latin, 4th c) B556; G157; AF188; AG104; AW415 104950
Joy fills our inmost hearts today (Dix) B552; D539; K534; BR 141 104951
Joy is a fruit that will not grow (Newton) G357; I546 104952
Joy to the world! The Lord is come (Watts) A319; B101; D324; G89; H141; I107; J15; K34; L 210; M346; N32; O201; P132; R161; S122; T331; U57; V118; Y360; Z190; AA158; AB109; AC 76; AD104; AE83; AF130; AG 65; AH264; AI60; AK120; AL55; AM149; AN163; AO129; AP165; AQ299; AR121; AS100; AT65; AU137; AV98; AW70; AX92; AY189; AZ191; BA160; BB189; BC89; BD207; BE164; BF290; BI10; BK142; BR140; BX195; BZ 104953
Joy to the world, the Lord will come (Watts) BC89 X Joy to the world, the Lord is come 104954
Joy to thee, O Queen of heaven (Latin, 14th c) BP33 104955
Joyful, joyful, we adore thee (Van Dyke) A281; G12; J438; R21; S5; U25; Y49; Z95; AB 12; AC43; AD9; AE10; AF8; AG5; AH200; AK21; AN42; AO79; AP148; AQ11; AR27; AS91; AT44; AV52; AW10; BA33; BD29; BF211; BZ 104956
Joyful, joyful will the meeting be (Root) R Come to the Saviour, make no delay 104957
Joys are flowing like a river (Ferguson) AE294; AI125; AU278; AW479; AX131; AY 466 104958
Jubilate! Jubilate! Jubilate! Amen (Moore) R Hark! the vesper hymn 104959
Jucundare, plebs fidelis (Adam of St. Victor) BT282 104960
Judean hills are holy (Stidger) AC456 104961
Judge eternal, throned in splendor (Holland) A518; B432; E423; J343; Q576; R517; S417; T448; W636; X552; Y277; Z545; AC277; AD432; AE397; AF435; AK 398; AL515; AM620; AN323; AP641; AS387; AW345; BV 662; BX381; BY643; BZ 104962
Judge me, God of my salvation (U. P. Psalter, 1912) T80; AJ120; AM539: AW499 104963
Judge me now, my God and Saviour (Zinzendorf, N. L.) AZ245 104964
Judge me, O God, and plead my cause (U. P. Psalter, 1912) AJ119 104965
Judge me, O Lord, for I have walked (Scottish Psalter, 1650) AP23 104966
Judge my integrity. The righteous Judge thou art (U. P. Psalter, 1912) T44; AJ70 104967
Just a few more days to be filled with His praise (Gabriel) AX569 104968
Just as I am, thine own to be (Hearn) R472; U280; W496;

Y136; Z297; AB160; AC145; AD486; AE452; AG310; AK 347; AO383; AR344; AS408; AT249; AU411; AW393; BA837; BF349; BV630; BY442; BZ 104969

Just as I am, without one plea (Elliott) A409; B139; D606; E316; F349; G198; H273; I 272; J370; K337; L494; M132; N427; O447; P248; Q388; R 272; S230; T388; U174; V296; W411; X253; Z295; AA318; AD 203; AE265; AF319; AG150; AH343; AI211; AK214; AL270; AM431; AO262, 699; AP410; AR258; AS201; AT240; AU162; AV169; AW458; AX303; AY213; AZ1144; BA433; BB222; BV472; BY443; BZ 104970

Just as seemeth good to thee (Reed) R Choose my path 104971

Just as Thou art, without one trace (Cook) N398; V256; AZ1145 104972

Just lean upon the arms of Jesus (Lewis) AX471; AY455 104973

Just now, your doubting give o'er (Morris) R If you are tired 104974

Just outside the door (Rowe) R O weary soul, the gate is near 104975

Just over the mountains in the Promised Land (Whitford arr) BB642 104976

Just when I need Him, Jesus is near (Poole) AI110; AS130; AT267; BB590 104977

K

Kee va-yom ha-zeh y'-cha-payr (Jewish traditional) BH322 104978

Keep by the mighty hand, O keep (Bonar) R Great Ruler of the land and sea 104979

Keep me near thee, blessed Jesus (Henry) AX506 104980

Keep me, O my blessed Jesus (Metzler) AY80 104981

Keep me, Saviour, near thy side (---) BR328 104982

Keep silence, all created things! (Watts) V112 104983

Keep thou my way, O Lord (Crosby) AO333 104984

Keep thyself pure! Christ's soldier, hear (Plumptre) AS 315 104985

Kimi ga yo wa Chi yo mi (Japanese national anthem) Y310 104986

Kind and loving to each other (Henry) R Let us ever love 104987

Kind Maker of the world, O hear (St Gregory the Great) A56 104988

Kinder, eilt euch zu bekehren (Unparth. G. B.) AY30d 104989

Kinder, lernt die Ordnung fassen (Unparth. G. B.) AY29d 104990

Kindle the taper like the stead-fast star (Lazarus) BH204 104991

Kindly spring again is here (Newton) E287; F607; X1 104992

King of glory, hear our cry (Caddell) R By the first bright Easter-day 104993

King of glory, King of peace (Herbert) E424; F367; X553; BJ22; BV539; BY12 104994

King of Glory! Saviour dear (Mitchell) D549 104995

King of my life I crown thee now (Hussey) AE295; AF453; AX 111 104996

King of my soul, a crown of thorns (Neumann) AK154 104997

King of saints, to whom the number (Ellerton) B287; D168; BV444 104998

King of the City Splendid (Coster) G473 104999

King Pharim sat a-musing, A-musing all alone (English trad carol) BG55(notes) 105000

Kingdom of God! The day how

blest (Beach) BX433 105001
Kingdom of light! Whose morning-star (Miller) I651 105002
Kingdoms and thrones to God belong (Watts) V104; AM67; AO88 105003
Kirken den er et gammelt Hus (Grundtvig) BT467 105004
Knock! but O most patient Lord (Holy songs, carols, and sacred ballads) BR294 105005
Know, my soul, thy full salvation (Lyte) AV215 X Jesus, I my cross have taken 105006
Know, O child, thy full salvation (Lyte) BE166 X Jesus, I my cross have taken 105007
Know this, that every soul is free (Gregg) BC90 105008
Knowledge, they say, drives wonder from the world (Noyes) AQ39 105009
Ko-dosh, ko-dosh, ko-dosh Adonoy (Jewish traditional) BH285 105010
Kol od balayvoy p'neemo (Imber) BH266 105011
Komm, du wertes Losegeld (Olearius) BT55 105012
Komm Gott Vater von Himmeln (Ausbund) BU37 105013
Komm, Heiliger Geist, Herre Gott (Luther) BT224 105014
Komm, o komm, du Geist des Lebens (Held) BT226; BW548 105015
Kommt, Brüder, steht nicht stille (Unparth. G. B.) AY31d 105016
Kommt und lasst uns Christum ehren (Gerhardt) BT90 105017
Kreutz, Verfolgung und Trübsal (Ausbund) BU80 105018
Kürzlich hab ich vorg'nommen (Ausbund) BU20 105019
Kürzlich vor wenig Tagen (Ausbund Suppl) BU2 105020
Kyrie, God Father in heaven above (Latin, ca 1100) Q6 105021
Kyrie, Gott Vater in Ewigkeit (Latin, ca. 1100) BT6 105022

L

Labor on, labor on. Keep the bright reward in view (Blackall) R In the harvest field 105023
Laborers of Christ, arise (Sigourney) V496 105024
Laboruing and heavy laden, Wanting help in time of need (Monsell) D436; O516; BR 308 105025
Lad denne Dag, o Herre Gud (Brun) BT337 105026
Lady in sorrow, silent thy womb ("M. J.", Father) BN 176 105027
Lady of the Visitation (Santeüil) BN150 105028
Laissez paître vos bêtes (French carol) R J'ai oui chanter le rossignol 105029
Lamb of God, all praise to thee (Gotter) AZ790 105030
Lamb of God beloved (Cook) AZ755; BA125 105031
Lamb of God, for sinners slain (Woodford) D543 105032
Lamb of God, I look to thee (Wesley) A251; D566; E591b; F451b; I374; X356b 105033
Lamb of God, I look to thee (Wesley) X Gentle Jesus, meek and mild 105034
Lamb of God, my Saviour (Cennick) AZ1076 105035
Lamb of God most holy (Decius) P99 X Lamb of God pure and holy 105036
Lamb of God, O Jesus! Thou who hearest all (St Gelasius' Sacramentary, 492) M411 105037
Lamb of God, pure and holy (Decius) M418; P99; Q146; AW540 105038
Lamb of God, thy precious blood (Zinzendorf, E. D.) AZ 1049; BA112 105039
Lamb of God, to thee we raise (Enman) BV446 105040
Lamb of God, we fall before thee (Hart) L162; Q358; AA

81 105041
Lamb of God, who thee receive (Dober) BA435 105042
Lamb of God, whose bleeding love (Wesley) AY260 X Lamb of God, whose dying love 105043
Lamb of God, whose dying love (Wesley) AO437; AY260; AZ 1468 105044
Lamb, the once Crucified! Lion, by triumph surrounded (Heusser-Schweizer) AZ531 105045
Lament, O man, thy pride of life (Bridges) BJ59 105046
Lamp of our feet, our path to light (Barton) BI41 X Lamp of our feet, whereby we trace 105047
Lamp of our feet, whereby we trace (Barton) A400; B60; D281; H93; I205; N221; O139; Q291; R254; U139; V71; W201; Z436; AA119; AB101; AC72; AD198; AE156; AF256; AG 133; AH237; AO245; AR242; AS 178; AV76; BD192; BF271; BI 41; BV302; BY248; BZ 105048
Land of our birth, we pledge to thee (Kipling) Y178, 286 X Father in heaven, who lovest all 105049
Land of the mountains high (---) BC140 105050
Land of the North where battling breezes sweep (Ingham) Y284; AB339; BF557 105051
Languéntibus in Purgatorio (Latin) BQ249 105052
Lapsus est annus: redit annus alter (Breviary. Meaux, 1713) BW382 105053
Lass mich dein sein und bleiben (Selnecker) BT334 105054
Lasset uns mit Jesus ziehen (Birken) BT409 105055
Lasst uns alle fröhlich sein (Langhans) BT97 105056
Late, late, so late! and dark the n ight, and chill (Tennyson) I743; AI205 105057
Laud, O Sion, thy salvation (St Thomas Aquinas) E317; F622 105058
Lauda Sion salvatorem (St Thomas Aquinas) BO253 105059
Laudate Dominum, laudate Dominum omnes gentes (Latin) BQ254 105060
Laudate, laudate, laudate Mariam (St Alphonso M. de Liguori) R Raise your voices, vales and mountains 105061
Launch out into the deep (Simpson) R The mercy of God 105062
Launch out into the deep And brave the stormy sea (Loy) M255 105063
L'-cho A-do-noy ha-g'-du-lo (Jewish traditional) BH291 105064
L'cho do'dee likras kalo (Jewish traditional) BH267 105065
Le vermeil du soliel (Denisot) BG101b 105066
Lead, holy Shepherd, lead us (St Clement of Alexandria) W569 105067
Lead, kindly Light, amid the encircling gloom (Newman) A430; B244; D423; E425; F298; G514; H347; I460; J523; L392; N344; O546; P 346; R331; S289; T399; U245; V419; W568; X554, app. 2; Y367; Z578; AB219; AC333; AD221; AE202; AF215; AG 157; AH404; AI299; AK315; AL436; AN239; AO327; AP 600; AR423; AS247; AT60; AU238; AV149; AW162; AY 465; AZ1502; BA685; BB403; BC112; BD250; BE169; BF 414; BJ11; BK89; BL67; BR 388; BX263; BY545; BZ 105068
Lead me gently home, Father (Thompson) AU123; AW449 105069
Lead me into life eternal (Widstoe) BC141 105070
Lead me, Lord, lead me in thy righteousness (Concord Anthem book, 1925) R539;

AE460; AF524; AG335; AR617; BZ 105071

Lead me safely on by the narrow way (Leslie) AX497; AY114 105072

Lead me to some soul today (Houghton) AU323 105073

Lead me to the living fountain (Latta) R O I long to see the beauty 105074

Lead on, lead on, mighty Man of Galilee (McKinney) R Lead on, O King of Glory 105075

Lead on, O King eternal (Shurtleff) A554; B534; G278; H 375; I408; J550; R332; S371; T373; U301; Y177; Z363; AB 220; AC199; AD309; AE247; AF375; AG191; AH445; AK299; AL402; AM488; AO403; AP540; AR324; AS255; AT417; AU236; AV210; AW399; BA578; BB362; BD87; BF470; BK78; BY375 105076

Lead on, O King of Glory (McKinney) AU460 105077

Lead on, O Lord! Above the New Year's gates (Kretzmann) M370 105078

Lead on, thou God of Hosts, lead on (Taylor) U302 105079

Lead them, my God, to thee (---) BB410 105080

Lead thou me on, and then my feet (Armstrong) BB406 105081

Lead us, great teacher Paul, in wisdom's ways (Elpis??) BQ99 105082

Lead us, heavenly Father, In our opening way (Herford) V655; BX521 105083

Lead us, heavenly Father, lead us (Edmeston) A567; B247; D421; E426; F311; K274; N 353; O215; R343; S304; T400; W563; X555; AD223; AE179; AF344; AK220; AL438; AP597; AY431; AZ621; BA604; BB87; BF418; BR302; BV583; BY43 105084

Lead us, heavenly Father, lead us, Shepherd Kind (Herford) BX521 X Lead us, heavenly Father, In our opening way? 105085

Lead us, O Father, in the paths of peace (Burleigh) A433; B248; D422; G271; I475; J 472; R341; S262; T409; U41; W566; X102; Z566; AD230; AF376; AG159; AL437; AN70; AO330; AP598; AR291; AW164; BF416; BY546; BZ 105086

Leader of faithful souls, and Guide (Wesley) I459; AL439; BV558 105087

Lean on his arms, trusting in his love (Lewis) R Just lean upon 105088

Lean on my ample arm (Curtis) BC260 105089

Leaning, leaning, leaning on the everlasting arms (Hoffman) R What a fellowship 105090

Leaning on Thee, my Guide and Friend (Elliott) AZ17 105091

Leave God to order all thy ways (Neumark) AB225 X If thou but suffer God to guide thee 105092

Leave starry heaven behind (Wheelock) AQ70 105093

Leave your burden at the place of prayer (Lillenas) R When the clouds 105094

Lebt friedsam, strach Christus der Herr (Ausbund) BU134 105095

Les anges dans nos compagnes (French trad) AD117; BG 119b 105096

Lest I forget Gethsemane (Hussey) R King of my life 105097

Let all exalt Jehovah's goodness (Westra) AJ427 105098

Let all men living in all lands (Patton) AQ225 105099

Let all mortal flesh keep silence (Liturgy of St James, 5th c) A197; B339; E318; F390; G 594; J281; R148; S112; X273; AD405; AE459; AF107; AG 337; AK336; AR120; AT80; BB685; BL52; BY102; BZ 105100

Let all on earth their voices raise (Latin, 10th c) F504; G19; I9; AT7; BN180; BZ 105101

Let all the earth Jehovah fear (U.P. Psalter, 1912) AJ86; AP30 105102

Let all the earth with songs rejoice (Latin, 10th c) BE168 X Let the round world with songs rejoice 105103

Let all the multitudes of light (MacNutt) F150; J113; X156; BV205 105104

Let all the world in every corner sing (Herbert) A290; E427; F375; G8; J418; K287; M600; R22; S9; W15; X556; AB43; AD8; AE20; AL38; BV243; BY13; BZ 105105

Let all together praise our God (Hermann) BZ 105106

Let all who enter here (---) R 528 105107

Let all who live in freedom (Patton) AQ171 105108

Let children hear the mighty deeds (Watts) M56; Q629; S479; V633; AB325; AM293; BR497 105109

Let Christian faith and hope dispel (Logan) AL415; AP 535 105110

Let Christian hearts rejoice today (St Jean de Brébeuf) BN 16 105111

Let Christians all with joyful mirth (Church-Gallery book) BG20 105112

Let Christians all with one accord rejoice (English trad carol, ca 18th c) BG65 105113

Let dogs delight to bark and bite. (Watts) BW11 105114

Let each man learn to know himself (---) BC91 105115

Let earth and heaven agree (Wesley) H230; I565; AZ1177 105116

Let earth's inhabitants rejoice (Clegg) BC93 105117

Let everlasting glories crown (Watts) V231; AL185 105118

Let every creature God has made (Bible. Psalm 148) BP99 105119

Let every creature hail the morn (Whittier) BE170 105120

Let every creature join (Watts) L87 105121

Let every ear attend (Watts) L375 X Let every mortal ear attend 105122

Let every heart exulting beat (Breviary, Sarum. 1495) BR162 105123

Let every lamp be burning bright (Belden) BB183 105124

Let every mortal ear attend (Watts) H237; L375; V266 105125

Let every tongue thy goodness speak (Watts) H117 105126

Let folly praise what fancy loves (Southwell) BL14 105127

Let God arise and by His might (U.P. Psalter, 1912) T123; AJ179 105128

Let God the Father, and the Son, and Spirit be adored (---) AZ140 X Let God the Father, God the Son, and Spirit be adored 105129

Let God the Father, God the Son, and Spirit be adored (---) AR627; AV409; AZ140 105130

Let hearts and tongues unite (Newton) AZ1347; BA173 105131

Let hearts awaken, now the night is ended (Latin, 6th c) F10; BV40 105132

Let heaven highest praises bring (St Bonaventura) BB297 105133

Let Him to whom we now belong (Wesley) I373 105134

Let Him who would excel (Confucius) AQ161 105135

Let hymns of joy to grief succeed (St Ambrose) BM83 105136

Let Israel trust in God alone (Hamburg Temple Hymnal)

BH139 105137
Let love arise and praise him (Crum) F627 105138
Let me be thine forever (Selnecker) J506; K271; L435; M538; N174; O410; P234; Q334; AA408 105139
Let me be with thee, where thou art (Elliott) AZ341 105140
Let me but hear my Saviour say (Watts) V437 105141
Let me dwell on Golgotha (Newton) AZ52 105142
Let me find a place with that happy band (Latta) R In the day of all days 105143
Let me go, I cannot stay (Baltzell) R On the shore beyond the sea 105144
Let me go, let me go, From the turmoil (Knak) M642 105145
Let me go where saints are going (Hartsough) AX614; AY 174 105146
Let me go where'er I will (---) AC489 105147
Let me with light and truth be blest (Tate & Brady) D662 105148
Let men their brethren know (Clarke) Y257 105149
Let my life be hid in thee (Bull) S318; AN223; BX96 105150
Let no hopeless tears be shed (Graduel de Paris, 1754) D245 105151
Let not such a thought e'er pain thee (Gerhardt) AA506 105152
Let not the wise their wisdom boast (Wesley) I308 105153
Let not thy hands be slack (Burrow) Y227; AB268; BA548 105154
Let not young souls be smothered out (Lindsay) AQ150 105155
Let not your heart be faint (LaTrobe) AZ1316 105156
Let not your weary heart be troubled (Warren) AX533 105157
Let, O my Soul, thy God direct thee (Neumark) N484 105158
Let others see Jesus in you (McKinney) R While passing thro' this world of sin 105159
Let others seek a home below (---) BB662 105160
Let our choir new anthems raise (St Joseph the Hymnographer) E187 X Let us now our voices raise 105161
Let party names no more (Beddome) AZ1373 105162
Let plenteous grace descend on thee (Newton) AR618; AS457 105163
Let saints on earth in concert sing (Wesley) A397; B299; D391; E428; F272; L285; W227; X557; BJ41; BV433 105164
Let sighing cease and woe (Coffin) E27 105165
Let Sion in her beauty rise (Partridge) BC262 105166
Let Sion's watchmen all awake (Doddridge) G399; H463; I223; L306; V560; AE322; AX160; BZ 105167
Let songs of praises fill the sky (Cotterill) K139; L170; M475; Q232; AA254; AZ94; BA254 105168
Let the beauty of Jesus (Orsborn) AU317 105169
Let the deep organ swell the lay (Pise) BO218; BQ105 105170
Let the earth exalt the Lord (Held) M362 X Let the earth now praise the Lord 105171
Let the earth now praise the Lord (Held) K32; M362; Q91; AA146 105172
Let the loud hosannas ring (Sisters of St Joseph, Toronto) BO214 105173
Let the lower lights be burning (Bliss) R Brightly beams our Father's mercy 105174
Let the round world with songs rejoice (Latin, 10th c) E176; BE168 105175
Let the saints new anthems raise (St Joseph the Hymnog-

rapher) AO413 X Let us now our voices raise 105176
Let the song go round the earth (Stock) B485; Z531; BV321; BY376 105177
Let the whole creation cry (Brooke) J414; S74; X558; Y 45; Z103; AB53; AC44; AF69; AN35; AQ10; AR28; AW49; BX61; BY14 105178
Let the whole creation sing, Joyous carols to our King (---) BR565 105179
Let the world their virtue boast (Wesley) AZ1466 105180
Let them praises give Jehovah (U. P. Bible songs hymnal, 1927) R Alleluia, praise Jehovah 105181
Let them that love Him (---) AZ 1207 105182
"Let there be light," at dawn of time (Wise) BH141 105183
Let there be light, Lord God of Hosts (Vories) R480; S402; U336; Z513; AB358; AC291; AD339; AE402; AF449; AG255; AK402; AN397; AQ201; AR393; AS360; AT444; AW353; BF565; BH232; BK116; BX434 105184
Let thine example, holy John, remind us (Paul the Deacon) E223; X230 105185
Let thoughtless thousands choose the road (Hoskins) Q608; AA 550 105186
Let thy blood in mercy poured (Greek) A190; B340; K188; AM362; AP200; AR516; AS 463 105187
Let thy grace, Lord, make me lowly (Goode) AY56 105188
Let thy presence go with me (Zinzendorf, N. L.) AZ1041; BA311 105189
Let thy Spirit, blessed Saviour (---) BB207 105190
Let us all in God rejoice (Langhans) M326; Q97; AA153 105191
Let us all press on in the work of the Lord (Stephens) BC98 105192
Let us all with gladsome voice (Langhans) Q97 X Let us all in God rejoice 105193
Let us awake our joys (Kingsbury) AZ1239 105194
Let us be faithful to our passing hours (Lysaght) AQ83 105195
Let us break bread together, On our knees (Negro spiritual) R447; AF288; AR489; BZ 105196
Let us choral anthems raise (St Joseph the Hymnographer) AB 242 X Let us now our voices raise 105197
Let us employ all notes of joy (Fox) F423 105198
Let us ever love each other (Henry) AX543 105199
Let us ever walk with Jesus (Birken) M220; Q409; AA333 105200
Let us go to Galilee (Paulsen) M630 105201
Let us joyfully give praise to our God (Chinese trad) Y311 105202
Let us keep steadfast guard (St Gregory the Great) AZ 1345 105203
Let us live, then and be glad (Latin) Y299 105204
Let us love, and sing, and wonder (Newton) AM127; AZ 616; BV267 105205
Let us now our voices raise (St Joseph the Hymnographer) A136; F518; J546; X215; AB 242; AM284; AO413; AZ864 105206
Let us now praise famous men (Bible. Ecclesiasticus) X432; AQ230 105207
Let us oft speak kind words to each other (Townsend) BC94 105208
Let us pray for each other (Kieffer) R There's a city of light 105209
Let us rejoice, the fight is won (Dearmer) X157 105210
Let us sing of Easter gladness (Hill) BE171 105211

Let us sing the King Messiah (Ryland) BY377 105212
Let us sing, with one accord (Thrupp) AZ1053 105213
Let us thank the Christ for all who did their duty (Crum) F455 105214
Let us wander where we will (Stevenson) AQ60 105215
Let us with a gladsome mind (Milton) A308; E532; F377; G81; J405; R28; S64; W11; X12; Y40; Z181; AC32; AD95; AE66; AF70; AG39; AH316; AI447; AK77; AL7; AM30; AP 120; AS82; AW64; BA25; BD25; BF220; BH58; BK53; BT570; BV20; BX20; BY15; BZ 105216
Let worldly minds the world pursue (Newton) V444 105217
Licht vom Licht! erleuchte mich (Schmolck) BW553 105218
Liebe, die du mich zum Bilde (Scheffler) BT397 105219
Liebster Jesu, wir sind hier, Dich und dein wort anzuhören (Clausnitzer) BT16; BW553 105220
Liebster Jesu, wir sind hier, Dienem worte nachzuleben (Schmolck) AW553b; BT16, 300 105221
Life and health are in the name (Darbyshire) X286; BV397 105222
Life has loveliness to sell (Teasdale) AC227 105223
Life is good, for God contrives it (Dearmer) G160; X158; Z248 105224
Life is the time to serve the Lord (Watts) L359; V658 105225
Life of ages, richly poured (Johnson) A373; G405; S95; X559; Y190; Z177; AB351; AC 214; AD330; AF236; AK82; AN 337; AQ172; BD33; BF427; BX 394; BY630 105226
Life of all that lives below! (Wesley) AN53; AW238; BX 93 105227
Life on earth is but a vapor (Schell) AX579 105228
Life-spring divine and bond of all (Latin, 6th c) BJ100 105229
Life without Thee would be dreary (Henry) R Keep me near Thee 105230
Life's day is ended, The battle fought and won (Brorson) O 591 105231
Lift high the cross, the love of Christ proclaim (Kitchin) F 633 105232
Lift high the triumph song today! (McGregor) G131; AK 137 105233
Lift Him up, lift Him up. (Oatman) R How to reach 105234
Lift Him up, the risen Saviour (Warren) R Lift Him up, 'tis He that bids you 105235
Lift Him up, 'tis He that bids you (Warren) BB520 105236
Lift the strain of high thanksgiving (Ellerton) D299; BT632 105237
Lift thine eyes, O lift thine eyes (Bible. Psalm 121) AH620; BC370 105238
Lift thy head, O Zion, weeping (Jeszensky) AF377; AK306 105239
Lift up, lift up your voices now! (Neale) D119; Z241; AB149; AE131; AM202 105240
Lift up the banner of salvation (Tamminen) M98 105241
Lift up the trumpet, and loud let it ring (Strout) BB541 105242
Lift up thy light, O man, arise and shine (Thaxter) BE172 105243
Lift up, ye princes of the sky (Aylward) BQ32 105244
Lift up your eyes, ye Christians (Solberg) M115 105245
Lift up your heads, eternal gates (Tate & Brady) V166 105246
Lift up your heads, Pilgrims aweary (Camp) AI97; AM687 105247
Lift up your heads, rejoice! Redemption draweth nigh

(Lynch) BI109 105248

Lift up your heads, ye gates of brass (Montgomery) E549; F 306; J308; K216; U399; W385; X301; AK368; AL260; AM384; AO514; AP389; BA359; BV319; BY378 105249

Lift up your heads, ye mighty gates (Weissel) A484; B186; D454; G126; J8; K7; M330; N2; O158; Q73; R152; S114; U54; Z224; AA138; AD176; AF114; AG108; AK92; AM146; AN179; AO195; AQ310; AR203; AT247; AW523; AY415; AZ1202; BA 151; BB294; BF321; BR191; BV80; BX200; BY82; BZ 105250

Lift up your heart! lift up your voice X Rejoice the Lord is King X On wings of living light X True lovers of mankind 105251

Lift up your hearts, O King of kings (Masterman) G472; R481; S405; AB278; AC295; AD342; AE379; AG253; AR290; BZ 105252

Lift up your hearts to things above (Wesley) I558 105253

"Lift up your hearts!" We lift them Lord, to thee (Butler) A482; E429; F341; S258; X560; Y176; Z372; AB178; AC3; AD 304; AF352; AK27; AL340; AN226; AR330; BF452; BV 474; BY444 105254

Lift up your hearts, ye people (Parr) AF189 105255

Lift up your voice, ye Christian folk (Lyon) F297 105256

Lift ye the Snow-white Banner (Kirby) R Forth to the fight, ye ransomed 105257

Lift your glad voices in triumph on high (Ware) I159; BR566 105258

Lift your heads, ye friends of Jesus (Wesley) H200 105259

Lift your hidden faces (Fyleman) X1; AQ319; BG156 105260

Light of ages and of nations (Longfellow) AN75; AQ248; BD183; BX453 105261

Light of Ages, shed my man (Chubb) Y149; AB294; BD140; BF422 105262

Light of conscience, clear and still (Chubb) AB294 X Light of Ages, shed by man 105263

Light of life, so softly shining (Bonar) AP775 105264

Light of life, the great Messiah (---) BR144 105265

Light of light, enlighten me (Schmolck) J186; L45; M4; N346; O33; R73; S21; U439; V32; Z445; AD34; AG17; AK42; AM333; AO15; AP345; AR63; AW553a; BF187; BR91 105266

Light of light, O Sun of heaven (Opitz) N347 105267

Light of light that shineth (Thring) R From the eastern mountains 105268

Light of the anxious heart (St Bernard of Clairvaux??) J475; K46; W249 105269

Light of the Gentile nations (Franck) K51; M378; N65; O203; Q138; AA190 105270

Light of the lonely pilgrim's heart (Denny) F209; H202; W381; AL243; AM232; AO 110; AP250; BA100; BV268 105271

Light of the world, come nigh and bless (Harvey) BA170 105272

Light of the world! for ever ever shining (Bonar) W171; AB75; AL119; BY209 105273

Light of the world, how long the quest (Poteat) Z320 105274

Light of the world, we hail thee (Monsell) G114; R138; S422; T370; U398; Y19; Z208; AB 72; AC9; AD467; AG277; AK 124; AO518; AR112; AT454; BF185; BZ 105275

Light of the world! whose kind and gentle care (Bateman) I505 105276

Light of those whose dreary dwelling (Wesley) B100; D

325; H199; I638; L212; AZ943; BA608 105277

Light, that from the dark abyss (Pirks) L187 105278

Light up this house with glory, Lord (Harris) AD28; BA328; BY272 105279

Lighten the darkness of our life's long night (Owen) E430; X103; AF386 105280

Light's abode, celestial Salem (St Thomas à Kempis) A587; B507; D399; F279; J591; O250; X199; AP632; AZ629; BR216; BV434 105281

Light's glittering morn bedecks the sky (Latin, 4th c) F602; BY159 105282

Like a river glorious (Havergal) W443; AM587; AT294 105283

Like a shepherd, true, Jesus leads (Clements) AY120 105284

Like a strong and raging fire (---) AH139 105285

Like as a father pities his child (Belden) BB66 105286

Like as a mother, God comforteth His children (Baum) BE174 105287

Like as the hart doth breathe and bray (Tate & Brady) BT525 X As pants the hart for cooling streams 105288

Like Enoch, let me ever walk with Thee (Hoppe) M207 105289

Like Mary at her Saviour's feet (Montgomery) AZ880; BA836 105290

Like Noah's weary dove (Muhlenberg) D486; H419 105291

Like pilgrims sailing thro' the night (Harris) AN361; BDp. 21; BX407 105292

Like radiant sunshine that comes after rain (Barratt) AT285; AU116 105293

Like shadows gliding o'er the plain (Taylor) BX180 105294

Like sheep we went astray (Watts) V250 105295

Like silver lamps in a distant shrine (Dix) B548 105296

Like Sion's steadfast mount are they (U.P. Psalter, 1912) AJ 354; AM585 105297

Like the deer that yearns for running streams (Ladies of the Grail) BL54; BSp. 16 105298

Like the eagle, upward, onward (Bonar) V502 105299

Like the golden sun ascending (Kingo) O325; Q207 105300

Like the stars of the morning (Cushing) R When He cometh, when He cometh 105301

Like the sunshine after rain (Lillenas) AU361 105302

Listen! the Master beseecheth (Punshon) AL506 105303

Listen to our prayer, O Lord; Hear our humble plea (Indian [Asia] Prayer) BZ 105304

Listen to the blessed invitation (Hewitt) AX252 105305

Listen to the gentle promptings (Montgomery) AX248; AY 373 105306

Listen to the Lambs (Negro spiritual) AH602 105307

Listen to those happy voices (Loy) M351 105308

Little Baby Jesus, born today (Kretzmann) M616 105309

Little children, Lord are we (---) BH249 105310

Little children, praise the Lord (Pollock) AY324 105311

Little children, praise the Saviour (Juvenile harmonist, ca 1837) AP747 105312

Little children, wake and listen (S.P.C.K. Appendix, 1869) W44; AL599; AN158; BD223; BX530 105313

Little David, play on your harp (Negro spiritual) Y317 105314

Little drops of water, Little grains of sand (Carney & Dearmer) E600; X365; AP778 105315

Little Jesus, sweetly sleep, do

not stir (Czeck trad.) X383; AF482; BG87 105316
Little King, so fair and sweet (A Sister of Notre Dame) BQ 125 105317
Little stars are shining (Leonard) AP805 105318
Little things that run and quail (Stephens) X305; AC243 105319
Little travelers Zionward (Edmeston) AZ1072 105320
Live in peace, where Christ doth shine (Dearmer) R Now thy earthly work is done 105321
Live out Thy life within me (Havergal) BB279 105322
Living below in this old sinful world (Coats) AX520 105323
Living for Jesus a life that is true (Chisholm) Z304; AT352; AU373 105324
Living Fountain, freely flowing (Rohr) M593 105325
Living, He loved me; dying, He saved me (Chapman) R One day when heaven was filled 105326
Living in Thee, Lord (Reitz) R Teach me to pray 105327
Lo, a gleam from yonder heaven (Berry) AR454; AS256 105328
Lo, as the potter molds the clay (Meir b. Baruch of Rothenburg) BH172 105329
Lo! Christ is risen, From the tomb's dread prison (Luther) M439 105330
Lo! for us the wilds are glad (Wesley) BR498 105331
Lo, from the desert homes (Coffin) F552 105332
Lo! God is here! let us adore (Tersteegen) E637; F249; H25; J162; X191; AF499; AL22; AM 308; AN495, 501; AO7; AW508; BX4; BY16 105333
Lo! God, our God, has come (Bonar) AZ1175; BA166 105334
Lo, God to heaven ascendeth (Sacer) O367; Q214; AA233; AM210 105335
Lo! golden light rekindles day (Prudentius) E55 105336
Lo! He comes, lo! Jesus comes (Palmer) R Watch, ye saints, with eyelids waking 105337
Lo! he comes, with clouds descending (Cennick) A5; B57; D39; E7; F51; H201; I601; K513; M320; N8; O166; R 234; S184; T351; U122; V 182; W160; X65; AE140; AG 121; AH243; AL136; AM237; AO114; AP246; AR212; AS 165; AT123; AV122; AW130; AZ1378; BA105; BB176; BV 81; BY185; BZ 105338
Lo, He cometh! countless trumpets (Cennick) AZ1378 X Lo! he comes with clouds descending 105339
Lo, He sent His word and healed them (Hay) BE175 105340
Lo, how a Rose e'er blooming (Speier Gebetbuch, 1599) J38; R162; Z194; AF131; AQ298; AR122; BD217; BN 17 105341
Lo! I come with joy to do (Wesley) AZ1481 105342
"Lo, in Cumorah's lonely hill." (Pratt) R An angel from on high 105343
Lo, in Sion a foundation (Cronenwett) M508 105344
Lo! in the clouds of heaven appears (Bryant) AR213 105345
Lo, in the wilderness a voice (Dearmer) X561 105346
Lo, Israel's gentle Shepherd stands (Doddridge) BR451 X See Israel's gentle Shepherd 105347
Lo, Judah's Lion wins the strife (Bohemian, 1650) Q211 105348
Lo, many shall come from the East and the West (Landstad) Q415 X Full many shall come. . . 105349
Lo! on a narrow neck of land

(Wesley) I579; V664; AZ558; BA411; BB384 105350
Lo! on the water's brink we stand (---) BC97 105351
Lo, our Father's tender care (Gutheim) BH82 105352
Lo, round the throne, a glorious band (Hill) F525; BJ3 105353
"Lo, she is not dead, but sleeping" (Brooks) AX620 105354
Lo! The Angels' Food is given (St Thomas Aquinas) E317b; F622b 105355
Lo! the clouds have burst asunder (Childs) BI6 105356
Lo, the day of days is here (Hosmer) AN199; AQ317; AW545; BD237; BX206 105357
Lo! The day of rest declineth (Robbins) BX34 105358
Lo, the earth awakes again (Longfellow) AQ318 X Lo, the earth is risen again 105359
Lo, the earth is risen again (Longfellow) AN200; AQ318; BD242; BK132; BX210 105360
Lo! the earth rejoices At the dawn of day (---) BH248 105361
Lo, the Easter-tide is here (Hosmer) AN201 105362
Lo! the heavens are breaking (---) AW434 105363
Lo, the mighty God appearing (Goode) BC264 105364
Lo, the pilgrim Magi leave their royal halls (Coffin) BR158 105365
Lo! the stone is rolled away (Scott) V160 105366
Lo! the voice of Jesus (Evans) D608 105367
Lo, they come in glad procession (Glenn) BI104 105368
Lo, upon the altar lies Bread of heaven from the skies (St Thomas Aquinas) M52; AA 433 105369
Lo, we tread on holy ground (Tressel) M507 105370
Lo! what a cloud of witnesses (Scottish Paraphrases, 1745) A569; B300; C393; BA808 105371
Lo! what a glorious sight appears To our admiring eyes (Watts) AM601; AP636 105372
Lo, what a pleasing sight (Watts) L289; AX545; AY116 105373
Lo, when the day of rest was past (Dearmer) X159 105374
Lobe den Herren, den mächtigen König der Ehren! (Neander) BW515 105375
Lobe den Herren, O meine Seele (Herrnschmidt) AW513b; BT 26; BW513 105376
Lobt Gott, ihr Christen allzugleich (Herman) BT105 105377
Long ago and far away (Horn) J44 105378
Long ago the lilies faded (Tarrant) BD62 105379
Long ago, there was born In the City of David (Blackmer) AR127 105380
Long ago, when heathen darkness (Callin) BY249 105381
Long ago when Jesus walked in Galilee (Bayly) BY751 105382
Long as I live I'll bless thy name (Watts) AY9; BR496 105383
Long did I toil, and knew no earthly rest (Quarles) E432; O396; W544; X104; AD263; AZ703 105384
Long for my Saviour I've been waiting (---) BB186 105385
Long hast thou stood, O Church of God (Grundtvig) BE176 105386
Long has thou wept and sorrowed (Heusser-Schweizer) N183; O465 105387
Long have I sat beneath the sound (Watts) I281; L388 105388
Long have they waited in the far distant lands (Schell) AX214 105389
Long have we sought eternal life

(Glasgow) AU131 105390
Long live the Pope! His praises sound (Henry) BO206; BQ122 105391
Long upon the mountains, weary (Smith) BB664 105392
Long years ago o'er Bethlehem's hills (Brewer) G99; I120 105393
Look down, O Lord, from heaven behold (Luther) O424; Q260 105394
Look down to us, Saint Joseph (McNaspy) BL64 105395
Look for the beautiful, look for the true (Belden) AR309; AS318 105396
Look for the waymarks (Belden) BB671 105397
Look from the sphere of endless day (Bryant) AP385 X Look from thy sphere 105398
Look from Thy sphere of endless day (Bryant) D251; H470; I 644; J325; K232; L340; N384; O115; P389; Q499; W340; AA 479; AD340; AE354; AI175; AK 375; AO537; AP385; BA347; BF 537; BX89; BY645 105399
Look! Look! Look and live (Hull) R There is life for a look 105400
Look to Jesus Christ thy Saviour (Franzén) N467 105401
Look to the Lamb of God (Jackson) R If you from sin 105402
Look up, by failure daunted (Dearmer) X232 105403
Look up, my soul, to Christ thy joy (Schade) AZ889; BA 692 105404
Look upon Jesus, sinless is He (Belden) BB593 105405
Look upon us, blessed Lord (Clausnitzer) J190; W203 105406
Look with mercy, Lord (Bible. Joel, 2) BM72 105407
Look, ye saints, the day is breaking (Kelly) BE177 105408
Look, ye saints, the sight is glorious (Kelly) A105; B185; D130; G165; H193; I169; J114; K121; L273; Q222; R133; S201; U111; V163; W134; Z256; AD172; AE124; AF 203; AH299; AK180; AL108; AM217; AO194; AP224; AS 161; AT148; AU425; AW119; AX121; AY267; AZ1403; BA 247; BV206; BY169; BZ 105409
Looking unto Jesus, in faith I come (Loes) AU132 105410
Looking upward every day, Sunshine on our faces (Butler) U220; W674; AL 326; AP786; BD95; BY477 105411
Lord, a little band and lowly (Shelly) W661; AP726; AX 564; AY340 105412
Lord, a Saviour's love displaying (Hawkins) D258 105413
Lord, accept into thy kingdom (Gabbott) BC100 105414
Lord, accept our true devotion (Alldridge) BC101 105415
Love, accept the alms we offer (Sedgwick) F406 105416
Lord, accept the gifts we offer (Latin) BM6 105417
Lord, all I am is known to thee (Watts) H106; L99 105418
Lord, and is thine anger gone (Wesley) AZ1471 105419
Lord and Master, who hast called us (Smith) F495; BV414 105420
Lord and Saviour, true and kind (Moule) G560 105421
Lord, as a pilgrim on earth I roam (Malmivaara) J536 105422
Lord, as of old at Pentecost (Gabriel) AT173 105423
Lord, as this solemn rite we keep (Kauffman) R We bow to thee 105424
Lord, as thou wilt, deal thou with me (Bienemann) Q406; AA383 105425
Lord, as to thy dear cross we flee (Gurney) A413; B125; D346; F334; J455; N170; O 392; S145; U87; W90; Z326;

AD152; AF347; AK222; AL78; AP510; AZ175; BA81; BF404; BR354; BV487 105426

Lord, as we thy Name profess (Parker) G295; AC176; AV207; BF450 105427

Lord, as we to thy Mercy flee (Gurney) BR354 X Lord, as to thy dear cross we flee 105428

Lord, at this closing hour (Fitch) L63; Z131; AY289; AZ1333; BB32 105429

Lord! at thy feet we humbly kneel (Browne) BB236 105430

Lord, at thy table we behold (Stennett) Z464 105431

Lord, be thy word my rule (Wordsworth) F327; BV299 105432

Lord, before thy Presence come (Taylor) BX31 105433

Lord, before thy throne we bend (Bowdler) BR103 105434

Lord, behold us with thy blessing (Buckoll) E523; F457; W677; X333 105435

Lord, bestow on us thy blessing (Swedberg) P65 105436

Lord, bless and pity us... That all the earth thy way may know (U.P. Psalter, 1912) R493; T122; AJ178 105437

Lord bless and pity us... That the earth thy way, and nations all may know (Scottish Psalter, 1650) AL657; AP57 105438

Lord, bless thy word to every heart (Howard) BB700 105439

Lord, cause thy face on us to shine (Cotterill) M94; AX 640 105440

Lord Christ, reveal thy holy face (Wilhelm II, duke) AZ321; BA374 105441

Lord Christ, when first thou cam'st to men (Bowie) A522; X562; AD146; AF325; AR366; BZ 105442

Lord Christ, who on thy heart, didst bear (Thomas) BY636 105443

Lord, dismiss us with thy blessing; Fill our hearts (Fawcett??) A489; B51; D34; G26; H37; I39; J191; K431; L66; M16; N 354; O48; P55; Q50; R79; S54; U448; V27; W299; Z 127; AA17; AD65; AE33; AF63; AG13; AH176; AI26; AK35; AL215; AM319; AN 470; AO49; AP340; AR48; AS62; AT31; AV23; AW45; AX79; AZ1395; BA378; BB 33; BC105; BF207; BK172; BV56; BX510; BY762; BZ 105444

Lord, dismiss us with thy blessing, Hope and comfort (Fawcett??) AN470 X Lord dismiss us ... Fill our hearts 105445

Lord, dismiss us with thy blessing, May our praise to thee (Fawcett??) BK172 X Lord dismiss us ... Fill our hearts 105446

Lord, dismiss us with thy blessing, Thanks for mercies (Buckoll) F458; W678; X 333b; BR105 105447

Lord, disperse the mists of error (Aström) N415 105448

Lord, do thou guide me on my pilgrim way (Lucas) BH22 105449

Lord, dost thou say, "Ask what thou wilt?" (Newton) V460; AZ333; BV622 105450

Lord, enthroned in heavenly splendour (Bourne & Dearmer) E319; F400; X274; AD407; AF291; AK344; BV382 105451

Lord, for ever at thy side (Montgomery) A451; B306; D649; L461; V320; AZ1066 105452

Lord, for grace we thee entreat (Zinzendorf, N.L.) AZ869 105453

Lord, for the mercies of the [this] night (Mason) K453; L7; R533; S9app.; AF501; AY280 105454

Lord, for thy coming us prepare (Gregor) AZ568; BA p.149 105455

Lord, for tomorrow and its needs (Mary Xavier, Sr. i.e. Sybil F. Partridge) B36; G314; I 510; U360; Z327; AC317; AE 236; AG222; AH388; AL433; AO315; AP514; AR292; AS 317; AT339; AU259; AV197; BB604; BD110; BN189; BO 194; BQ143 105456

Lord! from far-severed climes we meet (Hay) AV70 X Defend us, Lord 105457

Lord, from the depths to thee, I cried, My voice, Lord, do thou hear (Scottish Psalter, 1650) R277; S240; AL686; AP116 105458

Lord, from whom all blessings flow (Wesley) BY361 X Christ, from whom all blessings flow 105459

Lord, from whose hand we take our charge (Piggott) X346; BY349 105460

Lord, give me light to do thy work (Bonar) AX505; AY75; BR505 105461

Lord, give us a vision of souls gone astray (Davis) AX195 105462

Lord, give us light to do thy work (Bonar) BR505 X Lord, give me light 105463

Lord God almighty, in thy hand (Coster) BY62 105464

Lord God almighty, King of heaven (Kertzmann) M518 105465

Lord God, by whom all change is wrought (Gill) AN359; BX185 105466

Lord, God, from whom all life (Burroughs) X343; AD44; BY 503 105467

Lord God of hosts, by all adored (Gambold) L109; V517; AO52 105468

Lord God of hosts, how lovely (U.P. Book of Psalms, 1871) AK327; AP67 105469

Lord God of hosts, in mercy (U.P. Psalter, 1912) T154; AJ228 105470

Lord God of hosts, uplift thine hand (Ainger) R God of our fathers, unto thee 105471

Lord God of hosts, whose mighty hand (Oxenham) A529; B438; J359; U341; Y288; AH 208; AO591 105472

Lord God of hosts, whose purpose, never swerving (Knapp) R288; S368; Y209; Z497; AB 232; AC247; AD328; AF411; AH514; AK266; AR325; BF570 105473

Lord God of hosts, within whose hand (Housman) E219; X227 105474

Lord God of morning and of night (Palgrave) L1; AF500; AL534; AN89; AZ933; BX130; BY677 105475

Lord God Omnipotent, Lord God alone (Smith) AB54; BX66 105476

Lord God, our Father, thou our chiefest stay (Latin) O43 105477

Lord God, our Salvation (Swertner) AZ1027 105478

Lord God the Holy Ghost (Montgomery) F615; K141; L275; N160; U128; V213; AL158; AP274; AW132; AZ1484; BA 253; BV219; BY235 105479

Lord God, thy praise we sing (Latin, 5th c) AZ1112; BA p. 170 105480

Lord God, we all give praise to thee (Melanchthon) M483; Q254; AA286 105481

Lord God, we all to thee give praise (Melanchthon) Q254 X Lord God, we all give praise to thee 105482

Lord God, we worship thee! (Franck) A144; B440; D200; K496; M506; AZ785; BA875 105483

Lord God, who art my Father dear (Mathesius) AA517 105484

Lord God, whose breath the universe controls (Lucas) BH 37 105485

Lord, grant that we e'er pure retain (Melmbold) AA390 105486
Lord, grant thy servants grace (Heermann) AZ786; BA309 105487
Lord, grant us light that we may know (Tuttiett) BA887 X O grant us light, that we may know 105488
Lord, grant us, though deeply abased with shame (Schlicht) AZ494; BA312 105489
Lord, guard and guide the men who fly (Hamilton) Y187; AB 382; AC290; AH478; AN468; BZ 105490
Lord, hear me in distress, Regard my suppliant cry (U.P. Psalter, 1912) T281; AJ389 105491
Lord, hear me when I pray (U.P. Psalter, 1912) AJ72 105492
Lord, hear my prayer, and let my cry (Psalter, 1860 Kennedy) T186; AJ272 105493
Lord, hear my voice, my prayer attend (U.P. Book of Psalms, 1871) AP50 105494
Lord, hear the right, attend my cry (Scottish Psalter, 1650) AJ33; AP12 105495
Lord, hear the right, regard my cry (U.P. Psalter, 1912) T23; AJ31 105496
Lord, hear the voice of my complaint (Agricola) O275; AA365 105497
Lord, help me live from day to day (Meigs) AS338; AU77 105498
Lord, help us ever to retain (Helmbold) Q288 105499
Lord, her watch thy Church is keeping (Downton) B481; D 260; F267; K226; U397; W378; BB437; BY379 105500
Lord, how secure and blest are they (Watts) H285; I439 105501
Lord, how secure my conscience was (Watts) V280 105502
Lord, I am come! Thy promise is my plea (Newton) AZ462 105503
Lord, I am fondly, earnestly longing (Hoffman) AX371; AY339 105504
Lord, I am thine, entirely thine (Davies) G224; H309; I342; U186; V318; AZ381; BA456 105505
Lord, I believe a rest remains (Wesley) I356 105506
"Lord, I believe! help thou mine unbelief," (Gould) BR 332 105507
Lord! I believe, thy power I own (Wreford) U214; V349; AE194; AI234; AM428; AO 356; AR269 105508
Lord, I cannot let thee go (Newton) I514 105509
Lord, I care not for riches (Kidder) AX486 X I am bought not with riches 105510
Lord, I feel a carnal mind (Toplady) AZ1477 105511
Lord, I have made thy word my choice (Watts) V79; BV304 105512
Lord, I have passed another day (Taylor) AZ360 105513
Lord, I hear of showers of blessing (Codner) D589; H 57; I346; L399; N407; O268; U452; V579; W687; AH352; AI265; AL334; AM527; AO634; AP471; AS45; AU297; AV348; AW204; AX41; AY244; AZ 268; BA904; BB208 105514
Lord, I know thy grace is nigh me (Ganse) AO278 105515
Lord, I lift my soul to thee (U.P. Psalter, 1912) AJ64; AM 583 105516
Lord, I thank thee for thy love (Kauffman) R Worthy art thou, Lord divine 105517
Lord, I want to be a Christian in my heart (Negro spiritual) R317; AE454; AF353; AG318; AH608; AR486; BK167; BZ 105518

Lord I was blind: I could not see (Matson) AL337; BV486; BY 445 105519

Lord, I will praise thy name (U.P. Psalter, 1912) AJ78 105520

Lord, I would own thy tender care (Taylor) E601; F443; W655; BV538 105521

Lord, if at thy command (Wesley) I648; AA487; AX164 105522

Lord! in love and mercy save us (Symington) AZ275 105523

Lord, in the fullness of my might (Gill) AL352; AP563; AW397; BB BB386; BY446 105524

Lord, in the hollow of thy hand (Briggs) X337; AN467; BV 407 105525

Lord, in the morning thou shalt hear (Watts) H28; I41; L8; S28; V34; AD45; AM332; AO 21; AW20; AY281; BB39; BR9 105526

Lord, in the strength of grace (Wesley) G217; I352; AL363; BZ 105527

Lord, in thee am I confiding (U.P. Psalter, 1912) T68; AJ103 105528

Lord, in this blest and hallowed hour (Conder) BY321 105529

Lord, in this sacred hour (Bulfinch) L49; BH112 105530

Lord, in this thy mercy's day (Williams) A57; B122; D88; E76; F94; H283; W405; AL274; AO280; AP428; AZ1128; BA416; BR293 105531

Lord, in thy kingdom there shall be (Ansticc) AA461 105532

Lord in thy love abide with us (Latin) BI53-D 105533

Lord, in thy name tny servants plead (Keble) B183; D189; E140; F144; J362; W611; X171; BV 646 105534

Lord, in thy name we meet (Zinzendorf, E.D.) AZ1163; BA801 105535

Lord in thy presence dread and sweet (Catholic hymnal, 1860) B377; E342 105536

Lord, in thy presence here we meet (---) AS450; AX52; AY11 105537

Lord, in thy temple we appear (---) AJp.394 105538

Lord, into thy sacred dwelling (Berkowitz) BH144 105539

Lord, it belongs not to my care (Baxter) B392; D665; E433; F342; G516; H365; I470; J368; K403; L513; M 304; O502; Q527; V421; W549; X105; AA496; AL429; AO335; AP522; AW253; AZ1443; BY 612; BZ 105540

Lord, it is good for us to be (Stanley) B286; D166; E235; H159; I131; N204; W88; X 235; AB130; AO151; AZ931; BA72 105541

Lord Jesus, are we one with thee (Deck) V298; AZ1446; BV269 105542

Lord Jesus, bless thy witnesses (Zinzendorf, N.L.) AZ925 105543

Lord Jesus, blessed Giver (Wells) AO497 105544

Lord Jesus, by thy death (Zinzendorf, N.L.) AZ724 105545

Lord Jesus, by thy passion (Littlddale) D635; L236; O479; P171 105546

Lord Jesus Christ, all praise to thee (Latin, 11th c) BA 56 105547

Lord Jesus Christ, be present now (Wilhelm II, duke) J188; K419; M2; O36; P40; Q3; AF521; AK28; AM312; BZ 105548

Lord Jesus Christ, be with us now (Wilhelm II, duke) M2 X Lord Jesus Christ, he present now 105549

Lord Jesus Christ, I flee to thee (---) P279 105550

Lord Jesus Christ, I humbly pray (Pappus) AZ339 105551

Lord Jesus Christ, in thee alone (Schneesing) N410;

AA413; AZ1032 105552
Lord, Jesus Christ, in thee I trust eternally (Heermann) AZ 556 105553
Lord Jesus Christ, my life, my light (Behm) O584; Q148; AA 195 105554
Lord Jesus Christ, my Saviour blest (Sthen) M284; O278; P218; Q353 105555
Lord Jesus Christ, of Virgin born (Luther) M344 105556
Lord Jesus Christ, our Lord most dear (Laufenberg) E338 X O Jesus Christ, our Lord most dear 105557
Lord Jesus Christ, strong hero thou (Helder) AA230 105558
Lord Jesus Christ, the cause is thine (Preiswerk) M105 105559
Lord Jesus Christ, the Prince of peace (Ebert) M496 105560
Lord Jesus Christ, the children's friend (Hoppe) N394 105561
Lord Jesus Christ, the work is thine (Prieswerk) BV326 105562
Lord Jesus Christ, thou hast prepared (Kinner) Q306 105563
Lord Jesus Christ, thou highest good (Ringwaldt) O98 105564
Lord Jesus Christ, thou living Bread (Rist) Q312 105565
Lord Jesus Christ, to thee we pray (Luther) N240 105566
Lord Jesus Christ, to us attend (---) AA1 105567
Lord Jesus Christ, true man and God (Eber) K506; N594; O 587; AA527 105568
Lord Jesus Christ, we humbly pray (Jacobs) J265; K190; Q314 105569
Lord Jesus Christ, we seek thy face (Stewart) BV9 105570
Lord Jesus Christ, with us abide (Selnecker) M187; O427; Q292; S506; AA110 105571
Lord Jesus, for our call of grace (Zinzendorf, N. L.) AZ917; BA802 105572
Lord Jesus, from thy throne above (Darbyshire) A250 105573
Lord Jesus, God and man (Baker) AZ1369 X O Jesus, God and man 105574
Lord Jesus, God of heaven (Hymns of the English Conf. 1880) BR484 105575
Lord Jesus hath a garden full of flowers gay (Dutch carol, 17th c) BG105 105576
Lord Jesus, I have promised (Bode) BR384 X O Jesus, I have promised 105577
Lord Jesus, I long to be perfectly whole (Nicholson) P267; AI282; AO639; AR 445; AS452; AT201; AU9; AW469; AX407; AY233; BB 592 105578
Lord Jesus, I love thee, I know thou art mine (London hymn book, 1864) G234; BZ 105579
Lord Jesus, I pray, On Earth while I stay (J. F. Cammerhoff) AZ 105580
Lord Jesus, in the days of old (Noble) AE44; AL554 105581
Lord Jesus, in thy footsteps (Martin) BY295 105582
Lord Jesus, in thy presence we are blest (Schlicht) AZ 438 105583
Lord Jesus, Life eternal, before thy throne I bow (Hemminki) M64 105584
Lord Jesus, may I constantly (Watteville) AZ326 105585
Lord Jesus, 'mid thy flock appear (Swertner) AZ916; BA174 105586
Lord Jesus, on the holy mount (Anketell) N205 105587
Lord Jesus, Son of Mary (Crane) AB114; AC86; BF 298 105588
Lord Jesus, think of me (Synesius of Cyrene) A417; B393; D614; E77; F200; J365; K 320; O103; Q320; R270; S 239; X106; AF314; AG149; AL265; AW196; BV138; BY

565; BZ 105589
Lord Jesus, thou art going forth (Nachtenhöfer) Q150 105590
Lord Jesus, thou art truly good (Kinner) AA436 105591
Lord Jesus, thou the Church's Head (Mentzer) Q477 105592
Lord Jesus, though but two or three (Loy) M5; P41 105593
Lord Jesus, we give thanks to thee (Fischer) Q173 105594
Lord Jesus, when I think of thee (Richard Rolle of Hampole) BN36 105595
Lord Jesu, when we stand afar (How) F109; H167; I145; K64; L253; S160; AE115; AS139; BA221; BR177 105596
Lord Jesus, who art come (Fisher) Q485 105597
Lord Jesu, who at Lazarus' tomb (Rawnsley) E357 105598
Lord Jesus, who before thy passion (Rambach) AZ700; BA 303 105599
Lord Jesus, who, our souls to save (Latin, 14th c) K106; L262; M409; AA217 105600
Lord Jesus, with thy children stay (Selnecker) AZ363 105601
Lord Jesus, with thy presence bless (Watteville) AZ337; BA 535 105602
Lord, keep us in thy word and work (Luther) AA274 105603
Lord, keep us safe this night (Leland) A174; AS36; AV425; BB694 105604
Lord, keep us steadfast in thy word (Luther) J155; K167; L400; M29; N220; O138; P86 Q261; AM91 105605
Lord, lay some soul upon my heart (Weaver) AT332; AU 451 105606
Lord, lead the way my Saviour went (Croswell) AA359 X Lord, lead the way the Saviour went 105607
Lord, lead the way our Savior went (Croswell) AS343 X Lord, lead the way the Saviour went 105608
Lord, lead the way the Saviour went (Croswell) D270; Q 440; AA359; AS343; BA564 105609
Lord, let me know my end (Montgomery) AZ1368 105610
Lord, let mercy now attend us (Smith. Sacred harmonies, 1828) AP341 105611
Lord, let thy blest angelic bands (Schalling) AZ1110 105612
Lord, let thy goodness lead our land (Doddridge) L558; M502 105613
Lord, let thy Spirit, from earthly passion weaning (Briem) J128 105614
Lord, let us now depart in peace (---) S43app.; AE469; AH564; AR680; AV423 105615
Lord, lift me up (Oatman) R I'm pressing on the upward way 105616
Lord, like the publican I stand (Raffles) AI209; AM407; AO277 105617
Lord, my petition heed (U.P. Psalter, 1912) T158; AJ235 105618
Lord, my times are in thy hand (Taylor) AZ58; BA743 105619
Lord, my weak thought in vain would climb (Palmer) X563 AM93; BX238 105620
Lord of all being, throned afar (Holmes) A291; D313; E434; G62; H109; I82; R87; S87; T318; U14; V93; W24; X 564; Y1; Z151; AB187; AC 33; AD85; AE57; AF89; AG 44; AH215; AI33; AK74; AL 20; AN16; AO85; AP152; AQ38; AR74; AS80; AV40; AW53; AZ368; BA658; BB 20; BC287; BD55; BE319; BF231; BI27; BK54; BR36; BV245; BX50; BY63; BZ 105621

Lord of all hopefulness, Lord of all joy (Struther) A363; X565; AD484; AF217; AR53; BY631 105622

Lord of all majesty and might (Briggs) A295; X566; AN46; AQ32 105623

Lord of all power and might (Stowell) D328; G392; I206; K221; N211; AZ1243 105624

Lord of all, to thee we raise (Pierpoint) R For the beauty of the earth 105625

Lord of all, to whom alone (Alington) BY447 105626

Lord of beauty, thine the splendour (Alington) F174 105627

Lord of Creation, bow thine ear, O Christ, to hear (Latin, before 11th c) E174 105628

Lord of earth, thy forming hand (Grant) I469 105629

Lord of every land and nation (Robinson) AO203 X Mighty God, while angels bless thee 105630

Lord of glory, thou hast bought us (Alderson) O449; Q442; AA358; AZ247; BA565 105631

Lord of glory, who hast bought us (Alderson) Q442 X Lord of glory, thou hast bought us 105632

Lord of Good Life, the hosts of the undying ("The inner light") AD306 105633

Lord of grace and holiness (Benson) AO430 105634

Lord of harvest, send forth reapers (Thompson) R Far and near the fields are teeming 105635

Lord of health, thou life within us (Dearmer) R12; X567; Y193; AC167 105636

Lord of hosts! to thee we raise (Montgomery) H422; L296; AO465; AX644; AZ65 105637

Lord of hosts, whom all adore (Jewish hymn) BH178 105638

Lord of life and King of glory (Burke) E530; F498; G426; K418; W652; AR546; AS418; AW363; BA852; BY618; BZ 105639

Lord of life and light and blessing (Rohr) M622 105640

Lord of life! now sweetly slumber (LaTrobe) AZ940; BA207 105641

Lord of life, of love, of light (Hall) D301; N580; BA335 105642

Lord of life, who once wast cradled (Piggott) X342; BY619 105643

Lord of light, whose Name outshineth (Lewis) W337; Y222; Z504; AD324; AK268; AL377; AP568; AR376; AW 342; BF517; BY380 105644

Lord of loveliness, all beauty, Bears thy touch (Morse) AR386 105645

Lord of mercy and of might, God and Father of us all (Heber) AZ1274; BA647 105646

Lord of mercy and of might, Of mankind the life and light (Heber) B41; D527; K85; W159; AZ1138; BA 606 105647

Lord of my heart's elation (Carmen) Y131 105648

Lord of my Life! O, may thy praise (Steele) L13; AA27 105649

Lord of my life, whose tender care (Ω [Omega] Chelsea, England) Q24; AA18 105650

Lord of nations, bless in kindness (Farrell) BM95 105651

Lord of our highest love (Tickle) Z466 105652

Lord of our life, and God of our salvation (Löwenstern) A395; B469; D496; E435; F253; J157; K208; M489; O84; P14; Q258; U348; W 216; X349; Z430; AD389; AE399; AF379; AI150; AL 165; AM473; AN491; AO414; AP294; AR326; AV71; AW 278; AZ468; BA270; BB262; BF588; BI60; BR41; BV405;

BY261 105653
Lord of our life, God whom we fear (Smith, S. F.) G307; I 503 105654
Lord of spirits, I surrender (Welhaven) P383 105655
Lord of starry vasts unknown (Tweedy) BF354 105656
Lord of the Church, we humbly pray (Osler) D182; J303; K 210; L302; N284; O95; P110; Q489; S482; AA485; AX159; BA308 105657
Lord of the endless age! We raise to thee (McCook) AO608 105658
Lord of the harvest, bend thine ear (Hastings) V559 105659
Lord of the harvest, hear thy needy servants (Wesley) D185; H462; K215; L339; N369; P398; Q488; AA491; AZ1199; BA349; BV410; BZ 105660
Lord of the Harvest, it is right and meet (Stone) F378 105661
Lord of the harvest, once again (Anstice) W615; AZ660 105662
Lord of the harvest, thee we hail (Gurney) D190; M493; BH188 105663
Lord of the hearts of men (Coffin) D75; AO499 105664
Lord of the home, thine only Son (Bayly) BY620 105665
Lord of the lands, beneath the bending skies (Watson) AE391; AL511; AP648 105666
Lord of the living harvest (Monsell) D285; G401; H458; I219; J304; K211; N285; O94; Q492; U387; W335; AL234; AP368; AR558; BA317; BV324; BY381 105667
Lord of the mountain (Navajo prayer) Yp. 439; AC473 105668
Lord of the nations, Father of all (Pounds) AE406; AR394; AS361 105669
Lord of the ocean vast and deep (Harker) BB97 105670
Lord of the Sabbath and its light (---) BB455 105671
Lord of the Sabbath hear our vows (Doddridge) I73 X Lord of the Sabbath, hear us pray 105672
Lord of the Sabbath, hear us pray (Doddridge) H75; I73; AM322 105673
Lord of the Strong, when earth you trod (Hankey) X568; Y78; AB291; BF300 105674
Lord of the worlds above (Watts) F248; H421; J238; K239; L59; N322; Q480; R14; S50; V16; AA469; AL 198; AM302; AO9; AP66; AR574; AS190; AZ1168; BA376; BV559; BY273 105675
Lord of the worlds, unseen or seen (Blakeney) F492 105676
Lord of true light, we gratefully adore thee (Moxley) AF471; BY350 105677
Lord, on thee alone I stay me (---) BR338 105678
Lord, open thou both heart and ear (Olearius) M10 105679
Lord, open thou my heart to hear (Olearius) Q5; AA2 105680
Lord, our eyes unseal, to our minds reveal (Russell) AZ 536 105681
Lord, our High-priest and Saviour (Zinzendorf, N. L.) AZ571 105682
Lord, our Lord in all the earth (U. P. Psalter, 1912) R Lord, our Lord, thy glorious name 105683
Lord, our Lord, thy glorious name (U. P. Psalter, 1912) T10; AJ15; AM107 105784
Lord, pour thy Spirit from on high (Montgomery) A219; B 450; D183; F473; J302; M96; O90; P111; AA488; AO452; BR483 105685
Lord, rebuke me not in anger (U. P. Psalter, 1912) T8; AJ12 105686
Lord, save thy world (Bayly) AF452 105687

Lord, send a revival (McKinney) R Send a revival 105688
Lord, send the old-time power (Gabriel) R Lord, as of old at Pentecost 105689
Lord, send thy Spirit from above (Watts) BR208 X Come Holy Spirit, heavenly Dove, with all thy quickening 105690
Lord, send thy word, and let it fly (Gibbons) L334 105691
Lord, shall thy children come to thee (Hinds) B376 105692
Lord, speak to me that I may speak (Havergal) A574; B502; D586; G460; H389; I410; J538; K212; P323; R298; S399; T 374; U279; V499; W338; Y216; Z470; AB266; AC251; AD321; AE277; AF397; AG248; AH425; AI187; AK255; AL383; AO476; AP570; AR532; AS444; AT340; AV211; AW296; AX161; BA536; BB407; BD117; BF445; BK84; BV597; BY514; BZ 105693
Lord, take my heart just as it is (Stonehouse) AZ214 105694
Lord, teach us how to pray aright (Montgomery) E78; F317; J452; K279; N303; O360; P28; AF336; AZ122; BA607; BV609 105695
Lord, the God of my Salvation (U.P. Psalter, 1912) T162; AJ240 105696
Lord, the wind and sea obey thee (Dearmer) E543 105697
Lord, thee I love with all my heart (Schalling) Q429; AA366 105698
Lord, thee, my God, I'll early seek (Scottish Psalter, 1650) AL655; AP52 105699
Lord, thine ancient people see (Harland) M119; O127; P401; AO538 105700
Lord, thine appointed servants bless (---) AO458 105701
Lord, thine fore'er today I vow to be (Kretzmann) M549 105702
Lord, thine humble servants hear (Jewish liturgy: Yom Kippur) BH169 105703
Lord, this day thy children meet (How) H447; W238; AL617; AP801; AS395; BD 14; BX525 105704
Lord, thou hast been our dwelling place In every generation (Gill) AM287 105705
Lord, thou hast been our dwelling place Through all the ages (U.P. Psalter, 1912) R88; T167; AJ245 105706
Lord, thou hast been thy people's rest (Montgomery) AW 568; AZ743 105707
Lord, thou has favor shown thy land (U.P. Psalter, 1912) T156; AJ231 105708
Lord, thou hast greatly blessed our land (U.P. Psalter, 1912) AJ230 105709
Lord, thou hast known our joy (Mills) AF472 105710
Lord, thou hast promised grace for grace (Cox) I347 105711
Lord! Thou hast searched and seen me through (Watts) V96; AO84; BR278 105712
Lord, thou hast searched me, and dost know (U.P. Psalter, hymnal, 1927) S102; T275; AF576; AJ382; AM33 105713
Lord, thou hast taught our hearts to glow (Palmer) AO480 105714
Lord, thou hast told us that there be (Washbourne) X107 105715
Lord, thou lovest the cheerful giver (Murray) AK260; AM 368; AP562; AS354; BF607 105716
Lord, thou shalt early hear my voice (Scottish Psalter, 1650) AL631; AW576 105717
Lord! Thou Source of all perfection (Muenter) N190 105718
Lord, thou who gavest me all I have (Farjeon) X569 105719
Lord, thou wilt hear me when I pray (Watts) BC265

105720

Lord, through all the generations (U.P. Psalter, 1912) T166; AJ244 105721

Lord, through changing days, unchanging (Bowie) AW402; BF 637 105722

Lord through theis Holy Week of our salvation (Draper) F100; AF168 105723

Lord, thy children guide and keep (How) B374; D572; AZ1283; BB408 105724

Lord, thy death and passion give (Heermann) K95; N92; AI421 105725

Lord, thy glory fills the heaven (Mant) O62 X Round the Lord in glory seated 105726

Lord, thy Kingdom bring triumphant (Bayly) BY382 105727

Lord, thy mercy now entreating (Sidebotham) W404; AF332; AK216; AL277; AP429; AW 147 105728

Lord, thy omniscience I adore (Cronenwett) M155 105729

Lord, thy servants forth are going (Winks) BY383 105730

Lord, thy word abideth (Baker) A399; B59; D282; E436; F250; K168; L312; N224; O140; R252; V80; W199; X570; AF258; AG 298; AL186; AM266; AP288; AW292; AZ23; BI42; BJ4; BR 237; BV305; BY250 105731

Lord, thy word hath taught (Hunter-Clare) BV136 105732

Lord thy word, that sacred treasure (Zinzendorf, N.L.) M28 105733

Lord, thy word to me remember (U.P. Psalter, 1912) T231; AJ327 105734

Lord, 'tis not that I did choose thee (Conder) Q37; AA69 105735

Lord to me thy ways make known (U.P. Psalter, 1912) AJ67 105736

Lord, to our humble prayers attend (Greek liturgy: Great collect) E650; F588 105737

Lord, to thee alone we turn (Evans) AO654 105738

Lord, to thee I make confession (Franck) N405; O497; Q326; AA416; AZ433 105739

Lord, to thee I now surrender (Rambach) J293 105740

Lord, to thee, in whom is dwelling (---) BRp.467 105741

Lord, to thee my soul is lifted (Collier) AI441 105742

Lord, to whom except to thee (Monsell) K370 105743

Lord, unto thee we look for salvation (Sellers) AU441 105744

"Lord, we are able." (Marlatt) R "Are ye able" 105745

Lord, we ask thee, ere we part (Manwaring) BC119 105746

Lord we beseech thee (Huffman) AR655 105747

Lord, we come before thee now (Hammond) H59; I35; L197; P47; Q18; S11app.; U446; V17; Z116; AA7; AH164; AI17; AO4; AX53; AY54; BB 30; BC142 105748

Lord, we come with hearts aflame (Braley) AC250; BB229 105749

Lord, we confess our numerous faults (Watts) L417; N409; Q382; AA307 105750

Lord, we have come to thee (Sargent) BV631 105751

Lord, we humbly bow before thee (Thompson) O42 105752

Lord, we thank thee for our brothers (Powell) AF268 105753

Lord, we thank thee for the pleasure (Jex-Blake) BY17 105754

Lord, what a change within us one short hour (Trench) S250; AB223; AD286; AE237; AR 277; AW183; BF367 105755

Lord, what offering shall we bring (Taylor) AN281; BH

148; BR47; BX336 105756
Lord, when at thy command (Wesley) AA487 X Lord, if at thy command 105757
Lord! when before thy throne we meet (Nicholas) BR470 105758
Lord! when I all things would possess (Gill) I343 105759
Lord, when in Simon's house of yore (Henshaw) V634 105760
Lord, when the wise men came from far (Godolphin) X571 105761
Lord, when thou makest thy presence felt (Hardenberg) BR71 105762
Lord, when thy kingdom comes, remember me (Maclagan) E 113; F116; W98; AK157; AO 259; AZ449 105763
Lord, when we bend before thy throne (Carlyle) A410; B124; D354; E79; H52; Q22; U445; V462; X108; AA6; AO313; AP328; AZ197; BA602; BF 359; BR280; BV142; BX251 105764
Lord, when we have not any light (Matheson) G453 105765
Lord, while for all mankind we pray (Wreford) B431; E561; F581; G499; H531; I701; Q578; W633; X320; Z544; AA302; AD431; AH486; AL519; AN390; AO593; AP645; AZ158; BA870; BB509; BF562; BX425; BY646; BZ 105766
Lord, while I with thee remain (Loskiel) AZ1039 105767
Lord, who at Cana's wedding feast (Thrupp) A215; D237; J301; K414; N527; O536; Q620; AA443; BA842; BQ150 105768
Lord, who can be with thee compared? (Cramer) AW518 105769
Lord, who didst sanctify thyself, and hast thereby (Foster) AZ 548 105770
Lord, who didst send, by two and two before thee (Wilson) A575; X344 105771
Lord, who dost the voices bless (Williams) AN450; BX489 105772
Lord, who fulfillest thus anew (Mozley) B272 105773
Lord, who hast made me free (Briggs) X109 105774
Lord, who in thy perfect wisdom (Rees) BY647 105775
Lord, who left the highest heaven (Dudley-Smith) BV395 105776
Lord who lovest little children (Rowland) AH555 105777
Lord, who ordainest for mankind (Bryant) AN439 105778
Lord, who shall come to thee (Scrimger) AJ25; AK263; AM 445; AP10 105779
Lord, who shall sit beside thee (Romanis) E232; X234 105780
Lord, who throughout these forty days (Hernaman) A59; B134; D78; N84; R181; S144; AF153; AK141; BA198; BL19; BM75*; BV144 *major variant 105781
Lord, who thyself hast bidden us to pray (Briggs) X572 105782
Lord, whom winds and seas obey (Wesley) I103 105783
Lord, whose glory fills the skies BR12 X Christ whose glory fills 105784
Lord, whose love through humble service (Bayly) BZ 105785
Lord, wilt thou in this temple reign (Mudge) AD390 105786
Lord, with devotion we pray (Hay) AR456; AS13 105787
Lord, with glowing heart I'd praise thee (Key) A454; B233; D443; H61; J403; K291; L86; N296; O15; U315; AI5; AM69; AO54; AW511; AZ974; BA651; BB23 105788
Lord, written in rocks and in woodland (Hess) BH39 105789
Lost in the night doth the heathen yet languish (Finnish) P396 105790
Loud let the swelling anthems

rise (Hamburg Temple hymnal) BH78 105791

Loud lift your voices in triumph on high (Ware) R Lift your glad voices in triumph 105792

Lov og Tak og evig Ære (Kingo) BT401 105793

Love came down at Christmas (Rossetti) G94; J37; S133; W52; X92; BV105; BY103; BZ 105794

Love can tell, and love alone (Bridges) AQ162 105795

Love consecrates the humblest act (McManus) AX170; AY268 105796

Love divine, all loves [love] excelling (Wesley) A479; B226; D432; E437; F205; G372; H322; I355; J397; K276; L202; M158; N297; O295; P38; Q351; R399; S308; T326; U21; V323; W479; X573; Y356; Z379; AB193; AC 67; AD245; AE188; AF228; AG176; AH223; AK272; AL330; AM460; AN50; AO295; AP463; AR178; AS116; AT2; AU19; AV183; AW178; AX43; AY15; AZ948; BA490; BB142; BF256; BI3; BK52; BR24, 29; BV625; BX118; BY595; BZ 105797

Love divine, all loves excelling (Wesley) X Come, thou universal blessing (Wesley) 105798

Love divine, all loves excelling (Wesley) X Peace of God, which knows no measure (Book of hymns, 1846) 105799

Love from God our Lord, Ever forth has poured (Schjørring) M278 105800

Love is kind and suffers long (Wordsworth) Z386; BE173 105801

Love is life's true crown and glory (Grundtvig) BE178 105802

Love is the theme, love is supreme (Fisher) R Of the themes that men have known 105803

Love lifted me! (Rowe) R I was sinking deep in sin 105804

Love not the world! Its dazzling show (Flory) AX409; AY385 105805

Love of God, eternal love (Wine) AR88 105806

Love of Jesus, all divine (Bottome) B231; D607 105807

Love of love, and Light of light (Bridges) AN220; BJ97; BX 110 105808

Love of the Father, love of God the Son (Latin, 12th c) E 438; F238; J125; X574; BJ 28; BL99 105809

Love one another, -- word of revelation (Morrison) BE 179 105810

Love, the found of light from heaven (Grundtvig) O448; P293 105811

Love the Lord thy God! Love is staff and rod (Schjørring) BE180 105812

Love thyself last (Wilcox) AC 239 105813

Love, unto thine own who camest (Bridges) BJ92 105814

Love, who in the first beginning (Scheffler) AZ605 105815

Loved with everlasting love (Robinson) W434; BY448 105816

Lovely appear over the mountains (Bible, Isaiah 52) AH619 105817

Love's redeeming work is done (Wesley) X160 X Christ the Lord is risen today 105818

Loving Father, we thy children (Hackett) BE181 105819

Loving Jesus, gentle Lamb (Wesley) I374 X Lamb of God, I look do thee 105820

Loving Saviour, hear my cry (Crosby) AX249 105821

Loving Shepherd of thy sheep (Leeson) D552; E602; F444; W668; X366; AW429; BQ45; BV337; BY287 105822

Lovingly, tenderly calling to me (Ogden) R Jesus, the loving Shepherd 105823
Lovingly the Shepherd, Seeking the lost (Ukrainian trad.) AL 492 105824
Low at thy pierced feet, Saviour of all (Stephens) BB239 105825
Low in the grave He lay (Lowry) AE123; AH302; AI81; AM206; AR185; AS150; AT113; AU127; AV317; AW452; AX119; AY 265; BY160; BZ 105826
Löwen, lasst euch wieder finden (German. 1712) BT470 105827
Lowly entombed he lay (Hugg) AY265 X Low in the grave He lay (Lowry) 105828
Loyal and true and faithful (Toews) AX447 105829
Lucis creátor optime (St Gregory the Great) BO283; BQ26 105830
Lullay my liking, my dear son (English trad carol, 15th) R I saw a fair maiden, sitten and sing 105831
Lullay, thou little tiny child (Pageant of the Shearmen) BL 15 X Lully, lulla, thou little tiny child 105832
Lully, lulla, thou little tiny child (Pageant of the Shearmen. 15th c) BG22; BL15 105833
Lully, lulley, lully, lulley, The falcon hath borne my make away (English trad. 15th c) BG61 notes 105834

M

M.I.A. we hail thee (Fox) BC 111 105835
Mache dich, mein Geist, bereit, (Freystein) BT446 105836
Macht hoch die Tür, die Tor' macht weit (Weissel) BT73; BW523 105837
Make lowly wise, we pray no more (Hosmer) X575; AN274; AQ188; BF437; BX342 105838
Made of one blood with all on earth to dwell (Best) AD338 105839
Magdalene, thy grief and gladness (Grève) F556 105840
Magdalene, thy grief and gladness (Grève) X Sing we all the joys and sorrows 105841
Magnify Jehovah's name (Montgomery) D475; BH59 105842
Magnify th' Eternal's name (Montgomery) BH59 X Magnify Jehovah's name 105843
Maiden Mother, meek and mild (Latin, 13th c) BP75 105844
Majestic sweetness sits enthroned (Stennett) A353; B194; G220; H323; I135; J570; L152; O66; P8; R142; S197; T327; U71; V129; Z381; AB82; AE 100; AG111; AH311; AI106; AK183; AM143; AO202; AR 113; AS126; AT118; AU188; AV132; AW120; AX18; BA 493; BB159; BZ 105845
Make channels for the streams of love (Trench) AN276; AQ157; BD123; BE182; BX340 105846
Make haste, O God, to save (U.P. Psalter, 1912) AJ189 105847
Make haste, O man, to do (Bonar) BE183 X Make haste, O man, to live 105848
Make haste, O man, to live (Bonar) I390; U415; V667; BE183 105849
Make haste, O my God, to deliver (U.P. Psalter, 1912) T129; AJ188 105850
Make large our hearts with thine own love (Goforth) BK101 105851
Make me a blessing (Wilson) R Out on the highways 105852
Make me a captive, Lord (Matheson) G367; J508; R308; S 247; W464; X576; AB194; AE266; AF356; AG314; AI92; AK243; AL313; AO294; AR359; BB284; BF454; BV633; BY

478; BZ 105853
Make me a channel of blessing today (Smyth) R Is your life a channel 105854
Make me, O Lord, an instrument of thy peace (St Francis of Assisi??) BN60 105855
Make my calling and election (Gregor) AZ977; BA747 105856
Make use of me, my God (Bonar) AZ1290; BA553 105857
Make we joy now in this feast (English trad. carol, 15th c) BG23 105858
Make me merry, both more and less (English trad carol, ca 1500) BG172 105859
Make wide the door, unbar the gate! (Weissel) P115 105860
Maker, keeper, Thou, be my Guardian now (St Ambrose) AY288 105861
Maker of all things, Lord our God (Latin) AZ289 105862
Maker of all things, mighty Lord (Doddridge) L106 105863
Maker of earth and sea and sky (Lord) W350 105864
Maker of earth, to thee alone (Coffin) E64 105865
Maker of man, who from thy throne (Latin, ca 7th c) E62 105866
Maker of stars, Eternal King (Cross) Y232 105867
Man imperishably stands (Laing) AQ67 105868
Man is the earth upright and proud (Patton) AQ62 105869
Man lives not for himself alone (Shuttleworth) AN510; AQ151 105870
Man of Sorrows, now my soul (Zinzendorf, C.R.) AK152; AW 537 105871
Man of Sorrows! what a name (Bliss) AM175 X Man of Sorrows! wondrous name 105872
Man of Sorrows! wondrous name (Bliss) W693; AM175; AP213; AR166; AS135; AT163; AU257; AV321; BV159; BY187 105873
Man of Sorrows, wrapt in grief (Slovak hymal) AL88; BQ19 105874
Man's comradeship is very wide (Frank) AN403; AQ148 105875
Many and great, O God, are thy things (Dakota Indian Hymn) BZ 105876
Many souls today are dying (Teasley) AX217 105877
Many woes had Christ endured (Hart) AZ1261 105878
March, march onward, Soldiers true (Plumptre) BI5 105879
March on, march on to victory (Moultrie) BI7 X We march, we march to victory 105880
March on, my soul, with strength (Wright) W537; BY 716 105881
March on, O soul, with strength (Coster) G264; R351; S273; U300; Y110; Z359; AB249; AC184; AD290; AE251; AF 380; AH446; AK291; AO406; AR327; AT422; BD84; BF 478; BZ 105882
Marching home, we're marching home (---) R We are marching homeward with the blest 105883
Marching on, marching on, For Christ count everything R There's a royal banner given 105884
Marching with the heroes (Tarrant) U298; Y112; Z322; AC259; AH447; AN480; BD88; BF625; BX543 105885
Maria die wollt' wandern geh'n (German trad carol) BG93b 105886
Maria gin'g aus wandern (German trad carol) BG179b 105887
Maria, mater gratiae (Fortunatus??) BN148; BO84 105888
Marter Gottes, wer kann dein vergessen (C.R. v. Zinzendorf) BW537 105889
Martyr of God, whose strength

was steeled (Latin, 10th c) E 180 105890
Marvelous grace of our loving Lord (Johnston) AE224; AM705; AR457; AT200; AX321 105891
Mary! how sweetly falls that word (---) BO92 105892
Mary Immaculate, Mother and Maid (Currie) BN149 105893
Mary Immaculate, Star of the morning (Weatherell) BM56 105894
Mary the Dawn, Christ the Perfect Day (---) BM49 105895
Mary to the Saviour's tomb (Newton) AY315 105896
Mary, weep not, weep no longer (Grève) E231 105897
Master and Lord, 'tis good to be here (Pray) BE185 105898
Master, no offering (Parker) B 500; G464; N662; R299; S407; U277; Y229; Z303; AB263; AC252; AD322; AE281; AF 405; AG246; AK396; AN558; AO 493; AR377; AT401; AV214; BB478; BF502 105899
Master of eager youth (St Clement of Alexandria) A362 105900
Master, speak! Thy servant heareth (Havergal) G221; AW 219; AZ609; BA527; BR369; BV475; BY479; BZ 105901
Master, the tempest is raging (Baker) AM701; AU471; BB677; BC106 105902
Master, we thy footsteps follow (Jackson) BY296 105903
Masters in this hall, Hear ye news today (Morris) BG137 105904
May God be praised henceforth and blest forever (Luther) O156; AA431 105905
May God bestow on us His grace (Luther) O29; Q500; AA480 105906
May He, by whose kind care we meet (Newton) V613 105907
May He who kept us through the hours of night (Lucas) BH10 105908
May Jesus Christ, the spotless Lamb (Greek) AZ563 105909
May Jesus' grace and blessing (Mathesius) AZ565; BA773 105910
May my heart be turned to pray (---) R There is an hour of peace and rest 105911
May nothing evil cross this door (Untermeyer) AC530; AQ 159 105912
May the grace of Christ our Saviour (Newton) A216; F636; G27; I40; K436; L65; M14; N362; R76; S495; Z 126; AD512; AE468; AF539; AG334; AJp. 393; AK36; AP 338; AR682; AS68; AT538; AU497; AW613; AX75; AZ 953; BA913; BV21; BY763; BZ 105913
May the Lord depend on you (Martin) R In the warfare 105914
May the mind of Christ my Saviour (Wilkinson) BV634; BY596 105915
May the stream from Thee, the Rock, Gracious Jesus (Swertner) AZ725 105916
May we sow righteous seed for the reaping (Winsett) R There is coming a day 105917
May we thy precepts, Lord, fulfill (Osler) M214; Q412; AA339 105918
May we to thee, our Shepherd cleave (Horne) AZ682 105919
May you who enter here, Draw near to God (---) S 16app. 105920
Mee Cho-mo-cho bo-ay-leem A-do-noy (Jewish traditional) BH270 105921
Meet and right it is to sing (Wesley) AZ1479 105922
Mein frölich Herz das treibt mich (Ausbund Suppl.) BU4 105923
Mein frölich Herz das treibt

mich an zu singen (Ausbund) BU133 105924
Mein Gott! das herz ich bringe dir (Unparth. G. B.) AY13d 105925
Mein Gott dich will ich loben In meiner letzten Stund (L. Schneider) BU39 105926
Mein Heiland nimmt die Sünder an (Lehr) BT386 105927
Mein Herz will ich dir schenken (German. 1653) BT89 105928
Mein Jesu, wie du willt (Schmolck) BT420; BW250 105929
Mein Muth und Sinn steht mir dahin (M. Schneider) BU102 105930
Mein Schöpfer, steh mir bei (Rambach) BT335 105931
Meinen Jesum lass' ich nicht (Keimann) BT365 105932
Men and children everywhere (Moment) S4; Z96; BZ 105933
Men go out from the places where they dwelled (Turner) AQ216 105934
Men, my brothers, men the workers (Tennyson) AC522 105935
Men of England, who inherit (Campbell) X321 105936
Men of the Church of the Living God (Glasgow) U297 105937
Men true of heart and strong in faith (Boden) BY547 105938
Men who walk in folly's way (U. P. Psalter, 1912) T205; AJ294 105939
Men whose boast it is that ye (Lowell) X306; AF425; AN318; AQ173; BD159; BH121; BK104 105940
Mensch! wilt du nimmer traurig seyn (O. Rot) BU58 105941
Merciful Saviour, come and be my comfort (Ehrenberg-Posse) N460; P311 105942
Mercy there was great, and grace was free (Newell) R Years I spent in vanity 105943
Mercy thou art, Creator, Friend! (Dearmer) X577 105944
Merkt auf ein Sach und die ist wahr (Ausbund) BU54 105945
Merkt auf, ihr Christen all geleich (Ausbund) BU114 105946
Merkt auf ihr Christen allgemein (M. Schneider) BU 103 105947
Merkt auf, ihr Menschenkinder (Ausbund) BU94 105948
Merkt auf, ihr Völker alle (Ausbund) BU44 105949
Merkt auf, ihr Völker allgemein (M. Schneider) BU82 105950
Merkt auf, ihr Völker g'meine (H. Betz) BU109 105951
Merkt auf, ihr Völker überall (Ausbund) BU21 105952
Merkt auf mit Fleiss, ein Himmelspeiss. (H. Betz) BU92 105953
Merkt auf und nehmt zu Herzen (Ausbund) BU33 105954
Merry Christmas bells are ringing (---) BI80 105955
Met around the sacred tomb (Latrobe) AX1249 105956
Mich verlanget zu allen Zeiten (M. Schneider) BU93 105957
Michael, prince of all the angels (Lee) BN164 105958
'Mid all the traffic of the ways (Oxenham) G341; S322; U 237; AC159; AD265; AG204; AK232; BF391; BK88; BZ 105959
'Mid pleasures and palaces though wc may roam (Payne) P349; AS412; BB415; BC185 105960
'Mid scenes of confusion and creature complaints (Denham) L605; U428; V715; AI339; AX573; AY393 105961
'Mid the trials we experience (Foster) AZ979 105962
Mighty God, the First, the Last (Gaskell) BE186; BX175 105963
Mighty God, to thy dear name be given (Dass) J357 105964

Mighty God, we humbly pray (St Ambrose & N. L. Zinzendorf) AZ83; BA627 105965

Mighty God, while angels bless thee (Robinson) H101; I85; P21; R10; U114; V197; Z160; AD72; AE60; AG42; AH186; AM5; AO203; AR76; AT4; AV 50; AW46; BF238; BY210 105966

Mighty King of heaven, Our Redeemer, Saviour (Latin) R Incline thine ear, O Lord, and show us mercy 105967

Mighty King of righteousness (Bonar) AZ1127 X Blessed night, when first that plain 105968

Mighty Lord, extend thy kingdom (Cottle) N375 105969

Mighty Rock in a weary land (Charlesworth) R The Lord's our Rock, in Him we hide 105970

Mighty Rock, whose tow'ring form (Crosby) Z407; AI249 105971

Mighty Saviour, gracious King (Osler) AO5 105972

Mighty to save, mighty to save (Todd) R O who is this that cometh 105973

Mindful of our human frailty (U. P. Psalter, 1912) T193; AJ281 105974

Mine eyes have seen the glory (Howe) B434; J356; W155; X578; Y289; AC280; AF443; AH485; AN567; AO600; AT488; AV301; BD170; BX410; BZ 105975

Mine eyes look toward the mountains (Bible. Psalm 121: Swedish version) BE189 105976

Mine eyes unto the mountains (Olson) J398; N323 105977

Mine hour appointed is at hand (Herman) AZ746 105978

Mir mit Erbarmung widerfahren (Tersteegen) AW562b; BW562 105979

Mir nach! spricht Christus, unser Held (Scheffler) BT421; BW 565 105980

Miserere illi Deus (Latin) BQ 253 X Qui regnas in perpetum 105981

Mit Angst und Roth ruff ich dich an (M. Gerfass) BU41 105982

Mit einem zugeneigten G'müth (Ausbund) BU137 105983

Mit Ernst, o Menschenkinder (Thilo) BT75 105984

Mit Freuden woll'n wir singen (Ausbund: Fourteen Author) BU100 105985

Mit Fried' und Freud' ich fahr' dahin (Luther) BT 137 105986

Mit Lust so will ich singen (F. Mantzen) BU6 105987

Mit Lust so will ich singen Ein schöne Tageweiss (Ausbund) BU79 105988

Mit Lust und Freud will ich Gott lobsingen, Dem Vater gut. (M. Schneider) BU95 105989

Mitten wir im Leben sind (Luther) BT590 105990

Moment by moment I'm kept in his love (Whittle) R Dying with Jesus 105991

More about Jesus I would know (Hewitt) AH409 X More about Jesus would I know 105992

More about Jesus would I know (Hewitt) R316; AE296; AH 409; AI283; AM676; AR455; AS225; AT321; AV324; AX 373; AY48; BY597 105993

More and more like Jesus (Stillman) R I want to be more like Jesus 105994

More holiness give me (Bliss) U264; V412; AR404; AS222; AT338; AU217; AX429; AZ 496; BA633; BC114 105995

More light shall break from out thy word (Cross) AB392; AD436 105996

More like Jesus would I be (Crosby) AT316; AV190 105997

More like the Master I would

ever be (Gabriel) AT325 105998

More like thee, O Saviour, let me be (Davis) AR458; AS223; AX375; AY44 105999

More love to thee, O Christ (Prentiss) A461; D654; G364; H333; I317; J392; L198; N493; P310; R397; S315; T410; U 224; V372; Z390; AD256; AE 198; AF400; AG168; AH347; AI117; AK471; AL498; AM548; AO642; AP461; AR407; AS280; AT292; AU218; AV195; AW472; AX379; BA461; BB385; BF462; BZ 106000

More lovely than the noonday rest (Farjeon) X579 206001

More than all, one thing my heart is craving (Knapp) AZ 1005 106002

More than shepherd's faithfulness (Gregor) AZ585 106003

Morgenglanz der Ewigkeit (C.K. von Rosenroth) AW554b; BT539; BW554 106004

Morn of joy and morn of praise (Sewall) BI103 106005

Morning breaks upon the tomb (Collyer) N133; Q203 106006

Morning has broken Like the first morning (Farjeon) R464; X30; AD469; AF38; AN97; AQ266 106007

Morning has come, the table is spread (---) AR553 106008

Morning, so fair to see (Silliman) AN45; AQ14 106009

Morning Star, O cheering sight! (Scheffler) AZ1156; BA59 106010

Morn's roseate hues have decked (Breviary. Cluny) D120; AZ4; BR187 106011

Most ancient of all mysteries (Faber) F159; J138; X188 106012

Most fervent thanks I render (---) M563 106013

Most glorious Lord of life, that on this day (Spenser) E283; X22; BV73 106014

Most gracious God and Lord (Zinzendorf, N.L.) AZ782; BA122 106015

Most High, omnipotent, good Lord (St Francis of Assisi) A307 106016

Host Holy Lord and God, Holy, Almighty God (Breviary, Paris, 1531) AZ1205; BA 199 106017

Most holy Lord and God of heaven (Latin, 4th-5th c) E60 106018

Most holy Lord, mankind's Creator (Swertner) AZ1415 106019

Most holy Mary at thy feet (Caswall) R This is the image of our Queen 106020

Most perfect is the law of God (U.P. Psalter, 1912) R257; AF255; AI315; AJ41; AM 450* 106021

*refrain is unusual

Most wondrous is of all on earth (Grundtvig) P224 X O wondrous kingdom here on earth 106022

Mother dear, O pray for me (---) AH132; BO79 106023

Mother Mary, at thine altar (Faber) BO83; BP82 106024

Mother of Christ, Mother of Christ, What shall I ask of thee? (A Sister of Notre Dame) BQ89 106025

Mother of mercy, day by day (Faber) BO67; BQ77 106026

Motherhood, sublime, eternal (Cutler) Z604; AN557; AW 364 106027

Mount Sion -- where the Lamb of God (Swertner) AZ891 106028

Mount up with wings as eagles (Cross) AB414; BF670 106029

Mourn for the thousands slain (Brace) H526; I698; AZ1296; BB502 106030

Move in our midst, Thou Spirit of God (Morse) AR225 106031

Much in sorrow, oft in woe (White) W533 X Oft in danger, oft in woe 106032

Müde bin ich, geh' zur Ruh' (Unparth. G. B.) AY46d 106033

Muss es nun seyn gescheiden (Ausbund) BU136 106034

Must I go and empty-handed (Luther, C. C.) AT430; AU 296; AX345; AY527 106035

Must Jesus bear the cross alone (Shepherd) G276; H370; I428; L525; M394; N472; P314; R290; U416; V440, 766; Z366; AE219; AH294; AI317; AO384; AR317; AS330; AT428; AU153; AV204; AX426; AY113; AZ93; BA463; BB274; BZ 106036

Mute are the pleading lips of Him (Wallin) M424; N120 106037

My all for thee (McKinney) R All on the altar 106038

My all I to my God commend (Leon) O481 106039

My All-in-all, my faithful Friend (Zinzendorf, N. L.) AZ686 106040

My bark is wafted to the strand (Alford) I451 106041

My beautiful home is in heaven above (Poyry) M303 106042

My blest Redeemer and my Lord (Watts) BB140 X My dear Redeemer and my Lord 106043

My case to thee is fully known (Rose) AZ884 106044

My Church! My Church! My dear old Church (Lutheran Church. General Council S. S. Book, 1887) L286; M87; N276; P376 106045

My country is the world; My flag with stars impearled (Whitaker) Y271; Z514; AC294; AN402; AQ149; AR610 106046

My country 'tis of thee (Smith, S. F.) A141; B427; G489; H529; I702; J360; K490; L556; M505; N567; P410; R513; S412; T446; U338; Y293; Z548; AB334; AC279; AD440; AE393; AF437; AG274; AH474; AI363; AJp. 393; AK441; AN384; AO586; AQ242; AR611; AS383; AT487; AU458; AV302; AW344; AZ1230; BB510; BC 115; BD172; BF541; BH264; BI11; BK118; BR493; BX420; BZ 106047

My country, to thy shore (Williams) AN382; BDp. 56; BX 418 106048

My course is run. Praise God, my course is run (Gryphius) Q599 106049

My crucified Saviour, despised and contemned (Rutström) N114 106050

My days are gliding swiftly by (Nelson) L569; U417; V657; AS474; AV288; AW503; AX571; AY89; BR522 106051

My dear Jesus I'll not leave (Keimann) AA88 X Jesus I will never leave 106052

My dear Redeemer, and my Lord (Watts) H155; I140; K52; L 137; N188; U85; V138; Z207; AD136; AH234; AM171; AO 142; AR151; AS118; AT83; AZ417; BA84; BB140; BR165; BY124 106053

My dearest friends, in bonds of love (---) AX655; AY406 106054

My dearest Saviour I would fain (---) BO20 106055

My drowsy powers, why sleep ye so? (Watts) L199 106056

My end, Lord, make me know (U. P. Psalter, 1912) T71; AJ107 106057

My faith it is an oaken staff (Lynch) Y138; AC185; AF381; BK74; BY548 106058

My faith looks up to thee (Palmer) A449; B211; D345; E439; G213; H40; I334; J375; K360; L190; M234; N425; O456; P269; Q 394; R378; S285; T390; U194; V357; W415; X580; Z355; AA 351; AB172; AC155; AD218; AE193; AF348; AG211; AH 358; AI238; AK221; AL263; AM454; AO274; AP419; AR 261; AS270; AT257; AU209; AV168; AW150; AX453; AY60;

AZ1244; BA429; BB246; BF 369; BR303; BV507; BY549; BZ 106059

My faith shall be my rock of might (Abraham ibn Ezra) BH 200 106060

My faith shall triumph O'er the grave (Watts) AZ1460 106061

My faithful Shepherd is the Lord (U.P. Psalter, 1912) AJ54 106062

My Father bids me come (Wesley) BR290 X Ah! Whither should I go 106063

My Father! cheering name! (Steele) L522; V103; AA519; AS79 106064

My Father for another night (Baker) B6; D640; F5; K571; AP656; BV41 106065

My Father has many dear children (Graves) AU25 106066

My Father, hear my prayer (Horder. Book of praise for children. 1875) K573 106067

My Father is rich in houses and lands (Buell) AM720; AT270; AU47; AV342; BB614 106068

My Father, when I come to thee (Hart) AZ379 106069

My Father's house on high (Montgomery) M310 X Forever with the Lord 106070

My former hopes are fled (Cowper) H228 106071

My glorious Victor, Prince Divine (Moule) BB648 106072

My God, accept my heart this day (Bridges) A404; B372; D429; E341; F459; I369; J289; K178; L441; N253; O111; P257; Q336; S232; U185; X254; AA412; AE 269; AF321; AH351; AK346; AX166; AZ135; BA460; BL36; BQ132; BV363 106073

My God and Father, day by day (Elliott) AM575 X My God, my Father, while I stray 106074

My God and Father, while I stray (Elliott) U42; X My God, my Father, while I stray 106075

My God, and is thy table spread (Doddridge) O153 X My God, thy table now is spread 106076

My God, how endless is thy love (Watts) L12; S78; V36; AX 45; AY25; BB414; BR250; BV 42 106077

My God! how ought my grateful heart (---) BO200 X O God! how ought my grateful heart 106078

My God, how wonderful thou art (Faber) A284; B221; D441; E441; F169; I86; J181; K303; L101; N339; O64; P19; W27; X581; AI413; AL18; AM31; AO106; AP149; AS84; BA17; BN197; BO2; BP101; BV10; BY64; 106079

My God, I am determined (---) R In every waking moment 106080

My God, I am thine, what comfort divine (Wesley) AZ1420 106081

My God, I believe in thee (Latin) BQ145 106082

My God, I feel thy wondrous might (Cary) BX57 106083

My God, I know, I feel thee mine (Wesley) AY39 106084

My God, I know that I must die (Schmolck) N593; O586 106085

My God, I love thee; not because (St Francis Xavier??) A456; D653; E80; F106; G214; H324; I483; J489; K58; L451; S313; W433; X110; AD248; AF313; AL305; AO286; AV137; AZ152; BA496; BJ2; BO170; BY211 106086

My God I rather look to thee (Scudder) BX470 106087

My God, I thank thee! May no thought (Norton) BX247 106088

My God, I thank thee, who hast made (Proctor) B384; D624; G9; I29; J447; R409; S73; W441; X582; Y204; Z109; AB 213; AC51; AD270; AE19; AF 98; AG183; AH398; AL289;

AN263; AP440; AR31; AV49; AW177; BA36; BF389; BR423; BV581; BX316; BY504; BZ 106089

My God, I will extol thee (U.P. Psalter, 1912) AJ202 X In doubt and temptation 106090

My God, I will extol thee And ever bless thy name (U.P. Psalter, 1912) AJ399 106091

My God, is any hour so sweet (Elliott) H45; I501; P29; U362; V465; W449; AI224; AL335; AM529; AP487; AS48; AV17; AZ10; BA609; BB325; BR35 106092

My God, it was thy grace (U.P. Psalter, 1912) AJ79 106093

My God, my Father, blissful name (Steele) V103 X My Father! Cheering name 106094

My God! my Father! cheering name (Steele) AS79 X My Father! Cheering name 106095

My God, my Father, let me rest (Bickersteth) BV600 106096

My God, my Father, make me strong (Mann) Q424; X583; AK 208; BE190; BV574; BY480 106097

My God, my Father, while I stray (Elliott) A420; B391; D667; E440; F357; G306; H 362; I521 and 736; J465; K 408; L497; O238; Q418; U42; V435; W539; AA386; AE261; AL430; AM575; AO346, 702; AP504; AS237; AU103*; AV 237; AW245; AX390*; AY478; AZ16; BA695; BR345; BQ332; BX262 *Refrain 106098

My God! my God! and can it be (Faber) E101 106099

My God, my God, I cry to thee (U.P. Psalter, 1912) T32; AJ47 106100

My God, my God, O why hast thou ("Joint committee") AI72 106101

My God, my God, why dost thou me forsake? (Bridges) AL 635; AP17; BJ77 106102

My God, my King, thy various praise (Watts) AV42 106103

My God, my life, my love (Watts) H338 106104

My God, my portion, and my love (Watts) H340 106105

My God, my strength, my hope (Wesley) AS452 X Jesus, my strength, my hope 106106

My God, permit me not to be (Watts) D353; L434; V445; BR275 106107

My God! The covenant of thy love (Doddridge) V329; AO90; AP507; AZ130 106108

My God, the spring of all my joys (Watts) H291; I535; L456; V384; AI260; AL283; AO92; AS298; AZ109 106109

My God, thy table now is spread (Doddridge) A203; B329; D 231; E320; F396; H436; O153; W311; AA429; AE338; AH501; AL231; AP357; BA301; BR 471; BV390 106110

My God, whose gracious pity I may claim (Newton) BR 259 106111

My gracious Lord, I own thy right (Doddridge) G257; H311; I336; V317; AO388; BB21; BY 515 106112

My griefs of heart abound (Palmer??) AJ63 106113

My grieving soul revive, O Lord (U.P. Psalter, 1912) T228; AJ324 106114

My happy lot is here, The Lamb to follow (Gregor) AZ471 106115

My heart delights, O Lord, Upon thy works to ponder (French hymn) M157 106116

My heart doth overflow (U.P. Psalter, 1912) T84; AJ124; AM125 106117

My heart is filled with longing (Bridges) BJ82 106118

My heart is fixed, O God, A grateful song I raise (U.P. Psalter, 1912) T208; AJ299 106119

My heart is full of Christ, And longs (Wesley) H197 106120
My heart is longing to praise my Saviour (Eugenie, Princess of Sweden) P26 106121
My heart is resting, O my God (Waring) B220; R406; S300; W446; AD267; AL282; AP441; BA530; BB332; BX233; BY505 106122
My heart is so happy in Jesus my Lord (Buffum) AX305 106123
My heart its incense burning (Mathesius) O542; P51 106124
My heart lies dead; and no increase (Herbert) AZ13 106125
My heart looks in faith (Chao) AE197 106126
My heart prepare to give account (Brorson) M69 106127
My heart was distressed 'neath Jehovah's dread frown (Zelley) AU50 106128
My heart was glad to hear the welcome sound (U.P. Psalter, 1912) T251; AJ349 106129
My heavenly home is bright and fair (Hunter) I628; AU261; AX591; AY144 106130
My hiding-place, my refuge tower (---) BV526 106131
My hope is built on nothing less (Mote) D622; G244; H289; I330; J385; K331; L415; M190; N424; O236; P283; Q370; R 368; T391; U219; V354; W697; AA306; AE203; AH370; AI141; AM582; AP426; AR460; AS274; AT283; AU96; AV362; AW487; AX482; AY458; BA439; BB581; BT370; BV527; BZ 106132
My hope, my all, my Saviour thou (---) I444; K366 106133
My hope, my portion, and my God (Watts) L388 X Long have I sat beneath the sound 106134
My inmost heart now raises (Ngidius) N544; Q548; AA22 106135
My Jesus, as thou wilt (Schmolck) B395; D634; G330; H371; I524; J580; K395; L501; M273; N490 O233; P156; Q420; R367; S 280; T418; U247; V429; Z 408; AA387; AB241; AG214; AH392; AI291; AK313; AM 572; AO337; AR360; AS234; AT251; AU178; AV222; AW250; AX391; AY475; AZ486; BA 687; BB404; BR327; BZ 106136
My Jesus, I love thee, I know thou art mine (Featherstone) H321; P216; R405; U223; Z382; AE178; AH297; AI115; AM547; AO643; AR462; AS 275; AT289; AU154; AV323; AW216; AX396; AY195; BA 905; BB276 106137
My Jesus, if the Seraphim (Dessler) AZ992 106138
My Jesus, pierced for love of me (Paderborn G-B., 1726) S513 106139
My latest sun is sinking fast (Haskell) AU53; AV313; AX575 106140
My life flows on in endless song (Lowry) BB265 106141
My life is hid in Jesus (Vulpius. Ein schön geistliche G-B. Jena, 1609) O583; P420 106142
My life, my love I give to thee (Hudson) Z293; AH418; AR 341; AS245; AT359; AU168; AX408; AY103 106143
My life, O lord, I give to thee (Howard) R Since Jesus gave his life 106144
My life was lost in selfishness (Shank) AY507 106145
My life's a shade, my days Apace to death decline (Crossman) BJ73 106146
My Lord calls me (Negro spiritual) R Steal away 106147
My Lord, how full of sweet content (Guyon) G334; I518; L 467; AZ927 106148
My Lord, I do not ask to stand (Richardson) AI367; AR543; AS416 106149
My Lord, my God, my only King (Proud) BR56 106150

My Lord, my Life, my Love (Bridges) E442; S328; X584; BF35; BJ35 106151
My Lord, my love, was crucified (Mason) AI20; BJ38 106152
My Lord, my Master, at thy feet adoring (Bridaine) F103; K96; W95; AL91; AP195; AZ127 106153
My Lord, what a morning (Negro spiritual) BK171 X My Lord, what a mourning 106154
My Lord, what a mourning (Negro spiritual) AH599; BK171 106155
My Lord, who in the desert fed (Houghton) BV306 106156
My Maker and my King (Steele) BB71 106157
My Maker, be thou nigh (Rambach) Q335 106158
My Master was a worker, with daily work to do (Tarrant) Z500; AB179; BF435 106159
My Master was so very poor (Lee) S497; Z216; AC110; AD129; AR152; BK22 106160
My name's written there (Kidder) R I am bought not with riches 106161
My opening eyes with rapture see (Hutton) AZ372; BR94 106162
My own dear land (Oxenham) AH 473; AL512; BF552 106163
My people, give ear, attend to my voice (U.P. Psalter, 1912) T145; AJ213; AM301 106164
My portion is the Lord; I seek his favor (Gregor) AZ470; BA448 106165
My Redeemer knoweth me (Freylinghausen G-B.) AZ584 106166
My Redeemer, over-whelmed with grief (Zinzendorf, C.R.) BA214 X O delightful theme, past all expression 106167
My righteous God, who oft of old (U.P. Psalter, 1912) T4; AJ 6 106168
My Saviour, as thou wilt (Schmolck) BR327 X My Jesus, as thou wilt 106169
My Saviour guides me day by day (Bowman) AY127 106170
My Saviour, my almighty Friend (Watts) V189 106171
My Saviour needs helpers from day to day (Rowe) AX211 106172
My Saviour, on the word of truth (Waring) I364 106173
My Saviour sinners doth receive (Lehr) Q386; AZ1089 106174
My Saviour, that I without thee (Zinzendorf, A.N.) AZ409 106175
My Saviour, thou hast offered rest (Hamilton) BV489 106176
My Saviour was betrayed (Wobeser) BA215 106177
My Saviour, whom absent I love (Cowper) AZ1510 106178
My Saviour's pierced side (Watts) AZ1301 106179
My Saviour's praises I will sing ("J.E.A.") AI8; AM703 106180
My Shepherd is the Lamb (Beaumont) AZ1496 106181
My Shepherd is the living Lord (Rous) BT436 X The Lord's my Shepherd, I'll not want (Scottish Psalter, 1650) 106182
My Shepherd is the Lord, There is nothing I shall want (Ladies of the Grail) BS p.10 106183
My Shepherd is the Lord who knows my needs (U.P. Psalter, 1912) T39; AJ56 106184
My Shepherd's mighty aid (Roberts) AZ1195 106185
My sins and faults of youth, (U.P. Psalter, 1912) AJ61 106186
My sins, my sins, my Saviour (Monsell) U169; V282; AI 219; AM464; AO265; AV167

AY510 106187

My song forever shall record (U.P. Psalter, 1912) R516; T163; AJ241; AM101 106188

My song is love unknown (Crossman) F102; J65; X127; AF 169; AL96; BV155; BY143 106189

My song shall bless the Lord of all (Cowper) AZ329 106190

My soul, awake and render (Gerhardt) AN487; AZ36; BA 775 106191

My soul, be on thy guard (Heath) A555; B118; D504; G277; H384; I493; J559; K272; L538; M241; N455; O485; Q449; R363; U 295; V470; Y378; Z370; AA379; AD294; AE255; AH451; AI325; AN299; AO393; AR328; AS327; AT420; AU247; AV177; AX451; AY36; AZ1341; BA580; BB358; BD92; BF477; BX360; BZ 106192

My soul before thee prostrate lies (Richter) I273; AZ405; BA638 106193

My soul, bless the Lord! The Lord is most great (U.P. Psalter, 1912) T197; AJ285; AM110 106194

My soul complete in Jesus stands (Hinsdale) V313 106195

My soul doth magnify the Lord (Fünf auserlesene geistliche Lieder, Marburg, 1535) Q275 106196

My soul doth magnify the Lord (German, 1535) X Our souls shall magnify ... 106197

My soul for thy salvation waits (U.P. Psalter, 1912) T235; AJ331 106198

My soul glorifies the Lord (Ladies of the Grail) BSp.57 106199

My soul has found the sure foundation (Rothe) M131 106200

My soul, how lovely is the place (Watts) V10 106201

My soul in sad exile (Gilmour) AS301; AT228; AU79; AV353; AX524; AY125 106202

My soul in silence waits for God (U.P. Psalter, 1912) T111; AJ161; AM571 106203

My soul is grieved because my foes (U.P. Psalter, 1912) AJ155 106204

My soul, now bless thy maker (Graumann) M592; O7; P9; Q34; AA59 106205

My soul, praise the Lord, O God, thou art great (Bridges) BJ63 106206

My soul repeat his praise (Watts) H113; I94; K306; L73; M596; N293; V527; AA77; AP92 106207

My soul, there is a country (Vaughan, H.) F286; W463; X585; AN434 106208

My soul, thy great Creator praise (Watts) V520 106209

My soul, weigh not thy life (Swain) H383; V488 106210

My soul with expectation doth depend on God (Scottish Psalter, 1650) R113; S86; AL654; AP51 106211

My soul, with joy attend (---) AY400 106212

My soul with patience waits (Tate & Brady) A439; B 314; D334 106213

My soul's best Friend, what joy and blessing (Dessler) Q362 106214

My span of life will soon be done (Cowper) I426 106215

My spirit longs for thee (Byrom) E443; R321; S508; W456; X111; AL333; AP467; AZ474; BR325; BY481 106216

My spirit looks to God alone (Watts) L495 106217

My spirit on thy care (Lyte) B225; D664; K341; L508; N438; Q435; U213; V343; AA369; AG213; AO358; AZ 1356; BA715; BB252; BR251 106218

My stead fast heart, O God (U.P. Psalter, 1912) AJ298 106219

My times are in thy hand: My

God, I wish them there (Lloyd) G322; I449; K401; L506; N56; U198; V434; W551; Z395; AL 424; AM577; AO359; AP503; AU446; AZ1263; BA714; BV508 106220
My truest Friend abides in heaven (Schmolck) M631 106221
My trust is in the Lord, How say ye then to me (Psalms in meter, 1905) AM48; AP8 106222
"My yoke," saith Christ, "upon you take" (Scheffler) AZ617 106223
Mysterious Presence, source of all (Beach) S101; AD86; AN63; AQ130; AR226; BX80 106224

N

Naar Synderen ret ser sin Vaade (Landstad) BT65 106225
Näher, mein Gott zu Dir (Sarah F. Adams) AY38d 106226
Name of Jesus, softly stealing (---) N335 106227
Narodil se Kristus Pán, Veselme se (Tranovsky) BT86 106228
Nations, attend before his throne (Watts) BX27 X Before the Lord Jehovah's throne 106229
Nature, with open volume, stands (Watts) V229; BV156 106230
Naught have I gotten but what I received (Gray) AI131; AM698 106231
Nay, do not grieve though life be full of sadness (Naidu) AQ77 106232
Nay, speak no ill; a kindly word (---) BC116 106233
Near the cross her vigil keeping (Jacopone) G138 X At the cross her station keeping 106234
Near the cross was Mary weeping (Jacopone) N104 X At the cross her station keeping 106235
Nearer, dear Savior, to thee (Townsend) BC117 106236
Nearer, ever nearer (Thring) AZ763 X Saviour, blessed Saviour 106237
Nearer, my God to thee, Nearer to thee (Adams) A 465; B222; D344; E444; F 352; G362; H310; I315; J 577; K407; L428; M290; N 448; O466; P336; Q533; R 326; S261; T411; U265; V408; W475; X586; Y10; Z329; AA520; AC156; AD 308; AE201; AF351; AG173; AH359; AI266; AK318; AL 321; AN245; AO296; AP470; AQ126; AR397; AS210; AT 322; AU206; AV189; AW202; AX372; AY86; AZ1241; 1242; BA612; BB382; BC124; BD 109; BE192; BF376; BK86; BR357, 374; BT533; BX287; BY598; BZ 106238
Nearer my God to thee! Nearer to thee. Through word and sacrament (Jacobs) K336; N449; AA324; AB185; BT533 106239
Nearer, O God to thee! Hear thou our prayer (How) AZ 1242 X Nearer, my God, to Thee (Adams) 106240
Nearer, still nearer, close to thy heart (Morris) N494; U266; AI278; AR259; AS221; AT281; AV376; AX377; AY 310; BB390 106241
"Nearer the cross!" My heart can say (Crosby) AW491 106242
Nearer the cross of Jesus (Abbey) AS228 106243
'Neath the old olive trees (McKinney) R 'Neath the stars 106244
'Neath the stars of the night (McKinney) AU398 106245
Ne'er forget God's daily care (T.C. Chao) BZ 106246
Neighbour, what was the sound, I pray (French trad carol) BG88 106247
Nein, nein, das ist kein Sterben (Malan) BT602 106248
Never further than thy cross (Charles) G146; I144; AH

366; AL97; BV560; BZ 106249
Never grow old, never grow old (Moore) R I have heard of a land 106250
Never shone a light so fair (Crosby) AI64 106251
Never weather-beaten sail more willing bent to shore (Campian) X587 106252
New every morning is the love (Keble) A155; B1; D1; E260; F4; G35; I42; J201; K452; R45; S31; T304; V35; W259; X31; AD40; AE38; AF36; AG 22; AL530; AN98; AP654; AW 22; AZ357; BA766; BB42; BE 140; BF175; BR6; BV43; BX 135; BY678; BZ 106253
New every morning is thy love (Keble) BR6 X New every morning is the love 106254
New Russia rise and proudly stand (Stevens) Y312 106255
Night, with ebon pinion (Jameson) Z226 106256
Night's shadows falling, men to rest are calling (Russell) U 460; V48 106257
No change of time shall ever shock (Tate & Brady) D655; AA281 106258
No coward soul is mine (Brontë) X588 106259
No eye hath seen, nor tongue declared (Adams) BE188 106260
No farther go tonight, but stay (Cennick) AZ570; BA785 106261
No form of human framing (Van Dyke) G421; AK414; AR204 106262
No gospel like this feast (Charles) BY322 106263
No human eyes thy face may see (Higginson) BX239 106264
No longer forward nor behind (Whittier) AN254 X No longer forward or behind 106265
No longer forward or behind (Whittier) H121; AN254; AQ 187; BX232 106266
No longer, Lord, despise me (Collier) AI435; AM511 106267
No longer, Lord, thy sons shall sow (Marlatt) AC132; BF324 106268
No longer of him be it said (Kilmer) Y88; Z305 106269
No more, my God! I boast no more (Watts) V311 106270
No more we'll roam, no more we'll stray (Yoder) R Some time we all shall understand 106271
No mortal eye hath seen that land (Toews) AX601 106272
No mortal sense can still or stay (Greenwood) BE194 106273
No, never alone; no, never alone (---) R I've seen the lightning; R How many times discouraged (Rexford) 106274
No, no, it is not dying (Malan) L562; AO568 106275
No, not despairingly come I to thee (Bonar) G333; H282; I453; AM411; AT206; BA414 106276
No shadows yonder (Bonar) U429; AS480; AV293; BF 658 106277
No tears in heaven, no sorrows given (Arnold) AX600 106278
Noblest, truest, oldest, newest (Bonar) R Come and hear the grand old story 106279
Nobody knows like Jesus (Hugg) R When this poor heart 106280
Nobody knows the work it makes (---) AU40 106281
Nobody knows the trouble I've seen (Negro spiritual) Y320; AH612; BK169 106282
Nocte surgentes vigilemus omnes (St Gregory the Great) BJ49b 106283
Noël nouvelet, noël chantons ici (French trad carol) BG 149b 106284
Noiseless the morning flings its gold (---) AQ89 X Unheard the dews around me fall

106285
Non nobis, Domini, not unto us, O Lord (Kipling) A503 106286
None but Christ, my Saviour (Gregor) AZ1077 106287
None can satisfy but Jesus (Lear) AS294 106288
None e'er shall be ashamed (---) AZ1118 106289
None from God so distant are (Zinzendorf, N. L.) AZ582 106290
None God the Father's favor share (Zinzendorf, N. L.) AZ167 106291
None is like Jeshurun's God (Wesley) BR48 106292
None other Lamb, none other name (Rossetti) S504; W412; AL273; AM115; AP418; BV617; BY769 106293
Nor earth nor hell my soul can move (Mote) BT370 X My hope is built on nothing less 106294
Nor silver, nor gold hath obtained (Gray) AM721 106295
Not a thought of earthly things (Liturgy of St James) F392 106296
Not all the blood of beasts (Watts) K339; L232; N423; Q156; U98; V246; AA319; AM176; AP421; AU332; AX 109; AY22; AZ1293; BA436; BV157 106297
Not all the outward forms on earth (Watts) V303 106298
Not alone for mighty empire (Merrill) A145; G543; J345; R512; S416; Y239; Z597; AB343; AD 434; AE427; AF439; AG273; AK442; AN373; AQ239; AR612; AW355; BD160; BF555; BH229; BK105; BX415; BZ 106299
Not always on the Mount may we (Hosmer) A571; F561; I477; J535; X589; AN215; AQ90; AW 98; BD96; BV283; BX222 106300
Not by far-famed deeds alone (Phillips) F562 106301
Not by the martyr's death alone (Santeüil) AO387 106302
Not by the mighty hand (Woodford) B109; D72 106303
Not empty worship the benignant Father requireth (Whittier) BF507 X O brother man! fold to thy heart 106304
Not far from the Kingdom of heaven (Latta) AX262 106305
Not for more beauty would our eyes entreat thee (Bates) AC490 106306
Not for our sins alone (Twells) F324; BV490; BY449 106307
Not given to us from out the skies (Wendte) AN391; BX 431 106308
Not gold, but only men can make (---) AN312; AQ98 106309
Not half has ever been told (Atchinson) R I have read of a beautiful city 106310
Not haughty is my heart, Not lofty is my pride (U.P. Psalter, 1912) T262; AJ 366; AM578 106311
"Not I, but Christ," be honored, loved ("A.A.F." [Crosby??]) AS233 106312
Not in anger, mighty God (Albinus) O522; AZ787 106313
Not in dumb resignation we lift our hands on high (Hay) G467; Y234; Z368; AB289; AN317 106314
Not in Jerusalem alone (Montgomery) AZ171 106315
Not in the temples made with hands (Warner) AX433 106316
Not in vain the distance beacons (Tennyson) Y265; AC297; AN353; AQ195 106317
Not long on Hermon's holy height (Pease) AN211 X Not long upon the mountain's height 106318
Not long upon the mountain's

height (Pease) AB131; AN211; BD132; BX221 106319

Not, Lord, thine ancient works alone (Gill) BX188; BY65 106320

Not now, but in the coming years (Cornelius) AH386; AI292; AV388; AX619; BB495; BC267 106321

Not of the sunlight, Not of the moonlight (Tennyson) Y153; AC231 106322

Not one of Adam's race (Hammond) AZ1286; BA438 106323

Not only when ascends the song (Gill) I520 106324

Not only where God's free winds blow (Knapp) AN217 X Dear God, the sun whose light 106325

Not so in haste, my heart! (Torrey) G323; R382; S501; U215; V364; AD277; BK96 106326

Not to the strong is the battle (Crosby) R Conquering now and still to conquer 106327

Not to the terrors of the Lord (Watts) D392; Q478; V232; AA463 106328

Not unto us, O Lord (Bible, Psalm 115) E626 106329

Not unto us, O Lord of heaven (Norton) T215; AJ308; AM68 106330

Not what I am, O Lord, but what thou art (Bonar) W429; AZ451; BE195; BX282; BY583 106331

Not what my hands have done (Bonar) N175 X Not what these hands have done 106332

Not what these hands have done (Bonar) K332; N175; O414; Q 389; U187; V312; AA320; AI 134; AM403; AP420; AX318; AZ1324; BA437; BV491; BY 450 106333

Not with a crowd of angels without number (Gosse) X590 106334

Not with our mortal eyes (Watts) L426 106335

Not worthy, Lord, to gather up the crumbs (Bickersteth) H 444; J276; K184; O310; U 377; V548; AH503; AI165; AM356; AP355; AV162; AZ 440 106336

Not worthy, not worthy (Baker) AI220 X I am not worthy, Holy Lord 106337

Nothing between my soul and the Saviour (Tindley) AU66 106338

Nous allons, ma mie (French trad carol) BG147b 106339

Nous voici dans la ville (French trad carol) BG91b 106340

Now a new year opens (Clarke) D541 106341

Now all give thanks to God (Rinkart) BJ93 106342

Now all is still; Time holds his breath (Neumann) AK151 106343

Now all the heavenly splendor (Gerhardt) AQ268 106344

Now all the woods are sleeping (Gerhardt) BV57 X Now woods and wolds are sleeping 106345

Now another stage of travel (Carpenter) BA178 106346

Now April has come, The country grows sweet here (Dearmer) BG155 106347

Now are the days fulfilled (German, ca 1746) Q99 106348

Now are the days of humblest prayer (Faber) BO163 106349

Now are the woodlands resting (Gerhardt) AB21 106350

Now at the Lamb's high royal feast (Latin, 4th c) BO176; BQ30 106351

Now at the night's return we raise (Bright) BV58 106352

Now be the God of Israel blessed (Watts) AJp. 394 106353

Now be the gospel banner In every land unfurled (Hastings) N371; AI173; AO521; AZ830; BA342 106354

Now begin the heavenly theme (Madan. Collection: Appendix, 1763) L160; V388; AZ77 106355
Now bless the God of all (Abrahams) BH81 106356
Now blessed be Jehovah, God, The God of Israel (U.P. Psalter, 1912) T451; AJ197 106357
Now blessed be the Lord our God (Scottish Psalter, 1650) AM7 X His name for ever shall endure 106358
Now blessed be thou, Christ Jesu (Coverdale) BG131 106359
Now blessed thou, O Christ our Lord (---) BI7-D 106360
Now blessing, honor, glory, praise (Proud) BR213 106361
Now, brothers, lift your voices (Prost, Fr.) BG106 106362
Now cheer, our hearts this eventide (Selnecker) G58; W278; AF54; AL542; AW557; BJ13 106363
Now Christ, the very Son of God (Selnecker) AA403 106364
Now comes the light for which our souls have sought (Quin) AN355 106365
Now do we come, O God to worship (Knobel) AD411 106366
Now do we pray God, the Holy Ghost (Luther) AA260 106367
Now every child that dwells on earth (Farjeon) BG188 106368
Now for each yearning heart (---) AT527 106369
Now found is the fairest of roses (Brorson) P153 106370
Now from the altar of my heart (Mason) A170; B27; D20; I46; K470; L29; V55; AL565; AX69 106371
Now from the altar of our hearts (Mason) D20 X Now from the altar of my heart 106372
Now give heart's onward habit brave intent (Holmes) AQ178 106373
Now glad of heart be every one! (German trad carol, 16th c) BG95 106374
Now God be with us, for the night is closing (Herbert) G 49; I58; J225; K459; M571; N441; O565; Q556; R53; U 459; V47; W279; X48; Z147; AA38; AF59; AL567; AN116; AP675; AZ469; BA787; BB55; BD5; BR112; BX161; BY697 106375
Now, gracious Lord, thine arm reveal (Newton) AX630; AY 247 106376
Now hail we our Redeemer (St Ambrose) N21; P122 106377
Now hush your cries and shed no tears (Hermann) AA539 106378
Now I have found the firm foundation (Rothe) Q385 106379
Now I have found the ground wherein (Rothe) I302; K326; N441; O478; P281; AL272; AZ659; BA447; BV528; BY 451 106380
Now I have found the sure foundation (Rothe) AA312 106381
Now I recall my childhood when the sun (Tagore) AQ82 106382
Now I resolve with all my heart (Steele) BX374 106383
Now I'm resting, sweetly resting (James) R In the rifted Rock 106384
Now in holy celebration (Latin, 15th c) E228 106385
Now in joy we sing thy praises (Farrell) BM79 106386
Now in life's breezy morning (Myers) X591 106387
Now, in parting, Father, bless us (Bonar) L333; BA914 106388
Now in the days of youth (Mathams) R469; Z300; AB 233; AC146; AE447; AF490; AG308; AK446; AN474; AR 345; BD118; BF628; BY452 106389
Now in the tomb is laid (Colum)

AQ314 106390
Now is Christmas y-come, Father and Son together in one (English trad carol, ca 1500) BG173 106391
Now is the accepted time (Dobell) V277; AY24 106392
Now is the healing time decreed (Latin, before 12th c) E67 106393
Now is the hour of darkness past (Watts) BG148 106394
Now is the time approaching (Borthwick) AN326 X Hasten the time appointed 106395
Now Israel may say, and that in truth (U.P. Psalter, 1912) R357; T254; AJ353; AM514 106396
Now Israel may say, and that truly: -- If that the Lord had not our cause (Whittingham) AL683; AP112 106397
Now Israel's hope in triumph ends (Hedborn) N61 106398
Now it is evening; time to rest from labour (Herbert) A167 106399
Now Jesus at the door is knocking (Landstad) P119 106400
Now join, ye comrades true! (Dearmer) X592 106401
Now just a word for Jesus (Crosby) AX197; BB522 106402
Now lay we calmly in the grave (Weisse) O594; Q596; AA538; BA720 106403
Now let all loudly Sing praise to God the Lord (Lowenstern) Q28 106404
Now let every tongue adore thee! (Nicolai) Y352 X Wake, awake for night is flying 106405
Now let my soul, eternal King (Heginbothom) H96 106406
Now let our cheerful eyes survey (Doddridge) V174 106407
Now let our mourning hearts revive (Doddridge) AY175 106408
Now let the children of the saints (Watts) V542 106409
Now let the earth with joy resound (Latin, 10th c) BQ 110 106410
Now let the vault of heaven resound (Strodach) J103 106411
Now let us all arise and sing (Balch) AS358 106412
Now let us come before Him (Gerhardt) Q122; AA174 106413
Now let us join our hearts and tongues (Newton) AZ352 106414
Now let us praise the Lord (Rinkart) AZ783 X Now thank we all our God 106415
Now let us raise our Harvest song (Woods) AS421 106416
Now let us rejoice in the day of salvation (Phelps) BC118 106417
Now let us see thy beauty, Lord (Waugh) BY274 106418
Now Lord be with us, for the night is closing (Herbert) BR112 X Now God be with us 106419
Now, Lord, upon thy sea of air (Anderson) AD455 106420
Now, Lord, who in this vale of tears (Gregor) AZ892; BA 915 106421
Now may He who from the dead (Newton) G612; K434; L56; Q51; S41app.; W300; AA15; AL316; AM318; AP337; AZ 60; BY764 106422
Now may the light that shone in Jesus Christ our Lord (---) S44app. 106423
Now, my soul, thy voice upraising (Santeüil. Paris Breviary) D99; E623; K94; N113; AZ623 106424
Now, my tongue, the mystery telling (St Thomas Aquinas) A199; B338; F383 106425
Now none but Christ can satisfy ("B.E.") R O Christ, in thee my soul hath found 106426
Now, on land and sea descending (Longfellow) G45; R67; U462;

Z141; AD48; AE41; AF52; AG 27; AN111; AQ274; AR54; AT 28; AW28; BF192; BX154; BZ 106427

Now once again for help that never faileth (Stillman) A486 J382; AK311 106428

Now once again he heaven turns (Patton) AQ320 106429

Now our worship sweet is o'er (Schenck) M15; N357; Q45; AA10 106430

Now praise we Christ, the Holy One (Sedulius) Q104; AA148 106431

Now praise we great and famous men (Tarrant) S491; Y335; Z603; AB396; AD458; AF476; AN365; BF663; BY648; BZ 106432

Now quit your care (Dearmer) X98; BG144 106433

Now rest beneath night's shadow [s] (Gerhardt) K469; M572; O551; Q554; AA33 106434

Now rest in peace, Now rest in peace (---) AZ1204 106435

Now rest, ye pilgrim host (Raymond) N579 106436

Now shadows wane and hevy night departeth (St Gregory the Great) BJ75 106437

Now sing we a song for the harvest (Chadwick) W614; AP690; AS428; BY727 106438

Now sing we, now rejoice (Latin carol, 14th c) O199; P134; Q92 106439

Now sing we of the Paraclete (Dearmer) R When Christ blessed His disciples 106440

Now sweeping down the years untold (Nourse) BE198 106441

Now thank we all our God (Rinkart) A276; B422; D466; E533; F379; G7; H62; I30; J443; K283; L77; M492; N299; O31; P242; Q36; R9; S459; T300; V635; W29; X350; Y303; Z598; AA64; AB56; AC325; AD12; AE11; AF29; AG289; AH196; AI443; AK72; AL19; AM86; AN262; AO104; AP147; AQ19; AR601; AT491; AV44; AW514; AZ783; BA661; BB90; BC 120; BD200; BE199; BF169; BK62; BL56; BM14; BN198; BR492; BV22; BX187; BY18; BZ 106442

Now thank we all our God (Rinkart) X To Thee eternal God (Brueckner) 106443

Now that the day hath reached its close (Herzog) Q561 106444

Now that the daylight fills the sky (Latin, 6th c) A159; E254; F1; N538; O541; W 258; AL533; AP657; BR8; BV44 106445

Now that the day-star glimmers bright (Latin, 6th c) J211; W260 106446

Now that the sun is beaming bright (Latin, 6th c) P50 X Now that the sun is gleaming bright 106447

Now that the sun is gleaming bright (Latin, 6th c) B5; K451; L3; N547; P50; AZ 226; BR10; BY679 106448

Now the blessed Dayspring (Thomson) D157; N200 106449

Now the busy week is done (Jones) E282 106450

Now the day is over (Baring-Gould) A172; B364; D535; E603; F431; G53; I59; J231; K574; L17; M576; N540; O562; P67; Q654; R51; S 35; T309; U467; V41; W288; X49; Y94; Z149; AA45; AB 28; AC23; AD59; AE50; AF 51; AG33; AH170; AI379; AK56; AL545; AM666; AN 128; AO37; AP681; AR52; AS30; AT35; AU194; AV15; AW29; AZ767; BA788; BB52; BC122; BD6; BF198; BK45; BR519; BV59; BX144; BY 698; BZ 106451

Now the green blade riseth from the buried green (Crum) BG 149; BZ 106452

Now the holly bears a berry as

white as the milk (English trad carol) BG35 106453
Now the hour of worship o'er (Schenck) Q45 X Now our worship sweet is o'er 106454
Now the joyful bells aringing (Roberts) BG50 106455
Now the King in thy strength shall be joyful, O Lord (U.P. Psalter, 1912) T31; AJ45 106456
Now the laborer's task is o'er (Ellerton) A224; B411; D242; E358; F467; G526; J296; K509; S440; V678; W330; AH532; AL458; AO564; AP616; AW 315; BA731 106457
Now the light has gone away (Havergal) K472; Q653 106458
Now the morn new light is pouring (Albert) X32; BV47 106459
Now the shades of night are gone (Occom) L6; M554; O540; Q 538; AA26; AX60; AY282; AZ 78; BA774; BR7 106460
Now the spring has come again (Piae cantiones, 1582) AD 470; AQ323; BG98 106461
Now the Triune God confessing (---) AZ242 106462
Now the wings of day are furled (Brooke) AN118; BD11; BX 146 106463
Now the world is saved from darkness (Lee) BN161 106464
Now thy earthly work is done (Dearmer) X292 106465
Now to God, our Strength and Saviour (U.P. Psalter, 1912) T150; AJ222 106466
Now to heaven our prayer ascending (Hickson) T375; AN 555; AW371; BC171 106467
Now to Him who loved us (Waring) W708; AL624; AP812; AW617 106468
Now to Jesus Christ all glory and dominion (---) BI24-D 106469
Now to the great and sacred Three (---) Lp.741 106470
Now to the King of heaven (Doddridge) W710; AL626; AW615 106471
Now to the Lamb upon the Throne (Foster) AZ693 106472
Now to the Lord a noble song! (Watts & Wesley) H23; V 126; AT19; AV30; AZ330 106473
Now to those who search the deep (Noyes) Y186 106474
Now unto Jehovah, Ye sons of the mighty (U.P. Psalter, 1912) T49; AJ76; AM36 106475
Now upon the earth descending (Levy) BH236 106476
Now welcome, Summer, with thy sunne soft (Chaucer) BG 128 106477
Now we'll sing with one accord (Phelps) BC132 106478
Now when the dusky shades of night (St Gregory the Great) AB5; AN101; AZ1220; BR3; BX125 106479
Now while the day in trailing splendor (Hosmer) AN121; AQ269; BD8; BX149 106480
Now with angels round the throne (Conder) AZ1256 106481
Now with creation's morning song (Prudentius) AC10; AN102; BX137 106482
Now with joyful exultation (U.P. Psalter, 1912) T175; AJ255 106383
Now with joyful songs appear (Swertner) AZ581 106484
Now with the declining sun (Coffin) AZ73 106485
Now with the rising, golden dawn (Prudentius) AO24 106486
Now woods and fields are sleeping (Gerhardt) S505 X Now woods and wolds are sleeping 106487
Now woods and wolds are sleeping (Gerhardt) R66; S505; BV57 106488

Now yield we thanks and praise (Robbins) A14 106489
Nowell, Nowell, now sing a Saviour's birth (English trad carol) R The Babe in Bethlem's manger laid 106490
Nowell! Nowell! Nowell! Nowell sing we clear (Morris) R Masters in this hall 106491
Nowell, Nowell, Nowell, sing we with mirth (English trad) BG170 X Behold a simple tender Babe (Southwell) 106492
Nowell sing we, both all and some (English trad carol, 1450) BG 62 106493
Nu rinder Solen op Af Österlide (Kingo) BT542 106492
Nu singet und seyt fro (German trad carol, 14th c) BG86 notes X In dulci jubilo 106495
Nun bitten wir den Heiligen Geist (Luther) BT231 106496
Nun bringen wir den Leib zur Ruh (Unparth. G.B.) AY15d 106497
Nun danket all' und bringet Ehr' Ihr Menschen in der Welt (Gerhardt) BT581 106498
Nun danket alle Gott (Rinkart) Y303; BT36; BW514 106499
Nun freut euch, liebe Christen g'mein (Luther) BT387 106500
Nun Gott Lob, es ist vollbracht (Schenck) BT45 106501
Nun gute Nacht, ihr Liebsten mein (Unparth G.B.) AY14d 106502
Nun heben wir an in Röthen (Ausbund) BU42 106503
Nun hört, ihr Freund ehrsamen (Ausbund) BU28 106504
Nun hört mir zu in mein'm Gedicht (Ausbund) BU72 106505
Nun ist die Zeit erfüllt (German, 1746?) BT99 106506
Nun komm, der Heiden Heiland (St Ambrose) BT95 106507
Nun lasst uns den Leib begraben (Weisse) BT596 106508
Nun lasst uns gehn und treten (Gerhardt) BT122 106509
Nun, lob, mein' Seel', den Herren (Graumann) BT34 106510
Nun preiset alle Gottes Barmherzigkeit! (Lowenstern) BT 28 106511
Nun ruhen alle wälder (Gerhardt) AW556b; BT554; BW556 106512
Nun sich der Tag geendet hat (J.F. Herzog) AY21d; BT 561 106513
Nun sich die Nacht geendet hat (Unparth. G.B.) AY21d 106514
Nun singet und seid froh (Suso) BT92 106515
Nun wolt ich gerne singen (H. Betz) BU105 106516
Nunc sancte nobis spiritus (Latin, 4th c) BJ45 note 106517

O

NOTE: "O" has been made the acceptable form for both "O" and "Oh". Both spellings will be found in the same hymn, in different books. Only "O" is used herein. 106518

O all ye people, bless our God (U.P. Psalter, 1912) T120; AJ174 106519
O, alleluia, yes, 'tis heaven (Butler) R Since Christ my soul from sin 106520
O Allmächtiger Herre Gott! (Hut) BU8 106521
O Almighty Giver, bountiful and free (Monsell) R Earth below is teeming 106522
O, anywhere my Saviour leads (Moore) AX461; AY101 106523
O, at last I've found my Saviour (Janus) AZ983 106524
O awake! my slumbering minstrel (Snow) BC268 106525
O be joyful in the Lord (Beach) AF26 106526
O be not thou dismayed (Horn)

AZ842; BA269 106527
O, be saved, His grace is free (Crosby) R Troubled heart, thy God is calling 106528
O, be still, thou soul of mine (Ebel) AX394 106529
O be with us, gracious Father (Rooker) W244 106530
O beautiful for spacious skies (Bates) G491; J346; M504; P413; R510; S411; T447; U339; Y282; Z550; AB337; AC271; AD438; AE389; AF 440; AG270; AH483; AK443; AN383; AO592; AQ241; AR613; AS382; AT489; AU39; AV300; AW343; BA877; BB503; BC126; BD175; BF540; BH262; BK121; BX419; BZ 106531
O beautiful, my country (Hosmer) X322; Z542; AB344; AC275; AD433; AH472; AI355; AN388; AO596; AQ240; AV305; BD174; BF553; BX424 106532
O, beautiful Star of Bethlehem (Boyce) AX95 106533
O, behold the Bridegroom cometh (Oatman) R Time is gliding 106534
O Bethlehem, dear Bethlehem (Hugg) AY245 X Hark the hearld angels (Wesley) 106535
O Bethlehem of holy worth (Currie) BN18 106536
O Beulah land, Sweet Beulah land (Stites) R I've reached the land 106537
O bleeding Head, and wounded (St Bernard of Clairvaux) AA201 106538
O bless our God with one accord (Lamberts) AI448; AM348 106539
O bless the Lord, my Soul! His grace to thee proclaim (Montgomery) A293; B318; D474; H68; O65; AE17; AR29; AS5; BA653; BH62 106540
O bless, the Lord, my Soul! Let all within me join (Watts) K299; L71; N291; Q27; V524; Z105; AA76; AM72; AO86; AY23; BR45 106541
O bless, thou heavenly Potentiate (---) AA300 106542
O blessed are those who fear the Lord (Ladies of the Grail) BSp. 50 106543
O blessed Babe divine (Burmeister) O222 106544
O blessed by God, Saint Benedict (Schoehbechler) BN172 106545
O blessed day of Motherhood (McGregor) AC318; AH498; AT504; AU41; BF614 106546
O blessed day when first was poured (Besnault) Q115 X O happy day when first was poured 106547
O blessed faith! Its song of cheer (Hewitt) R "Have faith in God." 106548
O blessed Father! sent by God His mercy to dispense (Faber) BQ108 106549
O blessed Holy Trinity (Behm) Q541 X O holy blessed Trinity, Divine eternal unity 106550
O blessed home where man and wife (Landstad) Q624 X In house and home where man and wife 106551
O blessed hour, when evening comes (Squires) BB60 106552
O blessed house, that cheerfully receiveth (Spitta) K416; M262; AR541; AS414; AW358; AX558 106553
O blessed is the man who stays (Wallin) N495 106554
O blessed is the man whose sins (Scottish Psalter, 1650) AL 641; AP28 106555
O blessed life! the heart at rest (Matson) U414; BX88 106556
O Blessed Light from heaven (Solberg) M205 106557
O Blessed Light! O Trinity! Thou ever-blessed Unity (St Ambrose) AO238 106558
O blessed Saint Joseph, how great was thy worth (Faber)

BQ92 106559
O blessed Saviour, is thy love (Stennett) AZ150 106560
O blessed Son of God (Crain) Z520; AE378; AO468; AR368; AS341; BF487 106561
O blessed souls are they (Watts) V285 106562
O blessed Sun whose splendor (Spitta) J573; K362; O437; P327 106563
O blest communion with the saints at rest (Roberts) W226 106564
O blest Creator, God most high (St Ambrose) AO33 106565
O blest Creator of the day (St Gregory the Great) A163; E51 106566
O blest Creator of the light (St Gregory the Great) E51 X O blest Creator of the day; X Source of Light and Life divine 106567
O, blest memorial of our dying Lord (St Thomas Aquinas) BR478 X Thee we adore, O hidden Saviour 106568
O blest Redeemer, from thy radiant throne (Hymns of the English Conf. 1880) BR456 106569
O blest the house, whate'er befall (Pfeil) M264; N531; O234; P355; Q625; AA445 106570
O blest the souls that see and hear (Hosmer) AN404; BX399 106571
O bold, O foolish peasants (Lathrop) AN183; AQ309; AR 159 106572
O bona patria, lumina sobria (St Bernard of Cluny) BT614 106573
O bone Jesu! Miserere nobis (Latin) BQ256 106574
O boundless joy! There is salvation (Hiller) M137 106575
O boundless wisdom, God most high (Latin, ca 6th c) E58 106576
O bow thine ear, Eternal One (Pierpont) BB484 106577
O Bread of Heaven! beneath this veil (St Alphonso M de' Liguori) BO50 106578
O Bread of Life, for all men broken (Lew) R450; BZ 106579
O Bread of Life from heaven (Latin, 1661) D223; J271; O287; P90; S357; AZ559 106580
O Bread to pilgrims given (Latin, 1661) K186; L326; V554 106581
O breath of God, breathe on us now (Vine) AL150; BV294 106582
O Breath of life, come sweeping through us (Head) BV 298 106583
O breathe on me, thou Breath of God (Hatch) BN121 X Breathe on me 106584
O brethren, how this perfect love (Warner) R How sweet this bond 106585
O Bride of Christ, rejoice (Danish, ca 1600) M328; O 161; Q57 106586
O Brightness of the immortal Father's face (Greek, 3d c) A173; B12; D6; BL75 106587
O brother, be faithful! Soon Jesus will come (Smith) BB173 106588
O brother man, fold to thy heart thy brother (Whittier) A493; G466; J539; R474; S403; W485; X307; Y258; Z515; AC244; AD337; AE 407; AF410; AG254; AK393; AL366; AN348; AO469; AQ 144; AR378; AS340; AT447; AU403; AV275; AW229; BD 125; BE217; BF495, 507; BK110; BY662; BZ 106589
O brothers, lift your voices (Bickersteth) B495; D579; H400; R333; S372; BA549 106590
O Calvary! dark Calvary! (Darwood) R On Calv'ry's brow 106591
O can you sing the new song of salvation (Traasdal) P15

106592

O can we say we are ready, brother? (Crosby) R When Jesus comes to reward His servants 106593

O Canada! our home and native land! (Weir) BB508 X O Canada! our home, our native land! 106594

O Canada! our home, our native land! (Weir) Y295; BB508; BX544 106595

O cease, my wandering soul (Muhlenberg) V533; AI246; BR283 106596

O child of lowly manger birth (Blanchard) AB170 X O Jesus, youth of Nazareth 106597

O children, hither do ye come (Scottish Psalter, 1650) AL645; AP33; AW584 106598

O Christ, behind thy Temple's veil (Breviary) BO16 106599

O Christ, forget not them who stand (Sangster) S387; Y117; Z526; AB371; AC260; AD383; AK374; BY368 106600

O Christ, in thee my soul hath found ("B.E.") W699; AL482; AW451 106601

O Christ, my God, who seest the unseen (Rossetti) W545 106602

O Christ my Light, my gracious Saviour (Gerhardt) AZ993 106603

O Christ, of angel legions the bright crown (Herman) BP105 106604

O Christ, our hope, our heart's desire (Latin, 8th c) E144; J400; K128; L271; N144; O373; P204; AI425; AM120 106605

O Christ our joy, gone up on high (Latin, 5th c) F611 106606

O Christ, our joy, to whom is given (Latin, 5th c) Z142 106607

O Christ, our King, Creator, Lord (St Gregory the Great) J62; K59; AM134; AZ280 106608

O Christ, our Leader and our way (Kite) Y340 106609

O Christ, our Lord, who with thine own hast been (Bourne) BY323 106610

O Christ, our true and only Light (Heermann) K47; L 230; M109; N67; O221; P 147; Q512; AA475; AM296; AO533; AZ298; BA185; BR 40; BV325; BY384 106611

O Christ, the Way, the Truth, the Life (Squier) Z410; AC216; BF419 106612

O Christ, thou art our joy alone (Latin, 5th c) BN52 106613

O Christ, thou bright and Morning Star, now shed thy light (German, 1579) K350; L192 106614

O Christ, thou gift of love divine (Harmer) Z454 106615

O Christ, thou has ascended (Bickersteth) AZ819; BA 246 106616

O Christ, thou Lamb of God that takest away the sin of the world (Latin, 5th c [Agnus dei]) Q147 106617

O Christ, Thou Lord of worlds, Thine ear to hear us bow (Latin) F505 106618

O Christ, thy grace unto us lend (Wilhelm II, duke) N 305 106619

O Christ, thy guilty people spare (St Rabanus Maurus) BN185; BO219 106620

O Christ, thy love unbounded (Bosworth's hymns, 1865) N489 X Jesus, thy love unbounded 106621

O Christ, to thee we come (Hartman) AY276 106622

O Christ, we climb the hill with thee (Morse) AR408 106623

O Christ, what burdens bowed thy head (Cousin) AP198 106624

O Christ, who art the Light and Day (Latin, before 9th c) E81; F95; O557; Q559; BJ6

106625
O Christ who holds the open gate (Masefield) X593; Y81; AC 234; AD206 106626
O Christ, whom we may love and know (Cropper) F450; J453 106627
O Christ! with each returning morn (St Ambrose) AZ348; BB41 106628
O Christian, awake! 'tis the Master's command (Crosby) BB576 106629
O Christian, haste, thy mission high fulfilling (Thomson) AB367 X O Sion haste. . . 106630
O Christians, leagued together (Cassaday) J567; K578; L532; M524 106631
O Christmas tree, O Christmas tree (German) M618 106632
O Church of freedom, stand (Domer) N212 106633
O Church of God, divided (Ham) Z433 106634
O Church of God, our solitude forsaking (Schloerb) Z432 106635
O Church of God triumphant (Harlow) AR496 106636
O Church of God, united (Morley) AE312 106637
O Church, thy strength abide (Hayn) AZ472 106638
O come, all ye faithful, joyful and triumphant (Latin, 18th c (Oakeley tr) A12; B72; D49; E28; F59, 593; G96; H147; I 125; J42; Q102; R170; S116; T332; U56; V769; W55; X78; Y298; Z205; AB106; AC83; AD120; AE84; AF132; AG69; AH263; AI67; AK112; AL47; AM151; AN156; AO127; AP173, 174*; AQ288; AR143; AS110; AT66; AU143; AV90; AW80; AX94; BB105; BC129; BD205; BF291; BI83; BK149; BL11; BM63; BN11; BO150a; BP13; BQ4b; BV106; BX533; BY104; BZ 106639
*tr. by Mercer
O come, all ye faithful, joyfully triumphant (Latin, 18th c) (Mercer tr) AP174 X O come, all ye faithful, joyful and triumphant 106640
O, come, all ye that labor (McKinney) AU462 106641
O come, and dwell in me (Wesley) G377; H296; I362; BZ 106642
O, come, and let us all, with one accord (Hymns of the Spirit, 1864) BR99 106643
O come and mourn with me awhile (Faber) A74; B153; D105; E111; F113; G134; I 152; J86; K105; R192; S159; W96; X140; Z233; AF164; AH 126; AK146; AL90; AP193; AZ 422; BN37; BO168; BP32; BQ 21; BV173; BY144 106644
O come and sing unto the Lord (U.P. Psalter, 1912) R29 106645
O come and to Jehovah sing (U.P. Psalter, 1912) I176; AJ256 106646
O come, angel band (Haskell) R My latest sun is sinking 106647
O come before Jehovah! (Kretzmann) M530 106648
O come before the Lord, our King (U.P. Psalter, 1912) AJ 254 106649
O come, creator Spirit, come (Latin, 9th c) A108; BQ36; 106650
O come, Divine Messiah (Pellegrin, Abbé) BN7; BO147 106651
O come, if sinner be thy name (Lehr) O435 106652
O come, Immanuel, our King (Latin, 9th c) AB103 X O come, O come, Emmanuel 106653
O come in the might of the Lord of Light (Moultrie) B17 X We come in the might. . . 106654
O come let us adore Him (Mar-

tens) R When blossoms flowered 106655

O come, let us sing to the Lord (Scottish Psalter, 1650) S49; AK22; AL666; AM19; AP81 106656

O come, little children, O come, one and all (Schmidt) M615; AW413; BK152; BN19; BQ6 106657

O come, loud anthems let us sing (Tate & Brady) B308; D472; H64; AW18; BO4 106658

O come, my people, to my law (U. P. Psalter, 1912) R255; AJ215 106659

O come, my soul, bless thou the Lord thy Maker (U. P. Psalter, 1912) T195; AJ283; AM10 106660

O come, O come, Emmanuel (Latin, 9th c) A2; B66; D45; E8; F49; G83; H131; J2; K1; M117; N7; O172; P118; Q62; R147; S108; W149; X66; Z182; AB103; AC75; AD100; AE78; AF110; AG63; AI57; AK88; AL 137; AM147; AN150; AO107; AP 241; AQ280; AR214; AW67; AZ 677; BA106; BB109; BD203; BF275; BK140; BL3; BM61; BN6; BO149; BQ2; BR136; BV 83; BY83; BZ 106661

O come, O come, Immanuel (Latin, 9th c) BB109 X O come, O come, Emmanuel 106662

O come to the Lord today (Warren) AX288 106663

O come to the merciful Saviour who calls you (Faber) P260 106664

O come, ye happy children, and sings a gladsome lay (French trad) BD222 106665

O comfort to the weary? (Hymns of the English Conf., 1880 [J. Conder?]) BR373 106666

O Comforter, God Holy Spirit (Herbert) AZ374 106667

O cor, amoris victima (Latin) BO17 106668

O cor Jesu flagrans amor nostri (Latin) BQ236 106669

O cor Jesu, fons amoris (Latin) BO24 106670

O could I find from day to day (Cleveland) L432; V404; BB322 106671

O could I speak the matchless worth (Medley) B263; G118; H343; I540; K309; L148; R134; S203; U73; V130; Z 265; AE297; AG109; AH178; AI111; AL43; AM126; AO 205; AR115; AS114; AT146; AU17; AV126; AX7; AY29; BB161; BZ 106672

O could our thoughts and wishes fly (Steele) BB244 106673

O could we but love that Saviour (Boenisch) AZ952; BA497 106674

O cross, no stars thy glow outshine (Herman) BP31 106675

O darkest woe! Ye tears forth flow (Rist) J87; M397; O322; P185; Q167; AA215 106676

O dass ich tausend Zungen hätte (Mentzer) BT30, 243; BW509 106677

O daughter of Zion, awake from thy sadness (Fitzgerald. Collection) BE200 X Daughter of Zion, Awake. . . 106678

O daughter, take good heed (Scottish Psalter, 1650) AP40 106679

O daughters blest of Galilee (How) AO491 106680

O, David was a shepherd lad (Clarke) F449 106681

O day full of grace which we behold (Danish, 14th c) O379; P226 106682

O, day of awful story (Whittle) AU464 106683

O Day of God, draw nigh (Scott) A525; AF444; BY187; BZ 106684

O day of joy and wonder (Buchanan) BV220 106685

O day of light and gladness (Hosmer) AN196; AQ316; BD243; BX204 106686

O day of rest and gladness

(Wordsworth) A474; B43; D24; E284; F41; G396; H70; I68; J182; K441; L50; M8; N312; O471; P44; Q9; R70; S18; T 315; U438; V64; W268; Z443; AB9; AC15; AD30; AE52; AG 36; AH162; AI15; AK38; AL 188; AM321; AN130; AO13; AP344; AR64; AS38; AT36; AU11; AV8; AW285; AX65; AZ820; BA380; BB463; BF 168; BR86; BV72; BX15; BY 275; BZ 106687

O days of perfect happiness (Gregor) AZ902 X Whene'er we contemplate the grace 106688

O dear and lovely Brother (Dearmer) X367 106689

O dear little children, O come (Schmidt) BQ6 X O come, little children 106690

O dear Redeemer crucified (Hoppe) N138 106691

O dearest Jesus, thee I pray (Helder) AA188 106692

O dearest Jesus, what law hast thou broken (Heermann) Q143; AA198; AM181 106693

O dearest Lord, accept today the gifts (Bell) R554; S34app.; AD 509; AR675 106694

O dearest Lord, by all adored (Bell) E604 106695

O dearest Lord, receive from me (Kingo) M51 106696

O dearest Lord, thy sacred head (Hardy, Father Andrew) F436; BV153; BY516 106697

O dearest Love divine, my heart to thee I give (Henry) BQ65 106698

O dearly, dearly has He loved (Alexander) AK479 X There is a green hill 106699

O death, where is thy cruel sting? (Weissel) M448 106700

O, deem not that earth's crowning bliss (Burleigh) BH51 106701

O, deem not they are blest alone (Bryant) H357; I456; V427 106702

O delightful theme, past all expression (Zinzendorf, C.R.) AZ1018; BA214 106703

O depth of mercy! can it be (Baxter) R There is a gate that stands ajar 106704

O Deus, ego amo te (St Francis Xavier) BQ316 106705

O do not bar your mind (Parsons) BE201 106706

O do not let the word depart (Reed) AT234; AU465; AX237; AY217 106707

O draw me, Saviour, after Thee (Gerhardt) K356 106708

O dreamer, leave thy dreams for joyful waking (Turner) BE202 106709

O Du allersüsste Freude. (P. Gerhardt) BW134 106710

O du Liebe meiner Liebe (Savonarola) AW536b 106711

O Earth! thy past is crown'd and consecrated (Harris) AN354 106712

O Emmanuel, Rex et legifer (Latin, early) BQ153 106713

O enter, Lord, thy temple (Gerhardt) K155; M468; N 311; O266; Q228; AA252 106714

O esca viatorum, O panis angelorum (Latin, 1661) BN 90; BO34 106715

O Eternal Word, Jesus Christ, our Lord (Gregor) AZ539; BA48 106716

O everlasting Light! Giver of dawn and day (Bonar) BR17 X O everlasting Light! shine graciously 106717

O everlasting Light! Shine graciously within (Bonar) AY349; BR17; BX101 106718

O, exalt and praise the Lord (Herbert) AZ1035; BA751 106719

O, exult ye cherubim! (---) R Holy Mary, Mother mild 106720

O eyes that are weary, and hearts that are sore (Darby) L471; U203; V362; AO365; AZ498 106721

O fair Creator of the skies (Latin, 7th c) BP1 106722
O faith of England, taught of old (Lacey) E544; X246 106723
O faithful cross, O noblest tree (Fortunatus) BP30 106724
O faithful God, Thanks be to Thee (Selnecker) M73; Q321; AA425 106725
O faithful God, we worship Thee (Selnecker) AA425 X O faithful God, thanks be to thee 106726
O Father above us, our Father in might (Dearmer) X396a 106727
O Father, all creating (Ellerton) B381; E345; O534; Q621; W 326; AL237; AM628; AP705; AR538; BA845; BV391; BY622 106728
O Father almighty, to thee be addressed (---) Lp. 744; AZ 505 106729
O Father, bless the children (Ellerton) D208; N231 106730
O Father, by whose sovereign sway (Alington) F465 106731
O Father, for this little life (White) F426; BV341 106732
O Father, hear my morning prayer (Percy) AL536 106733
O Father in heaven, our Father on earth (Dearmer) X396b 106734
O Father, lead us gently by the hand (Cleator) AX491; AY119 106735
O Father, may thy word prevail (Brorson) O245; P159 106736
O Father, may we bear each hour (Castellain) BE203 106737
O Father mine, whose mercies never cease (Hoppe) N171 106738
O Father of goodness, thou art in each one (Dearmer) X396c 106739
O Father of mercy, be ever adored (Wesley) AZ500; BA9 106740
O Father of wisdom and friendship and peace (Dearmer) X 396d 106741
O Father, thou who givest all (Holmes) Z600; AC316; AH 552; AN268; BD201; BH250; BK36; BX132 106742
O Father, thou who hast created all (Knapp) O143; W308 106743
O Father, thy Kingdom is come upon earth (Berg) BE204 106744
O Father, we thank thee for Jesus thy Son (Sedding) F441 106745
O filii et filiae (Tisserand) BM 81; BN41; BO178; BP35; BQ 195; BT208 106746
O fill us with thy spirit ("L. J. L.") AY329 X From Greenland's icy mountains (Heber) 106747
O fix my heart, my God, my strength (Hymns of the English Conf. 1880) BR315 106748
O Food of exiles lowly (Latin, 1661) BN91 106749
O Food of men wayfaring (Latin, 1661) A192; E321; BL49 106750
O Food that weary pilgrims love (Latin, 1661) F389; BO47; BP57 106751
O Food to pilgrims given (Latin, 1661) BQ57 106752
O for a closer walk with God (Cowper) A416; B305; D660; E445; F325; G228; I492; J466; M217; N456; O501; P317; R 319; S259; U256; V414; W 457; X112; Z310; AD284; AE195; AF349; AG172; AH 357; AI279; AK319; AL308; AO299; AP474; AS213; AT 365; AU208; AV191; AW197; AX378; AY321; BA628; BB 383; BF368; BJ84; BR288; BV147; BY599; BZ 106753
O for a faith that will not shrink (Bathurst) G270; H363; I424; J395; K266; L422; M127; N 443; O243; Q396; U196; V348; W474; X594; AA354; AE192;

AI239; AL345; AO385; AP513; AT255; AU277; AV62; AW153; AX454; AY357; AZ188; BA708; BB245; BE205; BV502; BX277; BZ 106754
O for a glance of heavenly day (Hart) H276; I274 106755
O for a heart of calm repose (---) G363; I376; AR227 106756
O for a heart to love my God (Wesley) AS214 X O for a heart to praise my God 106757
O for a heart to praise my God (Wesley) A414; B260; D439; E82; F325; G370; H305; I354; J389; K264; L414; N453; R325; S260; U257; V403; W467; X113; AE181; AG177; AL309; AO300; AP473; AR398; AS214; AX387; AY7; AZ116; BA630; BB18; BJ 87; BR284; BV544; BY600; BZ 106758
O for a principle within (Wesley) AZ159; BA629 106759
O for a shout of sacred joy (Watts) V165 106760
O for a thousand tongues to sing (Wesley) A325; D440; E446; F196; G162; H300; I1; J428; K135; L139; M206; O446; P10; Q360; R141; S199; T328; U68; V203; W166; X595; Z262; AA 108; AD182; AE8; AF223; AG 112; AH374; AI13; AK181; AL 41; AM133; AO215; AP261; AR114; AS113; AT129, 140; AU5,279; AV128; AW12; AY 50; AZ200; BA121; BB155; BT360; BV270; BY212; BZ 106761
O for a thousand tongues to sings (with refrain: Blessed be the name) (Wesley) AT140; AU 279 106762
O for an overcoming faith (Watts) H494 106763
O for that flame of living fire (Bathurst) I187; BB210; BX398 106764
O for that tenderness of heart (Wesley) I278 106765
O for the death of those (Maxwell) V676 106766
O for the peace that floweth as a river (Crewdson) AN 550; AP477 106767
O, form us all while we remain (Gregor) BA915 X Now, Lord, who in this vale of tears 106768
O Fount of good, to own thy love (Doddridge) N388 106769
O Fount of grace that runneth o'er (Crewdson) BY339 106770
O Fount of truth and mercy (Nyström) N301 106771
O Fountain eternal of life and light (Koitsch) AZ777 106772
O Friend of sinners, Son of God (Hoppe) N185 106773
O Friend of souls, how blest am I (Dessler) AA109 106774
O Galilee! sweet Galilee! Where Jesus loved so much to be (Morris) R Each cooing dove 106775
O gentle one, we miss thee here (Warner) R A gentle hand 106776
O gentle presence, peace and joy and power (Eddy) BE 207 106777
O gentle Saviour, from thy throne on high (Birks) AR 683; AS66 106778
O gift of gifts! Oh grace of faith (Faber) H290; V351; AO379 106779
O Gift of God, we praise thee (Uhler) BB149 106780
O give me back my prophet dear (Taylor) BC137 106781
O, give thanks to Him who made (Conder) AZ1279; BX 14; BY19 106782
O give thanks to the Lord, for he is good, for his great love is without end (Ladies of the Grail) BSp. 54 106783
O give the Lord whole-hearted

praise (U.P. Psalter, 1912) T211; AI12; AJ304 106784

O give the Lord, you sons of God (Ladies of the Grail) BS p.14 106785

O, give us pleasure in the flowers today (Frost) AQ324 106786

O give us that good part (Schrautenbach) AZ1167 106787

O Giver of delightful fields (Morse) AR596 106788

O gladsome light, O grace (Greek, 3d c) A176; E269; J220; Q 101; R61; X50; AF49; AL551; AR55; AW34; BJ88; BY699 106789

O gloriosa virginum (Fortunatus) BN124; BO266; BQ210 106790

O glorious Head, thou livest now! (Tersteegen) AZ681 106791

O glorious hope of perfect love! (Wesley) I365 106792

O glorious King of Martyr hosts (Latin, ca 6th c) E183 106793

O Glorious Maid, exalted far (Latin, ca 9th c) E215 106794

O glory hallelujah, hallelujah, hallelujah (Lowry) R O worship the Lord 106795

O glory to Jesus! so sweet to me (Warner) R Not in the temples 106796

O God, above the drifting years (Buckham) AB395; AF297; AK 377; AN362; BF536 106797

O God, accept my heart this day (Bridges) N253; X O God, accept my heart this day 106798

O God, according to thy grace (U.P. Psalter, 1912) AJ143 106799

O God, all gracious! In thy gift (Moise) BH45 106800

O God, Almighty Father, creator of all things (German hymn) BM12; BN57 106801

O God, Almighty Father, thou Majesty divine (German hymn) BN57 X O God, Almighty Father creator of all things 106802

O God, arise! and by thy might (Collier) AI442 106803

O God, be merciful and bless (U. P. Psalter, 1912) AJ177 106804

O God, be merciful, be merciful to me (U.P. Psalter, 1912) T105; AJ151 106805

O God, be merciful to me, for men no mercy show (U.P. Psalter, 1912) AJ153 106806

O God, be merciful to me, My soul for refuge (U.P. Psalter 1912) T106; AJ154 106807

O God, be thy annointed Son (U. P. Psalter, 1912) T132; AJ198 106808

O God, be with us, for the night is falling (Herbert) Q556 X Now God be with us, for the night is closing 106809

O God, before whose altar (Lyon) F340; BZ 106810

O God, beneath thy guiding hand (Bacon) A148; G493; P416; R523; S462; T449; Y116; Z543; AB391; AC270; AD435; AE394; AF438; AG 290; AH477; AI362; AK436; AN369; AO594; AQ235; AR 605; AS386; AW367; BB507; BD167; BF543; BK120; BX 405; BZ 106811

O God, creation's secret force (St Ambrose) A162; E262 106812

O God Creator, in whose hand (Farrington) G555 106813

O God, Eternal Father, from thy high throne (---) BL80 106814

O God, Eternal God! thy name (Slemp) AU302 106815

O God, Eternal Source of love beyond our knowing (Heermann) J460 106816

O God, forsake me not (Franck) Q402; AA347 106817

O God, from heaven look down and see (Luther) AA278 106818

O God, give ear unto my cry, and to my voice attend (U. P. Psalter, 1912) AJ160

106819
O God, give ear unto my cry; Unto my prayer attend (Scottish Psalter, 1650) AL653; AP49 106820
O God, give thou ear to my plea (U.P. Psalter, 1912) T104; AJ150 106821
O God, great Father, Lord, and King (Hoss) I231 106822
O God-head hid devoutly I adore thee (Latin) BO44 106823
O God, hear thou the nation's prayer (Maurer) Y275; BF558 106824
O God, how good thou art To all the pure of heart (U.P. Psalter, 1912) T137; AJ203 106825
O God! how ought my grateful heart (---) BO200 106826
O God, how wonderful thou art (Faber) N339 X My God, how wonderful thou art 106827
O God, I cried, no dark disguise (Millay) Y166; AC40; AQ57 106828
O God, I love thee; not that my poor love (Spanish, 17th c) J489 X My God I love thee not because (St Francis Xavier) 106829
O God, I thank thee for each sight (Mason) AB190; AN91; BD35; BF179; BX38 106830
O God, I thank thee that the night (Pierpont) BX526 106831
O God, if thy beloved Son (Heermann) M173 106832
O God, in restless living (Fosdick) AB295; AD276; AR335; BF393; BK95 106833
O God! in thine autumnal skies (Brooks) BX169 106834
O God, in this hour of grace (Boutflower) F460 106835
O God, in whom we live and move, In whom we draw each breath (Briggs) X275; AQ24 106836
O God, in whom we live and move, Thy love is law, Thy law is love (Longfellow) Z179; AB186; BF224; BX83 106837
O God, in whose all-searching eye (Wordsworth) D211; BT332 106838
O God, in whose great purpose (Gilkey) Z607; AB317; AD 423; AK454; AR69 106839
O God, mine inmost soul convert (Wesley) BA411 X Lo, on a narrow neck of land 106840
O God, most holy are thy ways (U.P. Psalter, 1912) AJ211; AM41 106841
O God, most merciful and true (Wesley) I401 106842
O God, my days are dark indeed (Hojer) AA503 106843
O God, my ever constant Friend (Mayer) BH192 106844
O God, my heart is fixed; 'tis bent (Tate) AP48 106845
O God, my heavenly King (Hymns of the English Conf., 1880) BR329 106846
O God, my strength and fortitude (Sternhold) AD74; AL634; AM 524; AP13; BR139; BX313 106847
O God, no longer hold thy peace (U.P. Psalter, 1912) T152; AJ224; AM57 106848
O God, not only in distress (Smith) AB214; AD274; AP 528; BF410; BX261 106849
O God, O Spirit, Light of all that live (Tersteegen) AN69; BX44 106850
O God of ages, in whose light (Jarvis) BV60 106851
O God of Bethel, by whose hand (Doddridge) A497; B446; D417; E447; F299; H120; J519; K 254; L489; M236; O286; Q434; R342; S98; T401; U248; V420; W562; X596; Z174; AA364; AD89; AF389; AG52; AL446; AM498; AO99; AP599; AW167; BA30; BB88; BF225; BV561; BY550 106852
O God of earth and altar (Chesterton) A521; E562; J344; R511; S419; W638; X308; Y236; Z546;

AD347; AF436; AG271; AK370; AN381; AQ238; BK103; BX412; BZ 106853

O God of God! O Light of Light (Julian) B251; D455; I15; N71; O122; Q132; AO206 106854

O God, of good the unfathomed Sea (Scheffler) AL11 106855

O God of grace, thy mercy send (Greek: Litany of the Deacons) F589 106856

O God of heaven and earth, arise (Doddridge) AZ301 106857

O God of hosts, the mighty Lord (Tate & Brady) AM303 106858

O God of hosts, with thy strong hand (---) BI13 106859

O God of Jacob, by whose hand (Doddridge) Q434 X O God of Bethel, by whose hand 106860

O God of life, whose power benign (Russell) D138; AZ6; BA258; BY44 106861

O God of Light, thy word, a lamp unfailing (Taylor) J250; R247; AE160; AT185; BZ 106862

O God of love of truth (Kretzman) M526 106863

O God of love, O King of peace (Baker) A528; B436; D199; F490; G511; I705; J352; K499; N577; O483; S421; W646; Z557; AE401; AF447; AG279; AK404; AL523; AM622; AO604; AP652; AR389; AS364; AW352; BA881; BF579; BK113; BX432; BY663 106864

O God of love, to thee we bow (Jenkins) W325; AD416; BY623 106865

O God of love, whose spirit wakes (Tweedy) BY66 106866

O God of loveliness, O Lord of heaven above (St Alfonso M. de' Liguori) BQ38 106867

O God of mercies, Father mine (Hoppe) N193 106868

O God of mercy, God of might (Thring) D271; E448; J316; K237; L398; N181; O450; P405; Q439; U33; W487; AA362; AM 366; AP583; AS344; BA566; BF492 106869

O God of mercy! hearken now (Clark) B503; D275; N391; AK388; BD130 106870

O God of nations, God of men (Schmidt) AO583 106871

O God of nations, hear thy people's prayer today (Pyper) BY649 106872

O God of our fathers, we praise and adore thee (Pruden) AT 500 106873

O God of peace, thee we implore (Orwig) AE187 106874

O God of truth, O Lord of might (St Ambrose) A161; E261; F12; BR13b 106875

O God of truth, whose living word (Hughes) A547; B498; E449; F309; W531; X597; Y145; Z365; AC181; AK364; AL411; AM468; AN325; AP 548; BF559; BX384; BY517 106876

O God of wisdom, life and love (Brubacher) AX553 106877

O God of wondrous grace and glory (Reed) J353 106878

O God of youth, whose Spirit in our hearts is stirring (Burt) A508; J548; AF491 106879

O God, our dwelling-place (Wilson) AN43; BD133; BX 281 106880

O God, our Father-Mother, Love, Purge thou our hearts (Sinclair) BE206 106881

O God our Father, throned on high (Coster) W492; BV541 106882

O God our Father, who dost make us one (Jenkins) BY 765 106883

O God our help in ages past (Watts) A289; B445; D418; E 450; F165; G533; H104; I577; J168; K505; L518; M145; N57; O212; P142; Q123; R111; S77; T168; U19; V90; W601; X598; Y30; Z585; AA172; AB58; AC 28; AD1; AE65; AF1; AG40; AH218; AI412; AJ247; AK63; AL662; AM26; AN145; AO91;

AP74; AQ51; AR70; AS76; AT286; AU435; AV39; AW61; AX639; AZ126; BA29; BB81; BC123; BD60; BE213; BF221; BH47; BI36; BJ76; BK64; BL 95; BR268, 322; BV244; BX 396; BY71; BZ 106884

O God, our Lord, thy holy Word (Erfurt Enchiridion, 1527) Q266 106885

O God, our strength, to thee our song (Auber) H67 106886

O God, preserve me, for in thee (U.P. Psalter, 1912) T20; AJ27 106887

O God, regard my humble plea (U.P. Psalter, 1912) R329; T110; AJ159 106888

O God Supreme, who dost the world sustain (Bartlett) AO 523 106889

O God, the Eternal Father (Phelps) BC125 106890

O God, the Father, draw thou nigh (Latin) M139 106891

O God, the God that saveth me (U.P. Psalter, 1912) AJ144 106892

O God, the refuge of thy saints (Watts) BI43 106893

O God, the Rock of Ages (Bickersteth) I18; J176; K479; L78; O61; R92; S62; U413; V666; Z154; AB42; AD71; AE63; AG43; AH211; AI250; AL35; AM24; AN148; AP160; AS75; AZ815; BA172; BF241; BH32; BX395; BY67 106894

O God the Son eternal, thy dread might (Heber) E244 106895

O God, the world's sustaining force (St Ambrose??) F14 106896

O God, thou art my God alone (Montgomery) W473; AM556; AP53 106897

O God, thou art the Father (St Columba) R93; W454; AF 248 106898

O God thou art the object of my love (St Francis Xavier??) BL39 106899

O God, thou faithful God (Heermann) M215; O457; Q395; AA346; AN484; AW566 106900

O God, thou Giver of all good (Longfellow) BZ 106901

O God, thou hast rejected us (U.P. Psalter, 1912) T109; AJ158 106902

O God, thou righteous faithful Lord (Leon) M66; AA424 106903

O God, though countless worlds of light (Knowles) H409 106904

O God, thy judgments give the King, His Son thy righteousness (Reformed Presby. Book of Psalms, 1940) AM 230 106905

O God, thy name is love (Deck) AZ1358 106906

O God, thy power is wonderful (Faber) E451; I87; AZ1453 106907

O God, thy soldiers' crown and guard (Latin, 6th c) E181; F516; BN181 106908

O God, thy soldiers' faithful Lord (Latin, 6th c) BN181 X O God, thy soldiers' crown and guard 106909

O God, thy soldiers' great reward (Latin, 6th c) F516 X O God, thy soldiers' crown and guard 106910

O God, thy summons still is heard (Schloerb) Z449 106911

O God, thy world is sweet with prayer (Larcom) Z133; AB 4; AR40; AS21; BF183 106912

O God, to thy Anointed King (U.P. Psalter, 1912) AJ 193 106913

O God, to us show mercy (U. P. Psalter, 1912) T121; AJ176; AM385 106914

O God, unseen but ever near, Our blessed rest art thou (Osler) AN447; BX475 106915

O God, unseen yet ever near,

Thy presence (Osler) A198; B321; D221; F412; J263; K189; L328; O152; Z452; BR467; BV384 106916
O God, we have heard and our fathers have told (U. P. Psalter, 1912) T81; AJ121 106917
O God, we praise thee; and confess (Tate & Brady) H100; L80; AB45; AF18; AM90 106918
O God, we pray for all mankind (Conover) AT456; AV267; AW 350; AX365 106919
O God, we pray for faithful wills (Maurer) AB238 106920
O God, we pray thee, bless thy children (Gordon) AR619; AS 52 106921
O God, what offering shall I give (Lange) BY770 X Jesus, what offering 106922
O God, while generations flee (---) AN371; BX397 106923
O God, who saidst, "Let there be light" (Miller) N168 106924
O God, who to a loyal home (Fosdick) AE385 106925
O God, who workest hitherto (Freckleton) AC189 X The toil of brain, or heart, or hand 106926
O God, whom I delight to praise (U.P. Psalter, 1912) T209; AJ300 106927
O God, whom we as Father know (Knapp) M512 106928
O God, whose daylight leadeth down (MacDonald) AL546 106929
O God, whose law from age to age (Holmes) U20; AH224; AK79; BF226; BH97 106930
O God, whose love is over all (Holmes) U22; Z175; AB38; AD87; AK70; AR96; BF228 106931
O God, whose mighty works of old (Crum) F501 106932
O God, whose presence glows in all (Frothingham) AN60; BE214; BX81 106933
O God, whose smile is in the sky (Holmes) Z163; AN36; BF222; BX68 106934
O God, whose will is life (Rawnsley) BZ X Father, whose will is life 106935
O God, within whose sight (Oxenham) AE310; AF265; AR503; BF586 106936
O golden day, so long desired (Dickinson) BB434; 106937
O Good Saint Anne, we call on thy name (---) R To kneel at thine altar 106938
O Gott, du frommer Gott (Heermann) BT395; BW 566 106939
O Gott, du grosser her der Welt (Unparth. G. B.) AY5d 106940
O Gott Schöpfer, heiliger Geist (Ausbund) BU50 106941
O Gott Vater ins Himmels Throne (Ausbund) BU55 106942
O Gott Vater, wir loben dich (L. Clock) AY1d; BU131; BY362 106943
O gracious Father of mankind (Tweedy) G305; S85; Y34; Z338; AB198; AC66; AD215; AG175; AK235; AR73; BF 371; BK55; BZ 106944
O gracious God, forsake me not (U.P. Psalter, 1912) R396; T131; AJ192 106945
O gracious God, in whom I live (Steele) D338 106946
O gracious God, whose constant care (Stock) AF492; AK449 106947
O gracious Hand that freely gives (Russell) N186; O422 106948
O grant thy servants through thy grace (Gambold) AX 642; BA316 106949
O grant us light, that we may know (Tuttiett) R335; S210; U44; V738; W466; Z298; AD 422; AE375; AG129; AK187; AW389; BA887; BF429; BY 540 106950

O great Absolver, grant my soul may wear (Stone) AZ453 106951
O great High Priest, forget not me (Loy) M547 106952
O greatly blessed the people are (Scottish Psalter, 1650) AL661; AM38; AP73 106953
O guardian of the Church divine (Chamberlain) BR481; BV411 106954
O Guidet to every child of thine (St. Clement of Alexandria) BZ 106955
O happy band of pilgrims (St Joseph the Hymnographer) B 536; D511; E452; F289; W577; X599; AL443; AP602; AZ852; BA509; BB377; BV582; BY551 106956
O happy day, that fixed my choice (Doddridge) G212 X O happy day, that stays my choice 106957
O happy day, that stays my choice (Doddridge) D218; G212; H287; I312; L287; N255; O389; U192; V310; W499; AH345; AL361; AM589; AO652; AP564; AS454; AT389; AU461; AV251; AW465; AX331; AY271; AZ390; BA464; BB310; BR462; BY297; BZ 106958
O happy day, when first was poured (Besnault) E36; Q115; AA177; BN24 106959
O happy day when we shall stand (Wexels) J197; O52; P62 106960
O happy days, days marked with perfect blessings (Foster) AZ 710 106961
O happy home! O blest abode! (Morton) BC133 106962
O happy home, where thou art loved the dearest (Spitta) G427; I671; J336; N533; O537; P351; Q626; R455; U320; W648; Y382; Z601; AC313; AD 418; AE383; AH500; AK445; AL 393; AM624; AO562; AP707; AT373; AU445; BB412; BV394; BY621 106963
O happy homes among the hills (Stephens) BC337 106964
O happy is that man and blest (Scottish Psalter, 1650) AP 129 106965
O happy is the man who bears (Bruce) V233 X How happy are the young who hear 106966
O happy land, whose sons in youth (U.P. Board of Publ, 1909) T285; AJ393; AM289; AP126 106967
O happy rest, sweet happy rest (Crosby) R Will you come 106968
O happy time of reaping (---) AI349; AR591; AS430 106969
O hark! a glorious sound is heard (Robinson) BC134 106970
O haupt voll Blut und Wunden (Based on St. Bernard of Clairvaux) BT172; BW539 106971
O have you heard the wondrous story? (German) M611 106972
O have you not heard of that beautiful stream (Hull. The casket, 1865) AW232a 106973
O he who trusts in God's protection (Neumark) BE216 106974
O he who walked with fishermen (Iris) AC461 106975
O, he whom Jesus loved has truly spoken (Whittier) BE 217 X O brother man, fold to thy heart 106976
O Head so full of bruises (St Bernard of Clairvaux) BA 216 X O Sacred Head. . . 106977
O hear my cry, be gracious now to me (Crosby) AU289 106978
O hear my earnest prayer, dear Lord (Van Hoose) R Increase my faith 106979
O hear my prayer, Lord (Scottish Psalter, 1650) AP125 106980

O hear them marching, marching, the legions of good will (Ham) Z564 106981
O, hearken when we cry (Faber) R Now are the days of humblest prayer 106982
O Heart of God! Our home lies deep in thee (Stanfield) AW237; BO22 106983
O Heart of Jesus, Heart of God (Fullerton) BQ58 106984
O Heart of Jesus, purest Heart (Latin, 18th c) BP69; BQ64 106985
O heart of Mary, pure and fair (---) BN154; BO94 106986
O heavenly Beauty, lovelier far (Peers) X600 106987
O heavenly grace in holy rite descending (Spencer) A188 106988
O heavenly Jerusalem, of everlasting halls (Latin, 18th c) A592; B509; D401; E251; F569 106989
O heavens, send your rain upon us (Bible. Isaiah, 45) BN2 106990
O Heil'ger Geist, kehr bei uns ein (Schirmer) BT235; BW546 106991
O heilige Dreifaltigkeit, O hochgelobte Einigkeit (Behm) BT 541 106992
O heiliger Geist, O heiliger Gott (Niedling) BW547 106993
O help us Lord, each hour of need (Milman) B33; D337; E83; F320; K404; W455; X114; AP 464; AZ123; BA712 106994
O here, if ever, God of love (Taylor) BX481 106995
O Herr dich will ich loben (Ausbund) BU12 106996
O herre Gott, dein göttlich Wort (German. 1527) BT266 106997
O Herr Gott, gross ist die Roth (Ausbund) BU98 106998
O Herr! nicht stolz ist mein Herz doch (Ausbund. Psalm 130) BU130 106999
O Herr thu auf die Lefzen mein (Ausbund Suppl.) BU6 107000
O Herr! um dein Gnad ruff ich dich an (Ausbund) BU139 107001
O Herre Gott! hilf mir in deinem Namen (Ausbund. Psalm 54) BU83 107002
O Herre Gott in deinem Thron (M. Schneider) BU87 107003
O Herre Gott, in meiner Roth. (Ausbund) BU49 107004
O Herre Gott mein Roth thu ich dir klagen (Ausbund) BU115 107005
O Herre Gott vom Himmelreich (S. Hans & G. v. Ingersheim) BU59 107006
O hollow, soulless pomp, which decks (Howard) BR364 107007
O holy, blessed Trinity, Divine essential Unity (Behm) O545
X O holy, blessed Trinity, Divine, eternal Unity 107008
O holy, blessed Trinity, Divine, eternal Unity (Behm) M143; O545; Q541; AA20 107009
O holy city, seen of John (Bowie) A494; G474; J332; R508; S409; U354; Y63; AB 331; AD429; AF420; AG269; AK397; AL382; AP577; BF 509; BZ 107010
O holy day! O happy day! (Hoffman) R How calm and how bright 107011
O Holy Father, Holy Son (Kyle) Lp. 743; AZ310 107012
O holy Father, who in tender love (Bickersteth) AL222 107013
O Holy Ghost, eternal God (Helder) AA251 107014
O Holy Ghost, on this great day inspire (Rawlett) AZ 445; BA256 107015
O Holy Ghost, thou Fount of light (Adam of St Victor) AZ635 107016
O Holy Ghost, thou gift divine (Ringwaldt) O380; P225 107017
O Holy Ghost, thou God of peace

(Williams) D494 107018
O Holy Ghost, thy people bless (Baker) F234; BV221 107019
O Holy Ghost, to thee we pray (Luther) O39 107020
O Holy, Holy, Holy Lord (Eastburn) D137; L69; AS73 107021
O Holy Jesu, Prince of Peace (Brown-Borthwick) D232 107022
O holy joy that raises (---) BH 104 107023
O Holy Lord, content to fill (How) J334; K417; BB426 107024
O Holy Lord, our God (Young) L304; V564 107025
O Holy Name of majesty and power (O'Connell, Cardinal) BP21 107026
O holy night! the Stars are brightly shining (Adam) AH615; AU 468; AW86 107027
O holy Sabbath-day, draw near (Moses) BH117 107028
O Holy Saviour, Friend unseen (Elliott) D610; G327; H364; I478; R214; S306; T419; U195; V431; Z350; AB189; AD278; AG182; AI240; AP526; AT287; AV226; AZ1146; BF401; BR 377, 406; BZ 107029
O Holy Spirit, come to me (Blough) AR228 107030
O Holy Spirit, come, we pray (Luther) M467 107031
O Holy Spirit, Comforter (Holling) AL149 107032
O Holy Spirit, enter in (Schirmer) K153; M462; N156; O374; P53; Q235; AA247; AF244; AK186; AN493; AW546; AZ1095 107033
O Holy Spirit, God (Dearmer) A372; X601 107034
O Holy Spirit, gracious gift divine (Davis) AB90 107035
O Holy Spirit, grant us grace (Ringwaldt) O18; P56; Q293 107036
O Holy Spirit, lead us, we pray (Kelly) AU450 107037
O Holy Spirit, Lord of grace (Coffin) E453; F231; BJ14; BV291 107038
O Holy Spirit, Lord of life (Latin, 4th c) BJ45 107039
O Holy Spirit, making whole (Tweedy) AR229; BF264 107040
O holy words of truth and love (Townsend) BC135 107041
O home beloved, wher-e'er I wander (Stephens) BC335 107042
O how beautiful the sky (Grundtvig) P148 107043
O, how blessed is the Station (LaTrobe) AZ984; BA281 107044
O how blest are ye whose toils are ended! (Dach) K510; M294; O596; Q589; AA547 107045
O how deep are the riches of grace (Kennedy) R We are saved by the grace 107046
O how excellent and fair (Gregor) AZ788; BA746 107047
O how glorious, full of wonder (Beach) AF74; BZ 107048
O, how great, how rich, how free (Zinzendorf, N. L.) AZ1038 107049
O, how great is thy compassion (Olearius) Q384; AA317 107050
O how happy are they Who the Saviour obey (Wesley) G 356; H294; I311; V386; AS 300; AY205; AZ1421; BB 292; BZ 107051
O how happy are they Who their Saviour obey (Wesley) AS 300 X O how happy are they Who the Saviour obey 107052
O how holy is this place (Schmolck) O45 107053
O, how I love Jesus (Whitfield) R There is a name I love to hear 107054
O how I love thee Jesus! My soul aspires to thee (St Therese, of the Child Jesus)

BQ328 107055
O, how is the time so urgent (Mack) AR428 107056
O how love I thy law (U. P. Psalter, 1912) AM450 X Most perfect is the law of God 107057
O how lovely, O how sweet (Wengel) Z263 107058
O, how lovely was the morning (Manwaring) BC136 107059
O how marvelous, O how wonderful (Gabriel) R I stand amazed 107060
O how praying rests the weary (Kidder) R Ere you left your room 107061
"O how shall I keep Christmas?" (Westall) BR550 107062
O how shall I receive thee (Gerhardt) J11; K6; L258; M324; N4; O157; P112; AK100; AZ 800; BA149; BR137 107063
O how the thought of God attracts (Faber) G374; I363 107064
O how wondrous the grace of our God (Kennedy) AR430 X We are saved by the grace of our God 107065
O Hunter blessed, of hearts distressed (Herman) BP94 107066
O I long to see the beauty (Latta) AS451 107067
O, I long, yes, I long there to dwell (Newell) R A city awaits 107068
O, I love to talk with Jesus (---) AX366; AY198 107069
O, I love to tell the merits of my Saviour (Jones) R There is nothing in the world 107070
"O, I will give you glory," said God (Grimes) AC482 107071
O, I can hear you, God (Sarett) AC442 107072
"O, I have seen a king's new baby" (Colletet) BG108 107073
O ice and snow, O frost and cold (---) AC466 107074
O if the Lamb had not been slain (Cennick) AZ745 107075
O it is hard to work for God (Faber) I442; AZ202 107076
O, it is wonderful that he should care (Gabriel) R I stand all amazed at the love 107077
O it must be the breaking of the day (Sederquist) R 'Tis almost time for the Lord to come 107078
O Jehovah, hear my words (U. P. Board of Publ. 1909) T6; AI229; AJ9; AM47 107079
O Jerusalem, look toward the East (Latin) E618 107080
O Jesulein Süss, O Jesulein mild (Thilo) BG109b 107081

NOTE: "O Jesu" and "O Jesus" are interfiled. 107082

O Jesu, blessed Lord, to thee (Kingo) F419; J284; O155; P106; Q309 107083
O Jesus, blest is he (Russell) O482 107084
O Jesus, blest Redeemer (McAfee) R There is a place of quiet rest 107085
O Jesus, bruised and wounded more (Alexander) AA428 107086
O Jesus Christ, all praise to thee (Luther) O184 107087
O Jesus Christ, alone to thee (---) BI2D 107088
O Jesu Christ, Dein Kripplein ist (Gerhardt) BT81 107089
O Jesu Christ, from thee began (Latin, 9th c) E69 107090
O Jesus Christ, grow thou in me (Lavater) AL331; AO301; BV636; BY601 107091
O Jesus Christ, if aught there be (Caswall) AZ1456 107092
O Jesu Christ, mein schönstes Licht (Gerhardt) BT349; BW 170 107093
O Jesu Christ, mein's Lebens Licht (Behm) BT148 107094
O Jesus Christ, most holy (Zinzendorf, N. L.) AZ794 107095

O Jesus Christ, our Lord most dear (Laufenburg) A185; E338; F425; K175; R452; S351; W304; AF278; AM355 107096

O Jesus Christ, our only Lord (Sigstedt) BI15-D 107097

O Jesus Christ, Redeemer, Lord (Watts) BI37 107098

O Jesus Christ, remember, When thou shalt come (Caswall) BQ 55 107099

O Jesus Christ, the Holy One (Saxby) AP364 107100

O Jesus Christ, thou Bread of Life (Rist) N249 107101

O Jesus Christ, thy manger is (Gerhardt) Q81 107102

O Jesu Christe, wahres Licht (Heermann) AY3d; BT512 107013

O Jesus crowned with all renown (Benson) A101; B181 107104

O Jesus, crucified for man (How) A333; B52; D5; I326; K69; O475; U255; AG120; BF328 107105

O Jesus, crucified for me, And all whose sins (Sanger) AR 509 107106

O Jesu, der du felig macht (L. Ringmacher) BU74 107107

O Jesu, einig wahres Haupt (Mentzer) BT477 107108

O Jesus, ever present (Tuttiett) W176; BR394 107109

O Jesus, for thy matchless love (Zinzendorf, N. L.) AZ206 107110

O Jesus, full of pardoning grace (Wesley) W409 107111

O Jesu, gid du vilde (Kingo) BT 655 107112

O Jesus, God and Man (Baker) AO17; AZ1369 107113

O Jesus, I have promised (Bode) A570; B379; D615; E577; F331; G226; H316; I350; J515; M527; N259; O372; P108; R307; S268; T376; U253; W508; X255; Y 369; Z308; AB234; AC196; AD 244; AE263; AF218; AG165; AH428; AK271; AL354; AM552; AO389; AP554; AR346; AS455; AT386; AU187; AV193; AW 212; AZ841; BA465; BB288; BF443; BR384; BV365; BY 298; BZ 107114

O Jesus is a Rock (Charlesworth) R The Lord's our Rock 107115

O Jesus, Joy of loving hearts (St Bernard of Clairvaux) N241 X Jesus, thou Joy of loving hearts 107116

O Jesu, King most wonderful (St Bernard of Clairvaux??) E419b; F189b; J468; K352; L115; O292; Q361; W423; X547b; AA90; AL299; AO216; AP450; AZ196; BA109; BR 416; BV542; BY188 107117

O Jesus, King of glory (Behm) M372; P149; Q130; AA179 107118

O Jesus, Lamb of God, thou art (Helder) Q328; AA417 107119

O Jesus, Lamb of God, who art (Helder) AA417 X O Jesus, Lamb of God, thou art 107120

O Jesu! life-spring of the soul (St Rabanus Maurus??) BL 40 107121

O Jesus, Lord and Saviour, I give myself to thee (Chrisholm) R Living for Jesus 107122

O Jesus, Lord and Saviour, the soul's Eternal King (Bayley) BR31 107123

O Jesus! Lord most merciful (Hamilton) B131; D360 107124

O Jesus, Lord, most mighty King (St Bernard of Clairvaux) BO8 107125

O Jesus, Lord of heavenly grace (St Ambrose) K359; O444; AZ932; BV33; BY680 107126

O Jesus, Lord, to thee I cry (Hamilton) P254; AU86 107127

O Jesus, Master, when today (Newhall) G470; U278; Y212; Z517; AB282; AS1913; AT466;

BF493 107128

O Jesus my Lord, For ever adored (N. L. von Zinzendorf) AZ20; BA533 107129

O Jesus, my Redeemer (Belden) BB613 107130

O Jesus, once a Nazareth boy (---) Y135; Z505; AC174; AE 450; AH275; AR379; AS410; BF624 107131

O Jesus, our dear Master (Matters) BE221 107132

O Jesus, our Salvation (Hamilton) N191; O477 107133

O Jesus, Prince of life and truth (---) Z505 X O Jesus, once a Nazareth boy 107134

O Jesus, Saviour dear, how shall thy name be praised (Heermann) N250 107135

O Jesu, Saviour of the lost (Bickersteth) D85; L406; V242; BA441; BR359 107136

O Jesus, Saviour, Source of good (---) BR473 107137

O Jesus, shall it ever be (Grigg) N143 X Jesus, and shall it ever be 107138

O Jesu so meek, O Jesu so kind (Thilo) J501; AF135 107139

O Jesu, söde Jesu, dig (Kingo) BT309 107140

O Jesus, Source of calm repose (Freylinghausen) N486; O467 107141

O Jesus, strong and pure and true (How) W675 107142

O Jesu sweet, O Jesu mild (Thilo) AF135 X O Jesu so meek 107143

O Jesus, thou art standing (How) A407; B132; D357; E578; F355; G197; H281; I282; J386; K322; L360; M77; N401; R266; S228; T382; U170; V300; W397; Y375; Z279; AB157; AC148; AD205; AE169; AF329; AG139; AH325; AK211; AL469; AM414; AO257; AP395; AR252; AT346; AU242; AV179; AW144; AZ837; BA406; BB231; BF342; BR297; BV476; BY418; BZ 107144

O Jesu, thou the beauty art (St Bernard of Clairvaux??) E419c; X547c; BQ15 107145

O Jesu, thou the Virgin's crown (St Ambrose??) F521 107146

O Jesus, thou wast tempted (Park) BF301 107147

O Jesus, thy boundless love (Gerhardt) AR181 X Jesus, thy boundless love 107148

O Jesus Victim-Priest (Udulutsch) BM43 107149

O Jesu, we adore thee, Upon the cross (Russell) D364; R200; S156; V153; Z234; AI422; AK162; AM193; AZ 835; BA500 107150

O Jesus, we adore thee, Who in thy love (Udulutsch) BM 9 107151

O Jesus, were we through thy grace (Zinzendorf, N. L.) AZ1099 107152

O Jesus, when I think of thee (Bethune) Z218; AO146; AV 143 107153

O Jesus, youth of Nazareth (Blanchard) Z217; AB170; AC103; AE440; AR409; BF 299 107154

O, Joseph being an old man truly (English trad carol) BG115 107155

O joy, because the circling year (St Hilary of Poictiers) F151 107156

O joy of God, that comest in the morning (Boutflower) F 404 107157

O joyful hope, in weary hearts awaking (Bayly) BY84 107158

O joyful message, sent from heaven (Hoppe) M338 107159

O joyful sound of gospel grace! (Wesley) I371 107160

O joyous Easter morning, that saw the Lord of love arisen (---) AC125; AR187 107161

O kind Creator, bow thine ear. (St Gregory the Great??) E66 107162

O King enthroned on high (Greek: Pentacostarion, 8th c) A374; E454; F237 107163

O King most high of earth and sky (Latin, 17th c) E629 107164

O King of kings, before whose throne (Quarles) J175; W6 107165

O king of kings, beneath thy wings (Hymns of the English Conf. 1880) BR264 107166

O King of kings in splendor (Latin) BL60 107167

O King of kings, O Lord of hosts, whose throne is lifted high (Burton) I714 107168

O King of kings, whose reign of old (How) AP646 107169

O King of mercy, from thy throne on high (Birks) W453; AZ2; BR474 107170

O King of might and splendor (Manuale cantus sancti. Ratisbon, 19th c) BL100; BM8; BN205 107171

O King of nations, splendor, honor (Howard) BN99 107172

O King of saints, we give thee praise (Thomson) D177 107173

O König aller Ehren (Behm) BT130 107174

O Lamb of God, for sinners slain (Wesley) H270 107175

O Lamb of God, have mercy (Glenn) BI67 107176

O Lamb of God, most holy (Decius) N90; O147; AA203 107177

O Lamb of God, most lowly (Balfern) M392 107178

O Lamb of God, redeemer blest (Littledale) R O Lord, to whom the spirits live 107179

O Lamb of God, still keep me (Deck) A339; B149; D363; M425; U254; V400; W470; AI 281; AL320; AO341; AP475; AZ 838; BA526; BB290 107180

O Lamb of God, that takest away the sin of the world. (Latin, 5th c: Agnus Dei)

NOTE: This hymn will be found in the liturgical portion of many hymnals. Citation to AI 143 is to a single item within the normal congregational hymn section. 107181

O Lamb of God, unspotted (Decius) AZ731 107182

O Lamb of God who, bleeding (Decius) AK526 107183

O Lamb of God, who wast for sinners slain (Tersteegen) AZ520 107184

O Lamm Gottes, unschuldig (Decius) BT146; BW540 107185

O Lämmlein Gottes, Jesu Christ (Helder) BT328 107186

O land of our King! where harvest embraces (Grundtvig) M302; P345 107187

O land of rest for thee I sigh (Mills) AT284; AU167; AV 398; AX203; AY306 107188

O, land relieved from sorrow! (Duffield) AZ821 107189

O lead and guide us Lord (Plummer) BI59) 107190

O lead my blindness by the hand (Gladstone) E322; BY 324 107191

O leave your sheep, your lambs that follow after (French trad.) BV110 107192

O let him whose sorrow (Oswald) E455; V407; W542; X115; AO340; AP518; AZ 765; BA662; BR337, 340; BY771 107193

O let me walk with thee, my God (Stuttle) BB395 107194

O let my supplicating cry (U.P. Psalter, 1912) R323; T246; AJ342 107195

O let the children come to me (Wallin) B345; N232 107196

O let the heart beat high with bliss (Breviary, Sarum, 1495) E237 107197

O let triumphant faith dispel (Scottish Paraphrases, 1745) M122 107198

O let us praise the Christmas tree (German) M620 107199
O life that makest all things new (Longfellow) X602; AC219; AL 319; AN416; AQ54; AR530; AS 391; BD41; BE218; BX375 107200
O life that maketh all things new (Longfellow) BX375 X O life that makest all things new 107201
O Light, from age to age the same (Hosmer) J247; X192; AN464; AQ255; BF594; BX503 107202
O Light, O Trinity most blest! (St Ambrose) K462; L24 107203
O Light of God's most wondrous love (Boye) M459; O383 107204
O Light of life, O Saviour dear (Palgrave) S46 107205
O Light of Light, by love inclined (Latin, 10th c) E234 107206
O Light of Light, within us dwell (Gladden) AQ122 X Behold a Sower! 107207
O Light that knew no dawn (St Gregory Nazianzen) W458; AF 407; AM23 107208
O Light, whose beams illumine all (Plumptre) B40; D424; K 373; R145; S180; W172; AK244; AR293; AZ661; BI40 107209
O listen to our wondrous story (Gray) AU385 107210
O little Chid of Bethlehem (McKelway) U65 107211
O little flock, fear not the foe (Altenburg) Q263 107212
O little one sweet, O little one mild (Thilo) BG109 107213
O little town, O little town (Scollard) Y325 107214
O little town of Bethlehem (Brooks) A21; B78; D58; E15; F65; G 100; H145; I121; J27; K31; L 220; M605; N36; O196; P133; Q647; R171; S121; T334; U55; V741; W48; X79; Y330; Z184; AB107; AC82; AD121; AE85; AF134; AG64; AH250; AI66; AK108; AL51; AM152; AN 165; AO125; AP169; AQ286; AR126; AS103; AT75; AU 144; AV82; AW84; AX97; BA 157; BB104; BC165; BD226; BE222; BF292; BG138; BK 150; BR557; BV122; BX198; BY105; BZ 107215
O living Bread from heaven (Rist) J285; K193; N236; O148; P105; Q316; AA435 107216
O living Christ, chief Cornerstone (Cunniggim) G547; BZ 107217
O Lord, again in thy blest name we meet (Whitmore) BR101 X Father, again in Jesus' name we meet 107218
O Lord all glorious, Life of life (Harmony in praise, 1890) Y25; AB68; AC31; BR76 107219
O Lord, almighty God, thy works (The Whole Book of Psalmes) AF473 107220
O Lord almighty, thou whose hands (Newbolt) X323; Y238 107221
O Lord! and is thy table spread (Doddridge) BR471 X My God, thy table now is spread 107222
O Lord, and Master of us all (Whittier) A501; B496; E 456; W513; X603; AF223; AL348; AP184; AR390; BA 82, 634; BD70; BF332; BV 272; BX217; BY125 107223
O Lord, be near me when I pray (---) BH19 107224
O Lord, be thou my helper true (U.P. Psalter, 1912) T16; AJ21; AM45 107225
O Lord, be with us when we sail (Dayman) D305; K502; M266; N587; V643; W625; AP710; BA894; BR506; BY 669 107226
O Lord, by thee delivered (U. P. Psalter, 1912) R127; T 50; AJ77; AM526 107227
O Lord, devoutly I love thee

(Schalling) N465 107228
O Lord divine, we come to pray (Toews) AX554 107229
O Lord, encouraged by thy grace (---) BV343 107230
O Lord, give ear when with my voice (U.P. Psalter, 1912) T47; AJ74 107231
O Lord, give heed unto our plea (Swedberg) N348 107232
O Lord, hear thou my calling (Marot) O218 107233
O Lord, how are my foes increased! (Sternhold) T3; AJ5; AM469; AP3 107234
O Lord, how boundless is thy love! (Watts) BR250 X My God, how endless is thy love 107235
O Lord, how full of sweet content (Guyon) L467 X My Lord, how full of sweet 107236
O Lord, how happy should we be (Anstice) E457; I519; V361; W 543; X604; AL419; AP515; AW 255; BR335; BV510; BY482 107237
O Lord, how joyful 'tis to see (Coffin) F244; O412 107238
O Lord, how manifold the works (U.P. Psalter, 1912) T199; AJ288 107239
O Lord, how shall I meet thee (Gerhart) Q58; AA136; AM119 107240
O Lord, I am not worthy (---) AH133; BN100; BO49; BP66; BQ129 107241
O Lord, I love thee from my heart (Schalling) AA366 X Lord, thee I love with all my heart 107242
O Lord, I sing thy praises (Grant) W570 107243
O Lord, I sing with lips and heart (Gerhardt) Q569 X O Lord, I sing with voice and heart 107244
O Lord, I sing with mouth and heart (Gerhardt) AA292 X O Lord, I sing with voice and heart 107245
O Lord, I sing with voice and heart (Gerhardt) M495; Q569; AA292 107246
O Lord, I unto thee do cry (Scottish Psalter, 1650) AP 124 107247
O Lord, I would delight in thee (Ryland) AM543; BE224 107248
O Lord, in me fulfill Whatever is thy will (Claggett) AZ552 107249
O Lord, in me there lieth nought (Sidney & Pembroke) X605 107250
O Lord, in this great mystery (Gannon) BM5 107251
O Lord, it is a blessed thing (How) BX159 107252
O Lord Jesus, how long (Turner) R It may be at morn 107253
O Lord Jesus, I adore thee (Mauburn) F388 107254
O Lord, look down from heaven, behold (Luther) Q260 X Look down, O Lord, from heave behold 107255
O Lord, make haste to hear my cry (U.P. Psalter, 1912) R 392; T278; AJ386 107256
O Lord, may church and home combine (Buck) BZ 107257
O Lord most high, with all my heart (U.P. Psalter, 1912) R388; T13; AJ17; AM44 107258
O Lord, my best desire fulfil (Cowper) L505; AA389 107259
O Lord, my earnest cry, Thy listening ear (U.P. Psalter, 1912) T243; AJ339 107260
O Lord, my God, for thy name's sake (U.P. Psalter, 1912) AJ 301 107261
O Lord, my God, I cry to thee (Selnecker) O585; Q600; AA 543 107262
O Lord, my God, most earnestly (U.P. Psalter, 1912) R327; T114; AJ163 107263
O Lord, my God, my joyful heart (U.P. Psalter, 1912) AJ234 107264

O Lord, my God, thy holy law (Hoppe) M57 107265

O Lord, my God, to thee I pray (Hamburg Temple hymnal) BH29 107266

O Lord my God! When I in awesome wonder (Boberg) BZ 107267

O Lord, my inmost heart and thought (U.P. Psalter, 1912) R129; AI34; AJ384 107268

O Lord, now let thy servant (Ryden) M18; N590 107269

O Lord! of goodness so amazing (Spitta) AZ698 107270

O Lord of health and life, What tongue can tell (Phillimore) O235; AO150 107271

O Lord of heaven and earth and sea (Wordsworth) A305; B426; D477; E521; F480; G541; I692; J448; K385; L76; N573; O452; Q443; S398; T319; U481; W19; AA357; AB388: AC56; AD261; AK257; AL26; AO105; AP139; AR597; AS426; AZ7; BA567; BD131; BF649; BH66; BR487; BV599; BX331; BY68; BZ 107272

O Lord of hosts, all heaven possessing (Plumptre) E458; X606 107273

O Lord of hosts! Almighty King (Holmes) B437; D197; AH193; AO603 107274

O Lord of Hosts, how lovely the place where thou dost dwell (Asso. Reformed Presbyterian Psalter, 1931) AM305 107275

O Lord of Hosts, how lovely thy tabernacles are (U.P. Psalter, 1912) T153; AJ227 107276

O Lord of Hosts, in mercy (U. P. Psalter, 1912) AJ228 107277

O Lord of Hosts, the fight is long (Armitage) AP591 107278

O Lord of Hosts, to thee I cry (U.P. Psalter, 1912) T84; AJ226 107279

O Lord of Hosts, we now invoke (Dalrymple) BC271 107280

O Lord of Hosts, who didst upraise (Benson) E539; AL412 107281

O Lord of Hosts, whose glory fills (Neale) D291; H412; I658; L279; N275; Q633; AA 450; AF475; BA323 107282

O Lord of life, and love, and power (Armitage) U276; W 355; AL386; BY483 107283

O Lord of Life, the Truth, the Way (---) BI35; BR77 107284

O Lord of life, thy Kingdom is at hand (Ham) S370; Z491; AD341; AN332; BB198; BD 154; BF571; BX385 107285

O Lord of life, thy quickening voice (MacDonald) W264; Z132; AB3; AC13; AL537; BX140; BY681 107286

O Lord of life, to thee we lift (Gladden) R256; AD192; AE157; AR239; BE226 107287

O Lord of life where'er they be (Hosmer) J600; W331; Z575; AD459; AF469; AL459; AN 195; AW316; BF664; BX207; BY613 107288

O Lord of life, whose power sustains (Darbyshire) F585; BY650 107289

O Lord of love, compassionate (---) Y398 107290

O Lord of love! Shall we not understand (Burr) Y82 107291

O Lord of love, thou light divine (---) AT520 107292

O Lord of stars and sunlight (Holmes) AQ9 107293

O Lord our banner, God of might (Wordsworth) AP651 107294

O Lord, our Father, shall we be confounded (Heermann) Q269 107295

O Lord, our Father, thanks to thee (Schneegass) Q124; AA 170 107296

O Lord, our fathers oft have told (Tate & Brady) G498; I700; AS385; BZ 107297

O Lord, our God, accept, we pray (Schuette) M516 107298

O Lord, our God, Almighty King (Stratton) I664 107299
O Lord our God, arise (Wardlaw) K225; L277; N374; P395; W 376; AM375; AP379; BV331; BY385 107300
O Lord our God, in reverence lowly (Tersteegen) AZ1104 107301
O Lord, our God, in time to be (Whittier) AK413 107302
O Lord, our God, thy mighty hand (Van Dyke) S415; Y281; AB340; AC272; AH479; AO588; BA876; BD166; BF550 107303
O Lord, our God, to thee (Smith) BI11 X My country 'tis of thee 107304
O Lord, our help in ages past (Watts) BI36 X O God, our help 107305
O Lord our King how bright thy fame (Kennedy) BH72 107306
O Lord, our little ones to thee (Whiting) N228; O144; P97 107307
O Lord, our Lord, in all the earth (U.P. Psalter, 1912) R95; AJ14; BZ 107308
O Lord, our strength in weakness (Wordsworth) D278; N258 107309
O Lord, reprieve the lonely state (Currie) BN187 107310
O Lord, stretch forth Thy mighty hand (How) R To Thee our God we fly 107311
O Lord, the Holy Innocents (Alexander) B87; D575 107312
O Lord, thou art my God and King And I will ever bless thy name (U.P. Psalter, 1912) R5; T286 107313
O Lord, thou art my God and King, Thee will I magnify and praise (Craig) AL688; AP127; AW600 107314
O Lord, thou art the way (---) BR459 107315
O Lord, thou hast ascended (U. P. Psalter, 1912) T125; AJ183 107316
O Lord, thou hast me searched and known (Scottish Psalter, 1650) AP123 107317
O Lord, thou Judge of all the earth (U.P. Psalter, 1912) T174; AJ253; AM46 107318
O Lord, thou living Bread from heaven (---) M50 107319
O Lord, thy all discerning eyes (Adams) BH38 107320
O Lord, thy benediction give (Armstrong) AC218 X O Thou, who makest souls to shine 107321
O Lord, thy heavenly grace impart (Smucker) AY104 107322
O Lord, thy judgments give the King (Scottish Psalter, 1650) AP61 107323
O Lord, thy love through heavenly spheres descending (Plummer) BI78 107324
O Lord, thy people gathered here (Roberts) J258; K251; AN441 107325
O Lord, thy perfect righteousness (U.P. Psalter, 1912) T242; AJ338 107326
O Lord, thy work revive (Brown) H382; AZ1322; BA 907 107327
O Lord, to thee I cry (U.P. Psalter, 1912) T48; AJ75; AP26; AX540; AY77 107328
O Lord, to thee I cry (Link) AX540 X O Lord, to thee I cry (U.P. Psalter) 107329
O Lord! to thee who dwellest above (Jacobs) BH196 107330
O Lord, to us assembled here (---) AR6; AS57 107331
O Lord, to us thy mercy show (U.P. Psalter, 1912) T157; AJ232 107332
O Lord, to whom the spirits live (Littledale) A226; E359; F468 107333
O Lord, turn not away thy face (Marckant) E84; F93; O470; S503; W401; X116; AF580; AK213; BA421; BJ33 107334

O Lord, turn not thy face away (Marckant) O470 X O Lord, turn not away thy face 107335

O Lord, turn not thy face from me (Marckant) F93 X O Lord, turn not away thy face 107336

O Lord, we praise thee, bless thee, and adore thee (Luther) Q313 X Praise we the Lord and bless his name forever 107337

O Lord, we welcome thee (Ziegler) Q93 107338

O Lord what is man that Thou takest knowledge (Bible. Psalm 8) BH335 107339

O Lord when condemnation and guilt oppress my soul (Gosenius) O281 107340

O Lord, when we the path retrace (Deck) L247 107341

O Lord, where shall I find thee? (Judah ben Samuel Halevi) BH 21 107342

O Lord, where'er thy people meet (Cowper) BE227 X Jesus, where'er thy people meet 107343

O Lord, while we confess the worth (Peters) AE325; AX168; AY269 107344

O Lord, who by thy presence hast made light (Spitta) AZ461 107345

O Lord, who hast my place assigned (Loy) M254 107346

O Lord, who hast this table spread (Collier) AO439 107347

O Lord, who in thy love divine (Wordsworth) Q493 Thou who the night in prayer didst spend 107348

O Lord, who numberest all our days (Swertner) AZ365; BA848 107349

O Lord, whose bounteous hand again (---) Q567; AA291 107350

O Lord, with thankful hearts we meet (---) BA885 107351

O Lord, within my soul (Hoffman) AX333; AY190 107352

O Love divine, all else transcending (Tersteegen) M225; AW517a 107353

O Love divine and golden (Monsell) G430; O533; P350; R 454; S485; AO558; AR540; AS420; AY443; AZ827; BA 844 107354

O Love, divine and tender (Monsell) AZ827 X O Love, divine and golden 107355

O Love divine, how sweet thou art (Wesley) F195; G218; H344; I368; O459; W428; AL 301; AP452; AZ637; BB148; BV531; BY772; BZ 107356

O Love divine, of all that is (Chadwick) AN51; BX294 107357

O Love divine, that dwells serene (McKenzie) BE228 107358

O Love divine that stooped to share (Holmes) B400; D627; G273: H358; I457; R116; T 402; U212; V641; Z353; AD 236; AE212; AH214; AL124; AN188; AO369; AP232; AR 307; AS125; AW172; AY419; BB144; BF247; BX243; BZ 107359

O Love divine, what hast thou done! (Wesley) G137; H174; I153; AZ662; BB151; BZ 107360

O Love Divine, whose constant beam (Whittier) AN56; BE 229; BX73 107361

O Love, how deep, how broad, how high (St Thomas à Kempis) A344; E459; F187; K63; S139; AF150; AI419; AM121; AO144; BL90; BP103; BR169; BY126 107362

O Love! O Life! Our faith and sight (Whittier) I479; AB166; AN206; AQ121; BD65; BE 230; BX218 107363

O, love of God, how rich and pure (Lehman) R The love of God 107364

O Love of God, how strong and true (Bonar) I83; X607; AF

99; AI36; AM73; AN84; BB67; BX85; BY69 107365

O Love of God most full (Clute) R118; S84; AK275; AT52; BX 258 107366

O Love, our Mother, ever near (Matters) BE232 107367

O love that casts our fear (Bonar) A457; B235; D431; U23; AP 468; BV540 107368

O Love that lights the eastern sky (Benson) S433 107369

O Love that nothing can efface (Pados) BL46 107370

O Love that will not let me go (Matheson) AY468 X O Love that wilt not let me 107371

O Love that wilt not let me go (Matheson) A458; B236; F359; G318; I481; J402; K348; M208; N521; P288; R400; S307; T403; U26; V367; W424; Y37; Z388; AB181; AC154; AD249; AE262; AF399; AG181; AH221; AK278; AL311; AM594; AN243; AO289; AP465; AR271; AS266; AT290; AU231; AV232; AW175; AY468; BA492; BB145; BD115; BF245; BK90; BR422; BX286; BY20; BZ 107372

O Love, who formest me to wear (Scheffler) E460; F203; K364; O68; Q397; W496; X608; AA348; BJ12 107373

O Love, who madest me to wear (Scheffler) Q397 X O Love who formest me to wear 107374

O Love whose perfect path is known (Key) BE233 107375

O Loving Father, hear thou thy children (West) AR385 107376

O loving Father, to thy care (Alington) F427 107377

O loving Lord, who art for ever seeking (Jenkins) BY602 107378

O Lue fra Guds Kjärlighed (Boye) BT230 107379

O lux beata Trinitas (St Ambrose) BJ86b 107380

O make a joyful noise, ye lands (U.P. Psalter, 1912) AJ270 107381

O, make thy blest abode with me (Schell) R Humility, thou secret vale 107382

O Maker of the mighty deep (Van Dyke) U40; AB205 107383

O Maker of the sea and sky (Burton) B418; Y43; AB381; AC37; AH217 107384

O Maker of the stars of night (Latin, 9th c) BJ47 107385

O Maker of the world, give ear (Latin) F84 107386

O man, do never faint nor fear (English trad carol) R St Stephen was a holy man 107387

O man of God, arise (Fenner) L342 107388

O martyrs young and fresh as flowers (Prudentius) F538 107389

O Mary, dearest Mother (Russell) BO118 107390

O Mary, don't you weep (Negro spiritual) AH606 107391

O Mary, Mother full of grace (Fortunatus??) BN148 107392

O Mary! We crown thee with blossoms (---) R Bring flowers of the fairest 107393

O Master, it is good to be (Stanley) X235 X Lord, it is good for us to be 107394

O Master, let me walk with thee (Gladden) A572; B493; G259; H158; I411; J537; M223; P 324; R304; S364; T412; U271; W339; Y214; Z306; AB258; AC197; AD312; AE280; AF 418; AG245; AH371; AI185; AK205; AL388; AN208; AO 490; AP582; AR367; AS342; AT426; AU202; AV274; AW 223; AY467; AZ385; BA556; BB346; BD68; BE234; BF 375; BK99; BX225; BY518; BZ 107395

O Master, may my days be spent only for thee (Morse)

AE446; AR370 107396
O Master of all, come we to thy throne in praise (Emrick) AR30 107397
O Master of all grace and good (Brown) AR517 107398
O Master of the callous hand (Day) BF303 107399
O Master of the loving heart (Laufer) AE93 107400
O Master of the waking world (North) G480; AB376; AD388; AE409; AK382; AL261; AR575; BF533; BZ 107401
O Master! When thou callest (Stock) BB363; BV323; BY552 107402
O Master Workman of the race (Stocking) G118; R178; S140; U82; Y74; Z210; AB259; AC98; AD132; AE416; AF412; AG86; AK131; AN214; AR147; AS409; AT441; AW93; BF302; BK20; BZ 107403
O may we be still and seek Him (Linn) BE237 107404
O mean may seem this house of clay (Gill) K54; L449; AP181 107405
O men of God, go forth to win (Tiplady) Z471 107406
O Menschenkind, vernimm mich wohl (Ausbund) BU91 107407
O Merciful and Holy (Butler) BY276 107408
O merciful Redeemer, hear (St Gregory the Great) BM77 107409
O mighty God, Creator King (Thring) D310 107410
O mighty God of earth and heaven (Kretzmann) M151 107411
O mighty man, why wilt thou boast (U.P. Psalter, 1912) T100; AJ145 107412
O mind of God, broad as the sky (Huckel) Y31; BD128; BF377 107413
O Morning Star, how fair and bright (Nicolai) R415 X O Morning Star, so pure, so bright 107414
O Morning Star, so fair and bright (Nicolai) M175 X O Morning Star so pure, so pure 107415
O Morning Star so pure, so bright (Nicolai) K349; M175; R145; S321; AA103; AD285; AF145; AK122; BZ 107416
O mortal Man, remember well (English trad carol) BG45 107417
O most high, almighty, good Lord God (St Francis of Assisi) X434 107418
O most Holy, One and only God of earth (Hungarian Mass-Song, 1797) BL94 107419
O most Holy One, O most lowly One (Sicilian trad hymn) BN 126; BQ88 107420
O, most merciful! O, most bountiful (Heber) E323; F410; X276 107421
O most Mighty! O most Holy! (Smart) A320 107422
O Mother blest, whom God bestows on sinners (St Alfonso M. de Liguori) BN135; BO 113 107423
O mother dear, Jerusalem ("F. B.P." 16th c.) A584; B510; D403; H513; I610; K525; L593; S436; U431; V695; Z572; AH 522; AM603; AO547; AV277; BA762; BF656; BR433 107424
O mother dear, Jerusalem ("F. B.P." 16th c) X City of peace, our Mother dear (Prid) 107425
O Mother dear, Jerusalem, Jehovah's throne on high (Prid) BG132 107426
O Mother dear, this day in May (Hester) AH499 107427
O Mother Maid, be thou our aid (Newman) R Green are the leaves 107428
O Mother! most afflicted (---, 1873) BQ91 107429
O my dear heart, young Jesus sweet (Luther) BG181 107430
O my Father, I would know thee

(Munger) S395 107431
O my Father, thou that dwellest (Snow) BC138 107432
O my Immanuel, my wounded spirit heal (Zinzendorf, N. L.) AZ723 107433
O, my Saviour crucified (Batty) AU448 107434
O my Saviour, I adore thee (French) M196 107435
O my Saviour lifted (How) F360; S161; AL89; AP204; BV477; BY453 107436
O my soul, bless God, the Father (U. P. Book of Psalms, 1871) G80; AF100; AK83; AT51; BZ 107437
O my soul, bless thou Jehovah (U. P. Psalter, 1912) T194; AI352; AJ280; AX2* 107438
*slightly variant text
O my soul, on wings ascending (Wallin) J462 107439
O my soul, what means this sadness (Fawcett) AZ1384 107440
O my soul, why art thou grieving (U. P. Psalter, 1912) R Judge me, God of my salvation 107441
O mystery of love divine (Gill) AA330; AM436 107442
O Name, all other name's above (Hosmer) AN242; BX296 107443
O, Native Land, how fair you seem (Cherryman) Y278; AC281 107444
O North with all thy vales of green (Bryant) A541; B107; E550; AO529; BY386 107445
O, now I see the crimson wave (Palmer) H241; AX308; BB 598 107446
O now is the Time to remember our Creator (Cousin) AP757 107447
O one with God the Father (How) B97; D68; J56; K43; L203; O259; S137; AB73; AZ 805; BA663; BF424; BR367 107448
O Paradise, O Paradise, who doth not crave for rest? (Faber) A588; B167; D394; H516; I622; J589; L581; N 663; O616; T437; V705; AA 561; AB402; AO545; AP631; AV297; AZ1504; BA753; BF 659; BO204; BQ120; BR426 107449
O Paradise; O Paradise! Who would not win thy rest (Faber) AB402 X O Paradise, O Paradise, who doth not crave for rest? 107450
O, pardon me, Jesus, thy mercy I implore (Chadwick) R Jesus, my God, behold at length 107451
O Paschal feast, what joy is thine (Latin) J102 107452
O Pater sancte, mitis atque pie (Latin, 10th c) BT240 107453
O peace of all the faithful (St Bernard of Cluny) BR 436 X The world is very evil 107454
O peace of the world, O hope in each breast (Tomlinson) BE236 107455
O people blest, whose sons in youth (U. P. Bd. of Publ., 1909) AM289 X O happy land, whose sons in youth 107456
O perfect God, thy love (Greenway) F121; BV174 107457
O perfect life of love (Baker) F122; I155; J89; K103; N118; Q170; W102; AP208; AZ 1366; BA210; BV175 107458
O perfect love, all human thought transcending (Gurney) A214; B382; D238; E346; F 463; G431; I668; J300; K415; N528; O538; P354; Q623; R 453; S484; U484; V636; W 327; X283; AA444; AD417; AE386; AF465; AG296; AK 356; AL238; AM625; AN453; AO561; AP703; AR539; AS 419; AT501; AW312; BA843; BB416; BF613; BI77; BL65; BV393; BX486; BY624; BZ 107459
O pour thy Spirit from on high

(Montgomery) M96 X Lord pur thy Spirit from on high 107460

O power of love, all else transcending (Tersteegen) AW517 X O love divine, all else transcending 107461

O praise and bless the Lord, my soul (U.P. Psalter, 1912) T190, 453; AJ277 107462

O praise Him, Alleluia (St Francis of Assisi) R All creatures of our God and King 107463

O praise Jehovah! Who reigneth on earth and in heaven (Neander) AZ530; BA864 107464

O praise our God today, His constant mercy (Baker) AZ1338; BA569 107465

O praise our great and gracious Lord (Auber) E461; BE281 107466

O praise the Father, praise the Son (---) AP810 107467

O praise the Lord, all you nations (Ladies of the Grail) BSp. 19 107468

O praise the Lord, for He is good, His mercies still endure (U.P. Psalter, 1912) AJ297; AM84 107469

O praise the Lord, for He is good; Let all in heaven above (U.P. Psalter, 1912) AJ317 107470

O praise the Lord, His deeds make known (U.P. Psalter, 1912 T200; AJ289 107471

O praise the Lord! His name extol (Olearius) M482 107472

O praise ye the Lord and sing a new song (U.P. Psalter, 1912) AJ407; AM288 107473

O praise ye the Lord! Praise him in the height (Baker) F376; X 351; BV23 107474

O praise ye the Lord prepare your glad voice (Tate & Brady) D471; BI30; BR65 107475

O praise ye the name of Jehovah (U.P. Psalter, 1912) T268; AJ373 107476

O precious is the flow (Lowry) R What can wash away my stain? 107477

O precious Saviour, heal and bless (Hoppe) N393 107478

O precious sign and seal of heavenly union (Plummer) BI76 107479

O precious thought! Some day the mist shall vanish (Rosenius) N518 107480

O Prince of Peace, who man wast born (Lambeth 15th c ms) BJ23 107481

O prophet souls of all the years (Hosmer) AN421; AQ233; BD180; BX457 107482

O pure reformers! not in vain (Whittier) AN328; BX456 107483

O purest of creatures! Sweet Mother (Faber) AH135; BN 136; BO58; BQ79 107484

O Queen of peerless majesty Maria! (Molitor) BN159 107485

O Queen of the Holy Rosary (Shapcote) BN157; BO91 107486

O quickly come, dread Judge of all (Tuttiett) D42; E462; F227; AM243; AP243; AZ 655 107487

O rain depart with blessings (Solomon ibn Gabirol) BH 128 107488

O, rejoice, ye Christians, loudly (Keimann) Q96; AA 152 107489

O render thanks to God above (Tate & Brady) BH194; BI 111 107490

O rest in the Lord, wait patiently for Him (Bible, Psalm 37) AH618; AR684; AV424; BF 696 107491

O risen Christ, who from thy throne (Benson) U388; V 566 107492

O risen Lord! O Conquering King (Böhmer) O336; AZ895; BV189 107493

O Rock of ages, one Foundation (Martin) F554; O91; AZ990;

BA264 107494

O Royal Bride, give heed (U.P. Psalter, 1912) T85; AJ125 107495

O Sacrament most holy, O Sacrament divine (---) BQ330 107496

O sacred day, when first was poured (Besnault) AA177
X O happy day, when first 107497

O sacred head . . . (St Bernard of Clairvaux)

NOTE: All variant translations beginning "O Sacred head" are included here.
A75; B158; D102; E102; F111; G141; H176; I151; J88; K99; L243; M383; N116; O315; P 167; Q172; R194; S151; U103; V152; X128; Y350; Z231; AB 135; AD155; AE109; AF170; AG96; AH289; AI420; AK142; AL94; AM178; AN191; AO160; AP194; AQ311; AR168; AS136; AT91; AV107; AW539; AY490; AZ791; BA216-217; BB130; BF 312; BJ62; BL22; BM78; BN 38; BP26; BQ22; BR175; BV 158; BY145; BZ 107498

O Sacred Heart, O Heart of Jesus, hear! (Williams) BN 72; BO21 107499

O Sacred Heart of Christ aflame (---) BN71 107500

O Sacred Heart! Our home lies deep in thee (Stanfield) BO22
X O Heart of God! Our home lies deep 107501

O Sacred Heart with love benign (Latin) A priestly Heart, the Sacred Heart 107502

O sacrum convivium (Breviary, York, 1493) BQ235 107503

O safe to the Rock that is higher than I (Cushing) N600; P298; AE298; AH308; AL497; AM551; AP523; AR450; AS273; AT271; AU129; AV354; AX523; BB586; BY566 107504

O Saint of summer, what can we sing for you (Struther) X236 107505

O Saint Patrick, we proclaim thy heavenly glory (---)
R Hibernia's Patron Saint 107506

O saints of old! Not yours alone (Gill) BX459 107507

O salig den, Guds Ord har hört (Brun) BT48 107508

O salutâris hostia (St Thomas Aquinas) AH114; BM26; BN 78; BO273; BP55; BQ226 107509

O sanctissima, O piissima (Sicilian trad hymn) BN126; BO112; BP86; BQ206 107510

O save me by thy Name (U.P. Psalter, 1912) T102; AJ 147 107511

O Saving Victim, opening wide (St Thomas Aquinas) A209; B331; D227; E330b; F384b; J277; X277; BL53; BP56 107512

O Saviour, bless us ere we go (Faber) A182; B48; D22; E275; F28; H35; J199; K435; N361; O55; V28; W302; AA 12; AF542; AL213; AO45; AP 334; AW44; AZ673; BA617; BN195; BO192; BQ138; BR 116; BY700 107513

O Saviour dear, thy manger drear (Gerhardt) M360 107514

O Saviour, I have naught to plead (Crewdson) S512; W425; AL294; AP456; AS202; BY454 107515

O Saviour Jesu, not alone (Latin, 9th c) E249 107516

O Saviour, joy of loving hearts (St Bernard of Clairvaux) BR410 X Jesus, thou joy of loving hearts 107517

O Saviour of our race (Laurenti) K45; L222; N75; AZ1362; BA 52 107518

O Saviour, precious Saviour (Havergal) A349; B526; D 444; J419; K361; L110; M 209; N522; O204; P4; Q352; S200; U107; AE21; AI104;

AM118; AZ834; BA501; BB164; BR62; BV273 107519

O Saviour, the truest, the best of all friends (Koitsch) AZ778 107520

O Saviour Victim, opening wide (St Thomas Aquinas) X277 X O Saving Victim 107521

O Saviour, where shall guilty man (May) W111; AP202 107522

O Saviour, who for man hast trod (Coffin) D131 107523

O Saviour, who in love didst take (Monsell) O288 107524

O say can you see by the dawn's early light (Key) A142; B429; P414; Y291; Z651; AB341; AF 496; AH484; AO599; AT486; AU 457; AV303; BA939; BC131; BF 700; BH265 107525

O say, what is truth? (Jaques) BC143 107526

O scatter seeds of loving deeds (Pounds) AW498 107527

O scorned and outcast Lord, beneath (Coffin) AZ233 107528

O, see how Jesus trusts Himself (Faber) AZ1454 107529

O seek that beautiful stream (Hull. The casket) R O have you not heard 107530

O seek the Lord today! (Brorson) M22; P246 107531

O Seele, ich bitte dich komm (Hull. The casket) R Ich weis einen strom 107532

O selig Haus, wo man dich aufgenommen (Spitta) BT626; BW 358 107533

O send thy light forth and thy truth (Scottish Psalter, 1650) AL650; AP38; AW587; BY277 107534

O set ye open unto me (Scottish Psalter, 1650) AL677; AP106 107535

O, Shadow in a sultry land (Packard) BX157 107536

O Shepherd of the faithful (Latin) R O God-head hid devoutly 107537

O Shepherd of the nameless fold (Lathbury) BZ 107538

O Shepherd of the sheep (Coles) E190 107539

O sing a joyous carol ("M.B." Sr.) BQ10 107540

O sing a new song to the Lord, for wonders He hath done (Scottish Psalter, 1650) AL668; AP84 107541

O sing a new song to the Lord, Sing all the earth and bless His name (U.P. Psalter, 1912) AJ258 107542

O sing a new song to the Lord, Sing all the earth to God (Scottish Psalter, 1650) R37; S68; AJ257; AL667; AP82 107543

O sing a song of Bethlehem (Benson) R177; S138; W74; AE101; AL71; AP733; AW92 107544

O sing all ye lands with a jubilant voice (Vilhelm) J 423 107545

O sing the great Apostle (Latin, 17th c) BO216 107546

O, sing to me of heaven (Dana) AX612; AY137 107547

O sing to the Lord now, his greatness (Dearmer) X609 107548

O sing to the Lord, whose bountiful hand (Littledale) E291 107549

O sing with exultation (Arrebo) O341; Q217 107550

O sing with loud and joyful song (Blake) AN420; BX445 107551

O sing ye Hallelujah! 'Tis good our God to praise (U.P. Psalter, 1912) T290; AJ402 107552

O sinner, for a little space (Latin, 17th c) O309 107553

O sinner, lift the eye of faith (Latin, 17th c) AZ741 X O sinner, raise the eye of faith 107554

O sinner, raise the eye of faith (Latin, 17th c) E103; AZ741 107555

O sinner, we pray, will you come (---) R I know of a river 107556
O Sion, haste, thy mission high fulfilling (Thomson) A261; B474; D249; G475; I654; J314; K224; M102; N376; P392; R491; S382; T367; U395; V768; Y270; Z529; AB367; AC306; AD375; AE350; AF302; AG257; AH462; AK380; AL253; AO516; AP390; AR557; AS372; AT451; AU151; AV264; AW328; BA351; BB449; BF534; BZ 107557
O Sion, open wide thy gates (Santeüil) A116; F543 107558
O Sion, rise and brighten (Opitz) M373 107559
O Sion, rise in glory (New Churchman) BI17 107560
O Sion 'tis thy God's command (U. P. Psalter, 1912) AJ182 107561
O Sion's daughter, where art thou (Dutch trad carol) BG89 107562
O, Sion's songs are sweet to sing (Faber) R Blest is the Faith, divine and strong 107563
O sisters too, how may we do (Pageant of the Shearmen, 15th c) BG22 X Lully, lulla, thou little tiny child 107564
O solemn thought! and can it be (Cottrell) BB481 107565
O some times gleams upon my sight (Whittier) BH94 X O some-times gleams upon our sight 107566
O sometimes gleams upon our sight (Whittier) A502; X610; AN272; AQ177; BD32; BE238; BH94; BX37 107567
O sometimes the shadows are deep (Johnson) G245; I434; AH 376; AT320; AU133; AX517; BB 633; BZ 107568
O Son of God and man, receive (Wesley) AZ222; BA86 107569
O Son of God, in coeternal might (Loehe) K529; M183 107570
O Son of God incarnate (Tillett) G117; Z211; BF297; BZ 107571
O Son of God, our Captain of salvation (Ellerton) B280; D161; F550; S386; W360; AB265; AL368 107572
O Son of God, we wait for thee (Hiller) N198; O603; P430; AW524 107573
O Son of man, our hero strong and tender (Fletcher) A364; R217; S177; W146; X611; Y79; Z220; AB80; AC109; AD139; AL129; AW396; BF 634; BY127 107574
O Son of man, thou madest known (Littlefield) G121; J217; Y175; AC188; AE419; AK270; AR381; AW373; BD 69; BF438; BZ 107575
O Son of man, thyself once crossed (Thrupp) D145 107576
O Son of man, who walked each day (Turner) S182; AB151 107577
O sons and daughters, let us sing (Tisserand) A99; B555; F130; J96; R206; S167; W 124; AD164; AF191; AL106; AZ3; BL31; BN42; BR563; BZ 107578
O sons and daughters of the Lord (Tisserand) BP36 X Ye sons and daughters of... 107579
O sons of Sion, hear the voice (Rowe) BC152 107580
O sorrow deep! Who would not weep (Rist) A83; F126 107581
O soul in the far-away country (Frost) AU436 107582
O soul supreme above us (Newman) BH46 107583
O soul, you know the present and the past (Penner) AX463 107584
O source divine, and life of all (Sterling) X612; AL30; AN 26; BF232; BX48 107585
O speed thee, Christian, on the way (A "Lady" in Sacred melodies, 1840-41) V482 107586

O Spirit from on high, Thou comforter divine (Greek Pentecostarion, 8th c) BV218 107587

O Spirit of grace, thy kindness we trace (Moravian) AZ21; BA139 107588

O Spirit of Life, O Spirit of God (Niedling) K145; AR230; AW 547 107589

O Spirit of the living God! In all the fullness of thy grace (Montgomery) O125 X O Spirit of the living God! In all thy plenitude of grace 107590

O Spirit of the living God! In all thy plenitude of grace (Montgomery) A256; B475; D288; H464; I188; J306; K222; O125; Q504; R242; S207; V537; W386; AA473; AD190; AF299; AL239; AM253; AO224; AP371; AW330; AZ401; BA350; BI51; BV328; BY387 107591

O Spirit of the living God, Thou Light and Fire Divine (Tweedy) G182; Z273; AK190; AR231; BZ 107592

O Spirit, source of light (Beddome) BE240 X Come, blessed Spirit, source of light 107593

O Splendor of God's glory bright (St Ambrose) A158; E52; F2; G38, 638; J206; Q550; R46; S32; X33; AB1; AC11; AD39; AF39; AH623; AK48; AM56; AR364; BF182; BJ29; BY21; BZ 107594

O, spread the message far and wide (Buzzard) R As the dawn was calmly breaking 107595

O, spread the tidings round (Bottome) AX132; AY206; BB 526 107596

O stand beside us, Protect and guide us (Molitar) R O Queen of peerless majesty 107597

O star of truth, down shining (Savage) Y152; AC200; AN246; AQ115; AR294; BD111 107598

O star of wonder, star of night (Hopkins) R We three kings of orient are 107599

O still in accents sweet and strong (Longfellow) G289; H388; I395; AB378; AE323; AN449; AO459; AW294; BA 551; BE242; BX490 107600

O Stranger, with no place to lay thy head (Brown) AB 192 107601

O Strength and Stay upholding all creation (St Ambrose??) E271; F17; J219; K456; AN 435; AP662; AZ1218; BX124 107602

O, such wonderful love (McHose) R O, the great love 107603

O sweet and tender as the dawn (Stone) BE243 107604

O sweet Infant Jesus, we hail thee (A Carmelite Nun) BQ 333 107605

O sweeter than the marriage-feast (Coleridge) X613 107606

O take my hand, dear Father (Hausmann) J292; M548; P312; AR299; AW561a 107607

O teach thou us to count our days (U.P. Psalter, 1912) AJ246 107608

O tell me no more of this world's vain store (Gambold) AZ1418; BA469 107609

O, tell me, thou life and delight of my soul (Hastings) BB400 107610

O, tell what He's done for you (DeArmond) R Have you found rest? 107611

O tender and sweet was the Father's voice (Bradford) BB570 107612

O tender, loving Shepherd, We long to follow thee (Root) BE245 107613

O thank the Lord, the Lord of love (U.P. Psalter, 1912) AI377; AJ377 107614

O, that beautiful, beautiful land (Brenneman) R There's a beautiful, beautiful land 107615

O, that I as right and true might be ("A Calendar of country song") AC479 107616
O that I could repent (Wesley) I264 107617
O that I had a thousand voices (Mentzer) A302; Q30, 243; AA 62; AM11; AW509 107618
O, that I had wings of angels (Baring-Gould) R Daily, daily, sing the praises 107619
O that I knew the secret place (Watts) V411 107620
O, that last great day is coming soon (Warner) R The earth shall melt 107621
O that men to the Lord would give (Scottish Psalter, 1650) AP97 107622
O that my load of sin were gone (Wesley) H224; I381 107623
O, that the Comforter would come (Wesley) AZ665 107624
O that the Lord would guide my ways (Watts) K275; L425; N 180; O425; P320; Q416; V73; AA342; AZ113; BA631; BR300 107625
O that the Lord's salvation (Lyte) D266; K229; M118; N383; P 402; W368; AP375; AZ803 107626
O that thou wouldst rend the heavens (Tranovsky) M332 107627
O that thy fire now soon were kindled (German) M110 107628
O that we all could quite fulfill (Mueller) BA670 107629
O that we with gladness of spirit for ever (Gregor) AZ492 107630
O that will be glory for me, glory for me (Gabriel) R When all my labors and trials are o'er 107631
O! that will be joyful, joyful (---) R How pleasant thus to dwell 107632
O the agonizing prayer (MacKeller) AX179; AY254 107633
O the beautiful garden of prayer (Schroll) There's a garden 107634
O the beautiful old story! (Alcott) BX532 107635
O, the best Friend of all is the "Mighty to save" (Bills) R Do you seek for a friend 107636
O, the best friend to have is Jesus (Bilhorn) BB528 107637
O the bitter shame and sorrow (Monod) D612; G215; I380; AK215; AL323; AP478; AR 463; AS281; BA427; BV637; BY603 107638
O, the bliss of loves ones resting (Coffman) AY130 107639
O, the clanging bells of time (Gates) BE418 107640
O, the cleft of the Rock (Good) R There's a cleft in the Rock 107641
O, the crowning day is coming (Whittle) R Our Lord is now rejected 107642
O the deep, deep love of Jesus (Francis) AM453 107643
O, the delights, the heavenly joys (Watts) L156; BA45 107644
O the depth of love divine (C. Wesley) BZ 107645
O, the glory gates are ever open (Hott) R I am looking for the city 107646
O the golden glowing morning (LeJeune) Y348 107647
O, the great love the dear Saviour has shown (McHose) AX88; AY200 107648
O, the height and depth of mercy (Crosby) R Take the world 107649
O the kind words we give (Townsend) R Let us oft speak kind words 107650
O the land of cloudless day (Alwood) R O they tell me of a home 107651
O, the peace that Jesus gives (Lillenas) R Like the sun-

shine 107652
O the sunlight! beautiful sunlight! (Haughey) R There is sunlight on the hilltop 107653
O, the sweet wonders of that cross (Watts) L168 107654
O the unsearchable riches of Christ! (Crosby) AW454; AX 20 107655
O then, sail on, thou ship of state (Longfellow) Y290 107656
O then to the Rock let me fly (Johnson) R O sometime s the shadows are deep 107657
O, there's a sight that rends my heart (Gregor) AZ690 107658
O, there's sunshine (Hewitt) R There is sunshine 107659
O they tell me of a home far beyond the skies (Alwood) AH 539; AT484; AU81; AX608; AY150 107660
O think of the home over there (Huntington) AT480; AU43; AV 393; AX592 107661
O thou, at whose divine command (Alford) BR243 107662
O thou, before the world began (Wesley) D229; F395; BC274 107663
O thou, before whose Presence (Stone) D585; H525; O283; P412; W348; AE410; AP584; AZ839; BA561 107664
O thou best Gift of Heaven (Nicholls) K381; N504 107665
O thou blest Immanuel (---) M 235 107666
O thou by long experience tried (Guyon) AP524 107667
O, thou by whom we come to God (Montgomery) AF336 X Lord, teach us how to pray aright 107668
O thou essential Word, God from Eternity (Laurenti) BR161 107669
O thou Eternal Christ of God (Laufer) G130; BZ 107670
O thou eternal King most high (Latin, 5th c) F145; BN53; BO182 107671
O thou Eternal Source of Life (Schloerb) AD327 107672
O Thou, from whom all goodness flows (Haweis) B401; D663; E85; F117; H367; K394; L396; M288; Q515; V640; X117; AA497; AM457; AO409; AP484; AR197; BA 589; BJ53; BR321 107673
O thou God of all along desirous roaming (Brooke) Y133 107674
O thou God of my salvation (Olivers) H18; I25; AT164 107675
O thou God of our salvation (Clemens) AZ1102 107676
O thou great Friend to all the sons of men (Parker) S174; U83; Y219; Z347; AB78; AC 141; AD335; AF219; AN209; AQ120; AR205; AW224; AZ 454; BD71; BF425; BR395; BX216 107677
O thou great Shepherd of thy chosen race (U.P. Psalter, 1912) T148; AJ218 107678
O thou Holy Trinity! Undivided Unity! (---) R O God, Eternal Father From thy high throne 107679
O thou immortal holy Light (Carolla hymnorum. Cologne 1806) BN58; BO5 107680
O thou Immortal Light Divine (Corolla hymnorum, Cologne, 1806) BO5 X O thou Immortal holy Light 107681
O Thou in all thy might so far (Hosmer) A444; E463; I484; J480; R219; S176; U9; X614; Y5; AB169; AD84; AG115; AN241; BF236; BX295; BZ 107682
O Thou in lonely vigil led (Hosmer) AN171; BD139; BX439 107683
O Thou, in whom alone is found (Ware) D293 107684
O Thou, in whom thy saints repose (Ellerton) B462; D302; N585 107685
O Thou in whom we live and

move (Longfellow) BX83 X O God, in whom we live 107686

O Thou, in whose presence, my soul takes delight (Swain) G346; I530; AR199; AW470; BB160; BC195; BZ 107687

O Thou, Jehovah, Sovereign in battle (Bridgman) Y121 107688

O Thou joyful, O thou wonderful (Falk) AK117 107689

O thou kind and gracious Father (Denney) BC276 107690

O thou Love unbounded Grant to eyes enshrouded (Rambach) Q42 107691

O thou, my Judge and King (Watt) W402 107692

O thou, my light, my life, my joy (Montgomery) V623 107693

O thou my soul, bless God the Lord (Scottish Psalter, 1650) R121; S16; AL671; AM97; AP 90; AW596; BY70 107694

O thou, my soul, forget no more (Krishna Pal: Marshman tr) AV255; BY213 107695

O thou not made with hands (Palgrave) F259 X City not made with hands 107696

O thou, our God and Father (How) BR367 X O one with God the Father 107697

O thou pure light of souls that love (Latin, 7th-8th c) BQ33 107698

O thou Rock of our salvation (Townsend) BC130 107699

O thou sweetest source of gladness (Gerhardt) AD78 107700

O thou that art the Might One (Scottish Psalter, 1650) AP39 107701

O thou that hearest prayer (---) AF526 107702

O Thou that hearest the prayer of faith (Toplady) L496; V301 107703

O Thou that hear'st when sinners cry (Watts) D86; K318; L380; O99; Q325; AA419; AM413 107704

O thou that movest all, O Power (Duclaux) X616 107705

O Thou that rulest earth, and sky and sea (Neumark) BI 18D 107706

O Thou, the contrite sinners Friend (Elliott) C84; H266; K392; L393; U119; V173; AO 351; AZ1147; BA610 107707

O thou the Eternal Son of God (Dix) AM191 107708

O, thou the great eternal One (Byler) AY427 107709

O Thou, through suffering perfect made (How) D272; AK 132; AO145; BV400 107710

O Thou, to whom all creatures bow (Tate & Brady) V99 107711

O Thou to whom, in ancient time (Pierpont) I12; AN15; BX 438 107712

O Thou to whom in prayer and praise (Church) BX488 107713

O Thou, to whom the fathers built (Eliot) AQ116 107714

O Thou to whose all searching sight (Zinzendorf, N. L.) A 411; B119; D339; G360; H308; I359; K267; O246; V507; AD 310; AF324; AL317; AM525; AO306; BA619; BB330; BR 361; BZ 107715

O thou true Life of all that live (St Ambrose??) BR13c 107716

O thou who are my King (Badger) BX359 107717

O Thou, who art of all that is (Hosmer) AN270; BX293 107718

O thou who art the Shepherd (Shackford) BZ 107719

O Thou, who at thy Eucharist didst pray (Turton) E324 X Thou, who at thy first Eucharist didst pray 107720

O Thou, who by a star didst guide (Neale) J54; K40; AO 334; AZ179; BA182 107721

O Thou who camest from above (Wesley) A463; E343; F329; G344; I313; W471; X256; AL 344; AP492; BJ90; BV366; BY

519; BZ 107722
O Thou who didst prepare (Tonna) AZ1196 107723
O Thou, who didst the temple fill (Congregational collection) AZ 412 107724
O Thou, who didst with love untold (Toke) B269; D144; E206; BV458 107725
O Thou who dost accord us (Latin, ca 6th c) E86; O356 107726
O Thou who dost direct my feet (Houghton) BV580 107727
O Thou who dost to man accord (Latin, ca 6th c) BV145 107728
O Thou who driest the mourner's tear (Moore) H368; I522; BT 531 107729
O Thou who gavest power to love (Creighton) E347; F464; X 284 107730
O Thou, who gavest thy servant grace (Heber) B86; D146 107731
O Thou, who givest all their food (Conder) AZ1439; BA863 107732
O Thou, who hast at thy command (Cotterill) D428; I341; AN295; BX345 107733
O Thou who hast in every age (Dewart) BA883 107734
O Thou who hast redeemed of old (Wesley) BY455 107735
O Thou who hast thy servants taught (Alford) N488; BX514 107736
O Thou who hearest every heartfelt prayer (---) R532; S21app.; U491; AG333; AK503; AR615; BB684 107737
O Thou who hearest prayer (Edwards) AZ1198; BA613 107738
O Thou who in Jordan didst bow (Bethune) AT388; AV250 107739
O Thou, who in that last sad night (Zinzendorf, N.L.) BA 271 107740
O Thou, who lovest to send relief (Neale) AZ207; BA859 107741
O Thou, who madest land and sea (Thring) D276 107742
O Thou who makest souls to shine (Armstrong) B454; F471; R305; S480; W334; AC218; AE372; AK353; AO 423; AP366; AR529; AS393; BV412 107743
O Thou, who on earth didst children receive (Cennick) AZ489 107744
O Thou who once in Galilee (Hoppe) M586 107745
O Thou Who sealest up the past (Cole) AB399 107746
O Thou who sendest sun and rain (---) BR230 107747
O Thou who spreadest the heaven like a tent (Bible. Isaiah: Dutch) BE246 107748
O Thou who the Shepherd of Israel art (Asso. Refd. Presby. Psalter 1931) AM 279 107749
O Thou, who through this holy week (Neale) A73; D92; E 109; K89; N99; AF154; AO 157; BA218 107750
O Thou who turnest into morning (Loring) BX148 107751
O Thou who wouldst not have (Wesley) L382; AA338 107752
O Thou, whom all thy saints adore (Wesley) H24; I13 107753
O Thou, whom neither time nor space (Smith) BV655 107754
O Thou whom we adore (Wesley) AZ1493 107755
O Thou whose all-redeeming might (Latin, 8th c) E189 107756
O Thou, whose bounty fills my cup (Crewdson) I531; U77; AI353 107757
O Thou whose feet have climbed life's hill (Benson) A507; B365; G559; J454; K214; Q

486; R468; S490; U329; Y342; AD421; AE371; AG315; AK451; AO489; AR531; AS390; BD193; BF638 107758

O Thou whose glory shone like fire (Warburton) S477; AC309; AD394 107759

O Thou whose goodness words can ne'er express (Gregor) AZ518 107760

O Thou whose gracious presence blest (Benson) AC314; AD419; AE382; AK444; AR544; AT375 107761

O Thou whose gracious presence shone (Ham) AN448; AQ125; BX482 107762

O Thou, whose hand hath brought us (Goadby) G551; S473; AD 410; AK359; AR526; AT379; BF595; BX492; BY278 107763

O Thou, whose human life for us (Gregor) BA87 107764

O Thou, whose infant feet were found (Heber) N66 107765

O Thou whose love has brought us here (Robinson) BY717 107766

O Thou, whose mercy found me (Monsell) W426 107767

O Thou, whose mercy guides my way (Edmeston) AZ229 107768

O Thou, whose own vast temple stands (Bryant) U384 X Thou, whose unmeasured temple stands 107769

O Thou whose perfect goodness crowns (Chadwick) AN463; BX 507 107770

O Thou whose power o'er moving worlds presides (Boethius) AN 67; AQ128; BI69; BX42 107771

O Thou, whose Presence moved before (Holmes) BH216 107772

O Thou whose Spirit witness bears (Hosmer) AN52; AQ74; BX69 107773

O Thou, whose tender mercy hears (Steele) H279; V291 107774

O Thou with whom in sweet content (Foote) AN259; BX289 107775

O Thou within whose sure control (Munro) AL453 107776

O tidings of comfort and joy (English carol, 18th c) R God rest you merry 107777

O timely happy, timely wise (Keble) W259 X New every morning is thy love 107778

O, 'tis grace, 'tis wonderful grace (---) R Saved by grace 107779

O, to be there, where the songs of glory ("A.H.A.") AX349; AY239 107780

O, to have no Christ, no Saviour (Cushing) AX226; AY221 107781

O, to reflect His grace (Smith) R Christ the transforming Light 107782

O touch mine eyes, that I may see (Walton) BY604 107783

O, touch the hem (Root) R She only touched the hem 107784

O Traurigkeit, O Herzeleid! (Rist) BT167 107785

O Trinity, most blessed Light (St Ambrose) Q564 X O Trinity of blessed Light 107786

O Trinity, O blessed Light (St Ambrose) W4 X O Trinity of blessed Light 107787

O Trinity of blessed Light (St Ambrose??) A171; B11; E 164; F15; J133; Q564; R245; S59; W4; X51; AL4; AM339; BJ86 107788

O troubled heart, there is a home (Bellamy) AU440 107789

O troubled Sea of Galilee (Wilson) BX266 107790

O true Bread (St Thomas Aquinas) F622c X Very Bread, Good Shepherd 107791

O truly is the nation blest (U.P. Psalter, 1912) AP30 X Jehovah from His throne

on high X Let all the earth Jehovah fear 107792
O, trust ye in the Lord forever (Lathbury) H528 107793
O turn, great Ruler of the skies (Merrick) L381 107794
O turn to Jesus, Mother! turn and call Him (Faber) BO143; BQ115 107795
O turn ye, O turn ye (Hopkins) AI192; AZ508 107796
O 'twas a joyful sound to hear (Tate & Brady) A390; B307; D493; S19; AD33; AM277; BX 19 107797
O, 'twas love, love, love that moved (Gilmour) R When out in sin 107798
O valiant hearts, who to your glory came (Arkwright) A531; F584; G495; X293; Y123; AL 525 107799
O Vaterherz, das Erd' und Himmel schuf (Knapp) BT299 107800
O very God of very God (Neale) A442; B102; D326; K11; N11 107801
O Virgin all lovely, O Mother all gracious (DeDorz) BN160 107802
O, vision bright! The land of light (Faber) BO116 107803
O wait, meekly wait, and murmur not (Bellamy) R O troubled heart R The home where changes never come 107804
O walk with God along the road (Gill) BE247; BX353 107805
O walk with God, and thou shalt find (Coxe) BY553 107806
O walk with Jesus, wouldst thou know (Hood) BV635 107807
O watch and pray, my soul, the way (Brorson) M387; O430; P186 107808
O, we see the gleams of the golden morning (Graham) R The golden morning is fast approaching 107809
O weary pilgrim, lift your head (Wienland) BE425 107810
O weary soul, the gate is near BB562 107811
O weary wanderer, come home (Coffman) AX239; AY222 107812
O welcome in our midst (Dearmer) X335 107813
O welt, sieh hier dein Leben (Gerhardt) BT171 107814
O, what a change (Habershon) R Soon will our Saviour from Heaven appear 107815
O what amazing words of grace (Medley) H233; I292 107816
O what an act of majesty (Gregor) AZ689 107817
O what can little hands do? (Hinsdale) W670; AP780; BY752 107818
O what could my Jesus do more (---) AH144; BO53 107819
O what happiness divine (Hayn) AZ789 107820
O what if we are Christ's (Baker) D390; K388; AP501; BA809 107821
O what joy, O what joy awaiteth me (Gregor) AZ 716 107822
O what praise in highest strain (Gregor) AZ868 107823
O what praises shall we render (Burton) N645 107824
O what precious balm and healing (St Bernard of Clairvaux) O297; P181; Q144; AA194 107825
O what shall I do My Saviour to praise (Wesley) AZ1423 107826
O what songs of the heart (Townsend) BC87 107827
O, what tender, tender mercy (Gardiner) R When I see the way 107828
O what the joy and the glory must be (Abelard) V709 X O what their joy and their glory must be 107829
O what their joy and their glory must be (Abelard) A589; B544; D397; E281; J596; R 424; S430; V709; W224; X 200; AF310; AL173; BB202;

BL85 107830

O, when I think of that heavenly home (Kolb) AX595; AY136 107831

O, when shall I see Jesus (---) AY402 107832

O, when we see God's mercy (Burnett) BE249 107833

O where are kings and empires now (Coxe) A382; B471; G384; H408; I214; J154; K203; L288; N270; R431; S334; T362; U349; V539; Z427; AB319; AD395; AE343; AF264; AG230; AI430; AK326; AO425; AR497; AS186; AT383; AV242; AW276; AY429; AZ127; BA268; BB435; BF582; BZ 107834

O where are the reapers that garner in (Rexford) AP588; AU430; AX216; BB620 107835

O where is he that trod the sea (Lynch) H154 107836

O where is the home of the soul to be found? (Joergen) M641 107837

O where shall I be when the last trumpet sounds? (---) R When judgment day is drawing nigh 107838

O where shall rest be found (Montgomery) D513; H227; I250; L599; V221; AZ1343; BA 405; BR282 107839

O wherefore do the nations rage (U.P. Psalter, 1912) T2; AJ4; AM227 107840

O wherefore hast thou cast me off (U.P. Psalter, 1912) T 138; AJ205 107841

O who, in such a world as this (Montgomery) BB381 107842

O who is this that cometh (Todd) BB636 107843

O who like Thee, so calm, so bright (Coxe) D314; O225; U 70 107844

O who shall roll away the stone (Ham) A84 107845

O why not tonight (Reed) R O do not let the Word depart 107846

O, why should I be idle (Jeffrey) AX207 107847

O, why should you wander in darkness (Shoemaker) R Come, lost one 107848

O! wie ist die Zeit so wichtig (Mack) AR428 107849

O wie selig seid ihr doch, ihr Frommen (Dach) BT589 107850

O wie selig sind die (Unparth. G.B.) AY40d 107851

O Will of God beneath our life (Gordon) G78 107852

O with due reverence let us all (Tate & Brady) D479 107853

O with thy tender mercies, Lord (Scottish Psalter, 1650) AL663; AP75 107854

O wonderful prayer that Jesus prayed (Giffe) AS131 107855

O wonderful word of salvation (Hartsough) AS175 107856

O wonderful words of the gospel (Crosby) P258 107857

O wondrous Conqueror and great (Homburg) O366 107858

O wondrous Kingdom here on earth (Gruhdtvig) M81; P 224 107859

O, wondrous Name, by prophets heard (Crosby) BR527 107860

O wondrous type! O vision fair (Latin, 15th c) A119; B285; D167; F558; J147; N203; O253; R182; S142; W89; AO 152; AZ319; BA71; BV274 107861

O, wondrously sweet is the story (Hoffman) AX32; AY 517 107862

O word immortal of eternal God (Justinian, Emperor) E325 107863

O Word of God above (Guiet) E171; F475; 107864

O Word of God incarnate (How) A402; B58; D284; G386; H87; I200; J252; K169; L314; N216; O134; P89; Q294; R251; S215;

U134; V78; W198; Y364; Z434; AA113; AB100; AC68; AD193; AE158; AF252; AG131; AH233; AI151; AK199; AL182; AM267; AO240; AP289; AR240; AT183; AU75; AV75; AW289; AX90; AZ804; BA7; BB217; BE251; BF274; BI44; BR233; BV307; BY251; BZ 107865

O Word of God, most holy (How) BE251 X O Word of God incarnate 107866

O word of pity, for our pardon pleading (Greenaway) F115; W97; AF173; BV176 107867

O Word, that goest forth on high (Latin, ca 7th c) A8 107868

O world, behold! upon the tree (Gerhardt) O317; AZ576 107869

O world invisible, we view thee (Thompson) X617; Y192 107870

O world, see here suspended (Gerhardt) M427; P179 107871

O worship the King, all glorious above (Grant) A288; B255; D 459; E466; F167; G4; H13; I 106; J163; K294; L75; N333; O60; Q17; R26; S2; T297; U7; V13; W9; X618; Y59; Z94; AB 14; AC36; AD2; AE2; AF6; AG 6; AH187; AI11; AK10; AL21; AM13; AN6; AO58; AP93; AQ25; AR33; AS2; AT20; AU2; AV34; AW7; AX9; AY423; BA20; BB 75; BD27; BF167; BH60; BK65; BR408; BV248; BX10; BY22; BZ 107872

O worship the Lord in the beauty of holiness, Bow down before Him (Monsell) E42; F77; S7; U5; X93; Z106; AC12; AD27; AF31; AL201; AP314; AR39; AZ1153; BB6; BF217; BV11; BY35 107873

O worship the Lord in the beauty of holiness, in the beauty of holiness, in the beauty of holiness (Lowry) AR432; AS4 107874

O would, my God, that I could praise thee (Mentzer) N178; O 443; AZ697 107875

O would you be a blessing true (Ussery) AX436 107876

O ye heavens, bend and see ("H. 1708") K537 107877

O ye His angels, that excel strength (Scottish Psalter, 1650) AL673 107878

O ye mountains high, where the clear blue sky (Penrose) BC145 107879

O ye who dare go forth with God (Bowie) BD161 107880

O ye who taste that love is sweet (Rossetti) W358; AC 248; AN414; AQ141 107881

O yes, He cares for me (Presley) R I have a friend 107882

O, yes, He cares, I know He cares (Graeff) R Does Jesus care 107883

O yet we trust that somehow good (Tennyson) AN237 107884

O young and fearless Prophet (Harlow) G266; Z362; AB 288; AD325; AK391; AR 148; BF516; BK19; BZ 107885

O young mariner, you from the haven (Tennyson) AC231 X Not of the sunlight 107886

O Zion, haste, thy mission (Thomson) G475 X O Sion, haste, thy mission 107887

Obedient they but to a dream (Dillon) AQ228 107888

Obgleich die harf, ist gut und scharf (S. Franck) BU1 107889

Object of my first desire (Toplady) AZ1048 107890

"Observe ye" and "remember" still (Alkabetz) BH108 107891

Ocean Star, we greet you (Latin, 9th c) BN129 107892

O'er all the land have the signs now appeared (Gage) BB544 107893

O'er all the way green palms and blossoms gay (Faure?) AH622 107894

O'er continent and ocean (Holmes) AN400; AQ227 107895

O'er eras past I've pondered (Zinzendorf, C.R.) AZ560 107896

O'er field and forest stealing (Gerhardt) AL548 107897

O'er Jerusalem Thou weepest (Hoppe) N176; Q419 107898

O'er the distant mountains breaking (Monsell) D46; N187; O510; Q606; S189; AA548; AK98; AQ 111; AZ1398 107899

O'er the gloomy hills of darkness (Williams) H476; Q505; U401; V589; W387; AL247; AM373; AP380; AZ1404; BC127; BY 388 107900

O'er the realms of pagan darkness (Cotterill) AZ1405; BA352 107901

O'er the silent waters, Thro' the depths of night (---) BI72 107902

O'er the trackless ocean guided (Adams) AL449; AW165 107903

O'er those gloomy hills of darkness (Williams) W387 X O'er the gloomy hills of darkness 107904

O'er waiting harp-strings of the mind (Eddy) BE253 107905

O'erwhelmed in depths of woe (Breviary, Bologne, 1827) BQ25 107906

Of all the myriad moods of mind (Lowell) AB306; BF373 107907

Of all the thoughts of God that are (Browning) I541; BH224 107908

Of all things beautiful and good (Markham) AC521 107909

Of him who did salvation bring (St Bernard of Clairvaux??) G188; H231; I289 107910

Of His love I shall ever sing (Fisher) R There's a glad new song 107911

Of mercy and of judgment (U.P. Book of Psalms, 1871) AP88 107912

Of mercy and of justice, My thankful song shall be (U.P. Psalter, 1912) T185; AJ271 107913

Of my life the life, O Jesu (Homburg) O319 107914

Of omnipresent grace I sing (Cronenwett) M150 107915

Of one blood hath God created (Robins) Z510 107916

Of Sion's honor angels sing (Cronenwett) M91 107917

Of stones full previous are thy towers (Prid) X393b 107918

Of that branch in ancient Garden (Cummins) BL24 107919

Of the Father's heart begotten (Prudentius) X387 X Of the Father's love begotten 107920

Of the Father's love begotten (Prudentius) A20; B74; D52; E613; F58 and 591; J17; K 20; Q98; R7; W60; X387; AF 111; AK13; AL52; AM122; AP166; AR116; AZ898-899; BL5; BM46; BV109; BY85; BZ 107921

Of the glorious Body telling (St Thomas Aquinas) E326 107922

Of the themes that men have known (Fisher) AT293 107923

Of Thy love some gracious token (Kelly) W298; AL212 107924

Oft, as we run the weary way (Brooke) AB256; BX186 107925

Oft in danger, oft in woe (White & Fuller-Maitland) A558; B116; D506; E467; F291; I412; L546; M268; T 392; V489; W533; X619; AA 500; AL406; AM479; AO411; AP537; BA584; BR398; BV 584 107926

Oft in sorrow, oft in woe

107927

Oft to every man and nation (Lowell) BE258 X Once to every man and nation 107928

Oft when the waves of passion rise (Wesley) AZ631 107929

Often weary and worn on the pathway (Cosner) AX531; AY149 107930

NOTE: "Oh" has been eliminated as an entry word, See "O". 107931

O-lay-nu l'-sha bay-ach (Jewish traditional) BH329 107932

Om Salighed og Gläde (Arrebo) BT217 107933

Omnis mundus jucundetur nato Salvatori (Latin, 12th c) BT 82 107934

On a hill far away (Bennard) AE186; AH296; AT93; AU71; AV369; AX105; BB533; BZ 107935

On Calvary's brow my Savior died (Darwood) AI78; AU439 107936

On Calvary's height the Roman spear (Dollard) BO19 107937

On Christ, by faith, I would live (Hoskins) M218 X On Christ, by faith, my soul would live 107938

On Christ, by faith, my soul would live (Hoskins) L440; M218 107939

On Christ, the solid rock, I stand (Mote) R My hope is built 107940

On Christmas Eve the bells were rung (Scott) BG189 107941

On Christmas night all Christians sing (English trad carol) BG 24; BV114 107942

On Christ's ascension I now build (Wegelin) Q216 107943

On desert sands the vision comes (White) Y6 107944

On eyes that watch through sorrow's night (Hosmer) BX211 107945

On God alone my soul resides (U.P. Psalter, 1912) AJ149 107946

On hills and vales of heaven (Rowell) BB98 107947

On Jordan's bank the Baptist's cry (Coffin) A10; B282; D 44; E9; F50; J4; K2; L208; N13; O176; Q63; W78; X67; AF115; AK95; AZ318; BA 152; BL1; BM59; BN1; BV 79; BY86 107948

On Jordan's banks the Herald's cry (Coffin) O176 X On Jordan's bank the Baptist's cry 107949

On Jordan's stormy bank I stand (Stennett) G523; H 509; I617; L596; V702; AH 529; AT478, 479; AU249; AV282; AX567; AY142; BB 553; BR428; BZ 107950

On Mary, virgin undefiled (---) O290 107951

On mighty wings rush swiftly by, The hours, the days, the year (Hamburg Temple hymnal) BH161 107952

On mountains and in valleys (---) BR371 107953

On my heart imprint thine image (Kingo) O298; Q179 107954

On our way rejoicing (Monsell) A568; B432; D522; J195; P 382; R80; S56; Z417; AD483; AG15; AH213; AO361; AZ 757; BA510; BD18; BF617; BR511 107955

On the Cross is One uplifted (Collier) AO171 107956

On the good and faithful (U.P. Psalter, 1912) R52; T5; AJ7 107957

On the happy, golden shore (Blair) AX603 107958

On the moorland of life God's Shepherd is seen (Crum) X220 107959

On the mountain top appearing (Kelly) AW336 X On the mountain's top 107960

On the mountain's top appearing (Kelly) H404; I647; N269; U396; V590; AV245; AW336; AY241; BC273 107961

On the radiant threshold Of this dawning day (Wieand) AR65; AS18 107962
On the resurrection morning (Baring-Gould) D243; E136; AP617; BV404 107963
On the shore beyond the sea (Baltzell) BB657 107964
On the wood His arms are stretched (Latin, 12th c) BP28 107965
On Thee, our Guardian, God, we call (Davies) AZ300 107966
On this day earth shall ring (Piae Cantiones, 1582) AF136; BI85 107967
On this day everywhere (Piae Cantiones, 1582) AQ296 107968
On this day, O beautiful Mother (---) AH134; BO114 107969
On this day, the first of days (Breviary, Carcassonne, 1745) B47; F39; AA126; BL41; BN202; BV70 107970
On this glad day we dedicate (Lathrop) AR527 107971
On this stone now laid with prayer (Pierpont) G548; H423; I657; N274; AR528; BZ 107972
On thy Church, O Power Divine (Auber) AZ1276 107973
On thy ransomed congregation (Foster) AZ251; BA280 107974
On to victory (Cassell) R From over hill and plain 107975
On what has now been sown Thy blessing, Lord, bestow (Newton) J193; K430; N355; Q46; AA11; AZ1169; BT46 107976
On wings of living light (How) B559; S170; Z243; AC131; AK171; BB133; BY161 107977
Once again, dear Lord, we pray (Willcox) W374; AL619 107978
Once again, O blessed time (Bright) AZ863; BR556 107979
Once again to its close (Drury) AR583 107980
Once again we come to the house of God (Naylor) AX 51 107981
Once for all, O Christian receive it (Bliss) R Free from the law 107982
Once He came in blessing (Horn) K10; N10; Q74; AA 143; AZ550; BA154 107983
Once I thought my mountain strong (Newton) V484 107984
Once I wandered in darkness unsaved (Grisham) AX439 107985
Once in Jerusalem of old (Williamson) BB473 107986
Once in royal David's city (Alexander) A236; B349; D540; E605; F432; G442; J41; K535; M608; N633; R462; S454; W69; X368; AD474; AG302; AH242; AI 382; AL70; AM639; AO133; AP727; AR125; AV84; AW 412; AZ612; BA158; BB424; BF284; BR558; BV107; BY 106 107987
Once Mary would go wandering (German trad carol) BG93 107988
Once more before we part (Hart) AX78; AY397; AZ 1331; BA379 107989
Once more, my soul, the rising day (Watts) AY279 107990
Once more, O Lord, do I awaken (Weitzman) BH7 107991
Once more, O Lord, thy sign shall be (Doane) D38 107992
Once more the liberal year laughs out (Whittier) AC324; AN137; AQ275; BF651; BH 181 107993
Once more we come before our God (Hart) I33; AR7; AS55; AY8 107994
Once, only once, and once for all (Bright) E327; F398 107995
Once pledged by the cross, as children of God (Bode) F462 107996

Once to every man and nation (Lowell) A519; B433; E563; G263; J547; R361; S373; X 309; Y240; Z558; AB285; AC 220; AD349; AE376; AF441; AG 249; AH410; AK399; AL410; AN 319; AQ168, 220; AR569; AT 418; AW346; BB513; BD163; BE 258; BF480; BK82; BZ 107997

One cup of healing oil and wine (Drummond) BE259 107998

One day when heaven was filled with his praises (Chapman) AM689; AT85; AX309 107999

One gift, my God, I seek (Torrey) BX103 108000

One God! One Lord! One mighty King (Moise) BH140 108001

One holy Church of God appears (Longfellow) S335; Z424; AE 311; AF266; AK325; AN407; AQ261; AR498; BD189; BE261; BF590; BX452; BZ 108002

One is kind above all others (Nunn) AL473; AP737; AW447 108003

One is our God and Father (Ingemann) O468 108004

One Lord there is, call lords above (Rands) Y24; AN293; BX435 108005

One more day's work for Jesus (Warner) I419; AS27; AU55; AV387; BB622 108006

One prayer I have, -- all prayers in one (Montgomery) AN236; AZ160; BX278 108007

One precious boon, O Lord, I seek (Fitch) BB338 108008

One radiant morn the mists will all surrender (Wexels) P337 108009

One resolve, one resolve, you who falter and fear (Urseth) P247 108010

One sole baptismal sign (Robinson) B463; H421; I559; K206; AL169; AP304; AZ1187 108011

One sweetly solemn thought (Cary) B407; D676; G515; H497; I620; L563; O289; P338; T441; U425; V660, 762; AA531; AH533; AO 548; 704; AP615; AR416; AS 473; AU183; AV392; AW264; AX611; AZ476; BA727; BB 352; BC272 108012

One there is, above all others (Newton) H334; I174; J456; K389; L133; N430; U227; V375; W145; AL121; AM142 AO291; AP234; AV136; AY 26; AZ601; BA495; BY214 108013

One there is who loves thee (Ayres) AP406 108014

One thing I of the Lord desire (Smith) W461; A L324; AP 489; AU408; BB634 108015

One thing needful! This one treasure (Schroeder) O227 108016

One thing only, Lord, is needful (Schroeder) M222 108017

One thing's needful; Lord this treasure (Schroeder) Q366; AA83; AZ989 108018

One thing's needful! then Lord Jesus (Schroeder) AA83 X One thing's needful; Lord, this treasure 108019

One thought I have, my ample creed (Hosmer) AN77; AQ 50; AW248; BE260; BX74 108020

One Thy Light, the Temple filling (Keble) Q641 108021

One view, Lord Jesus, of thy passion (Bossart) AZ995; BA191 108022

One who us all unfit to count (Tilak) J384; S234; W406; AF330; AL279; BY456 108023

One world this, for all its sorrow (Silliman) AQ145 108024

Only a sinner saved by grace (Gray) R Naught have I gotten 108025

Only a step to Jesus (Crosby) AU432; AX254; AY503 108026

Only-begotten, Word of God eternal (Latin, ca 9th c) A228; E636; AL197 108027

Only believe, only believe (Rader) AU318 108028
Only God can bring us gladness (Wallin) BE263 108029
Only one prayer today (Dix) D594; AZ1287; BA202 108030
Only remembered, only remembered (Bonar) R Fading away like the stars 108031
Only sleeping, sweetly sleeping (Brooks) R "Lo, she is not dead" 108032
Only thine, only thine (Warner) R I heard the dear Redeemer say 108033
Only thy tender love, Saviour divine (Crosby) U226 108034
Only to follow Thee (Crosby) R Only thy tender love 108035
Only trust Him, and be still (Pierson) R Open wide thy heart 108036
Only trust Him, only trust Him (Stockton) R Come, every soul by sin oppressed 108037
O no A-do-noy, ka-per no (Jewish traditional) BH330 108038
Onward, brothers, march still onward (Ellis) AN351; BH230 108039
Onward, children onward, Fearless, firm and true (Sonnenschein) R Hark the voice of children 108040
Onward, Christian soldiers (Baring-Gould) A557; B530; D516; E643; F629; G280; H393; I383; J560; K379; L541; M242; N589; P374; Q658; R350; S365; T377; U294; V483; W535; X397; Y172; Z482; AB254; AC209; AD298; AE250; AF382; AG199; AH442; AI327; AK292; AL401; AM490; AN331; AO391; AP538; AT412; AU46; AV209; AW225; AX196; AZ772; BA582; BB360; BC128; BD145; BE264; BF471; BR512; BV562; BX542; BY520; BZ 108041
Onward, Christian! though the region (Johnson) D620; AN216; BE265; BF449; BX214 108042
Onward march, all-conquering Jesus (Williams) W384 108043
Onward, Onward, tho' the region (Johnson) AN216 X Onward, Christian! though the region 108044
Onward, then, and fear not (Havergal) R Standing at the portal 108045
Open, Lord, my inward ear (Wesley) BV639; BX63 108046
Open my eyes, that I may see (Scott) R390; AE200; AG 227; AI158; AR295; AS257; AT312; AU351; BZ 108047
Open now thy gates of beauty (Schmolck) J187; K420; M1; N306; O35; P45; Q1; R40; Z121; AA5; AF503; AK23; AM304; AW505; AZ606; BA 381; BZ 108048
Open our eyes, thy glory beholding (Sellers) R Lord unto thee 108049
Open the wells of grace and salvation (Hoffman) R Lord, I am fondly 108050
Open wide thy heart today (Pierson) AX251; AY505 108051
Oppressed by sin, O Lord, to Thee (Gellert) O102 X Crushed by my sin, O Lord to Thee 108052
Orémus pro pontifice nostro (Latin) BN201; BQ247 108053
Os er idag en Frelser föd (Boye) BT79 108054
Our babies' names are on the roll (Dearmer) X386e 108055
Our baptism first declares (Hart) AZ1313 108056
Our blessed bond of union (Murray) AP296 108057
Our blessed Saviour seven times spoke (Boschenstain) Q177; AA207 108058
Our blest Redeemer, ere He breathed (Auber) A368; B

199; D375; E157; F230; G177; H218; I189; K157; S205; T353; U131; W180; X182; AD188; AG 124; AH228; AL162; AO227; AP 272; AW138; AZ1142; BA141; BB214; BF261; BR203; BV223; BY236 108059
Our children, gracious Lord and God (Swertner) AZ918; BA 847 108060
Our children, Lord, in faith and prayer (Haweis) U485; W306; AI371; AM351; AP350; BV342 108061
Our Church proclaims God's love and care (Niedermeyer) Z425 108062
Our country is Immanuel's ground (Barbauld) L239 108063
Our country's voice is pleading (Anderson) H480; N382; P390; U410; AA472; AE362; AO530; AZ832; BA355 108064
One day of praise is done (Ellerton) A175; B49; D23; E38; W290; AP682; AY436; AZ1359; BA388; BB58; BF208 108065
One day of praise is ended (Tymms) BY701 108066
Our faith is in the Christ who walks with men today (Clark) Z351; AB167; AH320; BF329 108067
Our Father, by whose name (Tucker) A504; AF466 108068
Our Father, by whose servants (Briggs) A505; J248; X194; Y336; BY279 108069
Our Father, for our daily bread (Briggs) X403 108070
Our Father, God of life and light ("M. L. B.") BX136 108071
Our Father God! not face to face (Chapin) BX224 108072
Our Father God, thy name we praise (Clock) BY362 108073
Our Father, God, whose mercies still abide (Williams) Y397 108074
Our Father, hear our longing prayer (MacDonald) AZ220 108075
Our Father hears us when we pray (Burton) BV610 108076
Our Father in heaven, we hallow thy name (Hale) AT343; AV24; AX652 108077
Our Father, merciful and good (Petri) N166 108078
Our Father, our King (Jewish traditional) BH309 108079
Our Father, thou in heaven above (Luther) O359; Q458; AA396; AI437; AZ651 108080
Our Father, throned in heaven above (Guthrie) O4 108081
Our Father! through the coming year (Gaskell) U474; V628; AZ154 108082
Our Father thy dear Name doth show (Richards) A533; B 499; W486; Z522; BD126; BF496 108083
Our Father, unto Thee We now on bended knee (Russell) AN11 108084
Our Father, we adore Thee (Bowers) BR27 108085
Our Father, we beseech thy grace (Goldstein) BH145 108086
Our Father, while our hearts unlearn (Holmes) X620; AN 235; BX212 108087
Our fathers' God, from out whose hand (Whittier) Y339; AB345; AH471; BD162; BF 556; BK124 108088
Our Father's God! to thee (Smith) D196 108089
Our Fathers' God, to Thee we raise (Copeland) G494; I 713; AH207 108090
Our Father's home eternal (St Thomas à Kempis??) E252; F625 108091
Our fathers in the olden days (Bevier) AO658 108092
Our Father's wondrous works we see (Brooks) AX16 108093
Our fortress strong art thou, O Lord (Goulston) BH165 108094
Our friend, our brother, and

our lord (Whittier) AQ121 X O Love! O Life! Our faith and sight 108095
Our friends on earth we meet with pleasure (Chapman) AX 656 X With friends on earth 108096
Our glowing praise to thee (Morgan) AD443 108097
Our God, He is a God of might (Perkins) AI411 X Thou art, O God, the God of might 108098
Our God is all-in-all (Seal) BE 267 108099
Our God is good: in earth and sky (Gurney) BX86 108100
Our God is love; and all his saints (Cotterill) I552; J457; N500; AO82; BE266 108101
Our God is Love, and all His sons (Cotterill) BE266 X Our God is love, and all his saints 108102
Our God is Love, unchanging Love (Root) BE269 108103
Our God is truth, most faithful is His word (Herrnschmidt) AZ704 108104
Our God leads onward (Butler-Thwing) Y150 108105
Our God, our God, Thou shinest here (Gill) AN9; AQ36; BD30; BX29; BY262 108106
Our God, our help in ages past (Watts) L518 X O God, our help in ages past 108107
Our God shall reign where'er the sun (Watts) BE271 X Jesus shall reign where'er the sun 108108
Our God so loved the world that He (Olearius) AA327 108109
Our God, to whom we turn (Grubb) A283; J171; R128; X621; AF86; AK64; AN490; AR84 108110
Our God, we raise to thee (Snow) BC144a 108111
Our God, we thank thee, who hast made (Proctor) AB213 X My God, I thank thee, who hast made 108112
Our heavenly Father calls (Doddridge) AO444; AZ1310; BA 528 108113
Our heavenly Father hear (Montgomery) L191; M63; Q455; AA397; AZ1319; BA 614 108114
Our heavenly Father, Source of love (Wesley) AZ217; BA14 108115
Our highest joys succeed our griefs (---) I474 108116
Our hymns are sung, our prayers are said (Hawkes) BX509 108117
Our Jesus is the Rock where we safely rest (Jones) R We have a Rock 108118
Our life is ever on the wing (Watts) AY134 108119
Our life is hid with Christ (Bonar) AZ1325 108120
Our Lord and God, O bless this day (Brun) M537; O106; Q 337 108121
Our Lord Christ hath risen! (Plunkett) W125; AD163; AT112; AZ779 108122
Our Lord, his Passion ended (Burkitt) F155; X183; AW 572; BV224; BY237 108123
Our Lord is now rejected (Whittle) AU48; AV391; BY 189 108124
Our Lord is risen from the dead, And rays of glory crown his head (Boye) J101 108125
Our Lord is risen from the dead, Our Jesus has gone up on high (Wesley) L269 X Our Lord is risen from the dead, Our Jesus is gone up on high 108126
Our Lord is risen from the dead, Our Jesus is gone up on high (Wesley, J. & C.) B187; D132; F609; H180; I158; L269; W128; AA232; AO193; AZ934; BB132 108127
Our Lord the path of suffering trod (Santeüil) F517 108128
Our lot is fallen in pleasant

places (Spitta) AZ699 108129
Our loved Dominion bless (Murray: Canadian national anthem) AL509; AP640 108130
Our mountain home so dear (Wells) BC144 108131
Our pious fathers built their shrine (Mendes) BH215 108132
Our Redeemer rose victorious (Gregor) AZ1387 108133
Our rest will soon be given (Leatherman) R Some days are dark 108134
Our Saviour in his earthly life (Van Pelt) AX148; AY391 108135
Our Saviour to the Jordan came (Luther) M42 108136
Our Shepherd is the Lord (Hamburg Temple hymnal) AR272; BH84 108137
Our sins, our sorrows, Lord, were laid on thee (Eddis) N121; AK159; AO169; AZ448 108138
Our souls shall magnify the Lord (---) AJp.394 108139
Our souls with inmost shame (Allen) AZ1164 108140
Our table now with food is spread (Kingo) N542; O569; P352 108141
Our thanks and praise to Thee be given (Melanchthon) O24 108142
Our thought of Thee is glad with hope (Whittier) G506; I712; AB336; BF544 108143
Our thoughts go round the world (Moore) BK14 108144
Our times are in thy hand (Lloyd) L506 X My times are in thy hand 108145
Our wilful hearts have gone astray (Benson) Y42 108146
Ours be the poems of all tongues (Patton) AQ138 108147
Out from the camp-fire's red glowing (French) BB501 108148
Out in the darkness of sorrow and sin (McKinney) AU442 108149
Out in the desert the lost are straying (Evilsizer) AX219; AY224 108150
Out in the desert they wander (Wingate) R Dear to the heart of the Shepherd 108151
Out of James one twenty-two (Linthicum) AU326 108152
Out of my bondage, sorrow, and night (Sleeper) AE177; AH342; AI210; AM715; AR459; AT233; AV340; AX300 108153
Out of my need, you come to me, O Father (Sangster) AB312; AC445 108154
Out of our suffering, out of our sadness (Polish trad) Y309 108155
Out of the dark the circling sphere (Longfellow) AN99; AQ208; BD152; BX237 108156
Out of the deep I call (Baker) D349; F322; K315; Q327; AA423; AM412; BR352 108157
Out of the deep I cry to thee (Luther) AZ742 X Out of the depths I cry to thee 108158
Out of the depths I cry to Thee (Luther) J372; K317; L391; M65; N406; O273; Q329; W407; AA415; AK210; AM461; AW531; AZ742; BA413; BY457; BZ 108159
Out of the depths I cry to you, O Lord (Ladies of the Grail) BL20; BSp.52 108160
Out of the depths, O Lord, I cry to thee (Lucas) BH164 108161
Out of the depths of woe (Montgomery) AZ1291 108162
Out of the depths to Thee I cry (Marcy) I427 108163
Out of the depths to Thee, O Lord, I cry (Bible, Psalm 129) BN188; BP96; BQ117 108164
Out of the gloom and darkness (Shank) R My life was lost 108165

Out of the night that covers me (Henley) Y188 108166
Out of the orient crystal skies (English trad carol, 17th c) BG121 108167
Out of your sleep arise and wake (English trad carol, 15th c) BG177 108168
Out on an ocean all boundless we ride (Unitarian Collection) BB661; BR517 108169
Out on life's dark heaving ocean (Dewart) AP508 108170
Out on the highways and byways of life (Wilson) AT431; AU130 108171
Out on the mountain, sad and forsaken (Crosby) AI201 108172
Out on this dark world (Warren) AX502 108173
Outside the Holy City unnumbered footsteps throng (Gilkey) AD141; AH280; AK134; AR169; BF311 108174
Over Kedron Jesus treadeth (Kingo) N101; O302 108175
Over the land in glory (Hosmer) BD247 108176
"Over the line," hear the sweet refrain (Bradford) R O tender and sweet was the Father's voice 108177
Over the ocean wave, far, far away (Haskell) AX215; AY35 108178
Over there, over there, O think of the home (Huntington) R O think of the home 108179
Over yonder's a park which is newly begun (English trad carol) BG184 108180
Own thy congregation, O thou slaughtered Lamb (Zinzendorf) AZ758; BA805 108181

P

Palms of glory, raiment bright (Montgomery) E201; F530; L 582; AZ74 108182
Pange lingua gloriosi (St Thomas Aquinas) BN106; BO254; BQ 241 108183
Panis angelicus (St Thomas Aquinas) AH130; BN92; BO 33; BP51; BQ230 108184
Parce Domine, parce populo tuo (Bible, Joel 2) BM71; BN30; BO164; BQ239 108185
Pardoned through redeeming grace (Osler) L319; AO382; BA287 108186
Part in Peace! Christ's life was peace (Adams) R543; W303; AP339 108187
Part in peace! Is day before us? (Adams) AD63; AO50; BF209 108188
Partners of a glorious hope (Wesley) BE273 108189
Pass me not , O gentle Saviour (Crosby) G231; H43; I329; J461; N416; P13; U252; V 760; AE175; AH338; AI212; AL503; AM707; AO645; AP 495; AR464; AT219; AU230; AV349; AW474; AX380; AY 457; BA615; BB559; BZ 108190
Pass on the torch, pass on the flame (Cross) Y156; AB293; AC229 108191
Past are the cross, the scourge, the thorn (Jewitt) AN194; AQ 315; BD240; BX208 108192
Patapan, patapan, patapan (La-Monnoye) R Willie, take your little drum 108193
Patiently, tenderly pleading (Lillenas) AU433 108194
Patrick, Thee addressing (Lee) BN166 108195
Paul the preacher, Paul the poet (Sayle) F542 108196
Peace, be to this congregation (Wesley) AN24 X Peace be to this habitation 108197
Peace be to this habitation (Wesley) M263; AN24; AZ938; BA382; BE276; BI75; BR108; BX33 108198
Peace be to thy ever dwelling (Pohlman) O47; AZ1085 108199

Peace in our time, O Lord (Oxenham) A527; AE411; AW357; BK 114 108200

Peace is the mind's old wilderness cut down (Holmes) AQ179 108201

Peace of God, which knows no measure (Book of hymns: Unitarian 1846) BR206 108202

Peace on earth, Heaven is proclaiming (Lamb) AZ1396; BA 62 108203

Peace, peace, glorious peace (Teasley) R I came defiled 108204

Peace, peace on earth, good will to men ("H. L. W.") R So sweet and clear 108205

Peace, peace, sweet peace (Bilhorn) R There comes to my heart one sweet strain 108206

Peace! Peace! wonderful peace (Cornell) R Far away in the depths of my spirit tonight 108207

Peace, perfect peace have they who trust in God (Wine) AS 307 108208

Peace, perfect peace, in this dark world of sin (Bickersteth) A436; B405; D674; E468; F358; G354; I528; J571; K413; L465; R420; S301; T420; U231; V391; W444; AD268; AE229; AG205; AK245; AL285; AM590; AO364; AP438; AR337; AS309; AV298; AW256; AZ1; BA690; BB311; BF387; BR409; BV422; BY584; BZ 108209

Peace! perfect peace! the gift of God within (Hawkes) BX275 108210

Peace that passeth understanding (Montgomery) AZ982 108211

Peace through the cross shall come (Pounds) AS366 108212

Peace to soothe our bitter woe (Grundtvig) J200; O49; P210 108213

Peace, troubled soul, thou need'st not fear (Pocket hymn book, 1786) H127 108214

Peacefully lay her down to rest (---) AX618; AY169 108215

Peacefully round us the shadows are falling (Blatchford) AB 32; AC21; AE45; AL558; AR 57 108216

Peal out the watchword (Havergal) R True-hearted, whole-hearted 108217

People, look East, the time is near (Farjeon) AQ281; BG133 108218

People of the living God (Montgomery) V441; AX155; AZ 85 108219

Personent hodie voces puerulae (Piae cantiones) BG78 108220

Peter, faithless, thrice denies (---) AZ862 108221

Pie Jesu Domine (Henry) R Unto him, for whom, this day 108222

Pie Jesu Domine, dona eis requiem (Latin) BO212; BQ251 108223

Pilgrim on earth, home and heaven are within thee ("P. M.") BE278 108224

Pilgrims, on! The day is dawning (---) BB373 108225

Pity them, pity them, Christians at home (Haskell) R Over the ocean wave 108226

Place your hand in the nail-scarred hand (McKinney) R Have you failed 108227

Planted in Christ, the living Vine (Smith) AO449 108228

Pleasant are thy courts above (Lyte) A392; B467; D489; E469; F240; J184; K422; N326; O32; R441; V12; W 235; AL200; AO3; AP317; AZ1045; BA333; BR309; BV563; BY280 108229

Pleasure it is to hear (Cornish) AQ325; BG129 108230

Pledging our lives and our strength to the cause (Mayer) BH149 108231

Plunged in a gulf of dark despair (Watts) H225; I242; V222 108232

Ponder thou the cross all holy (Washburne) AZ644 108233
Poor soul, the centre of my sinful earth (Shakespeare) X622 108234
Popule meus quid feci tibi? (Breviary) BQ192 108235
Portal of the world's salvation (Latin, 15th c) E229 108236
Pour down thy Spirit from above (Romanis) BY521 X Pour forth thy Spirit 108237
Pour forth thy Spirit from above (Romanis) BV427; BY521 108238
Pour out thy Spirit from on high (Montgomery) Q490; W333; X298; AE345; AK351; AL236; AP367; AR521; AS446; AW295; AX636; AY437; AZ351; BA315; BV413; BY351; BZ 108239
Pour thy blessings, Lord, like showers (Kimball) I693 108240
Praise and honor to the Father (Kretzmann) Lp. 743; M519 108241
Praise be to the Father, to the Son, and Holy Spirit (---) R Praise ye the Father 108242
Praise for every scene distressing (West) AZ939; BA123 108243
Praise God for ever, Boundless is His favor (Augusta) AZ 1206 108244
Praise God from whom all blessings flow (Ken) A139; B25; D192; E257; F23; G616; Hp. 9; I718; J602; K449; L15; M568; N664; O655-5; P36; Q644; R544; S suppl. 94; T457; U487; W709; X413; Y387; Z611; AA578; AB11; AC334; AD5; AE473; AF514; AG324; AH570; AI448; AL625; AMp. 16; AN499; AP 816; AR632; AS497; AT514; AU481; AV408; AW618; AX11; AY410; AZ309; BA916; BB683; BC214; BF174; BL79; BM93; BRp. 467; BV64; BY694; BZ 108245
Praise God the Lord, ye sons of men (Hermann) Q105; AA157 108246
Praise God, the Love we all may share (Lyttle) AN500; AQ37 108247
Praise God, this hour of sorrow (Heermann) O600; P425 108248
Praise God, ye servants of the Lord (U. P. Psalter, 1912) R19; T213; AJ306 108249
Praise Him, praise Him, all his children praise Him (Dearmer) X386f; AE437; AL594; AR465; AT511; AU 306; AW426; BK2; BY753 108250
Praise Him, praise Him, all ye little children (Dearmer) EA437 X Praise Him, praise Him, all his children praise Him 108251
Praise Him! praise Him! Jesus our blessed Redeemer (Crosby) AH313; AM683; AS 112; AT137; AU355; AV326; AW438; BB645; BY215 108252
Praise, honor, majesty For Thy great victory (---) AZ 1113 108253
Praise Jehovah, all ye nations (U. P. Book of Psalms, 1871) AJ315; AM29; AP105 108254
Praise Jehovah for His love (U. P. Psalter, 1912) AJ376 108255
Praise, Lord, for thee in Zion waits (Lyte) L54; U478; V 618; AM114; AV67; BI117 108256
Praise, my soul, the King of heaven (Lyte) A282; B258; D458; E470; F365; G77; H 17; J160; K289; N327; O9; P2; R31; S14; U6; V513; W 21; X623; Z259; AD21; AE 22; AF16; AG8; AI3; AK3; AL17; AM70; AP91; AR34; AS7; AT18; AV31; AY424; BA652; BE280; BF213; BL 83; BR55; BV247; BY23; BZ 108257

Praise now creative Mind (McKenzie) BE275 108258
Praise now your God, all ye peoples (Brucker) BL43 108259
Praise, O my heart, to you (Torrence) AQ2 108260
Praise, O my heart, with praise from depth and height (Torrence) AQ3 108261
Praise, O praise our God and King (Baker) F481; K487; Q570; S463; W620; AA297; AF463; AY438; BA866; BB10; BR486; BV650 108262
Praise, O praise our God and King (Baker) X Let us with a gladsome mind (Milton) 108263
Praise, O praise our heavenly King (Trend) BR485 108264
Praise, O praise the Lord of the harvest (Hamilton) BV651; BY728 108265
Praise, O Sion, praise thy Master (St Thomas Aquinas) F622 X Laud, O Sion, thy salvation 108266
Praise our Father for this Sunday (Chao) R75 108267
Praise our glorious King and Lord (Thompson) Lp. 742; AZ1054; BA917 108268
Praise our God above (Chao) AF 487 108269
Praise our great and gracious Lord (Auber) BE281 X O praise our great and gracious Lord 108270
Praise the Almighty, my soul adore Him (Herrnschmidt) Q26 108271
Praise the Father, earth and heaven (---) Lp. 743; AZ262 108272
Praise the Father throned in heaven (---) Lp. 744 108273
Praise the God of all creation (Conder) Lp. 743; N669; AZ 254, 973; BA919 108274
Praise the God of our salvation (Conder) AZ254 X Praise the God of all creation 108275
Praise the Lord; bounteously He deals with thee (Foster) AZ714; BA262 108276
Praise the Lord, each tribe and nation (Franck) N289 108277
Praise the Lord, for He is good (U. P. Psalter, 1912) R115; T203; AJ292 108278
Praise the Lord! from the deeds of martyrs bold (---) AZ721 108279
Praise the Lord, His glories show (Lyte) R4; S12; W16; Z112; AD14; AE23; AF19; AL24; AP134; AR35; AZ68; BA659; BB16 108280
Praise the Lord in heavenly places (U. P. Psalter, 1912) AJ405 108281
Praise the Lord of heaven; praise Him in the height (Browne) E534; F381; J427; K288; M639; N652; X414; AN4; AP132; BM13 108282
Praise the Lord! one accord, sound throughout (Stein) BH130 108283
Praise the Lord, praise the Lord (Crosby) R To God be the glory 108284
Praise the Lord; Praise the Lord Bounteously He deals with thee (Foster) BA262 X Praise the Lord, bounteously He deals 108285
Praise the Lord that He has built (Aaberg) M88 108286
Praise the Lord through every nation (Feith) A351; B262; O364; AZ1107; BA912; BR 351; BV275 108287
Praise the Lord who reigns above (Wesley) AD15; BZ 108288
Praise the Lord with heart and voice (Cannon) BC149 108289
Praise the Lord with hearts and voices (Rist) AZ1084 108290
Praise the Lord! ye heavens,

adore Him (Foundling Hospital Coll. 1796) E535; F368; G11; H19; J407; K300; L84; N292; O12; R3; S10; U10; V515; W 35; X624; Z110; AB39; AC30; AD16; AE13; AF13; AG2; AL 31; AM16; AN2; AO57; AP133; AR36; AT9; AV38; AW16; BA 18; BE282; BF214; BI29; BK 50; BR59, 70; BV29; BX11; BY24; BZ 108291

Praise the Name of God most high (---) Lp. 742; AZ1255; BA920 108292

Praise the Rock of our salvation (Webb) O77; BR220 108293

Praise the Saviour, all ye nations (Francis) I649 108294

Praise the Saviour, now and ever (Fortunatus) J104; N135; P200; AI423; AM174 108295

Praise the Saviour, we who know Him (Kelly) AZ428 108296

Praise thou the Lord, O my soul, sing praises (Herrnschmidt) AF17; AK6; AW513a 108297

Praise to God, almighty Maker (Robinson) BY299 108298

Praise to God and thanks we bring (Gannett) AH492 X Praise to God, your praises bring 108299

Praise to God, immortal praise (Barbauld) A140; B420; D192; F485; H519; K485; L553; N572; Q572; U479; Z595; AA298; AE424; AF464; AH490; AK435; AM112; AN143; AO581; AR598; AS424; AT14; AU251; AX633; AY20; AZ43; BA865; BD26; BF652; BK138; BR488; BX176 108300

Praise to God in the highest! Bless us, O Father (Russian trad, 1815) BG107 108301

Praise to God, the great Creator (Fawcett) AZ248 108302

Praise to God who reigns above (Benson) F565 108303

Praise to God, your praises bring (Gannett) AF458; AH492; AN140; AQ308; BD199; BX178 108304

Praise to Mary, endless praise (St Alfonso M de' Liguori) R Uplift the voice and sing 108305

Praise to our God, who with love never swerving (Gray) W676 108306

Praise to our God, whose bounteous hand (Ellerton) W634 108307

Praise to the Father, the glorious King of creation (Neander) O387; P233 108308

Praise to the heavenly Wisdom (Ellerton) B275; D155 108309

Praise to the Holiest in the height (Newman) A343; B 259; D453; F185; J411; S 40app.; W32; X625; AF497; AL14; AP153; BA43; BL88; BN199; BO1; BQ142; BV160; BY216 108310

Praise to the living God (Jewish doxology) A286; Y300; Z124; AN1; AQ6; BH54; BX17; BZ 108311

Praise to the Lord! He is King over all creation (Neander) AO66 X Praise to the Lord, the Almighty 108312

Praise to the Lord, the Almighty (Neander) A279; E536; F382; G60; J408; K286; M490; N324; O5; P3; Q39; R1; S6; W22; X626; Z98; AA63; AB 40; AC35; AD13; AE1; AF15; AG3; AI1; AK8; AL9; AM50; AN7; AO66; AQ7; AR37; AT 6; AW515; BB12; BC150; BF172; BK49; BL84; BM1; BN62; BV246; BY25; BZ 108313

Praise to the man, who communed with Jehovah (Phelps) BC147 108314

Praise to Thee and adoration (Kingo) J194; O53; Q401 108315

Praise to Thee, O God, for cities (Schloerb) AE414 108316

Praise to Thee, O Lord, we render (---) AZ1389; BA644

108317
Praise to Thee, thou great Creator (Fawcett) V514; AZ246 108318
Praise waits for thee in Zion; All men shall worship there (U.P. Psalter, 1912) T116; AJ170; AM306 108319
Praise waits for thee in Zion, Lord; To thee vows shall be paid (Scottish Psalter, 1650) AL656; AP54; AW590 108320
Praise waits in Zion Lord, for thee, And unto thee shall vows be paid (U.P. Psalter, 1912) AJ166 108321
Praise waits in Zion, Lord, for thee, There we will pay our vow (U.P. Psalter, 1912) AJ172 108322
Praise we Christ, the King, the Strength of all (---) BQ335 108323
Praise we God the Father's name (Alington) BY45 108324
Praise we now the God of heaven (Moxley) BY729 108325
Praise we our God upon His throne (Weisse) BN51 108326
Praise we our God with joy (Grignon) BQ141 108327
Praise we the Lord and bless His name forever (Luther) M46; Q313 108328
Praise we the Lord, for His mercy endureth forever (Neander) BE283 108329
Praise we the Lord this day (Murray's Hymnal, 1852) A118; B276; D158; F546; Q274; BV 438 108330
Praise we the Lord, who made all beauty (Wilson) X627; AC224; BG164 108331
Praise ye Jehovah! praise the Lord most holy (Campbell) I20; O23; W34; AP157; AZ1223; BA 654 108332
Praise ye our Father for His loving kindness (Charles) BI20 X Praise ye the Father 108333
Praise ye, praise ye the Lord, All creation in accord (Lyon) AQ31 108334
Praise ye, praise ye the Lord, In yonder heavenly height (U.P. Psalter, 1912) R98; T292; AJ404; AM108 108335
Praise ye the Father for his loving kindness (Charles) J421; P17; AK14; AO76; BB9; BI20 108336
Praise ye the Father! Let every heart give thanks to Him (---) AU472 108337
Praise ye the Lord; all nature join (Watts) V522 108338
Praise ye the Lord among His saints (U.P. Psalter, 1912) T293; AJ406 108339
Praise ye the Lord, for He is good (Norton) T201; AJ290 108340
Praise ye the Lord! for it is good His mighty acts to magnify (Moise) AH156; BH 65 108341
Praise ye the Lord; for it is good. Praise to our God to sing (Scottish Psalter, 1650) AL690; AP130 108342
Praise ye the Lord, for it is good to sing unto our God (U.P. Psalter, 1912) R36; T291; AJ403 108343
Praise ye the Lord, His praise proclaim (U.P. Psalter, 1912) T289; AJ401 108344
Praise ye the Lord, His saints Who throng His courts (U.P. Psalter, 1912) AJ412 108345
Praise ye the Lord! My heart shall join (Watts) BC277 108346
Praise ye the Lord! Praise ye the Lord most holy (Campbell) BI45 108347
Praise ye the Lord; Praise ye the Lord; Praise ye [4 times] (Bible) AU474 108348
Praise ye the Lord, the Almighty (Neander) R1 X Praise to the Lord 108349
Praise ye the Lord! 'tis good to

raise (Watts) BB14 108350
Praise ye the Lord; with my whole heart (Scottish Psalter, 1650) AP99 108351
Praise ye the Lord, ye Gentiles all (Vulpius. Ein schöngeistliche G.B. 1609) M113 108352
Praise ye the Lord, he hosts above (U.P. Psalter, 1912) T455; AJ411 108353
Praise ye the Lord, ye saints below (U.P. Psalter, 1912) AJ 412 108354
Praise ye the Lord, ye immortal choirs (Watts) H107 108355
Praise ye the Lord, ye servants of the Lord (Apostolic constitutions, 3d c) J601 108356
Praises, thanks, and adoration (Swertner) AZ1105; BA918 108357
Praises to Him whose love has given (Bonar) AZ393 108358
Pray for the dead! at noon and eve (---) BO144 108359
Pray, pray in the old-time way (Brown) AX359 108360
Pray that Jerusalem may have (Scottish Psalter, 1650) X628 108361
Pray when the morn is breaking (Simpson) E473; X629; AW180 108362
Pray when the morn unveileth (Moise) BH8 108363
Pray, without ceasing, pray (Wesley) H53; AZ1321 108364
Prayer is appointed to convey (Hart) I502 108365
Prayer is the heart's sincere desire (Montgomery) BE284
X Prayer is the soul's sincere 108366
Prayer is the soul's sincere desire (Montgomery) A419; E474; G303; H47; I497; J458; M62; N307; O361; P18; Q454; R391; U358; V463; X630; Z335; AA398; AE239; AG225; AH354; AI227; AN234; AO314; AP493; AQ91; AR285; AS47; AT336; AU264; AV182; AW184; AX355; AY46; AZ157; BA603; BB319* BC220; BE284; BF362; BV 611; BX276; BY340; BZ 108367
*with Coleridge Refrain: "He prayeth best"
Prayer is the soul's sincere desire (Montgomery) with ref. He prayeth best (Coleridge) BB319 108368
Prayer to a heart of lowly dove (Tilak) BY341 108369
Prayer with our waking thought ascends (Brewer) BE287 108370
Previous Bible; what a treasure (Newton) AZ614 108371
Precious child, so sweetly sleeping (Hoppe) N42; P137 108372
Precious Jesus, O to love thee (---) AS208 108373
Precious memories, unseen angels (Wright) AX559 108374
Precious, more precious (Crosby) R O, the unsearchable 108375
Precious Name, O how sweet (Baxter) R Take the Name of Jesus with you 108376
Precious, precious blood of Jesus (Havergal) H245; L 420 108377
Precious promise God hath given (Niles) AU90; AV356; AX492 108378
Precious Savior, dear Redeemer (Palmer) BC109 108379
Precious word from God in heaven (Schmolck) M32 108380
Preist Gott, der allen Segen Gibt! (Thomas Ken) AY50d 108381
Prepare the way, O Zion! (Franzén) J9; M601; N1 108382
Prepare your lamps, stand ready (Laurenti) AZ1116 X Rejoice, rejoice believers 108383
Present with the two or three (Freer) W452; BV613

108384
Present your bodies to the Lord (Barton) AZ1429; BA467 108385
Preserve in fullest measure (Gryphius) M31 108386
Preserve thy word, O Saviour (Gryphius) Q264 108387
Press on, dear traveler, press thou on (Bell) BE288 108388
Press on, press on, ye sons of light (Gaskell) U293; Y151; AN315; BD151; BE290; BF636; BX370 108389
Primo dierum omnium (St Gregory the Great) BJ31b 108390
Prince of Peace, control my will (Dana) D613; G216; I337; L 472; V415; AX421; BB117 108391
Print thine image pure and holy (Kingo) J71 108392
Proclaim the tidings near and far (Smith) AR188; AS148 108393
Promptement levez-vous, mon voison (French trad carol) BG166b 108394
Prophets, teachers, true recorders (Dearmer) X212 108395
Prostrate, dear Jesus, at thy feet (Stennett) V292 108396
Protect and save me, O my God (U.P. Psalter, 1912) T108; AJ157 108397
Publish glad tidings (Thomson) R O Sion haste, thy mission high fulfilling 108398
Puer natus in Bethlehem (Latin, 14th c) BM66; BN8 108399
Puer nobis nascitur (Latin carol, 15th c) BG92; BQ159 108400
Pure and free from all corruption (Horn) AE180 108401
Purer in heart, O God, help me to be (Davison [or Davidson]) Z343; AR410; AS312; AT369; AU272; AX386; AY67 108402
Purer yet and purer, I would be in mind (Goethe) U260; V406; AE184; AH361; AK447; AO298; AR310; AS314; AV192; BB388; BD103 108403
Put down your feet and you shall feel (Wheelock) AQ156 108404
Put forth, O God, thy Spirit's might (Robbins) A380; J243; R477; AD396; AE318; AR 500 108405
Put on the armor of our God (---) AI324 108406
Put on the whole armour of pure consecration (Baum) BE292 108407
Put thou thy trust in God (Gerhardt) F310; J579; W547 108408
Put thou thy trust in God (Gerhardt) X Commit thou all that grieves 108409
Put your shoulder to the wheel (Thompson) R The world has need of willing men 108410

Q

Quae est ista (Latin) BQ222 108411
Queen and Mother, many hearts cast themselves (---) BO107 108412
Queen of the Rosary, Virgin thou fairest (---) BP83 108413
Queen, when the earth was first hurled into space (Latin, 20th c) BN147 108414
Quelle est cetter odeur agréable (French trad carol) BG164b 108415
Quem pastores laudavere (Latin, 1410) BG79 108416
Quest of the ages, goal of men (Patton) AQ203 108417
Qui creavit coelum. Lully, lully, lu (English trad carol, 1425) BG67 X He who made the starry skies 108418
Qui regnas in perpetum (Latin) BQ253 108419
Quick sympathy, hands that brought health (Dearmer) X341 108420
Quiet, Lord, my froward heart (Newton) U39; V392; AO616; AP499; AZ1263; BE291; BR

256 108421
Quittez, pasteurs, vos brebis (French trad carol) BG144b 108422
Quoi, ma voisine, est-tu fâchée? (Colletet) BG108b 108423

R

Raise the standard high, Sound the gathering cry (Belden) BB 500 108424
Raise your voices to the Lord (Stephens) BC154 108425
Raise your voices, vales and mountains (St Alfonso M de Liguori) BO70; BQ90 108426
Raised between the earth and heaven (Smith) D303; N583 108427
Rank by rank again we stand (Skrine) AN465; AQ258 108428
Reach out thy scepter, King of love (Zinzendorf, E.D.) AZ 678; BA544 108429
Ready to go, ready to stay (---) R Ready to suffer grief or pain 108430
Ready to suffer grief or pain (---) AT439; AU300; AX401 108431
Rebels, who had dared to show (U.P. Psalter, 1912) T204 108432
Receive, O Lord, in heaven above (St Ephraim the Syrian) E194 108433
Rede, liebster Jesu, rede (Anna Sophia, of Hesse-Darmstadt) BT296 108434
Redeemed from guilt, redeemed from fears (Lyte) AO307 108435
Redeemed, how I love to proclaim it (Crosby) AT203; AU92; AX316; BB635 108436
"Redeemed! redeemed!" O, sing the joyful strain (Whittle) AY 514 108437
Redeemed, restored, forgiven (Baker) O404; P282; Q32 108438
Redeemer of Israel, Our only delight (Swain) BC195 X O Thou, in whose Presence 108439
Redeemer of mankind, God of all grace (Meyer) AZ519 108440
Redemption! O wonderful story (Sayford) AX315 108441
Regard my grief and rescue me (U.P. Psalter, 1912) T244; AJ340 108442
Reges de Saba veniunt (Latin, 14th c) BM67 108443
Regîna caeli, jubila (Latin, 17th c) BN48; BQ207 108444
Regina caeli Laetâre (Latin, 14th c) BM86; BN47; BO 300; BP33; BQ204 108445
Regnum mundi (Breviary) BQ 217 108446
Rejoice, all ye believers (Laurenti) U120 X Rejoice, rejoice believers 108447
Rejoice and be glad! He lives who was slain (Dearmer) X161 108448
Rejoice and be glad! The Redeemer hath come (Bonar) BY170 108449
Rejoice and be merry in songs and in mirth (Church-Gallery Book) BG25 108450
Rejoice and be merry, set sorrow aside (English trad carol) R A virgin most pure, as the prophets 108451
Rejoice, and offer thanks to God (Mayer) BH259 108452
Rejoice, believer, in the Lord (Newton) BV529; BY567 108453
Rejoice in love we know and share (Lyttle) AQ42 108454
Rejoice, my heart, be glad and sing (Gerhardt) Q535 108455
Rejoice, O land, in God thy might (Bridges) A520; E 475; F582; X631; AF430; AN389; BJ54; BV663; BY 651 108456

Rejoice, O people, in the mounting years (Bayley) AF304; BY389 108457

Rejoice, our nature Christ assumes (St Ambrose) AZ292; BA60 108458

Rejoice, rejoice, believers (Laurenti) A4; B61; D43; H 206; K13; L207; M341; N17; O602; P113; Q72; R231; S 115; U120; V179; AE138; AK99; AM233; AO112; AR215; AS166; AZ810, 1116; BA102 108459

Rejoice, rejoice this happy morn (Boye) J32; O183; P139; Q79; AI417 108460

Rejoice, rejoice, ye Christians (Madegburg, Geistliche lieder. 1540) K30; N24; O197 108461

Rejoice, the Lord is King (Wesley) A350; B521; D457; E476; F216; G171; H185; I178; J436; K126; L124; O348; R140; S193; V201; W135; X632; Y346; Z260; AD179; AE24; AF204; AG110; AI90; AL112; AM226; AO70; AP223; AS156; AT108; AW121; AZ1183; BA251; BC151; BD121; BR193; BV210; BY190; BZ 108462

Rejoice! The year upon its way (St Hilary) E151; BY238 108463

Rejoice today with one accord (Baker) E537; O17; AZ1030; BR489; BV25; BX315 108464

Rejoice, ye dead, where'er your spirits dwell (Bridges) X208 108465

Rejoice, ye people, homage give (U.P. Psalter, 1912) AJ129; AM61 108466

Rejoice, ye pure in heart (Plumptre) A579; B537; D520; E644; F635; G358; I421; J555; N588; R407; S297; Y199; Z418; AB19; AC27; AD272; AE7; AF 345; AG209; AH183; AK7; AM502; AN13; AO62; AP608; AR336; AT17; AU285; AV47; AW156; BA124; BB17; BD119; BF170; BK66; BZ 108467

Rejoice, ye Saints of latter days (Gabbott) BC207 108468

Rejoice, ye sons of men (How) D152 108469

Rejoice, ye sons of men alway! (Freund) AA151 108470

Religion is the chief concern (Fawcett) I314; V227 108471

Remember all God's children (Dearmer) AW436 X Remember all the people 108472

Remember all the people (Dearmer) A262; J317; R495; X369; Z528; AE363; AF484; AW436; BW436; BY390 108473

Remember Him, the Only One (Lazarus) BH44 108474

Remember, holy Mary, 'Twas never heard or known (---) BQ85 108475

Remember, Lord, thy works of old (Baker) AI359 108476

"Remember me," the Master said (Frothingham) AH508; AN443; AQ165; BX477 108477

Remember not, O God, the sins of long ago (U.P. Psalter, 1912) AJ217; AM 417 108478

Remember, O thou man, O thou man, O thou man (Ravenscroft. Melismata) BG42 108479

Remember thy Creator now (Burton) V648; AS405; AZ 161; BA839 108480

Remember thy Creator, while thou art (Buerge) AX560 108481

Remember us poor Mayers all (English trad carol) BG49 108482

Renew me, O Eternal Light (Ruopp) Q398; AA350 108483

Repent, the kingdom draweth nigh (Hoppe) N15; P116 108484

Rerum Deus tenax bigor (Latin, 6th c) BJ100b 108485

Rescue the perishing, care for the dying (Crosby) G250; H 395; I697; V770; W681; AG 142: AH417; AL499; AO649; AP594; AR466; AS377; AT207; AU80; AV329; AW497; AX194; AY523; BB623; BY522; BZ 108486

Résonet in laudibus (Latin, 14th c) BN9; BP20; BQ156 108487

Rest for the toiling hand (Bonar) AZ1344 108488

Rest from thy labor, rest (Montgomery) AZ1300 108489

Rest in the Lord and be thou still (U.P. Psalter, 1912) AJ 96 108490

Rest in the Lord, my soul (Babcock) BH91 108491

Rest of the weary, joy of the sad (Monsell) E579; W174; AL130; AP233; BR320; BY217 108492

Rest of the weary! Thou thyself art resting now (Franck) K107 108493

Rest remaineth, O, so sweet (Hymns of the English Conf. 1880) BR334 108494

Rest, rest for the weary soul (Naisbitt) BC278 108495

Resting among the cattle mild (---) BP17 108496

Resting from His work today (Whytehead) B165; D107; F127; AO175; AZ1254; BA220 108497

Resting in the silent grave (LaTrobe) AZ1063 108498

Rett, o Herr Jesu, rett dein' Ehr' (Heerman) BT265 108499

Return, dear Lord, to those who look (Van Dyke) AB146; BF 333 108500

Return, my roving heart, return (Doddridge) BR276 108501

Return, O wanderer, return (Collyer) G195; H253; I255; L365; Q280; V259; AI193; AO 248; BB221 108502

Return! Return! O wanderer, now return (Collyer) AI193 X Return, O wanderer, return 108503

Reveal thy truth, O Lord (Hawkes) AN335; BX389 108504

Revealing Word, thy light portrays (Turner) AT177 108505

Reverently and meekly now (Townsend) BC280 108506

Revive thy work, O Lord (Midlane) B452; D618; F362; V 583; W679; AM297; AP326; BV139; BY391 108507

Rex summae majestátis (Manuale Cantus sancti. Ratisbon, 19th c) BN205 108508

Rich in mercy, Jesus reigns (Woodworth) BR211 108509

No entries 108510 - 108609

Ride on! ride on in majesty (Milman) A64; B145; D91; E620; F99; G125; H162; I150; J73; K88; L259; M 429; N98; O293; Q162; R188; S150; T340; W92; X137; Y 349; Z223; AB134; AC115; AD143; AE105; AF175; AH 282; AI71; AK133; AL85; AM 172; AN182; AO154; AP189; AR158; AT102; AV103; AW 101; AZ344; BA219; BB127; BF308; BI101; BR173; BV 167; BX199; BY128; BZ 108610

Ride on, ride on, O Saviour-King (Solberg) P187 108611

Ride on triumphantly! Behold we lay (Taylor) F599 108612

Ring, O ring, ye Christmas bells (Ham) AN169 108613

Ring, O ye bells, O ring out ere the daylight advances (Grundtvig) P124 108614

Ring out, O bell, thy welcome sound (Bruce) AO466 108615

Ring out the old, ring in the new (Tennyson) R526 X Ring out, wild bells, to the wild sky 108616

Ring out, wild bells, to the wild sky (Tennyson) B444; G537; R526; S466; U472; X

633; Y324; Z589; AB398; AC 327; AD448; AE423; AF453; AH495, 496; AK428; AN149; AO575; AQ305; AR585; AS436; AT496; AW379; BB514; BC279; BF646 108617

Ring out, wild bells, to the wild wild sky (Tennyson) G537 X Ring out, wild bells, to the wild sky 108618

Ring out, ye crystal spheres (Milton) W61; X634 108619

Ring the bells of heaven (Cushing) AU124 108620

Ringe recht, wenn Gottes Gnade (Winckler) AY10d; BW563 108621

Rise again, ye lion-hearted (German, 1712) Q470 108622

Rise, arise! Rise, arise! Zion rise to greet thy King (Hoppe) N6 108623

Rise, children of the kingdom (Rist) O162 108624

Rise, crowned with light, imperial Salem rise (Pope) A389; B466; D487; H484; Q503; S346; U347; V596; Z477; AA478; AD369; AI147; AZ455; BA277; BI46; BR 215; BT503 108625

Rise, exalt our Head and King (Hehl) AZ1034; BA113, 681 108626

Rise, glorious conqueror, rise (Bridges) I161; AE135; AH305; AZ1236; BR197 108627

Rise, God! Judge thou the earth in might (Milton) AN344; BX 383 108628

Rise, help and redeem us (U.P. Psalter, 1912) AM515 X If we have forgotten the name of our God 108629

Rise, Hero bold, from Golgotha! (Ewald) M246 108630

Rise in the strength of God (Greenaway) F302 108631

Rise, my soul, adore thy Maker (Cennick) AZ873; BA772; BV 45; BY682 108632

Rise, my soul, and stretch thy wings (Seagrave) B114; D512; G524; H512; I623; L438; N514; O409; R330; S264; V688; Z 573; AB196; AD303; AG122; AH363; AN62; AT122; AV 240; AW200; AZ1473; BA 754; BB668; BF381; BR424; BX322; BZ 108633

Rise, my soul, to watch and pray (Freystein) M243; Q446; AA381; AM476 108634

Rise, O Lord, lift up thine hand (Synnestvedt) BI8-D 108635

Rise, O my soul, pursue the path (Needham) I404; M 230 108636

Rise, O Salem, rise and shine (Rist) N68; O223 108637

Rise, thou Light of Gentile nations (Fick) Q498 108638

Rise, to arms, with prayer employ you (Arends) Q444 X Christians, prayer may well 108639

Rise to greet the sun (Chao) BZ 108640

Rise to the cry of battle (Greenaway) F497 108641

Rise up, O men of God! (Merrill) A535; B492; G267; J541; R352; S401; U274; W 344; X635; Y224; Z374; AB 279; AC254; AD332; AE252; AF300; AG252; AH459; AK 389; AL378; AN302; AO467; AP587; AQ218; AR329; AS 363; AT423, 445; AU91, 186; AW230; BA559; BC332; BD 122; BF482; BK115; BX362; BY523; BZ 108642

Rise up, O world, the light is on the hill (Stidger) AE351 108643

Rise up, rise up; you merry men all (English trad carol) BG55 108644

Rise ye children of salvation (Falckner) J556; K202; O87; Q472 108645

Rock of ages, cleft for me (Toplady) A471; B217; D336; E477; F210; G204; H244; I279; J379; K333; L402; M 181; N422; O27; P284; Q376;

R271; S237; T393; U100; V249; W413; X636; Y374; Z294; AA 325; AB165; AD209; AE284; AF358; AG147; AH356; AI137; AK217; AL267; AM421; AO260; AP416; AR180; AS211; AT103; AU171; AV236; AW148; AX521; AY312; AZ1280; BA434; BB 474; BC382; BE293*; BF353; BV492; BY458; BZ 108646
*deliberate variant

Rock of ages, let our song (Stein) AH150; AQ279; BH207 108647

Rock of ages, Truth divine (Root) BE293 X Rock of ages, cleft for me (Toplady) 108648

Roll on, thou mighty ocean (Edmeston) AS381; AZ831 108649

Roll on, ye stars, exult in youthful prime (Darwin) AQ52 108650

Roll out, O song, to God (Sewall) BI71; BR157 108651

Room for Jesus, King of glory ("L.W.M.") R Have you any room 108652

Rorate caeli desuper, et nubes pluant (Bible. Isaiah 45) BN2; BO146; BP7; BQ291 108653

Rorate caeli de super! Heavens distill (Dunbar) BG125 108654

Round me falls the night (Romanis) E272; F35; J237; K457; Q562; S502; X52; AL563; BV61 108655

Round Tabor heavenly glories shone (Zinzendorf, N.L.) AZ288 108656

Round the earth a message runs (Struther) X162 108657

Round the Lord in glory seated (Mant) A269; B207; D387; J177; K161; O62; S15; U13; V 11; W2; Z156; AD17; AI6, 30; AM42; AO55; AS6; BA650; BB 74; BI3-D; BY26 108658

Round the throne of glory (---) AI29 108659

Rouse, then soldiers! Rally round the standard (Sherwin) R Sound the battle cry 108660

Rouse, ye Christian workers, be ye up (MacKay) AX186; AY529 108661

Rouse ye, rouse ye, face the foe (Baum) R Rouse ye, soldiers of the cross 108662

Rouse ye, soldiers of the cross (Baum) BE296 108663

Ruler of the hosts of light (Breviary, Cluny, 1686) BR199 108664

Run scheiden wir, ihr herzensfreund (Unparth. G.B.) AY 36d 108665

Rüstet euch, ihr Christenleute! (Arends) BT444 108666

S

Sacred Heart in accents burning (Donnelly) BQ66 108667

Sacred Heart of Jesus, fount of love and mercy (---) BQ 59 108668

Sacred Name of Jesus, so great and holy (Hayn) AZ 526 108669

Sacred the place of prayer and song (Stephens) BC281 108670

Sacris solemniis juncta sint gaudia (St Thomas Aquinas) BQ230 108671

Safe home, safe home in port (St Joseph the Hymnographer) H501; AB406; AH536; AO556; AZ1190; BR441 108672

Safe in the arms of Jesus (Crosby) E580; N608; U207; V347; W707; AI311; AL507; AM608; AO637; AP791; AS 483; AU353; AV357; AW313; AX529; AY173; BB615 108673

Safe upon the billowy deep (Coppée) B417; D309 108674

Safe within the arms of Jesus (Robinson) AY96 108675

Safely, safely gathered in (Dobree) D246; N607; W328;

BA728 108676

Safely through another week (Newton) B46; G393; H80; I69; J185; K428; L38; M6; N 308; O38; Q11; R74; T299; U 437; V59; Z448; AA125; AE 53; AG35; AH161; AI16; AK39; AL190; AM320; AO12; AP346; AS37; AT37; AU10; AV9; AW 284; AX64; AY275; AZ1284; BA 385; BB462; BZ 108677

Saint Anthony, we turn to thee (---) BO140 108678

Saint Joseph, God has chosen you (Donohue) BM58 108679

Saint Joseph, pride of heaven's court (Herman) BP91 108680

Saint Mary goes a-seeking (German trad carol) BG179 108681

Saint of God, elect and precious (Latin, 11th c) E31 108682

Saint of the Sacred Heart, Sweet teacher of the Word (Faber) BQ103 108683

St Patrick's Breastplate (St Patrick) X I bind unto myself today 108684

Saint Stephen was a holy man (English trad carol) BG26 108685

Saints of God! Lo, Jesu's people (Riley) E239 108686

Saints of God! the dawn is brightening (Maxwell) D250; P386; Q502; AA470; AO510; AZ1393; BA357 108687

Salútis humánae sátor (Latin, 7th c) BP40 108688

Salvation and immortal praise (Watts) AL629; AP814 108689

Salvation is forever nigh (Watts) V237 108690

Salvation! O the joyful sound (Watts) H239; I287; L132; V 235; AY12 108691

Salvation unto us has come (Speratus) Q377 X To us salvation now is come 108692

Salve, Mater, misericordiae (Carmelite hymn) BM48; BN 125; BP73; BQ209 108693

Salve, Pater, salvatóris (Latin, 1874) BN167 108694

Salve Regina coelitum (Hermannus Contractus??) BQ 211 108695

Salve, Regina, Mater misericordiae (Hermannus Contractus??) BN142; BO301; BP76; BQ205 108696

Sancte, venite, corpus Christi sumite (Bangor Antiphoner, ca 680) BT307 108697

Sanctify me wholly, Soul of Christ adored (Latin, 14th c) BN101 108698

Save me, O God, because the floods (U.P. Psalter, 1912) T127; AJ184 108699

Save us waking, O Lord (---) AR556 108700

Saved by grace, I live to tell (---) AX324; AY234 108701

Saved by His power divine (Scholerfield) I've found a friend 108702

Saved to the uttermost; I am the Lord's (Kirkpatrick) AU51 108703

NOTE: "Savior" and "Saviour" are spelled as in the hymns, but filed as "Savior" 108704

Saviour, again to thy dear Name we raise (Ellerton) A487; B50; D32; E273; F31; G29; H31; I38; J198; K437; L62; M17; N363; O 54; P60; Q47; R77; S55; T 301; U451; V23; W301; X53; Y97; Z128; AA16; AB34; AC 24; AD64; AE34; AF60; AG 16; AH175; AI22; AK32; AL 214; AM316; AN126; AO42; AP333; AR62; AS61; AT27; AU252; AV22; AW43; AX74; AZ439; BA390; BB34; BD21; BF206; BH177; BK173; BR 109; BV63; BX162; BY702; BZ 108705

Saviour, all my sins confessing (Haweis) AA14 108706

Saviour and Regenerator (Cennick) BR75a 108707

Saviour, bless thy word to all

(Breay) AY408 108708

Saviour, blessed Saviour, Listen while we sing (Thring) A580; B527; D519; E645; I344; J425; K564; S202; U74; V405; W476; Z269; AL315; AM452; AO67; AP488; AZ761, 763; BA466, 468; BB287; BR510; BY459 108709

Saviour, breathe an evening blessing (Edmeston) A178; B24; D 17; G50; H32; I55; J221; K 467; L22; M577; N554; O559; P72; Q565; R54; S47; T310; U469; V40; W285; X54; AA37; AD55; AE49; AG29; AH173; AI48; AK60; AL559; AM340; AO30; AP684; AR58; AS28; AT34; AU221; AV20; AW38; AX70; AY285; AZ237; BA790; BB49; BF197; BI73; BR120; BZ 108710

Saviour, coming to thee (Warren) AX301 108711

Saviour eternal! Health and life of the world unfailing (Latin, before 11th c) E10 108712

Saviour, for the little one (Thomson) D247; N609 108713

Saviour, hear us, we pray (Ellsworth) G600; AX59 108714

Saviour, I follow on, Guided by Thee (Robinson) Q422; U202; V358; AA337; BR386 108715

Saviour, I look to Thee (Hastings) V355 108716

Savior, I would live for Thee (Schroll) AS348 108717

Saviour, keep us close to Thee (Lyon) AY76 108718

Saviour, lead me, lest I stray (Davis) AH407; AR467; AU104; AV370; AW502; AY121 108719

Saviour, let thy sanction rest (Raffles) N529 108720

Saviour, like a shepherd lead us (Thrupp. Hymns for the young. 1836) A247; B355; D573; G337; H449; I677; J524; K565; L201; M624; N644; O571; P361; R380; S458; U323; V332; W554; Z401; AD479; AE234; AF327; AG218; AH402; AI397; AK461; AL434; AM644; AO621; AP745; AR 296; AS250; AT344; AU13; AV377; AW395; AX496; AY 128; AZ1413; BA834; BB 394; BF623; BR298; BX529; BZ 108721

Saviour, more than life to me (Crosby) G236; H346; I490; V733; Z397; AH383; AT326; AU213; AV344; AX422; BZ 108722

Saviour, now the day is ending (Doudney) J229; K438; L36; O59; AH172; AL560; AP331; AZ613; BA791; BR111 108723

Saviour, now with contrite hearts (Hammer) BA786 108724

Saviour, O Saviour dear (Evilsizer) R Saviour, we come to Thee 108725

Savior of my soul, Let me choose thy goal (Naas) AR 361 108726

Saviour of sinners, now revive us (Gotter) O171 108727

Saviour of the heathen, come (St Ambrose) AA141 X Saviour of the nations, come 108728

Saviour of the nations, come (St Ambrose) Q95; AA141; AM165; BP6 108729

Saviour of thy chosen race (LaTrobe) AZ1251; BA417; 108730

Saviour, quicken many nations (Coxe) BY392 X Saviour, sprinkle many nations 108731

Savior, Redeemer, God of Love (Rose) BI70 108732

Savior, Redeemer of my soul (Whitney) BC155 108733

Saviour, Saviour, hear my humble cry (Crosby) R Pass me not, O gentle Saviour 108734

Saviour, send a blessing to us (Kelly) AZ1406 108735

Saviour, shed an evening blessing (Edmeston) W54 X

Saviour, breathe an evening blessing 108736

Saviour, source of every blessing (Robinson) B243; D442; G23; H5; I19; K298; L88; N320; P31; R379; S235; U368; V511; W435; Z111; AE220; AG9; AH181; AI 4; AK476; AL304; AM400; AO 273; AP447; AR438; AS14; AT 313; AU190; AV223; AW189; AX35; AY14; AZ961; BA479; BB291; BC70; BR246; BV17; BY494; BZ 108737

Saviour, sprinkle many nations (Coxe) B478; D257; E551; J312; K223; L337; M103; N365; O114; Q510; W382; AA477; AL242; AO520; AP378; AZ972; BA365; BY392 108738

Saviour, teach me, day by day (Leeson) A428; B354; D563; G449; H448; I676; J528; K568; M159; N654; R457; S452; U322; W437; X370; Z389; AD481; AE 436; AG299; AH551; AL611; AM654; AP767; AR403; AS276; AT291; AV196; AW424; AX418; AY53; BV545; BY484; BZ 108739

Saviour, thee my heart I tender (Burton) J549; P377; W495; AL355; AP762; AS406; AW394; BB427 108740

Saviour, thy dying love Thou gavest me (Phelps) G219; H319; I349; J463; L529; N499; P325; Q403; R311; S396; T378; U273; V398; Z387; AA353; AD 257; AE215; AF331; AG171; AH423; AK470; AL478; AM538; AO641; AP746; AR347; AS278; AT400; AU149; AV380; AW220; BA470; BB283; BF453; BV594; BY485; BZ 108741

Saviour, thy love hath guided (Mumford) BA804 108742

Saviour, to thee I come (Hott) AY237 108743

Saviour, visit thy plantation (Newton) V577; AO429 108744

Saviour, we come to thee (Evilsizer) AX34; AY210 108745

Saviour, when in dust to thee (Grant) A332; B130; D89; E87; F86; H268; I500; J72; K82; L235; M408; N96; O 305; Q166; V457; AA213; AK 219; AO270; AP238; AV111; AW145; AZ1070; BA422; BW 145 108746

Saviour, when night involves the skies (Gisborne) A469; B39; D641 108747

Saviour, when we call, O hear us (Kelly) O271; P177 108748

Saviour, while my heart is tender (Burton) P377 X Saviour, thee my heart I tender 108749

Saviour, who didst come to give (Bartlett) D226 108750

Saviour, who didst healing give (Rawnsley) E247; F567 108751

Saviour, who exalted high (Mant) BY176 X Son of man, to thee I cry 108752

Saviour, who thy flock art feeding (Muhlenberg) B343; D207; H450; J261; K174; L316; M 522; N646; O146; P96; Q631; S348; V544; AA449; AE328; AG238; AI161; AO433; AP351; AZ264; BA823; BF611; BR452 108753

Saviour, who thy life didst give (Lockwood) AB374 108754

Saviour, whom I fain would love (Toplady) D355 108755

Saviour, whose love is like the sun (Robbins) AD46; AR338 108756

Saw ye my Saviour? Heard ye the glad sound? (Eddy) BE298 108757

Saw ye my Saviour, Saw ye my Saviour, Saw ye my Saviour (---) AY253 108758

Saw ye never, in the twilight (Alexander) A50; B553; D 542; AH274 108759

Say not, "The struggle nought availeth" (Clough) W536; X637; Y125; AB301; AN306; AQ97 108760

Say not they die, those martyr souls (Quin) AN429; AQ76 108761
Say, sinner! hath a voice within (Hyde) U158; V276 108762
Scattering precious seed by the wayside (Ogden) AU399; AY 325 108763
Scattering sunshine all along our way (Smith) R In a world where sorrow Ever will be known 108764
Schenk mir ein sanft, zerbrochnes herz (Unparth. G.B.) AY44d 108765
Schier in allen G'schichten g' schreiben staht (Ausbund) BU 3 108766
Schmücke dich, o liebe Seele (Franck) BT305; BW552 108767
Schönster Herr Jesu, Herrscher aller Herren (Münster Gesangbuch. 1677) BT657; BW97 108768
School thy feelings, O my brother (Penrose) BC340 108769
Science, the angel with the flaming sword (Lynch) BE297 108770
Scorn not the slightest word or deed (Adams. Hymns for Christian devotion. 1846) U334; V494; AN286; BX341 108771
Seal my heart with thine impressure (Kingo) P64 108772
Seal us, O Holy Spirit (Meredith) R238; U287; V742; AT175; AU331 108773
Seal us, seal us, Seal us just now (Meredith) R Seal us, O Holy Spirit 108774
Search me, God, and know my heart (Wendell) J378; N496 108775
Search me, O God, and know my heart (Taylor) AZ165 108776
Search me, O God, my actions try (Bottome) BV148 198777
Search me, O Lord, and try this heart of mine (Crosby) AE233; AR297; AS224 108778
Searcher of hearts, from mine erase (Morris) AI354; AM 455; AR289; AS74 108779
See, amid the winter's snow (Caswall) K532; W51; AM 158; BG190; BO153; BQ5; BV119; BY107 108780
See, Father, thy beloved Son (Jervois) E328 108781
See from the rock the waters bursting (Hayn) AZ998 108782
See Him in raiment rent (Monro) E656 X In His own raiment clad 108783
See him in the garden lone (Sanders) AR162; AS133 108784
See how great a flame aspires (Wesley) G500; I643; AL246; AW339; BZ 108785
See how the rising sun (Scott) L11 108786
See! in yonder manger low (Caswall) W51 X See amid the winter's snow 108787
See Israel's gentle Shepherd stand [s] (Doddridge) G 407; H454; I230; M523; N 534; U321; V543; AE329; AL219; AM350; AO432; AP 349; AZ225; BA286; BB411; BR451; BT302; BZ 108788
See Jesus seated 'midst His own (LaTrobe) AZ894 108789
See, my soul, God ever blest (Hammond) AZ51; BA153 108790
See, O God, we children come (Philipson) BH147 108791
See the Conqueror mounts in triumph (Wordsworth) A103; B522; D126; E145; F148; J 112; K120; N147; P223; Q 218; S173; V170; X173; AA 231; AE137; AI89; AM211; AO190; AP226; AZ968-969; BA242; BR189; BV208; BY 171 108792
See the destined day arise! (Fortunatus) A67; B146; D 97; E110; F101 108793
See the leaves around us fall-

ing (Horne) BB491 108794
See the Lord, thy Keeper, stand (Wesley) BX323 108795
See the mighty angel flying (Thompson) BC342 108796
See the morning sun ascending (Parkin) BZ 108797
See the righteous marching on (Rivers) R As Sion's pilgrims in accord 108798
See the shining dewdrops (Major. Book of praise) AL591; AP724; AW407 108799
See what a living stone (Watts) 1869 L 123 108800
See, world, thy life assailed (Gerhardt) AA205 108801
See not afar for beauty (Savage) Y12; AB296; AC225; AN40; AQ174; BF384 108802
Seek where ye may to find a way (Weissel) Q383 108803
Seek ye a Patron to defend your cause (Breviary, Venice, 1798) BQ98 108804
Seek ye first, not earthly pleasure (Taylor) BV629 108805
"Seek ye first the Kingdom" (Elliott) BY554 108806
Seek ye who will some other way (Weissel) M536 108807
Seele, du musst munter werden! (Canitz) BW27 108808
Seems it in my anguish lone (Tietze) AA516 108809
Segne, Herr, mit deinem Geiste (Lieder-Perlen. Concordia Publ. 19th c) BT419 108810
Sei Lob und Ehr' dem höchsten Gut (Schütz) BT19; BW512 108811
Seliger Friede, Köstliche Gab' (Poppe) AW157b; BW157 108812
Send a great revival in my soul R Coming now to thee 108813
Send a revival, O Christ, my Lord (McKinney) AT333 108814
Send down thy truth, O God (Sill) G181; Y242; Z271; AB182; AC 268; AD333; AF237; AN288; AQ124; AR301; BD113; BF430; BX390 108815
Send forth, O God, thy light and truth (Adams) Y33; AD11 108816
Send forth the gospel! Let it run (Fox) BV329; BY393 108817
Send me light! Send me light (Bonar) R Lord, give me light 108818
Send, O God, a gentle shower (Kramer) AA248 108819
Send, O Lord, thy Holy Spirit (Lieder-Perlen. Concordia, 19th c) M534; Q491 108820
Send out thy light and thy truth (Bible. Psalm 43) Z624; AB416; AH556; AI25; AR631; BF674 108821
Send out thy light and truth, O God (Montgomery) AZ1029; BA348 108822
Send the light! the blessed gospel light (Gabriel) R There's a call comes ringing 108823
Send thou, O Lord, to every place (Gates) Q506; S383; U402; AA484; AK379; AM379; AP365; BV322; BY352 108824
Serene I fold my hands and wait (Burroughs) AQ186 108825
Serene will be our days and bright (Wordsworth) AQ158 108826
Servant of all, to toil for man (Wesley) BY632; BZ 108827
Servant of God, remember (Prudentius) E104 108828
"Servant of God, well done! Rest from thy loved employ" (Montgomery) I597; V670; AZ1339; BA314; BR379 108829
Servant of God, well done! Thy glorious warfare's past (Wesley) G518; H500; I593; AV295; BZ 108830
Servants of God, in joyful lays (Montgomery) H27 108831
Servants of God, or sons (Arnold) X213 108832

Servants of the Christ your Saviour (Evangelical Theological Seminary, Class of 1900) AE324 108833
Servants of the great adventure (Dearmer) X302 108834
Serve the Lord with gladness (McKinney) AT434; AU347 108835
Service and strength, God's angels and archangels (Rossetti) X240 108836
Serving the Lord with gladness (Sherman) AY524 108837
Set thou thy trust upon the Lord (Scottish Psalter, 1650) AL647; AP35 108838
Setze dich, mein Geist, ein wenig (Unparth G. B.) AY26d 108839
Seven last Words on the Cross (Breviary) BQ183 to 189 108840
Seven times our blessed Saviour spoke (Böschenstein) AA207 X Our blessed Saviour seven times spoke 108841
Shadows never darken heaven (Hostetler) AY161 108842
Shall God not share His children's care (Briggs) X638 108843
Shall hymns of grateful praise (Cummins) I26 108844
Shall I be ashamed of my Saviour and King (Naylor) AX343 108845
Shall I come just as I am (Hoffman) AX247; AY214 108846
Shall I, for fear of feeble man (Winckler) I225 108847
Shall I tell you what brought me to Jesus (---) AU384 108848
Shall man, O God of light and life (Dwight) I596 108849
Shall the youth of Sion falter (Stephens) BC157 108850
Shall we gather at the river (Lowry) AH534; AI409; AP637; AT481; AU434; AV394; AX597; BB555 108851
Shall we meet beyond the river (Hastings) AS482; AU85; AX602; AY163; BB557; BC156 108852
Shall we not love thee, Mother dear (Baker) F515 108853
Shalom, havayreem (Jewish trad) AQ160 108854
She loved her Saviour, and to him (Cutter) I694 108855
She only touched the hem of His garment (Root) AU287 108856
She who stood beside the cross (Briggs) BV182 108857
Shepherd divine, our wants relieve (Wesley) F318; X 118; BV564 108858
Shepherd divine, thou leadest me (Belden) BB391 108859
Shepherd, help thy chosen few (Zinzendorf, N. L.) AZ34 108860
Shepherd of eager youth (St Clement of Alexandria) R471 X Shepherd of tender youth 108861
Shepherd of mortals, here behold (Henderson) S15app 108862
Shepherd of one fold is He (Rankin) P349 108863
Shepherd of souls, refresh and bless (Montgomery) A213; B324; D235; G408; J269; L 323; R446; S356; Z465; AF 280; AG241; AK339; AM364; AT398; AZ153; BR466; BY 325; BZ 108864
Shepherd of souls, with pitying eye (Wesley) H472 108865
Shepherd of tender youth (St Clement of Alexandria) D 446; G429; I672; J179; K282; L317; M540; N535; O574; P 367; Q628; R471; T329; U 319; V652; Y353; Z266; AA 448; AB79; AC138; AD485; AE442; AI369; AK453; AM 117; AO628; AR548; AS399; AT162; AW398; AZ1238; BA 886; BB167; BF635; BR58; BY555; BZ 108866
Shepherd, show me how to go (Eddy) BE304 108867
Shepherd, with thy tenderest love (Wesley) D411 108868
Shepherds came, their praises

bringing (Latin, 1410) BV111 108869

Shepherds, in the field abiding (Woodward) F594; BP19 108870

Shepherds left their flocks astraying (Latin, 1410) BG79 108871

Shepherds now go we to yon fair Bethlehem town (Dickinson) BK148 108872

Shepherds, shake off your drowsy sleep (French trad) BD225; BG133b 108873

Shew me thy ways, O Lord (Scottish Psalter, 1650) AL639; AW 581 108874

Shine forth, O Sun of boundless love (Browne) BR13a X Come gracious Spirit, heavenly Dove 108875

Shine in me, yes, shine in me (Oatman) R In this world of sin and care 108876

Shine in my heart, Lord Jesus (Griffith) AX385; AY81 108877

Shine, mighty God, on Sion shine (Watts) V619 108878

Shine on our souls, eternal God! (Doddridge) L193; N471 108879

Shine on, thou Star of Bethlehem (Becker) M607 108880

Shine thou upon us, Lord (Ellerton) D587; K386; AL235; AM 631; AO451; AP369; AR533; AS389; AW293; BA888; BY353 108881

Shi-vee-see A-do-noy l'neg-dee (Jewish traditional) BH336 108882

Sh'ma Yisroayl! A-do-noy E-lo-hay-nu (Jewish traditional) BH269 108883

Sholom alaychem mal achay (Jewish liturgy) AH146; BH 278 108884

Should our minds to earthly objects cleaving (Foster) AZ1019; BA 625 108885

Should we meet no more till the judgment (Teasley) AX657 108886

Shout for joy, ye hosts of angels (Childs) R Lo! the clouds have burst asunder 108887

Shout, for the blessed Jesus reigns (Beddome) AI171; AM 298; AO207 108888

Shout, O earth! from silence waking (Havergal) AZ618 108889

Shout the glad tidings, exultingly sing (Muhlenberg) A15; B75; D53; I119; L349; O200; V120; AV97; BA145; BI100; BR150 108890

Show me myself, O holy Lord (Plymouth hymnal, 1893) BY773 108891

Show me thy ways, O Lord (Scottish Psalter, 1650) AW581 X Shew me thy ways, O Lord 108892

Show pity, Lord, O lord, forgive (Watts) H277; I270; L378; U172; V288; AO269; AZ378; BA415; BB240 108893

Show us thy way, O God (Holmes) AN437 108894

Showers of blessing (Whittle) R There shall be showers of blessing 108895

Shun, my heart, the thought forever (Gerhardt) N400 108896

Sieh! wie sein ist und lieblich schon (Ausbund. Psalm 133) BU84 108897

Silent night, holy night (Mohr) A33; B546; G106; I123; J16; K530; M603; 604; N46; P140; Q646; R154; S132; T339; U60; W49; Y302; Z188; AB116; AC 81; AD119; AE92; AF138; AG 74; AH125, 247; AI381; AK101; AL53; AM161; AN166, 167; AQ 289; AR135; AS102; AT72; AU 146; AW83; AX100; AY488; AZ1516; BA168; BB102; BC 160; BD218; BF288; BK151; BL12; BN20; BO151; BP9; BQ11; BV113; BX534; BY108; BZ 108898

Silent night! holy night! Golden

stars shed their light (Mohr) M604 X Silent night, holy night 108899

Silent night, holy night! Through the darkness beams a light (Mohr) P140 X Silent night, holy night 108900

Silent night, holy night! Bethlehem sleeps, yet what light (Mohr) AH125 X Silent night, holy night 108901

Silent night, holy night [etc] (Mohr) X Holy night, peaceful night 108902

Silent night! Peaceful night (Mohr) AI381 X Silent night, holy night 108903

Silently, silently, they pass away (---) AX616; AY186 108904

Silently the shades of evening (Coxe) I52 108905

Simply trusting every day (Stites) AM682; AP521; AT259; AU328; AX459 108906

Sin can never enter there (Naylor) R Heaven is a holy place 108907

Sin has a thousand treacherous arts (Watts) V225 108908

Sin, like a venomous disease (Watts) V223 108909

Since Christ has gone to heaven, His home (Wegelin) AA236 108910

Since Christ my soul from sin set free (Butler) AX335 108911

Since I have been redeemed (Excell) R I have a song 108912

Since I have felt the sense of death (Lyman) AQ81 108913

Since Jesus came into my heart (McDaniel) R What a wonderful change 108914

Since Jesus freely did appear (Berridge) I667; AX551; AY295; AZ168 108915

Since Jesus gave His life for me (Howard) AX398 108916

Since Jesus is my Friend (Gerhardt) J477; K342; L504; R218; S299; U233; V387; Y202; AD 269; AG207; AW236; AZ1318; BR257 108917

Since now the day has reached its close (Herzog) AA30 108918

Since o'er thy footstool here below (Muhlenberg) AR97; AS89 108919

Since to the Holiest none may enter in (Stoney) BB139 108920

Since we can't doubt God's equal love (Ken) AZ1440 108921

Since we, though unworthy (Foster) AZ752; BA616 108922

Since what we choose is what we are (Hyde) AQ108 X Creation's Lord, we give thee thanks 108923

Since with my God with perfect heart (U.P. Psalter, 1912) AJ35 108924

Since without Thee we do no good (Browning) I504 108925

Sinful, sighing to be blest (Monsell) B140; D347; E88; F87; BV150 108926

Sinful world, behold the anguish (Quirsfeld) N112 108927

Sing a new song to Jehovah (U.P. Psalter, 1912) T179; AJ261 108928

Sing about Jesus who died to save (Warren) AX5 108929

Sing, all good people gathered (French trad carol) X193; BG111 108930

Sing all ye Christian people (Struther) X163; AD165 108931

Sing alleluia, Christ doth live (Gregor) AZ1433; BA240 108932

Sing Alleluia forth in duteous praise (Mozarabic Rite, 5th-8th c) A583; B265; D462; F283; V616; X247; AB89; AD174; BL77; BY27 108933

Sing Alleluia forth in loyal

praise (Mozarabic rite, 5th-8th c) [Note: Great variation in these two cited versions] X247, AD174 X Sing alleluia forth in duteous praise 108934

Sing alleluia, honor, praise (---) AZ1098 108935

Sing alleluia, praise the Lord (Swertner) AZ893; BA755 108936

Sing aloud on this day! Children all (Piae cantiones. 1582) BG78b 108937

Sing, brothers, sing and praise your King (Alington) X164; app.1 108938

Song forth His high eternal name (Longfellow) AB59; AN308; BF 248; BX28 108939

Sing forth with gladsome voice (Latin carol, 14th c) M613 108940

Sing glory, glory, glory, alleluia (Smith) R Proclaim the tidings near and far 108941

Sing, good company, frank and free (Flemish trad carol) BG110 108942

Sing it o'er and o'er again (Neumeister) R Sinners Jesus will receive 108943

Sing loud alleluia in jubilant chorus (Agricola) O19 108944

Sing lullaby! Lullaby baby, now reclining (Baring-Gould) BV 115 108945

Sing, men and angels, sing (Masefield) A475; G152; J97; X165 108946

Sing, my soul, his wondrous love (Collection. Baltimore, 1800) A294; B257; D438 108947

Sing, my soul, to God who made thee (Gerhardt) AK16 108948

Sing, my tongue, the glorious battle (Fortunatus) A66; D98; E95; F97; J61; M402; W108; X129; AM194; BV161; BY146 108949

Sing, my tongue, the Mystery holy, of the Body of my Lord (St Thomas Aquinas) BN102 108950

Sing, my tongue, the Saviour's battle (Fortunatus) M402 X Sing, my tongue, the glorious battle 108951

Sing my tongue, the Savior's glory, Of His cross (St Thomas Aquinas) BL51; BM36; BO48; BQ52; BY326 108952

Sing Noel, sing noel, and merry be alway (Raymond) R There dwelt in old Judea 108953

Sing, O my lips, and loudly proclaim (---) R Mary! how sweetly falls that word 108954

Sing, O! sing of my Redeemer (Bliss) R I will sing 108955

Sing, O sing, this blessed morn (Wordsworth) A26; B77; D57; U53; BV116 108956

Sing, O ye ransomed of the Lord (Doddridge) H387 108957

Sing of Jesus, sing forever (Kelly) AO73 108958

Sing of Mary, pure and lowly (---) A117; BL63 108959

Sing of Mary, pure and lowly (---) X Sing the Holy Family's praises (Vaughan) 108960

Sing praise to God who reigns above (Schütz) E478; F366; G355; J422; K285; L85; M 594; N288; O3; Q19; R15; AB57; AF20; AM4; AW512; BV565; BY28; BZ 108961

Sing praise to God who spoke through man (Dearner) A299; X640 108962

Sing praises unto God on high (LaTrobe) AZ737 108963

Sing, sing, ye angel bands (Faber) BO66 108964

Sing the Holy Family's praises (Vaughan) BN122 108965

Sing the Holy Family's praises (Vaughan) X Sing of Mary (---) 108966

Sing the wondrous love of Jesus (Hewitt) AT483; AU281 108967
Sing them over again to me (Bliss) H88; R265; Z442; AE 306; AG141; AH241; AI406; AM722; AP761; AS184; AT181; AU233; AV314; AW494; AX36; BB574; BZ 108968
Sing to the great Jehovah's praise (Wesley) G538; H523; I575; Z590; AL572; BZ 108969
Sing to the Lord a joyful song (Monsell) W23; AB18; BF215; BY29 108970
Sing to the Lord most high (Dwight) AZ1178; BA26 108971
Sing to the Lord of harvest (Monsell) N571; O530; U482; AE 428; AL578; AP692; AZ851; BA 868; BG159; BI113; BY730 108972
Sing to the Lord, sing His praise, all ye peoples (U.P. Psalter, 1912) T177; AJ259; AM65 108973
Sing to the Lord the children's hymn (Hawker) E606; F446; J335; X371 108974
Sing to the Lord, who loud proclaims (Doddridge) L107 108975
Sing to the Lord with joyful voice (Watts) BW272 X Before the Lord Jehovah's throne 108976
Sing to the Sovereign of the skies (Hamburg Temple hymnal) BH67 108977
Sing we a song of the Saviour (Bennett) AY485 108978
Sing we all the joys and sorrows (Grève) E230 108979
Sing we now at parting (Manwaring) BC161 108980
Sing we the King who is coming to reign (Horne) BY191 108981
Sing we the praises of the great forerunner (Paul the Deacon) F551 108982
Sing we the song of those who stand (Montgomery) AZ141; BA383 108983
Sing we to our God above (Latin) 14th c) AZ80 X Jesus Christ is risen today 108984
Sing we triumphant hymns of praise (St Bede, the Venerable) E146; BM84; BP42 108985
Sing with all the sons of glory (Irons) D124; G150; I160; AK177; AO188; AS149; BR 188; BZ 108986
Sing with awe in strains harmonious (Gregor) AZ978; BA222 108987
Sing with humble hearts your praises (Mueller) BA123 108988
Sing with joy the Saviour's glory (St Thomas Aquinas) BM36 X Sing my tongue, the Savior's glory 108989
Sing ye faithful, Sing with gladness! (Ellerton) D517 108990
Sing, ye joyous children, sing, Glorious is the Christ (Dunn) BE310 108991
Singers, sing! The hoary world (Wightman) Y183 108992
Singing for Jesus, our Saviour and King (Havergal) N657 108993
Sink not yet, my soul, to slumber (Rist) AA31 X Father, merciful and holy 108994
Sinner, art thou still secure (Newton) V268 108995
Sinner, hear the Saviour's call (Newton) AZ1467 108996
Sinners, behold that downward road (Dobell. A new selection, 1806) AI208 108997
Sinners, behold the Lamb of God (Hoskins) V248 108998
Sinners, come, the Saviour see (Zinzendorf, N.L.) AZ1043 108999
Sinners, hear the joyful news (Dutton) AZ1475 109000
Sinners Jesus will receive

(Neumeister) (Bevan tr) J377; S227; AL477; AT195; AU113; AV330; AW466; AX264 109001

Sinners Jesus will receive (Neumeister: Bevan tr) J377 X Jesus sinners doth receive (Neumeister) 109002

Sinners may to Christ draw near (Neumeister) M125 109003

Sinners, the voice of God regard (Fawcett) H254; I246 109004

Sinners, turn: why will ye die (Wesley) G191; H261; I247; L373; U155; V272; AA48; AZ 1046; BA408; BZ 109005

Sinners, will ye scorn the message (Allen) V279 109006

Sion, founded on the mountains (U.P. Psalter, 1912) AJ237; AM369 109007

Sion mourns in fear and anguish (Heermann) Q268; AA505 109008

Sion, on the holy hills (U.P. Psalter, 1912) T161; AJ239 109009

Sion, praise thy Saviour, singing (St Thomas Aquinas) A193 109010

Sion, rise, Sion, rest. Sion, wake, arise, and shine (Schmidt) Q479 109011

Sion, Sion, lovely Sion (---) R Beautiful Sion, built above 109012

Sion stands with hills surrounded (Kelly) H403; I212; K200; L290; M83; N262; O83; Q474; U346; V538; AA465; AI149; AM275; AR499; AS188; AT378; AU364; AV246; AZ1391; BA266; BC 212 109013

Sion, the marvelous story be telling (Muhlenberg) R Shout the glad tidings 109014

Sion, to thy Saviour singing (St Thomas Aquinas) O311; P172; AM360; AZ649; BR464 109015

Sion's daughters! Sons of Jerusalem! (Adam of St Victor??) E172 109016

Sion's King shall reign victorious (Kelly) AL255; AP381 109017

Sister, thou wast mild and lovely (Smith) AX628; AY 170; BC381 109018

Sit down beneath His shadow (Havergal) AZ30; BV385 109019

Sitting at the feet of Jesus, O what words I hear ("J.H.") AX413; AY107; BB618 109020

Sitting at the feet of Jesus, Watching, waiting (Minter) AX47 109021

Skriv dig, Jesu, paa mit Hjerte (Kingo) BT179 109022

S'-lach no la-a-von ho-om (Jewish traditional) BH320 109023

Slain for my soul, for all my sins defamed (Young) BP 27 109024

Sleep, baby sleep! Thy mother watch doth keep (Buermeyer) K570; AW431 109025

Sleep, comrades, sleep, sleep and rest! (Longfellow) AH476 109026

Sleep, holy Babe, upon thy mother's breast (Caswall) BN21; BO152; BQ14 109027

Sleep, my little Jesus (Gannett) AH268 109028

Sleep on, beloved, sleep, and take thy rest (Doudney) H 486; AP620 109029

Sleep, sweet babe! My cares beguiling (Coleridge) BG 175b 109030

Sleep thy last sleep Free from care and sorrow (Dayman) N595; O598; V679; Z580; AZ1503; BA729 109031

Sleepers, wake, a voice is calling (Nicolai) BR132 109032

Sleepers, wake! the watch-cry pealeth (Nicolai) F55; BV 77 109033

Sleepers, wake! the watch-cry pealeth (Nicolai) X Wake, awake! for night is flying

109034
Slow comes the evening o'er the hill (Brooke) AN105 X The morning walks upon the earth 109035
Slowly, by thy hand unfurled (Furness) Y89; AB22; AC217; AD53; AN114; BD12; BF195; BX128 109036
Slowly sinks the setting sun (Lacy) V50 109037
Slowly, slowly darkening (Greg) I464 109038
Slumber, O slumber, dear Jesus my treasure (Polish trad carol) BN22 109039
Smiling skies will bend above us (Rowe) AU429 109040
Smite us not in anger, Lord (Albinus) K313; P264 109041
So brightly burns Love's holy glow (Key) BE311 109042
So fades the lovely, blooming flower (Steele) M297 109043
So gehst du nun mein Jesu, hin, (Nachtenhöfer) BT150 109044
So God send you all much joy (English trad carol) R Awake, awake, ye drowsy souls 109045
So here hath been dawning (Carlyle) S451; X34 109046
So I'll cherish the old rugged cross (Bennard) R On a hill far away 109047
So let our lips and lives express (Watts) L526; N459; R289; U313; V322; AO503; AT323; AX388; AY17; BE386 109048
So lowly doth the Saviour ride (Pennewell) BZ 109049
So merket auf ihr Christenleut (Bible. Maccabees) BU4 109050
So nimm denn meine Hände (Hausmann) AW561b; BW561 109051
So precious is Jesus, my Saviour (Gabriel) AE285; AT304 109052
So rest, my Rock (Franck) AA 216 109053
So sweet and clear, so sweet and clear ("H. L. W.") BI 89 109054
So wahr ich leb' spricht Gott der Herr (Herman) BT331 109055
So wash me, Thou, without, within (Smith) R One thing I of the Lord 109056
So we lift our hands and sing out thy praise (Dearmer) X396e 109057
So will ichs aber haben an (Bosch) BU69 109058
Soft as the voice of an angel (Hawthorne) AU466 109059
Softly and tenderly Jesus is calling (Thompson) G239; H262; J578; V753; Z283; AE165; AG135; AH331; AL 494; AM694; AP409; AR250; AT236; AU100; AV339; AW 456; AX221; AY502; BB563 109060
Softly beams the sacred dawning (Jacques) BC284 109061
Softly fades the twilight ray (Smith) G398; H85; I74; L30; U466; V62 109062
Softly I closed the Book as in a dream (Garrison) AC450 109063
Softly now the day is ending (Kingo) M570 109064
Softly now the light of day (Doane) A177; B19; D13; G 47; H30; I53; K465; L25; M 573; N539; O561; P71; R60; S34; T311; U458; V49; Z145; AB26; AD54; AE48; AG25; AH171; AI56; AK53; AM347; AN113; AO40; AP677; AR59; AS29; AT33; AU225; AV14; AW36; AZ70; BA789; BB48; BC162; BD9; BK46; BX127; BZ 109065
Softly the night is sleeping (Washburne) AZ859; BA57 109066
Softly the silent night falleth from God (Blatchford) AO38; BX151 109067

Soldier, go! Thy vow is spoken (Page) BY300 109068
Soldiers of Christ, arise (Wesley) A552; B346; D509; E479; F303; G282; H380; I382; J564; K384; L534; M245; N508; O489; Q450; R362; S269; U296; V490; W534; X641; Y171; AA380; AD287; AE248; AF384; AG187; AH441; AK289; AL404; AM 482; AO412; AP546; AT416; AW198; AZ1498; BA583; BB 366; BE312; BF481; BV585; BY508; BZ 109069
Soldiers of progress, manful and true (Perkins) R Gird on the armor, brave soul, today 109070
Soldiers of the cross, arise! Gird you [ye] with your armour (How) B115; D581; F 305; Q501; V602; W341; X 642; AA482; AB354; AL407; AP549; BA560; BF506; BV 601; BY524 109071
Soldiers of the cross, arise! Lo! your Leader from the skies (Waterbury) G281; I385 109072
Soldiers, true and faithful (Wiglesworth) AO397 109073
Soldiers, who are Christ's below (Breviary. Bourges, 1734) E480; F524; BV435 109074
Soldiers who to Christ belong (Breviary. Bourges, 1734) AM485 109075
Sollt' ich meinem Gott nicht singen? (Gerhardt) BT25 109076
Som den gyldne Sol frembryder (Kingo) BT207 109077
Somebody follows you (Henson) R Brother along on the highway 109078
Somebody needs your love (McKinney) R Out in the darkness 109079
Some day, I know, the mist that life is veiling (Wexels) M640 109080
Some day the silver cord will break (Crosby) AH455; AI135; AM726; AV395; AY494; BB 630 109081
Some day these conflicts will be o'er (Hoffman) AX536; AY140 109082
Some day you'll stand at the bar on high (Teddlie) AX 295 109083
Some days are dark and dreary (Leatherman) AX598; AY158 109084
Some near, near day (Hoffman) R Some day these conflicts 109085
Some of these mornings bright and fair (Negro spiritual) R O Mary, don't you weep 109086
Some-one will enter the pearly gate (McGranahan) AX291; BB568 109087
Some soul for thee (Weaver) R Lord, lay some soul upon my heart 109088
Some sweet day when life is o'er (Chord) AS479; AX 623; AY498 109089
Something every heart is loving (Tersteegen) AZ950 109090
Some time we all shall understand (Yoder) AX570; AY 345 109091
Sometimes a light surprises (Cowper) A443; F176; G351; I454; J495; L458; R418; S 296; U45; V385; W439; X643; Z581; AB201; AD231; AG208; AL287; AM520; AO332; AP 445; AZ843; BA684; BB254; BE313; BF417; BR20; BV530; BY585; BZ 109092
Son of a Virgin, maker of thy Mother (Latin, 8th c) E 191 109093
Son of God, eternal Saviour (Lowry) A500; E529; F207; J542; S393; W359; X339; Z 502; AD323; AE199; AF413; AR411; BF514; BY652 109094
Son of God! to Thee I cry (Mant) BA605 X Son of man, to thee I cry 109095

Son of Man, to Thee I cry (Mant) K83; AP479; AZ1269; BA605; BY176 109096
Son of the carpenter, receive (Wesley) BY632 X Servant of all, to toil for man 109097
Son of the Lord most high (Briggs) BY129 109098
Songs of immortal praise belong (Watts) M154; AA61 109099
Songs of praise exultant sing (---) BI11-D 109100
Songs of praise the angels sang (Montgomery) A292; B256; D476; E481; F369; H10; J432; K311; L178; M589; Q35; S11; V512; W38; X644; AA68; AO78; AP159; AZ49; BA660; BV26 109101
Songs of thankfulness and praise (Wordsworth) A53; B96; D67; E47; F81; J55; K37; L149; N76; Q134; AA184; BM70; BV131 109102
Sons of labor, dear to Jesus (Hole) AO506 109103
Sons of men, behold from far (Wesley) BI92 109104
Sons of Michael, he approaches (Harrison) BC163 109105
Soon as the morn with roses (Haweis) M560 109106
Soon falls the evening twilight (Metzler) AY74 109107
Soon may the last glad song arise (Vokes) A539; B484; H471; I630; V603; BB201 109108
Soon trials and conflicts of life will be o'er (Doughty) AX594; AY160 109109
Soon will our Savior from heaven appear (Habershon) AI95 109110
Soon will the heavenly Bridegroom come (Walther) O511 109111
Soon with angels I'll be marching (---) R Death shall not destroy my comfort 109112
Sooner or later; yet at last (Rossetti) S439; W586 109113
Soul, adorn thyself with gladness (Franck) Q305 X Deck thyself, my soul 109114
Soul of Jesus, make me whole (Latin, 14th c) E89 109115
Soul of mine, to God awaking (Rist) M579 109116
Soul of my Saviour, sanctify my breast (Latin, 14th c) BN103; BO29; BP68; BQ47 109117
Soul, what return has God, thy Saviour (Lochner) Q404; AA345 109118
Souls in heathen darkness lying (Alexander) D256; M114; AZ1397; BA364 109119
Souls of men! why will ye scatter (Faber) U146 X There's a wideness in God's mercy 109120
Souls of the Righteous in the hand of God (Bible. Wisdom 3) Y127; AB407 109121
Sound aloud Jehovah's praises (Martin) D142; F616 109122
Sound forth the tidings, long, loud, and clear (Gage) R O'er all the land have the signs now appeared 109123
Sound over all waters, reach out from all lands (Whittier) X327; AD359; AK408; AQ202; BI99 109124
Sound the battle cry, See! the foe is nigh (Sherwin) AH454; AI326; AM686; BB499; BY525 109125
Sound the chorus loud and clear (Whittle) R Who came down from heaven to earth 109126
Sound the loud anthem, to hail the blest morning (---) BR146 109127
Sound the loud timbrel o'er Egypt's dark sea! (Moore) BH131 109128
Sounds of joy have put to flight (Latin, 13th c) BN152 109129
Source of light and life divine (St Gregory the Great) K466 109130

Sovereign and transforming grace (Hedge) AN25; AQ127; BX30 109131
Sovereign of worlds, display thy power (Draper) V597 109132
Sovereign Ruler of the skies (Ryland) D669 109133
Sow in the morn thy seed (Montgomery) H377; I389; L549; U275; V495; AM299; AN248; AW1360; BA558; BE314; BV 598; BX307; BY526 109134
Sow the seed beside all waters (Murray) AP388 109135
Sowing in the morning, Sowing at the noontide (Ogden) R Scattering precious seed 109136
Sowing in the morning, Sowing seeds of kindness (Shaw) Z416; AH416; AP590; AT432; AU359; AX187; BB621 109137
Sowing the seed by the daylight fair (Oakey) AU404 109138
Sown in the darkness or sown in the light (Oakey) R Sowing the seed 109139
Spare your people, Lord (Bible. Joel, 2) BN30 109140
Speak gently, it is better far (Bates) BE315 109141
Speak gently to the erring ones (Lee) AX162; AY364 109142
Speak, I pray thee, gentle Jesus (Williams) W445; AL495 109143
Speak, Lord, in the stillness (Crawford) BB329; BV309 109144
Speak, O Lord, thy servant heareth (Anna Sophia of Hesse-Darmstadt) M381; O260; Q 296 109145
Speak to my heart, Lord Jesus (Routh) AT331; AU415 109146
Speak to us, Lord, thyself reveal (Wesley) BY486 X Talk with us, Lord, thyself reveal 109147
Speed away, speed away on your mission of light (Crosby) AR472; AS380 109148
Speed away! speed away! Take the gospel of light (Hackleman) AX208; AY331 109149
Speed thy servants, Saviour, speed them (Kelly) D264; K231; N373; P397; U394; AI177; AM382; AO527; AP 387; AZ1382; BA356 109150
Speis uns, O Gott, deine Kinder (Heermann) BT659 109151
Spirit blest, who art adored (Littledale) A234; B204; AI121 109152
Spirit divine, attend our prayers [prayer] (Reed) A370; B202; D382; F239; H210; I190; M 463; R243; S212; U127; W 183; Z275; AD189; AE142; AF241; AL153; AN55; AO221; AP282; AR234; AT171; AW 139; AZ212; BA329; BB213; BF258; BV297; BX77; BY 239; BZ 109153
Spirit Divine, Creator, come Dwell in our kindred souls (Latin, 9th c) U126 109154
Spirit of faith, come down (Wesley) G183; H212; I191; AZ1348; BA143; BZ 109155
Spirit of God, descend upon my heart (Croly) G179; H221; I197; J129; L394; R236; S204; T357; U125; V417; W195; Y99; Z272; AB95; AC62; AD 184; AE147; AF232; AG125; AH230; AI120; AK193; AL157; AN48; AO219; AP276; AR232; AS174; AT166; AV150; AW 133; AZ443; BA144; BF265; BK85; BX107; BY240; BZ 109156
Spirit of God, dwell thou within my heart (Croly) AI120 X Spirit of God, descend upon my heart 109157
Spirit of God, for every Good (Warmingham) AC64 109158
Spirit of God, in thunder speak (Chadwick) AN322; BX379 109159

Spirit of God, that moved of old (Alexander) W185; AM255; AP269 109160
Spirit of grace, and health and power (Wesley) BX349; BZ 109161
Spirit of grace and union (Adam of St Victor) BQ37 109162
Spirit of Grace, thou Light of life (Tersteegen) W192 109163
Spirit of holiness, descend (Smith) AE152; AV148 109164
Spirit of holiness, do thou (Holroyd) BV296 109165
Spirit of Jesus, who didst move (Phillips) F511 109166
Spirit of life, in this new dawn (Marlatt) G178; Y22; AC63; AE146; AR233; BK43; BZ 109167
Spirit of mercy, truth, and love (Foundling Hospital Coll. 1774) A111; B197; D136; E631; F153; J118; K140; M470; X184; AA 250; AZ416; BA255; BV222 109168
Spirit of peace, and holiness! (Smith) AZ419; BA321 109169
Spirit of power, and truth, and love (Alexander) BX319 109170
Spirit of the living God, Fall afresh on me (Iverson) AR656; AT523; AU329 109171
Spirit of the living God, Fall fresh on me (Iverson) AT523 X Spirit of the living God, Fall afresh on me 109172
Spirit of truth, come down (Wesley) AZ1348 X Spirit of faith, come down 109173
Spirit of truth, of life, of power (Westwood) AN507; AQ146 109174
Spirit of truth on this thy day (Heber) L274 109175
Spirit of truth, we call (White) D300; N572 109176
Spirit of truth, who makest bright (Gill) AN57; BX82 109177
Spirit of wisdom, turn our eyes (Catholic hymnal, 1860) O354 109178
Spirit so holy, Spirit of love (Whittle) AX133; AY203 109179
Spirit strength of all the weak (Pollock) AL159; AM244; AP280 109180
Splendid are the heavens high (Grundtvig) M606 109181
Splendor of the morning sunlight (Adler) BH9 109182
Splendor Paternae gloriae (St Ambrose) BJ29b 109183
Splendours three, from God proceeding (Goethe) R Everything changes 109184
Spouse of Christ, in arms contending (Contes) E253 109185
Spread, O spread, thou mighty Word! (Bahnmaier) A253; E552; J323; K166; M107; O119; Q507; X645; AW551; BV327; BY394 109186
Spread, still spread, thou mighty Word (Bahnmaier) X645 X Spread, O spread, thou mighty Word 109187
Spread the table of the Lord (Gregory) BY327 109188
Spring bursts today, for Christ is risen (Rossetti) X5 109189
Spring has now unwrapped the flowers (Piae cantiones, 1582) X4; AN135; AQ321; BG99; BK 131; BZ 109190
Springs and streams no longer bless (U.P. Psalter, 1912) T107; AJ296 109191
Stabat Mater dolorosa (Jacopone) BN33; BO262; BP24; BQ162 109192
Stalwart as pillars bearing high their burden (Phillips) F520 109193
Stand fast for Christ thy Saviour (Mathams) U311; AC180; BF455 109194
Stand fast, my soul, stand fast (Brorson) M249 109195
Stand like the brave (Crosby) R O Christian, awake! 'tis

the Master's command 109196
Stand, soldier of the cross (Bickersteth) D210; I413; AA 407; BA285; BY301 109197
"Stand still and see!" Yea, see, today (Fox) BB337 109198
Stand the omnipotent decree! (Wesley) I598 109199
Stand up and bless the Lord (Montgomery) F374; G39; H2; V9; W233; AF25; AL210; AM14; AP 318; AT16; AV28; AZ1306; BA 389; BV27; BX22; BY363; BZ 109200
Stand up, my soul, shake off thy fears (Watts) V479; AM478; AV199; AZ398; BA587 109201
Stand up, stand up for Jesus (Duffield) A562; B538; D582; E581; F307; G283; H379; I386; J551; L531; M250; N447; Q451; R349; S265; U288; V486; W532; X646; Y170; Z371: AA377; AB 253; AC201; AD288; AE217; AF385; AG188; AH443; AI329; AK290; AL405; AM477; AO394; AP541; AR468; AS323; AT415; AU31; AV205; AW193; AX437; AY303; AZ854; BA585; BB354; BF473; BV586; BY556; BZ 109202
Standing at the portal of the opening year (Havergal) M621; S468; U471; Z584; AI346; AK 427; AL571; AP697; AR584; AS434; AZ762; BA179; BF640; 109203
Standing by a purpose true (Bliss) AM660; AP773; AU322; AX563; BB497 109204
Standing forth on life's rough way (Bryant) BY342 109205
Standing in the market-place (Jackson) AL608 109206
Standing on the promises (Carter) AH391; AT266; AU115; AX474; BZ 109207
Star of Jacob, ever beaming (Breviary, Lisbon, 1786) BO 95 109208
Star of our hope! He'll soon appear (---) BB188 109209
Star of peace to wanderers weary (Simpson) W627; AL455; AP 712 109210
Star of the East, O Bethlehem Star (Cooper) AX96 109211
Star, Star, beautiful Star (Raymond) R There's a beautiful Star 109212
Star whose light shines o'er me (Krummacher) BY218 109213
Stars of glory shine more brightly (Husenbeth) BO156; BQ9 109214
Stars of morning, shout for joy (---) BC164 109215
Stars of the morning, so gloriously bright (St Joseph the Hymnographer) A121; B289; D170; E245; F288; F148; K 252; M485; N208; Q255; AA 285 109216
Stay, Master, stay upon this heavenly hill (Greg) G122 109217
Stay, thou insulted Spirit, stay (Wesley) H278; I269; V207 109218
Stay with us, Lord, the day is dying (Boye) P201 109219
Stayed upon Jehovah, Hearts are fully blest (Havergal) R Like a river glorious 109220
Steal away, steal away, steal away to Jesus (Negro spiritual) Y316; AG315; AH604; AR487; BK166 109221
Step by step, Ho-yo heave! (Russian trad) Y313 109222
Stern daughter of the Voice of God (Wordsworth) X647 109223
Still nigh me, O my Saviour, stand (Wesley) F90; BV149 109224
Still on the homeward journey (Borthwick) W602; AP700 109225
Still on thy loving heart let me repose (Spitta) AZ1025 109226

Still, still with thee, my God (Burns) BR124 X Still with thee, O my God 109227
Still, still with thee, when purple morning breaketh (Stowe) G40; I43; J496; O549; P335; S107; T305; U454; Y20; Z136; AB7; AC6; AD26; AF37; AG18; AH210; AK50; AL539; AN104; AO20; AR45; AS22; AT25; AV 4; AW23; BA776; BB326; BE 317; BF227; BK40; BR407; BX 123; BY683; BZ 109228
Still the night, holy the night (Mohr) W49, BY108 X Silent night, holy night 109229
Still will we trust, though earth seem dark and dreary (Burleigh) E482; I486; T394; V360; AL418 109230
Still with thee, O my God (Burns) H51; I525; S100; AP 472; BA622; BB315; BR124; BX102; BY774 109231
Stille, mein Wille! Dein Jesus hilft siegen (Schlegel) BT651; BW54 109232
Stille nacht, heilige nacht (Mohr) Y302; AD119; AF139; AK101b; AW83; BT646 109233
Storms of trouble may assail us (Herrnschmidt) AZ238; BA699 109234
Strait is the gate to all that come (Berg) M296; N631; O423 109235
Strait is the gate to heaven above (Berg) O423 X Strait is the gate to all that come 109236
Strengthen for service, Lord, the hands (Liturgy of Malabar, Syriac) A201; E329; J286; X278; BV386; BY328 109237
Stretched on the cross, the Saviour dies (Steele) V141 109238
"Stricken, smitten, and afflicted" (Kelly) L237; M399; N117; O316; P190; Q153; AA209; AM192 109239
Strike up, O harp and psaltery (Wallin) N345 109240
Strive aright when God doth call thee (Winckler) O255; AW 563 109241
Striving onward, pressing forward (---) AX435 109242
Strong Captain, in thy holy ranks (Crum) F461 109243
Strong of body, high of spirit (Felton) Y163; AC163; BF 627 109244
Strong, righteous Man of Galilee (Farrington) AD487; AR396; BF629 109245
Strong Son of God, immortal Love (Tennyson) A365; E 483; G206; I139; R228; S 175; W142; X648; Y70; Z349; AB173; AC215; AD235; AF 357; AG117; AK225; AL428; AN204; AP264; AR117; AS 264; AV124; AW149; BA 884; BF428; BK70; BZ 109246
S'u sh'-o-reem ro-shay-chem (Jewish traditional) BH288 109247
Sub tuum praesidium (Latin) BO78; BQ213 109248
Such love cannot be fathomed (Warren) R Behold what love 109249
Such love, such wondrous love (Bishop) R That God should love 109250
Such pity as a father hath (Scottish Psalter, 1650) AL 672; AP90C 109251
Such', wer da will, Ein ander Ziel (Weissel) BT383 109252
Suffer the children to come to me (Grundtvig) BE318 109253
Suffering Saviour, Lamb of God (Hart) AZ31 109254
Suffering Son of Man, be near me (Wesley) K81; N93 109255
Summer ended, harvest o'er (Phillimore) AF579 109256
Summer suns are glowing (How) P381; U249; V654; W613; X7; AB386; AL575; AN139; AO

577; AP688; AR587; AV51; AW 386; BA511; BB5; BD44; BF 643; BH155; BR405; BV647; BX520; BY722 109257

Sun of my soul, thou Saviour dear (Keble) A166; B20; D11; E274; F24; G56; H33; I47; J226; K 463; L21; M566; N563; O566; P77; Q551; R56; S37; T312; U457; V46; W292; X55; Y93; Z150; AA42; AB25; AC22; AD 57; AE44; AF50; AG28; AH174; AI50; AK55; AL556; AM346; AN108; AO31; AP666; AR56; AS34; AT15; AU177; AV239; AW30; AX68; AY129; AZ355; BA780; BB321; BF194; BJ85; BL73; BR125; BT551; BV62; BX139; BY703; BZ 109258

Sun of our life, thy quickening ray (Holmes) BE319 X Lord of all being, throned afar 109259

Sunk is the sun's last beam of light (Hermann) K477; N553 109260

Sunlight, sunlight in my soul today (Van Deventer) R I wandered in the shades 109261

Sunset and evening star (Tennyson) B412; G368; H499; I744; N591; S438; U419; W588; X649; Y129; Z574; AB413; AC536; AD 464; AH537; AL457; AO566; AP 614; AR427; AV290; AW265; AY497; BB678; BF669 109262

Sunset to sunrise changes now (St Clement of Alexandria) A81; AF165 109263

Supernae matris gaudia (Adam of St Victor) BJ 27 notes 109264

Suppliant, lo! Thy children bend (Gray) BR107 109265

Supreme and universal Light! (Moore) AN292; BX350 109266

Supreme in wisdom as in power (Watts) V506; BE320 109267

Surely Christ thy griefs has borne (Toplady) AO255 X Weary sinner keep thine eyes 109268

Surely Christ thy griefs hath borne (Toplady) AZ1262 X Weary sinner keep thine eyes 109269

Surrounded by unnumbered foes (Massey) BX368 109270

Suscipe Domine, universam libertatem meam (Latin) BQ218 109271

Sweet Agnes, holy child, all purity (Sister of Notre Dame) BQ106 109272

Sweet and clear those angel voices (Meigs) R Hark, a burst of heavenly music 109273

Sweet are the promises, kind is the word (Ogden) AR470; AW481; AX494 109274

Sweet baby, sleep! What ails my dear? (Wither) BG185 109275

Sweet be thy rest, and peaceful thy sleeping (Belden) BB 493 109276

Sweet day, so cool, so calm, so bright (Herbert) X650 109277

Sweet dreams form a shade (Blake) BG196 109278

Sweet feast of love divine (Denny) BA302 X Blest feast of love divine 109279

Sweet flowerets of the martyr band (Prudentius) Q273 109280

Sweet Gabriel, O blessed youth (Herman) BP98 109281

Sweet hour of holy, thoughtful prayer (Gilman) BE322 109282

Sweet hour of prayer (Walford) G302; H39; I516; N350; P11; R398; U359; Z337; AE232; AH349; AI228; AK475; AM 534; AN564; AO316; AR471; AS44; AT327; AU263; AV186; AW182; AX353; AY32; AZ923; BB316; BC166; BR524; BZ 109283

Sweet hymns and songs will I recite (Jewish trad., 13th c) BH23 109284

Sweet Infancy! O heavenly fire

(Traherne) X651 109285
Sweet is the breath of morning air (Smith) AL532 109286
Sweet is the hour when thus we meet (Stephens) BC12-a 109287
Sweet is the light of Sabbath eve (Edmeston) H72; BB460 109288
Sweet is the memory of thy grace (Watts) V620 109289
Sweet is the peace the gospel brings (Morton) BC191 109290
Sweet is the prayer whose holy stream (---) H44 109291
Sweet is the promise -- "I will not forget thee" (Gabriel) AT 278; AU438 109292
Sweet is the solemn voice that calls (Lyte) W239; AP321 109293
Sweet is the sunlight after rain (Punshon) AL195 109294
Sweet is the time of spring (Lloyd) H457 109295
Sweet is the work, my God, my King (Watts) B44; H71; I 71; J183; K444; S22; V523; AO16; AV45; AZ396; BA393; BB46; BC168; BV71; BY281 109296
Sweet is thy mercy, Lord (Monsell) H50; S251; AG226; AO 309 109297
Sweet promise is given to all who believe (Belden) BB548 109298
Sweet Sabbath! day of sacred joy (Maurice) BH116 109299
Sweet Sacrament divine! Hid in thine earthly home (Stanfield) BO38 109300
Sweet Sacrament, we thee adore (Faber) R Jesus, my Lord, my God, my All, How can I love 109301
Sweet Saviour, bless us ere we go (Faber) O55 X O Saviour bless us ere we go 109302
Sweet the lesson Jesus taught (Leeson) AP764 109303
Sweet the moments, rich in blessing (Shirley) A72; B157; D104; E105; G143; H168; J63; K61; L248; M423; N109; O323; P191; Q155; U102; V 555; AE117; AI80; AL99; AM 189; AO168; AP210; AR170; AS140; AV112; AX178; AY 250; AZ252; BA131 109304
Sweet the time, exceeding sweet (Burder) L51; BB516 109305
Sweet was the song the Virgin sang (Ballet) BG30 109306
Sweet was the time when first I felt (Newton) AY366 109307
Sweetened by the cross (Garrett) R Brother, here's a message 109308
Sweeter sounds than music knows (Newton) W170; AP263; AZ 81 109309
Sweetest note in seraph song (Hunter) R The Great Physician now is near 109310
Sweetly, Lord, have we heard (Slade) AS347; AT362; AU 228; AX508 109311
Sweetly the holy hymn (Spurgeon) BB40; BY684 109312
Sweetly the tones are falling (Slade) R Who at my door 109313
Swell the anthem, raise the song (Strong) I711; Q584; V622; AA299; AZ1052; BA 879 109314
Swiftly we're turning life's daily pages (Carruth) AX209 109315
Swing low, sweet chariot (Negro spiritual) Y321; AH610 109316

T

Take comfort, Christians, when your friends (Scottish Paraphrases, 1781) AP622 109317
Take courage, Saints, and faint not by the way (Crystal) BC 167 109317

Take heart, friends and neighbours (Dearmer) X166; BG 147a 109318
Take heart, the journey's ended (French trad carol, 15th c) BG91 109319
Take me, O my Father, take me (Palmer) U251; V399; AM410; AO279; AZ967; BA 418; BF350 109320
Take my hand and lead me, Father (Flory) AR298; AS 254 109321
Take my heart, O Father! take it (---) AR362; AV161; AW441; AX405; AY61 109322
Take my heart, O Jesus (Paulsen) M627 109323
Take my life, and let it be (Havergal) A408; E582; F361; G225; H302; I348; J510; K382; L408; M226; N655; P406; Q 400; R310; S242; T423; U268; V319; W512; X257; Y142; Z 296; AA355; AC198; AD260; AE267; AF404; AG166; AH 413; AI230; AK253; AL356; AM492; AN277; AO492; AP552; AR349; AS230; AT356; AU174; AV327; AW215; AX397; AY 223; AZ1071; BA471; BB273; BD116; BE324; BF446; BK97; BV641; BX332; BY527; BZ 109324
Take, my soul, thy full salvation (Lyte) AO375 X Jesus, I my cross have taken 109325
Take, O take me, holy Father (Schmidt) AO275 109326
Take the Name of Jesus with you (Baxter) G253; I508; N260; R411; AG152; AH430; AI100; AS297; AT305; AU424; AV320; AW485; AX27; AY460; BB523; BZ 109327
Take the world, but give me Jesus (Crosby) AX270; BB 596 109328
Take thou my hand and lead me (Hausmann) AK312; AX504 109329
Take thou my hand, O Father (Hausmann) AR299 X O take my hand, dear Father 109330
Take thou my heart, I would be thine alone (Gabriel) R More like the Master 109331
Take thou my life, dear Lord (Lehmann) M231 109332
Take thou our minds, dear Lord, we humbly pray (Foulkes) R306; S245; AB 164; AE374; AG311; AK252; AR535; BF352 109333
Take thou the heart I cannot give (Lathbury) BR306 109334
Take time to be holy (Longstaff) G251; H320; R300; Z 346; AE182; AH395; AI284; AL500; AM706; AR469; AS 50; AT367; AU291; AX428; AY111; BB603; BY509; BZ 109335
Take unto you the boughs of goodly trees (Lucas) AH149; BH187 109336
"Take up thy cross and follow me" (McKinney) AT347; AU99 109337
Take up thy cross, the Saviour said (Everest) E484; F333; G260; I433; O394; R293; U 270; W501; X119; Z285; AL 360; AM507; AO371; AP559; AR249; AS331; AZ345; BA 588; BE325; BV589; BY510; BZ 109338
Take us on the Quest of Beauty (Stock) AR415 109339
Take your burden to the Lord and leave it there (Tindley) R If the world from you 109340
Talk with us, Lord, thyself reveal (Wesley) G309; I499; AL314; BY486; BZ 109341
Tantum ergo Sacramentum (St Thomas Aquinas) AH114b; BM7; BN107; BO274; BP62; BQ241, 242 109342
Tarry with me, O my Saviour (Smith) B31; D642; U420; V639; AO46; AY290 109343

Tausend-tausendmal sei dir (Homburg) R Jesu, meines Lebens Leben 109344
Te, Joseph, celebrent agmina caelitum (Breviary, 1670) BN168; BO267 109345
Te, lucis ante terminum (St Ambrose) BJ91b; BQ261 109346
Teach me, Lord, the love that lives (Schroll) R Saviour, I would live for thee 109347
Teach me, my God and King (Herbert) A476; E485; F337; G320; H315; I417; J451; K262; L413; N503; W511; X652; AF 401; AM555; AN284; AO501; AW226; AZ1342; BA552; BF448; BV603; BX343; BY487 109348
Teach me, O Lord, the perfect way (Scottish Psalter, 1650) AL679; AP107c 109349
Teach me, O Lord, thy holy way (Matson) T413; AK262; AM456; AR300 109350
Teach me, O Lord, thy way of truth (U.P. Psalter, 1912) T229; AJ325; AM451 109351
Teach me, O Lord, to follow Him who trod (Lambert) W510 109352
Teach me the measure of my days (Watts) V663; AX420; AY166 109353
Teach me thy way, O Lord (Ramsey) BV642 109354
Teach me thy will, O Lord (Grimes) AX566 109355
Teach me to do the thing that pleaseth thee (Monsell) AZ460; BA476; BR376 109356
Teach me to pray, Lord, teach me to pray (Reitz) AT330 109357
Teach me yet more of thy blest ways (Hutton) AZ136; BA502 109358
Teach ye, O Lord, true brotherhood (Savage) U370; BF486 109359
Teach us what thy love has borne (Pollock) A231; B142c 109360
Tell how He pities the erring (Crosby) R Go as a witness 109361
Tell it again! Tell it again! (Slade) R Into the tent 109362
Tell it o'er and keep on telling (Lyon) R Go and tell the sweet old story 109363
Tell it out among the heathen that the Lord is King (Havergal) I634; AI170 109364
Tell it out among the nations (Havergal) AI170 X Tell it out among the heathen 109365
Tell it to every kindred and nation (de Fluiter) BB543 109366
Tell it to Jesus, Tell it to Jesus (Rankin) R Are you weary 109367
Tell me, my Saviour, where thou dost feed thy flock (Robinson) AO627 109368
Tell me the old, old story (Hankey) E583; N351; R403; U144; V239; W682; Z438; AH344; AL496; AM521; AO 633; AP433; AS181; AT222; AU370; AV345; AW495; AX 280; AY521; AZ806; BA420; BB524; BV481; BY420 109369
Tell me the stories of Jesus I love to hear (Parker) G441 R459; Z214; AE432; AG303; AH540; AL605; AP763; AR 474; AA400; AT505; AV405; AW419; BV356; BY130; BZ 109370
Tell me the story of Jesus (Crosby) AH276; AM685; AT211; AU367; AX317; BB 534 109371
Tell me, whom my soul doth love (Wolcott) AZ32 109372
Tell out, my soul, the greatness of the Lord (Dudley-Smith) BV439 109373
Tell the blessed tidings (Miller) G445; I652 109374
Tell us now, O Death, where is

thy sting? (Hanrahan) BN50 109375

Temper my spirit, O Lord (Untermeyer) Y182; AC173; AG307; AR657 109376

Ten thousand martyrs died for Israel's cause (Meyerhardt) BH135 109377

Ten thousand times ten thousand (Alford) A590; B541; D396; E486; F284; G531; I618; J595; K519; L351; M318; N617; O617; Q476; R427; S427; T352; U430; V706; W221; Z568; AA288; AB 415; AD457; AE308; AF311; AG285; AH524; AI341; AK416; AL175; AM234; AN547; AO553; AP308; AR426; AT476; AV292; AZ848; BA756; BB306; BD249; BF662; BR440; BV437; BX462; BY407 109378

Tender Shepherd, thou hast stilled (Meinhold) B414; D248; L570; O599; P423; Q595; AZ586 109379

Tent-like this day the King stretched out the sky (Kalir) BH160 109380

Thank and praise Jehovah's name (Montgomery) L95; V528; AE 18; AP96; BA16 109381

Thank God for the things of the spirit (Malloch) AC488 109382

Thank God! My Jesus cleanseth me (Olearius) AA189 109383

Thank the Lord! With bounteous measure (Fischer) AW376 109384

Thank we now the Lord of heaven (Hawkes) AN172; AQ290; BX 197 109385

Thank you for the world so sweet (Leatham) X404; BY754 109386

Thanks and praise, Jesus, unto thee are due (Moravian) AZ712 109387

Thanks be to God for His wonderful love (Emerson) AO64 109388

Thanks for the Sabbath School (Willes) BC177 109389

Thanks to the Man of sorrows be (Watteville) AZ684 109390

Thanksgiving, honor, praise and might (Arnold) AZ691 109391

That awful day will surely come (Watts) H492; V682 109392

That cause can neither be lost nor stayed (Ostergaard) Z493; AE377; AR534; BK28 109393

That day of wrath, that dreadful day (Latin 13th c Scott tr) E487; F228; H493; I603; J298; L578; M323; N613; O606; Q612; V683; W161; AA551; AL142; AM242; AP 247; BA736; BJ36 109394

That doleful night before His death (Hart) AX171 X That solemn night 109395

That Easter Day with joy was bright (Latin, 5th c) A98; J94; AO178 109396

That Easter-tide with joy was bright (Latin, 5th c) AO178 X That Easter Day with joy was bright 109397

That God should love a sinner such as I (Bishop) AX87 109398

That man a godly life might live (Luther) Q287; AA391 109399

That man hath perfect blessedness (Scottish Psalter, 1650) AL630; AP1; AW575 109400

That man is blest who, fearing God (U.P. Psalter, 1912) AJ1; AM446 109401

That mystic word of thine, O sovereign Lord (Stowe) BY 775 X Abide in me, O Lord 109402

That our Lord's views with us may be attained (Zinzendorf, N.L.) AZ522 109403

That solemn night before His death (Hart) AE331; AX171; AY257 109404

That we our will to Him might

yield (Luther) M59 109405
The abyss of many a former sin (St Joseph the Hymnographer) O400; AA420 109406
The advent of our God (Coffin) E11; F48; J3; K4; Q68; X68; AA137; BR130; BV88 109407
The advent of our King (Coffin) F48 X The advent of our God 109408
The ages one great minster seem (Lowell) AM417; BX448 109409
The amplitude of space comes down to your own door (Wheelock) AQ182 109410
The ancient law departs (Besnault) A113; B88; D148; F539; Q117; AA176; AZ1320 109411
The angel Gabriel from God Was sent to Galilee (English trad carol) BG37 109412
The angel sped on wings of light (How) D156 109413
The art, the science, and the lore (Trapp) AQ250 109414
The atoning work is done (Kelly) L143; AA241; AZ1188 109415
The Babe in Bethlem's manger laid (English trad carol) BG69 109416
The beam that shines from Zion hill (Bruce) AP383 109417
The beauteous day now closeth (Gerhardt) AD60 X The duteous day now closeth 109418
The best friend to have is Jesus (Bilhorn) R O, the best friend to have is Jesus 109419
The bird let loose in eastern skies (Moore) BR530 109420
The blasts of winter are fierce and cold (---) AC454 109421
The blessings of the earth and sky (Patton) AQ256 109422
The bliss for which our spirits pine (Hayne) AB410; BF667 109423
The boar's head in hand bear I (Queen's College, Oxford, 1812) BG19 109424
The body, Lord, is ours to keep (Stock) AC164 109425
The bread of life, for all men broken (Lew) BZ X O Bread of life 109426
The bread that bringeth strength I want to give (Fitch) Y231; AE279; AR380; AS357 109427
The bread that giveth strength (Fitch) AE279 X The bread that bringeth strength 109428
The breaking waves dashed high (Hemans) BX546 109429
The Bridegroom comes; Bride of the Lamb, awake (Bonar) BR222 109430
The Bridegroom soon will call us (Walther) M339; Q67; AA134; AX128 109431
The builders, toiling through the days (Ham) AN455 109432
The call to arms is sounding (Hernaman) AZ845 109433
The chariot! the chariot! its wheels rool on fire (Milman) BT162 109434
The Child of humble Virgin born (Schneegass) M352 109435
The Child sweetly rests (Cennick) AZ1417 109436
The children of the Hebrews, carrying palms and olive branches (Bible. Psalm 122) E617 109437
The chimes of the Sabbath reëcho abroad (Overby) P42 109438
The chosen three, on mountain height (Ela) I129 109439
The Christ- child lay on Mary's lap (Chesterton) BG143 109440
The Christ will our Pilot be (DeArmond) R We sail along 109441
The Christian warrior, see him stand (Montgomery) BE326 X Behold! The Christian warrior stand 109442

The Church above forever rings (Latin, 7th c) M511 109443
The Church has one foundation (Stone) BB443 X The Church's one foundation 109444
The Church has waited long (Bonar) AZ1485; BA101; BB177 109445
The Church of Christ, that He hath hallowed here (Spangenberg) AZ524; BA279 109446
The Church of God a Kingdom is (Muirhead) A387; E488; F254; X248; BJ61 109447
The Church of God is stablished (Thayer) AB322; BF585 109448
The Church on earth, in humble strain (Scheffler) AZ988 X Thy majesty, how vast it is 109449
The Church triumphant in thy love (Wesley) E639 109450
The Church's one foundation (Stone) A396; B464; D491; E 489; F255; G381; H401; I207; J149; K198; L278; M78; N264; O78; P80; Q473; R437; S333; T360; U345; V531; W205; X249; Y347; Z423; AA466; AB321; AC 308; AD391; AE314; AF260; AG228; AH511; AI144; AK322; AL164; AM270; AO416; AP295; AR491; AS185; AT380; AU406; AV244; AW273; AZ814; BA260; BB433; BF584; BL96; BR223; BV425; BY263; BZ 109451
The city, Lord, where thy dear life (Dudley) AD428; AR365; BF561 109452
The cleansing stream I see, I see! (Palmer) R O, now I see the crimson wave 109453
The clouds hang thick o'er Israel's camp (Drane) BO111 109454
The Comforter has come (Bottome) R O, spread the tidings round 109455
The coming King is at the door (Belden) BB546 109456
The corn is ripe for reaping (---) AO578 109457
The crest and crowning of all good (Markham) Y259; AN350; AQ 143 109458
The cross is not greater than His grace (Booth) R The cross that He gave 109459
The cross is on our brown (Dix) B369; D212 109460
The cross it standeth fast, Hallelujah (Bonar) AU470 109461
The cross, like pilgrim warriors, we follow (Gosse) X590b 109462
The cross that He gave may be heavy (Booth) AU372; AX 427; AY463 109463
The cross, the cross, O, that's my gain (Taylor) AZ279 109464
The dark night is ending (Whittier) R Sound over all waters 109465
The darkness now is over (Brock. The Children's hymn book, 1881) W270 109466
The dawn is sprinkling in the east (Latin, before 8th c) E57 109467
The dawn of God's dear Sabbath (Cross) I72; AL191; AR66; AS39; AW283; BB467; BR84 109468
The dawn of God's own Sabbath (Cross) BR84 X The dawn of God's dear Sabbath 109469
The dawn was purpling o'er the sky (Latin, 4th c) BO174 109470
The dawn-wind now is waking (Dearmer) BG157 109471
The day dawn is breaking (Townsend) BC179 109472
The day departs; Our souls and hearts (Freylinghausen) BY 704 109473
The day departs, yet thou art near (Franzén) M575; N564 109474
The day draws on with golden light (Latin, 4th-5th c) E 123 109475
The day is done, the night draws nigh (Weitzman) BH12

109476

The day is fast declining (Himmerich) P75 109477

The day is gently sinking to a close (Wordsworth) B13; D7; H36; I61; K461; L27; AO28; AV16; AZ702; BR127 109478

The day is past and gone (Leland) B21; D645; L31; V53; AA41; AO51; AY287 109479

The day is past and over (St Anatolius) A184; B23; D16; E276; F21; G52; J224; K458; L18; O555; Q555; S44; U465; V43; W287; AD50; AI54; AL 557; AM342; AN124; AO35; AP 670; AZ29; BA794; BF203; BV65; BX153; BY705; BZ 109480

The day is past; the shadows round are falling (Burton) AC19 109481

The day is slowly wending (Rowland) G57; BZ 109482

The day is surely drawing near (Ringwaldt) M321; N614; P 428; Q611; AA552 109483

The day is surely drawing near (Ringwaldt) X Dies irae (Latin, 13th c) 109484

The day, O Lord, is spent (Neale) K473; L23; AZ1315 109485

The day of resurrection (St John of Damascus) A96; B171; D 115; E137; F132; G159; H177; I164; J105; K115; L263; M441; N128; O327; Q205; R208; S166; T348; U106; W123; X146; Y301; Z247; AB144; AC127; AD160; AE125; AF192; AG99; AH300; AI83; AK165; AL103; AM197; AO184; AP220; AR189; AT111; AW115; AZ816; BA229; BB135; BD238, 239; BF322; BL29; BP 34; BR180; BV190; BY162; BZ 109486

The day of the Lord is at hand, at hand (Kingsley) X310; AF 417 109487

The day of wrath, that dreadful day (Latin 13th c Scott tr) L578 X That day of wrath, that dreadful day 109488

The day thou gavest, Lord, is ended (Ellerton) A179; B 29; E277; F33; G54; I60; J 227; R59; S45; T313; U464; W289; X56; Z140; AB33; AD 58; AE47; AF47; AG26; AK 54; AL568; AM338; AN120; AO32; AP671; AR60; BA395; BB57; BD10; BF191; BK47; BV52; BX147; BY706; BZ 109489

The day will bring some lovely thing (Crowell) AC430 109490

The daylight fades, the evening shades are gathering (Summers) K576 109491

The days that were, the days that are (Lewis) BY557 109492

The death of Jesus Christ, our Lord (Spegel) N234; Q163; AA434 109493

The doctrine of our dying Lord (Cennick) AZ652; BA446 109494

The duteous day now closeth (Gerhardt) A181; E278; F34; J228; N560; W284; X57; AD 60; AF53; AK58; AN112; AP 668; AW556a; BJ83; BY707 109495

The dying robber raised his aching brow (Lacey) E114 109496

The earth and the fullness with which it is stored (U.P. Psalter, 1912) T40; AJ57 109497

The earth is home and all abundant (Patton) AQ56 109498

The earth is hushed in silence (---) U441; AC7 109499

The earth, O Lord, is one great field (Neale) E168; F472 109500

The earth, O Lord, is one wide field (Neale) F472 X The earth, O Lord, is one great field 109501

The earth shall melt with fervent heat (Warner) AX287 109502

The earth with all that dwells therein (U.P. Psalter, 1912) R38; AJ59; AM66 109503

The ends of all the earth shall, hear (U.P. Psalter, 1912) R 501; T34; AI178; AJ49; AM295 109504

The eternal gates lift up their heads (Alexander) D129; X174; AZ97 109505

The eternal gifts of Christ the King! (St Ambrose) A132; E 175; F503 109506

The evning winds begin to blow (Long) BX143 109507

The evntide falls gently now (Brooks) AX110 109508

The ever-changing seasons (How) BX173 109509

The eye can naught but water see (Luther) AZ1031 109510

The fading day adorns the west (Steingrimur) J236 109511

The fast, as taught in holy lore (Latin, 6th c) E65 109512

The Father and the Son and Spirit we adore (---) AZ1328 109513

The fathers built this city (Tarrant) S408; Z503; AB330; AC266; AD425; AN395; BD138; BF508; BX538 109514

The fields are all white, and the reapers are few (Barrett. Book of praise for children, 1881) W362; BV360 109515

The fight is on, the trumpet sound (Morris) AH448; AU402 109516

The first fruits of the land we bring (Pendleton) BI110 109517

The first good joy that Mary had (English trad carol, 15th c) BG70 109518

The first Nowell [Noel] the angel did say (English carol) A30; B551; G97; J40; R156; S129; W45; X384; Y328; Z197; AB119; AC79; AD114; AE86; AF141; AG72; AH 124; AK118; AL65; AN174; AP730; AQ285; AR132; AT 63; AU140; AW76; BB108; BC39; BD231; BF281; BG27; BI82; BK160; BL8; BN23; BO159; BP15; BV117; BX 535; BY109; BZ 109519

The generations as they rise (Russell) AQ104 109520

The gloomy night will soon be past (Tregelles) AZ1143 109521

The glorious gates of righteousness (U.P. Psalter, 1912) R71; T224; AJ318 109522

The glorious gospel light has shone (Johnson) BC45 109523

The glorious universe around (Montgomery) AZ147; BA 675 109524

The glory of the Lord, The heavens declare (U.P. Book of Psalms, 1871) AP14a 109525

The glory of the spring how sweet (Gill) P228; W608; AE420; AI42; AK430; AL 574; AN134; AO576; AP687; AW385; BB95; BD42; BX 165; BY720 109526

The glory of these forty days (Latin, 6th c) A61; E68 109527

The God of Abraham praise (Jewish doxology) A285; B 253; D460; E646; F631; G5; H14; I4; J410; K284; Q40; R89; S8; V89; W571; X398; AD70; AF14; AG38; AK61; AL25; AM32; AP144; AR38; AW14; AZ1192; BA19; BB76; BF212; BI5-D; BK58; BL97; BV249; BY30; BZ 109528

The God of harvest praise (Montgomery) AO582; AS422; AY58; AZ1233; BA867; BI116 109529

The God of love my Shepherd is, And he that doth me feed (Herbert) E93; F178; X 653; BJ26 109530

The God of love my Shepherd

is, My gracious constant guide (Rawson) D413 109531

The God of mercy be adored (Watts) L p. 741; AZ1437 109532

The God of mercy warns us all (Heber) AO479 109533

The God of the ages your refuge (Kretzmann) M543 109534

The God that to the fathers revealed His holy will (Savage) BD147; BH234 109535

The God who made both heaven and earth (---) BE327 109536

The God who sits enthroned on high (U.P. Psalter, 1912) T18; AJ23; AM474 109537

The God, whom earth, and sea, and sky (Fortunatus) E214; F512; BL62; BV440 109538

The gold and silver are the Lord's (---) AZ388 109539

The golden gates are lifted up (Alexander) F439; H184; W130; AM214; AO192; BV 203 109540

The golden morning is fast approaching (Graham) BB547 109541

The good man's steps are led aright (U.P. Psalter, 1912) T64; AJ98 109542

The gospel bells are ringing (Martin) BY421 109543

The Gospel shows the Father's grace (Loy) M35; Q297; AA 116 109544

The grace of our Lord Jesus Christ, The love of God so highly prized (Watteville) AZ286; BA922 109545

The grave itself a garden is (Wordsworth) B166; D108 109546

The gray hillstaught me patience (Cross) Y161; AC186 109547

The great Creator of the worlds (Epistle to Diognetus) A298 109548

The great forerunner of the morn (St Bede, the Venerable) F553 109549

The great God of heaven is come down to earth (Bramley) E29 109550

The great Physician now is near (Hunter) P271; AH334; AI389; AP752; AS128; AT 86; AU226; AX535; BB530 109551

The great Redeemer we adore (Stennett) AS453 109552

The greatness of God in his love has been shown (Dearmer) X94; BG139 109553

The half has never yet been told (Havergal) R I know I love thee better 109554

The hand that was nailed to the cross (Pierson) AX106; AY 512 109555

The happy Christman comes once more (Grundtvig) J28; K23; M358; O193; AW411 109556

The happy day has rolled on (Dibble) BC250 109557

The happy morn is come! (Haweis) L260; AZ1176 109558

The happy sunshine now is gone (Hermann) AA32; BR119 109559

The harp at nature's advent strung (Whittier) Y47; AB 49; AD32; AN38; AQ93; BX 58 109560

The head that once was crowned with thorns (Kelly) A106; B188; D372; E147; F218; G163; H191; I173; J439; L145; M456; N150; O365; P211; Q 219; R211; S195; T330; U109; V162; W131; X175; AA237; AE122; AF200; AG107; AL 118; AM215; AO191; AP225; AR193; AS155; AT117; AV 117; BA249; BJ15; BV207; BY192; BZ 109561

The heaven of heavens cannot contain (Drennan) F619 109562

The heavenly child in stature grows (Santeuil) F78; BV

132 109563
The heavenly King must come (Martin) N201 109564
The heavenly word, proceeding forth (St Thomas Aquinas) X F384 The word of God proceeding forth 109565
The heavens are declaring the Lord's endless glory (---) AH179 109566
The heavens are thine, Thou King of Kings, Their glory shines for Thee (Plummer) BI6-D 109567
The heavens are thine, Thou King of Kings, Their glory thine (Odhner) BI12rD 109568
The heavens cannot thee embrace (Brueckner) M520 109569
The heavens declare His glory (Conder) BD37 109570
The heavens declare the glory Of Him who made all things (Root) BE329; BK57 109571
The heavens declare thy glory The firmament thy power (Birks) O8; Y50; AC41; AI 39; AK71; AS90 109572
The heavens declare thy glory, Lord (Watts) F252; H95; I202; R259; S217; U141; V230; Z441; AA114; AD194; AF257; AG263; AL28; AM263; AO95; AR32; AT187; AV73; AW291; BF268; BV308; BZ 109573
The heavens in their splendor declare (Collier) AI40 X The law that the Lord has ordained 109574
The heavens, O God, thy glory tell (Kennedy) BH57 109575
The heavens resound with His praises eternal (Hofer) AH616 109576
The hidden years at Nazareth (Cross) Y73; AB126; AC97; BB114; BK17 109577
The highest and the holiest place (Alford) E210; F545; BV451 109578
The holly and the ivy When they are both full grown (English trad carol) BG38; BV108 109579
The holly's up, the house is all bright (Cornelius) BG191 109580
The holy angels, When they to Christ draw near (Zinzendorf, N. L.) AZ545 109581
The holy Child Jesus (Cennick) AZ1115 109582
The Holy Ghost is here (Spurgeon) AT168; AZ1367 109583
The Holy Son of God most high (More) J34; X80 109584
The Holy Supper is kept indeed (Lowell) AC500 109585
The home where changes never come (Bellamy) BB616 109586
The Homeland, O the Homeland (Haweis) G530; I615; M307; T438; V693; AA562; AH520; AV284; BA757; BB639; BF 660 109587
The hour in dark Gethsemane (Norwegian) P175 109588
The hours' decline and setting sun (Herman) AZ399 109589
The hours of day are over (Ellerton) K575; L26; O567 109590
The hymn for conquering martyrs raise (St Bede, the Venerable) E35 109591
The joyous life that year by year (How) AH519 109592
The judgment has set, the books have been opened (Belden) BB482 109593
The King, O God, his heart to thee upraiseth (Bridges) E564; F580; X324; AL518; BJ74 109594
The King of Glory standeth (DeChenez) R410; S298; W 396 109595
The King of heaven His table spreads (Doddridge) G409; I233; BZ 109596
The King of love my shepherd is (Baker) A345; B326; D

412; E490; F197; G353; H118; I136; J530; K345; L490; M189; O420; Q431; R106; S99; T404; U80; V334; W438; X654; Y35; Z169; AB62; AC50; AD252; AE 69; AF79; AG51; AH219; AK304; AL280; AM141; AN87; AO324; AP146; AR80; AT280; AV224; AZ232; BA512; BB86; BD59; BE330; BF243; BR411; BV546; BX120; BY72; BZ 109597

The King rejoiceth in thy strength (U.P. Psalter, 1912) AJ46 109598

The King shall come when morning dawns (Greek hymn) A11; B70; J10; K14; R232; S187; AD 175; AF201; AM236; AR208; AW125; BB194; BZ 109599

The Kingdom is coming, O tell ye the story (Slade) R From all the dark places 109600

The kingdom Satan founded (Kingo) O280 109601

The Kings of the East are riding (Bates) G101; Y326; AC92 109602

The laborers are few, and still there's much to do (Jeffrey) R O, why should I be idle 109603

The laborers are few; Christ calleth for you (Evilsizer) R The time of the harvest 109604

The Lamb's high banquet called to share (Latin, 7th c) F129 X The Lamb's high banquet we await 109605

The Lamb's high banquet doth invite (Latin, 7th c) BJ30 109606

The Lamb's high banquet we await (Latin, 7th c) E125; F129 109607

The lamps of heaven are burning still (Benson) Y208 109608

The land we love is calling (Wilson) U409; Y279; AC276; AH470; BF554 109609

The Law commands and makes us know (Watts) Q289; V238 109610

The Law of God is good and wise (Loy) M33; O416; Q 295; AA115; AM449 109611

The law that the Lord has ordained (Collier) T29; AI40; AJ39, 40 109612

The lifted eye and bended knee (Scott) BE331; BX352 109613

The lifting of my hands, accept of me (Mordecai b. Sabbatai) BH174 109614

The Light along the ages (Tarrant) AC128; AN197; BD244; BF326; BX205 109615

The light, my light, world-filling light (Tagore) AQ59 109616

The light of God is falling (Benson) G468; R482; S400; U376; Z486; AB274; AG250; AR395; AT442; BF518 109617

The light of the morning is breaking (Lewis) AD334; BY193 109618

The light pours down from heaven (Gostick) AN408; BD 187; BR228; BX328 109619

The lights begin to twinkle from the rocks (Tennyson) AC495 109620

The little cares that fretted me (Guiney) AB307 109621

The little flowers came through the ground (Richards) BY 755 109622

The little while I linger here (Franzén) N457 109623

The living God my Shepherd is (Driscoll) BL89 109624

The lone, wild fowl in lofty flight (McFadyen) R540; S496; Y92; AC59; AD56 109625

The Lord Almighty is my light (U.P. Psalter, 1912) T46; AJ73 109626

The Lord Almighty reigns (U.P. Psalter, 1912) R94 109627

The Lord is King of all things

(St Anatolius) E32 109628

The Lord ascendeth up on high, Decked with resplendent wounds (Hart) AZ156 109629

The Lord ascendeth up on high, The Lord hath triumphed (Russell) E148; O362; R212; S172; W132; BV211; BY177 109630

The Lord at first did Adam make (English trad carol) BG1 109631

The Lord be praised! I'm homeward bound (Larsen) M311 109632

The Lord be with me everywhere (Hammond) AZ561 109633

The Lord be with us as each day (Ellerton) G28; Z125; AE36; AK33; AN473; AO47; AP336; AR61; AS65; AW42; AX76; BA 384; BB37; BC28; BD19; BX 515 109634

The Lord be with us as we bend (Ellerton) AK33 X The Lord be with us as each day 109635

The Lord be with us as we walk (Ellerton) BC28 X The Lord be with us as each day 109636

The Lord bless and keep thee in His power (Gregor) AZ1020; BA923 109637

The Lord bless thee and keep thee (Bible. Numbers) AU498 X The Lord bless you 109638

The Lord bless you and keep you (Bible. Numbers) G614; I748; AC25; AE474; AG340; AU498; AW614; BB695; BF 698; BY305a 109639

The Lord descended from above (Sternhold) BR139 X O God, my strength and fortitude 109640

The Lord doth reign and clothed is He (Scottish Psalter, 1650) AL665; AW593 109641

The Lord for ever doth endure (Scottish Psalter, 1650) AL 632 109642

The Lord for ever sits as King (Scottish Psalter, 1650) AP7 109643

The Lord God Jesus Christ doth reign (Bostock) BI53 109644

The Lord has heard and answered prayer (U.P. Psalter, 1912) AM25 X Thou, O Jehovah, shalt endure 109645

The Lord hath helped me hitherto (Amilie Juliane) M529; Q33; AA80 109646

The Lord hath reigned, and reigns: let earth (Keble) AP83 109647

The Lord hath said, "Seek ye my face" (Sadler) BX245 109648

The Lord hath yet more light and truth (Rawson) R We limit not the truth of God 109649

The Lord Himself gave forth the word (Zinzendorf, N.L.) AZ679 109650

The Lord I will at all times bless, In praise my mouth employ (U.P. Psalter, 1912) AJ88 109651

The Lord I will at all times bless, My mouth his praises (U.P. Psalter, 1912) R412; T57; AJ90 109652

The Lord imparted from above (Snow) BC298 109653

The Lord, in his righteousness, judges the people (Annin) Y27; AN327; BI14 109654

The Lord in Sion reigneth (Crosby) BB7 109655

The Lord into His Father's hands (Petursson) M390 109656

The Lord is come! On Syrian soil (Stanley) A327; E48; X95; AB129; AK125; BF339; BX196 109657

The Lord is coming! let this be (---) BB187 109658

The Lord is great; with worthy

praise (U.P. Psalter, 1912) T89; AJ131 109659
The Lord is in his holy place, In all things near and far (Gannett) X655; AD31; AN73; BD31; BX111 109660
The Lord is in his holy place, Let all the earth be still (Grundtvig) BE332 109661
The Lord is King! I own His power (Terry) BY488 109662
The Lord is King! lift up thy voice (Conder) F175; I90; L98; M144; R83; W25; AL8; AM58; AP162; AY422; BA24; BV239; BY194 109663
The Lord is King: -- upon His throne (Montgomery) AZ734; BA23 109664
The Lord is king, with majesty enrobed (Ladies of the Grail) BSp28 109665
The Lord is my light; then why should I fear (Nicholson) BB 577; BC103 109666
The Lord is my Shepherd, I shall not want (with refrain: His yoke is easy by Hudson) AX473 109667
The Lord is my Shepherd, I shall not want (Scottish Psalter, 1650) AX473 X The Lord's my Shepherd, I'll not want 109668
The Lord is my Shepherd, no want shall I know (Montgomery) I104; V509; Y365; Z170; AC57; AD234; AH212; AI304; AM663; AN261; AO321; AS260; AT57; AU22; AV66; AW62; AZ499; BA691; BB405; BC104; BD56; BF242; BI2; BR267; BX305 109669
The Lord is near! Why should we fear? (Kretzmann) M334 109670
The Lord is rich and merciful (Lynch) S82; W398; AB158; AF328; AM519; BY422 109671
The Lord is risen again, Ye heavens, exultant sing (Sigstedt) BI107 109672
The Lord is risen indeed (Kelly) E627; F142; H188; I157; W120; BV188 109673
The Lord is strong to help the weak (U.P. Psalter, 1912) T287; AJ396 109674
The Lord Jehovah lives, and blessed be my Rock! (Hastings) L486 109675
The Lord Jehovah reigns (Watts) G63; I81; V101; BB11; BZ 109676
The Lord my faithful Shepherd is (Arrebo) O345 109677
The Lord, my God, be praised (Olearius) Q38; AA272 109678
The Lord my pasture shall prepare (Addison) B317; D659; E491; F179; M149; Q368; X 656; AA85; BC113; BR252 109679
The Lord my pasture will prepare (Addison) BC113 X The Lord my pasture shall prepare 109680
The Lord my Shepherd holds me (U.P. Psalter, 1912) T38; AJ55 109681
The Lord my Shepherd is (Watts) J526; K255; N480; O346; Q426; V342; AA374; AK307; AO322; AS261; AY 117; BR258 109682
The Lord my Shepherd is and Guide (Meusslin) AZ744 109683
The Lord, my Shepherd still has been (Lucas) BH86 109684
The Lord of all, who reigns supreme (Jewish trad) BH76, 276 109685
The Lord of earth and sky (Wesley) AZ1171 109686
The Lord of glory is my light (Watts) AO74; AX490; AY 92 109687
The Lord of heaven confess (Wither) X657; AP131 109688
The Lord of life is risen (Lange) AK172; AO189; AZ 730; BT566 109689

The Lord of might, from Sinai's brow (Heber) O313; AZ749 109690

The Lord of Sabbath let us praise (Wesley, S., jr) H179 109691

The Lord our God alone is strong (Winchester) G561; I686; J502; AD424; AE370; BZ 109692

The Lord our God is clothed with might (White) G61; H105; I99; AZ137; BZ 109693

The Lord, our God, is full of might (White) AZ137; X The Lord, our God, is clothed with might 109694

The Lord, our God, is good to all (U.P. Psalter, 1912) AJ395 109695

The Lord our God we praise (Jewish doxology) BI5-D X The God of Abraham praise 109696

The Lord our Saviour is the way (Hymns of the English Conf. 1880) BR238 109697

The Lord prepared hath His throne (Scottish Psalter, 1650) AP 90d 109698

The Lord -- the Lord of glory reigns (Follen) BH71 109699

The Lord, The Lord reigneth (Jewish traditional Shofar) BH315 109700

The Lord Thee hear in time of grief (U.P. Book of Psalms 1871) AP16 109701

The Lord to thee appealeth To be his servant true (Grundtvig) M545 109702

The Lord unto His Christ hath said (U.P. Psalter, 1912) T 210; AJ303 109703

The Lord upholds the faltering feet (U.P. Psalter, 1912) AJ398 109704

The Lord who has remembered us (U.P. Psalter, 1912) T216; AJ309 109705

The Lord, who truly knows The heart of every saint (Newton) L411 109706

The Lord whom earth and air and sea (Fortunatus) BO100 X The Lord whom earth and stars 109707

The Lord whom earth and stars and sea (Fortunatus) BN137; BO100 109708

The Lord will come and not be slow (Milton) A312; E492; F52; I642; J327; R230; S185; W151; X658; AB347; AF95; AM294; AT126; BV89; BY195; BZ 109709

The Lord will grace and glory give (Montgomery) AZ915 109710

The Lord will I at all times bless (Scottish Psalter, 1650) AL644 109711

The Lord's is the earth and its fullness (Ladies of the Grail) BS12 109712

The Lord's my light and saving health (Scottish Psalter, 1650) AL640; AP24; AW582 109713

The Lord's my shepherd, I'll not want (Scottish Psalter, 1650) G70; H119; J522; L 105; P207; Q436; R104; S97; T37; U34; V330; AA367; AD 91; AF84; AG49; AJ53; AL 637; AM77; AN260; AP19; AQ49; AR273; AW579; AX 473; BB260; BK25, 94; BT 436; BV511; BX303; BY73; BZ 109714

The Lord's our Rock, in Him we hide (Charlesworth) AI 403; AX515; BB585 109715

The love of God is greater far (Lehman) AX82 109716

The loving friend to all who bowed Beneath life's weary load (Longfellow) BE333 109717

The maid of France, with visioned eyes (Henry) BQ 104 109718

The maker of the sun and moon (Housman) E16; AC87 109719

The man is ever blessed [blest] (Watts) M221; Q414; AA341 109720

The man of life upright (Campian) AQ107 109721
The man that fears the Lord (U.P. Psalter, 1912) AJ62 109722
The man who once has found abode (U.P. Book of Psalms, 1871) G74; T169; AF91; AJ 248; AM74; AP77; BZ 109723
The maple leaf our emblem dear (---) R In days of yore, from Britain's shore 109724
The mass of unborn matter knew Thee (Duclaux) X616b 109725
The Master comes! He calls for thee (Crawford) BV332 109726
The Master hath come, and He calls us (Doudney) AT427 109727
The men of the Church for the Master (Cooper) M528 109728
The mercies of my God and King (Lyte) AZ1438 109729
The mercy of God is an ocean divine (Simpson) AU45 109730
The merits of the saints (Latin, 8th c) E182 109731
The mighty God, Jehovah, speaks (U.P. Psalter, 1912) T94; AJ137 109732
The mighty God, the Lord, Has spoken unto all (U.P. Psalter, 1912) T96; AJ139 109733
The mighty God, the Lord, Hath spoken unto all (Scottish Psalter, 1650) AM239; AP44 109734
The moon shines bright, and the stars give a light (English trad carol) BG46 109735
The more thou puttest in the Lord thy trust (Howard) BR331 109736
The morning breaks; the shadows flee (Pratt) BC269 109737
The morning bright, with rosy light (Summers) K572; W653; AO629; AP804 109738
The morning hangs a signal (Gannett) AN90; AQ1 109739
The morning kindles all the sky (Latin, 4th c) AZ1445 109740
The morning light is breaking (Smith) A264; B479; D252; G487; H482; I653; J313; K 230; L347; M104; N366; O113; P391; Q497; R499; S389; U406; V587; Z524; AA471; AB375; AD376; AE 364; AF305; AG260; AH468; AK384; AL262; AN409; AO 511; AP386; AT448; AU12; AV271; AW324; AZ856; BA 354; BB453; BE335; BF531; BX329 109741
The morning Star upon us gleams (Nicolai) O220; P 146 109742
The morning sun illumes the skies (Hermann) M559 109743
The morning sun is brightly beaming (Finnish, 1836) Q545 109744
The morning walks upon the earth (Brooke) Y54; AB6; AN105; BD2; BX55 109745
The mouth of fools doth God confess (Luther) AA277 109746
The mystery hidden from the eyes (Gerhardt) AA264 109747
The Name of Jesus is so sweet (Martin) AM711; AU102; BB 643 109748
The new-born Child this early morn (Schneegass) AA169 109749
The new-born King who comes today (---) K538; N40 109750
The new church year again is come (Olearius) M342 109751
The night has a thousand eyes (Bourdillon) AQ164 109752
The night is come like to the day (Browne) X58 109753
The night is come wherein at last we rest (Herbert) AZ 528 109754

The night is ended and the morning nears (Tennyson, F) X328; AD365 109755
The night was dark and stormy (Eliot) BD216 109756
The nighty-nine within the fold (Schell) AX202 109757
The ocean hath no danger (Thring) K501 109758
The offering on the altar burned (U.P. Psalter, 1912) T73 AJ109 109759
The offerings to thy throne which rise (Bowring) BX499 109760
The old year now away is fled (New Christmas carols, 1642) BG28 109761
The old year now hath passed away (Steuerlein. Seiben und zwantzig...) M368; O207; P145; Q125; AA173 109762
The old year's long campaign is o'er (Stone) BY718 109763
The one thing needful, that good part (Ingham) AZ353; BA444 109764
The only Son from heaven (Cruciger) O167; P114 109765
The parson knew that he had lost the eyes (Jean Ingelow) BW 144 109766
The passion theme pursuing (Zinzendorf, C.R.) AZ796 109767
The past is dark with sin and shame (Higginson) AN321; BX380 109768
The past yet lives in all its truth, O God! (Appleton) BX442 109769
The peace of God protects our hearts (Grundtvig) M134 109770
The peace which God alone reveals (Newton) AZ924 109771
The people of the earth go down (MacLeish) AQ112 109772
The people that in darkness sat (Morison) F80; Q106; AM123; BR155; BV133; BZ 109773
The perfect world, by Adam trod (Willis) I660 109774
The pity of the Lord To those that fear His name (Watts) V 661 109775
The praises of that Saint we sing (Antoniano) E193; BN 184 109776
The praises of thy wonders, Lord (Scottish Psalter, 1650) AM38 X O greatly blessed the people are 109777
The praying spirit breathe (Wesley) H56 109778
The Prince of Peace His banner spreads (Fosdick) Z553; AB356; AD357; AK409; BF 576 109779
The Queen, O God (Bridges) AL518 X The King, O God 109780
The race that long in darkness sat (Morison) E43; N41; R153; X96; AL60; AP167; BJ71; BY110 109781
The radiant morn hath passed away (Thring) B14; D8; E279; F19; G41; J222; K460; N561; O553; P334; S38; V51; W279; AL566; AP679; AT32; AZ11; BY708 109782
The radiant morn shines in the skies (Hermann) Q547 109783
The reproach of Christ is glorious (Gotter) AZ234 109784
The restless day now closeth (Gerhardt) N560 X The duteous day now closeth 109785
The riches of God are eternal (Wine) AR475 109786
The righteous ones shall be forever blest (Thai Christian's paraphrase) BZ 109787
The river of death has brimmed his banks (Newboldt) Y159 109788
The roseate hues of early dawn (Alexander) D409; E493; N 513; AZ1465 109789
The royal banner is unfurled (Fortunatus) AZ180 X The royal banners forward go 109790

The royal banners forward go (Fortunatus) A63; B144; D94; E94; F96; H166; J75; K91; Q 168; X130; AZ180, 324; BY 147 109791

The royal standard forward goes (Fortunatus) K91 X The royal banners forward go 109792

The Sabbath day has reached its close (Elliott) BB61 109793

The Sabbath day was by (Robbins) A100 109794

The Sabbath light is burning bright (Sampter) BH106 109795

The saint who enters heaven (Heatwole) AX432; AY165 109796

The Saint who first found grace to pen (Housman) E220; X 228 109797

The saints of God! Their conflict past (Maclagan) A128; B294; D175; F572; J145; K247; T439; W219; AO539; AP306; BA764; BL71 109798

The saints on earth and those above Q478 X Not to the terrors of the Lord (Watts) X Come, let us join our friends above (Wesley) 109799

The saints who toiled from place to place (Frere) F522 109800

The sands have been washed in the footprints (---) AU26 109801

The sands of time are sinking (Cousins) O597; S434; T440; U418; V677; W581; AH521; AI 336; AL465; AM599; AO544; AP 612; BA758; BY776 109802

The Saviour calls; let every ear (Steele) L356; Q281; V278; AA47; BY423 109803

The Saviour died, but rose again (Church of Scotland, 1745) BV 276 109804

The Saviour in Gethsemane Bows low in bitter agony (Petursson) M422 109805

The Saviour is risen, Light bursts from the tomb (Franzén) M443; N123 109806

The Saviour kindly calls (Doddridge) L321; Q302; AA406 109807

The Saviour lives, no more to die (Medley) AZ294 X I know that my Redeemer lives what joy [comfort] 109808

The Saviour! O what endless charms (Steele) H234; U69; V131; AO357; AY51; AZ1436 109809

The Savior reigns, The Lord most high (Plummer) BI27d 109810

The Saviour who loves me (Gray) AU44 109811

The Saviour's blood and righteousness (Eber & Zinzendorf) AZ278; BA445 109812

The Saviour's precious blood (Korean hymn) BY664)109813

The sea withdraws and fetters break (Franciscan manual) R If, now, thou seekest miracles 109814

The seasons are fixed by wisdom divine (U.P. Psalter, 1912) T198; AJ286 109815

The Seer, the Seer, Joseph, the Seer! (Taylor) BC296 109816

The sepulcher is holding (St Cosmas) AZ27; BA213 109817

The Seraphim of God Exalt their voices (Gregor) AZ 1119 109818

The service of Jesus true pleasure affords (Huston) AU414 109819

The shadows lengthen, Lord, with me abide (---) BB698 109820

The shadows of the evening hours (Proctor) B22; D15; G46; I62; S36; T314; U456; V38; Z142; AB24; AD51; AH 165; AL543; AN122; AO26: AP 678; AS26; AV13; AZ1458; BA 793; BB54; BF204; BX156 109821

The shepherds had an angel

(Rossetti) G436; S448; X372; AH547; AL601; AP732 109822
The Shepherd's heart is saddened (Newton) AX267; AY219 109823
The ships glide in at the harbor's mouth (Sangster) U333; AC 226; AL592 109824
The sky can still remember (Brooks) S123; AB112 109825
The sky has gathered the flowers of sunset (Torrence) AQ197 109826
The snow in the street and the wind in the door (Morris) R From far away we come to you 109827
The snow lay on the ground (Sedulius of Liege) A41; BQ8 109828
The snow lies thick upon the earth (Image) BG192 109829
The soldiers led the Saviour out (Petursson) M391 109830
The solemn moment is impending (Amilie Juliane) AZ696; BA 733 109831
The solemn season calls us now (Breviary, Paris, 1736) AO 267 109832
The Son of Consolation (Coote) B281; D162; E222; BV443 109833
The Son of God goes forth for Peace (Allen) Z559 109834
The Son of God goes forth to war (Heber) A549; B85; D507; E202; F529; G285; H394; I416; J562; K383; L530; M382; O491; Q452; R354; S271; U290; V491; W530; X216; Y118; Z358; AB251; AC 262; AD296; AE249; AF388; AG 196; AH444; AK288; AL409; AM 489; AO396; AP543; AT414; AU21; AV198; AZ1427; BA586; BB361; BF469; BR402; BV457; BY558; BZ 109835
The Son of God, the Prince of Peace (Maurer) AB252 109836
The Son of Man goes forth to war (Heber) BR402 X The Son of God goes forth to war 109837
The Son of Man goes forth today (Barstow) AK267 109838
The soul wherein God dwells (Scheffler) AQ92 109839
The Sower goeth forth to sow (Hoppe) N82 109840
The sower went forth sowing (Bourne) F486; BV652 109841
The spacious firmament on high (Addison) A309; B252; D464; E297; F170; G66; H 111; I84; J442; R97; S69; U 8; V100; W10; X659; Z164; AB48; AC47; AD97; AF72; AG57; AH188; AI41; AK66; AL27; AM103; AN33; AO59; AP142; AQ47; AR98; AS88; AT10; AV53; AW50; BA32; BB91; BD36; BF230; BK129; BV232; BX52; BY74; BZ 109842
The spacious firmament on high (Addison) X occasionally includes The starry firmament on high (Grant) 109843
The spacious heavens declare (U.P. Psalter, 1912) T28; AJ37 109844
The Spirit and the Bride (---) BA104 109845
The Spirit breathes upon the word (Cowper) H94 X A glory gilds the sacred page 109846
The Spirit, in our hearts (Onderdonk) D596; K319; L362; M25; O486; V265; AZ1330 109847
The Spirit of God like a fire is burning (Phelps) BC213 109848
The Spirit of the Lord revealed (Briggs) J251; X660; Z437; AD199; AW570; AX147 109849
The Spirit's fruits are peace and love (Cronenwett) M228 109850
The spirits of the just (Hart) AZ1486 109851
The splendours of thy glory,

Lord (Coffin) X35 109852
The spring again is here (Benson) AC319 109853
The springs of salvation from Christ the Rock bursting (Foster) AZ1090; BA363 109854
The stable was old and rude and bare (Wagner) BK158 109855
The star proclaims the King is here (Sedulius) Q131; AA180 109856
The starry firmament on high (Grant) I203; BE336 109857
The stars shall light your journey (Kendon) R What songs are these 109858
The stars they sing together (Cross) Y64 109859
The stars were silent and the hills stood dark against the sky (Royce) AW77 109860
The steps of those whom He approves (U.P. Psalter, 1912) R422; T66; AJ101 109861
The storm-god of stern Sinai's hill (Farrington) AD356 109862
The story grows sweeter and sweeter (Hoffman) R O, wondrously sweet 109863
The story that never grows old (Yates) R How dear to my heart 109864
The strain upraise of joy and praise ((St Notker) D461; E 494; W14; AP151 109865
The strife is o'er, the battle done (Latin, 1695) A91; B173; D121; E625; F135; G156; J90; K109; M434; O324; P198; Q210; R203; S164; T346; U105; V737; W122; X147; Z238; AB142; AC 133; AD167; AE128; AF181; AG 103; AH312; AI84; AK173; AL 109; AM201; AO177; AP216; AR190; AT107; AW116; BA237; BF323; BP39; BR183; BV192; BY163; BZ 109866
The summer days are come again (Longfellow) E288; W612; X8; AC321; AD452; AF457; AK431; AL576; AN138; AQ326; BD 46; BX167 109867
The sun arises now in light and glory (Kingo) M562; Q542 109868
The sun ascending, To us is lending (Gerhardt) M557 109869
The sun declines; o'er land and sea (Walmsley) K464; S40; W273; AP672 109870
The sun goes down, the shadows rise (Jewish) BH179 109871
The sun has gone down (Bruun) O554; P74 109872
The sun in splendor rose (Currie) BN46 109873
The sun is on the land and sea (Benson) S29; AI44; AK195; BB45 109874
The sun is sinking fast (Latin, 1805) A183; B17; D10; E 280; F30; K474; O564; W 272; AL569; AP680; BY709 109875
The sun is sinking in the west (Bersagel) P68 109876
The sun rolls down The distant west (---) BB59 109877
The sun shines in splendor (---) BK1 109878
The sun's bright rays are lost in sight (Hermann) M578 109879
The sun's last beam of light is gone (Hermann) Q563 109880
The sweet June days are come again (Longfellow) AQ326 X The summer days are come 109881
The tempter to my soul hath said (Montgomery) BB253 109882
The tender love a father has (U.P. Psalter, 1912) T191; AJ278; AM85 109883
The tenor of the gospel word (Heatwole) AY297 109884
The things of the earth in the earth let us lay (St Joseph the Hymnographer) L572;

N606 109885
The thought of Jesus, O how sweet (St Bernard of Clairvaux) P 101 109886
The time for toil is past (Akers) AX581; AY131 109887
The time is far spent, there is little remaining (Snow) BC184 109888
The time is near when Zion's sons (Cottrell) BB307 109889
The time of the harvest is nigh (Evilsizer) AX204; AY333 109890
The time shall come when, free as seas of wind (Pope) AQ199 109891
The toil of brain, or heart or hand (Freckelton) I414; AC189; AS240; BF440; BX227 109892
The touch of human hands (Clark) Y207; AC237 109893
The trepass of the wicked man (U.P. Psalter, 1912) T60; AJ 94 109894
The tribute of our thanks we bring (Fischer) M395 109895
The true Messiah now appears (Watts) V134 109896
The trumpet call of duty (Miles) BD94 109897
The trumpet is sounding, we're off to the fray (Smith) R At home and abroad 109898
The turf shall be my fragrant shrine (Moore) Y53 109899
The twilight falls the night is near (Cheevers. Commonplace book; 1831) AI52 109900
The twilight shadows round me fall (Ryden) J233; M569; N556 109901
The unbounded love of my Creator (Zinzendorf, N.L.) AZ1009 109902
The uplifted eye and bended knee (Scott) BX352 X The lifted eye and bended knee 109903
The very Angels' Bread Doth food to man afford (St Thomas Aquinas) BQ46 109904
The voice of free grace cries, "Escape to the Mountain!" (Burdsall) L368; AZ504 109905
The voice of God again is heard (Stephens) BC289 109906
The voice of God is calling (Holmes) G454; P407; Y235; Z490; AB284; AF426; AK387; AN316; AQ214; AR251; BD 158; BF499; BH238; BX541 BZ 109907
The voice that breathed o'er Eden (Keble) B383; D240; E348; N530; Q622; AA442; AO559; AP704; AT502 109908
The Wallapai, the Navaho (Brink) AI174 109909
The wanderer no more will roam (Walker) AZ1148 109910
The war in which the soldier fights (---) AY387 109911
The water's going out to sea (Masefield) AC468 109912
The way is dark, I dare not go alone (Lear) AS217 109913
The way is long and dreary (Proctor) O267 109914
The way of the cross leads home (Pounds) R I must needs go home by way of the cross 109915
The way that I take He knoweth (Hoffman) R He knoweth the way 109916
The way that unto Jesus leads (Kingo) P121 109917
The way, we know, is rough and weary! (Howard) BR536 109918
The whole bright world rejoices now (German carol. 1623) X167; AF194; BG96 109919
The whole wide world for Jesus, This shall our watchword be (Johnson) AE355; AO524; AS368; AV270; AW340; BY395 109920
The whole wide world for Jesus Once more, before we part

(Johnson??) AV270 X The whole wide world for Jesus, This shall our watchword be 109921

The whole world was lost in the darkness of sin (Bliss) AE 301; AI392; AM679; AR473; AT88; AU330; AW467; AX273 109922

The wicked watching for their prey (U.P. Psalter, 1912) T65; AJ99 109923

The will of God is always best (Albrecht v. Brandenburg) Q517 109924

The winds and the waves shall obey thy will (Baker) R Master, the tempest 109925

The winged herald of the day (Prudentius) E53 109926

The winter night was dark and still (Benson) AC80; AD122 109927

The winter's sleep was long and deep (Dearmer) E221; X229 109928

The wintry day, descending to its close (Whitney) BC292 109929

The wise may bring their learning (Barrett. Book of praise for children, 1881) G439; J 545; P357; W363; X373; Z316; AH273; AL590; AM657; AP779; AT513; AW418; BF616; BG121b BH246; BV351; BY528 109930

The wise men from the East adored (Greek) AZ562 109931

The wonderful! The Counsellor! (Crosby) R O, wondrous Name, by prophets heard 109932

The wonders of redeeming love (Cottrell) BB143 109933

The Word, descending from above (St Thomas Aquinas) BQ50 109934

The Word of God, proceeding forth (St Thomas Aquinas) E330; F384 109935

The Word of God which ne'er shall cease (Moravian) AZ315; BA1 109936

The Word, whose word can make me whole (Govan) BB203 109937

The work is thine, O Christ our Lord (Preiswerk) AK 269; AR562; AW550a 109938

The works, O Lord, our hands have wrought (Wilson) BX 501 109939

The world has need of willing men (Thompson) BC206 109940

The world in condemnation lay (Montgomery) AZ986 109941

The world is glad, the world is bright (Howe) AR588 109942

The world is very evil (St Bernard of Cluny) A595; B 68; D405; E495; F276; J596; K526; Q605; V689; AZ812; BA750; BR436 109943

The world itself is blithe and gay (---) AD166 109944

The world itself keeps Easter Day (Neale) AH304; BG150 109945

The world looks very beautiful (Warner) W575; AP765; BV 359 109946

The world of sinners know not God (Naylor) AX442 109947

The world stands out on either side (Millay) AQ57 X O God, I cried 109948

The world's astir! The clouds of storm (North) G562; AR536 109949

The world's great age begins anew (Shelley) X311 109950

The worst of evils we can name (Worgan) AZ1430 109951

The year begins with Thee (Keble) AA175 109952

The year is gone beyond recall (Breviary, Meaux, 1713) AW382; BW382 109953

The year is swiftly waning (How) E294; W621; X15; AW387 109954

The year of jubilee has come (Wesley) R Blow ye the trumpet, blow 109955
The year's at the spring (Browning) X6; Y57; AC431 109956
The Yigdal (Daniel ben Judah) X Praise to the living God (Jewish doxology 109957
The young child, Christ, is straight and wise (Sandberg) AC455 109958
Thee, Father, Spirit, Son, We joyfully adore (---) Lp. 741 109959
Thee God we praise, Thy holy name we bless (Latin, 5th c: Te Deum) P12 X Thee God we praise, Thy name we bless 109960
Thee God we praise, Thy name we bless (Latin, 5th c: Te Deum) O1; P12, 16 109961
Thee, God's Anointed, hail we our King (Hacker) R Great King of Kings and Lord of Lords 109962
Thee, holy Father, we adore (Laufer) S13 109963
Thee, living Christ, our eyes behold (Morgan) F422 109964
Thee, Lord, before the close of day (St Ambrose) BL74 109965
Thee, O Christ, the Father's splendour (St Rabanus Maurus) E241 109966
Thee prostrate I adore, the Deity that lies (St Thomas Aquinas) BQ48 109967
Thee we address in humble prayer (Wesley) AZ117; BA898 109968
Thee we adore, eternal Lord, We praise thy name with one accord (Latin, 5th c: Te Deum) J415; K281; L94; M598; N319; AA66; AI19; AM18; BA22 109969
Thee we adore, O hidden Saviour, Thee (St Thomas Aquinas) E331; F385; J272; W319; X 279; BR478; BY330 109970
Thee we praise, eternal Lord (Latin, 6th c) BR80 109971
Thee will I love, my God and King (Bridges) X661; BJ 99; BY75 109972
Thee will I love, my strength, my tower (Scheffler) J505; K301; M233; N469; O474; P309; Q399; W431; AA349; AK276; AL293; AP455; AR 118; AZ672; BA494; BV547 109973
Their God and Saviour they forgot (U.P. Psalter, 1912) T202; AJ291 109974
Then away, haste away (Baird) R When the rosy light of morning 109975
Then away to the work I will go (Henry) R I cannot be idle 109976
Then come, wanderer, come (Pratt) R Afar on the mountain 109977
Then day by day along your way (Pounds) R O scatter seeds 109978
Then drink to the holly berry (English trad) BG189 R On Christmas Eve the bells were rung (Scott) 109979
Then let men and Angels praise thee (Sister of Notre Dame) R Hail! All hail, great Queen of heaven 109980
Then let us adore, His heart that loves (Dollard) R On Calvary's height the Roman spear 109981
Then Mary took her young Son (English trad carol) X Joseph was an old man 109982
Then sings my soul, my Saviour God to thee (Boberg) R O Lord my God! When I in awesome wonder 109983
Then trim your lamps, my brethren dear (Belden) R Let every lamp be burning bright 109984
Then trust Him in shine and shade (Homer) R Fear not, for God 109985

Then, O my Lord prepare my soul (Bonar) R A few more years shall roll 109986
Then praises bring our Lord and King (Woods) R Now let us raise 109987
Then sing you all, both great and small (English trad carol) R When righteous Joseph wedded was 109988
Then stand! stand firm! defy the foe! (---) R Put on the armor 109989
Then trust in God thro' all thy days (Cornelius) R Not now, but in the coming Years 109990
Then wake up, and do something more (Thompson) R Have I done any good 109991
Then welcome each rebuff (Browning) X662 109992
Then we'll be happy with Christ (Jacobs) R When the trump shall sound 109993
Then why will ye die? (Penn) R There is a Rock 109994
Then work, brothers, work, let us slumber no more (Punshon) R Listen! The Master. 109995
Theories, which thousands cherish, Pass like clouds (Waterston) BE337 109996
There are a myriad means, O Lord (Dearmer) X663; Y2 109997
There are ooming changes great (Matheson) BF575 109998
There are hearts that never falter (---) AS335 109999
There are lonely hearts to cherish (Cooper) AU394; AX182 110000
There are loved ones in the glory (Habershon) AX613 110001
There are none friendless, none afraid (McKenzie) BE339 110002
There came a little Child to earth (Elliott) K540; W68; AP728 110003
There came three kings, ere break of day (Moultrie) K543; AO137 110004
There comes a ship asailing (German trad carol, 1470-80) BG90 110005
There comes to my heart one sweet strain (Bilhorn) U230; AE300; AI256; AR476; AT 299; AU381; AX336; BB609 110006
There dwelt in old Judea (Raymond) AH249 110007
There is a Balm in Gilead (Negro Spiritual) BZ 110008
There is a better world, they say (Lyth) AP793 110009
There is a blessed home (Baker) A591; B515; D679; E496; O615; V713; W594; AP630; AZ482; BA759 110010
There is a blessed hope (---) BB379 110011
There is a blessed power, that shields us from all woe (Aaberg) M129 110012
There is a book that all may read (Keble) Z435 X There is a book, who runs may read 110013
There is a book who runs may read (Keble) E497; F168; W8; X664; Z435; AB46; AN39; AZ118; BB92; BF239; BR368; BV134; BX59; BY76; 110014
There is a calm for those who weep (---) AY176 110015
There is a city bright (Deck) W480; AM662; AP792; BV493 110016
There is a dear and hallowed spot ("Anne") L246 110017
There is a flower springing (Speier Gebetbuch, 1599) BG76 110018
There is a fountain filled with blood (Cowper) D593; E332; G140; H232; I291; J373; K77; L238; N97; O314; P277; Q157; R276; S241; U150; V 251; W692; AA200; AE183;

AG98; AH286; AI140; AL491; AM188; AO272; AP203; AR 477; AT92; AU37; AV154; AW 492; AX118; AY236; AZ92; BA 201; BB163; BV509; BY148; BZ 110019

There is a gate that stands ajar (Baxter) N616; P263; AI408; AX250; BB561 110020

There is a gentle Gardener Who owns a garden fair (German) M625 110021

There is a God who reigns above (Watts) V685 110022

There is a green hill far away (Alexander) A65; B159; D544; E106; F214; G135; H242; J77; K544; M419; N108; P174; R 202; S157; U91; V752, 149; W105; X131; Z230; AB139; AD153; AE111; AF171; AG92; AH288; AK149, 479*; AL87; AM184; AO162; AP734; AR172; AS145; AT98; AU98*; AV106*; AW104; AZ1449; BA226; BB 126; BC201; BF314; BV163; BY149; BZ 110023

*Ref. attached

There is a happy land, Far, far away (Young) E608; W587; AP795; AS471; AZ1247; BB 301 110024

There is a holy sacrifice (Elliott) W408; AP424; AZ18; BA428 110025

There is a house not made with hands (Watts) L448; AZ155 110026

There is a joy the heart can feel (Loveman) BH79 110027

There is a land immortal (MacKellar) L603 110028

There is a land mine eye hath seen (Robins) H504 110029

There is a land of corn and wine (Stites) BB554 X I've reached the land of joy 110030

There is a land of pure delight (Watts) A586; B513; D678; E498; F285; G528; H508; I 604; J583; K518; L586; M298; N620; O611; U423; V699; W 592; X201; AA560; AG286; AH 528; AI340; AL464; AM597; AO549; AP634; AU216; AV 281; AX596; AY141; AZ176; BA760; BB299; BR435; BV436; BX468; BY614 110031

There is a land whose sunny vales (Huish) BC72 110032

There is a mystic tie that joins (Meyerhardt) BH137 110033

There is a name I love to hear (Whitfield) P143; AI387; AT131; AU283; AW496; AX 46; AY47; BB171; BV548 110034

There is a place of quiet rest (McAfee) R318; AE225; AR478; AT301; AU273; AW 239; AX50; BB681 110035

There is a road, though narrow and obscure (Aufranc) BB374 110036

There is a Rock in a weary land (Penn) AU23 110037

There is a safe and secret place (Lyte) O70; U35; V341; AE228; AO354; AZ 211; BB399 110038

There is a sea of mercy (Solberg) P255 110039

There is a spot to me more dear (Hunter) AX327; AY318 110040

There is a story ever new (Snyder) AX374; AY202 110041

There is a stream whose waters rise (Neale) BR439 110042

There is a voice of sovereign grace (Watts) L405 110043

There is an arm that never tires (Burton) AS268 110044

There is an everlasting home (Bridges) BQ69, 70 110045

There is an eye that never sleeps (Wallace) P25; AE 242; BH68; BV615 110046

There is an hour of hallowed peace (Tappan) M282 X There is an hour of hallowed rest 110047

There is an hour of hallowed rest (Tappan) L590; M282 110048
There is an hour of peace and rest, Unmarred by (---) BC172 110049
There is an hour of peaceful rest To mourning wanderers (Tappan) H503; I609; L592; Q617; V704; AA564; AO55; AY133 110050
There is an unseen hand to me (Sims) AX467 110051
There is beauty all around (McNaughton) AE384; AS413; AW360; AX555; AY444; BC169 110052
There is coming a day when to judgment we'll go (Winsett) AX297 110053
There is life for a look at the Crucified One (Hull) AX328 110054
There is never a day so dreary (Russell) AT142; AU69; AV367 110055
There is no love like the love of Jesus (Littlewood) BY424 110056
There is no name so sweet on earth (Bethune) AI388; AM652; AO624; AS397; AV138; AW440; AX22 110057
There is no night in heaven (Knollis) K522; W590; AM598; AP624 110058
There is no other hope (Hoffman) R O Lord, within my soul 110059
There is no other name than thine (---) AZ371; BA69 110060
There is no sorrow, Lord, too light (Crewdson) S295; W148; X665; Z342; AL127; AM517; AP239; AW259; AZ228; BV614 110061
There is no unbelief; who ever plants a seed (Case) AC486 110062
There is not a friend like Jesus (Hendricks) AX526 110064
There is nothing in the world like Jesus (Jones) AX271 110065
There is one way, and only one (Alexander) D160 110066
There is One whom I love (Payn) AI267 110067
There is pow'r, pow'r, wonder-working pow'r (Jones) R Would you be free 110068
There is rest by and by (Cosner) R Often weary 110069
There is rest for the weary (Harmer) R In the Christian's home 110070
There is rest, sweet rest, at the Master's feet (Hewitt) AU109 110071
There is sunlight on the hilltop (Haughey) BB612 110072
There is sunshine in my soul (Hewitt) AT273; BB607; BC174 110073
There is sweet rest for feet now weary (Belden) BB380 110074
There is sweet rest in heaven (Bone) R Farewell, all earthly honors 110075
There is sweet rest in heaven (Metzler) R When trials and temptations 110076
There is within this heart of mine (Walther) AA460 110077
There lives a God! Each finite creature (Hamburg Temple hymnal) BH61 110078
There lives a voice within me (Massey) BB281 110079
There many shall come from the east and the west (Landstad) O239 X Full many shall come 110080
There shall be no night in heaven (Hostetler) R Shadows never darken heaven 110081
There shall be showers of blessing (Whittle) AH389; AI262; AM716; AT264; AU97; AX37; BB652 110082
There still is room! His house is not yet filled (German) Q509 110083
There was a star in David's land (English trad carol)

BG54 110084
There was a time when children sang (Taylor) I684 110085
There was One who was willing to die (Breck) AU345; BB123 110086
There were ninety and nine that safely lay (Clephane) E584; F247; W685; AH373; AI181; AL475; AM137; AP408; AU36; AY501; BB673; BR532; BY425 110087
There were three lights that night (Turner) AD113 110088
Therefore we, before him bending (St Thomas Aquinas) A200; B 338b; E326b; F383b; X280 110089
There'll be no shadows in heaven (Cook) AX606 110090
There'll be no sorrow there (Dana) R O sing to me 110091
There's a beautiful, beautiful land (Brenneman) AX589; AY135 110092
There's a beautiful land on high (Nicholson) AY159 110093
There's a beautiful star, a beautiful star (Raymond) AC93 110094
There's a blessing in prayer (Hewitt) R There is rest, sweet rest 110095
There's a breathless hush in the close tonight (Newbolt) Yp423 110096
There's a call comes ringing o'er the restless wave (Gabriel) AT457; AU117; AV381; AX212; AY330 110097
There's a church in the valley (Pitts) AG295; AH515 110098
There's a city of light 'mid the stars (Kieffer) AX370; AY 153 110099
There's a cleft in the Rock of Ages (Good) AX511; AY447 110100
There's a dear and precious book (Williams) AH239; AU380 110101
There's a deep settled peace in my soul (Brown) R I cannot tell thee whence it came 110102
There's a fountain free, 'tis for you and me (Slade) AX 230 110103
There's a Friend for little children (Midlane) B363; D553; E607; F452; I680; J592; K 558; P360; W593; AH542; AO625; AP789; AS396; BA 813; BV358; BY615 110104
There's a garden where Jesus is waiting (Schroll) AU342; AX362 110105
There's a glad new song ringing (Fisher) AT311 110106
There's a God who's standing at heaven's door (Ellis) AX 282 110107
There's a great day coming (Thompson) AU333 110108
There's a Kingdom fair and gently looming (Overby) P205 110109
There's a land beyond the river (DeMarbelle) AU360 110110
There's a land that is fairer than day (Bennett) N621; U424; AH535; AT471; AU344; AV396; AW504; AX587; BB 551 110111
There's a light upon the mountains (Burton) G123; Y248; Z249; AB155; AC285; AR216; AT124; BF338 110112
There's a Rose that is blooming for you, friend (Palmer) AR479 110113
There's a royal banner given (Whittle) AT408; AU59 110114
There's a song in the air! There's a star in the sky (Holland) G98; I112; R155; Z198; AC84; AD118; AE87; AH257; AI65; AR131; AT69; BB106; BZ 110115
There's a Stranger at the door (Atchinson) AH337; AU29; AX246; BB566 110116
There's a sweet and blessed story (Johnston) AU382

110117
There's a voice in the wilderness crying (Milligan) G503; AD 373; AK94; AL244; BZ 110118
There's a way that is free from sin (Brooks) AX363 110119
There's a wideness in God's mercy (Faber) A304; B240; E499; F364; G76; H243; I98; J493; K257; L89; N435; P259; R110; S93; T320; U18, 146; V240; W395; X666; Y39; Z172; AB71; AC55; AD82; AE74; AF 101; AG54; AH180; AI37; AK85; AL468; AN556; AO256; AP397; AQ44; AR91; AS87; AT48; AU 182; AV64; AW58; AZ250, 959; BA407; BB65; BD58; BE340; BF250; BK67; BV480; BW58; BY419; BZ 110120
There's but a small beginning made (Stach) AZ283; BA358 110211
There's heaven above, and night by night (Browning) X667 110122
There's no other name like Jesus (Belden) BB517 110123
There's not a bird with lonely nest (Noel) L487; AB69; AC52; AS 98 110124
There's not a friend like the lowly Jesus (Oatman) AI396; AY352 110125
There's sunshine in my soul (Hewitt) BB607 X There is sunshine 110126
There's within my heart a melody (Bridgers) AT307; AU391 110127
There's work for the hand and there's work for the heart (---) AX192; AY520 110128
These are the gifts I ask of Thee (Van Dyke) Y206; AC472 110129
These scenes, so bright, now take their flight (Oatman) AY404 110130
These things shall be: a loftier race (Symonds) G512; S423; W639; X312; Y189; Z507; AB 355; AC293; AD363; AE400; AF450; AG278; AK407; AL 514; AN360; AQ190; AR576; BD181; BF563; BH237; BK 106; BX408; BY196; BZ 110131
They all were looking for a king (MacDonald) X668 110132
They are all gone into the world of light (Vaughan, the Silurist) X294 110133
They are nailed to the cross (Breck) BB123 X There was one who was willing 110134
They brought their gifts to Jesus (Rexford) BB658 110135
They cast their nets in Galilee (Percy) A437; R421; AF 340; AQ111 110136
They come from the east and west (Landstad??) BB453 110137
They come from the thorny path (Landstad??) R They come from the east and west 110138
They come, God's messengers of love (Campbell) E246; F287; K253; L566 110139
They in the Lord that firmly trust (Scottish Psalter, 1650) AL684; AP113 110140
They sailed! They sailed! Then spake the mate (Miller) AC510 110141
They saw the light shine out afar (Dearmer) BG165 110142
They that traffic on the sea (U.P. Psalter, 1912) T206; AJ295 110143
They the builders of the nation (Alldredge) BC173 110144
They to my precepts are always true (McPhail) R All those who love 110145
They were nailed to the cross (Breck) R There was One 110146
They who hunger after Christ, are fed (Foster) AZ514 110147

They who Jesus' followers are (Gambold) BA677 110148
They who know our Lord indeed (Gambold) BA504 110149
They who on the Lord rely (Auber. Spirit of the Psalms. 1829) BR261 110150
They who seek the throne of grace (Holden) I515; U361; V468; AE240; AK233; AO310; AR71; AY341; AZ66; BE341; BF374 110151
They who tread the path of labour (Van Dyke) Z496; AD319 110152
They whose course on earth is o'er (Neale) E500; F273; X 295 110153
Thine advent, Lord, we hail (Odhner) BI55 110154
Thine agony, O Lord, is o'er (Wallin) N119 110155
Thine are all the gifts, O God (Whittier) X331; AO505; AP 575 110156
Thine arm, O Christ, in days of old (Plumptre) BY637 X Thine arm, O Lord 110157
Thine arm, O Lord, in days of old (Plumptre) A517; D273; E526; F478; J324; K236; N 385; R179; W86; X287; AC111; AD137; AE102; AI70; AL76; AO147; AP186; AR153; AS119; AW95; AZ1441; BA860; BV399; BY637 110158
Thine be the glory (Budry) BV193 X Thine is the glory 110159
Thine earthly Sabbaths, Lord, we love (Doddridge) L594; V57 110160
Thine for ever [forever] ! God of love (Maude) A427; B370; D216; E344; F330; H303; J511; K179; M546; N252; O107; Q338; S248; W504; X258; AA411; AK 348; AL357; AO348; AP555; BA 472; BB282; BR463; BV364; BY586 110161
Thine for ever! Thine for ever (Wordsworth) BR461 110162
Thine for service when the days are drear (Leech) R I have made my choice to follow 110163
Thine holy day's returning (Palmer) L43; BR85 110164
Thine honor rescue, Christ our Lord (Heermann) AA275 X Thine honor save, O Christ 110165
Thine honor save, O Christ, our Lord! (Heermann) Q 265; AA275 110166
Thine is the glory, Risen, conquering Son (Budry) J566; R209; Z244; AE127; AF193; AR194; BV193; BY164; BZ 110167
Thine is the glory, Thine O Lord the praise (Woods) BK30 110168
Thine is the power, Lord, humbly we crave (Sangster) AO303 110169
Thine, O Jesus, now and ever (Oldenburg) P305 110170
Thine own, O loving Saviour (Franzén) J264; N235 110171
Think gently of the erring one (Carney) I699; AE381; BH 239 110172
Think not when you gather to Zion (Snow) BC21 110173
Think on our brethren, Lord (---) AZ551 110174
Think on thy way, O thou storm-laden child (Scholfield) AI206 110175
Thirsting for a living spring (Appleton) AB184; AN221; BX92 110176
Thirsting for the living Fountain, Streaming from (Hungarian Mass-song, 1855) BL45 110177
Thirty years among us dwelling (Fortunatus) E96 110178
This body in the grave we lay Q596 X Now lay we calmly in the grave 110179
This child was born to men of God (German carol, 17th c) BG97 110180

This child we consecrate to thee (Neander) AO434 X This child we dedicate 110181
This child we dedicate to thee (Neander) I232; Q303; AA404; AE327; AK331; AO434; BH240 110182
This day at thy creating word (How) Q12 X This day the light of heavenly birth 110183
This day in thy dear name we meet (Daries) AK41 110184
This day is holy to the Lord (Foster) AZ887; BA386 110185
This day the first of days was made (St Gregory the Great??) E50; BJ31 110186
This day the light of heavenly birth (How) K440; L42; Q12; V58; AA127; AM324 110187
This endris night (English trad carol, 15th c) BG39 110188
This Feast of the Law all your gladness display (Jewish hymn) BH199 110189
This God is the God we adore (Hart) H129; BV30 110190
This house we dedicate to thee (Naisbett) BC176 110191
This is my body, which is given for you (Ford) AO441 110192
This is my Father's world (Babcock) G72; J487; R101; S70; U332; Y51; Z171; AB64; AC39; AD93; AE55; AF485; AG60; AH202; AI32; AK65; AL589; AM109; AR99; AS94; AT59; AV406; AW48; BB646; BF399; BK26; BZ 110193
This is my prayer! Give me the strength lightly to bear my joys and sorrows (Tagore) AC 477 110194
This is my song, O God of all the nations (Stone) BK37; BZ 110195
This is my story, this is my song (Crosby) R Blessed assurance 110196
This is not my place of resting (Bonar) V701; AX582 110197
This is the charge I keep as mine (Hill) AQ147 110198
This is the day of light (Ellerton) B45; D28; F42; G397; H79; K442; R72; S20; W 267; Z446; AB10; AD35; AE 51; AK37; AL189; AM327; AP343; AR42; AS41; AW287; AZ1355; BB461; BF189; BR 93; BV68; BY282 110199
This is the day of rest (Ellerton) BB461 X This is the day of light 110200
This is the day that our Father hath given (Grundtvig) M12 110201
This is the day the Lord hath made; Be glad, give thanks (Randall) BE342 110202
This is the day the Lord hath made. He calls the hours his own (Watts) F43; H178; K443; L46; Q10; R69; S23; U436; V67; X23; AA129; AF504; AG34; AM326; AT39; AU280; AV7; AX122; AY 356; AZ131; BA392; BV74; BZ 110203
This is the day we celebrate (Schuette) M649 110204
This is the day where-on the Lord's true witness (Latin, 8th c) BN182 110205
This is the hour of banquet and of song (Bonar) A206 110206
This is the hour of banquet and of song (Bonar) X Here, O my Lord, I see thee face to face 110207
This is the image of our Queen (Caswall) BO77; BQ82 110208
This is the image of the Queen (Caswall) BQ82 X This is the image of our Queen 110209
This is the message that I bring (Cassel) R I am a stranger here 110210
This is the truth sent from above (English trad carol) BG68 110211

This joyful Eastertide, Away with sin and sorrow (Cowley Carol Book, 1902) AL110; BN45; BV197 110212
This new Christmas carol Let us cheerfully sing (English trad carol) BG29 110213
This night a wondrous revelation (Nachtenhöfer) M345; Q88 110214
This night, O Lord, we bless thee (Burns) AM349 110215
This rite our blest Redeemer gave (Phelps) AT384 110216
This sanctuary of my soul (Sorley) Y141 110217
This ship, we now commend to thee (Fergusson) AZ338 110218
This solemn hour O let us be (Erikson) M580; N578 110219
This stone to thee in faith we lay (Montgomery) W253; AX646; AZ306 110220
This, this is Christ the King (Dix) R What child is this, who laid to rest 110221
This thought shall have our whole allegiance (Goethe) AQ176 110222
This was the song the angels sang (Stephens) BC359 110223
Those eternal bowers Man hath never trod (St John of Damascus??) A581; B540; D395; AL 460 110224
Those who love and those who labour (Dearmer) X669; AF403 110225
Thou art coming, O my Saviour (Havergal) B67; D317; L579; S186; W157; AM235; AO113; AP245; AW126; AZ1203; BB196; BV87 110226
Thou art gone up on high (Toke) B189; D373; E149; F149; K 123; O368; AP230; AZ1497; BA244; BR198 110227
Thou art my God, O God of grace (U.P. Psalter, 1912) T113; AJ164 110228
Thou art my hiding-place, O Lord (Raffles) B403; K396; L492; AM 553; AZ1442 110229
Thou art my life; if thou but turn away (Quarles) X670 110230
Thou art my portion, Lord (U.P. Psalter, 1912) T232; AJ328 110231
Thou art my Shepherd, caring in every need (Thalheimer & Haycraft) AC54; AI303 110232
Thou art, O Christ, the light and life (Rominger) BB389 110233
Thou art, O God, the God of might (Perkins) S67; AI411 110234
Thou art, O God, the life and light (Moore) E298; X20; AB52; AN31; BX40 110235
Thou art our comfort, blessed Jesus (Tranecker) AZ999 110236
Thou art the Christ, O Lord (How) D164; F555; BV454 110237
Thou art the everlasting Word (Conder) BY219 110238
Thou art the mighty King of Kings (Hymns of the English Conf. 1880) BR66 110239
Thou art the way: by thee alone (Doane) BR390 X Thou art the way, to thee alone 110240
Thou art the Way, the Truth, the Life from heaven (Krummacher) N428; P214 110241
Thou art the Way, to thee alone (Doane) A361; B279; D425; F199; G332; H151; I133; J 390; K368; L120; M164; N 429; O339; Q355; R221; S 254; U81; V137; W173; AA 94; AG167; AK238; AL339; AM116; AO217; AP185; AR 177; AS121; AV172; AW185; AX341; AY209; AZ181; BA85; BE343; BR390; BV455; BY 220; BZ 110242
Thou by heavenly hosts adored (Harbaugh) K495 X Christ

by heavenly hosts adored 110243

Thou camest down from heaven on high (Hoppe) N87 110244

Thou city of the angels, thou city of the Lord (St Bernard of Cluny) BR438 X For thee, O dear, dear country 110245

Thou dear Redeemer, dying Lamb (Cennick) I532; AZ1450 110246

Thou delightest, O Lord, when thy children draw near (Wells) U37; AI18 110247

Thou didst leave thy throne and thy kingly crown (Elliott) A321; B83; D319; E585; F363; G95; H146; I122; J433; K541; N47; R184; S231; U79; W67; Z292; AB115; AC101; AD131; AE94; AF326; AG84; AH254; AK126; AL68; AM170; AO130; AP180; AR142; AT82; AU138; AV123; AX99; BA88; BB103; BF304; BV277; BY111 110248

Thou didst live to God alone (Wesley) E591c; F451c 110249

Thou didst teach the thronging people (Ninde) AK129 X Thou who taught 110250

Thou dost not weep to weep alone (Snow) BC181 110251

Thou dost reign on high (Elliott) AM170 X Thou didst leave thy throne 110252

Thou, earth, art ours, and ours to keep (Howitt) AN44; AQ307 110253

Thou ever-present Perfect Friend (Newman) BH41 110254

Thou fairest Child Divine (Tersteegen) AZ1491 110255

Thou Father of us all (Clark) AR577 110256

Thou glorious God, before whose face (Chadwick) AL37; AN462; BX437 110257

Thou, God, all glory, honour, power (Tate & Brady) D456 110258

Thou God of all, whose spirit moves (Holmes) Z554; AF419 110259

Thou God, whose living voice was heard (Holmes) Y254 110260

Thou goest to Jerusalem (Hoppe) N83 110261

Thou Grace divine, encircling all (Scudder) AD83; AN224; AW57; BF251; BX116 110262

Thou gracious God, whose mercy lends (Holmes) F502; G432; I669; W649; Z602; AE 387; AL392; AN264; AP702; AW359; AX557; BX496 110263

Thou gracious Power, whose mercy lends (Holmes) W649 X Thou gracious God, whose mercy lends 110264

Thou, gracious Saviour, for my good (Zinzendorf, N. L.) AZ218; BA840 110265

Thou great mysterious God unknown (Wesley) I318 110266

Thou hallowed chosen dawn of praise (St John of Damascus) X168 X Thou hallowed chosen morn of praise 110267

Thou hallowed chosen morn of praise (St John of Damascus) A93; E138; X168 110268

Thou hast canceled my transgression (Rist) AZ980 110269

Thou hast indeed made manifest (Hoppe) N73 110270

Thou hast no shore, fair ocean (St Bernard of Cluny) X 459b 110271

Thou hast, O Lord, most glorious (Scottish Psalter, 1650) AP59 110272

Thou hast said, exalted Jesus (Giles) AT390 110273

Thou hidden Love of God, whose height (Tersteegen) A464; B227; D658; G375; I345; J 391; K346; N485; O476; W 459; X671; AK321; AL307; AN82; AP462; BR317; BV 494; BX288; BY460; BZ 110274

Thou hidden Source of calm repose (Wesley) G339; I466; R 423; AG203; AL284; AM426; AZ 664; BB169; BR318; BX306; BY 587; BZ 110275

Thou hidden Source of calm repose (Wesley) X Thou hidden Love of God, whose height (Tersteegen) 110276

Thou holy Church, God's city shine (Landstad) O79 110277

Thou, Jehovah, art my Shepherd (U.P. Psalter, 1912) T36; AJ52 110278

Thou, Jesus, art our King (Scheffler) AZ1160; BA127 110279

Thou, Jesus! art the way (Hymns of the English conf. 1880) BR 30 110280

Thou Judge by whom each Empire fell (Dearmer) X672; AF442; AR614 110281

Thou judge of quick and dead (Wesley) L576; AP244 110282

Thou knowest, Lord, the weariness and sorrow (Borthwick) B402; D630; O556; AZ1201; BR348 110283

Thou knowest, Lord! Thou knowest my life's deep story (Hawkes) BX267 110284

Thou knowest my tongue, O God (Solomon ibn Gabirol) BH31 110285

Thou Lamb of God, Thou Prince of Peace (Richter) BR351 110286

Thou Life within my life, than self more near (Scudder) S320 AD282; AN81; BF383; BX106 110287

Thou Light of Gentile nations (Franck) Q138 X Light of the Gentile nations 110288

Thou little flock, be not afraid (Altenburg) M90 110289

Thou living light of pentecostal glory (Goodenough) BE345 110290

Thou long disowned, reviled, oppressed (Scudder) X673; BX 78 110291

Thou, Lord, art Love (Burns) AI38 110292

Thou, Lord, by strictest search hast known (Tate) AP122; BR279 110293

Thou, Lord, hast dealt well with thy servant (U.P. Psalter, 1912) T233; AJ329 110294

Thou, Lord, has forsaken, to shame brought our boasts (U.P. Psalter, 1912) T82; AJ122 110295

Thou, Lord, hast given thyself for our healing (Browne) BY396 110296

Thou, Lord, hast power to heal (Greek: Paracletice) E349 110297

Thou, Lord, must for thy sake forgive (Wesley) AZ101 110298

Thou Lord of all above (Beddome) L387; AO268 110299

Thou Lord of Hosts, whose guiding hand (Frothingham) J305; AN310; BD77; BX376 110300

Thou Lord of life and death (Hoppe) N197 110301

Thou Lord of life, our saving health (Longfellow) Y218; Z309; AB261; AN469; AR 363; BX255 110302

Thou Lord of light, across the years (North) AC257; AK 365 110303

Thou lovely source of true delight (Steele) U136; V72; AO212 110304

Thou loving Saviour of mankind (St Gregory the Great) AO 158 110305

Thou mighty God who didst of old (Chadwick) AN422; BX 440 110306

Thou must be true thyself (Bonar) AS445 110307

Thou must increase, Lord, and I must decrease; yes, I offer (Jensen) M212 110308

Thou my everlasting portion (Crosby) G235; I332; Z413; AE299; AH324; AI269; AR

482; AS220; AT354; AU223; AV382; AX384; BZ 110309
Thou my sure portion art alone (Scottish Psalter, 1650) AP 107d 110310
Thou, O Almighty, knowest all, (Moses ibn Ezra) BH158 110311
Thou, O Christ of Calvary (Moore) AT189 110312
Thou, O Jehovah, shalt endure (U.P. Psalter, 1912) T187; AJ273; AM25 110313
Thou, O Lord, art God alone (U.P. Psalter, 1912) T102; AJ275 110314
Thou One in all, thou All in One (Beach) AN64; BX54 110315
Thou, our Light, our Guiding-star (Tribbechovius) AZ867 110316
Thou perfect Hero-Knight (Pullen) BY529 110317
Thou Power and Peace in whom we find (Alexander) S211; BX 373 110318
Thou rulest, Lord, the lights on high (Williams) AN37; BX 242 110319
Thou sayest, "Take up thy cross" (Palgrave) B246; X120; AB206; AL450; AN212; BX220 110320
Thou shalt arise, and mercy yet (Scottish Psalter, 1650) AL670; AP89; AW595 110321
Thou Shepherd of Israel, and mine (Wesley) AZ1509 X Thou Shepherd of Israel divine 110322
Thou Shepherd of Israel divine (Wesley, J & C) L431; AZ1509 110323
Thou Son of God, whose flaming eyes (Wesley) I245 110324
Thou, sore apprest, the sabbath-rest (Strauss) AZ509 110325
Thou spotless Lamb of God (Maurice) AX310 110326
Thou standest at the altar (Eddis) W315 110327
Thou Sun of love, whose radiant light (Stennett) BR57 110328
Thou sweet gliding Kedron, by thy silver streams (DeFleury) L244 110329
Thou that art so fair and bright (Latin, 13th c) BN139; BP 78 110330
Thou that once, on mother's knee (Palgrave) AP740 X Thou who once on Mother's knee 110331
Thou thinkest, Lord, of me (Mund) X Amid the trials which I meet 110332
Thou to whom the sick and dying (Thring) D274; E527; F477; J464; K234; N389; O274; W352; AO484; AP573; AW370; BA856; BR166; BY 638 110333
Thou true vine, that heals the nations (Dearmer) X674; AR206; AW234 110334
Thou very present Aid (Wesley) V366 110335
Thou virgin-born incarnate Word (Hoppe) N14 110336
Thou visitest the earth in love (U.P. Psalter, 1912) AJ169 110337
Thou visitest the earth with showers (U.P. Psalter, 1912) AJ167 110338
Thou warrior angel of the Lord, St Michael (---) BP89 110339
Thou wast, O God, and thou wast blest (Mason) X675 110340
Thou who a tender Father art (---) N536 110341
Thou who art enthroned above (Sandys) BX21 110342
Thou who art enthroned in glory (Pierson) AO532 110343
Thou who art three in Unity (St Ambrose) M476; AA266 110344
Thou, who at thy first Eucharist didst pray (Turton) A191; B337; D230; E324; F402 110345
Thou, who didst call thy saints of old (Welch) AZ1428 110346
Thou, who didst make and fash-

ion me (U.P. Psalter, 1912) T234; AJ330 110347
Thou who didst on Calvary bleed (Burns) W690; AZ1136 110348
Thou who didst stoop below (Miles) W147 110349
Thou who dost rule on high (Littlewood) BY670 110350
Thou who hast called us by thy word (Bode) AO261 110351
Thou who hast in Zion laid (Bulmer) AZ1482 110352
Thou who hast known the care-worn breast (Rawson) AP665 110353
Thou who, hero-like hast striven (Drane) BO138 110354
Thou, who on that wondrous journey (Alford) D77; AO471 110355
Thou who once on mother's knee (Palgrave) X374; AP740; BY 756 110356
Tho who rollest the year around (Palmer) Q111; U477; V630; AA165; AO572 110357
Thou, who sentest thine apostles (Ellerton) D173; E248; F568 110358
Thou who taught the thronging people (Ninde) AC113; AK129 110359
Thou who the night in prayer (Wordsworth) D184; N282; Q 493; AA492; BT493 110360
Thou who thyself didst sanctify (Rawson) AW297 110361
Thou who wast a child on earth (Doddridge) M521 110362
Thou who wast rich beyond all splendour (Houghton) BV101 110363
Thou, whom shepherds worshipped, hearing (Latin, 1410) F596 110364
Thou, whose almighty word (Marriott) A272; B104; D327; F266; G477; I629; J309; K217; L182; M111; N370; O123; Q508; S392; V82; W364; X303; Z536; AD384; AI176; AL240; AM376; AO522; AP372; AR566; AS371; AT461; AV259; AZ1235; BA13; BB451; BE346; BV333; BY46; BZ 110365
Thou whose birth on earth, Angels sang to men (Swinburne) X81 110366
Thou, whose coming seers and sages (Spitta) O191 110367
Thou, whose glad summer yields (Johnson) BX460 110368
Thou whose love brought us to birth (Foote) AN193 110369
Thou whose name is called Jesus (Pigott) BV278 110370
Thou whose spirit dwells in all (Chadwick) AN65; BX95 110371
Thou, whose unmeasured temple stands (Bryant) G549; I659; J246; L300; N278; S476; U 384; V568; Z605; AC525; AD412; AE346; AG294; AK 357; AN461; AO463; AP698; AS441; AX645; BA327; BX 498 110372
Thou Wind of God, whose coming stirred (Crum) F440 110373
Thou, with thy counsel, while I live (Scottish Psalter, 1650) AP62 110374
Though all my foes combine (---) BR311 110375
Though angels bright escape our sight (Loy) M484 110376
Though but a little child I am (Cennick) AZ328 110377
Though by nature I'm defiled (Gregor) AZ1086 110378
Though deepening trials throng your way (Snow) BC285 110379
Though faint, yet pursuing (Darby) D628; U47; V508; AI305; AO323; AY309; AZ502; BR383 110380
Though Fatherland be vast and fair (Cross) Y119; AB364; BF568 110381
Though I am poor and sorrow-

ful (U.P. Psalter, 1912) T126; AJ187 110382
Though I speak with angel tongues (Lange) AO370; AZ1272 110383
Though I'm in body full of pain (Cennick) AZ343 110384
Though in midst of life we be (Latin, 12th c) O240 110385
Though in the outward Church below (---) BC102 110386
Though lowly here our lot may be (Gaskell) AW374 X Though lowly here our work may be 110387
Though lowly here our work may be (Gaskell) W515; X676; AB 272; AW374; BD99 110388
Though man, the fiery element, sinks like fire (Holmes) AQ 61 110389
Though mighty foes assail me, Lord (U.P. Psalter, 1912) T245; AJ341 110390
Though mountains may depart from thee (Lias) BE347 110391
Though nature's strength decay (Jewish doxology) AZ1192 X The God of Abraham praise 110392
Though others may forsake the Lord (Childress) R Upon the first day 110393
Though our hearts dwell lovingly (Sternberg) BH228 110394
Though the angry surges roll (Martin) AH387; AM717 110395
Though the way we journey may be often drear (Jones) AT474 110396
Though troubles assail, and dangers affright (Newton) I92; N476; P300; W30; AI306; AM79; BR244; BY588 110397
Though troubles assail us, and dangers affright (Newton) N476 X Though troubles assail, and dangers affright 110398
Though troubles great o'ershadow me (U.P. Psalter, 1912) AJ 191 110399
Though we all in sinful blindness (Palgrave) N173; O402 110400
Though we long, in sin-wrought blindness (Palgrave) O402 X Though we all in sinful blindness 110401
Though your sins be as scarlet (Crosby) U159; AH384; AI198; AM465; AT213; AU350 110402
Thousand times by me be greeted (St Bernard of Clairvaux) AZ906 110403
Thousands, O Lord of hosts, today (Montgomery) BA858 110404
Three in One and One in Three (Rorison) B38; D389; E501; F163; AS70; AZ1134; BA259; BV230; BY47 110405
Three kings are here, both wealthy and wise (Flemish trad carol) BG80 110406
Three kings from Persian lands afar (Cornelius) BG193 110407
Three kings in great glory of horses and men (Image) BG 194 110408
Thrice blest is he to whom is given (Faber) AB237 X God's glory is a wondrous thing 110409
Throned upon the awful [awe-ful] tree (Ellerton) E116; F119; K104; Q174; R197; W100; X141; AF174; AL92; AM183; AP191; AW109; BV177 110410
Through all the changing scenes of life (Tate) E502; F290; G14; J420; L475; O454; Q29; S83; V105; X677; AA75; AF81; AL643; AM522; AO342; AP 31; AW583; AY365; AZ192; BA656; BV512; BY589; BZ 110411
Through all the long dark night of years (Massey) X313; AQ169 110412
Through all the various shifting scene (Collett) BX244

110413

Through all the years, may Israel say (U.P. Psalter, 1912) T259; AJ361 110414

Through good report and evil, Lord (Bonar) K259; L479; W514; AM503; AZ8; BA475; BR385 110415

Through Him who all our sickness felt (Wesley) B505; D588 110416

Through Jesus' blood and merit (Dach) Q372; AA323 110417

Through Jesus' bloody merit (Dach) AA323 X Through Jesus' blood and merit 110418

Through life's long day and death's dark night (Faber) R O Saviour bless us 110419

Through love to light! O wonderful the way (Gilder) G599; S499; AB230; BF196 110420

Through love to light! O wonderful the way (Gilder) BF196 X Hail gladdening light (Greek) 110421

Through midnight gloom from Macedon (Stone) O118; AZ 654 110422

Through north and south and east and west (Dearmer) A540; X415; AN506 110423

Through the dark the dreamers came (Marlatt) Y327; AC91; AD128 110424

Through the day thy love has kept us (Kelly) BR110 X Through the day thy love has spared us 110425

Through the day thy love has spared us (Kelly) B15; D646; E281; F25; K478; L35; M567; N562; O563; Q553; V52; AA 43; AL561; AO41; AP685; AZ603; BA792; BR110 110426

Through the day thy love hath spared us (Kelly) BA792 X Through the day thy love has spared us 110427

Through the love of God our Father (Peters) P296; W702; AV230; BE350; BF398; BY590 110428

Through the love of God our Saviour (Peters) W702 X Through the love of God our Father 110429

Through the night of doubt and sorrow (Ingemann) A394; B539; D521; E503; F292; H424; I567; J529; K201; L 301; O86; P82; Q481; R475; S345; W214; X678; Y305; Z481; AB239; AD219; AF 387; AG235; AH431; AK415; AL448; AN433; AO653; AP 603; AZ971; BA278; BD142; BE351; BF661; BV566; BX 446; BY559 110430

Through the night thy angels kept (Canton) E609; F429; X375 110431

Through thee as we together came (---) BR106 110432

Through willing heart and helping hand (Hosmer) AN457; BX494 110433

Through-out the night, O God above (Wise) BH244 110434

Throughout these forty days, O Lord (Hernaman) BM75 X Lord, who throughout these forty days 110435

Throw away thy rod, Throw away thy wrath (Herbert) AP485 110436

Throw out the life-line (Ufford) AH415; AT217; AU72; AX188; BB624 110437

Thus angels' Bread is made the Bread of man (St Thomas Aquinas) BP52 110438

Thus far the Lord hath [has] led me on (Watts) I51; V56; AA39; AO100; BR273 110439

Thus saith the mercy of the Lord (Watts) AI160 110440

Thus speaks the Lord to wicked men (U.P. Psalter, 1912) T95; AJ138 110441

Thy beauty, Lord, thou hast revealed (Brightman) Y32 110442

Thy blessing, Lord, on all vacation days (Haley) AD453

110443
The blood, so dear and precious (Praetorius) AZ795; BA498 110444
Thy blood, thy blood the deed hath wrought (Gersdorf) AZ230 110445
Thy bounties, gracious Lord (Scott) Z421 110446
Thy broken body, gracious Lord (---) BB471 110447
Thy ceaseless, unexhausted love (Wesley) H236; AL12; BY31 110448
Thy children, Lord, of many lands and nations (Stevenson) AB215 X Thy people, Lord, of many lands and nations 110449
Thy cross, O Jesus, thou didst bear (Geijer) M385; N105; P173 110450
Thy faithful servant, Lord, doth yearn (Solomon ibn Gabirol) BH167 110451
Thy glory thou didst manifest (Higbee) AO141 110452
Thy gospel, Jesus, we believe (---) A249 110453
Thy grace impart! In time to be (Whittier) Y263 X Forgive, O Lord, our severing ways 110454
Thy hand, O God, has guided (Plumptre) E545; F256; J159; W215; Y268; AC307; BV426; BY264 110455
Thy heaven, on which 'tis bliss to look (Moore) X679 110456
Thy holy day's returning (Palmer) BR85 X Thine holy day's returning 110457
Thy holy Sabbath, Lord (---) BB470 110458
Thy kingdom come! O Father hear our prayer (Seebach) J318 110549
Thy kingdom come, O God (Hensley) A544; B105; D329; F262; J329; V605; W152; Y262; AL140; AN 340; AP251; AW271; AZ483; BA107; BV334; BX388; BY397 110460
"Thy Kingdom come!" O Lord, we daily cry (Hawkes) AB 297; AN333; AW356; BX386 110461
Thy kingdom come, O Lord, wide-circling (Hosmer) A534; R488; S425; T443; Z562; AD 366; AE365; AF448; AK403; AL526; AN339; AO486; AQ 210; AR568; AS359; AW270; BD157; BF580; BX387 110462
Thy kingdom come! on bended knee (Hosmer) A391; B56; E504; F263; G463; J331; R484; S363; T371; U331; W153; X680; Z539; AD345; AK369; AL138; AN338; AP 249; AW268; BA360; BB193; BD155; BX458; BY398 110463
Thy kingdom, Lord, Thy kingdom (Scudder) Y237; AB 287; AD346; AR217; BF573 110464
Thy kingdom, Lord, we long for (Scudder) AB287 X Thy kingdom, Lord, Thy kingdom 110465
Thy law is perfect, Lord of light (Montgomery) AZ125; BA6 110466
Thy life was given for me (Havergal) B238; D604; J 513; K67; L233; O431; P329; R262; S229; U92; V154; Z 289; AA352; AM536; AP550; AR339; AZ553; BA473; BV 643 110467
Thy little ones, dear Lord, are we (Brorson) J49; M609; O179; P366; AI383 110468
Thy love, O gracious Lord and God (Kingo) O434 110469
Thy love to me, O Christ (Gates) AS284 110470
Thy loving-kindness, Lord, is good and free (U.P. Psalter, 1912) R393; T128; AJ187; AM510 110471
Thy majesty, how vast it is (Scheffler) AZ987-988; BA 130 110472

Thy mercy and thy truth, O Lord (U.P. Psalter, 1912) R82; T61; AJ94; AM55 110473
Thy mercy, Lord, is in the heavens (Rouse) V98; AL646; AP34 110474
Thy mercy, Lord, to us dispense (Luther) AZ1425; BA339 110475
Thy might sets fast the mountains (U.P. Psalter, 1912) R99; T 118; AJ171; AM111; BZ 110476
Thy mighty love, O God, constraineth me (Crawford) BB63 110477
Thy mighty power we sing (Hymns of the English Conf. 1880) BR 79 110478
Thy palm-trees fed with dew and sun (Bates) AC114 110479
Thy people, Lord, of many lands and nations (Stevenson) Y90; AB215 110480
Thy praise, O Lord, will I proclaim (Jewish: "A'ameer") BH183 110481
Thy oresence, gracious God, afford (Fawcett) AA4; AY3; AZ 316; BA394 110482
Thy promised mercies send to me (U.P. Psalter, 1912) T 230; AJ326 110483
Thy sacred word, O Lord, of old (Petri) M488; N215 110484
Thy saints are crowned with glory great ("F.B.P.") X395c 110485
Thy scepter, Jesus, shall extend (Franzén) N265 110486
Thy seamless robe conceals thee not (Chadwick) BX112 110487
Thy servant, blest by thee, shall live (U.P. Psalter, 1912) T 227; AJ323; AM260 110488
Thy soul, O Jesus, hallow me (Scheffler) M426; AA206 110489
Thy spirit, Lord, has stirred our souls (Kooyman) BC204 110490
Thy spirit, O Lord, makes life to abound (U.P. Psalter, 1912) AJ287 110491
Thy table I approach (Molanus) M47; Q310; AA430 110492
Thy temple is not made with hands (Alexander) D295; H413 110493
Thy tender mercies, O my Lord (U.P. Psalter, 1912) T74; AJ110 110494
Thy vineyards and thy orchards are ("F.B.P;") X395d 110495
Thy voice hath spoken, souls have heard (Maxwell) BB36 110496
Thy walls are made of precious stones ("F.B.P.") X395b 110497
Thy way and all thy sorrows (Gerhardt) O284 110498
Thy way is in the deep, O Lord (Martineau) AN186; AW242; BX250 110499
Thy way is in the sea (Fawcett) H125; L478; V416 110500
Thy way, not mine, O Lord (Bonar) B394; D632; E505; F356; I527; K393; L503; Q 532; U38; V430; W553; AA 384; AE268; AL425; AM573; AO339; AP506; AS243; AW 252; AZ473; BA688; BB396; BF406; BR324; BV644 110501
Thy way, O God, is in the sea (Fawcett) L478 X Thy way is in the sea 110502
Thy ways, O Lord! with wise design (Serle) L476; Q530; AA514 110503
Thy will, almighty Father, Thine and thine alone ("H") BE349 110504
"Thy will be done!" In devious ways (Bowring) AO700; BI 57 110505
Thy will be done in me (McKinney) AU103, AX390 X My God, my Father (Elliott) 110506
Thy will, O Lord, not mine (Daniels) BR307 110507
Thy wondrous testimonies,

Lord, my soul will keep (U.P. Psalter, 1912) T241; AJ 337 110508
Thy word is a lamp to my feet (Sellers) AI155; AM671; AT 180; AU389; AV372; AX141 110509
Thy word is like a garden, Lord (Hodder) P88; S219; AC70; AD191; AI159; AM257; AR241; AT182; AW290; BF273; BK24; BY253 110510
Thy word is to my feet a lamp (Tate & Brady) BH36 110511
Thy word, O God, declareth (Walther) J585; K523 110512
Thy word, O Lord, like gentle dews (Garve) J254; K171; N219; O136; P84; AI154; BR 240 110513
Thy word sheds light upon my path (U.P. Psalter, 1912) T238; AJ334 110514
Thy works, how beauteous, how divine (Coxe) BE352 X How beauteous were the marks divine 110515
Thy works, not mine, O Christ (Bonar) K68; N89; Q380; AA329; AM441; AZ1186 110516
Tibi, Christe, splendor Patris (St Rabanus Maurus) BT257 110517
Tidings true there be come new (English trad carol, 15th c) BG36 110518
"Till he come!" O, let the words (Bickersteth) H440; I240; T 365; V550; W321; AI162; AM357; AP359; AS462; AV257; AZ1252; BA305; BV388 110519
Till permitted hence to go (Gregor) AZ35 110520
Till we meet, till we meet (Rankin) R God be with you 110521
Time is filled with swift transition (Wilson) AX446 110522
Time is gliding like the shuttle of the weaver (Oatman) AX127 110523
'Tis a pleasant thing to see (Lyte) AZ1281; BA665 110524
'Tis a point I long to know (Newton) V481 110525
'Tis a sweet and tender story (Wight) AY522 110526
'Tis almost time for the Lord to come (Sederquist) BB 182 110527
'Tis by the faith of joys to come (Watts) L507; V363; BB242 110528
'Tis by thy strength the mountains stand (Watts) V621 110529
'Tis faith supports my feeble soul (Beddome) V350 110530
" 'Tis finished!" Jesus cries, He bows his head and dies (Foster) AZ547 110531
'Tis finished now, Redemption's finished now (Gregor) AZ 1228 110532
" 'Tis finished!" so the Saviour cried (Stennett) H160; I149; M421; N110; P189; U10; V 144; BB535 110533
'Tis finished! the Messiah dies (Wesley) H165; BZ 110534
'Tis from the mercy of our God (Watts) AP163 110535
'Tis God the Spirit leads (Beddome) BE354 110536
'Tis gone, that bright and orbéd blaze (Keble) AN108 X Sun of my soul 110537
'Tis good, Lord, to be here! (Robinson) E236; F560; K49; Q135; BV256; BY131 110538
'Tis hard to bear the heavy load (Hott) AY322 110539
'Tis midnight; and on Olive's brow (Tappan) G133; H163; I147; L241; N100; R189; T341; U96; V151; Z232; AD144; AE118; AF178; AG92; AH283; AK145; AM182; AO 161; AR163; AS132; AT104; AU295; AV105; AW103; AX 114; AY360; BA223; BB121; BZ 110540
'Tis midnight and the Saviour

calls (Buerge) AX242 110541
'Tis my happiness below (Cowper) V422; BB248 110542
'Tis not that I did choose thee (Conder) U156; V241; AI126; AM96; AZ840; BT37 110543
'Tis not the large, the huge, the vast (Cronbach) BH235 110544
'Tis not with eyes of flesh we see (Garber) AR275 110545
'Tis religion that can give (Masters) AS296 110546
'Tis so sweet to trust in Jesus (Stead) AE302; AI236; AM699; AR276; AS272; AT258; AU284; AV322; AW488; AX458; AY98; BB588; BZ 110547
'Tis sure that awful time will come (Ringwaldt) AZ747; BA735 110548
'Tis sweet to sing the matchless love (Manwaring) BC187 110549
'Tis the blessed hour of prayer (Crosby) Z332; AE238; AP 496; AR481; AS42; AT329; AU156; AX352; AY430; BB 324 110550
'Tis the day of Resurrection (St John of Damascus) BP34 X The day of Resurrection 110551
'Tis the grandest theme thro' the ages rung (Ogden) AT198 110552
'Tis the harvest time, 'tis the harvest time (Thomas) AX206; AY336 110553
'Tis the Lord! O wondrous story (Hanby) R Who is He in yonder stall? 110554
'Tis the month of our Mother (---) AH136; BN61 110555
'Tis the most blest and needful part (Zinzendorf, C.R.) AZ 879; BA532 110556
'Tis the promise of God full salvation to give (Bliss) AV 156; AW442 110557
'Tis thine alone, Almighty Name (Hatfield) AZ213 110558
'Tis true, O, yes, 'tis true (Morris) R For God so loved 110559
'Tis winter now; the fallen snow (Longfellow) E295; W623; X16; AF455; AL581; AN133; AP693; AQ301; AW384; BD54; BH198; BX 170; BY723 110560
To all the nations, Lord (Tiplady) Z552 110561
To avert from men God's wrath (Hus) AZ1260; BA 304 110562
To be alive in such an age! (Morgan) AC518 110563
To Bethel came the patriarch (Mendes) BH49 110564
To bless the earth God sendeth (U.P. Psalter, 1912) BZ X Thy might sets fast the mountains 110565
To bless thy chosen race (Tate & Brady) D500 110566
To Christ, the king of glory (---) AZ28 110567
To Christ, the Prince of Peace (Latin, 18th c) F198; BQ 63; BR184 110568
To Christ we homage pay (Benade) AZ1166; BA800 110569
To cloisters of the spirit (Gannett) AQ260 X God laid his rocks in courses 110570
"To Damascus!" Paul had shouted (Dearmer) X222 110571
To every man there openeth (Oxenham) AC232 110572
To Father, Son, and Holy Ghost, Be praise (---) Lp741 110573
To Father, Son, and Holy Ghost, One God, whom we adore (Tate & Brady) G617; Lp741; N665; X416; AL629; AO705; AZ144; BA925 110574
To Father, Son, and Holy Ghost, Our God forever (---) Lp743 110575
To Father, Son and Holy Ghost The God, whom we adore (Tate & Brady) AO705 X

To Father, Son, and Holy Ghost, One God, whom we adore 110576
To Father, Son, and Spirit blest, Supreme o'er (---) Lp744 110577
To Father, Son and Spirit, Eternal One in Three (---) AZ26 110578
To Father, Son, and Spirit, ever blest (---) AZ446 110579
To Father, Son, and Spirit, From earth let praise (---) Lp742 110580
To Father, Son, and Spirit, God ever Three in One (---) Lp742 110581
To God be glory, peace on earth (Tate & Brady. Suppl. 1700) M11; AA74 110582
To God be honor, laud and praise. (Darmstadt G-B. 1698) M146 110583
To God be the glory, great things he hath done (Crosby) AI142; AM667; AT41; BB647; BV280; BY32 110584
To God for help will I repair (U.P. Psalter, 1912) T141; AJ209 110585
To God I lift mine eyes, From God is all mine aid (Watts) L488; AO338 110586
To God I lift mine eyes, My trust is in His Name (---) BR32 110587
To God let all the human race (Melanchthon) AZ346 110588
To God my earnest voice I raise (U.P. Psalter, 1912) R387; T279; AJ387; AM509 110589
To God on high be thanks and praise For mercy ceasing never (Decius) I93; AH624 110590
To God on high be thanks and praise, Who deigns our bonds (Ball) AN488 110591
To God our Father, Builder and Creator (Mary Francis, Sr.) BN210 110592
To God our hearts we lift (Tiplady) Z176 110593
To God, our Immanuel, made flesh as we are (Gregor) AX491 110594
To God the anthem raising (Eber) O209; Q112 110595
To God the Ever-glorious (---) N668 110596
To God, the everlasting, who abides (Symonds) X681 110597
To God the Father, God the Son (Wilhelm II, Duke) Lp741, p743; AZ658; BA924 110598
To God, the Father of all love (Schütz) AA60 110599
To God the Father, Son and ever blessed Spirit (Hatfield) LP742 X To God the Father, Son, and Spirit ever blest 110600
To God the Father, Son, and Spirit, ever blest O(Hatfield) Lp742; AZ1184 110601
To God the Father, Son, and Spirit, One in Three (Wesley) Lp741; N667 110602
To God the Father, Son, and Spirit, The everlasting Three in One (---) Lp744 110603
To God -- the Father, Son, and Spirit -- Three in One (---) Lp742; AZ1246 110604
To God, the Father, Spirit, Son (---) BR544 110605
To God the Father's throne, Perpetual honors raise (---) AZ1307 110606
To God the Father's throne, Your highest honors raise (---) Lp741; AZ1185 110607
To God the only wise (Watts) G618; K305; L93; AL627; AO71; AP815; AW616; AZ 1297; BA117; BZ 110608
To God we render praise (Simpson) AZ1123; BA761 110609
To God who makes all lovely things (Crum) X376 110610
To God will I direct my prayer

(U.P. Psalter, 1912) AJ210 110611
To God, with heart and cheerful voice (Wither) X176 110612
To God your every want In instant prayer display (Wesley) I512 110613
To Him that loved the souls of men (Watts) AL628; AP811 110614
To Him who children blessed (Clarke) BF609; BR455 110615
To Him who for our sins was slain (Russell) D366 110616
To Him who hallows all our days (Rosser) AT499 110617
To Him who sits upon the throne (Watts) S35app; W711; AHp26 110618
To hold thy glory, Lord of all (Williams) BX493 110619
To Jesus Christ be glory given (Mason) BR49 110620
To Jesus Christ, our only Lord (---) BI1-! 110621
To Jesus' Heart all burning (Christie) AH138; BO25; BQ 61 110622
To Jordan came our Lord, the Christ (Luther) AA401 110623
To kneel at thine altar, in faith we draw near (---) BO133 110624
To make this earth, our hermitage (Stevenson) AQ306 110625
To me to live is Christ (Smith) BY605 110626
To Mercy, Pity, Peace, and Love (Blake) E506; X682; Y36; AN 285; AQ132 110627
To my heart in that dark lonely hour (Bobbitt) R I was once far away 110628
To my humble supplication (Bryan) E90; R536; X121; AF519 110629
To Nephi, seer of olden time (Townsend) BC186 110630
To our Redeemer's glorious name (Steele) D451; L150; M403; Q363; V380; AA101; AZ145; BA118 110631
To realms of glory I behold (Wallin) M458 X To realms of glory in the skies 110632
To realms of glory in the skies (Wallin) J116; M458; N146 110633
To render thanks unto the Lord (Scottish Psalter, 1650) AL 664; AP78 110634
To Shepherds as they watched by night (Luther) Q103; AA 162 110635
To Sion's hill I lift mine eyes (Tate & Brady) AO94 X To Sion's hill I lift my eyes 110636
To Sion's hill I lift my eyes (Tate & Brady) D648; AO94 110637
To suffer woes which hope thinks infinite (Shelley) AQ100 110638
To that Lord who unconstrained (Zinzendorf, N.L. & Anna) AZ424 110639
To the cross of Christ I'm clinging (Jackson) AY232 110640
To the God of all creation (Hull) BH20 110641
To the hills I lift mine eyes To the everlasting hills (Wesley) AZ1474; BA702 110642
To the hills I lift mine eyes To the God eternal (Bersagel) P286 110643
To the hills I lift my eyes; Whence shall help for me arise? (Wesley) T248; AJ 345 110644
To the knights in the days of old (Bryn Mawr College, 1923) Y147; AC230; AG306 110645
To the Lord in the hour of my distress I call (Ladies of the Grail) BSp38 110646
To the name of God on high (Bonar) L186 110647
To the name of our salvation Laud and honor let us pay (Latin, 15th c) A326; B89;

D321; E507; F190; G79; K36; O208; Q116; W164; AZ628; BA67; BN63; BO14; BQ16; BV282; BY221 110648

To the name that brings salvation (Latin 15th c) E507 X To the name of our salvation 110649

To the name that is salvation (Latin, 15th c) G79 X To the name of our salvation 110650

To the name that is salvation Praise and homage let us pay (Dearmer) X683; BF237 110651

To the name that is salvation Praise and homage let us pay (Dearmer) X To the name of our salvation (Latin, 15th c) 110652

To the promised home in glory (---) AX599; AY384 110653

To the regions beyond I must go (Simpson) AU76 110654

To the soul that seeks Him Christ is gracious (Foster) AZ1017 110655

To the work! to the work! (Crosby) AT435; AU64; AX185 110656

To Thee, above all creatures gaze (Hamburg Temple hymnal) BH 126 110657

To Thee all praise ascendeth (Rist) O385; P235 110658

To Thee alone our prayer and praise ascending (---) BRp467 110659

To Thee be glory, honor, praise (St Theodulph) AZ297 110660

To Thee be praise for ever (---) AZ829; BRp467 110661

To Thee before the close of day (St Ambrose) A164; AF507; BZ 110662

To Thee eternal God, Our fervent thanks we render (Brueckner) M531 110663

To Thee, Eternal Soul, be praise (Gilder) G10; I14; Y111; AB61; AD19; AN424; BF235; BX436 119664

To Thee, God Holy Ghost, we pray (Zinzendorf) AZ397; BA 142 110665

To Thee I lift my soul, In Thee my trust repose (U.P. Psalter, 1912) T41; AJ60 110666

To Thee I lift my soul; O Lord, I trust in Thee (Scottish Psalter, 1650) AP22 110667

To Thee I send my cry, Lord Jesus (Agricola) AZ994 110668

To Thee, Lord Christ, all praise be given (Swertner) AZ296 110669

To Thee, Lord Jesus, thanks we give (Vischer) AA193 110670

To Thee, most holy Lord (Oerter) BA362 110671

To Thee, my God and Saviour (Haweis) V187 110672

To Thee, my heart, eternal King (Exeter Collection) Z108 110673

To Thee my heart I offer (German, 1653) Q89 110674

To Thee, O blessed Saviour (---) AZ858; BA889 110675

To Thee, O Comforter divine (Havergal) D134; F613; K152; L276; AM252; AP285 110676

To Thee, O dear, dear Saviour (Monsell) I324; O480; AA 371; AI114; AO308; AP443; BA484; BB264 110677

To Thee, O Father, lamp of all the living (Gorell) F428 110678

To Thee, O Father, throned on high (Doane) D239 110679

To Thee, O God in heaven, This little one we bring (Clarke) BR454; BX516 110680

To Thee, O God, our hearts we raise (Dixon-Wright) Y134; BY302 110681

To Thee, O God, we bring our adoration (Mace) BE356 110682

To Thee, O God, we raise (Pierson) O44; AZ784 110683
To Thee, O God, we render thanks That thou to us hast given (Thring) W200 110684
To Thee, O God, we render thanks To Thee give thanks sincere (U.P. Psalter, 1912) T139 AJ206 110685
To Thee, O gracious Lord, we sing (Phillips) AY40 110686
To Thee, O heavenly Father (Welch) BY625 X We lift our hearts, O Father 110687
To Thee, O jesus Christ, we raise (---) BI29-D 110688
To Thee, O Lord, alone, Whom heaven (---) BRp467 110689
To Thee, O Lord, be glory given (---) BI28 110690
To Thee, O Lord, I fly (U.P. Psalter, 1912) T22; AJ29; AM581 110691
To Thee, O Lord, I humbly cry (U.P. Psalter, 1912) T280; AJ388 110692
To Thee, O Lord, I lift mine eyes (U.P. Psalter, 1912) AM 540 X To Thee, O Lord, I lift my eyes 110693
To Thee, O Lord, I lift my eyes (U.P. Psalter, 1912) T253; AJ351; AM540 110694
To Thee, O Lord, I yield my spirit (Senfft von Pilsach) O581 110695
To Thee, O Lord, my Saviour (---) BR419 110696
To Thee, O Lord, our hearts we raise, For all thy works (Plummer) BI9-D 100697
To Thee, O Lord, our hearts we raise, In hymns of adoration (Dix) D191; E292; F484; J445; K483; N570; O528; Q573; W616; X13; AA294; AK433; AP689; AW378; BV653; BY731; BZ 110698
To Thee, O Lord, the God of all (Landstad) J380 110699
To Thee, O Lord, will I sing praises (Crasselius) M587 110700
To Thee, our fathers' God, we bow (Cronenwett) M260 110701
To Thee our God we fly (How) B182; D187; E565; F606; O 518; Q580; W635; AA304; AI360; AM618; AP647; AZ 1180; BX413; BY653; 110702
To Thee, our loving Father, God (---) BE357 110703
To Thee our vows with sweet accord (Swertner) AZ888; BA853 110704
To Thee, Redeemer, King of highest heaven (Latin) F586 110705
To Thee, the Lord of all, I'll humbly sing (Freylinghausen, G-B. 1714) AZ447 110706
To Thee this temple we devote (Scott) L297 110707
To Thee we give ourselves today (Gottheil) BH166 110708
To Thee, who makest all (Dearmer) X417 110709
To Thee whose eye all nature owns (Hardy) X684 110710
To thine eternal arms, O God (Higginson) S90; BX246 110711
To thy brethren ever be propitious (Swertner) AZ1006 110712
To thy house, O Lord, with rejoicing we come (Naylor) R Once again we come 110713
To thy pastures, fair and large (Merrick) AX485; AY83 110714
To thy temple I repair (Montgomery) D30; K426; L52; Q2; V454; AA8; AM313; AP 324; AR8; AS59; BA391; BR89; BV12 110715
To thy temple we repair (Montgomery) L52 X To thy temple I repair 110716
To us a child of hope is born (Morison) H134; U52; V123; AA155; AM163; AO131; AR123; AS106; AX101; BB100; BE362 110717
To us a child of royal birth

(Wesley) F71; BV120 110718
To us from heaven's lofty height (German) M614 110719
To us in Bethlehem city (Cologne Psalter, 1638) X 685; BG112 110720
To us is born a blessed child (German before 1422) O189 110721
To us salvation now is come (Speratus) O205; Q377; AA 314 110722
To worship God in truth (Mayer) BH214 110723
To you have I lifted up my eyes (Ladies of the Grail) BSp44 110724
To you was given, O saint beloved (Merryweather) F537 110725
Tobias war ein frommer Mann (Ausbund Suppl.) BU1 110726
Today be joy in every heart (Hosmer) AN157; AW72; BD 214; BX190 110727
Today beneath benignant skies (Wortman) AO461 110728
Today I arise, Invoking the Blessed Trinity (St Patrick) W505 110729
Today the Saviour calls (Smith) V271; W686; AM388; AO646; AP398; AY313; AZ1372 110730
Today thy mercy calls me (Allen) H263 X To-day thy mercy calls us 110731
To-day thy mercy calls us (Allen) D590; H263; Q279; V264; W684; AA50; AP400; BA909 110732
Today we celebrate the birth (Luther) BA167 110733
Today, while the sun shines, work with a will (Douty) BC 215; BH258 110734
Together, Lord, we come to thee (Gilbert) AL318 110735
Toil on a little longer here (Smith) BB247 110736
Toiling on, toiling on (Crosby) R To the work 110737
Tollite hostias, et introite in atria ejus (Latin) BQ160 110738
Tomorrow, Lord, is thine (Doddridge) I253; V668 110739
Tomorrow shall be my dancing day (English trad carol) BG71 110740
Too soon we rise; the symbols disappear (Bonar) BR477 X Here, O my Lord, I see thee 110741
Torches, torches, run with torches (Spanish trad carol) BG81 110742
Tossed upon the raging billow (Bethune) V642 110743
Tota pulchra es, Maria (Latin, 15th c) BQ212 110744
Touch me, Lord Jesus, with thy love divine (Creamer) AU463 110745
Touch thou mine eyes, -- the somber shadows falling (Ham) AN230; BX270 110746
To-vo, to-vo l'-fo-ne-cho (Jewish traditional) BH324 110747
Trauren will ich stehen lassen (Ausbund) BU17 110748
Tread softly, tread softly, the Master is here (Crosby) R Be silent, be silent 110749
Trembling soul, beset by fears (Shepherd) AM670 110750
Trials dark on every hand (Tindley) AT473; AU134 110751
Triumph all ye cherubim (Hermannus Contractus) R Hail, holy Queen, enthroned above 110752
Triumph, ye heavens! rejoice ye with high adoration (Tersteegen) N37; O187 110753
Triumphant Lord, thy work is done (Irons) D370; H196

110754

Triumphant Sion, lift thy head (Doddridge) A381; B472; D488; H468; L346; AV243; BI47; BR 218 110755

Triumphantly doth Christ unfurl (Latin, 20th c) BN77 110756

Triumphs today the Lord of life (---) BI108 110757

Tröstet, tröstet meine Lieben (Olearius) BT61 110758

Troubled heart, thy God is calling, He is drawing (Crosby) AX 241; AY218 110759

Troubled soul, thy God is calling, Softly calling (Buerge) AX235 110760

Trudge on, singing praise for a spirit twice gifted (Clayton) X470b 110761

True Bread of life, in pitying mercy given (Bonar) AZ441 110762

True-hearted, whole-hearted (Havergal) G255; H396; I420; AH456; AS326; AT410; AV383; BY303; BZ 110763

True Light, that lightest all in heaven and earth (Thring) O613 110764

True lovers of mankind (Tweedy) BF520 110765

True Son of man, thou crown of human valour (Dearmer) X230 110766

True, the heart grows rich in giving (Charles) BE360 X Is thy cruse of comfort 110767

True to the faith that our parents have cherished (Stephens) R Shall the youth of Sion falter 110768

Truly, that eventful day (Gregor) AZ583 110769

Truly the light is sweet (Peabody) AQ136 110770

Trumpet of God, sound high (Brooks) F270 110771

Trust all to God, the Father, Confide thou in none other (Gerhardt) BE361 110772

Trust and obey (Sammis) R When we walk with the Lord 110773

Trust Me, try Me, prove Me (Leech) R Bring ye all the tithes 110774

Trust the Eternal when the shadows gather (McKenzie) BE359 110775

Trust your hand into His (Penner) R O soul, you know 110776

Trusting as the moments fly (Stites) R Simply trusting 110777

Truth comes alike to all (Avery) BE355 110778

Truth eternal, truth divine (Pratt) BC189 110779

Truth is the trial of itself (Jonson) AQ105 110780

Truth reflects upon our senses (Snow) BC188 110781

Try us, O God!and search the ground (Wesley) I555 X Help us to help each other, Lord 110782

Trying to walk in the steps of the Saviour (Hewitt) AX561 110783

Tu, Christe, nostrum gaúdium (Latin, 5th c) BN52 110784

Tu gloria Jerusalem (Latin) BQ223 110785

Turn back, O man, forswear thy foolish ways (Bax) A536; J348; R490; S424; X329; Y252; Z567; AB298; AD361; AE412; AF451; AK 410; AL520; AN342; AQ196; AR578; BF574; BK102; BL 92; BZ 110786

Turn, Lord, thy wrath away, in mercy spare us (Thymus) O104 110787

Turn us again, O God of hosts (Scottish Psalter, 1650) AP64 110788

Turn your faces toward the morning (Pounds) AY469 110789

Turned by thy grace, I look within (Bradley) D595

110790
Tut mir auf die schöne Pforte (Schmolck) BT1; BW505 110791
'Twas about the dead of night (Neale) BG151 110792
'Twas by thy Blood, immortal Lamb (Watts) F634 110793
'Twas Jesus died on Calvary (Manwaring) R 'Tis sweet to sing the matchless love 110794
'Twas like a dream, when by the Lord (Scottish Psalter, 1650) BH120 110795
'Twas on that dark, that doleful night (Watts) O312; Q164; V546; AA439; AF558 110796
'Twas on that night when doomed to know (Morison) R448; S360; W312; AD406; AH504; AL231; AM359; AP356; AR164; BY331 110797
'Twill all be joy up in heaven (Cook) R There'll be no shadows 110798
'Twixt gleams of joy and clouds of doubt (Shairp) W559; AB 210; AN251; BX236 110799
Two empires by the sea (Huntington) Z549; VX422 110800
Two little hands are sweetly folded (Warner) BX625 100801

U

Ubi caritas et amor Deus (Latin: Mandatum) BM15; BN87 110802
Ultima in mortis hora (Benedictine: Ultima) BN191 110803
Un flambeau, Jeannette (French trad.) Y304 110804
Unanswered yet? The prayer your lips have pleaded (Adams) BC 286 110805
Unbar the door! and let the Lord Christian (Oxenham) Y253; Z287 110806
Unchanging God, hear from eternal heaven (Stone) O126; P403 110807
Unchanging God, who livest (Wilder) F496 110808
Under His wings I am safely abiding (Cushing) AS263
X Under His wings I'm safely abiding 110809
Under His wings, I'm safely abiding (Cushing) P303; AS 263; AX525; BB587 110810
Under His wings, Under His wings (U.P. Board, 1917)
R Under the care of my God 110811
Under the care of my God, the Almighty (U.P. Board, 1917) AI307; AM78 110812
Under the feeble stable light (Keller) J43 110813
Under the shadows of Calvary (Minkler) R Grace, dear Lord 110814
Under the wide and starry sky (Stevenson) Y128 110815
Une vaine crainte trouble vos esprits (French trad carol) BG156b 110816
Ungnad begehr ich nicht von dir (Ausbund) BU32 110817
Unheard the dews around me fall (---) AN115; AQ89; AW39; BX70 110818
Unknown and unrewarded (Dearmer) X244 110819
Unless the Lord the house shall build (U.P. Psalter, 1912) T257; AJ359; AM291 110820
Unser Vater im Himmelreich, Dein Nam sei heilig ewiglich (Betz) BU104 110821
Unshaken as the sacred hill [hills] (Watts) V338; BB392 110822
Unto a thousand, yea, to eight thousand ages (Japanese national anthem) Y310 110823
Unto Caesar let us render (Cronenwett) M501 110824
Unto God our Saviour, Sing a joyful song (U.P. Psalter, 1912) T181; AJ262 110825
Unto God, our King, Joy and strength of Israel (Essenburg) AJ431 110826

Unto him, for whom this day (Juste judex ultionis) BQ116 110827
Unto him who hath loved us (Pierson) R With harps and with viols 110828
Unto him whose name is holy (Elliott) AZ874 110829
Unto Jesus' cross I'm now retiring (Zinzendorf, C.R.) AZ 1016 110830
Unto Mary, demon-haunted (Struther) X233 110831
Unto my Lord Jehovah said, "At my right hand" (Irish Psalter, 1898) AM229; AP98 110832
Unto the calmly gathered thought (Whittier) BK87 110833
Unto the hills around do I lift up (Campbell) J488; S96; T250; U201; Z166; AD79; AE64; AG 219; AJ347; AK86; AL681; AM 82; AO331; AP109; AR85; AW 598; BV567 110834
Unto the hills I lift mine eyes, O whence shall come (U.P. Psalter, 1912) BZ X I to the hills will lift my eyes 110835
Unto the hills I lift mine eyes, Whence comes my help (Lucas) BH13 110836
Unto the Lord lift thankful voices (Brondsema) AJ425 110837
Unto the Lord of all creation (Afzelius) N314 110838
Unto thee, most faithful Saviour (Gregor) AZ981 110839
Unto Thee my heart is sighing (Bridges) BJ58 110840
Unto Thee, unto Thee, Precious Saviour, now I flee (Crosby) R Mighty Rock, whose towering form 110841
Unto thy temple, Lord, we come (Collyer) AE27; AF276; AK328; AN14; AQ252; AR10; AW282; BX24 110842
Unto us a boy is born (Latin carol, 15th c) A34; X385; AF 142; BG92; BV121; BY112 110843
Unumschränkte Liebe (Rambach) BT42 110844
Unveil mine eyes that of thy law (Scottish Psalter, 1650) BH 202 110845
Unveil thy bosom, faithful tomb (Watts) H490; I586 110846
Unworthy to be called thy son (Furness) BX249 110847
Up and get us gone, to help the world along (Wilson) R Up, my neighbour 110848
Up! arouse thee, O beautiful Sion (Woodmansee) BC283 110849
Up, awake, ye defenders of Zion (Penrose) BC37 110850
Up Calvary's mountain, one dreadful morn (Christiansen) AT106; AU428 110851
Up from the grave He arose (Lowry) R Low in the grave He lay 110852
Up, my neighbour, come away (Wilson) BG166 110853
Up, my soul, gird thee with power (Freystein) M229 110854
Up now, laggardly lasses (Spanish trad carol) BG113 110855
Up to the bountiful Giver of life (Slade) AU128 110856
Up to the hills I lift mine eyes (Watts) BR265 X Up to the hills I lift my eyes 110857
Up to the hills I lift my eyes (Watts) L100; BR265 110858
Up to the throne on high (Blakeney) F315 110859
Up to those bright and gladsome hills (Vaughan, the Silurist) X686 110860
Up, ye Christians, join in singing (Arnschwanger) BR133 110861
Uplift the song of praise (Hosmer) AN378; AW366; BH261; BX404 110862
Uplift the voice and sing (St Alphonso M de' Liguori) BO 106 110863
Upon the cross downlying (Petursson) M389 110864

Upon the cross of Calvary (Raile) BC221 110865
Upon the cross the robber prayed (Peturrson) M412; P166 110866
Upon the first day of the week (Childress) AX67 110867
Upon the gospel's sacred page (Bowring) I199; AS180; BE 363 110868
Upon the mountain top alone I stand (Chippewa Indian trad) Y315 110869
Upon this happy morn (---) AZ 1170 110870
Upward I lift mine eyes (Watts) AO338 X To God I lift mine eyes 110871
Upward where the stars are burning (Bonar) S428; V711; AB 401; AZ650 110872
Urbs Sion aurea, patria lactea (St Bernard of Cluny) BT 613; BW262 110873
Urged by love, to every nation (Zinzendorf, N. L.) AZ896 110874
Use me, O my gracious Saviour (Woodrow) AX419; AY106 110875
Utah, Utah, beautiful beautiful land (Huish) R There is a land whose sunny vales 110876

V

Va-a-nach-nu ko-r'eem umishtachaveem (Jewish traditional) BH274 110877
Vain are the hopes the sons of men (Watts) V314 110878
Vain, delusive world, adieu (Wesley) H306 110879
Vainly, through night's weary hours (Auber) AZ259; BE364 110880
V'-al ku-lom, E-lo-a (Jewish traditional) BH325 110881
Valet will ich dir geben (Herberger) BT407 110882
Vanish doubt and hesitation (Schlegel) N440 110883
Vater unser im Himmelreich (Luther) BT458 110884
Va-y' -da-bayr Mo-she es moa-day (Jewish trad.) BH300 110885
Va-yo-mer A-do-noy (Jewish traditional) BH321 110886
Veiled in darkness Judah lay Rights (AN152; AQ284; AW 68 110887
Veni Creator Spiritus (Latin, 9th c) BJ48b; BN118; BO261; BP44; BQ199; BT233 110888
Veni, Jesu, amor me (Latin) AH131; BO35 110889
Veni, Redemptor gentium (St Ambrose) BT95 110890
Veni, Sancte Spiritus (Innocent III, Pope??) BN55; BO260; BQ198; BT227; BW131 110891
Veni Sponsa Christi (Breviary) BQ215 110892
Veni, veni, Emmanuel (Latin, 9th c) BN5; BP5; BQ152; BT62; BW67 110893
Venite adoremus, Dominum (Sedulius of Liege) R The snow lay on the ground 110894
Věříme v všemohoucího (Tranovsky) BT253 110895
Very Bread, good Shepherd, tend us (St Thomas Aquinas) A194; E317c; J280 110896
Very softly I will walk (Kellogg) AH554 110897
Verzage nicht, du Häuflein Klein (Altenburg) BT263 110898
Vexilla Regis prôdeunt (Fortunatus) BN28; BO287; BQ182; BT168 110899
Victim Divine, thy grace we claim (Wesley) E333; J274 110900
Victimae Paschali laudes immolent Christiani (Wipo??) BN39; BQ196; BT191 110901
Victoria! Victoria! Surrexit nostra gloria (Latin) BO171 110902
Victory, victory, through him that redeemed us (Crosby)

R Behold! a royal army 110903

Virgin-born, we bow before Thee (Heber) E640; F514 110904

Virgin wholly marvellous (St Ephraim the Syrian) BO117 110905

Virginis proles, opifex que Matris (Latin, 8th c) BN 183 110906

Virtue supreme, thy mighty stream (Dearmer) X214 110907

Viva! Viva! Gesù! che per mio bene (Italian, 18th c) BT158 110908

Vivat! vivat! vivat Pastor bonus! (Latin) BO210 110909

V'-nis-lach l'-chol a-das b'-nay (Jewish traditional) BH319 110910

Voison, d'ou venait ce grand bruit (French trad carol) BG88b 110911

Vom himmel hoch da komm' ich her (Luther) AW527b; AY24d; BT85; BW527 110912

Vom himmel hoch, o Engel, kommt (German trad carol, 15th c) BG118b 110913

Vom Himmel kam der Angel Schar (Luther) BT103 110914

Von Gott will ich nicht lassen (Helmbold) BT393 110915

Von Grönlands eis'gen Zinken. (R. Heber) BW333 110916

Von Herzen will ich loben (Ausbund) BU120 110917

Von Herzen woll'n wir singen (Ausbund) AY35d; BU119 110918

Vox clara ecce intonat (Latin, 6th c) BT60 110919

V'shom'ru V'-nay Yis-ro-ayl es ha-shab-bos (Jewish trad) BH272 110920

Vzkříšení čekame. (Slovak. 1674) BT603 110921

W

Wach auf, du Geist der ersten Zeugen (Bogatzky) BT494 110922

Wach auf, wach auf, o Menschenkind! Von deinem Schlaf stand auf geschwind (Ausbund) BU118 110923

Wachet auf! ruft uns die Stimme Der Wächter sehr hoch auf der Zinne (Nicolai) BT609; BW522 110924

Wacht auf, ihr Brüder werthe (Ausbund) BU113 110925

Waft [sic] my sould upon the Lord (Lloyd) AI285 X Wait my soul upon the Lord 110926

Wait, my soul! upon the Lord (Lloyd) V423; AI285; AO 349; BE365 110927

Wait, O my soul, thy Maker's will (Beddome) V425 110928

Wait on God, and trust Him through all thy days (Räder) AK478 110929

Waiting and watching, Waiting and watching ("S.M.H.") R We know not the time when He cometh 110930

Wake, arise! a voice appalling (Nicolai) N612 110931

Wake, awake for night is flying (Nicolai) A3; B62; D40; E 12; J7; K5; L214; N199; O 508; P426; Q609; W162; X 687; Y352; AA549; AB153; AD173; AF24,108; AI446; AK96; AL134; AM231; AN 486; AO115; AP242; AQ17; AR207; AW522; AZ1103; BA 103; BB197; BI17-D,52; BK 56 110932

Wake, harp of Sion, wake again (Edmeston) D267 110933

Wake, O wake, for night is flying (Nicolai) X687 X Wake, awake, for night is flying 110934

Wake, o wake! with tidings thrilling (Nicolai) E12 X Wake, awake for night is flying 110935

Wake, Spirit, who in times now olden (Bogatzky) W377

110936
Wake the song of joy and gladness (Sherwin) BB649 110937
Wake the song of jubilee (Bacon) L350; AZ76 110938
Wake! the welcome day appeareth (Freylinghausen) O160 110939
Waken, Christian children (Hamerton) BR531 110940
Walk daily with your Saviour (Hoffman) AX445; AY127 110941
Walk in the light, and thou shalt own (Barton) BY560 X Walk in the light, so shalt thou know 110942
Walk in the light, so shalt thou know (Barton) G378; I361; J474; L424; W482; Z479; AD224; AH 238; AN562; AR274; AT370; AW209; AX450; AY90; BA635; BB339; BD97; BE367; BF403; BK81; BV447; BX354; BY560; BZ 110943
Walk in the light, so thou shalt know (Barton) BE367 X Walk in the light, so shalt thou know 110944
Walk with the Lord! along the road (Gill) BX353 X O walk with God! 110945
Walking in sunlight all of my journey (Zelley) AU119; AX28; AY471 110946
Walking in the sunshine, beautiful and bright (Lindsay) AX440; AY479 110947
Walking, Saviour, close to Thee (Newell) AY95 110948
Walte, walte nah und fern (Bahnmeier) BT507; BW551 110949
Wanderer in sinful ways (Latta) AX238; AY220 110950
Wann der Herr die G'sägniss Zion (Ausbund. Psalm 126) BU86 110951
Wär' Gott nicht mit uns diese Zeit (Luther) BT267 110952
Wår Herres Jesu Kristi död (Spegel) BT163 110953
Warrior, at thy station stand (Zinzendorf, N. L.) AZ1042; BA554 110954
Warrior, on thy station stand (Zinzendorf, N. L.) BA554 X Warrior, at thy station stand 110955
Warum sollt' ich mich denn grämen? (Gerhardt) BT523 110956
Was ever grief like Thine (Wesley) AZ1488; BJ50 110957
Was frag' ich nach der Welt (Pfefferkorn) BT430 110958
Was gibst du denn, o meine Seele (Lochner) BT404 110959
Was Gott tut, das ist wohlgetan! Es bleibt gerecht sein Wille (Rodigast) BT521; BW567 110960
Was Gott tut, das ist wohl getan! So denken Gottes Kinder (Schmolck) BT571 110961
Was kann ich doch für Dank (Denicke) BT417 110962
Was mein Gott will, das G' scheh' allzeit (Albrecht, von Brandenburg) BT517 110963
Was mich auf diefer Welt betrübt (Unparth. G. B.) AY 8d 110964
Was the trial sore? Temptation sharp? Thank God a second time (Browning) AC474 110965
Was there ever kindest shepherd (Faber T320 X There's a wideness in God's mercy 110966
Was wend wir aber heben an (Ausbund) BU140 110967
Was woll'n wir aber singen (Ausbund) BU26 110968
Wash me, O Lamb of God, wash me from sin (Beegle) AY78 110969
Wassail, wassail, all over the town (English trad carol) (two versions) BG32, 31* 110970
*differing texts
Watch and pray, watch and pray (Brooks) R There's a way

that is free 110971
Watch, my soul, and pray (Wallin) N479 110972
Watch o'er me, O my Saviour (Plummer) BI61 110973
Watch, ye saints, with eyelids waking (Palmer) BB549 110974
Watchman, blow the gospel trumpet (Gilmour) BB619 110975
Watchman, tell me, does the morning (Brewer) AX129; AY 79; BB180 110976
Watchman, tell us of the night (Bowring) A440; B106; D331; G485; H483; I636; J525; L355; Q71; R149; S109; U393; V585; Y249; Z183; AB104; AC298; AD101; AE79; AF109; AG61; AH244; AK91; AN154; AO526; AQ283; AR124; AS99; AT462; AV263; AW66; AZ84; BA188; BD204; BE368; BF276; BI95; BK141; BR229; BX194; BZ 110977
Watchmen on the walls of Zion (---) BB184 110978
We all believe in one true God, Father, Son, and Holy Ghost (Clausnitzer) O76; Q252; AA393; AF250; BZ 110979
We all believe in one true God, Maker of the earth and heaven (Luther) M60; O71; Q251; AA394 110980
We are adventurers who come (Carmen & Hovey) Y167 110981
We are all blind, until we see (Markham) AK103 110982
We are all enlisted till the conflict is o'er (---) BC210 110983
We are building in sorrow or joy (Sargent) AX199; AY519 110984
We are but little children poor (Alexander) E610; W516; AP 769; BR538 110985
We are but little children weak (Alexander) W516 X We are but little children poor 110986
We are but strangers here, Heaven is our home (Taylor) L591; M312; N519; O462; Q660; V712; AA563; AM605; AS477; AX609; AY147; BB659; BR432 110987
We are children of one Father (Larcom) BX522 110988
We are climbing Jacob's ladder (Negro spiritual) Y318; AF495; AG319; AH597; BK165; BZ 110989
We are come with joy and gladness (Walmsley) BD48 110990
We are going down the valley, one by one (Pounds) AX615; AY496 110991
We are hid with Christ forever (Mace) BE370 110992
We are little gleaners, Little we can do (---) AY481 110993
We are little reapers, toiling all the day (---) AY483 110994
We are living, we are dwelling (Coxe) R356; S374; U310; Z494; AD348; AE259; AF427; AG275; AK297; AO482; AT 421; AV273; BB359; BF519 110995
We are marching homeward with the blest (---) AY145 110996
We are nearing home! We are nearing home! (Whitford, arr) R Just over the mountains in the Promised Land 110997
We are not here to play, to dream (Babcock) U269 X Be strong! we are not here to play, to dream 110998
We are not left to walk alone (Walker) AZ936 110999
We are saved by the grace of our God (Kennedy) AI132; AR430; AS291 111000
We are soldiers of Christ who is mighty to save (Pollock) AI328 111001
We are sowing, daily sowing (---) BC192 111002
We are standing in the great

dawn of a day (Shepard) AC 520 111003
We are that chosen nation, Lord (Bible. Joel 2) R Look with mercy, Lord 111004
We are the Lord's: His all-sufficient merit (Spitta) K410; O 226; Q453; AI255; AP561; AZ 1222 111005
We are Thy people, Thou art our King (Jewish traditional) BH 326 111006
We are waiting for the morning (Cushing) R We are watching we are waiting 111007
We are watching, we are waiting (Cushing) H205; U391; V601; AI93 111008
We are weary of life-long toil (Purchas) R Evensong is hushed in silence 111009
We bear the strain of earthly care (Davis) G471; R227; S179; U369; Y86; Z521; AB275; AC194; AF220; AG119; AK279; BF336; BX226; BZ 111010
We believe in One true God, Father, Son and Holy Ghost (Clausnitzer) BZ X We all believe 111011
We bid thee welcome in the name (Montgomery) I226; Q484; AA 489; AE342; AK350; AO460; BA319 111012
We bless the name of Christ, the Lord (Coffman) AX167 111013
We bless thee, for thy peace, O God (Church melodies, 1858) H361; U232; V393; Y103; AE 226; BF388; BX356; BY489 111014
We bless thee, Jesus Christ our Lord (Vischer) O308 111015
We bless thee, Lord, for all this common life (White) Y338; AC221 111016
We bow before thy throne (Simpson) AZ1122; BA44 111017
We bow to thee, O Lord, on high (Kauffman) AY379 111018
We bring no glittering treasures (Phillips) AZ857 111019
We build a sanctuary sure (Humbert) AE344 111020
We build an altar here, and pray (Martin) AC529 111021
We build our school on thee, O Lord (Meyer) B366; BD 194; BH254 111022
We cannot always trace the way (Bowring) BX260 X I cannot always trace 111023
We cannot build alone (Coles) U386; V567 111024
We cannot kindle when we will (Arnold) AQ86 111025
We cannot think of them as dead (Hosmer) G423; AL178; AN202; AQ73; AW318; BF666; BX231 111026
We care for our Lord's acres (Clarke) AR590 111027
We Christians may Rejoice today When Christ was born (Füger) Q107; AA156 111028
We Christians should ever consider (Spegel) N445 111029
We come in the might of the Lord of light (Moultrie) R We march, we march to victory 111030
We come, Lord, to thy feet (Whitmore??) D536; V651 111031
We come, O Christ, to thee (Clarkson) BV285 111032
We come, O Lord, before thy throne (Brown) L606 111033
We come unto our father's God (Gill) A303; B424; G385; R16; S342; W211; AF 271; AK361; AL170; AN363; AO610; AP301; AQ15; BX 403; BY265; BZ 111034
We come with songs and gladness (---) BD45 111035
We covenant with hand and heart (Benade) AZ886; BA 673 111036
We dedicate this temple (Emurian) R519 111037
We ever pray for thee, our Prophet dear (Stephen) BC 386 111038

We gather 'round your shrine today, Salve Regina (---) BM51 111039

We gather together to ask the Lord's blessing (Dutch trad.) A315; G20; R18; Y29; Z117; AD22; AF21; AG10; AH185; AM286; AR9; AT492; BB8; BD17; BF171; BK137; BL91; BZ 111040

We gather, we gather, dear Jesus, to bring (Harlingen) N660; O570; P356 111041

We give immortal praise (Watts) D141; AO60; AZ1181 111042

We give thee but thine own (How) A481; B319; D268; E 522; G456; H313; I688; J544; K387; L543; M252; N182; P 404; Q441; R312; S394; U337; V575; W346; X332; Y396; Z422; AA361; AB267; AC339; AD508; AE368; AF535; AG247; AH411; AI450; AK258; AL374; AM367; AN287; AO498; AP576; AQ131; AR343; AS353; AT402; AU492; AW213; AX648; AZ1361; BA568; BB477; BC180; BD129; BF503; BR231; BV605; BX363; BY530; BZ 111043

We give thee thanks, O God, this day (Offord) AR600; AS429 111044

We go not on a pilgrimage (Very) AN265; BX297 111045

We hail thee, Lord, thy Church's Rock (Zinzendorf, N. L.) N213; O525 111046

We hail thy Presence glorious (Parsons) F403 111047

We have a King who came to earth (Cropper) F434; BY531 111048

We have a Rock, a safe retreat (Jones) AM319 111049

We have a sure, prophetic word (Cronenwett) M30; P85; Q290; AA120 111050

We have an anchor (Owens) R Will your anchor hold 111051

We have heard a joyful sound (Owens) W680 X We have heard the joyful sound 111052

We have heard from the bright, the holy, land (Hyde) BB 305 111053

We have heard the joyful sound (Owens) R503; W680; Z537; AH408; AI103; AL259; AM370; AP798; AR480; AS293; AT 191; AU15; AW334; AX201; AY231; BB637; BV330; BY 399; 111054

We have not known thee as we ought (Pollock) AM418; BB 350; BY606 111055

We have not wings, we cannot soar (Longfellow) AN560 111056

We hear the call of Israel's children (Rosewater) BH256 111057

We honor those whose work began (Horton) BX504 111058

We hope in thee, O God (Hearn) G365; I328 111059

We in one covenant are joined (Swertner) AZ881; BA672 111060

We join to pray, with wishes kind (Gaskell) AX552; AY 296 111061

We join with all, in every place (Coster) AO446 111062

We journey through a vale of tears (Barton) I447; L498 111063

There is none other name than thine (---) BA69 X There is no other name 110063

We journey with a multitude (Patton) AQ66 110064

We knelt before Kings; we bent before lords (Merrill) BF498 111065

We know, by faith we know (Wesley) H506 111066

We know not a voice of that river (Rossetti) S432 111067

We know not the hour of the Master's appearing (Belden) BB540 111068

We know not the time when he cometh ("S. M. H.") BB542 111069

We know the paths where-in our feet should press (Drinkwater) AC187 X Grant us the will 111070
We know thee who thou art (Bright) AZ1374 111071
We leave thy house but leave not thee (Tiplady) Z130 111072
We lift our hearts in praise, O God of Life, to thee (Morrison) BE371 111073
We lift our hearts in thanks today (Chubb) AN12 111074
We lift our hearts, O Father (Welch) BV392; BY625 111075
We lift our hearts to thee (Wesley, J & C) G36; I45; L9; AA25; AO75; BZ 111076
We limit not the truth of God (Rawson) AF259; BY254 111077
We love the place, O God (Bullock) A398; B465; D484; E508; F242; J239; O41; W236; X688; AL199; AP325; AW281; AZ477; BC203; BR23, 95; BV13; BY 283 111078
We love the venerable house (Emerson) AN466; AO464; AP319; BX502 111079
We love thee, Lord, yet not alone (Elliott) AZ1447 111080
We love thy house, O God (Bullock) BC203 X We love the place, O God 111081
We love to sing around the king (Bethune) R There is no name 111082
We march, we march to victory (Moultrie) B533; D514; I418; L537; AH437; AO400; AP539; AV216; BA937; BD89; BF466; BI7; BR509 111083
We may not climb the heavenly steeps (Whittier) X Immortal love, forever full 111084
We meet again in gladness (---) BH255 111085
We meet again in Sabbath School (Manwaring) BC193 111086
We meet, as in that upper room they met (Briggs) AR513 111087
We men of earth have here the stuff (Markham) AC535 111088
We met them on the common way (Cardoza) AD311; AQ 237 111089
We mix from many lands (Swinburne) Z509 111090
We move in faith to unseen goals (Quin) AN357; AQ200 111091
We need not climb the heavenly steeps (Whittier) N196 X Immortal love forever full 111092
We nned not soar above the skies (Stockton) H103 111093
We now have met to worship thee (Shoemaker) AX54; AY5 111094
We now implore God, the Holy Ghost (Luther) M474; Q231 111095
We now return, each to his tent (Hartley) AZ882; BA387 111096
We, O Jesus, claim thy special care (Allen) AZ513 111097
We owe the Lord an evening song (Loewen) AX73 111098
We plough the fields and scatter (Claudius) X We plow the fields 111099
We plow the fields and scatter (Claudius) A138; B423; E293; F483; G544; I716; J364; K486; N569; P244; R524; S464; W 618; X14; Y46; Z594; AB387; AC323; AD445; AE417; AF460; AG288; AH489; AI351; AK432; AL579; AM614; AN142; AO580; AP141; AR592; AS425; AT493; AW375; AZ850; BA869; BD51; BF648; BH195; BR491; BV654; BX174; BY732; BZ 111100
We praise and bless thee, gracious Lord (Spitta) O386; BA424; BY607 111101
We praise thee, God, for harvests earned (Adams) Y157; AC206; AD301; AN314; AQ219; BD86; BX371 111102
We praise thee, Lord, for all the martyred throng (Heber)

F532 111103
We praise thee, Lord, for hours of bliss (Hopps) I550 111104
We praise thee, Lord, with earliest morning ray (Franck) AF502; AN94; BX43 111105
We praise thee, O God! For the days of our youth (Kuipers) AI376 X We praise thee, O God! for the Son of thy love (Mackay) 111106
We praise thee, O God! for the Son of thy love (Mackay & Kuiper) U27; AI376; AM634; AP718; AS16; AT205; AU155; AV328; AW437; AX417; AY420 111107
We praise thee, O God, our Lord and our King! (Schmidt) AI361 AO597 111108
We praise thee, O God, our Redeemer, Creator (Dutch hymn, 1626) J450; P20; Q568; R17; S461; AB63; AC29; AD76; AE25; AF21; AH204; AI7; AK19; AM 83; AO80; AT11; AW15; BF252 111109
We praise thy grace, O Saviour (How) B278; D159; BV449 111110
We praise thy name, all-holy Lord (Newell) E211; F575; X225 111111
We praise thy name, O Lord most high (---) B284 111112
We praise, we worship thee, O God (Gell's Psalms and hymns, 1815) W3; BY33 111113
We pray no more, made lowly wise (Hosmer) AN274 X Made lowly wise, we pray 111114
We pray thee, heavenly Father (Coles) E334; F401; BV389 111115
We pray thee, Jesus, who didst first (Phillimore) AS448; BA320 111116
We pray thee, wounded Lamb of God (Zinzendorf, N. L.) AZ 404; BA474 111117
We read of a place called heaven (Bridgewater) AX590 111118
We rear not a temple, like Judah's of old (Ware) I666 111119
We rest on thee, our shield and our defender (Cherry) BV569 111120
We sail along toward the harbor light (DeArmond) AU 299 111121
We saw not, when thou camest to die (Dearmer) X689b 111122
We saw thee not when, far away (Dearmer) X689a 111123
We saw thee not when thou didst come (Richter) E509; P162; W72; AP262; AS124; BR167; BV514; BY132 111124
We search the world for truth (Whittier) AC449 111125
We see him come, and know him ours (Herrick) R What sweeter music can we bring 111126
We see not, know not; all our way (Whittier) AB203 111127
We shall build on! (Studdert-Kennedy) AC483 111128
We shall know as we are known (Herbert) R When the mists 111129
We shall reach the river side (French) AU271 111130
We shall see the King some day (Jones) R Though the way we journey 111131
We shall sleep, but not forever (Kidder) N604; AY185 111132
We sing a song and then we part (Tilton) AZ1515 111133
We sing his love who once was slain (Hill) AO542 111134
We sing, Immanuel, thy praise (Gerhardt) Q108 111135
We sing now together our song of thanks giving (Buehrer) AQ22 111136
We sing of God, the mighty source (Smart) A314; X690

111137
We sing of golden mornings (Emerson) AQ40 111138
We sing the almighty power of God (Watts) L104; Q43; AA 293 111139
We sing the glorious conquest (Ellerton) A114; B271; D150; E207; F541; AM404; BV453 111140
We sing the praise of him who died (Kelly) A340; B160; D100; E510; F215; H161; J494; K66; O483; Q178; W109; X132; AL 102; AP211; AZ347; BA195; BB296; BV162; BY150 111141
We sing the rapture of the breath (Meredith) AQ139 111142
We sing to thee, Immanuel (Gerhardt) AZ320 111143
We speak of the realms of the blest (Mills) L600; N619; AZ1507; BB199 111144
We stand in deep repentance (Palmer) O100; AI432; BB235 111145
We thank thee and we bless thee (Dunn) BE374 111146
We thank thee, heavenly Father, for thy correcting rod (Whitney) BE376 111147
We thank thee, Jesus, dearest Friend (Praetorius. Musae sioniae 1607) Q223; AA239 111148
We thank thee, Lord, for eyes to see (Perkins) BK27 111149
We thank thee, Lord, for sending us (Curry) BL68 111150
We thank thee, Lord, for this fair earth (Cotton) AE425; AS97; BF233; BH193 111151
We thank thee, Lord, for this our food (Cennick) G564; N541; O568; P352; X691; AX651; BZ 111152
We thank thee Lord, for this our food (two versions) (Cennick) BZ 111153
We thank thee, Lord, for using us (Bonar) AO487; BY354 111154
We thank thee, Lord, thy paths of service lead (Laufer) G458; R294; S367; Y223; Z495; AC249; AF421; AK265; AR 383; BF501; BZ 111155
We thank thee, loving Father (---) X405 111156
We thank thee, O God, for a prophet (Fowler) BC196 111157
We thank thee, O our Father (---) AL586; AS95; AW422 111158
We thank you, Lord of Heaven (Struther) A313; X692; AN477; AQ29; BY34 111159
We three kings of orient are (Hopkins) A51; B554; G102; R176; Z204; AB122; AC96; AF143; AG82; AH269; AN 176; AO136; AQ300; AR141; AU139; AW90; BB107; BD229; BG195; BI88; BK161; BL17; BZ 111160
We, thy children, join the chorus (Cole) R Birds are singing 111161
We turn to thee, O Lord, and sing in sweet accord (Hill) BE378 111162
We walk by faith, and not by sight (Alford) B270; D426; AW152; BA710 111163
We welcome thee in Jesus' name (Palmer) L307 111164
We who here together are assembled (Zinzendorf, C.R.) AZ1011 111165
We, who would lead thy flock, must be (Symons) BV415 111166
We will carol joyfully (---) K547 111167
We will give, we will pray (Allen) R Christ for the whole wide world 111168
We will rest in the fair and happy land (unusual refrain) (Stennett) AT478 X On Jordan's stormy bank 111169
We wish you many happy returns of the day (Dearmer)

X386a 111170

We worship thee, almighty Lord (Wallin) J174; R25; S17; AF 28 111171

We worship thee, we bless thee (Havergal) R O Saviour, precious Saviour 111172

We would be building, temples still undone (Deitz) R470; Z489; AE441; AF494; AG313; AK452; AR384; BK117 111173

We would extol thee, everblessed Lord (Grieve) F380; BV28 111174

We would see Jesus; for the shadows lengthen (Warner) B406; D629; I323; N524; O294; P342; S263; U412; V665; Z400; AB229; AH393; AR413; AS215; AT324; AU220; AV219; AW201; AY476; AZ1216; BA531; BB 29 111175

We would see Jesus; lo! his star is shining (Park) G113; R183; U51; Y71; Z209; AB127; AC 100; AD471; AE95; AF152; AG 85; AK456; AL602; AR146; AT 89; BF305; BK18; BZ 111176

We would see Jesus, Mary's Son most holy (Park) AB127 X We would see Jesus; lo! His star is shining 111177

We would see Jesus, on the mountain teaching (Park) BK18 X We would see Jesus, Lo! his star 111178

Wearily at daylight's close (---) BR543 111179

Weary of earth, and laden with my sin (Stone) A58; B129; D82; E91; I284; J366; K324; L389; N404; O484; U181; V 283; AL268; AM467; AO258; AP411; AV160; AZ450; BA409; BB289; BR295 111180

Weary of self, and laden with my sin (Stone) B129 X Weary of earth, and laden 111181

Weary of wandering from my God (Wesley) B136; D83; AL264; AP415 111182

Weary sinner, keep thine eyes (Toplady) L252; AO255; AZ 1262 111183

Weary soul by sin oppressed (Grimes) AS51 111184

Weary souls that wander wise (Wesley) H258; I262 111185

Weep not for a brother deceased (Wesley) I594 111186

Weep not for Him who onward bears (Pollock) W94 111187

Weep, Sion, weep, in death's deep sleep (LaTrobe) AZ510 111188

Weeping endures but for a night (Smith) BB312 111189

Weighed in the balance of justice true (Warren) AX294 111190

Weil ich Jesus Schäflein bin (Hayn) BT648; BW430 111191

Weil nun die Zeit vorhanden ist (Ausbund) BU135 111192

Welcome among thy flock of grace (Zinzendorf, N. L.) AZ913; BA803 111193

Welcome be thou, heaven-king (English trad carol, 15th c) BG174 111194

Welcome, blessed Heavenly Stranger (Smart) AZ244 111195

Welcome, day of sweet repose (Evans) BB469 111196

Welcome, day of the Lord (Dearmer) G395; X390 111197

Welcome, delightful morn, Thou day of sacred rest (Hayward) G394; H77; I67; L47; U442; V61; Z444; AA124; AM 325; AT21; AU175; AV5; AZ 1172; BB465 111198

Welcome, happy morning! age to age shall say (Fortunatus) A87; B169; D109; G161; I 166; J93; K118; N122; Q202; R207; S169; V764; W115; Y 332; Z246; AB145; AC130; AD161; AE133; AI88; AK170; AL107; AM199; AO181; AP 217; AR191; AT110; AV119; AZ770; BA241; BD236; BF

320; BR513; BV195; BY165; BZ 111199
Welcome, morning, bright and blue (Tarrant) Y200; AC168 111200
Welcome, morning of joy, glad feast (Ascentiontide) (Fortunatus) F608 111201
Welcome, morning of joy, glad feast (Dedication) (Fortunatus) F618 111202
Welcome, morning of joy, glad feast (Easter) (Fortunatus) F 600 111203
Welcome, morning of joy, glad feast (Whitsunday) (Fortunatus) F612 111204
Welcome, sweet day of rest (Watts) D27; H78; I64; L39; V63; AO14; AY376; AZ1332; BR96 111205
Welcome, thou victor in the strife (Schmolck) K119; M436; N127; AA228; AW542 111206
Welcome to earth, thou noble guest (Luther) L223 111207
Welcome to earth, thou noble guest (Luther) L223 X From heaven high 111208
Welcome, wanderer, welcome (Bonar) R In the land of strangers 111209
Welcome, welcome, day of rest (---) AY272; BB459 111210
Welcome, welcome, ever welcome (Crosby) R Don't forget the Sabbath 111211
Welcome, welcome, Sabbath morning (Baird) BC190 111212
Welcome Yule, thou merry man (English trad carol) BG174 X Welcome be thou, heaven-king 111213
Well for him who, all things losing (---) BE379 111214
We'll be gathered home to Zion (Hayes) R Christ our Lord will soon be coming 111215
We'll build on the Rock, the living Rock (Belden) BB579 111216
We'll never say good-by in heaven (Chapman) R With friends on earth we meet 111217
We'll sing all hail to Jesus' name (Alldridge) BC218 11218
We'll sing and we'll shout (Phelps) R The Spirit of God like a fire is burning 111219
We'll sing the songs of Sion (Mills) BC205 111220
We'll to God's tabernacles go, and at his footstool bow (Scottish Psalter, 1650) AL687; AP117 111221
We'll walk in the light, beautiful light ("J. V. C.") [Crosby??] R All ye saints of light 111222
We'll work till Jesus comes (---) R Let others seek a home below 111223
We'll work till Jesus comes (---) R O land of rest (Mills) 111224
Wenn dein herzliebster Sohn, o Gott (Heermann) BT375 111225
Wenn mein Stündlein vorhanden ist (Herman) BT594 111226
Wenn meine Sünd' mich kränken (Gesenius) BT152 111227
Wenn wir in höchsten Nöten sein (Eber) BT522 111228
Wenn's doch alle Seelen wussten (Unparth. G. B.) AY45d 111229
Wer Christo jetzt will folgen nach (J. Wagner) BU11 111230
Wer Gott vertraut, hat wohl gebaut (Magdeburg) BT437 111231
Wer nur den lieben Gott lässt walten (Neumark) AW571b; BT518; BW571 111232
Wer weiss, wie nahe mir mein Ende! (Ämilie Juliane, countess) BT598 111233
Wer will mit uns nach Zion gehn (Unparth. G. B.) AY32d 111234
Were you there when they crucified my Lord (Negro

spiritual) A80; J500; R201; AE455; AF179; AG317; AH609; AR173; BK170; BL23; BZ 111235

We're bound for the land of the pure and the holy (---) BB368 111236

We're going home, no more to roam (Griswold) AX593 111237

We're marching on to glory (Chamberlain) BC194 111238

We're marching to Zion (Watts) R Come we that love the Lord 111239

We're nearing the shore of that beautiful land (Doughty) R Soon trials and conflicts of life 111240

We're not ashamed to own our Lord (Phelps) BC266 111241

We're not ashamed to own our Lord (Phelps) X I'm not ashamed to own my Lord (Watts) 111242

We've a story to tell to the nations (Nichol) G501; R504; U389; V740; Z532; AC302; AE353; AG261; AH464; AP797; AR564; AS370; AT455; AU379; AV261; AW335; BF525; BY400; BZ 111243

"We've no abiding city here" (Kelly) L597; AY390; BB308 111244

What a fellowship, what a joy divine (Hoffman) AH390; AI 401; AM718; AT371; AU276; AW489; AX49; BB611 111245

What a friend we have in Jesus (Scriven) A422; G240; H38; I551; J459; L427; M581; N343; O488; P33; Q457; R385; S257; U356; V469; W701; Z331; AA 395; AD214; AE303; AF335; AG224; AH319; AI107; AK472; AL502; AM533; AO318; AP 494; AR483; AS127; AT328; AU160; AV319; AW186; AX 350; AY55; AZ957; BA618; BB320; BF372; BV612; BY 343; BZ 111246

What a mighty God we serve (Brooks) R Our Father's wondrous works 111247

What a sea of tears and sorrows (Breviary, 1746) BQ146 111248

What a wonderful change in my life (McDaniel) AT310 111249

What a wonderful Saviour (Hoffman) R Christ has for sin 111250

What a wonderful, wonderful Saviour (---) AX107 111251

What affords the Christian warrior vigor (Zinzendorf, N. L.) AZ1022 111252

What are these in bright array (Montgomery) K246 X Who are these in bright array 111253

What are these that glow from afar (Rossetti) E203; X209 111254

What are they that are but one? (English trad carol, 1625) BG64 111255

What are those soul-reviving strains (Montgomery) AZ 332; BA224 111256

What beauteous sun-surpassing star (Coffin) BO161 111257

What brightness dawned in resurrection (McKenzie) BE 381 111258

What brought us together, what joined our hearts? (Schlicht) AZ493; BA678 111259

What can I give to Jesus (---) AT508 111260

What can wash away my sin (Lowry) AM677 X What can wash away my stain 111261

What can wash away my stain (Lowry) AI395; AM677; AT 204; AU456; AX115; AY511 111262

What can we offer thee, O Lord (Spangenberg) BA546 X High on his everlasting throne 111263

What cheering words are these

(Kent) K411; L470; N481; AZ1349 111264

What child is this, who, laid to rest (Dix) A36; G109; R159; Z200; AB121; AF140; AG300; AH255; AW78; BD220; BF295; BK162; BZ 111265

What conscience dictates to be done (Pope) X693; AQ133 111266

What contradictions meet In minister's employ (Newton) BT46 X On what has now been sown 111267

What do I owe! Nay, Lord what do I not? (Oxenham) BY490 111268

What doth the Lord require of thee (Cross) AD326 111269

What else is wisdom. What else man's endeavor (Euripides) AQ109 111270

What equal honors shall we bring (Watts) AV131 111271

What glorious scenes mine eyes behold (---) BC197 111272

What glory gilds the sacred page (Cowper) BR235 X A glory gilds the sacred page 111273

What God ordains is always good (Rodigast) M281 X Whate'er my God ordains is right 111274

What good news the angels bring (Hammond) AZ62; BA162 111275

What grace, O Lord, and beauty shone (Denny) G115; I126; R 180; S143; W87; Z219; AE97; AG87; AL79; AO148; AP187; AS 120; BR171; BZ 111276

What happiness can equal mine (Faber) BN104; BO39; BP67 111277

What happiness, what joy and happiness (Gregor) AZ1229 111278

What has drawn us thus apart (Chadwick) AN222; BX97 111279

What heroes thou hast bred (Menzies) X325 111280

What is it that makes us stand fast in one spirit (Schlicht) AZ1091 111281

What is our calling's glorious hope (Wesley) I358 111282

What is the thing of greatest price (Montgomery) I243; U149 111283

What is the world to me (Pfefferkorn) M195; Q430; AA385 111284

What is this life if, full of care (Davies) AQ183 111285

What is thy birthright, Man (Seal) BE382 111286

What joy to reach the harbor (Brorson) P330 111287

What joy, to think of that vast host (Wexels) BY408 111288

What laws, my blessed Saviour, hast thou broken (Heermann) AZ466 111289

What lovely Infant can this be (---) BO157 111290

What makes a city great and strong (---) AQ102 111291

"What means this glory round our feet" (Lowell) AN160; BX192 111292

What mercy and divine compassion (Tersteegen) AW 562a 111293

What mortal tongue can sing your praise (Santeüil) BN 158; BO82 111294

What, my soul, should bow thee down (Cennick) AZ33 111295

What offering shall I bring to thee (Toeltschig) AZ919; BA58 111296

What our Father does is well (Schmolck) K488; L480; M497; N466; O531; P301; Q571; AA301; AZ1267 111297

What praise to thee, my Saviour (Gambold) AZ566; BA897 111298

What purpose burns within our hearts (Savage) BY532 111299

What secret hand, at morning light (Montgomery) BA768 111300

What secret place, what distant star (Gill) BX91 111301

What service shall we render (Dodgshun) W644 111302

What shall I do, my God, to love (Wesley) H293; AP459; BZ 111303

What shall I do, my Lord, my God (Larcom) AB191 111304

What shall I render to my God For all His gifts to me (Mason) K302; L83; N334 111305

What shall I render to my God For all His kindness shown (Watts) V519; AM537; AR350; AS352 111306

What shall I render to my God For all his mercy's store (Wesley) BZ 111307

What shall I render to the Lord, For all his benefits to me (U.P. Psalter, 1912) T218; AJ311 111308

What shall I render to the Lord, What shall my offering be (U.P. Psalter, 1912) R32; T220; AJ313 111309

What shall I render unto thee O Lord, For all the gifts (Van Rensselaer) AH129 111310

What sinners value, I resign (Watts) L575; V680; AZ383 111311

What songs are these, faint heard and far (Kendon) BG140 111312

What Star is this, so radiant, More lovely than the Sun (Coffin) BN26 111313

What star is this, with beams so bright (Coffin) A47; E44; AF144; AW87; BJ8 111314

What sweet of life endureth (St John of Damascus) E360 111315

What sweeter music can we bring (Herrick) BG122 111316

What thanks and praise to thee we own (Maclagan) D172; BV448 111317

What thou wilt, O Father, give (Whittier) AN278; BX333 111318

What though I cannot break my chain (Toplady) AM398 111319

What though the arm of conquering death (Doddridge) I592 111320

What tidings bringest thou, messenger (English trad carol, 15th c) R A babe is born of high nature 111321

What time I am afraid (U.P. Psalter, 1912) AJ152; AM 564 111322

What tongue can tell thy goodness, Lord (---) BI19-D 111323

What various hindrances we meet (Cowper) H41; I496; V459; AZ407; BV616 111324

What voice salutes the startled ear (Naisbitt) BC275 111325

What wait I for but thee (U.P. Psalter, 1912) T70; AJ106 111326

What was witnessed in the heavens (Davis) BC299 111327

What wealth of joy thy presence lendeth (Dessler) M267 111328

What will it be? What will it be? (Teddlie) R Some day you'll stand at the bar on high 111329

What will you do with Jesus (---) R Jesus is standing at your heart's door (McKinney) R Jesus is standing in Pilate's hall (---) 111330

What within me and without (Francke) BR366 111331

What wondrous love is this, O my soul, O my soul (Negro spiritual) BZ 111332

What would you give in exchange (Berry) R Brother afar from the Saviour 111333
What, ye ask me, is my prize (Schwedler) S331; AM435 111334
Whate'er God will, let that be done (Albrecht of Brandenburg - Culmbach) AA494 111335
Whate'er I am, whate'er I do (Zinzendorf, N. L.) AZ680 111336
Whate'er my God ordains is right (Rodigast) D668; I487; J582; K402; M281; O370; Q521; R 366; S291; W540; AF96; AK 309; AM94; AW567; BA703; BR272; BV515 111337
Whate'er our God ordains is right (Rodigast) J582 X Whate'er my God ordains 111338
Whatever dims thy sense of truth (Hale) BE383 111339
Whatever God ordains is right (Rodigast) AA507 X Whate'er my God ordains ... 111340
When a deed is done for freedom (Lowell) AQ168 X Once to every man and nation 111341
When a knight won his spurs (Struther) X377 111342
When adverse winds and waves arise (Sigourney) AZ657 111343
When afflictions sore oppress you (Olearius) O277 111344
When all my labors and trials are o'er (Gabriel) AT485; BB641 111345
When all the world was cursed (Olearius) Q272 111346
When all thy mercies, gracious Lord (Addison) BR249 X When all thy mercies, O my God 111347
When all thy mercies, O my God (Addison) A297; B237; D657; E511; F177; G542; H67; I105; J440; K296; L108; M591; N328; O20; Q31; R119; S81; U36; V 518; W26; X694; AA72; AF94; AG48; AH220; AK84; AL23; AM 51; AN225; AO98; AP145; AR82; AS83; AV56; AZ186; BA35; BR249; BV568; BX 117; BY77; BZ 111348
When along life's thorny road (Deck) O503; AZ1069 111349
When at thy footstool, Lord, I bend (Lyte) D591 111350
When blooming youth is snatched away (---) AY178 111351
When blossoms flowered 'mid the snows (Martens) BQ 126 111352
When by fear my heart is daunted (Dearmer) G319; X 695 111353
When Caesar Augustus had raised a taxation (English trad carol) BG114 111354
When came in flesh the incarnate word (Anstice) E13; F56; BV75 111355
When children, blest by Jesus (Rothe) AZ572; BA730 111356
When Christ at evening hour (Jenkins) BV196 111357
When Christ beheld, in sinful night (---) AY442 111358
When Christ blessed his disciples (Dearmer) BG153 111359
When Christ had shown God's dawning Reign (Dearmer) X185 111360
When Christ, our Lord and Saviour, dwelleth (Swertner) AZ1416 111361
When Christ our Lord had passed once more (Latin, 4th c) E150 111362
When Christ, our Saviour, did ascend (Cennick) AZ575 111363
When Christ was born in Bethlehem, Fair peace of earth (Housman) A112; E 611; X221 111364
When Christ was born in Bethlehem, 'Twas night, but seemed the noon (Longfellow) BC295 111365

When Christ was born of Mary free (English trad. carol, 15th c) B547; BG178; BR560; BV118 111366
When Christ was born to set us free (English trad carol, 15th c) BP18 111367
When Christmas morn is dawning (Ehrenborg-Posse) J35; M610; N635 111368
When cold our hearts and far from thee (Monsell) M584 111369
When courage fails and faith burns low (Hosmer) Z356; AB228; AN238; AQ95; AW191; BF432 111370
When dark and drear the skies appear (Woodmansee) BC293 111371
When darkness gathers round thy way (Smith) BB314 111372
When day's shadows lengthen (Lee) BQ140; BR114 111373
When doomed to death, the Apostle lay (Bryant) D279 111374
When downward to the darksome tomb (Palmer) BA732 111375
When first the glorious light of truth (Clayton) BC198 111376
When from Egypt's house of bondage (Threlfall) W573; AP785 111377
When from the city of our God (Wordsworth) AO478 111378
When from the East the wise men came (Hopkins) D64 111379
When gathering clouds around I view (Grant) I134; V637; AI287; AO410; AZ656; BR 333 111380
When God is seen with men to dwell (Ballou) BE384 111381
When God of old came down from heaven (Keble) E158; F154; W181; AP277; AZ110 111382
When great Saint Patrick raised the cross (---) BN165 111383
When He cometh, when He cometh (Cushing) N651; W158; AL614; AM651; AP794; AU315; AW432; BB418; BV355 111384
When here, O Lord, we seek thy face (Montgomery) AX646 X This stone to thee 111385
When his salvation bringing (King) D558; F437; G129; K546; L257; N638; O577; P358; R186; S149; AE108; AH278; AI386; AK138; AL 83; AM646; AO156; AP750; AR175; AZ826; BA817; BF 620; BR537 111386
When I by faith my Saviour see (Newton) AZ361 111387
When I can read my title clear (Watts) H369; I440; L469; N618; U427; V698; AA368; AI337; AT468; AU 16; AV287; AY362 111388
When I fall on my knees (Negro spiritual) R Let us break bread together 111389
When I fear my faith will fail (Habershon) AI310 111390
When I get weary with toils of the day (Warren) AX532 111391
When I have reached earth's borderland (Jones) AX537 111392
When I read how my Saviour was nailed to the cross (Teasley) AX347 111393
When I see the blood (Foote) R Christ our Redeemer died on the cross 111394
When I see the way my Saviour leads me (Gardiner) AX26 111395
When I shall reach the more excellent glory (Spencer) AX568 111396
When I shall wake in that fair morn of morns (Bonar) H331 111397
When I survey the wondrous cross (Watts) A337; B154; D101; E107; F108; G148; H169; I141; J503; K97; L245; M420; N107; O306; P178; Q175; R198; S152; T342; U 88; V142; W106; X133; Y 376; Z228; AA204; AB137;

AC123; AD156; AE119; AF 177; AG97; AH291; AI77; AK 158; AL86; AM186; AO166; AP192; AR174; AS143; AT99; AU191; AV108; AW105; AX 113; AY259; AZ331; BA225; BB120; BF315; BJ70; BR176; BV164; BY151; BZ 111398

When I visit Jesus' grave in spirit (Zinzendorf, C.R.) AZ1012 111399

When I was a sinner (Negro spiritual) R Go tell it on the mountain 111400

When in His might the Lord arose to set us free (U.P. Psalter, 1912) AJ358; AM290 111401

When in his thoughts the stars and planets roll (Young) AQ 71 111402

When in the hour of utmost need (Camerarius) K498; M 276; N575; O524; Q522; AA 515; BR344 111403

When in the Lord Jehovah's name (Alford) D557 111404

When in the maddening maze of things (Whittier) AW241 X I know not what the future hath 111405

When in the night I meditate (U.P. Psalter, 1912) R68; T21; AJ28 111406

When in the wondrous realms above (Kooyman) BC199 111407

When Israel of the Lord beloved (Scott) H128; I95; W367; AP 604; BE385; BH119; BX36 111408

When Israel out of Egypt went (U.P. Psalter, 1912) T214; AJ307; AM39 111409

Then Israel through the desert passed (Beddome) AA118 111410

When Israel to the wilderness had fled (Meyerhardt) BH 127 111411

When Israel was in Egypt's land (Negro spiritual) AF428; AH611 111412

When I've gone the last mile (Oatman) R If I walk in the pathway 111413

When Jesus Christ was twelve years old (English trad carol) BG72 111414

When Jesus Christ was yet a child (Plechtchéev) BJ70 111415

When Jesus comes in glory (Miller) N615; P429 111416

When Jesus comes to reward his servants (Crosby) AI94; AT119; AU67; AX284 111417

When Jesus dwelt in mortal clay (Gibbons) I695; L443; V576 111418

When Jesus into Salem rode (Montgomery) AZ103 X When Jesus left his Father's throne 111419

When Jesus left his Father's throne (Montgomery) A331; B362; D561; AZ103; BA841 111420

When Jesus on the mountain, These sayings taught (Toews) AX48 111421

When Jesus our great Master came (Watts) BE386 X So let our lips and lives express 111422

When Jesus shall gather the nations (MacKeever) BB538 111423

When Jesus to our rescue drew (Bridges) BJ78 111424

When Jesus was a baby (Wilson) BG167 111425

When Judas did his Lord reject (Dearmer) X224 111426

When judgment day is drawing nigh (---) AX286 111427

When lamps are lighted in the town (Penstone) X378 111428

When like a stranger on our sphere (Montgomery) BE388 111429

When, Lord, to this our western land (Onderdonk) AO535 111430

When low in heaven the sun has

now descended (Gryphius) BJ37 111431

When marshalled on the nightly plain (White) H143; I124; V125; BI93 111432

When Mary brought her treasure (Struther) X223 111433

When Mary, immaculate, tender and mild (Currie) BN138 111434

When morning fills the skies (German, ca 1800) BN190 111435

When morning gilds the skies (German, ca 1800) A367; B37; D445; E512; F223; G31; H29; I32; J416; K310; M556; R41; S3; T323; V29; W167; Y201; Z135; AB77; AC2; AD43; AE40; AF35; AG21; AH158; AK43; AL 45; AM131; AN92; AO19; AP255; AR46; AS19; AT23; AU7; AV2; AW19; AZ554; BA128; BB43; BD4; BF176; BJ67; BK38; BO 10; BQ42; BR1; BV271; BY 685; BZ 111436

When morning lights the eastern skies (U.P. Psalter, 1912) R49; T283; AJ391 111437

When mothers of Salem (Hutchings) S446; W659; AL609; AP796; BY401 111438

When musing sorrow weeps the past (Noel) I455 111439

When my last hour is close at hand (Hermann) O582; Q594; AA528 111440

When my life-work is ended and I cross the swelling tide (Crosby) AT472; AV397; AX572; AY495 111441

When my lips can frame no sound (Comenius) BA854 111442

When my love to Christ grows weak (Wreford) BA227 X When my love to God grows weak 111443

When my love to God grows weak (Wreford) U89; X134; AF162; AN189; AQ313; AW102; BA227; BV165 111444

When, my Saviour, shall I be (Wesley) BB250 111445

When o'er my sins I sorrow (Gesenius) Q152; AA197 111446

When on my day of life the night is falling (Whittier) G519; I589; W589; X697; AB403; AD463; AK419; AL456; AN 436; AP625; BF668; BR425; BX471; BY777 111447

When on Sinai's top I see (Montgomery) AZ55 111448

When our heads are bowed with woe (Milman) A79; B409; D348; E513; K76; O464; W 329; AL131; BA664; BR346; BT162 111449

When out in sin and darkness lost (Gilmour) AX89; AY 201 111450

When, overwhelmed with grief (Watts) BR281 111451

When peace, like a river, attendeth my way (Spafford) L493; N525; P213; AE190; AH394; AI258; AM580; AR 484; AS310; AT265; AU73; AV363; AW484; AX484; AY 452; BB313 111452

When righteous Joseph wedded was (English trad carol) BG41 111453

When rising from the bed of death (Addison) E92; L390 111454

When Rome had shrouded earth in night (Luther) AA283 111455

When shadows gather on our way (Hosmer) S323; AN125; BX 104 111456

When shall thine hour,, dear Jesus come (Zinzendorf, N. L.) AZ282 111457

When shall we meet again? Meet ne'er to serve? (Watts & Smith) L598; AY 301 111458

When shepherds watched their flocks by night, In Bethlehem's fields so still (Westall) BR561 111459

When simplicity we cherish (Spangenberg) AZ235; BA636

111460

When sinners see their lost condition (Landstad) M343; O173; P270; Q65 111461

When sins and fears prevailing rise (Steele) V359 111462

When Sion in her low estate (U.P. Psalter, 1912) T256; AI264; AJ357 111463

When Sion's bondage God turned back (Scottish Psalter, 1650) AL685; AP114 111464

When sorrow and remorse (Gesenius) K75 111465

When spring unlocks the flowers to paint the laughing soil (Heber) E299; X21; Z592; AD451 111466

When Stephen, full of power and grace (Struther) X219; AF493; AN425; AQ155 111467

When storms of life are round me beating (Oatman) AX358 111468

When streaming from the eastern skies (Shrubsole) D638; N549; O550; Q543; AA19; AI47; AZ 671 111469

When sun rays crown thy pine clad hills (Boyle) AL524 111470

When the blind suppliant in the way (Bryant) H156 111471

When the book of life is opened (Snyder) R When your toils 111472

When the clouds are hanging low (Lillenas) AU334; AX364 111473

When the corn is planted In the dark deep bed (---) BY757 111474

When the day of toil is done (Ellerton) W584; AA546; AL466; AO29; AP619; AZ1137 111475

When the early morning breaking (Morris) AI308 111476

When the gladsome day declineth (Savage) AN123; AQ272 111477

When the golden evening gathered On the shore of Galilee (Dawson) Y76; Z212; AC108; AK 130; AR154 111478

When the great sun sinks to his rest (Babcock) S72 111479

When the heart is sad within (Milman) BR346 X When our heads are bowed 111480

When the herds were watching (Canton) X379 111481

When the King comes in, brother (Landor) R Called to the feast by the King are we 111482

When the light of day is waning (Geldart) BX155 111483

When the Lord of Love was here (Brooke) S141; U78; W85; Z215; AB128; AC104; AL80; AN207; BB115; BD66; BF306; BX215; BY133 111484

When the Lord turned the captivity of Sion (Ladies of the Grail) BSp46 111485

When the mists have rolled in splendor (Herbert) AU354 111486

When the night is still and far (Gannett) Y13 111487

When the paschal evening fell (Stanley) BV170; BX485 111488

When the roll is called up yonder (Black) R When the trumpet of the Lord 111489

When the rosy light of morning (Baird) BC200 111490

When the Sabbath, peace-inviting (Jastrow) BH114 111491

When the stars at set of sun (---) BH245 111492

When the storms of life are raging, Stand by me (Tindley) AU30; BZ 111493

When the storms of life are raging, Tempests wild on land and sea (Servoss) AU 409 111494

When the sun had sunk to rest (French) BF279 111495

When the sun shines bright and your heart is light (Reynolds) AT214; AV352 111496

When the trump shall sound and time (Jacobs) AY383 111497
When the trump shall sound (Jacobs) X When the trumpet of the Lord (Black) 111498
When the trumpet of the Lord shall sound (Black) AH530; AM727; AT482; AX577 111499
When the trumpet of the Lord (Black) X When the trump shall sound (Jacobs) 111500
When the unquiet hours depart (Russell i.e. "A.E.") X122 111501
When the weary seeking rest (Bonar) D609; I509; V758; W255; AB180; AK231; AL332; AM532; AP236; AW203; AZ 1505; BA611; BF365; BR25 111502
When the world around us throws (Williams) AN233; BF361; BX259 111503
When there is peace, Where praise hath been (Davis) BH 16 111504
When they bereaved his life so good (English trad carol) G72 X When Jesus Christ was twelve years old 111505
When this passing world is done (McCheyne) W582; AL302; AM 600; AP460; AZ1264; BY616 111506
When this poor heart is burdened with grief (Hugg) AY375 111507
When this song of praise shall cease (Bryant) AR47; BH103 111508
When Thou, my righteous Judge, shalt come (Huntingdom) H495; U422; V686; AI96; BB190 111509
When through the sail the wild tempest is streaming (Heber) N78; BR363 111510
When through the whirl of wheels, and engines humming (Studdert-Kennedy) X698; Y184; AC192; AD350; AF422; BF511 111511
When thy heart with joy o'er flowing (Williams) U371; Z508; AC 245; AE278; AH513; AN280; AO470; AQ226; AR373; AS345; AW227; BD134; BF608; BH 197; BK111; BX335 111512
When thy soldiers take their swords (Owen) AK345; AM 486; AO372; AP557; BX367 111513
When time seems short and death is near (Bethune) I296; BW440 111514
When trials and temptations around thee (Metzler) AX 530; AY386 111515
When upon life's billows you are tempest-tossed (Oatman) AT318; BC202 111516
When upon the raging waters (Kretzman) M174 111517
When very early in the dawn (Synnestvedt) BI106 111518
When vesper bells are calling (Franzén) N565 111519
When virgin morn doth call thee to arise (Herrick) X 36 111520
When warmer suns and bluer skies (---) BH134 111521
When waves of trouble round me swell (Elliott) AO355 111522
When we all get to heaven (Hewitt) R Sing the wondrous love of Jesus 111523
When we devote our youth to God (Watts) AZ166 111524
When we have ended searching (Patton) AQ181 111525
When we hear the music ringing (---) AY156 111526
When we walk with the Lord (Sammis) AE210; AH420; AI400; AM700; AR485; AS 269; AT260; AU390; AV373; AW486; AX465; AY454; BB582; BY491; BZ 111527
When wilt thou save the people (Elliott) A496; B501; E566; S375; X314; Y241; Z563; AB 290; AC288; AD352; AG280; AL527; AN324; AO483; AP 642; AR90; AV229; BB675;

BD165; BF577; BX382; BY654 111528

When winds are raging o'er the upper ocean (Stowe) P297; AB217; AN228; BF390; BX265; 111529

When wounded sore the stricken soul [heart] (Alexander) B138; F88; H226; L520; BV140 111530

When your toils below are ended (Snyder) AX293; AY389 111531

When came the armies of the sky (---) BB378 111532

Whence these sounds symphonious (Kelly) AZ759 111533

When-e'er I think of her so dear (Van de Venter) R I never can forget 111534

When e'er we contemplate the grace (Gregor) O344; AZ902 111535

Whenever war, with its red woes (Finley) Y228 111536

Where ancient forests widely spread (Norton) AN27; BX 35 111537

Where are the reapers? O who will come (Rexford) R O where are the reapers 111538

Where are you going, Greatheart? (Oxenham) AC499 111539

Where could I go, O where could I go (Coats) R Living below in this old sinful world 111540

Where cross the crowded ways of life (North) A498; B494; G465; I423; J351; K235; N387; P387; R507; S410; T442; U330; Y60; Z519; AB332; AC265; AD427; AE413; AF423; AG268; AH512; AI179; AK394; AL380; AN218; AO475; AP581; AQ189; AR198; AS339; AT464; AU405; AV276; AW222; BA555; BD136; BF522; BK80; BX223; BY533; BZ 111541

Where for safety shall I fly? (Hymns of the English conf. 1880) BR350 111542

Where He leads I'll follow (Ogden) R Sweet are the promises 111543

Where He leads me I will follow (Blandly) R I can hear my Saviour calling 111544

Where He may lead me I will go (Martin) AS249; AX507 111545

Where high the heavenly temple stands (Bruce) F204; K137; R389; V172; W140; AL122; AP231; AZ354; BA96; BB137; BV212; BY178 111546

Where is death's sting? We were not born to die (Bradby) A470; X296 111547

Where is he that came to save (Beach) BX209 111548

Where is my wandering boy (Lowry) AU89 111549

Where is our holy Church (Wilson) AN412; AQ259 111550

Where is the Friend for whom I'm ever yearning (Wallin) N517; S329 111551

Where is the true man's fatherland? (Lowell) AB359; BF 578 111552

Where is thy Lord, my soul? (Lynch) X699; Y16; AB188; BX100 111553

Where is thy hope, poor sinner (Warren) AX289 111554

Where is your God? they say (Martineau) Y3; AB35; AD 92; AN71; AQ87; BX109 111555

Where Judah's faithful sons are found (Mayer) BH210 111556

Where lies our path? We seek to know (North) AB316 111557

Where loyal hearts and true (Faber) R O paradise, O paradise 111558

Where, O God eternal, where art thou? (Kálmán) AK62 111559

Where restless crowds are thronging (Clark) J355;

BY655 111560
Where shall my wondering soul begin? (Wesley) BZ 111561
Where the angel-hosts adore thee (Santeüil) D171; N318; BA38 111562
Where the great ships, passing (Rowland) G556; AB383 111563
Where the mourner, weeping (Oswald) BR340 X O let him whose sorrow 111564
Where the olive grove stood darkly (Tiplady) Z229 111565
"Where two or three, with sweet accord" (Stennett) AY193; AZ406 111566
Where will I go? (Warren) R Eternity draws near 111567
Where will you spend eternity (Hoffman) AU290; AX268; AY 531 111568
Where wilt thou go, since night draws near (Homburg) M451; Q197; AA227 111569
Where winds the road o'er hill and dale (Mather) Z420; AR382 111570
Where'er have trod thy sacred feet (---) D315 111571
Where'er his creatures gather (U. P. Psalter, 1912) T151; AJ223 111572
Where'er I go, whate'er my task (Flemming) AA372 111573
Where-fore do the nations rage (Grant) AJ3 111574
Wherefore, O Father, we thy humble servants, Here bring before thee (Jervois) A205; E335; F416 111575
Wherefore, O Father, we thy humble servants Offer our praises (Dearmer) X281; AK 342; BV368 111576
Wherefore weep we over Jesus (Spitta) AZ958 111577
Wherever he leads I'll go (McKinney) R Take up thy cross 111578
Wherever men adore thee (Van Dyke) AK414 X No form of human framing 111579
Wherever through the ages rise (Whittier) AN442; BX483 111580
Wherewith, O Lord, shall I draw near (Wesley) I244 111581
Whether day my spirit's yearning (Goethe) AQ63 111582
Whether the end of earthly life (Zinzendorf, N. L.) BA711 111583
While filled with sadness and dismay (Newton) V581 111584
While humble shepherds watched their flocks (Tate) W42 X While shepherds watched their flocks 111585
While in sweet communion feeding (Denny) Z460; AI163; AS465 111586
While Jesus whispers to you (Witter) AU212; AX229; BB564 111587
While life prolongs its precious light (Dwight) H248; I254; V273 111588
While my Redeemer's near (Steele) BR262 111589
While o'er the deep thy servants sail (Burgess) D308 111590
While of these emblems we partake (Nicholson) BC217 111591
While passing thro' this world of sin (McKinney) AT348; AU423 111592
While shepherds kept their watching (Negro spiritual) R Go tell it on the mountains 111593
While shepherds watched their flocks by night (Tate) A13; B71; D54; E30; F62; G88; H136; I115; J24; K28; L225; M350; N44; O188; P131; Q 109; R169; S120; U50; V117; W42; X82; Z185; AD112; AE 88; AF146; AG80; AH260; AI 62; AK106; AL62; AM156; AN155; AO120; AP168; AQ 295; AR130; AT79; AU147;

AV89; AW73; AX98; AY489; AZ1462; BA161; BB101; BC222; BD210; BF283; BG33; BJ39; BK145; BR551; BV123; BY113; BZ 111594

While sinks our land to realms of night (Pattinson) BX142 111595

While successive years are wasting (Okely) AZ1383 111596

While the pilgrim travels (Zinzendorf, N. L.) AZ753; BA39 111597

While the sun is shining (Stowell) N507; AI183 111598

While the years of eternity roll (Gates) R I will sing to you a song 111599

While thee I seek protecting Power (Williams) B35; D671; H122; I517; L474; V426; Z334; AE243; AN255; AO89; AV41; AW199; AY43; AZ1452; BA901; BR247; BX304 111600

While thou, O my God, art my help and defender (Young) BE 389; BR312 111601

While we lowly bow before thee (Colesworthy) L206; 111602

While we pray and while we plead (Whittle) AT218; AV333; AX236 111603

While we take our seat (Zinzendorf, N. L.) AZ540 111604

While with ceaseless course the sun (Newton) H522; I574; L552; N53; Q113; V629; AA163; AM 613; AZ1073; BA180; BR500 111605

While yet the earth midst chaos whirled (Rypins) BH99 111606

While yet the morn is breaking (Mühlmann) M551; N543; Q544; AA21 111607

Whisper a prayer, whisper a prayer (McKinney) R Come linger here 111608

Whispering hope (Hawthorne) R Soft as the voice of an angel 111609

Whiter than snow, yes, whiter than snow (Nicholson) R Lord Jesus, I long to be perfectly whole 111610

Whither pilgrims, are you going (Golden chain, 1861) [Crosby?] W578; AP783 111611

Whither thus in holy rapture (Santeüil) BO96; BQ80 111612

Who are these arrayed in white (Wesley) I619 111613

Who are these in bright array (Montgomery) B298; D180; K246; L595; N209; AO557; AZ1059; BA752; BR443 111614

Who are these like stars appearing (Schenck) A130; B296; D178; E204; F570; K245; N630; O493; W222; X210; AM602; AZ607; BA810; BV465 111615

Who at my door is standing (Slade) AX245; AY374 111616

Who came down from heaven to earth (Whittle) AI385 111617

Who dares to bind to his dull sense (Rawson) AN368; BX 400 111618

Who dreads, yet undismayed (Darbyshire) F534; X218 111619

Who fathoms the eternal thought (Whittier) W558 X I know not what the future hath 111620

Who goes there, in the night (Clark) Y122; AC261 111621

Who has seen the wind (Rossetti) X386d 111622

Who hath believed after hearing the message (Oliver) AM673 111623

Who is he, in yonder stall (Hanby) E612; K560; W77; AE96; AL72; AP735; AW96; BV284; BY134 111624

Who is he whom crowds acclaim (Dearmer) X700b 111625

Who is like thee, O universal

Lord (Gutheim) BH69 111626
Who is on the Lord's side (Havergal) R355; S272; U292; V752; W519; Z367; AB349; AC202; AE272; AG190; AH434; AI331; AK286; AL365; AM493; AO373; AP551; AT413; AU63; AV208; AW190; BF475; BV592; BY534 111627
Who is she that stands triumphant (Vere) BM94 X Holy Church now stands 111628
Who is the man that shall ascend (Scottish Psalter, 1650) AP 20 111629
Who is the patriot? He who lights (Knowles) AQ243 111630
Who is there like thee, Jesus, unto me? (Freylinghausen) O30; AO381; AZ543 111631
Who is there that singeth so, Nowell? (Smart) BG21 111632
Who is this so weak and helpless (How) E514; L211; W73; AL74; AM169; AP260 111633
Who is this that comes from Edom (Kelly) D449; Q209; AA223; AM228; AZ604 111634
Who is this that comes in glory (Wordsworth) BR189 X See the Conqueror mounts in triumph 111635
Who is this, with garments dyed (Dayman) AZ557 111636
Who is this with garments gory (Coxe) E108 111637
Who is thy neighbor? He whom thou (Cutter) I690; AW228; BX339 111638
Who knows how near my end may be? (Amilie Juliana) L564; M301; O579; Q598; AA544 111639
Who knows how near my life's expended (Amilie Juliana) O579 X Who knows how near my end 111640
Who knows how soon my days are ended (Amilie Juliana) M301 X Who knows how near my end 111640a
Who knows when death may overtake me (Amilie Juliana) Q598 X Who knows how near my end 111641
Who made ocean, earth, and sky (Compton) BK4 111642
Who, O Lord, shall dwell with thee (U.P. Psalter, 1912) AJ26 111643
Who, O Lord, with thee abiding (U.P. Psalter, 1912) T19; AJ24 111644
Who overcometh shall abide forever (Moravian) AZ1023 111645
Who pits his trust in God most just (Magdeburg) AA511; AZ1093; BA698 111646
Who saved us from eternal loss (Gray) R O Listen to our wondrous story 111647
Who shall open for us the portals (Peter) M364 111648
Who shall the Lord's elect condemn (Watts) AA313 111649
Who taught the bird to build her nest (---) BH247 111650
Who thou art I know not (Kemp) AQ46 111651
Who trusts in God, a strong abode (Magdeburg) K334; N86; O282; Q437; R375; U 199; AB244; AF354; AM558; BF397 111652
Who will build the world anew (Clark) AE408; AR579 111653
Who will join the throng to heaven (Brorson) M70 111654
Who will now indict me (Franck) P272 111655
Who within that stable cries (Dearmer) X700a 111656
Who would true valor see (Bunyan) F293 X He who would valiant be 111657
Whole-hearted thanksgiving to thee will I bring (U.P. Psalter, 1912) T12; AJ16 111658
Who'll be the next to follow

Jesus (Hawks) AX258 111659
Whom have we, Lord, in heaven but thee, and whom on earth besides (Birks or Auber) (identification not possible) BR269 111660
Whom oceans part, O Lord, unite (Lewis) W628; Z525; AD454; AE366; AR504; BY656 111661
Who's on the Lord's side? Who? (Cornaby) BC175 111662
Whose works, O Lord, like thine can be (Lucas) BH222 111623
Whose in God alone confideth (Neumark) BR260 X He who would be in God confiding 111664
"Whosoever hearteh," shout (Bliss) AT238; AU126; AX 220; BB571 111665
"Whosoever" surely meaneth me (McConnell) R I am happy today 111666
Why art thou cast down my soul? (Schmolck) O237; P294 111667
Why art thou cast down my soul, why disquieted in me? (Hamburg Temple hymnal) BH171 111668
Why art thou heavey-hearted (Gerhardt) M270 111669
Why art thou sorrowful, servant of God (Faber) BQ144 111670
Why do the heathen rage (Kennedy) O217 111671
Why do we mourn departing friends (Watts) I595; L573; Q593; V673; AA542; AY168; AZ104 111672
Why do you wait, dear brother (Root) AT220; AU170; AX243 111673
Why dost thou stand afar (U. P. Psalter, 1912) AJ19; AM508 111674
Why, impious Herod, shouldst thou fear (Sedulius) E38 111675
Why is thy faith in God's great love so small (Sherwin) BE 390 111676
Why, my soul, thus trembling ever (Gerhardt) O342 111677
Why not now? (Whittle) R While we pray and while we plead 111678
Why not? why not? Why not come to Him now? (Root) R Why do you wait 111679
Why rage the heather? and vain things (Scottish Psalter, 1650) AP2 111680
Why search the future and the past (Barlow) BE391 111681
Why should cross and trial grieve me (Gerhardt) Q523 AA501; AM506 111682
Why should I fear the darkest hour (Newton) AP529; BV 578 111683
Why should I feel discouraged (Martin) AI312; AM725 111684
Why should I repine in sadness (Gerhardt) M275 111685
Why should our tears in sorrow flow (Bathurst) I591 111686
Why should sorrow ever grieve me (Gerhardt) AA501 X Why should cross and trial 111687
Why should the children of a king (Watts) I299; V304; AZ198 111688
Why should we start and fear to die (Watts) H489; I581; AZ 366 111689
Why sleep ye, my brethren? Come, let us arise (Hopkins) AY57 111690
Why standest thou afar, O Lord (U. P. Psalter, 1912) T14; AJ18 111691
Why this tumult among nations (Ladies of the Grail) BSp6 111692
Why those fears? Behold, 'tis Jesus (Kelly) O241 111693
Why will ye waste on trifling cares (Doddridge) U160; V274; AZ386 111694
Wide open are thy hands (St

Bernard of Clairvaux??) J66; K65; M417; P188 111695
Wide open are thy loving hands (St Bernard of Clairvaux??) P188 X Wide open are thy hands 111696
Wie bist du mir so innig gut (Unparth. G.B.) AY27d 111697
Wie gross ist des Allmächt'gen Güte! (Gellert) BW516 111698
Wie ich bin, komm' ich zu dir-- (Charlotte Elliott) BW458 111699
Wie schön geschmucht der festliche Raum (Cornelius) BG191b 111700
Wie schön leuchtet der Morgenstern, Voll Gnad' und Wahrheit von dem Herrn (Nicolai) BG 104b; BT343; BW529 111701
Wie schön leucht't uns der Morgenstern Vom Firmament des Himmels fern (Stegman) BT546 111702
Wie soll ich dich empfangen (Gerhardt) BT58 111703
Wie wohl hast du gelabet (Rist) BT316 111704
Wie wohl ist mir, o Freund der Seelen (Dessler) BT362 111705
Wild roars the blast, the storm is high (Cross) Y115; AC278 111706
Will the circle be unbroken (Habershon) R There are loved ones 111707
Will there be any stars, any stars in my crown (Hewitt) R I am thinking today 111708
Will you come to the fountain free (Slade) R There's a fountain free 111709
Will you come, will you come (Crosby) AX224 111710
Will your anchor hold in the storms of life (Owens) AU392; AW482; AX483; BB584; BY568 111711
Willie, take your little drum (LaMonnoye) BG82 111712
Willing to own thee Master and King (Fraser) AS231 111713
Willkommen, Held im Streite (Schmolck) BW542 111714
Wilt heden nu treden voor God den Heere (Dutch trad.) BT568 111715
Wilt thou forgive that sin, by man begun (Donne) E515; X123 111716
Wilt thou forgive that sin, where I begun (Donne) X123 X Wilt thou forgive that sin by man begun 111717
Wilt thou hear the voice of praise (Rice) I675 111718
Wilt thou not, my Shepherd true (Scheffler) O403 111719
Wilt thou, O man, live happily (Luther) AA392 111720
Winds of God unfailing fill the sunlit sails (Dearmer) BG 154 111721
Winning souls, winning souls (Mackay) R Rouse, ye Christian workers 111722
Winter creeps, nature sleeps (Dearmer) X380 111723
Winter is a cold thing (Dunham) AQ302 111724
Winter reigneth o'er the land (How) W622; AP694 111725
Winter reigns o'er many a region (Meisser) K228; N 377 111726
Wir bitten dich, ewiger Gott (Ausbund) BU31 111727
Wir Christenleut' Hab'n jetzund Freud (Füger) BT107 111728
Wir danken dir, Herr Jesu Christ Dass du für uns gestorben bist (Fischer) BT173 111729
Wir danken dir, Herr Jesu Christ Dass du gen Himmel g'fahren bist (Praetorius. Musae Sioniae 1607) BT223 111730
Wir danken dir, o treuer Gott (Selnecker) BT321 111731
Wir danken Gott von Herzen

(Ausbund) BU35 111732
Wir glauben all an einen Gott, Und lieben ihn (Athanasian Creed) BU2 111733
Wir glauben all'an einen Gott Vater, Sohn und Heil'gen Geist. (Clausnitzer) BT252 111734
Wir pflügen und wir streuen. (M. Claudius) BW375 111735
Wir sind des Herrn, wir leben oder sterben (Spitta) BT453 111736
Wir singen dir, Immanuel (Gerhardt) BT108 111737
Wir treten zum Beten vor Gott den Herren (Dutch traditional) BT568 111738
Wir warten dein, O Gottes Sohn (P. F. Hiller) BW524 111739
Wir werfen uns danieder (Unparth. G. B.) AY33d 111740
Wir wollen alle frölich sein (German trad carol, 16th c) BG95b 111741
Wir zieh'n nach dem verheiss'nen Land (Unparth. G. B.) AY 41d 111742
Wisdom and power to Christ belong (Wesley) AZ890; BA926 111743
Wisdom hath treasures greater far (Bruce) AN273; AQ96 111744
Wisdom, righteousness and power (Jones) R Jesus Christ is made to me 111745
Wise men seeking Jesus, traveled from a far (East) Z203; AD472; AL600; BF618; BY135 111746
With all my heart I love thee, Lord (Schalling) O393 111747
With all my heart will I record (Westra) AJ429 111748
With all my powers of heart and tongue (Watts) H63; BC216 111749
With all the power of heart and tongue (Watts) BC216 X With all my powers of heart and tongue 111750
With all the powers my poor heart hath (St Thomas Aquinas) K185 111751
With awe, and deeply bowed (Moravian) AZ1121 111752
With broken heart and contrite sigh (Elven) A60; B133; D87; H275; J367; K316; L376; M 72; N184; O441; Q323; U 171; V281; AA418; AI214; AM 416; AO263; BA419 111753
With Christ we share a mystic grave (Neale) E339 111754
With deep humility, O Lord (Trabert) N247 111755
With deeply humbled hearts we make confession (Simpson) AZ467 111756
With eternal day before us (Rowe) R Smiling skies will bend above us 111757
With firm resolve I held my peace (U. P. Psalter, 1912) AJ104 111758
With friends on earth we meet in gladness (Chapman) AU412; AX656; AY184 111759
With gladness we hail this blessed day (Grundtvig) M 348 111760
With gladsome feet we press (Singleton) AZ1194; BR516 111761
With gladsome hearts we come (MacLeod) D532 111762
With glorious clouds encompassed round (Wesley) I327 111763
With glory clad, with strength arrayed (Tate) AM64; AN489; BX53 111764
With God and his mercy, his Spirit, and word (Rosenius) N272; P43 111765
With God in grace I'm dwelling (Hauge) P326 111766
With golden splendour and with roseate hues of morn (Elpis??) E226 111767
With grateful heart my thanks I bring (U. P. Psalter, 1912) T274; AJ381; AM76 111768
With happy voices ringing

(Tarrant) R463; S441; Z113; AC320; AD468; AE31; AG301; AH201; AK455; AN478; AR11; AS93; AT507; AV407; BD16; BF619; BX519 111769

With happy voices singing (Tarrant) S441 X With happy voices ringing 111770

With harps and with viols (Pierson) AM714 111771

With heart and hand you now we own (Gregor) AX287 111772

With hearts and with voices, O praise ye the Lord (Herrnsschmidt) AZ495 111773

With heavenly power, O Lord, defend (Hill) V563 111774

With holy joy my heart doth beat (Hedborn) N243 111775

With humble prayer, O, may I read (---) AZ322 111776

With Jesus for hero, for teacher and friend (Dearmer) X69 111777

With joy and gladness in my soul (U.P. Psalter, 1912) AJ348 111778

With joy I heard my friends exclaim (U.P. Psalter, 1912) R439; T252; AJ350 111779

With joy we claim the growing light (Longfellow) AQ246 X Eternal One, thou living God 111780

With joy we hail the sacred day (Auber) D29; H84; I65; V69; AA128; AT38; AV6 111781

With joy we meditate the grace (Watts) L135; V176; AL125; BA98; BV281; BY179 111782

With joyful heart your praises bring (Günther) O13 111783

With joyfulness and longing (Ellis) BA336 111784

With love and peace and joy supreme (Nourse) BE392 111785

With loving hearts and hands we rear (Ames) BX497 111786

With mercy heart let all rejoice in one (Piae Cantiones) BG83 111787

With new life endowed by Christ our Saviour (Zinzendorf, N. L.) AZ1003 111788

With one consent let all the earth (Tate & Brady) D469 111789

With praise, O God, we worship thee (Froom) BB697 111790

With reverence let the saints appear (Watts) V108; BB4 111791

With silence only as their benediction (Whittier) AP 623 111792

With solemn joy we come, dear Lord (Ryden) J291; M542; N256 111793

With songs and honors sounding loud (Watts) H518; S 75; AB385; AF459; AH491; AM113; BI115; BR63; BX56 111794

With tearful eyes I look around (Elliott) D631; V294; AY 395 111795

With tears of anguish I lament (Stennett) L386; V476 111796

With tender greeting, Lo, thy children meeting (---) BP 93 111797

With thankful hearts, O Lord, we come (Mohler) AR599, AS423 111798

With thankful hearts we meet, O Lord (Peters) AY4 111799

With thankful voice praise ye the Lord (U.P. Psalter, 1912) T221; AJ314 111800

With the Lord begin thy task (Morgen-und Abendsegen. Waldenburg, 1734) Q540 111801

With the Lord thy task begin (Hohlfeldt) M646 111802

With the sweet word of peace (Watson) B419; AO509; AZ1197; BA892 111803

With the voice of sweet song (Mayer) BH70 111804

With Thee, O Lord, alone to go (Kretzmann) M535

111805
With thine own pity, Saviour, see (Palmer) AE320; BZ 111806
With thy presence, Lord, our Head and Saviour (Gregor) AZ1013; BA927 111807
With trembling awe the chosen three (How) O249 111808
With willing hearts we tread (Smith) BB439 111809
With wonderful deathless ditties (O'Shaughnessy) X315 111810
With wondering awe the wise men saw (---) BC209 111811
Withhold not, Lord, the help I crave (Spitta) O428 111812
Within the Father's house (Woodford) D69; N72; O228; Q133; AK128; AO153; BA73 111813
Within the maddening maze of things (Whittier) AF360 X I know not what the future hath 111814
"Within the veil!" Be this beloved (Allen) BB138 111815
Within this temple, reared of old (Blatchford) BX506 111816
Within thy house, O Lord, our God (Hymns adapted to the public worship, 1828) AS58 111817
Within thy tabernacle, Lord, be with us through this day (Hymns of the English Conf. 1880) BR88 111818
Within thy tabernacle, Lord, Who shall abide (Scottish Psalter, 1650) AL633; AP9; AW577 111819
Within thy temple, Lord, In that most holy place (U.P. Psalter, 1912) AJ134 111820
Within thy temple, Lord, We on thy mercies dwell (U.P. Book of Psalms, 1871) AM307; AP 43 111821
Within thy temple, Lord, We think on mercies past (U.P. Psalter, 1912) T90; AJ133 111822
Within thy temple's sacred courts (U.P. Psalter, 1912) R438; AJ132 111823
Without spot and blameless, O Saviour (Warren) AX150 111824
Witness, ye men and angels, now (Beddome) D217; AO 457; AY270; AZ151; BA462; BY304 111825
Wo ist Jesus, mein Berlangen (Unparth. G.B.) AY11d 111826
Wo kommt das her, o Jesu Christ (Ausbund) BU125 111827
Wo soll ich mich hin kehren (Ausbund) BU76 111828
Wo willst du him, weil's Abend ist (Homburg) BT197 111829
Woe unto him that has not known the woe of man (Binyon) AQ153 111830
Wohl einem Haus, da Jesus Christ (Pfeil) BT625 111831
Wohlauf, mein Herze, sing und spring (Gerhardt) BT535 111832
Wohlauf, Wohlauf, du Gottes G'mein (M. Schneider) BU97 111833
Wollt ihr hören, was ist geschehn (T. Drucker) BU 23 111834
Wonderful grace of Jesus (Lillenas) AM702 111835
Wonderful Jesus! glorious friend (Rowe) AX21 111836
Wonderful love! Wonderful love (Mund) R In Joyful high and holy lays 111837
Wonderful peace, beautiful peace (Barratt) R Like radiant sunshine 111838
Wonderful Saviour, Redeemer (Jacobs) AY392 111839
Wonderful story of love (Driver) AU349; AX281 111840
Wonderful the matchless grace of Jesus (Lillenas) R Wonderful grace of Jesus111841
Wonderful, wonderful Jesus (Russell) R There is never

a day so dreary 111842
Wonders still the world shall witness (Trapp) AN352; AQ191 111843
Wondrous gift! The word who fashioned (Breviary, Cluny, 1686) BM3-4 111844
Wondrous King, all-glorious (Neander) Q41; AM132 111845
Wondrous love that cannot falter (The Association of Perpetual Adoration) BQ56 111846
Wonn lächelt überall (Unparth. G.B.) AY48d 111847
Word of God, across the ages (Blanchard) AT176 111848
Word of God to earth descending (St Thomas Aquinas) BO41 111849
Word of Life, most pure, most strong (Bahmaier) AW329; BE 394 111850
Word supreme, before creation (Keble) E33; F536; Q271 111851
Work, for the night is coming (Coghill) D583; G293; H376; I422; L540; M647; R297; W357; AH414; AK477; AL390; AM728; AO507; AP595; AS334; AT424; AU243; AV272; AW221; AX189; AZ853; BA562; BB446 111852
Work is sweet, for God has blest (Thring) E516; BF433 111853
Work while it is today (Montgomery) AZ1346; BA74; BB347 111854
Workers on a building rare (Coats) AX191 111855
Working, O Christ, with thee (Ogden) BB345 111856
Working together, wary and strong (Dearmer) X345 111857
Workman of God! O lose not heart (Faber) I392; W520; Y173; AL 408; BB443; BF474; BX300; BY535 111858
Worship, glory, praise and honour (Wood) BV661 111859
Worship, honour, glory, blessing (Osler) F632; X418; 624b 111860
Worship the Lord in the beauty of holiness (Monsell) U5 X O worship the Lord 111861
Worthy art thou, Lord divine (Kauffman) AX6 111862
Worthy, O Lamb of God, art thou (Conder) R Thou art the everlasting Word 111863
Worthy, O Lord, art thou (Wesley) AZ1161; BA126 111864
Worthy, worthy is the Lamb (---) BB168 111865
Would men know you've been with Jesus (Sellers) AX438 111866
Would you be free from the burden of sin (Jones) AT193 X Would you be free from the guilt 111867
Would you be free from the guilt of your sin (Jones) AI394; AT193; AX278 111868
Would you be free from your burden of sin (Jones) AX 278 X Would you be free from the guilt 111869
Would you flee from sin and serve the Lord (Teasley) AX285 111870
Would you know the love of Jesus (Shacklock) AX351; AY52 111871
Would you live for Jesus and be always pure (Nussbaum) AS 239; AT239; AU122; AX277 111872
Would you lose your load of sin (Whittle) AI402 111873
Would you win a Saviour's blessing (Crosby) BB479 111874
Wouldst bring a gift to Jesus (Rexford) R They brought their gifts to Jesus 111875
Wunderbarer König (Neander) BT41 111876

Y

Ya-a-leh ta-cha-nu-nay-nu (Jewish traditional) BH323 111877

Ye angels round the throne (---) AZ1308 111878

Ye angels who stand round the throne (DeFleury) V708; AZ 1511 111879

Ye are the light of the world (Craig) AX157; AY382 111880

Ye baptized people, one and all (German) M41 111881

Ye bottomless depths of God's infinite love (Zinzendorf, N. L.) AZ1092 111882

Ye children, come, give ear to me (U.P. Board of Publ., 1909) AI405; AJ89; AM656 111883

Ye children of our God (Pratt) BC288 111884

Ye choirs of new Jerusalem (St Fulbert of Chartres) E122; 139; F128; V161; AZ185; BV 191 111885

Ye chosen twelve, to you are given (Pratt) BC211 111886

Ye Christian heralds, go, proclaim (Draper) A221; B453; D263; H459; R494; S381; U390; V595; AB370; AD383; AG262; AM380; AO453; AP565; AS374; AT459; AU235; AV265; AW337; BA361; BF528 111887

Ye Christians, sing a joyful lay (Hermann) M355 111888

Ye Christians, tune your noblest strains (Hymns of the English Conf. 1880) BR196 111889

Ye clouds and darkness, hosts of night (Prudentius) E54; X37 111890

Ye elders of Israel, come join now with me (Wheelock) BC344 111891

Ye fair green hills of Galilee (Conder) G124; W75; AC102; AD130; AG83; AL84; AW94 111892

Ye faithful, with gladness (Latin, 18th c) BQ4a 111893

Ye gates, lift up your heads on high (Scottish Psalter, 1650) AL638; AP21; AW 580; BY172 111894

Ye gates, lift your heads, the glad summons obey (U.P. Psalter, 1912) AJ58 111895

Ye gates of peace and joy untold (U.P. Psalter, 1912) T223; AJ320 111896

Ye heavens on high, praise ye the Lord. Angelic hosts to him accord (Grieve) AL691 111897

Ye holy angels bright (Baxter & Gurney) A600; B264; E517; F371; J409; W39; X701; AB67; AF23; AM17; AN5; AP158; BV24; BX62; BY36 111898

Ye humble souls, approach your God (Steele) L90 111899

Ye lands to the Lord make a jubilant noise (Koren) O11; P27; Q44 111900

Ye men and angels! witness now (Beddome) AY270 X Witness, ye men and angels; now 111901

Ye men of Christ awake (Schmidt) AI184; AO477 111902

Ye messengers of Christ (Vokes) BE396; BL86 111903

Ye must be born again (Sleeper) R A ruler once came 111904

Ye nations round the earth! rejoice (Watts) V4; AX19 111905

Ye parents, hear what Jesus taught (Helmbold) Q630 111906

Ye righteous in the Lord rejoice (Hopkins) T55; AJ85; AL642; AM40; AP29 111907

Ye saints, proclaim abroad (Ryland) L134; M401; AO68; 111908

Ye servants of God, your Master proclaim (Wesley) F226; G 169; H11; I11; J446; P32; R 27; S198; U110; V198; W168; Y 385; Z258; AB15; AD3; AE3; AF 206; AG106; AH194; AK11; AL 44; AM136; AO56; AP258; AR 119; AS3; AT147; AV325; AW 6; AZ503; BA129; BB342; BF 168; BV336; BY37; BZ 111909

Ye servants of the Lord (Doddridge) B456; D186; E518; F 229; H467; I429; L545; O429; V471; W156; X702; AA 382; AL141; AO456; AP580; AW128; AZ1314; BA557; BB351; BE398; BV606; BX361; BY 197 111910

Ye shepherd plains of Bethlehem (Crane) AN168; AQ291 111911

Ye simple souls that stray (Wesley) BC290 111912

Ye sons and daughters of the King (Tisserand) E626; Q208; X143 111913

Ye sons and daughters of the Lord (Tisserand) BM82; BO177; BP 36; BQ28; 111914

Ye sons of earth, prepare the plough (Cowper) BV479 111915

Ye sons of men, O hearken (Thilo) Q75 111916

Ye souls of the faithful! Who sleep in the Lord (Naketenus. Coeleste palmetum. 1669) BO145; BP95; BQ114 111917

Ye that do the Master's will (Wesley) BJ94 111918

Ye that have spent the silent night in sleep (Gascoigne) AL 531 X You that have spent 111919

Ye that know the Lord is gracious (Alington) F260; BV588 111920

Ye timid saints, fresh courage take (Cowper) BE399 X God moves in a mysterious way 111921

Ye tribes of Adam, join (Watts) V510 111922

Ye watchers and ye holy ones (Riley) A599; B266; E519; F6; J437; Q475; R34; AD66; AE29; AF30; AK9; BB77; BL27; BZ 111923

Ye who are banded as comrades and brothers (Lowry) BY536 111924

Ye who are called to labor (Page) BC345 111925

Ye who called to Christ's service are (Schlicht) AZ515; BA313 111926

Ye who called, ye who called to Christ's service are (Schlicht) BA313 X Ye who called to Christ's 111927

Ye who his temple throng, Jehovah's praise prolong (U.P. Psalter, 1912) T294; AJ408 111928

Ye who own the faith of Jesus (Coles) E218 111929

Ye who rose to meet the Lord (---) BB181 111930

Ye who the name of Jesus bear (Scottish Paraphrases, 1781) AL73; AP188 111931

Ye wretched, hungry, starving poor (Steele) V261 111932

Yea, as I live, Jehovah saith (Heermann) O401; Q331; AA426 111933

Yea, I will extol thee (Montgomery) AZ760 111934

Yea, o'er me soared the eternal sky (Larcom) Y205 111935

Years are coming -- speed them onward (Ballou) AN 554; AQ198 111936

Years I spent in vanity and pride (Newell) AT96; AX332; AY513 111937

Yes, for me, for me he careth (Bonar) U200; V352; AI251; AM688; AY99; AZ946 111938

Yes, he is risen who is the

first and last (Bonar) AZ456 111939
Yes, he knows the way is dreary (Havergal) AX611; BR370 111940
Yes, heaven is the prize (Vaughan) BO201 111941
Yes, I do feel, my God, that I am thine (Monsell) AZ452 111942
Yes, I'll sing the wondrous story (Rowley) R I will sing the wondrous story 111943
Yes, Jesus loves me (Warner) R Jesus loves me, this I know 111944
Yes, Lord, we thank thee for this day (Loewen) R We owe the Lord 111945
Yes, my heart says amen (Naylor) R I Have yielded myself to thy service 111946
Yes, others, Lord, yes others (Meigs) R Lord, help me to live 111947
Yes, since God himself hath said it (Newton) AZ602 111948
Yes, sleeping on guard (French) R Out from the camp fire's red glowing 111949
Yes, the redeemer rose (Doddridge) L267; AO185 111950
Yes, there is rest over Jordan's waters (---) R To the promised home in glory 111951
Yes, there remaineth still a rest (Kunth) AA566 111952
Yes, we'll gather at the river (Lowry) R Shall we gather at the river 111953
Yesterday with exultation (Adam of St Victor) F535 111954
Yet when the splendor of the earth (MacLeish) AQ113 111955
Yield not to temptation (Palmer) N648; U161; W704; AE258; AG195; AH452; AI404; AM658; AO631; AP770; AS320; AT364; AU338; AV371; AW477; AX441; AY445; BA835; BB498; BY569 111956
Yigdal Elohim chayveyish tabbach (Jewish doxology) Y300; AHp152; BH277 111957
Yim-loch A-do-noy l'olom (Jewish traditional) BH287 111958
You can make the pathway bright (Dungan) BC208 111959
You can't do wrong and get by (Ellis) R There's a God who's standing 111960
You have longed for sweet peace (Hoffman) AT350; AU54; AX402 111961
You that have faith to look with fearless eyes (Seaman) AQ 206 111962
You that have spent the silent night in sleep (Gascoigne) X38; AF505; AL531; AN485; AP655; AQ264 111963
Young and radiant, he is standing (Cross) AC99 111964
Your goal was not some island of the blessed (Clark) AC 509 111965
Your harps, ye trembling saints (Toplady) V369; W561 111966
Your little flame of life we guard (Sassoon) AQ263 111967
Youth of the world, unite (Davies) AC480 111968
Y'-vo-re-ch'-cho A-do-noy (Jewish traditional) BH301 111969

Z

Zeal of the lord, for ever burning (Dearmer) X703 111970
Zeuch ein zu meinen Toren (Gerhardt) BT228 111971
Zeuch uns nach dir (Funcke) BT215 111972

NOTE: "Zion" in English texts is spelled "Sion" in this index 111973

Zion klagt mit Angst und Schmerzen (Heermann) BT268 111974

Zoch-ray-nu la-cha-yeem (Jewish traditional) BH312 111975

Zu Bethlehem geboren (Cologne, Psalter, 1638) BG112b 111976

Zu Lob Gott Vater, Sohne (Ausbund) BU10 111977

Zu sing'n hab ich im Sinn: (Ausbund) BU138 111978

Zi singen will ich heben an (Ausbund) BU22 111979

II

Authors and First Lines

Anonymous

Anonymous hymns

NOTE: Satisfactory sources could not be identified for these first lines.

A glorious day is dawning
A holy stillness, breathing
A shepherd band their flocks
Afar upon a foreign shore;
R103026 Hail Blessed Saint
All glory be to thee, O Lord
All glory to God, the Father
All praise to the Father
All ye who grace inherit
Alleluia! Praise the Savior
Almighty Father, hear
And now may the courage
And now the sun hath sunk
And now to God the Father
Are you weary, heavy laden;
R101533 Come to Jesus, come
Arise, O Christian soldiers
As swiftly my days go out
Assist thy servant, Lord
At thy table, Lord of life
Be firm and be faithful
Be ye joyful, earth and sky
Beautiful Sion, built above;
R109012 Sion, Sion, lovely
Beauty around us, glory above
Behold the lilies of the field
Blessed art thou, O Lord
Bliss beyond compare
Bring flowers of the fairest;
R107393 O Mary! We crown thee
Brother, thou hast left us
Builder of mighty worlds
By angels in heaven
Can a mortal flee from sorrow
Can my soul find rest
Children of Jerusalem
Christ on the night He was;
X101198 Christ in the night
Christ went a building; R103910
I know, I know
Christian children must be
Christian, walk carefully
Cleanse my heart, O Father
Clear upon the night-air;
R100569 As the angels sang
Come all ye Saints and sing
Come, children, with singing
Come gentle peace
Come, Holy Spirit, from
Come, listen to a prophet's
Courage my soul! While God is
Dark and thorny is the desert
Daughter of a mighty Father
Daughter of God the Father
Day is done, gone the sun
Dear St Joseph, pure;
R103075 Hail St Joseph
Dear Saviour, we would know
Death shall not destroy;
R109112 Soon with angels
Do what is right; the day-dawn
Dona nobis pacem, pacem
Earth is waking, day is
Ere another day shall close
Fading, still fading, The last;
R102093 Father, have mercy
Farewell, my dear brethren
Father, fill us with thy love
Father, hear our prayer
Father, O hear us; Saviour
Father, Son, and Holy Ghost
Father, Son, and Holy Ghost, Three in One; from every coast
Father, Son, and Holy Spirit, Thou One in Three
Fling wide the gates
For Autumn's golden days
For flowers that bloom about
For health and strength
For Mother-love and Father-care

For sun and moon and stars
From the first man to climb
Gather around the Christmas;
R103601 Hosanna, Hosanna
Gentle Peace, from heaven
Give God the Father praise
Give thanks for the corn
Give thanks unto the Lord
Glory and praises ever be
Glory eternal be to thee
Glory, praise and blessing be
Glory to the blessed Jesus
God incarnate, veil thy
God is great, God is good
God of every land and nation
God of my heart! Its earliest
Gone from my heart, the world;
R103955 I love Him
Good morning to you
Gracious Father, guard
Gracious Father, hear our
Grant that we ask, Almighty
Grant us, Lord, the grace
Great Giver of all good
Great God in heaven, who by
Great God, to whom alone
Great God! whatever through
Great Jehovah! we adore thee
Great King of saints, enthroned
Hail! Christ, our Redeemer
Hail! holy guide of youthful
Hail, thou martyr host
Hail Virgin, dearest Mary!
Hark! hark! The organ loudly
Hark, listen to the trumpeters
Hark! the skies with music
Hark, what music fills
He knows the bitter weary way
Hear, O Lord, our humble
Hear our entreaties, Lord
Hear the royal proclamation;
R104807 Jesus reigns, He
Hear us, our Father! We know
Heart of Jesus I adore thee
Heart of Mary, heart all pure
Heir of the kingdom, O why
Hibernia's Patron Saint, all;
R107506 O St Patrick, we
His flock our Shepherd feeds
Holy habitations, after weary
Holy Jesus, be my light
Holy Love, from heaven
Holy Mary, mother mild;
R106720 O exult ye cherubim
Holy patron! thee saluting;
R103123 Happy Saint; in bliss
Holy Spirit, faithful guide
How cheering is the christian's
How happy are these little ones
How many were the silent
How pleasant thus to dwell;
R107632 O! that will be
How strong and sweet
How sweet are the tidings;
R103450 He's coming, coming
Humble praises, holy Jesus;
R100344 Alleluia, sweetly
I am dwelling on the mountain;
R104455 Is not this the land
I entered once a home of care
I have decided to follow
I know a soul that is steeped
I know of a river;
R107556 O sinner, we pray
I look not back; God knows
I look to Jesus, and the face
I love thee, I love thee
I love to hear the story
I ought to love my Saviour
I saw a mighty angel fly
I see my Jesus crucified
I will never, never leave
I'll thee exalt, my God
In a lonely graveyard
In days of yore, from Britain's;
R109724 The maple leaf
In every waking moment;
R106080 My God, I am determined
In from the highways;
R102448 Gather them in
In Oxford Town the faggots
In the still air the music
In this lone hour of deep
In yon blessed seats of heaven
Is there any pleasure, any joy
I've seen the lightning;
R106274 No, never alone
Jehovah, Jesus, Lord we own
Jehovah, Lord of heaven
Jerusalem, Jerusalem! Die du so
Jesus is standing in Pilate's;
R111330 What will you do
Jesus loves a little child
Jesus, our Saviour, only God

Jesus, rule my thoughts
Jesus, Savior, mighty Lord
Jesus, Savior, risen Lord
Jesus the glory of the holy
Jesus, to thee be endless;
R103607 Hosanna to our only
Keep me, Saviour, near
Land of the mountains high
Lead them, my God, to thee
Let all who enter here
Let each man learn to know
Let God the Father, God the
Son; X105129 Let God the
Father, and the
Let me go where'er I will
Let others seek a home below;
R111223 We'll work till
Let the whole creation sing;
R102860 Gone the night
Let them that love Him
Let thy Spirit, blessed
Light of life, the great
Like a strong and raging fire;
R100873 Bending low
Little children, Lord, are we
Lo! on the water's brink we
Lo! the earth rejoices at the
Lo! the heavens are breaking
Long for my Saviour I've been;
R104833 Jesus soon is coming
Lord in thy presence here we
Lord in thy temple we appear
Lord Jesus Christ, I flee
Lord Jesus Christ, to us
Lord, let us now depart in
Lord of the Sabbath and its
Lord, on thee alone I stay me
Lord, thine appointed servants
Lord, to thee, in whom is
Mary! how sweetly falls that;
R108954 Sing, O my lips
Mary the Dawn, Christ the
May you who enter here
Merry Christmas bells are
Morning has come,the table
Most fervent thanks I render
Mother dear, O pray for me
My dearest friends, in bonds
My dearest Saviour I would
My hope, my all, my Saviour
My hiding place, my refuge;
X101907 Engraved as in eternal (Watts)
My soul with joy attend
Name of Jesus, softly stealing
Nay, speak no ill; a kindly
Nobody knows of the work
None e'er shall be ashamed
Not gold, but only men can
Now blessed thou, O Christ
Now for each yearning heart
Now may the light that shone
Now rest in peace, now rest
Now to the great and sacred
Now the triune God Confessing
Now to Jesus Christ all glory
O bless, thou heavenly Potentate
O Father Almighty, to thee be
O for a heart of calm repose
O God, Eternal Father, from;
R107679 O thou Holy Trinity
O God! how ought my grateful;
X106078 My God! how
ought
O God of Hosts, with thy
O God, while generations flee
O happy time of reaping
O heart of Mary, pure and fair
O holy joy that raises
O, I love to talk with Jesus
O ice and snow, O frost
O Jesus Christ, alone to thee
O Jesus, once a Nazareth boy
X107134 O Jesus, Prince of
O Jesus, Saviour, Source of
O joyous Easter morning
O Lord, be near me when I
pray
O Lord, encouraged by thy grace
O Lord, I am not worthy
O Lord of Life, the Truth
O Lord of love, compassionate
O Lord of love, Thou light
O Lord, thou art the way
O Lord, thou living Bread
O Lord, to us assembled here
O Lord, whose bounteous hand
O Lord, with thankful hearts
O Mother! most afflicted
O praise the Father, praise
O Sacrament most holy
O Sacred Heart of Christ;
R101692 Dear Heart of
Jesus
O thou blest Immanuel
O thou that hearest prayer

O thou who hearest every
O thou who sendest sun and rain
O what could my Jesus do more
O, when shall I see Jesus
O'er the silent waters
On Mary, Virgin undefiled
On this day, O beautiful
On mountains and in valleys
Our highest joys succeed our
Our souls shall magnify;
X106197 My soul doth magnify
Peacefully lay her down
Peter, faithless, thrice denies
Pilgrims, on! The day is
Praise, honor, majesty, For thy
Praise the Father throned
Praise the Father, earth and
Praise the Lord! From the deeds
Praise the name of God most
Praise to thee, O Lord, we
Praise we Christ; the King
Praise ye the Father! Let;
R108242 Praise be to the Father
Pray for the dead! at noon
Precious Jesus, O to love;
R104689 Jesus, Jesus, precious
Put on the armor of our God;
R109989 Then stand! stand
Queen and Mother, many hearts
Queen of the Rosary, Virgin
Ready to suffer grief or pain
R108430 Ready to go
Resting among the cattle mild
Remember, holy Mary, 'Twas
Round the throne of glory;
R103535 Holy, Holy, Holy
Sacred Heart of Jesus, fount
St Anthony, we turn to thee
Save us waking, O Lord
Saved by grace, I live to tell;
R107779 O, 'tis grace
Saw ye my Saviour
Shall I tell you what brought;
R103252 He just put Himself
Silently, silently they pass
Sing alleluia, honor, praise
Sing of Mary, pure and lowly;
X108966 Sing the Holy Family's (Vaughan)
Songs of praise exultant sing
Sound the loud anthem, to hail
Star of our hope! He'll soon
Stars of morning, shout
Striving onward, pressing
Sweet is the prayer whose holy
Take my heart, O Father! take
The blasts of winter are fierce
The corn is ripe for reaping
The earth is hushed in silence
The Father and the Son
The God who made both heaven
The gold and silver are the
The heavens are declaring
The Lord is coming! let this
The Lord is my Shepherd, I
The new-born King who comes
The sands have been washed in
The shadows lengthen, Lord
The Spirit and the Bride
The sun rolls down the distant
The war in which the soldier
The sun shines in splendor
The world itself is blithe
Thee, Father, Spirit, Son we
There are hearts that never
There is a blessed hope
There is a calm for those who
There is an hour of peace;
R105911 May my heart be
There is no other Name than;
X110063 There is none other
There's work for the hand
Think on our brethren Lord
Thou warrior angel of the Lord
Thou who a tender Father art
Though all my foes combine
Though in the outward Church;
R102298 For soon the reaping
Through thee as we together
Thy broken body, gracious Lord
Thy Gospel, Jesus, we believe
Thy holy Sabbath, Lord
'Tis the month of our Mother;
R100217 All hail! to dear Mary
To Christ, the King of glory
To Father, Son, and Holy Ghost Be praise
To Father, Son, and Holy Ghost Our God forever
To Father, Son and Spirit
To Father, Son, and Spirit blest, Supreme o'er

To Father, Son, and Spirit, ever blest
To Father, Son, and Spirit From earth let praise
To Father, Son, and Spirit God ever Three in One
To God I lift mine eyes
To God the Ever-glorious
To God the Father, Son, and Spirit, the everlasting
To God -- the Father, Son, and Spirit -- Three in
To God, the Father, Spirit, Son
To God the Father's throne Perpetual honors raise
To God the Father's throne Your highest honors raise
To Jesus Christ, our only Lord
To kneel at thine altar, in;
R106938 O Good St Anne, we
To the promised home in glory;
R111951 Yes, there is rest
To thee alone our prayer
To thee be praise for ever
To thee, O blessed Saviour
To thee, O Jesus Christ, we
To thee, O Lord, alone
To thee, O Lord, be glory
To thee, O Lord, my Saviour
To thee, our loving Father
Triumphs today the Lord of life
Unheard the dews around me;
X106285 Noiseless the morning
Upon this happy morn
Watchmen on the walls of Zion
We are all enlisted till the
We are little gleaners
We are little reapers
We are marching with the blest
R105883 Marching home, we're
We are sowing, daily sowing
We come with songs of gladness
We gather 'round your shrine
We meet again in gladness
We praise thy name, O Lord
We thank thee, loving Father
We thank thee, O our Father
We will carol joyfully
Wearily at daylight's close
Welcome, welcome, day of rest
Well for him who, all things
We're bound for the land
What a wonderful, wonderful;
R103289 He was nailed
What can I give to Jesus
What glorious scenes mine eyes
What lovely Infant can this be
What makes a city great
What tongue can tell thy
When blooming youth is snatched
When Christ beheld, in sinful
When great St Patrick raised
When judgment day is drawing
R107838 O where shall I be
When the corn is planted
When the stars at set of sun
When warmer suns and bluer
When we hear the music ringing
Whence came the armies of the
Where'er have trod Thy sacred
Who taught the bird to build
With humble prayer, O, may I
With tender greeting, Lo, thy
With wondering awe The wisemen
Worthy, worthy is the Lamb
Ye angels round the throne
Ye who rose to meet the Lord

A

A.A.F. [Crosby??]
Not I, but Christ, be honored
A.E. pseud see
Russell, George William
A.E.E.
Jesus Christ the King of ages
A.H.A.
O, to be there, where the songs
A.N.
Jesus, my Saviour, to Bethlehem
Aaberg, J.C.
Praise the Lord that He has
There is a blessed power
The Abatal, 1532
Because you live again, O Rose
Abbey, Charlotte
Nearer the cross of Jesus
Abelard, Peter, 1079-1142

Alone thou goest forth, O Lord
O what their joy and their;
X107829 O what the joy
Abraham ibn Ezra
I hope for the salvation
My faith shall be my rock
Abrahams, Israel
How bless the God of all
Achrenius, Antti
Arise, my soul, new light
Ackley, A.H., 1887-
I serve a risen Saviour;
R103263 He lives, He lives
Adam of St Victor, 12th c
Christians, come, in sweetest
Come sing, ye choirs exultant
Jesus, kind above all others
Joy and triumph everlasting
Jucundare, plebs fidelis
O Holy Ghost, thou Fount of
Sion's daughters! Sons of
Spirit of grace and union
Supernae matris gaudia
Yesterday with exultation
Adam, A.
O holy night; the stars are
Adams. Hymns for Christian devotion, 1846
Scorn not the slightest word
Adams, Elizabeth C
Father, we thy loving children
God giveth light to all who
No eye hath seen, nor tongue
Adams, Jessie, 1863-1954
I feel the winds of God
Adams, John Coleman, 1849-
It swells upon the noon-day
We praise thee, God, for
Adams, John Greenleaf, 1810-87
Heaven is here, where hymns
Adams, John Quincy, 1767-1848
O Lord, thy all discerning
Send forth, O Lord, thy light
Adams, Ophelia G
Unransomed yet? The prayer
Adams, Sarah Flower, 1805-48
Näher, mein Gott zu Dir
Nearer, my God, to thee;
X106240 Nearer, O God to thee (How)
Part in peace: Christ's life
Part in peace! Is day before
Adams, William Henry, 1864-1932
O'er the trackless ocean
Adderley, James G., 1861-1942
Father, we greet thee, God of
Addison, Joseph, 1672-1719
How are thy servants blest
The Lord my pasture shall;
X109680 The Lord...will
The spacious firmament on high; X109857 The starry firmament (Grant)
When all thy mercies, O my God; X111347 When all... gracious
When rising from the bed of
Adler, Felix, 1851-1933
Hail the glorious Golden City
Splendor of the morning
Afzelius, Arvid August, 1785-1871
Unto the Lord of all creation
Agnes, of County Cork, Sr.
Hail, glorious St Patrick
Agricola, Johannes, 1492-1566
Lord, hear the voice of my
Sing aloud alleluia in jubilant
To thee I send my cry, Lord
Aguilar, Grace
Ah, well it is that God should
I bless thee, Father, for
Ahnfelt, Oskar Sanger, 1813-62
How blest are the moments
Ainger, Arthur Campbell, 1841-1919
God is working his purpose
God of our fathers, unto thee;
R105471 Lord God of hosts
Akers, Elizabeth
The time for toil is past
Albert, Heinrich, 1604-51
God, omnipotent creator
God who madest earth and heaven
Gott des Himmels und der Erden 1644
Now the morn new light is
Albinus, Johann Georg, 1624-79
All men living are but mortal
Alle Menschen müssen sterben 1652

Cast me not in wrath away
Death in all this world
Hark, a voice saith, all are
Not in anger, mighty God
Smite us not in anger, Lord
Albrecht von Brandenburg-Culmbach, 1522-57
The will of God is always
Was mein Gott will, das g' scheh' allzeit 1554
Whate'er God will, let that
Alcott, Louisa May, 1833-88
A little kingdom I possess
O the beautiful old story!
Alderson, Eliza Sibbald Dykes 1818-88
And now, beloved Lord, thy
Lord of glory, thou has bought; X105632 Lord of glory, who
Alexander, Cecil Frances, 1823-95
All things bright and; X101858 Each little flower
Do not sinful action, Speak
Every morning the red sun
For all thy saints, a noble
Forgive them, O my Father
Forsaken once, and thrice
From out the cloud of fiery
He is coming, he is coming
He is risen, he is risen
His are the thousand sparkling
Jesus call us; o'er the tumult
O Jesus, bruised and wounded
O Lord, the Holy Innocents
Once in royal David's city
Saw you never, in the twilight
Souls in heathen darkness
Spirit of God, that moved
The eternal gates lift up
The golden gates are lifted
The roseate hues of early
There is a green hill; R106699 O dearly, dearly
There is one way, and only one
Thou Power and Peace, in whom
Thy temple is not made
We are but little children; X110986 We are ... weak
When wounded sore the stricken
Alexander, William Lindsay, 1808-84
I'm kneeling at the threshold
Spirit of power, and truth
Alford, Henry, 1810-71
Come, ye thankful people, come
Forward! be our watchword; X102058 Far o'er yon horizon
Hark! through the courts
In token that thou shalt not
My bark is wafted to the strand
O thou, at whose divine command
O thou, who hast thy servants
Ten thousand times ten thousand
The highest and the holiest
Thou who on that wondrous
We walk by faith, and not by
When in the Lord Jehovah's
Alfred, Lord Tennyson see Tennyson, Alfred
Alington, Cyril Argentine, 1872-1955
Come, ye people, rise and sing
God, whose city's sure foundation
Good Christian men, rejoice
Lord of all, to whom alone
Lord of beauty, thine the
O Father, by whose sovereign
O loving Father, to thy care
Praise we God the Father's name
Sing, brothers, sing and praise
Ye that know the Lord is
Alkabetz, Solomon
"Observe ye" and "remember"; R101369 Come forth, my friend
Alldredge, Ida R.
They the builders of the nation
Alldridge, R
Lord, accept our true
We'll sing all hail to Jesus'
Allen, Ernest Bourner
The Son of God goes forth for peace
Allen, Freda Hanbury
"Within the veil!" Be this,

Allen, Hattie Bell
Christ for the whole wide; R111168 We will give
Allen, James, 1734-1804
Glory to God on high, Let; X102560 Glory to God on high (Boden)
Jesus, our risen King
Our souls with inmost shame
Sweet the moments see Walter Shirley
We, O Jesus, claim thy special
Allen, Jonathan??
Sinners, will ye scorn
Allen, Lillian Manker
For those who wrought
Allen, Oswald
Today thy mercy calls us; X110731 Today ... calls me
Allon. Children's worship, 1878
Hark, hark, my soul!
Alstyne, Frances Van see Crosby, Fanny
Altenberg, Johann Michael, 1584-1640
Be not dismayed, thou little
Fear not, O little flock, the
Fear not, thou faithful
O little flock, fear not
Thou little flock, be not
Verzage nicht, du häuflein
Alwood, J. K.
O they tell me of a home far; R107651 O the land of cloudless
"Am-a". 1769
And didst thou, Jesus, condescend
American carol
Away in a manger, no crib
American folk hymn
Note: In hymnal BZ all Negro Spirituals are cited as above. Within this index see Negro spirituals
Ames, Charles Gordon, 1828-1912
Father in heaven, hear us
With loving hearts and hands
Amilie Juliana, Countess of Schwarzburg-Rudelstadt, 1637-1706
Bis hieher hat mich Gott
The Lord hath helped me
The solemn moment is impending
Wer weiss, wie nahe mir mein Ende! 1688
Who knows how near my end may; X111640 Who ... my life's ; X111640A Who knows how soon; X111641 Who knows when death
Amis, Lewis R., 1856-1904
Jehovah, God, who dwelt of
Andersdatter, Elle, ca 1600-1650
In hope my soul, redeemed to
Andersen, Hans Christian, 1805-75
Child Jesus comes from
Anderson, Maria Frances, 1819-
Our country's voice
Anderson, Mary Louisa
Now, Lord, upon thy sea of air
Andrew, Father see Hardy, H. E. (Father Andrew) 1869-1946
Angelus Silesius see Scheffler, Johann, 1624-77
Anketell, John, 1835-1905
Lord Jesus, on the holy mount
Anna Sophia, Countess of Hesse-Darmstadt, 1638-83
Rede, liebster Jesu, rede
Speak, O Lord, thy servant
"Anne" (perhaps Anne Taylor, 1782-1866)
There is a dear and hallowed
Annin, Katharine Huntington, 1893-
The Lord, in his righteousness
Anstice, Joseph, 1808-36
Darkly rose the guilty morning
Lord, in thy kingdom there
Lord of the harvest, once
O Lord, how happy should we be
When came in flesh the incarnate

Anstruther, Joyce, see Struther, Jan pseud, 1901-53
Antoniano, Silvio, 1540-1603
Fortem virili pectore
The praises of that Saint we
Apostolic Constitutions. 3d c.
Praise ye the Lord, ye servants
Appleton, Francis Parker, 1822-1903
The past yet lives in all its
Thirsting for a living fountain
Arends, William Erasmus, 1677-1721
Christians, keep your banners
Christians, prayer may well; X108639 Rise, to arms
Rüstet euch, ihr Christenleute 1714
Arkwright, John Stanhope
O valiant hearts, who to your
Arlott, John, 1914-
God, whose farm is all creation
Armenian liturgy.
Holiness becomes thy house
Armitage, Ella Sophia, 1841-
In our dear Lord's garden
O Lord of hosts, the fight is
O Lord of life, and love, and
Armstrong, Harry
Lead thou me on, and then my
Armstrong, John, 1813-56
O thou, who makest souls to; X107321 O Lord, thy benediction
Arndt, Ernst Moritz, 1769-1860
Go and let my grave be made
I know whom I believe in
Arnold, of Louvain
Hail thee, Saviour and Atoner
Arnold, Gottfried, 1666-1714
All alone, and yet not lonely
Thanksgiving, honor, praise
Arnold, Matthew, 1822-88
Calm soul of all things, make
Servants of God, or sons
We cannot kindle when we will
Arnold, Robert S.
No tears in heaven, no sorrows
Arnschwanger, Johann Christoph 1625-96
Up, ye Christians, join in
Arrebo, Anders C., 17th c
O sing with exultation
Om salighed og glæde
The Lord my faithful shepherd
Arrhenius, Jacob, 1642-1725
Jesus is my best of friends
Jesus is my Friend most precious
Jesus, Lord and precious
Asper, Frank Wilson, 1892-
Hear thou our hymn, O Lord
Associate Reformed Presbyterian Psalter, 1931.
Come, let us sing unto the Lord
O Lord of hosts, how lovely
O thou who the Shepherd of Israel
The Association of Perpetual Adoration.
Wondrous love that cannot
Aström, Johan, 1767-1844
Lord, disperse the mists
Atchinson, Jonathan Bush, 1740-
I have read of a beautiful city; R106310 Not half has ever
In the shadow of his wings
There's a Stranger at the door
Athanasian Creed.
Wir glauben all an einen Gott, Und lieben ihn 1564
Atkins, George
Brethren, we have met to worship
Auber, Harriet, 1773-1862
Bright was the guiding star
Ere mountains reared their
Hasten, Lord, the glorious time
O God, our strength, to thee
O praise our great and gracious; X108270 Praise our great
On thy church, O Power Divine
Our blest Redeemer, ere he
They who on the Lord rely

(authorship in doubt)
Vainly, through night's weary
Whom have we Lord in heaven (authorship in doubt)
With joy we hail the sacred
Auerbach, Herbert
Blessed are they that have
Bring, heavy heart, your grief
Aufranc, D.A.R.
Alone with thee, my God
Far from all care we hail
Father, I yield to Thee my life
There is a road, though narrow
Augusta, Johann, ca 1500-1572
How blest and lovely thy
Praise God for ever! Boundless
Auryansen, Lucia Trevitt
Here, where the sun shines
Ausbund
Note: Cited as item BU within this index, it is the oldest Protestant hymnal which has been in constant use.
Ach fröhlich will ich singen
Ach Gott vom Himmelreiche!
All' die ihr Jetzund leidet
Ambrosius klärlich beschrieb
Christe, freundlicher Ritter, 1564
Christe mein Herr, ich bin ganz ferr
Christe thu dich erbarmen 1564
Dankt Gott in seinem hochsten Thron. 1522
Das Wort der Wahrheit Jesu Christ 1564
Der Glaub beschützt mich ganz und gar
Der Winter kalt, rauh ungestalt.
Die beste Freud aus Gottes Wort. 1553
Ein Grosse Freud ist ingemein. 1564
Ein Liedlein will ich singen. 1564
Ein Magdelein von Gleidern zart. 1564
Eins Morgens früh vor Tage 1564
Es waren auch zween Brüder gut 1564
Ewiger Vater im Himmelreich 1564
Ewiger Vater vom Himmelreich. 1529
Föhlich pfleg ich zu singen; X102365 Frölich pfleg ich zu
Für Gott den Herren woll'n wir gohn 1564
Gelobt sey Gott der Herre. 1564
Gott Vater, Sohn, Heiliger Geist. 1564
Gross sind die Merck des Herren. 1552
Gross Unbild thut mich zwingen. 1510
Herr Gott Vater im Himmelreich
Herr Jesu Christe, Starker Gott. 1564
Herr! starker Gott ins Himmels Thron. 1564
Herzlich thut mich erfreuen Die liebe Sommer-Zeit
Hilf Gott das ich mög singen. 1564
Hinweg ist mir genommen
Ich weiss, wer Gottes Wort bekennt 1564
Ich will von ganzem Herzen mein 1564
Ihr Kinder Gottes alle. 1564
In Gottes Namen heb'n wir an. 1564
Komm Gott Vater von Himmeln. 1564
Kreutz, Verfolgung und Trübsal 1564
Kurzlich hab ich vorg'nommen. 1529
Lebt friedsam, sprach Christus der Herr. 1564
Mein fröhlich Herz das treibt mich an zu singen. 1564
Merkt auf ein Sach und die ist wahr. 1564
Merkt auf, ihr Christen all geleich. 1564

Merkt auf, ihr Menschenkinder. 1564
Merkt auf, ihr Völker alle 1557
Merkt auf, ihr Volker überall
Merkt auf und nehmt zu Herzen. 1564
Mit einem zugeneigten G'müth. 1564
Mit Lust so will ich singen Ein schöne Tageweiss. 1564
Muss es nun seyn gescheiden. 1564
Nun heben wir an in Nöthen
Nun hört, ihr Freund ehrsamen. 1570
Nun Hört mir zu in mein'm Gedicht. 1564
O Gott Schöpfer, heiliger Geist. 1564
O Gott Vater ins Himmels Throne. 1564
O Herr dich will ich loben. 1550
O Herr! um dein Gnad ruff ich dich an. 1564
O Herre Gott, gross ist die Roth. 1564
O Herre Gott, in meiner Roth. 1564
O Herre Gott mein Roth thu ich der Klagen 1564
O Menschenkind, vernimm mich wohl. 1564
Schier in allen G'schichten g'schrieben staht
Trauren will ich stehen lassen 1564
Ungnad begehr ich nicht von dir. 1527
Von Herzen will ich loben. 1564
Von Herzen woll'n wir singen. 1564
Wach auf, wach auf, O Menschenkind! Von deinem Schlaf stand auf geschwind. 1564
Wacht auf, ihr Brüder werthe. 1564
Was wend wir aber heben an 1564
Was Woll'n wir aber singen
Weil nun die Zeit vorhanden ist. 1564
Wir bitten dich, ewiger Gott. 1528
Wir danken Gott von Herzen 1530
Wo kommt das her, o Jesu Christ. 1564
Wo soll ich mich hin kehren 1564
Zu Lob Gott Vater, Sohne 1559
Zu sing'n hab ich im Sinn:,: 1564
Zu singen will ich heben an 1564

Ausbund (Fourteen authors)
Mit Freuden woll'n wir singen. 1564

Ausbund (Seven Brothers)
Aus tiefer Noth schrey ich zu dir, Ach Gott erhör mein Rufen, Dein Heil' gen Geist fend du zu mir. 1564

Ausbund. Psalm 34.
Ich will loben den Herren. 1564

Ausbund. Psalm 35.
Herr Gott! streit wider meine Feind. 1564

Ausbund. Psalm 50.
Also redt der wahrhaftig Gott. 1564

Ausbund. Psalm 54.
O Herre Gott! hilf mir in deinem Namen. 1564

Ausbund. Psalm 86
Herr Gott! thu mich erhören. 1564

Ausbund. Psalm 126
Wann der Herr die G'sangniss Zion. 1564

Ausbund. Psalm 130
O Herr! nicht stolz ist mein Herz doch. 1564

Ausbund. Psalm 133
Sieh! wie sein ist und lieblich schon. 1564

Ausbund. Suppl.
Es ist eind wunder schöne
Es war ein Gottesfürchtiges

Kürzlich vor wenig Tagen
Mein fröhlich
Herz das treibt mich
O Herr thu auf die Lefzen mein
Tobias war ein frommer Mann

NOTE: Identified authors represented in Ausbund are:

Athanasian Creed.
Bappenheim, W.
Betz, H.
Bible, Maccabees.
Bilach, H. v.
Blaurock, G.
Bosch, S. v.
Büchel, H.
Clock, L.
Drucker, T.
Franck, S.
Gerfass, M.
Hans, S.
Hus, John
Hut, H.
Koch, H.
Landis, H.
Mantzen, F.
Ringmacher, L.
Rogel, H.
Rot, O.
Sattlers, M.
Schneider, L.
Schneider, M.
Schornschlager, L.
Straub, H.
Wagner, G.

Auslander, Joseph, 1897-
Blest is that man who sets his
Austin, John, 1613-69
Behold we come, dear Lord
Blest be thy love, dear Lord
Hark, my soul, how every thing
Hail, glorious spirits, heirs; X103037 Hail, glorious angels
Austin, William, 1587-1633
All this night shrill chanticleer; X100289 All this night bright
Avery, Benedict
Bowing low, then offer homage
Avery, Samuel J.
Truth comes alike to all
Ayers, Minny M.H.
I walk with love along the way
Aylward, James Ambrose, 1813-72
Lift up, ye princes of the sky
Ayres, H.C., ca 1894-
One there is who loves thee

B

"B.E.
O Christ, in thee my soul hath; R106426 Now none but Christ
Babcock, Maltbie Davenport, 1858-1901
Back of the loaf is the snowy
Be strong! We are not here; X110998 We are not here
God's boundless love and
Rest in the Lord, my soul
This is my Father's world
When the great sun sinks to
Babst. Geistliche lieder. Leipzig, 1545
All' Ehr' und Lob soll Gottes
All glory be to God alone
Bachelor, Mary A
Go bury thy sorrow
Bacon, Josephine Daskam, 1876-
Brother, sing your country's
Bacon, Leonard, 1802-81
Here, Lord of life and light
O God, beneath thy guiding
Wake the song of Jubilee!
Badger, George Henry, 1859-
O thou who art my king
Bahnmaier, Jonathan Friedrich, 1774-1841
Spread, O spread, thou mighty X109187 Spread, still spread
Walte, walte nah und fern 1827
Word of life, most pure, most
Baird, R.B.
Improve the shining moments
Welcome, welcome, Sabbath
When the rosy light of morning; R109975 Then away,

haste
Baker, Henry Williams, 1821-77
Almighty God, whose only Son
God made me for Himself, to
How welcome was the call
I am not worthy, holy Lord; R106337 Not worthy, not
Lord, thy word abideth
My Father, for another night
O God of love, O King of peace
O Holy Ghost, thy people bless
O Jesus, God and man; X105574 Lord Jesus, God
O perfect life of love
O praise our God today
O what if we are Christ's
Out of the deep I call
Praise, O praise our God; R102285 For his mercies aye
Redeemed, restored, forgiven
Rejoice today with one accord
Remember, Lord, thy works
Shall we not love thee
The King of love my shepherd
There is a blessed home
Baker, Mary A.
Master, the tempest is raging; R109925 The winds and the waves
Bakewell, John, 1721-1819
Hail, thou once despised Jesus; X104629 Jesus, hail!
Balch, Emily Greene
Now let us all arise and sing
Balfern, William Poole, 1818-87
O Lamb of God most lowly
Ball, William, 1784-1869
To God on high be thanks
Ballantine, William G., 1848-1937
God save America! new world
Ballet, William, 17th c
Sweet was the song the Virgin
Ballou, Adin, 1803-90
Years are coming -- speed
Ballou, Hosea, 1771-1852
When God is seen with me to
Baltzell, I.
On the shore beyond the sea; R105444 Let me go, I cannot
Baltzell, L.
I want to be a worker for the; R104109 I will work, I will
Bangor Antiphoner, ca 690
Draw nigh and take the Body; X101510 Come, take by faith
Sancti, venite, corpus Christi sumite
Banks, George Linnaeus, 1821-81
I live for those who love me
Bappenheim, Walpurg von
Du glaubigs Herz, so benedey. 1564
Barbauld, Anna Laetitia, 1743-1825
Blest is the man whose
Come, said Jesus' sacred voice; X101501 Come, says Jesus'
How blest the righteous when; X100987 Blest is the man
How blest the sacred tie
Our country is Immanuel's
Praise to God, immortal praise
Barber, Henry Hervey, 1835-
Far off, O God, and yet most
Baring-Gould, Sabine, 1834-1924
Daily, daily sing the praises; R107619 O, that I had wings
Hail the Sign, the Sign of Jesus
Now the day is over
On the resurrection morning
Onward, Christian soldiers
Sing lullaby! Lullaby baby!
Barlow, Charles H.
Why search the future and
Barnard, S., 18th c
Jehovah is our strength
Baron, Barclay, 1884-
Go forth with God! the day
Barratt, Alfred, 1879-
Like radiant sunshine that; R111838 Wonderful peace
Barrett. Book of praise for

children, 1881
The fields are all white
The wise may bring their
Barrows, Samuel J.
Enkindling Love, eternal Flame
Barstow, H.H.
The Son of Man goes forth
Barth, Christian Gottlob, 1799-1862
From distant shores returning
Go joyfully forth, To war
Bartholomew, Julia H.
From lands beyond the waters
Bartlett, Franklin Weston, 1843-
O God Supreme, who dost
Saviour, who didst come to
Barton, Bernard D., 1784-1849
Lamp of our feet, whereby we; X105047 Lamp ... our path to
Walk in the light! so shalt; X110942 Walk ... and thou; X110944 Walk ... so thou
We journey through a vale
Barton, William, 1603-78
Present your bodies to the Lord
Bateman, Christian Henry, 1813-89
Come, Christians, join to sing; X101351 Come, children, join
Bateman, Henry, 1802-72
Gracious Saviour, thus before
Light of the world! whose kind
Bateman, Mrs. L.M.B.
I will early seek the Saviour; R102282 For He loves me, yes
Bates, David, 1810-70
Speak gently, it is better far
Bates, Katharine Lee, 1859-1929
A little Child, a Joy-of heart
Dear God our Father, at thy
Not for more beauty would our
O beautiful for spacious skies
The Kings of the East are
The palm-trees fed with dew
Bathurst, William Hiley, 1796-1877
Hark, the distant isles
Holy Spirit, from on high
How blest are they whose hearts
Jesus, thy church, with longing
O for a faith that will not
O for that flame of living
Why should our tears in sorrow
Batty, Charles
O, my Saviour crucified
Batty, Christopher, 1715-97
Cheer thy chosen witnesses
Baum, Maria Louise
Here, O God, thy healing
High to heaven let song be
If the Lord build not the
In thee, my God and Saviour
Like as a Mother, God comforteth
Put on the whole armor of pure
Rouse ye, soldiers of the cross; R108662 Rouse ye, rouse ye
Bax, Clifford, 1886-
Turn back, O man, forswear
Baxter, Lydia, 1809-74
Take the name of Jesus; R108376 Precious Name, O how
There is a gate that stands; R106704 O depth of mercy
Baxter, Richard, 1615-91
Christ leads me through no
Christ who knows all his sheep
He wants not friends that hath
Lord, it belongs not to my
Ye holy angels bright
The Bay Psalm book see The Whole Booke of Psalmes, 1647
Bayley, Jonathan
O Jesus, Lord, and Saviour; R101498 Come, Saviour, come
Bayly, Albert F., 1901-
Long ago when Jesus, walked
Lord of the home, thine only
Lord, save thy world; in bitter
Lord, thy kingdom bring
Lord, whose love through

humble service c1961
O joyful hope, in weary hearts; R101579 Comfort ye, my people
Rejoice, O people, in the mounting
Baynes, Robert Hall, 1831-95
God Almighty, in thy temple
Holy Spirit, Lord of glory
Jesus, to thy table led
Beach, Curtis, 1914-
O be joyful in the Lord
O how glorious, full of wonder
Beach, Seth Curtis, 1837-1932
Kingdom of God! the day how
Mysterious Presence, source
Thou One in all, thou All in
Where is he that came to save
Beadon, Hyde Wyndham, 1812-
Fierce was the storm of wind
Glory to thee, O Lord, who by; X100266 All praise to thee
Beaumont, John, 1582-1628
My Shepherd is the Lamb
Beardsley, Monroe, 1915-
From all the fret and fever
Beck, Thomas, late 18th c
Jesus, we lift ourselves
Becker, Henry Albert
Back to the cross I go again
Christ is risen from the dead
Shine on, thou Star of Bethlehem
Beddome, Benjamin, 1717-95
Ascend thy throne, Almighty
Buried beneath the yielding
Come, blessed Spirit! source; X101348 Come, blessed Saviour; X107593 O Spirit, source
Come, Holy Spirit, come, with
Did Christ o'er sinners weep
Father of mercies, bow thine
God, in the gospel of his Son
If Christ is mine, then all is
In duties and in sufferings
Jesus, my love, my chief
Jesus, my Saviour, let me be
Let party names no more
Shout for the blessed Jesus
Thou Lord of all above
'Tis faith supports my feeble
'Tis God the Spirit leads
Wait, O my soul, the Maker's
When Israel through the desert
Witness, ye men and angels; X111901 Ye men and angels
Beeching, Henry Charles, 1859-1919
God who created me
Beegle, H.B.
Wash me, O Lamb of God, wash
Berry, Adaline Hohf, 1859-1929
Hail, blessed Trinity, Low
Lo, a gleam from yonder heaven; R104706 Jesus, Light, serene
Behm, Martin, 1557-1662
Lord Jesus Christ, my life
O heilige Dreifaltigkeit, O hochgelobte Einigkeit. 1593
O holy, blessed Trinity, divine; X106550 O blessed Holy; X107008 O holy ... essential
O Jesu Christ, mein's lebens
O Jesus, King of glory
O König aller ehren
Belden, F.E., 19th c
Blessed Lord, how much I need; R101999 Every hour
Eternal Father, God of love
Father, we come to thee
He's coming once again
Holy day, Jehovah's rest
I will sing of Jesus' love
I would be, dear Saviour
If any little word of mine; R102642 God help me speak
Let every lamp be burning; R109984 Then trim your lamps
Like as a father pities his
Look for the beautiful, look
Look for the waymarks
Look upon Jesus, sinless is He; R101609 Cover with His life
O Jesus, my Redeemer
Raise the standard high

Shepherd divine, thou leadest
Sweet be thy rest, and peaceful
Sweet promise is given to all; R103500 "Hold fast till I"
The coming King is at the door
The judgment has set, the books; R103744 How shall we stand
There is sweet rest for feet
There's no other name like
We know not the hour; R103305 He will come, let us
We'll build on the Rock
Belknap, Jeremy, late 18th c arr
Give ear, ye children to my
Bell, Charles Dent, 1818-98
Be with us, gracious Lord
Bell, George Kennedy Allen
Christ is the King! O friends; X101212 Christ ... friends rejoice
Bell, M. Bettie
Press on, dear traveller, press
Bell, Maud, 1868-1957
Father all-seeing, friend of
Bell, Maurice Frederick, 1862-1947
O dearest Lord, accept today
O dearest Lord, by all adored
Bellamy, W.H.
O troubled heart, there is; X107804 O wait, meekly wait
The home where changes never; X107804 O wait, meekly wait
Bement, Howard, 1875-1936
Clear is the call that bids
Benade, Samuel T., 1746-1830
Bless, O Lord, we pray, thy
Fountain of life and light
How needful, strictly to
To Christ we homage pay
We covenant with hand and heart
Benedictine "Ultima"
At our life's last moment
Ultima in mortis hora
Bennard, George
On a hill far away; R109047 So I'll cherish
Bennett, Archibald F
Holy temples on Mt Zion
Bennett, Henry, 1813-68
I have a home above
Bennett, Sanford Fillmore, 1836-1898
Sing we a song of the Saviour
There's a land that is fairer; R104386 In the sweet by and
Bennett, Wallace F.
God of power, God of right
Benson, Arthur Christopher, 1862-
Lord of grace and holiness
O Lord of hosts, who didst
The spring again is here
Benson, Edward White, 1829-96
O Jesus, crowned with all
Benson, Louis Fitzgerald, 1855-1930
A King might miss the guiding
For the bread, which thou hast
I name thy hallowed name
O Love that lights the eastern
O risen Christ, who from thy
O sing a song of Bethlehem
O Thou whose feet have climbed
O Thou whose gracious presence
Our wilful hearts have gone
The lamps of heaven
The light of God is falling
The sun is on the land
The winter night was dark
Benson, Richard Meux, 1824-1915
Praise to God who reigns
Berg, Carolina Vilhelmina Sandell, 1832-1903
Children of the heavenly
Jerusalem, Jerusalem, thou
O Father, thy kingdom is come
Strait is the gate to all; X109236 Strait ... to

heaven
Berkowitz, Henry
Lord, into thy sacred dwelling
Berlin, Irving, 1889-
God bless America
Bernstein, Christian Andreas, 1672?-1699
At last he's blest who by
Berridge, John, 1716-93
At Cana, Lord, thou didst
Jesus, cast a look on me
Since Jesus freely did appear
Berry, F.J.
Brother afar from the Saviour; R111333 What would you give
Bersagel, Andreas
The sun is sinking in the west
To the hills I lift mine eyes
Berwick hymnal, 1886
Father Almighty, bless us; X102079 Father Almighty, grant
Besnault, Sebastian, Abbe, ca ca1660-1724
Debilis cessent elementa legis
Felix dies, quam proprio
O happy day, when first was; X106547 O blessed day; X107497 O sacred day, when
The ancient law departs
Best, Nolan R.
Made of one blood with all
Betham-Edwards, Matilda B., 1836-1919
God make my life a little; X102701 God ... a shining
Bethune, George Washington, 1805-62
O Jesus, when I think of thee
O thou who in Jordan didst
There is no name so sweet; R111082 We love to sing
Tossed upon the raging
When time seems short and
Betz, Hans
Christus das Lamm auf Erden kam. 1564
Christus der Herr ist gangen. 1564
Gelobt sey Gott im höchsten Thron. 1564
Gott Zebaoth, der war, und ist
Herr Gott Vater im Himmelreich. 1564
Herr Gott Vater, von dir allein. 1564
Herr Gott Vater, zu dir ich schrey. 1564
Ihr Christen g'mein, die ihr seyd rein. 1564
Merkt auf, ihr Völker g'meine. 1564
Merkt auf mit Fleiss, ein Himmelspeiss. 1564
Nun wolt ich gerne singen. 1564
Unser Vater im Himmelreich, Dein Nam sei heilig ewiglich. 1564
Bevier, Louis
Our fathers in the olden
Bhagavad-Gita
Give me your whole heart
Bianco da Siena, d 1434
Come down, O Love divine
Bible.

NOTE: First lines of hymns are listed alphabetically, followed by citation when it is known.

Alleluia, alleluia: i.e. Hallelujah Chorus (Revelation)
Awake, Awake, Awake, Put on thy strength (Isaiah 52); R103624 How beautiful upon
Behold I stand at the door (Revelation 3)
Blessed, blessed, be Jehovah (Psalm 106)
Blessing and honour and glory (Revelation 5)
But the Lord is mindful (Psalms)
Cast thy burden upon the Lord (Psalm 55 or 16)
Down by the river's verdant (Psalm 137)
Give thanks to God (Psalm 136)
God so loved the world

(John 3)
Haec dies quam fecit Dominus (Psalm 117)
How wondrous is thy mercy (Psalm 36: Danish)
Let every creature God has (Psalm 148)
Let us now praise famous men (Ecclesiasticus 44)
Lift thine eyes, O lift (Psalm 121)
Look with mercy, Lord (Joel 2): R111004 We are that chosen
Lovely appear over the mountain (Isaiah 52)
Mine eyes look toward the mountains (Psalm 121: Swedish)
Not unto us, O Lord (Psalm 115)
O heavens, send your rain (Isaiah 45)
O Lord, what is man that Thou takest knowledge (Psalm 8)
O rest in the Lord, wait (Psalm 37)
O thou who spreadest the heaven (Isaiah: Dutch tr); R103218 Have ye not heard
Out of the depths to thee (Psalm 129)
Parce Domini, parce populo (Joel 2)
Praise ye the Lord
Rorate caeli desuper (Isaiah 45)
Send out thy light and thy truth (Psalm 43)
So merket auf ihr Christenleut. (Maccabees)
Souls of the righteous (Wisdom 3)
Spare your people, Lord (Joel 2)
The children of the Hebrews (Psalm 122)
The Lord bless you and keep (Numbers); X109638 The Lord bless thee

Bickersteth, Edward Henry, 1825-1906
Almighty Father, hear our
Arise and be baptized
Come ye yourselves apart
For My sake and the Gospel's
Hush! blessed are the dead
My God, my Father, let me rest
Not worthy, Lord, to gather
O brothers, lift your voices
O Christ, thou hast ascended
O God, the Rock of Ages
O holy Father, who in tender
O Jesu, Saviour of the lost
Peace, perfect peace, in this
Stand, soldier of the cross
"Till he come!" oh, let the

Bienemann, Kaspar, 1540-91
Lord, as thou wilt, deal thou

Bilach, Hanslein von
Einsmals spatziert ich hin und her

Bilhorn, Peter P., 1861-1936
O, the best friend to have; R109419 The best friend to
There comes to my heart one; R108206 Peace, peace, sweet

Bills, G.M.
Do you seek for a friend; R107636 O, the best Friend

Binney, Thomas, 1798-1874
Eternal Light! eternal Light!

Binyon, Laurence, 1869-1943
Down in the valley where
For mercy, courage, kindness
Woe unto him that has not

Bird, Thomas, 1780?-1828
In the lonely house of mourning

Birkedal, Wilhelm, 1809-92
I saw Him in childhood with

Birken, Sigismund von, 1626-81
Jesu, deine Passion will ich
Jesus, I will ponder now
Lasset uns mit Jesus ziehen 1653
Let us ever walk with Jesus

Birks, Thomas Rawson, 1810-83
O gentle Savior, from thy
O King of mercy, from thy throne
The heavens declare thy glory
Whom have we Lord in heaven (authorship in doubt)
Bishop, C.
That God should love a sinner; R109250 Such love, such
Black, James M.
When the trumpet of the Lord; R111489 When the roll is; X111498 When the trump shall (Jacobs)
Blackall, Christopher Ruby, 1830-
In the harvest field there is; R105023 Labor on, labor on
Blackie, John Stuart, 1809-95
Angels, holy, high and lowly
Blacklock, Thomas, 1721-91
Come, O my soul, in sacred
Blackmer, P.W.
Long ago, there was born
Blair, H.E.
On the happy, golden shore
Blaisdell, James Arnold, 1867-
Beneath the forms of outward
Christians, lo, the star
Blake, James Vila, 1842-1920
Father, thou art calling
O sing with loud and joyful
Blake, William, 1757-1827
And did those feet in ancient
Can a father see his child
Can I see another's woe
Every night and every morn
Sweet dreams form a shade
To Mercy, Pity, Peace and Love
Blakeney, E.H.
Lord of the worlds, unseen
Up to the throne on high
Blanchard, Ferdinand Q., 1876-
Before the cross of Jesus
O Jesus, youth of Nazareth; X106597 O child of lowly
Word of God, across the ages
Bland Tucker, Francis, 1895-
see Tucker, Francis B.
Blandly [Blandy], E.W.
I can hear my Saviour calling; R111544 Where He leads me
Blatchford, Ambrose Nichols, 1842-1924
A gladsome hymn of praise; R104276 In him rejoice with
Peacefully round us the shadows
Softly the silent night
Within this temple, reared
Blaurock, Georg
Gott führt ein recht Gericht. 1564
Herr Gott! dich will ich loben. 1528
Blaxill, E. Alex, 1873-1953
Father of all, we come to
Blenkhorn, Ada
In hymns of praise your voices
Bliss, Philipp, 1838-76
(sometimes written as Bliss, Philip Paul)
"Almost persuaded" now to
Brightly beams our Father's R105174 Let the lower lights
Free from the law, O happy; R107982 Once for all
God is always near me
Ho! my comrades, see the signal; R103502 Hold the fort
I know not the hour; R100452 And that will be
I will sing of my Redeemer; R108955 Sing, O! sing
Man of sorrows! wondrous Name; X105872 Man of Sorrows! what
More holiness give me
Sing them over again to me; R100763 Beautiful words
Standing by a purpose true; R101642 Dare to be a Daniel
The whole world was lost; R101539 Come to the Light
'Tis the promise of God; R100346 Alleluia 'tis done

"Who-so-ever heareth," shout
Blough, J.M., 1876-
O Holy Spirit, come to me
Blunt, Abel Gerald Wilson, 1827-1902
Here, Lord, we offer thee all
Boaden, Edward, 1827-
Here, Lord, assembled in thy
Bobbitt, J.P.
I was once far away from; R110628 To my heart in that
Boberg, Carl
O Lord my God! When I in; R109983 Then sings my soul
Bode, Alice M., ca 1850-
Once pledged by the cross
Bode, John Ernest, 1816-74
O Jesus, I have promised; X105577 Lord Jesus, I have
Thou who hast called us
Boden, J. Waugh, 1855-1943
Men true of heart and strong
Boden, James, 1757-1841
Come, all ye saints of God
Boe, V.E., 1872-
Jesus all glorious, Christ all
Boehmer, Justus Henning, 1674-1749
Courage, my sorely tempted
Boehnisch, Frederick, 1710-63
O could we but love that
Boethius, Anicius, M.S., 480-524
O thou whose power o'er moving
Bogatzky, Karl Heinrich von, 1690-1774
Awake, thou Spirit bold
Awake, thou Spirit of the
Awake, thou Spirit, who didst
Wach auf, du Geist der ersten Zeugen 1750
Wake, Spirit, who in times
Bohemian traditional, etc.
Aj, ten silný lev udatný (1650)
Come all ye shepherds; X101335 Come ... and be not
Lo, Judah's Lion wins (1650)
Bohemian Brethren see Moravian
Böhmer, Justus Henning, 1674-1749
O risen Lord! O conquering
Bonar, Horatius, 1808-89
A few more years shall roll; R109986 Then, O my Lord
A sinful man am I
All praise to Him, who built
All that I was, my sin, my
Angel voices, sweetly singing; R103351 Heaven at last
Begin the day with God
Beloved, let us love; love is X100870 Beloved ... love is
Beyond the smiling and the
Blessed night, when first; X100940 Blessed ... when Bethlehem's; X100942 Blessed ... first the; X105968 Mighty King of righteousness
Blessing and honor, and glory
By the cross of Jesus
Calm me, my God, and keep me
Church of the ever-living God
Come and hear the grand old; R106279 Noblest, truest
Come, Lord, and tarry not
Come, mighty Spirit, penetrate
Done is the work that saves
Fading away like the stars; R108031 Only remembered
Far down the ages now
Father, our children keep
For the bread and for the wine
From the cross the blood is
Give thou thy youth to God
Glory be to God the Father; X102568 Glory to the King
Go, labor on! spend and be
Go, labor on, while it is day; X102592 Go ... spend and be
Great King of kings, why

dost
Great master, touch us with
Great Ruler of the land and;
R104979 Keep by the mighty
He has come! the Christ of God
He liveth long, who liveth
Here, O my Lord, I see thee;
X103411 Here ... I'd see;
X110207 This is the hour;
X110714 Too soon we rise
Holy Father, hear my cry
I bless the Christ of God
I close my heavy eye
I did thee wrong, my God
I hear the words of love
I heard the voice of Jesus
I lay my sins on Jesus;
X103833 I bring my sins
I see a man at God's right
I see the crowd in Pilate's
I was a wandering sheep
In the land of strangers;
R111209 Welcome, wanderer
Jesus, Saviour, Son of God
Jesus, the Christ of God
Jesus, whom angel hosts adore
Light of life, so softly
Light of the world! for ever
Like the eagle, upward, onward
Lo! God, our God, has come
Lord, give me light to do;
X105463 Lord, give us light;
R108818 Send me light
Make haste, O man, to live;
X105848 Make haste ... to do
Make use of me, My God
No, not despairingly Come I to
No shadows yonder
Not what I am, O Lord
Not what these hands have done;
X106332 Not what my hands
Now, in parting, Father bless
O everlasting Light! Shine;
X106717 O ... Giver of dawn
O Love of God, how strong
O love that casts out fear
Our life is hid with Christ
Praises to Him whose love has
Rejoice and be glad!
Rest for the toiling hand
The Bridegroom comes; Bride of
The church has waited long
The cross it standeth fast
This is not my place of resting
This is the hour of banquet
Thou must be true thyself
Through good report and evil
Thy way, not mine, O Lord
Thy works, not mine, O Christ
To the name of God on high
True Bread of life, in pitying
Upward where the stars are
We thank thee, Lord, for
When I shall wake in that
When the weary, seeking rest; R103327 Hear then, in love
Yes, for me, for me He careth
Yes, He is risen who is
Bonar, Jane Catharine, 1821-84
Fade, fade, each earthly joy
Bone, Mary W.
Farewell, all earthly honors; R110075 There is sweet rest
Bonin, Ulrich Bogislaw von, 1682-1752
How great at last my joy
Bonn Gesangbuch, 1561
In God's name let us on our
Book of hours (French) 1490
God be in my head, and in my
Book of hymns (Unitarian) 1846
Peace of God, which knows no; X105799 Love divine (Wesley)
The Book of praise for children see Barrett, G.S. The Book of praise, 1881
Booth, Ballington, 1859-1940
The cross that He gave may be; R109459 The cross is not
Booth, Herbert

Blessed Lord, in Thee is refuge
Boreham, F.W., 1871-1959
Eternal Father, whose great
Borthwick, Jane Laurie, 1813-97
Come, labor on, who dares
Hasten the time appointed; X100434 And is the time; X106395 Now is the time
Still on the homeward journey
Thou knowest, Lord, the weariness
Bosch, Sigmund von
Fröhlich so will ich singen
So will ichs aber heben an 1564
Böschenstein, Johann, 1472-1540
Da Jesus an des Kreuzes Stamm
Our blessed Saviour seven; X108841 Seven times our blessed
Bossart, John Jacob, 1721-89
One view, Lord Jesus, of thy
Bostock, Edward C., arr
The Lord God Jesus Christ
Boswell, Robert, 1746-1804
Behold what love the Father
Bosworth's Hymns, 1865
Jesus, thy love unbounded; X106621 O Christ, thy love
Bottome, Francis, 1823-94
Love of Jesus, all divine
O, spread the tidings round; R109455 The Comforter has
Search me, O God, my actions
Bourdillon, Francis William, 1852-1921
The night has a thousand eves
Bourgignon, Antoinette, 1616-80
Come, Saviour Jesus, from above
Bourne, George Hugh, 1840-1925
Lord, enthroned in heavenly
O Christ, our Lord, who with
Bourne, William St Hill, 1846-1929
Christ, who once amongst us
The Sower went forth sowing
Boutflower, C.H., 1863-1942
O God, in this thine hour
O joy of God, that comest
Bowdler, John, 1783-1815
As, panting in the sultry
Lord, before thy throne we
To God I lift mine eyes
Bowers, J.E.
Our Father, we adore thee
Bowie, Walter Russell, 1882-
God of the nations, who from
Lord Christ, when first thou
Lord, through changing days
O holy city, seen of John
O ye who dare go forth with
Bowman, J.M.
My Saviour guides me day by
Bowring, John, 1792-1872
Father and Friend! Thy light
God is love; his mercy
How sweetly flowed the gospel
I cannot always trace the way; X111023 We cannot always
In the cross of Christ, I glory
The offerings to thy throne
"Thy will be done!" In devious
Upon the gospel's sacred page
Watchman, tell us of the night
Box, Howard, 1926-
Bells in the high tower
Boyce, R. Fisher
O, beautiful Star of Bethlehem; R100760 Beautiful Star of
Boye, Birgitte Cathrine, 1742-1824
He is arisen! Glorious word
Holy Spirit, God of Love
O Light of God's most wondrous
O Lue fra Guds Kjärlighed
Os er idag en Frelser föd
Our Lord is risen from the
Rejoice, rejoice this happy
Boye, Caspar Johannes, 1791-1853
Abide with us, the day is
Bliv hos os, Mester, Dagen

Stay with us Lord, the day
Boyle, Cavendish, 1849-1916
When sun rays crown thy pine-clad
Brace, Seth Collins, 1811-
Mourn for the thousands slain
Bradbury. Oriola, 1860
Go thou, in life's fair morning
Bradby, Godfrey Fox
Where is death's sting? We
Brady, Nicholas, 1659-1726, see Tate, Nahum 1652-1715 & Brady, Nicholas, 1659-1726
Bradford, Mrs. N.K.
O tender and sweet was; R108177 "Over the line"
Bradley, E.A.
Turned by thy grace, I look
Bradley, Mary
I need not care If days to
Brailsford, Edward John, 1841-1921
All things which live below
Braley, Berton, 1882-
Lord, we come with hearts
Bramley, Henry Ramsden, 1833-1917
The great God of heaven is
Breay, John George, 1796-1839
Saviour, bless thy word to all
Breck, Mrs. Frank A., 1855-1934
Face to face with Christ
Go to the deeps of God's
There was One who was willing; R110134 They are nailed; R110146 They were nailed
Brenneman, H.B.
There's a beautiful, beautiful; R107615 O, that beautiful
Brethren's Tune and hymn book. 1879
Is there a God? The rising sun
Breviary.

NOTE: First lines of hymns are listed alphabetically, followed by place and date of publication when known.

Adoremus te Christe, et benedicimus tibi
Beati mortui in Domino
Christi factus est pro nobis
Conquering kings their titles take (Nevers, 1727)
Cor, arca legem contenens (Bologna, 1827)
Glorious Virgin, thee we sing
He, who once in righteous vengeance (Bologna, 1827)
Holy Week Responsories
Inviolata integra et casta
Joseph our certain hope (1632)
Lapsus est annus: redit annus (Meaux, 1713)
Let every heart exulting beat (Sarum, 1495)
Morn's roseate hues have decked (Cluny, 1686)
Most holy Lord and God (Paris, 1531)
O Christ, behind the temple's
O let the heart beat high (Sarum, 1495)
O sacrum convivium (York, 1493)
O'erwhelmed in depths of woe (Bologna, 1827)
On this day, the first of days (Carcassonne, 1745)
Popule meus quid feci tibi
Regnum mundi
Ruler of the hosts of light (Cluny, 1686)
Seek ye a patron to defend (Venice, 1798); R100977 Blest holder of ... the keys
Seven Last Words on the Cross
Soldiers, who are Christ's below (Bourges, 1734)
Soldiers who to Christ belong (Bourges, 1734)
Star of Jacob, ever beaming (Lisbon, 1786)
Te, Joseph, celebrent (1670)

The solemn season calls us now (Paris, 1736)
The year is gone beyond recall (Paris, 1713)
Veni Sponsa Christi
What a sea of tears (1746)
Wondrous gift! The word who fashioned (Cluny, 1686); X103298 He who once to die
Brewer, Edith Gaddis
God of truth, eternal good
Prayer with our waking thought
Brewer, Leigh Richmond, 1839-1916
Long years ago o'er Bethlehem's
Brewer, Sidney S.
Watchman, tell me, does
Bridaine, Jacques, 1701-67
My Lord, my Master, at thy feet
Bridgers, Luther B., 1884-1948
There's within my heart; R104686 Jesus, Jesus, Jesus
Bridges, Matthew, 1800-94
Behold the Lamb of God
Crown Him with many crowns; X101626 Crown Him the Lord
My God, accept my heart; X106798 O God, accept my
Rise, glorious Conqueror, rise
There is an everlasting home; X103073 Hail, Rock of ages
Bridges, Robert Seymour, 1844-1930
All praise be to God
All-seeing Lord, whose power
Enter thy courts, thou Word
Eternal Father, who didst all
Gird on thy sword, O man
I love all beauteous things
Lament, O man, thy pride
Love can tell, and love alone
Love of love, and Light of light
Love, unto Thine own who
My God, my God, why dost thou
My heart is filled with longing
My Lord, my Life, my Love
My soul, praise the Lord
Rejoice, O land, in God
Rejoice, ye dead! Where'er
The King [The Queen], O God, his [her] heart to thee
Thee will I love, my God
Unto thee my heart is sighing
When Jesus to our rescue drew
Bridgewater, A.S.
We read of a place called; R103620 How beautiful heaven
Bridgman, Amy Sherman
O Thou, Jehovah, Sovereign
Briem, Valdimer, 1848-1930
How marvellous God's greatness
Lord, let thy Spirit, from
Briggs, George Wallace, 1875-1959
Christ is the world's true
Come, risen Lord, and deign
Dear Father, keep me through
For the brave of every race
God hath spoken -- by His
God my Father, loving me
Hark! a hundred notes are
I love God's tiny creatures
Lord, in the hollow of thy
Lord of all majesty and might
Lord, who hast made me free
Lord, who thyself hast bidden
O God, in whom we live and
Our Father, by whose servants
Our Father, for our daily
She who stood beside the cross
Shall God not share His children's
Son of the Lord most high
The Spirit of the Lord revealed
We meet, as in that upper room

Briggs, LeBaron Russell, 1855-1934
God of our fathers, who hast
Bright, William, 1824-1901
And now, O Father, mindful
And now the wants are told
At thy feet, O Christ, we lay
Behold us, Lord, before Thee
He sat to watch o'er customs
Now at the night's return we
Once again, O blessèd time
Once, only once, and once for
We know thee who thou art
Brightbill, Alvin Franz, 1903-
How lovely is thy dwelling
Brightman, Edgar Sheffield
Thy beauty, Lord, thou hast
Brink, L. P.
The Wallapai, the Navaho
Brock, Mrs. Carey. The Children's hymn book, 1881
The darkness now is over
Brondsema, S. G.
God Jehovah reigns, His are
Unto the Lord lift thankful
Brontë, Anne, 1820-49
Believe not those who say
Brontë, Emily, 1818-48
No coward soul is mine
Brooke, Rupert, 1887-1915
O thou God of all long desirous
Brooke, Stopford Augustus, 1832-1916
All lands and peoples, all
Eternal Peace, whose word of
Immortal Love, within whose
In our dark and doubtful
It fell upon a summer day
"It is finished," all the pain
Let the whole creation cry
Now the wings of day are
Oft, as we run the weary way
The morning walks upon; X109035 Slow comes the evening
When the Lord of Love was here
Brooks, Charles Timothy, 1813-83
God bless our native land see Mahlmann, S. A.
O God! in Thine autumnal
Brooks, Clara M.
"Lo, she is not dead; but--" R108032 Only sleeping, sweetly
Our Father's wondrous works; R111247 What a mighty God we
The eventide falls gently
There's a way that is free; R110971 Watch and pray
Brooks, Phillips, 1835-93
Everywhere, everywhere
God hath sent his angels; R100470 Angels sing his
O Little town of Bethlehem
The sky can still remember
Brorson, Hans Adolf, 1694-1764
Anxious heart be rid of sadness
Behold a host like mountain; X100800 Behold ... arrayed
Behold, they stand in robes
By faith we are divinely sure
Children of God, born again
I near the grave where'er I go
I see thee standing, Lamb
I walk in danger all the way
In this our happy Christmastide
Jeg gaar i Fare, hvor jeg gaar 1734
Jesus, name of wondrous grace
Life's day is ended, the battle
My heart, prepare to give
Now found is the fairest of
O Father, may thy word prevail
O seek the Lord today
O watch and pray, my soul
Stand fast, my soul, stand fast
Thy little ones, dear Lord
What joy to reach the harbor
Who will join the throng
Brown, Ann, 1908-
Grace, love, and peace abide
Brown, Elmer Elsworth
O Stranger, with no place

Brown, Howard I.
Jesus calls me, I must follow; R102247 Follow, I will follow
Brown, J.A.
Pray, pray in the old-time
Brown, J.S.
I cannot tell thee whence; R110102 There's a deep
Brown, Kathryn Wright, 1910-
O Master of all grace
Brown, Mary and C.E. Pryor
It may not be on the mountain's R104192 I'll go where you; X104489 It may not be on ... mountain
Brown, Phoebe Hinsdale, 1783-1861
I love to steal awhile away
O Lord, thy work revive
We come, O Lord, before thy
Brown-Borthwick, Robert, 1840-94
O Holy Jesu, Prince of Peace
Browne, R.D., 1905-
Thou, Lord, hast given Thyself
Browne, Simon, ca 1680-1732
And now, my soul, another
Come, gracious Spirit, heavenly; X101405 Come, Holy Spirit; X108875 Shine forth, O Sun
Frequent the day of God
Hail, happy day! Thou day of
Hail, Holy Spirit, bright
Lord! at thy feet we humbly
Browne, Sir Thomas, 1605-82
The night is come like to
Browne, Thomas Briarly, 1805-74
Praise the Lord of heaven
Browning, Elizabeth Barrett, 1809-61
Of all the thoughts of God
Since without thee we do no
Browning, Robert, 1812-89
I go to prove my soul
The year's at the spring
Then welcome each rebuff
There's heaven above, and night
Was the trial sore? Temptation
Brubacher, Menno M.
O God of wisdom, life and love
Bruce, Michael, 1746-1767
Behold, the mountain of the Lord
How happy are the young; X103698 How happy is the man; X106966 O happy is the man
The beam that shines
Wisdom hath treasure greater
Bruce, William, 1812-82
Holy Father, thou hast given
Bruce, William Patterson
Ring out, O bell, thy welcome
Brucker, H.F.
Accept from human hands
Accept this host, O God
Praise now your God, all ye
Brueckner, Hermann, 1866-1942
All hail, thou day of wondrous
Aloft in yonder belfry
The heavens cannot thee embrace
To thee eternal God, our fervent (Rinkart); X106443 Now thank we all our
Bruinengk, Heinrich von, 1738-85
Here in the name of Christ
Brun, Johan Nordahl, 1745-1816
Heavenly Spirit, all others
How blest are they who hear
In heaven is joy and gladness
Lad denne Dag, o Herre Gud 1786
O salig den, Guds Ord har
Our Lord and God, O bless
Bruun, Samuel O., d 1694
The sun has gone down
Bryan, Joseph
To my humble supplication
Bryant, William, 1850-1913
Standing forth on life's
Bryant, William Cullen, 1794-1878
Dear ties of mutual succor
Lo! in the clouds of heaven
Look from thyssphere; X105398 Look from the

sphere
Lord, who ordainest
O deem not they are blest; X101738 Deem not that they
O North, with all thy vales
Thou, whose unmeasured temple; X107769 O Thou, whose own
When, doomed to death, the
When the blind suppliant
When this song of praise
Bryn Mawr College, 1923.
To the knights in the days
Buchanan, Violet Nita, 1891-
Help me, dear Lord, to love
O day of joy and wonder
Büchel, Hans
Als man zählt tausend fünf hundert Jahr. 1557
Ein g'fahre Zeit vor nie erhört.
Es b'gab sich auf ein Zeite. 1564
Buck, Carlton C., d 1961
O Lord, may church and home combine c1961
Buckham, John Wright
O God, above the drifting
Buckholl, Henry James, 1803-71
Lord, behold us with thy
Lord, dismiss us with thy
Buddha, The Lord Gautama see Gautama Buddha, 5th c B.C.
Budry, Edmond, 1854-1932
Thine is the glory, risen; X110159 Thine be the glory
Buehrer, Edwin T., 1894-
We sing now together our song
Buell, Harriet E., 1834-1910
My Father is rich in houses; R104213 I'm the child of a King
Buerge, C.G.
Remember thy Creator, while
'Tis midnight and the Saviour
Troubled soul, thy God is
Buermeyer, Ferdinand F.
Sleep, baby, sleep! Thy mother
Buffum, Herbert
My heart is so happy in Jesus; R103901 I intend to go
Bugbee, Emily
Church of God, whose conquering
Bulfinch, Stephen Greenleaf, 1809-70
Hail to the Sabbath day; X103109 Hail to this holy
Hath not thy heart within
How glorious is the hour
Lord, in this sacred hour
Bull, John, 1777-1871
Let my life be hid in thee
Bullock, William, 1798-1874
We love the place, O God; X111081 We love thy house
Bulmer, Agnes Collinson, 1775-1837
Thou who hast in Zion laid
Bunyan, John, 1628-88
Blest be the day when moved
He that is down needs fear no
He who would valiant be; X111657 Who would true valor
Burder, George, 1752-1832
Sweet the time, exceeding
Burdsall, Richard, 1735-1824
The voice of free grace cries
Burgess, George, 1809-66
While o'er the deep thy servants
Burgess, Walter H.
Again as daylight fades
Burke, Christian, 1859-1944
Lord of life and King of glory
Burke, Herbert C.
I shall approach the altar
Burkitt, Francis Crawford, 1864-1933
Our Lord, his Passion ended
Burleigh, William Henry, 1812-71
Abide not in the realm
For the deep love that kept
From lips divine, like healing
Lead us, O Father, in the
O, deem not that earth's
Still will we trust though
Burmeister, Franz Joachim, d1672
O blessed Babe divine
Burnett, Vivian

O, when we see God's mercy
Burnham, Richard, 1749-1810
Jesus, thou art the sinner's
Burns, James Drummond, 1823-64
As helpless as a child
At thy feet, our God and
For thee, my God, for thee
Hushed was the evening hymn
Still with thee, O my God;
X109227 Still, still with thee
This night, O Lord, we bless
Thou, Lord, art love
Thou who didst on Calvary
Burntvedt, T.O.
God is faithful, He will never
Burr, Amelia Josephine, 1878-
O Lord of Love! shall we not
Burroughs, E.A., 1882-1934
Lord God, from whom all life
Burroughs, John, 1837-1921
Serene I fold my hands
Burrow, S.E.
Let not thy hands be slack
Burrowes, Elizabeth
God of the ages, by whose hand ca.1863
Burt, Bates Gilbert, 1878-1948
O God of youth, whose Spirit
Burton, Henry, 1840-1930
Break, day of God, O break
Come for the feast is spread
O King of kings, O Lord
O Maker of the sea and sky
There is an arm that never
The day is past; the shadows
There's a light upon
Burton, John, 1773-1822
Holy Bible, book divine
Burton, John, 1803-77
O what praises shall we render
Our Father hears us when we
Remember thy Creator now
Saviour, thee my heart I;
X108749 Saviour, while my
Busch, Calvin A.
Dear Lord, today, our child
Butcher, Edmund, 1757-1822
Great God, as seasons
Butcher, John Williams, 1857-1937
I thank thee, Lord, for life
Butler, C.J.
Since Christ my soul from sin; R106520 O alleluia, yes, 'tis
Butler, Henry Montagu, 1833-1918
"Lift up your hearts!" We lift
O merciful and holy
Butler, Mary
Looking upward every day
Butler-Thwing, Francis W.
Our God leads onward
Buzzard, Rufus
As the dawn was calmly; R107595 O, spread the message
Byler, Elsie
O, thou the great eternal One
Byrom, John, 1690-1763
"Cheer up, desponding soul."
Christians, awake, salute
My spirit longs for thee
Byron, George Gordon, Lord Byron, 1788-1824
Eternal spirit of the chainless

C

Caddell, Cecilia Mary, 1813-77
Behold the lilies of the field
By the blood that flowed; R104813 Jesus, Savior, hear
By the first bright Easter; R104993 King of glory, hear
I lift mine eyes unto the hills
Caird, George Bradford, 1917-
Almighty, Father, who for us
Calabrian Shepherds hymn:
As darker, darker see
Longfellow, Samuel (possible translator)
A Calendar of country song
O that I as right and true
Callin, R.W., 1886-1951
Long ago, when heathen darkness
Calvin, John, 1509-64
I greet thee, who my sure

Camerarius, Joachim, 1500-74
In tenebris nostrae et densa caligne mentis 15thc.
When in the hour of utmost
Camm, Bede, O.S.B.
Hail Mary, full of grace
Cammerhof, Johann Friedrich, 1721-51
Lord Jesus, I pray, on earth
Camp, Mabel Johnston
Lift up your heads, Pilgrims; R103242 He is coming again
Campbell, A. Christian hymn book.
Here, Saviour, we would come
Campbell, J. Comprehensive hymnbook, 1837
A glory in the word we find
Campbell, John, 1845-1914
Unto the hills around do I
Campbell, Margaret C., d1841
Praise ye Jehovah! praise
Campbell, Margaret C.
Praise ye the Lord! Praise ye
Campbell, Marion Susan
Angels at the Saviour's birth
Christ comes again with holy
Campbell, Robert, 1814-68
They come, God's messengers
Campbell, Susan F.
In Love divine all earth-born
Campbell, Thomas, 1777-1844
Men of England, who inherit
Campbell, Vera
God of the nations, hear our
Campian, Thomas, 1567-1620
Never weather-beaten sail
Sing a song of joy, praise
The man of life upright
Canadian national anthems, etc.
see ---. In days of yore; Murray. Our loved Dominion; Weir. O Canada
Canitz, Friedrich Rudolph Ludwig von, 1654-99
Come, my soul, thou must be
Seele, du musst munter werden!
Cannon, Tracy Y.
Come, rejoice, the King of
Praise the Lord with heart
Canton, William, 1845-1926
Hold thou my hands!
Through the night thy angels
When the herds were watching
Cardoza, Elizabeth C.
We met them on the common way
Carey, William
Jesus loves me, Jesus loves me
Carlyle, Joseph Dacre, 1758-1804
Lord, when we bend before thy
Carlyle, Thomas, 1795-1881
So here hath been dawning
Carmelite hymn.
Salve, mater misericordiae
A Carmelite Nun.
Hail, all hail, sweet youth
O sweet Infant Jesus, we hail
Carmen, Bliss, 1861-
Lord of my heart's elation
We are adventurers who come (with R. Hovey)
Carmichael, Amy Wilson, 1867-1951
Dear Lord, for all in pain
Carnett, Ellis L.
"It is finished," said
Carney, Julia A., 1823-
Little drops of water, little
Think gently of the erring
Carols will be found under headings such as: English traditional; German traditional; Traditional; etc.
Carpenter, Edward, 1844-1929
England, arise! The long, long
Carpenter, William Boyd, 1841-1918
Before thy throne, O God, we
Now another stage of travel
Carruth, Mrs. Roy
Swiftly we're turning life's; R104444 Into our hands
Carruth, William H., 1859-
A haze on the far horizon
Carter, Henry Child, 1875-1954
Give me, O Christ, the strength

Carter, R. Kelso,
Standing on the promises
Cary, Phoebe, 1824-71
One sweetly solemn thought
Cary, Alice, 1820-71
My God, I feel thy wondrous
Casartelli, Bishop.
Heart of Jesus! golden chalice
Case, Elizabeth York
There is no unbelief; whoever
Cassaday, Lillian Weaver, 1861-1914
O Christians, leagued together; R100210 All hail our glorious
Cassel, E. Taylor, 1849-1930
From over hill and plain; R107975 On to victory
I am a stranger here, within; R110210 This is the message
Castellain, Lewie Prittie
O Father, may we bear each
Caswall, Edward, 1814-78
Alleluia! alleluia! Let the holy anthem
Days and moments quickly
If thou wouldst life attain
O Jesus Christ, if aught there
O Jesus Christ, remember
See, amid the winter's snow; R103091 Hail, thou ever-blessed; X108787 See! in yonder manger
Sleep, holy Babe, upon thy
This is the image of our; R106020 Most holy Mary; X110209 This is the image
Caswall, Miss L. T.
I am the way, the truth, the
Catholic hymnal, 1860
Lord, in thy presence dread
Spirit of wisdom, turn our
Cawood, John, 1775-1852
Almighty God, thy word is; X100373 Almighty God ... sown
Hark! what mean those holy
Cennick, John, 1718-55
Be present at our table, Lord
Be with me, Lord, Where'er I
Blessed Lord, what shall we
Brethren, let us join to bless
Children of the heavenly King
Dear Saviour, we bless thee
Ere I sleep, for every favor
Go, follow the Saviour
Hail, Alpha and Omega, hail
Hail, Church of Christ, bought
How heart-affecting Christ to
I kneel in spirit at my Saviour's
I love the Lord who died for
I will a little pilgrim be
Jesus, my all, to heaven is
Jesus, thou art my salvation
Lamb of God, my Saviour
Lo! He comes with clouds; X105339 Lo, He cometh
No farther go tonight, but
O if the Lamb had not been
O Thou, who on earth didst
Rise, my soul, adore thy
Saviour and Regenerator
The child sweetly rests
The doctrine of our dying; X101207 Christ is our Master
The holy Child Jesus
Thou dear Redeemer, dying
Though but a little child, I
Though I'm in body full of
We thank thee, Lord, for this; X102959 Great God, we praise; X111153 We thank thee Lord
What, my soul, should bow
When Christ, our Saviour, did
Červenka, Matthias see Czerwenka, Matthias
Chadwick, James, 1813-82
Jesus, my God, behold at; X104756 Jesus, my Lord; R107451 O, pardon me, Jesus
Chadwick, John White, 1840-1904
Another year of setting suns
Backward looking o'er the past
Come, let us sing a tender
Eternal Ruler of the ceaseless
It singeth low in every heart
Now sing we a song for the
O Love divine, of all that is
O thou whose perfect goodness

Spirit of God, in thunder
Thou glorious God, before
Thou mighty God, who didst of
Thou whose spirit dwells in
Thy seamless robe conceals
What has drawn us thus apart
Chamberlain, John M.
We're marching on to glory
Chamberlain, Thomas, 1810-92
O guardian of the Church
Chandler, John, 1806-76
Above the clear blue sky
Chao, Tzu Ch'en, 1888-
Golden breaks the dawn
Jesus merciful, Jesus pitying
My hearts looks in faith
Ne'er forget God's daily care
Praise our father for this
Praise our God above
Rise to greet the sun
Chapin, Edwin Hubbell, 1814-80
Our Father God! Not face to
Chapman, Mrs. E.W.
Closer to thee, my Father; R101326 Closer with the cords
Go out and gather the golden
With friends on earth we meet; X108096 Our friends on earth; R111217 We'll never say
Chapman, J. Wilbur, 1859-1918
Jesus! what a Friend for; R100348 Alleluia! what a
One day when heaven was filled; R105326 Living, He loved me
Charles, David, 1762-1834
From heavenly Jerusalem's
Charles, Elizabeth Rundle, 1828-96
Come and rejoice with me
Is thy cruse of comfort; X110767 True, the heart
Never further than thy cross
No Gospel like this feast
Praise ye the Father for his; X108333 Praise ye our Father
Charlesworth, Vernon J., 1939-
The Lord's our Rock, in Him; R105970 Mighty Rock in a R107115 O Jesus is a Rock
Charteris, Archibald Hamilton, 1835-1908
Believing fathers oft have
Chatfield, Allen William, 1808-96
For ever we would gaze on thee
Chaucer, Geoffrey, 1340?-1400
Now welcome, Summer, with
Cheevers, Commonplace book of American poetry, 1831
The twilight falls, the night
Cheney, Ednah Dow, 1824-1904
At first I prayed for Light
Cherry, Edith Gilling, 1872-97
I have heard thy voice, Lord
We rest on thee, our shield
Cherryman, Myrtle Koon.
O, Native Land, how fair
Chester, Henrietta Mary, 19th c
Come, let us all with one
Chester ms., ca 1425
He who made the starry skies; X108418 Qui creavit, coelum
Chesterton, Frances, d 1938
How far is it to Bethlehem?
Chesterton, Gilbert Keith, 1874-1936
It is something to have wept
O God of earth and altar
The Christ-child lay on Mary's
Child songs.
For air and sunshine pure
Childress, J.H.
Upon the first day of the week; R110393 Though others may
Childs, R.W.
Lo! the clouds have burst; R108887 Shout for joy, ye
Chinese (authorship unknown)
Chaun dong whan lo tsan mei; R102656 God is forever
Father, long before creation
Let us joyfully give praise
Chippewa (Indians) traditional
Upon the mountain top alone
Chisholm, Thomas O., 1866-1960
"Great is thy faithfulness"

Living for Jesus, a life that; R107122 O Jesus, Lord
Chord, S.H.
Some sweet day when life is
Chorley, Henry Fothergill, 1808-72
God the Omnipotent! King, who; X102693 God, Lord of Sabaoth; X102811 God the All-merciful; X102812 God the All-terrible; X102813 God the Almighty One
Christiansen, Avis Burgeson, 1895-
Up Calvary's mountain one; R100945 Blessed Redeemer
Christie, A.J.
To Jesus' Heart all burning
Christierson, Frank von, 1900
As men of old their first fruits brought
Break forth, O living light of God.
Chubb, Percival, 1860-
Hail we now this happy morn
Light of Ages, shed by man; X105263 Light of conscience
We lift our hearts in thanks
Church, Edward Alonzo, 1844-1929
Almighty Builder, bless, we
O thou to whom in prayer and
Church-Gallery book, Dorset
Let Christians all with joyful
Rejoice and be merry in songs
Church melodies, 1858
We bless thee for thy peace
Church of Scotland, 1745
The Saviour died, but rose
The Churchman (?), 1858
Is this Jesus, then the Lord
Churton, Edward, 1800-74
God of grace, O let thy light
Earth, with all thy thousand
If our God had not befriended
Claggett, Martha, 1692-1773
O Lord, in me fulfill whatever
Clare, John, 1793-1864
A Stranger once did bless
Clare, Thomas Charles Hunter, 1910- see Hunter-Clare, T.C., 1910-
Clark, Alexander, 1835-79
Heavenly Father, bless me
Clark, Emily V.
O God of mercy! hearken now
Clark, Thomas Curtis, 1877-1953
God is not far from any one of
I sought his love in sun and
Our faith is in the Christ who
The touch of human hands
Thou Father of us all
Where restless crowds are
Who goes there, in the night
Who will build the world anew
Your goal was not some island
Clark, W.H.
All praise to Him who reigns; R100914 Blessed be the name
Clarke, C. Erskine, 1871-1926
O, David was a shepherd lad
Clarke, Dumont, 1883-
We care for our Lord's acres
Clarke, Harry D., 1888-
Into my heart, into my heart
Clarke, James Freeman, 1810-88
Brother, hast thou wandered
Father, to us thy children
To Him who children blessed
To thee, O God in heaven, this
Clarke, Samuel Childs, 1821-1903
Now a new year opens
Clarke, William Newton
Let men their brethren know
Clarkson, Edith Margaret, 1915-
We come, O Christ, to thee
Claudius, Matthias, 1740-1815
We plow the fields, and scatter; R100205 All good gifts; X111099 We plough the fields
Wir pflügen und wir streuen
Clausen, Martha
And now we must bid one

Clausnitzer, Tobias, 1619-81
Dearest Jesu, we are here
(see also the easily confused: Schmolck. Blessed Jesus, here are we)
Here in thy presence we appear
Liebster Jesu, wir sind hier
Look upon us, blessed Lord
We all believe in one True God; X111011 We believe in One
Wir glauben all' an einen
Clayton, Edith
Father, we come, with youth
Clayton, P.B.
Come, kindred, upstand in the
Trudge on, singing praise for
Clayton, William
Come, come, ye Saints, no toil
When first the glorious light
Cleator, Alice Jean
O Father, lead us gently by; R102212 Fears oft affright
Clegg, William
Let earth's inhabitants rejoice
Clemens, Christian Gottfried, ca 1750-1825
O thou God of our salvation
Clements, John R.
In the land of fadeless day; R102803 God shall "wipe away"
Like a shepherd, tender, true
Clephane, Elizabeth Cecilia, 1830-69
Beneath the cross of Jesus
There were ninety and nine
Cleveland, Benjamin, 1733-1811
O, could I find, from day to
Clock, Leenaert
O Gott Vater, wir loben dich. 1625
Our Father God, thy name we
Clough, Arthur Hugh, 1819-61
Say not, "The struggle naught"
Clough, Samuel O'Maley
I have a Saviour, He's pleading; R102324 For you I am praying
Clute, Oscar, 1837-1901
O Love of God most full
Coates, Florence Earle, 1850-
I thank thee that how-e'er we
Coates, J.B.
Living below in this old; R111540 Where could I go
Workers on a building rare
Coblentz, Stanton A.
I would not reach the mountain's
Cockburn-Campbell, Margaret
see Campbell, Margaret C. 1808-41
Codner, Eliza.
Lord, I hear of showers of; R101986 Even me, even me, Let
Coffin, Charles, 1676-1749
Another day is past and gone
As now the sun's declining
Christ is our Head, our Strength
Creator of the world, to thee
God from on high hath heard
Great mover of all hearts
Happy are they, they that love
His trial o'er, and now beneath
In the Light all light
Instantis adventum Dei
Jordanis oras praevia
Let sighing cease and woe
Lo, from the desert homes
Lo, the pilgrim Magi leave
Lord of the hearts of men
Maker of earth, to thee alone
Now with the declining sun
O Holy Spirit, Lord of grace
O Lord, how joyful 'tis to see
O Saviour, who for man hast
O scorned and outcast Lord
On Jordan's bank the Baptist's X107949 On Jordan's ... the Herald's
The advent of our God; X109408 The advent ... King
The splendours of thy glory
What beauteous sun-surpassing
What star is this, so radiant
What star is this, with beams

Coffman, J.S.
O, the bliss of loved ones
O weary wanderer, come home; R103382 Help me, dear Saviour
Coffman, S.F.
Extol the love of Christ
In thy holy place we bow
We bless the name of Christ
Coffman, see also Kauffman
Coghill, Anna Louisa (Walker), 1836-1907
Work, for the night is coming
Cohen, Aaron
Descend, descend, O Sabbath
Colby, Kate L.
Be true and list the voice
Cole, L.F.
Birds are singing, woods are; R111161 We, thy children, join
Cole, Samuel Valentine, 1851-
O thou who sealest up the past
Coleman, E.G., 1872-
Christian, let your burning
Coleridge, Samuel Taylor, 1772-1834
God! Let the torrents like a
He prayeth best who loveth
O sweeter than the marriage-feast
Sleep, sweet babe! My cares
Coles, Abraham
We cannot build alone
Coles, Vincent Stuckey Stratton, 1845-1929
Almighty Father, Lord most high
O Shepherd of the sheep
We pray thee, heavenly Father,
Ye who own the faith of Jesus
Colesworthy, Daniel C., 1810-93
While we lowly bow before thee
Collection. Baltimore, 1800
Sing, my soul, his wondrous
A Collection of Psalms and hymns for St Mary's and St Giles. Reading, 1830
"It is finished!" Shall we
Colletet, Francois
"O, I have seen a king's new"
"Quoi, ma voisine, est-tu"
Collier, Edward Augustus, late 19th c
As the hart when noon is
Bless, O Lord, we pray thee
I love the Lord, because
Lord, to thee my soul is
No longer, Lord, despise me
O God, arise! and by thy might
O Lord, who hast the table
On the cross is One uplifted
The law that the Lord has; X109574 The heavens in their
Collins, Henry, 1827-1919
Jesu, meek and lowly
Jesus, my Lord, my God, my All; X104762 Jesus, my Lord, my Life
Collyer, Robert, 1823-
Unto thy temple, Lord, we come
Collyer, William Bengo, 1782-1854
Deign this union to approve
Great God, what do I see and
Haste, traveler, haste! the
Morning breaks upon the tomb
Return, O wanderer, return; X108503 Return! Return! O
Cologne Psalter, 1638
To us in Bethlehem city
Zu Bethlehem geboren
Cologne Psalteriolium, 1710
I love thee, O thou Lord most
Colum, Padraic, 1881-
Now in the tomb is laid
Comenius, John Amos, 1592-1670
When my lips can frame no
Compton, Richard
God, our Father, made the
Who made ocean, earth, and sky
Concord Anthem book, 1925
Lead me, Lord, lead me in thy
Conder, Eustace Rogers, 1820-92
Ye fair green hills of Galilee
Conder, George William, 1821-74

All things praise thee, Lord
Conder, Josiah, 1789-1855
Alleluia! Raise, O raise
Be merciful, O God of grace
Beyond, beyond that boundless
Bread of heaven, on thee we
Day by day the manna fell
Father, now thy sinful child
Heavenly Father, to whose eye
How shall I follow Him I serve
Lord, in this blest and hallowed
Lord, 'tis not that I did
Now with angels round
O Comfort to the weary see Hymns of the English Conf.
O give thanks to Him who made
O thou, who givest all our
Praise the God of all creation: X108275 Praise ... our salvation
The heavens declare His glory
The Lord is King! lift up thy
Thou art the everlasting Word; R111863 Worthy, O Lamb
'Tis not that I did choose thee
Confucius, 551-497, B.C.
Let him who would excel
Congregational Church Hymnal. 1887
Behold the eternal King and
Congregational Collection
O thou, who didst the temple
Conover, Howard J., 1850-1922
O God, we pray for all mankind
Consterdine, James, 1852-1925
Hark, hark my soul! The voice; R102880 Gospel of Jesus
Contes, Jean-Baptiste de, 1601-79
Spouse of Christ, in arms
Conway, John Placid, 1855-
Hail full of grace and purity
Cook, Henry, 1788-1868
Jesus, Shepherd of the sheep
Cook, J., 1736-61
Lamb of God beloved
Cook, John T.
There'll be no shadows; R110798 'Twill all be joy
Cook, Russell Sturgis, 1811-64
Just as thou art, without one
Cooke, Greville, 1894-
Jesus Christ, my heart's true
Cooke, Rose Terry, 1827-92
I bring my hymn of thankfulness
Cooke, William, 1821-94
In exile here we wander
Cook, Joseph Simpson
Gentle Mary laid her child
Cooper, Arthur Eugene, 1872-1944
The men of the Church
Cooper, Edward, 1770-1833
Father of all, whose love; X102145 Father of heaven
Cooper, George, 1840-
Star of the East, O Bethlehem
There are lonely hearts to; R102854 Going by, going by
Coote, Constance, 1844-1936
For all who watch tonight
In the quiet consecration
Coote, Maude Oswell, 1852-1935
The son of consolation
Copeland, Benjamin, 1855-
Christ's life our code, His
Our fathers' God, to thee we
Copenhaver, Laura Scherer, 1868-1940
Heralds of Christ, who bear
Coppée, Henry
Safe upon the billowy deep
Corelli, Marie
In our hearts celestial voices
Cornaby, H.
Who's on the Lord's side? Who?
Cornelius, Carl A. Peter, 1824-74
Drei König wandern aus
The holly's up, the house is
Three kings from Persian lands
Wie schön geschmuckt der

Cornelius, Maxwell N.
Not now, but in the coming; R109990 Then trust in God
Cornell, W.D.
Far away in the depths of my; R108207 Peace! peace!
Cornish, William, d 1523
Pleasure it is To hear
Corolla Hymnorum, Cologne, 1806
O thou immortal, holy Light ; X107861 O ... Light Divine
Cosner, W.F.
Often weary and worn on the; R110067 There is rest by and
Coster, George Thomas, 1835-1912
From north and south and east
King of the City Splendid
Lord God Almighty, in thy hand
Collett, Samuel, 18th c
Through all the various shifting
March on, O soul, with strength
O God, our Father, throned
We join with all, in every
Cotterill, Jane Boak, 1790-1825
O Thou, who hast at thy command
Cotterill, Thomas, 1779-1823
Eternal Spirit, God of truth
Great God of Abraham, hear
Help us, O Lord, thy yoke
In memory of the Saviour's
Jesus! exalted far on high
Let songs of praises fill
Lord, cause thy face on us
O'er the realms of pagan
Our God is love; and all his; X108102 Our God ... his sons
Cottle, Joseph, 1770-1853
Mighty Lord, extend thy kingdom
Cotton, George Edward Lynch, 1813-66
We thank thee, Lord, for this
Cottrell, R.F.
O solemn thought! and can it be
The time is near when Zion's
The wonders of redeeming love
Cousin, Anne Ross, 1824-1906
O Christ, when burden bowed
O now is the time to remember
The sands of time are sinking
Coverdale, Miles, 1487-1569
Christ is now risen again
Now blessed be thou, Christ
Cowley Carol book, 1902
This joyful Eastertide; R103014 Had Christ, that once; R104147 If Christ who once
Cowper, Frances Maria Madan, 1727-97
My span of life will soon be
Cowper, William, 1731-1800
A glory gilds the sacred page; X111273 What glory gilds; X109846 The Spirit breathes
God moves in a mysterious way; X111921 Ye timid saints
God of my life, to thee I call; X102737 God ... on thee
Hark, my soul! it is the Lord
Heal us, Immanuel! Hear our
Hear what God the Lord hath
In thy holy contemplation
Jesus, where'er thy people; X107343 O Lord, where'er thy
My former hopes are fled
My Saviour, whom absent I love
My song shall bless the Lord
O for a closer walk with God
O Lord, my best desire fulfil
Sometimes a light surprises
There is a fountain filled
'Tis my happiness below
What various hindrances we
Ye sons of earth, prepare the
Cox, Christopher Christian, 1816-82
Silently the shades of evening

Cox, Luther J.
An alien from God and a
Cox, Samuel K.
Lord, thou hast promised grace
Coxe, Arthur Cleveland, 1818-96
How beauteous were the marks; X110515 Thy works, how beauteous
In the silent midnight
O walk with God, and thou
O where are kings and empires
O who like thee so calm so
Saviour, sprinkle many nations; X108731 Saviour, quicken
We are living, we are dwelling; R103183 Hark, the waking up
Who is this with garments
Craig, John, 1512-1600
O Lord, thou art my God
Craig, R. J.
Ye are the light of the world
Crain, Harry L.
O blessed Son of God
Cramer, Johann Andreas, 1723-88
Herr! Dir ist Niemand zu vergleichen!
Lord, who can be with thee
Crane, William Merriam, 1880-
Lord Jesus, Son of Mary
Ye shepherds plains of Bethlehem
Crashaw, Richard, 1613?-49
Gloomy night embraced
Crasselius, Bartholomäus, 1667-1724
Christ of holiness, the Fountain
Dir, dir Jehova, will ich
Holy Jesus! Fountain streaming
Jehovah, let me now adore
To thee, O Lord, will I sing
Crawford, Emily May Grimes, 1864-1927
Speak, Lord in the stillness
The Master comes! He calls
Thy mighty love, O God
Creamer, Louise
Touch me, Lord Jesus, with
Creighton, Mandell, 1843-1901
O thou who gavest power to love
Crewdson, Jane Fox, 1809-63
O for the peace that floweth
O Fount of grace, that runneth
O Saviour, I have naught to
O thou, whose bounty fills my
There is no sorrow, Lord, too
Croatian traditional
Hark, the angel voices singing
Croly, George, 1780-1860
Spirit of God, descend upon; X109157 Spirit ... dwell thou
Cronbach, Abraham
'Tis not the large, the huge
Cronenwett, Emanuel, 1841-1931
As by one's sin fell all
Faith is wisdom from on high
Invited, Lord, by boundless
Lo, in Sion a foundation
Lord, thy omniscience I adore
Of omnipresent grace I sing
Of Sion's honor, angels sing
The Spirit's fruits are peace
To thee, our Fathers' God we
Unto Caesar let us render
We have a sure prophetic Word
Cropper, Margaret Beatrice, 1886-
Jesus' hands were kind hands
O Christ, whom we may love
We have a King who came to
Crosby, Fanny, 1820-1915
NOTE: American books use this form of her name; British books use: Van Alystyne. She used many pseudonyms which are identified in Julian's Dictionary. Others presumed are: A.A.F., J.V.C., and Sallie Martin.

A wonderful Saviour is Jesus; R103239 He hideth my soul
A year of precious blessings

All the way my Saviour leads
Be silent, be silent; R110749 Tread softly, tread
Be with me all my journey; R100747 Be with me every
Behold! a royal army; R110903 Victory, victory
Behold me standing at the door
Blessed assurance, Jesus is; R110196 This is my story
Come with thy sins; R103200 Haste thee away, why
Conquering now, and still; R106327 Not to the strong
Don't forget the Sabbath; R111211 Welcome, welcome,
Go as a witness for Jesus; R109361 Tell how He pities
God of our strength enthroned
Great is the love that brought
Have you sought for the sheep
He is coming, the Man of Sorrows; R100319 Alleluia! Alleluia
Heavenly Father, we beseech; R100904 Bless the words we
Here from the world we turn
Hide me, O my Saviour, hide; R103458 Hide me, hide me
Hold thou my hand! so weak
Holy, holy, holy is the Lord
I am thine, O Lord; R101832 Draw me nearer
If I come to Jesus, He will
In thy cleft, O Rock of ages
Jesus is tenderly calling; R101126 Calling today
Jesus, keep me near the cross; R104347 In the cross
Keep Thou my way, O Lord
Loving Saviour, hear my cry; R101694 Dear Jesus, receive
Mighty Rock, whose towering; R110841 Unto Thee, unto Thee
More like Jesus would I be
"Nearer the cross!" My heart
Never shone a light so fair
Now just a word for Jesus
O Christian, awake! 'tis the; R109196 Stand like the brave
O hear my cry, be gracious now; R104521 I've wandered far
O the unsearchable riches; R108375 Precious, more precious
O wonderful words
O, wondrous name, by prophets; R109932 The wonderful!
Only a step to Jesus
Only thy tender love, Saviour; R108035 Only to follow Thee
Out on the mountain, sad; R101125 Calling to thee
Pass me not, O gentle Saviour; R108734 Saviour, Saviour,
Praise Him, praise him! Jesus
Redeemed, how I love to
Rescue the perishing
Safe in the arms of Jesus
Saviour, more than life; R101996 Every day, every hour
Search me, O Lord, and try
Some day the silver cord; R100431 And I shall see Him
Speed away, speed away on your
Take the world, but give me; R107649 O, the height
Tell me the story of Jesus
The Lord in Sion reigneth
The Lord's our Rock (see also Charlesworth, V. J.)
Thou my everlasting portion; R101323 Close to Thee
Though your sins be as scarlet
'Tis the blessed hour of prayer; R100926 Blessed hour
To God be the glory; R108284 Praise the Lord
To the work! to the work; R110737 Toiling on, toiling
Troubled heart, thy God is; R106528 O, be saved, His
When Jesus comes to reward; R106593 O can we say we

are
When my life-work is ended; R104027 I shall know Him
Whither, pilgrims, are you going (in Golden chain, 1861: presumed author)
Will you come, will you come; R106968 O happy rest, sweet
Would you win a Saviour's
Cross, Ada Cambridge, 1844-
The dawn of God's dear Sabbath; X109469 The dawn ... own
Cross, Allen Eastman, 1864-
America, America, the shouts
As stars come with the night
From out the Rock whence we
Guide of my spirit on its
Jesus, kneel beside me
Maker of stars, Eternal King
More light shall break
Mount up with wings as eagles
Pass on the torch, pass on
The gray hills taught me
The hidden years at Nazareth
The stars they sing together
Thou Fatherland be vast and
What doth the Lord require
Wild roars the blast, the storm
Young and radiant, he is
Cross, Frank
Go forth, strong word of God
Crossman, Samuel, 1624-83
Jerusalem on high, My song
My life's a shade, my days
My song is love unknown
Croswell, William, 1804-51
Lord, lead the way; X105607 Lord ... my Saviour; X105608 Lord ... our Saviour
Crowell, Grace Noll, 1877-
Because I have been given
The day will bring some
Cruciger, Elisabeth Meseritz, d 1535
The only son from heaven
Crum, J.M.C., 1872-
Let love arise and praise him
Let us thank the Christ for
Now the green blade riseth
O God, whose mighty works
On the moorland of life
Strong Captain, in thy holy
Thou Wind of God, whose coming
To God who makes all lovely
Crystal, James
Take courage, Saints, and
Cummings, A.
Father, in the morning, unto
Cummins, Evelyn Atwater
I know not where the road
Cummins, James John, 1795-1867
Jesus, Lord of life and glory
Shall hymns of grateful love
Cumins, Patrick
Bursting forth from Pharaoh's
Of that branch in ancient
Cuninggim, Maud M., 1874-
O living Christ, chief Corner
Currie, Edward C.
God most truly honored thee
Mary Immaculate, Mother
O Bethlehem of holy worth
O Lord, reprieve the lonely
The sun in splendor rose
When Mary, immaculate, tender
Curry, R. Donald
We thank thee Lord for sending
Curtis, Christine
As the hart with eager
Curtis, Theodore E.
Again, our dear redeeming Lord
I wander through the stilly
Lean on my ample arm
Curwen, John. Standard course, 1860
God is near thee, therefore
Curwen, John, 1817-80
I'm a little pilgrim, and a
Cushing, William Orcutt, 1823-
Beautiful valley of Eden
Down in the valley with my; R102246 Follow! follow! I
O safe to the Rock that is; R103460 Hiding in thee
O, to have no Christ
Ring the bells of heaven;

R102550 Glory, glory! how
Under His wings, I'm safely; X110809 Under ... I am safely
We are watching, we are waiting; R111007 We are waiting
When He cometh, when He; R105301 Like the stars
Cutler, J.S.
Motherhood, sublime, eternal
Cutter, William F., 1801-67
She loved her Saviour, and to
Who is thy neighbor? He whom
Czamanske, William Martin, 1873-
For many years, O God of
Czech traditional.
From out of a wood did a cuckoo
Little Jesus, sweetly sleep
Czerwenka, Matthias, 1521-69
How good it is, how pleasant

D

"D.S., 1920"
Holy, holy, holy, O thou love
Dach, Simon, 1605-59
Ich bin bei Gott in Gnaden 1651
O how blest are ye whose toils
O wie selig seid ihr doch, ihr Frommen 1635
Through Jesus' blood and merit; X110418 Through ... bloody
Dachstein, Wolfgang, 16th c
An wasserflüssen Babylon
Dahl, Christopher [Kristoffer] 1758-1809
Come, O sinner, all is ready
Dakota (Indians) hymn
Many and great, O God, are thy things
Dale, W.T.
"I am nearing the port"
Dalrymple, A.
O Lord of hosts, we now
Damrosch, Frank, jr
God, deigning man to be
Dana, Mary Stanley Bunce Shindler, 1810-
Flee as a bird to your mountain
I'm a pilgrim, and I'm a
O, sing to me of heaven; R110091 There'll be no
Prince of Peace, control
Daniel ben Judah, 14th c. "The Yigdal": see Jewish doxology
Daniels, E.D.
Thy will, O Lord, not mine
Danish traditional
Fryd dig, du Kristi Brud (ca 1600)
In God, my Saviour, I put my (1600)
In Jesus I find rest and peace (1740)
O Bride of Christ, arise (ca 1600)
O day full of grace, which we (14th c)
Darby, John Nelson, 1800-82
God and Father we adore thee
O eyes that are weary
Though faint, yet pursuing
Darbyshire, John Russell, 1880-1948
At eve, when now he breathed
Great is their joy who hide
Life and health are in the
Lord Jesus, from thy throne
O Lord of Life, whose power
Who dreads, yet undismayed
Daries, Frederick R.
This day in thy dear name we
Darmstadt. Gesangbuch, 1698
Alleluia! Let praises ring
Alleluia! Lob, Preis und Ehr'
To God be honor, laud
Darwin, Erasmus, 1731-1802
Roll on, ye stars, exult in
Darwood, W. M'K.
On Calvary's brow my Saviour; R106591 O Calvary! dark
Dass, Petter, 1647-1707
Mighty God, to thy dear Name
Davenport, T.

Come, all ye sons of God, who
Davies, Mary Carolyn
Youth of the world, unite
Davies, Samuel, 1723-61
Great God of wonders! all thy
Lord, I am thine, entirely
On thee, our Guardian, God, we
Davies, William Henry, 1871-1940
What is this life, if full of
Davieson, Eve
Hear us, Eternal King, hear
Davis, Corie F.
Have I need of aught, O
Davis, Frank M., 1839-96
More like thee, O Saviour, let
Saviour, lead me, lest I stray
Davis, John S.
What was witnessed in the
Davis, O.S. (c1947)
Lord, give us a vision
Davis, Ozora Stearns, 1866-1931
At length there dawns
O holy Spirit, gracious gift
We bear the strain of earthly
Davis, Robert, 1881-1950
I thank thee, Lord, for
Jesus, our brother, strong
Davis, T.A.
When there is peace, where
Davison [Davidson], Anna L.
Purer in heart, O God, help
Davison, W. Hope, 1827-94
Jesus, King of glory 1928
Dawson, William James, 1854-
Christ must be served indeed
When the golden evening
Day's Psalter, 1561
Al people yt on earth do dwel
Day, George E.
O Master of the callous hand
Dayan, Daniel ben Judah.
The Yigdal see Jewish doxology
Dayman, Edward Arthur, 1807-90
Almighty Father, heaven and
Christ has come for our
Honor and glory, thanksgiving
O Lord, be with is, when we
Sleep thy last sleep, free
"Who is this, with garments"
Dayton, Mary Alice
Eternal mind the Potter is
Dean, Joseph H.
Before Thee, Lord, I bow my
Dearmer, Geoffrey, 1893-
Those who love and those who
"To Damascus!" Paul had
When Judas did his Lord reject
Dearmer, Percy, 1867-1936
NOTE: A letter dated 28/4/64 from Oxford Univ. Pr. to the author listed the initials used as pseudonyms by Percy Dearmer. Frequently they are initials of hymnals in which his poems first appeared, Here they are: A.F., A.G., B.R., E.H., N.B.L., O.B.C., O.B.C.V., S.P., S.P.B.G., S.P.V., S.T., T.S.N. As the books are being reprinted, Oxford Univ. Pr. is replacing these initials with the author's name.

A brighter dawn is breaking
Ah! think not, "The Lord ..."
All hail to the Power who
Angels and ministers, spirits
As the disciples, when the
Be, Lord, the happy guide
Books of books, our people's
Christ to us across the water
Christian, do you see him
Come now, all people, keep
Crown him upon the throne
Draw us in the Spirit's tether
Father, who on man dost
God is love; his the care
God, we thank thee; not in
Good-bye! Our school is over
Good day to you all
Holy God, we show forth here
Holy Spirit, make us strong
How great the harvest is
In Asia born, from Asia

hailed
In God rejoice! his good
In the place of sorrow, waiting; X100620 At the cross her
Jesus, good above all others
Let us rejoice, the fight is
Life is good, for God contrives
Lo, in the wilderness a voice
Lo, when the day of rest was
Look up, by failure daunted
Lord of health, thou life
Lord, the wind and sea obey
Mercy thou art, Creator, Friend
Now April has come
Now join, ye comrades true
Now quit your care
Now thy earthly work is done; R105321 Live in peace, where
O dear and lovely Brother
O Father above us, our father
O Father in heaven, our father
O Father of goodness, thou art
O Father of wisdom and friendship
O Holy Spirit, God, all
O sing to the Lord now, his
O welcome in our midst
Our babies' names on the
Praise him, praise him, all; X108251 Praise ... all ye
Prophets, teachers, true
Quick sympathy, hands that
Rejoice and be glad! he lives
Remember all the people; X108472 Remember all God's
Servants of the great
Sing praise to God who spoke
So we lift up our hands and
Take heart, friends; X101159 Cheer up, friends
The dawn-wind now is waking
The greatness of God in his
The winter's sleep was long
There are a myriad means
They saw the lights shine out
Thou Judge by whom each Empire
Thou true Vine, that heals
Through north and south and
To the name that is salvation
To thee, who makest all
True Son of Man, thou crown
Unknown and unrewarded
Virtue supreme, thy mighty
We saw not, when thou cam'st
We saw thee not when, far
We wish you many happy returns
Welcome, day of the Lord
When by fear my heart is
When Christ blessed his; R106440 Now sing we of
When Christ had shown God's
Wherefore, O Father, we thy
Who is he whom crowds acclaim
Who within that stable cries
Winds of God unfailing
Winter creeps, Nature sleeps
With Jesus for hero, for
Working together, wary and
Zeal of the Lord, for ever

De Armond, Lizzie
Have you found rest and peace; R107611 O, tell what He's
If you only knew my Saviour
We sail along toward the; R109441 The Christ will our

DeChenez, Charitié Lees Bancroft, 1841-1923
Before the throne of God
The King of glory standeth

Decius, Nikolaus [Nicolaus] d 1541
All glory be to God on high; X100196 All glory ... most X100199 All glory be to thee
Allein Gott in der Höh sei
Alone to God on high be praise
Lamb of God, pure and holy; X105036 Lamb of God most holy
O Lamb of God, most holy
O Lamb of God, unspotted
O, Lamb of God, who, bleeding
O Lamm Gottes, unschuldig
To God on high be thanks

Deck, James George, 1802-84
Holy Saviour! we adore thee
How long, O Lord, our Saviour
Jesus, thy name I love
Lord Jesus, are we one with
O God, thy name is love
O Lamb of God, still keep me
O Lord, when we the path
When along life's thorny road
Deck, Mary Ann Sanderson, 1813-1902
There is a city bright
Deems, Charles F.
I shall not want! in deserts
DeFleury, Maria, d ca 1794
Thou sweet gliding Kedron
Ye angels who stand round
DeFluiter, Henry
God bless and keep thee
Tell it to every kindred and; R103046 Hail Him the King
Deitz, Purd E., 1897-
We would be building; temples
DeJong, Gerrit, jr.
Come, sing to the Lord, His
De la Mare, Walter, 1873-1956
It was about the deep of night
Deland, Margaret, 1857-1945
Blow, golden trumpets, sweet
DeMarbelle, Dion
There's a land beyond the river; R101815 Don't you hear
Denham, David, 1791-1848
'Mid scenes of confusion; R103591 Home, home, sweet
Denicke, [Denike], David, 1607-80
Almighty Lord of earth
By nature man cannot achieve
How can I thank thee, Lord
Was kann ich doch für Dank 1648
Denisot, Nicholas
All the gay gems of day
Le vermeil du soliel
Denney, Charles
O thou kind and gracious
Dennis, Amanda E.
Behold the shining Sabbath
Dennis, Ethel Wasgatt
A grateful heart a garden is
Dennis, Thomas
Have you read the story; R103233 He died of a broken
Denny, Edward, 1796-1889
Blest feast of love divine; X109279 Sweet feast of love
Children of light, arise
Hope of our hearts, O Lord
Light of the lonely pilgrim's
What grace, O Lord, and beauty
While in sweet communion
De Sola Mendes, Fred
see Mendes, Fred de Sola
Dessler, Wolfgang Christoph, 1660-1722
How blest am I, most gracious
I leave thee not, thou art my
Into thy gracious hands I fell
My Jesus, if the Seraphim
My soul's best Friend, what
O Friend of souls, how blest
What wealth of joy thy presence
Wie wohl ist mir, o Freund der Seelen 1692
Dewart, Edward Hartley, 1828-1903
Father, Supreme, by whom we
O Thou who hast in every age
Out on life's dark heaving
Dibble, Philo
The happy day has rolled on
Dickinson, Charles Albert, 1849-1906
Blessed Master, I have promised
O golden day, so long desired
Dickinson, Emily, 1830-86
If I can stop one heart from; X104154 If I can keep (Marlatt)
Dickinson, Helen A.
Shepherds now go we to yon
Dickson, William, 1817-89
Childhood's years are passing
Didache (Greek) ca 110
Father, we thank thee who hast

Dietrick, Emma G.
Abide with me, I need thee
Dillon, George, 1906-
Obedient they but to a dream
Dillingham, Frances Bent
All the happy children Gladly
Disciples Hymn book.
Father, the watches of the
Dix, William Chatterton, 1837-98
Alleluia! sing to Jesus
As with gladness men of old
Beauteous are the flowers
Come unto me, ye weary
In our work, and in our play
Joy fills our inmost hearts
Like silver lamps in a distant
O thou the Eternal Son of God
Only one prayer today
The cross is on our brow
To thee, O Lord, our hearts
What child is this, who, laid; R110221 This, this is Christ
Dixon-Wright, Henry Dixon, 1870-1916
To thee, O God, our hearts
Doane, George Washington, 1799-1859
Beloved, "It is well!" God's
Fling out the banner! let it
Once more, O Lord, thy sign
Softly now the light of day
Thou art the way, to thee; X110240 Thou ... by thee
Doane, William Croswell, 1832-1913
Ancient of Days, who sittest
To thee, O Father, throned on
Dobell, John. A new selection, 1806
Hark, 'tis the Saviour's
Now is the accepted time
Sinners, behold that downward
Dober, Anna Schindler, 1713-39
Lamb of God, who thee receive
Dober, Leonhard, 1706-66
Christ's love invites us
Dober, Martin, 1703-48
Jesus, Saviour, I implore
Dobree, Henrietta Octavia deLisle, 1831-94
Safely, safely gathered in
Dobson, Austin
All-wise, All-great whose
Doddridge, Philip, 1702-51
And art thou with us, gracious
And shall we still be slaves (with Watts)
And will the great eternal God
And will the Judge descend
Awake, my soul, stretch every
Awake, ye saints, and raise
Baptized into our Saviour's
Behold the amazing sight
Beset with snares on every
Come, sacred Spirit, from above
Dear Saviour, we are thine
Do not I love thee, O my Lord
Eternal and immortal King
Eternal source of every joy
Father of all, thy care we
Father of lights, we sing thy
Father of mercies, send thy
Father of peace, and God of
Fountain of good, to own thy
God of my life, through all
Grace! 'tis a charming sound
Great God, we sing that mighty; X102960 Great God ... guiding
Hail to the Prince of Life
Hark! the glad sound! The
High let us swell our tuneful
How gentle God's commands
How rich thy bounty, King of
How swift the torrent rolls
Jesus, I love thy charming
Jesus, my Lord, how rich thy; X104796 Jesus, our Lord, how
Jesus, thou Source of life
Let Sion's watchmen all awake
Lord, let thy goodness lead
Lord of the Sabbath, hear us; X105672 Lord ... hear our vows
Maker of all things, mighty
My God! the covenant of thy
My God, thy table now is;

X106076 My God, and is thy; X107222 O Lord! and is thy
My gracious Lord, I own thy
Now let our cheerful eyes
Now let our mourning hearts
Now to the King of heaven (with Watts)
O Fount of good, to own thy
O God of Bethel, by whose hand; X106860 O God of Jacob
O God of heaven and earth
O happy day, that stays my; R103119 Happy day, happy day; X103627 How blessed is the; X106957 O happy day, that
Our heavenly Father calls
Return, my roving heart, return
See Israel's gentle Shepherd; X105347 Lo, Israel's gentle
Shine on our souls, eternal
Sing, O ye ransomed of the
Sing to the Lord, who loud
The King of heaven his table
The Saviour kindly calls
Thine earthly sabbaths, Lord
Thou who wast a child on earth
Tomorrow, Lord, is thine
Triumphant Sion, lift thy
What though the arm of conquering
Why will ye waste on trifling
Ye servants of the Lord
Yes, the Redeemer rose
Dodge, Mary Mapes, 1831-1905
Can a growing child like me X101133 Can a little child
Dodgshun, Ernest, 1876-1944
What service shall we render
Dollard, James B. d 1946
Hail, glorious apostle, St Basil
On Calvary's height the Roman; R109981 Then let us adore
Domer, Harry Tennyson, 1877-
O Church of freedom stand
Domett, Alfred, 1811-87
It was the calm and silent
Donne, John, 1573-1631
Wilt thou forgive that sin, by X111717 Wilt thou ... where I
Donnelly, Eleanor C.
Sacred Heart in accents
Donnelly, F.P.
Ave, tu Rex Pácis nobiscum
Donohue, James J.
St Joseph God has chosen you
Döring, Carl August, 1783-1844
Father, Son, and Holy Ghost
Dorr, Julia Caroline Ripley, 1825-1913
Heir of all the ages, I
How can I cease to pray for
Doudney, Sarah, 1843-1926
For all thy care we bless
Saviour, now the day is
Sleep on, beloved, sleep
The Master hath come, and He
Dougall, Hugh W.
Jesus of Nazareth, Saviour and
Doughty, A.S.
Soon trials and conflicts of; R111240 We're nearing
Doughty, Nicholas
Today, while the sun shines
Downton, Henry, 1818-85
For thy mercy and thy grace
Lord, her watch, thy church
Drane, Augusta Theodosia, 1823-94
The clouds hang thick
Thou who, hero-like, hast
Draper, Bourne Hall, 1775-1843
Sovereign of worlds, display
Ye Christian heralds, go
Draper, William Henry, 1855-1933
All creatures of our God (see St Francis of Assisi)
From homes of quiet peace
Hush, all ye sounds of war
In our day of Thanksgiving
Lord, through this Holy Week
Drennan, William, 1754-1820
The heaven of heavens cannot
Drese, Adam, 1620-1701
Fairest Bridegroom mind
Jesus, call thou me, from the
Drinkwater, John, 1882-1937

A shining city, one happy
Grant us the will to fashion;
X111070 We know the paths
Driscoll, John, d 1940
Glorious Saint whose deeds
The living God my Shepherd is
Driver, J.M.
Wonderful story of love
Drucker, Thomas
Wollt ihr hören, was ist geschen, 1557
Drummond, William Hamilton, 1772-1856
One cup of healing oil
Drury, Miriam
Once again to its close
Dubois, Theodore, 1837-1924
Christ, we do all adore thee
Duclaux, Mme (nee A. Mary F. Robinson) 1857-1944
O thou that movest all
The mass of unborn matter knew
Dudley, William Ewart, 1887-
The city, Lord, where thy
Dudley-Smith, Timothy, 1926-
Christ be my leader by night
Lord, who left the highest
Tell out, my soul, the greatness
Duffield, George, jr., 1818-88
Blessed Saviour, thee I love
Stand up, stand up, for Jesus
Duffield, Samuel Willoughby, 1843-87
O, land relieved from sorrow
Dugmore, Ernest Edward, 1843-1925
Almighty Father of all things
Dunbar, William, ca 1465-1530
Rorate coeli de super
Duncan, Mary Lundie, 1814-40
Jesus, tender Shepherd, hear
Dungan, Helen
You can make the pathway;
R104170 If there's sunshine
Dunham, Barrows, 1905-
Winter is a cold thing
Dunkerley, William Arthur, 1852-1941, see Oxenham, John, 1852-1941
Dunn, John Randall
Sing, ye joyous children, sing
We thank thee and we bless
Durfey, Tom, 1653-1723
All hail to the days that
Dutch traditional
A message came to a maiden (1928)
Hours and days and years
Lord Jesus hath a garden (17th c)
O Sion's daughter, where art
We gather together to ask (1625)
We praise thee, O God, our
Wilt heden nu treden voor God den Heere 16th c
Wir treten zum Beten vor Gott den Herren tr. by Budde, 1897
Dutton, Thomas
Sinners, hear the joyful news
Dwight, Timothy, 1752-1817
How pleasing is thy voice
I love thy kingdom, Lord;
X103971 I love thy Church;
X103974 I love thy Zion
Shall man, O God of light
Sing to the Lord most high
While life prolongs its

E

Earle, J.C., 1821-99
I will arise and to my Father
East, James T., 1860-1937
Wise men seeking Jesus
Eastburn, James Wallis, 1797-1819
O Holy, Holy, Holy Lord
Ebel, William
O, be still, thou soul of mine
Eber, Paul, 1511-69
Helft mir Gott's Güte preisen
I fall asleep in Jesus'
In Christi Wunden schlaf' ich ein 1638
In thy dear wounds I fall
Jesus thy blood and righteousness (with Zinzendorf)
Lord Jesus Christ, true man
The Saviour's blood and (with Zinzendorf)
To God the anthem raising

Wenn wir in höchsten Nöten sein 1547
When in the hour of utmost need see Camerarius. When in the hour.
Lord Jesus Christ, the Prince
Eddis, Edward Wilton, 1825-1905
Our sins, our sorrows, Lord
Thou standest at the altar
Eddy, Mary Baker, 1821-1910
Blest Christmas morn, though
Brood o'er us with thy sheltering
It matters not what be thy lot
O gentle presence, peace and
O'er waiting harp-strings
Saw ye my Saviour? Heard ye
Shepherd, show me how to go
Edgar, Mary S., 1889-
God, who touchest earth with
I will follow the upward road
Edmeston, James, 1791-1867
Along my earthly way
As oft with worn and weary
Fountain of grace, rich, full
Lead us, heavenly Father lead
Little travelers Zionward
O thou, whose mercy guides my
Roll, on thou mighty ocean
Saviour, breathe an evening; X108736 Saviour, shed an
Sweet is the light of Sabbath; X103752 How sweet the light
Wake, harp of Sion, wake
Edwards, Annie, 1832-
He must reign, who won the
Edwards, Frank, 1898-
God of earth and sea
Edwards, Frederick
God of the nations, who hast
Edwards, Louise Betts
Christian Soul, the times are
Edwards, Robert Lansing
Declare, O heavens, the Lord
Edwards, William, 1798-1879
O thou who hearest prayer
Edworthy, Z.B.
Father, bless us as we part
Ehrenberg-Posse, Katarina Elizabeth, 1818-80
Merciful Saviour, come and be
When Christmas morn is dawning (arr.)
Ela, David Hough, 1831-
The chosen three, on mountain
Eldridge, Jay Glover
God of years, thy love hath
Eliot, Frederick May, 1890-1958
O thou, to whom the fathers
The night was dark and stormy
Ellerton, John, 1823-93
Again the morn of gladness; R102544 Glory be to Jesus
Before the day draws near its
Behold us, Lord, a little space
Day by day we magnify thee
God of the living, in whose
Hail to the Lord who comes
In the name which earth
King of saints, to whom the
Lift the strain of High
Now the laborer's task is o'er
O Father, all creating
O Father, bless the children
O Son of God, our Captain
O thou in whom thy saints
Our day of praise is done
Praise to our God, whose
Praise to the heavenly wisdom
Saviour, again to thy dear; X102073 Father, again to Thee; X102074 Father, again to thy
Shine thou upon us, Lord
Sing ye faithful, sing with
The day thou gavest, Lord
The hours of day are over
The Lord be with us as each; X109635 The Lord ... bend X109636 The Lord ... walk
This is the day of light; X110200 This ... day of rest

Thou, who sentest thine
Throned upon the awful Tree
We sing the glorious conquest
When the day of toil is done
Elliott, Charlotte, 1789-1871
Christian, seek not yet; X102471 Gird thy heavenly
Ever patient, gentle meek
God of my life, thy boundless
Jesus, my Saviour, look on me
Just as I am, without one
I need no other plea
Leaning on thee, my Guide
Let me be with thee, where
My God, is any hour so sweet
My God, my Father, while I; X106074 My God and Father, day by; X106075 My God and Father, while I; R 110506 Thy will be done
O Holy Saviour, Friend unseen
O thou, the contrite sinners'
The Sabbath day has reached
There is a holy sacrifice
When waves of trouble round
Wie ich bin, komm' ich zu dir--
With tearful eyes I look
Elliott, Ebenezer, 1781-1849
When wilt thou save the people
Elliott, Emily Elizabeth Steele, 1836-97
There came a little child
Thou didst leave thy throne; X110252 Thou dost reign
Unto Him whose name is holy
Elliott, Julia Anne, 1809-41
Father, who the light this
Hail thou bright and sacred
We love thee, Lord, yet not
Elliott, Norman, 1893-
"Seek ye first the kingdom"
Ellis, Frederick, 1835-
With joyfulness and longing
Ellis, G.E. Psalms and hymns. Boston, 1845
Ere to the world again we go
Ellis, Henry Havelock, 1859-1939
Onward brothers, march still
Ellis, Lethal A.
There's a God who's standing; R111960 You can't do wrong
Ellsworth, W.W.
Saviour, hear us, we pray; R104714 Jesus, Lord, hear
Elpis, ca 500
Lead us, great teacher Paul
With golden splendour and with
Elven, Cornelius, 1797-1873
With broken heart and contrite
Emerson, George D.
Thanks be to God for his
Emerson, Ralph Waldo, 1803-82
We love the venerable house
We sing of golden mornings
Emilie Juliana, countess ... see Amilie Juliane, countess ... 1637-1706
Emrick, Ernestine Hoff, 1918-
O master of all, come we to
Emurian, Ernest K., 1912-
We dedicate this temple
Enfield, William, 1741-97
Behold, where in a mortal form
English traditional, etc.
A babe is born all of a may (15th c)
A babe is born of high nature (15th c) R111321 What tidings
A child this day is born; R102519 Glad tidings to all
A virgin most pure, as the X100076 A virgin ... did tell; R108451 Rejoice and be merry
About the field they piped (ca 1450)
Adam lay abounden, Bounden in (15th c)
All under the leaves, the
All you that are to mirth (17th c)
As I passed by a riverside (13th-14th c)
As I sat on a sunny bank
As it fell out one May morning

As it fell out upon one day
As Jacob with travel was weary; R100347 Alleluia to Jesus
Awake, awake, good people all
Awake, awake, ye drowsy souls; X102625 God bless the ruler; X104500 It was early in the; R109045 So God send you all
Come all ye faithful Christians
Come all you worthy Christian men
Come all you worthy gentlemen
Deck the hall with boughs
Down in yon forest there stands; R100186 All bells in paradise
God bless the master of this
God rest you merry (18th c); R107777 O Tidings of comfort
God's dear Son without
Good people all, this Christmas
Green grow'th the holly
Here we come awassailing
I saw a fair maiden (15th c); R105831 Lullay my liking
I saw three ships come sailing
I sing of a maiden that is makèless (15th c)
In Bethlehem, that fair city (15th c)
It was on Christmas day
It was on Holy Wednesday
I've brought you here a bunch
Joseph was an old man; X100553 As Joseph was a-walking; X109982 Then Mary took her; X102010 Exortum est in love
King Pharim sat a-musing
Let Christians all with one (18th c?)
Lully, lulley, lully, lulley
Make we joy now in this feast (15th c)
Make we merry, both more and (ca 1500)
Now is Christmas y-come
Now the holly bears a berry
Nowell sing we, both all (ca 1450)
O, Joseph being an old man
O mortal man, remember well
On Christmas night all
Out of the orient crystal (17th c)
Out of your sleep arise and (15th c)
Over yonder's a park which; R100186 All bells in paradise
Remember us poor Mayers all
Rise up, rise up, you merry
St Stephen was a holy man; R107387 O man, do never
The angel Gabriel from God
The Babe in Bethlem's manger; R106490 Nowell, Nowell, now sing
The first good joy that Mary (15th c)
The first nowell the angel did
The holly and the ivy
The Lord at first did Adam
The moon shines bright, and
There was a star in David's (13th-14th c)
This endris night (15th c)
This is the truth sent from
This new Christmas carol
Tidings true there come new (15th c)
Tomorrow shall be my dancing X100775 Before Pilate; X104445 Into the desert
Wassail, wassail, all over
Welcome be thou, heaven-king (15th c); X111213 Welcome Yule, thou
What are they that are but one (1625, or earlier); R104412 In those twelve days
When Caesar Augustus had raised
When Christ was born of Mary (ca 1456); R104257 In excelsis gloria
When Christ was born to set

(15th c)
When Jesus Christ was twelve; X111505 When they bereaved
When righteous Joseph wedded; R109988 Then sing you all
Enman, William Edgar, 1869-1950
Lamb of God, to thee we
Epistle to Diognetus, ca 150
The great Creator of the
Erfurt Enchiridion, 1527
O God, our Lord, thy holy Word
Erikson, Gustaf
This solemn hour O let us be
Erskine, Ralph, 1685-1752
Faith comes by hearing God's
In thee I live, and move
Esling, Catherine H., 1812-97
Come unto Me, when shadows
Essenburg, B.
Unto God, our King, joy and
Estlin, John Prior, 1747-1817
Eternal Source of life
Eugenie, princess of Sweden
My heart is longing to praise
Euripides. The Bacchae, ca 407 B.C.
What else is wisdom? What else
Evangelical Theological Seminary. Class of 1900
Servants of the Christ your
Evans, Albert Eubule, d1896
Lo! the voice of Jesus
Lord, to thee alone we turn
Evans, I.H.
Welcome, day of sweet repose
Evans, Jonathan, 1748 or 49-1809
Come, thou soul-transforming; X101511 Come, thou all-transforming
Hark! the voice of love and
Evans, William Edwin, 1851-
Come, O thou God of grace
Everest, Charles William 1814-77
Take up thy cross, the Saviour
Evilsizer, Mrs. L.M.
Out in the desert the lost; R102606 Go to the lost
Saviour, we come to thee; R108725 Saviour, O Saviour
Evilsizer, R.A.
The time of the harvest; R109604 The laborers are few
Ewald, Johannes
Rise, hero bold, from Golgotha
Excell, Edwin O., 1851-1921
I have a song I love to sing; R108912 Since I have been
Exeter Collection
To thee, my heart, eternal
Extrait du Recuiel Louange et Prière. 4th ed., 1957
Great God who hast delivered

F

F.B.P., ca 16th c.
NOTE: An unidentified poet's version of St Augustine

Jerusalem, my happy home
O mother dear, Jerusalem
Thy saints are crowned with
Thy vineyards and thy orchards
Thy walls are made of precious
Faber, Frederick William, 1814-63
All hail, dear Conqueror, all
All praise to St Patrick
Blest is the faith, divine; R107563 O, Sion's songs are
Dear angel, ever at my side
Dear Guardian of Mary
Dear Jesus, ever at my side
Dear little One how sweet
Faith of our fathers! living; R102037 Faith ... holy faith; X102039 Faith ... (Catholic variant)
Full of glory, full of wonders

God's glory is a wondrous; X110409 Thrice blest is he
Hail bright Archangel, Prince
Hail, holy Joseph, hail! Chaste
Hark, hark my soul! angelic; R100467 Angels of Jesus; R100468 Angels of mercy
Have mercy on us, God most
Holy Ghost, come down upon
I was wandering and weary
I worship thee, most gracious; X104114 I worship thee, sweet
Jesus, all hail, Who for our; X102092 Father, gracious
Jesus, gentlest Saviour, God
Jesus is God! the glorious; X104669 Jesus ... the solid
Jesus my Lord, my God, my all; R109301 Sweet Sacrament
Most ancient of all mysteries
Mother Mary, at thy altar
Mother of mercy, day by day
My God, how wonderful thou; X106827 O God, how wonderful
My God! my God! and can it be; R106982 O hearken when we
Now are the days of humblest
O blessed Father! sent by God
O blessed St Joseph, how
O come and mourn with me; X104453 Is it nothing to you
O come to the merciful Saviour
O, gift of gifts! O, grace of
O God, thy power is wonderful
O how the thought of God
O it is hard to work for God
O Paradise, O Paradise, who; X107450 O Paradies ... would not win; R111558 Where loyal hearts
O purest of creatures! Sweet
O Saviour, bless us ere we go; X101713 Dear Saviour, bless; X109302 Sweet Saviour, bless; R110419 Through life's long
O, see how Jesus trusts himself
O turn to Jesus, Mother! turn
O, vision bright! the land of
Saint of the Sacred Heart
Sing, sing, ye Angel Bands
There's a wideness in God's; X109120 Souls of men! Why; X110966 Was there ever
What happiness can equal mine
Why art thou sorrowful
Workman of God! O lose not

Fahs, Sophia Lyon, 1876-
Divinity is round us

Falckner, Justus, 1672-1723
Auf, ihr Christen, Christi Glieder 1697
Christians, rise, put on your
Rise, ye children of salvation

Falconer, Hugh, 1859-1931
God and Father see Darby, J. N.

Falk, Johannes Daniel, 1768-1826
O thou joyful, O thou wonderful

Fan Cheng-ta, ca 1186
But for the cockerel calling

Farjeon, Eleanor, 1881-
Fields of corn, give up your
Lord, thou who gavest me all
More lovely than the noonday
Morning has broken Like the
Now every child that dwells
People look East The time is

Farningham, Marianne, pseud. see Hearn, Marianne, 1834-1909

Farrar, Frederick William, 1831-1903
In the field with their flocks

Farrell, Melvin
Christians, sound the name
Lord of nations, bless in
Now in joy we sing thy praises

Farrington, Harry Webb, 1880-1931
Dear Lord, who sought at dawn
I know not how that Bethle-

hem's
O God Creator, in whose hand
Strong, righteous Man of
The storm-god of stern
Sinai's
Faure, Jean Baptiste
O'er all the way green palms
Fawcett, John, 1739-1817
Behold the sin atoning Lamb
Blest be the tie that binds;
X103645 How blest the tie
How precious is the book
Lord, dismiss us with thy;
X105445 Lord, dismiss ...
Hope and comfort; X105446
Lord, dismiss ... My our
praise
O my soul, what means this
Praise to God, the great
Praise to thee, thou great
Religion is the chief concern
Sinners, the voice of God
Thy presence, gracious God
Thy way is in the sea; X110502
Thy way, O God, is
Featherstone, William R., 1842-
78
My Jesus, I love thee, I know
Feith, Rhijnvis
Praise the Lord through every;
X104721 Jesus, Lord, our
Fellows, John, d 1785
Jesus, mighty King in Zion
Felton, Richard
Strong of body, high of spirit
Fenner, Harlan K.
O man of God, arise
Ferguson, Mrs. Manie Payne
Joys are flowing like ariver;
R100944 Blessed quietness
Ferguson, Robert
This ship we now commend
Fick, Herman, 1822-85
Gehe auf, du Trost der Heiden
1917
Rise, thou Light of gentile
Fillmore, Charles M.
Abide in me, the true and
Fillmore-Bennett, S., see
Bennett, S. Fillmore
Finley, John
When-ever war, with its
red
Finnish traditional, etc
Aurinko armas vallolansa
(1836)
Lost in the night
The morning sun is brightly
(1836)
Fischer, Christoph, 1520-97
Lord Jesus, we give thanks
The tribute of our thanks
we
Wir danken dir, Herr Jesu
Fischer, Eberhard Ludwig,
1695-1773
Herr Jesu, der du selbst
1741
Lord Jesus, who art come
Fischer, Gottlob Nath., 1748-
1800
Dankt dem Herrn! mit fro-
hen Gaben
Thank the Lord! With bounteous
Fisher, Albert C., 1886-1946
Of the themes that men have;
R105803 Love is the theme
There's a glad new song;
R107911 Of His love I shall
Fitch, Charles
One precious boon, O Lord
Fitch, Eleazar Thompson,
1791-1871
Lord, at this closing hour
Fitch, W.R.
The bread that bringeth
strength; X109428 The
bread ... giveth
Fitzgerald. Collection, 1830
Daughter of Zion, awake from;
X106678 O daughter of
Zion
Fleming, Lucy Randolph
Awake, awake, O earth;
R103262 He lives again!
Our
Flemish traditional, etc.
A little child on the earth
Sing, good company, frank
Three kings are here, both
Flemming, Paul, 1609-40
Where'er I go, whate'er my
Fletcher, Frank, 1870-1954
O Son of Man, our hero
strong
Fletcher, Phineas, 1582-1650

Drop, drop, slow tears
Fliedner, Theodor, 1800-64
Blessed Fount of heavenly
Flint, Annie Johnson
God hath not promised skies; R101086 But God hath promised
Flint, James, 1779-1855
In pleasant lands have fallen
Flittner, Johann, 1618-78
Jesus, thou my heart's delight
Flory, Gertrude A.
Love not the world! Its
Take my hand and lead me
Flowerdew, Alice, 1759-1830
Fountain of mercy, God of; X102156 Father of mercies
Follen, Eliza Lee (Cabot), 1787-1860
How sweet upon this sacred
The Lord -- the Lord of glory
Foote, Henry Wilder, 1838-89
O thou with whom in sweet
Foote, Henry Wilder, II, 1875-1964
Thou whose love brought us
Foote, John G., ??
Christ our Redeemer died; R111394 When I see the blood
Forbush, William Bryon, 1868-1928
God of our boyhood, whom we; R102759 God of our youth, be; X102760 God of our youth, to
Ford, Charles Lawrence, 1830-
Earthly joys no longer please
"This is my body, which is"
Ford, David E.
How vain is all beneath
Forney, Lydia A.
If I would be a child of God
Förtsch, Basilius, d 1619
Jesus, thy name hath power
Fortunatus, Venantius Honorius Clementianus, 530-609
Hail thee, festival day: Sequences for Easter, Ascenciontide, Whitsunday Dedication
[But NOTE: First couplet is from Fortunatus. Balance is later writing.] X103031
Hail! festal day
Maria, Mater gratiae
O faithful cross, O noblest
O gloriosa virginium
O Mary, Mother full of grace
Praise the Saviour, now and
See the destined day arise
Sing, my tongue, the glorious X108951 Sing ... the Saviour's
The God whom earth, and sea,
The Lord whom earth, and stars; X109707 The Lord ... and air
The royal banners forward go; X109790 The royal banner is; X109792 The royal standard
Thirty years among us dwelling
Vexilla regis prodeunt
Welcome, morning of joy
"Welcome, happy morning!"
Fosdick, Harry Emerson, 1878-
God of grace and God of glory
O God, in restless living
O God, who to a loyal home
The Prince of Peace, his
Foster, Catherine, i.e. "C. F.", pseud.
Dread Jehovah! God of nations
Foster, Mrs. D.
'Mid the trials we experience
Foster, Frederick William, 1760-1835
Be this our happy destiny
Before thee we appear, thou
God, who art love, the same
In humble, grateful lays
Jesus, all our souls inspire
Jesus, hear our fervent
Join to render thanks and
Lord, who didst sancify thyself
Now to the Lamb upon the throne
O happy days, days marked
On thy ransomed congregation
Praise the Lord; bounteously; X108285 Praise the Lord; Praise the
Should our minds to earthly

Sing we, though unworthy
The springs of salvation from
They who hunger after Christ
This day is holy to the Lord
"Tis finished!" Jesus cries
To the soul that seeks him
Foulkes, William Hiram, 1877-
Gird us, O God, with humble
Take thou our minds, dear Lord
Foundling Hospital Collection, 1796
Praise the Lord! Ye heavens
Spirit of mercy, truth
Fowler, William
We thank thee, O God, for a
Fox, Adam, 1883-
Let us employ all notes of joy
Fox, Charles Armstrong
"Stand still and see!" Yea, see
Fox, Frances A.
In thee, O Spirit true
Fox, G.W.
Hard is now the constant woe
Fox, Henry Elliott, 1841-1926
Send forth the gospel! Let it
Fox, Ruth May
Firm as the mountains around
M.I.A., we hail thee
Frances, V., supposed pseud. of Fanny Crosby, q.v. "O, wondrous name"
Frances Raphael, Mother, O.S.D., see Drane, Augusta Theodosia, 1823-94
Francis, Benjamin, 1734-99
Great King of glory, come
In loud exalted strains
Praise the Saviour, all ye
Francis, Samuel Trevor, 1834-1925
Forward, christian, forward
Gracious God, we worship thee
O the deep, deep love of Jesus
Franciscan manual.
Blessed Francis, holy father
If, now, thou seekest miracles; R109814 The sea withdraws
Franck, Johann, 1618-77
Deck thyself, my soul, with; X101736 Deck ... with joy
X109114 Soul, adorn thyself
Herr Jesu, Licht der Heiden
Herr, ich habe missgehandelt 1649
In thine arm I rest me
Jesus, all my gladness
Jesus, best and dearest
Jesu, meine Freude 1655
Jesus, priceless Treasure
Light of the gentile nation; X110288 Thou Light of Gentile
Lord God, we worship thee
Lord, to thee I make confession
Praise the Lord, each tribe
Schmücke dich, o liebe Seele 1649
Who will now indict me
We praise thee, Lord, with
Franck, Salomo, 1659-1725
Ach Gott, verlass mich nicht 1714
Forsake me not, my God
I leave all things to God's
Ich halte Gott in allem stille 1685
O God, forsake me not
Rest of the weary! Thou thyself
So rest, my Rest!
Franck, Sebastian. 16th c
Obgleich die Harf, ist gut und scharf
Francke, August Hermann, 1663-1727
What within me and without
Frank, Florence Kiper, 1886-
Man's comradeship is very wide
Franz, Ignaz
God of might, we praise
Grosser Gott, wir loben dich
Holy God, we praise thy name; X103172 Hark! the loud celestial (Walworth)
Franzén, Frans Mikael, 1772-1847
Ajar the temple gates are
Awake! the watchman crieth
Come, O Jesus, and prepare me

Look to Jesus Christ thy
Prepare the way, O Zion
The day departs, yet thou art
The little while I linger
The Saviour is risen
Thine own, O loving Saviour
Thy scepter, Jesus, shall
When vesper bells are calling
Fraser, M.
I belong to Jesus
Willing to own thee Master
Frazer, George W., 1830-96
God, our Father, we adore
Freckelton, Thomas Wesley, 1827-1903
The toil of brain, or heart; X106926 O God, who workest
Freeman, Robert
Backward we look, O God
Braving the wilds all
For thy mercy aye pursuing
Freer, Frances, 1801-91
Present with the two or three
French, Arthur W.
Out from the camp-fire's red; R111949 Yes, sleeping on
We shall reach the river side
French traditional, etc.
Angels we have heard on high
Beautiful upon the mountain (1830-1850)
Bring a torch, Jeannette
Courons à fete, ne différons
Dans cette étable
Grand Dieu, Que de merveilles
Hearken all! what holy singing
Here, betwixt ass and oxen mild (13th c)
In stable lowly
In that poor stable
J'ai ouï chanter le rossignol (18th c); R105029 Laissez paitre vos
Je sais, vierge Marie, Ce que
Les anges dans nos compagnes
My heart delights, O Lord
Neighbour, what was the sound
Noël nouvelet, Noël chantons
O come, ye happy children
Nous allons, ma mie
Nous voici dans la ville
O leave your sheep, your lambs
O my Saviour, I adore thee
Promptement levez-vous; R100351 Allex, mon voison
Quelle est cette odeur
Quittez, pasteurs, vos brebis
Shepherds, shake off
Sing, all good people
Take heart, the journey's (15th c)
Un flambeau Jeannette
Une vaine crainte trouble vos
Voison, d'ou venait ce grand
When the sun had sunk to rest
Frere, W.H., 1863-1938
The saints who toiled
Freund, Cornelius
Rejoice, ye sons of men alway
Freund, Jacob
From Sinai's height a fountain
Freylinghausen, Johann Anastasius, 1670-1739
Jesus, who with thee
O Jesus, source of calm repose
The day departs; Our souls
Wake! the welcome day appeareth
Who is there like thee
Freylinghausen. Geist-reiches Gesang-buch. 1714
My Redeemer knoweth me
To thee, the Lord of all
Freystein, Johann Burkhard, 1671-1718
Mache dich, mein Geist, bereit 1697
Rise, my soul, to watch
Up, my soul, gird thee
Fries, Henry E., 1857-
Come, join the throng, on
Fritsch, Ahasuerus, 1629-1701
Jesus is my joy, my all
Froom, L.E.
Dismiss us, Lord, with blessing
With praise, O God
Frost, Mabel
O soul in the far-away;

R101408 Come home, come home
Frost, Robert Lee, 1875-1963
O, give us pleasure in
Frothingham, Nathaniel Langdon, 1793-1870
O God, whose presence glows
"Remember me," the Master said
Frothingham, Octavius Brooks, 1822-95
Thou Lord of Hosts, whose
Fry, Charles W., 1837-82
I have found a friend in Jesus; R103543 He's the Lily of the
Füger, Caspar, 16th c
We Christians may Rejoice today
Wir Christen leut' Hab'n
Fullerton, Georgiana Charlotte, Lady, 1812-85
O Heart of Jesus, Heart of God
Fullerton, William Young, 1857-1932
I cannot tell why He, whom
Funcke, Friedrich, 1642-99
Draw us to thee, for then
Draw us to thee in mind
Draw us to thee, Lord Jesus
Zeuch uns nach dir
Fünf auserlesene geistliche Lieder, Marburg, 1535
My soul doth magnify the Lord
Furness, William Henry, 1802-96
Feeble, helpless, how shall I
In the morning I will pray
Slowly, by thy hand unfurled
Unworthy to be called thy son
Furniss, John J., d 1865
In this Sacrament, Lord Jesus; X104405 In this Sacrament, sweet
Fyleman, Rose, 1877-1957
Lift your hidden faces; R100325 Alleluia, Alleluia

G

"G.M.J.", presumed pseud. of James McGranaham.
Someone will enter the pearly
Gabbott, Mabel Jones
In humility, our Saviour
Lord, accept into thy Kingdom
Rejoice, ye Saints of Latter Days
Gabirol, Solomon ibn see Solomon ibn Gabirol
Gabriel, Charles H., 1856-1932
I stand all amazed at the love; R107077 O, it is wonderful
I stand amazed in the presence; R107060 O how marvelous
Just a few more days; R104189 I'll exchange my
Lord, as of old at Pentecost; R105689 Lord, send the old-time
More like the Master I would; R109331 Take thou my heart
So precious is Jesus, my; R102281 For He is so precious
Sweet is the promise; R104100 "I will not forget"
There's a call comes ringing; R108823 Send the light
When all my labors and trials; R107631 O that will be glory
Gage, W.C.
O'er all the land have; R109123 Send forth the tidings
Gaines, Samuel Richards
From every clime and country
Gale, Norman, 1862-1948
Here in the country's heart
Gale, Zona, 1874-1938
Come, children of tomorrow
Gambold, John, 1711-71
Attend, O Saviour, to our
Dear Lord, my soul desireth
Go forth in spirit, go
Lord God of hosts, by all
O grant thy servants, through
O tell me no more Of this
They who Jesus' followers are
They who know the Lord indeed

What praise to thee, my Saviour
Gannett, William Channing, 1840-1923
Bring, O morn, thy music
From heart to heart, from
God laid his rocks in courses; X110570 To cloisters of
He hides within the lily
It sounds along the ages
Praise to God, your praises; X108299 Praise ... and thanks
Sleep, my little Jesus
The Lord is in his holy place
The morning hangs a signal
When the night is stall and
Gannon, Michael
O Lord, in this great mystery
Ganse, Hervey Doddridge, 1822-91
Eternal Father, when to thee
Lord, I know thy grace is nigh
Garber, Ora W., 1903-
'Tis not with eyes of flesh
Gardiner, William Henry
When I see the way my Saviour; R107828 O, what tender, tender
Garrett, Marguerite Bixler
Brother, here's a message; R109308 Sweetened by the cross
Hear, O hear us, Heavenly
Garrison, Winfred Ernest, 1874-
God of our fathers, the
Softly I closed the Book as in
Garve, Carl Bernhard, 1763-1841
Alleluia, Christus lebt
Alleluia! Jesus lives! He is
Alleluia! Jesus lives! Won
Thy word, O Lord, like gentle
Gascoigne, George, ca1525-77
You that have spent the silent; X111919 Ye that have spent
Gaskell, William, 1805-44
Calmly, calmly lay him down
Father, throughout the coming
Mighty God, the First, the Last
Our Father! through the coming
Press on, press on, ye sons
Though lowly here our work; X110387 Though lowly ... lot
We join to pray, with wishes
Gates, Ellen Huntington, 1835-1920
I will sing you a song of that; R111599 While the years
O, the clanging bells of time
Gates, Mary Cornelia, mid 19th c
Send thou, O Lord, to every
Thy love to me, O Christ
Gautama Buddha, 5th c B.C.
Be ye lamps unto yourselves
Gautier, Théophile, 1811-72
All things are doubly fair
Gedicke, Lampertus, 1683-1735
As God doth lead me, I will go
Deliver me, my God, from all
Geijer, Erick Gustaf
In triumph our Redeemer
Thy cross, O Jesus, thou didst
Geldart, Edmund Martin
When the light of day
Gellert, Christian Fürchtegott 1715-69
Crushed by my sin, O Lord; X108052 Oppressed by sin
How great, Almighty, is thy
Jesus lebt, mit ihm auch ich
Jesus lives and so shall I
Jesus lives! no longer now
Jesus lives! Thy terrors now; X104710 Jesus ... victory's
Wie gross ist des Allmächt'gen Güte!
Gell's Psalms and hymns, 1815
We praise, we worship thee
George, Hereford Brooke, 1838-1910
By every nation, race
Gerfass, Mattheiss.
Mit Angst und Roth ruff

ich dich an. 1566
Gerhardt, Paulus, 1607-76
A Lamb goes forth our griefs
A Lamb goes uncomplaining
A pilgrim and a stranger
All my heart this night; X100238 All ... this day
All ye who on this earth
Auf, auf, mein Herz, mit
Awake, my heart, and marvel
Awake, my heart, and render
Awake, my heart, with gladness
Befiehl du deine Wege 1656
Beside thy manger here I
Blessed is the man that
Blest is he that never
Come, your hearts and voices
Cometh sunshine after rain
Commit thou all that grieves; X108409 Put thou thy trust
Commit thou all thy griefs
Commit thou every grievance
Commit whatever grieves thee
Die güldne Sonne, Voll Freud' und Wonne
Ein Lämmlein geht und trägt
Emmanuel! we sing thy praise; X104221 Immanuel, to thee we; X104222 Immanuel, we sing
Evening and morning, Sunset
Extended on a cursed tree
Frohlich soll mein Herze
Give thy heart's love
Give to the winds thy fears
Go forth my heart and seek
Hab ich das Haupt zum Freunde
Hearts at Christmas time
Here I can firmly rest
Holy Ghost, dispel our sadness
Holy Spirit, Source of gladness
I know that my Redeemer lives
I sing to thee with voice
I will sing to my creator
I will sing my Maker praises
Ich bin ein Gast auf Erden 1666
Ich singe dir mit Herz und Mund 1653
If God be on my side
If God himself be for me
I'll praise thee with my heart
Is God my strong Salvation
Ist Gott für mich, so trete 1656
Jesus, I never can forget
Jesus, our Guardian, Guide
Jesus, thy boundless love; X107148 O Jesus, thy boundless
Kommt und lasst uns Christum
Let not such a thought
My soul, awake and render
Now all the heavenly splendor
Now are the woodlands resting
Now let us come before Him
Now rest beneath night's
Now woods and wolds; X106345 Now all the woods; X106487 Now woods and fields
Nun danket all' und bringet Ehr', Ihr Menschen in der Welt 1648
Nun lasst uns gehn und treten
Nun ruhen alle wälder
O Christ my Light, my gracious
O draw me, Saviour, after thee
O Du allersüsste Freude
O enter, Lord, thy temple
O how shall I receive thee; X103739 How shall I meet my
O Jesu Christ, dein Kripplein
O Jesus Christ, mein schönstes Licht 1653
O Jesus Christ, thy manger is
O Lord, how shall I meet thee
O Lord, I sing with voice; X107244 O Lord ... lips and; X107245 O Lord... mouth and
O sacred head, sore wounded (based on St Bernard of Clairvaux)

O Saviour dear, thy manger
O thou sweetest source
O welt, sieh hier dein leben
O world, behold! Upon the tree
O world, see here suspended
O'er field and forest stealing
Put thou thy trust in God
Rejoice, my heart, be glad
See, world, thy Life assailed
Shun, my heart, the thought
Since Jesus is my Friend
Sing, my soul, to God who made
Sollt' ich meinem Gott nicht
The duteous day now closeth; X109418 The beauteous day; X109785 The restless day
The mystery hidden from
The sun ascending, To us is
Thy way and all thy sorrows
Trust all to God, the Father
Warum sollt' ich mich denn grämen? 1653
We sing, Immanuel, thy praise
We sing to thee, Immanuel
Why art thou heavy-hearted
Why, my soul, thus trembling
Why should cross and trial; X111687 Why should sorrow
Why should I repine in sadness
Wie soll ich dich empfangen
Wir singen dir, Immanuel
Wohlauf, mein Herze, sing und spring 1653
Zeuch ein zu meinen Toren

German traditional, etc.
A babe is born in Bethlehem
A babe lies in the cradle
A boy was born in Bethlehem
A little child there is y-born (15th c)
Also hat Gott die welt geliebt (1791)
Bei frühem Morgenlicht (ca 1800)
Die ganze welt, Herr Jesu (1623)
Ein Kind geborn zu Bethlehem
Ein Kindlein in der Wiegen (1649)
Es ist noch Raum (19th c)
Es kommt ein Schiff geladen (1470-80)
Gebor'n ist uns ein Kindelein (17th c)
Gen Himmel aufgefahren ist (17th c)
God loved the world (1791)
God the Father, be our Stay (13-14th c)
Gott der Vater wohn' uns bei (13-14th c)
He smiles within His cradle (1649)
I have chosen thee, my Savior
I know a Kingdom without end (16th c or earlier)
Jesus, I long for thy blessed (1712)
Jesus, for thee and thy blessed (1712)
Jesus, with thy death
Joseph dearest, Joseph mine (16th c); R103228 He came among us
Joseph lieber, Joseph mein (16th c)
Löwen, lasst euch wieder (1712)
Maria die wollt' wandern
Maria ging aus wandern
Mein Herz will ich dir schenken (1653)
Now are the days fulfilled (1746 or earlier)
Now glad of heart (16th c)
Nun ist die zeit erfüllt (1746 or earlier)
O Christ thou bright (1579)
O Christmas tree, O Christmas
O God, Almighty Father, Creator; X106802 O God ... thou Majesty
O have you heard the wondrous
O Herre Gott, dein göttlich (1527)
O let us praise the Christmas tree
O that thy fire now soon
Once Mary would go wandering
Rise again, ye lion-hearted

(1712)
St Mary goes aseeking
The whole bright world (1623)
There comes a ship asailing (ms. 1470-80)
There is a gentle Gardener
There still is room!
This child was born to men (17th c)
To thee my heart I offer (1653)
To us from heaven's lofty
To us is born a blessed (before 1422)
Vom Himmel hoch, o Engel (before 1422)
When morning fills the skies (ca 1800)
When morning gilds the skies (ca 1800)
Wir wollen alle frölich sein (16th c)
Ye baptized people, one and
Gerok, Friedrich Karl von, 1815-90
Holy, holy, holy, blessed Lord
Gersdorf, Abraham von, 1704-84
Eternal thanks be thine
Thy blood, thy blood the deed
Gesenius, Justus, 1601-73
O Lord when condemnation
Wenn meine Sünd' mich Kränken
When o'er my sins I sorrow
When sorrow and remorse (with David Denicke)
Gibbons, Thomas, 1720-85
Great God, the nations of
Lord, send thy word, and let
When Jesus dwelt in mortal
Giffe, William T.
O wonderful prayer that Jesus
Giffin, Clare
Father, we thank thee, Father
Gilbert, Ann Taylor, 1782-1866
see Taylor, Ann. (This order retained to keep Ann and Jane Taylor together)
Gilbert, Edwin, 1859-
Together, Lord, we come
Gilbert, Rosa Mulholland, d 1921
Give me, O Lord, a heart
Gilder, Richard Watson, 1844-1909
God of the strong, God of the
If Jesus Christ is a man
Through love to light! O
To thee, Eternal Soul, be
Giles, John Eustace, 1805-75
Thou hast said, exalted Jesus
Giles, John Philip, 1905-
Here in this water I do vow
Gilkey, James Gordon, 1899-
O God, in whose great purpose
Outside the Holy City
Gill, Thomas Hornblower, 1819-1906
Break, new-born year, on glad
Come, Holy Ghost! in us arise
Dear Lord and Master mine
He who suns and worlds
I walk amidst thy beauty forth
Lord, God, by whom all change
Lord, in the fullness of my
Lord, thou hast been our
Lord! when I all things would
Not, Lord, thine ancient works
Not only when ascends the song
O mean may seem this house
O mystery of love divine
O saints of old! not yours
O walk with God along the road; X110945 Walk with the Lord
Our God, our God, thou shinest
Spirit of Truth, who makest
The glory of the spring
We come unto our fathers' God
What secret place, what distant
Gill, William Henry, 1839-1923
Hear us, O Lord, from heaven
Gillett, George Gabriel Scott,

1873-
It is finished! Christ hath
Gillman, Frederick John, 1866-1949
God send us men whose aim
Gilman, Caroline, 1794-1888
Sweet hour of holy, thoughtful
Gilman, Samuel, 1791-1858
Father, be thy blessing shed
Gilmore, Joseph Henry, 1834-1918
He leadeth me! O blessed
Gilmour, H. L.
My soul in sad exile; R104506 I've anchored my
Watchman, blow the gospel; R101004 Blow the trumpet
When out in sin and darkness; R107798 O, 'twas love, love
Gisborne, Thomas, ca 1760-
Saviour, when night involves
Gjertsen, M. Falk, 1847-1913
I know a way besieged
Gladden, Washington, 1836-1918
Behold a sower! from afar; X107207 O Light of Light
O Lord of life, to thee we
O Master, let me walk with
Gladstone, William Ewart, 1809-98
O lead my blindness by the
Glasgow, Samuel M.
Long have we sought eternal; R103706 How long? How long
Men of the Church of the
Glenn, Creda
Bow down in worship now
Chant your songs of glad
Lo, they come in glad
O Lamb of God, have mercy
Glenn, Grace
Jesus, I will follow thee
Glover, Ellen J.
In speechless prayer
Glover, Terrot Reaveley, 1869-1943
Jesus and Joseph day after
Goadby, Frederick William, 1845-80
O thou, whose hand hath
Godolphin, Sidney, 1610-43
Lord, when the wise men came
Goethe, Johann Wolfgang von, 1749-1832
Everything changes; R109184 Splendours three
Haste not! haste not! do not
Purer yet and purer
This thought shall have our
Whether day my spirit's
Goforth, Caroline
Make large our hearts
Golden chain, 1861 [Crosby?]
Whither, pilgrim, are you
Goldsmith, Peter Hair, 1865-
Holy, holy Lord, we with one
Goldstein, Ida
Our Father, we beseech thy
Good, S. E.
There's a cleft in the Rock; R107641 O, the cleft
Goode, William, 1762-1816
Crown His head with endless
Let thy grace, Lord, make me
Lo, the mighty God appearing
Goodenough, Lucy M.
Thou living light of pentecostal
Gordon, Adoniram Judson, 1836-95
Help me to be holy
Gordon, Anna A.
O God, we pray thee, bless
Gordon, George A., 1853-1929
Hail the day when Jesus rose
O Will of God beneath our life
Goreh, Ellen Lakshmi, 1853-
In the secret of His presence
Gorell, Ronald, 1884-
To thee, O Father, lamp of all
Gosse, Edmund, 1849-1928
Not with a choir of angels
The cross, like pilgrim
Gostick, Joseph, d 1887
The light pours down
Gothus, L. P.
Amid the world's deceitful cares

Gotter, Ludwig Andreas, 1661-1735
Friend of the weary, O refresh
I will ever sing thy praises
Lamb of God, all praise
Saviour of sinners, now
The reproach of Christ is
Gottheil, Gustav, 1827-1903
Come, O Sabbath day and bring
To thee we give ourselves
Gough, Benjamin, 1805-77
Awake, awake, O Sion
How beauteous on the mountains
Gould, Edwin
"Lord, I believe: help thou"
Goulston, Mrs.
Our fortress strong art thou
Govan, G.E.M.
I will not be afraid
Govan, W.J.
The Word, whose word can make
Gower, Jean Milne, 1867-
Dear Father, loud the ocean
Father, loving Father, hear
Graduel de Paris, 1754
Let no helpless tears be shed
Graeff, Frank E.
Does Jesus care when my heart; R107883 O, yes, He cares
Graham, Abbie
For the year that came from
Graham, S.J.
The golden morning is fast; R107809 O, we see the gleams
Gramann, Johann, see Graumann, Johann
Grant, Peter, 1783-1867
O Lord, I sing thy praises
Grant, Robert, 1785-1838
Lord of earth, thy forming
O worship the King
Saviour, when in dust to thee; X101116 By thy birth and by
The starry firmament on high; X109843 The spacious firmament
When gathering clouds around
Where-fore do the nations rage
Graumann, Johann, 1487-1541
My soul, now bless thy Maker
Nun lob, mein' Seel', den
Graves, F.A.
My Father has many dear; R103377 He'll never forget
Gray, Herbert Branston, 1851-1929
Praise to our God, who with
Gray, James M., 1851-1935
Naught have I gotten but what; R108025 Only a sinner saved
Nor silver nor gold hath; R103801 I am redeemed but
O listen to our wondrous; R111647 Who saved us from
The Saviour who loves me; R104665 Jesus is coming
Gray, Thomas, jr., 1803-49
Suppliant, lo! Thy children
Gt. Brit. National anthem. 17-18th c.
God save our gracious King
God save our gracious Queen
Greek traditional, etc. (chiefly from service and liturgical books)
Awaked from sleep, we fall (4th c)
Behold the Bridegroom cometh (8th c)
Behold the Bridegroom draweth (8th c); X100825 Behold ... cometh
God of all grace, thy mercy
Hail, gladdening Light (3d c) X110421 Through love to light (Gilder); X103036 Hail! ... of that pure
Here, while the cherubim (6th c)
Let thy Blood in mercy poured
Lord, to our humble prayers
May Jesus Christ, the spotless

O Brightness of the immortal (3d c)
O gladsome light (3d c); X103035 Hail Gladdening Light
O God of grace, thy mercy
O King enthroned on high (Pentecostarian 8th c)
O Spirit from on high (Pentecostarian, 8th c)
The King shall come when (Hymns of the Russian Church)
The wise men from the East
Thou, Lord, hast power to heal (Paracletice)
Greenaway, Ada Rundall, 1861-1937
O perfect God, thy love
O word of pity, for our pardon
Rise in the strength of God
Rise to the cry of battle
Greenwell, Dora, 1821-82
And art thou come with us
I am not skilled to understand
If ye would hear the angels
Greenwood, Annie Pike
Come, lay his books and papers
Greenwood, John Brooke, 1828-
Crown with thy benediction
Greenwood, Samuel
No mortal sense can still or
Greg, Samuel, 1807-77
Around my path life's
Slowly, slowly darkening
Stay, Master, stay upon this
Gregg, William C.
Know this, that every soul is
Gregor, Christian, 1723-1801
Be our Comfort, which ne'er
Bethany, O peaceful habitation
Glory to the Father, Who in
Holy Lord, Holy Lord, Holy and
Holy Lord, thanks and praise; X103553 Holy Lord, Holy Lord
I smite upon my guilty breast
In this sepulchral Eden
Jesus, bless us sensibly
Jesus, my Lord, thy nearness
Lord, for thy coming us
Make my calling and election
More than shepherd's
My happy lot is here
My portion is the Lord
None but Christ my Saviour
Now, Lord, who in this vale; X106768 O, form us all while
O Eternal Word, Jesus Christ, our Lord (Authorship very complicated: cf Julian 377)
O how excellent and fair; X101604 Countless hosts
O that we with gladness
O, there's a sight that rends
O Thou, whose goodness words
O Thou, whose human life
O what an act of majesty
O what joy, O what joy awaiteth
O what praise in highest strain
Our Redeemer rose victorious
Sing alleluia, Christ doth
Sing with awe in strains
The Lord bless and keep thee
The seraphim of God exalt
Though by nature I'm defiled
Till permitted hence to go
'Tis finished now, redemption's
To God, our Immanuel, made
Truly, that eventful day
Unto thee, most faithful
What happiness, what joy and
Whene'er we contemplate; X106688 O days of perfect
With heart and hand you now
With thy presence, Lord, our
Gregory, G.O., 1881-
Spread the table of the Lord
Gregory, Philip E., 1886-
Jesus, Friend, so kind and
Greiner, Minnie A.
Alleluia! Alleluia! Shout aloud
Grève, Philippe de, d 1236

Magdalene, thy grief and
Mary, weep not, weep no
Sing we all the joys and; X105841 Magdalene, thy grief
Grieve, Nichol, 1868-1954
We would extol thee
Ye heavens on high, praise ye
Griffith, F.P.
Shine in my heart, Lord Jesus
Grigg, Joseph, ca 1720-68
Behold! a stranger at the door; X100809 Behold a Stranger's; X100843 Behold the Saviour
Jesus, and shall it ever be; X107138 O Jesus, shall it
Grignon, Louis Marie, 1673-1716
Praise we our God with joy
Grimes, Katharine Atherton
"O, I will give you glory"
Teach me thy will, O Lord
Weary soul by sin oppressed
Grisham, R.N.
Once, I wandered in darkness; R104098 I will never turn
Griswold, Alexander Viets, 1766-1843
Holy Father, great Creator
Griswold, Mrs. E.W.
We're going home, no more to
Grodzki, Michal
Jesus Christ, our Lord most
Jezu Kriste, pane milý
Grose, Howard B., 1851-1939
Give of your best to the
Groser, William Howse, 1834-1925
A song of spring once more we
Grubb, Edward
Our God, to whom we turn
Gruenbeck, Esther, 1717-96
Grace, grace, O that's a
Grundtvig, Nikolai Frederik Severin, 1783-1872
Abide among us, we implore
All ye who like the birds can
As after the waterbrooks
As the rose shall blossom here
Bright and glorious is the sky
Built on a rock, the church; X101080 Built on the Rock
Chime, happy Christmas bells
Easter morrow stills our
Fair beyond telling, Lord, is
From the graves remove dark
God's word is our great
Golden light, serene and
Hast to the plow thou put
He who has helped me hitherto
Holy Spirit, come with light
I know a flower so fair
Kirken den er et gammelt Mus 1837
Long hast thou stood, O Church
Love is life's true crown
Love, the fount of light from
O how beautiful the sky
O land of our King! Where
O let thy Spirit with us tarry
O wondrous kingdom here on; X106022 Most wondrous is of
Peace to soothe our bitter
Ring, O ye bells, O ring out
Splendid are the heavens high
Suffer the children to come
The happy Christmas comes
The Lord is in His holy place
The Lord to thee appealeth
The peace of God protects
This is the day that our
With gladness we hail this
Gryphius, Andreas, 1616-64
Erhalt uns deine Lehre
Es ist vollbracht! Gott Lob, es ist vollbracht 1726
My course is run. Praise God
Preserve in fullest measure
Preserve thy word, O Saviour
Where low in heaven the sun

Guest, Benjamin, 1788-1869
Heavenly Father, may thy love
Guiet, Charles, 1601-64
O Word of God above
Guiney, Louise Imogen, 1861-1920
The little cares that fretted
Guiterman, Arthur, 1871-1943
Bless the four corners of
Hail Guest! We ask not what
Gunther, Cyriacus, 1649-1704
With joyful heart your praises
Gurney, Archer Thompson, 1820-87
Christ is risen! Christ is
Gurney, Dorothy Frances (Bloomfield), 1858-1932
O perfect love, all human
Gurney, John Hampden, 1802-62
Fair waved the golden corn
Great King of nations, hear
Lord, as to thy dear cross; X105428 Lord, as we to thy
Lord of the harvest, thee we
Our God is good! in earth and
Gustavus Adolphus, King of Sweden, see Altenburg,
Fear not, O little flock
Gutheim, James K.
Lo, our Father's tender care
Who is like Thee, O universal
Guthrie, John, 1814-78
Our Father, throned in heaven
Guyon, Mme., i.e. Jeanne Marie Bouvièrs de la Mothe, 1648-1717
I would love thee, God and
My Lord, how full of sweet; X107236 O Lord, how full
O thou, by long experience

H

"H"
In atmosphere of Love divine
O ye heavens, bend and see (1708)
Thy will, almighty Father
"H. L. W."
So sweet and clear, so sweet; R108205 Peace, peace on earth
Habershon, Ada Ruth, 1861-1918
Jesus Himself drew near
Soon will our Saviour from; R107815 O, what a change
There are loved ones in the; R111707 Will the circle
When I fear my faith will fail; R103308 He will hold me fast
Hacker, J. G.
Great King of Kings and Lord; R109962 Thee, God's Anointed
Hackett, Rosemary B.
Loving Father, we thy children
Hackleman, W. E. M.
Speed away! Speed away! Take
Haigh, Emily Waddington
In sunny days, when all is
Hale, Edward Everett, 1822-1909
And I? Is there some desert
From city and from prairie
Hale, Mary Whitwell, 1810-62
Whatever dims thy sense of truth
Hale, Sarah Josepha, 1795-1879
Our Father in heaven
Ha-Levi, Jehudah
Despise not, Lord, my lowly
Haley, Molly Anderson
Thy blessing, Lord, on all
Hall, Benjamin H.
Day of wonder, day of gladness
Lord of life, of love, of light
Hall, Christopher Newman, 1816-1902
Friend of sinners! Lord of
Hall, Elvina M., 1818-89
I hear the Saviour say; R104609 Jesus died for me
Hall, Joseph, 1574-1656
Immortal babe, who this dear
Halpine, Charles Graham, 1829-68
Comrades known in marches

Ham, Marion Franklin, 1867-1956
As tranquil streams that meet
From Bethany, the Master comes
Heir of all the waiting ages
I hear thy voice, within the
O Church of God, divided
O, hear them marching, marching
O Lord of life, thy kingdom
O thou whose gracious presence
O who shall roll away the stone
Ring, O ring, ye Christmas
The builders, toiling through
Touch thou mine eyes
Hamburg Temple Hymnal
Arise to praise the Lord
Father, see thy suppliant
Happy he that never wanders
Happy who in early youth
Let Israel trust in God alone
Loud let the swelling anthems
O Lord, my God, to thee I pray
On mighty wings rush swiftly
Our Shepherd is the Lord
Sing to the Sovereign
There lives a God! Each finite
To thee, above all creatures'
Why art thou cast down my soul
Hamerton, Samuel Collingwood, 1833-72
Waken, Christian children
Hamilton, Eliza H., fl. ca. 1888
My Saviour, thou hast
O Jesus, Lord, to thee I cry; R100451 And take me as I am; X104764 Jesus, my Lord, to
Hamilton, James, 1819-96
Across the sky the shades
O Jesus! Lord most merciful
O Jesus, our Salvation
Praise, O praise the Lord
Hamilton, Mary C.D.
Lord, guard and guide the men
Hammer, John Beck, 1856-80
Saviour, now with contrite
Hammond, William, 1719-83
A stranger and a pilgrim
Awake, and sing the song
Jesus, thy word is my delight
Jesus, who died a world
Lord, we come before thee now
Not one of Adam's race
See, my soul, God ever blest
The Lord be with me everywhere
What good news the angels
Hanaford, Phoebe A., 1829-
Cast thy bread upon the waters
Hanby, Benjamin Russell, 1833-67
Who is he, in yonder stall; R110554 'Tis the Lord! O
Hänel
God spake, my child, God spake
Hankey, Donald, 1884-1916
Lord of the strong, when earth
Hankey, Arabella Katherine, 1834-1911
Advent tells us Christ is near
I love to tell the story
Tell me the old, old story
Hanrahan, T. James
Tell us now, O Death, where
Hans, Schmit, & Georg v. Ingersheim
O Herre Gott vom Himmelreich. 1564
Harbaugh, John Henry, 1817-67
Christ by heavenly hosts; X102704 God, most mighty; X110243 Thou by heavenly
Hail, Jesus! Israel's Hope and
Jesus, I live to thee
Jesus, my Shepherd, let me
Jesus, to thy cross I hasten
Harbottle, Joseph, 1798-1864
Farewell, my friends beloved
Hardenberg, Georg Friedrich Philipp von, 1772-1801

I say to all men, far and near
If only I have thee
Lord, when thou makest thy
Hardy, Henry Ernest, i.e. Father Andrew, 1869-1946
O dearest Lord, thy sacred
Hardy, Thomas, 1840-1928
To thee whose eye all nature
Harker, A.
Lord of the ocean vast and
Harkness, Georgia, 1891-
God of the fertile fields
Hope of the world, thou Christ
Harland, Edward, 1810-90
And now this holy day
Behold, a humble train
Lord, thine ancient people see
Harlingen, J.N. van
We gather, we gather, dear
Harlow, S. Ralph, 1885-
O Church of God triumphant
O young and fearless Prophet
Harmer, Charles H., 1865-
O Christ, thou Gift of love
Harmer, Samuel Young, 1809-
In the Christian's home; R110070 There is rest
Harmony in praise, 1890
O Lord, all glorious, Life
Harris, Florence, 1891-1933
Like pilgrims sailing
Harris, John, 1802-56
Light up this house with glory
Harris, John Roy, 1891-
Great Redeemer, we adore thee
Harris, Thomas Lake, 1823-1906
O Earth! thy past is crowned
Harrison, Edward L.T.
Sons of Michael, he approaches
Hart, Joseph, 1712-68
Almighty Father, bless the
Christians, dismiss your fear
Come, Holy Spirit, come
Come, ye sinners, poor and needy; X101563 Come ... poor and wretched
Dismiss us with thy blessing
Great High-Priest, we view
Jesus, our triumphant Head
Lamb of God, we fall before
Many woes had Christ endured
O for a glance of heavenly
Once more before we part
Once more we come before our
Our baptism first declares
Prayer is appointed to convey
Suffering Saviour, Lamb of God
That solemn night before; X109395 That doleful night
The Lord ascendeth up on high
The spirits of the just
This God is the God we adore; X103678 How good is the God
Hart, Oliver, 1723-95
My Father, when I come to thee
Hartley, John, 1762-1811
Blessed Jesus, we implore thee
We now return, each to his tent
Hartman, George
O Christ, to thee we come
Hartsough, Lewis, 1828-1919
I hear thy welcome voice; R103788 I am coming Lord
Let me go where saints are
Hartsough, Palmer, 1844-1932
Give as the Lord hath prospered; R102478 Give, give with
I am resolved no longer to; R104094 I will hasten
O wonderful word of salvation
Hartzler, Henry B.
Go and seek the lost and dying
Harvard, Lionel deJersey, 1893-1916
Father of all, we lift to thee
Harvey, Charles E.W., 1846-1922
Light of the world, come nigh
Haskell, Jefferson, 1807-
My latest sin is sinking fast; R106647 O come, angel band
Haskell, Julia Sampson
Over the ocean wave, far,

far; R108226 Pity them, pity them
Hasloch, Mary, 1816-92
Christian, work for Jesus
Hasse, Evelyn R., 1855-1919
Almighty Lord, whose sovereign
Hastings, Horace Lorenzo, 1831-99
Shall we meet beyond the river
Hastings, Thomas, 1784-1872
Be tranquil, O my soul
Delay not, delay not
Drooping souls, no longer
Gently, Lord, O gently lead
God of mercy, hear our prayer
Hail to the brightness of
He that goeth forth with weeping
How calm and beautiful
Jesus, merciful and mild
Jesus, save my dying soul
Jesus, while our hearts are
Lord of the harvest, bend
Now be the gospel banner
O, tell me, thou life and
Saviour, I look to thee
The Lord Jehovah lives
Hatch, Edwin, 1835-89
Breathe on me, Breath of God; X106584 O breathe on me
Holy Spirit, breathe on me (arr by B.B. McKinney)
I dared not hope that thou
Hatfield, Edwin Francis, 1807-83
'Tis thine alone, Almighty
To God the Father, Son; X110600 To God ... and ever blessed Spirit
Hauge, Hans Nielsen, 1771-1829
With God in grace I'm dwelling
Haughey, Mrs. M.T.
There is sunlight on the hill; R107653 O the sunlight
Hausmann, Julia, 1825-1901
O take my hand, dear Father; X109330 Take thou my hand
So nimm denn meine Hände
Take thou my hand and lead me
Hautzmann, Julia von, see Hausmann, Julia, 1825-1901
Havergal, Frances Ridley, 1836-79
Another year is dawning; X100478 Another day is
As thy day, thy strength shall
Church of God, beloved and
From glory unto glory
God in heaven, hear our; X102721 God of heaven
Golden harps are sounding; R100224 All his suffering; R100225 All his work
Holy and infinite! viewless
How can she sing in the dark like this?
I am trusting thee, Lord Jesus
I could not do without thee
I gave my life for thee
I know I love thee better; R109554 The half has never
In full and glad surrender
Jesus, Master, whose I am; X104738 Jesus, Master, whom
"Jesus only!" in the shadow
Like a river glorious; R109220 Stayed upon Jehovah
Live out thy life within me
Lord, speak to me, that I may
Master, speak! thy servant
Now the light has gone away
O Saviour, precious Saviour; R111172 We worship thee
Precious, precious blood
Singing for Jesus, our Saviour
Sit down beneath his shadow
Standing at the portal; R108045 Onward, then
Take my life, and let it be
Tell it out among the heathen; X109365 Tell it out ... nations
Thou art coming, O my Sa-

viour
Thy life was given for me
To thee, O Comforter divine
True-hearted, whole-hearted; R108217 Peal out
Who is on the Lord's side; X104868 Jesus, thou hast
Yes, He knows the way
Havergal, William Henry, 1793-1870
Hosanna! raise the pealing
Shout, O Earth! from silence
Haweis, Hugh R., 1838-1901
The homeland, O the homeland
Haweis, Thomas, 1732-1820
Enthroned on high, almighty
From the cross uplifted high
O thou, from whom all goodness
Our children, Lord, in faith
Saviour, all my sins
Soon as the morn with roses
The happy morn is come
To thee, my God and Saviour
Hawkes, Henry Warburton, 1843-1917
Amid the din of earthly
"Give us each day our daily"
Our humns are sung, our
Peace! perfect peace! the gift
Reveal thy truth, O Lord
Thank we now the Lord
Thou knowest, Lord! Thou
"Thy kingdom come!" O Lord
Hawkes, Robert Stephen, of Morwenstow, 1804-75
Sing to the Lord the children's
Hawkins, Ernest, 1802-66
Lord, a Saviour's love
Hawkins, Hester Perriam, 1846-1928
Almighty Father, God of love
Heavenly Father, thou hast
Hawks, Annie Sherwood, 1835-72
I need thee every hour; R103990 I need thee (Lowry)
Who'll be the next to follow
Hawthorne, Alice[pseud] 1827-1902
Soft as the voice of an angel; R111609 Whispering hope
Hay, Edyth Hillery, d 1943
He loveth me, He loveth me
Lord, with devotion we pray; R102280 For great is the Lord
Hay, John, 1838-1905
Defend us, Lord, from every; X105457 Lord! from far-severed
Not in dumb resignation
Hay, Sara Henderson, 1906- (Mrs. N. Lopatnikoff)
It is a piteous thing to be
Hay, Violet, fl. ca. 1931
All glory be to God most high
Arise ye people, take your
From sense to soul my pathway
From these thy children
I love thy way of freedom
Jesus' prayer for all his
Lo, He sent His word and healed
Hayes, Oleta
Christ our Lord will soon be; R111215 We'll be gathered
Hayn, Henriette Luise von, 1724-82
Hail, all hail, victorious
I am Jesus' little lamb
Jesus makes my heart rejoice
O Church, thy strength abide
O what happiness divine
Sacred name of Jesus, so
See from the rock the waters
Weil ich Jesu Schäflein bin 1778
Hayne, Paul Hamilton, 1831-86
The bliss for which our spirits
Hayward, Thomas
Welcome, delightful morn
Hazard, Caroline, 1856-
Great western land, whose
Head, Bessie Porter, 1850-1936
O Breath of life, come
Hearn, Marianne Farningham, 1834-1909
Just as I am, thine own to

We hope in thee, O God
Heath, George, 1750-1822
My soul, be on thy guard
Heatwole, L. J.
The saint who enters heaven
The tenor of the gospel word
Heber, Reginald, 1783-1826
Bread of the world, in mercy
Brightest and best; X103077 Hail the blest
By cool Siloam's shady rill
From foes that would the land
From Greenland's icy mountains; R106747 O fill us (L. J. L.)
God, that madest earth; X102831 God, who madest
Holy, Holy, Holy, Lord God
Hosanna to the living Lord
I praised the earth, in beauty
In the sun, and moon, and stars
Lord of mercy and of might, God and Father of us all
Lord of mercy and of might, Of mankind the Life
O God the Son eternal
O, most merciful! O most
O thou, who gavest thy servant
O thou, whose infant feet
Spirit of truth, on this
The God of glory warns us all
The Lord of might, from Sinai's
The Son of God goes forth; X109837 The Son of Man goes
Virgin-born, we bow
Von Grönlands eis'gen Zinken
We praise thee, Lord, for all
When spring unlocks
When through the torn sail
Hebrew traditional, etc.
see Jewish traditional, etc.
Heck, Fannie E.S.
Come, women, wide proclaim
Hedborn, Samuel Johan, 1783-1849
Glorious Majesty, before thee; Z103556 Holy Majesty, before
Now Israel's hope in triumph
With holy joy my heart
Hedge, Frederick Henry, 1805-90
"It is finished!" Man of Sovereign and transforming
Heermann, Johann, 1585-1647
Ah, holy Jesus; X100162 Ah, dearest Jesus
Ah! Lord our God, let them
Be this henceforth my constant
Ere yet the dawn hath filled
Feed thy children, God most
God is known in loving-kindness
Herr, unser Gott, lass nicht
Herzliebster Jesu, was hast
Jesu, deine tiefen Wunden
Lord, grant thy servants
Lord, Jesus Christ, in thee
Lord, thy death and passion
O Christ, our true and only; X104801 Jesus, our true and
O dearest Jesus, what law; X100869 Beloved Jesus, what
O God, eternal source
O God, if thy beloved Son
O God, thou faithful God
O Gott, du frommer Gott 1630
O Jesu Christe, wahres Licht 1630
O Jesus, Saviour dear
O Lord, our Father shall we
Praise God, this hour
Rett, o Herr Jesu, rett
Sion mourns in fear
Speis uns, o Gott, deine Kinder 1656
Thine honor save, O Christ; X110165 Thine honor rescue
Wenn dein herzliebster Sohn, o Gott 1630
What laws, my blessed Saviour
Yea, as I love, Jehovah saith
Zion klagt mit Angst
Heginbothom, Ottiwell, 1744-68
Blest Jesus! when my soaring
Great God, let all our tune-

ful
Now let my soul, eternal King
Hehl, Matthäus Gottfried, 1704-87
Rise, exalt our Head and King; X101250 Christ, thy all-atoning
Heinrich of Laufenberg, 15th c
see Laufenberg, Heinrich von, 15th c
Held, Heinrich, ca 1600 - ca 1660
All the world give praises
Come, O come, thou quickening
Gott sei Dank durch alle Welt
Komm, o komm du Geist
Let the earth now praise; X105171 Let the earth exalt
Helder, Bartholomäus, d 1635
Lord Jesus Christ, strong Hero
O dearest Jesus, thee I pray
O Holy Ghost, eternal God
O Jesus, Lamb of God, thou art; X107120 O Jesus ... who art
O Lämmlein Gottes, Jesu Christ 1646
Helmbold, Ludwig, 1532-98
From God shall naught divide
Herr Gott, erhalt uns für
Höret, ihr Eltern, Christus spricht 1596
Lord, help us ever to retain
Von Gott will ich nicht lassen 1563
Ye parents, hear what Jesus
Helphingstone, Mary J.
A ransom for all my Saviour
Hemans, Felicia Dorothea, 1793-1835
Come to the Land of peace
The breaking waves dashed high
Hemminki, Maskun
Lord Jesus, Life eternal
Henderson, Daniel, 1880-
Constantine! Constantine!
Shepherd of mortals, here
Hendricks, Mrs. H.A.
There is not a friend
Hendrickson, H.N.
Father, source of life
Hengstenberg, Johann Heinrich Karl, 1770-1834
God is my Light! My soul
Gott ist mein Licht!
Henley, John, 1800-42
Children of Jerusalem; X103192 Hark! while infant
Henley, William Ernest, 1849-1903
A late lark twitters
Out of the night that covers
Henry, H.T.
Long live the Pope! His praises
O dearest Love divine, my heart
The maid of France, with
Unto him, for whom, this day; R108222 Pie Jesu Domine
Henry, S.M.I.
I know my heavenly Father; R103257 He knows, He knows
We know not the time when (authorship uncertain)
Henry, W.J.
I am fighting in the army; R104101 I will press
I cannot be idle, for Jesus; R109976 Then away to the work
Keep me near thee, blessed; R105230 Life without Thee
Let us ever love each other (with Luella E. Henry); R104987 Kind and loving
Henshaw, Sarah Edwards
Lord, when in Simon's house
Hensley, Lewis, 1824-1905
Thy kingdom come, O God
Henson, J.M.
Brother along on the highway; R109078 Somebody follows you
Herberger, Valerius, 1562-1627
Farewell I gladly bid thee; X102066 Farewell, hence-

forth; X102068 Farewell! I say with
Valet will ich dir geben 1613
Herbert, Annie
When the mists have rolled; R111129 We shall know as we
Herbert, George, 1593-1633
Come, my way, my truth
Enrich, Lord, heart, mouth
King of glory, King of peace
Let all the world in every
My heart lies dead
Sweet day, so cool, so calm
Teach me, my God and King
The God of love my shepherd
Throw away thy rod, Throw away
Herbert, Petrus, d 1571
Die Nacht ist kommen
Faith is a living power
Now it is evening; time to; X106419 Now Lord be with us; X106809 O God, be with us
O comforter, God Holy Ghost
O, exalt and praise the Lord
The night is come wherein
Herford, Brooke, 1830-1902
Lead us, heavenly Father; X105085 Lead us ... Shepherd Kind
Herman, Norbert, 20th c
Hail, noble Column, speak
O Christ, of angel legions
O Cross, no stars thy glow
O Hunter blessed, of hearts
St Joseph, pride of heaven's
Sweet Gabriel, O blessed
Herman, Nicolaus (or Hermann, Nikolaus), ca 1480-1561
Die helle Sonn' leucht't
Let all together praise our God
Lobt Gott, ihr Christen
Mine hour appointed is at hand
Hinunter ist der Sonnenschein 1560
Now hush your cries and shed
Praise God the Lord, ye sons
So wahr ich leb' spricht Gott der Herr 1560
Sunk is the sun's last beam
The happy sunshine now is gone
The hours' decline and setting
The morning sun illumes
The radiant sun shines
The sun's bright rays are
The sun's last beam of light
Wenn mein Stündlein vorhanden ist 1562
When my last hour is close
Ye Christians, sing a joyful
Hermannus Contractus, d 1054 (ascribed to)
Alma redemptoris Mater; X100352 Alma, Alma, Alma
Come, Holy Ghost, come, Lord
Hail holy Queen enthroned; R110752 Triumph all ye
Hail, O Holy Queen! Hail
Hail, Queen of the Heavens! Hail, Mistress
Hail, Queen of heaven, hail our Mother
Hail, Queen of heaven, the Ocean Star
Salve Regina coelitum
Salve Regina, Mater misericoridae
Hernaman, Claudia Frances, 1838-98
Lord, who throughout these forty; X110435 Throughout these
The call to arms is sounding
Herr, Amos
I owe the Lord a morning song
Herrick, Robert, 1591-1674
Down with the rosemary and bays
Here a little child I stand
In the hour of my distress
In numbers, and but these few
In this world, the Isle of
What sweeter music can we; R111126 We see him come
When virgin morn doth call
Herrnschmidt, Johann Daniel, 1675-1723

Lobe den Herren, O meine
Our God is truth, most faithful
Praise the Almighty, my soul
Praise thou the Lord, O my
Storms of trouble may assail
With hearts and with voices
Hertzog (or Herzog), Johann Friedrich, 1647-99
And now another day is gone see Isaac Watts, And now
Another day is at its close
Now that the day hath reached
Nun sich der Tag geendet hat 1670
Since now the day has reached
Hess, Isabella R., 20th c
A week within the sukko green
Father, as the day I greet
Father bless these [this] birthday children [child]
For the golden sun
Hear my prayer, O hear my
Lord, written in rocks
Hester, James McNaughton, 1924-
O Mother dear, this day in May
Heusser-Schweizer, Meta, 1797-1876
Lamb, the once Crucified! Lion
Long hast thou wept
Hewett, John William, 1824-86
In the name of God, the Father
Hewitt, Eliza E., 1851-1920
For Christ and the church let; R102267 For Christ our dear
"Give me thy heart," says
"Have faith in God," the Saviour; R106548 O blessed faith
I am thinking today; R111708 Will there be any
Listen to the blessed; R103478 Him that cometh unto
More about Jesus would I know; X105992 More ... I would know
Sing the wondrous love of; R111523 When we all get to
There is rest, sweet rest; R110095 There's a blessing
There is sunshine in my soul; R107659 O, there's sunshine; X110126 There's sunshine in
Trying to walk in the steps; R103623 How beautiful to walk
Hay, Johann Wilhelm, 1789-1854
As each happy Christmas
Hey, Wilhelm, 1789-1854
Aus dem Himmel ferne, Wo die Englein sind
Can you count the stars; X101140 Canst thou count
From yon distant heaven
Heyder, Friedrich Christian, 1677-1754
I come, O Saviour, to thy table
Ich komm' zu deinem Abendmahle 1710
Heywood, Florence L.
Breaking through the clouds
Hear our prayer, O gracious
Heywood, Thomas, 1574?-1641
I sought Thee round about
Hibbard, Agnus S.
Father in heaven, in thy love
Hickok, Francis Marion, 1844-1916
Come, Holy Spirit, Dove divine
Hickson, William Edward, 1803-70
God bless our native land
Now to heaven our prayer
Higbee, E.E., 1830-99
Jesus, o'er the grave
Thy glory thou didst manifest
Higginson, Thomas Wentworth, 1823-1911
From street and square, from
No human eyes thy face may see
The past is dark with sin
To thine eternal arms, O God
Hill, Frances Thompson
Let us sing of Easter glad-

ness
We turn to thee, O Lord
Hill, Leslie Pinckney, 1880-1959
This is the charge I keep
Hill, Rowland, 1744-1833
We sing His love, Who once
With heavenly power, O Lord
Hill, R. Psalms and hymns, 1783
Cast thy burden on the Lord
Lo, round the throne
Hiller, Philip Friedrich, 1699-1769
God, in human flesh appearing
Jesus Christ as King is
O boundless joy! there is
O Son of God, we wait for
Wir warten dein, O Gottes Sohn
Himmerich, Hans J., 1681-1735
The day is fast declining
Hinds, Samuel, 1793-1872
Lord, shall thy children come
Hingley, Joseph Beaumont
Come, Master workman, work
Hinkson, Katherine Tynan, 1859-1931
I would choose to be a door keeper
Hinsdale, Grace Webster, (Farin, pseud) 1833-1902
My soul complete in Jesus
O what can little hands do
Hjertén, Johan, 1781-1835
Jesus, in my walk and living
Hoatson, Florence
God whose Name is Love
Hodder, Edwin, 1837-1904
Jesus, tender Saviour, hast
Thy word is like a garden
Hodenberg, Bodo von, 1604-50
Before thy throne I now appear
Hodge, Dwight Munson, 1846-1906
Blow, winds of God, and bring
Hodges, George Samuel, 1827-99
Hosanna we sing, like the
Hodges, Leigh Mitchell
As when, in far Samaria
Hofer, Andreas, 1767-1810
The heavens resound with his
Hoffman, Elisha Albright, 1839-1929
Breathe upon us, Holy Spirit
Christ has for sin; R111250 What a wonderful
Down at the cross where; R102564 Glory to His name
Have thy affections been; R104461 Is thy heart right
Have you been to Jesus; R100496 Are you washed
He knoweth the way that I take; R109916 The way that I take
How calm and how bright; R107011 O holy day! O happy
I must tell Jesus all of my
I wonder, often wonder; R102269 Forever at His feet
Lord, I am fondly, earnestly; R108050 Open the wells
O Lord, within my heart; R110059 There is no other
O, wondrously sweet is; R109863 The story grows
Shall I come just as I am; R100595 As you are, just as
Some day these conflicts will; R109085 Some near, near day
Walk daily with your Saviour
What a fellowship; R105090 Leaning, leaning,
Where will you spend eternity; R101985 Eternity! eternity
You have longed for sweet; R104462 Is your all on the
Hoffmann, H.
Evening sun descending
Hofford, M. Lowrie
Abide with me, 'tis eventide
Hohlfeldt, Christoph Christian 1776-1849
Forsake me not! O thou my Lord
With the Lord thy task begin
Hojer, Conrad (or Cunrad Höier)

O God, my days are dark indeed
Holden, Oliver, 1765-1844
They who seek the throne
Hole, Samuel Reynolds, 1819-1904
Sons of labor, dear to Jesus
Holland, Henry Scott, 1847-1918
Judge eternal, throned in
Holland, Josiah Gilbert, 1819-81
There's a song in the air
Holling, T. Ernest, 1867-
O Holy Spirit, Comforter
Holm, Nils J., 1778-1845
How blessed is the little
Holme, James, 1801-82
God, my Father, hear me pray
Holmes, John, 1904-62
Now give heart's onward habit
O Lord of stars and sunlight
Peace is the mind's old
Though man, the fiery element
Holmes, John B., 1767-1843
At thy feet, at thy pierced
Holmes, John Haynes, 1879-
All hail, the pageant of
America triumphant! Brave land
God of the nations, near
O Father, thou who givest all
O God, whose law from age to
O God, whose love is over all
O God, whose smile is in the sky
O thou, whose Presence moved
O'er continent and ocean
Show us thy way, O God
The voice of God is calling
Thou God of all, whose Spirit
Thou God, whose living voice
Holmes, Oliver Wendell, 1809-94
Angel of peace, thou hast
Build thee more stately
Lord of all being, throned; X109259 Sun of our life, thy
O Lord of hosts! Almighty King
O Love divine, that stooped
Our Father, while our hearts
Thou gracious God, whose mercy; X110264 Thou gracious Power
Holroyd, James, 1850-1933
Spirit of holiness, do thou
Holy Family Hymns, 1860
Jesus, ever loving Saviour
Holy songs, carols, and sacred ballads, 1878
I sought the Lord, and afterward
Knock! but O most patient
Homburg, Ernst Christoph, 1605-81
Christ, the life of all
Jesus, meines Lebens Leben; R109344 Tausend-tausendmal
Jesus, source of my salvation
O wondrous Conqueror
Of my life the life, O Jesus
Where wilt thou go, since night
Wo willst du hin, weil's
Homer, Charlotte G.
Fear not, for God the Father; R109985 Then trust Him in
In loving kindness Jesus came; R102418 From sinking sand
Hood, Edwin Paxton, 1820-85
God, who hath made the daisies
I hear a sweet voice ringing
Jesus lives, and Jesus leads
O walk with Jesus wouldst
Hooker, Brian, 1880-
Filled full and flushed
Hopkins, John, 16th c
Ye righteous in the Lord
Hopkins, John Henry, 1820-91
Blow on, thou mighty wind
Christ our King to heaven
Come with us, O blessed Jesus
God of our fathers, bless
We three kings of Orient are; R107599 O star of wonder
When from the East the wise

men
Hopkins, Josiah, 1786-1862
O turn ye, O turn ye, for why
Why sleep ye, my brethren
Hoppe, Anna Bernardine Dorothy 1889-1941
Ascend, dear Lord! Thy earthly
By nature deaf to things divine
Desire of every nation
Eternal God, our Father
Have ye heard the invitation
He did not die in vain
Heavenly Sower, thou hast
How blest are they who through
I open wide the portals
Jesus, O precious name
Jesus, thine unbounded love
Like Enoch, let me ever walk
Lord Jesus Christ, the children's
O dear Redeemer, crucified
O Father mine, whose mercies
O Friend of sinners, Son
O God of mercies, Father mine
O joyful message, sent from
O Lord, my God, thy holy law
O precious Saviour, heal
O thou who once in Galilee
O'er Jerusalem thou weepest
Precious child, so sweetly
"Repent, the kingdom draweth"
Rise, arise! Rise, arise! Zion
The Sower goeth forth to sow
Thou camest down from heaven
Thou goest to Jerusalem
Thou hast indeed made manifest
Thou Lord of life and death
Thou virgin-born incarnate
Hopper, Edward, 1818-88
Jesus, Saviour, pilot me
Hopps, John Page, 1834-1911
Father, lead me day by day
Father, let thy Kingdom come
God of our fathers, hear
Hark, hark, my soul! Thy Father's voice; R102159 Father of mercy; X103148 Hark ... The Saviour's
We praise thee, Lord, for hours
Horace, i.e. Quintus Horatius Flaccus, 65 to 8, B.C.
Happy the man, and happy he
He who is upright, kind
Integer vitae
Horder. Book of praise for children, 1875
My father, hear my prayer
Horn, Edward Traill, III, 1909-
Long ago and far away; R103228 He came among us
Horn, Johann, i.e. Johann Roh, d 1547
Gottes Sohn ist kommen
O be not thou dismayed
Once He came in blessing
Horn, William W., 1773-1826
Pure and free from all
Horne, Charles Silvester, 1869-1914
For the might of thine arm; X102313 For the strength
Sing we the King who is coming; R101443 Come let us sing
Horne, George, 1730-92
See the leaves around us
Horne, William, 1716-
May we to thee, our Shepherd
Horton, Edward Augustus, 1843-
We honor those whose work
Hoskins, Joseph, 1745-88
In thy great name, O Lord
It shall be well, let sinners
Let thoughtless thousands
On Christ, by faith, my soul; X107938 On Christ ... I would
Sinners, behold the Lamb of God
Hosmer, Frederick Lucian, 1840-1929
All hidden lie the future
Father, to thee we look in all; X102187 Father ... turn away
Forward through the ages
From age to age how grandly

From age to age they gather
From many ways and wide apart
Go not, my soul, in search
Hear, hear, O ye nations
I came not hither of my will
I little see, I little know
I walk the unfrequented road
Immortal by their deed
Lo, the day of days is here
Lo, the Easter-tide is here
Made lowly wise, we pray no; X111114 We pray no more
Not always on the mount may we
Now while the day in trailing
O beautiful, my country
O blest the souls that see
O day of light and gladness
O Light, from age to age
O Lord of life, where'er they
O Name, all other names above
O prophet souls of all the years
O thou in all thy might so far
O thou in lonely vigil led
O thou, who art of all that is
O thou, whose Spirit witness
On eyes that watch through
One thought I have, my ample
Over the land in glory
Through willing heart and
Thy kingdom come! on bended
Thy kingdom come, O Lord
Today be joy in every heart
Uplift the song of praise
We cannot think of them; X103843 I cannot think
When courage fails and faith
When shadows gather on our way

Hoss, Elijah Embree, 1849-
O God, great Father, Lord

Hostetler, C.K.
Shadows never darken heaven; R110081 There shall be no

Hostetter, P.
A servant of God, the apostle

Hott, George P.
I am looking for the city; R107646 O, the glory gates
In from the highway, in from; R103389 Help us to win them
Saviour, to thee I come
'Tis hard to bear the heavy; R103256 He knows, He knows

Houghton, Frank, 1894-
Facing a task unfinished
My Lord, who in the desert fed
O thou who dost direct my feet
Thou who wast rich beyond

Houghton, Will H.
Lead me to some soul today

Housman, Laurence, 1865-1959
Fair is their fame who stand
Father eternal, Ruler of
Honor and glory, power and
Lord God of Hosts, within
The maker of the sun and moon
The Saint who first found
When Christ was born in

Hovden, A.
Help me, Lord, by thy great

Hovey, Richard, 1864-1900
See Carmen, Bliss. We are adventurers

How, William Walsham, 1823-97
Ashamed of thee, O dearest Lord
Behold a little child
Behold, the Master passeth by
Bowed low in supplication
Come, praise your Lord
For all the saints, who from; X102263 For all thy saints
For all thy love and goodness
It is a thing most wonderful
Jesus! Name of wondrous love
Lord Jesus, when we stand afar
Lord, this day thy children
Lord, thy children guide
O daughters blest of Galilee

O holy Lord, content to fill
O Jesus, crucified for man
O Jesus, strong and pure
O King of Kings, whose reign
O Lord, it is a blessed thing
O my Saviour lifted
O one with God the Father; X107697 O thou, our God and
O Jesus, thou art standing
O thou, through suffering
O Word of God incarnate; X107866 O Word ... most holy
On wings of living light; X105251 Lift up your heart
Rejoice, ye sons of men
Soldiers of the cross, arise
Summer suns are glowing; X102845 God's free mercy
The angel sped on wings
The ever-changing seasons
The joyous life that year by
The year is swiftly waning
This day the light of heavenly; X110183 This day at thy
Thou art the Christ, O Lord
To thee our God, we fly; R107311 O Lord, stretch
We give thee but thine own
We praise thy grace, O Saviour
Who is this so weak and helpless
Winter reigneth o'er the land
With trembling awe the chosen
Howard, D.H.
As above the darkest storm-cloud
Behold the heavenly city
Gone! yes, but for a little
In sorrow and affliction
O hollow, soulless pomp
The more thou puttest in
The way, we know, is rough
Howard, Mildred E.
Since Jesus gave his life; R106144 My life, O Lord
Howard, Pearl Waggoner
Lord, bless thy word to every
Howard, W. James
O King of nations, Splendor
Howe, Julia Ward, 1819-1910
Bid the din of battle cease
Mine eyes have seen the glory; X102549 Glory, glory!
The world is glad, the world
Howitt, Mary Botham, ca 1804-88
Thou, earth, art ours
Howson, John Saul, 1816-85
At all times praise the Lord
Hoyt, May P.
Here at thy table, Lord
Hubbell, Susan S.
For the summer's glowing
Huckel, Oliver, 1864-
O Mind of God, broad as
Hudson, Ralph E., 1843-1901
At the cross, at the cross see Watts. Alas and did my Saviour bleed
My life, my love I give; R104194 I'll live for Him
Huffaker, Perry L., 1902-
Father in heaven, lo, thine
Huffman, Nelson T., 1901-
Hear thou our prayer, Lord
Lord, we beseech thee
Hugg, George C.
When this poor heart is burdened; R106280 Nobody knows like
Hughes, J. Donald
Creator of the universe
Hughes, Thomas, 1823-96
O God of truth, whose living
Huish, O.P.
Come unto Jesus; ye heavy laden
Jesus, my Savior true
There is a land whose sunny; R110876 Utah, Utah, beautiful
Hull, Amelia Matilda, ca 1825-82
And is it true as I am told
There is life for a look; R105400 Look! Look! look

Hull, A. The casket, 1865
Ich weiss einen Strom;
R107532 O Seele, ich bitte
O have you not heard of that;
R107530 O seek that beautiful
Hull, William Winstanley, 1794-1873
To the God of all creation
Humbert, Harold
We build a sanctuary sure
Humphreys, Joseph, 1720-
Blessed are the sons of God
Hungarian Mass-song
O Most Holy, One and only God (1797)
Thirsting for the living (1855)
Hunter, J. Hymns of faith and life, 1889
How near to us, O God
Hunter, John, 1848-1917
Dear Master, in whose life
Hunter, William, 1811-77
In seasons of grief to my God
My heavenly home is bright;
R104208 I'm going home
The Great Physician now;
R109310 Sweetest note
There is a spot to me more
Hunter-Clare, Thomas Charles, 1910-
Fear not, my soul, alone to
God of the pastures, hear our
Lord, thy word hath taught
Huntingdon, Selina, countess, 1707-91
When thou, my righteous Judge
Huntington, DeWitt C., 1830-1912
O think of the home over there;
R108179 Over there, over
Huntington, George
Two empires by the sea
Hupton, Job, 1762-1849
Come ye faithful, raise;
X101559 Come, ye people
Hurditch, Charles Russell, 1839-
Come let us all unite to sing;
X101426 Come ... unite and
Hurn, William, 1754-1829
Arise, O Lord, and shine;
X100514 Arise, O God, and
Hus [Huss], John [Jean], 1373-1415 (authorship in some doubt)
Jesus Christ, our blessed
Jesus Christus, Gottes Sohn. 1415
Jesus Christus, nostra salus
Jesus Christus, unser Heiland
To avert from men God's wrath
NOTE: This is the oldest known Moravian hymn, ca 1400
Husenbeth, Frederic Charles, 1796-1872
Stars of glory shine
Hussey, Jennie E., 1874-
I stood alone at the bar of God
King of my life, I crown thee;
R105097 Lest I forget
Huston, Frank C.
The service of Jesus true;
R104494 It pays to serve
Hut, Hans.
O Allmächtiger Here Gott! 1564
Hutchings, William Medlen, 1827-76
When mothers of Salem
Hutchinson, Albert H.
For all the blessings of the
Hutton, James, 1715-95
Besprinkle with thy blood my
Come, faithful Shepherd, bind
My opening eyes with rapture
Teach me yet more of thy blest
Hyde, Abigail Bradley, 1799-1872
Dear Saviour, if these lambs
Say, sinner! Hath a voice
Hyde, W. H.
We have heard from the bright
Hyde, William DeWitt, 1858-1917
Creation's Lord, we give thee;
X108923 Since what we choose
Hymns adapted to the public

worship of the Christian Church. Princeton, 1828
Within thy house, O Lord
Hymns and Tunes, 1890
Follow the path of Jesus
Hymns of the English Conference [Swedenborgian] 1880
Built by Jehovah's hand
Cast upon the Lord thy care
Great God! thou dost all
Great God, we give thee praise
Great refuge of the weary soul
Jesus, in thee our hopes
Jesus, thou Shepherd of us all
Jesus, thou source of life
Lord Jesus, God of heaven
O blest Redeemer, from thy
O comfort to the weary
O fix my heart, my God
O God, my heavenly King
O King of Kings, beneath
Rest remaineth, O, so sweet
The Lord our Saviour is the way
Thou art the mighty King
Thou, Jesus, art the way
Thy mighty power we sing
Where for safety shall I fly
Within thy tabernacles, Lord
Ye Christians, tune your
Hymns of the Spirit, 1864
Come thou Almighty Will
Give forth thine earnest cry
God is in His holy temple
In this peaceful house; X104423 In thy peaceful
O, come, and let us all, with

I

Image, Selwyn
The snow lies thick upon
Three kings in great glory
Imber, N. H.
Kol od balayvov p'neemo
Indian (Asia) Prayer
Listen to our prayer, O Lord
Indians (American) traditional
see Chippewa, Dakota, Omaha
Ingelow, Jean, 1820-97
And didst thou love the race
The parson knew that he had
Ingemann, Bernhardt Severin, 1789-1862
As gold by fire is tested
As wide as the skies
Christmas brings joy
Christmas is here with joy
I live, and I know the span
Igjennem Nat og Trängsel 1825
Jesus, my Saviour, my Shepherd
One is our God and Father
Through the night of doubt
Ingham, Benjamin, 1712-72
The one thing needful
Ingham, John Hall
Land of the North, where
"The Inner Light"
Lord of Good Life, the hosts
Innocent III, Pope, 1161-1216
Veni, Sancte Spiritus BUT NOTE: Most translations of this hymn are filed within "Latin, 12th c" sequence
Innocent VI, Pope, d 1362
Ave verum Corpus natum; X100652 Ave, ave verum corpus
Hail to thee, true Body, sprung
Hail, true Body, born of Mary
Hail, true Body, truly born
Iris, Scharmel
O, he who walked with fishermen
Irish traditional, etc.
Christmas day is come; let's (17th c)
Be thou my Vision O lord (ancient)
Irish Psalter, 1898
Unto my Lord Jehovah said
Irons, Genevieve Mary, 1855-1928
Drawn to the cross, which thou
Irons, William Josiah, 1812-83
Father of love, our Guide
Sing with all the sons
Triumphant Lord, thy work
Irwin, Samuel Wesley, 1875-

For swinging wind, and tree-top birds
Isaacs, A.S., 1851-1920
A noble life, a simple faith
At midnight, so the sages
Italian traditional, etc.
Glory be to Jesus, who in (18th c)
Hail, Jesus, hail, who for my (18th c)
Viva! Viva! Gesù! che per mio (18th c)
Iverson, Daniel
Spirit of the living God; X109172 Spirit ... fall fresh

J

NOTE: Words, such as Iam, Iesù, etc., are herein spelled Iam, Jam, Jesù, etc., and are filed accordingly.
Jesu and Jesus are always interfiled.

"J.E.A."
My Savior's praises I will; R101997 Every day will I
"J.H."
Sitting at the feet of Jesus
"J.V.C." [Crosby?]
All ye saints of light; R111222 We'll walk in
Jackson, F.A., 1867-1942
Down the mines for buried; R103503 Hold the ropes, then
Master, we thy footsteps
Jackson, Frederick
Standing in the market-place
Jackson, H.G.
If you from sin are longing; R105402 Look to the Lamb
Jackson, Mary E.
Come forth, O Christian youth
Jackson, W.P.
To the cross of Christ I'm
Jacobs, George
O Lord! to thee who dwellest
Jacobs, Henry Eyster, 1844-1932
Lord Jesus Christ, we humbly
Nearer my God to thee ... Through word and sacrament; X101833 Draw me, O Lord
Jacobs, Henry S.
How goodly is thy house
Jacobs, W.K.
When the trump shall sound; R109993 Then we'll be happy; X111500 When the trumpet (Black)
Wonderful Saviour, Redeemer
Jacopone, i.e. Jacopone di Benedetti of Todi, d 1306
At the cross her station; X106234 Near the cross her; X106235 Near the cross was
By the cross her vigil
Stabat Mater dolorosa
Jahn, Martin, ca 1620-ca 82
see Janus, Martin
James, Annie L.
Is there a heart that is; R104676 Jesus is passing
James, Mary D.
All for Jesus! All for Jesus!
In the rifted Rock I'm; R106384 Now I'm resting
Jameson, Love H., 1811-92
Night, with ebon pinion
Janus, Martin, ca 1620-ca 82
Jesu, joy of man's desiring
O, at last I've found
Janvrin, Alice Jan, 1846-1908
He expecteth, He expecteth
Japanese national anthem
Kimi ga yo wa chi yo
Unto a thousand, yea
Jaques, John
O say, what is truth
Softly beams the sacred
Jarvis, Mary, 1853-1929
O God of ages in whose light
Jastrow, Marcus Mordecai, 1829-1903
Blessed, O blessed, moment
When the Sabbath peace-inviting
Jeffrey, H.R.
Come home, poor sinner, why; R104677 Jesus is pleading
O, why should I be idle; R109603 The laborers are

few
Jenkins, Rory Donaughmore, 1914-
When Christ at evening hour
Jenkins, William Vaughan, 1868-1920
O God of love, to thee
O God our Father, who dost
O loving Lord, who art for
Jensen, Gustav
Thou must increase Lord, and
Jensen, J. Marinus
A voice hath spoken from
Jervois, William Henry Hammond, 1852-1905
Father, see thy children
See, Father, thy beloved Son
Wherefore, O Father, we thy
Jeszensky, Karoly
Lift thy head, O Zion
Jewish traditional, etc.
Adon olom a'sher molach
A'do-noy, A'do-noy, Ayl rachum
A-do-noy, mo o'dom va-tay-do-ay-hu
A'do-noy yim-loch l'o-lom voed
All the world shall come to (Vaye-esayu)
All ye dwellers on earth (Shofar)
Ayn kay-lo-hay-nu
Ayn ko-mo-cho bo-e-lo-heem
Bo-r'chu es Adonoy
Boruch atoh adonoy
Bo-ruch shaym k'-vod mal-chu-so
B'ro-sh ha-sho-no yi-ko-say-vun
En Kelohenu (There is none like God)
Ere space exists, or earth (Adonoi melech)
For the mountains shall depart (Shofar call)
Fortress-Rock, my God, my aid
God of Might, God of Right
Har-nee-nu lay-lo-heem
Ha-yom t'-am' tsay-nu
Ho-du la-do-noy kee-tov
Kee va-yom ha-zeh y'-cha-payr
Ko-dosh, ko-dosh, ko-dosh Adonoy
L'-cho A-do-nay ha-g'-du-lo
L'cho do-dee likras kalo
Lord of Hosts, whom all
Lord, thine humble servants (Yom Kippur)
Mee-Cho-mo-cho bo-ay-leem A-do-noy
O-lay-nu l'-sha bay-ach
O-no A-do-noy, ka-per no,
Our Father, our King
Praise to the living God (Doxology)
Shi-vee-see A-do-noy l'neg-dee
Sh' ma Yisroayl! A-do-noy E-lo-hay-nu
Shalom, havay-reem
Sholom alaychem mal achay
S'-lach no la-a-von ho-om
S'u sh'-o-reem ro-shay-chem
Sweet hymns and songs (13th c)
The God of Abraham praise (Doxology); X100780 Before the great; X109696 The Lord our God we; X110392 Though nature's
The Lord of all, who reigned (Adon Olam)
The Lord, the Lord reigneth (Shofar)
The sun goes down, the shadows
This feast of the Law
Thy praise, O Lord, will I (A'ameer)
To-vo, to-vo l'-fo-ne-cho
Va-a-nach-nu ko-r'eem umishtachaveem
V'-al ku-lom, E-lo-a
Va-yo-mer A-do-noy
Va-y'-da-bayr Mo-she es mo-a-day
V'-nis-lach l'-chol a-das b'-nay
V'shom'ru V'-nay Yis-ro-ayl es ha-shab-bos
We are Thy people, Thou art our King

Ya-a-leh ta-cha-nu-nay-nu
Yigdal Eloheem chai (Doxology)
Yim-loch A-do-noy l'olom
Y'-vo-re-ch'-cho A-do-noy
Zoch-ray-nu la-cha-yeem
Jewitt, Alfred Charles, 1845-1925
Past are the cross, the scourge
Jex-Blake,Thomas William, 1832-1915
Lord we thank thee for
Joergen, L.
O where is the home of the soul
"John", pseud, see Foote, John G., supposed author
John, Duke of Argyll, see Campbell, John, Duke of Argyll, 1845-1914
Johns, John, 1801-47
Come, Kingdom of our God
Johnson, Catherine H., 1835-
The whole wide world for Jesus; X109921 The whole ... once more before we
Johnson, Erastus, 1826-1909
O sometimes the shadows are; R107657 O then to the Rock
Johnson, Henry Harrold, 1869-
Bring beams of oak
Johnson, Joseph, 1848-1926
God speaks to us in bird
Johnson, Joel H.
All hail the glorious day
High on the mountain top
The glorious gospel light
Johnson, Josephine, 1890-
In this stern hour
Johnson, Samuel, 1822-82
City of God, how broad
Father, in thy mysterious
God of the earnest heart
I praise thee, Lord, for; X103828 I bless thee, Lord
Life of ages, richly poured
Onward, Christian! though; X108044 Onward, Onward, tho'
Thou, whose glad summer yields
Johnson, William, 1906-
Deep are his wounds, and red
Johnson, Julia Harriette, 1849-1919
Here we come with gladness
Marvelous grace of our loving; R102902 Grace, Grace, God's
There's a sweet and blessed; R100349 Alleluia, what a
"Joint Committee".
My God, my God, O why hast
Jonae, Laurentius, d 1597
A Star is moving through
Jonas, Justus, 1493-1555
If God were not upon our side (Ps. 124, tr. by Winkworth)
Jones, Charles P.
Jesus Christ is made to me; R111745 Wisdom, righteousness
There is nothing in the world; R107070 O, I love to tell
Jones, Edith, 1849-1929
Father, who art alone
Jones, Edmund, 1722-65
Come, humble sinner, in whose
Jones, Harriet E.
We have a Rock, a safe; R108118 Our Jesus is the Rock
Jones, John Samuel, 1831-
I was made a Christian
Now the busy week is done
Jones, Lewis E., 1865-1936
Though the way we journey; R111131 We shall see the King
When I have reached earth's R101145 Carried away to
Would you be free from the; R110068 There is pow'r; X111867 Would you be free from the burden; X111869 Would you be free from your burden
Jones, R. Lawrence
Grant us, O God, a single aim
Jones, Samuel M.
Haste, O haste, delightful; R101993 Ever growing,

swiftly
Jonson, Ben, 1573-1637
I sing the birth was born
Truth is the trial of itself
Joseph of the Studium, d 883
see St Joseph, the hymnographer, d 883
Judah ben Samuel Halevi
O Lord, where shall I find
Judson, Adoniram, 1788-1850
Come, Holy Spirit, Dove divine
Jukes, Richard
By faith I view my Saviour
Julian, John, 1839-1919
Father of all, to thee
Hark! the voice eternal
O God of God! O Light of Light
Justinian, Emperor, 483-565
O Word immortal of eternal God
Juvenile Harmonist, 1837
Little children praise

K

"K", in Rippon. Selection of hymns, 1787
How firm a foundation, ye; X104252 In every condition
In songs of sublime adoration
Kahl, Johan, 1721-46
Arise, my soul, arise! Stretch
Kalir, Eleazer
Tent-like this day the King
Kålmån, Farkas
Where, O God eternal, where
Kauffman, Daniel
We bow to thee, O Lord, on high; R105424 Lord, as this solemn
Kauffman, Frieda
Worthy art thou, Lord divine; R105517 Lord, I thank thee
Kauffman, see also Coffman
Keats, John, 1795-1821
A thing of beauty is a joy
Keble, John, 1792-1866
Ave Maria! blessed Maid
Blest are the pure in heart
Draw, Holy Ghost, thy seven-fold
God, the Lord, a King remaineth
Lord, in thy Name thy servants
New every morning is thy love; X104162 If on our daily; X106254 New ... is thy love; X107778 O timely happy
One thy Light, the temple
Sun of my soul, thou Saviour; X110537 'Tis gone, that
The Lord hath reigned, and
The voice that breathed o'er
The year begins with thee
There is a book who runs may; X110013 There is ... that all
When God of old came down
Word supreme, before creation
Keegan, G. Kearnie
Are you tired of the life; R103251 He is watching
Keimann, Christian, 1607-62
Freuet euch, ihr Christen
I will leave my Saviour never
Jesus I will never leave; X106052 My dear Jesus I'll
Jesus will I never leave
Meinen Jesum lass' ich nicht 1658
O, rejoice, ye Christians
Keller, Arnold Frederick, 1890-
Under the feeble stable light
Kellogg, Caroline
Very softly I will walk
Kelly, Claire B.
O Holy Spirit, lead us
Kelly, Thomas, 1769-1854
Behold the temple of the Lord
Blessed fountain, full of grace
Boundless glory, Lord, be thine
Come, see the place where Jesus
Come, ye saints, look here
"Give us room that we may"
God of our salvation, hear us

Hark, ten thousand harps and
Hark! ten thousand voices
Hark! that shout of rapture
How sweet to leave the world
I hear a voice that comes
I love the sacred book of God
In thy name, O Lord, assembling
Jesus comes, his conflict over
Jesus, thou Shepherd of the
Look, ye saints, the day; R101625 Crown him! Crown him (Stebbins)
Look, ye saints, the sight
On the mountain's top; X107960 On the mountain top
Of thy love some gracious
Praise the Saviour, we who know
Saviour, send a blessing
Saviour, when we call, O hear
Sing of Jesus, sing forever
Sion stands with hills
Sion's King shall reign
Speed thy servants, Saviour
"Stricken, smitten, and"
The atoning work is done
The head that once was crowned
The Lord is risen indeed
Through the day thy love has; X110425 Through ... kept us; X110427 Through ... hath spared
We sing the praise of him
"We've no abiding city here"
Whence these sounds symphonious
Who is this that comes from
Why those fears! Behold, 'tis

Kemp, Harry, 1883-1960
I cannot put the Presence by
Joses, the brother of Jesus
Who thou art I know not

Ken, Thomas, 1637-1711
All praise to thee, my God; X102569 Glory to Thee, my
All praise to thee, who safe
Awake, my soul, and with; X102572 Glory to thee, who
Her Virgin eyes saw God
Praise God, from whom all
Preist Gott, der allen Segen Gibt!
Since we can't doubt God's

Kendon, Frank, 1893-
As we rode down the steep
What songs are these, faint; R109858 The stars shall

Kennedy, Benjamin Hall, 1804-89
How blest the man, who fears
O Lord our King how bright thy
The heavens, O God, thy glory
Why do the heathen rage

Kennedy, Gerald, 1907-
God of love and God of power

Kennedy, Mrs. W.J.
We are saved by the grace; R107046 O how deep are the; X107065 O how wondrous

Kent, John, 1766-1843
What cheering words are these

Kerr, Hugh Thomson, 1872-1950
Come thou my Light, that I may
God of our life, through all

Kethe, William, d ca 1593
All people that on earth

Key, Francis Scott, 1779-1843
Before the Lord we bow
Lord, with glowing heart
O say can you see by the dawn's

Key, Robert Ellis
O Love whose perfect path
So brightly burns Love's holy

Kidder, Mary Ann, 1820-1905
Ere you left your room this; R107061 O how praying rests
I am bought not with riches; X104454 Is my name written; X105510 Lord, I care not; R106161 My name's written
We shall sleep, but not

Kieffer, A.A.
There's a city of light 'mid; R105209 Let us pray
Killinghall, John, d 1740
In every trouble, sharp and
Kilmer, Joyce, 1886-1918
I think that I shall never
No longer of him be it said
Kimball, Edward P.
God loves us, so he sent
Kimball, Marriet McEwan, 1834-1905
Pour thy blessings, Lord
Kimball, Rosamond
Hark to the sound; it rings
King, John, 1789-1858
When his salvation bringing
Kingo, Thomas Hansen, 1634-1703
Dearest Jesus, draw thou
Enhver som tror og bliver döbt 1689
He that believes and is
How fair the church of Christ
I come, invited by thy Word
I pray thee, dear Lord Jesus
Like the golden sun ascending
Lov og Tak og evig Äre 1689
Nu rinder Solen op Af Österlide 1699
O dearest Lord, receive from
O Jesu, blessed Lord, to thee
O Jesu, gid du vilde 1699
O Jesu, söde Jesu, dig 1689
On my heart imprint thine
Our table now with food
Over Kedron Jesus treadeth
Praise to thee and adoration
Print thine image pure and
Seal my heart with thine
Skriv dig, Jesu, paa mit
Softly now the day is ending
Som den gyldne Sol frembryder
The kingdom Satan founded
The sun arises now in light
The way that unto Jesus leads
Thy love, O gracious Lord
Kingsbury, William, 1744-1818
Great Lord of all thy churches
Let us awake our joys
Kingsley, Charles, 1819-75
From thee all skill and
The day of the Lord is at
Kinner, Samuel, 1603-68
Herr Jesu Christ, du hast bereit't 1638
Lord Jesus Christ, thou hast
Lord Jesus, thou art truly
Kipling, Rudyard, 1865-1936
Father in heaven, who lovest; X105049 Land of our birth
God of our fathers, known of
Non nobis, Domine! Not unto
Kirby, W.H.
Forth to the fight, ye; R105257 Lift ye the Snow-white
Kirk, S.C.
Hear ye the Master's call; R102005 Every work for Jesus
Kirkland, Patrick Miller, 1857-1943
Jesus, Lord, Redeemer
Kirkpatrick, William J.
I've wandered far away from; R101580 Coming home, coming
Saved to the uttermost
Kitchin, G.W., 1827-1912
Lift high the cross, the love
Kite, Florence Lauer
O Christ, our leader and our
Klantendorfer, Paulus, d 1566
Another day is at an end
Klein, Max D.
All praise to thee we bring
Kleinman, Bertha A.
Come, hail the cause of Zion's
Klopstock, Friedrich Gottlieb, 1724-1803
Blessed are the heirs of heaven
Knak, Gustav Friedrich Ludwig, 1806-78
Jesus, Sun of gladness
Let me go, let me go, from
Knapp, Albert, 1798-1864

Dear Father, who hast made
Father of heaven, who hast
Father, who hast created all
More than all, one thing my
O Father, thou who hast
O God, whom we as Father
O Vaterherz, das Erd' und
Knapp, Edward Everett
From the Pilgrims' rock-bound
Knapp, Shepherd, 1873-1946
Dear God, the sun whose; X106325 Not only where God's
Lord God of Hosts, whose
Knight, Joel Abel
Fain would my soul with
Knight, William Allen
Come, my heart, canst thou
Knobel, Elizabeth
Now do we come, O God, to
Knollis, Francis Minden, 1815-63
There is no night in heaven
Knorr, Christian, Baron von Rosenroth, 1636-89 see Rosenroth, Christian Knorr von, 1636-89
Knowles, Frederick Lawrence, 1869-1905
Who is the patriot? He who
Knowles, James Davis, 1798-1838
O God, though countless worlds
Knowlton, Miss H.O.
Jesus loves the little children
Koch, Hans, & Leonhard Meister
Ach Gott Vater im Höchsten Thron. 1524
Kockritz, Ewald, 1876-1931
As fades the daylight splendor
Koitsch, Christian Jacob, 1671-1734
O Fountain eternal of life
O Saviour, the truest, the best
Kolb, A.B.
Christ who left his home in
Dear Saviour, when I think of
Kolb, A.C.
O, when I think of that
Kooyman, Frank I.
How beautiful thy temples, Lord
In memory of the crucified
Thy spirit, Lord, has stirred
When in the wondrous realms
Korean hymn
The Saviour's precious blood
Koren, Ulrik Vilhelm, 1826-1910
Al verden nu raabe for Herren
Ye lands to the Lord make a
Kramer, Edgar Daniel
His was no regal splendor
Kramer, Maritius
Send, O God, a gentle shower
Krause, Jonathan, 1701-62
Alleluia! Fairest morning!
Kretzmann, Paul Edward, 1883-
Ever content with the ways of
Father, hear thy child
Fervent in spirit, serving
I will bless thee, said the
Immanuel! God with us!
Immanuel! Our God and Lord
Lead, O Lord! above the
Little Baby Jesus, born today
Lord God Almighty, King of
Lord, thine fore'er today I
O come before Jehovah
O God of love and truth
O mighty God of earth and
Praise and honor to the Father
The God of the ages your refuge
The Lord is near! why should
When upon the raging waters
With thee, O Lord, alone to go
Krishna Pal, ca 1764-1822
O thou, my soul, forget no
Krummacher, Cornelius, 1824-84
Star whose light shines o'er

Krummacher, Friedrich Adolf, 1767-1845
Thou art the Way, the Truth
Kuhlmann, J.H.
Almighty God, I humbly ask
Bowed down beneath a weight
Fling wide thy gates, O church
God of nations, throned above
Hark! the King of heaven is
Kuipers, William
I hear in the air, 'neath the
I love the Lord, the fount of
In the good ship of our captain; R101886 E'en tho' the clouds
Kunth, Johann Sigismund, 1700-79
A rest remaineth for the weary
Es is t noch eine Ruh' vorhanden 1730
Yes, there remaineth still
Kurzenknabe, J.H.
Heavenly Father, I would pray
Kyle, R.W.
O Holy Father, Holy Son

L

"L.W.M."
Have you any room for Jesus; R108652 Room for Jesus
Lacey, Thomas Alexander, 1853-1931
O faith of England, taught of
The dying robber raised his
Lacy, William S., d ca 1900
Slowly sinks the setting sun
Ladies of the Grail, England
Come ring out our joy
Cry out with joy to the Lord
Defend me, O God, and plead
Have mercy on me, God, in
He who dwells in the shelter
How great is your name
I lift up my eyes to the mountains
I love the Lord for he has
I rejoiced when I heard them
I trusted even when I said
If the Lord does not build
Like the deer that yearns
My shepherd is the Lord
My soul glorifies the Lord
O blessed are those who fear
O give thanks to the Lord
O give the Lord, you sons
O praise the Lord, all you
Out of the depths I cry
The Lord is king, , with majesty
The Lord's is the earth and
To the Lord in the hour of
To you have I lifted up my
When the Lord turned the
Why this tumult among nations
"A Lady", in Sacred melodies, 1840-41
O speed thee, Christian, on
Laing, Dilys Bennett, 1906-60
Man imperishably stands
Lamb, Thomas, 1758-
Hail, thou wondrous Infant
Peace on earth, heaven is
Lambert, N.
Teach me, O Lord, to follow
Lamberts, L.J.
O bless our God with one
Lambeth Palace. 15th c ms
O Prince of Peace, who man
LaMonnoye, Bernard de, 1641-1728
Guillaume prends ton tambourin
Willie take your little drum; R108193 Patapan
Lamp, M. Willard, 1883-
God of our history, our fathers
Lancaster, Mary Ann Elizabeth (Shorey), 1851-
I have a Friend so precious
Landis, Hans
Ich hab ein schön neu Lied gemach. 1614
Landor, J.E.
Called to the feast by the King; R111482 When the King comes
Landstad, Magnus Brostrup, 1802-80
A slumber I know in Jesus'
Awake thou that sleepest
Before thee, God, who knowest
Darkness o'er the earth is

Der mange skal komme fra Öst og fra Vest. 1861
Full many shall come from the; X105349 Lo, many shall come; X110080 There many shall
I come to thee, O blessed Lord
I hus og Hjem, hvor Mand og Viv. 1861
I know of a sleep in Jesus'
In house and home where man; X106551 O blessed home
Jeg kommer her, o söse Gud. 1863
Jeg staar for Gud, som Alting veed. 1861
Jeg ved mig en Sovn i Jesu Navn. 1861
Naar Synderen ret Ser sin
Now Jesus at the door is
They come from the east and (authorship uncertain); R110138 They come from the thorny path
Thou holy Church, God's city
To thee, O Lord, the God of
When sinners see their lost
Lane, Franklin K.
I am whatever you make me
Lange, Ernst, 1650-1727
Though I speak with angel
Lange, Joachim, 1670-1742
Jesus, thy light again I view
Jesus, what offering shall; X106922 O God, what offering
Lange, Johann Peter, 1802-44
The Lord of life is risen
Langhans, Urban, fl 1540-62
Lasst uns alle frölich sein
Let us all in God rejoice; X105193 Let us all with
Larned, Augusta, 1835-
In quiet hours the tranquil
Lanier, Sidney, 1842-81
Into the woods my Master went
Lankton, Martha J.
Dwell in me, O blessed Spirit
Larcom, Lucy, 1826-93
Draw thou my soul, O Christ
I learned it in the meadow
I thank thee, Lord for precious
In Christ I feel the heart
O God, thy world is sweet
We are children of one Father
What shall I do, my Lord
Yea, o'er me soared the eternal
Larsen, Jens
Brothers and sisters, we now
The Lord be praised! I'm
Lathbury, Mary Ann, 1841-1913
All hail, all hail to the New
Arise, all souls, arise!
Break thou the Bread of life; X101033 Break thou, O Lord
Day is dawning in the east
Day is dying in the west; R103541 Holy, holy, holy
O Shepherd of the nameless fold
O, trust ye in the Lord
Take thou the heart I cannot
Lathrop, John Howland, 1880-
O bold O foolish peasants; R103602 Hosanna in the
Lathrop, Theodore B., 1881-
On this glad day we dedicate
Latin traditional, etc.
NOTE: Hymns within this section were either published anonymously or have had such a long acceptance within the office hymns and the liturgy of the Church that the author was forgotten centuries ago. Other hymns, of known source, are cited under that source. Translators have not been recognized.

A child is born in Bethlehem (14th c carol)
A messenger within the grave (4th-5th c)
A priestly Heart the Sacred Heart; R107502 O Sacred

with
Ad coenam Agni providi
Ad regias Agni dapes (4th c)
Adeste, fideles (18th c); X100134 Adeste fideles (English text)
Adoremus te, panem coelitum
All hail, adorèd Trinity (befor 11th c)
All praise to Jesus' hallowed (11th c)
All ye a certain cure (18th c)
All ye who seek a comfort sure (18th c); X100310 All ye ... sure relief; X100312 All you who seek
Alleluia! best and sweetest (11th c)
Alleluia, song of gladness (11th c); X100343 Alleluia ... sweetness
Almighty God, who from the flood (6th-7th c)
An image of that heavenly light (15th c)
Angelus ad virginem (14th c)
As the sun doth daily rise
At the Lamb's high feast (4th c)
Attende, Domine, et miserere X100131 Ad te Rex summe
Ave Maria gratia plena (13th c)
Ave, Maris stella, Dei Mater (9th c)
Ave, Regina caelorum (12th c)
Be joyful, Mary, Heavenly (17th c)
Be present, Holy Trinity (ca 10th c)
Behold! behold He cometh
Blessed be God! Blessed be
Blessed City, heavenly Salem (7th c)
Blessed feasts of blessed martyrs (12th c)
Blest creator of the light
Čas radosti, veselosti (12th c)
Child of a Virgin, Maker (8th c)
Christ above all glory (5th c)
Christ alone is our salvation (7th c)
Christ, enthroned in highest (13th c)
Christ is arisen From the grave's (11th-12th c)
Christ is made the sure (7th c); X101248 Christ, thou art
Christ is our corner-stone (7th c)
Christ ist erstanden (11th-12th c)
Christ the glory of the sky (5th c)
Christe, du Lamm Gottes (5th c)
Christe, qui lux es et dies (before 9th c)
Christus ist erstanden (11th-12th c)
Christus vincit! (8th c)
Claro paschali gaudio (4th c)
Come God Creator, Holy Ghost (11th c)
Come hither, ye faithful (18th c)
Come, Holy Ghost, Creator blest (9th c)
Come, Holy Ghost, Creator come (9th c)
Come, Holy Ghost, in love (9th c)
Come, Holy Ghost, our souls (9th c)
Come Holy Ghost, send down (9th c)
Come, Holy Spirit from above And from the realms (9th c)
Come Holy Spirit, from above And kindle in our breasts (9th c)
Come let us adore Him (18th c)
Come, O Creator Spirit blest (9th c)
Come, O Creator Spirit, come (9th c)
Come, pure hearts, in sweetest (12th c)
Come rejoicing, Faithful men (11th c or earlier)
Come rejoicing, Praises voicing

Come, thou Holy Paraclete (13th c)
Come, thou Holy Spirit, come (9th c)
Come thou now and be among us (7th c); X100921 Blessed city
Concordi laetitia (13th c)
Conditer alme siderum (9th c)
Cor dulce, cor amabile
Cor Jesu, salus in te
Confirma hoc Deus
Creator alme siderum (7th c)
Creator of the starry height (9th c)
Creator of the stars of night (9th c)
Creator Spirit, all divine (9th c)
Creator Spirit, by whose aid (9th c)
Creator, Spirit, heavenly Dove (9th c)
Creator Spirit, Lord of Grace (before 10th c)
Day of wrath! O day (13th c, perhaps by Thomas Celano) X101667 Day of judgment (Newton); X101669 Day ... doom impending; X101672 Day ... that day of
Day of wrath, O dreadful (13th c, Perhaps by Thomas Celano)
Dear crown of all the Virgin-choir (8th c)
Dear Maker of the starry skies (7th c)
Der Tag, der ist so freudenreich (14th c)
Deus, tuorum militum (6th c)
Dies est laetitia (14th c)
Dies irae, dies illa (13th c, perhaps by Thomas Celano) X109484 The day is surely (Ringwaldt)
Dormi Jesu! Mater ridet
Dost thou truly seek renown (14th-15th c)
Earth's mighty Maker, whose (7th c)
Eastern monarchs, Sages three (15th c)
Ecce nomen Domini Emmanuel (very early)
Ecce sacérdos magnus
En clára vox redarguit (5th-6th c)
Eternal glory of the sky (6th c)
Eternal Light, Divinity (18th c)
Eternal Monarch, King most high (5th c)
Eternal Son of God, O Thou (11th c)
Exsultet orbis gaudiis (10th c); X102014 Exultet orbis
Faithful cross! above all others
Far be sorrow, tears and sighing (13th c)
Fast sinks the sun to rest (18th c)
Father, most holy, merciful (ca 10th c); X102130 Father ... and tender
Finita iam sunt praelia (publ. Cologne, 1695)
Gabriel to Mary came (14th c)
Gaudeamus igitur
Gloriosi salvatoris (15th c)
Glory be to the Father, and to the Son (2d c)
Good Christian men, rejoice (14th c)
Guardian of virgins (19th c)
Hail, heavenly Queen! Hail; R103032 Hail, foamy ocean
Hail Mary, hail Mary, full of; (13th c); X103058 Hail Mary, full of
Hail, O Star that pointest (9th c)
Hail Ocean's beauteous Star (9th c)
Hail, our monarch, son of David
Hail the day so rich in cheer (before 1422)
Hail, thou living Bread (1815)
Hail thou living Victim blest
Hail thou Star of ocean (9th c)

Hail, thou who man's Redeemer (7th c)
Hark! a thrilling voice (ca 6th c); X103138 Hark! a herald voice; X103140 Hark! a mystic voice
Hark! the herald host (11th c)
Hark the hosts of heaven (11th c)
He who to Jesus manfully bore (8th c)
He whom joyous shepherds (1410)
He, whose confession God of old (8th c)
Heart of Christ my King (15th c)
Heart of our Lord, O loving
High Word of God, who once (10th c)
His cheering message from (4th-5th c)
Holy Ghost, my comforter (9th c)
Holy Spirit, come and shine (9th c)
Holy Spirit, gently come (9th c)
Holy Spirit, Lord of Light (12th c)
I give my heart to thee (9th c)
If great wonders thou desirest
Incline thine ear, O Lord; R105967 Mighty King of heaven
Ingrediente Domino in sanctam
Iste conféssor Dómini (8th c)
It is no earthly summer's ray (6th c)
Jesus Christ is risen today. Alleluia (14thc); X108984 Sing we to our God
Jesu, corôna Virginum (8th c)
Jesus, creator of the world (18th c)
Jesu Deus, amor meus
Jesu, grant me this, I pray (17th c)
Jesu, our hope, our heart's (7th c)
Jésu redémptor ômnium (6th c)
Jesu, the Father's only son (6th c)
Jesus, the Ransomer of man (6th c)
Jesu, thy mercies are untold
Jesu, who this our Lententide
Joseph, pure spouse (1670)
Joy because the circling year
Joy dawned again on Easter Day (4th c)
Joy to thee, O Queen of heaven (14thc)
Kyrie. God Father in heaven (ca 1100)
Kyrie, Gott Vater in Ewigkeit (ca 1100)
Latin Breviary see Breviary
Laudate Dominum, laudate
Languéntibus in Purgatorio
Let all on earth their voices (10th c)
Let hearts awaken, now the night (6th c)
Let the round world with songs (ca 10th c); X105103 Let all the earth
Let us live, then, and be glad
Life-spring divine and bond (6th c)
Light's glittering morn (4th c)
Lord, accept the gifts we offer
Lord God, our Father, thou
Lord God, thy praise we sing (5th c)
Lord in thy Love abide with
Lord Jesus Christ, all praise (11th c)
Lord Jesus, who our souls to save (14th c)
Lord of Creation, bow thine (11th c)
Love of the Father, love of God (12th c)
Maiden Mother, meek and mild (13th c)
Maker of all things, Lord
Maker of man, who from thy (7th c)
Martyr of God, whose strength

(10th c)
Most holy Lord and God (4th-5th c)
My God, I believe in thee
Now at the Lamb's high royal (4th c)
Now in holy celebration (15th c)
Now is the healing time (before 12th c)
Now let the earth with joy (10th c)
Now sing we, now rejoice (14th c)
Now that the daylight fills (6th c)
Now that the day-star glimmers (6th c)
Now that the sun is gleaming (6th c); X106447 Now that ... beaming
Nunc sancte nobis spiritus (4th c)
O bone Jesu! Miserere nobis
O Boundless Wisdom, God most (6th c)
O bread of Life from heaven (1661)
O bread to pilgrims given (1661)
O Christ, our hope, our heart's (8th c)
O Christ our joy, gone up on high (5th c)
O Christ, our joy, to whom (5th c)
O Christ, thou art our joy (5th c)
O Christ, thou Lamb of God (5th c)
O Christ, thou Lord of worlds
O Christ, who art the Light (before 9th c)
O come, all ye faithful (18th c); X100134 Adeste fideles (English text) ; X101328 Come, all ye; X106640 O come ... joyfully
O come, Creator Spirit, come (9th c)
O come, O come, Emmanuel (ca 9th c); X106653 O come, Immanuel; X106662 O come, O come, Immanuel; X101837 Draw nigh, draw nigh
O cor, amoris victima
O cor Jesu flagrans amore
O cor Jesu, fons amoris
O Emmanuel, Rex et legifer (early)
O esca viatorum, O panis (1661)
O fair Creator of the skies (7th c)
O food of exiles lowly (1661)
O Food of men wayfaring (1661)
O Food that weary pilgrims (1661)
O Food to pilgrims given (1661)
O glorious King of martyr-hosts (ca 6th c)
O glorious Maid, exalted far (ca 9th c)
O God-head hid devoutly; R107537 O Shepherd of
O God the Father, draw thou
O God, thy soldiers' crown (6th c); X106909 O God ... faithful Lord; X106910 O God ... great reward
O Heart of Jesus, purest heart (18th c)
O heavenly Jerusalem (18th c)
O Holy Spirit, Lord of life (4th c)
O Jerusalem, look toward the East
O Jesu Christ, from Thee began (9th c)
O King most high of earth (17th c)
O King of Kings in splendor; R101254 Christ we praise
O Lamb of God, that takest (5th c)
O Light of Light, by love (10th c)
O Maker of the stars of night (9th c)
O Maker of the world, give ear
O Paschal feast, what joy

O Pater sancte, mitis atque (10th c)
O Saviour Jesu, not alone (9th c)
O sing the great Apostle (17th c)
O sinner, for a little space (17th c)
O sinner, raise the eye (17th c); X107554 O sinner, lift
O thou eternal King most high (5th c)
O thou pure light of souls (7th-8th c)
O thou, who dost accord us (6th c)
O thou who dost to man accord (6th c)
O thou, whose all-redeeming (8th c)
O wondrous type! O vision (15th c)
O word, that goest forth (ca 7th c)
Ocean star, we greet you (9th c)
Omnis mundus jucundetur nato (12th c)
On the wood His arms (12th c)
Only-begotten, Word of God (ca 9th c)
Orêmus pro Pontifice nostro
Pie Jesu Dómine, dona eis
Portal of the world's salvation (15th c)
Puer natus in Bethlehem (14th c)
Puer nobis nascitur (15th c)
Quae est ista
Queen, when the earth was first hurled (20th c; 1955)
Quem pastores laudavere (1410)
Qui regnas in perpetuum; R105981 Miserere illi
Reges de Saba veniunt (14th c)
Regina caeli, jubila (17th c)
Regina caeli laetâre (14th c)
Rerum Deus tenax bigor (6th c)
Résonet in laudibus (14th c)
Saint of God, elect and precious (11th c)
Salútis humânae sátor (7th c)
Salve, pater Salvatoris (1874)
Sanctify me wholly, Soul of Christ (14th c)
Saviour eternal! health and life (before 11th c)
Shepherds came, their praises (1410)
Shepherds left their flocks (1410
Sing forth with gladsome (14th c)
Son of a Virgin, Maker of (8th c)
Soul of Jesus, make me whole (14th c)
Soul of my Saviour, sanctify my breast (14th c)
Sounds of joy have put to flight (13th c)
Spirit divine, Creator, come (9th c)
Sub tuum praesidium
Suscipe Domine universam
That day of wrath, that dreadful (13th c: Thomas of Celano); X109488 The day of wrath (Scott tr.)
That Easter Day with joy (5th c); X109397 That Easter-tide
The church above forever rings (7th c)
The dawn is sprinkling in the east (before 8th c)
The dawn was purpling o'er the sky (4th c)
The day draws on with golden (4th or 5th c)
The fast, as taught by holy (6th c)
The glory of these forty days (6th c)
The Lamb's high banquet doth invite (7th c)
The Lamb's high banquet we await (7th c); X109605 The Lamb's ... called to
The merits of the saints (8th c)
The morning kindles all the

sky (4th c)
The strife is o'er (publ. Cologne, 1695); X101904 Ended His strife
The sun is sinking fast (1805)
Thee God we praise, Thy name (5th c); X109960 Thee God ... holy name we
Thee we adore, eternal Lord (5th c)
Thee we praise, eternal Lord (5th c)
This is the day where-on (8th c)
Thou that art so fair (13th c)
Thou whom shepherds worshipped (1410)
Though in midst of life we be (12th c)
To Christ, the Prince of Peace (18th c)
To the Name of our salvation (15th c); X110649 To ... that brings; X110650 To ... that is; X110652 To the name that is (Dearmer)
To Thee, Redeemer, King; R103341 Hearken, O Lord
Tollite hostias, et introite
Tota pulchra es, Maria (15th c)
Triumphantly doth Christ (20th c: 1925)
Tu, Christe, nostrum gaudium (5th c)
Tu gloria Jerusalem
Ubi caritas et amor Deus
Unto us a boy is born (15th c)
Veni creator spiritus (9th c) X101385 Come, Holy Ghost
Veni, Jesu, amor mi
Veni, veni, Emmanuel (9th c)
Victoria! Victoria! Surrexit
Virginis proles, opifexque (8th c)
Vivat! vivat! Vivat Pastor
Vox clara ecce intonat (6th c)
When Christ our Lord had passed (4th c)
Ye faithful, with gladness (18th c); X100134 Adeste fideles (English text)

LaTrobe, Benjamin, 1725-86
I will rejoice in God
In this world so full of snares
Jesus' name, Source of life; X104778 Jesus' name, Jesus' name
O, how blessed is the station

LaTrobe, Christian Ignatius, 1758-1836
For our transgressions Thou
Let not your heart be faint
Lord of life! now sweetly
Met around the sacred tomb
Resting in the silent grave
Saviour of thy chosen race
See Jesus seated 'midst His
Sing praises unto God on high
Weep, Sion, weep, in death's

Latta, Eden Reeder, 1839-
He keepeth me ever
I have something I would tell
In the day of all days; R105143 Let me find a place
Jesus, thou hast promised; R104598 Jesus, come and
Not far from the Kingdom
O I long to see the beauty; R105074 Lead me to the
Wanderer in sinful ways; R103250 He is waiting

Laufenberg, Heinrich von, d ca 1458
I know a lovely angel-game
Ich weiss ein lieblich
O Jesus Christ, our Lord most; X105557 Lord Jesus Christ

Laufer, Calvin W., 1874-1938
O Master of the loving heart
O thou eternal Christ of God
Thee, holy Father, we adore
We thank thee, Lord, thy paths

Laurenti, Laurentius, 1660-1722
Ermuntert euch, ihr Frommen
O Saviour of our race
O thou essential Word, God
Rejoice, rejoice believers; X108383 Prepare your

lamps; X108447 Rejoice, all ye
Laurinus, Laurentius Laurentii, 1573-1655
In heaven above, in heaven
Lauterbach, Johann Michael, 1716-87
Bow down ye followers of the
Lavater, Johann Caspar, 1741-1801
O Jesus Christ, grow thou in
Lawson, James
I will follow thee, my Saviour
Lazarus, Emma, 1849-87
Kindle the taper
Remember Him, the Only One
Leachman, Edgecombe Walter, 1870-1945
Christian, unflinching stand
Lear, John W., 1870-
None can satisfy but Jesus
The way is dark, I dare not go; R103989 I need thee, Lord
Leatham, Edith Rutter, 1870-39
Thank you for the world so
Leatherman, Sarah C.
Some days are dark and dreary; R108134 Our rest will soon
LeDorz, F.
O Virgin all lovely, O Mother
Lee, Frederick George, 1832-
When day's shadows lengthen
Speak gently to the erring
Lee, Harry, 1877-1942
My Master was so very poor
Lee, M. Owen
As Victor in the strife
Dominic, our Lady's champion
Michael, prince of all
Now the world is saved
Patrick, thee addressing
Lee, Olav, 1859-
How blessed is the host in white
Lee, William Arthur
God of the circling realms
Leech, Lida Shivers, 1873-
Bring ye all the tithes; R110774 Trust Me, try Me
God's way is the best way
I have made my choice; R110163 Thine for service
Leeson, Jane Elizabeth, 1807-82
Gracious Saviour, gentle Shepherd; X102915 Gracious ... Little ones are; X102916 Gracious ... Our little ones
Loving Shepherd of thy sheep
Saviour, teach me, day by day
Sweet the lesson Jesus taught
Lehman, F.M.
The love of God is greater; R107364 O, love of God
Lehmann, W.H.
Beneath thy cross I stand
Take thou my life, dear Lord
Lehr, Leopold Franz Friedrich, 1709-44
Mein Heiland nimmt die Sünder an. 1732
My Saviour sinners doth; X101327 Come, all that
O come, if sinner be thy
Leiser, Joseph
For garnered fields
LeJeune, George Fitz-Curwood, 1842-1904
O the golden glowing morning
Leland, John, 1754-1841
Lord, keep us safe this night
The day is past and gone
O, when shall I see Jesus (authorship in doubt)
Leon, Johannes, d 1597
My all I to my God commend
O God, thou righteous
Leonard, George Hare
It is the day of all the year
Leonard, Julia
Little stars are shining
Leslie, J.H.
Lead me safely on the narrow
Levinger, Elma Ehrlich
In the candles' rays I see; R101898 Eleazer steadfast

Levy, David
Around the weary world
As birds unto the genial
Now upon the earth descending
Levy, J. Leonard
Come, ye faithful servants
Father, to thy dear name
Lew, Timothy T'ingfang (i.e. Liu T'ing-fang) 1892-1947
O Bread of Life, for all men; X109426 The bread of life
Lewis, Edgar
Just lean upon the arms; R105088 Lean on his arms
Lewis, Howell Elvet, 1860-1953
Friend of the home: as when
High Priest divine, from whom
Lord of light, whose Name
The days that were, the days
The light of the morning
Whom oceans part, O Lord, unite
Leyda, Ida F.
In the early morning dark
Liander, C.G.
A way to Calvary leadeth
Lias, Una R.
Though mountains may depart
Liebenberg, M.F.
Jesus, Master! at thy word
Lieder-Perlen. Concordia, 19th c
Segne, Herr, mit deinem Geiste
Send, O Lord, thy Holy Spirit
Lillenas, Haldor, 1885-
Like the sunshine after rain; R107652 O, the peace
Patiently, tenderly pleading; R101814 Don't turn him away
Wonderful grace of Jesus; R111841 Wonderful the matchless
Lillenas, Bertha Mae
When the clouds are hanging low; R105094 Leave your burden
Lindborn, Heinrich, 1712-50
Jesus Christ from death hath
Lindsay, Vachel, 1879-1930
An endless line of splendor
Let not young souls be
Lindsay, W. Robert
Walking in the sunshine; R102250 Follow, we will
Linn, Fay
O May we be still and seek
Linthicum, Blanche
Out of James one twenty-two; R100751 Be ye doers
Liscovius, Salomo, 1640-89
Jesus, my highest treasure
Litany of Loreto
Ave, Regina sacratissimi
Glorious Mary, Queen and Giver
Litany of the Sacred Heart
Cor Jesu sacratissium
Lithuanian traditional, etc.
Jesus, when we go to rest
Little, Velma G.
Great King of Peace, hear now
Littledale, Richard Frederick, 1833-90
God the Father, God the Son
God the Father, God the Word
God the Father, seen of none
Holy Spirit, heavenly Dove
I worship thee, Lord Jesus
In paradise reposing
Jesus, Saviour ever mild
Lord Jesus, by thy passion
O Lord, to whom the spirits; R107179 O Lamb of God
O sing to the Lord, whose
Spirit blest, who art adored
Littlefield, Milton Smith, 1864-1934
Come, O Lord, like morning
O Son of man, thou madest
Littlewood, R.W., 1908-
Thou who dost rule on high
Littlewood, William Edensor, 1831-86
There is no love like the love; R104724 Jesus' love
Liturgy of Malabar
Hands that have been handling
Strengthen for service, Lord

Liturgy of St James, 5th c
From glory to glory advancing
Let all mortal flesh keep
Not a thought of earthly
Livermore, Abiel Abbot, 1811-92
A holy air is breathing round
Livermore, Mary A., 1820-1905
Jesus, what precept is like
Lloyd, William Freeman, 1791-1853
My times are in thy hand; X108145 Our times are in thy
Sweet is the time of spring
Wait, my soul! upon the Lord; X110926 Waft [sic] my soul
Lobwasser, Ambrosius. Psalter, 1617
Audi, Deus me vacantem
Lochner, Karl Friedrich, 1634-97
Soul, what return has God
Was gibst du denn, o meine
Lock Chapel Collection, 1803
Come Holy Spirit, calm my mind
Lockwood, Amelia DeF.
Saviour, who thy life didst
Loehe, Wilhelm, d 1872
O Son of God, in coeternal
Loes, Harry Dixon
Looking unto Jesus, in faith
Loewen, Lois
We owe the Lord an evening song; R111945 Yes, Lord, we thank
Logan, John, 1748-88
Let Christian faith and hope (authorship disputed)
London Hymn book, 1864
Lord Jesus, I love thee, I know
Long, John Davis, 1838-
The evening winds begin
Longfellow, Henry Wadsworth, 1807-82
Ah! what a sound! The infinite
All are architects of fate
As torrents in summer
Down the dark future
I heard the bells on Christmas
I shot an arrow into the air
O then, sail on, thou ship
Sleep, comrades, sleep, sleep
We have not wings, we cannot
When Christ was born
Longfellow, Samuel, 1819-92
A voice by Jordan's shore
Again, as evening's shadow
Bless thou the gifts our hands
As darker, darker fall around
Beneath the shadow of the cross
Eternal One, thou living God; X111780 With joy we claim
Father, give thy benediction
Go forth to life, O child
God of the earth, the sky
God's trumpet wakes
Holy Spirit, Truth divine; X103564 Holy Saviour, truth
I look to thee in every need
In the beginning was the Word
Light of ages and of nations
Lo, the earth is risen again; X105359 Lo ... awakes again
Now, on land and sea descending
O God, in whom we live; X107686 O Thou in whom
O God, thou Giver of all good. 1864
O life that makest all things; X107201 O life that maketh
O still in accents sweet
One holy Church of God
Out of the dark the circling
Sing forth His high eternal
The loving friend to all
The summer days are come; X109881 The sweet June days
Thou Lord of life, our saving
'Tis winter now
Longstaff, William D., 1822-94

Take time to be holy
Lopatnikoff, Sara Henderson Hay (i.e., Mrs. Nikolai Lopatnikoff) 1906- see Hay, Sara Henderson, 1906-
Lord, Emily Bryant, 1839-86
Maker of earth and sea
Lorenz, S.E. (i.e. presumed identification of "S.E.L." signature)
Ready to suffer grief
Loring, Louisa Putnam, 1854-
O thou who turnest into
Loskiel, George Henry, 1740-1813
Lord, while I with thee
"Louisa E."
I love to think of my home; R103592 Home, sweet home
Louise Henriette von Brandenburg see Luise Henriette ...
Loveless, Robert C.
Every day with Jesus
Loveman, Robert
Here let thy people come
There is a joy the heart can
Lowell, James Russell, 1819-91
Great truths are portions
Men whose boast it is that ye
Of all the myriad moods
Once to every man and nation; X107928 Oft to every man; X111341 When a deed is done
The ages one great minster
The Holy Supper is kept
"What means this glory"
Where is the true man's
Löwenstern, Matthäus Apelles von, 1594-1648
Christe, du Beistand deiner
Christ, thou the champion
Jesus, our Captain, hope
Lord of our life, and God; X104793 Jesus, our Captain
Now let all loudly sing praise
Nun preiset alle Gottes
Lowry, Robert, 1826-99
I need thee, O I need thee (refrain only)
Low in the grave He lay; X105828 Lowly entombed; R110852 Up from the grave
My life flows on in endless
O worship the Lord in the beauty; R106795 O glory hallelujah
Shall we gather at the river; R111953 Yes, we'll gather
What can wash away my stain; R107477 O precious is; X111261 What ... my sin
Where is my wandering boy
Lowry, Somerset Corry, 1855-1932
Son of God, eternal Saviour
Ye who are banded as comrades
Loy, Matthias, 1828-1915
An awe-full mystery is here
At Jesus' feet our infant
Come, humble soul, receive
Give me, O Lord, a spirit
I thank thee, Saviour, for
Jesus, thou art mine forever
Jesus took the babes; X104898 Jesus ... the lambs
Launch out into the deep
Listen to those happy voices
Lord Jesus, though but two or
O Great High Priest, forget
O Lord, who hast my place
The Gospel shows the Father's
The Law of God is good
Though angels bright escape
Lucas, Alice, 20th c
Almighty God, who hearest
Behold, it is the springtide
How wondrous is thy world
Lord, do thou guide me
Lord God, whose breath
May He who kept us through
Out of the depths, O Lord
"Take unto you the boughs"
The Lord, my Shepherd still
Unto the hills I lift mine
Whose works, O Lord, like
Luce, Charles M.
It is so long a way

Ludämilia Elisabeth of Schwarzburg-Rudelstadt, 1640-72
Care for me, O God of grace
Jesus, Jesus, Jesus only; X104688 Jesus, Jesus, only
Jesus, Jesus, nichts als Jesus. 1687
Luise Henriette von Brandenburg, 1627-67
Jesus Christ, my sure Defence; X101223 Christ, my Rock
Jesus, meine zuversicht
Luke, Jemima, 1813-1906
I think when I read that sweet
Luther, Charles C., 1847-1924
Must I go, and empty-handed
Luther, Martin, 1483-1546
A mighty fortress is our God; X100047 A mighty ... our Lord; X100048 A mighty stronghold; X100251 All power is given (Root)
A safe stronghold our God is
A tower of strength our God
Ach Gott vom Himmel seih
Ah, dearest Jesus, holy child; X102480 Give heed, my heart
All praise to thee, eternal (from an ancient requiem, to which stanzas are added) X100262 All praise ... God
Almighty God, I call to thee
Aus tiefer Not schrei' ich zu dir. 1523
By help of God I fain would
Christ Jesus lay in death's
Christ Jesus, once to death
Christ lag in Todesbanden
Come, Holy Spirit, God; X101385 Come, Holy Ghost
Dear Christians, let us all
Dear Christians, one and all
Die Asche will nicht lassen
Dies sind die heil'gen zehn
Ein' feste Burg
Erhalt uns, Herr, bei, deinem
Es woll' uns Gott genädig sein. 1525
Flung to the heedless winds
From heaven high I come; X100161 Ah, dearest Jesus; X102393 From heaven above to; X111208 Welcome to earth
Gelobet seist du, Jesu Christ
Good news from heaven
Gott sei gelobet und gebenediet. 1524
Guds Ord det er vort Arvegods
Had God not come, may Israel
Happy the man who feareth
If God had not been on our
In death's strong grasps
In peace and joy I now depart
In the midst of earthly life
Isaiah, mighty seer, in days
Jesaia, dem Propheten, das
Komm, Heiliger Geist, Herre
Lo! Christ is risen from the
Look down, O Lord, from heaven; X107255 O Lord, look down
Lord Jesus Christ, of Virgin
Lord Jesus Christ, to thee
Lord, keep us in thy Word
Lord, keep us steadfast
May God be praised henceforth
May God bestow on us His grace
Mit Fried' und Freud' ich
Mitten wir im Leben sind. 1524
Now do we pray God, the Holy
Now let us all right merry
Nun bitten wir den Heiligen
Nun freut euch, liebe Christen g'mein. 1523
O God, from Heaven look down
O Holy Ghost, to thee we pray
O Holy spirit, come, we pray
O Jesus Christ, all praise
O my dear heart, young Jesus

Our Father, thou in heaven
Our Saviour to the Jordan
Out of the depths I cry; X102379 From ... I cry to; X102380 From ... I raise to; X108158 Out of the deep I
Praise we the Lord and bless; X107337 O Lord, we praise
That we our will to Him might
That man a godly life
The eye can naught but water
The mouth of fools doth God
Thy mercy, Lord, to us
To Jordan came our Lord
To shepherds as they watched
Today we celebrate the birth
Vater unser im Himmelreich. 1539
Vom Himmel hoch da Komm' ich
Vom Himmel kam der Angel Schar
Wär Gott nicht mit uns diese
We all believe in one true God
We now implore God the Holy
Welcome to earth, thou
When Rome had shrouded earth
Wilt thou, O man, live happily

Lutheran Church, General Council. S.S. Book, 1887
My Church! My Church! My dear

Lutheran Church, Ohio Synod. Gesangbuch, 1870
In thy dear name and by thy

Lyman, Helen Hoyt, 1887-
Since I have felt the sense

Lynch, Roberta B.
Science the angel with the flaming

Lynch, Thomas Toke, 1817-71
A thousand years have come
Christ in His word draws near
Dismiss me not thy service
Gracious Spirit! dwell with
How calmly the evening
Lift up your heads, rejoice!
My faith it is an oaken staff
O where is he that trod
The Lord is rich and merciful
Where is thy God, my soul

Lyon, Carrie Ward, 1879-
Praise ye, praise ye the Lord

Lyon, George W.
Go and tell the sweet old; R109363 Tell it o'er and
I am trusting in my Saviour
Jesus my Saviour, look on me
Saviour, keep us close

Lyon, P.H.B., 1893-
Lift up your voice, ye Christian
O God, before whose altar

Lysaght, S.R., 1870-1941
Let us be faithful to our

Lyte, Henry Francis, 1793-1847
Abide with me: fast falls; X100097 Abide ... fast breaks the morning (Woods)
Far from my heavenly home
God of mercy, God of grace
Jesus, I my cross have taken; X105006 Know, my soul, thy; X105007 Know, O child, thy; X109325 Take, my soul, thy
My spirit on thy care
O that the Lord's salvation
Pleasant are thy courts
Praise, Lord, for thee in
Praise, my soul, the King
Praise the Lord, His glories
Redeemed from Guilt, redeemed
Sweet is the solemn voice
The mercies of my God
There is a safe and secret
'Tis a pleasant thing to see
When at thy footstool, Lord

Lyth, John, 1821-86
There is a better world, they

Lyttle, Charles H., 1884-
Bring, O Past, your honor
Praise God, the Love we all
Rejoice in love we know

M

"M.A.", Fr., O.C.S.O.
In this your month, Creation's
M A L [pseud presumed to be Lathbury, Mary Ann. See her
Take thou the heart
"M.B.", Sr.
Heart of the Holy Child
O sing a joyous carol
"M.J.", Fr., O.C.S.O.
All of seeing, all of hearing
Lady in sorrow, silent
"M.L.B."
Our Father, God of life
NOTE ON FILING ORDER: Mac, Mc, and M' are interfiled as though spelled Mac

McAfee, Cleland B., 1866-1944
There is a place of quiet rest; R107085 O Jesus, blest
MacAlister, Edith F.B.
Father, hear us as we pray
McCheyne, Robert Murray, 1813-43
Chosen not for good in me
I once was a stranger to grace
When this passing world is
McComb (or M'Comb), William, 1793-
Chief of sinners though I be
McConnell, J. Edwin, 1892-1954
I am happy today; R111666 "Whosoever" surely
McCook, Henry C.
Lord of the endless age! We raise
McCrae, John, 1872-1918
In Flanders' fields
McDaniel, Rufus H., 1850-1940
What a wonderful change in my; R108914 Since Jesus came into
MacDonald, George, 1824-1905
O God, whose daylight leadeth
O Lord of life, thy quickening
Our Father, hear our longing
They all were looking for
MacDonald, Mary, 1789-1872
Child in the manger
McDonald, William, 1820-1901
I am coming to the cross; R103815 I am trusting, Lord
Macduff, John Ross, 1818-95
Christ is coming! let creation
Everlasting arms of love
Jesus wept! those tears are
Mace, Nellie B.
To thee, O God, we bring
We are hid with Christ
McFadyen, Henry Richard, 1877-
The lone, wild fowl
MacFarland, John T.
He is coming! He is coming!
MacFarlane, J.
Far, far away on Judea's; R102556 Glory to God
McFayden, Henry R., see McFadyen, Henry Richard, 1877-
McGranahan, James (i.e., G.M.J.)
Someone will enter the pearly
McGregor, Ernest F., 1879-
Lift high the triumph song
O blessed day of Motherhood
McHose, Irvine N.
O, the great love the dear Saviour; R107603 O, such wonderful
Mackay, J.B.
Rouse, ye Christian workers; R111722 Winning souls, winning
Mackay, Margaret, 1802-87
Asleep in Jesus! blessed
Mackay, William Paton, 1839-85
We praise thee, O God! for; X111106 We praise ... the Son (Kuipers); R100345 Alleluia! Thine the
MacKaye, Percy, 1875-1956
Holy, holy, holy, Lord thy
MacKeever, Harriet Burns, 1807-87
Jesus, high in glory
When Jesus shall gather; R103306 He will gather

Mack, Alexander, sr., 1679-1735
O how is the time so urgent
O! wie ist die Zeit so wichtig
Mack, Alexander, jr., 1712-1803
Bless, O Lord, this church
MacKellar, Thomas, 1812-99
All unseen the Master walketh
Book of grace and book of
Father! in my life's young
Give me a foot-hold on
Give me to know thy will
I thank the Lord, my Maker
In the vineyard of our Father
O the agonizing prayer
There is a land immortal
McKelway, A.J.
O little Child of Bethlehem
McKenzie, William P.
Happy the man whose heart
In mercy, in goodness, how
O Love divine, that dwells
Praise now Creative Mind
There are none friendless
Trust the Eternal when
What brightness dawned
McKinney, B.B., 1886-1952
All on the altar dear Jesus; R106038 My all for thee
As He heard his waiting; R104375 In the old-time way
Blessed Saviour, we adore; R102527 Glorious, Glorious
Christ the Saviour came; R103265 He lives on high
Come, linger here with; R111608 Whisper a prayer
Coming now to thee, O Christ; R108813 Send a great revival
Draw near, draw near
God give us Christian homes
Have faith in God when your
Have you failed in your plan; R108227 Place your hand
Holy Spirit, breath on me (cf: Hatch, Breath on me)
I am satisfied with Jesus
I know the Bible was sent
In thy holy temple
Jesus is standing at your heart's; R111330 What will you do
Lead on, O King of glory; R105075 Lead on, lead on
'Neath the stars of the night; R106244 'Neath the old olive
O, come, all ye that labor; R101542 Come to the Saviour
Out in the darkness of sorrow; R109079 Somebody needs
Send a revival, O Christ; R105688 Lord, send a revival
Serve the Lord with gladness
"Take up thy cross and follow"; R111578 Wherever he leads
While passing thro' this world; R105159 Let others see Jesus
Maclagan, William Dalrymple, 1826-1910
Be still, my soul, for God
Holy Spirit, Lord of love
It is finished! Blessèd Jesus
Lord, when thy kingdom comes
The saints of God! their
What thanks and praise to thee
MacLeish, Archibald, 1892-
The people of the earth
Yet when the splendor of
MacLeod, John, 1840-98
Blessèd Jesus, high in glory
MacLeod, Norman, 1812-72
Courage, brother! do not
With gladsome hearts we come
McManus, S.B.
Dear Lord, I come at last
I would that I might walk
Love consecrates the humblest
McNaspy, Clement
Look down to us, St Joseph
McNaughton, J.H.
There is beauty all around
McNeely, Edwin, 1891-
Jehovah the Lord, Our Sa-

viour
MacNutt, Frederick Brodie, 1873-1949
Let all the multitudes of light
McPhail, John
All those who love and obey; R110145 They to my precepts
McWhood, Leonard Beecher, 1870-
All people of the earth
Madan. Collection: Appendix 1763
Now begin the heavenly theme
Madison, Elizabeth Syle, 1883-
In sweet fields of autumn
Magdeburg, Joachim, 1525-1583 or later
Wer Gott vertraut, hat wohl gebaut. 1572
Who puts his trust in God
Who trusts in God, a strong
Magdeburg, Geistliche lieder, 1540
Rejoice, rejoice ye Christians
Mahlmann, Siegfried August, 1771-1826
God bless our native land
Gott segne Sachsenland
Major. Book of praise for home and school, 1869
See the shining dew drops
Malan, Henri Abraham César, 1787-1864
It is not death to die
Nein, nein, das ist kein
No, no, it is not dying
Malin, Annie
God, our Father, hear us
Malloch, Douglas
Thank God for the things
Malmivaara, Wilhelmi, 1854-1922
Lord, as a pilgrim on earth
Mann, Frederick, 1846-1928
My God, my Father, make me
Mant, Richard, 1776-1848
Bright the vision that delighted
For thy dear saints; X102262 For all thy saints; X102320 For thy dear saint
God, my King, thy might
Round the Lord in glory; X105726 Lord, thy glory fills
Son of man, to thee I cry; X108752 Saviour, who exalted; X109095 Son of God! to Thee
Mantzen, Felix
Mit Lust so will ich singen. 1526
Manuale cantus sancti. Ratisbon, 19th c
O King of might and splendor
Rex summae majestatis
Manwaring, George
Lord, we ask thee, ere we
O, how lovely was the morning
Sing we now at parting
'Tis sweet to sing; R110794 'Twas Jesus died
We meet again in Sabbath
March, Daniel, 1816-1909
Hark, the voice of Jesus; X103181 Hark ... Jesus crying
Marckant, John, 16th c
O Lord, turn not away thy face; X107335 O Lord ... thy face away; X107336 O Lord... thy face from me
Marcy, Elizabeth Eunice, 1822-
Out of the depths to thee I
Markant, John, see Marckant, John
Markham, Edwin, 1852-1940
He pressed on before
Here on the paths of everyday
Of all things beautiful
The crest and crowning
We are all blind, until we
We men of earth have here
Marks, Josephine Preston Peabody (Mrs. L.S. Marks) see Peabody, Josephine Preston
Marlatt, Earl Bowman, 1892-
Angels we have heard (French carol arr)
"Are ye able"; X100490

Are ye able, asked; R105745 "Lord, we are able"
Be of good cheer
God of the Spirit-Wind
If I can keep one spirit
No longer, Lord, thy sons
Spirit of Life, in this new
Through the night the dreamers
Marot, Clement, ca 1497-1544
O Lord, hear thou my calling
Marquis, Don, 1878-1937
A fierce unrest seethes
Marriot, John, 1780-1825
Thou, whose almighty word
Marsden, Joshua, 1777-1837
Go, ye messengers of God
Marshall, Louis
A new shrine stands
Martens, Frederick H.
When blossoms flowered 'mid; R106655 O come let us adore
Martin, Civilla D., 1868-1948
Be not dismayed whate'er; R102840 God will take care
Why should I feel discouraged
Martin, Henry Arthur, 1831-1911
O Rock of ages, one Foundation
Sound aloud Jehovah's praises
The heavenly King must come
Martin, Hugh, 1890-
Christ who welcomed little
Lord, Jesus, in thy footsteps
Martin, John
We build an altar here
Martin, Sallie (presumed pseud. of Fanny Crosby)
Conquering now and still to
Martin, Samuel Wesley, 1839-
The gospel bells are ringing; R102879 Gospel bells, how
Martin, W.C.
In the warfare that is; R105914 May the Lord depend
The name of Jesus is so sweet; R104784 "Jesus," O how sweet
Though the angry surges roll (arr); R100435 And it holds, my anchor
Where He may lead me I will; R104824 Jesus shall lead me
Martineau, Harriet, 1802-76
Faith grasps the blessing
Martineau, James, 1805-1900
A voice upon the midnight air
He who himself and God
Thy way is in the deep
Where is your God? they say
Mary Francis, Sr.
Accept, kind Father, bread and
Because thou hast made charity
Bringing our praise, we kneel
Holy is God! the light
To God our Father, Builder
Mary Teresine, Sr.
From the depths we cry
Mary Xavier, Sr. (secular name: Sybil F. Partridge)
Lord, for tomorrow and its
Masefield, John, 1878-
By weary stages, the old world
O Christ who holds the open
Sing, men and angels, sing
The water's going out to sea
Mason, Caroline Atherton, 1823-90
O God, I thank thee for each
Mason, Jackson, 1833-89
Forty days of Eastertide
Mason, John, ca 1645-94
Blest day of God! most calm
How shall I sing that majesty
I've found the pearl
Lord, for the mercies of
My Lord, my love, was crucified
Now from the altar of my heart; X106372 Now ... of our hearts
Thou wast, O God, and thou
What shall I render to my God
Mason, William, 1725-97
Again returns the day of

holy; X100153 Again the day returns
To Jesus Christ be glory
Massey, Gerald, 1828-1907
Surrounded by unnumbered foes
There lives a voice within me
Through all the long dark
Masterman, John Howard Bartram, 1867-1933
Almighty Father, who dost
Grant us thy peace; for thou
Lift up our hearts, O King
Masters, Mary
'Tis religion that can give
Mathams, Walter John, 1853-1931
Christ of the upward way
"God is with us, God is with"
Jesus, Friend of little
Now in the days of youth
Stand fast for Christ
Mather, Howard E.
Where winds the road
Mathesius, Johannes, 1504-65
Lord God, who art my Father
My Jesus' grace and blessing
My heart its incense burning
Matheson, Annie, 1853-1924
Dear Master, what can children
Lord, when we have not any
Matheson, George, 1842-1906
Gather us in, thou love
Jesus, Fountain of my days
Make me a captive, Lord
O Love that wilt not let me go; X107371 O Love that will not
There are coming changes
Mathews, Basil Joseph, 1879-1951
Far round the world thy
Matson, William Tidd, 1833-99
God is in His temple
Lord, I was blind; I could not
O blessed life! The heart at
Teach me, O Lord, thy holy
Matters, Margaret Glenn
O Jesus, our dear Master
O Love, our Mother, ever near
Matthias, John B.
I saw a way-worn traveler
Mauburn, Jean (John), d 1503
Dost thou in a manger lie
O Lord Jesus, I adore thee
Maude, Mary Fawler, 1819-87
Thine for ever! God of love
Maurer, Irving, 1878-
O God, hear thou the nation's
O God, we pray for faithful
Maurer, Oscar E., 1878-
Brother man, awake! Strength
The Son of God, the Prince (with Marion Maurer)
Maurice, Bertha Helena
Sweet Sabbath! day of sacred
Maurice, May
Thou spotless Lamb of God
Maxwell, James, 1720-1800
Didst thou, dear Jesus, suffer
Go forth, ye heralds, in my
Maxwell, Mary E.
Thy voice hath spoken, souls
Maxwell, Mary Hamlin, 1814-53
Saints of God! the dawn
Maxwell, William
Jesus, Master, hear me now
O for the death of those
May, Caroline Elizabeth, 1808-73
O Saviour, where shall guilty
Mayer, Harry H.
Bow down thine ear, Lord
Come, O holy Sabbath evening
God of Israel, keep us
In sunshine and in storm
O God, my ever constant
Pledging our lives and our
Rejoice, and offer thanks
To worship God in truth
Where Judah's faithful sons
With the voice of sweet song
Medley, Samuel, 1738-39
Awake, my soul, in joyful;

X100677 Awake ... to joyful
Come join, ye saints, with
I know that my Redeemer lives; X103929 I know ... O the sweet joy; X103930 I know ... comfort; X109808 The Saviour lives
Join, all who love the Saviour's
O could I speak the matchless
O what amazing words of grace
Meigs, Charles D.
Lord, help me to live; R111947 Yes, others, Lord
Meigs, Mrs. M.N.
Hark, a burst of heavenly; R109273 Sweet and clear
Meinhold, Johann Wilhelm, 1797-1851
Gentle Shepherd, thou hast
Guter Hirt, du hast gestillt. 1835
Tender Shepherd, thou hast
Meir b. Baruch of Rothenburg
Lo, as the potter molds
Meisser, Leonhard
Winter reigns o'er many
Melanchthon, Philip, 1497-1560
Dicimus grates tibi, summe
Herr Gott, dich loben alle
Lord God, we all give praise; X105482 Lord ... all to thee
Our thanks and praise to thee
To God let all the human race
Melmbold, Ludwig
Lord, grant that we e'er pure
Mencken, Lueder, 1658-1726
Come, be my heart's beloved
Mendes, Fred de Sola
Our pious fathers built their
To Bethel came the patriarch
Mentzer, Johann, 1658-1734
I praise thee, O my God
Lord Jesus, thou the Church's
O dass ich tausend Zungen
O Jesu, einig wahres Haupt. 1726
O that I had a thousand voices
O would, my God, that I could
Menzies, G.K., 1869-1954
What heroes thou hast bred
Mercedes, Sr.
Glorious Patron! Low before
Meredith, George, 1828-1909
In singing till his heaven
We sing the rapture
Meredith, Isaac H., 1872-
Seal us, O Holy Spirit; R108774 Seal us, seal us
Merrick, James, 1720-69
Eternal God! we look to thee
How sweet thy dwellings, Lord
O turn, great Ruler of the skies
To thy pastures, fair
Merrill, William Pierson, 1867-1954
Not alone for mighty empire
Rise up, O men of God; R100504 Arise, arise; X100519 Arise, O youth
We knelt before kings, we bent
Merrington, Ernest Northcroft, 1876-1953
God of eternity, Lord of
Merryweather, F.B., 1883-
To you was given, O saint
Mesechre, Mary I.
Arise, arise and shine
Metcalfe, L.C.
Holy, righteous, heavenly King
Metrical version of Psalms, 1909 see U.P. Board of Publication, 1909
Metzler, A.
Keep me, O my blessed Jesus
Soon falls the evening's
When trials and temptations; R110076 There is sweet rest
Meusslin, Wolfgang, 1497-1563
Christ, everlasting Source
The Lord my Shepherd is
Meyer, Sebastian W.
We build our school on thee
Meyer, Simon, ca 1720-60
Redeemer of mankind, God of
Meyerhardt, Max
Ten thousand martyrs died
There is a mystic tie
When Israel to the wilderness

Meyfart, Johan Matthaeur, 1590-1642
Jerusalem, du hochgebaute Stadt
Jerusalem! high tower thy
Jerusalem, thou city fair
Midlane, Albert, 1825-1909
How solemn are the words
Revive thy work, O Lord
There's a Friend for little
Miles, Alfred H.
The trumpet call of duty
Miles, C. Austin
I come to the garden alone; R100428 And He walks with me
Miles, Sarah Elizabeth, 1807-77
Thou who didst stoop below
Millay, Edna St Vincent, 1892-1950
O God, I cried, no dark; X109948 The world stands out
Miller, Emily Huntingdon, 1833-1913
I love to hear the story
Kingdom of light! whose
Tell the blessed tidings
Miller, Joaquin, 1839-1913
They sailed! they sailed!
Miller, John, see Mueller, John
Miller, Samuel Martin, 1890-
In the holy Father's keeping
O God, who saidst, "Let there"
When Jesus comes in glory
Milligan, James L., 1876-
There's a voice in the wilderness; X103143 Hark! a voice
Mills, Charles S., 1861-1942
Lord, thou hast known our joy
Mills, Elizabeth, 1805-29
O land of rest for thee; R111224 We'll work till
We speak of the realms
Mills, William G.
Arise, O glorious Sion
We'll sing the songs
Milman, Henry Hart, 1791-1868
Bound upon th'accursed tree
O help us Lord; each hour
Ride on! ride on in majesty
The chariot! the chariot! its wheels
When our heads are bowed; X111480 When the heart is
Milner-Barry, Alda M., 1875-1940
Good Joseph had a garden
It is the joyful Easter
Milton, John, 1608-74
God of our saving health
How lovely are thy dwellings; X103712 How ... dwellings, Lord
Let us with a gladsome mind; X108263 Praise, O praise (Baker); R102285 For his mercies aye
Ring out, ye crystal spheres
Rise, God! judge thou the
The Lord will come and not be
Minkler, Ross H.
Grace, dear Lord, grace; R110814 Under the shadows
Minter, K.C.
Sitting at the feet of Jesus
Mishler, Roy S.
Close to my Savior, there
Missionary minstrel, 1826
For the mercies of the day
Mitchell, E. Craige
Father, I come to thee; X102103 Father, I go to
Mitchell, Elizabeth Harcourt, 1833-
King of glory! Saviour dear
Mitchell, I.L.
Hark! I hear my Saviour say; R101800 Do not turn the lambs
Mohler, J.S.
With thankful hearts, O Lord
Mohr, Joseph, 1792-1848
Holy night! peaceful night; X108902 Silent night, holy
Holy Spirit, hear us; X103575 Holy Spirit, hear us
Silent night, holy night; X108901 Silent ... yet while; X108899 Silent ... golden; X108900 Silent

... through; X108903 Silent
... peaceful; X109229 Still the night
Stille nacht, heilige nacht
Moise, Penina, late 19th c
All living souls shall bless
Blest is the bond of wedded
Firm this corner-stone be
God supreme! to thee we pray (with Edward Calish)
Great Arbiter of human fate
In God the holy, wise and just
Into the tomb of ages past
O God, all gracious! In thy
One God! One Lord! One mighty
Praise ye the Lord! for it is
Pray when the morn unveileth
Molanus, Gerhard Walther, 1633-1722
Ich trete frisch
Thy table I approach
Molitor, Wilhelm
O Queen of peerless majesty; R107597 O stand beside us
Möller, Johann J.
I am content! My Jesus liveth
Ich hab g'nug: mein Jesus
Moller, Martin, 1547-1606
Help, Helper, help in fear
Moment, John James, 1875-
God of compassion, in mercy
Men and children everywhere
Monod, Theodore, 1836-1921
O the bitter shame and sorrow
Monro, Edward, 1815-66
In his own raiment clad; X108783 See Him in raiment
Monsell, John Samuel Bewley, 1811-75
Christ is risen! Alleluia
Christ is the foundation
Come and deck the grave
Earth below is teeming; R106522 O Almighty Giver
Fight the good fight with all
God is love! the heavens tell; X102669 God ... by Him upholden
God of that glorious gift
Holy offerings, rich and rare
I hunger and I thirst
Labouring and heavy laden
Light of the world, we hail
Lord of the living harvest
Lord, to whom except to thee
My sins, my sins, my Saviour
O Love divine and golden; X107355 O Love ... and tender
O Saviour, who in love didst
O thou, whose mercy found me
O worship the Lord in the; X111861 Worship the Lord in
O'er the distant mountains
On our way rejoicing
Rest of the weary, Joy of
Sinful, sighing to be blest
Sing to the Lord a joyful song
Sing to the Lord of harvest; X101505 Come, sing to the Lord
Sweet is thy mercy, Lord
Teach me to do the thing that
To thee, O dear, dear Saviour
When cold our hearts and far
Yes, I do feel, my God, that I
Montefiore, Florence
Come, let us praise our God
Forgive us Lord, we turn to
Montgomery, Ignatius, 1776-1841
At God's right hand in
Montgomery, James, 1771-1854
A poor wayfaring Man of grief
According to thy gracious
Almighty God, in humble
Angels from the realms of
At evening time, let there be
All hail, our church's Elder
Be joyful in God, all ye
Behold! the Christian warrior; X109442 The Christian warrior

Blessed be thy name Jesus; X102180 Father, throned on
Bright and joyful is the morn
Call Jehovah thy salvation; X101122 Call the Lord thy sure; X102275 "For-ever" ... Father; X104244 In darkness as in light; X106070 My Father's house
Come in, thou blessed of the
Come let us sing the song
Come to Calvary's holy
Command thy blessing from
Daughter of Zion, from the
Faith, hope, and charity
Father of eternal grace
Father! reveal thy Son in me
"Father, thy will, not mine"
For ever with the Lord
Friend after friend departs
Glad was my heart to hear
Glory to the Father give
Go to dark Gethsemane
Go to the grave in all thy
God is in his holy temple
God is my strong salvation
God is our refuge and defense
God made all His creatures free
Hail to the Lord's Anointed; X102629 God comes, with
Hark! the song of jubilee
Here, in thy name, eternal
Holy, holy, holy Lord God of
Hosanna! be the children's
How beautiful the sight of
I love the Lord! He lent an
In one fraternal bond of love
In the hour of trial
In time of tribulation
Jesus, our best beloved Friend
Lift up your heads, ye gates
Like Mary at her Saviour's
Listen to the gentle promptings
Lord, for ever at thy side
Lord God the Holy Ghost
Lord, let me know my end
Lord of hosts! to thee we
Lord, pour thy Spirit from on; X107460 O pour thy Spirit
Lord, teach us how to pray; X107668 O, thou by whom we
Lord, thou hast been thy people's
Magnify Jehovah's name; X105843 Magnify th' Eternal's
Not in Jerusalem alone
O bless the Lord, my soul!
O God, thou art my God
O Spirit of the living God; X107590 O ... the fullness
O thou, my light, my life
O where shall rest be found
O who, in such a world as
One prayer I have -- all
Our heavenly Father, hear
Out of the depths of woe
Palms of glory, raiment
Peace that passeth understanding
People of the living God
Pour out thy Spirit from on
Prayer is the soul's sincere; R103272 He prayeth best (Coleridge); X108366 Prayer ... heart's
Rest from thy labor, rest; X100716 Be known to us
Send out thy light and truth
"Servant of God, well done"
Servants of God, in joyful
Shepherd of souls, refresh
Sing we the song of those
Songs of praise the angels
Sow in the morn thy seed
Thank and praise Jehovah's
The glorious universe around
The God of harvest praise
The Lord is King: -- upon
The Lord is my Shepherd, no want; R103493 His yoke is easy
The Lord will grace and
The tempter to my soul hath
The world in condemnation lay
This stone to thee in faith; X111385 When here, O Lord
Thousands, O Lord of hosts
Thy law is perfect, Lord of
To thy temple I repair;

X110716 To thy temple we
We bid thee welcome
What are those soul-reviving
What is the thing of greatest
What secret hand, at morning
When Jesus left his Father's;
X111419 When ... into Salem
When like a stranger on our
When on Sinai's top I see
Who are these in bright array; X111253 What are these in
Work while it is today
Yea, I will extol thee

Moore, C. L.
O, anywhere my Saviour leads

Moore, Francis John
Father of mercy, Lover of all

Moore, Henry, 1732-1802
Supreme and universal Light

Moore, James C., 1888-
I have heard of a land; R106250 Never grow old
Thou, O Christ of Calvary

Moore, Jessie Eleanor
Our thoughts go round the

Moore, Leslie, H., 1909-
Far in the West the sunset's
Jesus, we love to meet thee

Moore, Thomas, 1779-1852
Come, ye disconsolate
Hark! the vesper hymn; X104959 Jubilate! Jubilate!
O thou who driest the mourner's
Sound the loud timbrel o'er
The bird let loose in eastern
The turf shall be my fragrant
Thou art, O God, the life
Thy heaven, on which 'tis

Moore, Thomas Vernon, 1818-71
Father, let thy smiling face

Moravian traditional, etc.
NOTE: Entry terms Unitas Fratrum and Bohemian Brethren are not used herein. However Bohemian traditional, Czeck traditional are used. They include some secular (folk) items, whereas Moravian is religious only.

Jesus hath procured salvation
Jesus, 'till my latest breath
O Spirit, of grace, thy kindness
Thanks and praise, Jesus
The word of God which ne'er
Who overcometh shall abide
With awe, and deeply bowed

Moravian Emigrants hymn
Blest be the day when I must

Mordecai b. Sabbatai
The lifting of my hands, accept

More, Henry, 1614-87
God is ascended up on high
The holy Son of God most high

Morell, Thomas, 1781-1840
Father of mercies, condescend

Morgan, Angela
Our glowing praise to thee
To be alive in such an age

Morgan, Edmund Robert, 1888-
Be thou exalted, holy Lord
Thee, living Christ, our eyes

Morgen- und Abendsegen. Waldenburg, 1734.
Fang dein Wek mit Jesu an
Go with Jesus to thy task
With the Lord begin thy task

Morison [Morrison] John, 1750-98
Come, let us to the Lord
The people that in darkness
The race that long in darkness
To us a Child of hope is born
'Twas on that night when doomed

Morley, Frederick B.
O Church of God, united

Morris, Mrs. C.H., 1862-1929
For God so loved this sinful; R110559 'Tis true, O, yes
Fully surrendered, Lord divine; R104086 I will be true
If you are tired of the load;

R104974 Just now, your
I've heard of a beautiful city; R104195 I'll make it my home
Jesus is coming to earth again; R102551 Glory, Glory! Joy to
Nearer, still nearer, close to
The fight is on, the trumpet
When the early morning; R103794 I am in my Father's
Morris, Eliza Fanny, 1821-74
God of pity, God of grace; X102763 God of pity, Lord of
Morris, George Perkins, 1802-64
Searcher of hearts, from mine
Morris, Robert, 1818-
Each cooing dove, and sighing; R106775 O Galilee! sweet
Morris, William, 1834-96
From far away we come to you; R109827 The snow in the street
He that dies shall not die
Masters in this hall; R106491 Nowell! Nowell! Nowell
Morrison [Morison] John, 1749-1798
see Morison, John, 1749-98
Morrison, Margaret
Love one another, word of
We lift our hearts in praise
Morse, Kenneth I., 1913-
God of the moving years
Lord of loveliness, all beauty
Move in our midst, thou Spirit
O Christ, we climb the hill
O Giver of delightful fields
O Master, may my days be spent
Morton, Mary Ann
O happy home! O blest abode
Sweet is the peace the gospel
Moser, Jessie F.
I come to thee, O Father
Moses, Isaac S.
O holy Sabbath-day, draw near
Moses ibn Ezra
God that doest wondrously
Thou, O Almighty, knowest all
Mote, Edward, 1797-1874
My hope is built on nothing; X106294 Nor earth nor hell; R107940 On Christ, the solid
Moule, Handley Carr Glyn, 1841-1920
Come in, O come! The door
Lord and Saviour, true
My glorious Victor, Prince
Moultrie, Gerard, 1829-85
Come, faithful people, come
There came three kings ere
We march, we march to victory; X106654 O come in the might; X105880 March on, march on; X111030 We come in the might
Moultrie, John, 1799-1874
All is o'er: the pain
Moxley, Henry R., 1881-
Father of Jesus, by whose
Lord of true light, we
Praise we now the God of
Mozarabic rite, 5th-8th c
Sing Alleluia forth in duteous; X108934 Sing ... loyal praise
Mozley, Henry Williams, 1842-
Lord, who fulfillest thus
Mudge, E. Leigh
Lord, wilt thou in this temple
Mudie, Charles Edward, 1818-
I lift my heart to thee
Jesus, who called'st little
Mueller, John, 1756-90
Christ the Lord, the Lord most
O that we all could quite
Sing, with humble hearts
Muenter, Balthasar, 1735-93
Behold the man! how heavy
Full of reverence at thy word
Lord! thou Source of all

Muhlenberg, William Augustus, 1796-1877
I would not live alway; I ask
Jesus' name shall ever be
Like Noah's weary dove
O cease, my wandering soul
Saviour, who thy flock
Shout the glad tidings;
X109014 Sion, the marvelous
Since o'er thy footstool here
Mühlmann, Johannes, 1573-1613
Dank sei Gott in her Höhe
While yet the morn is breaking
Muirhead, Lionel B.C.L., 1845-1925
The Church of God a kingdom is
Müller, Michael, 1673-1704
Good and pleasant 'tis to see
Mumford, Alfred H., 1864-
Saviour, thy love hath guided
Mund, E.D.
Amid the trials which I meet;
R110332 Thou thinkest, Lord
In joyful high and holy days;
R111837 Wonderful love
Munger, Harriet Osgood
O my Father, I would know
Munich. Mss. 15th c
In mitten in des lebens zeyt
Munro, Kathryn
O thou within whose sure
Munson, Ida Norton
His face? I know not whether
Münster Gesangbuch. 1677
Fairest Lord Jesus; X100757 Beautiful Saviour
Schönster Herr Jesu
Murray, Robert, 1832-1909
From ocean unto ocean
Our blessèd bond of union
Our loved Dominion bless
Sow the seed beside all waters
Murray, Robert D.
Lord, thou lovest the cheerful
Murray's Hymnal, 1852
Praise we the Lord this day
Myers, Ernest, 1844-1921
Now in life's breezy morning
Myers, Frederick William Henry 1843-1901
Hark, what a sound, and too divine

N

Nachtenhöfer, Caspar Freidrich, 1624-85
Dies ist die Nacht, da mir
Lord Jesus, thou art going
So gehst du nun mein Jesu, hin
This night a wondrous revelation
Naidu, Sarojini, 1879-1949
Nay, do not grieve though life
Naisbitt, Henry W.
For our devotions, Father
Rest, rest for the weary soul
This house we dedicate
What voice salutes the startled
Nakatenus, W. Coeleste palmatum, 1669
Ye souls of the faithful! Who
Narayan Vaman Tilak, 1862-1919 see Tilak, Narayan Vaman, 1862-1919
Nass, John, 1670-1741
Savior of my soul, Let me
Nathan, El. pseud see Whittle, Daniel W.
National anthems, hymns, etc. see these entry words:
Canadian
Great Britain
Japanese
Newfoundland
U.S.A.
Navajo (Indians) Prayer
Lord of the mountain
Navra, Sophia
I leave the burdens of my life
Naylor, C.W.
Are you adorning the doctrine
God's way is best
Heaven is a holy place;
R108907 Sin can never enter

I have yielded myself; R111946 Yes, my heart says
Once again we come to the house; R110713 To thy house, O Lord
Shall I be ashamed of my Saviour
The world of sinners; R100021 A gospel others

Neale, John Mason, 1818-66
A time to watch, a time
All is bright and cheerful
Around the throne of God
Art thou weary, art thou laden; X100532 Art ... heavy laden
Blessed Saviour, who hast; X100947 Blessed ... thou hast
Christ is gone up; yet ere
Earth today rejoices
Earthly friends will change
Good King Wenceslas
Holy Father, thou hast taught; X103523 Holy ... taught us
Lift up, lift up your voices
O Lord of hosts, whose glory
O thou, who by a star did'st
O thou, who lov'st to send
O thou, who through this holy
O very God of very God
The day, O Lord, is spent
The earth, O Lord, is one great; X109501 The earth ... one wide
The world itself keeps Easter
There is a stream whose
They whose course on earth
'Twas about the dead of night
With Christ we share a mystic

Neander, Christoph Friedrich, 1724-1802
Dir, Herr, sei dieses Kind
This child we dedicate; X110181 This .. consecrate

Neander, Joachim, 1650-80
All my hope on God is founded
For help, O whither shall I
Heaven and earth, and sea
Here behold me, as I cast me
Himmel, Erde, Luft und Meer
Lobe den Herren, den mächtigen König
O praise Jehovah! who reigneth
Praise to the Father, the
Praise to the Lord, the Almighty; X108312 Praise ... He is King; X108349 Praise ye the Lord
Praise we the Lord, for His
Wondrous King, all-glorious
Wunderbarer König

Needham, John, d 1787
Awake, my tongue, thy tribute
Holy and reverend is the name
Rise, O my soul, pursue the

Neele, Henry, 1798-1828
God of mercy, throned on high

Negro Spirituals

NOTE: Instead of this classification, hymnal BZ uses the term American folk hymn. This permits a blend with White Spirituals, and other melodies, which have long been especially known through such books as Sacred harp.

And I couldn't hear nobody
Deep river, my home is over
Go tell it on the mountain; R111400 When I was a sinner; R111593 While shepherds kept
Good-bye, mourner, I'm going
Great day! Great day, the; R101155 Chariot rode on the
Gwine to lay down my burden; X103780 I aint gwine study
I have a mother yonder
In-a this-a band we have; R102601 Go, tell, Mary and
It's me, it's me, it's me
I've got a robe
Let us break bread together; R111389 When I fall on my
Listen to the Lambs
Little David, play on your
Lord, I want to be a Christian
My Lord, what a mourning;

X106154 My Lord ... morning
No-body knows the trouble
O Mary, don't you weep; R109086 Some of these mornings
Steal away, steal away; R106147 My Lord calls me
Swing low, sweet chariot
There is a Balm in Gilead
We are climbing Jacob's ladder; X101816 Don't you want to go
Were you there when they crucified
What wondrous love is this
When Israel was in Egypt's land; R102579 Go down, Moses
Neibaur, Alex
Come, thou glorious day
Neisser, Friedrich Wenzel, 1716-77
From the doctrines, I'll never
Nelson, David, 1793-1844
My days are gliding swiftly; R102294 For now we stand
Nelson, Horatio, Earl, 1823-1913
As the sun doth daily rise
From all thy saints in warfare
Netherlands see Dutch
Neumann, Caspar, 1648-1715
From eternity, O God
God from all eternity
God of Ages, all transcending
Gott, du hast in deinem Sohn
Gracious God, again is ended
Herr, es ist von meinem Leben
Neumann, G. J.
Again, O Lord and Saviour
Healer Divine, who walkest
King of my soul, a crown
Now all is still; Time holds
Neumark, Georg Christian, 1621-81
He that confides in his
He who would be in God: X111664 Whoso in God alone
If thou but suffer God; X105092 Leave God to order
Let, O my soul thy God direct
O he who trusts in God's
O thou that rulest earth
Wer nur den lieben Gott Lässt
Neumeister, Erdmann, 1671-1756
I know my faith is founded
Ich weiss, an wen ich gläube. 1718
Jesus nimmt die Sünder an. 1718
"Jesus, sinners doth receive"; X109002 Sinners Jesus will
Sinners Jesus will receive; R108943 Sing it o'er
Sinners may to Christ draw
Nevill, E. Mildred, 1889-
God is good; we come before
Nevin, Edwin Henry, 1814-89
Always with us, always with
New Christmas carols, 1642
The old year now away is
New Church (English Conference) hymnal see Hymns of the English Conference, 1880
New Churchman.
O Sion rise in glory
Newbolt, Henry, 1862-1938
O Lord almighty, thou whose
The river of Death has
There's a breathless hush
Newell, Ebenezer Josiah, 1853-1916
We praise thy name, all-holy
Newell, Laura E.
A city awaits us we soon; R107068 O, I long, yes
I am trusting day by day
Walking, Saviour, close to
Newell, William R., 1868-
Years I spent in vanity; R105493 Mercy there was great
Newfoundland National anthem see Boyle, Cavendish. When sun rays crown
Newhall, Charles S., 1842-
O Jesus, Master, when today

Newman, Frederick William, 1856-1934
Jesus, Lord of our salvation
Newman, John Henry, 1801-90
Firmly I believe and truly
Green are the leaves; R107428 O Mother Maid, be
Help, Lord, the souls which
Lead, kindly Light
Praise to the Holiest
Newman, Louis I.
O soul supreme above us
Thou ever present Perfect
Newton, A. L.
My God, whose gracious pity
Newton, James, 1732-90
Let plenteous grace descend
Newton, John, 1725-1807
Amazing grace! how sweet
Approach, my soul, the mercy-seat
As the sun's enlivening eye
As when the weary traveller
Begone unbelief; for my; X100797 Begone ... my Saviour
Be still, my heart, these
Behold the throne of grace
Chief Shepherd of thy chosen
Come, my soul, thy suit; X101466 Come ... thy plea
Day of judgment -- day of wonders (Dies irae)
For a season called to part
For mercies, countless as
Glorious things of thee are; X102533 Glorious things are (Phelps)
Great Shepherd of thy people; X100151 Again our earthly; X101720 Dear Shepherd of; X102992 Great ... people, here
How lost was my condition
How sweet the Name of Jesus
How tedious and tasteless
I saw One hanging on a tree [perhaps another John Newton]
If to Jesus for relief
In evil long I took delight
In mercy, not in wrath
Jesus, hear our humble prayer
Jesus, who knows full well
Joy is a fruit that will
Kindly spring again is here
Let hearts and tongues unite
Let me dwell on Golgotha
Let us love, and sing
Let wordly minds the world
Lord, dost thou say, "Ask"; X100426 And dost thou say
Lord, I am come! Thy presence
Lord, I cannot let thee go
Mary to the Saviour's tomb
May He, by whose kind care
May the grace of Christ our
Now, gracious Lord, thine
Now let us join our hearts
Now may He who from the dead
On what has now been sown; X111267 What contradictions
Once I thought my mountain
One there is, above all
Precious Bible; what a treasure
Quiet, Lord, my froward heart
Rejoice, believer, in the
Safely through another week
Saviour, visit thy plantation
Sinner, art thou still secure
Sinner, hear the Saviour's
Sweet was the time when first
Sweeter sounds than music
The Lord, who truly knows
The peace which God alone
Though troubles assail and; X110398 Though ... assail us
'Tis a point I long to know
When I by faith my Saviour see
While filled with sadness
While with ceaseless course
Why should I fear the darkest
Yes, since God Himself hath
Newton, Martha Mills
The shepherd's heart is; R103276 He seeks His wandering
Newton, Maude deVerse
He sent His word, His holy
Nichol, Henry Ernest (Colin

Sterne, pseud) 1862-1928
We've a story to tell;
R102305 For the darkness
Nicholas, Tressilian George, 1822-91
Lord! when before thy throne
Nicholls.
O thou best Gift of heaven
Nicholson, James, 19th c
Lord Jesus, I long to be;
R111610 Whiter than snow
The Lord is my light
There's a beautiful land;
R104339 In that beautiful
Nicholson, John
"Come, follow me," the Savior
While of these emblems we
Nicholson, Mary Ann
Easter flowers are blooming
Nicholson, Sidney Hugo, 1875-1947
How joyful 'tis to sing
Nicolai, Philip, 1556-1608
How bright appears; X103649 How brightly beams; X103650 How brightly shines
How lovely shines
O Morning Star so pure; X107414 O Morning Star, how; X107415 O Morning Star, so fair
Sleepers, wake, a voice
Sleepers, wake, the watch-cry
The morning Star upon us
Wachet auf! ruft uns die Stimme
Wake, arise! a voice appalling
Wake, awake, for night; X106405 Now let every tongue; X109034 Sleepers, wake; X110934 Wake, O wake, for; X110935 Wake, O wake! with
Wie schön leuchtet
Niedermeyer, Mabel, 1899-
Our church proclaims God's
Niedling, Johann, 17th c
O Heiliger Geist
O Spirit of Life, O Spirit
Nigidius, Georg, 1525-88
Aus meines Herzens Grunde
My inmost heart now raises
Niles, John Jacob
In calm and cool and silence (from Whittier)
Niles, Nathaniel, 1835-
Precious promise God hath; R104093 I will guide thee
Ninde, Henry S.
Thou who taught the thronging; X110250 Thou didst teach
Nitschman, Anna see Zinzendorf, Anna Nitschman, 1715-60
Nitschmann, John, 1712-83
Christ is the Vine, we branches
Noble, James Ashcroft, 1844-96
Lord Jesus, in the days of old
Noel, Baptist Wriothesley, 1799-1873
Glory to God, whose Spirit
There's not a bird with
Noel, Caroline Maria, 1817-77
At the Name of Jesus, every; X104373 In the name of Jesus
Noel, Gerard Thomas, 1782-1851
If human kindness meets
When musing sorrow weeps
Norris, John W.
Give peace, O God, the nations
North, Frank Mason, 1850-1935
Jesus, the calm that fills
O Master of the waking world
The world's astir! the clouds
Thou Lord of light, across
Where cross the crowded ways
Where lies our path? We seek
Norton, Andrews, 1786-1853
My God, I thank thee! My no
Where ancient forests widely
Norton, Nathanael
"Come unto me," it is the
Norton, Thomas, ca 1532-

1583/4
Give thanks to God, for good
Not unto us, O Lord of heaven
Praise ye the Lord, for He is
Norwegian hymn
The hour in dark Gethsemane; R102468 Gethsemane, Gethsemane
Nourse, Laura C.
Now sweeping down the years
With love and peace and joy
Noyes, Alfred, 1880-1958
Knowledge, they say, drives
Now to those who search
Nunn, Marianne, 1778-1847
One is kind above all others
Nurnberg Gesangbuch, 1676
All depends on our possessing
Alles ist an Gottes Segen
Nussbaum [Nusbaum], Cyrus S.
Would you live for Jesus; R103487 His pow.r can make
Nyberg, Laurence T., 1720-92
Holy Trinity, we confess with; X103588 Holy ... thanks and
Nystrom, Per Olaf, d 1830
O Fount of truth and mercy

O

"O ---, Miss Mary"
God of the universe, to thee
Oakey, Emily Sullivan, 1829-83
I am so glad that our Father; R103805 I am ... Jesus loves
Sowing the seed by the daylight; R109139 Sown in the darkness
Oakley, Charles Edward, 1832-65
Hills of the north, rejoice
Oakley, Ebenezer Sherman, 1865-1934
Enduring Soul of all our life; X109180 Eternal Spirit, Source
In life's earnest morning
Oatman, Johnson, 1856-1926
A full surrender I have made; R104518 I've surrendered all
Christ will me His aid afford; R104674 Jesus is now
How to reach the masses, men; R105234 Lift Him up, lift
I am so happy in Christ today; R104662 Jesus included me
If I walk in the path-way; R111413 When I've gone
If thou wouldst have the dear; R103771 Humble thyself
I'm pressing on the upward; R105616 Lord, lift me up
In the blood from the cross; R101745 Deeper yet, deeper
In this world of sin and care; R108876 Shine in me, yes
There's not a friend like; R104695 Jesus knows all
These scenes, so bright, now; R102863 Good-by, good-by
Time is gliding like the shuttle; R106534 O, behold the Bridegroom
When storms of life are round; R100386 Alone with God
When upon life's billows; R101603 Count your blessings
Occum, Samson, 1723-92
Awaked by Sinai's awful sound
Now the shades of night are
O'Connell, William
O Holy Name of Majesty
Odhner, Vincent C.
The heavens are thine, thou
Thine advent, Lord, we hail
Oerter, Maurice Frederick, 1864-
To thee, most holy Lord
Offord, Robert M., 1846-
Jesus, heed me, lost and
We give thee thanks, O God

Ogden, Althea A.
Father, let thy blessing touch
Ogden, William A., 1841-97
Anywhere, dear Saviour, in thy
Baptize us anew with power
I've two little hands to work
Jesus, the loving Shepherd; R105823 Lovingly, tenderly
Scattering precious seed by; R109136 Sowing in the morning
Sweet are the promises; R111543 Where He leads I'll
'Tis the grandest theme thro'; R103240 He is able to deliver
Working, O Christ, with thee
Okely, William, 1762-1824
While successive years are
Ola Olude, A.T. see Olude, A.T. Ola
Oldenburg, Theodor V., 1805-42
Deep and glorious, word
Deep and precious, strong
God's eternal word is spoken
Thine, O Jesus, now and ever
Olearius, Johannes, 1611-84
Ach, wie gross ist deine Gnade
Again is come the new Church-year
Christ Himself, my Pride and; X104588 Jesus Christ, my Pride
Comfort, comfort ye, my people
Gelobet sei der Herr
God loved our erring mortal
Herr, öffne mir die Herzenstur
Jesus selbst, mein Licht, mein
Lord, open thou both heart
Lord, open thou my heart to
O, how great is thy compassion
O praise the Lord! His name
Our God so loved the world
Thank God! My Jesus cleanseth
The Lord, my God, be praised
The new Church year again is
Tröstet, tröstet meine Lieben
When afflictions sore oppress
Olearius, Johann Gottfried, 1635-1711
Come, thou precious Ransom
Es war die ganze Welt
Komm, du wertes Losegeld
When all the world was cursed
Olinger, Mrs. W.H.
I would not have my way
Oliver, Richard J.
Who hath believed after; R103290 He was wounded
Olivers, Thomas, 1725-99
O thou God of my salvation
The God of Abraham praise; see Jewish doxology ...
Olson, Ernst William, 1870-
Behold, by grace, and grace; X100813 Behold, by sovereign
Glorious Yule-tide, glad bells
God of peace, in peace preserve
Jesus, let my final rest
Mine eyes unto the mountains
Olude, A.T. Ola
Jesus, we want to meet
Omaha (Indians) traditional
Dha-ke-de hia-u-dha
Down through the ages
Ω [Omega]. Chelsea, 1838
Lord of my life, whose tender
Onderdonk, Henry Ustic, 1789-1856
Heirs of unending life
How wondrous and great
The Spirit, in our hearts
When Lord, to this our western
Opitz, Martin, 1597-1639
Arise and shine in splendor
Brich auf und werde lichte
Light of light, O Sun
O Sion, rise and brighten
Orr, C.E.
As pilgrims and strangers
Orsborn, Albert
Let the beauty of Jesus

Orthodox Eastern Church.
Liturgy and ritual see Greek traditional -- which is chiefly liturgical text
Orwig, Aaron W.
O God of peace, thee we
O'Shaughnessy, Arthur, 1844-81
With wonderful deathless
Osler, Edward, 1798-1863
Father, 'tis thine each day
Lord of the church, we pray
May we thy precepts, Lord
Mighty Saviour, gracious King
O God, unseen but ever near, Our blesséd rest (with S. Longfellow)
O God, unseen yet ever near, Thy presence may we feel
Pardoned through redeeming
Worship, honour, glory
Ostergaard, Christian
That cause can neither be lost
Oswald, Heinrich Siegmund, 1751-1834
O let him whose sorrow; X111-564 Where the mourner
Overby, Oscar R., 1892-
As the sunflower turns
God be with you now and ever
How oft, O Father, my heart
I would gather treasures
The chimes of the sabbath
There's a Kingdom fair
Owen, Frances Mary, 1842-83
Lighten the darkness of our
When thy soldiers take their
Owens, Priscilla Jane, 1829-1907
Give me the Bible, Star of
We have heard the joyful sound; X111052 We ... heard a joyful
Will your anchor hold; R111051 We have an anchor
Oxenham, John, 1852-1941
All labor gained new dignity
Forth to the fight he fared
In Christ there is no East
Lord God of hosts, whose
'Mid all the traffic of the ways
My own dear land
O God, within whose sight
Peace in our time, O Lord
To every man there openeth
Unbar the door! and let
What do I owe? Nay Lord
Where are you going, Great-heart

P

"P.M."
Pilgrim on earth, home and
Packard, Charlotte Mellen, 1839-1923
For common gifts we bless thee
O Shadow in a sultry land
Paderborn Gesangbuch, 1726
My Jesus, pierced for love of
Pados, Virginia Bogdan
Alleluia! Alleluia! Ye redeemed
O Love that nothing can efface
Page, Mary Judd
Ye who are called to labor
Page, T.E., 1850-1936
Soldier, go! Thy vow is
Pageant of the Shearmen and Tailors, 15th c
Lully, lulla, thou little tiny; X105832 Lullay, thou little; X107564 O sisters too, how
Palgrave, Francis Turner, 1824-97
Christ in his heavenly garden
City not made with hands; X107696 O thou not made with
Lord God of morning and of night
O Light of life, O Saviour
Thou say'st, "Take up thy"
Thou who once on mother's; X110331 Thou that once, on
Though we all in sinful; X110401 Though we long, in
Palmer, Alice Freeman, 1855-1902
How sweet and silent is

Palmer, Horatio Richmond, 1834-1907
Christ is knocking at my sad
My griefs of heart abound
Precious Saviour, dear
There's a Rose that is
Yield not to temptation; R100599 Ask the Saviour
Palmer, Phoebe
Blessed Bible, how I love it
O, now I see the crimson wave; R109453 The cleansing stream
Watch, ye saints, with eyelids; R105337 Lo! He comes, Lo!
Palmer, Ray, 1808-87
Come Jesus, from the sapphire
Come, Jesus, Redeemer, abide
Eternal Father, thou hast said
In thee, O God, the hosts
Jesus, Lamb of God, for me
Jesus, these eyes have never
Lord, my weak thought in vain
Lord, thou hast taught our
My faith looks up to thee
Take me, O my Father, take me
Thine holy day's returning; X110457 Thy holy day's
Thou who rollest the year
We stand in deep repentance
We welcome thee in Jesus'
When downward to the darksome
With thine own pity, Saviour
Pappus, Johann, 1549-1610
Lord Jesus Christ, I humbly
Park, J. Edgar, 1879-
O Jesus, thou wast tempted
We would see Jesus; X111177 We would ... Mary's; X111178 We would ... on the mountain
Park, Roswell, 1807-69
Jesus spreads His banner o'er
Parker, Edwin Pond, 1836-1925
Come to Jesus, ye who labor
Hail, holy Light! the world
Lord, as we thy name profess
Master, no offering
Parker, Theodore, 1810-60
O thou great Friend to all
Parker, William Henry, 1845-1929
Holy Spirit, hear us
Tell me the stories of Jesus
Parkin, Charles C., d 1953
See the morning sun ascending
Parnell, Thomas, 1679-1717
Holy Jesus! God of love
Parochial Hymn book, 1897
Immaculate Mary, your praises; X104215 Immaculate ... Our hearts; X104216 Immaculate ... Thy praises
Parr, Harriet, 1828-1900
Hear our prayer, O heavenly; X103319 Hear my prayer
Parr, Leonard A., 1880-
Lift up your hearts, ye people
Parsons, Charles
O do not bar your mind
Parsons, R.G., 1882-1948
We hail thy Presence glorious
Partridge, Edward
Let Sion in her beauty rise
Partridge, Samuel William, 1810-1903
How dearly God must love us
Partridge, Sybil F. (Lord, for tomorrow) see Mary Xavier, Sr.
Patton, A.B.
Faith of our mothers, living
Patterson, Adoniram Judson, 1827-1909
In thee, our Father, are we all
Pattinson, Janet Steel, 1848-
While sinks our land to realms
Patton, Kenneth L., 1911-
Before the stars a man is
Brief our days, but long for
Feet of the urgent pioneer
Let all men living in all lands
Let all who live in freedom
Man is the earth upright
Now once again the heaven
Ours be the poems of all
Quest of the ages, goal of men

The blessings of the earth
The earth is home and all
We journey with a multitude
When we have ended searching

Paul the Deacon, 8th c
E'en in thy childhood, 'mid
Let thine example, holy John
Sing we the praises of the great

Paulsen, P.C.
Blest is he who cries to
Let us go to Galilee
Take my heart, O Jesus

Pawels, E.
Great art thou, God!

Paxton, Thomas
God of the glorious sunshine

Payn, A.A.
There is One whom I love

Payne, John Howard, 1792-1852
'Mid pleasures and palaces; R103591 Home, home, sweet

Peabody, Josephine Preston (Mrs. L.S. Marks), 1874-1922
Truly the light is sweet

Pease, Theodore Claudius, 1853-
Not long upon the mountain's; X106318 Not long on Hermon's

Peckham, John, d 1294
Hail, true Victim, life

Pedersen, Bertel
Fear, my child, thy God
Jesus, let my soul be fed

Peers, E. Allison, 1890-1952
O heavenly Beauty, lovlier far

Pellegrin, Abbé, d 1745
O come, divine Messiah

Pembroke, Lady Mary Sidney
see Sidney, Sir Philip.
O Lord, in me there lieth

Pendleton, Eo.
The first fruits of the land

Pendleton, W.F.
City strong and mighty
Glory flaming in the cloud
Jesus, Saviour, heavenly

Penfield, Thornton B., 1867-
In loving adoration

Penn, W.E.
There is a Rock in a weary; R109994 Then why will ye die

Penn, William Joseph, 1875-1956
Enthrone thy God within thy

Pennefather, William, 1816-73
Jesus, stand among us

Penner, Edwin
O soul, you know the present; R110776 Trust your hand into

Pennewell, Almer T., 1876-
So lowly doth the Saviour ride

Penrose, Charles W.
Beautiful Sion for me
God of our fathers, we come
O ye mountains high, where
School thy feelings, O my
Up, awake, ye defenders of

Penstone, Maria M., 1859-1910
God has given us a book full
When lamps are lighted

Percy, Frances A.
O Father, hear my morning

Percy, William Alexander
They cast their nets in Galilee

Perkins, Emily S.
Thou art, O God, the God; X108098 Our God, He is a God

Perkins, H.S.
Gird on the armor, brave soul; R109070 Soldiers of progress

Perkins, Jeanette E.
We thank thee, Lord, for eyes

Perpetual Adoration, Asso. of see The Association of Perpetual Adoration

Perronet, Edward, 1726-92
All hail the power of Jesus'; X100213 All hail the great Immanuel's
Hail, Holy, Holy, Holy, Lord

Pestel, Thomas, 1584-1659
Behold the great Creator

Peter, P.A.
Who shall ope for us

Peters, Mary Bowly, 1813-56
Holy Father! we address thee
O Lord, while we confess
Through the love of God; X110429 Through ... our Saviour
With thankful hearts we meet
Petersen, H. H.
I'm a pilgrim; I'm a stranger
Petersen, Johann Wilhelm, 1649-1727
Jesus cometh to fulfill
Jesus, Lord of life and glory
Petri, Olavus, 1497-1552
Blest Easter Day, what joy
Our Father, merciful and good
Thy sacred Word, O lord, of
Petursson, Hallgrim, 1614-74
And then the Savior turned
Come, Lord, Thyself, in all
Come, Lord, Thyself with thine
Jesus, the mighty work
The Lord into his Father's
The Savior in Gethsemane
The soldiers led the Savior
Upon the cross down-lying
Upon the cross the robber
Pfeffel, Gottlieb Konrad, 1736-1809
Jehova! Jehova! Jehova! Deinem Namen sei Ehre
Jehovah, Jehovah, Jehovah, Thou art worthy
Pfefferkorn, Georg Michael, 1645-1732
Was frag' ich nach der Welt
What is the world to me
Pfeil, Christoph Carl Ludwig von, 1712-84
Blessèd Jesus all our hearts
O blest the house, whate'er
Wohl einem Haus, da Jesus
Phalen, Frank
Father in heaven, we wait
Phelps, Sylvanus Dryden, 1816-95
Saviour, thy dying love
This rite our blest Redeemer
Phelps, William W.
Awake! O ye people, The Savior
Come, all ye Saints who dwell
Come, all ye sons of Sion
Come, let us sing an evening
Gently raise the sacred strain
Glorious things are sung
If you would hie to Kolob
Now let us rejoice, in the day
Now we'll sing with one accord
O God, the Eternal Father
Praise to the man who communed; R103106 Hail to the Prophet
The Spirit of God like a fire; R111219 We'll sing and we'll
We're not ashamed to own
Phelps, William W. see paraphrases of; Watts, I'm not ashamed Newton, Glorious things
Philippson, L.
From heaven's height, Soft, vernal
Philipson, David
See, O God, we children come
Phillimore, Greville, 1821-84
Every morning mercies new
O Lord of health and life
Summer ended, harvest o'er
We pray thee, Jesus, who didst
Phillips, Charles Stanley, 1883-1949
Not by far-famed deeds alone
Spirit of Jesus, who didst
Stalwart as pillars bearing
Phillips, D. C.
To thee, O gracious Lord, we
Phillips, Harriet Cecilia, 1806-84
We bring no glittering
Piae cantiones, 1582
Gabriel's message does away
Now the spring has come again

On this day earth shall ring
On this day every where
Personent hodie voces
Sing aloud on this day
Spring has now unwrapped
With merry heart let all
Pictet, Benedict, ca 1650-ca 1710
Christians, sing out with
Faisons éclater notre joie
Pierpoint, Folliott Sandford, 1835-1917
For the beauty of the earth; X102308 For the joy of human; R105625 Lord of all, to thee
Pierpont, John, 1785-1866
Another day its course hath
God Almighty and All-seeing
Gone are those great and good
O bow thine ear, Eternal One
O God, I thank thee that
O thou to whom, in ancient
On this stone now laid with
Pierson, Arthur Tappan, 1837-1911
To thee, O God, we raise
With harps and with viols; R110828 Unto him who hath
Pierson, Hattie H.
Open wide thy heart today; R108036 Only trust Him
The hand that was nailed
Pierson, Lydia Jane
Thou who art enthroned
Piggott, William Charter, 1872-1943
For those we love within
Heavenly Father, may thy
In our work, and in our play
Lord, from whose hand we take
Lord of life, who once wast
Pigott, Jean Sophia, 1845-82
Jesus, I am resting, resting
Thou whose name is called
Pilcher, Charles Venn, 1879-
Father, in thy presence
Pilsach, L.R. Senfft von, see Senfft von Pilsach, L.R.
Pirks, Edward B.
Light, that from the dark
Pise, Charles Constantine, 1802-66
Let the deep organ swell
Pitts, William S.
There's a church in the valley; R101537 Come to the church
Plummer, Evelyn E.
I bow in utter need
O lead and guide us Lord
O Lord, thy love through
O precious sign and seal
The heavens are thine
The Savior reigns, The Lord
To thee, O Lord our hearts
Watch o'er me, O my Savior
Plumptre, Adelaide M.
Keep thyself pure! Christ's
Plumptre, Edward Hayes, 1821-91
Hark, the heaven's sweet melody
March, march onward, soldiers
O Light, whose beams illumine
O Lord of hosts, all heaven
Rejoice, ye pure in heart
Thine arm, O Lord, in days of; X110157 Thine arm, O Christ
Thy hand, O God has guided
Plunkett, William Conyngham, 1828-97
Our Lord Christ hath risen
Plymouth hymnal, 1893
Show me myself, O holy Lord
Pocket hymn book, 1786
Peace, troubled soul, thou
Pohjala, Jenny, 1899-
Jesus, hear my humble pleading
Pohlman, Charles Augustus, 1777-1843
Peace be to thy every dwelling
Polack, William Gustave, 1890-1950
Dear Lord, to thy true servants
God the Father, Son, and Spirit

Polish traditional, etc.
Infant holy, Infant lowly
Out of our suffering, out of
Slumber, O slumber, dear Jesus
Pollard, Adelaide Addison, 1862-1934
"But for a moment" -- this
Have thine own way, Lord
Pollard, Josephine, ca 1840-
Beyond the sunset's radiant
I have work enough to do
Joy-bells ringing, children
Pollock, Charles Edward
Come, ye wanderers, all (arr); R101571 Come, ye weary, heavy
Little children, praise the
Pollock, Thomas Benson, 1836-96
By the gracious saving call
Faithful shepherd, feed me
Father, hear thy children's
God the Father, God the Son
Great Creator, Lord of all
Jesus, from thy throne on high; X102089 Father from thy throne
Jesus, in thy dying woes; X104565 Jesus, all our ransom; X104567 Jesus, all thy labor; X104660 Jesus, in thy thirst; X104731 Jesus, loving to the; X104802 Jesus, pitying the; X104913 Jesus, whelmed in
Jesus, Son of God most high
Jesus, we are far away
Jesus, with thy church abide
Spirit, Strength of all
Teach us what thy love has
We are soldiers of Christ
We have not known thee as we
Weep not for Him who onward
Poole, William C., 1875-1949
Have you prayed all night; R101774 Did you pray till
Just when I need Him, Jesus
Pope [The Holy Father] see the given name used during incumbency
Pope, Alexander, 1688-1744
A herald voice the lonely
Rise, crowned with light
The time shall come when, free
What conscience dictates; X102136 Father of all, in
Poppe, Erhard Christoph, 1804-78
Jesus, our Savior, grant us
Seliger Friede, Köstliche
Posse, Katarina Elisabet see Ehrenberg-Posse, Katarina Elizabeth, 1818-80
Poteat, Edwin McNeill, 1892-1955
Eternal God, whose searching
Light of the world, how long
Pott, Francis, 1832-1909
Angel voices, ever singing
Potter, Thomas Joseph, 1827-73
Brightly gleams our banner
Pounds, Jessie H. Brown, 1861-1921
Anywhere with Jesus I can (with Mrs. C.M. Alexander)
I know that my Redeemer liveth
I must needs go home; R109915 The way of the cross
Lord of the nations, Father
O scatter the seeds; R109978 Then day by day
Peace through the cross
Turn your faces toward
We are going down the valley
Powell, Roger K., 1914-
Lord, we thank thee for our
Powell, Thomas Edward, 1823-1901
Bow down thine ear, Almighty
Poyry, Edla
My beautiful home is in heaven
Praetorius. Musae sioniae, 1607
We thank thee, Jesus
Wir danken dir, Herr Jesu
Praetorius, Johann, 1738-82
Thy blood, so dear and

Pratt, O. A.
Afar on the mountain; R109977 Then come, wanderer
He comes! He comes with
Pratt, Parley P.
An angel from on high; R105343 "Lo, in Cumorah's"
As the dew from heaven
Behold thy sons and daughters
Come, O thou King of Kings
Father in heaven, we do
Jesus, once of humble birth
The morning breaks, the shadows
Truth eternal, truth divine
Ye children of our God
Ye chosen Twelve, to you
Pray, Benjamin S.
Master and Lord, 'tis good to
Preiswerk, Samuel, 1799-1871
Das ist der Gemeinde Stärke
Die sach' ist Dein, Herr Jesu
Hark! the church proclaims
Lord Jesus Christ, the cause
Lord Jesus Christ, the work
The work is thine, O Christ
Prentiss, Elizabeth, 1818-78
More love to thee, O Christ
Presbyterian hymnal. Phila., 1874
Before thee, Lord, a people
Presbyterian sources see also United Presbyterian ... written as U.P. ...
Presley, L. G.
I have a friend in whom I; R107882 O yes, He cares for
Price, Mrs.
Above the trembling elements
Prid, William, 16th c
City of Peace, our mother; X107425 O mother dear (F.B.P.)
O mother dear, Jerusalem
Of stones full precious are
Prid, William, see also F.B.C. Jerusalem ...
Proctor, Adelaide Anne, 1825-64
I do not ask, O Lord, that
My God, I thank thee, who hast; X108112 Our God, we thank
The shadows of the evening
The way is long and dreary
Promnitz, Balthasar Friedrich von, 1711-44
Church of Jesus, sing
Proprium Officiorum. Prague, 1720
God in whom all graces dwell
Prost, Christen, d 1676
Fesans raijouissance
Now, brothers, lift your
Proud, Joseph, 1745-1826
Come in, thou blessed honored
Down from the worlds of
How shall we celebrate thy
I love the Lord; He heard my
I love the voice divine that
Jerusalem, arise, the heavenly
My Lord, my God, my only King
Now blessing, honor, glory
Pruden, Edward Hughes, 1903-
O God of our fathers, we praise
Prudentius, Aurelius Clemens, 348-413
All hail, ye little martyr
Bethlehem, of noblest cities
Blest martyr, let thy triumph
Corde natus ex parentis
Despair not, O heart, in thy
Earth has many a noble city; X100885 Bethlehem in land of; X100887 Bethlehem, of noblest
Father most high, be with us
Father of spirits, whose
Lo! golden light rekindles
Now with creation's morning
Now with the rising golden
O martyrs young and fresh; X100222 All hail, ye little
Of the Father's love begotten; X107920 Of ...

heart begotten; X103248
He is here, whom
Servant of God, remember
Sweet flowrets of the martyr
The wingèd herald of the day
Ye clouds and darkness, hosts
Prynne, George Rundle, 1818-1903
Jesus, meek and gentle
Psalms and hymns, 1858
Dear Lord, before we part
Psalms in meter, 1905
My trust is in the Lord
Psalter. New version see Tate & Brady
Psalter, 1860 (Kennedy)
Lord, hear my prayer, and let
Psalter, 1912 see U.P. Psalter, 1912 (i.e. United Presbyterian Psalter, 1912
Pugh, Alice
In the heart of Jesus
Pullen, Alice M., 1889-
At work beside his father's
For man's increasing quest
Thou perfect Hero-Knight
Pulsifer, Harold Trowbridge, 1886-
I shall go out as all men go
Punshon, William Morley, 1824-81
Listen! the Master beseecheth; R109995 Then work, brothers
Sweet is the sunlight after
Purchas, John, 1823-72
Evensong is hushed in silence; R111009 We are weary
Pye, Henry John, 1825-1903
In His temple now behold Him
Pyper, F.R., 1859-1915
O God of nations, hear thy

Q

Quarles, Francis, 1592-1644
Thou art my life; if thou but
Quarles, John, 1624-65
Fountain of light, and living
Long did I toil, and knew (with H.F. Lyte)
O King of kings, before whose
Queen's College, Oxford, 1812
The boar's head in hand
Quin, Malcolm, 1855-
Now comes the light for which
Say not they die, those martyr
We move in faith to unseen
Quirsfeld, Johann, 1642-86
Sinful world, behold
Plechtchéev
When Jesus Christ was yet a child

R

Rabanus Maurus see St Rabanus Maurus
Räder, Friedrich
Wait on God, and trust Him
Rader, Paul
Only believe, only believe
Radford, Benjamin J., 1838-1933
In homes where pride
Raffles, Thomas, 1788-1863
Blest hour, when mortal man
Eternal Father, throned above
Hark, ten thousand thousand
High in yonder realms of light; X103462 High ... realm of
Lord, like the publican
Saviour, let thy sanctions
Thou art my hiding-place
Raile, Vilate
Upon the cross of Calvary
Rambach, Johann Jakob, 1693-1735
A year again is now descending
Baptized into thy name most
Father, Son, and Holy Spirit
How great the bliss to be
I am baptized into thy name; X100711 Baptized into thy
Ich bin getauft auf deinen
Lord Jesus, who before thy
Lord, to thee I now surrender
Mein Schöpfer, steh mir bei
My Maker, be thou nigh
O thou Love unbounded,

grant
Unumschränkte Liebe
Ramler, Karl Wilhelm, 1725-98
Behold, how glorious is yon
Ramsey, Benjamin Mansell, 1849-1923
Teach me thy way, O Lord
Randall, Laura Lee
This is the day, the Lord hath
Rands, William B., 1827-82
One Lord there is, all lords
Rankin, Jeremiah Eames, 1828-1904
Are you weary, are you heavy-hearted; R109637 Tell it to Jesus
Beneath thy shadow hiding
God be with you till we meet; R110521 Till we meet
Gott mit euch, bis wir uns wiederseh'n
Shepherd of one fold is He
Ravenscroft, Thomas. Melismata, 1611
Remember, O thou man, O thou
Rawlett, John, 1642-87
O Holy Ghost, on this great
Rawnsley, Hardwicke Drummond, 1851-1920
Father, whose will is life; X106935 O God, whose will is
Lord Jesus, who at Lazarus'
Saviour, who didst healing
Rawson, George, 1807-89
By Christ redeemed, by Christ
Come to our poor nature's; X101535 Come ... dark nature's; X103529 Holy Ghost, the Infinite; X103578 Holy Spirit, in thy; X103579 Holy Spirit, lamp of; X104816 Jesus, Saviour, infinite
Father, in high heaven
Father of love and power
God the Lord is King; before
In the dark and cloudy day
The God of love my Shepherd
Thou who hast known
Thou who thyself didst sanctify
We limit not the truth; R109649 The Lord hath yet
Who dares to bind to his dull
Raymond, Rossiter Worthington, 1840-1918
Far out on the desolate
Now rest, ye pilgrim host
There dwelt in old Judea R108953 Sing Noel, sing Noel
There's a beautiful star; R109212 Star, Star, beautiful
Reed, Andrew, 1787-1862
Come, my Redeemer, come
Holy Ghost, with light divine; X103580 Holy Spirit, Light
Spirit divine, attend our
Reed, Eliza, 1794-1867
O do not let the Word depart; R107846 O why not tonight
Reed, Ida L.
Choose my path, O blessed; R104971 Just as seemeth good
Do life's storms above thee
He knoweth thy grief
Reed, Luther D., 1873-
O God of wondrous grace
Rees, Bryn Austin, 1911-
Have faith in God, my heart
Rees, Timothy, 1874-1939
God is love: let heaven adore
Lord, who in thy perfect
Reese, Lizette Woodworth, 1856-1935
Glad that I live am I
Reformed Presbyterian Church. Book of Psalms, 1940
O God, thy judgments give
Reitz, Albert S., 1879-
Teach me to pray, Lord, teach; R105327 Living in Thee, Lord
Reusner, Adam, 1496-ca 1575
In dich hab' ich gehoffet
In thee, Lord, have I put my
The Revival, 1859
Hark, 'tis the watchman's

cry
Rexford, Eben Eugene, 1848-
How many times, discouraged; R103721 No, never alone
O where are the reapers; R111538 Where are the reapers
They brought their gifts; R111875 Wouldst bring a gift
Reynolds, Isham E., 1879-1949
Jesus my Lord is real to me
When the sun shines bright; R104681 Jesus is the friend
Rhodes, Sarah Betts, 1829-1904
God who made the earth
Rice, Cale Young, 1872-1943
I have ridden the wind
Rice, Caroline Laura, 1819-
Wilt thou hear the voice of
Richard Rolle of Hampole, d 1349
Lord Jesus, when I think of
Richards, Charles Herbert
Dear land of liberty, Hope of
Our Father, thy dear Name
Richards, Laura E., 1850-1943
The little flowers came
Richardson, Norman E.
My Lord, I do not ask to stand
Richter, Anne Rigby, d 1857
We saw thee not when thou
Richter, Christian Frederick, 1676-1711
"Give me, my child," the Father
Jesus is my Light most fair
My soul before thee prostrate
Thou Lamb of God, thou Prince
Rights, Douglas LeTell, 1891-
Veiled in darkness Judah lay
Riley, John Athelstan Laurie, 1858-1945
Come, let us join the church
Saints of God! Lo, Jesus'
Ye watchers and ye holy ones
Ringmacher, Lorentz
O Jesu, der du felig mach. 1564
Ringwaldt, Bartholomäus, 1532-99
Es ist gewisslich an der Zeit
Gott Heil'ger Geist, hilf uns
Jesus, thou Source of every
Lord Jesus Christ, thou highest
O Holy Ghost, thou gift
O Holy Spirit, grant us grace
The day is surely drawing near (Dies irae)
'Tis sure that awful time will
Rinkart, Martin, 1586-1649
Now all give thanks to God
Now thank we all our God; R100252 All praise and thanks; X106415 Now let us praise
Nun danket Alle Gott
Rippon, John. Selection of hymns, 1787 "K" in Rippon, see "K"
Rist, Johann, 1607-67
All ye Gentile lands, awake
Arise my spirit, bless
Arise, the kingdom is at hand; X100506 Arise, arise, ye; X100520 Arise, sons of the
Auf, auf, ihr Reichsgenossen
Author of the whole creation
Break forth, O beauteous
Du Lebensbrot, Herr Jesu
Father, merciful and holy; X108994 Sink not yet, my soul
Glory, praise, to thee be
Help, Lord Jesus, let thy
Help us, O Lord, behold, we
Hilf, Herr Jesu, lass gelingen
Lord Jesus Christ, thou living
O darkest woe! Ye tears forth
O Jesus Christ, thou Bread of
O living Bread from heaven
O sorrow deep! Who would not
Praise the Lord with hearts
Rise, O Salem, rise and

shine
Rise, children of the Kingdom
Soul of mine, to God awaking
Thou hast canceled my
To thee all praise ascendeth
Wie wohl hast du gelabet
Ritchie, David Lake
As comes the breath of spring
Rivers, W.P.
As Sion's pilgrims in accord R108798 See the righteous
Robbins, Chandler, 1810-82
Lo! the day of rest declineth
Robbins, Howard Chandler, 1876-1952
And have the bright immensities
Now yield we thanks and praise
Put forth, O God, thy Spirit's
Saviour, whose love is like
The Sabbath day was by
Roberts, Daniel Crane, 1841-1907
God of our fathers, whose
Roberts, John, 1731-1806
O blest Communion with the
Roberts, Katherine Emily, 1877-
Awake were they only, those
Now the joyful bells aringing
O Lord, thy people gathered
Roberts, Richard, 1874-
For them whose ways are in the air
Roberts Robert Rowland, 1865-1945
Far off I see the goal
Roberts, Thomas
My Shepherd's mighty aid
Robertson, Nemi
Grace for today, O Love divine
Robertson, William, d 1745
Fair as a beauteous tender
Robertson, William, 1820-64
A little child the Saviour
Robilliard, H.W.
God of love, our Father, Saviour
Robins, Gurdon, 1813-
There is a land mine eye hath
Robins, Henry B.
Eternal Spirit, evermore
Of one blood hath God created
Robinson, Charles Seymour, 1829-99
Saviour, I follow on
Tell me, my Saviour, where
Robinson, Edith
Safe within the arms of Jesus
Robinson, Edwin Arlington, 1869-1935
Dark hills at evening
Robinson, George
One sole baptismal sign
Robinson, George Wade, 1838-77
Loved with everlasting love
Robinson, H. Wheeler, 1872-1945
O thou whose love has brought
Robinson, Joseph Armitage, 1858-1933
'Tis good, Lord, to be here!
Robinson, Paul M., 1914-
Here in our upper room with
Robinson, Richard Hayes, 1842-92
Holy Father, cheer our way
Robinson, Robert, 1735-90
Mighty God, while angels bless; X105630 Lord of every land
Saviour, source of every; X101518 Come, thou Fount
Robinson, W.O.
O hark! A glorious sound
Robinson, William, 1888-
Praise to God, almighty
Rodigast, Samuel, 1649-1708
Was Gott tut, das ist wohlgetan!
Whate'er my God ordains is; X111274 What God ordains; X111338 Whate'er our God; X111340 Whatever God ordains
Rogel, Hans
Ach Gott! verleih mir dein Genad. 1539
Roh, Johann, 16th c <u>see</u> Horn, John, 16th c
Rohr, A.F.
Eternal God, omnipotent

From afar, across the waters
Living Fountain, freely
Lord of life and light
Romanis, William, 1824-99
Lord, who shall sit beside
Pour forth thy spirit from; X108237 Pour down thy Spirit
Round me falls the night
Rome, James J.
Give me, O Lord, an understanding
Rominger, Charles H.
Thou art, O Christ, the light
Rooker, Alfred, 1814-75
O be with us, gracious Father
Rooper, W. J.
Dare to be brave, dare to be; R102228 Fight, then, good
Root, Frederic W.
All power is given unto
see Luther. A mighty . . .
O tender, loving Shepherd
Our God is love, unchanging
Rock of ages, Truth divine
see Toplady. Rock of ages
The heavens declare the glory
Root, George Frederick, 1820-95
Come to the Saviour, make no; R104957 Joyful, joyful, will
She only touched the hem; R107784 O, touch the hem
Why do you wait, dear brother; R111679 Why not? why not?
Rorison, Gilbert, 1821-69
Three in One, and One in Three
Roscoe, William, 1753-1831
Great God! beneath whose
Rose, D. F.
City of David, Bethlehem
Saviour, Redeemer, God of Love
Rose, Elizabeth Dorothy
My case to thee is fully known
Rosenius, Agata, 19th c
Abode of peace, my Father's
Rosenius, Carl Olof, 1816-68
I have a friend, so patient
O precious thought! Some day
With God and His mercy, His
Rosenroth, Christian Knorr von, 1636-89
Come, thou bright and morning-star
Dayspring of eternity, Light; X101515 Come, thou bright; X101674 Dayspring ... Brightness of the Father's; X101676 Dayspring ... Light of Light
Jesus, Sun of righteousness
Morgenglanz der Ewigkeit
Rosewater, Adeline R.
Dear Father, here thy children
We hear the call of Israel's
Ross, Ronald, 1857-1932
Before thy feet I fall
Rosser, John L., 1875-
To Him who hallows all our days
Rossetti, Christina Georgina, 1830-94
In the bleak midwinter
Love came down at Christmas
None other Lamb, none other
O Christ, my God, who seest
O ye who taste that love is
Service and strength, God's
Sooner or later: yet at last
Spring bursts today, For Christ
The shepherds had an angel
We know not a voice of that
What are these that glow
Who has seen the wind?
Rot, Othmar
Mensch! wilt du nimmer traurig seyn. 1564
Rothe, Johann Andreas, 1688-1758
Jesus, I know, hath died for
I now have found for hope
Ich habe nun den Grund
My soul has found the sure
Now I have found the ground
Now I have found the sure
Now I have found the firm
When children, blest by

Jesus
Rouse, Francis, 1579-1659
Thy mercy, Lord, is in the heavens
Routh, Gene
Speak to my heart, Lord Jesus
Rowe, Ed. M.
O sons of Sion, hear the voice
Rowe, James
Earthly pleasures vainly call; R100717 Be like Jesus, this
I was sinking deep in sin; R105804 Love lifted me
Jesus has taken a beautiful; R102450 Gathering buds
My Saviour needs helpers; R104191 I'll go, I'll go
O weary soul, the gate is near; R104975 Just outside the door
Smiling skies will bend above; R111757 With eternal day
Wonderful Jesus! glorious
Rowe, John, 1764-1833
From the table now retiring
Rowell, Eugene
On hills and vales of heaven
Rowland, May, 1870-
Come! Peace of God, and dwell
God of the shining hosts that
The day is slowly wending
Where the great ships, passing
Rowland, Mira
Lord who lovest little children
Rowley, Francis Harold, 1854-1952
I will sing the wondrous; R111943 Yes, I'll sing
Royce, E.
The stars were silent and the hills
Rube, Johann Christoph, 1665-1746
Him on yonder cross I love
Rumsey, Mrs. Mary
Jesus when He left the sky; (authorship disputed)
Runeberg, Johan Ludvig, 1804-77
I lift my eyes unto heaven
Ruopp, Johann Friedrich, d 1708
Erneure mich, o ew'ges Licht
Renew me, O eternal Light
Ruskin, John, 1819-1900
Bend back the lance's point
Russell, Anna B., 1862-1954
There is never a day so dreary; R111842 Wonderful, wonderful
Russell, Arthur Tozer, 1806-74
Give praise to God our King
Jesus, at thine invitation
Jesus, who for my transgression
Lord, our eyes unseal
Night's shadows falling
O God of life, whose power
O gracious Hand that freely
O Jesu, we adore thee
O Jesus, blest is he
The Lord ascendeth up on high
To Him who for our sins was
Russell, Byron G., 1850-
Our Father, unto thee, we now
Russell, Francis Albert Rollo, 1849-1914
Christian, rise, and act thy
Russell, George William, i.e. "A.E.", 1867-1935
The generations as they rise
When the unquiet hours depart
Russell, Matthew, 1834-
A message from the Sacred Heart
O Mary, dearest Mother
Russian traditional, etc.
As light, O Christ, thou
Ay-yukh-nyehm
Easter eggs! Easter eggs! Give to
Gloria, gloria! O come let us
Praise to God in the highest
Step by step (Volga boatmen)
Rutgers, Abraham, 1751-1809
Glory, honor, praise and pure
Rutilius, Martin, 1550-1618

Ach Gott und Herr, Wie gross
Alas, my God! my sins are
Rutström, Andreas Carl, 1721-72
Chosen seed of Zion's children
Come, Saviour dear, with us
My crucified Saviour, despised
Ryden, Ernest Edwin, 1886-
Behold what love, that God
Beyond the everlasting hills
Eternal God, before thy throne
Didst thou, dear Jesus, pray
How blessed is this place
O blessed is the man who stays see Wallin, O blessed is the man . . .
O Lord, now let thy servant
The twilight shadows round me
With solemn joy we come
Ryland, John, 1753-1825
Let us sing the King Messiah
O Lord, I would delight in
Sovereign Ruler of the skies
Ye saints, proclaim abroad
Rypins, Mrs. Isaac L.
Dim mine eyes with many
While yet the earth midst

S

"S.E.L." presumed to be Lorenz, E.S.
"S.M.H."
We know not the time when He; R110930 Waiting and watching
"S.N.D." i.e. Sister of Notre Dame, identified as Mary Xavier, Sr., whose secular name is Sybil Partridge. (There may, however be another person who has used these initials. No universal decision is made herein.)

Sacer, Gottfried Wilhelm, 1635-99
Gott, fähret auf gen Himmel
Lo, God to heaven ascendeth
Sadler, Thomas, 1822-91
The Lord hath said, "Seek ye"
Saint . . .
NOTE: Abbreviation St is used for canonized authors, whether men or women. Persons better known under other form of name are usually granted the alternative. Secular surnames beginning with St follow (the number is small).
St Alfonso de Ligouri, C.SS.R., 1696-1787
From starry heaven descending
Jesus, food of angels
Jesus Lord, be thou mine own
O Bread of Heaven! beneath
O God of loveliness, O Lord
O Mother blest, whom God
Raise your voices vales and; R105061 Laudate, laudate
Uplift the voice and sing; R108305 Praise to Mary
St Amandus, 1300-1365/6 see Suso, Henry
St Ambrose, 340-397
As fades the glowing orb
Before the ending of the day
Blest Spirit, one with God
Come, Holy Ghost, with God
Come, Holy Ghost, who ever One
Come, Holy Spirit, Godhead
Come, thou Saviour of our race
Come thou Redeemer of the earth
Creator of the earth and sky
Creator of the world, we pray
Ere yet in darkness ends
Jesus, the Virgin's crown, do
Let hymns of joy to grief
Maker, keeper, thou, Be my
Mighty God, we humbly pray
NOTE: This 4-line stanza precedes several Zinzendorf hymns.

Now hail we our Redeemer

Nun Komm, der Heiden Heiland
O blessed Light! O trinity
O blest Creator, God most high
O Christ! with each returning
O God, creation's secret force
O God of truth, O Lord of might
O God, the world's sustaining
O Jesus, Lord of heavenly
O Jesu, thou the virgin's
O light, O Trinity most blest
O lux beata trinitas
O Splendor of God's glory
O Strength and Stay upholding
O thou true Life of all that
O Trinity of blessed light; X107786 O Trinity, most; X107787 O Trinity, O blessed
Rejoice, our nature Christ
Saviour of the nations, come; X108728 Saviour of the heathen
Splendor paternae gloriae
Te deum, see Latin, 5th c
Te, lucis ante terminum
The eternal gifts of Christ
Thee, Lord, before the close
Thou who art Three in Unity
To thee before the close of day
Veni, Redemptor gentium

St Anatolius, late 6th c
A great and mighty wonder
Darkening night the land doth
Fierce was the wild billow; X102224 Fierce ... billow wild
The day is past and over
The Lord and King of all

St Andrew of Crete, 660-732
Christian, dost thou see them (ascribed to)

St Anselm of Canterbury, 1033-1109
Come thou, O come: Sweetest
Ah, holy Jesu, see Heermann

St Anselm of Lucca
Jesus, solace of the soul

St Augustine, see "F.B.P.", the Jerusalem hymns

St Bede, the Venerable, 673-735
A hymn of glory let us sing
Hail, harbinger of morn
Sing we triumphant hymns
The great forerunner of the morn; X103044 Hail, harbinger
The hymn for conquering

St Bernard of Clairvaux, 1091-1153
All my hope and consolation
Hail, thou King of saints
I see by rays surrounded
Jesu dulcis memoria
Jesus, highest heaven's
Jesus, how good the thought
Jesus, how sweet the thought
Jesu, Rex admirabilis
Jesu! the very thought is sweet
Jesus, the very thought of thee
Jesus, thou Joy of loving; X102179 Father, thou joy; X107116 O Jesus, Joy of X107517 O Saviour, joy of
Jesus thy memory divine
Light of the anxious heart
O bleeding Head, and wounded
O Haupt voll Blut und Wunden
O Jesu, King most wonderful
O Jesus, Lord, most mighty
O Jesu, thou the beauty art
O sacred head ... X106977 O Head so full
O what precious balm; X104626 Jesus, grant that
Of Him who did salvation
The thought of Jesus, O how
Thousand times by me be greeted
Wide open are thy hands; X111696 Wide ... thy loving

St Bernard of Cluny, 12th c
Brief life is here our portion
Daily sing in praise of Mary; X101635 Daily, daily sing to
For thee, O dear, dear country; X110245 Thou city of the angels
Hic breve vivitur, hic breve

Holy Queen, we come before; X103561 Holy Queen we bend
Hora novissima, tempora
Jerusalem, the glorious
Jerusalem the golden
O bona patria, lumina sobria
The world is very evil; X107454 O peace of all
Thou hast no shore, fair ocean
Urbs Sion aurea, patria
St Bonaventura, 1221-74
In the Lord's atoning grief
Let heaven highest praises
St Clement of Alexandria, ca 170-220
Lead, holy Shepherd, lead us
Master of eager youth
O Guide to every child
Shepherd of tender youth; X108861 Shepherd of eager
Sunset to sunrise changes
St Columba, 521-597
Christ is the world's Redeemer
O God, thou art the Father
St Cosmas, d ca 760
In days of old on Sinai
The sepulcher is holding
St Ephraim the Syrian, ca 307-373
Receive, O Lord, in heaven
Virgin wholly marvellous
St Francis of Assisi, 1181-1226
All creatures of our God; R107463 O praise Him, Alleluia; X101141 Canticle of the sun
Altissimo, omnipotente, bon
Make me, O Lord, an instrument
Most high, omnipotent, good; X101141 Canticle of the sun
O most high, almighty, good
St Francis Xavier, 1506-52
My God, I love thee not because; X106829 O God, I love thee (Spanish, 17th c)
O Deus, ego amo te
O God, thou art the object
St Fulbert of Chartres, ca 1000
Ye choirs of new Jerusalem
St Gelasius. Sacramentary, 492
Lamb of God, O Jesus (Agnus dei)
St Germanus, ca 634-734
A great and mighty wonder
St Gregory the Great, 540-604
Audi, benigne conditor
Christ's loving children
Ecce iam noctis tenuatur
Father we praise thee, Now the night
Kind Maker of the world
Let us keep steadfast guard
Lucis créator óptime
Nocte surgentes vigilemus
Now shadows wane, now hevy night
Now, when the dusky shades
O blest, Creator of the day; X106567 O blest ... of the light
O Christ, our King, Creator
O kind Creator, bow thine ear
O merciful Redeemer, hear
Primo dierum omnium
Source of light and life; X106567 O blest Creator
This day the first of days
Thou loving Saviour of mankind
St Gregory Nazianzen, 325-390
O light that knew no dawn
St Hilary of Poictiers, dd368
Again the slowly circling year
O joy, because the circling
Rejoice, the year upon its way
St Jean de Brebeuf, d 1649
Let Christian hearts rejoice
St John Chrysostom, 347-407
Come, let us worship and fall
St John of Damascus, 8th c
Come ye faithful, raise
The day of resurrection; X101506 Come, sing with holy; X110551 "Tis the day
Those eternal bowers
Thou hallowed chosen morn;

X110267 Thou ... dawn of praise
What sweet of life endureth
St Joseph of the Studium see St Joseph the Hymnographer
St Joseph the Hymnographer, 9th c
And wilt thou pardon, Lord
Let us now our voices raise; X101283 Christians, come, new anthems; X105161 Let our choir new; X105176 Let the saints new; X105197 Let us choral anthems
O happy band of pilgrims
Safe home, safe home in port
Stars of the morning
The abyss of many a former sin
The things of the earth
St Methodius, II, d 836
Are thy toils and woes
St Notker, d 912
The strain upraise of joy
St Patrick, 372-466
Christ be with me
I bind unto myself today; X108684 St Patrick's Breastplate
Today I arise, invoking
St Paulinus of Nola, 353-431
Another year completed
St Peter Damiani, ca 988-1072
From heaven's height Christ
From thee, illustrious Teacher
St Rabanus Maurus, 776-856
All prophets hail thee, from
Christ, the fair glory of
Jesus, Brightness of the Father
O Christ, thy guilty people
O Jesu! life-spring of the soul
Thee, O Christ, the Father's
Tibi, Christe, splendor Patris
Veni creator spiritus see Latin, 9th c
St Richard of Chicester, 1197-1253
Day by day, dear Lord of thee
St Stephen of Mar Saba, 8th c
Art thou weary, art thou see Neale, John Mason
St Theoctistus, ca 890
Jesus, Name all names above
St Theodulph of Orleans, d821
All glory, laud and honor; X100202 All glory, praise
Gloria, laus et honor
Glory and honor and laud
Glory and praise and dominion
To thee be glory, honor, praise
St Therese, of the Child Jesus
O how I love thee Jesus! My
St Thomas à Kempis, ca 1379-1471
Again the Lord's own day
If there be that skills
Light's abode, celestial Salem
O love, how deep, how broad
Our Father's home eternal
St Thomas Aquinas, 1227-74
Adoro te devote
Christ the Word to earth
Ecce panis angelorum
God-head here in hiding
Hail, angelic Bread of heaven
Humbly I adore thee
Humbly we adore thee
Laud, O Sion, thy salvation; X108266 Praise, O Sion
Lauda Sion Salvatórem
Lo! the Angel's Food is given
Lo, upon the altar lies, Bread
Now, my tongue the mystery
Pange lingua gloriosi
Panis Angelicus
O salutaris Hóstia
O saving Victim, opening wide; X107521 O Saviour Victim
Of the glorious Body telling
Sacris solemnis juncta sint
Sing, my tongue, the mystery
Sing, my tongue, the Savior's; X108989 Sing with joy
Sion, praise thy Saviour
Sion, to thy Saviour singing

Tantum ergo Sacramentum
The very Angels' Bread
The Word, descending from above
The Word of God, proceeding; X109565 The heavenly word
Thee prostrate I adore; R103054 Hail, Jesus, hail
Thee we adore, O hidden Saviour; X106568 O, blest memorial
Therefore we, before him
Thus angels' Bread is made
Very Bread, good Shepherd; X107791 O true Bread
With all the powers my poor
Word of God to earth descending

Saint (secular names)

NOTE: Only secular names beginning St follow. Religious names are above.

St John, Frank B.
I do not come because my soul

St Patrick's hymnal, 1862
Ave Maria! Thou Virgin; X100655 Ave Maria! O Virgin

Sammis, James H., d 1919
When we walk with the Lord; R110773 Trust and obey

Sampter, Jessie E.
Great Lord of Life who lives
In many a stone-bound city
The Sabbath light is burning

Sandburg, Carl, 1878-
The young child, Christ, is

Sanders, H.
See Him in the garden lone

Sandys, George, 1577-1643
Thou who art enthroned above

Sanger, Florence Ziegler, 1906-
O Jesus, crucified for me

Sangster, Margaret E., (Mrs. Gerrit van Deth), 1838-1912
Comes any good from Nazareth
For peace and for plenty
O Christ, forget not them; X102326 Forget them not
Out of my need, you come to me
The ships glide in at the harbor's
Thine is the power, Lord

Santee, L.D.
In the glad time of the harvest

Santeüil, Claude de, 1628-84
Blest Trinity, from mortal
Now, my soul, thy voice

Santeüil, Jean-Baptist de, 1630-97
All honor and praise, dominion
Captains of the saintly band
Christ in the highest heaven
Disposer supreme, and Judge; X100226 All honor and praise
Hail! princes of the host
In stature grows the heavenly
Lady of the visitation
Not by the martyr's death alone
O Sion, open wide the gates
Our Lord the path of suffering
The heavenly Child in stature
What mortal tongue can sing
Where the angel-hosts adore
Whither thus in holy rapture

Sarett, Lew, 1888-
God is at the anvil, beating
O, I can hear you God

Sargant, Edmund Beale
Be firm, ye sentinels of Truth
Dear Father-Mother, thou dost
Go forth and stand upon

Sargent, Edward Hewlett Gladstone, 1887-
Lord, we have come to thee

Sargent, Epes, 1813-80
All souls, O Lord, are thine

Sargent, Lucius Manlius, 1788-1867
Bondage and death the cup

Sargent, N.B.
We are building in sorrow

Sassoon, Siegfried, 1886-
Your little flame of life

Sattlers, Michael
Als Christus mit sein'r

wahren Lehr. 1564
Savage, Marion Dutton
Teach us, O Lord, true brotherhood
Savage, Minot Judson, 1841-1918
How shall come the Kingdom holy
O star of truth, down shining
Seek not afar for beauty
The God that to the fathers
What purpose burns within
When the gladsome day
Savile, W.H., 1859-1925
Far-shining names from age
Savonarola, Girolamo, 1454-98
Jesus, Refuge of the weary
Jesù, sommo conforto, Tu se'
O Du Liebe meiner Liebe
Saxby, Jane Euphemia, 1811-98
O Jesus Christ, the Holy One
Sayford, S.M.
Redemption! O, wonderful story; R100863 Believe it, O sinner
Sayle, Amy
Paul the preacher, Paul
Schade, Johann Caspar, 1666-98
Look up, my soul, to Christ
Schalling, Martin Mikael, 1532-1608
Herzlich lieb hab' ich dich
Lord, let thy blest angelic
Lord, thee I love with all my; X107242 O Lord, I love thee
O Lord, devoutly love I thee
With all my heart I love thee
Scheffler, Johann (Angelus Silesius), 1624-77
Begone! vain world, with all
Christ, the good Shepherd
Come, follow me, the Saviour
Dearest Jesus, come to me
Grant, most gracious Lamb
Earth has nothing sweet or fair
I am the Lord, O hear my voice
I thank thee, uncreated Sun
I will love thee, all my
Ich will dich lieben, meine
I'll glory in nothing but only
Jesus, Jesus, come to me
Jesu, komm doch selbst zu mir
Jesus' mercies never fail
Jesus, Saviour, come to me
Liebe, die du mich zum Bilde
Love, who in the first beginning
Mir nach! spricht Christus
Morning Star, O cheering sight
"My yoke," saith Christ
O God, of good the unfathomed
O Love, who formest me to wear; X107374 O Love, who madest
The soul wherein God dwells
Thee will I love, my strength
Thou, Jesus, art our King
Thy majesty, how vast it is; X109449 The Church on earth
Thy soul, O Jesus, hallow me
Wilt thou not, my Shepherd true
Scheidt, Christian Ludwig, 1709-61
Aus Gnaden soll ich selig
By grace I am an heir of heaven
By grace I'm saved, grace free
Schell, William G., 1869-
Humility, thou secret vale; R107382 O, make thy blest
Life on earth is but a vapor
Long have they waited; R103152 Hark, hear them
The ninety-nine within; R102599 Go search it out
Schenck, Hartmann, 1634-81
Now our worship sweet is o'er; X106454 Now the hour of worship
Nun Gott Lob, es ist vollbracht
Schenck, Theobold Heinrich (or, Heinrich Theobold), 1656-1727
Who are these like stars
Schirmer, Michael, ca 1606-

ca 35
O Heil'ger Geist, kehr bei
O Holy Spirit, enter in
Schjörring, Jens N. L., 1829-1900
Friends of Jesus in their parting
Love from God our Lord
Love the Lord thy God; Love is
Schlegel, Johann Adolf, 1721-93
Vanish doubt and hesitation
Schlegel, Katharina Amalia Dorothea von, 1697-
Be still, my soul: The Lord is
Stille, mein Wille! Dein Jesus
Schlicht, Ludolf Ernst, 1714-69
Blessèd Saviour with love's
Lord, grant us, though deeply
Lord Jesus, in thy presence
What brought us together, what
What is it that makes us stand
Ye who callèd to Christ's; X111927 Ye who callèd, ye who
Schloerb, Rolland W., 1893-
O Church of God, our solitude
O God, thy summons still is
O thou Eternal Source of Life
Praise to thee, O God, for
Schmidt, Ambrose M.
O God of nations, God of men
Take, O take me, holy Father
We praise thee, O God, our Lord
Ye men of Christ awake
Schmidt, Christian von, 1768-1854
Ihr Kinderlein, kommet
O come, little children, O come; X106690 O dear little children; X101380 Come hither, ye children
Schmidt, Johann Eusebius, 1670-1745
Christ crucified, my soul, by
Fahre fort, fahre fort
Sion, rise, Sion, rise, Sion, wake, arise
Schmolck, Benjamin, 1672-1737
Alleluia, lo, He wakes
Blessed Jesus, here are we; X100931 Blessed Jesu! here we stand
Blessed Jesus, we are here [Baptism]
Heavenward still our pathway; X103371 Heavenward stretch
Jesus, Saviour, wondrous mild
Lich vom Licht! erleuchte
Liebster Jesu, wir sind hier
Light of light, enlighten me
Mein Jesu, wie du willt
My God, I know that I must
My Jesus, as thou wilt; X106169 My Saviour, as thou
My truest Friend abides
O how holy is this place
Open now thy gates of beauty
Precious word from God in
Tut mir auf die schöne Pforte
Was Gott tut, das ist wohl
Welcome, thou Victor in the strife
What our Father does is well
Why art thou cast down
Willkommen, Held im Streite
Schneegass, Cyriacus, 1546-97
Herr Gott Vater, wir preisen
O Lord, our Father, thanks to
The child of humble Virgin
The new-born Child this early
Schneesing, Johannes, d 1567
Allein zu dir, Herr Jesu Christ
In thee alone, O Christ
Lord Jesus Christ, in thee
Schneider, Leopold
Mein Gott dich will ich loben. 1528
Schneider, Michael
Es hatt' ein Mann zween Knaben. 1564
Herr Gott in deinem Reiche. 1564
Herr Gott Vater in deinem

Thron! 1564
Ihr Christen rein, allkammt (with Hans Betz) 1564
Mein Muth und Sinn steht mer dahin. 1564
Merkt auf ihr Christen allgemein. 1564
Merkt auf, ihr Völker allgemein. 1564
Mich verlanget zu allen Zeiten. 1564
Mit Lust und Freud will ich Gott lobsingen, Dem Vater gut. 1564
O Herre Gott in deinem Thron. 1564
Wohlauf, Wohlauf, du Gottes G'mein. 1564
Schoenbechler, Roger
O blessed by God, St Benedict
Scholefield, Jack P., 1882-
I've found a friend who is all; R108702 Saved by His power
Think on thy way, O thou storm-driven
Schornschlager, Leopold
Die Lieb ist kalt jetzt in der Welt. 1564
Schrautenbach, Ludwig Karl, von 1726-83
O give us that good part
Schröder, Johann Heinrich, 1667-99
Eins ist not, ach Herr, dies
Jesus, my captain, to victory
One thing needful! This one
One thing only, Lord, is
One thing's needful; Lord this; X108019 One ... then Lord
Schroeder, Martin, 1888-
God calls to man, His acres to
Schroll, Eleanor Allen
Savior, I would live for thee; R109347 Teach me, Lord
There's a garden where Jesus; R107634 O the beautiful
Schuette, Conrad Herman Louis, 1843-
Another day has passed away
Great God, a blessing from
O Lord, our God, accept, we pray
Schuette, Walter E.
This is the day we celebrate
Schütz, Johann Jakob, 1640-90
All glory to the Sovereign
Give praise and glory unto
Sei Lob und Ehr' dem höchsten
Sing praise to God who reigns; X100254 All praise to God
To God, the Father of all love
Schwedler, Johann Christoph, 1672-1730
Ask ye what great thing I know
Do you ask what most I prize
What, ye ask me, is my prize
Scollard, Clinton, 1860-
O little town, O little town
Scott, Clara H., 1841-97
Open my eyes, that I may see
Scott, Elizabeth, 1708-76
Awake, ye saints, awake
See how the rising sun
Thy bounties, gracious Lord
Scott, Frederick G.
Cast thy care on Jesus
Scott, Jacob Richardson, 1815-61
To thee this temple we devote
Scott, Lesbia
I sing a song of the saints
Scott, Robert B. Y., 1899-
O day of God, draw nigh
Scott, Thomas, 1705-75
Angels, roll the rock away (with Thomas Gibbons); X100460 Angel, roll the rock
Hasten, sinner, to be wise; X103203 Hasten, O sinner, to
Imposture shrinks from light
Lo! the stone is rolled away
The lifted eye and bended knee; X109903 The uplifted eye
Scott, Sir Walter, 1771-1832
On Christmas Eve the bells; X109979 Then drink (Engl.

trad)
That day of wrath (Dies irae) see Latin, 13th c
When Israel of the Lord
Scott, William, tr. see Korean hymn: The Saviour's precious blood
Scottish hymnal, 1884
Great Shepherd of the sheep
Scottish paraphrases, 1745
Lo! what a cloud of witnesses
O let triumphant faith dispel
Scottish paraphrases, 1781
Ho! ye that thirst, approach
Take comfort, Christians, when
Ye who the Name of Jesus bear
Scottish Psalter, 1650

NOTE: Following the first line, the Psalm number is given parenthetically. Sixty-eight Psalms are included, fifteen of them several times.

After thy loving-kindness (Ps 51)
All lands to God, in joyful (Ps 66)
All nations whom thou mad'st (Ps 86)
Be merciful to me, O God (Ps 57)
Blessed are they that undefiled (Ps 119)
By what means shall a young man (Ps 119)
Earth thou dost visit (Ps 65)
Give ear unto me when I call (Ps 4)
Give ear unto my words (Ps 5)
Give praise and thanks unto (Ps 106)
Give thanks to God, call on (Ps 105)
God is of mine inheritance (Ps 16)
God is our refuge and our strength (Ps 46)
God reigneth, He is clothed (Ps 93)
God righteous judgement executes (Ps 103)
God will I bless all times (Ps 32)
God's law is perfect (Ps 19)
God's mercies I will ever sing (Ps 89)
Good unto all men is the Lord (Ps 145)
His name for ever shall endure (Ps 72); X106358 Now blessed be
How excellent in all the earth (Ps 8)
How lovely is thy dwelling (Ps 84)
I joyed when to the house (Ps 122)
I love the Lord, because (Ps 116)
I to the hills will lift mine (Ps 121)
I waited for the Lord my God (Ps 40)
I'll hear what God the Lord (Ps 85)
I'll of salvation take the cup (Ps 116)
In Judah's land God is well known (Ps 76)
Judge me, O Lord, for I have walked (Ps 26)
Lord bless and pity us (Ps 67)
Lord from the depths to thee (Ps 130)
Lord, hear the right, attend (Ps 17)
Lord, thee, my God, I'll early seek (Ps 63)
Lord, thou shalt early hear (Ps 5)
My soul with expectation doth (Ps 62)
O blessed is the man whose (Ps 32)
O children, hither do ye come (Ps 34)
O come, let us sing to the Lord (Ps 95)
O daughter, take good heed (Ps 45)

O God, give ear unto my cry (Ps 61)
O greatly blessed the people (Ps 89); X109777 The praises of thy
O happy is that man and blest (Ps 146)
O hear my prayer, Lord (Ps 148)
O Lord, I unto thee do cry (Ps 141)
O Lord, thou hast me searched (Ps 139)
O Lord, thy judgments give (Ps 72)
O send thy light forth (Ps 43)
O set ye open unto me (Ps 118)
O sing a new song to the Lord, For wonders He hath done (Ps 98)
O sing a new song to the Lord, Sing all the earth to God (Ps 96)
O that men to the Lord would (Ps 107)
O thou my soul, bless God the Lord (Ps 103)
O thou that art the mighty one (Ps 45)
O with thy tender mercies (Ps 90)
O ye His angels, that excel (Ps 103)
Praise waits for thee in Zion (Ps 65)
Praise ye the Lord: for it is good (Ps 147)
Praise ye the Lord: with my whole heart (Ps 111)
Pray that Jerusalem may have (Ps 122, 133, 116)
Set thou thy trust upon the Lord (Ps 37)
Shew me thy ways, O Lord (Ps 25); X108892 Show me thy ways
Such pity as a father hath (Ps 103)
Teach me, O Lord, the perfect (Ps 119)
That man hath perfect blessedness (Ps 1)
The Lord doth reign, and clothed (Ps 93)
The Lord for ever doth endure (Ps 9)
The Lord for ever sits as King (Ps 9)
The Lord preparèd hath his throne (Ps 103)
The Lord will I at all times (Ps 34)
The Lord's my light and saving (Ps 27)
The Lord's my shepherd, I'll not want (Ps 23); X106182 My Shepherd is (Rous); X109668 The Lord is my
The mighty God, the Lord (Ps 50)
They in the Lord that firmly (Ps 125)
Thou hast, O Lord, most glorious (Ps 68)
Thou my sure portion art alone (Ps 119)
Thou shalt arise, and mercy (Ps 102)
Thou, with thy counsel, while (Ps 73)
To render thanks unto the Lord (Ps 92)
To thee I lift my soul (Ps 25)
Turn us again, O God of hosts (Ps 80)
'Twas like a dream, when by (Ps 126)
Unveil mine eyes that by thy law (Ps 119)
We'll to God's tabernacles (Ps 132)
When Sion's bondage God turned (Ps 126)
Who is the man that shall ascend (Ps 24)
Why rage the heathen? and vain (Ps 2)
Within thy tabernacle Lord (Ps 15)
Ye gates, lift up your heads (Ps 24)

Scrimger, John, 1849-1915

Lord, who shall come to Thee
Scriven, Joseph, 1820-86
What a friend we have
Scriver, Christian, 1629-93
In peace will I lie down
Scudder, Eliza, 1821-96
Come, though with purifying
I cannot find thee! Still on
My God I rather look to thee
Thou Grace divine, encircling
Thou Life within my life
Scudder, Vida Dutton, 1861-
Thy kingdom Lord, thy kingdom; X110465 Thy kingdom, Lord, we
Seagrave, Robert, 1693-1759
Rise my soul, and stretch thy
Seal, Emily F.
Our God is All-in-all
What is thy birthright, man
Seaman, Owen, 1861-1936
You that have faith to look
Sears, Edmund Hamilton, 1810-76
Calm on the listening ear
Ho! ye that rest beneath
It came upon the midnight clear
Seaton. Church hymn book, 1855
God of eternal love
Sedding, Edward Douglas, 1884-
A work hath Christ for thee; X101193 Christ hath a work
O Father, we thank thee for
Sederquist, G.W.
'Tis almost time for the Lord; R107078 O it must be the breaking
Sedgwick, S.N., 1872-1941
Lord, accept the alms we offer
Sedulius of Liege, 15th c
The snow lay on the ground; R110894 Venite adoremus
Sedulius, Coelius, ca 450
A solis ortus cardine
Christum wir sollen loben
From east to west, from shore
Hostis Herodes impie
How vain the cruel Herod's fear
Now praise we Christ
The star proclaims the King
Why, impious Herod, shouldst
Seebach, Margaret Reynolds, 1875-1948
Thy Kingdom come! O Father hear
Seebass, Friedrich Wilhelm, d 1758
Jesus, I love thee fervently
Seelye, J.H.
God save our native land
Seiss, Joseph Augustus, 1823-1904
Jesus, Master, Son of God
Sellers, Ernest O.
Lord, unto Thee we look; R108049 Open our eyes, thy
Thy Word is a lamp to my feet
Would men know you've been; R101136 Can men tell that you
Selnecker, Nicolaus, 1528-92
Abide with us, O Saviour dear
Ach bleit bei uns, Herr Jesu
Lass mich dein sein und bleiben
Let me be thine for ever
Lord Jesus Christ, with us
Lord Jesus, with thy children
Now cheer our hearts this
Now Christ, the very Son of God
O faithful God, thanks be; X106726 O ... we worship Thee
O Lord, my God, I cry to thee
Wir danken dir, o treuer Gott
Seltzer, George Rise, 1902-
Come, all ye people, come
Senfft von Pilsach, L.R.
To thee, O Lord, I yield my
Serle, Ambrose, 1742-1812
Thy ways, O Lord! with wise
Service, Robert William,

1874-1958
Carry on! carry on! Fight the good fight
Servoss, Miss M.E.
When the storms of life; R103307 He will hide me
Sewall, Frank
Morn of joy and morn of
Roll out, O song, to God
Seymer, Violet Ker
As sings the mountain stream
In God I find a precious gift
Seymour, Aaron Crossley Hobart, 1789-1870
Jesus, immortal King, arise!
Shackford, John W., 1878-
O thou who art the Shepherd
Shacklock, Mrs. C.L.
Would you know the love; R100621 At the golden gate
Shairp, John Campbell, 1819-85
'Twixt gleams of joy
Shakespeare, William, 1564-1616
Blow, blow, thou winter wind
Poor Soul, the centre of my sinful earth
Shank, J.W.
My life was lost in selfishness; R108165 Out of the gloom and
Shanne, Richard. ms. 1611
Come, love we God, of might
Shapcote, Emily Mary, 1829-1909
Jesus, holy, undefiled
O Queen of the Holy Rosary
Shaw, Knowles, 1834-78
I am the vine and ye are
Sowing in the morning, sowing; R101062 Bringing in the sheaves
Shekleton, Mary, 1827-83
It passeth knowledge, that
Shelley, Percy Bysshe, 1792-1822
The world's great age begins
To suffer woes which hope
Shelly, Martha Evans Jackson, 1812-1901
Lord, a little band and lowly
Shenk, J.M.
Come, heaven-bound pilgrims
Shepard, Odell
We are standing in the great
Shepcote, Mrs. "E", see Shapcote, Emily Mary, 1829-1909
Sheperd, Anne Houlditch, 1809-57
Around the throne of God in heaven
Shepherd, Fred S.
Trembling soul beset by fears
Shepherd, Thomas, 1665- 1739
Must Jesus bear the cross
Sherman, Frank Dempster, 1860-1916
It is my joy in life
Sherman, H.H.
Serving the Lord with gladness
Sherwin, William Fisk, 1826-88
Galilee, bright Galilee
Sound the battle cry; R108660 Rouse, then, soldiers
Wake the song of joy
Why is thy faith in God's
Shillito, Edward, 1872-1948
Away with gloom, away with
Shindler, Mary S.B., see Dana, Mary S.B.S.
Shipton, Anna, ca 1815-1901
Call them in! the poor
Shirley, Walter, 1725-86
Sweet the moments, rich
Shirreff, E.L.
Gracious Saviour, who didst
Shoemaker, J.S.
Come, lost one, your Saviour; R107848 O, why should you
Father, we come in Jesus' name
We now have met to worship
Shrubsole, William, 1759-1829
Arm of the Lord, awake! awake
As every day thy mercy spares
When, streaming from the eastern
Shumate, Aurora M.
Every Sunday evening, To the
Shurtleff, Ernest Warburton, 1862-1917
Lead on, O King eternal

Shuttleworth, Henry Cary, 1850-1900
Father of men, in whom
Man lives not for himself
Sidebotham, Mary Anne, 1833-1913
Lord, thy mercy now entreating
Sicilian traditional, etc.
O most holy One, O most lowly
O sanctissima, O piissima
Sidney, Sir Philip, 1554-86 and Mary Sidney (his sister), i.e. Lady Mary Pembroke, 1561-1621
O Lord in me there lieth
Sigmond, Sven O, 1872-
Father Almighty, darkness now
Sigourney, Lydia Huntley, 1793-1865
Blest Comforter Divine, whose
Go to thy rest, fair child
Laborers of Christ, arise
When adverse winds and waves
Sigstedt, Cyriel O.
O Jesus Christ, our only Lord
The Lord is risen again! Ye
Sill, Edward Rowland, 1841-87
Send down thy truth, O God
Silliman, Vincent Brown, 1894-
As we leave this friendly
Earth arrayed in wondrous
Faith of the larger liberty
Morning, so fair to see
One world this, for all its
Silver, Rabbi Abba Hillel, 1893-
God built him a continent
Simonsson, Thomas, Bp. of Strängnos, Sweden, see Thomas, Bishop . . . d 1443
Simpson, A.B.
The mercy of God is an ocean; R105062 Launch out
Simpson, Jane Cross Bell, 1811-86
Go when the morning shineth
Pray when the morn is breaking
Star of peace to wanderers
Simpson, Margaret M.
To the regions beyond I must
Simpson, Robert, 1771-1843
From thy holy habitation
To God we render praise
We bow before thy throne
With deeply humbled hearts
Simpson, William James Sparrow, 1860-1952
Cross of Jesus, cross of
Sims, A.J.
There is an unseen hand; R104214 I'm trusting
Sinclair, Duncan
Help us, O Lord, to bear
O God, our Father-Mother, Love
Singleton, Robert Corbet, 1810-81
With gladsome feet we press
Sister of Notre Dame
Hail! all hail, great Queen; R109980 Then let men and Angels
Jesus, thou art coming
Little King, so fair and sweet
Lord for tomorrow see Mary Xavier, Sr., born Sybil F. Partridge
Mother of Christ, Mother of
Sweet Agnes, holy child, all
Sisters of St. Joseph, Toronto
Let the loud hosannas ring
Skavlan, Sigvald
As sinks beneath the ocean
Skemp, Ada, 1851-1927
I love to think that Jesus
Skrine, John Huntley, 1848-1923
Rank on rank again we stand
Slade, Mariana B. (perhaps: Mary B.C. Slade, 1826-82)
Up to the bountiful Giver; R102451 Gathering home
Slade, Mary B.C., 1826-82
From all the dark places; X102373 From ... needy races; R109600 The kingdom is coming
Into the tent where the gipsy; R109362 Tell it again
Sweetly, Lord, have we heard; R102252 Footprints of Jesus
There's a fountain free; R111709 Will you come to

the
Who at my door is standing;
R109313 Sweetly the tones
Sleeper, William T., 1819-1904
A ruler once came to Jesus;
R111904 Ye must be born
Out of my bondage, sorrow
Sleight, M.B.
Hark! the voice of Jesus
Slemp, John C.
Breathe o'er our waiting
In the quiet hours of morning;
R103415 Here we come
O God, Eternal God! Thy name
Slinn, Sarah
God with us! O, glorious name
Slovak traditional, etc.
In the resurrection
Man of sorrows, wrapt in grief
Vzkříšeni čekáme
Small, James Grindly, 1817-88
I've found a friend, O such
Smart, Christopher, 1722-71
All the scenes of nature
Awake, arise! lift up thy
Hosanna! music is divine
We sing of God, the mighty
Welcome, blessed Heavenly
Smart, Richard, 15th c
Who is there that singeth so
Smith, Annie R.
Blessed Jesus, meek and lowly
Hail, peaceful day! divinely
He sleeps in Jesus -- peaceful
How far from home? I asked
I ask not, Lord, for less
I saw one weary, sad, and
Long upon the mountains
Toil on a little longer here
Weeping endures but for a night
When darkness gathers round
Smith, Caroline Louisa Sprague, 1827-86
Tarry with me, O my Saviour
Smith, Eleanor, 1858-1942
In another land and time
Smith, Florence Margaret, 1886-1958
Lord and Master, who hast
Smith, Frederic, 1849-
O God, not only in distress
Smith, Fronia Savage
Proclaim the tidings near;
R108941 Sing glory, glory
Smith, G.N.
Holy, holy, holy Lord
Smith, Gipsy [pseud] see Smith, Rodney, 1860 -- [i.e. Gipsy Smith]
Smith, Horace, 1836-1922
O thou whom neither time
Smith, Horace, 1839-
Sweet is the breath of morning
Smith, Isaac Gregory, 1826-1920
By Jesus' grave on either hand
Smith, J.B.
At home and abroad, on life's;
R109898 The trumpet is sounding
In the early days of childhood; R100935 Blessed Jesus, we
Smith, Jay Holmes
Come forth, ye men of every
Smith, Joseph Denham, ca 1816-
Jesus Christ is passing by
Smith, Joseph Fielding
Does the journey seem long
Smith, L.J. Egerton, 1879-1958
For all the love that from
Smith, Lanta Wilson
I was wandering in a wilderness; R103822 I believe the promises
In a world where sorrow;
R108764 Scattering sunshine
Smith, M.J.
Cling to the Bible
Smith, Robert Archibald.
Sacred harmony, 1828
Lord, let thy mercy now
Smith, Rodney, 1860-
[i.e. Gipsy Smith]
Christ the transforming Light;
R107782 O, to reflect His
Smith, Samuel Francis, 1808-95
Auspicious morning, hail
Down to the sacred wave

Founded on thee, our only
Go, heralds of salvation
Lord of our life, God whom
My country, 'tis of thee;
X107304 O Lord, our God, to
Our Father's God! to thee
Planted in Christ, the living
Sister, thou wast mild
Softly fades the twilight
Spirit of holiness, descend
Spirit of peace and holiness
The morning light is breaking
Today the Saviour calls
When shall we meet again (with A.A. Watts)
With willing hearts we tread
Smith, Uriah
O brother, be faithful! Soon
Dark is the hour when death
Smith, Walter Chalmers, 1824-1908
Earth was waiting, spent
Immortal, invisible, God only
Lord God omnipotent, Lord God
One thing I of the Lord;
R109056 So wash me, Thou
To me to live is Christ
Smith, Wharton Buchanan, 1848-
Raised between the earth and
Smucker, S.J.
I've read of a world
O Lord, thy heavenly grace
Smyth, Clifford
Dear Saviour, stretch thy
Smyth, Harper G., 1873-1945
Is your life a channel;
R105854 Make me a channel
Smyth, Richard
Israel, Israel, God is
Smyttan, George Hunt, 1822-70
Forty days and forty nights
Snelling, J. Palmer
Dear God, how glorious is
Snow, B.
Our God, we raise to thee
Snow, Eliza R.
Again we meet around
Awake, ye Saints of God
Behold the great Redeemer die
Great is the Lord; 'tis good
How great the wisdom
O awake! My slumbering
O my Father, thou that dwellest
The Lord imparted from above
The time is far spent
Think not when you gather
Thou dost not weep to weep
Though deepening trials
Truth reflects upon our;
R100948 Blessed Saviour, thou
Snyder, F.L.
There is a story ever new;
R104077 I want to love him
When your toils below are;
R111472 When the book of life
S.P.C.K. Appendix, 1869
Little children, wake and
Söderberg, Erik Natanael, 1869-
In the temple where our
Sola Mendes, Fred de see Mendes, Fred de Sola
Solberg, C.K., 1872-
Arise, arise, united youth
Christian Leaguers, rally;
R102344 Forward, Christian Leaguers
Fellow Christians, let us
Lift up your eyes, ye Christians
O Blessed Light from heaven
Ride on, ride on, O Saviour-King
There is a sea of mercy
Solomon ibn Gabirol
Early will I seek thee, God
O rain depart with blessings
Thou knowest my tongue
Thy faithful servant, Lord
Songs of Zion, 1864
And is it so?"A little while"
Sonnenschein, S.H.
Hark, the voice of children;
R108040 Onward, children
Sorley, Charles Hamilton d 1915
This sanctuary of my soul
Southwell, Robert, ca 1561-94

Behold a simple tender babe;
R106492 Nowell, Nowell, Nowell (English trad)
Let folly praise what fancy
Sower, Christopher, jr., 1721-84
Death, death, thou hast
Spafford, Horatio Gates, 1828-88
When peace, like a river;
R104486 It is well with my
Spangenberg, Augustus Gottlieb, 1704-92
High on his everlasting throne;
X111263 What can we offer
The church of Christ, that He
When simplicity we cherish
Spanish traditional, etc.
Torches, torches, run with
Up now, laggardly lasses
Speece, Conrad, 1776-1836
Blest Jesus, when thy cross
Spegel, Haquin, 1645-1714
The death of Jesus Christ
War Herres Jesu Kristi död
We Christians should ever
Speier Gebetbuch, 1599
Behold a Rose of Judah
Es ist ein Reis (Ros')
I know a rose-tree springing
Lo, how a Rose e'er blooming
There is a flower springing
Spencer, Anna Garlin
Hail the Hero workers
Spencer, Robert Nelson
Eternal Father, strong to save
see Whiting, William
O heavenly grace in holy rite
Spencer, W.A.
When I shall reach the more;
R104025 I shall be like Him
Spengler, Lazarus, 1479-1534
All mankind fell in Adam's
Spenser, Edmund, 1553-99
Most glorious Lord of life
Speratus, Paul, 1484-1551
All blessing, honor, thanks
Es ist das Heil uns kommen
To us salvation now is come;
X100188 All blessing, honor; X108692 Salvation unto us has
Spitta, Karl Johann Philipp, 1801-59
Ah, this heart is void
Brethren, called by one
By the holy hills surrounded
Father, whose hands hath led
How blessed from the bonds
I know no life divided
I place myself in Jesus' hands
In thy service will I ever
O blessed house, that
O blessed Sun whose splendor
O happy home, where thou art
O Lord! of goodness so
O Lord, who by thy presence
O selig Haus, wo man dich
Our lot is fallen in pleasant
Still on thy loving heart let
Thou, whose coming seers
We are the Lord's: His all-sufficient
We praise and bless thee
Wherefore weep we over Jesus
Wir sind des Herrn, wir leben
Withhold not, Lord the help
Spring-Rice, Cecil, 1859-1918
I vow to thee, my country;
X104062 I vow ... all earthly
Spurgeon, Charles Haddon, 1834-92
Sweetly the holy hymn
The Holy Ghost is here
Squier, George L.
O Christ, the Way, the Truth
Squires, N.J.
O blessed hour, when evening
St, see above as if spelled Saint
Stach, Matthew, 1711-87
There's but a small beginning
Stainer, J R.L., 1866-1939
Daystar on high, bright

Stammers, Joseph, 1801-85
Breast the wave, Christian
Stanfield, Francis, 1836-
Hear thy children, gentle Jesus
Hear thy children, gentlest Mother
O Heart of God! Our home lies; X107501 O Sacred Heart! Our
Sweet Sacrament divine! Hid in
Stanley, Arthur Penrhyn, 1815-81
All the toil and sorrow done
He is gone; a cloud of light; X103247 He is gone - beyond
Lord, it is good for us to be; X107394 O Master, it is good
The Lord is come! On Syrian
When the paschal evening fell
Statler, Ruth B., 1906-
God eternal, in thy presence
Stead, Louisa M.R.
'Tis so sweet to trust in; R104684 Jesus, Jesus, how I
Steele, Anne, 1716-86
Alas! what hourly dangers
Almighty Lord, before thy
Come, Lord, and warm each
Come, ye that love the Saviour's name
Dear Father, to thy mercy-seat
Dear refuge of my weary soul
Deep are the wounds which sin
Enslaved by sin and bound
Eternal Source of joys
Far from these scenes of night
Father of mercies! in thy
Father, whate'er of earthly
Great God, to thee my evening
He lives! the great Redeemer
How helpless guilty nature
How lovely, how divinely
How oft, alas! this wretched
In vain would boasting
Jesus, in thy transporting
Lord of my life! O, may thy
My Father! cheering name; X106094 My God, my Father, blissful; X106095 My God! my Father! cheering
My maker and my King
Now I resolve with all my
O could our thoughts and wishes
O gracious God, in whom
O thou, whose tender mercy
So fades the lovely, blooming
Stretched on the cross, the
The Saviour calls; let every
The Saviour! O what endless
Thou lovely source of true
To our Redeemer's glorious
When sins and fears
While my Redeemer's hear
Ye humble souls, approach
Ye wretched, hungry, starving
Stegmann, Josua, 1588-1632
Abide among us with thy grace
Abide in grace, Lord Jesus
Abide, O dearest Jesus
Abide with us, our Saviour; X100102 Abide ... Lord Jesus
Ach bleib mit deiner Gnade
Come, Rain from the heavens
Wie schön leucht't uns der
Stehn, Hans Christenson, 16th c, see Sthen, Hans Christenson, 16th c
Stein, Leopold, 1810-82
Praise the Lord! One acoord
Rock of ages, let our song
Stennett, Joseph, 1663-1713
Another six days' work
Come, lowly souls that mourn
Lord, at thy table we behold
O blessèd Saviour, is thy
The great Redeemer we adore
Stennett, Samuel, 1727-95
Come every pious heart
Here at thy table, Lord, we
How charming is the place
Jesus, my Saviour and my God
Majestic sweetness sits

On Jordan's stormy banks I; R103787 I am bound for the; R111169 We will rest in the
Prostrate, dear Jesus, at thy
Thou Sun of love, whose
" 'Tis finished!" So the Saviour
Where two or three with sweet
With tears of anguish I lament
Stephens, Evan
Father, thy children to thee
In remembrance of thy suffering
Let us all press on
O happy homes among the hills
O home beloved, where'er
Raise your voices to the Lord
Sacred the place of prayer
Shall the youth of Sion; R110768 True to the faith
Sweet is the hour when thus
The voice of God again is
This was the song the angels
We ever pray for thee
Stephens, James, 1882-1950
Little things that run
Low at thy pierced feet
Stephenson, Isabella S., 1843-90
see Stevenson, Isabel S., 1843-90
Sterling, John, 1806-44
O Source divine, and life
Stern, Louis
Come let us sing in sweet
Sternberg, Sadye
Though our hearts dwell
Sternhold, Thomas, d 1549
How long wilt thou forget me
O God, my strength; X109640 The Lord descended
O Lord, how are my foes
Steuerlein, Johann. Sieben und zwantzig newe geistliche Gesange. Erfurt, 1588
Das alte Jahr vergangen ist
The old year now hath passed
Stevens, David
New Russia, rise and proudly
Stevenson, Isabel Stephana, 1843-90
Holy Father, in thy mercy
Stevenson, Robert Louis, 1850-94
Let us wander where we will
Thy people, Lord, of many; X110449 Thy children, Lord
To make this earth, our hermitage
Under the wide and starry sky
Stewart, Alexander, 1843-1923
Lord Jesus Christ, we seek
Sthen, Hans Christenson, 16th c
Herre Jesu Krist! Min Freiser
I know a Kingdom without end
Lord Jesus Christ, my Saviour
Stidger, William L.
Judean hills are holy
Rise up, O world, the light
Stiles, E.P., see Stites, E.P. [printing error]
Stillman, J.M.
I want to be more like Jesus; R105994 More and more like
Stillman, Mildred Whitney, 1890-
Now once again for help that
Stites, Edgar Page
I've reached the land of joy; R106537 O Beulah land; X110030 There is a land
Simply trusting every day; R110777 Trusting as the moments
Stock, Eleanor B.
Take us on the Quest of Beauty
The body, Lord, is ours
Stock, Harry T., 1891-1958
O gracious God, whose constant
Stock, Sarah Geraldina, 1838-98
Let the song go round
O Master! when thou callest
Stocker, John
Gracious Spirit, Dove divine; X102922 Gracious ... Love divine
Stocking, Jay T., 1870-1936
O Master Workman of the

race
Stockman, Paul, 1602-36
Jesus, thou who knowest death
Jesus, thou who once wast dead
Stockton, John Hart, 1813-77
Come, every soul by sin; R108037 Only trust Him
Stockton, Martha, 1821-85
God loved the world of sinners
Stockton, Thomas H., 1808-68
Can truth divine fulfillment
Stokes, E.H.
Hover o'er me, Holy Spirit; R102229 Fill me now
Stone, Ella A.
O sweet and tender as the dawn
Stone, Lloyd
This is my song, O God of all
Stone, Samuel John, 1839-1900
Lord of the Harvest, it is
O great Absolver, grant my
O thou, before whose Presence
The Church's one foundation; X109444 The Church has one
The old year's long campaign
Through midnight gloom
Unchanging God, hear from
Weary of earth, and laden with; X111181 Weary of self
Stonehouse, Maria Th., 1722-51
Lord, take my heart just as it
Stoney, C. Butler
Since to the Holiest none may
Stowe, Harriet Beecher, 1812-96
Abide in me, O Lord, and I in; X100093 Abide ... o'er shadow; X109402 That mystic word
Still, still with thee, when
When winds are raging o'er
Stowell, Hugh, 1799-1865
From every stormy wind that
Jesus is our Shepherd
Lord of all power and might
Stowell, Thomas Alfred, 1831-
While the sun is shining
Stratton, Mrs. F.K.
O Lord, our God, Almighty King
Stratton, Maggie
Holy Bible, how I love it
Straub, Hans
Durch Gnad so will ich singen. 1564
Straub, Maria, 1838-98
God sees the little sparrow; R103269 He loves me too
Strauss, Victor Friedrich von 1809-99
Thou, sore opprest, the sabbath
Strodach, Paul Zeller, 1876-1947
God of our life, all-glorious
Now let the vault of heaven
Strong, Nathan
Almighty Sovereign of the skies, see Watts, Isaac Almighty Sovereign ...
Swell the anthem, raise the
Strout, Jessie E.
Lift up the trumpet, and
Struther, Jan, 1901-53
Daisies are our silver
God, whose eternal mind
High o'er the lonely hills
Lord of all hopefulness
O Saint of summer, what can
Round the earth a message
Sing, all ye Christian people
Unto Mary, demon-haunted
We thank you, Lord of heaven
When a knight won his spurs
When Mary brought her treasure
When Stephen full of power
Stryker, Melanchthon Woolsey, 1851-1929
Almighty, Lord, with one accord
God speed the gospel! O Father
Stubbs, Charles William, 1845-
Fair the night in Bethlem land
Studdert-Kennedy, Geoffrey Anketell, 1883-1929
Awake, awake to love and

work
Close by the heedless worker's
We shall build on!
When through the whirl
Stutsman, Grace M.
In Bethlehem 'neath starlit
Stuttle, Mrs. L. D. Avery
O let me walk with thee, my
Summers, Thomas Osmund, 1812-82
The daylight fades, the evening
The morning bright, with rosy
Suso, Henry, 1300-66
In dulci jubilo; X106495 Nu singet und seyt
Nun singet und seid froh
Sutton, Amos, 1802-54
Hail! sweetest, dearest tie
Swahili hymn
Jesus, Son of Mary, Fount of
Swain, Joseph, 1761-96
Brethren, while we sojourn
Come, let our hears and voices
Come, ye souls by sin afflicted
How sweet, how heavenly is
O Thou, in whose presence my; X108439 Redeemer of Israel
Swain, Leonard, 1821-69
My soul, weigh not thy life
Swayne, Amelia W.
For all the souls who sought
Swedberg, Jesper, 1653-1735
Lord, bestow on us thy blessing
O Lord, give heed unto our
Swedenborg, Emanuel, 1688-1772
in boundless mercy, gracious
Swertner, John, 1746-1813
Believing souls, rejoice and
Grace and peace from God our
Gracious Lord, our Shepherd
Highly favored congregation; X103473 Highly favored (Benade)
Holy Lord, by thy body given
Jesus, my King, thy kind and
Lord God, our Salvation
Lord Jesus, 'mid thy flock
May the stream from thee
Most holy Lord, mankind's
My Sion where the Lamb of God
Now with joyful songs appear
O Lord, who numberest all our
Our children, gracious Lord
Praises, thanks, and adoration
Sing alleluia, praise the Lord
To thee, Lord Christ, all praise
To thee our vows with sweet
To thy brethren ever be
We in one covenant are joined
When Christ, our Lord
Swinburne, Algernon Charles, 1837-1909
For no sect elect
Thou whose birth on earth
We mix from many lands
Switton, Florence
A message sweet the breezes
Symington, Andrew James, 1829-
Lord! in love and mercy save
Symonds, John Addington, 1840-93
These things shall be
To God, the everlasting, who
Symons, Emily, 1842-1924
I give myself to thee
We, who would lead thy flock
Synesius of Cyrene, ca 375-430
Lord Jesus, think on me
Synnestvedt, Elsa
Father all-holy, Lord of
Rise, O Lord, lift up thine
When very early in the dawn

T

Tagore, Rabindranath, 1861-1941
Now I recall my childhood
The light, my light, world-filling light,

This is my prayer: Give me
Tailour, F. Robert. Fiftie select Psalms, 1615 see Bridges, Robert.
The King, O God, his heart
Talley, Thomas
Behold that star
Tamminen, K. V.
Lift up the banner of salvation
Tappan, William Bingham, 1794-1849
There is an hour of hallowed; X110047 There ... Peace
There is an hour of peaceful
'Tis midnight; and on Olive's
Tarrant, William George, 1853-1928
Come, let us join with faithful
"Draw nigh to God, he will"
I saw the city of the Lord; X100070 A temple of the Lord
Long ago the lilies faded
Marching with the heroes
My Master was a worker
Now praise we great and famous
The fathers built this city
The Light along the ages
With happy voices ringing; X111770 With ... voices singing
Welcome, morning, bright and
Tate, Nahum, 1652-1715, & Brady, Nicholas, 1659-1726 usually cited as Tate and Brady
As pants the hart for cooling; X105288 Like as the hart
Be thou, O God! exalted high
Defend me, Lord, from shame
Give ear ye children (with Watts), see Belknap, Jeremy. Give ear ye children
Have mercy, Lord, on me
He that hath God his guardian
Let me with light and truth
Lift up your heads, eternal
My soul with patience waits
No change of time shall ever
O come, loud anthems let us
O God, my heart is fixed
O God of hosts, the mighty
O God, we praise thee, and (Te Deum)
O Lord, our fathers oft have
O praise ye the Lord
O render thanks to God above
O thou, to whom all creatures
O 'twas a joyful sound to hear
O with due reverence let us
Thou, God, all glory, honor
Thou, Lord, by strictest
Through all the changing scenes
Thy word is to my feet a lamp
To bless thy chosen race
To Father, Son and Holy Ghost; X110576 To ... The God, whom
To God be glory, peace on
To Sion's hill I lift my eyes; X110636 To ... lift mine eyes
While shepherd's watched; X111585 While humble shepherds
With glory clad, with strength
With one consent let all
Taylor, Ann, i.e. Ann Taylor Gilbert, 1782-1866
Great God! and wilt thou (with Jane Taylor)
Lord, I have passed another
There is a dear and hallowed (authorship questioned)
Taylor, C. T.
Cross of Christ, O sacred tree
Taylor, Clare, d 1778
Lord, my times are in thy hand
The cross, the cross, O that's
Taylor, E. G.
Fear not! God is thy shield
Taylor, Emily, 1795-1872
God of the changing year
O here, If ever, God of love
Taylor, George Lansing, 1835-
Dare to do right
Taylor, Georgiana Mary, 1848-1915
Seek ye first, not earthly

Taylor, James H.
Lead on, thou God of hosts
Taylor, Jane, 1783-1824
Lord, I would own thy tender
Taylor, Jeremy, 1613-67
Draw nigh to thy Jerusalem; X101765 Descend to thy
Ride on triumphantly
Taylor, John, 1750-1826
God of mercy! God of grace; X102729 God ... penitential songs
Like shadows gliding o'er
Lord, before thy presence
Lord, what offering shall we
Taylor, John (dates unknown)
Go, ye messengers of glory
O give me back my prophet
The Seer, the Seer, Joseph
Taylor, M.
Search me, O God, and know my
Taylor, Sarah E., 1883-1954
O God of Light, thy word
Taylor, Thomas Rawson, 1807-35
Earth, with her ten thousand
There was a time when children
We are but strangers here; X104207 I'm but a stranger
Teasdale, Sara, 1884-1933
Life has loveliness to sell
Teasley, D.O.
Farewell, dear friends, I bid
I came defiled and guilty; R108204 Peace, peace
I stood at the time-beaten
Many souls today are dying; R100185 All because we do not
Should we meet no more till
When I read how my Saviour; R103912 I know in my heart
Would you flee from sin and; R100728 Be ready, Be ready
Teddlie, Tillit S.
Earth holds no treasures but; R103352 Heaven holds all
Some day you'll stand at the; R111329 What will it be
Tennyson, Alfred Tennyson, Lord, 1809-92
Flower in the crannied wall
I am a part of all that I have
Late, late, so late! and dark
Men my brothers, men the workers
Not in vain the distance
Not of the sunlight; X107886 O young mariner
O yet we trust that somehow
Ring out, wild bells; X108616 Ring out the old; X108618 Ring out ... wild wild sky
Strong Son of God, immortal
Sunset, and evening star
The lights begin to twinkle
Tennyson, Lady Emily Seelwood, 1813-96
Great God who knowest each
Tennyson, Frederick, 1807-98
The night is ended
Terry, Darley, 1848-1934
The Lord is King! I own His
Terry, Richard R., 1868-1938
Christ the Lord is my true
Tersteegen, Gerhard, 1697-1769
Come, brethren, let us hasten!
Conquering Prince and King; X101594 Conquering ... Lord of Glory
God calling yet! Shall I not
God himself is with us; X102644 God ... is present; X102664 God is in His temple; X102794 God reveals His
God is in his temple: O let X102662 God is ... Let us fall
Gott ist gegenwärtig
I sing the praise of love
Ich bete an die Macht
Jesus, whom thy church doth
Lo! God is here! let us adore

Mir ist Erbarmung widerfahren
O glorious Head, thou livest
O God, O Spirit, Light of all
O Lamb of God, who wast for
O Lord our God, in reverence
O Love divine, all else; X107461 O power of love
Something every heart is
Spirit of Grace, thou Light
Thou fairest Child divine
Thou hidden love of God, whose; X110276 Thou hidden Source (Wesley)
Triumph, ye heavens! rejoice
What mercy and divine compassion
Thai Christian
The righteous ones shall be
Thalheimer, Elsie, & Margaret Scott Haycroft
Thou art my Shepherd
Thaxter, Celia, 1836-94
Lift up thy light, O man
Thayer, Lucius H.
The Church of God is stablished
Thilo, Valentin, 1607-62
Mit Ernst, o Menschenkinder
O Jesulein süss, o Jesulein
O Jesu so meek, O Jesu so; X107143 O Jesu sweet, O Jesu
O little one sweet, O little
Ye sons of men, O hearken
Thoburn, Helen, 1885-1932
Father of lights, in whom see Elizabeth Wilson
Thomas, Bp. of Strängnas, Sweden, d 1443
Freedom is the finest gold
Thomas of Celano, 13th c may have been the author of Dies Irae; but see Latin, 13th c
Thomas, Alexcenah
Hark, 'tis the Shepherd's; R101060 Bring them in
'Tis the harvest time; R102521 Gleaning on the hillside
Thomas, Carrie S.
Great King of heaven, our
Thomas, H. Arnold, 1848-1924
Lord Christ, who on thy heart
Thompson, Alexander Ramsay, 1812-95
Hail! kingly Jesus, to thy
Praise our glorious King
Thompson, Francis, 1859-1907
O world invisible, we view
Thompson, Henry
Lord, we humbly bow before
Thompson, J. O.
Far and near the fields are: R105635 Lord of harvest, send
Thompson, Robert B.
See, the mighty angel flying
Thompson, Will Lamartine, 1847-1909
Have I done any good in the; R109991 Then wake up, and do
Jesus is all the world to me
Lead me gently home, Father
Softly and tenderly Jesus is; R101409 Come home, come home
The world has need of willing; R108410 Put your shoulder
There's a great day coming; R100494 Are you ready
Thomson, John, 1783-1818
Jehovah God! Thy gracious
Thomson, Mary Ann, 1834-1923
Now the blessèd Dayspring
O King of saints, we give thee
O Sion, haste, thy mission; X106630 O Christian, haste; X107887 O, Zion, haste; R108398 Publish glad tidings
Saviour, for the little one
Thorsteinsson, Steingrimur, d 1913
The fading day adorns the
Threlfall, Jeannette, 1821-80
Hosanna, loud hosanna
When from Egypt's house of
Thring, Godfrey, 1823-1903
All that's good and great

Fierce raged the tempest
From the eastern mountains; R105268 Light of light
God the Father, God the son (Children's litany)
Grant us, O our heavenly Father
Hail! sacred day of earthly
Heal me, O my Saviour, heal
Hear us, thou that broodest
I heard a sound of voices; X104013 I saw the holy city
Jesus came, the heavens
O God of mercy, God of might
O mighty God, Creator, King
O thou, who madest land and
Saviour, blessed Saviour, listen; X106237 Nearer, ever nearer
The ocean hath no danger
The radiant morn hath passed
Thou to whom the sick and
To thee, O God, we render
True Light, that lightest
Work is sweet, for God has

Thrupp, Adelaide
Lord, who at Cana's wedding

Thrupp, Dorothy Ann, 1779-1847
Come, Christian children, come
Come, Holy Spirit, come
Let us sing, with one accord

Thrupp, Dorothy Ann. Hymns for the young, 1836
Saviour, like a shepherd lead; X103366 Heavenly Shepherd

Thrupp, Joseph Francis, 1827-67
Awhile in spirit, Lord, to
O Son of man, thyself once

Thymus, G.
Turn, Lord, thy wrath away

Tickle, G.Y.
Lord of our highest love

Tietze, Christoph, 1641-1703
By sin weighed down
Seems it in my anguish lone

Tiffany, Emma A.
Jesus dear, I come to thee

Tilak, Narayan Vaman, 1862-1919
Heart and mind, possessions
One who is all unfit to count
Prayer to a heart of lowly

Tillett, Wilbur Fisk, 1854-1936
O Son of God incarnate

Tilton, Theodore, 1835-
We sing a song and then we

Timm, H.A.
Abide with me, my Saviour

Tindley, Charles A., 1856-1937
If the world from you; R109340 Take your burden
Nothing between my soul and
Trials dark on every hand; R101090 By and by, when the morning
When the storms of life

Tiplady, Thomas, 1882-
Above the hills of time
Awake, O church of God
Beyond the wheeling worlds
I may not climb the heights
O men of God, go forth
To all the nations, Lord
To God our hearts we lift
We leave thy house but leave not
Where the olive grove stood

Tisserand, Jean, 15th c
O filii et filiae
O sons and daughters let us
Ye sons and daughters of the King; X107579 O sons and daughters
Ye sons and daughters of the Lord

Titius, Christophe, 1641-1703 see Tietze, Christophe

Todd, R.W.
O who is this that cometh; R105973 Mighty to save

Toeltschig, Johann, 1703-64
What offering shall I bring

Toews, Jacob D.
Come, ye weary ones, come; R101543 Come tonight
Far, far beyond the starry
Jesus, bless us with thy
Loyal and true and faithful; R102516 Giving our best
No mortal eye hath seen

O Lord divine, we come to
When Jesus on the mountain
Toke, Emma Leslie, 1812-72
Glory to thee, O Lord, who
O thou, who didst with love
Thou art gone up on high
Tomlinson, Irving C.
A Voice from heaven we have
O peace of the world, O hope
Tonna, Charlotte Elizabeth Brown, 1790-1846
O thou who didst prepare
Toplady, Augustus Montague, 1740-78
A debtor to mercy alone
Christ to know is life
Fels des Heils, geöffnet mir
Fountain of never-ceasing
Happiness, delightful name
How vast the benefits divine
If, on a quiet sea; X104175 If, through unruffled
Inspirer and hearer of prayer; X100066 A sovereign Protector
Lord, I feel a carnal mind
O thou that hearest the prayer
Object of my first desire
Rock of ages, cleft for me; X108648 Rock ... Truth divine (Root)
Saviour, whom I fain would
Weary sinner, keep thine eyes; X109268 Surely Christ thy ... has; X109269 Surely Christ thy ... hath
What though I cannot break
Your harps, ye trembling
Torrence, Ridgely 1875-1951
Consider well your ways
Praise, O my heart, to you
Praise, O my heart, with praise
The sky has gathered
Torrey, Bradford, 1843-1912
Not so in haste, my heart!
One gift, my God, I seek
Townsend, Joseph L.
Choose the right, when a choice
Hope of Israel, Zion's army
Let us oft speak kind words; R107650 O the kind words
Nearer, dear Saviour, to thee
O holy words of truth and love
O thou Rock of our Salvation
O what songs of the heart
Reverently and meekly now
The day dawn is breaking; R100756 Beautiful day
To Nephi, seer of olden time; R103507 Hold to the rod
Traasdal, J.
O can you sing the new song
Trabert, George Henry
Here we often are perplexed
With deep humility, O Lord
Traherne, Thomas, 1637-73
Sweet Infancy! O heavenly
Tranecker, G., 1717-1802
Thou art our Comfort, blessèd
Tranoscius, Georgius, 1591-1637 see Tranovsky, Juraj, 1591-1637
Tranovsky, Juraj, 1591-1637
Christ the Lord to us is born
In one true God we all believe
Narodil se Kristus Pán
O that thou woulds't rend
Věříme v všemohouciho
Trapp, Jacob, 1899-
The art, the science, and
Wonders still the world shall
Trask, Harold
God, the Hope of those who
Tregelles, Samuel Prideaux, 1813-75
The gloomy night will soon
Trench, Richard Chevenix, 1807-86
Good cheer! Let all men know that all; R102866 Good cheer! good cheer! good cheer
Lord, what a change within
Make channels for the streams
Trend, Henry, 1804-69
Praise, O praise our heaven-

ly; R102285 For his mercies aye
Tressel, W. E.
Lo, we tread on holy ground
Tribbechovius, J., 1678-1712
Thou, our Light, our Guiding-star
Tritton, Joseph, 1819-87
Head of the Church and Lord
Tucker, Francis Bland, 1895-
All praise to thee, for thou
Our Father, by whose name
Tuckerman, Joseph
Father divine, the deadening
Turner, Daniel, 1710-98
Beyond the starry skies
Jesus, full of all compassion
Turner, H. L.
It may be at morn, when the; R107253 O Lord Jesus, how
Turner, M. Elmore, 1906-
Revealing word, thy light
Turner, Nancy Byrd, 1880-
Men go out from places
O Son of man, who walked
There were three lights that
Turner, Mrs. R. N.
How blest was that life; R103924 I know that He liveth
Turner, Rosa M.
O dreamer, leave thy dreams
Turton, William Harry, 1856-1938
At that first Eucharist
Thou, who at thy first Eucharist; X107720 O Thou, who at thy
Tuttiett, Laurence, 1825-97
Father, let me dedicate; X102099 Father, here we
Go forward, Christian soldier
O Grant us light, that we; X102931 Grant us thy light; X105488 Lord, grant us light
O Jesus, ever present
O quickly come, dread Judge
Tuttle, Emma
I think of a city; R100547 As I dream of a city
Tweedy, Henry Hallam, 1868-1953
All ye who love the Lord
Eternal God, whose power
Lord of starry vasts unknown
O God of love, whose spirit
O gracious Father of mankind
O Holy Spirit, making whole
O Spirit of the living God
True lovers of mankind; X105251 Lift up your heart
Twells, Henry, 1823-1900
At even, when the sun was set; X100606 At even, ere the sun
Awake, O Lord, as in the time
Not for our sins alone
Tymms, Thomas Vincent, 1842-1921
Our day of praise is ended

U

U. P. Psalter, see below as if spelled United Presbyterian Psalter (or alternate specific name)
Udulutsch, Irvin
O Jesus Victim-Priest
O Jesus, we adore thee
Ufford, Edwin S.
I believe the Bible
Throw out the life-line
Uhler, Grace Elma
O Gift of God, we praise
Ukranian traditional, etc.
Lovingly the Shepherd
Underwood, Lizzie
I've heard them sing again; R104504 It will open wide
Unitarian collection
Out on an ocean all boundless
United Presbyterian sources which follow are cited as U. P. followed by the distinctive term. The order is chronoligical, beginning with 1871
U. P. Book of Psalms, 1871
NOTE: Following the first

line, the Psalm number is given parenthetically. Eleven Psalms are represented.

Behold all ye that serve (Ps 134)
Blest the man who fears Jehovah (Ps 128)
Give ye to Jehovah, O sons (Ps 29)
God's perfect law restores (Ps 19b)
Great is the Lord, and greatly (Ps 48)
How blest the man that fears (Ps 112)
Lord God of hosts, how lovely (Ps 134)
Lord, hear my voice, my prayer (Ps 61)
O my soul, bless God, the Father (Ps 103)
Of mercy and of judgement (Ps 101)
Praise Jehovah, all ye nations (Ps 117)
The glory of the Lord (Ps 19a)
The Lord thee hear in time of grief (Ps 20)
The man who once has found (Ps 91)
Within thy temple, Lord (Ps 48)

U.P. Board of Publication, 1909

O happy land, whose sons (Ps 144); X107456 O people blest
O Jehovah, hear my words (Ps 5)
Ye children come, give ear (Ps 34); R101166 Children, come, hither

U.P. Psalter, 1912

NOTE: Following the first line, the Psalm number is given parenthetically. All Psalms are represented, except #3 and #13, both of which are credited to Sternhold.

A little that the righteous (Ps 37)
All lands, to God, in joyful sounds (Ps 66)
All men on earth that live (Ps 117)
All nations clap your hands (Ps 47)
All people that dwell on the earth (Ps 100)
All that I am I owe to thee (Ps 139)
All who with heart confiding (Ps 125)
All ye that fear God's holy name (Ps 22); X100303 All ye ... Jehovah's
All ye that fear Jehovah's name (Ps 22)
Alleluia! Alleluia! Earth and heaven in sweet (Ps 150)
Alleluia! Alleluia! In his temple God be praised (Ps 150)
Alleluia, praise Jehovah (Ps 146)
Almighty God, thy lofty throne (Ps 89)
Amid the thronging worshipers (Ps 22)
Among His people, God is known (Ps 76)
Arise, O Lord, our God, arise (Ps 132)
As pants the hart for streams (Ps 42)
As thirsts the hart for cooling (Ps 42)
As thirsts the hart for waterbrooks (Ps 42)
As thou, O Lord, hast made (Ps 18)
Be thou my helper in the strife (Ps 35)
Be thou my judge, O righteous Lord (Ps 26)
Because thy trust is God alone (Ps 91)
Before my journey is complete (Ps 102)
Before thy people I confess (Ps 40)
Behold, how pleasant and how good (Ps 133)

Blest be the Lord! for us He cares (Ps 68)
Blest be the Lord, my rock (Ps 144)
Blest be the Lord, our fathers' God (Ps 72); X100112 Abundant fields
Blest is he who loves God's (Ps 1)
Blest the man that fears Jehovah (Ps 128)
Bow down thy ear, O Lord (Ps 86); X101019 Bow down thine ear
By all whom thou hast made (Ps 86)
By Babel's riverside we sat (Ps 137)
By Babel's streams we sat (Ps 137)
Christ shall have dominion (Ps 72)
Come, all ye people, bless (Ps 66)
Come, all ye servants of the Lord (Ps 134)
Come, let us sing before the Lord (Ps 98)
Come, ye that fear Jehovah (Ps 22)
Come, ye that fear the Lord (Ps 66)
Deceit and falsehood I abhore (Ps 119)
Deliver me from evil, preserve me, Lord (Ps 140)
Do ye, O men, speak righteousness (Ps 58)
Dust to dust, the mortal dies (Ps 49)
Established in the highest heavens (Ps 103)
Ever are my longing eyes (Ps 25)
Exalt the Lord, His praise (Ps 135)
Fools in their heart have said (Ps 53)
For ever settled in the heavens (Ps 119)
For ever trusting in the Lord (Ps 37)
Fret not thyself, nor envious (Ps 37)
From out the depths I cry, O Lord (Ps 130)
From out the depths I cry to thee (Ps 130)
From the depths do I invoke (Ps 130)
From the depths my prayer (Ps 130)
Give thanks and praise to God (Ps 118)
God be merciful to me (Ps 51)
God guards the good with watchful eye (Ps 34)
God is King forever: let the nations (Ps 99)
God is known among his people (Ps 76)
God is our refuge and our strength, A helper ever (Ps 46)
God is our refuge and our strength, our everpresent (Ps 46)
God loveth the righteous (Ps 73)
God saved his people from distress (Ps 68)
God will our strength and refuge (Ps 46)
Grace and truth shall mark (Ps 25)
Gracious God, my heart renew (Ps 51)
Gracious Lord, remember David (Ps 132)
Great Shepherd who leadest (Ps 80)
Had not the Lord been Israel's (Ps 124)
He waters the hills with rain (Ps 104)
Hear, Lord, the voice of my complaint (Ps 64)
Hear my words, O gracious Lord (Ps 5)
Hear this, all ye people (Ps 49)
His saints shall live, and to (Ps 72)
His wide dominion shall extend (Ps 72)

How blest is he whose trespass (Ps 32)
How blest the man who fears (Ps 112)
How blest the man who thoughtfully (Ps 41)
How blest the perfect in the way (Ps 119)
How dear to me, O Lord of hosts (Ps 84)
How good and pleasant is the sight (Ps 133)
How good it is to thank the Lord (Ps 92)
How great the goodness kept (Ps 31)
How I love thy law, O Lord (Ps 119)
How lovely, Lord of hosts, to me (Ps 84)
How pleasant and how good it is (Ps 133)
How shall the young direct their way (Ps 119)
I constant care will take (Ps 39)
I cried to God in my distress (Ps 120)
I graciously will teach thee (Ps 54)
I have followed truth and justice (Ps 119)
I know that the Lord is almighty (Ps 135)
I love the Lord, for my request (Ps 116)
I love the Lord, his strength (Ps 18)
I love the Lord who heard my cry (Ps 116)
I thought upon the days of old (Ps 77)
I to the hills will lift my eyes (Ps 121); X110835 Unto the hills
I waited for the Lord Most High (Ps 40)
I waited for the Lord my God (Ps 40)
I will extol thee, O my God (Ps 145)
If we have forgotten the Name of our God (Ps 44); R108629 Rise, help and redeem
In doubt and temptation (Ps 73); R106090 My God, I will extol
In full assurance of thy grace (Ps 69)
In God will I trust, though my counsellors (Ps 11)
In sweet communion, Lord, with thee (Ps 73)
In the fullness of thy grace (Ps 5)
In the heavens the Lord Almighty (Ps 103)
In thee, O Lord, I put my trust, I call upon thy name (Ps 31)
In thee, O Lord, I put my trust, Shamed let me never (Ps 71)
In thy heritage the heathen (Ps 79)
In thy wrath and hot displeasure (Ps 38)
In vision to his saints God spake (Ps 89)
It is good to sing thy praises (Ps 92)
Jehovah from his throne on high (Ps 33); X107792 O truly is the nation
Jehovah hear thee in thy grief (Ps 30)
Jehovah is my light (Ps 27)
Jehovah, my God, on thy help (Ps 7)
Jehovah reigns in majesty (Ps 99)
Jehovah reigns; let earth be (Ps 97)
Jehovah reigns supreme: Let nations (Ps 99)
Jehovah sits enthroned (Ps 93)
Jehovah, to my prayer give ear (Ps 55)
Jehovah's perfect law (Ps 19)
Judge me, God of my salvation (Ps 43); R107441 O my soul, why art
Judge me, O God, and plead my cause (Ps 43)

Judge my integrity, the righteous judge (Ps 26)
Let all the earth Jehovah fear (Ps 33); X107792 O truly is the nation
Let God arise, and by His might (Ps 68)
Like Sion's steadfast mount (Ps 125)
Lord, bless and pity us (Ps 67)
Lord God of hosts, in mercy (Ps 84)
Lord, hear me in distress (Ps 143)
Lord, hear me when I pray (Ps 27)
Lord, hear the right, regard (Ps 17)
Lord, I lift my soul to thee (Ps 25)
Lord, I will praise thy name (Ps 30)
Lord, in thee am I confiding (Ps 38)
Lord, my petition heed (Ps 86)
Lord, our Lord, thy glorious name (Ps 8); R105683 Lord ... in all the earth
Lord, rebuke me not in anger (Ps 6)
Lord, the God of my salvation (Ps 88)
Lord, thou hast been our dwelling place (Ps 90)
Lord, thou hast favor shown (Ps 85)
Lord, thou hast greatly blessed (Ps 85)
Lord, through all the generations (Ps 90)
Lord, thy word to me remember (Ps 119)
Lord, to me thy ways make known (Ps 25)
Make haste, O God, to save (Ps 70)
Make haste, O my God, to deliver (Ps 70)
Men who walk in folly's way (Ps 107)
Mindful of our human frailty (Ps 103)
Most perfect is the law of God (Ps 19); R107057 O how love I thy law
My end, Lord, make me know (Ps 39)
My faithful Shepherd is the Lord (Ps 23)
My God, I will extol thee (Ps 145)
My God, it was thy grace (Ps 30)
My God, my God, I cry to thee (Ps 22)
My grieving soul revive (Ps 119)
My heart doth overflow (Ps 45)
My heart is fixed, O God (Ps 108)
My heart was glad to hear (Ps 122)
My people, give ear, attend (Ps 78)
My righteous God, who oft (Ps 4)
My Shepherd is the Lord who knows my needs (Ps 23)
My sins and faults of youth (Ps 25)
My song forever shall record (Ps 89)
My soul, bless the Lord! The Lord is (Ps 104)
My soul for thy salvation (Ps 119)
My soul in silence waits for God (Ps 62)
My soul is grieved because (Ps 57)
My steadfast heart, O God (Ps 108)
Not haughty is my heart (Ps 131)
Now blessed be Jehovah, God (Ps 72)
Now Israel may say, and that in truth (Ps 124)
Now the King in thy strength (Ps 21)
Now to God, our Strength and Saviour (Ps 81)

Now unto Jehovah ye sons of (Ps 29)
Now with joyful exultation (Ps 95)
O all ye peoples, bless our God (Ps 66)
O come and sing unto the Lord (Ps 95)
O come and to Jehovah sing (Ps 95)
O come before the Lord, our King (Ps 95)
O come, my people, to my law (Ps 78)
O come, my soul, bless thou (Ps 103); R100897 Bless Him, ye angels
O give the Lord whole-hearted (Ps 111)
O God, according to thy grace (Ps 51)
O God, be merciful and bless (Ps 67)
O God, be merciful, Be merciful to me (Ps 56)
O God, be merciful to me, For men (Ps 56)
O God, be merciful to me, My soul for refuge (Ps 57)
O God, be thy anointed Son (Ps 72)
O God, give thou ear to my plea (Ps 55)
O God, how good thou art (Ps 73)
O God, give ear unto my cry (Ps 61)
O God, most holy are thy ways (Ps 77)
O God, no longer hold thy peace (Ps 83)
O God, preserve me, for in thee (Ps 16)
O God, regard my humble plea (Ps 61)
O God, the God that saveth me (Ps 51)
O God, thou hast rejected us (Ps 60)
O God, to thy anointed King (Ps 72)
O God, to us show mercy (Ps 67)
O God, we have heard and our (Ps 44)
O God, whom I delight to praise (Ps 109)
O Gracious God, forsake me not (Ps 71)
O let my supplicating cry (Ps 119)
O Lord, be thou my helper true (Ps 12)
O Lord, by thee delivered (Ps 30)
O Lord, give ear when with my voice (Ps 27)
O Lord, how manifold the works (Ps 104)
O Lord, make haste to hear (Ps 141)
O Lord, most high, with all my heart (Ps 9)
O Lord, my earnest cry, thy listening (Ps 119)
O Lord, my God, for thy name's (Ps 109)
O Lord, my God, my joyful (Ps 86)
O Lord, my God, most earnestly (Ps 63)
O Lord, my inmost heart (Ps 139)
O Lord of hosts, how lovely (Ps 84)
O Lord of hosts, in mercy (Ps 84)
O Lord of hosts, to thee I cry (Ps 84)
O Lord, our Lord, in all the earth (Ps 8)
O Lord, thou art my God and King (John Craig may be author. See Julian p 1022b) (Ps 145)
O Lord, thou hast ascended (Ps 68)
O Lord, thou Judge of all (Ps 94)
O Lord, thy perfect righteousness (Ps 119)
O Lord, to thee I cry (Ps 28); X107239 O Lord (close variant)
O Lord, to us thy mercy show (Ps 85)

O make a joyful noise, ye lands (Ps 100)
O mighty man, why wilt thou (Ps 52)
O my soul bless thou Jehovah (Ps 103)
O praise and bless the Lord (Ps 107)
O Praise the Lord, for he is good, His mercies still (Ps 107)
O praise the Lord, for he is good, Let all in heaven (Ps 118)
O praise the Lord, his deeds (Ps 105)
O praise ye the Lord, and sing (Ps 149)
O praise ye the name of Jehovah (Ps 135)
O Royal Bride, give heed (Ps 45)
O save me by thy name (Ps 54)
O sing a new song to the Lord (Ps 96)
O sing ye Alleluia! 'Tis good (Ps 147)
O Sion, 'tis thy God's command (Ps 68)
O teach thou us to count our days (Ps 90)
O thank the Lord, the Lord of love (Ps 136); R103489 His tender mercies
O thou great Shepherd of thy chosen race (Ps 80)
O wherefore do the nations (Ps 2)
O wherefore hast thou cast (Ps 74)
Of mercy and of justice (Ps 101)
On God alone my soul relies (Ps 55)
On the good and faithful (Ps 4)
Praise God, ye servants of the Lord (Ps 113)
Praise Jehovah for his love (Ps 136)
Praise the Lord, for He is good (Ps 107)
Praise the Lord in heavenly places (Ps 148)
Praise waits for thee in Sion (Ps 65)
Praise waits in Sion, Lord, for thee, And unto thee (Ps 65)
Praise waits in Sion, Lord, for thee, There we will (Ps 65)
Praise ye, praise ye the Lord (Ps 148)
Praise ye the Lord among His (Ps 149)
Praise ye the Lord, for it is good (Ps 147)
Praise ye the Lord, His praise proclaim (Ps 146)
Praise ye the Lord, His saints who throng (Ps 150)
Praise ye the Lord, ye hosts (Ps 150)
Praise ye the Lord, ye saints (Ps 150)
Protect and save me, O my God (Ps 59)
Rebels, who had dared to show (Ps 107)
Regard my grief and rescue me (Ps 119)
Rejoice, ye people, homage (Ps 47)
Remember not, O God, the sins (Ps 79)
Rest in the Lord and be thou (Ps 37)
Save me, O God, because the floods (Ps 69)
Since with my God with perfect heart (Ps 18)
Sing a new song to Jehovah (Ps 98)
Sing to the Lord, sing His praise (Ps 96)
Sion founded on the mountain (Ps 87)
Sion, on the holy hills (Ps 87)
Springs and streams no longer (Ps 107)
Teach me, O Lord, thy way of truth (Ps 119)
That man is blest who, fear-

ing God (Ps 1)
The earth and the fulness (Ps 24)
The earth with all that dwell (Ps 24)
The ends of all the earth (Ps 22); R100192 All earth to Him
The glorious gates of righteousness (Ps 118)
The God who sits enthroned (Ps 14); X102395 From heav'n the Lord
The good man's steps are led (Ps 37)
The King rejoiceth in thy strength (Ps 21)
The Lord Almighty is my light (Ps 27)
The Lord Almighty reigns (Ps 93)
The Lord I will at all times bless, In praise my mouth (Ps 34)
The Lord I will at all times bless, My mouth his praises (Ps 34)
The Lord is great; with worthy praise (Ps 48)
The Lord is strong to help (Ps 145)
The Lord my Shepherd holds me (Ps 23)
The Lord, our God, is good to (Ps 145)
The Lord unto his Christ hath (Ps 110)
The Lord upholds the faltering (Ps 145)
The Lord who has remembered us (Ps 115)
The man that fears the Lord (Ps 25)
The mighty God, Jehovah, speaks (Ps 50)
The mighty God, the Lord (Ps 50)
The offering on the altar burned (Ps 40)
The seasons are fixed by wisdom (Ps 104)
The spacious heavens declare (Ps 19)
The steps of those whom He (Ps 37)
The tender love a father hath (Ps 103)
The trespass of the wicked man (Ps 36)
The wicked watching for their prey (Ps 37)
Their God and Saviour they forgot (Ps 106)
They that traffic on the sea (Ps 107)
Thou art my God, O God of grace (Ps 63)
Thou art my portion, Lord (Ps 119)
Thou Jehovah, art my Shepherd (Ps 23)
Thou, Lord, hast dealt well (Ps 119)
Thou, Lord, hast forsaken, to shame brought (Ps 44)
Thou, O Jehovah, shalt endure (Ps 102); X109645 The Lord has heard
Thou, O Lord, art God alone (Ps 102)
Thou visitest the earth in love (Ps 65)
Thou, who didst make and fashion me (Ps 119)
Though I am poor and sorrowful (Ps 69)
Though mighty foes assail me (Ps 119)
Though troubles great o'ershadow me (Ps 71)
Through all the years, may Israel say (Ps 129)
Thus speaks the Lord to wicked (Ps 50)
Thy loving-kindness, Lord, is good (Ps 69)
Thy mercy and thy truth (Ps 36)
Thy might sets fast the mountains (Ps 65); X110565 To bless the earth
Thy promised mercies send to me (Ps 119)
Thy servant, blest by thee (Ps 119)

Thy Spirit, O Lord, makes life (Ps 104)
Thy tender mercies, O my Lord (Ps 40)
Thy wondrous testimonies, Lord (Ps 119)
Thy word sheds light upon my (Ps 119)
To God for help will I repair (Ps 77)
To God my earnest voice I raise (Ps 142)
To God will I direct my prayer (Ps 77)
To thee I lift my soul (Ps 25)
To thee, O God, we render thanks (Ps 75)
To thee, O Lord, I fly (Ps 16)
To thee, O Lord, I humbly cry (Ps 142)
To thee, O Lord, I lift my eyes (Ps 123); X110693 To thee ... mine eyes
Unless the Lord the house (Ps 127)
Unto God our Saviour, Sing a (Ps 98)
What shall I render to the Lord, For all his benefits (Ps 116)
What shall I render to the Lord, What shall my offering (Ps 116)
What time I am afraid (Ps 56)
What wait I for but thee? (Ps 39)
When in his might the Lord (Ps 126)
When in the night I meditate (Ps 16)
When Israel out of Egypt went (Ps 114)
When morning lights the eastern skies (Ps 143)
When Sion in her low estate (Ps 126)
Where'er his creatures gather (Ps 82)
Who, O Lord, shall dwell with thee (Ps 15)
Who, O Lord, with thee abiding (Ps 15)
Whole-hearted thanksgiving to thee (Ps 9)
Why dost thou stand afar (Ps 10)
Why standest thou afar, O Lord (Ps 10)
With firm resolve I held my peace (Ps 39)
With grateful heart my thanks (Ps 138)
With joy and gladness in my soul (Ps 122)
With joy I heard my friends (Ps 122)
With thankful voice praise ye (Ps 117)
Within thy temple, Lord, In that (Ps 48)
Within thy temple, Lord, We think (Ps 48)
Within thy temple's sacred courts (Ps 48)
Ye gates lift your heads (Ps 24)
Ye gates of peace and joy (Ps 118)
Ye who his temple throng (Ps 149)

U.P. Board of Publication, 1917
Under the care of my God (Ps 91); R110811 Under His wings

U.P. Bible songs hymnal, 1927
Alleluia, praise Jehovah (Ps 148); R105181 Let them praises give

U.P. Psalter hymnal, 1927
Lord, thou hast searched me (Ps 139)

U.S.A. National anthems, etc.
see Smith, S.F. My country; Key, F.S. O say, can

Unpartheyisches Gesangbuch. (Mennonite) 1804
Auf, Seele, auf und säume nicht
Aus Gnaden wird der Mensch gerecht
Bedenke, Mensch, das Ende
Der Heiland rufet mir und dir
Der herr uns segne und

behüt
Du unbegreislich höchstes Gut
Es gibt ein wunderschönes Land
Freudenvoll, freudenvoll walle ich fort
Geh, Selle frisch im Glauben fort
Glucksel'ger Tag, da ich erkor
Gott, der du alles wohl bedacht
Gott, ist die Liebe, lässt mich erlösen
Gute Nacht, ihr meine Lieben
Heut Fänget an das neue Jahr
Ich will lieben und mich üben
Ihr jungen Helden, aufgewacht
Kinder, eilt euch zu bekehren
Kinder, lernt die Ordnung fassen
Kommt, Brüder, steht nicht stille
Mein Gott! das herz ich bringe dir
Müde bin ich, geh' zur Ruh'
Nun bringen wir den Leib zur Ruh
Nun gute Nacht, ihr Liebsten mein
Nun sich die Nacht geendet hat
O Gott, du grosser herr der Welt
O wie selig sind die
Run scheiden wir, ihr herzensfreund
Schenk mir ein sanft, zerbrochnes herz
Setze dich, mein Geist, ein wenig
Was mich auf diefer Welt betrübt
Wenn's doch alle Seelen wussten
Wer mit uns nach Zion gehn
Wie bist du mir so innig gut
Wir werfen uns danieder
Wir zieh'n nach dem verheiss'nen Land
Wo ist Jesus, mein Berlangen
Wonne lächelt überall
Untermeyer, Jean Starr, 1882-
Temper my spirit, O Lord
Untermeyer, Louis, 1885-
God, though this life is but
May nothing evil cross
Upham, Thomas Cogswell, 1799-1872
Happy the man who knows His Master
Urseth, Hans A., 1866-1909
Alone with thee, O Lord, when
One resolve, one resolve
Ussery, M.D.
O would you be a blessing; R101813 Don't let your light

V

Van Andel, Henry, tr
Jesus, Saviour, Thou art mine
Van DeVenter, Judson W., 1855-1939
All to Jesus I surrender; R104045 I surrender all
I never can forget the day; R111534 When-e'er I think
I wandered in the shades; R109261 Sunlight, sunlight
Van Dyke, Henry, 1852-1933
By the breadth of the blue
Four things a man must learn
Jesus, thou divine Companion
Joyful, joyful we adore thee
No form of human framing; X111579 Wherever men adore
O Lord, our God, thy mighty
O Maker of the mighty deep
Return, dear Lord, to those
These are the gifts I ask
They who tread the path
Van Hoose, H.W.
Increase my faith, dear Lord; R106979 O hear my earnest
Van Pelt, R.A.
Our Saviour in his earthly
Van Rensseler, H.
What shall I render unto thee
Vaughan, Edmund, 1827-1908
God of mercy and compas-

sion; R104715 Jesus, Lord, I ask
Happy we, who thus united; R104733 Jesus, Mary, Joseph
Sign the Holy Family's praises; X108960 Sing of Mary, pure
Yes, heaven is the prize
Vaughan, Henry, the Silurist, 1621-95
My soul, there is a country
They are all gone into the world
Up to those bright and gladsome
Venantius Fortunatus, see Fortunatus, Venantius Honorius Clementianus, ca 530-609
Vere, Thomas Aubrey de, 1814-1902
Holy Church now stands triumphant; R103446 Hers the Kingdom; X111628 Who is she that
Versteeg, John M.
Does thy soul leap up within
Very, Jones, 1813-80
Father, thy wonders do not singly
We go not on a pilgrimage
Vig, P.S.
How gladly I my place have
Vilhelm, Ulrik, 1826-1910
O sing, all ye lands, with
Vine, Alfred Henry, 1845-1917
O breath of God, breathe on
Vischer [or Fischer], Christoph, 1520-97
To thee, Lord Jesus, thanks
We bless thee, Jesus Christ
Voice of praise, 1887
"Follow Me," the Master said
Vokes, Mrs.
Soon may the last glad song
Ye messengers of Christ
Von

NOTE: von is placed in its usual filing position at the end of the personal name.

Voorsanger, Jacob
Happy he who walketh ever
Vories, William Merrill, 1880-
Let there be light, Lord God
Vulpius. Ein schön geistliche Gesangbuch, 1609
Christus, der ist mein Leben
For me to live is Jesus
My life is hid in Jesus
Praise ye the Lord, ye gentiles

W

"W.W.D." presumed to be D.W. Whittle
Wagner, Georg
Den Vater woll'n wir loben 1527
Wer Christo jetzt will folgen nach. 1527
Wagner, Ida Tyson
The stable was old and rude
Walford, William W.
Sweet hour of prayer
Walker, Anna L., see Coghill, Anna L. Walker
Walker, C.L.
Dearest children, God is near
Walker, Mary Jane, 1816-78
Jesus, I will trust thee
The wanderer no more will roam
We are not left to walk alone
Wallace, James Cowden, 1793-1841
There is an eye that never
Wallin, Johan Olof, 1779-1839
A voice, a heavenly voice
Again thy glorious sun doth
All hail to thee, O blessed
Almighty God, eternal Lord
Behold, the joyful day is nigh
Blessed, blessed he who knoweth
By thy cross, O Christ
Father of lights, eternal Lord
From peaceful slumber waking
Great joy and consolation
Guardian of pure hearts
He lives! O fainting heart
Heavenly Light, benignly
I know in whom I trust

In my quiet contemplation
Jehovah, thee we glorify
Jerusalem, lift up thy voice
Mute are the pleading lips; (paraphrase by E. E. Ryden)
O blessed is the man who stays
O let the children come to me
O my soul, on wings ascending
Only God can bring us gladness
Strike up, O harp and psaltery
Thine agony, O Lord, is o'er
To realms of glory in the skies; X110632 To realms ... I behold
Watch, my soul, and pray
We worship thee, almighty Lord
Where is the Friend for whom
Wallis, James H.
Come, ye children of the Lord
Wallis, Sydney James
Hail thee! Spirit, Lord eternal
Walmsley, Douglas, 1848-1940
Father, O hear us, seeking
Walmsley, Robert, 1831-1905
Come, let us sing of a wonderful
The sun declines; o'er land
We are come with joy
Walter, Howard Arnold, 1883-1918
I would be true, for there are those
Walther, B.
There is within this heart
Walther, Carl Ferdinand Wilhelm, 1811-87
Erstanden, erstanden ist Jesus Christ
He's risen, He's risen, Christ
Walther, Johann, 1496-1570
Der Bräut'gam wird bald rufen
Soon will the heavenly Bridegroom
The Bridegroom soon will call
Thy word, O God, declareth
Walton, W. Spencer, 1850-1906
In tenderness He sought me
O touch mine eyes, that I may
Wandersleben, Martin, 1608-68
As we begin another week
Heut' fangen wir in Gottes
Warburton, George Augustus, 1859-
O thou whose glory shone
Ward, J. W. G.
And whate'er the need may be
Wardlaw, Ralph, 1779-1853
Christ of all my hopes
O Lord our God, arise
Ware, Henry (the younger) 1794-1843
All nature's works His praise
Around the throne of God
Great God, the followers
Happy the home when God is; X100985 Blest is the home
Lift your glad voices; R105792 Loud lift your voices
O thou, in whom alone is
We rear not a temple, like
Waring, Anna Laetitia, 1820-1910
Beneath thy wing, O God, I rest
Father, I know that all my life
Go not far from me, O my
I ask thee for the daily
In heavenly love abiding; X104289 In Jesus' love
My heart is resting
My Saviour, on the word of truth
Waring, Samuel Miller, 1792-1827
Now to him who loved us
Warmingham, Osbert Wrightman, ca 1890-
Spirit of God, for every Good
Warner, Anna Bartlett, 1821-1915
Jesus loves me! this I know
One more day's work for Jesus
The world looks very beauti-

ful
We would see Jesus; for the shadows
Warner, D.S.
A gentle hand unseen by us; R106776 O gentle one, we
By thy blessed word obeying; R101710 Dear Redeemer, we
Church of God, thou spotless
Fill me with thy spirit, Lord; R101480 Come, O Spirit, seal
How sweet this bond; R106585 O brethren, how this
I heard the dear Redeemer say; R108033 Only thine, only thine
I've found my Lord and He is R103493 His yoke is easy
Not in the temples made with; R106796 O glory to Jesus
The earth shall melt with fervent; R107621 O, that last great
Two little hands are sweetly
Warner, John Allan, 1851-1928
Brothers, joining hand
Warner, Susan, 1819-85
Jesus bids us shine; R111944 Yes, Jesus loves me
Warren, Arthur
Glorious are the lofty
Warren, B.E.
Behold, what love, yes; R109249 Such love cannot be
Do you love the world
Eternity draws near, as time; R111567 Where will I go
Glory to God in the highest
I would be closer my Saviour
Let not your weary heart
O come to the Lord today
Out on this dark world
Saviour, coming to thee
Sing about Jesus who died
Weighed in the balance
When I get weary with toils; R101324 Closer, my child
Where is thy hope, poor sinner
Without spot and blameless
Warren, May E.
Lift Him up, 'tis He that bids; R105235 Lift Him up, the risen
Warren, William Fairfield, 1833-1929
I worship thee, O Holy Ghost
Washbourne, Thomas, 1606-87
Lord, thou hast told us that
Washburne, Edward Abiel, 1819-81
Ponder now the Cross, all holy
Softly the night is sleeping; R102557 Glory to God
Waterbury, Jared Bell, 1799-1876
Soldiers of the cross, arise
Waterston, Robert Cassie, 1812-93
Theories, which thousands cherish
Watson, Albert Durant, 1859-1926
Lord of the lands, beneath
Watson, George, 1816-98
With the sweet word of peace
Watson, William, 1858-1935
Great and fair is she, our land
Watt, Lauchlan MacLean, 1867-1957
Dark the day on Calvary's
I bind my heart this tide
O thou, my Judge and King
Watteville, Johannes de, 1718-88
Jesus, thyself to us reveal
Lord Jesus, may I constantly
Lord Jesus, with thy presence
Thanks to the Man of Sorrows
The grace of our Lord Jesus
Wattles, Willard Austin, 1888-1950
"Against my second coming"
I cannot think or reason
Watts, Alaric Alexander, 1797-1864
When shall we meet again
Watts, Isaac, 1674-1748
A broken heart, my God
Above the heavens, eternal
Ah, how shall fallen men

Alas! and did my Saviour; R103268 He loves me; R103382 Help me, dear Saviour (Coffman); R100618 At the cross, at the (Hudson)
Almighty sovereign of the skies
Am I a soldier of the cross; R100455 And when the battle's; R104278 In His name I'll
And must this body die
And now another day is gone; X104304 In mercy, Lord
Arise, O King of grace
As when the Hebrew prophet
At thy command, our dearest
Awake, my soul, to sound His
Awake, our souls! away, our
Be thou exalted, O my God
Before the heavens were
Before the Lord Jehovah's; X100772 Before Jehovah's awful; X100773 Before Jehovah's glorious; X106229 Nations, attend before; X108976 Sing to the Lord
Begin, my tongue, some
Behold the amazing gift of love
Behold the glories of the Lamb
Behold the morning sun
Behold the sure foundation-stone
Behold, what wondrous grace
Beneath th'amazing gift of love
Bless, O my soul! the living
Blest are the humble souls
Blest are the sons of peace
Blest are the undefiled
Blest be the everlasting God
Blest is the man, for ever blest
Blest is the man who shuns
Blest morning, whose first
Broad is the road that leads
Christ hath a garden, walled (paraphrase by Bridges)
Come, dearest Lord, descend; X101375 Come, gracious Lord
Come hither, all ye weary
Come, Holy Spirit, heavenly; X105690 Lord, send thy Spirit
Come, let us join our cheerful; X101432 Come ... sacred songs
Come, sound his praise abroad
Come, we [ye] that love; X101549 Come we who love; X101568 Come, ye that love; R111239 We're marching to
Come, worship at Immanuel's
Dearest of all names above
Deep in the dust before thy
Early, my God, without delay
Eternal power, whose high
Eternal Spirit! we confess
Faith is the brightest evidence
Far as thy name is known
Far from my thoughts, vain
Father, how wide thy glory
Father, I long, I faint to see
Father of glory, to thy name
From all that dwell below; X102376 From all who dwell
Give me the wings of faith; X102513 Give us the wings
Give thanks to God; He reigns
Give thanks to God most high
Give to our God immortal
"Go, preach my gospel," saith
God in his earthly temple
God is the name my soul adores
God is the refuge of his saints
God, my supporter and my hope
God of the morning, at whose
Great God, attend, while
Great God, how infinite art
Great God, indulge my humble
Great God! to what a glorious

Great is the Lord our God
Had I the tongues of Greeks
Happy the heart where graces
Hark! from the tomb a doleful
Hark, how the adoring hosts; X100830 Behold the glories
Hast thou not known, hast thou
He dies! the Friend of sinners; X103234 He died! the Great
He reigns! The Lord, the Saviour
He that hath made his refuge
Hear what the voice from heaven
Here's love and grief beyond
High in the heavens, Eternal
Hosanna to the Prince of grace
Hosanna to the Royal Son
Hosanna with a cheerful
How beauteous are their feet
How bright these glorious spirits
How condescending and how kind
How did my heart rejoice
How glorious Zion's courts; X103675 How glorious is the sacred
How large the promise, how divine
How oft have sin and Satan
How pleasant, how divinely
How pleased and blest was I
How sad our state by nature is
How shall the young secure
How short and hasty is our life
How sweet and awful is the place
How vast the treasure we
Hush! my dear, lie still and slumber; X103777 Hush! dear child, lie
I love the Lord: he heard my
I pray thee, Lord, to guide
I sing the almighty power of; Z104034 I sing the mighty
I wait for thy salvation, Lord
I'll praise my Maker while I've; X104198 I'll praise ... whilst; X104199 I'll praise ... with
I'll speak the honours of my King
I'm not ashamed to own my Lord; X111242 We're not ashamed (Phelps)
In all my vast concern with
In vain we seek for peace
Jehovah reigns! He dwells in
Jesus, dear name! how sweet it
Jesus invites his saints
Jesus shall reign where'er; X108108 Our God shall reign
Jesus, thy love exceeds by far
Jesus who died, is now seated
Join all the glorious names; X104753 Jesus, my great High
Joy to the world! the Lord is; X104954 Joy ... the Lord will
Keep silence, all created
Kingdoms and thrones to God
Let children hear the mighty
Let dogs delight to bark
Let everlasting glories crown
Let every creature join
Let every mortal ear attend; X105122 Let every ear attend
Let every tongue thy goodness
Let me but hear my Saviour say
Life is the time to serve
Like sheep we went astray
Lo! what a glorious sight
Lo, what a pleasing sight
Long as I live I'll bless thy
Long have I sat beneath the sound; X106134 My hope, my portion
Lord, all I am is known
Lord, how secure and blest
Lord, how secure my conscience
Lord, I have made thy word

Lord, in the morning thou shalt
Lord of the worlds above
Lord! thou hast searched and
Lord, thou wilt hear me when
Lord, we confess our numerous
My dear Redeemer, and my Lord; X106043 My blest Redeemer
My drowsy powers, why sleep
My faith shall triumph o'er
My God, how endless is thy; X107235 O Lord, how boundless
My God, my King, thy various
My God, my life, my love
My God, my portion, and my love
My God, permit me not to be
My God, the spring of all my
My Lord, my life, my love see Bridges. My Lord . . .
My Saviour, my Almighty Friend
My Saviour's pierced side
My soul, how lovely is the place
My soul repeat his praise
My soul, thy great Creator praise
My spirit looks to God alone
Nature, with open volume, stands
No more, my God! I boast no
Not all the blood of beasts
Not all the outward forms on earth
Not to the terrors of the Lord; X109799 The saints on earth
Not with our mortal eyes
Now be the God of Israel blessed; X100913 Blessed be the Lord (Psalter version)
Now is the hour of darkness; X101240 Christ the Lord is
Now let the children of the saints
Now to the Lord a noble song (with C. Wesley)
O bless the Lord, my soul
O blessed souls are they
O for a shout of sacred joy
O for an overcoming faith
O God, our help in ages past; X107305 O Lord, our help in; X108107 Our God, our help in
O God, the refuge of thy saints
O Jesus Christ, Redeemer, Lord
O that I knew the secret place
O that the Lord would guide
O, the delights, the heavenly
O, the sweet wonders of that cross
O thou, that hearest when
Once more, my soul, the rising
Our life is ever on the wing
Plunged in a gulf of dark
Praise ye the Lord; all nature
Praise ye the Lord! My heart
Praise ye the Lord! 'tis good
Praise ye the Lord, ye immortal
Salvation and immortal praise
Salvation is forever nigh
Salvation! O the joyful
See what a living stone
Shine, mighty God, on Sion
Show pity, Lord, O Lord
Sin has a thousand treacherous arts
Sin, like a venmous disease
So let our lips and lives; X111422 When Jesus our great
Songs of immortal praise
Stand up, my soul, shake off
Supreme in wisdom as in power
Sweet is the memory of thy grace
Sweet is the work, my God
Teach me the measure of my

That awful day will surely
The God of mercy be adored
The Law commands and makes us
The Lord Jehovah reigns
The Lord my Shepherd is
The Lord of glory is my light
The man is ever blessed
The pity of the Lord, to those
The true Messiah now appears
There is a God who reigns
There is a house not made
There is a land of pure delight
There is a voice of sovereign
This is the day the Lord hath
Thus far the Lord hath led me
Thus saith the mercy of the Lord
'Tis by the faith of joys
'Tis by thy strength the mountains
'Tis from the mercy of our God
To God I lift mine eyes; X110871 Upward I lift mine
To God the only wise
To Him that loved the souls
To Him who sits upon the throne
'Twas by thy blood, immortal
'Twas on that dark, that doleful
Unshaken as the sacred hill
Unveil thy bosom, faithful tomb
Up to the hills I lift my eyes; X110857 Up ... lift mine eyes
Vain are the hopes the sons
We give immortal praise
We sing the almighty power
Welcome, sweet day of rest
What equal honors shall we
What shall I render to my God
What sinners value, I resign
When I can read my title
When I survey the wondrous
When overwhelmed with grief
When we devote our youth
Who shall the Lord's elect
Why do we mourn departing friends
Why should the children
Why should we start and fear
With all my powers of heart; X111750 With all the power
With joy we meditate the grace
With reverence let the saints
With songs and honors sounding
Ye nations round the earth! rejoice
Ye tribes of Adam, join

Waugh, Benjamin, 1839-1908
Now let us see thy beauty

Wayland, John W.
Gracious King enthroned above

Weatherell, F.
Mary Immaculate, Star of the morning

Weaver, Mack
Lord, lay some soul upon my; R109088 Some soul for thee

Webb, Benjamin, 1820-85
Behold, He comes, thy King
Praise the Rock of our salvation

Wegelin, Josua, 1604-40
Auf Christi Himmelfahrt allein
On Christ's ascension I now
Since Christ has gone to

Weingartner, Sigismund
Auf meinen lieben Gott
In God, my faithful God

Weir, Robert Stanley, 1856-
O Canada! Our home, our native; X106594 O Canada! our home and

Weisberg, Florence
How good it is to thank

Weisse, Michael, ca 1480-1534 (various spellings: Weys, Weyss, etc.)
Christ the Lord hath risen
Christ the Lord is risen again
Now lay we calmly in the grave; X110179 This body in the grave

Nun lasst uns den Leib begraben
Praise we our God upon his throne
Weissel, Georg, 1590-1635
Lift up your heads, ye mighty
Macht hoch die Tür
Make wide the door, unbar
O death, where is thy cruel
Seek where ye may to find a way
Seek ye who will some other
Such', wer da will, Ein ander
Weitzman, Lily
Create in this weak form
Grant me strength when skies
Once more, O Lord, do I awaken
The day is done, the night
Welch, Edward Ashurst, 1860-1932
Thou, who didst call thy saints
We lift our hearts, O Father; X110687 To Thee, O heavenly
Wellhaven, Johan S.C., 1807-73
Lord of spirits, I surrender
Wells, Amos R., 1862-1933
God help our country to be
Lord Jesus, blessed Giver
Thou delightest, O Lord, when
Wells, Emmeline B.
Our mountain home so dear
Wells, Marcus B., 1815-95
Holy Spirit, faithful Guide
Welsh traditional, etc.
All poor men and humble
Dark the night lay, wild and
Wendell, Claus August, 1866-1950
Search me, God, and know my
Wendte, Charles William, 1844-1931
Not given to us from out the skies
Wengel, Paul, 1892-
In his love abiding, wait on
O how lovely, O how sweet
Wesley, Charles, 1707-88
A charge to keep I have
A thousand oracles divine
Ah! whither should I go; X106063 My Father bids me
All praise to our redeeming
All praise to the Lamb!
All ye that pass by, to Jesus
And am I born to die
And are we yet to live; X100417 And are we yet alive
And can I yet delay
And can it be that I should
And let our bodies part
And let this feeble body fail
And must I be to judgment
Angels, where'er we go, attend
Arise, my soul, arise, And with a cheerful voice
Arise, my soul, arise, Shake off thy guilty fears
Author of faith, eternal Word
Author of faith, to thee
Author of life divine
Awake, Jerusalem, awake
Away, my needless fears
Away with our fears, our troubles
Before the Father's awful
Behold, how good a thing
Behold the Lamb of God, who
Blessing, honour, thanks and
Blest be that sacred covenant-love
Blest be the dear uniting love
Blow ye the trumpet, blow; R109955 The year of jubilee
Captain of Israel's host
Christ, from whom all blessings; X105459 Lord, from whom all
Christ the Lord is risen today; X105818 Love's redeeming
Christ, whose glory fills the skies; X105784 Lord, whose glory
Come, Father, Son, and Holy Ghost; X101982 Eternal Sun of Righteousness
Come Holy Ghost, our hearts; X101390 Come ... our

souls
Come, Holy Spirit, raise our songs
Come, let us anew our journey
Come, let us join our friends; X109799 The saints on earth
Come, let us join with one
Come, and let us sweetly join
Come, let us rise with Christ
Come, let us use the grace
Come, let us who in Christ
Come, let us with our Lord
Come, O thou all-victorious Lord
Come, O thou Traveler unknown
Come, on my partners in distress
Come, sinners, to the gospel
Come, thou everlasting Spirit
Come, thou long-expected Jesus; X101490 Come, Redeemer, blessed; X103095 Hail, thou long-expected
Come, thou universal Blessing; X105798 Love divine, all loves
Come, ye weary sinners, come
Depth of mercy! can there be
Draw near, O Son of God
Equip me for the war
Eternal Beam of Light divine; X101976 Eternal Source
Ever gracious Lord, I fly
Father, at thy footstool see
Father, God, thy love we
Father, I dare believe thee
Father, I stretch my hands to
Father, in whom we live
Father of Jesus Christ, my
Father, Son, and Holy Ghost; In solemn power
Father, Son, and Holy Ghost, One in three
Father, Son, and Spirit, hear
For ever here my rest shall
Forth in thy Name, O Lord I go; X102336 Forth ... we go
From my own works at last
Gentle Jesus, meek and mild; X105304 Lamb of God, I look
Give me a new, a perfect heart
Give me the faith which can
Giver of concord, Prince
Glory be to God on high (Gloria in excelsis, paraphrased)
God is gone up on high
God of all power, and truth
God of Israel's faithful
God of love, that hearest; X102727 God of love, who
God of my life, whose gracious
God of my salvation, hear
Granted is the Saviour's prayer
Hail! Holy, Holy, Holy Lord
Hail the day that sees him
Happy soul, thy days are
Happy the man that finds
Happy the souls to Jesus joined
Hark! a voice divides
Hark! the herald angels sing; R106535 O Bethlehem, dear; X103153 Hark, how all the welkin
Head of the Church triumphant; X103311 Head of thy Church
Heavenly Father, God of love
Help us to help each other; X110782 Try us, O God! and
Holy, and true, and righteous
Holy as thou, O Lord, is none
Holy Lamb, who thee confess
Hosanna in the highest
How can a sinner know
How glorious is the life
How happy every child of grace
I know that my Redeemer lives, And ever prays for me
I know that my Redeemer lives; He lives, and on

the earth
I know that my Redeemer lives; He lives, who once was dead
I long to behold him arrayed
"I the good fight have fought"
I want a principle within
If thou impart thyself to me
In age and feebleness extreme
In that sad memorable night
In weariness and pain
Infinite God, to thee we raise
Jesus, from whom all blessings
Jesus, let all thy lovers
Jesus, let thy pitying eye
Jesus, let thy sufferings
Jesus, Lord, we look to thee
Jesus, Lover of my soul
Jesus, Master of the feast
Jesus, my Lord, my God
Jesus, my Saviour, Brother
Jesus, my strength, my hope; X106106 My God, my strength
Jesus, my truth, my way
Jesus, the all-restoring Word
Jesus, the conqueror, reigns
Jesus! the Name high over all
Jesus, the sinner's Friend
Jesus, the truth and power
Jesus, the weary wanderer's
Jesus, thine all-victorious
Jesus, thou all-redeeming Lord
Jesus, thou art my righteousness
Jesus, to thee I now can fly
Jesus, united by thy grace
Jesus, we look to thee
Jesus, we thus obey
Join, all ye ransomed sons
Join, earth and heaven
Lamb of God, I look to thee; X102462 Gentle Jesus, meek; X105820 Loving Jesus, gentle
Lamb of God, whose dying love; X105043 Lamb ... bleeding love
Leader of faithful souls
Let earth and heaven agree; X104899 Jesus, transporting
Let him to whom we now belong
Let not the wise their wisdom
Let saints on earth in concert
Let the world their virtue
Life of all that lives below
Lift up your hearts to things
Lift your heads, ye friends
Light of those whose dreary
Lo! for us the wilds are glad
Lo! He comes with clouds descending (a very complicated text) see Cennick, Charles. Lo! He comes . . .
Lo! I come with joy to do
Lo! on a narrow neck of land; X106840 O God, mine inmost
Lord, and is thine anger
Lord, I believe a rest remains
Lord, if at thy command; X105757 Lord, when at thy
Lord, in the strength of grace
Lord of the harvest, hear thy
Lord, whom winds and seas
Love divine, all loves excelling; X104717 Jesus, Lord, of all
Meet and right it is to sing
My God, I am thine; what comfort
My God, I know, I feel thee
My heart is full of Christ
None is like Jeshurun's God
O come, and dwell in me
O Father of mercy, be ever adored
O for a heart to praise my; X106757 O ... to love my God
O for a principle within
O for a thousand tongues; R100914 Blessed be the name; X102555 Glory to God and praise
O for that tenderness of heart

O glorious hope of perfect
O God, most merciful and true
O how happy are they who the; X103693 How happy are they who Jesus; X103694 How happy are they, who their [the] X107052 O how ... their Saviour
O Jesus, full of pardoning
O joyful sound of gospel grace
O Lamb of God, for sinners
O Love divine, what hast
O Son of God and man, receive
O that I could repent
O that my load of sin were
O, that the Comforter would
O the depth of love divine
O thou, before the world began
O thou who camest from above
O thou who hast redeemed of old
O thou who wouldst not have
O thou, whom all thy saints
O thou whom we adore
O what shall I do, my Saviour
Oft when the waves of passion
Open, Lord, my inward ear
Our heavenly Father, Source
Partners of a glorious hope
Peace be to this habitation; X108197 Peace ... congregation
Praise the Lord who reigns
Pray, without ceasing, pray
Rejoice, the Lord is King!; X105251 Lift up your heart
See how great a flame aspires
See the Lord, thy Keeper, stand
Servant of all, to toil; X109097 Son of the carpenter
Servant of God, well done
Shepherd divine, our wants
Shepherd of souls, with pitying eye
Shepherd, with thy tenderest; X103124 Happy soul, secure
Sing to the great Jehovah's
Sinners, turn: why will ye die
Soldiers of Christ, arise
Sons of men, behold from far
Spirit of faith, come down; X109173 Spirit of truth
Spirit of grace and health; X101971 Eternal Son, eternal Love
Stand the omnipotent decree
Stay, thou insulted Spirit
Still nigh me, O my Saviour
Suffering Son of Man, be near
Talk with us, Lord, thyself; X109147 Speak to us, Lord
The Church triumphant in thy
The Lord of earth and sky
The praying spirit breathe
Thee we address in humble prayer
Thou didst live to God alone
Thou great mysterious God
Thou hidden Source of calm
Thou Judge of quick and dead
Thou, Lord, must for thy sake
Thou Son of God, whose flaming
Thou very present Aid
Through Him who all our sickness
Thy ceaseless, unexhausted
'Tis finished! the Messiah
To God your every want
To the hills I lift mine eyes, To the everlasting hills
To the hills I life my eyes: Whence shall help for me
To us a Child of royal birth
Vain, delusive world, adieu
Victim Divine, thy grace we
Was ever grief like thine
We know, by faith we know
Weary of wandering from my
Weary souls that wander wide
Weep not for a brother deceased
What is our calling's glorious
What shall I do, my God
What shall I render to my God
When, my Saviour, shall I be

Where shall my wandering soul
Wherewith, O Lord, shall I
Who are these arrayed in white
Wisdom and power to Christ
With glorious clouds encompassed
Worthy, O Lord, art thou
Ye servants of God, your Master
Ye simple souls that stray
Ye that do the Master's will
Wesley, E.G.
Christ the Lord cometh; R104667 Jesus is coming
Wesley, John, 1703-91
How happy is the pilgrim's lot
To God the Father, Son, and Spirit, One in Three
Wesley, John and Charles
Ho! every one that thirsts
Our Lord is risen from the dead; X108126 Our Lord ... has gone
Thou Shepherd of Israel divine; X110322 Thou Shepherd ... and mine
We lift our hearts to thee
Wesley, Samuel, sr., 1662-1735
Behold the Saviour of mankind
Wesley, Samuel, jr., 1691-1739
The Lord of Sabbath let us praise
West, Lewis Renatus, 1753-1826
Praise for every scene
West, Robert Athow, 1809-65
Come, let us tune our loftiest
West, Russell Greene, 1894-
O loving Father, hear thou
Westall, J.
"O how shall I keep Christmas"
When shepherds watched their flocks by night, In Bethlehem's fields
Weston, Rebecca J.
Father, we thank thee for the night
Westra, Dewey
Alleluia! Praise ye God
How blessed are the perfect
Let all exalt Jehovah's
With all my heart will I
Westwood, Horace, 1884-
Spirit of Truth, of Life
Wetzel, F.G.
How good it is for brethren
Wexels, Wilhelm Andreas, 1797-1866
O happy day when we shall stand
One radiant morn the mists
Some day, I know, the mist
What joy, to think of that
Wexelsen, Marie, 1832-1911
I am so glad each Christmas; X103671 How glad I am each
Wheelock, Cyrus H.
Come, go with me, beyond
Ye elders of Israel, come join
Wheelock, John Hall, 1886-
How little our true majesty
Leave starry heaven behind
Put down your foot and you
The amplitude of space comes
Whitaker, Robert, 1863-1944
My country is the world
Whitcomb, George W.
Jesus may come today; R102517 Glad day! Glad day
White, Frederick M.
We bless thee, Lord, for all
White, Gilbert, 1859-1933
Hail, O Mary, full of grace
O Father, for this little life
White, Henry Kirke, 1785-1806
Come, Christian brethren, ere
Oft in danger, oft in woe; X106032 Much in sorrow, oft; X107927 Oft in sorrow, oft
The Lord our God is clothed; X109694 The Lord ... full of
When marshalled on the nightly
White, Hinton
On desert sands the vision
White, W.A.
Spirit of truth, we call

White spiritual
I am a poor wayfaring; R104209 I'm going there to meet
Jesus walked this lonesome
Whitfield, Frederick, 1829-1904
I need thee, precious Jesus
I saw the cross of Jesus
There is a name I love to hear; R107054 O, how I love Jesus
Whitfield, George
Hymnbook, 1757
Come thou almighty King
Whitford, C.P.
Just over the mountains in; R110997 We are nearing home
Whiting, William, 1826-78
Eternal Father, strong to save; X100364 Almighty Father (Missionary service book)
O Lord, our little ones to thee
Whitman, Walt, 1819-92
All the past we leave behind
Away, O soul, hoist up the anchor
Whitmore, Lucy Elizabeth Georgiana, 1792-1840
Father, again in Jesus' name; X107218 O Lord, again in thy
We come, Lord, to thy feet
Whitney, M. Fannie
We thank thee, heavenly Father
Whitney, Orson F.
Saviour, Redeemer of my soul
The wintry day descending
Whittier, John Greenleaf, 1807-92
All as God wills, who wisely
All things are thine; no gifts
All through the long bright
Blest land of Judea! Thrice
Blow, winds of God, awake
Dear Lord and Father of mankind; X101698 Dear Lord ... of us
In calm and cool and silence see Niles, John Jacob
Forgive, O Lord, our severing; X110454 Thy grace impart
He stood of old, the holy
Heap high the farmer's wintry
I bow my forehead in the dust; X103831 I bow my forehead to
I know not what the future; X103948 I long for household; X111405 When in the maddening; X111814 Within the maddening; X111620 Who fathoms the eternal
I see the wrong that round me
Immortal Love, for ever full; X103231 He cometh not a King; X111084 We may not climb; X111092 We need not climb
It may not be our lot to wield
Let every creature hail
No longer forward or behind; X106265 No ... nor behind
O brother man, fold to thy; X106304 Not empty worship; X106976 O, he whom Jesus
O Lord, and Master of us all; X103231 He cometh not a King
O Lord our God, in time to be
O Love Divine, whose constant
O Love! O Life! our faith and; X108095 Our friend, our brother
O pure reformers! not in vain
O sometimes gleams upon our; X107566 O sometimes gleams upon my
Once more the liberal year
Our thought of thee is glad
Our fathers' God, from out
Sound over all waters, reach; X109465 The dark night
The harp at nature's advent
Thine are all the gifts, O

God
Unto the calmly gathered
We search the world for truth
We see not, know not; all our
What thou wilt, O Father, give
When on my day of life the night
Wherever through the ages rise
With silence only as their benediction
Whittingham, William. d 1579
Now Israel may say, and that truly:- If that the Lord
Whittle, Daniel W., 1840-1901
Be ye strong in the Lord; R102237 Firmly stand
Dying with Jesus, by death; R105991 Moment by moment
Fierce and wild the storm (by W.W.D., Pseud); R104947 Joy, behold the Saviour
"For God so loved!" O wondrous; R102561 Glory to God
I know not why God's wondrous; R101087 But I know whom I
In grace the holy God did full; R101099 By grace are ye saved
O, day of awful story; R100847 Behold the stone
Our Lord is now rejected; R107642 O, the crowning day
"Redeemed! redeemed!" O, sing
Spirit so holy, Spirit of love
There shall be showers of blessing; R108895 Showers of blessing
There's a royal banner given; R105884 Marching on
While we pray and while we; R111678 Why not now
Who came down from heaven to; R109126 Sound the chorus
Would you lose your load of sin; R104923 Jesus, who on the cross
The Whole Booke of Psalmes, 1647, i.e. The Bay Psalm Book
O Lord, Almighty God, Thy works
Whytehead, Thomas, 1815-43
Resting from his work today
Widstoe, John A.
How long, O Lord, most holy
Lead me into life eternal
Wieand, Albert Cassel, 1871-
On the radiant threshold; R104371 In the morning, noon
Wienland, M.M.
O weary pilgrim, lift your head; R104949 Joy cometh in the morning
Wiesenmeyer, Burkhard, d before 1691
How lovely shines the morning star; X103717 How lovely now the
Wight, Almeda E.
'Tis a sweet and tender story; R104492 It must be told
Wightman, Richard
Singers, sing! The hoary world
Wiglesworth, Esther, 1827-1904
Almighty Father, God of love (authorship uncertain)
Soldiers, true and faithful
Wigner, John Murch, 1844-
Come to the Saviour now
Wilcox, Ella Wheeler, 1855-1919
Love thyself last
Wilder, H.C., 1860-1948
Unchanging God, who livest
Wile, Frances Whitmarsh, 1878-1939
All beautiful the march of days
Wiley, Hiram Ozias, 1831-73
He leads us on by paths we; X103260 He leads ... through childhood's
Wilhelm II, duke of Saxe-Weimar, 1598-1662
Herr Jesu Christ, dich zu uns

Lord Christ, reveal thy holy face
Lord Jesus Christ, be present; X105549 Lord .. be with us
O Christ, thy grace unto us
To God, the Father, God the Son
Wilkinson, Katie Barclay, 1859-1928
May the mind of Christ my
Willcox, Mary Jane, 1835-1919
Once again, dear Lord, we
Willes, William
Come along, come along, is the call
Thanks for the Sabbath School; R104936 Join in the jubilee
Williams, Benjamin, 1725-95
Holy, holy, holy Lord!
Williams, Corinne
Forgive the things I've said
Williams, Edith
Jesus so lowly, Child of the earth
Williams, Helen Maria, 1762-1827
While thee I seek, protecting
Williams, Irena F.
Our Father, God, whose mercies
Williams, Isaac, 1802-65
Be thou my Guardian; X100743 Be thou our Guardian
Lord, in this thy mercy's day
O Holy Ghost, thou God of Peace
Williams, Isabel, d 1911
O Sacred Heart, O Heart of Jesus, hear
Williams, M.B.
There's a dear and precious Book; R100919 Blessed book, precious
Williams, Roger, ca 1604-83
God makes a path, provides a
Williams, Sarah, 1838-68
Because I knew not when my life
Williams, Theodore Chickering 1855-1915
As the storm retreating
By law from Sinai's clouded
Glory be to God on high
God be with thee! Gently; X102686 God is with me
Hast thou heard it, O my brother
In the lonely midnight
Lord, who dost the voices bless
My Country, to thy shore
Thou rulest, Lord, the lights
To hold thy glory, Lord of all
When the world around us throws
When thy heart with joy
Williams, Thomas
Father in heaven, thy children
Williams, William, 1717-91
Arglwydd, arwain trwy'r anialwch
Guide me, O thou great Jehovah; X103005 Guide ... great Redeemer; X103008 Guide us, O thou
O'er the gloomy hills; X107904 O'er those gloomy
Onward march, all-conquering
Speak, I pray thee, gentle Jesus
Williamson, T.R.
Once in Jerusalem of old
Willis, Love Maria Whitcomb, 1824-1908
Father, hear the prayer we
Willis, Nathaniel Parker, 1807-67
The perfect world, by Adam
Willman, F.A.
Hark! Are they not angels
Wills, Whitfield Glanville, 1841-91
In our work and in our play
Wilson, Edwin Henry, 1898-
Where is our holy church
Wilson, Elizabeth, 1867- and Helen Thoburn, 1885-1932
Father of lights, in whom
Wilson, Ira B., 1880-1950

Out on the highways and byways; R105852 Make me a blessing
Wilson, Jennie
Time is filled with swift transition; R103506 Hold to God's unchanging
Wilson, Lewis Gilbert, 1858-1928
America, awake! Behold the glory
O God, our dwelling-place
O troubled sea of Galilee
The works, O Lord, our hands
Wilson, Sarah Josselyn, 1893-
The land we love is calling
Wilson, Stewart, 1889-
In every town and village
Lord, who didst send by two
Praise we the Lord, who made
Up, my neighbour, come away; R110848 Up and get us gone
When Jesus was a baby
Winchester, Caleb Thomas, 1847-1920
The Lord our God alone is
Winckler, Johann Joseph, 1670-1722
Ringe recht, wenn Gottes Gnade
Shall I, for fear of feeble man
Strive aright when God doth
Wine, Mary Stoner, 1885-
I believe in thee, Lord Jesus
Love of God, eternal love
Peace, perfect peace have they
The riches of God are eternal
Wingate, Mary B.
Dear to the heart of the Shepherd; R108151 Out in the desert
Wingrove, John, 1720-93
Hail! my ever blessed Jesus
Winks, William Edward, 1842-1926
Lord, thy servants forth are
Winsett, R.E.
Built on the Rock, without spot
There is coming a day when to; R105917 May we sow righteous
Wipo of Burgundy, d ca 1048
Christ the Lord is risen today, Christians haste
Christians, to the Paschal Victim
Victimae Paschali laudes
Wise, Isaac Mayer, 1819-1900
From heaven's heights the thunder
In mercy, Lord, incline thine
"Let there be light", at dawn
Wise, Isidore
Through-out the night, O God
Wiseman, Nicholas Patrick Stephen, 1802-65
Full in the panting heart of Rome
Wither, George, 1588-1667
Behold the sun, that seemed
Come, O come in pious lays
The Lord of Heaven confess
Sweet baby, sleep! What ails
To God, with heart and cheerful
Witter, W.E.
While Jesus whispers to you
Wobeser, Ernst Wilhelm von, 1727-95
I see my Saviour languish
My Saviour was betrayed
Wolcott, Samuel, 1813-86
Christ for the world we sing
Content, O Lord, and free
Goodly were thy tents
Tell me, whom my soul doth love
Wolf [Wolff], Jakob Gabriel, 1684-1754
Blest are they, supremely
Wolfe, Aaron Roberts, 1821-1902
A parting hymn we sing
Wood, Maurice Arthur Ponsonby, 1916-
Worship, glory, praise and honour
Woodbury, Isaac B.
Ho! reapers of life's harvest

Wood, Basil, 1760-1831
Hail, thou Source of every
Woodford, James Russell, 1820-85
Lamb of God, for sinners slain
Not by thy mighty Hand
Within the Father's house
Woodhouse, Charles Goddard 1835-76
Heavenly Shepherd, thee we pray (rewritten by G. Thring)
Woodhull, Alfred Alexander, 1810-36
Great God of nations, now
Woodmansee, Emily H.
Up! arouse thee, O beautiful
When dark and drear the skies
Woodrow, Fred
Use me, O my gracious Saviour
Woods, Amy S.
Now let us raise our Harvest song; R109987 Then praises bring
Woods, Bertha H.
Abide with me;fast breaks the morning light see Lyte, H. F. Abide with me
Woods, Isabel
Thine is the glory, thine
Woodward, George Ratcliffe, 1849-1934
Shepherds, in the field abiding
Woodworth, Samuel
Rich in mercy, Jesus reigns
Wordsworth, Christopher, 1807-85
Alleluia! Alleluia! Hearts and voices; X100320 Alleluia! ... voices heavenward raise; X100322 Alleluia! ... to heaven and voices
Arm these thy soldiers
Come, ever blessed Spirit
Father, of all, from land
Glory be to God the Father
Gracious Spirit, Holy Ghost
Hark! the sound of holy voices
Heavenly Father, send thy blessing
Holy, holy, Holy, Lord God
In thy glorious resurrection
Lord, be thy word my rule
Love is kind and suffers long
O day of rest and gladness
O God, in whose all-searching eye
O Lord of heaven and earth
O Lord, our strength in weakness
See the Conqueror mounts in triumph; X103527 Holy Ghost, Illuminator; X111635 Who is this that
Sing, O sing, this blessed morn
Songs of thankfulness
The day is gently sinking
The grave itself a garden is
Thine for ever! Thine for ever
Thou, who the night in prayer; X107348 O Lord, who in thy
When from the city of our God
Wordsworth, Elizabeth, 1840-
God is our stronghold and our stay
O Lord our Banner, God of might
Wordsworth, William 1770-1850
Blest are the moments, doubly
Serene will be our days
Stern daughter of the Voice of God
Worgan, Ann
The worst of evils we can
Worthington, John, 1725-90
Go, my soul, go every day
Wortman, Denis, 1835-1922
God of the prophets, bless
Today beneath benignant skies
Wotton, Henry, 1568-1639
How happy is he born and taught; X103697 How happy ... born or taught
Wreford, John Reynell, 1800-81
Lord! I believe; thy power
Lord, while for all mankind
When my love to God grows weak; X111443 When ... to Christ
Wright, J. B. F.

Precious memories, unseen angels
Wright, William, 1859-1924
March on, my soul, with strength
Writer, Clara, 1859-1915
A little seed lay fast asleep
Wyse, John, 1825-98
I'll sing a hymn to Mary

Y

Yates, John H.
Encamped along the hills of light; R102035 Faith is the victory
How dear to my heart is the story; R109864 The story that never
Yattendon hymnal, 1899 was edited by Robert Bridges who did much of the writing. See his name.
Yigdal, see Jewish doxology.
The God of Abraham praise
Yoder, Silvanus
Some time we all shall understand; R106271 No more we'll roam
Young, Alfred
Slain for my soul, for all my
Young, Andrew, 1807-89
There is a happy land, far
Young, Edward, 1683-1765
When in his thoughts the stars
Young, J.
O Holy Lord, our God
Young, William
While thou, O my God, art my

Z

Zelley, H. J.
I do not ask to choose; R100898 Bless me, Lord
My heart was distressed; R103227 He brought me out (Gilmour)
Walking in sunlight all my; R103369 Heavenly sunlight
Ziegler, Caspar
Ich freue mich in dir. 1648
O Lord, we welcome thee
Zihn, Johann Friedrich, 1650-1719
God liveth still! Soul despair
Zinzendorf, Anna Nitschmann, 1715-60
Deeply moved and duly heeding
My Saviour, that I without thee
Zinzendorf, Christian Renatus, 1727-62
I am needy, yet forgiven (with Anna N. Zinzendorf)
Man of sorrows, now my soul
Marter Gottes, wer kann dein vergessen
O delightful theme, past all; X106167 My Redeemer, overwhelmed
O'er eras past I've pondered
The passion theme pursuing
'Tis the most blest and needful
Unto Jesus' cross I'm now retiring
We who here together are
When I visit Jesus' grave
Zinzendorf, Erdmuth Dorothea, countess von, 1700-56
Jesus, God of our salvation
Lamb of God, thy precious blood
Lord, in thy name we meet
Reach out thy scepter, King
Zinzendorf, Nicolaus Ludwig von, 1700-60
A messenger of peace
All the bliss which we possess
Are you formed a creature new
As long as Jesus Lord remains
Be present with thy servants
Bread of life, Christ by whom
Christ will gather in his own
Christian hearts, in love united
Christ's love produces love

Come, sing, thou happy Church
Destroy, O Lord, the carnal
Ere we know our lost condition
Eternal depth of love divine
Faithful Lord, my only joy
Fit us for thy service, Lord
From land to land the Christian
From place to place the Christian
Glory to God! Whose witness
Had we naught, naught beyond; X103018 Had we naught, had we
Happy race of witnesses
Hold o'er thy church, Lord
High-Priest before the Father's
I thirst, thou wounded Lamb
If our all on Christ we
In mercy, Lord, this grace
In spirit I am waiting
In these our days exalt thy grace; X100517 Arise, O Lord, exalt
In thy love and knowledge
Jesus, by the Holy Spirit
Jesus Christ, thou Leading-Star; X104593 Jesus ... Guiding-Star
Jesu, geh voran auf der Lebensbahn
Jesus, great High-Priest
Jesus, hear our prayer
Jesus, hear the way; X104603 Jesus, day by day; X104628 Jesus, guide our way; X104699 Jesus, lead thou on; X104837 Jesus, still lead on
Jesus, Lord, most great and glorious
Jesus' love unbounded
Jesus, thou wounded Lamb
Jesus thy blood and righteousness (with Paul Eber)
Jesus, truest Friend, unite
Judge me now, my God and
Let thy presence go with me
Lord, for grace we thee entreat
Lord Jesus, bless thy witnesses
Lord Jesus, by thy death
Lord Jesus, for our call of grace
Lord, our High-priest and Saviour
Lord, thy word, that sacred
Mighty God, we humbly pray
Most gracious God and Lord
My All-in-all, my faithful friend
None from God so distant are
None God the Father's favor share
O, how great, how rich, how free
O Jesus Christ, most holy
O Jesus, for thy matchless
O Jesus my Lord, for ever
O Jesus, were we, through thy love
O my Immanuel, my wounded
O thou to whose all-searching
O thou, who in that last, sad
Own thy congregation, O thou
Round Tabor heavenly glories
Shepherd, help thy chosen few
Sinners, come, the Saviour see
That our Lord's views with us
The holy angels when they to Christ
The Lord Himself gave forth
The unbounded love of my Creator
Thou, gracious Saviour, for my good; X103781 I am a little child
To that Lord who unconstrained (with Anna N. Zinzendorf)
To thee, God Holy Ghost, we pray
Urged by love, to every nation
Warrior, at thy station stand; X110955 Warrior, on thy
We hail thee, Lord, thy

Church's Rock
We pray thee, wounded Lamb
Welcome among thy flock
What affords the Christian warrior
Whate'er I am, whate'er I do
When shall thine hour, dear Jesus
Whether the end of earthly life
While the pilgrim travels
While we take our seat
With new life endowed by Christ
Ye Bottomless depths of God's

Zions Herfen (Das kleine geistliche Harfe der Kinder Zions) 1803
Ach Gott, ein manches herzeleid

Zwick, Johannes, 1496-1542
Each morning brings us fresh

Zwingli, Ulrich [Huldreich], 1484-1531
Guide, O Lord, thy chariot now

PART TWO: THE TUNES

Index III

Tune Names and Variants, with Citations

A babe is born (English trad) [LLMRMDTL, MLTDTLSL] BG116 1

A blessing in prayer (Kirkpatrick) [DRMSSMRDDM, MMR FFM] AU109 2

-----. R [MFSSSDSSLLS, MS SFF] 3

A call for help (Motte) [SDM MFMMRDDRD, LSDR] AY327 4

-----. R [DFFFFLLLSF#S, MRRMF] 5

A charge to keep (Mason) X Laban 6

A child of a king (Sumner) X The child of a king 7

A child of the King (Sumner) X The child of a king 8

A child this day (English trad) X Sandys 9

A clean heart (Byshe) [MFF# SMMRD, SMSTTRLL] AU408; BB634 10

-----. R [DTLSMSMS, TLSTL SLM,] 11

A Danish tune (Balle) X Emmanuel 12

A few more years (Dunbar) [DMRDSTRD, SSMMDRMR,] AS475; AX612; AY137 13

A few more years shall roll (---) [DMMRFM, RDDDMR, RMSM] AX576; AY252 14

A full surrender (Hugg) [DMF LSDST, LSSLSMR, D] AX 399; AY109 15

-----. R [DTRDS, LS#TLS, MFF#SDS] 16

A gallery carol (Church-gallery book) [SDTDRMFSFMR, MF MFS] BG25 17

A great and mighty wonder (Geistliche kirchengesang: Cologne, 1599) X Rosa mystica 18

A hymn anthem (Beethoven) [SDSSMDMMRDDT, SFRT] AH179; BH77; BI37 19

-----. V [SDSMDMMRDDT, SFRTS] BH77 20

-----. V [SDSMDSMRDDT, SFMRD] BI37 21

A little child (Flemish trad) [DMRDDMSSLS, DMRDDM] X352; BG74 22

A little kingdom I possess (Rogers) [MSMMMSRR, TD DMMS, SS] BH251 23

A little while (Tarbutton) [DD DDDDDDDDTRD, LLL] H 502; U435; V696 24

A message from the Sacred Heart (Montani) [DTDLS# LMM, LTDRDT, DT] BQ68 25

A message sweet (Hecht) [SSMFSDDTLLS, SSTDR] BH133 26

A mighty fortress (Luther) X Ein feste burg 27

A morning hymn (Clarke) [DMFRTDRT, RMSF#SLF#S,] F145b 28

A new dial (English trad) [MLLS#MDDT, TLLS#MDLT,] BG64 29

A new shrine (Heller) [SDSM MMRDS, SLTDRDT] BH213 30

A noble life (Grimm) [SFMRD SS#LLR, RMRSRR#] BH225 31

A poor wayfaring man of grief (---) [SFMSDDTDRRRM, FMDD] BC153 32

A prayer for grace (Minkler) [SFMTLL, LSLSSFM, SSF]

AX325 33
-----. R [DDDDTLLSS, SLS FSFM] 34
A priestly Heart (Mitterer) [SDTLSLSS, SDDRDTDM] BQ337 35
-----. R [SMRDTTLL, LRDTS DRM,] 36
A ransom for all (Warren) [SSMFSDMDRD, MFFFFS] AX319 37
-----. R [SSM, DDS, MFFFFS FMMF] 38
A safe stronghold (Luther) X Ein feste burg 39
A shelter in the time of storm (Belden) [SMRFMRLR, DTT DDRSM,] BB585 40
-----. R [SSLFLLSSM, DDMD DDR] 41
A shelter in the time of storm (Rosche) [SSDMDLDS, SDD DDMDR,] AY319 42
-----. R [DMMMMMRDDLS, DTTTL] 43
A shelter in the time of storm (Sankey) [SDDDRMFS, MMM MMFMR,] AI403; AM719; AX515 44
-----. R [SLLLLLTLSSS, MF FFS] 45
A shepherd band (Hutchins. S. S. Hymnal) [SSLTSLTDT, RRRRRRR] BR546 46
-----. R [SSLTSLTDT, SSDT TLS] 47
A solis ortus cardine (Plainsong, M 3) [RMFSLRMFSFMM, SL DD] E18; J20a 48
A stronghold sure (Luther) X Ein feste burg 49
A Succoth prayer (Jassinowsky) [MMMDFMMRDRFMRD, DS] BH184 50
A virgin most pure (I English carol) [MFSLL#LSFM, RSF MRD, M] BG4a 51
-----. R [MSFMRFMRDD, TD RMSF] 52
A virgin most pure (II English carol) [DDMSSMMSFMRD, DDMS] BG4B 53
-----. R [MRRFMRD, MSSLLS, MFSL] 54
A virgin most pure (III English carol) [LTDRSF#SMLSMRD LTL,] BG4C 55
-----. R [MF#SSLSMR, RL SMSF#M, L] 56
A virgin most pure (IV English carol) [MFSLSFMR, SMFS LSD, M] AD134; BP14; BQ 12 57
-----. V [MFSLSFMR, SM FSLTD, M] AD134 57a
-----. V [MFSLSFMR, MF SLSD, MF] BQ12 58
A virgin unspotted (English trad) [SDMSSFMDRMFMRD, SD] E29; AT427 59
A virgin unspotted (II English trad) X Bramley 60
A virgin unspotted (III English trad) X No room in the inn 61
A voice hath spoken (Keeler) [SDRMSFMRDR, MFMRDT] BC291 62
A week within the Sukko green (Schalit) [LLSLTDRTL, LM MDRM, M] BH189 63
A week within the Sukko green (Weinberg) [SMRDTLDS, SD DRDM, LF] BH190 64
A wonderful Saviour (Kirkpatrick) X He hideth my soul 65
Aaberg (Crueger) X St Nicholas 66
Abbey (Hopkins) [SSLSSDRDRM, MFMRMD] D380b 67
Abbey (Scottish Psalter, 1615) [DDMRDDTD, FMRRD#RSM] W455; X492; AF311; AL 652b; AP114; BR306 68
Abbot's Leigh (Taylor) [SMD DDTLLS, LMFSLSF] F257a; BV424; BY17a 69
Abend [ist est wieder] (Rinck) X St Lucian 70
Abendlied (Ebeling) X Shining day 71
Abendlied (Schubert) [SMSFM RDSR, MFRLDTR] BE43 72
Abendruh (Schultz) [SSMFLSM,

SDDRRMSDT] BK14 73

Abends (Oakeley) [SDTLLFMR, RMFSDTLS, T] A120; B291; C400; D33b; F24a; G42; I48; J334; K417; O258; Q280; R 62; S46; T58a; V437; W292a; AB328; AC218; AD86; AE223; AJ91a; AL556c; AP666a; AR 529; AS393; BA415; BB56; BE133; BF179; BV62; BY703; BZ 74

Aber (Monk) [DTLSFM, MSF MRM, MMMF#] I155; O103; AZ582-S; BA210 75

Aberavon (Davis) [SFMRFM, SFMRRD, TDTD] D187b 76

Aberdeen (Chalmers' Collection) [DRMSDRTD, MRSFMR, DR] E561; F581; R328; W481b; X320; AL327; AN303; AP38; AW596; BY550b 77

Aberdour (Essex) [SDSSLSM, FMDRMD, DFF] K545 78

Abergele (Lloyd) [SLTDDMRD, DTDRRM, MM] G328; W183; Z599; AL300; AM351; BY 203b 79

Aberystwyth (Ouseley) [MRDTTL, TDMMRM, MSMR] M221; Q591; V676; AA533 80

Aberystwyth (Parry) [LLTDRMD TL, DTLS#LT] A415a; B130b; C130b; E87; F86; G338c; J 393a; K371b; R216a; S233c; T417; W414; X542; Y249; Z415; AB104; AC298a; AD101; AF 109; AG61b; AK317; AL88; AM 427; AP238; AR406; AT158; BA408; BF276; BK141; BV 506b; BY441b; BZ 81

Abglanz aller majestaet (Lüneburg G-B. 1686) X Meinhold 82

Abide among us (Lindeman) X O lad din Aand nu med os voere 83

Abide in grace (Vulpius) X Cana 84

Abide in me (Fillmore) [MD RMSLDTLS, RTDRRM] AY87 85

Abide with me (Monk) X Eventide 86

Abide with me, I need thee (Pollock) [MMFSSLSF#SM, DTLSMR] AX368; AY70 87

Abide with me; 'tis eventide (Millard) [MMMSMMRR, RFFFFM, MM] BC2 88

-----. R [STTLSLSS, MSRF FM, SD] 89

Abiding (Mendelssohn) X Heavenly love 90

Abiding grace (Camp) [DFM RDDTDR, DMSLF#S, R] I504 91

Abingdon (Routley) [MFSLSDR S, SFMFMSDL] BV558; BY 230 92

Abinger (Williams) [DMFSML S, SLTDTLLSF] X319b 93

Above the heavens, eternal God (Schumann) X Canonbury 94

Abridge (I. Smith) [DSDDTLSF MMR, MLSSF#] E369; F300; K443; L130; R413; T152; V 103; W483b; X100; AJ172; AL156a; AP32; AW266; AZ 14-L; BA383; BE333; BV146; BY600b 95

Abschied (Müller) [SF#SLRFT D, SF#STLSFM] AM39 96

Acadia (Morson) [MMMMMS FMRRD, SSSFM] Z515; AO 469; AR378; AS340 97

Accept, kind Father (Kelly) [MLLSSFMRDRM, MF#S#LT] BN206 98

-----. R [DRDRMFFFSFM, MF#S#LL] 99

According to thy gracious word (Wilson) X Martyrdom 100

Accrington (Sewall) [MLSMRD RM, SDT, DLS, MM] BR75 101

Ach, alles was himmel und erde (Darmstaedt G-B) X Gregor's 39th metre - B 102

Ach bleib bei uns (Calvisius) X Calvisius 103

Ach bleib mit deiner gnade (Vulpius) X Cana 104

Ach Gott und Herr (As hymnodus sacer, 1625) [DTLSSLT D, RDTLTLLS,] D197a; E329; F588; J286; M454; N411; O58; Q215; S326; W698; X278; AA 234; AF476; AN365; AQ169; BA323; BE393; BV386; BX572; BY204a; BZ 105

-----. V [DTLSSLTD, RDTLT DLS,] E329 105a

-----. V [DTLSSLTD, DRTDTLS, D] N411 106

-----. V [DTLSSLTD, RDTLTLS, D] Q215 106a

Ach Gott, verlass mich nicht (Neu ordentlich G-B. Hanover, 1646) X Steadfast 107

Ach Gott, verlass mich nicht (Meiningen G-B. 1693) X O Gott, du frommer Gott 108

Ach Gott vom himmel (Erfurt G-B. 1524) [TDTLMRDT, RDTLRDTL,] O424; Q260; AA278 109

-----. V [MFMRLLFM, MFM RSFMR] Q260 110

Ach Gott vom himmelreiche (Praetorius) X Praetorius II 111

Ach Gott! was hat vor herrlichkeit (Grimm's Choral buch. 1755) X Gregor's 172nd metre 112

Ach Gott, wie (As hymodus sacer) X Breslau 113

Ach Herr (Praetorius) [MRMFS MRD, MRMFSMRD,] F70 114

Ach Herr, wo sind nun meine vor'gen kroefte (Grimm's Choral buch) X Grimm's 552nd metre 115

Ach Jesu, dessen treu (Lüneburg G-B. 1648) [MLSLTD, RMT DLSM, MLS] N434 116

Ach! Wan doch Jesu, liebster mein (Spee. Trutz nachtigall, 1649) X Nachtigall 117

Ach, wann werd ich dahin kommen (Witt) [DTLTDRM, MF SFMRDLT] AA58; AN114; AQ163 118

Ach, was soll ich sünder machen (Flittner) X Flittner 119

Ach wie sehnlich wart ich (Briegel) [MMLFMMRM, S# LDDTD, TD] AA210 120

Achill (Wesley) [MFMRDFML, TDRDTD, SM] BA424 121

Achnasheen (Lloyd) [SLSMRD RFM, MRDTLTD] S432 122

Ack, bliv hos oss (Swedish Koralbok. 1697) X Pax 123

Ack, saliga stunder (Ahnfelt) [SSDMSDDTLTD, DDTLS] N272; P43 124

Ackley (Ackley) X He lives 125

Ad astra (Ley) [SSSDTLSM, FSLSMDRR] F492 126

Ad cenam agni providi (Sarum plainsong M 8) [SDLSDTD RDTL, LLSMF] E125; F 129a; BJ30 127

Ad perennis (French church mel) [LTDRMLRT, DDRM FFM,] A587b; E350; W524b; X274b 128

-----. V [LLDRMLRT, DDRM FFM,] E350 129

Ad sacratissimum cor Jesu (Piel) [DRMMFMMR, RM FFFFFM,] BO24 130

Adam lay ybounden (Warlock) [LDTLMM, LDTLM, FMMRD,] BG180 131

Adam's song (Sanders) [SSSS FMR, DRRM, SSSSF] AQ2 132

Addeer hu (Jewish trad) [MSSMSS, LTDTLLS, SDD] AH147; BH125 133

Addison (Emerson) [MMMFM R#M, DTLLSSMR, M] L516; V670 134

-----. V [MMMFMRM, DTLL SSMR, M] V670 135

Addison's (Sheeles) [DMMRS FMRDR, SDRMR] B252; E 297; F170; X659; AQ116; BV217 136

Adelaide (Stebbins) [MRMFMD TDR, RD#RMR, RD] R302; Z324; AE270; AH426; AI280; AM574; AR351; AS241; AT 355; AU254; AV384; AW217; AX395; BB272; BZ 137

Ades domine (---) [DDRMFM, SFMRFM, MMF#S] BR114 138

Ades Pater supreme (Melodiae Prudentianae) [MSLTDTL, RD LSLFM, SS] F112 139

Adeste fideles (Wade's Cantus diversi) [DDSDRS, MRMFMRD, DTL] A12; B72; C72; D49; E28; F59; G96; H147; I125; J42; K21; L216; M237; N33; O195; P125; Q102; R170; S 116; T40; U56; V325a; W55; X78; Y298; Z205; AA159; AB 106; AC74; AD120; AE84; AF 132; AG69; AH123; AI67; AJ 57; AK112; AL47; AM36; AN 156; AO127; AP27; AQ288; AR143; AS110; AT66; AU143; AV90; AW80; AX94; AZ39-F; BA155; BB105; BC129; BD56; BE123; BF291; BI83; BK149; BL11; BM63; BN10; BO150, 150a; BP13; BQ4, 158; BR 73; BV106; BX305; BY104; BZ 140

-----. V [DSDRS, MRMFMR, DTLDR] BO150a 141

-----. V [DDSDRTS, MRMFMR, DDT] BQ158 142

Adesto sancta trinitas (Chartres Antiphoner. 1784) [DDSDDRRD, DFFMMRDS,] E159b; R245b; S59; X51b 143

Adesto sancta trinitas (Plainsong M 3) [MRSLDDDTLSLS FM, FF] E159 144

Adjutor (Lewars) [SSLFMR, DMR T, DSLFMR,] K48 145

Admah (Mason) [DDTDRMFMR DTD, MFSL] H197 146

Adon olam (Jewish trad) [MLT DLTS# L, MLTDMRDT] BH157, 311 147

Adon olom (Gerovitch) [MMFM RDTL, MMTLSF#SL] AH154; BH276 148

Adonoy adonoy (Gerovitch) [MD TL, LLS# LT, D# RRD# L, LM] BH313 149

Adonoy hy ho-eloheem (Jewish trad) [DRMRMLLLL, MR SDSSF] BH340 150

Adonoy mo odom (Halpern) [LLDRTMLRRRMR, MMMR] BH334 151

Adonoy yimloch (Binder) [SLTDS, DTLSSFMFR, MF] BH294 152

Adoramus (Spencer-Palmer) [SDTLSMDF, FMFSLTDT,] BV30 153

Adoramus te, panem (Catholic) [SSFMSLSFMR, SSFMSL] BQ232 154

Adoration (Elvey) [MMSSDDS S, LLSDFMMR,] D123b; J 177a; K161 155

Adoration (Hanby) [SSSSSSL, LLSSDDR, DR] K560; W77; AE96; AP735; AW96 156

----. R [DRMMFMMR, TDR RMRRD] 157

Adoration (Havergal) X St John 158

Adoration (Haydn) X O come, loud anthems ... 159

Adoration (Stewart) [SF#SM R#MDTLS, LTDSMD] H24 160

Adoration (Torrance) [SSDTDF RM, MMTLTSSS] O98 161

Adoration (Tufts) [DDDMRDR M, MMMLSF#S, S] BX61 162

Adoration (Woodman) [DSLTLS SDRMMR, RMRD] BF181 163

Adoro (Barnby) X St Chrysostom 164

Adoro te (Barnby) X St Chrysostom 165

Adoro te devote (Benedictine Plainsong M 5) [DMSSSLS FMRDD, DMS] A204; E331; F385a; J272; K183a; W319; X279; AD472; AF557; AL 214b; AN173; AQ128; BL50; BM10; BN88; BO32; BP48; BQ227a; BR331; BY330a 166

-----. V [DMSSLSFMRDD, DMSSL] K183a 167

-----. V [FLDDDRD, L# LS FF, FLDD] BL50 168

Adoro te devote (Gounod) X

Jesus, Food of angels 170
Adoro te (No. 2) (Van Damme) [SFMMFMRSSF#S, SFMMS] E308; X7; AN139 171
Adowa (Gabriel) [SDDDRMMM, FSSSMFMR,] AJ175 172
Adrian (Gould) [DRMFMRMRD, SDTRFLS] AI246 173
Adrian (Rinehart) [DDDDRDTLT RD, MMMMM] G350a; H372a 174
Adrian (Stewart) [SMRDMDLS, DTRDSLR, M] W609a 175
Adsis Jesu (Monk) [MMSMRD, RDTLS, LLDRM] W248 176
Adsum (Leslie) [MRMLSF, LTDRD, MRMF#M] BY538 177
Advent (Beecher. Plymouth coll. 1855) [MMRDRMSSS, LMMFM RD] E342; X604b 178
Advent (Garrett) [SSLDDDS, FM RDMRR,] B116b 179
Advent (Goss) [SDMSLS, MRD RFM, MRDS] V9; W267b 180
Advent (Knox) [SDMMMLLR, S DLDRRM, R] C67b; D317b 181
Advent (Monk) X Beverly 182
Advent (Moulton) [DDDSSD, SSS SMS, MMMF#] Y267 183
Advent (Tours) X The wise men 184
Advent (Wolle) [DDRMMSM, FFMMRD, DDR] AZ72-C; BA 154 185
Adventurers (Thompson) [DSSL SSSS, SDRMRDRR,] Y167 186
Aeterna caeli gloria (Guisbourough hymnal Plainsong M 4) [MDRFMFSFM, MDRFMFS] E56 187
Aeterna Christi munera (Guidetti) X Guidetti 188
Aeterna Christi munera (Plainsong M 7) [SSLTTSLTDTLSS, ST] A132a; F503a; AC11 189
-----. V [SSLTSLTDTLSS, SLTD] AC11 190
Aeterna Christi muneri (Rouen church mel.) [SFMRMDRMR DD, MSSMD] E151b; J133b; W4b 191
Aeterna Rex (Sarum plainsong M 8) [SSLTDLSFLSLTDTL SL] B331b; E141 192
Aethelwold (Nicholson) [SSDD RDRMFF, MRDMRL] F143; BV465b 193
Af dybsens nød (Walther) X De profundis 194
Af himlens (Swedish) X Praise 195
Af høiheden oprunden er (Nicolai) X Frankfort 196
Afar upon a foreign shore (Breton trad) [SDDRMFMR, DRMRDRRR] BQ107 197
Affection (Greenwood's Psalmody) [SDTDFMRD, RMSDLTDT] E343; W471a; X284; AQ275; BE219; BY56 198
Afternoon (Barnby) [DRMSMDRD T, RMFLSFL] BX148 199
Again, as evening's shadow falls (Binder) [SSF#SMFFF, FM R#MDRRR] BH11 200
Again, our dear redeeming Lord (Durham) [DRMSFM RR, RMFLLSFM,] BC251 201
Again the slowly circling year (Richardson) [DMRFMSFM, MRDFMR, DR] BN54; BO188 202
-----. V [MMRFMRSM, MRD FMR, RR] BO188 203
Again we meet around the board (Careless) [SDMSFLMRDTLT D, MMR] BC242 204
Agape (Dickinson) [SLTDMMRL DT, DTLSDR] D225b; G412; S359; Z463; AB301; AL224b; AP358c; AR518 205
Agape (Sherwin) X Mason 206
Agatha (Harding) [MFSMDDRM DL, SLTDFM] AP732 207
Agatha (Södergren) [DTLSRFFM, SLTDSRSM] N263 208
Agawam (Bradbury) [MMMMMSS S, SLLSSS, SD] T24a; AJ33a 209
Agincourt (English trad) [LLS LSSFM, LLSMRMRL] B439b; E249b; F501; R182; S139;

W634a; X684; AF151 210

-----. V [RRDRDDTL, RRDLS LSR] F501 211

-----. V [LLSLSSF#M, LLSM RMRL] R182 212

Agnes (Bunnett) [MSFMMRD, FM LSSF#S, D] B142c; S238; W 399; AK212; AP196b 213

Agni (Conant) [MDRMRDM, SM DTDM, FMF] Y182; AC173; AG307; AR657 214

Agnus (Danish trad) X Release 215

Agnus Christi (Grimm's Choral buch) X Gregor's 115th metre 216

Agnus dei (---) [MDTLT, TRDT LTLLLS#, L] AI143 217

Agnus dei (Blow) X St Agnes 218

Agnus dei (Bugenhagen. Liturgy Braunschweig. 1528) [DRM SFM, MRMFSFM, MRD] M411; Q147; AK525 219

-----. V [DRMMFFM, MMRRM FSFFM] Q147 220

Agnus dei (Decius) X O Lamm Gottes 221

Agnus dei (Mozart) [MMSMR RFR, DTDRMSFM] BR24 222

Ah, well it is that God should read (Neumark) X Neumark 223

Ahnfelt (Ahnfelt) [SSMDDSMMR MD, DDTLS] P158 224

Ainger (Kingham) X Benson 225

Ainger (Davies) [DDRDRMDR, LSMSFMRM,] B483b; BE82 226

Ainsworth 97 (Genevan Psalter. 1562) [SMFSSMFRRD, DMFSFM] AF502; AI416; AJ426; AQ52 227

Airedale (Stanford) [MRSLTDRTL L, FMMLTD] F205a 228

Airlie (Nicholson) [SDTLSDRMF RS, MMFSL] F453 229

Ajalon (Redhead) X Petra 230

Ak Fader, lad dit ord din aand (Lindeman) [DMRDMFSFM, RDRTLS, D] O245; P159 231

Ak, Herre form (As hymnodus sacer. 1625) X Ach Gott und Herr 232

Akdamos mode (Jewish trad) X Sinai's height 233

Akdamus (Jewish trad) [SM DDDDSS, DDTDRLL, L] BH 56 234

Alas! and did my Savior bleed (Hudson) X At the cross 235

Albano (Novello) [MSFMRDR T, TDDRRM, M] A360b; B300; D588b; E327; F398; J216; K470; V610; W345; AA330; AJ354b; BV153; BY125 236

Albany (Jeffery) [SSSSLSDTM LS, SLLT] A274; B519b; c519a; D311a; G59; I76; J 137; M481; R246; S58; U 4; V84; Y21; Z99; AB16; AC1; AD67; AE160; AF249; AG46; AH191; AK197; AO 235; AR14; AS72; AT185; AV27; BB680; BD28; BF180; BK59; BZ 237

Albany (Oliver) [SDTLSMDR, MLSMRMR, M] D299a 238

Albert (Albert) X Waltham 239

Alberta (Harris) [DDRMRFM RDL, SDRM, DM] F298a; X 554a; BV567; BY545a 240

Albertson (Knapp) [MMMMFFF, RRSFFMM, DD] AO638 241

Albinus (Gauntlett) X St Albinus 242

Alcaic ode (Lowenstern) X Nun preiset alle 243

Alcester (Wesley) [SMRDSD LS, FMLSFMR, D] AM49; AP101 244

Aldeby (Shaw) [MMMMMLTDT DL, SMLTD] X396b 245

Aldersgate (Merrick) [MMM SFM, SSSLTS, SSSL] D626; K401; V434; Y16 246

Aldersgate Street (Horner) [MRMFLRM, MFSLRRMR, S] AD329 247

Aldwinkle (Wessnitzer) [LS# F#MDRDTTL, TDRMLR] AQ185 248

Alene Gud i Himmerig (Plainsong. 1539) X To God on high 249

Alene til dig, Herre Jesus Krist (Nürnberg, 1541) X Allein zu dir, Herr Jesu Christ 250

Aletheia (Hall) [MLTS#S#F#S#, LTDT, TLSS] B416b 251

Aletta (Bradbury) [MSDRRRDR M, MSDRRRM] G146; H303; I144; L252; T237; V441; AE 330; AH366; AI407; AJ333; AM 674; AO230; AS177; AT179; AU237; AV80; AW311; AX421; BB234 252

Alexander (Everest) [MMR#MD DDRMF, FFMFRR] L421 253

Alexander (Gibson) [MR#MFD# MR, DTRSFM, MF#M] Y152 254

Alexander (Smart) [SMDLRDTD, FMRSDTLS,] V536 255

Alexandria (Arnold) [MMRMSF MRD, MRMSFMR,] D660a; L57; T139b; V73; AJ89; AO 300; AS343 256

-----. V [DMRMSMFMRD, MR MSFM] AO300 257

Alford (Dykes) [MFFDRMD, MSMDRD, MR] A590; B541; C541; D396; F284; G421; I618; J595b; K519; L351; M318; N617; O617; Q476; R427; S427; T352; U311; V706; W221b; Z568; AA 288; AB415; AC266; AD141; AE308; AF311; AG285; AH280; AK414; AL175; AM234; AN547; AO553; AP308; AR69; AT476; AV292; BA756; BB306; BD138; BE65; BF311; BR440; BV437; BX462; BY407 258

Alfreton (New version Supplement. 1708) [DMFRMDRT, RMF#SRMRD] E240; F95b; X189b 259

Algiers (Herbert) [DDTLTRDS, DMRLRR, DD] AJ223 260

Alice (Roberts) [LMRDTLTLS#, RDFMMRM,] W404; AM408 261

Alida (American trad) [SDDMR DLLDT, LSSSDM] G522; H336; BB473 262

Aline (Bergquist) [MRDTDRM FMMR, FMRD#R] J336; N533 263

All and some (English trad, ca 1450) [LLLMMSFM, M MMRRRDTL.] BG62 264

-----. R [MMMSFMRD, SS SSLMFRD,] 265

All as God wills (Barnby) X Holy Trinity 266

All because we do not love them (Teasley) [DRMSS FMD, DMRFMRM, D] AX217 267

-----. [MFSMDLSM, DRMSFMR, D] 268

All bells in Paradise (Shaw) [LTDTLS, MMF#LS#L, SSLS] BG184 269

All creatures of our God (Cologne G-B) X Vigiles et sancti 270

All' ehr' und lob (Kirchen G.-B. Strassbourg. 1541) [DDRMDFFM, RMFSMFRD,] Q236 271

All for Jesus (Lough) [MFSL SMMR, RMFLSFM, M] AX 403; AY108 272

All for Jesus (Stainer) X Oxford 273

All glory be to God most high (As hymnodus sacer. 1625) X Ach Gott und Herr 274

All glory be to thee (Plainsong, 1539) X To God on high 275

All glory, laud (Lindeman) [DDRMDSS, LSMDMR, SFM] P34 276

All glory, praise [laud] and honor (Teschner) X St Theodulph 277

All hail, dear conqueror (Bragers) [SDTRDTLS, SR MFMRDR,] BP37 278

All hail the glorious day (Stephens) [MFSDTLSFMFS, LSMRM] BC223 279

All hail the great Immanuel's name (Holden) X Coronation 280

All hail the power (Holden) X

Coronation 281

All hallows (Brown) [MRMDMSF M, LSMDRR, SS] AB302; AP 198; BX157; BY512b 282

All hallows (Martin) [SDDDSSR D, TLTDTL] A96b; B509b; C171b; D115b; Y279; AC276; AD370; AK134 283

All hallows (Wiseman) [DTSLLSM F, FDRMSLTD] S504; AL273 284

All I need (Jones) [DDDSDRM, MRRRMD, DDD] AX314 285

-----. [SSLLSSM, FFRRMFS, SS] 286

All in the morning (English carol) [LLLDTLS, DTLLRM, TDM] BG17 287

All morgen ist (German. Wittenberg, 1537) [DDTDSMFRD, DMFSLTD] AF498 288

All my heart this night (Ebeling) X Ebeling I 289

All of seeing (A monk of Gethsemani) [MMSSRRMM, LLRMFF M, S] BN143 290

All on the altar (McKinney) [MMMMRDMR#R, FFFFSFM,] AU83 291

-----. R [SMLSFDFM, SRMF LSFM,] 292

All praise to our redeeming Lord (Gläzer) X Azmon 293

All praise to St Patrick (Catholic) [SDTLSMSLFLLSS, DTD] BO 135 294

-----. R [SDTLSLTLTD, TDTL ST] 295

All saints (Meiningen G-B.) X St Leonard 296

All saints (Croft) [MMLS#LTTL, DTMLLS#, MS] AZ590D 297

All saints (Cutler) X All saints new 298

All saints (Darmstadt G-B. 1698) [DSLLSFMD, SLTDTLLS] A 130; B296; C296; D178; E204; F570; J456a; K245; N630; V 164a; W222; X210a; AM127; BN178; BV267; BY214a 299

All saints (later form: Darmstadt G-B.) X Weisseflagen (Tochter Sion. 1741) 300

All saints (Davies) [MDRT TDFMRM, SMF#R#F#T] S250 301

All saints (Knapp) X Wareham 302

All saints (Stainer) X Beati 303

All saints (Wilson) X Martyrdom 304

All saints new (Cutler) [SM FSDDTT, DRMFMR, R] A549; B85b; C85a; G285; H154; I 416; J562; K383; L530; M 382; O491; P187; Q452; R 354; S271a; T210; U290; V491; Y118; Z358; AB251; AC262; AD296; AE249; AF 388; AG196; AH444; AJ303; AK288; AL409b; AM384; AN309; AO397; AP543c; AQ213; AR379; AS410; AT 414; AU21; AV198; AW194; BA586; BB361; BD91; BE 374; BF469; BK20; BX28; BZ 305

All saints old (Darmstadt G-B. 1698) X All saints 306

All souls (Yoakley) [MRDFM LLSRM, MF#SDTL] Eap58; W202a; AD230; BE195; BY 243b 307

All the way (Lowry) [MMMM RDSD, DMRTDRM, M] N464; R365; T263; U211; V736; Z396; AE207; AG154; AH375; AI289; AJ367; AL445; AM 505; AP606; AR434; AS253; AT268; AU369; AV360; AX 466; BB259; BY537; BZ 308

All the world (Binder) [SSDT LTDS, SLSLLTM, S] AH152; BH63 309

All the world (McCutchan) [SDTLSFMRMF, LSMD, MF] G8; AE20; BZ 310

All things are thine (Allgemeines katholisches G-B, Vienna, 1774) X Hursley 311

All things are thine (Pensum sacrum) X Herr Jesu Christ dich zu uns wend

312

All things bright (Monk) X All things bright and beautiful 313

All things bright (Ouseley) [DD MFSLS, SDMSFMR, FF] W18b; BY472a 314

All things bright (Spohr) X Gerald 315

All things bright and beautiful (Danish trad) [SDDRRMRD, RM SRMD, SD] AM636 316

-----. R [MSLSMFMR, MFSFRM, SD] 317

All things bright and beautiful (Monk) [DMFLSMD, MRTTLS, DMF] F442; K554; AP724; BY733a 318

-----. R [LSDDTDD, LSDDTD, D#RM] 319

All things bright and beautiful (Shelley) [DRMDRRD, DDRMDRS, RM] BH252 320

All this night (Maker) [DRMMFS LSR, MMR, DDT, R] D538b; BY88a 321

All this night (Sullivan) [DRM FSLS, DRMFSLS, SS] BR555 322

All through the night (Welsh trad) X Ar hyd y nos 323

All to Christ I owe (Grape) [DMSLSMD, DRRDRM, DMS] Z284; AM690; AT225; AU258; AV337; AW462; AX320; AY 235; BB527 324

-----. R [SLSMD, SLSMR, SL SMDT] 325

All waters (Shaw) [SFMRDSDRM RD, SFMRD] X327 326

-----. R [TSFR#RR#FR#RDS, SLDRM] 327

All wise, All great (Singer) [SLSSDDTT, SLSSRRDD,] BH218 328

All ye dwellers (Jewish trad) [SSDDDD, DDMMDSR, R#T, S] BH317 329

All ye who seek (Montani) [MM DRMFMRD, SSMFSLR,] BQ67 330

All ye who seek (Tozer) X Jazer 331

All ye who seek (Lee) [SSS LSFSM, DRMFFM, SL] BN 70 332

Alla trinita beata (Laudi spirituali) X Alta trinita beata 333

Alle deine gaben (Gregor) X Gregor's 7th metre 334

Alle jahre wieder (Rinck) [MMSSFR, DRMFR, FFMML] K539; N634 335

Alle menschen (Hintze) X Salzburg 336

Alle menschen müssen sterben (Weimar G-B. 1681) X Jesu, meines lebens leben 337

Alle vögel (German) X Jesus lives, and Jesus leads 338

Allegiance (Sampaix) [SMDL SMFMDRD, SMDDT] H396 339

-----. R [MFSLTLSFMFSFF, MFS] 340

Allein Gott in der höh sei ehr (Plainsong) X To God on high 341

Allein zu dir, Herr Jesu Christ (Nürnberg, 1541) [DSLDM RRD, MDLRDTTL,] N410; O96; Q319; AA413; AZ202-a 342

-----. V [DSLDMRRD, MRDT DTL, D] O96 343

-----. V [DSLDMRDTD, MRD TSLR] Q319 344

-----. V [DSLTDRMRRD, SL TDRT] AZ202-a 345

Alleluia

NOTE: Other spellings of this word are not used herein, no matter the language.

Alleluia (Lowe) X Praise 346

Alleluia (Wesley) [DDTDLSLT, DRMSLLS, S] A281; B193; C193b; D368a; F399a; J417; K127; S10a; W138; AB39; AL377; AP148; BE171; BI

3-D; BV383b; BY168 347
Alleluia! Alleluia! (Catholic) [MFSSMRDDTLSRSFM, M] AH127; BO173 348
(H) Alleluia chorus (Handel) [DSLS, DSLS, DDDD, DDDD] AU477 349
Alleluia, Christ is risen (Kestel) [SDMFRMDS, SDMSMRM, S] BL26 350
Alleluia, dulce carmen (Essay on the Church plain chant. 1782) X Dulce carmen 351
Alleluia, dulce carmen (LaFeilleé. Methode. 1808) [MMRFRDRF FRM, RFLSF] F82a 352
Alleluiah for the cross (McGranahan) [SDTDRMFS, DRDTRMR D,] AU470 353
Alleluia! Gott zu loben (Baessler) [SDRMLSSFM, RMFSMRD,] AA223 354
Alleluia, Jesus lives (Wonnberger) [DSMDSTD, RRMMF#MF# SR,] M449 355
Alleluia, let the holy anthem rise (Terry) X Holy church 356
Alleluia perenne (Monk) [SMMM FSDLDS, SLSTD] B265a; C265; D262b; V616; AB89 357
Alleluia piis edite (Hodges) [DF MRDDDRMR, RSFMS] B265b 358
Alleluia! Praise the Savior (Sullivan) X Lux eoi 359
Alleluia! Sing to Jesus (French Paroissien mel) X Daily, daily 360
Alleluia song (Hungarian trad) [SFMFSMRD, RMFFMLS, S] BL33 361
Alleluia, 'tis done (Husband) X We praise thee, O God 362
Alleluia, what a Saviour (Bliss) X Man of sorrows 363
Alleluias. (Cologne G-B. 1623) X Vigiles et sancti 364
Alleman (Alleman) [SSSSF#SM, S LLLDS, SSM] L528 365
-----. R [SRRRMD, SLTDRM, MMMM] 366
Allen (Allen) X Joyful song 367
Allen (Prout) [DMFSLS, MRD DTL, LSDD] BA867 368
Allerton (Mann) [SDDTLSLS, DRMSFMR, S] D435 369
Alles ist an Gottes segen (Koenig) X Evangelists 370
Allgüter, mein preisgesang (Weimar) [SMRDDRMFSM, SLSFMR] F611; J303; W 428a; X521; AL301a; BY482; BZ 371
Allhallows (Brown) X All hallows 372
Allington (Hopkins) [MRDFFM, MSMDRT, RFMR] C49a; D 23a; F38 373
Alma (Brackett) [SMSLDRMSL D, RMMSRM] BE154 374
Alma (Webbe) X Consolation 375
Alma mater (Hendrickson) [SSMFMRRD, SSMF#SLLS,] P49 376
Alma mater (Redhead) [SMDM RD, MRSSF#S, MFFM] D71b 377
Alma redemptoris mater (Gounod) [SSSDRMFMRMM, SMMMS] BQ202 378
Alma redemptoris mater (Plainsong M 5) [DMFSLS, SSL TDSMMMF] BN140; BQ277 379
Alma redemptoris [mater] (Webbe) X Consolation 380
Almighty Father (Mendelssohn) X Almighty Father, hear 381
Almighty Father (Schalit) [LLSLDMRDRDT, DLLLT] BH6 382
Almighty Father, hear (Lysberg) [SDRMMSFDRM, MM RRRD] AV418 383
Almighty Father, hear (Mendelssohn) [SLRDT, DFFFMM RLTDD] R542; Sap19; AE 462; AH563; AR651; AT529; AU488; AV415; BB687; BF 689; BY305-C 384
-----. V [SLRDT, TDFFF, FMMRLT] Sap. 19 385

Almighty Father, hear (Mendelssohn) X Intercession (Callcott) 386
Almighty God (Lewandowski) [DTLSFMFS, LSFMRMFM,] BH53 387
Almost (Bliss) X Almost persuaded 388
Almost persuaded (Bliss) [MF FMD, DRRM, MFFMD, RM] P256; U154; AH341; AI191; AT248; AU169; AV335; AX263; AY506; BB228 389
Almsgiving (Dykes) [MMRDSDR M, SDMSFM] A305; B426; C 426a; D477a; F480; H45; I501; J448a; K385; L76; N573; P427; S398; T319; U362; V465; W19b; AA357; AB338; AC56; AD261; AI225; AK257; AL26b; AM575; AO105; AP139; AS48; AV17; AZ3-C; BA475; BB325; BD131; BE190; BF649; BR35; BV599b; BX262a; BY68 390
Almsgiving (Wesley) [SMDSFMMR DFMLSDFM] F204; I401 391
Aloha (Hawaiian trad) X He lives on high 392
Alone with God (Kirkpatrick) [SDDDDMDMS, LSSSSMD] AX 358 393
-----. R [MMFSSLLSM, MRMF RMF] 394
Alone with thee (Conradi) [DMM FFMRSFM, MMMMRD] P332 395
Alpha (Leslie) [SSSF#SLS, SS DRLT, DDD] D583b 396
Alphege (Gauntlett) X St Alphege 397
Alsace (Beethoven) [SDRMMM FMR, SFMRMTLS] C460; H166; I518; AA332; AB358; AM52; BE422 398
-----. V [SDRMMMFMR, SFMR MTDLS] I518 399
Alston (Burleigh) [MFSLSFMM R, DRMSSLS] AP727b 400
Alstone (Willing) [SSLSDMRD, RMFSLSM] B87; C87; D575a; F435; I203; J4; K2; L208; M 515; O176; T123; W516; Y69; AB410; AJ179; AK332; AP769; AS453; AW300; BA37; BD35; BF232; BR381; BX192; 401
Alta trinita beata (Laudi spirituali. Florence) [DDRMRD FMRMM, RMFMM] A135; E184; G615; R557; Sap. 45; X669; AD511; AF403; AN3; AP338; AR678; BQ240; BZ 402
Altenburg (German trad) [SM MFMRDTDR, SFFSFM] M645 403
Althorp (Green. Psalmody. 1744) [SDRMRDFMR, RSFM RDR] F249 404
Althorp (Lomas) [DRMFMRRD, MFSDTLS, S] AO256 405
Altid frejdig naar du gaar (Weyse) X Cheerfulness 406
Alvan (Mason) [SMMDRDRDM S, SMMDRD] L205; V279 407
Alverstoke (Barnby) X Caritas 408
Alverstroke (Barnby) X Caritas 409
Alveston (Harwood) [SDTLTD RRSSSMFMFS] W380 410
Am I a soldier (Sankey) [DM MFMFLS, MSDTLS, FM] AI 322a 411
-----. R [SDTSLTD, TDRDTLS, FM] 412
Am I a soldier of the cross (Arne) X Arlington 413
Amadeus (Warner) [MRLTDRMF, MRSMDDTD] AZ606-A 414
Amara (Perkins) DRMMSFMR R, RMFFLSF] T80; AJ120; AW499 415
-----. R [SSLLFSLSM, SFM RRRD] 416
Amazing grace (American trad) [SDMDMRDLS, SDMDMRS,] G209; R275b; AH335; AM402; AR433; AT188; AU161; AW 463; AX108; AY251, 257; BZ 417
-----. V [SLDMDMRDLS, SLD MDM] AX108 418
-----. V [SLDMDMRDLSS, SLDMD] AY257 419

Amberg (Church of Scotland Hymn tune book.) [MFSLSDRTD, DTLRDTL] W449; AK255 420

Ambleside (Lowe) [MRDLTDRD, DDRRM, MSS] C523a; D531a; BR405 421

Ambrose (Ambrose) [SSSSSS, LLLSMR, MMFF#] B407; C407; G515; H497; L563; O289; P338; T70; U425; AA531; AH533; AJ 106; AO548; AR416; AS473; AW 264; BA727; BB352; BC272 422

-----. V [SSSSSSSLLLSMR, MM FF#] L563 423

Amelia (Bradbury) [SDDMMS, MRDMRD, SDDM] T292; AJ 404 424

Amen Court (Bower) [DRMFM S, MRDRLS, SLDR] F237; BV 218 425

Amen, Jesus han skal raade (Berggren) [SMRRMFFM, DTLR SFM, L] G221; J456b; K389a; N430; O35; P45; AW219; BZ 426

Amen sjunge hvarje tunga (Berggren) X Amen, Jesus han skal raade 427

America* (Thesaurus musicus, 1740) [DDRTDR, MMFMRDRD] A141; B427; C427; D196; E 560; F577; G489; H529; I702; J358; K489; L556; M498; N 566; O519; P410; Q577; R513; S412; T446; U338; V652; W631; X318; Y293; Z548; AA305; AB 334; AC279; AD440; AE392; AF437; AG274; AH474; AI363; AK439; AL508; AN384; AO585; AP639; AQ242; AR611; AS383; AT487; AU458; AV302; AW344; AZ579-a; BA872; BB506; BC 115; BD172; BF541; BH264; BI11; BK118; BR493; BX420; BY641; BZ 428

* British texts call it "National anthem"

America (Thesaurus musicus, 1740) X Remember (Ravenscroft. Melismata) 429

America befriend (Merrill) [SS MLMSFM, DRMFLS, DT] S415; AB340; AC272; AH 479; AO588; BF550 430

America, the beautiful (Brown) [MMRRLLSS, DTLFLS, FM] AO592 431

American hymn (Keller) [SD RMSSSLSFM, RRMFS] J166; K295; L146; P22; AO602; BD184 432

Americus (Gabriel) [SSLSM MFM, MFSLSFMR,] T113; AJ164 433

Ames (Neukomm) [SSDTDRT D, MRTDLSF#S,] M30; R 412; T57; AJ90; AN237 434

Amesbury (Burnap) [SSLTD DLT, DD#MRSM, MM] N414; R178; U31; Z210; AB210; AC98; AE385; AG86; AI218; AR222; AT441; BA530; BF 262 435

Amherst (Billings) [DMSFMR D, SDSLSFMR, S] AQ31 436

Amicus (Swedish trad) [SSDD DDDMDDT, DTLSF] M626; N468 437

Amid the trials (Lorenz) [SS MMDRDTT, SSFFRMR] AI288; AS311; AX488; AY88 438

-----. R [SSMSLR, FFRFSM, SSMM,] 439

Amnos (Benbow) [DRMSSFMR, RMFMRDRD,] K188 440

Amor Dei (Kirchen gesang. Bremen, 1707) [DSFMMRRD, RMF#SSSF#S,] W425; AN459 441

Amsterdam (Nares) [DSDRM RMF, SLSFMR, DS] B114a; C114a; D512a; G524; H512; I623; L438; N514; R330; S 264; V688; X286; Z573; AB 196; AD15; AG122; AH363; AN62; AT122; AV240; AW200; AZ56-a, 591-d; BA313, 702; BB668; BE296; BF381; BR 500a; BX322; BZ 442

-----. V [DSDRMRMFSSSFM R, DS] AZ56-a 442a

-----. V [DSDRMRMF, SFM

R, DSDR] T375 443
An angel from on high (Tullidge) [MMFMDRMF, FRRSFMR, M] BC224 444
-----. R [SSMDRMFMR, SSMD RMF] 445
An die freude (Schiller. Ode. 1799) [SSDDRRMFS, SMMRFR D] AQ168 446
An wasserfleussen Babylon (Teutsch kirchenampt. Strassburg, 1525) X Passiontide 447
Angola (Crossley) [SSSDSSFM, MRMFFS, SS] AB45; BF263; BR551a 448
Anastasius (Freylinghausen) X Macht hoch die tür 449
Anatolius (Dykes) X St Anatolius 450
Ancient of days (Jeffery) X Albany 451
Ancient of days (Parker) [DMSS DDTDMMR, DRRMF#] B519b; C519b; D311b; BE202 452
Ancyra (Unseld) [MMDDDDTT, FFLTLLS, M] R296; T120; AJ174 453
And are we yet alive (Naegeli) X Dennis 454
And I couldn't hear nobody pray (Negro spiritual) [MRMMDM SMS, SSLLLDD] AH607 455
And now, my soul, another year (Kieffer) [DSMLSFMR, RMS SF#S, SS] AX629; AY246 456
And now we must bid (Lindeman) X Saa vil vie nu sige 457
Andernach (Andernach G-B) [DDDTSLTD, MRFMRDRM,] E50b; W230; X130; AL6b; BN24; BY147b 458
Andre (Bradbury) [DDMDMMRD TD, DMSMSS] R19; T213; AJ 306; BB308 459
Andreas Hofer (Tyrolese national song) [SDTDRDTL, SDTDRS, SR] Y237 460
Anfield (---) [DDDMRRD, DDD FMR, SSS] D357c 461
Angel choir (Gower) [DTLSLTD RMFS, SLSMF] AS105 462
Angel voices (French carol mel) X Gloria 463
Angel voices (Monk) [MSLS DLSM, DRMFR, MS] B461b; F246; W252; AL202; AP320; BV234; BY4 464
Angel voices (Sullivan) [MMMFM RD#RS, DDRRM, MM] B461a; C461; G15; H7; I27; J240; K240; N584; R30; S455; U15; V87; Y203; Z101; AC228; AD18; AE12; AG297; AH203; AI21; AK457; AM8; AO6; AR 15; AV46; BA641; BB19; BF 218; BZ 465
Angelic songs (Walch) X Tidings 466
Angelica (Gilbert) [DDDSLTDS, DDDTLRS, D] AO128; BR159; BX326 467
Angels (Gibbons) X Angel's song 468
Angels, from the realms (French trad) X Gloria 469
Angels! from the realms (Hastings) X Sion 470
Angels, from the realms (Smart) X Regent Square 471
Angels holy (Farmer) [MFSM, LSFM, DTLSSF#S, R] AB55a 472
Angels holy (Flemish trad) X Flanders 473
Angels' hymn (Gibbons) X Angel's song 474
Angels of Jesus (Barnby) [MTD LLDTLTLS, LTDTM] D398c; O607; BR447b 475
-----. R [MDRMMMDRM, DSSFMRD] 476
Angels, roll the rock (Gilbert) X Maidstone 477
Angels' song (Dykes) X Vox angelica 478
Angel's song (Gibbons) [DDDRM FRS, DMFSRSF#S,] A573; B490; C291; D339b; E259; F336; J214; M256; W651; X 29; AA286; AL322; AN26; AP264; AZ22-K; BA885; BB 2; BJ25; BN120; BV294; BY 360a 479
-----. V [DMDRMFMRD, DMF#SRSF#] C291 480

-----. V [DMDRMFRD, DMF# SRSF#S,] AA286 481
-----. V [DDDRMFRM, DMF SRSF#S] AN26 482
Angels' song (Mendelssohn) [FMRDDTLS, LFSMSFMR,] BE342 483
Angel's story (Mann) X Watermouth 484
Angels we have heard (French carol) X Gloria 485
Angels we have heard (Montani) [SSDSFML, RRSFMRM, SS] BQ7 486
Angelus (German chorale) [MS FRMDRR, SSDTLLS, S] AO293 487
Angelus (Joseph) [DDRMF#SS F#S, SLTDTLLS,] A168; B 399; C399; D14; E266; F20; I313; J232; K79; Q115; R55; S43; T30b; U468; V313; W 277; X42b; Z602; AA177; AB 132; AD135; AE99; AF55; AG 24; AJ234b; AK57; AL392b; AM88; AN211; AP348a; AR 149; AV100; AW37; AZ22-N; BA69; BB296; BD96; BE214; BF205; BO176; BP70; BR170; BV49b; BX180; BY688 488
Angelus (Rider) [DDDDDD, SSS SSS#LT, DL] D535b 489
Angelus ad Virginem (Dublin Troper) [SMSSFMR, RMDFR MDD, S] F547; BG52 490
-----. V [SMSSFMR, RMDRD TDD, S] BG52 491
Angers (Croft. Collection) X Iste confessor 492
Anglia (Lyra Davidica) X Easter hymn 493
Anglorum apostolus (Murray) [DMFSLSFMRM, SLTDTL] BY39b 494
Angmering (Parry) [MDMLSFM R, MF#SLTLS, S] F251 495
Anima Christi (English trad) [MLLSLSFM, SFMRDTL,] A582; E89 496
Animae hominum (Blanchet) [SLDTSLDT, SLTDRRR, F] BV480b; BY419b 497
Annapolis (---) [MMDFMMR, RD#RMRD, MMD] D603b 498
Annetta (Kirkpatrick) [SDTD STLS, FMLSDFMR,] AJ85 499
Annisquam (Noble) [RMMRDRM FS, RMMLLSF] AK73 500
Anniversary (Sankey) [DRMSTL SM, DRMFRDD, D] BB480 501
Anniversary song (Sherwin) [MRDSLFMRD, TDRRMRR,] BB649 502
-----. R [TDRDRMMFFFLSM, DRM] 503
Annue Christe (Paris Antiphoner. 1681) [DDRMMMRMFMR DD, MMF] E174b; F505; V 713; W594; X688; AD367; AP 630; BV591a; BY639 504
-----. V [DDRMMMRMFMRD D, DMF] AD367 505
Annue Christi, saeculorum Domini (Plainsong. M 1) [RLLTSLTDTL, RDTLSD] E174 506
Annunciation (Barry) [SSLFMM, DTSLSS, SRMF] F546 507
Annunciation (Dutch trad. 1896) [SSDDRMFMRDT, SSLMF] A 317; X226; BG100 508
Another day is dawning (McKinney) [SSFMRDS, SLDRDS, SS F] AU275 509
-----. R [SSRRMR, SSMMFM, SDDM] 510
Another year is dawning (Wesley) X Aurelia 511
Anthes (Anthes) [SDTDRMD, DL FMRD, SDT] Q276 512
Antioch (Handel) [DTLSFMR D, SLLTTD, DD] C101c; G89; H141; I107b; J15; K34; L210; M346; N32; O201; P132; Q87; R161; S122; T331; U57; V 118b; Y360; Z190; AB109; AC76; AD104; AE83; AF130; AG65; AH264; AI60; AK120; AL55; AM149; AN163; AO 129; AQ299; AR121; AS100; AT65; AU137; AV98; AW70; AX92; AY189; BA160; BB189; BC89; BD207; BE417; BF290;

BI10; BK142; BX195; BZ 513
Antiphoner (Paris. Gradual. 1685) [DRMFMDRD, MSLSMFS, S] F590; BV19 514
Anton (Gersbach) [SSMFSL, LSD MRD, DTLT] T243; AJ339 515
Antwerp (Smallwood) [SSSDDRMF M, RRRMF#SL] BV235; BY 29 516
Anvern (Mason) [SSDMDRTD, D DMSMFRM,] L340; T13; V60; AJ17a; AO424; AV243; BB307 517
Anxious heart (Norwegian folk) [MTDLLFMD, MTDLTSL, M] P168 518
Anywhere (Towner) [SSLLSMDRM FS, FMRMF] AI399; AM680; AS271; AX470; BB589 519
-----. R [RMFMFS, LLSF#S, DD DST] 520
Anywhere, dear Saviour (Ogden) [MRDSLD, RRMDR, MRDSL] BB344 521
Anywhere with Jesus (Towner) X Anywhere 522
Apolutrosis (Bach) [MFMRRSFM RD, RRDTLS] AA405 523
Appeal (Tomissön. Psalmebog, 1569) X Franzen 524
Appleton (Boyce) [SSSSSDRM, SSS DTLLS,] M201; T223b; AJ 320; AO423 525
April (Welsh carol) [DMFSD, DMRDRD, TDSLS] BG155 526
Ar det ringa kall (English trad) [MRDDRFMR, SDTTDMRR#,] N28 527
Ar hyd y nos (Welsh trad) [DTLDRDTS, LTTD, DTL] A 169a; E268; F26a; G43; J230; P73; R58; S41; T308; X46; Y 306; Z143; AB29; AC18; AD52; AF58; AG30; AH167; AI51; AL 547b; AN100; AO43b; AS33; AT30; AV230; AW35; BE350; BF201; BK48; BY590b; BZ 528
Ara (Matthison-Hansen) [DTLSFM RDRM, RMF#SLT] M12 529
Arabia (Wilson) [SDRMFLSFM, SLSFMMR,] X454; Z591 530
Arator (Schulz) X Claudius 531
Arcadelt (Arcadelt) [MRMDR MM, SSSFMR, MRM] O94; AP 160; BP87; BQ200b 532
Arcadia (Hastings) [SSSDDRM D, SLFDLS, SS] L513 533
Arden (Thalben-Ball) [DMDSM FMRM, LRMDTLT,] BV268; BY304 534
Ardgowan (Finlay) [SRMLSL DRSM, SLMMRD] F33a 535
Ardudwy (Roberts) [MMMRDRD L, SSSF#MR#M, L] W108b; X695; AM43; AN471; BY146b 536
Ardwick (Gauntlett) [SMDLS, DDTRRD, MSFMR,] BV213; BY223 537
"Are ye able" (Mason) X Beacon Hill 538
Are you adorning the doctrine (Byers) [SMRMDRDS, SDDDR DRM,] AX158 539
Are you washed in the blood? (Hoffman) X Washed in the blood 540
Arfon (major: Welsh hymn) [SDDTLSDRM, FMRDMRD] BZ 541
Arfon (minor: Welsh hymn) [MLLS#F#MLTD, RDTLDTL] E116; R197; W100; X141; AF174; AM183; BV370; BY 616; BZ 542
Argyle (Ewing) X Ewing 543
Argyle (Turpin) [MSMRDMRD, FMLSFMR, R] D159 544
Ariel (Mozart) [SSMMMDDDT DMMR, RMF] C263a; G19; H343; I9; L148; R134; S203; T52; U73; V130; Z265; AE 297; AG109; AH178; AI111; AJ81; AL43; AM126; AO205; AR115; AS114; AT7; AU17; AV126; AX7; AY29; BB161; BZ 545
-----. V [SSMMMDDTRFFM, SSDT] BC102 546
Arimathea (Roper) [MMFMFLLS, DMMRDRSS] C177; D116a; AH303 547
Arimathaea (Wurzburger G-B

1628) X O traurigkeit 548
Arise (American trad) [LDLSL DDLSM, SSLSLD] AT241: AU 229; AV341 549
Arise, my soul, arise (Careless) [DMSLSLTD, DDTLLSFF] BC227 550
Arise, my soul arise (Edson) X Lenox 551
Arise, O glorious Sion (Careless) [SDSMDFM, MMRRDT, SDS] BC225 552
Arise, O Lord (Whittington) [SDTLRSFM, MMF#SLLS, L] BI51 553
Arise, O youth of God (McKinney) X Leavell 554
Arise to praise the Lord (Binder) [MFSMFRD, MFSMDLS, MF] BH74 555
Arizona (Earnshaw) [MMMMMSF M, DDTDRMRD] R87; Y276; AC59; AE366; AL20b; AP152b; BY532 556
Arles (Gabriel) [SDDDDSDMMM MD, MSSS] T49; AJ76 557
Arlington (Arne) [DMMMRDDD, RMSFMR, F] A325b; B270; C237a; D426; G270; H151; I354b; J554; L46; M230; N454; P278; R69; S23; U143; V233; Z435; AE231; AG34; AH295; AI 136; AL349b; AM116; AN55b; AO241; AP33b; AR177; AS121; AT39; AU176; AV7; AW152; AX55; AY356; AZ14-S; BA392; BB355; BE372; BR238; BX78; BZ 558
Armageddon (German mel.) [SSMRDS, LLDDS, S#S#LDM] C523b; R355; S272; U292; V752; W519; Z367; AB349; AC202; AE272; AG190; AH434; AI331; AK286; AL365; AM493; AO373; AP551; AT413; AU63; AV208; AW190; BF475; BY534; 559
-----. R [DSMDLS, DRMFS, DDDDM] 560
Armagh (Turle) [SMFRDDFLS, DDTLMLS#] V292; AB378 561
Armenia (Pond) [DDTDRRRDRM, RMRDTD] G417; H427; I553; L437; V134; AO409; AW322; AX160; BZ 562
Armenian hymn (Armenian liturgy) [SLSFMRD, MFSMS FMRM] BE113 563
Armes (Armes) [SMRDDLLS, SDLTLSLM] A539a; B480; F220b; W647a; AP374a; BE 259; BV156b; BY184a 564
Armonia biblica (Pisani) [SL DRMSLS, MRDDRTL, S] AC 240 565
Arms of Jesus (Doane) [MRD SDMFM, SLSMDR, MR] E 580; N608; U207; V347; W 707; AI311; AL507; AM608; AO637; AP791; AS483; AU 353; AV357; AW313; AX529; AY173; BB615 566
-----. R [RRMRRRS, F#F# F#MRRS, RR] 567
Armstrong (Armstrong arr) [MMFSSF#RFFMD, MRDMR] AO546b 568
-----. R [SLSF#RFSFM, MF MRLRR] 569
Armstrong (Chadwick) [MMM RLTRDS, MMRSMRD] U78; AB128; AC104; BB115; BD 66; BF306; BX215 570
-----. V [MMMRLTRD, MM RSMRDT] AB128 571
Armstrong (Richards) [MFSS LSSM, MMSRD#RM, M] J 493b; K256; L89a; T166; U200; Z172; AI80; AJ244; AM688; AR595 572
Arncliffe (Statham) [DDMSDT LSLRS, FLSFM] F381 573
Arnheim (Ahle) X Liebster Jesu 574
Arnold (Arnold) [SSMSFRFM F, MR, RMFSL] AL645; AM 276; AP33a; AW584 575
Arnold (Johnson) [MRMFMRM D, DTDMRR, RM] N505 576
Arnold (Murrill) [SMDLSSLT, TDRMLR, RF] BV608b 577
Arnsberg (Neander) [MMMM RR, DDDDTT, LLSD] J164; K424; M9; Q4; R13; S51; W234; Z123; AD24; AE4;

AF3; AG11; AK29; AL196; AM 132; AP315; AW506; AZ195-A; BA375; BR12; BY41; BZ 578

-----. V [MMMMRR, DDDDTT, LLLL] Q4 579

-----. V [MMMFMRR, DDDRDT T, LL] AZ195-A 580

Arnstadt (Drese) X Rochelle 581

Around the weary world (Norden) [MMMSSFFMDR, R#MSDDT] BH17 582

Art (Clarke) [SLSMFS, SL#DL SF, LS, SR] AQ135 583

Art thou weary (Bullinger) X Geneva 584

Art thou weary? (Warner) [SLSDDRDT, DRMRR, MFS] AZ269-F 585

Artavia (Hopkins) [SSDDTLSDR M, SSFFMRD] A405; B398; C398; AB161; AD281; AK237; AL126; AM397b; BF355; BY 140b 586

Arthur's seat (Goss) [SDDTLS, LTDRMRDR, SM] A237; G264; L87; R351; S273; U300; Y110; Z359; AB249; AC184; AD290; AE24; AF380; AH446; AI259; AJ37; AK291; AM226; AO60; AR327; AT422; AW121; BA26; BD84; BF478; BZ 587

Arundel (Dykes) [SDTDRMMR, MLTDLLS, M] D125a; J407; K300; M577; O164; W495a 588

As after the water-brooks (Lindeman) X Som torstige hjort 589

As fades the glowing orb (Webbe) X Melcombe 590

As God wills (Levenson) [MRD TDRMR, DTLSLTDT,] BH90 591

As pants the hart (Kaiser) [SD DRRMDLS, STDTLS, S] BH40 592

As sinks beneath the ocean (Christiansen) [LSMRSSF, DTLS FM, MMM] P422 593

As swiftly my days (---) [DMRD RRRDRM, MMRMFM] BC5 594

-----. R [RDDRMDRRMF, FM RDRM] 595

As the dawn was breaking (Buzzard) [SSLSF#SMM, MMRR DRM, M] AY492 596

-----. R [SSSSMRDS, RMFR MFM, M] 597

As the dew from heaven (Daynes) [SLTDDTSLTRRD, LTDM] BC232 598

As the hart (Bourjeois) X Bourgeois 599

As the sun doth daily rise (Parish choir) X Innocents 600

As wide as the skies (---) [SMRMDTDRDLS, SDDDD] P292 601

Asaph (Stubbs) [MMMRDL, SSL SS, SSSF] B527a; AO67 602

Asa's death (Grieg) [MLT, MLT, DTLTDRDT, ML] Y122; AC261 603

Asbury (Harrington) [MRD SRDRMRD, FMRDTD] I143a 604

Ascalon (Silesian mel) X St Elizabeth 605

Ascending King (Bourgeois) [SMDRM, FMRRD, SSLTD, S] AJ418 606

Ascending song (Walthall) [MMMMFSSS, SLTDRDT, T] I520 607

Ascendit (Morice) [SDSMRDRF M, SDTDFLS,] X676 608

Ascendit Deus (Schicht) [SLT DTDRM, MSFMDFMR,] J156b; R212; S172; W132; BY177a 609

Ascension (Bancroft) [SFMDR MRDRS, LTDRMF] AK94 610

Ascension (Gauntlett) X Ascension tide 611

Ascension (Monk) [MSDDRFM, MSDRD, MSDDR] A104a; D128a; F147a; J111; S171; AD169; AH306; AK175; AL 104; BR192; BV203; BY167a 612

Ascension, No. 1 (Monk) X Ascension 613

Ascension, No. 2 (Gauntlett)

X Ascension tide 614
Ascension tide (Gauntlett) [SM MRDS, SFFMRM, MRMR] O 368; AB233; BR200 615
-----. V [MMMRDS, SFFMRM, MRMR] AB233 616
Ascham (Carter) X Slingsby 617
Ascription (Emerson) [SSMD LSMS, SDDMDR, RM] T103; AJ149 618
Ase's death (Grieg) X Asa's death 619
Ash grove (English trad) X A virgin unspotted 620
Ashbourne Road (Morgan) [DRR DDFMRM, SF#SLTMS] BY246 621
Ashburn (Hildebrand) [LLLTD TL, LTDMRDT, DT] AY341 622
Ashburton (Jackson) [MMMRM FFF, FFFMRSSS,] BR256 623
Ashburton (Wesley, S.S.) [MM FMRLLS#, LSFMLTDT] W392 624
Ashford (Thiman) [MRDRTDTLT, S#LTDRDS,] BV636; BY741b 625
Ashland (Smith) [MMSFMDRMS FM, MMRMR] AC105 626
Ashray yod'ay (Jewish trad) [SDDRMSMDMR, MSSLSM] BH 315 627
Ashville (Everett) [SSSSSDRM, LLLDLS, SS] AS450 628
Ashwell (Mason) [MMMMMFMR, SF#SMLSF#S,] L61; T259; AJ361 629
Askenazi tune (Lyra Anglo-Judaica) [LLLDTLTM, LLLD TLS#, S#] BH214 630
Asleep in Jesus (Bradbury) X Rest 631
Asleep in Jesus (Bull) [MMLSS FMRDLT, MMLSS] P421 632
Asleep in Jesus (Wolle) [MMR# MFMMRD, DLSFSMR#] BA936 633
Aspinwall (Gabriel) [SDDDDSMRD S, SRRRRD] T198; AJ287 634
Aspiration (Barnby) X St Sylvester 635
Aspiration (German trad) X Mendon 636
Aspiration (Mendelssohn) [M MRDFMRDTDMR, RRRM] D661a; F463 637
-----. V [MRDSFMRDTDMR, RRMF] F463 V Brightest and best G40 638
Aspiration (Thompson) [SMS DRM, SLSMDR, RSF#L] AZ 341-C 639
Aspurg (Frech) X Wittenberg 640
Assisi (Smith) [DDDRDTTL, LDRMMR] A307 641
Assiut (Stebbins) [DMMFSDR DT, DRRMFSL] T104b; AJ 150 642
Assurance (Knapp) [MRDSSFS LS, SMSDTTL] G238; H298; I548; R139; V731; Z412; AE 208; AG216; AH209; AR436; AS285; AT269; AU120; AV 359; AW480; AX477; AY207; BB608; BY493; BZ 643
-----. R [SSSDSLLLS, SSS LDTT] 644
Aston (Heywood) [DTLLS#S, SSMRTD, DTLS] BR352 645
Astra matutina (Thorne) [MM FSFMLSFM, SSLTLS] D170b 646
At Calvary (Towner) X Calvary 647
At midnight, so the sages tell (Handel) X Christmas 648
At sunset (Boe) [SDMRDFLS, STDRRMFM,] P68 649
At the cross (Hudson) [DMR DMSFM, SLSFMR, RM] U97; AE289; AI74a; AS142; AT94; AU112; AX311 650
-----. R [DRMMMM, FMM RRDR, RMF] 651
At the golden gate of prayer (Showalter) [MRDMLDSD, RMRTDRM, M] AX351; AY 52 652
-----. R [DRMDLS, DDRRDR M, DRM] 653
At the Lamb's high feast (Hintze) X Salzburg 654

At the Saviour's right hand (Holsinger) [DRMR#MDRMFM FR, MFSL] AX292; AY152 655

-----. R [SDTLSMSFMR, MSDT LS,] 656

At thy feet (Smart) X Bethany 657

Athanasius (Hopkins) X St Athanasius 658

Athens (Giardini) [DSFMRDRD, SLTDSFFM,] M87; N276 659

Athens (Greek mel) X Luke 660

Athens (Piae Cantiones) [MMR MDTL, LDRMSMM, MM] BG 151 661

Athlone (Quaile) [SSFFMSSDD RDDT, TDT] S446; W659 662

Athol (Harrison) X Cambridge 663

Atkey (Dyson) [MMSDDRFM, DLFSLSMR,] BE157 664

Atonement (---) [DRMFSSLRDT LS, DTDR] AY253 665

Attende (Plainsong M 5) [DMSSS DTSLS, DSRFSM] E736; F586; BM73; BN29; BQ279 666

Attende, Domini (Plainsong. M 5) X Attende 667

Attercliffe (Mather) X Medfield 668

Attolle paulum (Plainsong. 1539) X To God on high 669

Attwood (Attwood) [SSDTLSMD RM, MRSLT] A371; B198b; D289a; E156; J124a; W184; X 181; BY226b 670

Au clair de la lune (French trad) [DDDRMR, DMRRD, DDDRM] BV352 671

Au fort de ma détresse (Genevan Psalter) [MLTDTLS, DL TDRM, MRM] E252; X244 672

Auburndale (Parker) [SDDDTT, DRRRSM, MMM] B458; C458; D294a 673

Auch jetzt macht Gott (Koch. Choralbuch. 1816) [SLSFMFMRD, RMF#SSF#S,] E550; AR213; BE74 674

Auchincairn (Scott) [SMLSMFF RSFM, SLDSD] AP157c 675

Auctor omnium bonorum (König) X Evangelists 676

Auctor vitae (Davies) [DMS SLL, MRMFMM, DMSS] W 317 677

Auctoritate saeculi (Poitiers Antiphoner, 1746) [MLDTLT LSL, LDRMDRR] E176b; F 387a; J155a; X67; AN218 678

Audi, benigni conditor (Plainsong, M 2) [RDRFMFRM MRDRR, FMF] E66; F84a; BN27 679

Audi, benigni conditor (Plainsong, M 3) [LSLDTLSL, D RDTLSLL,] BM77 680

Audite audientes me (Sullivan) [MMMRMFFM, MLMDTL, MM] D673b; T155; AJ226; BB319; BR277; BX230 681

Audley (The Hallelujah, 1849) X Malvern 682

Auf, auf, mein herz (Crueger) [SMSFMRD, SLTDTLT, LS] Q192; AA218 683

Auf, auf, weil der tag erschienen (Fabricius) X Gregor's 133rd metre - B 684

Auf, auf, weil der tag erschienen (Filitz) X Mannheim 685

Auf meinen lieben Gott (Regnart) X Gottingen 686

Auf, seele, sei geruest't (Darmstadt G-B) X Darmstadt 687

Aughton (Bradbury) [SMRDS LFF, LSMMRDM] A426; B 245; C245; D616a; G242; H 130; I489; J478; L544; N497; P328; R338; S106; U46; V 346; Z405; AD222; AE292; AF370; AG53; AH405; AI301; AK466; AL483; AM500; AN 565; AO632; AP519; AR442; AS251; AT58; AU422; AV59; AW478; AX495; BA686; BB393; BD120; BE95; BF415; BI6-D; BZ 688

-----. R [SSDTRDTLS, LSM MRD] 689

Augsburg (Ahle) [DRRM, SDD RRM, RMSSF#S,] M370;

AW560 690

Augsburg (Neumark) X Neumark 691

Augusta (Bohemian Br.) [MS SFMRDSLMSFM, SLT] AZ 69-A; BA334 692

Augustana (Norrbom) [MMMSTD FMR, FFFMSSF#] M575; N 564 693

Augustine (Abelard) X Gildas 694

Auld lang syne (Shield) [SDDD MRDR, MDDMSL, LS] G521; T144; AJ212b; AY409 695

Aurelia (Wesley) [MMMFMMR, DDLSFM, FSD] A396; B464; C464; D491; E489; F255; G 324; H70; I207; J149; K42; L203; M78; N16; O61; P44; Q473; R437; S333; T121; U 191; V531; W205; X249b; Y347; Z423; AA466; AB321; AC308; AD391; AF260; AG228; AH497; AI144; AJ176; AK322; AL35; AM224; AN130; AO240; AP 295; AR66; AS39; AT210; AU 406; AV153; AW273; AX631; AZ151-L; BA260; BB279; BD 244; BE75; BF584; BK130; BL96; BR223; BV425; BX15; BY263; BZ 696

Aurora (Benson) [SLTDMSFM, MMRDMRD, S] BY422 697

Aurora lucis rutilat Pt I (Sarum Antiphonal M 8) [SSLTDTLS, DDDTSLDD] E123I; J94b; X148 698

Aurora lucis rutilat Pt II (Plainsong. M 4) [FFFMRMSLFM, SLSLDD] E123II 699

Aus dem himmel ferne (Gesangbuch mit noten) [DDMMSM, FFM RMR, RMFM] AW421 700

Aus der tiefe (Herbst) X Heinlein 701

Aus gnaden soll ich (Knecht) X Salvation by grace 702

Aus meines herzens grunde (Wolder. Catholic G-B. 1598). X Wolder 703

Aus tiefer not (Bierman) [MS FMRDTD, SDTLSFMF] AW532 704

Aus tiefer not (Teutsch. Kirchenampt. 1525) [DTDRRDRM, FMRDTDRD,] J372; K317; L391; M384; O380; P225; Q 312; AA383; AK210; AW531 705

-----. V [DTDRRDRM, FMRD DRD, D] L391] 706

Aus tiefer not [noth] schrei ich zu dir (Walther) X De profundis 707

Austin (Bristol tune book. 1876) X St Austin 708

Austin (Sewall) [MMLDTL, LSL FFFM, MMS] BR330 709

Austria (Haydn) [DRMRFMRTD, LSFMRMD] A385; B468; C 468; D299b; E393; F368; G 382; H193; I210; J152b; K 197b; L588; O12; P21; R434; S339; T179; U352; V529; W 206; X500; Y61; Z431; AB 248; AC264; AD348; AE137; AF267; AG231; AH518; AI 145; AJ261; AK323; AL31; AM269; AN75; AO360; AP133; AQ248; AR495; AS192; AT176; AV127; AW274; BA276; BB 304; BD183; BE71; BF519; BI29; BK50; BR72; BV29; BX 416; BY24a; BZ 710

Austrian hymn (Haydn) X Austria 711

Author of faith, Eternal Word (Careless) [SLTRDMFSFM, SDMLRF] BC228 712

Author of life (Powell) [LLTDR M, SFMRRM, SMSL] BZ 713

Author of life (Stainer) [DRM FLS, MMRLTDT, RMF] F394b; BV361a 714

Autumn (Barthélémon) [DRM RDLSM, DRMRMSR,] B42b; C42b; D414b; G166; H101; I 171; L196; M366; N129; R10; S292; T194; U113; V197; Z 160; AA335; AB110; AD323; AE60; AG42; AH318; AI139; AJ280; ALSuppl.; AM566; AN 23b; AO326; AP388; AR192; AT4; AV50; AW2; BA565; BB268; BF238; BR143; BX

118b; BZ 715

Autumn, No. 2 (Iliffe) [MMFS LSRM, SSRMF#S, SD] BR480b 716

Avalon (Doane arr) [SDSLSSM, SLSDMS, SDS] AJ78 717

Avanti (Loy) [SSLDRSDDTLS, SLTDR] BD146 718

Ave (Hoffman) [DSMRDTTL, R LFMRDDT,] M202 719

Ave Maria (Arcadelt) X Arcadelt 720

Ave Maria (Bottazzo) [SDSSSDLTR DT, TF#MMD] BQ313 721

Ave Maria (Franck) [MSFRT, D MMRDT, MDRML] BQ200c 722

Ave Maria (Plainsong. M 1) [DSLLMFM, MRDRMM, MRD] BN123; BP72; BQ200a 723

Ave Maria klare (Psalteriolum harmonicum) [DTSLTDD, MRT DLS, SSS] X223 724

Ave Maria! O maiden, O mother (Slovak hymnal) [SSSFMMDDT TL, FFFMR] BQ74 725

-----. R [RMMFFFMRMFMR, MFFS] 726

Ave Maria! Thou Virgin and mother (Tozer) [SLSDTLSMF SMR, DRDS] BP77 727

Ave Maris stella (Balthasar) [MRDMMSFM, RMDMSLS, M] BQ201b 728

Ave, Maris stella (Est) X Winchester old 729

Ave, Maris stella (Ett) X St Martin 730

Ave Maris stella (Grieg) [MRD RMSS, MRDRMSS, S#F#] BQ 201d 731

Ave, Maris stella (Italian mel) [SSSSFMFSM, RLSSF#S, D] BO264 732

Ave Maris stella (Mohr) [MMSD RM, RMFFMR, DDLR] BQ201c 733

Ave, Maris stella (Plainsong M 1) [RLLTSLTRDTLSL, LLR] E213; BN127; BQ201a 734

-----. V [RLTSLTRDTLSL, LLR M] BN127 735

Ave Maris stella (St Peter Damian) [DDRRMRR, FFMRDTD, MR] BQ314 736

Ave, Maris stella (Arundel hymns) [DDRMRD, MRMFS LS, SSL] E213b; O140; AL 186b; AP288b 737

Ave radix (Sens processional) [DSMFSLS, DLTDTLS, MF] F213a 738

Ave, Regina (---) [SFMRDTD, DLTDTLSFM,] BO299 739

Ave, Regina caelorum (Plainsong. M 6) [DTLSLDRD, M SFRMRDM] BN141; BQ278 740

-----. V [FMRDRFSF, LDL# SLSFL] BQ278 741

Ave, Regina coelorum (Montani) [SSSL#L#LSFSS, DSM SFM] BQ203 742

Ave, tu Rex pacis (Bragers) [MRDRDLDDRD, DTLTLS] BP107 743

Ave verum (Rouen mel. M 6) [DRMDRRDFMRMM, RDTD] E311; F407a; BN85; BP50; BQ233e 744

-----. V [DRMDRDFMRM, RDTDRM] F407a 745

Ave verum corpus (Gounod) [MTRDTLSLLSFM, DDTR] BQ233a 746

Ave verum corpus (Guilmant) [SF#LSDTDRFFM, DLRDT] BQ233d 747

Ave, verum corpus (Mozart) [SDMSF#F, FLSFFMM, RR M] BO36; BQ233c 748

Ave verum corpus (Saint Saëns) [DRMFMMRDRD, MFSLSS] BQ233b 749

Ave virgo (Horne) X Gaudeamus pariter 750

Ave virgo virginum (Horne) X Gaudeamus pariter 751

Ave virgo virginum (Leisentritt. G-B. 1584) [DDSSDR M, LSFMRD, DDS] E131; X 144; AF186; BN94; BQ136; BY155 752

-----. V [DDSSDRMM, LSFM RRD, D] BQ136 752a

Ave vivens Hostia (Leisentritt G-B. 1584) X Ave virgo

virginum 752b
Aviemore (Hickman) [SDMMRD, DMSSFM, RRF#S,] R117; T 159 753
Avis (Hartmann) [DDDMRDTRD, DLDLDSF] M636 754
Avison (Avison) [SLSLSDRMF MRMFS, LSL] A15; B75; C75; D53; I119; L349; V120; AV97; BA145; BI100 755
-----. V [SLSLSDRMFS, SSLS LS] BI100 756
Avon (Wilson) X Martyrdom 757
Avondale (Booth) [SMRFMRDTL S, SSDTDL] V393 758
Avondale (Gabriel) [MMDFMMR D, DDDFDM, MS] T191; AI 209; AJ278; AM85 759
Avondale (Shepherd) [DRMSLD TD, SDTLSDMD] BY82 760
Awake, arise (Nicolai) X Sleepers, wake 761
Awake, my soul (Handel) X Christmas 762
Awake, my soul, in joyful lays (Caldwell) X Loving kindness 763
Awake, O earth (Showalter) [SDRMRD, SLDTLS, SLTD] AX120; AY347 764
-----. R [MFFM, MRLTDR, SDRMFS,] 765
Awake! O ye people (Mitton) [SSDMFMMRMFSFM, DDT] BC183 766
Awake, put on thy strength (McKinney) [SDDMMSFMRDFM RD, SL] AU473 767
Awake, ye saints of God (Stephens) [SDSLRDTTD, SF# SLDTT] BC229 768
Away in a manger (American, 19th c) X Müller 769
Away in a manger (Spilman) [SDDMRDDSLDLS, SDDR] AS 107; AY482 770
Axson (Campbell) [MSDTLSFM, RDMLSFMR] V664 771
Ayl nora aleelah (Jewish trad) [MMRDRSM, MMRDRSM, MM] BH176 772
Aylesbury (Camp) [SMRDTLS, SD DDRMR, FM] T69; AJ105; AM48 773
Aylesbury (Chetham. Psalms.) [LMRDTL, MSFMRM, DTLM] F236; R118; W194b; X120a; AL148a; AZ582-A; BA202; BV 491; BY187b 774
Ayn kay-lo-hay-nu (Freudenthal) X En kelohenu 775
Ayn kay-lo-hay-nu (Lewandowski) [DSDMRD, SMSFMR, DL DM] BH275 776
Ayn komocho (Binder) [MML LLLLLLS# LDT, MMM] BH 304 777
Aynhoe (Nares) [DTLSLTD, TRTDTLS, SD] O489; Q450; V364; BB32; BE16 778
-----. V [DDLSTD, RRTDLS, SDRM] Q450 779
-----. V [DDTLSLTD, TRTDT LS, S] BB32 780
Ayrshire (Finlay) [SSMSLSLD D, RMRRDLS,] BZ 781
Aysgarth (Cobb) [DDDRMFS L, TDRSSFR, R] D318c 782
Az yasheer (Jewish trad) [DRMRMFM, RMFSMFR, RR] BH62, 121 783
Azmon (Gläzer) [SDDRRMRD, RMMFMR, SS] G162; H300b; I1; J428b; L125; O386; P18; Q281; R141; S179; T219; U 68; V162; Z262; AA47; AD 182; AE8; AF223; AG107; AH374; AI13; AJ312; AL 352b; AM133; AO282; AP 804; AR114; AS113; AT117; AU5; AV117; AW12; AX360; AY41; BA115; BB438; BE 320; BZ 784
Azmon new (Gläzer) X Azmon 785

B

Babylon's streams (Campian) [LDRMMRDT, TDRMMRRD,] A60; E487; F228; L378; W 366; X124; AN184; AP247; AZ22-M; BE353; BJ36 786

Baca (Bradbury) [MMMMDDDR, RRMFFMRM,] L367; M193; T76; AI268; AJ114; AM549b; AO287; AX44; AY2 787
Baca (Havergal) X Haver 788
Badea (German mel) [SSMDR M,SFMRRD,SSLF] L134; T44b; AJ146; AZ582-T; BA621; BB 470; BR82 789
Baden (Gastorius) X Was Gott tut 790
Baginton (Gooch) [DMRDLSFM, MRDRMR,DT] W246b 791
Bairn (Danish folk mel) [DDR MRDSSS,RRMFRSF] BE318 792
Baker Chapel (Sampaix) [SSFM MMMRD,SLTDFMR,] H375 793
Bala Cynwyd (Barnes) [DDDRM FMRM,MMMF#SLS] AD439 794
Balcom (Aylward) [DMSSFMRD, RMF#STTLS] O412 795
Baldwin (Silcher) X Lorelei 796
Balerma (Barthélémon) X Ballerma 797
Balfern (---) [SF#SLSSM,RD#RF LLS,DT] M392 798
Balfour (Knowles) [DSSDMRLS, SRMFRD,] A312b; E186; X 620 799
Ballards Lane (Hawkins) [LTDT LLS#LT,DRDT,LTL] BV45 800
Balle (Balle) X Emmanuel 801
Ballerma (Barthélémon) [DMR DLSLD,DMRMSMMR,] A127; E199; H120; I242; J289; L164; R386; S226; T126a; U367; V293; W313b; X207; AD217; AE275; AJ186; AL180; AM77b; AN224a; AO90; AP36; AR374; AS214; AT169; AU208; AV147; AX177; AW57; AY255; BB221; BE126; BR288; BV420; BZ 802
-----. V [DMRDLSLD,RMRMSM R,R] AS214 803
Balm in Gilead (Negro spiritual) [MRMRDSDRM,DMMFMRF,] BZ 804
-----. R [DMDMMFS,FMMSMR, DMD 805
Baltimore (Schumacher) [SS DTLTDS,DRMDFMR,S] Q 481 806
Balty (Thommen's Christenschatz.) X Batty 807
Balulalow (Warlock) [DRMFLS FM,SLDTTLLS,] BG181 808
Bamberg (--- 17th c) [SMFS DSLTDT,SLTDTL] X6 809
Bamberg (Meiningen G-B.) X St Leonard 810
Bangor (Tans'ur) [MDTLMLS FM,MMSF#MR#M,] A68; B102; E300; F345; W313a; X259; AF149; AL660b; AN 51; AP68b; BE348; BV1; BY 139a 811
-----. V [MDTLMLSFM,MM F#SF#MR#] BY139a 812
Bankfield (Harrison) [DMSD RTD,MRSTLS,SSF] D27b; H54; V63 813
-----. V [DMSDRTD,MRSS F#S,SSF] H54 813a
Banner (Lissant) [SDMSMMRD RM,FMRSDM] D253a 814
Baptism (Lutkin) [MMMLSTDR, SMDDLLTS] I231 815
Baptiste (Calkin) X Welcome, happy morning 816
Baptize us anew (Ogden) [MR DDD,SLDDD,LSDRMM] BB 525 817
-----. R [MFFFLDRMMMM, MFSMD] 818
Baptized into our Saviour's death (Havergal) X Evan 819
Baptizien (German trad) [RF SLSDTL,SDTLSFMR,] M42 820
Barby (Tans'ur) [DMMRMRDT D,MSFMRDM] V223; AL 349a; AM585; AO220; AP15; AW578 821
-----. V [DMMRMDTD,MS FMDMR,S] AM585 822
Barmouth (Macfarren) [DRMM MFS,LTDTLTS,SS] J203b; W265 823
Barnabas (Goudimel) X Gregor's 205th metre 824

Barnard (Barnard) X Give of your best 825
Barnby I (Barnby) [DDTLTS, SDTDR, RMF# LS] D50 826
Barnby II (Barnby) [DRMFLSFM, SLTDLS, SL] I87; AZ14-Ee; BA656 827
Barnby III (Barnby) [LLDTLS# T L, DDMRDTTD,] V155; BR178 828
Barnby (Barnby) X Just as I am 829
Barnby (Barnby) X Merrial 830
Barnby (Barnby) X St Andrew 831
Barnby (Barnby) X Sarum 832
Barnby (Barnby) X Stand up 833
Barnby's Hymnary, Tune 53 (Stainer) X Laus matutina 834
Barnby's hymnary, Tune 59 (Stainer) X Lux prima 835
Barnby's hymnary, Tune 91 (Barnby) X Kirkdale 836
Barnby's hymnary, Tune 101 (Barnby) [SSSDDDRMRD, MMM RTS] AZ298-C 837
Barnby's hymnary, Tune 140 (Smart) [SMLSLTDS, MFSDTL RT,] AZ95-D 838
Barnby's hymnary, Tune 148 (Gounod) X Lux prima 839
Barnby's hymnary, Tune 154 (Goss) X St Casimer 840
Barnby's hymnary, Tune 222 (Sullivan) X Lacrymae 841
Barnby's hymnary, Tune 224 (Langran) X Langran 842
Barnby's hymnary, Tune 225 (Sullivan) X Lux mundi 843
Barnby's hymnary, Tune 237 (Barnby) X St Andrew 844
Barnby's hymnary, Tune 285 (Sullivan) X St Kevin 845
Barnby's hymnary, Tune 291 (Smart) [MMRMFLLS, DSMFS DMR,] AZ95-E 846
Barnby's hymnary, Tune 474 (Smart) X Sion 847
Barnby's hymnary, Tune 475 (Smart) [SSSLSS, LTMD, DD TLS] AZ141-K 848
Barnby's hymnary, Tune 525 (Winn) [SLTDRM, SFMRDT, TDRM] K332; N293 849
Barnby's hymnary, Tune 590 (Barnby) X Edinburgh 850
Barnby's hymnary, Tune 633 (Barnby) X Nightfall 851
Barnekow I (Barnekow) [MM SLSMMS, DDDFMMR, R] J 210 852
Barnekow II (Barnekow) [MS FMDRMD, RMFLSDMR,] M134 853
Barnekow III (Barnekow) [MM MSFMRMD, DLSFMRD] M179 854
Barnet (Jesson) [SDRMSL, SM DRMS, SLMM] F223a 855
Barnett (Campbell) [MMRLTD RD, DDRMFFFM,] V708 856
Barony (Sullivan) X Courage, brother 857
Barre (Clark) [MMFSDTLL, LSDTLS, FM] T201; AJ290 858
Bartholdy (Mendelssohn) X Selwyn 859
Bartimaeus (Pilsbury. U.S. Sacred harm. 1799) V308; AQ44; BZ 860
-----. V [DRMRMSMRD, SLTDLSM] BZ 860a
Bartley (Hastings) [MMMRDD D, DRRMMR, MMM] L327 861
Barton (---) [SSSDSLSS, DRM FMRM, S] I205; AL153b; BY239 862
Barton (Knecht) X Knecht 863
Bassett (Stair) [SDTDLSRM, DLDFMRM, D] Y86; AC169 864
Bath (Cooke) [MMMRFM, MM MFRM, MMMF#] I587 865
Bath (Sewall) [MDRMRMSFM RD, MMF#SF#] BR41 866
Battell Chapel (Jepson) [SDS LTDRSM, MMMF#S#LTD,] Y151; BF636 867
Battenberg (Henry, Prince of Battenberg) [DDMMMRD,

DDFFLLS, SR] AO430 868
Battishill (Battishill) [SMRDRRM, FMLSFMR, SM] W668; X538; BY754 869
Battle (Lawes) [DDTLTS#TDR M, MRMDRT] E432; X290; AN 95 870
Battle cry (Gray) [LLLDDTL, DSLSFM, SDD] F497 871
Battle cry (Sherwin) [SSMFSLF MRD, RMRTSL] AH454; AI326; AM686; BB499; BY525 872
-----. R [MDMDRD#RFMD, MT DLRD] 873
Battle hymn (Steffe) [SSSSFMSDR MMMRD, D] B434; C434; J356; Y289; AC280; AF443; AH485; AN566; AO600; AT488; AV301; BD170; BX410; BZ 874
-----. R [SFMSDRMD, LTDTDLS] 875
Battle hymn of the Republic (Steffe) X Battle hymn 876
Battle hymn (---) X When the battle's over 877
Battle song (Shaw) [MLSLTDRMS TLLSL, MS] W155b; X578; Y 155 878
Batty (Thommen's Christen-Schatz) [DRMRMFSM, LSFM RRMS] A72; B100; C157; D 104; E105; F124a; J63b; K61; L560; M14; N109; O146; P318; Q155; AA449; AF332; AK216; AL99; AN85; AP115; AW147; AZ16-A; BA263; BN93 879
-----. V [DRMDRMFSM, LSSM FFM,] AW147 880
-----. V [DRMRMSFM, LSFMR RM, S] BN93 881
Bavaria (Gale) [MMMRSFM, LR MFM, RRSL] D518a 882
Bavaria (Thommen's Christen-Schatz) X Cassel 883
Baxter (Burnap) [DMRFMLS, DTLSFM, MMM] V430; AO451; BA888; BF406 884
Bayeaux (Huet) X Diva servatrix 885
Baynard (Booth) [SSLSSDRM, M MRDLSFM,] D622b 886
Be not afraid (Temple Star) [SM MRMFM, RDDRRM, SMM] AX 530; AY386 887
-----. R [DRMMMS, FMRRR MF, MRD] 888
Be not dismayed (German trad 15th c) X Kommt her zu mir 889
Be present at our table, Lord (Mason) X Rockingham 890
Be ready when He comes (Teasley) [DRMMMFMRD, DRRDRM, D] AX285 891
Be silent (Doane) [SSMDDS, MSSSS, SLDDD] AR437; AS 43; AU485; AX39; AY448; BB601 892
Be strong (Eaton) [SD, MRD TLSSF#LS, STMR] AB176b 893
Be strong, O men (Fillmore) [SLTDDDTDRM, LTD#RRR] U269; Y185 894
Be thou exalted (Geistliche lieder. 1535) X Wo Gott zum haus 895
Be thou faithful (Hughes) [MS DSDRM, DRMFMRDMR] BY 305c 896
Be thou faithful (Mendelssohn) X Almighty Father, hear 897
Be Thou King (Sisters of St Joseph, Toronto) [DDMM SSS, RRFFLLL, SM] BO214 898
-----. R [SLSFMRD, FMRDT LS, SD] 899
Be Thou our guide (Holsinger) [SDMDLSDMRFM, MMFML] AR65 900
-----. R [TDRRDRMMMMF MR, MFS] 901
Be with me (Ackley) [SLTDRD TRSM, SLTDRD] U364 902
-----. R [MR#MFMMR, RD# RMRD, DTD] 903
Be ye doers of the word (McKinney) [SDMMR#MD, TDRM RDL, DL] AU326 904
-----. R [MFMRRRR, RMRD DDD, DT] 905
Be ye joyful (Bohemian trad) [DRMFSSS, FSLS, SSFFM] P129; Q86 906

-----. V [DRMF#SLS, F#SLS, SSFFM] Q86 907

Be ye strong in the Lord (Sankey) [SSDDDTSSFFFFM, SSL] AX448; AY461 908

-----. R [SLSSLS, DDLSFMRD R, S] 909

Beachley (Cottman) [MRDSTLS, LSLDRR, MRD] AS333 910

Beacon Hill (Mason) [SSSMDTTL, FFFRTLS, S] G268; Y174; Z 360; AC205; AE443; AG189; AR311; AT351; AU396; AW392; BZ 911

-----. R [MMMMM, MFDRM, SLTDMR] 912

Bealoth. (Mason. Sacred harp. 1843) [MMMMRD, DRRRMRD, SMM] G183; I191; Z428; AI 146; AR490; AS191; AX149; AY 380; BZ 913

-----. V [SMMMRD, DRRRMRD, SMM] I191 914

Beata (Stotzel. Choralbuch. 1744) X O wie selig seid ihr doch 915

Beata nobis gaudia (Plainsong M 1) X Veni, Redemptor gentium 916

Beata nobis gaudia (Psalterium chorale. Constance) [SMDRM FMRDLTD, DMFS] E185; F391; X44b 917

Beati (Stainer) [MMRDSSFM, SDT LSRD] A128b; B198; C198; D 175a; F572; I459; K247; L320; O476; Q370; T439; W219b; AA 306; AO539; AP306; BA764; BB 247; BE427; BX40; BY460a 918

Beatitudo (Dykes) [DRMSMDFM, LTDMRR, R] A416b; B27; C35a; D391; F528; G419; H122; I79; J213; K87; L101; M253; N57; Q360; R249; S218; T192; U256; V66; W592b; Y103; Z334; AA 108; AB169; AC216; AD195; AE 36; AF350; AG130; AH357; AI 279; AJ195; AK319; AL179b; AM 259; AN236b; AO89; AP312; AR 61; AS65; AW42; AY416; BA2; BB18; BE284; BF368; BR445a; BV297a; BX74; BY405 919

Beatrice (Coe) [MMSMRMF FM, DLSMRMF#] N335 920

Beatus (Dunhill) [SLTLSFM RM, FSMRMDT] E650 921

Beaufort (Wild) [MR#MFMMR D, SF#STLS, SS] D15b; AB 307 922

Beaumaris (Gauntlett) [SLSS TDDRML, LL#L#LD#R] BR 479 923

Beaumont (Strom) [SDDRRMD, FMDDTD, MRR] N382 924

Beauteous day (Root) [MRR DDTTL, FMMRDRM, M] H205; U391; V601; AI93 925

-----. Beauteous day (Root) R [SSLSMMSM, DDRRMSMR,] 926

Beautiful homeland (Holsinger) [SSLSSMDMSRD, MFFFL] AY403 927

-----. R [SSSRRRMFM, MMM RRLT] 928

Beautiful land on high (Haven) [MFSF#SMRD, MFSF#SSF# S,] AY159 929

Beautiful river (Lowry) [MMM RMFSM, FFFSFMRS,] AH534; AI409; AP637; AT481; AU 434; AV394; AX597; BB555 930

-----. R [LLDTDLSM, MFMFM FMF] 931

Beautiful Sion, built above (Fones) [DDDDSDMRD, MMM MDMS] BC78 932

Beautiful Sion for me (Thomas) [SLSMFSL, TDRFMFLS, S] BC6 933

Beautiful star (Schilling) [SS SLTDRMFMR#M, D#MRL] AC93 934

-----. R [SLLSF#S, SRSDRM, MFDR] 935

Beautiful star of Bethlehem (Boyce) [SDRMSSSMD, MRD LDDL] AX95 936

Beautiful valley of Eden (Sherwin) X Kelley 937

Beauty of holiness (Lowry)

[SSMDSSSSMDMRRRMF] AR 432; AS4 938

-----. R [TDDTLSM, SSSFR, LLLS] 939

Because you live again (French trad) [LMRDLDRM, MLSFMR MR] BN162; BY126 940

Bechler (Bechler) [SDDRRMFSF MMRRD, SD] AZ159-D; BA 755 941

Beck (Beck) X Just as I am 942

Beddome (Statham) X Thanksgiving 943

Bede (Handel) [DTDSFMRDTDRD T, DTD] F75a; W676 944

Bedford (Bishop) X Leicester 945

Bedford (Wheall) [SMDLSFMR, SDTLLS, M] A116; B10; C321; D221a; E83; F320; K404; Q284; S75; W242; X114; AA117; AL73; AP5; AZ14-C; BA132; BR87; BY306 946

Beecher (Zundel) [SSLSMRMRD, TLDLSF] A304; B240; C240; G372; H190; I355b; J312; K 276b; L202; M116; N149; P38; R399; S308a; T175; U21; V323; Y356; Z379; AB193; AC67; AD 245; AE188; AF228; AG176; AH 223; AJ255; AK272; AL449; AM 368; AN50b; AO295b; AP562; AR178; AS116; AT2; AU19; AV 183; AW165; AX43; AY516; BA 490; BB142; BD58; BE276; BF 256; BK52; BX532; BZ 947

Beechmont (Burrowes) [SSMDLD SD, RMRDRMR, S] C81 948

Beechwood (Booth) [MRDRTSDDR RM, MSMDT] W20; AC58 949

Beecroft (Mallary) [MMMRSLTD S, DTLLRDT,] H424 950

Beeding (Thiman) [MSDRMRD, RFMLSF#S, RD] BV573b 951

Beeforth (Mann) [MMMFFLFM, MLLDLS, SM] O395 952

Beethoven (Beethoven) [MMFSSF M, RDDRMMRR, MM] B114b; C114b; D512b; G12; I160; R 21; S5; U25; Y49; Z95; AB12; AC43; AD9; AE10; AF8; AG 5; AH200; AK21; AN42; AO 79; AQ11; AR27; AS91; AT 44; AV52; AW10; BA33; BB 29; BE58; BF211; BH230; BI34; BK109; BR188; BX63; BZ 953

Beethoven (Mason arr) [MFS LSFMR, MFSLDTLS,] AO 542 954

Befiehl du deine wege (German trad) X Commit thy way 955

Befiehl du deine wege (Rostocker G-B) X Gregor's 151st metre-H 956

Before the Menorah (Binder) [DSDSLTD, RRMDMF#S, RL] BH206 957

Before Thee, Lord, I bow my head (Dean) [SLTDMDLT, STDRFMRM,] BC231 958

Begin the day with God (Read) X Lisbon 959

Behold a branch (Geistliche K-G. Cologne 1599) X Rosa mystica 960

Behold a host (Norwegian trad) [DMSSLSMDMSR, RMFRD] J599; M313; N207; O492b; P434; Q656; BE19 961

Behold, a rose (Geistliche K-G. Cologne. 1599) X Rosa mystica 962

Behold! a royal army (Geibel) [SDTDRTS, SDTDRM, MRM] BC7 963

-----. R [SSSSSS, SSMRDT LS, SS] 964

Behold a simple, tender Babe (Monaghan) [MLTDTLSLM, MLLSFM, M] BN13 965

Behold! behold He cometh (Webbe) [SMMMMMRR, RMR DTD, LF] BQ3 966

Behold, I stand at the door (Gabriel) [DMMMR#MFFM, MMRDTRD,] AI273 967

Behold it is the springtime of the year (---) [MSMDRM FMLSLS, SDTL] BH129 968

Behold me standing (Knapp) [SSDTDRLR, DTDRD#RMD,]

BY410 969

-----. R [STDRD#RMDS, DM FSMRD] 970

Behold the great Redeemer die (Careless) [MMMLLSFM, S SSLDTLS,] BC230 971

Behold, the mountain of the Lord (Daynes) [SDMFSDRMMRD, DLSFM] BC297 972

Behold the Saviour of mankind (American trad) X Amazing grace 973

Behold the star (Negro spiritual) [MMSRD, FFLRDSL, MMSRD,] Y323; BK164 974

-----. R [DDDSLMMRD, MM RDLDR] 975

Behold thy sons and daughters (Schreiner) [SDDRRMRDR, RMSFMMR,] BC24 976

Behold what love (Teasley) [MS LSMMFM, MSLSMR, MS] AX 84 977

-----. R [SLLLLLS, MSLSMR, MSS] 978

Behold, where, in a mortal form (Arne) X Arlington 979

Belden (Belden) [SLSMRDRMRD, DTLSFM] AR309; AS318 980

Belfry praise (Matthews) [DTLSFM RD, DTLTLS, DL] F496 981

Belgrave (Horsley) [DMSDMFSLR, SFMF#SLT] E511; F479; J 440a; W26; X694; AN225; BY 567 982

-----. V [SMSDMFSLR, SMF# STLS] F479 983

-----. V [SMSDMFSLR, SFM F#SLT] X694 984

Belhaven (Pritchard) [DRRMMFF MRDS, SLTDS] W34; BE356 985

Belief (American trad) X Camp-meeting 986

Believe me if all those endearing (Irish trad) X Sweet story 987

Believe not those (Alman) [RR RMFM, DDDRMR, RRMF] BH 231 988

Bell carol (French trad) [MLT DRMRD, LTDT, MLTD] BG162 989

Belleville (Jones) [DMMFRD DL, LSRM, SLTR] C36a; U360; AC317; AP514b; BO 194 990

Belleville (Lutkin) [SSSSSLSS, SSMRDDTT,] I347 991

Bellwoods (Hopkirk) [DTLSML, SMRDRM, MF#S#] A525; BY187a 992

Belmont (Gardiner's Sacred mel. 1812) [SMRDTTLDS, SSFMMR] A328; B166; C27; D20; F189b; G28; H82; I36; L92; N81; P50; Q436; R104C; T73; U34; V69; W309; Z125; AA367; AB327; AE269; AG49; AI38; AJ109; AK395; AL269b; AM265; AN251b; AO47; AP 436; AR78; AS79; AV56; AW 197; BA4; BB295; BF359; BH202; BO8; BR269; BV342; BY339 993

Beloit (Reissiger) [SSLTDRM MFD#R, SSLTD] G470; I145; Z179; AC316; AI367; AJ377; AM46; AR543; AS416 994

Beloved (Lewis) [DDRMFSLS FMRRD, SDD] G346; I530; AR199; AW470; BB160; BC 195; BZ 995

-----. V [DDRMFSLFMRRD, SDDR] AW470 996

Belsize (Elliott) [MSDMRD, DMLDTL, MRRS] D187a; V 510; AA304 997

Belsize (Shaw) [MSFMLR, RFMRS, DDRMM] E415; X543 998

Belstead (Taylor) [MDRMSD, TLSDMR, SMSL] F315 999

Bemerton (Filitz) X Caswall 1000

Bemerton (Greatorex) [MRD TLSDD, DMRDFMRD] U136; V99; AO148; BR264 1001

Bemotzoay (Jewish trad) [LT DTDLMM, LTDTDRM, M] BH 173 1002

Ben Avon (Stebbins) [SSFM RDTD, SDTLSMDR] AJ269 1003

Ben Jonson's carol (Boughton) [LRDLSFSLR, LRDLSFS]

BG168 1004

Ben Rhydding (Reinagle) [DMFS LTD, TLMSF#M, MFR] D69b; I94; N423; V524; AA319; BA 73 1005

Beneath the cross (Sankey) [SS SF#SDS, MSSFRM, SSS] Eap. 22 1006

Beneath thy shadow hiding (Tenney) [DRMMMR#MSS, SDDRD RM,] AY93 1007

-----. R [SSFMMRDMR, SSFMM RD] 1008

Benedic anima mea (Goss) X Lauda anima 1009

Benediction (---) [MMMSFMDRM RD, MSLS, D] AP623 1010

Benediction (Barraclough) [MMM MMMDRMSFM, FFFF] Sapp44 1011

Benediction (Brunk) [SSSSLSDRM, MMRLT, SS] AY412 1012

Benediction (Froom) [MR#MFM SSSS, RD#RMRDM] BB702 1013

Benediction (Hopkins) X Ellers 1014

Benediction (Ledington) [MMMM MMRS, DFMRRR, MM] BB700 1015

Benediction (Lutkin) X The Lord bless you 1016

Benediction (McKinney) X Bryson City 1017

Benediction (Mann) X Orient morning 1018

Benevento (Webbe) [DDDDMRD, RRRRFMR, MM] E469; H522; I574; L552; M108; U155; V272; X256; AL246; AM613; AN140; AW339; AZ205-M; BE72 1019

Benevolence (Greenwood) [DTDLS DRD, TDRRR, R#RR#] BE309 1020

Benison (---) [MMRDMSFM, MF FMRD#RM] BR191 1021

Benison (Hullah) [MRMRLSMS, MRMRLSMS,] H131 1022

Benjamin (Chitty) [DMRRFFMM, RMRRMR, SF] AZ590-G 1023

Benson (Kingham) [SSLDDTLS, SLRDTD, MM] B483a; C483; Eap63; F271; AP394; BV315a; BY371 1024

Bentley (Hullah) [MRMFLLS, DTSFLS, MM] B224; C381; D437b; I454; J495a; L361; R268; S284b; U45; V255a; W439; Z581; AB201; AD231; AG208; AH377; AL287; AM 520; AO332; AP445; BA401; BE251; BF412; BY251 1025

Benton Harbor (Hoffman) X Hoffman 1026

Bera (Gould) [MMRDSSRMFM, DDLSMR] G196; H250; I 249; L523b; S225; T89; U 158; V276; AG143; AH326; AI319; AJ104; AM525; AO 247; AR255; AS194; AV36; AW141; BB330; BE99 1027

-----. V [MMRDSSRMFM, MMRDSS] BE99 1028

Bereden (Swedish mel. 16th c) X Messiah 1029

Bereden väg för herran (Swedish mel. 16th c) X Messiah 1030

Berggren I (Berggren) [SFMM R, RLLSFFM, MRDD] J128; M640; P297; BE209 1031

-----. V [SFMRRLLSFFM, MRDDT] M640 1032

Berggren II (Berggren) [SST DRMFFM, MFSRMFR] M69 1033

Berkshire (Stark) [MFLSSDM MR, RMFLSFS] AR47; BH103 1034

Berkshire (Wesley, C., the younger) [SDMLFMRDR, SDM RSLT] BV240 1035

Berlin (Bourgeois) X Bourgeois 1036

Berlin (Crueger) X Ratisbon 1037

Berlin (Mendelssohn) X Brightest and best 1038

Bernard (---) [DDTDLLLS, SLTDMR, SS] D537; L144 1039

Berne (Beery) [DMDMDSSM, DRRRFM, DM] AI260; AS 298 1040

Berno (Mann) [SMRDDTLS, FMFSLR, SM] J182a; W268;

BE249 1041
Berry Down (Bullock) [MRDRM SDLSFMRD, RMS] X590 1042
Bertha (Tours) X Groningen 1043
Berthelsdorf (Herrnhut ms.) X Gregor's 141st meter-A 1044
Berthold (Tours) X Tours 1045
Berwick Street (Shaw) [MRFM RDS, SLDTRD, DTL] X372 1046
Berwyn (Roberts) [SMRDDRMSF FM, MMMF#F#] BY209 1047
Besançon carol (French trad) [DDDSSLTD, DDTTLSLS,] AQ281; BD225; BG133 1048
Bethabara (Stainer) X Beati 1049
Bethany (Mason) [MRDDLL, SDM R, MRDDL] A465; B222; C222; D344a; G362; H310; I315b; J577; K407b; L428a; M290; N 448; O466; P336; Q533; R326; S261; T411; U265; V408a; Y10; Z329; AA520; AB185; AC156; AD308; AE201; AF351; AG173; AH359; AI266; AK318; AL321c; AN245; AO296a; AP470b; AQ126; AR397; AS210; AT322; AU206; AV189; AW202; AX372; AY86; BA612; BB382; BC124; BE192; BF376; BK86; BR374a; BX287; BZ 1050
Bethany (Smart) [MLSMDRDT,LSDM SFMR,] D292b; H139; I211; K 228; O77; S274; T320; U61; V 115; W502; AB70; AI347; AM 593; AN358; AO375; AP568; AR573; AW46; BA457; BE277; BF254; BI56; BY595b 1051
Bethel (Cornell) [SSDDTT, SSRR DD, DRLD] I184 1052
Bethel (Mason) X Bethany 1053
Bethel (Roberts) [DDTDRM, MFMRDT, RDLS,] BY693 1054
Bethlehem (Barnby) [MSLTDRMR, FLTDRS, MM] C78a; D58a; I121b; O196; AB126; AO125b 1055
Bethlehem (Fink) [SDDTLSLS, S LRDTD, S] A533; B499; C71a; D54a; F575; G391; J24; K28; M350; N38; P88; Q109; R23; S478; W42; Y135; Z505; AC 70; AD10; AE16; AH275; AI42; AK131; AL71; AM257; AN129; AO120; AP733; AR 12; AW92; BD126; BF190; BK24; BR551b; BZ 1056
-----. V [SDDTLSFM, SLRDT D, SL] F575 1057
Bethlehem (French trad) X Old French noël 1058
Bethlehem (Mendelssohn) X Mendelssohn 1059
Bethlehem (Redner) X St Louis 1060
Bethlehem (Wesley, S) X Doncaster 1061
Bethlehem (Woodman) [MMSF MMRR, MFLSFM, MM] AB411; BF654 1062
Bethlehem lullaby (Brahms) X Lucy 1063
Bethlehem, of noblest cities (Witt) X Stuttgart 1064
Bethlem Land (Noble) [SSS DSSS, DMFSLTL, RL] AB117 1065
Bethsaida (Barnby) X Longwood 1066
Betracht'n wir heut zu dieser frist (Bohemian Br. G-B. 1544) DDMSSSMFS, TDLD SSL] AQ151; BG95 1067
Better land (---) [DDRMFSFM R, RMMRSTR] H504 1068
Better land (Sherwin) [SSSDT DR, SSRRDRM, MR] T205; AJ376 1069
Beulah (Garrett) [MRMDSFSM, STLSMR, M] B470; C470; F32; BD191; BE131; BV436b 1070
Beulah (Hemy) [SDDTDR, SRR DRM, SMMF] A591; B515b; C515; D679b; T105; AR533; AS389 1071
Beulah (Smith) [DRMDFMMD, TDRDRRM, D] AY486 1072
-----. R [SSDSLSSM, SSFRSF M, S] 1073
Beulah land (Sweney) [SMMMR DDD, SFFFMRRR,] AU114; BB554 1074
-----. R [SRRRSMMM, SLSFR SFM,] 1075

Bevan (Goss) [DDRMFS, SSSFMR, RMF] B463; D152; M172; O 357; Q220; W635; AM222 1076

Beverly (Baermann) [DMSLTDLS, DRMF#SLS, S] BX158 1077

Beverly (Monk) [SSDSFMRD, SF MMRDS,] B67; C67a; D317a; W157; AM235; AO113; AP245; AW126; BB196; BV87 1078

Bewdley (Ouseley) [SSLRTDR, MS RSLTS, LL] F295 1079

Beweley (Taylor) [LSMRDRM, DTSLMFS, SL#] BV299; BY 481a 1080

Bexfield (--) [SMMSSFF, STRFM, SMMS] AP575 1081

Beyond (Harrington) [SSS#LTD RMF, MDRM, SSS#] I627 1082

-----. R [DDRMSFM, DDRMRD.] 1083

Beyond the sunset (Perkins) [DRMMMRMFLS, MRMFFM] AU88 1084

-----. R [SLTDDTLS, MRMFFM RM,] 1085

Bickersteth (Caldbeck) X Pax tecum 1086

Bid them look to Christ (Perry) [DDRMMFSLSM, DTDRMS] AX219; AY224 1087

-----. R [SSF#SMRDMFM, SLS MDM] 1088

Billesley (Mullinar) [DRFSLMRM DS, MSRFMD] X497 1089

Billing (Terry) X Newman 1090

Bilsdale (Slater) [SDDFMRDTD, RMDSLS, S] X361; BY115 1091

Binchester (Croft) [MRDTSFMR, RMSSF#S, RR] E398; F261; W440; X509; AD255; AL290; AP442; BJ34; BV250b; BY496 1092

Bingham (---) [SDDRMSLLTD, MRTSDM] T3; AI34; AJ384a 1093

Binghampton (Alexander) [MMMM SMSM, MRRRMFM, M] Y400 1094

Binghamton (Sumner) X The child of a King 1095

Binney's (Thiman) [LMMMDFMRM, RDTLTS#, S#] BV4a 1096

Binti hamari (India mel) [LTRRTRMFM, MLSLM, DD] BZ 1097

Binyon (Sanders) [LLLTLTDM MRDT, DDRM] AQ153 1098

Birchington (Butcher) [DRMF SLTD, RMDLDT, LS] C346b 1099

Birds are singing (Hymns for children) [SF#SMMR#MD, RMRTDRM, S] AL587; AP 723; AW409 1100

-----. R [FRTSDMSM, FFF MMMRD] 1101

Birdstown (Gabriel) [SDDDRM DL, RDDTTDD, S] AJ302 1102

Birkdale (Barnby) X Diadema 1103

Birkdale (Hiles) [MRDMFLDD, DTLL, SFMF] O547 1104

Birling (---) [MRDDTLSFMR, MRDMRD] C20b; E274; X55; BE91; BV245; BY521 1105

Birmingham (Cunningham's Selection of Psalm tunes) [DMDSMLSLTD, SLSFMR] A531a; E429; X266; AD430; AR513; AW307; BY626 1106

Birmingham (Mendelssohn) [DDRMLLSFM, MSSFRD, D] AR626; AU478; BB692; BC 235 1107

Birthday (Shaw) [SLSLTDM LSRMD, SLSL] X386c 1108

Bis willkommen (Kittel) [DM SDTDRR, DMRTLLS, D] Q576; AA186 1109

-----. V [DMFSDTDRR, DM RDTLLS] AA186 1110

Bishop (Bishop) X Illsley 1111

Bishop (Holbrook) [MMMSMDR M, MMMRDLRR,] T229; AJ 325; AM451 1112

Bishopgarth (Sullivan) [SMMM MFMR, RSLMRDRD] J445; K334a; R375; T266; U199; W370; AB244; AF355; AJ 371; AK433; AM377; AP384; BF373; BY302 1113

Bishopthorpe (Clarke) [SFMR

DTLFMDTD, RMFS] A360a; B351; E408; F208; J476a; W 137; X536; AB303; AF274; AL664; AN132; AP78; BE142; BJ5; BV517; BY121 1114

-----. V [SMRDTLFMDTD, RM FSS] BJ5a 1115

Bishopthorpe (Parry) [MSDMFS LR, FMRLDRT, S] D41b 1116

Bist willkommen, liebster freund (Grimm. Choral buch) X Tabor 1117

Bithynia (Essay on the church plain chant) X Dulce carmen 1118

Blackbourne (Harrison. Sacred harmony) [LMRDRDTL, LLTD RM, SD] E456; W531a; X575 1119

Blackburn (Aitken) [MRDFMMRD RM, SFMMRR] L523a; T18; AJ 23a; BB82 1120

Blackie (Ouseley) [SSLL, TTDS, MMRSDRT, T] K280 1121

Blaencefn (Thomas) [DMRDSLTD RMR, DMLTD] W387b; X222 1122

Blaenhafren (Welsh trad) [LLSF MDTLTLS#, LLS#LT] R356; S374; Z494; AF427; AM539 1123

Blaenwern (Rowlands) [SSLLS DMMR, DTLSSTL] BV612; BY 595b 1124

Blairgowrie (Dykes) [MRMFLSM, MSMDRM, MRM] D240c; G266; H263; I219; R454; S485; T290; U169; V302; Z362; AB42; AD 325; AH211; AI109; AJ402; AO 497; AR148; AS420; AT502; AY 443; BA844; BF516; BZ 1125

Blairgowrie (Thompson) [MS FMSMRD, RMSDLSFM,] G158; BY181 1126

Blake's cradle song (Williams) [MSRMD, MRMSLSMS, TTL] BG196 1127

Blencathra (Somervell) [SLDRMF R, MDLSFS, SLDR] A546; X394 1128

-----. R [SLSDTLS, DLTDFR, MD] 1129

Blenden (Kettle) [MFMRLTTD, M MMMFR, MF] AB211; BR393 a 1130

Blendon (Giardini) [DMFSSDT LS, SLDLSFM] L70; AA281 1131

Bless Jehovah (Vail) X Close to Thee 1132

Bless the words (Pollock) [MSSMDMMR, RMFRSFM, M] AX77; AY61 1133

Blessed are they that have the faith (Lund) [SMR#MFRD#R, SRD#RMDRM] BC233 1134

-----. R [SLRSDFTM, MMTD DRMR,] 1135

Blessed assurance (Knapp) X Assurance 1136

Blessed be the name (Havergal) X Evan 1137

Blessed be the name (Hudson) X Blessed name 1138

Blessed Bible (Landis) [SMD TLSLSSM, SRMFLS] AX143; AY194 1139

Blessed Bible, how I love it (Beery) [SSDDMRDL, LLSD MMR, S] AS183 1140

Blessed, blessed (Binder) [MFFMSD, TLDLLS, MFFF] BH153 1141

Blessed communion (Schörring Koralbog. 1781) X Contentment 1142

Blessed Francis holy father (Slovak hymn) [MFSDTDRS, LTDFMRM, M] BQ102 1143

Blessed Francis holy father (Theophane) [SLTDDRRMD, DRMFMRD] BN179 1144

Blessed home (Stainer) [MR LTSD, MRLTSD, DTLT] B394; C394; D632b; I527; K386; O615; AZ38-D; BA 31 1145

Blessed hope (Alexis) [SSDST LS, RRDLSF#S, TT] N609 1146

Blessed host (Norwegian trad) [STRTDRMFSMDT, SDRM] P432 1147

Blessed host (Norwegian trad) X Behold a host (Norwegian) 1148

Blessed hour (Doane) X Doane II 1149
Blessed Jesus, at thy word (Ahle) X Liebster Jesu 1150
Blessed light (Russian mel) [LDMRMFMRDT, TDRTMD] AL303 1151
Blessed Lord, how much I need thee (Belden) [MRDSLDLS, TDRRDRM, M] BB578 1152
-----. R [SFMRDDL, DLSDMDMR, S] 1153
Blessed Lord, in thee (Owen) X Bryn Calfaria 1154
Blessed morn (Roper) [SSMRRDLS, SSTLSLSF#] C77b; D57b; U53 1155
Blessed name (Bradbury) X There is no name 1156
Blessed name (Hudson) [SSDMDRDDLS, SSDRMF] AT140; AU279; AX3 1157
Blessed night, when first the plain (M. B. F.) X Melford 1158
Blessed, O blessed (Kaiser) [MFMMRD, SLSSFM, RMFF] BH154 1159
Blessed quietness (Marshall) X Marshall 1160
Blessed Redeemer (Loes) X Redeemer 1161
Blessin (Blessin) [SDRMSSDFMR, FMTDDR] M183 1162
Blessing and honour (Bach, School of) [DTTDSSLSFM, LS#S#LMM] BY305-B 1163
Blessing and honor (Parker) X Pro patria 1164
Blessings (Excell) [MMMFSSSMFMF, RMFST] AT318; BC202 1165
----. R [SSDSSMFFF, FFTLSFM] 1166
Blessings over Chanukkoh lights (Jewish trad) [SDRMRDD, DRMMSFMMR,] BH297 1167
Blessings over the Lulav (Jewish trad) X Kiddush 1168
Blest be the dear uniting love (Chetham. Psalmody. 1718) X Marlow 1169
Blest be the tie (Naegeli) X Dennis 1170
Blest is the bond (Heller) [SF#FMRDTL#L, LLS#SFMR] BH219 1171
Blest is the Faith (Montani) [DMSSSLFLD, LSMRDML] BQ123 1172
-----. R [DDDSFMDLFS, SLLLFL] 1173
Blest moments (Baxter) [DDRMMRRM, SFRMMDRM,] J217b 1174
Bletchley (Bedford) [DMMMFSSDRM, SLTDDD] BY594a 1175
Bliss (Bliss) [SSFMMRMFLSFM, SDTL] L493; N525; P213; AE190; AH394; AI128; AM580; AR484; AS310; AT265; AU73; AV363; AW484; AX484; AY452; BB313 1176
-----. R [SSSSSS, MSLLDDTDD] 1177
Bliv med din store naade (Vulpius] X Cana 1178
Blodyn (Roberts) [MRDSFMMRDDT, RMRDS] W347 1179
Blomstertid (Swedish Koralbok. 1697) J449; N543 1180
Bloomfield chant (Bradbury) [SSSDDDRM, MMMMMMF#S,] T214; AJ307 1181
Blow (Blow) X St Agnes 1182
Blumenthal (Blumenthal) [MMMMSFM, DDRRFMR, MM] I500b; V457; AJ275; AO427; BA11; BH43; BR103 1183
Boardman (Devereaux) [DSFMRDDTLS, SSDDMR] H327; I129; L310; N334; R38; T200; AJ289a; AO267; BF590; BR314 1184
Boar's head carol (English trad) [SDDDTDS, MFFLFSSD, S] BG19 1185
-----. R [DDTTDDS, FFLLSSD.] 1186
Bod Alwyn (Jenkins) [MMMFRM, DDDRLT, DDDR] BY318 1187
Bodley (Horsley) [DMRDDLRFM, MDTLSTL] BV440 1188

Bodlondeb (Arthur) [SMDRMLS DRDT, MR#TTF#] W427; BY438b 1189
Bodmin (Scott-Gatty) [MRDTLS LFM, MFSLLLT] BV486; BY 213 1190
Bohemia (Bohemian Br. G-B.) X O mensch sieh 1191
Bohemia (German trad) [SS SSLS, DDTLS, SSSSL] J425; K552 1192
Bohemia (Thommen. Christen-schatz. 1745) X Cassel 1193
Bohemia #11 (Thommen. Christen-schatz. 1745) X Cassel 1194
Bohemian Brethren (Bohemian Brethren) [DMFSDTLS, LSF MRMFRD,] A522; E604; F 423; G355; R15; Sap. 34; X214; Z637; AB57; AD146; AF20; AN 363; AQ15; AR366, 675; AW 512; BC158; BV565; BY362; BZ 1195
-----. V [DMFS, DTLSDTLS, SDRM] Sap. 34 1196
Bohemian hymn (Bohemian Brethren) X Far off lands 1197
Böjd under korset (Blomqvist) [LLMTDTLS# L, DDRMDRL] N576 1198
Bolton (Bolton) [MMMFFFFMF SS, LLSMM] BB271 1199
Bona patria (Sacred hymns and tunes. Bristol. 1876) [DMSLSF M, MRFMDR, DMS] Q614 1200
Bonar (Calkin) X Civitas dei 1201
Bonar (Mason) [DMMRMF, MRR DRM, DMMR] L195; BB372 1202
Bonaventura (Gower) [MMRRLL SS, MMRRDMRR,] BB297 1203
Bone pastor (Dykes) X Faith 1204
Bone pastor (Plainsong sequence. M 7) [SSLSTDRMR, MFMRMT L] A194a; E317c; BQ231b 1205
Bone pastor (Polleri) X Ecce panis angelorum 1206
Bonifacio (Evans) [DMLSMDRM DL, TDLM, DM] W568a 1207
Bonn (Beethoven) X Alsace 1208
Bonn (Rosenmüller) X Nassau 1209
Bonn (Ebeling) X Ebeling I 1210
Bonn (Freylinghausen's G-B) X Festus 1211
Bonn (Gardiner's Sacred melodies) X Gardiner 1212
Bonnie Doon (Scottish trad) X Candler 1213
Bont-newydd (Roberts) [MRM SMRDFMR, MFMSMR] W 243a; BY583 1214
Book divine (Schnyder) X Horton 1215
Booker (Ruebush) [SMFSMRD L, DSDMDR, RM] AY270 1216
Bor'chu (Jewish trad) [SLSMFS, LSSLTTDS, DM] BH305 1217
Bor'chu (Sulzer) [SSDRDRM, LTDRD, SDDD] BH268, 279 1218
-----. V [LLMMRDR, LLDRTL, LLL] BH279 1219
Born again (Stebbins) [DMM MMFSLSF#S, SSFMR] AT215; AU68; AW461; AX326; AY 509 1220
-----. [SSSMFSL, LLLRMFS, FM] 1221
Bortniansky (Bortniansky) X St Petersburg 1222
Bortniansky (Bortniansky) X Vesper hymn 1223
Boruch shaym I (Jewish trad) [SDDDTDFMMRDTLS#, SM] BH331, 332 1224
-----. V [SDDDDDTDFMMRDT LS#] BH332 1225
Boruch shaym II (Jewish trad) [LLSFMMR, LRDTLLS#, LT] BH339 1226
Boruch shaym (Sulzer) X Sh'ma Yisroayl II 1227
Bossiney (Holst) [DSLDFMRM RD, SFMMRM] E571 1228
-----. R [RSF#MDLRDT, MM RRDRM] 1229
Bost (Bost) [DMDSDMFSM, DSMDRMF] M84 1230

Boston (Burnap) [MMR#MDML S,SLDMRDR,M] L505; T 139a; AJ206 1231
Boston (Plainsong M 1: arr by Mason) X Hamburg 1232
Boston (Siedhoff) [DMFSLDRM, RDTLTS,DS] BE429 1233
Boughs (Jewish trad) [MMMMM RDTLDRM,MMMM] AH149; BH187 1234
Bound Brook (Hymns and tunes. 1890) X Follow the path of Jesus 1235
Boundary (Shaw) [DRMLF#S, RSMMFF,LSDR] E99 1236
Bounding heart (Brightbill) [MFSLLTDRTS,LDLSMR] AR330 1237
Boundless mercy (Union harmony. 1793) [DDRRMSMR,DDMMR D,DD] R39; AY320 1238
Bourbon (Hesperian harp. 1848) [MLLDRDLSL,LLLDLDRM,] AF558 1239
Bourdillon (Gibbons) [DMRDSMF FS,FMR,RDTL] AQ164 1240
Bourgeois (Bourgeois) [DRMRD TLS,DRMFMRD] A129; E200; J12; K8; M337; N347; O53; P64; Q61; S227; W359; X291; AA130; AD78; AF104; AI415; AJ416; AK234; AL147; AM148; AO197; AP275; AR333; AZ165-a; BA781; BI104; BJ27; BR 338; BV199 1241
Bourne (Currier) [LTDMMRDTL, LTDTLS#] A263b 1242
Bournemouth (Parry) [MFSRFM, RMDLT,TTDMR] F418 1243
Bouwerie (Goldsworthy) [SDRTDR MFMR,MRDTL] A330 1244
Bovina (Tate) [DDMRDRMSFM, SDLSMR,] AJ51 1245
Bow Brickhill (Nicholson) [DTLD SLMFRD,DFMLSD] F215; BV162 a; BY357 1246
Bow Church (Bullivant) [DRMSD, DRMSD,RMFLSF] F206 1247
Bow down in worship (Purcell) [DTDRRLTDRM,MRDT,SR] BI50-D 1248
Bow down thine ear (Poteat) [SDRMFSSLTD,SLTSLF] AR652 1249
Bow down thine ear, Lord (Beimel) [DTLSLMRDT,DRM FMRD] BH35 1250
Bowden (Wesley, S.S.) [SMF MRD,MSDTLS,SLSF] W518 1251
Bowen (Haydn) [DTDRDTRFM MR,MRMDT] AA450; AJ131; AN91; BE185; BI570; BR 196 1252
-----. V [DTDRDTFMMR, MRMDTT] AJ131 1253
Bowring (---) [SLSMDTLTDS, SDMRST] AV48 1254
Boxted (R.E.) [MRLDTL,TD TLSM,MSLD] AN300b 1255
Boyce (Boyce) [MDSDRFM, LSTDFMR,MD] E201; F 186; G560; L461b; W435a; X375; AP397a; AZ16-H; BR 232; BV198 1256
-----. V [MDSDRMFFM, LSTDFMM] F186 1257
-----. B [MDSMRFM,LSTDF MR,MD] L461b 1258
Boyce (Boyce) X Kingsland 1259
Boye (Hohenfurth ms. 1410) X Dies est laetitiae 1260
Boylston (Mason) [SMFSLS, DDTLLS,SM] A495a; B489; C489; D672; G287; H227; I275; L527; M47; N501; O486; Q225; R301; S343; T96; U178; V312; Y383; Z131; AA462; AB324; AC 312; AD408; AE274; AF 273; AG161; AH419; AJ139; AK280; AM285a; AO445; AP 482b; AR312; AS328; AT168; AU157; AW214; AX109; AY 22; AZ582-N; BA74; BB205; BF490a; BX516; BZ 1261
Boynton (Malan) [SDRDTSRMR D,MFLLDT] L478; AJ352 1262
Bracondale (Booth) [MFMSS LSD,DTLSLFM,M] I209; Y28; AD75 1263
Bradbury (---) [MMMSSM,MR MFSM,MMMS] AJ389b

1264
Bradbury (Bradbury) X Pleasant pastures 1265
Bradbury (Bradbury) X Rest 1266
Braden (Bradbury) [SMDSLTD, SFFMDR, SMR#] H271; L522 1267
Bradfield (Calkin) [SDMSSDRM, FSDLLS, TM] V482; AA452; AB3; BV258 1268
Bradford (Handel) X Messiah 1269
Bradford (Haydn) [SDTRDMRD, DRMFRDT, S] D579b; AS411; AV227; BA549 1270
Brady (Spohr) X Gerald 1271
Brahms (Brahms) [SDTDLSDRM RMDR, SDT] Y23; AR30 1272
Braint (Welsh trad) [LM, MSF# MRDLM, MF#LMRD] W226; X505a 1273
Bramley (English trad) [DDSS FMMMR, DRMRD, DD] X94; BG139 1274
Brandenberg (Crueger. Praxis pietatis melica) X Ratisbon 1275
Brandenburg (German trad) X Mendon 1276
Branksome (Thorn) [SLSMDRM, FSMRDRT, DT] BY431a 1277
Branson (Miller) [MMSLSDRM, MS#LTDL, DT] BB236 1278
Brasted (Weimar) [DSLTDRMR D, MRDTLLS,] A578a; B304; C304; D452b; L457; AA56; AN 201 1279
Brattle Street (Pleyel) [SSDSMFFR, RDRMDSMM] C35b; D671b; V 426; AN569; AV41; AW199; BR247; BX304 1280
Braun (Braun) [MMMRRD, SSMLT D, DDRM,] T329; X662; AJ316; AM117; AO628 1281
Bread of heaven (Dykes) X Dies dominica 1282
Bread of heaven (MacLagan) [SF MMRDRM, FSFMMRR,] A212; B332; C374; D224b; Eap. 43; F 411b; J377; M521; O257; T365; AB92; BA293 1283
Bread of life (Sherwin) [MDMSLS, MDMR, MDMSLS] G387; H 89; I325; J491; L309; M36; P87; R250; S216; T405; U 381; V553; Y101; Z451; AB 99; AC71; AD197; AE162; AF254; AG132; AH236; AK 204; AL187; AM256; AO243; AP291b; AR236; AS182; AT 178; AU192; AV81; AW288; AX144; AY439; BA367; BB 218; BF270; BR301; BV 303b; BZ 1284
Bread of life (Warren) [SLL SDTDR, SDDFMMR, R] S357 1285
Break, day of God (Armistead) X Pro patria 1286
Break forth, O beauteous heavenly light (Schop) X Schop 1287
Break thou, O Lord, the bread (Vulpius) X Der tag bricht an 1288
Break thou the bread of life (Sherwin) X Bread of life 1289
Breathe o'er our waiting Spirits (McKinney) [DDDTTLDLS, MMMRDR, F] AU286 1290
Breathe on me (McKinney) X Truett 1291
Breathe upon us, Holy Spirit (Showalter) X Showalter 1292
Brecknock (Wesley) [MDTLS#L DTL, FMRD#RRD] F468 1293
Brecon (Heins) [DDDRMSFF, MMMRDT, TD] U127; AJ80; AO221; AT172; AW139; BF 258 1294
Bremen (Hastings) [SDDMRDRR F, RMMSFML] L352; T16; AJ21; AX159 1295
-----. V [DDDMRDRRF, RM MSFML] T16 1296
Bremen (Neumark) X Neumark 1297
Bremen (Storl's Wurtemberg G-B.) [DRMLSFMM, SSFRRD, DR] E195; X255b 1298
Bremen (Vulpius) X Cana 1299

Brent (Weeks) [SDSDSLTD, RM MRDT, TD] AO192 1300
Breslau (As hymnodus sacer. Leipzig) [DDDLDRTL, LTDRS LTS] A6b; B108; C108; 328; D100; E484; F333; J374; K64; L259b, 418; M5; N15; O221; Q7; R293; W501b; X132; AA 350; AF67; AL360a; AM296; AN321a; BA619; BR169a; BV 162b; BX380; BY136 1301
-----. V [DDDLDRTL, LTDRST LS,] L418 1301a
-----. V [DDDLTDRDTL, LTD RSL] C328 1302
-----. [DDDLTDRTL, LTDRDT D] M5 1303
-----. V [DDDLDRTL, TDRDS TLS,] BZ 1304
Brethren, we have met to worship (Moore) X Holy manna 1305
Brich durch mein angefachtnes herz (Gregor. Chorale book) X Gregor's 54th metre 1306
Bridgewater (Edson) [DMDRRDT L, MRDFMRDM] AQ232 1307
Bridgewater (English trad) [M MRDLS, RDRM, MRDLSF] E 656 1308
Bridgewater (Fisher) [SDMFLSF MF#F#S, SSSS#] AR304 1309
Brief life is here our portion (Wesley) [DRMFMMR, MRD RMRD, MS] O612 1310
Brierly (Hart) [MRDSFMMRDR, MRDSFM] D33a 1311
Briesen (Freylinghausen) [MDSL SFMD, LRTLSF#, SL] AZ157-B; BA169 1312
Briggs (Tarbutton) [SLSDDTDR, RMRDMRTD,] T14a; AJ18 1313
Brightest and best (Mendelssohn) [MRDSFFMRDTDMR, RRM] D66a; G40; H6; I43; N523; P342; R455; S107; T79; U412; V15; Y144; Z136; AB229; AC 6a; AD26; AF37; AG18; AH 210; AJ117; AL539; AM356; AN 104; AO435; AP477; AR45; AS 22; AT25; AU220; AV4; AW23; AY476; BA531; BE174; BF 266; BH96; BI87; BK40; BX 271; BZ 1314
Brightest and best (Thrupp) X Epiphany hymn 1316
Brightly beams (Bliss) X Lower lights 1317
Brightly gleams (Storer) [SDT RRD, SSSFMR, RFMR] D515c 1318
-----. R [DDDTLTRD, FMRD TLS, S] 1319
Bring a torch (French trad) X Un flambeau 1320
Bring flowers of the fairest (Catholic) X Flowers of the fairest 1321
Bring, heavy heart, your grief (Lund) [SMRDRDTT, SFMRS DRM,] BC349 1322
Bring them in (Ogden) [SSLSM MRR, SSLSRRDD,] AM684; AT429; AU266; AX213; BB625 1323
-----. R [MSMRLR, MMMRD MRRR, M] 1324
Bringing home our sheaves (Rupp) [DDRMRMRDLS, DD RMFM] AX581; AY131 1325
Bringing in the sheaves (Minor) [SSSLSM, DDDRDL, SSSL] Z416; AH416; AP590; AT432; AU359; AX187; BB621 1326
-----. R [MSSLS, LDDLS, SS DRMD] 1327
Bringing our praise (Francis) [DTRDRMMRFMM, SMRLS] BN203 1328
Bristol (Hodges) [SDMLFMRD, SMRDTLS, MF] B54; C54a; D47a; BE347 1329
Bristol (Ravenscroft's Psalter) [SFRMDRRD, FMRRD#R, RM] A7; E6; F53; W260; X62; AP279; BJ50; BR131; BV74; BY81a 1330
Bristol (Wesley) [MMFMRDFM RM, SDTLSF#] W472 1331
Bristol, No. 1 (Ravenscroft's Psalter) X Bristol 1332
Broadbent (Sheldon) [LSLTDR D, LSLFRM, LSL] BV152

1333

Broadlands (Lausanne Choral buch) [SMLSFMMFLSMR, SSSL] D277a 1334

Broadwalk (Ashfield) [SMRDSLD MRMD, LDRMS] BV125b 1335

Broadway (Showalter) [SMRDDRR SSF, FMRSMD] AR291 1336

Broadwood (Strover) [SMFSSLTD TLS, DRMFS] BV368 1337

Brockham (Clark) [SDRMTDRT, RFFMDMF#S,] E220; F45b; W3; X228; AN133; BB132; BE 235; BJ9; BY533 1338

Brocklesbury (Barnard) [MRDSTLL S, DDMMRMR,] A241b; B360; C343; D207a; J261; K174; L 212; M167; N295; O323; P96; S348; T350b; U469; V642; AD 480; AG238; AH548; AI161; AJ400; AM642; AO433; AP762; BA608; BB427; BF611 1339

Brocklesby (Barnard) X Brocklesbury 1340

Bromham (Matthews) [DTLSDMR DRM, MRDSMD] M224; N657 1341

Bromley (Clark) [DMFRDMSSL SFFM, DFM] A163b; B11b; AB167; AL231; AP357; BE388; BJ6 1342

Bromley Common (Shaw) [MMF# F#SRSLLTS, LLDTL] X187b; Y75; AN18 1343

Brompton (Schachner) [MFLSDTR S, LSMDDSFM] BR19 1344

Bromsgrove (Psalmodia evangelica 1789) [DDSLSLTDFMRDT D, DR] E144; W381; X23; BE 106 1345

-----. V [DDSLTDFMRDTDRM DT] W381 1346

-----. V [DDSLTDFMRDTD, DRMD] BE106 1347

Brookend (Holst) [DRSDRML, SMRDRML, SL] X348 1348

Brookfield (Southgate) [SMMMRLT DRD, DFMRDT] D308; G121; H335; I70; N143; T241; V136; Z217; AB183; AC188; AE387; AG120; AI359; AJ337; AK270; AM73; AP564a; AR381; AS123; AW373; AY515; BA96; BB426; BF328; BY142b 1349

Brooklyn (Kasschau) [MMRDDR RS, SDRMFLS, S] AD428 1350

Brooklyn (Zundel) [SDDMSD, S DSDRM, MRTD] U386; V567 1351

Broome (Dawes) [MMRDSFM MRMRD, DRMF#] BY696 1352

Brorson (Berggren) [SLTDDRR MD, FMRMRDL] M70 1353

Brother, here's a message (Garrett) [SSMSDSMSSFFM, SSM S] AS308 1354

-----. R [SSSSS, LSFMLS, DDS L#L] 1355

Brother James' air (Bain) X Marosa 1356

Brotherhood (Reay) [SMDTDMR D, SFMLRR, RR] AB269 1357

Brotherland (Horner) [SLSMRD ST, LSMSFM, MS] AB364 1358

Broughton (Hastings) [SSSFMM R, FFFMRM, SSS] C395; AL 235; AP506b; AW293 1359

Brown (Bradbury) [SDRMDLTD, LSSDMR, SM] H184; L469; U259; V44; Z475; AE181; AI 275; AR82; AS83; AT38; AV 6; AX71; AY292; BA121; BB 317 1360

Brown (Brown) X St Anatolius 1361

Browne (Browne) [SDDTTD, SF MFSLR, RMM] BX546 1362

Brownell (Haydn) [SMSDDTR SRFFM, SDMS] D638; N549; O550; AB52; BR333 1363

Browning (Branscombe) [MDRM FSLS, SDRMFS, LS] Y57 1364

Browning (Burnap) [SMMFMR MD, TLRTLTD, S] L3; AN 235b 1365

Brownwell (Haydn) X Brownell 1366

Brunswick (Handel) [DMFSDL# LS, LRMFFSLS] E555; X297 1367

Bryan (Bryan) [MMRMFTD, DT DRSSF#S, S] L599; AP22b; BR207 1368

Bryant (Alcock) [SSDRMMRR, RTDMRD, M] B107; C107; W 685b; AB205 1369

Bryd frem, mit hjertes trang at lindre (Lindeman) [SLDSL FSMR, MSF#STDL] K347; O171 1370

Bryn Calfaria (Owen) [MMLTDD DT, DDMRDTTL,] E319; J114b; R90; X274a; AD407; AF291; AI248; AK344; AM187; BV473; BZ 1371

-----. V [MMLTDDDT, DRMRD TTL,] AD407 1372

Brynhyfryd (Williams) [DMRDT DRMDR, DRMLRD] X241; BY 648 1373

Brynland (Spencer-Palmer) [DSL MRMFSSDTL, LRRF] BV581b 1374

Brynteg (Lloyd) [LDRMLTDTL, DRMFMMR] W623a; AM59 1375

Bryntirion (Lutteroth) [MFSS LLSM, MRDDRRM, M] E248; W310 1376

Bryson City (McKinney) [MFMD SLSM, DDRFMRM, M] AT540; AU497 1377

Bucer (Mason & Webb's Cantica laudis) X Heath 1378

Buckland (Haynes) [SMRDRRM, SDTSSF#S, D] A428; B354; D552a; Eap. 67; F444; Q51; W193; AA15; AF236; AH551; AL154a; BD140; BV141c; BY 118b 1379

Bucklebury (Harmonia perfecta. 1730) [DSDTSLSFM, MMRMF SS] X189 1380

Buddugoliaeth (Hughes) [MMRDT RRDTL, TDRMMR] BY455a 1381

Bude (Wesley, S.S.) [DMRDDFM MR, SDRFMRD,] W515; AP 287a 1382

Budleigh (Mudie) [MMMFMMRDR MM, MMMFM] H337; L453; AS277; BA482 1383

Buffham (Hopkins) [DRMMRDFF FMRDLS, DD] F455 1384

Bugail Israel (Price) [MFSSLS SF, MRSRMRR, S] W465 1385

Builders Porter) [DMFSDL, SM SSF#M, MF#ST] Y65 1386

Building for eternity (Coats) [MMSMFLS, SSMDRMR, MM] AX191 1387

Building for eternity (Sargent) [DRMMMMMRD, MFSSSLL] AX199; AY519 1388

-----. R [MFSMMSD, DRRRR MFM, D] 1389

Built on the Rock (Lindeman) X Kirken 1390

Bullinger (Bullinger) X Geneva 1391

Bulstrode (Sharpe) [SDRMSFMR, MDTDRTS, S] X367 1392

Bunessan (Gaelic trad) [DMSD R, TLSLS, DRMSL, S] R464; W53; X30; AD469; AF38; AN97; AQ266; BV96; BY92 1393

Bunyan (English trad) [DDRM FS, FMRDTD, RMDF] BY759 1394

Bunyan (Mendelssohn) X Stukeley 1395

Bunyan (Thommen. Christenschatz) [DSLSFM, DRMRD, RRMRD] F293; BV551 1396

Bunyan (Thommen. Christenschatz) X Gregor's 37th metre (Herrnhut ms) 1396a

Burber (Tenney) X Go to thy rest, fair child 1397

Burford (Purcell) [LLTDRMR DT, S#LTDRMM] A410a; B 385b; E447; F117; K321; Q 454; V376; W274b; X596; AA 303; AL79b; AN236a; AP187; AW228; AZ14-D; BA858; BE 321; BY211a 1398

Burg (Perkins) [DDRRMFMRM, MFSLTDD,] S67; AI411 1399

Burke (Burke) [DMMFLSM, RD DRMR, RMM] AE21 1400

-----. R [TDSMDLL, LLLTDTL, SD] 1401

Burleigh (Barnby) [DSMRDFFSL S, FMF#SRR] G271; I475 1402

Burleigh (Weekes) [MDDTDMS, LSDSFMSFM] AB22 1403

Burlington (Burrowes) [DRMFM RLSDR, SF#STLS] D429; G 388; I198; M456; V620; AR 238; AT186; AV79 1404

Burning light (Coleman) [DDD SDRM, LSFMRDR, DD] AR435 1405

-----. R [SSSSSMLSFMR, FF FFF] 1406

Burnley (Barnby) X Diadema 1407

Burton (Woodbury) [SDDDDRTD, RMMMDTLS,] BB24 1408

Burwell (Herbert) [SMRDDLLLS, LFRSDRF] D190; AW363; BO50; BY700b 1409

-----. V [SMRDDLLLS, LFRSDR M] AW363 1409a

Bushmead (Taylor) [MFLSDRFM, MTDFMR, MF] BV318 1410

"But for a moment" (Stebbins) [MR#MSDMMR#MFT, RD#R SR] AY450 1411

-----. R [SF#SLSMR#MFM, MRLDTD] 1412

But the Lord (St Paul) (Mendelssohn) [SLSSF#LDDDT, SDMSFM] AH621; AR685 1413

Butler (English trad) [DDMSFLM FSMR, MFSLS] X378 1414

By and by (Tindley) [DRMMMMM, RMRDDLD, DR] AT473; AU134 1415

-----. R [SLMDRDDLD, SLM DRRR] 1416

By grace are ye saved (McGranahan) [SSSLTD, DDDTLS, S# LLL] AU469 1417

-----. R [SSMFSLS, DTLTLS, S LL] 1418

By the blood that flowed (Montani) [MMRMDDTD, LLSLTTT, T] BQ20 1419

-----. R [SLDTSFS, SS#DL#SFS, SL] 1420

By the blood that flowed (Richardson) X Tichfield 1421

By the cross (Mainz G-B. 1661) X Mainz 1422

By the first bright Easter Day (Mendelssohn) X Mendelssohn 1423

By the first bright Easter Day (Slovak hymnal) [DRMMFM MR, MRDTDRMR] BQ137 1424

Byfield (Hastings) [MMMMMFF M, RDDRMR, RR] M62; V 462; AH354; AO314; BF362 1425

Byrd (Peery) [SDDDDTLS, SD LSF#S, SS#] G555; J519a 1426

Byzantium (Jackson) X Jackson 1427

C

Caddo (Bradbury) [SDMSMR DMRD, DTLDRD] H235; L 444; R82; T61; AJ94; AM 55 1428

Caergybi (Roberts) [LLTDD TLT, TDRMMMRM,] K237; BY430 1429

Caerlleon (Welsh hymn mel) [LSFMRDRMDT, LSFMRD] E334; X193a 1430

Caersalem (Edwards) [DSDM DMSFMRD, MRDFM] E397; W564b; X508; AL441b; AM 369; AP404; BB409; BY388 1431

Cairnbrook (Prout) [MMSFMR DT, DDTDMR, MM] D77; F488; J337; K500; N586; AK129; AM630; AO471; AP713a; BV498; BY668a 1432

Caithness (Scottish Psalter, 1635) [DMFSDTDR, MFSLLS, S] A353; E445; F325; J384b; M217; O501; P317; W481a; X112; AF349; AN19; AP459; AQ74; BE215; BV147b; BY 593; BZ 1433

Calcutta (Heber) [DRMMMMMD, DRRTTD, DR] E547; L499;

M196; N418; P273; R127; T50a; AI126b; AJ77; AN144b; AT190; AU20; AW380 1434

Caledonia (Scottish trad) [SSS MSLD, LLLSLTD, MM] G281; I385; AX541; BB181 1435

-----. V [SSSMSLD, LLLSLTD, MF] AX541 1436

Calkin I (Calkin) [SSMMRRD, DDFFMR, RRL] D208a; I295; U48; V241; Z368; AI114; AM96; AO271; BA317; BB264 1437

Calkin II (Calkin) [MMRDRM, MSFMFS, SLLR] V110; BY 143b 1438

Callcott (Callcott) X Elim 1439

Calling to thee (Main) [SLSMSDT LLS, SRMFSL] AI201 1440

-----. R [SMDMRDLS, MMMM SLSM] 1441

Calling today (Stebbins) X Jesus is calling 1442

Calm (Dykes) [MMMFFMRR, RRMFRLTD,] I305; T58b; U160; AJ234a; AL150; AP361; AS139 1443

Calm (Hastings) X Hastings 1444

Calm on the listening ear (Blackman) [DRMRMFSMD, RMFSLS F#] BI98 1445

Calon Lân (Hughes) [SDMDRMD S, LTDLFMMR,] BY343b 1446

Calvary (Hurst) [SSSLLL, LSFM, LLLD] B163b; C163b; D106b 1447

Calvary (Rosenmüller) [LTDTLL S#L, MMRRDDT, T] M416 1448

Calvary (Stanley) [DRMRDTLSSD D, RMF#SD] E530; L250; W652; X333a; AO167 1449

Calvary (Sweney) [MRDSMSDT, FMRLTLSM,] AI78; AU439 1450

-----. R [SRD#RMDLS, SLLFMR DR] 1451

Calvary (Towner) [SSSFMFSLS, TTTLSFM] AT96; AX332; AY 513 1452

-----. R [DTDTDLLSS, TLTLTL S] 1453

Calvary (Wolff) X Naar tid og stund den 1454

Calvert (R. J. C.) [DDRMLTD RTS, LDTLDT] AS428 1455

Calvin (Bourgeois) X St Michael 1456

Calvin (Bushey) [DRMMMMR# MD, MSSSMRF] AT234; AU 465; AX237; AY217 1457

-----. R [DRMTRD, MSRFM, SDTLS] 1458

Calvin College (Van Andel) [SMLSDFMR, MMFMDMRD,] AI438 1459

Calvisius (Calvisius) [MMFSM DRMF, MRDDRMM] E510; Q197; S506; W278; X42a; AA110; AF54; AL542; AW 557; BJ13 1460

-----. V [MMSMDRMF, MRDT MRDT] Q197 1461

Camber (Shaw) [DTDLTS, LTD RM, RMFSL] X365; BY135 1462

Camberwell (Harrison) X Cambridge 1463

Cambria (Bristol Tune book. 1876) [DDMMRDRLTD, DD MMRR] AM345; AP330 1464

Cambridge (Harrison) [DMRDM RDTD, RMSFMR, S] B319; C319; D268a; H428; L191; Q519; W679a; AA518; AI 450; AM254; AN210; AP92; BB172; BE124; BY54 1465

-----. V [DMRDRDTD, RMSF MR, SD] C319 1466

-----. V [DMDRTD, RMSFM R, SDDL] Q519 1467

-----. V [DSDMRDTD, RMSF MR, SD] AN210 1468

Cambridge (Randall) [DMMRD FMR, DMFRDTD, D] H239; L554; AL120; AW17 1469

-----. V [DMMRDFMR, DRM FRDTD] AL120 1470

Cambridge (Wood) [DMSLSFS, DDRMRDLL, D] X288 1471

Cambridge new (Randall) X

Cambridge 1472
Camden (Calkin) X Waltham 1473
Cameronian midnight hymn (Scottish hymn mel) [SDMRDSL DR, MFSRFMR] E401; J147b; X514 1474
Camp (Lutkin) [SDRMDFFM, M LRSDTLS,] I686 1475
Campfields (Monk) [MRMFMRMF, RSSSFM, MF#] W245; BE104 1476
Campian (Campian) [LMDTLLT, DSMDRRD, R] A459; AN452; AQ313 1477
Campian 2 (Campian) [DTLSF#S, SFFMMF#, SSSL] AQ107 1478
Campmeeting (American trad) [DTRRRDMM, MRMFLS, MS] G303; T75; U180; V449; AI 160; AJ69; AM458; AR281; AT 336; AW99; AX355, 490; AY 45; BB670; BZ 1479
Campmeeting (American trad) X X The Lord of glory (refrain: Mosley) 1479a
Can a little child (Bassford) X Thanksgiving 1480
Cana (---) [MMMMMR, RDDDDT, TLLL] AJ151 1481
Cana (Mozart) [SSDTDRMSFMR, TRDLR] D662; I80; AR3; BE 93; BH1; BR71 1482
-----. V [SDTDRMSFMR, TRD LRM] BE93 1483
Cana (Vulpius) [DMRMFSM, LSFMRM, SLT] A252; B383; D511b; E232; F114a; G534; J192; K433; L60; M13, 164; N183; O57, 144; P57; Q53; R347; S92; V411; W368; X 585; Y292; Z365; AA9; AD248; AF373; AK34; AL398; AM568; AN274; AP25; AQ188; AW559; AZ8-A; BA590; BB377; BM58; BR249; BV385; BX341; BY575; BZ 1484
-----. V [DMRMLSFM, LSFM RM, DS] M164 1485
-----. V [DMRMFSFM, LSFMR M, SL] V411 1486
-----. V [DMRMFSSM, LSFM RM, SL] Y292 1487
-----. V [DMRMLSFM, LSF MRM, SL] AZ8-A 1488
-----. V [DRMRMLSFM, LS FMRM, S] BR249 1489
Canaan (Bailey) [SDDRRML S, MFSMFRDD,] AL593; AW 403 1490
-----. R [MFSSSLSFFF, SMD SMM] 1491
Canaan (Baker) [DSMDRTLS, SDDRRM, SF] AA155 1492
Canaan (Rupp) X Jerusalem, my happy home 1493
Candlemas Eve (Church Gallery book) [SDDMDLTD, MS FMRDR, M] BG126 1494
Candler (Scottish trad) [SDD RDRMSMRD, RMRDD] G311; BZ 1495
Cannock (Stanton) [MDRSDFM RM, MRDRSLS] R359b; BV 329; BY470 1496
Cannons (Handel) X Canons 1497
Canon (Tallis) X Tallis' canon 1498
Canon VIII (Ryley) [MLSDD RFM, MFRSDRLT,] F244 1499
Canonbury (Schumann) [SMM MFMRDRM, SLTDRT] B44; C7; D499; G116; H389; I42; J538; K18; L230a; M559; N502; O24; P323; R298; S78; T217; U279; V5; Y216; Z133; AB4; AC251; AD321; AE277; AF46; AG248; AH 425; AI45; AJ310; AK256; ALsuppl; AM93; AN508; AO44; AP661; AR40; AS21; AT84; AU298; AV101; AW 296; AY456; BA50; BB407; BD69; BE322; BF183; BH2; BI43; BK70; BR6; BZ 1500
-----. V [SMMMFRDRM, SLTD RTL] L230a 1501
Canons (Handel) [LMS#LTDRT, DSTDRMFR] E66b; F84b; R392; S421a; X337a; Y188;

AB382; AN106a; 1502
Cantate domino (Barnby) X Jordan 1503
Cantate domino (Schop) X Sollt ich meinen gott 1504
Canterbury (Gauntlett) X Hatfield 1505
Canterbury (Gibbons) X Song 13 1506
Canticum refectionis (Williams) [DSLSMFMRRM, DSLS] A206 1507
Cantionale (Pensum sacrum. Goerlitz. 1648) X Herr Jesu Christ, dich zu uns wend 1508
Cantus ubique (Hohenfurth ms. 1410) X Dies est laetitiae 1509
Capel (English trad) [SFMMRMM RMRD, DRRSS] A586; E488; G450; X248; BE242; BG55; BY720 1511
-----. V [DRMMRMMRMRD, DRRSS] BE242 1512
Capello (Mason) [DDDDRM, MMM MF#S, SSSL] T102a; AJ147 1513
Capetown (Filitz) [SMLSFFM, DT DSFMR, SD] A275; B38; C41; D76b; E501; F163; H208; J119; O498; S252; V215; W282; X 507; Z386; AA356; AK189; AL 161b; AP667b; AS70; AW174; AZ265-B; BA259; BE67; BR 121; BV230; BY47 1514
Captain of Israel's host (Rossini) [MMMSSDDM, MRSRDMLS] BC236 1515
Cara patria (Higgs) [SLFMRRD, MFLSMS, SLF] BY701b 1516
Carden Place (Nisbet) [DTLSLSM, LSFDRM, MF#S#] W315 1517
Care for me (Lindeman) X Spring of souls 1518
Caress (Stewart) X Mount Calvary 1518a
Carey (Carey) [SMLTDFMRM, MRF#SSDT] A306; B317; C 317; D659; E491; F179; J359b; Q368; V354; W172; X656; AD 130; AL213b; AW44; AZ96-H; BA494; BB337; BE139; BV 496; BY55a 1519
-----. V [SFMLDTDFMRM, MRF#SS] C317 1520
-----. V [SFMRDTDFMRM, MRF#SR] Q368 1521
Carey's (Carey) X Carey 1522
Carillon (Ross) [DTSLMS, DTS LMS, F#MF#S] W61 1523
Carinthia (Freylinghausen's G-B) X Luebeck 1524
Caritas (---) [SLTDRDDT, RD# RMRDLL] AI274; AO472 1525
Caritas (Barnby) [MR#MS, TT DRMML, LTD#R] B382b; G427; I671; N524; T305; U 454; Y382; Z220; AB7; AD 337; AE383; AR308; AT373; BA776; BB412; BF227; BX 123 1526
Caritas (Beaty) [DRMSLSSM, MMRD, DRMS] AL473; AW 447 1527
Caritas (Gordon) X Gordon 1528
Caritas perfecta (Atkinson) [DRMFMRRSFFM, SMRDR] Q623 1529
Carlisle (Lockhart) [DSDMRDT D, DFSLSDFMR,] A579a; E190; F362; I362; J451b; K 151; L426; O93; W344; X458; AA289; AC315; AF25; AN 299a; BE396; BV27; BY523 1530
-----. V [DSDRDTD, DFSLSDF MR,] AN299a 1531
Carlton (Barnby) [SSLSMDMR, DDRMSFR, R] I85; V181; BX446 1532
Carman (Lutkin) [MSSFRLLS, SDDTTLS] A154b; B3b 1533
Carmel (Hemy) X Conqueror 1534
Carmel (Smart) X Nachtleid 1535
Carmelite litany (---) [MF SDTL#T, TLRFLSM, MF] C142Ib 1536
Carmen Coeli (Barnby) X

Angels of Jesus 1537
Carmen naturae (Donizetti) X Savery 1538
Carmichael (Spencer-Palmer) [MMLRDTTL, LTDRFM, MF#] BV326b 1539
Carnarvon (Martin) [SFMRFMRD, TLSLDTD, S] Y62 1540
Carne (Joseph) X Keine schönheit hat die welt 1541
Carol (---) [MMMRDSFMR, DR MLSF#S,] BR145 1542
Carol (Corner. 1649) X Corner 1543
Carol (Willis) [SMRRDLSLS, SL TDDRMR,] A13b; B79; C79; D59a; G92; H135; I110; J23; K29b; L215; N39; P135; R160; S127; T338; U58; V116; Y245; Z191; AB108; AC78; AD107; AE82; AF129; AG73; AH245; AI159; AK107; AL58b; AM157; AN162; AO122; AP170b; AO 287; AR136; AS104; AT71; AU 141; AV85; AW75; AX98; AY 489; BA156; BB99; BC82; BD 206; BF289; BK146; BR548b; BX191b; BZ 1544
-----. V [SMTRDLSLS, SLTDDR M] L215 1545
Carol melody, 14th c. (Hohenfurth ms.) X Quem pastores 1546
Carol of beauty (French carol) X Fragrance 1547
Carol of service (French trad) [MLLSLSFM, MLSLSFM, S] BG166 1548
-----. R [LTDRMLLS#LTL, LTD RM] 1549
Carol of the advent (French trad) X Besançon carol 1550
Carol of the kingdom (Manx carol) [MLTDRDL, MMRDTL, MLT] BG167 1551
Carolina (Johnson) [MRLSMDRM, MMLSF#S, FM] N210; AI436 1552
Carr (Monk) X St Ethelwald 1553
Carrick (Finlay) [MDRDTSL, LD TRDM, MDR] BV639 1554
Carrington (Pollock) X Bless the words 1555
Carrow (Sullivan) [MMMMRD DF, MRDT, SSSS] B384; D624a; BX316 1556
Carry on (Conant) [MMR, MMR, DTDRRM, DMDM] Y160 1557
Carson (Meredith) X Meredith 1558
Carter (Carter) X Slingsby 1559
Carter (Updegraff) [SSLDTS, SSLDT, DDTDM] AJ202 1560
-----. R [SSRRMRDM, MRRM RR, SS] 1561
Carthage (Root arr) [SLSSMD DTLSLS, FSFM] H189 1562
Cary (Tourjée) [MSSDRM, MR MFFM, MMSS] I620; AV392 1563
Caryl (Lutkin) [SSSSSSLS, M F#STLSFM,] I583b 1564
Caskey (Perkins) [SMRDLSD, DRRDRM, SMR] H325; L 603 1565
Cassel (Cassel) X The King's business 1566
Cassel (Thommen. Christenschatz.) [DRMSFMR, MR DRDTD, TD] F119; J69; K 92a; L162; M28, 39; N92; Q37; V511a; W187; AI410; AL152; AO200; AP479; AW 536; AX449; AY388; AZ167-A; BA192; BR460a; BY309a 1567
-----. V [DRMSFMRR, MRDRD TD, T] V511 1568
-----. V [DRMSFMRR, MRD MRTD, D] AO200 1569
Cassidy (Main) [MSTDLSFMR M, SDMFSL] U83; Y219 1570
Cast thy burden on the Lord (Mendelssohn) X Birmingham 1571
Castle Rising (Hervey) [MFM RLDTLT, TDDRRM, M] D409b; O66 1572
Castleford (Sacred harmony. Leeds. 1720) [DMRDLSFM, MSDTLS, SMD] W197; BV

646 1573
Caswall (Filitz) [MMRRDT, DDR RM, SSFFMR,] A335; B162; C162b; D362b; E315b; F107; J76; K90; N639; Q158; R222; Sap. 13; W542; Y107; AA208; AE457; AK485; AL205; AM190; AP323; BA92; BN73; BO28; BR337; BV154; BY771 1574
Caswell Bay (Havergal) [SMRDD TLS, FMFSLRRR,] D586b 1575
Cathcart (Bell) [SDRMMMML, SMRDDDTL,] E546; M383; Y232 1576
Catherine (Clark) [SSSSSLSD, D TDRRDRM,] T59; AJ92 1577
Caton (Miller) X Rockingham 1578
Cavell (Fowles) [SMSTLSDM, R TRFMRM, F] Y119; AC111 1579
Cecil (Hall) [DSTLSSMRDR, SD MFLS] B75b 1580
Cecile (Johnson) [DMMR#MFF M, DMRDTD, MR] J233; M569; N556 1581
Cecilia (Dykes) X Domines regit me 1582
Cecilia (Hayne) X St Cecilia 1583
Celeste (Swedish Koralbok, 1697) X Laurinus 1584
Celestia (Danish trad) [DRMFSD S, LSFMSSR, RM] J57; M606; O148 1585
Celestial voices (Lloyd) [MMRM FML, TDMR, MMFSS] S493; AL621; BB419 1586
Cennick (Hutton. Tunes for the hymns) [SFMRD, SRRDT, SDTL SM] AZ587-A 1587
Ceres (English trad) [SMMRDR D, DSSLLR, RMM] BY725 1588
Chadwick (Webster) [DRMFMLSS FM, MFSLSD] BX443 1589
Chalice (Branscombe) [SDFFM RD, SDFFMRD, RR] Y147; AC 230a 1590
-----. R [SLDTLSM, SLDTLSM, RM] 1591
Chalvey (Hayne) [SLSSRF, MMR RLT, RSF#] A452; B443; C189; D203a; I340a; K480; N579; V631; AP230; BA265 1592
Chamber music (Bach) [SDR MR, SRMFM, SSSSFM] BK9 1593
Chamouni (Lomas) X Althorp 1594
Chant (Boyce) [DDDDDSFM, M RSSF#S, SS] AP61b 1595
Chant (Dupuis) [DDDDDTDL, FMRDTDR, R] AP107d 1596
Chant (Mornington) [SSSSSS FM, SLTTLS, DD] AP65c 1597
Chant (Hayes) [MMMMMMRD; FFMRDT, SS] AP11b 1598
Chant (Jacobs) X Hope 1599
Chant (Norris) [DDDDDMSD, DLTDFMR, R] AP41c 1600
Chant (Randall) X Randall 1601
Chant: Troyte, No. 1 (Troyte) X Troyte, No 1 1602
Chant: Troyte, No. 2 (Troyte) X Troyte, No. 2 1603
Chant your songs (Gluck) [MS DDRRFMRR, DTLSLS] BI 114 1604
Chanticleer (English trad) [DDMSLSLTD, MFSDRMR,] BG123 1605
Chapel (Wesley's Foundery Collection. 1742) X Savannah 1606
Chapel Royal (Boyce) [DDD RMFRM, DMSLSFMR,] F316; AL301b 1607
Chapin (Dykes) X Esca viatorum 1608
Chapman (Marsh) X One day 1609
Charing (Russell) [DRMRMSL S, DLSMLFMR,] E531; X 340 1610
Charity (Jaehnigen) [DRMRS, FSMDR, RSSF#MR] BE180 1611
Charity (Lutkin) [MFMSMDLS M, MRMRLS, M] Y226; AC 242 1612

Charity (Stainer) [DFMRDRS, LT DLRDDT, D] B121; C38; D 76a; F233; V424; W484a; BA 671; BV543; BY232b 1613

Charleston (Pilsbury. U.S. Sacred harmony, 1799) X Bartimaeus 1614

Charlestown (Pilsbury. U.S. Sacred harm. 1799) X Bartimaeus 1616

Charlotte (Biggs) [SMFSSLMS, FRFMDR] A215 1617

Charlotte (Maclean) [MMRDRM, MLLSFM, SSDT] V429a 1618

Charterhouse (Evans) [SDRMDF MRMDL, DTLSS] A188; R217; S177; W146; X283; AB80; AD 139; BE345; BY350 1619

Chartres (French, 15th c) [LLMMTDRR, LLDRTDL,] A50a; W44; AL599; AN158; BG91 1620

-----. V [LLMMTDRR, LTDRTD L, L] AN158 1621

-----. V [LMMTDRR, LDRTDL, LMM] BG91 1622

Chatham (Weber) X Seymour 1623

Chautauqua (Sherwin) [DDDLSF# S, DDDLSF#S, TT] G44; I57; J234; L20; M637; N559; R65; S39; T10; U463; V54; Y96; Z 144; AB23; AC17; AD47; AE43; AF45; AG31; AH168; AI53; AK 481; AL562; AM343; AO27; AR 50; AS25; AT29; AU87; AV12; AW31; AY440; BA782; BB51; BD13; BF202; BK44; BY689; BZ 1624

-----. R [DSDSMD, SFRD, DTD LSD] 1625

Chebar (Smart) [SMDFMLS, DF FMRM, SMD] W198; BB363 1626

Cheerful (Shaw) [DDDRDTSLT D, MRTDTL] E376; J413b; X472; Y195 1627

Cheerfulness (Weyse) [SSFMRFM, SLTDTLLS, R] BE141 1628

Chelmsford (Chapin) X Melody 1629

Chelsea (Hutton. Tunes for the hymns) [DDTDRMMR, DFMRRD, DM] AZ590-F 1630

Chelsea (Ireland) [SMFSSDLS, MRMLSRR, S] X164 1631

Chelsea Square (Robbins) [SM RDSDTLS, MLSFMR,] A380; J243a 1632

Chenies (Matthews) [SSMMRD S, SLDDTD, SSM] D252b; K 169; L147; M563; R251; S 123; T151; U134; V78; W 470a; Y50; Z211; AB330; AC41; AG131; AI151; AL83; AP289; AS90; BB290; BO118; BR502b 1633

Cherith (Spohr) X Spohr 1634

Cherry tree (English trad) [SDTLSDR, MFSFMRDTL,] E285; W463; X599; BG66a; BV582b; BY551b 1635

Cherry tree carol (English trad) X Cherry tree 1636

Cherubic hymn (Bortniansky) X St Petersburg 1637

Cherubic hymn (Psalterium chorale. Constance) X Beata nobis gaudia 1638

Cheshire (Est. Whole book of Psalms) [LLTDDTTL, LDD RSM, MM] E109; F342; J 368; K89; S503; W457a; X 105; AP181a; AR670; BE 286; BJ87 1639

-----. V [LLLTDTTL, LDD DRRSM,] AR670 1640

Cheshire tune (Est. Whole book of Psalms) X Cheshire 1641

Chester (Chester) [SSSLTDTT L, LLLTD#R] A566a 1642

Chester (Dykes) X St Bees 1643

Chester ("Oratory hymns") [MMR#MFMMRR, MDDRR M, M] C403; L247; M482 1644

Chesterfield (Haweis) X Richmond 1645

Chesterton (Beaumont) [SLDT MR, TDMRLS, SDTL] BY 250b 1646

Chichester (Whitehead) [MM L, LF#S#LMRRT, MLT] A 429a 1647

Chief of sinners (Ekström) X Jesus för varlden gifvet sitt lif 1648
Chief shepherd (Bradbury) X Brown 1649
Chignell (Edwards) [MFSMFSM DD, MFSSSSM,] D407b 1650
Child Jesus (Gade) [SLSMFMRR, MSLFMRD, S] BR547 1651
Child of a virgin (Mailloux) [DDMSSLSLTDD, MMF#SS] BN183 1652
Child service (Button) [MMMSF MMR, MFFLSFM, M] W670; BY752 1653
Childhood (Wales. Univ. 1923) [DMSLSFMRDDD, SLTDR] E227; G443; R461; S444; W80; X668; Z180; AD476; AF480; AG88; AL77; BV322; BY122; BZ 1654
Children all (Shaw) [DTLSLSFM, FMRDMLF#S,] X386e 1655
Children of Jerusalem (Root) [DTDSLLS, MRDSLTD, DT] BI1 1656
-----. R [RRRRRMFMMMR DMR, RR] 1657
Children of Jerusalem (Curwen's Tunebook. 1842) [DDMMRFRDT D, MMSSMD] W658; AL607; AP751; AW404; BA822; BY735 1658
-----. R [DRM, TDDRRM, MF S, RMMF#F#S,] 1659
Children of the heavenly Father (Swedish mel) X Sandell 1660
Children of the light (Smyth) [SSSFMMMMRD, DLSDMS] BR 461 1661
Children's friend (---) [MFSDTL SM, MSMSMR, MF] AO625 1662
Children's litany (St Alban's Tune book) X Lebbaeus 1663
Children's offerings (Stainer) [SMLSFMFMR, SMLSFMF#] I673 1664
Children's praise (Barnby) [MM DMSLS, SDTLSMR, MM] I675 1665
Children's praises (Matthews arr) [SDDTDRRD, RMRMFS, SL] K553; L583; N653; P362; S450; U326; V653; AH550; AL615; AM648; AP790; AW 405; BA818 1666
-----. R [TSDD, RR, MFSFM RD.] 1667
Children's prayer (Novello) [MRDRMFMRMF, SFMFRD] AH555; BK5 1668
Children's song (Walton) [DM MMRDFFM, DRD, MSSS] W 68b; AP728 1669
Children's song of praise (Showalter) X When I see the blood 1670
Children's song of the nativity (English trad) X Stowey 1671
Children's voices (Hopkins) [MFMRMD, TLTDRS, MFM] B353; C353; D570; W37; AP 714; BD195 1672
Child's evening prayer (Ephros) [SDRMRMRD, DSFMFMRR,] BH244 1673
Child's morning hymn (Batchellor) X Onslow 1674
Chilswell (Holst) [DSLL#LSDR RD, MFSLFD] X498 1675
Chilton Foliat (Martin) [SDSM FSSLTD, RMRTST] W503; BY222 1676
Chimes (Mason) [MMSSDLRTD, RMDLSTL] L308; T60; V105; Z464; AJ93; AO94 1677
China (Bradbury) X Renar 1678
China (Swan) [MRRDDMLLM, SSSLLTD,] H491; V673 1679
Chinese melody (Chinese trad) X P'u T'o 1680
Chios (Gabriel) [SDDDDMSSSS, MFRSMD] T145; AJ213 1681
Chisago (Malstrom) [MFSSSL TDS, MFSLSFM,] N537 1682
Chiselhurst (Barnby) [SDFMR D, MRSTLS, SSLL] I688; L 459b; T414b; Y255 1683
Chislehurst (Nicholson) [MRD SLDR, DRMS, MRDMR] F610

1684
Choose the right (Tuckett) [MF SSSLDTLSM, RMFST] BC110 1685
-----. R [LTDTLS, RRMFLSFM FS,] 1686
Chope (Chope's carols) [SSSLT DMFSRS, LTLSL] I117 1687
-----. R [R#MMMMMSR, MFMF LFMR,] 1688
Chopin (Woodbury) [SSSDSMRD, MDMSMDMR,] R29b; T176; AJ256; AO108; AS58; BB339 1689
-----. V [SSSDDMRD, MDMSM DMR,] AS58 1690
Choral (Vulpius) X Weimar 1691
Chorley (Reay) [SMSDMFSLS, SR SMF#SR] M258; O354 1692
Chorus angelorum (Somervell) X Somervell 1693
Chorus novae Jerusalem (Sarum plainsong, M 3) [MFSFMRMMR DRFRMFM,] B556b; E122 1694
Christ arose (Lowry) [SSLLSS, SFLLS, LTDDS] AE123; AH 302; AI81; AM206; AR185; AS150; AT113; AU127; AV317; AW452; AX119; BY160; BZ 1695
-----. R [DDDMSSD, DRMDRD TLS,] 1696
Christ by heavenly hosts (Williams) X Gloucester 1697
Christ Church (Steggall) X Christchurch 1698
Christ, der du bist der helle tag (Bohemian Br.) X Gregor's 54th metre 1699
Christ for the whole wide world (McKinney) [SDTDRM, MFFDR M, MMRR] AU444 1700
-----. R [SDMRMD, TDRRR SFM, MF] 1701
Christ has for sin (Hoffman) X Hoffman 1702
Christ in His word draws near (Bunnett) X Kirby Bedon 1703
Christ in the night He was betrayed (Mason) X Hebron 1704
Christ is all (Williams) [DMM MRDDD, MSSSSLLS,] AY 110 1705
Christ is born in Bethlehem (Hugg) [DDDSMFSLS, MMM MMMF] AY246 1706
-----. R [SDSDRMRD, FFF DRM, MF] 1707
Christ is knocking (Palmer) [MMMRDSSM, RRDRM, MMM] AS195; BB565 1708
Christ is my life (Vulpius) X Cana 1709
Christ is our Head (La scala santa) X Coleraine 1710
Christ is risen (Kolb) [SMD STLSLSM, LSSFMR] AY266 1711
Christ ist erstanden (Latin. 12th c) [MMRMSLM, MRM DTDLL, R] E134; F601; J107; K114a; M439; Q187, 190; W121a; X155a, 162; AA225; AF183; AL116b; AW543; BG148; BQ329 1712
-----. R [MRDRFM, SMSMR D, MDLT] 1713
-----. V [LSLDRL, LSLFM FR, MMR] M439 1714
-----. V [LLSLDRL, LSLF MFR, SS] Q190 1715
-----. V [DDDTDRMD, SDDD TLSF] X162 1716
-----. V [MMRMSLM, MRMD TDL, RR] BQ329 1717
Christ lag in todesbanden (Latin. 12th c. [Bach arr]) [MR#MF#SLSF#M, MDRMRD T] J98b; O330; AA224; BZ 1718
-----. V [MRMSLSF#M, MD RMRDTL,] O330 1719
Christ lag in todesbanden (Latin. 12th c) X Christ ist erstanden (Latin. 12th c) X Victimae paschali (Plainsong sequence M 1 ascribed to Wipo) 1720
Christ lag in todesbanden (Latin. 12th c.: minor) [LSLDRDTL, LFSLSFMR]

J98a; K110; M432; Q195; AM 207; AZ154-a; BY153 1721

Christ, my life! (Pincott) [MF F#SMRMFRDT, RMRSL] BB139 1722

Christ receiveth sinful men (McGranahan) X Neumeister 1723

Christ returneth (McGranahan) [DMRDSLSMRDMR, RMMS] AT120; AU49; AV389; AW455; BB536 1724

-----. R [SMMFSLLD, DDD TLS, TT] 1725

Christ, the glory of the sky (Scheffler's Heilige seelenlust) X Culbach 1726

Christ the King (English trad) X Greensleeves 1727

Christ the Lord cometh (Bentley) [SF#SLSMSFMR, FMFRMF] AX125; AY532 1728

-----. R [RRRFFFMMLS, DDDDTL] 1729

Christ the Lord hath risen (Latin. 12th c) X Christ ist erstanden 1730

Christ the Lord is my true Shepherd (Currie) [DSLTDMRD, F MRMDRM, M] BN59 1731

Christ the Lord is my true Shepherd (Terry) [SSLSSDRD, SM MRDRM, M] BO11 1732

Christ the Lord is risen (Allgemeinisches Katholisches G-B. 1774) X Te Deum 1733

Christ, the Lord, is risen today (---) [SDLRDTD, DMRDTLS, DL#] BN40; BO175 1734

Christ the Lord is risen today (Bragers) [SMLSLTD, DTDSLL S, FF] BP38 1735

Christ the Lord is risen today (Strattner) X Posen 1736

Christ the Lord is risen today (Lyra davidica) X Easter hymn 1737

Christ the Lord is risen today (Montani) [SSDSSFFM, RMFS MRDR,] BQ31 1738

Christ unser herr zum Jordan kam (Walther. G-B) [RFSLSDTL, L DTLSFMR] AA401; AZ201-A 1739

-----. V [RFSLTDTL, S#D TLSFMR,] AZ201-A 1740

Christ, we do all adore (Dubois) [DDDTTLS, LLLDDDD TD,] AR634 1741

Christ will me his aid (Entwisle) [DDMLSMD, DRMR RMFM, M] AS299 1742

-----. R [RMFMRMFLS, LTDTLSM] 1743

Christbaum (Cornelius) X The Christmas tree 1744

Christchurch (Ouseley) [DDM SLSMR, SSFMLF#F#M,] E 460 1745

Christchurch (Steggall) [DM SDRS, DLSSFM, RMSL] B182; D259; E411; F280; I178; W 537; X197b; AL528; AP633a; AZ342-I; BR193; BV202; BX 62; BY716 1746

Christe, der du bist tag und licht (Plainsong, ca 600) X Christe, qui lux es it dies 1747

Christe du beistand (Loewenstern) [LLTDTMF#SLFM, SF#MRR] E160; X349a 1748

Christe, du lamm Gottes (Bugenhagen liturgy. 1528) X Agnus dei 1749

Christe fons jugis (Rouen church mel) [MMRMDMFSMFM, MRMDT] E335; F416; X281; AB215; AK342; AL456a; AN 436; AP625a 1750

Christe, qui lux es et dies (Plainsong, ca 600) [RFRD# RMFMR, FFFFDRF] Q559; AA34; AZ22-D 1751

-----. V [LDTLS#LTDTL, DDDDSD] AZ220-D 1752

Christe qui lux es et dies (Plainsong, M 2) [MMRDRM FRR, RRFMDRF] Eap. 1; F95a 1753

Christe Redemptor (Sarum Plainsong, M 1) [DRMSS FMRFMRDR, DM] A485b; B328b; E17; F188a; J483a; W421; X549a; AL297c; BJ

32; BP10; BQ155a 1754

-----. V [DRMSSFMRMFMR, DMSL] BP10 1755

Christe, redemptor omnium (Sarum Plainsong, M 1) X Christe redemptor 1756

Christe sanctorum (Paris Antiphoner. 1681) [SMFMRD, MFSS LS, SLTD] A157b; E165b; F 10b; J134; R43; S24; W263; X48b; Z102; AC26; AD41; AF 41; AK44; AL567b; AN116; AW 24; BV40; BY675; BZ 1757

Christe sanctorum (Sarum plainsong, M 1) [LSLSFMFRDSS FSLL] A123a; E242 1758

Christe, sanctorum decus angelorum (Plainsong, M 8) [DRF MFSSSSSLDTLS, D] F564a 1759

Christe, wahres seelenlich (Freylinghausen G-B. 1704) [DDRMMLLS#LMFMRRD, D] K82b; M408; Q113 1760

-----. V [DDMMLLS#, LMFM RRD, DD] Q113 1761

Christi blut (As hymnodus sacer. Leipzig) X Breslau 1762

Christi mutter stund von [mit] schmerzen (Corner. G-B.) [SSLSFMSM, SFMMFMRR,] E115b; G139; X138b; AN185b; AP197 1763

Christian home (McKinney) [MR# MFTD, MMMSFMRMF, F] AT 377 1764

Christian soldier (Hugg) [MMMM RRDD, DRRRDRM, M] AY387 1765

Christian soldiers (Fuller) [SLT DMRDS, TD#R#MSF#MS] C 530b; D516c 1766

Christian, walk carefully (Stebbins) [SDMMRDRDTD, SDM SFM] AX444 1767

Christians, awake (Fuller) [MD LSSLTDRM, DFMRDT] D56b; Y213 1768

Christine (Kroeger) [MFSSDLSM S, SLLRDTL] AJ250 1769

Christmas (Gilchrist) [DRMSLTD SM, SDDRDM, D] BR548a 1770

Christmas (Handel) [MFSDTLS DRM, MFSSSF] A577; B111; C111; D503; G88; H84; I115; J552; K380; L112; N20; R 169; S120; T293; U291; V493; Y165; Z185; AA378; AB241; AC195; AD112; AE88; AF362; AG80; AH260; AI321; AJ406; AK106; AM156; AN155a; AO 401; AQ223; AR130; AS325; AT79; AU147; AV89; AW73; AZ14-Y; BA161; BB100; BD 90; BE362; BF283; BH175; BK 145; BR435; BX364; BZ 1771

Christmas (Handel) X Innocents (Parish choir) 1772

Christmas (Mendelssohn) X Mendelssohn 1773

Christmas brings joy (Weyse) [MDMSMDRM, DLLSFMRS,] J46; M617 1774

Christmas carol (Davies) [MR MDMRMD, MLSMRDM, M] J27b; W48a; X79b; AC80; AD122; BE223; BV122; BY 105a 1775

Christmas dawn (German trad) [SMMRMDS, SSSLSM, DLL] J35; W610, 643; N635; AW 436 1776

-----. V [SMMRMDS, SSSFSM, DLL] M643 1776a

Christmas Eve I (English carol) [MF#SF#MRDFMR, DTLMML,] BG1a 1777

-----. R [TDTDRMRDT, SDD SRM, L] 1778

Christmas Eve II (English carol) [LMMRDTMLSS, LTTDRF] BG1b 1779

-----. R [MLTDRMRDT, TDTL TDR] 1780

Christmas Eve (Knudsen) [SDD MRDTDR, SRMFMRM,] J45; P369 1781

Christmas hymn (Wainwright) X Yorkshire 1782

Christmas joy (Crueger) [DRM SFMRD, FMR, MF#S, FS] M 353; Q77; AA145 1783

Christmas morn (Conant) [MFMS TDRM, SLSFMR, RM] BE24 1784

Christmas morn (Freylinghausen. Geistliche G-B. 1704) X Mocht hoch die tür 1785

Christmas morn (Hopkins) [DMM MRMSM, DRRRDRM, D] J545; W363 1786

Christmas song (Harrington) [SL SDLT, SSSDMS, SLSD] G98; I112b; R155; Z198; AC84; AD 118; AE87; AR131; AT69; BB 106; BZ 1787

Christopher (Maker) X St Christopher 1788

Christopher (Peter) [LTDRMFS#, LTDDRRD, LT] E304; X636a 1789

Christopher Sower (Gottshall) [MFMMMMR, RDDTTL, LMM] AR418 1790

Christ's return (Hayes) [MR#M DMSLS, MRDDRMR, M] AX 130 1791

-----. R [MSLDTLLS, MRDDLL S, M] 1792

Christum wir sollen loben schön (Geistliche lieder. W'burg.) [RFSLRSFM, SLDDTLTD,] J20b; Q104; AA148 1793

Christum wir sollen loben schön. (German trad) X Cyriacus 1794

Christus der ist mein leben (Vulpius) X Cana 1795

Christus ist auferstanden (Cologne G-B. 1623) X Cologne 1796

Christus ist erstanden (Latin. 12th c) X Christ ist erstanden 1797

Christus Rex (Putnam) [DSLM FSTD, FMRDRTLS,] C145c 1798

Christus Rex (Williams) [DMSDT LSLLS, SFMLS] A543 1799

Christus urunknak (Hungarian carol) [RRRLLSSLSFM, LLT SD,] AQ303 1800

Christus vincit (Ambrosian: ancient) [LLSLL, TLSLL, LSL MM, S] BP106 1801

Christus vincit (French trad) [MFMRRMM, MFMRRMM, MF] BQ248 1802

Christus vincit (Italian Asso. of St. Cecilia) [MMSSDDMM, LRSDFMRD.] BQ310 1803

Chrysostom (Barnby) X St Chrysostom 1804

Church (Holbrook) [SSMDRSRM RD, MSMFRD] L239; T242; AJ338 1805

Church (Lindeman) X Kirken 1806

Church of God (Rogers) [MR DDDDDD, TDRRMMR, M] AX 151 1807

Church of God, awake (O'Kane) [SLSF#SSMRD, LS#LTDTL] AY518 1808

-----. R [DRMFMRD, TDRDF MR, DR] 1809

Church triumphant (Elliott) X Triumphant 1810

Church vigilant (Ziegler) [DM FSSLDDS, MSLSFMR#] AC 224 1811

City bright (Tyler) [MSFMRD, RMSFMR, MMFS] W480; AM662; AP792; BV493 1812

City of David, Bethlehem (French carol) [DDTLSDRM, SSFMRDRD] BI84 1813

City of light (Coster) [SMSDR M, MSFDFM, MSS] G473 1814

City Road (Lutkin) [DDRDRM, MSFMFS, SS#LL] I311 1815

City strong and mighty (Whittington) [DDDSDD, RRRLRR, MMMF#] BI16-D 1816

Civitas dei (Caldicott) [SLDFM MR, MDTDRT, DRM] AB289; BF508 1817

Civitas dei (Calkin) [SSDDTLT LS, SSDDDTD] N104; S428; V711; AB401; BR464a 1818

Claflin (Kotzschmar) [SDRMRR SM, SDRMRRM, M] AS95 1819

Clairvaux (Loyd) [SFMRDTDR, M LDTRS, SL] AL565 1820

Clairvaux (Polack) [MRDSMFM RM, MMMF#F#S, S] Q350; AA98 1821

Clare Market (Palmer) [MRDT LLSDRDT, SMDTM] AO500

1822

Clarence (Sullivan) [LLLTDTL, TTTDRDT, D] B140; D347; W622; BR7 1823

Claribel (Mitchell) [SSSMMRD SLTT, SSSFF] AN550 1824

Clarion (Rembault) [DSDMDTLS, SLTDTDMR] D111a 1825

Clark (Main) [SMSDSLSS, DTST LS, SR] L170b 1826

Clarke's (Clarke) [SSLSSDMMR DRMS, SSM] L368 1827

Clarksville (Bradbury) [SSFMFS, LSFMRMFM, SS] AJ79 1828

Claro paschali gaudio (Plainsong, M 8) X Aurora lucis rutilat 1829

Clarum decus jejunii (Plainsong, M 2) [DRRRFDRFFMRMM, SFM] E68 1830

Claudius (Fink) X Bethlehem 1831

Claudius (Mann) [DDTLMMRD, LTDTLS#, S#L] I595 1833

Claudius (Schulz) [SDDSSMD, SFMRDS, DT] A138; B423; C423; E293; F483; J364; K 486; N638; R524; S464; W237; X14; Y46; Z594; AB387; AC 323; AD445; AE417; AF460; AG288; AH489; AI351; AK432; AL193; AM614; AN142; AO580; AP141; AR592; AW375; BA869; BD51; BF548; BV654; BX174; BY732; BZ 1834

-----. [DDDDRR, RMSFMR,] 1835

Clausnitzer (Darmstadt G-B. 1699) [MMSFMRRM, RMFM RRD, M] M61; O76; Q252; AA393; AF250 1836

Cleansing (Doane) [SSSMFSLS, S DTDTLS, S] U159; AH384; AI198; AM465; AT213; AU350 1837

Cleansing fountain (American trad) [DMSLSDDLS, DMSSLS M] G140; I291a; R276; T112; U151; V251b; AE183; AG98; AI140; AJ162; AM188; AR477; AT92; AU37; AV154; AW492; AX 118; AY236; BB163; BZ 1838

Cleansing wave (Knapp) [DM SMDLDD, LLSSMR, DM] H 241; AX308; BB598 1839

-----. R [SLLLDDSS, MRMF LLSS,] 1840

Clearway (Baker) X St Timothy 1841

Clemm (Clemm) [MMMRDDD RDL, SSDDMR] AI188; AM668; AW325; AX210; AY334; BB 448 1842

-----. [SMSMFFFMR, MMFSS LS] 1843

Clevedon (Wesley, S.S.) [MD STDTLLS, FMRDRMR] AP 684a 1844

Cleveland (Burnap) [MRDSLT, RD#RMRD, MRDS] AA369 1845

Clewer (Filitz) [DDRMFM, SSF MR, SMLS] B357; E455; AL 545b; AP518 1846

Cliff Town (Routley) [MRD RSLSDRM, MRDSMR] AQ83; BV168 1847

Clifton (Burnap) [SLTDRDTRL, LS, DDDDM] AB217; BF390 1848

Clifton (Clifton) [DMRDTDRM F, RSMF#SLT] W418b; BV135 1849

Clifton (Jordan) X Rhodes 1850

Clifton (Monk) [SSDMMRD, MM LSFMR, MM] C312; D332; L176; W266 1851

Cliftonville (Maker) [MSSSLTD SS, MSFMRM, M] AP765 1852

Cling to the Bible (Murray) [DDDDTLSLMSF, RRRRD] AX140; AY500 1853

-----. R [DDRMDRRMFR, MMFSSF] 1854

Clinging (Torrance) X Moredun 1855

Clinton (Holbrook) [MMRDSDRM, MFFMSR, MM] T109; AJ14 1856

Cloisters (Barnby) [MMMMM SFMRRM, MMMM] A395; B469; C469; D496; F253b; J157; K208; M489; U348; W216a; Z430; AD389; AF

371; AM473; AO414; AR326; AV71; BA270; BB262; BF588; BI60; BV405b 1857

Clolata (Palmer) [DDDDMRDD, FFFFMMRD] D595b; I251; T26; AJ35; AK473; AO254 1858

Clonmel (Irish trad) [SDRDTLS SLS, FMDMRD] AT182; BE136; BY743; BZ 1859

Close to my Savior (Mishler) [MFMMRFSFM, SLSSMMR] AS219 1860

-----. R [RMFMSFSFM, LFLSM, SF] 1861

Close to Thee (Vail) [SDMDTRD S, DMSMDMR, S] G235; I332; T19; Z413; AE299; AH324; AI 269; AJ24; AR482; AS220; AT 354; AU223; AV382; AX2 ; BZ 1862

-----. R [TDRFTD, MFSSMR, SDMM] 1863

-----. R [TDRRFTDD, MFSSS MR, S] AX2 1864

Closer cling to Jesus (Hugg) [MFMRDTLS, SDMSLSR, M] AX516; AY311 1865

Closer to Thee, my Father (Tenney) [DDRMMFFMD, DLLD LS, T] BB632 1866

-----. R [SSLLLLL, SMRRMMF, MD] 1867

Clovelly (Parker) [LSLMRDTL, TDRMF#F#S, S] AN187; BX 248 1868

Cluff (Sankey) X I am praying for you 1869

Clymer (Root) [DMRDTDRD, DDTLSMDR,] L232 1870

Cobb (Cobb) [DRMMMFMRD, MFSSSL] A134; B288; D497b; L34; AM361 1871

Cobbold ("S. M. W. V. R.": Shaw & Williams) [DDSDRMDM, FSLF MRD, D] Xapp. 1 1872

Cobern (Gauntlett) [SMDLSSMD LS, DFFRSM] I92; W168b; Y388; AJ407; ALsuppl; AM110; AP93c; AZ39-E; BR244; BV519 1873

-----. V [SMDLSSSMDLS, DFF RS] AZ39-E 1874

Cobham (Finlay) [DSMSLS, FMSFM, STLSD] BV592b 1875

Coblentz (Bourgeois) X Bourgeois 1876

Coburg (Enckhausen) X Schönste sonne 1877

Cochran (Burnap) [MRMSLTT LSM, MRLR, MT] I505 1878

Coelestis aula (Whitney) [DD SLMSDR, MSDTLTLS] D387b 1879

Coeli (Stewart) X Coeli enarrant 1880

Coeli enarrant (Stewart) [DM FSLLS, DRRMFM, MRS] W335; AB179 1881

Coelites plaudant (Rouen mel., 17th c) [DSLSFMLTSDDTD, DRR] A123b; E242b; F564b; G16; Sap. 42; X262a; AL540; BY345 1882

Coena Domini (Sullivan) [MRD FMRMDRTDFMRLS] C330b; D220b; J273; K187; L325; W453; AO442; AR683; AS66; AZ1-C; BA296; BR474; BY 323 1883

Colchester (Tans'ur. Compleat melody) [DDTLSFMRDS, SLT DRT] AA129; AB237; AN 134; AP51; AQ327; BE182; BX165 1884

Colchester (Wesley, S. S.) [MSDFRDTD, SDTLRSFM] F90; N441; O347; W332; BV 332b; BY349 1885

Cole (Munson) [LSLTL, DLTR M, SRMRR, T] AQ134 1886

Colebrooke (Smart) [MFMRLS FM, MSRMTDRT,] AZ92-D 1887

Coleman (McKinney) [SMFSD TLL, LSF#SMRR, S] AT348; AU423 1888

-----. R [SMRDMRDT, SFMR FMRD,] 1889

Coleraine (La scala santa. 1681) [DSSLDDTD, MLLRTLLS,] E333; BN204 1890

Coleshill (Barton. Psalms) [LLSDSLLM, DMRDSD, DM] E492; W31a; X658; AL671b;

AP90b 1891

Collaudemus (French carol) [DRDTDRRMD, MFSFMRD] E229b; W554 1892

College (March) [DMSSLMSF, M RDRM, MFS] AC113 1893

College cross (Grundy) [MRDT LS, LTTD, MRDRTS,] BV85 1894

Collegedale (Miller) [MMMSFM RMD, MFSLL# LS,] BB147 1895

Collingwood (Bate) [DSMRSDRM FSFFMRDF] F180 1896

Cologne (Cologne G-B. 1623) [DLSDMRD, DLSDMRD, SL] X163; AD165 1897

Columba (Irish trad) X St Columba 1898

Columbia (Blanton) [SDSDMS, FM MRDRD, SDS] R98; AM108 1899

Columbia (Jackson) [DTLSMS, DTLSMS, F# TLS,] AB335 1900

Columbia (Löhr) X St Frances 1901

Columbia College (Warren) [DD DTLTLS, DRMSFMRD] S487 1902

Columbia the gem of the ocean (Becket) X Red, white and blue 1903

Colwinstone (Lloyd) [MTDFMRR R, MFLMSRDR,] W408 1904

Colwyn Bay (Linekar) [DMRR FMRD, MSSLSMF# S,] AM45; AP452 1905

Colyton (Monk) [MSLTDD, TLS FMMMFMM] W66 1906

Comavon (James) X Cwmafon 1907

Combe Martin (Harwood) [MR SDTDT, DLSFSMR, S] A174 1908

Come (Garrett) X Forgiveness 1909

Come, all ye faithful (Wade's Cantus diversi) X Adeste fideles 1910

Come all ye saints (Wheelwright) [SMMRDLSSFM, SLTDRM] BC 11 1911

Come, all ye saints who dwell (---) [SSSSSSDT, TDLSFM, MM] BC12 1912

Come, all ye sons of God (Huish) [SDDMFS, SLLLLS M, SDD] BC302 1913

Come, all ye sons of Zion (Tullidge) [SDMFLSM, MF SSLFS, SD] BC303 1914

Come along, come along (Smyth) [SSSMRDTLSLTD, SDDD] BC19 1915

-----. R [SFMMRDDTRDTL, FMRR] 1916

Come and hear the grand old story (Ohl) [SDDTSRRD, SMMRRLR, S] K531 1917

-----. R [MMFMRLTL, SLTD RMSF,] 1918

Come children (Sewall) [SMS SLMMFLLTS, SMMM] BR 549 1919

Come closer to me (Warren) [MMMMMMMRDR, RRRRRR] AX532 1920

-----. R [MMMFMMD, RRR MRDS, MM] 1921

Come, come ye saints (English trad) [DDRMDTDRMF, MDR, DTD,] BC13 1922

Come dearest Lord (Stephens) [MDFMRDMRDTDRMRDM,] BC237 1923

Come, every soul (Stockton) X Stockton 1924

Come, faithful people (Bicknell) [MSF#SMLSF#M, MDTLRLT] E619; X136 1925

Come, follow me (McBurney) [MDFMSDTLS, SLMFFFS] BC14 1926

Come, go with me, beyond the sea (--- arr by Griggs) [SDRMSDRM, MRDMRD, SD] BC15 1927

Come, gracious Spirit, heavenly dove (Bradbury) X Baca 1928

Come, great deliverer (Doane) [SFMSDDRDTLL, STDTD] AU289 1929

-----. R [DTLTDRTLSD, DDTDRM] 1930

Come, hail the cause (German trad) X Evergreen 1931
Come, heaven-bound pilgrim (Shenk) [SSFMLSMFMRDS, SDD R] AX56; AY323 1932
Come, Holy Ghost (Gibbons) X Angel's song 1933
Come, Holy Ghost (Hopkins) [SSSSSLSFS, SLLL# L#] A217b; B455; C455; D289c 1934
Come Holy Ghost (Sarum plainsong, M 8) X Veni creator 1935
Come, Holy Ghost, creator blest (Lambillotte) X Veni, creator spiritus 1936
Come, Holy Ghost, in love (Beery) [SSMDRM, SDSLFM, SFMR,] AS170 1937
Come, Holy Ghost, send down (---) [SLTDDDDD, SDRMMMR M] BO187 1938
-----. R [SMDDDDTDRD, SSS MDD] 1939
-----. [MMMRMRDTLTDR, MMMR] 1940
Come, Holy Ghost, who ever one (Pieraccini) X Santa Trinita 1941
Come home (McKinney) [SSF# SMRDLD, LSDDDRM] AU436 1942
-----. R [SMRD, DLTDRDS, SMDF, L] 1943
Come home, poor sinner (Jeffrey) [MRDLD, RDRM, MRDLD, RD] AX232 1944
-----. R [SSMFL, SSMMR, SSM FL, S] 1945
Come, humble sinner (---) [LTDL SMS# LLTD, RMMRD] AU454 1946
Come, just as you are (Showalter) [MMMMFFM, DDDDRRM, MF] AX247; AY214 1947
-----. R [SSDDTLS, SSLLSF#S, SS] 1948
Come, lay his books and papers by (Edwards) [SDDDDDDD, M RDMRD, SF] BC338 1949
Come, let us anew (---) [SFM MRDRMMF#S, SLSF#S,] BB 369 1950
Come, let us anew (Lucas) X Lucas 1951
Come, let us praise (Grimm) [SDRMDFMRD, SLSLLTL] BH201 1952
Come, let us sing an evening hymn (Cannon) [MSDR DMFMRRD, FFMSF] BC238 1953
Come, let us sing in sweet accord (Grauman) [SDDTTLT S, SSLTDSFM] BH217 1954
Come, let us worship (Russian mel., 19th c) [MRMFMSFM RRDTD, DTL] BL44 1955
Come, listen to a prophet's voice (Daynes) [DMSSF#SLSD MM, MFSSF] BC46 1956
Come, lost one (Shoemaker) [DMSSSMRDFF, LSFMMR] AX225; AY230 1957
-----. R [SLLLDTLLS, MFMFSSR] 1958
Come, love we God (Shann ms.) [DSSSSLFS, SL# L# LFSLS] BG10 1959
Come, my way (La Montaine) [LLMMF# F# L, LLMMF# F# L, LL] BL32 1960
Come, O Lord, Jesus (Polish folk song) [SFMMMMMRM SF, FFMRR] P311 1961
Come, O Sabbath day (Binder) X Sabbath hymn 1962
Come, O thou King of Kings (---) [SMFMRDTD, SLTD TDLS,] BC20 1963
Come, rejoice (Cannon) [SSDD RDRMD, FFMDR, SS] BC1 1964
Come, ring out your joy (Gelineau) [FFLD, DDRD, DLT L, LSLF, RFSF, FL#S] BSp. 30 1965
Come, Saviour, come (Work) [MMRDMSDDTL, SSLSMD] BB544 1966
-----. R [RRDTR, DMRD, LLTDTLS] 1967
Come, sing to the Lord (de Jong) [DMDRMSFMRD, DLFLSM] BC32 1968
Come, sing to the Lord (Gei-

bel) X Trumpet call 1969
Come, sinner, come (Palmer) [MDRMFLMR, DRDRM, MDR] AU212; AX229; BB564 1970
Come, thou fount (Wyeth) X Nettleton 1971
Come, thou glorious day (Smyth) [MSDMRMFFM, RDDTLST] BC 240 1972
Come, thou Holy Spirit, come (Webbe) X Veni sancte spiritus 1973
Come, Thou, O come (---) [MFLS, SDTTLL, SMFMRD] BR201 1974
Come, thou quickening Spirit (Meiningen G-B) X St Leonard 1975
Come to Jesus (Pollock) [MFSS SDDL, LLSLSFM, M] AX223; AY226 1976
-----. R [TDRRDRMD, SSLDTL S, M] 1977
Come to me (Brunk) [SMRDDSF M, SLDSDLRR,] AY395 1978
Come to the fountain (Stebbins) [SMFSMRDS, DTDRFMR, S] AX231 1979
-----. R [FFFFMMMM, LLLS FMRF#] 1980
Come to the Saviour (Maker) X Invitation 1981
Come to the Saviour (Root) [SL SMSDRDL, TTDRMDT] N647; AI391; AM693; AP758; AX233 1982
-----. R [MMFMMRRLR, RRM RRDD] 1983
Come unto Him and rest (Verdi) [SSF#SLSMFM, SSF#SLSM] AU462 1984
Come unto Jesus (Huish) [MF MLS, SMTRD, LLLSDT] BC22 1985
Come unto Me (Dykes) [DDDLT DD, RMDRDD, MMM] B387a; C387a; D437a; F350; T433; V255b; W390a; AB156; AL470; AP396; BF343; BY412 1986
Come unto me (Handel) X Messiah 1987
Come unto Me (Stebbins) [MDRM MFFFFM, SLSMDD] AI194; AS193 1988
-----. R [MRMS, SLSD, DTLS MFFF] 1989
Come, we that love the Lord (Lowry) [DMDSLTD, RMDSF MR, RM] AS287; AT308; AU 8; AV343; AW443; AX29; BB 640 1990
-----. R [MSMMMD, MRDSFM RS, FM] 1991
Come, we that love the Lord (Williams) X St Thomas 1992
Come, ye disconsolate (Webbe) X Consolation 1993
Come, ye faithful servants (Levenson) [MRDTTLD, MR DTL, MSFM] BH101 1994
Come, ye sinners (Ingalls) X Invitation 1995
Come, ye sinners (Rousseau) X Greenville 1996
Come, ye thankful people (Elvey) X St George's Windsor 1997
Come, ye wanderers (Pollock) [MFSDMRDDL, DTLSDRM] AX222; AY225 1998
-----. R [TDRRRDRMD, RM RDTLS,] 1999
Come, ye weary ones, tonight (Toews) [MFSSLSM, RDRD LDS, MF] AX234 2000
Comfort (---) [SLSSMFRSFFM, SLSSM] AN570; AW229 2001
Comfort (English mel) [MM MRMFF#S, RRRDRMD, M] AJ9; BR442 2002
Comfort (Garratt) [MRDSFMR DRRM, MFSLT] W681 2003
-----. R [SLSDTL, SFMMRD, DRDS] 2004
Comfort (Rich) [SMRTDDTT, L SDRMMRR,] BE424 2005
Comfort ye (Genevan Psalter. 1551) X Donne secours 2006
Comforter divine (Reay) [MMM MMRRS, SSSSSLLT,] D134b 2007
Coming home (Kirkpatrick) X Lord, I'm coming home

2008

Coming now, O Lord, to thee (Kieffer) X Something for Jesus (Lowry) 2009

Coming to the cross (Fischer) [SDMDRMD, MFSLSMR, DR] G246; H272; I351; L464; R 278; U177; V747; AH339; AP 430; AR257; AT243; AU260; AV 173; AX60; AY282; BA903; BB 600; BZ 2010

Commandemens (Bourgeois) X Commandments 2011

Commandments (Bourgeois) [DDRMMFFMR, MFMRD] A179a; D380a; E277; F554; K498; M54; N50; O56; P104; Q141; R59; V683; W289a; X 56; AA424; AF47; AL568b; AN 120; AP211; AQ97; BJ3; BR 119; BZ 2012

-----. V [DDRMRFMRD, MFM RDTD] K498 2013

-----. V [DDRMRFRD, MFMRDT DR,] M54 2014

-----. V [DDRMDFRD, MFMRD TDR,] N50 2015

-----. V [DDRMMFMR, MFMR DTDR] AP211 2016

Comme un cerf attere brame (Bourgeois) X Bourgeois 2017

Commemoration (Gesius) [SMSLS FM, MRMRRD, SMS] A505; E 345; J248; Q544; X194a; AA21; AN197; BY552 2018

-----. V [SMSLSFM, MRDDTD, SMS] Q544 2019

Commit thy way (German) [SM FMRMRDSS, SLSLTL] M129; AW558 2020

Common ways (Swabian trad) X Miserere nobis 2021

Commonwealth (Booth) [LLL DDMD, LTDLTDLM, M] S375; Y241; Z563; AB290; AC288; AD352; AG280; AL527; AN324; AO483; AP642; AR90; AV229; BD165; BF577; BX382; BY654 2022

-----. R [DDRFMRLS, SSFMRD RT] 2023

Communion (Brackett) [MRM FM, SLSMRR, MSDTT] BE 298 2024

Communion (Garrett) [SLSDM RDT, TDRMSSF#S,] AB379 2025

Communion (Gilchrist) [SSS LLDDD, SS#LTDRR, S] BR 467b 2026

Communion (Jenks) [SDMRDM RDLS, SDMRDR] H172; I 146a; BB399 2027

Communion (Ledington) [MM RFMRLSF, MMMMRDF] BB 476 2028

Communion (Mason & Webb. Cantica Laudis.) X Heath 2029

Communion (Mendelssohn) X Brightest and best 2030

Communion (Miller) X Rockingham 2031

Communion (---) [MDMSMRM FM, FFFMDSM] L136 2032

Communion hymn (Brightbill) [MSFMMMRD, DDRMFSLF] AR517; BH196 2033

Communion hymn (Gesius) X Herrnhut 2034

Communion meditation (Sanger) [MMMMSFMDRD, DFLSMD] AR509 2035

Communion processional (Biggs) [DMMMMFMMRM, MSSSSL] BN208 2036

Communion spiritual (Negro spiritual) [SLDDDDMRRDD DD, MFS] R447; AF288; AR489; BZ 2037

-----. R [DMSSSS, LSFRM FFF, SM] 2038

-----. V [SLDDDDMRRD, MF SSSS] AF288 2039

Companion (Newman) [MFSLDT SL, SMRDSLRR,] AL554 2040

Compassion (Doane) X Cleansing 2041

Compassion (Rich) [DTDRMRT D, MMMFMR, DT] BE420 2042

Complainer (Southern harmony. 1835) [SDDMSLS,

MSMRDM, SDD] AQ40; BZ 2043

-----. V [DDDMSLS, SMMRD M, DDD] BZ 2044

Comrade heart (Hyatt) [DRMD RMSSF, LLLSRM, F#] Y207; AC237 2045

Comrades of the cross (Barnes) [MFSMRMM, MFSMRM, MF# S] Y72; AC122 2046

Concord (---) [MMMR#MSRR, RRRD#RFM, M] C505 2047

Concord (Johnson) [DDRMFMM, RMRDD, RRFF] BE306 2048

Concordi laetita (Corbeil) X Orientis partibus 2049

Conditor alme (Sarum antiphonal, M 4) [MDMSLLFS, SLFSFM RM] A6a; E1; F45a; J147a; R245a; X51a; AF113; BJ47; BL4; BM96; BN3; BO283; BP 2; BZ 2050

-----. V [MDMSSLFS, SLFSFM RM,] BN3 2051

Conditor alme siderum (Sarum antiphonale, M 4) X Conditor alme 2052

Confession (Moravian) X Gregor's 39th metre 2053

Confession (Walther) [LMRMTD TL, MMLSF#MSF#] M60; O71; Q251b; AA394 2054

-----. V [LMRMTDTRDTLS# L, MMF] Q251b 2055

-----. V [RLSLMFMSFMRD# R, LLR] Q251b 2056

Confidence (Barnby) X Kirkdale 2057

Confidence (Chamberlain) [SM LSSLDD, SFMLSSMR] V256 2058

Confidence (Crueger. Praxis pietatis melica) X Ratisbon 2059

Confidence (Moore) [MMRDML RDTD, MRRRSR] I286 2060

Confirmation (Hayden) X Father, I come to thee 2061

Confirmation (Rosenmüller) X Nassau 2062

Congaudeat (Piae cantiones) [RRMFMR, DRL, LSFF#FMF] BG83 2063

-----. V [LLTDTLSLM, MRM FMRMD,] BG83 2064

Congleton (Wise) [LDTDLS#L SFM, SSMLTD] E312; W98; X622; AQ69 2065

Congregation (Zinck) [SMD SSDDT, SDMFMRD, S] BE130 2066

Conisborough (Sanderson) [MF SLDTLDLLS, SLMSF] Z317; AC222; AR401; BK92 2067

Coniston (Barnby) X Holy Trinity 2068

Conjugal love (Gould) [DMF RSSFM, MRDFMR, RM] BR 480a 2069

Conjugial love (?) (Gould) X Conjugal love (Gould) 2070

Conquering love (Willcocks) [LLTDRMDR, LDMF#RMM, M] BV205b 2071

Conquering now (Sweney) X Victory through grace 2072

Conqueror (Freylinghausen G-B. 1704) [DRMRMF#SS, D DTLTLLS,] J435b; M450; O15; P120; Q129; AA182 2073

-----. V [DRMRMF#SS, DDTD TLS, D] Q129 2074

Conqueror (Hemy) [DSLSMRD S, LLFMRMR, D] D126b; H 204; U310; BD160 2075

Conquest (Barrows) [SDLSMD RM, SLTDRT, DS] A541; BY 219b 2076

Conquest (BridgeP [SLTDMSF, MRMFFM, SLT] BF585 2077

Conquest (Croft) X Hanover 2078

Conquest (Stainer) [SDTLTDS, LSMSFM, F#SS] D278a; I448 2079

Conquest (Thommen. Christenschatz) X Cassel 2080

Consecration (---) [MDSDLDSD, MDSDRRRR#] I348a; U268 2081

No entry 2082

Consecration (Byers) [SSSMSDDT T, DRSSLTD,] AX398 2083
-----. R [SMMMRDRLS, SRRR MRD,] 2084
Consecration (Brown) [MMMSS LLFLD, DTLSMS] U261 2085
Consecration (Havergal) [DRM LSFM, MFSDTLS, ST] F361; H302; J520; K382; M226; P 406; Q400; W512b; AA355 2086
-----. V [DRMLSFM, MF#SD TLS, ST] H302 2087
Consecration (Lowry) X Something for Jesus 2088
Consecration (Malan) X Hendon 2089
Consecration (Morse) [DDRFM RDR, MLTDRMF] A458a 2090
Consecration (Rounsefell) X I'll go where you want me to go 2091
Consecration hymn (Steinel) [DRMFMLS, SDMTLS, FMF] BB286 2092
Consecration to Our Lady (Roman hymnal) [MMMSSDD, DF FFSFM, MM] BO115 2093
-----. R [MMF#SF#T, TDDTLSS FMM] 2094
Consolation (Beethoven) X Emmanuel 2095
Consolation (Grimm. Choral buch) [LTDMRDT, SDRMFFM, LT] AZ581-F 2096
Consolation (Lindeman) X Holy mountain 2097
Consolation (Mendelssohn) X Brightest and best 2098
Consolation (Webbe) [SMDLSS, FSLTDS, MMMFF] A483; B 388; C388; D637; G312; H441; I526; J569; K412; L366; M27; N477; O438; P266; Q531; R373; S293; U229; V428; W688; Z398; AA512; AD264; AE163; AG134; AH382; AI293; AK303; AL435; AM518; AO250; AP532; AR247; AS198; AT297; AU449; AV280; AW243; AY350; BA693; BB223; BC18; BE40; BO298; BQ117; BR339; BZ 2099
----- . V [SMDLS, FMFSLTDSS, MM] BO298 2100
Consolation (Wyeth ...) X Morning song 2101
Consolator (Arundel hymns) X Ave, Maris stella 2102
Consolator (Bradshaw) [MSF MMMRMFDT, RDTDM] BR 348 2103
Consolator (Falconer) [SSDTD RM, MMSMRDR, MM] D135b 2104
Consolator (Webbe) X Consolation 2105
Constance (Doane) [SSDS MFSRFM, SMRDTS] AV54 2106
Constance (Gauntlett) [SLTDR MFR, SFMRMRRD,] K106 2107
Constance (Sewall) [MMMSS M, MMMDRM, MMMF#] BR 324 2108
Constance (Sullivan) [MMMFR SLS, FMMFRRD, M] H342; K334b; R220; T271; U188; AB396; AG162; AJ378; AK 474; AL128; AM433; AP235; BA337; BF459; BY440b 2109
Constancy (Mendelssohn) [MF SLSMRFM, SMRDDDT] BE 229 2110
Constantia (Morris) [LLSFM RMFSLTT, DDTL] X501a 2111
Contemplation (Beethoven) X Emmanuel 2112
Contemplation (Mendelssohn) X Trust 2113
Contemplation (Ouseley) [MS RMSFMRD, MLSMFR, M] F 177; BV489; BY77b 2114
Contentment (Schörring. Koralbog. 1781) [DRMMRSLSLS FM, RMFM] M287; O377; P229 2115
Contrast (Edson) [DDSDMDMS, FMFSSFMR,] G349; I538; V371; AH368; AI271; AT306; AU24; AV180; BB199 2116
-----. V [DDSDMDMS, FMS MRDRD,] AH368 2117
Contrition (Bourgeois) X Du

fort de ma detresse 2118
Contrition (Dykes) X Almsgiving 2119
Contrition (Oakley) X Penitence 2120
Contrition (Persichetti) [LDTLDM RL, DSMRDR, RS] AF580 2121
Contrition (Rosenroth) X Old 29th 2122
Contrition (Stainer) [MRRDFM MR, MFSLSFM, S] D612a 2123
Converse (Converse) X Erie 2124
Convert (---) X O how happy are they 2125
Conway (Lawes) X Farley Castle 2126
Cooling (Abbey) [MFSSF#SLSS, FMRMSFF] G174; I186; T245; V329; Z571; AD465; AJ144; AL127b; AW259; BZ 2127
Coolinge (Taylor) [SDRFFMDLR S, SDRFLS] AQ84 2128
Copeland (Harrington) [SDRMM SFM, MMDMFMRD,] G331; I138 2129
Copenhagen (Lutkin) [MMFSDTFL, LSSSFMMR,] I107a 2130
Copenhagen (Zinck) [DDSLTDT, SDDMRD, DDS] J506; K271; O148; P75; Q655; AA377 2131
Copley Square (Smyth) [DMRD TLDS, SSSSDR, LF] BR557 2132
Coppee (Minshall) [SSMRDRDT, TDFMMRM, M] D309a; L175 2133
Cor, arca legem continens (Slovak trad) [MLTDTLFM, S SFMLLS#L,] BN66 2134
Cor dulce, cor amabile (German, 1669) [SSFMSDRM, SLTDTLLS,] BN68; BO15; BQ182c 2135
Cor Jesu, cor purissimum (Catholic) [DRMRDTDRD, DRM RDTD] BP69 2136
Cor Jesus sacratissimum (Plainsong, M 1) [MMMRFMRDD, RMRDTDT] BN67; BO23 2137
-----. V [LLLSL#LSFF, SL SFMFM] BO23 2138
Cor Jesu, salus (Schulthes) X Raise your voices, vales and mountains 2139
Corbeil (Corbeil) [LLLLSF# M, RLLF#SF#MR, S] F507a 2140
Corde natus (Piae cantiones. 1582) X Divinum mysterium 2141
Corde natus (Smart) [DRMSFL LS, DSMFSLR, M] C74b; D52b 2142
Corde natus ex parentis (Piae cantiones. 1582) X Divinum mysterium 2143
Cordis donum (Clausen. G-B) [SDTDRMR, RSFMRD, SDT] Q89 2144
Corelli (Nichol) [SLTDDTLTD, RFM, SSSF] AP809 2145
Corfe mullen (Matthews) [DM SSSLTDD, DRMSFFM,] BY 169 2146
Corinth (An essay on the church plain chant) X Dulce carmen 2147
Cormac (Irish trad) [SSDMDR TDTS, MFSMDD] G492; W 212; X495; BZ 2148
Cornell (Cornell) [SDDMDLDS, SDMRDDT, R] I223 2149
Corner (Corner. Geistliche nachtigall. 1649) [MMFSDD RDRM, DRMFSF] A39; E578; X369; BE9; BG84 2150
Corner-stone (Baker) [DMSSLL SS, LSFMRRR, D] D483b 2151
Cornerstone (Bourgeois) X Rendez a Dieu 2152
Cornfields (Hohenfurth ms. 1410) X Dies est laetitiae 2153
Cornhill (Darke) [SLSMDRMD R, SLTDSMS] E46; X41; BV 132b 2154
Cornish (Swisher) [MMR#MSL S, SDSFML, DSS] BD39 2155
Cornish carol (English trad)

X Eastertime 2156
Cornwall (Wesley) [MSMRDDTL S, MRDFMLS] F195; BV531b; BY65 2157
Corona (Stewart) [DSSLSFS, DFSMFR, RMD] E381b; F224a; BY452 2158
Coronae (Monk) [MMSSDDMM, LTDRMSR, M] A105; B185; C 185a; D130; H200; K121; N 375; Q222; R133; S201a; T36; U111; V163; AE28; AF203; AH 299; AI98; AJ52; AK180; AM 217; AO194; AS161; AW119 2159
Coronation (Holden) [SDDMMRD R, MRDMRD, R] A355a; B192; C192a; D450a; H192; I180; J 426b; K131c; L114a; M184; N153; O6; P7; Q339; R132a; S192a; T325; U116; V196a; Y 362; Z252; AA93; AB87a; AC 135b; AD180a; AE130; AF195; AG114; AH197; AJ197; AK184; AL46b; AM218a; AN9; AO208a; AP254c; AQ36; AR101; AS159; AT132; AU1; AV133; AW4; AX 13; AY1; AZ14-R; BA90a; BB 156; BC83; BD30; BE86; BF 327a; BI23; BR53b; BX29; BZ 2160
Coronet (Hews) [MRMDRFMMR, MRMDFMR] AO367 2161
Corpus domini (Malet) [LLLLLLL S#F#S#L, DDDDD] Eap. 47 2162
Corwin (Lerman) [SDSMDSMD, DFMRDT, SD] G262 2163
Costa (Costa) [DSSMDDFMR# M, RLTDDM] AB51; AR412 2164
-----. V [DSSMDFFMR#M, R LTDMS] AR412 2165
Cotham (Jenkins) [DDTLTDRS, SM RD, DDTL] BV80b 2166
Cöthen (Bach) [MRDRSDMRDT S, LSFMR] X150a 2167
Cottingham (Pullen) [SSMDRMFL S, SDTLSMR] BK32 2168
Cottman (Cottman) X Morn of gladness 2169
Country lanes (Vibbard) [MMM RLSLF, FMMDLS, SM] Y191; AC172 2170
Courage (Hume) X Dare to be brave 2171
Courage (LaTrobe) [DSDTLS, SFMRMFM, DMF#] AZ 595-B 2172
Courage (Parker) [SMDLLLT DRS, SMDLL] B113b; C113a; D505a; S270b; AB240a; AK 298; BF467a 2173
Courage (Wales. Univ. Student hymnal) [MSLSMRDMM, S MSLSDM] BE380 2174
Courage, brother (Sullivan) [SSDDDTLTDS, LTDRMS] G298; I513; AO402; BA573; BB263; BF627 2175
Courons a la fete (French trad) X The Spirit 2176
Courtland (Methfessel) [SDS DRMRD, MRDTLS, SD] M475 2177
Coutances (Rouen Antiphoner. 1728) X Because you live again 2178
Covenant (German trad) X Gregor's 185th metre-A 2179
Covenant (Stainer) [SDMRD S, FMDRTD, MRS] A285b; B253b; C253b; D460b; K 284b; BF460 2180
Covenant hymn (Canning) [DD MSSLSFS, DSFMRRM,] BZ 2181
Covenanters (Scottish trad) [SDDDRMDLLLS, MSDDM] R153; AT468; AU16; AV 287; BZ 2182
-----. V [SDDDRMDLLLS, MSSLD] AT468 2182a
Coventry (Cuzens) [SSDDTD LSFFM, SSSLS] H349; L170a; V76; AO97; BB244; BE327 2183
Coventry (Howard) [LMTDRDT L, DRMFMRM, M] AN328; BX313 2184
Coventry carol (English carol, 1591) [LLS#LDTTLS#, LTD RTL, M] BG22; BL15 2185
Cover with His life (Belden) [MMR#MDSSF#SM, MMR#

MDR] BB593 2186

-----. R [TLSDSLLLLS, F#M RD#F#F] 2187

Coverdale's carol (English trad) [MLTDRTLTLSM, MMRTL] BG131 2188

Covert (Tochter Sion. Cologne, 1741) X St Bernard 2189

Cowley (Vale) [DSFMRDRD, DSF#MRSL] A110 2190

Cowper (Mason) [MFSLSMDLS, DRMFMMR,] H232; I291a; L238; M135; N97; Q157b; S 241; T138; U150; V251a; AA 200; AH286; AJ205; AO272a; BA201 2191

Crackington (Sheldon) [MDRM SDTLSLM, F#SLTL] BV316 2192

-----. R [RRDRSFSLS, DLTDD SL] 2193

Cradle hymn (Harmonia sacra, 1753) [MS#LTDTLS#LT, LTDR M] A242 2194

Cradle song (Kirkpatrick) [SDD RMDD, MFSSLF, RMF] A43; S126; W657; X353; AL598; AO630; AP729; AQ276; BK 154; BV95b; BY734a 2195

Craig (Maclean) [DDTLSDDDT LS, LTDRM] V386 2196

Cranham (Holst) [MFSMRD, RMRLR, MFSM] A44; E25; F67; G104; J36; W50; X75; AF128; AL56; BG187; BV100; BY99; BZ 2197

Crasselius (Bach) [SDMRMDLFF SDFRRD, R] X93a 2198

Crasselius (Wittwe. Hamburger Musikalisches handbuch. 1690) [SDSLLSFMD, RMF#SLTD] A255; J255; M98; Q21; AA67; AW569; AZ106-B, 110-A 2199

----. V [SDSLLSFMRD, RMF# SLT] M98 2200

-----. V [SDSLLSLSFMRD, RMF#S] AW569 2200a

-----. V [SDSLLSFMRD, RMMR SL] AZ106-B 2200b

Crasselius (Wittwe. Hamburger Musikalisches handbuch. 1690) X Winchester New (Wittwe. Hamburger ...) X Wer weiss, wie nahe (Bronner. Choral-buch. 1715) 2201

Create in me (Reynolds) [LLL DTLR, DTTSSLTDR] AT518 2202

Create in this weak form of mine (---) [MRDSLDTT, FM RDRM, MM] BH170 2203

Creation (Haydn) [SDDRRMDL RDT, SLTDR] A309; C252; D464; G66; H111; I84; J442; M493; R97; S69; T270; U8; V100; Z164; AA114; AB48; AC47; AD97; AF72; AG57; AH188; AI41; AJ375; AK66; AL27; AM12; AN33; AO59; AP142; AQ47; AR98; AS88; AT10; AV53; AW50; AY422; BA32; BB91; BD36; BE170; BF230; BI31; BK129; BR 219; BX52; BZ 2204

-----. V [DDRRMDLRDT, TDRMFM] BI31 2205

Creator, alme siderum (Sarum antiphonale) X Conditor alme 2206

Creator alme siderum (Thermignon) [DTLSLLSFM, SLTD MRL] BQ151, 309 2207

Creator Spirit, Lord of grace (Bragers) [DDRMDRDT, R RTDRDTL,] BP43 2208

Crediton (Clark) [SDTDSLSF, MSLTDFMR] E206; J54a; W40; X35; AM98; AN238; AP39; BV458 2209

Credo (Stainer) [MMMMLS# LM, RDMSFMRD,] B462; W72; AP262; BV514; BX368; BY132 2210

Creevelea (Davis) [MSFMSFF M, MFSLFMR, R] Y34 2211

Cressbrook (Jackson) [DDD SLTD, RRRMFMR, MM] AO 504 2212

Crete (Dykes) X St Andrew of Crete 2213

Crieff (Finlay) [MSLDTL, SM RF, LRDTLD,] BV303a 2214

Crigglestone (Grundy) [MLTD

MRDL#, LDTLTM, ML] BV509 2215

Crimea (Harris) [MMMFMRMD, MMMSF#MF#S,] I124 2216

Crimond (Irvine) [SMFRSFRDTD, MMRRF#F#] J522; R104b; AF84; AL663b; AM77c; BV 511a; BY73 2217

Crimson (Doane) X Cleansing 2218

Crispinian (Ivimey) [DDDTSLLS, MDRMFSFM] BE56 2219

Croatia (Croatian carol) [DRM RMFMDRS, DRMRMF] AK110 2220

Croft (Croft) X Crofts 136th 2221

Croft (Croft) X Hanover 2222

Crofton (Crofton) [SDTLLLFM RDT, DD#D#RR] U320; AM624; AS414 2223

Croft's (Croft) X Crofts 136th 2224

Croft's 136th (Croft) [SDTDSL, SMFSMRDD, MF#] D565; F248; J238a; L158; Q580; W 39; X657; AA124; AF229; AP 14a; AZ342-F; BJ43; BV196b; BY175a 2225

-----. V [SDTDSL, SMSRRD, MF#RS] AA124 2226

Croft's 148th (Croft) X Croft's 136th 2227

Cromer (Lloyd) [SDMLFRDTD, RMSDFMR] E237; J62a; X531; BV252; BY384 2228

Crosby (Doane) X I am thine 2229

Cross and crown (Booth) [MSLTDT LM, LSDFMRM, S] Y256 2230

Cross and crown (Houseley) [SS LLDDTT, LSRRR#M, MM] V766 2231

Cross-bearer (Nachtenhöfer) [MM MRRDDT, TDRMFRD, M] M385; N105; P173; Q150 2232

Cross of Christ (Breedlove) [LDMTRTLLSM, SLTRMT] AQ68 2233

Cross of Christ, O sacred tree (Grove) [MSDSLDS, MRDTDM R, MS] AX117; AY199 2234

Cross of Christ, O sacred tree (Holsinger) [SSSSLM S, SDTRLTD, SS] AS137 2235

Cross of Jesus (Stainer) X Crucifixion 2236

Crossing the bar (Barnby) [M MMSSD, DFFLLR, RMFS] B412; C412; G368; I744; N591; S438; W588; Z574; AB413; AD464; AH537; AO 566; AP614; AR427; AV290; AW265; BB678; BF669 2237

Crossing the bar (Maker) [MR RDSS, SSFDRM, MMMS] Y129 2238

Crossing the bar (Root) X Rialto 2239

Crossing the bar (Worden) [MDRFFM, RDMSFM, MLSF] AY497 2240

Crossings (Gibbs) [DMRTSLLS, DDRMSDRS,] X661b 2241

Crowle (Green. Book of psalmody. 1724) [LMRDTDTLS#L; DT LTDR] E463; N248; W94; X 482; AL310b; AP490a 2242

Crown Him (---) X Hark! What mean those holy voices (---) 2243

Crown Him (Hughes) X Cwm Rhondda 2244

Crown Him (Monk) X Coronae 2245

Crown Him (Montani) [DMM LRDT, TDRMDMR, RM] BQ 43 2246

Crown Him (Terry) [SFMR RD, MRSSF#S, DLTS] BN75 2247

Crowned or crucified? [SMMRR DFM, MFSDDRMM,] AU447 2248

Croydon (Foss) [DSLSFMRM, FSLTDRT, M] X170b; BY 671 2249

Croyland (LaTrobe) X LaTrobe 2250

Croyland (Statham) X Thanksgiving 2251

Crucifer (Irons) [SMMTDDT, DLLFLS, SSS] D582b 2252

-----. R [SSSDLLS, SRD#RR# M, DDD] 2253
Crucifer (Mozart) X Ellesdie 2254
Crucifer (Nicholson) [SDSFSMFS LR, RMSDLS] F633 2255
Crucifer (Smart) X Bethany 2256
Crucifix (Heber) X Calcutta 2257
Crucifixion (Schumann G-B. 1539) X Old 112th 2258
Crucifixion (Stainer) [MDSSSDDT, DMLTDFMM] B152a; C152b; D201b; E54; I98; J64b; K62a; N435; R196; S155; V555; Y39; AD81; AE113; AK163; AM189; AO173; AP199a; AR171; AW111; BE102; BV86; BY227 2259
Crucifixion (Zinck. Koralbog. 1801) X Naglet til et kors paa Jorden 2260
Crucis (Garrett) [SLDDTD, TDM MR#M, SFMR] N75 2261
Crucis milites (Foster) [SMRD FLS, DSLSMRDR, R] D581a; F305; BV435; BY524b 2262
Crucis umbra (Barnby) [SDDTT LL, LLMRDT, TDR] B150; C150 2263
Crucis victoria (Foster) [DMF SMFSL, SSLFMR, RM] F306; BV319b; BY378 2264
Crudwell (Stanton) [SDRMRDFSL SM, RMF#SL] BY396b 2265
Crueger (Crueger) [SLSFMRM, MDDRSM, SLS] D323b; E45; F219; J495b; K526; W154; X 87; AL139; AN76; BN71; BO19; BV129; BY80 2266
-----. V [SLSFMRRM, MDDRSM, SL] BN71 2267
Crueger (Crueger) X Graefenberg 2268
Crueger (Crueger) X St Nicholas 2269
Crueger (Crueger) X Nun danket 2270
Crugybar (Welsh hymn mel) [DMMMMSMDR, DSLSLSM] W596; X609; AD334; BY193 2271
-----. V [DMMMMSMDR, DMSL SLS] AD334 2272
Crusader (Whitney) [SDSLTDRM, SSMRDL, LR] B85a; C85b; D507d; S271b; Y274; AC241; BD161; BF485 2273
Crusader's hymn (Silesian folk) X St Elizabeth 2274
Crux (Lewis) [DRMMRDMMR R, RMFSMD,] C163a; D 106a 2275
Crux beata (Miller) X Rockingham 2276
Crux Christi (Mann) X Watermouth 2277
Crux crudelis (Peace) [MMM MSSFF, FMMMDMRR,] D 575b 2278
Crux salutifera (Stainer) [RD TLLS#L, FMRDTDLM, M] O305 2279
Cry out with joy (Gelineau) X The Lord is King 2280
Cuddesdon (Ferguson) [SLT DFF, MDDRM, SLTDF] W178a; BV128b; BY199a 2281
-----. V [SLTDFF, MRDRM, SLTDM] BV128b 2282
Culbach (Scheffler's Heilige seelenlust) [DMSSFSM, DD TTLLS, ST] A373; D30b; E286; F73; K481; Q121; W 38b; X1; AA536; AN479; AW 528; BN192; BO117; BV417; BY327 2283
Culford (Hopkins) [MMSSDDS, LLSLFMM, MM] G500; I640; W512a; AZ205-L; BA751; BI 5 2284
-----. V [MMSSDDS, LLSLF FM, MM] BI-5 2285
Cullingworth (Moss) [MFLSDD DFMMR, MF#RST] AB207 2286
Culross (Scottish Psalter 1634) [MLDTLSLT, MLSLTD, LD] E525b; W353a; X530 2287
-----. V [MLDTLS#LT, ML S#LTD, SD] W353a 2288
Cultor dei, memento (Plainsong, M 8) [DDDTLTDL, D DDTSTSL] Eapp. 2 2289
Cumnor (Williams) [LDRMLS,

SMRDRTL, DRM] X213 2290

Cumulus (Nicholson) [DTLDTLL S#, LTDDRMFM] F622 2291

Cura dei (Barrowes) [DRMFS, LRMFSM, MDTLSF,] A248; R466 2292

Curfew (Maker) [MMMMRMFFFF MR, SSLT] Z336; AB32; AC21; AE45; AR57 2293

Cushman (Turner) [MFSLS, SLT DMR, DDTLL] G113; R183; U51; Y71; Z209; AB127; AC 100; AD471; AE95; AF152; AG85; AK456; AL602; AR146; AT89; BF305; BK18; BZ 2294

Cutler (Cutler) X All saints new 2295

Cutting (Sherwin) [MRDSLS, MRDTDR, MLF#S,] J311a; AI176; AJ298; AK372; AO517; AT458; AU367; AV262 2296

Cuttle Mills (Griffith) [MMRMFLS F, MDLFR, SDT] E366; W667; BV651a; 2297

Cuyler (Brewer) [SDMRDMSR, RLSMMDRR,] V249a 2298

Cwm Rhondda (Hughes) [SLSD DTDRMR, MDLFMR] F296b; G165; J520a; R339a; S104b; Z256; AD220; AE246; AF93; AG158a; AK80; AL441a; AM 501; AQ27; AR287; AT55; AU 425; BC56; BK77; BV555b; BY 541; BZ 2299

------. V [SLSDDTDRMR, MFSFRD] AU425 2300

Cwmafon (James) [LDRMRFMRD, MRDTMRT] R540; S496; Y92; AD56 2301

Cwmdu (Evans) [MMMMLDDT, T DL, SLF, ML] S511b; W294b 2302

Cyprus (Mason) [DDDDDRTD, R RRMDTLS,] AP265 2303

Cyprus (Mendelssohn) [DDMMSF M, MMFLDDD, RM] AB294; AO 304; BF422; BR350 2304

Cyriacus (German trad. 15th c) [DSSLSFRM, SSSSMFRD,] M352; AA169 2305

D

Da Christus geboren war (Doles) X Lichfield 2306

Da Jesus an des kreuzes (Babst. G-B. 1545) [TDTLTRDT, TDTDLLFM,] Q177; AA207 2307

Da zu dir der heiland kam (Wagner) [DSLTDRMFM, SD TTDTL] E313; X271 2308

Dabney (Maclean) [MMMSFM RD, RMFSDTLS,] V361 2309

Daily, daily (French Paroissien mel) [SSDDMDRR, F LSMFRD, S] E568; AW124; BO59 2310

-----. R [MFSMSSFR, FF MDMMR, S] 2311

Daily, daily (Hemy) X Conqueror 2312

Daily, daily, sing to Mary (Catholic) [SMFSDDTLTDS, FSFMM] BO60 2313

-----. R [LLSMRMFSFM, LTDMSF] 2314

Daily, daily sing to Mary (French Paroissien mel.) X Daily, daily 2315

Daily, daily sing to Mary (Montani) [DDDTLTLS, M MMRDRT, D] BQ76 2316

Daily, daily sing to Mary (Piel) [SSDTLSSFM, LDM RDTL] BP79 2317

Daily, sing in praise of Mary (Trier G-B.) X Sunrise 2318

Dakota hymn (Dakota Indian hymn) [LLLMFMMRD, RR TLTL, L] BZ 2319

Dalalin (Russian trad) X Easter eggs 2320

Dalarne (Swedish trad) [MLL LLTDDTLT, RMFMR] M303 2321

Dalehurst (Cottman) [MRDFM MRD, DRMFFF, RM] C166a; D108a; H253; I278; J593b; L441; R319a; S143; T24b; U370; V298; Y137; Z219; AA359; AB209; AD431; AE

97; AG87; AH486; AJ5; AL385b; AM360; AN276b; AO277; AP 183a; AR197; AS392; AW218; BA81; BE410; BF486; BR418; BX142 2322

Dalkeith (Hewlett) [SMRDDRM SFM, MMMDDT] D422a; Eap. 25; O235; W429; AB296; AL 268; AP411a; BE297; BI78; BX386 2323

Dallam (Hungarian folk song) [SLTDLS, SDLSFM, LSFM] AN92b 2324

Dallas (Cherubini) [SLSTDLSFF M, SLSTDS] V415; AJ68; BR 328 2325

Dalliba (Bradbury) [DDDDDRRM, MMMSMRRR] AO107b 2326

Damascus (---) [MMMMMRDR, MMMLSSF#S,] AP348b 2327

Dana (Berggren) X Amen, Jesus han skal raade Sardis 2328

Danbury (Gibbs) [MMSLMDD RMS, DDTDS, L] X81 2329

Danby (English trad) [SDTDSL#L S, SDTDRMFMR,] E295; W 623b; X16; AF455; AN291a; AQ90; BY331 2330

Dane (Beethoven) X Sardis 2331

Daniel (Bliss) [MMRDSDD, RM RSM, FFFF] AM660; AP773; AU322; AX563; BB497 2332

Daniel (Irish trad) [DRMFMRDD, SLTDTLSS,] E246; X376; BV 407; BY488 2333

Daniel's band (Bliss) X Daniel 2334

Dank sei Gott [in der höhe] (Gesius) X Commemoration 2335

Danket dem herrn (Bohemian Br.) X Saelir 2336

Dans cette etable (French trad) X Old French noël 2337

Dantzig (Filitz) X Capetown 2338

Dare to be a Daniel (Bliss) X Daniel 2339

Dare to be brave (Hume) [MMM FTLTD, RMFSMRDT] AH613; AT411; AU320; AV401 2340

Dare to do right (Bradbury) [MRMDMRMS, LSFMRDTD] AP772 2341

-----. R [SDTLTD, LSTLTD, DDTL] 2342

Dark and thorny (Thommen. Christen-schatz) X Cassel 2343

Dark the night (Jones, O.) [LTDMMRDDT, LTDRMRD] BG9 2344

Darkness to dawning (Nichol) X Message 2345

Darmstadt (Darmstadt G-B.) [MDLMRM, TDRDTL, LM F#S] AZ71-A 2346

Darmstadt (Fritsch) [SMRDS SL, LRRSFMRD] A14; J171; Q99; R128; X621; AA385; AB35; AF198; AN71; AQ87; AR84; AW566 2347

-----. V [SMDSSL, LRRSFM RD, SL] Q99 2348

Darmstadt (Maker) [SSSDDD, MFFS, LTDRMM] AB54; BX66 2349

Darmstadt (Meiningen G-B. 1693) X O Gott, du frommer Gott 2350

Darmstadt (Weimar G-B. 1681) X Jesu, meines lebens leben 2351

Darwall (Darwall) [DMDSMD, TLSFMR, RMDL] A600; B 264; C264; D482b; E517; F371; G171; H185; I26; J 238b; K68; L266; N89; O 130; Q46; R14; S50; V101; W135a; X701; Z260; AA457; AF23; AG110; AL112a; AM 17; AN5; AO9; AP66; AS442; AT108; AW9; AZ342-D; BA 166; BB485; BV24; BX413; BY36; BZ 2352

-----. V [DMDSMD, SLSFMM R, RMD] H185 2353

Darwall's 148th (Darwall) X Darwall (Darwall) 2354

Das alte jahre ist nun dahin (Praetorius) [SDDTDLTD, D RRMRDDT,] AA173 1355

Das herrlich hohe fest (Peter) [DMSLTD, DMDTLT, RRRM] E182b 2356

Das ist meine freude (Freylinghausen) [DSMDLTD, MRMLF# S, RSR] E97 2357
Das ist unbeschreiblich (Herrnhut ms.) X Gregor's 141st metre-A 2358
Das leiden des herrn (German trad) [LLLMFMMRDT, RRRRDT] E387; W5a; X119; AL3b 2359
Das neugeborne (Vulpius) [LLL MRDMRDT, MMF#SF#M] C494b; E67b; F395; J274a; W304; X80 b; AF235; AN429; AQ76; BI 47-D; BJ90; BV149 2360
Das neugeborne kindelein (Vulpius) X Das neugeborne 2361
Das wahre christenthum (Herrnhut ms.) X Gregor's 37th metre 2362
Das walt' Gott [Vater] (Vetter) X Vetter 2363
Dauchy (Mendelssohn) [SSF#SL TDRM, MRMFMRD] AO557 2364
Daughter of a mighty Father (---) [MFSMDLSM, MRMSFM R, M] BO81 2365
-----. R [SLRMFSM, SLRMFS M, SS] 2366
Daughter of Zion (---) [DRMMD DTDRRT, TDRMM] BB303 2367
Daughter of Zion (Mason) [MFS FMRDDRMR, RMFSF] L353 2368
-----. R [SLSDTLSLSFM, RMFS F] 2369
Daughter of Sion (Smart) X Pilgrims 2370
David (Briggs) [LTDRM, MRDT LS#S#, LTDT] X501b 2371
David (Dearle) [SDSLSFMFS, FMDRRD, D] F449; BY483 2372
David (Handel) X Thatcher 2373
David (Morley) X St Alban's 2374
David's harp (---) [MSDTDLRSM, MMMMRDT] BR56 2375
David's harp (King) [MRDTDRMF M, RMF#SSSF#S,] A295; B230; E378; J471; K346; W432; X476; AP415a; BE100; BY 466 2376
Dawn (Foster) [MSDSMDMR, DDLSSFMR,] V757 2377
Dawn (Ingham) [MRDRMR, DLS L, DRMFM] A473; X63; AD 102; AF42; AN96; AQ267; BY485b 2378
Dawn (Jewish trad) X Rosh Hashanah I 2379
Dawn (Parker) [SLTDRM, FSF MRR, RRMF,] L547 2380
Dawn (Stainer) X Laus matutina 2381
Dawn (Wesley) [MSDSLS, MRD FFMLSFM] Y257 2382
Dawning (Dadman) X Is not this the land of Beulah 2383
Dawning (Sydnor) [SMMRDFF M, MMRDRM, MS] U65 2384
Day (Abbott) [SSDMRMFM, MFSLSMDM] BB252 2385
Day by day (Carter) X Slingsby 2386
Day by day (Somervell) X Stonethwaite 2387
Day of grace (Elliott) [DRRM FLS, SMMLSF#M, TD] D356b 2388
Day of praise (Parker) X Garden City 2389
Day of praise (Steggall) [SM DLRT, DLTDFMRM, MM] D70b; W290; AP682b; BA 388; BV255b 2390
Day of rest (Elliott) [DMSLS F#SM, RDRMFLR, R] A570 b; B379; C43a; D24a; G352; I452; K441; M8; S268a; W 508b; Z222; AB234; AD243; AL188b; AO473; AP344b; BA380; BE196; BR141; BY 298a 2391
Daymer (Sheldon) [DTSLFSMR, RFMLS#L, LD] BV134 2392
Dayspring (Lloyd) [MFSMDRM D, RMF#SLT, DS] F434 2393
Dayspring (Freylinghausen) X

Gregor's 77th metre 2394
Dayspring (Freylinghausen) X Morgenglanz der ewigkeit 2395
Daystar (Miller) [SSMMRRD, DDDTTL, MMR] N615 2396
Dayton (Showalter) X God moves in a mysterious way 2397
Dayton (Wilson) [DTLSDRDRM, DFMRMDR] J330b 2398
De boodschap (Dutch trad) X Annunciation 2399
De Fleury (Edson) X Contrast 2400
De liefde voortgebracht (Oudean. Amsterdam Psalter) X Vreuchten 2401
De profundis (English trad) [LTDDRRDD, LTDRMFRM] E90 2402
De profundis (Walther) [TMTDT SLT, TDRDLSFM,] M65; O102; Q329; AA415; BY457; BZ 2403
-----. V [MLMFMDRM, MFSF RDTL,] M65 2404
-----. V [TMTDTLS#LT, TRRDT LS] AZ132-E 2405
-----. [TMTDTLSLT, TDRDTLS] BY457 2406
De turlu turlutu (French trad) X So, Brother 2407
Dear Angel, ever at my side (Bragers) [DMMFRDTD, DFSL SFMR] BP88 2408
Dear angel! ever at my side (Catholic) [SDRMRDTLS, DTD RMD, S] BO195 2409
Dear Angel! ever at my side (Crookall) [SSSMDTLS, SLTD DLFM] BO195a 2410
Dear angel, ever at my side (Day's Psalter) X St Flavian 2411
Dear Angel! ever at my side (Montani) [MMDRMFRDTD, SSM FSL] BQ112 2412
Dear crown of all the virgin choir (Piel) [MMMSFMRDFFM, MFSLR] BQ109 2413
Dear guardian of Mary (Bonitus, Brother) [SDTLSMSDRRM, DDT LR] AH141; BO128 2414
Dear little One (Walters) [MR MSSLFM, MSMDRR, FF] BO 155 2415
Dear little One! how sweet (Montani) [SFMRLSFMDTLS LF#S, S] BQ127 2416
Dear Lord, I come (Kolb) [DM FMRD, MSLSMR, RRRM] AY227 2417
Dear love (Smallman) [SMRDST LSDF, LSLTDD] BY594b 2418
Dear Maker of the starry skies (Piae cantiones, 1582) X Ein kind gebor'n 2419
Dear St Joseph, pure (Sisters of Notre Dame) [MFSSMDRR, FLSDMRD, M] BO132 2420
-----. R [RMFFSFMR, MFSL SMR, M] 2421
Dear Saviour, when I think of thee (Kolb) [SLSFSMFMR, STLSLFS] AY248 2422
Dear to the heart (Kirkpatrick) [MR#MFMR#MD, DTDRDLS, M] BC26 2423
-----. R [DTLDTLTM, DDDRD RM, M] 2424
Dearest children God is near you (Macfarland) [SMDSMRD TL, SMDMMRR,] BC170 2425
Dearhurst (Langran) X Deerhurst 2426
Dearmer (Hohenfurth ms.) X Quem pastores 2427
Debenham (Redhead) X St Nicholas 2428
Decision (Day) [TMRTRDTLT DDRDRM, M] AC232 2429
Decius (Plainsong, 16th c) X To God on high 2430
Deck the halls (Welsh trad) X Nos galan 2431
Deck thyself (Crueger) X Schmuecke dich 2432
Declare, O heavens (Laubenstein) [SDMLRSFM, RMF# SLTLS] BL76 2433
Decree (English trad) [MLS# LTDMMDT, DLS#LTD] X484; BG65a 2434

-----. V [MLS#LTDMMDL, MLS#LTD] BG65a 2435

Dedham (Gardiner) [DRRMSFMR, RMRDTLS, R] B183b; D189b; H388; J428a; K135; L157; V34; AA94; AN39; AO210; AR501; AW209; AY432; BE105; BR88; BX498 2436

Dedicatio anni (Coules) [DRM SLLS, DMSMR, DMLS] BR501 2437

Dedication (Bentley) [SMRDSSL DLS, DTDRMF] AO458 2438

Dedication (Calkin) X Golden corn 2439

Dedication (Flittner) X Gregor's 124th metre 2440

Dedication (Foster) [DRMSSFMF, FMRRM, DMS] B448 2441

Dedication (Franz) [MRDFMRDM R, SFMRRFM] AR307 2442

Dedication (Gilding) X St Edmund 2443

Dedication (Macfarren) [SMFSL LL, TLSFM, FLRD] C448; F72b; BV657; BY713 2444

Dedication (Sea) X I belong to Jesus 2445

Deed (Mason) [MRDTLSDRMR, MRDFMR] Y181 2446

Deed (Whitmer) [MRDLTDRMF R, MRDLTD] AC187 2447

Deep and glorious (Crueger) X St Nicholas 2448

Deep harmony (Parker) [MDMF MMMM, MLLSMMRR,] BY281a 2449

Deep river (Negro spiritual) [MMRDRL, DDDDLSMR, MM] AR488 2450

Deeper life (Longacre) [MMFSSLT DRDT, TDLSL] G361 2451

Deeper yet (Kirkpatrick) [SSSDD D, RRRDRM, SSSD] BB275 2452

-----. R [MRDDTL, SSSDMR, MRDD] 2453

Deerhurst (Langran) [MSMDTD RM, FMRSTLS, M] D292a; E ap. 32; F526; J143; K41; M380; O121; W2a; AA358; AL177; BB 237; BE370; BY370 2454

Defend me, O God (Gelineau) [MLSM, MRM, MTLT, TSM.] BSp. 20 2455

Deganwy (Williams) [SMRST LDS, DTDRMMR, R] W28; BY328a 2456

Deilig er Jorden (Silesian mel) X St Elizabeth 2457

Deirdre (Irish trad) [DLDSL RDD, DDFMRDM] A268b; B525b; C525b; E212b; BN61; BY433b 2458

Deirdre (Irish trad) X St Patrick (St Patrick) 2459

Delay not (Croft) X Hanover 2460

Delhi (Rimbault) [SMDLFM RD, MRLSDTLS,] W493a; AC248; BY44a 2461

Delight (French) [MFSLSFMF SLTDFMRD,] M157 2462

Deliverance (Barnby) X St Sylvester 2463

Deliverance (Ogden) [SSDDDD RDTT, TDTLLL] AT198 2464

-----. R [SSDMRDDTT, TD RFMRR] 2465

Deliverance will come (Mathias) [MRDDDDDD, DRRRR M, RM] AY132 2466

Deliverer (---) [MMMMRMSM, RRSSFRM, M] AR104; AX 413; AY107; BB618 2467

Delphine (Danks) [DMRDMRD DTLS, SLLLS] T129; AJ188 2468

Dem heiligen blute des herrn zu gefallen (Schlicht) X Gregor's 243rd metre 2469

Demmin (Schop) [DRMDFMR, RRMSSF#S, SM] N329 2470

Den blomstertid nu kommer (Swedish Koralbok, 1697) X Blomstertid 2471

Den des vaters sinn geboren (Freylinghausen) [DRMFSS MD, LSFMRRD, M] E218 2472

Den die Engel droben (Gregor) X Gregor's 6th metre 2473

Den Herre Krist i dødens baand (Latin, 12th c) X Christ lag

in todesbanden 2474
Den signede dag (Weyse) X Weyse 2475
Den store hvide flok (Lindeman) [SDDTLSSM, MFFSRMSR,] O492a 2476
Den store, hvite flokke (Norwegian trad) X Behold a host 2477
Den store mester kommer (Hoffman) X Fulfillment 2478
Denbigh (Welsh hymn mel) [LLTDTL, TDRMRM, MRDT] E439; W415b; X580; AM376 2479
Denby (Dale) [SLSDRM, MFMRLT, SLS] B395; J580; M273; N490; O233; Q259; AB96; AL151; BD157; BF580 2480
Denfield (Gläzer) X Azmon 2481
Denham (Damon's Psalter, 1579) X Southwell 2482
Denmark (---) [MFSMM, RDLDD, TLSDRM] M278; BC145 2483
Dennis (Naegeli) [MMDMRTRD, DDLDDSDT,] A495b; D502; G69; H124; I100; J543; L63; M21; N294; P58; R105; S279; T41; U373; V608; Y384; Z399; AB208; AD239; AE67; AF76; AG50; AH226; AI276; AJ60; AL376; AM285b; AN563; AO103; AP571; AR505; AS67; AT366; AU239; AV77; AW41; AX489; AY399; BB379; BC67; BE402; BF395; BK174; BR123; BX312b; BY355a; BZ 2484
Dennis (Thalben-Ball) [MDRMSLS MRDM, MFSTL] BE22 2485
Denny (Mason) [MFSSSLTDDD, LRDTLS,] I126; L423 2486
Dent Dale (English trad) [DDDD TDR, DRMMFMRDS,] E23; X88 2487
Denver (Houseley) [MMMSMM RR, RDDFFM, MM] U22; Z175; AR96 2488
Deo gracias (English trad) X Agincourt 2489
Deo gratias (Crueger) X Nun danket 2490
Deo gratias (Ponsonby) [DMMFM RSSL, SFMFSMR] U333; AC226; AL592 2491
DePauw (McCutchan) [SMRDD MSD, DTLSMMDS,] G82; S423a; AK407 2492
Dependence (Lowry) X Need 2493
Depth of mercy (Beethoven) [MDRMFLR, RMFSSF#S, MR] AY216 2494
Der am kreuz (Koenig) [LMLTDTLS#M, TDRDTTL,] Q144; AA194 2495
Der Freyschuetz (Weber) X Jewett 2496
Der Heilige Geist herniederkam (Schein) [LLLMMFFM, DRMFMRRD,] AA239 2497
Der lieben Sonne licht und pracht (Freylinghausen. Geistriches G-B. 1704) X Se solens skjøune lys og pragt 2498
Der mange skal komme (Then Swenska Psalmboken 1695) X Stockholm 2499
Der Sabbath ist um's menschen will'n (German trad) X Gregor's 159th metre 2500
Der tag bricht an (Vulpius) [LMMFMRLDTL, LDLMF#S] E101; X563; BI66 2501
Der tag der ist [so freuden reich] (Hohenfurth ms. 1410) X Dies est laetitiae 2502
Der tag mit seinem lichte (Ebeling) X Shining day 2503
Derbe (Sacred harmony. 1780) [DRMDSFM, RMFRLSFM, S] AL573; BY712a 2504
Derry (Dykes) [MMRDLSDR, RRMFMRD#D#] F323 2505
Derwent (Adcock) [SMLSFM, SDFMRD, MRSF#] O405 2506
Descend, O sabbath princess (Nowakowsky) [SSMRDDMS TLMS, SLFM] BH107 2507
Desire (Geistliche volkslied, 1850) [LTDDRDTT, DTLTLS#LL] M399; N117; Q153;

AA209; AM192; AO279 2508

Desire (Minor: Geistliche volkslied, 1850) X Cassel (Major) 2509

Desire (Smart) [DDFMRS, DRR M, MMF#SLT,] D654a 2510

Desire (Woodbury) [SDRMDRDTD, RMMSMRRR] L575a; AA460 2511

Desiring to love (Handel) [DM FSFMRFM, DMFSLTD] AZ 92-E 2512

Despair not, O heart (Luther. Christlich G-B. 1542) X Jam moesta 2513

Despise not, Lord (Miller) X Sweet Sabbath 2514

Dessau (Ahle) X Liebster Jesu 2515

Dessler (Bach) [DMFSMLSLF M, DTLF#SL] X703 2516

Destiny (French trad) [DDDDDR RMR, DFFMMMD] Y125 2517

Det kimer nu til julefest (Balle) X Emmanuel 2518

Detroit (Fishwick) [DRMDSFM RM, MFSMTTD] M616 2519

Detroit (Hastings) [MMFMRM, S SLSF#S, SSSL] L251; BR96 2520

Detroit (Suppl. to Kentucky harmony, 1820) X Detroy 2521

Detroy (Suppl. to Ky. Harmony, 1820) [LDRMDRDLS#L, LDR MS#L,] AR106; BZ 2522

-----. V [LDRMDRDLSL, LDRM SL,] BZ 2523

Detroy (Suppl. to Kentucky Harmony, 1820) X Morning song (Wyeth Repository, 1813) 2524

Deus creator omnium (Ambrosian) [RFMSSSFM, RMFSRMRD,] BJ91 2525

Deus creator omnium (Sarum Antiphonal. M 4) [FMSLSFS LSFMM, RRLL] E49; X44a 2526

-----. V [FMSLSFSLSFMM, RLLL] X44a 2526a

Deus fortis (Norwegian mel) [DR DSLTDMRD, DRDSLT] J357; P205 2527

Deus tuorum militum (Grenoble Antiphoner, 1753) [DMSDS FMRD, DMDLTDS] A344; E181b; F129b; J494a; R83; Sap. 29; W356; X633; AD 448; AE465; AF150; AH568; AK438; AL8a; AN149; AP 152a; AQ305; AR585; BN52; BO269; BV35; BY238; BZ 2528

Deus, tuorum militum (Plainsong, M 8) X Exultet caelum laudibus 2529

Deus vitae (Thurman) [SSMF SDDTT, LSLFSM, S] U276 2530

Deus vobiscum (Tomer) X God be with you 2531

Deva (Hopkins) [MRMFSS, LDTLS, SLSFM] D35a; G 445; I652; AP697b 2532

Deventer (Tours) [SSDTLSFM, SDLRSLTL] I708; V613; AB276; AC257 2533

Devereaux (Devereaux) X Boardman 2534

Devizes (Tucker) [DDRMFM RDTD, RMSFRM] H83; L 447; N483 2535

Devonshire (English trad: Devonshire) [DMMMMMRD, RMSSFMR, R] E294; W270; X459a 2536

Devonshire (Lampe) X Kent 2537

Devotion (Doane) X More love to thee 2538

Devotion (Gower) [SSSF#FM, MMDRRM, SSLS] AM536 2539

Devotion (Hall) [SLDLSLDD, SDRMDRLD,] AQ183 2540

Devotion (Johnson) [SMRDRD TD, MRDTDTLS,] B34; C 34; D643b; L32; N619 2541

Devotion (Meiningen G-B. 1693) X Munich 2542

Dexter Street (Douglas) [SM RDMSLSFM, LLSLT] A100 2543

Diadem (Ellor) [SDRMFSDRD

TD, TLSSS] G164c; AM218c; AO208b; AT134; AU255; AW5; BZ 2544

-----. R [SFMRFMRDMRDTRD D, F] 2545

Diadema (Barnby) [MSDTLSMDRRM, FFMLS] I486; T394; V360; BX471 2546

Diademata (Barnby) [DTLTTL, S DTDRSM, MMM] K123; M452 2547

Diademata (Elvey) [DDDMML, LSDFMR, RMSL] A352; B190; C190; D374a; F224b; G170; H198; I179; J431; K134a; L153; N341; P30; Q341; R213; S190; T91; U115; V195; W136; Y171; Z250; AA104; AB88; AC136; AD170; AE132; AF199; AG100; AH328; AJ134; AK176; AL115; AM216; AN248; AO198; AP 227; AR105; AS157; AT152; AU 18; AV141; AW118; AZ595-C; BA228; BB162; BD118; BE312; BF325; BK114; BL58; BV209; BX307; BY182; BZ 2548

Dian (Shaw) [MFSLRMF, FSLS MDR, MM] E396 2549

Diana (English trad) [DRMDFMR MFM, SFMR] A585b 2550

Dibden (Jackson) [DMMLSFMF, MS#LRDT, S#S#] E433; X 254 2551

Dich bit ich, trautes Jesulein (Helder) [DMDSRFMR, RMD LSLTD,] AA188 2552

Dich, Jesu, loben vir (Freylinghausen) X Gregor's 341st metre 2553

Dickinson (Austrian trad) X The Shepherd 2554

Dickson (Warner) [SSLTDDRM, MSRMRTDT,] AZ606-C 2555

Did you think to pray (Perkins) [MMFMRDSD, RRFMR, RRR] AU335; AX361; BC31 2556

-----. R [SSLSF#SDS, MSLSFM R, M] 2557

Die ganze welt (Cologne G-B) X Hilariter 2558

Die Gottes seraphin (Eberhard) X Gregor's 249th metre 2559

Die güldne sonne (Ebeling) X Philippi 2560

Die helle sonne (Staden) [DDDLFMRD, SLDSFM, MM] J6; K9; AW542 2561

Die helle sonn' leucht't (Vulpius) [DMFSDTLS, SSF#SL DTD,] Q547; AA266 2562

Die König (Cornelius) X The Kings 2563

Die nacht ist kommen (Nigidius) [DRMFMRRD#RMR, FFFRS] Q556; X48a 2564

Die sach' ist dein (Haydn, J. M.) X Salzburg II 2565

Die seele Christi heil'ge mich (Geistliche gesang. Wittenburg, 1544) X Rhau[w] 2566

Die wanderschaft in dieser zeit (Herrnhut ms.) X Gregor's 166th metre 2567

Dies dominica (Dykes) [MSFM RDD, DTLFLS, MSF] D24c; F401; K186; V554; BA500; BV391 2568

Dies est laetitiae (Hohenfurth ms. 1410) [DDRMFRD, RRLT DD, DDRM] A29a; C485; M 459; O185; P165; Q78; X11; AZ215-a; BG158; BQ294 2569

-----. V [DDRMFRD, RDLTD RD, DD] Q78 2570

-----. V [DDDRMFRD, MRR LTDRD] M459 2571

-----. V [DDRSFMRD, RRLT DRD, D] AZ215-A 2572

-----. V [DDRMFRD, RRLTD TD, DD] X11 2573

-----. V [DDRMFSFM, DDTD LS, DD] BQ294 2574

Dies irae (Dykes) [DTLTDRM L, FFMLRDTD#,] B65a; C65; D36; I747; K515 2575

Dies irae (Latin mel. ca 1200) [DRMDFMRD, RRMRDTLS,] Q607; AA555 2576

Dies irae (Lindeman) [LLD LTDRMM, DRMRMF#S] O601 2577

Dies irae (Parry) X Merthyr

tydvil 2578

Dies irae (Plainsong sequence, M 2-1) [FMFRMDRR, FFSFM RDM] A468; B65b; E351; F466; BMp.162; BN243; BQ270d 2579

-----. V [DTDLTSLL, DDRDTL ST] BN243 2580

Dies irae I (Wolle) [LSFMD LSFMD, LTDRMM] AZ608-A; BA929 2581

Dies irae II (Wolle) [DRMSFM RMM, MFMDTLS] AZ608-A 2582

Dies ist der tag (Sohren) [DD SDMRRD, RRTDTLS,] E138 2583

Dies sind die heil'gen (German, ca 1200) [SSSSSSLTD, DRR DSLT] Q287; AA391] 2584

Dieses ist der tag dei wonne (Dretzel. Musicalische harmonie. 1731) [DSLFRSMD, RRMLSF#S, D] N173 2585

Dig, Jesus, min dyraste Jesus (Stolpe) [MSFFMRRMF#F# LS, SDMM] N78 2586

Dijon (Fliedner. Liederbuch, 1842) [DDDDTDMR, RRRRDR M, M] G452; K472; Q653; S449a; AK459; AL622b; AO5; AP808; AW254 2587

-----. V [DDDDTDR, RRRRDR M, MM] K472 2588

Diligence (Belden) [SDDDMSMS, LSMDTDMR,] BB183 2589

-----. R [SDDDSLLS, SDDDSMDR] 2590

Diligence (Mason) [SMFSSLS, DD DDRM, SMF] D583a; G293; H 376; I422; L540; M647; R297; W357; AH414; AK477; AL390; AM728; AO507; AP595; AS334; AT424; AU243; AV272; AW221; AX189; BA562; BB446 2591

Dim mine eyes with many teardrops (Jewish trad) X Bemotzoay 2592

Diman (Sweetser) [SDMSMRLTS D, MFLSMR] Sap. 15; Y53 2593

Dinard (Chepmell) [SMMMMSSS, RDDSFMR, S] D559b 2594

Dinas Bethlehem (Hughes) [MLTDRMMR, LDDTLSL, M] BY105b 2595

Dinbych (Parry) [LMMMRDT, TDRMRSM, ML] X479; BV 522 2596

Dir, dir, Jehova, will ich singen (Wittwe. Hamburger Musikalisches handbuch. 1690) X Crasselius 2597

Dirge (Handel) [MMMMMMRM FMR, FFSLF] I586 2598

Disciple (Mozart) X Ellesdie 2599

Disciples (Lynes) [DMSSLSS FM, MRMFLR, S] BX497b 2600

Disconsolate (Webbe) X Consolation 2601

Dismiss us with thy blessing (Bourgeois) X Old 100th 2602

Dismissal (Sicilian mel) X Sicilian mariners 2603

Dismissal (Viner) [DTLSMLD LSM, MRDLR] A489b; E523; L204b; N353; S104a; W678; X333b; AI296; AL434; AM 354; AP352; AW160; BA378; BY762 2604

-----. V [DTLSMLDSM, MR DLRDT] S104a 2605

Dismissal (Whelpton) [SSSLLS SS, SDTLLLRD] AE469; AH p. 11; AR680; AV423 2606

Distress (Southern harmony. 1835) [LDRMRDLSL, RMSLL SM] AQ64 2607

Diva servatrix (Huet) [MMFM DRDRMRD, MMSF] A167; E208b; F519; W280; X262b; Y44; AF59; AI150; BY666 2608

Dives and Lazarus (English trad) [DDSSFMRRD, SSMSSL S,] BG57a 2609

Dives and Lazarus (English trad) X Eardisley 2610

Divine compassion (---) X Sweet the moments 2611

Divinum mysterium (Piae cantiones: Plainsong, M 5, 13th c) [DRMFMRMRD, MF

SLSMFS,] A20; B74; C74a; D 52a; E613; F58; J17; K20a; Q 98; R7; W60; X387; AF111; AK13; AL52; AN172; AP166; AQ290; AR116; BL5; BV109; BY85a; BZ 2612

-----. V [DDRMFMRD, DMSL SMR, D] BL5 2613

Dix (Kocher) [DTDRDFFM, LTD LSSS, D] A52; B94; C94; D65; E39; F79; G18; H148; I28; J52; K38; M6; N50; O219; Q127; R2; S71b; T204; U16; V113; W63; X83; Y357; Z167; AA 183; AB120; AC46; AD94; AE14; AF66; AG59; AH206; AI46; AJ 293; AK12; AL15a; AM154; AN32; AO119; AP58; AQ12; AR92; AS111; AT14; AU246; AV88; AW51; AX634; AZ581-H; BA181; BB22; BD40; BE35; BF257; BK126; BL78; BR156; BV126; BX13; BY90; BZ 2614

Djupt sjun ker aret i sin gang (Beethoven) X Emmanuel 2615

Do what is right (Kaillmark) [MRDMRDRDMD, DTLSDM] BC27 2616

----. R [SSSLSSSSSLS, SDM SM] 2617

Do you love the world (Hunter) [DRMMMDMSSM, DRMMSF] AX265 2618

-----. R [SSLLFLLSSM, SSFFF M] 2619

Doane (Calkin) X Waltham 2620

Doane I (Doane) [DRMRDLSD, DRRRMR, DD] W679b 2621

Doane II (Doane) [DRMR#MFS, SSDTLS, SSS] Z332; AE238; AP496; AR481; AS42; AT329; AU156; AX352; AY430; BB 324 2622

-----. R [MSSSSMSDTLS, SSLDL] 2623

Dr. Steggall's Tune 172 (Stephens) [MSDMRMF, LSMDRM, MSD] AZ591-E 2624

Doers (Costa) X Costa 2625

Does Jesus care (Hall) [SMRDL LSFM, MRD#RSFM,] AX528; AY464 2626

-----. R [DTFTRDMS, MRTL MF#S, T] 2627

Does the journey seem long? (Pyper) [MFSF#SM, DRMR# MD, DRMR] BC245 2628

Dolberrow (Stanton) [DSMRDT DLS, DRMRDTL,] F616 2629

Dolce domum (Ambrose) X Ambrose 2630

Dole (Rees) [MRDTDL, DTM MR#M, MFMR] W190b 2631

Doles (Doles. Choral-buch) [SMFSDLSFM, MFMRDFM] AA400 2632

Dolgelly (Welsh hymn mel) [LMRDTL, MSF#MR#M, MMR M] E349; J268b; X263; AL 226b; BX484b 2633

Dolomite chant (Austrian trad) [MMMFMR, FFFSFM, MMMF] G323; R382; S501; AD277; AP618; BK96 2634

Dolut (Meyer) [DTLSDTLS, T DRMRDRT,] Y339; AC164 2635

Dolwyddelan (German, 1693) [MMLSFM, SRFMRD, MMLS] BY649 2636

Domenica (Oakeley) X Dominica 2637

Domine, clamave (Knecht) [LT MRDTLS#L, TDDRRM, M] Q593; AA542 2638

Domine, nobiscum (Barnby) [MMLSMRDR, MDTLTTS, M] BR506 2639

Dominic, Our Lady's champion (Goss) X Lauda anima 2640

Dominica (Oakeley) [SSSDRM, MRMFRT, SLTD] C45b; D28b; F42; G397; K442; V496; W 267a; AD35; AL189b; AP343b; BE92; BV68; BX100 2641

Dominus misericordiae (Stainer) [MMMMMMMMSSM, MMMMM] D630b 2642

Dominus regit (Dykes) X Dominus regit me 2643

Dominus regit me (Dykes) [MSFMMRRD, SSLTDMR,] A345b; B326; C326a; D412a;

F197; G353; I136; J530a; K 345; L490; M189; O420; R106 a; S99; T404; U80; V334; W 438a; X654b; Y35; Z169; AB 62; AC50; AD252; AE69; AF 79; AG51a; AH219; AK304; AL280b; AM141; AN87b; AO324; AP146a; AR600; AS429; AT280; AV224; AZ15-C; BA295; BB86; BD59; BE330; BF243; BR411; BV546b; BX120; BY72a; BZ 2644

Dominus sanctus (Pierre) [DS LTD, MMFRD, SSMF#S, M] AJ 432 2645

Dominus vobiscum (Somervell) [DDRMSFMRRM, DDTDLS] F489 2646

Domus Domini (Jordan) [SMD LTD, TLLLRT, SDDR] D484a 2647

Dona (Goss) [SDMSFMRD, TL DTLS, DL] D25b; W200 2648

Dona nobis pacem (---) [DSMRS FMRDDT, LSFMS] BK34 2649

Dona nobis pacem (Mozart) [MM MMSFMFMFLFMR, MM] AP 807 2650

Donald (Bergquist) [MDDRMSMR, DRMSMRR, M] N656 2651

Doncaster (Wesley) [SDMFLS, SLSTDR, SSDT] A293; D181a; F310; J3; K4; M335; N72; O 469; W490; AA504; AZ582-I; BA 557; BV525; BY530b 2652

Donne secours (Genevan Psalter, 1551) [MDRMSMDRDTL, MM RML] E564; F17a; R285; S 386; W360; X324; AD210; AF 334; AL91; AN230; AP157a; AQ 72; BJ74; BY84 2653

Donora (Doane) X Jesus, thy name I love 2654

Don't forget the Sabbath (Bradbury) [DDTLSM, MRMFLLS, SDD] BB653 2655

-----. R [MMRRDDLL, SMRM FLS, M] 2656

Don't forget to pray (Perkins) X Did you think to pray 2657

Don't let your light burn low (Williams) [SSSSSLTD, LSD RDRM, S] AX436 2658

-----. R [DMMMDRD, DDD RDLS, SS] 2659

Don't turn Him away (Lillenas) [MMMFMRDS, LDDRDLS, T] AU433 2660

-----. R [MRDRMD, MRDRM D, LLLR] 2661

Donum Dei (True) [DMMR#MF M, RSDDTL, LSS] BB149 2662

Donum Dei (Vincent) [MRRR MFFMRM, MMLSF#M] D228a 2663

Door keeper (Shaw) [DRMM MRSMD, DRMRDL, M] X196 2664

Dorian mode (Latin, 18th c) X Christ lag in todes banden 2665

Dorking (English trad) [SDSD SDRMFS, MFSLSF] X205; AN157; AW72; BY681 2666

-----. V [SDSDRMFS, MFS LSFMR] AN157 2667

Dorothea (Johnson) [MFSD MRDS, LDSDTLS, T] N318 2668

Dorothy (Pratt) [SSSLTDRM, MRMFSM, DL] AH321; BF 330 2669

Dorothy (Sampaix) [MMRRD TLS, SSSRSS, MM] H102 2670

Dorrnance (Woodbury) [MM MDRRMM, SLSMDMR, M] G143; H32; L133; T193; U379; V556; Z468; AD512; AE117; AH507; AJ281; AO 168; AR362; AT538; AV112; AW441; AX582; BA701; BF 606; BR34 2671

Dort (Mason) [DMDSLS, STS RMR, DTLS,] H530; I161; K217; L342; N211; S413; AC283; AD384; AE135; AH 305; AI369; AO582; AR523; AS371; AW348; BA871; BB 512; BZ 2672

Doudney (Bonner) [MDSTLSD RFM, MTRDMM] H486 2673

Dove (Bradbury) X Lottie 2674
Dover (Williams. Psalmody, ca 1700) X Durham 2675
Doversdale (Stanley) [SDFMRD SSLTD, DDDTL] W639; AL391 2676
Down Ampney (Williams) [DRM SLS, SLSDTLS, S] A376; E152; J123; W191; X177; AF239; BL 34; BV214; BY224 2677
Down by the river's verdant side (---) [MFSSSMFSSS, MMMMRM] BC55 2678
Down in yon forest (English trad) [LTLSLTDTLT, MLTLSL] BG 61 2679
Downing (Lloyd) [SDDRMRD, DRRDTLS, SL] BY574b 2680
Downs (Mason) [DMSLSSFM, S LDSF#S, DT] L425; R422; T66; V339; AI366; AJ101; AM 422; AR545; AS415; AV55; BA 138; BB233 2681
Downshire Hill (Shaw) [SDDDTD RMMF, MLSDRF] X328a; AD 365 2682
Doxford (Terry) [DMFSFMR, DR MFMFSLS,] BY364 2683
Doxology (Bourgeois) X Old 100th 2684
Dransfield (Thalben-Ball) [MR MLSDRM, MSDTSLDT] BE26 2685
Draw me nearer (Doane) X I am thine 2686
Draw near (McKinney) [SDMFS, DTDLSS, SLLDS] AU304 2687
Draw nigh (Buck) [DRMFRSLSD FFM, F#S#TL] E307; BE255 2688
Draw us to thee (Norwegian) [MMRMLLSM, SFMRDRM, L] P215 2689
Dreamers (Daniels) [LMMMFRM, SLMDTM, LMM] Y327; AC91; AD128 2690
Dresden (Dresden G-B. 1632) [DDSSFRM, RRMSLS, SLS] M326; Q97; AA153 2691
Dresden (Dresden, 1694) X So giebst du 2692
Dresden (Redhead) X Redhead No. 46 2693
Dresden (Schmidlin) X Swiss tune 2694
Dresden (Schulz) X Claudius 2695
Drese (Drese) X Rochelle 2696
Dretzel I (Dretzel, abr. by Monk) [DSSFMRDD, DTLTL LS, D] E281; F25; O463; BY479b 2697
Dretzel II (Dretzel) [DMDRSF MRD, RRRMSSF#] M494; Q243; AA62 2698
Drink to me only with thine eyes (Melish) X I heard the voice of Jesus say 2699
Drumcondra (Wilson) [DRMFS MRMD, MFSLL#L#L] X601 2700
Du bist ja, Jesu, meine freude (Grimm. Choral buch) X Old 466th (alt) 2701
Du ewiger abgrund der seligen liebe (Freylinghausen) X Gregor's 221st metre 2702
Du fort de ma detresse (Bourgeois) (MLTDTLS, DT LDRM, RMF#] O100; AI 432 2703
-----. V [LRMFMRD, FRM FSL, LS#L] AI432 2704
Du friedensfürst, Herr Jesu Christ (Gesius) [MDRMSFM, SFMRRM, MDR] G52; AN 124a; BZ 2705
Du lifvets bröd (Sohren) X Elbing 2706
Du meine seele singe (Ebeling) [DMSDMRR, TDSSFM, DMS] J176b; AF189 2707
Du meiner seelen' (Hungarian chorale mel 16th c) [MMSF RMDR, SSSDTLLS,] AK276; AN16; AQ38; AW98 2708
Du, O schönes weltgebaeude (Hintze) X Salzburg 2709
Du, O schönes weltegebaudes (Crueger) [LMLLTSF#M, DMRDTTL, L] O42; AZ 168-C 2710
Du vaere lovet, Jesus Krist

(Trad., ca 1400) X Redeemer 2711

Duane Street (Coles) [SDMMDRF F, RMDTDRSS,] G199; H251; I306; AM264; AW468; AX156; AY62; BB371 2712

Düben (Düben) X Jesu 2713

Dublin (---) [LLSDTLS# L, DM RDTD, DM] AY178 2714

Dublin (Howard) X Smith 2715

Dublin (Lutkin) [DDTTLLS, SL LSSFFM, D] AC243 2716

Dublin (A collection of hymns... Dublin, 1749) X Irish 2717

Duke Street (Hatton) [DMFSLTDT LS, SSSLS] A148; B32; C187; D132; E167; F268; G17; H22; I5; J307; K136b; L79; M106; N368; O28; P24; Q200; R5; S377; T286; U392; V363; W 517b; X298; Y116; Z152; AA 229; AB373; AC278; AD6; AE342; AF202; AG267; AH461; AI167; AJ397; AK350; AL249a; AM3a; AN14; AO53; AP89; AQ 43; AR22; AS9; AT19; AU150; AV30; AW341; AY426; AZ22-Q; BA34; BB1; BC52; BD34; BE325; BF527; BK120; BL59; BR46; BV577b; BX24; BY184b; BZ 2718

Dulce (Barnby) [MRMFRRD, SF MF#SF#M, LS] V217 2719

Dulce carmen (Essay on the church plain chant) [DRMFSFMR, D DDFMRD, L] A54; B110; C110; D73a; E63; F82b; G319; J58; K57; M379; N254; O295; R343; S304; T361; V513; W563; X 199; Z259; AD223; AE22; AF 344; AK3; AL515b; AN323; AO 111; AP341; AY431; AZ167-G; BA123; BB87; BE90; BF213; BQ52; BR55; BV124; BX381; BY494a; BZ 2720

Dulce domum (Ambrose) X Ambrose 2721

Dulce nomen (Tours) X Gouda 2722

Dulcetta (Beethoven) [MRDDFM MR, RRMFLDTM] I88b 2723

Dulcimer (Lewis) X Beloved 2724

Dulcina (English trad) [MFSS FMRD, LTDDTLS, M] W244 2725

Dulcis Jesu memoria (Andernach, 1608) X Jesu dulcis memoria 2726

Dulcis memoria (Dykes) X Faith 2727

Dulwich (McWilliam) [LTDR MT, RMF#SLM, SF#RT,] BV507 2728

Dummerston (Herron) [SS MDSMSLFRM, SDDMR] C220 2729

Dumpton Gap (Grundy) [MLDT LSFMFS, DRMFSL] BV335 2730

Dunaha (Irish trad) [MMMSS RMFRM, RDDDDT] W438a 2732

Dunbar (Dunbar) X A few more years 2733

Dunbar (Dunbar) X I'll live for Him 2734

Dunblane Cathedral (Barnes) [DTLSSSDTLS, MMMMLS] W373; AC8; AD369; AL251 2735

Dundee (Scottish Psalter, 1615) [DMFSDRMF, MRDDTD, SD] A397; B269; C269; D417; E43; F80; G68; H52; I96; J181; K502; L97; M49; N 242; O64; P19; Q49; R112; S98; T216a; U11; V91; W 227; X557; Y372; Z162; AA13; AB102; AD88; AE58; AF85; AG45; AH225; AI414; AJ247b; AK75; AL176; AM7; AN80; AO99; AP108; AQ34; AR500; AS441; AT398; AW 60; AY49; AZ14-P; BA83; BB84; BD193; BF225; BI 36; BJ10; BK71; BR155; BV75b; BX70; BY53; BZ 2736

Dundee (Damon's Booke of musicke, 1591) X Windsor (Tye) 2737

Dunelm (Vincent) [MFLSDM RD, FFMLLSDT] BY540 2738

Dunfermline (Scottish Psalter)

B431; E64; F209; R95; W295; X517; AF395; AL40; AM317; AN203; AP61a; AW575; BB 509; BV304; BX383; BY501; BZ 2739

Dunn Aluinn (Irish trad) [MLL TDL, TTLSL, MMMDR] E356; W525a; X115b 2740

Dunstan (Barnby) X Just as I am 2741

Dunstan (English trad) [MLLD RMRDTL, SSMRMS] E638d; X393b 2742

Durch Adam's fall (German, 1525) [MMRTRDTL, LDRMSF#M, M] O296 2743

Durch Adam's fall ist ganz verderbt (German mel) X Gregor's 212th metre 2744

Durham (Dykes) X St Agnes 2745

Durham (Ravenscroft's Psalter) [DSMLSMDR, FMSLLS, S] A297; W274a; X525; AL203a; AP107b; AW279 2746

Durham (Williams. Psalmody, ca 1770) [SMFSTD, DTDTLS, MFSL] J564b; K141; L123; M82; Q241; W376; AA270; BR 329; BY428 2747

During (Bradbury) [SSSSSSSSM, DLLDLS, D] L539a 2748

Durrow (Irish trad) [MLTDTLS M, RTLTDRM, M] R93; W454; AF248 2749

Dusseldorf (Havergal) [SDRMFS DT, RSLTDLLS,] V94 2750

Dusseldorf (Mendelssohn) [SMRT DLSM, SDTRDLS, S] BY210b 2751

Dusseldorf (Neander) X Neander 2752

Dutch carol (Dutch carol, 1599) [LDRMSMRD, MSMDRDTL,] BG73 2753

Duties of today (Jewish trad) [SSFMFSD, DTLTD, SSFM] BH258 2754

Dwell in me (Berky) [MFSLSDD T, TDRTLTD, D] AI124; AK 464; AO650 2755

-----. R [DDDDTLSS, SSSSSSS, M] 2756

-----. R [MSLLSFMM, MMR FMRM] 2757

Dwelling place (Mozart) X Cana 2758

Dwight (---) [MMMFFM, MDM SSS, SFMR] L574 2759

Dyb af kjaerlighed (Hartmann) [DDDTLS, MMMRDT, RLLS,] K218a 2760

Dykes (Dykes) X Blairgowrie 2761

Dykes (Dykes) X Mary Magdalene 2762

Dykes (Dykes) X Nicaea 2763

Dykes (Dykes) X St Oswald I 2764

Dymchurch (Shaw) [DSLSMRDD RDLSF, MFS] X93b 2765

E

Each cooing dove (Palmer) X Memories of Galilee 2766

Eagley (Walch) [SSLTDRMMR D, LLDFLS,] C513b; I406; J440b; M591; T108a; AC189; AJ157; AL243; AM232; AP62; AS240; BA100; BF440 2767

-----. V [SLTDRMMRD, LLD FLS, S] M591 2768

Ealing (Oakeley) [DTDRRDRM, MFMRMDLS,] F387b; BV 380a 2769

Eardisley (English trad) [DRMM RDRMFFMR, DRMF] E601; X393c; BG57 2770

Eardisley (English trad) X Noel 2771

Earl (Turner) [SSDTLS, SLLLL L, LRTL] AB182b 2772

Earlham (Booth) [SMSDML, LS MMRR, RSTT] AA469; AB406; AH536 2773

Early will I seek thee (Sabel) [MMTDLS, DSFMSR, FFD#R] BH18 2774

Earth with all thy thousand voices (Lewandowski) [DRMM FMRDRS, LTDDRD] BH64 2775

Earth, with her ten thousand flowers (Griggs) [SDTSLRTD, RMRDTDL] BC30 2776

Earthly friends (German, 16th c) [DMSSFLSM, SFMDRD, DM] BG135 2777

Earthly pleasures (Ackley) [MM R#R#MMRD, SDRDDT, FF] AS236 2778

-----. R [MMFMMRL, RRMRR DS, MS] 2779

East Church (Freeman) [DMM SFMRLS, SSMDDRR] V435a 2780

East Hill (Bowcher) [MMSSFRD RFFMM, DDTL] AL201b 2781

East Horndon (English trad) [SD DDLTDRTLS, SDDDR] E595; S442a; AP738b; BY120b 2782

East Peckham (Ryley) [SLTDFM RM, LMRMSFM, M] F319b 2783

Eastbourne (Hardy) [MFMRDRF M, MFLSMRDR] O459 2784

Easter (Dykes) X Resurrection 2785

Easter (Gilchrist) [SDRMFSM, RDRMFR, SDR] BR564 2786

Easter (Lyra Davidica) X Easter hymn 2787

Easter alleluya (Cologne G-B. 1623) X Vigiles et sancti 2788

Easter angels (Parker) X God hath sent his angels 2789

Easter carol (Foote) [SLSF#SM SMRDFDM, MRD] BD247 2790

Easter carol (French trad) X Nous allons 2791

Easter eggs (Russian trad) [RR RRRR, SSFMRD, MRRM] BG 94 2792

Easter Eve (Krauth) [MMMMMS, MDDDRM, MLSF] K107 2793

Easter flowers (Custance) [MRD RMFSLDT, TLFLLS] C558 2794

-----. R [SSMFSLL, LLF#SLTT, DD] 2795

Easter flowers (Hutchins. S.S. Hymnal) [SDMDLDSM, SDMDDT DR,] BR562 2796

Easter flowers (Stebbins) [MM MDRMSS, LLLFSLDD,] AC 126 2797

-----. R [LRTLSTMDTL, L DRFMR] 2798

Easter glory (Lindeman) [DS MS, FMDR, MSF#STLS, D] J100; M588; O22; P150; Q8; AA123 2799

Easter hymn (Lyra Davidica) [DMSDFLLS, MFSDFMFM RD] A85; B172; C172; D 112a; E133; F134; G154; H181; I156a; J92; K113; L 261; M442; O334; P197; Q 199; R204; S163; T347; U 118; V756; W119a; X145, 172; Y331; Z239; AB143; AC129; AD158; AE121; AF 182; AG102; AH298; AI82; AK167; AL105; AM198; AN 192; AO176; AP215; AQ318; AR182; AS146; AT115; AU33; AV115; AW114; AZ11; W; BA 234; BB134; BC10; BD245; BE413; BF318; BK135; BL30; BN44; BR190; BV194; BY 157; BZ 2800

-----. V [DMSDFLS, MFSDM FRD,] X172 2801

Easter hymn (Monk) [SLDDTLS, LDRD, SLDDT] D112b; BO 180 2802

Easter morrow (Lindeman) X Our Lady, Trondhjem 2803

Easter song (Cologne G-B.) X Vigiles et sancti 2804

Easter song (Russian trad) X Praise to God 2805

Easter-tide (Oudean. Amsterdam Psalter) X Vreuchten 2806

Easter time (Hancock) [SSS DTLSMS, MFRRMFM] BY755 2807

Eastergate (Ireland) [MMLLL TDD, TLRTS#, LLL] E520 2808

Eastern monarchs (Lang) [LL MMFSM, LLMMFSM, LM] BL16 2809

Eastertime (English trad) [SD TDRMFSFMR, MDTDR] AL 618; BG71; BY745 2810

Eastham (Hutton. Tunes for

the hymns) [SDRMFSM, DL SFFM, MRS] BA952 2811

Eastman (Perkins) [SMMRSDDS, SDDRSM, MR] AB309 2812

Eastnor (King) [MSMDTL, LFMR DT, RMMS] D300a 2813

Easton (Mozart) [SDTDRMFMR, RDLRMSTL] H196; T223a; V427; AJ208 2814

Easton (Nevin) [MMMMRS, DRM FFM, SDDR] C465b 2815

Eastview (Lee) [MSMDRS, SDR MFR, RMRM] BV266; BY129b 2816

Eastwell (Oakeley) [DRMFMMM RDDT, RMF#SD] O224; P151 2817

Eastington (Croft) [DMFRTDRM, RDTLRT, RS] E639; F201; X192 2818

Eaton (Chadwick) [MR#MSDRM RD, LTLRMTL] AC103; AE 440; AR409; BF233 2819

Eaton Square (Fischer) X Hankey 2820

Ebeling I (Ebeling) [DRMRMSLS, SLF, FSM, MS] A32; B545; C545; D538c; J26; K22; M275; N30; O177; P130; Q523; R172; S125; W41; X89; Z186; AA501; AB113a; AD111; AF123; AG77; AI68; AK119; AL48; AM150; AR140; AW525; AZ157-A; BD 224; BR552; BV92; BY88b; BZ 2821

-----. V [DRMRMSSF#S, SLF, F SM, D] AW525 2822

-----. V [DRMRMF#SSF#S, SLSF, FS] AZ157-A 2823

Ebeling II (Ebeling) [DTLTDRRT, DTRMRRD, D] AA296 2824

Ebeling (Ebeling) X Philippi 2825

Ebeling (Ebeling) X Nicht so traurig, nicht so sehr 2826

Ebenezer (Williams) [LLTDTLTT DRDTL, MR] A519; B433; C433; E108; G263; J547; R361; S373; W701a; X309; Y240; Z558; AB 285; AC220; AD349; AE376; AF441; AG249; AI87; AK399; ALsuppl; AM42; AN319; AP508; AQ220; AR569; AW346; BB513; BE258; BF480; BK82; BY 494b; BZ 2827

Ecce agnus (Dresden. Neues G.B., 1593) [LDDTTL, M RRDDT, TDDR] Q165; X638 2828

-----. V [LTDTL, LTDTL, MRDT, TD] X638 2829

Ecce agnus (Dykes) X St John 2830

Ecce agnus (Trad. mel) [SS DRTD, DMSFMR, TDMR] D96b 2831

Ecce agnus (Warren) [MMRDT L, TDRMFR, MMMM] S153; AK148 2832

Ecce jam noctis (Sarum plainsong, M 4) [MFMRMMRDR MM, MDMS] A71b; B155b; BJ75 2833

Ecce nomen domine Emmanuel (Plainsong) [SFMFSFMFS FS, DRMFS] BQ157 2834

Ecce panis (Dykes) [DDTDF MMDR, DDTDFMM] J280 2835

Ecce! Panis angelorum (Plainsong, M 8) [RDRTDTLSFS S, STRRM] E317b; BP53; BQ231b 2836

-----. V [RDRTDLFS, STRR MDRR,] BP53 2837

Ecce panis angelorum (Polleri) [MFSSLLLS, DRMMFFFM,] BQ317 2838

Ecce panis angelorum (Portuguese mel) [SSDDTRDTLSD S, DRMR] BQ231a 2839

Ecce tempus idoneum (Plainsong, M 3) [SLTTLDTLSLT, STSLM] E67 2840

Eccles (Selby) [LS#LTTD, DTD RRM, MRSF] F89 2841

Ecclesfield (Scott-Gatty) X Spirit divine 2842

Ecclesia (---) [MFSDDLSM, LLSLSSFM] AO186 2843

Ecclesia (Gower) [MLLLLT DLL, SFMMMMM] Y9; AB 300 2844

Ecclesia (Schafer) [SSSLRMF FM, MMLSFM, F#] K236 2845

Ecclesia (Terry) X Holy Church 2846

Eden (---) [SSDRMRDL, TDR MFMR, S] AY130 2847

Eden (Feilden) [SMSDTL, SMD MF#S, SLDT] F327 2848

Eden (Gregor) [DSLSSFFM, DR LSFMRR] AZ597-B; BA212 2849

Eden (Havergal) [DMRDTDLS, LDTLS#L, DD] AM469; AP3; AY85 2850

Eden (Mason, T.B.) [DMRDDTL SMRD, SSFMM] C11; D95; AL 275; AP100; BA221; BR230; BY604 2851

-----. V [MMRDDTLSMRD, SS FMM] D95 2852

Eden (Sacred hymns and tunes. Boston, 1850) [DMFSLSM, RM SLFR, DMF] Q621 2853

Eden (Stainer) X St Giles 2854

Eden, W. (Wesley) [MMRRDD, DDDM, SSFFMM,] BR386 2855

Edengrove (Smith) [MFSDDTTL, SFMFSM, MM] B363b; C363a; D553a; I680; J592; K558; U 387; AH542; AI348 2856

Edgbaston (Tilleard) [MMRDTRF LLS, SDTLSL] D646a 2857

Edina (Oakeley) [SLTDFM, MSD RM, RMFSL] A580; B527b; C527a; D519a; V405; AL315a; AP488a; BB287; BR510; BY 459 2858

Edinburgh (Barnby) [MMFSDTLS FFM, MFSLS] B402; C402; D630a; O556; AZ383-B 2859

Edmeston (Woodbury) [MMSMM FRM, SDSLSSF#S,] AJ119 2860

Edmund (Dykes) [MMRLSFM, DTLSMF#S, MM] B231 2861

Edom (Peace) [DTDDDTDD, DMR DTLS, S] AM228 2862

Edsall (Day) [LLTDTLSLLL, DD RFM] A207a 2863

Edwards (Kingsley) [DRMMMRM FS, DSMRDFM] V176 2864

Edwin (Deale) [SDSFSLS, DF MRDR, SLS] BV139a 2865

Edyfield (Wesley's Foundery collection. 1742) X Savannah 2866

Eeuwig dank en eere (German trad) X Gregor's 185th metre - A 2867

Effie (Click) X God is love, His mercy 2868

Effingham (English) [DSFMM RDSFMMR, SDTD] H308; L 174; V57 2869

Egbert (Hall) [DLDFMR, DTD RRRTDRM] B117 2870

Egerton (Thalben-Ball) [DRM SLSM, FMRDRD, DRM] BE 308 2871

Egham (Turner) [MRDFML, TDSMFR, RMSF] BA314 2872

Egli (Egli) [SDTDLSFM, MR RRDTLS,] M35; AA116; AN264; AW359 2873

Eia, Eia (Nordstern. Fuhrer ...) [SDRMRDTD, DRMSF MR, S] X685; BG112 2874

Eia, Jesu adorande (Plainsong, M 3) [FRMFSLSF, SLSFM RM, M] F388a 2875

Eifionydd (Lloyd) [LLTDTLS# LTML, S#LTLT] AL74; AM169; AP260 2876

Eighmey (Pontius) [SDDSMRD TD, FMRDTLR] I412 2877

Ein' feste burg (Luther) [DD DSLTDTLS, DTLSLF] A551; B213; C213; E362; F183; G67; H405; I101; J150; K195; L343; M487; N266; O17; P 91; Q262; R91; S266; T87; U308; V530; W526; X436; Y351; Z155; AA273; AB243; AC210; AD289; AE59; AF363; AG41; AH378; AI309; AJ128; AK281; AL397; AM81; AN304; AO606; AP542; AQ16; AR75; AS258; AT40; AU38; AV37; AW549; AZ199-A; BA348; BB261; BC3; BD78; BE10; BF396; BI-1-D; BK75; BR 365; BV25; BX314; BY562; BZ 2878

-----. V [DDDSTDTLS, DTLS LFM] P91 2879

-----. V [DDDSLDTLS, DTLS

LFM] Q262 2880
-----. V [DDDSTDLS, DTLSLF RD,] BX314 2881
Ein' feste burg ist unser Gott (Luther) X Ein' feste burg 2882
Ein kind gebor'n (Piae cantiones, 1582) [LLLTTDLS, SDMRRDDD,] E44; S134; X91; BG85, 120; BN4 2883
-----. V [LLLTTDLS, SDRDTD, DD] BG85 2884
Ein kindlein in der wiegen (Corner. 1649) X Corner 2885
Ein lamm geht hin (Teutsch kirchenampt. Strassburg, 1525) X Passiontide 2886
Einer, ach nur einer (Gregor. Choral buch) X Gregor's 208th metre-C 2887
Einer ist König (Hille) [DSDM RDMMF#SS, SSSDS] J319b 2888
Eins ist not (Bach) X Cöthen 2889
Eins ist not (Layriz) [MFSSLT DD, LSFLSFM, M] Q366; AA83 2890
Eins ist noth (Crueger) X Ratisbon 2891
Eintracht (German trad) X Christmas dawn 2892
Eintracht (Mathias) [SSLTDTLDT LS, SSDRM] AQ46 2893
Eirene (Havergal) [MFRD, DRD TLSS, DRMSF] D161; O226; Q453; V765; AI255; AP561; BR425 2894
Eirene (Taylor) [LDRMMLMRDT L, DMF#SL] BV405a 2895
Eisenach (Meiningen G. B.) X St Leonard 2896
Eisenbach (Schein) [DMMSSFM R, SLTDTL] A93; B86; C133b; D119b; E138; F187; G344; J 116; M232; N82; O68; Q421; V237; W241; X168; AA334; AB68; AF99, 500; AI419; AL 344b; AM474; AN31; AO144; AQ156; AW508; AZ90-A; BA 140; BE80; BL62; BM88; BN 104; BO141; BV283; BY293; BZ 2897
-----. V [DRMFSSFMSSLTD TLL] C133b 2898
-----. V [DMFSSFMR, SLT DTLLS,] D119b 2899
-----. [DRMFSSFMR, SLTD TLL] G344 2900
-----. V [DMFSLSFMR, SLT DTLS,] AZ90-A 2901
Eisleben (German trad) [LS MFSM, LSMFSM, LS#LT] AZ 519-A; BA199 2902
Eisleben (Wolder. Catechismus G-B. 1598) X Wolder 2903
El Kader (---) [SSSLTD, MRM FSM, SSSL] BB71 2904
El Nathan (McGranahan) [DM MFMRDLSS, MSSLSF] AE 221; AH385; AI252; AM712; AR447; AT275; AW450; AX 478; AY459; BY437 2905
-----. R [DDDDDTLLS, SLSS FFS] 2906
El paran (Mason) [DRMMFMM RD, MFSSLSS] L41 2907
Elation (Rossini) [SMMMR# MSM, MDDRDRR#M] L289 2908
Elbe (König. Harmonischer lieder schatz. 1738) X Mentzer 2909
Elberfeld (Plainsong. 1539) X To God on high 2910
Elberton (Harwood) [DMFRS SFFMR, SLTDSF] F386b 2911
Elbing (Sohren) [SDRMLRDT, SLTDMRD,] A287; N83; O336; Q306; AA436 2912
-----. V [SDRMLRRT, SLTDM RD, S] O336 2913
Eldora (Sateren) [SDSLFMRR D, RMF#SSF#S,] J342a 2914
Eleanor (---) [DSLTDRM, FL SMRDT, DS] D551; BA819 2915
Electus (German) [MFSDRMR SFMRD, MRMF#] M550 2916
Elgin (Beery) [LDDRDDT, S#L TDTRD, LT] AR323 2917

Elgin (Dyson) [MMFSDRMFF MR, RMF#SL] BE64 2918
Elgin (Scottish Psalter, 1625) [DTLTMRDT, LRDTLT, MD] W246a; X665 2919
Eli (Costa) [DMSFMRD, RMFM RR#M, MS] D581b 2920
Elijah (Mendelssohn) [MDLSDR M, FFMMMRLDT,] BE118; BR323a 2921
Elijah (Stainer) [MMMMMFR, SFMRM, SSSS] D609a 2922
-----. R [MSMRMFSM, MLSFL DDR] 2923
Elim (Calkin) [SMFSLDT, LS LSFM, MRM] D605b; K338; BR394; BX466; V282 2924
Elim (Callcott) [MMMFMRSD, DRMFLS, SD] B403; AP441 2925
Eliyahu hanavi (Jewish trad) [DTLLS#MLL, DTLLS#TM, M] BH42 2926
Elizabeth (Kroeger) [SSSTLS, SD DRRD, MSMD] T44a; AJ70 2927
Elizabeth (Sampaix) [SSSSSSDDT, DLSMDR, S] H103 2928
Elizabeth (Thompson) X He's my friend 2929
Elizabethtown (Kingsley) [MM MMMSMDR, RDDDRM, R] G357; H454; I546; T72; U182; V438; AJ108; AX378; AY321; BB458 2930
Ella (Woodbury) [DRMMMDMSS S, MSDDTL] T127; AJ184 2931
Ellacombe (Würtemberg G-B. 1784) [SDTLSDMFS, SLTDRRM,] A96a; B381; D533; E137; F132; G85; I650; J308; K216; M38; P376; Q9; R84a; S65; U267; W 93; X193b; Y33; Z522; AB385; AC117; AD11; AE75; AF68; AG 89; AH279; AI277; AJ265; AK 93; AL82; AM526; AN74; AO515; AP220; AQ236; AR95; AS119; AT499; AW47; AZ151-R; BA 184; BB254; BD111; BE226; BH239; BK68; BL14; BN157; BO9; BR63; BV190; BX64; BY558; BZ 2932
-----. V [SDTLSDMF#S, SLTD RRM] M38 2933
Ellah (Rendle) [MMMRLSFMR M, MMMF#TT] AC289 2934
Ellasgarth (Spencer-Palmer) [MRDFFMRS, F#SLSTRDT] BV617; BY769 2935
Ellerker (Thommen's Christenschatz. 1745) X Batty 2936
Ellers (Hopkins) [SSLSDDTDR M, DDRDM] A487; B50; C50; D12b; Eap. 38; F31a; G29; H31; I38; J198; K437; L62; M17; N363; O54; P37; Q47; R77; S55; T273; U125; V23; W301a; Y97; Z128; AA16; AB34; AC24; AD64; AE34; AF60; AG16; AH175; AI22; AJ380; AK32; AL214; AM316; AN81; AO42; AP333; AR62; AS61; AT27; AU252; AV22; AW43; AZ32-D; BA390; BB 34; BD21; BE208; BF206; BI76; BK173; BR109; BV63a; BX106; BY702; BZ 2937
-----. V [SSLSDDTDRMM, DDRDM] BI76 2938
Ellerton (Barnby) X St Chrysostom 2939
Ellerton (Hopkins) X Ellers 2940
Ellerton (Hoyte) [SDMRDMSF, MSDDRRM, D] D517a 2941
Ellesdie (Mozart) [DDDDMRR DD, RRRRFMR,] G261; H351; I458; R20; T172; U281; V446b; Z375; AD258; AE264; AG192; AH422; AI316; AJ251; AK249; AM691; AN554; AO374; AR 357; AS235; AT387; AU34; AV136; AX423; AY112; BA 345; BB267; BE109; BH229; BR460c; BZ 2942
Elleston (Mozart) X Ellesdie 2943
Ellingham (Godfrey) [MDFM MRD, RLRDTDR, MD] T423; Y142; AC198; AS350; AV104; BF427; BK97 2944
Ellingham (Wesley, S.S.) [MMRDDRMFSM, SDTLSS] J318; S262; AB223; AL437;

AP411b 2945

Elliott (Dykes) X Almsgiving 2946

Elliott (Emerson) [DRMMMRDLD, DRRRSSM] L393 2947

Elliott (Matthews) X Margaret 2948

Ellon (Root) [SDDDDMRD, DRR DTD, DM] G439; AH273; AL 590; AM657; AO623; AP779; AS402; AT513; AW418; BA 816; 2949

Elm (Roberts) [MMRSMMRS, LTSSF#S, FF] I522 2950

Elmcourt (Simper) [MMFSDD TT, LSS#LFMR, M] AS421 2951

-----. R [SSLTDLSMS, SLTD RDT,] 2952

Elmhurst (Drewett) [MMMFMSR M, DLSFMMRR,] B283; C283; D271b; S383b; U33; V173; W 487b; AA484; AD416; AK379; AM180; AO351; AP365a; AS 344; BA566; BF492 2953

Elmic (Strom) [SMMRDDD, LS FMDMRR, S] N548 2954

Eltham (Harmonia perfecta, 1730) X Wondrous cross 2955

Eltham (Mason) [SDMDSSM, SD MDRMRD, S] L555a; V714; BR69 2956

Elton (Bower) [DRMSLS, MDR RM, MSMSL] F534 2957

Elton (Maker) X Rest 2958

Elton (Mason) [SLTDRMDL, L RTDLSF#S,] AF449 2959

Elven (St Alban's tune book, 1866) X Holborn Hill 2960

Elven (Mendelssohn) [MLTDTRL S#T, MMMMRDT] I273 2961

Elvet (Dykes) [MFFSDDLS, DTL SF#S, MF] L90; V314; W201; AA389; AO245 2962

Elvey (Elvey) [DMSFMR, SLD TLS, SDRM] W147 2963

Elvey (Elvey) X St George's Windsor 2964

Ely (Turton) [DDRMDLTD, RMD TDTLS,] B292; D172a; F74b; W334; AJ260b; AP342; BA71; BE387; BV450; BY351 2965

Ely Cathedral (Noble) [SDS DMSM, DRMDRMSD,] A598c; B512c; J534b; Y266 2966

Emilia (Bergquist) [MSMMRD RM, SDTLSSLS,] N437 2967

Emilie (Baume) [MMMSDTDRM FM, MMMDL] I197 2968

Emmanuel (Balle) [MMMDMSL SM, MFRMDRM] J28; K23; M53; N31; O193; AH494; AI257; AM591; AW411; BK 119 2969

-----. V [DRMMDMSLSM, MFRMDR O193 2970

Emmanuel (Beethoven) [SDD DDMRD, SRRFMR, SM] L139; N228; P97; AZ14-Bb; BA14; BE194; BR171; BY272b 2971

Emmanuel (Himmels-lust, 1675) X Liebster Immanuel 2972

Emmanuel (Main) [SMRRMR, SMDDRM, DRMM] AH257 2973

Emmanuel (Sewall) [DMDFRTD D, MSMTLSSS,] BR136a 2974

Emmaus (---) X Barton 2975

Emmaus (Allchin) [MSFMRD, DLFR, DTDFML,] BY709b 2976

Emmaus (Barnby) [DDRMFS, SL#LSSS, LFSM] B225a; V651 2977

Emmaus (Cooke) [MLTDLSLF MM, MRDTSR] F585 2978

Emmelar (Sullivan) [DRRMM SSDRRMS, FSLS] AV404 2979

Emmons (Burgmüller) [SDDD MDSM, SMDMRRTD,] I532 2980

Emulation (Cutler) X All Saints, new 2981

En clara vox redarguit (Antiphonale romanum. Plainsong, M 1) [MDMSLTLL, SLTDTSLT] BQ154 2982

En framling klappar pa din dorr (German) [SDDRSMF MR, DLFMRDT] N387 2983

En kelohenu (Freudenthal) [DD DRMD, MMMFSM, SMDL] AH 151; BH292 2984

Encamped along the hills of light (Sankey) X Victory 2985
Endearing young charms (Irish trad) X Sweet story 2986
Endor (Marsh) [DSSSLLS, DT DMRD, DSS] AY260 2987
Endsleigh (Ferretti) X Salvatori 2988
Energy (Monk) X St Ethelwald 2989
Engadine (Canzuns spirituaelas. 1765) [MDRTTDMRMM, MRD MRD] X516b 2990
Engedi (Beethoven) X Salome 2991
Engedi (Wesley) [DRSMRDRDT, DRSMRDS,] F184b 2992
Engelberg (Stanford) [SDMRSLTD LS, SSFMR] A366; F527a; AF 147; BV253; BY198 2993
England's Lane (English trad) [DMRDSMDS, DSRMRTLS] A26; C425; E309; X494; Y 200; AC168; AL608; BV18; BY8a 2994
-----. V [DMRDSMDS, DSRM RDTL] AL608 2995
Enniskerry (Boyle) [LLSLTLDTLL, LSLTL] X240 2996
Enon (Feilden) [SLSFMM, RMF FFM, SDTL] D550; BY453a 2997
Enon (Widdeman) X Saviour, again to thy dear name 2998
Enon's Isle (Woodbury) [SMRDR DRM, MSFMRDRD,] L431 2999
Enos (Burnap) [SSDRMRL, DT LTSD, SMR] L562 3000
Entbinde mich, mein Gott (Freylinghausen) X Gregor's 118th metre 3001
Eola (Sellers) X Thy word have I hid 3002
Ephraim (Leslie) [DSDSDRM, FRMDTDR, MF] BY367 3003
Epiphany (Filby) [SLSMRDDTLS, MMFSLT] I159 3004
Epiphany (Hopkins) [MFMRLLRM FFM, RSF#ML] F75b; AP178 3005
Epiphany II (Hopkins) [SSMFSDD TLS, SSFMRF] D55b; BX168 3006
Epiphany (Smith) X There came three kings 3007
Epiphany (Thrupp) X Epiphany hymn 3008
Epiphany hymn (Thrupp) [MR DSLTDTLSFM, RDDF] C 95c; Eap. 9; W64b; AL49a; AW91; BV125a; BY91a 3009
Epsom (Arnold. Complete Psalmodist) [DRMRDLTD, DRMFSMR, R] E506; X682; AN296; BE3 3010
Epworth (Wesley) [DMSDMRL SFM, SDTLSF#] W264; X 224; BV204 3011
Epworth (Wesley, S.S.) [SL SDTLLS, SMRDRMRD,] AP 558 3012
Epworth Church (Copes) [ML TDTLSTL, TDRMRDL,] BZ 3013
Er ist mein himmel, meine wonne (Freylinghausen) X Gregor's 109th metre 3013a
Er wird es thun, der fromme, treue Gott (Gregor) X Gregor's 112th metre 3014
Erbarmung (Schicht) X Mir ist erbarmung widerfahren 3015
Ere you left your room (Perkins) X Did you think to pray 3016
Erfreut euch (German mel., 1536) [DDTDRTLS, RMRD TLS, D] F625; O259 3017
Erfurt (Ilse) [SLTDRMRD, M SFMDR, SL] Q232; AA254 3018
Erfurt (Luther) X From heaven high 3019
Erfurt (Weimar) X Allgütiger, mein preisgesang 3020
Erfyniad (Welsh hymn mel) [LDRMRDTLS#L, TDLTMR] E430; X270; AN341; AQ39 3021
Erhalt uns, herr (Luther) X Spires 3022
Erie (Converse) [SSLSMDDL, SDMDSMR, S] A422; G240;

H38; I551; J459; L427; M581; N343; P33; Q457; R385; S257; U356; V469; W701; Z331; AA 395; AD214; AE303; AF335; AG224; AH319; AI107; AK472; AL502; AM533; AO318; AP494; AR483; AS127; AT328; AU160; AV319; AW186; AX350; AY55; BA618; BB320; BC81; BF372; BY343a; BZ 3023

Erin (Irish trad) X St Columba 3024

Eripe me (Crossley) [MMMRD MM, MFSRRM, SSS] AR196 3025

Erling (Stubbs) X Asaph 3026

Ermuntert euch, ihr frommen (Freylinghausen) X Gregor's 151st metre-I 3027

Ermuntre dich [mein schwacher Geist] (Schop) X Schop 3028

Ernan (Mason) [SMFSDDTLTD, LLLSST] G292; L566; P409; T246; V582; AD313; AE276; AH412; AI165; AJ342; AL384b; AN204b; AO502; AP579; AR 253; AV252; AW231; BA540; BB60; BR410; BX351 3029

Ernstein (Swift) [SMMRDS, LFF MR, SDRMF] G438; W189; AL616; AM638; AP756 3030

Erschienen ist der herrlich tag (Hermann) [RRRLTDTLS, LTD# RLDT] F609; Q108; X159; AA161; BV201 3031

-----. V [LLLMF#SF#MR, MF# S#LMSF#] X159 3032

Erskine (Gabriel) [SDDTLLSS, DMRRSM, SD] AJ225 3033

Erskine (Gladstone) [SFMRFM RD, DRFMLSF#M,] Eap. 34; W325 3034

Es flog ein kleins waldvöglein (German trad) X Woodbird 3035

Es geh, wies woll (Praetorius) [LLDTSLTD, TDRMDRD, L] O163 3036

Es ist das heil (Etlich Christliche lider 1524) X Wittenberg 3037

Es ist ein born (American trad) X Campmeeting 3038

Es ist ein ros' entsprungen (Geistliche K-G. Cologne 1599) X Rosa mystica 3039

Es ist genung (Ahle. Geistliche arien) [DRMF#F#SRRFM, MFLLS#L,] Q196; AA226 3040

-----. V [DRMF#F#SRRFM, RMSSF#S,] AA226 3041

Es ist gewisslich (Geistliche lieder. Wittenberg, 1535) X Luther 3042

Es ist kein tag (Meyer. Geistliche seelenfreud) [SDTLSLS FMRD, MFSSL] E521; F589; G425; J448b; Q417; W19a; X289; AL26a; BE191; BV372; BY62 3043

-----. V [SDLSLFRD, MSSLTD DT,] Q418 3044

Es ist noch raum (---) [SLSM, SLLDLS, MRMFSM,] N152 3045

Es kam die gnadenvolle (Egli) X Egli 3046

Es kommt ein schiff (Andernach G-B. 1608) X Song of the ship 3047

Es liegt ein schloss (German trad., 16th c) X Freiburg 3048

Es muss die ganze Christenschar (Waldis) [MMLDRMRD TL, MSF#M, LD] AQ325; BG 129 3049

-----. V [MMLDRMRDTL, MSFM, LD] BG129 3050

Es spricht der unweisen mund (Walther) [DDTSDRMD, TDR MFRD, D] AA277 3051

Es woll' uns Gott genädig sein (Teutsch kirchenampt ...) N166; Q500; AA480 3052

-----. V [TDTLTRMRDT, RDT DLS] Q500 3053

Esca viatorum (Dykes) [DMSF RDRM, DFMLSTDS] B377; C377; AB256; BO139 3054

-----. V [DMSFRDRM, DFM LSTDF,] BO139 3054a

Eschol (Garrett) [DMSDMLLS, DMSDTLLS,] BE111 3055

Eshtemoa (Mason) [MR#MFMLSM R, MR#MLSSF] L385; U378; V551 3056
Eskdale (Joseph) [MMMM, MFM RDTLS# L, LMF] X651 3057
Eskridge (Stebbins) [SMMMRDTD, SSLTDFMR,] T29; AJ40 3058
Essex (Clark) [DLSMRSFM, SSL TDRDT,] I162; L95; AO172; AS154; AV38 3059
Essex (English trad) [MRDSDRM FR, MFSSMSM] X637b 3060
Essex (Holst) [SLDTSLLL, SMS MRM, DR] W180a; BY236b 3061
Esslingen (Krieger) X Nun sich der tag 3062
Esterhazy (Schubert) [SDMLFRD RM, LSFMRDD] Y205 3063
Et barn er født i Bethlehem (Lindeman) [SDSLSSFM, MSFM, MRTS] O194 3064
Et er nødigt (Crueger. Praxis pietatis melica) X Ratisbon 3065
Et lidet barn saa lystetigt (Hohenfurth ms. 1410) X Dies est laetitiae 3066
Et trofast hjerte, Herre min (Praetorius) X Es geh, wies woll 3067
Eternal Light (Runkel) [DDTLM FLS#, S#LFMLT, T] A478 3068
Eternal Light (Willan) [MMRRLL SS, SDDTSF, MM] AP155 3069
Eternal Source (Holsinger) [SD RMFRMD, DDMSLSMR,] AS 431 3070
Eternity (Bliss) [MFSSSSS, SF MMMMM, RD] BE418 3071
Eternity (Gauntlett) [SSDTLS, SSMFMR, SSDT] V369; BA 405 3072
Eternity (Hutton) [MMRDTLS, SS LRDT, SSL] W591 3073
Eternity (Schop) [DMFSSLTD, DMFSSFMR,] M124; N444; BI15-D 3074
-----. V [DRMFS, SLTDDRMFS SF] BI15-D 3075
Eternity (Teasley) [MFSSSLS F#SM, RMFFMF] AX296 3076
Eternity (Wesley, S.S.) [SLLSDFFM, RDFMLDDT,] AL204; AM466; AP327 3077
Etherington (Davies) [SSDLS MFRD, D#RMFSMR,] BE 132 3078
Ethnol (English trad) [SDTLS LFSM, FSDFMRD,] Y238 3079
Etiam et mihi (Dykes) [MMRM FFFSM, SLTDDTL] D589b; O268; V579a; AP471a 3080
Eton (Barnby) [DTLSMRDT, F MRMRDLT,] I39 3081
Eton College (Barnby) [MRR DFMMR, SFMRDRT, F] I212; V27a; BA825 3082
Etona (Goodhart) [MDRMLSM D, TLTDRMDT,] E559 3083
Eucharist (Brown-Borthwick) [DMSFMRRM, MDTLSFMR] D232 3084
Eucharist (Hodges) X Eucharistic hymn 3085
Eucharist (Sewall) [SDRMSF RD, MMFMDSDR,] BR471 3086
Eucharist (Woodbury) [MMMS SLSFSM, MRMFMF] G148; H169; I141; T244; AJ340; AO288; AS143 3087
-----. V [MMMSSLSF#SM, MRMFRR] T244 3088
Eucharistic hymn (Hodges) [SSFMSFMRMFS, SSFMDR] A196; B336; C336; D225a; G414; H442; I238; J279; K194; L332; R445; S353; V552; Z453; AD403; AE 339; AF283; AG239; AH502; AM358; AN121; AO443; AR 514; AS460; AT394; AV254; AW304; BD10; BF603; BZ 3089
Eucharistica (Elliott) [SDRDS MFM, SMDRMFS, S] D368c 3090

Eucharistica (Stewart) [DMMSD RMFSFM, MSSTM] BE172 3091
Eucharisticus (Stainer) [MMRM FR, SDRMF, DLSFF] F418b; BN96; BO42 3092
-----. V [MMRMFR, DLSFM, MSDLS] BN96 3093
Euclid (Pfautsch) [LLLMRDTLT DDRRM, MF] BZ 3094
Euclid (Smyth) [SSDDDTDRL, LLTTTTL] AT438; AU61 3095
-----. R [SLTDMRDTLT, LTDS DM] 3096
Eudora (Murray) [MMMFMRMF, FFFSFMFS,] U480; Z168; AC53; AI224; AM529; AO96; AR81 3097
Eudoxia (Baring-Gould) [MMFFS M, FFMMR, MMR] A172a; B322; C322; D576b; E315; F 431; G308; K574a; N540a; Q654; R225; S494; X49; Z328; AF510; AL545a; AN128a; BV59b; BY 698 3098
Euphemia (Unseld) [MRDSLLSS, SLTDRMR, M] AJ88 3099
Euroclydon (Noble) [LLLDLL, LSFL, LLLDTL,] B416; AD 138 3100
Evan (Havergal) [SSDMRDLS, SSDMDR, FM] C10; H119; I 356; J373; K77; L432; M45; N180; O111; P25; Q416; R 104a; S97; T37a; U321; V278; W692; AA342; AB320; AE228; AH332; AI227; AJ53; AL194b; AM77a; AN38; AO239; AP49 AR268; AS302; AV76; AW153; AX52; AY10; BB411; BE357; BR163; BX58; BZ 3101
-----. V [SDRMRDLS, SDRMDS, RM] AV76 3102
-----. V [SSDMDDLS, SSDMDR] AY10 3103
Evan new (Havergal) X Evan 3104
Evangel (Doane) X Tell me the old, old story 3105
Evangel (Fink) X Bethlehem 3106
Evangel (Hopkins) [DDRMRRMF, MRDTDLS, D] B127b; D 250b 3107
Evangel (Stainer) [MMFMRM DD, RMFSMLS, S] C363b; D553b; F452; W593; X373; AP789; BA813; BV358; BY 615 3108
Evangelist (Mendelssohn) [SDTLSFMR, DTDRSSS, S] G538; Z590; BH3 3109
Evangelists (Koenig) [DDSSFSM D, MMRRDRTS,] C288; D497a; F508; M280; Q282; X212; AA363; AF112; BV50 3110
-----. V [DDSMFSMD, MMR MDRTS,] M280 3111
Evangelium (Oakeley) [MRTD MSF, MRSDRT, RMF] D364a 3112
Evans (Steinel) [MLSMRMF, MMMRDTD, RS] BB469 3113
Evanston (Harrington) [MMRD RMSS, SFFFMR, FF] G203; I632 3114
Evarts (Mason) [MFSMLSSM SFSMFR, MF] J401; K363; L458; M339; N216; O533; P350; AX128 3115
Evelyn (Ashford) [DTLTDRD, FFMRDTLS, S] I515 3116
Evelyn (Sullivan) [MMMMSF M, RRRRFMR, D] A234b; B204; C204; AI121 3117
Evelyns (Monk) [MSLSDSFM RDD, DMF] A356b; B428; C528; D518b; F225; J430a; W178b; BV254a; BY199 3118
Even at the door (Belden) [SD DDRMFS, LMFMRDRM] BB546 3119
-----. R [MFSDRM, DRM MMRMFS, S] 3120
Even me (Bradbury) [MFSD FMMR, RMFRDTD, M] D589a; H57; I346; L399; N407; U 452; V579b; AH352; AI265; AL334b; AO634; AP471b; AS45; AU297; AV348; AW 204; AX41; BA904; BB208 3121

-----. R [SMSMDM, MFSDMRD.] 3122
Even song (Berggren) [SSDDRF MM, DDMMLLSS,] M570 3123
Even song (Flotow) [SSDDFMRD, DRMMMRDR,] AO57, 574 3124
-----. V [SDDFMRD, DRMMM RDR, S] AO574 3125
Even song X Evensong 3126
Evening (Barnby) X Merrial 3127
Evening (Gilchrist) [DRMRMSFM R, DRSM, DRM] BR540 3128
Evening (Good) [SSDDDMMR, DRMDMRD, S] AY290 3129
Evening (Ohl) [SSSL, LTTD, MMR MF#S, SD] K576 3130
Evening and morning (Ebeling) X Philippi 3131
Evening blessing (Kjerulf) [MD LTDRDS, DRMMFMR, M] P72 3132
Evening hymn (Barnby) [MMMMM SSFDM, FFFFFF] D7b 3133
Evening hymn (Gounod) [MRDFM MRS, SLTDLSF#M,] Q558b; AA36a; BQ66*
*(Rare ref.) 3134
-----. R [LFMRRL#SFMM, DTMLLT] BQ66 3135
Evening hymn (Jackson) [MMFMM RDTD, FMRMSFM] W283; AL 549; AP683 3136
Evening hymn (MacFarren) [MFSMDTLS, SRRMFSM, M] M 567 3137
Evening hymn (Maude) [DLTDLT DRMD, MDRMDM] E569 3138
-----. R [DRDLDRMR, RMFM MLS, S] 3139
Evening hymn (Tallis) X Tallis' canon 3140
Evening praise (Loewen) [SDD MMFMRM, DRMFRM, M] AX 73 3141
-----. R [SDDDTLSMD, SLFD TLS,] 3142
Evening praise (Sherwin) X Chautauqua 3143
Evening prayer (Binder) [MMRD SSFM, L#L#LSFS, SL] BH243 3144
Evening prayer (Nowakowsky) [LDTMM, MMLS#TL, MLDT M] BH15 3145
Evening prayer (Randegger) [DDDDTDMR, RRRRDRM, S] T42; AJ65 3146
Evening prayer (Reinecke) [SFMRMSFR, RMFRMSFM,] BR543 3147
Evening prayer (Stainer) [SS SFMMMR, DRMMSFMR] A241a; B343; C360; J235; K577; N661; R76; S495; W654; AG334; AH549; AK36; AW425; 3148
Evening prayer (Stebbins) [SLLSSDDT, DLSSLTLR] G50; I55; J221; K467; M263; N554; Q565b; R54; S47; T 261a; V40; Y95; AA37; AD 55; AE49; AG29; AI48; AJ 363; AL559c; AM340; AO30; AP684b; AR58; AS28; AT34; AU221; AV20; AW38; BA790; BB49 3149
Evening shadows (Musgrave) [DTLSFM, MMMMRR, MFRS] AB206 3150
Evening song (Hall) X Saviour, breathe an evening blessing 3151
Evening sun descending (Rinck) X St Lucian 3152
Evensong (Heberden) [MDRM FSDMRD, MDRMFS] BE156 3153
Evensong (Wade) X St Thomas 3154
Evensong X Even song 3155
Eventide (Holmes) [SDTLLSS LTLS, MLFMR] BB353 3156
Eventide (Monk) [MMRDSLSSF M, MFSLSF] A467; B18; C18; D12a; E363; F27; G520; H 34; I50; J576; K476; L16; M289; N550; O126; P340; Q552; R64; S33; T128; U 470; V42a; W286; X437; Y 368; Z138; AA40; AB31; AC 20; AD61; AE42; AF209; AG 23; AH169; AI49; AJ187; AK

51; AL550; AM335; AN127; AO25; AP663a; AQ79; AR417; AS35; AT295; AU179; AV296; AW40; AX356; AY441; AZ32-K; BA516; BB50; BC51; BE7; BF 193; BI62; BK72; BR326; BV 500; BX163; BY686; BZ 3157

Eventide (Smart) [MMMMFSLR, FMRDRM, SD] N170; BA384 3158

Ever faithful (Strattner) X Posen 3159

Ever faithful (Sullivan) [DDRRMFR, MRDTLLS, SL] AL7a; BA824; BR486b 3160

Ever faithful, ever sure (Sullivan) X Ever faithful 3161

Ever lead me (Warren) [SLSDSD TLS, SLSDMRD] AX502 3162

Ever will I Pray (Tenney) [MM RDLS, DRRSM, MMRDL] AY69 3163

Everett (Everett) [MMMMSDRM, DTLSMR, MM] AR51; AS49 3164

Evergreen (---) [SMRDMRSD, S MRDMRSD,] N524 3165

-----. R [MFRMFR, MFSDFM RD.] 3166

Evergreen (German trad) [SDD DRMMM, MRMFTRD, S] M618; BC16 3167

Evermore (Gauntlett) [MSRMDRT, TDFMRRM, S#S#] D216a; V 423; BR463 3168

Eversley (Cottman) [SMSDDTLS, SDMRDT, RM] BF437 3169

Everton (Smart) [MFSDLTDS, FSMDRRR, M] B481; C481; D260; Eap. 27; F207; K226; W609b; AO506; BE29; BV178b; BY379 3170

Every day (Doane) X Every day and hour 3171

Every day (McGranahan) [SSD MSSFR, FMDTDR, SS] AI8; AM 703 3172

-----. R [MMMTRRD, SSSRFFM, SS] 3173

Every day and hour (Doane) [MRDRDLS, SSLDSDMRR] G236; H346; I490; V733; Z397; AH383; AT326; AU213; AV344; AX422; BZ 3174

-----. R [DRMMFS, MRDDR MR, MRD] 3175

Every morning (Hopkins) X Kelso 3176

Every morning mercies new (Hastings) X Toplady 3177

Everyland, No. 1 (Rendle) [SDRMDMFSL, SFMRM, DM] G476 3178

Ewhurst (Allen) [MRMDDFFM, MLLSDMRR,] BV624 3179

Ewing, (Ewing) [DRDFMRD, MSDTS# L, LS] A597; B511; C511a; D408a; E412; F278; G529; H514; I612; J584; K528; L585; M306; N48; O480; P431; Q448; R428; S435a; T38; U432; V690; W599; X198a; Z569; AA 556; AB408; AD466; AE307; AF309; AG283; AH523; AI 338; AJ55; AK422; AL463; AM604; AN144a; AO550a; AP628; AR425; AS469; AT 477; AU219; AV285; AW262; AZ151-N; BA748; BB300; BD57; BE148; BF657a; BI18; BR437; BV432; BX183; BY 295; BZ 3180

Ex more docti mystico (Plainsong, M 2) [MSSLLSFSSL, SMFSFM] E65 3181

Excelsior (Booth) [MFSTDRM, MTDFMR, MF#S] W674; AL326; BY477 3182

Excelsior (Mason) X Bethany 3183

Excelsius (Cornell) [DSLTD RM, RMFMRDDT, D] O409 3184

Exeter (Jackson) [DMSMRDR MFM, DMSDTL] E528; X 338 3185

Exeter (Mason, H. L.) [MRD TDRRM, MSMMF#S, MR] R 224; S181; AG118 3186

Exhortation (Hibbard) [DM SMSMFSFMRD, RMRM] BB 387 3187

Exile (English trad) [FFMFSD TD, MFSLSFRR,] X573b 3188

Exmouth (Brown) X Purleigh 3189
Exodus (Rötscher) [MMFSDR MRD, SSLTDTL] F605 3190
Exon (Armstrong) [DRMFMLLS, SLTDRTLS] X469 3191
Expectation (---) [DDSLTDRMR, MRDLTDR] BB186 3192
Expectation (Berggren) X Berggren I 3193
Expostulation (Hopkins, J.) [DMRDMRDLSLS, MSLSM] AI 192; AY407 3194
Extol the love of Christ (Root) X Varina 3195
Exultation (---) [SDMMRD, LRF FMR, RMLS] L74 3196
Exultation (Bourgeois) X Rendez à Dieu 3197
Exultation (Kettle) [SDMSFMR, RDDRMR, RRF#] D208b 3198
Exultet caelum laudibus (Plainsong, M 4) [FFSFFMRDRMMM, SSLL] F504a 3199
Exultet caelum laudibus (Plainsong, M 8) [SLTDTLSLFS, TRDTRD] E176; F516a 3200
Exultet cor praecordiis (Antiphonale romanum Plainsong M 1) [LLLLRFMR, LLTSLDT L,] E237; BM28; BN64; BP 22; BQ161c 3201
Eyre (MacElree) [DDTSLLS, DDRMFFM, DD] AR579 3202

F

Faben (Willcox) [SSSMRMDS, SSFLSFFM,] D443b; H19; I638a; L142; M211; R3; S 10b; U10; V515; Z110; AC30; AD17; AG2; AI5; AM16; AO 54; AS6; AW16; BA18; BB 74; BX119 3203
Face to face (Tullar) [SSLSM DDT, RDTLSLS, S] AH527; AT475; AU106; AV390; AX 126; BB545 3204
-----. [RRMRDTDM, RMRDTLS, M] 3205
Fade, fade, each earthly joy (Bradbury) [MFMMRD, RSF M, MFMMRD,] N601 3206
Fade, fade, each earthly joy (Perkins) X Lundie 3207
Fahre fort (Schmidt) [DMSLTD, MRDRDTD, SSL] N6; Q479; AK200; AW520; AZ119-A; BA3 3208
-----. V [DRMFSLTD, MRD RDTD, S] AK200 3209
Fahre fort! Zion, fahre fort (Schmidt) X Fahre fort 3210
Fairest Lord Jesus (Münster G-B. 1677) [MLTS#S#, LTD RMM, SDDRM] A346a; B356; E323; R135b; X276; AG113 3211
-----. V [MLTS#S#S#, LTD RMMM, SDR] E323 3211a
Fairest Lord Jesus (Silesian mel) X St Elizabeth 3212
Fairfield (Turle) [MRMDDRM F, RMSDTLT, L] W354 3213
Fairford (Schubert) X Schubert 3214
Fairlight (Shaw) [LLDLM, FMRDL, LRRDRM] X386d 3215
Faith (Dykes) [MRDFMLTD, RMFSLR, RR] C138; D434b; I228; T126b; V350; AJ156a; BD72; BX279 3216
Faith (Fairlamb) [SMDTRD, LDLLSS, SLSS,] K360b; L190b; O382 3217
Faith (Herrmann) [SDTLSF F#SFM, SF#SLTL] K136a 3218
Faith (O'Connor-Morris) [MDRMFS, LSMFSS, LDTS] BE301 3219
Faith (Rossini) [MFMMRR, DRDT, LTLDRM,] AZ140-D; BA76 3220
Faith is a living power (Emerson) X Sessions 3221
Faith is the victory (Sankey) X Victory 3222
Faith of our fathers (Catholic) X Jesus, my Lord, my God 3223
Faith of our fathers (Hemy) X St Catherine 3224
Faith of our fathers (Montani)

SLDLTDTDRD, DRMTDR] BQ121 3225
----. [MMMMRD, FMR, MM MMRDL] 3226
Faith triumphant (James) [DTLL LSDRM, RMSMRDR] Y268 3227
Faithful (---) [SSLSSDDDTLS, S LDDD] BB173 3228
Faithful (Bach) [SSMFSDTLS, SSMFSDT] Y64; AC125; AE 31; AI39; AM104; AR11 3229
Faithful (Scottish trad) [DDD RMSMSFMRD, DDDR] X282 3230
Faithful guide (Wells) X Holy Spirit, faithful guide 3231
Faithful legions (Barnes) [MMRS DLSDFMR, MMRSL#] AD328 3232
Faithfulness (MacFarren) X Luffenham 3233
Faithfulness (Runyan) [MMMM RRFFFFM, LTLSF] Z165; AE 68; AM27; AR429; AT47; BV 238; BY576 3234
-----. R [SSRFMM, LLMSFF, SLTD] 3235
Falan-tidings (Tyrolese trad) [SDDMDTRTS, LSMFTD, S] BG121; BV351; BY390 3236
Falckner (Antes) X Hope 3237
Falcon Street (Smith) X Silver Street 3238
Falconer (Morton) [MMLSMDRM, MMMMDLMR#] AJ46a 3239
Falfield (Sullivan) [MRDDRMFF, FFMSSF#S, M] D127; J512b; K223; AB348 3240
Falkirk (Arne) [DRMFMRDTD, RMSSFMM] I598 3241
Falkland (Lawes) [SMDFMRRD, DTSDRMFS] E219; X227; BL 35; BN195 3242
Fall fresh on me (Iverson) X Spirit of the living God 3243
Falls Creek (McKinney) [SMM FFSSD, RMMRDR, S] AT347; AU99 3244
-----. R [SMMMMRD, MSSSMSR, SM] 3245
Falmouth (Young) [DMSDMMRDT D, RMSLSF#] BE36 3246
Famous men (Williams) [DRM SLSMR, MSLDTLSL] X432; AQ230 3247
Fanad Head (Irish trad) [MLT DTLTTLSMRMM, ML] X 294 3248
Fang dein werk (Franck) X Schwing dich 3249
Far and near the fields (Clemm) X Clemm 3250
Far, far away on Judea's plains [DDRMMFSSFM, RRMFMS] BC33 3251
Far, far beyond the starry sky (Melish) X I heard the voice of Jesus say 3252
Far Hills (Conant) [SSLLDTLT, DDFMMRR, R] Y193 3253
Far off lands (Bohemian Br. mel) [SDSFMRDSS, FMSFR D] A262; J317; R495; AF 484; AQ247; AR496; BE189; BZ 3254
Far verden, far vel (Norwegian folk) [MMDTL, MS#L TDLMS#TL,] O554; P74 3255
Fareham (Goss) X Advent 3256
Farewell (Tomer) X God be with you 3257
Farewell, all earthly honors (Bradbury) [DMMRMFM, RD DRRM, SMM] BC35 3258
-----. R [DRMMMSFMRRMF, MRDMDDR] 3259
Farley Castle (Lawes) [DMF SMFSLTD, DTLDSL] E217; F414; L27; W510; X22; AQ 3; BV73; BY660 3260
-----. V [DMFSMFSLTD, DTSDSL] L27 3261
Farmborough (Warrell) [LDM LSMRM, MFSMRDRL,] E509; X689; BV69 3262
Farmer (Farmer) [DDDMSLS, S MDTRD, DDD] U409; AH 470; AI349; AO578; AR591; AS430; BA577; BF554 3263
Farnaby (English trad) [FD FSLSLS, FDFSLLS,] A231; E591; X362 3264
Farnboro (Naylor) [MRDLSSF

M, SDTTLS, SF] V133 3265
Farnell (Finlay) [MMSFMRDR MM, SLDDTL] BY546 3266
Farnham (English trad) [MLTD TLLM, MDDRMRM, D] E525; X285 3267
Faroon (Barnby) [DDRMDTLLS L, DDR#MSF] BR102 3268
Farrant (Tye) [DDRMRDFR, RMF#SSF#S, D] E339; J10; K14; Q440; R533; Sap. 9; V 112; W625; X275; AA524; AD 32; AF501; AJ158; AL650b; AP75; AQ121; AS405; AW587; AZ14-U; BA316; BR242; BY 354 3269
-----. V [DDRMRDFR, RMSSF# S, DF] AA524 3270
Fast to thine arm (Lyon) [MR DLD, TDRM, MRDLD, TD] AX522; AY139 3271
Father all-holy (Gluck) [DDRTD, RRMFM, SSLFFS] BI24 3272
Father Almighty, we bow before Thee (Handel) X Father, O hear us 3273
Father hear (Jewish trad) X Eliyahu hanavi 3274
Father, I come to thee (Hayden, V.) [DDDTDRD, MMMRMFM, RD] BI22; BR457 3275
Father, I stretch my hands to thee (Glazer) X Azmon 3276
Father in heaven (Flemming) X Flemming 3277
Father in heaven (Handel) [SM RDD, DTLSS, LTDRMR] AH617 3278
Father in heaven, we do believe (Crawford) [MMMMMFMM, R DDRR#M, MM] BC41 3279
Father! in life's young morning (Brunk) [MSRMDLSD, DDRMM RF#S,] AX562; AY64 3280
Father, lead us (Hugg) [DMSDR MFMDRD, RRMRT] AX491; AY119 3281
-----. R [RRRTLS, FFFFM, SSSDR] 3282
Father, let me dedicate (Macfarren) X Dedication 3283
Father, let thy blessing (Miller) [SDDTTL, DFFMR, DSFMR] BH102 3284
Father most holy (Crueger) X Herz liebster Jesu 3285
Father, O hear us (Handel) [MMMFF, RSFFM, LLTDRS] AR616; AV417; AW609 3286
Father, see thy suppliant children (Binder) [MMRDFFFR, MMRDDF#S, S] BH152 3287
Father, see thy suppliant children (Munn) [MDLDSDRMD, MMFMMRL] BH150 3288
Father, see thy suppliant children (Rubin) [MRDSSLSF# SM, MF#SLTL] BH151 3289
Father, thy children to thee now raise (Stephens) [DTLS FMRDRM, FFMRMF] BC 43 3290
Father, to thee we look (Lutkin) [SSDMDTLDLLS, SSLSM] AV221 3291
Father, to thee we look in all our sorrow (Mendelssohn) X Brightest and best 3292
Father, to thy dear name (Binder) [MFSSF#SRMFFM F, DRMM] BH85 3293
Father, to us (Barnby) X Sandringham 3294
Father, we come (Arne) X Arlington 3295
Father, we come to thee (Bostwick) [SMDTRF, LSFMFS, DSMR] BB599 3296
----. R [MMMFFF, SSSL, DT LSS#L] 3297
Father, whate'er of earthly bliss (Naegeli) X Naomi 3298
Fatherland (Edwards) [MMFLL S, MRDRM, MMSSS] D420b 3299
Fatherland song (Crieg) [DRM FSLSD, MF#SDTS, RF] BY 408a 3300
Fealty (Conant) [MMMRMF, RMFLSFM, MMD] R286; Y 143; Z302; AC121; AE444; AG169; AR356 3301
Fear my child, thy God (Ger-

man, 1544) X Singen wir aus herzens grund 3302

Fear not (Stebbins) [SDSDRM, MFMRDR, SDSD] BR521 3303

Federal Street (Oliver) [MMM FMSSFM, FFFMMF#F#] A423; B135; C135; D183b; G185; H 158; I271; J514; K52; L137; M 96; N124; O90; P265; Q346; R518; S90; T264; U175; V436; Z207; AA91; AD136; AE348; AF290; AG137; AH234; AI318; AJ368; AK331; AL489b; AM34; AN188; AO378; AR353; AS279; AT83; AV125; AW192; AZ22-Z; BA84; BB152; BD55; BE352; BK87; BR36; BX50; BZ 3304

Felix (Mendelssohn) X Brightest and best 3305

Felix (Mendelssohn) X Selwyn 3306

Felix dies (Plainsong, M 2) [DDRMRRDT, RTDLSDDD,] F151a 3307

Fellowship (Lint) [MMSMRMFFM, SSMFMRM,] AR682; AS68 3308

Fellowship (Wathall) [MMRMMM RM, MSMF#F#S, ST] I450 3309

Feniton (Nicholson) [DLDRM SS, LSMDRDLS, D] F392 3310

Feniton Court (Hopkins) [SSDD MRDT, LTDMSFMM] D421a; AZ91-F; BA67; BE177 3311

Feodore (Haynes) [SDDDTD, MSS SF#S, MLSF] AI360 3312

Ferdinand (Marks) [MLSMMRD, LTDSLTS, ML] K547 3313

Ferguson (Kingsley) [SSMDDTL S, MFSMFR, MM] G322; I172; L411; N206; T208; U145; V527; Z395; AJ299; AM576; AO93 3314

Ferniehurst (Church hymnal) [DRMFFM, MMMSF#M, MRTD] I250 3315

Fernshaw (Booth) [SFMRDMRD, SSDTDR, ML] D31b 3316

Ferree (Price) [MMFSDMRDLS, FMF#SSR] AE71; AK78 3317

Ferrier (Dykes) [MMMDSLS, SL TDTLTLS,] D552b; J528; K568; L584; M159; N654; W 665; AJ135b; AP803; BX126b 3318

Ferry (Green. Psalmody. 1731) [DTDRSFMR, MFSDFMRD,] X39; BY634 3319

Fesans raijouissance (French trad) X So, brother 3320

Festal day (Lewars) [DDRM DMFS, MDMSMSF#S] J249a 3321

Festal song (Walter) [SDSMSL, SLTDTLS, RM] A535; B314; C492; G267a; I413; J541; L 121; R352; S401; U274; Y225; Z374; AB279; AD332; AE252; AF300; AG252; AH459; AK 389; AO467; AQ207; AR329; AS363; BA559; BF463; BV 508; BZ 3322

Festgesang (Mendelssohn) X Mendelssohn 3323

Festgesang (Wathall) [MMRMFS DS, MDDRFFM, M] I120a 3324

Festival (Heywood) [DTLSLRM, DTDRSM, MRM] BR515 3325

Festival carol (Oudean. Amsterdam Psalter.) X Vreuchten 3326

Festum matris gloriosae (Plainsong, M 2) [DDRRRDFMRD, FSLSFS] E228 3327

Festus (Freylinghausen, G-B. 1704) [SDTLSLRFM, MRSMF# SL] D167b; W170b; AB190; AQ219; AZ155-A; BA542; BD138; BV228; BY297 3328

-----. V [DTLSLRFM, RSMF# SLDT] W170b 3329

Ffigy-sbren (Welsh hymn mel) [DMMMSFMRRM, DMMMSF] E324; G406; S320; X560; AD286; AF219; AL340; AN 226; AW183; BY285 3330

Fiat lux (Dykes) [SDRMRD, SF MRRM, RTLS,] D328a; I206; S392; V82; Z536; AO522; AP 372; BA13; BB451 3331

Fiat lux (Hiles) [MSDFSM, DRM FLR, DDTD,] K143 3332

Fidei defensor (Nevin) [SDDDD RRR, RSF#FFMRR,] Y120

3333
Fidei unitas (Walther, G-B) X Soldau 3334
Fidelis ad mortem (Müller) [SMLSFMSFRM, SMLSFM] AH142 3335
-----. R [DTLSSLSFM, RRMFM RMF] 3336
Fides (Davis) X Goshen 3337
Fides (Scholefield) [DTDRMLSF, MMMSFMRM,] D142 3338
Field (Laufer) [SDRMSFMRM D, RDRMSL] G458; R294; S 367; Y223; Z495; AC249; AF 421; AK265; AR383; BZ 3339
Fierce was the wild billow (Cambra) [SDRMRD, LDRD, SDR MRD,] BP100 3340
Fifth mode melody (Tallis) [DM FSSLFS, FMRM, DMFS] W250; X483 3341
Fight of faith (Peace) [DTLSDTL S, TDDRRM, MD] BR402a 3342
Filia (Shearer) [MFMLSFFM, S LTDTLLS,] J265b 3343
Filius dei (Gaul) [DMFSSLTD, RMFSRM, DM] AB158 3344
Fill me now (Sweney) [MMRDS LDR, MFSLSMR, M] AE149; AS173; AX136; AY204; BB212; 3345
-----. R [SSDLLD, RRDLDLS, LLS] 3346
Fill me with thy spirit (Byers) [MMMRDRDL, DLSDDTDR,] AX137 3347
-----. R [SMDRMDFM, SSSFMM DR,] 3348
Fillmore (Belden) [SMDRMFLS, DLSMFMR, S] BB447 3349
Fillmore (Fillmore) X Pounds 3350
Fillmore (Ingalls) [DMRDRMRDR, MSSSLSM] G229; H159; I310; T142; AI287; AJ210; AQ8; BZ 3351
Final rest (Bergquist) [MRDRMFR, SSFMRMRR, S] N605 3352
Fine flowers(Scottish trad) [LLLS MMLLSM, MDDTDR] AH304 3353
Fingal (Anderson) [MFMRDDTD, SDDFFM, MD] B404; C404b; W141; AJ301; AK33; BE260; BY456 3354
Fingal (Irish trad) [MMMMDR M, RDLLDRMR, M] R321; S508; W456b 3355
Finlandia (Sibelius) [MRMFMR MDRRM, MRMFM] G73; P 12; Q651; R374; S281; W 556a; Z161; AB231; AD80; AE211; AF77; AG215; AH 403; AK87; AR263; AU479; AW54; BF255; BK37; BY683; BZ 3356
Finlay (Friedell) [MMSLSLLD R, MRMDLSMS,] AF27 3357
Finnart (Finlay) [DMRDSLDRM, MSLSDRL] F583; W491a; AL581; BV49a; BY657 3358
Finnish song (Suomen Koraalikirja, 1738) [DSDRMRDT S, DRMFMRR] J191b 3359
Firenze (Longacre) [SDDRTD LS, MFSMSLTS,] AK208 3360
Firm as the mountains around us (Durham) [SMSFMRTLS, DTDFDM, M] BC42 3361
Firm foundation (Schumacher) [SDTDMRDRDTD, RMFSS] Q427 3362
Firm this cornerstone be laid (Stark) [DTDSTLS, LLSSS FM, DD] BH212 3363
Firmament (Davies) [SSSSLT DMRD, DDTLSD] W10; BE 203; BV232b; BY74 3364
Firmament (Root) [MFF#SLT DR, DTLSLSFM,] BR76 3365
First Church (Lester) [MMM RDSLLS, DRRM, MMM] Y206 3366
First mode melody (Tallis) [LLLS#LDTT, TTMMR#M, MM] E78; F106a; W433b; X625; BJ2 3367
Firth (Firth) [SSMRDTD, SS SSLTDT, S] D116c 3368
Fischer (Fischer) X Whiter than snow 3369
Fisher (Fisher) [SSDTLSRDT,

SSRTLST] AT293 3370
-----. R [DRDTRMRD, RDLTRD# RM,] 3371
Fishwick (Fishwick) [MMRSFM RD, DDRM, MRSF#] M535 3372
Fisk (Harrington) [SLSMFMRDR M, SLSMFM] I185; AJ135a 3373
Fitzwilliam (English trad) [DRM MFFMFM, SFMRDTD] E448; X539 3374
Flanders (Flemish trad) [LLSM SFMRMM, LLSMSF] X440; BG 160 3375
-----. R [DDLLMML, DDRRM ML.] 3376
Flavian (Day's Psalter) X St Flavian 3377
Flee as a bird (Dana arr) [LM MMFMMT, LDDRR#MT, L] AI 244; AU459; BB232 3378
-----. V [LMMMFMMRDT, LDD RR#R#MT, L] BB232 3379
-----. V [LMMMFMMRDT, LDDRR#R#] BB232 3380
Fleming (Flemming) X Flemming 3381
Flemish carol (Flemish carol) X A little child 3382
Flemming (Flemming) [DDDRRM DDRDT, MMMMR] G327; H266; I478; J421; M161; N428; O565; P17; R53; S306; T419; U195; V48; Y297; Z147; AB189; AD 278; AE241; AF333; AG182; AH350; AI240; AJ112; AK14; AL165b; AM179b; AN117; AO 76; AP625b; AR79; AT287; AV 226; AW59; AZ36-E; BA787; BB9; BC34; BD5; BE179; BF 364; BK175; BR377; BX160; BY261b; BZ 3383
Flensburg (Spohr) [SMSDDDTLS, FMFSLR, S] D673b; I465; AB 304; BR140 3384
Fletcher (Gibbons) X Song 46 3385
Fling wide the gates (Halevy) X Min hamaytsar 3386
Flittner (Flittner) [LLDDRRMD, SSFMRRD, R] M191; Q384; AA317; AQ170 3387
-----. V [LLDDRRM, MSFMR RD, RR] AQ170 3388
Flora (Sheldon) [DRSLTDRM, DFMRLS, SM] BV495 3389
Flow gently sweet Afton (Spilman) X Away in a manger 3390
Flower (Fillmore) [MRDFFF MRS, LTDDSMF] AS316; BB117 3391
Flower of love (Christiansen) [SMRMFMRDLS, SSFFSM] P380 3392
Flowers of the fairest (Catholic) [SDTDMDMRMFTL, MMRL] AH137; BO105 3393
-----. R [SSF#SLSSSDRM, MRTSR,] 3394
Foel fras (Harding) [SMRDR MFRM, SLSSMDM] AR300 3395
Folkingham (New version. Supplement. 1708) [MLTDLL FM, DFMRDRTL,] E558; W 637b; X317; AF431; AN380 3396
Follow all the way (Norris) X Where He leads me 3397
Follow, I will follow thee (Brown) [MMRDTSLD, TSL FM, MMR] AU443 3398
-----. R [MDSDMLSFT, FM RD#RR#M,] 3399
Follow me (Garrett) X Forgiveness 3400
Follow me (German trad) X Jesus lives, and Jesus leads 3401
Follow me (Palmer) [MMMMF MMD, MRRFMM, MM] AX 255 3402
Follow on (Lowry) [SDRMMR DDDTLS, STTT] AU118; AX 412 3403
-----. R [MSMRD, DRDLLS, TTTDD] 3404
Follow the gleam (Douglas) [SSF#SLFM, MMMRTSRD, S] AC230b; AG306 3405
-----. R [TL#LFFMSM, MR SR, RDSD,] 3406
Follow the path of Jesus

(Hymns and tunes. 1790) [DD RMSMD, RRRRSM, DDR] AX 498; AY305 3407
Folsom (Mozart) [SSSSMSFMF SFM, DRRM] AV94 3408
Fons sempiternus (Olds) [STLT SM, FSLSLRMF, SR] AB305 3409
Font Hill (Emerson) [SMRDTLSD, RMRMF#S, SS] L71 3410
Footsteps (Everett) X Sweetly Lord, have we heard 3411
Footsteps of Jesus (Everett) X Sweetly Lord, have we heard 3412
For all the saints (Barnby) X Sarum 3413
For Christ and the Church (Kirkpatrick) [SSMFSMRDDD, TL SSLS] AR494; AS324; AX153 3414
-----. R [STTLTDS, SLDTLS, SS D] 3415
For God so loved (McGranahan) [SDMMRDRFFMRMSSFM] AI9 3416
-----. R [SMFSLSS, SMFSLSS, SM] 3417
For health and strength (---) [SSSSFMMMRDDDTD. DD] AR552 3418
For our devotions, Father (Fones) [DRRMSFMRFTRD, RFRM] BC107 3419
For peace and for plenty (Knowlton) [MSMDSS, SDTLS, SSMSL] BI112 3420
For the beauty of the earth (Kocher) X Dix 3421
For the mountains (Jewish trad) [LLMMMRMFM, MMSDRMF] BH316 3422
For the Sabbath (Ledington) [MMRFMRDRT, DFMLSF#S] BB46 3423
For the strength of the hills (Stephens) [SSDMDSSLS, SFFM DR, T] BC241 3424
-----. R [RRMSSDSLS, DRFM RD] 3425
For thee, O dear, dear country (Pierson) [MMFMMMR, DT LTRD, MMF] BR449b 3426
For thee, O dear, dear country (Sullivan) X Homeland 3427
For you and for me (Thompson) X Softly and tenderly 3428
Ford (Musgrave) [DRMFLSM, MSDDRM, MF#F#] D437c 3429
Ford Cottage (Maker) [DMSD DRMFM, SLSFMR, R] G474; J332 3430
Ford Place (Finlay) [DLSFSL SM, SFMRMFM, M] BV359 3431
Forest (Chapin) [DLSDDMRD, DMSMDRMR,] H126; L515; AQ147 3432
-----. V [DSLDDMRD, DMSM DMRD] AQ147 3433
Forest Green (English trad) [SDDDRMRMFS, MFMDRRD,] A21a; C78c; E15; F65a; R 96; S471; W612; X79a; Y250; Z316; AD191; AE344; AF456; AG56; AK201; AL51a; AN 138; AP169; AQ304; AR586; AW290; BD46; BE5; BF273; BG138; BV122a; BY718; BZ 3434
Forest Hill Church (Smith, R. A. L.) [MM, SLTDRMSDR M, MRRD#] BF400b 3435
Forever here my rest (American trad) X Belief 3436
Forever here my rest (Pollock) [MFSSLSF#SM, MRDRMFM,] AX172; AY258 3437
Forgive (McKinney) [SDDDLT TTDLDS, SDDD] AU416 3438
Forgive us, Lord (Jewish trad) X Yom Kippur mode 3439
Forgiveness (Garrett) [MLSR MFM, SDTF#SLS, SL#] D592; V467; BR391; BX30a 3440
Förlossningen är vunnen (Erfurt Enchiridion, 1524) [DDMRDTL, MFRMRD, DDM] N21; O167; P114 3441
Fortem virili pectore (Catholisches G-B. Strassburg 1697) [SDDRRMRMD, MFSS

FMR,] X183; AW572 3442
Fortitude (Filby) [SLSMD, LTD SM, SLSSMD] A565; B112; C112; D656a; H354; BR400 3443
Fortitude (Palmer) X Yield not to temptation 3444
Fortitude (Smith) [MM, RRDFM RDLSFM, MMM] G300; I407; AB176; AC182; AD488; AH449; BF400a; 3445
Fortitude (Young) [MFSLSFMR, DRFM, MF#SL] BE161 3446
Fortitudo (Miller) [SDRMFSSS, MRMFMRDR,] J502a 3447
Fortress (Luther) X Ein' feste burg 3448
Fortress-Rock, my God, my aid (Jewish trad) X Rock of ages 3449
Fortunatus (English trad: old) [LLTDTLMRDT, LLTDTL] E579; W174b; AL130a; AP233a 3450
Fortunatus (Sullivan) [DTDRMFM RDDTD, MFSL] A87; B169; C 169b; D109b; J93; K118; N122; R207; V764; W115; Y332; Z 246; AC130; AD161; AI88; AO 181; AP217; AR191; AV119; BD236; BR513; BY165 3451
Fortune (English trad: old) X Fortunatus 3452
Forward (Edwards) [SDSDDMR, DDTLSSS, SD] D510c 3453
Forward (Smart) X Sion 3454
Foundation (American trad) [SL DLDSD, DMDMS, SLDL] G315b; I461b; R369b; T15; U206; V325b; Z406; AD234; AG212b; AH380; AI306; AJ20; AQ21; AR260; AT 263; AU199; AX146; AY33; BF 242; BZ 3455
-----. V [SDLDSDRMRMS, SD LDS] R369b 3456
-----. V [SLDLDSDDMRMS, SLDL] AQ21 3457
Foundation (Parker) [SDDDDTLS LSFMMR, RL] B212b; D628a 3459
Fount of glory (Landis) X Blessed Bible 3460
Fountain (American trad) X Cleansing fountain 3461
Fountain of grace (Balle) X Emmanuel 3462
Fountain's Abbey (Slater) [DMRDSLTDRMDLR, LLT] X579 3463
Four seas (Roberts) [LLDT LS, DDLTDR, TDMR] AQ161 3464
Four winds (Foote) [DDRMSM RDLDM, LDTLS] AQ202 3465
Fowler (McCutchan) [MMM SDTDRD, MRSFM, RR] G9b 3466
Fra himlen hoit (Luther) X From heaven high 3467
Fragment (Sarum Gradual, 1527) X The rosy sequence 3468
Fragrance (French carol) [MM RDSDSLMF, SDRMSM] X627; BG164; BV101 3469
Frainsby (Dyson) [MMMMRL DD, SSSTLMSS,] BE39 3470
Frälsta värld! i nadens under (Swedish Koralbok, 1697) [LLMDRDTL, DDTDDRM, L] N101 3471
Frances (McGranahan) [SD RDSMFS, DMFMSLTD,] T55; AJ86; AM40 3472
Franck (Franck) X Schwing dich 3473
Franconia (Ebeling) X Philippi 3474
Franconia (German) [SSFMM R, FFMRM, SSLTD] BR389 3475
Franconia (Koenig) [DRMFSM, SLDFMR, SDTS] A418; B88b; C277; D210; E370; F48b; J 394; K369; N201; O228; Q133; R94; V583; W190a; X455; Z 466; AA406; AF214; AG221; AK247; AL146a; AN253; AP 343a; AW205; BA135; BE44; BR30; BV88; BX312a; BY 463; BZ 3476
Frankfort (Gill) [SMRLTLS, SDLDFLMR, S] D335c; N 165 3477
-----. V [SMRLTSS, SDLD

FLMR, S] N165 3477a

Frankfort (Nicolai) [DSMDSLLS, SLTDTLLS,] A329; B98; C98; J33; K153; M146; N25; O183; P53; Q23; R415; S321; X90; AA24; AB76; AD285; AF145; AI417; AK122; AM434; AN493; AW529; AZ228-a; BA54; BG104; 193; BI19-D; BL13; BR135; BV 130; BZ 3478

-----. V [DSMRDSLLS, SLTDTLL S.] BI19-D 3479

Frankscot (Barnby) [SSFMRRD, LLLSFM, DTL] O439; U239; V397; AG217; BA663 3480

Franzen (Tomissön. Psalmebog. 1569) [DMMFMFSS, SSMFRD; DM] J264; M545; N235 3481

-----. V [DMMFFSS, SSMFRD, DMM] N235 3482

Fred til bod (Hartmann) X Peace of God 3483

Fred til bod (Lindeman) X Easter glory 3484

Frederick (Kingsley) [SDDRML, SMRDRM, SDDR] H320; I584a; L565; T12; V674; AA535; AJ 16 3485

Fredricton (Schuman) [SSDDMM R, MFRLTD, MRR] Y131 3486

Free waters (Everett) [DRMMM FMRRR, MRDDDT] AX230 3487

-----. R [MFSFMRRR, RMFM RMMM,] 3488

Freedom (Greenwood) [MSLMR, RFSL#L, TSF#TTD#] BE302 3489

Freedom (Shaw) [SDRDMSLSM, SMDS, SDR] X322a 3490

Freely give (Perkins) [MMMFSLSD, TLSFM, MMM] BB479 3491

Freeport (---) [SFMFMRDTDM R, MSFMF] BB464 3492

Freeport (Shoemaker) [SDMDLST D, DTDFMR, RM] AY6 3493

Freiburg (German trad. 16th c) [MRDSSLMS, SMMDRRM, D] J63a; M81; O523; P117 3494

-----. V [MMRDSSLM, SLSMDR M, M] M81 3494a

-----. V [MMRDSSLM, SSMMDR M, D] O523 3495

Fremont (Lehmann) [LMRDDT, DRDTTL, DLSF] M393 3496

French (Scottish Psalter. 1615) X Dundee 3497

French carol (French trad) X Love is come again 3498

French carol (French trad) X Picardy 3499

Freshwater (Parry) [MDRMS D, LSMRMM, MDRM] AL457 3500

Freshwater (Statham) [MDM LSFSM, SLSF#F#M, ML] BA 591 3501

Freu dich sehr (Bourgeois) X Bourgeois 3502

Freuen wir uns (Bohemian mel. 1457) [LTDTLSL, DR MMFMFRM,] E314; X510; AF579; BV141a 3503

Freuen wir uns all in ein (Bohemian mel. 1457) X Freuen wir uns 3504

Freuet euch, ihr christen (Minor: Hammerschmidt) [LLSFMMRR, FSLLSSF, M] Q96; AA152; AZ210-A 3505

-----. [Major) V [MMRDDTL, DRMMRRD, TD] AZ210-A 3506

Freut euch, ihr lieben (Schröter) [DDDRMFM, MRDDTD, DDD] Q59; AA132 3507

Freylinghausen (Freylinghausen) X Gregor's 341st metre 3508

Freylinghausen (Freylinghausen) X Macht hoch die tür [thür] 3509

Friend (Converse) X Erie 3510

Friend (Mendelssohn) [SSS FMRRD, DRRRDRM, M] P360 3511

Friend (Stebbins) [SSMMFM RR, DTLSLSD, S] G241; V 763; Z290; AE305; AH323; AI108; AR449; AT261; AU28; AV318; AW445; AX527; BB 531; BZ 3512

Friend after friend (Grimm) [DTLDTL, FTRMMM, LTS#L] BH223 3513
-----. R [DMRDMRD, DLRF SSS, DR] 3514
Friend of sinners (Crozart) [SMSDMDLD, SMSDTRR, S] AI378 3515
Friends of Jesus (Swedish trad) X Jesus, lat din rädda dufva 3516
Friendship (Converse) X Erie 3517
Frilford (Ferguson) [MLSMRDR M, LDTL, MLSM] BV490 3518
Frisk op, min sjael (Breitendich. Koralbog) [SMRDRMFS, MFSLS F#S, S] O282 3519
Fritwell (Brockless) [SDRMFRSM L, FSMRDFM] BY368 3520
Froebel (Lewars) [DSLTDFMMR, MSFRDRM,] K563 3521
Fröhlich soll mein herze (Crueger) X Christmas joy 3522
Fröhlich soll mein herze springen (Freylinghausen) X Briesen 3523
Frohlock', liebe christenheit (Grimm. Choral buch) X Grimm's 265th metre 3524
From all that dwell below the skies (Hatton) X Duke Street 3525
From all that dwell beneath the skies (Bourgeois) X Old 100th 3526
From every stormy wind (Hastings) X Retreat 3527
From Greenland's icy mountains (Mason) X Missionary hymn 3528
From heaven above (Luther) X From heaven high 3529
From heaven high (Luther) [DT LTSLTD, DDSSMFSF] A22; B484; E17b; F151b; J22; K19; L2; M 51; N27; O133; P106; Q70; R 173; S118; V335; W56; X80a; AA150; AD123; AF121; AG75; AI 418; AK114; AM166; AN160; AQ 42; AW527; AZ22-B; BA60; BB 201; BE168; BI86; BK156; BV98; BX53; BY308; BZ 3530
-----. V [DTLTSLTD, DDSSM SFM,] V335 3531
-----. V [DTLTLSLTD, DD SSMFS] X80 3532
-----. V [DTLTSLTD, DDSSF MFS] BB201 3533
From heaven's height (Jacobsohn) [SSFM, DLTDLS, MF MR, SM] BH124 3534
From heaven's heights the thunder peals (Jewish trad) X Mee chomocho 3535
From Sinai's height a fountain gushes (Jewish trad: Akdamos mode) X Sinai's height 3536
From starry heaven (Italian carol) [SDTDRMM, RMFSS FMR, M] BN14 3537
From strength to strength (Naylor) [DSSDRM, DDFMR D, MRDT] J564a; W534b; X 641a; AC146; AD287; AL 404a; BV585b; BY508a 3538
From the depths we cry (Herbst) X Heinlein 3539
From the eastern mountains (Sullivan) X St Gertrude 3540
From thee, illustrious teacher Paul (French trad) X The praises of that saint 3541
Frondeg (Evans) [MLLS#LT DL, TLSF#M, LTD] W391b 3542
Fryd dig, du kristi brud (Regnart) X Göttingen 3543
Fulbert (Gauntlett) X St Fulbert 3544
Fulda (Gardiner's Sacred melodies) X Gardiner 3545
Fulfillment (Hoffman) [SMSD FMRD, MFSMFLS, L] BE15 3546
Full in the panting heart (Catholic) [DMFSMLTD, SSLSSMRD] BO205 3547
-----. R [SLDTLSMFLSFM, DTLS] 3548
Full of glory (Montani) [DM SSLTDS, LSSFMR, DM] BQ 40 3549

Full of glory (Terry) [DRMSDTL S, FMRRD, DRM] BL81 3550
Full salvation (Pollock) [MRD DRRMS, LLSMRDR, M] AY232 3551
Fulton (Bradbury) [MRDLTDSD MR, MRDLTD] H220 3552
Fulton (Kroeger) [DDTTRRDD, M FMRDDT, S] AJ396 3553
Für dein empfangen speis und trank (Praetorius) X Praetorius I 3554
Furry Day carol (English trad) [DDDRDMFSSLS, LTDSS] BG 49 3555
-----. R [SLLLSFMFSLS, LTD SS] 3556

G

Gaa nu hen og grav (Swedish) [SSFMRRD, RRMRMLF#S, D] O413 3557
Gabriel (Funk) X Bethlehem 3558
Gabriel (Gabriel) X Just when I need Him 3559
Gabriel (Ouseley) x St Gabriel 3560
Gabriel's message (Piae cantiones. 1582) [LSDRMRM, RMFMMRD, RM] BG102 3561
Gade (Gade) [LFRMMLLS, DTMSF# M, LF] M246 3562
Gainsborough (Tans'ur) X St Martin's 3563
Gairney Bridge (Kroeger) [MR DFFMRS, SLTDSFMR,] T215; AJ308; AM68 3564
Gaisberg (Gale) X Galsberg 3564a
Galdan (Danish trad) [MRRDT DR, FMMRDRM, DD] M630 3565
Galilean (Barnby) [MRMSFRDT, DLSMRDR, M] Q469; AA476 3566
Galilee (Armes) X Armes 3567
Galilee (Jude) [MSRRRSDD, DD DLDRM,] A566b; B268b; C 268c; D143; G233; I545a; J553; M200; N172; R269; S223; T258; U284; V735; Y106; Z281; AB 159; AC144; AD201; AE164; AF322; AG144; AH327; AI 297; AJ360; AK207; ALSuppl; AM491; AO376; AP553a; AR 243; AS229; AT360; AU159; AV188; AW140; AX40; AY474; BA404; BB421; BD62; BF348; BK67; BZ 3568
Galilee (Sherwin) X Sherwin I 3569
Galliard (Dowland) [MRDTLDR, MSFMRMR, MR] E649; X461; BE53 3570
Galsberg (i.e. Gaisberg] (Gale) [SDRMSL, LRMFS, SDRMS] D515d 3571
Galway (Miller) [DFMMRDTD, DRMF#SLTL] F328; AP593; BV602 3572
Gamble (Gamble. Collection) [SSDRMS, MMRDL, SSDRM] X379 3573
Gambold (---) [SDDMR, SRRFM, DMSMFL] AZ587-C; BA469 3574
Ganador (Sanders) [DDRTLSDR MFMR, DRMD] AQ136 3575
Ganges (American Musical misc., 1798) [DMMMRSSS, SDSLSL MR,] T63; V305; AJ97; AP 530 3576
-----. V [DMMMRSSS, SDSLSS MR,] AP530 3576a
Gannett (Loy) [SLTDRDTTTLS LS, SLT] AC5; BD23 3577
Garden (English trad) [MMFSM LSFMR, MFSLT] A202a; X36; BY475b 3578
Garden City (Parker) [SLDM RD, SLDMRD, MSRR] A175; B21; C21b; D23b; G181; S 404; V53; Y242; AC268; AD 331; AR301; BB58; BR208 3579
Gardiner (Gardiner's Sacred melodies 1815) [SDTDRSL TD, DTLRTTL] A227; B460; C86; D146; G260; H75; I339; J206; K26; L442; N29; O180; P387; S410; T211; U93; V93; W109; Y60; Z108; AA115; AB 332; AC10; AD413; AE413; AF423; AG268; AH512; AI179; AJ304;

AK394; AL8b; AM262; AN102b; AP16; AR198; AS339; AT403; AU405; AV45; AW222; AZ22-R; BA55; BB519; BD141; BE238; BF224; BK80; BV504; BX137; BY680; BZ 3580

Garelochside (Finlay) [SMRDRMD, RMSDTDL, LR] BV255a 3581

Garfirth (Stewart) [DRDFMLS, SSMDRM, MMD] AB322; BA172 3582

Gartan (Irish trad) X Garton 3583

Garton (Irish trad) [DRMLSS, SSSMRMSSSM] G94; J37; W52; BY103a; BZ 3584

Gastorius (Gastorius) X Was Gott tut 3585

Gates ajar (Vail) [SSMSDDLS, MLSMDMR, S] N616; AI408; AX250; BB561 3586

-----. R [DRD#RMDLD, MSSLSMDR,] 3587

Gather the golden grain (Davis) [MFSSSDRMFM, MRRMFL] AY337 3588

Gather them into the fold (Showalter) X In from the highways 3589

Gathering buds (Vaughan) [MMMSMDRDLD, SSSLSM] AX624 3590

-----. R [DRMSLSMS, SSSMRDR, M] 3591

Gathering home (McIntosh) [MMMMRMSLSM, RFFFSL] AU128 3592

-----. R [DMSD, LTDS, SLSSMDRR] 3593

Gaude, regina gloriae (Bohemian Br. G-B) [SLSFMFRMFS, LTDTLS] E55 3594

Gaudeamus igitur (---) [DSSDLLL, TDRTDMD, DS] Y299 3595

Gaudeamus pariter (Horne) [DDSSDRM, LSFMRD, DD] A94a; E131; F294; X144; AF186; BN94; BQ136; BY155; BZ 3596

-----. V [DDSSDRMM, LSFMRRD, D] BQ136 3596a

Gaudeo (Crueger) X Jesus, all my gladness 3597

Gaudete (Smith) [MRFMLSFM, SLTDRS, SF#] C552a; D539; K534; BR141 3598

-----. R [SSDDTSSRRD, SLLFMR,] 3599

Gaudia matris (Baker) [SDSLDRRD, MFFMDRS, F] D156b 3600

Gaul (Gaul) X Holy City 3601

Gauntlett I (Gauntlett) [MSMRDDMDLS, SSFMLD] F376b; X351; BY588b 3602

Gauntlett II (Gauntlett) [SMSLDS, LDTLS, SLTDR] L541b 3603

Gauntlett III (Gauntlett) [SMDMSL, DFMRRD, RMRM] AO454 3604

Gauntlett (Gauntlett) X St George 3605

Gaza (Jewish trad) [LLLLTDRM, LSFMLLT] A222; C14b; E279; X650 3606

Gebauer (Gebauer) X Maria, hun er en jomfru ren 3607

Gebor'n ist uns der heil'ge Christ (Gregor. Choral book) X Old 271st 3608

Gebor'n ist uns ein kindelein (Cologne G-B. 1634) X The secret flower 3609

Geduld, die soll's wir haben (Gesius) X Commemoration 3610

Geer (Greatorex) [SSMDSSSFRS, SSMDDT] H202; I376; L511; V477; AN571; AV137; BA254; BX278b 3611

Geht, erhoeht die majestaet (Goudimel) X Gregor's 205th metre 3612

Geibel (Geibel) X Trumpet call 3613

Gekreuzigter, mein herz sucht (Freylinghausen) X Gregor's 102d metre 3614

Gelobet seist du (Traditional, 14th c) X Redeemer 3615

Gelobt sei Gott (Vulpius. G-B. 1609) [DTLSSLTD, DDRSDTLS,] F135a; J109; Q208; W

331; X154; AD459; AF184; AL 109a; BN51; BV192b; BY156a; BZ 3616

-----. R [DDTDTL, SSF#SFM, RDTD,] 3617

Gelobt sei Gott, der unsre noth (Bohemian Br.) X Gregor's 2d metre 3618

Gems of day (Muret) [MFSMFS, DTLSLSFM, MF] BG101 3619

Gen himmel auf gefahren ist (German, 16th c) X God is ascended 3620

Genesis (Garrett) [MMRMFSD, DLSFSM, MMR] D601b 3621

Geneva (Bullinger) [SLSDMRLTL S, DDMRLR,] C386b; D342b; Eap. 18; G223; I293b; L420; R102; S221a; U152; V267b; Z 282; AC245; AD490; AE278; AG 140a; AH397; AI242; AJ365a; AL471b; AM389b; AN280a; AO 171; AP401b; AR373; AS265; AT246; AV202; AW227; AY446; BA891; BB256; BD134; BF346; BK111; BX335a; BY432; BZ 3622

Geneva (Cole) [DDRMMFSDTD, LTRDTL] H69; L108; U36; V518 3623

Geneva (Day) [MDRMLRTDRM, DLTDLD] A145; J345; R512; BK105 3624

Geneva (Geneva Psalter. 1551) [LFFMDRMFMRD, MSLTS] AQ 109 3625

Geneva (Lowden) [MTRDFDMR, DTSSS, SS#L] Z315; AC223; AE451; AR355; AT45 3626

Geneva (Wissmer) [DDDRRSFM, M RDDTD, DD] AK70 3627

Geneva 119 (Bourgeois) X Royal law 3628

Geneva 124 (Bourgeois) X Old 124th 3629

Geneva 61 (Genevan Psalter, 1562) [LRRDFMRD, FMRD#, LDLR] BJ92 3630

Genevan 137th (Strassburg Psalter. 1539) [LDRMMMRM F#SM, SMRDR] BJ37 3631

Genevan Psalm 12 (Genevan Psalter. 1551) X Donne secours 3632

Genevan Psalm 22 (Bourgeois) [DLRDDFFMRD, SDRMMR] AF408; AL636; AP17; BJ77 3633

Genevan Psalm 42 (Bourgeois) X Bourgeois 3634

Genevan Psalm 86 (Bourgeois) X Mon Dieu, prête moi l'orielle 3635

Genevan Psalm 110 (Bourgeois) X L'Omnipotent 3636

Genevan Psalm 118 (Bourgeois) X Rendez a Dieu 3637

Genevan Psalm 119 (Bourgeois) X Royal law 3638

Gennesaret (James) [MMRDMS FM, DTLSLR, RS] Y74 3639

Gentle Jesus (Roe) [MMRMRD LS, DDFMRR#MM] C361b; D567b 3640

Gentle Jesus (Shaw) [MFSMFM R, MFSDMRD, D] A251; E602; G444; W662a; X356; BY739a 3641

Gentle Saviour (Rider) [SSFSM R, MSSLS, DDTLS] C361a; D567a 3642

Gently, Lord, Oh gently (Jacobs) [DRMDFMMD, TDR D#RR#M, D] AY351 3643

Gently raise the sacred strain (Griggs) [DSMDSTRFM, SMD RMSF] BC92 3644

Georgetown (Williams) [SDMFM RMDLL, TDRMDR,] A437; R421; AF340; AQ111 3645

Gerald (Spohr) [SSFMDTLL, LSMSFM, SS] G299; I320; L 475; AE429; AI70; AK480; AO 246; AT8; AV400; BB226; BE 51; BZ 3646

-----. V [SFMDTLL, SMSFM, SFMD] AE429 3647

Gerar (Mason) [DMDSTD, MMR SSF#LS, SS] I264; L375; T85; U98; V246; AJ125; AX545; AY116 3648

Gerard (Cobb) [SSSDDMD, DR MFMRD, MS] D590a 3649

Gerard (English trad) X Noel 3650

Gerhardt (Magdeburg. Christ-

liche tischgesange. Erfurt, 1572) X Guds Godhed vil vi prise 3651
Gerhardt (Holbrook) [SMRFMRD, SFMSRM, SMR] L243b; V153; AO160 3652
-----. V [SMRFMRD, SFMFSR M, SM] V153 3653
Gerhardt (Ohl) [MFMMLLS#, S# LDTS# L, SSD] K517b 3654
Germania (German) [DDRMFS, SLT DLS, DDRM] D650b 3655
Germany (Beethoven) X Gardiner (Gardiner's Sacred melodies 1815) 3656
Geronimo (Stanford) [SDTDSFMS, SDTDSFMS,] F46 3657
Gerontius (Dykes) [MMRDSDMS, MRSSSS, LRM] A343b; B259; C259; D234a; F185a; J411; W 32b; AA228; AB59; AL14b; AP153; BA43; BE408; BF248; BV160; BX190 3658
Gerrans (Brown) [SLSLTD, SFM SFMR, SF#M] F9b 3659
Gertrude (Sullivan) X St Gertrude 3660
Gesius (Gesius) [DDRMRDTD, DDDRDTLS#] E417; Q397; X 533; AA348; BI108 3661
Gether (Gether) [SSDDT, SRFF M, SMDR, SS] M23 3662
Gethsemane (Bliss) X Man of sorrows 3663
Gethsemane (Brunk) [MRDSLDS, TDRRMMR, MR] AX179; AY 254 3664
Gethsemane (Carr) X Spanish chant 3665
Gethsemane (Dykes) X Rock of ages 3666
Gethsemane (Redhead) X Petra 3667
Gethsemane (Tye) [MMMLLS# L, LDTLTMLS#, M] F110b; AL93; AW107; BR174 3668
Gevaert (French noel, 13th c) [LLTDLMMM, LMMRDRM, L] A38; BP17 3669
Ghent (Van Damme) X Adoro te, No. 2 3670
Gibbons (Gibbons) X Angel's song 3671
Gibbons (Gibbons) X Song 13 3672
Gibbons (Gibbons) X Song 46 3673
Gibbons (Gibbons) X Song 67 3674
Giessen (Gauntlett's Comprehensive tune book. 1851) [MM DSSMDDTLS, FMRDL] W 409; BY347 3675
Gifford (Pritchard) [MDRMSL DSMRR, MDRMS] W589 3676
Gift of grace (Lindeman) [MD LLTDDRMD, MFSMDR] P54 3677
Gilbert (Gilbert) X Angelica 3678
Gilberts (Gilbert) X Angelica 3679
Gildas (Abelard) [SDRMRD, MSSFMR, MDFM] D75; L459a; AL172b; AP281; BR502a; BY 301 3680
Gilder (Oldberg) [MFSDRMFF M, SDSLMF#S] I14a 3681
Gilead (Mehul) [SLTDDDDD, DRRMMDFR,] I202; T180; AJ264; AO7; BR60 3682
Gillam (Shaw) [LTDRTM, RTD LTL, LLTD] X649 3683
Gird us, O God (Singer) [LL LLLDTL, LS# LDMS, FF] BH24 3684
Give (Grigg) X Grigg 3685
Give me a foothold (Rupp) [SMRDRDLL, DRDRMR, SM] AX519; AY72 3686
Give me Jesus (Sweney) [DRM MRMSF, FMRDRMD, D] AX 270; BB596 3687
-----. R [SSLLFLSM, MMRR MF#S, D] 3688
Give me the Bible (Lorenz) [MS DMFMRRMDS, LLTDF] AX 138; BB655 3689
-----. R [SMFSDFMRDLD, SDRMS] 3690
Give me thy heart (Bourne) [SDRMMMFDRM, SRMFMF] AI196; AM723; AX260 3691
-----. R [MSMS, DMDM, L

LLSMDDT] 3692
Give of your best (Barnard) [MM MFMRSS, SDRMFMR, M] AS 407; AT353; AU366; AV375; AW400 3693
Give thanks (Simper) [MRDSLR DT, TDRMFR, MR] AS425 3694
-----. R [SMMFSLSM, RMLS F#MF#S,] 3695
Give thanks to God (Plainsong. 1539) X To God on high 3696
Give to the Lord (Fillmore) [DR MFMMRR, SRMFM, DRM] AX 647 3697
-----. R [SMRDMRR, SRMFFM M, SS] 3698
Give us room that we may dwell [Shepherd) [MFF#SMSDTLS, SRMFMR] BC256 3699
Giver of all (Norden) [SMMM RRDD, TLLFMMRR,] BH250 3700
Giving (Leech) [DDDDDTDRMS, LLLLSM] AT404; AU393 3701
-----. R [DSMDSF#SLSMFSL, T TD] 3702
Glad tidings (Goss) [DDMSMS DDRM, DDDLSD] O200 3703
Gladdening light (Harris) [DDMR SSSDRT, SLTDRM] BV54 3704
Glade Jul (Grueber) X Holy night 3705
Gladje utan Gud ej finnes (Düben) X Jesu 3706
Gladness (Barnby) X St Anselm 3707
Gladness (Bliss) [SSSSSSSDRM, RRRRRD] G435; AH543; AL 480; AM647; AP742; AT508; AU319; AX38; AY484; BB423; BY498 3708
-----. R [SSSSMRDLL, SSSRSDR] 3709
Gladness (Bohemian trad) [DDRM FFMM, RRMMRD, DD] Q82 3710
Gladness (Düben) X Jesu 3711
Glan Geirionydd (Welsh hymn mel) [LDRMLMRDTL, LDRM LS] X592 3712
Glan'rafon (Davies) [DS, LSFM RDMR, RMLSFM] X505b 3713
Glaser (Glaser) [SMRDMSLS, MLSTDMR, R] M259 3714
Glasgow (Moore. Psalm singer's ... 1756) [DMRMRDMSLS FM, MRFM] R257; W365; AL661a; AM272; BV416; BY 658 3715
Glastonbury (Dykes) [MMRDL DS, SSSMRDR, R#R#] D247 3716
Gleams of the golden morning (Graham) [DRMMMMMMR DD, RRMRD,] BB547 3717
-----. R [MFSSSSMDDDD, RRRDM] 3718
Gleason (Lutkin) [MMMMMRR, RSRMFM, MMM] I464b; 3719
Glebe Field (Dykes) [DDDRM FFM, SMFSLRR, S] C417a; D204d; K561; BX209 3720
Glenfinlas (Finlay) [SDRMRDL, SDRMS, SLSM] F433a; W663; X354; BV59a; BY751; BZ 3721
Glenluce (Scottish Psalter, 1635) [DMFSLSFM, RMSSF#S, RR] X523; AW206 3722
-----. V [MMFSLSFM, RMSS F#S, RR] AW206 3723
Glenmont (Harris) [MRDTRD TL, RMFLTDRD] BR360 3724
Glenn (Rosecrans) [SMFMMR R, SRMRRDD, SM] BB429 3725
-----. R [SDDTT, SRRDD, SMRDT, L] 3726
Glezen (Glezen) [DDRMFMRS, SLSMMRDR,] N56 3727
Gloaming (Stainer) [MFRMM FRM, DTLR, MFRM] K464; W273; BE160 3728
Gloria (French carol mel) [MMMSSFM, MRMSMRD, MM] A42; F594; G108; J30; R158; X71; Z187; AD117; AE89; AF116; AH256; AK105; AN 175; AQ294; AR138; AT64;

AW82; BD227; BF279; BG119; BK143; BL9; BM65; BN12; BO 154; BP16; BV93; BY89; BZ 3729

-----. R [SLSFMFSFMRMFMR] 3730

-----. V [MMRMSSFMD, MMRM SSF] F594 3731

-----. V [MMMMSSFMD, MMRMM SS] AN175 3732

Gloria (Pearsall) [SRMFLSFM, R MF#SLTLS,] E567 3733

Gloria (Pierre) [DMRDMF#S, DMRDMF#S, ML] AJ430 3734

Gloria dei (Johnson) [DMFMRDR D, TLLLRDT, D] N141 3735

Gloria in excelsis (Elliott) [DM RDMSLS, RMRDMSLS,] W231 3736

Gloria, laus et honor (Plainsong, M 1) [MRRMRRDRRMRDT, RRT] BN31 3737

Gloria, laus et honor (Ravanello) [MMMMSFM, SLTDTSLT, T] BQ168 3738

Gloria, laus et honor (Sarum Processional, M 1) [RLL#L SSLSSFSSLSFMR,] E621; F598 3739

Gloria patri (Greatorex) X Glory be to the Father 3740

Gloria patri (Meineke) [DDDDD RR, RRSRRRMDT] AE471; AK 492; AMp.xv; AR637; AT524; AU494; AV430; AW607 3741

Glorification (Tscherlitzky) [DS DDRRM, MRDMR, DSDM] Q118; AA166 3742

Glorious Mary (Florian) [DRMM FSLSS, LLDLSSM] BN156 3743

Glorious name (McKinney) [SSS MLLSM, DRMSFMRM,] AT138 3744

-----. R [SFMFSLSFM, FMRM FSF] 3745

Glorious patron (Browne) [MFSM DRMD, DTTLLFMR,] BQ101 3746

Glorious peace (Teasley) [SMM RMFMD, DRRRRMFM] AX337 3747

-----. R [MMMRDR, RFFFMR M, MSM] 3748

Glorious saint whose deeds immortal (Darmstadt G-B) X All saints 3749

Glorious things (LeJeune) [MDRMFSLTDT, LSSFMM] D490b; Y208 3750

Glorious things are sung (Daynes) [DMSDLF#LS, LSRS F#FM, D] BC243 3751

Glorious things of thee are spoken (Conkey) X Rathbun 3752

Glorious things of thee are spoken (Hall) X Saviour breathe an evening blessing 3753

Glorious things of thee are spoken (Hanecy) [SDFMRD TLSD, DDRMRF#] BC244 3754

Glorious Virgin, thee we sing (German hymn arr) [DMF SDDTD, RMRDRF#SS] BO89 3755

Glory (Harrison) X Cambridge 3756

Glory (Matthews) X Children's praises 3757

Glory (Curwen's Tune book. 1842) [DDMFSSLLS, DLR SSTD,] W600; BY608 3758

Glory be to Jesus (Filitz) X Caswall 3759

Glory be to Jesus (Montani) [LLDMLM, SSRRM, LLDMF] BQ72 3760

Glory be to the Father (Greatorex) [DDDDDDT, DRSSSS LTL] R546; T458; U488; Y389; AC335; AE472; AG 323; AHp.9; AI449; AK493; AMp.xv; AR637; AS488; AT 525; AU495; AV428; AW606; BA944; BB689; BF680 3761

Glory flaming (Whittington) [DMSSLLM, DDTF#R#D#T, DM] BI54 3762

Glory gates (Hott) [DRMSS LSLSMD, DRMSM] AX269; AY146 3763

-----. R [DSDDSLSLSMD, DR MSS] 3764
Glory in the highest (Ouseley) [MDSDLDS, MFSLSDRMR,] B558; K548 3765
Glory, praise and blessing (Smith, B. E.) [SMMFSDTLS, F#F#SLTDT] BI20-D 3766
Glory song (Gabriel) [SDTLSFMS DM, MRD#MRT] AT485; BB 641; BY191a; 3767
-----. R [MMMMMRMF, FF FFFSRM,] 3768
Glory to God in the highest (Stephens) [DTLSLTLS, SML SFMR, R] BC359 3769
-----. R [SSSFMSFLS, DR# R#MDR#R#] 3770
Glory to God in the highest (Warren) [MMFSDLSM, SDTL RMFL] AX103 3771
-----. R [MMRDMFSD, DDTRM F#S, F] 3772
Glory to God on high (Giardini) X Moscow 3773
Glory to his name (Stockton) [M MRDDTLDS, MMMSSMD] AT 95; AU185; AV386; AW464; AX4 3774
-----. R [DDDLSLD, MMMDR MR, MM] 3775
Gloucester (Ravenscroft's Psalter) [DSMRDFSL, MRMFSM, SM] W223b; AP698b 3776
Gloucester (Williams) [MR#MS DLS, DFMLSRFM, R] D611a; BI12 3777
Gloucestershire wassail (English trad) [SDDDRMFMRMS, SF RRR] BG31 3778
Glovernia (Brewer) [DMMMFS MSLT, SDDTLS] AP569 3779
Glück zu kreuz (Halle, 1697) X Petersen 3780
Glynthorpe (Shaw) [FSRDLS, FFMTRRDTLM,] X588 3781
Go as a witness (Ackley) [MM MMR#MSS, SF#SMSDT, F] U314 3782
Go bury thy sorrow (Bliss) [DDTLLSFFLSM, DDTLL] AU293 3783
Go down Moses (Negro spiritual) [MDDTTDDL, MMS#S#L, M DD] AF428; AG611 3784
-----. R [LL, RR, MMRMMRD L, DLLD] 3785
Go tell it on the mountain (Negro spiritual) [MMRDLSD, RRRDRMRMRD,] AK488; BK163; BZ 3786
-----. R [DMSSLSM, DRRDR M, DMS] 3787
Go to the deeps (Gabriel) [SF#SLSDMM, RDFLDTLS,] AI241 3788
-----. R [DDDDTLSS, MSR MFSFM,] 3789
Go to thy rest, fair child (Tenney) [MMMSFM, MRM FSM, SLSM] AX627; AY 177 3790
Go, ye messengers (Robertson) [MMMDFMRMD, RMFSDDM] BC247 3791
Gobaith (Davies) X Hope 3792
God (Haile) [SMSDDTTD, MDMLSS, SR] BH68 3793
God be in my head (Davies) [SSSMR, TLTRTLS, SSSM] R395; AF543; AL364; AR 679; BV623; BY471; BZ 3794
God be with you (Tomer) [M MMMMMSRM, LLLLLLL] G557; H434; I564; L67; M 650; N364; R78; U449; V26; Z129; AF62; AG14; AH177; AI344; AM632; AN472b; AO 48; AP701; AR506; AS63; AT372; AU480; AV235; AW 365; AX654; AY405; BA932; BB35; BC47; BY761a; BZ 3795
-----. R [MFSDMRDLD, TLSLSMD] 3796
God bless America (Berlin) [DTLTLS, RDRM, RMFL, FM] AH488 3797
God bless our native land (Mason) X Dort 3798
God cares (Martin) X Martin 3799
"God hath sent his angels" (Parker) [SMDMSDS, SDMR

D, LMDM] C557; AO187 3800

-----. R [SMDRMFSDS, SDM RD, FF] 3801

God in heaven (Fuller) [MRDSLD TLLS, DRMFSL] D578 3802

God in nature (Stainer) [SDFFMRS, SDFFMR, RRS] W18a 3803

God incarnate, veil thy splendor (Smart) X Bethany 3804

God is ascended (Edmunds) [DM FSLTDRS, DTLS, LSF] BL38 3805

God is ascended (German, 16th c) [LLRD#RMRDL#L, RFSLTD#] AD166; BG127 3806

-----. V [LLRD#RMRDTL, RFSLTD#] BG127 3807

God is good (Bontrager) [SSLS TLLMS, SDDDTLS] AY427 3808

God is great, God is good (Allgemeines katholisches G-B. Vienna, 1744) X Te deum 3809

God is in his holy temple (Asper) [MDFMRRDTS, DRMFRDT] BC246 3810

God is in his holy temple (Hawkes) [MMRDTDMR, FFMR DRM, S] BH4 3811

God is love (Bailey) X Praise him 3812

God is love (Lorenz) [DMFSS LTD, RTD, DMFSS] AE70; AW439; AX81 3813

-----. R [SLF, FSM, DDDDDRD TLS] 3814

God is love (Mendelssohn) X Trust 3815

God is love, his mercy (Click) [SSSDRRMS, SSLSDMR, M] AX86; AY372 3816

God is my strong salvation (Binder) [DTTDSMRD, MSMD RR, LR] BH95 3817

God is near thee (Curwen's Standard course) [SSSMDDDSM R, RMFMRM] AP536 3818

God is the giver of all (Grauman) [MMMSFMLLS, SDSSFM M] BH66 3819

God knows what is best (Ruebush) [SSF#SMRDL, DSDDMMRR] AY322 3820

-----. R [SSDMDRDL, LSDM DMRR,] 3821

God loved us so he sent his Son (Schreiner) [DDDDDRFM, SSSSSDLS,] BC178 3822

God most truly (Daley) [DRM RDTL, LSLDRTD, DR] BN 175 3823

God moves in a mysterious way (Binder) [MMDLDTTT, TRM RDR, MM] BH83 3824

God moves in a mysterious way (Bradbury) X Harvey's chant 3825

God moves in a mysterious way (Showalter) [MFSSSDM RD, SLDDLS, M] AX85; AY 84 3826

God of grace (Haile) [DRMM SLTD, TTLLSFM, R] BH75 3827

God of hosts (Hopkins) X St Athanasius 3828

God of Israel (Binder) [SSD TLSFMRMRDS, SSL] BH52 3829

God of love (Hugg) [DRMDT LTD, MF#STLSF#S] AY 34 3830

God of mercy and compassion (Montani) [MMFRDTMD, TLRTLTDM,] BQ134 3831

-----. R [MMMRFMRD, SSS FLFMR] 3832

God of might (Jewish trad) X Addeer hu 3833

God of our fathers (Warren) X National hymn 3834

God of our fathers, known of old (Robertson) [SSSSLSFS, SSSLDTLT,] BC77 3835

God of our fathers, known of old (Woodbury) X Selena 3836

God of our fathers, we come unto thee (Beesley) [MDRMFM RDTD, MMMSFM] BC50 3837

God of our strength (Doane) X Vision 3838

God of power, God of right

(Cannon) [MLSDRRM, FMRM DTLS, R] BC36 3839
God of the nations, near and far (Lutkin) X Upham 3840
God our Father (Silcher) X Gott ein vater 3841
God, our Father, hear us pray (Gottschalk) X Mercy 3842
God our Father made the daylight (English trad) X Song of praise 3843
God rest you merry (Minor: English mel., 18th c) [LLMM RDTL, SLTDRM, L] A40; R166; S131; AD109; AF122; AG67; AH259; AL66; AM160; AP731; BC222; BG12; BV91; BY96; BZ 3844
-----. (Major) V [DDSSFMRD, TDRMFS, DD] BC222 3845
God rest you merry II (English carol) [DDLSFMRD, LSDTTD, DS] BG11 3846
-----. R [DRMFS, DTLSMFS LTD, D] 3847
God save America (Lvov) X Russia 3848
God save our gracious king (Thesaurus musicus, 1740) X America 3849
God save the queen (Thesaurus musicus, 1740) X America 3850
God! send us men (Levenson) [MRMSMFMRMD, RDRMDR] BH233 3851
God so loved the world (Stainer) [MMRRS, SSF# F# TLSDTLS] AU476 3852
God speed the right (Arndt) [SS DSMMSM, DRRM, SSDS] AN555; AW371; BC171 3853
God supreme (Achron) [DDMDR DLL, DDMDRDLD] AH155; BH 93 3854
God, that doest wondrously (Jewish trad) X Ayl nora allelah 3855
God the all-merciful (Lvov) X Russia 3856
God will take care (Martin) X Martin 3857
God with us (Barnes) [LSFMRS, DTLSLSFMRR] AD113 3858
Goderich (Darley) [SDDTD SSLSFFM, SDDD] BA368 3859
Godesberg (Albert) X Waltham 3860
Godfrey (Trebel) [SMRDDTLT D, RMF#SRDT] M599 3861
Godfrey (West) [SMDRMS, LDTLS, MSDRM] I344; AC 65 3862
-----. V [SSMDRM, SLDTLS, SMSD] AC65 3863
Godhead here in hiding (French trad) X Love is come again 3864
God's dear Son (English carol) [LFMRDLTS#, LTDDRRM, L] BG13 3865
God's glory (Langford) [SSSS FMRRR, RRMFSLS] AR364 3866
God's heaven (Negro spiritual) [DDDMDDDM, MMMMRDD M,] Y319; AH601 3867
-----. R [TRDM, MMMMMRD RRRRD] 3868
God's love (Sherwin) [SLTD RDT, STDRMRD, DD] AC42 3869
God's mariner (Smyth) [MMM SSMMSSMMDRMR, M] BR 525 3870
God's plan (Nellemann) [SMR DTDSRM, RDDFMRR,] AE 377; AR534 3871
God's presence (West) [MF SLSMD, RMFSFMR, MF] AH 554 3872
God's way (Leech([MDRMFM, RTMRD, MDRMF] AI290 3873
-----. R [SSMSLS, FFTLLS, DSMD] 3874
God's way is best (Hunter) [SSSSSLSSM, DRRRRDR] AX 389 3875
-----. R [DRRRFMRMS, SSRRFMR] 3876
Godwin (Blanchard) [MFMRSR FFM, MMMMSLL] G457; Z311 3877

Goeldel (As hymnodus sacer. 1625) X Ach Gott und Herr 3878

Goetchius (Maclean) [MSDFM R, MSSF#SS, LLSD] V80 3879

Going home (Dvorák) [MSSMRD, RMSMR, MSSMR] AI267 3880

Going home (Miller) [DMMM DRMR, DMSSDMRD,] I628; AU261; AX591; AY144 3881

Golden (English trad) X The merchants' carol 3883

Golden chain (Barnby) X The golden chain 3884

Golden corn (Calkin) [MRDDTT, FMRRDD, DLLL] D569a; I 196; T122b; AJ61 3885

Golden Grove (Cooke) [MFSM RDMLS, DRMSFMR] F307a 3886

Golden Grove (Littlewood) [DRMSFFRMFM, MF#SLSF#] Y338 3887

Golden Hills (Chapin) [DMRDLRR D, SLSLDLS, S] AY368 3888

Golden mornings (English trad) [MDTDLSSM, MRMFMRM, M] BG165 3889

Golden sequence (Langton) X Veni sancte spiritus (Langton) 3890

Golden sheaves (Basque trad) [LTDRMRDT, RDLDTSL, L] BG159 3891

Golden sheaves (Sullivan) [SMS SFMRD, DRMFLTD, S] D191a; Eap. 17; F484; N570; O525; W616; BE392; BV653; BX428; BY731 3892

Golden trumpets (LWhitmer) [MSSSLTDR, MSSSLTLS,] AC134 3893

Golders Green (Fowles) [DTSL TDRMRDTR, DTSL] BY765 3894

Goldschmidt (Darmstadt G-B) [LTDTDRMM, LTDTLLS# L, D] C268b; E382; Q60; X217b; AA133; AZ16-B 3895

-----. V [LTDTDRMM, LTDTLLS# L, L] P200 3895a

Golgotha (Harrington) [MMRM, M RMFFMRM, MRDT] AK151 3896

Gone to bloom above (Teasley) [SMR#MRDRM, RDDRDLS, S] AX626 3897

-----. R [MFFDFMR#M, R DDDRMR, S] 3898

Gonfalon Royal (Buck) [SLD FMRMDL, LRTSDFM] E 141b; W23; X593; BE271; BV33b; BY147a 3899

Good-bye (Hugg) [SMMMDDLD, DTDRRDRM,] AY404 3900

-----. R [MFMFFMR#M, MSF#SDMRR,] 3901

Good-bye (Shaw) [SDSFSMM, MMLS#TL, SDS] X386g 3902

Good bye, mourner (Negro spiritual) [DMDMDMMMD, DMDDLDDL] AH598 3903

Good cheer (Perkins) [SDMS LTD, DRMDFMRTD] Y194 3904

Good King Wencelas (Piae cantiones, 1582) X Tempus adest floridum 3905

Good morning to you (---) [SLSDT, SLSRD, SSMDTL,] AU308 3906

Good news from heaven (Luther) X From heaven high 3907

Good Shepherd (Barnby) [SDS MRDRMSRM, DFFMR] I104a; AJ122 3908

Good Shepherd, Rosemont (Miller) [SMRDMLSM, S LTDTLS] A378a 3909

Goodwell (Emerson) [SDRMM SDRMM, RMFMMR] L65 3910

Goodwill (Roberts) [SLSDMM RDT, D RDTLS, F] AR270 3911

Goodwin (Webb) X Webb 3912

Gopsal (Handel) [SLSMF#S, DF MRRD, SSML] D457a; E476; F216; V201; W135b; X632; BV210; BY190 3913

Gor porten hög (Swedish Koralbok, 1697) [LDRMLLS# L,

DRMFMRDT,] N2 3914
Gordon (Barnby) X St Ignatius 3915
Gordon (Gordon) [DMFFMRD MRTTD, DMFF] G234; H321; P216; R405; T149; U203; Z382; AE178; AH297; AI115; AJ211; AM547; AO643; AR462; AS275; AT289; AU154; AV323; AW216; AX396; AY195; BA905; BB276; BZ 3916
Gordon (Smart) [SSSDMFLS, DRFMRM, SM] J362a; W611; BV288 3917
Goring (Thiman) [SMFSLDTD, RMSSF#S, SD] BY274 3918
Gorran (Dussek) [DSMTDRMLT DR, MLSM, D] C244b 3919
Gorton (Beethoven) [SSSLLS, SSSDDR, RMMD] J89; K46; N582; T102b; AJ217; AM417; AO153; AS36; AV425; BB694 3920
Gorton (Brunk) X Father! in life's young morning 3921
Goshen (Davis) [DDTLSM, SMR DR, DDTLS] Eap. 70; K564; W552; AH541; AP741; BV505 3922
Goshen (Haydn) X St Michel's 3923
Goss (Goss) X St Casimer 3924
Gosterwood (English trad) [DD LTDRMD, SFMRDRD, D] E299; R410; S298; W70; X21; Y76; Z592; AD451; AL576; BE377; BV220 3925
-----. V [DDDLTDRMD, SFMRD RD,] Y76 3926
Gotha (Knecht) [DDMDMMSM, RSMDTDR, D] M400; AK18; AW 511 3927
Gothenburg (Crueger) X Schmuecke dich 3928
Gott der vater wohn' (Walther. Geistliche G-B. 1524) [SSLTD DT, LDSMFMRD, S] Q247; AA 271; AN480 3929
-----. V [SSLTDT, DSMFR, SSLTD] AN480 3930
Gott des himmels [und der erden] (Albert) X Waltham 3931
Gott des himmels und der erden (Meiningen G-B) X St Leonard 3932
Gott ein Vater (Silcher) [SL SFMR, DRMFMR, MSLS] E600; F415; W666; AM661; AP585; BV7; BY336a 3934
Gott ist gegenwärtig (Neander) X Arnsberg 3935
Gott ist getreu (Ahle) X Augsburg 3936
Gott ist mein hort (Egli) [SD DTTDRM, MDLRDTLS,] AA461 3937
Gott sei dank (Freylinghausen. Geistriches G-B.) X Luebeck 3938
Gott sei gelobet (Walther) X Walther 3939
Gott sprach zu dir (---) [MM FSDTLSFMM, MMLLS] K551 3940
Gott will's machen (Steiner) X Steiner 3941
Gott woll'n wir loben (Bohemiam Br.) X Gregor's 520th metre 3942
Gottes lamm ruft gnade (Tscherlitzky) X Glorification 3943
Gottes sohn ist kommen (Weisse) X Ravenshaw 3944
Göttingen (Regnart) [LLMM RM, MMRDDT, TDRM] M328; N18; O161; Q526; AA508; AZ75a 3945
-----. R [MSMMDRR, RMR DDTL.] 3946
-----. V [LLTDRM, MMRDR T, TDRM] O161 3947
-----. V [LLTDRM, MMRDD T, TDRM] Q526 3948
-----. V [LLTDRM, MRRDDT, TDRM] AZ75-a 3949
Gottlieb (Maker) X Word of life 3950
Gottlob (Wagner. Sammlung ...) X Gottlob, es geht nun mehr zu ende 3951
Gottlob, es geht nun mehr zu

ende (Wagner. Sammlung ...) [MDMFMRDR, MMMLTDDT,] Q163; W271b; X637a; Y111; AA66; AB8; AD446; AF468; AN82; BE32; BN97; BY315 3952

-----. V [MDMFMRDRR, MMMLTDD] X637 3953

-----. V [MDMFMRMR, MMMLTDDT] Y111 3954

-----. V [MDMFMRDR, MLTDDT, MD] BE32 3955

Gottschalk (Gottschalk) X Mercy 3956

Gouda (Tours) [SLTDRMRD, DDMDFR, SL] I447; BR368 3957

Goudimel (Goudimel) [SLDDTD, DLTTLS, SDLT] AA338 3958

-----. V [SLDDTD, DLTDLS, SDLT] AJ423 3958a

Goudimel (Goudimel) X Gregor's 205th metre 3959

Gould (Burnap) [SSMMMSFR, FMSDLS, SS] L519 3960

Gould (Gould) X Hymn 3961

Gould (Warren) [DMFSSSLLTDS, MRDTS] BR152 3962

Gouldie (Pollock) [DRMRMFSM, LSFMRDR, M] AY256 3963

Gounod (Gounod) [SMRDDLSFFM, SLTDMR] V344 3964

Gounod (Gounod) X Lux prima 3965

Gounod's Evening hymn (Gounod) X Evening hymn 3966

Gower (Gower) X Gower's Litany 3967

Gower's Litany (Gower) [MMRMSRR, FFMFLSS, SS] AB162; AI223; AL159b; AM244; AO276; AP280b; AR280; AV413; BF360; BK31 3968

Gower's Recessional (Gower) X Recessional 3969

Grabesruhe (Rau) [SLTDSMDRD, DTLSTLS] AZ89-C; BA70 3970

Grace (American traditional) X Amazing grace 3971

Grace (Berggren) [SDDTFLLS, MSFSLRDT,] M188 3972

Grace (Nitzsche) [MMR#MLSSF, MRD#RSFM, S] BA465 3973

Grace (Stenhammer) [MSFMRMSF, FLSFMSFM] BE76 3974

Grace (Warren) [DDRRR#R#FR, RRMMFFSM,] D595a 3975

Grace after meals (Jewish trad) [MMSFMRMF, FFLSFMFS,] BH111 3976

Grace Church (Pleyel) [MMRDTDRM, SSFMRDTD,] A108b; B119; C119; D297a; H207; J62b; K59; L181; N126; S22; T428b; V247; Y43; Z309; AA488; AD310; AF324; AK74; AM134; AN64; AO85; AR363; BA706; BR40; BX54; BY258 3977

Grace Church, cananoque (George) [MMRSF#MRM, SLTDTLLM,] BZ 3978

Grace dieu (Wesley, S.S.) [SDMRSDRRD, SSSDTLF] W536 3979

Grace greater than our sin (Towner) X Marvelous grace 3980

Grace soit (French trad) [SSLTDS, DDRTD, SSLTD] X3; AQ319; BG156; BM13 3981

Grace soit rendue (French carol) X Grace soit 3982

Grace, 'tis a charming sound (Link) [MMFMRMRD, SSLSFSFM] AX323; AY77 3983

Graceham (Chitty) [DDRMMRD, DRMRDRR, DD] AZ581-K; BA434B 3984

Gracias (Beaumont) [SSMRLT, SDDDDLS, FMD] BY18a 3985

Gracious Father, O Lord hear us (Beethoven) [SSSS, SLSS, SSSSSSSL] AU487; AV414 3986

Gracious God whose mercy lends (Allgemeines katholisches G-B. Vienna, 1774) X Hursley 3987

Gracious King, enthroned (Unseld) [MRDSLDS, DRMRR, MRDS] AI217; AS206 3988

Graefenberg (Crueger) [DLSD

RMMR, MSFMRD, SM] A370; E421; F347; G389; J413a; K15; M11; N127; P8; Q10; R243; S 197a; W351; X38; Z275; AD 189; AE142; AF241; AG229; AH235; AK183; AL153a; AN 159a; AP4; AQ96; AR234; AS 167; AW242; BE287; BV534; BY206a; BZ 3989

-----. V [DLSDRMMR, MSFM RD, SF] AS167 3989a

Grafton (Chants ordinaires ... Paris) [DRMDMRMFSM, SSFF MR] E33; F383b; W207; X 129b; BO274c; BV161b; BY326 3990

Grafton (Clark) [SSSSFMRD, RMSLDTLS,] AQ251 3991

Grand Dieu! que de merveilles (French trad) X The builders 3992

Grand Isle (Hopkins) [SDDDMFS LS, MFSDRM,] A243; AF481; BY259 3993

Grandpont (Stainer) [MMRDLD, DTFMMR, SSFM] S500; W488; BE21 3994

Grange (Brown-Borthwick) [SSMRDRDT, DDLSFMR, S] BR70a 3995

Grant me strength (Weinberg) [MFS#S#S#LTT, DTLS#TS#, TT] BH48 3996

Grasmere (Barnby) X Edinburgh 3997

Grasmere (Freylinghausen) [MM FSSFFM, MRDRTTDD,] F567 3998

Grassmere (Traditional mel) [DMSSSDLDS, SFM, FMR, D] L502; AP717 3999

Grateful praises (Kaiser) [SSMD RMRD, RMSSF#S, RM] BH104 4000

Grateful submission (Kolb) [SM FMSSRM, SSDDRDT, D] AY 379 4001

-----. R [SSSSSSDD, LSMSFMR, R] 4002

Gratia (Freylinghausen. G-B. 1704) X Luebeck 4003

Gratitude (Bost) [SSDMMSMRF TD, SSDMM] G460; I410; L12; V36; AO24 4004

Gratitude (German trad) X Gregor's 185th metre-A 4005

Gratitude (Crueger) X Nun danket 4006

Gratitude (Dykes) X Beatitudo 4007

Gratitude (Herr) X I owe the Lord a morning song 4008

Gratitude (Wesley, S.S.) [MS MMRDFMR, RMF#SLTL] C 426b; D477b; W322; AL229a 4009

Gratitude (Whitmer) [SLTSSL TDRM, FMRMRD] AC233; AD341 4010

Gravity (Mason) X Rockingham 4011

Great Arbiter of human fate (Samuel) [SDTLSFMR, MFSDRMM, S] BH209 4012

Great day (Negro spiritual) [SLD, DDSLSSSSLM, MMM] AH605 4013

Great God, attend (Daynes) [MFSDRDDTTDRFMRRD,] BC248 4014

Great God, to thee my evening song (Kimball) [DMFSLSFMR D, SLTDDT] BC59 4015

Great God! whatever through thy church (LaSalle hymnal) [SDSMSDSM, SDDRMR, RR] BO209 4016

Great God, whatever through thy church (Slovak hymnal) [DDDDMMSSF, MRMFRDT] BQ128 4017

Great High Priest (Gregor's Chorale book. 1784) X Gregor's 12th metre 4018

Great is the Lord; 'Tis good (Beesley) [DSFMLSFMRD, SLTDDT] BC234 4019

Great is the love (Kirkpatrick) [SSSDTLS, FFFSSM, SSS] AE 291 4020

-----. R [TTTDDRS, DDRRM, MMMD] 4021

Great is thy faithfulness (Runyan) X Faithfulness 4022

Great King of heaven (Robertson) [SDMLSSFMLS, SDRTSL] BC 53 4023
Great King of Kings (Kreitmaier) [DMFSMFLS, SLTDSSFM] BQ 336 4024
-----. R [DTSLSSFMMR, LSM FMM] 4025
Great King of peace (Roff) [DM FSMFLSRM, SMRDDL] BL57 4026
Great King of saints (Bourgeois) X Old 100th 4027
Great Physician (Stockton, arr) [SSMDRMFS, SSDMDRD, S] P271; AH334; AI389; AM144; AP752; AS128; AT86; AU226; AX535; BB530 4028
-----. R [SLTDSTLS, SLTDSTLS,] 4029
Great Redeemer! (Conte) X Redentore 4030
Great St Joseph (Bragers) [MD SSFMRMD, DRMFRDT] BP90 4031
Great St Joseph (Slovak hymn) [MMLSFMMR, RRMRMFMR,] BQ93 4032
Great St Joseph (Stein) [DTLS LRSFMRD, SLF#SL] BN170; BO126 4033
Great white host (Norwegian trad., arr by Grieg) X Behold a host 4034
Greatorex (Allen) [SLSMDRDLS, DMSFRDR] T207; AJ296; AO 285 4035
Greek folksong (Greek mel) X Luke 4036
Greek hymn (Holbrook) [DTLDRD, MRDMR, DTLDR] C162a; G 275b; I616b 4037
Green are the leaves (Catholic hymn mel) [SMRDTTLS, SDDMR DRM,] BO110 4039
Green grow'th the holly (Henry VIII, King) [MLSMM, MLSM M, MLLSFM] BG63 4040
Green Hill (Comley) [DMSFMM RD, DLSSMR, TD] K544b; P174 4041
Green Hill (Peace) [MMMRDFFM, RSSFML, LL] I314; O70; U35; V75; AB82; AE323; AJ224; AL427; AM498; BA226 4042
Green Hill (Stebbins) X The green hill 4043
Greenland (Haydn) [MSSSS DM, MRRFFM, RMSS] A4; B171b; C61; D43a; H206; I18; M558; N312; R482; S400; U107; V710; Y280; Z486; AB284; AD242; AE63; AF190; AG250; AR395; AS166; AT111; BA868; BB164; BD 94; BE120; BF411; BQ26; BX541 4044
-----. V [SSSSSDS, MRRSFM, RMM] BQ26 4045
Greensleeves (English trad., before 1642) [LDRMFMRTS L, TDLLS#LT] A36; G109; J48; R159; Y326; Z200; AB 121; AF140; AG300; AH255; AW78; BD220; BF295; BG 28; BK162; BZ 4046
-----. R [SSF#MRTSL, TD LLS#LTS] 4047
-----. V [SSFMRTSL, TDLL S#LTS] Y326 4048
Greenville (Rousseau) [MMRD DRRMRD, SSFMMR] G187; H446; I39; L66; N365; V253; W661; AI195; AL476; AP726; AT390; AW459; AX240; BC 105; BR78; BY286 4049
-----. V [MMRDDRRMD, SSF MMRD] V253 4050
Greenwell (Leslie) [MDLSMDT LS, DTDFMMR] BY204b 4051
Greenwood (Prout) X Allen 4052
Greenwood (Sweetser) [MRDS LS, TLTDMS, RDRM] G217; H203; I352; L504; R218; S 299b; T71; U222; V365; Y 202; AA541; AB246; AD269; AG207; AJ107; AM327; AO569; AV121; AW236; BA99; BB40; BR257 4053
Greeting (Shaw) [SDSMF, SDS MF, SDSMFS] X386a 4054
Greeting (Wathall) [DSFMDS FM, MLDTMS#F, F] I572

4055

Gregor (Gregor) [MLS# LRDT, DLRDTTL, ML] AZ581-E 4056

Gregor (Herrnhut ms.) X Gregor's 37th metre 4057

Gregor's 2d metre (Bohemian Br.) [SLTDRMFS, FMRMRDTD,] AZ2-A 4058

Gregor's 6th metre (Gregor) [SDRMFM, SDRMFM, SSFF] AZ6-B 4059

Gregor's 7th metre (Gregor) [SDTDRRM, SDTDRRM, SD] AZ7-B 4060

Gregor's 9th metre (Gregor. Choral buch) [LDTDLTDR, MMRDTL, MM] AZ9-a 4061

Gregor's 10th metre (Selnecker) X Selnecker 4062

Gregor's 12th metre (Gregor. Choral buch, 1784) [DTDLSFM, DLRDTLS, DS] AZ11-l; BA453 4063

Gregor's 15th metre (Praetorius) X Ich dank' dir schon 4064

Gregor's 16th metre (Darmstadt G-B) X Goldschmidt 4065

Gregor's 20th metre (---) [DM SMFLSR, MSFRDLTS,] AZ 20-A 4066

Gregor's 22d metre-A (Geistliche G-B. Wittenberg 1544) X Rhau[w] 4067

Gregor's 22d metre-C (Crueger) X Lob sei dem allmachtigen Gott 4068

Gregor's 22d meter-D (Plainsong, ca 600) X Christe, qui lux es et dies 4069

Gregor's 36th metre (Crueger) X Herzliebster Jesu 4070

Gregor's 37th metre (Herrnhut ms) [DSLSFM, DRMMRD, MRMR] AZ37-A; BA448 4071

Gregor's 37th metre (Herrnhut ms) X Bunyan (Thommen. Christen-schatz) 4071a

Gregor's 39th metre-A (Moravian) [DDSMSFMRDTDD, DDSM] AZ39-A; BA312 4072

Gregor's 39th metre-B (Darmstadt G-B) [DMDMSSDDRTD, DMDMS] AZ39-B 4073

Gregor's 39th metre-C (Grimm's Chorale book) [DSSSSLTDDDT, TLLLS] AZ39-C 4074

Gregor's 45th metre (Wurzberger G-B 1628) X O traurege-keit 4075

Gregor's 46th metre (Drese) X Rochelle 4076

Gregor's 54th metre (Bohemian Br.) [LLTDLTDRM, MMM SMRR] AZ54-A 4077

Gregor's 54th metre-D (Gregor. Chorale book) [MRDSLTD, DTLTLLS, SD] AZ11-Q 4078

Gregor's 56th metre (Nares) X Amsterdam 4079

Gregor's 58th metre (Walther G-B.) X Soldau 4080

Gregor's 58th metre, Pt. II (Walther. G.-B.) X Soldau Pt. II 4081

Gregor's 61st metre (Stralsund G-B) X Praise to the Lord 4082

Gregor's 70th metre (Lowenstern) X Nun preiset alle 4083

Gregor's 74th metre (Gregor) [LLTDRM, MRRDDT, TDRM MR] AZ74-B 4084

Gregor's 75th metre (Regnart) X Göttingen 4085

Gregor's 77th metre (6-line stanza: Freylinghausen) [SSDDRRM, RMRDTLS, SS] AZ77-A; BA46 4086

Gregor's 79th metre (Crueger) [DSSLTDDTD, DDTLSLL] AZ79-B 4087

Gregor's 82d metre (Herrnhut ms.) [SDRMFSFM, SDRMFS FM,] AZ82-D; BA486 4088

Gregor's 83d metre (Freylinghausen. G-B. 1704) X Tu vins, Jesus 4089

Gregor's 95th metre (Freylinghausen) [DDRDFSFMR, MSLSDTD] AZ95-A 4090

Gregor's 97th metre (Freylinghausen. G-B. 1704)

[SDRMFMRD, SDRMFMRD,] AZ97-A; BA544 4091

Gregor's 99th metre (Gregor) [MRDLSSFM, SMDRMFMR,] AZ99-B 4092

Gregor's 101st metre (Darmstadt. G-B. 1698) [DMF#SSLTD, RMD TSLDT] AZ101-A 4093

Gregor's 102d metre (Freylinghausen) [MFSMMLTS#, TTT DTLSS] AZ102-A 4094

Gregor's 106th metre (Wittwe. Hamburger Musikalisches handbuch. 1690) X Crasselius 4095

Gregor's 107th metre (Gregor) [MMRDSLSSFM, DFMRDT] AZ107-C; BA303 4096

Gregor's 109th metre (Freylinghausen) [MMMMRDTLS#LL, MMMMR] AZ109-C 4097

Gregor's 112th metre (Gregor) [MSTDDLFMRD, RMMF#F#S] AZ112-B 4098

Gregor's 114th metre (Richter) [SSFMSLSDMFSFM, DTL] AZ114-A 4099

Gregor's 115th metre (Grimm's Choral buch) [SMLSDTLSFM RR, SDDT] AZ115-B; BA499 4100

Gregor's 118th metre (Freylinghausen) [LMRDTLMLFMRM DTL, L] AZ118-A 4101

Gregor's 119th metre (Schmidt) X Fahre fort 4102

Gregor's 124th metre (Flittner) [MMFSFMRRR, SFMRD, TT] AZ124-A 4103

Gregor's 126th metre-B (Gregor) [DDMRFMR, FMDRTD, DDM] AZ126-B 4104

Gregor's 132nd metre-B (Christliche lieder, 1524) X Nun freut euch 4105

Gregor's 132d metre-F (Geistliche lieder. Wittenberg, 1535) X O Jesu, när jag ... 4106

Gregor's 133d meter-B (Fabricius) [SLSMFFMM, FMRDDTLS] AZ133-B 4107

Gregor's 141st metre-A (Herrnhut ms) [DTLSFMM, SDTLS, DTLS] AZ141-A; BA125 4108

Gregor's 151st metre-H (Rostocker G-B. 1659) [SMSD FMR, RMF#SSF#S, SM] AZ 151-H; BA682 4109

Gregor's 151st metre-I (Freylinghausen) [DMDSRMRD, M SSSFMR, D] AZ151-I; BA102 4110

Gregor's 152d metre-B (Vulpiüs) X Weimar 4111

Gregor's 155th metre (Freylinghausen G-B.) X Festus 4112

Gregor's 156th metre (8-line stanza: Freylinghausen) [SSDDRRM, RMRDTLS, SS] AZ156-A 4113

Gregor's 159th metre (German trad) [DDSLTDLS, FMSFM RD, D] AZ159-A; BA532 4114

Gregor's 160th metre-B (Gastorius) X Was Gott tut 4115

Gregor's 161st metre (Hille) [SDRMFSFMD, SSFMFMR] AZ161-A 4116

Gregor's 163d metre (Gregor's Choral buch) [DSFMDRMFSM, RSF#SSF#] AZ163-A 4117

Gregor's 166th metre (Herrnhut ms) [DRMRMFMRDR, MDRMFM] AZ166-A; BA58 4118

Gregor's 167th metre-B (French trad) [DMRFMRDRF, MLF# SSF#S,] AZ167-B 4119

Gregor's 167th metre-D (Freylinghausen) [MMMS#LTLS#S#, TTDLSF#M,] AZ167-D 4120

Gregor's 167th metre-E (Darmstadt. G-B. 1698) [LTDMLD TL, DRMMRRD, L] AZ167-E 4121

Gregor's 168th metre-B (German trad) [MMTDRDTL, DDT LS#LT, M] AZ168-B 4122

Gregor's 168th metre-C (Crueger) X Du, O schönes welt gebaudes 4123

Gregor's 172d metre (Grimm's Choral buch) [SDDDTDRRR, RMMMRDR] AZ172-B; BA130 4124

Gregor's 183d metre (Dessler) [SLTDRMRD, MRMDTLLS,] AZ183-A 4125

Gregor's 184th metre-A (Freylinghausen) [SDRMDSSFMRD, MRMRS] AZ184-A; BA264 4126

Gregor's 184th metre-C (Grimm. Choral buch) [MLTDTDRMM, SSFMSFM] AZ184-C 4127

Gregor's 185th metre-A (German trad) [DDLRDTDSMD, DDLFM R] AZ185-A; BA89; BE73 4128

Gregor's 189th metre-B (Darmstadt. G-B. 1697) [DDRTLSLS FMD, SSSLT] AZ189-B 4129

Gregor's 192d metre (Darmstadt G-B. 1697) [DTLSLTDLFMRD, DTLS] AZ192-A 4130

Gregor's 201st metre (Walther. G-B.) X Christ unser herr zum Jordan kam 4131

Gregor's 202d metre (Nurnberg, 1541) X Allein zu dir, Herr Jesu Christ 4132

Gregor's 205th metre (Goudimel) [SFMLSFM, SFMRMRD, SF] AZ205-A; BA111; BZ 4133

-----. V [SFMLSFM, SFMRRD, SFM] BZ 4133a

Gregor's 208th metre-A (Crueger) X Jesus, all my gladness 4134

Gregor's 208th metre-C (Gregor. Choral buch) [DSLLSFM, LL RDTLS, DT] AZ208-C 4135

Gregor's 210th metre (Hammerschmidt) X Freuet euch, ihr christen 4136

Gregor's 211th metre (Darmstadt G-B. 1687) [LS#LTDLTM, S SFMRRM, S] AZ211-A; BA 935 4137

Gregor's 212th metre (German mel) [LLLSLSFMR, LDRLTDT] AZ212-A 4138

Gregor's 215th metre (Hohenfurth ms) X Dies est laetitiae 4139

Gregor's 217th metre-B (Hille) [SDTLSLRMFM, RMDF#RS] AZ217-B 4140

Gregor's 218th metre (Freylinghausen. G-B. 1704) X Sinner's friend 4141

Gregor's 221st metre (Freylinghausen) [DRMMF#SSSL LTDD, RMR] AZ221-A; BA363 4142

Gregor's 223rd metre (Calvisus) [DDRMSFMR, RDR MRDR, R] AZ223-B 4143

Gregor's 225th metre (Joseph) [SDL, RDT, SSLTDDTD, MM] AZ225-A 4144

Gregor's 232d metre (Schmid) X Herzlich lieb habich ... 4145

Gregor's 243d metre (Schlicht) [MSDTDDRMDFRR, SF#MR] AZ243-A 4146

Gregor's 244th metre (Grimm) [DDRMMFM, RMF#SSF#S, DD] AZ244-A 4147

Gregor's 249th metre (Eberhard) [DSFMRD, SMDTDR, RRRS] AZ249-A; BA44 4148

Gregor's 298th metre (Joseph) [MMRDDSLDTDD, LLTRD] AZ298-A 4149

Gregor's 310th metre (Freylinghausen) [DRMFSDDTD, LLLSSF#S,] AZ310-A 4150

Gregor's 341st metre (Freylinghausen) [DSLSFM, SLR MRD, MDSS] AZ341-A; BA 126 4151

Gregor's 483d metre (Molthar) [MLDMLLS#L, DTRDMFRT] AZ1204 4152

Gregor's 520th metre (Bohemian Br.) [SSSLS, DDDTLS, LTDSM] AZ520-A 4153

Gregory (Knorr. Neuer helicon, 1684) X St Gregory 4154

Greiter (Greiter) X Psalm 68 4155

Grenfell (Hayman) X Lanherne

4156

Grenoble (Grenoble Antiphoner, 1753) X Deus tuorum militum 4157

Gresham (Shaw) [MRDRMRD, MFSFMR, M] A593a; W221a; AD457; AK454 4158

Grey (---) [DDDSDRM, MMLL SF#S, DD] M240 4159

Greyfriars (Scottish Psalter. 1635) [LDDRRMMFRMM, SDDRR] W645 4160

Greystone (Waghorne) [DSDRMR D, DFFMRMFR, D] B358; C358; Eap. 66; AR93; AW410; BK10 4161

-----. R [SSMFSLLS, SDTLM F#S, S] 4162

-----. V [SDSDRMRD, DFFM RMFR,] BK10 4163

Grice (McKinney) [SDDDTLSSM, SDDDTDR] AT184 4164

-----. R [SRDTD, TLLLTDR, SMR#M] 4165

Grigg (Grigg) [SDMSMRDRM, RDRMFMR,] L403; T108b; AJ148; AO426 4166

Grimm's 253d metre (Grimm. Choral buch) [DMRSSF#S, DSLSFMR, SM] AZ253-A; BA 136 4167

Grimm's 265th metre (Grimm. Choral buch) [LTDTLS#L, DR MFMRM, FM] AZ265-A 4168

Grimm's 315th metre (Grimm. Choral buch) [MSDDRFM, RS MDTLS, DD] AZ315-A 4169

Grimm's 349th metre (Grimm. Choral buch) [DMSSLTD, TR DTLLS, DM] AZ349-A 4170

Grimm's 480th metre (Grimm. Choral buch) [DMSSLTDD, M RDTTLS, F] AZ480-A 4171

Grimm's 552d metre (Grimm. Choral buch) [LTTDS#LTDR DTL, TDTD] AZ552-A 4172

Gring (Hollingshead) [MSFMM RDF, FLSFFMRS,] AO86 4173

Griswold (Griswold) [MMMMSMR FM, LLLSMSS] BR94 4174

Groeswen (Lloyd) [DSLTDRMD, FLRDTLS, D] W448b; AL334a 4175

Gröningen (Neander) X Arnsberg 4176

Groningen (Tours) [MRDLTD FM, MRSLLS, SL] K378; M247; V557a 4177

Groombridge (Whitwell) [LD MRDRDT, LRDTL, LDM] E 592 4178

-----. R [MMRDTDRDL, MMSMSF#M] 4179

Grosser Gott [wir loben dich] (Allgemeines katholisches G-B. Vienna, 1774) X Te deum 4180

Grostette (Greatorex) [MMM RDTLS, S#S#S#S#S#LTD] H471; I139; V186; AS73; AV124; BA15 4181

Groton (Zeuner) [DDDMDSRM, LSMFMDS, S] L115 4182

Grüber (Grueber) X Holy night 4183

Guardian of virgins (Cecilia Miriam, Sr.) [MRMFFFR FMRDTL, LTD] BN169 4184

Gud Faders Søn enbaarne (German Enchiridion, 1524) X Forlossningen ar vunnen 4185

Gud har af sin . . . (Etlich christlich lider 1524) X Wittenberg 4186

Gud skal alting mage (Lindeman) X Lindeman 4187

Gud var Gud (Lagergren) [DS DRMFR, DMRTDLS, MM] K238; M268; N85; AA500 4188

Gud vaere lovet evig nu (Walther) X Walther 4189

Guds Godhed vil vi prise (Magdeburg. Christliche tischgesange. Erfurt. 1572) [LLTDRTS, SLLTTM, LLT] M 468; O209; Q393; AA509 4190

-----. V [RRMFRMD, DRRM ML, RRM] Q393 4191

-----. V [LLTDLTS, SLLTT M, LLT] AA509 4192

Guds menighed, syng (Hoff) X Hoff 4193

Guds Søn er kommen (Etlich Christliche lider) X Wittenberg 4194
Guernsey (Perkins) [MRDDRD TLS, TDRRRDRM,] T161; AJ239 4195
Guernsey (Pescott) [DDTDRM, MFLSFM, MMTD] AL526 4196
Guidance (Brackett) [DRMLSMR, MLSDT, DLSM] BE304 4197
Guidance (Dahle) [DTDRMFRRD, SMDFMRL] O216 4198
Guidance (Flotow) [MFLSMDRMD, MMSFMDR,] L248; AO532 4199
Guide(Wells) X Holy Spirit, faithful Guide 4200
Guide me (Viner) X Dismissal 4201
Guide me (Warren) [DRMSDTLS LSFMMRMR,] Q54; AA340 4202
Guide me, O thou great Jehovah (Beethoven) X Beethoven 4203
Guide me, O thou great Jehovah (Hastings) X Sion 4204
Guide us, O thou great Jehovah (Hughes) X Cwm rhondda 4205
Guidetti (Guidetti) [DDRMDRM FMRDD, DMF] A132b; E175b; X37a; AD39 4206
Guiding star (Freylinghausen. G-B.) X Festus 4207
Guild (Peace) [SSDDTTLL, LSS LSS, SS] W521 4208
Guildford (Haynes) [MMFMMRD, SSLSSFM, SD] K450 4209
Guildford (Williams) [DDRMSL DTSLS, DRMLS] X316 4210
Guildhall (Barnby) X Westcott 4211
Gulworthy (Hurst) [SSLDMRRD, DDRMFFM, M] K20b 4212
Gun Hill (Shaw) [SLSRRMFMR M, MSLSF#S] X486 4213
Gustavus Adolphus (Johnson) [SDDDDDS, SLLTRD, MRR] N231 4214
Gute bäume bringen (Sohren) [LLTDRMM, SMLS#L, LLTD] E72; F91b; J68a; X466; BV 137b; BY218b 4215
Gute baume bringen (Sohren) X Sohren 4216
Guter hirte [willst du night] (Freylinghausen. G-B) X Tu vins, Jesus 4217
Gwalchmai (Welsh mel) [MS DRMFMR, MFRD, MSDR] A95b; E424; F367b; X553; Z100; AD14; AF65; AL24; AN164; AP134; AR35; BV 539; BY12 4218
Gwalia (Welsh trad) [MFSFM RDRMRM, FMRSF] S186; W384; X54; AD150; AL448c 4219
Gweedore (Wesley) [MFMRLS, DDSMRDD, RML] F394a 4220
Gwyneth (Price) [DTLDTLTLL S#, S#LTDRM] S512; W411b AM431b 4221

H

Habakkuk (Hodges) [SSDDDTLS LFM, SLTDR] I368 4222
Haddam (Mason, arr) [SDS LTD, SLSFMR, SDSL] H431; L486; T28; AJ38; AM448; AO209 4223
Haec dies (Willan) [DDDDRMF FR, SFMDMRD] BN43 4224
Haf trones lampa färdig (Swedish trad) X Vigil 4225
Hagerstown (Brunk) [SMDLS LTDTMR, RDRMS] AY212 4226
Hagerup (Grieg) [MLTDRML S#, SDRMFSDT,] Y278; AC 281; BI13 4227
Hague (Wilms) [SDDMRDTLS, DTDFMR, S] L596; W644; AI20; AO612; BR526 4228
Hail, all hail, sweet youth (Egbert) [MFSDDTLSM, RLS DRMR] BP97 4229
-----. R [SFMRMFSM, SLFRS FM, S] 4230
Hail, blessed Trinity (Beery) [SSMFSM, DTDR, MSDRMF,] AS71 4231

Hail! Bright archangel (Schulthes) X Lambeth 4232
Hail! Christ, our redeemer (Koenen) [MDLTDS, DMSMLS, SSRF] BP104 4233
Hail, full of grace (Montani) [SSDDRDTT, DRDRRM, SS] BQ86 4234
Hail, glorious St Patrick (Hemy) [MMFMRLDTMRD, DDLTD] BO137 4235
Hail! Glorious St Patrick (Paderborn G-B. 1765) X O purest of creatures 4236
Hail glorious St Patrick (St Patrick) X St Patrick 4237
Hail, glorious St Patrick (Slovak hymnal) [SDDDDDRMRDTD, DMMM] BQ96 4238
Hail, guest (Welsh carol) [MF SMLSFMRDRM, MFSM] BK8 4239
Hail harbinger of morn (Bell) [SDMSSL, SDLMFS, SLTD] E225 4240
Hail, heavenly Queen (Goule) [MMRMD, MMRMSFR, RFMR] BO57 4241
-----. R [SMDRMR, SMDR, MFSLSL] 4242
Hail Him the King of glory (de Fluiter) [MMR#MR#DDRDL, SDTDR, R] BB543 4243
-----. R [MMMMRDL, SDTDFM R, MR] 4244
Hail! holy guide (Dykes) X Esca viatorum 4245
Hail! holy Joseph (Pearsall) X Pearsall 4247
Hail, holy Joseph (Whitehead) [MMRLTD, SSFDRM, MMFM] BO131 4248
Hail, holy Queen (Bansbach) [SSSLLDDD, MRDT, SSSL] BQ334 4249
Hail, holy Queen (Hildesheim, 1736) [MFSSSLSFM, FMMRD, MF] BM50; BN153; BO75; BP84; BQ83 4250
-----. R [DTLRDTLS, DTLRDTL S,] 4251
-----. V [MFSSSLSFM, FMRD, MFS] BP84 4252
Hail! Jesus, hail! (Novello) [MSFMSDL#L, RSMDFMMR,] BO27 4253
Hail, Jesus, hail! (Montani) [SDSSFMFS, SLTDSFMR,] BQ71 4254
Hail Mary (Willan) [DFRMSL, SLTDRL, TDLT] BN145 4255
Hail, Mary, full of grace (Montani) [MMFSLD, SLF LSFM, MMM] BQ749 4256
Hail, Mary, Pearl of grace (Terry) [DDFMRM, RMSFM R, SDTL] BO68 4257
Hail noble column (Bragers) [DMSSSSLSFS, RMFMSS] BP29 4258
Hail, ocean's beauteous Star (Jenner) X Quam dilecta 4259
Hail, Queen of the heavens! (Catholic) [SDDMRRFTTRD, SDDMR] BO90 4260
Hail, Queen of heaven, the ocean star (Hemy. Easy hymn tunes) X Stella 4261
Hail, Rock of ages (Montani) [MRDSSLLS, SLLSDR, MM] BQ70 4262
Hail the glorious golden city (---) [SMSSSDMD, DLSM DRM, S] BH227 4263
Hail! thou living Bread (Milgrove) X Harts 4264
Hail, thou living Victim (Catholic) [SSLTDLS, DSMFMRD, MS] BO46 4265
Hail, thou Star of ocean (Richardson) [SSDLSM, FM RDR, MMFLS] BM55; BO76 4266
-----. V [SMDLSM, FMRDMR, SMFL] BO76 4267
Hail, thou Star of ocean (Taddei) [SDFMRDTD, RMFSD MR, S] BQ73 4268
Hail to the brightness (Mason) X Wesley 4269
Hail to the brightness (Parry) [DMSDTLSLDFLSM, MRD] BC182 4270

Hail to thee! true Body (Kloss) [SLTDRMFRDT, RMFSDT] BQ51 4271
Hail, true Victim (Leisentrit) X Ave virgo virginum 4272
Hail Virgin, dearest Mary (Yenn) [SDTDRMR, FMDRRMR, SR] BQ81 4273
Hakafos melody (Jewish trad) [SDDRMRDSFMMR, RSSL] BH199 4274
Hakes (Belden) [MR#MDSLFLLS, DMSMFM] BB380 4275
Halifax (Handel) [MLLLTDRMM, RDTLTL] A354b; AF294; BZ 4276
Hall (Laufer) [SMRDRMFSLS, RDRMFS] R306; S245; AE374; AK252; AR535 4277
Halle (Algemeines katholisches G-B. Vienna, 1774) X Te deum 4278
Halle (Freylinghausen. G-B. 1704) X Se solens skjønne lys ... 4279
Halle (Plainsong, 1539) X To God on high 4280
Halle (Schneider) [DDDTLSLTD, DRDTDTLS,] V359 4281
Halle (The Psalmist, 1830) [LLTTDDS, LLMMFSSF] A67 4282
Hallel (Jewish trad) [LTDRMM FMFRM, MDDRR] BH138, 266 4283
-----. V [LTDRMMFMFLM, RRTDD] BH266 4284
"Hallelujah" in all languages is spelled and filed as "Alleluia" 4285
Hallett (Shepherd) [SSDSTLS, MFSLS FMR,S] L185;AO237 4286
Hallon (Schulthes) X Lambeth 4287
Halton Holgate (Boyce) X Boyce 4288
Hambridge (English trad) [MF MLSMRMD, DTRRMFS,] E355; X15; BV184 4289
Hamburg (Franck) X Komm, selle 4290
Hamburg (Plainsong, M 1) [DD RMRMFMRM, MMMF] A219; B52b; D5b; G334; H165; I225; J503a; K69; L168; M58; N 255; O99; P183; Q175a; R 198; S152b; T279; U88; V144; Y376; Z228; AB137; AC123; AD156; AE119; AF177; AG 97a; AH291; AI77a; AJ387; AK158; AL208a; AM186; AN 272; AO248; AP321; AQ146; AR174; AS331; AT99; AU 191; AV108; AW106; AX113; AY259; AZ22-P; BA315; BB220; BD32; BE386; BF315; BR42; BV173a; BX26; BZ 4291
-----. V [DRMMRMFMRM, MFFMRR] BV173a 4292
Hamburg (Schop) X Sollt ich meinem . . . 4293
Hamden (Mason) [SSDRMDR R, MRDRDTD, S] H201; L 333 4294
Hamilton (Finlay) [SSLDRDRM, LSDMFMRD] BV12 4295
Hamilton (Swisher) [MMMM RD, DRMR, MMMMRD,] BD 7 4296
Hamilton (White) [SDMRMFSS FM, RDMSSD] AQ57 4297
Hammersmith (Gladstone) [MS MRDLMDTL, RDLFFM,] E ap. 50; W111; AB333; AL286 a; BE428 4298
Hampden-Sidney (St Alban's Tune book, 1866) X Lebbaeus 4299
Hampstead (Davies) [SDMMSF RMD, DTLDLLT] BE232; BY20b 4300
Hampstead (Horner) [MMMFL DTT, LSDRMR, RM] I563 4301
Hampton (Williams. Psalmody) X Durham 4302
Hampton Lucy (Stanton) [SSDR MFMRS, DRMSDRD,] BY45 4303
Han lefver! o min ande känn (Haeffner. Koralbok. 1819) [MDSMRDTD, DDFRSSF#S,] N136 4304
Hand in hand (Naff) X We join to pray 4305

Handel (Handel) [DMSSLTD, RSMDTLS, SS] N332 4306

Handy (Holbrook) [MMFSDLSM, MSMRMRMF] T239; AJ335; AO39 4307

Hanford (Gabriel) [SLSSMSFFM F, LTLLRS] AT325 4308

-----. R [DTLMSLSLDT, DTL FSL] 4309

Hanford (Sullivan) [SSSSSFMR, LLLLLSF] A412; B390; C390a; D341a; G306; H437; I239; K 259; L497; U42; V487; AE261; AJ364; AM140; AO408; AS237; AV237; AW245; AZ3-E; BA12; BB475; BF410; BR385; BX262b 4310

Hankey (Fischer) [SDSSDMRD, DDLRDLS, S] G249; H240; I 544; J326; P388; R383; S443; U312; V236; Z532; AD253; AF 317; AG186; AH346; AI390; AK467; AL504; AM387; AO635; AP592; AR440; AS295; AT141; AU371; AV385; AW493; AX200; BA906; BB518; BE414; BY415; BZ 4311

-----. R [SSTRMRD, DDFFFFM, MS] 4312

Hanna (Laufer) [MSRDFFM, SD FMRRR, MS] S350 4313

Hannah (Fillmore) X Pounds 4314

Hanover (Croft) [SDDRMSDRTD, RMRDTD] A288; B255; C255; D459; E466; F167; G169; I11; J163; K294b; M541; O60; Q17; R27; S2; V198; W9; X618; Y 385; Z258; AA57; AB15; AD2; AE2; AF206; AG106; AH194; AK10; AL21a; AM301; AP93a; AR119; AS3; AW6; AZ39-D; BA9; BB342; BE236; BF168; BJ52; BV248; BY22; BZ 4316

-----. V [SDDRMMSDRTD, RMRDT] AA57 4317

Hansome place (Lowry) X Beautiful river 4318

Happy day (Rimbault) [SDRMSDRM, MFMRDMRD,] G212; H287; I312; L287; U192; V310; AH345; AO 652; AS454; AT389; AU461; AV251; AW465; AX331; AY 271; BA464; BB310 4319

-----. R [MFSDRM, MFMRD MRD, SS] 4320

Happy he that never wanders (Binder) X Happy he who walketh 4321

Happy he who walketh (Binder) [LTDLFFFM, LLSFMRDT,] AH153; BH26 4322

Happy he who walketh ever (Fabisch) [SSDDRTDS, DRMF MRDD] BH25 4323

Happy home (Niemeyer) X O selig haus 4324

Happy home (Bunnett) [MSFM RDDTDMR, MMMLT] AP707 4325

Happy land (Hindu air) [MMRM SS, MMRD, MMRMSS,] E608; W587; AP795; AS471; AZ580-A; BB301 4326

Happy Sion (Woodbury) [SDRM DLDLS, SDRMDRT] AI149; AR499; AS188 4327

Happy spirits (Burkett) [MSLS MDFL, SSLSMDR, M] AY191 4328

-----. R [DDRDTLLS, SSDSMDR, M] 4329

Happy the home when God is there (Havergal) X Evan 4330

Happy, we who thus united (Herbert) X Holy Queen, we come 4331

Happy we who thus united (Leisentrit G-B.) X Ave virgo virginum 4332

Happy who in early youth (Gottschalk) X Mercy 4333

Happy with Christ (Jacobs) [SD MMFMRDRDL, LSDDM] AY 383 4334

-----. R [MSSLSMF, RFF SFMRDR] 4335

Hardwick (English trad) [MRR SMRD, DSSLS[M]FSL] S451; X34 4336

Hardy Norse men (Norwegian trad) [SSSSDTLL, LFRDTRD, S] AW391 4337

Harewood (Wesley, S.S.) [SLTD RDT, SFMRDMRD, R] B559; C559; D294b; F243; W458; X464b; AA453; AF407; AP303; AZ342-G; BA811; BV456; BY 267 4338

Harington (Harington) [SDTLSFMF SLLS, SSF#S] E85; X613; AL 659; AP65a; BY607 4339

Hark, a herald voice (Francis) [MRDTLTDS, SSSMDLS, D] BO148 4340

Hark, hark my soul (---) [SSFM MMMRMSF, STRSS] BO198 4341

-----. R [LTDDSFSFM, LTDD SSS] 4342

Hark, hark, my soul (Hummel) [SMRD, TLLLLLS, DDTRR] BI74 4343

Hark! hark! my soul (Montani) [DSLDRRMDRMFSR, RMD] BQ111 4344

-----. R [MRDRMS, RDTDRS, DTLT] 4345

Hark! listen to the trumpeters (Careless) [SSSSSSSS, SSLTDR M,S] BC253 4346

Hark! a mystic voice (Montani) [SSLMMRMM, MMFRDRM, S] BQ1 4347

Hark! are they not angels ("K") [SDTDRSSRD#RMD, SMRM] AX91 4348

Hark ten thousand thousand voices (Daynes) [DSDSDDTDS, MMFSLSF] BC249 4349

Hark! the herald angels (Mendelssohn) X Mendelssohn 4350

Hark! the herald host (Humperdinck) [SLSFMRDL, DRMSDLS, L] BQ13 4351

Hark, the song of jubilee (Haydn) X Creation 4352

Hark, the voice of children (Blunt) X Merrial 4353

Hark! the voice of Jesus calling (Holsinger) [SLSFMRMS, LLDLS MR, S] AS379 4354

Hark! the voice of Jesus calling (Van Arsdale) X Mission song 4355

Hark! the voice of Jesus crying (Mozart) X Ellesdie 4356

Hark! what mean those holy voices (---) [MR#MDSF#SM, RD#RFMRD, M] AX93; AY 267 4357

Hark! what mean those holy voices (Weber) X Wilmot 4358

Harlech (Welsh trad) [SDTLT DRM, DFMRDTLT,] K132; M455; BZ 4359

Harlem (Drese) X Rochelle 4360

Harmony Grove (Oliver) [MM MMSDRM, MMMMMF#F#S,] L311; M260; O234; P355; AA122 4361

Harneenu (Binder) [SDSLSMFS, LSLTDS, SR] BH308 4362

Harre meine seele (Malan) X In His love abiding 4363

Harris (Hawley) [DTLSLSM, MF SLTD, DDT] D284b 4364

Harrogate (Cobb) [DDRMSDLS, MDMRRD, DD] BY386 4365

Harrowby (Gillespie) [LSLTD TL, DTLTDRM, FM] BV150 4366

Hart (Stevenson) [DTLTFTLFM, SSFMRFL] D316b 4367

Hartel (Mason) [DMMMRMFS, SLSSMFMM,] BB227 4368

Hartford (Dykes) X Blairgowrie 4369

Hartford (Milgrove) X Harts 4370

Hartland (Hopkins) [MDDMS, LFFLD, DTL, SRM] AP485 4371

Hartmann (Hartmann) [MFSDRM F, MRSSFMRFM,] M88 4372

Hartmann (Hartmann) X Peace of God 4373

Harts (Milgrove) [SSDDRRM, DDFMRDRMR,] E177; F191a; W11a; X520; AL154b; AP120 b; BV14; BY630a 4374

-----. V [SSDDRRM, DDFMR DMR, S] AH316 4374a

-----. V [SSDDRRMM, DDFM RDMR] BO-54 4374b

Hartville (Bixler) [SDRMDDLS,

TTDTLS, SD] AY435 4375
Harvard (Berridge) [MMMFRSDT, DSLFFM, RM] U66; Y8; Z385; AC142; AR89 4376
Harvard hymn (Paine) [SDLSFMR MFLS, RFMLD] B539b; C539b; D521b; Y239; AN433; BX415 4377
Harvest (Clemm) X Clemm 4378
Harvest (Frost) [DMMLSFSMF R, SFMRDM] D262a; F378 4379
Harvest (Minor) X Bringing in the sheaves 4380
Harvest (Singer) [SDDTLSLLD, DRRRDRM,] BH186 4381
Harvest home (Elvey) X St George's Windsor 4382
Harvest home (Root) [SDDDDRM SLS, DRRRRM] AP588; AU430 AX216; BB620 4383
-----. R [SSSSSSDRM, MFFFF MS] 4384
Harvest Home (Storer) [MRDDTLS RM, FSMLFRR,] D191b 4385
Harvest hymn (St Gall G-B., 1863) [DSLSMFRM, RMFSFMR, D] Q573 4386
Harvest song (Cringan) [SDTDRD TDS, MRDTLTD] AP690 4387
Harvest song (Thomas) [LLTDTLS, SDMRRM, LLT] BY730 4388
Harvest-tide (Falconer) [SSLSDR MMR, DTDRSLF#] T269; AJ373 4389
Harvey's chant (Bradbury) [DDDDD TDR, RRRRRM, MM] L281; T51; AI164; AJ348; AR510; AS466; BB4; BC48 4390
Harwell (Mason) [SSDSDMRR, SSSDMRD, S] G167; I177; J152a; L154; M85; N271; U112; V164b; Z268; AA451; AE139; AI30; AM 225; AO55; AR210; AS158; AT 70; AU227; AV93; AW123; AY 425; BC138 4391
Harwich (Crueger) X Nun danket 4392
Harwich (Milgrove) [MRDDLSMR DDLS, RMFR] X161 4393
Hasidim (Jewish trad) [LMRMDTL, LLRSSLM, L] AQ175 4394
Haslemere (Songs and tunes for education. 1861) [DDMMR, RRFFM, MMSSL,] A244; X359 4395
Hassler (Hassler) X Passion chorale 4396
Hast du denn, Jesu (Stralsund G-B. 1665) X Praise to the Lord 4397
Hast du Jesus ruf vernommen (Sweney) [MMFMRDMD, RS FTDRM, M] AW342 4398
Haste not! Haste not! Do not rest (Blumenthal) X Blumenthal 4399
Hastings (Hastings) [MFSS MRDTLSF, MLSSF] L265; T 23; V158b; AJ31; AM209; AR184; AS147 4400
Hatfield (Gauntlett) [MSLS MFMMR, RSLSDTD] D517b; AV248 4401
Hatikvo (Jewish trad) X Hallel 4402
Hauge (Norwegian trad) [SD MSTRDLS, FMDMRDT] J 146b; P433 4403
Have faith in God (McKinney) X Muskogee 4404
Have faith in God (Rosche) [MRDSLSDT, FMRLTDRM,] AY359 4405
-----. R [DMSSLLMS, SMST LLS#S,] 4406
Have I done any good? (Thompson) [SSDDDDRMRTD, DR MRD] BC58 4407
Have mercy on me (Gelineau) [LFSM, RFSL, RDRL, LDT L,] BSp. 22 4408
Have mercy on us (Haydn) [SSDTLSTLS, SSFMRDM] BO7 4409
Have Thine own way (Stebbins) X Adelaide 4410
Have you any room for Jesus (Williams) [SLSDTLLS, FM FSLSSM,] AX259 4411
-----. R [RRRRMRDS, LLLLT DR, M] 4412
Have you prayed it through (Ackley) [DMSSSMSDDD, SDTLSF] AU121 4413
-----. R [SF#FFMFSF, SFM

MR#MLS,] 4414
Have you sought? (Sankey) [SD MMMMMMMFS, SSRMF] AX 198; AY526 4415
Haven (Hastings) [MMRDSFMRM, MRSLSF#S,] T228; AJ160; AV279 4416
Haven (Lemare) [MFMRLRMRD, LTDFMMR] D309b; V83; AH 232 4417
Haven of rest (Moore) X My soul in sad exile 4418
Haver (Havergal) [SDRMFS, MLS FSM, SDRM] L233; AZ74-C 4419
Havergal (Barnby) X St Olave 4420
Havergal (Bliss) X I gave my life for thee 4421
Havewood (Wesley, S.S.) X Harewood 4422
Hawarden (Wesley, S.S.) [SD TTLS, SDRMRD, SDTT] E496b; J97; W336; AP369; BY353 4423
Hawes (Wesley arr) X Streatley 4424
Hawkhurst (Gauntlett) [MFMRR SFM, SF#SLMRDT,] F232; BV215; BY656 4425
Hawkridge (Wesley) [SLTDMMRD, FFMRMRR, R] AZ159-C 4426
Haydn (Haydn) [MFRMFSLRDS, SSSFMM] B3a; C3a; D3a; G 30; J207a; K445; R44; T302; V37a; Y359; Z134; AB2; AD 36; AE39; AG19; AH160; AK46; AM334; AO18; AP 660; AR43; AV10; AW27; BF 177; BK39; BZ 4427
-----. V [MFRMFSLRTDS, SSSFM] G30 4428
Haydn (Haydn) X St Michel's 4429
Haydn (Haydn) X Petition 4430
Haydn (Haydn) X Salzburg II 4431
Haydn, No. 1 (Haydn) X Bowen 4432
Haydn, No. 2 (Gardiner's Sacred mel. 1812) X Belmont 4433
Haydn's hymn (Haydn) X Austria 4434
Hayes (Beethoven) X Sardis 4435
Hayn (Herrnhut ms) X Gregor's 82d metre 4437
Hayom t'am'tsaynu (Lewandowski) [LMDDRFTLLS#, LS#, DS#LR#] BH333 4438
Hazard (MacDougall) [SMMR# MFT, TFFMRS, SSS#] Y38; AB202 4439
Hazel (Harewood) [MRDRM LMRDRM, MRDRM] W330b 4440
-----. R [MRDDFMRDS, DT LSMFS] 4441
He arose (Hugg) [MRDTFF, FMRMM, SSLSM] AY265 4442
-----. R [DMRDMFS, SSLL SMDMR,] 4443
He brought me out (Gilmour) [DMMMMRDSSSS, SLLLS] AU50 4444
-----. R [DDDDTLSMS, DD DDTLT] 4445
He comes (Neff) [SMRDFMDM, SSRMFMRR,] AX124 4446
He died for me (McKinney) [SMFMDMR#R, SFFFFM, SM] AU410 4447
-----. R [MRD#RFMR#M, S FMRF#LS, F] 4448
He died for thee (Vail) [DMS MMRRD, FFMMRDR, D] AX 241; AY218 4449
-----. R [LLSMSSM, FFM MRF#S, DM] 4450
He died of a broken heart (Dennis) [SDMMDRMFMD, MMRDTD,] AU383 4451
-----. R [SRRMFMRDRM, MSFMMR] 4452
He died! The great Redeemer (Careless) [SSLSMFLSFM, STLTRD] BC263 4453
He hideth my soul (Kirkpatrick) [SSFMMRDLLLS, SSFMM] AE283; AI270; AM675; AS 289; AT272; AX510; BB651 4454
-----. R [STTTTLTDTLS,

SFMFR] 4455

He is coming again (Camp) [SM LS, TLSDS, LDLSSLS] AI97; AM687 4456

-----. R [SSDTLT, SSRDTD, SMRD] 4457

He is not here, but is risen (McGranahan) [MMMRDFMR, DRRM, MMMR] AU464 4458

-----. R [SSSSSSLTD, LLLL LLT] 4459

He is risen (Neander) X Neander 4460

He is so precious (Gabriel) [SM MMFMRRDLS, STTTT] AE285; AT304 4461

-----. R [MSLTDRDM, SRRRR MFM,] 4462

He just put Himself in my place (Hammontree) [MFSLTDRDM D, DDTDRD] AU384 4463

-----. R [SSDDDTLT, SSRRRDT D,] 4464

He keepeth me ever (Rosche) [MDRMFM, DRMFM, SRMFL] AY316 4465

-----. R [SSSSLS, MMMMFM, DMFS] 4466

He keeps me singing (Bridgers) X Sweetest Name 4467

He knoweth the way that I take (Pollock) [DMMMMRDS, FMM MMRDR,] AX487; AY118 4468

-----. R [FMMMMFSLS, MRRRR MF] 4469

He knoweth thy grief (Hall) [MM R#MFM, RRMRRD, MMR#M] AY317 4470

-----. R [SMFSLS, MSFMMR, MMR#M] 4471

He leadeth me (Bradbury) X Aughton 4472

He leads us on (Webster) [DD DMMRRSFM, FMFRML] BX 264 4473

He lifted me (Gabriel) [SSLLSMM F, MMRSRRDD,] AI130; AM 672; AT202 4474

-----. R [MMMMMSSL, SFFFFF MM] AI130 4475

-----. R [SSDMSSTT, STRFLLS S, S] 4476

He lives (Ackley) [SSLLDDL, FSSLLM, SMM] AE287; AT279 4477

-----. R [SMSMRDDRDLS, SSFFL] 4478

He lives on high (Hawaiian trad) [SDMRDTDLSS, MRRD#RM] AU336 4479

He loves me (---) [SSMDDLD D, DMDSMR, SS] AX116; AY 249 4480

He loveth me (Keeny) [DDRM MMFS, SLSMDRMR,] AS122 4481

-----. R [SSDT, RFLS, DMF SLSMR,] 4482

He ransomed me (Henderson) [MFSSSSLS, MSDDDDRD,] AU382 4483

-----. R [TDRRRRRT, LT DDDRDS,] 4484

He seeks His wandering sheep (Showalter) [SMSFMRL, DT LSFM, MSF] AX267; AY219 4485

-----. R [MSSLSM, RDRMF#S, SDTL] 4486

He that believes (Etlich Christliche lider 1524) X Wittenberg 4487

He was nailed to the cross (Graves) [DRMRDFMMMR, TDRRRD] AX107 4488

He was wounded (Oliver) [LM MLMMSRRSR, MLTDM] AM 673 4489

-----. R [MRRDLFMMR, DLT SD#RR#] 4490

He who dwells (Gelineau) [TT LT, TTSL, DDTD, DDLT,] BSp. 25 4491

He who once, in righteous vengeance (Mohr) [DSDR MSFMR, RMFRDRM,] BQ18 4492

He will gather the wheat (Sweney) [MFSLSMDMRDL, LSDD D] BB538 4493

-----. R [MMFFFFLLSMS, MM RSS] 4494

He will hide me (McGranahan) [SDRMMFMRMD, SDMSSL] AU409 4495

-----. R [LDFLF, SDMSM, STRFSF] 4496

He will hold me fast (Harkness) [MSMRRSMR, DMDTL, FLS 4497

Hear our prayer (Chopin) [SLLSLDTD, RMFMRRD.] AT531; AV416 4498

Hear our prayer (Excell) [SL LTLSSSM, DLLSSSD] AS487 4499

Hear our prayer (Whelpton) [MM MMR, FFFFM, MSSSMF,] R535; U494; AE461; AH561; AI451; AMp. xiv; AR662; AT530; AU489; AW604; BB688; BF688 4500

Hear thou our hymn (Asper) [MLSFSM, SDTLLS, SLTD] BC96 4501

Hear thy children (Haydn) [SSDD DMSMMR, FFMFRD] BQ87 4502

Heart of God (McAfee) X McAfee 4503

Heart of Jesus (Forrest) [MMRL DT, DDTLS, MMRRS] BB348 4504

Heart of Jesus (Montani) [MM RMSFMRD, FFMFLSF] BQ331 4505

Heart of Jesus! golden chalice (Gounod) X Lux prima 4506

Heart of Mary (Herold) [DRM DTDR, MSFMRD, DRM] BM53 4507

Heart of our Lord (Slovak trad) [DRMFMRRD, SMSDTLLS,] BN69 4508

Heart of the Holy Child (Birtchnell) [MRMDLS, DRFS, MRM DLS,] BO160 4509

Hearthfire (Barnby) [MMMFFFLS FM, DTF#S, SS] AB192 4510

Heart's desire (Cologne G-B. 1623) X Hosmer 4511

Heath (Mason & Webb's Cantica laudis) [SDSLTD, DFMRDDT, T] A555; B118; C21a; D72a; G456; H313; I66; J559; L23; N74; O 65; P398; Q449; R312; S362; U215; V77; W561; Z422; AA41; AB267; AC339; AD367; AG247; AH411; AK258; AN363; AO 17; AR342; AS40; AW213; AX648; AY436; BA49; BB 461; BC180; BD92; BE183; BF487; BZ 4512

Heathfield (Perkins) [DMSSS DTL, SMMFMR, DM] BR25 4513

Heathlands (Smart) [SDTSLL S, FRMFSFMR, S] B46; C77a; D57a; E395; F264; J444; K 423; V145; W509; X170a; AB 313; AL379; AR598; AS96; BA543; BR68; BV46; BY231; 4514

Heaton Norris (Grimshaw) [SDMFSLSFMRM, MSDTDR] W499 4515

Heaven (Cook) [DMMMR#MS M, DRRRMFM, D] AX606 4516

-----. R [SLLDTLSM, SRSTT LS, D] 4517

Heaven (Franck) X Melchior 4518

Heaven (Wilson) [SSSDMFSLS M, FFFMRM] AT483; AU 281 4519

-----. R [MSDTLSM, SSDDD DDTD] 4520

Heaven at last (Kirkpatrick) [SLSMDLSM, DRMFSLSF] BB556 4521

-----. R [SMDLDS, MFSLSD DTLS] 4522

Heaven holds all to me (Teddlie) [MR#MRDRDTLLS, MSLSM] AX604 4523

-----. R [MRDSLSD, MSLSM DR, MR#] 4524

Heaven is my home (Mason) X Oak 4525

Heaven is my home (Sullivan) X St Edmund 4526

Heavenly city (Trebel) [SDTLS LSRMFSM, SLRD] M316 4527

Heavenly father (Kurzenknabe) [SSDDRTD, MMFMR, SSMD] AO325 4528

Heavenly father (Lowry) [DR MDFMMR, TDRDMRD, D] N360; AI345 4529

-----. R [SSFMFSMM, MMMTD LR, S] 4530
Heavenly fold (Sherwin) [DRMFM MRD, MDTLS#L, TD] AJ317 4531
Heavenly friend (Silesian trad) [DSSSFMSFMRD, SFMRM] M539 4532
Heavenly guide (Drese) X Rochelle 4533
Heavenly Jerusalem (Franck) X Melchior 4534
Heavenly love (Mendelssohn) [SMDTDMR, DFMLLS, SDS] J573; O343; P199; Z384; AE 222; AR266; AS262; AV231; BB674; BC125; BE376; BO201 4535
Heavenly sunlight (Cook) [SLTDDM RDRS, SLSMDM] AU119; AX28; AY471 4536
-----. R [SSSLFFSLSM, SSSS MM] 4537
Heavenly treasures (Norwegian) [DRMMFMRDS, DRMSSFM] P378 4538
Heavenly voices (Irons) [DMM RRSD, DLLSFM, MMM] D404b 4539
Heavenward (Irish trad) X Clonmel 4540
Hebdomadal (Strong) [DSMDDLLS, SDTSLLS, M] Sap. 40; W175 4541
Heber (Barnes) [DDDDDDTD, RRRRDTLS,] BB293 4542
Heber (Hopkins) X Evangel 4543
Heber (Kingsley) [MFSSSMLLL, SMRDLSM] H368; I424; L165; R255; T265b; U75; V374; AA101; AJ215; AO301; AV182 4544
Heber (Mason) X Missionary hymn 4545
Hebron (Barnby) [MDLTDTL, R D#RMFFM, MM] B411b; D242b; K509b 4546
Hebron (Crueger) [LTDTLTS#M, MLRDTTL, L] BY652 4547
Hebron (Mason) [SMSLSLTD, D TRMDTLS,] B459; C292; D 296a; H74; I51; J533; L262; M 94; N49; R289; T32; U172; V20; Z115; AA39; AJ47; AL350b; AN 21; AO100; AS447; AW13; AX175; AY261; BA142; BB 456; BX244; BZ 4548
Heidelberg (Vulpius) X Cana 4549
Heiliger Geist (Corner. Geistliche nachtigall) [LLD MRDTD, MMSMDTD, M] X 391 4550
Heiliger Geist (Crueger) X Holy Ghost 4551
Heil'ger Geist do tröster mein (Grimm. Choral buch) X Grimm's 253d metre 4552
Heiliger Herre Gott (German trad) X Eisleben 4553
Heineken (Heineken) [MMSSS F#S, SSFMDFMR, R] BR18 4554
Heinlein (Herbst) [MMLTDRM, MMSSF#F#M, MM] A55; B123; C123; D79; E92; F92; K78; Q111; V409; W79; X97; AF148; AK143; AL97a; AO 143; BA743; BM76; BR366; BV141b; BY118a; BZ 4555
-----. V [MMLTDRM, MMF# SSF#MM, M] X97 4556
Hela världen fröjdes herren (Swedish Koralbok) X Kalmar 4557
Helder (Helder) X Wohlauf thut nicht verzagen 4558
Helen (Vail) X Close to thee 4559
Helena (Bradbury) [MMMMRD LL, LSDRDRM, M] BA77 4560
Helensburgh (Finlay) [DTLTDR TS, SDTDRMFM] W358 4561
Helfer meiner armen seele (Scheffler. Heilige seelenlust, 1657) X Scheffler 4562
Helft mir Gott's Güte (Figulus) [LLLDDTDR, MDLLS#L, LL] Q112 4563
Helig, helig, helig Herre Gud (Stolpe) [SSLLLLLLS, SSDT LLT] N337 4564
He'll never forget (Graves) [MMFMDRMFM, DRRRDDF] AU25 4565

-----. R [SSSSMSDD, DDSMSDM R] 4566

Helmsley (Olivers) [DMSDTLSLT DTLSFM,] A5b; E7; F51; W 160; X65; AP246; BV81; BY185 4567

Help, Lord, the souls (Dutch trad., 1500) [LSMLTDDT, MR DTLT, TD] BN186 4568

Help, Lord, the souls (Gardiner's Sacred mel.) X Belmont 4569

Help, Lord, the souls (Slovak hymnal) [MLTDLS#TDR, R# MTRDTL] BQ113 4570

Help us, O God (Steggall) [DL LSMRLTDD, DTLMSS] BI43-D 4571

Help us, O God (Weber) [MSS LSMSFMR, SLTRDL] BI52-D 4572

Helsingfors (Nyberg) [LTDDRDT L, DRMMLSLM] W402 4573

Hemans (---) [MMFSLS, DRMFM R, DTLS,] M540; N535 4574

Hemel (Thomas) [MDRMSLTD, RMSMRD, MD] BY553a 4575

Hemingford (Emerson) [MMMSFMR, DDRMRD, TTT] L9; AO75 4576

Hendon (Malan) [DDDSDMSFM, MMMRFRD] C219; G147; H59; I507; L197; M433; N23; P123; R310; S312; U272; V17; Z116; AD260; AE267; AG166; AH413; AI17; AK239; AM437; AN278; AO179; AR331; AS230; AT161; AU184; AV129; AW215; AX53; AY83; BA480; BB30; BE186; BI26; BZ 4577

Henham (Shaw) [MRDRMDTLM, MFSLSMR] X616 4578

Henley (Mason) [SMMMRDDRRM D, SMMMD] G350b; H372b; I462; L358; R384; S256; Z345; AD211; AG223; AH348; AK445; AO253; AR439; AW188; BB323; BF363; BR26; BX273 4579

Henllan (Evans) [SSLLSDDT, DRM DTLS, S] W298; AL212 4580

Henry (Pond) [DDDDTDSLTD, RRMRDT] L354; N19; T119; V119; AJ173; AO386 4581

Henryd (Lloyd) [MMMRDMRT, LDTMRDT, M] W73 4582

Her kommer dine arme smaa (Schulz) X Paedia 4583

Her vil ties (Hoff) [MMRDTL TRD, SSFMDTD] O571 4584

Her vil ties (Lindeman) X Our Lady, Trondhjem 4585

Herald (Shaw) [LLLLLLLT, DD DL#LSF, M] E205 4586

Herald angels (Dykes) [SSSMSD MR, DLSSDRR, R] D51b 4587

Herald angels (Mendelssohn) X Mendelssohn 4588

Herbert (Chope) [MMMMMSF M, RRRLSSF#S,] AP487; BR304 4589

Herbert (Hodge) [SLSMRMFM, SLTLSF#SF#] D613 4590

Herbert (Mason) [DDSLTDRM, FSRDMR, RR] BB251 4591

Here at thy table (Hall) [MM FMSDRM, SSLSMRR, R] AS 461 4592

Here behold me (Neander) X Sieh hier bin ich, Ehrenkönig 4593

Here let thy people (Binder) [MLTDRMFM, LSMDRM, MS] BH5 4594

Here, Lord of life and light (Holsinger) X Wayland 4595

Hereford (Evans) [DRMFSLRS M, MFMRDMR,] Y335 4596

Hereford (Gauntlett) [SMFSS DRM, SLSDDT, SM] O495; AB 91; BX167 4597

Hereford (Heins) [SSDDDDTDS M, DRFFMR] G503; AD373; AL244; BZ 4598

Hereford (Ouseley) [LLS#LTDR M, MRDTLS#, TD] F88 4599

Hereford (Wesley) [MMRDRFM MRDRRM, SS] A463; F329a; BV366; BY207 4600

Hereford carol (English carol) [SDRFMDTRD, SFMRDS, S] BG7 4601

Hermann (Hermann) [DSSSMLS FM, MFSLLS,] A435a; B270b;

J197; M154,327; O52; P62; Q105; V90b; X481b; AA157; AF492; AI425; AJ33b; AK97; AM123; AN217; AQ118; AZ14-B; BE101; BI110; BR495; BY408b; BZ 4602

-----. V [DSSSSLSFM, MFSLLS, S] M327 4603

-----. V [DSSSSLSM, RMSLF#S, MS] O52 4604

-----. V [DSSSMLSFM, RMF# SLLS] V90b 4605

-----. V [DSSSSLSFM, RMF# SLLS,] AN217 4606

-----. V [DSSSSLSFM, RMF#SS LS] AZ14-B 4607

-----. V [DSSSSLSM, RMSLLS, RM] BR495 4608

Hermann (Hermann) X Erscheinen ist der herrlich tag 4609

Hermann (Strachauer) [DRMDM FF#, DDTSMF#M, MM] BR214 4610

Hermannsburg (Meiningen G-B.) X St Leonard 4611

Hermas (Havergal) [MMMRDL, FMRDT, SRMD, R] A568; B532; C532; D522a; G161; I175; J115; K549; M457; P222; R80; S56; V750; W133; AD483; AG15; AH213; AK170; AL107; AM213; AO199; AP488b; AS152; AT110; BA245; BD43; BR195; BV592a; BY166; BZ 4612

Hermitage (Morris) [LTDTLL, DDTLSLLM, SL] S133; X92; BV105a 4613

Hermon (Clark) [MLTDTLTLS#, TDTDRM, M] AF220; BJ61 4614

-----. V [MLTDTLDTLS#, T DTDRM,] BJ61 4615

Hermon (Gastorius) X Was God tut? 4616

Hermon (Mason) [SMFSDLDS, DDDTDRTD,] L477; T283a; V287; AJ54; AM21; AO459 4617

Hernlein [sic] (Herbst) X Heinlein 4618

Heroes hymn (Minor: Swedish folk) [LTDMM, LTDMM, FM RTLL] Y121 4619

-----. (Major) R [DRMSS, DRM SS, LSSSMD] 4620

Herongate (English trad) [SS DLSSMRD, SDDMSLS] E597; W550a; X602; Z216; AD129; AR152; BV350; BY142a 4621

Herr Christ der einig nicht lassen (German. Enchiridion, 1524) X Förlossningen är vunnen 4622

Herr, deinen zorn (Crueger) X Oblation 4623

Herr, dir ist niemand zu vergleichen (Knecht) [DD DMDFMRD, MMMRMFM] AW 518 4624

Herr Gott Vater (Besler) [DD DRRMFS, SSMLTDTL] E 274b; W292b; AL556b 4625

Herr, ich habe missgehandelt (Crueger) X St Nicholas 4626

Herr Jesu Christ dich zu uns wend (Pensum sacrum. Goerlitz, 1648) [DMSMRM F#S, LSFMRDRM] A159b; E173; G611; J188a; K419; L230b; M2; N98; O36; P40; Q3; R555; S475; W254; X40; Z636; AA1; AE464; AF521; AK28; AM100; AN489; AT 536; AU493; AZ22-F; BA1; BZ 4629

-----. V [DMSMRMF#S, LSM RDDTD,] N98 4630

Herr Jesu Christ, du hast bereit't (Sohren) X Elbing 4631

Herr Jesu Christ, du höchstes Gut (Sohren) X Elbing 4632

Herr Jesu Christ, meines (As hymnodus sacer. 1625) X Breslau 4633

Herr Jesu Christ, meines lebens licht (Nürnberg G-B. 1676) X O Jesus Christ, meins lebens licht 4634

Herr Jesu Christ, wahr'r mensch und Gott (Eccard) [DDDLTDRMRD, MMMLSS]

AA527; AN84 4635

Herr Jesu, ewig's licht (Gregor) X Gregor's 74th metre 4636

Herr und aeltster deiner kreuzgemeine (German trad) X Gregor's 185th metre-A 4637

Herr und Gott der tag und noechte (Freylinghausen) X Gregor's 167th metre-D 4638

Herr, wie du willst, so schick's mit mir (Teutsch kirchen ampt. Strassburg, 1524 or. 25) X Aus tiefer not 4639

Herra (Danish hymn) [LLLMFSM RD, RMMFSM, D] AN122a 4640

Herre Gud Fader, du vor høi' ste trøst (Tomisson. Psalmebog. 1569) [DMDRMRFMRD, MSMSFM] O43 4641

Herre, jeg har handlet ilde (Crueger) X St Nicholas 4642

Herre, jeg har handlet ille (Lindeman) X Repentance 4643

Herre Jesus Krist min frelser du est (Lindeman) [SDLS, DMRDR, TRRDTSL] O278; P218; Q353 4644

Herren sig i nad förklarer (Stenhammer) X Grace 4645

Herrick's carol (Cologne G-B. 1623) [DTLSSLTD, DTLSSLTD,] BG122 4646

Herrick's ode (Gibbs) [MLMSD RM, FSMRDTLL, T] BG176 4647

Herrnhut (Gesius) [MLS#LTRDT, TDRMDRTD,] J376a; M177; N234; O153; P101; AA434; AQ189 4648

-----. V [MLSLTDLT, TDRM DDTD,] N234 4649

-----. V [MLS#LTDLT, TDRMD DTD,] AA434 4650

Herrnhut (Nicolai) X Sleepers, wake 4651

Herrnhut (Wesley's Foundery collection) X Savannah 4652

Hershey (Hershey) [SSRDTLSDM, SSRDTLS] M528 4653

-----. R [SSMMRDTF, MRDD RR#M, M] 4654

Hervey (Hervey) X Hervey's litany 4655

Hervey's litany (Hervey) [SL TDDLT, RFMRDLS, MF] A233b; B473b; C473b; D89b; G380; U179; AB136b; AHp. 27; AI148; AL168; AO657; AP280a; AS187; BF313b; BX259 4656

Herz und herz vereinst zusammen (French trad) X Gregor's 167th metre-B 4657

Herzlich lieb hab ich dich, O Herr (Schmid. Orgelbuch. Strasburg, 1577) [DTLS MLLS, DTLSMLLS,] N465; O393; Q429; AA366; AZ232-A 4658

-----. V [DTLSFMLLS, DTLSFML] AA366 4659

-----. V [DTLSMLLS#, DT LSMLLS#] AZ232-A 4660

Herzlich thut mich erfreuen (German trad: mediaeval) [DDDMDSSDTSLSM, DSL] E284; X249a; AA371 4661

-----. V [DDRMFSSDTSLSM, DSL] AA371 4662

Herzlich thut mich erfreuen (Crueger) X St Simon 4663

Herzlich thut mich verlangen (Hassler) X Passion chorale 4664

Herzliebster Jesu (Crueger) [LLLSM, LTDDRT, TDRMD,] A71a; B155; C155; E70; J 85; K100; M413; N115; O75; P14; Q143; R191; S158; W 216b; X99; AA198; AD147; AF163; AK147; AM181; AN491; AW534; AZ36-A; BI67; BJ 42; BV151; BY137; BZ 4665

-----. V [LLLS#F#M, LTD DRDT, TDR] AN491 4667

-----. V [LLLS#M, LTDDRDT, TDRM] W216b 4667

He's coming (---) [MFSF#SD TLSLDRM, MFS] BB669

4668

-----. R [SLFDTLLSSMS, MFSL S] 4669

He's my friend (Thompson) [MR DFMMRD, SDDRRM, SS] AI398; AM664; AS282; AT155; AV351; AX23; BZ 4670

Heslington (Peel) [SDDTDR, MLL LRDT, LSD] D632a 4671

Heslington II (Peel) [MFSSSSS M, DDRMRRD, M] AS396 4672

Hesperus (Baker) [MMMSDRRM, SSSFSMFR] A469; B39; C25b; D18b; G273; H214; I372; J370a; K337a; L1; M132; N391; R215; S89; T278; U44; V311; W501a; Y22; Z353; AA479; AB173; AC63; AD404; AE212; AF447; AG129; AH193; AJ386; AK187; AL360b; AM507; AN572; AO369; AP232b; AR389; AS364; AT136; AV134; AW171; BA79; BE244; BF247; BK43; BR8; BX88; BY 515; BZ 4673

Heut' ist o mensch (Lowenstern) X Lowenstern 4674

Heut' triumphiret (Gesius) X Gesius 4675

Hezekiah (Gibbons) X Song 22 4676

Hibernia's patron saint ("B. S.") [MFSDMSFMRD, MFRFS, M] BO136 4677

-----. R [DDTLSFMSD, SD SMDMS] 4678

Hic breve vivitur (Pettet) [MS DFMRD, MFSLLR, SDM] F569a 4679

Hickling Broad (Shaw) [DRMDLS FMFSLRM, DRM] X18 4680

Hide me (Doane) X Hide me, O my Saviour 4681

Hide me, O my Saviour (Doane) [MMMRDSLD, SDMRR, MMM] V761; AI247; AW483; AX513; AY71 4682

-----. R [MDFLSDRMSSR, MRDDL] 4683

Hide thou me (Lowry) X Keller 4684

Hiding [in Thee] (Sankey) X O safe to the Rock 4685

Hier legt mein sinn sich vor dir nieder (Rosenroth) X Old 29th 4686

Hierapolis (Wesley) [DMRDD RRM, MRDFMRDT] W239 4687

High on the mountaintop (Beesley) [SDDDRM, RMSFMR, RMRM] BC62 4688

High road (Shaw) [SDDDRDT LSLT, SDLS, SD] A290a; E 427; R22; X556; AL38 4689

Higher ground (Gabriel) [SSD MMRDL, RDLSDMDR,] AT 319; AU269; AV374; AX382; AY462; BB631; 4690

-----. R [SDMSSFMF, STR FFMRM,] 4691

Higher than I (---) [SDDDD TDRSSS, MMFMR] AY328 4692

Highest lauds (LeJeune) [DDD TTLLS, LTLSLTLS,] Y348 4693

Highland Avenue (Fisher) [MMMMMDRMM, SSSSSMF#] AR386 4694

Highwood (Terry) [SLMRTD LSMDR, MF#LRS] AD103; BV569; BY127 4695

Hilariter (Cologne. G-B. 1623) [RFMRLDTL, SSDTLLS#L,] E164b; X167; AF194; BG96 4696

Hilda (Barnby) X St Hilda 4697

Hilderstone (Hart) [DMFSLSF M, DMLRSSF#S,] F8 4698

Hildesheim (Koenig) X Evangelists 4699

Hiles (Hiles) X St Leonard 4700

Hilf Gott, dasz mir's gelinge! (Gregor) X Gregor's 126th metre 4701

Hill Bourne (Skeffington) [DR MFLDM, F#SMDRM, MFF] D43b 4702

Hill Crest (Holst) [RFMRM, DTDRSRFMRD, T] X86 4703

Hillery (Hay) [SSSLLLS, MMMM SFMR, M] AR456; AS13 4704
-----. R [SDDDDDRDLS, SSRM FT] 4705
Him that cometh unto Me (Kirkpatrick) [MMMRDTDLSM, SSSSDD] AX252 4706
-----. R [MMMRMFS, RRRRDR M, FF] 4707
Himlens Gud og Jordens Herre (Meiningen G-B.) X St Leonard 4708
Himmel (Himmel) [SSLSFSFM, RRTLSF#S, S] J464; W352 4709
Himmel, erde, luft und meer (Strattner) X Posen 4710
Hin maeta morgunstunden (Pålssan) [SLTDLSMSFMRD, SLTD] AD320; AN279 4711
Hinchman (Burnap) [MDSMFMR, RDTDRMRD, M] R73; S21; U439; V32; Z445; AD34b; AG 17; AM333; AO15; AR63; BF 187 4712
Hingham (Holyoke) [DDRMDFMM R, RMFSLSF] V658 4713
Hinman (Lovelace) [SMDLTD, SMDLTD, RMF#S,] R471; BZ 4714
Hinton-Martell (Evans) [SLR SSFM, DRMDRRD, MF#] W321 4715
Hintze (Hintze) X Salzburg 4716
Hir oesi fair (Welsh carol) X April 4717
His bride (---) [MMRDRSDR M, MMFMRDT] AY442 4718
His eye is on the sparrow (Gabriel) [SLSMDRM, FS LDDS, SFM] AI312; AM715 4719
His forever (Barnby) [SSSDTRD D, DDFMRSM, M] V306; W705 4720
His tender mercies (McGranahan) [SSDMMRDS, SDMSSDMR] AI377 4721
-----. R [SSSSSF#SM, MMMMM R#MD,] 4722
His way with thee (Nusbaum) X Would you live with Jesus 4723
His yoke is easy (Warren) [SSSDTLSLSM, SSFFFM] AX348 4724
-----. R [SSSMFSLLLS, MFR RMF] 4725
Hitchen carol (English trad) [TDTLTDRDTLS#MLTDR] AP168b; BG46a 4726
-----. V [TDTLTDRDTLS#, MLLTD] BG46a 4727
Hjem jeg laenges (Lindeman) [LTDLDRMD, MFSMRRD, M] K81; O316; P190 4728
Hobart (Tucker) [DMSLSS, SLSDMR, RMSL] T232; AJ 328 4729
Höchster priester (Wesley's Foundery collection. 1742) X Savannah 4730
Höchster priester, der du dich (Gregor. Choral buch, 1784) X Gregor's 12th metre 4731
Hodges (Hodges) [DMFSLSM, SFMRSM, MFS] B43a; C43b; D24b; L257 4732
Hodu and Ono (Halevy) X Min hamaytsar 4733
Hoff (Hoff) [SSLTDTDMRTD, TRDLS,] J423; O11; P27; Q44 4734
Hoffman (Hoffman) [SDDSSTLS, FFMRDSS, S] AE174; AS144; AT130; AW473; BB644 4735
-----. R [DRMRDSMDRDRMS, SSD] 4736
-----. V [SDDSSTLS, FFMR RMFM] AS144 4737
Hoffman II (Hoffman) [DRM MMDMFSSSM, DDMR] AT 350; AU54; AX402 4738
-----. R [SSLLLLTLLSMS, SLLL] 4739
Holborn (Adams) [MSFFMMR, DTLSSS, SLT] D585a 4740
Holborn (Morley) [DTLSMRD SFM, LTDMRR] K200; Q 474; AA465 4741
Holborn (Paisiello) X Vigil 4742
Holborn (Thiman) [DDRMDFM RRD, MMFSML] BY312

4743

Holborn Hill (St Albans Tune book. 1865) [MMMFMMRD, DDDRMF# F#S,] C133a; D87a; G257; I199; L376; O115; S160; T174b; V22; AA419; AB177; AD454; AJ166; AL318; AM308; AS180; BA393; BB69; BR278 4744

Holcomb (McKinney) [MMMFF# SR, DDDFDM, MMM] AT331; AU415 4745

-----. R [LLLFLSF#SM, RRRF# MRS,] 4746

Holcombe (Sykes) [MSFMMRRD, DTLSMLRR,] BA195 4747

Hold fast till I come (Belden) [SSDRMSLSMR, MFMRMR] BB548 4748

-----. R [MSSSSSSLSMR, MFF FF] 4749

Hold oppe, Gud, hos os dit ord (Luther) X Spires 4750

Hold the fort (Bliss) [SLSMDRDL SLSMR, SLS] E570; AU303 4751

-----. R [DDDDDSMSLLLDT, DDD] 4752

Hold thou my hand (Main) [SF# SLSSMRDDT, RTDRM] AP527; AU207; AX469 4753

Hold to God's unchanging hand (Eiland) [DDDSLSLD, MMRDD MS, S] AX446 4754

Holiness (Bliss) [MMLSF#S, DDTDMR, MMLS] U264; V412; AR404; AS222; AT338; AU217; AX429; BA633; BC114 4755

Holiness (Stebbins) [MMRMFM, DRDTD, MMRMF] G251; R300; Z346; AE182; AH395; AI284; AL500; AM706; AR469; AS50; AT367; AU291; AX428; AY111; BB603; BY509a; BZ 4756

Holland (Wilms) X Hague 4757

Holland (Tours) [MRRSMDRM, MMF#SLTLS,] V499 4758

Holley (Hews) [MR#MDMRMFS M, SF#SMM] A574b; B502; C8; D272b; G398; H85; I74; L25; N396; R372; S209; T43; U89; V62; W550b; Z470; AA 411; AB261; AD53; AE336; AH 229; AI175; AJ66; AL97b; AN 113; AO4; AP283; AR221; AS446; AT395; AU232; AV 14; AX161; AY437; BA175; BB250; BD12; BE419; BF 195; BR204; BX127 4759

Hollingside (Dykes) [MSLSS FM, DTLSMDR, MS] A408; B223; C223a; D335a; E414; F193; G191; H435; I247; J393b; K371a; L149; O92; S233b; T416; V331a; W414a; Y373; AB204; AC157a; AD 212a; AG153b; AL266b; AM 459; AO655; AP417a; AW 159; AZ205-I; BA422a; BB 402; BD199; BF370; BR43, 261; BV506a; BX485; BY 441a 4760

-----. V [MSLSSFM, MMRSS F#S, MS] BR261 4761

Holly Springs (Maclean) [MM FLSFFM, MSDLSF#S, M] V52 4762

Hollywood (Wade) X St Thomas 4763

Holmbush (Richards) [DSMR DDRTLS, LTDDRR] AK85 4764

Holmes (Holmes) X Eventide 4765

Holmes (Shippen) [MFSLLRS FM, DTLSFMR,] AD354 4766

Holmfirth (Gill) [MMFSS LTD, TLSFMMR, M] I611 4767

Holsinger (Holsinger) [DRMSL FMDRRDRM, MMS] AR265 4768

Holy Bible, book divine (Bradbury) X Aletta 4769

Holy Church (Brown) [DMRD SLS, SMRDMR, SMR] D605; J304; K211; L26; V299; AB 288; BR84 4770

Holy Church (Terry) [DSDSM RDR, MFSLTDR, D] BL66; BM87; BN200; BY365 4771

Holy City (Dale) [SMRRD, DDLS, SRMRD, DM] AV293 4772

Holy City (Gaul) [SSFMFSM R, MFFLFM, SF#] D406c;

O608; AT508 4773
Holy City II (Gaul) [MRLTS,D RRM, LSMFR, RT] U429; BF 658 4774
Holy City (Gaul) X Sanctus 4775
Holy comfort (Genge) [LLTDRTD, LLTDRTM, DD] E410 4776
Holy cross (Brown) [MFMRSD FMR, STLDF#S, S] W269; BY 773 4777
Holy cross (Wade, arr) [SMRD STLS, DRSRR#M, SM] G347; H304; I137; L152; V303; Y47; Z483; AC328; AE371; AH317; AJ194; AO311; AP787b; AW 381; BA5 4778
Holy cross (West) [DTLSSLDR, MRDTDRDT,] C122b; D88b 4779
Holy day (Parker) [SSTDRMSFM, RMMMLSF#] D26 4780
Holy day, Jehovah's rest (Belden) [MRDDFMR, RRRRRDRM, M] BB654 4781
-----. R [SMLSFFRSFM, MRDD FM] 4782
Holy desire (Stebbins) X Adelaide 4783
Holy faith (Martin) [MMMSFM RD, SSSTLSF#S,] Y78; BV535 4784
Holy Ghost (Crueger, arr., Voll standige Psalmen. Bremen, 1639) [LDTD#RDT, DRMFMRD, MD] A57a; E76; W405a; AL 160b; AP362 4785
-----. V [LDTDRDT, DRMFM RD, MD] AP362 4786
Holy Ghost, with light divine (Gottschalk) X Mercy 4787
Holy God, we praise thy name (Allgemeinisches katholisches G-B. 1774) X Te deum 4788
Holy guide (Burnap) [SSLTDDT, LSMMRDT, TM] U38; AJ152; AM564 4789
Holy Hill (Bourgeois) [DRRDD FFMR, DRFMRDT] AJ417 4790
Holy Hill (Pontius) [DMSSS DTD, SDTDSFMR] I13 4791
Holy, holy, holy (Dykes) X Nicaea 4792
Holy, holy, holy Lord (Barnby) [SSDSLLS, MRDTLLS, SS] BI38 4793
Holy, holy, holy Lord (Malan) X Hendon 4794
Holy innocents (Gray) [DRMM RDTLTDRT, LSS] A112 4795
Holy is God (Currie) [MMM SMFMRDMR, MF#F#SL] BN 207 4796
Holy is the Lord (Bradbury) X Saboath 4797
Holy Jesus (Lissant) [MRDD TDRFMR, SMRDTD] D572 4798
Holy Lord (Schmidt) X Fahre fort 4799
Holy Love (Schumann) [DTRD FMMRR, RRMRTSS,] BR528 4800
Holy manger (Keller) [MFM SDRLR, RMRSSLSM] J43 4801
Holy manna (Moore) [SSLDD RRDMRDL, SSLD] AT368; AU198; AX33 4802
Holy Mary, mother mild (Dressler) [DDTDRMRD, SMDMR, RRD] BO101 4803
-----. R [SSMDRMR, SSMDR MR, SM] 4804
Holy mountain (Lindeman) [S MRDDTLTS, SMDRTLS,] J82; M405; N106; O274; P217; Q149; AA212 4805
Holy Name (Genevan Psalter, 1562) [SSDRMFS, MSFMDR D, MR] A323a; W62a 4806
Holy Name (Major reading: Genevan Psalter, 1562) X Louez dieu (Minor reading) 4806a
Holy night (Grueber) [SLSMSLS M, RRTDDS, LL] A33; B546; C546; G106; I123; J16; K530; M603; N46; O178; P140; Q 646; R154; S132; T339; U60; V749; W49; Y302; Z188; AB 116; AC81; AD119; AE92; AF138; AG74; AH125; AI381; AK101; AL53; AM161; AN166;

AO132; AP172; AQ289; AR135; AS102; AT72; AU146; AV87; AW 83; AX100; AY488; AZ1516; BA 168; BB102; BC160; BD218; BF288; BI97; BK151; BL12; BN20; BO151; BP9; BQ11; BV 113; BX534; BY108; BZ 4807

Holy offerings (Redhead) [MRFM MRD, SRMSSF#LS,] A480; B504; C504; D478a; AO496; AZ156-D; BR296 4808

Holy Offerings (Spinney) [MRR DDTT, FMMRRDD, DT] D478b 4809

Holy Patron! thee saluting (Catholic) [SDDTDLTDS, LSSSFMM] BO124 4810

-----. R [DTLSSDTLLS, FMM RDD] 4811

Holy Queen, we bend (Herbert) X Holy Queen, we come 4812

Holy Queen! we bend before thee (Hurley) [MSDTLSLFS, MSDR MFM] BP85 4813

Holy Queen, we come (Herbert) [DSMLSFFM, MFSDFMR, D] BN134; BO55 4814

Holy quietness (Marshall) X Marshall 4815

Holy Rood (Brown) [SDRMFS, M FLRDT, SDTL] AM297; BY282b 4816

Holy Sepulchre (Thorne) [DDDD MSRM, SSSLMSFM] F125; AZ2-C 4817

Holy Spirit (Campbell) [MMRDD TT, FFMRRDD, SS] BB701 4818

Holy Spirit (LeJeune) [DRMFMRD, SLTDTTLS, L] B371 4819

Holy Spirit, come and shine (Catholic) [SDDTLTDRMF#S, MFRMM] BO185 4820

Holy Spirit, faithful guide (Wells) [SSDDMRDR, MMSDTDRD,] G243; H213; I193; L462; N53; T248; U132; V212; Z276; AE 150; AG126; AH227; AJ345; AO232; AP346; AR443; AS252; AT165; AU245; AV152; AW137; AX135; AY196; BB211; BZ 4821

Holy Spirit, lead us (Kelly) [MFFMDFFFM, LTLSMMR] AU450 4822

Holy Spirit, Lord of light (Webbe) X Veni Sancti Spiritus 4823

Holy Spirit, truth divine (English trad) X Lew Trenchard 4824

Holy temples on Mount Zion (Schreiner) [DMSSLTDS, LLSDSFMR,] BC63 4825

Holy Trinity (Barnby) [DTLS F#LLS, FMMMRDT, M] B30; C30; D270; H210; I299; V 368; AB280; AM517; AN202 b; AO216; AP239; AZ14-Dd; BA862; BB386; BD234; BE147; BF513; BH88; BX 228 4826

Holy voices (Geer) [DDDD RRRR, MRDDLDR, M] D61a 4827

Holy war (Booth) [LLLLDTL, LLSFM, LLLL] C126b; D81b; K73b; AK295; AO390; BY 506a 4828

Holy Well (English trad) [SMFMFSDTL, SLRDTD, S] F277; BG56a 4829

-----. V [SMRMFSDTL, SS LLRRDTD,] BG56a 4830

Holy Word (Barnby) X St Sylvester 4831

Holyrood (Stewart) [MFSLTDS, LLSMRMFFM,] C340 4832

Holyrood (Watson) [DMSSLS, SLDTLS, SSLD] D376; F338; T355a; W494; AL146b; AP10; BV649a 4833

Holywell (Joy) [SDTLSFMRD, MSDTLS, S] V97b 4834

Holywood (Wade) X St Thomas 4835

Homburgh (German trad) [DR MDFMRD, RRMSSF#S, D] D361 4836

Home I (---) [MDRM, MFFM, RRMFMFSL,] D676a 4837

Home II (---) [SSMSSMSFRFM, MMFLS] M641; AI199 4838

Home (Bishop) X Home, sweet home 4839
Home (Emerson) [DDDRRM, MMLSMRD, SSM] L601 4840
Home (McNaughton) [SMMRDLD, SLSMR, MFSM] AE384; AS413; AW360; AX555; AY444; BC169 4841
-----. V [SDMRDLD, SLSMR, MFSM] AX555 4841a
Home (Mozart) [SDRMFRDRTD, MSRTMR] BE34 4842
Home (Stotzel. Choralbuch. Stuttgart, 1744) X So fürst du doch 4843
Home (Thompson) [SDRMSDRM, LSMRDR, MR] G433; AD420 4844
Home of the blest (Brenneman) X There's a beautiful, beautiful land 4845
Home of the soul: new (Doughty) X Soon trials and conflicts 4846
Home of the soul (Phillips) [DMSF#SM, SSLTDS, SSF#S] G525; AM729; AS472; AU42; AV399; BB552 4847
Home of the soul (Pollock) [MFSSLSMSDTLS, SDDD] AX588; AY164 4848
-----. R [TDRRRRDRM, SSLLLDT] 4849
Home over there (O'Kane) [SDDDDMRD, TDRRRRFM] AT480; AU43; AV393; AX592 4850
-----. R [TDRDRM, MFFFMSMR, SF] 4851
Home, sweet home (Bishop) [DMFSSMSFMFRM, DMFS] H511; L605; P349; U428; V715; AI339; AS412; AX573; AY393; BB415; BC185 4852
-----. R [SFRDRM, SDTLSMSFMF] 4853
-----. V [DRMFFLSMSFMFRM, DR] P349 4854
-----. V [DMFLSMSFMFRM, DMFL] U428 4855
-----. V [DMFSSMMSFMFRM, DDM] BC185 4856
Homeland (Sullivan) [DMMLLSS, FMDDTD, DMM] A598b; B281; C281; D162; G530; I615; J543a; M307; N450; T436; V691; AA562; AH520; AV284; BA757; BD174; BE245; BF553; BO202; BR449a; BX254 4857
Homeward (Traditional) [DMMDMFMRD, MSSFMRR] Y42 4858
Homeward bound (---) [MMRDDTLDRM, RRRR, MRD] BB661; BR517 4859
Homeward bound (---) X No, not one (Hugg) 4860
Homines christi (Lowden) [SDDDSDRM, SFMRDS, SL] AI184; AO477 4861
Hominum amator (Ferguson) [MSMDRMM, TDRMLM, MSM] E276; BV65a 4862
Honor (---) [SSMRDDT, DRD#RR#M, DDS] M428 4863
Hope (Antes) [LDTLMFT, DRMMRRD, SS] AQ129; AZ11-K 4864
Hope (Davies) [DSMDFMMR, MDFMRMR] E551; AZ167-L; BA242 4865
Hope (Gastorius) X Was Gott tut 4866
Hope (Irons) [MMMSTDRM, SLSDMLLR,] W522; Y54; AB37; AP693 4867
Hope (Jacobs) [MRMS, SSSSF#S, MRMD, DD] D676b; AP615 4868
Hope (Remsberg) [DRMMMMFMR, TDRRMFM] L600 4869
Hope of Israel (Clayson) [DDDSMFSLSD, RMRSLT] BC64 4870
-----. R [DSMSDRM, RRRDRMDS, D] 4871
Hopkins (Beethoven) X Alsace 4872
Hopkins (Hopkins) X Twilight 4873
Hopkins (Monk) [DMSSFMRMF, FLFSMDF#] D64 4874
Horbury (Dykes) [DRMSFM, MRMFM, MLLSF#] B500; C500; E444; F352; X586c;

AC324; AL321a; AP470a; AZ 579-D; BE193 4875
Horeb (Barnby) X Nightfall 4876
Horeb (Barnby) X Jordan 4877
Horeb (Polack) [DSLTDMRDT, LTDRM, MM] AA69 4878
Horeb (Smart) [SSSLLS, MSLDT, TDLSF#] BY709a 4879
Horsfield (Rusbridge) [SDRMDRM FRS, MRDLTD] BY542 4880
Hornsey (Wesley, S.S.) [SSDMR MFS, MRDRSLDT,] Eap. 28 4881
Horsham (English trad) [MMFS MRD, MMSSSMRDR,] E344; R538; S95; X258; AK348 4882
Horsley (Horsley) [DRMFMSFMR, SMDTLS,] A65a; B159; C159b; D544; E106; F214; J77b; K544 a; L315b; M419; Q157a; S157b; V149; W105; X131; Y87; AF171; AJ384b; AL87; AM191; AP290b; BB126; BE383; BV163; BY149; BZ 4883
Horton (Minshall) [MSFMMRD, FMLSRRR, MM] AB98 4884
Horton (Schnyder) [SDMDDLS, SF RMDLSTL] H10; I248b; L364; N158; P385; U357; V468; AA 243; AO231; AT244; AV158; AX145; AY499; BB219; BR47 4885
Hos Gud är idel glädje (Ahnfelt. Sanger) [SDDDMSM, LSSFRM, SDD] N632 4886
Hosanna (Campbell) [MFRDRRM M, MFRDRRMM,] AC114 4887
-----. R [SLL, LTT, SSLDMSL, MFM] 4888
Hosanna (Dykes) [DSFMMRRD, SSSSLTDRR,] A318; B53; C53; D316a; J424; K425; S53; V14; AD168; AM314; AO63; AR200; BA373; BF334 4889
Hosanna (Dykes) X Hosanna we sing 4890
Hosanna (Elliott) [DSMFRDTD, DRMFSLRR,] F241b 4891
Hosanna (Gray) [SDDDTTLL, LFM RDDTT,] BY269 4892
Hosanna (Kettle) [SDMSDMRD, DRMF#SRDT] D557 4893
Hosanna in excelsis (Nicholson) [SDSMFSLT, SLLRDTDR] F421 4894
Hosanna we sing (Dykes) [MM DMSSSLTDD, SSDDT] D560; AP753 4895
Hosmer (Bullard) [MMRDRMR, MFSFMFS, SS] BD149; BF 465; BX409 4896
Hosmer (Cologne G-B. 1623) [DDSDRM, SFMRRM, MMMR] A534; E443; X111; AK263; AL333; AN335; AP467; AQ92; AW308; BY481b 4897
Hostis Herodes impie (Plainsong, M 3) [SSLTDLSFM RRFMFSS,] E38; F74a 4898
Houghton (Gauntlett) X Cobern 4899
Houghton (Wesley) X Sebastian 4900
Hour of need (Bourgeois) X Commandments 4901
Hour of prayer (Doane) X Doane II 4902
Hour of prayer (Hansen) [LM MMRTDTL, TDDRDRM] P29; BD74 4903
-----. V [MMMMRTDTL, DD RDRM, M] BD74 4904
Hover o'er me, Holy Spirit (Sweney) X Fill me now 4905
How beautiful heaven must be (Bland) [SMMMMRDMD, MSSSMDM] AX590 4906
-----. V [SDDDMDRD, MSS SMDMR,] 4907
How beautiful thy temples, Lord [Cannon) [SMDRMFFM, SL LSMR, SM] BC65 4908
How blessed is the little flock (Lindeman) X Ludwig 4909
How blest (Kirkpatrick) [SS LSDDDTLS, SSLTDT] AI102 4910
-----. R [SSSSSS, DTDRD, DM RDD] 4911
How blest are they (Tomissön. Psalmebog. 1569) X Island

4912
How blest the man (Kinross) [LDTLS#LMM, F#SMSFM, LD] BH27 4913
How brightly beams (Nicolai) X Frankfort 4914
How can I leave thee? (Thuringen folk song) X Lynde 4915
How fair the Church (Schumann. G-B. 1539) X Old 112th 4916
How far from home? (---) [DDD DTLDDM, SSFRLLS] BB665 4917
How firm a foundation (---) [SDDM SSLSFMSD, SDDD] BC66 4918
How firm a foundation (American trad) X Foundation 4919
How gentle God's commands (Naegeli) X Dennis 4920
How gladly (Traditional) [TDMS SLSDM, SFRTFMR] P280 4921
How good it is to thank the Lord (Gideon) [MRFLSFMMM, ML TD#RLT] BH109 4922
How good it is to thank the Lord (Lewandowski) [MMSDSLDS, SRMFSLSF] BH110, 267 4923
How goodly is thy house (Mozart) X Cana 4924
How great is your Name (Gelineau) [FFLD, DDRD, DLTL, LSLF.] BSp. 8 4925
-----. R [FDLDRDRFD, LDSF.] 4926
How great the wisdom (McIntyre) [SMRDDTFFMRM, SLRFS] BC68 4927
How I Love Jesus (---) X O, how I love Jesus 4928
How long must we wait? (Caldwell) [MDRMMFMR#M, MRD#RMRD] AU131 4929
-----. R [SSL, SSFMF, FFS, FF MR#M,] 4930
How long, O Lord, most holy (Gates) [MLTDTMRDD, TMFF MMR] BC69 4931
How lovely are thy dwellings (Mendelssohn) X Evangelist 4932
How lovely are thy dwellings (Schumann) X Canonbury 4933
How marvelous (Gabriel) [SS MSDRMDDTTTDRD, S] AE 304; AT139; AX24 4934
-----. R]MMRDSSFM, RRR MFMR, M] 4935
How oft, alas (Pollock) [SM MMDDDL, SSMMDR, SS] AX 339; AY208 4936
How pleasant and how good (American trad) X Camp-meeting 4937
How reads your life-book? (Byers) [SDDDTLSFM, SLD TDRD,] AX442 4938
-----. R [SMMMDFMMRR, SRMFFF] 4939
How sweet, how heavenly (Bradbury) X Brown 4940
How tedious and tasteless (Edson) X Contrast 4941
How wondrous (Jewish trad) X Akdamus 4942
How wondrous and great (Haydn) X Lyons 4943
Howard (Cuthbert) [MFSLSDLS FFM, MRSLS] H233; I338; L390; R121; T190; V280; AJ277; BB155 4944
Howard (Howard) X Smith 4945
Hoylake (Roberts) [DDRMFM RL, MR, RSMRDT] W487a 4946
Hoyte (Hoyte) X St Columba 4947
"Hozanna", see "Hosanna" in all languages 4948
Hsuan P'ing (Confucian temple chant) [LSMSL, DLSLM, LD LDR, M] AF487 4949
Hubbard (Chinese folk tune) [DSLDRM, MSMRDR, RMRD] R223 4950
Hubert (Darwall) X St Hubert 4951
Huddersfield (Parratt) [MSFM RMDR, MFSS#LTT, D] Eap. 37; W240; AP667a; BE173; BY447 4952
Huddersfield (Williams. Psalmody, ca 1770) X Durham

4953
Huddleston (Berridge) [SSLSST MRDTLS, SSDR] AL603 4954
Hudson (Hudson) X At the cross 4955
Huger (American trad) X Foundation 4956
Huguenot hymn (Darms) X My Lord and I 4957
Hull (American Musical misc., 1798) X Ganges 4958
Humble thyself to walk (Rogers) [SDRMRDRDLLS, SDMSF] AX430 4959
-----. R [MMMMMMMRDDT, SSSSS] 4960
Humility (---) X Deliverer 4961
Humility (Goss) X See, amid the winter snow 4962
Humility (Hunter) [SDDDRMMM, SSMDMR, MF] AX431 4963
-----. R [MFSSSMRDDD, MRR SRM,] 4964
Humility (Mainzer) [DTDRMRD, RD#RMFMR, MR] AP764 4965
Humility (Tuckerman) [DRMSFM DRM, SF#SLSMR] D86; T225; U278; Y212; Z517; AJ321; AS 337; AT466; AV70; BX135 4966
Hummel (Zeuner) [SDDDRMFM, SFMRDT, TT] I292; Z512; AF 369; AR107; AS401; BB443; BX211 4967
Hunnys (Seven sobs of a sorrowful soul. 1585) [LDRTDTLS#, LRDDTD, DR] E79; X108 4968
Huntingdon (Beery) [DRMSDMLD, DRMDSLR, D] AR298; AS254 4969
Huntingdon II (Beery) [DMDRDDD TDR, MRMFMM,] AY78 4970
Huntington (Huntington) [SSMR DDLF#S, SLLLTDR,] L99 4971
Hurdus (Downes) X Solitude 4972
Hurlbut (Bird) [MFMMRDDTD, MFSSFMM] Y196 4973
Hursley (Allgemeines Katholisches G.B. Vienna, 1774) [DDD DTDRMRD, MMMMRM] A166; B20; C20a; D11a; Eap.39; F24b; G56; H33; I47; J209; K463; L21; M525; N563; O 566; P77; Q551; R57; S37; T132; U457; V46; W292c; Y93; Z150; AA42; AB25; AC 22; AD57; AE44; AF50; AG 28; AH174; AI50; AJ198; AK 55; AL556a; AM346; AN108; AO31; AP666b; AR56; AS34; AT15; AU177; AV239; AW30; AX68; AY129; AZ22-L; BA 780; BB321; BE227; BF194; BK54; BL73; BX139; BZ 4974
Hursley (Allgemeines Katholisches G-B. Vienna, 1774) X Te deum 4975
Hurstmonceaux (Prout) [MR DS, DRFMRR, SFMMRR] AB97 4976
Hus (Pensum sacrum) X Herr Jesu Christ, dich zu uns wend 4977
Hushed was the evening hymn (Sullivan) X Samuel 4978
Hussite hymn (Moravian trad) [LMMRMT, LMMRMT, DTDR] BE378 4979
Hvad hör jäg? (Schulz) [SDD MSFMR, MDRDTLS,] N223 4980
Hvad kan os komme til for Nød (Geistliche lieder. Wittenberg, 1535) X Luther 4981
Hvad ljus öfver griften (Jespersön. Gradual, 1573) X Jespersön 4982
Hvad röst, hvad ljuflig röst jag hör (Ahlstrom) X St James' Stockholm 4983
Hvo ene lader herren raade (Neumark) X Neumark 4984
Hvo ved, hvor naer mig er min ende (Bronner. Choral buch. 1715) X Wer weiss, wie nahe 4985
Hvor salig er den lille flok (Lindeman) X Ludwig 4986

Hyatt (Sweney) [MMSF#FMDDL LDS, RSFM] AO142b 4987
Hyfrydol (Prichard) [DRDRM FMRDR, SFMMR] A347b; C 226b; E301; F260; G11; J397a; Q423; R123; S113a; W479; X260; AB343; AD16; AE13; AF13; AG62; AK174; AL117; AM145; AN50a; AO651; AP76; AQ192; AR36; AT9; AW69; BC49; BE 175; BF214; BV259; BY173; BZ 4988
Hymn (Gould) [SDRMMFRRTD, SLSSF#S] H293; I575; AN159b; AJ193; BD67; BX189 4989
Hymn for Day of Atonement (Weinberg) [LLLTDRM, MMMRDDT, TT] BH169 4990
Hymn for Memorial Day (Fulton) [MMMMRSLS, FSFMF#SFM,] AH476 4991
Hymn for month of May (Matthews) X Chenies 4992
Hymn for Tabernacles (Alman) [MRDRFMDT, LRMFSM, MM] BH185 4993
Hymn for the golden age (Beimel) [DRMFLSSFM, RMSMR, DR] BH236 4994
Hymn for glory (Garrett) [DDDMRD FM, MMMSMRTL] AS153 4995
Hymn of glory (Jewish trad) X Omnom kayn 4996
Hymn of nations (McWhood) [DM SLF#S, DMSLF#S, DTLS,] G508 4997
Hymn of praise (Schubert) [SDD RDTRRDRM, SMMFM] BK1 4998
Hymn of spring (Norden) [SDD DDTTLLL, SDDRDR] BH134 4999
Hymn of thanksgiving (Hauser) [DTDRMFLSFM, MRSSF#M] AH129 5000
Hymn of the harvest (Grimm) [DSLDRD, MDS, FMRSMRD] BH188 5001
Hymn to joy (Beethoven) X Beethoven 5002
Hymn to mothers (Binder) [SSS SSMRD, MSDDTLSL] BH260 5003
Hymn to St Joseph (Vulpius) X Cana 5004
Hymn to the Cross (Bragers) [LDTS#TLDRM, MRTRDLD] BP31 5005
Hymn to the Holy Cross (Wiltberger) [SSLSDTLS, LSFMR RM, S] BM79 5006
Hymn to the Holy Name (O' Connell) [MRDSSSLSRFM, MRDLD] BP21 5007
-----. R [SMDLLLF#RT, TLSDRFM] 5008
Hymn to the sorrowful Mother (Walther, G-B. 1524) X Venit hora 5009
Hymnus eucharisticus (Rogers) [LLTDRMRDTLLS#,S#S#LT] E328; W471b; X607a 5010
Hyndland (Finlay) [DTRMRDM, SDLSFMSDR,] BV446 5011

I

I am a stranger (Cassel) X The King's business 5012
I am coming, Lord (Hartsough) X I hear thy welcome voice 5013
I am coming to the cross (Fischer) X Coming to the cross 5014
I am not worthy (Converse) [SMRDSMRD, DFFLLS, SM] AI220 5015
-----. R [SSMSLF, LSDRMR, R MMF] 5016
I am praying for you (Sankey) [SSDMDMMRLTDS, SSDM] G237; AE166; AH435; AS 197; AT232; AU78; AV332; AW460; AX367; BB575 5017
-----. R [MSSLSM, MMMFM R, DDTL] 5018
I am resolved (Fillmore) X Resolution 5019
I am so glad (Bliss) X Gladness 5020
I am the vine (Shaw) [DMSS MRDRMD, DMSDSL] AX414 5021
-----. R [DDDDSLLLSM, DDDDSL] 5022
I am Thine (Doane) [MFMRR

RMRDD, DTLLLD] G252; H 345; R320; U217; V734; Z312; AE191; AG148; AH361; AI272; AL490; AM713; AO648; AP483; AR444; AS232; AT349; AU56; AV368; AW475; AX411; AY473; BB594; BZ 5023

-----. R [MFSMRDTLS, DTLDM RD,] 5024

I am Thine, O Lord (Doane) X I am Thine 5025

I am trusting (Fischer) X Coming to the cross 5026

I am trusting in His word (Moon) [SSDDMRDRDL, LLSSDR] AX460; AY97 5027

-----. R [SSLDTLSM, MFSS DRMR] 5028

I am trusting in my Saviour (Mosley) [SSLSMDDT, SLSFTLS,] AX462; AY94 5029

-----. R [MFMRSRMRD, DDDTD RM,] 5030

I believe the Bible (Ufford) [MM MMRDMSSSLS, MMRD] AX139 5031

-----. R [DDDDLS, LSMFS, DDDDL] 5032

I belong to Jesus (Sea) [SMRD LD, TDRSM, SMRMF] AI253; AM649 5033

I bless thee, Father, for the grace (Epstein) [MTDS#LFMR, LDTLTLS, D] BH115 5034

I bow in utter need (Whttington) [DTTTDRRRDTL, DFMMR] BI65 5035

I bring my sins to Jesus (Pollock) [MFSSLDLS, DTDRMR, RM] AY228 5036

I can hear my Savior calling (Norris) X Where He leads me 5037

I cannot be idle ("A. L. B.") [SDRMMRDRDLS, SDRMM] AX190 5038

-----. R [MMSSSLSMS, MSSS LSM] 5039

I cannot tell thee (Brown) [SDD DRMMM, FMDTRD, SD] AS 306 5040

-----. R [DDFFFFDRM, MMRRR F#M] 5041

I come into thy house (Whittington) [MSMRMDTLSSTDMMR, S] BI44-D 5042

I come to thee (Hugg) [SDFMM RR, DDDDRRM, MF] AY215 5043

I denne verdens sorger saenkt (Lindeman) [LDMLSFFM, R DTLLDDT,] O391 5044

I djupet af mitt jhärta (Ahnfelt) [SMTDMLS, FMSRSD, MLS] N516 5045

I do believe (American trad) X Belief 5046

I gave my life for thee (Bliss) [SSSMSLDT, LSSFSM, SS] N512; R262; U163; V748; Z289; AE171; AG145; AH287; AI138; AS244; AT399; AU222; AV378; AX312; BA473 5047

I have a mother over yonder (Negro spiritual) [DDDLDLL DL, DDDLSSS] AH596 5048

I have a Savior (Sankey) X I am praying for you 5049

I have a song (Excell) X Othello 5050

I have decided to follow Jesus (Hart) [DDMSSSLSMD, DDDD DD] AX304 5051

I have made my choice (Leech) [SSDDDMDSLDS, DRMSS] AS336; AX181 5052

-----. R [SSLSMSFFF, FFSFRFM] 5053

I have work enough to do (Kirkpatrick) [DRMMMMS, MRDMR, RMFF] BC71 5054

I hear in the air (---) X Home II 5055

I hear the Saviour say (Grape) X All to Christ I owe 5056

I hear thy welcome voice (Hartsough) [DMSMRDD, DR FLSM, SDT] E573; P262; W 689; AH240; AL481; AM406; AP435; AR446; AS204; AT224; AU265; AV170; AX299; BA908; BB224 5057

-----. R [DTLSL, SMRDR, SLMRDR] 5058

I heard the bells on Christmas

Day (Calkin) X Waltham 5059
I heard the voice of Jesus say (Brunk) [SSFMLSFM, DTLSFM, SS] AX329; AY472 5060
I heard the voice of Jesus say (Melish) [MMMFFSFMRM, FS DFMR] AU163; AX607 5061
I himmelen, i himmelen (Lindeman) [DMLSMDFM, DLTDMR, RR] O263 5062
I himmelen, i himmelen (Swedish Koralbok, 1697) X Laurinus 5063
I hoppet sig min frälsta själ förnöjer (---. 16th c. Northern mel) X Sweden 5064
I intend to go through with Him (Morris) [MSLSMRDMMFM, MSMDT] AX305 5065
I Jesu havn skal al vor gjerning ske (Kingo. Gradual. 1699) [DTLS#, S#LTDRM, TDLRDT] O247 5066
I Jesus söger jeg min fred (Lindeman) [MSFMRDRS, SLLSF MR, M] O370 5067
I know a kingdom (German trad. 16th c) X Freiburg 5068
I know a way (Sandström) [SDRM MMRDMR, RMRDDR] P306 5069
I know God's promise is true (Morris) [SSMRDSSMFS, DTL FST] AX476 5070
-----. R [SMDTDRD, SMRDDT DR, S] 5071
I know I love thee better (Hudson) [DMFSSLDD, DDDTLS, DM] AS283; AU94; AX479 5072
-----. R [SMDRDDLS, STTLSD, SM] 5073
I know in my heart what it means (Teasley) [SSDDDDTLSF#LS, SSTL] AX347 5074
-----. R [MRRMFMRMS, SLLL LTD] 5075
I know that my Redeemer lives (Edwards) [SSSTLTLSD, SSST LLL] BC95 5076
I know that my Redeemer lives (Fillmore) X Pounds 5077
I know whom I have believed (McGranahan) X El Nathan 5078
I Kristi sar jag somnar in (Swedish, 1698) [LDRMT DRT, SLTF#SMR#M,] N596 5079
I lift mine eyes (Achron) [LTLTDRDT, LDTTLSL, L] BH33 5080
I lift my eyes (Lagi) [DMR DRMFMR, RMFSFMM] J396 5081
I lift up my eyes (Gelineau) [DDDR, RRM, MMMF, RFM.] BSp. 40 5082
I long to be there (Schmucker) [SSSSSSDS, SSSSMRDR] AY 59 5083
I love Him (Foster) [DMFSS LDTLS, DMFSSL] AU210 5084
I love the Lord (Gelineau) [LFSM, FSL, RDRL, LDTDT] BSp. 34 5085
I love the Lord (Genevan Psalter. 1562) X Ainsworth 97 5086
I love thee (Ingall. Christian harmony) [SDDMSSLSMDR M, SDDM] AT150; BB343 5087
I love thee, O thou Lord (Cologne. Symphonia ... 1695) [SDRMFSDFMR, RM FSFM] BN209; BQ316 5088
I love thy kingdom, Lord (Mason. Sacred harp, 1843) X Bealoth 5089
I love to hear the story (Gauntlett) [MMMMRMFMR, LSFM RMF] F445b 5090
-----. R [LTDTLRMFFM, MMRDTL] 5091
I love to hear the story (Root) X Ellon 5092
I love to steal awhile away (Pollock) [MMMSMFMR, RR RDRM, SS] AX72; AY291 5093
I love to tell the story (Fischer) X Hankey 5094
I love to tell the story (Jacobs) [DMSSLSSM, SSRMFM, DM]

AY348 5095

I love to think of my home (Pollock) [SSDDDDTRR, RRDMM DR,] AS478; AX586; AY151 5096

-----. R [RMD,SSLDS,DMMM RDR, S] 5097

I must tell Jesus (Hoffman) X Orwigsburg 5098

I name thy hallowed Name (Spiess) X Swabia 5099

I need thee [every hour] (Lowry) X Need 5100

I need thee, precious Jesus (Showalter) [DRMMFMMR, T DRFMRD, D] AS216 5101

I need thee, precious Jesus (Slovak hymn) [MFSSDTLLS, MSDMRDT,] BQ41 5102

I need thee, precious Jesus (Webb) X Webb 5103

I owe the Lord a morning song (Herr) [DDSDRMFMRDTD, RMRD] AX58; AY278 5104

I praegtige himle (Lindeman) [DMMFSSSMRDLS, DTMM] O19 5105

I pray thee, Lord (Mather) X Medfield 5106

I rejoiced when I heard (Gelineau) [MLSM, MRM, MTLT, TSMF# M,] BSp. 42 5107

I remember Calvary (Black) X Where He may lead me 5108

I saw a mighty angel (Careless) [SSLTDRMSFRFM, MRLF] BC255 5109

I saw three ships (English carol) X Sunny Bank 5110

I see by rays surrounded (Haller) [DMFSMLS, DTLSRM, RMF] BP71 5111

I see my Jesus crucified (Montani) [MLTDDTTS, LFMRMSLT] BQ 24 5112

I see thee standing, Lamb of God (Danish trad.) X Release 5113

I shall approach the altar (Track) [MMMSMDDRRM, MDTLSD] BL42 5114

I shall be like Him (Spencer) [MMMMRMSSSSM, RRRRD] AX568 5115

I shall know Him (Sweney) [DRMMMMMRDMDDLS, SS] AT472; AV397; AX572; AY 495 5116

-----. R [MMRTLTDS, DRM MMFMR] 5117

I sing of a maidin (Shaw) [LL LTDTLSLL, LLTDTL] BG 183 5118

I stand all amazed (Gabriel) [SSDLSMFSDLTLS, SSR] BC80 5119

I surrender all (Weeden) X Surrender 5120

I thank the Lord my Maker (Webb) 5121

I think when I read (Cornell) [DRMMMMFMRMRR, RMFS] BR539 5122

I think when I read (Gifford) [SMTDRDLSMLS, SLLLR] U325; AI384b 5123

I think, when I read that sweet story (Greek mel) X Luke 5124

I trusted even when I said (Gelineau) X I love the Lord 5125

I wander through the stilly night (Dougall) [SSLTDTLS, MFD# RLSR#M,] BC294 5126

I want to be a Christian (Negro spiritual) [DDMMSM RD, DDMSLSM, D] R317; AF353; AG318; AH608; AR 486; BK167; BZ 5127

-----. V [DDMMSMRD, DDD MSSLS] AH608 5128

I want to be a worker (Baltzell) [SDDDRMMRDR, SRRRMF] AX184 5129

-----. R [SFMSMD, DRMMM MSMRD] 5130

I want to be more like Jesus (Stillman) [SSLSDRMFMR, DTDRMR] AS226; AX376 5131

-----. R [LS# LTDSMS, FMF MRMFS,] 5132

I want to love Him more (Smith) [DMRDSLDS, DM

MSSR, DM] AX374; AY202 5133

-----. R [MSSLLS, DMMFMR, MSSL] 5134

I was a wandering sheep (Zundel) X Lebanon 5135

I was glad when they said (McKinney) [SFMMRDMLS, FM RRRMF] AU309 5136

I will arise and go to Jesus (American trad) X Arise 5137

I will be true to thee (Morris) [MR#MFMMRD, DDDMMR, MR#] AX400 5138

-----. R [SSSSLSM, DDDFFM, MFM] 5139

I will early seek my Saviour (Fillmore) [SMRDMLLS, SFMDL TD, S] BB417 5140

-----. R [DDTRRRDM, MMM RDLS, S] 5141

I will never turn back (Grisham) [DRMMR#MMRD, DMSMR#MM] AX439 5142

-----. R [DRMMRD, DRSFFM, DRMM] 5143

I will not forget thee (Gabriel) X Sweet promise 5144

I will sing (Bilhorn) [MFSSLSDS, SSSSLSS, M] AE293; AM709; AT144; AU377; AV315 5145

-----. R [SLTDDTLSM, SSSSL SS,] 5146

I will sing (McGranahan) X My Redeemer 5147

I will sing (Phillips) X Home of the soul 5148

I will sing of Jesus' love (Belden) [MFSMMRD, RMFL LSM, MF] BB529 5149

-----. R [DDDTLSDM, DRMFMM RR] 5150

I will sing you a song (Phillips) X Home of the soul 5151

I wonder (Pollock) [MFSMFLSM, SFMRFM, MF] AX30; AY346 5152

-----. R [SDTLSSFM, SFMRFM, SD] 5153

I would be closer to thee (Warren) [SSSDDDDL, LTTTDRM, S] AX381 5154

I would be true (Peek) X Peek 5155

I would love thee (Hymns and tunes. 1890) X May the grace of Christ 5156

I would not have my way (Byers) [SSF#LSMRDLD, LSSDRM] AX393 5157

-----. R [SLLFLDLSMS, MMRD#RS] 5158

"Iam" (latin) is written and filed as "Jam" 5159

Ibstone (Tiddeman) [DMFSRM, SDTLTLS, SSF] F356; I641; BV631; BY317b 5160

Iceland (Icelandic mel) [DMM SLS, SRRMF#S, LTSD] AN 247 5161

Ich armer mensch, ich armer suender (Wittwe. Hamburger Musikalisches handbuch. 1690) X Crasselius 5162

Ich blicke nach der hoehe (Grimm) X Gregor's 244th metre 5163

Ich dank' dir, lieber herre (Gerle. Musika teutsch) [DDTDRTS, RMRDLS, DDT] Q32; AA408 5164

Ich dank' dir schon (Praetorius) [DDDFRMF#S, SLTD TLS, S] Q431; AN394; AQ 204; AZ15-A 5165

-----. V [DDDFRMF#S, MFS LFSF, S] AN394 5166

-----. V [DDDFRMFS, SLTD TDLS,] AQ204 5167

Ich fahr dahin (German trad) [SDDSFMRD, DTDRSTLS,] X667; Y24 5168

Ich halte treulich still (Bach) [SMRDSLSS, DRMSFMRD] E644; F635; Q532; W547; X480; AD271; AF337; BI107; BV219; BY435; BZ 5169

-----. V [SMDSLS, SRMFRD, RMLF#] Q532 5170

Ich lass dich nicht (Doles) [SMRDRMFSLSFM, MMFR,] AA87 5171

Ich liebe dich herzlich, O Jesu (Grimm's Choral buch) X Gregor's 39th metre -

C 5172
Ich ruehme mich einzig (Moravian) X Gregor's 39th metre 5173
Ich ruf zu dir (Geistliche lieder. Wittenberg, 1535) X Jeg raaber, Herr Jesus Krist 5174
Ich seh'in bangen Busz-ideen (Grimm. Choral buch) X Saxony 5175
Ich singe dir (Gesangbuch mit noten. 1890) [DMSDDRDTD, DRDTLS, R] AR542; AW362 5176
Ich singe dir (Koenig. Harmonisches lieder) [SSSSDRTD, RLTLLS, SD] Q29; AA292 5177
Ich steh an deiner krippe (Schemelli. G-B. 1736) X Wonnberger 5178
Ich sterbe täglich (Leipzig ms.) [DTLSLFSMRD, MRSF#DT] Q120; AA171 5179
Ich weiss an wen ich glaube (Gesangbuch mit noten, 1890) [SDDRRMF, RMFRDTD, SD] AR246; AW240 5180
Ich weiss ein lieblich engelspiel (German, 14th c) X Mothering Sunday 5181
Ich weiss einen strom (Hull. The Casket) [SDDDDTDRDTD, DMDDD] AW232; AX257 5182
Ich will dich lieben (Koenig) [DMSDSLSFM, RMF#SDTL] J505; K213; M142, 233; N380; O225; Q399; AA349; AR118 5183
Ich will's wagen (Nares) X Amsterdam 5184
Idag er naadens tid (Neu ordentlich, G-B. Hanover, 1646) X Steadfast 5185
If any little word of mine (Hakes) [SMMFFDRM, MRRD RMS, S] BB629 5186
-----. R [SSSSSFMR, RMMF#F# SS, S] 5187
If great wonders (Slovak hymn) [DRMRMFMRR, MFSFMRD,] BQ100 5188
If I come to Jesus (Doane) [DSSSLD, TDRMDS, DSSS] AP759b 5189
-----. R [TTRTDT, LDTLS, DSSSL] 5190
If I would be a child of God (Hastings) X Retreat 5191
If, now thou seekest miracles (Vehe. G-B. 1537) X Wer da wonet 5192
If our God had not befriended (Weinberg) [MMTLTDDT, LTD LTML, S] BH123 5193
If the Lord does not build (Gelineau) [SSLD, DDDR, DD DL, LFSL] BSp. 48 5194
If thou but suffer God (Neumark) X Neumark 5195
If ye would hear (Souter liedekens. 1539) [DDDMMFFS, DDMMFFSL,] BG134 5196
If you could hie to Kolob (Daynes) [MFSSF#SLSD, TLSMSRM,] BC257 5197
If you only knew Him (Moore) [MFSDMDTL, RDTRLTD, M] AU421 5198
-----. R [MRDSDSTL, RDTD RR#M, M] 5199
Ignatius (English trad) [DFM RDTD, DRMF#STLS, S] AZ 582-O; BA52 5200
Ihr gestirn' (Peter) X Christopher 5201
Ihr kinderlein kommet (Schulz) X Tekna 5202
Ihr seelen, sinkt, ja sinket hin (Moravian) X Old 26th 5203
Il buon pastor (Canzuns spirituals, 1765) [SDRMFSFMR D, SSFMFS] R12; X567; AC167 5204
Ilfracomb (Schulthes) X Lambeth 5205
Ilkley (Dykes) X Calm 5206
I'll go where He sendeth me (Tinsley) [MSSSMFSLSM, SLLDTL] AX211 5207
-----. R [SSMDDL, LSSDTLS, SSM] 5208
I'll go where you want me to go (Rounsefell) [MMMSMMFF

L, LSFMSMR,] H398; AH427; AT425; AV379; AY105; BC75 5209

-----. R [SSRRRD#RMDM, SSRRRD] 5210

I'll live for Him (Dunbar) [SM MMSMMM, SDMSDRMR,] Z293; AH418; AS245; AT359; AU168; AX408; AY103 5211

I'll make it my home (Stafford) [DMR#MDRMSF#LS, DMR#M D] AX605 5212

-----. R [MDDDDDD, MSSSSSS, SL] 5213

I'll praise my Maker (Fones) [DMFSMDLSFMRD, RMSF] BC254 5214

I'll sing a hymn (German trad) X Woodbird 5215

I'll sing a hymn to Mary (German trad) [SDDTDRR, SRRDRM, SMM] BO64 5216

I'll stand by (McGranahan) [SF# SF#SF#SM, LSFMR, FMF] AU431 5217

-----. R [SMFSLTDS, LFLDT LS, D] 5218

I'll Thee exalt (Praetorius) X Praetorius II 5219

Illa (Mason) [DDDTDMMRD TD, RRRMD] L53; T252a; V460; AJ350; AN79b; AO479; AW63; BX90 5220

Illinois (Spilman) [DRMFSLSMR MFM, RMSD] I399; AQ59 5221

Illsley (Bishop) [DDSDRMFMRD, DDSDRM] E62; F1b; J133c; R335; X610; AB355; AN266; AW176; BE129; BV58; BY360b 5222

Illuminatio (Elvey) [MMFMMRD, RLTSDMR, MM] W204; AK 345 5223

Ilona (Lerman) [DRMFMMRSM RD, DFMLS] G466; AT447; AV275 5224

Ilsley (Bishop) X Illsley 5225

Ilsley (Ilsley) [MMDDDTLL, SFMRDTL, L] U146; V240; BE97 5226

I'm a pilgrim (Italian mel) [DRM DDDRMSFR, SFMMM] V662; AI314; BB666; BE415 5227

-----. V [DRMDDRMSFR, SFRRRR] BE415 5228

I'm a pilgrim (Ahnfelt) X Jag är främling 5229

I'm a pilgrim, I'm a stranger (Robertson) [MMMRSLSF, MSFMRFM, M] BC261 5230

I'm going home (Miller) X Going home 5231

I'm not ashamed (Arne) X Arlington 5232

I'm pressing on the upward way (Gabriel) X Higher ground 5233

Immaculate Mary (Lourdes Pilgrims hymn) [SDDMDDMRR MRD, SDDM] BM54; BN144; BO62; BP80 5234

-----. R [FFMMRRRSD, FFM MMRM] 5235

Immanuel (---) [MMRDRDLS, SDRMDR, RM] AS60 5236

Immense caeli conditor (Sarum plainsong, M 2) [FFSLSSFM, SMFRDFFF,] E58; X33a 5237

Immortal Babe (German carol) X Tredeca 5238

Implicit trust (Wathall) [MM MMMM, MSSSLLSM, MM] I 464a 5239

Improve the shining moments (Baird) [SDDDRMD, SRRMFM, SMR] BC73 5240

In-a this-a band (Negro spiritual) [DLSMSSSDTD, DLS MFF] AH600 5241

-----. R [DMMMRDR, DDRM MRDD, D] 5242

In a world where sorrow (Excell) [SSLSTL, SSFFM, SSLS T] BC74 5243

-----. R [MSSLSMSLTDDT, FLLT] 5244

In aeternum (Tchaikowsky) [MMRFMRRDRM, MMLRRS] Y127 5245

In allen meinen thaten (Davidisches harfen) [MMSFMRD, RRRMF#SSF#S,] E321 5246

In answer to my prayer (Jewish trad) X Sheer hasheerem II 5247

In Babilone (Dutch trad) [DTL SDRDRMD, FMRMRDT] A103a; B191b; C522a; E145; J542; R 110a; S93; X173a; Z502; AD 434; AE76; AF74; AG54a; AK 89; AN352; AQ191; AR612; AW 122; BD48; BE98; BV463; BY 647; BZ 5248

In Bethlemen, that fair city (Piae cantiones, 1582) X Ein kind gebor'n 5249

In Christo gelebt (Neander) X Neander II 5250

In corde meo (Baumbach) [MM MSFMMMRDTDRMD, D] U493; AC338; AE463; AH562; AN568; AR663; AS490; AT532; AV412; AW608; BB691; BX555 5251

In dark Gethsemane (Hull) [MM RRFFMM, SSMDMR, MF] P175; AL101b; AW323; AX239; AY 222 5252

In der wiegen (Corner. Geistliche nachtigall. 1649) X Corner 5253

In dich hab'ich gehoffet (Sunderreiter. Himmlische harfen) [DDSSDLTD, DRMFRS F#S,] Q524; AA494 5254

"In dich hab ich gehofft, Herr" (Plainsong arr) [LLMTRDTL, MMF#SF#MF#R] BL47 5255

In dulce jubilo (German mel, 14th c) [DDDMFSLS, SDDMFSL] A31; B549; C549; G110; J39; M613; O199; P134; Q92; R165; S130; W58; Z193; AB118; AD 110; AE80; AF125; AG70; AH258; AK116; AL61; AM159; AN177; AR129; AT74; AZ121-A; BD230; BF278; BG86; BK159; BN15; BP18; BV99; BY97; BZ 5256

-----. V [DDDMFSLS, DDDM FSLS] AL61 5257

-----. V [SDDRMFSLS, SDDRM FS] AZ121-A 5258

In einem kripplein lag ein Kind (Laufenberg) [DTLTDLSS, DTLMSF MM,] E338 5259

In excelsis gloria (Brown) X When Christ was born 5260

In excelsis gloria (Ouseley) X Glory in the highest 5261

In excelsis gloria (Shaw) [DMFSLSMD, MFMRDLDR,] BG178b 5262

-----. R [DRMFMRDRRRSL L#LS.] 5263

In excelsis gloria (Stokowski) [LRLLFSLTD, LRLLFSL] B547b 5264

In from the highways (Showalter) [SSLSDRMDLS, TTDRMR,] AS376; AX218; AY338 5265

-----. R [RRMRSLSDRM, FMMRDR,] 5266

In God, my Saviour (Zinck. Koralbog, 1801) X Paa Gud alene 5267

In God, the holy (Shelley) [SMFFLF#SS, DDLTSLS, S] BH73 5268

In heaven above (Norwegian trad) X Hauge 5269

In heaven is joy (Norwegian trad) [SDMSLSFM, DLRDLT D, S] P113 5270

In heavenly love abiding (Mendelssohn) X Heavenly love 5271

In His keeping (Morris) [SL SMRDTS, SLSFMRD, S] AI 308 5272

-----. R [DRMMFMMR, TDR FMRM, M] 5273

In His kingdom (Norwegian mel) X Deus fortis 5274

In His love abiding (Malan) [SSLSMD, RMFS, SSLS MD] Z391; AK478 5275

In His name (Showalter) [MF SSLSMSD, SLLDLS, F] AY 354 5276

-----. R [LTDDTLS, FMRLS FMFS,] 5277

In humility, our Saviour (Prichard) X Hyfrydol 5278

In hymns of praise (Beirly) [SMDRDTLSLTD, RMFFM] BC9 5279

-----. R [DTDRTDRM, MRRM F#S, SD] 5280

In manus tuas (Plainsong, M 6) [DDDDRRRDRRM, MDRMR] BN193 5281

In manus tuas (Plainsong, M 6) [FFFFSLLS, FSLSFRFS] E 739 5282

In manus tuas (Eastertide: Plainsong, M 6) [FFFSFFFFFMS L, LLSS] E740 5283

In medio bello (Layard) [SMFS LSMFSL, SSLTST] C243b 5284

In memoriam (Campbell) [MS MFMRDRM, FSMLSMD] V545 5285

In memoriam (Maker) [MMRDD FFM, SSFMDMRD] C335; D236; AL229b; AO448; AS467; AW 310; BX260 5286

In memoriam (Stainer) X Evangel 5287

In memoriam (Sullivan) [MMMM RDS, MMMMRDR, SF] B21b 5288

In memory of the Crucified (Schreiner) [DRMFMRDTD, MF#SLSF#F#] BC99 5289

In memory of the Saviour's love (Barthélemon) X Ballerma 5290

In mercy, Lord, incline thine ear (Binder) [MMRDTRTL, LLL SFM, RM] BH211 5291

In mercy, Lord, remember me (Bradbury) X Brown 5292

In morgenrot gekleidet (Beutler) [MMMFMMRD, SDSFMR, TT] AA322 5293

In natali domini (Andernach, G-B., 1608) [LDTLSLTD, DRMFDTL, T] X478 5294

In palmis (Tours) X Tours 5295

In remembrance of thy suffering (Stephens) [MSF#LSSDTTL, LRM SFF] BC258 5296

In tenderness (Gordon) [SSDDRD T, DRD#RMD, SSM] U167; AU 65 5297

-----. R [SDDRDT, SRRMRD, MFSM] 5298

In that day (McPhail) [SSSMMRD LS, SDDMMR, S] AX585; AY 307 5299

-----. R [RRRRDRMSS, LS MSMRD] 5300

In the cross of Christ (Conkey) X Rathbun 5301

In the field (Farmer) [MFS MRDRSLS, DRMMMF] W43 5302

In the garden (Miles) [SSMF SDRM, RDDDRDLD] AH329; AU356; BB606 5303

-----. R [MRDDDTLTTT, SS MMMR] 5304

In the gloaming (Harrison) [SLSMS FFM, DLDMSFM, S] AI397b; AS406; BC57 5305

In the good ship (---) [DMSSSLS M, DSLLLDS, D] AI393 5306

-----. R [RMMMRRDD, DR RRDRMS,] 5307

In the harvest field (Doane) X Labor on 5308

In the hour of trial (Lane) X Penitence 5309

In the land of fadeless day (Danks) X No night there 5310

In the light all light excelling (Elgar) [MMSMMRRM, FF LFMRM, S] BO6 5311

In the lonely midnight (Howard) X Lonely midnight 5312

In the old-time way (McKinney) [MFSSLMSS, DTLLDLS, L] AU305 5313

-----. R [DMSSS, MSDDD, SSLDTL] 5314

In the rifted rock (Bentley) [DRMMRDMS, LLSMRDR, D] AX512; AY453 5315

-----. R [SSDSMMSM, MMR MFMR, S] 5316

In the shadow of His wings (Excell) [MFSLSFMMRDRD, DDTT] AU135 5317

-----. R [MMF, MFS, MSD, SFMSRSD,] 5318

In the silent midnight watches (Root) [MMMMMMFM, RRM RD, MMM] AX244 5319

In the town (French, 15th c)

X Chartres 5320

In this sacrament (Catholic) [SFMMRMSF, FMRRDRM, S] BO40 5321

In this sacrament (Marsh) [SS SFMRRM, MSLLSFM, M] BN95 5322

In this your month (A Monk of Gethsemani) [MRDSSDDT, LSMFSMLS] BN146 5323

In thy holy place (Brunk) [MR#M LSSFM, RRRRLTS, M] AY434 5324

In thy holy temple (McKinney jr.) [SSSSSS, DRDM, MMMRDM] AU365 5325

In vernali tempore (Piae cantiones, 1582) [LTRLTRDTDL, DRMMRD] AQ323; BG98 5326

Inasmuch (Burnap) [SSDRMMLL, LLRMFFTT,] AO491 5327

Incarnation (Barnby) X To victory 5328

Incarnation (Wooler) [SDTDMMR, LLSLFM, MMM] G117 5329

Incense (German) [DSMLFRFMD, MRDSSTL] M110 5330

Increase my faith (Van Hoose) [SDDMDDLS, SDDMDRMR,] AX457 5331

-----. R [MSSMRDRMMM, MSSMRD] 5332

Industry (Lester) [DDDTTLLTTSS, SSSMM] Y184; AC192; AD350 5333

Infant holy (Polish carol) X W Zlobie Lezy 5334

Infant praise (Curwen's Tune Book, 1842) X Children of Jerusalem 5335

Infantium laudes (Parry) [MSS LLSFM, FSSLDS, FM] F437 5336

Infinitas (Whitlock) [SFMRMDT L, SDRM, LRDT] BE27 5337

Infinite light (English trad) X Bramley 5338

Ingemann (Hartmann) [DMDD SSSLLTD, DSSLF] M147 5339

Ingrave (English trad) [DMSM DLFM, DRMFMDDD,] E607 5340

Ingrediente domino (Montani) [M RDFMLLS, SLTDLSF#S,] BQ300 5341

Ingrid (Alexis) X St Ingrid 5342

Inita (Wonnberger) [MFSD MRD, TLSLSFFM, M] M646 5343

Innellan (Evans) [SDSLDFM RM, MLSDMRT] W424a 5344

Innocents (Parish choir) [MF SDTLS, DRMSFMR, MF] A235; B91; C91; D322a; E37; F191b; G81; H475; J511; K179; L186; Q35; R42; S25; V512; W574b; X366; Y40; Z114; AA68; AB260; AC32; AD95; AE 66; AF33; AH266; AJ26; AK77; AL612; AM392; AN 277a; AO22; AP263; AR41; AS82; AT291; AW64; AX 62; AZ11-M; BA162; BB516; BD3; BE83; BF220; BK53; BV552; BX332; BY739b; BZ 5345

Innsbruck (Isaak) [MDRMSFM, MSSRMDT, TD] J271; K469; L276; M373; N169; O287; P48; Q126; AA33; AK52; AL548; AZ79-A; BA411; BJ82; BR335; BV57, 145; BX185; BY455b 5346

-----. V [DDRMSFM, MSSR MDT, DR] K469 5347

-----. V [MDRMSFFM, MSSR MDDT] L276 5348

-----. V [MDDMSFM, MS RMRDT, SD] N169 5349

-----. V [MDRMSSFM, MSS RMDT, S] AK52 5350

-----. V [MDRMSFM, MSFM RMFMR,] AZ79-A 5351

-----. V [DDRMSFM, MSFRM DT, DR] BJ82 5352

-----. V [MRDRMSFFM, MD SSRMR] BR335 5353

-----. V [MDRMFSFFM, MF SSRMR] BV145 5354

Innsbruck (Isaak: Bach) [MDR MFSFM, MFSSRMDT,] A181; B174; C174a; E86; F34; J228; R66; S505; W284; X57; AB

21; AD60; AF53; AN112; AP668; AQ268; AW556; BE361; BJ83; BL49; BN91; BQ57; BY707 5355

-----. V [MDRMFSFM, MFSS RMRDT] BJ83 5356

Innsbruck (Isaak) X Gregor's 79th metre (Crueger) 5357

Innsbruck, ich musz dich lassen (Isaak) X Innsbruck 5358

Innsbruck new (Isaak) X Innsbruck 5359

Innspruck (Isaak) X Innsbruck 5360

Ins feld geh (Layriz Collection) X Layriz 5361

Integer [vitae] (Flemming) X Flemming 5362

Intercession (Callcott) [SMMRD DD, TDRMR, SMMR] D609b; I509; V758; W255; AB180; AL332; AM532; AP236; AW 203; AZ604-A; BA611; BF365 5363

Intercession [refrain] (Callcott) X Almighty Father, hear (Mendelssohn) 5364

Intercession (Dykes??) [DMRDFM RDRTD, TDRM] A333; B52; C52a; D5a; I477; K477; L24; V562; AB310; AL30; AO145 5365

Intercession (Sankey) X I am praying for you 5366

Intercession New (Callcott) X Intercession 5367

Intercession Old (Dykes) X Intercession 5368

Intercessor (Parry) [LSFMMFLDD TL, LSFMM] A493; F115; X307; AF410; AL341; AQ55; BV176; BY662 5369

Into my heart (Clarke) [MMMD, MMMD, MSFMRFFM,] AR653; AU321 5370

Into our hands (Teddlie) [SDRMDM R#MFL, DTLSDM] AX209 5371

-----. R [SSSSMSLSSF, FMFRRS] 5372

Into the tomb of ages (Heller) [SMRMMSMRD, DLFMFRM] BH156 5373

Into the tomb of ages past (Jewish trad) X Adon olom II 5374

Into the woods (McKinney) [MMMLTDRMFM, DTLTTM,] AU420 5375

Into thy hands (Hartog) [SMF SSLTDMMR, RMRDR] BH 14 5376

Invermay (Lamb) [SSMLS, MM MRFM, SDTLT] W362 5377

Invitation (Ingalls) [DRMDR MRDRMFMR, DTL] H255; AY229 5378

Invitation (Hastings) [SMRDSLD LS, SLTDRFM] L514 5379

Invitation (LaTrobe) [SMLDSF M, RMF#SLLS, SM] AZ591-A 5380

Invitation (Maker) [MMMMRR, MFFMRM, LLLL] G190; R 261; S220; T281; U166; V 263; Z278; AE268; AG138; AJ389a; AK463; AM395; AO 644; AR245; AS359; AT226; AW270 5381

Invitation (Root) X Come to the Saviour 5382

Invitation (Sophr) X Gerald 5383

Invitation (Wallace) X Serenity 5384

Invocation (Burnap) X Seelye 5385

Invocation [sentence] (Harrington) X The Lord is in His holy temple 5386

Invocation (Landahl) [MDLSS DDRRM, MMRDMR] J178 5387

Invocation (Wagner) X Pilgrim chorus 5388

Iona (Stainer) [DMSFMRFM, RDMRDTD, D] B287; C287; D168 5389

Ionia (Belcher) [SDMRDMR, RMFFMRM, DT] L51 5390

Ionia (Everett) [MMMMMRM FSM, LSFMRD] AS62 5391

Irae (Barnby) [MDTLLLLL, L FMRRFFM,] I603 5392

Irby (Gauntlett) [STDDDTDRR D, DMSMMR] A236; B349;

D540; E605; F432; G442; J41; K535; M608; N633; R462; S 454; W69; X368; AA287; AD 474; AG302; AH242; AI382; AL70; AM639; AO133; AP727a; AR125; AV84; AW412; AZ89-D; BA158; BB424; BF284; BR558; BV107; BY106 5393

Irene (Hopkins) X Ellers 5394

Irene (Scholefield) [SSLSDDT, RRMFTDR, MM] C203a; D 135a; K85; W584; AL161a; AM248; AP271; BY229 5395

Iris (French carol) X Gloria 5396

Irish (Collection of hymns ... Dublin, 1749) [DDSDRMFMRM, SMFSDR] A444; E504; F263; G14; J331; R29a; S49; V79; W153; X680; AK22; AL138; AM19; AP29; AW268; AZ14-M; BA118; BE145; BV221b; BY398; BZ 5397

Irish carol (Irish trad) [DDMD MS, DDDMRDR, SDD] BG6 5398

Irish melody (Irish trad) X Londonderry 5399

Irmer (Haeussler) [DDRMRD, FLTDD, RDTLD] AK67 5400

Irons (Irons) [SFMRRD, MSL R, SSMRM] A183; B17; C17a; D10a; Eap. 42; F30; K474; W 272; AL569; AP680a 5401

Irons (Irons) X Southwell 5402

Irvin (Langden) [SDDTSRD, RRFMRD#R, DM] L472a 5403

Irvine Waterside (Finlay) [SM RDMFSLS, TDLSFMF] BY265b 5404

Irving (Hartshorn) [SFMRMRDM S, SLSMMRD] T162; AJ240 5405

Is it the crowning day (Marsh) [SLSDRM, SRSM, FSLMRS] AM692 5406

-----. R [DLTS, FMRMRS, SDTDRD] 5407

Is my name written there (Davis) X My name's written there 5408

Is not this the land of Beulah (Dadman) [SDMDRDDL, D LSSLDD, S] AU27; AX129; AY79, 353; BB180 5409

-----. V [SDMDRDDL, DLS SLTD, S] AX129 5409a

-----. V [SDMDRDDL, LLSS LTD, S] BB180 5409b

Is there any pleasure (Naegeli) [MFSFMR, DDRSM, LSFMS] AX539 5410

Is thy heart right with God? (Hoffman) [SSSMFSLLLD, MMDRMD,] AX274 5411

-----. R [SSSLLS, DDDDDR, MMMD] 5412

Is your all on the altar? (Hoffman) X Hoffman II 5413

Isca (Wood) [DSFMDMRD, DLSFMMRD] D239; AO141 5414

Ishpeming (Alexis) [SMTRD TLS, SDDRRM, MM] J301; N557 5415

Island (Tomissön. Psalmebog, 1569) [LLLDLSFM, DTLSM FRD,] J253; M19; O46; P 59; Q48 5416

Isleworth (Howard) [MLMFRD TL, TDRMLSF#] A77; B156; E557; Q439; S383a; W101; X253 5417

Israel (Goss) [SDSDRMRD, RM RMFSFM,] BA236 5418

Israel (Martin) [SSSSFMRD, LLLLSSFL] W110; AP455 5419

Israel, Israel, God is calling (Converse) X Erie 5420

Israel's song (Levenson) [SM RDMRDRT, SFMRFM, L] BH 79 5421

Iste confessor (Croft. Collection) [SDTLSDTDRMM, SSM FM] E188b; F158b; X231; AD216; AK227; BV226 5422

Iste confessor (Plainsong) [RDRFFMRMRRDRFF, SF] BO268 5423

Iste confessor (Plainsong, M 2) [RFRRDR, FFRMMR, RLL#L] E188 5424

Iste confessor (Plainsong, M 8:

mediaeval) [SLSMFSSLFLDT LS, D] A228a 5425
Iste confessor (Poitiers vesperale, 1740) X Rouen I 5426
It came upon the midnight (Willis) X Carol 5427
It is finished (Carnett) [DRMRM LSM, SSSFMR#M, M] AU427 5428
-----. R [SSSFMR#R#M, DDLDR DM, M] 5429
"It is finished" (Redhead) X Redhead, No. 1 5430
It is no earthly summer's ray (Schein) X Eisenach 5431
It is well (Bliss) X Bliss 5432
It may be at morn (McGranahan) X Christ returneth 5433
It may not be on the mountain height (Rounsefell) X I'll go where you want me 5434
It must be told (Marquis) [DRM MFMMR, RMFFSFM, D] AY522 5435
It pays to serve Jesus (Huston) [SMR#MMSFMDLS, DDTLT] AU414 5436
-----. R [MSRMFLTDMLS, SSRSL] 5437
It singeth low (Grimm) [SDDT SSLLSM, MTLSLS] BH220 5438
Itala (Paris Antiphoner, 1681) X O quanta qualia 5439
Italian hymn (Giardini) X Moscow 5440
It's me (Negro spiritual) [MM MMDD, DDDDRRM, MMM] AH 603 5441
-----. R [MMMSMMMDD, DD DDRRM,] 5442
I've enlisted in the service ("A. L. B.") [SSDDDRMMRMD, RM RRR] AX180 5443
-----. R [MMRRRMFSFMRDR M, DT] 5444
I've found a friend (Stebbins) X Friend 5445
I've wandered far away (Kirkpatrick) X Lord, I'm coming home 5446
Ives (Beecher. Plymouth collection) [DRMDMSD, LSMLSMDRM] E582; X306; AF425 5447
Ivinghoe (Cooke) [SMRSDRD TS, DRMFSFM] BY294 5448
Ivyhatch (Selby) [MFSSSDRMF M, MMRDTD] F175; BV430 5449

J

Jabez (Welsh hymn mel) [LS# LTDTDT, DRMRDTL, L] W 597 5450
Jackson (Jackson) [SSDTLSFSF M, MF#SDTL] E210; W507b; X445; Z132; AL111; AP56; AQ93; BV276; BY404 5451
-----. V [SSDTLSFSFM, MSDTLS] Z132 5452
-----. V [SSDLSFSM, MSDTL S, SM] BY404 5453
Jacobs (Jacobs) X Hope 5454
Jacob's ladder (English trad) [SDDDMRDRRRFMRDDD] AD124; AR133; BF294; BG58 5455
-----. V [SDDDDMRDRRRR FMRD] BG58 5456
Jacob's ladder (Grauman) [SD DTLSDRM, FSMLFS, M] BH 49 5457
Jacob's ladder (Negro spiritual) [MMMMSSSM, RRRRFLLS,] Y318; AF495; AG319; AH 597; BK165; BZ 5458
Jag är främling (Ahnfelt) [MRRDSSFFM, DTTLDLS] N526; P348 5459
Jag gar mot döden, hvar jag gar (Gotha Cantional. 1726) [MLTDMMR#M, MRDTDTL, M] N603 5460
Jag har en vän (Swedish trad) X Amicus 5461
Jag tror pa Gud, och vet (German, 1523) [DDDTLDLS, MSLSDMRD,] O29 5462
Jam Christus astra ascenderat (Plainsong, M 1) [RRFRR DFSL, LSDDRDD] E150 5463

Jam lucis (Benedictine plainsong, M 6) [DDDDDRDD, DDDDTRR] A164b; B28b; C28; D21; F11a; G58; W258; AD390; AF507; BZ 5464

Jam lucis orto sidere (Bendeictine plainsong, M 8) [SSLSFSLSL, DDDDRD] A159a; E254; F]a 5465

Jam moesta (Luther. Christlich G-B. 1542) [DFRRMRDRD, DRMFSFMR] J297; O595; P153 5466

-----. V [DFRRMRDRD, DRMMSFM] P153 5467

Jam as moesta quiesce querela (Luther. Christlich G-B. 1542) X Jam moesta 5468

James Quinter (Frederick) [SSSSFMRS, SLLLSS, SS] AR110 5469

Jamison (Smart) [SMDMSD, LSDSFMR, SML] V321; BY385 5470

Janes (Mozart) X Cana 5471

Janet (Stebbins) [SSF#SDRDDT, LSTDRMF] T268; AJ374 5472

January carol (Piae cantiones, 1582) [DDRMFMRM, DMRDTDLS,] BG141 5473

Jasmine flower (Chinese trad) [MMSLDDLSSLS, MMSLS] Y197 5474

Jazer (Bradbury) [SSFMMRDDTLS, SLTDF] AJ59 5475

Jazer (Tozer) [SSLTDRFFM, DDMRDTL] I245; BO18 5476

Je sais, vierge Marie (French trad) X Bell carol 5477

Jeg beder dig (German. 1525) X Durch Adam's fall 5478

Jeg er rede til at bede (Neander) X Sieh hier bin ich, Ehrenkönig 5479

Jeg har dig hjerteligen kjaer (Schmid. Orgelbuch. 1577) X Herzlich lieb hab ich dich, o Herr 5480

Jeg har min sag til Gud Hjemstilt (Lindeman) [LMMDLLLS#, MLSFMRRM] O481 5481

Jeg raaber fast, O Herre (Bourgeois) X Du fort de ma detresse 5482

Jeg raaber, Herr Jesus Krist (Geistliche lieder. Wittenburg, 1535) [MDRDLDRM, MSMDRFM, M] O275; AA365 5483

Jeg ser dig, søde Lam staa (Danish trad) X Release 5484

Jeg synger Julekind (German, 14th c) X In dulce jubilo 5485

Jeg ved et evigt himmerig (German trad. 16th c) X Freiburg 5486

Jeg vil din pris unsjunge (Hamburg. Neu Catholisches G-B. 1598) X Eisleben 5487

Jeg vil mig Herren love (Zinck) X Copenhagen 5488

Jehovah (Gerold) [DRMM, MFSS, SDSLSFM, R] AK494; AW507 5489

Jehovah (Hopkins) [DDDRDDDRMFM, MSFMR] O23; BA654; BE426 5490

Jehovah, Jesus, Lord (Dixon) X Lanesboro 5491

Jehovah, Lord of heaven and earth (Holden) X Coronation 5492

Jehovah nissi (Crawford) [MSFMMMRD, SLTDRMRR,] AM470; AP126 5493

Jena (Vulpius) X Das Neugeborne 5494

Jenkins (Miller) [DDRMDS, SLSFMR, RMTD] BB170 5495

Jericho tune (Handel) X Milites 5496

Jersey (Boyce) X Boyce 5497

Jerusalem (Chauvenet Collection) [DDDTDR, MRDFMR, RRRM] BR212 5498

Jerusalem (Dykes) [SFMRMFRD, MFSLLR, SL] F438 5499

Jerusalem (Franck) X Melchior 5500

Jerusalem (Haydn, F.J.) X

St Michel's 5501
Jerusalem (Parry) [DMSLDLSFS, LSFSMRD] F578; W640; X446; Y162; AC269; AL522 5502
Jerusalem (Roper) [DDRMFSLSMS, MSMDRM] C510b; D403b; H 505; L13; AO547b; AZ14-W; BA763a 5503
Jerusalem (Spohr) X Gerald 5504
Jerusalem (Stainer) X Conquest 5505
Jerusalem (Staniforth) [DMMFM RMD, LSMMRRSD] B510; C510c; D403c; Eap. 69; L593b 5506
-----. V [SMMFMRMD, LSMMRR, SD] C510c 5507
Jerusalem, du Herrens hya stad (English) [SMTDDDDRTD, DR RRRM,] N626 5508
Jerusalem, du hochgebaute stadt (Franck) X Melchior 5509
Jerusalem et Sion filiae (Plainsong, M 5) [SDRDFMDR DD, MSMDFM] E172 5510
Jerusalem, Jerusalem (Haydn) X St Michel's 5511
Jerusalem, my happy home (Italian hymn mel) [SDTLS LLSFM, MSLTDM] BQ119 5512
Jerusalem, my happy home (Rupp) [SSFMMMRD, MFM RDR, SD] AX610; AY143 5513
Jerusalem, the golden (Ewing) X Ewing 5514
Jerusalem the golden (Grabowski) [SMMRDFM, RDDMRDT, SR] BQ118 5515
Jerusalem the golden! (Sullivan) X Lux mundi 5516
Jervaulx Abbey (Genevan Psalter, 1562) [DSFMRDRM, MLLSM SF] A128a; W219a; AJ421 5517
Jesaia, dem propheten (Luther) [SSMDMSSLLS, SSFSDF] Q249 5518
Jeshurun (Gauntlett) [SDMMMRS, SSDDTD, SDM] BR48 5519
Jesmian (Thalben-Ball) [MRD FMRSLMDRM, RSMD] BY721 5520
Jespersön (Jespersön) [DSS LTS, SDTLS, MFSSL] M443; N123 5521
"Jesu" and "Jesus" are interfiled 5522
Jesu (Düben) [SDTDRSMD, MSD TLDR, S] J59; M55; N64; BE263 5523
-----. V [SDTDRMFSMD, MF SDTD] BE263 5524
Jesus a wedding guest (Good) X Since Jesus did appear 5525
Jesus all glorious (Boe) [SLS MRD, RDRSFM, RMFL] P208 5526
Jesus, all my gladness (Crueger) [MMRDTL, MF#SMLS#, LTD] A453; J575a; M213; Q347; R414; X544; AA82; AF222; AK240; AW564; AZ208-A; BJ57; BV640; BY768; BZ 5527
-----. V [MMRDTL, MMF#S# LS#, LDTT] J575a 5528
-----. V [MMRDTL, MF#SM LS#LDTS#] AZ208-A 5529
-----. V [MMRDTL, MF#S SLS#, LTDT] BZ 5530
Jesus allt mitt goda är (Arrhenius) [DSLTDRT, DRMSFM RR, M] N68 5531
Jesus är min van den bäste (Düben) X Jesu 5532
Jesus, be our Guide (Drese) X Rochelle 5533
Jesus bids us shine (Excell) [DSSSSDRDTT, RSSSSR] AL 613; AM653; AP768; AW420; BY746a 5534
Jesu, bone Pastor (Willcox) [MDDTFRRD, SMMRMFMR] D573; BR298; BX511 5535
Jesus calls us (Jude) X Galilee 5536
Jesus Christ is risen today (Monk) X Easter hymn 5537
Jesus Christ is risen today (Montani) [LLLLDTL, LSFS LL, MMM] BQ27 5538

Jesus Christ, my sure defense (Crueger. Praxis pietatis melica) X Ratisbon 5539
Jesus Christ, the King of ages (Goss) X Lauda anima 5540
Jesus Christus blick dich an (Gregor's choral buch, 1784) X Gregor's 9th metre 5541
Jesus Christus, unser heiland (Geistliche lieder. 1535) [DSMDRMFM, DSMLSFSM,] Q311; AA441 5542
Jesus, come to me (Sletten) [LMFMRDT, MLDTS#LT, DD] P341 5543
Jesus comes (Kirkpatrick) [DD DRMSLS, RRRMFSLS] BB549 5544
-----. R [DRMMRDR, DDDSLS MS, D] 5545
Jesu corona (Rouen church mel) [LDRMRMDTL, LSLTLSF#] E65 5546
Jesu, corona Virginum (Grenoble Antiphoner, 1753) X Deus tuorum militum 5547
Jesus, Creator of the world (d'Hooghe) [SSSDRMFRD, MF# F#SMDD] BQ60 5548
Jesu, deine passion (Vulpius) X Weimar 5549
Jesu, der du meine selle (German trad) X Gregor's 168th metre-B 5550
Jesu Deus, amor meus (Catholic) [DDMRRRFM, MMRDTLS, T] BQ315 5551
Jesu dilectissimi (McCartney) [MFMRLDT, LSTMRS, SSD] B387 b; C387b; D444a; S311 5552
Jesus, din lhukommelse (Gesius) X Herrnhut 5553
Jesus, din søde forening et smage (Schorring. Koralbog, 1781) X Contentment 5554
Jesus, dine dybe vunder (Bourgeois) X Bourgeois 5555
Jesus! du dig själf uppväkte (Swedish, 1675) [DSMRDTDD, MFRSSF#S, D] X325 5556
Jesu, du hoffnung (Joseph) X Gregor's 298th metre 5557
Jesu, dulcedo cordium (Fisher) [MR#MLDRDM, MFSLSMD R,] AR202 5558
Jesu, dulcedo cordium (Poitiers Antiphoner, 1746) X Auctoritate saeculi 5559
Jesu dulcis memoria (Andernach, 1608) [LSLTTDTLT, LSLTSLS] A56; E238b; W 420b; X549b 5560
Jesu dulcis memoria (Murphy) [MTDRMRFMRM, MMMLSF] BQ296 5561
Jesu dulcis memoria (Antiphonale romanum. M 1) X Exultet cor praecordiis 5562
Jesu dulcis memoria (Sarum plainsong, M 1) X Christe redemptor 5563
Jesu dulcis memoria (Schmuck) [SSLTDLSFM, MMSDTLL] BQ161b 5564
Jesu dulcis memoria (Vittoria) [LTLS#LDTLLS#, S#LLSLS] BQ161a 5565
Jesus er mit haab og trøst (Crueger. Praxis pietatis melica) X Ratisbon 5566
Jesus er mit liv i live (Crueger) X Du, o schönes weltegebäude 5567
Jesus, ever loving Saviour (Schubert) [DSMDFMMR, MRDRTLS, D] BQ135 5568
Jesus, food of angels (Gounod) [SSFFMMDRMRDD, SSFF] BQ54, 227b 5569
-----. V [SSSFFMMDRMRDD, SSF] BQ227b 5570
Jesus för världen gifvet sitt lif (Ekström) [DDTMDDT, LLSMMMRD, D] N421; AI 434 5571
Jesus from whom all blessings flow (Coles) X Duane Street 5572
Jesus, gentlest Saviour (Montani) [MDSLLS, DLDMR, MDSLL] BQ49 5573
Jesus, gentlest Saviour(Stainer) X Eucharisticus 5574
Jesus has died for me ("A. H. A.") [MMMMRDLDLS, TTTTLS] AX349; AY239

5575
Jesus, hear (Maasalo) [LMLTD LTD, RRDTLS#L, L] J383 5576
Jesus, highest heaven's completeness (Dykes) X St Oswald I 5577
Jesus, how good the thought (Tochter Sion, 1741) X St Bernard 5578
Jesus, I am resting (Mountain) X Resting 5579
Jesus, I come (Stebbins) [SF# SMRDTLS, DTDR, RDR] AE 177; AH342; AI210; AM715; AR459; AT233; AV340; AX300 5580
Jesus, I my cross (Barnby) X St Polycarp 5581
Jesus, I my cross have taken (Mozart) X Ellesdie 5582
Jesus is all the world to me (Thompson) X He's my friend 5583
Jesus is calling (Stebbins) [SS SSMFSLTD, DTLT, LS] R267; Z280; AE168; AH330; AI200; AM697; AT229; AU57; AV334; AX228; BB569; BY417; BZ 5584
-----. R [DTLT, RDTD, MRDDT LSS] 5585
Jesus is coming (Trowbridge) [SDDDDTLSLSM, RMFMF] AU 44 5586
-----. R [DDDDSDRSRMD, LTDSD] 5587
Jesus is God (Wurtemberg G-B.) X Ellacombe 5588
Jesus is passing this way (Doane) [MR#MFMRDS, DDDDTDR, M] AU93 5589
-----. R [MFSLLLSM, MFRSSM, MF] 5590
Jesus is tenderly calling thee home (Stebbins) X Jesus is calling 5591
Jesus is the name (Scholfield) [SMMMSDRM, FMDMRD, SM] AI387 5592
-----. R [SMDRM, RSMD, DDDRMMS] 5593
Jesus ist das schönste licht (Freylinghausen) [MRMFSL SFFMM, MRDDR] E247 5594
Jesus ist das schoenste licht (Freylinghausen) X Gregor's 156th metre 5595
Jesu, Jehovah! ich such' und verlange (Grimm. Choral buch) X Old 193d 5596
Jesus, Jesus, come to me (Catholic) [MMRMSFF, FF MFLSS, DD] BQ131 5597
Jesus, Jesus, come to me (Marsh) X Martyn 5598
Jesu, Jesu du mein hirt (Heinlein) [MMLSFFM, MSF# MMR#M, MS] E655; F110a; X506; BE89 5599
Jesus, Jesus, nichts als Jesus (Bronner. Choral buch, 1715) [DDSSLTDS, LSFMRRD, D] Q348; AA 86 5600
Jesu joy of man's desiring (Schop) [MFSSFMRR, MFS MRFMR] A211; E418; F275a; J67b; M381, 534; N3; O37; P 39; Q207; X101; AA31; AI 440; AK90; AQ28; AR111; AZ165-C; BA665; BI41*
*distinct variant 5601
-----. V [MFSSFMR, MFSF MRD, MF] E418 5602
-----. V [MFSSFMRR, MFSM RRD, M] M381 5603
-----. V [MFSSFMRR, MFS DRRD, M] M534 5604
-----. V [MMFSSFMRR, MF SMRRD,] AK90 5605
-----. V [MMFSSFMR, MFSM RRD, R] BA665 5606
-----. V [DDMSSFMR, RMF RRM, DD] BI41 5607
Jesu, joy of man's desiring (Schop) X Angelus (German choral) 5608
Jesus, keep me near the cross (Doane) X Near the cross 5609
Jesus knows (Hugg) [MMMMR RDDD, RRRDRMS,] AY375 5610
-----. R [SSSSFMS, LLLSM

MR, MM] 5611
Jesus, kom dog selv til mig (Lindeman) [DSDDRSM, MS F#STLLS, F] O169 5612
Jesu, komm doch selbst zu mir (Wesley's Foundery Collection, 1742) X Savannah 5613
Jesu Kreuz, leiden und pein (Vulpius) X Weimar 5614
Jesus, lat din rädda dufva (Swedish trad) [SDMMRDR, RMFFMRM, S] N262; P66 5615
Jesus leads (Sweney) [MFMR SRD, DRDTRMRD, M] AY120 5616
Jesu leiden, pein und tod (Vulpius) X Weimar 5617
Jesus lives, and Jesus leads (German) [DMSDLDS, FSMDMR, DMS] AI101; AP766; BV116b 5618
-----. V [DMSDLDLS, FSMDRR D, S] BV116b 5619
Jesus, Lord and precious Saviour (Swedish) X Kalmar 5620
Jesus, Lord, be thou mine own (Perosi) X L'Emmanuello 5621
Jesus, lover of my soul (Barnby) X St Polycarp 5622
Jesus, lover of my soul (Holbrook) X Refuge 5623
Jesus, lover of my soul (Marsh) X Martyn 5624
Jesus loves me (Bliss) X Gladness 5625
Jesus loves me (Bradbury) X Renar 5626
Jesus loves the little children (Root) [MMMRDLSD, RRMR DMR, S] AU311 5627
Jesu, magister bone (Dykes) [MMRLTDD, RMDSFR, MMR] D363a; O567; V400 5628
Jesu, meine freude (Crueger) X Jesus, all my gladness 5629
Jesu meine lust und wonne (Lüneburg G-B. 1686) [MFSLFF MM, SRDTDR, S] N389 5630
Jesu, meine zuversicht (Crueger. Praxis pietatis melica. 1653). X Ratisbon 5631
Jesu meines glaubens zier (Freylinghausen G-B.) X Sebastian 5632
Jesu meines herzens freud (Lüneburg G-B. 1686) [MDS SFMR, MRRD, TRMMR] AA89 5633
Jesu, meines lebens leben (Weimar G-B. 1681) [DDTS LTDD, MSFMRDR, D] J79; K98; N91; Q151; W379; Z510; AK155; AL258; AW535; AZ 168-A; BA196 5634
-----. V [DDTSLTDD, MMF FMMR, D] N91 5635
-----. V [DDTSLTD, MMFFMM R, MF] W379 5636
-----. V [DDTLSLTDD, MMFF MMR,] Z510 5637
-----. V [DDTSLTDD, RMFF MMR, D] AZ168-A 5638
Jesus, mighty King of Sion (Cannon) [MMFSLLSM, DDT LSF#S, L] BC108 5639
Jesus, my God; behold (Brydaine) [DDRDDRDRRM, DRR DDR] BO167; BQ133 5640
-----. R [SMRDFM, RMRDRD T, DRM] 5641
Jesus my life (As hymnodus sacer, Leipzig) X Breslau 5642
Jesus my Lord is real to me (Reynolds) [DTDRDSLT, RD# RMRRDS,] AU346 5643
-----. R [RRRSRMFM, MMMR, F#MF#S,] 5644
Jesus, my Lord, my God (---) [SMDDTDRSFFM, MRDFR] BP59 5645
Jesus, my Lord, my God (Cath olic) [DMSSSDMLSFR, LSS MS] AH143; BO43 5646
-----. V [DMSSSDMLSFR, LSMSF] BO43 5647
Jesus, my Lord, my God (Montani) [MMRFMRTDRS, SSFLSF] BQ53 5648
-----. R [RDRMMRMSF, FSL LSFR] 5649
Jesus, my Lord, my God (Wagner) X Gottlob, es geht 5650

Jesus, my Saviour true (Huish) [DRRSF#F, DMRD, DRDSF#F,] BC85 5651
Jesus nimmt die sünder an (Neumeister) [MMSRDRMR, RRMSLSFM,] AM394 5652
Jesus of Nazareth (---) [SLSMD M, FDRM, MLTDTL,] BC86 5653
Jesus of the manger (Flemish trad) [MMMRMFRM, RMFFM RM, M] BG110 5654
Jesus, once of humble birth (English chorister) [SMSMSFL R, RMFMRDRM,] BC88 5655
Jesus only (Lindeman) X Holy mountain 5656
Jesus our Brother (Corbeil) X Orientis partibus 5657
Jesus paid it all (Grape) X All to Christ I owe 5658
Jesu pastor (Willcox) X Jesu, bone Pastor 5659
Jesus, priceless treasure (Lindeman) X Lindeman) 5660
Jesu, quadragenariae (Plainsong, M 4) [FMFSLSFRFMFMM, SLT] E69; F558a; BP40 5661
-----. V [FMFSLSFRFMFSFM, SL] BP40 5662
Jesu redemptor (Sarum plainsong, M 1) X Christe redemptor 5663
Jesu redemptor omnium (Taler) [LLTTTDRM, MRRLLTDD] BQ155b 5664
Jesu redemptor saeculi (La Feillée. Méthode du plain chant) [DRDRMFRM, RMFR DRFM] Eap. 26 5665
Jesus, revealed in me (Young) [SF#SLFM, SF#STRD, SF#SL] AU418 5666
-----. R [SFLMRD, D#D#D#RM F, TDRS] 5667
Jesu, rufe mich (Drese) X Rochelle 5668
Jesu, salvator saeculi (York Breviary) [RLLSFMRSLTDTL, RSL] E249 5669
Jesus saves (Kirkpatrick) X Salvation 5670
Jesus Saviour, blessed centre (Mountain) [MRDRMFSM, MMRDR, MRD] Z229 5671
Jesus, Saviour, heavenly Father (Costa) [DDDDRDRM M, FMLSDTD] BI64 5672
Jesus, Saviour, pilot me (Gould) X Pilot 5673
Jesus, Savior, risen Lord (Freylinghausen. Geistreiches G-B) X Luebeck 5674
Jesus, still lead on (Drese) X Rochelle 5675
Jesus, Sun of righteousness (Lindeman) X Easter glory 5676
Jesus the glory (French mel) [DTDLSDDLMMRD, SLSD] BO199 5677
Jesus, the Light of the world (---) [MSSSMRD, MMMLSM R, MS] AX272 5678
-----. R [SMSSSMSSS, MSSLSMM] 5679
Jesus the Teacher (Brunk) [MSFMRDRM, MRRSSF#LS,] AX148; AY391 5680
Jesus, the very thought of Thee (---) [DMFSDRRD, SDTLT LS, R] BQ17 5681
Jesus the very thought of Thee (Dykes) X St Agnes 5682
Jesus, thou art coming (Bainbridge) [DTLMLS, RDTLS, MTMRR] BO51 5683
Jesus, thou art coming (Schubert) [MMRMFM, RRRMD R, MMRM] BN98 5684
Jesus, thou art coming (Slovak hymnal) [SSDTLS, SSFFM, SLTDD] BQ130 5685
Jesus, thou hast promised (Perkins) [DSSDLD, TDRSM, DSSDL] BB602 5686
-----. R [SMMFSFR, MMM RDR, MMM] 5687
Jesus, thy boundless love (Bortniansky) X St Petersburg 5688

Jesus, thy name I Love (Doane) [MSFMRD, DFLLSS, SLF#S,] U225; AJ236 5689
Jesus, united by thy grace (Hastings) X Ortonville 5690
Jesus, when we go to rest (Lithuanian trad) [MRMFSFM, SFMFMRMR, M] BN194 5691
Jesus, while our hearts are bleeding (Mason) X Mount Vernon 5692
Jesus will bear me o'er (Nickle) [MMMMRDFFF, MMMSMDR,] AX537 5693
-----. R [FFFFFFMMM, MMMSMR, M] 5694
Jesus with thy Church abide (Hintze) X Salzburg 5695
Jewels (Root) X When He cometh 5696
Jewett (Weber) [SMDMRFMR, MDMSSFM, S] G330; H371; I524; K395; L331; M80; P156; R367; S280; T282; U247; V429b; Z408; AA387; AD241; AG214; AH392; AI291; AJ390; AK313; AM572; AO337; AR360; AS234; AT251; AU178; AV222; AW250; AX391; AY475; AZ38-E; BA687; BB404 5697
-----. V [SMDRFMR, MDMSSFM, SL] AV222 5698
Jewish tune (Jewish trad) [DDRM DSRM, MMSSLFRSM,] BK36 5699
Joachimsthal (Hermann) X Hermann 5700
Joanna (Welsh mel) X St Denio 5701
Job I (English trad) [MFSSLSLTD TL, SLTSL] BG60a 5702
Job II (English trad) [MLTDMLLL S, MDRRMF#S] BG60b 5703
Job III (English trad) [SDRTDRM FR, MFSSFRD,] BG50d 5704
John Nass (Beery) [MMRDRD, SSFMRM, DDSS] AR361 5705
John Three Sixteen (McKinney) [MSSLLS, MDDFFM, MRMF] AU324 5706
Joldwynds (Stanford) [DRFMSD RTD, MRTLSLT] X56b 5707
Jonathan (Sheldon) [DDDRMD, DTDRMS, FSLT] BV349 5708
Jones (Jones) [SLSFMSSFF MF, TL#TLS] AT474 5709
-----. R [MFSLSDT, RMFSL TS, DR] 5710
Jordan (Barnby) [MSLSMRDRM, SMF#SLT] A327; B251; D 211; E48; I158; S466; V125; W128; X95; AB18; AH496; AK125; AR596; BB514; BF 215; BX196 5711
Jordan's Banks (American trad) [DRMMMFSFFFM, RMMMF] AH529; AT479; AU249; AV282; BB682; BZ 5712
-----. R [DRMMMMFSFSFM, RRMM] 5713
Joseph (Mehul) [SDMRDDTTL L, RDDTLT] D558; AO156; 5714
Joseph (Price) [MSDSTLSF, MFSRMFMR] Y221 5715
Joseph and Mary (English trad) [MLTDMSMRMSL, LTDDT] BG115 5716
Joseph lieber, Joseph mein (German carol, 14th c) X Resonet in laudibus 5717
Joseph, our certain hope (Dykes) X St Agnes 5718
Joseph, pure spouse (Mattoni) [SFMSFLLSFFM, SLTDT] BQ94 5719
Josephine (Kroeger) [MMMRD SFF, FFFMRLSS,] T62; AJ 95 5720
Joshua (Lutkin) [MMTTTRLD, LTDRLTDR] I403a 5721
Josie (Kieffer) [DRMSFMR, RMFRDTD, SS] AY408 5722
Journey's end (Anderson) [DDDDDDDRDDD#, RFFFD] G519; AK419 5723
Joy (Beethoven) X Beethoven 5724
Joy (Gadsby) [SLSDMRDT, LSSLMS, SM] B552; C552b 5725
Joy (Poppen) [MDMRLTRS, S

LSLTDMM] M171 5726
Joy-bells (Tucker) [SSLSF#SD SLSF#S,SFFF] AP774 5727
-----. R [SDRM,RDTLSFMS, SDRM] 5728
Joy cometh in the morning (Lorenz) [DRMSSDLDS,MSLSM DM] BE425 5729
-----. R [RMRDRMS,LFLDLSM, SL] 5730
Joy of man's desiring (Schop) X Jesu joy of man's desiring 5731
Joy to the world (Handel) X Antioch 5732
Joyful song (Allen) [MSDMRMRDT LSD,MSDM] AH313; AM683; AS112; AT137; AU355; AV326; AW438; BB645; BY215 5733
Joys are flowing (Marshall) X Marshall 5734
Joys seven (English trad) [SD DDRMRD,DRRTTD,SD] BG70 5735
-----. R [DRRRRRMFM,RMM MRMF] 5736
Jubilate (Dahle) [DDDLTDRTS, RRDTDRM] O358 5737
Jubilate (Farrer) [SDTLSLRSF M,F#SSLTLS,] D440 5738
Jubilate (Parker) [SDSMDL,SFM FSRM,MMMF#] A350a; B521; C521a; J436a; S193b; Y346; AC131; AD179; BB133; BC151; BD121; BF520 5739
-----. R [SRMFSMFS,LFLRDT] 5740
Jubilate (Parry) [DMDSMLM, FSMDRM,MSM] BY67 5741
Jubilation (Genevan Psalter) X Psalm 138 5742
Jubilee (Mozart) [MMMSDRM, FMLSSFFMM] V599 5743
Jubilee (Sullivan) X Bishopgarth 5744
Judah (Doty) [SSDLSDMRRD,RM SMRD] L575b 5745
Judah's Lion (Bohemian trad) [DMSDSLTD,DSLSSFMR] Q211 5746
Judas Maccabaeus (Handel) [SM FSD,RMFSFMR,MFSL] J566; R209; Y285; Z244; AE127; AF 193; AR194; BK30; BV193b; BY164; BZ 5747
Jude (Jude) X Galilee 5748
Judea (Arnold) X Alexandria 5749
Judea (Dykes) [DMRDDTDFF MR,RSFMR] I104b 5750
Judge eternal, throned in splendor (Smart) X Regent Square 5751
Judgment (LaTrobe) [SSDDM DRD,MRDTLLS,S] AZ585-A; BA364 5752
Judson (Baker) X St Saviour 5753
Julian (Maker) [DDDTMLLS, DFFMSSF#S,] C251 5754
Julian (Richards) [SDMMRDRM FSLS,MMRR] AK293 5755
Julius (Shaw) [MRDRSDTLTS, SLTDRM] F584a; BV3 5756
Juniata (Beery) [DMSSLSSM, DDDRDLS,D] AR454; AS 256 5757
-----. R [SSSSLSSM,DDDLT LS,D] 5758
Juniata (Wood) X St Stephen's Church 5759
Just as I am (Barnby) [SLDT SDRM,MMMFMRDT,] H173; I272a; J316a; L398; N181; O450; P405; Q390; R472; T 389; U280; V296b; Y136; Z 297; AA321; AB160; AC145; AD486; AE452; AG310; AJ 111; AK347; AM523; AO262 a; AP410a; AR344; AS408; AT249; AU411; AW393; BF 349; BY442a; BZ 5760
Just as I am (Beck) [MMLSFM RD,MSRMMMRD] AZ277-B; BA934 5761
Just as I am (Bradbury) X Woodworth 5762
Just as seemeth good to thee (Hugg) [MFSSLSMS,LLSMM RDR,] AX493; AY123 5763
-----. R [RMFFFMRM,SSLL SMR,M] 5764
Just for today (Jones) X Belleville 5765
Just for today (Lee) [SLTDSM

FS, DFMMR, SLT] BN189 5766

Just for today (Montani) [MLL SDFFM, DDRR, MLLS] BQ143 5767

Just for today (Palmer) X Vincent 5768

Just outside the door (Ackley) [SMR#MRDLS, DTTDRD, SM] BB562 5769

-----. R [SFMD#RSMRDD, SDT TLS] 5770

Just when I need Him (Gabriel) [SSSSMRDRM, FSLDLLS] AI 110; AS130; AT267; BB590 5771

-----. R [LLLLFD, SSSSMS, F#MRL] 5772

Jutland (Rung) [DSDRMRDS, LL SSDMR, D] M447 5773

K

Kabzeel (Crueger) X Graefenberg 5774

Kaerlighen fra Gud (Jaehnigen) X Charity 5775

Kalman (Kálmán) [SSLSMRDTD, DMRTRDT] AK62 5776

Kalmar (Swedish mel) [DDLLTS DD, MFRSSF#S, M] J485; K357; N289; P316 5777

Kane (Mason) [SDRMRD, SLTDLS, SDRM] J165; K308; N474 5778

Kathrine (Gabriel) [SDMMMSFF, F RTLTD, SM] AJ116a 5779

Keble (Dykes) [SSLLSDRM, MSF MRDRM] D167a; F85; G62; I 82; V535; AA360; AB149; AO 152; AS355; BX493; BZ 5780

Keble (Sewall) [MMMMFMRD, MMMSMDFM] BR125 5781

Kedron (Dare) [DTLLMMRDT, DTLLLTL] A81; AF165; AQ 114; BZ 5782

Kedron (Spratt) [MMMMRR, FFF M, SFMR#MM,] D344b; G333; H282; I453; L428b; N449; V408b; AM411; AT206; BA414 5783

Kee hinay kachomer I (Jewish trad) [MLLMMSLSFM, MSSLTD] BH166 5784

Kee hinay kachomer II (Jewish trad) [SSLSFMFS, SRDDFF MM] BH172 5785

Kee vayom (Lewandowski) [S SF#SRSSR#DSR#R#FSR#D,] BH322 5786

-----. R [DSLLSSDRRMD, DSSLT] 5787

Keep me near thee (Warren) [MMRDMSLS, MMRDSMR, M] AX506 5788

-----. R [SSSSLLLL, TTTT DDD, M] 5789

Keep thou my way (Main) [MRDSDT, SDRMRFM, MRD] AO333 5790

Keep us close to thee (Showalter) [DRMMFSLS, MRDSS LSM] AY76 5791

-----. R [SLSLTDD, LLSSM RDR, M] 5792

Keine schönheit hat die welt (Joseph: in Scheffler's Seelenlust) [MFSFMRRD, MR MF#SSF#S,] E586; F429; X559; BE366; BY484 5793

Keith (Sanders) [MMLMLDM FMRDTL, DRD] AQ101 5794

Keller (Lowry) [SSDMRDSD, R DRM, RDDL] L419; AE286; AX514 5795

Keller's American hymn (Keller) X American hymn 5796

Kelley (Sherwin) [SFMMRDLS, MRDSMR, SF] AU166; AV 312; AX578; BB550 5797

-----. R [DDDDTLSM, RMFL SMS, D] 5798

Kelso (Hopkins) [DDDFMRD, DLSDMRR, DD] D4; K448; AD247; AM328; AS20; BA 770; BF184; BR5 5799

Kemerton (Spohr) X Leyden 5800

Kemper (Morse) [DMSSLSFMR, MFSDRM] A490 5801

Kendal (Cottman) [MMRDDFD M, MDTTLS, SL] AB74 5802

Kendal (Somervell) [MRMFRS D, FMDRDTD, MLL] A496;

B501; C501; E566; X314; BB 675 5803

Kenosis (Bliss) X I gave my life for thee 5804

Kensington new (Tilleard) [SDM RDMSF, MMRLDRD, D] K513; N8; Y329 5805

-----. V [SSDMRDMSF, MMRLD RD,] Y329 5806

Kent (Lampe) [SMTDLSFM, MRSF#SLTL] E347; F71; W 225; X524; BV120; BY178; BZ 5807

Kent (Stanley) [DDLSMRTD, DRMRTLS, D] AL329 5808

Kerr (Laufer) [MTDFMRLTD T, DRMLSF] S324; Z403 5809

Kerry (Jowett) [DSDRMFFM, SDMFSLMR,] W233 5810

Keston (Stainer) X Oxford 5811

Keynsham (Spencer-Palmer) [MDMLSFMR, RMRSMLMT,] BV578 5812

Khanta zagun (Basque trad) X Golden sheaves 5813

Kiddush (Jewish trad) [SDDDD DD, SSDDDDTDR,] AHp. 148; BH303 5814

Kidlington (Reinagle) [MRDFRD TD, MMMF#LSFM,] V102 5815

Kiel (Lutkin) [MMMMFLLS, F MMMF#LLS,] I140 5816

Kildrostan (Evans) [LLMLTDRD TDL, MRDTL] W461 5817

Kilgetty (Irish trad) [DSSLTLS MDRMS, DSSL] BV356; BY 130b 5818

Killin (Gaelic trad) [LDTMDTL, TDTLDTL, LD] W570 5819

Kilmarnock (Dougall) [DMSLSMMR D, LSDLSDR] A414; E542; F69; R125; S28; W400; X522; AD91; AK230; AL672; AP97; AW338; BV143; BY423 5820

Kilmorey (Lloyd) [LLTDRMT, TDTLDT, S#LT] W470b; AL 320b 5821

Kimigayo (Japanese trad) [SLSTR TL, TRMRMLF#MR,] Y310 5822

Kindle the taper (Binder) [DDDD SDFMMRRD, MFSM] BH205 5823

Kindle the taper (Singer) [MM MSSRRRRF, FDRDRM] BH 204 5824

King Edward (Sydenham) [SM DSRD, DFDMMR, SDSD] C 261a; D369a; Y243; AC183; AD293 5825

King Herod and the cock (English trad) [MLLDRDLS, MLL DRD, DR] BG54 5826

King of glory (Parker) [DM FSDT, LSDFMFM, MRM] D482a 5827

King of love (Malim) [DFM RFMRD, MLDFRDT, S] D156a 5828

King of my life (Kirkpatrick) X Lest I forget 5829

King Olaf (Webbe) [DDTDLS, LMLS#LT, D#TD#L] Y15 5830

Kingdom (Copes) [SLSDDTLS, LTDRMRDR,] BZ 5831

Kingdom (German trad. 16th c) X Freiburg 5832

Kingdom of God (English mel) [SSDFMR, DDTLS, LLTDR] BY554 5833

Kingly Vale (Allen) [SMRD LSLTD, TLSLMRD] BE81; BY729 5834

Kingo (---) [SSMFRDDFMRM, MRF#SL] J284 5835

King's College (Mann) [MFST DD, LSFMR, MFSTD] B524; C524a; D133b 5836

King's College (Walker) [DT LSMRRD, SSDLTDRR,] AP 452b 5837

Kings in glory (Shaw) [SDD RMMRMDLS, RMDLS,] BG 194 5838

King's Land (Lindeman) [SD LDS, MRSFMRDLLLS,] M302; P345 5839

King's Langley (English trad) [MFSSMMFFMR, RMMF S[S]D] E221; W608; X229; AX574a; AW385 5840

King's Lynn (English trad) [MRMLTDRS, FMRDLSL,]

A521; E562; J344b; X308; Y 236; AN381; AQ214; BE78; BV 323b; BX412 5841

King's Norton (Clark) [DLTS#M LTDRM, MFMRDD] E419b; X547a; BJ7 5842

-----. V [DLTS#MLTDRM, MM FMRD] BJ7 5843

Kings of orient (Hopkins) X Three kings of orient 5844

Kings of the East (English trad) X Greensleeves 5845

King's Weston (Williams) [LTDTLS, LTDRL, DRMM] A356a; E368; R143; X392; AF197; AL113a; BZ 5846

Kingsfold (English trad) [DT LLLSDDR, DRMMRDLS,] A101; E574; R177; S138; W74; X529; Y83; Z301; AE101; AF412; AL 271b; AP150b; BE270; BG60b; BK16; BV513; BY436a 5847

-----. V [DTLLLSLTDDR, DR MMR] BG60b 5848

Kingsford (English trad) X Kingsfold 5849

Kingsland (Boyce) [SDSLSFM, DMFSLTDT, S] E554; X452; AZ342-B 5850

-----. V [SDSLFM, DMFSLTDT, SL] AZ342-B 5851

Kingsley (Kingsley) [SSFMMMR D, MFSLLSMR,] L245; T372 5852

Kingston (Hayes) X Magdalen College 5853

Kington (Edwards) [MDRMSLSM S, RMFMRDR,] S323a; BE25 5854

Kinross (Stebbins) [MMRDFMM RD, LTDMMRD] AJ315 5855

Kinsman (McGranahan) [SSDMM FMRR, SSTRFFF] AI315; AJ 42; AM450 5856

-----. R [SSSF#SM, MMMR#MD, DDDT] 5857

Kirby Bedon (Bunnett) [MMM RDF, FFFMRS, SMF#S] B486b; C486; D580; G429; J179; L317; T368; U319; Y353; Z146; AB 79; AC138; AD485; AE442; AI 152; AM261; AR548; AT162; AW398; BA252; BB167; BF635 5858

Kirk Ella (Nichol) [SFMMRLTD RFM, RMRD, T] AL555 5859

Kirkdale (Barnby) [MMMMFM SD, FFFMLLR, S] D646b; L35; AA43; AZ89-F; BA792 5860

Kirken (Lindeman) [LLMD LDRM, MF#SMDRTL,] J151; M92; O132; P81; Q467; R432; AF270; BE176; BZ 5861

Kirken dener et gammelt hus (Lindeman) X Kirken 5862

Kirkland (Evans) [DRMSLSMD, RML, DRMSL] W127; AM 208; BV55 5863

Kirkpatrick (Kirkpatrick) [SS DSDRMRD, MFSSFMR,] AM 105 5864

-----. R [MFSFMFSM, SSLS FMR, S] 5865

Kirkpatrick (Kirkpatrick) X He hideth my soul 5866

Kirkstall (Carr) [MMRDDDLS, SSDFMMMR] D610a 5867

Kirn (Taylor) [SDDRTD, LSD RM, MRMFS] W125; AD163; AT112 5868

-----. R [SDDRMRD, LRRM FMR, RS] 5869

Kjaemp alvorlig nu, Guds naade (Thommen. Christenschatz. 1745) X Batty 5870

Kjaerlighed er lysets kilde (Lindeman) [DSLSDMSR, MMRSLTS, D] O363; P293; BE178 5871

Klug (German, 14th c) X In dulce jubilo 5872

Knecht (Knecht) [DDTDRRRD, MMRMFRT, DDRR] B536; C536; E451; F289; K17; N30; W577; AL443; AP67; BV582a; BY551a 5873

Knickerbocker (Owen) [MRD TLSLDRM, MMRDT] A207b 5874

Knightsbridge (Baden-Powell) [DRMSLDLS, LSFMRRR, D] C193a; D368b; V707; AH 410 5875

Knocking at the door (Everett) [MMMMRDDL, SDMSMR, MM] AX245; AY374 5876

-----. R [LLLLLSM, SLSSMR, MMM] 5877

Know this, that every soul is free (Stephens) [SDSLTDRM, MFMRDTLS,] BC90 5878

Knowhead (Gabriel) [SSSLTLS, SD DRRM, MFF] AJ356 5879

Knowlton (Harding) [SSLTDRDT, DDRRFMRM,] AP743 5880

Knowsley (Hopkins) [MRDRMLSSFM, RMF#SLT] Z460 5881

Knox (Havergal) X Evan 5882

Kocher (Knecht) X Knecht 5883

Kodosh (Sulzer) [SMSFSSSSSM, RRMFMR] BH285 5884

Koenigsberg (Albert) X Waltham 5885

Kol nidre (Jewish trad) [MLS# MMS#LDLM, LS#LTDT] BH318 5886

Kolding (Lutkin) [MMMRDM, RRR DMT, LLSF] I112c 5887

Kom, du folkefrelser sand (Walther, G-B. 1524) X Veni, redemptor 5888

Kom helligaand, Herre Gud (Erfurt G-B. 1524) X Komm Heilege Geist, Herre Gott 5889

Komm helligaand, med skabermagt (Sarum plainsong, M 8) X Veni creator 5890

Kom hid til mig, enhver isaer (German. 15th c) X Kommt her zu mir 5891

Kom, huldaste forbarmore (Hedberg) [DMFSDTLS, MFLSMRD, D] N298 5892

Komm, Gott schöpfer Heiliger Geist (Sarum plainsong M 8) x Veni creator 5893

Komm Heilige Geist, Herre Gott (Erfurt G-B. 1524) [SLSMSR MF#S, SLSRFMR] J122a; K146a; M471; N154; O375; Q224; AA257; AZ203-A 5894

-----. V [SLSMRMFS, SLSRFMR D,] N154 5895

-----. V [SLSFMRMF#S, SLSR FMR] AZ203-A 5896

Komm, o komm, du Geist des lebens (Meiningen G-B. 1693) X St Leonard 5897

Komm, seele (Franck) [SDSL SFMM, SFMRRDD, M] E486; F340; J182b; W176; X255a; AN316 5898

-----. V [SDSLSFMM, SFMRDD, MR] AN316 5899

Kommet ihr hirten (Bohemian trad) [SSMLFSSMLFSMSRMD,] Y308; AD108; AK111; AW79; BD221 5900

Kommt her zu mir (German, 15th c) [LLLMRMDT, LDT DRMRD] J156b; K196; M90; O85; P110; Q263; AA276 5901

-----. V [LLLMRMDT, LDT DMRDT,] P110 5902

Kommt, ihr seelen, nehmt zu herzen (German, Old) X Stabat mater 5903

Kommt seelen (Bach) X Rinkart 5904

Korea (Tai Jun Park) [MS FRDM, SLSMFR, DDSF] BY664 5905

Koschat (Koschat) X Poland 5906

Kozeluch (Kozeluch) [MFS MDTLSSM, DRMFSS] L28 5907

Kremser (Dutch trad) [SSLS MFSFMRMD, SS] A315; G20; J450; P20; Q468; R17; S461; Y27; Z117; AB63; AC29; AD 22; AE25; AF21; AG10; AH 185; AI7; AK19; AM83; AN 327; AO80; AQ22; AR9; AT 11; AW15; BB8; BD17; BE 292; BI14; BK137; BL91; BZ 5908

Kreuznach (German mel) X Er freut euch 5909

Kücken (Kücken) [MRDMSLSM, MRDDRMRD,] L461a; U39; V392; AC227; AO255; 5910

-----. V [MRDMSLSM, MRD DRMMR] U39 5910a

Kybald Twychen (Harris) [SS

LSLDTD, MMRSLTDT,] F614 5911

Kyrie, Gott Vater (Latin, ca 800) [SLT, LDDTLLS, LLSFMM] Q6 5912

L

Laban (Mason) [MFSSSDS, MR DTLS, MFS] C118; D504b; G277; H296; I429; K272b; L 538; R363; T122a; U295; V 470; Y378; Z370; AA379; AD294; AE255; AH451; AI325; AJ178; AM14; AN299a; AO393; AR328; AS327; AT397; AU247; AV177; AX163; AY36; BA580; BB358; BD113; BF477; BX360; BZ 5913

Labor (Smith) [LDRMMFRM, DM FSSLF] A510 5914

Labor on (Doane) [DRMMMRDRDL DLSDDT] AU327; AX183; AY 528 5915

-----. R [DRMRDL, TDRRMDR, MFS] 5916

Lacrymae (Sullivan) [MMMFSDR M, SSDTLLS, L] B137; C327; D222a; H283; W314b; AZ253-C; BA300; BF597; BR292 5917

Lacy (Campbell) [MSMRMFM, FSMLFR, SSF] V668 5918

Lady in sorrow (A Monk of Gethsemani) [DRTDMSSLF#S, MFS FMR] BN176 5919

Lady of the visitation (Mainz G-B. 1661) [SFMMFMRR, MRDRDTL, D] BN150; BO96 5920

Ladywell (Ferguson) [SDRMSFM R, DRMRDSFM,] F297; W139b; BV265b; BY180a 5921

Laetabundus (Gatty) [SSSSSMLSF MRMDRMF] E22b 5922

Laetabundus (Hopkins) [SSLTDLT, DRMRD, SSLT] D114b 5923

Laetabundus (Plainsong, 11th c. M 5) [DRDRMD, FSLSFS LFSF] E22 5924

Lafayette (Herbert) [SSFMMMRD, DTLDFLS, S] T168a; AJ247a; AM26b 5925

Lafayette (Stewart) X St Helen's 5926

Lagergren (Lagergren) X Gud, var gud 5927

Lahee (Lahee) X Wimbledon 5928

Laissez paître vos bêtes (French, ancient) X The band of children 5929

Lake Enon (Woodbury) [SSMM RD, SSFFMR, RMSS] G335; L470; S246a; Z314; AE271; AK254; AO377; AR451 5930

Lamb of God (Decius) X O Lamm Gottes 5931

Lambdin (Cassel) [SDDDD, RMMMMM, SDDD] AT407; AU374 5932

-----. R [LLLFL, DDDSS, F#F#F#F#SF#] 5933

Lambeth (Akeroyd) [DMMM FSSLSF#S, LLSSF] E340; X346 5934

Lambeth (Schulthes) [MMMFTL TD, DRMSFMR, M] B279b; C85d; D346b; H386; I190; J246; L80; N278; R32; T220; U81; V137; Y5; Z436; AB 101; AC72; AD84; AE156; AG115; AH237; AJ313; AM 428; AO146; AP734b; AR 242; AS178; AW185; BA86; BB213; BF236; BO196; BR 402b; BX477 5935

Lamb's Hill (Lee) [SMFMRD, SDLSFM, SDTL] AZ71-B 5936

Lambs of Jesus (German) [MF SDMDLD, FLSDTLS, M] M 39 5937

Lament (Persichetti) [MRR MRDSRMTLF#, F#SF#M] AQ314 5938

Lammas (Brown) [MRDDTDSFM R, RMFTL] A202b; B330; D220a; O150; BR475 5939

Lamp of our feet (Schop) X Jesu joy of man's desiring 5940

Lancashire (Smart) [SSMFLS M, DDFSLR, SSM] A257;

B61; C477; D255; G278; H177; I387; J550; K13; L129; M101; N590; Q205; R208; S115; T373; U120; V179; W123; Y177; Z 247; AB144; AC127; AD160; AE 125; AF192; AG99; AH278; AI 357; AK99; AL182; AM197; AN196; AO112; AP296; AQ316; AR215; AS255; AT417; AU236; AV210; AW115; AZ151-M; BA 229; BB135; BD47; BF297; BI 44; BK78; BR62; BX204; BZ 5941

Lancaster (Howard) [SDRMDFM R, RMDTLS, SL] J211; K205; M20; O454; W116; AP99a; AQ 106 5942

Land of our birth (Floyd) [SSSDS TLS, MDRMDTLS,] C367a; BY 644 5943

Land of our hearts (Lester) [DR MRDRLSFM, MFLSMM] Y284 5944

Land of rest (American trad) [SDDRMSDDLS, SDDRM] A585a; J587a; AF312 5945

Land of rest (Miller) [DRMMMM SMMR, DRDRRM] AT284; AU167; AV398; AX203; AY306; BB662 5946

-----. R [SSSLSMR, DMRMSS, SSS] 5947

-----. V [DRMMMMSMMD, RD RRMS] BB662 5948

Land of rest (Newman) [SMM FMRLS, MDDTDR, SM] V615; AC321 5949

Land of the mountains high (Stephens) [SDMMR#M, MRFFM, SDMMR#] BC140 5950

Landskron (Bohemian hymnal, 1531) [SDRDTLSLTD, MSLSMD] Sap. 38 5951

Lane (Lane) X Penitence 5952

Lanesboro (Dixon) [DSSLTDSFM, SLFRDTD,] H104; V68; BI23-D; BR37 5953

-----. V [SDSLTDSFM, SLFRDTD] BR37 5954

Langa (Soto) [MMFSSSMFSLL, RRMFF] Eap. 60; Y90; AD463; BY777 5955

Langdale (Somervell) [MMSDRM FM, F#SLTLSF, M] E590 5956

Langdon (Campbell) [MRLLS S, MDDTLS, LRDT] V660 5957

Langdon (Langdon. Divine harmony) [DDDDDDRM, MM MRDFMR,] AO306; AP90c; BA670 5958

Langemarck (Jones) [SSFM RDTDFMR, FMLF#F#] C491; AP566 5959

Langford (Langford) [MMR# MMSFMR#M, SMSFMF] M203; O484 5960

Langham (Shaw) [MRDTLDRM DSM, LSMS] A532; R486; X326; Y247; AD362; AF445; AK401 5961

Langport (English trad) [MM MMRD, SSSS, MMMMRD] E 656b 5962

Langran (Langran) [MDRMSF MMRD, MMRSRF] A58; B 129; C129; D82; F116; G495; I284; J366; K324a; L389; N 121; R341; S174; T148; U 41; V283; W323; Y11; Z347; AB311; AD399; AE326; AF 287; AG159; AH510; AI23; AJ218; AK31; AL220; AM 467; AN40; AO1; AP354; AR550; AW303; AZ32-F; BA 256; BB289; BD71; BE390; BF384; BR295; BX41; BZ 5963

Langstaff (Stebbins) X Holiness 5964

Langton (Streatfeild) [MMMSF M, DDDRFFM, MMM[L345; BR307 5965

Languentibus in purgatorio (Plainsong) [LDRDFMRDT DD, MSLSF] BQ249 5966

Lanherne (Hayman) [MMFSS DDTLSM, MRDFM] Y209; AB265; BF507 5967

-----. V [MMFSSSDTLSM, MRDFM] BF507 5968

Lanier (Hansen) X Hour of prayer 5969

Lanier (Lutkin) [MMMMRDRL L, DTLS#L, MM] G132; I745;

U99; Y84; Z225; AC119; AD 145; AH277; AR161; AT90; AV 114; BB128 5970

Lansdowne (Greenwood) [DSFM RDRLS, LTDRFMS] BE220 5971

Lansing (Gabriel) [SMRDMFSLT DS, DTSRD] AJ58 5972

Laramie (Bode) [LSMDLDRM, SDRMRDL, L] A432 5973

Larghetto (Beethoven) X Alsace 5974

Larue (Pleyel) X Seasons 5975

Lassen (Danish mel) [MRMDSDR M, SFMLSSMR,] M311 5976

Lasset uns mit Jesu ziehen (Bolze) X Walk with Jesus 5977

Lasst uns alle (Dresden. G-B., 1632) X Dresden 5978

Lasst uns erfreuen (Cologne G-B.) X Vigiles et sancti 5979

Last hope (Gottschalk) X Mercy 5980

Last sleep (Barnby) X Requiem 5981

Lasus (Mann) [SLTDDRMFM, SFMRMRD] D315; AA70 5982

Latakia (Taylor) [DRMMMMFMM RDRM, MFS] T31; AJ45; AX 328 5983

Lathbury (Sherwin) X Bread of life 5984

LaTrobe (LaTrobe) [MMLLTT D, DLSMRFM, MM] K83; AZ 581-A; BA204 5985

LaTrobe's 121st metre (LaTrobe) [MDLSFM, LRFDTL, MR#MS] AZ121-C 5986

LaTrobe's 166th metre (LaTrobe) [LLTDMRDT, DRFMRDTD,] AZ166-B 5987

LaTrobe's 578th metre (LaTrobe) [SFMR, DSDTLS, TDLFMR,] AZ578-B 5988

LaTrobe's 586th metre (English trad) [DDDDTLSFMFS, DDLLS] AZ586-A 5989

Latter day (Beecher. Plymouth collection) [SLSMDLSM, DLS MDRM, R] AO482; BB359 5990

Laud (Dykes) [SDDDRMRD, SFMMRR, RM] D559a; I34; K131b; L105; V202; AA102 5991

Lauda anima (Andrews) [SM RDDFLLS, SMSDTLSF#] AR34 5992

Lauda anima (Goss) [SSSSDTLS, FMLSMFR] A282; B258; C258; D421b; E470; F365; J160a; K289; L273; O129; R31; S14; W21; X623; AD21; AF16; AL17; AM63; AP91; AR76; AS7; AY424; BA652; BE280; BL83; BM45; BN177; BV247; BY23; BZ 5993

Lauda, Sion (Catholic) [SDSM RFMRD, RSRFMSF] BO253 5994

Lauda Sion (Cobb) X Cobb 5995

Lauda Sion (Plainsong sequence, M 7) [MSLSDTLS, LTSMFMR] A193a; E317 5996

-----. V [RSLSDTLS, LTSMF MR] E317 5997

Lauda Sion (Plainsong, M 7) X Ecce panis angelorum 5998

Lauda Sion salvatorem (Cobb) X Cobb 5999

Laudate dominum (Gauntlett) X Cobern 6001

Laudate dominum (Gauntlett) X Gauntlett I 6002

Laudate dominum (Parry) [SM DRS, DLSFM, SMRSD, T] F376a; W168a; AL44; AM288; BV23; BY37 6003

Laudate dominum (Schubert) [SDTLSLLS, DMDSMSFM] BQ254 6004

Laudate dominum (Stralsund G-B. 1665) X Praise to the Lord 6005

Laudes domini (Barnby) [MF SLDTL, SLTDMR, DTD] A367; B37; C37a; D445a; F223b; G31; H29; I32; J416; K310; M556; R41; S3; T323; U453; V29; W167; Y201; Z 135; AB77; AC2; AD43; AE40; AF35; AG21; AH158; AK43;

AL45b; AM131; AN92a; AO19; AP255b; AR46; AS19; AT23; AU7; AV2; AW21; BA128; BB 43; BD4; BF176; BI116; BK38; BR2; BV271; BY685a; BZ 6006

Laudon (Thalben-Ball) [DSS MD, FMRMD, SDMRTL] BE 300 6007

Lauds (Redhead arr) [SLSSDRRD, SLSSDMRR,] D160b; T14b; AJ23b; AP653a 6008

Laufer (Perkins) [MMFSDDT, DRMFFM, MR#M] G468; AB 375 6009

Launch out into the deep (Carter) [DDMFSSSLDLS, SLLLS] AU45 6010

-----. R [SDSTLS, SSMDMR, MRDM] 6011

Lauree (Huffaker) [SSRFMRDTM RRD, TLMM] AR86 6012

Laurel Hill (---) [MFSMSDDTT, RMFSLSS] BB72 6013

Laurinus (Swedish Koralbok, 1697) [LMMRRDDT, LTDRDT, TD] J146a; M317; N628 6014

Laus deo (Bach) [DSLSFMRDT DRS, LTDR] F422 6015

Laus deo (Gower) [MMMSSF, TDDRRM, SSSL] AP633b 6016

Laus deo (Redhead) X Redhead, No. 46 6017

Laus matutina (Stainer) [MSM DRMSDTLS, SMRDD] AB5; AZ 552-B; BI45; BR3; BX270 6018

Laus regis (Fischer) [DMDMSD, SSMFSM, MRSF#] J436b; K126; L589; AS156 6019

Laus sempiterna (Prout) [SDDDS DDD, SMFSLMR, S] W211b 6020

Laus sempiterna (Reay) [MMM SDLS, DFMRD, MMMS] D128b 6021

Laus sempiterna (Scottish Presbyterian hymnal) [MMMMSDDD, SMFSLMR, S] AO610b 6022

Laus tibi (German processional) X Laus tibi Christi 6023

Laus tibi Christi (German processional) [SSSSLS, FMRRD, SSSSL] E534; X388; AN430 6024

Lausanne (Lausanne Choral buch) X Broadlands 6025

Lausanne (Haydn) X Greenland 6026

Lawes' Psalm 47 (Lawes) X Psalm 47 6027

Lavington (Congregational Church Music. 1871) [DRMM FSLSFM, MFSDFM] AP578 6028

Lawes (Lawes) X Psalm 32 6029

Lawson (Lawson) [SSMMRRDD, LLDDLLS, S] BB266 6030

-----. R [TDRRDRMM, RMFF MDR, S] 6031

Layriz (Layriz Collection, 1853) [LDTLDMRM, MDDFMRD# R] E440; F357 6032

L'cho adonoy (Ephros) [SDDRM MFSLS, MMMLSF] BH291 6033

L'cho dodee (Lewandowski) X How good it is to thank the Lord 6034

Le P'ing (Chinese trad) [DRM DLSLS, DRMSMS, DR] AF 486; BZ 6035

Le vermeil du soliel (Muret) X Gems of day 6036

Lea (Summers) [SMDLSDRM, SMDLLS, RM] M56 6037

Leach (English trad) [DSL SFMRDFMRDTD, RM] H179 6038

Lead, kindly light (Dykes) X Lux benigna 6039

Lead me (Davis) X Lead me, Saviour 6040

Lead me gently home (Thompson) [MFF#SLSMDDTLS, FSRT] AU123; AW449 6041

-----. R [SMDLSTRSSMDLS TRS] 6042

Lead me into life eternal (Schreiner) [DDRSMRDS, LTDDDTDR,] BC141 6043

Lead me, Lord (Wesley, S. S.) [MRDFMRDMMR, SMRD

RM] R539; AE460; AF524; AG335; AR617; AT522; BZ 6044

Lead me on (Pollock) [SSDDDD RMMM, MMRRRM] AX497; AY114 6045

-----. R [MFSLSM, MFSSSMR, MFS] 6046

Lead me, Saviour (Davis) [SMSDTLS, FMRLSFM, SS] AH407; AR467; AU104; AV 370; AW502; AY121 6047

-----. R [SMDS, MRDLSMRMF, MMM] 6048

Lead me to Calvary (Kirkpatrick) X Lest I forget 6049

Lead me to some soul today (Loveless) [DMMRDFF, LSDM SRMR, D] AU323 6050

Lead on, lead on (McKinney) [SSMRDSLS, DRMFRDD, S] AU460 6051

-----. R [SLSSLS, SSLSDRM, RM F] 6052

Lead on, thou God of hosts (Gillis) [MMRDMFMR, LSD SFM, MR] U302 6053

Lead us, great teacher Paul (Slovak hymn) [SFFMFSLFM MR, MRRDD] BQ99 6054

Leaf (---) [SSSSLLSS, DDTLTD, SM] T130; AJ190 6055

Leamington (Nicholson) [MRD DDRMSFMR, RRMFM] F385b 6056

Lean on His arms (Jones) [SM MMR#MFMRD, SRRD#RF] AX471; AY455 6057

-----. R [MMR#MFMRDR, FF MFSFM] 6058

Lean on my ample arm (Stephens) [MR#MSFM, TDRS, MR#MS SS#,] BC260 6059

Leaning on Jesus (Showalter) [MMMRDRRRDL, SSDTDR] AH390; AI401; AM718; AT371; AU276; AW489; AX49; BB611 6060

-----. R [MDDL, SDTDRMMR, MDDL] 6061

Leaning on the everlasting arms (Showalter) X Leaning on Jesus 6062

Leave it there (Tindley, arr) X The roll (Black) 6063

Leave your burden (Lillenas) [SDMR#MRD, DDRDTLS, SD] AU334; AX364 6064

Leave your burden at the place of prayer (Lillenas) X Leave your burden 6065

Leavell (McKinney) [SDDDMFS, DTDRTD, SDD] AT423; AU 91 6066

-----. R [SFMFSMRM, DTDR MRR, S] 6067

Lebanon (Allen) [SLSMDRMRD, MSMLSSF#] BB21 6068

Lebanon (English) [SSLTDSS, FMFLSMS, SM] BR498 6069

Lebanon (Zundel) [SDDDTDR, SRRRDRM, SM] H212; L128; V382; AI222; AJ82; AM396; AV171; BA454 6070

Lebbaeus (St Alban's Tune Book, 1866) [MMMRDDS, DD RRMMR,] A229; B141; C141; D528; K84b; L256; M398; V132; W469; AB136a; AK542; AP432; BF313a; BR503 6071

Ledbury (---) [SDTLSFM, FLS RFFM, SD] BR33 6072

Lee (McKinney) [SSSLTDS, LLDTLS, SRR] AT434; AU 347 6073

----. R [SMSDS, LTDDTLS, FRST] 6074

Lee (Nash) [SSDMDDLSSS, DSFMSD] AN86 6075

Lee (Swisher) [MSDMLSDMRD, TDRMFS] BD52 6076

Legion (Brown) [DLSMFRDT, DSSSFMR, D] D620a 6077

Leicester (Bishop) [MMLS#LR DTLS#, S#LSFML] E322; J 175; W6; X605; AQ86; BE289; BJ12 6078

Leicester (Hurst) [SSMRDDRM FM, SDRMSF] S498; V70; W316; AL223; AP363a; BA 298 6079

-----. V [SMRDDRMFM, SDRM SFM] V70 6080

Leigh (Reinagle) [MMRDLSFM, MSMLSFMR,] AA455 6081

Leighton (Greatorex) [MMRDRM, SSFMRD, SSLS] C408b; D333b; H113; I493a; L277b; U128; V 213; AE72; AO68; AW230; BB 174 6082

Leighton (Leighton) [DRMFM RDRM, MRMF#SRS] E180b; X245; AL389; AM273; AP302; BJ96 6083

Leila (McKinney) [SSFMDRMD, DFFDRM, SS] AT332; AU451 6084

-----. R [DFFLFMMS, MRSF#M F#S, S] 6085

Leinbach (Leinbach) [DMFSDMR D, DRMRSLTL] BA931 6086

Leipsic (As hymnodus sacer) X Breslau 6087

Leipsic (Schein) X Eisenach 6088

Leipzig (Mendelssohn) [SDTDRM FRSFM, RDDMR] AC290 6089

Leithead (Pritchard) [MFSDDTLS, MSDRD, MFS] W576b 6090

LeJeune (LeJeune) X Love divine 6091

Leland (Fosbery) [MMMMMS, SF#FMFR, DDDL] L31 6092

Lella (Pollock) X I love to steal awhile away 6093

L'Emmanuello (Perosi) [MRSLF SMR, MSFMRMD, S] B31a; BQ44 6094

Lemon's Farm (Shaw) [SDRMRS, SLSLDR, RRRR] X165 6095

Lenoir (Maclean) [DTLSML, LFM RDT, DDDR] V490 6096

Lenox (Edson) [DDDSLS, SDR MRD, DMSM] G189; H229; I 294; L249; N70; V234; AH365; AM223; AO116; AP392; AR 574; AS190; AT250; AV165; AX112; AY263; BA91; BZ 6097

Leominster (---) [MR#MFMD, RMFSFM, SF#SL] K168b; L312 6098

Leominster (Martin) [MMMMM F, FRRRMR, RMMS] D203b; E361; G367; I283; J66; M365; N175; O352; S247b; T22; W 464a; AA487; AB194; AE266; AH526; AI92; AJ29; AK243; AL313; AM125; AO294; AR 359; AZ595-B; BA101; BB 284; BF454; BR289; 6099

Leon (Mason) X Denny 6100

Leonard (Hiles) X St Leonard 6101

Leonburg (German) [DMRFM RRD, MDLRDTLS,] O557 6102

Leoni (Jewish trad) [MLTDR M, DRMFSM, TDR] A285a; B253; C253a; D460a; E646; F631; G5; H14; I4; J410; K284a; Q40; R89; S8; V89; W571; X398; Y300; Z124; AD70; AF14; AG38; AHp. 152; AK61; AL25; AM32; AN1; AP144; AQ6; AR38; AW14; AZ345-A; BA19; BB 76; BE371; BF212; BH54, 277; BI5-D; BK58; BL97; BR311; BV249; BX17; BY 30; BZ 6103

-----. V [MLTDRM, DRMFR M, TDDD] BH54 6104

-----. V [MLTDRM, DRMFS M, DDDD] BH277 6105

Les anges dans nos compagnes (French carol) X Gloria 6106

Les commandemens de Dieu (Bourgeois) X Commandments 6107

Leslie (Campbell) [DMFSS LLS, SFMRMFM, F#] V158 6108

Lest I forget (Kirkpatrick) [MMRDDFFM, MRDSMRMM] AE295; AR453; AX111 6109

-----. R [RRMFLSFM, RRM FLSFM,] 6110

Lest we forget (Blanchard) [DTSLMSFM, MMMMMMRL] U340; V745; Y288; Z560; AC162; AH208; BB505; BF 633 6111

Let all on earth their voices (Sheehan) [DDDSSLFS, SDRM FSFM] BN180 6112

Let Christian hearts (French, 16th c) [MLTDRDTL, SLL TSL, ML] BN16 6113

Let each man learn (---) [SS

DDRMFM, SMFRSRMR] BC91 6114

Let earth's inhabitants rejoice (Robertson) [SDMLSFMRM, SDRTSLS] BC93 6115

Let every creature (Bragers) [DSFMDFMR, SDRMRDR, D] BP99 6116

-----. R [SRMFRMSS, DFFMR DMR] 6117

Let Him in (Excell) [MFSM DLS, SLS, MFSMDL] AH337; AU29; AX246; BB566 6118

Let hymns of joy (Cologne G-B.) X Vigiles et sancti 6119

Let Israel trust in God alone (Lowenberg) [SDTDSMDL, SFMFSRM, M] BH139 6120

Let Jesus come into your heart (Morris) X McConnelsville 6121

Let me go (Hartsough) [DMMSDR MS, LLSMSMR, D] AX614; AY 174 6122

Let not your heart be troubled (Warren) [SSSF#SLSSD, DRDTL SF] AX533 6123

-----. R [SFMDDMMR, RMFRRT DS,] 6124

Let others see Jesus in your (McKinney) X Coleman 6125

Let Sion in her beauty rise (Edwards) [DMSDTLSFM, SDD RR#M, R] BC262 6126

Let the beauty of Jesus (Jones) [MMMRDMRDSSS, FFFMR] AU317 6127

Let the deep organ swell (Montani) [DLLDTLTD, SDRFMRDR,] BQ105 6128

Let the deep organ swell (Raymond-Barker) [SLDTLSFM, R MSFMRDT,] BO218 6129

Let the lower lights be burning (Bliss) X Lower lights 6130

Let the whole creation ring (Richards) [SLTDSLSD, TLS MDLS, M] BR565 6131

Let the words of my mouth (Baumbach) X In corde meo 6132

Let them come to see (Hildebrand) [SLSFMSD, TLSFMLS, SL] AY370 6133

Let there be light (Mombach) [SSFMDTLS, LSMFRRM, M] BH141 6134

Let there be light I (Singer) [MFSLLRDTDS, SLSFSF] BH99 6135

Let there be light II (Singer) [DDDSDMRD, MMMDMSFM,] BH232 6136

Let the words abide (Dyson) [DDRMFMRDR.] R547 6137

Let us all press on (Stephens) [MFSDMSF#SLFMF, FMRT] BC98 6138

Let us break bread together (Negro spiritual) X Communion spiritual 6139

Let us oft speak kind words (Beesley) [SSDDDMRDTL, LRSTRS] BC94 6140

-----. R [MFSSLSDRMMFM, SDDM] 6141

Leuchars (Hately) [MMSFMR, MDDRRM, MFMR] W553; AP125 6142

Levabo (---) [LLSMDRM, MM LDT, RDTL] BR340 6143

Lew Trenchard (English trad) [MFMRMDRM, LLTDTLS#] A177a; B417; C140; E591b; X493; BM90 6144

-----. V [DMFMRMDRM, LLT DTLS#] X493 6145

Lewars (Ohl) [MSDTLSSFM, RDFMRF#S] K478 6146

Lewes (Randall) [MFRSDRTD, FMLSFMFM] E250; F64; W65a; X555a; AL64; AP 179 6147

Lexington (Smart) [DRRSSD, LRMSFM, MF#SL] V466 6148

Leyden (Spohr) [MMRMFRS, DTLSSFM, MM] I619; AB 53; BR237 6149

Leyden (Wilms) X Hague 6150

Libera nos (Taylor) [DLTDMLS MM, SFMRDRR] BY413 6151

Liberation (German trad) [DS LTDFMMR, MDTLLS, S]

AA6 6152
Liberty Hall (---) [MLS#LTDRDT L, DMDTLT] AY182 6153
Liberty Hall (---) X Martyrdom (Wilson) 6153a
Lichfield (Doles) [DRMFSLFSFM, DTLSLT] C180b; E287; W574a; X2 6154
Lichfield (LaFeille. Methode .... 1782) X Milan 6155
Lichfield (MacLagan) [SDMMRD TD, TDRRDTLS,] W340 6156
Liddon (Jeffery) [SDMTLSMD, DLSDRMFR] I15; Y254; AO 206 6157
Liebe die du mich zum bilde (Meiningen G-B.) X St Leonard 6158
Lieblich, dunkel, sanft und stille (Walther) [MSFMRDDTLS, FM FMSL] AD319 6159
Liebster Immanuel (Himmels-lust. 1675) [DDDTLSLFMRD, SSM LT] E41; F409b; J53b; Q582; W64c; X85; BY91b 6160
-----. V [DDDTLSLFMRRD, SSML] F409b 6160a
Liebster Jesu (Ahle) [MRDRS MDR, DDDDRMRD,] A186; D547; E336; F408; G310; H181b; I103; J190; K412; L550; M3; N225; O34; P46; Q16; R248; S31a; V484; W203; X457; AA3; AB374; AD34a; AE32; AF212; AH490; AK26; AM112; AN143; AQ245; AW553; AZ84-A; BA282; BB27; BE85; BF652; BR100; BV2; BX126a; BY241; BZ 6161
-----. V [MDRSFMMR, DTLTD RMR] G310 6162
-----. V [MDRSFMRDR, DTLTD RM] N225 6163
-----. V [MDRSMDR, DDTDRM RD, M] AE32 6164
-----. V [MDRSMDR, DDDD RMRD, S] AQ245 6165
-----. V [MDRSFMDR, DDLTD RMR] AZ84-A 6166
-----. V [MRDRSMRDR, DDDD RMR] BR100 6167
Liebster Jesu (Briegel) [LTDMRDT, MF#SMLSF#M, L] N302 6168
Liebster Jesu, liebstes lieben! (Darmstadt G-B. 1687) X Gregor's 211th metre 6169
Liebster Jesu, wir sind hier (Ahle) X Liebster Jesu 6170
Liefeld (Liefeld) [DDDSLD RD, DMDDRT, DD] M649 6171
Life line (Ufford) [SMMMRDRM FM, SLSSMM] AH415; AT217; AU72; AX188; BB624 6172
-----. R [SSSLS, MMMFM, RRRRDR] 6173
Life's harvest (Woodbury) [SDDTLSS, SDDLDS, SDD] BB444 6174
Lift Him up (Beall) [SSDDD TTTLTD, DRMMM] AU60 6175
Lift Him up (Hakes) [DRMM FFMD, MFSSLLS, F] BB520 6176
-----. R [DDLS#LFMS, SSS RMFM, D] 6177
Lift thine eyes (Mendelssohn) [SSSDMRDLDDT, SLLLR] AH620; BC370 6178
Lift up (Naylor) [DMDDMSRR, FMRDTDRS] D119a 6179
Lift up, ye princes (Slovak hymn) [SDDTDRRD, MRDT RLLS,] BQ32 6180
Lift up your heads (Mendelssohn) [DTDRDF, MRDTDDR, RSS] BI109 6181
Lift up your heads (Singer) [MLLTTTD, MLLTTTD, LL] BH289 6182
Lift up your heads (Stobaeus) [MSFMRMFS, MFSLFSSF,] O158; Q73a; AA138 6183
Lift your glad voices (Leslie) [DTLSMFSDRT, TDDRMT] BR566 6184
Light (Grimm's Choral buch) X Grimm's 253d metre 6185
Light (Leavitt. Christian lyre, 1832) [LMLSSDLS, DMDR DTL,] A443 6186

Light (Lindeman) X Kjaerlighet er lysets kilde 6187
Light divine (Gibbons) X Angel's song 6188
Light of ages (Lloyd) [MMMMFR T, DDRMSF#M, LL] Y149 6189
Light of life (Mason) X Star of peace 6190
Light of light (MacMillan) [MDRMFMRM, LSTDFMMR,] AP345 6191
Light of the soul (Freylinghausen G-B, 1704) X Christe, wahres seelenlichte 6192
Light of the world (---) [SDRMD LS, DFMRDR, SDR] AK124; AO518 6193
Light of the world (Bliss) [SDR MMRDRDRM, MSSSS] AE301; AI392; AM679; AR473; AT88; AU330; AW467; AX273 6194
-----. R [RRMRSF#MF#S, RRMRSF#M] 6195
Light of the world (Himmel) [MDSSSLSSM, SDTLLLR] I192 6196
Light of the world (MacFarren) [DTLSMDRMFMR, SMRDL] AB75 6197
Like a river (Mountain) X Remo 6198
Like a strong and raging fire (Root) [SSSSLSSD, SSSSLSR, S] AH139; AI65b; BC340 6199
-----. V [SSSLSD, SSSLSR, SS SL] AI65b 6199a
Like as a father (Hakes) [MR# MFMRMRD, DSMRMRD,] BB66 6200
Like the deer that yearns (Gelineau) [SSLD, DDR, DDD L, LRD, SS] BL54; BS p. 16 6201
Lilies of the field (Brunk) [SSFMDRMF, FFFFLSFM,] AY361 6202
Lille (French trad) [MRDRMFS LSFM, MRFM, M] AL355; AP799; AW394 6203
Lille Guds barn (Danish folk mel) X Bairn 6204
Lily of the valley (Hays) X Salvationist 6205
Lime Street (Shaw) [DDRTTD, LDTSM, LLLSL] X85b; BE 279 6206
Limpsfield (Booth) [SSSLRMF M, DFR, SSSLR] W680; AL 259a; BV330; BY399 6207
Limpsfield (Freeman) [MDRSS LTDRFF, RMDLS] AD306; BE210 6208
Lincoln (Paine) [MMFSSLLS, SDLSRFMR,] AZ277-D 6209
Lincoln (Ravenscroft's Psalter) [DRMRDDTD, DSFFMF, FM] E140; F144; X171 6210
Lincoln (Vulpius) X Cana 6211
Lincoln's Inn (Steggall) [MF SMFMRM, FSLSMRDR,] D384 6212
Lind (---) [MMMMMMFM, RRRRDRM, S] AI163; AS465 6213
Lindeman (Lindeman) [MRD SLS, SFMDMR, MSSF#] J575b; O351; P163; AI428; AM550 6214
Lindesfarne (Dykes) [SSDSLD R, MRDMRLTS, S] V169b 6215
Lindsey House (Hutton. Tunes for the hymns) [DMFSDDTD, MRDTLS, DM] AZ590-A, BA240 6216
Lingham (Funk) [SDRMFSLSF MDRTD, MF] AY421 6217
Lingwood (Gibbs) [DDRFMM FL, SLLTDRM, M] BV662b 6218
Linton (Holmes) [MMRRDFFM, MMSFMR, SS] AP347b 6219
Linton (Stanton) [MDFMRSD, RMSFMR, SSL] BY233 6220
Linwood (Rossini) [MDRMSFM RMD, SDMSLS] I496; AO223; BE416; BH140 6221
Lisbon (Read) [DLSDRM, MRD FMR, SDDD] H78; I64; L39; T173b; V7; AE356; AJ25; AM445; AO14; AX61; BR17

6222
Lischer (Schneider) [SDRMFLS, DMSSFSFM, S] G394; H77; I 67; L47; U442; V61b; Z444; AI90; AM325; AO185; AT21; AU175; AV5; BB465; 6223
Lisle (Brethren hymnal, 1901) [DMMRDTLDT, TLTDRM, T] AQ148 6224
Listen to the gentle promptings (Weber) X Wilmot 6225
Listen to the lambs (Negro spiritual) [MRMDLD, MRM DLD, MRMD] AH602 6226
-----. R [SSSSSMSSS, SSSSTTL] 6227
Litany (---) [SLSMMRD, LLDDFM R, SL] AL606; AP776 6228
Litany (Brown) [MRDTDFM, RMDTDRLT, T] E651 6229
Litany (Bunnett) X Agnes 6230
Litany (Carr) X Spanish chant 6231
Litany (Gower) X Gower's litany 6232
Litany (Hervey) X Hervey's litany 6233
Litany (Monk) [DDTDTLS, DDTD TLS, MM] J153b; K207 6234
Litany (St Alban's Tune book, 1866) X Lebbaeus 6235
Litany (Scheffler. Heilige seelenlust. 1657) X Scheffler 6236
Litany (Scholefield) X Litany, No. 9 6237
Litany No. 1 (Bunnett) [SSLDFM MR, SDTDRF#S, S] BR221 6238
Litany, No. 1 (Turpin) [SSLSDMR, RRMFMRM, SF] D524 6239
Litany, No. 2 (St Alban's Tune book, 1866) X Lebbaeus 6240
Litany, No. 2 (Turpin) [SSLSDSL, LLTDTLS, TT] D525 6241
Litany, No. 3 (---) [SSF#SDLS, DDTDRRR, SS] D526 6242
Litany, No. 4 (Whiting) [DDMSL LS, MFSLRMFM, M] D527 6243
Litany, No. 5 (Hoyte) X Lebbaeus (St Alban's Tune book, 1866) 6244
Litany, No. 6 (Stainer) [MM MMFRM, MRDTLLT, DT] C142Ia; D529Ia 6245
Litany, No. 7 (Turpin) X Turpin's litany 6246
Litany, No. 8 (Turpin) [TT DMMRM, MRD#RLLL, LL] C142IIb; D529IIb 6247
Litany, No. 9 (Scholefield) [MMSMRDR, FFLFMRM, SS] C142IIIa; D529IIIa; AP196a 6248
Litany, No. 10 (Monk) X Words on the cross 6249
Litany of the Passion (Dykes) [MMMMSRR, RRRRFDD, D] A233a; B142b 6250
Litany of the Passion (Nicholson) [MRFMRDR, RMSFMR RD#, R] F587 6251
Litlington Tower (Barnby) [DMLSDDRD, FMRDSSF#S,] L69; AB6 6252
Little Baddow (Gibbs) [MLL SMFM, MRMDDT, MLL] X 646a 6253
Little brown church (Pitts) X Wildwood 6254
Little clusters (---) [MFSDM DDT, RMFTRFFM,] D577; V332 6255
Little Cornard (Shaw) [LDRM ML, SMDRML, DTLS] A131; F269; J321; R478; W372; X 64; AF106; AL248; BV314; BY374 6256
Little David (Negro spiritual) [SSMSMDLS, DDMS, SSMS] Y317 6257
Little flock (German, 15th c) X Kommt her zu mir 6258
Little flower (Moskowski) [MMR#R#MMS, SDDRRRSS, M] Y14 6259
Little hands (Thomson) [DDSS DR, RMFMFSM, SST] AP 780 6260
Little King, so fair (Slovak) hymn) [DRMDTLTS, LTDMRD TD] BQ125 6261
Little ones like me (Holsinger) [MMMDFMR, RDRDRMD, MM]

AY396 6262

Little reapers (---) [MSSSDS, SL SFM, MSSSL] AY483 6263

Little town (Chadwick) [MFSMM RRDL, DLDMFS, S#] Y325 6264

Livermore (Gower) [DDTDD# R, MMMFMR, SSMM] Z325 6265

Liverpool (Roberts) [LMSLLS, LDTL, DDSLTD,] W475a; X 586b; BY598b 6266

Liverpool (Wainwright) [DMSD SFMRD, LSF#SLDT] Y6; BE127 6267

Living (Lowden) X Living for Jesus 6268

Living for Jesus (Lowden) [MF MSRMFDRM, MRMRDT] Z 304; AT352; AU373 6269

-----. R [SSMMRRD, LLFFMR, DTS] 6270

Livingston (Oliver) [SSLF#SDM R, FFMRRLL, L] AO188 6271

Livorno (Sullivan) [MRDFMRMD RT, DRMLSM] AE279; AR380; AS357 6272

Llandaf (Evans) [MSDFMMRLS, SDTLMF#S] W247; BV616 6273

Llandaff (Moss) [MRDFMLRR, MSFMRM, SL] I358 6274

Llandinam (Williams) [MSTDMS LDTRD, MRFMR] W65b 6275

Llanfair (Williams) [DDMMSFMR, SFMFMRD, D] A104b; E143; F147b; G155; J99; Q191; R4; S12; W16; X149; Z112; AD159; AE23; AF19; AK166; AL114; AM205; AN193; AO222; AQ 317; AU32; AW117; BE307; BV 203; BY154; BZ 6276

-----. V [DDMMSFMR, SMFM RD, DD] BE307 6277

Llanfyllin (Welsh trad) [SDD RRMRD, DFFMMR, S] A570a; BZ 6278

Llangan (Welsh trad) [MRDMFSM D, MFSSFMRM] W445; AL495 6279

Llangloffan (Evans. Hymnau a thonaw, 1865) [MLLTTDTL, LRRDDT, ML] E207; G467; J334a; K367a; R231; S222; W397; X643a; Y234; Z546; AD232; AF436; AG271; AK 370; AL469; AM305; AN317; AP395; AQ227; AR507; BA 509; BK103; BV313; BY375; BZ 6280

-----. V [MMLLTTDTL, LRRDDT, M] AR507 6281

Llangoedmor (Welsh hymn mel) [DSMDFMFLD, DMDSRDT] E539; G418; W493b; X242; BY356 6282

Llangollen (Welsh hymn mel) X Lledrod 6283

Llangristiolus (Parry) [LMD LTLS#L, LDTLMRDT,] W 703; AM99 6284

Llanherne (Thalben-Ball) [DS LSDTDRMD, SFMFRD] S76; AF73; BY5b 6285

Llanilar (Welsh hymn mel) [LTDRMSF#M, MMMRDRM, L] E75b; X508a 6286

Llanllyfni (Jones) [LMMRDT, DTLLS#L, TDTL] E391; S247a; W464b; X453; AF356; AG314; BY478 6287

Llansamlet (Arthur) [MSDRS LTDRM, DFMRSM] W192 6288

Llansannan (Welsh hymn mel) [MLSLSMDR, MLSM RDTL,] E514; W337; X666; AF316; AN392; BE116 6289

Lledrod (Welsh hymn mel) [DDRDSMSD, MRRRSDLS,] A506; E556; Sap. 30; W634b; X488; AL534; BV31; BY208 6290

Llef (Jones) [LLLDRDTL, DRRMMRDT,] J298a; W161; AL142; AM75; BY514 6291

Lo, a gleam (Beery) X Juniata 6292

Lo, as the potter molds the clay (Jewish trad) X Kee hinay kachomer II 6293

Lo! He comes, with clouds descending (Pollock) X Parousia 6294

Lo! on the water's brink [MM

RDDDTL, LSSDRR, SS] BC97 6295

Lo, our Father's tender care (Rogers) [MMMDSSS, FFFRM S, MMM] BH82 6296

Lo! the clouds have burst (Cobb) X Moultrie 6297

Lo! the earth rejoices (Binder) [DDTDRR, MMRMF, SSFSL] BH248 6298

Lo! the heavens are breaking (German mel) [MMMFSM, FRMMR, MFSMF] AW434 6299

Lo! the mighty God (Stephens) [SSDRMRDSS, RMFFFFM,] BC264 6300

Lo, they come in glad procession (Bourgeois) X Bourgeois 6301

Lo, what a pleasing sight (Mason) X Gerar 6302

Lob sei demm allmächtigen Gott (Crueger) [DDRMSFMR, SDTL SSF#S,] J102; M513; N73; AZ 22-C 6303

Lobe den Herren (Stralsund G-B. 1665) X Praise to the Lord 6304

Lobe den Herren, o meine (Anhang der Seelen-harpff) [DSDDTDRMFFMR, RRMF] Q26; AF17; AK6; AW513 6305

Lobet den Herren (Crueger) X Oblation 6306

Lobet den Herren, ihr (Vulpius) [SSSMRDTDLS, SSMLSF] Q19; X475; AM4 6307

Lobet und preiset (German trad) [SSSSFMFMRD, MMMMRD] BK11 6308

Lobt den Herrn, die morgensonne (Evangelisches choralbuch Halle, 1829) [DMSDFMRR, RMRSTLST] Q461; AA160; AN24; AQ63 6309

Lobt Gott (Hermann) X Hermann 6310

Lobt Gott (Vulpius) X Lobet den Herrn, ihr 6311

Lobt Gott, ihr Christen (Hermann) X Hermann 6312

Lodsworth (English trad) [DM DFLSMRD, DMDFLSM] E275; X336 6313

Lofsongur (Bohemian Br., 1531) [MDMSLSF#S, FLFSFMRM,] M412 6314

Log College (Warren) [MMRLD TRD, MRSLDT, TD] C365; U 329 6315

Logan (Modern harp) [SMRDDT LSDMR, RMRDT] BR291 6316

Lohengrin (Wagner) [SSMDM DDTL, LLSF#FMR] Y25 6317

Lombard Street (Russell) [LD MMRDRMRDLL, LDM] A575; X698; AF422; AN72; AR400 6318

L'Omnipotent (Bourgeois) [LSL TDRMRDTL, DTLSL] E538; F100; W95; X347; AF467; AN232; AQ234 6319

London (Sheeles) X Addison's 6320

London new (Scottish Psalter, 1615) [DSMDSLDT, SDMSR D, SD] A310; B216; C216; D427; E394; F181; J369; N408; W520b; X503; AD89; AP34; AZ14-I; BA85; BD50; BJ40; BR263; BV319a; BY 77a 6321

Londonderry (Irish trad) [TD RMRMLSMRDL, DMFS] C280 b; G145; X230; Y79; Z236; AB394; AC109; AH473; AL 512; AN559a; AW396; BE412; BF447; BV262; BY183 6322

Londonderry air (Irish trad) X Londonderry 6323

Lone Acre (Mueller) [MMMMMM RM, MLLLTT, ML] AK127 6324

Lonely midnight (Howard) [SS SLLSFMRD#RS, SSSL] Z203; AC89; AH251; BD215; BF287; BX531 6325

Lonesome Valley (American trad) [LDDMRDLD, DDD MMSLS,] BK168 6326

Long have they waited (Warren) [SMFSSSSLDDD, SSSDR] AX 214 6327

-----. R [SSSLSSDDDD, RRRR DD] 6328

Long live the Pope! (Ganss) [SDDDTLTDRM, MFMRDR,] BO206; BQ122 6329

Long Milford (Barnby) [SLRDTD RM, DFFMRDRT] BX507 6330

Long Mynd (Thatcher) [DDRDDTD, LSLSMFS, SL] X465 6331

Longden (Thompson) [SLDLSMRD, MSLSMDR, M] G153 6332

Longfellow (Bullard) [MMRRFF MM, MSMDRM, SS] AJ32 6333

Longstaff (Stebbins) X Holiness 6334

Longwood (Barnby) [MMFSMRDT D, MMF#STL] D422b; J320; S 48; T357a; W566; AD23; AM311; AN69; AO330; AR205; AS174; AT166; AV150; AW164; BF416; BI69; BX44 6335

Lonsdale (Troyte) [DDRMDFMR, RMSFMRDT,] AJ98 6336

Look down on us (Gibson) [SM RDFMRLSSF#, FFSRF] AV 420a 6337

Look for the beautiful (Belden) X Belden 6338

Look for the waymarks (Belden) [DMFSDMRDRM, MLTDDR] BB671 6339

-----. R [SSSSMRDDDRMM, LLTD] 6340

Look to the Lamb of God (Black) [MMFMSDRMFS, SSMDMR,] AX256 6341

-----. R [SSLSDT, RFSTLS, MMFS] 6342

Look up and see (Graun) [SDLS TD, RFMRDTTDD, L] AZ578-A 6343

Looking to Jesus (Keegan) [SSS SSSSLTDS, DTLLL] AU357 6344

-----. R [SSSM, MRDL, DLSSS DRM] 6345

Looking unto Jesus (Loes) [MM R#MSRRDRM, LLS#LDS] AU 132 6346

-----. R [SSF#SLSMSF#F, LLS#LTL] 6347

Lord, a little band (Showalter, arr) X When I see the blood 6348

Lord, accept our true devotion (Daynes) [SLSDTLLS, FMFL SFM, S] BC101 6349

Lord, accept into thy kingdom (Schreiner) [DRMSFMRD, MF#SSLSF#S,] BC100 6350

Lord, be thou with us still (Heller) [SDRMSMSLM, SDRMSMS] BH39 6351

Lord, cause thy face on us to shine (Mason) X Hebron 6352

Lord, dismiss us (Rousseau) X Greenville 6353

Lord, dismiss us (Sicilian mel.) X Sicilian mariners 6354

Lord, do thou guide me (Heller) [SMDTLSTRFM, SLL TLS,] BH22 6355

Lord, for tomorrow (Palmer) X Vincent 6356

Lord, give us a vision (Davis) [DMMMRDMSSLS, SMMMD] AX195 6357

-----. R [SDDDDTLS, DMM DRMR, S] 6358

Lord, I believe (Gould) [MD RMMMMMFS, SFMRFM] BR332 6359

Lord, I hear of showers of blessing (Bradbury) X Even me 6360

Lord, I want to be a Christian (Negro spiritual) X I want to be a Christian 6361

Lord, I'm coming home (Kirkpatrick) [SMMDDLDLS, DD MMR, SM] AI213; AL474; AP431; AS203; AT237; AX 302; BB560 6362

-----. R [MMDDDL, SMMDR, SMMDD] 6363

Lord, in this sacred hour (Shelley) [MSMFMF, RRR DTM, MRDT] BH112 6364

Lord, in thy presence (Havergal) X Evan 6365

Lord, into thy sacred dwelling (Grauman) [LTDRMFFM, M RDTLLS#, L] BH144 6366
Lord Jesus, by thy Passion (Kingo. Gradual, 1699) X O Jesu, for din pine 6367
Lord Jesus Christ, be present now (Pensum sacrum. Goerlitz, 1648) X Herr Jesu Christ 6368
Lord Jesus Christ, my Saviour blest (Lindeman) X Herr Jesus Krist, min Frelser du est 6369
Lord Jesus, I long to be perfectly whole (Fischer) X Whiter than snow 6370
Lord Jesus, when I think of thee (A Monk of Gethsemani) [LD RMMMDR, MTDRMDTL,] BN36 6371
Lord, keep us safe tonight (Beethoven) X Gorton 6372
Lord keep us steadfast (Luther) X Spires 6373
Lord, lay some soul upon my heart (McKinney) X Leila 6374
Lord of all being (Linley) [SLT DDRRMFM, MRDRSS] BI27 6375
Lord of all being (Robertson) X God of our Fathers, known of old 6376
Lord of hosts (---) X Purity 6377
Lord of life (Darmstadt G-B. 1687) X Gregor's 211th metre 6378
Lord of life and king of glory (Herbert) X Burwell 6379
Lord of light, whose name outshineth (Sweney) X Hast du Jesus 6380
Lord of might (Page) [SDTLSDM RD, RMMFMRD,] AM229; AP83 6381
Lord of nations (Woollen) [SLTDT DRMFM, FSMDRL] BM95 6382
Lord of our life (Barnby) X Cloisters 6383
Lord of spirits (Reissiger) [SD DTLSLS, SSSFMRM, S] P383 6384
Lord of the Church (Hastings) X Bremen 6385
Lord of the nations (Fillmore) [DDDRRMRDR, DDDRMFM] AE406; AR394; AS361 6386
Lord, speak to me (Hews) X Holley 6387
Lord, this day thy children meet (Showalter) [MMRRD RM, MFSMRMF#S, S] AS 395 6388
Lord, thou wilt hear me (Daynes) [MFSLSMRMFSFR, MFSL] BC265 6389
Lord, thy word abideth (Blunt) X Merrial 6390
Lord, to thee (Bourgeois) [DTLSDRMD, MMFMDRD, D] AI441; AJ415 6391
Lord victorious (Freylinghausen G-B. 1704) X Conqueror 6392
Lord, we ask thee (Beesley) [SSDDRRM, SSFMRRMR, S] BC119 6393
Lord, we come before thee (Dean) [LTDDTLS#L, LLS MSFM, L] BC142 6394
Lord, we come before thee now (Malan) X Hendon 6395
Lord, what offering shall we bring (Weinberg) [SMRDSM RD, RMSMRMS, S] BH148 6396
Lord, when at thy command (Woodbury) X Nearer home 6397
Lord, who at Cana's wedding feast (Browne) [SDMMDD LL, SRFFMR, RS] BQ150 6398
Lord, with devotion (Hay) X Hillery 6399
Lord's Day (Mendelssohn) [SSMFSMDR, FMRMFLS, M] AC7 6400
Lord's Supper (Naegeli) X Dennis 6401
Lorelei (Silcher) [SSLSDTLSF, FMMRDRM,] P372; AI35; AV159 6402

Lorica patricii (Irish trad) [MF MRSFMRD, MFMRSDT] W505 6403

-----. R [LDTLLTTDDRDTL SL, L] 6404

Lorraine (Darmstadt G-B. 1698) X All saints 6405

Los Angeles (Smith) [DDMMRD SS, FMDDRTLT,] I664b 6406

Lost and found (Tilleard) [SLLSS DDT, LLSDSFM, S] M634; O 338 6407

Lost forever (Warren) [SSSLSM D, DDDRDLS, SS] AX289 6408

Lost in the night (Finnish folk) [MMMDTLLLSMD, RRRSL] P 396 6409

Lostwithiel (Turle) [SSSSSSS, SL LLTDT, DS] AB85 6410

Lottie (Bradbury) [SSMMRM, SSMMRD, SLLD] AY262; BB64 6411

Loud let the swelling anthems rise (Norden) [SDDTTLLS, SMRDTL, LF] BH78 6412

Louez dieu (Genevan Psalter, 1562) [DDFSLL#D, LDL#LFSF, LS] E377; X473 6413

Louez dieu (Minor reading: Genevan Psalter, 1562) X Holy Name (Major reading) 6414

Loughborough (Briggs) [MSMRLT D, RMSLLR, RMF#] X194b; Y336 6415

Loughborough College (Briggs) [DMSDRTD, MRDTLLS, DM] X243; AN426 6416

Louisville (Zundel) [SDMRTD, SL DTLS, DTDR] AJ412 6417

Louvan (Taylor) [SSDRMDRDRM, MFMRMD] G307; H109; I266; J170; L526; S87; T188; U14; V208; Y1; Z151; AA235; AB 187; AC31; AD85; AE57; AF90; AG44; AH215; AI33; AJ274; AK375; AO320; AR74; AS80; AV40; AW53; BB242; BF231; BZ 6418

-----. V [SDRMDRDRM, MFM RMDM] AD85 6419

Love (Gordon) X Gordon 6420

Love (Richardson) [DMRDFLSF M, SF#STLS, S] L156; AO82; BA66 6421

Love (Young) [SSFFMMRD, DRMFLS, FM] BE30 6422

Love at home (McNaughton) X Home 6423

Love consecrates the humblest act (Showalter) X God moves ... 6425

Love divine (Hiller) [MMMRR DDT, DRMFMRRD,] AZ96-F 6426

Love divine (LeJeune) [DRM MFMMR, RMSFRMD,] A479 b; B226; C226a; D432c; J 397b; L189; N192; O114; S 308b; Y85; AB277; AC191; AE415; AG243; AK392; AM 460a; AO164; AR150; BA 547; BF442 6427

Love divine (Sicilian mel) X Sicilian mariners 6428

Love divine (Stainer) [DDDRM RDTS, DSSF#SMR,] D207b; F205b; V701; BV625a; BX 118a 6429

Love divine (Zundel) X Beecher 6430

Love divine, No. 2 (LeJeune) X Love divine 6431

Love each other (Byers) [MM DMLSSM, DDRRMFM, M] AX543 6432

-----. R [SDTLDLSM, SDT RDLS, M] 6433

Love found me (Gilmour) [DM SSSSSS, DSS, SLSSS] AX89; AY201 6434

Love incarnate (Pettman) [SL MRMDS, DRMFSDRMR,] BV105b; BY103b 6435

Love is come again (French trad) [LMF#RMD, RRMDTL, LMF#R] BG149; BN89; BZ 6436

Love lifted me (Smith) [SLS MSLS, SLTDRT, LTL] AH 340; AT212; AU352; AX 330 6437

-----. R [MSRD, DMTL, LLTD SDD, R] 6438

Love not the world (Holsinger) [MRDSMRMD, DDDFFM, MR] AX409; AY385 6439

-----. R [RRMFLSFM, DDMSM R, MR] 6440
Love of God (Beery) [MMMRDRD T, RRRMDRM, S] AR88 6441
Love of the Father (Edmunds) [LS#S#LTDTLLS#, LLSFMM] BL99 6442
Love that will not let me go (Peace) X St Margaret 6443
Love, the fount of light (Lindeman) X Kjaerlighed er lysets kilde 6444
Love unknown (Ireland) [MSLM RD, RMFSML, LTLS] F192; W76 a; X127a; BV155; BY143a 6445
Lovely (Edwards) X Rhosymedre 6446
Lovely appear (Gounod) [MMSSLL DDS, DDLLDS, M] AH619 6447
Lover den Herre (Stralsund G-B., 1665) X Praise to the Lord 6448
Love's consecration (Kolb) [SM FMDDLS, DTDFMR, SM] AY268 6449
Love's offering (Parker) [MRDD TT, DRSM, MRTRDD,] G464; N662; R299; S407; U277; Y229; Z303; AB263; AC252; AD322; AE281; AF405; AG246; AK396; AN558; AO493; AR377; AT401; AV214; BB478; BF502 6450
Loving kindness (Caldwell) [SD DDRMDRRR, MFSFMD] H284; I539b; L163; U148; V190; AI2; AM138; AO404; AS15; AT26; AV 11; AX17; AY28; BB667; 6451
-----. V [SDDDMRRR, MFSFM RDR] V190 6452
Loving Shepherd of thy sheep (Catholic Hymn tunes, 1849) X Lugano 6453
Lovingly, tenderly calling (Ogden) [DRMFLSM, RMFM RD, DRM] BB572 6454
-----. R [SMMMRDTSSS, SFFF MR] 6455
Lowe (Lowe) X Praise 6456
Lowell (Bortniansky) X St Petersburg 6457
Lowell (Mason) X Diligence 6458
Lowell (Nichol) [DSMSDRMF, SDRMRDT, D] AI189 6459
Löwen, lasst euch wiederfinden (Klein) [RRFSLTDL, LTDRDTL, R] Q470 6460
Lowenstern (Lowenstern) [MS LTDTLRDT, MRDTLS] X 670 6461
Lower lights (Bliss) [SLS MRDTL, LLRDTDR, S] G254; U316; Z313; AC253; AE290; AH438; AI186; AS351; AT 300; AU262; AW448; AX193; AY525; BB628; BC159; BZ 6462
-----. R [DDFFFFFM, MMM RLRR, S] 6463
Lower Marlwood (Harwood) [DMSDDRMF, LSFMS, TDR] BV80a 6464
Lowliness (Hanby) X Adoration 6465
Lowrance (Campbell) [MMSFR M, DDMRTD, MSF#M,] V355 6466
Lowry (Lowry) X All the way 6467
Lowry (Lowry) X Need 6468
Lowry (Lowry) X Something for Jesus 6469
Loyal and true (---) [MSLM RDD, MSLMRDR, MS] AX447 6470
-----. R [SLTDTLSM, DFLSM DS, S] 6471
Loyalty to Christ (Cassel) X Lambdin 6472
Lubbock (McKinney) [SDMR# MDMFSSM, DMRRM] AT231; AU397 6473
-----. R [SSLLLFLS, SSF# RRMF#S] 6474
Lucas (Lucas) [SDDDDTDRR RR, SMMDR] I568; BC17 6475
Lucas (Wilson) [SSLSDTRD, MRFMMRL, L] AI85 6476
Luccombe (Fuller-Maitland) [MMFSMRDRMM, SLTDTL] E641b 6477
Lucerna, laudoniae (Arthur)

[SSMDRML, SDFMDMR, MD] W17; AL15b 6478

Lucerne (Strassburg Psalter, 1539) X Psalm 68 (Greiter) 6479

Lucerne (Willis) [SSMDTRRD, DTTLDLS, S] C93b; N12; AC 14; AO50; BA643; BF209; BK 42 6480

Lucia (Donizetti) [SSSDMRDS, DTLTDRSM] AI352 6481

Lucile (Gabriel) [DTLSDFMRD, DTDFMRR] AJ258 6482

Lucis creator (Angers church mel) [LLDLSDRM, RSLSF#M RM] E51b; X37b; AN61; AQ 273 6483

Lucis creator (Sarum plainsong, M 4) X Conditor alme 6484

Lucis creator (Sarum plainsong, M 8) [SLSFLDDSLSFSS, SR] A163a; E51 6485

Lucis creator optime (Plainsong, arr. 1539) X To God on high 6486

Lucius (Kingsley) [SSMDTTLL, LRRSFM, SS] BA840 6487

Luckington (Harwood) [DMSDDRL SFM, SLRT, DL] F375; W15a; BV243; BY13 6488

Luconer (Coleridge-Taylor) [SSLSMMMFMT, DRMTLD] Y36 6489

Lucy (Brahms) [MMSMMS, MS DTLLS, RMF] G600; AI205; AR127; AX59 6490

-----. V [MSMSMSDDTLLS, RMFR] AI205 6491

Ludborough (Matthews) [DMFSLS FM, MMRDDTLS,] B8; F473; W188b 6492

Ludovica (Lindeman) X Easter glory 6493

Ludwig (Lindeman) [DSLSFMRM, SLDTLS, DS] M86; O50; P268 6494

Ludwigsburg (Bourgeois) X Bourgeois 6495

Luebeck (Freylinghausen. Geistreiches G-B. 1704) [DMSSLTD, TDRTLLS, MF] A253; B47; C 47; D322b; E552; F39; J323; K32; M107; O63; Q2; R6; S27; V602; W170a; X645; AA106; AD99; AF75; AI447; AK45; AL342a; AN222; AW510; AZ 11-B; BA855; BB178; BI22-D; BL41; BN202; BV70; BX 96; BY234 6496

-----. V [DMFSSLTD, TDR DTLSS,] E552 6497

-----. V [DMSSLTD, TRST LLS, SD] M107 6498

-----. V [DRMFSSLTD, TDR SLTL] R6 6499

-----. V [DMFSSLTD, TRDT LLS, D] BI22-D 6500

Luebeck (Darmstadt G-B. 1699) [DDTDLTD, MMRSFMRD, D] M435; Q55; AA414 6501

Luella (Whitney) [MDSF#SDR D#RMDS, MDSF#] AO618 6502

Lueneburg (Ebeling) X Ebeling II 6503

Luetzen (Hermann) X Hermann 6504

Luffenham (Macfarren) [SSS LTDRSD, MMRRMFL] K440; AC52; AS98 6505

-----. V [SSSLTDRSS, MM RRMFL] AC52 6506

Lugano (Catholic Hymn tunes, 1849) [DDTDLLDD, DTLT DRDT] E529; W285a; AL 559a; AP684c; BQ45 6507

-----. V [DDTDTLLTT, DTDLTDR] AL559a 6508

Luise (Crueger) X Ratisbon 6509

Luke (Greek folk mel) [DRMM MMRMFLSSS, MR] A246; B350; C350; D562; G440; H452; I682; J497; K557; L450; P359; R460; S442b; V645; W82; Z213; AD475; AE433; AF483; AH553; AK 460; AM650; AO622; AP738a; AR549; AS398; AT506; AV86; AW427; BA832a; BB422; BD 64; BV346; BY120a 6510

-----. V [DRMRMSFMFLSSS, MFS] I682 6511

-----. V [DRMRMSFMRLSSS, MFS] W82 6512

-----. V [DRMMMMRMFLS

SS, FMR] AT506 6513
Lullaby (Geibel) [MMMRRD, SSSFM, LLLSS] AH268 6514
Lullay my liking (Holst) [DLT DLTDRTLS, LTDMR] BG182 6515
-----. R [MMF#STL, RDTL, LLTDTL] 6516
Lumetto (Arthur) [MDRMLDM SMS, SSLDMM] W671 6517
Lumina (Sarum plainsong, M 1) X Splendor paternae 6518
Lundie (Perkins) [SLSMRD, RDR MS, SLSMR] I529; AS288; AU 205; AX404; BB277 6519
Lüneburg (Ebeling) X Ebeling 6520
Lura (Reynolds) [SSDDDDRMSS, SFMRDR] AT214; AV352 6521
----. R [SSSLSMF, FFFSFRM, SS] 6522
Lusatia (Vulpius) [MRDTLTDD, RMFRMF#S, R] O105 6523
Lute-book lullaby (Ballet) [RRM FFSFM, LDLL#LSFF,] BG30 6524
Luther (Geistliche lieder. Wittenberg, 1535) [DDMRDRRM, D MFSMRD, D] B64; C64, 236a; D37; E4; F366b; G385; J113; K514; L580; M173; N265; O18; P56; Q293; R16; S342; V687; W211a; X672; AA552; AE15; AF271; AK361; AL170; AM240; AP301; AR13, 203, 614; AW521; AZ132-L; BA734; BB195; BJ 16; BV78; BX181; BY28; BZ 6525
-----. V [DDMRDRRM, DRMFS FMRD,] AR13 6526
-----. V [DDRMRDRRM, DRMFS FM] AR203 6527
-----. V [DDMRDRRM, DMFSFM RD,] AZ132-L 6528
Luther (Hastings) [SSLSFMRD, MRDFMR, MF] H238; L126 6529
Luther (Luther) X Spires 6530
Luther (Luther) X Ein feste burg 6531
Luther (American, 19th c) X Müller 6532
Luther League hymn (Haas) [DMDFRLS, MDDRMR, RMM] J567; K578; L532; M524 6533
-----. R [SDSMSDD, SLFRDT, SMT] 6534
Luther Seminary (Dahle) [DTL SSLTD, DRMFMR, RM] J287; O361 6535
Luther's chant (Zeuner) [SLTD LSFM, MRTDRDLT,] AV310; BX73b 6536
Luther's cradle hymn (Kirkpatrick) X Cradle song 6537
Luther's hymn (Geistliche lieder. 1535) X Luther 6538
Luther's hymn (Geistliche lieder. Wittenberg, 1531) X Luther (1535) 6539
Luther's hymn (Teutsch kirchenampt. Strassburg, 1525) X Aus tiefer not 6540
Luton (Burder) [SSLSFMRD, DDTLSFMF] D44b; H27; I217; M144; T100; V206; AA144; AJ145; AN15; AO 533 6541
Lutzen (Hermann) X Hermann 6542
Lux aeterna (Gounod) X Radiant morn 6543
Lux beata (Peace) [SLSSSSS LTD, TLTS, SL] D423b; S 303; T250; U201; AB221; AG219; AJ347; AM82; AP 600b 6544
Lux benigna (Dykes) [SDRM MRDLDLS, DTDR,] A430b; B244; C244a; D423a; E425; F298b; G514a; H347; I460; J523a; L392; N344; O546; P346; R331; S289; T39; U 240; V419; W568c; X554b; Y367; Z578; AB219a; AC 333; AD221; AE202; AF215; AG157; AH404; AI299; AJ56; AK315; AL436a; AN239; AO 327a; AP600a; AR423; AS 247; AT60; AU238; AV149; AW162; AY465; AZ601-A; BA685; BB403; BC112; BD

250; BE169; BF414; BK89; BR388a; BX263; BZ 6545

Lux coelestis (Basford) [SSSSFM R#M, DTLSSLDT] T164; AJ 242 6546

Lux dei (Miller) [DDSRSMFR, SSFMMRLS,] N168 6547

Lux eoi (Sullivan) [SSDSSFFM, LLSMRDR, S] A92; B520; C 520; D123a; F137; I402; J108; K116; M174; T345; U104; V 180; W126; AL387; AV268; AZ 167-H; BA233; BE115; BI4-D; BR189; BV178a; BY17b 6548

Lux fiat (Gounod) X Orient 6549

Lux mundi (Sullivan) [MMRDM RDSR, MDTLMR, S] D357b; AO341; AZ151-P; BA431; BO 203; BR419 6550

Lux noel (German trad) [SMD FRSFM, RDSFMMR, S] M620 6551

Lux perpetua (Whelan) [DMMMF S, SFFMMR, RMMM] K522 6552

Lux prima (Gounod) [DDDMRDT DS, MMMSFMR] B425; D312a; G334; J229; K438; L5; N466; R47; S26; V375; Z270; AB197; AD42; AG20; AH172; AL561; AM247; AO291; AW26; AZ89-E; BA495; BQ62; BR110; BY214b 6553

Lux prima (Macfarren) [MMMMM RR, FFSRFMM, MF#] AP659 6554

Lux prima (Stainer) [DDMSFLDS, MMRTDDTS] L4; V37b; AZ 86-D; BA769 6555

Lux vera (Gounod) X Lux prima 6556

Lux vitae (Barnby) X Barnby III 6557

Lydbrook (Spencer-Palmer) [MLDTLLSFFM, DMLSFM] BV637 6558

Lydia (Phillips) [SSDMRMSDFMR, SLSFM] L517; BY212b 6559

Lydia (Stebbins) [SLSDRLTLS, DSFMRSF#] AJ405 6560

Lyle Road (Finlay) [DRFMRD, MFSLS, SLDTL] BV195 6561

Lymington (Jackson) [SDDRMDS M, DLLSFM, SD] BY381 6562

Lynchburg (Hallstrom) [DRM DRMDR, MFSLSL, LD] A526b 6563

Lynde (Thuringian trad) [MDLSDRDRMLS, SF#SLF] AC54; AO627 6564

Lyndhurst (Blunt) X Merrial 6565

Lyndhurst (Lane) X Penitence 6566

Lyndhurst (Maker) [DRMFMM RD, D#D#D#RR#M, MR] L 386 6567

Lyne (Magdalen Hospital hymns, 1760) [DRMRDMF#S, SLSFM FRD,] E296; F454; S445; W565; X19; AK458; AN68; AQ152; BD106; BY719 6568

-----. V [DDRMRDMFS, SS LSFMF] AQ152 6569

Lyngham (Jarman) [DMFSLSFM FMDRTD, MF] ALSuppl; BY 200b 6570

Lynne (Burt) [DDRMMMRMS FMRD, MM] A508; J548; AF 491 6571

Lynton (Jamouneau) [MMMRM SFM, SSS#LMF, TT] AJ391a 6572

Lyons (Haydn) [SDDRMDFFM R, SDDRMF] A260; B254; C 254; D467; F226; G4; H11; I106; J446; K294a; L75; M 24; N333; P32; R26; S198; T197; U7; V13; Y59; Z94; AB14; AC36; AD3; AE3; AF 6; AG6; AH187; AI11; AJ285; AK11; AM13; AN6; AO56; AP258; AQ25; AR33; AS2; AT20; AU2; AV34; AW7; AX 9; AY423; BA20; BB75; BC 146; BD27; BE18; BF167; BH60; BI30; BK65; BR65; BX10; BZ 6573

-----. V [SDDRMMDFFMR, SDDRM] M24 6574

Lyons (Haydn) X O purest of creatures (Paderborn G-B. 1765) 6576

Lyra (Lyra Davidica, 1708)

X Easter hymn 6577
Lyra (Root) [SFMMMMMRM, SMRRDRM,] AP645b 6578
Lystra (Wesley) [SMFMRSDRTD, RMFSL] A447 6579
Lyte (Holbrook) [MFLSFM, SDMRLTS, SDR] L118; AJ204 b; AO284 6580
Lyte (Temple star) [MFSLSSMD FMMR, MFSL] AY309 6581
Lyte (Wilkes) [DLMFFM, MMM LTD, DDDD] B408; C408a; D333a; K340; V703 6582
Lytham (Lightwood) [MRDSDDTT, LSLTDRM, M] G453 6583
Lytham (Malley) [MR#MFMMRDR M, FSLSMM] AJ253 6584
Lytlington (Nicholson) [MRDM SDFMRDRD, SMR] A466; F332b; AF393 6585

M

M.I.A. we hail thee (Robinson) [SSLSMT, RDSDT, RRD#RF] BC111 6586
-----. R [MSRDDT, FTMRDS, SMRD] 6587
Mabon (Murray) X Eudora 6588
Mabyn (Brown) X St Mabyn 6589
McAfee (McAfee) [MMR#MM FMF, RRRSFM, MM] R318; AE225; AR478; AT301; AU 273; AW239; AX50; BB681 6590
-----. R [DLLFLLS, SFMFSM, DLL] 6591
Maccabaeus (Handel) X Judas Maccabaeus 6592
McCabe (Gabriel) [SSDDDSDRM MM, FMRMR] AT457; AU117; AV381; AX212; AY330 6593
-----. R [MFSLSFMMM, FMRFMRM,] 6594
McCabe (Widdeman) [DRMFMM RDRDTD, MFSF] BB120 6595
McComb (Sims) [SDRMFMRD, SLTDLLS, S] AT384 6596
McConnell (McConnell) [MFSD RMFMRLR, DTTLS] AT209 6597
-----. R [MSDMRMRDL, TDTLSFM] 6598
McConnelsville (Morris) [SS SSMSDRMS, DTTTTD] AT230; AX261 6599
-----. R [MDLSMLS, MFMR LMR, MS] 6600
McDaniel (Gabriel) [MFSLT DDRMMFM, RDDL] AT310 6601
-----. R [SMMRMDM, RDDL DDDS, M] 6602
Macfarren (Macfarren) [MF MLSDRM, MRSTLS, SL] M 565 6603
McGranahan (McGranahan) [SSDSMLSS, SDTTLTD, S] AT114 6604
Mach hoch die tür (Lemke) [SMDDTDRTS, SSLTDLS] Q73a 6605
Mache dich, mein geist, bereit (Rosenmüller) X Nassau 6606
Mach's mit mir Gott (Schein) X Eisenach 6607
Macht hoch die tür (Freylinghausen. Geistliche G-B. 1704) [MSFMRDRMR, SFF MRMR] J8b; K7; M330; Q73b; X77; AK92; AM146; AW523; AZ459-A; BA151 6608
-----. V [DSFMRDMR, SFF MMRRD,] AK92 6609
Macht hoch die Thür (Stobaeus) X Lift up your heads 6610
McIntosh (American trad) X Amazing grace 6611
Mack (Frederick) [DMSSFF, RFLLSS, RSF#S] AR606 6612
McKee (Negro mel) [DMSS SSLL#L#L, SLDDLSLD,] A263a; R479b; AF415 6613
Maclagan (Maclagan) X Newington 6614
McPherson (Fisher) [MFSLL RMFSS, DRMSMR] AR385 6615
Madagascar (Ruud) [DMRM

F#SSF#S, SLSLTDT] J494b 6616

Maddermarket (Shaw) [SMSSDRDT LTD, RMRDR] X396a 6617

Madison (Willis) [SFMRDTL, LLTDTLS, SL] AS381 6618

Madison Avenue (Bingham) [DDLDRMD, RMDMFSM, DT] AR577 6619

Madrid (Carr) X Spanish chant 6620

Madrid (Matthews) [DTLSFMFS DDTD, MRDT] BY451 6621

Maelor (Hughes) [LLDFRM, MSM RDT, TMF#S] BY175b 6622

Maer Down (Sheldon) [SLSFMDR M, TDRMFTLR,] BV53 6623

Maesgwyn (Edwards) [LMDLRM, LDTLT, RTDRM] BY506b 6624

Magda (Williams) [SDLSMDRMF SM, SDLRS] A482b; E273; F341; W243b; X53; AQ78; BY 344 6625

Magdalen (Stainer) X Beati 6626

Magdalen College (Hayes) [DM SDLFFM, RMFSLTDR,] A314; E457; F389a; S482; W543b; X690; AJ96; AZ92-C; BV531a 6627

Magdalen Tower hymn (Rogers) X Hymnus eucharisticus 6628

Magdalene (German. 16th c) [DSSSSLLDTLSFM, MSF] E 392; X591 6629

Magdalena (Stainer) [DFMRDSS, LSDDRM, F#SD] B239; C239a; D603a; I200; M162; O203 6630

Magdalena (Spohr) X Spohr 6631

Magdeburg (Bourgeois) X Commandments 6632

Magherafelt (Hogan) [MMRDRM D, TDRMFLS, TD] AP550 6633

Magi (Lahee) [SDDTDS, FMR RD, MLLTD] D362a 6634

Magill (Perkins) [DRMDLSDDRDR MDRMD] L244 6635

Magister (Mason) [DRMDFMMR, DFMRDTD, D] BY479a 6636

Magnae deus potentiae (Plainsong, M 2) [RRRMMFRD, DFSLFFMF] E61 6637

Magnificence (Everett) [SDSM RDTL, LSSSFM, SD] AR97; AS89 6638

Magnus (Herbert) [DMMMRDM SSLS, MRRMF] AJ123; AM515 6639

-----. R [SMRDRD, SLTDS, DRDLS] 6640

Magyar (Eneke) [LMLTRDTL, DSDRMRD, L] AF377; AK306 6641

Maidstone (Gilbert) [SLTDRM FMRM, SFMRM] A392; B467; C467; D301; Eap. 20; F240b; I469; J184; K422; N326; R441; V12; W235; AL200a; AO3; AP 317; BA333; BI105; BR309; BV563a; BX197; BY280; 6642

Mainz (Mainz G-B. 1661) [DR MRMSFM, MRDTLTLS,] A76a; B161; C161b; D103c; E115; F 118; G138; J84; W99; X138a; AD151; AH113; AK150; AL95; BL21; BM80; BN33; BO262; BP24; BQ23 6643

-----. V [DRMRMSFM, MRDR LTLS,] BL21 6644

Mainz (Cologne G-B. 1623) X Hosmer 6645

Mainzer (Mainzer) [SSSDTLLS, LFSMDTLS,] B284; C367b; D279a; K253; V3; W333; AB 395; AL353; AP269b; AS97; BA767; BX193; BY33; BZ 6646

Mainzer (Mainzer) X Humility 6647

Maitland (---) [MSSLSMDLS, SLTDMRL] D543 6648

Maitland (Allen) [MFSSDM RDLD, LSSDMR,] G276; H225; I428; L525; M394; N472; R68; T21; U196; V440; Z366; AE219; AH294; AI317; AJ28; AO384; AR317; AS330; AT428; AU153;

AV204; AX426; AY113; BA463; BB274; BZ 6649

-----. V [MFSSDMRDL, LSSDMR, M] M394 6650

Majestic sweetness sits enthroned (Hastings) X Ortonville 6651

Majesty (Neander) X Sieh hier bin ich, Ehrenkönig 6652

Majesty (Llewellyn) [LLLTLS, LLLTLS, LTDT] BV5 6653

Majesty (Schicht) [SSDFMRRD, SLRRMR, SS] BA795 6654

Make me a blessing today (Gilmour) [SDDDMDLS, SDDDMR, SD] AX416 6655

-----. R [SSMDRDLLS, SDDD MRD] 6656

Make me a blessing (Schuler) X Schuler 6657

Make me a channel (Smyth) X Euclid 6658

Make we joy (English carol. 15th c) [MMMSFMRD, MSMRDTL, M] BG23 6659

Make we merry (Shaw) [RMFSFM RD, DRMFSFMR] BG172 6660

Maker (Maker) [SSLSMMSFD# R, MDDSFM] I89; Z218 6661

Maker (Maker) X St Christopher 6662

Malabar (Williams) [SFMLLSS D, DTLSMSS,] A201 6663

Maldwyn (Welsh, ca 1600) [MLLT DDTLTS# L, TDDRT] Q278; X 69 6664

-----. V [MLLTDDTLDTLLS#, TDD] X69 6665

Mallett (Hall) [MSFMRFFM, MMRTLSMR,] B236; AB361 6666

Malone (Emerson) [SDDDMFSL, LLLLLTTD,] T117; AJ168 6667

Malvern (The Hallelujah, 1849) [SMSDRD, DLDRMR, DTLS,] J121; V564a; W364b; AL145; AW131; BY640 6668

-----. V [SMSDRD, DLDRMR, SSFM] V564a 6668a

Malvern (Mason) [MMMMMMRMF S, SLLSMF] G24; I37b; M26; AE26; BB515; BZ 6669

Mamre (Scholinus) [SLSLTDS, DTRDMR, SMR] W569 6670

Man of sorrows (Bliss) [SSS MDDT, LLSDTLS, SS] W693; AM175; AN213; AR166; AS 135; AT163; AU257; AV321; BV159; BY186 6671

Man of sorrows (Slovak hymn) [LLS# LTDLT, MMRDTLS#, L] AM464; AY510; BQ19 6672

-----. V [LLS# LTDT, MMR DDT, LL] AM464 6672a

Manchester (Rounsefell) X I'll go where ... 6673

Manchester (Stebbins) [SSFRM DS, DMRMFRS, SS] Y161; AC 186 6674

Manchester (Wainwright) [DMRD DLSFM, DSFMLTD] E168; F472; L356a; V248; X673; BV281 6675

Manchester new (Wainwright) X Manchester 6676

Mandor (Emerson) [SMDTLSLS MMR, MSDLD] L84 6677

Manger (Crueger) [MDDR, MFFM, SLSMRMSF] M360; Q81; AA156 6678

Manger (Esmond) [MMFFSRMS, DDT, LLS, SS] D538a 6679

Manger (Garrett) [MRDMRDT D, SFMMR# M, MR] BR142 6680

Manger Throne (Steggall) [DSLSMRMD, RMLSDT, SD] B548; C548 6681

Manitou (Chippewa Indian mel) [DDDLLFFFLFFF, LLLL] Y315 6682

Mann (Mann) [SLSMRD, SMR DR, RMFLS] M621; AS434 6683

Manna (Barnby) [MRDLSSFM, MF# SDTLS, F#] BR27 6684

Manna (Gottschalk) X Mercy 6685

Manna (Schicht) [DMDLLRRT, SDDRRMMR,] F389b 6686

Mannheim (Filitz) [DMSSLSFM, MFSDMRD, S] A524; E426; F311; J142; K274; O215; W564a; X555b; AL216; AP

597; AW298; AZ585-C; BA852; BN111; BR500b; BV583; BY43 6687

Manoah (Rossini) [DRMRDTTLL, RMFMRDDT,] B401; C401; D663b; G378; H67; I105; L138; M277; N303; P375; R86; S94; T235; U69; V24; Z153; AB65; AD7; AE226; AG242; AH192; AJ331; AK213; AM436; AN224b; AO312; AR17; AS12; AT49; AV 35; AY134; BA35; BB25; BE121; BF251; BK81; BR356; BX116; BZ 6688

Manor Street (Shaw) [SDLDSLSF MS, DRMSFM,] X386f 6689

Mansfield (Barnby) [SDTRDM, RDLSSS, SDTR] S170; Z243; AK171 6690

Mansfield (Turpin) [SSSSLDRD, D TLMTDRM,] D243b; AP617 6691

Mansfield Road (Baker) [SMRDM S, SDRDLFRT, SD] BY500 6692

Mant (Morgan) [SDLSDRMFS, LF MRDTD] V11 6693

Mant (Barthélémon) X Autumn 6694

Mantegna (Williams) [MRDRMFM DL# L, MMSFL, M] X126 6695

Maple leaf for ever (Muir) [SM SMDLDS, TDRDTLS, F] P415 6696

-----. R [SMSDSLDS, SSSFMMR, S] 6697

Mar Saba (Barnby) X Hebron 6698

Mara (Wesley, S.S.) [MRFMRS, DRMFMR, SDDT] AZ577-A 6699

Marathon (Williams) [MMRMDLS L, DRMRDLSL,] X302; BV208 6700

Marburg (Crueger) [MMDTRDTL, TDRMFMMR,] AA204 6701

March to victory (Barnby) X To victory 6702

Marchfield (Collier) [SMRDTLTD S, STDRMSF] T234; AJ330; AO439 6703

Marching (Shaw) [MFSSLTDT, D RMRDLS, R] C63b; E503; F182; J529b; W214b; X678; Y163; AL448a; AN83a; BE364; BV414; BY559 6704

Marching home (Bushey) [DRM MMRDMS, SLDTLS, D] AY 145 6705

Marching to Zion (Lowry) X Come, we that love the Lord 6706

Marcus Whitman (Merrill) [SD RMSLML, LFSLLTST,] S418; AB346 6707

Marenzo (Crueger) X Nun danket 6708

Margaret (Matthews) [DRMM FMRDRM, MFSSM] A321; B83; C83; D319a; E585; F 363; G95; I122; J433; K541; N47; R184; S231; U79; W67; Z292; AB115; AC101; AD131; AE94; AF326; AG84; AH254; AK126; AL68; AM170; AO 130; AP180; AR142; AT82; AU138; AV123; BA88; BB 103; BF304; BV277; BY111 6709

-----. R [SSMFSDDT, LLSDRM RD] 6710

Margaret (Peace) X St Margaret 6711

Margaret (Roberts) [MMM MFMRDRM, SSSSLS] BY775 6712

Margaret Street (Hoyte) [SD LDRMRD, SMDFMRR, R] D99 6713

Margaretting (Brown) [DTLS# LT, LSFM, TTTTR#M,] C416 6714

Marguerite (Walker) X St Marguerite 6715

Maria (Alexis) [MSFMRRD, DT DFMR, RMM] N569 6716

Maria, hun er en Jomfru ren (Gebauer) [MMRDSSFM, MR SDTLS, M] O290 6717

Maria jung und zart (Cologne G-B. 1623) X Hosmer 6718

Maria mater gratia (German, 1669) X Cor dulce, cor amabile 6719

Maria, mater gratia (A Monk

of Gethsemani) [LTDTTLLSM, LTDTTLL] BN148 6720
Marias Wallfahrt (Brahms) X The quest 6721
Marias wanderschaft (German trad) X Mary's wandering 6722
Maribah (Mason) X Meribah 6723
Marietta (White) [SFMRDLS, MRDFMR, RMF] BB235 6724
Mariners (Rendle) [MRDMSS, LL MLS, SF#MST] G556; AB383 6725
Mariners (Sicilian mel) X Sicilian mariners 6726
Marion (Messiter) [DSMRDRM, MMDRMF#S, S] A579b; B537; C537; D520a; G358; I421; J555; N588; R407; S297; Y199; Z418; AB19; AC27; AD272; AE7; AF 345; AG209; AH183; AK7; AM 502; AN13; AO62; AP608; AR 336; AT17; AU285; AV47; AW 156; BA124; BB17; BD119; BF170; BK66; BZ 6727
-----. R [SS, SS, SFMRMRD] 6728
Markell (Keiffer) X And now, my soul, another year 6729
Marken (Tours) X Deventer 6730
Market Street (English) [DMFMR DTD, SDTLSF#S, S] L339 6731
Marlborough (Sullivan arr) [MM MMMSLSFFM, MDDTL] AB 312; BR417; BX108 6732
Marlee (Sateren) [LDTLTM, LR MFMLS#L, LD] J80; 6733
Marlow (Chetham's Psalmody) [DMMMDSSS, SMDFMR, DM] A547b; B488; C488; D508; H365; I8; L106; M57; T371; U474; V266; AA368; AM481; AO405; AR7; AS55; AW501; AX168; AY269; BA451; BB 486; BR239 6734
Marosa (Bain) [DMSDSLDS, FM DDTD, DM] BK25; BL89 6735
Marshall (Geer) [SSDLDS, MMM FDRM, SSS] C246b 6736
Marshall (Marshall) [MF SDDMRDLD, TLSMSDR,] AE 294; AI125; AU278; AW479; AX131; AY466 6737
-----. R [MFSF#SDTLS#L, TLSMSD] 6738
-----. R [MFSMS, DTLFL, DLSMSD] AI125 6739
-----. V [MFSDMRDLD, TLSMSDR,] AU278 6740
Marter christi (Gnadauer Choral buch, 1735) [DDTL RDTDSFMRD, DDT] AK152; AW537 6741
Martha (Clelland) [DSMRDTLS, LTDRMF#S, L] AM130 6742
Martha (Hammer) [MDFMMRD, LLSMRMR, MD] AZ205-S; BA786 6743
Martham (Maunder) [SSMRD LLS, SSSLDTLS,] I73; BY 69 6744
Marthina (Marks) [MFF#SD LSFM, MLTDTLS] AJ249 6745
Martin (Martin) [MFF#SDRM RD, STLFLSM,] R124; AH 381; AM696; AT274; AV366; AX480; BZ 6746
-----. R [DTLLSS, STLF, FLSM, SD] 6747
Martineau (Fairlamb) [SSSSLLS, SRRRDRM, SS] C534; AC 200; BD81 6748
Martins (Buck) [SLSFSDTLS MD, RMRMF#] A583; F283; X247; AD174; BL77; BY27 6749
Marton (Iszlai) [SSFMFSLS, LS FMRD, SS] AN131 6750
Martyn (Marsh) [MMMDRRR, MMSFMRD, M] A415c; B 223b; C223b; D335b; G338a; H348; I463c; J393c; K371c; L122b; M204; N419; O244a; P154; Q345; R216b; S233a; T6; U263; V331c; Y373b; Z414; AA107; AC157b; AD 212b; AE173; AF210; AG153a; AH355; AI245b; AJ10; AK316; ALsuppl; AM427b; AO336a;

AP417b; AR405; AS212; AT156; AU172; AV233b; AW158; AX 509; AY314; AZ205-K; BA523B; BB401; BC84; BF370; BP48; BR323b; BZ 6751

Martyr dei (Plainsong: medieval M 6) [DDRMMRMRRD, MSSS] A209a 6752

Martyr dei qui unicum (Hereford Hymnal) [RMFSFMRMM, MRM FMSS] E180 6753

Martyrdom (Wilson) [SDLSDRMR D, MSMDMR,] A410b; B124b; C124; D85; E367; F299b; G70; H48; I102; J388; K101; L242; M406; N111; P184; Q154; R 199; S16b; T37b; U101; V72; W457b; X449; Z163; AA214; AD 200; AE112; AF285; AG95; AH 285; AI74b; AJ192; AK153; AL 101a; AM195; AN20; AO170; AP19a; AR167; AT101; AU244; AV109; AW108; AX69; AY166, 182; AZ14-X; BA203; BB124; BD185; BE266; BV561a; BY292a; BZ 6754

-----. V [SDLSDRMRD, MSM RDMR,] M406 6755

Martyrdom (Wilson) X Liberty Hall (---) 6756

Martyrs (Scottish Psalter, 1615) X Plaintive martyrs 6757

Marvelous grace (Towner) [DT DRDRMRD, TTDRTDD] AE224; AM705; AR457; AT200; AX321 6758

-----. R [MDFM, RRRRMRD FM, MDF] 6759

Mary (Lewis) [DMRDTD, DRM FMR, RMFS] AJ30 6760

Mary! How sweetly falls that word (English hymnal: old) [SMSMR DTL, DSDDMR, SM] BO92 6761

-----. R [RRRRRRRFR, RFR DDTD] 6762

Mary Immaculate, Mother and Maid (Kittel) X Quedlinburg 6763

Mary Immaculate, Star (Udulutsch) [DDDRMD, RTDTL, DDDRM] BM56 6764

Mary Madgadele (Dykes) [DDRM FM, MMRDT, DDRMF] D 340b; Q516; S255a; W525b; AJ263; AP240; AV192; BA 662; BB388 6765

Mary the Dawn (Cross) [LL SL, SLTSL, LSLL, SLT] BM49 6766

Marylebone (Irish trad) [RM MMDTLSFM, RMDLTD] X 315a 6767

Marylebone (Parry) [MMRM DRMDS, FFMLLFM] I746 6768

Mary's wandering (German trad) [MLTDTLTLS, DTM F#SF#M,] BG93 6769

Maryton (Smith) [MMMFMRR R, SSFMDDT] A572; B197b; C493; G178; I232; J537; M 223; N94; P324; R304; S 364; T163; U271; W420a; Y214; Z307; AB258; AC 197; AD90; AE146; AF418; AG245; AH371; AI185; AJ 241; AK205; AL297a; AM 101; AN208c; AP448b; AR 233; AS342; AT385; AU 202; AV274; AW223; AY 467; BA443; BB346; BD 68; BE234; BF249; BK99; BR169b; BV380b; BX225a; BY63; BZ 6770

Masefield (McCutchan) [SLTD RD, SLTDRM, TDRM] G 152 6771

Mason (Belden) [MSFMRDRT D, SLSFMSF] BB31 6772

Mason (Harmonia sacra) [MM LTS# LTDRTL, MRDTL] X 220 6773

Mason (Mason) X Hebron 6774

Mason (Sherwin) [MRDDTT, DRMSFM, RDLS,] L304; T158; AJ235; BR58 6775

Mason's Chant (Bradbury) [SSSSSSSSD, SLLLDS, D] AJ153 6776

Massachusetts (Davis) [LLM MRMDR, TDRTLTL, L] BZ 6777

Massachusetts (Miller) [MM MRMFSM, LLLSDSFR,]

BB80 6778
Master, the tempest (Palmer) X Peace, be still 6779
Masters in the hall (French trad) [LMMRDR, MRDTDTLS#, LM] BG137 6780
-----. R [DTLS#LM, DTLS#L, MSFRM] 6781
Mater (Depew) [MMFSMDRM, FSDFFM, MM] AC318; AH498; AT504; AU41; BF614 6782
Mater dolorosa (Corner. G-B. 1625) X Christi Mutter 6783
Mater misericordiae (Scott-Gatty) X Spirit divine 6784
Materna (Ward) [SSMMSSRR, MFSLTS, SS] A584b; B510b; C510a; D403a; G491; H513; I605; J346; K525; L593a; M 504; N40; P413; R510; S411; T86; U339; V695; Y282; Z535; AB337; AC271; AD132; AE357; AF440; AG270; AH483; AJ126; AK443; AM37; AN383; AO514; AQ241; AR613; AS382; AT489; AU39; AV277; AW343; BA762; BB265; BC126; BD175; BF496; BH262; BI115; BK121; BR433; BX419; BZ 6785
Matheson (Davies) X Hampstead 6786
Mathilda (Strom) [SSSLSFSM, SFMRDR, RM] N623 6787
Matins (Hodges) [SSSFMRDM, S DDT, DTLS] C3b; D3b; AN88a; BD1; BX150a 6788
Matins (Shepherd) [SSDRSM, RDD RDT, TLSS] BR1 6789
Matthews (McKinney) [MRDRDLS LD, TTTTDRD] AT333 6790
-----. R [MMRDTDR, FFMRDRM, SS] 6791
Matthias (Monk) X St Matthias 6792
Mattie (Everett) [MMMSSLSM, MRMSFM, DS] AR6; AS57; AX503; AY367 6793
Mauburn (Noble) [MFSFMRM, DRMFMM,] A29b; B550; C 550 6794
Maud (Scott-Gatty) [MSFMMRD, RMFMRLS, MS] AO329 6795
Maxon (Glynn) [SLTDML, SM RDLM, DRM] A475 6796
May (Pollock) X How oft, alas 6797
May carol (English trad) [LL MRDDRMRT, RDTLSF#] BG47 6798
May-day garland (English trad) [DDMSMRTD, DDMSLFM, S] BH48 6799
May God depend on you? (Wilson) [MFSSDTTL, LDTLSFM, M] AU358 6800
-----. R [MSDTRDT, STRD# MRD, DD] 6801
May He who kept us (Rogers) [MMMFFRRMFM, SSLTSS] BH10 6802
May Hill (Watson) [MMSMDRM F, SSTSMF#S, L] BV442b 6803
May song (English trad) [SSM SSDRM, MRDMRDL, D] G436; S448; AH547; AL601 6804
May the Christ-life shine in me (Hugg) [SDMDTDRD, SS TTLLS, S] AX410; AY66 6805
-----. R [SMRDLSDRM, SMRDLSD] 6806
May the grace of Christ (Hymns and tunes, 1890) [DDDSDM MR, RMFFDRM, D] AX75; AY82 6807
May the words (Binder) [MR DRMDSRDTLTDMRR] BH 273 6808
May the words (Jewish trad) [MMMRDRM, LLLRLRM, FF] Sap. 18; AR668 6809
May the words (Serbian trad) [DDDDDDDDDTDLTDLT] Sap. 20 6810
Mayer (Mayer) [SDTDRMRD, MRDTLTDT,] M614 6811
Mayfield (Macey) [SDTDSLDS, MLSSMDMR,] BY476 6812
Mead House (Taylor) [SSDS DRMD, FMRDTLS, S] BV383 a; BY247 6813
Meadow Cove (Geneva Psalter, 1551) [DRMFMRDDTD, MR

MF#S, L] AQ166 6814
Meadows (White) [SMRDTDRDS, SLTDRMR,] D511d 6815
Mear (Williams) [DSSMMDMR, RMDSF#S, SL] C300; D393a; G617; H226; I592; L573; T216b; V290; AA354; AJ391b; AO584; AW299; AY183; BA808; BB39; BR213; BX112 6816
-----. V [DSSFMMRDRMR, RMDSM] AY183 6817
Mecklenburg (German) [DDRDMMF M, SFMRMRRR] BR452c 6818
Med sorgen og klagen hold maade (Luther. Christliche gesang. 1542) X Jam Moesta 6819
Medfield (Mather) [SDMRFMRD, TDRTLDTL] L334; X118; AM 38; AO140; BI4 6820
Meditation (Gower) [MMMMMM DD, DFFMRS, SSS] A65b; B 159b; C159a; G135; J77a; N108; R202; S157a; T143; U91; AB139; AD153; AF172; AG93; AH508; AJ1; AK149; AM184; AO162; AW104; BC201; BD99; BF314; BX111; BZ 6821
Meditation (Lewis) X Beloved 6822
Meditation (Perkins) X Lundie 6823
Mee chomocho (Binder) [MS#FM FS#, S#LTLS#LFS#M,] BH283 6824
Mee chomocho I (Jewish trad) [SSSLMRDTLS, MRDTLS] BH 142, 295 6825
-----. V [SLMRDTLS, MRDTLS DD] BH295 6825
Mee chomocho II (Jewish trad) [LMRMFM, LLD#TD#RD#, S#ML] BH298 6827
Mee chomocho III (Jewish trad) [SSLSSMMFFS, SSLSSL] BH307 6828
Mee chomocho (Jewish trad) X Rock of ages 6829
Mee chomocho (Kaiser) [SDMMRL DTLS, SDMSFL] BH281 6830
Mee chomocho (Lewandowski) [MMFMRRDTLS, LLFRDT] BH 270 6831
Meet me there (Kirkpatrick) [DR MMMMM, DMSSSSS, SS] AX603 6832
-----. R [SSSLSMD, TLSS SSLS, S] 6833
Meet Mother in the skies (---) [MR#MFMDLDDLS, MR# MFM] AY504 6834
Mehul (Mehul) X Gilead 6835
Mehul (Mehul) X Joseph 6836
Mein G'mut ist mir verwirret (Hassler) X Passion chorale 6837
Mein heiland (Thommen. Christen-schatz) [MSSSLMRD, R MRF#SDT] Q386 6838
Mein heiland nimmt de suender an (Hille) X Gregor's 217th metre-B 6839
Mein Jesu, dem die seraphinen (Dessler) X Gregor's 183d metre 6840
Mein Jesu, der du vor dem scheiden (Gregor) X Gregor's 107th metre 6841
Mein leben (Vulpius) X Cana 6842
Mein Salomo, dein freundliches regieren (Richter) X Gregor's 114th metre 6843
Mein Schöpfer, steh mir bei (Meyer) [DDRMMR, SFM RRD, DDRM] Q335; AA384; AQ210 6844
Mein Seel, o Herr, muss loben dich (Gesius) X Herrnhut 6845
Meine armuth (Freylinghausen) X Richter 6846
Meine hoffnung (Neander) [L S#LTDDTM, LSFMRRD, L] W448a; X442; AF339; AN219; AQ35; BJ69; BM3; BY492 6847
-----. V [LS#LTDDTM, LSFM RRM, L] BM3 6847a
Meine liebe lebet noch (Freylinghausen) X Jesus ist das schönste licht 6848
Meinen Jesum lass' ich nicht (Darmstadt G-B. 1699) X Luebeck 6849

Meinen Jesum lass ich nicht (Hammerschmidt) [SSLLTTD, RRDDTTLS, S] K325; M125; AA88 6850

Meinen Jesum lass ich nicht (Ulich. Lüneburg G-B. 1686) [MM FSRDRMR, RRMFSLS] AK42 6851

Meinhold (Lüneburg G-B. 1686) [MMMSFFM, MMRMFMRD, M] B414; C414; D248a; J186; K516; L570; N346; O33; V671; AI333; AO570; AP200; AR516; AS463; AZ83-A 6852

-----. V [MMFSSFFM, MMRM FMRD,] AZ83-A 6853

Meiningen (Meiningen G-B. 1693) X Munich 6854

Meiringen (Neefe) [SDMSMRFM, DTLSF#S, SD] J540; K139; U 40; AD364; AO529; BF491; BX 445 6855

Meirionydd (Lloyd) [SFMMRDR MM, SFMFMRD] A598a; C224; E473; G194; J355; M319; O504; R200; S156; W598; X629; Y235; Z234; AB287; AF426; AI221; AK305; AM118; AN90; AP627; AQ1; AT227; AW180; BE313; BK19; BV389; BY275; BZ 6856

Meirionnydd (Lloyd) X Meirionydd 6857

Meiromydd (Lloyd) X Meirionydd 6858

Meistersinger chorale (Wagner) X Da zu dir der heiland kam 6859

Melanchthon (Meiningen G-B.) X St Leonard 6860

Melanesia (Smith) [DMFSSLDS, LSSFMRLT,] D253c 6861

Melchior (Franck) [DSMDMFSLL S, LSRMF#] A594; B543; C543; J588; K521; M315; O610; Q619; AA559; AZ576-A 6862

-----. V [SSMRDMFSLLS, LSR MF#] M315 6863

-----. V [SMRDMFSLLS, LSRM F#S] Q619 6864

-----. V [DSMRDMFSLLS, LS RMF#] AZ576-A 6865

Melchior (Vulpius) X Lobet den herrn, ihr 6866

Melcombe (Webbe) [SSFMRD LS, SDTLSSF#S,] A111; B1; C1; D1; E260; F4; G35; I95; J201; K232; L82; M150; O 67; Q504; R45; S31; T449b; V35; W259; X31; AA167; AB 186; AD40; AE38; AF36; AG 22; AK353; AL207; AM121; AN37; AO84; AP122; AQ158; AS64; AW22; BA40; BB42; BD2; BE6; BF175; BN83; BO5; BQ139; BR126; BV43; BX239; BY268; BZ 6867

Melford ("M. B. F.") [MMSSF# SLS, MMMMSFMR,] S361; BI81 6868

Melita (Dykes) [DMMSSLLS, SDRTSSF#S,] A512; B415; C415; D184; E540; F487; G 480; J124b; K331; M190; R521; S492; T157; U363; V 644; W626; Z610; AA19; AB 380; AD456; AE61; AF429; AH216; AJ232; AK382; AL 261; AM243; AN574; AO410; AP709; AR67; AS358; AT61; AV69; AW169; AZ96-L; BA 890; BE12; BF264; BK124; BR507; BV408; BX289; BY 288; BZ 6869

Melling (Fawcett) [DSDRMFM RD, RMDLRDT] E373; W11b; X463; BV550; BY394 6870

Melmore (Martin) [SSSF#SLS M, MFMRMFSM,] T256; AI 264; AJ357 6871

Melody (Chapin) [SDRMRDLS, SDRMF#S, SF] H91; L151; V473; AY175; BZ 6872

Melody (Praetorius. Musae sionas. 1610) [DDDSSLTD, SFSMRR, DD] BK27 6873

Melrose (Maker) [DMSDTLS, MMRDRMF#S,] Y198; Z377; AB352; AC165; AD351; AE 398; AF434; AH460; AR604; AS388; AW384; BA881; BF 560; BK125 6874

Melrose (Scottish Psalter, 1635) [DSMFSFRM, FMDR MR, SL] E451; X686 6875

Melton (Mason) [DRMFMDMRR

DTD, TDRM] AO441 6876

Memoria (Wesley, S.S.) X Gratitude 6877

Memorial (Hodges) [MMFMRM RD, MMFMRDT, D] L402b 6878

Memories of Galilee (Palmer) [SDSMSRSF, STSRSDSM,] AU 437; BC38 6879

-----. R [SDRMSDRM, MRM FRMFS,] 6880

Memory (Harmer) [DMMRDTDF, SFFMRM, SM] Z454 6881

Mendebas (German trad) X Mendebras 6882

Mendebras (German trad) [DRM MMRDRDS, DMSSSF] G396; I68; L50; R70; S18; T116; U438; Z 443; AB9b; AD30a; AE52; AG 36; AH162; AI15; AJ170; AK 38; AM321; AO13b; AS38; AT 36; AU11; AV8; AW285; AX65; BB463; BR86; BZ 6883

Mendelssohn (Mendelssohn) [SDD TDMMR, SSSFMRM, S] A27; B 73; C73; D51a; E24; F60; G86; H138; I111; J25; K25; L224; M168; N34; O198; P136; Q94; R163; S11; T333; U59; V121; W46; X74; Y361; Z189; AA154; AB111; AC77; AD105; AE81; AF120; AG66; AH253; AI59; AJ3; AK102; AL59; AM168; AN169; AO126; AP171; AR128; AS101; AT81; AU142; AV83; AW85; AZ 205-R; BA163; BB111; BC60; BD211; BE310; BF286; BI94; BK 144; BL10; BO153a; BR147; BV112; BX206; BY98; BZ 6884

Mendelssohn (Mendelssohn) X Brightest and best 6885

Mendelssohn (Mendelssohn) X Trust 6886

Mendip (English trad) [SSFMSD TL, LSMDDR, DR] E498; W592a; X201; AN265; BE87; BY205 6887

Mendon (German trad) [DTDSDTDR, DMDLRDRT] A218; B201; C201; D313; G509; H97; I669; J415; K142c; L446; M218; N13; Q119; R370; S474; T25; V522; Y 189; Z120; AA4; AC293; AD29; AE30; AF238; AJ34; AK328; AL316; AM64; AN 290a; AO603; AP337; AR525; AS438; AV67; AW211; BA 350; BB210; BE228 6888

Mendota (---) [SSSMRDLS, SSSDTDR, R] AR350; AS352; AX162; AY364 6889

-----. V [SSSMRDLLD, LSSDTDR,] AY364 6890

Mensch, willt du leben selig lich (Walther) [MSSLTDTL, TDSLMSFM,] AA392 6891

Mentzer (Koenig's Harmonischer lieder schotz) [SMSLSFMRD, MRDRMFMR,] A302; K355a; L485b; M123; O10; Q30; AA 311; AM11; AW509 6892

Mer helighet gif mig (Pilgrimsharpan) [DDMMSDDTTLS, STTTD] N660 6893

Mercersburg (Woodbury) X Lake Enon 6894

Merciful Saviour (Traditional) [SDMFRDTDRMFSMR, SD] P260 6895

Mercy (Gottschalk) [SLSDMMR D, DDDTDRMR] C447; G47; H216; I53; L184; M546; N 162; P47; R240; S208; T289; U133; V218; Y100; Z274; AA259; AB94; AC60; AD185; AE141; AF242; AG127; AH 231; AI122; AJ276; AK188; AM245; AN25b; AO380; AP 286; AR219; AS29; AT170; AU204; AV151; AW136; AX 134; AY451; BA137; BB206; BC8; BE46; BF267; BH253; BK98; BR270; BX30b; BZ 6896

-----. V [SLSDMMRD, DTDD SMRM] Z274 6897

-----. V [SLSDMMRD, DTD DMRMR] BE46 6898

Mercy's free (Auber) [SFMMM MMFSLS, SFMRF] AX313 6899

Meredith (Knecht) X St Hilda 6900

Meredith (Meredith) [MMMFLSM, SRMFMRM, MM] R238; U287; V742; AT175; AU331 6901

-----. R [SMDL, SLSMDR, MMM MSS] 6902

Meribah (Mason) [DMMMRMFS, MLLLSFMR,] B263; C174b; H270; I365; K269; L302; M214; Q412; R329; T110; U422; V301b; AA339; AI96; AJ159; AL301c; AM563; AO535; AP50; AW255; BB384 6903

Meridian (Sims) [DMMRSDMMR, SDSSFMR] AT539 6904

Merlin (Conant) [SSSLM, MMM SM, DDDS#D, D] Y153 6905

Merlo (Emerson) [SMMRDRDLS M, SFMRMF] L206 6906

Mernle (Symonds) [SMRDRDLS, S DSMRS, SM] F445a; BV347 6907

-----. R [SFMRMDTL, RSMLS F, RM] 6908

Meroe (Bradbury) [DDDTDRDTD, DRMMMRD] L169a; T209; AJ 300 6909

Merrial (Barnby) [SSSSSS, LLS# LTLD, DDT] A172b; B364; C 364a; D535a; G53; I59; J231a; K574b; M575; N540b; O562; P67; R51; S35; T309; U467; V41; Y94; Z149; AA45; AB28; AC23; AD59; AE50; AF51; AG 33; AH170; AJ8; AK56; AL545c; AM666; AN128b; AO37; AR52; AS30; AT35; AU194; AV15; AW29; BA788; BB52; BC122; BD 6; BF198; BK45; BR519; BX 144; BZ 6910

Merrial (Blunt) [SLTDDT, SSL SS, LTDMM] L17; U260; V406; AE184; AH360; AI379; AJ262; AK447; AO225; AR310; AS314; BA39; BD103; BH146; BI42 6911

Merry Christmas (Shaw) [LRTD LTSL, DRTDLTSS,] BG189 6912

-----. R [RMLLLSML, TMLLSM L, T] 6913

Merry Christmas bells (Gilchrist) [SMFSFFSDTLSM, SFRS] BI80 6914

Merthry Tydvil (Parry) [ML S#LMSRM, LTDTMSF#M,] X312; AN375; AQ200; BY 196b 6915

Merton (Barnard) X Brocklesbury 6916

Merton (Jewson) [DRMSFMR M, MMMFMR, RD] M584 6917

Merton (Monk) [DMSSFLLS, MF#SSLLS, S] A9; B63; C 63a; D41a; E5; F47; J1; K 3; X61; AA14; BE79; BV76; BY249 6918

Merton (Oliver) [SLTDRMDD, MRDTLS, RD] AO74 6919

Message (Nichol) [DRMMMFM R#MD, MFSSLS] G501; R 504; U389; V740; Z530; AC302; AE353; AG261; AH 464; AP797; AR564; AS370; AT455; AU379; AV261; AW 335; BF525; BY400; BZ 6920

-----. R [SSDDDRMMR, RM FFFMR] 6921

Messengers (St Alban's Tune book) [SDRDTDFSFM, MRT DFM] D182; E216 6922

Messiah (Handel) [SDMRDLFM FM, SDRTLS] H183; I370; L150; M438; V175; Z245; AA245; AH310; AI254; AJ 354a; AM120; AO214; AS 163; AV118 6923

-----. V [SDMRDLSFMFM, SDRTL] L150 6924

Messiah [Come] (Handel) [SS FMRDS, TDRMFSS, SS] AH614; AI250; AS75; BR353b 6925

-----. V [SSFMRDS, TDRM FR, SSF] AS75 6926

Messiah (Herold) [MRDDFMR, SLLSMDR, MR] C231; D 607b; G225; I348b; L408; V592; AO654; AY155; BR 211; BZ 6927

Messiah (Hult) [SSSSDLLS, DD TSLSF#M,] N426 6928

Messiah (Swedish. 16th c) [DDDDLSS, SLDDTD, DDD] J9; M601; N1 6929

Metcalfe (Metcalfe) [MMFSFM R, SMFFMRS, MM] BB70 6930

Metzler (Redhead) X Metzler's Redhead, No. 66 6931

Metzler's Redhead No. 66 (Redhead) [MRDDSLLS, SLTDTL, LL] Eap. 29; F146; J453; K 128; M288; W423; AP249; BE367; BV200; BY272a 6932

Meyer (Meyer. Geistliche seelenfreud. Ulm, 1692) X Es ist kein tag 6933

Michael (Weisse) [DDDTTDLS, SLDTLSFM,] E652 6934

Michael, prince (Marsh) [DDD RMSFMR, DDRFMRM,] BN 164 6935

Michaelmas (Davis) [SSLSDRMFR TD, MRDRM] BY706b 6936

'Mid pleasures and palaces (Bishop) X Home, sweet home 6937

Middlesex (---) [MMRDRMFMR, RSFMFRD] AL440; AW168 6938

Middleton (Arnold) [DRMMMRRD RR, DMSMRD] H199; L22; AO520 6939

Middletown (Winchester) [MMM FMMRRMRLS, SSST] I451 6940

Midhurst (Gatty) [SSLSSFMRR, MFSDRRM,] X152 6941

Midian (Allen) [LLTDTLDFMLL, DDRR#R] BV137a 6942

Midt i livit ere vi (Walther) X Mitten wir im leben sind 6943

Mid-winter (Holst) X Cranham 6944

Mig hjertelig nu laenges (Hassler) X Passion chorale 6945

Mig kläd i helig prydnad (Lindström) [SMRDTRL, DDTLSS, SMR] N311 6946

Migdol (Mason) [SSDLRDTD, M RMRDTDR] H182; I630; L10; M95; T289; V19; AJ401; AM 114; AO16; BB154 6947

Mighty rock (O'Kane) [MFSLSDM, MRDDTLLS, M] Z407; AI249 6948

-----. R [STRFMRD, DRDTL TSF, M] 6949

Mighty to save (Sanders) [SS MRTDS, SLDFLS, DDT] BB 636 6950

-----. R [STDR, SDRM, F#F# F#S, SDMS] 6951

Milan (LaFeille. Methode ... 1782) [DRMRMSFM, MRDTL RDT] AP813; BR89 6952

-----. V [DRMRMSFM, MRD TLRT, D] BR89 6952a

Milburn (Price) [DTDFMMRD R, RSSSFMF,] AK154 6953

Mildred (Johnson) [DMSFMR, RRSLTLS, F#MS] N229 6954

Miles animosus (Shaw) [SDLR MDM, SDLRMD, MRS] J551a; S265b; AL405a 6955

Miles' Lane (Shrubsole) [SDDD RMRDR, SLSFMRD,] A355b; B192b; C192b; D450b; E364; F217; G164b; I167; J426a; K131a; L114b; R132b; S192b; T324; U117; V196b; W139a; X440; Z253; AB87b; AC135a; AD180b; AE129; AF196; AG 114b; AH198; AI337; AK185; AL46a; AM218b; AO208a; AP254a; AR102; AS155; AT 133; AU256; AW3; AZ14-Q; BA90-B; BB157; BF327B; BR53a; BV265a; BY180b; BZ 6956

Militant (Barnby) X Sarum 6957

Milites (Handel) [DSDDDDD, RMDMF#S, DSM] E381; X 343; AD44; BY503 6958

-----. V [DSDDDDD, RMRDM F#S, SS] BY503 6958a

Milites crucis (Corbeil) X Orientis partibus 6959

Mill Brow (Routley) [LLDTLS DR, MMSFR, RRS] BV406b 6960

Mill Lane (St Alban's Tune book, #10) [DRMFMRLTD, MFSMDTL] C473a 6961

Millenium (American trad) [SDDDTLS, SLDTRD, DRM]

G63; I81; AJ71; BB11; BZ 6962

Miller (Miller) X Rockingham 6963

Miller Chapel (Jones) [DDRMSL LS, DRMSLDS, L] R107 6964

Millet (Stevens) [SDSDRMSS, L SMDMRDD,] Y259 6965

Millikan (Cottman) [SMTDRT, TD LSSS, SLTD] AB41 6966

Milster (Campbell) [SSFMLSFM RFM, MMMLL] V307 6967

Milton (King) [SDDTDDSLSFM, SDDRM] AQ194 6968

Milton (Mason. Hallelujah, 1854) [DDDDSLSS, RMRDTLS, M] AP282b 6969

Milton Abbas (Thiman) [DDDSLM, MFRMFS, DTLS,] bY555 6970

Min blodige konung (Rutström) [DSSSSLSSFMR, RFFFF] N114 6971

Min hamaytsar (Halevey) [SSM DTDMRTS, SLSTRF] BH132, 302 6972

-----. V [SSMDTDMRTS, LSTRF T] BH302 6973

Min ljufva tröst (Lindström) [SDSTLLMF, LRDTLLSM,] N459 6974

Min sjael, min sjael, lov Herren (Lindeman) [MSFMDLS, SFFM SDMR, M] O7; P9 6975

Min sjael, min sjael, lov Herren (Kugelman. Concentus novi. 1540) X Tabor 6976

Min sjael og aand opmuntre dig (Tomissön. Psalmebog, 1569) X Island 6977

Minerva (Stockton) X Stockton 6978

Ministres de l'Eternel (Genevan Psalter. 1562) [DLSSLTD, SLS FMRD, DM] E258; W261; X26; AL535a 6979

Ministry (Gower) [DRMSMDRMD, SDRM, MF#S] Y211; BD135; BX334 6980

Minna (Koch) [MFRTDS, FSMDR, MMF#F#S] BY218a 6981

Minto (Crook) [SDTLTS, LTDFM R, RMRD] B293 6982

Minto (Monk) [MMSSDDMM, LLT DRM, MS] W629; BY668b 6983

Mir ist erbarmung widerfahren (Schicht) [SLTDMRDRMR, RMFSFM] AK224; AW562 6984

"Mir nach, " Spricht Christus unser Held (Schein) X Eisenach 6985

Mirabile (Hartmann) [DMFS, MRDTLSLS, LFRS] M152 6986

Miracle (König) X Franconia 6987

Mirfield (Cottman) [SDDDMF SSS, SDRMMRM,] C513a; S 338; Y173; AD292; AM66; AR18; BF474 6988

Miriam (Holbrook) [SSDRDDT, LSSLFM, SSD] H246; J176a; K479; L78; R92; S62b; T 255; U413; V666; Z154; AD 71; AG43; AI219; AJ355; AM430; AO265; BF241; BR 371 6989

Mirken (Lindeman) X Kirken 6990

Miron (Wissmer) [SSSSLFMR M, MMMRRD, D] AK241 6991

-----. R [SLTDRMDDTTD, DTTLT] 6992

Miserere mei (Seven sobs of a sorrowful soul.) [DTLS#, LT RD#LTTL, LSLT] E403; W 555; X519 6993

Miserere nobis (Swabian folk song) [MRMMMRMM, MMFS FMR, R] Y398; AR431 6994

Misericorde (Sanders) [LLTLT DRT, LDMRMFMR,] AN207 6995

Miséricordia (Smart) [MRDFM LLS, STDRMDFM] F349; W411a; AL270a; AP410b; BY443a 6996

Mission (Parker) [SDRMSSF, MMRLTD, SSL] B535; AH 432 6997

Mission song (Van Arsdale) [MRDRMRMS, LSSLSMR, M] H392; AX205; AY332 6998

Missionary (Mason) X Missionary hymn 6999

Missionary chant (Zeuner) [MM MMDRRT, TDDDDMRM,] A221; B453b; C453; D263; H411; I397; R494; S211; T133a; U285; V104; Y380; Z526; AB370; AD382; AG 198; AI180; AJ199a; AK352; AM 67; AN290b; AO453; AR393; AS 360; AU235; AV131; AW337; BA361; BE218; BF528; BR78; BX35 7000

Missionary hymn (Mason) [DMS SLSM, DTDFMMR, DMS] A254; B476; C476; D254; E577; G401; H479; I655; J310; K220; L338; M100; N367; M120; P357; Q 495; R509; S385; T125; U405; V586; W371a; Z541; AA474; AD371; AG265; AH467; AI168; AJ183; AL256; AM383; AN408a; AO528; AP376; AR558; AS93; AT442; AU35; AV269; AW333; AX90; AY329; AZ151-0; BA341; BB445; BC40; BD187; BE2; BF 301; BR225; BX328a; BY57b 7001

Missionary's farewell (Baltzell) [MFSSDRM, RDLDTDR, MF] BB657 7002

-----. R [RDTLSDMD, FFLDTDR, S] 7003

Misströsta et att Gud är god (Swedish, 1695) [SMRDDTLS, SLMF#SSF#S,] N594; AQ310 7004

Mit freuden zart (Bohemian Br.) X Bohemian Brethren 7004a

Mit fried' und freud' (Walther. Geistliche G-B. 1524) [RLL SRDTL, DLDTL, LDT] Q137; AA 185 7005

Mit haab og Trøst og al Tillid (Tomissön. Psalmebog. 1569) [LLLMLSF#M, MLSFMR#M, L] O428 7006

Mitchell (Mitchell) [SDSTLL, SRF M, SDTLL,] BB239 7007

Mitt hjerta, Jesu! denna dag (Swedish Koralbok, 1884) [SM RDFMRM, SLDDTDD, S] N14 7008

Mitten wir im leben sind (Walther) [SSLTDDTL, TDRLSFM, S] O240; Q590 7009

Mittit (Malim) X King of love 7010

Mittler, schau auf sie hernieder (Schicht) [SSSDFMMRD, RRMDSFM,] AA290 7011

Mixolydian (Mason) X Boylston 7012

Mizpah (de Fluiter) [SLSMRD RDM, SLL#TSMF#] BB38 7013

Mizpah (Tomer) X God be with you 7014

Moab (Roberts) [LLDTLS, LD DTT, DDLTD] R337; S183; W572 7015

Mobile (Campbell) [MFMRSDRM FRMD, RMFS] V362; AJ201a 7016

Moccas (Reinagle) [DTDRF#S, SLSSFM, MFFM] K504; AZ 582-M 7017

Modena (Woodbury) [SSMMDDL, LSMMDR, SSM] T54; AJ84 7018

Moel Llys (Stock) [DRMSLTD, DDRRD, DRMS] B485; BV321; BY376 7019

Mohler (Showalter) [DDDDRD TD, RRRMDTLS,] AR599; AS 423 7020

Moline (Kirkpatrick) [SSMRR DLSMS, SSRDTF] T199; AI 368; AJ288 7021

Molleson (Fletcher) [SDDDTLS RM, SDRMRDR] G214 7022

Moment by moment (Moody) [SDRMMMFDRM, MRD#RMR] AH401; AI313; AM708; AU58; BB583 7023

-----. R [MFSMRDTDRM, MFSMRD] 7024

Mon Dieu, prête-moi l'orielle (Bourgeois) [LLSLTDTL, LLSLTDTL,] E640; F514; R536; X121; AF519; BJ58 7025

-----. V [LLS#LTDTL, LLS# LTDTL,] BJ58 7026

-----. V [RRDRMFMR, RRD RMFMR] F514 7027

Monica (Foster) [MMSSSFFM,

MMLSSFM, F#] D246 7028
Monk (Monk) [MDRMF#S, SF# MR#F#M, MRMF] BX258 7029
Monk (Monk) X Eventide 7030
Monk (Monk) X St Philip 7031
Monk (Monk) X Waltham 7032
Monk Street (Holst) [DRMRDLS DRSMFRD, DR] X534 7033
Monkland (Antes) [DMSMFSLTD, MMRDTLS,] A308; B175; C 175b; E532; F377; H144; J405; K311; L350; Q570; R28; S64; V127; W38a; X12; AA297; AD 477; AF463; AG39; AL7b; AM 30; AP120a; BA25; BB10; BD25; BK132; BV20; BX20; BY15 7034
-----. R [RRDTSDMR, MRDTDD] 7035
Monks Gate (English trad) [DRM DMFSL, SSDTD, DRM] A362; E402; G265; J563a; S276a; W 576a; X515; AN213; AQ94; BV 587; BY561 7036
Monk's march (Welsh trad) X Ymdaith Mwnge 7037
Monmouth (Davis) [MDLSMRMFM, FMFSLST] I534a; BY60a 7038
Monmouth (Geistliche lieder. Wittenberg, 1535) X Luther 7039
Monod (Vincent) [SLTDRDDT, RSSS#LFM, L] D612b; G215; AL323; AP478; BA427 7040
Monora (Bradbury) [SSMSDDSD, MRDMRD, SS] T115; AJ165 7041
Monroe Place (---) [DTLLSS, FMRD, SFMMRR,] AA337 7042
Monsell (Barnby) X St Andrew 7043
Monsell (Sherwin) [DTLSMSLFLL SS, DTDR] U5; Z106; AC12; AD27b; AF31; AR39; BF217 7044
Monsell (Slovak hymn) X Man of sorrows 7044a
Monson (Brown) [SSMRDSSFMMR, SDRML] V10 7045
Mont Richard (Buck) [MLTDTLSMM, MLTDTL] A571a; E633; X148b 7046
Montague (Barnes) [MMMMMM M, MLLLLL, LSS] W638 7047
Monte Cassino (Italian hymn) [DSSDRMRD, SRMFMRDD,] E150b; AN360a 7048
Montesano (Law) [LS#LMLR DTL, LSFMFSD] E122b; X 491 7049
Montgomery (Champness) [DD SLLSFMRDS, SMRDM] E632; F549; X612 7050
Montgomery (Hopkins) X Nukapu 7051
Montgomery (Jarvis) X Stanley 7052
Montgomery (Woodbury) X Nearer home 7053
Montreat (Adams) [STDMRDTL SS, TMRDLD] Y397 7054
Montrose (Gilmour. Psalm-singer's assistant. 1793) [D MSDMRDSD, DDTDTLS,] BV 241 7055
Montrose (Smyth) [SSLTDM DTLSLSRS, SS] BR545 7056
Moody (Towner) X Marvelous grace 7057
Moore (Harrington) [MMMM MM, MRMFS, SSS#S#L] I685 7058
Moore (Moore) [SSSMFLS, DDTLSF#S, SS] AT189 7059
Moorehead (Stebbins) [MMM RDDTT, DRMFFM, SS] T398; AR422 7060
Mooz [t]zur (Jewish trad) X Rock of ages 7061
Moravia (West) [DMSDLS, FM DMF#S, SRDT] D71a; V343; AA388; AZ582-C; BA117; BY235 7062
-----. V [DMSDLS, FMDRM F#S, SRD] AZ582-C 7063
Moravia (Weisse) X Ravenshaw 7064
Moravia (Wolder. Catechismus G-B. 1598) X Wolder 7065
Moravian (Emerson) [DMLSM MRDRRMFMR, DM] L113 7066
More about Jesus (Sweney) [SSSSLDDD, RRRRFMMM,]

R316; AE296; AH409; AI283; AM676; AR455; AS225; AT321; AV324; AX373; AY48; BY597 7067

-----. R [MSLSDD, RRMFMM, SSSS] 7068

More holiness give me (Bliss) X Holiness 7069

More like Jesus (Doane) [MMM RRDD, RRRDFMR, MM] AT316; AV190 7070

More like Jesus (Stillman) X I want to be more like Jesus 7071

More like thee (Showalter) [DM SLSMRMD, DDRRDRM,] AR 458; AS223; AX375; AY44 7072

-----. R [MFSLSD, DDRRDRM, DMS] 7073

More love to thee (Doane) [SLS DRM, MRDR, SLSDRM,] G364; I317; J392; L198; N493; R397; S315; T410; U224; Z390; AD 256; AE198; AF400; AG168; AH 347; AI117; AK471; AL498; AM 548; AP461; AR407; AS280; AT 292; AU218; AV195; AW472; AX379; BA461; BB385; BF462 BZ 7074

More love to thee (Perkins) [MR MDLS, RDRM, MRMDLS,] P 310; AO642 7075

Morecambe (Atkinson) [MMMFM LSFFM, DTLSLT] D219b; G 179; H221; J129; L329; N171; R236; S204; T251; U377; V548; Y99; Z272; AB95; AC62; AD 184; AE137; AF232; AG125; AH230; AJ349; AK193; AM310; AN48b; AO219; AP276; AR232; AV162; AW133; AY433; BA144; BB336; BE207; BF265; BK85; BZ 7076

Moredun (Smart) [MSRMFSLSFM RD, SFMR] W232; AL201c; AP 314 7077

Moredun (Torrance) [MFMMRDR FM, SSDDTLS] D610b; Sap. 43; AA265; AL294; AP365b; AZ 277-A; BA837; BY454 7078

Morewellham (Steggall) X Morwellham 7079

Morgan (Gould) [SSDDMMMMRD, SLDSLL] BR299 7080

Morgan (Lyra Davidica) X Easter hymn 7081

Morgenglanz der ewigkeit (Freylinghausen) [MRDSLSFM, D TLTDTLS,] C128b; E374; J212; K454; M160; O548; P52; Q539; S30; W262; X27; AA125; AK47; AL538; AR 414; AW554 7082

-----. V [MDSLFMM, DTLTD TLS, M] P52 7083

-----. V [MRDSLFMM, DTLT DTLS,] Q539 7084

-----. V [MDSLSFM, DTLT DTLS, M] AK47 7085

Morgenglanz der ewigkeit (Grimm's Choral buch) X Grimm's 349th metre 7086

Morgenlied (Maker) [DDDSD RMD, LLSDFMR, R] K117; BY152 7087

Morgenstern auf finstre nacht (Freylinghausen) X Gregor's 310th metre 7088

Moriah (Welsh hymn mel) [MFSLSMD, SSFMLLSMD] E437; W435b; X573a 7089

Moring (Moring) [MFSDTDM R, SFFMRDTD] J207b 7090

Morlaix (Knecht) X Knecht 7091

Morley (Morley) X St Alban's 7092

Morley (St Patrick) X St Patrick 7093

Morn of gladness (Cottman) [SDTRDFM, MMRRDT, SDT] B352; C352; U440; V746; AH163; BD45; BR491 7094

-----. [SMRMRD, DRMFLS, S SSF] 7095

Morn of joy (Sewall) [SMFRD MM, SMFRDMM, RS] BI103 7096

-----. R [SMFSLS, FRMSFM, SMFS] 7097

Morning (Gilbert) [MMTDLS, LLTDLS, MRSR] D445b 7098

Morning (Haydn) X Haydn 7099

Morning (Monk) X Clifton 7100

Morning (Silcher) [SDRMR, SRM FM, SSMSFM] K572; AO629 7101

Morning (Wesley) [MRDDTDRMR D, SFMMRD] W374; AB257; AL532 7102

Morning has come (---) [SMDSDR SM, SMDSSRMD.] AR553 7103

Morning hymn (Barthélémon) [DRMMMFMRRR, SF#SF#M] A151; B2; C2; D2; E257; F3; I44; J202; K449; M552; N546; O 539; Q536; R50; V33; W256; X25a; AA29; AB282; AD37; AE37; AF 32; AL529a; AM331; AN89; AP 653b; AQ265; AS24; AV3; AW25; BA765; BE384; BF178; BR4; BV34; BX129; BY672 7104

-----. V [DMMMFMRRR, SF# SF#MRD] M552 7105

Morning hymn (Boyce) [DMMFM RRM, DLTDRMFR,] R439; T 252b; AJ199b 7106

Morning light (Webb) X Webb 7107

Morning praise (Geneva Psalter, 1551) X O Seigneur 7108

Morning prayer (Jassinowsky) [SMMRRDM, RMRRRDDLD,] BH241 7109

Morning prayer (Leyda) [SSSSDR M, SSRD, MMSMD] AL620 7110

Morning prayer (Reinecke) [DTD MRDTD, RMMLFR, RM] BR542 7111

Morning sacrifice (Störl) X Storl I 7112

Morning song (Wyeth. Repository. 1813) [MLTDRDTLSM, MLTD RM,] A156; R508; AF34; AQ 203; BZ 7113

Morning song (Wyeth Repository, 1813) X Detroy (Supplement to Kentucky Harmony, 1820) 7114

Morning Star (Franck) [SLTDRM F#S, LSFSM, SFR] M376 7115

Morning Star (Harding) [MRDT LSSDTDMR, SFM] A46a; B 95b; C95a; D66c; G119; I114; J53a; K39; L228; M377; N62; Q128; R175; S136; T337; U62; V114; Z202; AA181; AB125; AC239; AD126; AF126; AG 81; AH272; AI63; AK121; AM167; AO138b; AR144; AS109; AT67; BA183; BD 212; BZ 7116

Morning Star (Meinecke) [SS MDDTLLSFM, MMLTD] BR 361 7117

Morning Star (Nicolai) X Frankfort 7118

Mornington (Howard) X Lancaster 7119

Mornington (Mornington) [SSFM RD, DTLSLSFM, FF] C314; D300b; G25; H219; I45; K 520a; L277a; T355b; V214; AA258; AF401; AJ124; AN 284; AO377; AW226; BE70; BF448; BX310; BZ 7120

Morris (Barnby) X Just as I am 7121

Morris (Morris) X Nearer, still nearer 7122

Morris chant (Bradbury) [MM MMMMMF, FMDLRDT, M] L274; AJ100 7123

Morrow's Hill (Pollock) [SM R#MDDRDLS, SSF#SMR] AY39 7124

Morton (Barnes) [SSSDMRLTD, DDDDDDT] BB395 7125

Morwellham (Steggall) [MFSL SMDFM, LTDRMFR,] O256; S409; U354; W548; Y63; AB 331; AG269; AI298; AK397; AL382; AM444; AP577; AW 166; BF509; BY468b 7126

Moscow (Calkin) X Elim 7127

Moscow (Giardini) [SMDRTD, DRMFMR, SMDS,] A271; B 104; C104; D327; E553; F266; G2; H15; I2; J136; K164; L 179; M480; N164; O73; P237; Q227; R244; S52; T294; U3; V81; W364a; X303; Y354; Z122; AA262; AB13; AC38; AD20; AE154; AF246; AG12; AH189; AI24; AJ408; AK4; AL240; AM89; AN10; AO2; AP373; AQ26; AR21; AS1; AT12; AU4; AV32; AW8; AX 1; AY27; AZ579-B; BA10;

BB3; BC44; BD24; BE346; BF 216; BH136; BI39; BK63; BR 79; BV333; BX8; BY46; BZ 7128

-----. V [SMDRDTD, DRMFS FMR, S] N164 7129

Moscow (Lvov) X Russia 7130

Moseley (Smart) [DRMFLS, LFSMDR, SMDT] A457; B235; C325; D343; U23; V455; AB 163; BA299; BE267; BX389 7131

-----. V [DRMFLS, LLFSMDR, SMD] AB163 7132

Mosley (Showalter) [DMMFFSTD, RMFSF#S, SL] AR497 7133

Mother dear, O pray for me (Catholic trad) [MDRDLSMS, DRRRDRM, S] AH132; BO79 7134

Mother knows (Cassel) [MR#MD RMFFM, MSRRMFF] AU40 7135

Mother, Mary, at thy altar (Trier G-B. 1695) X Sunrise 7136

Mother of Christ (Montani) [DD DDT, FFFFM, SMRDTL,] BQ89 7137

Mother of mercy (Catholic) [MM MFFSFM, MMMRSF# F#S,] BO67; BP32 7138

Mother of mercy (Yenn) [SMFSR MDFMR, RMF#SLT] BQ77 7139

Motherhood (Moore) [MDFMRM RD, TDRMSFM, M] Z604; AN 557; AW364 7140

Motherhood (White) [MMSFMRRD, RMFLSFM, M] AO563; AR547; AS417; AT503 7141

Mothering Sunday (German, 14th c) [SLTDRLTD, DMFSFSR, R] BG145 7142

Motherland (Andrews) [DMSLMSM RM, DMSLMF#S] Y286 7143

Moultrie (Cobb) [SDDTMRRD, SFMDRMD, S] A125; B207; C207; D179b; J177b; BF521; BI6 7144

Mount Airy (Reed) [SDTLSSLSR FM, RMF#SD] J353 7145

Mount Auburn (Kingsley) [MSMSL MRD, DTLSMMR, R] T283b; AJ41 7146

Mount Calvary (Owen) X Bryn Calfaria 7147

Mount Calvary (Stewart) [MR DTLLSS, SLTDRR, FM] B272; C102a; D326; G289; I65; V 541; Y342; BE144; BF404; BO140; BX276 7148

Mt Elliot (Fishwick) [MFF#SS L, LDLS, MFMMDT] M549 7149

Mt Ephraim (Milgrove) [DMR DSFMRD, DTLSRDT] E196; F531a; W447; X203; BY495b 7150

Mt Holyoke (Wostenholm) [SS MMRMDS, SSMMRMD, L] G 123; Y248; Z249; AB155; AC285; AR216; BF338 7151

Mt Olive (Harrison) X Bankfield 7152

Mount Sion (Parker) [SSSSLTD MRD, SLLLT] A390; B307; C307; D493a; S19; AD33; BD 144; BF626; BX19a 7153

Mt Sion (Spielman) [DMSSLTD D, SSDLSF#S, D] M83 7154

Mount Sion (Sullivan) [MFSL DTD, SMLLLRR, RM] W582; AM600; BY19 7155

Mount Vernon (Mason) [MMSM FLLS, DMMRMFMR,] L571; M501; T68; AJ103; AO275; AX622; AY170; BB269 7156

Mt Zion X Mt Sion 7157

Mountain Christians (---) [SSDDTTDS, SLTDDTD, D] BY256 7158

Mountain wave (Beethoven) [MMMMMMMMMM, MMF#SSS] Y77 7159

Mountain's height (Rounsefell) X I'll go where you want me to go 7160

Moville (Irish trad) [LLSLL TDD, TDRFMRD, R] R136; W179 7161

Mozart I (Mozart) [MFRDSDRM FRD, MMMFR] C175a; D111b 7162

Mozart II (Mozart) [DDDTSFF M, SSMSFRDM] C444; D428; R388; S242; T27; U472; V231; Y187; AC327; AD339; AI230; AJ36; AL356b; AM484; AO 575; AR318; AW329; BA471; BE47; BF646; BR499; BY527b 7163

-----. V [DDTSFFM, SMSFRDM RR,] S242 7164

-----. V [DDDTLSFFM, SSMSFR D] Z376 7165

-----. V [DDTLSFFM, SMSFRD MR] AI230 7166

-----. V [DDTSFFM, SMSFRDM R, D] BR499a 7167

Müde bin ich geh zur reh (Fliedner. Liederbuch. 1842) X Dijon 7168

Müller (American, 19th c) [SS FMMRDDTLS, SSLSS] G434; J47; K536; N637; P363; R157; Z199; AD116; AE435; AF137; AG76; AH265; AK109; AM641; AR137; AT77; AU314; AV92; AW414; BK153; BZ 7169

Müller (Müller) [SSFMRDRD, R RMF#SSF#S,] X642; BY448 7170

Mundays (Shaw) [MTRDLSLSFM, MTRDLS#] X447 7171

Mundi salus affutura (Plainsong, M. 8) [SSSMFSMR, SLTDTLSF] E229 7172

Munich (Meiningen G-B. 1693) [DRMLSFMM, MSFMRRD,] A114; B58; C58; D150; G386; H87; I151a; J252; M527; O134; P89; Q294; R251a; S215; W694; Y364; Z434; AA113; AB100; AC 68; AD193; AE158; AF252; AH 233; AK193; AM263; AN29; AO 474; AP413; AR240; AT183; AU75; AV75; AW289; AZ146-C; BA7; BB217; BD232; BE77; BF 274; BR137; BY701a; BZ 7173

-----. V [DRMLSFMM, MSFRRD, DR] BR137 7174

Munich (Meiningen G-B. 1693) X O Gott, du frommer Gott 7175

Munich (Dresden. Neues G-B. 1593) X Ecce Agnus 7176

Munus (Calkin) [MFSDDTD, LTDSLRR, MF] I438; V622; Y190 7177

Muriel (Bergquist) [MRDTDR FM, SLSFMR, MR] N432 7178

Muriel (Gounod) X Lux prima 7179

Muriel (Morley) [SMRDSTL, STDRSM, MML] U441 7180

Music-makers (Nicholson) [SLTDFMLR, DTDDRSLS,] X315b 7181

Muskogee (McKinney) [SMFSLT DTLLS, SFMRM] AT253; AU 52 7182

-----. R [SLDT, STRD, DTLS, DDLT] 7183

Must I go, and empty-handed (Stebbins) X Providence 7184

Must Jesus bear the cross alone? (Allen) X Maitland 7185

Muswell Hill (English trad) [SDDMRRFMSDLS, FMFR] Y138; AC185; AF381; BK 74; BY548 7186

Muswell Hill (Bonner) [DRM SFLSDT, LSMSFMR,] BK 139 7187

My anchor holds (Towner) [SSDSMFS, SSLLLLS, SS] AH 387; AM717 7188

-----. R [SSDDDDD, SSRRRRR, SS] 7189

My beloved (Lewis) X Beloved 7190

My country 'tis of thee (Thesaurus musicus) X America 7191

My cross (Norwegian folk) [LDMRDMMRTD, LTDTLT] P314 7192

My dancing day (English trad) X Eastertime 7193

My days are gliding (Root) X Shining shore 7194

My dearest friends, in bonds of love (Ingalls) X The mid-

night call 7195
My dearest Saviour (---) [DMSSS MDMR, RMFFFLS] BO20 7196
My faith (Levenson) [MMS#S#MR MF, MMLLS#FMF] BH221 7197
My faith looks up to thee (Mason) X Olivet 7198
My Father knows (Excell) [SDTL MSFF, STLSFMFS,] BB591 7199
-----. R [SFRD, STLSFMFS, SFRD,] 7200
My Father knows (McKinney) [S MMMMFDM, MRMRLTDR,] AU452 7201
My God, accept my heart (Montani) [MMMFMDLS, DFFMDR, RR] BQ132 7202
My God, accept my heart (Walch) X Sawley 7203
My God, how endless is thy love (Pollock) [SDSLSDMFMRM, SDSLS] AX45; AY25 7204
My God! how ought my grateful heart (---) X My God, how wonderful thou art 7205
My God, how wonderful (Croft) X St Anne 7206
My God, howwwonderful (Hassler) X Passion chorale 7207
My God, how wonderful thou art (---) [SSFMDDSS, SLSFMR, SS] BO2 7208
My God, I am determined (---) [SDRMSSF, RRRSFM, SDR] AX344 7209
-----. R [DLFFSLS, MRRSFM, D LF] (---) 7210
My God, I love thee not because (Reinagle) X St Peter 7211
My God, my Father (Troyte) [DDTDLSFFM, DDTDLSF#] BQ332 7212
My God, my Father (Troyte) X Troyte, No 1 7213
My heart its incense burning (Hamburg. Neu Catholisches G-B. 1598) X Eisleben 7214
My heart says Amen (Hunter) [SDMMMMRDLD, LLSDRM] AX392 7215
-----. R [TDRRRRFMRDS, DR MMM] 7216
My heavenly home is bright and fair (Miller) X Going home 7217
My home above (Pollock) X I love to think of my home 7218
My hope is built (Bradbury) X The solid rock 7219
My Jesus, as thou wilt (Weber) X Jewett 7220
My Jesus, I love thee (Gordon) X Gordon 7221
My latest sun (Bradbury) [SS SSSLDD, LSDMRD, SS] AU53; AV313; AX575 7222
-----. R [RRMRD, RRRMRD, SDDDR] 7223
My life, my love, I give to Thee (Dunbar) X I'll live for Him 7224
My Lord and I (Darms) [SD SDRMD, LSTRFM, SDS] AO 611 7225
My Lord and I (Main) [SLSSM RD, DDLDRM, SLS] BB532 7226
My Lord and I (Shepard) [MM MRDLD, RRRDMR, MMM] AY 326 7227
My Lord, I'll go (Nafziger) [SSSLLDTLS, DMRDRTD,] AY507 7228
-----. R [SLTDRDT, TFLTL S, SLT] 7229
My Lord, what a morning (Negro spiritual) X My Lord, what a mourning 7230
My Lord, what a mourning (Negro spiritual) [MMRMD D, SSMSRRSMFR] AH599; BK171 7231
My Master (Day) [MLS#LTS# F#M, MDTDRTLS#] AC110; BK22 7232
My Master (Harrington) [ML SMRDRM, RDRDLDRD,] S 497 7233
My mother's Bible (Tillman) [DDMMMMD, DDDDDLS, SF] AH239; AU380 7234
-----. R [SDTSRD, DTLTDM RLTD] 7235

My mother's prayer (Weeden) [MMFSDTDR, FFFTLLSS,] AU95 7236
-----. R [DDTTLLSS, DDTT LSF#S,] 7237
My name's written there (Davis) [SDDRMD, SSLDFM, DRMM] AU337; AX486; AY371; BB 617 7238
-----. R [DRMMRD, DRMMSR, MFSS] 7239
-----. V [SSDDRMD, SSLDFM, DRM] AX486 7240
My prayer (Bliss) X Holiness) 7241
My redeemer (McGranahan) [SD RMMMRDRR, STRFFF] AI10; AM681; AT143; AU388; AX8; BC139, 270 7242
-----. R [DRMFFLDFMM, SD MRRR] 7243
-----. V [SDRMMMRDRR, SR MFFF] BC270 7244
My Saviour cares for me (De Vaughan) [DMMSSMRD, MSLS MR, DM] AX538 7245
-----. R [SLLFLS, MSLSMR, DMMS] 7246
My Saviour first of all (Sweney) X I shall know Him 7247
My Saviour guides me (Bowman) [SDRMDTRS, SLDFMMRR,] AY127 7248
-----. R [MSLSDFMR, STRFLS RR#] 7249
My Saviour's love (Gabriel) X How marvelous 7250
My Shepherd is the Lord (Gelineau) [DMSL, LSMRM, MSLD, SLS] BSp. 10 7251
My song (Hakes) [SMMRDLSD, RMMSFMR, F] BB613 7252
-----. R [MRRRMFLS, MRRRM FM, S] 7253
My soul be on thy guard (Mason) X Laban 7254
My soul in sad exile (Moore) [SMMMMRDDLDS, SDDDD] AS301; AT228; AU79; AV353; AX524; AY125 7255
-----. R [DFFFFFFMMMM, MDDDD] 7256
My soul, now bless (Lindeman) X Min sjael, min sjael lov herren 7257
My testimony (Arterbury) [D RMMMMDMRD, MFSSSM] AX340 7258
-----. R [SSLLLFSLSM, MFSSSM] 7259
Mylor (Stanton) [LTDMRDTT T, RDRMFMR] BV171 7260

N

Naar mig min synd vil kraenke (German, 1790) [MLTDLSFM, SLDRRD, ML] O281 7261
Naar mit øie, traet af møie (Lindeman) X Holy mountain 7262
Naar synderen ret ser sin vaade (Meyer) X Rudolstadt 7263
Naar tid og stund den er forhaand (Wolff) [DSDTDRM D, MSSMSFM, M] O206; Q 594; AA528; AZ132-K 7264
-----. V [DSLTDRMD, MSS MSFM, M] Q594 7265
Naar vi i største nøden staa (Bourgeois) X Commandments 7266
Nachtigall (Spee. Trutz-Nachtigal) [MLTDLSFM, SLTDFM RD,] X313; BV626 7267
Nachtlied (Smart) [MMMFMLS DRMR, SFMLS] B13; C13a; D7a; I61; K461; AB230; AV 16; BF196; BR127 7268
Nadolig (Lloyd) [LDMLSFM RDR, MLSL, LD] W68a 7269
Naglet til et kors paa Jorden (Zinck. Koralbog, 1801) [LTDDRRMM, MDTDRDTT,] O271; P172 7270
Nailed to the cross (Tullar) [MMMDRMMMFDRM, MMMR] AU345; BB123 7271
-----. R [SSSF#LS, MMMR# FM, MMMR] 7272
Nain (Mason) X Today 7273
Name (Chevenix-Trench) [DRM MMRDRRR, RMFFFM] BB 171 7274

Name of Jesus (Spinney) [MMRF MRLL, RRD#MRD, SS] D433c 7275

Name of Jesus (Strom) [MMM RFMRD, SSLSFMR, M] J67a 7276

Nanini (Nanini) [MFMMRRMM, SSSSSF#SS,] BJ1 7277

Nannie (Pollock) X Thou art the way 7278

Nannini (Nanini) X Nanini 7279

Nantmel (Williams) [DMLSFM, SSFMLSSF, MR] BY549b 7280

Naomi (Naegeli) [MMMSFMRMF M, MLLSF#] A170; B396; C 396; D670a; G202; H44; I277; J458; L324; N239; O442; T47; U246; V390; Z310; AE145; AH 396; AI166; AJ74; AL156b; AM 562; AN444; AO345; AP278; AR515; AS200; AV57; AW251; BA602; BB322; BI19; BR245; BX 479; BZ 7281

Naphill (Darke) [SDRMFRR, SL SMRDRD, M] F155; BV224; BY237 7282

När juldags-morgon glimmer (German trad) X Christmas dawn 7283

Nar mit öie (Lindeman) X Holy mountain 7284

Narenza (Leisentrit. Catholicum hymnologium. 1584) [DTSLTD, MRTDLS, SSSL] D185; E518; J579; K204; O429; W546a; AK 308; AL141b; AP8; BV605; BY197 7285

Nares (Nares) X Aynhoe 7286

Nashville (Mason, arr) [DMFSS LLS, SMSDSLLS,] I534b; V516; BB457 7287

Nassau (Rosenmüller) [MMSSDR M, LTDMRRD, SR] A95a; B561; C561; D114a; Eap. 12; F136; I240; K114b, 313; L268a; M67, 229; O108; P107; Q446; V370; AA381; AD149; AM476; AP353; AS462; AW544; AZ149-A; BA 746; BI11-D; BK7; BR181; BV 179; BY167b 7288

-----. V [MMFSSDRM, LTDM RD, MM] K313 7289

-----. V [MMFSSDRM, LTDMR RD, M] BI11-D 7289a

-----. V [MFSSDRM, LTDM RD, MFS] AP353 7290

-----. V [MMSSDRM, LTDM RRD, MM] AW544 7291

-----. V [MFSSDRM, LTDM SF#S, MF] BK7 7292

Nathaniel (Sullivan) X St Nathaniel 7293

National anthem (Smith) [SMD MSDMRDMF#S, SMRD] A142; B429; C429; P414; Y291; Z 651; AB341; AF496; AH484; AO599; AT486; AU457; AV 303; BA939; BC131; BF700; BH265 7294

National anthem (Thesaurus musicus. 1740) X America 7295

National hymn (Warren) [DD RMFMDDTD, MMMSLT] A 143; B430; C430a; G482; I 704; J521; K493; M648; R 498; S379; T450; U342; V 744; Y283; Z533; AB338; AC273; AD374; AE359; AF 433; AG264; AH480; AI358; AK385; AM616; AN376; AO 523; AR567; AT54; AU240; AV26; AW347; BA874; BB504; BC54; BD169; BF529; BH 263; BK123; BZ 7296

Nativity (Danish trad) [SDSD RMFMRD, SFM, FMR] M612 7297

Nativity (Lahee) [MMMSSDD M, RDLLRDT, S] B27b; C101 b; D324b; Eap. 48; F221; I 108; V203; W617; Y32; AO 457; AP165b; BA187; BE164; BV16; BX19b; BY200a 7298

Nativity (Maker) X All this night 7299

Nativity (Minke) [SSSMDTLS, SLLTRR, SS] L220a 7300

Nature (Parry) [DMFSSLFD, LSMMRDFR,] F173 7301

Nature's praises (Danish trad) [DRMRDSSS, LTDLRDTL] P23 7302

Nauford (Sullivan) X Hanford 7303

Navarre (Bourgeois) X Rendez

à Dieu 7304
Navarre (Bourgeois) X Toulon 7305
Nay, speak no ill (---) [MM RDTDRMS, MMRDRMF] BC 116 7306
Nazareth (Harts) [SLTDMSTT, SL LFFM, MM] AC97; BB114; BK 17 7307
Nazareth (Malan) [SDRMSFLLS, SDRMSFR] BR167 7308
Nazareth (Perkins) [SSDDRMFS, LSMDTDRM] AJ398 7309
Nazareth (Plain song) [DSFMRSL S, SDTLSSF#S,] M476 7310
Nazareth (Thalben-Ball) [SLTD RMSFMR, MRDLTD] BY123 7311
Nazareth (Webbe) X Melcombe 7312
Neale (Barnby) X Emmaus 7313
Neander (Neander) [DRMDMFS S, DTLSMRRD,] A90; B179; C179; D117; E241b; F222; J 187; K202; L40; M1; N306; P219; Q1; R40; V538a; W163; X477; Z121; AA5; AF503; AK23; AL135; AM238; AW127; AZ91-A; BA61; BC61; BR182; BV257; BY85b; BZ 7314
-----. V [DRMDRMF#SS, DT LSDDT] AZ91-A 7315
Neander II (Neander) [SMMRD, RMMF#S, SDSFM, S] AZ4-A; BA139 7316
Near the cross (Doane) [MFMRD LL, SDDMMR, MFM] G248; N461; P182; R376; U218; V732; Z339; AE172; AH293; AI79; AK462; AL485; AM704; AO647; AP212; AR452; AS227; AT97; AU 294; AV350; AW490; AX383; AY470; BB595; BZ 7317
-----. R [MSSFLL, SLSMMR, MFMR] 7318
Near to the heart of God (McAfee) X McAfee 7319
Nearer, dear Savior to thee (Clayson) [MDMSMRD, DLFM DR, MDM] BC117 7320
Nearer home (Woodbury) [SSS MRD, DRRDRM, MFFF] D675b Eap. 51; F346; H517; I590; K 520b; L604; V656; W583a; AE448; AL462; AP629; AW261; AX164; BA721; BY 609a 7321
Nearer, my God (Mason) X Bethany 7322
Nearer, still nearer (Morris) [MMMSS, DFFM, LLLSMMM] N494; U266; AI278; AR259; AS221; AT281; AV376; AX 377; AY310; BB390 7323
Nearer the cross (Knapp) [MRDRMSSS, DSSMMR, MR] AW491 7324
Nearer the cross of Jesus (Showalter) [MFMRMRDS, LTDMMR, MF] AS228 7325
-----. R [FFFLSSMS, MRD SMMR, M] 7326
Nearing the port (Pollock) [S SSMFSSSLFLS, SSSF] AY 162 7327
'Neath the old olive trees (McKinney) [SSSMFS, DDD TLS, SSSR] AU398 7328
-----. R [MMMRDT, FFFM R#M, MMRL] 7329
Neckar (German) [MSDDRSFM RD, SMLDRM] BR444a 7330
Need (---) [MFMMRRD, DRRF FM, MFM] N258 7331
Need (Farjeon) [MFSMDRML, DRDMMF#MS,] X569 7332
Need (Lowry) [DMRDTD, DDR DLS, SRM] A438a; B131; D602; G232; H55; I506; J479; L401; M629; N462; P319; R324; S332; T407; U303; V 492; W700; Z341; AC150; AD275; AE196; AF342; AG 170; AH322; AK469; AL493; AM710; AO640; AP480; AR 306; AS218; AT334; AU193; AV346; AW187; AX354; AY 68; BB258; BC79; BE137; BF364; BY475a; BZ 7333
-----. R [MMDFMMR, RDM RRD, DD] 7334
N'eelah hymn (Jewish trad) X Ayl nora allelah 7335
N'eelah melody I (Jewish trad) [SSMMDDSLTLSLTLS, S]

BH177 7336
N'eelah melody II (Jewish trad) [SLLSSLRRMR, TLTDRT] BH 179 7337
Neilson (Gower) [SLSMDSF, TD DMRDR, SL] U137; AC180 7338
Nenthorn (Hately) [MSLSFM, MRDTD, RMF#SL] W475b 7339
Nestling (Winding) X Winding II 7340
Netherlands (Dutch trad) X Kremser 7341
Netherlands folksong (Dutch trad) X Kremser 7342
Nettleton (Wyeth) [MRDDMSRR, MSLSMRD, M] G23; H5; I19; L88a; P31; R379; S235; U368; V511b; Z111; AE220; AG9; AH181; AI4; AK476; AM400; AO273; AP447; AR438; AS14; AT313; AU190; AV223; AW189; AX35; AY14; BA479; BB291; BC70; BZ 7343
Neuadd Wen (Evans) [DLMLSFM L, TMSF#TDRT,] W393 7344
Neumark (Neumark) [MLTDTLT S#M, SSF#MLLS#] E458; G 272; I476; J568; K398; L485a; M68; N484; O230; P141; Q194; R344; S105; V139; W541; X 606; Z404; AA498; AB225; AF 83; AG156; AI439; AK300; AL 423; AM567; AP500; AZ106-A; BA718; BE216; BH89; BI46-D; BL48; BR260; BV523; BX182; BY580; BZ 7345
-----. V [MLTDTLTS#M, SSFM LLS#] Q194 7346
-----. V [MLTDTLTLS#, SSFM LLS#] V139 7347
-----. V [MLTDTLTLS#M, SSF MLL] BH89 7348
-----. V [MLTDTLTSM, SSSFM LT] BR260 7349
Neumeister (McGranahan) [MFSL MLS, SDTLSFM, MF] AT195; AU113; AV330; AW466; AX264 7350
-----. R [MFSLDDTLS, SLMSS SL] 7351
Never alone (---) [SSSMSDMR#M, RD DRDLS,] AU400; AX543; AY 91 7352
-----. R [SMSDMR#MR, DRD LS, SSS] 7353
Never shone a light (Lowry) [SLSMSLS, MFMDRMD, SL] AI64 7354
Nevin (Nevin) [DTLFLS, FMR DRSS, DTL] AL112b 7355
New 113th (Hayes) [DTLSDRM MRDDT, TDRM] E298; G375; W431; X20; BY460 7356
New America (Longacre) [DS LSFM, LTDDTD, RMRS,] Z514 7357
New Calabar (Farrer) [MRDTT LS, DRMFMRDR, S] D651b; L463; W238; AD213; AL596; AP788; BA596 7358
New England (Noble) [SLDTDRS S, MFMRDR] A84 7359
New every morning (Schumann) X Canonbury 7360
New Grange (MacAlister) [MR DTLLSS, MRDTLS, SD] W 610 7361
New Haven (Hastings) [DDDMRD, RRRFMR, MF#F#S,] L119; U129; V210; BA63 7362
New Orleans (Sellers) [SSSSSSS SS, SSLLLLL] AT142; AU69 7363
-----. R [MRDSLDDT, TDR D#RSTF] 7364
New Prince, new pomp (Ireland, J.) [RLTSLTDRDTSL, RRDR] BG170 7365
New Russia (Gretchaninoff) [SDDDRTDTRL, SDDDRM,] Y312 7366
New Sabbath (Phillips) [DSLS FMFSDLRDTD, MR] X691 7367
New St Andrew (Gill) X Frankfort 7368
New Ulm (Reuter) [MDLLRDD T, DRMFMSMR,] Q50b 7369
New year (Barnby) X St Ignatius 7370
New year (Booth) [MMSLSM, D DMFR, MDLSD] D541b 7371
New Year (Mann) X Mann 7372

New York (Noble) [DSSLSFMFS, SDTLSLT] B437 7373
Newark (---) [SLDDLSMSLD, DR DMRD,] AY402 7374
Newbold (Kingsley) [SSLSDTRD, DRMFLSM, S] I24; L217 7375
Newbury (English trad) [DMSS LFSMRD, MRRMFM] E16; W655; X395c; BE146; BG46c 7376
-----. V [DMSSFLLSMRD, MR RMF] BG46c 7377
Newcastle (Everett) [SSLSMDLS, DRRDTD, RR] AR285; AS47; AU264 7378
Newcastle (Morley) [DDTTRRDD, MSFDRM, MM] B120; C241; V739; W36; Y67; AL36; AP 202; BB85; BE206; BV4b; BY 51a 7379
Newcastle (Sankey) [DMSMDLDSD, DRMFMR, D] AT121 7380
-----. R [SSRRSSMM, MMRSF# S, MF] 7381
Newcombe (---) [DDDTMRD, DD DTTLS, FM] AO305 7382
Newell (Bradbury) [SSMMSSFF, FFMRMFM, S] AM84 7383
Newell (Swisher) [DMSDMRRD, RMFSLTLS,] BD237 7384
Newfoundland (Parry) [DMDSFM RD, SLFDTLS, R] AL524 7385
Newington (Jones) X St Stephen 7386
Newington (Maclagan) [MMFRLTD, RRMRRDT, RM] B180; C180a; F330; AL357a; AP555; BA472; BB282; BV364; BY586 7387
Newland (Armstrong) [SDTLSM, F MRDMR, SDTL] E589; F433b 7388
Newland (Gauntlett) [SDMRRM, MFLSMR, MMRD] B261; D410b; V396; W102a; BX344b 7389
Newman (Calkin) [SSSLMFFSRM, DDRM, MS] AB219b 7390
Newman (Terry) [DMSDLSRM, M LDTLS,] A343a; C70a; BY206b 7391
Newnham (Barnby) [MMMMMMM FMRM, MMMMM] BX267 7392
Newton Ferns (Smith) [SMLFRSM D, DTLSFRT, M] D465b; W59; Y148 7393
Niagara (Jackson) [SMSDDRR M, DTDFMRRR,] AO460; BY194b 7394
Nicaea (Dykes) [DDMMSS, LLLSM, SSSSD] A266; B 205; C205; D383; E162; F 160; G1; H1; I78; J131; K158; L177; M140; N163; O72; P232; Q246; R11; S57; T182; U1; V88; W1; X187a; Y18; Z107; AA263; AB17; AC4; AD25; AE155; AF251; AG1; AH159; AI27; AJ266; AK1; AL1; AM87; AN8; AO 234; AP135; AQ4; AR1; AS 17; AT1; AU6; AV1; AW1; AX12; AY30; AZ144-C; BA 8; BB73; BD22; BE117; BF 186; BI25; BK41; BL37; BM 92; BR35; BV227; BX5; BY 42; BZ 7395
Nicholls (Pollock) X My God, how endless is thy love 7396
Nicht so traurig (Bach) [DT LMRDTDRS#, LTDFMR] E100; F411a; W413c; X264; AF281; AL267b; AP191; BE 295; BV388; BY309b 7397
Nicht so traurig (Freylinghausen) X Pressburg 7398
Nicht so traurig, nicht so sehr (Ebeling) [DRDSDRM, MSF MRRD, DR] AA28; AN152; AQ284; AW68 7399
Nicht so traurig, nicht so sehr (Grimm. Choral buch) X Consolation 7400
Nicolai (Rosenmüller) X Nassau 7401
Nicolai (Nicolai) X Frankfort 7402
Nicolai (Nicolai) X Sleepers, wake 7403
Nicolaus (Hermann) X Hermann 7404
Nielsen (Nielsen) [SSFM SMTRD, DLFDLSF] M338 7405
Nigerian tune (Olude) [SDM SDMR, DDSLSLDD, M] BZ 7406
Nightfall (Barnby) [SFDMRDM

SDDT, LSLSF] G49; I58; J225; K459; N551; U459; V47; AA38; AZ36-F; BI20; BR112 7407

-----. V [SFDMRDMSDDTL, SSSL] BI20 7408

Nightfall (Rau) [SSLSDRMFMR, MDLSDR] AZ58-D 7409

Nightingale (Staples) [SDTLSM RDRM, FLSRMS] BY746b 7410

Nil nisi labore (Webster) [DFSM, SDLFSMDTLS, RT] BY511 7411

Niles (Cooke) [DTLLSDTLS, SF RDRM, R] D234b 7412

Niles (Niles) [MMMMMMRDTLS, SDMMR] BK100 7413

Nilus (Gabriel) [MSSSSSSDL, LSFMSFM] T233; AJ329 7414

Ninety and nine (Bridge) [SLL DTRDMR, MFSSLSS,] BR533 7415

Ninety-third [Psalm] (---) [SLD LRDLS, SLDLDRMR] AY289 7416

Ninety-fifth [Psalm] (Hopkins, arr) [DDRMFMRD, RMFSF#S, SD] AY362 7417

Ninth Street (Main) [DRMFRDTD, RMSDLSF#S,] L54 7418

Nishmas (Alman) [DLSLSLSMS, SLRRDLD,] BH55 7419

No abiding city here (Brunk) [SSSF#SLTD, MMMRDTLT,] AY390 7420

No friend like Jesus (Teasley) [MMMR#MFSM, FFFMRSM, M] AX526 7421

-----. R [LLLTDTLSM, FFFM RSM,] 7422

No hope in Jesus (Lowry) [DRMS LLSM, DMSRMD, DR] AX226; AY221 7423

-----. R [SSSSMRRD, SSSMRRD, D] 7424

No mortal eye hath seen (---) [SSMMRDLL, DSDDRMR, S] AX601 7425

No night in heaven (---) [MMM DRDLSD, SSSSLF#S,] AY161 7426

-----. R [SSSSMFSLS, MMMSSF M] 7427

No night there (Danks) [DRMMFRS, DRMDRD, DRM] AI342; AM730; AS470; BB558 7428

-----. R [SSSMLSF, FFFRSF M, SS] 7429

No, not one (Hugg) [MMRDDT LDLS, MMRMRD,] AI396; AY352 7430

-----. R [MSSLSMMRD, MSS LSMM] 7431

No, not one (Hugg) X Homeward bound (---) 7432

No room in the Inn (English trad) [SSSLSMMDFMRD, DM SS] BG114 7433

No shadows yonder (Kirkpatrick) [SMRRD, DFLS, DTLLS, DF] AS480 7434

No tears in heaven (Arnold) [DDDDDMMMRD, DDDMMR] AX600 7435

Nobody knows (Negro spiritual) [MSLDRMMMM, SSLDDLS,] Y320; BK169 7436

-----. R [MSSSMSSM, SMR, MSSSM] 7437

Nocte surgentes (Sarum plainsong, M 6) [RFMRFF, RMD RFF, FFF] A157a; E165; F10a; X28a; BJ49 7438

-----. V [LDTLDDLTSLDD, DDD] X28a 7439

Nocturn (Burstall) [SMRDDD TLS, SMRDDDT] D11b; AJ 260a 7440

Noel (English mel) [DRMRDRM FMR, SSMFSLS,] A19a; B 362; C362b; E26; F66; I236; K29a; L225; S128; W47; X76; AB390; AE157; AI62; AJ394; AL58a; AP170a; AR239; AZ 590-I; BA53; BB95; BE373; BF269; BV104; BY101 7441

Noël nouvelet (French trad) X Love is come again 7442

Noelsch (Noelsch) [SLSDFM R, RMLSF#S, SLS] AO568 7443

Nomen (Murray) [DMLSMMRD, SLDDRMR, M] D433b 7444

Nomen Jesu (Corbeil) X Orientis partibus 7445

Nomina (Smart) [DSSMDLLS, SDDTLS, MF] AZ14-Ff; BA 882 7446

Non nobis, Domini (Plainsong) [TRMRDTLTT, SLTTTTT] E626 7447

Non nobis, Domini (Williams) [LLLLS# L, LLTDRM, DRD] A503 7448

Non-resistance (Heatwole) [SDDD SMSD, SLLLLDLS,] AY297 7449

None but Christ (McGranahan) [SDMMMDMSSS, SMRRDRM,] W699; AL482; AW451 7450

-----. R [SSSSMLSSFM, DRMMM S] 7451

-----. V [SDMMMDMSSS, SM RRRD] AW451 7452

None can satisfy (Showalter) [MF SDTLSM, SLSRSLS, M] AS294 7453

None other Lamb (Ridsdale) [RM MFFSSL, LL#DLSL#LS] W412 7454

Nonington (Grundy) [SLTDSDRM D, MLSMRDL,] BV404 7455

Nor silver nor gold (Towner) [SSMSDSMSFSFR, FFRF] AM721 7456

-----. R [SLTDDTLTF, FFTT LFM,] 7457

Norelius (Johnson) [DMFSLSFMD, SLDSM, FM] N88 7458

Norfolk Park (Coward) [DTLSDMS FM, RLFMRDT,] D519c 7459

Noricum (James) [DDDTLSFM, STDRMSFR,] BY8b 7460

Norman (Doles' Choral buch, 1785) [SDTDRDTD, DMMRDT LL] W529b 7461

Normandy (French trad) [MLL LTDDDTLLSM, MSL] BY734b 7462

Normanton (Vulpius) X Cana 7463

Norris (Norris) X Where He leads me 7464

Norrland (---. 16th c. northern mel) X Sweden 7465

Norse (Lindeman) X Spring of souls 7466

Norse air (Norwegian folk mel) [SSLSDTLL, LFRDTTD, S] BZ 7467

North Coates (Matthews) [SSLLDD, TTDLS, DDMMS] D541a; F360; K566; S161; W343; AL89; AP204; BA831; BV353; BY 453b 7468

North Petherton (Harris) [SL SDTD, MLTDDT, SLTD] F235 7469

Northampton (King) [MRFM RLT, DSDRMF#S, SF] F369; BV26 7470

Northfield (Ingalls) [DSFMSDM R, RMMRDR, SD] H300; BB 245 7471

Northrepps (Booth) [DDRMLL SF, FMRDRR, RS] D652b; V304; AB228; AJ324; AP 181b 7472

Northrop (Northrop) [DRRM FSFMRD, MRSTLS] Eap. 8; X82b; ALSuppl 7473

Northumberland (Smart) [SS LSMFSDT, LSDFRM, M] W 531b 7474

Northumbria (English trad) [SD TDRFMRD, FFMSRRD,] X 382; BG130 7475

-----. R [MDTDLSSFM, MDT DLSS] 7476

Northumbria (Stanton) [SDDRM FSLSFS, SFRMF] BY389 7477

Norton (Brackett) [SSDDMSLS, MFLDLS, MM] BE254 7478

Norwich (Crespin. Psalms, 1556) [DTLSDMRD, DRM FRM, MR] D38; E404; Q583; W643; X526; Z437; AA521; AD199; AL32; AN58a; AP 122a; AQ88; BJ84 7479

Norwich (Mann) X Lasus 7480

Norwich (Mann) X Watermouth 7481

Norwich (Mason) [LTDTLS# L, DRMRDTD, MM] V268 7482

Norwich (Ravenscroft's Psalter, 1621) [LDRMMFFM, MFDR RD, DM] X577 7483

Norwick (Woods) [SMDLRTS, DLTSMF, SMF#] BY276 7484

Nos Galan (Welsh trad) [SFM RDDRMD, RMFRMRD] BG50 7485

Nostre Dieu (Calvin. Psalter, 1539) [DDDLRLDTL, LTD RLDTL,] E233b 7486
Not all the blood of beasts (Mason) X Boylston 7487
Not alone for mighty empire (Mozart) X Ellesdie 7488
Not dead, but sleeping (Warren) [SFMSSFFM, MMMRRSS, S] AX620 7489
-----. R [SSSMMFSLS, SSSRFM R] 7490
Not far from the kingdom (Tenney) [SSMFSLLSD, DRRRRDR] AX 262 7491
-----. R [SSMSL, LSSSDRRM, FMM] 7492
Not half has ever been told (Presbrey) [MFSF#SLTRDS, DDDTDR] AU386 7493
Not I, but Christ (Burke) [MRD FMMRLRDT, SRRSL] AS233 7494
Not made with hands (---) [DM MRDMMR, DSSS, SLSS] AX481 7495
-----. R [DMDS, MSLSMRD, DM DS, D] 7496
Not now, but in the coming years (McGranahan) X Some time we'll understand 7497
Not what these hands have done (Runyan) [SMDTDRD, MSMRMF M, SM] AX318 7498
-----. R [MSRSFFM, MMTMRD, DLL] 7499
Nothing between (Tindley) [MMM MDRDLLS, DDDDMM] AU66 7500
-----. R [DDLSMRDRMD, DDLS MR] 7501
Nothing but the blood (Lowry) [DDDRMSM, DDDRMMRD, D] AI395; AM677; AT204; AU456; AX115; AY511 7502
-----. R [SMRMSM, RRDRRMS, SMR] 7503
Nothing like Jesus (Jones) [DRM MMMMDRD, MFSLSM] AX271 7504
-----. R [SSLLLLLDTLLS, MF SL] 7505
Notting Hill (Purday) [SSLDRM DL, SLSDMR, SS] H416 7506
Nottingham (Clark) X St Magnus 7507
Nottingham (Mozart) X Mozart II 7508
Nous allons (French carol) [DMFSLSFMRMFRD, DMF] E645; X166; BG147 7509
Nous allons, ma mie (French carol) X Nous allons 7510
Nous voici dans la ville (French, 15th c) X Chartres 7511
Nova vita (Peace) [MMMM RR, SSSSF#F#, TT] A375b; B380; C380 7512
Novalis (Mozart) X Cana 7513
Novello (Wade) X St Thomas 7514
Now are the days (Catholic) [LDRMMFMD, DTLS#LRMF] BO163 7515
-----. R [SDRMFMR, MDDR DT, SDR] 7516
Now at the Lamb's high royal feast (Joseph) X Angelus 7517
Now at the Lamb's high royal feast (Montani) [LTRDSSFM, MF#LSDTLS,] BQ30 7518
Now bless the God of all (Cowen) [SLSMFS, MRDTD TL, LLR] BH81 7519
Now blessed thou (Bach) [DD RMFSRMF#S, FMRMFS] BI7-D 7520
Now for each yearning heart (Bigelow) [MFMMRR, RMF MRD, FRRD,] AT527 7521
Now from the altar of my heart (Wilson) X Martyrdom 7522
Now glad of heart (Bohemian Br. G-B. 1544) X Betracht'n wir heut zu dieser frist 7523
Now, gracious Lord, thine arm reveal (Wilson) X Martyrdom 7524
Now just a word for Jesus (Doane) [DMRDDDL, LSMM

RR, FMR] AX197; BB522 7525

-----. R [SDRDLSM, SDTDMMR, FM] 7526

Now let every tongue adore thee (Nicolai) X Sleepers wake 7527

Now let the earth with joy (Spevnicek) [DRRMRSF#MR, DRRMRSF#] BQ110 7528

Now let us rejoice (---) [MRDM SLSSDMFLS, SSF] BC118 7529

Now the day is over (Baring-Gould) X Eudoxia 7530

Now the day is over (Barnby) X Merrial 7531

Now the shades of night (Fischer) X Coming to the cross 7532

Now the world is saved from darkness (Hintze) X Salzburg 7533

Now to heaven our prayer (Arndt) X God speed the right 7534

Now to Jesus Christ (Root) [SS DDRRMD, MMSSFMR, L] BI24-D 7535

Now we'll sing with one accord (Daynes) [DMSLTDRM, MFRRR MD, D] BC132 7536

Nox et tenebrae et nubila (Sarum plainsong M 1) X Splendor paternae 7537

Nox praecessit (Calkin) [MMM DRMMF, RDMSFM, DL] B60; C60; D281b; H93; I246; S469; V8; W482; Y66; Z426; AA119; AC267; AD198; AE388; BA6; BD97; BE261; BF403; BX353; BY248 7538

Noyon (Lowden) [SSSFMRD, DT LSMDR, RR] T92 7539

Nu bede vi den helligaand (Walther. G-B. 1524) X Soldau 7540

Nu er frelsens dag oprundet (Lindeman) [MDSSLTRD, FMR DTDR, M] O191 7541

Nu fryde sig hver kristen mand (Christliche lieder. Wittenberg, 1524) X Nu freut euch 7542

Nu hviler mark og enge (Isaak) X Innsbruck 7543

Nu lader os da grave ned (Hermann) [DDDRTDTLS, SDR MRDT] O594 7544

Nu lukker sig mit oege (Korssing) [SSDDRDT, LLRRFTD, MM] N504 7545

Nu rinder solen op (Zinck. Koralbog, 1801) X Zinck 7546

Nu skal du, min sjael (Crueger) X Schmuecke dich 7547

Nu takker alle Gud (Crueger) X Nun danket 7548

Nu wol Gott das unser gesang (Traditional, 16th c) [DSLS DDRM, MFMRDLTD,] S513 7549

Nukapu (Hopkins) [MFSMDRM D, LTDDRMFM,] D173; V647 7550

Nun bitten wir den heiligen Geist (Walther. G-B. 1524) X Soldau 7551

Nun danket (Crueger) [SSSLLS, SFMRMRD, SS] A144; B422; C422; D200; E533; F379; G7; H62; I30; J443; K283; L77; M22; N299; O31; Q36; R9; S459; T300; V635; W29; X350; Y303; Z173; AA64; AB56; AC325; AD12; AE11; AF29; AH196; AI443; AK72; AL19; AM86; AN262; AO104, 338; AP147; AQ19; AR601; AT491; AV44; AW514; AZ 146-A; BA122; BB90; BC120; BD200; BE199; BF169; BI55; BJ93; BK62; BL56; BM14; BN198; BR492; BV22; BX187; BY18b; BZ 7552

-----. V [SSSLLS, MFMRMRD, SSS] N299 7553

-----. V [SSSLLS, MFMRDTD, SSS] Q36 7554

-----. V [SSSLLS, SMFMRD, RRRM] AO338 7555

-----. V [SSSLLS, SFMRSFM RD, S] AZ146-A 7556

Nun danket all' (Crueger) X Graefenberg 7557

Nun danket all' und bringet ehr (Crueger) X Graefenberg 7559

Nun danket all' und bringet ehr

(Störl) X Stoerl I 7560
Nun danket alle Gott (Crueger) X Nun danket 7561
Nun freut euch (Christliche lieder. 1524) [DDSDFMRD, DRMFMRLT] E148; F150; M113; O3; Q124; X640; AA310; AZ132-B 7562
-----. V [DDSDFMRD, DRFMRLT D] O3 7563
Nun freut euch (Geistliche lieder. 1535) X Luther 7564
Nun freut euch lieben christen g'mein (Christliche lieder. 1524) X Nun freut euch 7565
Nun komm der heiden heiland (Walther, G-B. 1524) X Venit hora 7566
Nun kommt das neue (Darmstadt G-B) [SSSSSLTD, TDTLTLLS,] AA140 7569
Nun lasst uns den leib (Geistliche Gesäng. Wittenberg, 1544) X Rhau 7570
Nun lasst uns geh'n (Kirchen-und haus buch. Dresden) [SFMRD RD, MFSLSFMMR] E104 7571
Nun lasst uns Gott dem herren (Burgk) X Selnecker (Selnecker) 7572
Nun lob' mein' seel' (Kugelmann. Concentus novi. 1540) X Tabor 7573
Nun preiset alle (Lowenstern) [DDRMD, RRMFFF, MMFSR,] Q28; X236; AZ70-A 7574
-----. V [DDRMD, RRMFMF, MMFSR] AZ70-A 7575
Nun ruhen alle wälder (Isaak) X Innsbruck 7576
Nun seht (Bohemian Br.) X Stettin 7577
Nun sich der tag (Krieger) [MLTDDRRM, MRMDDT, MD] C496; Q561; AA30; AZ14-A; BA859 7578
-----. V [MLTDDRRM, MLDT LS#, TD] Q561 7579
Nun sich der tag geendet hat (Williams) X Mear X Nun sich der tag (Krieger) 7580
Nunc dimittis (Bourgeois) [SLS FMR, FMDRRD, DS] A176; E 269; J220; Q101; R61; X50; AF49; AL551; AR55; AW 34; BJ88; BY699 7581
Nunc sancte (Plainsong: early M 8) [LLLLLLLS, LLLL SLLL] A160a 7582
Nunc sancte nobis (Latin: old) [FFSLFSFM, SFFMRFSF,] BJ45 7583
Nunc, sancte, nobis, spiritus (Plainsong, M 4) [MMMR MRDRRMM, FFMRR] E255 7584
Nuremberg (Ahle) X Liebster Jesu 7585
Nusbaum (Nusbaum) X Would you live for Jesus 7586
Nutfield (Monk) [MMFSLTDS, SRSM, MMF] A169b; B26; C26; D19a; Eap. 15; F26b; V39; W702; AL547c 7587
Nyberg (Nyberg) [SDMSFM FS, TLSFMFSF] J145 7588
Nyland (Finnish trad) [SMR DRDLS, SSLSFM, SM] A431; J574; R417; S284a; W442; AD433; AE343; AK301; AL 281; AM306; AN246; AQ115; AR294; AT303; BV307; BY 581b; BZ 7589

O

O amor quam ecstaticus (Plainsong M 1) [RLSFMRFSL, LRDL#LSL] E214b; W143; X607b; BV580 7590
O amor quam exstaticus X O amor quam ecstaticus 7591
O anblick der mir's herz bricht (Gregor) X Gregor's 99th metre 7592
O awake! my slumbering minstrel (Stephens) [MFSLSSF MRS, SF#SFFF] BC268 7593
O, be still (Goerz) [DRMRD LS, SSDDMR, DRM] AX394 7594
O beautiful for spacious skies (Ward) X Materna 7595
O Bethlehem (Irish trad) [SS

MSMDSD, RMRSMRDR,] BN18 7596

O bless the Lord, my soul (Jewish trad) X Az yasheer 7597

O blessed are those (Gelineau) [DDDR, RRM, MMMS, MDR, MM] BSp. 50 7598

-----. R [DSSSLSMRMDDLLLM.] 7599

O blessed by God (Benedictine trad) [DRDTLTSD, DRRDRFRM,] BN 172 7600

O blessed day, when first was poured (Andernach G-B) X Andernach 7601

O blessed Father! sent (Montani) [DMFSDRDL, DTDRMFM, D] BQ108 7602

O blessed St Patrick (Paderborn G-B. 1765) X O purest of creatures 7603

O bone patria (Sullivan) X Homeland 7604

O Bread of heaven (Herbert) X Burwell 7605

O Bread of life (Isaak) X Innsbruck 7606

O breathe on me (Irish trad) X St Columba 7607

O Brightness (Hume) [SLSLTDTDRS, SMRDRS,] BL75 7608

O can you sing the new song (Norwegian trad) [DSDTLFLTDSFM, DTDR] P15 7609

O Canada (Lavalle) [MSSDRMFSLR, MF#F#SLT] Y295; AE 391; AL511; AP648; BB508; BX544 7610

O Christ, behind thy temple's veil (Gardiner. Sacred melodies) X Belmont 7611

O Christ, of angel legions (Bragers) [SLMFSLTDDRD, RRMDT] BP105 7612

O Christ, thy guilty people spare (Whitehead) [MFMRMDDTL, TDRMSFM] BN185; BO219 7613

-----. V [MFMRMDRDTL, TDRMSF] BO219 7614

O Christe, morgensterne (Gesius) [DDDDLSRR, RMFRRD, MF] K 350 7615

O Christliche herzen (Portnersches G-B. 1831) [MLLDTLLDDMRD, MFMR] BE389 7616

O come, all ye faithful (Wade. Cantus diversi.) X Adeste fideles 7617

O come, and mourn (Catholic) [SDDTDRTS, SDDFMRDR] AH126; BO168 7618

-----. R [TDRRFMRDR, SRRFMRD] 7619

O come, and mourn (Catholic) X Mother of mercy 7620

O come and mourn (Crookall) [MMRMSFRDRM, MFMFLS] BO168a 7621

O come and mourn (Montani) [MMDTLDMSFM, MFRTDR] BQ21 7622

O come and mourn (Slovak trad) [LMMTRDTL, LFFMLSF#M,] BN37 7623

O come, Divine Messiah (French mel) X The band of children 7624

O come, let us worship (Barnes) [SLLLRRRSD, DDFFFLS] Sap. 3 7625

O come, let us worship (Tschaikowsky) [LTDLTDL, DDRMRDT, RR] Sap. 4 7626

O come, loud anthems (Haydn) [DDSMMRDDTDR, DDSMM] AW18; BO4; BR287 7627

-----. R [MMRDSFMR, SSLSMFRD] 7628

-----. V [DDSMMRDDTDR, DSMMR] BO4 7629

-----. V [DSMMRDDTDR, RDSMMR] BR287 7630

O come, O come, Immanuel (Plainsong M 1) X Veni (Emmanuel) 7631

O cor, amoris victima (Planque) [MMMMRMRD, DMFSMFFM,] BO17 7632

O cor Jesu (Perosi) [SFMR, MSSDTLT, DLTSD] BQ236 7633

O, could I speak (Mozart) X Ariel 7634

O darkest woe (Wurzburg G-B. 1628) X O traurigkeit 7635

O dass ich tausend (Dretzel) X Dretzel II 7636

O dass ich tausend (Gnadaeur choralbuch) [DDSLDMRD, RM F#SDTLS,] AA420; AZ96-E 7637

-----. V [DDSLTDRMR, RM F#SDTL] AZ96-E 7638

O dass ich tausend zungen hätte (Gnadaeur choralbuch) X O dass ich tausend 7639

O dass ich tausend zungen hätte (Koenig. Harmonischer liederschatz. 1788) X Mentzer 7640

O day full of grace (Weyse) X Weyse 7641

O day of rest and gladness (German trad) X Mendebras 7642

O dear little children (Schulz) X Tekna 7643

O dearest love divine (Montani) [MMMMMSF, FRRDRFM, RD] BQ65 7644

O der alles [hoett' verloren] (Darmstadt G-B.) X Goldschmidt 7645

O Deus, ego amo te (Cologne. Symphonia ... 1695) X I love thee, O thou Lord 7646

O du Guds Lam (Söderberg) [SM RDMLSMDMR, RMRDM] N517 7647

O du hueter Israel (Freylinghausen) X Festus 7648

O du Liebe (Thommen. Christenschatz. Basel, 1745) X Cassel 7649

O du Liebe meiner Liebe (Darmstadt G-B.) X Gregor's 167th metre-E 7650

O du Liebe meiner Liebe (Thommen. Christen-schatz. Basel, 1745) X Cassel 7651

O, du mitt hjartas trangtau (Haeffner) [SSMFSLSM, SLLTTD, MR] N371 7652

O du store seierherre (Freylinghausen. G-B. 1704) X Conqueror 7653

O durchbrecher (Freylinghausen) X Conqueror 7654

O Emmanuel (Plainsong M 2) [SDTDLTLSLL, TLLTDL] BQ153 7655

O esca viatorum (Bourgeois) [LLLSSLDTD, MMSFM] A192; W543a; AI435; AM 511 7656

-----. V [LLLSLDTD, MMSFM RRD,] W543a 7657

O esca viatorum (Haydn) [SM DDLLLS, DTDRFFM, D] BN 90; BO34, 47; BQ42 7658

-----. V [SMDDLLLSS, DTD RFFM] BO47 7658a

O esca viatorum (Isaak) X Innsbruck 7659

O everlasting Light (Hallman) [DDTDRLTD, DFMMRDR, S] AY349 7660

O Fader var, barmhertig god (Teutsch kirchenampt. Strassburg, 1525) X Es woll' uns Gott genädig sein 7661

O Fader vor i himmerig (Schumann. G-B. 1539) X Old 112th 7662

O fair Creator of the skies (Bragers) [MDMSSLSFS, SRFFMMR] BP1 7663

O faithful cross (Catholic) [DD RMLSFM, MFSMMRDD,] BP30 7664

O Father, may thy word prevail (Lindeman) X Ak Fader, lad dit ord din aand 7665

O filii et filiae (French plainsong, 15th c: Solesmes version M 2) [LDRMRDRDT L, LDRMR] A99; B555; C555; E626; F130; J96; R206; S167; W124; X143; AD164; AF191; AL106a; AN194; AQ315; BM 81; BN41; BO178; BP35; BQ 28; BR563; BY163b; BZ 7666

-----. R [LLTLS, LDTLM, TDTL.] 7667

-----. V [LLTLS#, LTDTLTM, TDRM] X143b 7668

-----. V [LDRMDRDTL, LDR MDRD] AQ315 7669

O food that weary pilgrims

love (Bragers) [SDSLTDRM, DRTDRMFS,] BP57 7670
O food that weary pilgrims love (Haydn) X O esca viatorum 7671
O food to pilgrims (Isaak) X Innsbruck 7672
O for a closer walk with God (Kingsley) X Elizabethtown 7673
O for a faith that will not shrink (Havergal) X Evan 7674
O for a heart to praise my God (Showalter) [SLSDSDMR, RMR DLS, SL] AX387; AY7 7675
O gentle Savior (Sullivan) X Coena Domini 7676
O give me back my prophet dear (Careless) [MMRDSSFM, DDL FMMRR,] BC137 7677
O give thanks (Gelineau) [SLD DLDR, MRMDRDRT, T] BSp. 54 7678
O give the Lord, you sons of God (Gelineau) X How great is your Name 7679
O gloriosa virginum (Jacobsen) [MRDSFMRD, RRRFRDRM,] BO266 7680
O gloriosa virginum (Davidisches harfen, 1744) [SDRMFSRMFM, RMF#SLS] BQ210a 7681
O gloriosa virginum (La Tombelle) [LDTDTDRMFM, RDRMRD] BQ210b 7682
O gloriosa virginum (Plainsong M 2) [LLSMRSLDDTLT, LRRT] BN124 7683
O God all gracious (---) [SDRMF SRMFM, RMSSMF#] BH50 7684
O God, all gracious (Dunkley) [DMRDSMDRM, DDTSLTS,] BH45 7685
O God, almighty Father (Mainz, G-B. 1833) X O God, eternal Father 7686
O God eternal (McKinney) [SS MRRDLLSS, SSFRMR] AU302 7687
O God, eternal Father (Mainz G-B. 1833) [SDTDRMRSLTD RRD, SD] BL80; BM12; BN57 7688
O God of hosts (Grieg) X Hagerup 7689
O God of love (The Divine Companion) [MSFMRMF# SS, RMRDRT, M] E446; X 595 7690
O God of wisdom (American trad) X Campmeeting 7691
O God, our help (Croft) X St Anne 7692
O God, the eternal Father (Mendelssohn) X Heavenly love 7693
O God, the refuge (Schumann) X Canonbury 7694
O God, the Rock of ages (Achron) [RMRMRRR, RM RMLL, MSD] BH32 7695
O God thou art (French church mel., 16th c) [DTLSLSDSF M, MFMRSL] BL39 7696
O God, thou faithful God (Meiningen G-B. 1693) X O Gott, du frommer Gott 7697
O God, thy soldiers' faithful Lord (A Monk of Gethsemani) [SDDDRMFS, SLLLSFFS,] BN181 7698
O God, we pray for all mankind (Hastings) X Ortonville 7699
O God, whose law from age to age (Singer) [FMRRMRDD, LSFRMFM, F] BH97 7700
O Godhead hid (Terry) [SSFM RDTLFMR, MSF#MF#] BO 44 7701
O Gott, du frommer Gott (Fritsch) X Darmstadt 7702
O Gott, du frommer Gott (Meiningen G-B. 1693) [MM LSFM, MSDRMRD, MML] K 397; M195; N55; O41; P246; Q395; AA346; AK64; AZ146-C 7703
O Gott, du frommer Gott (Meiningen G-B. 1693) X Munich 7704
O Gottes Lamm (Mozart) [DM RDMSFM, DRMFMRM, R]

BQ35 7705

O Gottessohn (Spaeth) [DSFMMFF SSL, SFMMMM] K529 7706

O grant thy servants through thy grace (Glazer) X Azmon 7707

O grant us light (Roberts) [MS FMMRDT, RDTLDTTT,] W466 7708

O grosser Gott (Gesang - und notenbuch) [SMFSSLTD, TDTL SLLS,] Q132 7709

O Gud! ditt rike ingen ser (Waldis) X Waldis 7710

O Gud, du fromme Gud (Meiningen G-B. 1693) X O Gott, du frommer Gott 7711

O Guds Lam uskyldig (Decius) X O Lamm Gottes 7712

O happy day (Hermann) X Hermann 7713

O happy home! O blest abode (Robertson) [SMFSSLFS, SDDD TLDS,] BC133 7714

O happy home, where thou art loved (Niemeyer) X O selig haus 7715

O happy homes among the hills (Stephens) [MDRMRDRM, DTD RDTDTSD] BC337 7716

O happy is the man (Everett) X Mattie 7717

O hark! a glorious band (Asper) [SDRMFSMD, MLSFMR, SD] BC134 7718

O haupt voll blut und wunden (Hassler) X Passion chorale 7719

O heart of God (Stevenson) [SLSS, MMMFMM, SLTDSF] AW237 7720

O heart of Jesus (---) [DDSLTDR D, DMRDTDLLS,] BQ64 7721

O heart of Jesus (Montani) [MF SMDRMD, DTDFMMR, M] BQ58 7722

O heart of Mary (Piel) [SDM SFMRMRD, MFSMRD] BO94 7723

-----. R [SLMFSFMR, FM SLTDLS,] 7724

O heart of Mary (Staniforth) [D MSDSLSFM, SDDDFMR,] BN154 7725

O heilige dreifaltigkeit (Hermann) [DMFSSLLS, SSDTS LLS,] M59; Q340; AA-20, 120; AM339 7726

-----. V [DDDSSLLS, SSDT SLLS,] Q340 7727

O Heiliger Geist, O Heiliger Gott (Scheidt) X O Jesulein Süss 7728

O helligaand, du skat (Teutsch kirchenampt. Strassburg, 1524 or 25) X Aus tiefer not 7729

O Herre Gott (Enchiridion. Erfurt, 1527) [DDLLSDRM, R SFMRFMR] Q266; AA494 7730

O Herre Gott, in meiner not (Reiman) [LDTLSDRM, MMMRMDDT,] AA543 7731

O Herre Gott, in meiner noth (Gregor) X Old 96th 7732

O Herre Gud, oändelig (Crespin) [DDTLSDRM, DMFSM FRD,] N167 7733

O hjertens ve (Wurzburger G-B. 1628) X O traurigkeit 7734

O holy day (Pollock) [SSDRM, DDRDLS, SSDMS] AX66; AY 274 7735

-----. R [MFSLSM, DRDRM, SLSML] 7736

O Holy Ghost, thou gift (Teutsch kirchenampt. Strassburg, 1524-25) X Aus tiefer not 7737

O holy night (Adam) [MMMSS LLFLDS, SMRDM] AH615; AU468; AW86 7738

-----. V [MMLSSLLFLDS, SMRDM] AW86 7739

O holy words of truth and love (Parry) [SMR#MRDTD, SL S#LRT, SF] BC135 7740

-----. R [SLSMFLS, DRDLT RD, DM] 7741

O home beloved, where're I wander (Parry) [SDDDDRDD T, DRRRRMR] BC335 7742

O how beautiful the sky (Danish trad) X Celestia 7743

O how happy are they (---) [SS SSLDR, MRDLSMS, DR] AY205; BB292 7744

-----. V [SSSLDR, MDDDLS, DRMR] BB292 7745

O, how I love Jesus (---) [DM MMRMDDD, DRRRDRM] AT131; AU283; AW496; AX46; AY100 7746

-----. R [MMRMDD, RRDRM SF, MMR] 7747

-----. V [DMMMRRDD, DRRRD RMS,] AY100 7748

O, how I love Jesus (---) X O save me at the cross (---) 7749

O how I love thee Jesus (Montani) [DMFSDLS, SSMRDMRR, R] BQ328 7750

O how lovely (Milgrove) X Harts 7751

O, how lovely was the morning (Smyth) [MFSSSDDT, TDRRR FFM,] 7752

O Hunter blessed (Bragers) [DM DSMFSLS, STDRDMR] BP94 7753

O hvor salig er I dog I fromme (Crueger) [MLSMFMRDRD, MSF#SLS] O596 7754

O I long to see the beauty (Showalter) [SDMDRDLD, D MSDRMR, S] AS451 7755

-----. R [RMFFMRMS, MRD DDRMR, M] 7756

O, I love to talk with Jesus (Fischer) [DRMMFMMR, RM FLSFM, D] AX366; AY198 7757

O ihr ausewoehlten kinder (Hille) X Gregor's 161st metre 7758

O invidenda martyrum (Dijon church mel) [SDRMRFMRD, SLSLTDT] E58 7759

O Jerusalem, du schöne (Störl) X Storl II 7760

O Jesu (Reimann. Hirschberg G-B.) [SDRMFSFMR, RMF#SS F#S,] E406; G325; J490; Q24; R114; S79; X532; Z499; AB200; AD237; AF92; AN146; AQ205; AR83; AW244; BB492; BE311; BF402; BZ 7761

O Jesu! än de dina (Tomissön. Psalmebog. 1569) X Franzen 7762

O Jesu Christ (Reinigius) [LLLSSDRM, MFMRDRRD,] Eap. 46; F419 7763

O Jesus Christ, alone to thee (Gastorius) X Was Gott tut 7764

O Jesu Christ, dein kripplein ist (Crueger) X Manger 7765

O Jesu Christ, du höchstes Gut (Crueger) [DLSDRMFR, SMD FMRD, D] N134 7766

O Jesu Christ, meins lebens licht (Nürnberg G-B. 1676) [DDRMSDRMR, RMFSMRR] J376b; K16; N9; O125; Q64; Z600; AA195; AF208; AN268; AQ208 7767

O Jesus Christ, our only Lord (Schop) X Eternity 7768

O Jesus Christ, Redeemer (Beethoven) X A hymn anthem 7769

O Jesus Christ, remember (Montani) [DRMFLLS, SLTD RDT, TD] BQ55 7770

O Jesu Christe, wahres licht (Nurnberg G-B. 1676) X O Jesu Christ, meins lebens licht 7771

O Jesus, for din pine (Kingo. Gradual, 1699) [LLTDMTL, TMRDDT, TMT] O479; P171 7772

O Jesu! life-spring (Peloquin) [LFMFMRMDR, MSFLSDT] BL40 7773

O Jesu mi dulcissimi (Clausener. G-B.) [MDLMLSF#M, DRMFMRDD] E635; X184 7774

O Jesu, när jag hädan skall (Geistliche lieder. 1535) [D TLDMRRD, DTLRDTL, D] N406; AA284; AZ132-F 7775

-----. V [DDLDMRRD, DTLD RTL, D] AA284 7776

-----. V [DDLTDMRRD, D TLTDRD] AZ132-F 7777

O Jesus, thou the beauty art

(Montani) [MMRRMRDD, FFMMFR, SS] BQ15 7778

O Jesus victim-priest (Bach) X Potsdam 7779

O Jesu, warum legst du mir (Reimann) X O Jesu 7780

O Jesulein süss (Scheidt) [DDTD RTDTLS, MRRDRS] F425; J501; K145; X600; AF135; AR230; AW 547; BG109 7781

-----. V [DDDDR, TDTLS, MRR DRS] K145 7782

O King of kings (Cologne G-B. 1623) [SSDLTDS, SLLSFM, MFS] BL60 7783

-----. R [DMRTS, DMRTS, SD DRRM] 7784

O King of might (Murray) [MLT DTLSM, MLTDRM, ML] BL100 7785

O King of might and splendor (Mohr) [MMRSFMRM, MSDRR D, MM] BN205 7786

O King of nations (Maclean) [SD TLSLTDRMFRDD, DT] BN99 7787

-----. R [MDLRDT, LSDDRM, FMRD] 7788

O kom dog hver, som synd har gjort (Lindeman) [DMSFMLLS, SFMRRMFM] O435 7789

O lad din aand nu med os vaere (Lindeman) [SMDMRFMRM, DT DRSLT] O91; P95 7790

O Lamb of God, have mercy (Crueger) X Herzliebster Jesu 7791

O Lamm Gottes (Decius) [DM FSSLS, SDRMFMD, DM] J70; M418; N90; O147; P99; Q146; AA203; AK526; AW540; AZ127-A 7792

-----. V [DMFSSLS, SDRMFRD, DM] N90 7793

-----. V [DMSSSLS, SDRMFMR D, D] P99 7794

-----. V [DMSSSLSLS, SDRMF RD,] Q146 7795

-----. V [DMMSSLS, SDRMMFR D,] AA203 7796

-----. V [DRMFSSLS, SDRMFM RD,] AW540 7797

O Lamm Gottes unschuldig (Decius) X O Lamm Gottes 7798

O land of our King (Lindeman) X King's land 7799

O, land of rest, for thee I sigh (Miller) X Land of rest 7800

O lead and guide us (Beethoven) [MRDTTL, TDRMR, SFMRR] BI59 7801

O leide, leide gern (Gesangbuch mit noten) [SSMSSFMF, FFM RLSFM,] AW252 7802

O liebe meiner liebe (Thommen. Christen-schatz) X Cassel 7803

O Light, whose beams (Barnby) X St Chrysostom 7804

O little one (Scheidt) X O Jesulein süss 7805

O little town (English trad) X Forest green 7806

O little town of Bethlehem (Redner) X St Louis 7807

O living Bread (Zinck) X Copenhagen 7808

O Lord, be near me (Shelley) [MMMFTDRM, MSMRMD, RM] BH19 7809

O Lord, Divine, we come (Hull) X In dark Gethsemane 7810

O Lord, I am not worthy (Bragers) [SSSLSFM, RMDFM R, RFM] BP66 7811

O Lord, I am not worthy (Catholic trad) [MFSLSDDT, TDRFLSM, M] AH133; BN 100; BO49 7812

O Lord, I am not worthy (Montani) [MDRMSDLS, LFS MSFMR,] BQ129 7813

O Lord, in this great mystery (Andriessen) [LTDRMRDRT, LTDTLLS] BM5 7814

O Lord, my God (Sulzer) [ML MFLSFM, MRDFFF, RM] BH29 7815

O Lord of hosts (Careless) [SSDMRDDTLS, FMDLSF#] BC271 7816

O Lord, open thou our eyes

(Camidge) [DDDDDDD, MMM MMFFMM] R548; Sap. 22 7817

O Lord, our God (Thesaurus musicus) X America 7818

O Lord, our King (Alman) [LL DMLMF#M#F#RM, DLDML] BH72 7819

O Lord, our little ones (Beethoven) X Emmanuel 7819a

O Lord, reprieve (Irish; ancient) [DDDTTLLT, TDDRDTLS] BN187 7820

O Lord, save thy people (Clemens) [SMRMRD, DSLSSFFFMR] BI42-D 7821

O Lord, save thy people (Vitale) [LDDDTS, MLLS#LTDTT, T] BI49-D 7822

O Lord, thy all discerning eyes (Shelley) [MMDRDRMFF, MRDR MD, D] BH38 7823

O Lord, thy love (Hewlett) X Dalkeith 7824

O Lord, to thee I cry (Link) X Grace, 'tis a charming sound 7825

O Lord! to thee who dwellst above (Brightbill) X Communion hymn 7826

O Lord, what is man! (Heller) [MMMMFFFFFSFML, LLL] BH335 7827

O Lord, where shall I find Thee? (Weinberg) [SMMMMML, DDDTLD, MSS] BH21 7828

O Lord, while we confess (Chetham. Psalmody) X Marlow 7829

O Lord, within my soul (Hoffman) [SMMRRD, SFFMMR, SSSF] AX 333; AY190 7830

-----. R [MSSSMS, DMMFMR, MFFF] 7831

O Love divine (Brunk) [MMRD SLDT, TRR#MMFF#S,] AY419 7832

O Love how deep (Schumann G-B. 1539) X Old 112th 7833

O Love, how deep (Walter) [SD TLDRDT, SLLTSDLS,] BL90 7834

O love that nothing can efface (Pados) [SSSDTLSSM, SLTDR DD] BL46 7835

O lux beata trinitas (Sarum plainsong M 8) [SLSFMFRM FSLLSS, S] A171a; B11; E164; F15a; J133a; W4a; AL4; BJ86 7836

O Mary, don't you weep (Negro spiritual) [MFFMMMRRR, RMMRRRD] AH606 7837

-----. R [MMMFMMRR, RRMRRDD, L] 7838

O mein Jesu, ich muss sterben (Geistliche volkslied. 1850) X Desire 7839

O mensch sieh (Bohemian Br. G-B. 1566) [MMMRDRFM, SLMSMRMD] E121; R476; S344; W114; X142; Z484; AD392; AF262; AN414; AQ 141 7840

-----. V [MMMRDRFM, M SLMSMRM] R476 7841

O mentes perfides (Piae cantiones. 1582) [RSLFMRM, RSLLSFM, LD] X272; AQ 70 7842

O most holy (Hungarian hymn) [DSMFSMRDTDRFRMDRTD,] BL94 7843

O Mother blest (Roman hymnal, 1884) [SDDRRMFM, DFMR DR, SD] BN135; BO113 7844

-----. R [MSFMMFMR, MFM RDTLS,] 7845

-----. V [SDDRRMFM, MRD DRRD, S] BO113 7846

O Mother! most afflicted (---. 1638) [MLTDLTT, TLTDD T, MRR] BQ91 7847

O my Father (McGranahan) X My Redeemer 7848

O my Father (Mason) X Harwell 7849

O, my Saviour crucified (Hammontree) [DRMSFFM, MM SSDRM, MM] AU448 7850

O nata lux de lumine (Plainsong M 4) X Jesu, quadragenariae 7851

O Paradise (Barnby) X Paradise 7852

O Paradise (Hemy) X Paradise 7853

O Paradise! O Paradise (Slovak hymnal) [DDTTRRDD, MDDFM R, RR] BQ120 7854

O Pater sancte (Sarum Antiphonal. Plainsong M 4) [FRMMMMMS LLSLL#LSS] E160; F158a; X186a 7855

O perfect love (Barnby) X Sandringham 7856

O perfect love (Smith) [MDMLS FMRDMR, SLLTD] BI77 7857

O praise the Lord (Gelineau) [MS LR, LTRDL, LTRDL, RL] BSp. 19 7858

O praise ye the Lord (Haydn) X Lyons 7859

O precious sign and seal (Hopkins) X Ellers 7860

O purest of creatures (Montani) [MMMMRFTDRMR, RMMMR] BQ79 7861

O purest of creatures (Paderborn G-B. 1765) [SDDRMMFLSFMR D, SDD] AH135; BN136; BO58; BP92; BQ92; BV336; BY573b 7862

-----. V [SDDRMMFSMRD, SDDRM] BN136 7863

-----. V [SDDRMMMFSMRD, SDDR] BP92 7864

O purest of creatures (Paderborn G-B. 1765) X Lyons (Haydn) 7865

O quanta qualia (Paris Antiphoner. 1681) [DDRMDDFMRRD, SMDF] A589; B544; C544; D397; E465; F281; J596b; K184; N208; Q255; R122; S290; V709; W224; X200; AD178; AF310; AK178; AL173; AM219; AP253; AR103; BB202; BL85; BR98; BY191b 7866

-----. V [DDRMDFFMRRD, SM DFM] K184 7867

O Queen of peerless majesty (Benz) [SDSLSDRM, MRM RD, SDS] BN159 7868

O Queen of the Holy Rosary (Wurtemberg G-B. 1784) X Ellacombe 7869

O render thanks (Binder) [SSFM SLTD, DDTLDTLS,] BH194 7870

O render thanks (Sullivan) X Valete 7871

O rest in the Lord (Mendelssohn) [DMFRD, DLLTDS, S SFMF] AH618; AR684; AV 424; BF696 7872

O sacrament most holy (Fulda mel) [SDMRDLS, SLDRRD, SDM] BM9 7873

O sacrament most holy (Gounod) [DTDRMRD, SFMRMFM, M R#] BQ330 7874

O sacred Heart of Jesus, hear (Bourgeois) X Old 124th 7875

O Sacred Heart! our home (Ampleforth) [SMRDDRMFF M, MFSLDT] BO22 7876

O sacrum convivium (Perosi) [MFMRRSFM, SLTDTLSF#] BQ320 7877

O sacrum convivium (Remondi) [SSSSLLL, LLDLDTTTT] BQ235 7878

O safe to the Rock (Sankey) [SSFMMRDDTLTD, DFML] N600; P298; T135; AE298; AH308; AJ220; AL497; AM 551; AP523; AR450; AS273; AT271; AU129; AV354; AX 523; BB586; BY566 7879

-----. R [RRMF, MMFS, SDTL SMDM] 7880

O sälla land (Ahnfelt) [SSFM MMFSLSFR, RRDT] N431; AI235 7881

O salutaris (Duguet) [DMRM FMRDD, MMRMSF#S] E330b; AN60; AQ140; BM26; BN82; 82; BO273d; BP61; BQ226b 7882

O salutaris Hostia (Beethoven) [SMRDFMRDRTD, TDRMF] BO273c; BR248 7883

-----. V [SMRDFMRDRTD, TDDRM] BR248 7883a

O salutaris Hostia (Bourgeois) X Old 100th 7884

O salutaris Hostia (Lee) [LL TDLDRM, SLSMDRRM,] BL53 7885

O salutaris Hostia (Montani)

X The Word descending 7886
O salutaris Hostia (Antiphonale romanum M 1) X Exultet cor praecordiis 7887
O salutaris Hostia (Plainsong M 7) [SLSFSLSLTDTLSS, TR] BN79 7888
O salutaris Hostia (Plainsong M 8) [SSLDTLSFLSLTLSFS,] BN80; BQ226c 7889
O salutaris Hostia (Rheinberger) [MRMSSFMM, SFMRDTDR,] BQ226d 7890
O salutaris Hostia (Webbe) X Melcombe 7891
O salutaris Hostia (Werner) [SLSDSLLS, SDMRTDTL] AH114; BN84; BO273e; BP60; BQ226g 7892
O sanctissima (Sicilian mel) X Sicilian mariners 7893
O, save me at the cross (---) [SSSMSDDD, RRRDMMM, S] AX249 7894
-----. R [MRDLSD, RRDRMD, MRDL] 7895
O, save me at the cross (---) X O how I love Jesus (---) 7896
O say, can you see! (Smith) X National anthem 7897
O say, what is truth (Melling) [SMMRDDTLDS, SSDDRM] BC143 7898
O Seigneur (Genevan Psalter, 1551) [DSSLTDDTLSFS, MMDF] C37b; E512; W167; X696; AJ414; AL 45a; AP255a; AW19; BJ67; BY 685b 7899
-----. V [DSSLTD, DTLSF#S, MMDF] AJ414 7900
O selig haus (Neimeyer) [DMS DDTLSFFM, SMSLS] Q626; AO562; AW358; AX558 7901
O sing a joyous carol (Geistliche kirchengesang. 1599) X Rosa mystica 7902
O sing the great apostle (German trad) X Woodbird 7903
O, sing to me of heaven (Dunbar) X A few more years 7904
O Sion, haste (Storer) [SLDDTLS S#LFFM, MRMF] D249b; 7905
-----. R [SLTDRS, LTDR, SMTDLS] 7906
O Sion, haste (Walch) X Tidings 7907
O so bright (Traditional) X Grassmere 7908
O sometimes the shadows are deep (Fischer) X The Rock of refuge 7909
O sons of Sion (Manookin) [SD TDLSFMFS, DLTDRD] BC152 7910
O soul Supreme (Binder) [MM RDTTL, LFRTLS#, S#LT] BH 46 7911
O spirit of the living God (Est's Psalter) X Old 25th 7912
O store Gud (Swedish folk mel) [SSSM, SSSLLFL, LLLSM] BZ 7913
-----. R [SSDMRDTDLS, DDTR, FL] 7914
O such wonderful love (McHose) [SSSLSMRDLD, LSDDMR] AX 88; AY200 7915
O sueszer Stand, O sel'ges leben (Freylinghausen. 1704) X Gregor's 184th metre-A 7916
O sweet Infant Jesus (Bansbach) [MFSSSLSLSF, FSLLLS] BQ333 7917
O take my hand (Silcher) X So nimm denn meine Hände 7918
O, the best Friend to have is Jesus (Bilhorn) [SDMMR#MF LR, DDTDTLS] BB528 7919
-----. R [SSMFSLSF, FFRM FSFM,] 7920
O the bitter shame (Mountain) [DDDDTDRRD, MMMRRRM] AR463; AS281 7921
O the unsearchable riches (Sweney) X Unsearchable riches 7922
O think of the home over there (O'Kane) X Home over there 7923
O thou, before the world began (Asper) [MSFMMRMFMRM, MMDTT] BC274 7924

O thou eternal King (---) [DMRD SLTD, MRTDLS, MR] BN53; BO182 7925
O thou immortal holy Light (Tallis) X Tallis' Canon 7926
O thou immortal Light divine (Webbe) X Melcombe 7927
O thou kind and gracious Father (Careless) [DDRRMDTLS, SSLTDTL] BC276 7928
O thou pure Light (Slovak hymn) [MMFSDTDRTDS, LDLSM] BQ33 7929
O thou that rulest earth (Bourgeois) X Toulon 7930
O thou Rock of our salvation (Clayson) [MFSMDLSM, RMFLS FM, S] BC130 7931
O thou who hearest prayer (Welsh mel) [LLS#LTD, DTMMR#M, LLS#L] AF526 7932
O thou whose power o'er moving worlds (Barnby) X Longwood 7933
O thou, whose presence (Heller) [MMMSSDDF, FMS#LLSFM,] BH216 7934
O thou, whose temple stands (Arne) X Arlington 7935
O traurigkeit (Würzburger G-B. 1628) [MDLT, S#LLS#, MMM FMRDT] A83; F126; J87; M387; O322; P185; Q167; AA 215; AZ45-A 7936
-----. V [MDDT, DLLS#, M MMFMRD, T] O322 7937
-----. V [MDDT, DLLS#, M MSFMRD, T] AZ45-A 7938
O traurigkeit! O herzeleid! (Wurzburger G-B. 1628) X O traurigkeit 7939
O turn to Jesus (Slovak hymn) [MLTDMRDT, RRRMRDTL,] BQ115 7940
O turn to Jesus, mother! (---) [SSSF#SLMSF, FMFLSFM] BO143 7941
O ursprung des lebens (Selle) X Zoerbig 7942
O Virgin all lovely (Brun) [LD DDTL, LDDDTL, LTLS] BN160 7943
-----. R [DRRSF, MRMRD, DRD TD.] 7944
O, Vision bright (Bowen) [DD RM, RMFS, SLSMDRMR,] BO116 7945
O welt, ich muss dich lassen (Isaak) X Innsbruck 7946
O welt, sieh hier (Friese) [LFRSFMM, MFFSSLL, LT] Q171a; AA205 7947
O welt, sieh hier dein leben (Crueger) X Gregor's 79th metre 7948
O what a change (Harkness) [SLDTFFFLTS, MRDSLD] AI95 7949
-----. R [DTLTLSF#S, MF SLLLTD] 7950
O what could my Jesus do more (Sweney) X Story of Jesus 7951
O what precious balm (Bourgeois) X Bourgeois 7952
O what songs of the heart (Clayson) [SSDDDDMRDLD S, SSDD] BC87 7953
O, where are the reapers (Root) X Harvest home 7954
O why not tonight (Bushey) X Calvin 7955
O wie sehr lieblich! (Bohemian Br.) X Augusta 7956
O wie selig seid ihr doch (Stötzel. Choralbuch. 1744) [DMFSSLSFMSFM, DMFS] K510; M294; Q589; AA547 7957
O wie selig seid ihr doch ihr frommen (Crueger) X O hvor salig er I dog I fromme 7958
O wie selig sind die seelen (Freylinghausen) X Gregor's 95th metre 7959
O wonderful prayer (Giffe) [SS MMMRDLRR, TTTTLS] AS 131 7960
O wonderful word of salvation (Fillmore) [SSFMMRDDL, DSSDMMS] AS175 7961
O wonderful words (Swedish trad) [MLLTDTLTM, MMRRDDL] P258 7962

O wondrous name (Sankey) [SS FMDDTL, LSLSMR, SS] BR 527 7963
-----. R [SRTSSMDS, SFMRDDT, S] 7964
O word of God incarnate (Mason) X Missionary hymn 7965
O word of God incarnate (Smart) X Lancashire 7966
O, worship the King (Haydn) X Lyons 7967
O worship the Lord (Gaul) [SSFM FMMFSDTTLL, LM] AR630 7968
O worship the Lord (Lowry) X Beauty of holiness 7969
O ye mountains high (---) X Denmark 7970
Oak (Mason) [DDRMRD, RDTD, DDRMRD] L591; AX609; AY 147; BB659 7971
Oak Hill (Kidner) [SSSFMRDRM, L, SDDMMS,] BV326a 7972
Oakland (Belden) [SDRMDRMF, FMRDMRTD,] BB441 7973
Oakley (Williams) [LDRMRDRML, SDRMRDR] X58 7974
-----. R [DRFMRRD#, MM FMSSF#, SS] 7975
Oakridge Lynch (Shaw) [MRMFM R, DRMRS, L# LSFM] X518 7976
Oaksville (Zeuner) [DDSMDDDTD R, RMDRMF#] V380 7977
Obedience (Byers) [DRMSFMMR, RMFLRFM, D] AX415 7978
-----. R [SSDTFFLS, SSDTTLS, D] 7979
Oberammergau (Oberammergau) [MSSDMSSD, SDTLSSF# S] W 92b 7980
Oberlin (Demuth) [SLDDTLSTRTLS, MRDD] Y20; AC6b; BB326 7981
Obiit (Parratt) [DDRDFMLS, DTL SFSM, M] BV555a 7982
Oblation (Crueger) [SDTLSMFSS FM, SLT] A205; E223b; F551b; J225b; X186b 7983
Oblation (Whitlock) [SLSDRMSRM RDRL, LRM] BE257 7984
Oblations (Stainer) [DSSLDS, LTDR MRR, RMT] B215 7985
Ocean Star, we greet you (Ett) X St Martin 7986
Ockbrook (Hutton. Tunes for the hymns) [LDLRDFFM, RLDTTL, MM] AZ590-E 7987
Odumin (Hartmann) X Hartmann 7988
O'er the gloomy hills of darkness (Petersen) [MRDSFM DTLLS, SFMLS] BC127 7989
O'er the silent waters (German mel) [MMSSDD, LFFSLS, SR RM] BI72 7990
O'erwhelmed in depths of woe (Montani) [DDTLTS#, MMRD RT, TDRM] BQ25 7991
Of all the thoughts of God (Deutsch) [DMMSFMRMD, DDTDRMF] BH224 7992
Offertorium (Haydn, J. M.) [MFSDDTLTDS, SMRMFM] F176; BV72 7993
Often weary and worn (Pollock) [DRMMMMMFSSS, SSLL] AX531; AY149 7994
-----. R [MFSMSD, SSLLL SSMFS] 7995
Ohne rast und unverweilt (Knecht) X Vienna 7997
Oikoumenikos (Poteat) [MMM SSFMMRD, MMMRSD] AR 572 7998
O'Kane (O'Kane) [DMSLSMD RD, DRRRSFM,] AT478; AU250; AX567; BB553 7999
-----. R [DRMMMMRMFS, SSLLLS] 8000
Olaynu (Jewish trad) [SMD DDTLTLSSSLTD, S] BH329 8001
Old Black Joe (Foster) X I love him 8002
Old Bohemian carol (Bohemian trad) X Kommet ihr hirten 8003
Old Commons (Campbell) [SSSSMDRD, DFSLFR, RR] BV436a 8004
Old French carol (French trad) [SDRMFSS, LSMFSD, SDR]

BD222 8005
Old French mel (French carol) X Gloria 8006
Old French noël (French trad) [DRMDD, SLLSFM, RMFSS,] BD213; BG75 8007
Old French melody (Corbeil) X Orientis partibus 8008
Old German (Harmonia sacra) X Mason 8009
Old hundred twenty-fourth (Bourgeois) X Old 124th 8010
Old Judea (Jackson) [MLDTS#LM, FMRDRM, MSR] AH249 8011
-----. R [SDDSMFMRD, DTLLLR D] 8012
Old martyrs (Scottish Psalter, 1615) X Plaintive martyrs 8013
Old, old story (Doane) X Tell me the old, old story 8014
Old rugged cross (Bennard) [MF SF#LSSSLS#TL, LSFM] AE186; AH296; AT93; AR71; AV369; AX105; BB533; BZ 8015
-----. R [TDRRRRDTD, DTLLL DT] 8016
Old-time power (Gabriel) [MR DDRDTT, SFFFFM, MR] AT173 8017
-----. R [SMMMRRDMDDDLLS, DD] 8018
Old --- Psalms, etc. by number follow here 8019
Old First [1st] (Genevan Psalter, 1542) [SLSMSFMFRD, DMFSSL] AN41 8020
Old 18th (Anglo-Genevan Psalter, 1561) [LLS#LDTTM, MLDTTL, LL] W586b; X43 8021
Old 22d (Anglo-Genevan Psalter, 1556) [DDRMSFFMDFMRRD, SL] E163; S85; X176; AF259 8022
Old 23d (Divine musical misc. 1754) [SDSMRDFMMR, MMRM FM] AL272 8023
Old 25th (Anglo-Genevan Psalter) [DMRMFS, MMDFRD, MRDS] B189; E149; F149; W583b; X195 8024
Old 25th (Est's Psalter, 1592) [DMRDDFRM, MRDSFFRM,] BI51 8025
Old 26th (Moravian) [DMFRM FMRM, SSMRMFM] AZ22-Aa 8026
Old 29th (Rosenroth) [SMFSLS SFM, SMRMFSM] AZ22-U; BA289 8027
Old 30th (Est's Psalter, 1592) [MMR#MLDTL, MSMRDM, M R] X693 8028
Old 38th (Bourgeois) [DTLT DRMR, MRDTRRMD] AN88b; BJ64; BX150b 8029
Old 42d (Bourgeois) X Bourgeois 8030
Old 44th (Anglo Genevan Psalter, 1556) [DDTDLSSD, SFMRRD, DD] E211; W530b; X655; AP2 8031
Old 71st (Bourgeois) X Genevan Psalm 22 8032
Old 72d (Weisse) X Ravenshaw 8033
Old 77th (Este's Whole book of Psalms, 1592) X Old 120th 8034
Old 77th-A (Freylinghausen) X Gregor's 77th metre 8035
Old 80th (Scottish Psalter, 1564) X Psalm 80 8036
Old 81st (Old 77th: Day's Psalter, 1562) [DMFSSLLS SLTDLT, SD] E461; F529; W355a; X216 8037
Old 81st (Este's Whole book of Psalms, 1592) X Old 120th 8038
Old 96th (Gregor) [MDTLLS FM, SDRMFMRD,] AZ97-B 8039
Old Hundred (Bourgeois) X Old 100th 8040
Old hundred (Bourgeois) X Tabor (Kugelmann) 8040a
Old 100th (Bourgeois) [DDTLS DRM, MMMRDFMR,] A139; B249; C249; D468; E365; F 166; G3; H20; I6; J161; K 492; L68; M10; N275; O1; P16; Q13; R24; S1; T184; U487; V1; W229; X443; Y296; Z104; AA78; AB11; AC334;

AD4; AE5; AF4; AG7; AH182; AI448; AJ268; AK24; AL6a; AM 1; AN496; AO8; AP86; AQ13; AR2; AS8; AT13; AU3; AV33; AW594; AX11; AY410; AZ22-E; BA21; BB13; BC214; BDp. 1; BF174; BI29-D; BJ79, 80; BK 61; BL79; BM93; BN81; BO 273b; BR49; BV231; BX1; BY2; BZ 8041

-----. V [DDTLSDRM, MMMRMFM R,] BJ80 8043

Old 104th (Ravenscroft's Whole book of Psalms.) [LDTLMDRF MR, RMSF#S, D] A260a; E178; F167a; W30; X211; AL21b; AP 93b; BJ63; BV459; BY573 8044

Old 106th (Gnadaeur choral buch) X O dass ich tausend 8045

Old 107th (Bourgeois) [LLMLLSS M, MFMDRD, LL] E493; R230; S185a; W151; X512; BZ 8046

-----. R [LMF#SLSF#M, LTLMF# M, MS] 8047

Old 112th (Schumann G-B. 1539) [MMDRMDTL, MMRSMDRM,] A147; B410b; C229; E462; F227; J359a; K506; M390; N 593; O97; P79; Q318; W459a; X566; AA396; AF44; AI437; AL 22; AM41; AN46; AP243; AQ 32; AZ96-A; BA951; BP103; BV468a; BY16; 8048

-----. V [MMDRMRDTL, MMRS MRD] M390 8049

-----. V [MMDRMRDTL, MMF# SMRD] AZ96-A 8050

Old 113th (Strassburg Psalter) X Psalm 68 (Greiter) 8051

Old 117th (Genevan Psalter, 1551) [SDDTSLTD, DTLSFMRD,] E637; X191 8052

Old 120th (Est's Whole Book of Psalms) [DMFSLS, SLTDLT, SDTLS] A115; B274; C274; E209; F259; Q405; S229; X615; Z478; AN396; BL18; BV643; BY449a 8053

Old 124th (Meter: 10 10 10 10 10) (Bourgeois) [DRMFMRDDTD, MFSLS] A536; D280a; E114; F380; J348; Q307; R357; S424; T254; X329; Y176; Z372; AB298; AC287; AD361; AE412; AF451; AJ353; AK410; AL520; AM 514; AN342; AP112; AQ196; AR578; AW354; BF574; BK 102; BL92; BM11; BN72; BO21; BV28; BX202; BZ 8054

Old 124th (Bourgeois) X Toulon 8055

Old 127th (Bourgeois) [DFFM DRMF, FMRDTLSF,] AD183 8056

Old 130th (Strassburg Psalter, 1539) [LRMFMRD, FMRFSL, SLT] J398; N191 8057

Old 134th (Bourgeois) X St Michael 8058

Old 136th (Bourgeois) [LTSDT LSL, MLTLDDTD,] BJ70 8059

Old 136th (Est's Psalter, 1592) [DSDDTD, LDDLFF, DRTD] X197a 8060

Old 137th (Crespin. Psalms) X Norwich 8061

Old 148th (---) [DMSDSFM, SLLSFMR, SD] BY161 8062

Old 168th (Hintze) X Salzburg 8063

Old 193d (Grimm's Choral buch) [LDMLMLTMRDTL, MMMR] AZ298-B 8064

Old 197th (Neander) X Sieh, hier bin ich, Ehrenkönig 8065

Old 271st (Gregor's Choral buch) [SDSLFM, SDTTLS, RTSL] AZ38-A; BA857 8066

Old 466th (Grimm. Choral buch) [DMSSLSFMRD, RMF#SSL] AZ185-D (app.) 8067

Old 583d (Hutton. Tunes for the hymns) [SDRMLSFMRD, MR DTDR] AZ32-C; BA668 8068

Oldbridge (Quaile) [MMMMDRMD, SSSFRMDR] Eap. 72; G41; O605; W213; AQ159; AT495; AU301; BZ 8069

Olden (Mason) [SDSDDRRM, MFFMRDMR,] BB535 8070

Oldown (Harwood) [DTDFFFMS, DMRM, MMRR] W441a; BE

256; BV581a; BY717 8071
Olena (Herbert) [SMRDDTLLS, SSLTDTD] T104a; AJ39 8072
Oliphant (Baillot) [SSLSMDSLS M, FSLSTD] U32; V333b; BR 453b 8073
Oliva (Morton) [SSDFMMRD, TLD FLS, SS] T17; AJ22 8074
Oliva speciosa (Italian) [SMFSD TLS, LSFMFMRM,] Eap. 49 8075
Olivarius (Lutkin) [SSLTDMLSS, SSDTLLT] I712 8076
Oliver (Oliver) [DMTDFMMRD# RL, LLLSF] AC221 8077
Oliver (King) [MLTDMRDTL, S#LDRRM, M] X117 8078
Olive's Brow (Bradbury) [SSS LLSSS, DDDRMRRD,] G133; H163; I147; L241; M66; T272a; U96; V151; Z232; AD144; AE 118; AF178; AG92; AH283; AJ379; AK132; AL209b; AM182; AO161; AP332b; AR163; AS132; AT104; AU295; AV105; AW103; AX114; AY360; BA223; BB121; BZ 8079
Olivet (Dykes) [SSDDMS, DFMMR D, DSSD] D373b 8080
Olivet (Mason) [DMSSFM, RRF FMR, MRFS,] A449; B211; C211; D345a; Eap. 58; G176; I184; J375; K360a; L172; M 234; N212; O456; P269; Q394; R378; S285; T137; U194; V357; W415a; Z355; AA351; AB172; AC155; AD218; AE193; AF348; AG211; AH358; AI238; AJ204a; AK221; AL263; AM454; AN11; AO274; AP419; AR261; AS270; AT257; AU209; AV168; AW150; AX453; AY60; BA429; BB246; BF369; BR303; BY549a; BZ 8081
Olivet (Woodbury) X Eucharist 8082
Olmutz (Plainsong M 7) [SLSDRD, DTDLLS, SLSD] C456; D186; H228; I227; L387; T262a; V277; AJ366; AM176; AO444; AS304; AV256; BE404; BF605; BR251; BX343b 8083
Olney (Gounod) [SSSLMSFF, FTLS FM, SD] I696 8084
Olney (Mason) [SSFMFS, DTD FMR, SSFM] L362; V342; AA382 8085
Olrig Grange (Bridge) [DMDDM DSFFM, MSSF#MF#] BX39 8086
Olwen (Welsh carol) X Poverty 8087
Omaha peace song (Omaha Indian trad) [MRDDLS, MRR DLSLL, LS] Y314 8088
Ombersley (Gladstone) [MRD FFFFM, MFSLLRDT,] G205; J118; W24; Y217; AB83; AC 212; AL20a; AR399; BA658; BB67; BE243; BV635; BY 393 8089
Omega and alpha (Piae cantiones, 1582) X Puer nobis 8090
Omni dei (Corner. G-B) [DD RDMSFM, DRMSSF#S, S] E120; J282; W395b; X217a; AF539; BY416b 8091
Omnia (Barnby) X Edinburgh 8092
Omnipotence (Anderson) [DTD RDFDRM, MMRDDRD] BB 97 8093
Omnom kayn (Jewish trad) [DDRMFSSLTD, DDTLSR] BH23 8094
On Jordan's Bank (Vehe. G-B. 1537) [MSSLTDTL, SDRM RDRT] BM59 8095
On Jordan's Bank (Wittwe. Musikalisches handbuch.) X Winchester New 8096
On Jordan's banks (American trad) X Jordan's Bank 8096a
On Jordan's stormy banks (O'Kane) X O'Kane 8097
On mighty wings (Jewish trad) X Oveenu malkaynu 8098
On parting (Jewish trad) X N'eelah mel I 8099
On the mountain's top appearing (---) [MMSFRDTDMR, FML SDR] BC273 8100
On the radiant threshold (Perkins) [SLTDFF, MRDTM, RRMRS] AS18 8101
-----. R [SSLSFLTL, SSFMLT,

DF] 8102
On the wood His arms (Traditional: mediaeval) [MFSSLLS, DTLS, MFSSL] BP28 8103
On this day earth shall ring (Piae cantiones, 1582) X Theodoric 8104
On this day, O beautiful Mother (Lambillotte) [MRMSSFMFLS, MRMSSR] AH134; BO114 8105
-----. R [DTLSLSS, DTLSFRM, SF#] 8105a
On this day, the first of days (Freylinghausen) X Luebeck 8106
Once again (Dykes) [SF#SMMRD TL, SLTDTTL] BR556 8107
Once again to its close (Drury) [DRMDRS, DRMDRS, DDRM] AR583 8108
Once again we come (Naylor) [DRMMMRDSSS, LSMMRD] AX51 8109
-----. R [SSLLLLLSSSS, MRDDS] 8110
Once for all (Bliss) [DMLSMM RDMR, RD#RFLL] AI129; AT 199; AU340 8111
-----. R [SLTDDDTLLS, SLTDDD] 8112
Once more before we part (Unseld) [DDDDRM, MMMSSS, MMMS] AX78; AY117 8113
Once more, O Lord (Weinberg) [DDDDDDRRM, DFFMDMF] BH7 8114
Once more the liberal year (Heller) [SSSLLDTD, DDDRMFMR] BH181 8115
One day (Marsh) [SMFSLTDTLS M, FRMFM] AM689; AT85; AX 309 8116
-----. R [DLDTF, LTLSM, SFMLLL] 8117
One God! One Lord (Rossini) X Linwood 8118
One more day's work (Lowry) [SSSLSDS, DRMDLS, SLS] I419; AS27; AU55; AV387; BB622 8119
-----. R [SSSLSSD, SSSLSSR, SM] 8120
One radiant morn (---) X Taenk, naar engang den taage (---) 8121
One resolve (Christiansen) [MMMMMSLSSDDM, MMMR] P247 8122
One sweetly solemn thought (Ambrose) X Ambrose 8123
One sweetly solemn thought (Phillips) [SMDRDLS, SLL SLSM, SM] V762; AU183; AX611 8124
-----. R [RMRDS, MFMR, MRDDTLS] 8125
One thing needful (Crueger) X Ratisbon 8126
Oneanta (Hall) [MSSDFFMRS, DTLSLS] A571b; B28; J 535b 8127
Onido (Pleyel) [SSSMFRM, FSLTDSSFF] L272 8128
Only a sinner (Towner) [SMF SDTLDLS, FRMTLS] AI131; AM698 8129
-----. R [SSSLSDRM, MDDR DDRM,] 8130
Only a step (Doane) [MMMFM RD, LSDDMR, MMM] AU432; AX254; AY503 8131
-----. R [LLLDSSSM, MFSM R, RRR] 8132
Only a step to Jesus (Doane) X Only a step 8133
Only believe (Rader) [SF#SM DTDL, SSLSMMMR] AU318 8134
Only remembered (Sankey) [SF#SDSMSFRFM, LTTDS] AX584; AY530 8135
-----. R [RRMFF, MMFSS, S F#SLTD] 8136
Only thee (Blosser) [MFSMLS F#SM, DRMFMRM] AY197 8137
Only thee (Perkins) [SSSDTDR D, RMFMR, DRM] BB580 8138
-----. R [SDMDLS, SSSDMDR, SDM] 8139
Only thine (Byers) [SSDMDLDS, DRSSDRM, M] AX406 8140
-----. R [SSMMMD, DRSRMF M, SSM] 8141

Only thy tender care (Ackley) [SF#LSDM, MFMRL, TLSDR] U226 8142
-----. R [MDLSF#S, LDFMDS, MFMR] 8143
Only trust him (Stockton) X Stockton 8144
Ono adonoy kaper no (Jewish trad) [DMDDD, LTDTDRD, LLLT] BH330 8145
Onslow (Batchellor) [SF#SLSM DLS, SSSLDTD] R467; AE438; AF479; AL585; AM659; AP720; AR554; AT341; AU310; AW423; BK6 8146
Ontario (American mel) [SLSDDDT LS, STRFRMD] AP492b 8147
Onward (---) [SSSMDDDS, SSLLL LS, S] BB373 8148
Onward (Barrington) [SSLSMD, RLTLS, SSLSM] D516b; U374; AC263; AO391b; AW267; BF 515 8149
Onward (Filby) X Fortitude 8150
Onward (Gauntlett) X University College 8151
Onward (Roe) [MMRDLS, SMR DR, MMRDL] K562 8152
Onward brothers, march still onward (Beethoven) X Beethoven 8153
Onward, Christian soldiers (Jude) [MMMMMRDRM, FMRDR, MF] AU475 8154
Onward, Christian soldiers (Sullivan) X St Gertrude 8155
Op alle som paa Jorden bor (Hermann) X Hermann 8156
Op, thi dagen nu frembryder (Lindeman) [DDMRDSLS, DRMM SFMR,] O160 8157
Open my eyes (Scott) [DTLSLLSS, RTLSTLSS,] R390; AE200; AG227; AI158; AR295; AS257; AT312; AU351; BZ 8158
Open our eyes, thy glory beholding (Sellers) [SDRMMMFMMR, STRFFL] AU441 8159
-----. R [SF#FMSLSF#SM, FFM RFS] 8160
Open the wells of salvation (Pollock) [SDRMDRDLSD, DTDRRR] AX371; AY339 8161
-----. R [SMFSSLSF#S, MM RDRRR] 8162
Open thou mine eyes (Fillmore) [DSFMLLTDT, DDDDD DD] AS495 8163
Open wide thy heart (Owen) [M MMRDSL, RDTD, RRRRR] AX251; AY505 8164
-----. R [MMMFMRD, FFF SFMR, SS] 8165
Opening song (Heller) [SDM SSLSLS, MRDDRDR] BH 257 8166
Oppidans Mews (Shaw) [SLL# SLF, RMFSM, TDRMD] X 386b; BV345; BY757 8167
Optatus votis (Plainsong M 4: Barking hymnal) [MSLLSS FM, DRFMRFRM] F14 8168
Optimism (Hunnewell) [DDTLS DRM, DRRRM, DDT] BF575 8169
Ora labora (Noble) [SLSS, DT LSMLLSFS, M] A576; B497; C497; R287; S366; AB262; AD317; AF293 8170
Oremus (Freylinghausen) X Morgenglanz der ewigkeit 8171
Oremus pro pontifice (Plainsong M 1) [SLSSDTDRMRD TDLSS] BN201 8172
Oremus pro pontifice (Schubert) [MMRDRMMMSFMRDFM, M] BQ247 8173
Orford (Mason) [MFSLSSMR MFM, MFSLS] BR504a 8174
Oriel (Bradbury) [MRDSDTDR, MRDLDDTD,] L468; T186; AJ272; AO118 8175
Oriel (Ett) [DDDDRMFM, MMRDTLS, D] A326; B89; C89; D321a; E228b; F190a; G79; K36; O131; W164; X 190b; AL163; AP85a; BM31; BN110; BO14; BR464b; BV 282; BY79 8176
Orient (Gounod) [MMMSMFM DRRD, SF#SMF#] D66b; U492; AB416; AH556; AI25;

AR631; AS496; BF674 8177
Orient (Stanford) [SSDTLSFM, MMSDMRMD,] BY756 8178
Orient (Steggall) [DRMLSS, DDR RM, DMFMR] BR158 8179
Orient morning (Mann) [SDFMRL DT, SFMDTLR, S] N233; O241; V25 8180
Orientis partibus (Corbeil) [DR MDRTD, SSLMFSSM, M] A324; B115; C90b; D149b; E129; F524; G405; J509; L159; Q193; R457; W341; X153; AA221; AB354; AG 299; AL407; AN25a; AP549; AW 102; BA68; BD14; BE114; BF 506; BK157; BN151; BO123; BP74; BQ197; BV601b; BY48, 469; BZ 8181
-----. V [DRMDRTD, SSLMSSM, MR] X153 8182
-----. V [DDRMDRTD, DSSLF SSM,] BK157 8183
-----. V [DRMDRTDSSLFSSM, MR] BQ197 8184
Orison (Custance) [MMMRLSMR R#, MMMLDTF#] C16b 8185
Orisons (Evans) [SDMMRS, SDM MRS, FMLT] W673 8186
Orisons (Kocher) X Dix 8187
Orisons (Wesley, S.S.) [MMDL, LLLLLLL, MMDLL] Y251; AD360; AP663b 8188
Ormiston (Spielman) [SDDDRMR D, RSSSLTLS,] M331 8189
Orono (Harrington) [MR#MFMSF LFM, RDRM, SS] I542 8190
Orpheus (Gluck) [SMFSDDTL, S LSFSFMR,] AR620 8191
Ortonville (Hastings) [SDDRRMR D, SLLSLS, SD] C194a; D648; G220; H94; I135; J570; M296; N194; R142; S197b; T327; U71; V129; Z381; AE100; AG111; AH311; AI43; AL666; AM106; AO202; AR108; AS176; AT118; AU188; AV62; AW120; AX18; AY21; BA493; BB159; BZ 8192
Orwell (Newton) [MSSLMS, SMD TDR, MFFM] BY605 8193
Orwigsburg (Hoffman) [DRMSSDR MRD, DRMSSD] AT298; AV347; AX357; AY499 8194
-----. R [DDDDS, DDDDL, FSLSSS] 8195
Osborne (Carey) [LLTDFMRDT L, MLTDRM,] S319b; X550 8196
Osgood (Mason) [SSLSSTLTD SS, MSDLS] AO353 8197
Oslo (Norwegian trad) [LLM MRDTLS#, LTDDRR] A596 a; J586; X232 8198
Oss Kirstna bör tro och besinna (Swedish, before 1540) [ML LTDDTS# L, TMMRDDT] N445 8199
Ostend (Mason) [SMFSSLSS, MRMFSM, SM] T287; AJ297; AM230 8200
Ostergaard (Danish folk mel) [SMRDTDSRM, TDDFMRR] Z493; BK28 8201
Oswald (Dykes) X St Oswald I 8202
Oswald's Tree (Davies) [SS LSTLSDTLSM, RDRM] F247; BV6 8203
Oswestry (Dykes) [MRMSFMR MFMR, FMFLS] BR407 8204
Oswin (Dykes) [DSFMRDRT, SDRMFR, SF] V439; AA74 8205
Othello (Excell) [SDRMFSLSF M, DMMRDS,] AT208; AU 108; BB638 8206
-----. R [MFSSMDS, RMFFFF F, LT] 8207
Others (Hackleman) [MSLDRD LDT, SFFMRDT] AS338 8208
-----. R [SSFLFFM, MMRLF LS, SD] 8209
Others (Shields) [SFMMMRMF, FTLLTLSS,] AU77 8210
-----. R [MM, MMFF, FFF TLS, MMMR] 8211
Otterbourne (Haydn) X Bowen 8212
Ottery St Mary (Ley) [LLLL TTDL, DRMRDTT, L] BV379 8213
Otto (English trad) X Comfort 8214

Our best (Tullar) X Tullar 8215
Our brother is born (Fargeon) [LDTSLDSM, MLFTSD, DT] BG188 8216
Our Christ (Overby) [DMRDRD RMSS, MFFMDM] J593a; P206 8217
Our Father (Heys) [DSFMRDRM, MRDDTD, SD] AJ434 8218
Our Father (Plainsong arr) [MR MFMRM, MRDRMRD, MR] AW 610 8219
Our Father, our King (Jewish trad) X Oveenu Malkaynu 8220
Our Father, we beseech thy grace (Schalit) [LLLLTDTRT, TLT DRTR] BH145 8221
Our fortress strong (Dunkley) X O God, all gracious 8222
Our guiding star (Mendelssohn) X Trust 8223
Our Lady, Trondhjem (Lindeman) [DSLLFTRD, SMMRMFRM,] J160b; O9; P2; AA470; BE 291 8224
Our Lord is now rejected (McGranahan) X The crowning day 8225
Our mountain home so dear (Stephens) [MMMSFM, RSF MFS, LTDT,] BC144 8226
Our Pilot (Wilson) [SLSMRDFFF, RMFTLS, S] AU299 8227
-----. R [SDTLSLT, FTLSFSM, MF] 8228
Our pious fathers (Grauman) [ML DTLS#LTM, MDDRDRM] BH215 8229
Our prayer (Garrett) [SSDMRDDT, SSTFMRMD,] AS53 8230
Our Shepherd is the Lord (Lutkin) X Psalm 23 8231
Our times are in thy hand (Hammontree) [MRDLDS, LTDDRD, MRDF] AU446 8232
Out of my bondage, sorrow and night (Stebbins) X Jesus I come 8233
Out of the depths (Bragers) [LL TDDT, DTLSL, DDRMM] BP96 8234
Out of the depths (Gelineau) [MMMS, SSMSL, LLLD, DTS] BL20; BSp. 38 8235
Out of the depths (Ronan) [SSSLLSSFRM, SDTDRM] BN188 8236
Out of the depths, O Lord (Binder) [MR#MFMRD, MLS#LM, MMMR] BH164 8237
Out of the depths, O Lord (Webbe) X Consolation 8238
Out of your sleep (Shaw) [LR MDLDRM, LRMDLDRM,] BG 177 8239
Oveenu malkaynu (Jewish trad) [MLS#LTDTTLLMM, SDSD] BH161, 309 8240
-----. V [MLS#LTDTTLLM M, MDSD] BH309 8241
Over Kedron (Lindeman) [MR DLDTS#M, LTDTMRD, M] O302 8242
Over the line (Belden) [SSF# SMRDDDTT, SSSLT] BB570 8243
-----. R [MR#MDSSMR#MD, RTSRTS] 8244
Over the ocean wave (Bradbury) [MRDDTLSDMR, MRDDTL] AX215; AY35 8245
Overberg (Rinck) [MMFSMSFM RM, MRSMDT] H72; I366; AI215; AS305 8246
Overdale (Williams) [MFMSM RDDTD, RMRSFM] Z566 8247
Overlook Park (Mueller) [DDD RMFRDTD, MMFSSL] AK264 8248
Over X O'er 8249
Ovio (Mason) [SSSMDDDS, DRMRDMR, R] L548; AY26 8250
-----. V [SSSMDDDS, DDMR DMR, R] AY26 8250a
Owen (Sweetser) [MMLDTL, SDSMDRM, MMM] I698 8251
Oxenbridge (Shaw) [SDRMRFM RDR, RMFSFM] X104 8252
Oxford (Stainer) [MSDTLSSF, MSDMRDR, R] C100a; D258b; L231b; AA510; AL13b; AP156;

BF449; BV17; BY141b 8253

Oxford New (Smith, I. Collection) [DSDTLTDRMRD, MRDTL] F 196a; BV302 8254

Oxnam (McCutchan) [SMRDTD, SLTDDRT, STL] G267 8255

Ozrem (Woodbury) [MMMSFMRM, SSDMLSF#S] H457 8256

P

Pa jorden är allting föränderlight (Mozart) [SSMDDSMSFRM, SSMDD] N476 8257

Paa Gud alene (Zinck. Koralbog. 1801) [DSFMR, DSSLTD, DSFM R,] O350; P287 8258

Paa sit kors i Dødens smerte (Zinck. Koralbog. 1801) [DT LTDDDT, DTLTDDDT] O311 8259

Pactum (Haas) X Luther League hymn 8260

Paddington (Wood) [SDLSFM, MRS SF#S, SDLS] H2 8261

Paddocks (Shaw) [SMFSFMDR, SMFSFMDT] X402 8262

Paderborn (Katholische kirchengesang) [DDRMFSSS, FMFSF M, MM] E251; X234 8263

Paderborn (Paderborn G-B. 1765) X O purest of creatures 8264

Paean (Weber) [SMFSLTDD, LSD RMRD, S] B267; C267; D174; K251; AB105; AQ9; BA806 8265

Paedia (Schulz) [DRMMFFMRD, DMSSLLS] J49; M308; O179; P366; AI383 8266

Palestine (---) [MMRDDFFM, MRSSF#S, SM] BR359 8267

Palestrina (Palestrina) X Victory 8268

Palgrave (Blackith) [SDTLSSS, LLSMFMR, SD] I195; BA417 8269

Palisades (Sowerby) [DLLDRMF RD, DMMRM] A365 8270

Palm Sunday (Carter) [SDSMRDLS, SSFMRDTD] AE105 8271

Palm Sunday (Harrington) [MM RDMRDRDM, MMMR#MS] I684 8272

Palm Sunday (Schulz) X Claudius 8273

Palm Sunday Anthem (Plainsong M 1) [RFRRDFSFSLL, FLDLS] E617 8274

Palmarum (Wolle) [LTDDRMDS SS, MRDDL] A259a; Y233; AE35; AZ22-I; BA219 8275

Palmer (---) [SDDMDLLD, LSS DDR, RM] V476 8276

Palmer (Palmer) X Yield not to temptation 8277

Palmer (Sweezy) [DDMRDTD, MMSFMRM, SS] T48; AJ63 8278

Palms of glory (Maclagan) [SSDRDTD, RMRDTLS, FF] Eap. 33; F499; K209; AO538; BE395 8279

Palmyra (Summers) [DRMSFM RD, SLTDDT, LS] C397; AB 86; BR470; BY218a 8280

Panem vivum (---) [SSFMSSLS FMMRMMF#F#] BQ319 8281

Pange lingua (Ett) X Oriel 8282

Pange lingua (Sarum plainsong M 3) [MMMRSSLDDDRDDD LD] A66; B338; C338b; D98; E95, 326b; F97a, 383a; J61a; W108a; X129a, 280a; BL51; BM32; BN106, 107; BO264; BQ241a, 241b; BV161; BY 146a 8283

-----. V [MMMRSSLTDD, DRD TLD] E326b 8284

-----. V [LLLSDDRMM, MFS FFMR] F97a 8285

-----. V [MMFMRSSLDD, DR DDTL] J61a 8286

Pange lingua gloriosa (Essay on the church plainchant. 1782) x Dulce carmen 8287

Panis angelicus (Franck) [MM RRDD, MMRRDD, LLSF] Y262 8288

Panis angelicus (Lambillotte) [MMMSFMLSFMMRR, RRR] AH130; BN92; BO33; BQ 229b 8289

Panis angelicus (Meurers) X

The very Angels' Bread 8290
Panis angelicus (Mohr) [DSDRMR, FMDRRD, MRMS] BQ230 8291
Panis angelicus (Sarum plainsong M 7) X Sanctorum meritis 8292
Panis angelicus (Tomadini) [DTDR RR, MDDDTD, RMRD] BQ318 8293
Panis vitae (Hodges) X Eucharistic hymn 8294
Panoply of light (Parker) [DSM SDMRDS, LTDRMRD] BD76 8295
Paraclete (Burnap) [SDMFMRD# R, STRFFMR#M,] L194; AI118; AO229; AS346 8296
Paraclete (Erfurt. G-B. 1524) X Komm Heilige Geist, Herre Gott 8297
Paraclete (Harker) [MMMR#MS, DFMMRR, SSST] BB679 8298
Paraclete (Maker) X Maker 8299
Paradise (Barnby) [MFMMMSFF, MRDRFM, MM] A588; B167; C167a; D394a; H516; I622b; J589; L581b; N663; O616; T437; V705; AA561; AB402; AO545a; AV297; AZ603-B; BA753; BF 659; BR426 8300
-----. R [SDSTLS, SF#LSF#S, SDM] 8301
Paradise (Dykes) X Paradise, No. 1 8302
Paradise (Hemy) [SSSDSTLL, FF MFLSM, S] C167b; BO204 8303
Paradise (Smart) [MSMRDDTT, D RMFSM, SL] B167b; D394c; L 581a; AL149; AO545b; AP631 8304
Paradise (Weber) X Paean 8305
Paradise No. 1 (Dykes) [MRDRM RDD, DRDFML, SD] D394b; I 622a; AZ603-A 8306
Paradise, No. 2 (Barnby) X Paradise 8307
Paran (Neander) X Neander 8308
Parce domini (Day) [SMMSDRRM, DFFMMR, SM] AO583 8309
Parce, domini (Plainsong M 1) [MMMRRD, MMMRRDRDTL,] BM71; BN30; BO164 8310
Park Square (Loomis) [SDRFMLS MDRM, SDTLS] Y231 8311
Park Street (Venua) [DDDDR MRDTD, MMMMF#S] B308; C308a; D472a; H26; I23; J110; K122; L94; N319; R8; S63; T33; U17; V95; AB 134; AD68; AE54; AF10; AG47; AH282; AI19; AJ48; AK25; AM6; AN313; AO154; AR16; AS78; AV29; AW272; AZ22-S; BA880; BB20; BD 139; BE59; BZ 8312
Parker (Harrington) [MRDSLT L#T, DRD#RR#M, MM] I46 8313
Parker (Parker) [SSSLTDTLS, LFSMSDT] A63b; B144b; C144a; D94; J75b 8314
Parker (Parker) X Pro patria 8315
Parker (Parker) X Stella 8316
Parole (Lane) X Penitence 8317
Parousia (Pollock) [MMFSSLLD LSM, SSLSD] AR212; AS165 8318
Parousia (Stainer) X St Giles 8319
Parratt (Parratt) [SLFMRS, DTLS, LFMRD] A438b 8320
Parry (Maunder) [MMSSSFM MR, DDFFMRM,] D548 8321
Parsifal (Wagner) [SDTLSLTL SF, SLSFSM] E629 8322
Parsons (Hubbard) [SDRDSDR MRD, MFSMDM] H280 8323
Parting hand (Ingalls) X The midnight call 8324
Parting hymn (---) [SDDDTDM DDT, DRRTLT] AY398 8325
Parting hymn (Danish trad) [SMSLFRFSMDMSR, SMS] P69 8326
Pascal (Allgemainisches katholisches G-B. Vienna ca 1774) X Te deum 8327
Pascal (Hopkins) X Pascal, No. 1 8328

Pascal No. 1 (Hopkins) [MMM SDRRM, MMMLMMRR,] AZ 277-C; BA610; BB61; BR406 8329

Paschal (Lindeman) X Our Lady, Trondhjem 8330

Paschale gaudium (Stainer) [SSM SDRD, LSDSSFM, SS] I156b 8331

Paskemorgen slukker sorgen (Lindeman) X Our Lady, Trondhjem 8332

Pass me not (Doane) [MRDTDLS D, RRDRM, MRD] G231; H43; I329; J461; N416; P13; U252; V760; AE175; AH338; AI212; AL503; AM707; AO645; AP495; AR464; AT219; AU230; AV349; AW474; AX380; AY457; BA615; BB559; BZ 8333

-----. R [SMRDL, SDMDR, MR DTDL] 8334

Pass me not, O gentle Saviour (Doane) X Pass me not 8335

Passion (Van der Werp) [MMR DDDTD, LDRMLLS# L,] AI72 8336

Passion chorale (Hassler) [MLSF MRM, TDDTLTL, ML] A75; B158; C158a; D102a; E102; F 111; G141; I151b; J88; K99; L243a; M269; N116; O231; P 155; Q172; R194; S151; V152; W107; X128; Y350; Z231; AA 201; AB135; AC48; AD155; AE109; AF170; AG96; AH289; AI420; AK142; AL94; AM178; AN191; AO160; AP194; AQ311; AR168; AT91; AW539; AY490; AZ151-A; BA215; BB130; BE 252; BF312; BI32; BJ62; BK73; BL22; BM8; BN38; BP26, 101; BQ22; BR175; BV158; BX309; BY145; BZ 8337

-----. V [MLSFMRM, TDDTTL, MLS] N116 8338

-----. V [MLSFMRM, TDTLS# L, MLS] AZ151-D 8339

-----. V [MLSFMRRM, TDDTLT L, M] BI32 8340

-----. V [MLSFMRRM, TDDTTL, ML] BP101 8340a

Passiontide (Teutsch kirchenampt. Strassburg, 1525) [SLSM SFFM, RMFSFMRD,] M396; Q142; AA191; AW533 8341

-----. V [SLSFMFSFFM, RMFSFM] AW533 8342

Pastor (Abt) [SSSSDSSS, DRR LLSFM,] L161 8343

Pastor (Wood) [DSLDFFFM, RDTMLTS, D] D290 8344

Pastor benignus (Witt) X Stuttgart 8345

Pastor bonus (Davis) X Goshen 8346

Pastor bonus (Caldicott) [DD TLSLTL, SDTLSLTL,] I300; T298 8347

Pastor bonus (Smyth) [SMR# MFMDRDRM, SMR#MF] BR 267 8348

Pastor bonus (Stainer) [DDRM LTD, RFMDMR, DDR] F447; I683 8349

Pastor pastorum (Silcher) X Gott ein Vater 8350

Pastor regalis (Bonner) [SF MMRR, LSRLSSF#, MF#R#] Y271; AC294 8351

Pastoral (---) [DMMRMRD, MSSFSFM, MR] D571 8352

Pastoral chant (Cuff) [MSS S, LSMFFM, MMMF, F#D] BR532 8353

Pastorale (Naegeli) [SDDRM FMDRD, SMRDTL] AR588 8354

Patapan (French trad) [LLM MRMD, TDRT, MDT, TD] BG82 8355

Pater noster (Buck) [LSDRM SFM, DRMFRD, DT] BE4 8356

Pater omnipotens (Dickey) [MMRDRMRMFS, SDTLS] A530 8357

Pater omnium (Holmes) [DR MSFRDRM, FMLSDDT] I466; L234; N469; AB360; AK68; AL264; AM71; AP415b; AR 256; AS403; BA75; BB146; BE357; BV547; BY770 8358

-----. R [RTSMMRTSS, SFR

DFMR] 8359

Pathway (Bourgeois) X Lord, to thee 8360

Patmos (Havergal) X Consecration 8361

Patmos (Storer) [SSLTDDT, DRD#RR#M, SM] A593b; D542; C542a; D404a; I626; J597; S408; U433; Z503; AD425; AO552 8362

Patmos (Wesley, S.S.) [SMM MMMMRLL, LSFM, MS] W568b; AL436b 8363

Patricroft (Heaton) [MR#MFMMRR, DTDRR#M, MR#] AH509; BF 602 8364

Patten (Lutkin) [SSSDDLLL, L LLRDDT, S] G558; I687; AK 450; AO488; AW390 8365

Paule, doctor egregie (Plainsong M 7) [DDDRFMFS, SSSLLSFM] F145a 8366

Paulina (Donizetti) [SMMMR#MM DDRM, SMMMM] L471; N606; T9; AJ13; AO365 8367

Pax (Kilgore) [MTDSLTDMMR, DLSDDT] J349 8368

Pax (Public School hymn book. 1928) [LTDTLSM, LSFMDRM,] A224a 8369

Pax (Rendle) [MMMMRDLDRM, SSSSLT] G510; Z555 8370

Pax (Swedish koralbok. 1697) [LDTLMRDT, TDTLMMR#M,] J352a; N110 8371

Pax caelestis (Gould) [SDDTDRM RD, DMMRMFS] BR536 8372

Pax celeste (Celestial harps. Edinburgh, 1824) [DRMFMRRD, MFSLFR, ST] Q617 8373

Pax dei (Dykes) [DMSSFM, DMR DDT, DMSD] B313; C313; D32a; F31b; J489; K58; V417; W301b; AA427; AB78; AL214c; AO11; AZ32-G; BA476; BB26; BR395; BX184; BY330b 8374

Pax dei (Hopkins) X Ellers 8375

Pax orbi (Milligan) [SLSMDR, RMF#SSFS, SDT] Z552 8376

Pax tecum (Caldbeck) [SSSSSLLL SS, SDRMRD] A436b; B405; C 405a; D674; F358b; G354; I528; J571; K413; L465; R420; S301; T420; U231; V391; W444a; AD268; AE229; AG205; AK 245; AL285b; AM590; AO364; AP438a; AR337; AS309; AV 298; AW256; BA690b; BB 311; BF387; BR409; BX274 8377

Pax veritatis (Bornschein) [MFRSDLSFMR, RMRSLF] Y253; Z287 8378

Pax veritatis (Parker) [SDTT LRMF, LSFMSTTT,] B442; C442 8379

Pax vobiscum (Arthur) [DLD, SMDR, FMLSFMF#S, F] R543; W303 8380

Paxtang (Lowry) [DMMSSSLS M, DDDMMRM] T253; AJ351 8381

Peace (Baermann) [DMSRR DD#RFM, SDRDTL] BX75b 8382

Peace (Bohemian Br.) X Saelir 8383

Peace (Chadwick) [SSSDDTD RMRD, MMMFM] G316; J 473; R274; U193; AG220; AI133; AM397a; AR179 8384

Peace (Dykes) X Requiescat 8385

Peace (Fesca) [MMMSFMR, MDDRRRSF#, F] AO102 8386

Peace (Hodges) [DMFRMD, RMLSF#S, SMSD] D614 8387

Peace (Mozart) X Cana 8388

Peace (The revivalist, 1869) [SLLDMRDLLL, SLLDLS] AF578; AQ206 8389

Peace, be still! (Palmer) [SLSSDMRL, DTLSFSM, S] AM701; AU471; BB677; BC106 8390

-----. R [MMMMMMMFFF, RRM, MMM] 8391

Peace be to this congregation (Beethoven) [SLSLSSSS, D DDDDTD, S] BI75 8392

Peace I leave with you (Vassar College) [SDMRD, SSDMMR DT, MMM] AK511 8393

Peace makers (German) [MLTD MDTLT, DDRM, DRM] AD356 8394

Peace of God (Hartmann) [MM SLDRM, SMDTDFMR, T] J200; M497; O40; P210; AA71 8395

Peace, perfect peace (Miller) [MR#MSSDDDFM, SLTDSL] AS307 8396

Peace through the cross (Jerusalem's gates reopened) [MRMF MRD, DRRM, RRMRD] AS366 8397

Peace to soothe (Hartmann) X Peace of God 8398

Peacefield (Irish mel) [MMFSMM R, MMMFSRDD, M] A232; B609; X541; BE341; BV545; BY742 8399

Peaceful rest (Emerson) [SSDRM MMRDDT, SSLTD] AY176 8400

Pearsall (Pearsall) [SDTDMLS, SFMRRM, DM] A595; B68; C68; D405; E495; F276; S62a; V689; W396; X198b; AB141; AD346; AK 71; AP18; BN171; BQ95; BV 323a; BY278 8401

Peek (Peek) [MRDSSLTRDDT, FMRTL] Y180; Z361; AB236; AC177; AD489; AE445; AF489; AG309; AH433; AK448; AS319; AT315; AU368; AW207; BB425; BD101; BF457; BK29; BZ 8402

Peel Castle (Manx trad) [SM RDTDDMRDD, DMS] A208b; AC19; AL338 8403

Pekin (German chorale) [MFSD RTD, DRMFFM, MRS] V285 8404

Pelham Street (Covell) [DMRDT LLS, RMDMF#S, SL] AQ24 8405

Pembroke (Foster) [DMRDSSFM RM, MRLSDF] BB36; BY772 8406

Pembroke (Hadley) [LTDRMRDTD T, LTDDRM] X311 8407

Penfield (Pierce) [SDDTLSM, DRMSMRD, SD] AH184 8408

Peniel (Booth) [MMRSSFFM, ML LSMMRR,] C230; D42; AB 345; AH471; AL312b 8409

Peniel (Hastings) [SMRDFM RLTD, MSTLRF#] V384 8410

Peniel (Wesley, S.S.) X Wrestling Jacob 8411

Penitence (Lane) [MMFMLS, DMSRM, MMFM] A334; B 147; C147; D340a; G274; H 373; I431; J561; K391; L524; M272; N257; P169; R52; S 255b; T5; U238; V171; Y104; Z333; AA409; AB195; AC178; AD148; AE245; AF374; AG 151; AH439; AI286; AJ7; AK 160; AM475; AO340; AP406; AR303; AS321; AT317; AU 467; AV187; AW195; AY477; AZ141-E; BA466; BB327; BD108; BF479; BR347; BZ 8412

Penitence (Oakley) [DSMRDDTL S, SLLSTD, M] H264; I491; L397 8413

Penitence (St Alban's tune book, 1866) X Holborn Hill 8414

Penitentia (Dearle) [MMFSDR RMFM, MRDLSS] A208a; B334; C334; D219a; G415; I237; J275; U382; V549; Y 261; AB164; AC300; AD282; AG311; AP355; AR519; AT 391; BE423; BF352; BR259; BZ 8415

Penlan (Jenkins) [MSFMRDT, DRMSFM, MSF] W684; BV 524; BY581a 8416

Pentatone (Davies) [DRMSDLS MM, LSMMRMD,] R109; S282; W446; AD267; BE159 8417

Pentecost (Boyd) [MMMMMRDF, MMMMRRD] A560b; B113; C113b; D505b; F304b; G286; I409; J557; N384; R283; S 270a; T106; U299; W517a; Y158; AB240b; AC207; AD492; AE257; AF367; AG201; AH 453; AJ91b; AK355; AL384a; AM496; AN397b; AO392; AP 544a; AS315; AT406; AU270;

AV200; AW353; BA574; BD85; BE60; BF434; BK116; BX434; BZ 8418

Pentecost (Lomas) [MRRMFS, SLSFSM, STLS,] BY225a 8419

Pentecost (Sewell) [SLSMRMM, SMFSLDD, MR] BR205 8420

Pentecost (Spielman) [DMSSFMR, MF#SDTLS, DR] M466 8421

Pentonville (Mason) [SMDRTD, MRDTLS, RTSD] L255; V250; AO368 8422

People of the living God (Harmonia sacra) [MRDDTDR, SFMRDTD, MR] AX155 8423

Peoria (Bradbury) [SSDMSMSFRSM, SLFLS] AR24; AS10 8424

Per pacem (Martin) [SDTTLLMMRD, TTLS, SD] D633a 8425

Percival-Smith (Laufer) [MMDRMFFM, MLDRMML, M] G130 8426

Percivals (---) [MRDSLTD, RMRDTLS, DD] C354; D563; I676; AO251; BA676 8427

Perfect love (Barnby) X Sandringham 8428

Perkins (Perkins) [DSDMRD, SLTDRDT, DMF#] AS422 8429

Perkins (Perkins) X Lundie 8430

Perranport (Wilson) [SLTDMSSS, DMMFS, SLT] F72a 8431

Perry (Sowerby) [DTDRMFSM, MLSMF#S, FM] BZ 8432

Personent hodie (Piae cantiones. 1582) X Theodoric 8433

Peterboro (Harrison) [DMMFFMRD, MSSFMR, MR] H292; I404; V98; AA255; AL572; AO508; BX140 8434

Peterborough (Goss) [SSSDSLLS, SDRMDRDT] H180; M139; N71; O122; AB393 8435

Peterborough (Harrison) X Peterboro 8436

Peterborough Old (Harrison) X Peterboro 8437

Petersen (Halle, 1697) [SSFMRMRDRR, MFMLSF] A216; BE103 8438

Petersham (Poole) [DMSDLSFM, MRSLLS, SS] S82; W398; Y73; AB318; AK409; BX444; BY254 8439

Peterson (Perkins) [MMFRTLLS, MMFRTLLS,] BF350 8440

Petition (Gower) [MMMRDRMF, MDRR, SSMF] Z330 8441

Petition (Haydn) [SMRDTTLS, DFMRDDT, S] G351; H123; L543; T277; AI104; AJ385; AO135; AZ582-R; BA714 8442

-----. V [SMRDTLS, DFMRDDT, SM] H123 8443

Petra (Redhead) [DDRMFFM, DDRMRRD, DMS] A70; B151; C151; D93; E477; F127; I280; J78; K93; N102; O27a; P170; Q159; R193; S214; T97; V147; W413a; X636b; Z227; AA199; AE114; AF158; AH284; AJ140a; AK144; AL92; AM357; AO159; AP190; AR160; AS172; AT105; AW109; AZ581-G; BA220; BB122; BD26; BF612; BV177; BX367; BY458; BZ 8444

Petrie (Irish trad) [SDRMFSFMRDRMFR, SD] X102 8445

Petrograd (Tschaikowsky) [DDDDLTD, RMRDTLTD, S] Y390 8446

Pevensey (Aufranc) [SLTDMMRDTRD, MMRDM] BB468 8447

Philadelphia (Bradbury) X Zephyr 8448

Philadelphia (Wesley arr) [DSDMRDFMRM, SLSFMR] BY663 8449

Philippi (Ebeling) [SSLSFM, SFRMRD, RMF#S,] D367; J215; K447; M557; P291; AK49; AN402; AW555; AZ607-A; BY225b 8450

-----. V [SSLSFM, SFRMRD, MFSL1 J215 8451

-----. V [SSLSFM, SFRMMR, DTLS,] AN402 8452

Philippine (Roberts) [MMRDSMRDRM, SDTLSM] J258; X251; BE363; BV622; BY174 8453

Phoenix (Fowles) X Cavell 8454
Phuvah (Vulpius) X Cana 8455
Picardy (French trad) [LTDRMM RMM, MMFSFM] A197; B339; C339a; E318; F97b; G594; J 281; R148; S112; W636; X273; AC277; AD405; AE459; AF107; AG337; AK336; AL515a; AN178; AQ293; AR120; AT80; BB685; BL52; BY102; BZ 8456
Picton (Branscombe) [MLTDRM LSFM, MDTLSF#] Y272; AC 118 8457
Pie Jesu (Michel) [MFFMMLS# LLS#, MFRTDD] BO212 8458
Pie Jesu (Montani) [MMMRRFFF M, SSSFMRD] BQ251 8459
Pie Jesu (Vanden Plas) [LLT TDDT, LTDDDTLS#, L] BO213 8460
Pierre (Pierre) [DMFSDTDLS, SDTLSMD] AJ425 8461
Pietas (---) [SDMSTDRM, F#SL TRDTL] D134a 8462
Pilesgrove (Mitchell) [DMSSM RDTD, MSFMRDS] H73; L551 8463
Pilgrim (Italian mel) X I'm a pilgrim 8464
Pilgrim (Mozart) X Ellesdie 8465
Pilgrim (Ohl) [SMDTLSMRD, LLSMMRM,] J520b; K261 8466
Pilgrim (Sewell) [MMMFRSS, MMMFLS, SF#M] BR39 8467
Pilgrim band (Stainer) [MRDSLRT S, DTLTDMR, M] W578 8468
-----. R [MRDSLRTS, SF#MRM LF#S] 8469
Pilgrim chorus (Wagner) X Pilgrim's chorus [sic] 8469a
Pilgrim song (Hagfors) [SDRMDDTD R, SRMFRRD] J536 8470
Pilgrim song (Catholic) [MFSDD LSM, SLSMFSM, S] P82 8471
Pilgrimage (Barnard) [SLSMMRD, LTDSFMR, SL] C348 8472
Pilgrimage (Elvey) [MSDDRMFM, FSLDFMR, S] F296; BY40 8473
Pilgrimage (Freylinghausen G-B. 1704) X Se solens skjønne lys og pragt 8474
Pilgrimage (Herrnhut ms.) X Gregor's 166th metre 8475
Pilgrims (Smart) [MSFMRDR MFMR, SDTL] A472; B290; C290a; D398a; F354; G532; I621a; J498; L587a; P347; R426; S431; T196; U434; V 694a; W580; Y343; Z582; AB 404a; AC329; AD462; AG282; AH369; AJ284; AK420; AL 442; AN549; AO546a; AP601; AR421; AS476; AT469; AU62; AV286; AW260; BB376; BD 153; BF385; BI50; BX464 8476
-----. R [RMFS, DLSFM, DT LSMD] 8477
-----. V [MSFMMRDRMFM R, RSDT] BI50 8478
Pilgrim's chorus (Wagner) [S DSMMFSSLSSSF, LRD] Y252; AH623; AR619; AS52 8479
Pilgrim's mission (Phillips) [DMSLSMRD, RRRRDRM, M] AL506 8480
-----. R [DTTTTLTDDDDT, DRRR] 8481
Pilgrims of the night (Recueil de cantiques) X Swiss melody 8482
Pilot (Gould) [MRDTRDLS, F MMRDTD, R] G269; H350; I482; J531; K270; L240; M 169; N340; P161; Q649; R 336; S286; T249; U235; V 340; Y371; Z409; AB227; AC160; AD225; AE254; AF 213; AG155; AH309; AI302; AJ346; AK468; AL444; AM 497; AO328; AP607; AR288; AS248; AT337; AU158; AV 238; AW161; AX501; AY308; BA704; BB398; BC121; BY 543; BZ 8483
Pimlico Road (Shaw) [SLDSM RDRR, MFSLSFM] X617 8484
Pine Glen (Huffaker) [MMMMM FMRD, SSSSSLS] AR225 8485
Pioneer (Ewing) [DMSDDTLS, DRMRDTLS,] AR77 8486
Pioneers (Lowens) [MMLLLSL,

LTDLLSFM, M] AQ211 8487
Pioneers (Olds) [SSDRMF#S, SS SMLMSR, S] AB308 8488
Pioneers (Shaw) [FMRRRLR, MF SLSLFMR] X304; Y164; AC211; AD491 8489
Pisani (Pisani) [SDTLSFMFSFM, RLSS#L] AC163 8490
Pisgah (Evans) [LMDRMLDTLSM, LMDRM] X233 8491
Pisgah (Scottish trad) X Covenanters 8492
Pitts (Pitts) X Princethorp 8493
Pittsburgh (Russell) [DMDFRS, FMMRRD, DLDT] D457c 8494
Pixham (Parker) [MFSSSDTLS, FMMMTLS] A150; B7; J122b; Y130; BB47; BD102; BE20 8495
-----. V [MMFSSSDTLS, FMMM TL] Y130 8496
Plainfield (Lowry) X Nothing but the blood 8497
Plainsong (Sarum Antiphonal. M 4) X Deus creator omnium 8498
Plainsong M 4) (Sarum Antiphonale M 4) X Conditor alme M 4) 8499
Plainsong M 6 (Sarum plainsong M 6) X Nocte surgentes 8500
Plaintive martyrs (Scottish Psalter, 1615) [RFRLFMRL, LDLTDRL,] A547a; E449; F 309; W520a; X597; AL668b; AP 63a; BY517a 8501
-----. V [LDLMDTLM, MSMF# SLM, M] X597 8502
-----. V [LDLMDTLM, MSMFLM, MS] AP63a 8503
Plaistow (Magdalen Hospital hymns. 1760) [LMTDLRMFM, TDRMSF M] E69b; W491b; X122; AN 208b 8504
Platt's Lane (Sharpe) [MDMFS, S LSMFR, SDTLS] X358 8505
Plea (German, 16th c) [DDSDRM FM, SMDFMRD, D] M424 8506
Pleading (Bourgeois) X O esca viatorum 8507
Pleading (Link) X Grace, 'tis a charming sound 8508
Pleading Saviour (Leavitt. Christian lyre) [MRDLDRM SMR, MRDLD] A117; E593; R210; X516a; Z504; AD318; AF409; AK179; AP198; AR206; AW234; BL63; BZ 8509
Pleasant pastures (---) X Little clusters 8510
Pleasant pastures (Bradbury) [MMMRMFSDSM, RMFLSF] C355; G337; H449; I677; J524; K565; L201; N644; R380; U323; Z401; AD479; AE234; AF327; AG218; AH 402; AI397a; AK461; AM644; AO621; AP745; AR296; AS 250; AT344; AU13; AV377; AW395; AX496; BA834; BB 394; BF623; BZ 8511
-----. R [SSLDTLSM, MMR LSFM, S] 8512
Pleasant Street (Johnson) [MM MMDRMFMM, RDDTD, D] BE 253 8513
Pleasure it is (Waldis) X Es muss die ganze Christenschar 8514
Pledging our lives (Epstein) [DMFSMDLSFM, DLLDLL] BH149 8515
Plenitude (Davis) [DSDMMRDT, DLLLSL, DL] BE165 8516
Pleyel (Pleyel) X Pleyel's hymn 8517
Pleyel's hymn (Pleyel) [MSRM FRM, MSRMFRD, R] A578; B370; C370; D452a; G326; H256; I35; K277; L160; M 336; N133; O458; P333; R 340; S347; U243; V504; Z 267; AD229; AE18; AG236; AH399; AI334; AL342b; AM 499; AN53; AO541; AP481a; AR315; AU251; AV212; AW 238; AZ11-T; BA626; BB 459; BD20; BE394; BI33; BK 138; BR434; BX92; BZ 8518
Plumer (Maclean) [SDSLSFFM, RMSLDT, SD] V123 8519
Plumptre (Monk) [SLDDTD, DRRDLS, SLLD] C261b; D 369b 8520
Plymouth (Wathall) [MMRRFM

RR, SSMLLR, SD] I474 8521
Poacher (Weber) X Jewett 8522
Poland (Koschat) [SMMMMD, DMMMF, SFFFF] Y365; Z170; AC57; AH212; AI304; AM663; AS260; AT57; AU22; AW62; BA691; BC104; BI2; BR529 8523
-----. R [SDTLSM, MSMFSMDT, SD] 8524
Poland (Polish mel) [SSFMMMM RMSF, FFMRR] AB224; AD418; AL393; AR372; BQ36 8525
-----. V [SSFMMMRMSF, FFM RRL] BQ36 8525a
Polish carol (Polish trad) X W. Zlobie Lezy 8526
Pollard (Stebbins) X Adelaide 8527
Polycarp (Barnby) X St Polycarp 8528
Polzeath (Kidner) [MTDMFS, LM FSLT, DLSR] BV287b 8529
Pomerania (Wagner. G-B. ms. 1742) X Wir glauben all' an einen Gott 8530
Pone luctum (Catholic, 1750) [DMRDSDRMD, MFSLSFF] BQ 78 8531
Pont Neuf (Sanders) [SDSRDR, MF MRDRS, SDS] AQ137 8532
Pontiac (Haynes) [MMMFMRLSS, MFSLTDS] BB699 8533
Poplar (Strong) [LTDRMLRDT SLSL, LSD] F332a 8534
Poppen (Poppen) [SSLSDMRD, MRDMMRR, S] M622 8535
Porter (McCutchan) [SMMRDSSL DRDTT, DMS] AT521 8536
Porth Kerry (Lloyd) [SDMSLSMD, MRRLRR, S] W575 8537
Portland (Taylor) [SSSDSMFS, SLDTDRLT,] BV599a; BY480 8538
Portsea (Boyce) [LSFMFRMDT, LTDRMLT] F124b 8539
Portuguese (Wade. Cantus diversus) X Adeste fideles 8540
Portuguese hymn (Wade. Cantus diversus) X Adeste fideles 8541
Posen (Strattner) [DDDDRMFM, S SSSLTDT,] D549; M589; R458; S452; V159; Z177; AB351; AD330; AE434; AG305; AM 654; AN34; AO617; AQ33; AR282; AV196; AW424; AX 123; AZ11-C; BA232; BB331; BF423; BR485; BX60 8542
Potsdam (Bach) [DRFMRD, SL DTLS, MFLS] B109; C109b; Q117; V471; AA175; AF233; AL422; AN437; AO228; BE14; BM43; BY320 8543
Pounds (Fillmore) [SSMDDTL SFM, MRMFRS] Z255; AR 448; AT127; AU413; AW453; AY491 8544
-----. R [SF#SRTLTDSS, SF#SRTL] 8545
Pour out thy spirit (Allgemeines katholisches G-B. Vienna, 1774) X Hursley 8546
Poverty (Welsh carol) [SDDR DTD, RMMFMR, DMD] BG34; BV94 8547
-----. V [SDDRDTD, RMMFM R, DRM] BV94 8548
Power in the blood (Jones) X There is power . . . 8549
Praeneste (Palestrina) [MMM FMRRDDT, SDRMRD] BR 477 8550
Praetorius I (Praetorius) [DS SLSSFM, DRMFFM, MM] E549; W130; X174; Y31; AN 77a; AW248; BI21-D 8551
-----. V [DSSLSSSM, DRMF FM, MM] BI21-D 8552
Praetorius (--- 1536, Praetorius arr) [SDDRFMRMR, RDDF MR,] A133; E179; F509; G71; Q67; X146; AA134 8553
Praetorius (Geistliche Kirchengesang Cologne, 1599) X Rosa mystica 8554
Prague (Plainsong, ca 600) X Christe, qui lux es et dies 8555
Prague (Pensum sacrum) X Herr Jesu Christ 8556
Praise (Goss) X Lauda anima 8557
Praise (Harrington) [DTLLSSL

TDFM, RMFSM] I20 8558
Praise (Hopkins) X Kelso 8559
Praise (Lowe) [DDRRRFFM, MMD TLTM, M] K27; AD72; AH186; AM5; AO203; BF238; BR61 8560
Praise (Sewall) [MMMSSDRM, MMMFMRRD,] BR54 8561
Praise (Shaw) [LSLTLDRMRFM RLL, MF] E535; X624 8562
Praise (Stralsund G-B. 1665) X Praise to the Lord 8563
Praise (Swedish) [DMFSLFFM, RDDFMRD, D] J422; N288 8564
Praise and prayer (Fisher) [DR MFMDRD, MFSLSMF#S,] AR 493 8565
Praise God from whom (Bourgeois) X Old 100th 8566
Praise Him (Bailey) [DDMSLTDL SM, DDFMSS,] AE437; AL594; AR465; AT511; AU306; AW426; BK2; BY753 8567
Praise Him! praise Him (Allen) X Joyful song 8568
Praise Jehovah (Stralsund G-B. 1665) X Praise to the Lord 8569
Praise, Lord, for thee in Zion waits (Haydn) X Bradford 8570
Praise my soul (Goss) X Lauda anima 8571
Praise now your God (Kern) [LTTDLLRTDLL, DDRMD] BL 43 8572
Praise the Lord (Bechler) [DSM SDRMD, FMRDTDR, M] BA171 8573
Praise the Lord (Jewish trad) X Addeer hu 8574
Praise the Lord (Pollock) [SSS MLSS, FRRLSS, SSS] AY324 8575
Praise the Lord (Rolle) [DMS, MDRTD, SLTDLLS, M] AZ16-M 8576
Praise the Lord in heaven (French carol) X Grace soit 8577
Praise the Lord with heart and voice (Cannon) [MSDTTLS, MS DDTLS, TD] BC149 8578
Praise the Lord! ye heavens (Haydn) X Austria 8579
Praise the Saviour (Darmstadt G-B.) X Goldschmidt 8580
Praise to God (Russian trad) [DSDRMMMFM, RDRMD, R M] BG107; BK13 8581
-----. V [DDS, DRM, MMSF MRDRMD,] BK13 8582
Praise to God, immortal praise (Abbot) X 'Tis religion that can give 8583
Praise to the Holiest (Montani) [DDDFMDLTD, SDTLTDR,] BQ142 8584
Praise to the Holiest (Somervell) X Somervell 8585
Praise to the Holiest (Tallis) X Tallis' Ordinal 8586
Praise to the Lord (Stralsund G-B. 1665) [DDSMRDTL SLTDRD, DD] A279; E536; F382; G60; J408; K286; M 212; N37; O5; P3; Q39; R1; S6; W22; X626; Z98; AA63; AB40; AC35; AD13; AE1; AF15; AG3; AI1; AK8; AL9; AM50; AN7; AO66; AQ7; AR37; AT6; AW515; AZ61-A; BA864; BB12; BC150; BE283; BF172; BK49; BL 84; BM1; BN62; BV246; BY25; BZ 8587
-----. V [DDSMRDTLS, DR MRD,] AA63 8588
Praise to the man (---) [DD DMDMSDMRDS, FLFM] BC 147 8589
-----. R [DDDTLSSDDDTLS, DDD] 8590
Praise we Christ, the King (Michaud) [MMRMFS, SDT SLS, SFRM] BQ335 8591
Praise we our God (Montani) [LTDRTLS, DRMFMRD, LT] BQ141 8592
Praise ye our Father (Barnby) X Nightfall 8593
Praise ye the Father (Gounod) [SSSDF, FFMRDSFM, MMM] AU472 8594
Praise ye the Lord (Isaacs)

[SMFSDTLS, MFMFSMFR,] AH156; BH65 8595
Praise ye the Lord (Sherwin) [DDDD, MFFM, SFFMRDLR] AU474 8596
Praise ye the Lord (Stainer) X Laus matutina 8597
Praise ye the Lord (Stephens) [DRMFMRSFM, RRRSRDT] BC277 8598
Praises (Selby) [SLMSLTDDR, SMRDTLS] F241a 8599
Praxis pietatis (Stralsund G-B. 1665.) X Praise to the Lord 8600
Pray (Brown) [MMRDRMMD, DRRRMR, MM] AX359 8601
-----. R [SSLSMD, MRDDDRMR, SS] 8602
Pray for the dead (---) [LTTD, DD RM, FMMRDTTL,] BO144 8603
-----. R [MFMR, RSFM, MMFM RMRD] 8604
Pray when the morn unveileth (Brandeis) [MRDFMRSMDL, SDTLSF] BH8 8605
Prayer (---) [SMLSDDTLTDS, DTLSM] AO317 8606
Prayer (Abbott) X 'Tis religion that can give 8607
Prayer (Babcock) [SLTDMSFM, RDDTLS, SS] V463 8608
Prayer (Butcher) [SSMSLLDTL S, SSSDSM] R126; T136; AJ 203 8609
Prayer (D'Andreiux) [DSDSDRDT LS, MSMSMF] BH37 8610
Prayer (Dykes) X Almsgiving 8611
Prayer (Greenwood) [MFSLSMRD, MMFSMRM, M] BE285 8612
Prayer (Marshall) [SFMSMRMMRD RM, FFFM] L382 8613
Prayer for a holy death (Plainsong M 1) [SDDMSFMR, SDD MSFMR] BN191 8614
Prayer for all men (Hastings) X Ortonville 8615
Prayer for wisdom (Grimm) [SD DTTLRR, MFMFSRM, M] BH28 8616
Prayer is the soul's desire (American trad) X Camp-meeting 8617
Prayer is the soul's sincere desire (Careless) [DSLSM SFRD, RMLSF#S, L] BC220 8618
Prayer of St Francis (A Monk of Gethsemani) [SMFSSSDDR MFS, SMFS] BN60 8619
Prayers (Milford) [MMSDTL, SLSMRDRM, MS] X504 8620
Praying for you (Sankey) X I am praying for you 8621
Precious child (Norwegian trad) [DRDSDRDS, DMSFMRSF] P137 8622
Precious Jesus, O to love thee (Pollock) [MFSMRDLS, SS DSFMR, M] AS208 8623
-----. R [SSDSMFSM, SDTTLL S, M] 8624
Precious memories (Wright) [SSLDDDLS, MRDDDMR, S] AX559 8625
-----. R [SMSM, MMRD, DDR DRDMD,] 8626
Precious name (Doane) [SDM RDRDS, LDTLDLS, S] G253; I508; N260; R411; AG152; AH430; AI100; AS297; AT 305; AU424; AV320; AW485; AX27; AY460; BB523; BZ 8627
-----. R [DTLDLS, DRMSDMR, MRD] 8628
Precious promise (Bliss) [SL TDDDRMLL, LTDRRR] AU 90; AV356; AX492 8629
-----. R [SFMMRRMFFM, MRMSMM] 8630
Precious Savior, dear Redeemer (Palmer) [MRDDMRDD, SMR RMFM, M] BC109 8631
Precious to me (Gabriel) X He is so precious 8632
Preis, lob, ehr', ruhm, dank (Darmstadt G-B. 1698) X Gregor's 101st metre 8633
Prentiss (Doane) X More love to thee 8634
Presbyter (Gautnlett) [SFMRF

MRD, MLSTDFMR,] AB381; AH217 8635
Presbyter (Wilkinson) [SDDTTLL S, SMMRRR, MF] U399; Y281 8636
Prescott (Lutkin) [MRMFMMRR, LRTLSM, MR] I263 8637
Prescott (Stewart) [SSSLTDSMS, DDRRFFM,] D449; K133; M196; N42; O496; AA238; BA93 8638
Presence (Whitlock) [SLSDRMRS MR, LRMFMD] BE211 8639
Preservation (Störl) X Störl I 8640
Press on (---) [DDSDRM, DLS S, RRLRRF] Y227 8641
Pressburg (Freylinghausen) [LS# LMDTLS#, SLMFSRMR] E358; W112; X292; AW538 8642
Pressly (Gabriel) [DMMMDLSS, MSFRRMFM,] T284; AJ370 8643
Preston (Doane) [SSSDSSFMRM, SSSDRM] R258; T226; AJ322 8644
Preston (Maclean) [SSMMMRDDT, LSSDRDT,] V659 8645
Preston (Miller) [DSDRMDMF, SLFRDRM, D] BB23 8646
Priestly benediction (Binder) [MM LTDDRMS, FMRDTL, L] BH301 8647
Primo dierum omnium (Sarum plainsong M 4) [RMFSMSFMF, RMFSMSF] E50; BJ31 8648
Primrose (Chapin) X Melody 8649
Prims (Sheldon) [DRDSMRML, T DRFMRDR,] BV306 8650
Prince (Hemy) X St Catherine 8651
Prince of peace (Dykes) [MSMDR MDL, DSDRMR, MS] D59b 8652
Prince of peace (Maclagan) [SSLS FMRD, MLDTLS, LM] V421; BA30 8653
Prince of peace (Smythe) [SDD RMMFSLS, SFMMRD] BR173b 8654
Prince of peace, control my will (Bradbury) X Aletta 8655
Prince Rupert (English march, 1648) [LMLTDRD, TLLS# L, LM] A316; X397; Y113 8656
-----. R [DSMSDS, DRMFM R, DSMS] 8657
Princess Eugenie (Norwegian trad) [MLLS#MMDDTL, TD LTS#M] P26 8658
Princethorp (Pitts) [MD FRSFM, RMFMRD, MDF] D608; N279; T321; V654; AL113b; AO399; AP132; AW89; BA110; BN101; BR 389b; BY95 8659
Pro me perforatus (Barnby) X St Olave 8660
Pro nostris liberis (Lloyd) [DTSMSLS, SDTLRTSLS,] W650; AL395 8661
Pro omnibus sanctis (Barnby) X Sarum 8662
Pro patria (Armistead) [MS DFMRM, MLRFMRM, MS] F606b; AD355 8663
Pro patria (Parker) [DRMS SSSSDTDMR, MMM] B430b; C430b; D194; S370; AB270; AC258; BB198; BF571; BX 42 8664
-----. V [DRMSSSDTDMR, MMMMT] S370 8665
Pro patria (Warren) X National hymn 8666
Proclaim the tidings (Mason) X Sing glory, hallelujah 8667
Proclamation (Walch) X Tidings 8668
Proclamation (Warner) [SSDS MFSLLS, SDTSTR] AZ23-C 8669
Promise (---) [SMLSSMRMS FFM, SMLS] BB397 8670
Promise (Sanders) [SDRMSL TDTLS, SDRMS] AN240 8671
Promised land (American trad) X Jordan's Banks [Variants follow:] 8672
-----. V [DRMMDMFSFFFM, RMMD] AV282 8673
-----. V [DDDDRMRRR, TDD DRMT,] BB682 8674
-----. V [DRMMDMFSFFSF M, RMM] BZ 8675
Promises (Carter) [SSSLSFM

FSDD, LLLTD] AH391; AT266; AU115; AX474; BZ 8676

Promptement levez-vous (French trad) X Carol of service 8677

Prompto gentes animo (Rouen church mel) [DSLSFMFS, DRM FMRDR,] E653; S141; AL80 8678

Propior Deo (Sullivan) [MRMDSL, STRM, MRMDS] A461; D654b; H333; V372; W475c; AL321b; AP470c; BR357; BY598a 8679

Protection (Abbott) [DDDRTDRM, MRRRDTLS,] BB490 8680

Protection (American trad) X Foundation 8681

Protection (Filitz) X Mannheim 8682

Protection (Kolb) [DDMSSMF LS, MRDDTDR,] AY148 8683

Protection (Dutch trad) X Kremser 8684

Protection (Pearce) [SMRMFM FS, FMFSLFMR] D643a 8685

Protector (Rostocker G-B) X Gregor's 151st metre-H 8686

Providence (Stebbins) [SSSFMD LSM, FFFMRSF] AT430; AU296; AX345; AY527 8687

-----. R [DDDTLSLSM, DDDT LTL] 8688

Providence (Straub) [SDDRRMSR, FMMRDR, SD] AL588; AM635; AP721; AW408 8689

-----. R [SLSMSLSM, SLSMSR, SD] 8690

Pruen (Ouseley) [MSDLSFM, RSSLTLS, SL] D30a; V454; AA 8 8691

-----. V [MSDLSFM, RSSSLTL S, S] V454 8692

Prysgol (Owen) [DMMMRMFSM, SFMFMRM] E575; AL486; AM 462; AP414; AW444 8693

P'sach lonu (Stark) [LMDDTLS#LT DTLRDRM,] BH337 8694

Psallat fidelis concio (Piae cantiones) [MSSMDRMFMRD, DRR DS] BV360 8695

Psalm 3 (Genevan Psalter, 1551) X O Seigneur 8696

Psalm 6 (Bourgeois) X O esca viatorum 8697

Psalm 12 (Genevan Psalter, 1551) X Donne secours 8698

Psalm 23 (Crespin, Psalms, 1556) [SDRMDFRD, TDMRR M, MS] BJ41 8699

Psalm 23 (Lutkin) [SMRDLS, DTDFMMR, SMR] AR272; BH84 8700

Psalm 32 (Lawes) [DRDFFM, MSRFMR, RRMD] E505; W 456a 8701

Psalm 36 (Greiter) X Psalm 68 8702

Psalm 42 (Bourgeois) X Bourgeois 8703

Psalm 42 (Rinder) [DDLRDD LL, SSLLTD, DR] BH30 8704

Psalm 47 (Genevan Psalter, 1551) X Meadow Cove 8705

Psalm 47 (Lawes) [MRSDRM, MRSSF#S, SSSL] BJ73; BV 196a; BY129a 8706

Psalm 67 (Scottish Psalter, 1615) X 67th Psalm 8707

Psalm 68 (Greiter) [DDRMDM FS, SFMRDMFS,] E544; G513; T56; W217; X246; AF577; AI 442; AJ87, 420; AL10; BJ72; BV211; BY177b; BZ 8708

-----. V [DDRMDMFS, SFM RDMF#S,] G513 8709

Psalm 80 (Scottish Psalter, 1564) [LMMRMLDRDTL, LR DLD] W97; X269; AF168; AN229 8710

Psalm 84 (Genevan Psalter mel. 1562) X Jervaulx Abbey 8711

Psalm 86 (Bourgeois) X Mon Dieu, prête moi l'orielle 8712

Psalm 88 (Bourgeois) [RRD#R MFRM, LRDFMRD#R] W460 8713

Psalm 93 (Genevan Psalter, 1562) [SMFSSLDDTD, DLD TSL] X208 8714

Psalm 107 (Bourgeois) X Old 107th 8715

Psalm 110 (Bourgeois) X L'-

Omnipotent 8716

Psalm 118 (Bourgeois) X Rendez à Dieu 8717

Psalm 119 (Weinberg) [MS# LTRD TL, LDDRRM, MS] BH191 8718

Psalm 135 (Genevan Psalter, 1562) X Ministres de l'Eternal 8719

Psalm 136 (Braham. Hebrew melodies) [MSSSMDR, RRMSMDR, RR] BH58 8720

Psalm 136 (Genevan Psalter) X Louez Dieu 8721

Psalm 138 (Genevan Psalter) [DMFSDTLS, SLSMMFMRD] X661a; AJ429; BJ99; BY75 8722

Psalm 146 (Genevan Psalter 1602) [MFMDRDTL, LDTLLSL, D] X210b 8723

Psalm of Sion (English trad) X St Austin 8724

P'u T'o (Chinese mel) [MDDRM SSLMRD, MDDRM] R75; Y311; AF71 8725

Puer natus (Piae Cantiones, 1582) X Ein kind geborn 8726

Puer natus in Bethlehem (Plainsong M 1) [LDDTDRDT, LDTL, LDRM] BL6; BM66; BN8 8727

-----. V [RFFMFSFMRFMR, RF SL] BM66 8728

Puer nobis (Piae cantiones, 1582) [DDRMFMRD, DSSSLTDD] A34, 47; B556; C556; E14; F430; G157; J94; M395; Q63; R46; S119; X 33d, 385; Y157; AA162; AB152; AD301; AF39; AG78; AK48; AN 56a; AQ125; AW87; BE323; BG 92; BV121; BY112; BZ 8729

-----. V [DRMFMRD, DSSLTDD, DR] A34 8730

-----. V [DDRMFMMD, DSLTS LTD] M395 8731

-----. V [DRMFMRD, SSLTDD, DRT] BG92 8732

Puer nobis nascitur (Piae cantiones, 1582) X Puer nobis 8733

Puer nobis nascitur (Scheidemann) [SMDSLLS, LTDTLS, SMD] BQ159 8734

Purer in heart (Fillmore) [MFM MRD, DTLS, RRRMFS,] Z 343; AT369; AU272; AX386; AY67 8735

Purer in heart (Holsinger) [MRMDDS, SFMR, MRMDDS,] AS312 8736

Puritan (Dunham) [DDTLTLSF M, RDFMLSF#] I713a 8737

Purity (---) [DDMDTRD, MM SMMRDR, F] AR8; AS59; AX418; AY53 8738

Purity (Norwegian trad) X Behold a host 8739

Purleigh (Brown) [DDSLDDTD, MMDRSDTL,] K210; N185; O95; V301a; AA485; AJ392; AP30; BA308; BX188 8740

Purleigh (Calkin) X Golden corn 8741

Purpose (Davies) X Ainger 8742

Purpose (Shaw) [LTDTLSM, SDTLSL, LTD] A538; E548; R500; X300; AF298; BV315b 8743

Q

Quam dilecta (Jenner) [MFMM RD, SLMRDR, RMSSL] A398; B465; C465a; D484b; E508; F242; J239; K393; W236; AL199; AP325; AW281; BE 268; BO122; BR23; BV13; BY283 8744

Quam dilecta (Root) [MMMMM MMMFM, MSSSSS] N673; U490; AE456; AG320; AR623; AT515; AU482; AV411; BB 690 8745

Quebec (Baker) X Hesperus 8746

Quedlinburg (Kittel) [DMFSS DLSFM, RSFMRD] E245; J596a; X238; BN149 8747

Queen and mother (Catholic) [SDDTSFFM, SSLSFMMR,] BO107 8748

Queen of the rosary (Haller) [SMFSMS, DTLSFM, SLLT] BP83 8749

Queen, when the earth (Andrews) [MMRDDMSSFM,

FFMRRF] BN147 8750

Queen's College) (Davenport) [MMFSDDTLSS, MRRMFS] AP364 8751

Queenswood (Hann) [LLTDTLFL, TDRMRS, SL] Y145; AC181 8752

Quelle est cette odeur agreable? (French carol) X Fragrance 8753

Quem pastores (Hohenfurth ms.) [DMSMFSLSR, MFSFM] A35; B506; C506; E543; F456; N195; O500; Q90; W349; X540; AC 171; AE380; BD105; BE237; BG79; BV111; BY617 8754

-----. V [DMSMFSLSR, MSFMRD L] Q90 8754a

Quem pastores laudavere (Hohenfurth ms) X Quem pastores 8755

Quem terra, pontus (Plainsong M 2) [RRDTDLSDRFFMRM, SS] E214; F512a 8756

Quest (Spencer-Palmer) [LMFFM LLS#, LMFFSRFM,] BV629 8757

Quest (Poteat) [SLTDDRMFM, SFMRMDT] Z320 8758

Qui laborat orat (Allen) [DDD S, SLTRDTDFMM, SF] F339; BE41 8759

Qui tenet (Barnes) [SDTLSLM RM, MLSFMLD] Y81; AC234; AD206 8760

Quietude (Green) X The quiet hour 8761

Quinquagesima (Jones) [MM SMDRMR, MSSF#S, LSF] BY472b 8762

Quinta (Wales. Univ. Students' hymnal.) [DMSDSM, DSLSFM, SMRD] W120b 8763

Quittez, pasteurs (French trad) [SMRDSDRMFSD, SMRDS] X98; BG144; BV110 8764

-----. V [SMRDSDRMFSS, SM RDS] BG144 8765

Quoi, ma voisine? (French trad) X The Kingdom 8766

R

Rabenlei (Rinck) X St Lucian 8767

Rachel (Sewall) [DSLSSD, MR MDDDTLT, D] BR198 8768

Rachie (Roberts) [SDLRDT, TMDFMR, RSSF] BY539 8769

Racine (Diggle) [SMDDSLSFM, RSDDLT] A529 8770

Racine (Edwards) [SDTLSSDT, SDTTLLRD] D506b 8771

Racine (Lutkin) [SLSMDDTT, RRDSMMR, L] I484 8772

Radford (Wesley) [SDRMDFMM R, RMFSMMR] W289b; AL 568a 8773

Radiance (Smith) [MMMRDSLS, RMSTLR, R#M] I537 8774

Radiant morn (Freylinghausen) X Morgenglanz der Ewigkeit 8775

Radiant morn (Gounod) [MRM FSFMRD, SF#SLTLS] I566; S38; AB214; AT32; BX331b 8776

Radlett (Greenwood) [SSFMRM LSL, TDMSFM, R] BE231 8777

Radwell (Chadwyck-Healey) [RMFSLTDRDTL, FRMFS] F441 8778

Raglan (Clemens) [MMMMRDTD, SFMRLDT, F] BA768 8779

Raise your voices to the Lord (Stephens) [MDSMDRM, FM RMRDT, FR] BC154 8780

Raise your voices, vales and mountains (English hymnal: old) [SSDDRFMM, DMRRT RDD,] BO70 8781

-----. R [SMMFLS, MSFRFM, SMMR] 8782

Raise your voices, vales and mountains (Schulthes) [MMM RMFMRDDT, DD#RST] BQ 90, 237 8783

-----. V [SMMMRMFMRDDT, DD#RS] BQ237 8784

Rakem (Woodbury) [MMMSMDR M, MFMFLSFM,] T95; AJ 138 8785

Raleigh (Prout) [MRMLLS, DTD FFM, SDTL] W630; BY667 8786

Ralston (Barnby) X Barnby II 8787

Ramaulx (Selby) [DRMFMRDTDR M, RDTLT] B195b 8788

-----. R [MFSLRSSFMF, MRFM RD] 8789

Ramoth (Calkin) [SSDDTLS, MM SDDRD, SS] D355; W328; AP 339; AZ205-B; BA521 8790

Ramoth (English trad) [SDDDRMMM, RMFSSFMR,] T64; AJ169 8791

Ramoth (Jones) [SMDDTLS, MF SLFMRD, S] X464a 8792

Ramwold (Warner) [DTSLFMRD, DFMLSDDT,] AF303 8793

Randall (Randall) [SSSDRM, SFM MRD, MSSD] M182; AP82b 8794

-----. V [SSSSSDRM, SDTTLS, MF] AP82b 8795

Randall (Randall) X Cambridge 8796

Randolph (Williams) [MSLSFMRDD, MF#SSLTD] E524; R78a; W624; X334; AF61; AN472a; BY761b; BZ 8797

Rangoon (Wood) [DMMSSD, SML SMFSM, MM] F270 8798

Ransom (Bunnett) [SSMLSSRR, MFSLTDSS,] D366; BX186 8799

Raphael (Hopkins) X St Raphael 8800

Raphael (Smith) [DRMFMRDTDR, DDDL#LS] BV396 8801

Rapture (Harwood) [DDSLTDRDT D, MRDTRM] T65; AJ99 8802

Rapture (Haydn) [MRDDMSFM, R MFFRDTD,] C298; D180a 8803

Rapture (Humphreys) [DRMMMSFM RRMF, MRDDRMR] G356 8804

Rapture (Scholefield) [SMMMRD TRD, TLRFRMR,] AT197; AU339 8805

-----. R [DTLTDR, RDTDRM, SMMM] 8806

Rathbon (Crueger) X Ratisbon 8807

Rathbun (Conkey) [SDMDTLSDS, SLMRMF#] A336; B152b; C152a; D48b; G149; H175; I143b; J64a; K62b; L231a; M166; N103; O262; P193; Q354; R195; S154; T288; U 64; V143; Y377; Z237; AA 95; AB140; AC124; AD157; AE116; AF157; AG94; AH 292; AI76; AJ282; AK76; AL100b; AN190b; AO165; AP 199b; AR176; AS138; AT100; AU180; AV113; AW110; AY 188; AB197; BB125; BE379; BF316; BI49; BR59; BX213a; BZ 8808

Ratisbon (Crueger. Praxis pietatis melica) [SSLTDDT, LD SMFRD, MM] A153, 190; B4, 340; C4; D224a; E282; F7; G32; J294b; K511; L264; M4, 222; O45, 227; P209; Q20, 201; S465; V30, 681, 352; W 394; X24; AA220; AF43; AK 168; AM362; AN220; AR23; AZ83-D, 173-A; BA238; BJ 97; BR12; BV36; BX110; BY 673; BZ 8809

-----. R [DRMMMRR, RMFFF MM, ML] 8810

-----. V [SMLTDDT, LDSMFM RD, S] A190 8811

-----. V [SFMLTDDT, LTDS FMFM] E282 8812

-----. V [SMLTDDT, LDLSFM RD, S] J294 8813

-----. V [SSLTDDTT, LLSM FRD, S] M222 8814

-----. V [SSLTDDDT, LLSFM FRM] V352 8815

-----. V [SSLTDDTT, LDSFM FRD,] AZ173-A 8816

Rau (Rau) X Grabesruhe 8817

Ravendale (Stokes) [SMRDDTLS, SFMSMRDR,] I445; K309 8818

Ravenna (Knecht) X Vienna 8819

Ravensbourne (Maker) [DDD RR#MMS, FMDMRR, MF] AB 146; BF333 8820

Ravenscroft (Ravenscroft. Whole

book of Psalms) X Old 104th 8821
Ravenshaw (Schein) [MSSSFMMR, FLRMMR, SF] AZ159-B 8822
Ravenshaw (Weisse. Ave hierarchia, 1531) [DDMFSS, LTDSM F#S, FR] A399; B59; D282a; E436; F250; K10; N10; Q74; W199; X570; AA143; AF258; AL186a; AP288a; AW292; AZ581-C; BA305; BV305; BY250 8823
-----. V [DDRMF#SLS, LTDSFM F#S,] AZ581-C 8824
Ravensworth (Lloyd) [SSSFMSSS, SMMRMFSM] AL356a; AP96 8825
Raymond (Noble) [MMMSSLTD, LSFM, MMML] B36; C36b 8826
Raynolds (Mendelssohn) X Brightest and best 8827
Ready (Tillman) X Tillman 8828
Ready token (Stanton) [MRDSM DRMFMR, SMDRS] BY536 8829
Rebecca (Shenk) X Come, heaven-bound pilgrims 8830
Recessional (Blanchard) X Lest we forget 8831
Recessional (Gower) [DDSDTLM S, SDMSMDSR] Y287; Z561; AB342; AD442; AO590; BF549 8832
Recessional (Lynes) [SSSLDTLS, SSSLDTDR, MDD] C439; Y179 8833
-----. R [SMRDDLSF, FMRD TDRD] 8834
Recessional (Noble) [SSSSSSLTD, DTLSSMD] B439; C438 8835
Recessional (Wood) [MLLMRMM L, TDRMLDTM,] W637a 8836
Rector potens (Plainsong M 2) [RDRFSFMR, SSFSFMRD] E261 8837
Rector potens (Sewall) [DRMSDM FRRD, MFSLFS] BR13 8838
Red Cross (Lutkin) [SLSDTLSF, MRDSFMRF] Y228 8839
Red, white and blue (Becket) [SSDDDRSFMD, SLLSFM] BC37 8840
Red Wing Seminary (Dahle) [MFS FMRMFM, SMLSFMR,] J185; O38 8841
Redal (Bradbury) [DMFSSLTD, DDDTTDLT,] T156; AJ231 8842
Redcliff (Hopkins) [SDTDSLLS, SLTDTRDT,] D120a; BR187 8843
Rede selber uns zu gut (Grimm. Choral buch) X Grimm's 315th metre 8844
Redeemed (Kirkpatrick) [SSSS SLTDS, DRRRRDR] AT203; AU92; AX316; BB635 8845
-----. R [DFFMDRRRRDRM, SLFL] 8846
Redeemed (McGranahan) [MFS LS, MFSDTLS, SLSL] AY514 8847
-----. R [SDSDSDTDSL, LR LRLR] 8848
Redeemer (Emerson) [SDMRD LLS, SSLSDDR, M] T1a; AJ 2a 8849
Redeemer (Keller) [MMRMDRT L, MSLDRM, MM] J480b 8850
Redeemer (Loes) [SSSSMSFMR, FFFFRLS] AT106; AU428 8851
-----. R [LLLLFLLLSM, SSS SRS] 8852
Redeemer (Traditional, 1400) [SSSLSDRD, TRMRDLS, S] M344; O184; Q80; AA147 8853
-----. V [SSSLSDRD, DTRM RDLS,] O184 8854
Redeemer of Israel (Lewis) X Beloved 8855
Redeemer's praise (Richards) [MFSSSDDT, RMFFFLLS,] AP750 8856
Redeeming love (Fisher) [MRR DDRDDTT, FMMRTL] AT311 8857
-----. R [SDMFMRLL, TDRM RDSS,] 8858
Redemption (Bilhorn) [SSMDD RMSF, FMRDMDR] AX315 8859
-----. R [DLS#LDTLSM, SDT LTSL] 8860
Redemption (Cherubini) [MMMM

MMFRM, SSFMLTD] AA250 8861

Redentore (Conte) [MMMMFMM R, DRMSFMR, R] AT154; AU 362 8862

Redhead (Redhead) [DRMLSRM, DFSLFMR, RM] AA25 8863

Redhead (Redhead) X Metzler's Redhead, No. 66 8864

Redhead (Redhead) X Petra 8865

Redhead (Redhead) X St Prisca 8866

Redhead, No. 1 (Redhead) [DM SSLLLS, MSFMRDD, D] D39b; BA209 8867

Redhead, No. 12 (Redhead) X Jam lucis (Benedictine plainsong M 6) 8868

Redhead, No. 45 (Redhead) X Orientis partibus (Corbeil) 8869

Redhead, No. 46 (Redhead) [DT DMRDDT, LRSDLLS, S] E372; F161; W35; X460; AZ16-G; BA600; BV15; BY24b 8870

Redhead, No. 47 (Redhead) X St Prisca 8871

Redhead, No. 66 (Redhead) X Metzler's Redhead No. 66 8872

Redhead, No. 76 (Redhead) X Petra 8873

Reed (Campbell) [SMFSDT, LSDFSM, FSDT] V61a 8874

Refuge (---) [SFMSDSRTSFM, SSDMR] P211 8875

Refuge (Buck) X Draw nigh 8876

Refuge (Doane) X Arms of Jesus 8877

Refuge (Holbrook) [SSSMLSSM, MFSLDTLS,] L122a; M128; T99; U262; V331b; AI245a; AJ142; AM427c; AO336b; AT 157; AU173; AV233a; AX518; BC259 8878

-----. R [MMMDFMMD, DRM FLSFM,] 8879

Regensburg (Crueger) X St Nicholas 8880

Regensburg (Schop) X Jesu, joy of man's desiring 8881

Regent Square (Smart) [SMDSMRD S, LLSDSFM, S] A28; B80; C80; D60; E431; F279; G77; H17; I25; J31; K231; L188; M32; N26; O48; P55; Q50a; R168; S61; T335; U6; V122; W7; Z192; AA452; AC88; AD 106; AE91; AF117; AG8; AH 246; AI3; AJ238; AK104; AL 2; AM60; AN345; AO236; AP 79; AR139; AS108; AT18; AU 145; AV31; AW81; AZ585-D; BA164; BB113; BD228; BE 42; BF237; BI96; BK147; BR706; BV172; BX325; BY 377; BZ 8882

Regi litania (Hungarian trad. litany) [MRDFMRD, SFMLS FM, DD] AN233 8883

Regina caeli jubila (Leisentrit, G-B. 1584) [DDSMDR RM, SFMRD, FFF] BM85; BN49; BQ207 8884

Regina caeli jubila (Praetorius) X Rosa mystica (Geistliche kirchengesang. Cologne, 1599) 8885

Regina caeli laetare (Antonio) [DDTDDRMRDTDS, DMMM] BQ204 8886

Regina caeli laetare (Mauro-Cottone) [MRDMRD, SFMSF M, LSFM.] BQ302 8887

-----. R [DTTLS, DTTLS, LS MFMRM] 8888

Regina caeli laetare (Plainsong M 6) [DRDRMFMRFMRD, DSSL] BM86; BN47; BO300; BP33; BQ279 8889

-----. V [FSFSLL#LSL#LSF, FDDR] BQ279 8890

Regnart (Regnart) X Göttingen 8891

Regnator orbis (Paris Antiphoner) X O quanta qualia 8892

Rehoboth (Van der Werp) [SLS MMRD, SLFMRDT, SL] AI 229; AM47 8893

Reigate (Hall) [MMRDMSFFM MRDRM, MM] B385 8894

Reimann (Reimann) X Reimann's 315th metre 8895

Reimann's 315th metre (Reimann) [SSMDFLS,

SSMDFLS, DS] AZ315-B; BA 231 8896
Reitz (Reitz) [MFF#LSDTSF, RMFTLSR] AT330 8897
-----. R [SLTDSMR#MF, FSLSF RR#] 8898
Rejoice (Barnby) [SDTDRSLTDS MRDD, DF] D457b 8899
Rejoice (Freylinghausen) X Gregor's 151st metre-I 8900
Rejoice, all ye believers (Laurenti) [SDDSSMRD, SFMRDS, TD] M341 8901
-----. R [DDDDR, RRMMFMR, RMRM] 8902
Rejoice and be glad (Husband) X We praise thee, O God 8903
Rejoice and offer thanks to God (Singer) [SDMFSLSS, SLLSLSF M,] BH259 8904
Rejoice, O people (Thiman) [DT LSDRMFSM, RMF#SLT] BV520 8905
Rejoice, the Lord is King (Parker) X Jubilate 8906
Rejoice, ye saints of latter-days (Asper) [SDTDRMFS, DLSFMM DR,] BC207 8907
Rejoicing (Wolder) X Wolder 8908
Rejoicing of the law (Jewish trad) X Simchas torah 8909
Release (Danish trad) [SLSMSS FR, MDDRSM, SL] J60; M407; O136; P84; AI154 8910
Reliance (Gower) [SSLSDRM, SSLSFMF, MM] N142; AI162; AM486; AO372; AS292 8911
Reliance (Mendelssohn) X Heavenly love 8912
Relief (Fawcett) [MLS#LSMDTL, DMRDTLT] E497; X614 8913
Remember (Ravenscroft. Melismata) [LLLDTL, SSLTS#M, LLLD] BG42 8914
Remember Him, the only One (Henle) [MDLTS#LTRDTL, DMDLS] BH44 8915
Remember, holy Mary (Slovak hymn) [MFSDTDLS, MFSDFMR, M] BQ85 8916
Remember me (Hull) X In dark Gethsemane 8917
Remember the poor (Irish trad) [STDDRMRMDTLTS, SLL#] X310; AF417 8918
Remember thy Creator (---) [SDDDMSLS, FMDRMD, SD] AX560 8919
Remembrance (Booth) [SLTDRDT, DDLFMRM, MS] W682; AL 496b 8920
-----. V [SLTDRDT, DLFMR M, MSM] AL496b 8921
Remembrance (McCartney) [SD RDTDRRD, MSFMRDR,] D 233b; T363; AA412 8922
Remembrance (Wesley) [MSMR DLSFM, SDSLSSF] BE349 8923
Remission (Blake) [LLTDMRDT LSSL, TDRM] F324a 8924
Remo (Mountain) [DDRRMSFF RRM, DDRRM] T181; W443; AM587; AT294 8925
-----. R [SSSSLS, FFMMR, MMRRD] 8926
Remsen (Holbrook) [SMMMRDL D, FMMMRDRS,] H92; L246; T20; V225; AJ279; BA564 8927
Renar (Bradbury) [SMMRMSS, LLDLLSS, SM] L491; R465; W660; AH546; AL623; AM633; AP746; AT512; AU307; AW 428; BA833; BV354; BY749 8928
-----. R [SMSLD, DMDMD, SMSLD, L] 8929
Renascence (Porter) [SLMM DTLS, MRMFLSRM,] Y166; AC40 8930
Rendez à Dieu (Bourgeois) [DL SDDRFMR, SMMDFMR] A 195; E305; F409a; Q100; W 318; X265; AF282; AI444; AJ424; AK337; AL224a; AM 512; AN306; AP358a; AQ 269; AW306; BJ19; BV371; BY310b 8931
Renova (---) [DTRDFM, RRRR R, DMRSD] M627 8932
Repentance (Lindeman) [MRR LFMMR, DRMSRMD, M] BE 84 8933

Repentance (Perkins) [DDRMDR DTD, RRMFRSM] T238; AJ334; AV255 8934
Repose (---) [SSF#TLSM, DTLSF, MRMT] AZ22-V 8935
Repose (Blunt) X Merrial 8936
Repose (Dickinson) X Agape 8937
Repose (Kücken) X Kücken 8938
Repose (Stainer) [SSDMRLLS, SFMSF#MR#M,] B15; AS418 8939
Repose (Statham) X Thanksgiving 8940
Repton (---) [DSSLSMFSSD, DFM TDS,] E383; F184a; X481a; BE50; BF608a; BY50a 8941
Republic (Merrill) X America befriend 8942
Requiem (Barnby) [DDDD, FFM RRM, MMMM, LL] N595; O598; V679; Z580; AZ602-A; BA729 8943
Requiem (Barnby) X Sarum 8944
Requiem (Hyatt) [MMMLLLS#S#, LLDDDTT, L] Y128 8945
Requiem (Schulthes) [MRDDFMRD DT, RMDDDM] D555; Eap. 21; F477b; K234; N113; AP573; BA 856; BR166 8946
Requiescat (Barnby) X Requiem 8947
Requiescat (Dykes) [MSDTTLS, DDTLSMM] A224b; B411; C411; D242a; F467; G526; J 296; K509a; S440; V678; W330a; AH532; AL458; AO564; AP616; AW315; BA731 8948
Rerum Deus tenax vigor (Ambrosian) [RDRFFMRMRD, RDRFFM] BJ 100 8949
Rerum Deus tenax vigor (Plainsong M 4) [FSFMSSLLSFRM, FRFM] E262 8950
Rescue (Doane) [SMFSSS, DTL LS, SLTDR] G250; H395; I697; V770; AG142; AH417; AL499; AO649; AP594; AR466; AS377; AT207; AU80; AV329; AW497; AX194; AY523; BB623; BY522a; BZ 8951
-----. R [RDRMRD, RDRMD, DT LSD] 8952
Rescue the perishing (Doane) X Rescue 8953
Resignation (---) [SSMRDTRD LS, SLRDTD,] M496; N227 8954
Resignation (---) [SSLSSMSL DLS, SDRML] T81; AJ121 8955
Resignation (Campbell) [SSLS MRMFM, MDTLSF#S,] V418 8956
Resignation (Cross) [SSDFFM, RRSDDT, TDDR] G365; I 328 8957
Resignation (Heller) [LLLLLT TLSL, LLLSSS] BH92 8958
Resignation (Hullah) X Salisbury 8959
Resignation (Kettle) [MSDTD F, MRLSFM, MRTT] D634 8960
Resolution (Fillmore) [SMFS DDLTDL, SMFSDR,] AT216; AU105; AX298 8961
-----. R [MDRDLD, SMRMM R, MDRD] 8962
Resolven (Rees) [LDMRDT, DMLSF#M, F#MR#M,] K 381b 8963
Resonet in laudibus (German carol mel. 14th c) [SMD MSLS, SMDDMSLS, F] A45; E612; J44; X700; AL72; BG77; BK155; BN9; BP20; BQ156; BV284; BY134 8964
-----. R [DSSSSSDTL, SDT LSS] 8965
-----. V [SMDMSLS, SMDM SLS, FF] AL72 8966
Resonet in laudibus (Jaspers) [SFMFSSDSS, LSFSLLR] BQ293 8967
Response (Froom) [SDRMSLS M, DRSMDLRR,] BB697 8968
Rest (Bradbury) [SSSDSSMR, FFFRTLTD,] B413; C413; D244a; H487: I583b; K507b; L568; M293; Q587; T4; U 421; V672; AA540; AH538; AJ6; AM25; AO565a; AS483; AU165; AV299; AW314; AX

621; AY179; BA719; BB489 8969
Rest (Callcott) X Elim 8970
Rest (Goodrich. Service and tune book) [MMMFDRM, MM RLTD, DDT] N492 8971
Rest (Maker) [MMMR#MSSF#, FMDDRR, MM] A435b; B120b; C120; G342; I543; J467; N331; R416; S302; T406; U242; V410; Y80; Z411; AA564; AB212; AC 152; AD279; AE176; AF341; AG202; AH400; AK226; AL 286c; AN250; AO366; AP437; AQ119; AR334; AS303; AT 335; AU401; AV63; AW181; BA 514; BB116; BD112; BE49; BF 421; BK83; BX285; BY50b; BZ 8972
Rest (Redhead) X St Prisca 8973
Rest (Stainer) X Beati 8974
Rest by and by (Pollock) X Often weary and worn 8975
Rest for the weary (Dadmun) [M FSSLSSD, DRMRDLS, M] AU84; AV358; AX574 8976
Rest in the Lord, my soul (Binder) [MSFMSDL, LRSFRRM, MM] BH91 8977
Rest over Jordan (Holsinger) [DD LSDDLS, DDRMRDRS] AX599; AY384 8978
-----. R [SLSMMRDDLS, DDRM RD] 8979
Rest, rest for the weary soul (Careless) [SMDDMRD, LSMM RRR, MD] BC278 8980
Resting (Mountain) [SSLSLTTD, SSLSTDR, M] S327; AL505; AM139; AP525; BY582 8981
Resting-place (Van der Werp) [DRMFFMRD, MRDDTD, SS] AI431 8982
Resurgam (Adams) [DDRFLSFTT LSFSRM, D] D241 8983
Resurgam (Sewall) [MFSSLRDT, DSLLLSFF] BR316 8984
Resurgenti nazareno (Bohemian, 1505) [DDTLSMMR, DRMRM FRM,] Q253 8985
Resurrection (Dykes) [MRDSDRM, SFMRDTTD,] B177; D116; H 187 8986
Resurrection (Harmonia sacra, 1753) [MFSSSLTD, DRMFS LS] A350b 8987
-----. R [RRMFMMFS, FM RDLS] 8988
Resurrection (Neander) X Neander 8989
Resurrection (Nevin) [SDSD RMM, SFMRDR, SDS] AK 172; AO189 8990
Resurrection (Slovak, ca 1600) [LS#LTDT, DMRDTL, DDT, M] Q603 8991
Resurrection hymn (Gauntlett) [SLSDDRM, MRDSMRD, MR] K112 8992
Resurrection morning (Buck) [MRFMRMLL, MRFMRDR, S] E136 8993
Resurrection morning (Warren) [DRMDLTDR, MFSDTLS, D] D243a 8994
Resurrexit (Sullivan) [MMMM SSFMR, DDRMFFM, M] D 113; U108; V168; Z240 8995
Retirement (Harington) X Harington 8996
Retreat (Hastings) [MFSSS FMLLS, TDRRR] A421; B 32b; C32; D481; G317; H42; I495; L466; M516; N531; R419; T247; U365; V458b; Z394; AG210; AH353; AI 231; AJ343; AL426; AM528; AO319; AP498; AR262; AS 46; AT296; AU189; AV185; AX167; AY180; BA593; BB 241; BZ 8997
Return, O wanderer (Root) [DMD M, DFFDRM, MRRM, SS] AI193 8998
Reunion (Wales. Univ. Students hymnal) [DDDRMRDR, MSL SFMRD] AN465; AQ258 8999
Reuter (Reuter) [DMRDLSFM, MSSFMDR, D] Q283 9000
Revelation (Berggren) X Berggren I 9001
Revelation (Handel) X Messiah [Come unto me] 9002
Reverence (Neander) X Arnsberg 9003
Reverently and meekly now (Beesley) [MRDDSFMR, DR MFRDTD] BC280 9004

Reverently and meekly now (Marsh) X Martyn 9005

Revive us again (Husband) X We praise thee, O God 9006

Rex gloriae (Smart) [DSDRMFM R, SDRMFMR] A103b; B522; C522b; D126a; E616; F148; J112; K120; N147; O62; P223; Q218; V170; X173b; AA231; AI6; AO190; AP226; BY171 9007

Rex gloriose (Andernach G-B. 1608) [DMFSSLTD, SDTLSL] A8b; E183b; F504; AN102a 9008

Rex gloriose martyrum (Andernach G-B. 1608) X Rex gloriose 9009

Rex regum (Lissant) [SDTDRMRD, LFMDMR, RS] D110b 9010

Rex regum (Stainer) [MRDDRMFS, SDDTLS, SS] I607; AB292 9011

Rex triumphans (Hill) [MSLLFFS S, MDTLSLFM] S201b 9012

Reykjavik (Traditional, 15th c) [RRFMRD#R, RLFSFM, RRF] M388 9013

Reynolds (Mendelssohn) X Brightest and best 9014

Reynoldstone (Matthews) [SLS MRRM, DTLSSF#S, RR] C371; I599; AL232; AP359 9015

-----. V [MMMSRRM, DTLSSF# S, RR] I599 9016

Rhau (Geistliche Gesang. Wittenberg. 1544) [DRDTDRMD, D RMFMDRM,] M409; Q596; AA538; AZ22-A; BA445 9017

Rheidol (Roberts) [LS#LTDRTL, MFMDRDT, L] W687; AM527 9018

Rhiw (Wales. Univ. Students' hymnal) [DMMMRS, DRRRDR M, MMM] S100; AM555 9019

Rhodes (Jordan) [SSMDTLS, MF RMFLSSM,] I303; T262b; V453; AJ19; AM508 9020

-----. V [SMDTLS, MFRMFLSS M, S] V453 9021

Rhosymedre (Edwards) [SDDRRM, DFFMRD, SDD] A504; E303; J65; X127b; AF169 9022

Rhuddlan (Welsh trad) [DDDD MDRS, TTDDTLS, D] E423; F556; J343b; R517; S417; X552; Y277; AE397; AF435; AK398; AM620; BV662; BY 372b 9023

Rhyddid (Welsh hymn mel) [DSDMMRDR, DMLSFMRD,] E222; X643b 9024

Rhyd-y-groes (Edwards) [MM MLTDTLLS#L, MMF#SL] BY55b 9025

Rhys (Evans) [DDDDDMRDT RD, MMMMM] BY578b 9026

Rhys (Thomas) [SLDRMSLDR M, RRDTLS] G296 9027

Rialto (Root) [DMFSSS, SLTD DD, DDRM] H499; I157; T 173a; AE378; AJ252; AO468; AR368; AS341 9028

Riber (Beatson) [MRMDDRMF SM, SFSMRD] BB63 9029

Richard (Owen) [DLDLSMRDR, FRMFMRR] E57; X25b 9030

Richards (Richards, i.e. Emmelar) X Armstrong 9031

Richemont (Hervey) [MRDRTD, FRMDR, MRDRT] D133a 9032

Riches of God (Fitzwater) [SD MRDTDRDS, DRRRRD] AR 475 9033

Riches of grace (Showalter) X We are saved 9034

Richmond (Everett) [SDDDD R, MSFMRD, SDDD] G343; I340b 9035

Richmond (Haweis) [SDMSFM FRD, MRSDTDLS,] A319; B101; C101a; D31a; E375; F258; H407; I63; J330a; K 302; L132; M206; N309; O 446; P10; Q66; R436; S199; V74; W32a; X468; Z539; AA 139; AD345; AF261; AK181; AL14a; AN410; AP165a; BE 38; BR234; BV270b; BY255a; BZ 9036

Richmond Hill (Lloyd) [MFSM RDSLDLS, SDRMR] BY588a 9037

Richter (Freylinghausen) [DR

MFSSLSFMD, FMRR] A154a; BV38b; BY674 9038

Ridderholm (Swedish Koralbok, 1697) [DRMDMFSM, FSLSSF# S, D] J104; N135; AI423; AM 174 9039

Ride on, ride on (Dykes) X St Drostane 9040

Ridgefield (Main) [MTDFMRTD MR, STD#RMR] AR297; AS 224 9041

Righini (Righini) [DSMRTD, MDSFRM, SMDR,] G477; I629; AR566; BR197 9042

Righteous Joseph (English trad) [DDRMFSFMR, RMFSLS, S] BG41 9043

Righteous Judge (Goudimel) X Goudimel 9044

Riley (Shaw) [MDLSDDR, MDLS DDD, L] A292a; E481; X644; Y183; BV563b 9045

Rimington (Duckworth) [MRDSM RRD, MMLSMDFR,] G345; S32; AL249b; BB14; BY9 9046

Ring out (Shaw) [SDSLSD, RMT DRMR, RSF] X634 9047

Ring out, wild bells (Gates) [LLT DMMMFMRM, MRMFM] BC279 9048

Ring the bells of heaven (Root) [SSLSMDRDLTD, TDRDM] AU124 9049

-----. R [MMSFRTDDM, LLRM RDT] 9050

Ringe recht (Thommen's Christen-Schatz 1745) X Batty 9051

Ringland (Naylor) [MDDFMSSS, SDTDRFTT] D120b 9052

Rinkart (Bach) [SMRDDTLS, MF#SLRSDT] X60; BV418; BY659 9053

Ripley (Mason) [DMSMFLSM, S DFMRRD, D] J403b; K291a; L141; M103; N251; O109; P 109; AI372; AM53; AR415 9054

Ripon (Haydn) X St Michel's 9055

Ripponden (Cocker) [DMSSFMRF, MRDLSDRM,] BY311 9056

Risby (Rooper) [DDRMRDRMF S, SLSLSM] X568 9057

Rise, crowned with light (Lvov) X Russia 9058

Rise, O Lord (Wagner) [DMLL TDD, DTDSMDRM, M] BI8-D 9059

Rise up, O men of God (Asper) [DMFSLTD, MFMRMF#S, SS] BC332 9060

Riseholme (Gauntlett) [SSLDD DRR, DRFFMRRM,] D495a; AP424b 9061

Risveglio (Loy) [SSSSRD, TLTD TDFMRD,] BD178 9062

Rittman (Smucker) [SSMMMDD RDLS, SSDMS] AY104 9063

Rivaulx (Dykes) [SSSSSLLS, DDLRMFFM,] B206; C206; D80a; F164b; I244; J140; K63; O388; T317; V294; W 5b; Y55; AA269; AB27; AJ 17b; AL3a; AN56b; AP138; BA347; BD201; BE319; BV 483; BX73a; BY39a 9064

Riverdale (Perkins) [SMMRT SD, DFFMDR, R#MR] Y124 9065

Robinson (---) [SDMRTDS, DM SFRFM, MR] D628b; T83; V508 9066

Robinson (Belden) [MDSTLR M, FTRDS, MDST] BB410 9067

Robinson (Hastings) [SSSLSM MR, FFFMRDTD,] T240; AJ336 9068

Robyn (Cornysshe) [DLTTDTLT, TTMMRRD, M] X467 9069

Rochelle (Drese) [DDTDR, DRM RD, MFSFM] A425; B449; C449; E272; F35; G336; J532; K260; L533; M194; N458; O 30; Q410; R334; S502; W567; X52; AA331; AB226; AD228; AK284; AL447; AO381; AP 613; AR305; AW574; AX500; AZ46-A; AZ68-A; BA47, 930; BB676; BR67; BV61; BY544 9070

-----. V [DDTDRMFMRD, MFSFMR] AX500 9071

-----. V [DRMRD, MFMRD, MF SFMR] AZ46-A 9072

Rochester (Day) [SMSLMS, MRM FSMRD, DR] AC166 9073
Rochester (Holdroyd) [DDRMDR TD, MFSLLS, SF] V232; AQ 50 9074
Rochester (Stewart) [DRMFMRD RM, F#SRDTLS,] W422; X594; BV296 9075
-----. V [DDRMFMRDRM, F# SRDTL] W422a 9076
Rock of ages (Dykes) [MMMRDDT, DMSLSSDMR,] D336; T98; AJ 141; AO260b; BF433 9077
Rock of ages (Hastings) X Toplady 9078
Rock of ages (Jewish trad) [DS DFMRD, SLRFMRD, DS] S4; Z96; AF26; AH150; AQ179; BE 281; BH207, 208; BZ 9079
-----. V [DSDFMRD, DSLRFM RD, D] BH208 9080
Rock of refuge (Fischer) X The Rock of refuge 9081
Rockbridge (Chapin) X Forest 9082
Rocking (Czeck mel) [DMSSLL F#S, LLF#S, FFRM] X383; AF 482; BG87 9083
Rockingham (Mason) [DTDRMSM R, MRDLSDRD,] G188; H155; I71; L100; M155; T236; U85; V138; AA309; AJ332; AO142a; AS464; AV42; AY192; BB140; BZ 9084
Rockingham (Miller arr) [DMFR DMSLS, SDTLSS] A203; B154; C154; D101; E107; F108; H 110; I17; J503b; K97b; L253; M420; N241; O306; P178; Q175b; R387; S152a; T187; V142; W106; X133; Y41; Z492; AB191; AD 406; AE27; AF357; AG97b; AH 501; AI77b; AJ230; AK262; AL86; AM44; AN311; AO166; AP192; AR10; AS118; AW105; AZ22-G; BA225; BB89; BE188; BF581; BR176; BV164; BX82; BY151 9085
Rockingham [New] (Mason) X Rockingham 9086
Rockingham Old (Miller) X Rockingham 9087
Rocklands (Hopkins) [MSFM RD, DLLSFM, RMMF#] D532a 9088
Rockport (Noble) [MLLDTLM D, LLLDTLS# L,] R146; AF105; AK366 9089
Rodigast (Gilbert) [SMMMRL TD, RMFSFMR, S] D668; I487 9090
Rodman (Mason) [DTLSMSS FRFFM, DTLS] BB185 9091
Rodmell (English trad) [SDT LRDTLTS, SDMSFM] E611; X221; BY49 9092
Rodney (Lefebvre) [MRMSMR M, SDDTLS, MRM] AD470 9093
Roepper (Warner) [MSFMRM RD, RMLSF#TLS,] AZ606-D 9094
Rogers (Miller) [SSSDSFM R, FFFTLSFM,] BB28 9095
Roland (Simper) [DRMSLDS, FLSDFMR, DR] D67b; L595; Y45; AC44; AW49 9096
Roll call (Black) X The Roll 9097
Roll out, O song, to God (Smyth) [DMSDDD, MSDMM M, MMMF] BI71; BR157 9098
Rolland (Bradbury) [DDDD RMDL, LSSDRMDR,] T178; V238; AJ233; AO224 9099
Romberg (Hastings) [DMRDL SSS, DLRRDTD, D] L7; V 204 9100
Rominger (Skinner) [DRMSFM MRD#R, LRMFFF] BB389 9101
Rondthaler (Peterson) [DMS SLLS, SSSDTLTLS,] BA491 9102
Room for thee (Sankey) [DMS SSDMMRDTD, DDFS] AX99 9103
-----. R [SFMMMRMFL, LLSSLSF] 9104
Rorate (Scottish trad) [SMR DDRMSMSL, TDSMF] BG125

9105
Rorate caeli (Lewars) [DSMDDT D, MRDTLLS, RR] K537 9106
Rorate caeli (Plainsong M 1) [DRMMLSSFMMR, MFMRD] E735; BN2; BO146; BP7; BQ 291 9107
-----. V [FSLLRDDL#LLS, LL# LLS] E735 9108
Rorate coeli (Lewars) X Rorate caeli 9109
Rosa (Hartmann) [SSMFSMM, DDMRTD, SSM] M602 9110
Rosa mystica (Geistliche kirchengesang. Cologne, 1599) [SSS LSSM, FMRDTD, SSS] A17; B82; C82; E19; F68; J38; K533; P138; Q76; R162; W81; X70; Z194; AF131; AK113; AM153; AQ298; AR122; AW526; BB672; BD216; BE152; BG76; BM62; BN17, 48; BQ10; BV90; BY87 9111
-----. V [SSSLSSM, FMRRDDT D, S] P138 9112
-----. V [SSSLSSSM, MRDRMM, SS] BN48 9113
Rose Hill (Sweetser) [MMMMFSS FM, RRRRSTD] L434; T257; V4; AJ359; AM291 9114
Rose of Sharon (Ledington) [MRD SLMR, DRMFFM, MRD] BB98 9115
Rose of Sharon (Palmer) [DRM MMRMRDS, DMSSSS] AR479 9116
-----. R [SSLFLSF#SM, MMRRR RD] 9117
Roseate hues (Barnby) [SSFMMM RD, DFFFMRM, M] B181; C181; D409a; BD124; BE228 9118
Rosedale (Root) [MMMMSMRFR M, MSFMMR] H41; I596; L365 9119
Rosefield (Malan) [SSDDRDRM, LDLSDMRT] H258; I262; M 367; T206; V315; AJ295; AM 443; AO77; AR332; AV257; BB408 9120
Rosenmüller (Hintze) X Salzburg 9121
Rosenmüller (Rosenmüller) [MM SSFRMR, DDDTDRMR] O408 9122
Rosh Hashanah I (Jewish trad) [MRMLLDTL, LDTLSF#SL] BH158 9123
Rosh Hashanah II (Jewish trad) [MMRMLLLLD, LMRDTL, M] BH159 9124
Roslyn (Macmillan) [DRMSDL SR, MMMFMRRS,] AP351 9125
Rosmore (Trembath) [MDSLTD T, FRTLS, MDSL] C92b; U63; Y112; Z322; AC94; AH 270; AI346; BA186; BF625 9126
-----. R [SLTDD#RS, SLTD MRFFM] 9127
Rossetti (Jeater) [SFFMSFFM, MMSDTLSM] AM115; AP 418 9128
Rosslyn (English trad) [DDRM DRRR, RRMFTDMS,] G448; AW417 9129
Rosslyn (Simper) [SSDRMSS, FMRDRDTL, S] D188b 9130
Roswell (Cottman) X Morn of gladness 9131
Rothley (Goss) X Dona 9132
Rothwell (Shaw) [LLLSMR, DTTL, LLLSMR,] C222c; X586a 9133
Rothwell (Tans 'ur) [DMSDS FMRD, RMF#SSLS] H410; L269; M502; T165; V177; AJ243; AV116; BB62 9134
Rotterdam (Tours) [MSDFFM D, LSDMRD, MSD] B171a; C171a; D115a; G159; I164; J56; K43; L263; M441; O 327; S137; T185; U106; V 64a; Y301; Z433; AB9a; AC 15; AI281; AR189; BA246; BF188 9135
Rouen (Gounod) [MMMFRDT RD, SSSLFMR] D73b; V182; BQ146 9136
Rouen (Poitiers Vesperale, 1740) [LMDRMLTDRDTL, LMDR] A228b; E435; F253 a; X349b; AF378; AL165a; AM179a; AP201; BY261a

9137
Rouen (Rouen church mel) [LDTL SLMLL, DRDTLTD] E18b 9138
Rouen (Rouen church mel) X Christi fons jugis 9139
Rouen (Rouen mel. 17th c) X Coelites plaudant 9140
Round the throne of glory (Mortimer) [MMMMSRM, FFT LS, SSDD] AI29 9141
-----. R [DMSF#SLS, DSTLS, DMSL] 9142
Rousseau (Rousseau) X Greenville 9143
Routh (McKinney) [MMMM RDSS, LLLLDRM, M] AT436; AU375 9144
-----. R [DTTLF, TLLSM, RM FSLT] 9145
Rowe (Matthews) X Children's praises 9146
Rowley (---) [DRMRDS, MSFMR M, SSSM] AS300 9147
Roxbury (Smyth) [MMMMFFFF#, SSDSMFMR,] BR420 9148
Royal banner (McGranahan) [MFSSS DMFSLS, DDTRL] AT408; AU 59 9149
-----. R [STRMRD, DFFMRDM R, SS] 9150
Royal law (Bourgeois) [DRMDMS SFMR, MDTLSD] AJ428; AQ229 9151
Royal Oak (English trad) [SMS SFMFL, LTDRTD] A311; E587; F442; G447; R456; X444; AF 478; AL582; BB421; BV233; BY733b; BZ 9152
-----. R [SMFMRDTLS, MFLTL] 9153
Royden (Shaw) [RMDRML, DDTDR S, SSMR] X335 9154
-----. R [MMRD, FMFR, SMLS MDLT] 9155
Rudolfstadt (German trad) [SMRD SLSFFM, SLTDTL] AB273 9156
Rudolstadt (Meyer) [DTDRMFMR D, RMRDTLL] M50; O173; Q65; AA544 9157
Rugby (Candlyn) [MRMDRM, LTT DRS, SDTL] Y140; AC170 9158
Rugby (Somervell) [SMRDRT, DRRMFS, RSMR] BY11 9159
Rugged cross (Bennard) X Old rugged cross 9160
Ruhe ist das beste gut (Stötzel) [DSLLSSFM, DRMRRD, DS] AK231 9161
Ruhetag (Daries) [SMFMRRM D, SLDTLS, SM] AK41 9162
Ruhe ist des todes schlummer (Rau) X Grabesruhe 9163
Rung I (Rung) [SFMLSFRDR M, MRDFRM] M43 9164
Rung II (Rung) [DMDFSLLS, SRFMDMF, F] M120 9165
Rushford (Ley) [DDRMSDLS, DDRMSDLT,] A560a; BV 577a; BY289b 9166
Rusper (English trad) [DRM DSMDMRD, SDDMDL] E379 9167
Russell (Barnes) [SSSLSS LSM, MMMMMSF] BB494 9168
Russia (Bortniansky) X St Petersburg 9169
Russia (Lvov) [SLLSMD, DTLS L, FSSMM] A523; B435; C 435; D487; F491; G505; I 707; J354; K497; N43; R487; S346; U347; V596; W641; Y 264; Z477; AB366; AC284; AD368; AE404; AF446; AG 281; AH481; AI147; AK405; AL517; AM617; AN 374; AO88; AP650; AR608; AT42; AU387; AV72; AW351; AZ32-I; BA277; BB78; BF551; BH265b; BI46; BK122; BR 215; BX43; BZ 9170
-----. V [SLLSMD, DDDTLS, LFSM] S346 9171
-----. V [SLLSM, DDTLS, LFS MMM] BI46 9172
-----. V [SLLSMD, DDTLS, LF SMM] BR215 9173
Russian anthem (Lvov) X Russia 9174
Russian Contakion (Kieff mel) [LS#LDTLS#, DDTLS#LS#LT] E744 9175
Russian hymn (Lvov) X Russia

9176
Russian vesper (Bortniansky) X Vesper hymn 9177
Rustington (Parry) [DDFMRDTS, DDLSFSM, R] F292a; Y265; BE360; BY380 9178
Ruth (Hartshorn) [SMR#MFMMRD, DDTLSMR,] T74; AJ110 9179
Ruth (Smith) [DDDRMS, FFFLD, DDTLS] P381; U249; W613; AB 386; AL575; AO577; AP688; AR 587; AV51; AW386; BA511; BB 5; BD44; BF643; BR448b; BX 520; BY722 9180
Ruth (Webster) [DMMSSDDF, FM RDRM, MM] I492a 9181
Rutherford (Urhan) [MMMRRDD, DFFMFR, RSS] I614a; O597; R281; S434; T53; U418; V677; W581; AB295; AD276; AH521; AI204; AJ83; AL320a; AM599; AO544; AP612; AR335; AV278; BA758; BB605; BE151; BF393; BK95; BR373a; BY776 9182
Ryburn (Cocker) [DMFSSLSD, FFMRDMRD,] BV494; BY324 9183
Ryden (Crueger) X Lob sei dem allmächtigen Gott 9184

S

Sa är fulkomnadt (Swedish Koralbok, 1697) X Pax 9185
Saa vil vi nu sige hverandre farvel (Lindeman) [DMRDDTLS LFM, DTDRR] O51; P63 9186
Sabaoth (Bradbury) [MMMMRDTL S, DDRDTRR] Z97; AH205; AI 31; AS11 9187
Sabaoth (Hopkins) [SDRMRDRMF# S, SDRMRD] D195 9188
Sabbata (Hemy) X Siloam 9189
Sabbath (Mason) [DRMMFMR, TD RFMRD, DR] C46; G393; H80; I69; L38; R74; T299; U437; V 59a; Z448; AE53; AG35; AH161; AI16; ALSuppl; AM320; AO12; AS37; AT37; AU10; AV9; AW 284; AX64; AY275; BB462; BZ 9190
Sabbath bell (Tenny) [SSDMDLTD, RRDTLSFM,] T221; AJ314 9191
Sabbath blessing (Binder) [MLL DMRDTL, LRMFLSL] BH106 9192
Sabbath chimes (Norwegian trad) [SMDRMSLMFRD, DSL TD] P42 9193
Sabbath Eve (Jewish trad) X Sheer hasheereem I 9194
Sabbath evening (Perkins) [MF SDDLSMDRM, MFSFM] T455; AJ411 9195
Sabbath hymn (Binder) [MMMM RDRM, MLSDRDRM,] AHp. 150; BH118 9196
Sabbath hymn (Grauman) [SS DMRDTDRMFFM, MMR] BH113 9197
Sabbath hymn (Nowakowsky) [MMTRD, FMTRD, MLMSFM] BH108 9198
Sabbath morn (Mason) X Sabbath 9199
Sabbatsdag, hur skön du är (Blomqvist) [SMMRRDD, LD DLLSS, SF] N640 9200
Sacrament (Gregor) X Gregor's 107th metre 9201
Sacrament (Hopkins) [MMMSMD RFM, LLLSDFM] AP358b; AZ184-F; BY310a 9202
Sacramentum unitatis (Lloyd) [MRMFRSDDRM, MLLSM] A191; B337; C337; D230 9203
Sacred crown (---) [DMRMFSS, SFMFSM, DMR] AS136 9204
Sacred Heart! in accents burning (Gounod) X Evening hymn 9205
Sacred Heart of Jesus (Slovak hymn) [DDTLLS, RTSFFM, MSSL] BQ59 9206
Sacred morn (Squires) [MSD RMFS, LSFMRLS, SS] AJ 294 9207
Sacred the place of prayer (Stephens) [MMMR#MSFF, MRMSFM, SS] BC281 9208
Sacrifice (Bliss) X I gave my life for thee 9209
Sacrifice of praise (Genevan

Psalter. 1562) X Ainsworth 97 9210
Sacris solemnis (Mohr) X Panis angelicus 9211
Sadie (Pollock) X Forever here my rest 9212
Saelir (Bohemian Br) [LDTDRM, MRDTT, TMRRD] M410; AZ 1-A 9213
Safe home (Hymns of the Eastern Church) [SMDFRD, DRRMMF, RMMM] BR441a 9214
Safe home (Sullivan) [MMSMSS, RRSRSS, DMMS] H501; AO556; BR441b 9215
Safe in he arms of Jesus (Doane) X Arms of Jesus 9216
Safe with Jesus (Gabriel) [MRDR MDLS, SMMR, FMRM] AY96 9217
-----. R [SSSSLLSM, SMRMR, MRD] 9218
Safely through another week (Mason) X Sabbath 9219
Safety (Smith) X Love lifted me 9220
Saffron Walden (Brown) [MRDSDD TLS, SFMRTDF] A409a; C156; E117; F120; W497; AP205; BE 48; BV472; BY442b 9221
Sag was hilft (Speer) X Speer 9222
Sagina (Campbell) [DDRMSFLTR D, MFRLSD] BY426 9223
SAINT: General note
Many melodies having prefix Saint are frequently named without prefix. However, the references in this file allow for either designation. 9224
St Aëlred (Dykes) [MMMMMFFM, LDTLSFFM,] Eap. 62; F313; I485; O242; W83; AL75; AP182; AZ270-C; BA78; BR168; BV 553b; BY117 9225
St Agatha (Cramer) [SDDTLTLS, LTDDRRM, M] BR302b 9226
St Agatha (Southgate) [DRMFM RM, FFMSSF#S, DR] W690 9227
St Agnes (Blow) [MFMRRRMRD, DDRMFML] AL270b; AR341; AS202 9228
-----. V [MFMRRRMRD, DR MFMLR] AR341 9229
St Agnes (Dykes) [MMMRMFT D, SSSMRR] A24; B84; C84; D55a; Eap. 55; F515b; G341; H47; I33; J256; K172; L167; M170; N139; O139; Q361; R239; S206; T354; U76; V 205; W422b; Y358; Z201; AA90; AB81; AC159; AD251; AE214; AF225; AG128; AH 372; AI112; AJ344; AK103; AL298; AM364; AN77b; AO 124; AP449; AR109; AS141; AT46; AU241; AV58; AW155; AY417; AZ14-Cc; BA120; BB 158; BC148; BD155; BE37; BF222; BK88; BO127; BR 300; BX68; BY486; BZ 9230
St Agnes (Langran) X Langran 9231
St Agnes (Statham) X St Joseph 9232
St Agnes School (Jeffery) X Liddon 9233
St Aidan (Ayres) [MDSMRM, DMSLS, LDTSR] BV309b 9234
St Aidan (Grey) [MMMFFTRD, DDTLSMSS] AP529; BY44b 9235
St Aidan (Popple) [SMFSDRD TL, SLTDLR, M] X331 9236
St Alban (Haydn) [MMRRDS, SSLLR, FFMMR] D531b; E643; H399; L127; N642; V759; Z417; AB281; AE133; AL571; AM199; AN334; AO 571; AP697a; AR584; AV220; AZ141-G; BA241; BD18; BF 436; BK108; BR508; BX377 9237
St Alban (St Alban's Tune book, 1865) X Messingers 9238
St Alban (St Alban's Tune book, 1866) X Holborn Hill 9239
St Alban, No. 1 (St Alban's Tune book, 1866) X Holborn Hill 9240
St Alban, No. 2 (Haydn) X St Alban 9241

St Alban's (Haydn) X St Alban 9242

St Alban's (Morley) [MSMRDL, DTDMS, SS#L] A581; B540; C527b; D157; J427; K288; M 632; N507; S202; U121; Y139; Z269; AB314; AC213; AI99; BF 630 9243

St Albans (Steggall) [MDTLDMRT, DLTS#LFM, M] AZ15-D 9244

St Albinus (Gauntlett) [MDSMLL S, MRDTLDDS,] A88; B176; C176; D122; E134b; F140; V 169a; W121b; X155b; AL116a; AM203; AO182; AP229; BR185; BV187; BY158 9245

St Alkmund (Dykes) X Intercession 9246

St Alkmund (Parker) [SDTLSFM, MLSTDR, TDR] D364b; W305 9247

St Alphage (Gauntlett) X St Alphege 9248

St Alphege (Gauntlett) [DMFSDT D, DTDFMR, DMF] A596b; B69; C69; D240a; E348; F275b; J18; K229; M118; N530; V692; W 597a; X459b; AA442; AB414; AO554; AP88a; BA741; BF670; BR436; BV449; BX173; BY439 9249

St Amand (Sewall) [SSLMSLSM, SSLMSLSM,] BR241 9250

St Ambrose (Gauntlett) [SLDDD RD, DDTDLLS, SL] W484b 9251

St Ambrose (La Feillée. Methode du plain chant.) [DDRMFMRD, SSLSMSFM,] E193; F512b; AA550; AP332a 9252

St Ambrose (Monk) [DRFMRS, DDLSFM, LSF#S,] D345b; AA 448; AB479-E 9253

St Ambrose (Sewall) [DMFSDLSS, SMRMFRDD,] BR544 9254

St Ambrose (Steggall) [DDRM DDTD, MRTLLS, RF] W276a 9255

St. Ambrose, No. 2 (Monk) X St Ambrose 9256

St Anatolius (Barnby) [SMRDDDD, DRMFMRM, MR] D16a 9257

St Anatolius (Brown) [SLSDFMR, DRMFLS, SL] A184; B23; C23; D16b; Eap.40; F21; J224; K458a; L18; O555; Q555; S44; U465; W287; AD50; AI54; AL557; AM342; AN 124b; AO35; AP670; BA794; BF203; BV65b; BX153; BY705 9258

St Anatolius (Dykes) [DTDFMM R, MLLTDRD, MM] D16c; K 458b; V43 9259

St André (Davies) [MLTDTLT M, MDRMFMR, D] BE344 9260

St Andrew (Barnby) [MMFSRM, MMLSF#M, SDTL] B218; C369; D212; G610; H50; I 276; J451a; K262; M322; S251; V356; Y396; AB188; AD508; AE466; AK128; AO 309; AP326; AR676; AT402; AU492; AZ522-Q; BA97; BD 129; BF503; BX102 9261

St Andrew (Barnby) X Carlton 9262

St Andrew (Tans'ur) X Barby 9263

St Andrew (Thorne) [MMRMFM LS, DDTLSLS, S] B268; F533; W500; AP553b; BV442a; BY 416a 9264

St Andrew of Crete (Dykes) [MMMMMM, MMMMM, LLS S] A556b; B126; C126a; D81a; F91a; G275a; I616a; J68b; K73a; R360; S275; U 305; V474; Y168; AB245; AC 179; AD295; AF364; AG194; AI323; AK294; AM483; AO 390a; AR319; AV194; AZ 141-F; BA570; BB367; BD79; BF472; BR401; BV137c; BX 537 9265

-----. R [SDRSMD, MRDLS, SSDDF] 9266

St Andrews (Barnby) X Carlton 9267

St Anne (Croft) [SMLSDDTD, S DSLF#S, TD] A289; B85c; C85c; D392; E450; F165; G 384; I214; J168; K203; L213; M145; N144; O212; P142; Q123; R111; S77; T168b; U19; V90a; W530a; X598;

Y30; Z427; AA172; AB58; AC 28; AD1; AE65; AF1; AG40; AH218; AI412; AJ309; AK63; AL 409a; AM26a; AN145; AO91; AP71; AQ51; AR70; AS76; AT 53; AU435; AV39; AW61; AX 639; AY429; AZ14-H; BA29; BB81; BC123; BD60; BE213; BF221; BH47; BJ76; BK64; BL 95; BN197; BR496; BV244; BX 396; BY71; BZ 9268

St Ann's (Croft) X St Anne 9269

St Anselm (Barnby) [SSMRMRD, D#RMFLS, FMM] B43b; C97; D68b; G544; I72; J585; K523; L43; AB344; AD30b; AO13a; AR64; AT493; BE329; BK57; BR85; BX65 9270

St Anselm (Hayne arr) [DDRMFM RD, MSLSDTLS] W386 9271

St Ansgar (Strom) [SFMRDTDD, RRMFSLSFM,] N399 9272

St Anthony chorale (Haydn) [MFMMFMRD, RMFMMR, MF] AR392; BZ 9273

-----. V [MFMMFMRD, RMFR MDMR,] BZ 9274

St Anthony, we turn (Stewart) X Mount Calvary 9275

St Anthony's choral (Haydn) X St Anthony chorale 9276

St Apollos (Morgan) [DSLDTLS, LTDMRDR, MR] W523b; AL 396b 9277

St Asaph (Bambridge) [MMMFSS SD, DLSLSMR,] A394; B539; C539a; D521c; G37; J529a; K 197a; M93; R475; S173; Y305; Z137; AB239; AD219; AE414; AF387; AG235; AH195; AK268; AM211; AO653; AP533; AR4; BA278; BB664; BD142; BE351; BF219; BZ 9278

St Asaph (Giornovichi) [SDDRRM SFM, SFFMMR, S] W223; AP 311; BE158 9279

St Asaph (Mann) [SSDTLRDDTLT DS, MMR] BR312 9280

St Asaph (Shrubsole) X Miles' Lane 9281

St Athanasius (Hopkins) [SLTDM RD, FMRDTLS, S] A270; B77; C208; D385; I77; J135; K159; N338; S71a; U2; V86; AA99; AC73; AK39; AO65; BA257; BB229; BF272 9282

St Audoen (Stewart) [MSFMRD, DRMFLR, MFML] O89; W 210 9283

St Audrey (Harwood) [DRMRD DRMRR, MSDMFT] F174; AP632; BV488 9284

St Audrey (Noble) [DMDMFS, MLMLTT, TDLT] B253c 9285

St Augustine (Chorale songs for four voices, 1769) X Gildas (Abelard) 9286

St Augustine (Goss) [DMSSLS, SMFMRD, DMSL] O414 9287

St Augustine (Yon) [DTLS# DTLS#, LTDTLDT, M] AK 215 9288

St Austell (Brown) [SLSFMFM R, MFMRSLSF#] D216b; AM313 9289

St Austin (Bristol Tune book, 1876) [MMMRFMRD, RRRLD TL, M] K94; L577; V140a; AM241; AP466 9290

St Austin (English trad) [SDRM DMRD, MFMRD#R, RF] E 638a; X395a; BG132; BV596 9291

St Austin (Lord) [DDTDRDRM, MSFMMRDR,] BY355b 9292

St Avold (Haydn) [DDMMRRD D, D#RMFLMR, S] D74; V 264 9293

St Baldred (Bell) [DRMSLDDT, DTLMSFM, M] D556 9294

St Barbara (Lutkin) [MMM SRMMSF, MFSSFLL] I456 9295

St Barnabas (---) [DMSTLSD, SLLLSS, MFF] D373a; BA 244 9296

St Barnabas (Buck) [SLDDTRDT DLSS, SLDD] BE149 9297

St Bartholomew (Duncalf) [SD SRSMRDR, SDTLSLS] E81; W672; X256; BV412b; BY513 9298

St Bartholomew (Smith. Harmonious companion 1732) [MSMFSL RD, RSMFRM, SM] BJ26 9299

St Bartholomew's (Williams) [SD DDDD, RMDLLL, SLTD] AD443 9300

St Basil (German) [MMMMFFM, LLSSFFM, SS] BR476 9301

St Basil (Martin) X Leominster 9302

St Basil (Willan) [SDRTDRMFR DD, MRSF#M] AD359; AL34; BN174; BOp. 4 9303

St Bavon (Horsley) [MFRDMSLS, SLSDMR, R] A387 9304

St Beatrice (Bridge) [MFFLFFM, RSSTLS, SLL] F486; BV652 9305

St Beatrice (Moulton) [SDRMSSD RMS, SDMSLL] Y134 9306

St Bede (Dykes) [DSSLTDDM, LRMFFM, MM] U209; AC139; AD259; AV60; AZ129-D; BA697; BF451; BX291 9307

-----. V [DMSSLTDDM, LRMFFM, M] AZ129-D 9308

St Bees (Dykes) [DDDTLTD, RRMSLRT, RFM] A294; B90; C90a; D149a; Eap. 52; F344b; G192; I257; K370; L472b; M 180; N330; R263; S224; T384; U28; V373; W417a; AA178; AB176; AG136; AH164; AK253; AL292b; AM492; AN118b; AO 252; AP284; AZ11-U; BA95; BB298; BD11; BE273; BF394; BR413; BV533b; BX146; BY414 9309

St Benedict (Stainer) [SSFMFM RD, LSFRMFR, S] W437 9310

St Bernard (Gardiner. Sacred mel.) X Belmont 9311

St Bernard (Monk) [SMSDLSRM, M RF#SLTDF#] B328; F188b; AB 238; BV33a 9312

St Bernard (Tochter Sion. Cologne. 1741) [SDRMRDFMR, SMLF#F# S, S] A413; B125; C234; D267; E71; F104; G332; I133; J371; K406; Q378; V451; W87; X537; AA496; AB148; AD152; AF347; AK222; AL79a; AN73; AP 68a; BA839; BE358; BN65; BO13; BV140; BY253; BZ 9313

-----. V [DDRMDFMR, SML F#F#SLT] BN65 9314

St Blane (Scholefield) X Litany No. 9 9315

St Boniface (Barnby) [MMFS MRMD, DTLSSLSF#,] I290; AB405; BF671 9316

St Boniface (Gadsby) [SDMSS F, MDDTD, LTDF] A561; B 531; C531; D523a 9317

St Boniface (Smart) X Sion 9318

St Botolf (Gower) [MSMMRD RM, DLSMDRMR,] AM252; AP285 9319

St Botolph (Slater) [DMDSM RDTD, RMSLSFS,] E419; F450; X527a; BV548; BY 557 9320

St Botolph (Smart) X Sion 9321

St Bride (Howard) [LMLDTL, DSDMRD, MRD] A417; B 246; C246a; D351; E74; F 322; J365b; K315; M71; O592; Q322; R233; S188; V221; W403; X699; AA422; AD238; AE253; AF338; AL 265b; AN59; AP22a; AQ 224; AR209; AW581; AZ 582-B; BJ65; BR281; BV 174; BX344a; BY322; BZ 9322

St Brides (Howard) X St Bride 9323

St Bride's (Howard) X St Bride 9324

St Casimer (Goss) [SMFSDD TT, LSDRMMRR,] B286; C286; D166; AB130; AO151; AZ166-F; BA72 9325

St Catherine (Dale) [DMMSS DT, SLFSMR, RMM] Eap. 65; F355; W348; BV476; BY418 9326

St Catherine (Hemy) [MRDDTD RLTD, DTLSD] A185; B136; C227; G256; H318; I194; J 516; K355; L155; M149; N

214; O474; P212; R88; S267; T167; U210; V324; W697; Y109; Z348; AB168; AC49; AD262; AE216; AF365; AG164; AH429; AI237; AJ245; AK282; AL399; AM487; AN546; AO297; AP161; AR94; AS92; AT252; AU201; AV184; AW154; AX434; BA275; BB349; BD148; BF456; BK69; BL87; BR252; BX401; BY606; BZ 9327

-----. R [FFFMMRRM, MRDLD RR] 9328

St Catherine's Court (Strutt) [DR MDRMDRMFSLS, LTD] F476 9329

St Cecilia (Hampton) [SMRDDTL S, TDLRTLLS,] F96b; Q168 9330

St Cecilia (Hayne) [SFMMRD, MRTTLS, RRMF] A544; B105; C105; D329; Eap. 64; F262; J 329; R488; S425; V605; W152; AF448; AK403; AL140; AN339; AO486; AP251; AS243; AW271; BA107; BB396; BE382; BV334; BX387; BY317a 9331

St Cecilia (Sewall) [MMMFF RRRM, MMMSSF#F#] BR320 9332

St Cephas (Crosbie) [DDTRDT, RD#RFM, SSLSD] AM124 9333

St Chad (Redhead) [SDTLSMRM, SSDTLLS, S] A454; B233; C 233; D443a; BA651 9334

St Christopher (Maker) [SSSF# LSM, DRMFFM, MD] A339; B 149; C149; D102b; G144; J482; K362; M425; N69; O321; P180; R190; S162; T344; U95; V252; W691; Y105; Z235; AB138; AC120; AD154; AE110; AF160; AG91; AH290; AI75; AK161; AL98; AM177; AO163; AP209; AR165; AS332; AT345; AU234; AV110; AW112; BA189; BB280; BD82; BF317; BR373b; BY427a; BZ 9335

St Chrysostom (Barnby) [MMMM RDRM, SSSSF#MF#] A460; B228; C228; D600; Eap. 19; F202; I10; J274b; K351; O 116; T171; V219; W430; Z 383; AB291; AD246; AJ229; AK244; AL295; AM355; AO 446; AP426; AR358; AS129; BA488; BB350; BF253; BI40; BX114; BY611 9336

St Chrysostom (Irons) [MRD DTLSS, MFMMRDTD] D271a 9337

St Chrysostom (Ohl) [MMRD MSFM, SSSRRLS, L] J507; K375 9338

St Clement (Scholefield) [SMFM SMRDRLDT, LSS] A179b; B 29; C29; Eap. 16; F33b; G54; I60; J227; R59; S45; T313; U464; W289c; Z140; AB33; AD58; AE47; AF48; AG26; AK54; AL568c; AM338; AO 32; AP671; AR60; BA395; BB57; BD8; BE381; BF191; BK47; BV52b; BX147; BY 706a 9339

St Clement (Steggall) [SLSM RRM, RMLDDTD, MS] D213b 9340

St Clothilde (Franck) [SDMMS, SLSFFM, MMSSD] Y391 9341

St Colomb (Hoyte) X St Columba 9342

St Columba (Hoyte) [DMSDSLS, SDTDRM, MRD] D205b; I 573; K30; S467 9343

St Columba (Irish trad) [DRM FSFSMRD, DRMFSFSL] A345a; C326b; E490; F29; J530b; R106b; S145; W196; X654a; Z326; AF80; AG51b; AL280a; AM271; AN87a; AP 146b; AR80; BE339; BN121; BV546a; BY72b 9344

-----. V [DRMFSFMRD, DRMF SFS] BN121 9345

St Columba (Irons) X Irons 9346

St Columbia (Irons) X Irons 9347

St Constantine (Monk) [MRFM RD, RSF#LS, FMLFM,] A358; B361; Eap. 53; F194; K567; W462; AA256; AP491; BR305;

BV477b 9348

St Crispin (Elvey) [MMMSDRRM, SSSDTLL] A409b; B139; C139a; D606a; Eap. 36; I258; J325; N184; Q245; R116; S175; T276; U86; V96; Y70; Z349; AA326; AB151; AC33; AD46; AF320; AG117; AJ383; AK225; AL351; AO263; AP579a; AR117; AS264; AW149; BA419; BD136; BF426; BX223 9349

St Croix (Garrett) [SMSDMMR, DDTLTD, SMS] K575 9350

St Cross (Dykes) [DDRMLSFM, MMFSDM] A74; B153; C153; D105; E111; F113; G134; H164; I152; J86; K105; M72; N100; O441; Q164; R192; S159; W96; X140; Z233; AA439; AF164; AK146; AL90; AM242; AO174; AP193; BV173b; BY144 9351

St Cuthbert (Dykes) [DDDRMFF M, SDMMF#S,] A368; B199; C199; D375; Eap. 31; F230a; G177; H76; I189; K157; S205; T353; U131; W180b; AD188; AG124; AH228; AL162; AN125; AO227; AP272; AW138; AZ272-A; BA141; BB214; BF261; BR 92; BV223b; BX104; BY236a 9352

St Cyprian (Chope) [SSLTDS, MD LRDT, SSFM] C59; D282b; K168a; N224; R252; AG298; AM266 9353

St Cyprian (Goss) [SDTLSMFS, SDRMFSLR,] I594 9354

St Cyril (Bliss) [SDTLSM, FLS FM, SSDDR] W664 9355

St Darerca (Macalister) [DTSLM SDRMS, DRMS, SL] S9; W15b 9356

St David (Ravenscroft's Psalter) [DSDMSFMR, DSDFLS, SL] E166; F470; W31b; X301; AL674; AP 6; BJ60 9357

St David (Thomas) [SSDRDTDMR DT, DLTDD] AP405a 9358

St David's (Ravenscroft's Psalter) X St David 9359

St Denio (Welsh mel) [DLFRTSD MMRD, DLFRTS] A301; E407; F372; G64; J172; R85; S66; W 12; X535; Z159; AD73; AF7; AJ201b; AK408; AL403; AM 35; AN30; AQ41; AR20; AT43; BE150; BL93; BV 242; BY61; BZ 9360

St Denys (Spinney) [DTLSMS F, RDD#RLS, FMF] B235b; C235; D431; BR95 9361

St Drostane (Dykes) [SDSDR MRD, SFMRRRF#S] A64c; B145; C145a; D91; F99; G 125; I150; J73a; K88; L259 a; M429; O293; R188; S150 a; T340; Z223; AC115; AD 143; AF175; AJ46b; AK133; AL85b; AM172; AN182b; AP189a; AR158; AV103; AW 101; BB127; BD73; BF308; BI101; BR173a; BV167a; BX 199; BY128 9362

St Dunstan (Redhead) X St Prisca 9363

St Dunstan's (Douglas) [DDS DRM, FMDMR, DDSDRM,] A563; B117b; C117; J563; R345; S276; Y169; Z364; AB175; AC204; AD226; AF 371; AG193; AK296; AR 322; BF409; BK79; BZ 9364

St Eanswyth (Sidebotham) [SSSDDLS, SSSMMRR, TD] BA51 9365

St Ebbe (Redhead) [DSSSLS, MFMRRD, DSSS] AZ342-H 9366

St Edith (Knecht) X St Hilda 9367

St Edmund (Gilding) [DDMRDT D, RMSFMR, RRM] E171; K49; W551b; X120b; BE241 9368

-----. V [DDRMRDTD, RMF SFMMR] BE241 9369

St Edmund (Steggall) [MSRMD LS, LDRMRRR, MS] B298; D67; E47; F81; K37; AA 184; BV131 9370

St Edmund (Sullivan) [DDDD TR, SSLS, SMMMRS,] B222b; C222b; D344c; G297; I315a; M312; N77; O462; P251; Q 660; R284; U202; V712; Y

370; Z299; AA563; AB264; AC 149; AE273; AF318; AG160; AK 206; AM605; AN43; AO38; AR 348; AS242; AT314; BA548; BB345; BD109; BR374b; BX151a; BZ 9371

St Edward (Steggall) X St Edmund 9372

St Elizabeth (Silesian mel) [DD DRTD, MMMMFRM, SD] A238; B356b; C356; G111; I118; J 434; K129; L111; M623; N317; O576; P6; Q657; R135a; S194; U72; V751; Y58; Z261; AB84; AC137; AD181; AE103; AF227; AG113a; AH314; AI105; AK182; AM129; AN45; AO211; AQ14; AR100; AT159; AU211; AV102; AW97; AX565; AZ33-C; BA119; BB165; BD63; BE274; BF331; BK21; BQ38; BY270; BZ 9373

-----. V [DDDRTD, MMMFRM, SDLS] M623 9374

St Elwyn (Hopkins) [SDDTLSLS, FMSLRDT, S] D273; AB38 9375

St Enoch (Gilbert) [SSSSLDSM, MRDRMF#S,] D256 9376

St Enodoc (Lang) [LDTLLRTM, D RMFSM, ML] BV250a 9377

St Erik (Swedish trad) [DSDRMD, TDLLS, SSLTD] J430b 9378

St Etheldreda (Turton) [DDRMRD TD, RMSFMR, MF] F318; J295; K170; O502; W467; AE192; AG 177b; AI413; AM31; AP329; BA 182; BV564b 9379

St Ethelreda (Turton) X St Etheldreda 9380

St Ethelwald (Monk) [SFMRMFM, MRSLLS, SLT] C346b; D268b; E479; F303; K272a; M241; Q 374; W534a; X641b; AA361; AB 182a; AL404b; AM595; AP111; BE398; BV585a; BY508b 9381

St Fabian (Barnby) X St Polycarp 9382

St Fidelis (Barnby) X St Boniface 9383

St Finbar (Hemy) X St Catherine 9384

St Flavian (Day's Psalter) [DDT DMRRD, DFMDRM,] A59; B56; C56a; D78; E161; F159; G 423; J138; K53; N84; Q22; R113; S86; V600; W8; X188; AA463; AD74; AE337; AF153; AI433; AJ185; AK141; AL 178; AM557; AN54; AP47; AW318; BA198; BB193; BL 19; BM75; BN163; BV148; BX76; BY195; BZ 9385

St Frances (Lohr) [DFMRDS FM, MRSLLS, SD] D29a; M122; V227; W90; AM282; AP589; BX226 9386

St Francis (Briggs) [MLLM RDTL, MLLMDRML,] X439 9387

St Francis (Diggs) [MMSSFF M, SSLSMRR, LL] U197 9388

St Francis (Moschetti) [MM SMRMSFMMR, MFSLD] J276 9389

St Francis (Sullivan) [MDR MMMMSFM, RDDRFM,] B 342; C342; D206; K173 9390

St Francis II (Sullivan) [MSF MRDDRFM, MSSFMR] W308 9391

St Francis Xavier (Stainer) X Xavier 9392

St Frideswide (Lloyd) [MRD RMFSM, LLSMFSM, S] D619a 9393

St Fulbert (Gauntlett) [SSDRL SFM, SMSLDT, DS] A456; C302b; D372b; E139; F128; J196; K296; V161; W675; X151; AK364; AP282a; AZ 14-V; BA550; BV191; BX355; BY628a 9394

St Gabriel (Braun) X Braun 9395

St Gabriel (Greatorex) [SSMF LSMRDTLS, FMSD] I224 9396

St Gabriel (Ouseley) [MSFM FMRD, DLSFSMF#S,] A180; B14; C14; D8a; F19; J222; K460; N561; O452; V51a; W 279; AD274; AL566; AP424a; BY708 9397

St Gabriel, O blessed youth

(Bragers) [DDTTRRDD, SLLTD RRR,] BP98 9398

St Gall (St Gall G-B. 1863) [SM LSMFSFMRD, RMRMS] E292; X13; AW378 9399

St George (Elvey) X St George's Windsor 9400

St George (Gauntlett) [MFLSFM, MRDDTD, SLF#S] A118; B276; C276; D69a; F63; I390; K387; V604; W590; AA430; AL420; AM560; AP516; AS313; BA302; BE201; BR45; BV157; BY131 9401

St George of Windsor (Elvey) X St George's Windsor 9402

St George's (Elvey) X St George's Windsor 9403

St George's Bolton (Walch) [MMR STRD, SLDTLS, MMR] C131; D360a; I614b; L607; AE410; AP368; AV167; BA519; BB467; BR353a 9404

St George's, Edinburgh (Thomson) [DDRMFSSS, SFMRDMR, R] AL638; AP21; AW580; BY172 9405

St George's Windsor (Elvey) [MM SMDRM, MMSMDRM, MM] A137; B421; C106a; D118b; E289; F 131b; G545; H481; I636a; J91; K111; L348; M430; N130; Q71; R149; S109; T444; U474; V528; W118; X9; Z593; AA295; AB389; AC322; AD447; AE79; AG287; AH482; AI350; AK91; AL250; AM365; AN141; AO218; AP214; AQ10; AR594; AT462; AU136; AV307; AW377; AZ205-F; BA861; BB496; BC29; BD159; BE369; BF650; BI95; BK136; BL55; BR490; BV183; BX18; BY724; BZ 9406

St Germans (Maker) [DMMMRDS, FMMMRDDT, D] Z509; AB350 9407

St Gertrude (Sullivan) [SSSSSLS, RRDRM, DMS] A557; B530; C530a; D516a; E643a; F629; G280; H393; I383; J560; K379; L541a; M242; N589; P373; Q 658; R350; S365; T134; U294; V483; W535; Y172; Z482; AB 254; AC209; AD299; AE250; AF382; AG199; AH442; AI 327; AJ200; AK292; AL401; AM490; AN329; AO391a; AP 538; AQ215; AR502; AT412; AU46; AW225; AX196; AZ 141-H; BA582; BB360; BC 128; BD145; BE264; BF471; BI91; BR512; BV562; BX378; BY520; BZ 9408

-----. R [DDDDDTLTD, RR RDRM] 9409

St Giles (Bell) [MRDDRM, DTL LTS, SSFM] J544a; W346; BR231; BV381 9410

St Giles (Stainer) [MMFSSR FF, MMRDRM, SD] D635; AB114; AC86; AO559; BF 298 9411

St Godric (Dykes) [MRDLTD, RMSFMR, MRSD] C182; D141; J193; K138; L59; N145; AL 169; AM283; AP118; AZ342-E; BA376; BX484a; BY653 9412

St Gregory (Knorr. Neuer helicon 1684) [SMSLDSFM, SDM FMRDR,] D199b; E49b; F83 J352b; K482; V192; AL185; AP654; BA324; BE239; BY 473 9413

St Gregory (Plainsong, Barnby arr) [DDDRDD, DTDLSS, DDDR] AB67 9414

St Helen (Hately) [MFFMDTL SLS, MRRMLS] W556b; AP 512 9415

St Helen (Martin) [DDDMLSMR, DDLSSLT, S] F400; BV382 9416

St Helen (Stewart) X St Helen's 9417

St Helena (Allen) [SMRRDD, MDTL, SLTDRM] AM513 9418

St Helena (Milgrove) [DMDRRD, STSLLS, FMDL] D70a; F475; K249; M25; AA137 9419

St Helen's (Stewart) [MRFMLS SF, MRDRM, MMR] S395; U176; V353; W695; AP502a;

AS443; AZ269-D; BF351 9420

St Hilary (Ganther) [MMSSDRMR, FMLSFMR, M] J5; K12; M340; N22; Q640; AA242; BR108 9421

St Hild (Ellis) [MSLTDRM, FLR DTDR, SF] W159 9422

St Hilda (Barnby) [DDRMLSSF, MRSMDRM, D] C191; D365; V156; AM128; AZ167-I; BR 206 9423

St Hilda (Knecht & Husband) [DD TDRRRD, MMRMFRT, DTD] A407; B132; C132; D357a; G 197; H281; I282; J386; K322; L360; M77; N401; R266; S228; T153; U170; V300; Y375; Z 279; AA435; AB157; AC148; AD205; AE169; AF329; AG 139; AH325; AJ227; AK211; AM414; AO257; AR252; AT346; AU242; AV179; AW144; AZ151-Q; BA269; BB231; BE221; BF 342; BR297; BX536; BZ 9424

St Hildred (Pearsall) [SFMRDDLS FM, SDSLLT] C301b 9425

St Hill (Stainer) X Pastor bonus 9426

St Hubert (Darwall) [SSLLSMM DRM, RMFRMF] D420a; J237; K457; Z357; AV225; BR387; BX324 9427

St Hugh (English trad) [DDDLLS FM, SLLLLS, MF] E606; J335; W557; X371; BE248 9428

St Hugh (Hopkins) [DDRMDSRM, MFLSDR, SD] F317; W549a; AB353; BE303; BR16; BV66; BX75a; BY325a 9429

St Ignatius (Barnby) [DDRDMFS, MRDDD, DDRD] W606; AS433; AT498 9430

St Ignatius (Cooke) [SSDTLDDS, MMRDTLS, S] C378b; D358c 9431

St Ingrid (Alexis) [SFMFMMRD, MRDTRDTL] J391a; N485 9432

St Ishmael (Vincent) [SDTLTS, FMFSLR, RMF#S] BY609b 9433

St Issey (English trad) [DRMRD LS, DRMRD, TDRM] E388; R 528; Sap. 16; X490 9434

St James (Courteville) [SDRM DRFM, MLTDLS, RM] A361; B279; D144; E341; F199; J247; K279; R221; S254; W173; X96; Z424; AF266; AJ341; AK325; AL339; AP 185; AZ14-E; BA607; BR390; BV445; BY110 9435

St James' Stockholm (Ahlström) [DMSRFMRD, RMR DTLLS,] J270; N238 9436

St James the Less (Dykes) X Hollingside 9437

St Jerome (Champneys) [SLS FMFSRRD, MRMF#SR] B438 9438

St Joan (Coller) [DMSDLS, L DLSMRM, D] A258; R492 9439

St John (Calkin) X Calkin II 9440

St John (Dykes) [LMRDTL, LSLFFM, LSLF] B148; C 148; D96a; K102; O265; BB129 9441

St John (Havergal) [DMMSSD, DTLSF#S, SLTD] Q380; V 167; W710; AA329; AL626; AM307; AP43; AW615 9442

St John (Turle) X St John's Westminster 9443

St John (Wade) X St Thomas 9444

St John Baptist (Calkin) X Bradfield 9445

St John Damascene (Barker) [SSMFLS, SSFRM, DDTDR] D395a; AL460 9446

St John Damascene (Brown) [SLDDDRM, DRMFSS, SLD] F133; K70 9447

St John's (Havergal) X St John 9448

St John's College (Garrett) [SLSDMFML, RSDFMR, MF] V67 9449

St John's, Highlands ("W. C. B.") [MFF#SDDTF, MMMMLLR R,] D244; R438; T170; AJ 132; AO565b 9450

St John's, Westminster (Turle) [DTDRMFFM, MRSSF#S, SS] D233a; G410; I234; AW305

9451

St Joseph (Calkin) [MFMSFMRD, RMFSDTLS,] W361 9452

St Joseph (Hopkins) [SSSDMRDT, DRMDLRRS,] B226b 9453

St Joseph (Parry) [MLSMDRMFM RM,MDTLS] X441 9454

St Joseph (Statham) [MMMMSFM R,DDRMFRD,M] I132; L363; AP685 9455

St Joseph, be our guide (Jenkins) [DRDSLDRMSFMDRF,MR] BL 64 9456

St Joseph, pride of heaven's court (Bragers) [SMDDTLSDR M,MFMRRD] BP91 9457

St Jude (Vincent) X Monod 9458

St Katrine (Williamson) [DRMSS FM,F#STLSF#S,SL] BY260b 9459

St Kentigern (Arthur) [SDRMSLM S,TDRMDFMR,] W218; AD460 9460

St Kerrian (Dresden mss. 1761 Stainer arr) [DDRMFRM,RR DSSF#S,RM] D222b; W314 9461

St Keverne (Lang) [MLLLTTDRT DRMFLS#L,] A492 9462

St Kevin (Patton) [MMFMRLTDR MR,RMF#SS] AZ596-A; BA 832b 9463

St Kevin (Sullivan) [MMMRDMFS, DRMFMR,RR] A94b; B170; C170; D110a; G151; I163; J 106a; K108; M445; N131; R 205; S168; U220; V767; Z242; AB242; AD162; AE136; AF185; AG101; AH301; AK169; AM200; AO180; AR183; AT109; AW113; AZ152-H; BB136; BD95; BF319; BR179; BZ 9464

St Kilda (Broomfield) [LLTDMRDT, DLTDRM,MR] W558 9465

St Lawrence (Hayne) [MMRDTT LS,SSSFMRDT,] B454; C454; D169b; F471; AP366; BV412a 9466

St Lawrence (Smith) [DMMFSLM RD,SLDSFFM] W633 9467

St Lawrence (Steggall) [MSLDSM MR,DRMLSMR,M] AZ585-F 9468

St Lawrence, Lund (Swedish, 17th c) [SDRMRDTD,MRM DTLLS,] J302 9469

St Leonard (Meiningen G-B.) [MRDRSDRDTS,LTDDRS] A 518; B273; C15; D151; E527; J126; K149; M465; N157; O 59; P231; Q226; X32b; Z545; AA246; AD432; AL560a; AW 548; AZ89-B; BA288; BN63; BR444b; BV475; BY638 9470

----. V [MDRSDRTS,LTDDR SM,M] M465 9471

-----. V [MDRSDRDTS,LTD DRRM] AZ89-B 9471a

St Leonard (Davis) [DDDRDDT, LSSDMR,MFS] C536b 9472

St Leonard (Hiles) [DRFMRR DD,DRRRRR,RM] C22; D 15a; G46; I62; J54b; K40; N219; S36; T314; U20; V38; Z142; AB24; AC66; AD51; AG175; AH165; AJ257; AK79; AL282; AM553; AN122b; AO 26; AP678; AR73; AS26; AV 13; AZ590-H; BA793; BB54; BD31; BE224; BF204; BK55; BR122; BX156 9473

St Leonard (Irons) [SMRDLFMR, SLDTLSF#S,] Eap. 41; W 514 9474

St Leonard (Smart) [SSMLSLT D,RMDTLS,RT] F443; K 266; N41; W474; BE247; BV 502; BY446 9475

St Leonard's (Barham-Gould) [MSFMRDDT,DDRMMF#S,D] BV634; BY596 9476

St Lo (Breton trad) [SDRMDM RD,RMRDRMLS,] S489; AK 413; AL369; AN510; AW388 9477

St Louis (Redner) [MMMR#MS FL,RDTDRSM,M] A21b; B 78; C78b; D58b; G100; H145; I121a; J27a; K31; L220b; M605; N36; P133; Q647; R171; S121; T334; U55; V 741; Y330; Z184; AB107; AC82; AD121; AE85; AF134; AG64; AH250; AI66; AJ399;

AK108; AL51b; AM152; AN165; AO125a; AQ286; AR126; AS103; AT75; AU144; AV82; AW84; AX 97; BA157; BB104; BC165; BD 226; BE222; BF292; BK150; BX198; BZ 9478

St Lucian (Rinck) [MMRRDS, LT DMR, MMFMR] J231b; K550; P70; AP744; AZ141-C; BA637 9479

St Lucy (Poole) [DDRMFMRD, SSLTDTLS,] AP497 9480

St Luke (---) [SDSLLSMFMRM, MMFML] M300; O580 9481

St Luke (Clark:Clarke) X Uffingham 9482

St Luke, No 1 (Beethoven) X O salutaris Hostia 9483

St Luke, No. 2 (Gilmore) [DMM RDFSFM, MMMR#MF#F#] BR 472 9484

St Luke's (---) X St Luke 9485

St Mabyn (Brown) [MMRDSMMR, FFMLTDT, R] W395a; AA467; AL468b; BE337; BY419a 9486

St Mabyn (Humphreys) [SMMMRD LS, DMRRMR, RF] D240b 9487

St Magnus (Clark) [SDRTSDRM, RMDMF#S, RM] A106; B188; C188; D129; E147; F218; G78; H191; J439; K11; N11; O175; Q219; R211; S185b; T202; V109; W131a; X175; AA237; AB347; AD326; AE122; AF78; AG315; AH11; AI429; AJ291; AK451; AL118; AM113; AN251a; AO 191; AP24; AQ98; AT126; AW 582; BA249; BE328; BF638; BJ21; BR139; BV207; BX236; BY58b; BZ 9488

-----. V [SDRDTSDRM, RMDR MF#S,] BJ21b 9489

St Margaret (Dunman) [SDRMSL, LRMRDT, SMRD] L413 9490

St Margaret (Masser) [MMMSFM RD, DRMFRSFM,] AP489 9491

St Margaret (Peace) [SSSSLTDDT, TTTTDR] A458b; C236b; G318; I481; J402; K348; M208; N521; P288; R400; S307; T46; U26; V 367; W424b; Y37; Z388; AC154; AD249; AE262; AF399; AG181; AH221; AJ73; AK278; AL311; AM594; AN243; AO289; AP 465; AR271; AS266; AT290; AU231; AV232; AW175; AY 468; BA492; BB145; BD115; BE406; BF245; BK90; BR 422; BX286; BY20a; BZ 9492

St Margaret (Statham) [LMM MMMD, DMMMRR, RFF] F 114b 9493

St Marguerite (Walker) [MD RDSTLS, SLTDRR, FM] C 56b; D338; I369; U286; V 378; AB166; BA360; BF439; BR428 9494

St Maria (Haydn) X St Michel's 9495

St Mark (Bell) [MMSFMRD R, MMRDRRS, M] Eap. 71 9496

St Mark (Crowfoot) [MSLSF MFRD, RMF#SDTL] F405 9497

St Mark (Elliott) [MLS#LDTL S#, LSFMLLS#L,] O236 9498

St Mark (Gauntlett) [MSSSFF FM, MMMMRR, RF] I699; U232; BA109 9499

St Mark (Mozart) X Mozart II 9500

St Mark (Teschner) X St Theodulph 9501

St Mark's (Haas) MMMRM F, LSFM, MMMF#F#S,] K 336 9502

St Martin (Briggs) [MLTDRM MSFM, RDLT, TD] X572; AQ58 9503

St Martin (Corbeil) X Orientis partibus 9504

St Martin (Ett) [SMFMRD, DMSSLS, LTDT] E416; F 213b; K74; BN129; BO265 9505

St Martin's (Tans'ur) [DDRD SDRM, MFSFMDR, M] C71c; D54b; G172; H105; I183; L 193; T227; V117; AD327; AI370; AJ323; ALsuppl; AM 260; AN366; AO215; AW74; AY418; AZ14-Aa; BD190; BR497; BX402; BZ 9506

St Mary (Prys. Psalms, 1621) [LDTLLSFM, MSDMRD, MS] E84; F93; O318; W401; X 116; AF497; AL127a; AP206; AZ14-G; BA421; BJ33; BV144; BY139b 9507

St Mary Magdalene (Dykes) X Mary Magdalene 9508

St Mary Magdalene (Jeboult) [DT DRDTLS#LTM, MLSFM] E112; W426 9509

St Mary's (Prys) X St Mary 9510

St Matthew (Croft) [SMSDMRDTD, MRSLSF#S,] A517; C499; E 526; F478; J254a; M186; N385; O470; R179; W86; X287; AB356; AD87; AE102; AK190; AL76; AM57; AN270; AP186; AR153; AW95; AZ590-B; BA230; BE52; BV399; BY277a; BZ 9511

St Matthias (Gibbons) X Song 67 9512

St Matthias (Monk) [MRDFMR MD, MRDRSMF#] A182; B40; C40; D22; F28; H35; J199; K 175; O55; V28; W302a; AB376; AL213a; AP268; BA617; BF 533; BV60a; BY700a 9513

St Medan (Monk, arr) [DDTLSLS, SLSMRMR, DD] B368 9514

St Michael (Bourgeois) [SDMRRM, SFMRRD, DTLS] A113; B88; C88; D148; E27; F142; G39; H81; J141; K215; N438; Q310; R493; T101; V452; W120a; X 702; AA490; AF237; AJ189; AL141a; AM72; AN300a; AP 40; AQ259; AT16; AW128; AZ 582-F; BA349; BB270; BD98; BJ66; BR130; BV188; BY363a; BZ 9515

St Michael New (Wesley, S.S.) [MSMDTDRMRD, RMFSSL] E244 9516

St Michel's (Haydn) [SSFMSFMR, FMDLRDT, S] G118; I584b; J 322; K414; L371; N625; T82; U47; V270; AI207; AL531; AM 519; AO321; AR371; AT343; AV 24; AW93; BB405; BE269; BR 383; BY505a; BZ 9517

St Millicent (Sullivan) [MMSFMR MR, RRFMRDRD] D245a 9518

St Nathaniel (Sullivan) [DSLDD RRM, RMRMF#S, SS] B220; V461 9519

St Nicholas (Crueger) [LS#LT DRTL, DTLTDRM, M] J139; M34; N405; O251; P160; Q 326; AA416; AF368; AZ91-D 9520

-----. V [LMS#LTDTL, DTLT DRM, L] N405 9520a

-----. V [LS#LTDRTL, DTLT DRM, L] O251 9520b

-----. V [LS#LTDDTL, DTLT DRM, M] AF368 9521

-----. V [LS#STDRDTL, DTL TDRM,] AZ91-D 9521a

St Nicholas (Ellis) [DTDRMFS SFMRD, FMRS] F190b 9522

St Nicholas (Havergal) X Eden 9524

St Nicholas (Greene) [LDMLM FMRDT, DLTDRM,] E265; S16a; X395d; AD311; AM97; AP117a; AZ14-Hh; BY277b 9525

-----. V [LDMLMFMRD, TLTDRM, M] S16a 9526

St Nicholas (Redhead) [SLLSFM MR, DRMSDLS, S] C55b; O 190; W150; AI69; BA572; BO 95 9527

St Nicholas (Scholefield) [MMM SMRMFSM, MMLSF] A173; B12; C12; D6a 9528

St Nicolai (Rosenmüller) X Nassau 9529

St Nicolas (Nicholson) [MFSRM FLR, DTLSLFMM,] F576 9530

St Nicolas (Redhead) X St Nicholas 9531

St Ninian (Dykes) [DDDDDRM RDTD, MMMF#S] BF277 9532

St Ninian (Monk) [SLSMDRM, FLSMSFR, MD] K428 9533

St Ninian (Prothero) [DMMSSTL S, MDDRRM, MS] C239b 9534

Saint of the Sacred Heart

(Montani) [MMMMRD, SDDRM R, FFFF] BQ103 9535
St Olaf (Dahle) [MMRDMSFMR, M, MRFMRD,] O143 9536
St Olaf (Haydn) X Petition 9537
St Olaf's sequence (Koralbok for den Norske Kirke. 1926) [LT DRDTLDTLSLL, LMS] X59 9538
St Olave (Barnby) [DDTLSM, MMRDTD, DFFM] J513; O431; P329; U92; V154; AA352 9539
St Olave (Gauntlett) X St George 9540
St Olave (Hudson) [DMFSLDTDF MRM, DMLS] W257; BE140 9541
St Oswald I (Dykes, 1857) [SM LDTLSM, DDRMSLS, S] A434; B42; C42; D125b; Eap. 61; F 292b; I109; V309; W214a; AB 44; AL358b; AM29; AP105; AZ16-E; BA131; BD61; BE33; BO12; BV444; BX213b; BY141a 9542
St Oswald II (Dykes, 1862) [DS SSSDTLS, SDDTTLL] K47 9543
St Oswin (Dykes) X Oswin 9544
St Osyth (Wood) [SLSM, DRMFM SM, DLSM,] A509; F550; X511; BY602 9545
St Pancras (Smart) [DTDSMFMR, MFSDRSM, M] D318b; K242; L229; BA150 9546
St Patrick (Gaelic trad) [DDRMM R, RMFMRD, DMFS] BN166 9547
St Patrick (Irish trad) [SDRDDMF SLSSM, DRDR] AH140 9548
St Patrick (St Patrick) [MLL SMSDMRDDT, TRTS] A268a; B525; C525; E212; F162; W 506; X528a; BQ97; BV229; BY 433 9549
-----. R [LDRRDRFS, DTLFMM RD,] 9550
-----. V [MSLLSLDR, SF#MDT TLS,] X528b 9551
-----. V [MLLLSMSDMRDDT, TDR] BQ97 9552
St Patrick (St Patrick) X Deirdre (Irish trad) 9553
St Patrick (Sullivan) [DDD MSSL, SMRDDTDR, R] AB 150; BA250 9554
St Patrick's Breastplate (St Patrick) X St Patrick 9555
St Paul (Chalmers. Collection, 1749) X Aberdeen 9556
St Paul (Etlich Christliche lider.) X Wittenberg 9557
St Paul (Goss) X Lauda anima 9558
St Paul (Goss) X Tarsus 9559
St Paul (Johnson) [SDRMRDLS, SLTDRMR, M] N189 9560
St Paul's (---) [DMRDLSRM, MRSF#SLTL] V520 9561
St Paul's (Clarke) X Bishopthorpe 9562
St Paul's (Erskine) [SMRMSM RM, SLTLSMR, D] B31b; Y222 9563
St Paul's (Stainer) [SSFMFR, LSFMRM, DTRD] F200; BV 138; BY565b 9564
St Peter (Plainsong arr 1539) X To God on high 9565
St Peter (Reinagle) [SDTLSS FM, MRDFMR, MF] A455; B5; C5; D281a; E405; F13; G424; H430; I241; J291; K178; L388; M236; N54; O417; P93; Q286; R130; S81; T424; U375; V189; W419; X527b; Y273; Z 264; AA96; AB357; AC299; AD254; AE56; AF221; AG48; AI427; AJ27; AK406; AL252; AM51; AN255; AO101; AP52; AR387; AS362; AT393; AW 320; AZ14-T; BA65; BB150; BD19; BE125; BF432; BK 112; BL36; BO170; BV260; BX232; BY203a; BZ 9566
St Peter's (Ross) X St Peter's Manchester 9567
St Peter's (Turle) X St Peter's, Westminster 9568
St Peter's, Manchester (Ross) [SSSSDDTLT, SDRMDR, D] J412; K44; L143 9569
St Peter's, Oxford (Reinagle) X St Peter 9570

St Peter's, Westminster (Turle) [DDDRMFMR, MFSSLLS, M] D318b; S60; AK194; AZ585-G; BA356 9571

St Petersburg (Bortniansky) [SM FSDRDTD, SLDLSM] A499; G 339; H174; I134; J399; L116; M225; N7; O172; P118; Q493; R145; S180; T94; W459b; AA 84; AE148; AG203; AI47; AJ 137; AK17; AL11; AM76, 494; AO591; AP556; AQ56; AR275; AS124; AT177; AW517; AX42; BB153; BC113; BV9, 478; BY 321; BZ 9572

-----. V [MMFSDRDTD, SLDL SMS] L116 9573

-----. V [SSMFSDRDTD, SLDLSM] AL11 9574

-----. V [SMFSDRDTD, LDLSM SF] AP556 9575

St Philip (Barnby) X Sarum 9576

St Philip (Hopkins) [MRMFRM, SLTDLT, TDSL] BA253 9577

St Philip (Monk) [DDRMFMRD, MFSSLSFM,] A57b; B122; C 122a; D88a; Eap. 10; F94; O 378; W186; AL160a; AO280; AP428; AZ263-B; BA274; BV 613b; BY319a 9578

St Piran (Hopkins) [SLTDDTR, DD TSM, MRDT] AO505 9579

St Polycarp (Barnby) [LTLS#TD TL, DRMDRMD, D] B378; C 378a; D358a; I463b; V446a; BR323c 9580

St Polycarp (Pleyel) X Grace Church 9581

St Prisca (Redhead) [MMRMFFM, SSDLF#F#S] A79; B146; C146a; D97; E513; F105b; K76; M74; O540; T7; W329; AJ11; AL131; AP434; BA27; BR346; BX257 9582

St Quintin (Parr) [SSFMDDT, DTLSLLS, SS] S243; AK251 9583

St Raphael (Hopkins) [DDTDLTDS, LTDFRDD, D] B127; C127; D 264; E75; F321; K80; M624; N187; O25; V1; W524a; AS164; BA377; BR286 9584

St Regulus (Macmeikan) [MR DSFMRDR, FMLRF#S, S] D670 9585

St Sacrament (Monk) [SFSLSM RDRM, MRDSFM] AB222 9586

St Saviour (Baker) [DDTDLSFM, SLDRRR, SM] C54b; D47b; L209; Q434; V327; AA364; AE420; AL574b; AM162; AP73; BA147; BV472; BY 81b 9587

-----. V [SDTDLSFM, SLDRR R, SM] Q434 9588

St Sebastian (Buck) X Martins 9589

St Sebastian (Cecil) [SLSDTDRD, RMRDTLS, S] D358b 9590

St Sechnall (Irish trad) [SDTL SDSFMFMRDDD, D] F386a; X268 9591

St Sepulchre (Cooper) [DSLS DFSM, SDRMFFFM] E422; F109; BA292; BE331; BY 334 9592

St Serf (Lahee) [SMMDDRRS, LTDDDRMF] D455 9593

St Silas (Lancaster) [MRDFM RDT, TDRMSSF, F] Y154; AD429; AL381; BR380; BY 468a 9594

St Simon (Crueger) [DMMFSSF M, SMMRRD, DM] AZ151-C, 590-C; BA889, 594 9595

-----. V [DMFSSFFM, FM DRRD, DM] AZ590-C 9596

Saint Stephen (English trad) [LS#LMFMRDRMRDR, DRM] BG26 9597

-----. R [S#LTDRMDRDT, TDTDRM,] 9598

St Stephen (Jones) [DSMDRD TDR, MFSDRMRD,] A11; B70; C70b; D29b; E337; F52; H209; I86; J327; K268; L173; R49; S187; V65; W483a; X 250; AA128; AD175; AF201; AK346; AL328; AM236; AN 305; AO92; AP188; AQ261; AR208; AZ14-N; BA332; BB 194; BD123; BE334; BF559; BR284; BV339; BX301; BY 179; BZ 9599

-----. V [DSMRDRDTDR, MFS DRM] V65 9600

-----. V [DSMDRTDR, MSDMRD, MF] AZ14-N 9601

St Stephen (Smith) X Abridge 9602

St Stephen the Sabaite (Hymns of the Eastern Church) [DRM RFMFM, MRDRM, SFF] AZ 269-E; BA178 9603

St Stephen's Church (Miller) [MMFRSRRD, MRDTL, SMM] AD300 9604

St Stephen's Church (Wood) [MM RFMLSS, DTLSMMRR,] M219; Y210; AJ180 9605

St Sulien (Arthur) [SMMDRDRMD, SRTSMDM] W614; BY727 9606

St Sylvester (Barnby) [DDDRMM RR, MFSLTS, SD] W559a;AB46; AD137; AS390; BD166; BF239; BX16 9607

St Sylvester (Dykes) [MMMMRM FSM, MMMMMRR,] C31; D 534a; T67; U420; V632; W585; AJ102; AN277b; AO46; AP429; AZ16-K; BA742; BD15; BR308; BX32 9608

St Sylvester, No. 2 (Dykes) X St Sylvester 9609

St Theoctistus (Ouseley) [MMDD LLS, SMDFMR, R] A342 9610

St Theodulph (Teschner) [DSSLTD D, MRDDTD, SSSL] A62; B560b; C143; D90; E622; F98; G128; H525; I31; J11; K6; L207; M 18; N24; O8; P112; Q58a; R 187; S146; T322; U318; V157; W91; X135; Z221; AA179; AB 133; AC116; AD140; AE106; AF155; AG90; AH281; AK100; AL81; AM119; AN181; AO155; AP60a; AQ20; AR155; AS115; AT151; AV142; AW100; AZ 151-G; BA149; BB15; BE153; BF309; BI102; BK134; BL25; BN32; BR172; BV166; BY114; BZ 9611

-----. V [DSSLTDD, MRDLTD, DSS] Q58 9612

St Theresa (Sullivan) [MRMFSS, MRMFS, LSFL] A359; B560; C560a; D545b; G446; I681; S457; U306; V485; AC208; AD482; AH440; AO398; AV 218; BD83; BF621; BR514; BY464 9613

St Thomas (Ashworth. Collection. 1760) [DMRDSLTDS, SDRMFMR] AL654; AP20 9614

St Thomas (Wade) [DRMDRMF M, LSFMRRD, DT] A5a; B57; C57; D39a; E623; F388b; I 601; J61b; K177; R234; S184; T351; V184; W299; X342; AE140; AG121; AH114b; AL 136; AM237; AN351; AP85b; AW130; AZ585-E; BA105; BB176; BM6; BN113; BO48; BP64; BQ242b; BR453a; BV 56; BY619 9615

St Thomas (Williams) [SDDMRD R, MFSFMFMR,] A388; B 315; C315; D474a; E11; F48a; G227; H12; I22a; J158; K199; L292; M 79; N261; P83; Q27; R408; S337; T183; U208; V193; X68; Y224; Z105; AA 76; AB323; AC254; AD333; AE17; AF269; AG233; AH 199; AJ267; AK30; AL210; AM588; AN212; AO72; AP 444; AQ124; AR441; AT382; AU186; AV247; AW269; AZ 582-P; BA108; BB442; BC 25; BD156; BE354; BF591; BK115; BR224; BV649b; BX 219; BY478; BZ 9616

St Timothy (Baker) [SDDTDR RD, DTSLLS, RM] B6; C6; D640; F5; BE400; BV41; BY252 9617

St Ulric (Brown) [SDDDMRD, SLTDFMR, SM] D223 9618

St Ursula (Westlake) [MSFMD MRD, SLDDRT, RS] B79b; C 362a; D237; W355b 9619

St Venantius (Rouen church mel) [DMSFMRMDRM, SLSFMF] G638; S72a; W142; X571; AD340 9620

St Veronica (Champneys) [SM RMFRT, SDMRDT, SMR] D 154; F544b; BV441 9621

St Victor (Redhead) [SDMDTLS, SDRMSR, MFM] W342a 9622
St Vigian (Falconer) [MMSFFM, DTDFMR, RMSS] D604b 9623
St Vincent (Neukomm) [SSF#SM DRFMRRD, DSFM] A209b; B331; C331a; D227; I221; J 277b; AO33; BE155; BR127 9624
St Werburgh (Dykes) [DDMSDDL S, SDSFMRMR] D314a; L91; AA291 9625
St Wilfred (Hall) [SLTDRFM, RD LSS, RRSF] B449b 9626
St Winifred (Dykes) [DDDDRM FSLSM, SSLFS] F103b 9627
St Wystan (Butler) [MRRDFM, RMRDS, SMDLS] C357a 9628
Saints' days (Smith) X Edengrove 9629
Saints of God (Stainer) X Beati 9630
Saints of God (Sullivan) [MSSSS DTL, LSFMSRRD,] C462; D175b; W75; AA481; AC102; BX306 9631
Saints' reward (Hunter) [MMMRM SLSM, MMMMRDR,] AX579 9632
Salamis (Greek mel) X Luke 9633
Salem (Methfessel's Song book, 1818) [SDTLSSSLSLTDS, SLS] AL609; AP757; BC184; BY401 9634
-----. V [SDTLSSSLSLTDSS, SL] BC184 9634a
Salisbury (Barnes) [MMMSDRM, FFMDDTDR, M] BB216 9635
Salisbury (Hullah arr) [MMSFRL TD, RRMFMRDR] D667c; O238; AZ3-D 9636
Salisbury (Ravenscroft's Psalter, 1621) [DRFMSSF#S, MLSFFM, SM] W296; BY262b 9637
Säll du, som dig at Gud betror (Waldis) [DSLSDTLS, SLDSMR D, D] N495 9638
Salome (Beethoven) [SDTDRMRDDT, MRDTDL] I204; AL564; BY 262b 9639
Salome (Bradbury) [SMSLSDSM, S FSLSTSR,] AJ254 9640
Salonica (Pollock) [MRDRDLLS, DRMRFMR, M] T147; AJ 216 9641
Salonica (Scott) [DSLR, DRSR DLTDMS, SL] X471; BV593 9642
Salus aeterna (Plainsong, before 11th c M 7) [TRM TSS, LDTLSTSLS,] E10 9643
Salus mortalium (Gesangbuch. Erfurt, 1663) [SMDRMFMRD, SLSFMRD#] F517 9644
Salutas (Silcher) X Lorelei 9645
Salutis humanae sator (Plainsong M 4 trad) X Jesu, quadragenariae 9646
Salvation (Etliche Christliche lieder, 1524) X Wittenberg 9647
Salvation (Kentucky Harmony. 1816) [MDLTS#LLTD, RMD RDTL] AQ53 9648
Salvation (Kirkpatrick) [SSDSD RM, SSSMDR, SSD] R503; Z537; AH408; AI103; AL259b; AM370; AP798; AR480; AS 293; AT191; AU15; AW334; AX201; AY231; BB637 9649
Salvation (Weisenthal) [MMMM SSFMFRFM, DTDS] AS32 9650
Salvation by grace (Knecht) [SDTRDFRTD, DTLRMDT] M137; AF499; AM399 9651
-----. V [SDTRDFRTD, DTL RMTL] AM399 9652
Salvationist (Hays) [MFSSLSS M, DRDDLS, DR] AT87; AU 363; AW446; AX25 9653
Salvator (Danish) [SMFSLMFS, LSMFSFM, S] M284 9654
Salvator (Foster) [MRDTLDD, RRMDFMR, RS] W85; Z215; BY133 9655
Salvator (Goss) [MDSFMFMR, DTLFMRD, S] D17b 9656
Salvator amicus (Hirst) [DMS SLSSM, FMRDRMR, D] D46 9657
Salvator natus (Bohemian trad) X Be ye joyful 9658

Salvator No. 1 (Sullivan) X Lacrymae 9659

Salvatori (Ferretti) [MRDDRRM D, DTLRDTD, M] N128; T348; AI83; AL191; AO184; AP748; AR580; AW283; BA485; BY57a 9660

Salve cordis gaudium (Ahle) [MMFSFMRRR, MFMRD, MM] F367a 9661

Salve Domini (Watson) [MSSLTD S, DDLDRM, SRD#] G114; R138; T370; U398; Y19; Z208; AB72; AC9; AD467; AG277; AH472; AR112; AT454; BD87; BF185 9662

Salve, festa dies (Baden-Powell) [DMFSSLTDDT, TTDRDT] B168; C168 9663

Salve, festa dies (Sarum processional. M 4) [FSMSLFRM, S LDLSLSF] E624; F600; X389 9664

Salve festa dies (Williams) [DS FMRD, MRDTDRTLS] A86; B168; E624b; X390 9665

Salve Jesu (Lewars) [MRMDTL, MSFMRD, TDRF] K65 9666

Salve, Mater (Plainsong M 5) [DSDDDTLSLS, MMSSFM] BM 48; BN125; BP73; BQ209 9667

Salve, Pater salvatoris (Andrews) [SSSMFMMR, SSSMFMMR] BN167 9668

Salve Regina coelitum (Hildesheim, 1736) X Hail, holy Queen 9669

Salve Regina (Plainsong M 5) [D MSLSLDTLSLSS, DSL] BL61; BN142; BO301; BP76; BQ280 9670

Salve, Regina (Schubert) [MMFM RD, SSSFMRMR, MM] BQ205 9671

Salzburg (Haydn) [DMSSFMMRD, DDTDSFM] G383; W562a; Z 462; AL12b; AP12; AR228; AW 167; BV615; BY550a; BZ 9672

Salzburg II (Haydn) [SDDDMMR, RMFRDTD, SD] L303; M105; AK269; AR562; AW550 9673

-----. V [SDDDMMRR, FMFRD TD, S] M105 9674

Salzburg (Hintze) [SDSLSFM, SSFMRRD, SDS] A53; B96; C96; D118a; E128; F139; J95a; M305; O532; Q601; W129; X558; AA513; AF69; AL200b; AM623; AN199; AQ 173; AR428; AW545; AZ205-H; BE11; BI58; BK104; BL 28; BM2; BN161; BO175a; BV317; BY14 9675

-----. V [SDSLSFMM, SSFMR RD, S] M305 9676

-----. V [DMRD, SSLSFFM,] AA513 9677

-----. V [SDSSSFMD, SSFMR RD, S] BN161 9678

Samaria (Bullinger) [MFSDLDS M, DRMSFMR, M] BA407 9679

Samos (Havergal) [DSMRDLS, LDFMRDS, MD] BY507b 9680

Sampford (Ireland) [DTLDSFM, MFSLSMR, MF#] F131a; BV170 9681

Sampson (Handel) X Samson 9682

Samson (Handel) [DMFSMLTD, DSLSMRDT] D131; G472; I298; L219; V85; X451; AA 376; AB61; AL28; AR290; AW258; BA224; BB484; BR 81; BV570; BX86; BY290 9683

-----. V [DMFSMLTD, DSLS MDRM] AR290 9684

-----. V [DMFSMLTD, DSLSM RDR] BA224 9685

Samuel (Sullivan) [MMSFM F, LSF#SDDT, DLS] B359; C359; D568; G451; I559; T45; W251; Z609; AH364; AI374; AJ72; AL211; AM655; AO626; AP806; AR264; AW416; BB 428; BC252; BD196; BK23; BV361b; BX518; BY474 9686

San Remo (Barber) [SSLDRFM R, DDTDRLS, S] D546 9687

San Vincente (Barnes) [SMDSS DRM, DFMRDTDR,] AK248 9688

Sanctissimus (Cooke) [MRMSFM RMFMRD, DDTL] BY35a 9689

Sanctorum meritis (Sarum plainsong M 7) [STDRMDR, SLTD TLSLS,] E182; BP51 9690

Sanctuary (Dickinson) X Agape 9691

Sanctuary (Dykes) [SDMRDLSS, S SSMRDR, R] B207b; C297a; D179a; I174; J403a; K248; L 86; V501; AB286; AM607; AO 495; AP307a; BA650; BD137; BF510; BR271; BX427 9692

Sanctus (Cooper) [MMSSDSFMF MMR, SSLT] AW601 9693

Sanctus (Gaul) [SLSMFR, MDM RLR, SLSM] Z615; AG322; BF 682 9694

Sanctus (Richards) [DDTLSLSM, SSSSLDT, D] S15; W2b; BY26 9695

Sanctus (Wesley, S.) [DD, MM, LSMFSM, RRSLTL] H99 9696

Sandell (Swedish) [DRMMSMMR, RMFLSFFM,] J572; N487; P 368; AE256; BZ 9697

Sandford (Stephenson) [SDMMRD, SFMLRR, MDRT] O232; BR161 9698

Sandon (Purday) [MMMFMMRDR M, DRTD, M] A430a; F298c; G514b; J488; O572; R108; S88; T260; W568d; Z166; AB400; AD79; AE62; AF97; AJ362; AK86; AL436c; AM463; AO327b; AP109; AR68; AW163; BF641; BL67; BR388b; BY545b; BZ 9699

Sandringham (Barnby) [DMSSSSS DTTL, RMFSM] A214; B382; C 382; D238; G431; I668; J300; K415; N528; O538; P354; R453; S484; T77; U484; V636; W327; Z291; AA444; AD417; AE386; AF465; AG296; AJ115; AK50; AL238; AM625; AN453; AO20; AP662; AR539; AS419; AT282; AW312; BA843; BB416; BF358; BI63; BL65; BX486; BY624; BZ 9700

Sands (Kirkpatrick) [SDRMRDTD, SDMSMRDR] AJ246 9701

Sandwith (Micklem) [DMRMFS, DLSFFM, MF#MF#] BY738 9702

Sandys (English trad) [SSDTSL T, RDTDTLS, SS] A476; E 485; F337; W511; X652; BE 184; BG2; BR554; BV102; BY38 9703

Sandys Psalm 8 (Lawes) X Whitehall 9704

Sanglier (German) [SDMMSSFF, FMFRDTD, S] BR321 9705

Sankey (Sankey) [SDDRDTLTD S, SRRMFM] BZ 9706

Sankey (Sankey) X O safe to the Rock 9707

Sankey (Sankey) X Victory 9708

Sans Day carol (English trad) [DMSSSFMDMFRTD, DMS] BG35 9709

-----. R [DMSSLTDDSSSSLT D, D] 9710

Santa Monica (Noble) [DMRF MSFM, RDDMRS, S#L] AK 140 9711

Santa Trinita (Pieraccini) [SS LTDTRDLS, MMRRRD] D379b; AC37; BA370; BO183; BR15 9712

Santolius (Geistliche volkslied. 1850) X Desire 9713

Santwat (Manx trad) [LLMRDR MDL, LTDRMDT] X647 9714

Sarah (Gabriel) [SSDMFMRR, SSTRMD, SS] T230; AI119; AJ326 9715

Sarah (Thomas) [DMFSMFMR M, DLTDFMR,] AB369; AK367; AR560 9716

Sardis (Beethoven) [DTDRMSFM R, MMMLSF#S,] B700b; C 100b; D325; G27; I40, 131; T 1b; V544; Y220; AB71a; AC 90; AE468; AJ2b; BA38; BE 181; BF489; BH20; BI73; BR246 9717

-----. V [SDTDRMFR, SSSS S#LLR,] I131 9717a

Saron (Hughes) [MR#MFDMR D, DTDFDRM, M] Y132 9718

Sarratt (Ryley) [MMDFMRSLS, SLMFSMR] E34; W436a; Y 215; AM556 9719

Sarum (Barnby) [SMFSSLLLLL S, SDDT] A126b; B295; C295a; D176; Eap. 23; F527b; G527; H 433; I430; J144b; K250; N629; R425b; S429a; T379; U309; V 614; Z576; AB412; AC330b; AD 461b; AE309; AF307; AG284a; AH525; AK417; AL174b; AM281; AN428b; AO540; AR420; AV283; AW317; AZ58-E; BA740; BB365; BD248; BE421; BF655; BR446; BX463; BZ 9720

Sarum (Hullah) X Salisbury 9721

Sarum New (Lloyd) [SSRDMFLS, RMSDTLF#R,] BV659 9722

Satis (Whitlock) [DRFFMRLL, S DTL, MSFF] BE162 9723

Satisfied with Jesus (McKinney) X Routh 9724

Satterlee (Hopkins) [DMFSSSLTD R, SMDLTD] H484 9725

Sauveur (Baker) X St Saviour 9726

Savannah (Pleyel) [SDRMMMSFM R, SDRMMM] BR97 9727

Savannah (Wesley's Foundery Collection. 1742) [SSFMRDRMR, SSFMRDR] A427; E135; F141; G295; Q507; R529; S288; W504; X160; AA26; AF458; AL292a; AN200; AQ60; AZ11-A; BA42; BV340; BZ 9728

Save us waking (Plainsong) [DRM MRMFSFMMRM, MFS] AR556 9729

Saved by grace (Stebbins) [MMFM RSRD, DTDFMRLR,] AH455; AI135; AM726; AV395; AY494; BB630 9730

-----. R [MMSSLMSS, SSFFSTLS,] 9731

Saved, saved (Scholfield) X Rapture 9732

Saved to the uttermost (Kirkpatrick) [MMMMRDDTDR, FFFF MR] AU51 9733

-----. R [SLSMFSMD, RSSF#MF# S, S] 9734

Savery (Donizetti) [SMMFTRDDT, LSF#SLSS] L117; AB49; AW 235 9735

-----. V [MFTR, DDTLSF#SL SSM, S] AW235 9736

Saving health (Etlich Christliche lider, 1524) X Wittenberg 9737

Saviour (Young) [DDTLS, DRMF MR, SFMLS] BE299 9738

Saviour, again to thy dear name (Widdeman) [SSDMDRMRM R, SSDMDM] AX74; AY293 9739

Savior, breathe an evening blessing (Beethoven) X Sardis 9740

Saviour breathe an evening blessing (Hall) [SSMFSLSM, LLLDDLS, S] AX70; AY 285 9741

Saviour, hear us, we pray (Brahms) X Lucy 9742

Savior, I would live (Fillmore) [DSFMMRRM, FSLTLS, DS] AS348 9743

-----. R [SSLLTLS, LLTTDL R, DT] 9744

Saviour, I'm coming (Warren) [MDRDLS, RRFRM, MDRDL] AX301 9745

Saviour, lead me lest I stray (Davis) X Lead me, Saviour 9746

Saviour, like a Shepherd (Jacobs) [SFMRDLSFMR, MFSLSL] AY128 9747

Savior, like a Shepherd lead us (Bradbury) X Pleasant pastures 9748

Saviour, more than life (Doane) X Every day and hour 9749

Saviour of the nations, come (--- 16th c) [DRFRRDM, F RDRMDD, RL] BP6 9750

Savior, Redeemer, God of Love (Palestrina) X Victory 9751

Savior, Redeemer of my soul (Dean) [DMFSSLTD, LRDT SLF#S,] BC155 9752

Savior, Redeemer of my soul (Stephens) [MDMFMRTD, R MRDSDDD,] BC282 9753

-----. R [SMSLSFSM, SDTLTS F#S] 9754
Savior! teach me (Converse) [S SSMDLD, SSSMRRR, SS] AS 276 9755
Saviour, teach me day by day (---) X Purity 9756
Savior, thy dying love (Lowry) X Something for Jesus 9757
Saviour, we come to thee (Perry) [MFDMRR, RMTRDD, DTLS] AX34; AY210 9758
-----. R [SLMSFF, FSRFMM, MF MR] 9759
Savior, while my heart is tender (Harrison) X In the gloaming 9760
Savonarola (Benbow) [MLSMRD RTL, RMLRRMF,] K92b 9761
Savoy Chapel (Calkin) X Calkin 9762
Sawley (Walch) [DTLSMFTLS, MRDTDL] A462b; B316b; C 316; D92; G374; H211; I363; J583; K518; S319a; T111; U142; V295; Z352; AC158; AD280; AE161; AI116; AJ161; AM545; AO363; AP106b; AS179; AX166; BA218; BB37; BD104; BE315; BF558; BK107; BY741a 9763
-----. V [SDTLSMFTLS, SMRD TD] BE315 9764
Saxby (Matthews) X Storrs 9765
Saxony (Grimm. Choral buch) [MDLFMRMDT, DTLS#LRD] AZ184-B; BA190 9766
Saxony (Hammerschmidt) X Meinen Jesum lass ich nicht 9767
Saxony (Kirkpatrick) [SSDRMM FDRM, MMRLTD] AJ212a 9768
Saxony (Oliver) [SSMDRDRMDS, SSMDRD] AO201 9769
Scarborough (Glynn) [RFLSLDLS, LFLRDL, S] A298b 9770
Scattering precious seeds (Hugg) [SSSLSDMRDS, SSSLSD] AU399; AY325 9771
-----. R [SDSDMRL, TSRFLSM, SD] 9772
Scepter (Freylinghausen. G-B. 1704) X Gregor's 97th metre 9773
Scheffler (Koenig) X Ich will dich lieben 9774
Scheffler (Scheffler. Heilige Seelenlust. 1657) [MRDDRR M, TDRTLLS, S] A234a; E 648; J153a; W208; AL159a 9775
Schein (Schein) X Eisenach 9776
Schilling (Schilling) [SSF#SLS DSM, SMRMFML] AO134 9777
Schlaf, Kindlein, schlaf (Reichardt) [MRRD, DMSSF FM, DFFRR] K570; AW431; BN21; BO152a; BQ14 9778
-----. V [MRRD, MSSFFM, M FFRRS] BN21 9779
Schlaf, liebes Kind (Molthar) X Gregor's 483d metre 9780
Schmuecke dich (Crueger) [MRDRMSFM, SMFMRDMR] A210; E306; F393; J262; K 182; M48; N246; O149; P76; Q305; W324; X267; AA432; AI426; AK334; AL221; AN 494; AQ145; AW552; BY314; BZ 9781
-----. V [MRDRMSFM, SMFM DMRD,] N246 9782
-----. V [MRDRMFSFM, SM FMRDR] AN494 9783
-----. V [MRDRMSFM, SSLS FMRD,] AZ23-A 9784
Schmuecke dich, O liebe seele (Crueger) X Schmuecke dich 9785
Schönheit (Joseph) X Keine schönheit hat die welt 9786
Schönste Sonne (Enckhausen) [DRDRMLS, SFMRDRRD, M] AA253 9787
Schönster Herr Jesu (Münster G-B. 1677) X Fairest Lord Jesus 9788
Schönster Herr Jesu (Silesian mel) X St Elizabeth 9790
Schönster Immanuel, Herzog der Frommen (Darmstadt G-B.) X Gregor's 189th metre -B 9791
School house (Wood) [MFSDT

LSLDRMR, TDRM] E271; X 344 9792
School thy feelings (Root) X Like a strong and raging fire 9793
Schop (Schop) [DDRMF#SSF#S, MFMRMR, D] A25; J29; W492; AF118; AN492; AQ297; AZ169-A; BC239; BE13; BI90; BL7; BV 541; BY440a; BZ 9794
-----. V [MRDRMF#SSF#S, MF MRMRD] AZ169-A 9795
Schop (Schop) X Jesu, joy of man's desiring 9796
Schörring (Schörring) X Contentment 9797
Schroeder (Miller) [DDRMFSL TD, SDDTSLM] BB79 9798
Schubert (Schubert) [SMMR#R# MD, DRRFFM, SMM] AM24; AR251; BR421 9799
Schubert II (Schubert) [SLF#SDR MMR, DTLSSLS] AO81 9800
Schuler (Schuler) [MR#MSFMRMR D, FSLDTL] AT431; AU130 9801
-----. R [MSMFL, TMRDS, LD LSMM] 9802
Schulz (Schulz) X Paedia 9803
Schumann (Mason & Webb. Cantica laudis) X Heath 9804
Schumann (Schumann. G-B. 1539) X Old 112th 9805
Schwing dich (Franck) [DSDSLSM, MRMSLS, DSD] F518; M216; Q540 9806
Schwing dich auf zu deinem Gott (Crueger) [MMLSLTD, TDRMD TL, MM] N286 9807
Science (Brackett) [SDLSDRFM, MRSLDTS, S] BE197 9808
Scientia salutis (Stainer) [DRM RD, FMRDTRS, SMDL] F604 9809
Scotch stilt (Scottish Psalter. 1615) X York 9810
Scotstown (Finlay) [DLSTLSMSF MRM, MF#LL] BV591b 9811
Scott (Naegeli) [DRMMFMMR, MRDDRSM, S] AP26 9812
Scott (Scott) X Open my eyes 9813
Scudamore (Chope) [DTDSLTD, RRRDTLS, DR] BA248; BB248 9814
Se solens skjønne lys og pragt (Freylinghausen. G-B. 1704) [SDMRFMDT, SFMFSMR, S] O269; P313; Q413; AZ164-A; BA724 9815
Seabury (Means) [MSSDRMRD, RMLSSLD] A548 9816
Seal (Russell) [MSDTLS, MRM FSM, SDTL] D72b 9817
Seal us, O Holy Spirit (Meredith) X Meredith 9818
Search me, O God (Vulpius) X Das neugeborne 9819
Search me, O Lord (Main) X Ridgefield 9820
Search the Scriptures (Freylinghausen) [S#LTDTLLS#LTD TDLTD] BI35-D 9821
Seasons (Mendelssohn) X Heavenly love 9822
Seasons (Pleyel) [SMRDDRM FM, RMRDRDT] H357; V262; AO387; BR250 9823
Sebaste (Stainer) [MFSM, LS DMRR, DDTLSD] F18; G637; W281; AL552; AP664; BY 695 9824
-----. V [MMMMMMMFSM, LLLLLL] F18 9825
Sebastian (Bach) X Nicht so traurig 9826
Sebastian (Freylinghausen G-B.) [MRFMRMRD, MMRMFFS] A78; E118; X139 9827
Sebastian (Hodges) [SSSFFMM R, MFSMRRR, M] B81 9828
Sebastian (Wesley) [MMFMRDTD, MLSFRDTD,] V550; BE294 9829
Sebastian (Wesley, S.S.) X Almsgiving 9830
Seccomb (Morse) [MMMFMMR DTRD, MFMLS] BE217 9831
Second coming (Morris) [MMM SSSLMS, SLTDLT, F] AT125 9832
-----. R [DTLMSLTRDR, TRFLLT] 9833
Second mode melody (Tallis) [LLTDLTTLLSLTTL, LR] E3; O512 9834

-----. V [LDTDLTTLLSLTTL, LR] O512 9835
Second Parish (Busch) [SSDDRDT, DRD#RR#M, SSD] AM353 9836
Security (Widéen) [SLSMFMDRD, MDTMMLS] BE112 9837
Sedgwick (Bristol) [SMMMFSDTL, SLTDRRM,] J515b 9838
Sedulius (Nürnbergisches G-B.) [LDRMSDRMR, RMFSMRR] F57a 9839
Sedulius (Piae cantiones) X Puer nobis 9840
See, amid the winter snow (Goss) [DRDTLSS, DRFMMRR, DR] K532; W51; AM158; BG190a; BV119; BY107 9841
-----. R [SSFMRDT, SSFMRDT, DR] 9842
See! amid the Winter's snow (---) [DRMFMRD, SLSDLTD, DR] BO153 9843
-----. R [SSSFMFS, SSSFMFS, DR] BO153 9844
See, amid the winter's snow (Catholic) [SFMSDLS, RMLSSFMR, S] BQ5 9845
-----. R [SLL#SL#LFLLS, SLL#SL#L] 9846
See! amid the winter's snow (Mendelssohn) X Mendelssohn 9847
See He comes (Young) [MMMDRMRD, RFFSLLS, M] BP8 9848
See Him in the garden lone (Showalter) X The garden 9849
See, O God, we children come (---) [LMMMMRDRD, DTLSLLM] BH147 9850
See, the mighty angel flying! (Stephens) [SSDTRDTD, TDRR#MFT, S] BC342 9851
See the shining dewdrops (Kleiner liederschatz, 1901) [MMRRDS, DDTDR, FRTSS] AW407 9852
Seeds of promise (Fillmore) [SSLTDRMDL, RDTLTDT,] AW498 9853
-----. R [SSTRFTDMS, SSTRFSM,] 9854
Seedtime (Wilson) [MRDTTLTDSSS, DTRDT] U74 9855
Seedtime and harvest (Hunter) [MSLSMSFMMRD, DFDRM] AX583 9856
Seek ye a Patron? (Montani) [MMMSDTDR, RRRFTD, DD] BQ98 9857
Seek ye the Lord (Laufer) [SDRSM, LRMLF, MTRDTL] AE458; AR625 9858
Seeking for me (Hasty) [SFMMRDRDLL, SDDDRM] AU 14; AX31 9859
-----. R [STRSFMD, STRFLSM, SF] 9860
Seelenbrautigam (Drese) X Rochelle 9861
Seelye (Burnap) [SDDTFLLS, DMMRFMD, S] AO233; AW134 9862
Sefton (Calkin) [MMRDSSFM, DTLSF#F#SS,] B366; C366; D279b; I326; AY415 9863
Sefton (Crosbie) [SMDTTLSD, FMRDTDR, S] W375; BY210a 9864
Segne uns (Rosenmüller) X Nassau 9865
Segur (Holbrook) [SMDTRDLSM, MFSRRSF] L204a; R339b; U29; V333a; Y366; AG158b; AI73; AR546 9866
Sei du mir gegrüsset (Enchiridion. Lubeck) [DRMDFM, RDDTD, MFSML] Q202 9867
Seir (Mason) [MFMDRDRD, RRSTLSLS,] H295; L11 9868
Selby (Eyre) [MMMMFSTD, DLSFMMR, R] F196b 9869
Selena (Woodbury) [SSSLSSF#S, TTDRDDTD,] G137; I153; T374b; AJ273; AS365; BB243; BC76; BZ 9870
Seliger friede (Gesangbuch mit noten) [MR#MFMDTDR, MR#MFMDT] AW157 9871
Selma (Scottish trad: Isle of Aaron) [DMRDRMS, SLSMSLL, LS] E290; S299a;

W249; X10; AG226; AL657; AP57; BE314; BN46 9872

Selnecker (Selnecker) [DDTLDR D, DDRTSDT, T] A149; E126; Q122; X435; AA174; AN487; AZ10-A; BA775 9873

-----. V [DDTLDTD, DDRTTDT, TD] Q122 9874

-----. V [DDTLTDRD, DDRTLS DT] X435 9875

-----. V [DDTLTDRD, DDRTRD T, T] AZ10-A 9876

Selvin (German trad) [MMRMSFF, MRMFLSS, DD] G321; I446; AI335; BB249 9877

Selwood (Staniforth) X Jerusalem 9878

Selworthy (Greenwood) [DMLSM RDRM, SLSF#S, MS] BE28 9879

Selwyn (Mendelssohn) [SDRMR FMMR, DDDDTRR] D265a; I379; T272b; V317; AJ154 9880

Semper (Casson) X Semper aspectimus 9881

Semper aspectimus (Casson) [S SFMMMRD, SLTDTLS, L] O 490; BA441 9882

Send me light (Hugg) [SSDMMDL S, DRRDRM, MS] AX505; AY 75 9883

-----. R [MRDDLS, DRMMRDR, MFS] 9884

Send the light (Gabriel) X McCabe 9885

Sennen (Sherwin) X Chautauqua 9886

Sennen Cove (Harris) [SMDFRD RTD, MRMTDLS,] F528a; BV 655; BY661 9887

Sentinel (Cooke) [MSDRMRDTL, LTDTLDR] F308a 9888

Septem verba (Schumacher) [LTD DRRM, DRMMF#F#S, LS] Q180 9889

Septem voces (Hoyte) X Lebbaeus (St Alban's Tunebook, 1866) 9890

Septem voces I (Lewars) [LLDD RRM, MRFMRRM, MS] K84a1 9891

Septem voces II (Lewars) [LMM RDTL, DSSFMRM, DR] K84a2 9892

Septem voces III (Lewars) [MMSMMRD, MMFSLFFM, M] K84a3 9893

Septem voces IV (Lewars) [LDDSLSFM, LDRMRDTD,] K84a4 9894

Septem voces V (Lewars) [MR DRMMR, FMRDDRRD, S] K84a5 9895

Septem voces VI (Lewars) [DDRDDTD, MRDTLLT, TD] K84a6 9896

Septem voces VII (Lewars) [DDDRDTDR, RMDDRMRD,] K84a7 9897

Septem voces (St Alban's Tune book, 1866) X Lebbaeus 9898

Seraph (Fink) X Bethlehem 9899

Seraphim (Alexis) [MRDFM DMR, SSLSFMR, M] J512a; N627 9900

Seraphim (Eberhard) X Gregor's 249th metre 9901

Seraphim (Smart) [MRFMLS FM, DTLSLTLS,] AB55b; AD96; BX67; BY603 9902

Serenity (Bryan) X Bryan 9903

Serenity (Wallace) [MMMFMM RR, RSRMFM, SS] C404a; G120; H152; I128; J476b; L 131; N196; P152; R229; S178; T265a; U9; V135; Y68; Z254; AB171; AC140; AD250; AE 93; AF230; AG116; AH424; AI113; AJ369; AK242; AN 561; AO213; AR201; AS84; AT277; AV178; AW173; BA 82; BB141; BD70; BE23; BF 246; BK91; BZ 9904

-----. V [MMMFMMRR, RS RMFM, FS] T265a 9905

Sering (Sering) [SMDRDLLSS D, MRMRRM] M625 9906

Serug (Wesley. European Palmist) [DTDRDTD, MRDFMR, DTL] AF265; AK5; AL5; AN364; BE355 9907

Serve the Lord with gladness (McKinney) X Lee 9908

Service (Nares) X Amsterdam

9909
Service (Webster) [SSMLSSFF, MMRDRM, SL] I414 9910
Serving the Lord in song (Hildebrand) [SLTDRMD, DMLSF# S, SSS] AY524 9911
-----. R [DDDLLSM, DDDSD R, RRR] 9912
Sessions (Emerson) [SLSDSLSDRM, RRMRRM] G224; H157; I342; L58; T141; U186; V318; AJ209; AO595; AX455; BB179 9913
Sevenfold Amen (Lutkin) [MSDTL, DFMR, TMRDMSF] AMp. xvii 9914
Seventh mode melody (Tallis) [DSRMFS, SLSSF#S, DSRM] E496 9915
Severn (Howells) [DSFMFSDR, FMRD, DSFS] X582 9916
Sewell (Sewell) [SMFSDRMR#M, MRDTDRD] AT194 9917
-----. R [MFMMRL, RMRRDSD, DDT] 9918
Sewey (Weyse) X Christmas brings joy 9919
Seymour (Weber) [MRFMLSMR, MMMMFTD, M] A177b; B19; C19a; D13; G200; H30; I267; K465; L30; M573; N379; O561; P71; R60; S34; T311; U173; V49; Y89; Z145; AA7; AB26; AC217; AD54; AE48; AG25; AH171; AI56; AJ67; AK53; AM347; AN66; AO40; AP677; AR59; AS199; AT33; AU225; AV164; AW36; AY438; AZ11-S; BA287; BB48; BC162; BD9; BE 365; BF374; BK46; BR107; BX98; BZ 9920
Shackelford (Cheeswright) [SLS MDRLL, TLSFFM, SL] U50; Y48; AB259; AC326; BB94; BD53; BK128 9921
Shaddick (Burt) [SMRDDRRM, RMSLLT, S] A419; BZ 9922
Shakespeare's carol I (Arne) [SFMRDLDDT, DRMFRSF] BG171a 9923
Shakespeare's carol II (Stevens) [SDDDRMFMR, TDRMFSL] BG171b 9924
Shall I be ashamed (Byers) [DM MR#MSSLSF#S, MMRDR] AX343 9925
Shall I let Him in (Palmer) X Christ is knocking 9926
Shall the youth of Sion falter? (Stephens) [SDMMMRDFM, MRDDRR#M] BC157 9927
-----. R [MMMMMMFFFFM R, FFFF] 9928
Shall we gather (Lowry) X Beautiful river 9929
Shall we know each other there (Showalter) [SSDDRDRMS, SLSMMRD] AY150 9930
Shall we meet (Rice) [DRMSLS SDT, DRRMRDS,] AS482; AU85; AX602; AY163; BB 557; BC156 9931
-----. R [DMRRFM, MMRMF MMR, DR] 9932
Shall you? shall I? (McGranahan) [MMMMRMDDM, SMLS SML] AX291; BB568 9933
Shalom (Jewish trad) [LRRM FRMMFS, SRDL, LR] AQ160 9934
Shamokin (Fischer) X Laus regis 9935
Shanghai (Chinese mel) [LLDL SMSDDLSM, SSLS] X17 9936
Shanghai (Chinese mel) X P'u T'o 9937
Sharon (Boyce) X Boyce 9938
Sharon (Hemy) X Siloam 9939
Sharon (Ouseley) [DDSDFM RD, MRS#LDTLS,] F617 9940
Shawmut (Mason) [MMMSSM, LLLLS#L, MMMM] I265 9941
Shawnee (Angell) [MMMMMM MMM, MMMMMMM] AT516 9942
Shechem (---) [DMRDMSFM, DRMFSFMR] H118 9943
Sheen (Holst) [SLDRMDTLS DFMRDD, D] E310; F417; X496 9944
Sheer hamaalos (Jewish trad) [LTDTLLRMFMR, RDMTM] BH122 9945
Sheer hasheereem I (Jewish

trad) [MSLLSF#SLM, DMSM RDR] BH105 9946
Sheer hasheerem II (Jewish trad) [DDMLDSSSM, DDMSFMR] BH192 9947
Sheffield (English trad) [SDSDR MR, MFSDMRDTD,] Y244; Z257; AD177 9948
Sheffield (Mather) X Medfield 9949
Sheffield (Root) [SSSLSSD, DR RRRDRM, S] AT220; AU170; AX243 9950
-----. R [MDDLSSTLSSD, MD DL, S] 9951
Sheldonian (Taylor) [MMSMRD RMSL, SLTDTL] BY240 9952
Shelter (Ohl) [MMMMMRRS, SSMRDDF, F] K396 9953
Shelter (Sankey) X O safe to the Rock 9954
Sheltered Dale (German trad) [SMMMRMFRT, SDDDTDR,] G455; Z323; AD273; AR369; BF392 9955
Sheltering wing (Barnby) X Westcott 9956
Sheng en (Su Yin-lan) [DDRMDR MDLL, LDDLDD] R450; BZ 9957
Shepherd (Bradbury) X Pleasant pastures 9958
Shepherd (Ogden) X Bring them in 9959
Shepherd (Sullivan) [SSLSMFSF, RSDTLT, SS] AA560 9960
Shepherd care (Ukranian mel) [LTDTLTL, DDRMDR, RMF] AL492 9961
-----. R [MLLTD, TRRRR, DTLFM, R] 9962
Shepherd true (---) [SFMSDDDT, RLRFFFM, D] AL484; AP422 9963
Shepherds in the field (French carol mel) X Gloria 9964
Shepherds in the field abiding (Traditional) [LTDTLDTLSLM, LTDTL] BP19 9965
Shepherds left their flocks a-straying (Hohenfurth ms) X Quem pastores 9966
Shepherds' pipes (Gay) [MLDT SLLSM, MLDTSL, M] AF328; BZ 9967
Shepherds, shake off your drowsy sleep (French trad) X Besançon carol 9968
Shepton-Beauchamp (English trad) [DTTDMRRMR, RRMRSRM] E389; AP544b 9969
Sherborne (Mendelssohn) X Cyprus 9970
Shere (Thiman) [DMSDRM, MRS DTSLS, DF] BV331; BY434 9971
Sherwin I (Sherwin) [DSSDDTT, RSSRRDD, MS] AC106; AV 402 9972
Sherwin II (Sherwin) [MRDS DTDRMSFM, DTDR] BB375 9973
-----. R [RMFMSLSMR, SFM RDTL] 9974
Shield (Barnby) X Kirkdale 9975
Shields (---) [DRMMMRRDM M, DMSMRD] AY243 9976
Shiloh (Anderson) [MRDTLS# TL, DTLTDRFM,] W104 9977
Shine in my heart, Lord Jesus (Kolb) [SLTDTTL, LSSDDR, SRR] AX385; AY81 9978
Shining day (Ebeling) [SDRMS RD, SDRMSRD,] A313; X 692; AN477 9979
Shining Shore (Root) [SSDDRM DR, MDMRDLD, L] L569; U417; V657; AS474; AV288; AW503; AX571; AY89; BR 522 9980
-----. R [MSMSLSMR, MSM LSMR, S] 9981
Ship of State (Kinder) [SDSFM RDDT, LSLTDRM] Y290 9982
Shipston (English trad) [DMSL SFMRMD, DMSLSM] E390; W495b; X364; AD38; AL622a; AN123; AQ272; BB430; BV 348; BY726 9983

Shirland (Stanley) [DRMFRSTD, DTRSMLSF#] D501; H56; I512; L93; V316; AM280b; AW129 9984

Shirleyn (Harper) [SSLTDRDRM, MFMRMDR,] G112; Z206; BZ 9985

Shiveesee (Sulzer) [LLL, LLL, LLDDRM, MMDL] BH336 9986

Sh'ma Yisroayl (Binder) [MMMM MMLMMSFFFDFM,] BH280 9987

Sh'ma Yisroayl I (Jewish trad) [MDRM, DDFDRMR, DRMRR,] BH290 9988

Sh'ma Yisroayl II (Jewish trad) [MMRDTL, MSRRMD, MLRM,] BH314 9989

Sh'ma Yisroayl III (Jewish trad) [MMRDTL, MSFMMRMLTD] BH338 9990

Sh'ma Yisroayl I (Sulzer) [MM MDS, SDRMRMSM, DDR] BH 269 9991

Sh'ma Yisroayl II (Sulzer) [MM MMMR#, MMSSSSSF, FF] BH 306 9992

Sh'meenee atseres (Schalit) X A week within the sukko green 9993

Sh'meenee atseres (Weinberg) X A week within the sukko green 9994

Shoemaker (Pollock) [MRDSRM FM, MRDRDTD, R] AY40 9995

Sholom Alaychem (Goldfarb) [MD TLLS# LTLS#FMMS#S#L] AH146; BH278 9996

Shoreham (Dykes) [MMMFMRLS, SDTLSFFM] O553 9997

Shortle (Goodrich) [DMSSLTD SS, MSLLTDR] I664a; T285; AJ393; AM289 9998

Should we meet here no more (Teasley) X The last farewell 9999

Should you feel inclined to censure (Bliss) X Lower lights 10000

Shout the glad tidings (Avison) X Avison 10001

Showalter (Showalter) [MMFFMRR D, MFSSLLS, M] AR218; AS169 10002

Showalter (Showalter) X Leaning on Jesus 10003

Showers of blessing (McGranahan) [SSSSLTDS, TTTTDRD, L] AH389; AI262; AM716; AT 264; AU97; AX37; BB652 10004

-----. R [MR#MDS, MRDRTDR, MMMR] 10005

Shrewsbury (Hunt) [MSMRDTL LS, SLTDRR, S] F230b; BV 223a 10006

Sialkot (Stebbins) [SMRDSTL S, DLTDFMRD,] AJ177 10007

Siberia (German mel) [SFMDR TDS, LTDLSMR, S] D61b; AO123 10008

Sicilian hymn (Sicilian mel) X Sicilian mariners 10009

Sicilian mariners (Sicilian mel) [SLSFMFSLSFM, SSLT D] A247; B51; C51; D34; F410; G26; H37; J191a; K 431; L44; M16; N354; R79; S54; T456; U448; V27b; Z 127; AA17; AD65; AE33; AF 63; AG13; AH176; AI26; AJ 413; AK35; AL304; AM319; AN470; AO49; AP782; AR 48; AS140; AT31; AV23; AW 45; AX79; AZ16-L; BA165; BB33; BE119; BF207; BI3; BK172; BN126; BO112; BP 86; BQ88; BR120; BX510; BZ 10010

-----. V [SLSFMSLSFM, SSLTDT] BP86 10011

Sicilian mariners' hymn (Sicilian mel) X Sicilian mariners 10012

Sicily (Sicilian mel) X Sicilian mariners 10013

Sidmouth (Dale) [MLTRDFMM, RSLSFMDR] BY633 10014

Sidney (Poppen) [SLSMSMFM DM, RD#RMFS] M446 10015

Sidon (Crotch) [MLSFMLRDT D, DSFMRM] W549b 10016

Sidwell (Beethoven) [SSSSS# LSFFM, SSS#LMR] BR265

10017

Sieh hier bin ich, Ehrenkönig (Neander) [MMLLSSFMD, SMLSFFM,] K273; M114; N 352; O276; P397; Q56; AA131; AZ585-H 10018

-----. V [MMLLSSMD, SMLS FFM, R] P397 10019

-----. V [MMLLSFMD, SMLSFF M, R] Q56 10020

Sienna (Deane) [SLSDTLS, SS# S#LFR, MR#M] U123; V185 10021

Silas (Silas) [LRTDTLS#LT M, LLSSFF] W84 10022

Silcher I (Freylinghausen G-B., 1704) X Luebeck 10023

Silcher II (Silcher) [MDSSDRMM, MMF#SSLLS,] AA464 10024

Silcher (Silcher) X So nimm denn meine hände 10025

Silchester (Malan) [SSMFSLS, SLDTLSFM, D] AP318 10026

Silchester (Stanton) [MRDRS, DRM SFM, LSTDR] BY202 10027

Silent (Bixel) [LDLLS# LTS#M RDTLS# F#S#] AW77 10028

Silent night (Gruber) X Holy night 10029

Silently bury the dead (Leslie) X Silently, they pass away 10030

Silently, they pass away (Leslie) [SMDMDD, DTRD, SMD, MSS] AX616; AY186 10031

Silesius (Mann) [MRMSFMRD, RMF#SDTLS,] I367 10032

Silesius (Schein) X Eisenach 10033

Silksworth (Vincent) [DRMDRMFM, LTDRMF#S, R] Z531 10034

Siloam (Hemy) [SSSDTDRSD, DL TDMRD] C351; D565; I588; L83; V623; AO432 10035

Siloam (Horsman) [SLDFMRMR, RSDDDF, FM] B401b 10036

Siloam (Woodbury) [MFSMLSM DMR, RMSMRF] H451; I281; L606; M282; S349; T131; V650; AD400; AI375; AJ191; AL218; AN438; AO431; AR618; AS394; AY363; BA838; BB340; BX517 10037

Silver Street (Smith) [DSS MSD, MRSDLSF#S,] A552; B346; C346a; D509a; G22; H4; I3; K384b; L81; M255; N508; T88; U147; V106; X 635; Z118; AA328; AI14; AJ 130; AM102; AO69; AS77; AV28; BA285; BD100; BX 22; BY282a 10038

Silverton (Bradbury) [SDMRDTL S, SDRMDR, RR] AJ395 10039

Simchas Torah (Jewish trad) [DSSLSFSMD, DSTDDFM] BH200 10040

Simcoe (Cringan) [SLTDDLTDF MR, DRMFM] AP157b 10041

Simeon (Stanley) [SSFMFMRD, DFMSFTDR,] E320; Sap. 12; X551; AL514; BV575; BY 196a 10042

Simon (Strover) [DTSLMRDM SL, RDTLSD] BV193a 10043

Simonside (Harker) [DTRDFM LS, DDRRR, SFM] BB420 10044

Simplicity (Stainer) [SLSMFS M, MRDDSFMR, S] F451; W662b; AP760; BA820 10045

Simpson (Spohr) X Spohr 10046

Sin can never enter there (Warren) [SSDDDRMSSLLLTD, LL] AX283 10047

-----. R [DDDTTRD, MMM RRFM, SS] 10048

Sinai (Barnby) [SDDTDLLS, MRRDTLT, S] I600 10049

Sinai's Height (Jewish trad, "Akdamos mode") [SMDD DDRDTLL, LLMRL] AH148; BH143 10050

Since I have been redeemed (Excell) X Othello 10051

Since Jesus did appear (Good) [SDMFMRMD, TLLMRR, SD] AX551; AY295 10052

Since o'er thy footstool (Everett) X Magnificence 10053

Sine nomine (Williams) [SM RDSLDRSM, MRRDT] A126a;

C295b; E641; G527; J144a; Q 463; R425a; S429b; W220; X 202; Y345; Z577; AC330a; AD461a; AF306; AG284b; AK 418; AL174a; AN428a; AP310c; AQ75; AR419; BB364; BE66; BK76; BL70; BV460; BY7; BZ 10054

Sing about Jesus (Warren) [SS SLSSDRM, FMRMDRS] AX5 10055

-----. R [MMMSLSDRM, FMRM RDT] 10056

Sing aloud on this day (Piae cantiones, 1582) X Theodoric 10057

Sing glory, hallelujah (Mason) [SDTDLSSS, SLLFMMR, R] AR188; AS148 10058

Sing my tongue (Essay on the church plain chant. 1782) X Dulce carmen 10059

Sing my tongue (A Monk of Gethsemani) [LLDDMFSR, MMDT LLR, T] BN102 10060

Sing my tongue, the Saviour's glory (Wade) X St Thomas 10061

Sing praise to Him (Bohemian Br) X Bohemian Brethren 10062

Sing, sing, ye angel bands (Catholic) [DMRDLS, SMM DMMR, RRR] BO66 10063

Sing the Holy Family's praises (Andachtige ...) X Wurzburg 10064

Sing them over again to me (Bliss) X Wonderful words 10065

Sing to the Sovereign of the skies (Levenson) [DSSLMFMRS, SM SLSFM,] BH67 10066

Sing we now at parting (Beesley) [MRDSSM, DSLSMR, MRDS] BC161 10067

Sing we triumphant (Bragers) [S SMRDSLLS, LTDSLSF] BP42 10068

Sing with joy (Bamberg) [DS LTDRMD, DLRDTLLS,] BM 36 10069

Singen wir aus herzens grund (German, 1544) [LDTLS#LT, TDRMDTL, TD] O110; P103 10070

Singt dem Herrn, nah und fern (Joseph) X Gregor's 225th metre 10071

Sinner's friend (Freylinghausen. G-B. 1704) [DMMRSDFMR, MSRRMDT] M267; Q362; AA109; AZ218-A 10072

Sinners Jesus will receive (McGranahan) X Neumeister 10073

Sinners' Redeemer (Hutton. Tunes for the hymns) X Old 583d 10074

Sion (Hastings) [SSSMDSLS, DDRRDTD, S] H114; I91; L290; T160; U122; V140b; Z393; AE235; AH406; AI177; AJ237; AM275; AO114; AR 286; AS246; AT56; AU181; AV43; AW336; AX102; AY 211; BA694; BB184 10075

Sion (Mason's Companion) [SF MRDSLTD, DTLSLSF] X 341 10076

Sion (Morley) X Holborn 10077

Sion (Smart) [SSMRDS, DDRS M, SSM] A559; B523; C529b; D523b; J565; L542; S369; W579; AB218; AD227; AH 362; AZ141-I; BA575; BF382 10078

-----. R [SSMRDS, DFSDL, LSFS] 10079

Sion quadrata (Docker) [MMSDR MRD, LTDMRDT, T] BR220 10080

Sion stands with hills surrounded (Hastings) X Sion 10081

Sion stands with hills surrounded (Smyth) [SLSMFMMRSRD, LFLSM] BC212 10082

Sion's daughter (Dutch trad) [SSLSDDTD, DSLSDDTL] BG 10083

Sion's daughters (French) [DRM DSLSMFS, LTDSLS] Eap. 7 10084

Sion's glad morning (Harmonia sacra) [SSMSLDRMRDDLS, SSM] AX104; AY487 10085

Sion's praise (Bourgeois) [MM

MLMFMRD, RMRDTL, M] AJ 419 10086

Sir Christèmas (English carol) [DDDTLTLSMF#S, DRMRD] BG21 10087

-----. R [DDTLSS, DRMRDLTD, SL] 10088

Sister, thou wast mild (Lewis) [DDTRMLRDT, FMRSMDR] BC381 10089

Sister, thou wast mild (Mason) X Mount Vernon 10090

Sitting at the feet of Jesus (---) X Deliverer 10091

Sitting at the feet of Jesus (Davis) [MMMMFFMD, DDDDDRM, M] AX47 10092

-----. R [SSSSLLSM, RRRRDRM, S] 10093

67th Psalm (Scottish Psalter, 1615) [SDRRMRMFFS, FMRDTD] E 291; BJ89 10094

Skader, skader nu här alle (Swedish koralbok. 1697) [TM S#LTRDT, TDLTS#LT, T] N112 10095

Skara (Sewall) [MRDFMRDTD R, MFRSMR] BR38 10096

Skara (Widéen) [LMRDTLDRM, F#S#LTDTL] J218a 10097

S'lach no (Lewandowski) [DDLTD, MMRSLTD, DTLT] BH320 10098

Slain for my soul (Young) [DMF# SDFMMRD, DLTDLR] BP27 10099

Slane (Irish trad) [DDRDLSSLD DRM, RRR] A122; R303; S325; W477; X565; Z321; AD307; AE 449; AF217; AG174; AL336; AR53; AT62; BF386; BV571; BY462; BZ 10100

-----. V [DDRDLSLDDRM, RRR RM] R303 10101

-----. V [DDRDLSSLDDRM, SMRR] AR53 10102

Sleep (Lee) [MR#MFMRMFFM, LLSMRR] BB491 10103

Sleep, downy sleep (Clark) X Uffingham 10104

Sleep, holy Babe (---) [MMMS, MDDRRMD, MMMSM] BO152 10105

Sleep, holy Babe (Reichardt) X Schlaf, Kindlein, schlaf 10106

Sleep till that morning (Showalter) [MR#MDSLDS, DDDDT DRR] AX618; AY169 10107

-----. R [DTDR, RFFFM, RDTRD.] 10108

Sleepers, wake (Nicolai) [DM SSSSLS, SDSDRMRDTLS] A3; B62; C62; D40a; E12; F55; J7; K5; L214; M199; N199; O80; P426; Q444; W 162; X687; Y352; AA549; AB153; AD173; AF24; AI 446; AK96; AL134; AM231; AN486; AO115; AP242; AQ 17; AR207; AW522; AZ230-A; BA103; BB197; BI17-D; BK56; BR132; BV77 10109

-----. V [DMSSSSLS, SDT DMRMR] N199 10110

-----. V [DMSSSSLL, SDTD MRDR] P426 10111

-----. V [DMSSSSLSLS, SDS DMR] Q444 10112

-----. V [DMF#SSLDTL, SSDT DMR] AZ230-A 10113

-----. V [DMSSSSLS, SDSDRM RD] BR132 10114

Sleeping on guard (Davis) [SS SSMDSM, FFFSFRM, S] BB 501 10115

Slingsby (Carter) [SSSDTLLLR, TTDRMMR] D574b; I88a; U 24; V649; Z178; AE244; AP 716; BE340; BF244; BR499b 10116

Slingsby (Dykes) X St Bede 10117

Slovakia (Slovak trad) [DDMF# SLS, F#SLS, SSFFM] M359 10118

Slumber, O slumber (Polish carol) [MMRMFFMRRFLS, MMRM] BN22 10119

Smart (Smart) X Eventide 10120

Smart (Smart) X Sion 10121

Smiley (Summers) X Palmyra 10122

Smith (Howard) [MMSFMRDRL TD, RMF#SD] L271; AL687;

AM571; AP218; BV479 10123

-----. V [MMSFMRDRLTD, RM F#SR] AL687 10123a

Smithville (---) [SFMRDTDR, DSSS#LF#S, S] AY99 10124

Smitten Rock (Spencer-Palmer) [MFLDTL, RDTDLS, SLMF] BV378 10125

Snow in the street (Williams) [LDRMLSMR, DFSMRDDF] BG186 10126

Snowden (Robertson) [MMMMMFFF, MRRRRSFM,] AJ118 10127

Snowdon (Halstead) [DMFSSDDRD T, LLSMMR] BB96 10128

So, brother (French trad) [ML DTRDL, DTLS#TL, MLD] BC 106 10129

So fuehrst du doch recht selig (Darmstadt G-B.) X Gregor's 192d metre 10130

So fürst du hoch Stötzel. (Choralbuch. Stuttgart) [SDRMDFM RMRD, MRDTR] K416; M262 10131

So gehst du nun, mein Jesu, hin (Nachtenhöfer) X Cross-bearer 10132

So giebst du (Dresden G-B. 1694) [DMRDMRDDTD, MSFMMD] E515; X123 10133

So lange Jesus bleibt der Herr (Gesangbuch mit noten) [SSSSS LLS, DDDTLSF#S,] AW301 10134

So let our lips and lives confess (Mason) X Uxbridge 10135

So nimm denn meine hände (Silcher) [SLSFMMR, MFSM, SLSFM] J292; M548; P312; AK312; AR299; AW561; AX504 10136

So sweet and clear (Strachauer) [SLSDRDTDMDDT, SLSR] BI89 10137

-----. R [SDTR, SRDM, MMMM RMFR] 10138

So wahr ich leb spricht Gott der Herr (Schott) [LLTDRMRD, MSFMRDTL,] AA426 10139

Søode Jesu, vi er her (Ahle) X Liebster Jesu 10140

Softly and tenderly (Thompson) [MRDDTDRDLLS, DDDMR] G239; H262; J578; V753; Z283; AE165; AG135; AH331; AL494; AM694; AP409; AR 250; AT236; AU100; AV339; AW456; AX221; AY502; BB 563 10141

-----. R [SRMDRM, RRRMM F#SF#F, M] 10142

Softly beams the sacred dawning (Careless) X O thou kind and gracious Father 10143

Softly now the light of day (Weber) X Seymour 10144

Softly the night is sleeping (Warner) [SF#SDSMFS, MRR MFSM, S] AZ151-W; BA57 10145

-----. R [RDMS, SMSD, DMD SMFSL] 10146

Soho I (Barnby) [SSLTDDTDR, FMSF#MRS,] D554a; G309; I285; N534; W653; AC13; AM350 10147

Soho II (Silcher) X Morning 10148

Sohren (Sohren) [LLTDRMM, MLLS#L, LLT] A556a 10149

Sohren (Sohren) X Gute baume bringen 10150

Sojourner (Mallary) [DRMFMR D, RMFSLS, SDD] T50b; AJ 271 10151

Sol justitiae (Margetson) [MM SFMRD, RRRMF#LS, DT] BR 90 10152

Sol praeceps rapitur (Paris. Antiphoner, 1681) [MFMRSS LD, DLDTLSS, L] F37 10153

Soldau (Walther G-B. 1524) [DRRDLSLD, MSLSMDLD] J236; M474; O39; Q231; R389; S102; W140; AA260; AL122b; AM33; AP269a; AZ58-A, 58-B; BA 279 10154

-----. V [DRRDLSLTD, MSL SMDL] M474 10155

-----. V [DRRDSLTD, MSLS

MDTL] O39 10156
-----. V [DRRDLSDDTD, MSLSM D] AZ58-B 10157
-----. V [DRRDLSDDTD, MSLS MR] AZ58-A 10158
Soldau Pt II (Walther G-B) [MMM RMRD, RRRMRD, RRR] AZ58-C 10159
Soldiers of Christ (Merrill) [SS SDSL, LLLRLT, SSSD] S269; AM482; BA583 10160
Soldiers of the cross (Negro spiritual) X Jacob's ladder 10161
Solemnis haec festivitas (Paris. Gradual, 1689) [DMFSSLSFS, SLTDSMM] E123c; M78; X33b; AN293; BY21 10162
-----. V [DMFSSLSFS, SLTDSM F] AN293 10163
Solid Rock (Bradbury) X The solid Rock 10164
Solitude (Downes) [SF#SMDTLS, SRMFMRLS,] G612; H153; I307; L319; N359; Sap. 41; V 320; AA126; BR255 10165
Solitude (Everett) X Everett 10166
Solitude (Showalter) X O for a heart to praise my God 10167
Soll en nun die gruenen jahre (Thommen. Christen-schatz) X Cassel 10168
Soll's sein (Drie schöne neue geistliche lieder. 1637) [MSFM RDRT, TDRMFRD, M] E288; X8; BD38; BE96; BY66 10169
Sollt es gleich bisweilen scheinen (Fritsch) [MMLLSFM, SLSDDT D, SM] AA516 10170
Sollt' ich meinem Gott nicht singen (Schop) [LLMLS#S#LL, DTLSLF#M, L] Q25; AA65; AK16; AZ214-A; BA28 10171
-----. V [LDRMLLS#LL, DTLS FFM,] AK16 10172
-----. V [LTDRMLLS#LL, DTLSFF] AZ214-A 10173
Solomon (Handel) [DMFSSLLS, SLSTDR, SL] E80; S313; X110; AA267; AL346a; BR415; BX56; BY58a 10174
Solon (American trad) X Amazing grace 10175
Solothurn (Swiss trad) [DDRM DSRD, SSLTSDLS,] E243; F448; R305; S477; W436b; X239; AB131; AD394; AN 79a; BE385; BV452; BY677 10176
Som hønen klukker mindelig (Winding) X Winding II 10177
Som torstige hjort (Lindeman) [DSSFMRDLS, SDDTTLS] O453; P250 10178
Some day the silver cord will break (Stebbins) X Saved by grace 10179
Some near, near day (Pollock) [SMR#MRDLD, LSSDRM RD] AX536; AY140 10180
-----. R [DRD#RMDLD, LSS DRMRD] 10181
Some sweet day (Chord) [MR DDRRM, SLSMR, MRDD] AS 479; AX623; AY493 10182
-----. R [FFM, SMR, MRD DRMFMRD,] 10183
Some sweet day (Towner) [DR MDRMD, DMSMDR, DRM] AU271 10184
Some time we'll see (King) [SMMMRDRM, FSLSMMRD] AX570; AY345 10185
-----. R [MSLSMMRD, DRM FRMFS,] 10186
Some time we'll understand (McGranahan) [SMRDMSDT, TTFLTLSM,] AH386; AI 292; AV388; AX619; BB495; BC267 10187
-----. R [RRRRRMRS, SRS F#RDLS,] 10188
Somebody follows you (Henson) [MMRDMMSSLS, MMRDMR,] AX443 10189
-----. R [SSLSMS, MMRDMR, MMRD] 10190
Somebody needs your love (McKinney) [MR#MSLSDRR# M, SRMFSF] AU442 10191
-----. R [DMLSF#F, LRMF SLS, DTR] 10192
Somerset (Barnes) [DDTLLTD RSS, MMRDMR] AD453

10193
Somerset (Hewlett) [DMSDTLFM, RDMLTS, LL] G313; AL203b 10194
Somerset carol (English carol) [DDSSLSMD, TDTMFS, DS] BG8 10195
Somerset wassail (English trad) [DDLSFMRDDRMFS, DDL] BG32 10196
-----. R [SSDRS, SSDRMF, MFSDL] 10197
Somervell (Somervell) [DRMFM LSDT, LTDSFMF] F185b; BL 88; BO1; BV270a; BY217b 10198
Something for Jesus (Garrison) [DRMMMRMSM, MRRRDRM,] BB658 10199
-----. R [SLLDTLSM, DRRRDR MS,] 10200
Something for Jesus (Lowry) [MFMRLR, DTLTDS, MFMR] G219; H319; I349; J463; L529; N499; P325; R311; S396; T378; U273; V398; Z387; AD257; AE 215; AF331; AG171; AH423; AI 202; AK470; AL478; AM391; AO 641; AP476; AR347; AS278; AT 400; AU149; AV380; AW220; AY237; BA470; BB283; BF453; BY485a; BZ 10201
-----. V [MFMRLR, DTLTD, MF MRL] AY237 10201a
Something for Thee (Lowry) X Something for Jesus 10202
Something I would tell you (Duncan) [DRMDMSLS, MRDDRMR, D] AX334; AY344 10203
-----. R [SSMSLSM, DRMDMM R, D] 10204
Something to do (Ruebuch) [SS MMMRDRMFL, TLSFF] AX192; AY520 10205
-----. R [DTDRFMRMDFM, DDTLS] 10206
Sommerlied (Bonner) [MDTDLL, FRTDTS, DRMS] AL595; AM 637; AP722; BV237; BY744 10207
Son of man (Coerne) [MMSSLT LS, MSDTLTS, M] AC99 10208
Sonata (Mozart) [MFMSSRMRFF, DDRRMS] AW179 10209
Sonata (Mozart) X Stars of glory 10209a
Song (German) [DMSSSLTDS, DMSSSMD] AN73 10210
Song 1 (Gibbons) [SSSDRMMRR D, MMFSSD] A470; E302; F402; J350; W489; X296; AD240; AF275; AL370; BV 419; BY358 10211
Song 3 (Gibbons) [MMRMLDTL, MFMRDT, TD] BJ38 10212
Song 4 (Gibbons) [MLS#LTD SLFM, MSF#MRD] E113; X261 10213
Song 5 (Gibbons) [MMMFRM DT, TDRMLRD#R,] E483; F164a; X648; AD235; AF509; AN204a; BJ23 10214
Song 13 (Gibbons) [MFSLRRM, SLTDLLS, MF] A451; B219; D204a; E413; F105a; J130; K156; O515; Q234; W604; X134; AF162; AL570a; AN22; AP695a; BJ24; BR199; BV 165; BY333; BZ 10215
-----. V [MFSLRDM, SLTD LLS, MF] AN22 10216
Song 18 (Gibbons) [MMDRMDT L, DDRMMMR#M,] E357; W428b; X604a; BN74 10217
Song 20 (Gibbons) [MMF#S#LT, LDLSFM, SSF#S] E442; W 546b; X584; BE397; BJ35; BV503 10218
-----. V [LLTD#RM, RFRD L#L, DDTD] BJ35 10219
Song 22 (Gibbons) [SSMLSS FMSR, RMDFRS] A433; D 280b; E438; F238; J125; W 195; X574; AD207; AN48a; AR254; BE212; BJ28; BV 374 10220
Song 24 (Gibbons) [DDRMM-RDTTL, MMF#SSF#] E325; F397a; R530; S488; W545; X103; AF207; AN70; AQ167; BE69; BY564 10221
-----. V [FFSLLSFMMR, LLT DDT] F397a 10222
-----. V [LM, DDRMMRDTTL, MMF#S] S488 10223

Song 31 (Gibbons) [MLSMSFM, SMLSF#F#M, SR] BJ94 10224

Song 34 (Gibbons) X Angel's song 10225

Song 46 (Gibbons) [DMDS, DFFF MR, RTDLS,] A69; E98; F358a; W444; X125; AL285a; AP438b; BV373; BY584 10226

Song 46 (Gibbons) X Bourdillon 10227

Song 67 (Gibbons) [DSMFSLLS, SDLTTL, D] A404; E197; F 325a; R37; S68; W433a; X204; AB326; AF336; AL667a; AN202a; AP82a; AQ73; BE262; BJ56; BV367; BY599 10228

Song of joy (Campian) [SMLRMF FFSL, LSFSFM] X639 10230

Song of praise (English trad) [M SMDDRDRM, MSMDDRM] Z447; AD186; BK12 10231

-----. V [MSMDDRDRMD, MSMDDR] BK12 10232

Song of Songs (Baden-Powell) [DTLSMFSLTD, RMRDTL] D448b 10233

Song of the branches (Kestel) [S LDTLSLL, SLDRTDTL,] BL24 10234

Song of the crib (German carol, 14th c) X Resonet in laudibus 10235

Song of the dew (Jewish trad) X Tal 10236

Song of the Nuns of Chester (Chester ms. ca 1425) [DRM RDMSL, DTTSLLS, T] BG67 10237

Song of the pilgrims (Alexander) [SMSMSMRDRMM, SMSMM] Y133 10238

Song of the Saviour (Gabriel) [SS LTDRMF, MRDTLTD, S] AY485 10239

Song of the ship (Andernach G-B. 1608) [LLLTTDRM, MRRLTD, DM] BG90 10240

Song of the Spirit (Dutch trad) [SDRMRDD, SSMFSL, DTL] BG153 10241

Song of the Yangtze Boatmen (Chinese chantey, trad.) [LDRDLLDRDL, MRDMRD] AE197 10242

Songs of praise (Rosenmüller) X Nassau 10243

Sons of light (Lynes) [SMMM RDTLTL, SMMMRD] U293 10244

Sons of men, behold (Flood) [DMSDTLS, FMRDFMR, MS] BI92 10245

Sons of Michael, He approaches (Thomas) [DRMDRMFMMR, SFMFRD] BC163 10246

Soon trials and conflicts (Doughty) [DMMMMRMFF FF, MRRRR] AX594; AY 160 10247

Sørg, O kjaere Fader, du (Lindeman) X Spring of souls 10248

Sorrows (Powell) [MMMMSM, LSDRM, MMMMS] Z226 10249

Soto (Mason) [SDDDSDRM, MSMRTLRS,] AJ410 10250

Soul of my Saviour (Bragers) [DTLLSLTDMR, DTLLSD] BP68 10251

Soul of my Saviour (Dobici) [MFMRRRMDRM, SLSFMM] BQ47 10252

Soul of my Saviour(Maher) [S DDDTD, DRRM, MRMDT, T] BN103; BO29 10253

Sound over the waters (Gilchrist) [MDLDMD, MDLDM, FRL#RF] BI99 10254

Sound the battle cry (Sherwin) X Battle cry 10255

Sound the loud timbrel (Weinberg) [LMFMDDMRRD, TLDFML] BH131 10256

South Cerney (Hadow) [MFSS FMRRM, MRSSLTL] E359; W496 10257

Southampton (---) [SSDDT, SRM RD, MSSSFM] U355; Y102; AC161; AR283; AS54 10258

Southampton (Barnes) [SSS LSDRMMRMFS, LLL] BB6 10259

Southampton (Croft) [DMRMDRT D, DSRMF#S, SF] AZ14-F; BA41 10260

Southgate (Southgate) [DSDRMSF M, RLTD, DSDR] BY590a 10261

Southill (English trad) [DRM RDLRMT, RDTDRSM,] E638b; X395b 10262

Southport (Kingsley) [DRMMM SLFF, LSRRMFM,] L498; AJ 113 10263

Southport (Lomas) [MMFSMRRM, SDDTSTLS,] C390b; D341b; AA386; BR341 10264

Southwark (Tye) [SDRMFSFM, FMRDDT, RR] W166; AP11a 10265

Southwell (Damon's Psalter, 1579) [LDDTTL, LDDRRM, MSSF] D349; E77; F122; J365a; K 75; Q156; R270; S239; W102b; X106; AA554; AF314; AG149; AL265a; AM412; AP44; AW196; AZ582-L; BA737; BJ51; BV175; BY565a; BZ 10266

Southwell (Irons) [DMMSDDLS, S DMRRR, SS] A584a; B301; C 514b; D283b; F282; I268; J469; K524; L602; M314; O609; V55; W418a; AA558; AL461b; AP635; BE399; BF388; BR445b; BV300; BX164; BY76 10267

Southwick (Vincent) [SMRDLLLS, DTLMTLS, R] AZ480-B 10268

Sovereign grace (Pierre) [DLSDR MMSFMRD, DLSD] AJ422 10269

Sovereignty (McManiman) [SLTD FMRD, SFRSSF#LS,] H309 10270

Sowing in the morning (Minor) X Bringing in the sheaves 10271

Spain (Carr) X Spanish chant 10272

Spain (Dana arr) X Flee as a bird 10273

Spanish carol (Spanish carol) [LTDTLSM, SLTLSL, LTD] BG113 10274

Spanish chant (Carr arr) [DDTD LDS, MDFRDTD, DD] A332; B130; C130a; D89a; H268; I500; J72; K82a; L235; M 431; N96; Q166; R131; S191; U157; V254; W177; AA213; AE206; AI182; AJ64; AK198; AL597; AN281b; AO270; AP 740, 755; AQ127; AR25; AS 69; AT22; AU195; AV111; AW145; AZ581-M; BA452; BB238; BC23; BI10-D; BX 336a; BZ 10275

-----. V [DTDLDS, MDFRDT D, DTD] R131 10276

Spanish hymn (Carr) X Spanish chant 10277

Spanish melody (Carr) X Spanish chant 10278

Sparta (Mason) [SSSDDDDR, RRRMFSMR,] L199 10279

Spazier (Spazier) [SDSMD SFM, RDSDMR, SR] M544 10280

Speak gently (---) X Mendota 10281

Speak to my heart (McKinney) X Holcomb 10282

Speed away (Woodbury) [SSS SSSSSSF#SM, MMMR#] AR472; AS380; AX208; AY 331 10283

Speer (Speer) [DMRMFS, SFM R, RRDRMF,] E280 10284

Spencer Lane (Lane) X Penitence 10285

Speranza (Sewall) [SMMRM FLS, MSMDRMRD] BR439 10286

Speratus (Etlich Christliche lider) X Wittenberg 10287

Spes mea in deo (Warburton) [MFRSS#LTDFMR, MMF#SL] Y12; AB90; AC235; AD305; BF380 10288

Spes unica (Perry) [MSLSS DFM, MRFMMRR, M] AA447 10289

Spetisbury (Knapp) [DMFSD, SLDTD, SFMMDR,] F566 10290

Spicer (Hultman) [MMRDSLM, MMRDSLF, FR] BB453 10291

Spire (Drese) X Rochelle

10292

Spires (Luther) [LTDTLS#LTD TL, DRRMDRRM,] A61; E68b; J155b; L400; M29; N220; O138; P86; Q5; X277b; AA274; AM91 10293

-----. V [LDLSLDTL, DRRMDRR M] J155b 10294

-----. V [LDLS#LDTL, DRRMD RRM] N220 10295

Spirit Divine (Scott-Gatty) [MRM SLTDR, FMFLTDRM,] U126; Y175; AC310; AR522 10296

Spirit of grace and union (Montani) [DDRMDDTD, MMFSMRDR,] BQ37 10297

Spirit of the living God(Iverson) [MMMMRMF, MDDRM, MMMM] AR656; AT523; AU329 10298

-----. V [MMMMRMF, MDRM, MMMMR] AT523 10299

Spirit so holy (Stebbins) [SMF SLSMSFMRS, SMFS] AX133; AY203 10300

Spirit-wind (Frederick) [MFSM RR, FSLSS,LLLSF] AR223 10301

Spiritus (Walther. G-B. 1524) X Soldau 10302

Spiritus domini (Wilson) [SDSLDR DRM, DFFMRDR,] J243b 10303

Spiritus sancti gratia (Triller) [LLLMMFFM, MTDRMRDTD] AA32 10304

Spiritus vitae (Hammond) [DTSL FMRSS, DDRMSMR] BV298 10305

Spitta (Danks) [SDSDMSS, LSMR MD, SLL] H317; AV174; BR 367 10306

Splendour (Piae cantiones. 1582) X Puer nobis 10307

Splendor of the morning sunlight (Tintner) [SSDSMFLS, DRMFLS FM] BH9 10308

Splendor paternae (Sarum plainsong M 1) [FFSLL#LSL, LSDDSLL#] A158a; E52; F2a; J206a; K359a; X33c; AF40; AQ 110; BJ29 10309

-----. V [DDRMFMRM, MRSSRM FM] F2a 10310

-----. V [FSLL#LSLL, SDD SLL#LS] AQ110 10311

Splendor paternae gloriae (Sarum plainsong M 1) X Splendor paternae 10312

Spohr (Spohr) [SMMSDMRD, MLSMFSM, M] B303; C303; D652a; G363; H332; I309; L120; N44; Q456; R322; S 317; T78; V401; W451a; AA 399; AB275; AD283; AE205; AG178; AJ116b; AL649b; AM554; AN575; AO302; AP 402; AR227; AS120; AV409; AW586; BA410; BD65; BE230; BH51; BR358; BX234 10313

-----. V [SMMSDMRD, DLS MFSM, M] N44 10314

-----. V [DMMSDMRD, DLSM FSM, M] Q456 10315

Spohr (Sophr) X Gerald 10316

Sponso (Nottingham) [SLDDTD RD, FFMRDRM, S] AS149 10317

Sponsa Christi quae per orbem (Plainsong sequence M 1-2) [RDRFSFMR, LSLFSLL, L] E253 10318

Sprague Hill (Baumgartner) [LTDRMLRMFML, LLSSS] Y52 10319

Spring (Everett) [SLSSDMRD, D RMSLS, DR] I331 10320

Spring (Shaw) [DRLS, MDRM DLSLRD, DR] X5 10321

Spring Gardens (---) [MSMDD RMFM, FSDLTDT,] BB203 10322

Spring has come (Piae cantiones. 1582) X In vernali tempore 10323

Spring of souls (Lindeman) [S MMRDDF, RRMF#STLS, S] J106b; O328; P195; AZ205-G 10324

-----. V [SMMRDDF, RRMF# STLLS,] AZ205-G 10324a

Spring Run (Huffaker) [MMMM RR, FFFFMM, SSSS] AR72 10325

Spring-tide hour (Barnby) X

Soho 10326
Springfield (Gauntlett) [SFMMRD RMFFM, RFMLL] W64a; BP800; BY396a 10327
Springfield (Grieg) [DMFSSLLDL LS, SMDMS] AC292 10328
Springfield (Minshall) X Coppee 10329
Springhill (Hurndall) [DRFMRDDT, DLSDTDR, D] D647b 10330
Springs of salvation (Freylinghausen) X Gregor's 221st metre 10331
Springtime (Briggs) [DMSSFLD LSMS, DMSSF] X360 10332
Springtime (Keller) [MSMRFMDR, DTRDLS, DL] J362b 10333
Sri Lampang (Asian mel) [SS SSLDLSMSLD, MRDL] BZ 10334
Stabat mater (Dykes) [DRMDFM MRD, DRMDFMM] D103a; AM 185; AN576; BX203 10335
Stabat mater (German: old) [DRMMFSFMM, SSFFMMR] AZ95-C; BA211 10336
Stabat mater (Knight) [SSDSMFM R, RMRTDRDT,] I154 10337
Stabat mater (Mainz G-B. 1661) X Mainz 10338
Stabat mater (Mechlin plainsong M 4) [DTDRMRTDT, MMRDT SL] A76b; C161a; D103b; E 115c; BJ44 10339
Stabat mater (Nanini) [DMMRDT RD, DTRDDTLS,] BQ162c 10340
Stabat mater (Tartini) [MMFSLS LSLSFM, SFML] BQ162a 10341
Staincliffe (Dixon) [MMR#MF MMRD, SSF#SDSS] D172b; L 169b; V581; AB271; AO34; BA 80; BB648 10342
Stainer (Stainer) X Beati 10343
Stainer (Stainer) X Evangel 10344
Staines (Attwood) [SSMRDD#RFM R, RSFMRD] D588a 10345
Stalham (English trad) [LTDRM SMRTL, RMLDRM,] E638c; X393a 10346
Stand by me (Tindley) [DRMMM RDSLTD, DMSSS] AU30; BZ 10347
-----. V [DRMMMRDS, LDD, DMSSS] BZ 10348
Stand firm (Tozer) [SDRDSM SD, RMRDMR, SD] AI324 10349
-----. R [MFDMMFDM, MS MDRTTL] 10350
Stand like the brave (Bradbury) [SSMSDDRMDRM, MRRRS] BB576 10351
Stand up (Barnby) [SSSDRMD, LSDRTD, DRR] D582c; AB 317 10352
Stand up (Thalben-Ball) [SD DRSMD, LSDDRD, SDD] BV 586b 10353
Stand up, stand up for Jesus (Geibel) X Trumpet call 10354
Stand up, stand up for Jesus (Webb) X Webb 10355
Standard (Hakes) [MFSF#SM FSLS, MMFMRS] BB500 10356
-----. R [DDFFLFMS, SRRR MFM, D] 10357
Standing on the promises (Carter) X Promises 10358
Standish (Bower) [LTDTLSLS, DRMDRRD, D] F407b 10359
Staniforth (Staniforth) X Jerusalem 10360
Stanley (Barnby) [MSMRDRTD, SDTLSLF#S,] I170 10361
Stanley (Lutz) [SSDSMMRD, DR MFLTRD,] AB129; BF339; BR273 10362
Stanley (Mann) [SSSLTDSS, DMFMRLRD#] I651 10363
Stanley (Jarvis) [SDSLLSFMR DS, SMRDS] AJ286; BY579 10364
Stanstead (Russell) [DTLMMM MRDTL, DRMSS] E482; X 697 10365
Stanton (Hamilton-Gell) [DSM FLS, DDDRM, DDTLR] D62b 10366
Star of Jacob (Redhead) X St Nicholas 10367
Star of peace (Mason) [DDDD RRMR, MMMF#SLT, D]

W627; Z439; AL455; AP712; BY 242 10368

Star of the East (Kennedy) [MR# MDMFLFM, MR#MDMFM] AX96 10369

Star-spangled banner (Smith) X National anthem 10370

Starlight (Hedges) [MFSLFS, MRD TLT, TRMR] BV540 10371

Stars in my crown (Sweney) [MF SF#SDMRDTDR, RMFT] AT 470; AY508; BB626 10372

-----. R [MRDRDSMSDDRM, MFSM] 10373

Stars of glory (Mozart) [MFMSMR MRFR, DDRRMS] BO156 10374

Stars of glory (Mozart) X Sonata 10374a

Stars of glory (Janowska) [DRM DRMRRMRD, TLSFR] BQ9 10375

Stars of morning, shout for joy (Durham) [DMSDDTD, LLLSF MMRR] BC164 10376

State Street (Woodman) [MMRDLS, DTDRMR, RMRD] H53; L321; M310; V284; Y381; Z446; AA 458; AE213; AH517; AM530; AO499; AS189; AU282; AV291; AW246; BA592 10377

Statham (Statham) X St Joseph 10378

Staunton (Main) [DSDSDRMFMR, SRTSTL] L460b 10379

Steadfast (Neu ordentlich G-B. Hanover, 1646) [MLS#LTD, D RDTLS#F#M, M] A283; O217; AF86 10380

-----. V [MLS#LTD, DRDTLSF M, ML] O217 10381

Steal away (Negro spiritual) [DD DMMM, SSSLRM, DDDL] Y316; AG316; AH604; AR487; BK166 10382

-----. R [LLSLS, MSMSMSM, DMSS] 10383

Stearndale (Emerson) [DDDDSLLS, SDMRDTLS,] L104 10384

Stebbins (Stebbins) X Adelaide 10385

Stebbins (Stebbins) X Jesus is calling 10386

Stebbins (Stebbins) X The Green Hill 10387

Steele (---) [MMMRDDTDR, DTLSFMR] L166 10388

Stegman (Hartmann) [SSLSFM RMFSLT, DSSF] M473 10389

Steiner (Kolb) X Dear Lord, I come 10390

Steiner (Steiner) [DMRSSDMR SS, SFMRMF] A320; E253b; F364; X487; BE55; BV579a; BY467b 10391

Stella (Hemy. Easy hymn tunes) [SSMSSDDTLS, SSFMRM] C48b; D22b; Eap. 54; F203b; G124; L567; S314; T146; AB 283; AC83; AJ214; AK273; AL84; AM426; AO45; AP334 b; AR181; AW94; BB151; BN133; BO102; BP81; BQ84; BV468b 10392

-----. V [SSMSSDDTLS, SFM RMF] BN133 10392a

-----. V [SSMFSLTDTLS, SS FMR] T146 10393

Stella (Hull. The casket) [MS SSLSFM, MFMRDR, RR] M 607 10394

-----. R [SMSMMFMRDR, RRRRMF] 10395

Stella (Parker) [MMMRDTLSS, MLS, RLS, R] B454b; C545b; G91; Y344; AB113b; AC85; AH262; AO121; BB110; BF 280 10396

Stella (Wathall) [SMSLLD, SMS LLD, DRMM] I112a 10397

Stella maris (Hemy. Easy hymn tunes) X Stella 10398

Stella orientis (Willan) [MRDF MRFMLS, DTLSR] AL49b 10399

Stephanos (Baker) [MMMRM SSF, MMRDR, SL] A406; B386; C386; D342a; F348; G193; H245; I293a; J517; K72; L357; Q428; R264a; S221b; U153; V267a; W391a; Z286; AA370; AB154; AC151; AD208; AE167; AG140b; AJ 365b; AK302; AL471a; AM 389a; AO249b; AP401a; AR

302; AT245; AU426; AV157; AW143; AZ269-C; BA477; BB341; BF347; BR396; BV467a; BX335b; BY296; BZ 10400

Stephens (Jones) X St Stephen 10401

Stephenson (Shoemaker) X We now have met 10402

Stepney (Holst) [DDRMFSDDSTL S, DSTL] X325 10403

Stepping in the light (Kirkpatrick) [SSLSMFSDRDL, SSLSF] AX561 10404

-----. R [DTLLLLLLLSSSSM, FF] 10405

Sterling (Harrison) X Stirling 10406

Steterburg (Decius) X O Lamm Gottes 10407

Stettin (Bohemian Br.) [LLLDR RDT, LDTLS# L, LL] E202; X 225 10408

Stewart (Lowden) [SS, SMSSF# FM FSM, MLMM] AO395 10409

Stewart (Strohm) [SMRDDDFMR SS, DTS] A46b 10410

Stiastny (Stiastny) [SDMSFMRD, SDMRDTLS,] T318b; V275; AJ 167 10411

Still water (Hastings) [MFSSLTD SSSMDR, MFS] BB400 10412

Stilla, ja, allt mera stilla (Wetterling) X Wetterling 10413

Stilla jag pa dig vill akta (German, 18th c) [DSDRMRTS, DRMFRR D, D] N498 10414

Stilla jag pa dig vill akta (Tilleard) X Lost and found 10415

Stille nacht (Grueber) X Holy night 10416

Stillingfleet (Swiss) [SMSLSS, SFM RRD, SMSD] M63; P339 10417

Stirewalt (Peery) [MRDFMMRD RM, SLSFMR] Y108; Z130; AC112; AR279; BF307 10418

Stirling (Harrison) [DDDDDRRM, MMMFMRRD,] L440; AO226 10419

Stobel (Müllers Choralbuch) [SL TDRM, SDSFMR, STLS,] D446; K221; AM546 10420

Stockholm (Then Swenska Psalmboken. 1695) [LMMMLLSDT LS, TDTLS#] J333; O239; P157; Q415 10421

Stockport (Wainwright) X Yorkshire 10422

Stockton (Stockton) [SSLSDM MR, DSSMDR, MS] G184; I261; R36; T291; AE209; AH 333; AI190; AJ403; AM724; AR244; AS196; AT235; AU 197; AV331; AW457; AX227; AY102; BB567; BZ 10423

-----. R [SMMRDDLLS, SDMDR, SM] 10424

Stockton (Wright) [DMFSDFM R, RMF#SF#S, DM] E82; F325b; X113; BV451; BY402 10425

Stockwell (Jones) [DSSDTDRDT, DMRFMRD,] H133; I52; L102; T150; U102; V500; Z126; AH173; AJ222; AN 83b; AW55; BB207; BD93; BX121 10426

Stockwell New (Laufer) [SLS FMRDT, DRMFSMR, S] Z212; AC108; AK130; AR154 10427

Stokesay Castle (Thiman) [SDDDRMFSM, DSMFMRD,] BY279 10428

Stonefield (Stanley) [DMFMRD SSLTD, DDDTS] H21; L55; T222; AJ319 10429

Stonethwaite (Somervell) [SLS DRMFSMRDR, SDTL] R541; Sap. 39; X399; AG336; AR 555 10430

Stonor (Watson) [SMFSDFSLTD S, SSLTT] F404 10431

Store Gud, som dig til aere (Weyse) [DSDMLSFMR, SSLT DFR] O47 10432

Stories of Jesus (Challinor) [SMFSTLSM, FSRM, SMFS] G441; R459; Z214; AE432; AG303; AH540; AL605; AP763; AR474; AS400; AT505; AV 405; AW419; BY130a; BZ 10433

Störl I (Störl) [SMSLSFRM, S

DTLLS,SD] A516; F239; M561; N56; AA27; AN55a; BV297a; BY560 10434

-----. V [SMSLSFMRM,SDTLLS, S] AN55a 10435

Störl II (Störl) [SDTLLLRDTS, DRMFMR] J13; K439; M320; O166; Q606; V684; AA548; AK 98 10436

-----. V [SDLLLRDTS,DRMFMR R] Q606 10437

Storm-tossed (Sullivan) [SSSSS SDSSSSLS,SLL] BR363 10438

Storrington (Thiman) [SSDTSRFM, DTLRSLS,S] BY704 10439

Storrs (Matthews) [MMMRDDTD, RRRMSSF#S,] I165; K55; N 394; T280; U414; V321; Y141; Z306; AA514; AC175; AF392; AJ388; AK335; AO436; AR461; AT460; BA556; BB460; BF444; BY445a 10440

Story of Jesus (Sweney) [MMRD MFSM,SRMFMRM,M] AH144; 276; AM685; AT211; AU367; AX317; BB534; BO53 10441

-----. V [SMMMFSLS,MSRM FMRM] AH144; BO53 10442

Story of love (Root) X Ellon 10443

Story of the cross, Pt. 1 (Brown) [MMMMFS,DFMR,SSFMRD,] B163a 10444

-----. V [MDRMFM,DTLS#,LSF MRD,] B163a 10445

-----. V [DLFFMM,RRFD, L#LSLDR,] B163a 10446

Stover (Bowman) [MRDFMSLS,R MFLLSF#S,] AY54 10447

Stow (Mason) [SDDDRM,MRD FMR,RMRM] L267; AP14b 10448

Stowe (Mason) X Stow 10449

Stowell (Meredith) [DMSDDD,ML DMMM,DTTM,] G392 10450

Stowey (English trad) [DRMRDLS FRRRR,DRMR] X377; BG142; BY509b 10451

Stracathro (Hutcheson) [DMRDRM DTL,DSMDMRD,] A325a; E 445a; F299a; G340; R327; W451b; X438; AB272; AD31; AF255; AL 12a; AN52; BE343; BK94; BV 147a; BY70 10452

Straf mich nicht (Rosenmüller) X Nassau 10453

Strasburg (Teutsch kirchenampt. Strassburg, 1524 or 25) X Aus tiefer not 10454

Strassburg (Strassburger Kirchen G-B. 1616) [DDDMF SSS,SLSMFS,SL] X400 10455

Stratford (Dykes) X Jesu, magister bone 10456

Strattner (Strattner) X Posen 10457

Streatham (Dykes) X Keble 10458

Streatley (Wesley, S.S. arr) [MRDTDRM,SFMRDTD,RM] AP552b; BA291 10459

-----. V [MRDTDRM,SFM RDTRD,M] BA291 10459a

Strength and stay (Dykes) [MMFSLSMDFMRM,MF#F# S] B280; C280a; D177; F17b; J219; K410; Y4; AB232; AC 244; AH514; AN227; AR325; AU403; AW249; BD125; BE 317; BF356; BK110; BV393; BX124; BY578a 10460

Stricken, smitten (Lindeman) X Hjem jeg laenges 10461

Strive aright (Thommen's Christen-schatz. Basle, 1745) X Batty 10462

Striving, onward, pressing forward (---) [MRRDDMSFFM M,MRFRD] AX435 10463

Stroudwater (Wilkins Psalmody) [DSDSMFMRD,DRMFMR,M] E158; X185; AL632; AP7 10464

Struther (Foote) [SDRMRFMD, LSMFMRDD] AQ29 10465

Study song (Milgrove) X Harts 10466

Stukeley (Mendelssohn) [MSLS MDRM,MRSSF#S,SD] BA763b; BR414 10467

Sturges (Parsons) [LDMRDTLT, DMRDRM,M] A445 10468

Stuttgart (or Stuttgard, or Stuttgardt) (Witt) [SSDDRRMD, SSLFRSM,] A1; B55; C55a;

D48a; E40; F76; G75; J51; K 297; L404; M156; N386; O516; Q83; R151b; S113b; T350a; V 124; W113; X84; AB124; AD 507; AE6; AF100; AG55; AK83; AL13a; AM2; AN23a; AP397b; AQ117; AR5; AS86; AT50; AW 88; AZ16-F; BA899; BE265; BF695; BL2; BN25; BO162; BR154; BV127; BX214; BY78; BZ 10469

Stuyvesant (Gilbert) [MMRFMRL T, DRSMRD, MR] AA443 10470

S'u Sh'oreem (Naumburg) [MM MMDLLMDL, LTDRMF] BH288 10471

Suabia (Spiess) X Swabia 10472

Sub tuum praesidium (Haller) [MLSSDTTTLS#S#, LTDLT] BQ213a 10473

Sub tuum praesidium (Lambillotte) [SSDDRRM, DTLSLSFM, S] BO78 10474

Sub tuum praesidium (Plainsong M 7) [STDRRTDRMMR, RRD LD] BQ213b 10475

Submission (Lomas) [DDMSSSDT LS, TTLS, RS] C385b; D633b 10476

Submission (Peace) [DDRMM RMFFM, RDRM, MF] C385a; S305; U43; Z340; AD266; AE 204; AL431; AP505; AR402; AW 471; BA507; BF420 10477

Succos (Jewish trad) X The lulav 10478

Succoth hymn (Jassinowsky) [MM SMRRDMDTL, LRLMR] BH 182 10479

Such a friend (Stebbins) X Friend 10480

Such love (Harkness) [SMMDDRDT LS, SLTDMM] AX87 10481

Such', wer da will (Stobaeus) [SMFS, DTLS, SMFSMRD, S] Q383 10482

Sudeley (Stainer) [SMRDSDTL, SLMFMR, MF] F154a 10483

Suffer the children to come (Ogden) [DDDDMDL, SSSRDTDR M] AY343 10484

-----. R [MMSFMRMF, RRFM RDRM,] 10485

Suffering Savior (Crueger) X Herz liebster Jesu 10486

Sullivan ("C.A.P." 1855) [SL SMRDTL, DLSDDTDR,] M89 10487

Sullivan (Sullivan) X St Gertrude 10488

Sullivan (Sullivan) [SDDDDD TDRM, DFMRDT,] AH519 10489

Summer carol (French trad) [SDDRTDD, MRFMRD, SDD] BG157 10490

Summer in winter (Cantiques de Strasbourg, 1697) [DRMDS DRMDS, DRMFSD] BG124 10491

Summer suns are glowing (Binder) [SFMSDL, FMDFL S, SFMS] BH155 10492

Summercourt (English trad) [DRMSFMRMRDLD, DRMS] BY94 10493

Summerford (Grimley) [SSDT DRMFRM, SFMRMR] AB397; AC274; AH469; BF653 10494

Summer time (French carol) X Grace soit 10495

Sumner (Biggs) [MFM, SFFM RDRR, RFMR] A429b 10496

Sumus tibi (Button) [SMRDDT, LFMRS, SDDTM] AL451 10497

Sun of grace (Groos) [SMDSL S, MDTDMR, SMDS] M198 10498

Sun of my soul (Allgemeines katholisches G-B. 1774) X Hursley 10499

Sun of my soul (Smith) X Maryton 10500

Sunderland (Smart) X Jamison 10501

Sundown (Gower) [SDTTLLTL MS, SLTLSL] C13b; AB20; AC231; AD49; AJ219; AO28; BF494 10502

-----. V [DTTLLTLMSS, SLTLSL] AC231 10503

Sundridge (Filby) [DSSLSSDS, MDDRMFLR,] K152 10504

Sunlight (Weeden) [SDDDRMM

M, FSSSLS, SL] AU376 10505
-----. R [DTLSFFFFF, TLSF MFS] 10506
Sunning Hill (Elvey) [SMTDSLSF M, SLTDRDT,] D402c 10507
Sunny Bank (English carol) [SD DDMSMD, DRMRDRTS,] BG3, 18 10508
-----. V [SDDRMSMR, FMDDM RTS,] BG18 10509
Sunrise (Stainer) X Lux prima 10510
Sunrise (Trier G-B. 1695) [MM RSDRT, DSLTDDTD, T] F6; BM52; BN132; BQ75 10511
-----. V [MMRSDRTS, DSLTDD TD,] BM52 10512
Sunrise (Zinck) X Zinck 10513
Sunset (Ambrose) X Ambrose 10514
Sunset (Barnby) [MMRRDSFM, MF#STLSF#M,] D8b; V51b; BI57 10515
Sunset (Herbert) X Burwell 10516
Sunset (Howard) [DRMFMMRDM SLS, SDDT] AP672 10517
Sunset (Lutz) X Stanley 10518
Sunset (Stocks) [DRMFMRDRS, DRMFMRD] S509; W271a; BV52a 10519
Sunset and evening star (Stone) [DTDRDT, DRMMRDF, RMF] U419 10520
Sunshine (Sweney) [DRMSLTDR M, MFMRSRD,] AT273; BB607; BC174 10521
-----. R [SFMDRDLSM, MFSDM SF] 10522
Suo-gân (Welsh trad) [DRMRDR, DRMRMD,] X380 10523
Suomi (Finnish cavalry march) [SDDTTLDLS, DSDSFMR] G 131 10524
Suomi II (Finish trad) [MLDTS# L, TDLDMRM, MF#S] J180 10525
Suppliant (Stainer) [DSLSDRMD, RMFMRD#R, R] D274b 10526
Supplication (Monk) [LTDRMLSF, MMRDTT] A500; B191; J435a; K60; O264; V399 10527
Supplication (Vincent) [MMRDLTD, SSFDRM, MRR] D277b; AD 366 10528
Surette (Davis) [SMFSLS, MFR MRDRD, SS] BZ 10529
Surrender (Stebbins) X Adelaide 10530
Surrender (Weeden) [MMFMR RMR, DDFMRMD, M] AT363; AU82; BB573 10531
-----. R [DTLSF, TLSFM, MFLSDT] 10532
Surrexit (Murray) [SMRDMD RDTL, LSLTDM] BY156b 10533
Surrey (Carey) X Carey 10534
Surrey (Costellow) [SDTDMLS FM, MRDSFMM] M369 10535
Sursum corda (Handel) X Solomon 10536
Sursum corda (Lomas) [DDRM FS, FMRM, SDRMFM,] O398; R295; S277; AE439; AG312; AI320; AK250; AR278; BR 336; BY438a 10537
Sursum corda (Smith) [DMSFM RDRRD, SLTDTL] A482a; AF286; AQ71; BV376; BY 316 10538
Sursum corda, No. 1 (Sewall) [MSSLLD, DMRD, DTLSF#S,] BR186 10539
Sursum corda, No. 2 (Lomas) X Sursum corda 10540
Sursum voces (Button) [SLDTM RRD, FMRDTLLS,] BE282 10541
Susanni (German trad) [MMRD SMDRMD, SMSM, DR] BG118 10542
Sussex I (English trad) [DSS FMRMFMR, DRMRMF] B345; C345; BG45 10543
Sussex II (English trad) [MMM RDRMRDL, FFMRDM] C311b; E239; R103; S80; W33; X321; AL559b; BE338; BV579b; BY 467a 10544
Sussex carol (English carol) [SSMFSMRDR, TDDRMFM] BG24a; BV114 10545
Sussex carol (Irish trad) [ML

TDTLSLM, MRDTMLT] BG24b 10546

Sussex mummers carol (English trad) X Sussex I 10547

Sutherland (Ashford) [DDMRDD TD, DTDRLDTL,] I377 10548

Sutherland (Bradbury) [SDTDSLLD, TLSFMRD, S] L103 10549

Sutton Courtenay (Routley) [SL DTD, RMSF#S, MFSSFM,] BY 712b 10550

Sutton Volence (Russell) [DTDTLL, SLDTD, DRMRF] E615; X115a 10551

Swabia (Spiess) [SMFRRD, RMF# SSF#S, SLSL] A375a; B45; C 45a; D28a; H79; I648; Q274; R72; S20; W478; AA373; AB10; AE51; AK37; AN287; AQ131; AR42; AS41; AX63; AZ582-K; BA613; BF189; BR93; BV51; BX362; BY329 10552

Swabia No. 1 (Spiess) X Swabia 10553

Swahili (Schulz) [DDTTLS, SDT DR, MMF#F#S] F469; W476; AN4; BX521 10554

Swainsthorpe (Booth) [DDMRFFM, RMSFLS, SDD] D664; AO560 10555

Swanage (Greenwood) [SMRDRSRM RDRS, SMFM] BE200 10556

Swanmore (Blackall) [MSLMSMDR M, MLDTRDL] F396a 10557

Swansea (Basque church mel) [DSMRDRMRDLS, DMSLS] Y 337; AC69 10558

Swanwick (Lucas) [SDDRMDM RDTD, MFMRD] H9; L192; M 403; T107; V348; AJ156b 10559

Swanwick (Shaw) [LTDRLTLTD, DTLSMMF#] X546 10560

Sweden (---. 16th c) [LDDRRMM RDTL, LDDRR] M292; N602; Q432 10561

Sweden (Hiles) [MMMSDSFM, MMLF#STLS,] C39; D641; U351 10562

Swedish litany (Swedish mel., 1697) [MDTLLS#L, DMRDDTD,] A82a; J81; AF166 10563

Sweet Agnes, holy child (Slovak hymn) [SLSMFMRDRM, FSMR, SL] BQ106 10564

Sweet are the promises (Ogden) [DMFSSSLFLS, SFFFFM] AR470; AW481; AX494 10565

-----. R [DDFLSM, SRMFM, DDFLS] 10566

Sweet be thy rest (Hakes) [M SF#SM, SLDTLLS, SF#SD,] BB493 10567

Sweet by and bye [by] (Webster) [DRMRDRDLS, DRMMMSS] N621; U424; AH535; AT471; AU344; AV396; AW504; AX 587; BB551 10568

-----. R [MFSSMR, RMFFF FMRM, M] 10569

Sweet chariot (Negro spiritual) [MDMDDLS, DDDDMMSS, L] Y321; AH610 10570

-----. R [MSDLDDDDDDLS, DDDD] 10571

Sweet day (Unseld) X Once more before we part 10572

Sweet home (Bishop) X Home, sweet home 10573

Sweet hosannas (Handel) [MRD RMFMMR, SLSMFRM,] AP 747 10574

-----. R [SLSFMFMRMS, SLSFMF] 10575

Sweet hour (Bradbury) [DMF SSLTD, LSMMRDRM] G302; H39; I516; N350; P11; R 398; U359; Z337; AE232; AH349; AI228; AK475; AM 534; AN564; AO316; AR471; AS44; AT327; AU263; AV 186; AW182; AX353; BB316; BC166; BR524; BZ 10576

Sweet hour of prayer (Bradbury) X Sweet hour 10577

Sweet hour of prayer (Hall) [SSSLDTLS, SSSDDTDR, SSS] AY32 10578

Sweet is the peace the Gospel brings (Durham) [MMMFM SRR, MFFMRR, SD] BC191 10579

Sweet is the story (Giffe) [SSLSMRDDM, SSLSMRD] AX32; AY517 10580

-----. R [SDDDDTLSM, SDDD SMR,] 10581
Sweet is the work, my God, my King (McClellan) [SLTDRMF# S, SLTDRMDR,] BC168 10582
Sweet peace (Bilhorn) [SMRDMSD T, SFMRLTLS,] U230; AE300; AI256; AR476; AT299; AU381; AX336; BB609 10583
-----. R [MDFMRRRRDLS, S DDDD] 10584
Sweet peace, the gift of God's love (Bilhorn) X Sweet peace 10585
Sweet promise (Gabriel) [SDRM MMFRMDS, DRMFS] AT278; AU438 10586
-----. R [SFMRDRMDLS, STT RRF] 10587
Sweet rest in heaven (Leatherman) [DMMR#MSF, RDDRRM, DMM] AX598; AY158 10588
-----. R [DRRDRMS, MRRDR M, DMM] 10589
Sweet Sabbath (Miller) [MMMMMM RMFS, SDTLSS] BH116 10590
Sweet sacrament divine (Stanfield) [MSFRMD, MLTDRMR, MSF] BO38 10591
Sweet Saviour, bless us (Catholic) [SSSDDTDRDDT, SSSRR] BO192 10592
-----. R [MMMDMMMMF, FMRDDTT] 10593
Sweet Saviour! Bless us (Herbert) X Burwell 10594
Sweet Saviour, bless us (Lawes) X Falkland 10595
Sweet Saviour! bless us (Montani) [MMRDFMRLSMR, RMRDF] BQ138 10596
-----. R [FFFFMSDDDT, TT TTDL] 10597
Sweet story (Gifford) X I think, when I read 10598
Sweet story (Irish trad) [MRD RDDMSFLDD, TLSF] N649; AI384a 10600
Sweet the moments (---) [DDRR MMRR, MSFMRRD, D] AX178; AY250 10601
Sweeter sounds (LaTrobe) [SM LSFMR, MFSFMRD, RM] BA 503 10602
Sweeter than the day before (Loveless) [SLTDMMMSF#S F#SF#F, SL] AU325 10603
Sweetest hosannas (Brunk) [SF#SLSTDRRD, DTDRMR] AY480 10604
-----. R [DRMFLLTDSD, DTDRMR] 10605
Sweetest name (Bradbury) X There is no name 10606
Sweetest name (Bridgers) [M MR#MFMMRL, TDD#RSFM] AT307; AU391 10607
-----. R [SLTDFT, SRSR#M, SLTDR] 10608
Sweetest name (Stockton) X Great Physician 10609
Sweetly, Lord, have we heard (Everett) [MMMMRDLLS, S MDR, MMM] AS347; AT362; AU228; AX508 10610
-----. R [LFLLSSSLSMR, MMMMR] 10611
Sweetly resting (Bentley) X In the rifted rock 10612
Sweney (Sweney) X Fill me now 10613
Sweney (Sweney) X More about Jesus 10614
Swiss melody (Recueil de cantiques) [MMRMD, SMMMRM SF, FFM] C290b; E399 10615
Swiss tune (Schmidlin) [SMSD TDRM, SLTDRMFR,] AA73; AB359; BY60 10616
Switzerland (Schmidlin) X Swiss tune 10617
Sycamore (Hostetter) [SDSLSDR MDRD, SLLLD] AY299 10618
Sychar (Dykes) X St Oswald I 10619
Sykes (Hall) [MFSSSSLLS, SM MMMFM] AY193 10620
Sylvester (Camp) [DRMFMM R, RDMSLSE,LT] I571 10621
Sylvester (Dykes) X St Sylvester 10622
Sympathy (Stockton) X Great Physician 10623
Symphony (Norwegian trad) X

Behold a Host 10624
Synge vi af hjertens grund (German, 1544) X Singen wir aus herzens grund 10625

T

Tabernacle (Arthur) [DMMSMDTD FFM, MRSSF#] W544 10626
Tabernacles (Genevan Psalter, 1562) X Jervaulx Abbey 10627
Tabler (Frost) [MMMMFMRMRD, RRRRSF] T452; AJ196 10628
Tabor (Grimm. Choral buch) [DSLTDRRM, SFRMMR, DS] AZ591-C 10629
Tabor (Kugelmann. Concentus novi. 1540) [DDTLSDRM, MM RDDD, DD] D360b; M592; N345; O385; Q34; AA59 10630
-----. V [DDTLSDRM, MMMMRD TD,] M592 10631
-----. V [LDTLSDRM, MMMM RDTD,] Q34 10632
Tabor (Kugelmann. Concentus novi. 1540) X Old 100th (Bourgeois) 10633
Taconic (Harris) [MMLLDRM, MMFRDTL, MM] BR194 10634
Tadcaster (Hopkins) [DSLTDS, MMFLS, DSLTD] C518b 10635
Taenk, naar engang den taage (---) [SLSSMMMFMMR, SLSS R] O537; P295 10636
Taenk, naar engang ... (Berggren) X Berggren I 10637
Take courage, saints (Asper) [DMSMRDDTDR, MFLSMS] BC167 10638
Take me as I am (Sankey) [DM MMFMRD, MSSSLSRM,] P 254; AU86 10639
-----. R [DMMMRD, MSSSFM, SLLL] 10640
Take my hand and lead me (Beery) X Huntingdon 10641
Take my heart, O Father (Pollock) X Bless the words 10642
Take my life and let it be (---) X Consecration 10642a
Take my life, and let it be (Bradbury) X Yarbrough 10643
Take the name [of Jesus with you] (Doane) X Precious name 10644
Take the world, but give me Jesus (Sweney) X Give me Jesus 10645
Take thou my hand and lead me (Silcher) X So nimm denn meine hände 10646
Take time to be holy (Stebbins) X Holiness 10647
Take unto you (Jewish trad) X Boughs 10648
Tal (Jewish trad) [MFMDD RMRL, LRMSS, MF] BH128 10649
Tallis (Tallis) X Tallis' Ordinal 10650
Tallis' Canon (Tallis) [DDTDD RRM, DFFMMRRD,] A165; B25; C25a; D18a; E267; F23; G51; I49; J21; K471; M568; O4; Q558a; R63; S42; U461, 495; V45a, b; W291; X45; Z 148; AA36b; AB30; AD62; AE46; AF56; AG32; AI55; AK59; AL529b; AM341; AN 110; AO36; AP77a; AQ85; AR49; AS31; AV19; AW33; AZ22-T; BA778; BB53; BE 272; BF200; BJ54, 55; BK35; BL72; BN58; BR117; BV37; BX131; BY694; BZ 10651
-----. V [SDDDDRRM, DFFMM RRD,] M568 10652
-----. V [SDDDDRRMFM, D FFMMR] U495 10653
-----. V [SSSS, DDTDDRRM, DDTD] BJ54 10654
Tallis' Evening hymn (Tallis) X Tallis' Canon 10655
Tallis' Lamentation (Day's Psalter, 1562) [LDRDTDTL, DMMRDRTL,] E235; X235; BJ59 10656
Tallis' Ordinal (Tallis) [DMF SSLLS, SDTLLS, D] A298a; B237; C237b; D209; E453; F78; G478; H150; J154; K 54; M304; R119; V261; W 353b; X664; AE381; AF18; AK84; AL125; AN49; AP1;

AQ133; AW326; BA98; BB92; BJ14; BN199; BV132a; BY332; BZ 10657

Tallis' Hymn (Tallis) X Tallis' Canon 10658

Talmar (Woodbury) X Dorrnance 10659

Talyllyn (Welsh trad) [SDTLDTLS, RMDRTD, SD] AK69; BY556b 10660

Tana mana dhana (Marathi trad) [DRMRDRDDLLSSL, MMM] AF394 10661

Tantum ergo (---) [SFMLSLTDD, DLSF#SLT] BO274E 10662

Tantum ergo (---) [SSLSFMDLLS, SSLSFM] BO274g 10663

Tantum ergo (Balthasar) [SLDDR DTT, LTDRRDD, R] BQ242c 10664

Tantum ergo (Beltjens) [MSDLSF FM, LLSLSFMR] BQ242a 10665

Tantum ergo (Essay on the church plain) X Dulce carmen 10666

Tantum ergo (Dooner) [SLSLDTD LS, SLMSLTT] BQ326 10667

Tantum ergo (Dubois) [SDMMRR MFFM, SLTLSM] BQ242i 10668

Tantum ergo (Ett) X Oriel 10669

Tantum ergo (Filitz) X Mannheim 10670

Tantum ergo [sacramentum] (Chants ordinaires ... Paris) X Grafton 10671

Tantum ergo (Miller) [MMMRFFFM LLSMRDR, M] BO274 10672

Tatum ergo (Mohr) X He who once in righteous vengeance 10673

Tantum ergo I (Montani) [MMM LTRMM, MSFMRDDT,] BQ242j 10674

Tantum ergo II (Montani) [MSL DTSLS, LTDSFMMR,] BQ323 10675

Tantum ergo (Mozarabic plainsong M 5) [DRMMMRMFMFMRM RD,] A200c; B338c; BN109; BP62; BQ325 10676

-----. V [FSLLLSTDLSLSF, FSL] BQ325 10677

Tantum ergo (Perosi) [SDDLS FFM, RMSDTLLS,] BQ321 10678

Tantum ergo (Plainsong M 5) [DRRMRDRMSSFM, LSSF] BN108 10679

Tantum ergo (Ravanello) [MR MDRDDTD, MF#SLF#F#M,] BQ242d 10680

Tantum ergo (Rush) [SSSDD RMM, MFMDRRD, S] BN112; BO274F 10681

Tantum ergo (Slovak hymn) [DTDLSMFMRD, MFSRMD] BQ242g 10682

Tantum ergo (Smit) [DTLSM, LSFMR, MF#STLS] BQ242E 10683

Tantum ergo (Sullivan) [MMM LTDTLM, DDMRDDT] BQ 324 10684

Tantum ergo (Wade) X St Thomas 10685

Tantum ergo No. 2 (Palestrina?) [S#S#LLSSSS, DDDRDDT, T] E326c; X280b 10686

Tanycastell (Jones) [DDDTTRR MDFFFMMFM] W502b; AP 228 10687

Tappan (Kingsley) [SSSMRDLS, SSSFMRDR,] G61; I99; L 448; V702; AO110 10688

Taps (---) [SSDSDMSDMSDM SDM, D] AC344; AG339; AH 566; BB370 10689

Tarsus (Goss) [SDTDRMFR, MFSLRMFM,] O467; AB60 10690

Task sublime (English trad) [DRMRDRMFMR, MRDTLS,] AE311; AR365 10691

Task sublime (English trad) X Noel 10692

Taylor Hall (Sowerby) [MFSL SM, RMFSLTS, DT] A527 10693

Tchaikowsky's "Legend" (Tchaikowsky) X The crown of roses 10694

Te deum (Allgemeinisches Katholisches G-B. 1774) [DDDTDRMRD, MMMRDSM] A273; J167; L96; Q250; R115;

T203; W413b; AF247; AH145; AJ292; AK20; AS23; AW519; AX10; BE88; BL82; BM91; BN196; BO3; BQ39; BR80; BZ 10695

-----. V [DDDTDRDRM, MMM FSSF] J167 10696

-----. V [DDDDRDRD, MMM FSSFM] L96 10697

-----. V [DMSMRDRD, MMMFS SFM] R115 10698

Te deum (Allgem. Kath. G-B. 1774) X Hursley X Halle 10699

Te deum laudamus (Barnby) [MDMRDDDFFFFMRS, DD] AR635; AS494 10700

Te, Joseph, celebrent (Catholic) [SLDLTDDSLSFMR, SLD] BO267 10701

Te, Joseph, celebrent (Plainsong M 1) [RFMFSLRDFMFRDDR, R] BN168 10702

Te laudant omnia (Swift) [MSDRDT D, LSTDFMR, MS] BY3 10703

Te lucis (Plainsong arr) [LLLSL DTL, DRRDRMMM,] BR118 10704

Te lucis (Sarum plainsong M 8) [LDDDDRDT, LLLLTTL] A164a; E264b; F16 10705

Te lucis ante terminum (Andernach G-B. 1608) [SLMFMRRD, MFSLLSFM,] E264c 10706

Te lucis ante terminum (Gastorius) X Was Gott tut 10707

Te lucis ante terminum (Plainsong M 8) [LDLLTDLL, LLTD TLSL] E264 10708

Teach me, O Lord (Hewlett) [M MMMRMDLTDR, MFSLS] Sap. 25; AR671 10709

Teach me the measure (Wilson) X Martyrdom 10710

Teach me thy will, O Lord (Runyan) [SFMMRD, RMFM, SFMMRD,] AX566 10711

Teilo Sant (Dobbs) [SMFSLTDTL S, SDRMLS] BY51b 10712

Tekna (Schulz) [SSMSSMSFRFM, SSMSS] M615; AW413; BK152; BN19; BQ6 10713

Tell it again (McIntosh) [MMMM RDRDLS, SDDDTD] AU378 10714

-----. R [FFFR, MMMD, DDDDTDRM] 10715

Tell it out (Sankey) [SSDTDRM RMFSMD, MFS] I634; AI 170 10716

Tell it to Jesus (Lorenz) [DMMRDRDLSD, RRMRS, M] AU110: AW476 10717

-----. R [RRMRS, MMFMD, FFFMRD] 10718

Tell me the old, old story (Doane) [MMFSSLS, SDDD MF#S, SD] E583; N351; R 403; U144; V239; Z438; AH 344; AL496a; AM521; AO633; AP433; AS181; AT222; AU 370; AV345; AW495; AX280; AY521; BA420; BB524; BV 481; BY420 10719

-----. R [MMFSSLS, TTDRR RD, MM] 10720

Tell me the story (Sweney) X Story of Jesus 10721

Tell the story (Fischer) X Hankey 10722

Tell the sweet old story (Showalter) [MFSSLSMD, DDDDT LS, M] AY369 10723

-----. R [DRMMMRDSD, TD RMRDL] 10724

Tell us now, O Death (Cologne G-B.) X Vigiles et sancti 10725

Tell what He's done for you (Byers) [SDMMRDTRR, SR FFMRD] AX346 10726

-----. R [MFSFMFSLS, RMFMRMF] 10727

Tempest (Huxtable) [DRMFMR, DTDR, MMMMMT] BR343 10728

Tempest (Koenig) [DTLMRDTD LS#, TTTDRM] F312 10729

Temple (Bartlett) [DMFSFMRM FM, FSLTLS,] I665 10730

Temple (Davies) [DSSLMS, STSF#MM, MF] A374; E454 10731

Temple (Hopkins) [MMFMM RRD, LSRM, MMFM] D19b; K468; L19; W293; AA44;

AO43a; AV21; AZ605-A; BX 152 10732

Temple (Wagner) [SSLDMMRDR RDSFMFF] Y401 10733

Temple Boro (Pindar) [SDDTDLLS, MSFRMFM, S] T140; AJ207 10734

Temple Bryan (Macalister) [MSL TDDMMRM, SLTDMR] S330; W144; BY140a 10735

Tempus adest floridum (Piae cantiones. 1582) [DDDRDDS, LS LTDD, DD] A136; G107; R167; S453; X4; AD115; AG68; AH 252; AL57; AM640; AN135; AQ321; AT73; BG99; BK131; BZ 10736

Ten thousand martyrs (Weinberg) [LRDTLDLDTL, LDLDLS] BH135 10737

Ten thousand times ten thousand (Sankey) [SDDMDSFM, SLTDRDT, L] AI341 10738

-----. R [SSRDTLSFMD, DDRD MR] 10739

Tenbury (Nicholson) [SDDTLSM, SLSMRDD, RM] F627 10740

Tenbury (Ouseley) [DRMFSMS, LSLFM, DRMF] D656a 10741

Tenbury (Ouseley) X Aberystwyth 10742

Tenbury (Statham) [MSMRDDRMS MR, SLRTL,] X328b 10743

Tender Shepherd (Barnby) [DDTDRM D, FMRDTLTLS,] D248b 10744

Tender thought (Kentucky harmony, 1816) [RMRDLDRMSMR, RMRD L] AF576 10745

Tenderness (Reinecke) [MFSFM FLS, MFSDT, TRD] AL604 10746

Tenebrae (Redhead) X St Prisca 10747

Tent-like this day (Samuel) [MD TLTDDRRM, LSSDDF] BH160 10748

Tenterden (Bullinger) [DMSFMRD MRD, DMSF#MR#] O396 10749

Ter sanctus (Cruickshank) [MM, MM, MM, MRDL, RMFSSM] U489 10750

Ter sanctus (Rostockerhandboken, 1529) [MFMRMDRM, SMD RMFFM,] J174; N316; R25; S17; AF28 10751

Terra beata (English trad) [DRMSMRD, RMFLSMR, LS] G72; J487; R101; S70; Y51; Z171; AB64; AC39; AD93; AE55; AF485; AG60; AH202; AI32; AK65; AL589; AM109; AR99; AS94; AT59; AV406; AW48; BB646; BF399; BK 26; BZ 10752

Terra patris (English trad) X Terra beata 10753

Teschner (Teschner) X St Theodulph 10754

Teshiniens (Polish trad) [LT LS#LTDT, TDRMRDTL,] Q 169; AM196 10755

Tetworth (Garrett) [MLLDTLL S#, LSSMRRD, M] I380 10756

Thacher (Handel) X Thatcher 10757

Thalberg (Thalberg) [SSSLF# SS, MMMSTD, SSS] H176 10758

Thanet (Jowett) [MRDDFMMR, MF#SMF#S, FS] S511a; W 294a; AM337; BV48 10759

Thankful hearts (Rogers) [MM SSDTT, FFTTRDD, SS] BH 249 10760

Thankfulness (MacFarren) X Luffenham 10761

Thanks for the Sabbath School (Murray) [SLSSMRDRDL, LSDRMR] BC177 10762

-----. R [RRMFFFMMFS, SSLTLS] 10763

Thanksgiving (Baker) [SDTLLSS, SLTDMRDT, T] BY34 10764

Thanksgiving (Basswood) [SD DDDTT, TLTLLSS, SD] AE 431; AH544; AL584; AM645; AP719; AW435; BK15 10766

-----. R [DSSTL, RLLDT, D MMMLR] 10767

Thanksgiving (Carter) [SSM DDDRMFM, MMRDTL] AO 64 10768

Thanksgiving (Crueger) X

Graefenberg 10769
Thanksgiving (Dykes) X Trinity College 10770
Thanksgiving (Gilbert) [DTDSLSFM, MF#SLTLS, D] B103; C103; T11; W389; AA299; AJ15; AM 107; BA344; BB16 10771
Thanksgiving (Quaile) X Oldbridge 10772
Thanksgiving (Schop) X Sollt ich meinem Gott 10773
Thanksgiving (Statham) [SSSDFMR S, SDLRSLTL] I216; V565; Y 218; AA437; AB293; AC219; AD344; AR530; AS391 10774
Thanksgiving carol (Hohenfurth ms.) X Dies est laetitiae 10775
Thanksgiving hymn (Balle) X Emmanuel 10776
That cause can neither be lost (Danish trad) X Ostergaard 10777
That doleful night (American trad) X Amazing grace 10778
That heavenly home (Kolb) [MR# MDSSLTDS, MR#MDTD] AX595; AY136 10779
That will be glory for me (McGranahan) [SSF#SMRDDTL S, SSFMF] AU341 10780
-----. R [SDDDDRML, LRRRR DLS,] 10781
Thatcher (Handel) [DMRDSFMR, SDRMLTD, D] C225a; D27a; H129; I182; J526; K265; L49; M401; N374; O346; P395; T84; V265; Z457; AA341; AJ62; AO 359; AY428; BE240; BR32 10782
Thaxted (Holst) [MSLDTSDRDT LTLSM, M] F579; X379a; BY 642 10783
The alarm (Beecher. Plymouth coll.) X Latter day 10784
The angel Gabriel (English trad) [DMSMRDTR, MDLDTL, DM] BG37 10785
-----. R [SLTDMRDT, TDTLS SM, D] 10786
The armor of light (Lynes) [SSS SSLLS, SLTDTLL, T] BX540 10787
-----. R [MMMRDTLTLS, MMMRDT] 10788
The band of children (French, 16th c) [SDRMMFM, RDTLD TLS, S] BG140; BN7; BO 147 10789
-----. R [RDTD, RDTD, DFM RSFMR,] 10790
The banner of the cross (McGranahan) X Royal banner 10791
The battle hymn of the republic (Steffe) X Battle hymn 10792
The beatitudes (Toews) [SFM SSSLS, SLTD, DTLL] AX48 10793
The beautiful garden of prayer (Fillmore) [MFSMSLDLSM, DRMDRM] AU342; AX362 10794
-----. R [SLTLSFMRDMLS, SLTL] 10795
The bell cadence (Tearne) [DS, RMFS, SM, SM, SM, SM, MD,] AT553 10796
The bellman's song (English trad) [SFMRMDRMFLRS, SFMF] BG46b 10797
The bellman's song (English trad) X Hitchen carol 10798
The bellman's song (English trad) X Newbury 10799
The best friend of all (Bills) [DRMRMDDTLDLS, SSDD] AX279 10800
-----. R [SFMMRDDTLDLS, SDDD] 10801
The bird let loose ("Franklin Square") [SMRDMLSS, MSF RMD, SM] BR530 10802
The birds (Czech trad) [SMR DDTDRMD, SM, SMRD] X381; BG103 10803
The blameless church (Speck) [SFMMMMRMFSS, MFSSS] AX150 10804
-----. R [MSDDDDTLSM, S LLLDT] 10805
The blessed home (Stainer) X Blessed home 10806
The blessed name (Barnby)

[DMMRDSLS, SSDTLSM, D] AP689 10807
The blessed rest (Barnby) [MMM SSDDRFM, FFMRLS] AP620 10808
The blood of the Lamb (Showalter) X When I see the blood 10809
The bond of perfectness (Warren) [SSLSMDRM, SSMDMMR, S] AX550 10810
-----. R [DTLSSLSD, DRMFS LS, S] 10811
The bread that giveth strength (Sullivan) X Livorno 10812
The breaking of the day (Sederquist) [SMMMSMFFLD, LSSS DS] BB182 10813
-----. R [SFMMMMFSLS, FM RRRM] 10814
The Bridegroom soon will call us (Mason) X Evarts 10815
The builders (French trad) [SD DRSFMRDRRMRD, SD] BG111 10816
The call (Williams) [DMSSLSF S, DMSSLSFS,] AQ123 10817
The call for reapers (Clemm) X Clemm 10818
The canticle of the Blessed Virgin I (Gelineau) [DDRL, LDLS L.] BSp. 57 10819
The canticle of the Blessed Virgin II (Gelineau) [SLDLDL, LSL DLDL, RDT] BSp. 58 10820
The carnal and the crane (English trad) [MSLLTDMSSM, MLLTDR] BG53 10821
The cherry tree carol I (English trad) X Cherry tree 10822
The cherry tree carol II (English trad) [MDLS#TLM, LLSFLM, DRD] BG66b 10823
The cherry tree carol III (English trad) [DMSLTDSM, SLDTLS, LT] BG66c 10824
The cherry tree carol IV (English trad) [DDTLDTLS, MFMRFM, MR] BG66d 10825
The Child Jesus (Scheidt) X O Jesulein süss 10826
The child of a King (Sumner) [M SSSMMMMMD, DRRRRM] AM 720; AT270; AU47; AV342; BB614 10827
-----. R [DMSSSM, MMMMS, SDTLS] 10828
-----. V [MSF#SMMMR#MD, DRRRRM] AU47 10829
The children's King (MacLeod) [SSMRDDT, LSFMRRD, TL] D532b 10830
The Christian home (McKinney) [SF#SMMSFDRMR, FMFRS] AU445 10831
The Christian's Guide (Warren) [DMMRRMFR, MFSLSMD, D] AX142 10832
The Christian's passport (Heatwole) [MFSMDRM, MFSMF MR, MF] AX432; AY165 10833
The Christmas manger hymn (Spilman) X Away in a manger 10834
The Christmas tree (Cornelius) [SMDFRSLFM, STDRTSD] BG191 10835
The Church of the living God (Winsett) [SSLSDRMMRD, LTDDRD] AX152 10836
-----. R [SMFSDRMMD, LTD DRDL] 10837
The church's one foundation (Wesley) X Aurelia 10838
The city of light (Kieffer) [SD MDMSLSMDMR, MFSF] AX 370; AY153 10839
-----. R [MFSSLSFMFMR M, MFSD] 10840
The cleansing wave (Knapp) X Cleansing wave 10841
The cleft of the rock (Good) [SSDDDDMDS, SSLLDTL] AX511; AY447 10842
-----. R [SSSMDS, DTLFM, SSMSD] 10843
The cleft of the rock (Kirkpatrick) X He hideth my soul 10844
The clouds hang thick (Catholic) [SDSDRMMR, MFRDTD, MR] BO111 10845
The Comforter has come (Kirkpatrick) [SSLSMS, DDRDLD, LSLS] AX132; AY206; BB 526 10846

-----. R [DMRDRM, DDRD LD, LSLS] 10847
The coming day (Gaines) [SSMFSS DS, SLSMDR, SS] Y260 10848
The convert (---) [SSRDR, MRD DLS, DRMRM] H294 10849
The cradle (Corner. 1649) X Corner 10850
The cross is not greater (Booth) [SSF# SLMSFR, RMFSTLS] AU 372; AX427; AY463 10851
The crown of roses (Tchaikowsky) [LLSDRMML, MLSDRMML,] BG197 10852
The crowning day (McGranahan) [SSDDRMR, DLDDLS, SSS] AU 48; AV391; BY189 10853
-----. R [DDDFFFFL, LLSSMS MR] 10854
The cry of Israel (Heller) [MMMM SMR, RLSS, SDDTM] BH31 10855
The cry of Israel (Schalit) [LRD TLSFS, RRRM, MFFS] BH34 10856
The dawn was purpling (Haworth) [SSSSDTLL, LLLLRDTT,] BO174 10857
The day dawn is breaking (Clayson) [SDSSMSSDDRMD, SLLL] BC179 10858
-----. R [SMSMDRDLS, SMSDDM R] 10859
The day is done (Levenson) [MM MRMRRD, RDDTLDTL] BH12 10860
The decree (English trad) [DMFS LSMRFM, DMFSLS] BG65b 10861
The decree (English trad) X Decree 10862
The Divine praises (Bragers) [SL DD, DDDRMRDD, RRRR] BP 102 10863
The eventide (Warren) [MMFSMFM R, RRMFMRDM,] AX110 10864
The 5th tune (Tallis) [SDRMDFRM RDTD, SDRM] BJ98 10865
The fight is on (Morris) [SDDD SLSSSLSS, SRRR] AH448; AU 402 10866
-----. R [SLTDTLMSS, SLTDTL M] 10867
The first fruits of the land (Hermann) X Hermann 10868
The first noël (English trad) X The first nowell 10869
The first nowell (English trad) [MRDRMFSLTDTLS, LT] A30; B551; C551; G97; J40; R156; S129; W45; X384; Y 328; Z197; AB119; AC79; AD114; AE86; AF141; AG 72; AH124; AK118; AL65; AN174; AP730; AQ285; AR 132; AT63; AU140; AW76; BB108; BC39; BD231; BF281; BG27; BI82; BK160; BL8; BN23; BO159; BP15; BV117; BX535; BY109; BZ 10870
The five lesser joys (Irish trad) [LTDDTSLLLTDDRM, MR] BN138 10871
The fountain (American trad) X Cleansing fountain 10872
The garden (Showalter) [SSLL SRD, DDTLLS, MMM] AR162; AS133 10873
The garden of Jesus (Dutch, 1633) [SDRMFSSSMRRD, SD RM] BG105 10874
The gate ajar for me (Vail) X Gates ajar 10875
The glorious gospel light (Robertson) [SDDDDRTD, DMRDDT, SS] BC45 10876
The glory song (Gabriel) X Glory song 10877
The God of harvest praise (Barnby) X Laudes domini 10878
The God that to our fathers (Isaacs) [LDDTLRD, DTTT DLS#, MT] BH234 10879
The golden carol (Williams) [DDTSLSM, DDDTLSLLT] BG 173 10880
-----. V [SDDTSLSM, SDDD TLSL] BG173 10881
The golden chain (Barnby) [MM MMMSSS, SDLFLSS, M] AM 287; AO610a; BX403; BY265a 10882
The golden harvest (Jeffrey)

[SDDDRMD, DRRDTD, SDD] AX207 10883

-----. R [MSSSMS, DMMMRM, SDDD] 10884

The good fight (Barnby) X To victory 10885

The Good Shepherd (Heinlein) X Jesu, Jesu du mein hirt 10886

The Good Shepherd (Hunter) [SS SSDDDMD, MSSSFFM] AX253 10887

-----. R [SDDDDM, MRRRFMR M, SL] 10888

The gospel bells (Martin) [SDD DMLS, SSLSDRM, MS] BY421 10889

-----. R [MDSFRS, SSLSDRM, MSD] 10890

The Great Physician [now is near] (Stockton) X Great Physician 10891

The great reaping day (Winsett) [MFSMRDMRDDLS, MFSS] AX297 10892

-----. R [DDFFFLLLSM, MMR SSS] 10893

The green hill (Stebbins) [MMM FMMRD, MSSSFM, MM] T114; V755; Z230; AE111; AH288; AI52; AJ163; AK479; AR172; AS145; AT98; AU98; AV106 10894

-----. R [STLSFMFS, SLLSF#S, FM] 10895

The hallowed spot (---, arr by O'Kane) [DDRFDFLS, FLFSFR D, D] AX327; AY318 10896

The hand that was wounded (Towner) [SSMFSLMSF#F, FFRMFT] AX106; AY512 10897

The happy Christmas (Balle) X Emmanuel 10898

The happy day has rolled on (Beesley) [SDDDTDLSDTD, MRTSL] BC250 10899

The happy story hour (Truss) [SMMRRD, LFFML, TSSFF] AU 312 10900

The haven of rest (Moore) X My soul in sad exile 10901

The heart's refuge (Doane) X Arms of Jesus 10902

The heavens (Pond) [SMDDRT TD, DSMMFRRM] AI40 10903

The heavens are thine (Peruchot) [MLSDTDRRM, SLTDTLS] BI12-D 10904

The heavens, O God (Beethoven) X A hymn anthem 10905

The heavens, O God (Isaacs) [DMDFRSF#S, DFFMRDRD] BH57 10906

The hem of His garment (Root) [SSSSSSF#SLS, MRMSFM,] AU287 10907

-----. R [SDDTLSLS, SLDSM R, RM] 10908

The highway (Lutkin) [SSSLTD S, SSSLTDS, LL] Y13 10909

The holly and the ivy (English trad) [DDDDLSM, DDDDLS, SFM] BG38; BV108 10910

The Holy City (Ward) X Materna 10911

The Holy Well (English trad) [SDDRMFMRD, MFSSMRD] BG56b 10912

The Holy Well (English trad) X Holy Well 10913

The home over there (O'Kane) X Home over there 10914

The homeland (Stebbins) [SM MFMMR, DDTDRMM, SM] T438; BB639 10915

The hundredth Psalm (Bourgeois) X Old 100th 10916

The Infant King (Basque carol) [DRTD, RMFSLSFMRM, DR] BV115 10917

The judgment has set (Belden) [SSF#SDMMR#MFM, MRD#R L] BB482 10918

The Kingdom (French trad) [MLTDTLLSLTL, SLSM, M] BG108 10919

The Kingdom coming (McIntosh) [DMMMMD, MSSSSM, SDTL] G483; I633; AT409; AU125 10920

-----. R [SLLLLTDSSSSM, SLLL] 10921

The Kingdom is coming (McIntosh) X The Kingdom coming 10922
The Kings (Cornelius) [SMTRDM FLSS, SDRMRD] BG193 10923
The King's business (Cassel) [SLD MMMMRDFFF, FMRF] AI197; AM695; AT433 10924
-----. R [SSSTTLSD, MRMFSTLS,] 10925
The King's majesty (George) [LD RFMLDRDTL, LTDM] A64a; J 73b; AF176; BZ 10926
The Lamb of God (English trad) [MLMRF#MRDLTL, DRMRS] BG44 10927
-----. R [DRMLSMF#RDRMRD TL, D] 10928
The last farewell (Teasley) [MF SSLSMD, SLLTDLS, M] AX617, 657 10929
-----. V [DRMMSMDRMD, SS LLLR] AX657 10930
The last great day (Warren) [SL SMDLDD, DRRRRDMS,] AX 287 10931
-----. R [SSLLFLLSSMS, MMR MF] 10932
The last mile of the way (Marks) [DRMMMMRDTR, RMFFFF] AX580 10933
-----. R [MFSSSLSMF, RMFFF SF] 10934
The last sleep (Barnby) X Requiem 10935
The lifting of mine hands (Alman) [DDRDTLTD, DDRDTLTD,] BH174 10936
The Light of the world [is Jesus] (Bliss) X Light of the world 10937
The light of the world (Brunk) X Ye are the light 10938
The Lily of the valley (Hays) X Salvationist 10939
The long way home (Sullivan) [DRRMSMR, DRMSDTLS, S] BR91 10940
The Lord be with us (Arne) X Arlington 10941
The Lord be with us (Cannon) [SLDRFMRD, DMFSDR, RM] BC28 10942
The Lord bless thee (Hughes) [SLDS, SLDFMRM, DFFRR] BY305-A 10943
The Lord bless thee (McKinney) [SDDTDRDS, SDDDTT DR] AT541; AU498 10944
The Lord bless thee (Purcell) [MMMRDFM, RD#LRRDTLS#] BY305-A 10945
The Lord bless you (Lutkin) [SSMDDRFM, SSMSDTLM] G614; I748; AC25; AE474; AG340; AT542; AV426; AW 614; BB695; BF698 10946
The Lord God Jesus Christ (Wagner) [DRR#MRDSMR, FMRDDRR#] BI53 10947
The Lord imparted from above (Careless) [SSLTDDTDRMF M, MSFM] BC298 10948
The Lord in his righteousness (Dutch trad) X Kremser 10949
The Lord in Zion reigneth (Danks) [SMDRTDD, MSDT S#L, SDS] BB7 10950
The Lord is in His holy temple [DMMMRMFSS, DMMMRDM] AS485 10951
The Lord is in His holy temple (Harrington) [SDDDDDMRD T, SDRMFR] G589; I734; Z 616; AHp. 7; BB703 10952
The Lord is in His holy temple (Laufer) [SSSLLMFSS, DRMSMFM] Sap. 5 10953
The Lord is in His holy temple (Myers) [DDDDLSSSS, SLLL LTT] AU483 10954
The Lord is King (Gelineau) [SSLD, DDDL, LLLS.] BSp. 28 10955
The Lord is King (Jewish trad) X Rosh hashanah II 10956
The Lord is my light (Bischoff) [SMFMRSRMRD, DDTLSD] BB577 10957
-----. R [DSMDRSSMDR, MMT TDM] 10958
The Lord is my light (Sweney) [SSDRMMSFDRM, MMFLT] BC103 10959
-----. R [SMRDTDLS, SDMSR

RM, S] 10960
The Lord is my Shepherd (Hudson) [SSLSMDLTDS, SLTDSM] AX473 10961
The Lord is my Shepherd (Hudson) X His yoke is easy (Warren) 10962
The Lord is my Shepherd (Koschat) X Poland 10963
The Lord is our leader (Koschat) X Poland 10964
The Lord is risen again (Bach) X Ich halte treulich still 10965
The Lord my Shepherd is (Showalter) [DRMSSMRD, RMSLSMR, M] AS261 10966
The Lord, my Shepherd still has been (Binder) [MMMRMFML M, MSFMRDR] BH86 10967
The Lord of all (Jewish trad) [SDDDMRRR, RMFSLSFM] BH80 10968
The Lord of all (Sulzer) [SSDTTT LTD, SLTDRDT] BH76 10969
The Lord of glory (Mosley) [SS MMDRDLS, SDDMDR, S] AX490; AY92 10970
-----. R [DTRRRDMM, MRMFLS, DD] 10971
The Lord of the harvest calls (Showalter) [SDDDDTLS, MRMF FMRM,] AX204; AY333 10972
The Lord our God we praise (Jewish trad) X Leoni 10973
The Lord reigneth (Jewish trad) X Ashray Yod'ay 10974
The Lord -- The Lord of glory reigns (Rappaport) [SDSDRMRD, TLTDRR, SS] BH71 10975
The Lord whom earth (St Gall Cantarium, 1845) [DMFSSLLS, SLSFMFMR,] BN137; BO100 10976
The Lord's is the earth (Gelineau) [SSLD, DDDR, DDDL, LLLS,] BSp. 12 10977
The Lord's prayer (Hays) [SSLLS DDT, DTDRSM, MF] AJ433 10978
The Lord's prayer (Schuman. G-B. 1539) X Old 112th 10979
The Lord's prayer (Toews) [SSM FSSSLDLS, SSMFS] AX652 10980
The love of God (Lehman) [DDRMSLSSM, SSMRFMR] AX82 10981
The love of Jesus (Perkins) [SMMMRMFMRD, RRRRDT,] BY424 10982
-----. R [FLDMSD, RRRRDT, SMMM] 10983
The lulav (Jewish trad) [DM RDRTDRDS, MMSSFM] BH 180 10984
The Magdalen Tower hymn (Rogers) X Hymnus eucharisticus 10985
The Maid of France (French trad. noël) [LLMLTDTDL M, DRMFMR] BQ104 10986
-----. R [TTTDTLTDR, DRM LTDR] 10987
The merchants' carol (English trad) [MLTDS# LLM, FMRDT LL, M] BG146 10988
The message (Dutch trad) X Annunciation 10989
The midnight call (Ingalls) [D MRDDDRDR, MSMSSMR] AX 248; AY406 10990
The midnight cry (Winsett) [MFSSSSLSDRMD, DTLL] AX127 10991
-----. R [DTLTDLLS, DD RRRRDR] 10992
The miraculous harvest (English trad) X Capel 10993
The morning breaks; the shadows flee (Careless) [SSMDTLM RDT, RTSMRD] BC269 10994
The morning star (Hagen) [SDMDTLTSDR, MF#SMMR] AZ310-B; BA59 10995
The morning watch (Price) [SSLDRSSLDMS, RFFMS] G34; BB44 10996
The mulberry bush (English carol) X Sunny Bank 10997
The Mystic (Barnes) [SDRMFS, SDRMFS, SDRM] Y7 10998
The nail-scarred hand (McKinney) X Lubbock 10999
The name of Jesus (Lorenz)

[SDTLMSF#F, TRDTFLSS,] AM711; AU102; BB643 11000

-----. R [DSLSSFF, RTDTLS S, MD] 11001

The New Year (Mann) X Valour 11002

The ninety and nine (Sankey) [SSDDDDDTTD, DDMMDD] E584; G247; W685a; AH373; AI181; AL475; AM137; AP408; AU36; AY501; BB673; BY425 11003

The ninety-nine (Warren) [DMM MDRMD, SSSSRMFM,] AX202 11004

-----. R [SSSSDTLS, DMMMSF MR,] 11005

The Old Hundredth (Bourgeois) X Old 100th 11006

The old rugged cross (Bennard) X Old rugged cross 11007

The only Son from heaven (German Enchiridion, 1524) X Förlössningen är vunnen 11008

The open gate (Hanson) [MSF#S MDDTDS, SSDMSM] AY154 11009

-----. R [SSLFFLSMM, MRR RRMF#] 11010

The palms (Faure) [SSSMDDTL DS, RRRRRR] AH622 11011

The peace that Jesus gives (Lillenas) [MRDDTLS, FSMS MRR, MR] AU361 11012

-----. R [LSFMFMF, SFMR# MR#M, DD] 11013

The pilgrim (---) X A few more years shall roll 11014

The pilgrims' chorus (Wagner) X Pilgrim chorus 11015

The ploughboy's dream (English trad) X Forest green 11016

The praise of Christmas (English trad) [LDTLMLSFMD, DRM FSF] BG5 11017

The praises of that saint (French trad) [SDRMMFMRM, MRDTDR M] BN184; BO217 11018

-----. V [SDRMMFMRM, MR DTDRD] BO217 11019

The precious name (Doane) X Precious name 11020

The Prince of Peace (Barker) [SF#FMRD, MSSLLS, FMMR#] Z195 11021

The promised land (American trad) X Promised land 11022

The promises of God (Kirkpatrick) [MFSSSLSFMRDRD LS, S] AX472; AY124 11023

-----. R [SLSMDDDLS, SLS MRRR] 11024

The quest (Brahms) [MLDLS MFS, LSFMRDT, L] BG179 11025

The quiet hour (Green) [DDRL SM, MMF#F#S, DDSS#L] BB 329; BV309a 11026

The radiant morn (Gounod) X Radiant morn 11027

The regions beyond (Simpson) [MFSSLSMRDDLS, MFSD] AU76 11028

-----. R [DRMRDS, TDRDRM, RDDL] 11029

The righteous marching home (---) [SLDDDMDLS, SDDDMS, S] AY157 11030

The river of life (Hull. The casket) X Ich weiss einen strom 11031

The Rock of refuge (Fischer) [SDMDSLDLS, SSDRMFM] G245; I434; AH376; AT320; AU133; AX517; BB633; BZ 11032

-----. R [DRRRMMMR, RR MMFSMD] 11033

The Rock that is higher (Fischer) X The Rock of refuge 11034

The roll (Black) [DRMMMMM RDDRDDLS, D] AH530; AM 727; AT482; AX468 11035

-----. R [MFSFMFSM, MMF MRMFR,] 11036

------. V [DRMMMMMRD RDDLS, DR] AX468 11037

The rosy sequence (Sarum Gradual) [SLDTLSMD, DRM FMRMD] E238c; X548; BE 316 11038

The Sabbath Bride (Jewish trad) [LMMFMRDRL, LMSFMRD]

BH117 11039
The Sacred Heart (Dykes) [MM MRMFRMFSM, SSSSD] Eap. 44 11040
The saints of God (Hurd) [MR DTLTLSD, MRSFMRD] BL71 11041
The salutation carol (English trad., 15th c) [RRMFSFM, RFMDRM, LDD] BG36 11042
-----. R [RRFMDMRDTL, LD DRRM] 11043
The sanctity of sorrow (Spohr) X Spohr 11044
The Saviour reigns (Smith, B.E.) [DRRDDFFM, MRDSFM, SD] BI27-D 11045
The Saviour's work (English trad) [MLDTS#LDM, DLDTS#M, ML] BG69 11046
-----. R [MMMFMFSF, MRDTD RMR,] 11047
The Second tune (Tallis) [LDTL LLS#L, DTLLS#L, DF] BJ78 11048
The secret flower (Cologne G-B. 1634) [SDRMFSDRMRDRD, DSS] BG97 11049
The seer, Joseph, the seer (Neukomm) [SDSMDRSD, SRTD LTSL] BC296 11050
The seven virgins (English trad) [LDDTLSTRRML, SLSFRD] BG43 11051
The sheaves (Minor) X Bringing in the sheaves 11052
The Sheltering Rock (Penn) [SD DDMRDLS, DRRRDRM] AU23 11053
-----. R [MDLDSD, DRRMR, DRMMM] 11054
The Shepherd (Austrian trad) [DSMDSMSMDRFRD, DSM] BG161; BK148 11055
The sinner's redemption (English trad) [LLLTDTLSF#M, MMRDT L] BG51 11056
The 6th tune (Tallis) [DDDDDRR M, MRDDTD, DR] BG68 11057
The sleep of the Child Jesus (French noel, 13th c) X Gevaert 11058
The snow lay on the ground (Grieg) [MMFSLSLSM, MDS MDS, M] BQ8 11059
The snow lies thick (Shaw) [LDRDLSLL#L, SLDFSMR] BG192 11060
The Solid Rock (Bradbury) [SDMSMMRR, MFFFRDTD,] G244; H289; I330; L415; R368; T274; U219; AE203; AH370; AI141; AJ381; AR 460; AS274; AT283; AU96; AV362; AW487; AX482; AY 458; BA439; BB581; BZ 11061
-----. R [SSSSSLLL, LSMM DMMR,] 11062
The soul's Bridegroom (Drese) X Rochelle 11063
The Spirit (French trad) [MF SLSSDRMRD, MFSLS] BG154 11064
The Spirit of God like a fire (---) [SDRRMRDDTLSLS, FMS] BC213 11065
-----. R [SSMSSMSDMRDT LSL, T] 11066
The Spirit of the Lord revealeth (Wolder. Catechismus G-B. 1598) X Wolder 11067
The spiritual sailor (Southern harmony, 1835) [LMLLTDT, DLLSFM, MLM] AQ240 11068
The staff of faith (English trad) X Muswell Hill 11069
The star (German trad) [SDD RMFRMD, RMFSLFS] BK158 11070
The star-spangled banner (Smith) X National anthem 11071
The stars watch you (Grauman) [SMRFMDS, DRMLSFMF, L] BH245 11072
The story of Jesus (Jutson) [DRMRMFMRSM, DDLTLS] BY740 11073
The story that never grows old (McPhail) [MFSLSMRDRDLS, DRMR] AY355 11074
-----. R [DDTLDTLSDM, MM RDMR] 11075

The sun goes down (Jewish trad) X N'eelah melody II 11076
The sun has gone down (Norwegian folk mel) X Far verden far vel 11077
The sun in splendor rose (Scottish trad) X Selma 11078
The sweet story of old (Englebrecht) [SDDDDTDRDTD, DMRDD] AU316; AY342 11079
The sweetest name (Bradbury) X There is no name 11080
The temple of God (Warren) [S SSLSMRD, DRFMRDS, S] AX 433 11081
-----. R [MMRDSD, TTLTDS, MMRD] 11082
The three traitors (English trad) [SDRMRDTLTS, RMF#SMD] BG163 11083
The time is far spent (Methfessel's Song book, 1818) X Salem 11084
The Torah (Jassinowsky) [SFM DRMFR, SSLDRMRD] BH203 11085
The torch of Israel (Jewish trad) [MLLLLLSDTL, LMRDDT] BH256 11086
The tribes (DeRoo) [SMMMFM RRR, MRDDRRM] AI174 11087
The Trinity (Giardini) X Moscow 11088
The truth from above (English trad) [MLTDTLSLM, TDDTLSL] BG68 11089
The unclouded day (Alwood) X Unclouded day 11090
The Unity's march (Grimm's Choral buch. 1755) X Gregor's 172d metre 11091
The unseen city (Clark) [SMMM MMMFMM, MRRRDR] AY187 11092
The unseen hand (Sims) [SDD DRDLS, DMDMDRMR,] AX 467 11093
-----. R [DMSSMMRD, RDLS DMDR,] 11094
The upper room (McKinney) [SMLSMRDS, DTLDTLS, S] AU107 11095
-----. R [SSRRMRDS, SSLDTDR, S] 11096
The venite (Collection of hymns and sacred poems. Dublin. 1749) X Irish 11097
The very Angels' Bread (Meurers) [MFLSFM, LTLTDDT, LSF] BQ46 11098
The Virgin's cradle hymn (Rubbra) [SLTR, TLMRM F#, SLTRMR] BG175 11099
The voice of God again is heard (Stephens) [SMMSM DRM, RMSDMRS, S] BC289 11100
The voice of God is calling (Levenson) [SSTDRMR, SS TDMR, SSM] BH238 11101
The way is dark (Hay) [DRM MMR#MFMR#MD, DDFF] AS217 11102
-----. R [DLLSSFFM, MRL SFM, DL] 11103
The way of the cross leads home (Gabriel) X Way of the cross 11104
The wayfaring stranger (American trad) [LDRMMRMDL, LRRRLDR] AU74 11105
The whole wide world (Kirkpatrick) X Whole wide world 11106
The whole wide world (Maunder) [SSSLSSM, MMRMFFM, SS] AS368; AW340; BY395 11107
-----. R [DDMS, DFLD, DTLS F#LSM,] 11108
The whole wide world (Thompson) [SSLDLDT, TRLTLS, SSL] AV270 11109
-----. R [MMMMMFF, FFF FFM, MMM] 11110
The whole world was lost (Bliss) X Light of the world 11111
The wintry day, descending (Kimball) [SF#STLSFMFM, MR#MFST] BC292 11112
-----. R [MR#MSFMRD#RS, SF#SLTR] 11113
The wise may bring their learning (Rogers) [DDRM SFF, TTDRSM, DDR] BH246

11114
The wise men (Tours) [SMRD SMMR, DRMMSF#S,] A50b; B553; C553; D542; AH274
11115
The Word, descending (Montani) [MMRDSSFM, MMRDRTLS,] BQ50 11116
The world has need of willing men (Thompson) [SMMFMSFM, SLT DRM, MR] BC206 11117
-----. R [SSDRMFSLMSM, SSDR M] 11118
The world itself (Piae cantiones. 1582) [DRMMMRDTLS, LMF SSF] BG150 11119
The world's desire (Negro trad) [SDDDRMLTD, LSLSLTD,] BG 143 11120
The worth of suffering (Rogers) [SSSLTDSM, MSSFFM, SL] BH98 11121
Thee, Lord (Bales) [DDRMFM RDTD, MMFSMR] BL74 11122
Thee prostrate I adore (Montani) [SLSDRMR, FMRDRT, SLS] BQ48 11123
Theoctistus (Calkin) [LTDLMM M, MMRDTL, LTD] O307
11124
Theodora (Handel) [SDDTLSLR, MRFMRDS, D] D438b; H423; L296; V326; BA16; BE324
11125
Theodora (Legge) [DRMFMRM FM, SSDLSTL] W174a; AL130b; AP233b; BY217 11126
Theodore (Lutkin) [MMSLTD MS, FFMRDRLR,] G494; I713b; AH207; AR408 11127
Theodoret (Ohl) [SLTLSRDS, M MRSDRT, T] K276a; N377
11128
Theodoric (Piae cantiones. 1582) [RRLSSL, LLRTDL, SLD, S] X502; AF136; AQ296; BG78; BI85 11129
Theodulph (Teschner) X St Theodulph 11130
Theophilus (Ohl) [DMSSLMSS, MSDDTS#L, L] K389b 11131
There are hearts that never falter (Pollock) [MRDMSDTL, DLSLS MR, M] AS335 11132
There came a little child to earth (Havergal) [SSLTDM FRM, SFM, SSLT] K540
11133
There came three kings (Smith) [SSLSSDSLSS, DLTDRF] K543; AO135 11134
There comes to my heart (Bilhorn) X Sweet peace
11135
There is a flower (Geistliche kirchengesang. Cologne, 1599) X Rosa mystica
11136
There is a gate that stands ajar (Vail) X Gates ajar
11137
There is a green hill (Gower) X Meditation 11138
There is a green hill (Stebbins) X The green hill 11139
There is a happy land (Hindu air) X Happy land 11140
There is a land of pure delight (Root) X Varina 11141
There is a land where sunny vales (Huish) [MMFSDTRD, TTLSRMLS,] BC72 11142
-----. R [DSDSDTDRDLT, TF STF] 11143
There is a mystic tie (Achron) [DL#LDDRSS, DFFMMRDR] BH137 11144
There is a mystic tie (Jewish trad) X Hallel 11145
There is a place (McAfee) X McAfee 11146
There is an arm (Showalter) [MRDSMRDT, LSFFFM, SD] AS268 11147
There is an everlasting home (Mattoni) [DRMRDRRM, MF MDMSM, M] BQ69 11148
There is an hour of peace (Peterson) [DRMMMRMFF F, MFSMRD] BC172 11149
-----. R [SFMSLSF, FMRRS FM, MF] 11150
There is beauty all around (McNaughton) X Home 11151
There is life for a look (Taylor) X Latakia 11152

There is never a day so dreary (Tours) X Tours 11153
There is no name (Bradbury) [SDDMDLLD, LSDMDMR, S] AI388; AM652; AO624; AS397; AV138; AW440; AX22 11154
-----. R [SLLLLSMS, SLLSMMR, S] 11155
There is power in the blood (Jones) [SSSSSSLLLS, DTRD# R, D] AI394; AT193; AX278 11156
-----. R [SDMMRDDLS, TDRDRM, S] 11157
There is sunlight on the hilltop (Haughey) [SSMSRMDL, LDSDT DR, S] BB612 11158
-----. R [MFSMRMRDS, MFSMD MR,] 11159
There lives a God (Lob) [SLSMD FMMR, RMRDRMS] BH61 11160
There many shall come (Then Swenska Psalmbok. 1695) X Stockholm 11161
There shall be showers (McGranahan) X Showers of blessing 11162
Therefore give us love (Scottish trad) X Caledonia 11163
There's a beautiful, beautiful land (Brenneman) [DRMRDRDL S, DRMSMR, M] AX589; AY135 11164
-----. R [SSLSSSMDM, SMM RDR, S] 11165
There's a great day coming (Thompson) [SSDDDD, DMM RD, LSDDD] AU333 11166
-----. R [SSLS, MMFM, DDDDDD MR] 11167
There's a land (Webster) X Sweet by and bye 11168
There's a song (New: Martin) [SSSLTDRMRDLS, SSTL] AI65a 11169
There's a song (Root) X Like a strong and raging fire 11170
There's a stranger at the door (Excell) X Let Him in 11172
There's no other name like Jesus (Belden) [SDMR#MSMD, TDR D#RFM, S] BB517 11173
-----. R [SMMD, TDRD#RLS M, SMMD,] 11174
There's sunshine in my soul today (Sweney) X Sunshine 11175
Theresa (Sullivan) X St Theresa 11176
These things shall be (Levenson) [SSDMMRFM, MRFMRDTD] BH237 11177
Thessalonica (German) [SDLS FM, DRMRRD, MRMR] K400 11178
Thetford (Atkinson) [DDDRRM, SFMMRR, RRLS] BR379 11179
Thetford (Aufranc) [MFFMR DDDFMR, TDRDS] BB374 11180
They the builders of the nation (Durham) [SSLDDRMD, LL SDDMR, M] BC173 11181
Thine advent Lord (Crueger) X Nun danket 11182
Thine arm, O Lord (Hassler) X Passion chorale 11183
Thine for service (Leech) X I have made my choice 11184
Thine forever, God of love (Pleyel) X Pleyel's hymn 11185
Thine house (Barnes) [SMDS SSLTDR, SMDL, LR] AD411 11186
Thine is the glory (Handel) X Judas Maccabaeus 11187
Thine the glory (Husband) X We praise thee, O God 11188
Think gently of the erring one (Wurtemberg G-B. 1784) X Ellacomb 11189
Think not, when you gather (Tullidge) [SDMLSLSFR, R MMMMDD] BC21 11190
Think on thy way (Scholfield) [MDLS, DMSMDT, FRTSSR] AI206 11191
Third mode melody (Tallis) [MSSSSLLT, TTTTDT, MT] A424b; E92; J499a; W559b; X675; BY505b 11192

Thirsk (Wrigley) [SSDTLSMM, RDDMRDLS,] D430 11193
Thirsting (Bourgeois) X Bourgeois 11194
Thirsting for the living fountain (Hungarian mel) [MMDSLTDDS, RRDTLSF#] BL45 11195
This child we dedicate (Singer) [MSMMFSLRR, RFMRMFS] BH240 11196
This endris nyght (English carol, 15th c) [DMFSSLTLS, SDTLSLF] E20; G115; R180; W595; X72; AL194a; AN168; AQ291; BG39; BV377; BY531 11197
This feast of the Law (Jewish trad) X Hakafos melody 11198
This house we dedicate (Asper) [SDRMFMRTD, RMLSF#S, R] BC176 11199
This is not my place of resting (Woodbury) X Dorrnance 11200
This is the day (A Monk of Gethsemani) [DDTDMMRRDTT, LTDSD] BN182 11201
This is the day the Lord hath made (Arne) X Arlington 11202
This is the image of our Queen (Catholic) [SLTDSRMD, DTLSRFM, S] BO77 11203
-----. R [SMLSMDLS, MMMLS#LT, D] 11204
This is the image of our Queen (Slovak hymn) [SDDTDRDRMD, MRMSFM] BQ82 11205
This joyful Eastertide (Oudean. Amsterdam Psalter) X Vreuchten 11206
This new Christmas carol (English trad) [LDDRMMLTDTTL, LTDT] BG29 11208
Thomissön (Thomissön) [RRRDRTDL, FMRD#TDR, R] M389 11209
Thomisson (Tomissön. (Psalmebog, 1569) X Island 11210
Thompson (Thompson) X Softly and tenderly 11211
Thornbury (Harwood) [SMTDLDT, RSLFMRM, SM] E545; F256; J159; W215; X255c; AC307; BE375; BV426; BY264 11212
Thornes House (Grundy) [MRDRLS, SDRMFR, TMSF] BV186 11213
Thorney Abbey (---) [MMSRRRMF, FFMRRM, ML] BR315 11214
Thou art the way (Pollock) [MMFSSFMR, RRMFSM, MM] AX341; AY209 11215
Thou delightest, O Lord (Brown) [SSSLTDTDFLDM, MMRL] U37; AI18 11216
Thou dost not weep alone (Careless) [SDMMRFFLFFM, MMMDD] BC181 11217
Thou ever present Perfect Friend (Rinder) [SDDRRMRD, SLTDTLS, S] BH41 11218
Thou, my everlasting portion (Vail) X Close to thee 11219
Thou spotless Lamb of God (Kirkpatrick) [DMMMFS, SSMRDR, DMMM] AX310 11220
Thou that art so fair (Pothier) [DRMFSLS, DSLSFM, RFM] BN139; BP78 11221
Thou thinkest, Lord, of me (Lorenz) X Amid the trials 11222
Thou warrior of the Lord (Catholic) [DMMRMDLS, MRMFM, MSM] BP89 11223
-----. R [SLTDRMRRRMFSLS, SF] 11224
Thou who, hero-like (Catholic) [MFRMDRTD, RLRDDTLS] BO138 11225
Thou, whose almighty word (Trebel) [DDRMRD, RRMFMR, MTLS,] M111 11226
Though deepening trials (Careless) [SFMRLSFM, DLSFFMF#S,] BC285 11227
Though in the outward Church below (Mozart) X Ariel 11228
Though our hearts dwell lovingly (Blumenthal) X Blumenthal 11229
Though your sins be as scarlet (Doane) X Cleansing 11230

Three kings (Flemish trad) [ML TDRMRFM, MRMDTDL] BG80 11231

Three kings of orient (Hopkins) [MRDLTDTL, MRDLTDT] A51; B554; C554; G102; R 176; Z204; AB122; AC96; AF 143; AG82; AH269; AN176; AO136; AQ300; AR141; AU 139; AW90; BB107; BD229; BG195; BI88; BK161; BL17; BZ 11232

-----. R [TRDDDSDLD, DDD SDL] 11233

Through the day (Barnby) X Kirkdale 11234

Throw out the life-line (Ufford) X Life line 11235

Thule (German folk song) [ML LMMFD, DRMFRM, MLL] E371 11236

Thuringia (Drese) X Rochelle 11237

Thuringia (German trad) X Christmas dawn 11238

Thy brother (Heller) [SDDRMFSF M, MLLRMF, T] BH197 11239

Thy faithful servant, Lord, doth yearn (Shelley) [MR#TTRDL L, S#LTDRDRT,] BH167 11240

Thy God reigneth (McGranahan) [SF#SMFSLTD, DLSS, SF#S] AM670 11241

Thy great bounty (Byles) [MMM SSDDMMRFM, MMMF] AD314; AK259; AR340; BF500 11242

Thy kingdom come (Wennerberg) [MDTLTMMLSFS, SDTDR] BE204 11243

Thy life (MacFarren) [DFRM DL, LSMFRRM, DDD] B238; C238; D604a 11244

Thy life was given (MacFarren) X Thy life 11245

Thy little ones (Schulz) X Paedia 11246

Thy love to me (Avis) [MFMM RD, RDRR#M, MFMMR] AS284 11247

Thy praise, O Lord (Norden) [SDDDTLSSS, SMMMFMR] BH 183 11248

Thy spirit, Lord, has stirred (Schreiner) [MMMMDRRT, TDRMFMRM,] BC204 11249

Thy testimonies (Whittington) [SMMMMMSDM, MDDRMDR] BI38-D 11250

Thy will be done (Barnby) X Sunset 11251

Thy will be done (McGranahan) [SMMMRMFMRR, SRRRDR] AX390; AY478 11252

-----. R [LLLDMRDR, SMS FMRDT] 11253

Thy will be done! (McKinney) [SDDDRMMRR, SRRRMFF] AU103 11254

-----. R [SLTDSDRDT, SLT RTRD] 11255

Thy word have I hid (Beale) [MMMMSFFM, MRRMFFFM,] AW605 11256

Thy word have I hid (Sellers) [SDDDMRDS, FMRDRRM, S] AI155; AM671; AT180; AU 389; AV372; AX141 11257

-----. R [SFMMMMRMF, FFFFFLS] 11258

Thy word is a lamp to my feet (Sellers) X Thy word have I hid 11259

Thy word is to my feet a lamp (Jassinowsky) [SDDDDTMRD, DRMFMDR,] BH36 11260

Tibberton (Williams) [DDDMFS, MLLSRM, MMMM] D374b 11261

Tichfield (Richardson) [MSFM SDTLS, SDFMMRR,] D188a; J55; K495; O32; V624; W434; AP137; BA873; BN35; BO169; BY361 11262

-----. V [MFMSDTLS, SDFM MRR, M] BN35 11263

Tideswell (Hopkins) [SMMRDD FM, DMF#SLRDL,] D84 11264

Tidings (Llewellyn) [SDRMFSM RDRD, SLTDR] BV439 11265

Tidings (Walch) [DMFSSSDM RRD, DTLSST] A261; B474; C474; D249a; G475; I654;

J314; K224; M102; N376; P392; R491; S382; T195; U395; V768; Y270; Z529; AB367; AC306; AD 375; AE350; AF302; AG257; AH 462; AJ283; AK380; AL253; AM 10; AO516; AP390; AR557; AS372; AT451; AU151; AV264; AW328; BA351; BB449; BF534; BR382; BZ 11266

-----. R [TLSDL, TLSM, MFMM RD] 11267

Til fridens hem (Gustaf) [SMRDS, SMMFMMR, LFD#R] N624 11268

Tilak (Bonner) [MFSLFRMFS, DRMFLTD] BY341 11269

Tillkomme ditt rike (Wennerberg) X Thy kingdom come 11270

Tillman (Tillman) [MMMMDSS S, SRMFSM, MM] AT439; AU 300; AX401 11271

-----. R [LLLLSSSS, SRMFSM, LL] 11272

Tiplady (McCutchan) [SSRRDRM RD, SSRRDRM,] G404 11273

'Tis midnight (Bradbury) X Olive's Brow 11274

'Tis not the large, the huge the vast (Heller) [SSSSSFSLTD, DTLLSF] BH235 11275

'Tis religion that can give (Abbot) [SSSMFSM, SSLLSMR, FF] AS296; AX633; AY20 11276

'Tis so sweet (Kirkpatrick) X Trust in Jesus 11277

'Tis sweet to sing (Asper) [SD TLSDRDRM, SSFMMR] BC187 11278

-----. R [SRDDTRDRM, DDTLLTD] 11279

'Tis the blessed hour of prayer (Doane) X Doane II 11280

'Tis the day of Resurrection (Bragers) [DMSSLTDS, MRM DRM, DM] BP34 11281

'Tis the harvest time (Hall) [SSDMMDDDLL, LSDMFM] AX206; AY336 11282

-----. R [MRDRDS, MFSMR, MRDRD] 11283

'Tis the month of our Mother (French hymnal) [MMMRMSLS, MRRRRDRM,] AH136; BO 61 11284

-----. R [SSMSMSLSF, FFR FRFS] 11285

'Tis winter (Heller) [LTLTD DRDRM, MSFMMR] BH198 11286

Tiverton (Grigg) [SDRMRDTL TD, MRSDTLS,] D382b; L 37; W57; X456; BA329; BY 292b 11287

-----. V [SDRMDTLTD, MRSD TLS] W57 11288

To Christ, the Prince of Peace (Montani) [MSDFMR, RMLR DT, TDDR] BQ63 11289

To God be the glory (Doane) [SSLTDSDRSRM, MFLFM] AI142; AM667; AT41; BB 647; BV280; BY32 11290

-----. R [MFSMFS, SMDRM R, RMF] 11291

To God on high (Plainsong. 1539) [DRMFSFMRM, MMRMFR] A303; B424; C424; D303; E103; I93; J 132; K160; M141; N300; O2; P1; Q33; W407; X561; AA80; AF2; AH624; AI28; AK2; AM 92; AN488; AW568; AZ132-A; BA648; BI21; BQ200; BR 153 11292

-----. V [DMFSFMRM, MMR FRDTD] O2 11293

-----. V [DMFSFMRM, MM RFMRDT] P1 11294

-----. V [DMFSFMRM, MRM FMRD#D,] BO260 11295

To God our Father (Becker) [SSFSDLLSFSD, RRRMF] BN210 11296

To Jesus' heart all burning (Catholic trad) [MFSSF# LSDM, MRMFSSF] AH138; BO25 11297

-----. R [STTTTDS, SRDTL SFM, M] 11298

To Jesus' heart, all burning (Montani) [DSLRFTDM, MSF MRDR, R] BQ61 11299

-----. R [MMMF#S#LM, DD DRMF, LMM] 11300

To kneel at thine altar (Lourdes

Pilgrim hymn) X Immaculate Mary 11301
To Nephi, Seer of olden time (Clayson) [DSSSFMFS, MRDSF M, SL] BC186 11302
-----. R [SMFSLSFMRD, SMS DLS,] 11303
To the God of all creation (Beethoven) X Sardis 11304
To the Lord in the hour (Gelineau) X Out of the depths 11305
To the Name that brings salvation (Meiningen G-B.) X St Leonard 11306
To the Name that brings salvation (Ett) X Oriel 11307
To the Name that brings salvation (Montani) [SDLRDTDS, LTSFM LLR,] BQ16 11308
To the work (Doane) X Toiling on 11309
To Thee, above all creatures' gaze (Haile) [MRLSMRLS, MRDTDTLS,] BH126 11310
To Thee, O Jesus Christ (Bourgeois) X Old 100th 11311
To Thee, O Lord (Burney) X Truro 11312
To Thee, O Lord (Schemelli. G-B.) [MSFMRRMF#S, RMRDRDT] BI9-D 11313
To Thee we give ourselves (Jewish trad) X Kee hinay kachomer 11314
To thy pastures, fair and large (Malan) X Hendon 11315
To us a child of hope (Mason) X Zerah 11316
To us is born (Hohenfurth ms.) X Dies est laetitiae 11317
To victory (Barnby) [SSLMSSL M, MFSLLTDR] B533; C533; D514; I418; L537; AH437; AO 400; AP539; AV216; BA937; BD 89; BF466; BI7; BR509 11318
-----. R [SSSSSSSSSS, SLLDRM] 11319
To You have I lifted (Gelineau) X I lift up my eyes 11320
Toc H (Shaw) [DTLMRDRM, SLS MSLSM,] F500 11321
Today (Mason) [SSMMDR, SLF#S, SSMMSL,] V271; W686; AM 388; AP398; AY313 11322
Today, while the sun shines (Stephens) [SSDRMDLS#LTL, RRTDR] BC215 11323
-----. R [DMDMMRDRM, DR TRMFM] 11324
Toiling on (Doane) [MFSSSS DRMMMM, RMFF] AT435; AU64; AX185 11325
-----. R [MFSDMR, RMFSFM, MFSD] 11326
Tollite hostias (Saint Saëns) [SSSDSS, LSFMRFMLLS] BQ160 11327
Tomer (Tomer) X God be with you 11328
Ton-mân (Evans) [MDRMSMR, MLS#LTDT, D] A82b; E270; X47; AD397; AF167 11329
Tonus peregrinus (Pre-reformation mel) X St Austin (Bristol Tune book, 1876) 11330
Ton-y-botel (Williams) X Ebenezer 11331
Too late (Lindsay) [MMRMDR RMRD, SSF#SDR] I743 11332
Too late, too late (Brahms) X Lucy 11333
Toplady (Hastings) [SLSMD LS, DRMRDTD, T] A471b; B217b; C217a; D336b; G204; H244; I279; J379b; K333b; L402a; M181; N422; O27b; P284; Q376; R271; S237a; T393; U100; V249b; Y374a; Z294; AA325; AB165; AD209; AE284; AF358; AG147; AH 356; AI137; AJ140b; AK217; AL267c; AM421a; AO260a; AR180; AS211; AT103; AU 171; AV236; AW148; AX57; AY312; AZ581-L; BA434a; BB474; BC382; BE293; BF 353; BR313; BZ 11334
Torchbearers (Hyatt) [DTLTS LSL, MFSLDRTS,] Y156; AC229 11335
Torches (Spanish trad) [DDD TTTLS, SLTTTLTL] BG81 11336

Torgau (Grobe) [MMSFRDMRD, MRDDDRM] AA482 11337
Torgau (Latin, 12th c) X Christ lag in todes banden 11338
Toronto (---) [SSDMSLSSM, MFMMRLS] D589c 11339
Toronto (Hopkins) [MSDMRM FM, FLSMRDTD] L226; BA 385 11340
Tota pulchra es (Balthasar) [SM DRM, SLDD, STTSSMM] BQ212 11341
Totteridge (Nicholson) [MFSLDR, SDSLSFS, DRS] F302 11342
Touch me, Lord Jesus (McKinney) [MRLDT, FFMRM, MMRDSF,] AU463 11343
-----. R [FFDRMM, RRDRM, MMRDS] 11344
Touch not the cup (---) X Ye elders of Israel 11345
Toulon (Meter: 10 10 10 10: Bourgeois) [DRMFMRDDTD, MFSLS] A220; B451; C451; K183b; Q483; R144; S481; Z472; AA486; AB329; AD77; AE321; AF432; AK157; AM135; AN67; AO259; AR520; AV160; BA310; BD154; BE108; BF545; BI18-D; BJ20; BR376; BY316 11346
Tourjèe (Tourjèe) X Wellesley 11347
Tours (Tours) [MFSDTLSM, DRMDRMRD,] B495; C495; D205a; G129; M205; P358; R 186; S111; T35; V187; Z113; AB 112; AC320; AD468; AE77; AG301; AH201; AJ50; AK138; AM646; AR175; AT507; AV367; BA817; BB281; BD16; BF619; BR537; BX329 11348
Tovo l'fonecho (Jewish trad) [DT DL, MRRRRRRDRDTL] BH324 11349
Town of Bethlehem (Davies) X Christmas carol 11350
Towner (Towner) [MFMR#MD, RR DTD, MFMR#M] AE185 11351
Tozer (Tozer) [SLSMMRRD, LDSD MRR, S] AO278 11352
Trackless ways (Williams) [DDRM SSFM, SLLLDDTL,] AD455 11353
Traeder nu til Herrens Bord (Rosenmüller) X Nassau 11354
Tranmer (Hayes) [DMSFMLS FM, SLSFMR, R] F168 11355
Tranoscius (Slovak trad) [LLLMSF#M#R, RF#MF#S# LM, L] M332 11356
Tranquillity (Gregor's Choral buch) X Old 271st 11357
Transfiguration (Goss) X St Casimer 11358
Transfiguration (Lutkin) [MM LLSFSLR, RMSLTS, S] I479 11359
Transfiguration (Olsson) [SLT DMRDTD, SDRMSFM] J316b 11360
Transylvania (Hungarian chorale mel. 16th c) X Du meiner seelen 11361
Travis Avenue (McKinney) [MF SLSDDTT, RMFSLTL] AT342 11362
-----. R [DDDDDSLDT, RRRRR ST] 11363
Tread softly (Doane) X Be silent 11364
Treasure (König. Choralbuch. 1738) X Ich will dich lieben 11365
Trebel (Trebel) [SDSMDLRDT, RMSFRDT] M309 11366
Tredeca (German carol. 13th c) [DRRDLSTD, DMSLSMDL] M467; BG117 11367
-----. V [DRRDLSLD, MSL SMRDL] BG117 11368
Trefaenan (Welsh trad) [SLS MSLSM, SLSMRDR, S] G160; X158; Z248 11369
-----. V [SLSMSLSM, DDMDL TD,] X158 11370
Tregaron (James) [RLSLMFSL, TDRDTL] A354a 11371
Trentham (Jackson) [MMMFDM, SFMRMR, MFLS] G180; J470; N182; R235; S84; T414a; U 213; Z450; AB93; AC61; AD 187; AE143; AF234; AG123; AK191; AL148b; AM438; AP

270b; AR220; AT52; AV146; AW135; BF260; BZ 11372

Tres magi de gentibus (Andernach G-B. 1608) [SSMFSSM, SSMFSSM, MM] E647; W468; X305; BY260a 11373

-----. V [SSMFSSM, MSSMFSS M, M] X305 11374

Treuer heiland (Kocher) X Dix 11375

Trewen (Evans) [LDTLS#LTL, TDTDRDRM,] W560; BY570 11376

Trewks (Fischer) [MMRDLS, RRMFMR, DDDT] L180 11377

Tribute (Hopkins) [DDDFMRD, DLSDMRRS, D] D140 11378

Trinity (Hermann) X O heilige dreifaltigkeit 11379

Trinity (Giardini) X Moscow 11380

Trinity (Pieraccini) X Santa Trinita 11381

Trinity (Wesley, S.S.) [MDFR SM, DDDFFM, DTDR] Y17; AC107; AD133 11382

-----. V [MDFRSM, DDFFM, R DDRM] AD133 11383

Trinity College (Dykes) [DMSDSF SM, RMF#SSTLS,] F57b; J117b; K235; W339; AA118 11384

Trisagion (Smart) [SSLSMRDRR M, MRDSF] A121; B289; C289; D170a; F288; J148; M485; W 169; AA285; AL42 11385

Tristitia (Barnby) X St Chrysostom 11386

Triumph (Cornell) [SDTDSLLRD# R, RRRMFT] BR150 11387

Triumph (Gauntlett) [DMSSSLS M, SSDTLLS, M] D321b; J114a; K50; W134; AD172; AL108; AP 812; AW617; AZ91-E; BA235; BY221 11388

Triumph No. 2 (Vibbert) [SDTDRM D, DFFFFM, SDT] U304 11389

Triumphant (Elliott) [SDSMRDLS, MFSLTDMR] C484; D463a; E 40; I90; L341; R497; T133b; V191; W25; AJ155; AM58; BE 290; BF631; BR77; BV67; BY 194a 11390

Triumphant Sion (Knapp) X Wareham 11391

Triumphantly doth Christ (Biggs) [SSFMRMRD, TDRM FS, SL] BN77 11392

Triumphs today the Lord of Life (Gesius) X Gesius 11393

Troas (Maclagan) [DMFSDTL S, MFSLSMDR] D229 11394

Troubled soul, thy God is calling (Davis) X Sitting at the feet of Jesus 11395

Troyte (Troyte) [MMMMMM FS, FFFFFMRM,] B391; C 391b; F357b; AO149 11396

Troyte, No. 1 (Troyte) [MMF S, FMRM, MMRD, RDTD] D 667a; Eap. 59; I736; K408b; V42b; AL430b; AP504b 11397

Troyte, No. 2 (Troyte) [MMR D, FFMR, SSFM, RRD.] D461; E494; W14; AL174c; AP151; BR129 11398

True freedom (Jewish trad) X Az yasheer 11399

True happiness (Southern harmony) [MSSLDR, MRDLSM S, RRM] BZ 11400

True-hearted (Booth) [SSLSM FSDTLS, MRDTT] BY303 11401

-----. R [FDRDLLLLTDL, MRDTR] 11402

True-hearted, whole-hearted (Stebbins) [DSDMDMSLSF# SM, FSSL] G255; I420; AH 456; AS326; AT410; AV383; BZ 11403

-----. R [SF#SLS, MR#MFM, LSF#SMM] 11404

Truett (McKinney) [MR#MF DMRD, SF#SLSR, MR#] AT 174; AU417 11405

-----. R [SMFSFDRM, LLS MF#MF#S,] 11406

Truman (Holbrook) [SMTRDLSM S, SLRMFLS,] G210b; I304b 11407

Trumpet (Pierre) [SSLTD, DTLSLS, SSLTD,] AJ431 11408

Trumpet call (Geibel) [SMMMM

MM, MMDTDFSFF] C538a; G 283; U288; AE218; AI329a; AO 394; AT419; AV365; BA933; BF473; BI113 11409

-----. R [SMMSF, SRD#RLS, SLMFF] 11410

Truro (Burney) [DMFSSLTD, SDS FMRDFM] A484; B187; C308b; D265; E420; F220a; G126; H 143; I7; J8a; K444; L346; M91; R152; S114; V126; W369; X 337b; Y115; Z224; AA428; AB 336; AC260; AD363; AE120; AF 82; AG108; AJ129; AK363; AM 61; AN103; AO178; AQ54; AR 186; AS151; AT102; BA177; BB 440; BD77; BE326; BF544; BI 28; BK106; BV39; BX133; BY 645; BZ 11411

Trust (Dykes) X Rock of ages 11412

Trust (Kettle) [MMMFMRMFFF M, RRMFF] AB403; BF668 11413

Trust (Mendelssohn) [SSLSDMRD T, LTDFMRD,] A448; B243; C243 a; D415; G33; G33; L88b; V502; W382; AA81; AB66; AD324; AN 2; BB257; BD208; BF517; BH87; BI8; BR160; BX11 11414

Trust (Ohl) [MRDSLS, FMRS, SFM RDL,] K407a 11415

Trust (Stockton) X Stockton 11416

Trust (Torrance) X Moredun 11417

Trust and obey (Towner) [DRMM RDDMSSFM, MMFL] AE210; AH 420; AI400; AM700; AR485; AS 269; AT260; AU390; AV373; AW 486; AX465; AY454; BB582; BY 491; BZ 11418

-----. R [SRSMMMLMSF, FFF MRM] 11419

Trust him (Gabriel) [SSMRDSS, DDLFLD, TLS] AX464 11420

-----. R [MRDRMSS, LLLRDT, LSD] 11421

Trust in Jesus (Kirkpatrick) [MR DTLDLS, DMSMRDR, M] AE302; AI236; AM699; AR276; AS272; AT258; AU284; AV322; AW488; AX458; AY98; BB588; BZ 11422

-----. R [MSSMRDMR, MSS MRDR, M] 11423

Trust in Jesus (Moore) [SDD MDLDS, MSLSMMR, S] AX 461; AY101 11424

-----. R [SMLS, SLSMMR, SD DMDL] 11425

Trust, No. 1 (Mendelssohn) X Trust 11426

Trust, No. 2 (Wilms) X Hague 11427

Trust, try, and prove me (Leech) X Giving 11428

Trust your hand into His (Penner) [SSLDMSFMRM, MSLSMR] AX463 11429

-----. R [SSDTLS, SSLSFM, MFSS] 11430

Trusting (Fischer) X Coming to the cross 11431

Trusting (Kirkpatrick) X Trust in Jesus 11432

Trusting in Jesus (Hall) [SD MRDLS, TDRSLSM, SD] AY 95 11433

-----. R [MD, DL, RSTLSF#S, SDMRD] 11434

Trusting Jesus (Sankey) [MRFM MRD, DLDLSDMR, M] AM682; AP521; AT259; AU328; AX 459 11435

-----. R [SMSMMRR, MTDD RLT, DD] 11436

Truth (Freylinghausen) [SMF SLSFM, RRMMRDT, T] AZ82-C(app) 11437

Truth (Troup) [MRDRMS, FMD TRD, SFMS] AS445 11438

Truth eternal (Schreiner) [MFS SDRM, SLTDTLLS, S] BC189 11439

Truth reflects upon our senses (Tillman) [MMMDRMRD, DD DRDLS, S] BC188 11440

-----. R [FFFFDRMM, SSS MRDR, M] 11441

Tryggare kan ingen vara (Swedish) X Sandell 11442

Tryggare kan ingen vara (Widéen) X Security 11443

Tu, Christe, nostrum gaudium (Grenoble church mel) X

Deus tuorum militum 11444
Tu vins, Jesus (Freylinghausen. G-B. 1704) [LMRDTLS#LL, DD RMFMR] AD63; AQ48; AZ83-B 11445
-----. V [LMRDTLS#L, DRMFM RDD,] AZ83-B 11446
Tubingen (---) [SSDTLSFM, M MRSSF#S, S] BR151 11447
Tucker (Abbey) [MMFMMRDR, RMFMRDTD,] L508 11448
Tudor (Jewson) [MFMMRDTD, RMTD RS, SL] BA563; BY31 11449
Tugwood (Gatty) [SSSSSLLS, SDR MSFMR,] E146; BV362 11450
Tullar (Tullar) [SF#FMSD, DTL S, STLLSD,] AT437; AU343 11451
-----. R [RD#MRTSDLS, RD# MRTSD] 11452
Tunbridge (Clark) [LDTMFRM, DMRSLTD, ML] E88; F87; X 474; BE187; BJ95; BV533a 11453
Tunbridge (Walch) X Tidings 11454
Turin (Giardini) [SSSSLDTLS, FMLSSFM] M479 11455
Turle (Turle) X Armagh 11456
Turn your faces toward the morning (Fillmore) [DDDRMFSLSM, DDDRMF] AY469 11457
-----. R [DDTLSLLSFM, DDTLS L] 11458
Turner (---) [DMMFRSSS, MFRFM RD, D] ALSuppl 11459
Turpin's Litany (Turpin) [SSLDT LS, DDRMFMRM, M] B142a; C142IIIb; D529Ib 11460
Tviflan ur min sjal försvinne (Wessnitzer) [DRMSFMRD, RRMS SF#S, D] N79 11461
'Twas like a dream (Schumann) X Canonbury 11462
Twilight (Barnby) X Merrial 11463
Twilight (Hopkins) [MRDTLS, SLD S, SLTDRM] C17b; D10b; O564 11464
Twilight (Judefind) [SSDDTTLFTL S, SDRMD] H36 11465
Twinkling stars (German trad) [DRMMFRLS, MSSFFSF] A245 11466
Two fatherlands (Lester) [SM SLDTS, FMDRRM, SFM] Y 126; AC331 11467
Two little hands (Ogden) [DMM RDRMRMS, SSLSMR] AY300 11468
-----. R [MSDFLD, SLSMRRR F, MS] 11469
Two little hands (Warren) [MM MFMMRDD, DRRSFM, M] AX 625 11470
Twyford (Blake) [DRFMRDTLS, LTDMSMR,] F36; BV482 11471
Tyholland (German trad) [DM SLSMFS, DLTDSSFM,] W452a; BV613a; BY319b 11472
Tynemouth (Choron) [DDRMF SFM, LF#SSF#S, RT] Y2 11473
Tynemouth (Hemy) X St Catherine 11474
Tyrley, tyrlow (Warlock) [LM MRRDDT, TDRMDRTS] BG169 11475
Tyrolean cradle song (Tyrolese trad) [SDDRMSSFMMRD, SDDR] BV95a 11476
Tyrolese (Tyrolese trad) X Falan-tidings 11477
Tysk (German mel. sung at Tysk Church, Stockholm) [DSLSFM, SSLTDT, RSL] A 477 11478
Tytherton (West) X Moravia 11479

U

Ubi caritas (Plainsong M 6) [DDRMMRMFMRMRDDDR] BM15; BN87 11480
Uffingham (Clark) [LLSFMTD TLS#, MMMRDR] E434; F274; Q323; V289; W275a; X564; AA418; AF89; AL124a; AM 416; AP232a; BE94; BJ81; BY338 11481
-----. V [LSFMDTLS#, MMRD RDTD,] Q323 11482
Ulster (Lowry) X All the way 11483

Ultima (Moffatt) [MDRMDLTD, RMDDRD, MD] S439; W586a 11484

Ultor omnipotens (Sullivan) [SS SSSSSDTLL, LSFMR] D198 11485

Un flambeau (French trad) [SDD TDRMFMR, SDDTDR] Y304; AF124 11486

Unafraid ("G. E. M. G.") [SSLSFM, SSLSFM, MFSL] AE453 11487

Unami (Rau) [MSDTTLLS, DRMF SMRR] AZ858-I 11488

Unanswered yet? the prayer (Tillman) [MR#MDMSFDRMM, MMMFM] BC286 11489

Unclouded day (Alwood) [SSDDDD DMRDLS, SSDD] AH539; AT484; AU81; AX608; AY150 11490

-----. R [SLSMDMD, SLSMRDM MR,] 11491

Unde et memores (Monk) [MMDDR MMMFS, MRMFF] A189; B333; C333; D228b; J278; S355; W320; AD263; AH222; AK340; AL222; AM579; AR589; BY307 11492

Under his wings (Sankey) [MFF# SSSSLMSF, RMFLS] AI307; AM78; AS263; AX525; BB587 11493

-----. R [SMSDTLTD, DSMLSM MR,] 11494

Underbar en st'jarna blid (Berggren) [MDDTDLS, LTDFM RDT, M] N52 11495

Undique gloria (Elvey) [SSSDD RRRRM, DTLS, SL] J418; K287; M600 11496

Undique gloria (Reay) [SDSSFMDT LS, FMRM, LR] AB43 11497

Une vaine crainte (French carol) X Grace soit 11498

Union Square (Dykes) X Blairgowrie 11499

Unitas Fratrum (Bohemian Br., 1566) [DTLSSDRD, DSLSDT] A194b 11500

Unity (Mason) [DMMFMM, MRRF FM, MSSL] L598; AY301 11501

Unity (Warren) [DMMSSLLS, SRFM, DMMS] AS85 11502

Unity (Woodman) [SDDMSD, DTS SLS, SSDD] S472 11503

Universal praise (Whinfield) [DDRMFSSLTDMR, SSF#] A290e; Eap. 56; AD8 11504

University (Collignon) [SFM RDDRMSFM, SMDLS] E93; F178; W498; X653; AL352a; AP254b; BY212a 11505

University College (Gauntlett) [MDLSFMR, MDSSSF#S, MR] A558; B116; C116; D506a; E467; F291; H90; J50; K35; L270; T392; V489; W533; X 619; AB184; AK233; AL406; AM479; AN65; AO411; AP 537; AS449; BA584; BR398; BV584; BX94; BY524a; 11506

University hymn (Smith) [SSSS DT, DTLSF#S, FFSM] Y150 11507

Un'saneh tokef (Jewish trad) [DMDDD, LLLTDRDTDLD] BH328 11508

Unsearchable riches (Sweney) [SSSSMSDDDD, RRRDDR] AW454; AX20 11509

-----. R [RSFMD, MRDTDLS, MMMM] 11510

Unser Herrscher [unser König] (Neander) X Neander 11511

Unter lilien jener freuden (G-B mit noten. 1890) [ML SSRRSFFM, DTLSF#S] AW 32 11512

Unto him, for whom, this day (Montani) [MDRMFRM, MSS FRMMRD] BQ116 11513

Unto the hills (Beimel) [LTT DLTSL, LTRDTDLT,] BH13 11514

Unto us a boy is born (Piae cantiones. 1582) X Puer nobis 11515

Unveil mine eyes (Gardiner's Sacred melodies. 1812) X Belmont 11516

Up! Arouse thee, O beautiful Zion (Robertson) [MRFMRRM FSF, MSSDSL] BC283 11517

Up, awake, ye defenders of Zion (Becket) X Red, white

and blue 11518
Upham (Lutkin) [MDLLSSDMS, FMDMRR, R] I297; BH226 11519
Uplift the song of praise (Rogers) [SMMMSS, FMDDTD, MRRS] BH261 11520
Uplift the voice and sing (Seymour) [SDDMDS, FMRDRMR, TDD] BO106 11521
-----. R [FDDDFFM, LMMMLLT, LL] 11522
Upon the cross of Calvary (Robertson) [SLSDRMFS, DFMRDR, FM] BC221 11523
Upon the first day (Taylor) [SDD TLSLS, SSSLLSFM,] AX67 11524
-----. R [DRFMRDTD, MRMRD TLS,] 11525
Upp, min tunga (Swedish Koralbok. 1697) X Riddarholm 11526
Uppfaren är var herre (Swedish, 17th c) X St Lawrence, Lund 11527
Upsala I (Crueger) X Schmuecke dich 11528
Upsala II (Crueger) X Schmuecke dich 11529
Upwick (Whinfield) [SSLSMRDRM SDTLS, SS] E642 11530
Urania ("Oratory hymns") X Chester 11531
Urbs beata (LeJeune) [SDDRMDS, SLLRLRD, RM] C511b; D408b; S435b; Y341; Z570; AB409; AO 550b; AW263; BF657b 11532
-----. R [SRD#RMDD, SFMFFM, MSS] 11533
Urbs beata (Sarum plainsong M 2) [LLLSFSLLR, FSMFRD] A383; B508; C508b; E169; F474a; J245b; X190a 11534
Urbs caelestis (Hodson) [MRDRM FMRDTDRD, MRD] E169b 11535
Urquell aller seligkeiten (Kocher) [SSDRMSFMR, MF#SDTSL] E640b 11536
Urswicke (Elvey) [DMMRDS, LTDRM, MRMF#S] N200; O371; V200; W696; AP511 11537
Use me, Saviour (Gabriel) [SMLS MDFM, MRDTDRM, S] AX 419; AY106 11538
-----. R [SMLS, SMLSMDR, SMRF, D] 11539
Ut queant laxis (Plainsong M 2) [DRFRMRRRDRMM, MFS M] F551a 11540
Ut queant laxis (Rouen church mel) [LSLDDTLTLSLTDD, RD] E191b; X28a 11541
Utah, Utah, beautiful, beautiful land (Huish) X There is a land whose sunny vales 11542
Uttingen (Rheinhardt ms) X Was lebet, was schwebet 11543
Uxbridge (Mason) [DDRMRD TD, MSSLTDLS,] C144b; G 186; I256; Q303; R259; S217; T2; U141; V230; Z441; AA 403; AD194; AE115; AF257; AG263; AJ4; AM74; AN422; AO95; AR32; AT396; AV73; AW291; AX388; AY17; BB 83; BF268; BX46 11544

V

Vaagn op, du, som sover (Lindeman) [MSMRDMSLDT LDMRTL] O159 11545
Va-anachnu (Goldstein) [DDMRR, RFMM, DTL#LSFM] BH274 11546
Va-a-nachnu (Sulzer) [MMMLL TS#S#L, DDTTLLS] BH310 11547
Vaer nu glad og vel tilmode (Schop) X Jesu, joy of man's desiring 11548
V'al Kulom [melody] (Jewish trad) [DRMLDRML, DRMMM RDTL,] BH171, 325 11549
-----. V [LDRMLDRML, DRM MRDT] BH325 11550
Valentia (Eberwein) [SSMSD DLD, TLSMFRM, L] H290; L424; V351; AO157; BB381 11551
Valerius (Dutch hymn: old) [MDRMMRDDTD, MDRMMR] BE246 11552

-----. R [DDDDRMRMDRMRM FMR] 11553
Valet will dich dir geben (Teschner) X St Theodulph 11554
Valete (Sullivan) [MMSDMLTD, DRFMLSF#S,] AA410; BE288; BI111; BR279 11555
Valiant hearts (Holst) [DFRSMFM RRD, DFRSD] A531b; X293a 11556
Valley (Knight) [DMFSSDDS, SLS MFS, DM] F446 11557
Valley Forge (Clarke) [MDTLTS, LTDRMSF#M, DL] AQ302 11558
Valour (Allen) [DDRMDMLS, DDRMMSFR,] BE61 11559
Valour (Mann) [DSDRDT, DRM FMR, MMM] A49; B92; C92a; D62a; S380; AB123; AD127; AK427; AO139; BF293 11560
Valor (Irish trad carol) [DMFS LSMFSFM, SDMFS] E91; X 293b; Y123; BG128 11561
-----. V [DMFSLSMFSFM, DMF SL] BG128 11561a
Van der Werp (Van der Werp) [SSLSDSFMRD, MRSSLT] AI 12 11562
Varina (Root) [SSSSDMMM, SDDDRM, SS] G523; H508; I604; L586; U184; V297b; AG286; AH 528; AI340; AO549; AU216; AV 281; AX173; AY141; BA760; BB93 11563
Varndean (Routley) [DSMSLLS, M FSDRM, LMD] BV264 11564
Vater unser [im Himmelreich] (Schumann. G-B. 1539) X Old 112th 11565
Vaterland, in deinen gauen (Mendelssohn) X Mendelssohn 11566
Vaudois (Swiss trad) [MFSLTDMLS M, DTDFMR,] Y334 11567
Vaughan (Hopkins) [LDTLM, RDTL T, MMFSLT] L374 11568
Va-y'dabayr Moshe (Binder) [SSDRMFFSSS, SLL#L, SF] BH 300 11569
Vayomer Adonoy (Lewandowski) [SMMMMS, DTDFMMR, RFF] BH321 11570
Veni (Elliott) [MFSMDRMFM R, MMFMRM] D319b 11571
Veni (Stainer) [MMRFRT, SDRMSR, MMRF] I389; T 359b; AM280a; BV289 11572
Veni, anima mea (Dickey) [SSDDRMFM, SSSFMRDT] AF506 11573
Veni Creator (Sarum plainsong M 8) [SLSFSLSDRDD, DSLD R] A108a; B375; D289b; E 154; F157; G636; J117a; K 142a; M464; O355; P111; Q 233; R237; W182; X179; AA 249; AF575; AL143; AP267; AZ22-O; BA133; BJ48; BN 118; BO261; BP44; BQ199b; BV216; BY226a; BZ 11574
-----. V [SLSFSLSDRRD, DS LDR] D289b 11575
-----. V [SLSFSDRD, DSTD RMMR,] M464 11576
-----. V [DRDTDFSF, FDM FSLLS,] M464 11577
-----. V [SLSFSDRD, DSLTD RMM] AZ22-O 11578
Veni Creator (Tallis) [LLS#LM MRM, MF#SLTLSF] E153; X 178 11579
Veni Creator, No. 1 (Attwood) X Attwood 11580
Veni Creator, No. 2 (Dykes) [SSMFSLSSS, LMF#SRDT] F152; K142 11581
Veni Creator, No. 3 (Hopkins) X Come, Holy Ghost 11582
Veni Creator Spiritus (Polish mel.) X Poland 11583
Veni, Creator Spiritus (Lambillotte) [SSSDRRRM, MRMSFM MF] AH128; BM89; BN119; BO186 11584
Veni Creator Spiritus (Montani) [LDTSMLLM, MF#SLF#TTS,] BQ199a 11585
Veni Creator Spiritus (Sarum plainsong M 8) X Veni Creator 11586
Veni Creator Spiritus (Thermignon) X Creator alme siderum 11587
Veni, Domini Jesu (Barnby)

[MMFSMLLSRM, SSDTLT] H146 11588

-----. F [SSLSFDDS, MMDTD RMD] 11589

Veni Emmanuel (Gounod) [MSFMD MRD, STLSMSFM] D45b; AO 107a; BA106 11590

Veni Emmanuel (Plainsong M 1) [LDMMMRFMRD, RMDLDR] A2; B66; C66; D45a; E8; F49; G83; J2; K1; M117; Q62; R147; S108; W149; X66; Z182; AB103; AC75; AD100; AE78; AF110; AG63; AK88; AL137; AM147; AN150; AP241; AQ280; AR214; AW67; BB109; BD203; BF275; BK140; BL3; BM61; BN5; BO 149; BP4; BQ152; BR136b; BV 83; BX200; BY83; BZ 11591

Veni, Immanuel (Plainsong M 1) X Veni Emmanuel 11592

Veni, Jesu, amor mi (Cherubini) [MMMMMFRS, DDRRMDSM] AH131; BO35 11593

Veni lux (Brown) [DMMRDSLLS, DTLSMSF#] L187 11594

Veni, O Sapientiae (Plainsong) [MMMMFSFMR, MFMRDRR] BQ2 11595

Veni, redemptor (Walther G-B. 1524) X Venit hora 11595a

Veni, Redemptor gentium (Plainsong M 1) [DRRLL#LLLSS LSSF, LL] E14 11596

Veni Redemptor gentium (Walther G-B. 1524) X Venit hora 11597

Veni Sancte Spiritus (Langton: Plainsong M 1) [DRMFMRDR, FSLL#LSFS] A109a; B196a; E155; X180a; BN55 11598

Veni Sancte Spiritus (Webbe) [DDDRMRD, RMRSSF#S, LS] A109b; B196b; C196; D378; E 155; F156; K144; W186b; X180b; AL144; AP266; BN56; BO189; BQ34; BV225; BY228 11599

Veni Spiritus (Stainer) [MRDDRM, LSF#MR#M, MDDT] W194a; AP270a; BY592a 11600

Veni, veni Emmanuel (Plainsong M 1) X Veni Emmanuel 11601

Venice (Amps) [SLSFMRMFM, DDRMFMR] A372; F510; K45; L222; AP370; BV139b; BZ 11602

Venice (Haydn) X St Avold 11603

Venit hora (Walther, G-B. 1524) [LLSDTLTL, LTDRDR MD,] C146b; E110; F101; M52; O186; Q91; W417b; X 295; AA141; AM165; AQ67; AZ11-D; BA153; BM57 11604

-----. V [LLSDTTL, LDRDR MD, DR] M52 11604a

-----. V [LLSDTLTL, LDRD RMD, D] Q91 11604b

Venite ad me (Sullivan) [DTRD FMRD#, RTDLS, DTL] BV 651b 11605

Venite adoremus (Traditional) [SMRDTD, SFMR, RDTL] A41 11606

-----. R [MSFRRMSFMF, FFMR] 11607

Venting (Reynolds) [SSSSMF SLLLL, RRRRR] AT285; AU 116 11608

-----. R [DTLF, TLSM, RF# LDTLRS] 11609

Ventnor (Barnby) X Caritas 11610

Verbum pacis (Lomas) [MRM SFM, RDMLTDT, SLT] AO 509; BA892 11611

Verbum pacis (Monk) [MDMS FM, RDLSF#MF#S, SL] B419 C419; AZ345-B 11612

Verbum supernum (Mechlin. Antiphonarium romanum. M 8) [SLSLDTLSMFS, STDRD] E2; F384a; J277a; W188a; X277a; BY124 11613

Verbum supernum (Sarum plainsong M 2) [MDMSLTLL, SL DDTS] A8a; E2 11614

Verbum supernum (Sarum plainsong M 1) X Vexilla regis 11615

Verdi (Belden) [MFSMSDM, RDLDDLS, MF] BB191 11616

Veritas (Burnham) [DDMFSDFRR D, DDFMRS] U203; AC143 11617
Vermont (Floyd) [SSFMRLLSFM, SDTMF#S] AD19 11618
Vermont (Miller) [LMRMDRDTL, LLSFFM,] A526a 11619
Vernham Dean (Alleyne) [SMRD SLTDT, DSLSFMR] F522 11620
Vernon (Lacy) [MRDDTLSLTD, RMRTRD] V50 11621
Vernon (Lowry) X Need 11622
Verona (Deane) [SDDTTLLS, DSF MMRR, M] BR302a 11623
Veryan (Knight) [DMSLSDTLSMDR M, DMS] F9a 11624
Vesalius (Perry) [SLSSSLTDMRD T, RDTD] AC313 11625
Vesper (Acfield) [MMR#MFM, SDDFM, MMMF#S] BF345 11626
Vesper (Ingalls) [DLDLSLTD, D MSMRDR, S] AY277 11627
Vesper (Mann??) [SMSMSM, MSF RM, LFFLS] G593 11628
Vesper (Miller) [MMMMFSSFM R, MDMLSF#] BB59 11629
Vesper (Parkyn) [DMMMRDLLS FM, MMMLL] BB698 11630
Vesper (Stainer) [MFSLTDSF, MR DRMFR, M] B16; D9b; F22; K475; BV286; BY431b 11631
Vesper hymn (Bortiansky) [MS FSMSRS, MSFRDTD] A178; B24; C24; D17a; G45; M349; N643; R67; Y91; Z141; AC16; AD48; AE41; AF52; AG27; AH 166; AI380; AK60; AM410; AN 111; AQ274; AR54; AT28; AW 28; BF192; BK176; BX154; BZ 11632
Vesper hymn (Halstead) [DRMSF MMRSLTLS, SSD] BB696 11633
Vesper hymn (Rendle) [DRMFSM M, MFSLTDS, SL] G57; BZ 11634
Vesperi lux (Dykes) [SLLSDRM, SRMFMRDDT,] C16a; D9a; I56; AA546; AO29 11635
Vespers (Brunk) [SDTLSFM, SL RDLS, SMR] AY287 11636
Vespers (Elliott) [MMMMRDF FM, SSRMDMS] BR431 11637
Vespers (Stewart) [DMSSS SSL#LS, MDDRMS] AP680b 11638
Vetter (Vetter) [DMSSMDRM, DSSLTDLS,] A160b; E36; F384b; M143; O545; Q273; W89; X679; AA300; AF231; AN291b; BE233; BJ85 11639
-----. V [DMSFMDRM, DSS LDTLS,] AA438 11640
-----. V [DMSSMDRM, DSSLT DTLS] BJ85 11641
Vetters (Vetter) X Vetter 11642
Vexilla regis (Hampton) X St Cecilia 11643
Vexilla regis (Lewars) [DMF SLDTD, LLLTRDTL] K91 11644
Vexilla regis (Parker) X Parker 11645
Vexilla regis (Sarum plainsong M 1) [DRFFMRDRR, MRDT L,] A63a; B144; E94; F96a; J75a; X130a; BN28; BP55; BQ182a 11646
-----. V [DRMFMRDR, RMRDT L, RR] BN28 11647
Vexilla regis prodeunt (German) X Cor dulce, cor amabile 11648
Vexilla regis prodeunt (Sarum plainsong M 1) X Vexilla regis 11649
Vexillum (Smart) [MFSSDS, MFSRM, DRMSD] C529a; D 515a; I384; W538; AB145; BD241 11650
-----. R [SSSSDS, MFSRM, MSDTL] 11651
Vi lofve dig, o store Gud (Rostockerhandboken. 1529) X Ter sanctus 11652
Vi tro og trøste paa en Gud (Walther) X Confession 11653
Via bona (Dykes) [SDRDTDR RM, FFRMRMR] V458a 11654

Via dolorosa (Dykes) [DMSSLSM, MMRMFFM, DM] O267 11655
Via dolorosa (Liander) [MLLMR DML, TDMLLT, MD] P176 11656
-----. R [MMLDMRDLT, TTMM DTL,] 11657
Via lucis (Prout) [SFMRDTDLR S, DTRSF#S,] D6b 11658
Via pacis I (Barnby) [DMRDDD, RMSLLS, FMMF] L503; AZ38-C; BA688 11659
Via pacis II (Barnby) [MMMSS F, MRDRRM, MLLS] V16 11660
Viator (---) [DRMMFMLS, FM MSMR, SD] M644 11661
Viborg (Barnekow) [MMSFMLS, S#S#LDRMRD, L] M472 11662
Vicar (Copes) [DMFSLSFMDRM, MFSLS] BZ 11663
Vicaria (Fairlamb) [SMFSSLSF#S M, MRTRDT] N107 11664
Vicenza (La Scala Santa) X Coleraine 11665
Victimi paschali (Wipo. Plainsong sequence M 1) [RDRFSF MR, LSMSFMR,] A97; E130; F138 11666
Victimi paschali (Plainsong, 12th c M 1) [LSLDRDTLMRTRDTL, M] BN39; BQ196 11667
Victimi paschali (Plainsong, 12th c M 1) X Christ ist erstanden X Christ lag in todesbanden 11668
Victor (Darmstadt. G-B) [MRD TLSLTDRD, DRMRD] M251 11669
Victor King (Allgemeinisches Katholisches G-B. 1774) X Te deum 11669a
Victor King (Latin 12th c) X Christ ist erstanden 11670
Victoria (Catholic) [SSFMMRR D, SLTDSLLS,] BO171 11671
-----. R [SRMFMRD, SLTDSM F#S, L] 11672
Victorious (Brahms) X Brahms 11673
Victors (Perkins) [SDRMDLLTD, DTDRDRM,] BD80 11674
-----. R [MMFMDRDRM, MMM RDLS] 11675
Victor's crown (Parker) [SS SSLTDRMD, LTRDLS] B185b; C185b 11676
Victory (Link) [DDDTDR, RRR DRM, MMRD] AY276 11677
Victory (Palestrina) [SSSLSSF MS, MMMMMMR] A91; B173; C173; D121; E625; F135b; G 156; J90; K109; M231var; M434; O324; P198; Q210; R203; S164; T346; U105; V737; W122; X147; Y263; Z238; AA307; AB142; AC 64; AD167; AE128; AF181; AG103; AH312; AI84; AK 173; AL106b; AM201; AN195; AO177; AP107c, 216, 292; AR 190; AS107; AW116; BD188; BF323; BI70; BK133; BL31; BN42; BO177; BP39; BQ29; BR183; BV192a; BX159; BY 163a; BZ 11678
-----. R [MMFMSSLSSDTD] 11679
-----. V [SLSSFMS, MMMM RDR, SS] M231 11680
-----. V [SSSLSFMS, RMMRD R, DR] AA307 11681
Victory (Sankey) [SSDDRDTT, FFRSFM, SS] AH450; AT 256; AV355; AX456 11682
-----. R [SLMSFF, FSRFM M, LLTD] 11683
Victory (Whitehead) [DDDRSM, MMMFMR, SSFM] I391; AV 295 11684
Victory through grace (Sweney) [DMSDSMSDMD, DRMRDT] AI330; AM665; AV361 11685
-----. R [SLTDDTDRS, SSS RMFM,] 11686
Vienna (German trad) X Ich fahr dahin 11687
Vienna (Knecht) [MRDMSFM, LTDRTLS, DT] A239; C115b; D476b; E500; F44; I374; K56; L52; M165; O16; P144; Q18; V319; W450; X357; Z 103; AA433; AF243; AN35; AP176; AQ172; AR28; AZ11-P; BA504; BB131; BE274;

BR254; BV423; BY764 11688

View me, Lord (Campian) X Campian 11689

Vig (---) [DMSDDMRDS, DTLFLLS] M138 11690

Viggo (Kalhauge) [DRMDFMMR, MRRDDRM, D] M178 11691

Vigil (Paisiello) [SMMRDRD, MFSMLFR, RM] H355; I625; L545a; M460; N481; V533; AM577; AR29; AS5; AW210 11692

Vigil (Patton) [MLDDTL, FFFF, MLDDTL,] AZ580-B; BA545 11693

Vigil (Swedish trad) [SDMSSFM, SLRDTD, SDM] J14; N17 11694

Vigil (Thalben-Ball) [DSDRM FMRDRD, RMDMR] BY300 11695

Vigilate (Monk) [MMFMLLS, MM MMMFR, MM] B128; C128a; F308b; I494; V503; W523; AB 247; AL396a; AM471; AP547; BA571; BB357; BE68; BV573a; BY507a 11697

Vigiles et sancti (Cologne G-B.) [DDRMDMFS, DRMDMF] A599; B266; C266; E519; F172; G6; J103; Q15; R33; S13; W13; X 157; Y307; Z157; AB47; AC45; AD66; AE9; AF12; AG4; AH 190; AK9; AL29; AM3b; AN198; AP121b; AQ23; AR19; AT3; AW 11; BB77; BC4; BF173; BI106; BK51; BL27; BM83; BN50; BV 32; BY1; BZ 11698

-----. R [FMRD, FMRD, DTLS, DT] 11699

-----. V [DDDRMDMFS, DTLS, DDD] BN50 11700

Vigilia (Smyth) X Roll out, O song, to God 11701

Vigils (Gardiner's Sacred melodies) X Belmont 11702

Village (Stocks) [SFSMRDLSLDLDR D, SF] W48b; AC87 11703

Ville de Havre (Bliss) X Bliss 11704

Vincent (Palmer) [MMMFMMRD, DDRM, SSSL] G314; I510; S40; Z327; AE236; AG222; AH388; AL433; AO315; AP514a; AR 292; AS317; AT339; AU259; AV197; BB604; BD110 11705

Vincenzo (Sewall) [MRDTLLF# S, DRMFMMR, M] BR262 11706

Vindex (Cutler) X All Saints New 11707

Viola (Bradbury) [SDMRDLS, MSFRDTD, SD] M44; N76 11708

Violet (Pollock) [MMRDRM, SF MRDR, FMRD] AY294 11709

Virgin unspotted II (English trad) X A Virgin most pure X Bramley X No room in the inn 11710

Virgin most pure (Davies. Some ancient Christmas carols) X A virgin most pure IV (English carol) 11711

Virgin wholly marvellous (Scheffler's Heilige seelenlust) X Culbach 11712

Virginis proles (Plainsong M 8) [SLSSMFMRRM, DMSLLS] E191 11713

Visio Domini (Dykes) [MDRR D, DRDTDMR, SFMR] B406; C406; D629; I323; O294; V665 11714

Vision (Campbell) [SDRMMM MRML, LRMFFF] AC236; BK93 11715

Vision (Davies) [DRMRMSL SMDRMFMM, D] W155a 11716

Vision (Doane) [MRDSSLDS, MRDSLSMR,] R501; T34; AI178; AJ49; AM295; AV25 11717

-----. R [SSSSLTDD, DTLS MDFM] 11718

Vision (Mason, S) [LSLMRM LLS, DRMSMRD] E198; X 206 11719

Visions of Christ (Norwegian folk) [MSSFFMSDTLLS, MSSF] P308 11720

Vita (Berggren) [DMMSDDRTS

FM, MFSSL] M239 11721
Vita (Faning) [MRDSFMRD, DLS FLM, MS] BE31 11722
Vita (Gauntlett) [MMMRMFMR, FMRDRMRM] D245b 11723
Vita aeterna (---) [DDTRDTLLS, MMMRDSF] D124 11724
Vita aeterna (Barnby) [SSSLFSM, SSSTLS, SSS] AB147 11725
Vita lampada (Candlyn) [MLLTD RMFM, TDDDRMF] Y159 11726
Vittel Woods (Keeler) [SMMMMM RF, LDTDMRR, S] S433 11727
Viva! viva! Gesu (Filitz) X Caswall 11728
Vivat! vivat! (Catholic) [DDRR MSMDDTRTS, DDR] BO210 11729
Vivit (Handel) X Messiah 11730
Vladimir (Sewall) [DDDDRMRD, MMMMMRLD] BR216 11731
V'nislach (Jewish trad) [DDDRMR, SSMSLSFMFM] BH319 11732
Voice divine (Plainsong M 1: arr by Mason) X Hamburg 11733
Voison, d'où venait? (French trad) X Waking-time 11734
Vola (Voigtländer) [SFFMDLLS, MSSFRFFM,] M642 11735
Volga boatman (Russian trad) [DLRL, DLRL, DFMFMR, DL] Y313 11736
Voller wunder (Ebeling) [DSLDD TD, TDRSLTLS, D] E256; J 203a; Q11; W706; X374; AA315; BV295 11737
-----, V [DSLDDTD, TDRS LLS, DS] Q11 11738
Vom himmel hoch (Luther) X From heaven high 11739
Von Gott will ich nicht lassen (Crueger) [SLSFMRR, MF MRMD, SLS] AA233 11740
Von Gott will ich nicht lassen (Madgeburg. Christliche Tischgesange. Erfurt, 1572) X Guds Godhed vil vi prise 11741
Vox aeterna (Lutkin) [DSDMM R, FLMRDT, DRMM] D35b 11742
Vox aeterna (Parker) [MDSLL S, SMFMM, MDSLT] B518; C518a 11743
Vox angelica (Dykes) [DMM SSLSMDMRD, MMML] B290b; C290c; D398b; H510; I621b; L587b; U426; V694b; AB404 b; AZ189-E; BA745; BR447a; BX465 11744
-----. R [MDMSSSDLS, SSS SDSS] 11745
Vox angelica (Smart) X Pilgrims 11746
Vox celestis (Foster) [DLTD RM, MMMMLS#M, MDL] Y3; AD92; BX109 11747
Vox dilecti (Dykes) [MMLLT DDT, TLLLLS#, M] A424a; B242; C242; D673a; F351; G210a; H297; I304a; J499b; K365; M163; Q277; R280; S236; T385; U183; V297a; W410; Z288; AA46; AB199; AC147; AD204; AE170; AG 163; AI203; AJ143; AK236; AL271a; AM221; AO246a; AP412a; AR267; AV175; AW 142; AZ590-K; BA505; BB 225; BF344; BR393b; BV 513b; BY436b; BZ 11748
Vox Jesu (Spohr) X Flensburg 11749
Vreden di n afvend (Crueger) X Herzliebster Jesu 11750
Vreuchten (Oudaen. Amsterdam Psalter 1685) [SDRMFS, SLS FLSFMRD] X169; AL110; BG152; BN45; BV197 11751
-----. R [DRMFMRMFSLSS F#S, SF] 11751a
V'shom'ru (Lewandowski) [MS SSSLL#LFSLSSSSS] BH272 11752
Vulpius (Vulpius) X Gelobt sei Gott 11753
Vulpius (Vulpius) X Cana 11754

W

W. Zlobie Lezy (Polish carol) [SSDD, TDRRMFSFMRD, S]

G105; R164; AE430; AL63; BV 103; BY100; BZ 11755

Wach auf, mein Geist! erhebe dich (Schop) X Eternity 11756

Wach auf, mein herz, und singe (Selnecker) X Selnecker 11757

Wachet auf! (Nicolai) X Sleepers, wake 11758

Wachet auf, ihr mueden geister (Grimm. Choral buch) X Grimm's 480th metre 11759

Wachet doch: erwacht (Crueger. Praxis pietatis. 1662) [MRDT MRTL, DDTLS#LT, M] AA163 11760

Wachet, wachet, lieben kinder (Gregor's Choral buch. 1784) X Gregor's 163d metre 11761

Wachovia (Chitty) [SFMMR, RR RMRD, MFMMR,] AZ70-B 11762

Wachterlied (German, 16th c) [SMSDSDRM, RMFSFMRD,] X562 11763

Wachuset (Davis) [LMMMTRDLS L, DRRMSF] BZ 11764

Waddell (Crueger) X Ratisbon 11765

Wainwright (Wainwright) [DDMRL SFM, SSSDLFF] A240; W473; X355; AN27; AP53 11766

Wait, and murmur not (Kirkpatrick) [SSSF#SLSD, MFMRLS FM,] AU440; BB616 11767

-----. R [SSMSSFFFF, FTLTDS S] 11768

Wait on God (Malan) X In His love abiding 11769

Waiting and watching (Pontius) [SSF#SLSF#SM, DDTDRDL] BB 542 11770

Waits' carol (Stutsman) [SDRMFSS LLS, MFSMFM] G103; BZ 11771

Wake, arise (Nicolai) X Sleepers, wake 11772

Wake, awake (Nicolai) X Sleepers, wake 11773

Wake! awake! (Thorne) [DTDLS FMS, SLTDTDMR] D40b 11774

Wakeman (Thayer) [MRDSMDRFM RD, MRDRM] L261b 11775

Waken, Christian children (---) [SLSFMM, FSFMR, SLSFM] BR531 11776

Waking-time (French trad) [DDRMDSSS, FMFSLLSF] BG 88 11777

Walden (Jones) [SSMFSDTTL S, SSRMFF] AL78; AP19b; BB260; BV511b 11778

Walder (Walder) [SMRDLSFM, SDDTLS, TR] Q285; AA111 11779

Waldis (Waldis) [SSSMSLLS, SMSFMRD, S] M488; N86 11780

Waldrons (Miller) [DMMSDRM FM, SSSLTDT,] AP130 11781

Walenn (Walenn) [SLTDMRSD, DRMF#SF#M, T] C339b 11782

Walford (Bradbury) X Sweet hour 11783

Walford (Thalben-Ball) [MMM SMDRM, SSSDTLSM] BY443b 11784

Walk daily with your Saviour (Pollock) [DRMMFMMR, RD DRRM, DR] AX445; AY126 11785

-----. R [MFSSLLSM, SLLS F#S, DR] 11786

Walk in the light (Showalter) [SSLSMMRD, DRRSRM, DM] AX450; AY90 11787

-----. R [SMDT, FRLS, SMDT, LSSS] 11788

Walk with Jesus (Bolze) [DRM FMRR, DRMFMRD, S] M220; Q409; AA333 11789

Walking in the sunshine (Sankey) [SF#SLSSMSDRM, LS#LTD] AX440; AY479 11790

-----. R [MSLTDRDL, SDMM RDR, M] 11791

Wallace (Baker) [MMMSMRMFS M, SSF#SDT] T218; AJ311 11792

Wallace (Hamilton) [SMSLDRD, DTDLSS, SMS] G101; AC92 11793

Wallace (Wallace) [SSMDSMFM RFLS, SSMD] L572 11794

Wallin (Rostockerhandboken,

1529) X Ter sanctus 11795
Wallog (Davies) [DDLSMRRDR MLS,SSMM] BE278 11796
Walmisley (Walmisley) [MRDTTL, DL#LSSF,LTTD] F121 11797
Walsall (Purcell) [LDTLMMRDT L,DLS#LTD] A501; E13; F56; N99; R129; S232a; W148; X603; AD458; AF154; AL348b; AP124a; AR390; BE17; BV75a; BY687 22798
-----. V [LDTLMMRDTL,DTL S#LT] AL348b 11799
Waltham (Albert) [DRMFSDTLS, LTDRMFR] D274a; E132; F 406,636; J205; K446; M553; O87; Q549; W145; X32a; AA 23; AF323; AK40; AL121; AM 142; AO41; AP234; AR44; AW 370; AZ89-a; BA193; BE166; BV21,47; BY763 11800
-----. V [DRMSFMDTLS,LTDR MR] E132 11801
-----. V [DRMSDTLS,LTDRMFR D,] F636 11802
-----. V [DRMSDTLS,LTDRMR D,D] M553 11803
-----. V [DRMFSDTLS,LTD RMRR] AW370 11805
Waltham (Calkin) [DMR#MMFMF, F#SDTLLSS,] A259b; C285; D253b; G502; H63; I12; J315; N509; R506; S384; T174a; U54; V58; Y269; Z241; AA127; AB 372; AC304; AD379; AE131; AF296; AG256; AH267; AI172; AJ127; AK354; AL245; AM202; AN315b; AO466; AP48; AS369; AT78; AU148; AV258; AW331; BA340; BB450; BC219; BD86; BF526; BI93; BK60; BX370 11806
Waltham (Monk) [MMRMFSM,SSFM FFM,MF#] F324b; K67; AP 305; AR339; BY449b 11807
-----. V [MMRMFFM,SSFMFSM, MF#] AR339 11808
Walther (Walther, C) [DDSMMDSSF MR,RRSF#M] Q198 11809
Walther (Walther) [SSSLSDRDTLS, LDSFM] M46; O156; Q313; AA 431 11810
Walton (Gardiner's Sacred melodies. X Gardiner 11811
Wansted (German) [DMRSFM DR,DDTLTDRM] N51 11812
Wär Gott nicht mit uns (Walther. Geistliche G-B. Wittenburg, 1524) [RLLMSF MR,RLTDRDTL,] Q267; AA 282 11813
War no more (Negro spiritual) [MMMSLDM,MMMMRD, RRM] Y322 11814
-----. R [MMMMRD,DRMRF MRD,DR] 11815
Waratah (Cross) [MRDSMSF M,MTLSSF#SL] I549 11816
Ward (Scottish mel) [SSDTDSL S,SSSSDRMR] D80b; H65; I218; L481; M279; T30a; V 336; AB371; AE375; AJ43; AM292; AN106b; AO87; AV 68; BA307; BB137; BD152; BE128; BR274; BX84 11817
Wardlaw (Booth) [MSDDRM, DTLSFM,MMLL] D569b 11818
Ware (Kingsley) [SSSLSDMR, RDDDMSRS] H112; L487; T124; V443; AJ181; BB204 11819
Wareham (Knapp) [DDTLSDR DTD,RMRDTD] A119; B9; C9; D137; E53; F245; G38; H95; I215; J127; K66; L279; N511; O475; Q608; R527; S470; V18; W253; X631; Z 285; AD449; AF430; AI362; AK425; AL37; AN63; AO594; AP143; AQ99; AR226; AT323; AW208; AY414; AZ22-H; BA 56; BB188; BE391; BF303; BI47; BR218; BV8; BX80; BY138; BZ 11820
Warfare (Chadwick) [DDRMFM, RSDFR,MMMML] D523c 11821
Warfare (Hutton) [DDDTLSS, LLLTDR,MMM] C357b; AP 771 11822
Waring (Barnby) X Frankscot 11823
Waring (Dykes) X St Bede

11824
Waring (Spohr) X Flensburg 11825
Warner (Bradbury) X Renar 11826
Warner (Rossini) [SSLFMMMFR D, SDRMMF] H160; L380; M228; V281 11827
-----. V [DSLFMMMFRD, SDRMM F] M228 11828
Warner (Warner) X Softly the night is sleeping 11829
Warren (Campbell) [SMMMMSD D, MLTDRM, MR] AC332 11830
Warren (Taylor) [SMMMRDRM, DTLSFMFS] H71 11831
Warren (Warren) X Bread of life 11832
Warrington (Harrison) [SSFMSD DRTD, MRRMRD] C480; D251; E263; F11b; O389; V211; W388; X25c; AK196; AL33; AM20; AN 57; AO537; AP322; AW257; BA 306; BB187; BE163; BR462; BY 150 11833
Warrior (MacDonald) [SDDDRM RD, RMSLSFMR] Y146; AB255; AC203 11834
Warsaw (Clark??) [DSFMDS, M FSLTDRDDT,] E386; I67; L 510; W165; X252 11835
Warsaw (Polish) [MMMRRDDDT T, LTDSSF] Y309 11836
Wartburg (Erfurt G-B. 1524) X Komm, Heiliger Geist, Herre Gott 11837
Wartburg (Isaak) X Innsbruck 11838
Warum sind der Thränen (Schulz) X Swahili 11839
Warum sollt ich (Ebeling) X Ebeling I 11840
Warwick (Stanley) [DMSDLSLSM RD, MSLTD] H28; I41; L8; N 328; V108; W385a; X513; AD45; AI153; AL537b; AM332; AO21; AV144; AW20; BY188 11841
-----. V [DMSDLSLSMRD, MSL DT] N328 11842
-----. V [DMSDLSFLSMRD, MF#SL] W385a 11843
Warwick (Thalben-Ball) [MRSFM RDLS, LTDLFMR] BV38 11844
Was frag' ich nach der welt (Fritsch) X Darmstadt 11845
Was fuerrecht du feind Herodes (Franck) [DMRDTLSS, SLTDTRRT,] AA180 11846
Was Gott thut das ist wohlgethan (Gastorius) X Was Gott tut 11847
Was Gott tut [thut] (Gastorius) [SDRMFSFM, LSFMFMRD,] J582; K402; M281; O603; P 430; Q521; R366; S291; W540; X403; AA507; AF96; AK309; AM94; AN44; AQ30; AW524; AZ160-A; BA703; BI2-D; BQ 261; BR240; BV189 11848
-----. V [SDRMFSFM, LSFM MRD, S] M281 11849
-----. V [SDRMLSFM, LSFM FMRD,] O603 11850
-----. V [SDRMFSSM, LSFM MRD, S] AM94 11851
-----. V [SDRMFSFM, LSFM MRRD,] AQ30 11852
-----. V [SDRMLSFM, LSFM FSRD,] BI2-D 11853
-----. V [SDRMLSFM, LSMRRD, SD] BR240 11854
Was kann es schön'res geben (G-B. mit noten) [SMMRRD S, SLLDLS, SDD] AW387 11855
Was lebet; was schwebet (Rheinhardt. Choralbuch ms) [SD DRMMSFMRMMM, RDR] E42; F77; S7; X470; AD27a; AL 201a; BV11; BY35b 11856
-----. V [DDRMMSFMRMMM, RDRM] AD27a 11857
Was mein Gott will (Sermisy) [MSLSDDTD, DTLRTLS#L] Q437; AA511; AF354 11858
-----. V [MFSLSDDTD, DTLR DTT] AF354 11859
Washed in the blood (Hoffman) [MSDDDSMSDDD, DRMMM] AT192; AU111; AX276 11860
-----. R [MRDDTL, TLSDRM FMR, M] 11861
Washington (Price) [DDDRRFM

RM, MFMMLSF#] I444 11862
Washington Square (Greenfield) [DDDDDDDD, DRRRRRRD,] Y340 11863
Wassail song (English carol) [DR MRDRM, RDSSSS, SLL] BG15a 11864
-----. R [MFSDLS, MFSDLS, MF S] 11865
Wassail song (English carol) X God rest you merry 11866
Watch o'er me (Barnby) [MMFS SLDDTD, DTLSSL] BI61 11867
Watch unto prayer (Warren) [SS DMRDLD, SSDLSSMR,] AX363 11868
-----. R [SSMDDL, SSDDRMMR, SS] 11869
Watching (Doane) [SSLSDRMDL D, SF#SLSD] AI94; AT119; AU 67; AX284 11870
-----. R [RRMRSLSDMD, LDTLS D] 11871
Watchman (Ingham) X Dawn 11872
Watchman (Leach) [DMSDMR, SF#SDTLS, SDR] BY363b 11873
Watchman (Mason) [DRMRMFS, SMSLSMR, D] A440a; B106; C106b; D331b; G485; H483; I 636b; J525; L355; T93; U393; V585; Z183; AC298b; AG61a; AH244; AJ136; AN154; AO526; AQ283; AR124; AS99; AV263; AW66; BA188; BD204; BE368; BR229; BX194 11874
Watchman, blow the gospel trumpet (Kirkpatrick) [DRDSMSDM, LTDTDMR, D] BB619 11875
-----. R [FRTSMRDS, DDDTDR M, M] 11876
Watchman, tell me (Dadman) X Is not this the land of Beulah 11877
Watchman, tell us (Elvey) X St George's Windsor 11878
Watchman! Tell us (Mason) X Watchman 11879
Watchman's call (---) [DSDDRS SDDRM, MDDDS] AY57 11880
Watchword (Smart) X Sion 11881
Watchword (Stainer) [DDLDDS, SLSFM, SSLTT] D523d 11882
Water-End (Shaw) [SMDRMS, LTDRD, SMDRM] X499 11883
Watermouth (Mann) [MMMRDD T, SFFMRM, M] A349; B526; C526b; D444b; G226; H316; I350; J419; K361; L110; M 209; N259; O204; P4; Q352; R307; S200; T154; U253; W 71; Y369; Z308; AB73; AC 196; AD244; AE263; AF218; AG165; AH428; AJ228; AK271; AL69; AM541; AO389; AP 400; AR346; AS455; AT386; AU187; AV193; AW212; BA 526; BB288; BF424; BY119; BZ 11884
-----. R [R#MMRDDT, SFFM RM,] 11885
Waterspring (Bourgeois) X Bourgeois 11886
Waterstock (Goss) [SMFSDS, SMFSLR, RMMD] O124; W 117 11887
Watts (Brunk) [DMRDTLTD, RMSFMRLS,] AY413 11888
Watts' Cradle song (English trad) x Northumbria 11889
Waugh (Harrison) X Cambridge 11890
Waveney (Redhead) X Metzler's Redhead, No. 66 11891
Waverton (Jackson) [MMMFFF, FMMLLR, MMMM] AM23 11892
Wavertree (Shore) [MMMSFFF MRD, LLLSSS] C136; D83; AA492 11893
Way of the cross (Gabriel) [SLDDDRDMMFM, RDTDF] AT196; AX424 11894
-----. R [SMMMMFM, DMSS SSLS, M] 11895
Wayland (Becket) [MRDFMRSM, MFMLSSF#S,] AP570b 11896
Wayland (Holsinger) [MMM SSDRM, MFSLSFMR,] AQ217; AX637; AY298 11897
We all believe in one true

God (Darmstadt G-B. 1699) X Clausnitzer 11898

We are all enlisted (Bradbury) [DRMRDTLSSMLS, STDR,] BC210 11899

We are going down the valley (Fillmore) [DRMMMMMMFRM, DDRRR] AX615; AY496 11900

We are little gleaners (Fillmore) [MMRRDS, DDRRM, MMRRD] AY481 11901

We are nearing home (Sweney) [MFSSLSMRDRMD, MSDD] BB642 11902

-----. R [MFSLS, MSDRD, DTTLLL] 11903

We are saved (Showalter) [SSDD DTLLS, SSDDDTD] AI132; AR 430; AS291 11904

-----. R [SSFFMRDRM, DRMM FSF#] 11905

We are soldiers of Christ (Edwards) [SSDTLSFMMRFL, TD TR] AI328 11906

We are sowing (Tuckett) [DRM MFMMD, DRMFSM, D] BC192 11907

We are thy people (Beimel) [LLT DDTRDTLM, LLTDD] BH326 11908

We bless the name of Christ, the Lord (Hastings) X Retreat 11909

We build our school on thee (Rogers) [MMMMMFMM, FFFFFLSS,] BH254 11910

We ever pray for thee (Stephens) [SSSSFMRMFM, LTLSFM] BC386 11911

We give thee but thine own (Bradley) [MMMMMM, MMRDR M, MFFM] AS353 11912

We give thee but thine own (Mason & Webb. Cantica laudes.) X Heath 11913

We have an anchor (Kirkpatrick) X Will your anchor hold? 11914

We have heard (---) [SSMRMFM MRD, SSDDDD] BB305 11915

We have heard the joyful sound (Kirkpatrick) X Salvation 11916

We join to pray (Naff) [SD TDRMRD, DDRMFFMR] AX 552; AY296 11917

We love thy house, O God (Robertson) [DRMSLFS, SDTLSFM, MF] BC203 11918

We march to victory (Barnby) X To victory 11919

We meet again in gladness (Hecht) [SDDTTDTLS, DMDTDR, S] BH255 11920

We meet again in Sabbath School (Beesley) [SDD RRMFS, MRDDRRM, S] BC 193 11921

We now have met (Shoemaker) [SDRMDFMR, STDRFMRD,] AX54; AY5 11922

We plough [plow] the fields

NOTE: Plough and plow are interfiled as spelled plough

We plow the fields (Bay) [SM DMSDD, DRRDTD, SMD] P 244 11924

We plough the fields (Cottman) X Morn of gladness 11925

We plough the fields (Grimm) [DDLTSLSF#S, SLFFMRD,] BH195 11926

-----. R [MDTLDT, LLSRS M, SDTD] 11927

We praise thee, O God (Husband) [SDDDDDRMMMM, DM SSS] U27; AI376; AM634; AP718; AS16; AT205; AU155; AV156, 328; AW437; AX417; AY420; BY170 11928

-----. V [SSDDDDRMMRDR, SSRR] AV156 11929

-----. R [SSLSMRDD, SSLS MR, SS] 11930

-----. V [SSSSSLS, MMMMM FM, RR] AV156 11931

We shall sleep, but not forever (Vail) [SSSSMFLS, DTLLS FM, S] N604; AI300; AY185 11932

-----. R [SFMMFLSFM, SS DDRRM] 11933

We thank thee (Batchellor) X Onslow 11934

We thank thee (Rogers) [SSSS LLLS, SSSLLTLS,] BH242 11935

We thank thee (Singer) [SDMLSFM RD, DLLSDSF] BH193 11936

We thank thee Lord (Curry) [DM FSRMRDFMMRMFS, L] BL68 11937

We thank thee, O God, for the prophet (Norton) [DRMMRDRM FSM, DRMMR] BC196 11938

We three kings of orient (Hopkins) X Three kings of orient 11939

We would see Jesus (Belden) [DRMFMMRDTRD, RMF#SL] BB29 11940

We would worship (Bigelow) [DD RRR, RSFMM, FFMRDS] AT519 11941

Wearmouth (Steggall) [MSMFRMDR M, FSMLSMF#] D138; AB315; BA258 11942

Weary soul by sin oppressed (Excell) [MMMRDLS, DDRDM R, MMM] AS51 11943

Weather-beaten sail (Campion) [MMRSFFMLSDRRD, MMR] X587 11944

Webb (Webb) [SDDMDDL, DSDRMR, SDM] A264; B99b; C479; D252a; E581; F307b; G487; H137; I386; J313; K230; L347; M104; N264; O113; P255; Q455; R99; S265a; T118; U406; V 486; W532; X646b; Y170; Z371; AA471; AB253; AC201; AD288; AE217; AF305; AG105; AH443; AI329b; AJ171; AK290; AL262; AM111; AN151; AO394; AP386; AQ209; AR468; AS323; AT379; AU12; AV95; AW65; AX338; AY 73; AZ151-T; BA354; BB354; BD37; BE335; BF337; BR20; BV586a; BX201; BY556; BZ 11945

Webbe (Essay on the church plain chant. 1782) X Dulce carmen 11946

Webbe (Miller) [MFRDMFSSLLS, DDTLL] B95; C95b 11947

Webbe (Webbe) X Consolation 11948

Weber (Flotow) X Even song 11949

Weber (Weber) X Jewett 11950

Weber (Weber) X Seymour 11951

Wedlock (Sacred harp. 1844) [LTLTRMMR, TLLSMS, SL] BZ 11952

Weeping One of Bethany (Bushey) [MDMSSSMSDD, DL SMMR] AY211 11953

Weighed in the balance (Warren) [SMMDRMMRD, DDDM RDR,] AX294 11954

Weihnacht (Harrington) [MMS# MSSRR, MFMFRS, MM] G99; I120 11955

-----. R [DTLDTLDT, LSF# SLSFM,] 11956

Weil die worte wahrheit sind (Freylinghausen) X Truth 11957

Weil die worte wahrheit sind (Herrnhut ms) X Gregor's 82d metre 11958

Weil ich Jesu schäflein bin (Brüder. Choral buch. 1784) [SDLLSFM, SDLLSFM, SD] Q648; AM643; AW430 11959

Weil ich Jesu schäflein bin Dölker. (Geistliche lieder. 1876) [DDDMRDTDR, MRM FMRM] K556; N650 11960

Weimar (Bach, C.P.E.) [SSDTL SFM, MRDFRMMR,] Q328; V603; AA417; BR553 11961

Weimar (Nares) X Amsterdam 11962

Weimar (Pensum sacrum. Goerlitz, 1648) X Herr Jesu Christ 11963

Weimar (Vulpius) [MRDRMFS, LSFMRD, MSFMR] A37; E 187; J546; Q140; S318; X215; AA192; AB362; AZ152-B; BR429 11964

-----. V [MRDRMFS, LSFM RRRD, M] S318 11965

Weimar (Vulpius) X Cana 11966

Weisse (Wagner. Sammelung) X Gottlob, es geht nun mehr

zum ende 11967
Weisse flaggen (Tochter Sion. Cologne, 1741) [DSLLSFMRD, DTLRDTL] AF180; BV301 11968
Weisse flaggen (Tochter Sion. Cologne, 1741) X All Saints. (Darmstadt G-B. 1698) 11969
Welcome (English trad) [SLTDRM, SDLDMRD, SLT] H438 11970
Welcome (Leach) [MDRMDLD, M FSMDLSMR] G395 11971
Welcome (Linton) [MMDDDLS, SDMDRDTD, M] AY272 11972
Welcome (Sankey) [MMMMSS DDDDM, LDTLS] AP407 11973
Welcome (Smart) X Vexillum 11974
Welcome, happy morning (Calkin) [SSLDDS, SFMRD, LDFFF] C169a; D109a; I166; BF320 11975
-----. R [SSDDRR, MRDTTL, RRRL] 11976
Welcome, happy morning (Sullivan) X Fortunatus 11977
Welcome, summer (Irish trad carol) X Valor 11978
Welcome voice (Hartsough) X I hear thy welcome voice 11979
Welcome, welcome Sabbath morning (Beesley) [SF#SMDTLS, FM FRSFM, S] BC190 11980
Welcome Yule (Nicholson) [DLT DRDT, DLTDLSF, FD] BG174 11981
-----. R [DTL, DTLS, SFMRD SLS.] 11982
We'll build on the Rock (Belden) [SDDRMDRDLS, SDDRMD] BB579 11983
-----. R [MFSDRM, FMRDRM, MMMM] 11984
We'll never say good-by (Tenney) [SSMSDMDDT, LSMSDR, S] AU412; AX656; AY184 11985
-----. R [SSMDSLLL, LLRRMR, RM] 11986
We'll sing all hail (Coslett) [SM RDDTLSLSFFM, SLL] BC218 11987
We'll sing the songs of Zion (Mendelssohn) X Heavenly love 11988
We'll work till Jesus comes (Miller) X Land of rest 11989
Wellard (Whitehead) [MRDLS LS, SSDMR, SFMR] AL591; AP724 11990
Wellerd (Main) [DMSDDRTD, M MMRTSLS,] AO195 11991
Wellesley (Elvey) [DRMFMM RD, LLSSRM, DD] D615b; W 602 11992
Wellesley (Swisher) [DSFMDRFM, MFSMDRMR] BD54 11993
Wellesley (Tourjée) [SDRDTS RMRD, LSFMRF#] G76; I98; L89b; R110b; T295; U18; Z 173; AB71b; AC55; AD82; AE74; AG54b; AH180; AI37; AJ409; AL117; AR91; AS87; AT48; AU182; AV64; AW58; BB65; BF250 11994
Wellingham (Bullinger) [SMF SDRFM, SLSTDFML,] BY 369 11995
Wellington Square (Warrack) [MLTDTLSM, LMRDTL, M] A265; X219; AF493; AN 425 11996
Wells (Bortniansky) X St Petersburg 11997
Wells (Holdroyd) [DMSDTDLS, SSSSMFRD,] L439 11998
Wells (Johnson) [MFMSFMRD, SLSRDTLS,] BV236b 11999
Wells (Wells) X Holy Spirit, faithful guide 12000
Welsh carol (Welsh trad) [ML LLS# LTDDDTR, TDLL] BG 59 12001
Welsh hymn (Welsh trad) X Ar hyd y nos 12002
Welton (Malan) [SSSDMRRM, LDLSDMRD] I322; L15; T 212; V207; AJ305; AO158 12003
Welwyn (Scott-Gatty) [MRDTDR FMRDT, DLLSD] A486; E 346; G592; J382; R150; S110; W648; Z497; AB36; AE407; AF411; AG254; AK266; AL 129; AR211; BE57; BY621; BZ 12004

Wem in leidenstagen (Filitz) X Caswall 12005
Weman (Weman) [MMSDRRMM, SSLLSM] A193b 12006
Wengen (Davies) [SLTDFMFMR D, SLDSDL,] F65b 12007
Wenn erblick ich doch einmal (Flittner) X Gregor's 124th metre 12008
Wenn in leidenstagen (Filitz) X Caswall 12009
Wenn meine seel' den tag bedenket (Grimm. Choralbuch) X Gregor's 184th metre-C 12010
Wenn mein stündlein vorhanden ist (Wolff) X Naar tid og stund den er forhaand 12011
Wenn meine sund' (Praetorius) [LFLLDL#L, MSSRMFM, LD] Q152 12012
Wenn wir in höchsten nöthen sein (Bourgeois) X Commandments 12013
Wennerberg I (Wennerberg) [DS MSLTD, SMFMRM, DSM] J378; N496 12014
Wennerberg II (Wennerberg) [MD LTDRMSF, MSSFRDR] P322 12015
Wentworth (Cluett) [MMMRFML, SFMMMF#S, MM] L56 12016
Wentworth (Maker) [SDDTLSMD, RMLR, MMMD] C384; D624b; G9; I29; J447; R409; S29; W 441b; Y204; Z109; AB213; AC 51; AD270; AE19; AF98; AG 183; AH398; AI44; AK195; AL 289; AN263; AP440; AR31; AV 49; AW177; BA36; BB45; BF 389; BR423; BY504; BZ 12017
Wer da wonet (Vehe. G-B-lein. 1537) [DDMSMFSLS, DTLSMSF] E35; W88; AN350; AQ143; BN 173; BY587 12018
Wer Gott vertraut, hat wohl gebaut (Calvisius) X Gregor's 223d metre 12019
Wer hier fuer Gott will sein (Hermann) X O Heilege Dreifaltigkeit 12020
Wer nur den lieben Gott (---) [SDDMDDLLS, DTDRMFM] AW 571 12021
Wer nur den lieben Gott (Neumark) X Neumark 12022
Wer weiss, wie nahe (Bronner. Choral-buch. 1715) [SDSLL SFMD, MFMRSLL] N59; O 445; P98 12023
-----. V [DDSLLSFMD, MFM RSLL] O445 12024
Wer weiss, wie nahe (Bronner. Choral-buch. 1715) X Winchester New (Wittwe. Musikalisches handbuch. 1690) X Crasselius (Wittwe. ibid) 12024a
Wer weiss, wie nahe mir mein ende (Meyer) X Rudolstadt 12025
Wer weist wie nahe mir mein ende. (Bronner. Choral-buch. 1715) X Wer weiss wie nahe 12026
Werde munter (Schop) X Jesu, joy of man's desiring 12027
We're going home tomorrow (Bliss) [SMR#MDDRD, LSDD, MMR, S] AX593 12028
-----. R [MSMMDRRRFFM, MSMM, D] 12029
We're marching on to glory (Chamberlain) [MRDSDRDTL, DRMMSDR,] BC194 12030
We're marching to Zion (Lowry) X Come, we that love the Lord 12031
We're not ashamed to own our Lord (Daynes) [SDMSLSFM, MLDMFMR, S] BC266 12032
Were you there (Negro mel) [SDMMMRDMRD, DMSSSL] A80; J500; R201; AE455; AF179; AG317; AH609; AR 173; BK170; BL23; BZ 12033
-----. V [DDMMMRDMRD, MMSSSL] AE455 12034
Wesley (---) [DMRDSFMR, MFSLMRD, D] E588; W76b; AL96; AW309 12035
Wesley (Hastings) [SSSFMRS MD, SSLSLTD,] L6 12036

Wesley (Mason) [DTLSSSLDL LS, MRRDT] G488; H132; J 319a; M99; N381; O112; P399; R505; S391; T177; U408; V598; Z523; AC303; AD380; AG259; AH466; AJ259; AK378; AM65; AO138a; AR561; AT453; AU248; AV266; BA343; BB302; BF524; 12037

Wessex (Hopkins) [MMRDSSFM, RMSLDT, TD] I473; AA18; BE134; BR272; BX284 12038

West (West) X Moravia 12039

West Burn (Finlay) [DDRMTDLSF M, SLSDTL] BV310, 447 12040

-----. V [DRMTDLSFM, SLS DTLT,] BV447 12041

West Heath (Hopkins) [SMSDSLT D, RMTDLSFM,] BA267 12042

West Milton (American trad) X Campmeeting 12043

Westall (Worcester) [SDDDRM FMD, DDDDLLL] BR550 12044

Westcott (Barnby) [DTLTSLSMF, SLTDTLT] I37a; V273; Y88; Z305; AB50; AJ182; AW52; BF234 12045

Westgate (---) [SMMFMRMD, TL DTLS, SM] AO147 12046

Westerly (Hopkins) [SSMFSRM, RRDRMTD,] A230 12047

Westminster (Cooke) [SSLSFMRD, DRMFMRDS,] F15b 12048

Westminster (Sullivan) X Propior Deo 12049

Westminster (Turle) [MSSDDTLS, SMTDRS, ST] B183; C183; D 189a; E441; F169; I700; W27; X581; AL18; AP63b; AS385; BA17; BE54; BV10; BY64 12050

Westminster Abbey (Purcell) [MSMDFRTS, DRMRDTLS,] F574; BV660b; BY372a 12051

Westminster College (Greiter) X Psalm 68 12052

Westminster New (Nares) [DMMM RMFSLLS, FMRDD] F334b; AP350 12053

Westmoreland (Plainsong, arr by Barnby) [MMMFMR, MDRMRD, MMMF] L557; AB384 12054

Westmoreland (Steggall) [MFSM SDT, DLSMMF#S, SM] Y114 12055

Weston (Roe) [MMFMRMRD, MSSFLMR, M] D432b; I130; M585; N140; AN553; BR28 12056

Weston (Wesley) [LTDTLTS# L, DRMLSFM, T] W452b 12057

Westridge (Shaw) [MFSMRDL S, DRMDR, FSL] A514; X363; BV357; BY747 12058

Westron Wynde (Llewellyn) [DRMFS, MSFMR, DRMRMF] BV136 12059

Westwood (McCartney) [MFM LMMR, DTLSLS, MFM] D68a; J328; M325; AB274; AH315; AV305; BF518 12060

Wetherby (Wesley) [LDLSFDR RD, DFMMRD] A73; W513 12061

Wetterling (Wetterling) [SSD DDDDTT, SSRRRRM,] M238; N95 12062

Wexford carol (English carol) [SDDTDRMFS, SFMDSLL#] BG14 12063

Weymouth (Ferris) [SDTDR MFS, FMDDTD, S] A401 12064

Weyse (Weyse) [DMMMSSDL S, MLSSFRM] J299; M299; O379; P226; Q592; AA565 12065

Weyse II (Weyse) [SDTDDRRM, SMRDLS, DS] O611 12066

What a friend (Converse) X Erie 12067

What a mighty God (Warren) [SDDRRMSS, SLSMDMR, S] AX16 12068

-----. R [DDDDRRM, MMM MFF#S, SS] 12069

What a sea of tears (Gounod) X Rouen 12070

What a wonderful Saviour (Hoffman) X Hoffman 12071

What beauteous sun surpassing star (Schmidt) X What star is this 12072

What did He do? (Owen) [DSL

SDTLSS, MSLRDTD,] AU385 12073

-----. R [SMSSLSFM, DDTL, RRDT,] 12074

What do I owe? (Powell) [SD RMSSF#MR#M, FMRSSL] BY490 12075

What glorious scenes mine eyes behold (Beesley) [MMRDSFMMR DTD, MRSF#] BC197 12076

What God hath promised (Runyan) [MDRMMFFFM, MRDTRFM] AX475 12077

-----. R [DMSFMDDFFM, MRD TRF] 12078

What happiness can equal mine (German trad) [DTLSLFMRD, DTSF#LTL] BO39; BP67 12079

What happiness can equal mine (Schein) X Eisenach 12080

What joy to reach (Norwegian) [SDDRRMF, SMMFRD, SDD] P330 12081

What lovely Infant (---) [DMMMR DLS, SMMSFMRM] BO157 12082

What mortal tongue can sing (Roman hymnal) [DMRDSFMR, RMRDRDT, F] BN158; BO82 12083

What shall the harvest be? (Bliss) [MFF#SMDDTT, TLLLSSS] AU404 12084

-----. R [SMFSLTDTLS, FMFRM F] 12085

What star is this (Schmidt) [MSM DRMFS, SLDDTD, SL] BN26; BO161 12086

What tender mercy (Ogden) [MR DMRDLDSD, RRDRMM] AX26 12087

-----. R [RMRSMFMD, FFMM RDR, M] 12088

What tongue can tell (Nicolai) X Frankfort 12089

What voice salutes the startled ear (Beesley) [SSLSDDTT, SST LFM, SS] BC275 12090

-----. R [SDSLL#LLL, LRLTDT TT,] 12091

What was witnessed in the heavens? [SLTDMMRDSS, SLSRMF] BC 299 12092

What will you do with Jesus (McKinney) [SSSMMMFFR, FFFRRRS] AU101 12093

-----. R [DTLSMLR, TLSRM FLS, D] 12094

What will you do with Jesus? (Stocks) [MMMMMMFMM, DTLLSFF] AX266 12095

-----. R [MFSDLSM, DTLTDT, DDD] 12096

What will your answer be? (Teddlie) [SSSSSSLLL, SSSDT DR,] AX295 12097

What would you give in exchange? (Carr) [SDMSLSMDRD, SDDMSF] AX275 12098

-----. R [MDRM, SF#SM, M R#MSLSMD] 12099

Wheeler (Hardy) [DRMFLS, LFSMDR, RMMF#] BY116 12100

Wheelock (Sanders) [SSSLSMDM SLSM, DRDR] AQ182 12101

Whelpton (Whelpton) X Hear our prayer 12102

When blossoms flowered (Yon) [SSFMFMRMRDR, SDDRM] BQ126 12103

-----. R [SDTDRDS, MMRMF MR, MF] 12104

When Christ was born (Brown) [DSMDRMFMRM, MRRMSL] B547; C547; BG178; BV118 12105

When Christ was born (German mel. 14th c) X In dulce jubilo 12106

When Christ was born in Bethlehem (Beesley) [DTLSFMR D, RMLSMRDM] BC295 12107

When dark and drear (Daynes) [MFSF#SLSDTLSF#LSM, M] BC293 12108

When day's shadows lengthen (Catholic) [MMRDFR, SSF RDT, SSSD] BQ140 12109

When first the glorious light of truth (---) [SMSSSMSS, SLD TLS, SM] BC198 12110

When great St Patrick (Kelly) [SDSMFSLS, MLMRDRMM]

BN165 12111
When He cometh (Root) [DRMM MFSS, LMMRDD, DR] N651; W158a; AL614; AM651; AP794; AW432; BB148; BV355 12112
-----. R [DTLLDSS, LSDDRMS, DT] 12113
When here, O Lord (Allgemeines katholisches G-B. Vienna, 1744) X Hursley 12114
When I get to the end (Tillman) [SDDDMFSTL, LLSTLSL] AU26 12115
When I see the blood (Foote) [S SLSMLLSS, SFSFRLS] AU70 12116
-----. R [MFSLSD, SDTLSS, MFSD] 12117
When I see the blood (Showalter) [MMRDSLDLS, SDRMDRR] AX307, 564; AY240, 340 12118
-----. V [MRDSLDDS, DRMDR RD, M] AX564 12119
-----. R [DRMDLS, DDRDRM, MFDR 12120
-----. V [DMSSSLSSM, DMSSS LS] AX564 12121
When I survey the wondrous cross (Plainsong M 1: arr by Mason) X Hamburg 12122
When in the hour of utmost need (Bourgeois) X Commandments 12123
When in the wondrous realms (Schreiner) [MRDFMRRM, MF# SLSF#F#S,] BC199 12124
When Israel, of the Lord beloved (Beimel) [SDTDRMFM, DSFMRD TD] BH119 12125
When Israel to the wilderness (Beimel) [DMSRMDRLTD, DFM RDT] BH127 12126
When, marshalled on the nightly plain (Calkin) X Waltham 12127
When morning fills the sky (German trad) [DMFSMD, DRM FSM, MRTD] BN190; BO10 12128
-----. V [DMFSSD, DRMFSM, MRTD] BO10 12129
When morning gilds the skies (Haydn) X O esca viatorum 12130
When morning gilds the skies (German trad) X When morning fills the sky 12131
When my life-work is ended (Sweney) X I shall know Him 12132
When peace, like a river (Bliss) X Bliss 12133
When the battle's over (---) [SDDMMSFM, MFMRRD, SD] AU395; AY122 12134
-----. R [SDDDRMFSSSFM, SFFF] 12135
When the book is opened (Smith) [SSDDLSSD, DRMSM DR, S] AX293; AY389 12136
-----. R [MMRMFRMD, TT LLRMR, S] 12137
When the King comes in (Lorenz) [SLSMRDRMD, LS LDTLS] BB537 12138
-----. R [RRRDRMMS, LSLD LS, DD] 12139
When the King shall claim His own (Darnes) [SDMSDSTL, TDRTDRM, D] BB539 12140
When the Lord turned the captivity (Gelineau) X Defend me, O God 12141
When the mists have rolled away (Sankey) [MFSSSSSD, TLSSSSS, S] AU354 12142
When the morning comes (Tindley) X By and by 12143
When the roll is called (Black) X The roll 12144
When the rosy light of morning (Baird) [MFSSLSLTDS, TLS SFM] BC200 12145
-----. R [TDRDRM, MRDDD MDR, SS] 12146
When the Sabbath (Jewish trad) [MSLSSFMFM, SDL# LSFM] BH114 12147
When the shadows flee (Sellers) [MFSMRMDS, MFSRDMFS] AU429 12148
-----. R [SSDDTLTT, SSRRD TRD,] 12149
When the sun (French carol

mel) X Gloria 12150
When the sun shines bright (Reynolds) X Lura 12151
When there is peace (Binder) [SLTDDFFM, MLLSMDL#L,] BH16 12152
When they ring the golden bells (DeMarbelle) [SFMR#MR#MS, MDLTDLSD,] AU360 12153
-----. R [SSLFDLFL, DLSLSM MS,] 12154
When this song of praise shall cease (Stark) X Berkshire 12155
When upon life's billows (Excell) X Blessings 12156
When very early in the dawn (Cologne G-B.) X Vigiles et sancti 12157
When we all get to heaven (Wilson) X Heaven 12158
When we walk with the Lord (Towner) X Trust and obey 12159
Where could I go? (Coats) [MMMMDRDDRD, DDRMMF] AX520 12160
Where He leads I'll follow (Ogden) X Sweet are the promises 12161
Where He leads me (Norris) [SDMMFMMR, STRDMRRD,] AH336; AR248; AS207; AT361; AU164; AV338; AW500; AY115 12162
Where He may lead me (Black) [MMMMDSSS, LLLSMRMR,] AS249; AX507 12163
-----. R [DRMFFFFM, MFSL LLDT,] 12164
Where is my boy tonight (Lowry) [MMMFMMRD, DDDDFFM, M] AU89 12165
-----. R [MFDDDRM, SSRRR MR, RM] 12166
Where Jesus is, 'Tis heaven (Black) [SDRMSLDD, DTLSMM DR,] AX335 12167
-----. R [SFFFFMDM, MMM SMMDR,] 12168
Where Judah's faithful sons are found (Alman) [SDSDL#LSF, LSRSFRM, D] BH210 12169
Where shall I be? (---) [SD DMMDDM, DLLS, SDDM] AX 286 12170
-----. R [MSDDMDMRDLS, DSDDM] 12171
Where the gates swing outward never) [SSDDDDRMMM, MRDRDL] AX569 12172
-----. R [SFMMMMRDDD, TLSSDM] 12173
Where we'll never grow old (Moore) [DRMR#MD, MFSF#S M, SSLD] AU348 12174
-----. R [SMSDLDLS, SSSM MMRD] 12175
Where will I go? (Warren) [MRMRDD, DRDLS, DTRDR] AX290 12176
Where will you spend eternity (Tenney) [MRDFMMDM, SFM RRMFM] AU290; AX268; AY 531 12177
-----. R [MFMMSLSS, DDRM DRDD] 12178
Wherever He leads I'll go (McKinney) X Falls Creek 12179
While Jesus whispers to you (Palmer) X Come, sinner, come 12180
While of these emblems we partake (McBurney) [MSFM DMRD, SF#MTSF#RM,] BC226 12181
While of these emblems we partake (Schreiner) [MMM SFMDR, MMLLSF#M,] BC 217 12182
While shepherds watched (English mel., 18th c) X God rest you merry 12183
While shepherds watched their flocks (Willis) X Carol 12184
While the days are going by (Sankey) [MFSSLSSD, DRM DRRD, M] AU394; AX182 12185
-----. R [DRM, DLS, DMS, MDR, DRMM] 12186
Whisper a prayer (McKinney) [DTLSF#SLS, DTDMRDR, D] AU453 12187

-----. R [SDRM, RSRD, DTLSD, LTD] 12188
Whispering hope (Hawthorne, pseud) [SSSDTLSM, FFFLSFM, M] AU466 12189
-----. R [SLTDTDRDRMS, LTDSS] 12190
Whitburn (Baker) X Hesperus 12191
White (White) [SMMMRDLS, SDD MRDR, S] BB230 12192
White fields (Bruning) [DSLMSL LS, DDDDDRM, D] AK383 12193
White gates (Williams) [LLSLM DTL, LLSMRDRM] E541; X 489; BV553a 12194
White Ladies Aston (Atkins) [LTDRDTDLT, DTLSFML] E 400; X370 12195
White Lent (French trad) X Quittez, pasteurs 12196
White ribbon (Sampaix) [SMFM DMRRD, LDLSDMR] H528 12197
-----. R [SSLSMMRRD, LTDSD RM,] 12198
Whitefield (Miller) [DDSLTD, SM DLSFMMR, S] H68; I22b 12199
Whitehall (Lawes) [DTLDMFLS, SLTDTLMR,] E234b; F525; W297; X589; AN91a; BV274 12200
Whitehead (Whitehead) [SDRMM SMR, MDTLTDRS] B441 12201
Whiteland (German) [DRDDTD MRDTD, SSFMM] BR243 12202
Whiter than snow (Fischer) [SS DRMRDRMRD, SSDRM] P267; AI282; AO639; AR445; AS452; AT201; AU9; AW469; AX407; AY233; BB592 12203
-----. R [RRRRDMDLS, SLDFM RD] 12204
Whitfield (Heber) X Calcutta 12205
Whitford (Lloyd) [MRDTLLS#, MLTDRT, MRD] W390; AF315 12206
Whither, pilgrims (Bradbury) [SDDTRFLS, SDTSLTD, S] AP783 12207
Whither thus in holy rapture (Mainz G-B. 1661) X Lady of the visitation 12208
Whither thus in holy rapture (Slovak hymnal) [DMLSF# SDS, LSFFSFM, D] BQ80 12209
Whitner (Campbell) [MRMDSL DS, SDTDMRDT,] V573 12210
Whitney (Andrews) [DTSLM FLRDT, DTLRTS] AD377 12211
Whitstable (Vincent) [DSMD SFMD, FMRLT, MTR] BY 728 12212
Whitsun (Selby) [DDRMRDTLS, SLTDFMR] F613 12213
Whitsuntide (Gilchrist) [MLT DML, TDTLTSM, MFS] BR 209 12214
Whittier (Maker) X Rest 12215
Whittingham (Parker) [SSDDM FSLDT, LSMDRR,] B543b; C543b 12216
Who came down (McGranahan) [MMRDSLT, DMSMMR, MMR] AI385 12217
-----. R [SSSSLLL, SLSMMR R, MM] 12218
Who givest all (LeSaint) [DM MMMMRR, MFFFFFMM,] AR597; AS426 12219
-----. R [SDTLSDTT, DRDT RRDD,] 12220
Who is He (Hanby) X Adoration 12221
Who is like Thee (Binder) [SM SDDDTLTD, SMSLSL] BH69 12222
Who knows how near (Bronner. Choralbuch. 1715) X Wer weiss wie nahe 12223
Who made ocean (Finnish trad) [DDTTLDT, MMS#TLL, DDT] BK4 12224
Who taught the bird (Binder) [SSLSMMFR, MFSTLS, SS] BH247 12225
Whole wide world (Kirkpatrick) [SDSMDSS, SLSFMR, SMD] AE355; AO524 12226

-----. R [SSSSLTDRDT, SSLT DR] 12227
Who'll be the next (Lowry) [SS SSSDMRDS, LLTDTL] AX258 12228
-----. R [DSSS, DLLL, TTDRM RDS] 12229
Wholly thine (Belden) [DRMDSD MRD, TDRDRM, D] BB597 12230
-----. R [SMSMDM, FMRRD RM, SMS] 12231
Who's on the Lord's side? (---) [SSDDRM, MMMFMR, TSTR] BC175 12232
Whose works, O Lord, like thine (Warren) [DMMRRSLS, SFFMDR, RS] BH222 12233
Whosoever (Bliss) [SLSMDDLDL S, SLSMDM] AT238; AU126; AX220; BB571 12234
-----. R [TTTDR, DDDLS, MMM SLS] 12235
Whosoever will (Bliss) X Whosoever 12236
Why art thou cast down (Crueger. Praxis pietatis melica. 1653) X Ratisbon 12237
Why art thou cast down? (Jewish trad) X V'al Kulom mel 12238
Why art thou sorrowful (Yenn) [SSDTDMMRLDTLS, SLT] BQ 144 12239
Why carelessly wait? (Warren) [DMRDSLS, DMRDRMR, DM] AX288 12240
Why do you wait? (Root) X Sheffield 12241
Why not now? (Case) [SDTRTLSM, LSFRSFM, S] AT218; AV333; AX236 12242
-----. R [DTLTLS, LSFMFSM, DTL] 12243
Why this tumult (Gelineau) [RR FR, RRSM, RLDL, LTSL,] BSp. 6 12244
Wiant (Chinese mel) [LLSSDSDR, SLDRMSRR] BZ 12245
Wickliffe (Hastings) [SSDMMRFRD TD, SLLDT] L29 12246
Wicklow (Irish trad) [DRMLSMRD LLS, DRMRD] E157; X182 12247
Wie gross ist des Allmächt' gen Guete (Bach) X Apolutrosis 12248
Wie gross ist des Allmächt'gen Güten (Richter) [SDRMDSSMD, MRSMLSF#] AW516 12249
Wie herrlich ist's ein schoeflein Christi werden (Grimm's Choralbuch) X Gregor's 115th metre 12250
Wie schön ist unser Königs Braut (Freylinghausen G-B. 1704) X Gregor's 97th metre 12251
Wie schön leuchtet [der Morgenstern] (Nicolai) X Frankfort 12252
Wie soll ich dich empfangen (Crueger. 1653) [DMFSSF M, FMDRRD, DMF] K51; N65; Q58b; AA136 12253
Wie wohl ist mir (Bach) X Dessler 12254
Wie wohl ist mir [O freund der seelen] (Freylinghausen. Geistreiches G-B. 1704) X Sinner's friend 12255
Wigan (Wesley) [LDTRDF, MR DTLS#L, DT] A338; F212; J83 12256
Wigton (Scottish Psalter) [MMMFMRDRD, MMRMFS, R] E354; J384a; S234; W406; X630; Z342; AF330; AN234a 12257
Wigtown (Scottish Psalter) X Wigton 12258
Wild bells (Lahee) [DDDTLSFM RDDTLSFM] G537; AB398; AW379 12259
Wilderness (Thatcher) [LDLM MLTD, SSSTSRT] A574a; BV595 12260
Wildersmouth (Hopkins) [DRM MRMSF, MRDDRRM, M] U401; V589; W573; AO429 12261
Wildwood (Pitts) [SSSLSSSDRM R, RSTDR] AG295; AH515 12262
Will Jesus find us watching

(Doane) X Watching 12263
Will the circle be unbroken (Gabriel) [MFSSDRMM, MRD RDLS, M] AX613 12264
-----. R [DRMSMRDM, DTLR DLS, S] 12265
Will there be any stars (Sweney) X Stars in my crown 12266
Will you go? (---) [DRMMMM FLSRFMD, SDT] BB368 12267
-----. R [SFMMFSFMRDRM, SDTD] 12268
Will you go to Jesus (Showalter) [DDDRMSLS, MDSMMR, SM] AX238; AY220 12269
-----. R [LFFSLSMS, FRRMFM F#S] 12270
Will your anchor hold (Kirkpatrick) [DRMDLRRDTD, MMRRST] AL501; AU392; AW482; AX 483; BB584; BY568 12271
-----. R [SSSSSSLSS, MMMSSMD] 12272
Williams (Kingsley) X Kingsley 12273
Williams (Williams) [SDTRDM RF, MSSFMRDT,] L109a; AO 52 12274
Williamson (German) [SMRDDTD R, SFMRRSFM,] AK307; AO 322 12275
Willing (Willing) X Alstone 12276
Willing to own thee (Sea) [SDRMMDTLS, STRFFFD] AS231 12277
Willingham (Abt) [MMMRDMF F#SRFM, MF#RR] J496; N515; O549; P303; Y258; AC225; AH 500; BB406; BE359 12278
Willington (Williams) [SDMSMDM LTD, RMSRSD] V260 12279
Wilma (Smyth) [SMMMMRMFM, SRFMRD, S] BR534 12280
Wilmar (Minns) [DMSSFRDTD, DDTLSLT] AB69 12281
Wilmot (Weber) [DMRDSDMRDS, LDSMMR] H116; I545b; L218; T231; U227; V107; AJ327; AO 83; AX248; AY373; BI79 12282
Wilson (Mendelssohn) [SMRDTRD LSM, SLDTTR] I116 12283
Wilson (Wilson) X Martyrdom 12284
Wilton (Mann) [SMRDRMSFLLS, SDTLS] W171; AL119 12285
Wilton (Stanley) [DDDRMFM RD, DDMRDTL] BY519b 12286
Wilton Square (Watts-Hughes) [MDDTLSFM, MLLLTS#, MD] BY427b 12287
Wiltshire (Smart) [SMSDDTD FMRRM, SS] A441; C301a; E 502; F290; J420; N270; S83; X677; AF81; AL537a; AM77d; AP19c; AW583; BV512; BY 589 12288
-----. V [SSDDTDFMRRM, SSSSM] F290 12289
Wimbledon (Lahee) [SLSDDTT, MRDTTL, LLT] AP786 12290
Wimbledon (Wesley) [SDRFM RRM, FSLSFMM] A420a; W539; AL430a; AP504a 12291
Wimborne (Whitaker) [DDRM DSLFRDT, SDRMD] H64; I439; L171 12292
Winchcombe (Calkin) [SDDD, MMMMDS, SLLTDR,] BR222 12293
Winchester (Ests's Whole booke of Psalmes) X Winchester Old 12294
Winchester New. (Wittwe. Hamburger Musikalisches handbuch. 1690) [SDSLLSFM, MF MRSSF#S,] A10; B145b; C 145b; D44a; E9; F2b; J162; K326; L109b; Q12; R242; S 150b; V480; W92; X137; Y 349; Z471; AB1; AD176; AF 9; AH552; AK95; AL16; AM 56; AN28; AP104; AQ246; AR352; AW369; AZ22-X; BA 152; BE336; BF182; BL1; BN 1; BR11; BV79; BX48; BY86; BZ 12295
-----. V [SDSLLSFM, MFM RSLSS,] J162 12295a
Winchester Old (Est's Whole booke of Psalms) [DMMRD FFMRMSSF#S, MLS] A13a

B71; C71b; D657; E30; F62; G175; I181; J389; K265; L14; O20; Q31; R381; S91; V166; W181; X82a; AA72; AD28; AF 146; AK228; AL23; AN155b; AP41a; AW191; AZ14-Z; BA 841; BB101; BD180; BE122; BJ39; BN128; BO263; BR9; BV123; BX252; BY113; BZ 12296

-----. V [DMMRDFM, RMSS F#S, MLS] BN128 12297

Winchester Old (Wittwe. Musikalisches handbuch) X Winchester New 12298

Windermere (Kroeger) [MSLSDLS, DMMFFM, MSL] T90; AJ133 12299

Windermere (Maker) [MRMFSS FMFSLL, SSLT] BY5a 12300

Windermere (Somervell) [SLSFS LS, DFMRMDR, SL] E522; R553; Sap. 31; X332; AH567; BE143; BV499; BY530a 12301

Windham (Read) [LDRMMDTL, LDTDMRDT,] J298b; M323; Q612; V447; AA551; AQ154; AY394; BZ 12302

Winding I (Winding) [MMSFM RDDRMD, FFMLS] M130 12303

Winding II (Winding) [SSLTSDLS, MFFFSMM, D] M286; BE332 12304

Windrush (Rouen church mel) X Prompto gentes animo 12305

Windsor (Barnby) X Caritas 12306

Windsor (Tye) [LLTDTLLS#, DM RDTD, DM] A284; B124a; E332; F334a; G136; J269; M136; O314; Q176; V682; X547b; AA502; AF 226; AM22; AN115; AP45; AQ 89; AW39; AZ14-O; BE107; BJ 53; BR280; BV142; BZ 12307

Windsor and Eton (Tye) X Windsor 12308

Windsor Forest (Clarke) [SFSDRL SLFM, TMF#SLD] AQ199 12309

Windy Ridge (Aufranc) [SSF#FTL TD, SSLTLSTD,] BB335 12310

Winkworth (Barnby) [MMF#S#LL S#L, LSLTDD] A226; B229 12311

-----. R [S#LTDRMMRM, MRDTD] 12312

Winning souls for Jesus (Mackay) [SSMFSMRDDLSM, RMFS] AX186; AY529 12313

-----. R [SSSSSSDDMRDS, LLLL] 12314

Winscott (Wesley, S.S.) [MM RDLSFM, MFMRDTDR,] J 218b; W338; AL297b; AP385 12315

Winsted (Dutch trad) [SDDM RDTLLF, RDDRMD,] Y275; Z553 12316

Winston (Hildebrand) [MSFM RDRM, DLTDRMRR,] AY 273 12317

Winterbourne (Barnes) [DRM FMMRR, MFSLLRDR] BB 391 12318

Winter's snow (Goss) X See, amid the winter's snow 12319

Winter's snow (Morris) [MRM SLSL, LTDTLSFM, M] BG 190b 12320

Winterton (Barnby) [SLTDMM, LRFM, SLTDMM,] Q403; V358; AA353; AB268 12321

Winton (Lloyd) [SMSDDRD, DFMRDMR, RM] AP256 12322

Wir christenleub (Dresden. Neues G-B. 1593) X Ecce agnus 12323

Wir danken dir, Herr Jesu Christ (Bergkreyen. 1551) [RFFMRFSL, LFSSFMMR,] AA193 12324

Wir danken dir, Herr Jesu Christ (Erfurt. 1663) [LTSML LS#L, DRMRDDTD,] AA217 12325

Wir glauben all' an einen Gott (Darmstadt G-B. 1699) X Clausnitzer 12326

Wir glauben all 'an einen Gott (Wagner. G-B. ms) 1742) [DDTLSLRSM, RSF#SDTL] Q251a; AA394b 12327

Wir glauben all an einen Gott (Walther) X Confession 12328
Wir pflügen (Schulz) X Claudius 12329
Wir wollen alle fröhlich sein (Nürnberg G-B. 1544) X Betracht'n wir heut zu dieser frist 12330
Wirak (Miller) [SLMSDRM, FSLSMFMR, M] BB215 12331
Wireless (Barnes) [SMMRDRM, SMDLSMDR, M] Y186 12332
Wirksworth (Chetham. Psalms, 1718) X Aylesbury 12333
Wirtemburg (Rosenmüller) X Nassau 12334
Wirth (Bradbury) [SSDMDDLS, DTDRDDT, S] AJ44 12335
Wisdom (Thalben-Ball) [SMRD TLSFM, SLTDMRD] BE198 12336
Wishart (Smart) X Nachtlied 12337
Wismar (Schein) X Eisenach 12338
With all the power of heart (Durham) [DMFSSLLS, SDTLS LTL] BC216 12339
With gladsome feet (MacFarren) [DDRMDS, SLTDLD, LTSD] BR516 12340
With God and His mercy (Ahnfelt) X Ack, saliga stunder 12341
With happy voices (Mason) X Missionary hymn 12342
With harps and with viols (Bliss) [MFSSLTDDTDRDLS, SS] AM714 12343
-----. R [MRDDDTLLLRRMR, RRM] 12344
With songs and honors sounding (Ward) X Materna 12345
With tender greeting (Piel) [SFMLS, RFMSFMR, MLSF#] BP93 12346
With thankful hearts, O Lord (Showalter) X Mohler 12347
With the voice of sweet spring (Cowen) [DRMSSM, DRMLS M, RDMS] BH70 12348
With wondering awe (---) [SSDD, TLSDD, SLLFLLS,] BC209 12349
----. R [SLSMMFRRDMRDT D.] 12350
Wither's Rocking hymn (Williams) [MFSMRLSM, MFSMR LTS,] BG185 12351
Within the veil (---) [DMRDD RMFFFM, MMMMF#] BB138 12352
Wittenberg (Frech) [SDSFMLS SFM, RDMF#SL] L451b; AJ 270 12353
-----. V [SDSMLSFM, RDM F#SLS, S] AJ270 12354
Wittenberg (Ilse) [SDRMLSFM, RDRTDTLS,] AA316 12355
Wittenberg (Etlich Christliche lider. 1524) [SSSSL#LS F, SMDRMF#SL] E478; F 366a; J259; K285; L85; M41, 594; O141; P94; Q301; X156; AA314; AB203; AR659; AZ 132-D; BA23; BV205a 12356
-----. V [SSSSLL#LSF, SMD RMF#LS] M594 12357
-----. V [SSSSL#LSF, SMDM F#SLS,] M41 12358
-----. V [SSSSL#LSF, SMDM FSLS] Q301 12359
Wittenberg (Luther) X From heaven high 12361
Wittenberg (Luther) X Spires 12362
Wo Gott der Herr nicht bei uns hält (Geistliche lieder. Wittenberg, 1535) X O Jesu, nar jag häden skall 12363
Wo Gott züm haus (Geistliche lieder. 1535) [DSSMRMF#S, SMSFSMRD,] Q131; AA445; BI15 12364
-----. V [DSSFMRMF#S, SM SFSMR] BI15 12365
Wo ist Jesus, mein verlangen (Thommen. Christen-Schatz. Basel, 1745) X Desire 12366
Wo soll ich fliehen hin (Stiller) [MSLRRM, SDTLLS, SMLL] Q57 12367
Wohlauf, thut nicht verzagen (Helder) [DMMRDFM, SLS

FRM, DMM] E32; X322b 12368
Woking (Glynn) [DMSLSLTD, LRT MDTL] A502 12369
Woking (Spencer-Palmer) [SDSL FMRS, DTSLMRDR] BV332a 12370
Wolder (Wolder. Catechismus G-B. 1598) [DDSMRDDRMR, MSFMRD,] J251; M329; O162; P51; Q69; W306; X660; AA22; AL331; AM210; AW570; AX147 12371
-----. V [DDSMDTDRMSMRRD, DD] M329 12372
-----. V [DDSMDDMR, MSFM RD, DD] O162 12373
-----. V [DDSMDDMR, MSFMRD, MS] W306 12374
-----. V [DDSFMRDMR, MFSF MRD,] AW570 12376
Wolder (Wolder) X Walder (Walder) 12377
Wolff (Wolff) [DSLDRDTL, SDRM FRD, D] M391 12378
Wollt ihr wissen ... (Cammin. Melodienbuch ...) [DTLSLTD, MRDRTLS, LS] S331; AM435 12379
Wollt ihr wissen was mein Preis (Reimann) X Reimann's 315th metre 12380
Wolvercote (Ferguson) [SDFMRM DLS, MFSMRDR] F331; W508a; AD171; BE250; BV365; BY271 12381
Wolverhampton (Redhead) [SSM RDRFFM, DMSLLS, S] J395; M127; O243 12382
Womit soll ich dich wohl loben (Knecht) X Gotha 12383
Wonder (Bax) [LTDTLLSL, LFSM RFMR] X107 12384
Wonder (Poppen) [SDMFMMRD, TLRMRD, SM] M363 12385
Wonder tidings (English trad. 15th c) [SSTLTDRTDLS, SSLSF] BG40 12386
Wonderful grace (Lillenas) [SSS SSLS, DMFSFM, MMM] AM702 12387
-----. R [DRMFSLSMSR, DRMSDT] 12388
Wonderful grace (Pollock) [SSDT LDS, DRMDRMR, MR] AX 324; AY234 12389
-----. R [MRDDRDLS, SDR MDRMR] 12390
Wonderful Jesus (Denton) [MR DMDRDLS, DRMSMSF] AX21 12391
-----. R [SF#SLF, FSLSM, MR#MSMS] 12392
Wonderful love (Watson) [MMM MDRMDFM, MRLRMR] AL 488; AM669; AP399 12393
Wonderful love (Wiseman) [M MMSFMRMRD, LFMR, MR#] BY411 12394
Wonderful love of Jesus (Lorenz) [SSDDTTLL, LRSSF FMM,] BB650 12395
-----. R [SSSSLLLL, SSSS FMS, D] 12396
Wonderful peace (Cooper) [DR MMMMRDRDLS, DRMM] BB610 12397
-----. R [MDRDLS, SSDDDM RMR, M] 12398
Wonderful peace of my Saviour (Reynolds) X Venting 12399
Wonderful Saviour (Jacobs) [SLSMSDDT, RMFTLS, SL] AY392 12400
Wonderful story of love (Driver) [DDDDTLS, DDDTRD, DDD] AU349; AX281 12401
Wonderful, wonderful Jesus (Sellers) X New Orleans 12402
Wonderful words (Bliss) [MMM FMMRR, SRRMRDS, M] H88; R265; Z442; AE306; AG141; AH241; AI406; AM722; AP 761; AS184; AT181; AU233; AV314; AW494; AX36; BB 574; BZ 12403
-----. R [SFFFFMMM, MRD RTDMS,] 12404
Wonderful words of life (Bliss) X Wonderful words 12405
Wondrous cross (Harmonia perfecta, 1730) [LMDTMRD T, MSF#MMR#M, L] AP192b; BV156a 12406
------. V [LMDTMRDT, MTS F#MMR#M,] BV156a 12406a

Wondrous gift (Neander) X Meine hoffnung 12407
Wondrous grace (McGranahan) X El Nathan 12408
Wondrous love (Fischer) [DDMSL SMRD, DDFLLS, M] AL479; AP425; AX83 12409
-----. R [SLSMMRDS, SLLDLS, SS] 12410
Wondrous love that cannot falter (Gounod) [MMMRRFMRDRM, SMSML] BQ56 12411
-----. R [SLSFRMFSFM, SSLF MRD.] 12412
Wondrous story (Bilhorn) X I will sing 12413
Wondrous story (Theiss) [SSMMR MFLS, SDRMRMF] M611 12414
-----. R [SMSFM, MRMFR, DTLSTL] 12415
Wondrous works (English trad) [SSMRTFFF, LSMRTDRM] BG72 12416
Wonnberger (Wonnberger) [SD RMFMRD, MRTDLLS,] M619 12417
Wood (Jones) [MRDLDR, MSM DRM, RDRM] AJ75 12418
Woodbird (German trad) [DDSM DTDR, SLDDTD, DD] A474; AQ181; BN155; BO216; BV324; BY585 12419
Woodbrook (Adcock) [MMSDRD, LLDLS, FLSFM] W669; AP759a 12420
Woodbury (Woodbury) X Eucharist 12421
Woodbury (Woodbury) X Nearer home 12422
Woodchester (Napleton) [SMMRS MMR, DDFMR, SSD] B347; C 347 12423
Woodchurch (Nicholson) [SDRM RDDRMF, FMRSMD] F532 12424
Woodhall (Crossley) [MMMMFM RDRM, SLSDDT] Y82 12425
Woodland (Gilchrist) [SMRDSFMR, MLTDRMLS] AZ606-B 12426
Woodland (Gould) [DMMSMRMR, MSSDRM, MR] H328; I609; L 592; V704; AO555; AY133; BB 143 12427
Woodlands (Greatorex) [SSS DSLMFSRM, SDDDR] A389a; S148; X299; Y246; AB178; AC3; AD142; AF156; AK27; AQ61; BF310; BV474; BY 366 12428
Woodlawn (Sanders) [DLSDF FMR, SDRRM, TTD] AN280b; AQ226 12429
Woodleigh (Barnby) [SDSMRR DD, DLLTDRDT,] D310 12430
Woodlynn (Stainer) [MMRRDFM LSSF, FFMMR] K96 12431
Woodman (Woodman) [MMMM DRM, MMMRMF#S, SS] AP694; BF341 12432
Woods (Miller) [MMMMMSRR, FSLSMMRR,] BB240 12433
Woodside (Emerson) [MRDLS MRDMR, RMSSMD] L414 12434
Woodstock (Doane) X Watching 12435
Woodstock (Dutton) [DMMMSR RR, MFSLSFMM] G55; H46; I498; L429; V402; AJ289b; AO217; AV18 12436
Woodworth (Bradbury) [DRMM SFMRMFM, SSRM] A409c; B139b; C139b; D606b; G195; H273; I255; J370b; K337b; L 494a; M133; N398; O447; P 248; Q388b; R272; S230b; T 275; U174; V296a; Z295; AA318; AD203; AE265; AF319; AG 150; AH343; AI211; AJ382; AK214; AL270c; AM431a; AO262b; AP410c; AR258; AS201; AT223; AU162; AV 169; AW458; AX303; AY213; BA433; BB222; BZ 12437
Woodworth (Margetson) [MMM SLTDDRDT, DSMDR] BR146 12438
-----. R [DTSLTS, DTSLTS, DDRM] 12439
Woolich (Kettle) X Woolwich 12440
Woolmer's (Ouseley) [DDRTTD RM, SFRMDTLS,] F287; W 275b 12441
Woolsey (Steggall) [SMDRMD,

RMLSMR, RMSL] AB250 12442

Woolwich (Kettle) [MR#MFMR, RD#RMRD, DRDF] L254; N503; Y98; BB328 12443

Worcester (Playford's Whole book of Psalms) [LTDTLRRD#, LMRSF#M, MM] X323 12444

Worcester (Whinfield) [DMSD MRDDT, DTLSFMR] D617b; P236; Q244; AA268 12445

Word of God to earth (Elgar) X In the Light and light excelling 12446

Word of life (Maker) [MMDRM SFM, MRMFM, DLS] AP291a; BY243a 12447

Words of life (Bliss) X Wonderful words 12448

Words on the cross: The litany (Monk) [DDRDTLL, LDTLRDT, TM] B164; D530 12449

Wordsworth (---) [MMRMMDRM RD, SLLSSM] BR113 12450

Wordsworth (Monk) [MSMFMRD, RMSLLS, SDS] F41; BE135 12451

Worgan (Lyra Davidica, 1708) X Easter hymn 12452

Work (Mason) X Diligence 12453

Work, for the night is coming (Mason) X Diligence 12454

Work song (Mason) X Diligence 12455

Working (Shaw) [DMLSRFMRD, DMLSRFM] X345 12456

World invisible (Haile) [MSLLL SSSM, STDDDTT] Y192 12457

World to come (Hindu air) X Happy land 12458

Worley (Rosecrans) [MFSDM RDTD, SRMFMR, M] AS267 12459

Worship (German trad) [SDDRRM SR, RSSFMRD,] A250 12460

Worship (German trad) X Gregor's 159th metre 12461

Worship (Harrington) [MMFSFM RD, MRFMSSF#S,] G10; I14 12462

-----. V [MMFSFMMRD, MRFM SSF#] I14 12463

Worship (Hopkins) X Jehovah 12464

Worship (Meineke) [MMRDMR DTD, MRMTLS, R] BR106 12465

Worthy (---) [DDDDTLS, LLLL SFM, DD] BB168 12466

-----. R [SMDTLS, FMRSMD, SMDT] 12467

Worthy art thou, Lord (---) [SSDDDDD, TDRRRRR, FF] AX6 12468

-----. R [MFSMLSM, SMRFM RM, MF] 12469

Would men know (Sellers) [SL TDRDMD, DDTDRDS, S] AX438 12470

-----. R [MRDSF#SDT, F FFFFFM, S] 12471

Would you live for Jesus (Nusbaum) [SDDRMMMMMRRMF, STR] AS239; AT239; AU 122; AX277 12472

-----. R [SSRSSRFFMM, SS RSSR] 12473

Would you lose your load of sin [DSDRMFM, SMMRDMR, DS] AI402 12474

------. R [SF#SLSSFF, FMF SFFMM,] 12475

Wraysbury (Hopkins) [MRDMRS MRD, DMRSSLF#] L33; BY 10 12476

Wreford (Carter) [MMSFMMR D, D#RMFLR, SD] D25a; AL192; AP347a; AS448; AZ 272-B 12477

Wrestling Jacob (Wesley) [DM SRMRDRM, MMRDFFM] F 343; W416; AL312a; BY767 12478

Write these words (---) [DDD DDR, DDDLTD.] R550 12479

Wulfrun (Briggs) [DSDRMFRM, SLLSMRDR,] X401; AF527 12480

Wunderbarer König (Neander) X Arnsberg 12481

Würtemburg (Rosenmüller) X Nassau 12482

Wurzburg (Andächtige und auserlesene gesänger) [SDTDRM RDTS, DTDRMR] E127; X

150b; BN122; BY392 12483
Wych Cross (Routley) [DRMSM RDLLDLSMRDM,] BV60b; BY650 12484
Wychbold (Whinfield) [DSLSFMR MD, RSLTDLS,] E409; O262b; BY299 12485
Wycliff (Stainer) X Oxford 12486
Wye Valley (Mountain) X Remo 12487
Wyke (Heward) [MSRFMRDT, FMLSDTLS] F359 12488
Wylde Green (Cutts) [MMMRDRM FR, SSSFMRD] BZ 12489
Wynnstay (Lloyd) [DMSSLSSM, DRRM, DMSS] AL547a; AM344; AP674 12490
Wyoming (Carter) [MMFMMRD, DDRDRR#M, MM] BR334 12491
Wyoming (Perkins) [DDDDDTDR TD, DFFFMR] T267; AJ372 12492
Wytham (Watson) [DSSLDRM, RFMRDR, RLR] BV397 12493
Wyvill (Wyvill) [DDRMSFMRD, RMF#SDTL] AV304 12494

X

Xavier (Champneys) [DSLFRSM, MMRSTLS, LR] F485 12495
Xavier (Stainer) [DRMLSFSM, R FMRDR, RM] D653a; F106b; BA496; BY211b 12496

Y

Yaa'leh (Beimel) [MMS#MMMLLL S#FMS#, MMT] BH323 12497
Yarbrough (Bradbury) [SDMMM RDR, STRFFMRM,] AT356; AU174; AX397; AY223 12498
Yattendon (Tye) X Yattendon 15 12499
Yattendon 4 (Wooldridge) [DRFM RD, RMSFMR, MSLS] BJ4 12500
Yattendon 8 (Clark) [LLTDTDRDT LM, SFMRM] BJ8 12501
Yattendon 11 (Wooldridge) [MMM MRRDFFM, SSF#S, SL] BJ11 12502
Yattendon 12 (Bishop) X Leicester 12503
Yattendon 15 (Tye & Wooldridge) [SDRMFSSF#S, RFMDDT, R] W528b; BE225; BJ15 12504
Yattendon 17 (Wooldridge) [S SLTDDTT, DRMRRM, SM] BJ17 12505
Yattendon 18 (Wooldridge) [FLLSLTD, RRTDLLS, TT] BJ18 12506
Yattendon 22 (Wooldridge) [M DSFMRM, MF#SS, SMLSS] BJ22 12507
Yattendon 46 (Wooldridge) [DRMFFM, LSDMRD, SFM] A481; AJ535; BJ46 12508
Ye are the light (Brunk) [DD DDTLSM, FFFFSFM, D] AX157; AY382 12509
Ye children, come (Sprague) [SSMMDLFF, LSMMDR, SS] AI405; AM656 12510
-----. R [DMSMRD, RMFFSM R, MRD] 12511
Ye children of our God (Careless) [SSLSSFM, MDDTLS, MMF] BC288 12512
Ye chosen Twelve (Fox) [DSF MRDLSFM, RSFMMF] BC211 12513
Ye elders of Israel (---) [SDT DRMRMFSLSM, MSF] BC 344 12514
Ye lands, to the Lord (Hoff) X Hoff 12515
Ye messengers (Edmunds) [SM FRMD, RMFSLR, SMFS] BL 86 12516
Ye must be born again (Stebbins) X Born again 12517
Ye simple souls who stray (Stephens) [MMMSFMR, RRM FRSFM, M] BC290 12518
-----. R [SSSMRDT, TTDRTMR D, D] 12519
Ye sons and daughters (Palestrina) X Victory 12520
Ye souls of the faithful (Bragers) [MMDRMLTDRDT, RR TRM] BP95 12521
Ye souls of the faithful (Cath-

olic) [DRMMRDM, SDTLS, RM FF] BO145 12522

Ye souls of the faithful (Italian hymn mel) [SMRDDTSFMRRD, MSFM] BQ114 12523

Ye who are called to labor (---) [SF#SDSTL, LSLFLS, SF#S] BC 345 12524

Yearning (Norwegian) [MS#LTRDLL SM, MRTDDD] P343 12525

Years of youth (Morse) [DTRDRM FM, SFMR, MFRM] AE446; AR 370 12526

Yes, for me He careth (Richards) X Armstrong 12527

Yes, heaven is the prize (Mendelssohn) X Heavenly love 12528

Ygdrasil (Clarke) [MSFMRMFL MM, SDTDRD] AQ197 12529

Yield not to temptation (Palmer) [MMFMRR, DDRDT, LLTDS] N648; U161; W704; AE258; AG195; AH452; AI404; AM658; AO631; AP770; AS320; AT364; AU338; AV371; AW477; AX441; AY445; BA835; BB498; BY569 12530

-----. R [SSSLSSD, RRRDRMD, DD] 12531

Yigdal (Jewish trad) [MMMS#LT LS#DTLS#FM, MM] BH327 12532

Yigdal (Jewish trad) X Leoni 12533

Yimloch (Sulzer) [SMMMRRD, D#D#RMFMRDT,] BH287 12534

Yimloch Adonoy (Jewish trad) X Boruch Shaym I 12535

Ymdaith Mwnge (Welsh trad) [DLTDDSMFS, MLLMRDT] E203; X209 12536

Yn y Glyn (Evans) [LLMMLSLTL L, MF#SMDR] E563; W529a; X339 12537

Yoakley (Yoakley) [DRMMFSMDR MFFM, DMS] G222; I333; AJ 211; AZ96-K 12538

Yoeman's carol (Church Gallery book) [SDRMFSLS, SRMFMRD S,] BG20 12539

-----. R [FMSDLTDRTLS, DRM FS] 12540

Yom Kippur mode (Jewish trad) [DDDRMMRR, SDDRMSMR,] BH163 12541

Yom Kippur prayer (Weinberg) X Lord, what off'ring shall we bring 12542

York (Barnes) [MMRDMFFM, SSFMFRMF] BB144 12543

York (Harris) [SSMRDTL, SS DTDR, SSM] D585b 12544

York (Scottish Psalter, 1615) [DMSFLMSR, RMSSF#S, DM] A312a; E472; F301; V92; X628; AB325; AF95; AL630b; AP13; BA317; BJ71; BR138; BV89 12545

Yorkshire (Wainwright) [DDRM FSMFSL, SLTDRMRD] A16; B76; C76; D56a; E21; F61; G93; J19; K24; Q84; U344; W54; X73; Z506; AD336; AF 127; AK115; AL67; AN349b; AP175; AR134; AW71; AZ 600-A; BA159; BR148; BV 97; BY93 12546

You can make the pathway bright (Dungan) [SDFMR#M D, TDMRD#RLRM] BC208 12547

-----. R [SSSFLFM, FMMR RSR, MF] 12548

You can't do wrong and get by (Ellis) [MFSSLSDRMRD, DLLLD] AX282 12549

-----. R [DLLDDLS, SDDDDR MR, D] 12550

Youth (Lynes) X Recessional 12551

Yule (Luther) X From heaven high 12552

Z

Zachary (French trad) [SFM FRDMR, MRDRMF#SF#] X576 12553

Zeal (Marshall) [DDMDS, RD# RMRDMLS, RD#] BF512 12554

Zebulon (Mason) [SSFMRD, RMMFMR, SSFM] L48; AA11; AJ358 12555

Zeige mir dein angesicht (Freylinghausen) X Gregor's 77th metre 12556
Zelotes (Mozart) X Mozart II 12557
Zennor (Maker) [SMRDTLDTL S, SFFMDT] U30; AI295 12558
Zeno (Morton) [MRDTDRLTR DS, LFMRL] T8; AJ12 12559
Zephyr (Bradbury) [SSSLDLSMR, FMRMSFM] D87b; H86; I457; L330; T169; U70; V141; AA51; AE327; AI214; AJ248; AO567; AP77b; AS125; BB41; BR22 12560
Zerah (Mason) [SDDDMRSS, SSMF RM, SL] H8; L227; R71; T224; U12; V97a; AG37; AJ318; AM 163; AO131; AR123; AS106; AX101; BB175 12561
Zeuch ein (Crueger) [MDSFMRD, MRDTDR, MDS] Q228; AA252 12562
Zeuch ein zu meinen toren (Crueger) X Zeuch ein 12563
Zeuch meinen geist (Knorr, Neuer helicon. 1684) X St Gregory 12564
Zinck (Zinck, Koralbog. 1801) [DSFMRM, SDTLS, DSFMR] M249; O26; P5; Q542 12565
Zinck (Zinck. Koralbog. 1801) X Paa Gud alene 12566
Zinzendorf (Drese) X Rochelle 12567
Zion
NOTE: In English language entries, Zion is always spelled Sion within this index. 12568
Zion klagt (Schein) [LMMSFMR D#, MFSFMMR, L] Q268; AA 505 12569
Zions vaegter (Nicolai) X Sleepers, wake 12570
Zoan (Havergal) [DMRDTDD, DF MFRM, M] A545b; B99; C99; D323b; V584; AP60b; BR233; BV273 12571
Zochraynu (Jewish trad) [MRM LLLDTL, MRMTTTR] BH312 12572
Zoerbig (Selle) [DSFMRDSLTDT, SLLTD] AZ142-A 12573
Zu Bethlehem geboren (Nordstern. Fuhrer ...) X Eia, Eia 12574
Zu meinem herrn (Schicht) [SLTDTDDRRMD, MRDTS] E119; W103; AF173; AN 101 12575
Zum frieden (Bach) [MDLLF MFM, RDFMRDT, M] E499; W285b; X674; BE110 12576
Zundel (Zundel) [MRDTLTD, DMRDDT, MRD] Eap. 68 12577
Zundel (Zundel) X Beecher 12578
Zurich (Weimar. G-B. 1681) X Jesu, meines lebens leben 12579
Zuversicht (Crueger. Praxis pietatis melica. 1653) X Ratisbon 12580
Zwingli (Knecht) [SDDDLSFM, SLLLRDT, S] BR416 12581
Zwingli (Zwingli) [DDRMFRD, MFSSRMF, MF] AO605 12582

IV

Composers and Tune Names

Anonymous

Anonymous tunes
NOTE: Satisfactory sources could not be identified for these melodies.

A few more years shall roll; X11014 The pilgrim
A poor wayfaring man of grief
Ades domine
Agnus dei
Anfield
Annapolis
As swiftly my days
As wide as the skies
Atonement
Ave, Regina (19th c)
Balfern
Bamberg (17th c)
Barton X2975 Emmaus
Behold, it is the springtime of the year
Benediction
Benison
Bernard
Better land
Bexfield
Bingham
Birling (19th c)
Bowring
Bradbury
Cana
Caritas
Carmelite litany
Carol
Carthage
Children's friend
Christ, the Lord, is risen today
Come, all ye saints who dwell
Come, go with me, beyond the sea
Come, Holy Ghost, send down (19th c)
Come, humble sinner
Come, let us anew
Come, O thou King of Kings
Come, thou O come
Comfort
Communion
Concord
Consecration; X10642a Take my life and let it be
Create in this weak form of mine
Damascus
Daughter of a mighty Father
Daughter of Zion
David's harp
Deliverer; X4961 Humility; X10091 Sitting at the feet
Denmark; X7970 O ye mountains high
Dona nobis pacem
Down by the river's verdant side
Dublin
Dwight
Ecclesia
Eden
El Kader
Eleanor
Es ist noch raum
Evergreen
Expectation
Exultation
Faithful
For health and strength
Freeport
Gambold
Gaudeamus igitur
Good morning to you
Gott sprach zu dir
Gregor's 20th metre (before 1400)
Grey
Hail the glorious golden city
Hark, hark my soul
Hark! what mean those holy

voices; X2243 Crown Him
He loves me
Hemans
He's coming
Higher than I
His bride
Home I
Home II; X5055 I hear in the air
Homeward bound; X7432 No, not one (Hugg)
Honor
How far from home
How firm a foundation
Immanuel
In the good ship
Jesus, my Lord, my God
Jesus of Nazareth
Jesus, the Light of the world
Jesus the very thought of thee
Kingo
Laurel Hill
Leaf
Ledbury
Leominster
Let each man learn
Levabo
Liberty Hall; X6756 Martyrdom (Wilson)
Light of the world
Lind
Litany
Litany No. 3
Little clusters; X8510 Pleasant pastures
Little reapers
Loyal and true
Maitland
Meet mother in the skies
Mendota; X10281 Speak gently
Middlesex
Monroe Place
Morning has come
Mountain Christians
My dearest Saviour
My God, how wonderful thou art; X7205 My God! how ought
My God, I am determined
My Shepherd
Nay, speak no ill
Need
Never alone
Newark
Newcombe
Ninety-third [Psalm]
No mortal eye hath seen
No night in heaven
Not made with hands
Now let us rejoice
O God all gracious
O Heart of Jesus
O how happy are they; X2125 Convert
O, how I love Jesus; X4928 How I love Jesus; X7896 O, save me
O Mother! most afflicted (1638)
O save me at the cross; X7749 O, how I love Jesus
O thou eternal King
O turn to Jesus, Mother
Old 148th
On the mountain's top appearing
Onward
Palestine
Palmer
Panem vivum
Parting hymn
Pastoral
Percivals
Pietas
Praise to the man
Prayer
Press on
Promise
Purity; X6377 Lord of hosts; X9756 Saviour, teach me
Refuge
Remember thy creator
Renova
Repose
Resignation (adapted by Sieboth)
Resignation
Robinson
Rowley
Sacred crown
St Barnabas
St Luke; X9485 St Luke's
St Paul's
Saviour of the nations, come (16th c)
See! amid the winter's snow
See, O God, we childrenccome
Shechem
Shepherd true
Shields

Sleep, holy Babe
Smithville
Southampton (1870)
Spring gardens
Steele
Striving onward, pressing forward
Sweden (16th c North Europe)
X5064 I hoppet sig min;
X7465 Norrland
Sweet the moments; X2611 Divine compassion
Taenk, naar engang den Taage;
X8121 One radiant morn
Tantum ergo
Tantum ergo
Taps
The convert
The hallowed spot
The righteous marching home
The Spirit of God like a Fire
Thorney Abbey
Toronto
Tubingen
Turner
Viator
Vig
Vita aeterna
Waken, Christian children
Watchman's call
We have heard
Wer nur den lieben Gott
Wesley
Westgate
What lovely infant
When first the glorious light of truth
When the battle's over; X877 Battle hymn
Where shall I be?
Who's on the Lord's side?
Will you go?
With wondering awe
Within the veil
Wordsworth
Worthy
Worthy art thou, Lord
Write these words (ancient melody)
Ye elders of Israel; X11345 Touch not the cup
Ye who are called to labor

A

A.H.A. (A.H. Ackley?)
Jesus has died for me
A.L.B.
I cannot be idle (1907)
I've enlisted in the service
Abbey, Alonzo J., 1825-87
Cooling
Abbey, Horatio G.
Tucker
Abbot, Asahel
'Tis religion that can give;
X8583 Praise to God;
X8607 Prayer
Abbot, H.
Day
Protection
Abelard, Peter, 1079-1142
Gildas; X694 Augustine;
X9286 St Augustine
Abt, Franz, 1819-85
Pastor
Willingham
Acfield, W.
Vesper
Achron, Joseph, 1886-1943
God supreme
I lift mine eyes (1932)
O God, the Rock of Ages (1932)
There is a mystic tie (1932)
Ackley, A.H. (A.H.A.?)
He lives; X125 Ackley
Ackley, B.D.
Be with me (1917)
Earthly pleasures (1911)
Go as a witness (1917)
Have you prayed it through? (1915)
Just outside the door (1912)
Only thy tender care (1916)
Adam, Adolphe-Charles, 1803-56
O holy night
Adams, Mrs. Crosby
Montreat
Adams, Thomas, 1785-1858
Holborn
Resurgam
Adcock, John, 1838-1919
Derwent (1882)

Woodbrook
Ahle, Johann Rudolph, 1625-73
Augsburg (1662); X3936 Gott ist getreu
Liebster Jesu (1664); X574 Arnheim; X1150 Blessed Jesus, at thy; X2515 Dessau; X6170 Liebster Jesu, wir; X7585 Nuremberg; X10140 Søode Jesu, vi er
Salve cordis gaudium
Ahle. Geistliche arien, 1672
Es ist genung
Ahlström, Olof, 1756-1835
St James' Stockholm; X4983 Hvad röst, hvad
Ahnfelt, Oskar, 1813-82
Ack, saliga stunder; X12341 With God and His
Ahnfelt
I djupet af mitt hjärta
Jag är främling; X5229 I'm a pilgrim
O sälla land
Ahnfelt, O. Sanger.
Hos Gud är idel gladje
Aitken, William M. H.
Blackburn
Akeroyd, S. Divine companion, 1701
Lambeth
Albert, Heinrich, 1604-51
Waltham; X239 Albert; X3860 Godesberg; X3931 Gott des himmels; X5885 Koenigsberg
Alcock, Walter G., 1861-
Bryant
Alexander, Ian
Binghampton (1927)
Song of the pilgrims (1927)
Alexis, Gerhard Theodore, 1889-1927
Blessed hope (1924)
Ishpeming (1924)
Maria (1924)
St Ingrid) X5342 Ingrid
Seraphim (1923)
Allchin, William Thomas Howell, 1843-83
Emmaus
Alleman, Benjamin F.
Alleman
Allen, Alfred R.
St Helena (1911)
Allen, Cecil John, 1886-
Ewhurst
Allen, Chester G., 1838-78
Greatorex
Joyful song; X367 Allen; X8568 Praise Him! praise
Lebanon
Allen, George Nelson, 1812-77
Maitland (1840); X7185 Must Jesus bear
Allen, Hugh Percy, 1869-1946
Kingly vale
Midian
Qui laborat orat
Valour
Alleyne, A. 1867-1949
Vernham Dean
Allgemeines Katholisches gesangbuch. Vienna, 1774
Halle
Hursley (Long meter); X311 All things are thine; X 3987 Gracious God whose; X8546 Pour out thy spirit; X10499 Sun of my soul; X10699 Te deum; X12114 When here, O Lord
Te deum (78. 78. 77 meter) X1733 Christ the Lord is risen; X3809 God is great; X4180 Grosser Gott; X 4278 Halle; X4788 Holy God, we praise; X4975 Hursley; X8327 Pascal; X11669a Victor King
Alman, Samuel
Believe not those (arr, 1932)
Hymn for tabernacles (1932)
Nishmas (1932)
O Lord, our King (1932)
The lifting of mine hands (1932)
Where Judah's faithful sons are found (1932)
Alsatian traditional see German traditional, if anonymous source
Alwood, J. K.
Unclouded day; X11090 The unclouded day

Ambrose, Robert S.
Ambrose (1876); X2630 Dolce domum; X2721 Dulce domum; X8123 One sweetly solemn; X10514 Sunset
Ambrosian (ancient melody)
Christus vincit
Deus creator omnium
Rerum deus tenax vigor
"American folk hymn"
NOTE: Hymnal BZ uses this phrase for Negro Spirituals.

American Indian tribal tunes
see Chippewa, Dakota, Omaha

American musical miscellany, 1798
Ganges; X4958 Hull
American traditional
Alida (early 19th c)
Amazing grace (1805); X973 Behold the Saviour; X3971 Grace; X6611 McIntosh; X10175 Solon; X10778 That doleful night
Arise (A southern mel.); X5137 I will arise and go
Campmeeting; X986 Belief; X3038 Es ist ein born; X3436 Forever here my rest; X4937 How pleasant and how; X5046 I do believe; X7691 O God of wisdom; X8617 Prayer is the soul's; X12043 West Milton
Cleansing fountain (early 19th c); X3461 Fountain; X10872 The fountain
Foundation; X4919 How firm a foundation; X4956 Huger; X8681 Protection
Jordan's Banks; X8096a On Jordan's banks; X8672 Promised land; V8673-75 misfiled as Promised Land; X11022 The promised land
Land of rest
Lonesome Valley
Millenium (before 1850)
Müller (19th c); X769 Away in a manger; X6532 Luther
Ontario
The wayfaring Stranger
Ampleforth, Laurence
O Sacred Heart! Our home
Amps, William, 1824-1910
Venice (1858)
Andächtige und auserlesene gesänger. Würzburg, 1703
Würzburg; X10064 Sing the Holy Family's
Andernach Gesangbuch, 1608
Andernach; X7601 O blessed day, when
In natali domini
Jesus dulcis memoria; X2726 Dulcis Jesu memoria
Rex gloriose; X9009 Rex gloriose martyrum
Song of the ship; X3047 Es kommt ein schiff
Te lucis ante terminum
Tres magi de gentibus
Anderson, A.W.
Omnipotence (1940)
Anderson, James Smith, 1853-1945
Fingal
Shiloh (arr)
Anderson, William K., 1888-
Journey's end (1930)
Andrews, Carroll T.
Queen when the earth (1958)
Salve, Pater salvatoris (1958)
Andrews, Mark, 1875-
Lauda anima
Motherland (1927)
Whitney (1910)
Andriessen, Hendrik, 1892-
O Lord, in this great mystery
Angell, Warren M., 1907-
Shawnee (1951)
Angers church melody
Lucis creator
Anglo-Genevan Psalms, 1558
Old 25th
Anglo-Genevan Psalter (by John Day), 1561
Old 18th
Anglo-Genevan Psalter, 1556.
Old 22d

Old 44th
Anhang der Seelen-Harpff. Onolzbach, 1665
Lobe den herren, o meine
Anonymous tunes see beginning of this index (p. 909)
Antes, John, 1740-1811
Hope; X3237 Falckner
Monkland
Anthes, Friedrich, Konrad, 1812-
Anthes (1847)
Antiphonale romanum
En clara vox redarguit M 1
Exultet cor praecordiis M 1
X5562 Jesu dulcis memoria; X7887 O salutaris Hostia
Antonio.
Regina caeli laetare (1667)
Arcadelt, Jacques, ca 1505 - ca 60
Arcadelt (1572); X720 Ave Maria
Armenian liturgy
Armenian hymn
Armes, Philip, 1836-1908
Armes (1875); X3567 Galilee
Vigilantes
Armistead, John, 1877-1935
Pro patria; X1286 Break, day of God
Armstrong, James, 1840-1928
Armstrong (arr)
Newland
Armstrong, Thomas
Exon (1931)
Arndt, E.M.
God speed the right; X7534 Now to heaven our
Arne, Thomas Augustine, 1710-78
Arlington (1762); X413 Am I a soldier; X979 Behold, where, in a; X3295 Father, we come; X5232 I'm not ashamed; X7935 O thou, whose temple; X10941 The Lord be with us; X11202 This is the day
Falkirk
Shakespeare's carol I
Arnold, Robert S.
No tears in heaven (1935)
Arnold, Samuel, 1740-1802
Arnold
Arnold, William
Alexandria; X5749 Judea
Middleton
Arnold. Complete psalmodist, 1756
Epsom
Arran, Isle of see Scottish traditional: Isle of Arran
Arrhenius, Jakob
Jesus allt mitt goda är
Arsdale, P.P. van see Van Arsdale, P.P.
Arterbury, Joel
My testimony
Arthur, Edward, 1874-1948
Bodlondeb (1927)
Llansamlet
Lucerna laudoniae (1927)
Lumetto
Pax vobiscum (1927)
St Kentigern (1927)
St Sulien (1927)
Tabernacle
Arundel hymns
Ave, maris stella; X2102 Consolator
As hymnodus sacer, Leipzig, 1625
Ach Gott und Herr; X232 Ak, Herre form; X274 All glory be to God; X 3878 Goeldel
Breslau; X113 Ach Gott, wie; X1762 Christi blut; X4633 Herr Jesu Christ; X5642 Jesus my life; X6087 Leipsic
Ashfield, Robert James, 1911-
Broadwalk
Ashford, Emma L.
Evelyn (1905)
Sutherland (1905)
Ashworth, C. Collection, 1760
St Thomas
Asian melody
Sri Lampang
Asper, Frank Wilson, 1892-
God is in His holy temple
Hear thou our hymn
O hark! a glorious sound
O thou, before the world began
Rejoice, ye Saints of Latter-

days
Rise up, O men of God
Take courage, Saints
This house we dedicate
'Tis sweet to sing
Atkins, Ivor, 1869-1953
White Ladies Aston
Atkinson, Frederick Cook, 1841-97
Caritas perfecta (1885)
Morecambe (1870)
Thetford
Attwood, Thomas, 1765-1838
Attwood (1831); X11580 Veni Creator, No. 1
Staines
Auber, D. F.
Mercy's free
Aufranc, D. A. R.
Pevensey (1940)
Thetford (1940)
Windy Ridge (1940)
Austrian traditional
Dolomite chant
The shepherd; X2554 Dickinson
Avis, E. C.
Thy love to me
Avison, Charles, 1709-70
Avison; X10001 Shout the glad tidings
Aylward, T. E., 1844-
Balcom
Ayres, James Caiger, 1933-
St Aidan

B

B E W see Warren, B. Elliott
B. S.
Hibernia's patron saint
Babcock, Maltbie Davenport, 1858-1901
Prayer (1889)
Babst. Gesangbuch, 1545
Da Jesus an des kreuzes
Bach, Karl Philipp Emanuel, 1714-88
Apolutrosis; X12248 Wie gross ist des
Weimar (1784)
Bach, Johann Sebastian, 1685-1750
Chamber music
Cöthen; X2889 Eins ist not
Crasselius
Dessler; X12254 Wie wohl ist mir
Faithful
Ich halte treulich still; X10965 The Lord is risen
Laus deo (1736)
Nicht so traurig; X9826 Sebastian
Now blessed thou
Potsdam; X7779 O Jesus victim-priest
Rinkart; X5904 Kommt seelen
Zum frieden
Bach, Johann Sebastian, The School of
Blessing and honour
Baden-Powell, James
Knightsbridge
Salve, festa dies
Song of songs
Baermann, Carl, 1839-1913
Beverly (1903)
Peace (1905)
Baessler, J. G.
Alleluia! Gott zu loben (1826)
Bailey, E. R., 1859-1938
Canaan
Praise him; X3812 God is love
Baillot, Pierre Marie Francois de Sales, 1771-1842
Oliphant
Bain, James Leith Macbeth, 184?-1925
Marosa (1932); X1356 Brother James' air
Bainbridge, Leslie
Jesus! thou art coming
Baird, R. B.
Improve the shining moments
When the rosy light of morning
Baker, A. S., 1868-96
Canaan
Corner-stone
Gaudia matris
Baker, Benjamin Franklin, 1811-89

Wallace
Baker, David, 1940-
Thanksgiving
Baker, Frederick G., 1840-76
St Saviour (1876); X5753 Judson; X9726 Sauveur
Baker, Henry, 1835-1910
Hesperus (1866); X8746 Quebec X12191 Whitburn
Baker, Henry Williams, 1821-77
St Timothy (1875); X1841 Clearway
Stephanos (1868)
Baker, Reginald, 1904-
Mansfield Road
Bales, Richard
Thee, Lord (1964)
Balle, Carl C.N., 1806-55
Emmanuel (1860); X12 A Danish tune; X801 Balle; X2518 Det kimer nu til; X3462 Fountain of grace; X10776 Thanksgiving hymn; X10898 The happy Christmas
Ballet, W.
Lute-book lullaby (17th c)
Balthasar.
Ave maris stella
Tantum ergo
Tota pulchra es
Baltzell, I. and Baltzell, L. may be the same individual. Note carefully.
Baltzell, I.
Missionary's farewell
Baltzell, L.
I want to be a worker
Bamberg (no initials)
Sing with joy (1732)
Bambridge, William S.
St Asaph
Bancroft, H. Hugh.
Ascension (1938)
Bansbach, Philip A.
Hail, holy Queen (1940)
O sweet Infant Jesus (1940)
Barber, E.W.
San Remo
Barham-Gould, Arthur Cyril, 1891-1953
St Leonard's
Baring-Gould, Sabine, 1834-1924
Eudoxia; X7530 Now the day is over
Barker, Cyril
The Prince of Peace
Barker, E.R.
St John Damascene
Barnard, Mrs. Charles
Give of your best; X825 Barnard
Barnard, Charlotte Alington, (Claribel, pseud), 1830-69
Brocklesbury (1868); X10340 Brocklesby; X6916 Merton
Pilgrimage
Barnby, Joseph, 1838-96
Afternoon (1896)
Angels of Jesus; X1537 Carmen Coeli
Barnby I
Barnby II; X8787 Ralston
Barnby III (1872); X6557 Lux vitae
Barnby's Hymnary, Tune 101
Bethlehem
Burleigh (1872)
Caritas; X408 Alverstoke; X409 Alverstroke; X11610 Ventnor; X12306 Windsor
Carlton; X9262 St Andrew; X9267 St Andrews
Children's praise (1896)
Chiselhurst
Cloisters (1868); X6383 Lord of our life
Crossing the bar (1892)
Crucis umbra (1890)
Diadema (1883); X1103 Birkdale; X1407 Burnley
Diademata (1872)
Domine, nobiscum
Dulce, (1883)
Edinburgh (1872); X850 Barnby's hymnary, Tune 590; X3997 Grasmere; X8092 Omnia
Emmaus; X7313 Neale
Eton
Eton College

Evening hymn
Faroon
Frankscot (1883); X11823 Waring
Galilean (1883)
Good Shepherd
Hearth fire (1868)
Hebron (1874); X6698 Mar Saba
His forever (1890)
Holy, holy, Holy Lord
Holy Trinity (1861); X266 All as God wills; X2068 Coniston
Irae
Jordan (1872); X1503 Cantate domino; X4877 Horeb
Just as I am; X829 Barnby; X2741 Dunstan; X7121 Morris
Kirkdale; X836 Barnby's hynary, Tune 91; X2057 Confidence; X9975 Shield; X11234 Through the day
Laudes domini (1868); X10878 The God of harvest
Litlington Tower
Long Milford
Longwood; X1066 Bethsaida; X7933 O thou whose power
Manna
Mansfield (1893)
Merrial (1868); X830 Barnby; X3127 Evening; X7531 Now the day is over; X11463 Twilight
Newnham
Nightfall (1897); X851 Barnby's hymnary, Tune 633; X4876 Horeb; X8593 Praise ye our Father
Paradise (1866); X7852 O Paradise; X8307 Paradise, No 2
Rejoice
Requiem (1869); X5981 Last sleep; X8947 Requiescat; X10935 The last sleep
Roseat hues
St Anatolius
St Andrew (1866); X831 Barnby; X844 Barnby's hymnary, Tune 237; X7043 Monsell
St Anselm (1869); X3707 Gladness
St Boniface; X9383 St Fidelis
St Chrysostom (1871); X164 Adoro; X165 Adoro te; X1804 Chrysostom; X2939 Ellerton; X7804 O Light, whose beams; X11386 Tristitia
St Hilda (1861); X4697 Hilda
St Ignatius; X3915 Gordon; X7370 New year
St Olave (1897); X4420 Havergal; X8660 Pro me perforatus
St Polycarp (1869); X5581 Jesus, I my cross; X5622 Jesus, lover of my soul; X8528 Polycarp; X9382 St Fabian
St Sylvester; X635 Aspiration; X2463 Deliverance; X4831 Holy Word
Sandringham (1889); X3294 Father, to us; X7856 O perfect love; X8428 Perfect love
Sarum (1868); X832 Barnby; X3413 For all the saints; X6957 Militant; X8662 Pro omnibus sanctis; X 8944 Requiem; X9576 St Philip
Sinai
Soho (1881); X10326 Springtide hour
Stand up; X833 Barnby
Stanley (1894)
Sunset; X11251 Thy will be done
Te deum laudamus
Tender Shepherd
The blessed name
The blessed rest
The golden chain (1887); X3884 Golden chain
To victory (1872); X5328 Incarnation; X6702 March to victory; X10885 The good fight; X11919 We march to victory
Veni, Domini Jesu

Via pacis I
Via pacis II (1889)
Vita aeterna (1868)
Watch o'er me
Westcott (1872)
X4211 Guildhall; X9956 Sheltering wing
Winkworth (1869)
Winterton (1892)
Woodleigh
Barnekow, Christian, 1837-1913
Barnekow I
Barnekow II
Barnekow III
Viborg
Barnes, Archie Fairbairn, 1878-
Dunblane Cathedral
Montague
Barnes, Edward Shippen, 1887-
Bala Cynwyd (1937)
Comrades of the cross (1927)
Faithful legions (1936)
God with us (1936)
Holmes (1936)
O come, let us worship (1926)
Qui tenet (1927)
San Vicente (1939)
Somerset (1937)
The Mystic (1927)
Thine house (1937)
Wireless (1927)
Barnes, Edwin, fl. 1886
Heber
Morton
Russell
Salisbury
Southampton
When the King shall claim His own
Winterbourne
York
Barraclough, Henry
Benediction (1932)
Barrington, J.W.
Onward
Barrows, Donald S., 1877-1951
Conquest (1941)
Cura dei (1941)
Barry, Charles Ainslie, 1830-1915
Annunciation
Barthélémon, Francois Hippolyte, 1741-1808
Autumn (1785); X6694 Mant Ballerma; X797 Balerma; X5290 In memory of the Saviour's
Morning hymn (1789)
Bartlett, Maro L.
Temple(1905)
Barton. Psalms, 1706
Coleshill
Basford, Henry
Lux coelestis
Basque traditional, etc.
Golden sheaves; X5813 Khanta zagun
Swansea
The Infant King
Bassford, William Kipp, 1839-1902
Thanksgiving; X1480 Can a little child
Basswood, W.K. see Bassford, William K.
Batchellor, Daniel
Onslow (1885); X1674 Child's morning hymn; X11934 We thank thee
Bate, H.A., 1899-
Collingwood
Battishill, Jonathan, 1738-1801
Battishill
Baumbach, Adolph, 1830-80
In corde meo; X6132 Let the words
Baume, John W.
Emilie (1905)
Baumgartner, Hope Leroy
Sprague Hall (1927)
Bax, Arnold Edward Trevor, 1883-1953
Wonder (1931)
Baxter, Catherine Deisher, 1914-
Blest moments (1958)
Bay, R.
We plow the fields
Beale, E.D.
Thy word have I hid
Beall, B.B.
Lift Him up
Beatson, C.S.
Riber
Beaty, Richard William, 1799-

1883
Caritas
Beaumont, Geoffrey, 1903-
Chesterton
Gracias
Bechler, John Christian, 1784-1857
Bechler
Praise the Lord
Beck, Abraham Reinke, 1833-
Just as I am (1861); X942 Beck
Becker, Arthur C.
To God our Father
Becket, Robert Anderson, 1834-1910
Wayland
Becket, Thomas à, 1843-1918
Red, white and blue; X1903 Columbia the gem; X11518 Up, awake, ye defenders
Bedford, G. L., 1912-
Bletchley
Beecher, H. W. Plymouth collection, 1855
Advent
Ives
Latter day; X10784 The alarm
Beery, Adaline H.
Hail, blessed Trinity (1894)
Beery, William, 1852-
Berne
Blessed Bible, how I love it (1901)
Come, Holy Ghost, in love
Elgin (1950)
Huntingdon; X10641 Take my hand and lead
Huntingdon II
Juniata (1896); X6292 Lo, a gleam
John Nass
Love of God (1951)
Beesley, Ebenezer
God of our fathers, we come to thee
Great is the Lord; 'tis good
High on the mountain top
Let us oft speak kind words
Lord, we ask thee
Reverently and meekly now
Sing we now at parting
The happy day has rolled on
We meet again in Sabbath School
Welcome, welcome Sabbath morning
What glorious scenes mine eyes behold
What voice salutes the startled ear
When Christ was born in Bethlehem
Beethoven, Ludwig van, 1770-1827
A hymn anthem; X7769 O Jesus Christ, Redeemer X10905 The heavens, O God
Alsace
X1208 Bonn; X4872 Hopkins; X5974 Larghetto
Beethoven (from 9th symphony); X4203 Guide me, O thou great; X5002 Hymn to joy; X5724 Joy; X8153 Onward brothers, march
Depth of mercy
Dulcetta
Emmanuel; X2095 Consolation; X2112 Contemplation; X2615 Djupt sjun ker aret; X7819a O Lord, our little ones
Gorton; X6372 Lord, keep us safe
Gracious Father, O Lord, hear us
Mountain wave
O lead and guide us
O salutaris hostia; X9483 St Luke, No 1
Peace be to this congregation
Salome; X2991 Engedi
Sardis; X2331 Dane; X4435 Hayes; X9740 Savior, breath an evening; X11304 To the God of all
Sidwell
Beimel, Jacob
Bow down thine ear, Lord (1932)
Hymn for the golden age (1932)

Unto the hills (1932)
We are thy people
When Israel, of the Lord beloved (1932)
When Israel to the wilderness (1932)
Yaa'leh
Beirly, A.
In hymns of praise (1896)
Belcher, John W.
Ionia
Belden, Franklin E.
A shelter in the time of storm (1899)
Belden (1900); X6338 Look for the beautiful
Blessed Lord, how much I need thee (1886)
Cover with His life (1899)
Diligence (1886)
Even at the door (1886)
Fillmore (1886)
Hakes (1878)
Hold fast till He come (1886)
Holy day, Jehovah's rest (1886)
I will sing of Jesus' love (1886)
Look for the waymarks
Mason (1886)
Oakland (1886)
Over the line (1895)
Robinson (1886)
The judgment has set (1886)
There's no other name like Jesus (1886)
Verdi (1886)
We would see Jesus (1899)
We'll build on the Rock (1886)
Wholly thine (1886)
Bell, John Montgomerie, 1837-1910
St Baldred
St Giles
Bell, M. F.
St Mark
Bell, William Henry, 1873-1946
Cathcart
Hail harbinger of morn
Beltjens, Joseph H.
Tantum ergo
Benbow, William
Amnos (1914)
Savonarola (1915)
Benedictine plainsong, mode and date indicated when known
Adoro te devote M 5 (13th c); X8868 Redhead, No. 12 (Redhead)
Jam lucis M 6
Jam lucis orto sidere M 8
O blessed by God (Monte Cassino trad)
Bennard, George
Old rugged cross (1913); X9160 Rugged cross; X11007 The old rugged cross
Benson, H. Ford, 1859-1933
Aurora
Bentley, William W.
Christ the Lord cometh
Dedication
In the rifted rock; X10612 Sweetly resting
Benz, Johann B.
O Queen of peerless majesty (1861)
Berggreen, Andreas Peter (or Anton Peter Berggren) 1801-80
Amen, Jesus hanskal raade (1849); X427 Amen sjunge hvarje; X2328 Dana
Berggren I; X3193 Expectation; X9001 Revelation; X10637 Taenk, naar engang
Berggren II
Brorson
Even song
Grace
Underbar en stjarna blid
Vita
"Berg kreyen", 1551
Wir danken dir, Herr Jesu Christ
Bergquist, John Victor, 1877-1935
Aline
Donald (1924)
Emilia (1924)
Final rest (1903)
Muriel (1924)
Berky, Georgia Guiney
Dwell in me

Berlin, Irving (real name Isidor Balin), 1888-
God bless America (1939)
Berridge, Arthur, 1855-
Harvard (1905)
Huddleston
Besler, Samuel, 1574-1625
Herr Gott Vater
Beutler, J. B.
In morgenrot gekleidet (1799)
Bicknell, C., 1842-1918
Come faithful people
Bierman, J. B.
Aus tiefer not (ca 1876)
Bigelow, James, 1920-
Now for each yearning heart
We would worship (1951)
Biggs, Arthur H.
Charlotte (1941)
Sumner (1941)
Biggs, Richard Keys
Communion processional (1958)
Triumphantly doth Christ (1958)
Bilhorn, Peter P.
I will sing (1887); X12413 Wondrous story
O, the best Friend to have is Jesus
Redemption
Sweet peace (1887); X10585 Sweet peace, the gift; X11135 There comes to my
Billings, William, 1746-1800
Amherst (1770)
Bills, G. M.
The best friend of all
Binder, Abraham Wolfe, 1895-
Adonoy yimloch
Again as evening's shadow falls (1932)
All the world (1932)
Arise to praise the Lord (1932)
Ayn komocho
Before the Menorah (1932)
Blessed, blessed
Evening prayer (1932)
Father, see thy suppliant children (1932)
Father, to thy dear name (1932)
God is my strong salvation (1932)
God moves in a mysterious way (1932)
God of Israel (1932)
Happy he who walketh (1932); X4321 Happy he that never
Harneenu
Here let thy people (1932)
Hymn to mothers (1932)
In mercy Lord, incline thine ear (1932)
Kindle the taper (1932)
Lo! the earth rejoices (1932)
May the words
Mee chomocho
O render thanks (1932)
O Soul Supreme (1932)
Out of the depths, O Lord (1932)
Priestly benediction
Rest in the Lord, my soul (1932)
Sabbath blessing (1932)
Sabbath hymn; X1962 Come, O Sabbath day
Sh'ma Yisroayl
Summer suns are glowing (1932)
The Lord, my Shepherd still has been (1932)
Va-y'dabayr moshe
When there is peace (1932)
Who is like thee (1932)
Who taught the bird (1932)
Bingham, Seth, 1882-
Madison Avenue (1943)
Bird, James
Hurlbut (1927)
Birtchnell, Frank N.
Heart of the Holy Child
Bischoff, J. W.
The Lord is my light
Bishop, Henry Rowley, 1786-1855
Home sweet home; X4839 Home; X6937 'Mid pleasures and; X10573 Sweet home
Bishop, John, 1665-1737
Illsley; X1111 Bishop; X 5225 Ilsley
Leicester (ca 1700); X945

Bedford; X12503 Yattendon 12
Bixel, James W., 1913-
Silent (1938)
Bixler, Marguerite
Hartville
Black, James M.
Look to the Lamb of God (1918)
The roll; X6063 Leave it there (Tindley, arr); X9097 Roll call; X12144 When the roll is
Where He may lead me (1900); X5108 I remember Calvary
Where Jesus is, 'tis heaven
Blackall, A.K., 1877-
Swanmore
Blackith, H. de la Haye
Palgrave (1893)
Blackman, G.A.
Calm on the listening ear
Blake, Leonard James, 1907-
Remission
Twyford
Blanchard, George F., 1868-
Lest we forget (1898); X8831 Recessional
Blanchard, William G., 1905-
Godwin (1934)
Blanchet, Alfred Tom, 1868-1926
Animae hominum
Bland, A.P.
How beautiful heaven must be
Blanton, Leonard Cooper
Columbia (1951)
Blessin, G.
Blessin
Bliss, Philipp, becomes Bliss, Philip P., or Bliss, P.P. or Bliss, Philip Paul, 1838-76
Almost persuaded; X388 Almost
Bliss; X5432 It is well X11704 Ville de Havre; X12133 When peace, like a
Daniel; X2334 Daniel's band; X2339 Dare to be a Daniel
Eternity
Gladness (1870); X5020 I am so glad; X5625 Jesus loves me
Go bury thy sorrow
Hold the fort
Holiness (1875); X7069 More holiness give me; X7241 My prayer
I gave my life for thee (1874); X4421 Havergal; X5804 Kenosis; X9209 Sacrifice
Light of the world; X10937; The Light of the world; X11111 The whole world was
Lower lights; X1317 Brightly beams; X6130 Let the lower lights; X10000 Should you feel
Man of sorrows; X363 Alleluia, what a Saviour; X3663 Gethsemane
Once for all
Precious promise
St Cyril
We're going home tomorrow
What shall the harvest be?
Whosoever; X12236 Whosoever will
With harps and with viols
Wonderful words; X10065 Sing them over again; X12405 Wonderful words of life; X12448 Words of life
Blomqvist, Joel
Böjd under korset
Sabbatsdag, hur skön du är
Blosser, H.C.
Only thee
Blow, William
St Agnes; X218 Agnus dei; X1182 Blow
Blumenthal, Jacob (or Jacques), 1829-1909
Blumenthal; X4399 Haste not! Haste not!; X11229 Though our hearts
Blunt, F.W., 1939-1921
Merrial; X4353 Hark, the voice; X6390 Lord, thy word abideth; X6565 Lyndhurst; X8936 Repose
Bode, Arnold G.H.
Laramie (1941)
Boe, V.E.

At sunset (1914)
Jesus all glorious (1931)
Bohemian Brethren.
NOTE: Publication date or source given, when known.

Augusta (1566); X7956 O wie sehr lieblich!
Betracht'n wir heut zu dieser frist (1544); X7523 Now glad of heart; X12330 Wir wollen alle fröhlich sein
Bohemian Brethren (1566); X7005 Mit freuden zart; X10062 Sing praise to Him
Far off lands (Hemmets Koralbok); X1197 Bohemian hymn
Gaude, regina gloriae (1544)
Gregor's 2d metre (1531); X 3618 Gelobt sei Gott, der
Gregor's 54th metre (before 1566); X1699 Christ, der du bist
Gregor's 520th metre (1541); X3942 Gott woll'n wir loben
Landskron (1531)
Lofsungur (1531)
O mensch sieh (1566); X1191 Bohemia
Saelir (1544); X2336 Danket dem herrn; X8383 Peace
Savannah, see Wesley, J. Foundery collection, 1742
Stettin (1566); X7577 Nun seht
Unitas Fratrum (1566)
Bohemian traditional, etc.
NOTE: Wisely see also Czeck traditional titles.

Be ye joyful; X9658 Salvator natus
Freuen wir uns (1457); X3504 Freuen wir uns all in
Gladness (12th c)
Judah's Lion (ca 1600)
Kommet ihr hirten; X8003 Old Bohemian carol
Resurgenti Nazareno (1505)
Bolton, Fannie E.
Bolton (1900)
Bolze, G.
Walk with Jesus (1788); X5977 Lasset uns mit Jesu
Bonitus, Brother
Dear Guardian of Mary
Bonner, Carey, 1859-1938
Doudney
Muswell Hill II
Sommerlied
Tilak
Bonner, Robert
Pastor regalis (1887)
Bontrager, Sylvia
God is good
Booth, Ballington, 1959-1940
The cross is not greater
Booth, Josiah, 1852-1930
Avondale (1887)
Baynard
Beechwood
Bracondale
Commonwealth (1888)
Cross and crown
Earlham
Excelsior
Fernshaw
Holy war
Limpsfield
New year
Northrepps
Peniel (1909)
Remembrance
Swainsthrope
True-hearted
Wardlaw
Bornschein, Franz Carl, 1879-1948
Pax veritatis (1927)
Borthwick, R. Brown see Brown-Borthwick, R.
Bortniansky, Dmitri Stepanovich, 1751-1825
St Petersburg (1825); X1222 Bortiansky; X1637 Cherubic hymn; X5688 Jesus, thy boundless; X6457 Lowell; X9169 Russia; X11997 Wells
Vesper hymn (1818); X1223 Bortiansky; X9177 Russian vesper
Bost, Paul A.I.D., 1790-1874
Bost
Gratitude (1837)
Bostwick, W.J.
Father, we come to thee
Bottazzo, L.

Ave Maria (1940)
Boughton, Rutland, 1878-
Ben Jonson's carol
Bourgeois, Loys (Louis), ca 1510-ca 1561
NOTE: See also Genevan Psalter, 1551 and Goudimel (who republished Bourgeois, etc.)

Ascending King (1551)
Bourgeois (1551); X599 As the hart; X1036 Berlin; X1876 Coblentz; X2017 Comme un cerf attere; X3502 Freu dich sehr; X3634 Genevan Psalm 42; X5555 Jesus, dine dybe; X6301 Lo, they come in glad; X6495 Ludwigsburg; X8030 Old 42d; X8703 Psalm 42; X11194 Thirsting; X11886 Waterspring
Commandments (1543); X2011 Commandemens; X4901 Hour of need; X6107 Les commandemens; X6632 Magdeburg; X7266 Naar vi i største; X12013 Wenn wir in höchsten; X12123 When in the hour of
Du fort de ma detresse (ca 1545); X2118 Contrition; X5482 Jeg raaber fast, O Herre
Genevan Psalm 22 (1549); X8032 Old 71st
Holy Hill (1543)
L'Omnipotent (1551); X3636 Genevan Psalm 110; X8716 Psalm 110
Lord, to thee (1551); X8360 Pathway
Mon Dieu, prête-moi l'orielle (1543); X3635 Genevan Psalm 86; X8712 Psalm 86
Nunc dimittis (1549)
O esca viatorum (1542); X8507 Pleading; X8697 Psalm 6
Old 38th (1542)
Old 100th (1551); X2602 Dismiss us with thy; X2684 Doxology; X3526 From all that dwell; X4027 Great King of saints; X7884 O salutaris Hostia; X8040 Old Hundred; X8566 Praise God from whom; X10633 Tabor (Kugelmann. Concentus novi, 1540); X10916 The hundredth Psalm; X11006 The Old Hundredth; X11311 To Thee, O Jesus Christ
Old 107th (1643); X8715 Psalm 107
Old 124th [10.10.10.10.10 metre] (1551); X3629 Geneva 124; X7875 O sacred Heart of Jesus; X8010 Old hundred twenty-fourth
Old 127th
Old 136th (1551)
Psalm 88 (1543)
Rendez à dieu (1543); X2152 Cornerstone; X3197 Exultation; X3637 Genevan Psalm 118; X7304 Navarre; X8717 Psalm 118
Royal law (1551); X3628 Geneva 119; X3638 Genevan Psalm 119
St Michael (1551); X1456 Calvin; X8058 Old 134th
Sion's praise (1543)
Toulon [10.10.10.10 metre] (1551); X7305 Navarre; X7930 O thou that rulest; X8055 Old 124th
Bourne, Annie F. (Fanny Crosby??)
Give me thy heart
Bowcher, J.
East Hill
Bowen, J.C.
O vision bright
Bower, John Dykes, 1905-
Amen Court
Elton
Standish
Bowman, J.M.
My Saviour guides me
Stover
Boyce, R. Fisher
Beautiful star of Bethlehem (1940)
Boyce, William, 1710-79
Appleton (1740)

Boyce (1765); X4288 Halton
Holgate; X5497 Jersey; X 9938 Sharon
Chant
Chapel Royal
Kingsland; X1259 Boyce
Morning hymn
Portsea
Boyd, William, 1816-68
Pentecost (1864)
Boyle, Ina
Enniskerry
Brackett, Lyman
Alma
Communion
Guidance (1887)
Norton (1887)
Science
Bradbury, William Batchelder, 1816-68
Agawam
Aletta (1860); X4769 Holy Bible, book; X8655 Prince of peace, control
Amelia
Andre
Aughton (1864); X4472 He leadeth me
Baca; X1928 Come, gracious Spirit
Bloomfield chant
Braden
Brown; X1649 Chief shepherd; X4940 How sweet, how heavenly; X5292 In mercy, Lord
Caddo
Clarksville
Dalliba
Dare to do right
Don't forget the Sabbath
During
Even me; X6360 Lord, I hear of showers
Fade, fade, each earthly joy
Farewell, all earthly honors
Fulton
Harvey's chant; X3825 God moves in a
Helena
Jazer
Lottie; X2674 Dove
Mason's chant
Meroe
Monora
Morris chant
My latest sun
Newell
Olive's Brow (1853); X11274 'Tis midnight
Oriel
Over the ocean wave
Peoria
Pleasant pastures (1859); X1265 Bradbury; X9748 Savioir, like a Shepherd; X9958 Shepherd
Redal
Renar; X1678 China; X5626 Jesus loves me; X11826 Warner
Rest (1843); X631 Asleep in Jesus; X1266 Bradbury
Rolland
Sabaoth; X4797 Holy is the Lord
Salome
Silverton
Stand like the brave
Sutherland
Sweet hour (ca 1860); X10577 Sweet hour of prayer; X11783 Walford
The solid rock; X7219 My hope is built; X10164 Solid Rock
There is no name; X1156 Blessed name; X10606 Sweetest name; X11080 The sweetest name
Viola (1849)
We are all enlisted
Whither, pilgrims
Wirth
Woodworth (1849); X5762 Just as I am
Yarbrough; X10643 Take my life, and let
Zephyr; X8448 Philadelphia
Bradley, F. L.
We give thee but thine own (1920)
Bradshaw, M. L.
Consolator
Bragers, Achille P.
All hail, dear Conqueror

Ave, tu rex pácis
Christ the Lord is risen today
Creator Spirit, Lord of grace
Dear Angel, ever at my side
Great St Joseph (1953)
Hail noble column
Hymn to the Cross
Let every creature
O Christ, of Angel legions
O fair Creator of the skies (1954)
O food that weary pilgrims love (1953)
O Hunter blessed
O Lord, I am not worthy (1953)
Out of the depths
St Gabriel, O blessed youth
St Joseph, pride of heaven's court
Sing we triumphant (1953)
Soul of my Saviour (1953)
The divine praises (1939)
'Tis the day of resurrection (1953)
Ye souls of the faithful (1953)

Braham and Nathan. Hebrew melodies.
Psalm 136

Brahms, Johannes, 1833-97
Brahms; X11673 Victorious
Lucy; X1063 Bethlehem lullaby; X9742 Saviour, hear us, we; X11333 Too late, too late
The quest; X6721 Marias Wallfahrt

Brandeis, Frederick, 1832-99
Pray when the morn unveileth

Branscombe, Gena, 1881-
Browning (1927)
Chalice (1927)
Picton (1927)

Braun, Johann G.
Braun; X9395 St Gabriel

Breedlove, Leonard P., d ca 1879
Cross of Christ (1844)

Breitendich. Koralbog, 1764
Frisk op, min sjael

Brenneman, Henry B.
There's a beautiful, beautiful land; X4845 Home of the blest

Brethren hymnal, 1901
Lisle

Breton traditional
Afar upon a foreign shore
St Lo

Brewer, Alfred Herbert, 1865-1928
Glovernia

Brewer, John Hyatt, 1856-1931
Cuyler

Bridge, John Frederick, 1844-1924
Conquest
Ninety and nine
Olrig Grange (1905)
St Beatrice

Bridgers, Luther B., 1884-1948
Sweetest name (1909); X4467 He keeps me singing

Briegel, Carl Wolfgang, 1626-
Ach wie sehnlich wart ich (1687)
Liebster Jesu (1687)

Briggs, George Wallace, 1875-1959
David (1929)
Loughborough
Loughborough College
St Francis
St Martin (1931)
Springtime
Wulfrun (1929)

Brightbill, Alvin Franz, 1903-
Bounding heart
Communion hymn: X7826 O Lord! to thee who

Bristol, Lee H., Jr., 1923-
Sedgwick

Bristol Tune book, 1876
Cambria
St Austin; X708 Austin; X11330 Tonus peregrinus (Pre-reformation mel)

Brockless, George Frederick, 1887-1957
Fritwell

Bronner. Choral-buch, 1715
Jesus, Jesus, nichts als Jesus
Wer weiss, wie nahe mir

mein ende; X2201 Crasselius (Wittwe. Hamburger Musikalisches handbuch, 1690); H4985 Hvo ved, hvor naer mig; X12026 Wer weist wie nahe; X12223 Who knows how near
Broomfield, William Robert, 1826-88
St Kilda
Brown, Arthur Henry, 1830-1926
All hallows (1862); X372 Allhallows
Gerrans
Holy church (1862)
Holy cross
Holy rood (1863)
Lammas (1868)
Legion
Litany
Margaretting
Purleigh (1856); X3189 Exmouth
Saffron Walden (1890)
St Anatolius (1862); X1361 Brown
St Anstell
St John Damascene
St Mabyn; X6589 Mabyn
St Ulric
Story of the cross
Veni lux
When Christ was born (1859); X5260 In excelsis gloria
Brown, Charles S.
America, the beautiful (1906)
Consecration (1901)
Thou delightest, O Lord
Brown, Howard L.
Follow, I will follow thee (1937)
Brown, J.A.
Pray (1922)
Brown, L.O.
I cannot tell thee (1899)
Brown, S.R.
Monson (before 1938)
Brown-Borthwick, Robert, 1840-94
Eucharist
Grange
Browne, John Lewis, 1864-1933
Glorious Patron (1913)
Lord, who at Cana's wedding feast
Browne, Mary A.
Browne
Bruder Choral-buch, 1784 (probably Bohemian Brethren)
Weil ich Jesu schafflein bin
Brun, Fritz, 1878-1943
O Virgin all lovely
Bruning, David
White fields (1915)
Brunk, C.H.
Father! In life's young morning; X3921 Gorton
Gethsemane
Brunk, J. Claude
O Love Divine
Brunk, J.D.
Benediction
Come to me
Hagerstown
I heard the voice of Jesus say (1911)
In thy holy place
Jesus the teacher
Lilies of the field
No abiding city here
Sweetest hosannas
Vespers
Watts (1910)
Ye are the light; X10938 The light of the world
Bryan, Cornelius
Bryan; X9903 Serenity
Brydaine, Father
Jesus, my God; behold
Buck, Percy Carter, 1871-1947
Draw nigh; X8876 Refuge
Gonfalon Royal
Martins (1913); X9589 St Sebastian
Mont Richard
Pater noster
Resurrection morning
St Barnabas
Bugenhagen. Liturgy. Braunschweig, 1528
Agnus dei; X1749 Christe, du lamm
Bull, Ole Bornemann, 1810-80
Asleep in Jesus
Bullard, Frederick Field,

1864-1904
Hosmer (1902)
Longfellow
Bullinger, Ethelbert William, 1837-1913
Geneva; X584 Art thou weary; X1391 Bullinger
Samaria (1874)
Tenterden
Wellingham
Bullivant, G., 1883-1937
Bow Church
Bullock, Ernest
Berry Down (1925)
Bunnett, Edward, 1834-1923
Agnes (1877); X6230 Litany
Happy home
Kirby Bedon (1887); X1703 Christ in His word
Litany, No. 1
Ransom
Burder, G.
Luton
Burgmüller, Friedrich
Emmons
Burke, J.H.
Burke
Not I, but Christ (1896)
Burkett, J.C.
Happy spirits
Burleigh, Henry Thacker, 1866-1949
Alston
Burnap, Uzziah Christopher, 1834-1900
Amesbury (1895)
Baxter (1871)
Boston
Browning
Cleveland
Clifton
Cochran
Enos
Gould
Hinchman (1869)
Holy Guide (1895)
In-as-much
Paraclete
Seelye (1869)
X5385 Invocation
Burney, Charles, 1726-1814
Truro (1769); X11312 To Thee, O Lord
Burnham, John N.
Veritas (1923)
Burrowes, John Freckleton, 1787-1852
Beechmont
Burlington (1830)
Burstall, F.H.
Nocturn
Burt, Bates, G., 1878-1948
Lynne (1940)
Shaddick (1941)
Busch and Bushey
NOTE: Composers cited with these names are probably from the same family, variant spelling

Busch, Calvin A.
Second Parish (1954)
Bushey, J. Calvin
Calvin; X7955 O why not tonight
Marching home
Weeping One of Bethany
Butcher, Frank C.
Birchington
Butcher, William U., fl 1860
Prayer
Butler, L.T.
St Wystan
Button, Henry Elliot, 1861-1925
Child Service
Sumus tibi
Sursum voces
Buzzard, Rufus
As the dawn was breaking
Byers, A.L.
Are you adorning the doctrine?
Consecration
Fill me with thy Spirit (1918)
How reads your life-book?
I would not have my way
Love each other
Obedience
Only thine (1918)
Shall I be ashamed
Tell what He's done for you (1922)
Byles, Blanche Douglas
Thy great bounty (1925)

Byshe, Fred H.
A clean heart

C

C.A.P.
Sullivan (1855)
Caldbeck, George Thomas, 1852-1912?
Pax tecum (1877); X1086 Bickersteth
Caldicott, Alfred James, 1842-97
Civitas dei
Pastor bonus
Caldwell, C.T.
How long must we wait (1917)
Caldwell, William
Loving kindness (before 1830); X763 Awake, my soul, in
Calkin, Jean Baptiste, 1827-1905
Bradfield (1872); X9445 St John Baptist
Calkin I (1887); X9762 Savoy Chapel
Calkin II (1887); X9440 St John
Civitas dei; X1201 Bonar
Elim (1867); X7127 Moscow
Golden corn; X2439 Dedication; X8741 Purleigh
Munus
Newman (1867)
Nox praecessit (1873)
Ramoth
St Joseph
Sefton (1872)
Theoctistus (1872)
Waltham (1872); X1473 Camden; X2620 Doane; X5059 I heard the bells; X12127 When marshalled on
Welcome, happy morning; X816 Baptiste
Winchcombe
Callcott, William Hutchins, 1807-82
Elim (1867); X1439 Callcott; X8970 Rest
Intercession (1865); X386 Almighty Father, hear (Mendelssohn); X5367 Intercession New
Calvin, J. Psalter, 1539
Nostre dieu
Calvisius, Sethus, 1556-1615
Calvisius (1589); X103 Ach bleib bei uns
Gregor's 223d metre (1598); X12019 Wer Gott vertraut
Cambra, A.
Fierce was the wild billow
Camidge, John, 1735-1803
O Lord, open thou our eyes
Cammin, J. Melodienbuch von Rautenburg.
Wollt ihr wissen was mein preis
Camp, Harvey
Aylesbury
Camp, John Spencer, 1858-1946
Abiding grace (1905)
Sylvester (1905)
Camp, Mabel Johnston
He is coming again (1913)
Campbell, John P.
Axson (1899)
Barnett (1901)
In memoriam (1899)
Lacy (1899)
Langdon (1900)
Leslie (1899)
Lowrance (1899)
Milster (1899)
Mobile (1899)
Reed (1899)
Resignation (1900)
Whitner (1899)
Campbell, Leroy B.
Hosanna (1929)
Vision (1929)
Warren (1930)
Campbell, Paul O.
Holy Spirit (1939)
Campbell, Sidney Scholfield, 1909-
Old Commons
Campbell, Thomas, 1825-
Sagina
Campian (or Campion), Thomas 1567-1620
Babylon's Streams (1613)
Campian (1613); X11689

View me, Lord
Campian 2 (ca 1613)
Song of joy
Weather-beaten sail
Candlyn, Frederick H.
Rugby (1927)
Vitai lampada (1927)
Canning, Thomas, 1911-
Covenant hymn (1961)
Cannon, Tracy Y.
Come, let us sing an evening hymn
Come, rejoice
God of power, God of right
How beautiful thy temples, Lord
Jesus, mighty King of Sion
Praise the Lord with heart and voice
The Lord be with us
Cantica laudis, see Mason & Webb. Cantica laudis
Cantiques de Strasbourg, 1697
Summer in winter
Canzuns spirituaelas. Upper Engadine, 1765.
Engadine
Il buon pastor
Careless, George
Again we meet around the board
Arise, my soul, arise
Arise, O glorious Sion
Author of faith, Eternal Word
Behold the great Redeemer die
Hark! listen to the trumpeters
He died! the great Redeemer
I saw a mighty angel
O give me back my Prophet dear
O Lord of Hosts
O thou kind and gracious Father; X10143 Softly beams the sacred
Prayer is the soul's sincere desire
Rest, rest for the weary soul
The Lord imparted from above
The morning breaks: the shadows flee
Thou dost not weep alone
Though deepening trials
Ye children of our God
Carey, Henry, ca 1687-1743
Carey (1723); X1522 Carey's; X10534 Surrey
Osborne
Surrey
Carnett, Ellis L.
It is finished (1940)
Carr, Benjamin, 1768-1831
Spanish chant (arr 1824); X3665 Gethsemane; X6231 Litany; X6620 Madrid; X 10272 Spain; X10277 Spanish hymn; X10278 Spanish melody
Carr, F.
Kirkstall
Carr, J.H.
What would you give in exchange?
Carter, A. Norman
Palm Sunday (1882)
Carter, Edmund S., 1845-
Slingsby (1865); X617 Ascham; X1559 Carter; X2386 Day by day
Wreford (1865)
Carter, J.H.
Wyoming
Carter, Olen S.
Thanksgiving (1885)
Carter, R. Kelso
Launch out into the deep
Promises (1886); X10358 Standing on the promises
Case, Charles C., 1843-1918
Why not now?
Cassel, Flora Hamilton, 1852-1911
NOTE: See also Flora H. Good. May be the same individual.
Lambdin; X6472 Loyalty to Christ
Mother knows (1890)
The King's business; X1566 Cassel; X5012 I am a stranger
Casson, J.H.
Semper aspectemus (1875); X9881 Semper

Catholic traditional, etc.
NOTE: These tunes are usually modern, anonymous, and found within the Catholic hymnals.

Adoramus te, panem
All praise to St Patrick
Alleluia! Alleluia
Cor Jesu, cor purissimum
Daily, daily, sing to Mary
Dear Angel! ever at my side
Flowers of the fairest; X1321 Bring flowers of the
Full in the panting heart
Green are the leaves
Hail, Queen of the Heavens
Hail, thou living Victim
Holy Patron! thee saluting
Holy Spirit, come and shine
In this sacrament
Jesu deus, amor meus
Jesus, Jesus, come to me
Jesus, my Lord, my God; X3223 Faith of our fathers
Lauda Sion
Mother dear, O pray for me
Mother of mercy; X7620 O come and mourn
Now are the days
O come, and mourn
O faithful cross
O Lord, I am not worthy
Pilgrim song
Pone luctum (1750)
Pray for the dead!
Queen and Mother
See, amid the winter's snow
Sing, sing, ye angel bands
Sweet Saviour! bless us
Te, Joseph, celebrent
The clouds hang thick
This is the image of our Queen
Thou warrior of the Lord
Thou who, hero-like
To Jesus' heart all burning
Victoria
Vivat! vivat!
When day's shadows lengthen
Ye souls of the faithful

Catholic Hymn tunes, 1849
Lugano; X6453 Loving Shepherd of thy sheep

Catholisches gesangbuch. Strasbourg, 1697
Fortem virili pectore

Catholische Geistliche gesänge. Andernach, 1608 see Andernach Gesangbuch 1608

Catholische Kirchengesang. Cologne, 1623 see Cologne Gesang-buch. 1623 and
NOTE: Most hymnals published before 1650 are cited under place of publication. Later books are by title or compiler, whichever applies.

Cecil, R.
St Sebastian

Cecilia Miriam, Sr. S.N.J.M.
Guardian of Virgins (1958)

Celestial harps. Edinburgh, 1824
Pax celeste

Chadwick, George Whitefield, 1854-1931
Armstrong (1887)
Eaton (1888)
Little town (1927)
Peace (1890)
Warfare

Chadwyck-Healey, H.P., 1889-
Radwell

Challinor, Frederic Arthur, 1866-1952
Stories of Jesus (ca 1904)

Chalmers' Collection, 1749
Aberdeen; X9556 St Paul

Chamberlain, G.B.
Confidence (1870)

Chamberlain, John M.
We're marching on to glory

Champness, W.
Montgomery (1762)

Champneys, Francis Henry, 1848-1930
St Jerome (1889)
St Vernonica
Xavier

Chants ordinaires de l'office Divin. Paris, 1881.
Grafton; X10671 Tantum ergo [sacramentum]

Chapin, Aaron and Chapin,

Amzi have not been absolutely identified as composers or compilers of these three tunes. Both men are cited as "A. Chapin" in some books. Their active years were the same period in U.S. history.
Chapin, Aaron
Forest; X9082 Rockbridge
Golden Hills (1832)
Chapin, Amzi, 1768-1835
Melody (1823); X1629 Chelmsford; X8649 Primrose
Chartres Antiphoner, 1784
Adesto, sancta trinitas
Chauvenet Collection
Jerusalem
Cheeswright, Frederick H.
Shackelford (ca 1889)
Chepmell, E.
Dinard
Cherubini, Maria Luigi Carlo Zenobio Salvatore, known as Luigi Cherubini, 1760-1842
Dallas
Redemption
Veni, Jesu, amor mi
Chester, William Sidell
Chester (1898)
Chester ms., ca 1425
Song of the Nuns of Chester
Chetham, J. Psalmody, 1718
Aylesbury; X12333 Wirksworth
Marlow; X1169 Blest be the dear; X7829 O Lord, while we confess
Chevenix-Trench, May
Name
Chinese traditional, etc.
Hsuan P'ing see below Confucian Temple chant
Hubbard
Jasmine flower
Le P'ing
P'u T'o; X1680 Chinese melody; X9937 Shanghai
Shanghai
Song of the Yangtze boatmen (chantey)
Wiant
Chippewa (Indian) melody
Manitou
Chitty, Simon Comenius, 1831-1902
Benjamin
Graceham
Wachovia (1890)
Chope, Richard Robert, 1830-
Herbert
St Cyprian
Scudamore
Chope's Carols
Chope
Chopin, Francois-Frédéric, 1810-49
Hear our prayer
Chord, S.H.
Some sweet day
Choron, Alexandre Etienne, 1771-1834
Tynemouth (1822)
Christiansen, Frederik Melius, 1871-1955
As sinks beneath the ocean
Flower of love (1919)
One resolve (1891)
Christliche lieder. Wittenberg, 1524
NOTE: See also Geistliche Gesangbüchlein. Wittenberg, 1524 and Etliche Christliche lieder. Wittenberg, 1524
Nun freut euch; X4105 Gregor's 132d metre-B; X7542 Nu fryde sig hver; X7565 Nun freut euch lieben christen ...
Church-Gallery book
A Gallery carol
Candlemas Eve
Yoeman's carol
Church Hymnal
Ferniehurst
Church of Scotland Hymn tune book, 1862
Amberg
Clark (no initials)
The unseen city
Clark, Edward, 1888-
Barre
Clark, E.M.
Catherine
Clark, Jeremy or Clarke,

Jeremiah, ca 1673-1707
A morning hymn
Bishopthorpe (1700); X9562 St Paul's
Brockham
Bromley (1700)
Hermon
King's Norton
St Magnus; X7507 Nottingham
Tunbridge
Uffingham; X9482 St Luke; X10104 Sleep, downy sleep
Yattendon 8
Clark, Thomas, 1775-1859
Crediton
Essex
Grafton
Warsaw
Clarke, Harry D., 1888-
Into my heart
Clarke, Henry Leland, 1907-
Art (1959)
Valley Forge (1958
Windsor Forest (1960)
Ygdrasil (1960)
Clarke, John, 1770-1836
Clarke's
Clausener. Gesangbuch, 1653
Cordis donum
O Jesu mi dulcissimi
Clayson, William
Hope of Israel
Nearer, dear Savior to thee
O thou Rock of our Salvation
O what songs of the heart
The day dawn is breaking
To Nephi, seer of olden time
Clelland, Wilfred G.
Martha (1957)
Clemens, Charles Edwin, 1858-1923
O Lord, save thy people
Clemens, Theodor L., 1858-
Raglan
Clemm, J.B.O.
Clemm (1895); X3250 Far and near the fields; X4378 Harvest; X10818 The call for reapers
Click, D.M.
God is love, His mercy; X2868 Effie
Clifton, John Charles, 1781-1841
Clifton
Cluett, John W.A.
Wentworth
Coats, J.B.
Building for eternity (1941)
Where could I go? (1940)
Cobb, Gerard Francis, 1838-1904
Aysgarth
Cobb; X5995 Lauda Sion; X5999 Lauda Sion salvatorem
Gerard
Harrogate
Moultrie; X6297 Lo! the clouds have
Cocker, Norman, 1889-1953
Ripponden
Ryburn
Coe, William Wallace, 1862-
Beatrice (1895)
Coerne, Louis Adolphe, 1870-1922
Son of Man
Cole, John
Geneva
Coleman, E.G., 1872-
Burning light
Coleridge-Taylor, Samuel, 1875-1912
Luconer
Coles, George, 1792-1858
Duane Street (1835); X5572 Jesus from whom all
A Collection of hymns and sacred poems. Dublin, 1749
Irish; X2717 Dublin; X11097 The venite
Coller, Percy E.B.
St Joan (1941)
Collier, Edward A.
Marchfield
Collignon, C., 1725-85
University
Cologne Gesangbuch, 1623
Cologne; X1796 Christus ist auferstanden
Herrick's carol
Hilariter; X2558 Die ganze welt
Hosmer; X4511 Heart's desire; X6645 Mainz; X6718

Maria jung und zart
O King of Kings
Vigiles et sancti; X270 All creatures of our; X364 Alleluias; X2788 Easter alleluya; X2804 Easter song; X5979 Lasst uns erfreuen; X6119 Let hymns of joy; X10725 Tell us now, O Death; X12157 When very early
Cologne Gesangbuch, 1634
The secret flower; X3609 Gebor'n ist uns ein kindelein
Cologne, Symphonia Sirenum, 1695
I love thee, O thou Lord; X7646 O Deus, ego amo te
Comley, J.
Green Hill
Conant, Albert F.
Christmas Morn
Conant, Grace Wilbur, 1880-1948
Agni (1927)
Carry on (1927)
Far Hills (1927)
Fealty (1927)
Merlin (1927)
Confucian Temple chant
Hsuan P'ing
Congregational Church music, 1871
Lavington
Conkey, Ithamar, 1815-67
Rathbun (1851); X3752 Glorious things of thee; X5301 In the cross of Christ
Conradi, Johan G., ca 1830-96
Alone, with Thee
Conte, Paolo, 1891-
Redentore (1940); X4030 Great Redeemer
Converse, Charles Crozart, 1832-1918
Erie (1868); X2124 Converse; X3510 Friend; X3517 Friendship; X5420 Israel, Israel, God is; X12067 What a friend
Friend of sinners (1896)
I am not worthy
Savior! teach me
Cook, G. H.
Heavenly sunlight
Cook, John T.
Heaven
Cooke, Benjamin, 1734-93
Westminster
Cooke, Greville, 1894-
Emmaus
Golden Grove
Ivinghoe
Sentinel
Cooke, H. E.
Niles
St Ignatius
Cooke, William Henry, 1820-1912
Bath
Sanctissimus
Cooper, Alexander Smith, 1835-
Sanctus
Cooper, George, 1820-76
St Sepulchre (1836)
Cooper, W. G.
Wonderful peace
Copes, V. Earle, 1921-
Epworth Church (1964)
Kingdom 1960)
Vicar (1963)
Corbeil, Pierre de, d 1222
Corbeil
Orientis partibus (ca 1210); X2049 Concordi laetitia; X5657 Jesus our Brother; X6959 Milites crucis; X7445 Nomen Jesu; X8008 Old French melody; X8869 Redhead, No. 45 (Redhead); X9504 St Martin
Cornelius, Peter, 1824-74
The Christmas tree; X1744 Christbaum
The Kings; X2563 Die König
Cornell, John Henry, 1828-94
Bethel
Cornell
Excelsius (1872)
I think when I read
Triumph
Corner, D. G. Geistliche nachtigall, 1649
Corner; X1543 Carol; X2885

Ein kindlein in der; X5253 In der wiegen; X10850 The cradle
Heiliger Geist
Corner, D.G. Gesangbuch, 1625
Christi mutter stund vor schmerzen; X6783 Mater dolorosa
Corner, D.G. Gesangbuch, 1631
Omni dei
Cornish folksong see English traditional: Lew Trenchard
Cornysshe, William, early 16th c
Robyn
Coslett, Joseph
We'll sing all hail
Costa, Michael, 1806-84
Costa; X2625 Doers
Eli
Jesus, Saviour, Heavenly Father
Costellow (no initials)
Surrey (ca 1810)
Coster, Arthur V., 1864-1931
City of light (1909)
Cottman, Arthur, 1842-79
Beachley
Dalehurst (1874)
Eversley
Kendal
Millikan
Mirfield (1874)
Morn of gladness (1877); X 2169 Cottman; X9131 Roswell; X11925 We plough the fields
Coules, Reginald F.
Dedicatio anni
Courteville, Raphael
St James (1697)
Covell, William King, 1906-
Pelham Street (1960)
Coward, Henry, 1849-1944
Norfolk Park
Cowen, Frederic Hymen, 1852-1935
Now bless the God of all
With the voice of sweet spring (1932)
Cramer, Francis, 19th c
St Agatha
Crawford, Edward Patrick, 1846-1912
Jehovah nissi
Crawford, Jane Romney
Father in heaven, we do believe
Crespin, Jean
O Herre Gud, oändelig (1551)
Crespin. Psalms, 1556
Norwich; X8061 Old 137th Psalm 23
Cringan, Alexander Thom, 1860-
Harvest song
Simcoe
Croatian carol
Croatia (14th c)
Croft, J.B. Collection.
Iste confessor; X492 Angers
Croft, (or Crofts) William, 1678-1727
All Saints (1703)
Binchester
Croft's 136th; X2221 Croft; X2224 Croft's; X2227 Croft's 148th
Eatington
Hanover (1708); X2078 Conquest; X2222 Croft; X2460 Delay not
St Anne (1708); X7206 My God, how wonderful; X7692 O God, our help; X9269 St Ann's
St Matthew (1708)
Southampton (1727)
Crofton, Edward Lord
Crofton (1893)
Crook, George C.
Minto (1918)
Crookall, Msgr.
Dear Angel! ever at my side
O come and mourn
Crosbie, Howard Augustus, 1844-1918
St Cephas
Sefton
Cross, Moses S., 1854-1911
Resignation
Waratah (1905)
Cross, Paul
Mary, the Dawn (20th c)
Crossley, Hastings, 1846-
Eripe me

Crossley, Thomas H.
Anagola (1876)
Crossley, W. J.
Woodhall (1905)
Crotch, William, 1775-1847
Sidon
Crowfoot, W., 1724-83
St Mark
Crueger, Johann, 1598-1662
NOTE: Crueger's Praxis pietatis melica, originally published in Berlin, 1644, contained many of these chorales. Reprints and other compilations were issued during his lifetime. Publication date, when known, is the limit of the citation herein.

Auf, auf, mein Herz (1648)
Christmas joy (1653); X3522 Fröhlich soll mein
Crueger
Du, o schönes Weltegebäude (1649); X4123 Gregor's 168th metre-C; X5567 Jesus er mit liv i live
Graefenberg (1653); X2268 Crueger; X5774 Kabzeel; X7557 Nun danket all'; X7559 Nun danket all' und bringet ehr; X10769 Thanksgiving
Gregor's 79th metre (1653); X5357 Innsbruck (Isaak); X7948 O welt, sieh hier dein
Hebron
Herzliebster Jesu (1640); X3285 Father most holy; X4070 Gregor's 36th metre; X7791 O Lamb of God, have; X10486 Suffering Savior; X11750 Vreden din afvend
Holy Ghost (1639); X4551 Heiliger Geist
Jesus, all my gladness (1653); X3597 Gaudeo; X4134 Gregor's 208th metre-A; X5629 Jesu, meine freude
Lob sei dem Allmachtigen Gott; X4068 Gregor's 22d metre-C; X9184 Ryden
Manger (1653); X7765 O Jesu Christ, dein Kripplein
Marburg
Nun danket (1647); X2270 Crueger; X2490 Deo gratias; X4006 Gratitude; X4392 Harwich; X6708 Marenzo; X7548 Nu takker alle Gud; X7561 Nun danket alle Gott; X11182 Thine advent Lord
O hvor salig er I dog I fromme (1649); X7958 O wie selig seid ihr
O Jesu Christ, du höchstes Gut (1658)
Oblation (1653); X4623 Herr, deinen zorn; X6306 Lobet den Herren
Ratisbon (1653); X1037 Berlin; X1275 Brandenberg; X2059 Confidence; X2891 Eins ist noth; X3065 Et er nødigt; X5539 Jesus Christ, my sure; X5566 Jesus er mit haab og; X5631 Jesu, meine zuversicht; X6509 Luise; X8126 One thing needful; X8807 Rathbon; X11765 Waddell; X12237 Why art thou cast; X12580 Zuversicht
St Nicholas (1649); X66 Aaberg; X2448 Deep and glorious; X2269 Crueger; X4626 Herr, ich habe missgehandelt; X4642 Herre, jeg har handlet; X8880 Regensburg
St Simon (1549); X4663 Herzlich thut mich erfreuen
Schmuecke dich (1649); X2432 Deck thyself; X3928 Gothenburg; X7547 Nu skal du, min sjael; X9785 Schmuecke dich, O liebe seele; X11528 Upsala I; X11529 Upsala II
Schwing dich auf zu deinem Gott (1653)
Von Gott will ich nicht lassen (1640)
Wachet doch; erwacht (1662)

Wie soll ich dich empfangen (1653)
Zeuch ein (1653); X12563 Zeuch ein zu meinen
Cruickshank, W. A. C.
Ter sanctus
Cuff, C. R.
Pastoral chant
Cunningham, F. Selection of Psalm tunes, 1834
Birmingham
Currie, Edward C.
Christ the Lord is my true Shepherd (1958)
Holy is God (1958)
Currier, Everett R.
Bourne (1941)
Curry, R. Donald
We thank thee Lord (1963)
Curwen's (John) Standard course, 1860
God is near thee
Curwen's (John) Tune book, 1842
Children of Jerusalem; X6335 Infant praise
Glory
Custance, A. F. M.
Easter flowers
Orison
Cuthbert, Elizabeth H.
Howard
Cutler, Henry Stephen, 1824-1902
All Saints new (1872); X298 All saints new; X2295 Cutler; X2981 Emulation; X11707 Vindex
Cutts, Peter, 1937-
Wylde Green
Cuzens, Benjamin
Coventry
Czeck traditional, etc.
NOTE: See also entries under Bohemian and Moravian
Rocking (1931)
The Birds (1928)

D

Dadman, J. W.
Is not this the land of Beulah; X2383 Dawning; X11877 Watchman, tell me
Rest for the weary
Dahle, John, 1853-1931
Guidance (1911)
Jubilate (1911)
Luther Seminary
Red Wing Seminary
St Olaf (1911)
Dakota (Indian) hymn
Dakota hymn
Dale, Benjamin James, 1885-1943
Sidmouth
Dale, Charles J.
Denby (1904)
Dale, Reginald Francis, 1845-1919
St Catherine (1867)
Dale, W. T.
Holy City (1913)
Daley, James E.
God most truly (1958)
Damon's Psalter, 1579
Southwell; X2482 Denham
Dana, Mary S. B. (later, Mary S. B. D. Shindler)
Flee as a bird (arr); X10273 Spain
D'Andrieux (17th c)
Prayer
Daniels, Mabel Wheeler, 1878-
Dreamers (1927)
Danish traditional, etc.
All things bright and beautiful
Bairn; X6204 Lille Guds barn
Celestia; X7743 O how beautiful the sky
Galdan
Herra
Lassen
Nativity
Nature's praises
Ostergaard; X10777 That cause can neither
Parting hymn
Release; X215 Agnus; X5113 I see thee standing; X5484 Jeg ser dig, søde Lam
Salvator
Danks, Hart Pease, 1834-1903
Delphine (1901)
No night there; X5310 In the

land of fadeless
Spitta
The Lord in Zion reigneth (1886)
Dare, Elkanah Kelsay, 1782-1826
Kedron
Darius, Frederick R.
Ruhetag (1916)
Darke, Harold Edwin, 1888-
Cornhill
Naphill
Darley, W. H. W.
Goderich
Darms, Antonius
My Lord and I; X4957 Huguenot hymn
Darmstadt Gesang-buch,
NOTE: Several editions indicated by date at end of tune name.

All saints (1698); X306 All saints old; X3749 Glorious saint whose deeds immortal; X6405 Lorrain; X11969 Weisse flaggen (Tochter Sion, Cologne)
Clausnitzer (1699); X11898 We all believe in one; X12326 Wir glauben all' an einen
Darmstadt (1698); X687 Auf, seele, sei geruest't
Goldschmidt (1698); X4065 Gregor's 16th metre; X7645 O der alles [hoett' verloren]; X8580 Praise the Saviour
Gregor's 39th metre-B (1698); X102 Ach, alles was himmel
Gregor's 101st metre(1698); X8633 Preis, lob, ehr, ruhm
Gregor's 167th metre-E (1698); X7650 O du Liebe meiner Liebe
Gregor's 189th metre-B (1697); X9791 Schönster Immanuel, Herzog der Frommen
Gregor's 192d metre (1698); X10130 So fuehrst du doch
Gregor's 211th metre (1687); X6169 Liebster Jesu, liebstes lieben!; X6378 Lord of life
Luebeck (1699); X6849 Meinen Jesum lass' ich nicht
Nun kommt das neue (1698)
Victor
Darwall, John, 1731-97
Darwall (1770); X2354 Darwall's 148th
Darwall, Leicester, 1813-
St Hubert; X4951 Hubert
Davenport, F. S. S.
Queen's College
Davidisches Harfen-un Psalterspiel, 1744
In allen meinen thaten
O gloriosa Virginum
Davies, David, 1810-75
Glan'rafon
Davies, Edward Thomas, 1878-
All saints
Michaelmas
Davies, Henry Walford, 1869-1941
Ainger (1915); X8742 Purpose
Auctor vitae
Christmas carol; X11350 Town of Bethlehem
Etherington
Firmament
God be in my head (1910)
Hampstead; X6786 Matheson
Oswald's Tree
Pentatone (1923)
Plentitude
St André
Temple (1906)
Vision
Wallog
Wengen
Davies, Robert, 1814-67
Hope (1860; X3792 Gobaith
Davis, Arthur
Creevelea (1927)
Davis, F. W.
Aberavon
Davis, Frank M.
Gather the golden grain
Lead me, Saviour; X6040 Lead me; X9746 Saviour, lead me lest
My name's written there; X5408 Is my name written
Sleeping on guard
Davis, G.

Monmouth
Davis, J.W.
Sitting at the feet of Jesus; X11395 Troubled soul, thy God
Davis, Katherine K., 1892-
Massachusetts (1964)
Surette (1964)
Wachuset (1964)
Davis, Marchel, fl. ca 1848
Goshen (1860); X3337 Fides; X8346 Pastor bonus
Davis, O.S.
Lord, give us a vision
Davis, W.B.
St Leonard
Dawes, Eric, 1902-
Broome
Day, George Henry, 1883-
Decision (1929)
Edsall (1940)
Geneva (1940)
My Master (1929)
Parce domine (1917)
Rochester (1929)
Day, John. Psalter, 1562
Old 81st
St Flavian; X2411 Dear Angel, ever at; X3377 Flavian
Tallis' Lamentation
Daynes, Joseph J.
As the dew from heaven
Behold, the mountain of the Lord
Come, listen to a prophet's voice
Glorious things are sung
Great God, attend
Hark ten thousand thousand voices
If you could hie to Kolob
Lord, accept our true devotion
Lord, thou wilt hear me
Now we'll sing with one accord
We're not ashamed to own our Lord
When dark and drear
Deale, Edgar Martin, 1905-
Edwin
Dean, Harry A.
Lord, we come before thee
Savior, Redeemer of my soul
Dean, Joseph H.
Before thee, Lord, I bow my head
Deane, John H.
Sienna (1869)
Verona
Dearle, D.W.
David (1926)
Dearle, Edward
Penitentia (1880)
Decius, Nikolaus, ca 1490-1541
O Lamm Gottes; X221 Agnus dei; X5931 Lamb of God; X7712 O Guds Lam uskyldig; X7798 O Lamm Gottes unschuldig; X10407 Steterburg
De Fluiter, Henry
Hail Him the King of Glory
Mizpah
De Jong, Gerrit, jr.
Come, sing to the Lord
de Lloyd, David, 1883-1948
see Lloyd, David de
De Marbelle, Dion
When they ring the golden bells
Demuth, John Arthur, 1848-1920
Oberlin (1900)
Dennis, T.
He died of a broken heart
Denton, J.P.
Wonderful Jesus
Depew, Arthur
Mater (1925)
De Roo, Cornelia J.
The tribes
Dessler, W.C., 1660-1722
Gregor's 183d metre; X6840 Mein Jesu, dem dei seraphinen
Deutsch, M.
Of all the thoughts of God
Deutsch kirchenampt see Teutsch Kirchenampt
De Vaughan, W.M.
My Saviour cares for me
Devereux, L.
Boardman; X2534 Devereaux
D'Hooghe, J.
Jesus, Creator of the world
Dickey, Mark, 1885-

Pater omnipotens (1941)
Veni, anima mea
Dickinson, Charles J., 1822-83
Agape (1861); X8937 Repose; X9691 Sanctuary
Diggle, Roland
Racine (1941)
Diggs, T. Lloyd
St Francis (1906)
Dijon Church melody
O invidenda martyrum
The Divine companion, 1709
O God of love
Divine Musical miscellany, 1754
Old 23d
Dixon, R.W.
Staincliffe
Dixon, William, 1750-1825
Lanesboro; X5491 Jehovah, Jesus, Lord
Doane, William Howard, 1832-1915
Arms of Jesus; X8877 Refuge; X9216 Safe in the arms of; X10902 The heart's refuge
Avalon (arr)
Be silent (1903); X11364 Tread softly
Cleansing; X2041 Compassion; X2218 Crimson; X11230 Though your sins be
Come, great Deliverer
Constance
Doane I
Doane II; X1149 Blessed hour; X4902 Hour of prayer; X11280 'Tis the blessed hour
Every day and hour (1899); X3171 Every hour; X9749 Saviour, more than life
Hide me, O My Saviour; X4681 Hide me
I am thine; X2229 Crosby; X2686 Draw me nearer; X5025 I am Thine, O Lord
If I come to Jesus
Jesus is passing this way
Jesus, thy name I love; X2654 Donora
Labor on; X5308 In the harvest field
More like Jesus
More love to thee (1870); X2538 Devotion; X8634 Prentiss
Near the cross; X5609 Jesus, keep me near
Now just a word for Jesus
Only a step; X8133 Only a step to Jesus
Pass me not; X8335 Pass me not, O gentle
Precious Name (1899); X10644 Take the name [of Jesus with you]; X11020 The precious name
Preston
Rescue (1870); X8953 Rescue the perishing
Tell me the old, old story; X3105 Evangel; X8014 Old, old story
To God be the glory (1903)
Toiling on; X11309 To the work
Vision (1873); X3838 God of our strength
Watching (1904); X12263 Will Jesus find us watching; X12435 Woodstock
Dobbs, Jack Percival Baker, 1922-
Teilo sant
Dobici, L.
Soul of my Saviour
Docker, F.A.W.
Sion quadrata
Doles, Johann Friedrich, 1715-97
Ich lass dich nicht (1780)
Lichfield; X2306 Da Christus geboren
Doles, J.F. Choralbuch. Leipsic, 1785
Doles
Norman
Dölker. Geistliche lieder, 1876
Weil ich Jesu schäflein bin
Donizetti, Gaetano, 1797-1848
Lucia
Paulina
Savery; X1538 Carmen naturae
Dooner, Albert J.
Tantum ergo

Doty, Abraham
Judah
Dougall, Hugh W.
I wander through the stilly night
Dougall, Neill
Kilmarnock (1831)
Doughty, A.S.
Soon trials and conflicts; X4846 Home of the soul (new)
Douglas, Charles Winfred, 1867-1944
Dexter Street (1940)
St Dunstan's (1917)
Douglas, Sallie Hume
Follow the gleam (1915)
Dowland, John, 1562-1626
Galliard
Downes, Lewis Thomas, 1827-1907
Solitude; X4972 Hurdus
Drei schöne neue geistliche lieder. München, 1637
Soll's sein
Dresden. Neuesgesangbuch, 1593
Ecce agnus; X7176 Munich; X12323 Wir christenleub
Dresden Gesangbuch, 1632
Dresden; X5978 Lasst uns alle
Dresden Gesangbuch, 1694
So giebst Du; X2692 Dresden
Dresden mss., 1761
St Kerrian
Drese, Adam, 1620-1701
Rochelle (1698); X581 Arnstadt; X2696 Drese; X4076 Gregor's 46th metre; X4360 Harlem; X4533 Heavenly guide; X5533 Jesus, be our Guide; X5668 Jesu, rufe mich; X5675 Jesus, still lead on; X9861 Seelenbrautigam; X10292 Spire; X11063 The soul's Bridegroom; X11237 Thuringia; X12567 Zinzendorf
Dressler, W.
Holy Mary, Mother mild
Dretzel, Cornelius Heinrich, 1698-1775
Dretzel I
Dretzel II; X7636 O dass ich tausend
Dretzel, C.H. Musicalische harmonie, 1731
Dieses ist der Tag der wonne
Drewett, Edwin, 1850-1924
Elmhurst (1887)
Driver, J.M.
Wonderful story
Drury, Miriam
Once again to its close (1940)
Düben, Gustaf, 1671-1730
Jesu; X2713 Düben; X3706 Glädje utan Gud ej finnes; X3711 Gladness; X5532 Jesus är min van den bäste
Dublin Troper, ca 1360
Angelus ad Virginum
Dubois, Clément-Francois Theodore, 1837-1924
Christ, we do all adore thee (1867)
Tantum ergo
Duckworth, Francis, 1862-1941
Rimington (1904)
Duguet, Abbe
O salutaris
Dunbar, C.R.
I'll live for him; X2734 Dunbar; X7224 My life, my love, I give to
Dunbar, E.W.
A few more years: X2733 Dunbar; X7904 O, sing to me of heaven
Duncalf, Henry
St Bartholomew (1762)
Duncan, S.E.
Something I would tell you
Dungan, J.M.
You can make the pathway bright
Dunham, Henry Morton, 1853-1929
Puritan (1905)
Dunhill, Thomas Frederick, 1877-1946
Beatus
Dunkley, Ferdinand Luis, 1869-1956
O God, all gracious; X8222 Our fortress strong
Dunman, S.J.P.

St Margaret
Dupuis, Thomas Sanders, 1730-96
Chant
Durham, Alfred M.
Again, our dear redeeming Lord
Firm as the mountains around us
Sweet is the peace the Gospel brings
They the builders of the nation
Durham, Lowell M.
With all the power of heart
Durham, Thomas
Stars of morning, shout for joy
Dussek, Ronald
Gorran
Dutch traditional, etc.
NOTE; Holland and Netherlands are unused herein. Melodies are gathered under Dutch.

Annunciation (1896); X2399 De boodschap; X10989 The message
Dutch carol (1599)
Help, Lord, the souls (1500)
In Babilone
Kremser (1625); X7341 Netherlands; X7342 Netherlands folksong; X8684 Protection; X10949 The Lord in His righteousness
Sion's daughter
Song of the Spirit
The garden of Jesus (1633)
Valerius (old hymn)
Winsted
Dutton, Deodatus, jr., 1808-32
Woodstock (ca 1830)
Dvorâk, Antonin, 1841-1904
Going home
Dykes, John Bacchus, 1823-76
Alford (1875)
Almsgiving (1865); X2119 Contrition; X2946 Elliott; X8611 Prayer
Arundel
Beatitudo (1875); X4007 Gratitude
Blairgowrie (1872); X2761 Dykes; X4369 Hartford; X11499 Union Square
Calm; X5206 Ilkley
Come unto me (1875)
Derry
Dies Dominica; X1282 Bread of heaven
Dies irae (1861)
Dominus regit me (1868); X1582 Cecilia; X2643 Dominus regit
Ecce panis
Edmund
Elvet
Esca viatorum (1868); X1608 Chapin; X4245 Hail! holy guide
Etiam et mihi
Faith; X1204 Bone pastor; X2727 Dulcis memoria
Ferrier
Fiat lux (1875)
Gerontius (1868)
Glastonbury
Glebe Field
Herald angels
Hollingside (1861); X9437 St James the Less
Horbury (1861)
Hosanna (1865)
Hosanna we sing; X4890 Hosanna
Intercession, arr (1853); X5368 Intercession old; X9246 St Alkmund
Jerusalem (1862)
Jesu, magister bone; X10456 Stratford
Judea
Keble (1875); X10458 Streatham
Laud
Lindisfarne (1862)
Litany of the Passion
Lux benigna (1865); X6039 Lead, kindly light
Mary Magdalene; X2762 Dykes; X9508 St Mary Magdalene
Melita (1861)
Nicaea (1861); X2763 Dykes; X4792 Holy, holy, holy
Olivet (1870)

Once again
Oswestry
Oswin (1862); X9544 St Oswin
Paradise, No. 1; X8302 Paradise
Pax dei (1868)
Prince of Peace
Requiescat (1875); X8385 Peace
Resurrection; X2785 Easter
Rivaulx (1866)
Rock of Ages; X3666 Gethsemane; X11412 Trust
St Aelred
St Agnes (1866); X2745 Durham; X5682 Jesus the very thought; X5718 Joseph, our certain
St Anatolius (1862); X450 Anatolius
St Andrew of Crete (1868); X2213 Crete
St Bede (1867); X10117 Slingsby; X11824 Waring
St Bees (1862); X1643 Chester
St Cross (1861)
St Cuthbert (1861)
St Drostane (1862); X9040 Ride on, ride on
St Godric (1862)
St John (1864); X2830 Ecce agnus
St Ninian (1866)
St Oswald I (1857); X2764 Dykes; X5566 Jesus, highest heaven's; X8202 Oswald; X10619 Sychar
St Oswald II (1862)
St Sylvester (1862); X9609 St Sylvester, No. 2; X10622 Sylvester
St Werburgh (1862)
St Winifred
Sanctuary (1871)
Shoreham
Stabat mater
Strength and Stay (1875)
Trinity College (1857); X10770 Thanksgiving
Veni creator, No. 2
Vesperi lux (1873)
Via bona (1862)
Via dolorosa
Visio domini (1868)
Vox angelica (1868); X478 Angels' song
Vox dilecti (1868)

Dykes, John St. O.
The Sacred Heart

Dyson, George, 1883-
Atkey
Elgin
Frainsby
Let thy word abide

E

Earnshaw, Robert Henry, 1856-1929
Arizona

Eaton, Edward D.
Be strong (1917)

Ebeling, Johann Georg, 1637-76
Du meine Seele singe
Ebeling I (1666); X289 All my heart this night; X1210 Bonn; X6520 Lüneburg; X11840 Warum sollt ich
Ebeling II; X6593 Luneburg
Nicht so traurig, nicht so sehr; X2826 Ebeling
Philippi; X2560 Die güldne sonne; X2825 Ebeling; X3131 Evening and morning; X3474 Franconia
Shining day (1666); X71 Abendlied; X2503 Der tag mit seinem lichte
Voller wunder

Eberhard, Karl Otto, d 1757
Gregor's 249th metre; X2559 Die Gottes seraphin; X9901 Seraphim

Eberwein, Max
Valentia

Eccard, Johannes, 1553-1611
Herr Jesu Christ, wahr'r mensch und Gott (1597)

Edmunds, John, 1913-
God is ascended (1961)
Love of the Father (1961)
Ye messengers (1957)

Edson, Lewis, 1748-1820
Bridgewater (1782)
Contrast; X2400 De Fleury

X4941 How tedious and tasteless
Lenox; X551 Arise, my soul arise
Edwards, A. Morris
We are soldiers of Christ
Edwards, F. Llewellyn
Kington (20th c)
Edwards, J.
Fatherland
Edwards, John, 1878-1928
Maesgwyn
Edwards, John David
Rhosymedre (ca 1840); X6446 Lovely
Edwards, Lewis D.
Come, lay his books and papers by
I know that my Redeemer lives
Let Sion in her beauty rise
Edwards, P.C., jr.
Chignell
Forward
Racine
Edwards, R., 1797-1862
Caersalem
Edwards, T.D., 1875-1930
Rhyd-y-groes
Egbert, Father
Hail, all hail, sweet youth
Egli, Johann Heinrich, 1742-1810
Egli (1790); X3046 Es kam die gnadenvolle
Gott ist mein hort (1787)
Eiland, F.L.
Hold to God's unchanging hand
Ekström, A.
Jesus för varlden gifvet sitt lif; X1648 Chief of sinners
El Nathan, pseud. see Whittle, Daniel W., 1840-1901
Elgar, Edward William, 1857-1934
In the Light all light excelling; X12446 Word of God to earth
Elliott, E.S.
Veni
Elliott, James William, 1833-1915
Belsize
Day of grace
Day of rest
Eucharistica
Gloria in excelsis
Hosanna
St Mark
Triumphant; X1810 Church triumphant
Vespers
Ellis, Lethal A.
You can't do wrong and get by (1929)
Ellis, William, 1868-1947
St Hild
St Nicholas
Ellor, James, 1819-99
Diadem (1838)
Elvey, George Job, 1816-93
Adoration
Diademata (1868)
Elvey
Illuminatio
Pilgrimage
St Crispin (1862)
St George's Windsor (1858); X1997 Come, ye thankful; X2964 Elvey; X4382 Harvest home; X9400 St George; X9402 St George of Windsor; X9403 St G George's; X11878 Watchman, tell us
Sunninghill
Undique gloria
Urswicke
Wellesley
Emerson, Luther Orlando, 1820-1915
Addison
Ascription
Elliott
Font Hill
Goodwell
Hemingford
Home
Malone
Mandor
Merlo (composer's acrostic)
Moravian
Peaceful rest
Redeemer
Sessions (1847); X3221 Faith is a living power
Stearndale
Woodside
Emmelar, pseud. see Richards, Henry Brinley, 1817-89
Enchiridion. Erfurt, 1524 see

Erfurt Gesangbuch, 1524
Enchiridion. Erfurt, 1527
O Herre Gott
Enchiridion. Lübeck, 1545
Sei du mir gegrüsset
Enckhausen, Heinrich Friedrich, 1799-1885
Schönste Sonne; X1877 Coburg
Enke, Gâlyarabok. Hungarian Galley slaves hymn, 1674
Magyar
Englebrecht, J.C.
The sweet story of old
English chorister
Jesus, once of humble birth
English hymnody see early sources, as Day's Psalter, Est's Psalter, Anglo-Genevan Psalter, New Version, etc. Traditional tunes will be found under English traditional, which follows.
English traditional, including many carols.
A babe is born
A new dial
A Virgin most pure I; X11710 Virgin unspotted II
A virgin most pure II
A virgin most pure III
A virgin most pure IV; X11711 Virgin most pure
A virgin unspotted; X620 Ash grove
Agincourt (ca1415); X2489 Deo gracias
All and some (ca 1450)
All in the morning
Anima Christi
Ar det ringa kall att tjäna
Boar's Head carol
Bramley; X60 A virgin unspotted II; X5338 Infinite light; X11710 Virgin unspotted II
Bridgwater
Bunyan
Butler
Capel; X10993 The miraculous harvest
Ceres
Chanticleer
Cherry tree; X1636 Cherry tree carol; X10822 The cherry tree carol I
Christmas Eve I
Christmas Eve II
Come, come ye Saints
Comfort; X8214 Otto
Coventry carol (1591)
Coverdale's carol
Danby
De profundis
Decree; X10862 The decree
Dent Dale
Devonshire
Diana (16th c)
Dives and Lazarus
Dorking
Down in yon forest
Dulcina
Dunstan
Eardisley; X2610 Dives and Lazarus
East Horndon
Eastertime; X2156 Cornish carol; M7193 My dancing day
Effingham
England's Lane
Essex
Ethnol
Exile
Farnaby
Farnham
Fitzwilliam
Forest Green; X7806 O little town; X11016 The ploughboy's dream
Fortunatus; X3452 Fortune
Furry Day carol
Garden
Gloucestershire wassail
God rest you merry (18th c); (London carol); X11866 Wassail song; X12183 While shepherds watched
God rest you merry II (Cornwall carol)
God's dear son
Golden mornings
Gosterwood
Green growth the holly see Henry VIII, King of England
Greensleeves (before 1642); X1727 Christ the King; X5845 Kings of the East

Hambridge
Hardwick
Hereford carol
Herongate
Hitchen carol; X10798 The bellman's song
Holy Well; X10913 The Holy Well
Horsham
Ignatius
Ingrave
Jacob's Ladder
Jerusalem, du Herrens nya stad
Job I
Job II
Job III
Joseph and Mary
Joys seven
King Herod and the cock
Kingdom of God
King's Langley (a May Day carol)
King's Lynn
Kingsfold; X5849 Kingsford
Langport
La Trobe's 586th metre
Leach
Lebanon
Lew Trenchard; X4824 Holy Spirit, truth
Lodsworth
Make we joy
Market Square
Mary, how sweetly falls that word
May carol
May-day garland
May song
Mendip
Monks Gate (Sussex trad)
Muswell Hill; X11069 The staff of faith
Newbury; X10799 The bellman's song
No room in the Inn; X11710 Virgin unspotted II; X61 A virgin unspotted III
Noel; X2771 Eardisley; X3650 Gerard; X10692 Task sublime
Northumbria; X11889 Watts' Cradle song
Prince Rupert (1648 march)
Raise your voices, vales and mountains
Ramoth
Righteous judge (19th c)
Rodmell
Rosslyn
Royal Oak
Rusper
St Austin; X8724 Psalm of Sion
St Hugh
St Issey
St Stephen
Sandys (publ 1833); X9 A child this day
Sans Day carol
Sheffield
Shepton-Beauchamp
Shipston
Sir Christèmas
Somerset carol
Somerset wassail
Song of praise; X3843 God our Father made
Southill
Stalham
Stowey; X1671 Children's song of the nativity
Summercourt
Sunny Bank: X5110 I saw three ships; X10997 The mulberry bush
Sussex I; X10547 Sussex mummers carol
Sussex II
Sussex carol
Task sublime
Terra beata; X10753 Terra patris
The Angel Gabriel
The bellman's song
The carnal and the crane
The cherry tree carol I is entered as Cherry tree. See above
The cherry tree carol II
The cherry tree carol III
The cherry tree carol IV
The decree I is entered as Decree. See above
The decree II
The first nowell; X10869 The first noël

The holly and the ivy
The Holy Well
The Lamb of God
The merchants' carol; X3883 Golden
The praise of Christmas
The salutation carol (15 c)
The Saviour's work
The seven virgins
The sinner's redemption
The three traitors
The truth from above
This endris night (15th c)
This new Christmas carol
Wassail song
Welcome (a Celtic carol)
Wexford carol
Wonder tidings (15th c)
Wondrous works

Entwisle, J. Howard
Christ will me His aid (1900)

Ephros, Gershon
Child's evening prayer (1932)
L'cho adonoy

Epstein, A.
I bless thee, Father, for the grace
Pledging our lives

Erfurt Gesangbuch, 1524
Ach Gott vom Himmel
Förlossningen ar vunnen; X4185 Gud Faders Søn enbaarne; X4622 Herr Christ der einig; X11008 The only Son from heaven
Komm heiliger Geist, Herre Gott; X5889 Kom Helligaand, Herre Gud; X8297 Paraclete; X11837 Wartburg

Erfurt Gesangbuch, 1663
Salus mortalium
Wir danken dir, Herr Jesu Christ

Erskine, John, 1870-1951
St Paul's (1917)

Esmond, A.
Manger

Essay on the Church Plain Chant, 1782
Dulce carmen; X351 Alleluia, dulce carmen; X1118 Bithynia; X2147 Corinth; X8287 Pange lingua gloriosa; X10059 Sing my tongue; X10666 Tantum ergo; X11946 Webbe

Essex, George
Aberdour

Est, T. Whole book of Psalms, 1592
Cheshire; X1641 Cheshire tune
Old 25th; X7912 O spirit of the living God
Old 30th
Old 120th; X8034 Old 77th; X8038 Old 81st
Old 136th
Winchester Old; X729 Ave, Maris stella; X12294 Winchester

Etlich Christliche lieder. Wittenberg, 1524 see also Walther, Johann. Geistliches Gesangbuchlein. Wittenberg, 1524
Wittenberg; X3037 Es ist das heil; X4186 Gud har af sin; X4194 Guds Søn er kommen; X4487 He that believes; X9557 St Paul; X9647 Salvation; X9737 Saving health; X10287 Speratus

Ett, Kaspar. Cantica sacra. Munich, 1840
Oriel; X8282 Pange lingua; X10669 Tantum ergo; X11307 To the Name that brings
St Martin; X730 Ave, Maris stella; X7986 Ocean Star, we greet you

Evangelisches choralbuch. Halle, 1829
Lobt den Herrn, die morgensonne

Evans, Daniel. Hymnau a Thonau, 1865
Llangloffan

Evans, David, 1874-1948
Bonifacio (1927)
Charterhouse (1927)
Frondeg

Henllan (1927)
Hinton-Martell
Innellan (1927)
Kildrostan (1927)
Kirkland (1927)
Llandaf
Neuadd wen
Orisons (1927)
Pisgah
Ton-mân (1912)
Yn y Glyn (1927)
Evans, David Emlyn, 1843-1913
Cwmdu
Hereford
Trewen
Evans, W.J., 1866-1947
Rhys
Everest, Charles
Alexander
Everett, Asa B., 1828-75
Ashville
Free waters
Ionia
Knocking at the door
Magnificence; X10053 Since o'er thy footstool
Newcastle
Richmond (1859)
Sweetly, Lord, have we heard; X3411 Footsteps; X3412 Footsteps of Jesus
Everett, L.C., 1818-67
Everett; X10166 Solitude
Mattie; X7717 O happy is the man
Spring
Ewing, Alexander C., 1830-95
Ewing (1853); X543 Argyle; X5514 Jerusalem, the golden
Ewing, J.C., 1849-1937
Pioneer
Excell, Edwin Othello, 1851-1921
Blessings; X12156 When upon life's
Hear our prayer
In a world where sorrow
In the shadow of His wings
Jesus bids us shine
Let Him in; X11172 There's a stranger
My Father knows (1896)
Othello; X5050 I have a song; X10051 Since I have been
The Lord is in His holy temple
Weary soul by sin oppressed (1912)
Eyre, A.J., 1853-1919
Selby

F

Fabisch, H.
Happy he who walketh ever
Fabricius, Werner, 1633-79
NOTE: Real name, Peter Schmid, was discarded
Gregor's 133d meter-B (1659)
X684 Auf, auf, weil der tag
Fairlamb, James Remington, 1838-1908
Faith
Martineau
Vicaria (1864)
Falconer, A. Croil
Consolator
Harvest-tide
St Vigian
Faning, Joseph Eaton, 1850-1927
Vita
Far eastern sources see Asian, Chinese, etc.
Farjeon, Harry, 1878-1948
Need (1931)
Our brother is born
Farmer, Henry, 1819-91
Angels holy
Farmer
In the field
Farrer, John Downing, 1829-1919
Jubilate
New Calabar
Faure, Jean-Baptiste, 1830-1914
The Palms
Fawcett, John, 1789-1867
Melling (1822)
Relief (1822)
Feilden, Oswald Mosley, 1837-1924
Eden
Enon

Felton, William M.
Hymn for Memorial Day
Ferguson, William Harold, 1874-1950
Cuddesdon
Frilford
Hominum amator
Ladywell
Wolvercote
Ferretti, Salvatore, 1817-74
Salvatori; X2988 Endsleigh
Ferris, Theodore P.
Weymouth (1941)
Fesca, Alexander Ernst, 1820-1849
Peace
Figulus, Wolfgang, 1520-91
NOTE: Real name, Töpfer
Helft mir Gott's Gute (1575)
Filby, William C., 1836-
Epiphany
Fortitude (1874); X8150 Onward
Sundridge
Filitz, Friedrich, 1804-76
Capetown (1847); X2338 Dantzig
Caswall (1847); X1000 Bemerton; X3759 Glory be to Jesus; X11728 Viva! viva! Gesu; X12005 Wem in leidenstagen; X12009 Wenn in leidenstagen
Clewer (1847)
Mannheim (1847); X685 Auf, auf, weil der tag; X8682 Protection; X10670 Tantum ergo
Fillmore, Charles M.
Abide in me
Fillmore, Fred A.
I will early seek my Saviour
Seeds of promise
Fillmore, James H., 1849-1941
Be strong, O men (1920)
Flower
Give to the Lord
Lord of the nations
O wonderful word of salvation (1915)
Open thou mine eyes
Pounds; X3350 Fillmore; X4314 Hannah; X5077 I know that my Redeemer
Purer in heart
Resolution; X5019 I am resolved
Saviour, I would live (1923)
The beautiful garden of prayer (1920)
Turn your faces toward the morning
We are going down the valley
We are little gleaners
Fink, Gottfried Wilhelm, 1783-1846
Bethlehem (1842); X1831 Claudius; X3106 Evangel; X3558 Gabriel; X9899 Seraph
Finlay, Kenneth George, 1882-
Ardgowan
Ayrshire
Carrick
Cobham
Crieff
Farnell
Finnart
Ford Place
Garelochside
Glenfinlas
Hamilton
Helensburgh
Hyndland
Irvine Waterside
Lyle Road
Scotstoun
West Burn
Finnish traditional, etc.
Lost in the night
Nyland
Suomi (a 17th c cavalry march)
Suomi II
Who made ocean
Fischer, William E., 1849-1936
Laus regis; X9935 Shamokin Trewks
Fischer, William Gustavus, 1835-1912
Coming to the cross; X5014 I am coming to the cross; X5026 I am trusting; X7532 Now the shades of night; X11431 Trusting
Hankey (ca 1872); X2820 Eaton Square; X5094 I

love to tell the story; X 10722 Tell the story
O, I love to talk with Jesus
The Rock of refuge; X7909 O sometimes the shadows are deep; X9081 Rock of refuge; X11034 The Rock that is higher
Whiter than snow (1872); X3369 Fischer; X6370 Lord Jesus, I long to
Wondrous love

Fisher, Albert C., 1886-1946
Fisher (1912)
Redeeming love (1956)

Fisher, Nevin W., 1900-
Bridgewater (1951)
Highland Avenue (1950)
Jesu, dulcedo cordium (1951)
McPherson (1951)
Praise and prayer (1951)

Fishwick, William
Detroit (1930)
Fishwick (1930)
Mt Eliot (1930)

Fitzwater, A.J., 1886-
Riches of God (1951)

Flemish traditional, etc.
A little child; X3382 Flemish carol
Flanders; X473 Angels holy
Jesus of the manger
Three Kings

Flemming, Friedrich F. 1778-1813
Flemming (1811); X3277 Father in heaven; X3381 Fleming; X5362 Integer [vitae]

Fletcher, Douglas, 1884-
Molleson (1924)

Fliedner. Liederbuch fur Klein-kinder-schulen, 1842
Dijon; X7168 Müde bin ich geh zur reh

Flittner, Johann, 1618-78
Flittner (1653); X119 Ach, was soll ich
Gregor's 124th metre (1661); X2440 Dedication; X12008 Wenn erblick ich doch

Flood, Edwin
Sons of men, behold

Florian, Sr. Mary, S.S.J.
Glorious Mary (1958)

Flotow, Friedrich Ferdinand Adolf, 1812-83
Even Song; X11949 Weber Guidance

Floyd, Alfred E., 1870-
Land of our birth
Vermont

Fluiter, Henry de see De Fluiter, Henry

Fones, J.G.
Beautiful Sion, built above
For our devotions, Father
I'll praise my Maker

Foote, Arthur William, 1853-1937
Easter carol

Foote, Arthur, II, 1911-
Four winds (1958)
Struther (1949)

Foote, J.G.
When I see the blood

Forrest, C.H.
Heart of Jesus

Fosbery, L.M.
Leland

Foss, Hubert James, 1899-1953
Croydon

Foster, J.
Pembroke

Foster, Myles Birket, 1851-1922
Crucis milites
Crucis victoria
Dawn
Dedication (1890)
Medford (by M.B.F., presumed to be M.B. Foster)
Monica
Salvator (1905)
Vox celestis (1905)

Foster, Stephen Collins, 1826-64
I love Him; X8002 Old Black Joe

Fowles, Leonard N., 1871-1939
Cavell (1918); X8454 Phoenix
Golders Green

Fox, A.M.
Ye chosen Twelve

Francis, M., Sr., P.C.

Bringing our praise (1958)
Francis, Philip
Hark, a herald voice
Franck, César-Auguste, 1822-90
Ave Maria
Panis Angelicus
St Clothilde
Franck, Johann Wolfgang, 1644-ca 1710
Komm, seele (1681); X4290 Hamburg
Franck, Melchior, ca 1579-1639
Melchior (1663); X4518; Heaven; X4534 Heavenly Jerusalem; X5500 Jerusalem; X5509 Jerusalem, du hochgebaute stadt
Morning Star (1628)
Was fuerrechst du Feind Herodes (1616)
Franck, Peter, 1616-75
Schwing dich (1657); X3249 Fang dein werk; X3473 Franck
Franklin Square (perhaps by S.B. Pond, 1850)
The bird let loose
Franz, Robert, 1815-92
Dedication
Frech, Johann G.
Wittenberg; X640 Aspurg
Frederick, Donald, 1917-
James Quinter
Mack (1951)
Spirit-wind
Freeman, Andrew, 1876-
Limpsfield
Freeman, Elizabeth W.
East Church (1899)
French Psalter, 1562 see Genevan Psalter, 1562
French traditional, liturgical, etc.
Ad perennis (16th c church)
Au clair de la lune
Bell carol; X5477 Je sais, vierge Marie
Besançon carol; X1550 Carol of the advent; X9968 Shepherds, shake off
Carol of service; X8677 Promptement levez-vous
Chartres (15th c); X5320 In the town; X7511 Nous voici dans la ville
Christus vincit
City of David, Bethlehem
Collaudemus
Daily, daily; X360 Alleluia! Sing to Jesus; X2315 Daily, daily sing to Mary
Delight
Destiny (16th c)
Fragrance; X1547 Carol of beauty; X8753 Quelle est cette odeur agreable?
Gevaert (13th c noel); X11058 The sleep of the Child Jesus
Gloria; X463 Angel voices; X469 Angels, from the; X485 Angels we have heard; X5396 Iris; X6106 Les anges dans nos; X8006 Old French melody; X9964 Shepherds in the field; X12150 When the sun
Grace soit; X3982 Grace soit rendue; X8577 Praise the Lord in heaven; X10495 Summer time; X11498 Une vaine crainte
Gregor's 167th metre-B (1558); X4657 Herz und herz vereinst
Jesus the glory
Let Christian hearts (16th c)
Lille
Love is come again; X3498 Love is come again; X3864 Godhead here in hiding; X7442 Nöel nouvelet
Masters in the hall
Normandy (a Norman carol)
Nous allons; X2791 Easter carol; X7510 Nous allons, ma mie
O filii et filiae (15th c plainsong, Solemes version, M 2, or modern version)
O God thou art (16th c)
Old French carol; X1058 Bethlehem; X2337 Dans

cette etable
Old French noël
Patapan
Picardy (17th c); X3499 French carol
Quittez, Pasteurs; X12196 White Lent
Sion's daughters
So, brother; X2407 De turlu turlutu; X3320 Fesans raijouissance
Summer carol
The band of children (16th c); X5929 Laissez paitre vos betes; X7624 O come, Divine Messiah
The builders; X3992 Grand Dieu! que de merveilles
The kingdom; X8766 Quoi, ma voisine?
The Maid of France (used by Bizet in L'Arlésienne suite)
The praises of that saint; X3541 From thee, illustrious
The Spirit; X2176 Courons, a la fete
'Tis the month of our Mother
Un flambeau; X1320 Bring a torch
Waking-time; X11734 Voison, d'où venait?
Zachary

Freudenthal, Julius
En kelohenu; X775 Ayn kay-lo-hay-nu

Freylinghausen, Johann Anastasius, 1670-1739
NOTE; Both composer and compiler. Melodies not completely identified, but they may be attributed to these publication dates: Gesangbuch. Halle, 1704; Neues Geistriches Gesangbuch, 1714; with several intervening and unidentified dates also cited.

Briesen (1704); X3523 Fröhlich soll mein herz springen
Christe, wahres seelenlicht (1704); X6192 Light of the soul
Conqueror (1704); X6392 Lord victorious; X7653 O du store seierherre; X7654 O durchbrecher
Das ist meine freude
Den des vaters sinn geboren
Festus (1704); X1211 Bonn; X4112 Gregor's 155th metre; X4207 Guiding star; X7648 O du hueter Israel
Grasmere
Gregor's 77th metre (Trochaic: 7. 6. 7. 6. 7. 7) (1705); X2394 Dayspring; X8035 Old 77th-A; X12556 Zeige mir dein angesicht
Gregor's 95th metre (1710); X7959 O wie selig sind die
Gregor's 97th metre (1704); X9773 Scepter; X12251 Wie schön ist unsers
Gregor's 102d metre (1704); X3614 Gekreuzigter, mein herz sucht
Gregor's 109th metre (1710); X3013a Er ist mein himmel
Gregor's 118th metre (1704); X3001 Entbinde mich, mein Gott
Gregor's 151st metre-I (1704); X3027 Ermuntert euch, ihr frommen; X8900 Rejoice
Gregor's 156th metre (Trochaic: 7. 8. 7. 8. 7. 8. 8. 7) (1704); X5595 Jesus ist das schoenste licht
Gregor's 167th metre-D (1704); X4638 Herr und Gott der tag
Gregor's 184th metre-A (1704); X3458 Foundation; X7916 O suezer Stand, O sel'ges leben
Gregor's 221st metre (1704); X2702 Du ewiger abgrund der seligen liebe; X10331 Springs of salvation
Gregor's 310th metre (1704); X7088 Morgenstern auf finstre nacht
Gregor's 341st metre (1704); X2553 Dich, Jesu, loben

vir; X3508 Freylinghausen
Jesus ist das schönste licht; X6848 Meine liebe lebet noch
Luebeck (1704); X1524 Carinthia; X3938 Gott sei dank; X4003 Gratia; X5674 Jesus, Savior, risen; X8106 On this day, the first; X10023 Silcher I
Macht hoch die tür (1704); X449 Anastasius; X1785 Christmas morn; X3509 Freylinghausen
Morgenglanz der Ewigkeit (1704); X2395 Dayspring; X8171 Oremus; X8775 Radiant morn
Pressburg (1714); X7398 Nicht so traurig
Richter (1706); X6846 Meine armuth
Se Solens skjønne Lys og Pragt (1704); X2498 Der lieben Sonne licht und pracht; X4279 Halle; X8474 Pilgrimage
Search the Scriptures
Sebastian (1714); X5632 Jesu meines glaubens zier
Sinner's friend (1704); X4141 Gregor's 218th metre; X12255 Wie wohl ist mir [O freund der seelen]
Truth (1704); X11957 Weil die worte wahrheit sind
Tu vins, Jesus (1704); X4089 Gregor's 83d metre; X4217 Guter hirte [willst du nicht?]
Friedell, Harold W., 1905-58
Finlay
Friese, Heinrich
O Welt, sieh hier (1703)
Fritsch, Ahasuerus, 1629-1701
Darmstadt (1679); X7702 O Gott, du frommer Gott; X11845 Was frag' ich nach
Sollt es gleich bisweillen scheinen
Fromm, L.E.
Benediction (1934)
Response (1939)
Frost, Charles Joseph, 1848-1922
Harvest
Frost, E.H.
Tabler
Fulda melody
O sacrament most holy
Fuller, H.R.
Christian soldiers
Christians, awake
God in heaven
Fuller Maitland, John Alexander, 1856-1936
Luccombe
Funk, Joseph
Lingham

G

G.E.M.G. (melody originated in Occupied China, World War II; & sung by students and teachers)
Unafraid
Gabriel, Charles H., 1856-1932
Adowa
Americus
Arles
Aspinwall (1912)
Avondale (1901)
Behold, I stand at the door (1917)
Birdstown
Chios (1912)
Erskine
Glory song (1900); X10877 The glory song
Go to the deeps (1907)
Hanford (1906)
He is so precious (1902); X8632 Precious to me
He lifted me (1905)
Higher ground; X5233 I'm pressing on the upward way
His eye is on the sparrow
How marvelous; X7250 My Saviour's love
I stand all amazed (1898)
Just when I need Him (1908); X3559 Gabriel
Kathrine
Knowhead
Lansing
Lucile
McCabe; X9885 Send the

light
McDaniel (1914)
Nilus
Old-time power (1912)
Pressly
Safe with Jesus (1900)
Sarah (1901)
Song of the Saviour (1893)
Sweet promise; X5144 I will not forget thee
Trust Him
Use me, Saviour
Way of the cross (1906); X11104 The way of the cross
Where the gates swing outward never (1920)
Will the circle be unbroken
Gade, Niels Vilhelm, 1817-90
Child Jesus
Gade
Gadsby, Henry Robert, 1842-1907
Joy
St Boniface (1875)
Gaelic traditional, etc.
Bunessan
Killin
St Patrick
Gaines, Samuel Richards, 1869-1945
The coming day (1927)
Gale, Clement R.
Bavaria
Galsberg; X3564a Gaisberg
Gamble, J. Collection, 1659
Gamble
Ganss, H.G.
Long live the Pope!
Ganther (no initials)
St Hilary
Gardiner, William. Sacred melodies, 1812-15
Belmont; X4433 Haydn, No. 2; X4569 Help, Lord, the souls; X7611 O Christ, behind the temple's veil; X9311 St Bernard; X11516 Unveil mine eyes; X11702 Vigils
Dedham
Gardiner; X1212 Bonn; X3545 Fulda; X3656 Germany (Beethoven); X11811 Walton
Garratt, Charles A.
Comfort (19th c)
Garrett, George Mursell, 1834-97
Advent (1891)
Beulah
Communion
Crucis (1872)
Eschol
Forgiveness; X1909 Come; X3400 Follow me
Genesis
Hymn of glory
Manger
St Croix (1889)
St John's College (1872)
Tetworth
Garrett, Margueritte Bixler
Brother, here's a message
Our prayer (1925)
Garrison, Joseph
Something for Jesus
Gastorius, Severus, d 1678
Was Gott tut (1670); X790 Baden; X3585 Gastorius; X4115 Gregor's 160th metre-B; X4616 Hermon; X4866 Hope; X7764 O Jesus Christ, alone to thee; X10707 Te lucis ante terminum; X11847 Was Gott thut das ist
Gates, B. Cecil
How long, O Lord, most holy
Gates, Crawford M.
Ring out, wild bells
Gatty, Nicholas Comyn, 1874-1946
Laetabundus
Midhurst
Tugwood
Gaul, Alfred Robert, 1837-1913
Filius dei
Holy City; X3601 Gaul
Holy City II; X4775 Holy City
Sanctus
O worship the Lord
Gauntlett, Henry John, 1805-76
Ardwick
Ascension tide; X611 Ascension; X614 Ascension, No.

2
Beaumaris
Cobern; X4899 Houghton; X 6011 Laudate dominum
Constance (1875)
Eternity (1849)
Evermore
Gauntlett I; X6002 Laudate dominum
Gauntlett II
Gauntlett III
Hatfield; X1505 Canterbury
Hawkhurst
Hereford
I love to hear the story
Irby (1858)
Jeshurun
Newland (1858)
Presbyter
Resurrection hymn
Riseholme
St Albinus (1852); X242 Albinus
St Alphege (1852); X397 Alphege; X9248 St Alphage
St Ambrose (based on plainsong M 8)
St Fulbert (1852); X3544 Fulbert
St George (1848); X3605 Gauntlett; X9540 St Olave
St Mark
Springfield
Triumph
University College (1852); X8151 Onward
Vita

Gauntlett's Comprehensive tune book, 1851
Giessen

Gawler. Harmonia perfecta, 1730 see Harmonia perfecta, 1730

Gay, Annabeth McClelland, 1925-
Shepherds' pipes

Gebauer, J.C.
Maria, hun er en Jomfru ren X3607 Gebauer

Geer, G.J.
Holy voices
Marshall

Geibel, Adam, 1855-1933
Behold! a royal army
Lullaby
Trumpet call; X1969 Come, sing to the Lord; X3613 Geibel; X10354 Stand up, stand up for

Geistliche gesangbuchlein- Wittenberg, 1524 was edited by Johann Walther. See note under his name

Geistliche gesänge. Leipzig, 1625 see As hymnodus sacer. Leipzig, 1625

Geistliche kirchengesang. Cologne, 1599
Rosa mystica (usually cited as harmonized by Michael Praetorius, 1609); X18 A great and mighty wonder; X960 Behold a branch; X962 Behold a rose; X3039 Es ist ein ros' entsprungen; X7902 O sing a joyous carol; X8559 Praetorius; X8885 Regina caeli jubila; X11136 There is a flower

Geistliche lieder. Wittenberg, 1535 (often cited as Klug ...)
Christum wir sollen loben schon
Jeg raaber, Herr Jesu Krist; X5174 Ich ruf zu dir
Jeus Christus, unser Heiland
Luther; X3042 Es ist gewisslich; X4981 Hvad kan os komme til; X6538 Luther's hymn (1535); X6539 Luther's hymn (1531); X7039 Monmouth; X7564 Nun freut euch
O Jesu när jag häden skall; X4106 Gregor's 132d metre-F; X12363 Wo Gott der Herr nicht bei uns
Wo Gott zum Haus; X895; Be thou exalted

Geistliches gesange. Wittenberg, 1544
Rhau; X2566 Die seele Christi; X4067 Gregor's 22d metre-A; X7570 Nun lasst uns den leib

Geistliches volkslied, 1850
Desire; X2509 Desire (min-

or reading); X7839 O mein Jesu, ich muss; X9713 Santolius

Geistreiches gesangbuch. Darmstadt. 1698 see Darmstadt gesangbuch, 1698

Gelineau, Joseph, S.J.
Come ring out your joy (1953)
Defend me, O God (1953); X12141 When the Lord turned
Have mercy on me (1953)
He who dwells (1953)
How great is your name (1953); X7679 O give the Lord, you
I lift up my eyes (1953); X11320 To You have I lifted
I love the Lord (1953); X5125 I trusted even when
I rejoiced when I heard (1953)
If the Lord does not build (1953)
Like the deer that yearns (1953)
My Shepherd is the Lord (1953)
O blessed are those (1953)
O give thanks (1953)
O praise the Lord (1953)
Out of the depths (1953); X11305 To the Lord in the hour
The canticle of the Blessed Virgin I (1953)
The canticle of the Blessed Virgin II (1953)
The Lord is King (1953); X2280 Cry out with joy
The Lord's is the earth (1953)
Why this tumult (1953)

Genevan Psalters
NOTE: Several psalters are included. Date gives the edition essential to melody publication.

Ainsworth 97 (1562); X9210 Sacrifice of praise; X5085 I love the Lord
Au fort de ma détresse (1542)
Autumn (1551) NOTE: This is usually attributed to Barthélémon.
Donne secours (1551); X2006 Comfort ye; X3632 Genevan Psalm 12; X8698 Psalm 12
Geneva (1551)
Geneva 61 (1562)
Holy Name [being the minor reading of Louez dieu] (1562); X6414 Louez dieu (minor reading)
Jervaulx Abbey (1562); X8711 Psalm 84; X10627 Tabernacles
Louez dieu [being the major reading of Holy Name] (1562); X4806a Holy Name (major reading); X8721 Psalm 136
Meadow Cove [being the latter portion of Psalm 47] (1551); X8705 Psalm 47
Ministres de l'Eternel (1562); X8719 Psalm 135
O Seigneur (1551); X7108 Morning praise; X8696 Psalm 3
Old First (1542)
Old 117th (1551)
Psalm 93 (1562)
Psalm 138; X5742 Jubilation
Psalm 146 (Delft ed., 1602)

Genge, R.S.
Holy Comfort

George, Graham, 1912-
Grace Church, Cananoque (1964)
The King's majesty (1940)

Gerle, Hans. Musica Teutsch. Nürnberg, 1532
Ich dank' dir, lieber Herre

German traditional, including many church melodies.
All morgen ist (1537)
Altenburg
Angelus; X5608 Jesu, joy of man's desiring (Schop)
Armageddon
Badea
Baptizien (adapted by Luther and Walther)
Bohemia (14th c)
Christmas dawn (1823); X2892 Entracht; X7283 När juldags-morgon glimmer; X11238 Thuringia
Commit thy way; X955

Befiehl du deine wege
Cor dulce, cor amabile (1669); X6719 Maria mater gratia; X11648 Vexilla regis prodeunt
Cyriacus (15th c); X1794 Christum wir sollen loben schön
Das Leiden des Herrn
Dies sind die heil'gen (ca 1200)
Dolwyddelan (1693)
Durch Adam's fall (1525); X 5478 Jeg beder dig
Earthly friends (16th c)
Eisleben (15th c); X4553 Heiliger Herre Gott
Electus
En främling klappar pa din dörr
Erfreut euch (1536); X5909 Kreuznach
Evergreen; X1931 Come, hail the cause
Franconia
Freiburg (16th c); X3048 Es liegt ein schloss; X5068 I know a kingdom; X5486 Jeg ved et evigt himmerig; X5832 Kingdom
Germania
Glorious Virgin, thee we sing
God is ascended (16th c); X3620 Gen himmel auf gefahren ist
Gregor's 159th metre; X2500 Der Sabbath ist um's menschen will'n; X12461 Worship
Gregor's 168th metre-B (1642); X5550 Jesu, der du meine seele
Gregor's 185th metre-A (1740); X2179 Covenant; X2867 Eeuwig dank en eere; X4005 Gratitude; X4637 Herr und aeltster deiner
Gregor's 212th metre (before 1540); X2744 Durch Adam's fall ist
Herzlich thut mich erfreuen (mediaeval mel)
Homburgh
Ich fahr dahin; X11687 Vienna
In dulci jubilo (14th c); X5485 Jeg synger Julekind; X5872 Klug; X12106 When Christ was born
Incense
I'll sing a hymn to Mary
Jag tvor pa Gud, och vet (1523)
Jesus lives, and Jesus leads; X338 Alle vögel; X3401 Follow me
Komm, Gott Schöpfer, heiliger Geist (1524)
Kommt her zu mir (15th c); X889 Be not dismayed; X5891 Kom hid til mig, enhver isaer; X6258 Little flock
Lambs of Jesus
Laus tibi Christi (14th c); X6023 Laus tibi
Leonburg
Liberation
Lo! the heavens are breaking
Lobet und preiset
Lux noel
Magdalena (16th c)
Mary's wandering; X6722 Marias wanderschaft
Mecklenburg
Mendebras; X6882 Mendebas; X7642 O day of rest and gladness
Mendon; X636 Aspiration; X1276 Brandenburg
Mothering Sunday (14th c); X5181 Ich weiss ein lieblich engelspiel
Naar mig min Synd vil kraenke (1790)
Neckar
Nu wol Gott das unser gesang (16th c)
O'er the silent waters
Peace makers
Pekin
Plea (16th c)
Resonet in laudibus (14th c); X5717 Joseph lieber, Joseph mein; X10235

Song of the crib
Rudolfstadt
St Basil
Sanglier
Selvin
Sheltered Dale
Siberia
Singen wir aus Herzens Grund (1544); X3302 Fear my child, thy God; X10625 Sunge vi af hjertens grund
Song
Stabat mater (old German); X5903 Kommt, ihr seelen, nehmt zu herzen
Stilla jag pa dig vill akta (18th c)
Susanni (16th c)
The Star
Thessalonica
Thule
Tredeca; X5238 Immortal Babe
Twinkling stars
Tyholland
Tysk
Wachterlied (16th c)
Wansted
What happiness can equal mine
When morning fills the sky; X12131 When morning gilds
Whiteland
Williamson
Woodbird; X3035 Es flog ein kleins waldvöglein; X5215 I'll sing a hymn; X7903 O sing the great apostle
Worship

Gerold, Johan Carl
Jehovah (1800)

Gerovitch, Eliezer
Adon olom
Adonoy adonoy

Gersbach, Anton
Anton

Gesang-und Notenbuch. Stuttgart, 1744
O Grosser Gott

Gesangbuch. Erfurt, 1663 see Erfurt Gesangbuch, 1663

Gesangbuch mit noten, 1890
Aus dem himmel ferne
Ich singe dir
Ich weiss an wen ich glaube
O leide, leide gern
Seliger friede
So lange Jesus bleibt der Herr
Unter lilien jener freuden
Was kann es schön'res geben

Gesius, Bartholomaeus, 1555-1613
Commemoration; X2335 Dank sei Gott [in der höhe]; X3610 Geduld, die soll's
Du Friedensfürst, Herr Jesu Christ
Gesius; X4675 Heut' triumphiret; X11393 Triumphs today the Lord
Herrnhut; X2034 Communion hymn; X5553 Jesus, din lhukommelse; X6845 Mein Seel, o Herr, muss
O Christe, Morgensterne (1605)

Gether, A.
Gether

Giardini, Felice de, 1716-96
Athens
Blendon
Moscow; X3773 Glory to God on high; X5440 Italian hymn; X11088 The Trinity; X11380 Trinity
Turin

Gibbons, Orlando, 1583-1625
Angel's song (1623); X468 Angels; X474 Angels' hymn; X1933 Come, Holy Ghost; X3671 Gibbons; X6188 Light divine; X10225 Song 34
Bourdillon; X10227 Song 46
Song I (1623)
Song 3 (1623)
Song 4
Song 5
Song 13 (1623); X1506 Canterbury; X3672 Gibbons
Song 18
Song 20
Song 22 (1623); X4676 Hezekiah
Song 24
Song 31 (1623)

Song 46 (1623); X3385 Fletcher; X3673 Gibbons
Song 67 (1621)
NOTE: The bass is attributed to Gibbons; the melody is from Prys, Psalms, 1621; X3674 Gibbons; X9512 St Matthias
Gibbs, Cecil Armstrong, 1889-1960
Crossings (1930)
Danbury (1925)
Herrick's Ode (1928)
Lingwood
Little Baddow (1930)
Gibson, Alexander S., 1843-1919
Alexander (1915)
Look down on us
Gideon, Henry
How good it is to thank the Lord (1932)
Giffe, William T.
O wonderful prayer
Sweet is the story
Gifford, Philip A.
I think, when I read; X10598 Sweet story
Gilbert, Walter Bond, 1829-1910
Angelica; X3678 Gilbert; X3679 Gilberts
Maidstone (1862); X477 Angels, roll the rock
Morning
Rodigast
St Enoch
Stuyvesant
Thanksgiving
Gilchrist, William Wallace, 1846-1916
Christmas
Communion
Easter
Evening
Merry Christmas bells
Sound over the waters (1920)
Whitsuntide
Woodland (1891)
Gilding, Edmund
St Edmund (1762); X2443 Dedication
Gill, Benjamin
Holmfirth (1905)
Gill, John
Frankfort; X7368 New St Andrew
Gillespie, James, 1929
Harrowby
Gillis, Emma Hanford
Lead on, thou God of Hosts (1914)
Gilmore, H. C.
St Luke, No. 2
Gilmour, H. L.
He brought me out
Love found me
Make me a blessing today
Gilmour, Robert. Psalm-Singer's assistant, 1793
Montrose
Giornovichi (real name Jarnowick), Giovanni Marie, 1745-1804
St Asaph
Gladstone, William Henry, 1840-91
Erskine
Hammersmith
Ombersley (1872)
Glaser, Joseph
Glaser
Gläser, Carl G., 1784-1829
Azmon (ca 1839); X293 All praise to our redeeming Lord; X785 Azmon new; X2481 Denfield; X3276 Father, I stretch my hands; X7707 O grant thy servants
Glezen, E. K.
Glezen
Gluck, Christoph Willibald, 1714-87
Chant your songs
Father all-holy
Orpheus
Glynn, Franklin
Maxon (1941)
Scarborough (1941)
Woking (1941)
Gnadauer choralbuch, 1735
Marter Christi
Gnadauer choralbuch, 1784
O dass ich tausend; X7639 O das ich tausend zungen hätte; X8045 Old 106th
Godfrey, Nathaniel S., 1817-83

Ellingham
Goerz, P.J.
O, be still
Goldfarb, I.
Sholom alaychem
Goldstein, M.
Va-anachnu
Goldsworthy, W.A.
Bouwerie (1941)
Gooch, Frederick
Baginton (1858)
Good, Flora H.
Since Jesus did appear; X5525 Jesus a wedding guest
Good, P.S.
Evening
Good, S.E.
The cleft of the Rock
Goodhart, A.M.
Etona
Goodrich, Charles G.
Shortle (1905)
Goodrich. Service and tune book
Rest
Gordon, Adoniram Judson, 1836-99
Gordon (1864); X1528 Caritas; X6420 Love; X7221 My Jesus, I love thee
In tenderness
Goss, John, 1800-80
Advent (1872); X3256 Fareham
Arthur's Seat (1874)
Bevan (1853)
Dona; X9132 Rothley; X840 Barnby's hymnary,Tune 154; X3924 Goss; X11358 Transfiguration
Glad tidings
Israel
Lauda anima (1869); X1009 Benedic anima mea; X2640 Dominic, Our Lady's champion; X5540 Jesus Christ, the King of ages; X8557 Praise; X8571 Praise my soul; X9558 St Paul
Peterborough
St Augustine (1854)
St Casimer
St Cyprian
Salvator
See, amid the winter snow (1870); X4962 Humility; X12319 Winter's snow
Tarsus; X9559 St Paul
Waterstock
Gotha Cantional, 1726
Jag gar mot döden, hvar jag gar
Gottschalk, Louis Moreau, 1829-69
Mercy (1854); X3842 God, Our Father, hear; X3956 Gottschalk; X4333 Happy who in early youth; X4787 Holy Ghost, with light; X5980 Last hope; X6685 Manna
Gottshall, Henry G., 1903-46
Christopher Sower (1938)
Goudimel, Claude, 1508-72
Goudimel; X9044 Righteous Judge
Gregor's 205th metre; X824 Barnabas; X3612 Geht, erhoeht die majestaet; X3959 Goudimel
Gould, Edwin
Conjugal love; X2070 Conjugial love
Lord, I believe
Pax caelestis
Gould, John Edgar, 1822-75
Adrian
Bera (1849)
Hymn; X3961 Gould
Morgan
Pilot (1871); X5673 Jesus Saviour, pilot me
Gould, Nathanael D.
Woodland
Goule (no initials)
Hail, heavenly Queen
Gounod, Charles François, 1818-93
Alma redemptoris mater
Ave verum corpus
Evening hymn; X3966 Gounod's Evening hymn; X9205 Sacred Heart! in accents
Gounod
Jesus, food of angels; X170 Adoro te devote

Lovely appear
Lux prima (1872); X839 Barnby's hymnary, Tune 148; X3965 Gounod; X4506 Heart of Jesus! golden chalice; X6556 Lux vera; X7179 Muriel
O sacrament most holy
Olney
Orient; X6549 Lux fiat
Praise ye the Father
Radiant morn; X6543 Lux aeterna; X11027 The radiant morn
Rouen; X12070 What a sea of tears
Veni Emmanuel
Wondrous love that cannot falter

Gower, Jean Milne, 1867-
Livermore

Gower, John Henry, 1855-1922
Angel choir (1896)
Bonaventura
Devotion (1895)
Ecclesia
Gower's Litany (1890) X3967 Gower; X6232 Litany
Laus Deo
Meditation (1890); X11138 There is a green hill
Ministry (1909)
Neilson (1894)
Petition
Recessional (1903); X3969 Gower's Recessional
Reliance (1895)
St Botolf (1890)
Sundown

Grabowski, J.
Jerusalem

Graham, S. J.
Gleams of the golden morning

Grape, John T., 1833-
All to Christ I owe; X5056 I hear the Saviour say; X5658 Jesus paid it all

Grauman, Max
Come let us sing in sweet accord (1932)
God is the giver of all (1932)
Jacob's ladder (1932)
Lord, unto thy sacred dwelling
Our pious fathers (1932)
Sabbath hymn (1932)
The stars watch you (1932)

Graun, Karl Heinrich, 1704-59
Look up and see

Graves, F. A.
He was nailed to the cross
He'll never forget

Gray, Alan, 1855-1935
Battle cry
Hosanna

Gray, D. Vincent
Holy Innocents (1941)

Greatorex, Henry Wellington, 1811-58
Bemerton (1849)
Geer
Glory be to the Father (1851); X3740 Gloria patri
Grostette
Leighton (1849)
St Gabriel

Greatorex, Walter, 1871-1930
Woodlands (1919)

Greek melody
Luke; X660 Athens; X4036 Greek folksong; X5124 I think when I read; X9633 Salamis; X10599 Sweet story

Green, Harold, 1871-1931
The quiet hour; X8761 Quietude

Green, James. Book of Psalmody, 1724
Crowle

Green, James. Psalmody, 1731
Ferry

Green, James. Psalmody, 1744
Althorp

Greene, Maurice, 1696-1755
St Nicholas

Greenfield, Alfred M.
Washington Square (1927)

Greenwood, E. Norman
Benevolence (1932)
Freedom (1932)
Lansdowne (1932)
Prayer (1932)
Radlett (1932)
Selworthy (1932)
Swanage (1932)

Greenwood's Psalmody, Halifax, 1838
Affection
Gregor, Christian Friedrich, 1723-1801
Eden (1763)
Gregor (1784)
Gregor's 6th metre (1784); X2473 Den die Engel droben
Gregor's 7th metre (1784); X334 Alle deine gaben
Gregor's 9th metre (1784); X5541 Jesus Christus blick dich an
Gregor's 12th metre (1784); X4018 Great High Priest; X4731 Höchster priester, der du dich
Gregor's 54th metre-D (1784); X1306 Brich durch mein angefachtnes herz
Gregor's 74th metre (1784); X4636 Herr Jesu, ewig's licht
Gregor's 99th metre (1784); X7592 O anblick der mir's herz bricht
Gregor's 107th metre; X6841 Mein Jesu, der du vor dem scheiden; X9201 Sacrament
Gregor's 112th metre; X3014 Er wird es thun, der fromme, treue Gott; X4701 Hilf Gott, dasz mir's gelinge!
Gregor's 126th metre-B (1784)
Gregor's 163d metre (1784); X11761 Wachet, wachet, lieben kinder
Gregor's 208th metre-C (1784); X2887 Einer, ach nur einer
Old 96th (1784); X7732 O Herre Gott, in meiner noth
Old 271st (1784); X3608 Gebor'n ist uns der heil'ge Christ; X11357 Tranquillity
Greiter, Mattaeus, ca 1490-1550
Psalm 68 (ca 1525); X4155 Greiter; X6479 Lucerne; X8051 Old 113th; X8702 Psalm 36; X12052 Westminster College
Grenoble Antiphoner, 1753
Deus tuorum militum; X4157 Grenoble; X5547 Jesu, corona Virginum; X11444 Tu, Christe, nostrum
Gretchaninov, Alexander Tikhonovitch, 1864-1956
New Russia
Grey, Francis Richard, 1813-90
St Aidan
Grieg, Edvard Hagerup, 1844-1907
Asa's death; X619 Ase's death
Ave maris stella
Fatherland song
Hagerup; X7689 O God of hosts
Springfield
The snow lay on the ground
Griffith, William, 1867-1929
Cuttle Mills
Grigg, Joseph
Grigg; X3685 Give
Grigg, Thomas
Tiverton
Griggs, Thomas C.
Earth, with her ten thousand flowers
Gently raise the sacred strain
Grimley, John T.
Summerford (1887)
Grimm, Carl Hugo, 1890-
A noble life (1932)
Come, let us praise (1932)
Friend after friend (1932)
Hymn of the harvest (1932)
It singeth low (1932)
Prayer for wisdom (1932)
We plough the fields (1932)
Grimm, D.J. Choralbuch, 1755
Consolation; X7400 Nicht so traurig, nicht so sehr
Gregor's 39th metre-C; X5172 Ich liebe dich herzlich, O Jesu
Gregor's 115th metre; X216 Agnus Christi; X12250 Wie herrlich ist's ein schoeflein
Gregor's 172d metre; X112 Ach Gott! was hat vor

herrlichkeit; X11091 The Unity's march
Gregor's 184th metre-C; X 12010 Wenn meine seel' den tag bedenket
Gregor's 244th metre; X5163 Ich blicke nach der hoehe
Grimm's 253d metre; X4552 Heil'ger Geist do tröster mein; X6185 Light
Grimm's 265th metre; X3524 Frohlock', liebe christenheit
Grimm's 315th metre; X8844 Rede selber uns zu gut
Grimm's 349th metre; X7086 Morgenglanz der ewigkeit
Grimm's 480th metre; X11759 Wachet auf, ihr mueden geister
Grimm's 552d metre; X115 Ach Herr, wo sind nun meine vor'gen kroefte
Old 193d; X5596 Jesu, Jehovah! ich soch' und verlange
Old 466th; X2701 Du bist ja, Jesu, meine freude
Saxony; X5175 Ich seh'in bangen Busz-ideen
Tabor; X1117 Bist willkommen, liebster freund
Grimshaw, John, d 1819
Heaton Norris
Grisham, R.N.
I will never turn back
Griswold (no initials)
Griswold
Grobe, J.
Torgau (1840)
Groos, C.
Sun of grace
Grove, Albert H.
Cross of Christ, O sacred tree
Grueber, Franz Xaver, 1787-1863
Holy night (1818); X3705 Glade Jul; X4183 Grüber; X10029 Silent night; X10416 Stille nacht
Grundy, David Heywood, 1934-
College Cross
Crigglestone
Dumpton Gap
Nonington
Thornes House
Guidetti, Giovanni Domenico, 1530-92
Guidetti; X188 Aeterna Christi munera
Guilmant, Alexander Felix, 1837-1911
Ave verum corpus
Guisborough hymnal
Aeterna caeli gloria (a plainsong M 4)
Gustaf, Prince of Sweden, 1827-52
Till fridens hem
Gwyllt Ieuan, 1822-77 see Roberts, John, 1822-77

H

Haas, George C.F., 1854-1927
Luther League Hymn (1893); X8260 Pactum
St Mark's (1915)
Hackleman, W.E.M.
Others (1915)
Hadley, Patrick Arthur Sheldon, 1899-
Pembroke (1925)
Hadow, William Henry, 1859-1937
South Cerney
Haeffner, Johann Christian Friedrich, 1759-1833
O, du mitt hjärtas trängtan (1808)
Haeffner, J.C.F. Koralbok 1819
Han lefver! o min ande, känn
Haeussler, Theodore C.
Irmer (1938)
Hagen, Francis Florentine, 1815-1907
The Morning Star (1842)
Hagfors, Ernest August, 1827-1913
Pilgrim song
Haile, Eugen, 1873-1933
God (1932)
God of grace (1932)
To thee, above all creatures' gaze (1932)
World invisible (1927)

Hakes, D. S.
If any little word of mine (1908)
Lift Him up
Like as a father
My song (1900)
Standard
Sweet be thy rest
Halévy, Jacques-François Fromental-Elie, 1799-1862
Min hamatsar; X3386 Fling wide the gates; X4733 Hodu and Ono
Hall, Americk, 1785-1827
Devotion
Hall, Jacob Henry, 1855-
He knoweth thy grief (1897)
Here at thy table
Saviour, breathe an evening blessing; X3151 Evening song; X3753 Glorious things of thee
Sweet hour of prayer
Sykes
'Tis the harvest time
Trusting in Jesus (1896)
Hall, J. Lincoln
Does Jesus care?
Hall, Walter Henry, 1862-1935
Aletheia (1918)
Cecil (1917)
Egbert (1917)
Mallett (1918)
Oneonta (1918)
Reigate (1918)
St Wilfred (1900)
Halle melody
Petersen (1697); X3780 Glück zu kreuz
The Hallelujah, 1849
Malvern; X682 Audley
Haller, Michael, 1840-1915
I see by rays surrounded
Queen of the Rosary
Sub tuum praesidium
Hallman, E.S.
O everlasting Light
Hallstrom, Henry
Lynchburg (1941)
Halpern, M.
Adonoy mo odom
Halstead, E.
Snowdon (1940)
Vesper hymn (1938)
Hamburg. Neu Catechismus-Gesangbuch, 1598
Eisleben; X5487 Jeg vil din pris unsjunge; X7214 My heart its incense burning
Hamburger Musikalisches handbuch. 1690 see Wittwe, Georg. Musikalische handbuch, 1690
Hamilton, Clarence Grant, 1865-1935
Wallace (1914)
Hamilton-Gell, A.W.
Stanton
Hammer, John Beck
Martha (1876)
Hammerschmidt, Andreas, 1612-75
Freuet euch, ihr Christen (1646); X4136 Gregor's 210th metre
Meinen Jesum lass ich nicht (1658); X9767 Saxony
Hammond, Mary Jane, 1878-
Spiritus vitae
Hammontree, Homer
He just put Himself in my place (1921)
O, my Saviour crucified (1940)
Our times are in thy hand
Hampton, John, 1834-1921
St Cecilia (1875); X11643 Vexilla regis
Hanby, Benjamin Russell, 1833-67
Adoration (1866); X6465 Lowliness; X12221 Who is He
Hancock, B.J., 1862-1937
Easter time
Handel, Georg Friedrich, 1685-1759
[H] Alleluia chorus (1742)
Antioch (1836); X5732 Joy to the world
Bede (1733)
Brunswick
Canons; X1497 Cannons
Christmas (1728); X648 At midnight, so the sages tell; X762 Awake, my soul
Desiring to love
Dirge
Father in heaven

Father, O hear us; X3273 Father Almighty, we bow before thee
Gopsal (1750)
Halifax (1748)
Händel
Innocents (source in doubt)
Judas Maccabaeus (1747); X6592 Maccabaeus; X11187 Thine is the glory
Messiah (1742); X1269 Bradford; X11730 Vivit
Messiah [Come unto me, ye weary] (1742); X1987 Come unto Me; X9002 Revelation
Milites (1727); X5496 Jericho tune
Samson (1742); X9682 Sampson
Solomon; X10536 Sursum corda
Sweet hosannas
Thatcher (ca 1874); X2373 David; X10757 Thacher
Theodora

Hanecy, J.S.
Glorious things of Thee are spoken

Hann, Sidney
Queenswood

Hansen, H. Matthias
Hour of prayer; X5969 Lanier

Hanson, S.C.
The open gate

Harding, H.A.
Foel fras

Harding, James P., ca 1860-1911
Morning Star (1892)

Harding, R.Y., 1859-
Agatha
Knowlton

Hardy, B.E.
Wheeler

Hardy, H.W.
Eastbourne

Harington, Henry, 1727-1816
Harington; X8996 Retirement

Harker, J.
Paraclete (1914)
Simonside (1940)

Harkness, Robert
He will hold me fast
O, what a change (1905)
Such love (1929)

Harmer, Charles H., 1865-
Memory

Harmonia perfecta, 1730
Bucklebury
Wondrous cross; X2955 Eltham

Harmonia sacra, 1753
Cradle hymn
Mason; X8009 Old German
People of the living God
Resurrection
Sion's glad morning

Harper, Earl Enyeart, 1895-
Shirleyn (1928)

Harrington, Calvin S.
Fisk

Harrington, Claude W.
Asbury (1905)

Harrington, Karl Pomeroy, 1861-1953
Beyond (1905)
Christmas song (1904)
Copeland (1905)
Evanston (1905)
Golgotha (1938)
Moore (1905)
My Master (1927)
Orono (1905)
Palm Sunday (1905)
Parker (1905)
Praise (1905)
The Lord is in His Holy Temple (1905); X5386 Invocation [sentence]
Weihnacht (1903)
Worship (1905)

Harris, E.A.
York

Harris, T.W.
Glenmont
Taconic

Harris, Thoro
Crimea (1905)

Harris, William Henry, 1883-
Alberta
Gladdening light
Kybald Twychen
North Petherton
Sennen Cove

Harrison, Annie F.

In the gloaming; X9760 Savior, while my heart is tender
Harrison, Ralph, 1748-1810
Bankfield; X7152 Mt Olive
Peterboro; X8436 Peterborough; X8437 Peterborough Old
Stirling; X10406 Sterling
Warrington
Harrison, Ralph. Sacred harmony, 1784
Blackbourne
Cambridge; X663 Athol; X 1463 Camberwell; X3756 Glory; X11890 Waugh
Hart, Dorothea, arr
I have decided to follow Jesus (1950)
Hart, Philip, d 1749
Hilderstone (1713)
Hart, W.H.
Brierly
Hartmann, Emil, 1836-98
Avis
Hartmann, Johann Peder Emilius, 1805-1900
Dyb af Kjaerlighed
Ingemann
Hartmann; X7988 Odumin
Mirabile
Peace of God; X3483 Fred til bod; X4373 Hartmann; X8398 Peace to soothe
Rosa
Stegman
Hartog, Cecile
Into thy hands
Hart's Psalter, 1615 see Scottish Psalter, 1615
Harts, Harry L.
Nazareth (1927)
Hartshorn, W. Irving
Irving
Ruth
Hartsough, Lewis, 1820-72
I hear thy welcome voice; X5013 I am coming, Lord; X11979 Welcome voice
Let me go
Harwood, Basil, 1859-1949
Alveston
Combe Martin (1908)
Elberton
Hazel
Lower Marlwood
Luckington
Oldown
St Audrey
Thornbury
Harwood, Edward
Rapture
Hassler, Hans Leo, 1564-1612
NOTE: Certainly more than this single Hassler melody is within 20th century church music! Others are probably in compilations cited elsewhere herein.

Passion chorale (1601); X4396 Hassler; X4664 Herzlich thut mich verlangen; X6837 Mein G'mut ist mir; X6945 Mig hjertelig nu laenges; X7207 My God, how wonderful; X7719 O haupt voll blut; X11183 Thine arm, O Lord
Hastings, Eurotas P.
Detroit
Hastings, Thomas, 1784-1872
Arcadia
Bartley
Bremen; X6385 Lord of the Church
Broughton
Byefield
Hastings; X1444 Calm
Haven
Invitation
Luther
Ortonville (1837); X5690 Jesus, united by the grace; X6651 Majestic sweetness; X7699 O God, we pray for all; X8615 Prayer for all men
New Haven
Peniel
Retreat (1842); X3527 From every stormy wind; X5191 If I would be a child; X11909 We bless the name of
Robinson
Romberg

Sion; X470 Angels! from the realms; X4204 Guide me, O thou great; X10081 Sion stands with hills surrounded
Still water
Toplady (1832); X3177 Every morning mercies new; X9078 Rock of ages
Wesley
Wicliffe
Hasty, E.E.
Seeking for me
Hately, Thomas Legerwood, 1815-67
Leuchars
Nenthorn
Hately, Walter, 1843-1907
St Helen
Hatton, John C., d 1793
Duke Street (1793); X3525 From all that dwell below the skies
Haughey, M.T.
There is sunlight on the Hilltop
Hauser, Carl
Hymn of thanksgiving
Haven, C.A.
Beautiful land on high
Havergal, Frances Ridley, 1836-79
Caswell Bay
Eirene
Hermas (1871)
There came a little child to earth
Havergal, William Henry, 1793-1870
Consecration; X8361 Patmos
Dusseldorf (1849)
Eden; X9524 St Nicholas
Evan (1847); X819 Baptized into our Saviour's death; X1137 Blessed be the name; X3104 Evan new X4330 Happy the home when God is there; X5882 Knox; X6365 Lord, in thy presence; X7674 O for a faith that will not shrink
Haver; X788 Baca
St John (1851); X158 Adoration; X9448 St John's
Samos
Zoan (1859)
Hawaiian traditional
He lives on high [Aloha]; X392 Aloha
Hawarden, Viscountess, see Maude, Caroline
Haweis, Thomas, 1734-1820
Richmond (1792); X1645 Chesterfield
Hawkes, H.W.
God is in His holy temple
Hawkins, Gordon, 1911-
Ballards Lane
Hawley, W.A.
Harris
Haworth, F.
The dawn was purpling
Hawthorne, Alice (pseud. of Septimus Winner) 1827-1902
Whispering hope
Hay, Edyth Hillery, d 1943
Hillery; X6399 Lord, with devotion
The way is dark (1923)
Hayden, Victoria (or Victoire)
Father, I come to thee; X2061 Confirmation
Haydn (no initials)
Have mercy on us
O come, loud anthems; X159 Adoration
Rapture
Haydn, Franz Joseph, 1732-1809
Austria (1797); X711 Austrian hymn; X4434 Haydn's hymn; X8579 Praise the Lord! ye heavens
Bowen; X4432 Haydn, No. 1 X8212 Otterbourne
Bradford; X8570 Praise, Lord, for thee in Zion waits
Brownell; X1366 Brownwell
Creation (1798); X4352 Hark, the song of jubilee
Haydn (1791); X7099 Morning
Petition (1801); X4430 Haydn X9537 St Olaf
St Alban; X9241 St Alban, No. 2; X9242 St Alban's
St Anthony chorale; X9276

St Anthony's choral
Haydn, Johann Michael, 1737-1806
Greenland (1819); X6026 Lausanne
Hear thy children
Lyons (from the Paderborn Gesangbuch, 1765 text); X4943 How wondrous and great; X7859 O praise ye the Lord; X7865 O purest of creatures; X 7967 O, worship the King
O esca viatorum; X7671 O food that weary pilgrims love; X12130 When morning gilds the skies
Offertorium
St Avold; X11603 Venice
Salzburg
Salzburg II; X4431 Haydn; X2565 Die sach' ist dein
St Michel's; X3923 Goshen; X4429 Haydn; X5501 Jerusalem; X5511 Jerusalem, Jerusalem; X9055 Ripon; X9495 St Maria
Hayes, Oleta
Christ's return (1935)
Hayes, William, 1705-77
Chant
Magdalene College; X5853 Kingston
New 113th
Tranmere
Hayman, Henry, 1820-94
Lanherne; X4156 Grenfell
Hayne, Leighton George, 1836-83
Buckland (1863)
Chalvey (1868)
St Anselm
St Cecilia (1863); X1583 Cecilia
St Lawrence (1863)
Haynes, D. F.
Pontiac (1934)
Haynes, William, 1829-1902
Feodore
Guilford (1876)
Hays, William Shakespeare, 1837-1907
Salvationist; X6205 Lily of the valley; X10939 The Lily of the valley
Heaton, Walter
Patricroft (1923)
Heatwole, L. J.
Non-resistance
The Christian's passport
Heber, Reginald, 1783-1826
Calcutta; X2257 Crucifix; X12205 Whitfield
Heberden, Arthur C.
Evensong
Hebrew melodies see Jewish Traditional, etc.
Hecht, Simon
A message sweet
We meet again in gladness (1932)
Hedberg, Fredrik Gabriel, 1811-93
Kom, huldaste förbarmare
Hedges, Anthony John, 1931-
Starlight
Heineken, N. S.
Heineken
Heinlein, Paul, 1626-80
Jesu, Jesu du mein hirt; X10886 The Good Shepherd
Heins, Francis D., 1878-
Hereford (1930)
Heins, Nicholas
Brecon (1900)
Helder, Bartholomäus, 1585-1635
Dich bitt ich, trautes Jesulein (1635)
Wohlauf, thut nicht verzagen; X4558 Helder
Heller, James G., 1892-
A new shrine (1932)
Blest is the bond (1932)
Into the tomb of ages (1932)
Lord, be thou with us still (1932)
Lord, do thou guide me (1932)
O Lord, what is man!
O Thou, whose Presence (1932)
Once more the liberal year
Opening song (1932)
Resignation (1932)
The cry of Israel (1932)
Thy brother (1932)

'Tis not the large, the hjge, the vast (1932)
'Tis winter
Hemy, Henri Frederich, 1818-1901
Beulah (1864)
Conqueror; X1534 Carmel; X2312 Daily, daily
Hail, glorious St Patrick
Paradise; X7853 O Paradise
St Catherine (1864); X3224 Faith of our fathers; X8651 Prince; X9384 St Finbar; X11474 Tynemouth
Siloam; X9189 Sabbata; X9939 Sharon
Hemy, H. F. Easy hymn tunes ... for Catholic schools. London, 1851
Stella; X4261 Hail, Queen of heaven; X10398 Stella maris
Henderson, J. W.
He ransomed me (1916)
Hendrickson, H. N.
Alma Mater
Henle, M.
Remember Him, the only One
Henry, Prince of Battenberg, 1858-
Battenberg
Henry VIII, King of England, 1491-1547
Green grow'th the holly
Henson, J. M.
Somebody follows you
Herbert, George, 1817-1906
Burwell; X6379 Lord of life and king; X7605 O Bread of Heaven; X10516 Sunset; X10594 Sweet Saviour! Bless
Holy Queen, we come; X4331 Happy we, who thus; X4812 Holy Queen, we bend
Herbert, John B.
Algiers
Lafayette
Magnus
Olena (1912)
Herbst, Martin, 1654-81 (probable composer)
Heinlein (1676); X701 Aus der tiefe; X3539 From the depths we cry; X4618 Hernlein [sic]
Hereford Hymnal
Martyr Dei qui unicum (plainsong M 4)
Hermann, Nikolaus, ca 1485-1561
Erscheinen ist der herrlich tag (major reading) (1560); X4609 Hermann
Erscheinen ist der herrlich tag (minor reading) 1560)
Hermann (1554); X5700 Joachimsthal; X6310 Lobt Gott; X6312 Lobt Gott, ihr Christen; X6504 Luetzen; X6542 Lutzen; X7404 Nicolaus; X7713 O happy day; X8156 Op alle som paa Jorden; X10868 The first fruits of
Nu lader os da grave ned
O Heilige Dreifaltigkeit (1560); X11379 Trinity; X12020 Wer hier fuer Gott
Herold, Louis-Joseph-Ferdinand, 1791-1833
Heart of Mary (1808)
Messiah (1839)
Herr, Amos
I owe the Lord a morning song (1890); X4008 Gratitude
Herrmann, Christopher F.
Faith (1882)
Herrnhut ms Choral buch, 1735-45
Gregor's 37th metre; X1396a Bunyan (Thommen. Christen-schatz); X2362 Das wahre christenthum; X4057 Gregor
Gregor's 82d metre; X4437 Hayn; X11958 Weil die worte wahrheit sind
Gregor's 141st metre-A; X1044 Berthelsdorf; X2358 Das ist unbeschreiblich
Gregor's 166th metre; X2567 Die wanderschaft in; X8475 Pilgrimage
Herron, J. D.
Dummerston
Hershey, Urban Henry, 1876-1952

Hershey
Hervey, Frederick Alfred John, 1846-1910
Castle Rising
Hervey's Litany; X4655 Hervey X6233 Litany
Richemont
Heseltine, Philip, 1894-1930
see his pseudonym: Warlock, Peter
Hesperian harp, 1840
Bourbon
Heward, Leslie H., 1897-1943
Wyke
Hewlett, Thomas, 1845-74
Dalkeith; X7824 O Lord, thy love
Hewlett, William Henry, 1873-1940
Somerset (ca 1915)
Teach me, O Lord
Hews, George, 1806-73
Coronet
Holley (1835); X6387 Lord, speak to me
Hays, John A.
Our Father (1947)
The Lord's Prayer (1947)
Heywood, John
Aston
Festival
Hibbard, S.
Exhortation
Hickman, Roger M. fl 1917
Aviemore
Higgs, H.M., 1855-1929
Cara patria
Hildebrand, E.T.
Ashburn
Let them come to see
Serving the Lord in song (1907)
Winston
Hildesheim melody
Hail, holy Queen (1937); X9669 Salve Regina coelitum
Hiles, Henry, 1826-1904
Birkdale (1865)
Fiat lux
St Leonard (1867); X4700 Hiles; X6101 Leonard
Sweden
Hill, G. Everett
Rex triumphans
Hille, Johann Georg
Einer ist König (ca 1730)
Gregor's 161st metre (1739); X7758 O ihr auserwoehlten
Gregor's 217th metre-B; X6839 Mein heiland nimmt de
Hiller (or Hüller), Johann Adam, 1728-1804
Love divine
Himmel, Friedrich Heinrich, 1765-1814
Himmel
Light of the world
Himmels-Lust. Leipzig, 1675
Liebster Immanuel; X2972 Emmanuel
Hindu (Indian) air
Happy Land; X11140 There is a happy land; X12458 World to come
Hintze, Jakob, 1622-1702
Salzburg (1678); X336 Alle menschen; X654 At the Lamb's high feast; X2709 Du, o schönes weltegebaeude; X4716 Hintze; X5695 Jesus with thy Church; X7533 Now the world is saved; X8063 Old 168th; X9121 Rosenmüller
Hirst, G.
Salvator amicus
Hodge, C.R.
Herbert
Hodges, Edward, 1796-1867
Bristol (1841)
Habakkuk
Peace
Hodges, John Sebastian Bach, 1830-1915
Alleluia piis edite
Eucharistic hymn (1868); X3085 Eucharist; X8294 Panis vitae
Hodges (1869)
Matins
Sebastian
Memorial
Hodson, Henry E.
Urbs caelestis (1880)

Hoff, Erik Christian, 1830-94
Her vil ties
Hoff; X4193 Guds menighed, syng; X12515 Ye lands, to the Lord
Hoffman, C. Christian, 1839-93
Ave
Fulfillment; X2478 Den store mester kommer
Hoffman, Elisha A., 1939-1929
Hoffman; X1026 Benton Harbor; X1702 Christ has for sin; X12071 What a wonderful
Hoffman II; X5413 Is your all on the altar?
Is thy heart right with God?
O Lord, within my soul
Orwigsburg; X5098 I must tell Jesus
Washed in the blood; X540 Are you washed in the blood?
Hogan, Frederick William, 1845-
Magherafelt
Hohenfurth ms. 1410
Dies est laetitiae; X1260 Boye; X1509 Cantus ubique; X2153 Cornfields; X2502 Der tag der ist [so freuden reich]; X3066 Et lidet barn saa; X4139 Gregor's 215th metre; X10775 Thanksgiving carol; X11317 To us is born
Quem pastores; X1546 Carol melody, 14th c; X2427 Dearmer; X8755 Quem pastores laudavere; X9966 Shepherds left their flocks astraying
Holbrook, Joseph Parry, 1822-88
Bishop
Church
Clinton
Gerhardt
Greek hymn (1870)
Handy
Lyte
Miriam
Refuge; X5623 Jesus, lover of my soul
Remsen
Segur
Truman
Holden, Oliver, 1765-1844
Coronation (1793); X280 All hail the great Immanuel's name; X281 All hail the power; X5492 Jehovah, Lord of heaven and earth
Holden, O. Union harmony, 1793
Boundless mercy
Holdroyd, Israel
Rochester (1753)
Wells
Holland see Dutch
Hollingshead, D.S.
Gring
Holmes, Henry James Ernest, 1852-1938
Eventide; X4765 Holmes
Linton
Pater omnium
Holsinger, George Blackburn, 1857-1908
At the Saviour's right hand
Be thou our guide
Beautiful homeland (1902)
Cross of Christ, O sacred tree
Eternal source
Hark! the voice of Jesus calling (1901)
Holsinger (1901)
Little ones like me
Love not the world
Purer in heart
Rest over Jordan
Wayland (1902); X4595 Here, Lord of life and
Holst, Gustav Theodore, 1874-1934
NOTE: Real name was Gustavus Theodore von Holst, but changed after 1914.

Bossiney
Brookend
Chilswell (1927)
Cranham (1906); X6944 Midwinter
Essex
Hillcrest (1928)
Lullay my liking
Monk Street

Sheen
Stepney
Thaxted
Valiant hearts (1925)
Holyoke, Samuel, 1762-1820)
Hingham
Hopkins, D.E., 1902-
Buffham
Hopkins, Edward John, 1818-1901
Abbey
Artavia (1887)
Children's voices (1875)
Culford
Christmas Morn
Deva (1887)
Ellers (1869); X1014 Benediction; X2940 Ellerton; X5394 Irene; X7860 O precious sign and seal; X8375 Pax dei
Epiphany
Epiphany II
Evangel; X4543 Heber
Feniton Court
Hartland
Jehovah; X12464 Worship
Kelso; X3176 Every morning; X8559 Praise
Knowsley
Laetabundus
Nukapu; X7051 Montgomery
Pascal, No. 1; X8328 Pascal
Redcliff
Rocklands
Sacrament
St Athanasius (1872); X658 Athanasius; X3828 God of hosts
St Elwyn
St Hugh (1862)
St Joseph
St Philip (1852)
St Piran
St Raphael (1862); X8800 Raphael
Tadcaster
Temple (1867)
Tideswell
Toronto
Tribute
Vaughan
Wessex
West Heath
Wildersmouth (1879)
Wraysbury
Hopkins, J., 1822-1900
Allington
Hopkins, John Henry, jr., 1820-91
Come Holy Ghost; X11582 Veni Creator, No. 3
Ninety-fifth [Psalm]
Sabaoth
Satterlee
Three Kings of Orient (1857); X5844 Kings of orient; X11939 We three Kings of orient
Twilight; X4873 Hopkins
Hopkins, John Henry
Grand Isle (1940)
Westerly (1941)
Hopkins, Josiah, 1786-1862
Expostulation
Hopkirk, James
Bellwoods (1938)
Horne, Johann, d 1547
Gaudeamus pariter (1544); X750 Ave virgo; X751 Ave virgo virginum
Horner, B.W.
Brotherland
Horner, E.F., 1864-1928
Aldersgate Street
Hampstead (1904)
Horsley, Charles Edward.
Eighty-four church tunes, 1857
Bodley
St Bavon
Horsley, William, 1774-1858
Belgrave
Horsley (1844)
Horsman, Edward, 1873-1918
Siloam (1903)
Hostetter, P.
Sycamore
Hott, G.P.
Glory gates
Houseley, Henry, 1852-1925
Cross and crown (1896)
Denver (1896)
Howard, Alonzo Potter, 1838-1902
Lonely midnight; X5312 In the lonely midnight
Howard, Samuel, 1710-82
Coventry (1762)

Isleworth (1765)
Lancaster; X7119 Mornington
St Bride (1762); X9323 St Brides; X9324 St Bride's
Smith; X2715 Dublin; X4945 Howard
Howard, Samuel, 1846-
Sunset
Howells, Herbert Norman, 1892-
Severn (1931)
Hoyte, William Stevenson, 1844-
Ellerton
Margaret Street
St Columba; X4947 Hoyte; X9342 St Colomb
Hubbard, S.
Parsons
Hudson, Ralph E., 1843-1901
At the cross (1885); X235 Alas! and did my Saviour bleed; X4955 Hudson
Blessed Name; X1138 Blessed be the name
I know I love thee better (1881)
The Lord is my Shepherd
Hudson, Robert, 1732-1815
St Olave
Huet, Pierre Daniel, 1630-1721
Diva servatrix; X885 Bayeaux
Huffaker, Perry L., 1902-
Lauree (1951)
Pine Glen
Spring Run (1951)
Hugg, George C.
A full surrender
Christ is born in Bethlehem
Christian soldier
Closer cling to Jesus
Father, lead us
God of love
Good-bye (1898)
He arose (1892)
I come to thee (1898)
Jesus knows (1892)
Just as seemeth good to Thee
May the Christ-life shine in me
No, not one; X4860 Homeward bound
Scattering precious seed
Send me light
Hughes, G.W., 1861-1941
Buddugoliaeth
Hughes, John (Glandŵr), 1872-1914
Calon Lân
Hughes, John (Pontypridd), 1873-1932
Cwm Rhondda (1905); X2244 Crown Him; X4205 Guide us, O thou great
Hughes, John (Dolgelly), 1896-
Be thou faithful
Dinas Bethlehem
Maelor
The Lord bless thee
Hughes, Thomas
Saron
Huish, O.P.
Come, all ye sons of God
Come unto Jesus
Jesus, my Saviour true
There is a land whose sunny vales; X11542 Utah, Utah, beautiful
Hull, Asa, 1828-
In dark Gethsemane; X7810 O Lord, Divine, we come; X8917 Remember Me
Hull, Asa. The casket of Sunday School melodies, 1865
Ich weiss einen strom; X11031 The river of life
Stella
Hullah, John Pyke, 1812-84
Benison
Bentley (1866)
Salisbury (arr); X8959 Resignation; X9721 Sarum
Hult, Adolf, 1869-
Messiah (1899)
Hultman, J.A.
Spicer
Hume, Duncan
Dare to be brave; X2171 Courage
Hume, Paul, 1915-
O Brightness (1964)
Hummel, Johann Nepomuk, 1778-1837
Hark, hark, my soul
Humperdinck, Engelberg, 1854-1921
Hark the herald host (1893)
Humphreys, F.L.

St Mabyn
Humphreys, R.D., 1826-
Rapture
Hungarian traditional, etc.
Alleluia song (1855)
Christus Urunknak (carol)
Dallam (folk)
Du meiner seelen' (16th c chorale); X11361 Transylvania
Magyar see Éneke, Gâlyarabok.
O most Holy (hymn)
Regi litania (litany)
Thirsting for the living Fountain
Hunnewell, Frank S.
Optimism (1916)
Hunt, John Eric, 1903-58
Shrewsbury
Hunter, C.E.
Do you love the world?
God's way is best
Humility
My heart says Amen
Saints' reward
Seedtime and harvest
The Good Shepherd
Huntington, C.W.
Huntington
Hurd, Peter Wyeth
The Saints of God (1957)
Hurley, E.G.
Holy Queen! we bend before thee
Hurndall, W.F.
Springhill
Hurst, John, 1859-
Calvary (1890)
Gulworthy
Hurst, William, 1849-
Leicester
Hus, John, 1369-1415 supposed composer
Herr Jesu Christ
NOTE: See Pensum sacrum, Görlitz, 1648.
Husband, John J., 1760-1825
We praise thee, O God; X362 Alleluia, 'tis done; X8903 Rejoice and be glad; X9006 Revive us again; X11188 Thine the glory
Huston, Frank C.
It pays to serve Jesus (1909)
Hutcheson, Charles, 1792-1860
Stracathro (1832)
Hutchins. Sunday School hymnal
A shepherd band
Easter flowers
Hutton, James. Tunes for the hymns, 1740-44
Cennick
Chelsea
Eastham
Lindsey House
Ockbrook
Old 583d; X10074 Sinners Redeemer
Hutton, Laura Josephine, 1852-88
Eternity
Warfare
Huxtable, F.
Tempest
Hyatt, Nathaniel Irving
Comrade heart (1927)
Requiem (1927)
Torchbearers (1927)
Hymns and tunes, 1890
Follow the path; X1235 Bound Brook
May the grace of Christ; X5156 I would love thee
Hymns for children
Birds are singing
Hymns of the Eastern Church
Safe home
St Stephen the Sabaite

I

Icelandic melody
Iceland
Iliffe, Frederick, 1847-1928
Autumn, No. 2
Ilse, Ludwig Herman, 1845-1931
Erfurt (1910)
Wittenberg (1910)
Illsley, Frank G.
Ilsley (1887)
Indian traditional
NOTE: See also Marathi, and Hindu
Binti hamari
Ingall. Christian harmony,

1805
I love thee
Ingalls, Jeremiah, 1764-1828
Invitation; X1995 Come, ye sinners
Fillmore
Northfield
The midnight call (1863); X7195 My dearest friends in bonds; X8324 Parting hand
Vesper (1804)
Ingham, Thomas H., 1878-1948
Dawn (1931); X11872 Watchman
Ireland, John Nicholson, 1879-1962
Eastergate
Chelsea
Love unknown (1948)
New Prince, new pomp
Sampford (1948)
Irish traditional, etc.
Clonmel; X4540 Heavenward
Cormac
Daniel
Deirdre; X9553 St Patrick (St Patrick)
Dun Aluinn
Dunaha
Durrow
Fanad Head
Fingal
Garton; X3583 Gartan
Irish carol
Kilgetty
Londonderry; X5399 Irish melody; X6323 Londonderry air
Lorica Patricii
Marylebone
Moville
O Bethlehem
O Lord, reprieve (ancient)
Peacefield (ancient)
Petrie
Remember the poor
St Columba; X1898 Columba; X3024 Erin; X7607 O breathe on me
St Patrick; X2459 Deirdre
St Sechnall
Slane
Sussex carol
Sweet story; X987 Believe me if all those; X2986 Endearing young charms
The five lesser joys
Valor; X11978 Welcome, summer
Wicklow
Irons, Herbert Stephen, 1834-1905
Crucifer
Heavenly voices
Hope
Irons (1861); X9346 St Columba; X9347 St Columbia
St Chrysostom (1860)
St Leonard (1916)
Southwell (1861); X5402 Irons
Irvine, Jessie Seymour, 1836-87
Crimond
Isaacs, Lewis C.
Praise ye the Lord (1932)
The God that to our fathers
The heavens, O God (1932)
Isaak, Heinrich, ca 1450-1527
NOTE: Spelling varies greatly, as: Isaac, Izak, Yzacm Ysack; Arrigo Tedesco, Arrighus Tedesco
Innsbruck; X5358 Innsbruck, ich musz dich lassen; X 5359 Innsbruck new; X 5360 Innspruck; X7543 Nu hviler mark og enge; X7576 Nun ruhen alle wälder; X7606 O Bread of life; X7659 O esca viatorum; X7672 O food to pilgrims: X7946 O welt, ich muss dich lassen; X11838 Wartburg
Innsbruck (Bach arr); NOTE: See previous entry for variant tune names.
Iszlai, Marton (19th c)
Marton
Isle of Arran see Arran, Isle of
Italian Association of St Cecilia
Christus vincit
Italian traditional, liturgical, etc.
Ave, maris stella

From starry heaven (1755)
I'm a pilgrim; X8464 Pilgrim
Jerusalem, my happy home
Monte Cassino
Oliva speciosa (18th c)
Ye souls of the faithful
Iverson, Daniel
Spirit of the living God; X3243 Fall fresh on me
Ivimey, John W.
Crispinian

J

J.H.H. here identified as Hopkins, John Henry, jr.
Jackson, George K., 1745-1822
Dibden
Jackson, Robert, 1842-1914
Ashburton
Columbia
Cressbrook
Lymington
Niagara
Old Judea
Trentham (1888)
Waverton (1876)
Jackson, Thomas, ca 1715-81
Jackson; X1427 Byzantium
Jackson, William (of Exeter), 1730-1803
Exeter
Jackson, William, 1815-66
Evening hymn
Jacobs, W.K.
Gently, Lord, O, gently
Happy with Christ
I love to tell the story (1896)
Saviour, like a shepherd
Wonderful Saviour
Jacobs, William, 1796-1872
Hope; X1599 Chant; X5454 Jacobs
Jacobsen (no initials)
O gloriosa Virginum
Jacobsohn, B.
From heaven's height
Jaehnigen, C.F.
Charity; X5775 Kaerlighen fra Gud
James, Frederick, 1858-1922
Gennesaret
Noricum
James, Philip, 1890-
Cwmafon (1927); X1907 Comavon
Faith triumphant (1927)
Tregaron (1941)
Jamouneau, Arthur J.
Lynton
Janowska, S.
Stars of glory
Japanese melody
Kimigayo
Jarman, Thomas, 1782-1862
Lyngham
Jarvis, Samuel (probable composer)
Stanley (1762); X7052 Montgomery
Jaspers, C.
Resonet in laudibus
Jassinowsky, Pinchos
A Succoth prayer (1932)
Morning prayer (1932)
Succoth hymn (1932)
The Torah (1932)
Thy word is to my feet a lamp (1932)
Jeater, William, 1838-
Rossetti (1907)
Jeboult, H.A., 1871-1925
St Mary Magdalene
Jeffery, John Albert, ca 1854-ca 1929
Albany (1886); X451 Ancient of days
Liddon; X9233 St Agnes School
Jeffrey, H.R.
Come home, poor sinner
The golden harvest
Jenkins, David, 1848-1915
Bod Alwyn
Penlan
Jenkins, Joseph W.
St Joseph, be our Guide (1963)
Jenkins, Rory Donaughmore, 1914-
Cotham
Jenks, S.
Communion
Jenner, Henry Lascelles, 1820-98
Quam dilecta (1861); X4259

Hail, ocean's beauteous Star
Jepson, Harry Benjamin, 1870-1952
Battell Chapel
Jerusalem's Gates reopened, 1919
Peace through the cross
Jespersön, Niels. Gradual, 1573
Jespersön; X4982 Hvad ljus öfver griften
Jesson, R. H., 1929-
Barnet
Jewish traditional, including many temple melodies arranged for congregational use.
NOTE: Numerous items are indexed elsewhere under composer's name, but notice the traditional names in Hebrew-transliterated-to-roman letters in this section.

Addeer hu; X3833 God of might; X8574 Praise the Lord
Adon olam; X5374 Into the tomb of ages
Adonoy hu ho-eloheem
Akdamus; X4942 How wondrous
All ye dwellers
Ashray yod'ay; X10974 The Lord reigneth
Ayl hora aleelah; X3855 God, that doest wondrously; X7335 N'eelah hymn
Az yasheer (Sephardic mel); X7597 O bless the Lord, my; X11399 True freedom
Bemotzoay; X2592 Dim mine eyes with many teardrops
Blessings over the Chanukkah lights
Bor-chu
Boruch shaym I; X12535 Yimloch Adonoy
Boruch shaym II
Boughs (Succos mel); X10648 Take unto you
Come, ye faithful servants
see Levenson, Boris
Duties of today
Eliyahu hanavi; X3274 Father hear
For the mountains
Gaza
Grace after meals
Hakafos melody; X11198 This feast of the Law
Hallel; X4402 Hatikvo; X 11145 There is a mystic tie
Hasidim
Jewish tune
Kee hinay kachomer; X11314 To Thee we give ourselves
Kee hinay kachomer II; X6293 Lo, as the potter molds the clay
Kiddush (Lewandowski version); X1168 Blessings over the Lulav
Kol nidre
Leoni; X10973 The Lord our God we praise; X12533 Yigdal
May the words
Me chomocho I; X3535 From heaven's heights the thunder peals
Me chomocho II
Me chomocho III
N'eelah melody I; X8099 On parting
N'eelah melody II; X11076 The sun goes down
Olaynu
Omnom kayn; X4996 Hymn of glory
Ono adonoy kaper no
Oveenu malkaynu; X8098 On mighty wings; X8220 Our Father, our King
Rock of Ages; X3449 Fortress-Rock, my God; X6829 Mee chomocho; X7061 Mooz [t]zur
Rosh Hashanah I; X2379 Dawn
Rosh Hashanah II; X10956 The Lord is King
Shalom (arr as a round)
Sheer hamaalos
Sheer hasheersem I; X9194 Sabbath Eve
Sheer hasheereem II; X5247 In answer to my prayer
Sh'ma Yisroayl I
Sh'ma Yisroayl II
Sh'ma Yisroayl III

Simchas Torah; X8909 Rejoicing of the law
Sinai's Height (Akdamos mode arr); X233 Akdamos mode; X3536 From Sinai's height a fountain gushes
Tal; X10236 Song of the dew
The Lord of all
The lulav; X10478 Succos
The Sabbath Bride
The torch of Israel
There is a mystic tie see Achron, Joseph
Tovo l'fonecho
Un'saneh tokef
V'al kulom; X12238 Why art thou cast down?
V'nishlach
When the Sabbath
Yigdal
Yom Kippur Mode; X3239 Forgive us, Lord
Zochraynu

Jewson, James Pentland, 1825-89
Merton
Tudor (1876)

John Gamble's Collection, 1659 see Gamble, John. Collection, 1659

Johnson, Arthur Basil Noel, 1861-1950
Wells

Johnson, James A.
Devotion

Johnson, Peter, 1870-
Arnold (1923)
Carolina (1922)
Cecile
Dorothea (1923)
Gloria dei (1923)
Gustavus Adolphus (1923)
Mildred (1923)
Norelius
St Paul (1924)

Johnson, William Lyman
Concord (1905)
Pleasant Street (1905)

Jones, Charles P.
All I need
Nothing like Jesus (1913)

Jones, Darius Elliott, 1815-81
Stockwell
Wood

Jones, David Hugh, 1900-
Miller Chapel (1954)

Jones, Griffith Hugh (Gutyn Arfon), 1849-1919
Llef

Jones, J.R., 1762-1822
Ramoth

Jones, James Edmund, 1866-1939
Belleville; X5765 Just for today
Langemarck
Walden

Jones, John (Talysarn), 1797-1857
Llanllyfni
Tanycastell

Jones, Lewis E,
Jones (1906)
Lean on His arms (1903)
There is power in the blood; X8549 Power in the blood

Jones, Owen (canon)
Dark the night

Jones, T.E.
Quinquagesima

Jones, Tom
Let the beauty of Jesus

Jones, William ("Oriental Jones"), 1726-1800
St Stephen; X7386 Newington; X10401 Stephens

Jordan, Charles Warwick
Domus domini
Rhodes; X1850 Clifton

Joseph, Georg
Angelus (1657); X7517 Now at the Lamb's high royal feast
Gregor's 225th metre (1668); X10071 Singt dem Herrn, nah und fern
Gregor's 298th metre (1668); X5557 Jesu, du hoffnung
Keine Schönheit hat die welt (1657); X1541 Carne; X9786 Schönheit

Joseph, J.M., 1894-1929
Eskdale

Jowett, Joseph, 1784-1856
Kerry
Thanket

Joy, W.
Holywell
Jude, William Herbert, 1851-1922
Galilee (1887); X5536 Jesus calls us; X5748 Jude
Onward, Christian soldiers
Judefind, W.B.
Twilight
Jutson, Charles Bentley, 1870-1930
The story of Jesus

K

"K"
Hark! Are they not angels
Kaillmark, E.
Do what is right
Kaiser, Alois
As pants the hart
Blessed, O blessed (1932)
Grateful praises
Mee chomocho
Kalhauge, Sophus Viggo Harald, 1840-1905
Viggo
Kálmán, Farkas
Kalman
Kasschau, Frank
Brooklyn (1929)
Katholische Kirchengesänge. Paderborn, 1616
Paderborn
Keegan, G. Kearnie
Looking to Jesus (1940)
Keeler, Bradley
Vittel Woods (1924)
Keeler, J.J.
A voice hath spoken
Keeny, David E.
He loveth me
Keller, Arnold Frederick, 1890-
Holy manger (1958)
Redeemer (1958)
Springtime (1958)
Keller, Matthias, 1813-75
American hymn; X5796 Keller's American hymn
Kelly, Richard A.
Holy Spirit, led us (1940)
Kelly, Thomas C.
Accept, kind Father (1958)
When great St Patrick (1958)
Kennedy, Amanda
Star of the East
Kentucky Harmony, 1816
NOTE: see also Supplement to Kentucky Harmony.

Salvation
Tender thought
Kern, Jan
Praise now your God (1964)
Kestel, Edmund, O.S.B.
Alleluia, Christ is risen (1946)
Song of the Branches (1946)
Kettle, Charles E.
Blenden (1876)
Exultation
Hosanna
Resignation
Trust
Woolwich; X12440 Woolich
Kidner, Frank Derek, 1913-
Oak Hill
Polzeath
Kieff melody
Russian Cantakion of the departed
Kieffer, Aldine S.
And now my soul, another year; X6729 Markell
Josie
The city of light
Kilgore, Clive Harold, 1889-
Pax (1958)
Kimball, Edward P.
Great God, to thee my evening song
The wintry day, descending
Kimball, Jacob, 1761-1826
Milton (1793)
Kinder, Ralph, 1876-1952
Ship of State (1927)
King, A.
Eastnor
King, Charles John, 1859-1934
Northampton
King, Chauncey J.
Some time we'll see
King, Oliver A., 1855-1923
Oliver
King, Robert
David's Harp (1722)

Kingham, Millicent Douglas, 1866-1927
Benson (1894); X225 Ainger
Kingo, Gradual, 1699
I Jesu Navn skal al vor Gjerning ske
O Jesus, for din Pine; X6367 Lord Jesus, by thy passion
Kingsley, George, 1811-84
Edwards (1847)
Elizabethtown; X7673 O for a closer walk
Ferguson
Frederick
Heber (ca 1873)
Kingsley; X12273 Williams
Lucius
Mount Auburn
Newbold
Southport
Tappan (1839)
Ware
Kinross, J.
How blest the man (1932)
Kirchen Gesange. Bremen, 1707
Amor dei
Kirchengesangbuch. Strassburg, 1541
All' Ehr' und Lob
Kirchen-und haus Buch. Dresden, 1694
Nun lasst uns geh'n
Kirkpatrick, William J., 1838-1921
A blessing in prayer
Alone with God
Annetta (1901)
Cradle song; X6537 Luther's cradle hymn
Dear to the heart (1899); X65 A wonderful Saviour; X5866 Kirkpatrick; X10844 The cleft of the rock
Deeper yet (1896)
For Christ and the Church
Give me thy heart
NOTE: Here filed under Annie F. Bourne, who may have been Fanny Crosby. Kirkpatrick published many melodies which he did not write, without mentioning that fact.
Great is the Love
He hideth my soul
Heaven at last
Him that cometh unto me
How blest
I have work enough to do
Jesus comes
Kirkpatrick
Lest I forget (1921); X5829 King of my life; X6049 Lead me to Calvary
Lord, I'm coming home (1892); X2008 Coming home; X5446 I've wandered far away
Meet me there
Moline (1901)
No shadows yonder (1903)
Redeemed
Salvation (1882); X5670 Jesus saves; X11916 We have heard the joyful sound
Sands (1901)
Saved to the uttermost
Saxony
Stepping in the light
The Comforter has come
The promises of God
Thou spotless Lamb of God
Trust in Jesus (1881); X11277 'Tis so sweet" X11432 Trusting
Wait, and murmur not
Watchman, blow the gospel trumpet
Whole wide world; X11106 The whole wide world
Will your anchor hold; X11914 We have an anchor
Kittel, Johann Christian, 1732-1809
Bis willkommen (1790)
Quedlinburg; X6763 Mary Immaculate, Mother and Maid
Kjerulf, Halfdan, 1815-68
Evening blessing
Klein, Bernhard, 1793-1832
Löwen, lasst euch wiederfinden (1817)
Kleiner Liederschatz, 1901
See the shining dewdrops

Kloss, J. F.
Hail to thee! true Body
Klug, Joseph. Gesangbuch, 1535 or Geistliche Lieder, Wittenberg, 1535 see Geistliche Lieder, Wittenberg, 1535
Knapp, Mrs. Joseph F., 1839-1908
NOTE: Possibly is Mary A. Bachelor Knapp (See Julian, p. 1609, 1641)

Albertson
Assurance (1873); X1136 Blessed assurance
Behold me standing
Cleansing wave; X10841 The cleansing wave
Nearer the cross
Knapp, William, 1698-1768
Spetisbury
Wareham (1738); X302 All saints; X11391 Triumphant Sion
Knecht, Justin Heinrich, 1752-1817
Domini clamavi (1797)
Gotha (1797); X12383 Womit soll ich dich
Herr, dir ist niemand zu vergleichen
Knecht (1799) [Meter 7.6.7.6.] X863 Barton; X5883 Kocher; X7091 Morlaix
St Hilda (1799, arr by Husband 1871) [Meter 7.6.7.6.D]; X6900 Meredith; X9367 St Edith
Salvation by grace (1796); X702 Aus gnaden soll ich
Vienna (1797); X7997 Ohne rast und unverweilt; X8819 Ravenna
Zwingli
Knight, G.H., 1908-
Valley
Veryan
Knight, H.
Stabat mater
Knorr. Neuer helicon, 1684
St Gregory; X4154 Gregory; X12565 Zeuch meinen geist
Knowles, G.J.
Balfour (18th c)
Knowlton, F.S.
For peace and for plenty
Knox, J.C.
Advent
Knudsen, Peder, 1819-63
Christmas Eve
Koch, H.C. Choralbuch, 1816
Auch jetzt macht Gott
Koch, Minna, 1845-1924
Minna
Kocher, Conrad, 1786-1872
Dix (1838); X3421 For the beauty of; X8187 Orisons; X11375 Treuer heiland
Urquell aller Selig keiten
Koenen, Father
Hail! Christ our Redeemer
Koenig, Johann Balthasar, 1691-1758
Evangelists; X370 Alles ist an Gottes; X676 Auctor omnium bonorum; X4699 Hildesheim
Tempest
Koenig, J.B. Choralbuch, 1738
NOTE: Title of book varies considerably.

Der am Kreuz
Franconia; X6987 Miracle
Ich singe dir
Ich will dich lieben; X9774 Scheffler; X11365 Treasure
Mentzer; X2909 Elbe; X7640 O dass ich tausand zungen hätte
Kolb, A.B.
Christ is risen (1896)
Dear Saviour, when I think of thee
Grateful submission
Love's consecration
Kolb, A.C.
Dear Lord, I come; X10390 Steiner
Protection
Shine in my heart, Lord Jesus
That heavenly home
Koralbok for den Norske Kirke, 1926

St Olaf's Sequence
Koschat, Thomas, 1845-1914
Poland; X5906 Koschat; X10963 The Lord is my Shepherd; X10964 The Lord is our Leader
Kotzschmar, Hermann, 1829-1909
Claflin
Kozeluch (or Kotzeluch), Leopold Anton, 1752-1818
Kozeluch
Krauth, Harriet Reynolds (Mrs. Adolph Spaeth), 1845-1925
Easter Eve (1869)
Kreitmaier, J., S.J., arr
Great King of Kings
Krieger, Adam, 1634-66
Nun sich der Tag (1667); X3062 Esslingen; X7580 Nun sich der tag geendet (Williams)
Kroeger, Ernest Richard, 1862-1934
Christine
Elizabeth
Fulton
Gairney Bridge (1901)
Josephine (1901)
Windermere
Krossing, Peter Casper
Nu lukker sig mit oege
Kücken, Friedrick Wilhelm, 1810-82
Kücker; X8938 Repose
Kugelmann, Johann. Concentus novi, 1540
Tabor; X6976 Min sjael, min sjael; X7573 Nun lob' mein' seel'; X8041 Old hundred (Bourgeois)
Kurzenknabe, J.H.
Heavenly Father

L

Lacy, William S.
Vernon (1891)
LaFeillée. Methode du plain chant
Alleluia, dulce carmen (1808)
Jesu redemptor saeculi (1782)
Milan (1782); X6155 Lichfield
St Ambrose (1782)
Lagergren, Johan Frederik, 1826-
Gud var Gud; X5927 Lagergren
Lagi, Rudolf, 1823-68
I lift my eyes
Lahee, Henry, 1826-1912
Magi
Nativity (1855)
St Serf
Wild bells (ca 1875)
Wimbledon; X5928 Lahee
Lamb, James, 1835-1904
Invermay
Lambillotte, Louis, 1796-1855
On this day, O beautiful Mother
Panis Angelicus
Sub tuum praesidium
Veni, Creator Spiritus; X1936 Come, Holy Ghost, creator blest
LaMontaine, John, 1920-
Come, my way
Lampe, John Friedrich, 1703-51
Kent (1746); X2537 Devonshire
Lancaster, J.
St Silas (1860)
Landahl, Carl Wilfred, 1908-
Invocation
Landis, A.L.
Blessed Bible; X3460 Fount of glory
Lane, Spencer, 1843-1903
Penitence (1875); X5309 In the hour of trial; X5952 Lane; X6566 Lyndhurst; X8317 Parole; X10285 Spencer Lane
Lang, Craig Sellar, 1891-
Eastern monarchs
St Keverne (1936)
St Enodoc
Langden, W.A.
Irvin
Langdon, Richard. Divine harmony, 1774
Langdon
Langford, Samuel
God's glory
Langford
Langran, James, 1835-1909

Deerhurst; X2426 Dearhurst
Langran (1862); X842 Barnby's hymnary, Tune 224; X9231 St Agnes
Langton, Stephen
NOTE: "The golden sequence" is ascribed to Langton: an 11th c plainsong M 1
Veni Sancte Spiritus; X3890 Golden sequence
La Salle hymnal
Great God! whatever through thy church
La Scala santa, 1681
Coleraine; X1710 Christ is our Head; X11665 Vicenza
Latin (mediaeval) melodies
Christ ist erstanden (12th c); based on Victimae Paschali); X1720 Christ lag in todesbanden; X1730 Christ the Lord hath risen; X1797 Christus ist erstanden; X11668 Victimi paschali; X11670 Victor King
Christ lag in todesbanden (12th c; in Geistliches Gesangbüchlein. Wittenberg, 1524); X2474 Den Herre Krist i dødens baand; X2665 Dorian mode (Latin, 18th c; X11338 Torgau; X11668 Victimi paschali
Christ lag in todesbanden (12th c; in Geistliches Gesangbüchlein. Wittenberg, 1524. Bach harm.)
Dies irae (ca 1200)
Kyrie, Gott Vater (ca 800; hymn, "Kyrie fons bonitatis")
Nunc sancte nobis
La Tombelle, Ferdinand de, 1854-1928
O gloriosa virginum
LaTrobe, Christian Ignatius, 1758-1836
Invitation (1795)
Judgment (1795)
LaTrobe; X2250 Croyland
LaTrobe's 121st metre (1824)
LaTrobe's 578th metre
LaTrobe, Peter, 1795-1863
Courage (1852)
LaTrobe's 166th metre (1825)
Sweeter sounds (1854)
Laubenstein, Paul F.
Declare, O heavens (1964)
Laudi spirituali. Florence, 14th c (adapted by Charles Burney, 1782)
Alta trinita beata; X333 Alla trinita beata
Laufenberg, H., von ms. ca 1430
In einem Krepplein lag ein Kind
Laufer, Calvin Weiss, 1874-1938
Field (1919)
Hall (1918)
Hanna (1927)
Kerr (1932)
Percival-Smith (1933)
Seek ye the Lord (1927)
Stockwell, New
The Lord is in His holy temple (1926)
Laurenti, Laurentius, 1660-1722
Rejoice, all ye believers (ca 1700)
Lausanne Choral book
Broadlands; X6025 Lausanne
Lavallée, Calixa, 1842-91
O Canada (1880)
Law, John
Montesano
Lawes, Henry, 1596-1662
Battle
Falkland; X10595 Sweet Saviour, bless us
Farley Castle; X2126 Conway
Psalm 32; X6029 Lawes
Psalm 47 (1638); X6027 Lawes' Psalm 47
Whitehall; X9704 Sandys Psalm 8
Lawson, James
Lawson
Layard, E.B.
In medio Bello
Layriz, Friedrich, 1809-59
Eins ist not (1849)
Layriz Collection, 1853
Layriz; X5361 Ins feld geh
Leach, James, 1762-98
Watchman

Leach, Rowland, 1885-
Welcome (1933)
Leatherman, M. Janie
Sweet rest in heaven
Leavitt, Joshua. Christian lyre, 1830-31
Light
Pleading Saviour
Ledington, Stanley
Benediction (1939)
Communion (1939)
For the Sabbath (1938)
Rose of Sharon (1940)
Lee, George E.
Sleep
Lee, James Vernon, 1892-1959
Eastview
Lee, John
All you who seek (1958)
Just for today (1958)
O salutaris hostia (1964)
Leech, Lida Shivers, 1873-
Giving (1923); X11428 Trust, try, and prove me
God's way (1911)
I have made my choice (1915); X11184 Thine for service
Lees, John
Lamb's Hill (ca 1805)
Lefebvre, Channing
Rodney (1935)
Legge, Alfred, 1843-1919
Theodora
Lehman, F.M.
The love of God (1917)
Lehmann, W.H.
Fremont (1929)
Leighton, William, d before 1614
Leighton (1614);
NOTE: Probably in his The teares or lamentacions of a sorrowfull soule. 1614
Leinbach, E.W., 1823-1901
Leinbach (1870)
Leipzig, Library ms., 1756
Ich sterbe täglich
Leisentrit, J. Catholicum Hymnologium, 1584
Ave virgo virginum; X752b Ave vivens Hostia; X4272 Hail, true Victim; X4332 Happy we who thus united
Narenza
Regina caeli jubila
Le Jeune, George Fitz-Curwood, 1842-1904
Glorious things
Highest Lands
Holy Spirit (1894)
Love divine (1887); X6091 Le Jeune; X6431 Love divine, No. 2
Urbs beata (1887)
Lemare, Edwin Henry, 1865-1934
Haven
Lemke, August, 1820-1913
Mach hoch die tür (1849)
Lerman, Joseph W., 1865-1935
Corwin (ca 1908)
Ilona (1908)
Le Saint, Louis
Who givest all (1920)
Leslie, C.E.
Silently, they pass away; X10030 Silently bury the dead
Leslie, E.
Lift your glad voices
Leslie, Ernest B.
Adsum
Greenwell
Leslie, Henry, ca 1825-76
Ephraim
Leslie, J.H.
Alpha
Lester, Thomas William, 1889-1956
First Church
Industry (1927)
Land of our hearts (1927)
Two fatherlands (1927)
Levenson, Boris, 1884-1947
As God wills (1932)
Come, ye faithful servants (1932)
God! send us men (1932)
Israel's song (1932)
My faith (1932)
Sing to the Sovereign of the skies (1932)
The day is done (1932)
The voice of God is calling (1932)
These things shall be (1932)

Lewandowski, Louis, 1821-1904
Almighty God
Ayn kay-lo-hay-nu (1932)
Earth with all thy thousand voices (1932)
Hayom T'am'tsaynu
How good it is to thank the Lord; X6034 L'cho dodee
Kee vayom
Mee chomocho
S'lach no
Vayomer adonoy
V'shom'ru
Lewars, Harold, 1882-1915
Adjutor (1914)
Froebel (1909)
Rorate caeli (1914); X9109 Rorate coeli
Salve Jesu (1914)
Septem voces, 1st (1914)
Septem voces, 2d (1914)
Septem voces, 3d (1914)
Septem voces, 4th (1914)
Septem voces, 5th (1914)
Septem voces, 6th (1914)
Septem voces, 7th (1914)
Vexilla regis (1913)
Lewars, Ralph P., 1883-
Festal day (1958)
Lewis, Freeman, 1780- 1859
Beloved (1913); X2724 Dulcimer; X6822 Meditation; X7190 My beloved; X8855 Redeemer of Israel
Lewis, John S.
Sister, thou wast mild
Lewis, Henry A.
Mary
Lewis, T.C.
Crux
Ley, Henry George, 1887-1962
Ad astra
Ottery St Mary
Rushford (1936)
Leyda, Ida F.
Morning prayer
Liander, C.G.
Via dolorosa
Liefeld, Albert D.
Liefeld (1911)
Lightwood, James Thomas, 1856-
Lytham (1910)
Lillenas, Bertha Mae
Leave your burden (1934); X6065 Leave your burden at the place of prayer
Lillenas, Haldor, 1885-
Don't turn Him away
The peace that Jesus gives (1931)
Wonderful grace (1918)
Lindeman, Ludvig Matthias, 1812-87
Ak, Fader, lad dit Ord, din Aand; X7665 O Father, may thy word prevail
All glory, laud
Bryd frem, mit hjertes trang at lindre
Den store hvide Flok
Dies irae
Easter glory; X3484 Fred til bod; X5676 Jesus, Sun of righteousness; X6493 Ludovica
Et Barner født i Bethlehem
Gift of grace
Herre Jesus Krist, min Frelser du est; X6369 Lord Jesus Christ, my Saviour blest
Hjem Jeg Laenges; X10461 Stricken, smitten
Holy mountains; X2097 Consolation; X5656 Jesus only; X7262 Naar mit øie, traet af møie; X7284 Nar mit öie
I denne Verdens Sorger saenkt
I Himmelen, i Himmelen
I Jesus søger jeg min Fred
I praegtige Himle
Jeg har min Sag til Gud hjemstilt
Jesus, kom dog selv til mig
King's land; X7799 O land of our King
Kirken; X1390 Built on the Rock; X1806 Church; X5862 Kirken den er et gammelt hus; X6990 Mirken
Kjaerlighed er Lysets Kilde; X6187 Light; X6444 Love,

the fount of light
Lindeman; X4187 Gud skal alting mage; X5660 Jesus, priceless treasure
Ludwig; X4909 How blessed is the little flock; X4986 Hvor salig er den lille
Min Sjael, min Sjael, lov Herren; X7257 My soul, now bless
Nu er Frelsens Dag oprundet
O kom dog hver, son Synd har gjort
O lad din Aand nu med os vaere; X83 Abide among us
Op, thi Dagen nu freymbryder
Our Lady, Trondhjem; X2803 Easter morrow; X4585 Her vil ties; X8330 Paschal; X8332 Paskemorgen slukker sorgen
Over Kedron
Repentance; X4643 Herre, jeg har handlet
Sal vil vi nu sige hver-andre Farvel; X457 And now we must bid
Som Tørstige Hjort; X589 As after the water-brooks
Spring of souls; X1518 Care for me; X7466 Norse; X10248 Sørg, O kjaere Fader
Vaagn op, du, som sover
Lindsay, Miss
Too late
Lindstrom, Albert Esaias, 1853-
Mig klädd i helig prydned
Min ljufva tröst
Linekar, Thomas Joseph, 1858-
Colwyn Bay
Link, C.U.
Grace, 'tis a charming sound; X7825 O Lord, to thee I cry; X8508 Pleading
Victory
Linley, Francis
Lord of all being
Lint, Conrad G., 1834-
Fellowship
Linton, G.W.
Welcome
Lissant, G.B.
Banner
Holy Jesus
Rex regum
Lithuanian melody
Jesus, when we go to rest
Littlewood, Ernest
Golden Grove
Llewellyn, William Benjamin James, 1925-
Majesty
Tidings
Westron Wynde
Lloyd, Charles Francis Ambrose, 1852-1917
Ravensworth
Lloyd, Charles Harford, 1845-1919
Dayspring
Sacramentum Unitatis (1885)
Achnasheen (1903)
St Frideswide
Lloyd, David de, 1883-1948
Richmond Hill
Lloyd, John Ambrose, 1815-74
Abergele (1873)
Brynteg
Cromer
Downing
Eifionydd
Groeswen
Henryd
Kilmorey
Wynnstay
Lloyd, John Morgan, 1880-
Colwinstone (1927)
Nadolig (1927)
Perth Kerry (1927)
Pro nostris liberis (1927)
Lloyd, Richard Francis, 1871-
Celestial voices
Clairvaux
Light of ages
Winton
Lloyd, Richard Hey, 1933-
Sarum New
Lloyd, William, 1786-1852
Meirionydd (1840); X6857 Meirionnydd; X6858 Meiromydd
Lob, Otto
There lives a God
Lockhart, Charles, 1745-1815
Carlisle (1769)

Loes, Harry Dixon, 1892-
Looking unto Jesus (1933)
Redeemer (1921); X1161 Blessed Redeemer
Loewen, Lois
Evening praise
Lohr, George Augustus, 1821-97
St Frances; X1901 Columbia
Lomas, George, 1834-84
Althorp; X1594 Chamouni
Pentecost
Southport
Submission
Sursum corda; X10540 Sursum corda, No. 2
Verbum pacis
Longacre, Lindsay Bartholomew, 1870-
Deeper life (1928)
Firenze (1941)
New America
Loomis, Harvey Worthington, 1865-1930
Park Square (1927)
Lord, A.E.
St Austin
Lorenz, Edmund S. (or Edward S.), 1854-
Amid the trials; X11222 Thou thinkest, Lord, of me
Give me the Bible
God is love (1886)
Joy cometh in the morning
Tell it to Jesus
The name of Jesus
When the King comes in
Wonderful love of Jesus
Lough, A.D.
All for Jesus
Lourdes Pilgrims Hymn, Grenoble, 1882
Immaculate Mary; X11301 To kneel at thine altar
Lovelace, Austin C., 1919-
Hinman (1953)
Loveless, Wendell P.
Lead me to some soul today (1936)
Sweeter than the day before (1936)
Lowden, C. Harold, 1883-
Geneva
Homines Christi (1914)
Living for Jesus; X6268 Living
Noyon (1917)
Stewart
Lowe, Albert, ca 1840-86
Ambleside
Praise (1876); X346 Alleluia; X6456 Lowe
Lowenberg, William
Let Israel trust in God alone (1932)
Lowens, Irving, 1916-
Pioneers (1955)
Löwenstern, Matthias Appelles von, 1594-1648
Christe du beistand
Lowenstern; X4674 Heut' ist o mensch
Nun preiset alle (1644); X 243 Alcaic ode; X4083 Gregor's 70th metre
Lowry, Robert, 1826-99
All the way (ca 1888); X 6467 Lowry; X11483 Ulster
Beautiful river; X4318 Hansome place; X9929 Shall we gather
Beauty of holiness; X7969 O worship the Lord
Christ arose (1874)
Come, we that love the Lord; X6706 Marching to Zion; X12031 We're marching to
Follow on
Heavenly Father (1878)
Keller; X4684 Hide thou me
Need (1872); X2493 Dependence; X5100 I need thee [every hour]; X6468 Lowry; X11622 Vernon
Never shone a light (1882)
No hope in Jesus
Nothing but the blood (1876); X8497 Plainfield
One more day's work
Paxtang (1917)
Something for Jesus (1899); X2009 Coming now, O Lord, to; X2088 Consecration; X6469 Lowry; X9757 Savior, thy dying love; X10202 Something for Thee

Where is my boy tonight
Who'll be the next?
Loy, Harvey
Avanti (1924)
Gannett (1924)
Risveglio (1922)
Luard-Selby, Bertram, 1853-1919 see Selby, Bertram Luard, 1853-1919
Lucas, James, ca 1762-
Lucas (1832); X1951 Come, let us anew
Swanwick
Lund, Anthony C.
Blessed are they that have the faith
Bring, heavy heart, your grief
Lüneburg Gesangbuch, 1648
Ach Jesu, dessen Treu
Lüneburg Gesangbuch, 1686
Jesu meine Lust und Wonne
Jesu meines herzen freud
Meinhold; X82 Abglanz aller magestaet
Luther, Martin, 1483-1546
Ein' feste Burg (1529); X27 A mighty fortress; X39 A safe stronghold; X49 A stronghold sure; X2882 Ein' feste burg ist unser Gott; X3448 Fortress; X6531 Luther
From heaven high (1539); X 3019 Erfurt; X3467 Fra himlen hoit; X3529 From heaven above; X3907 Good news from heaven; X11739 Vom himmel hoch; X12361 Wittenberg; X12552 Yule
Jesaia, dem Propheten (1526)
Luther, M. Christliche Gesang. Wittenberg, 1542
Jam moesta
Spires (based on Plainsong M 2, Jesu dulcedo cordium) X3022 Erhalt uns, Herr; X4750 Hold oppe, Gud, hos os dit ord; X6373 Lord keep us steadfast; X6530 Luther; X12362 Wittenberg
Lutkin, Peter Christian, 1858-1931
Baptism (1905)
Belleville (1905)
Camp (1905)
Carman (1895)
Caryl (1905)
Charity (1927)
City Road (1905)
Copenhagen
Dublin (1927)
Father, to thee we look (1897)
Gleason (1905)
Joshua (1905)
Kiel (1905)
Kolding (1905)
Lanier (1905)
Olivarius (1905)
Patten (1902)
Prescott (1905)
Psalm 23; X8231 Our Shepherd is the Lord
Racine (1905)
Red Cross (1927)
St Barbara (1902)
Sevenfold Amen
The Highway (1927)
The Lord bless you; X1016 Benediction
Theodore (1905)
Transfiguration (1905)
Upham (1905); X3840 God of the nations, near and far
Vox aeterna
Lutteroth, Ascan Henri Théodore, 1802-89
Bryntirion
Lutz, Wilhelm Meyer, 1822-1903
Stanley; X10518 Sunset
Lvov, Alexey Feodorovitch, 1798-1870
Russia (1833); X3848 God save America; X3856 God the all-merciful; X7130 Moscow; X9058 Rise, crowned with light; X9174 Russian anthem; X9176 Russian hymn
Lwoff, Alexis Feodorovich, 1798-1870 see Lvov, Alexey Feodorovitch, 1798-1870
Lynes, Frank, 1858-1913

Disciples
Sons of light
The armor of light
Lynes, T.
Recessional; X12551 Youth
Lyoff, Alexis Theodore, 1798-1870 see Lvov, Alexey Feodorovitch, 1798-1870
Lyon, G. W.
Fast to thine arm
Lyra Anglo-Judaica
Askenazi tune
Lyra Davidica, 1708
Easter hymn; X493 Anglia; X1737 Christ, the Lord is risen; X2787 Easter; X6577 Lyra; X7081 Morgan; X12452 Worgan [sic]
Lysberg, Charles-Samuel (real name Bovy-Lysberg) 1821-73
Almighty Father, hear

M

M. B. F.
NOTE: See also Foster, Myles B., 1851-1922

Melford (1886); X1158 Blessed night, when first the plain
Maasalo, Armas, 1885-
Jesus hear
McAfee, Cleland Boyd, 1866-1944
McAfee; X4503 Heart of God; X7319 Near to the heart; X11146 There is a place
Macalister, Robert Alexander Stewart, 1870-1950
New Grange (1927)
St Darerca (1927)
Temple Bryan (1927)
McBurney, S.
Come, follow me
While of these emblems we partake
McCartney, Robert Hyslop, 1844-95
Jesus dilectissimi
Remembrance
Westwood
McClellan, John Jasper, 1874-1925
Sweet is the work, my God, my King
McConnell, J. Edwin, 1892-1954
McConnell (1914)
McCutchan, Robert Guy (John Porter, pseud), 1877-
All the world (1930)
De Pauw (1928)
Fowler (1929)
Masefield (1933)
Oxnam (1929)
Porter
Tiplady (1931)
MacDonald, Archibald
Warrior (1877)
MacDougall, Hamilton Crawford, 1858-
Hazard (1907)
MacElree, Mary Eyre
Eyre (1947)
Macey, J.D., 1860-1933
Mayfield
Macfarlane, J. M.
Dearest children, God is near you
MacFarlane, James
NOTE: This may be same composer as above.
Far, far away on Judea's plains
Macfarren, George Alexander, 1813-87
Dedication (1889); X3283 Father, let me dedicate
Evening hymn (1870)
Light of the world
Luffenham (1872); X3233 Faithfulness; X10761 Thankfulness
Lux prima
Thy life (1875); X11245 Thy life was given
With gladsome feet
Macfarren, Walter Cecil, 1826-1905
Barmouth (ca 1875)
Macfarren (1870)
McGranahan, James, 1840-1907
Alleluia for the cross
By grace are ye saved
Christ returneth; X5433 It

may be at morn
Christ returneth; X5433 It may be at morn
El Nathan (1885); X5078 I know whom I have believed; X12408 Wondrous grace
Every day
For God so loved
Frances (1901)
He is not here, but is risen
He will hide me
His tender mercies (1890)
I'll stand by
Kinsman (1897)
McGranahan
My Redeemer; X5147 I will sing; X7848 O my Father
Neumeister; X1723 Christ receiveth sinful men; X10073 Sinners Jesus will receive
None but Christ
Redeemed (1907)
Royal banner; X10791 The banner of the cross
Shall you? shall I?
Showers of blessing; X11162 There shall be showers
Some time we'll understand; X7497 Not now, but in the coming years
That will be glory for me
The crowning day; X8225 Our Lord is now rejected
Thy God reigneth
Thy will be done
Who came down
Would you lose your load of sin?

McHose, Irvine N. (late 19th - early 20th c)
O, such wonderful love

McIntosh, Robert M.
Gathering home
Tell it again
The Kingdom coming; X10922 The Kingdom is coming

McIntyre, Thomas
How great the wisdom

Mackay, J.B.
Winning souls for Jesus

McKinney, B.B., 1886-1952
NOTE: McKinney jr and Mc Kinney sr, both B.B. McKinney, are not clearly identified. But one set of dates is known. Melodies are interfiled.

All on the altar (1936)
Another day is dawning (1940)
Awake, put on thy strength (1940)
Be ye doers of the Word (1940)
Breathe o'er our waiting spirits (1936)
Bryson City (1940); X1017 Benediction
Christ for the whole wide world (1938)
Christian home (1949)
Coleman (1924); X6125 Let others see Jesus in you
Come home (1940)
Crowned or crucified (1940)
Draw near (1940)
Falls Creek (1936); X12179 Wherever He leads I'll go
Forgive
Glorious Name (1942)
Grice
He died for me
Holcomb (1927); X10282 Speak to my heart
I was glad when they said
In the old-time way (1937)
In thy holy temple (1940)
Into the woods (1940)
John three-Sixteen
Lead on, lead on (1940)
Leavell; X554 Arise, O youth of God
Lee (1931); X9908 Serve the Lord with gladness
Leila (1940); X6374 Lord, lay some soul upon my heart
Lubbock (1924); X10999 The nail-scarred hand
Matthews
Muskogee (1934); X4404 Have faith in God
My Father knows (1940)
'Neath the old olive trees (1929)
O God eternal (1936)

Routh (1926); X9724 Satisfied with Jesus
Somebody needs your love (1940)
The Christian home (1940)
The Lord bless thee
The upper room (1939)
Thy will be done! (1937)
Touch me, Lord Jesus (1940)
Travis Avenue
Truett; X1291 Breathe on me
What will you do with Jesus (1940)
Whisper a prayer (1940)

Maclagan, William Dalrymple, 1826-1910
Bread of heaven (1875)
Lichfield
Newington (1875); X6614 Maclagan
Palms of glory
Prince of Peace (1884)
Troas

Maclean, Joseph
Charlotte (1899)
Craig (1899)
Dabney (1899)
Goetchius (1901)
Holly Springs (1899)
Lenoir (1899)
Plumer (1899)
Preston (1898)

Maclean, Quentin Stuart Morvaren, 1896-
O King of nations (1958)

MacLeod, D. B.
The children's King

McManiman, G. E.
Sovereignty

Macmeikan, J. A.
St Regulus

MacMillan, Ernest Campbell, 1893-
Light of Light

Macmillan, Margaret, 1863-1903
Roslyn

McNaughton, J. H.
Home (1863); X6423 Love at home; X11151 There is beauty all around

McPhail, John
In that day

McPhail, M. L.
The story that never grows old (1898)

McWhood, Leonard Beecher, 1870-
Hymn of nations (1933)

McWilliams, Clement Charles, 1934-
Dulwich

Magdalen Hospital Hymns, ca 1760
Lyne
Plaistow

Magdeburg, Joachim. Christliche Tischgesänge. Erfurt, 1572
Guds Godhed wil vi prise; X3651 Gerhardt; X11741 Von Gott will ich nicht lassen

Maher, William J., S.J. d 1677
Sing of my Savior

Mailloux, Thomas B., C.S.B.
Child of a Virgin (1958)

Main, Hubert Platt, 1839-1926
Calling to thee
Cassidy (1895)
Clark
Emmanuel
Hold thou my hand
Keep thou my way
My Lord and I
Ninth Street
Ridgefield; X9820 Search me, O Lord
Staunton
Wellerd

Mainz Gesangbuch, 1661
Lady of the visitation; X12208 Whither thus in holy rapture
Mainz; X1422 By the cross; X10338 Stabat mater

Mainz Gesangbuch, 1833
O God, eternal Father; X7686 O God, almighty Father

Mainzer, Joseph, 1801-51
Humility; X6647 Mainzer
Mainzer (1841)

Maker, Frederick Charles, 1844-1927
All this night; X7299 Nativity
Cliftonville
Crossing the bar
Curfew
Darmstadt
Ford Cottage (1909)
In memoriam
Invitation (1881); X1981 Come to the Saviour
Julian
Lyndhurst
Maker; X8299 Paraclete
Melrose
Morgenlied (1876)
Ravensbourne
Rest (1887); X2958 Elton; X12215 Whittier
St Christopher (1881); X1788 Christopher; X6662 Maker
St Germans
Wentworth (1876)
Windermere
Word of life; X3950 Gottlieb
Zennor
Malan, Henri Abraham César, 1787-1864
Boynton
Hendon (1827); X2089 Consecration; X4794 Holy, holy, holy Lord; X6395 Lord, we come before thee now; X11315 To thy pastures, fair
In His love abiding(1827); X4363 Harre meine seele; X11769 Wait on God
Nazareth
Rosefield
Silchester
Welton
Malet, G.E.W., 1839-1918
Corpus domini
Malim, A.W.
King of Love; X7010 Mittit
Mallary, R. DeWitt
Beecroft
Sojourner
Malley, James
Lytham
Malmstrom, Carl Sigurd, 1886-
Chisago (1924)
Mann, Arthur Henry, 1850-1929
Allerton
Beeforth (1885)
Berno
Claudius
King's College
Lasus (ca 1900); X7480 Norwich
Mann; X7372 New Year
Orient morning (1885); X1018 Benediction
St Asaph
Silesius
Stanley
Valour (1889); X11003 The New Year
Vesper
Watermouth (1889); X484 Angel's story; X2277 Crux Christi; X7481 Norwich
Wilton
Manookin, Robert P.
O sons of Sion
Manx traditional, etc.
Carol of the Kingdom
Peel Castle
Santwat
Marathi (India) traditional
Tana mana dhana
March, F.K.
College (1905)
Margetson, E.J.
Sol justitiae
Woodworth
Marks, Clement A., 1864-1912
Ferdinand (1895)
Marks, J. Christopher
Marthina
Marks, William Edie
The last mile of the way
Marquis, Robert C.
It must be told (1893)
Marsh, Charles H., 1886-
Is it the crowning day (1910)
One day; X1609 Chapman
Marsh, Simeon Butler, 1798-1875
Endor
Martyn (1834); X5598 Jesus, Jesus, come to me; X5624 Jesus, lover of my soul;

X9005 Reverently and meekly now
Marsh, William J.
In this sacrament (1958)
Michael, prince (1958)
Marshall, John Patton, 1877-1941
Zeal
Marshall, Leonard
Prayer
Marshall, W.S.
Marshall (1876); X1160 Blessed quietness; X4815 Holy quietness; X5734 Joys are flowing
Martin, George Clement, 1844-1916
All Hallows (1892)
Carnarvon
Chilton Foliat
Holy Faith
Israel
Per pacem
St Helen
Martin, George E.
There's a song (New) (1899)
Martin, George William, 1828-81
Leominster (1862); X9302 St Basil
Martin, S. Wesley, 1839-
The gospel bells
Martin, W.
Melmore
Martin, W. Stillman, 1862-1935
Martin (1905); X3799 God cares; X3857 God will take care
Mary (religious)
NOTE: The name Mary is considered as secondary in this index: e.g., Sister Mary Florian, S.S.J. will become: Florian, Sr. Mary, S.S.J. The secular surname is ignored.

Mason, Daniel Gregory, 1873-1953
Deed (1927)
Mason, Harry Silvertone, 1881-
Beacon Hill (1925); X538 "Are ye able"
Mason, Henry Lowell, 1864-
Exeter (1923)
Mason, John. Companion, 1847
Sion
Mason, Lowell, 1792-1872
NOTE: Some of these tunes are associated with Mason's name as compiler and publisher rather than as composer. Cf. Baker's Biographical dictionary for list of his collections.

Admah
Alvan
Anvern
Ashwell
Bealoth (1843); X5089 I love thy kingdom, Lord
Beethoven
Bethany (1856); X1053 Bethel; X3183 Excelsior; X7322 Nearer, my God
Bonar
Boylston (1832); X7012 Mixolydian; X7487 Not all the blood of beasts
Capello
Chimes
Cowper
Cyprus
Daughter of Zion
Denny; X6100 Leon
Diligence (1864); X6458 Lowell; X12453 Work; X12454 Work, for the night is coming; X12455 Work song
Dort (1832); X3798 God bless our native land
Downs
El Paran
Eltham
Elton
Ernan (1850)
Evarts; X10815 The Bridegroom soon
Gerar; X6302 Lo, what a pleasing
Haddam
Hamburg (arr) see Plainsong M 1, "Hamburg"
Hamden
Hartel
Harwell (1841); X7849 O my Father
Heath (1850); X1378 Bucer X2029 Communion; X9804

Schumann; X11913 We give thee but thine
Hebron (1850); X1704 Christ, in the night; X6352 Lord, cause thy face; X6774 Mason
Henley (1854)
Herbert
Hermon
Illa
Kane
Laban (1830); X6 A charge to keep; X7254 My soul be on thy guard
Magister
Malvern (1847)
Melton
Mendebras (arr) see German traditional, Mendebras
Meribah (1839); X6723 Maribah
Migdol
Milton
Missionary hymn (1823); X3528 From Greenland's icy; X4545 Heber; X6999 Missionary; X7965 O word of God incarnate; X12342 With happy voices
Mount Vernon; X5692 Jesus, while our hearts; X10090 Sister, thou was mild
Nashville
Norwich (1825)
Oak; X4525 Heaven is my home
Olden
Olivet (1833); X7198 My faith looks up
Olney
Orford
Osgood
Ostend
Ovio
Pentonville
Ripley
Rockingham (1830); X890 Be present at our table; X4011 Gravity; X9086 Rockingham (New)
Rodman
Sabbath (1824); X9199 Sabbath morn; X9219 Safely through another week
Seir
Shawmut
Soto
Sparta
Star of peace; X6190 Light of life
Stow; X10449 Stowe
Today (1831); X7273 Nain
Unity
Uxbridge (1830); X10135 So let our lips and
Watchman (1830); X11879 Watchman! Tell us
Wesley (1833); X4269 Hail to the brightness
Zebulon
Zerah; X11316 To us a child of hope
Mason, Sam
Sing Glory, Hallelujah (1920); X8667 Proclaim the tidings
Vision (1925)
Mason, Timothy Battle, 1801-61
Eden
Eshtemoa
Masser, John Thornton, 1855-
St Margaret
Mather, William, 1756-1808
Medfield; X668 Attercliffe; X5106 I pray thee, Lord; X9949 Sheffield
Mathias, Franz Xaver, 1871-1939
Eintracht
Matthews, Henry E., arr, 1820.-
Children's praises (ca 1853); X3757 Glory; X9146 Rowe
Matthews, J.H., 1859-
Belfry praise
Matthews, Timothy Richard, 1826-1910
Bromham (1886)
Chenies (1855); X4992 Hymn for the month of May
Corfe Mullen
Ludborough (1846)
Margaret (1876); X2948 Elliott
North Coates (1862)
Reynoldstone
Storrs; X9765 Saxby
Matthews, William, 1759-1830

Madrid
Matthias, John B.
Deliverance will come (1836)
Matthison-Hansen, L.
Ara
Mattoni, M.
Joseph, pure spouse
There is an everlasting home
Maude, Caroline, i.e. Viscountess Hewarden
Evening hymn
Maunder, John H.
Martham (1897)
Parry
The whole wide world (1894)
Mauro-Cottone, Melchiorre
Regina caeli laetare (1918)
Mayence see Mainz
Mayer, Frederick Christian, 1882-
Mayer (1930)
Means, Claude
Seabury (1941)
Mechlin plainsong
Stabat Mater, M 4
Verbum supernum, M 8
(in Antiphonarium romanum)
Méhul, Etienne-Nicholas, 1763-1817
Gilead; X6835 Mehul
Joseph; X6836 Mehul
Meineke, Charles, 1782-1850
Gloria Patri (1840)
Morning Star
Worship
Meiningen Gesangbuch, 1693
Munich (Mendelssohn arr); X2542 Devotion; X6854 Meiningen; X7704 O Gott, du frommer
O Gott, du frommer Gott; X108 Ach Gott, verlass mich; X2350 Darmstadt; X7175 Munich; X7697 O God, thou faithful; X7711 O Gud, du fromme Gud
St Leonard (Bach arr); X296 All saints; X810 Bamberg; X1975 Come, thou quickening Spirit; X2896 Eisenach; X3932 Gott des himmels und der erden; X4611 Hermannsburg; X4708 Himlens Gud og Jordens Herre; X5897 Komm, o kom, du Geist; X6158 Liebe die du mich zum; X6860 Melanchthon; X11306 To the Name that brings
Melish, R.
I heard the voice of Jesus say; X2699 Drink to me only with; X3252 Far, far beyond
Melling, Ellen Knowles
O say, what is truth
Melodiae Prudentianae, 1553
Ades pater supreme
Mendelssohn, Felix, 1809-47
NOTE: Full name, Jacob Ludwig Felix Mendelssohn-Bartholdy.

Almighty Father, hear (1846); X381 Almighty Father; X897 Be thou faithful; X5364 Intercession ([refrain] Callcott)
Angels' song
Aspiration
Birmingham; X1571 Cast thy burden on the Lord
Brightest and best; X1038 Berlin; X2030 Communion; X2098 Consolation; X3292 Father, to thee we look; X3305 Felix; X6885 Mendelssohn; X8827 Raynolds; X9014 Reynolds
But the Lord (from St Paul)
Constancy
Cyprus; X9970 Sherborne
Dauchy
Dusseldorf
Elijah
Elven
Evangelist (1836); X4932 How lovely are thy dwellings
Friend
Heavenly love; X90 Abiding; X5271 In heavenly love abiding; X7693 O God, the eternal Father; X8912 Reliance; X9822 Seasons; X11988 We'll sing the songs of Zion; X12528 Yes, heaven is the prize
Holy cross, see Wade, arr

Intercession (refrain only) (1846)
Leipzig
Lift thine eyes (from Elijah)
Lift up your heads
Lord's Day
Mendelssohn (1840); X1059 Bethlehem; X1423 By the first bright Easter Day; X1773 Christmas; X3323 Festgesang; X4350 Hark! the hearld angels; X4588 Herald angels; X9847 See! amid the winter's snow; X11566 Vaterland, in deinen gauen
O rest in the Lord (from Elijah)
Selwyn; X859 Bartholdy; X3306 Felix
Stukeley; X1395 Bunyan
Trust (1840); X2113 Contemplation; X3815 God is love; X6886 Mendelssohn; X8223 Our guiding star; X11426 Trust, No. 1
Wilson

Meredith, Isaac Hickman, 1872-
Meredith (1900); X1558 Carson; X9818 Seal us, O Holy Spirit
Stowell (1935)

Merrick, George Purnell, 1840-
Aldersgate

Merrill, William Pierson, 1867-
America befriend (1912); X8942 Republic
Marcus Whitman (1927)
Soldiers of Christ (1895)

Messiter, Arthur Henry, 1834-1916
Marion (1883)

Metcalfe, L. C.
Metcalfe (1925)

Methfessel, Albert Gottlieb, 1785-1869
Courtland

Methfessel, A. G. Song book, 1818
Salem; X11084 The time is far spent

Meurers, P.
The very Angels' Bread; X8290 Panis angelicus

Meyer, Franz Heinrich Christoph, 1705-67
Mein Schöpfer, steh mir bei (1740)

Meyer, J.D. Seelenfreud, Ulm, 1692
Es ist kein tag; X6933 Meyer Rudolstadt; X7263 Naar synderen ret ser; X12025 Wer weiss, wie nahe

Meyer, S. W.
Dolut

Michaud, Joseph
Praise we Christ; the King (1940)

Michel, Abbe
Pie Jesu

Micklem, Thomas Caryl, 1925-
Sandwith

Miles, C. Austin
In the garden (1912?)

Milford, Robin H., 1903-60
Prayers (1925)

Milgrove, Benjamin, 1731-1810
Harts; X4264 Hail! thou living Bread; X4370 Hartford; X7751 O how lovely; X10466 Study song
Harwich (1812)
Mt Ephraim
St Helena (1861)

Millard, Harrison, 1829-95
Abide with me; 'Tis eventide

Miller (no initials)
Tantum ergo

Miller, Anne L.
Vermont (1941)

Miller, Charles Edward, 1856-
Waldrons

Miller, Edward, 1731-1807
Galway
Rockingham, arr (1790); X1578 Caton; X2031 Communion; X2276 Crux beata; X6963 Miller; X9087 Rockingham Old
Webbe, arr (ca 1790)
Whitefield

Miller, Harold A.
Branson (1939)
Collegedale (1939)
Jenkins (1939)
Massachusetts (1939)
Preston (1939)
Rogers (1939)
Schroeder (1939)
Vesper (1939)
Wirak (1939)
Woods (1939)

Miller, L. David, 1919-

Fortitudo (1958)
Miller, Robert B.
Good Shepherd, Rosemont
Miller, Russell King
Father, let thy blessing
Sweet Sabbath (1932); X2514 Despise not, Lord
Miller, Samuel Martin, 1890-
Daystar (1922)
Lux dei (1923)
Miller, Selden
St Stephens' Church
Miller, Walter L.
Peace, perfect peace
Miller, William
Going home; X5231 I'm going home; X7217 My heavenly home is bright
Land of rest; X7800, O land of rest, for thee I sigh; X11989 We'll work till Jesus
Milligan, Cleo Cannon
Pax orbi (1941)
Miner, George A. See Minor, George A.
Minke, Emma L.
Nativity (1899)
Minkler, Ross H.
A prayer for grace (1936)
Minns, G.
Wilmar
Minor, George A.
Bringing in the sheaves; X4380 Harvest; X10271 Sowing in the morning; X11052 The sheaves
Minshall, Edward
Coppee; X10329 Springfield
Horton
Mishler, Roy S.
Close to my Savior
Mitchell, Mrs. E.T.
Claribel, arr
Mitchell, J.S.
Mitchell
Mitchell, S.
Pilesgrove
Mitterer, Ignaz Martin, 1850-1924
A priestly heart (1929)
Mitton, Samuel B.
Awake! O ye people
Modern harp
Logan
Moffatt, James, 1870-1944
Ultima
Mohr, Joseph, S.J., d 1892
Ave maris stella
He who once in righteous vengeance; X10673 Tantum ergo
O King of might and splendor
Panis angelicus; X9211 Sacris solemnis
Molthar, Philip Henry
Gregor's 483d metre (1750); X9780 Schlaf, liebes Kind
Mombach, J.S.
Let there be light
Monaghan, Francis E., C.S.B.
Behold a simple tender Babe (1958)
A Monk of Gethsemani [Monastery]
All of seeing
In this your month (1958)
Lady in sorrow (1958)
Lord Jesus, when I think of thee (1958)
Maria, mater gratia (1958)
O God, thy soldiers' faithful Lord (1958)
Prayer of St Francis (1958)
Sing, my tongue (1958)
This is the day (1958)
Monk, Edwin George, 1819-1900
Angel voices (1861)
Hopkins
Monk
St Ninian (1862)
Monk, Mark James, 1858-
Campfields
Monk, William Henry, 1823-89
Aber
Adsis, Jesu
All things bright and beautiful; X313 All things bright
Alleluia perenne (1868)
Ascension (1861); X613 Ascension, No. 1
Beverly (1875); X182 Advent
Clifton; X7100 Morning
Colyton
Coronae (1871); X2245 Crown Him

Easter hymn; X5537 Jesus Christ is risen today
Evelyns (1875)
Eventide (1861); X86 Abide with me; X7030 Monk
Litany
Merton (1850)
Minto
Nutfield (1861)
Plumptre
St Ambrose (1874); X9256 St. Ambrose, No. 2
St Bernard
St Constantine (1861)
St Ethelwald (1861); X1553 Carr; X2989 Energy
St Matthias (1861); X6792 Matthias
St Medan (arr)
St Philip (1861); X7031 Monk
St Sacrament
Supplication
Unde et memores (1875)
Verbum pacis (1889)
Vigilate (1868)
Waltham; X7032 Monk
Words on the cross: The Litany (1889); X6249 Litany, No. 10
Wordsworth

Montani, Isabella
Hail, full of grace (1920)

Montani, Nicola Aloysius, 1880-1948
A message from the Sacred Heart (1920)
All ye who seek
Angels we have heard (1920)
Ave, regina coelorum (1920)
By the blood that flowed (1920)
Christ the Lord is risen today (1920)
Crown Him (1920)
Daily, daily sing to Mary (1920)
Blest is the Faith
Dear Angel! ever at my side
Dear little One! how sweet (1920)
Full of glory (1920)
Faith of our Fathers (1920)
Glory be to Jesus
God of mercy and compassion (1920)
Hail, Jesus, hail! (1920)
Hail, Mary, full of grace (1920)
Hail, Rock of Ages (1920)
Hark! a mystic voice (1920)
Hark! hark! my soul (1920)
Heart of Jesus (1940)
I see my Jesus crucified
Ingrediente domino (1940)
Jesus Christ is risen today (1920)
Jesus, gentlest Saviour (1920)
Jesus, my Lord, my God
Just for today
Let the deep organ swell (1920)
Mother of Christ (1920)
My God, accept my heart (1920)
Now at the Lamb's high royal feast (1920)
O blessed father! sent (1920)
O come and mourn (1920)
O dearest Love divine (1920)
O Heart of Jesus
O how I love thee Jesus (1925)
O Jesus Christ, remember (1920)
O Jesus, thou the beauty art (1920)
O Lord, I am not worthy
O purest of creatures
O'erwhelmed in depths of woe
Pie Jesu (1936)
Praise to the Holiest (1920)
Praise we our God
Saint of the Sacred Heart (1920)
Seek ye a Patron (1920)
Spirit of grace and union (1920)
Sweet Saviour! bless us
Tantum ergo
Tantum ergo (1910)
The Word, descending (1920); X7886 O salutaris Hostia
Thee prostrate I adore
To Christ, the Prince of Peace
To Jesus' Heart, all burn-

ing
To the Name that brings salvation (1920)
Unto him, for whom, this day
Veni Creator Spiritus
Moody, May Whittle, 1870-
Moment by moment
Moon, Robert M.
I am trusting in His word
Moore. Psalm singer's pocket companion, 1756
Glasgow
Moore, C. L.
Trust in Jesus
Moore, George D.
My soul in sad exile; X4418 Haven of rest; X10901 The haven of rest
Moore, James C., 1888-
If only you knew Him (1940)
Moore (1956)
Where we' ll never grow old
Moore, W.
Confidence
Moore, William
Holy manna; X1305 Brethren, we have met
Moore, Willis A.
Motherhood
Moravian traditional hymns
Gregor's 39th metre-A; X2053 Confession; X5173 Ich ruehme mich einzig
Hussite hymn
Old 26th; X5203 Ihr seelen, sinkt, ja sinket hin
Morgan, Alfred Phillips, 1857-
St Apollos
Morgan, G.A., 1892-1957
Ashbourne Road
Morgan, Irvin J.
Mant (1895)
Morice, F.D.
Ascendit (19th c)
Moring, Karl Johan, 1832-68
Moring
Morley, Henry L.
Newcastle (1875)
Morley, Thomas, 1845-91
Holborn (1891); X10077 Sion
Muriel
St Alban's; X2374 David
X7092 Morley
Mornington, Garret Colley Wellesley, Earl of, 1735-81
Chant
Mornington
Morris, Mrs. C.H., 1862-1929
I know God's promise is true
I will be true to thee (1913)
In His keeping (1898)
McConnelsville; X6121 Let Jesus come into
Nearer, still nearer (1898); X7122 Morris
Second coming
The fight is on (1905)
Morris, Homer F.
I intend to go through with Him
Morris, Reginald Owen, 1886-1948
Constantia
Hermitage
Winter's snow
Morse, Anna J.
Consecration (1941)
Kemper (1941)
Morse, Charles Henry, 1853-1927
Seccomb (1893)
Morse, Kenneth I., 1913-
Years of youth (1951)
Morson, W.C.T.
Acadia
Mortimer, Alfred G.
Round the throne of glory (1879)
Morton, Alexander B.
Falconer
Oliva
Zeno (1901)
Moschetti, Giuseppi, 1908-
St Francis
Mosley, T.B.
I am trusting in my Saviour
The Lord of glory; X1479a Campmeeting (American trad)
Moss, Edwin, 1838-
Cullingworth (1877)
Llandaff
Moszkowski, Moritz, 1854-1925

Little flower
Motte, Amanda
A call for help
Moulton, W. Fiddian
Advent
St Beatrice
Mountain, James, 1843-1933
Jesus, Saviour, blessed centre
O the bitter shame
Remo; X6198 Like a river; X12487 Wye Valley
Resting; X5579 Jesus, I am resting
Mozarabic plainsong, M 5
Tantum ergo
Mozart, Wolfgang Amadeus, 1756-91
NOTE: Full name, Johannes Chrysostomus Wolfgangus Theophilus.

Agnus dei
Ariel; X7634 O, could I speak; X11228 Though in the outward Church
Ave, verum corpus
Cana; X2758 Dwelling place; X4924 How goodly is thy house; X5471 Janes; X7513 Novalis; X8388 Peace
Dona nobis pacem
Easton
Ellesdie; X2254 Crucifer; X2599 Disciple; X2943 Elleston; X4356 Hark! the voice of Jesus crying; X5582 Jesus, I my cross; X7488 Not alone for mighty; X8465 Pilgrim
Folsom
Home
Jubilee
Mozart I
Mozart II; X7508 Nottingham; X9500 St Mark; X12577 Zelotes
O Gottes Lamm
Pa jorden är allting forander-ligt
Sonata; X10374a Stars of glory
Stars of glory; X10209a Sonata
Mudie, Thomas Mollison, 1809-76
Budleigh
Mueller, Carl F.
Lone Acre (1941)
Overlook Park (1939)
Muir, Alexander
Maple leaf forever
Müller, Hermann von, 1859-1938 see Bonner, Carey, 1859-1938
Müller, I.
Fidelis ad mortem
Müller, J.M., 1683-
NOTE: Associated with a Choralbuch of the Norwegian Church.

Müller
Stobel
Müller, Wenzel, 1767-1835
Abscheid
Mullinar, Michael
Billesley (1927)
Munn, Mrs. S.E.
Father, see thy suppliant children
Munson, Kenneth, 1916-
Cole
Münster Gesangbuch, 1677
Fairest Lord Jesus; X9788 Schönster Herr Jesu
Muret, Marc-Antoine, 1526-85
Gems of day; X6036 Le vermeil du soliel
Murphy, Joseph A.
Jesus dulcis memoria (1937)
Murray, A. Gregory, O.S.B., 1905-
Anglorum apostolus
O King of might (1963)
Surrexit
Murray, J. McCrombie
Nomen (1894)
Murray, James R., 1841-1905
Cling to the Bible
Eudora; X6588 Mabon
Thanks for the Sabbath School
Murrill, Herbert Henry John, 1909-52
Arnold
Musgrave, John T.

Evening shadows (1900)
Ford
Musikalisches handbuch Hamburg, 1690 see Wittwe, Georg ...
Myers, S.S.
The Lord is in His holy temple

N

Nachtenhöfer, Casper Friedrich, 1624-85
Cross-bearer (1651); X10132 So gehst du nun, mein Jesu, hin
Naegeli, Johann (Hans) Georg, 1773-1836
Dennis; X454 And are we yet alive; X1170 Blest be the tie; X4920 How gentle God's; X6401 Lord's Supper
Is there any pleasure
Naomi; X3298 Father, whate'er of earthly bliss
Pastorale
Scott
Naff, Edward D.
We join to pray; X4305 Hand in hand
Nafziger, Olive
My Lord, I'll go
Nanini (or Nanino), Giovanni Maria, ca 1545-1607
Nanini; X7279 Nannini
Stabat mater
Napleton, John, 1850-
Woodchester
Nares, James, 1715-83
Amsterdam (1742); X4079 Gregor's 56th metre; X5184 Ich will's wagen; X9909 Service; X11962 Weimar
Aynhoe; X7286 Nares
Westminster New (1762)
Nash, Charles Ellwood, 1855-1932
Lee
Naumburg, S.
S'u Sh'oreem
Naylor, C.W.
Once again we come (1907)
Naylor, Edward Woodall, 1867-1934
Farnboro (1894)
From strength to strength
Naylor, John, 1838-97
Lift up
Ringland
Neander, Joachim, 1650-80
Arnsberg; X3935 Gott ist gegenwärtig; X4176 Gröningen; X9003 Reverence; X12481 Wunderbarer König
Meine Hoffnung; X12407 Wondrous gift
Neander (1680); X2752 Dusseldorf; X4460 He is risen; X8308 Paran; X8989 Resurrection; X11511 Unser Heerscher [unser König]
Neander II (1679); X5250 In Christo gelebt
Ratisbon, see Werner's Choralbuch, 1815
Sieh hier bin ich, Ehrenkönig (1679); X4593 Here behold me; X5479 Jeg er rede til at bede; X6652 Majesty; X8065 Old 197th
Neefe, Christian Gottlob, 1748-98
Meiringen
Neff, J. Raymond
He comes
Negro spirituals
NOTE: Called American folk melodies in citation Z. See books on Southern (U.S.) traditional and Southern spirituals for further information on this very complicated traditional melodic heritage.

And I couldn't hear nobody pray
Balm in Gilead
Behold the Star
Communion spiritual (a Calhoun melody); X6139 Let us break bread
Deep River
Go down Moses
Go tell it on the mountains

God's heaven
Goodbye, Mourner
Great day
I have a mother over yonder
I want to be a Christian; X6361 Lord, I want to be a Christian
In-a this-a band
It's me
Jacob's ladder; X10161 Soldiers of the cross
Listen to the lambs
Little David
McKee
My Lord, what a mourning; X7230 My Lord, what a morning
Nobody knows
O Mary, don't you weep
Steal away
Sweet chariot
The world's desire
NOTE: Contributed by one of the Theological Seminaries in Atlanta, Georgia. It is presumed to be a Negro traditional spiritual.

War no more
Were you there?
Nellemann, J.
God's plan
Netherlands . . . see Dutch
Neu Ordentlich Gesangbuch, 1646
Steadfast; X107 Ach Gott, verlass mich nicht; X5185 Idag er naadens tid
Neues Geistreiches Gesangbuch. Halle, 1704 see Freylinghausen. Neues Geistreiches Gesangbuch. Halle, 1704
Neukomm, Sigismund Ritter von, 1778-1858
Ames
St Vincent
The Seer, Joseph, the Seer
Neumark, Georg, 1621-81
Neumark (1657); X223 Ah, well it is that God should read; X691 Augsburg; X1297 Bremen; X4984 Hvo ene lader herren raade; X5195 If thou but suffer; X12022 Wer nur den lieben Gott
Neumeister, Erdmann, 1671-1756
Jesus nimmt die sünder an (1718)
Nevin, Alice, 1837-1925
Resurrection
Nevin, George Balch, 1859-1933
Easton
Fidei defensor (1927)
Nevin
New Version. Supplement, 1708
Alfreton
Folkingham
Newman, Richard S., 1850-
Companion
Land of rest (1877)
Newton, Frank E.
Orwell
Nichol, Henry Ernest, 1862-1928
NOTE: Used an acrostic pseudonym, Colin Sterne.

Corelli
Kirk Ella
Lowell (1905)
Message (1896); X2345 Darkness to dawning
Nicholson, Sidney Hugo, 1875-1947
Aethelwold
Airlie
Bow Brick Hill
Chislehurst
Crucifer
Cumulus
Feniton
Hosanna in excelsis
Leamington
Litany of the Passion
Lytlington
Music-makers (1919)
St Nicholas
Tenbury
Totteridge
Welcome Yule
Woodchurch
Nickle, W.S.
Jesus will bear me o'er
Nicolai, Philip, 1556-1608
Frankfort (1599); X196 Af

høiheden oprunden er; X4914 How brightly beams; X7118 Morning Star; X7402 Nicolai; X12089 What tongue can tell; X12252 Wie schön leuchtet [der Morgenstern]
Sleepers, wake (1599); X761 Awake, arise; X4651 Herrnhut; X7403 Nicolai; X7527 Now let every tongue; X11758 Wachet auf!; X11772 Wake, arise; X11773 Wake, awake; Z12570 Zions vaegter
Nielsen, Ludolf, 1876-1939
Nielsen
Niemeyer, Edward
O selig Haus (1854); X4324 Happy home; X7715 O happy home, where thou art
Nigidius, Petrus, 1501-83
Die nacht ist kommen (1550)
Niles, John Jacob, 1892-
Niles (1955)
Nisbet, John MacDonnell, 1857-
Carden Place
Nitzschke, F.R., 1871-
Grace (1908)
Noble, Thomas Tertius, 1867-1953
Annisquam (1938)
Bethlem Land
Ely Cathedral (1895)
Euroclydon (1918)
Mauburn (1918)
New England (1941)
New York (1917)
Ora labora (1918)
Raymond (1917)
Recessional (1918)
Rockport (1938)
St Audrey (1894)
Santa Monica (1938)
Noelsch, William
Noelsch
Norden, Norris Lindsay, 1887-1956
Around the weary world (1932)
Giver of all (1932)
Hymn of spring (1932)
Loud let the swelling anthems rise (1932)
Thy praise, O Lord (1932)
Nordstern. Führer zur Selig-keit, 1671
Eia, Eia; X12574 Zu Bethlehem geboren
Norrbom, August, 1860-
Augustana (1924)
Norris, J.S.
Where He leads me; X3397 Follow all the way; X5037 I can hear my Savior; X7464 Norris
Norris, Thomas, 1741-90
Chant
Northrop, A.
Northrop
Norton, Mrs.
We thank thee, O God, for the Prophet
Norwegian traditional, etc.
NOTE: Several melodies have been specially arranged by Overby. These are marked with an asterisk (*) before the date

Anxious heart (*1931)
Behold a host (Grieg arr)
Blessed host (*1932)
Deus fortis; X5274 In His kingdom
Draw us to Thee
Far verden, far vel; X11077 The sun has gone down
Hardy Norsemen
Hauge; X5269 In heaven above
Heavenly treasures (*1931); X1148 Blessed host; X2477 Den store, hvite flokke; X4034 Great white host; X8739 Purity; X10624 Symphony
In heaven is joy
My cross
Norse air
O can you sing the new song (*1932)
Oslo
Precious child (*1931)
Princess Eugenie
Sabbath chimes (*1931)
Visions of Christ (*1932)
What joy to reach (*)
Yearning (*1931)

Nottingham, S.
Sponsa
Novello, Francis Vincent, 1781-1861
Albano (1800)
Children's prayer
Hail! Jesus, Hail!
Nowakowsky, David
Descend, O Sabbath Princess (1932)
Evening prayer (1932)
Sabbath hymn (1932)
Nürnberg. [Broadside publication] 1541
Allein zu dir, Herr Jesu Christ; X250 Alene til dig, Herre Jesus Krist; X4132 Gregor's 202d metre
Nürnberg Gesangbuch, 1676
O Jesu Christ, mein lebens licht; X4634 Herr Jesu Christ, meines lebens licht; X7771 O Jesu Christe, wahres licht
Sedulius
Nusbaum, Cyrus S.
Would you live for Jesus (1899); X7586 Nusbaum; X4723 His way with thee
Nyberg, Berndt Mikael, 1871-1940
Nyberg
Nyberg, Hugo, 1873-
Helsingfors
Nyland. Piae cantiones, 1582
see Piae cantiones. Griefswald, Finland, 1582

O

Oakeley, Herbert Stanley, 1830-1903
Abends (1873)
Dominica (1875); X2637 Domenica
Ealing
Eastwell
Edina (1868)
Evangelium
Oakley, W. H.
Penitence; X2120 Contrition
Oberammergau. Passion Play.
Oberammergau
O'Connell, William Henry, Cardinal, 1859-1944
Hymn to the Holy Name
O'Connor-Morris, G.
Faith (1932)
Ogden, William A., 1841-97
Any where, Dear Saviour
Baptize us anew
Bring them in; X9959 Shepherd
Deliverance
Lovingly, tenderly calling
Suffer the children to come (1894)
Sweet are the promises; X12161 Where He leads I'll follow
Two little hands
What tender mercy
Ohl, Jeremiah Franklin, 1850-1941
Come and hear the grand old story (1886)
Evening (1884)
Gerhardt (1915)
Lewars (1893)
Pilgrim
St Chrysostom (1910)
Shelter (1912)
Theodoret (1887)
Theophilus (1885)
Ohl, Wesley Jacob, 1864-
Trust (1887)
O'Kane, Tullius C., 1830-1912
Church of God, awake
Home over there; X7923 O think of the home; X10914 The home over there
Mighty rock
O'Kane; X8097 On Jordan's stormy banks
Ola Olude, A. T. see Olude, A. T. Ola
Oldberg, Arne
Gilder (1905)
Olds, William B.
Fons sempiternus (1937)
Pioneers (1937)
Oliver, George Edgar
Albany
Livingston
Oliver

Oliver, Henry Kemble, 1800-85
Federal Street (1832)
Harmony Grove
Merton
Saxony
Oliver, Richard J.
He was wounded
Olivers, Thomas, 1725-99
Helmsley
Olsson, Otto Emanuel, 1879-
Transfiguration
Olude, A.T. Ola
Nigerian tune
Omaha (Indian) traditional
Omaha Peace song
Oratory hymns [Chester?]
Chester; X11531 Urania
Oudaen, J. Amsterdam Psalter, 1685
Vreuchten; X2401 De liefde voortgebracht; X2806 Eastertide; X3326 Festival carol; X11206 This joyful Eastertide
Ouseley, Frederick Arthur Gore, 1825-89
Aberystwyth (1861); X10742 Tenbury
All things bright
Bewdley
Blackie
Christchurch
Contemplation
Glory in the highest (1877); X5261 In excelsis gloria
Hereford
Pruen
St Gabriel (1868); X3560 Gabriel
St Theoctistus (1882)
Sharon (1875)
Tenbury
Woolmer's
Overby, Oscar Rudolph, 1892-
Our Christ
Owen, Frank K.
Knickerbocker (1941)
Owen, Morfydd, 1892-1918
Richard
Owen, R.T.
Open wide thy heart
Owen, William, 1814-93
Bryn Calfaria; X1154 Blessed Lord, in thee; X7147 Mount Calvary
Prysgol
What did He do?

P

Paderborn Gesangbuch, 1765
O purest of creatures; X4236 Hail! Glorious St Patrick; X6576 Lyons (Haydn); X7603 O blessed St Patrick; X8264 Paderborn
Pados, Virginia Bogdan
O love that nothing can efface (1943)
Page, Arthur, 1846-
Lord of might
Paine, John Knowles, 1839-1906
Harvard Hymn
Lincoln (1873)
Paisiello, Giovanni, 1741-1816
Vigil; X4742 Holborn
Palestrina, Giovanni Pierluigi, ca 1525-94
Praeneste
Tantum ergo, No. 2
Victory (1588); X8268 Palestrina; X9751 Savior, Redeemer, God of Love; X12520 Ye sons and daughters
Palmer, Horatio Palmer, 1834-1907
Christ is knocking (1879); X9926 Shall I let Him in
Come, sinner, come; X12180 While Jesus whispers
Follow me; X2766 Each cooing dove
Memories of Galilee
Peace, be still!; X6779 Master, the tempest
Precious Saviour, dear Redeemer
Rose of Sharon
Vincent (1887); X5768 Just for today; X6356 Lord, for tomorrow
Yield not to temptation (1868); X3444 Fortitude; X8277 Palmer

Palmer, M.
Clair Market
Palmer, Peggy Spencer, 1900-
see Spencer Palmer, Florence Margaret, 1900-
Palmer, W. St Clair
Clolata
Palssan, Bjarna, 1857-87
Hin maeta morgunstunden
Paris Antiphoner, 1681
Annue Christe
Christi sanctorum
O quanta qualia; X5439 Itala X8892 Regnator orbis
Sol praeceps rapitur (plainsong, M 3)
Paris Gradual, 1685
Antiphoner
Paris Gradual, 1689
Solemnis haec festivitas
The Parish choir, 1850
Innocents; X600 As the sun doth daily; X1772 Christmas (Handel)
Parker, Edwin Pond, 1836-1925
Dawn
Love's offering (1888)
Parker, Handel, 1857-1929
Deep harmony
Parker, Horatio William, 1836-1919
Ancient of Days (1903)
Auburndale (1893)
Clovelly (1903)
Courage
Foundation (1903)
Garden City (1893); X2389 Day of praise
Holy Day
Jubilate (1894); X8906 Rejoice, the Lord is King
King of Glory
Mission (1894)
Mount Sion (1886)
Parker (1894); X11645 Vexilla regis
Pax veritatis (1918)
Pixham (1901)
Pro patria (1900); X1164 Blessing and honor; X8315 Parker
Stella (1893); X8316 Parker
Victor's crown (1893)
Vox aeterna (1903)
Whittingham (1887)
Parker, James Cutler Dunn, 1828-1916
God hath sent his angels; X2789 Easter angels
Parker, Leonard
Panoply of light
Parker, Robert
St Alkmund (1868)
Parkyn, Walter A.
Vesper
Parr, Henry, 1815-
St Quintin (1834)
Parratt, Walter, 1841-1924
Huddersfield
Obiit
Parratt (1904)
Parry, Charles Hubert Hastings, 1848-1918
Angmering
Bishopthorpe
Bournemouth
Freshwater
Infantium laudes
Intercessor (1904)
Jerusalem
Jubilate
Laudate dominum
Marylebone
Nature
Newfoundland
Repton
Rustington
Parry, Edwin F.
Hail to the brightness
O holy words of truth
Parry, Joseph, 1841-1903
Aberystwyth (1879)
Dinbych
Llangristiolus
Merthry Tydvil; X2578 Dies irae
O home beloved, where'er I wander
St Joseph
Parsons, Ernest J.
Sturges (1941)
Patton, Arthur St George, 1853-92
St Kevin
Vigil
Peace, Albert Lister, 1844-

1912
Crux crudelis
Edom (1885)
Fight of faith
Green Hill (1885)
Guild
Lux beata
St Margaret (1885); X6443 Love that will not let me go; X6711 Margaret
Submission
Peace, Lister R., 1885-
Nova vita (1914)
Pearce, James
Protection
Pearsall, Robert Lucas de, 1795-1856
Gloria
Pearsall (1863); X4247 Hail! holy Joseph
St Hildred
Peek, Joseph Yates, 1843-1911
Peek; X5155 I would be true
Peel, Frederick
Heslington (1893)
Heslington, No. 2 (1894)
Peery, Rob Roy, 1900-
Byrd (1929)
Stirewalt (1927)
Peloquin, C. Alexander
O Jesu! life-spring (1959)
Penn, W.E.
The sheltering rock
Penner, Edwin
Trust your hand into His
Pensum Sacrum. Görlitz, 1648
Herr Jesu Christ, dich zu uns wend
NOTE: John Hus is the supposed composer, cf books AZ and BA herein; X312 All things are thine; X1508 Cantionale; X4977 Hus; X6368 Lord Jesus Christ, be present now; X8566 Prague; X11963 Weimar
Perkins, C.W.
Heathfields
Perkins, E.A.
Perkins
Perkins, Emily Swan, 1866-
Burg (1921)
Eastman (1937)
Good cheer (1927)
Laufer (1925)
Peterson (1921)
Riverdale
Perkins, Henry Southwick, 1833-1914
Victors
Perkins, Theodore Edson, 1831-1912
Caskey
Freely give
Lundie; X3207 Fade, fade, each earthly joy; X6823 Meditation; X8430 Perkins
Magill
More love to Thee (1875)
Nazareth
Repentance
Sabbath Evening
The love of Jesus
Wyoming
Perkins, Thomas E.
On the radiant threshold (1923)
Perkins, William Oscar, 1831-1902
Amara
Beyond the sunset
Did you think to pray; X2657 Don't forget to pray; X3016 Ere you left your room
Guernsey
Jesus, thou hast promised
Only thee
Perosi, Don Lorenzo, 1872-1956
L'Emmanuello; X5621 Jesus, Lord, be thou mine own
O cor Jesu
O sacrum convivium
Tantum ergo (1937)
Perry, E. Cooper
Spes unica (1889)
Vesalius (1895)
Perry, J.C.
Bid them look to Christ
Perry, S.J.
Saviour, we come to thee
Persichetti, Vincent, 1915-
Contrition
Lament (1956)
Peruchot, Luigi
The heavens are Thine

Pescott, Frank Denty, 1880-
Guernsey
Peter, Christopher, 1626-69
Christopher; X5201 Ihr gestirn'
Das herrlich hohe fest (ca 1674)
Petersen, H.H.
O'er the gloomy hills of darkness
There is an hour of peace
Peterson, Samuel E., 1869-
Rondthaler
Pettet, A., ca 1785- ca 1845
Hic breve vivitur
Pettman, Charles Edgar, 1866-1943
Love incarnate
Pfautsch, Lloyd, 1921-
Euclid (1964)
Phillips, H.
New Sabbath (ca 1806)
Phillips, Philip, 1834-75
Home of the soul; X5148 I will sing; X5151 I will sing you a song
One sweetly solemn thought
Pilgrims mission
Phillips, Thomas, 1735-1807
Lydia
Piae Cantiones. Griefswald, Finland, 1582
NOTE: See Oxford book of carols, p. 291, for the history of this book.

Athens
Congaudeat
Divinum mysterium (13th c plainsong M 5); X2141 Corde natus; X2143 Corde natus ex parentis
Ein kind geborn; X2419 Dear Maker of the starry skies; X5249 In Bethlehem, that fair city; X8726 Puer natus
Gabriel's message
In vernali tempore; X10323 Spring has come
January carol
O mentes perfidas
Psallat fidelis concio
Puer nobis nascitur; X8090 Omega and alpha; X8733 Puer nobis nascitur; X9840 Sedulius; X10307 Splendour; X11515 Unto us a boy is born
Tempus adest floridum; X3905 Good King Wenceslas
The word itself
Theodoric; X8104 On this day earth shall ring; X8433 Personent hodie; X10057 Sing aloud on this day
Piel, P.
Ad sacratissimum cor Jesu
Daily, daily sing to Mary
Dear crown of all the virgin choir
O heart of Mary
With tender greeting
Pieraccini, Emilio, 1828-1902
Santa Trinita; X1941 Come, Holy Ghost, who ever one; X11381 Trinity
Pierce, Jason Noble, 1880-
Penfield
Pierre, Maitre, see also French Psalter, 1562 and Genevan Psalter, 1562
Dominus sanctus (1562)
Gloria (1562)
Pierre (1562)
Sovereign grace (1562)
Trumpet (1562)
Pierson, Hugo
For thee, O dear, dear country
Pilgrimsharpan
Mer helighet gif mig
Pilsbury. United States' harmony, 1799
Bartimaeus; X1614 Charleston; X1616 Charlestown
Pincott, Frank
Christ, my Life
Pinder, F.
Temple Boro
Pisani, Umberto
Armoria Biblica
Pisani
Pitts, William S., 1829-1903
Princethorpe; X8493 Pitts
Wildwood; X6254 Little brown church

Plainsongs

NOTE: It has seemed more practical to arrange by traditional tune name (followed by mode number), than numerically by mode. Few source notes are given.

It must be remembered that countless additional plainsongs are cited under place name, rite, publication, or personal name (when presumed accurate).

A solis ortus cardine M 3
Adesto, Sancta Trinitas M 3
Aeterna Christi munera M 7
Alma redemptoris Mater M 5
Annue Christi, saeculorum Domini M 1
Attende M 5; X667 Attende, Domini
Audi, benigne conditor M 2 (major reading)
Audi, benigne conditor M 3 (minor reading)
Aurora lucis rutilat, Pt. I, M 4; X1829 Claro paschali gaudio
Ave Maria M 1
Ave, maris stella M 1
Ave, Regina caelorum M 6
Bone pastor M 7 (12th c)
Christe, qui lux es et dies (ca 600); X1747 Christe, der du bist tag und licht; X4069 Gregor's 22d metre-D; X8555 Prague
Christe qui lux es et dies M 2
Christe sanctorum decus angelorum M 8
Clarum decus jejunii M 2
Cor Jesu sacratissimum M 1
Cultor dei, memento M 8
Dies irae (13th c)
Ecce nomen Domine Emmanuel
Ecce! Panis angelorum M 8; X5998 Lauda Sion
Ecce tempus idoneum M 3
Eia, Jesu adorande M 3
Ex more docti mystico M 2
Exultet caelum laudibus M 4
Exultet caelum laudibus M 8; X2529 Deus, tuorum militum
Felix dies M 2
Gestum matris gloriosae M 2
Gloria, laus et honor M 1
Hamburg M 1 (Lowell Mason arr, 1844); X1232 Boston; X11733 Voice divine; X12122 When I survey the wondrous cross
Hostis Herodes impie M 3
In dich hab ich Gehofft, Herr (Jan Kern arr, 1964)
In manus tuas M 6
In manus tuas M 6
In manus tuas (Eastertide) M 6
Iste confessor
Iste confessor M 2
Iste confessor M 8
Jam Christus astra ascenderat M 1
Jerusalem et Sion filiae M 5
Jesu, quadragenariae M 4; X7851 O nata lux de lumina; X9646 Salutis humanae sator
Laetabundus M 5 (11th c)
Languentibus in purgatorio
Lauda Sion M 7 (12th c)
Magnae Deus potentiae M 2
Martyr Dei M 6
Mundi salus affutura M 8
Nazareth (arr by S. Webbe)
Non nobis, Domini
Nunc Sancte M 8
Nunc Sancte, nobis, Spiritus M 4
O amor quam ecstaticus M 1
O Emmanuel (major antiphon) M 2
O gloriosa virginum M 2
O salutaris Hostia M 7
O salutaris Hostia M 8
Olmutz M 7 (arr by Lowell) Mason, 1834)
Optatus votis M 4
Oremus pro Pontifice M 1
Our Father
Palm Sunday anthem M 1
Parce, Domini M 1
Paule, doctor egregie M 7
Prayer for a holy death M 1
Puer natus in Bethlehem M 1
Quem terra, pontus, aethera

M 2
Rector potens, verax Deus M 2
Regina caeli laetáre M 6
Rerum Deus tenax vigor M 4
Rorate, caeli M 1
St Gregory (arr by Joseph Barnby)
Salus aeterna M 7 (before 11th c)
Salve, Mater M 5
Salve Regina M 5
Save us waking
Sponsa Christi quae per orbem M 1-2
Sub tuum praesidium M 7
Tantum ergo M 5
Te, Joseph, celebrent M 1
Te lucis, arr
Te lucis ante terminum M 8
To God on high (adapted, in Schumann, Gesangbuch, 1539) X249 Alene Gud i Himmerig; X275 All glory be to thee; X341 Allein Gott in der höh sei ehr; X669 Attolle paulum; X2430 Decius; X2910 Elberfeld; X3696 Give thanks to God; X4280 Halle; X6486 Lucis creator optime; X9565 St Peter
Ut queant laxis M 2
Veni Emmanuel M 1; X7631 O come, O come, Immanuel; X11592 Veni, Immanuel; X11601 Veni, veni Emmanuel
Veni, O Sapientiae
Veni, Redemptor gentium M 1; X916 Beata nobis gaudia
Victimi Paschali M 1 (major reading) (12th c); X1712 Christ ist erstanden; X1721 Christ lag in todesbanden
Victimi Paschali M 1 (minor reading) (12th c)
Virginia proles M 8
Westmoreland (arr by Barnby)
Planque (no initials)
O cor amoris victima
Playford, John. Whole book of Psalms, 1677
Worcester
Pleyel, Ignaz Joseph, 1757-1831
Brattle Street
Grace Church (1815); X9581 St Polycarp
Onido
Pleyel's Hymn (1791); X8517 Pleyel; X11185 Thine forever; God of love
Savannah
Seasons; X5975 Larue
Plymouth collection see Beecher, H. W. Plymouth collection
Poitiers Antiphoner, 1746
Auctoritate saeculi; X5559 Jesu, dulcedo cordium
Poitiers Vesperale, 1740
Rouen; X5426 Iste confessor
Polack, Herman Adolph, 1862-1930
Clairvaux (1910)
Horeb (1910)
Polish traditional, etc.
Come, O Lord Jesus
Poland; X11583 Veni Creator Spiritus
Slumber, O slumber
Teshiniens (ca 1500)
W Zlobie Lezy; X5334 Infant holy; X8526 Polish carol
Warsaw
Polleri, G. B.
Ecce panis angelorum; X1206 Bone pastor
Pollock, Charles Edward, 1853-
Abide with me, I need thee
Bless the words; X1555 Carrington; X10642 Take my heart, O Father
Come to Jesus
Come, ye wanderers
Forever here my rest; X9212 Sadie
Full salvation
Gouldie
He knoweth the way that I take
Home of the soul
How oft, alas; X6797 May
I bring my sins to Jesus
I love to steal awhile away; X6093 Lella
I love to think of my home; X7218 My home above
I wonder

Lead me on
Morrow's Hill
My God, how endless is thy love; X7396 Nicholls
Nearing the port
O holy day
Often weary and worn; X8975 Rest by and by
Open the wells of salvation
Parousia; X6294 Lo! He comes, with clouds descending
Praise the Lord
Precious Jesus, O to love thee (1901)
Salonica
Shoemaker
Some near, near day
There are hearts that never falter (1901)
Thou art the way; X7278 Nannie
Violet
Walk daily with your Saviour
Wonderful grace

Pond, Sylvanus Billings, 1792-1871
Armenia (1835)
Henry (1835)
The bird let loose see Franklin Square (perhaps by S. B. Pond, 1850)
The heavens

Ponsonby, A. B.
Deo gratias (1913)

Pontius, William H.
Eighmey (1905)
Holy Hill (1905)
Waiting and watching

Poole, Clement William 1828-1924
Petersham

Poole, Henry James, 1843-97
St Lucy

Poppen, Emmanuel, ca 1870-1950
Joy (1904)
Poppen (1910)
Sidney
Wonder (1907)

Popple, Herbert
St Aidan (1931)

Porter, Hugh Boring, 1897-
Builders (1927)
Renascence (1927)

Porter, John, pseud see McCutchan, Robert Guy, 1877-

Portnersches Gesangbuch, 1831
O Christliche herzen

Portugal (or Portogallo), Marcos Antonio da Fonseca (real name Ascençao) 1762-1830.
Sicilian Mariners (1794)
NOTE: Sometimes attributed to this author. The dates correspond, but Baker's Biographical dictionary makes no mention.

Portuguese melody
Ecce panis angelorum

Poteat, Edwin McNeill, 1892-1955
Bow down thine ear
Oikoumenikos
Quest

Pothier, Joseph, O. S. B., 1835-1923
Thou that art so fair

Powell, C., 1855-1931
What do I owe?

Powell, James Baden, see Baden-Powell, James

Powell, Joseph P.
Sorrows

Powell, Robert J., 1932-
Author of life (1964)

Praetorius, Michael, 1571-1621
NOTE: Name, originally Schultheiss, was Latinized.

Ach Herr
Das alte Jahre ist nun dahin (1609)
Es geh, wies woll (1610); X3067 Et trofast hjerte, Herre min
Ich dank' dir schon (1610); X4064 Gregor's 15th metre
Melody (1610)
Praetorius I (1599); X3554 Für dein empfangen speis und trank
Praetorius II (1536 mel.

arr. 1609); X111 Ach Gott vom himmelreiche; X5219 I'll Thee exalt
Wenn meine sünd (1609)
Pratt, John Barnes, 1865-
Dorothy (1929)
Presbrey, O. F.
Not half has ever been told
Price, Carl Fowler, 1881-
Ferree
Milburn (1941)
The Morning Watch (1913)
Washington (1905)
Price, John (Beulah), 1857-
Gwyneth
Price, Tom, 1857-1925
Bugail Israel
Joseph
Prichard, Rowland Hugh, 1811-87
Hyfrydol (1830); X5278 In humility, our Saviour
Pritchard, Thomas Cuthbertson Leithead, 1885-
Belhaven (1927)
Gifford (1927)
Leithead (1927)
Prothero, H.A.
St Ninian
Prout, Ebenezer, 1835-1909
Allen; X4052 Greenwood
Cairnbrook
Hurst Monceaux
Laus sempiterna
Raleigh
Via lucis
Prys, Edmund. Psalms, 1621
St Mary; X9510 St Mary's
The Psalmist, 1830
Halle
Psalmodia Evangelica, 1789
Bromsgrove
Psalteriolum harmonicum, 1642
Ave Maria klare
Psalterium chorale. Constance, 1510
Beata nobis gaudia; X1638 Cherubic hymn
Public School hymn book, 1929
Pax
Pullen, Alice M.
Cottingham (20th c)
Purcell, Henry, ca 1659-95
Bow down in worship
Burford
The Lord bless you
Walsall (1699)
Westminster Abbey
Purday, Charles Henry, 1799-1885
Notting Hill
Sandon (1860)
Putman, L. G.
Christus rex
Pyper, George D.
Does the journey seem long?

Q

Quaile, Robert Newton, 1867-
Athlone (1911)
Old Bridge (1903); X10772 Thanksgiving

R

R. E.
Boxted (1935)
R. J. C.
Calvert (1910)
Rader, Paul
Only believe (1921)
Randall, John, 1715-99
Cambridge; X1472 Cambridge new; X8796 Randall
Lewes
Randall; X1601 Chant
Randegger, Alberto, 1832-1911
Evening prayer
Rappaport, S.
The Lord -- The Lord of glory reigns
Rau, Albert George
Unami (1889)
Rau, Robert, 1844-1906
Grabesruhe (1864); X8817 Rau; X9163 Ruhe ist des todes schlummer
Nightfall (1877)
Ravanello, Oreste, 1871-1938
Gloria, laus et honor
Tantum ergo
Ravenscroft's Psalter, 1621
Bristol; X1332 Bristol, No. 1

Durham
Gloucester
Lincoln
Norwich
Old 104th; X8821 Ravenscroft
Remember; X429 America
(Thesaurus musicus, 1740)
St David; X9359 St David's
Salisbury
Raymond-Barker, C., S.J.
Let the deep organ swell
Read, David (or Daniel), 1757-1836
Lisbon; X959 Begin the day with God
Windham
Reay, Samuel, 1822-
Brotherhood
Chorley (1876)
Comforter Divine
Laus sempiterna
Undique gloria (1872)
Recueil de cantiques
Swiss melody; X8482 Pilgrims of the night
Redhead, Richard, 1820-1901
Alma Mater
Holy Offerings (1870)
Lauds (1850)
Metzler's Redhead No. 66 (1859); X6931 Metzler; X8864 Redhead; X8872 Redhead, No. 66; X11891 Waveney
Petra (1853); X230 Ajalon; X3667 Gethsemane; X8865 Redhead; X8873 Redhead, No. 76
Redhead
Redhead, No. 1 (1870); X5430 "It is finished"
Redhead, No. 46; X2693 Dresden; X6017 Laus deo
St Chad
St Ebbe (1853)
St Nicholas (1859); X2428 Debenham; X9531 St Nicholas; X10367 Star of Jacob
St Prisca (1853); X8866 Redhead; X8871 Redhead, No. 47; X8973 Rest; X9363 St Dunstan; X10747 Tenebrae
St Victor
Wolverhampton
Redner, Lewis Henry, 1831-1908
St Louis (1868); X1060 Bethlehem; X7807 O little town of Bethlehem
Reed, Luther Dotterer, 1873-
Mount Airy (1958)
Rees, Gomer Christmas, 1872-
Resolven (1915)
Rees, John Thomas, 1858-1912
Dole
Regnart (or Regnard), Jacob, ca 1540-99
Göttingen (1574); X686 Auf meinen lieben Gott; X4085 Gregor's 75th metre; X 8891 Regnart; X3543 Fryd dig, du kristi brud
Reichardt, Louise (or Luise), 1779-1826
Schlaf, Kindlein, schlaf; X10106 Sleep, holy Babe
Reimann, John Balthasar, 1702-49
O herre Gott, in meiner Not (1747)
O Jesu (1741); X7780 O Jesu, warum legst
Reimann's 315th metre (1747); X8895 Reimann; X12380 Wollt ihr wissen was
Reinagle, Alexander Robert, 1799-1877
Ben Rhydding
Kidlington (1865)
Leigh
Moccas
St Peter (1836); X7211 My God, I love thee; X9570 St Peter's, Oxford
Reinecke, Carl Heinrich Carsten, 1824-1910
Evening prayer
Morning prayer
Tenderness
Reinigius, P. Haus Kirchen Cantorie, 1587
O Jesu Christ
Reissiger, F.A., 1809-83
Lord of spirits
Reissiger, Karl Gottlieb, 1798-1859

Beloit
Reitz, Albert S., 1879-
Reitz (1925)
Remondi, R.
O sacrum convivium
Remsberg, Wilson L.
Hope
Rendle, Lily, 1875-
Ellah (1928)
Everyland, No. 1 (1933)
Mariners (1935)
Pax (1928)
Vesper hymn (1930)
Reuter, Friedrich Otto (Fritz), 1863-1924
New Ulm (1910)
Reuter
The Revivalist, 1869
Peace
Reynolds, Isham E., 1879-1949
Jesus, my Lord, is real to me (1933)
Lura; X12151 When the sun shines bright
Venting (1925); X12399 Wonderful peace
Reynolds, William J., 1920-
Create in me
Rheinberger, Josef Gabriel, 1839-1901
O salutaris hostia
Rheinhardt, J.H. Choralbuch. Uttingen, 1754
Was lebet, was schwebet; X11543 Uttingen
Rice, Elihu S.
Shall we meet (1866)
Rich, C.B.
Comfort (1932)
Compassion
Richards, B.
Let the whole creation ring
Richards, Charles H.
Redeemer's praise
Richards, G. Darlington
Holmbush (1938)
Julian (1939)
Richards, Henry Brinley, 1817-89
NOTE: Used pseud Emmelar.
Armstrong; X9031 Richards; X12527 Yes, for me He careth
Richards, John (Isalaw), 1843-1908
Sanctus
Richardson, John J., 1816-79
Again the slowly circling year
Hail, thou Star of Ocean
Love
Tichfield; X1421 By the blood that flowed
Richter, Christian Friedrich, 1676-1711
Gregor's 114th metre (1714); X6843 Mein Salomo, dein freundliches
Wie gross ist des allmacht' gen güten (1703)
Rider, H. deK.
Angelus
Gentle Saviour
Ridsdale, Charles Joseph, 1840-
None other Lamb
Righini, Vincenzo, 1756-1812
Righini
Rimbault, Edward Francis, 1816-76
Delhi
Happy day (1854)
Clarion
Rinck, Johann Christian Heinrich, 1770-1846
Alle jahre wieder
Overberg
St Lucian; X70 Abend [ist es wieder]; X3152 Evening sun descending; X8767 Rabenlei
Rinder, Reuben R.
Psalm 42 (1932)
Thou ever present Perfect Friend (1932)
Rinehart, Thomas Franklin, 1860-
Adrian (1901)
Robbins, Howard Chandler, 1876-1952
Chelsea Square (1941)
Roberts, Arthur Owen, 1869-1952
Blodyn
Hoylake
Roberts, Caradog, 1878-1935
Berwyn
Margaret

Rachie
Roberts, David E., 1863-
Goodwill (1925)
Roberts, J. Varley
Elm
Roberts, John (Ieuan Gwyllt) 1822-77
Ardudwy
Bethel
Bont-Newydd
Four Seas (1859)
Liverpool
Moab (1870)
Rheidol
Roberts, John Dryhurst, 1862-
Caergybi (1883)
Roberts, John Henry, 1848-1924
O grant us light
Roberts, Robert, 1863-
Alice
Roberts, Robert Edwin, 1878-1940
Philippine
Robertson, Leroy J., 1896-
Go, ye messengers
God of our fathers, known of old; X6376 Lord of all being
Great King of heaven
I'm a pilgrim; I'm a stranger
Let earth's inhabitants rejoice
Lo! on the water's brink
O happy home! O blest abode
The glorious gospel light
Up! arouse thee, O beautiful Zion
Upon the cross of Calvary
We love thy House, O God
Robertson, Robert B.
Snowden
Robinson, W. O.
M.I.A. we hail thee
Roe, John Edward, 1838-71
Gentle Jesus
Onward (1870)
Weston
Roff, Joseph
Great King of Peace (1959)
Rogers, Benjamin, 1614-98
Hymnus eucharisticus; X6628 Magdalen Tower hymn; X10985 The Magdalen Tower hymn
Rogers, H. E.
Church of God
Rogers, James Hotchkiss, 1857-1940
A little kingdom I possess (1932)
Lo, our Father's tender care (1932)
May He who kept us (1932)
Thankful hearts (1932)
The wise may bring their learning (1932)
The worth of suffering (1932)
Uplift the song of praise (1932)
We build our school on thee (1932)
We thank thee (1932)
Rogers, W. J.
Humble thyself to walk
Roh, Johann, d 1547 see
Horne, Johann, d 1547
Rolle, Johann Heinrich, 1716-85
Praise the Lord
Roman hymnal (date unknown)
Consecration to Our Lady
What mortal tongue can sing
The Roman hymnal, 1884
O Mother blest
Ronan, John E.
Out of the depths (20th c)
Rooper, J. B.
Risby (1925)
Root, George Frederick, 1820-95
NOTE: Pseud Friedrich Wurzel
Beauteous day
Children of Jerusalem
Clymer
Come to the Saviour (1870) X5382 Invitation
Ellon (1871); X5092 I love to hear the story; X10443 Story of love
Firmament
Harvest home; X7954 O, where are the reapers
In the silent midnight watches

Jesus loves the little children
Like a strong and raging fire; X9793 School thy feelings; X11170 There's a song
Lyra
Now to Jesus Christ
Quam dilecta
Return, O wanderer
Rialto; X2239 Crossing the bar
Ring the bells of heaven
Rosedale
Sheffield; X12241 Why do you wait?
Shining Shore; X7194 My days are gliding
The hem of His garment
Varina (1856); X3195 Extol the love of Christ; X11141 There is a land
When He cometh (1866); X5696 Jewels
Roper, Charles F.
Arimathea
Blessed morn (1883)
Jerusalem (1872)
Rosche, George F.
A shelter in the time of storm (1894)
Have faith in God
He keepeth me ever (1891)
Rosecrans, James H.
Glenn (1890)
Worley
Rosenmüller, Johann, ca 1620-84
Calvary (1655)
Nassau; X1209 Bonn; X2062 Confirmation; X6606 Mache dich, mein geist; X7401 Nicolai; X9529 St Nicolai; X9865 Segne uns; X10243 Songs of praise; X10453 Straf mich nicht; X11354 Traeder nu til Herrens Bord; X12334 Wirtemburg; X12482 Würtemburg
Rosenmüller (1649)
Rosenroth, Christian Knorr von, 1636-89
Old 29th; X2122 Contrition; X4686 Hier legt mein sinn
Ross, Roger Rowson, 1817-99
St Peter's, Manchester; X9567 St Peters'
Ross, William Baird, 1871-1951
Carillon (1925)
Rossini, Gioachino Antonio, 1792-1888
Captain of Israel's host
Elation
Faith
Linwood; X8118 One God! One Lord
Manoah (1851)
Warner
Rostacker Gesangbuch, 1659
Gregor's 151st metre-H; X956 Befiehl du deine wege; X8686 Protector
Rostockhandboken, 1529
Ter sanctus; X11652 Vi lofve dig, o store Gud; X11795 Wallin
Rötscher, J. F.
Exodus (1790)
Rouen church melodies
Aeterna Christi munera
Ave verum, M 5
Because you live again (1728); X2178 Coutances
Christi fons jugis; X9139 Rouen
Coelites plaudant (17th c); X9140 Rouen
Jesu corona
Prompto gentes animo; X12305 Windrush
Rouen
St Venantius
Ut queant laxis (1681)
Rounsefell, Carrie E., 1861-1930
I'll go where you want me to go (1894); X2091 Consecration; X5434 It may not be on the mountain; X6673 Manchester; X7160 Mountain's height
Rousseau, Jean-Jacques, 1712-78
Greenville (1825); X1996 Come, ye sinners; X6353 Lord, dismiss us; X9143 Rousseau

Routley, Erik Reginald, 1917-
Cliff Town (1951)
Abingdon
Mill Brow
Sutton Courtenay
Varndean
Wych Cross
Rowlands, William Penfro, 1860-1937
Blaenwern
Rubbra, Edmund, 1901-
The Virgin's cradle hymn (1925)
Rubin, A.
Father, see thy suppliant children
Ruebush, J. H.
Booker
God knows what is best (1897)
Ruebush, W. H.
Something to do
Rung, Henrik, 1807-71
Jutland
Rung I
Rung II
Runkel, Kenneth E.
Eternal Light (1941)
Runyan, William M., 1870-
Faithfulness; X4022 Great is thy faithfulness
Not what these hands have done (1935)
Teach me thy will, O Lord (1935)
What God hath promised
Rupp, H. S.
Bringing home the sheaves
Give me a foothold
Jerusalem, my happy home; X1493 Canaan
Rusbridge, A. Ewart, 1917-
Horfield
Rush, E. Leonard, C.S.B.
Tantum ergo (20th c?)
Russell, E. H.
Pittsburgh
Seal
Russell, Frederick George, 1867-1929
Lombard Street (1929)
Russell, S. L.
Charing (1931)
Stanstead (1931)
Sutton Valence (1931)
Russian traditional, etc.
Blessed light
Come let us worship (19th c ?)
Easter eggs; X2320 Dalalin
Praise to God; X2805 Easter song
Volga boatman
Rutström, Andreas Carl, 1721-72
Min blodige konung
Ruud, Gordon C., 1920-
Madagascar (1958)
Ryley, Geoffrey Charles Edward, 1866-1947
Canon VIII
East Peckham
Sarratt

S

S. M. W. V. R.
NOTE: This is a joint initial pseud of Martin Shaw and Ralph Vaughan Williams; used for melody "Cobbold". The order, W. V. R., seems to indicate this composer's preference to be known as "Williams", rather than "Vaughan Williams".

Sabel, S.
Early will I seek thee
Sacred harmony. Leeds, ca 1720
Castleford
Sacred harmony, 1780
Derbe
Sacred harp, 1844
Wedlock
Sacred hymns and tunes. Boston, 1880
Eden
Sacred hymns and tunes. Bristol, 1876
Bona patria
St Alban's Tune Book, 1866
Holborn Hill; X2960 Elven; X9239 St Alban; X9240 St Alban, No. 1; X8414 Penitence
Lebbaeus; X1663 Children's litany; X4299 Hampden-

Sidney; X6235 Litany; X6240 Litany, No. 2; X6244 Litany, No. 5 (Hoyte); X9890 Septem voces (Hoyte); X9898 Septem voces
Messengers; X9238 St Alban
Mill Lane (No. 10)
St Gall Cantarium, 1845
The Lord whom earth
St Gall Gesangbuch, 1863
Harvest hymn
St Gall
St Patrick (ascribed to) 372-466 A.D.
St Patrick; X4237 Hail glorious St Patrick; X7093 Morley; X9555 St Patrick's Breastplate
St Peter Damian, †1072
Ave Maris stella
Saint-Saëns, Charles Camille, 1835-1921
Ave verum corpus
Tollite hostias
Sampaix, Leon
Allegiance
Baker Chapel
Dorothy
Elizabeth
White ribbon
Samuel, Edward
Great Arbiter of human fate
Tent-like this day
Sanders, Harry
Mighty to save
Sanders, Robert L., 1906-
Adam's Song (1961)
Binyon (1961)
Ganador (1958)
Keith (1958)
Misericorde (1932)
Pont Neuf (1961)
Promise (1932)
Wheelock (1961)
Woodlawn (1934)
Sanderson, Wilfred
Conisborough
Sandström, Israel
I know a way
Sanger, Florence Ziegler, 1906-
Communion meditation
Sankey, I. Allen
Anniversary (1907?)
Sankey, Ira David, 1840-1908
A shelter in the time of storm
Am I a soldier
Be ye strong in the Lord
Beneath the cross
Have you sought?
I am praying for you; X1869 Cluff; X5049 I have a Savior; X5366 Intercession; X8621 Praying for you
Newcastle
O safe to the Rock; X4685 Hiding [in Thee]; X9707 Sankey; X9954 Shelter
O, wondrous Name (1886)
Only remembered
Room for Thee (1881)
Sankey
Take me as I am
Tell it out, arr (1881)
Ten thousand times ten thousand
The ninety and nine
Trusting Jesus
Under His wings (1896)
Victory; X2985 Encamped along the hills; X3222 Faith is the victory; X9708 Sankey
Walking in the sunshine
Welcome
When the mists have rolled away
While the days are going by
Sargent, N.B.
Building for eternity
Sarum plainsongs
NOTE: Tune name is followed by mode, source and approximate date (when known).

Ad cenam agni providi, M 8 (11th c)
Aeterna Rex, M 8 (Sarum Antiphonal)
Aurora lucis rutilat, Pt I, M 8 (Sarum Antiphonal)
Chorus novae Jerusalem, M 3
Christe redemptor, M 1; X1756 Christe, redemptor omnium; X5563 Jesu dulcis memoria; X5663 Jesu redemptor

Christe sanctorum, M 1
Conditor alme, M 4; X2052 Conditor alme siderum; X2206 Creator, alme siderum; X6484 Lucis creator; X8499 Plainsong M 4
Deus creator omnium, M 4 (Sarum Antiphonal); X8498 Plainsong
Ecce jam noctis, M 4
Gloria, laus et honor, M 1 (Sarum Processional)
Immense caeli conditor, M 2
Lucis creator, M 8
Nocte surgentes, M 6; X8500 Plainsong M 6
O lux beata Trinitas, M 8
O Pater Sancte, M 4 (Sarum Antiphonal)
Pange lingua, M 3
Primo dierum omnium, M 4 (6th c)
Salve, festa dies, M 4
Sanctorum meritis, M 7; X8292 Panis angelicus
Splendor paternae, M 1; X6518 Lumina; X7537 Nox et tenebrae et nubila; X10312 Splendor paternae gloriae
Te lucis, M 8
The Rosy Sequence (Sarum Gradual, 1527, 28, & 32); X3468 Fragment
Urbs beata, M 2
Veni creator, M 8
Verbum supernum, M 2
Vexilla regis, M 1; X11615 Verbum supernum; X11649 Vexilla regis prodeunt

Sateren, Leland Bernhard, 1913-
Eldora (1958)
Marlee (1958)

Schachner, J.R.
Brompton

Schafer, Norman W.H., 1858-
Ecclesia (1900)

Schalit, Heinrich
A week within the Sukko green (1932); X9993 Sh'meenee atseres
Almighty Father (1932)
Our Father, we beseech thy grace (1932)
The cry of Israel (1932)

Scheffler, Johann. Heilege Seelenlust, 1657
Culbach; X1726 Christ, the glory of the sky; X11712 Virgin wholly marvelous
Scheffler; X4562 Helfer meiner armen seele; X6236 Litany

Scheidemann, David, 1570-1625
Puer nobis nascitur

Scheidt, Samuel, 1587-1654
O Jesulein süss (1623); X7728 O Heiliger Geist, O Heiliger Gott; X7805 O little one; X10826 The Child Jesus

Schein, Johann Hermann, 1586-1630
Der Heilige Geist hernierderkam (1627)
Eisenach (1629); X5431 It is no earthly summer's ray X6088 Leipsic; X6607 Mach's mit mir Gott; X6985 "Mir nach," Spricht Christus, unser; X9776 Schein; X10033 Silesius; X12080 What happiness can; X12338 Wismar
Ravenshaw
Zion Klagt (1623)

Schemelli, G.C. Gesangbuch, 1736
To Thee, O Lord

Schicht, Johann Gottfried (i.e. "Theophil"), 1753-1823
Ascendit Deus
Majesty (1819)
Manna
Mir ist erbarmung Widerfahren; X3015 Erbarmung
Mittler, schau auf sie hernieder (1819)
Zu meinem herrn

Schiller, Friedrich von. Ode an die Freude, 1799
An die freude

Schilling, Frederick
Beautiful Star
Schilling (1865)

Schlicht, Ludolf E.
Gregor's 243d metre (1744); X2469 Dem heiligen blute des herrn zu gefallen
Schmid, Bernhardt. Orgelbuch. Strassburg, 1577
Herzlich liebe hab ich dich, o Herr; X4145 Gregor's 232d metre; X5480 Jeg har dig hjerteligen kjaer
Schmidlin, Jean, fl 1796
Swiss tune; X2694 Dresden; X10617 Switzerland
Schmidt, C.
What star is this; X12072 What beauteous sun surpassing star
Schmidt, Johann Eusebius
Fahre fort; X3210 Fahre fort! Zion, fahre fort; X4102 Gregor's 119th metre; X4799 Holy Lord
Schmuck, Cornelius
Jesu dulcis memoria
Schneider (or Schnyder), Friedrich J.C., 1786-1853
Halle (1829)
Lischer
Schnyder von Wartensee, Xaver, 1786-1868
NOTE: Variously cited as: Schnyder, Xavier; Wartensee, X.S. von; or Schneider, with above variations.

Horton; X1215 Book divine
Scholefield, Clement Cotterill, 1839-1904
Fides
Irene (1874)
Litany, No. 9; X6237 Litany; X9315 St Blane
St Clement (1874)
St Nicholas (1870)
Scholfield, Jack P., 1882-
Jesus is the Name
Rapture (1911); X9732 Saved, saved
Think on thy way
Scholinus, Friedrich Karl Ludwig, 1772-1816
Mamre
Schop, Johann, d 1664
Demmin
Eternity (1642); X7768 O Jesus Christ our only Lord; X11756 Wach auf, mein Geist!
Jesu joy of man's desiring (1642); X5731 Joy of man's desiring; X5940 Lamp of our feet; X8881 Regensburg; X9796 Schop; X11548 Vaer nu glad og vel; X12027 Werde munter
Schop (1641); X1287 Break forth, O beauteous heavenly light; X3028 Ermuntre dich [mein schwacher Geist]
Sollt' ich meinem Gott (1641); X1504 Cantate domino; X 4293 Hamburg; X10773 Thanksgiving
Schorring. Koralbog, 1781
Contentment; X1142 Blessed communion; X5554 Jesus, din søde forening et smage; X9797 Schörring
Schott, J.G.
So wahr ich leb, spricht Gott der Herr (1603)
Schreiner, Alexander, 1901-
Behold thy sons and daughters
God loved us, so He sent His Son
Holy temples on Mount Zion
In memory of the Crucified
Lead me into life eternal
Lord, accept into thy Kingdom
Thy Spirit, Lord, has stirred
Truth eternal
When in the wondrous realms
While of these emblems we partake
Schröter, Leonhart, ca 1532-ca 1601
Freut, euch, ihr lieben (1587)
Schubert, Franz Peter, 1797-1828
Abendlied
Esterhazy
Hymn of praise
Jesus, ever-loving Saviour
Jesus, thou art coming (ascribed to Schubert)
Laudate Dominum

Oremus pro Pontifice
Salve, Regina
Schubert; X3214 Fairford
Schubert II
Schuler, George S., 1882-
Schuler (1924); X6657 Make me a blessing
Schulthes, Wilhelm August Ferdinand, 1816-79
Lambeth (1871); X4232 Hail! Bright archangel; X4287 Hallon; X5205 Ilfracomb
Raise your voices, vales and mountains; X2139 Cor Jesu, salus
Requiem
Schultz, Ferdinand
Abendruh (20th c)
Schulz, Johann Abraham Peter, 1747-1800
Claudius (1800); X531 Arator; X2695 Dresden; X8273 Palm Sunday; X12329 Wir pflügen
Hvad hör jäg?
Paedia; X4583 Her kommer dine arme; X9803 Schulz; X11246 Thy little ones
Swahili; X11839 Warum sind der Thränen
Tekna; X5202 Ihr kinderlein kommet; X7643 O dear little children
Schumacher, Bernhard, 1866-
Baltimore (1910)
Firm foundation (1931)
Septem verba (1939)
Schumann, Robert Alexander, 1810-56
Canonbury (1839); X94 Above the heavens, eternal God; X4933 How lovely are thy dwellings; X7360 New every morning; X7694 O God, the refuge; X11462 'Twas like a dream
Fredricton
Holy love
Schumann, V. Gesangbuch, 1539
Old 112th; X2258 Crucifixion; X4916 How fair the Church; X7662 O Fader vor i himmerig; X7833 O Love how deep; X9805 Schumann; X10979 The Lord's prayer; X11565 Vater unser [im Himmelreich]
Scott, Clara H., 1841-97
Open my eyes (1895); X9813 Scott
Scott, J.S.
Salonica
Scott, James King, 1839-83
Auchincairn
Scott-Gatty, Alfred, 1847-1918
Bodmin
Maud
Spirit Divine (1899); X2842 Ecclesfield; X6784 Mater misericordiae
Welwyn (1902)
Scottish Presbyterian hymnal
Laus sempiterna
Scottish Psalters, various dates
Abbey (1615)
Caithness (1635)
Culross (1634)
Dundee (1615); X3497 French
Dunfermline (1615)
Elgin (1625)
Glenluce (1635)
Greyfriars (1635)
London New (1635)
Melrose (1635)
Plaintive martyrs (1615); X6757 Martyrs; X8013 Old martyrs
Psalm 80 (1564); X8036 Old 80th
Wigton (1635); X12258 Wigtown
York (1615); X9810 Scotch stilt
67th Psalm (1615); X8707 Psalm 67
Scottish traditional, etc.
Caledonia; X11163 Therefore give us love
Cameronian Midnight hymn
Candler (i.e. "Bonnie Doon", in Hesperian Harp, 1847); X1213 Bonnie Doon
Covenanters; X8492 Pisgah
Faithful (1931)
Fine flowers

Rorate
Selma (from Isle of Arran); X11078 The sun in splendor rose
Ward
Sea, M.A.
I belong to Jesus; X2445 Dedication
Willing to own thee (1896)
Sederquist, G.W.
The breaking of the day
Selby, Bertram Luard, 1853-1919
Eccles
Ivyhatch
Praises
Ramaulx (1904)
Whitsun
Selle, Thomas, 1599-1663
Zoerbig (1655); X7942 O ursprung des lebens
Sellers, Ernest O., 1869-1952
New Orleans: X12402 Wonderful, wonderful Jesus
Open our eyes, thy glory beholding (1940)
Thy word have I hid (1908); X3002 Eola; X11259 Thy word is a lamp
When the shadows flee (1909)
Would men know
Selnecker, Nicolaus. Christliche Psalmen, 1587
Selnecker; X4062 Gregor's 10th metre; X7572 Nun lasst uns Gott; X11757 Wach auf, mein herz, und singe
Sens. Office de la circoncision attributed to Pierre de Corbeil, d 1222.
Orientis partibus
Sens Processional, 1728
Ave radix
Sephardic melodies are filed as Jewish traditional
Serbian traditional
May the words
Sering, Friedrich Wilhelm, 1822-1901
Sering
Sermisy, Claude (or Claudin) de, ca 1490-1562
Was mein Gott will (1529)
Seven sobs of a sorrowful soul, 1585
Hunnys
Miserere mei
Sewall, Frank
Accrington (1893)
Austin (1893)
Bath (1893)
Come children, arr (1893)
Constance (1893)
Emmanuel (1893)
Eucharist
Keble (1893)
Morn of joy (1893)
Pentecost
Pilgrim (1893)
Praise (1893)
Rachel (1893)
Rector potens (1893)
Resurgam (1893)
St Amand (1893)
St Ambrose (1893)
St Cecilia
Skara (1893)
Speranza
Sursum corda, No. 1 (1893)
Vincenzo (1893)
Vladimir (1893)
Sewell, Hampton H., 1874-1937
Sewell
Seymour, Joseph
Uplift the voice and sing
Shann, Richard. Ms., 1611
Come, love we God
Sharpe , Evelyn
Bulstrode (1931)
Platt's Lane (1929)
Shaw, Geoffrey Turton, 1879-1943
Dymchurch (1915)
Fairlight (1929)
Freedom (1919)
Gillam (1915)
Glynthorpe (1925)
Gresham (1915)
Hickling Broad (1931)
Langham (1925)
Lime Street
Miles animosus
Paddocks
Praise
Ring out (1925)
Rothwell

The snow lies thick
Water-end (1925)
Shaw, Knowles
I am the vine
Shaw, Martin, 1875-1958
Aldeby (1929)
All bells in Paradise
All waters (1931)
Battle Song (1915)
Belsize
Berwick Street (1929)
Birthday (1915)
Boundary
Bromley Common (1915)
Camber (1931)
Cheerful
Children all (1915)
Cobbold (with Vaughan Williams, and signed: S.M.W.V.R.)
Dian
Door keeper (1931)
Downshire Hill (1925)
Gentle Jesus (1915)
Good-bye (1915)
Greeting (1915)
Gun Hill (1929)
Henham (1931)
Herald (melody appears for alto voice)
High Road (1915)
I sing of a Maiden (1928)
In excelsis gloria
Julius
Kings in glory
Lemon's Farm
Little Cornard (1915)
Maddermarket (1929)
Make we merry (1926)
Manor Street (1915)
Marching
Merry Christmas
Mundays (1931)
Oakridge Lynch (1925)
Oppidans Mews (1915)
Out of your sleep
Oxenbridge (1931)
Pimlico Road (1925)
Pioneers (1925)
Purpose (1931)
Riley (1915)
Royden (1929)
Swanwick (1931)
Spring (1930)
Toc H
Westridge (1929)
Working (1930)
Shearer, Winifred Jacobs, 1882-
Filia
Sheehan, Peter E., C.S.B.
Let all on earth their voices (1958)
Sheeles, John, 1688-1761
Addison's (ca 1720); X6320 London
Sheldon, Robin Treeby, 1932-
Broadbent
Crackington
Daymer
Flora
Jonathan
Maer Down
Prims
Shelley, Harry Rowe, 1858-1947
All things bright and beautiful (1932)
In God, the Holy (1932)
Lord, in this sacred hour (1932)
O Lord, be near me (1932)
O Lord, thy all discerning eyes (1932)
Thy faithful servant, Lord, doth yearn (1932)
Shenk, J.M.
Come, heaven-bound pilgrims; X8830 Rebecca
Shepard, F.S.
My Lord and I (1898
Shephard, H.F.
Matins
Shepherd (or Shepard), James Hallett, 1835-79
Hallett
Shepherd, Jehu, 1899-
Avondale
Shepherd, William N.B.
Give us room that we may dwell
Sherwin, William Fisk (or Fishe) 1826-88
Anniversary song
Battle cry; X10255 Sound the battle cry

Better Land
Bread of Life (1877); X1289 Break thou the bread; X5984 Lathbury
Chautauqua (1877); X3143 Evening praise; X9886 Sennen
Cutting
God's love
Heavenly fold
Kelley; X937 Beautiful valley of Eden
Mason; X206 Agape
Monsell
Praise ye the Lord
Sherwin I (1880); X3569 Galilee
Sherwin II
Shield, William, 1748-1829
Auld Lang Syne (ca 1782)
Shields, Elizabeth McE.
Others (1917)
Shoemaker, Joseph Shellenberger, 1854-1936
Come, lost one
Freeport
We now have met (1889); X10402 Stephenson
Shore, W.
Wavertree
Showalter, Anthony J., 1858-1924
God moves in a mysterious way; X2397 Dayton; X6425 Love consecrates the humblest act
Leaning on Jesus; X6062 Leaning on the everlasting arms; X10003 Showalter
O for a heart to praise my God; X10167 Solitude
Showalter, B. F.
Sleep till that morning
Showalter, J. Henry, 1864-1947
At the golden gate of prayer
Awake, O earth
Broadway
Come, just as you are
He seeks His wandering sheep
I need thee, precious Jesus
In from the highways; X3589 Gather them into the fold
In His Name (1900)
Keep us close to Thee
Lord, this day thy children meet
Mohler; X12347 With thankful hearts
More like Thee
Mosley
Nearer the cross of Jesus
None can satisfy
O I long to see the beauty
Shall we know each other there
Showalter; X1292 Breathe upon us, Holy Spirit
Tell the sweet old story
The garden (1922); X9849 See Him in the garden
The Lord my Shepherd is
The Lord of the harvest calls
There is an arm
Walk in the Light
We are saved (1899); X9034 Riches of grace
When I see the blood; X1670 Children's song of praise; X6348 Lord, a little band; X10309 The blood of the Lamb
Showalter, Jacob M.
Will you go to Jesus
Shrubsole, William, 1760-1806
Miles' Lane (1779); X9281 St Asaph
Sibelius, Jan (or Jean), 1865-1957
NOTE: Christened Johan Julius Christian Sibelius
Finlandia (1894)
Sicilian melody
Sicilian Mariners (1794, in Merrick's Psalms); X2603 Dismissal; X6354 Lord, dismiss us; X6428 Love divine; X6726 Mariners; X7893 O sanctissima; X10009 Sicilian hymn; X10012 Sicilian mariners' hymn; X10013 Sicily
Sidebotham, Joseph W., 1830-
St Eanswyth (1881)
Siedhoff, E. Elizabeth
Boston

Silas, Edouard, 1827-1909
Silas
Silcher, Friedrich, 1789-1860
Gott ein Vater; X3841 God our Father; X8350 Pastor pastorum
Lorelei; X796 Baldwin; X9645 Salutas
Morning; X10148 Soho II
Silcher II (1825)
So nimm denn meine Hände; X7918 O take my hand; X10025 Silcher; X10646 Take thou my hand and lead me
Silesian traditional
Heavenly Friend
St Elizabeth (1842); X605 Ascalon; X2274 Crusader's hymn; X2457 Deilig er Jorden; X3212 Fairest Lord Jesus; X9790 Schönster Herr Jesu
Simper, Caleb
Elmcourt
Give thanks
Roland
Rosslyn
Simpson, Margaret M.
The regions beyond
Sims, A. J.
The Unseen Hand
Sims, W. Hines, 1907-
McComb (1956)
Meridian (1951)
Singer, Jacob
All wise, All great (1932)
Gird us, O God (1932)
Harvest (1932)
Kindle the taper (1932)
Let there be light I (1932)
Let there be light II(1932)
Lift up your heads
O God, whose law from age to age (1932)
Rejoice and offer thanks to God (1932)
This child we dedicate (1932)
We thank thee (1932)
Sisters of Notre Dame
Dear St Joseph, pure
Sisters of St Joseph, Toronto
Be thou King
Skeffington, W. S.
Hill Bourne
Skinner, T. Stanley
Rominger
Slater, Gordon, 1896-
Bilsdale (1931)
Fountain Abbey (1931)
St Botolph
Sletten, Jacob Hveding
Jesus, come to me (1923)
Slovak traditional, etc.
NOTE: Hymnal BQ quotes from a "Slovak Hymnal" with no further identification. Many melodies below are there named.

Ave Maria! O Maiden, O Mother
Blessed Francis, holy father
By the first bright Easter Day
Cor, arca legem continens
Great God, what ever through thy church
Great St Joseph
Hail, glorious St Patrick
Heart of our Lord
Help, Lord, the souls
I need thee, precious Jesus
If great wonders
Jesus, thou art coming
Lead us, great teacher Paul
Lift up, ye princes
Little King, so fair
Man of Sorrows; X7044a Monsell
O come and mourn
O Paradise! O Paradise
O Thou pure light
O turn to Jesus
Remember, holy Mary
Resurrection (1600 ms)
Sacred Heart of Jesus
Slovakia
Sweet Agnes, holy child
Tantum ergo
This is the image of the Queen
Tranoscius
Whither thus in holy rapture
Smallman, C. Stanley, 1894-
Dear love
Smallwood, Williams, 1831-97
Antwerp

Smart, George Thomas, 1776-1867
Wiltshire (1795)
Smart, Henry, 1813-79
Alexander (1872)
Barnby's Hymnary, Tune 140
Barnby's Hymnary, Tune 291
Barnby's Hymnary, Tune 475
Bethany (1867); X657 At thy feet; X2256 Crucifer; X3804 God incarnate, veil thy splendor
Chebar
Colebrooke
Corde Natus
Desire
Eventide (1876); X10120 Smart
Everton (1867)
Gordon
Heathlands (1866)
Horeb
Jamison (1866); X10501 Sunderland
Lancashire (1836); X7966 O word of God incarnate
Lexington (1881)
Misericordia
Moredun
Moseley (1881)
Nachtlied (1872); X1535 Carmel; X12337 Wishart
Nomina
Northumberland
Paradise (1868)
Pilgrims (1868); X2370 Daughter of Sion; X111746 Vox angelica
Regent Square (1867) X471 Angels, from the realms; X5751 Judge eternal, throned in splendor
Rex gloriae (1868)
St Leonard (1867)
St Pancras
Seraphim
Sion (1872); X847 Barnby's hymnary, Tune 474; X3454 Forward; X9318 St Boniface; X9321 St Botolph; X10121 Smart; X11881 Watchword
Trisagion (1868)
Vexillum (1868); X11974 Welcome
Smit, W.A.
Tantum ergo
Smith, Alfred M.
Assisi (1940)
Labor (1941)
Sursum corda (1941)
Smith, Besse E.
Glory, praise and blessing
O perfect love
The Saviour reigns
Smith, Beulah
Beulah (improvised when a child of five years)
Smith, David Stanley, 1877-1949
Fortitude (1904)
Los Angeles (1905)
Smith, Edward J.
University hymn (1911)
Smith, Henry Percy, 1825-98
Maryton (1874); X10500 Sun of my soul
Smith, Howard E., 1863-1918
I want to love Him more
Love lifted me (1912); X9220 Safety
When the Book is opened
Smith, Isaac. Collection, ca 1770
Abridge; X9602 St Stephen
Oxford New
Silver Street; X3238 Falcon Street
Smith, John Stafford, 1750-1836
National anthem, arr (1771); X7897 O say, can you see!; X10370 Star-spangled banner; X11071 The star-spangled banner
Smith, Joseph
Radiance
Smith, Kenneth Donald, 1928-
Raphael
Smith, Lucia May
Ashland (1918)
Smith, R.A. Laslett, 1873-
Forest Hill Church
Smith, R.F.
There came three Kings (1875); X3007 Epiphany
Smith, Robert Archibald, 1780-1829

St Lawrence
Smith, Samuel, 1821-1917
Edengrove (1874); X9629 Saints' days
Gaudete
Melanesia
Newton Ferns
Ruth (1870)
Smith. Harmonious companion, 1732
St Bartholomew
Smucker, S.J.
I long to be there
Rittman
Smyth, A.C.
Come along, come along
Come, thou glorious day
O, how lovely was the morning
Sion stands with hills surrounded
Smyth, Harper G., 1873-1945
Euclid; X6658 Make me a channel
Smyth, Julian K.
Children of the light
Copley Square
God's mariner
Montrose
Pastor bonus
Prince of Peace
Roll out, O song, to God; X11701 Vigilia
Roxbury
Wilma
Söderberg, Th[eodor?]
O du Guds Lam
Södergren, Carl Johannes, 1870-
Agatha (1924)
Sohren, Peter, ca 1630- ca 1692
Dies ist der Tag (1676)
Elbing (1668); X2706 Du lifvets bröd; X4631 Herr Jesu Christ, du hast bereit't; X4632 Herr Jesu Christ, du höchstes Gut
Gute bäume bringen, arr; X10150 Sohren
Sohren (1668), arr (by W. Douglas (1938); X4216 Gute baume bringen
Somervell, Arthur, 1863-1937
Blencathra (1925)
Dominus vobiscum
Kendal (1906)
Langdale
Rugby
Somervell; X1693 Chorus angelorum; X8585 Praise to the Holiest
Stonethwaite (1931); X2387 Day by day
Windermere
Songs and tunes for education, 1861
Haslemere
Soto de Langa, Francisco, 1539-1619
Langa
Souter Liedekens Ghemaect ter Eeren Gods. Antwerp, 1539
If ye would hear
Southern harmony (Walker's); 1835
Complainer
Distress
The spiritual sailor
Southern harmony, 1855
True happiness
Southgate, Frederic, 1824-85
St Agatha
Southgate, Thomas Bishop, 1814-68
Brookfield (1887)
Southgate
Sowerby, Leo, 1895-
Palisades (1941)
Perry
Taylor Hall (1941)
Spaeth, Adolph, 1939-1910
NOTE: Christened, Philipp Friedrich Adolph Theodor
Spaeth.
O Gottessohn (1885)
Spaeth, Mrs. Adolph, see Krauth, Harriet Reynolds, 1845-1925
Spanish traditional
Spanish carol
Torches
Spanish plainsong, see Mozarabic Rite
Spazier, Johann Karl Gottlieb (or Johann Gottlieb Karl), 1761-1805
Spazier

Speck, A. L.
The blameless Church
Spee, Friedrich von. Trutz-Nachtigal, 1649
NOTE: See also Corner. Geistliche Nachtigall, 1649

Nachtigall; X117 Ach! Wan doch Jesu liebster mein
Speer, Daniel, 1636-1707
Speer; X9222 Sag was hilft
Spencer, W. A.
I shall be like Him
Spencer Palmer, Florence Margaret (i.e. Peggy) 1900-
Adoramus
Brynland
Carmichael
Ellasgarth
Keynsham
Lydbrook
Quest
Smitten Rock
Woking
Spevniček, Lachmannov
Now let the earth with joy
Spielman, John H.
Mt Zion (1881)
Ormiston (1881)
Pentecost (1881)
Spiess, Johann Martin, 1715-ca 66
Swabia (1745); X5099 I name thy hallowed Name; X10472 Suabia; X10553 Swabia No. 1
Spilman, Jonathan
Illinois
Spilman, Jonathan E.
Away in a manger (1834); X3390 Flow gently sweet Afton; X10834 The Christmas manger hymn
Spinney, Frank, 1850-88
Holy offerings
St Denys
Spinney, Walter
Name of Jesus (1890)
Spohr, Louis (or Ludwig), 1784-1859
Flensburg; X11749 Vox Jesu; X11825 Waring
Gerald (1834); X315 All things bright; X1271 Brady; X 5383 Invitation; X5504 Jerusalem; X10316 Sophr
Leyden; X5800 Kemerton
Spohr (1835); X1634 Cherith; X6631 Magdalene; X10046 Simpson; X11044 The sanctity of sorrow
Sprague, P. J.
Ye children, come
Spratt, Ann Baird
Kedron (1866)
Squires, William H.
Sacred morn
Staden, Sigmund Gottlieb [Theophilus?] ca 1605-55
Die Helle Sonne
Stafford, C. C.
I'll make it my home
Stainer, John, 1840-1901
Author of life
Beati (1873); X303 All saints; X1049 Bethabara; X6626 Magdalen; X8974 Rest; X9630 Saints of God; X10343 Stainer
Blessed Home (1875); X 10806 The blessed home
Charity (1868)
Children offerings
Conquest (1875); X5505 Jerusalem
Contrition (1882)
Covenant (1889)
Credo (1875)
Crucifixion (1887); X2236 Cross of Jesus
Crux salutifera
Dominus misericordiae
Elijah
Eucharisticus; X5574 Jesus, gentlest Saviour
Evangel; X5287 In memoriam; X10344 Stainer
Evening prayer (1898)
Gloaming (1898)
God in nature (1897)
God so loved the world
Grandpont
Iona (1868)
Laus matutina (1872); X834 Barnby's hymnary, Tune 53; X2381 Dawn; X8597

Praise ye the Lord
Litany, No. 6 (1875)
Love Divine (1889)
Lux prima; X835 Barnby's hymnary, Tune 59; X10510 Sunrise
Magdalena (1868)
Oblations
Oxford; X273 All for Jesus; X5811 Keston; X12486 Wycliff
Paschale gaudium
Pastor bonus (1875); X9426 St Hill
Pilgrim band
Repose (1875)
Rex Regum
St Benedict
St Giles; X2854 Eden; X8319 Parousia
St Paul's
Scientia salutis
Sebaste
Simplicity
Sudeley
Suppliant
Veni
Veni Spiritus
Vesper (1875)
Watchword
Woodlynn (1889)
Xavier (1875); X9392 St Francis Xavier

Stair, Patty, 1869-1926
Bassett (1915)

Stanfield, Francis, 1836-
Sweet Sacrament Divine (1860)

Stanford, Charles Villiers, 1852-1924
Airedale
Engelberg (1904)
Geronimo (1909)
Jolwynds (1904)
Orient

Staniforth, Thomas Worsley, 1845-1909
Jerusalem (1866); X9878 Selwood; X10360 Staniforth
O heart of Mary

Stanley, Samuel, 1767-1822
Calvary
Doversdale
Kent
Wilton
Shirland
Simeon
Stonefield
Warwick

Stanton, Walter Kendall, 1891-
Cannock (1951)
Crudwell
Dolberrow
Hampton Lucy
Linton
Mylor
Northumbria
Ready token
Silchester

Staples, H. J., 1891-1943
Nightingale

Stark, E. J.
Berkshire; X12155 When this song of praise shall cease
Firm this cornerstone

Stark, Josef
P'sach Lonu

Stratham, Francis Reginald, 1844-
Freshwater (1872)
Thanksgiving; X943 Beddome; X2251 Croyland; X8940 Repose

Statham, H. D., 1889-
Arncliffe

Statham, Heathcote
Tenbury (1925)

Statham, Henry Heathcote, 1839-
St Joseph; X9232 St Agnes; X10378 Statham

Statham, W., 1832-98
St Margaret

Stebbins, George Coles, 1846-1945
Adelaide (1907); X4410 Have Thine own way; X4783 Holy desire; X8527 Pollard; X10385 Stebbins; X10530 Surrender
Assiut (1912)
Ben Avon
Born again; X12517 Ye must be born again
"But for a moment" (1906)
Christian, walk carefully

Come to the fountain
Come unto Me
Eskridge
Evening prayer (1876)
Fear not
Friend (1878); X5445 I've found a friend; X10480 Such a friend
Holiness (1890); X5964 Langstaff; X6334 Longstaff; X10647 Take time to be holy
Janet (1912)
Jesus, I come (1886); X8233 Out of my bondage
Jesus is calling; X1442 Calling today; X5591 Jesus is tenderly calling; X10386 Stebbins
Kinross (1901)
Lydia
Moorehead (1927)
Providence; X7184 Must I go, and empty-handed
Saved by grace; X10179 Some day the silver cord
Sialkot
Spirit so holy
The Green Hill; X4043 Green Hill; X10387 Stebbins; X11139 There is a green hill
The Homeland (1920)
True-hearted, whole-hearted (1890)

Stebbins, George Waring, 1869-1930
Easter flowers (1913)
Manchester (1927)

Steffe, John William
Battle hymn (1852); X876 Battle hymn of the Republic; X10792 The battle hymn of the Republic

Steggall, Charles H., 1826-1905
Christchurch (1858); X1698 Christ Church
Day of praise
Help us, O God
Lincoln's Inn (1892)
Manger Throne (1867)
Morwellham; X7079 Morewellham
Orient
St Albans
St Ambrose
St Clement (1849)
St Edmund (1849); X9372 St Edward
St Lawrence
Wearmouth (1890)
Westmoreland
Woolsey (1872)

Stein, A. Gereon
Great St Joseph (1852)

Steinel, Irving A.
Consecration hymn (1940)
Evans (1939)

Steiner, Johann Ludwig, 1688-1761
Steiner (1735); X3941 Gott will's machen

Stenhammer, Per Ulrik, 1829-75
Grace; X4645 Herren sig i nad förklarer

Stephens, Charles Edward, 1821-92
Dr. Steggall's Tune 172 (1865)

Stephens, Evan
All hail the glorious day
Awake, ye Saints of God
Come, dearest Lord
Father, thy children to thee now raise
For the strength of the hills
Glory to God in the highest
In remembrance of thy suffering
Know this, that every soul is free
Land of the mountains high (commemorating Utah's statehood)
Lean on my ample arm
Let us all press on
Lo! the mighty God
O awake! my slumbering minstrel
O happy homes among the hills
Our mountain home
Praise ye the Lord
Raise your voices to the Lord

Sacred the place of prayer
Savior, Redeemer of my soul
See, the mighty angel flying!
Shall the youth of Sion falter?
The voice of God again is heard
Today, while the sun shines
We ever pray for thee
What was witnessed in the heavens?
Ye simple souls who stray
Stephenson, J.
Sandford
Stevens, David
Millet (1921)
Stevens, Richard John Samuel, 1757-1837
Shakespeare's Carol II
Stevenson (no initials)
O Heart of God (1918?)
Stevenson, Frederick
Hart (1892)
Stewart, Charles Hylton, 1884-1932
Corona
Rochester
Stewart, J.W.
Adoration
Stewart, Robert Prescott, 1825-94
Adrian
Coeli enarrant; X1880 Coeli
Eucharistica
Garfirth (1868)
Holyrood (1873)
Mount Calvary (1874); X1518a; Caress; X9275 St Anthony, we turn
Prescott (ca 1873)
St Audoen
St Helen's; X5926 Lafayette; X9417 St Helen
Vespers
Stiastny, Johann
Stiastny
Stieler, Kaspar. Der Busfertige Sünder. Nürnberg, 1679
Wo soll ich fliehen hin
Stillman, J.M.
I want to be more like Jesus (1878); X7071 More like Jesus
Stobaeus, Johann, 1580-1646
Lift up your heads (1634); X6610 Macht hoch die Thür
Such', wer da will (1613)
Stock, Sarah Geraldina, 1838-98
Moel Llys (1899)
Stocks, George Gilbert, 1877-1960
Sunset
Village
Stocks, M.L.
What will you do with Jesus?
Stockton, John Hart, 1813-77
Glory to His name
Great Physician, arr; X10609 Sweetest name; X10623 Sympathy; X10891 The Great Physician [now is near]
Stockton (1875); X1924 Come, every soul; X6978 Minerva; X8144 Only trust him; X11416 Trust
Stokes, Walter
Ravendale
Stokowski, Leopold Antoni Stanislaw, 1887-
In excelsis gloria (1908)
Stolpe, Gustav, 1833-1901
Dig, Jesus, min dyraste Jesus (1892)
Helig, helig, helig Herre Gud (1892)
Stone, Frank Leslie
Sunset and evening star (1901)
Storer, Henry Johnson, 1860-1935
Brightly gleams (1890)
Harvest home (1890)
O Sion, haste (1894)
Patmos (1891)
Störl, Johann Georg Christian, 1675-1719
Störl I; X7112 Morning sacrifice; X7560 Nun danket all' und bringet ehr; X8640 Preservation
Störl II; X7760 O Jerusalem du schöne
Störl's Wurtemberg Gesangbuch, 1710

Bremen
Stötzel, Johann Georg
Ruhe ist das beste gut (1777)
Stötzel, Choralbuch. Stuttgart, 1744
O wie selig seid ihr doch; X915 Beata
So führst du hoch; X4843 Home
Strachauer, H.
Hermann
So sweet and clear
Stralsund Gesangbuch, 1665
Praise to the Lord; X4082 Gregor's 61st metre; X4397 Hast du denn, Jesu; X6005 Laudate dominum; X6304 Lobe den Herren; X6448 Lover den Herre; X8563 Praise; X8569 Praise Jehovah; X8600 Praxis pietatis
Strassburg Psalter, 1539
Genevan 137th
Old 130th
Strassburg Kirchenampt, 1524
see both Teutsch Kirchenampt, Strassburg, 1525 and Kirchengesangbuch. Strassburg, 1541
Strassburger Kirchengesangbuch, 1616
Strassburg
Strattner, Christoph Georg (or Georg Christoph), 1650-1705
Posen (1691); X1736 Christ the Lord is risen today; X3159 Ever faithful; X4710 Himmel, erde, luft und meer; X10457 Strattner
Straub, S.W., 1842-1899
Providence
Streatfeild, Charlotte
Langton
Strohm, Albert J.
Stewart (1933)
Strom, Ralph Alvin, 1909-
(sometimes 1901-
Beaumont (1924)
Elmie (1924)
Mathilda (1924)
Name of Jesus
St Ansgar (1924)
Strong, Thomas Banks, 1861-1944
Hebdomadal
Poplar
Strover, Martin Christian Tinne, 1932-
Broadwood
Simon
Strutt, R., 1848-1927
St Catherine's Court
Stubbs, G. Edward, 1857-
Asaph (1894); X3026 Erling
Stutsman, Grace May
Waits' carol (1935)
Su Yin-lan, 1915-37
Sheng en (1934)
Sullivan, Arthur Seymour, 1842-1900
All this night
Angel voices (1872)
Audite audientes me (1874)
Bishopgarth (1897); X5744 Jubilee
Carrow (1873)
Clarence (1874)
Coena Domini (1874)
NOTE: "Livorno" is an enlargement of this melody; X7676 O gentle Savior
Constance
Courage, brother (1872); X857 Barony
Emmelar
NOTE: This name refers to Henry Brinley Richards, Sullivan's contemporary in London.
Evelyn (1874)
Ever faithful; X3161 Ever faithful, ever sure
Falfield (1874)
Fortunatus (1872); X11977 Welcome, happy morning
Golden sheaves
Hanford (1874); X70303 Nauford [sic]
Homeland (1867); X3427 For thee, O dear, dear country; X7604 O bone patria
In memoriam
Lacrymae (1872); X841 Barnby's hymnary, Tune 222; X9659 Salvator No. 1
Livorno (see Coena Domini, above); X10812 The bread that giveth strength

Lux Eoi (1874); X359 Alleluia! Praise the Savior
Lux mundi (1872); X843 Barnby's hymnary, Tune 225; X5516 Jerusalem the golden!
Marlborough, arr
Mount Sion
Propior Deo (1872); X12049 Westminster
Resurrexit (1874)
Safe home
St Edmund (1872); X4526 Heaven is my home
St Francis (1874)
St Francis II
St Gertrude (1871); X3540 From the eastern mountains; X3660 Gertrude; X8155 Onward, Christian soldiers; X10488 Sullivan
St Kevin (1872); X845 Barnby's hymnary, Tune 285
St Millicent
St Nathaniel; X7293 Nathaniel
St Patrick (1874)
St Theresa (1874); X11176 Theresa
Saints of God (1874)
Samuel (1874); X4978 Hushed was the evening hymn
Shepherd
Storm-tossed
Sullivan
The long way home
Ultor omnipotens (1874)
Valete; X7871 O render thanks
Venite ad me

Sullivan, E.M.
Tantum ergo (1940)

Sulzer, Salomon (or Solomon) 1804-90
Bor'chu
Kodosh
O Lord, my God
Shiveesee
Sh'ma Yisroayl I
Sh'ma Yisroayl II; X1227 Boruch shaym
The Lord of all
Va-a-nachnu
Yimloch

Summer, John B., 1838-1918
see Sumner, John B.

(Accuracy of spelling is not established: both forms in publications)

Summers, J.
Palmyra (1863); X10122 Smiley

Summers, James Lea, 1837-81
Lea

Sumner, John B., 1838-1918
The Child of a King; X7 A child of a king; X8 A child of the king; X1095 Binghamton

Sunderreiter, G. Himmlischen Harfen. Augsburg, 1581
In dich hab' ich gehoffet

Suomen Koraalikirja, 1738
Finnish Song

Supplement to Kentucky Harmony, 1820
Detroy; X2521 Detroit; X7114 Morning song (Wyeth Repository, 1813)

Sussex traditional see English traditional

Swabian folk song
Miserere nobis (Brahms arr); X2021 Common ways

Swan, Timothy, 1758-1842
China

Swedish Koralbok, 1697
see the 1697 items filed with Swedish traditional melodies just below.

Swedish traditional, liturgical, etc.
NOTE: The 1697 items were published in the Swedish Koralbok, 1697. And see Then Swenska Psalmboken. Stockhom, 1695

Amicus; X5461 Jag har en vän
Blomstertid (1697); X2471 Den blomstertid nu kommer
Dalarne
Frälsta värld! i nodens under (1697)
Gaa nu hen og grav min Grav
Gor porten hög (1697)

Heroes hymn
I Kristi sar jag somnar in (1689)
Jesus! du dig själf uppväckte (1675)
Jesus, lat din rädda dufva; X3516 Friends of Jesus
Kalmar (1676); X4557 Hela världen fröjdes herren; X5620 Jesus, Lord and precious Saviour
Laurinus (1697); X1584 Celeste; X5063 I himmelen, i himmelen
Messiah (16th c); X1029 Bereden; X1030 Bereden väg för herran
Misstrosta ej att Gud är god (1695)
Mitt hjerta Jesu! denna dag (in Swedish Koralbok, 1884)
O store Gud
O wonderful words
Oss Kristna bör tro och besinna (before 1540)
Pax (1697); X123 Ack, bliv hos oss; X9185 Sa är fullkomnadt
Praise (1697); X195 Af himlens
Riddarholm (1697); X11526 Upp, min tunga
St Erik (1697)
St Lawrence, Lund (17th c) X11527 Uppfaren är var herre
Sandell; X1660 Children of the heavenly Father; X11442 Tryggare kan ingen vara
Skader, skader nu här alle (1697)
Swedish Litany (1697)
Vigil; X4225 Haf trones lampa färdig

Sweetser, Joseph Emerson, 1825-73
Diman
Greenwood (1894)
Owen
Rose Hill

Sweezy, Israel B.
Palmer

Sweney, John R., 1837-99
Beulah Land
Calvary
Fill me now; X4905 Hover o'er me, Holy Spirit; X10613 Sweney
Give me Jesus; X10645 Take the world, but give
Hast du Jesus ruf vernommen; X6380 Lord of light, whose name outshineth
He will gather the wheat
Hyatt
I shall know Him; X7247 My Saviour first of all; X12132 When my lifework
Jesus leads (1893)
More about Jesus (1887); X10614 Sweney
Stars in my crown; X12266 Will there be any stars
Story of Jesus; X7951 O what could my Jesus do more; X10721 Tell me the story
Sunshine; X11175 There's sunshine in my soul
The Lord is my Light
Unsearchable riches; X7922 O the unsearchable riches
Victory through grace; X 2072 Conquering now
We are nearing home

Swift, James Frederick, 1847-1931
Ernstein
Te laudant omnia

Swisher, Walter S.
Cornish (1923)
Hamilton (1923)
Lee (1924)
Newell (1923)
Wellesley (1924)

Swiss traditional
NOTE: See also the Tyrolese traditional tunes.

Solothurn
Stillingfleet
Vaudois

Sydenham, Edwin Augustus, 1847-91
King Edward

Sydnor, G.G.

Dawning (1926)
Sykes, Frederick H., 1826-
Holcombe
Symonds, Daniel Philip, 1929-
Mernle

T

Taddei, M.
Hail, Thou Star of Ocean (1920)
Tai Jun Park
Korea
Taler (a Dominican, Monastery of Strasbourg, 1361)
Jesu Redemptor omnium
Tallis (or Tallys, Talys), Thomas, ca 1505-95
Fifth mode melody
First mode melody
Second mode melody
Seventh mode melody
Tallis' Canon (ca 1567); X1498 Canon; X3140 Evening hymn; X7926 O thou immortal holy Light; X10655 Tallis' Evening hymn; X10658 Tallis' Hymn
Tallis' Ordinal (ca 1567); X8586 Praise to the Holiest X10650 Tallis
The Second tune
The 5th tune (1560)
The 6th tune (1560)
Third mode melody (1567)
Veni Creator (ascribed to)
Tans'ur (originally Tanzer), William, 1706-83
Bangor (1734)
Barby (1755); X9263 St Andrew
St Martin's (1740); X3563 Gainsborough
Rothwell
Tans'ur, W. Compleat melody, 1734
Colchester
Tarbutton, William A.
A little while
Briggs
Tartini, Giuseppe, 1692-1770
Stabat Mater
Tate, Laura A.
Bovina
Taylor, B.M.
Upon the first day
Taylor, Cyril Vincent, 1907-
Abbot's Leigh
Belstead
Beweley
Bushmead
Coolinge
Eirene
Libera nos
Mead House
Portland
Sheldonian
Taylor, E.G.
Latakia; X11152 There is life for a look
Taylor, John Prentice, 1871-
Kirn
Taylor, Virgil Corydon, 1817-91
Louvan (1847)
Warren
Tchaikowsky, Peter Ilitch, 1840-93
NOTE: Great variation in transliteration of spelling. Baker uses Tchaikovsky, Piotr Ilyitch.

In aeternum
O come, let us worship
Petrograd
The Crown of Roses; X10694 Tchaikowsky's "Legend"
Tearne, T.S.
The bell cadence
Teasley, D.O.
All because we do not love them
Be ready when He comes
Behold what love
Eternity
Glorious peace
Gone to bloom above
I know in my heart what it means
No friend like Jesus
The last farewell; X9999 Should we meet here no more
Teddlie, Tillet S.
Heaven holds all to me
Into our hands (1939)

What will your answer be? (1935)

Temple Star

Be not afraid

Lyte

Tenney, John H.

Beneath thy shadow hiding

Closer to thee, My Father

Ever will I pray

Go to thy rest, fair child; X1297 Burber

Not far from the Kingdom

Sabbath bell

We'll never say good-by (1889)

Where will you spend eternity

Terry, Richard Runciman, 1865-1938

Christ the Lord is my true Shephard

Crown Him

Doxford

Full of glory

Hail, Mary, Pearl of Grace

Highwood

Holy Church; X356 Alleluia, let the holy anthem rise; X2846 Ecclesia

Newman (1912); X1090 Billing

O Godhead hid

Teschner, Melchior, 1584-1635

St Theodulph (1615); X277 All glory, praise [laud] and honor; X9501 St Mark; X10754 Teschner; X11130 Theodulph; X11554 Valet will dich dir geben

Teutsch Kirchenampt. Strassburg, 1525

Aus tiefer not; X4639 Herr, wie du willst, so schik's mit mir; X6540 Luther's hymn; X7729 O helligaand, du skat; X7737 O Holy Ghost, thou gift; X10454 Strasburg

Es woll' uns Gott genädig sein; X7661 O Fader var, barmhertig god

Passiontide; X447 An wasserfleussen Babylon; X2886 Ein lamm geht hin

Thalben-Ball, George Thomas, 1896-

Arden

Dennis

Dransfield (1932)

Egerton (1932)

Jesmian

Laudon (1932)

Llanherne

Nazareth

Stand up

Vigil

Wisdom

Walford

Warwick

Thalberg, Sigismond, 1812-71

Thalberg

Thatcher, Reginald Sparshatt, 1888-1957

Long Mynd (1931)

Wilderness (1936)

Thayer, M.C.

Wakeman

Theiss, J.A.

Wondrous story

Then Swenska Psalmboken. Stockholm, 1695.

NOTE: See also Swedish traditional melodies, 1695 items may be from this book.

Stockholm; X2499 Der mange skal komme; X11161 There many shall come

Theophane, M., Sr., O.S.F.

Blessed Francis, holy father (1958)

Thermignon, D.

Creator alme siderum; X11587 Veni Creator Spiritus

Thesaurus musicus, 1740

America; X3849 God save our gracious king; X3850 God save the queen; X7191 My country 'tis of thee; X7295 National anthem; X7818 O Lord, our God

Thiman, Eric Harding, 1900-

Ashford

Beeding

Binney's

Goring

Holborn

Milton Abbas

Rejoice, O people
Shere
Stokesay Castle
Storrington
Thomas, Charles J.
Sons of Michael, He approaches
Thomas, J. Harries, 1875- 1950
Hemel
Thomas, J. Lyddon, 1910-
Harvest song
Thomas, J.R. [perhaps John Rogers Thomas, 1829-96]
Beautiful Sion for me
Thomas, John, 1839-1922
Blaencefn
Thomas, Rhys, 1867-1932
Rhys (1932)
St David (1916)
Sarah (1929)
Thomissön, H. see Tömisson, H.
Psalmebog, 1569
Thommen. Christen-schatz Basel, 1745
NOTE: Full title, Erbaulicher, musikalischer Christenschatz. Basel, 1745

Batty; X807 Balty; X2936 Ellerker; X5870 Kjaemp alvorlig nu; X9051 Ringe recht; X10462 Strive aright
Bunyan; X4071a Gregor's 37th metre (Herrnhut ms)
Cassel (major reading)
Desire (minor reading); X12366 Wo ist Jesus, mein verlangen
Mein Heiland
Thompson, J.H.
Aspiration
Thompson, John Winter, 1867-1951
Adventurers (1927)
Thompson, Robert George, 1862-1934
Blairgowrie (1933)
Thompson, Van Denman, 1890-
Home (1935)
Longden (1933)
Thompson, Will Lamartine, 1847-1909
Have I done any good?
He's my Friend (1904); X2929 Elizabeth; X5583 Jesus is all the world
Lead me gently home, Father
Softly and tenderly; X3428 For you and for me; X11211 Thompson
The whole wide world (1908)
The world has need of willing men
There's a great day coming
Thomson, Andrew Mitchell, 1778-1831
St George's, Edinburgh
Thomson, John, 1841-
Little hands
Thorne, Edward Henry, 1834-1916
Astra matutina
Holy Sepulchre
St Andrew (1875)
Wake! Awake
Thorne, Gilbert C., 1890-
Branksome
Thrupp, Francis Joseph (or Joseph Francis), 1827-67
Epiphany hymn; X1316 Brightest and best; X3008 Epiphany
Thuringian traditional
Lynde; X4915 How can I leave thee?
Thurman, E. Lester
Deus vitae (1914)
Tiddeman, Maria, 1837-1911
Ibstone
Tilleard, James, 1827-76
Edgbaston
Kensington New (1866)
Lost and found; X10415 Stilla jag pa dig
Tillman, Charles D., 1861-1943
My Mother's Bible (1893)
Tilman; X8828 Ready
Truth reflects upon our senses
Unanswered yet? The prayer
When I get to the end
Tindley, Charles A., 1856-1933
By and by; X12143 When the

morning comes
Leave it there, arr.
NOTE: Apparently a variant of James Black's 'The roll".

Nothing between
Stand by me
Tinsley, W.C.
I'll go where He sendeth me
Tintner, M.
Splendor of the morning sunlight
Tochter Sion. Cologne, 1741
St Bernard; X2189 Covert X5578 Jesus, how good the thought
Weisse flaggen; X300 All saints (later form) (Darmstadt G-B.)
Toews, Aaron
The Lord's Prayer
Toews, Jacob D.
Come, ye weary ones, tonight (1943)
The Beatitudes
Tomadini, Jacopo, 1820-83
Panis angelicus
Tomer, William Gould, 1832-96
God be with you (1882); X2531 Deus vobiscum; X3257 Farewell; X7014 Mizpah; X11328 Tomer
Tomissön, Hans. Psalmebog, 1569.
Franzen; X524 Appeal; X7762 O Jesu! än de dina
Herre Gud Fader, du vor høi' ste Trøst
Island; X4912 How blest are they; X6977 Min sjael og aand opmuntre dig; X11210 Thomisson
Mit Haab og Trøst og al Tillid
Thomissön
Torrance, George William, 1835-1907
Adoration
Moredun; X1855 Clinging; X11417 Trust
Tourjée, Eben, 1834-91
Cary
Tourjée, Lizzie Esterbrook, 1858-1913
Wellesley (1877); X11347 Tourjée
Tours, Berthold, 1838-97
Deventer; X6730 Marken
Gouda; X2722 Dulce nomen
Groningen (1872); X1043 Bertha
Holland (1875);
Rotterdam (1875)
The Wise Men (1881); X184 Advent
Tours (1872); X1045 Berthold; X5295 In palmis; X11153 There is never a day
Towner, Daniel B., 1850-1919
Anywhere; X522 Anywhere with Jesus
Calvary; X647 At Calvary
Marvelous grace (1910); X3980 Grace greater than our sin; X7057 Moody
My anchor holds
Nor silver nor gold
Only a sinner (1905)
Some sweet day
The hand that was wounded (1905)
Towner
Trust and obey; X12159 When we walk with the Lord
Tozer, A. Edmonds
Ave Maria! Thou Virgin and Mother
Jazer
NOTE: This appears to be a misprint of word "Tozer"; X331 All ye who seek
Tozer, Ferris
Stand firm
Tozer
Track, Gerhard
I shall approach the altar (1964)
Traditional melodies
IMPORTANT NOTE: These might have been placed in the anonymous section, but because of their long use within Church or Folk music this category was made. For traditional melodies which may be attributed to a national or cultural community, see the name of

that culture or community.

Ecce Agnus
Grassmere; X7908 O so bright
Homeward
How gladly
Merciful Saviour
On the wood His arms (Mediaeval mel)
Redeemer (ca 1400); X2711
Du vaere lovet, Jesus; X3615
Gelobet seist du
Reykjavik (15th c)
Shepherds in the field abiding (ancient)
Venite adoremus

Trappist Monks' contributions are entered as: A Monk of Gethsemani

Trebel, G.H.
Godfrey (1910)
Heavenly City (1883)
Thou, whose Almighty Word (1903)
Trebel

Trembath, Henry G., 1844-1908
Rosmore (1893)

Trier Gesangbuch, 1695
Sunrise; X2318 Daily, sing in praise of Mary; X7136
Mother, Mary, at thy altar

Triller (no initials)
Spiritus Sancti gratia (1555)

Troup, E. Josephine
Truth

Trowbridge, J.C.
Jesus is coming

Troyte, Arthur Henry Dyke, 1811-57
Lonsdale
My God, my Father
Troyte (1860)
Troyte, No. 1; X1602 Chant (Troyte, No. 1); X7213 My God, my Father
Troyte, No. 2; X1603 Chant (Troyte, No. 2)

True, Latham
Donum Dei

Truss, Ida T.
The happy story hour (1936)

Tschaikowsky, Peter Ilitch, see Tchaikowsky, P.I.

Tscherlitzky, Johann H.
Glorification (1832); X3943
Gottes lamm ruft gnade

Tucker, Henry
Hobart
Joy-bells (1850)

Tucker, Isaac
Devizes

Tuckerman, Samuel Parkman, 1819-90
Humility

Tuckett, Henry A.
Choose the right
We are sowing

Tufts, John Wheeler, 1825-1908
Adoration

Tullar, Grant Colfax, 1869-1950
Face to face (1899)
Nailed to the cross
Tullar (1912); X8215 Our best

Tullidge, John
An angel from on high
Come, all ye sons of Zion
Think not, when you gather

Turle, James, 1802-82
Armagh (1861); X11456
Turle
Fairfield
Lostwithiel (1854)
St John's Westminster (1862); X9443 St John
St Peter's Westminster (1862); X9568 St Peter's
Westminster (1835)

Turner, Herbert B., 1852-1927
Cushman (1905)
Earl (1893)

Turner, William, 1651-1740
Egham

Turpin, Edmund Hart, 1835-1907
Argyle (1866)
Litany No. 1 (1875)
Litany No. 2 (1875)
Litany No. 7 (1875)
Litany No. 8 (1875)
Mansfield (1889)
Turpin's Litany; X6246
Litany, No. 7

Turton, Thomas, 1780-1864

Ely (1844)
St Etheldreda; X9380 St Ethelreda
Tye, Christopher, 1500-72
Farrant
Gethsemane (1553)
Southwark
Windsor (1553); X2737 Dundee (Damon's Booke of musicke, 1591); X12308 Windsor and Eton
Yattendon 15 (arr by H.E. Wooldridge); X12499 Yattendon
Tyler, James Sherman, 1842-1917
City bright
Tyrolese traditional
NOTE: See also the Swiss traditional tunes.

Andreas Hofer (National song of the Tyrol)
Falan-tidings; X11477 Tyrolese
Tyrolean Cradle song

U

Udulutsch, Irvin, O.F.M.
Mary Immaculate, Star
Ufford, Edwin S., 1851-1929
I believe the Bible
Life line; X11235 Throw out the life-line
Ukranian melody
Shepherd care
Ulich, Johann
Meinen Jesum lass ich nicht (1674)
Union harmony, 1793 see Holden, Oliver. Union Harmony, 1793
Unitas Fratrum (as author) see Bohemian Brethren
Unseld, Benjamin C., 1843-1923
Ancyra (1901)
Euphemia (1901)
Gracious King enthroned (1901)
Once more before we part X10572 Sweet day
Updegraff, E. Grace
Carter
Urhan, Chrêtien, 1790-1845
Rutherford (1834)

V

Vail, Silas Jones, 1818-84
Close to Thee; X1132 Bless Jehovah; X4559 Helen; X11219 Thou, my everlasting
Gates ajar; X10875 The gate ajar for me; X11137 There is a gate that stands ajar
He died for thee
We shall sleep, but not forever
Vale, Walter S.
Cowley (1935)
Van Andel, Henry
Calvin College (1928)
Van Arsdale, P.P.
Mission song; X4355 Hark! the voice of Jesus
Van Damme, P.J., Canon of Ghent
Adoro te, No. 2; X3670 Ghent
Vanden Plas, E.
Pie Jesu
Van der Werp, H.
Passion (1911)
Rehoboth (1911)
Resting-place (1911)
Van der Werp
Van Hoose, H.W.
Increase my faith
Vassar College
Peace I leave with you (1937)
Vaudois traditional see Swiss traditional
Vaughan, James D.
Gathering buds
Vaughan Williams, Ralph see Williams, Ralph Vaughan
Vehe. Gesangbuchlein, 1537
On Jordan's bank
Wer da wonet; X5192 If, now, thou seekest miracles
Venua, Frederick Marc Antoine, 1788-1872
Park Street (1810)
Verdi, Fortunino Giuseppe Francesco, 1813-1901

Come unto Him and rest
Vetter, Daniel, d 1730
Vetter (1713); X2363 Das walt' Gott [Vater]; X11642 Vetters
Vibbard, Harry
Country lanes (1927)
Vibbert, W. H.
Triumph, No. 2 (1896)
Vincent, Charles John, jr., 1852-1934
Donum Dei
Dun Elm
Monod (1877); X9458 St Jude
St Ishmael
Silksworth
Southwick
Whitstable
Vincent, G. F.
Supplication (1890)
Viner, William Letton, 1790-1867
Dismissal (1845); X4201 Guide me
Vitale, Tomaso
O Lord, save thy people, arr
Vittoria, T. L., da
Jesu dulcis memoria
Voigtländer, J.
Vola
Vulpius, Melchior, 1560-1616
NOTES: Unlatinized name was Fuchs.
The 1609 date following tune name indicates its inclusion in Vulpius' Gesangbuch, Jena, 1609

Cana (1709); NOTE: This is one of several tunes having 14 name variants in this index; X84 Abide in grace; X104 Ach bleib mit deiner gnade; X1178 Bliv med din store naade; X1299 Bremen; X1709 Christ is my life; X1795 Christus der ist mein; X 4549 Heidelberg; X5004 Hymn to St Joseph; X6211 Lincoln; X6842 Mein leben; X7463 Normanton; X8455 Phuvah; X11754 Vulpius; X11966 Weimar
Das Neugeborne (1609); X2361 Das neugeborne kindelein; X5494 Jena; X9819 Search me, O God
Der tag bricht an; X1288 Break thou, O Lord, the bread
Die Helle Sonn' leucht't (1609)
Gelobt sei Gott (1609); X11753 Vulpius
Lobet den Herrn, ihr (1609) X6311 Lobt Gott; X6866 Melchior
Lusatia
Weimar (1609); X1691 Choral; X4111 Gregor's 152d metre-B; X5549 Jesu, deine passion; X5614 Jesu Kreuz, leiden und pein; X5617 Jesu leiden, pein und tod

W

W. C. B.
St John's, Highlands
Wade, J. F. Cantus diversi, 1751
Adeste fideles; X1910 Come, all ye faithful; X7617 O come, all ye faithful; X8540 Portuguese; X8541 Portuguese hymn
St Thomas; X3154 Evensong; X4763 Hollywood; X4835 Holywood; X7514 Novello; X9444 St John; X10061 Sing my tongue, the Saviour's glory; X10685 Tantum ergo
Wade, James Clifft, 1847-
Holy Cross, arr
Waghorne, William Richard, 1881-
Greystone (1906)
Wagner, J. G. MS Gesangbuch. Langenäls, 1742
Wir glauben all' an einen Gott; X8530 Pomerania
Wagner, J. G. Sammlung alter und neuer, 1742
Gottlob, es geht nunmehr zu Ende; X3951 Gottlob; X5650 Jesus, my Lord, my God; X11967 Weisse

Wagner, Wilhelm Richard, 1813-83
Da zu dir der Heiland kam; X6859 Meistersinger chorale
Lohengrin (1850)
Parsifal (1882)
Pilgrim's chorus [sic] (1845); X5388 Invocation; X8469a; Pilgrim chorus; X11015 The pilgrim's chorus
Rise, O Lord
Temple (1868)
The Lord God Jesus Christ
Wainwright, John, 1723-68
Yorkshire (1750); X1782 Christmas hymn; X10422 Stockport
Wainwright, Robert (or Richard), 1748-82
Liverpool
Manchester (1791); X6676 Manchester new
Wainwright (1790)
Walch, James, 1837-1901
Eagley
St George's Bolton (1875)
Sawley (1860); X7203 My God, accept my heart
Tidings (1876); X466 Angelic songs; X7907 O Sion, haste; X8668 Proclamation; X11454 Tunbridge
Walder, Johann Jakob, 1750-1817
Walder (1788); X12377 Wolder (Wolder)
Waldis, Burkard
Es muss die ganz Christenschar (1553); X8514 Pleasure it is
Säll du, som dig at Gud betror (1553)
Waldis (1553); X7710 O Gud! ditt rike ingen
Walenn, J. F.
Walenn
Wales, Univ. of. Student's hymnal, 1923
Childhood
Courage
Quinta
Reunion
Rhiw
Walker, Edward Charles, 1848-72
King's College
St Marguerite (1876); X6715 Marguerite
Walker, William. Southern harmony, 1835 see Southern harmony, 1835
Wallace, William Vincent, 1814-65
Serenity (1856); X5384 Invitation
Wallace
Walmisley, Thomas Attwood, 1814-56
Walmisley
Walter, Samuel
O love, how deep (1964)
Walter, William Henry, 1825-93
Festal song (1894)
Walters, E.
Dear little One
Walther, Carl Ferdinand Wilhelm, 1811-87
Walther (1860)
Walther, Johannes, 1496-1570. Geistliches Gesangbuchlein. Wittenberg 1524.
NOTES: Walther's original name was Blanckenmüller.
This was the first Protestant singing-book: containing eight hymns (four by Luther), and with music edited and prepared by Walther. Cf. both Baker (on Walther) and Julian (on Luther).

Christ unser Herr zum Jordan kam; X4131 Gregor's 201st metre
Confession; X11653 Vi tro og trøste paa; X12328 Wir glauben all an
De profundis; X194 Af dybsens nød; X707 Aus tiefer not [noth]
Es spracht der Unweisen Mund
Gott des Vater wohn'
Lieblich, dunkel, sanft und stille (date uncertain)
Mensch, willt du leben seliglich

Mit Fried' und Freud'
Mitten wir im Leben sind; X6943 Midt i livit ere vi
Soldau; X3334 Fidei unitas; X4080 Gregor's 58th metre; X7540 Nu bede vi den helligaand; X7551 Nun bitten wir den; X10302 Spiritus
Soldau, Pt. II; X4081 Gregor's 58th metre, Pt. II
Venit hora (Bach arr); X3334 Fidei unitas; X5009 Hymn to the sorrowful Mother; X5888 Kom, du folkefrelser; X7566 Nun komm der heiden; X11595a Veni, redemptor; X11597, Veni redemptor gentium
Walther; X3939 Gott sei gelobet; X4189 Gud vaere lovet evig
Wär Gott nicht mit uns

Walton, Herbert Francis Raine, 1869-
Children's song

Warburton, J.S.
Spes meo in deo

Ward, Samuel Augustus, 1847-1903
Materna (1882); X7595 O beautiful for spacious skies; X10911 The Holy City; X12345 With songs and honors

Warlock, Peter (pseud of Philip Heseltine), 1894-1930
Adam lay ybounden (1925)
Balulalow
Tyrley, Tyrlow

Warner, Massah M., 1836-1900
Amadeus
Art thou weary? (1890)
Dickson
Proclamation
Roepper
Softly the night is sleeping; X11829 Warner

Warner, Richard, 1908-
Ramwold

Warrack, Guy, 1900-
Wellington Square (1931)

Warrell, Arthur Sydney, 1883-1939
Farmborough

Warren, B. Elliott
A ransom for all
Come closer to me
Ever lead me
Glory to God in the highest
His yoke is easy; X10962 The Lord is my Shepherd (Hudson)
I would be closer to thee
Keep me near thee
Let not your heart be troubled
Long have they waited (1900)
Lost forever
Not dead, but sleeping
Saviour, I'm coming
Sin can never enter there
Sing about Jesus
The bond of perfectness
The Christian's Guide
The eventide
The last great day
The ninety-nine
The temple of God
Two little hands
Watch unto prayer
Weighed in the balance
What a mighty God!
Where will I go?(1923)
Why carelessly wait?

Warren, George William, 1828-1902
Ecce agnus
Columbia College (1886)
Grace
Guide me (1884)
Log College
National hymn (1892); X3834 God of our fathers; X8666 Pro patria
Resurrection morning

Warren, Ivor
Whose works, O Lord, like Thine

Warren, Samuel Prowse, 1841-1914
Bread of life; X11832 Warren
Gould
Unity (1886)

Wartensee, Xavier Schnyder von, see Schnyder von Wartensee, Xavier.

Wathall, Alfred G.

Ascending song (1905)
Fellowship (1905)
Festgesang (1905)
Greeting (1905)
Implicit trust (1905)
Plymouth (1905)
Stella (1905)
Watson, Adam, 1845-1912
Wonderful love
Watson, James, 1816-80
Holyrood (1867)
Watson, Lawrence White, 1860-1927
Salve Domini (1909)
Watson, Sydney, 1903-
May Hill
Stonor
Wytham
Watts-Hughes, Megan, 1842-1907
Wilton Square
Weale, William, ca 1690-1727
see Wheall, William
Webb, George James, 1803-87
NOTE: See also Mason and Webb. Cantica laudis.

Webb (1837); X3912 Goodwin; X5103 I need thee, precious Jesus; X5121 I thank the Lord my maker; X7107 Morning light; X10355 Stand up, stand up for
Webbe, Samuel, 1740-1816
Behold! behold He cometh
Benevento (1792)
Consolation (1792); X375 Alma X380 Alma redemptoris [mater]; X1993 Come, ye disconsolate; X2105 Consolator; X2601 Disconsolate; X8238 Out of the depths; X11948 Webbe
Melcombe (1782); X590 As fades the glowing orb; X7312 Nazareth; X7891 O salutaris Hostia; X7927 O thou immortal Light
Veni Sancte Spiritus (1782); X1973 Come, thou Holy Spirit, come; X4823 Holy Spirit, Lord of light
Webbe, Samuel, jr., 1770-1843
is often cited as composer in Gardiner's Sacred melodies
Webbe, William Y.
King Olaf
Weber, Carl Maria Friedrich Ernst von, 1736-1826
Help us, O God
Jewett (1820); X2496 Der Freyschuetz; X7220 My Jesus, as thou wilt; X8522 Poacher; X11950 Weber
Seymour (1826); X1623 Chatham; X10144 Softly now the light; X11951 Weber
Wilmot; X4358 Hark! what mean those holy voices; X6225 Listen to the gentle promptings
Weber, Frederich Wilhelm, 1813-94
Paean; X8305 Paradise
Webster, Harry, 1878-
Nil nisi labore
Webster, Joseph Philbrick, 1819-75
Sweet by and bye (1868); X11168 There's a land
Webster, Lorin
Ruth (1905)
Service (1905)
Webster, Mary Phillips, 1858-
Chadwick (1913)
He leads us on (1913)
Weeden, Winfield S., 1847-1908
My mother's prayer
Sunlight
Surrender; X5120 I surrender all
Weekes, Samuel, 1843-
Brent
Burleigh
Weimar, Georg Peter, 1734-1800
Allgütiger, mein Preisgesang; X3020 Erfurt
Brasted (1780)
Weimar Gesangbuch, 1681
Jesu, meines lebens leben; X337 Alle menschen müssen sterben; X2351

Darmstadt; X12579 Zurich
Weinberg, Jacob, 1879-1956
A week within the Sukko green (1932); X9994 Sh'meenee atseres
Grant me strength (1932)
Hymn for Day of Atonement (1932)
If our God had not befriended (1932)
Lord, what offering shall we bring (1932); X12542 Yom Kippur prayer
O Lord, where shall I find Thee? (1932)
Once more, O Lord (1932)
Psalm 119 (1932)
Sound the loud timbrel (1932)
Ten thousand martyrs (1932)
Weisenthal, T.V. (or F.V.)
Salvation (1830)
Weisse, Michael, ca 1480-1534
Michael
Weisse, M. Ave hierarchia, 1531
Ravenshaw; X3944 Gottes sohn ist kommen; X7064 Moravia; X8033 Old 72d
Wellesley, Garrett, 1735-81 see Mornington, Earl of
NOTE: Sometimes written "Wesley", by other members of the large family.
Wells, Marcus Morris, 1815-95
Holy Spirit, faithful Guide X3231 Faithful guide; X4200 Guide; C12000 Wells
Welsh traditional, and traditional hymn tunes (marked *)
April; X4717 Hir oesi fair
Ar hyd y nos; X323 All through the night; X12002 Welsh hymn
Arfon (major reading)*
Arfon (minor reading)*
Ash Grove, see English traditional, etc.
Blaenhafren
Braint
Caerlleon*
Crugybar*
Denbigh*
Dolgelly* (19th c)
Erfyniad*
Ffigysbren* (1840)
Glan Geirionydd*
Gwalchmai
Gwalia
Hail, Guest
Harlech
Jabez*
Llanfyllin (1865)
Llangan
Llangoedmor * (1826)
Llanilar*
Llansannan*
Lledrod* (1859); X6283 Llangollen
Maldwyn (ca 1600)
Moriah*
Nos Galan; X2431 Deck the halls
O Thou who hearest prayer
Poverty; X8087 Olwen
Rhuddlan
Rhyddid*
St Denio; X5701 Joanna
Suo-gân
Talyllyn
Trefaenan
Welsh carol
Ymdaith mwnge; X7037 Monk's march
Weman, Henry
Weman (1937)
Wennerberg, Gunnar, 1817-1901
Thy Kingdom come; X11270 Tillkomme ditt rike
Wennerberg I
Wennerberg II
Werner, Arno, 1865-1955
O salutaris hostia
Wesley, Charles, the younger, 1757-1834
Berkshire
Epworth
Lystra
Wesley, John. Foundery collection, 1742
Savannah (from a MS choralbuch. Herrnhut, ca 1740)
Wesley, Samuel, 1866-1837
Bristol

Doncaster (1837); X1061
Bethlehem
Hierapolis
Sanctus
Wesley, Samuel Sebastian, 1810-76
NOTE: His European Palmist, 1872 melodies are included below.

Achill (1872)
Alcester, arr
Alleluia (1868)
Almsgiving; X9830 Sebastian
Ashburton
Aurelia (1864); X511 Another year is dawning; X10838 The church's one foundation
Bowden, arr
Brecknock
Brief life is here our portion
Bude
Clevedon
Colchester (1872)
Cornwall
Dawn
Eden, W.
Ellingham
Engedi
Epworth
Eternity
Grace Dieu
Gratitude; X6877 Memoria
Gweedore
Harewood (1839); X4422 Havewood
Hawarden
Hawkridge
Hereford (1872)
Hornsey
Lead me, Lord
Mara
Morning (see also his Streatley)
Orisons
Patmos
Philadelphia, arr
Radford
Remembrance
St Michael New
Sebastian (1872); X4900 Houghton
Serug (1872)
Streatley, arr (see also his morning); X4424 Hawes
Trinity
Weston
Wetherby (1872)
Wigan (1872)
Wimbledon (1864)
Winscott
Wrestling Jacob; X8411 Peniel
Wessnitzer, Wolfgang
Aldwinkle (1665)
Tviflan ur min sjal försvinne (1661)
West, Dorothy
God's presence
West, John A.
Godfrey
West, John Ebenezer, 1863-1929
Holy Cross
West, Lewis Renatus, 1753-1826
Moravia (1795); X11479 Tytherton; X12039 West
Westlake, Frederick, 1840-98
St Ursula (1863)
Wetterling, Hampus, 1830-70
Wetterling; X10413 Stilla, ja, allt mera
Weyse, Christoph Ernst Freidrich, 1774-1842
Cheerfulness; X406 Altid frejdig naar du
Christmas brings joy; X 9919 Sewey
Store Gud, som dig til Aere
Weyse; X2475 Den signede dag; X7641 O day full of grace
Weyse II (1837)
Wheall, William, ca 1690-1927
Bedford (1723)
Wheelwright, Lorin F.
Come all ye saints
Whelan, Ernest H.
Lux perpetua (1891)
Whelpton, George, 1847-1930
Dismissal
Hear our prayer (1897); X12102 Whelpton
Whinfield, Wallis Grenville,

1865-1919
Universal praise (1906)
Upwick
Worcester
Wychbold
Whitaker, John, 19th c.
NOTE: Perhaps John Whitaker, 1820-95 of Whitaker's Almanack
Wimborne
White, Benjamin Franklin
Hamilton (1844)
White, L. Meadows
Meadows
Motherhood (1899)
White, J.E. [probably John White, 1855-1902]
Marietta (1878?)
White
White Spirituals.
Herein filed under "American traditional" are melodies from the Appalachian and Piedmont: as
Foundation
Amazing grace
Cleansing fountain
See also file, "Negro spirituals", etc.
Whitehead, Alfred, 1887-
Wellard
Whitehead, Alfred E.
Chichester (1941)
Whitehead, H., O.P.
Hail, holy Joseph (20th c)
O Christ, thy guilty people (20th c)
Whitehead, H.A.
Victory
Whitehead, J. Brinton, 1869-
Whitehead (1909)
Whiting, Arthur Battelle, 1861-1936
Litany No. 4
Whitlock, Percy
Infinitas
Oblation (1932)
Presence (1932)
Satis (1932)
Whitmer, Thomas Carl, 1873-
Deed (1930)
Golden trumpets (1930)
Gratitude (1929)
Whitney, H.N.
Luella
Whitney, Samuel Brenton, 1842-1914
Coelestis aula
Crusader (1889)
Whittington, C.J.
Arise, O Lord
City strong and mighty
Glory flaming
I bow in utter need
I come into thy house
Thy testimonies, arr
Whitwell, W.J.
Groombridge
Widdeman, E.S.
McCabe
Saviour, again to thy dear Name; X2998 Enon
Widdemer, E.S., see Widdeman, E.S.
Widéen, Karl Ivor Natanael, 1871-1951
Security; X11443 Tryggare kan ingen
Skara
Wilcox, J.H., see Willocx, John H.
Wild, A.A.
Beaufort
Wilkes, John Bernard, 1785-1869
Lyte (1861)
Wilkin's Psalmody, 1669
Stroudwater
Wilkinson, Walter Olivant, 1852-
Presbyter (1895)
Willan, Healey, 1880-
Eternal Light
Haec Dies
Hail Mary
St Basil
Stella orientis
Willcocks, David Valentine, 1919-
Conquering love
Willcox, John Henry, 1827-75
Faben (1849)
Jesu, bone pastor; X5659 Jesu pastor
Williams, Aaron, 1731-76
Mear; X7580 Nun sich der tag
St Thomas (1763); X1992 Come, we that love

Williams, Benjamin, 1839-1918
Deganwy
Williams, C.C.
Have you any room for Jesus?
Williams, Charles Lee, 1853-1935
Gloucester (1890); X1697 Christ by heavenly hosts
Tibberton (1885)
Williams
Williams, David McKinley, 1887-
Canticum refectionis (1941)
Christus rex (1941)
Georgetown (1941)
Malabar (1941)
Non nobis Domine (1942)
St Bartholomew's
Trackless ways (1936)
Williams, F.W.
Willington (1851)
Williams, J.E.
Don't let your light burn low
Williams, J. Rhosyd, 1885-
Overdale
Williams, John (Dolgelley), 1740-1821
Brynhyfryd
Williams, Ralph Vaughan, 1872-1958
Abinger (1931)
Blake's Cradle hymn (1928)
Cumnor (1925)
Down Ampney (1906)
Famous men (1923)
Guildford (1925)
King's Weston (1925)
Magda (1925)
Mantegna (1931)
Marathon (1928)
Oakley (1925)
Randolph
Salve festa dies (1906)
Sine nomine (1906)
Snow in the street
The call (1911)
The golden carol (1928)
White gates
Wither's Rocking hymn (1928)
Williams, Robert, ca 1781-1821
Llanfair (1817)
Williams, Thomas. Psalmody, ca 1770
Durham; X2675 Dover; X4302 Hampton; X4953 Huddersfield
Williams, Thomas (Hafrenydd), 1807-94
Llandinam
Nantmel
Williams, Thomas John, 1869-1944
Ebenezer (1890); X11331 Ton-y-botel
Williams, W.A.
Christ is all
Williamson, J., 1868-1947
St Katrine
Willing, Christopher E., 1830-1904
Alstone (1868); X12276 Willing
Willis, J.A. (or T.A.?)
Lucerne
Willis, Richard Storrs, 1819-1900
Carol (1850); X5427 It came upon the midnight; X12184 While shepherds watched their
Madison
Wilms, Jan Willem, 1772-1847
Hague; X4757 Holland; X6150 Leyden; X11427 Trust, No. 2
Wilson, A.W., 1869-
Perranporth
Wilson, David Frederick Ruddell, 1871-1957
Drumcondra
Wilson, Emily D., 1865-1942
Heaven; X12158 When we all get to heaven
Wilson, Hugh, 1764-1825
Lucas
Martyrdom (ca 1800); X100 According to thy gracious word; X304 All saints; X757 Avon; X6153a Liberty Hall (---); X7522 Now from the altar of my heart; X7524 Now, gracious Lord, thine arm; X10710 Teach me the measure; X12284 Wilson
Wilson, Ira B.
May God depend on you?

(1878)
Our Pilot (1907)
Wilson, Robert H.
Seedtime
Wilson, Roger Charles, 1912-
Dayton (1958)
Spiritus domini (1958)
Wilson, W (?)
Arabia (1833)
Wiltberger, August, 1850-1928
Hymn to the Holy Cross (1908)
Winchester, Caleb Thomas, 1847-1920
Middletown (1905)
Winding, August Henrik, 1835-99
Winding I
Winding II; X7340 Nestling; X10177 Som hønen klukker mindelig
Winn, William, 1828-88
Barnby's Hymnary Tune 525 (1872)
Winner, Septimus, 1827-1902
see Hawthorne, Alice, pseud.
Wilson, Selection of Psalm Tunes. 1825
Smith
Winsett, R. E.
The Church of the living God (1918)
The great reaping day
The midnight cry
Wise, Michael, ca 1648-87
Congleton
Wiseman, Frederick Luke, ca 1859-1944
All Hallows
Wonderful love
Wissmer, Pierre, 1915-
Geneva (1939)
Miron (1939)
Witt, Christian Friedrich, 1660-1716
Ach, wann werd ich dahin kommen (1715)
Stuttgart (1715); X1064 Bethlehem, of noblest; X8345 Pastor benignus
Wittwe, Georg. Musikalisches Handbuch. Hamburg, 1690
Crasselius; X2597 Dir, dir, Jehova, will ich singen; X4095 Gregor's 106th metre; X5162 Ich armer mensch, ich armer suender; X12024a Wer weiss, wie nahe (Bronner. Choralbuch, 1715)
Winchester New; X2201 Crasselius; X8096 On Jordan's bank; X12024a Wer weiss, wie nahe (Bronner. Choral-buch, 1715); X12298 Winchester old
Wolder. Catechismus-Gesangbüchlein, 1598
Wolder; X703 Aus meines herzens grunde; X2903 Eiselben; X7065 Moravia; X8908 Rejoicing; X11067 The Spirit of the Lord revealeth
Wolff, J.
Naar Tid og Stund den er forhaand (1560); X1454 Calvary; X12011 Wenn mein stündlein vorhanded ist
Wolff (1568)
Wolle, John Frederick, 1863-1933
Advent
Dies Irae I (1890)
Dies Irae II (1890)
Palmarum (1923)
Wolle, Theodore Frederick, 1832-85
Asleep in Jesus (1877)
Wonnberger, C.
Alleluia, Jesus lives
Inita
Wonnberger (in Schemelli. Gesangbuch, 1736); X5178 Ich steh an deiner krippe
Wood, Basil
Paddington
Wood, Charles, 1866-1926
Cambridge (1925)
Rangoon
Recessional
Wood, D. J.
Isca
Pastor
Wood, David Duffle, 1838-1910
St Stephen's Church (1895); X5759 Juniata
Wood, Thomas, 1892-1950
St Osyth (1925)
School house (1931)
Woodbury, Isaac Baker, 1819-58

NOTE: Original spelling as Woodberry.

Burton
Chopin
Desire
Dorrnance (1845); X10659 Talmar; X11200 This is not my place
Edmeston
Ella
Enon's Isle
Eucharist (1856); X8082 Olivet; X12421 Woodbury
Happy Sion
Lake Enon (1854); X6894 Mercersburg
Life's harvest
Modena
Nearer home (1852); X6397 Lord, when at thy command; X7053 Montgomery; X12422 Woodbury
Ozrem
Rakem
Selena; X3836 God of our fathers, known of old
Siloam
Speed away

Woodman, Jonathan Call, 1813-94
State Street (1844)

Woodman, Raymond Huntington, 1861-1943
Adoration (1893)
Bethlehem
Unity (1895)
Woodman

Woods, Bertram Ernest, 1900-
Norwick

Wooldridge, Harry Ellis, 1845-1917
Yattendon 4 (1891)
Yattendon 11 (1890)
Yattendon 17 (1899)
Yattendon 18 (1899)
Yattendon 22 (1887)
Yattendon 46 (1899)

Wooler, Alfred, 1867-1937
Incarnation (1920)

Woollen, Russell, 1923-
Lord of nations

Worcester, John
Westall (1893)

Worden, B. T.
Crossing the bar (1905)

Work, Henry Clay, 1832-84
Come, Saviour, come

Wostenholm, Maurice L., 1887-
My Holyoke (1910)

Wright, J. B. F.
Precious memories

Wright, Thomas, 1763-1829
Stockton

Wrigley, W. A.
Thirsk

Würtemberg Gesangbuch, 1784
Ellacombe; X5588 Jesus is God; X7869 O Queen of the Holy Rosary; X11189 Think gently of the erring one

Würzburg Gesangbuch, 1628
O Traurigkeit; X548 Arimathaea; X4075 Gregor's 45th metre; X7635 O darkest woe; X7734 O hjertens ve; X7939 O traurigkeit! O herzeleid

Wyeth, John, 1770-1858
Nettleton (1825); X1971 Come, thou fount

Wyeth, J. Repository of sacred music. Pt. II; 1813
Morning song; X2101 Consolation; X2524 Detroy (Suppl. to Kentucky Harmony, 1820)

Wyvill, Z., 1762-1837
Wyvill

Y

Yenn, S. M.
Hail Virgin, dearest Mary
Mother of mercy (1920)
Why art thou sorrowful?

Yoakley, John, 1860-1915
All souls

Yoakley, William, 1820-
Yoakley (1841)

Yon, Pietro Alessandro, 1886-1943
St Augustine (1939)

When blossoms flowered (1917)
York Breviary
Jesu, Salvator saeculi
Young, Alfred
See, He comes (1953)
Slain for my soul
Young, E. Edwin
Jesus, revealed in me (1931)
Young, Walter E.
Falmouth (1932)
Fortitude (1932)
Love (1932)
Saviour (1932)

Z

Ziegler, Charles L.
Church vigilant (1902)
Zeuner, Charles, 1795-1857
see his real name, Zeuner, Heinrich Christoph, 1795-1857
Zeuner, Heinrich Christoph, 1795-1857
Groton
Hummel
Luther's Chant
Missionary Chant
Oaksville (1839)
Zinck, Hartnack Otto Konrad, 1746-1832
Congregation
Copenhagen; X5488 Jeg vil mig Herren love; X7808 O living Bread
Zinck, H.O.K. Koralbog, 1801
Naglet til et Kors paa Jorden; X2260 Crucifixion
Paa Gud alene; X5267 In God, my Saviour; X12566 Zinck
Paa sit Kors i Dodens Smerte
Zinck; X7546 Nu rinder solen op; X10513 Sunrise
Zundel, John, 1815-82
Beecher (1870); X6430 Love divine; X12578 Zundel
Brooklyn (1852)
Lebanon; X5135 I was a wandering sheep
Louisville
Zundel (ca 1855)
Zwingli, Huldrich (or Ulrich) 1484-1531
Zwingli

V

Melodies, a Systematic Index

DDD - (Multiple)

DDDDDDDDDDTRD, LLL 24
DDDDDDDD, DRRRRRRD, 11863
DDDDDDDDDTDLTDLT 6810
DDDDDDDRDDD#, RFFFD 5723
DDDDDDD, MMMMMFFMM 7817
DDDDDDRRM, DFFMDMF 8114
DDDDDDRM, MMMRDFMR, 5958
DDDDDD, SSSSSS#LT, DL 489
DDDDDDTD, RRRRDTLS, 4542
DDDDDDT, DRSSSSLTL 3761
DDDDDRDD, DDDDTRR 5464
DDDDDR, DDDLTD. 12479
DDDDDRR, RRSRRRMDT 3741
DDDDDRRMRDFFMMMD 2517
DDDDDRRM, MRDDTD, DR 11057
DDDDDRRM, MMMFMRRD, 10419
DDDDDRRM, MMMSMRRR, 2326
DDDDDRMRDTD, MMMF#S 9532
DDDDDRFM, SSSSSDLS, 3822
DDDDDRTD, RRRMDTLS, 2303
DDDDDMRDTRD, MMMMM 9026
DDDDDMMMRD, DDDMMR 7435
DDDDDMSD, DLTDFMR, R 1600
DDDDDSMSLLLDT, DDD 4752
DDDDDSFM, MRSSF#S, SS 1595
DDDDDSLDT, RRRRRST 11363
DDDDDTDR, RRRRRM, MM 4390
DDDDDTDRMS, LLLLSM 3701
DDDDDTDRTD, DFFFMR 12492
DDDDDTDL, FMRDTDR, R 1596
DDDDDTLLS, SLSSFFS 2906
DDDDDTLTD, RRRDRM 9409
DDDDRDRD, MMMFSSFM 10697
DDDDRDRMM, FMLSDTD 5672
DDDDRDTD, RRRMDTLS, 7020
DDDDRDTLTRD, MMMMM 174
DDDDRRRDRRM, MDRMR 5281
DDDDRRRRMRDDLDR, M 4827
DDDDR, RRMMFMR, RMRM 8902
DDDDRR, RMSFMR, 1835
DDDDRRMR, MMMF#SLT, D 10368
DDDDRRM, MMMMFF#S, SS 12069
DDDDRMDL, LSSDRMDR, 9099
DDDDRMRD, MMMMMRLD 11731
DDDDRMRDTD, MMMMF#S 8312
DDDDRMRRR, TDDDRMT, 8674
DDDDRMRMDRMRMFMR 11553
DDDDRM, MMMMF#S, SSSL 1513
DDDDRM, MMMSSS, MMMS 8113
DDDDRMFM, MMRDTLS, D 8176
DDDDRMFM, SSSSLTDT, 8542
DDDDRMFFR, SFMDMRD 4224
DDDDRMFSLSM, SSLFS 9627
DDDDR, TDTLS, MRRDRS 7782
DDDDMDRS, TTDDTLS, D 9023
DDDDMDL, SSSRDTDRM 10484
DDDDMRDD, FFFFMMRD 1858
DDDDMRD, RRRRFMR, MM 1019
DDDDMRRDD, RRRRFMR, 2942
DDDDMMSSF, MRMFRDT 4017
DDDD, MFFM, SFFMRDLR 8596
DDDDMSRM, SSSLMSFM 4817
DDDD, FFMRRM, MMMM, LL 8943
DDDDS, DDDDL, FSLSSS 8195
DDDDSDRSRMD, LTDSD 5587
DDDDSDMRD, MMMMDMS 932
DDDDSDFMMRRD, MFSM 5823
DDDDSLSS, RMRDTLS, M 6969
DDDDSLLS, SDMRDTLS, 10384
DDDDSLLLSM, DDDDSL 5022
DDDDLSRR, RMFRRD, MF 7615
DDDDLSM, DDDDLS, SFM 10910
DDDDLSSSS, SLLLLTT 10954
DDDDLSS, SLDDTD, DDD 6929
DDDDLS, LSMFS, DDDDL 5032
DDDDLTD, RMRDTLTD, S 8446
DDDDTDR, DRMMFMRDS, 2487
DDDDTDRRD, MMMRRRM 7921
DDDDTDR, RRRRDRM, MM 2588
DDDDTDRMRD, MMMMRM 4974
DDDDTDMR, RRRRDRM, M 2587
DDDDTDMR, RRRRDRM, S 3146
DDDDTDSLTD, RRMRDT 4581
DDDDTR, SSLS, SMMMRS, 9371
DDDDT, FFFFM, SMRDTL, 7137
DDDDTLDDM, SSFRLLS 4917
DDDDTLS, DDDTRD, DDD 12401

DDDDTLSM, RMFLSMS, D 5798
DDDDTLSM, FFFFSFM, D 12509
DDDDTLSMS, DDDDTLT 4445
DDDDTLSFMFS, DDLLS 5989
DDDDTLSS, MSRMFSFM, 3789
DDDDTLSS, SSSSSSS, M 2756
DDDDTLSLMSF, RRRRD 1853
DDDDTLS, LLLLSFM, DD 12466
DDDDTLLSS, SLSFSFM 34
DDDRDDDRMFM, MSFMR 5490
DDDRDD, DTDLSS, DDDR 9414
DDDRDDS, LSLTDD, DD 10736
DDDRDDT, LSSDMR, MFS 9472
DDDRDMFSSLS, LTDSS 3555
DDDRDTDR, RMDDRMRD, 9897
DDDRDTSLTD, MRTDTL 1627
DDDRDTTL, LDRMMR 641
DDDR, RRM, MMMF, RFM. 5082
DDDR, RRM, MMMS, MDR, MM 7598
DDDRRMDDRDT, MMMMR 3383
DDDRRMRDR, DDDRMFM 6386
DDDRRM, MMLSMRD, SSM 4840
DDDRRMFS, SSMLTDTL 4625
DDDRRM, SFMMRR, RRLS 11179
DDDRRFMRM, MFMMLSF# 11862
DDDRRSFM, MRDDTD, DD 3627
DDDRR#MMS, FMDMRR, MF 8820
DDDRMD, DTDRMS, FSLT 5708
DDDRMD, RTDTL, DDDRM 6764
DDDRMD, MMMFSM, SMDL 2984
DDDRMDMFS, DTLS, DDD 11700
DDDRMRD, RMRSSF#S, LS 11599
DDDRMRDR, MSLSFMRD 8999
DDDRMR, DMRRD, DDDRM 671
DDDRMRDTS, DSSF#SMR, 6429
DDDRMR, SSMSLSFMFM 11732
DDDRMMRR, MFSLTS, SD 9607
DDDRMMRR, SDDRMSMR, 12541
DDDRMFRD, MRRLTDRD 2571
DDDRMFRDTD, MMFSSL 8248
DDDRMFRM, DMFSRSF#S 482
DDDRMFRM, DMSLSFMR, 1607
DDDRMFRS, DMFSRSF#S, 479
DDDRMFMRD, DDMRDTL 12286
DDDRMFMRM, MMMF#SLS 794
DDDRMFMR, MFSSLLS, M 9571
DDDRMFM, MRDDTD, DDD 3507
DDDRMFFM, SDMMF#S 9352
DDDRMFFM, SMFSLRR, S 3720
DDDRMFSLSM, DDDRMF 11457
DDDRMFSL, TDRSSFR, R 782
DDDRMSM, DDDRMMRD, D 7502
DDDRMS, MSFMRD, DDDR 3230
DDDRMSFMR, DDRFMRM, 6935
DDDRMSFF, MMMRDT, TD 1294
DDDRMS, FFFLD, DDTLS 9180
DDDRMSLS, RRRMFSLS 5544
DDDRMSLS, MDSMMR, SM 12269
DDDRFMFS, SSSLLSFM 8366
DDDRSM, MMMFMR, SSFM 11684
DDDRTDRM, MRRRDTLS, 8680
DDDRTD, MMMMFRM, SD 9373
DDDRTD, MMMFRM, SDLS 9374
DDDRTDTLS, SDRMRDT 7544
DDDMDDDM, MMMMRDDM, 3867
DDDMDMSDMRDS, FLFM 8589
DDDMDFMRD, MMMRMFM 4624
DDDMDSRM, LSMFMDS, S 4182
DDDMDSSDTSLSM, DSL 4661
DDDMRD, RRRFMR, MF#F#S, 7362
DDDMRDRRF, RMMSFML 1296
DDDMRDRM, MMMLSF#S, S 162
DDDMRDFM, MMMSMRTL 4995
DDDMRDTD, MRMFMRM 11960
DDDMRDTDS, MMMSFMR 6553
DDDMRDTRD, DLDLDSF 754
DDDMRRD, DDDFMR, SSS 461
DDDMMRRSFM, FMFRML 4473
DDDMMM, SSSLRM, DDDL 10382
DDDMMFFS, DDMMFFSL, 5196
DDDMML, LSDFMR, RMSL 2548
DDDMFS, MLLSRM, MMMM 11261
DDDMFSSS, SLSMFS, SL 10455
DDDMFSLS, DDDMFSLS 5257
DDDMFSLS, SDDMFSL 5256
DDDMSSD, DRMDRDTLS, 1696
DDDMSSL, SMRDDTDR, R 9554
DDDMSLSSMDTRD, DDD 3263
DDDMSLS, SMMRDM, DDD 2044
DDDMLSMR, DDLSSLT, S 9416
DDDFRMFS, SLTDTDLS, 5167
DDDFRMF#S, MFSLFSF, S 5166
DDDFRMF#S, SLTDTLS, S 5165
DDDFMDLTD, SDTLTDR, 8584
DDDFMRD, DLSDMRR, DD 5799
DDDFMRD, DLSDMRRS, D 11378
DDDFFFFL, LLSSMSMR 10854
DDDSDD, RRRLRR, MMMF# 1816
DDDSDRMD, LLSDFMR, R 7087
DDDSDRM, MRRRMD, D, DD 285
DDDSDRM, MMLLSF#S, DD 4159
DDDSDRM, LSFMRDR, DD 1405
DDDSDMRD, MMMDMSFM, 6136

DDDSDMMR, RMFFDRM, D 6807
DDDSDMSFM, MMMRFRD 4577
DDDSMFSLSD, RMRSLT 4870
DDDSMFSLS, MMMMMMF 1706
DDDSFMDLFS, SLLLFL 1173
DDDSSD, SSSSMS, MMMF# 183
DDDSSLFS, SDRMFSFM 6112
DDDSSLLS, SSDTSLLS, 7727
DDDSSLTD, DDTTLSLS, 1048
DDDSSLTD, SFSMRR, DD 6873
DDDS, SLTRDTDFMM, SF 8759
DDDSLDRD, DMDDRT, DD 6171
DDDSLDTLS, DTLSLFM 2880
DDDSLMMRD, MMRDLDR 975
DDDSLM, MFRMFS, DTLS, 6970
DDDSLS, SDRMRD, DMSM 6097
DDDSLSLD, MMRDDMS, S 4754
DDDSLTD, RRRMFMR, MM 2212
DDDSLTDS, DDDTLRS, D 467
DDDSLTDTLS, DTLSLF 2878
DDDSTDLS, DTLSLFRD, 2881
DDDSTDTLS, DTLSLFM 2879
DDDLDRTL, LTDRSLTL 1301
DDDLDRTL, LTDRSTLS, 1301a
DDDLDRTL, TDRDSTLS, 1304
DDDLDLLDL, DDDLSSS 5048
DDDLRLDTL, LTDRLDTL, 7486
DDDLFMRD, SLDSFM, MM 2561
DDDLSF#S, DDDLSF#S, TT 1624
DDDLSLD, MMMDRMR, MM 3775
DDDLLFFFLFFF, LLLL 6682
DDDLLSM, DDDSDR, RRR 9912
DDDLLSFM, SLLLLS, MF 9428
DDDLTDD, RMDRDD, MMM 1986
DDDLTDRDTL, LTDRSL 1302
DDDLTDRMD, SFMRDRD, 3926
DDDLTDRMRD, MMMLSS 4635
DDDLTDRTS, RRDTDRM 5737
DDDLTDRTL, LTDRDTD 1303
DDDTDRDRM, MMMFSSF 10696
DDDTDRD, MMMRMFM, RD 3275
DDDTDRDTD, DRMMMRD 6909
DDDTDR, RRRDRM, MMRD 11677
DDDTDRMD, SDDDTLSF 1716
DDDTDRMRD, MMMRDSM 10695
DDDTDR, MRDFMR, RRRM 5498
DDDTDMMRDTD, RRRMD 5220
DDDTMRD, DDDTTLS, FM 7382
DDDTMLLS, DFFMSSF#S, 5754
DDDTSFFM, SSMSFRDM 7163
DDDTSLLS, MDRMFSFM 2219
DDDTSLTD, MRFMRDRM, 458
DDDTLDLS, MSLSDMRD, 5462
DDDTLSDM, DRMFMMRR 5150
DDDTLS, MMMRDT, RLLS, 2760
DDDTLSFMRDDTLSFM 12259
DDDTLSFM, STDRMSFR, 7460
DDDTLSFFM, SSMSFRD 7165
DDDTLSSDDDTLS, DDD 8590
DDDTLSS, LLLTDR, MMM 11822
DDDTLSLFMRD, SSMLT 6160
DDDTLSLFMRRD, SSML 6160a
DDDTLSLSM, DDDTLTL 8688
DDDTLSLTD, DRDTDTLS, 4281
DDDTLTD, RRMSLRT, RFM 9309
DDDTLTDL, DDDTSTSL 2289
DDDTLTRD, FMRDTLS, S 1319
DDDTLTLS, DRMSFMRD 1902
DDDTLTLS, MMMRDRT, D 2316
DDDTLTLSMF#S, DRMRD 10087
DDDTTDLS, SLDTLSFM, 6934
DDDTTRD, MMMRRFM, SS 10048
DDDTTRRMDFFFMMFM 10687
DDDTTLDLS, MMMRDR, F 1290
DDDTTLS, LLLDDDDTD, 1741
DDDTTLLS, LTLSLTLS, 4693
DDDTTLLT, TDDRDTLS 7820
DDDTTLLTTSS, SSSMM 5333
DDDTTTLS, SLTTTLTL 11336

DDR

DDRDDRDRRM, DRRDDR 5640
DDRDDTD, MRDTLLT, TD 9896
DDRDDTD, LSLSMFS, SL 6331
DDRDRMDR, LSMSFMRM, 226
DDRDRM, MSFMFS, SS#LL 1815
DDRDMMFM, SFMRMRRR 6818
DDRDMFS, MRDDD, DDRD 9430
DDRDMSFM, DRMSSF#S, S 8091
DDRDFMLS, DTLSFSM, M 7982
DDRDFSFMR, MSLSDTD 4090
DDRDSDRM, MFSFMDR, M 9506
DDRDSMSD, MRRRSDLS, 6290
DDRDLSSLDDRM, RRR 10100
DDRDLSSLDDRM, SMRR 10102
DDRDLSLDDRM, RRRRM 10101
DDRDTLLS, SSDSMDR, M 4329
DDRDTLL, LDTLRDT, TM 12449
DDRDTLTD, DDRDTLTD 10936
DDRRRDFMRD, FSLSFS 3327
DDRRR, RSFMM, FFMRDS 11941
DDRRRFFM, MMDTLTM, M 8560
DDRRR#R#FR, RRMMFFSM, 3975

DDRRMDLRDT, TDRMFM 2205
DDRRMDTLS, SSLTDTL 7928
DDRRMRR, FFMRDTD, MR 736
DDRRMMRR, MSFMRRD, D 10601
DDRRMFR, MRDTLLS, SL 3160
DDRRMFMRM, MFSLTDD, 1399
DDRRMSMDDTRTS, DDR 11729
DDRRMSMR, DDMMRD, DD 1238
DDRRMSFFRRM, DDRRM 8925
DDRMDDFMRRD, SMDF 7866
DDRMDDTD, MRTLLS, RF 9255
DDRMDDTD, MMFSMRDR, 10297
DDRMDRDTD, RRMFRSM 8934
DDRMDRDT, RRTDRDTL, 2208
DDRMDRRR, RRMFTDMS, 9129
DDRMDRRMFR, MMFSSF 1854
DDRMD, RRMFMF, MMFSR 7575
DDRMD, RRMFFF, MMFSR, 7574
DDRMDRMDLL, LDDLDD 9957
DDRMDRMFMRDD, DMF 4206
DDRMDRTD, DSSLFSSM, 8183
DDRMDRTD, MFSLLS, SF 9074
DDRMDMFS, DDRMDMF 11698
DDRMDMFS, MDMSMSF#S 3321
DDRMDMFS, SFMRDMFS, 8708
DDRMDMFS, SFMRDMF#S, 8709
DDRMDMLS, DDRMMSFR, 11559
DDRMDFRD, MFMRDTDR, 2015
DDRMDFMRRD, MMFSML 4743
DDRMDFMR, RMSFMRDT, 6336
DDRMDFMR, SMLF#F#SLT 9314
DDRMDFMMR, RMFSLSF 4713
DDRMDFFMRRD, SMDFM 7867
DDRMDFFM, RMFSMFRD, 271
DDRMDSRD, SSLTSDLS, 10176
DDRMDSRM, MFLSDR, SD 9429
DDRMDSRM, MSSLFRSM, 5699
DDRMDSSS, FMFSLLSF 11777
DDRMDSS, LSMDMR, SFM 276
DDRMDS, SLSFMR, RMTD 5495
DDRMDS, SLTDLD, LTSD 12340
DDRMDSLFRDT, SDRMD 12292
DDRMDLTD, RMDTDTLS, 2965
DDRMDTDRMF, MDR, DTD, 1922
DDRMDTLLSL, DDR#MSF 3268
DDRMRD, RDTD, DDRMRD 7971
DDRMRDRRM, DRMFSFM 6527
DDRMRD, RRMFMR, MTLS, 11226
DDRMRDRMF, SLSLSM 9057
DDRMRD, MRMFSLS, SSL 737
DDRMRDMFS, SSLSFMF 6569
DDRMRDFR, RMF#SSF#S, D 3269
DDRMRDFRRMSSF#S, DF 3270
DDRMRDFMRMM, RMFMM 402
DDRMRD, FLTDD, RDTLD 5400
DDRMRDSSS, RRMFRSF 792
DDRMRDTD, DDDRDTLS# 3661
DDRMRDTD, RMFSFMMR 9369
DDRMRDTD, RMSFMR, MF 9379
DDRMRDTD, MSSLTDLS, 11544
DDRMRDTLS, SLTDFMR 12213
DDRMRRDT, RTDLSDDD, 3307
DDRMRRMF, MRDTDLS, D 3107
DDRMRMRDLS, DDRMFM 1325
DDRMRMFMRM, MMMF 4291
DDRM, RMFS, SLSMDRMR, 7945
DDRMRFRD, MFMRDTDR, 2014
DDRMRFMRD, MFMRDTD 2013
DDRMRFMRDL, SDRM, DM 240
DDRMMRD, DRMRDRR, DD 3984
DDRMMRDTTL, MMF#SSF# 10221
DDRMMR, RMFMRD, DMFS 9547
DDRMMRRM, SFRMMDRM, 1174
DDRMMRMRRD, MSSS 6752
DDRMMRMFMRMRDDDR 11480
DDRMMRMFFM, RDRM, MF 10477
DDRMMR, SFMRRD, DDRM 6844
DDRMMMRMFMRDD, DMF 505
DDRMMMRMFMRDD, MM 504
DDRMMMRMSFMRD, MM 6571
DDRMMMFS, SLSMDRMR, 4481
DDRMMFMR, MFMRDTDR 2016
DDRMMFM, RMF#SSF#S, DD 4147
DDRMMFFMD, DLLDLS, T 1866
DDRMMFFMR, MFMRD 2012
DDRMMFSDTD, LTRDTL 3623
DDRMMFSSFM, RRMFMS 3251
DDRMMFSLSM, DTDRMS 1087
DDRMMSM, FFMMRD, DDR 185
DDRMMSFMRMMM, RDRM 11857
DDRMMLLS#LMFMRRD, D 1760
DDRMFRD, RDLTDRD, DD 2570
DDRMFRD, RRLTDD, DDRM 2569
DDRMFRD, RRLTDTD, DD 2573
DDRMFRD, MFSSRMF, MF 12582
DDRMFRM, RRDSSF#S, RM 9461
DDRMFMDDTD, MMMSLT 7296
DDRMFMRD, DMSLSMR, D 2613
DDRMFMRD, DSSSLTDD 8729
DDRMFMRDR. 6137
DDRMFMRD, RMFSF#S, SD 7417
DDRMFMRDRM, F#SRDTL 9076
DDRMFMRD, MFSSLSFM, 9578

DDRMFMRD, MSLSDTLS 9271
DDRMFMRD, SSLSMSFM, 9252
DDRMFMRD, SSLTDTLS, 9480
DDRMFMRDTD, RMSFRM 2535
DDRMFMRDTD, MMFSMR 11122
DDRMFMRM, DMRDTDLS, 5473
DDRMFMRM, MRSSRMFM 10310
DDRMFM, RSDFR, MMMML 11821
DDRMFMRS, SLSMMRDR, 3727
DDRMFMRLMR,RSMRDT 4946
DDRMFMMD, DSLTSLTD 8731
DDRMFMM, RMRDD, RRFF 2048
DDRMFM, MMRDT, DDRMF 6765
DDRMFM, SFMRFM, MMF#S 138
DDRMFM, SSFMR, SMLS 1846
DDRMFFM, DDRMRRD, DMS 8444
DDRMFFMM, RRMMRD, DD 3710
DDRMFSDDSTLS, DSTL 10403
DDRMFSRMF#S, FMRMFS 7520
DDRMFSMFSL, SLTDRMRD 12546
DDRMFSFM, DDTDLS, DD 2574
DDRMFS, FMRDTD, RMDF 1394
DDRMFSFMR, RMMRSTR 1068
DDRMFSFMR, RMFSLS, S 9043
DDRMFS, FMRM, SDRMFM, 10537
DDRMFSFM, LF#SSF#S, RT 11473
DDRMFSSDTSLSM, DSL 4662
DDRMFSSM, MLSSF#S, SM 2739
DDRMFSSS, FMFSFM, MM 8263
DDRMFSSS, SFMRDMR, R 9405
DDRMFS, SSSFMR, RMF 1076
DDRMFSSLTD, DDTLSR 8094
DDRMFSSLTDMR, SSF# 11504
DDRMFS, SLTDLS, DDRM 3655
DDRMFS, SL#LSSS, LFSM 2977
DDRMFSLFMRRD, SDDR 996
DDRMFSLSMS, MSMDRM 5503
DDRMFSLSFMRRD, SDD 995
DDRMFSLTD, SDDTSLM 9798
DDRMF#SSF#S, MFMRMR, D 9794
DDRMF#SSF#S, SLTDTLLS, 488
DDRMF#SLS, LTDSFMF#S, 8824
DDRMSDRMR, RMFSMRR 7767
DDRMSDLS, DDRMSDLT, 9166
DDRMSDLS, MDMRRD, DD 4365
DDRMSMD, RRRRSM, DDR 3407
DDRMSMRDLDM, LDTLS 3465
DDRMSFM, DDRMRD. 1083
DDRMSFMRD, RMF#SDTL 12494
DDRMSFMR, RDRMRDR, R 4143
DDRMSFMRRM, DDTDLS 2646
DDRMSFMR, SDTLSSF#S, 6303
DDRMSFM, MSFRMDT, DR 5352
DDRMSFM, MSSRMDT, DR 5347
DDRMSFFMDFMRRD, SL 8022
DDRMSFF, TTDRSM, DDR 11114
DDRMSFLTRD, MFRLSD 9223
DDRMSSFM, SLLLDDTL, 11353
DDRMSLDTSLS, DRMLS 4210
DDRMSLSSM, SSMRFMR 10981
DDRMSLLS, DRMSLDS, L 6964
DDRMLSFM, MMFSDM 9351
DDRMLSFM, MFSMMRDD, 7664
DDRMLSSF, MRSMDRM, D 9423
DDRMLLSFM, MSSFRD, D 1107
DDRMLLSF, FMRDRR, RS 7472
DDRMLTD, RFMDMR, DDR 8349
DDRMLTDRTS, LDTLDT 1455
DDRMTDLSFM, SLSDTL 12040
DDRFDFLS, FLFSFRD, D 10896
DDRFMMFL, SLLTDRM, M 6218
DDRFMRDR, MLTDRMF 2090
DDRFMRLS, SSFMRDRT 2023
DDRFLSFTTLSFSRM, D 8983
DDRSMRDS, LTDDDTDR, 6043
DDRSFMRD, RRLTDRD, D 2572
DDRLSM, MMF#F#S, DDSS#L 11026
DDRL, LDLSL, 10819
DDRTD, RRMFM, SSLFFS 3272
DDRTDR, MMFMRDRD 428
DDRTLS, DRMFMR, DRMD 3575
DDRTLSLSFMD, SSSLT 4129
DDRTTDRM, SFRMDTLS, 12441
DDRTTD, LDTSM, LLLSL 6206

DDM

DDMDRDLL, DDMDRDLD 3854
DDMDMMRDTD, DMSMSS 459
DDMDMMSM, RSMDTDR, D 3927
DDMDMS, DDDMRDR, SDD 5398
DDMDS, RD#RMRDMLS, RD# 12554
DDMDTRD, MMSMMRDR, F 8738
DDMRDDTD, DTDRLDTL, 10548
DDMRDDTD, FMRRD#RSM 68
DDMRDRRM, DRMFSFMRD, 6526
DDMRDRRM, DMFSMRD, D 6525
DDMRDRRM, DMFSFMRD, 6528
DDMRDRMSFM, SDLSMR, 1245
DDMRDSLS, DRMMSFMR, 8157
DDMRDTD, RMSFMR, RRM 9368

DDMRDTD, MMSFMRM, SS 8278
DDMRDTL, MFRMRD, DDM 3441
DDMRR, RFMM, DTL#LSFM 11546
DDMRRRFM, MMRDTLS, T 5551
DDMRFMR, FMDRTD, DDM 4104
DDMRFFM, RMSFLS, SDD 10555
DDMRSSSDRT, SLTDRM 3704
DDMRLSFM, SSSDLFF 11766
DDMMRDRLTD, DDMMRR 1464
DDMMRDSS, FMDDRTLT, 6406
DDMMRRDD, D#RMFLMR, S 9293
DDMMR, RRFFM, MMSSL, 4395
DDMMRFRDTD, MMSSMD 1658
DDMMMRD, DDFFLLS, SR 868
DDMMMRDMRD, MMSSSL 12034
DDMMMMD, DDDDDLS, SF 7234
DDMMSDDTTLS, STTTD 6893
DDMMSMRD, DDDMSSLS 5128
DDMMSMRD, DDMSLSM, D 5127
DDMMSM, FFMRMR, RMFM 700
DDMMSFMR, SMFMRD, DD 6277
DDMMSFMR, SFMFMRD, D 6276
DDMMSFM, MMFLDDD, RM 2304
DDMMSSS, RRFFLLL, SM 898
DDMMSS, LLLSM, SSSSD 7395
DD, MM, LSMFSM, RRSLTL 9696
DDMMLLS#, LMFMRRD, DD 1761
DDMFMSDFRRD, DDFMRS 11617
DDMFSSSLDLS, SLLLS 6010
DDMFSSLLS, DLRSSTD, 3758
DDMFSS, LTDSMF#S, FR 8823
DDMFSLS, SDMSFMR, FF 314
DDMF#SLS, F#SLS, SSFFM 10118
DDMSDDLS, SDFMRMR 9625
DDMS, DFLD, DTLSF#LSM, 11108
DDMSDTLSLRS, FLSFM 573
DDMSMRTD, DDMSLFM, S 6799
DDMSMFSLS, DTLSMSF 12018
DDMSMSDDRM, DDDLSD 3703
DDMSFLDS, MMRTDDTS 6555
DDMSFLMFSMR, MFSLS 1414
DDMSSMMSFMRD, DDMS 53
DDMSSMFLS, MRDDTDR, 8683
DDMSSFMR, RMFRRM, DD 5607
DDMSSSDTLS, TTLS, RS 10476
DDMSSSMFS, TDLDSSL 1067
DDMSSSLSMD, DDDDDD 5051
DDMSSLSFS, DSFMRRM, 2181
DDMSSLSLTDD, MMF#SS 1652
DDMSLSMRD, DDFLLS, M 12409
DDMSLSMR, SSFMLF#F#M, 1745
DDMSLSLTD, MFSDRMR, 1605
DDMSLLS, MFSLRMFM, M 6243
DDMSLTDLSM, DDFMSS, 8567
DDMLDSSSM, DDMSFMR 9947
DDMLSMD, DRMRRMFM, M 1742
DDFMRDTS, DDLSFSM, R 9178
DDFMRM, RMSFMR, SDTL 4257
DDFMRS, DRRM, MMF#SLT, 2510
DDFFFFDRM, MMRRRF#M 5041
DDFFFFFM, MMMRLRR, S 6463
DDFFFLLLSM, MMRSSS 10893
DDFFLFMS, SRRRMFM, D 10357
DDFSLL#D, LDL#LFSF, LS 6413
DDFLSM, SRMFM, DDFLS 10566
DDSDDRRD, DFFMMRDS, 143
DDSDRMDM, FSLFMRD, D 1872
DDSDRM, DLSS, RRLRRF 8641
DDS, DRM, MMSFMRDRMD, 8582
DDSDRM, FMDMR, DDSDRM, 9364
DDSDRMFMRD, DDSDRM 5222
DDSDRMFMRDTD, RMRD 5104
DDSDRMFMRM, SMFSDR 5397
DDSDRMFM, SMDFMRD, D 8506
DDSDRM, SFMRRM, MMMR 4897
DDSDRS, MRMFMRD, DTL 140
DDSDRTS, MRMFMR, DDT 142
DDSDMDMS, FMFSSFMR, 2116
DDSDMDMS, FMSMRDRD, 2117
DDSDMRRD, RRTDTLS, 2583
DDSDFMRD, DRMFMRLT 7562
DDSDFMRD, DRFMRLTD 7563
DDSDFMRD, MRS#LDTLS, 9940
DDSDTLMS, SDMSMDSR 8832
DDSRSMFR, SSFMMRLS, 6547
DDSMDDDTDR, RMDRMF# 7977
DDSMDDMR, MSFMRD, DD 12373
DDSMDDMR, MSFMRD, MS 12374
DDSMDRRM, SFMRD, FFF 8884
DDSMDTDRMSMRRD, DD 12372
DDSMDTDR, SLDDTD, DD 12419
DDSMRDDRMR, MSFMRD, 12371
DDSMRDTLS, DRMRD, 8588
DDSMRDTLSLTDRD, DD 8587
DDSMMDSSFMR, RRSF#M 11809
DDSMMRDDTDR, DDSMM 7627
DDSMMRDDTDR, DSMMR 7629
DDSMFSMD, MMRMDRTS, 3111
DDSMSFMRDTDD, DDSM 4072
DDSFMRDMR, MFSFMRD, 12376
DDSSDR, RMFMFSM, SST 6260
DDSSDRMM, LSFMRRD, D 3596a

DDSSDRM, LSFMRD, DD 3596
DDSSDLTD, DRMFRSF#S, 5254
DDSSFRM, RRMSLS, SLS 2691
DDSSFMRD, TDRMFS, DD 3845
DDSSFMRRD, SSMSSLS, 2609
DDSSFMMMR, DRMRD, DD 1274
DDSSFSMD, MMRRDRTS, 3110
DDSSLSMD, TDTMFS, DS 10195
DDSSLTDS, LSFMRRD, D 5600
DDSLDDTD, MMDRSDTL, 8740
DDSLDMRD, RMF#SDTLS, 7637
DDSLMSDR, MSDTLTLS 1879
DDSLSLTDFMRDTD, DR 1345
DDSLLSFMD, MFMRSLL 12024
DDSLLSFMRDS, SMRDM 7050
DDSLTDRD, DMRDTDLLS, 7721
DDSLTDRDTD, MRDTRM 8802
DDSLTDRMR, RMF#SDTL 7638
DDSLTDRMR, MRDLTDR 3192
DDSLTDRM, FSRDMR, RR 4591
DDSLTDFMRDTD, DRMD 1347
DDSLTDFMRDTDRMDT 1346
DDSLTD, SMDLSFMMR, S 12199
DDSLTDLS, FMSFMRD, D 4114
DDSLTDT, SDDMRD, DDS 2131
DDLDDS, SLSFM, SSLTT 11882
DDLDRMD, RMDMFSM, DT 6619
DDLDMRRD, DTLDRTL, D 7776
DDLRDTDSMD, DDLFMR 4128
DDLRDDLL, SSLLTD, DR 8704
DDLSDDLS, DDRMRDRS 8978
DDLSMRDRMD, DDLSMR 7501
DDLSMRRDRMLS, SSMM 11796
DDLSMRTD, DRMRTLS, D 5808
DDLSFMRDDRMFS, DDL 10196
DDLSFMRD, LSDTTD, DS 3846
DDLSTD, RRTDLS, SDRM 779
DDLS#LFMS, SSSRMFM, D 6177
DDLLMML, DDRRMML. 3376
DDLLSDRM, RSFMRFMR 7730
DDLLTSDD, MFRSSF#S, M 5777
DDLTDRMD, SFMRDRD, D 3925
DDLTDMRRD, DTLTDRD 7777
DDLTD, MMRSLTD, DTLT 10098
DDLTSLSF#S, SLFFMRD, 11926
DDTDDRRM, DFFMMRRD, 10651
DDTDDRMRDTDS, DMMM 8886
DDTDD#R, MMMFMR, SSMM 6265
DDTDR, DRMRD, MFSFM 9070
DDTDRDRM, MSFMMRDR, 9292
DDTDRRRDRM, RMRDTD 562
DDTDRRRD, MMRMFRT, DDRR 5873
DDTDRRRD, MMRMFRT, DTD 9424
DDTDRR, MMRMF, SSFSL 6298
DDTDRMD, FMRDTLTLS, 10744
DDTDRMRD, SMDMR, RRD 4803
DDTDRMMR, DFMRRD, DM 1630
DDTDRM, MFMRDT, RDLS, 1054
DDTDRM, MFLSFM, MMTD 4196
DDTDRMFMRD, MFSFMR 9071
DDTDRMFMRDTD, MFSL 146
DDTDRLTD, DFMMRDR, S 7660
DDTDRTDTLS, MRRDRS 7781
DDTDRTS, RMRDLS, DDT 5164
DDTDRTLS, RMRDTLS, D 3017
DDTDMMRRDTT, LTDSD 11201
DDTDMRRD, DFMDRM, 9385
DDTDFMMDR, DDTDFMM 2835
DDTDSMFRD, DMFSLTD 288
DDTDLDS, MDFRDTD, DD 10275
DDTDLSFM, SLDRRR, SM 9587
DDTDLSFFM, DDTDLSF# 7212
DDTDLSSD, SFMRRD, DD 8031
DDTDLS, LMLS#LT, D#TD#L 5830
DDTDLSLT, DRMSLLS, S 347
DDTDLLDD, DTLTDRDT 6507
DDTDLLLS, SLTDMR, SS 1039
DDTDLTD, MMRSFMRD, D 6501
DDTDLTDS, LTDFRDD, D 9584
DDTDTLS, DDTDTLS, MM 6234
DDTDTL, SSF#SFM, RDTD, 3617
DDTDTLLTT, DTDLTDR 6508
DDTRDT, RD#RFM, SSLSD 9333
DDTRDTLLS, MMMRDSF 11724
DDTRRRDM, MMMRDLS, S 5141
DDTRMLRDT, FMRSMDR 10089
DDTMDDT, LLSMMMRD, D 5571
DDTSDRMD, TDRMFRD, D 3051
DDTSFFM, SMSFRDMR, D 7167
DDTSFFM, SMSFRDMRR, 7164
DDTSLSM, DDDTLSLLT 10880
DDTSLLS, DDRMFFM, DD 3202
DDTSLTDD, RMFFMMR, D 5638
DDTSLTDD, MMFFMMR, D 5635
DDTSLTDD, MSFMRDR, D 5634
DDTSLTD, MMFFMMR, MF 5636
DDTLDRD, DDRTSDT, T 9873
DDTLDTD, DDRTTDT, TD 9874
DDTLDTLSDM, MMRDMR 11075
DDTLDTLS, MFMRFM, MR 10825
DDTLRDTDSFMRD, DDT 6741
DDTLMMRD, LTDTLS#, S#L 1833

DDTLMFLS#, S#LFMLT, T 3068
DDTLSDDDTLS, LTDRM 2196
DDTLSDRDTD, RMRDTD 11820
DDTLSDRM, DRRRM, DDT 8169
DDTLSDRM, DMFSMFRD, 7733
DDTLSDRM, MMMRDFMR, 8041
DDTLSDRM, MMRDDD, DD 10630
DDTLSDRM, MMMMRDTD, 10631
DDTLSDRM, MMMRMFMR, 8043
DDTLS, DRMFMR, SFMLS 9738
DDTLSDRM, SSFMRDRD 1813
DDTLSMMR, DRMRMFRM, 8985
DDTLSM, MRMFLLS, SDD 2655
DDTLSM, MMRDTD, DFFM 9539
DDTLSM, SMRDR, DDTLS 3922
DDTLSFMRDS, SLTDRT 1884
DDTLSFMSD, SDSMDMS 4678
DDTLSFFM, SMSFRDMR 7166
DDTLSS, DRMRDLTD, SL 10088
DDTLSLRSM, RSF#SDTL 12327
DDTLSLSM, SSSSLDT, D 9695
DDTLSLS, SLSMRMR, DD 9514
DDTLSLLSFM, DDTLSL 11458
DDTLSLTDD, MMFFMMR, 5637
DDTLSLTD, TRTDTLS, S 780
DDTLSLTL, SDTLSLTL, 8347
DDTLLS, RTSFFM, MSSL 9206
DDTLLSFFLSM, DDTLL 3783
DDTLLTDRSS, MMRDMR 10193
DDTLTDRD, DDRTRDT, T 9876
DDTLTDRD, DDRTLSDT 9875
DDTLTDRS, SMRD, DDTL 2166
DDTLTRDS, DMRLRR, DD 260
DDTLTS, SDTDR, RMF#LS 826
DDTLTS#, MMRDRT, TDRM 7991
DDTLTS#TDRM, MRMDRT 870
DDTLTLSFM, RDFMLSF# 8737
DDTTDDS, FFLLSSD. 1186
DDTTRRDD, MDDFMR, RR 7854
DDTTRRDD, MFMRDDT, S 3553
DDTTRRDD, MSFDRM, MM 7379
DDTTRRDD, SLLTDRRR, 9398
DDTTLDT, MMS#TLL, DDT 12224
DDTTLS, SDTDR, MMF#F#S 10554
DDTTLLSS, DDTTLSF#S, 7237
DDTTLLS, SLLSSFFM, D 2716
DRDDTDMRDTD, SSFMM 12202
DRDRMD, FSLSFSLFSF 5924
DRDRMFRM, RMFRDRFM 5665
DRDRMFMRDR, SFMMR 4988
DRDRMFMRFMRD, DSSL 8889
DRDRMFFSFM, MF#S#LL 99
DRDRMLS, SFMRDRRD, M 9787
DRDFMRD, MSDTS#L, LS 3180
DRDFMLS, SSMDRM, MMD 3582
DRDFFM, MSRFMR, RRMD 8701
DRDSDRDS, DMSFMRSF 8622
DRDSDRM, MSFMRRD, DR 7399
DRDSMRML, TDRFMRDR, 8650
DRDSMSDM, LTDTDMR, D 11875
DRDSF#F, DMRD, DRDSF#F, 5651
DRDSLDRMSFMDRF, MR 9456
DRDSLTDMRD, DRDSLT 2527
DRDLDRMR, RMFMMLS, S 3139
DRDTDRRMD, MFSFMRD 1892
DRDTDRMD, DRMFMDRM, 9017
DRDTDFSF, FDMFSLLS, 11577
DRDTRMRD, RDLTRD#RM, 3371
DRDTLSS, DRFMMRR, DR 9841
DRDTLTSD, DRRDRFRM, 7600
DRD#RMDLD, LSSDRMRD 10181
DRD#RMDLD, MSSLSMDR, 3587
DRRDDFMRM, SF#SLTMS 621
DRRDDFFMR, DRFMRDT 4790
DRRDDFFM, MRDSFM, SD 11045
DRRDRMS, MRRDRM, DMM 10589
DRRDSLTD, MSLSMDTL 10156
DRRDLSDDTD, MSLSMD 10157
DRRDLSDDTD, MSLSMR 10158
DRRDLSLD, MSLSMDLD 10154
DRRDLSLD, MSLSMRDL 11368
DRRDLSLTD, MSLSMDL 10155
DRRDLSTD, DMSLSMDL 11367
DRRRRRMFM, RMMMRMF 5736
DRRRMMMR, RRMMFSMD 11033
DRRRFDRFFMRMM, SFM 1830
DRRRFMRMS, SSRRFMR 3876
DRRMRDRMSSFM, LSSF 10679
DRRMRSF#MR, DRRMRSF# 7528
DRRMMFFMRDS, SLTDS 985
DRRMMSSDRRMS, FSLS 2979
DRRMFSFMRD, MRSTLS 7473
DRRMFLS, SMMLSF#M, TD 2388
DRRM, SDDRRM, RMSSF#S, 690
DRRMSMR, DRMSDTLS, S 10940
DRRMSFMR, RMRDTLS, R 2436
DRRMSFMRFTRD, RFRM 3419
DRRSF, MRMRD, DRDTD. 7944
DRRSSD, LRMSFM, MF#SL 6148
DRRLL#LLLSSLSSF, LL 11596
DRR#MRDSMR, FMRDDRR# 10947
DRMDDDRMSFR, SFMMM 5227

DRMDDRMSFR, SFRRRR 5228
DRMDD, SLLSFM, RMFSS, 8007
DRMDRDFMRM, RDTDRM 745
DRMDRRD, DDRMDRS, RM 320
DRMDRRDFMRMM, RDTD 744
DRMDRMD, DMSMDR, DRM 10184
DRMDRMDR, MFSLSL, LD 6563
DRMDRMDRMFSLS, LTD 9329
DRMDRMRDRMFMR, DTL 5378
DRMDRMRRMRD, TLSFR 10375
DRMDRMFMMR, SFMFRD 10246
DRMDRMFM, LSFMRRD, DT 9615
DRMDRMFM, LTDRMF#S, R 10034
DRMDRMFSM, LSSMFFM, 880
DRMDRMF#SS, DTLSDDT 7315
DRMDRMSSF, LLLSRM, F# 2045
DRMDRS, DRMDRS, DDRM 8108
DRMDRTD, SSLMFSSM, M 8181
DRMDRTD, SSLMSSM, MR 8182
DRMDRTDSSLFSSM, MR 8184
DRMDMRMFSM, SSFFMR 3990
DRMDMFF#, DDTSMF#M, MM 4610
DRMDMFSM, FSLSSF#S, D 9039
DRMDMFSS, DTLSMRRD, 7314
DRMDMFSL, SSDTD, DRM 7036
DRMDMSD, LSMLSMDRM 5447
DRMDMSSFMR, MDTLSD 9151
DRMDMSLS, MRDDRMR, D 10203
DRMDFM, RDDTD, MFSML 9867
DRMDFMRD, RRMRDTLS, 2576
DRMDFMRD, RRMSSF#S, D 4836
DRMDFMR, RRMSSF#S, SM 2470
DRMDFMRMFM, SFMR 2550
DRMDFMMD, TDRDRRM, D 1072
DRMDFMMD, TDRD#RR#M, D 3643
DRMDFMMRD, DRMDFMM 10335
DRMDFMMR, DFMRDTD, D 6636
DRMDFMMR, MRRDDRM, D 11691
DRMDFMMR, TDRDMRD, D 4529
DRMDSDRMDS, DRMFSD 10491
DRMDSDMRD, TDRDRM, D 12230
DRMDSMDMRD, SDDMDL 9167
DRMDSFMRM, MFSMTTD 2519
DRMDSFM, RMFRLSFM, S 2504
DRMDSLSMFS, LTDSLS 10084
DRMDLRRDTD, MMRRST 12271
DRMDLSDDRDRM, DRMD 6635
DRMDLS, DDRDRM, MFDR 12120
DRMDLS, DDRRDRM, DRM 653
DRM, DLS, DMS, MDR, DRMM 12186
DRMDLSFMFSLRM, DRM 4680
DRMDLSLS, DRMSMS, DR 6035
DRMDLTDR, MFSDTLS, D 8994
DRMDTDR, MSFMRD, DRM 4507
DRMDTLTD, MF#STLSF#S 3830
DRMDTLTS, LTDMRDTD 6261
DRMRDDRMRR, MSDMFT 9284
DRMRDDTD, DSFFMF, FM 6210
DRMRDRDDLLSSL, MMM 10661
DRMRDR, DRMRMD, 10523
DRMRDRDLS, DRMMMSS 10568
DRMRDRDLS, DRMSMR, M 11164
DRMRDRRM, MFMDMSM, M 11148
DRMRDRM, RDSSSS, SLL 11864
DRMRDRMFMR, MRDTLS, 10691
DRMRDRMFMR, SSMFSLS, 7441
DRMRDRLSFM, MFLSMM 5944
DRMRD, MFMRD, MFSFMR 9072
DRMRDMF#S, SLSFMFRD, 6568
DRMRDMSL, DTTSLLS, T 10237
DRMRD, FMRDTRS, SMDL 9809
DRMRDFMMMR, TDRRRD 4488
DRMRDSMDRDRMS, SSD 4736
DRMRDS, MSFMRM, SSSM 9147
DRMRDSSS, LTDLRDTL 7302
DRMRDS, TDRDRM, RDDL 11029
DRMRDLRMT, RDTDRSM, 10262
DRMRDLSD, DRRRMR, DR 2621
DRMRDLS, DRMRD, TDRM 9434
DRMRDLSDRSMFRD, DR 7033
DRMRDLSM, DRMRMSR, 715
DRMRDLSFRRRR, DRMR 10451
DRMRDLS, SSDDMR, DRM 7594
DRMRDLTD, DRMFSMR, R 3010
DRMRDL, TDRRMDR, MFS 5916
DRMRDTDRD, DRMRDTD 2136
DRMRDTLS, DRMFMRD, 1241
DRMRDTLSSDD, RMF#SD 1449
DRMRDTLSSMLS, STDR, 11899
DRMRDTL, LSLDRTD, DR 3823
DRMRDTTLL, RMFMRDDT, 6688
DRMRMDDTLDLS, SSDD 10800
DRMRMFMDRS, DRMRMF 2220
DRMRMFMRDR, MDRMFM 4118
DRMRMFMRR, MFSFMRD, 5188
DRMRMFM, RMFSMFR, RR 783
DRMRMFMRSM, DDLTLS 11073
DRMRMFSMD, RMFSLSF# 1445
DRMRMFSM, LSFMRDR, M 3963

DRMRMFSM, LSFMRRMS 879
DRMRMFS, SMSLSMR, D 11874
DRMRMF#SS, DDTDTLS, D 2074
DRMRMF#SS, DDTLTLLS, 2073
DRMRMF#SSF#S, SLSF, FS 2823
DRMRMSMRD, SLTDLSM 860a
DRMRMSFMR, DRSM, DRM 3128
DRMRMSFMRLSSS, MFS 6512
DRMRMSFM, MRDRLTLS, 6644
DRMRMSFM, MRDTLRDT 6952
DRMRMSFM, MRDTLRT, D 6952a
DRMRMSFM, MRDTLTLS, 6643
DRMRMSFMFLSSS, MFS 6511
DRMRMSFM, LSFMRRM, S 881
DRMRMSSF#S, SLF, FSM, D 2822
DRMRMSLS, DLSMLFMR, 1610
DRMRMSLSMDRMFMM, D 11716
DRMRMSLS, SLF, FSM, MS 2821
DRMRMLSM, SSSFMR#M, M 5428
DRMRMLSFM, LSFMRM, S 1489
DRMRMLLLLMR, SDSSF 150
DRMRFMRTD, LSFMRMD 710
DRMRFMFM, MRDRM, SFF 9603
DRMRSMRD, SLTDLSMR, 860
DRMRS, FSMDR, RSSF#MR 1611
DRMR#MDRMFMFR, MFSL 655
DRMR#MD, MFSF#SM, SSLD 12174
DRMR#MFS, SSDTLS, SSS 2622
DRMMDDTDRRT, TDRMM 2367
DRMMDMSLSM, MFRMDR 2970
DRMMDMFSFFM, RMMD 8673
DRMMDMFSFFSFM, RMM 8675
DRMMRD, DRMMSR, MFSS 7239
DRMMRD, DRSFFM, DRMM 5143
DRMMRDDMSSFM, MMFL 11418
DRMMRDR, DDDSLSMS, D 5545
DRMMRDRMFFMR, DRMF 2770
DRMMRDRMFSM, DRMMR 11938
DRMMRDMMRR, RMFSMD, 2275
DRMMRDM, SDTLS, RMFF 12522
DRMMRDMS, LLSMRDR, D 5315
DRMMRDFFFMRDLS, DD 1384
DRMMRDTLTDRT, LSS 4795
DRMMRMMRMRD, DRRSS 1512
DRMMRMFMRM, MFFMRR 4292
DRMMRMFSFMMRM, MFS 9729
DRMMRMSF, MRDDRRM, M 12261
DRMMRMSF, FMRDRMD, D 3687
DRMMRSLSLSFM, RMFM 2115
DRMMR#MMRD, DMSMR#MM 5142
DRMMMDMFSSSM, DDMR 4738
DRMMMDMSSM, DRMMSF 2618
DRMMMDMSSS, MSDDTL 2931
DRMMMRDRDS, DMSSSF 6883
DRMMMRDRDL, DLSDDT 5915
DRMMMRDRRR, RMFFFM 7274
DRMMMRDMS, SLDTLS, D 6705
DRMMMRDSD, TDRMRDL 10724
DRMMMRDSSS, LSMMRD 8109
DRMMMRDS, LDD, DMSSS 10348
DRMMMRDSLTD, DMSSS 10347
DRMMMRDLD, DRRRSSM 2947
DRMMMRDTLS, LMFSSF 11119
DRMMMRRDRR, DMSMRD 6939
DRMMMRRDMM, DMSMRD 9976
DRMMMRR, RMFFFMM, ML 8810
DRMMMRMRDS, DMSSSS 9116
DRMMMRMFMFMRMRD, 10676
DRMMMRMFFF, MFSMRD 11149
DRMMMRMFS, DSMRDFM 2864
DRMMMRMFLS, MRMFFM 1084
DRMMMRMSM, MRRRDRM, 10199
DRMMMRSMD, DRMRDL, M 2664
DRMMMR#MFMR#MD, DDFF 11102
DRMMMR#MSS, SDDRDRM, 1007
DRMMMMDMRD, MFSSSM 7258
DRMMMMRDRDLS, DRMM 12397
DRMMMMRDTR, RMFFFF 10933
DRMMMMRMFS, SSLLLS 8000
DRMMMMRMFLSSS, MR 6510
DRMMMMRMFLSSS, FMR 6513
DRMMMMR#MD, MSSSMRF 1457
DRMMMMMD, DRRTTD, DR 1434
DRMMMMMDRD, MFSLSM 7504
DRMMMMM, DMSSSSS, SS 6832
DRMMMMMRDDRDDLS, D 11035
DRMMMMMRDRDDLS, DR 11037
DRMMMMMRDMDDLS, SS 5116
DRMMMMMRD, MFSSSLL 1388
DRMMMMM, RMRDDLD, DR 1415
DRMMMMMMRDD, RRMRD, 3717
DRMMMMMMFRM, DDRRR 11900
DRMMMMMFSSSS, SSLL 7994
DRMMMMFMRMRR, RMFS 5122
DRMMMMFMR, TDRRMFM 4869
DRMMMMFMMRDRM, MFS 5983
DRMMMM, FMMRRDR, RMF 651
DRMMMMFSFSFM, RRMM 5713
DRMMMMFLSRFMD, SDT 12267

DRMMMMS, MRDMR, RMFF 5054
DRMMMMSMMD, RDRRMS 5948
DRMMMMSMMR, DRDRRM 5946
DRMMMFMRD, DRRDRM, D 891
DRMMMFMRD, MFSSSL 1871
DRMMMFMRRR, MRDDDT 3487
DRMMMFMRRR, SF#SF#M 7104
DRMMMFMR#MD, MFSSLS 6920
DRMMMFSFFFM, RMMMF 5712
DRMM, MFSS, SDSLSFM, R 5489
DRMMMFSS, LMMRDD, DR 12112
DRMMMFS, LTDTLTS, SS 823
DRMMMS, FMRRRMF, MRD 888
DRMMMSFMRRMF, MRDDRMR 8804
DRMMMSFMRRMF, MRDMDDR 3259
DRMMMSLFF, LSRRMFM, 10263
DRMMFRS, DRMDRD, DRM 7428
DRMMFRLS, MSSFFSF 11466
DRMMFMRDRM, MFSSM 6709
DRMMFMRDRS, LTDDRD 2775
DRMMFMRDS, DRMSSFM 4538
DRMMFMR, TDRFMRD, DR 9190
DRMMFMMD, DMRMFSM, D 11907
DRMMFMMRD, MFSSLSS 2907
DRMMFMMR, RDDRRM, DR 11785
DRMMFMMR, RMFFFFFM, 130
DRMMFMMR, RMFFSFM, D 5435
DRMMFMMR, RMFLSFM, D 7757
DRMMFMMR, RMSFRMD, 6427
DRMMFMMR, MRDDRSM, S 9812
DRMMFMMR, MRDTDRMR 1424
DRMMFMMR, TDRRMRRD 157
DRMMFMMR, TDRFMRD, D 5101
DRMMFMMR, TDRFMRM, M 5273
DRMMFMLS, FMMSMR, SD 11661
DRMMFFMD, MFSSLLS, F 6176
DRMMFFMRD, DMSSLLS 8266
DRMMFFM, MMRRMFSFFM 220
DRMMFFMFM, SFMRDTD 3374
DRMMFSMDRMFFM, DMS 12538
DRMMFS, MRDDRMR, MRD 3175
DRMMFSFMM, SSFFMMR 10336
DRMMFSLSR, MMR, DDT, R 321
DRMMFSLS, MRDSSLSM 5791
DRMMFSLSFM, MFSDFM 6028
DRMMFSLSS, LLDLSSM 3743
DRMMF#SSSLLTDD, RMR 4142
DRMMSMDRMD, SSLLLR 10930
DRMMSMMR, RMFLSFFM, 9697
DRMMSFMRR, RMFFLSF 415
DRMMSFMRMFM, SSRM 12437
DRMMSLTD, TTLLSFM, R 3827
DRMMLSSFMMR, MFMRD 9107

DRMF

DRMFRDTD, RMSDLSF#S, 7418
DRMFRSLSDFFM, F#S#TL 2688
DRMFRSTD, DTRSMLSF# 9984
DRMFMDRD, MFSLSMF#S, 8565
DRMFMDRD, MSLSMFS, S 514
DRMFMDMRRDTD, TDRM 6876
DRMFMRD, DSSLTDD, DR 8730
DRMFMRDD, SLTDTLSS, 2333
DRMFMRDDTD, MRMF#S, L 6814
DRMFMRDDTD, MFSLS 11346
DRMFMRDDTD, MFSLS 8054
DDMFMRDRRRSLL#LS. 5263
DRMFMRDR, RMRDTL, RR 11647
DRMFMRDRM, MRMF#SRS 6083
DRMFMRD, RMFSLS, SDD 10151
DRMFMRDRM, F#SRDTLS, 9075
DRMFMRDR, FSLL#LSFS 11598
DRMFMRDRS, DRMFMRD 10519
DRMFMRD, SSLTDD, DRT 8732
DRMFMRD, SLSDLTD, DR 9843
DRMFMRD, SLTDTTLS, L 4819
DRMFMRDTDR, DDDL#LS 8801
DRMFMRD, TDRDFMR, DR 1809
DRMFMRDTDRM, RDTLT 8788
DRMFMR, DTDR, MMMMMT 10728
DRMFMRDTD, RMSSFMM 3241
DRMFMRDTD, MF#SLSF#F# 5289
DRMFMRRD, MFSDTLS, S 405
DRMFMRRD, MFSLFR, ST 8373
DRMFMRRD, SMSDTLLS, 4508
DRMFMRRD#RMR, FFFRS 2564
DRMFMRRSFFM, SMRDR 1529
DRMFMRMRD, MFSLSMFS, 2612
DRMFMRMRD, SDTRFLS 173
DRMFMRMFM, SSDLSTL 11126
DRMFMRM, FFMSSF#S, DR 9227
DRMFMRMFSLSSF#S, SF 11751a
DRMFMRSFM, RRRSRDT 8598
DRMFMRLSDR, SF#STLS 1404
DRMFMRLTD, MFSMDTL 6961
DRMFMMRD, D#D#D#RR#M,MR 6567

DRMFMMRDRD, MFSLSS 749
DRMFMMRDRDTD, MFSF 6595
DRMFMMRD, MDTLS#L, TD 4531
DRMFMMRDMSLS, SDDT 10517
DRMFMMRD, LLSSRM, DD 11992
DRMFMMRDTRD, RMF#SL 11940
DRMFMMR, RDMSLSF, LT 10621
DRMFMMRR, MFSLLRDR 12318
DRMFMMRR, SRMFM, DRM 3697
DRMFMMR, MRDRMRD, MS 1310
DRMFMMRSMRD, DFMLS 5224
DRMFMMMRDDT, RMF#SD 2817
DRMFMS, MRDRLS, SLDR 425
DRMFMSFMR, SMDTLS, 4883
DRMFMLSDT, LTDSFMF 10198
DRMFMLS, SDMTLS, FMF 2092
DRMFMLSSFM, MFSLSD 1589
DRMFMLLS, SLTDRTLS 3191
DRMFFMRD, MRDDTD, SS 8982
DRMFFM, MMMSF#M, MRTD 3315
DRMFFM, LSDMRD, SFM 12508
DRMFFFFM, MFSLLLDT, 12164
DRMFFLDFMM, SDMRRR 7243
DRMFFLSMSFMFRM, DR 4854
DRMFSDDTD, LLLSSF#S, 4150
DRMFSDS, LSFMSSR, RM 1585
DRMFS, DTLSMFSLTD, D 3847
DRMFSDTLS, LTDRMRR 11805
DRMFSDTLS, LTDRMFR 11800
DRMFSMRMD, MFSLL#L#L 2700
DRMFSMM, MFSLTDS, SL 11634
DRMFS, MSFMR, DRMRMF 12059
DRMFSM, SLDFMR, SDTS 3476
DRMFSMS, LSLFM, DRMF 10741
DRMFSFMR, DDDFMRD, L 2720
DRMFSFMRD, DRMFSFS 9345
DRMFSFMRM, MMRMFR 11292
DRMFSFSMRD,DRMFSFSL 9344
DRMFSSMD, LSFMRRD, M 2472
DRMFSSFMR, SLTDTLL 2900
DRMFSSFMSSLTDTLL 2898
DRMFSSS, FSLS, SSFFM 906
DRMFSSLRDTLS, DTDR 665
DRMFSSLSFMD, FMRR 9038
DRMFSSLS, SDRMFMRD, 7797
DRMFS, SLTDDRMFSSF 3075
DRMFSSLTD, TDRSLTL 6499
DRMFS, LRMFSM, MDTLSF, 2292
DRMFSLRSM, MFMRDMR, 4596
DRMFSLFSFM, DTLSLT 6154
DRMFSLS, DRMFSLS, SS 322
DRMFSLSD, MF#SDTS, RF 3300
DRMFSLS, DSLSFM, RFM 11221
DRMFSLSMRMFM, RMSD 5221
DRMFSLSMSR, DRMSDT 12388
DRMFSLTD, RMDLDT, LS 1099
DRMFSLTD, MRDRDTD, S 3209
DRMFLDM, F#SMDRM, MFF 4702
DRMFLSM, RMFMRD, DRM 6454
DRMFLS, MMRLTDT, RMF 714
DRMFLSM, MSDDRM, MF#F# 3429
DRMFLSFM, SLDTTLLS, 808
DRMFLSFM, SLTDLS, SL 827
DRMFLSSFM, RMSMR, DR 4994
DRMFLS, LFSMDR, RMMF# 12100
DRMFLS, LFSMDR, SMDT 7131
DRMFLS, LLFSMDR, SMD 7132
DRMFLLS, SLTDRDT, TD 7770
DRMFLLTDSD, DTDRMR 10605
DRMF#F#SRRFM, RMSSF#S, 3041
DRMF#F#SRRFM, MFLLS#L, 3040
DRMF#SLS, F#SLS, SSFFM 907
DRMSD, DRMSD, RMFLSF 1247
DRMSDRTD, MRSFMR, DR 77
DRMSDMFRRD, MFSLFS 8838
DRMSDMLD, DRMDSLR, D 4969
DRMSDLSR, MMMFMRRS, 9125
DRMSDLSMM, LSMMRMD, 8417
DRMSDTLS, FMRRD, DRM 3550
DRMSDTLSLSFMMRMR, 4202
DRMSDTLS, LTDRMRD, D 11803
DRMSDTLS, LTDRMFRD, 11802
DRMSMDRDT, RMFLSFL 199
DRMSMDRMD, SDRM, MF#S 6980
DRMSMDFM, LTDMRR, R 919
DRMSMRD, RMFLSMR, LS 10752
DRMSMRDM, DTLRDLS, S 12265
DRMSMRDL, LDLSMRDM, 12484
DRMSFRDRM, FMLSDDT 8358
DRMSFMDRM, SF#SLSMR 4966
DRMSFMDTLS, LTDRMR 11801
DRMSFMRD, RRMSSF#S, D 11461
DRMSFMRD, MF#SSLSF#S, 6350
DRMSFMRD, FMR, MF#S, FS 1783
DRMSFMRD, SLTDDT, LS 8280
DRMSFMRR, RMFLLSFM, 201

DRMSFMRR, MRDRDTD, T 1568
DRMSFMRR, M RDMRTD, D 1569
DRMSFMR, RMFRDTD, SS 5722
DRMSFMR, MRDRDTD, TD 1567
DRMSFMRMRDLD, DRMS 10493
DRMSFMRM, MMMFMR, RD 6917
DRMSFMRMM, MFMDTLS 2582
DRMSFMMRD#R, LRMFFF 9101
DRMSFMMR, RMFLRFM, D 7978
DRMSFM, MRMFM, MLLSF# 4875
DRMSFM, MRMFSFM, MRD 219
DRMSFMMRSLTLS, SSD 11633
DRMSFFRMFM, MF#SLSF# 3887
DRMSFFM, MMSSDRM, MM 7850
DRMSFLSDT, LSMSFMR, 7187
DRMSFLLS, DSMFSLR, M 2142
DRMSSDRMRD, DRMSSD 8194
DRMSS, DRMSS, LSSSMD 4620
DRMSSDLDS, MSLSMDM 5729
DRMSSM, DRMLSM, RDMS 12348
DRMSSMRDDM, MMRFFM 2
DRMSSMRD, RMSLSMR, M 10966
DRMSSFMD, DMRFMRM, D 267
DRMSSFMR, RMFMRDRD, 440
DRMSSFMRMFMR, DMSL 1755
DRMSSFMRFMRDR, DM 1754
DRMSSFMF, FMRRM, DMS 2441
DRMSSFM, F#STLSF#S, SL 9459
DRMSSSDTDMR, MMMMT 8665
DRMSSSSSDTDMR, MMM 8664
DRMSSLSLSMD, DRMSM 3763
DRMSLDDT, DTLMSFM, M 9294
DRMSLDS, FLSDFMR, DR 9096
DRMSLDLS, LSFMRRR, D 5875
DRMSLDTD, SDTLSDMD 760
DRMSLFMDRRDRM, MMS 4768
DRMSLFS, SDTLSFM, MF 11918
DRMSLS, MDRRM, MSMSL 2957
DRMSLSMD, RML, DRMSL 5863
DRMSLSMR, MSLDTLSL 3247
DRMSLSM, FMRDRD, DRM 2871
DRMSLSMS, SSSMRDR, M 3591
DRMSLSSDT, DRRMRDS, 9931
DRMSLSSM, MMRD, DRMS 1527
DRMSLS, SLSDTLS, S 2677
DRMSLLS, DMSMR, DMLS 2437
DRMSLLSM, DMSRMD, DR 7423
DRMSLTD, DDRRD, DRMS 7019
DRMSLTDRM, MFMRSRD, 10521
DRMSLTDSM, SDDRDM, D 1770
DRMSTLSM, DRMFRDD, D 501
DRMLDRML, DRMMMRDTL, 11549
DRMLF#S, RSMMFF, LSDR 1236
DRMLSRM, DFSLFMR, RM 8863
DRMLSMRDLLS, DRMRD 12247
DRMLSMR, MLSDT, DLSM 4197
DRMLSMF#RDRMRDTL, D 10928
DRMLSFMM, MSFRRD, DR 7174
DRMLSFMM, MSFMRRD, 7173
DRMLSFM, MFSDTLS, ST 2086
DRMLSFM, MF#SDTLS, ST 2087
DRMLSFMM, SSFRRD, DR 1298
DRMLSFSM, RFMRDR, RM 12496
DRMLSS, DDRRM, DMFMR 8179
DRMLSS, SSSMRMSSSM 3584
DRM, TDDRRMMFS, RMMF#F#S, 1659
DRMTDLSFM, SLSDTLT, 12041
DRMTRD, MSRFM, SDTLS 1458
DRFRRDM, FRDRMDD, RL 9750
DRFRMRRRDRMM, MFSM 11540
DRFMRDDT, DLSDTDR, D 10330
DRFMRD, RMSFMR, MSLS 12500
DRFMRD, MFSLS, SLDTL 6561
DRFMRD, SLDTLS, MFLS 8543
DRFMRDTD, MRMRDTLS, 11525
DRFMRDTLS, LTDMSMR, 11471
DRFMRRDD, DRRRRR, RM 9473
DRFMRRD#, MMFMSSF#, SS 7975
DRFMRS, DDLSFM, LSF#S, 9253
DRFMFSSSSSLDTLS, D 1759
DRFMSDRTD, MRTLSLT 5707
DRFMSSF#S, MLSFFM, SM 9637
DRFFMRDRR, MRDTL, 11646
DRFFMRLL, SDTL, MSFF 9723
DRFSLMRMDSMSRFMD 1089
DRSDRML, SMRDRML, SL 1348
DRSMRDRDT, DRSMRDS, 2992
DRSLTDRM, DFMRLS, SM 3389
DRLS, MDRMDLSLRD, DR 10321
DRTD, RMFSLSFMRM, DR 10917
DRTDMSSLF#S, MFSFMR 5919

DMD

DMDDD, LLLTDRDTDLD 11508
DMDDMDSFFM, MSSF#MF# 8086
DMDDD, LTDTDRD, LLLT 8145
DMDDMSRR, FMRDTDRS 6179

DMDDSSSLLTD, DSSLF 5339
DMDRDDDTDR, MRMFMM, 4970
DMDRRD, STSLLS, FMDL 9419
DMDRRDTL, MRDFMRDM 1307
DMDRMRFMRD, MSMSFM 4641
DMDRMFRD, DMF#SRSF#S, 481
DMDRMFMRD, DMF#SRSF# 480
DMDRMSFMRD, DLFLSM 1968
DMDRSFMRD, RRRMSSF# 2698
DMDRTD, RMSFMR, SDDL 1467
DMDMDMMMD, DMDDLDDL 3903
DMDM, DFFDRM, MRRM, SS 8998
DMDMDSSM, DRRRFM, DM 1040
DMDMMRDRM, DRTRMFM 11324
DMDMMFS, FMMSMR, DMD 805
DMDMFS, MLMLTT, TDLT 9285
DMDMSD, SSMFSM, MRSF# 6019
DMDMSSDDRTD, DMDMS 4073
DMDFRS, FMMRRD, DLDT 8494
DMDFRSF#S, DFFMRDRD 10906
DMDFRLS, MDDRMR, RMM 6533
DMDFRTDD, MSMTLSSS, 2974
DMDFSLLS, SRFMDMF, F 9165
DMDFLSMRD, DMDFLSM 6313
DMDSDMFSM, DSMDRMF 1230
DMDS, DFFFMR, RTDLS, 10226
DMDSRMRD, MSSSFMR, D 4110
DMDSRFMR, RMDLSLTD, 2552
DMDSMD, SLSFMMR, RMD 2353
DMDSMD, TLSFMR, RMDL 2352
DMDSMRDTD, RMSLSFS, 9320
DMDSMFMRM, LRMDTLT, 534
DMDSMFSLS, STDRDMR 7753
DMDS, MSLSMRD, DMDS, D 7496
DMDSMLM, FSMDRM, MSM 5741
DMDSMLSLTD, SLSFMR 1106
DMDSFMRD, SLFDTLS, R 7385
DMDSLS, STSRMR, DTLS, 2672
DMDSLTD, RMDSFMR, RM 1990
DMDSTD, MMRSSF#LS, SS 3648
DMDLLRRT, SDDRRMMR, 6686
DMRDDDRDR, MSMSSMR 10990
DMRDDD, RMSLLS, FMMF 11659
DMRDDDL, LSMMRR, FMR 7525
DMRDDRRM, MRDFMRDT 4687
DMRDDRMFFFM, MMMMF# 12352
DMRDDMSSLS, DMRDDM 22
DMRDDFRM, MRDSFFRM, 8025
DMRDDFMMR, SDRFMRD, 1382
DMRDDLRFM, MDTLSTL 1188
DMRDDLSFM, DSFMLTD 6675
DMRDDTDFFMR, RSFMR 5750
DMRDDTLSMRD, SSFMM 2851
DMRDDTLSLFM, DTDRR 9186
DMRDRDRMSS, MFFMDM 8217
DMRDRDTD, RMSFMR, SD 1466
DMRDRRRDRM, MMRMFM 594
DMRDRM, DDRDLD, LSLS 10847
DMRDRMDTL, DSMDMRD, 10452
DMRDRMRDR, MSSSLSM 3351
DMRDRMFMR, RMFSFMM 5081
DMRDRMS, SLSMSLL, LS 9872
DMRDRTDRDS, MMSSFM 10984
DMRDMRD, DLRFSSS, DR 3514
DMRDMRDDTD, MSFMMD 10133
DMRDMRDDTLS, SLLLS 2468
DMRDMRDLSLS, MSLSM 3194
DMRDMRDTD, RMSFMR, S 1465
DMRDMFSFM, RDRTLS, D 231
DMRDMFS, SSLLSMDMR, 4443
DMRDMF#S, DMRDMF#S, ML 3734
DMRDMSFM, DRMFMRM, R 7705
DMRDMSFM, DRMFSFMR 9943
DMRDMSFM, SLSFMR, RM 650
DMRDMSLS, RMRDMSLS, 3736
DMRDFMRDRTD, TDRM 5365
DMRDFLSFM, SF#STLS, S 6421
DMRDSDRMD, MFSLSFF 8531
DMRDSDMRDS, LDSMMR 12282
DMRDSMDRM, DDTSLTS, 7685
DMRDSMDS, DSRMRDTL 2995
DMRDSMDS, DSRMRTLS 2994
DMRDSMFFS, FMR, RDTL 1240
DMRDSFMRD, DTLSRDT 7150
DMRDSFMR, RMRDRDT, F 12083
DMRDSFMR, MFSLMRD, D 12035
DMRDSFMR, SDRMLTD, D 10782
DMRDSSFMRM, MRLSDF 8406
DMRD, SSLSFFM, 9677
DMRDSLDRM, MSLSDRL 3358
DMRDSLDS, DMMSSR, DM 5133
DMRDSLS, DMRDRMR, DM 12240
DMRDSLSMRDMR, RMMS 1724
DMRDSLS, SMRDMR, SMR 4770
DMRDSLTDRMDLR, LLT 3463
DMRDSLTDRMR, DMLTD 1122
DMRDSLTD, MRTDLS, MR 7925
DMRDSLTDS, SDRMFMR 9614
DMRDSTRD, SSMMDRMR, 13
DMRDLRRD, SLSLDLS, S 3888
DMRDLSRM, MRSF#SLTL 9561
DMRDLSFM, MRDRMR, DT 791
DMRDLSFM, MSDTLS, SMD 1573
DMRDLSFM, MSSFMDR, D 9000

DMRDLS, SMMDMMR, RRR 10063
DMRDLSSS, DLRRDTD, D 9100
DMRDLSLD, DMRMSMMR, 802
DMRDLSLD, RMRMSMR, R 803
DMRDTD, DDRDLS, SRM 7333
DMRDTDD, DFMFRM, M 12571
DMRDTD, DRMFMR, RMFS 6760
DMRDTDRD, DDTLSMDR, 1870
DMRDTDRMDR, DRMLRD 1373
DMRDTDRMF, RSMF#SLT 1849
DMRDTDLS, LDTLS#L, DD 2850
DMRDTLDS, SSSSDR, LF 2132
DMRDTLSS, SLTDTRRT, 11846
DMRDTLLS, RMDMF#S, SL 8405
DMRDTLTD, RMSFMRLS, 11888
DMRRFMRD, MSSLSMF#S, 1905
DMRRFM, MMRMFMMR, DR 9932
DMRRFFMM, RMRRMR, SF 1023
DMRMDRTD, DSRMF#S, SF 10260
DMRMFMRDD, MMRMSF#S 7882
DMRMFS, DLSFFM, MF#MF# 9702
DMRMFS, MMDFRD, MRDS 8024
DMRMFSM, LSFMRM, SLT 1484
DMRMFSFM, LSFMRM, SL 1486
DMRMFSSM, LSFMRM, SL 1487
DMRMFS, SFMR, RRDRMF, 10284
DMRMFSS, SFMFSM, DMR 9204
DMRMF#SSF#S, SLSLTDT 6616
DMRMSMFMRD, MRMSFM 257
DMRMLSFM, LSFMRM, DS 1485
DMRMLSFM, LSFMRM, SL 1488
DMRFMRDRF, MLF#SSF#S, 4119
DMRFMRRD, MDLRDTLS, 6102
DMRFMSFM, RDDMRS, S#L 9711
DMRFMSFM, MRDFMR, DR 202
DMRFMLS, DTLSFM, MMM 884
DMRSFMDR, DDTLTDRM 11812
DMRSSDMRSS, SFMRMF 10391
DMRSSF#S, DSLSFMR, SM 4167
DMRTS, DMRTS, SDDRRM 7784
DMRTSLLS, DDRMSDRS, 2241
DMR#MDRMSF#LS, DMR#MD 5212
DMR#MMFMF, F#SDTLLSS, 11806
DMMDMFMRD, MSSFMRR 4858
DMMRDRDLSD, RRMRS, M 10717
DMMRDRMRMS, SSLSMR 11468
DMMRDMMR, DSSS, SLSS 7495
DMMRDFMR, DRMFRDTD 1470
DMMRDFMR, DMFRDTD, D 1469
DMMRDFM, RMSSF#S, MLS 12297
DMMRDFM, SLSFRM, DMM 12368
DMMRDFFM, RMSSF#S, MLS 12296
DMMRDFF, LSDMSRMR, D 6050
DMMRDFSFM, MMMR#MF#F# 9484
DMMRDSLS, SSDTLSM, D 10807
DMMRDSLLS, DTLSMSF# 11594
DMMRDS, LTDRM, MRMF#S 11537
DMMRDTDF, SFFMRM, SM 6881
DMMRDTRD, DTRDDTLS, 10340
DMMRDTLDT, TLTDRM, T 6224
DMMRRMFR, MFSLSMD, D 10832
DMMRRSD, DLLSFM, MMM 4539
DMMRRSLS, SFFMDR, RS 12233
DMMRMDLS, MRMFM, MSM 11223
DMMRMDTD, MSFMDMR, S 822
DMMRMRD, MSSFSFM, MR 8352
DMMRMRDTD, MSFMRDM 821
DMMRMFM, RDDRRM, SMM 3258
DMMRMF, MRRDRM, DMMR 1202
DMMRFM, RDDDMR, RMSM 14
DMMRSDMMR, SDSSFMR 6904
DMMRSDFMR, MSRRMDT 10072
DMMRSFMRDR, SDRMR 136
DMMR#MFM, RSDDTL, LSS 2662
DMMR#MFFM, DMRDTD, MR 1581
DMMR#MSF, RDDRRM, DMM 10588
DMMR#MSSLSF#S, MMRDR 9925
DMMMDRD, DDDRDLS, SS 2659
DMMMDRMD, SSSSRMFM, 11004
DMMMDRMR, DMSSDMRD, 3881
DMMMDSSS, SMDFMR, DM 6734
DMMMDLSS, MSFRRMFM, 8643
DMMMRDDD, RMSFMR, F 558
DMMMRDDD, MSSSSLLS, 1705
DMMMRDR, DDRMMRDD, D 5242
DMMMRD, MSSSFM, SLLL 10640
DMMMRDMSSLS, MRRMF 6639
DMMMRDMSSLS, SMMMD 6357
DMMMRDFFM, DRD, MSSS 1669
DMMMRDS, FMMMRDDT, D 9407
DMMMRDLS, SMMSFMRM 12082
DMMMRDLLSFM, MMMLL 11630
DMMMRRDD, DRRRDRMS, 7748
DMMMRMDDD, DRRRDRM 7746
DMMMRMFSM, SFMFMRM 8693
DMMMRMFS, MLLLSFMR, 6903

DMMMRMFSS, DMMMRDM 10951
DMMMRMFS, SLSSMFMM, 4368
DMMMRMFSLLS, FMRDD 12053
DMMMRMSM, DRRRDRM, D 1786
DMMMRS, DRRRDRM, MMM 9019
DMMMRSSS, SDSLSSMR, 3576a
DMMMRSSS, SDSLSLMR, 3576
DMMMR#MFFM, MMRDTRD, 967
DMMMR#MSM, DRRRMFM, D 4516
DMMMMD, MSSSSM, SDTL 10920
DMMMMRDS, FMMMMRDR, 4468
DMMMMRDSSSS, SLLLS 4444
DMMMMRMFFFF, MRRRR 10247
DMMMMMRDDLS, DTTTL 43
DMMMMMRD, RMSSFMR, R 2536
DMMMMMRR, MFFFFFMM, 12219
DMMMMFMMRM, MSSSSL 2036
DMMMMFSLSF#S, SSFMR 1220
DMMMMSMDR, DMSLSLS 2272
DMMMMSMDR, DSLSLSM 2271
DMMMFMRD, MSSSLSRM 10639
DMMMFMRRR, SF#SF#MRD 7105
DMMMFSMSLT, SDDTLS 3779
DMMMFSSDRM, SLTDDD 1175
DMMMFS, SFFMMR, RMMM 6552
DMMMFS, SSMRDR, DMMM 11220
DMMMFSSLSF#S, LLSSF 5934
DMMMSRRR, MFSLSFMM 12436
DMMMSFMRRM, DMMMSF 3330
DMMMSSDLS, MLSSFRM 12065
DMMFRDDL, LSRM, SLTR 990
DMMFRDTD, DFSLSFMR 2408
DMMFRSSS, MFRFMRD, D 11459
DMMFMRDLSS, MSSLSF 2905
DMMFMRRM, DLTDRMFR, 7106
DMMFMRMD, LSMMRRSD 5506
DMMFMRSSL, SFMFSMR 2491
DMMFMM, MRRFFM, MSSL 11501
DMMFMFSS, SSMFRD, DM 3481
DMMFMFLS, MSDTLS, FM 411
DMMFFMRD, MSSFMR, MR 8434
DMMFFMRSFM, MMMMRD 395
DMMFFSS, SSMFRD, DMM 3482
DMMFFSTD, RMFSF#S, SL 7133
DMMFSDRDT, DRRMFSL 642
DMMFSSFM, SMMRRD, DM 9595
DMMFSSSMRDLS, DTMM 5105
DMMFSLMRD, SLDSFFM 9467
DMMFLSM, RDDRMR, RMM 1400
DMMSDDRTSFM, MFSSL 11721
DMMSDDLS, SDMRRR, SS 10267
DMMSDRMFM, SSSLTDT, 11781
DMMSDRMFSFM, MSSTM 3091
DMMSDRMS, LLSMSMR, D 6122
DMMSDMRD, DLSMFSM, M 10315
DMMSMDTDFFM, MRSSF# 10626
DMMSMRMR, MSSDRM, MR 12427
DMMSFMRMD, DDTDRMF 7992
DMMSFMRLS, SSMDDRR 2780
DMMSSDDF, FMRDRM, MM 9181
DMMSSD, DTLSF#S, SLTD 9442
DMMSSD, SMLSMFSM, MM 8798
DMMSSDT, SLFSMR, RMM 9326
DMMSSMRD, MSLSMR, DM 7245
DMMSSFMR, SLTDTL 2897
DMMSSSLSM, DDDMMRM 8381
DMMSSLSMDMRD, MMML 11744
DMMSSLS, SDRMMFRD, 7796
DMMSSLLS, SDRTSSF#S, 6869
DMMSSLLS, SRFM, DMMS 11502
DMMSSTLS, MDDRRM, MS 9534
DMMSLS, SRRMF#S, LTSD 5161
DMMLRDT, TDRMDMR, RM 2246
DMMLSFMF, MS#LRDT, S#S# 2551
DMMLSFSMFR, SFMRDM 4379
DMMLLSS, FMDDTD, DMM 4857
DMFRD, DLLTDS, SSFMF 7872
DMFRDMSSLSFFM, DFM 1342
DMFRDMSLS, SDTLSS 9085
DMFRMD, RMLSF#S, SMSD 8387
DMFRMDRT, RMF#SRMRD 259
DMFRMFMRM, SSMRMFM 8026
DMFRSSFM, MRDFMR, RM 2069
DMFRSSFFMR, SLTDSF 2911
DMFRTDRM, RDTLRT, RS 2818
DMFRTDRT, RMSF#SLF#S, 28
DMFMRDRD, TLLLRDT, D 3735
DMFMRD, MSLSMR, RRRM 2417
DMFMRDSSLTD, DDDTS 10429
DMFMRDTD, SDTLSF#S, S 6731
DMFMRMDRM, LLTDTLS# 6145
DMFFMRDMRTTD, DMFF 3916
DMFSD, DMRDRD, TDSLS 526
DMFSDDTD, RMRDRF#SS 3755
DMFSDDTD, MRDTLS, DM 6216
DMFSDRDL, DTDRMFM, D 7602
DMFSDRRD, SDTLTLS, R 5681
DMFSDRMF, MRDDTD, SD 2736
DMFSDMRD, DRMRSLTL 6086
DMFSDMRDRM, MLTDDR 6339
DMFSDFMR, RMF#SF#S, DM

10425
DMFSD, SLDTD, SFMMDR, 10290
DMFSDL, SMSSF#M, MF#ST 1386
DMFSDLS, SSMRDMRR, R 7750
DMFSDLSS, SMRMFRDD, 9254
DMFSDL#LS, LRMFFSLS 1367
DMFSDTD, DTDFMR, DMF 9249
DMFSDTDRR, DMRDTLLS 1110
DMFSDTDR, MFSLLS, S 1433
DMFSDTDLS, SDTLSMD 8461
DMFSDT, LSDFMFM, MRM 5827
DMFS, DTLSDTLS, SDRM 1196
DMFSDTLS, MFSLSMDR 11394
DMFSDTLS, MFLSMRD, D 5892
DMFSDTLS, SSF#SLDTD 2562
DMFSDTLS, SLSMMFMRD 8722
DMFSDTLS, LSFMRMFRD, 1195
DMFSRMRDFMMRMFS, L 11937
DMFSRM, SDTLTLS, SSF 5160
DMFSMD, DRMFSM, MRTD 12128
DMFSMDLSFM, DLLDLL 8515
DMFSMDLSFMRD, RMSF 5214
DMFS, MRDTLSLS, LFRS 6986
DMFSMFMRM, DLTDFMR, 9716
DMFSMFSL, SSLFMR, RM 2264
DMFSMFSLTD, DTSDSL 3261
DMFSMFSLTD, DTLDSL 3260
DMFSMFLSRM, SMRDDL 4026
DMFSMFLS, SLTDSSFM 4024
DMFSMLS, DTLSRM, RMF 5111
DMFSMLS, SLTDTLLSF 93
DMFSMLSLFM, DTLF#SL 2516
DMFSMLTD, DSLSMDRM, 9684
DMFSMLTD, DSLSMRDR 9685
DMFSMLTD, DSLSMRDT 9683
DMFSMLTD, SSLSSMRD 3547
DMFSFMR, DRMFMFSLS, 2683
DMFSFMRM, MRMFMRD#D,
11295
DMFSFMRM, MMRFRDTD 11293
DMFSFMRM, MMRFMRDT 11294
DMFSFMRMFM, FSLTLS, 10730
DMFSFMRFM, DMFSLTD 2512
DMFSSDDRDT, LLSMMR 10128
DMFSSD, DRMFSM, MRTD 12129
DMFSSDDS, SLSMFS, DM 11557
DMFSSDLSFM, RSFMRD 8747
DMFSSDTLS, SLDLSFM 1131
DMFSSMMSFMFRM, DDM 4856
DMFSSMSFMFRM, DMFS 4852
DMFSSFMR, SLTDTLLS, 2899
DMFSSFM, FMDRRD, DMF 12253
DMFSSFFM, FMDRRD, DM 9596
DMFSSSDMRRD, DTLSST 11266
DMFSSS, SLTDDD, DDRM 9028
DMFSSSLFLS, SFFFFM 10565
DMFSSSLLTDS, MRDTS 3962
DMFSSSLTDR, SMDLTD 9725
DMFSSLDD, DDDTLS, DM 5072
DMFSSLDDS, MSLSFMR# 1811
DMFSSLDS, LSSFMRLT, 6861
DMFSSLDTLS, DMFSSL 5084
DMFSSLFD, LSMMRDFR, 7301
DMFSSLFS, FMRM, DMFS 3341
DMFSSLSD, FFMRDMRD, 9183
DMFSSLSFMSFM, DMFS 7957
DMFSSLSFS, SLTDSMM 10162
DMFSSLSFS, SLTDSMF 10163
DMFSSLS, SDRMFRD, DM 7793
DMFSSLS, SDRMFMD, DM 7792
DMFSSLLDLLS, SMDMS 10328
DMFSSLLS, SDTLSLTL 12339
DMFSSLLS, SDTLLS, D 10657
DMFSSLLS, SMSDSLLS, 7287
DMFSSLLS, SFMRMFM, F# 6108
DMFSSLLS, SSDTSLLS, 7726
DMFSSLLS, SLSFMFMR, 10976
DMFSSLLS, SLSTDR, SL 10174
DMFSSLLS, SLTDLT, SD 8037
DMFSSLTD, DDDTTDLT, 8842
DMFSSLTD, DMFSSFMR, 3074
DMFSSLTDDT, TTDRDT 9663
DMFSSLTD, RMFSRM, DM 3344
DMFSSLTD, RTD, DMFSS 3813
DMFSSLTD, SDSFMRDFM 11411
DMFSSLTD, SDTLSL 9008
DMFSSLTD, LRDTSLF#S, 9752
DMFSSLTD, LSMMRDRM 10576
DMFSSLTD, TDRDTLSS, 6497
DMFSSLTD, TRDTLLS, D 6500
DMFSSLTLS, SDTLSLF 11197
DMFSLDRM, RDTLTS, SD 1233
DMFSLDTDFMRM, DMLS 9541
DMFSLDTD, LLLTRDTL 11644
DMFSLFFM, RDDFMRD, D 8564
DMFSLSMD, MFMRDLDR, 5262
DMFSLS, MRDDTL, LSDD 368
DMFSLSM, RMSLFR, DMF 2853
DMFSLSMRFM, DMFSLS 10861
DMFSLSMFSFM, DMFSL 11561a
DMFSLSMFSFM, SDMFS 11561
DMFSLSM, SFMRSM, MFS 4732
DMFSLSFMDRM, MFSLS 11663
DMFSLSFM, DMLRSSF#S, 4698
DMFSLSFMD, SLDSM, FM 7458
DMFSLSFMRD, SLTDDT 4015

DMFSLSFMRMFRD, DMF 7509
DMFSLSFM, RMSSF#S, RR 3722
DMFSLSFMRM, SLTDTL 494
DMFSLSFMR, SLTDTLS 2901
DMFSLSFM, MMRDDTLS, 6492
DMFSLSFMFMDRTD, MF 6570
DMFSLS, SSLTDSMMMF 379
DMFSLS, SLTDLT, SDTLS 8053
DMFSLLS, DRRMFM, MRS 1881
DMFSLTDRS, DTLS, LSF 3805
DMFSLTD, MFMRMF#S, SS 9060
DMFSLTD, TLMSF#M, MFR 1005
DMFSLTDTLS, SSSLS 2718
DMFLSDST, LSSLSMR, D 15
DMFLSMD, MRTTLS, DMF 318
DMFLSMSFMFRM, DMFL 4855
DMF#SDFMMRD, DLTDLR 10099
DMF#SSLDTL, SSDTDMR 10113
DMF#SSLTD, RMDTSLDT 4093

DMS

DMSDDD, MSDMMM, MMMF 9098
DMSDDD, MLDMMM, DTTM, 10450
DMSDDRDTD, DRDTLS, R 5176
DMSDDRMFM, SLSFMR, R 3430
DMSDDRMF, LSFMS, TDR 6464
DMSDDRLSFM, SLRT, DL 6488
DMSDDRTD, MMMRTSLS, 11991
DMSDDMRDS, DTLFLLS 11690
DMSDDTD, LLLSFMMRR 10376
DMSDDTLS, DRMRDTLS, 8486
DMSDDTLSFFM, SMSLS 7901
DMSDRM, MRSDTSLS, DF 9971
DMSDRMFMDRD, RRMRT 3281
DMSDRS, DLSSFM, RMSL 1746
DMSDRTD, MRDTLLS, DM 6416
DMSDRTD, MRSSF#S, SSF 813a
DMSDRTD, MRSTLS, SSF 813
DMSDR, TLSLS, DRMSL, S 1393
DMSDMRDDT, DTLSFMR 12445
DMSDMRDSD, DDTDTLS, 7055
DMSDMRRD, RMFSLTLS, 7384
DMSDMRR, TDSSFM, DMS 2707
DMSDMR, SF#SDTLS, SDR 11873
DMSDMRLSFM, SDTLSF# 3011
DMSDMMRDTD, RMSLSF# 3246
DMSDMFSLR, SFMF#SLT 982
DMSDMLLS, DMSDTLLS, 3055
DMSDFMRR, RMRSTLST 6309
DMSDFLS, MFSDMFRD, 2801
DMSDFLLS, MFSDFMFMRD 2800
DMSDSM, DSLSFM, SMRD 8763
DMSDSMSDMD, DRMRDT 11685
DMSDSFMRD, DMDLTDS 2528
DMSDSFMRD, RMF#SSLS 9134
DMSDSFMRD, LSF#SLDT 6267
DMSDSFM, SLLSFMR, SD 8062
DMSDSFSM, RMF#SSTLS, 11384
DMSDSLDS, FMDDTD, DM 6735
DMSDSLSFM, RMF#SDTL 5183
DMSDSLSFM, SDDDFMR, 7725
DMSDSLS, SDTDRM, MRD 9343
DMSDSLTD, DSLSSFMR 5746
DMSDSTLS, MMRDRMF#S, 6874
DMSDLDSFSMDMR, DMS 5618
DMSDLDLS, FSMDRRD, S 5619
DMSDLFFM, RMFSLTDR, 6627
DMSDLF#LS, LSRSF#FM, D 3751
DMSDLSRM, MMLDTLS, 7391
DMSDLS, FMDRMF#S, SRD 7063
DMSDLS, FMDMF#S, SRDT 7062
DMSDLSFM, MRSLLS, SS 8439
DMSDLSFLSMRD, MF#SL 11843
DMSDLS, LDLSMRM, D 9439
DMSDLSLSMRD, MSLDT 11842
DMSDLSLSMRD, MSLTD 11841
DMSD, LTDS, SLSSMDRR 3593
DMSDTDRR, DMRTLLS, D 1109
DMSDTDLS, SSSSMFRD, 11998
DMSDTLFM, RDMLTS, LL 10194
DMSDTLS, FMRDFMR, MS 10245
DMSDTLSFM, SDDRR#M, R 6126
DMSDTLSLDFLSM, MRD 4270
DMSDTLSLLS, SFMLS 1799
DMSDTLSLTDTLSFM, 4567
DMSRRDD#RFM, SDRDTL 8382
DMSRMDRLTD, DFMRDT 12126
DMSRMRDRM, MMRDFFM 12478
DMSRFMRD, RMRDTLLS, 9436
DMS, MDRTD, SLTDLLS, M 8576
DMSMDLDD, LLSSMR, DM 1839
DMSMDLDSD, DRMFMR, D 7380
DMSMDLFM, DRMFMDDD, 5340
DMSMRDD, DRFLSM, SDT 5057
DMSMRDDTDR, MFLSMS 10638
DMSMRDRD, MMMFSSFM 10698
DMSMRDRMFM, DMSDTL 3185
DMSMRD, RMFFSMR, MRD 12511
DMSMRDTR, MDLDTL, DM 10785
DMSMRMF#S, LSMRDDTD, 4630
DMSMRMF#S, LSFMRDRM 4629
DMSMMRRD, FFMMRDR, D 4449
DMSMFSLSR, MFSFM 8754

DMSMFSLTD, MMRDTLS, 7034
DMSMFLSR, MSFRDLTS, 4066
DMSMFLSM, SDFMRRD, D 9054
DMSMSMFSFMRD, RMRM 3187
DMSFRDRM, DFMLSTDF, 3054a
DMSFRDRM, DFMLSTDS 3054
DMSFMDDFFM, MRDTRF 12078
DMSFMDRM, DSSLDTLS, 11640
DMSFMRDRRD, SLTDTL 10538
DMSFMRD, RMFMRR#M, MS 2920
DMSFMRDMRD, DMSF#MR# 10749
DMSFMRD, SDSLSFMR, S 436
DMSFMR, RRSLTLS, F#MS 6954
DMSFMRRM, MDTLSFMR 3084
DMSFMRMDRM, SLSFMF 9620
DMSFMRFM, RDMRDTD, D 5389
DMSFMR, SLDTLS, SDRM 2963
DMSFMMRD, DLSSMR, TD 4041
DMSFMLSFM, SLSFMR, R 11355
DMSFMLLS, SFMRRMFM 7789
DMSFLMSR, RMSSF#S, DM 12545
DMSF#SM, SSLTDS, SSF#S 4847
DMSF#SLS, DSTLS, DMSL 9142
DMSSDDTDMMR, DRRMF# 452
DMSSMDRM, DSSLTDLS, 11639
DMSSMDRM, DSSLTDTLS 11641
DMSSMRDRMD, DMSDSL 5021
DMSSMRDTD, MSFMRDS 8463
DMSSMMRD, RDLSDMDR, 11094
DMSSFRDTD, DDTLSLT 12281
DMSSFM, DMRDDT, DMSD 8374
DMSSFMRD, RMF#STTLS 795
DMSSFM, RRFFMR, MRFS, 8081
DMSSFMRMF, FLFSMDF# 4874
DMSSFMR, MF#SDTLS, DR 8421
DMSSFMRF, MRDLSDRM, 9056
DMSSFMMRD, DDTDSFM 9672
DMSSFF, RFLLSS, RSF#S 6612
DMSSFSM, DDTTLLS, ST 2283
DMSSFLDLSMS, DMSSF 10382
DMSSFLSM, SFMDRD, DM 2777
DMSSFLLSMRD, MRRMF 7377
DMSSFLLS, MF#SSLLS, S 6918
DMSSF#SLSDMM, MFSSF 1956
DMSSSDMMRDTD, DDFS 9103
DMSSSDMLSFR, LSMSF 5647
DMSSSDMLSFR, LSSMS 5646
DMSSSDLDS, SFM, FMR, D 3999
DMSSSDTD, SDTDSFMR 4791
DMSSSDTSLS, DSRFSM 666
DMSSSDTL, SMMFMR, DM 4513
DMSSSMDMR, RMFFFLS 7196
DMSSSMRDFF, LSFMMR 1957
DMSSSM, MMMMS, SDTLS 10828
DMSSSMSDDD, SDTLSF 4413
DMSSS, MSDDD, SSLDTL 5314
DMSSSFMDMFRTD, DMS 9709
DMSSSSSDTTL, RMFSM 9700
DMSSSSSS, DSS, SLSSS 6434
DMSSSSSL#LS, MDDRMS 11638
DMSSSS, LSFRMFFF, SM 2038
DMSSSSLSFS, RMFMSS 4258
DMSSSSLS, SDSDRMRD 10114
DMSSSSLS, SDSDRMRDTLS 10109
DMSSSSLS, SDTDMRMR 10110
DMSSSSLSLS, SDSDMR 10112
DMSSSSLL, SDTDMRDR 10111
DMSSSSLL#L#L, SLDDLSLD, 6613
DMSSSLFLD, LSMRDML 1172
DMSSSLSM, DSLLLDS, D 5306
DMSSSLSM, SSDTLLS, M 11388
DMSSSLSFMRDD, DMS 166
DMSSSLS, SDRMFMRD, D 7794
DMSSSLSSM, DMSSSLS 12121
DMSSSLSLS, SDRMFRD, 7795
DMSSSLTDD, DRMSFFM, 2146
DMSSSLTDS, DMSSSMD 10210
DMSSLMSF, MRDRM, MFS 1893
DMSSLMSS, MSDDTS#L, L 11131
DMSSLFSMRD, MRRMFM 7376
DMSSLSM, DRRDRM, DMS 3787
DMSSLSMDMSR, RMFRD 961
DMSSLSM, DTDFMMR, DMSS 7001
DMSSLSM, MMRMFFM, DM 11655
DMSSLSFMRDD, DMSSL 167
DMSSLSFMRD, RMF#SSL 8067
DMSSLSFMR, MFSDRM 5801
DMSSLSFM, MFSDMRD, S 6687
DMSSLSFS, DMSSLSFS, 10817
DMSSLSSM, DDDRDLS, D 5757
DMSSLSSM, DRRM, DMSS 12490
DMSSLS, SMFMRD, DMSL 9287
DMSSLSSM, FMRDRMR, D 9657
DMSSLSSM, SSRMFM, DM 5095
DMSSLSSFM, MRMFLR, S 2600
DMSSLS, SLDTLS, SSLD 4833
DMSSLLM, DDTF#R#D#T, DM 3762
DMSSLL, MRMFMM, DMSS 677
DMSSLLMS, SMSTLLS#S, 4406
DMSSLLF#S, LLF#S, FFRM 9083

DMSSLLS, SSSDTLTLS, 9102
DMSSLLSS, LSFMRRR, D 2151
DMSSLLLS, MSFMRDD, D 8867
DMSSLTDD, MRDTTLS, F 4171
DMSSLTDDM, LRMFFM, M 9308
DMSSLTDD, SSDLSF#S, D 7154
DMSSLTDDSSSSLTD, D 9710
DMSSLTD, RSMDTLS, SS 4306
DMSSLTDS, MRMDRM, DM 11281
DMSSLTDSS, MSLLTDR 9998
DMSSLTDS, LSSFMR, DM 3549
DMSSLTDS, LLSDSFMR, 4825
DMSSLTD, TDRTLLS, MF 6496
DMSSLTD, TRDTLLS, DM 4170
DMSSLTD, TRSTLLS, SD 6498
DMSLDLSFS, LSFSMRD 5502
DMSLMSMRM, DMSLMF#S 7143
DMSLF#S, DMSLF#S, DTLS, 4997
DMSLSDDLS, DMSSLSM 1838
DMSLSDTLSMDRM, DMS 11624
DMSLSMD, DRRDRM, DMS 324
DMSLSMDRD, DRRRSFM, 7999
DMSLSMRD, RRRRDRM, M 8480
DMSLSMRMD, DDRRDRM, 7072
DMSLSMMRD, LSDLSDR 5820
DMSLSMFS, DLTDSSFM, 11472
DMSLSFMRDDD, SLTDR 1654
DMSLSFMRMD, DMSLSM 9983
DMSLSFM, MRFMDR, DMS 1200
DMSLSFS, DDRMRDLL, D 1471
DMSLSF#SM, RDRMFLR, R 2391
DMSLSSFM, SLDSF#S, DT 2681
DMSLSS, SLSDMR, RMSL 4729
DMSLSLDTLSLSS, DSL 9670
DMSLSLTD, DDTLLSFF 550
DMSLSLTD, LRTMDTL 12369
DMSL, LSMRM, MSLD, SLS 7251
DMSLTD, DMDTLT, RRRM 2356
DMSLTDRM, MFRRRMD, D 7536
DMSLTD, MRDRDTD, SSL 3208
DMSLTDSM, SLDTLS, LT 10824
DMSLTDLS, DRMF#SLS, S 1077
DMSTLSD, SLLLSS, MFF 9296
DMLSDDRD, FMRDSSF#S, 6252
DMLSRFMRD, DMLSRFM 12456
DMLSMDRMDL,TDLM, DM 1207
DMLSMDFM, DLTDMR, RR 5062
DMLSMRDRM, SLSF#S, MS 9879
DMLSMMRDRRMFMR, DM 7066
DMLSMMRDMR, RD#RFLL 8111
DMLSMMRD, SLDDRMR, M
7444
DMLSFM, SSFMLSSF, MR 7280
DMLSF#F, LRMFSLS, DTR 10192
DMLSF#SDS, LSFFSFM, D 12209
DMLLTDD, DTDSMDRM, M 9059
DMTDFMMRD#RL, LLLSF 8077
DFRRMRDRD, DRMMSFM 5467
DFRRMRDRD, DRMFSFMR 5466
DFRMDL, LSMFRRM, DDD 11244
DFRMSL, SLTDRL, TDLT 4255
DFRSMFMRRD, DFRSD 11556
DFMRDDDRMR, RSFMS 358
DFMRDDTDR, DMSLF#S, R 91
DFMRDRS, LTDLRDDT, D 1613
DFMRDSFM, MRSLLS, SD 9386
DFMRDSS, LSDDRM, F#SD 6630
DFMRDTD, DRMF#STLS, S 5200
DFMRFMRD, MLDFRDT, S 5828
DFMMRDTD, DRMF#SLTL 3572
DFFMDRRRRDRM, SLFL 8846
DFFMDRMF, FMRDTLSF, 8056
DFFFFFFMMMM, MDDDD 7256
DFFFFLLLSF#S, MRRMF 5
DFFLFMMS, MRSF#MF#S, S 6085
DFSM, SDLFSMDTLS, RT 7411

DSD

DSDDDDD, RMRDMF#S, SS 6958a
DSDDDDD, RMDMF#S, DSM 6958
DSDDRRM, MRDMR, DSDM 3742
DSDDRSM, MSF#STLLS, F 5612
DSDDRSSDDRM, MDDDS 11880
DSDDSLSLSMD, DRMSS 3764
DSDDTDRMFFMR, RRMF 6305
DSDDTD, LDDLFF, DRTD 8060
DSDDTLSFMMR, MLSSF# 95
DSDRDTD, DFSLSDFMR, 1531
DSDRDT, DRMFMR, MMM 11560
DSDRMDMF, SLFRDRM, D 8646
DSDRMD, TDLLS, SSLTD 9378
DSDRMRD, DFFMRMFR, D 4161
DSDRMRDS, LLSSDMR, D 5773
DSDRMRDTS, DRMFMRR 3359
DSDRMRMF, SFMR, DSDR 443
DSDRMRMFSSSFMR, DS 442a
DSDRMRMF, SLSFMR, DS 442
DSDRMR, FMDRRD, MRMS 8291
DSDRMRTS, DRMFRRD, D 10414
DSDRMMMFM, RDRMD, RM 8581
DSDRMFR, DMRTDLS, MM 4188
DSDRMFRM, SLLSMRDR, 12480
DSDRMFMRDRD, RMDMR 11695
DSDRMFMRD, RMDLRDT 6870
DSDRMFMR, SDRMFMR 9007

DSDRMFM, SMMRDMR, DS 12474
DSDRMFFM, SDMFSLMR, 5810
DSDRMSFMR, RMFRDRM, 4492
DSDRMSFM, RLTD, DSDR 10261
DSDRS, MRMFMR, DTLDR 141
DSDMDMSFMRD, MRDFM 1431
DSDMDMSLSF#SM, FSSL 11403
DSDMDTLS, SLTDTDMR 1825
DSDMRDMMF#SS, SSSDS 2888
DSDMRDFMRM, SLSFMR 8449
DSDMRD, SMSFMR, DLDM 776
DSDMRD, SLTDRDT, DMF# 8429
DSDMRDTD, DFSLSDFMR, 1530
DSDMRDTD, RMSFMR, SD 1468
DSDMMRDR, DMLSFMRD, 9024
DSDMMRDT, DLLLSL, DL 8516
DSDMMR, FLMRDT, DRMM 11742
DSDMSFMR, DSDFLS, SL 9357
DSDMLSFMR, SSLTDFR 10432
DSDFMRD, DSLRFMRD, D 9080
DSDFMRD, SLRFMRD, DS 9079
DSDSDDTDS, MMFSLSF 4349
DSDSDRDTLS, MSMSMF 8610
DSDSDRM, FRMDTDR, MF 3003
DSDSDRMFMR, SRTSTL 10379
DSDSDTDRDLT, TFSTF 11143
DSDSMD, SFRD, DTDLSD 1625
DSDSMRDR, MFSLTDR, D 4771
DSDSMFMRD, DRMFMR, M 10464
DSDSLSM, MRMSLS, DSD 9806
DSDSLTD, RRMDMF#S, RL 957
DSDTDRMD, MSSMSFM, M 7264
DSDTSLSFM, MMRMFSS 1380
DSDTLFLTDSFM, DTDR 7609
DSDTLS, SFMRMFM, DMF# 2172
DSDTLTDRMRD, MRDTL 8254
DS, RMFS, SM, SM, SM, SM, MD, 10796
DSRMFS, SLSSF#S, DSRM 9915
DSMDDLLS, SDTSLLS, M 4541
DSMDDTD, MRDTLLS, RR 9106
DSMDRDTDR, MFSDRMRD, 9599
DSMDRMFM, DSMLSFSM, 5542
DSMDRMFMRM, MRRMSL 12105
DSMDRSSMDR, MMTTDM 10958
DSMDRTDR, MSDMRD, MF 9601
DSMDRTLS, SDDRRM, SF 1492
DSMDMFSLLS, LSRMF# 6862
DSMDFMMR, MRDRTLS, D 5568
DSMDFMFLD, DMDSRDT 6282
DSMDSMSMDRFRD, DSM 11055
DSMDSFMD, FMRLT, MTR 12212
DSMDSFMMR, MDFMRMR 4865
DSMDSF#SLSMFSL, TTD 3702
DSMDSLDT, SDMSRD, SD 6321
DSMDSLLS, SLTDTLLS, 3478
DSMDSTD, RRMMF#MF#SR, 355
DSMDSTRFM, SMDRMSF 3644
DSMDLS, DRMFS, DDDDM 560
DSMDLTD, MRMLF#S, RSR 2357
DSMRDDRTLS, LTDDRR 4764
DSMRDDTLS, SLLSTD, M 8413
DSMRDRDTDR, MFSDRM 9600
DSMRDRMRDLS, DMSLS 10558
DSMRDRM, MMDRMF#S, S 6727
DSMRDMFSLLS, LSRMF# 6865
DSMRDFFSLS, FMF#SRR 1402
DSMRDFSL, MRMFSM, SM 3776
DSMRDSLLS, SLTDTLLS 3479
DSMRDLS, LDFMRDS, MD 9680
DSMRDTDD, MFRSSF#S, D 5556
DSMRDTDLS, DRMRDTL, 2629
DSMRDTLS, LTDRMF#S, L 6742
DSMRDTTL, RLFMRDDT, 719
DSMRSDRMFSFFMRDF 1896
DSMRSFMRDDT, LSFMS 2649
DSMRTD, MDSFRM, SMDR 9042
DSMMRDDTDR, RDSMMR 7630
DSMFRDTD, DRMFSLRR, 4891
DSMFSMRDTDRFRMDRTD, 7843
DSMFSFRM, FMDRMR, SL 6875
DSMFSLS, DLTDTLS, MF 738
DSMFSLLS, SDLTTL, D 10228
DSMFLS, DDDRM, DDTLR 10366
DSMSDRMD, FMRDTDR, M 8573
DSMSDRM, RRRDRMDS, D 4871
DSMSDRMF, SDRMRDT, D 6459
DSMSDMRDS, LTDRMRD 8295
DSMSDS, DRMFMR, DSMS 8657
DSMS, FMDR, MSF#STLS, D 2799
DSMSLS, FMSFM, STLSD 1875
DSMSLLS, MFSDRM, LMD 11564
DSMSLTD, SMFMRM, DSM 12014
DSMLFRFMD, MRDSSTL 5330
DSMLSMDR, FMSLLS, S 2746
DSMLSFMR, RMSSF#S, SS 456
DSMLSFFM, MFSDFMR, D 4814
DSMTDRMLTDR, MLSM, D 3919
DSFMDRMFSM, RSF#SSF# 4117
DSFMDRFM, MFSMDRMR 11993
DSFMDMRD, DLSFMMRD 5414
DSFMDFMR, SDRMRDR, D 6116
DSFMDS, MFSLTDRDDT, 11835
DSFMDSFM, MLDTMS#F, F 4055
DSFMRDDTLS, SSDDMR 1184
DSFMRDRD, DSF#MRSL 2190

DSFMRDRD, SLTDSFFM, 659
DSFMRDRM, MRDDTD, SD 8218
DSFMRDRM, MLLSMSF 5517
DSFMRDRLS, LTDRFMS 5971
DSFMRDRT, SDRMFR, SF 8205
DSFMRD, MRDTDRTLS 9665
DSFMRDMR, SFFMMRRD, 6609
DSFMRD, SMDTDR, RRRS 4148
DSFMRDSSLTD, DDDTL 2676
DSFMR, DSSLTD, DSFMR, 8258
DSFMRDSLTDT, SLLTD 12573
DSFMRDLSFM, RSFMMF 12513
DSFMRM, SDTLS, DSFMR 12565
DSFMRSLS, SDTLSSF#S, 7310
DSFMMRDSFMMR, SDTD 2869
DSFMMRRD, RMF#SSSF#S, 441
DSFMMRRD, SSSSLTDRR, 4889
DSFMMRRM, FSLTLS, DS 9743
DSFMMFFSSL, SFMMMM 7706
DSFMFSDR, FMRD, DSFS 9916
DSFMSDMR, RMMRDR, SD 7471
DSFMLSFMRD, SLTDDT 4019
DSFMLLTDT, DDDDDDD 8163
DSSDDTT, RSSRRDD, MS 9972
DSSDRM, DDFMRD, MRDT 3538
DSSDRMRD, SRMFMRDD, 7048
DSSDMRLS, SRMFRD, 799
DSSDLD, TDRSM, DSSDL 5686
DSSDLLL, TDRTDMD, DS 3595
DSSDTDRDT, DMRFMRD, 10426
DSSMDDFMR#M, RLTDDM 2164
DSSMD, FMRMD, SDMRTL 6007
DSSMDFFMR#M, RLTDMS 2165
DSSMDLLS, SDDTLS, MF 7446
DSSMRMF#S, SMSFSMRD, 12364
DSSMMDMR, RMDSF#S, SL 6816
DSSMSD, MRSDLSF#S, 10038
DSSFMRDD, DTLTLLS, D 2697
DSSFMRDLS, SDDTTLS 10178
DSSFMRMFMR, DRMRMF 10543
DSSFMRMF#S, SMSFSMR 12365
DSSFMMRDRMR, RMDSM 6817
DSSS, DLLL, TTDRMRDS 12229
DSSSMLSFM, RMF#SLLS 4605
DSSSMLSFM, MFSLLS, 4602
DSSSFMFS, MRDSFM, SL 11302
DSSSFMSFMRD, SFMRM 4532
DSSSSDRDTT, RSSSSR 5534
DSSSSDTLS, SDDTTLL 9543
DSSSSSDTL, SDTLSS 8965
DSSSSLFS, SL#L#LFSLS 1959
DSSSSLSM, RMSLF#S, MS 4604
DSSSSLSM, RMSLLS, RM 4608
DSSSSLSFM, RMF#SSLS 4607
DSSSSLSFM, RMF#SLLS, 4606
DSSSSLSFM, MFSLLS, S 4603
DSSSSLSSFMR, RFFFF 6971
DSSSSLLDTLSFM, MSF 6629
DSSSSLTDDDT, TLLLS 4074
DSSSLD, TDRMDS, DSSS 5189
DSSSLSMRMDDLLLM. 7599
DSSSLS, MFMRRD, DSSS 9366
DSSSLLS, DTDMRD, DSS 2987
DSSLDDTD, MLLRTLLS, 1890
DSSLDRM, RFMRDR, RLR 12493
DSSLDS, LTDRMRR, RMT 7985
DSSLMFMRS, SMSLSFM, 10066
DSSLMS, STSF#MM, MF 10731
DSSLSMFSSD, DFMTDS, 8941
DSSLSFRM, SSSSMFRD, 2305
DSSLSFMFS, SDTLSLT 7373
DSSLSFS, DFSMFR, RMD 2158
DSSLSFSMD, DSTDDFM 10040
DSSLSSDS, MDDRMFLR, 10504
DSSLSSFM, DRMFFM, MM 8551
DSSLSSSM, DRMFFM, MM 8552
DSSLSSSS, SDRMRDRR, 186
DSSLTDD, MRDDTD, SSLS 9611
DSSLTDD, MRDLTD, DSS 9612
DSSLTDDM, LRMFFM, MM 9307
DSSLTDDTD, DDTLSLL 4087
DSSLTDDTLSFS, MMDF 7899
DSSLTD, DTLSF#S, MMDF 7900
DSSLTDSFM, SLFRDTD, 5953
DSSLTS, SDTLS, MFSSL 5521
DSSLTLSMDRMS, DSSL 5818
DSSTL, RLLDT, DMMMLR 10767
DSLDDRRM, RMRMF#S, SS 9519
DSLDDMRD, DMSMDMRD 3433
DSLDDTD, TDRSLLS, DS 11738
DSLDDTD, TDRSLTLS, D 11737
DSLDRD, MDS, FMRSMRD 5001
DSLDRDTL, SDRMFRD, D 12378
DSLDRRMDRMFSR, RMD 4344
DSLDRM, MSMRDR, RMRD 4950
DSLDMRDTD, MRDTSLR 344
DSLDMRRD, MDLRDTTL, 342
DSLDMRRD, MRDTDTL, D 343
DSLDFMRMRD, SFMMRM 1228
DSLDFFFM, RDTMLTS, D 8344
DSLDTLS, LTDMRDR, MR 9277
DSLR, DRSRDLTDMS, SL 9642
DSLRFTDM, MSFMRDR, R 11299
DSLMRMFSSDTL, LRRF 1374

DSLMFSTD, FMRDRTLS, 1798
DSLMSLLS, DDDDDRM, D 12193
DSLFRSMD, RRMLSF#S, D 2585
DSLFRSM, MMRSTLS, LR 12495
DSLFMMMFRD, SDRMMF 11828
DSLSDDRM, MFMRDLTD, 7549
DSLSDRMD, RMFMRD#R, R 10526
DSLSDMSR, MMRSLTS, D 5871
DSLSDFSM, SDRMFFFM 9592
DSLS, DSLS, DDDD, DDDD, 349
DSLSDTDRMD, SFMFRD 6285
DSLSDTLSS, MSLRDTD, 12073
DSLSDTLS, SLDSMRD, D 9638
DSLSMRDDRDLSF, MFS 2765
DSLSMRDS, LLFMRMR, D 2075
DSLSMRMD, RMLSDT, SD 6681
DSLSMFRM, RMFSFMR, D 4386
DSLSMFMRRM, DSLS 1507
DSLSMSFRD, RMLSF#S, L 8618
DSLSFM, DRMRD, RRMRD 1396
DSLSFM, DRMMRD, MRMR 4071
DS, LSFMRDMR, RMLSFM 3713
DSLSFMRDFMRDTD, RM 6038
DSLSFMRDTDRS, LTDR 6015
DSLSFMRMD, RSLTDLS, 12485
DSLSFMRM, FSLTDRT, M 2249
DSLSFMRM, SLDTLS, DS 6494
DSLSFMFS, DRMFMRDR, 8678
DSLSFMFSDLRDTD, MR 7367
DSLSFM, SSLTDT, RSL 11478
DSLSFM, SLRMRD, MDSS 4151
DSLSFM, LTDDTD, RMRS, 7357
DSLSFMLTSDDTD, DRR 1882
DSLSSD, MRMDDDTLT, D 8768
DSLSSFF, RTDTLSS, MD 11001
DSLSSFFM, DRLSFMRR 2849
DSLLMFM, MRDRMM, MRD 723
DSLLFTRD, SMMRMFRM, 8224
DSLLSFMD, SLTDTLLS 299
DSLLSFMRD, DTLRDTL 11968
DSLLSFM, LLRDTLS, DT 4135
DSLLSSDRRMD, DSSLT 5787
DSLLSSFM, DRMRRD, DS 9161
DSLL#LSDRRD, MFSLFD 1675
DSLTDRRM, SFRMMR, DS 10629
DSLTDRMD, DLRDTLLS, 10069
DSLTDRMD, MSSMSFM, M 7265
DSLTDRMD, FLRDTLS, D 4175
DSLTDRMRD, MRDTLLS, 1279
DSLTDRMRRD, SLTDRT 345
DSLTDRM, RMFMRDDT, D 3184
DSLTDRMFM, SDTTDTL 2308
DSLTDRM, FLSMRDT, DS 2915
DSLTDRT, DRMSFMRR, M 5531
DSLTDMRD, FMRMDRM, M 1731
DSLTDMRDT, LTDRM, MM 4878
DSLTD, MMFRD, SSMF#S, M 2645
DSLTDFMMR, MDTLLS, S 6152
DSLTDFMMR, MSFRDRM, 3521
DSLTDS, MMFLS, DSLTD 10635
DSLTLSSDRMMR, RMRD 163
DSTLSSMRDR, SDMFLS 1580
DLDRMSS, LSMDRDLS, D 3310
DLDFMR, DTDRR, RTDRM 2870
DLD, SMDR, FMLSFMF#S, F 8380
DLDSLRDD, DDFMRDM 2458
DLDLSMRDR, FRMFMRR 9030
DLDLSLTD, DMSMRDR, S 11627
DLDTF, LTLSM, SFMLLL 8117
DLRDDFFMRD, SDRMMR 3633
DLRL, DLRL, DFMFMR, DL 11736
DLMFFM, MMMLTD, DDDD 6582
DLMLSFML, TMSF#TDRT, 7344
DLFRTSDMMRD, DLFRTS 9360
DLFFMMRRFD, L#LSLDR, 10446
DLFFSLS, MRRSFM, DLF 7210
DLSDDRFMR, SMMDFMR 8931
DLSDDMRD, DMSMDRMR, 3432
DLSDRM, MRDFMR, SDDD 6222
DLSDRMMR, MSFMRD, SM 3989
DLSDRMMR, MSFMRD, SF 3989a
DLSDRMMSFMRD, DLSD 10269
DLSDRMFR, SMDFMRD, D 7766
DLSDMRD, DLSDMRD, SL 1897
DLSDFFMR, SDRRM, TTD 12429
DLSMRSFM, SSLTDRDT, 3059
DLSMFRDT, DSSSFMR, D 6077
DLSMSSSDTD, DLSMFF 5241
DLSFSLSM, SFMRMFM, M 3431
DLSSLTD, SLSFMRD, DM 6979
DLSLSLSMS, SLRRDLD, 7419
DLSTLSMSFMRM, MF#LL 9811
DLS#LDTLSM, SDTLTSL 8860
DLLDDLS, SDDDDRMR, D 12550
DLLDRMFRD, DMMRM 8270
DLLDTLTD, SDRFMRDR, 6128
DLLFLLS, SFMFSM, DLL 6591
DLLSMRLTDD, DTLMSS 4571
DLLSSFFM, MRLSFM, DL 11103
DLTDDSMFS, MLLMRDT 12536
DLTDRDT, DLTDLSF, FD 11981

DLTDRM, MMMMLS#M, MDL 747
11747
DLTDMLSMM, SFMRDRR 6151
DLTDLTDRMD, MDRMDM 3138
DLTDLTDRTLS, LTDMR 6515
DLTS, FMRMRS, SDTDRD 5407
DLTS#MLTDRM, MMFMRD 5843
DLTS#MLTDRM, MFMRDD 5842
DLTTDTLT, TTMMRRD, M 9069
DL#LDDRSS, DFFMMRDR 11144

DTD

DTDDDTDD, DMRDTLS, S 2862
DTDRDRMRD, TTDRTDD 6758
DTDRDFDRM, MMRDDRD 8093
DTDRDF, MRDTDDR, RSS 6181
DTDRDFFM, LTDLSSS, D 2614
DTDRDSLT, RD#RMRRDS, 5643
DTDRDT, DRMMRDF, RMF 10520
DTDRDTD, MRDFMR, DTL 9907
DTDRDTRFMMR, MRMDT 1252
DTDRDTFMMR, MRMDTT 1253
DTDRDTLS#LTM, MLSFM 9509
DTDRRDRM, MFMRMDLS, 2769
DTDRRDRM, FMRDDRD, D 706
DTDRRDRM, FMRDTDRD, 705
DTDRRR, MDDDTD, RMRD 8293
DTDR, RFFFM, RDTRD. 10108
DTDRRLTDRM, MRDT, SR 1248
DTDRMRD, RD#RMFMR, MR
4965
DTDRMRD, SFMRMFM, MR# 7874
DTDRMRTD, MMMFMR, DT 2042
DTDRMRTDT, MMRDTSL 10339
DTDRMFRRD, SMDFMRL 4198
DTDRMFMRDDTD, MFSL 3451
DTDRMFMRD, RMRDTLL 9157
DTDRMFFM, MRSSF#S, SS 9451
DTDRMFSM, MLSMF#S, FM 8432
DTDRMFSSFMRD, FMRS 9522
DTDRMFLSFM, MRSSF#M 5000
DTDRMSMR, MRDLSDRD, 9084
DTDRMSFMR, MMMLSF#S, 9717
DTDRMLSF, MMMSFMRM, 3338
DTDRFMRMDFM, DDTLS 10206
DTDRF#S, SLSSFM, MFFM 7017
DTDRSFMR, MFSDFMRD, 3319
DTDRTDRM, MRRMF#S, SD 5280
DTDMRDDT, LRSDLLS, S 8870
DTDMRDTD, RMMLFR, RM 7111
DTDFMMRDR, RSSSFMF, 6953
DTDFMMR, MLLTDRD, MM 9259
DTDFFFMS, DMRM, MMRR 8071
DTDSDTDR, DMDLRDRT 6888
DTDSMFMR, MFSDRSM, M 9546
DTDSFMRDTDRDT, DTD 944
DTDSLSFM, MF#SLTLS, D 10771
DTDSLLS, MRDSLTD, DT 1656
DTDSLTD, RRRDTLS, DR 9814
DTDSTLS, LLSSSFM, DD 3363
DTDLDS, MDFRDTD, DTD 10276
DTDL, MRRRRRRDRDTL 11349
DTDLSDDLMMRD, SLSD 5677
DTDLSDRD, TDRRR, R#RR# 1020
DTDLSMFMRD, MFSRMD 10682
DTDLSFM, DLRDTLS, DS 4063
DTDLSFMS, SLTDTDMR 11774
DTDLS#LMM, LTDRDT, DT 25
DTDLTSLL, DDRDTLST 2580
DTDLTS, LTDRM, RMFSL 1462
DTDTDLLSS, TLTLTLS 1453
DTDTLL, SLDTD, DRMRF 10551
DTRDRMMRFMM, SMRLS 1328
DTRDRMFM, SFMR, MFRM 12526
DTRDFMRD#, RTDLS, DTL
11605
DTRDFM, RRRRR, DMRSD 8932
DTRDFMMRR, RRMRTSS, 4800
DTRDFMLS, DDRRR, SFM 10044
DTRDS, LS#TLS, MFF#SDS 16
DTRRRDMM, MRMFLS, DD 10971
DTRRRDMM, MRMFLS, MS 1479
DTRMRDM, SDLSFMSDR, 5011
DTFTRDMS, MRTLMF#S, T 2627
DTSMSLS, SDTLRTSLS, 8661
DTSLMRDMSL, RDTLSD 10043
DTSLMFLRDT, DTLRTS 12211
DTSLMSDRMS, DRMS, SL 9356
DTSLMS, DTSLMS, F#MF#S 1523
DTSLMSFM, MMMMMMRL 6111
DTSLFMRD, DFMLSDDT, 8793
DTSLFMRSS, DDRMSMR 10305
DTSLFSMR, RFMLS#L, LD 2392
DTSLSSFMMR, LSMFMM 4025
DTSLLSMF, FDRMSLTD 284
DTSLTDD, MRTDLS, SSS 724
DTSLTDRMRDTR, DTSL 3894
DTSLTD, MRTDLS, SSSL 7285
DTSLTS, DTSLTS, DDRM 12439
DTLDRD, MRDMR, DTLDR 4037
DTLDRDTS, LTTD, DTL 528
DTLDMRRD, DTLRDTL, D 7775
DTLDMFLS, SLTDTLMR, 12200
DTLDSFM, MFSLSMR, MF# 9681
DTLDSLMFRD, DFMLSD 1246

DTLDLS, DRMSDMR, MRD 8628
DTLDTLDT, LSF#SLSFM, 11956
DTLDTL, FTRMMM, LTS#L 3513
DTL, DTLS, SFMRDSLS. 11982
DTLDTLLS#, LTDDRMFM 2291
DTLDTLTM, DDDRDRM, M 2424
DTLDTLTLLS#, S#LTDRM 4221
DTLRDTLS, DTLRDTLS, 4251
DTLMRDRM, SLSMSLSM, 11321
DTLMRDTDRS#,LTDFMR 7397
DTLMRDTDLS#, TTTDRM 10729
DTLMMMMRDTL, DRMSS 10365
DTLMSLSLDT, DTLFSL 4309
DTLMSLTRDR, TRFLLT 9833
DTLMLS, RDTLS, MTMRR 5683
DTLFLS, FMRDRSS, DTL 7355
DTLF, TLSM, RF#LDTLRS 11609
DTLSDRDRM, DFMRMDR 2398
DTLSDRDRMD, FMRMRDT 5248
DTLSDRMD, MMFMDRD, D 6391
DTLSDRMMRDDT, TDRM 7356
DTLSDRMFSM, RMF#SLT 8905
DTLSDMRD, DRMFRM, MR 7479
DTLSDMRDRM, MRDSMD 1341
DTLSDMSFM, RLFMRDT, 7459
DTLSDFMRD, DTDFMRR 6482
DTLSDTLS, TDDRRM, MD 3342
DTLSDTLS, TDRMRDRT, 2635
DTLSRFFM, SLTDSRSM 208
DTLSMDRMFMR, SMRDL 6197
DTLSMRDSFM, LTDMRR 4741
DTLSMRDT, FMRMRDLT, 3081
DTLSMRRD, SSDLTDRR, 5837
DTLSMFSDRT, TDDRMT 6184
DTLSMFSLTD, RMRDTL 10233
DTLSMFTLS, MRDTDL 9763
DTLSMS, DTLSMS, F#TLS, 1900
DTLSMSMS, TLSTLSLM, 11
DTLSMSF, RDD#RLS, FMF 9361
DTLSMSSFRFFM, DTLS 9091
DTLSMSLFLLSS, DTDR 7044
DTLSMLDSM, MRDLRDT 2605
DTLSMLDLSM, MRDLR 2604
DTLSMLR, TLSRMFLS, D 12094
DTLSML, SMRDRM, MF#S# 992
DTLSM, LSFMR, MF#STLS 10683
DTLSML, LFMRDT, DDDR 6096
DTLSMLLS, DTLSMLLS, 4658
DTLSMLLS#, DTLSMLLS# 4660
DTLSFMRD, DTLTLS, DL 981
DTLSFMRDRM, RMF#SLT 529
DTLSFMRDRM, FFMRMF 3290
DTLSFMRD, RMLSMRDM 12107
DTLSFMRD, SLLTTD, DD 513
DTLSFM, MMMMRR, MFRS 3150
DTLSFMM, SDTLS, DTLS 4108
DTLSFM, MSFMRM, MMMF# 75
DTLSFMFSDDTD, MRDT 6621
DTLSFMFS, LSFMRMFM, 387
DTLSFMLLS, DTLSFML 4659
DTLSFFFFF, TLSFMFS 10506
DTLSF, TLSFM, MFLSDT 10532
DTLSF#S, SFFMMF#, SSSL 1478
DTLSF#SLS, DTDMRDR, D 12187
DTLSF#LLS, FMMMRDT, M 4826
DTLSSDRD, DSLSDT 11500
DTLSSDTLLS, FMMRDD 4811
DTLSSSDTLS, MMMMLS 2735
DTLSSSLDLLS, MRRDT 12037
DTLSSLDR, MRDTDRDT, 4779
DTLSSLSD, DRMFSLS, S 10811
DTLSSLSFM, RRMFMRMF 3336
DTLSSLTD, DDRSDTLS, 3616
DTLSSLTD, DRMFMR, RM 6535
DTLSSLTD, DRTDTLS, D 106
DTLSSLTD, DTLSSLTD, 4646
DTLSSLTD, RDTLTDLS, 105a
DTLSSLTD, RDTLTLS, D 106a
DTLSSLTD, RDTLTLLS, 105
DTLSLDRD, MSFRMRDM 740
DTLSLRM, DTDRSM, MRM 3325
DTLSLRFM, RSMF#SLDT 3329
DTLSLRSFMRD, SLF#SL 4033
DTLSLMRDT, DRMFMRD 1250
DTLSLFMRD, DTSF#LTL 12079
DTLSLFSMRD, MRSF#DT 5179
DTLSLSDSFM, MFMRSL 7696
DTLSL, SMRDR, SLMRDR 5058
DTLSLSM, MFSLTD, DDT 4364
DTLSLSM, LSFDRM, MF#S# 1517
DTLSLSFM, FMRDMLF#S, 1655
DTLSLSS, DTLSFRM, SF# 8105a
DTLSLLSFM, SLTDMRL 2207
DTLSLLSS, RTLSTLSS, 8158
DTLSLTDRMFS, SLSMF 462
DTLSLTD, MRDRTLS, LS 12379
DTLSLTDLFMRD, DTLS 4130
DTLSLTD, TRTDTLS, SD 778

DTLSLTLS, SMLSFMR, R 3860
DTLS#DTLS#, LTDTLDT, M 9288
DTLS#, S#LTDRM, TDLRDT 5066
DTLS#LM, DTLS#L, MSFRM 6781
DTLS#, LTRD#LTTL, LSLT 6993
DTLS#LT, LSFM, TTTTR#M, 6714
DTLLDSS, LSDDRMS, DT 12113
DTLLMMRDT, DTLLLTL 5782
DTLLSDTLS, SFRDRM, R 7412
DTLLSS, FMRD, SFMMRR, 7042
DTLLSS, STLF, FLSM, SD 6747
DTLLSSLTDFM, RMFSM 8558
DTLLSLTDMR, DTLLSD 10251
DTLLS#MLL, DTLLS#TM, M 2926
DTLLS#L, SSMRTD, DTLS 645
DTLLLSDDR, DRMMRDLS, 5847
DTLLLSDRM, RMSMRDR 3227
DTLLLSLTDDR, DRMMR 5848
DTLLLLLLLSSSSM, FF 10405
DTLTDDDT, DTLTDDDT 8259
DTLTDRD, FFMRDTLS, S 3116
DTLTDR, RDTDRM, SMMM 8806
DTLTDRRT, DTRMRRD, D 2824
DTLTDRMR, MRDTRRMD 8029
DTLTDRM, MFSFMRDLT 118
DTLTDRML, FFMLRDTD#, 2575
DTLTDRTS, SDTDRMFM 4561
DTLTDRTLSD, DDTDRM 1930
DTLTDLSS, DTLMSFMM, 5259
DTLTDLLS, DDRRRRDR 10992
DTLT, RDTD, MRDDTLSS 5585
DTLTMRDT, LRDTLT, MD 2919
DTLTFTLFM, SSFMRFL 4367
DTLTSLSMF, SLTDTLT 12045
DTLTSLSL, MFSLDRTS, 11335
DTLTSLTD, DDSSMFSF 3530
DTLTSLTD, DDSSMSFM, 3531
DTLTSLTD, DDSSFMFS 3533
DTLTLS, RDRM, RMFL, FM 3797
DTLTLSF#S, MFSLLLTD 7950
DTLTLS, LSFMFSM, DTL 12243
DTLTLSLTD, DDSSMFS 3532
DTLTTL, SDTDRSM, MMM 2547
DTTDMRRMR, RRMRSRM 9969
DTTDSMRD, MSMDRR, LR 3817
DTTDSSLSFM, LS#S#LMM 1163
DTTLF, TLLSM, RMFSLT 9145
DTTLS, DTTLS, LSMFMRM. 8888
DTTLLTLMSS, SLTLSL 10503
DTTTDRRRDTL, DFMMR 5035
DTTTTLTDDDDT, DRRR 8481

RDD

RDDRMDRRMF, FMRDRM 595
RDRMRD, RDRMD, DTLSD 8952
RDRMMRMSF, FSLLSFR 5649
RDRFMFRMMRDRR, FMF 679
RDRFFMRMRD, RDRFFM 8949
RDRFFMRMRRDRFF, SF 5423
RDRFSFMR, SSFSFMRD 8837
RDRFSFMR, LSMSFMR, 11666
RDRFSFMR, LSLFSLL, L 10318
RDRTDLFS, STRRMDRR, 2837
RDRTDTLSFSS, STRRM 2836
RDMS, SMSD, DMDSMFSL 10146
RDTD, RDTD, DFMRSFMR, 10790
RDTLSDMD, FFLDTDR, S 7003
RDTLLS#L, FMRDTDLM, M 2279
RD#MRTSDLS, RD#MRTSD 11452
RRDRDDTL, RRDLSLSR 211
RRDRMFMR, RRDRMFMR 7027
RRDRSFSLS, DLTDDSL 2193
RRDTDLSDRFFMRM, SS 8756
RRDTR, DMRD, LLTDTLS 1967
RRDTSDMR, MRDTDD 7035
RRD#RMFRM, LRDFMRD#R 8713
RRRDRMMS, LSLDLS, DD 12139
RRRDRTDL, FMRD#TDR, R 11209
RRRRDRMSS, LSMSMRD 5300
RRRRDMDLS, SLDFMRD 12204
RRRRRRRFR, RFRDDTD 6762
RRRRRR, SSFMRD, MRRM 2792
RRRRRMRS, SRSF#RDLS, 10188
RRRRRMF, MMMRDMR, RR 1657
RRRRMRDS, LLLLTDR, M 4412
RRRMMFRD, DFSLFFMF 6637
RRRMFM, DDDRMR, RRMF 988
RRRFFFMMLS, DDDDTL 1729
RRRSRMFM, MMMR, F#MF#S, 5644
RRRLLSSLSFM, LLTSD, 1800
RRRLTDTLS, LTD#RLDT 3031
RRRTLS, FFFFM, SSSDR 3282
RRMRD, RRRMRD, SDDDR 7223
RRMRDTDM, RMRDTLS, M 3205
RRMRRRS, F#F#F#MRRS, RR 567
RRMRS, MMFMD, FFFMRD 10718
RRMRSF#MF#S, RRMRSF#M 6195
RRMRSLSDRM, FMMRDR, 5266

RRMRSLSDMD, LDTLSD 11871
RRMFRMD, DRRMML, RRM 4191
RRMFMR, DRL, LSFF#FMF 2063
RRMFMMFS, FMRDLS 8988
RRMF, MMFS, SDTLSMDM 7880
RRMFF, MMFSS, SF#SLTD 8136
RRMFFFMMFS, SSLTLS 10763
RRMFFSFM, LDLL#LSFF, 6524
RRMFSFM, RFMDRM, LDD 11042
RRMFLSFM, DDMSMR, MR 6440
RRMFLSFM, RRMFLSFM, 6110
RRMSSDSLS, DRFMRD 3425
RRFRRDFSL, LSDDRDD 5463
RRFR, RRSM, RLDL, LTSL, 12244
RRFMDMRDTL, LDDRRM 11043
RRFMRD#R, RLFSFM, RRF 9013
RRFSLTDL, LTDRDTL, R 6460
RRLSSL, LLRTDL, SLD, S 11129
RMDRML, DDTDRS, SSMR 9154
RMDSSLDS, DMMMRDR, S 5097
RMRDRMS, LFLDLSM, SL 5730
RMRDS, MFMR, MRDDTLS 8125
RMRDLDRMSMR, RMRDL 10745
RMRMRRR, RMRMLL, MSD 7695
RMRSMFMD, FFMMRDR, M 12088
RMMRDRMFS, RMMLLSF 500
RMMMDTLSFM, RMDLTD 6767
RMMMRRDD, DRRRDRMS, 5307
RMMFFFMRMFMR, MFFS 726
RMMFFSSL, LL#DLS, L#LS 7454
RMFMRMFLS, LTDTLSM 1743
RMFMFS, LLSF#S, DDDST 520
RMFMSFSFM, LFLSM, SF 1861
RMFMSLSMR, SFMRDTL 9974
RMFFMRMS, MRDDRMR, M 7756
RMFFFMRM, SSLLSMR, M 5764
RMFFSFMR, MFSLSMR, M 2421
RMFS, DLSFM, DTLSMD 8477
RMFSMSFMF, RMFSMSF 8648
RMFSFMRD, DRMFSFMR 6660
RMFSFMRMM, MRMFMSS 6753
RMFSLRMFSFMM, SLDD 48
RMFSLTDRDTL, FRMFS 8778
RMLLLSML, TMLLSML, T 6913
RFRD#RMFMR, FFFFDRF 1751
RFRRDR, FFRMMR, RLL#L 5424
RFRRDFSFSLL, FLDLS 8274
RFRLFMRL, LDLTDRL, 8501
RFMRM, DTDRSRFMRD, T 4703
RFMRFF, RMDRFF, FFF 7438
RFMRLDTL, SSDTLLS#L, 4696
RFMFSLRDFMFRDDR, R 10702
RFMSSSFM, RMFSRMRD, 2525
RFFMRFSL, LFSSFMMR, 12324
RFFMFSFMRFMR, RFSL 8728
RFSLRSFM, SLDDTLTD, 1793
RFSLSDTL, SDTLSFMR, 820
RFSLSDTL, LDTLSFMR 1739
RFSLTDTL, S#DTLSFMR, 1740
RFLSLDLS, LFLRDL, S 9770
RSFMD, MRDTDLS, MMMM 11510
RSF#MDLRDT, MMRRDRM 1229
RSLFMRM, RSLLSFM, LD 7842
RSLSDTLS, LTSMFMR 5997
RLSFMRFSL, LRDL#LSL 7590
RLSLMFMSFMRD#R, LLR 2056
RLSLMFSL, TDRDTL 11371
RLLMSFMR, RLTDRDTL, 11813
RLLSRDTL, DLDTL, LDT 7005
RLLSFMRSLTDTL, RSL 5669
RLLTSLTDTL, RDTLSD 506
RLLTSLTRDTLSL, LLR 734
RLL#LSSLSSFSSLSFMR, 3739
RLTSLTDRDTSL, RRDR 7365
RLTSLTRDTLSL, LLRM 735
RTSMMRTSS, SFRDFMR 8539
R#MMRDDT, SFFMRM, 11885
R#MMMMMSR, MFMFLFMR, 1688

MDD

MDDDDDD, MSSSSSS, SL 5213
MDDR, MFFM, SLSMRMSF 6678
MDDRMSMR, DRMSMRR, M 2651
MDDRMSSLMRD, MDDRM 8725
MDDMSFM, MSRMRDT, SD 5349
MDDMS, LFFLD, DTL, SRM 4371
MDDFMSSS, SDTDRFTT 9052
MD, DL, RSTLSF#S, SDMRD 11434
MDDL, SDTDRMMR, MDDL 6061
MDDLSSTLSSD, MDDL, S 9951
MDDTDMS, LSDSFMSFM 1403
MDDTDLS, LTDFMRDT, M 11495
MDDT, DLLS#, MMMFMRD, T

7937
MDDT, DLLS#, MMSFMRD, T 7938
MDDTFRRD, SMMRMFMR 5535
MDDTLSFM, MLLLTS#, MD 12287
MDDTTDDL, MMS#S#L, MDD 3784
MDRDSTLS, SLTDRR, FM 9494
MDRDLDRM, MSMDRFM, M 5483
MDRDLD, SMRMMR, MDRD 8962
MDRDLS, RRFRM, MDRDL 9745
MDRDLSMS, DRRRDRM, S 7134
MDRDLS, SSDDDMRMR, M 12398
MDRDTSL, LDTRDM, MDR 1554
MDRRD, DRDTDMR, SFMR 11714
MDRM, DDFDRMR, DRMRR, 9988
MDRMDLD, MFSMDLSMR 11971
MDRMDLTD, RMDDRD, MD 11484
MDRMRDRM, DTDRDTSD, 7716
MDRMRDM, SMDTDM, FMF 214
MDRMRMSFMRD, MMF#SF# 866
MDRMMRDDTD, MDRMMR 11552
MDRMMMDRM, DSSFMRD 476
MDRMMMMMFS, SFMRFM 6359
MDRMMMMSFM, RDDRFM, 9390
MDRMMFMR#M, MRD#RMRD 4929
MDRM, MFFM, RRMFMFSL, 4837
MDRMMFFFM, MRDTRFM 12077
MDRMMFFFFM, SLSMDD 1988
MDRMFRM, MSSFRMMRD 11513
MDRMFM, DRMFM, SRMFL 4465
MDRMFM, DTLS#, LSFMRD, 10445
MDRMFMRDTD, MMMSFM 3837
MDRMFMRM, LSTDFMMR, 6191
MDRMFM, RTMRD, MDRMF 3873
MDRMFSDMRD, MDRMFS 3153
MDRMFSFM, MFSSRMDT, 5355
MDRMFSFM, MFSSRMRDT 5356
MDRMFSFFM, MFSSRMR 5354
MDRMFS, LSMFSS, LDTS 3219
MDRMFSLS, SDRMFS, LS 1364
MDRMFSLTDT, LSSFMM 3750
MDRMFLR, RMFSSF#S, MR 2494
MDRMFLMR, DRDRM, MDR 1970
MDRMF#S, SF#MR#F#M, MRMF 7029
MDRMSD, LSMRMM, MDRM 3500
MDRMSDLS, LFSMSFMR, 7813
MDRMSD, TLSDMR, SMSL 999
MDRMSDTLSLM, F#SLTL 2192
MDRMSMDRDTL, MMRML 2653
MDRMSMR, MLS#LTDT, D 11329
MDRMSFMRMD, SDMSLS 6221
MDRMSFMMRD, MMRSRF 5963
MDRMSFM, MSFMRMFMR, 5351
MDRMSFM, MSSRMDT, TD 5346
MDRMSFM, SFMRRM, MDR 2705
MDRMSFFM, MSSRMDDT 5348
MDRM, SF#SM, MR#MSLSMD 12099
MDRMSSFM, MSSRMDT, S 5350
MDRMSLDSMRR, MDRMS 3676
MDRMSLDTLS, RTDRRM 85
MDRMSLSMRDM, MFSTL 2485
MDRMSLSMS, RMFMRDR, 5854
MDRMSLTD, RMSMRD, MD 4575
MDRMLDMSMS, SSLDMM 6517
MDRMLRTDRM, DLTDLD 3624
MDRMLSMD, TLTDRMDT, 3083
MDRFMFSFM, MDRFMFS 187
MDRMFFM, RDMSFM, MLSF 2240
MDRSDRDTS, LTDDRRM 9471a
MDRSDRTS, LTDDRSM, M 9471
MDRSDFMRM, MRDRSLS 1496
MDRSMDR, DDDDRMRD, S 6165
MDRSMDR, DDTDRMRD, M 6164
MDRSFMDR, DDLTDRMR 6166
MDRSFMRDR, DTLTDRM 6163
MDRSFMMR, DTLTDRMR 6162
MDRSSLTDRFF, RMDLS 6208
MDRTTDMRMM, MRDMRD 2990
MDRTTDFMRM, SMF#R#F#T 301
MDMDDLS, DDDDMMSS, L 10570
MDMDRD#RFMD, MTDLRD 873
MDMRLTRS, SLSLTDMM 5726
MDMFMRDRR, MMMLTDD 3953
MDMFMRDR, MMMLTDDT, 3952
MDMFMRDR, MLTDDT, MD 3955
MDMFMRMR, MMMLTDDT 3954
MDMFMRTD, RMRDSDDD, 9753
MDMFMMMM, MLLSMMRR, 2449
MDMFS, SLSMFR, SDTLS 8505
MDMSMDRM, DLLSFMRS, 1774
MDMSMRD, DLFMDR, MDM 7320
MDMSMRMFM, FFFMDSM 2032
MDMSFM, RDLSF#MF#S, SL 11612
MDMSSSDLS, SSSSDSS 11745
MDMSSSMSDD, DLSMMR 11953
MDMSSLFS, SLFSFMRM, 2051
MDMSSLSFS, SRFFMMR 7663

MDMSLS, MDMR, MDMSLS 1284
MDMSLSF#S, FLFSFMRM, 6314
MDMSLLFS, SLFSFMRM 2050
MDMSLTLL, SLDDTS 11614
MDMSLTLL, SLTDTSLT 2982
MDMLSFMRDMR, SLLTD 7857
MDMLSFMR, RMRSMLMT, 5812
MDMLSFMR, MF#SLTLS, S 495
MDMLSFSM, SLSF#F#M, ML 3501
MDFRSM, DDDFFM, DTDR 11382
MDFRSM, DDFFM, RDDRM 11383
MDFRSFM, RMFMRD, MDF 8659
MDFMRDMRDTDRMRDM, 1923
MDFMRRDTS, DRMFRDT 3810
MDFMRRRRDLS, SDDDD 10584
MDFM, RRRRMRDFM, MDF 6759
MDFMRMRD, TDRMSFM, M 7140
MDFMRSD, RMSFMR, SSL 6220
MDFMMRD, RLRDTDR, MD 2944
MDFMMRD, LLSMRMR, MD 6743
MDFMSDTLS, SLMFFFS 1926
MDFLSDRMSSR, MRDDL 4683
MDSDRMFFM, LSTDFMM 1257
MDSDRFM, LSTDFMR, MD 1256
MDSDMLSFT, FMRD#RR#M, 3399
MDSDLDSD, MDSDRRRR# 2081
MDSDLDS, MFSLSDRMR, 3765
MDSMDRM, FMRMRDT, FR 8780
MDSMRDTD, DDFRSSF#S, 4304
MDSMRM, DMSLS, LDTSR 9234
MDSMRFM, LSTDFMR, MD 1258
MDSMFMR, RDTDRMRD, M 4712
MDSMLLS, MRDTLDDS, 9245
MDSFRS, SSLSDRM, MSD 10890
MDSFMRD, MRDTDR, MDS 12562
MDSFMRM, MF#SS, SMLSS 12507
MDSFMFMR, DTLFMRD, S 9656
MDSF#SDRD#RMDS, MDSF# 6502
MDSSDRMM, MMF#SSLLS, 10024
MDSSFMRMD, DRMFRDT 4031
MDSSFMR, MRRD, RTMMR 5633
MDSSSDDT, DMLTDFMM 2259
MDSSSLSSM, SDTLLLR 6196
MDSSLTRD, FMRDTDR, M 7541
MDSLFMM, DTLTDTLS, M 7083
MDSLSFMD, LRTLSF#, SL 1312
MDSLSFM, DTLTDTLS, M 7085
MDSLLS, DLDMR, MDSLL 5573
MDSLLS, SMFMM, MDSLT 11743
MDSLTDT, FRTLS, MDSL 9126
MDSTDTLLS, FMRDRMR 1844
MDSTLRM, FTRDS, MDST 9067
MDSTLSDRFM, MTRDMM 2673
MDLDMD, MDLDM, FRL#RF 10254
MDLDSD, DRRMR, DRMMM 11054
MDLDSDRMD, MMFMMRL 3288
MDLRDT, LSDDRM, FMRD 7788
MDLMRM, TDRDTL, LMF#S 2346
MDLMLSF#M, DRMFMRDD 7774
MDLFMRMDT, DTLS#LRD 9766
MDLSDDR, MDLSDDD, L 9045
MDLSDRDRMLS, SF#SLF 6564
MDLSDRM, FFMMMRLDT, 2921
MDLS, DMSMDT, FRTSSR 11191
MDLSMDTLS, DTDFMMR 4051
MDLSMRMFM, FMFSLST 7038
MDLSMLS, MFMRLMR, MS 6600
MDLSFMR, MDSSSF#S, MR 11506
MDLSFM, LRFDTL, MR#MS 5986
MDLSF#S, LDFMDS, MFMR 8143
MDLSSDDRRM, MMRDMR 5387
MDLSSLTDRM, DFMRDT 1768
MDLS#TLM, LLSFLM, DRD 10823
MDLLRDDT, DRMFMSMR, 7369
MDLLFMFM, RDFMRDT, M 12576
MDLLSSDMS, FMDMRR, R 11519
MDLLTDDRMD, MFSMDR 3677
MDLTDRDS, DRMMFMR, M 3132
MDLTDRMSF, MSSFRDR 12015
MDLTDS, DMSMLS, SSRF 4233
MDLTDTL, RD#RMFFM, MM 4546
MDLT, S#LLS#, MMMFMRDT 7936
MDLTS#LLTD, RMDRDTL 9648
MDLTS#LTRDTL, DMDLS 8915
MDTDLSSM, MRMFMRM, M 3889
MDTDLSSFM, MDTDLSS 7476
MDTDLL, FRTDTS, DRMS 10207
MDTLDMRT, DLTS#LFM, M 9244
MDTLDT, LLSRSM, SDTD 11927
MDTLMLSFM, MMF#SF#MR# 812
MDTLMLSFM, MMSF#MR#M, 811
MDTLS#LDTL, FMRD#RRD 1293
MDTLLSFM, SDRMFMRD, 8039
MDTLLS#L, DMRDDTD, 10563
MDTLLS#LTLS#FMMS#S#L 9996
MDTL, LLS#LT, D#RRD#L, LM 149

MDTLLLLL, LFMRRFFM, 5392
MDTLTDDRRM, LSSDDF 10748
MDTLTMMLSFS, SDTDR 11243
MDTLTS, LTDRMSF#M, DL 11558
MDTLT, TRDTLTLLLS#, L 217

MRD

MRDDDDDD, DRRRRM, RM 2466
MRDDDDDD, TDRRMMR, M 1807
MRDDDRMSFMR, RRMFM 6056
MRDDD, SLDDD, LSDRMM 817
MRDDDTLLLRRMR, RRM 12344
MRDDDTLTTT, SSMMMR 5304
MRDDRDLS, SDRMDRMR 12390
MRDDRDTLS, TDRRRDRM, 4195
MRDDRDTT, SFFFFM, MR 8017
MRDDRRMD, DTLRDTD, M 9660
MRDDRRM, SLSMR, MRDD 10182
MRDDRRMS, LLSMRDR, M 3551
MRDDRRM, TDRTLLS, S 9775
MRDDRM, DTLLTS, SSFM 9410
MRDDRMFF, FFMSSF#S, M 3240
MRDDRMFS, SDDTLS, SS 9011
MRDDRM, LSF#MR#M, MDDT 11600
MRDDRFMR, SDTTDMRR#, 527
MRDDMRDD, SMRRMFM, M 8631
MRDDMSRR, MSLSMRD, M 7343
MRDDMSFM, RMFFRDTD, 8803
MRDDFMRDDT, RMDDDM 8946
MRDDFMRDS, DTLSMFS 4441
MRDDFMR, RRRRRDRM, M 4781
MRDDFMR, SLLSMDR, MR 6927
MRDDFMMR, RRMFLDTM 2723
MRDDFMMR, MF#SMF#S, FS 10759
MRDDSFMR, DRMFRDTD 9004
MRDDSLLS, SLTDTL, LL 6932
MRDDLS, DRMMRDR, MFS 9884
MRDDLSMRDDLS, RMFR 4393
MRDDLS, MRRDLSLL, LS 8088
MRDDLL, SDMR, MRDDL 1050
MRDDTDRDLLS, DDDMR 10141
MRDDTDRMRD, SFMMRD 7102
MRDDTDRFMR, SMRDTD 4798
MRDDTDR, SFMRDTD, MR 8423
MRDDTDRLTD, DTLSD 9327
MRDDTDSFMR, RMFTL 5930
MRDDTLSDMR, MRDDTL 8245
MRDDTLSRM, FSMLFRR, 4385
MRDDTLSFMR, MRDMRD 1105
MRDDTLS, FSMSMRR, MR 11012
MRDDTLSS, MFMMRDTD 9337
MRDDTL, SSSDMR, MRDD 2453
MRDDTLSLTD, RMRTRD 11621
MRDDTL, TLSDRMFMR, M 11861
MRDDTT, DRMSFM, RDLS, 6775
MRDDTT, DRSM, MRTRDD, 6450
MRDDTT, FMRRDD, DLLL 3885
MRDRDDMSFLDD, TLSF 10600
MRDRDS, MFSMR, MRDRD 11283
MRDRDSMSDDRM, MFSM 10373
MRDRDLDDRD, DTLTLS 743
MRDRDLS, SSLDSDMRR 3174
MRDRDLSLD, TTTTDRD 6790
MRDRDLLS, DRMRFMR, M 9641
MRDRMD, MRDRMD, LLLR 2661
MRDRMDSRDTLTDMRR 6808
MRDRMDLS, SMMR, FMRM 9217
MRDRMDTLM, MFSLSMR 4578
MRDRMRDD, DRDFML, SD 8306
MRDRMRD, MFSFMR, M 4158
MRDRMR, DLSL, DRMFM 2378
MRDRMRMS, LSSLSMR, M 6998
MRDRMMR, FMRDDRRD, S 9895
MRDRMFR, SSFMRMRR, S 3352
MRDRMFMDL#L, MMSFL, M 6695
MRDRMFMRDTDRD, MRD 11535
MRDRMFMRMF, SFMFRD 1668
MRDRMFMMR, SLSMFRM, 10574
MRDRMFSM, MMRDR, MRD 5671
MRDRMFSM, LLSMFSM, S 9393
MRDRMFSFM, SMFMRDR 9783
MRDRMFSLDT, TLFLLS 2794
MRDRMFS, LSFMRD, MSFMR 11964
MRDRMFS, LSFMRRRD, M 11965
MRDRMFSLSFM, MRFM, M 6203
MRDRMFSLTDTLS, LT 10870
MRDRMF#SSF#S, MFMRMRD 9795
MRDRMSDLSFMRD, RMS 1042
MRDRMS, RDTDRS, DTLT 4345
MRDRMS, FMDTRD, SFMS 11438
MRDRMSFM, SMFMDMRD, 9782
MRDRMSFM, SMFMRDMR 9781
MRDRMSFM, SSLSFMRD, 9784
MRDRMSFFM, MDSSRMR 5353
MRDRMSS, MRDRMSS, S#F# 731
MRDRMSSS, DSSMMR, MR 7324
MRDRMSS, LLLRDT, LSD 11421
MRDRMLMRDRM, MRDRM 4440
MRDRMLSSFM, RMF#SLT 5881

MRDRFMDT, LRMFSM, MM 4993
MRDRFM, SMSMRD, MDLT 1713
MRDRSDRDTS, LTDDRS 9470
MRDRS, DRMSFM, LSTDR 10027
MRDRSDMRDTS, LSFMR 2167
MRDRSDTLTS, SLTDRM 5756
MRDRSMDR, DDDDRMRD, 6161
MRDRSMRDR, DDDDRMR 6167
MRDRSLSDRM, MRDSMR 1847
MRDRLS, SDRMFR, TMSF 11213
MRDRTD, FRMDR, MRDRT 9032
MRDRTDTLT, S#LTDRDS, 625
MRDRTSDDRRM, MSMDT 949
MRDMDRDRMD, DTLSDM 2616
MRDMDRDLS, DRMSMSF 12391
MRDMRD, SFMSFM, LSFM. 8887
MRDMRDLDSD, RRDRMM 12087
MRDMRDTD, SFMMR#M, MR 6680
MRDMRSMRD, DMRSSLF# 12476
MRDMMSFM, RMDMSLS, M 728
MRDMFSMD, MFSSFMRM 6279
MRDMFLDD, DTLL, SFMF 1104
MRDMSDFMRDRD, SMR 6585
MRDMSDTL, DLSLSMR, M 11132
MRDMSFM, LTDRTLS, DT 11688
MRDMSS, LLMLS, SF#MST 6725
MRDMSLSM, MRDDRMRD, 5910
MRDMSLSM, MRDDRMMR 5910a
MRDMSLSSDMFLS, SSF 7529
MRDMLDSD, RMRTDRM, M 652
MRDFRDTD, MMMF#LSFM, 5815
MRDFMDMR, SSLSFMR, M 9900
MRDFMRDMR, SFMRRFM 2442
MRDFMRDMMR, SMRDRM 6044
MRDFMRD, SFMLSFM, DD 8883
MRDFMRDTDR, MFRSMR 10096
MRDFMRDT, TDRMSSF, F 9594
MRDFMRRM, MF#SLSF#F#S 12124
MRDFMRMDRT, DRMLSM 6272
MRDFMRMDRTDFMRLS 1883
MRDFMRMD, MRDRSMF# 9513
MRDFMRSMDL, SDTLSF 8605
MRDFMRSM, MFMLSSF#S, 11896
MRDFMRSFMLS, DTLSR 10399
MRDFMRSLMDRM, RSMD 5520
MRDFMMDM, SFMRRMFM 12177
MRDFMMRD, DRMFFF, RM 2322
MRDFMMRDRM, SFMMRR 1120
MRDFMMRDRM, SLSFMR 10418
MRDFMMRD, SDDRRM, SS 4670
MRDFMMRS, SLTDLSF#M, 3134
MRDFMMRLRDT, SRRSL 7494
MRDFMSLS, RMFLLSF#S, 10447
MRDFMLRR, MSFMRM, SL 6274
MRDFMLLSRM, MF#SDTL 307
MRDFMLLS, SLTDLSF#S, 5341
MRDFMLLS, STDRMDFM 6996
MRDFMLTD, RMFSLR, RR 3216
MRDFML, TDSMFR, RMSF 2872
MRDFFMRS, F#SLSTRDT 2935
MRDFFMRS, SLTDSFMR, 3564
MRDFFM, MSMDRT, RFMR 373
MRDFFFMRS, LTDDSMF 3391
MRDFFFFM, MFSLLRDT, 8089
MRDSDDTLS, SFMRTDF 9221
MRDSDDTT, LSLTDRM, M 6583
MRDSDRDTL, DRMMSDR, 12030
MRDSDRMFR, MFSSMSM 3060
MRDSDRM, SFMRDTTD, 8986
MRDS, DRFMRR, SFMMRR 4976
MRDSDMFM, SLSMDR, MR 566
MRDSDSTL, RDTDRR#M, M 5199
MRDSDTDR, MRDLDDTD, 8175
MRDSDTDRMSFM, DTDR 9973
MRDSDT, SDRMRFM, MRD 5790
MRDSRDRMRD, FMRDTD 604
MRDSRMFM, MRDRDTD, R 9995
MRDSMDRMFMR, SMDRS 8829
MRDSMDRFMRD, MRDRM 11775
MRDSMRDT, LSFFFM, SD 11147
MRDSMRRD, MMLSMDFR, 9046
MRDSMRMD, DDDFFM, MR 6439
MRDSMFMRM, MMMF#F#S, S 1821
MRDSMSDT, FMRLTLSM, 1450
MRDSMSFM, MTLSSF#SL 11816
MRDSFMDTLLS, SFMLS 7989
MRDSFMRD, DLSFLM, MS 11722
MRDSFMRD, RRRFRDRM, 7680
MRDSFMRDRRM, MFSLT 2003
MRDSFMRDR, FMLRF#S, S 9585
MRDSFMRDTDMR, RRMF 638
MRDSFMMRDDT, RMRDS 1179
MRDSFMMRDR, MRDSFM 1311
MRDSFFMRDTDMR, RRM 1314
MRDSF#SDT, FFFFFFM, S 12471
MRDSSDDT, LSMFSMLS 5323
MRDSSM, DSLSMR, MRDS 10067

MRDSSFSLS, SMSDTTL 643
MRDSSSLSRFM, MRDLD 5007
MRDSSLDS, MRDSLSMR, 11717
MRDSSLMS, SMMDRRM, D 3494
MRDSSLSF#SM, MF#SLTL 3289
MRDSSLLS, SLLSDR, MM 4262
MRDSSLTRDDT, FMRTL 8402
MRDSLDDS, DRMDRRD, M 12119
MRDSLDDT, TDRD#RSTF 7364
MRDSLDR, DRMS, MRDMR 1684
MRDSLD, RRMDR, MRDSL 521
MRDSLDS, DRMRR, MRDS 3988
MRDSLDS, TDRRMMR, MR 3664
MRDSLDLS, TDRRDRM, M 1152
MRDSLDTLLS, DRMFSL 3802
MRDSLDTT, FMRDRM, MM 2203
MRDSLRDT, TDRMFR, MR 3694
MRDSLRTS, DTLTDMR, M 8468
MRDSLRTS, SF#MRMLF#S 8469
MRDSLMR, DRMFFM, MRD 9115
MRDSLFMRD, TDRRMRR, 502
MRDSLFMM, DTLTDTLS, 7084
MRDSLSD, MSLSMDR, MR# 4524
MRDSLSDT, FMRLTDRM, 4405
MRDSLS, MRDTDR, MLF#S, 2296
MRDSLSFM, DTLTDTLS, 7082
MRDSLS, FMRS, SFMRDL, 11415
MRDSLS, SFMDMR, MSSF# 6214
MRDSLS, TLTDMS, RDRM 4053
MRDSLLSS, SLTDRMR, M 3099
MRDSLTD, DTLTLLS, SD 4078
MRDSLTD, RMRDTLS, DD 8427
MRDSLTDTLSFM, RDDF 3009
MRDSLT, RD#RMRD, MRDS 1845
MRDSLTL#T, DRD#RR#M, MM 8313
MRDSTLS, LSLDRR, MRD 910
MRDSTLLS, DDMMRMR, 1339
MRDLD, RDRM, MRDLD, RD 1944
MRDLDR, MSMDRM, RDRM 12418
MRDLDRMSMR, MRDLD 8509
MRDLDS, LTDDRD, MRDF 8232
MRDLD, TDRM, MRDLD, TD 3271
MRDLDTS#M, LTDTMRD, M 8242
MRDLFMMR, DRMSRMD, M 8933
MRDLSD, RRDRMD, MRDL 7895
MRDLSMRDMR, RMSSMD 12434
MRDLSSFM, MF#SDTLS, F# 6684
MRDLSSFM, SDTTLS, SF 3265
MRDLSSFM, SMDRMFMR, 4092
MRDLSLS, SSDMR, SFMR 11990
MRDLTDRD, DDRRM, MSS 421
MRDLTDRMFR, MRDLTD 2447
MRDLTD, RMSFMR, MRSD 9412
MRDLTDFM, MRSLLS, SL 4177
MRDLTDSDMR, MRDLTD 3552
MRDLTDTL, MRDLTDT 11232
MRDTDRRM, MSMMF#S, MR 3186
MRDTDRMR, DTLSLTDT, 591
MRDTDRMFM, RMF#SSSF#S, 2376
MRDTDRMFMMR, FMRD#R 263
MRDTDRM, SFMRDTD, RM 10459
MRDTDRM, SFMRDTRD, M 10459a
MRDTDRFMRDT, DLLSD 12004
MRDTDRFM, SLSFMR, MR 7178
MRDTDRLTRDS, LFMRL 12559
MRDTDFM, RMDTDRLT, T 6229
MRDTDL, DTMMR#M, MFMR 2631
MRDTDLSD, RRDRM, MRD 8333
MRDTRDLS, FMMRDTD, R 8483
MRDTRDTL, RMFLTDRD 3724
MRDTMRTL, DDTLS#LT, M 11760
MRDTFF, FMRMM, SSLSM 4442
MRDTSFMR, RMSSF#S, RR 1092
MRDTLDD, RRMDFMR, RS 9655
MRDTLDRMDSM, LSMS 5961
MRDTLDR, MSFMRMR, MR 3570
MRDTLDLS, DMSMRDR, M 11422
MRDTLSDD, DMRDFMRD 1001
MRDTLSDRMR, MRDFMR 2446
MRDTLSSDTDMR, SFM 7116
MRDTLS, SLDS, SLTDRM 11464
MRDTLSLDRM, MMRDT 5874
MRDTLSLFM, MFSLLLT 1190
MRDTLSLTDRD, DRMRD 11669
MRDTLS, LTTD, MRDRTS, 1894
MRDTLS#TL, DTLTDRFM, 9977
MRDTLLF#S, DRMFMMR, M 11706
MRDTLLSDRDT, SMDTM 1822
MRDTLLSS, MRDTLS, SD 7361
MRDTLLSS, SLTDRR, FM 7148
MRDTLLS#, MLTDRT, MRD 12206
MRDTLTDD, RMFRMF#S, R 6523
MRDTLTD, DMRDDT, MRD 12577
MRDTLTDS, SSSMDLS, D 4340
MRDTLTLSD, MRSFMRD 11041
MRDTTLD, MRDTL, MSFM 1994
MRDTTL, DL#LSSF, LTTD 11797
MRDTTLS, DRMFMRDR, S 7358

MRDTTL, TDRMR, SFMRR 7801
MRDTTL, TDMMRM, MSMR 80
MRDTTLTDSSS, DTRDT 9855
MRD#RFMR#M, SFMRF#LS, F 4448
MRRDDRDDTT, FMMRTL 8857
MRRDDMSFFMM, MRFRD 10463
MRRD, DMSSFFM, DFFRR 9778
MRRDDMLLM, SSSLLTD, 1679
MRRDDTT, FMMRRDD, DT 4809
MRRDDTTL, FMMRDRM, M 925
MRRD, MSSFFM, MFFRRS 9779
MRRDFMRMRDS, SMDLS 9628
MRRDFMMR, MFSLSFM, S 2123
MRRDFMMR, SFMRDRT, F 3082
MRRDSSFFM, DTTLDLS 5459
MRRDSS, SSFDRM, MMMS 2238
MRRDLFMMR, DLTSD#RR# 4490
MRRDTDR, FMMRDRM, DD 3565
MRRRMFFMRM, MMLSF#M 2663
MRRRMFLS, MRRRMFM, S 7253
MRRMRDSRMTLF#, F#SF#M 5938
MRRMRRDRRMRDT, RRT 3737
MRRMFMRMS, SLLLLTD 5075
MRRMFS, SLSFSM, STLS, 8419
MRRFMRD, MSSLLS, MFSL 54
MRRSMDRM, MMF#SLTLS, 4758
MRRSMRD, DSSLS[M]FSL 4336
MRMDDRMF, RMSDTLT, L 3213
MRMDDRMFSM, SFSMRD 9029
MRMDDFFM, MLLSDMRR, 3179
MRMDDS, SFMR, MRMDDS, 8736
MRMDRDDTD, MF#SLF#F#M, 10680
MRMDRMM, SSSFMR, MRM 532
MRMDRM, LTTDRS, SDTL 9158
MRMDRFMMR, MRMDFMR 2161
MRMDMRMD, MLSMRDM, M 1775
MRMDMRMS, LSFMRDTD 2341
MRMDMSFM, LSMDRR, SS 282
MRMDSDRM, SFMLSSMR, 5976
MRMDSFSM, STLSMR, M 1070
MRMDSLDS, SDTDMRDT, 12210
MRMDSL, STRM, MRMDS 8679
MRMDLD, MRMDLD, MRMD 6226
MRMDLS, DRFS, MRMDLS, 4509
MRMDLS, RDRM, MRMDLS, 7075
MRMDTL, MSFMRD, TDRF 9666
MRMRDD, DRDLS, DTRDR 12176
MRMRDSDRM, DMMFMRF, 804
MRMRLSMS, MRMRLSMS, 1022
MRMMDMSMS, SSLLLDD 455
MRMMMRMM, MMFSFMR, R 6994
MRMFRRD, SFMF#SF#M, LS 2719
MRMFRM, SLTDLT, TDSL 9577
MRMFRSDDRM, MLLSM 9203
MRMFRSD, FMDRDTD, MLL 5803
MRMFMDTDR, RD#RMR, RD 137
MRMFMRD, DRRM, RRMRD 8397
MRMFMR, DRMRS, L#LSFM 7976
MRMFMRMD, DTDMRR, RM 576
MRMFMRMDRRM, MRMFM 3356
MRMFMRM, MRDRMRD, MR 8219
MRMFMRMF, RSSSFM, MF# 1476
MRMFMMRR, LRTLSM, MR 8637
MRMFMSFMRRDTD, DTL 1955
MRMFM, SLSMRR, MSDTT 2024
MRMFFFRFMRDTL, LTD 4184
MRMFSMRD, MRMFSMRD, 114
MRMFSFMRD, SF#SLTLS 8776
MRMFSFM, SFMFMRMR, M 5691
MRMFSS, MRMFS, LSFL 9613
MRMFSSFMFSLL, SSLT 12300
MRMFSS, LDTLS, SLSFM 2532
MRMFSLSFFMM, MRDDR 5594
MRMFLRM, MFSLRRMR, S 247
MRMFLSM, MSMDRM, MRM 1125
MRMFLLS, DTSFLS, MM 1025
MRMSMRDFMR, MFMSMR 1214
MRMSMRM, SDDTLS, MRM 9093
MRMSMFMRMD, RDRMDR 3851
MRMSFRDT, DLSMRDR, M 3566
MRMSFMRD, RMF#SDTLS, 10032
MRMSFM, RDMLTDT, SLT 11611
MRMSFMRMFMRD, DDTL 9689
MRMSFMRMFMR, FMFLS 8204
MRMSSFMM, SFMRDTDR, 7890
MRMSSFMFLS, MRMSSR 8105
MRMS, SSSSF#S, MRMD, DD 4868
MRMSSLFM, MSMDRR, FF 2415
MRMS, SLSD, DTLSMFFF 1989
MRMSLSF#M, MDRMRDTL, 1719
MRMSLSL, LTDTLSFM, M 12320
MRMSLTDR, FMFLTDRM, 10296
MRMSLTTLSM, MRLR, MT 1878
MRMLSDRM, MSDTSLDT 2685
MRMLSF, LTDRD, MRMF#M 177
MRMLLDTL, LDTLSF#SL 9123
MRMLLS, DTDFFM, SDTL 8786
MRMLLLDTL, MRMTTTR 12572
MRMLTDRS, FMRDLSL, 5841

MRFMRDR, RMSFMRRD#, R 6251
MRFMRD, RSF#LS, FMLFM, 9348
MRFMRDS, SLDTRD, DTL 1046
MRFMRRMFSF, MSSDSL 11517
MRFMRMRD, MMRMFFS 9827
MRFMRMLL, MRFMRDR, S 8993
MRFMRS, DRMFMR, SDDT 6699
MRFMRLT, DSDRMF#S, SF 7470
MRFMMRD, DLDLSDMR, M 11435
MRFMMRD, SRMSSF#LS, 4808
MRFMLSMR, MMMMFTD, M 9920
MRFMLSFM, DTLSLTLS, 9902
MRFMLSFM, SLTDRS, SF# 3598
MRFMLSSF, MRDRM, MMR 9420
MRFLSFMMM, MLTD#RLT 4922
MRSDRM, MRSSF#S, SSSL 8706
MRSDTDT, DLSFSMR, S 1908
MRSFMRDLS, LTDLFMR 11844
MRSLDDDTLSLSFM, FF 144
MRSLFSMR, MSFMRMD, S 6094
MRSLTDRTLL, FMMLTD 228
MRLDT, FFMRM, MMRDSF, 11343
MRLDTL, TDTLSM, MSLD 1255
MRLSMDRM, MMLSF#S, FM 1552
MRLSMRLS, MRDTDTLS, 11310
MRLLSS, MDDTLS, LRDT 5957
MRLTDRMF, MRSMDDTD 414
MRLTS, DRRM, LSMFR, RT 4774
MRLTSD, MRLTSD, DTLT 1145
MRTDMSF, MRSDRT, RMF 3112
MR#MDRMFFM, MSRRMFF 7135
MR#MDMRMFSM, SF#SMM 4759
MR#MDMFLFM, MR#MDMFM 10369
MR#MDMSFDRMM, MMMFM 11489
MR#MDMSLS, MRDDRMR, M 1791
MR#MDS, MRDRTDR, MMMR 10005
MR#MDSF#SM, RD#RFMRD, M 4357
MR#MDSSMR#MD, RTSRTS 8244
MR#MDSSLTDS, MR#MDTD 10779
MR#MDSLDS, DDDDTDRR 10107
MR#MDSLFLLS, DMSMFM 4275
MR#MRDRDTLLS, MSLSM 4523
MR#MFDMRD, DTDFDRM, M 9718
MR#MFDMRD, SF#SLSR, MR# 11405
MR#MFD#MR, DTRSFM, MF#M 254
MR#MFMD, RMFSFM, SF#SL 6098
MR#MFMDLDDLS, MR#MFM 6834
MR#MFMDTDR, MR#MFMDT 9871
MR#MFMRD, MLS#LM, MMMR 8237
MR#MFMRDS, DDDDTDR, M 5589
MR#MFMR, RD#RMRD, DRDF 12443
MR#MFMRMRD, DSMRMRD, 6200
MR#MFMRMFFM, LLSMRR 10103
MR#MFMR#MD, DTDRDLS, M 2423
MR#MFMMRD, DDDMMR, MR# 5138
MR#MFMMRDRM, FSLSMM 6584
MR#MFMMRD, SF#STLS, SS 922
MR#MFMMRR, DTDRR#M, MR# 8364
MR#MFMMR, RD#RMRD, DTD 903
MR#MFMSFLFM, RDRM, SS 8190
MR#MFMSSSS, RD#RMRDM 1013
MR#MFMLSMR, MR#MLSSF 3056
MR#MFTD, MMMSFMRMF, F 1764
MR#MF#SLSF#M, MDRMRDT 1718
MR#MSDRMRD, LTLRMTL 2819
MR#MSDMMR#MFT, RD#RSR 1411
MR#MSDLS, DFMLSRFM, R 3777
MR#MSFMRD#RS, SF#SLTR 11113
MR#MSFMRMRD, FSLDTL 9801
MR#MSFM, TDRS, MR#MSSS#, 6059
MR#MSSDDDFM, SLTDSL 8396
MR#MSLSDRR#M, SRMFSF 10191
MR#MS, TTDRMML, LTD#R 1526
MR#MLDRDM, MFSLSMDR, 5558
MR#MLSSFM, RRRRLTS, M 5324
MR#TTRDLL, S#LTDRDRT, 11240

MMDDDDTT, FFLTLLS, M 453
MMDDDL, SMMDR, SMMDD 6363
MMDDDLS, SDMDRDTD, M 11972
MMDDDTLL, SFMRDTL, L 5226
MMDDRMMMFS, MRMFF 11492
MMDDLLS, SMDFMR, R 9610
MMDRDRMFF, MRDRMD, D 7823
MMDRMDTL, DDRMMMR#M, 10217
MMDRMDTL, MRSMDRM, 8048
MMDRMRDTL, MMRSMRD 8049
MMDRMRDTL, MMF#SMRD 8050
MMDRMFRDTD, SSMFSL 2412
MMDRMFMRD, SSMFSLR, 330
MMDRMFFM, MLDRMML, M 8426
MMDRMSFM, MRMFM, DLS 12447
MMDRMLTDRDT, RRTRM 12521
MMDMRTRD, DDLDDSDT, 2484
MMDMSSSLTDD, SSDDT 4895
MMDMSLS, SDTLSMR, MM 1665
MMDMLSSM, DDRRMFM, M 6432
MMDFMRSLS, SLMFSMR 9719
MMDFMMRD, DDDFDM, MS 759
MMDFMMR, RDMRRD, DD 7334
MMDFMMR, RD#RMRD, MMD 498
MMDSSMDDTLS, FMRDL 3675
MMDSLTDDS, RRDTLSF# 11195
MMDLDTTT, TRMRDR, MM 3824
MMDL, LLLLLLL, MMDLL 8188
MMDTRDTL, TDRMFMMR, 6701
MMDTLDMSFM, MFRTDR 7622
MMDTL, MS#LTDTLMS#TL, 3255
MMRDDDLS, SSDFMMMR 5867
MMRDDDTD, LDRMLLS#L, 8336
MMRDDDTL, LSSDRR, SS 6295
MMRDDRRMD, SSFMMRD 4050
MMRDDRRMRD, SSFMMR 4049
MMRDDRRS, SDRMFLS, S 1350
MMRDDRMFSM, SDTLSS 2945
MMRDDMSSFM, FFMRRF 8750
MMRDDFDM, MDTTLS, SL 5802
MMRDDFFM, MRDSMRMM 6109
MMRDDFFM, MRSSF#S, SM 8267
MMRDDFFM, SSFMDMRD 5286
MMRDDSLDTDD, LLTRD 4149
MMRDDTLDRM, RRRR, MRD 4859
MMRDDTL, DRMMRRD, TD 3506
MMRDDTLDS, MMMSSMD 3774
MMRDDTLDLS, MMRMRD, 7430
MMRDDTLSMRD, SSFMM 2852
MMRDDTT, FFMRRDD, SS 4818
MMRDRD, SSFMRM, DDSS 5705
MMRDRDLS, SDRMDR, RM 5236
MMRDRMD, TDRMFLS, TD 6633
MMRDRMR, MFSFMFS, SS 4896
MMRDRMRMFS, SDTLS 8357
MMRDRMMD, DRRRMR, MM 8601
MMRDRMMMSFMRDFM, M 8173
MMRDRM, MSFMFS, SLLR 1438
MMRDRM, MLLSFM, SSDT 1618
MMRDRMFRR, RRFMDRF 1753
MMRDRMFMR, RSFMFRD 6938
MMRDRM, SFMRDR, FMRD 11709
MMRDRM, SSFMRD, SSLS 6082
MMRDRMSS, SFFFMR, FF 3114
MMRDRMSSS, LMMFMRD 178
MMRDRFMMRDRRM, SS 4600
MMRDRSDRM, MMFMRDT 4718
MMRDRSM, MMRDRSM, MM 772
MMRDRL, DDDDLSMR, MM 2450
MMRDMRDRDM, MMMR#MS 8272
MMRDMRDSR, MDTLMR, S 6550
MMRDMRDTD, MRMTLS, R 12465
MMRDMMSSLS, MMRDMR, 10189
MMRDMFMR, LSDSFM, MR 6053
MMRDMFFM, SSFMFRMF 12543
MMRDMFSD, DDTRMF#S, F 3772
MMRDMFSM, SRMFMRM, M 10441
MMRDMSDDTL, SSLSMD 1966
MMRDMSFM, DTLSLR, RS 3639
MMRDMSFMRM, MRFMRD, 9536
MMRDMSFM, MFFMRD#RM 1021
MMRDMSFM, SSSRRLS, L 9338
MMRDMSFFMMRDRM, MM 8894
MMRDMSLS, MMRDSMR, M 5788
MMRDMLRDTD, MRRRSR 2060
MMRDFR, SSFRDT, SSSD 12109
MMRDFMRDTDMR, RRRM 637
MMRDFMRLSMR, RMRDF 10596
MMRDFMMRD, LTDMMRD 5855
MMRD, FMFR, SMLSMDLT 9155
MMRD, FFMR, SSFM, RRD. 11398
MMRDFFFR, MMRDDF#S, S 3287
MMRDSDD, RMRSM, FFFF 2332
MMRDSDRM, MFFMSR, MM 1856
MMRDSDRM, SDMSFM 390
MMRDSDMS, MRSSSS, LRM 3658
MMRDSDSLMF, SDRMSM 3469
MMRDSD, TTLTDS, MMRD 11082

MMRDSMDRMD, SMSM, DR 10542
MMRDSMRDRM, SDTLSM 8453
MMRDSMMR, FFMLTDT, R 9486
MMRDSFMRM, MRSLSF#S, 4416
MMRDSFMR, SSLSMFRD 7628
MMRDSFMMRDTD, MRSF# 12076
MMRDSFMMRMRD, DRMF# 1352
MMRDSSRMFM, DDLSMR 1027
MMRDSSRMFM, MMRDSS 1028
MMRDSSFM, DDLFMMRR, 7677
MMRDSSFM, DTLSF#F#SS, 9863
MMRDSSFM, RRRMFMR, M 4935
MMRDSSFM, RMSLDT, TD 12038
MMRDSSFM, MRSDTLS, M 6717
MMRDSSFM, MMRDRTLS, 11116
MMRDSSFM, SDTLSRD 918
MMRDSSFM, L#L#LSFS, SL 3144
MMRDSSLM, SSMMDRM, D 3495
MMRDSSLM, SLSMDRM, M 3494a
MMRDSLDR, MFSLSMR, M 3345
MMRDSLDLS, SDRMDRR 12118
MMRDSLDT, TRR#MMFF#S, 7832
MMRDSLM, MMRDSLF, FR 10291
MMRDSLSSFM, DFMRDT 4096
MMRDSLSSFM, MFSLSF 3157
MMRDSLT, DMSMMR, MMR 12217
MMRDLD, DTFMMR, SSFM 3994
MMRDLDS, SSSMRDR, R#R# 3716
MMRDLS, DDRSM, MMRDL 3163
MMRDLSD, RRRDRMRMRD, 3786
MMRDLSDR, RRMFMRD#D# 2505
MMRDLS, DTDRMR, RMRD 10377
MMRDLS, RDRM, MRDLSF 1308
MMRDLS, RRMFMR, DDDT 11377
MMRDLSFM, MFMRDTDR, 12315
MMRDLSFM, MSMLSFMR, 6081
MMRDLS, SMRDR, MMRDL 8152
MMRDLTD, SSFDRM, MRR 10528
MMRDTDD, MSSFFM, MMR 1180
MMRDTDRDL, MMSMSF#M 4179
MMRDTDRMS, MMRDRMF 7306
MMRDTDRM, SSFMRDTD, 3977
MMRDTDR, FFMRDRM, SS 6791
MMRDTDMR, FFMRDRM, S 3811
MMRDTRRDTL, TDRMMR 1381
MMRDTRFLLS, SDTLSL 2857
MMRDTRTL, LLLSFM, RM 5291
MMRDTSLD, TSLFM, MMR 3398
MMRDTL, MMF#S#LS#, LDTT 5528
MMRDTL, MF#SMLS#LDTS# 5529
MMRDTLMF#SMLS#, LTD 5527
MMRDTL, MF#SSLS#, LTDT 5530
MMRDTL, MSRRMD, MLRM, 9989
MMRDTL, MSFMMRMLTD 9990
MMRDTLS, SSLRDT, SSL 3073
MMRDTL, TDRMFR, MMMM 2832
MMRDTLTRD, SSFMDTD 4584
MMRDTTLS, SSSFMRDT, 9466
MMRDTTL, LFRTLS#, S#LT 7911
MMRRDD, DDDM, SSFFMM, 2855
MMRRDD, MMRRDD, LLSF 8288
MMRRDDLL, SMRMFLS, M 2656
MMRRDRM, MFSMRMF#S, S 6388
MM, RRDFMRDLSFM, MMM 3445
MMRRDFMLSSF, FFMMR 12431
MMRRDFFM, MMSFMR, SS 6219
MMRRDS, DDRRM, MMRRD 11901
MMRRDS, DDTDR, FRTSS 9852
MMRRDSFM, MF#STLSF#M, 10515
MMRRDS, SSLLR, FFMMR 9237
MMRRDS, LTDMR, MMFMR 9479
MMRRDT, DDRRM, SSFFMR, 1574
MMRRDTLS, SSSRSS, MM 2670
MMRRRMFSFMRDRM, DT 5444
MMRRMRDD, FFMMFR, SS 7778
MMRRFMRR, SSMLLR, SD 8521
MMRRFFMM, MSMDRM, SS 6333
MMRRFFMM, SSMDMR, MF 5252
MMRRS, SSF#F#TLSDTLS 3852
MMRRLLSS, DTLFLS, FM 431
MMRRLLSS, MMRRDMRR, 1203
MMRRLLSS, SDDTSF, MM 3069
MMRMDD, RRDRMSF, MMR 7747
MMRMDD, SSMSRRSMFR 7231
MMRMDDTD, LLSLTTT, T 1419
MMRMDRRMRD, SSF#SDR 11332
MMRMDRMDS, FFMLLFM 6768
MMRMDRTL, MSLDRM, MM 8850
MMRMD, MMRMSFR, RFMR 4241
MMRMDMFSMFM, MRMDT 1750
MMRMD, SMMMRMSF, FFM 10615
MMRMDLSL, DRMRDLSL, 6700
MMRMDTL, LDRMSMM, MM 661
MMRMRDLS, DDFMRR#MM 3640
MMRMMDRMRD, SLLSSM 12450
MMR, MMR, DTDRRM, DMDM 1557
MMRM, MRMFFMRM, MRDT 3896

MMRMMMRM, MSMF#F#S, ST 3309
MMRMFR, DLSFM, MSDLS 3093
MMRMFRMD, TTLLRMR, S 12137
MMRMFR, SDRMF, DLSFF 3092
MMRMFRS, DTLSSFM, MM 6149
MMRMFM, DRDTD, MMRMF 4756
MMRMFM, RRRMDR, MMRM 5684
MMRMFMLS, DDTLSLS, S 9264
MMRMFML, TDMR, MMFSS 1586
MMRMFFMRRFLS, MMRM 10119
MMRMFFM, SSDLF#F#S 9582
MMRMFFM, SSFMFSM, MF# 11808
MMRMFFFSM, SLTDDTL 3080
MMRMFSD, DLSFSM, MMR 3621
MMRMFSDS, MDDRFFM, M 3324
MMRMFSM, SSFMFFM, MF# 11807
MMRMFS, SDTSLS, SFRM 8591
MMRMFLSF, MDLFR, SDT 2297
MMRMFLLS, DSMFSDMR, 846
MMRMFTD, DTDRSSF#S, S 1368
MMRMSRR, FFMFLSS, SS 3968
MMRMSFRDRM, MFMFLS 7621
MMRMSFMRD, MRMSFMR, 256
MMRMSFMRD, FFMFLSF 4505
MMRMSFF, MRMFLSS, DD 9877
MMRMSFF, FFMFLSS, DD 5597
MMRMSS, MMRD, MMRMSS, 4326
MMRMSSFMD, MMRMSSF 3731
MMRMSLM, MRMDTDL, RR 1717
MMRMSLM, MRMDTDLL, R 1712
MMRMLDTL, MFMRDT, TD 10212
MMRMLLSM, SFMRDRM, L 2689
MMRMLLLLD, LMRDTL, M 9124
MMRFRDRFFRM, RFLSF 352
MMRFRT, SDRMSR, MMRF 11572
MMRFMRDRT, DFMLSF#S 3423
MMRFMRRDRM, MMLRRS 5245
MMRFMRSM, MRDFMR, RR 203
MMRFMRLSF, MMMMRDF 2028
MMRFMRLL, RRD#MRD, SS 7275
MMRFMRLT, DRSMRD, MR 10470
MMRFMRTDRS, SSFLSF 5648
MMRFMLSS, DTLSMMRR, 9605
MMRSDRT, DSLTDDTD, T 10511
MMRSDRTS, DSLTDDTD, 10512
MMRSDLSDFMR, MMRSL# 3232
MMRSMMRS, LTSSF#S, FF 2950
MMRSFMRD, DDRM, MRSF# 3372
MMRSFMRM, MSDRRD, MM 7786
MMRSFFMLSDRRD, MMR 11944
MMRSF#MRM, SLTDTLLM, 3978
MMRSSFFM, MLLSMMRR, 8409
MMRSTRD, SLDTLS, MMR 9404
MMRLDT, DDTLS, MMRRS 4504
MMRLDTRD, MRSLDT, TD 6315
MMRLSFM, DTLSMF#S, MM 2861
MMRLTDD, RMDSFR, MMR 5628
MMRLTDRD, DDRMFFFM, 856
MMRLTD, SSFDRM, MMFM 4248
MMRTRDTL, LDRMSF#M, M 2743
MMRTLTDS, DRMMMFMR 5117
MMR#R#MMS, SDDRRRSS, M 6259
MMR#R#MMRD, SDRDDT, FF 2778
MMR#MDDDRMF, FFMFRR 253
MMR#MDMLS, SLDMRDR, M 1231
MMR#MDSSF#SM, MMR#MDR 2186
MMR#MR#DDRDL, SDTDR, R 4243
MMR#MMFMF, RRRSFM, MM 6590
MMR#MMSFMR#M, SMSFMF 5960
MMR#MFMRDR, FFMFSFM 6058
MMR#MFM, RRMRRD, MMR#M 4470
MMR#MFMMRD, DLSFSMR# 633
MMR#MFMMRD, SSF#SDSS 10342
MMR#MFMMRR, MDDRRM, M 1644
MMR#MFMMRL, TDD#RSFM 10607
MMR#MFM, SDDFM, MMMF#S 11626
MMR#MSRRDRM, LLS#LDS 6346
MMR#MSSRR, MFMFRS, MM 11955
MMR#MSLS, SDSFML, DSS 2155
MMR#MLDTL, MSMRDM, MR 8028
MMR#MLSSF, MRD#RSFM, S 3973

MMMDRDLSD, SSSSLF#S, 7426
MMMDRRR, MMSFMRD, M 6751
MMMDRRMM, SLSMDMR, M 2671
MMMDRMRD, DDDRDLS, S 11440
MMMDRMRD, RFFSLLS, M 9848
MMMDRMMMFDRM, MMMR 7271
MMMDRMMF, RDMSFM, DL 7538
MMMDRMSS, LLLFSLDD, 2797
MMMD, MMMD, MSFMRFFM, 5370
MMMDMMMMF, FMRDDTT 10593
MMMDMSLSM, MFRMDRM 2969
MMMDFMR, RDRDRMD, MM 6262
MMMDFMRMD, RMFSDDM 3791
MMMDFMMD, DRMFLSFM, 8879
MMMDFMMRDRFMRD, DS 50
MMMDS, SDRMRMSM, DDR 9991
MMMDSSS, FFFRMS, MMM 6296
MMMDSLS, SLTDTLTLS. 3318
MMMDTLLLSMD, RRRSL 6409
MMMRDDD, DRRMMR, MMM 861
MMMRDDDRDL, SSDDMR 1842
MMMRDDS, DDRRMMR, 6071
MMMRDDTDR, DTLSFMR 10388
MMMRDDTD, RRRMSSF#S, 10440
MMMRDDT, DMSLSSDMR, 9077
MMMRDDT, SFFMRM, M 11884
MMMRDDTT, DRMFFM, SS 7060
MMMRDRDL, DLSDDTDR, 3347
MMMRDRDL, SSSF#MR#M, L 536
MMMRDRDT, RRRMDRM, S 6441
MMMRDRRRDL, SSDTDR 6060
MMMRDR, RFFFMRM, MSM 3748
MMMRDRMRDL, FFMRDM 10544
MMMRDRMFR, SSSFMRD 12489
MMMRDRMF, MDRR, SSFM 8441
MMMRDRM, LLLRLRM, FF 6809
MMMRDRFM, MSLMSMRM 7841
MMMRDRFM, SLMSMRMD 7840
MMMRDMRDSSS, FFFMR 6127
MMMRDM, RRRDMT, LLSF 5887
MMMRDMRT, LDTMRDT, M 4582
MMMRDMM, MFSRRM, SSS 3025
MMMRDMFF#SRFM, MF#RR 12278
MMMRDMFS, DRMFMR, RR 9464
MMMRDFMR, DRRRM, MMMR 4458
MMMRDFM, RD#LRRDTLS#10945
MMMRDFFM, RSSFML, LL 4042
MMMRDF, FFFMRS, SMF#S 5858
MMMRDSFMR, DRMLSF#S, 1542
MMMRDSFF, FFFMRLSS, 5720
MMMRDSSM, RRDRM, MMM 1708
MMMRDS, SFFMRM, MRMR 616
MMMRDSLD, SDMRR, MMM 4682
MMMRDSL, RDTD, RRRRR 8164
MMMRDSLS, RMSTLR, R#M 8774
MMMRDSLLS, DRRM, MMM 3366
MMMRDLD, RRRDMR, MMM 7227
MMMRDL, FMRDT, SRMD, R 4612
MMMRDLS, DDRDMR, MMM 11943
MMMRDLSD, RRMRDMR, S 5627
MMMRDL, SSLSS, SSSF 602
MMMRDTDLSM, SSSSDD 4706
MMMRDT, FFFMR#M, MMRL 7329
MMMRDTLSS, MLS, RLS, R 10396
MMMRDTLS, S#S#S#S#S#LTD 4181
MMMRDTLTLS, MMMRDT 10788
MMMRRDD, DFFMFR, RSS 9182
MMMRRDDDTT, LTDSSF 11836
MMMRRDD, RRRDFMR, MM 7070
MMMRRDDT, DRMFMRRD, 6426
MMMRRDDT, TDRMFRD, M 2232
MMMRRD, MMMRRDRDTL, 8310
MMMRRD, SSMLTD, DDRM, 1281
MMMRRD, SSSFM, LLLSS 6514
MMMRRFMRDRM, SMSML 12411
MMMRRFFFM, SSSFMRD 8459
MMMRMRD, RRRMRD, RRR 10159
MMMRMRDRRMM, FFMRR 7584
MMMRMRDTLTDR, MMMR 1940
MMMRMRRD, RDDTLDTL 10860
MMMRMFRM, RMFFMRM, M 5654
MMMRMFRMFSM, SSSSD 11040
MMMRMF, RMFLSFM, MMD 3301
MMMRMFMRDDT, DD#RST 8783
MMMRMFMR, FMRDRMRM 11723
MMMRMFMLM, MSFMRDR 10967
MMMRMFFM, MLMDTL, MM 681
MMMRMFFF, FFFMRSSS, 623
MMMRMFF#S, RRRDRMD, M 2002
MMMRMFSDSM, RMFLSF 8511
MMMRMFS, RRRRDRM, FF 4707

MMMRMFSM, FFFSFMRS, 930
MMMRMFSM, LLLSDSFR, 6778
MMMRMF, LSFM, MMMF#F#S, 9502
MMMRMFTD, SSSMRR 9230
MMMRMSFM, SSS#LMF, TT 6572
MMMRMSSF, MMRDR, SL 10400
MMMRMSLS, MRRRRDRM, 11284
MMMRMSLSM, MMMMRDR, 9632
MMMRFMRDD, RMRDTDT 2137
MMMRFMRD, RRRLDTL, M 9290
MMMRFMRD, SSSFLFMR 3832
MMMRFMRD, SSLSFMR, M 7276
MMMRFM, MMMFRM, MMMF# 865
MMMRFML, SFMMMF#S, MM 12016
MMMRFFFMLLSMRDR, M 10672
MMMRSFM, LRMFM, RRSL 882
MMMRSSLDDDRDDDLD 8283
MMMRSSLTDD, DRDTLD 8284
MMMRSLSF, MSFMRFM, M 5230
MMMRSLTDS, DTLLRDT, 950
MMMRLSMRR#, MMMLDTD# 8185
MMMRLSFMRM, MMMF#TT 2934
MMMRLSLF, FMMDLS, SM 2170
MMMRLTRD, MMRSMRDT 571
MMMRLTRDS, MMRSMRD 570
MMMR#MFSM, FFFMRSM, M 7421
MMMR#MS, DFMMRR, SSST 8298
MMMR#MSRR, RRRD#RFM, M 2047
MMMR#MSFF, MRMSFM, SS 9208
MMMR#MSFL, RDTDRSM, M 9478
MMMR#MSSF#, FMDDRR, MM 8972
MMMMDD, DDDDRRM, MMM 5441
MMMMDDDR, RRMFFMRM, 787
MMMMDRDDRD, DDRMMF 12160
MMMMDRDLLS, DDDDMM 7500
MMMMDRRT, TDDDDMRM, 7000
MMMMDRRT, TDRMFMRM, 11249
MMMMDRMDFM, MRLRMR 12393
MMMMDRMD, SSSFRMDR 8069
MMMMDRM, RDLLDRMR, M 3355
MMMMDRM, MMMRMF#S, SS 12432
MMMMDRMFMM, RDDTD, D 8513
MMMMDSSS, SRMFSM, MM 11271
MMMMDSSS, LLLSMRMR, 12163
MMMMDLLMDL, LTDRMF 10471
MMMMRD, DRRRMRD, SMM 913
MMMMRD, DRMR, MMMMRD, 4296
MMMMRD, DRMRFMRD, DR 11815
MMMMRDDF, MRDT, SSSS 1556
MMMMRDDL, SDMSMR, MM 5876
MMMMRDDTDR, FFFFMR 9733
MMMMRDRDLS, SDDDTD 10714
MMMMRDRM, MLSDRDRM, 9196
MMMMRDRM, SSSSF#MF# 9336
MMMMRDRLL, DTLS#L, MM 5970
MMMMRDMR#R, FFFFSFM, 291
MMMMRDMSSSLS, MMRD 5031
MMMMRD, FMR, MMMMRDL 3226
MMMMRDFFM, SSRMDMS 11637
MMMMRDFFF, MMMSMDR, 5693
MMMMRD, SDDRMR, FFFF 9535
MMMMRDSD, DMRTDRM, M 308
MMMMRDS, MMMMRDR, SF 5288
MMMMRD, SSSS, MMMMRD 5962
MMMMRDSS, LLLLDRM, M 9144
MMMMRDLDRM, SSSSLT 8370
MMMMRDLDLS, TTTTLS 5575
MMMMRDL, SDTDFMR, MR 4244
MMMMRDLLS, SMDR, MMM 10610
MMMMRDLL, LSDRDRM, M 4560
MMMMRDTD, SFMRLDT, F 8779
MMMMRDTLS, DDRDTRR 9187
MMMMRDTLS#LL, MMMMR 4097
MMMMRR, DDDDTT, LLSD 578
MMMMRR, DDDDTT, LLLL 579
MMMMRRDD, DRRRDRM, M 1765
MMMMRRDDD, RRRDRMS, 5610
MMMMRRDFFM, SSF#S, SL 12502
MMMMRR, MFFMRM, LLLL 5381
MMMMRR, FFFM, SFMR#MM, 5783
MMMMRR, FFFFMM, SSSS 10325
MMMMRRFFFFM, LTLSF 3234
MMMMRR, SSSSF#F#, TT 7512
MMMMRMDDM, SMLSSML 9933
MMMMRMDLTDR, MFSLS 10709

MMMMRMRD, DMFSMFFM, 7632
MMMMRMF, MDDRM, MMMM 10298
MMMMRMF, MDRM, MMMMR 10299
MMMMRMFMR, LSFMRMF 5090
MMMMRMFFFFMR, SSLT 2293
MMMMRMFSM, MMMMMRR, 9608
MMMMRMSM, RRSSFRM, M 2467
MMMMRMSSSSM, RRRRD 5115
MMMMRMSLSM, RFFFSL 3592
MMMMR, FFFFM, MSSSMF, 4500
MMMMRFTDRMR, RMMMR 7861
MMMMRS, DRMFFM, SDDR 2815
MMMMRSLS, FSFMF#SFM, 4991
MMMMRLDD, SSSTLMSS, 3470
MMMMRTDTL, DDRDRM, M 4904
MMMMR#MSS, SF#SMSDT, F 3782
MMMMMDRMM, SSSSSMF# 4694
MMMMMRDR, MMMLSSF#S, 2327
MMMMMRDRM, FMRDR, MF 8154
MMMMMRDF, MMMMRRD 8418
MMMMMRDTLDRM, MMMM 1234
MMMMMR, RDDDDT, TLLL 1481
MMMMMRR, RSRMFM, MMM 3719
MMMMMRR, FFSRFMM, MF# 6554
MMMMMRRS, SSMRDDF, F 9953
MMMMMRRS, SSSSSLLT, 2007
MMMMMRMF, FFFFFSRM, 3768
MMMMMRMFSM, LSFMRD 5391
MMMMMR#, MMSSSSSF, FF 9992
MMMMMMDD, DFFMRS, SSS 6821
MMMMMMDRMSFM, FFFF 1011
MMMMMMRD, FFMRDT, SS 1598
MMMMMMRDTLS, SDMMR 7413
MMMMMMRM, MLLLTT, ML 6324
MMMMMMRMFMR, FFSLF 2598
MMMMMMRMFS, SDTLSS 10590
MMMMMMRMFS, SLLSMF 6669
MMMMMMRS, DFMRRR, MM 1015
MMMMMMMRDDT, SSSSS 4960
MMMMMMMRDR, RRRRRR 1920
MM, MM, MM, MRDL, RMFSSM 10750
MMMMMM, MRMFS, SSS#S#L 7058
MMMMMM, MMRDRM, MFFM 11912
MMMMMMMMM, MMMMMMM 9942
MMMMMMMMMM, MMF#SSS 7159
MMMMMM, MMMMM, LLSS 9265
MMMMMMMFMRM, MMMMM
MMMMMMMMFM, MSSSSS 8745
MMMMMMMMSSM, MMMMM 2642
MMMMMMM, MLLLLL, LSS 7047 7392
MMMMMMMF, FMDLRDT, M 7123
MMMMMMMFFF, RRM, MMM 8391
MMMMMMMFSM, LLLLLL 9825
MMMMMM, MSSSLLSM, MM 5239
MMMMM, MFDRM, SLTDMR 912
MMMMMMFRM, SSFMLTD 8861
MMMMMMFM, RRRRDRM, S 6213
MMMMMMFM, RRMRD, MMM 5319
MMMMMMFMM, DTLLSFF 12095
MMMMMMFFFFMR, FFFF 9928
MMMMMMFS, FFFFFMRM, 11396
MMMMMMSRM, LLLLLLL 3795
MMMMMMLMMSFFFDFM, 9987
MMMMMFRS, DDRRMDSM 11593
MMMMMFR, SFMRM, SSSS 2922
MMMMMFMRD, SSSSSLS 8485
MMMM, MFMRDTLS#L, LMF 3057
MMMMMFMR, SF#SMLSF#S, 629
MMMMMFMM, RDDRR#M, MM 3279
MMMMMFMM, FFFFFLSS, 11910
MMMMMF, FRRRMR, RMMS 6099
MMMMMFFM, RDDRMR, RR 1425
MMMMMFFM, LDTLSFFM, 9225
MMMMMFFF, MRRRRSFM, 10127
MMMMMFF, FFFFFM, MMM 11110
MMMMMSRR, FSLSMMRR, 12433
MMMMMS, MDDDRM, MLSF 2793
MMMMMSMDR, RDDDRM, R 2930
MMMMMSFM, DDTDRMRD 556
MMMMMSFMRRD, SSSFM 97
MMMMMSFM, RRRLSSF#S, 4589
MMMMMSFMRRM, MMMM 1857
MMMMMSF, FRRDRFM, RD 7644

MMMMMSSFDM, FFFFFF 3133
MMMMMS, SF#FMFR, DDDL 6092
MMMMMSSS, SDLFLSS, M 10882
MMMMMSSS, SLLSSS, SD 209
MMMMMSSL, SFFFFFMM 4475
MMMMMSLSFFM, MDDTL 6732
MMMMMSLSSDDM, MMMR 8122
MMMMMLTDTDL, SMLTD 245
MMMMFRM, MRDTLLT, DT 6245
MMMMFRT, DDRMSF#M, LL 6189
MMMMFMRDRM, SSSSLS 6712
MMMMFMRDRM, SLSDDT 12425
MMMMFMRD, MMMSMDFM 5781
MMMMFMRMRD, RRRRSF 10628
MMMMFMMD, MRRFMM, MM 3402
MMMMFMMR, DRMSFMR, R 8862
MMMMFMSD, FFFMLLR, S 5860
MMMMFFMD, DDDDDRM, M 10092
MMMMFFM, DDDDRRM, MF 1947
MMMMFFM, LLSSFFM, SS 9301
MMMMFFF, RRSFFMM, DD 241
MMMMFFFFFSFML, LLL 7827
MM, MMFF, FFFTLS, MMMR 8211
MMMMFFFF#, SSDSMFMR, 9148
MMMMFS, DFMR, SSFMRD, 10444
MMMMFSFMR, MFMRDRR 11595
MMMMFSSFM, RRRRSTD 9114
MMMMFSSFMR, MDMLSF# 11629
MMMMFSSS, SLTDRDT, T 607
MMMMFSLR, FMRDRM, SD 3158
MMMMFSTD, DLSFMMR, R 9869
MMMMFLLS, FMMMF#LLS, 5816
MMMMSDDD, SMFSLMR, S 6022
MMMMSDRM, DTLSMR, MM 3164
MMMMSDRM, MMMMMF#F#S, 4361
MMMMSRR, RRRRFDD, D 6250
MMMMSRM, FFTLS, SSDD 9141
MMMMSMR, RLSS, SDDTM 10855
MMMMSMRFRM, MSFMMR 9119
MMMMSMRFM, LLLSMSS 4174
MMMMSMSM, MRRRMFM, M 1094
MMMMSM, LSDRM, MMMMS 10249
MMMMSFM, DDRRFMR, MM 1183
MMMMSFMDRD, DFLSMD 2035
MMMMSFMR, DDRMFRD, M 9455
MMMMSFMR, DDRMFFM, M 8995
MMMMSFM, RRRRFMR, D 3117
MMMMSFMFMFLFMR, MM 2650
MMMMSFM, SLTDTSLT, T 3738
MMMMSFFM, MRRMFFFM, 11256
MMMMSSDDDDM, LDTLS 11973
MMMMSSFMD, MMRMMSS 3732
MMMMSSFMFRFM, DTDS 9650
MMMMSSFF, FMMMDMRR, 2278
MMMMSSSM, RRRRFLLS, 5458
MMMMLDDT, TDL, SLF, ML 2302
MMMMLS#LM, RDMSFMRD, 2210
MMMFDRM, MMRLTD, DDT 8971
MMMFDM, SFMRMR, MFLS 11372
MMMFRDTRD, SSSLFMR 9136
MMMFRM, DDDRLT, DDDR 1187
MMMFRMDT, TDRMLRD#R, 10214
MMMFRSDT, DSLFFM, RM 4376
MMMFRSS, MMMFLS, SF#M 8467
MMMFRSLS, FMMFRRD, M 2109
MMMFMDLS, DFFMDR, RR 7202
MMMFMRDRD, MMRMFS, R 12257
MMMFMRD, FFFSFMR, SS 8165
MMMFMRDS, LDDRDLS, T 2660
MMMFMRD, LSDDMR, MMM 8131
MMMFMRD#RS, DDRRM, MM 465
MMMFMRR, DDDRDTT, LL 580
MMMFMRRDDT, SDRMRD 8550
MMMFMRRR, SSFMDDT 6770
MMMFMR, MDRMRD, MMMF 12054
MMMFMRMD, MMMSF#MF#S, 2216
MMMFMRM, DTLLSSMR, M 135
MMMFMRMFFFM, RRMFF 11413
MMMFMRMF, FFFSFMFS, 3097
MMMFMR, FFFSFM, MMMF 2634
MMMFMRSD, DRMFLS, SD 2925
MMMFMRSS, SDRMFMR, M 3693
MMMFMRLS, SDTLSFFM 9997
MMMFMRLSS, MFSLTDS 8533
MMMFMR#M, DTLLSSMR, M 134
MMMFMMD, RRRMRDS, MM 1921
MMMFMMRD, DDDDFFM, M12165
MMMFMMRD, DDDRMF#F#S, 4744
MMMFMMRDD, DRRSFM, M 11470
MMMFMMRD, DDRM, SSSL 11705

MMMFMMR, DDLSFM, FSD 696
MMMFMMRDRM, DRTD, M 9699
MMMFMMRDRMM, MMMFM 1383
MMMFMMRD, MSSSFM, MM 10894
MMMFMMRD, SDSFMR, TT 5293
MMMFMMRDTRD, MFMLS 9831
MMMFMMRR, RRMRRDD, L 7838
MMMFMMRR, RSRMFM, FS 9905
MMMFMMRR, RSRMFM, SS 9904
MMMFMMRRMRLS, SSST 6940
MMMFMMRR, SRRMRDS, M 12403
MMMFMFSF, MRDTDRMR, 11047
MMMFMSRR, MFFMRR, SD 10579
MMMFMSRM, DLSFMMRR, 2953
MMMFMSSFM, FFFMMF#F# 3304
MMMFMLSDRMR, SFMLS 7268
MMMFMLSFFM, DTLSLT 7076
MMMFFRRRM, MMMSSF#F#9332
MMMFFRRMFM, SSLTSS 6802
MMMFF, RSFFM, LLTDRS 3286
MMMFFMRR, RRMFRLTD, 1443
MMMFFM, MDMSSS, SFMR 2759
MMMFFF, FMMLLR, MMMM 11892
MMMFFFFMFSS, LLSMM 1199
MMMFFF, SSSL, DTLSS#L 3297
MMMFFFLSFM, DTF#S, SS 4510
MMMFFSFMRM, FSDFMR 5061
MMMFFSFM, MMMRSF#F#S, 7138
MMMFFLFM, MLLDLS, SM 952
MMMFFTRD, DDTLSMSS 9235
MMMFF#SR, DDDFDM, MMM 4745
MMMFSDRM, SSDTLLS, L 5917
MMMFSM, FRMMR, MFSMF 6299
MMMFSSSD, DLSLSMR, 9278
MMMFSSSMFMF, RMFST 1165
MMMFSLSD, TLSFM, MMM 3491
MMMFLDTT, LSDRMR, RM 4301
MMMFLSM, SRMFMRM, MM 6901
MMMFTDRM, MSMRMD, RM 7809
MMMFTLTD, DRMSFMR, M 5935
MMMFTLTD, RMFSMRDT 2340
MMMF#S#LM, DDDRMF, LMM 11300
MMMSDRRM, MMMLMMRR, 8329
MMMSDRRM, SSSDTLL 9349
MMMSDRRM, SSSFSMFR 4673
MMMSDRM, FMLSSFFMM 5743
MMMSDRM, FFMDDTDR, M 9635
MMMSDSFM, MMLF#STLS, 10562
MMMSDLS, DFMRD, MMMS 6021
MMMSDTDRD, MRSFM, RR 3466
MMMSDTDR, RRRFTD, DD 9857
MMMSDTDRMFM, MMMDL 2968
MMMSRRM, DTLSSF#S, RR 9016
MMMSRMMSF, MFSSFLL 9295
MMMS, MDDRRMD, MMMSM 10105
MMMSMDDRRM, MDTLSD 5114
MMMSMDRDLD, SSSLSM 3590
MMMSMDRM, MMMRDLRR, 1112
MMMSMDRM, MFMFLSFM, 8785
MMMSMDRM, SSSDTLSM 11784
MMMSMDRFM, LLLSDFM 9202
MMMSMRMFSM, MMLSF 9528
MMMSMRMFSM, SSF#SDT 11792
MMMSMMRR, RDDFFM, MM 2488
MMMSMMRR, RFFFFM, MM 88
MMMSMMMDD, DDDDRRM, 5442
MMMSMMFFL, LSFMSMR, 5209
MMMSMFMDRRD, SF#SMF# 8177
MMMSMFMRDMR, MF#F#SL 4796
MMMSMFMR, RRRDRM, SS 5093
MMMSFM, DDDRFFM, MMM 5965
MMMSFMDRMRD, MSLS, D 1010
MMMSFMDR, MMMLLSF#M, 12182
MMMSFMR, DDRMRD, TTT 4576
MMMSFMRD, DRMFRSFM, 9491
MMMSFMRD, RMFSDTLS, 2309
MMMSFMRD, MSMRDTL, M 6659
MMMSFMRDFFM, MFSLR 2413
MMMSFMRD, SSSSLMFRD, 265
MMMSFMRD, SSSTLSF#S, 4784
MMMSFMR, RRMFRSFM, M 12518
MMMSFMR, MDDRRRSF#, F 8386
MMMSFMRMD, DLSFMRD 854
MMMSFMRMD, MFSLL#LS, 1895
MMMSFMRMRD, LFMR, MR# 12394
MMMSFMRMFM, MLLSF# 7281
MMMSFMRM, SSDMLSF#S, 8256
MMMSFM, RSFMFS, LTDT, 8226
MMMSFMMR, MFFLSFM, M 1653
MMMSFM, MRMFSM, SLSM 3790
MMMSFMMMRDTDRMD, D 5251

MMMSFM, SSSLTS, SSSL 246
MMMSFMLSFMMRR, RRR 8289
MMMSFMLLS, SDSSFMM 3819
MMMSFFM, MMRMFMRD, M 6852
MMMSFFFMRD, LLLSSS 11893
MMMSSDD, DFFFSFM, MM 2093
MMMSSDDRFM, FFMRLS 10808
MMMSSDDM, RDLLRDT, S 7298
MMMSSDDMMRFM, MMMF 11242
MMMSSDDM, MRSRDMLS 1515
MMMSSDDF, FMS#LLSFM, 7934
MMMSSD, DFFLLR, RMFS 2237
MMMSSDRM, MMMFMRRD, 8561
MMMSSDRM, MFSLSFMR, 11897
MMMSS, DFFM, LLLSMMM 7323
MMMSSRRRRF, FDRDRM 5824
MMMSSRMFRM, RDDDDT 2732
MMMSSM, MRMFSM, MMMS 1264
MMMSSM, MMMDRM, MMMF# 2108
MMMSSMMSSMMDRMR, M 3870
MMMSSM, LLLLS#L, MMMM 9941
MMMSSF, MRDRRM, MLLS 11660
MMMSSFMMRD, MMMRSD 7998
MMMSSFM, MRMSMRD, MM 3729
MMMSSFFMDR, R#MSDDT 582
MMMSSF, TDDRRM, SSSL 6016
MMMS, SSMSL, LLLD, DTS 8235
MMMSSSLMS, SLTDLT, F 9832
MMMSSLSM, MRMSFM, DS 6793
MMMSSLSFSM, MRMFMF 3087
MMMSSLSF#SM, MRMFRR 3088
MMMSSLLFLD, DTLSMS 2085
MMMSSLLFLDS, SMRDM 7738
MMMSSLTD, LSFM, MMML 8826
MMMSLDM, MMMMRD, RRM 11814
MMMSLSDRM, FMRMRDT 10056
MMMSLTDDRDT, DSMDR 12438
MMMSTDRM, SLSDMLLR, 4867
MMMSTDFMR, FFFMSSF# 693
MMMS#LTLS#DTLS#FM, MM 12532
MMMS#LTLS#S#, TTDLSF#M, 4120
MMMLMFMRD, RMRDTL, M 10086
MMMLSTDR, SMDDLLTS 815
MMMLLSFM, SSSLDTLS, 971
MMMLLS#L, LDTLTMLS#, M 3668
MMMLLLS#S#, LLDDDTT, L 8945
MMMLLTS#S#L, DDTTLLS 11547
MMMLTDRMFM, DTLTTM, 5375
MMMLTDTLM, DDMRDDT 10684
MMMLTDTLLS#L, MMF#SL 9025
MMMLTRMM, MSFMRDDT, 10674
MMMTRRD, SSSRFFM, SS 3173

MMF

MMFRDTMD, TLRTLTDM, 3831
MMFRSRRD, MRDTL, SMM 9604
MMFRLTD, RRMRRDT, RM 7387
MMFRTLLS, MMFRTLLS, 8440
MMFMDRDRMRD, MMSF 2608
MMFMDRDRM, MMMRDLS 11675
MMFMDRMFM, DRRRDDF 4565
MMFMDRMF, FRRSFMR, M 444
MMFMRDMD, RSFTDRM, M 4398
MMFMRDFMRM, SDTLSF# 1331
MMFMRDSD, RRFMR, RRR 2556
MMFMRD, SSSFMRMR, MM 9671
MMFMRDTD, MLSFRDTD, 9829
MMFMRDTL, MMTLSF#SL 148
MMFMRR, DDRDT, LLTDS 12530
MMFMRRDTLS, LLFRDT 6831
MMFMRRMR, DDFMRMD, M 10531
MMFMRMDD, RMFSMLS, S 3108
MMFMRMRD, MMFMRDT, D 6878
MMFMRMRD, MSSFLMR, M 12056
MMFMRMRD, SSLSFSFM 3983
MMFMRM, SSLSF#S, SSSL 2520
MMFMRSRD, DTDFMRLR, 9730
MMFMRSSLDD, DRDDTL 8286
MMFMRLDTMRD, DDLTD 4235
MMFMRLLS#, LSFMLTDT 624
MMFMRLTDRMR, RMF#SS 9463
MMFMRLTL, SLTDRMSF, 1918
MMFMMRD, DDRDRR#M, MM 12491
MMFMMRDR, RMFMRDTD, 11448
MMFMMRD, RLTSDMR, MM 5223
MMFMMRD, SSLSSFM, SD 4209
MMFMMRDTD, FMRMSFM 3136
MMFMMRRD, LSRM, MMFM 10732
MMFMMRRLR, RRMRRDD 1983
MMFMMRL, RRMRRDS, MS 2779
MMFMMMR, DTLTRD, MMF 3426

MMF, MFS, MSD, SFMSRSD, 5318
MMFMFLLS, DMMRDRSS 547
MMFMSDRMFS, SSMDMR, 6341
MMFMSDRM, SSLSMRR, R 4592
MMFMSSLSSDTD 11679
MMFMLS, DMSRM, MMFM 8412
MMFMLLS, MMMMMFR, MM 11697
MMFFMRRD, MFSSLLS, M 10002
MMFFFFLLSMS, MMRSS 4494
MMFFSRMS, DDT, LLS, SS 6679
MMFFSM, FFMMR, MMR 3098
MMFSDDRDRM, DRMFSF 2150
MMFSDDT, DRMFFM, MR#M 6009
MMFSDDTLSS, MRRMFS 8751
MMFSDDTT, LSS#LFMR, M 2951
MMFSDRDTD, SLDLSMS 9573
MMFSDRRMFM, MRDLSS 8415
MMFSDRMRD, SSLTDTL 3190
MMFSDRMFFMR, RMF#SL 2918
MMFSDMRDLS, FMF#SRR 3317
MMFSDLSM, MSMRMRMF 4307
MMFSDLSM, SDTLRMFL 3771
MMFSDTDR, FFFTLLSS, 7236
MMFSDTDRTDS, LDLSM 7929
MMFSDTRD, TTLSRMLS, 11142
MMFSDTFL, LSSSFMMR, 2130
MMFSDTLSFMM, MMLLS 3940
MMFSDTLSFFM, MFSLS 2859
MMFSDTLL, LSDTLS, FM 858
MMFSRDRMR, RRMFSLS 6851
MMFSRM, MMLSF#M, SDTL 9261
MMFSMDRMF, MRDDRMM 1460
MMFSMDRM, FSDFFM, MM 6782
MMFSMRDDTD, MMF#STL 6335
MMFSMRDRMM, SLTDTL 6477
MMFSMRD, MMSSSMRDR, 4882
MMFSMRRM, SDDTSTLS, 10264
MMFSMRMD, DTLSSLSF#, 9316
MMFSMMR, MMMFSRDD, M 8399
MMFSMFMR, RRMFMRDM, 10864
MMFSMSFMRM, MRSMDT 8246
MMFSMLSFMR, MFSLT 3578
MMFSMLLSRM, SSDTLT 11588
MMFSFMRD, MRFMSSF#S, 12462
MMFSFMRRR, MFMRD, MM 9661
MMFSFMRRR, SFMRD, TT 4013
MMFS, FMRM, MMRD, RDTD 11397
MMFSFMR, SMFFMRS, MM 6930
MMFSFMMRD, MRFMSSF# 12463
MMFSFMLSFM, SSLTLS 646
MMFSSDDTLSM, MRDFM 5967
MMFSSDRM, LTDMRD, MM 7289
MMFSSDRM, LTDMRRD, M 7289a
MMFSSRFF, MMRDRM, SD 9411
MMFSSFM, RDDRMMRR, MM 953
MMFSSFMR, RRMFSM, MM 11215
MMFSSFMRR, MFSMRRD, 5605
MMFSSFMR, MFSMRRD, R 5606
MMFSSFFM, MRDRTTDD, 3998
MMFSSFFM, MMRMFMRD, 6853
MMFSSF#RFFMD, MRDMR 568
MMFSSSDTLSM, MRDFM 5968
MMFSSSDTLS, FMMMTL 8496
MMFSSSMFSLL, RRMFF 5955
MMFSSLDDTD, DTLSSL 11867
MMFSSLSF#SM, DTLSMR 87
MMFSSLS, SDDDMF#S, SD 10719
MMFSSLS, TTDRRRD, MM 10720
MMFSSLLDLSM, SSLSD 8318
MMFSSLLSM, MRMFRMF 394
MMFSSLLS, SDLSRFMR, 6209
MMFSSLTDRDT, TDLSL 2451
MMFSSLTD, TLSFMMR, M 4767
MMFSLD, SLFLSFM, MMM 4256
MMFSLS, DRMFMR, DTLS, 4574
MMFSLSRM, SSRMF#S, SD 716
MMFSLSMDFMRM, MF#F#S 10460
MMFSLSFM, RMSSF#S, RR 3723
MMFSLSLSM, MDSMDS, M 11059
MMFSLSLSLSFM, SFML 10341
MMFSLLSM, DDTLSF#S, L 5639
MMFSLTDS, SRSM, MMF 7587
MMFLSFFM, MSDLSF#S, M 4762
MMFLLS, MRDRM, MMSSS 3299
MMF#F#SRSLLTS, LLDTL 1343
MMF#SF#T, TDDTLSSFMM 2094
MMF#STL, RDTL, LLTDTL 6516
MMF#S#LLS#L, LSLTDD 12311
MMF#S#LT, LDLSFM, SSF#S 10248
MMSDDRFM, DLFSLSMR, 664
MMSDRD, LLDLS, FLSFM 12420
MMSDRRMM, SSLLSM 12006
MMSDRMRD, LTDRDT, T 10080
MMSDRM, RMFFMR, DDLR 733
MMSDRMFM, F#SLTLSF, M 5956
MMSDMLTD, DRFMLSF#S, 11555
MMSDSLDS, SRMFSLSF 4923
MMSDTL, SLSMRDRM, MS 8620
MMSRDRMR, RRMSLSFM, 5652
MMSRD, FFLRDSL, MMSRD, 974
MMSRRRMF, FFMRRM, ML 11214

MMSMDRMR, MSSF#S, LSF 8762
MMSMDRM, MMSMDRM, MM 9406
MMSMDRMF, MRDTMRDT 1461
MMSMDRMF, SSTSMF#S, L 6803
MMSMRD, RDTLS, LLDRM 176
MMSMRDRMSL, SLTDTL 9952
MMSMRDR, FFLFMRM, SS 6248
MMSMRRDMDTL, LRLMR 10479
MMSMRRFR, DTDRMSFM 222
MMSMRMFFM, DLSMRMF# 920
MMSMRMFFM, SSMFMRM, 3308
MMSMRMSFMMR, MFSLD 9389
MMSMMRD, MMFSLFFM, M 9893
MMSMMRRM, FFLFMRM, S 5311
MMSMMFRM, SDSLSSF#S, 2860
MMSMMS, MSDTLLS, RMF 6490
MMSMFLS, SSMDRMR, MM 1387
MMSMFLLS, DMMRMFMR, 7156
MMSMSS, RRSRSS, DMMS 9215
MMSFRDMRD, MRDDDRM 11337
MMSFRDTDMR, FMLSDR 8100
MMSFRM, DDMRTD, MSF#M, 6466
MMSFRMDR, SSSDTLLS, 2708
MMSFRLTD, RRMFMRDR 9636
MMSFRTDDM, LLRMRDT 9050
MMSFMDRMSFM, MMRMR 626
MMSFMRDDRMD, FFMLS 12303
MMSFMRD, RRRMF#SSF#S, 5246
MMSFMRD, RRRMF#LS, DT 10152
MMSFMRDR, MMRDRRS, M 9496
MMSFMRDRMM, SLDDTL 3266
MMSFMRDRLTD, RMF#SD 10123
MMSFMRDRLTD, RMF#SR 10123a
MMSFMRDT,DDTDMR, MM 1432
MMSFMRRD, RMFLSFM, M 7141
MMSFMRRM, RMFMRRD, M 1836
MMSFMR, MDDRRM, MFMR 6142
MMSFMRMR, RRFMRDRD 9518
MMSFMRMF, RRFMRDRM, 10485
MMSFMRMF, FFLSFMFS, 3976
MMSFMMRD, D#RMFLR, SD 12477
MMSFMMRR, MFLSFM, MM 1062
MMSFMF, LSF#SDDT, DLS 9686
MMSFMLS, S#S#LDRMRD, L 11662
MMSFFM, DTDFMR, RMSS 9623
MMSF#FMDDLLDS, RSFM 4987
MMSSDDMM, LRSDFMRD. 1803
MMSSDDMM, LLTDRM, MS 6983
MMSSDDMM, LTDRMSR, M 2159
MMSSDDSS, LLSDFMMR, 155
MMSSDDS, LLSLFMM, MM 2284
MMSSDDS, LLSLFFM, MM 2285
MMSSDD, LFFSLS, SRRM 7990
MMSSDRMR, FMLSFMR, M 9421
MMSSDRM, LTDMRRD, MM 7291
MMSSDRM, LTDMRRD, SR 7288
MMSSDSFMFMMR, SSLT 9693
MMSSDLRTD, RMDLSTL 1677
MMSSDTT, FFTTRDD, SS 10760
MMSSRRMM, LLRMFFM, S 290
MMSSFR, DRMFR, FFMML 335
MMSSFRDRFFMM, DDTL 2781
MMSSFRMR, DDDTDRMR 9122
MMSSFFM, SSLSMRR, LL 9388
MMSSF#SLS, MMMMSFMR, 6868
MMSSSFMMR, DDFFMRM, 8321
MMSSSFFM, MMLSSFM, F# 7028
MMSSSF#S, SSFMDFMR, R 4554
MMSSSLSMS, MSSSLSM 5039
MMSSLMSS, SSFFSTLS, 9731
MMSSLLDDS, DDLLDS, M 6447
MMSSLTLS, MSDTLTS, M 10208
MMSLDDLSSLS, MMSLS 5474
MMSLDRM, SMDTDFMR, T 8395
MMSLMDDRMS, DDTDS, L 2329
MMSLSDRM, MS#LTDL, DT 1278
MMSLSM, DDMFR, MDLSD 7371
MMSLSMMS, DDDFMMR, R 852
MMSLSLLDR, MRMDLSMS, 3357
MM, SLTDRMSDRM, MRRD# 3435
MMSLTDMS, FFMRDRLR, 11127
MMS#MMMLLLS#FMS#, MMT 12497
MMS#S#MRMF, MMLLS#FMF 7197
MMLDRMRDTL, MSFM, LD 3050
MMLDRMRDTL, MSF#M, LD 3049
MMLDMRDLT, TTMMDTL, 11657

MMLDTL, SDSMDRM, MMM 8251
MMLDTL, LSLFFFM, MMS 709
MMLRDTTL, LTDRFM, MF# 1539
MMLMLDMFMRDTL, DRD 5794
MMLFMMRM, S#LDDTD, TD 120
MMLSMDRM, MMMMDLMR# 3239
MMLSMRDR, MDTLTTS, M 2639
MMLSFMRD, MSRMMMRD 5761
MMLSFMMR, RRMRMFMR, 4032
MMLSFM, MSDRMRD, MML 7703
MMLSFM, SRFMRD, MMLS 2636
MMLSFFM, MSF#MMR#M, MS 5599
MMLSF#S, DDTDRM, MMLS 4755
MMLSSFMRDLT, MMLSS 632
MMLSSLLFLDS, SMRDM 7739
MMLSLTD, TDRMDTL, MM 9807
MMLS#LRDTLS#, S#LSFML 6078
MMLS#LTTL, DTMLLS#, MS 297
MMLLDRM, MMFRDTL, MM 10634
MML, LF#S#LMRRT, MLT 1647
MMLLSFMD, SMLSFFM, R 10020
MMLLSFM, SLSDDTD, SM 10170
MMLLSFSLR, RMSLTS, S 11359
MMLLSSMD, SMLSFFM, R 10019
MMLLSSFMD, SMLSFFM, 10018
MMLLLSL, LTDLLSFM, M 8487
MMLLLLLLS#LDT, MMM 777
MMLLLTDD, TLRTS#, LLL 2808
MMLLTDDT, TLLLLS#, M 11748
MMLLTTD, DLSMRFM, MM 5985
MMLLTTDTL, LRRDDT, M 6281
MMLTDDDT, DDMRDTTL, 1371
MMLTDDDT, DRMRDTTL, 1372
MMLTDDRMS, FMRDTL, L 8647
MMLTDRDT, LTDLTML, S 5193
MMLTDRM, MMF#SSF#MM, M 4556
MMLTDRM, MMSSF#F#M, MM 4555
MMLTS#LTDRTL, MRDTL 6773
MMTDRDTL, DDTLS#LT, M 4122
MMTDLS, DSFMSR, FFD#R 2774
MMTDLS, LLTDLS, MRSR 7098
MMTRD, FMTRD, MLMSFM 9198
MMTTTRLD, LTDRLTDR 5721

MFD

MFDDDRM, SSRRRMR, RM 12166
MFDMRR, RMTRDD, DTLS 9758
MFDMMFDM, MSMDRTTL 10350
MFRD, DRDTLSS, DRMSF 2894
MFRDRRMM, MFRDRRMM, 4887
MFRDMFSSLLS, DDTLL 11947
MFRDMSLS, SLSDMR, R 9304
MFRDSDRMFRD, MMMFR 7162
MFRMDRTD, RLRDDTLS 11225
MFRMMFRM, DTLR, MFRM 3728
MFRMFR, MFSDFMRD. 3166
MFRMFFSLRDS, SSSFMM 4427
MFRMFSLRTDS, SSSFM 4428
MFRSDRTD, FMLSFMFM 6147
MFRSDLSFMR, RMRSLF 8378
MFRSS#LTDFMR, MMF#SL 10288
MFRTDS, FSMDR, MMF#F#S 6981
MFMDDRMRL, LRMSS, MF 10649
MFMDRDRD, RRSTLSLS, 9868
MFMDRDTL, LDTLLSL, D 8723
MFMDSLSM, DDRFMRM, M 1377
MFMRDDDFFFFMRS, DD 10700
MFMRDDTD, SDDFFM, MD 3354
MFMRDRFM, MFLSMRDR 2784
MFMRDFML, TDRDTD, SM 121
MFMRDLL, SDDMMR, MFM 7317
MFMRDTLS, SDMSLSR, M 1865
MFMRRRR, RMRDDDD, DT 905
MFMRRRMDRM, SLSFMM 10252
MFMRRRMRD, DDRMFML 9228
MFMRRRMRDD, DTLLLD 5023
MFMRRRMRD, DRMFMLR 9229
MFMRRMM, MFMRRMM, MF 1802
MFMRRSFMRD, RRDTLS 523
MFMR, RSFM, MMFMRMRD 8604
MFMRRSFM, SF#SLMRDT, 4425
MFMRRSFM, SLTDTLSF# 7877
MFMRMDDTL, TDRMSFM 7613
MFMRMDRDTL, TDRMSF 7614
MFMRMDRM, SMDRMFFM, 10751
MFMRMDRM, LLTDTLS# 6144
MFMRMD, TLTDRS, MFM 1672
MFMRMRDS, LTDMMR, MF 7325
MFMRMMRDRMM, MDMS 2833
MFMRSDRMFRMD, RMFS 7016
MFMRSDFMR, STLDF#S, S 4777
MFMRSRD, DRDTRMRD, M 5616
MFMRSRMRD, DDDTDRM, 5030
MFMRSRFFM, MMMMSLL 3877
MFMRSFMRD, MFMRSDT 6403
MFMRSSLD, DLDTLSS, L 10153
MFMRLDT, LSTMRS, SSD 5552
MFMRLDTLT, TDDRRM, M 1572

MFMRLR, DTLTD, MFMRL 10201a
MFMRLR, DTLTDS, MFMR 10201
MFMRLRMRD, LTDFMMR 4417
MFMRLS, DDSMRDD, RML 4220
MFMRLSFM, MSRMTDRT, 1887
MFMRLLRMFFM, RSF#ML 3005
MFMRLLFM, MFMRSFMR 110
MFMRLTTD, MMMMFR, MF 1130
MFMR#MD, RRDTD, MFMR#M 11351
MFMMRDDTD, MFSSFMM 4973
MFMMRD, DTLS, RRRMFS, 8735
MFMMRD, RDRR#M, MFMMR 11247
MFMMRDRFM, SSDDTLS 7078
MFMMRD, RSFM, MFMMRD, 3206
MFMMRD, SLMRDR, RMSSL 8744
MFMMRD, SLSSFM, RMFF 1159
MFMMRDTD, RMTDRS, SL 11449
MFMMRRD, DRRFFM, MFM 7331
MFMMRR, DRDT, LTLDRM, 3220
MFMMRR, RMFMRD, FRRD, 7521
MFMMRRMM, SSSSSF#SS, 7277
MFMMRFSFM, SLSSMMR 1860
MFMMRL, RMRRDSD, DDT 9918
MFMMMMR, RDDTTL, LMM 1790
MFMMMSFF, MRDRFM, MM 8300
MFMMFMRD, RMFRMDMR, 9274
MFMMFMRD, RMFMMR, MF 9273
MFMMSLSS, DDRMDRDDD 12178
MFMMLLS#, S#LDTS#L, SSD 3654
MFMFFMR#M, MSF#SDMRR, 3901
MFMSDRLR, RMRSSLSM 4801
MFMSDTLS, SDFMMRR, M 11263
MFMSRMFDRM, MRMRDT 6269
MFMSMDLSM, MRMRLS, M 1612
MFMSMRDDTD, RM RSFM 8247
MFMSMRMRFR, DDRRMS 10374
MFMSFMRD, RMFSDTLS, 9452
MFMSFMRD, SLSRDTLS, 11999
MFM, SFFMRDRR, RFMR 10496
MFMSSRMRFF, DDRRMS 10209
MFMSSLSD, DTLSLFM, M 1263
MFMSTDRM, SLSFMR, RM 1784
MFMLMMR, DTLSLS, MFM 12060
MFMLSDRM, MRSTLS, SL 6603
MFMLSMRMD, DTRRMFS, 4289
MFMLSFFM, SLTDTLLS, 3343
MFMLS, SMTRD, LLLSDT 1985
MFFDRMD, MSMDRD, MR 258
MFFDFMR#M, RDDDRMR, S 3898
MFFMD, DRRM, MFFMD, RM 389
MFFMDFFFM, LTLSMMR 4822
MFFMDTLSLS, MRRMLS 9415
MFFMRDDDFMR, TDRDS 11180
MFFM, MRLTDR, SDRMFS, 765
MFFMMMRRR, RMMRRRD 7837
MFFMMLS#LLS#, MFRTDD 8458
MFFMSD, TLDLLS, MFFF 1141
MFFFLDRMMMM, MFSMD 818
MFFSDDLS, DTLSF#S, MF 2962
MFFLFFM, RSSTLS, SLL 9305
MFF#SDDTF, MMMMLLRR, 9450
MFF#SDRMRD, STLFLSM, 6746
MFF#SDLSFM, MLTDTLS 6745
MFF#SMDDTT, TLLLSSS 12084
MFF#SMRMFRDT, RMRSL 1722
MFF#SMMRD, SMSTTRLL 10
MFF#SMSDTLS, SRMFMR 3699
MFF#SSSSLMSF, RMFLS 11493
MFF#SSL, LDLS, MFMMDT 7149
MFF#SLSMDDTLS, FSRT 6041
MFF#SLTDR, DTLSLSFM, 3365
MFF#LSDTSF, RMFTLSR 8897
MFSDDMRDLD, TLSMSDR, 6737
MFSDDLSMDRM, MFSFM 9195
MFSDDLSM, SLSMFSM, S 8471
MFSDDLSM, LLSLSSFM 2843
MFSDDTD, LTDSLRR, MF 7177
MFSDDTLSM, RLSDRMR 4229
MFSDDTLS, MSDRD, MFS 6090
MFSDDTLTDS, SMRMFM 7993
MFSDDTTL, SFMFSM, MM 2856
MFSDRDDTTDRFMRRD 4014
MFSDRM, DRMMMRMFS, S 3120
MFSDRMRSFMRD, MRMF# 2916
MFSDRM, MFMRDMRD, SS 4320
MFSDRM, FMRDRM, MMMM 11984
MFSDRMF, MRSSFMRFM, 4372
MFSDRMFMRLR, DTTLS 6597
MFSDRMFFM, SDSLMF#S 3681
MFSDRTD, DRMFFM, MRS 8404
MFSDMDDT, RMFTRFFM, 6255
MFSDMDLD, FLSDTLS, M 5937
MFSDMDTL, RDTRLTD, M 5198
MFSDMRDDL, DTLSDRM 1998
MFSDMRDS, LDSDTLS, T 2668
MFSDMRDLD, TLSMSDR, 6740
MFSDMRDLD, TLSLSMD 3796
MFSDMRDTD, SRMFMR, M 12459
MFSDMRD, TLSLSFFM, M 5343
MFSDMR, RMFSFM, MFSD 11326
MFSDMSFMRD, MFRFS, M 4677
MFSDMSF#SLFMF, FMRT 6138
MFSDFMMR, RMFRDTD, M 3121

MFSDLDSM, DRMSFMR, M 9679
MFSDLSM, DTLTDT, DDD 12096
MFSDLS, MFSSDLS, MFS 11865
MFSDLTDS, FSMDRRR, M 3170
MFSDTDRS, LTDFMRM, M 1143
MFSDTDMR, SFFMRDTD 7090
MFSDTDLS, MFSDFMR, M 8916
MFSDTLSDRM, MFSSSF 1771
MFSDTLS, DRMSFMR, MF 5345
MFSDTLSM, DRMDRMRD, 11348
MFSDTLSM, MSMSMR, MF 1662
MFSDTLSM, SLSRSLS, M 7453
MFSDTLSFMFS, LSMRM 279
MFSDTLSLDRMR, TDRM 9792
MFSDTL#T, TLRFLSM, MF 1536
MFSRMFLR, DTLSLFMM, 9530
MFSRFM, RMDLT, TTDMR 1243
MFSMDDRMDL, SLTDFM 207
MFSMDRMD, DTDFMMR, M 7722
MFSMDRMD, DTTLLFMR, 3746
MFSMDRMD, RMF#SLT, DS 2393
MFSMDRMD, LTDDRMFM, 7550
MFSMDRM, MFSMFMR, MF 10833
MFSMDRMFMR, MMFMRM 11571
MFSMDRML, DRDMMF#MS, 7332
MFSMDLSM, DRMSFMR, D 268
MFSMDLSM, RMFLSFM, S 7931
MFSMDLSM, MRMSFMR, M 2365
MFSMDLS, SLS, MFSMDL 6118
MFSMDTLS, SRRMFSM, M 3137
MFSMDTLSSM, DRMFSS 5907
MFSMRD, RMRLR, MFSM 2197
MFSMRDRSLS, DRMMMF 5302
MFSMRDMRDDLS, MFSS 10892
MFSMRDMLS, DRMSFMR 3886
MFSMRDSLDLS, SDRMR 9037
MFSMRDLS, DRMDR, FSL 12058
MFSMRDLS, SSDSFMR, M 8623
MFSMRDTDRM, MFSMRD 7024
MFSMRDTLS, DTLDMRD, 5024
MFSMRR, FSLSS, LLLSF 10301
MFSMRMDS, MFSRDMFS 12148
MFSMRMRDS, MFSMDMR, 11159
MFSMRMM, MFSMRM, MF#S 2046
MFSMRLSM, MFSMRLTS, 12351
MFSMMRD, RMFLLSM, MF 5149
MFSMM, RDLDD, TLSDRM 2483
MFSMMRRDLDLDMFS, S# 6264
MFSMMSD, DRRRRMFM, D 1389
MFSMMLTS#, TTTDTLSS 4094
MFSMFRD, MFSMDLS, MF 555
MFSMFMR, MFSDMRD, D 3641
MFSMFMRM, FSLSMRDR, 6212

MFSMFS, DTLSLSFM, MF 3619
MFSMFSMDD, MFSSSSM, 1650
MFSMFS, SMDRMR, RMF 11291
MFSMFLSM, SFMRFM, MF 5152
MFSMSDDTT, RMFSLSS 6013
MFSMSDM, RDLDDLS, MF 11616
MFSMSD, SSLLLSSMFS 7995
MFSMSDT, DLSMMF#S, SM 12055
MFSMS, DTLFL, DLSMSD 6739
MFSMSSFR, FFMDMMR, S 2311
MFSMSLDLSM, DRMDRM 10794
MFSM, LSDMRR, DDTLSD 9824
MFSMLSMDMR, RMSMRF 10037
MFSMLSM, SMRFMRM, MF 12469
MFSM, LSFM, DTLSSF#S, R 472
MFSMLSFMRDRM, MFSM 4239
MFSMLSF#SM, DRMFMRM 8137
MFSMLSSMSFSMFR, MF 3115
MFSFMRDDRMR, RMFSF 2368
MFSFMR, DDRSM, LSFMS 5410
MFSFMRDRMRM, FMRSF 4219
MFSFMRRD, MRMF#SSF#S, 5793
MFSFMRRR, RMFMRMMM, 3488
MFSFMRM, DRMFMM, 6794
MFSFMRMMRDRFRMFM, 1694
MFSFMRMFM, SMLSFMR, 8841
MFSFMFSM, MMFMRMFR, 11036
MFSFMFSM, SSLSFMR, S 5865
MFSFMFSLS, RM FMRMF 10727
MFSFMFLS, MFSDT, TRD 10746
MFSF#SDMRDTDR, RMFT 10372
MFSF#SDTLSLDRM, MFS 4668
MFSF#SDTLS#L, TLSMSD 6738
MFSF#SM, DRMR#MD, DRMR 2628
MFSF#SMRD, MFSF#SSF#S, 929
MFSF#SMFSLS, MMFMRS 10356
MFSF#SLSDTLSF#LSM, M 12108
MFSF#SLTRDS, DDDTDR 7493
MFSF#LSSSLS#TL, LSFM 8015
MFSSDRM, RDLDTDR, MF 7002
MFSSDRMM, MRDRDLS, M 12264
MFSSDRM, SLTDTLLS, S 11439
MFSSDRM, LTDMRD, MFS 7290
MFSSDRM, LTDMSF#S, MF 7292
MFSSDMRDLD, LSSDMR, 6649
MFSSDMRDL, LSSDMR, M 6650
MFSSDS, MFSRM, DRMSD 11650
MFSSDLSMS, SLLRDTL 1769
MFSSDTLLS, MSDMRDT 5102
MFSSDTTL, LDTLSFM, M 6800
MFSSMDRR, FLSDMRD, M 2420
MFSSMDS, RMFFFFF, LT 8207

MFSSMRDDTLSRSFM, M 348
MFSSMRDTLSF, MLSSF 4400
MFSSMR, RMFFFFMRM, M 10569
MFSSMMFFMR, RMMFS[S]D 5840
MFSSFMRD, LTDDTLS, M 2725
MFSSFMRRM, MRSSLTL 10257
MFSSFMRR, MFSDRRD, M 5604
MFSSFMRR, MFSMRRD, M 5603
MFSSFMRR, MFSMRFMR 5601
MFSSFMR, MFSFMRD, MF 5602
MFSSF#SRMFFMF, DRMM 3293
MMFSSF#SLSD, TLSMSRM, 5197
MFSSF#SLSS, FMRMSFF 2127
MFSSF#LSDM, MRMFSSF 11297
MFSSSDDL, LLSLSFM, M 1976
MFSSSDDT, RMFFFLLS, 8856
MFSSSDDT, TDRRRFFM, 7752
MFSSSDRMFM, MRRMFL 3588
MFSSSDRMFM, MMRDTD 5449
MFSSSDMRD, SLDDLS, M 3826
MFSSSDMFSLS, DDTRL 9149
MFSSSDS, MRDTLS, MFS 5913
MFSSSDSSLLS, MSSFF 3
MFSSSDTLS, FMMMTLS 8495
MFSSSMRDDD, MRRSRM, 4964
MFSSSMFSSS, MMMMRM 2678
MFSSSMLLL, SMRDLSM 4544
MFSSSFMLLS, TDRRR 8997
MFSSSSDRMMMM, RMFF 11325
MFSSSSMDDDD, RRRDM 3718
MFSSSSSD, TLSSSSS, S 12142
MFSSSSSM, DDRMRRD, M 4672
MFSSSSS, SFMMMMM, RD 3071
MFSSSSLSDRMD, DTLL 10991
MFSSSSLS, MSDDDDRD, 4483
MFSSSSLLS, SMMMMFM 10620
MFSSSLDTLSM, RMFST 1685
MFSSSLSMF, RMFFFSF 10934
MFSSSLSFMRDRDLS, S 11023
MFSSSLSFM, FMRD, MFS 4252
MFSSSLSFM, FMMRD, MF 4250
MFSSSLSFFF, SMDSMM 1491
MFSSSLSF#SM, RMFFMF 3076
MFSSSLSLSF, FSLLLS 7917
MFSSSLTDDD, LRDTLS, 2486
MFSSSLTD, DRMFSLS 8987
MFSSSLTDS, MFSLSFM, 1682
MFSSLDLS, DTDRMR, RM 5036
MFSSLRDT, DSLLLSFF 8984
MFSSLMSS, DTLLDLS, L 5313
MFSSLSDRMRD, DLLLD 12549
MFSSLSDRMMFM, SDDM 6141
MFSSLSDS, SSSSLSS, M 5145
MFSSLSMD, DDDDTLS, M 10723
MFSSLSMD, SLLTDLS, M 10929
MFSSLSMRDDLS, MFSD 11028
MFSSLSM, RDRDLDS, MF 2000
MFSSLSMRDRMD, MSDD 11902
MFSSLSMSD, SLLDLS, F 5276
MFSSLSMSDTLS, SDDD 4848
MFSSLSMS, LLSMMRDR, 5763
MFSSLSFMFMRM, MFSD 10840
MFSSLSF#SM, MRDRMFM, 3437
MFSSLSSD, DRMDRRD, M 12185
MFSSLSSD, DRMRDLS, M 8976
MFSSLSSM, DRDDLS, DR 9653
MFSSLSSM, MMSRD#RM, M 572
MFSSLSSF, MRSRMRR, S 1385
MFSSLSLTDS, TLSSFM 12145
MFSSLSLTDTL, SLTSL 5702
MFSSLLS, DTLS, MFSSL 8103
MFSSLLSM, MRDDRRM, M 1376
MFSSLLSM, SLLSF#S, DR 11786
MFSSLLLS, DRMMFFFM, 2838
MFSSLTDD, LSFLSFM, M 2890
MFSSLTDDTDRDLS, SS 12343
MFSSLTDSSSMDR, MFS 10412
MFSSLTDT, DRMRDLS, R 6704
MFSLDDTLS, SLMSSSL 7351
MFSLDR, SDSLSFS, DRS 11342
MFSLDTD, SMLLLRR, RM 7155
MFSLDTSL, SMRDSLRR, 2040
MFSLDTLDLLS, SLMSF 2067
MFSLDTL, SLTDMR, DTD 6006
MFSLRDM, SLTDLLS, MF 10216
MFSLRRM, SLTDLLS, MF 10215
MFSLRMF, FSLSMDR, MM 2549
MFSLRSSFMF, MRFMRD 8789
MFSLMLS, SDTLSFM, MF 7350
MFSLFRMFS, DRMFLTD 11269
MFSLFFMM, SRMDTDR, S 5630
MFSLFS, MRDTLT, TRMR 10371
MFSLSD, DDRRDRM, DMS 7073
MFSLSDDTD, DTLRDTT 11859
MFSLSDDT, TDRFLSM, M 7812
MFSLSDDT, TDRTLTD, D 2755
MFSLSDDTT, RMFSLTL 11362
MFSLSDRS, SFMFMSDL 92
MFSLSDRTD, DTLRDTL 420
MFSLSDM, MRDDTLLS, M 6948
MFSLSD, SDTLSS, MFSD 12117
MFSLSDLSFFM, MRSLS 4944
MFSLSDT, RMFSLTS, DR 5710
MFSLSM, DRDRM, SLSML 7736
MFSLSMD, RMFSFMR, MF 3872
MFSLSMDMRDL, LSDDD 4493

MFSLSMDFM, LTDRMFR, 7126
MFSLSMD, SSFMLLSMD 7089
MFSLSMDLS, DRMFMMR, 2191
MFSLSMRDRDLS, DRMR 11074
MFSLSMRD, MMFSMRM, M 8612
MFSLSMRMFSFR, MFSL 6389
MFSLSM, RMFSLTS, DT 10693
MFSLSMRFM, SMRDDDT 2110
MFSLSMMR, RMFLSFM, M 272
MFSLSM, MFSSSMR, MFS 6046
MFSLS, MFSDTLS, SLSL 8847
MFSLS, MSDRD, DTTLLL 11903
MFSLSFMR, DRFM, MF#SL 3446
MFSLSFMR, MFSLDTLS, 954
MFSLSFMR, MFSLSD, MF 58
MFSLSFMR, SMFSLSD, M 57
MFSLSFMR, SMFSLTD, M 57a
MFSLSFMMRDRD, DDTT 5317
MFSLSFMMR, DRMSSLS 400
MFSLSFMMM, FMRFMRM, 6594
MFSLSFMFSLTDFMRD, 2462
MFSLSSDRMRD, MFSLS 11064
MFSLSSMDFMMR, MFSL 6581
MFSLSSMRMFM, MFSLS 8174
MFSLSSFMRS, SF#SFFF 7593
MFSLS, SLTDMR, DDTLL 2294
MFSLLRDTDS, SLSFSF 6135
MFSLLRMFSS, DRMSMR 6615
MFSLLRSFM, DTLSFMR, 4766
MFSLLLSM, MFRSSM, MF 5590
MFSLLTDRTS, LDLSMR 1237
MFSLL#LSFM, RSFMRD, M 51
MFSLTDDRMMFM, RDDL 6601
MFSLTDRDMD, DDTDRD 4463
MFSLTDMLSM, DTDFMR, 11567
MFSLTDSF, MRDRMFR, M 11631
MFSLTDS, LLSMRMFFM, 4832
MFSLTLSFMFSFF, MFS 340
MFSTDD, LSFMR, MFSTD 5836
MFSTDRM, MTDFMR, MF#S 3182
MFS#S#S#LTT, DTLS#TS#, TT 3996
MFLDTL, RDTDLS, SLMF 10125
MFLSDDDFMMR, MF#RST 2286
MFLSDRFM, MTDFMR, MF 1410
MFLSDMRD, FFMLLSDT 2738
MFLSDTRS, LSMDDSFM 1344
MFLSMDRMD, MMSFMDR, 4199
MFLSFM, MRDDTD, SLF#S 9401
MFLSFM, SDMRLTS, SDR 6580
MFLSFM, LTLTDDT, LSF 11098
MFLSSDMMR, RMFLSFS 1034
MFLS, SDTTLL, SMFMRD 1974
MFTR, DDTLSF#SLSSM, S 9736
MF#SF#MRDFMR, DTLMML, 1777
MF#SSLSMR, RLSMSF#M, L 56

MSD

MSDDDDTLSM, SLLLDT 10805
MSDDDSMSDDD, DRMMM 11860
MSDDRRFMRR, DTLSLS 1604
MSDDRM, DTLSFM, MMLL 11818
MSDDRMFM, FSLDFMR, S 8473
MSDDRFM, RSMDTLS, DD 4169
MSDDRFM, MSDRD, MSDDR 612
MSDDRSFMRD, SMLDRM 7330
MSDDMDMRDLS, DSDDM 12171
MSDRDMFMRRD, FFMSF 1953
MSDRDTD, LSTDFMR, MS 10703
MSDRRRDRM, MSDRRRM 252
MSDRMRD, RFMLSF#S, RD 951
MSDRMRDTL, LTDTLDR 9888
MSDRMFMR, MFRD, MSDR 4218
MSDRMFS, LSFMRLS, SS 9207
MSDRSLTDRM, DFMRSM 6288
MSDMRD, DMLDTL, MRRS 997
MSDMRMRDL, TDTLSFM 6598
MSDMRMRDTLSD, MSDM 5733
MSDMRMFM, FLSMRDTD 11340
MSDMRMFFM, RDDTLST 1972
MSDMRMF, LSMDRM, MSD 2624
MSDMFMRRMDS, LLTDF 3689
MSDMFSLR, FMRLDRT, S 1116
MSDMLSDMRD, TDRMFS 6076
MSDFRDTD, SDTLRSFM 1885
MSDFMRD, MFSLLR, SDM 4679
MSDFMR, RMLRDT, TDDR 11289
MSDFMRM, MLRFMRM, MS 8663
MSDFMR, MSSF#SS, LLSD 3879
MSDFMMRLS, SDTLMF#S 6273
MSDFFMD, LSDMRD, MSD 9135
MSDFSM, DRMFLR, DDTD, 3332
MSDFLD, SLSMRRRF, MS 11469
MSDSDRM, DRMFMRDMR 896
MSDSMDMR, DDLSSFMR, 2377
MSDSLDS, MRDTDMR, MS 2234
MSDSLS, MRDFFMLSFM 2382
MSDSTLSF, MFSRMFMR 5715
MSDLDDDDDDLS, DDDD 10571
MSDLSFM, RSSSLTLS, S 8692
MSDLSFM, RSSLTLS, SL 8691
MSDLSFFM, LLSLSFMR 10665
MSDTDDRMDFRR, SF#MR 4146
MSDTDF, MRLSFM, MRTT 8960

MSDTDLRSM, MMMMRDT 2375
MSDTRDT, STRD#MRD, DD 6801
MSDTL, DFMR, TMRDMSF 9914
MSDTLSMDRRM, FFMLS 2546
MSDTLS, MRMFSM, SDTL 9817
MSDTLSM, SSDDDDDTD 4520
MSDTLSFM, RDMLSFMR 771
MSDTLSSFM, RDFMRF#S 6146
MSDTLSSF, MSDMRDR, R 8253
MSDTLSLFS, MSDRMFM 4813
MSDTTLS, DDTLSMM 8948
MSDTTLS, MSDDTLS, TD 8578
MSDTTLLS, DRMFSMRR 11488
MSRD, DMTL, LLTDSDD, R 6438
MSRDDT, FTMRDS, SMRD 6587
MSRDFFM, SDFMRRR, MS 4313
MSRRRSDD, DDDLDRM, 3568
MSRMDRT, TDFMRRM, S#S# 3168
MSRMD, MRMSLSMS, TTL 1127
MSRMDLSD, DDRMMRF#S, 3280
MSRMDLS, LDRMRRR, MS 9370
MSRMFRM, MSRMFRD, R 8518
MSRMFSLSFMRD, SFMR 7077
MSRMFLTDMLS, SSRSL 5437
MSRMSFMRD, MLSMFR, M 2114
MSRFMRDT, FMLSDTLS 12488
MSRSFFM, MMTMRD, DLL 7499
MSMDDRDRMD, MSMDDR 10232
MSMDDRDRM, MSMDDRM 10231
MSMDDRMFM, FSDLTDT, 10322
MSMDRMDL, DSDRMR, MS 8652
MSMDRMM, TDRMLM, MSM 4862
MSMDRMFMLSLS, SDTL 968
MSMDRMFS, SLDDTD, SL 12086
MSMDRMSDTLS, SMRDD 6018
MSMDRS, SDRMFR, RMRM 2816
MSMDFRTS, DRMRDTLS, 12051
MSMDSS, SDTLS, SSMSL 3420
MSMDTDRMRD, RMFSSL 9516
MSMDTDRM, FMRSTLS, M 2454
MSMDTL, LFMRDT, RMMS 2813
MSMRD, DRDLLS, TTTDD 3404
MSMRDDRMSMR, SLRTL, 10743
MSMRDDMDLS, SSFMLD 3602
MSMRDDTLS, MRDFMLS 2157
MSMRDDTT, DRMFSM, SL 8304
MSMRDRTD, SDTLSLF#S, 10361
MSMRDMRD, FMLSFMR, R 544
MSMRDMSLDTLDMRTL 11545
MSMRDL, DTDMS, SS#L 9243
MSMRDLMDTL, RDLFFM, 4298
MSMRDLSFM, SDSLSSF 8923
MSMRDTLLS, SLTDRR, S 10006
MSMRRSMR, DMDTL, FLF 4497
MSMRMDTLSSTDMMR, S 5042
MSMRMFM, FSMLFR, SSF 5918
MSMRMFSM, MLSFLDDR 2923
MSMRFMDR, DTRDLS, DL 10333
MSMRLR, MMMRDMRRR, M 1324
MSMRLTD, RMSLLR, RMF# 6415
MSFMMFMR, MFMRDTLS, 7845
MSMMDRR, RMRDDTL. 3946
MSMMDRRRFFM, MSMM, D 12029
MSMMRDRM, DLSMDRMR, 9319
MSMMRDRM, SDTLSSLS, 2967
MSMMRDFMR, RMF#SLTL 4009
MSMMMD, MRDSFMRS, FM 1991
MSMMMSRR, TDDMMS, SS 23
MSMMFSLRR, RFMRMFS 11196
MSMFRMDRM, FSMLSMF# 11942
MSMFMRDRM, FSMLSMD 5285
MSMFMRD, RMSLLS, SDS 12451
MSMFMF, RRRDTM, MRDT 6364
MSMFSLRD, RSMFRM, SM 9299
MSMFL, TMRDS, LDLSMM 9802
MSMS, DMDM, LLLSMDDT 3692
MSMSMSDDTLLS, RMFR 6491
MSMSLMRD, DTLSMMR, R 7146
MSMSLSMR, MSMLSMR, S 9981
MSFRDM, SLSMFR, DDSF 5905
MSFRRMSFMF, FFMR 11607
MSFRMDRR, SSDTLLS, S 487
MSFRMD, MLTDRMR, MSF 10591
MSFRT, DMMRDT, MDRML 722
MSFMDRMD, RMFLSDMR, 853
MSFMDMRD, SF#MTSF#RM, 12181
MSFMDMRD, SLDDRT, RS 9619
MSFMDMRD, STLSMSFM 11590
MSFMDLS, SFFMSDMR, M 6975
MSFMRDD, DTLFLS, MSF 2568
MSFMRD, DRMFLR, MFML 9283
MSFMRDDRFM, MSSFMR 9391
MSFMRD, DFLLSS, SLF#S, 5689
MSFMRD, DLFR, DTDFML, 2976
MSFMRD, DLLSFM, RMMF# 9088
MSFMRDDT, DDRMMF#S, D 9476
MSFMRDDTDMR, MMMLT 4325
MSFMRDDTLS, FMFMSL 6159
MSFMRDRM, DLTDRMRR, 12317
MSFMRDRMR, SFFMRMR 6608
MSFMRDRM, MRRSSF#LS, 5680
MSFMRDRMFMR, SDTL 8476
MSFMRD, RMSFMR, MMFS 1812
MSFMRDRS, SLLSFMR, M 5067

MSFMRDRTD, SLSFMSF 6772
MSFMRDRT, TDDRRM, M 236
MSFMRDRT, TDRMFRD, M 10169
MSFMRDT, DRMSFM, MSF 8416
MSFMRDTD, SDTLSFMF 704
MSFMRRD, DTDFMR, RMM 6716
MSFMRRMF#S, RMRDRDT 11313
MSFMRMDR, MFSS#LTT, D 4952
MSFMRMRD, RMLSF#TLS, 9094
MSFMRMFS, MFSLFSSF, 6183
MSFMRMFLMM, SDTDRD 12529
MSFMRMF#SS, RMRDRT, M 7690
MSFMRMSF, FLSFMSFM 3974
MSFMRFMRDD, TDRMSF 52
MSFMRFFM, MMRTLSMR, 6666
MSFMMRDRMFMR, RSDT 8478
MSFMMRD, RMFMRLS, MS 6795
MSFMMRD, FMLSRRR, MM 4884
MSFMMRD, FMLSSF#S, D 213
MSFMMRDF, FLSFFMRS, 4173
MSFMMRDT, RDTLDTTT, 7708
MSFMMRRD, DTLSMLRR, 4747
MSFMMRRD, SSLTDMR, 2644
MSFMMRMFMRM, MMDTT 7924
MSFMMMRD, DDRMFSLF 2033
MSFMMMRD, SLTDRMRR, 5493
MSFMMMRMFDT, RDTDM 2103
MSFMFMRD, DLSFSMF#S, 9397
MSFMSDL, LRSFRRM, MM 8977
MSFMSDL#L, RSMDFMMR, 4253
MSFMSDTLS, SSDFMMRR, 11262
MSFMSMRD, RMSDLSFM, 1126
MSFMSFFM, MFSLFMR, R 2211
MSFMLR, RFMRS, DDRMM 998
MSFFMRRMF#F#LS, SDMM 2586
MSFFMMR, DTLSSS, SLT 4740
MSFSMSRS, MSFRDTD 11632
MSF#SMDDTDS, SSDMSM 11009
MSF#SMMMR#MD, DRRRRM 10829
MSF#SM, SLDTLLS, SF#SD, 10567
MSF#SMLSF#M, MDTLRLT 1925
MSF#LSSDTTL, LRMSFF 5296

MSS

MSSDDTLS, SMTDRS, ST 12050
MSSDRM, MRMFFM, MMSS 1563
MSSDRMRD, RMLSSLD 9816
MSSDRMFSLR, MF#F#SLT 7610
MSSDMSSD, SDTLSSF#S 7980
MSSDFFMRS, DTLSLS 8127
MSSMDRMFMRD, DRRDS 8695
MSSMDMMR, RMFRSFM, M 1133
MSSMRDRMMM, MSSMRD 5332
MSSMRD, RMSMR, MSSMR 3880
MSSMRDMR, MSSMRDR, M 11423
MSSMSS, LTDTLLS, SDD 133
MSSFRLLS, SDDTTLS 1533
MSSFMRDSLMSFM, SLT 692
MSSFFMSDTLLS, MSSF 11720
MSSFLL, SLSMMR, MFMR 7318
MSSSDS, SLSFM, MSSSL 6263
MSSSMDR, RRMSMDR, RR 8720
MSSSMRD, MMMLSMR, MS 5678
MSSSMMMMMD, DRRRRM 10827
MSSSMFSLSM, SLLDTL 5207
MSSSMS, DMMMRM, SDDD 10884
MSSSMS, DMMFMR, MFFF 7831
MSSSMSSM, SMR, MSSSM 7437
MSSSFMMR, FLRMMR, SF 8822
MSSSFFFM, MMMMRR, RF 9499
MSSSSDM, MRRFFM, RMSS 4044
MSSSSDTL, LSFMSRRD, 9631
MSSSSMSDTLS, SSLDL 2623
MSSSSSSDL, LSFMSFM 7414
MSSSSSSLSMR, MFFFF 4749
MSSSSLLT, TTTTDT, MT 11192
MSSSSLL#LFSLSSSSS 11752
MSSSLMRD, RMRMF#SDT 6838
MSSS, LSMFFM, MMMF, F#D 8353
MSSSLSFM, MFMRDR, RR 10394
MSSSLTDR, MSSSLTLS, 3893
MSSSLTDSS, MSFMRM, M 1852
MSSLDR, MRDLSMS, RRM 11400
MSSLMS, SMDTDR, MFFM 8193
MSSLSMDLS, SLTDMRL 6648
MSSLSM, RDRMF#S, SDTL 4486
MSSLSMMRD, MSSLSMM 7431
MSSLSM, MMMFMR, DDTL 5018
MSSLSMF, RFFSFMRDR 4335
MSSLSMSFMR, SLTRDL 4572
MSSLSMSLTDDT, FLLT 5244
MSSLS, LDDLS, SSDRMD 1327
MSSLLD, DMRD, DTLSF#S, 10539
MSSLLS, DMMFMR, MSSL 5134
MSSLLS, MDDFFM, MRMF 5706
MSSLLSFM, FSSLDS, FM 5336
MSSLLSFSSL, SMFSFM 3181
MSSLTDS, DDLDRM, SRD# 9662
MSSLTDTL, SDRMRDRT 8095
MSSLTDTL, TDSLMSFM, 6891
MSLDRDLDT, SFFMRDT 8208
MSLDRMMMM, SSLDDLS, 7436
MSLDSMMR, DRMLSMR, M 9468

MSLDTSDRDTLTLSM, M 10783
MSLDTSLS, LTDSFMMR, 10675
MSLDTL, SMRF, LRDTLD, 2214
MSLDTLLS, MRDDLLS, M 1792
MSLRRM, SDTLLS, SMLL 12367
MSLR, LTRDL, LTRDL, RL 7858
MSLMRDD, MSLMRDR, MS 6470
MSLMRD, RMFSML, LTLS 6445
MSLMR, RFSL#L, TSF#TTD# 3489
MSLMSMDRM, MLDTRDL 10557
MSLSDD, RRMFMM, SSSS 7068
MSLSDDTD, DTLRTLS#L 11858
MSLSDFMR, STRFLSRR# 7249
MSLSDSFMRDD, DMF 3118
MSLSDLS, DMMFFM, MSL 12299
MSLSDLSM, DRMFR, MS 464
MSLSDTLS, LTSMFMR 5996
MSLSMDRM, MRSSF#S, SD 10467
MSLSMDFL, SSLSMDR, M 4328
MSLSMRDRM, SMF#SLT 5711
MSLSMRDMMFM, MSMDT 5065
MSLSMRDMM, SMSLSDM 2174
MSLSMMRD, DRMFRMFS, 10186
MSLSMMFM, MSLSMR, MS 977
MSLSMFMR, MFSFRM, SD 317
MSLSMFMMR, RSLSDTD 4401
MSLSMSFMMRD, DFDRM 9856
MSLSFMRDD, MF#SSLTD 8797
MSLSFM, MRDTD, RMF#SL 7339
MSLSFMFRD, RMF#SDTL 9497
MSLSSDFM, MRFMMRR, M 10289
MSLSSFM, DTLSMDR, MS 4760
MSLSSFM, MMRSSF#S, MS 4761
MSLSSFMFM, SDL#LSFM 12147
MSLLFFSS, MDTLSLFM 9012
MSLLSFMM, MMRFMRM, 2757
MSLLSF#SLM, DMSMRDR 9946
MSLLSSFM, DRFMRFRM 8168
MSLLSLDR, SF#MDTTLS, 9551
MSLLLSSSM, STDDDTT 12457
MSLLTDMSSM, MLLTDR 10821
MSLTDDMMRM, SLTDMR 10735
MSLTDD, TLSFM, MMFMM 1906
MSLTDRDM, SRRRRMFM, 4462
MSLTDRDL, SDMMRDR, M 11791
MSLTDRMR, FLTDRS, MM 1055
MSLTDRM, FLRDTDR, SF 9422
MSLTDTL, RDLSLFM, SS 139
MSLTDTLRDT, MRDTLS 6461
MSLTDTLM, LSDFMRM, S 2230
MSTDDLFMRD, RMMF#F#S 4098
MSTDMSLDTRD, MRFMR 6275
MSTDLSFMRM, SDMFSL 1570
MS#FMFS#, S#LTLS#LFS#M, M 6824
MS#LTDTLS#LT, LTDRM 2194
MS#LTRDLLSM, MRTDDD 12525
MS#LTRDTL, LDDRRM, MS 8718
MLDDTL, FFFF, MLDDTL, 11693
MLDMLLS#L, DTRDMFRT 4152
MLDLSMFS, LSFMRDT, L 11025
MLDTRDL, DTLS#TL, MLD 10129
MLDTSLLSM, MLDTSL, M 9967
MLDTS#LDM, DLDTS#M, ML 11046
MLDTS#LM, FMRDRM, MSR 8011
MLDTS#L, TDLDMRM, MF#S 10525
MLDTLSFMFS, DRMFSL 2730
MLDTLSLT, MLSLTD, LD 2287
MLDTLS#LTM, MDDRDRM 8229
MLDTLS#LT, MLS#LTD, SD 2288
MLDTLLSFFM, DMLSFM 6558
MLDTLTLSL, LDRMDRR 678
MLMRF#MRDLTL, DRMRS 10927
MLMFRDTL, TDRMLSF# 5417
MLMFMDRM, MFSFRDTL, 2404
MLMFLSFM, MRDFFF, RM 7815
MLMSDRM, FSMRDTLL, T 4647
MLSDDRFM, MFRSDRLT, 1499
MLSDRRM, FMRMDTLS, R 3839
MLSDTDRRM, SLTDTLS 10904
MLSRMFM, SDTF#SLS, SL# 3440
MLSMDRDT, LSDMSFMR, 1051
MLSMDRMFMRM, MDTLS 9454
MLSMRDRM, RDRDLDRD, 7233
MLSMRDRM, SDT, DLS, MM 101
MLSMRDRM, LDTL, MLSM 3518
MLSMRDRTL, RMLRRMF, 9761
MLSMRMF, MMMRDTD, RS 3113
MLSMMRD, LTDSLTS, ML 3313
MLSM, MRM, MTLT, TSM. 2455
MLSM, MRM, MTLT, TSMF#M. 5107
MLSMM, MLSMM, MLLSFM 4040
MLSMFMRDRD, MSF#SLS 7754
MLSMSFM, SMLSF#F#M, SR 10224
MLSFMRRM, TDDTLTL, M 8340
MLSFMRRM, TDDTTL, ML 8340a
MLSFMRM, TDDTLTL, ML 8337
MLSFMRM, TDDTTL, MLS 8338
MLSFMRM, TDTLS#L, MLS 8339
MLSFMLRDTD, DSFMRM 10016

MLSFSM, SDTLLS, SLTD 4501
MLSSDTTTLS#S#, LTDLT 10473
MLSSRRSFFM, DTLSF#S 11512
MLSLSMDR, MLSMRDTL, 6289
MLSLTDRMSTLLSL, MS 878
MLSLTD, RMTDLSM, MLS 116
MLSLTDLT, TDRMDDTD, 4649
MLS#MMS#LDLM, LS#LTDT 5886
MLS#LDTLS#, LSFMLLS#L, 9498
MLS#LRDT, DLRDTTL, ML 4056
MLS#LMSRM, LTDTMSF#M, 6915
MLS#LSMDTL, DMRDTLT 8913
MLS#LTD, DRDTLSFM, ML 10381
MLS#LTD, DRDTLS#F#M, M 10380
MLS#LTDRDTL, DMDTLT 6153
MLS#LTDMMDL, MLS#LTD 2435
MLS#LTDMMDT, DLS#LTD 2434
MLS#LTDSLFM, MSF#MRD 10213
MLS#LTDLT, TDRMDDTD, 4650
MLS#LTDTTLLMM, MDSD 8241
MLS#LTDTTLLMM, SDSD 8240
MLS#LTRDT, TDRMDRTD, 4648
MLS#LTS#F#M, MDTDRTLS# 7232
MLLDRDLS, MLLDRD, DR 5826
MLLDRDLSL, LLLDLDRM, 1239
MLLDRMRDTL, SSMRMS 2742
MLLDMRDTL, LRMFLSL 9192
MLLDTLMD, LLLDTLS#L, 9089
MLLDTLLDDMRD, MFMR 7616
MLLDTLLS#, LSSMRRD, M 10756
MLLMRDML, TDMLLT, MD 11656
MLLMRDTL, MLLMDRML, 9387
MLLMRMML, TDRMLDTM, 8836
MLLMMFD, DRMFRM, MLL 11236
MLLMMSLSFM, MSSLTD 5784
MLLSDFFM, DDRR, MLLS 5767
MLLSMFM, MRMDDT, MLL 6253
MLLSMSDMRDDT, TRTS 9549
MLLSSFMRDRM, MF#S#LT 98
MLLSLSFM, MLSLSFM, S 1548
MLLSLSFM, SFMRDTL, 496
MLLS#MDDT, TLLS#MDLT, 29
MLLS#MMDDTL, TDLTS#M 8658
MLLS#F#MLTD, RDTLDTL 542
MLLS#LTDL, TLSF#M, LTD 3542
MLLLSMSDMRDDT, TDR 9552
MLLLS#LTDDDTR, TDLL 12001
MLLLLLSDTL, LMRDDT 11086
MLLLLTDDTLT, RMFMR 2321
MLLLLTDLL, SFMMMMM 2844
MLLLTDDDTLLSM, MSL 7462
MLLLTDRMM, RDTLTL 4276
MLLLTTDRTDRMFLS#L, 9462
MLLTDDTS#L, TMMRDDT 8199
MLLTDDTLDTLLS#, TDD 6665
MLLTDDTLTS#L, TDDRT 6664
MLLTDRMFM, TDDDRMF 11726
MLLTDL, TTLSL, MMMDR 2740
MLLTD, TRRRR, DTLFM, R 9962
MLLTDTLTM, MMRRDDL 7962
MLLTTDTL, LRRDDT, ML 6280
MLLTTTD, MLLTTTD, LL 6182
MLTDDRRM, MRMDDT, MD 7578
MLTDDRRM, MLDTLS#, TD 7579
MLTDDTTS, LFMRMSLT 5112
MLTDRDL, MMRDTL, MLT 1551
MLTDRDTLSM, MLTDRM, 7113
MLTDRDTL, SLLTSL, ML 6113
MLTDRM, DRMFRM, TDDD 6104
MLTDRM, DRMFSM, DDDD 6105
MLTDRM, DRMFSM, TDR 6103
MLTDRMRD, LTDT, MLTD 989
MLTDRMRDT, TDTLTDR 1780
MLTDRMRFM, MRMDTDL 11231
MLTDRMMR, LDDTLSL, M 2595
MLTDRMMSFM, RDLT, TD 9503
MLTDRMFM, LSMDRM, MS 4594
MLTDRMLSFM, MDTLSF# 8457
MLTDRMLS#, SDRMFSDT, 4227
MLTDRTLTLSM, MMRTL 2188
MLTDMDTLT, DDRM, DRM 8394
MLTDMRDL#, LDTLTM, ML 2215
MLTDMRDT, RRRMRDTL, 7940
MLTDMRDTL, S#LDRRM, M 8078
MLTDMMR#M, MRDTDTL, M 5460
MLTDMSMRMSL, LTDDT 5716
MLTDMLLLS, MDRRMF#S 5703
MLTDML, TDTLTSM, MFS 12214
MLTDS#LLM, FMRDTLL, M 10988
MLTDLSFM, SLDRRD, ML 7261
MLTDLSFM, SLTDFMRD, 7267
MLTDLSLFMM, MRDTSR 2978
MLTDLS#TDR, R#MTRDTL 4570
MLTDLLFM, DFMRDRTL, 3396
MLTDLTS#L, MLTDMRDT 147
MLTDLTT, TLTDDT, MRR 7847
MLTDTDRMM, SSFMSFM 4127
MLTDTRLS#T, MMMMRDT 2961

MLTDTMRDD, TMFFMMR 4931
MLTDTLDTLS#, TDTDRM, 4615
MLTDTLFM, SSFMLLS#L, 2134
MLTDTLS, DLTDRM, MRM 672
MLTDTLS, DTLDRM, RMF# 2703
MLTDTLSM, RTLTDRM, M 2749
MLTDTLSMM, MLTDTL 7046
MLTDTLSM, MLTDRM, ML 7785
MLTDTLSM, LMRDTL, M 11996
MLTDTLSLM, MRDTMLT 10546
MLTDTLSLM, MLLSFM, M 965
MLTDTLSLM, TDDTLSL 11089
MLTDTLSTL, TDRMRDL, 3013
MLTDTLLM, MDDRMRM, D 3267
MLTDTLLSLTL, SLSM, M 10919
MLTDTLTM, MDRMFMR, D 9260
MLTDTLTSM, SSSFMLT 7349
MLTDTLTS#M, SSFMLLS# 7346
MLTDTLTS#M, SSF#MLLS# 7345
MLTDTLTLS, DTMF#SF#M, 6769
MLTDTLTLS#M, SSFMLL 7348
MLTDTLTLS#, SSFMLLS# 7347
MLTDTLTLS#, TDTDRM, M 4614
MLTDTLTTLSMRMM, ML 3248
MLTRDFMM, RSLSFMDR 10014
MLT, MLT, DTLTDRDT, ML 603
MLTS#S#F#S#, LTDT, TLSS 251
MLTS#S#S#, LTDRMMM, SDR 3211a
MLTS#S#, LTDRMM, SDDRM 3211
MTDRMRFMRM, MMMLSF 5561
MTDMFS, LMFSLT, DLSR 8529
MTDFMRRR, MFLMSRDR, 1904
MTDFMRLTDT, DRMLSF 5809
MTDFMRTDMR, STD#RMR 9041
MTDSLTDMMR, DLSDDT 8368
MTDS#LFMR, LDTLTLS, D 5034
MTDLLDTLTLS, LTDTM 475
MTDLLFMD, MTDLTSL, M 518
MTRDFDMR, DTSSS, SS#L 3626
MTRDLSLSFM, MTRDLS# 7171
MTRDTLSLLSFM, DDTR 746

FDD

FDDDFFM, LMMMLLT, LL 11522
FDRDLLLLTDL, MRDTR 11402
FDFSLSLS, FDFSLLS, 3264
FDLDRDRFD, LDSF. 4926
FRMMMMMSLLSLL#LSS 7855
FRMFSLSF, SLSFMRM, M 2875
FRTSDMSM, FFFMMMRD 1101
FRTSMRDS, DDDTDRM, M 11876
FMRDDTLS, LFSMSFMR, 483
FMRDRFSF, LDL#SLSFL 741
FMRD, FMRD, DTLS, DT 11699
FMRRRLR, MFSLSLFMR 8489
FMRRMRDD, LSFRMFM, F 7700
FMMMMFSLS, MRRRRMF 4469
FMFRMDRR, FFSFMRDM 2579
FMFSLSFRFMFMM, SLT 5661
FMFSLSFRFMFSFM, SL 5662
FMSDLTDRTLS, DRMFS 12540
FMSLSFSLSFMM, RRLL 2526
FMSLSFSLSFMM, RLLL 2526a
FFDRMM, RRDRM, MMRDS 11344
FFMMRRRSD, FFMMMRM 5235
FFMFSDTD, MFSLSFRR, 3188
FFM, SMR, MRDDRMFMRD. 10183
FFFR, MMMD, DDDDTDRM 10715
FFFMRMSLFM, SLSLDD 699
FFFMMRRM, MRDLDRR 9328
FFFFDRMM, SSSMRDR, M 11441
FFFFMMMM, LLLSFMRF# 1980
FFFFMSDDDT, TTTTDL 10597
FFFFFFMMM, MMMSMR, M 5694
FFFFSLLS, FSLSFRFS 5282
FFFSFFFFFMSL, LLSS 5283
FFFLSSMS, MRDSMMR, M 7326
FFSFFMRDRMMM, SSLL 3199
FFSLFSFM, SFFMRFSF, 7583
FFSLSSFM, SMFRDFFF, 5237
FFSLLSFMMR, LLTDDT 10222
FFSLL#LSL, LSDDSLL# 10309
FFLD, DDRD, DLTL, LSLF. 4925
FFLD, DDRD, DLTL, LSLF, RFSF, FL#S 1965
FSRDLS, FFMTRRDTLM, 3781
FSMSLFRM, SLDLSLSF 9664
FSFMSSLLSFRM, FRFM 8950
FSFSLL#LSL#LSF, FDDR 8890
FSLLRDDL#LLS, LL#LLS 9108
FSLLLSTDLSLSF, FSL 10677
FSLL#LSLL, SDDSLL#LS 10311
FLDDDRD, L#LSFF, FLDD 168
FLDMSD, RRRRDT, SMMM 10983
FLLSLTD, RRTDLLS, TT 12506

SDD

SDDDDDDD, MRDMRD, SF 1949
SDDDDDD, SSDDDDTDR, 5814
SDDDDDRDLS, SSRMFT 4705
SDDDDD, RMDLLL, SLTD 9300
SDDDDDRMRDTD, DMMM 4238

SDDDDDRMRDTD, DMMM 4238
SDDDDDRMMMM, DMSSS 11928
SDDDDD, RMMMMM, SDDD 5932
SDDDDDMRDT, SDRMFR 10952
SDDDDDS, SLLTRD, MRR 4214
SDDDDDTDRM, DFMRDT, 10489
SDDDDDTDF, MMRDTLS# 1225
SDDDDRDDT, DRRRRMR 7742
SDDDDRRR, RSF#FFMRR, 3333
SDDDDRRM, DFFMMRRD, 10652
SDDDDRRMFM, DFFMMR 10653
SDDDDR, MSFMRD, SDDD 9035
SDDDDRMSLS, DRRRRM 4383
SDDDDRML, LRRRRDLS, 10781
SDDDDRTD, DMRDDT, SS 10876
SDDDDRTD, RMMMDTLS, 1408
SDDDDMDMS, LSSSSMD 393
SDDDDMRD, DRRDTD, DM 2949
SDDDDMRDRRRRFMRD 5456
SDDDDMRD, SRRFMR, SM 2971
SDDDDMRD, TDRRRRFM 4850
SDDDDM, MRRRFMRM, SL 10888
SDDDDMSSSS, MFRSMD 1681
SDDDDSDMMMMD, MSSS 557
SDDDDSMRDS, SRRRRD 634
SDDDDTDRDTD, DMDDD 5182
SDDDDTDRDTD, DMRDD 11079
SDDDDTDRRRR, SMMDR 6475
SDDDDTDRSSS, MMFMR 4692
SDDDDTMRD, DRMFMDR, 11260
SDDDDTLS, DMMDRMR, S 6358
SDDDDTLS, MRMFFMRM, 10972
SDDDDTLSM, SDDDSMR, 10581
SDDDDTLS, SDLSF#S, SS# 1426
SDDDDTLSLSM, RMFMF 5586
SDDDDTLSLSFMMR, RL 3459
SDDDDTTLL, SDDRDR 4999
SDDDDTT, TLTLLSS, SD 10766
SDDDRDLS, DMDMDRMR, 11093
SDDDRDTLSLT, SDLS, SD 4689
SDDDRMD, DRRDTD, SDD 10883
SDDDRMDRRR, MFSFMD 6451
SDDDRMD, SRRMFM, SMR 5240
SDDDRMDL, RDDTTDD, S 1102
SDDDRMDLLLS, MSDDM 2182
SDDDRMDLLLS, MSSLD 2182a
SDDDRMRD, DRRTTD, SD 5735
SDDDRMRD, RMSLSFMR 11834
SDDDRMRD, RSSSLTLS, 8189
SDDDRMRDR, SLSFMRD, 6956
SDDDRMRD, SFMMRR, RM 5991
SDDDRMRMFS, MFMDRRD, 3434
SDDDRM, RMSFMR, RMRM 4688
SDDDRMMRDR, SRRRMF 5129
SDDDRM, MRDFMR, RMRM 10448
SDDDRMMRR, SRRRMFF 11254
SDDDRMMM, RMFSSFMR, 8791
SDDDRMMM, MRMFTRD, S 3167
SDDDRMMM, FMDTRD, SD 5040
SDDDRMMM, FSSSMFMR, 172
SDDDRMMM, FSSSLS, SL 10505
SDDDRMMM, SSMDMR, MF 4963
SDDDRMFMD, DDDDLLL 12044
SDDDRMFMRMS, SFRRR 3778
SDDDRMFMR, TDRMFSL 9924
SDDDRMFM, SFMRDT, TT 4967
SDDDRMFSM, DSMFMRD, 10428
SDDDRMFS, MMMMMFMR, 44
SDDDRMFSSSFM, SFFF 12135
SDDDRMFS, SLLLSFFS, 7698
SDDDRMFS, LMFMRDRM 3119
SDDDRMLTD, LSLSLTD, 11120
SDDDRTDTRL, SDDDRM, 7366
SDDDMDRD, MSSSMDMR, 4907
SDDDMDSM, SMDMRRTD, 2980
SDDDMDLS, SDDDMR, SD 6655
SDDDMRDRRRFMRDDD 5455
SDDDMRDR, MDDMSL, LS 695
SDDDMRDS, FMRDRRM, S 11257
SDDDMRD, SLTDFMR, SM 9618
SDDDMRDLS, DRRRDRM 11053
SDDDMRRR, RMFSLSFM 10968
SDDDMRRR, MFSFMRDR 6452
SDDDMRSS, SSMFRM, SL 12561
SDDDMMR, RMFRDTD, SD 9673
SDDDMMRR, FMFRDTD, S 9674
SDDD, MMMMDS, SLLTDR, 12293
SDDDMFS, DTDRTD, SDD 6066
SDDDMFSSS, SDRMMRM, 6988
SDDDMFSLS, MFSDRM, 3993
SDDDMFSL, LLLLLTTD, 6667
SDDDMFSTL, LLSTLSL 12115
SDDDMSMD, DRMRDRTS, 10508
SDDDMSMS, LSMDTDMR, 2589
SDDDMSM, LSSFRM, SDD 4886
SDDDMSLS, FMDRMD, SD 8919
SDDDMLS, SSLSDRM, MS 10889
SDDDSDDD, SMFSLMR, S 6020
SDDDSDRM, MSMRTLRS, 10250
SDDDSDRM, SFMRDS, SL 4861
SDDDSMSD, SLLLLDLS, 7449
SDDDSSRD, TLTDTL 283
SDDDSLSSSLSS, SRRR 10866
SDDDSLLS, SDDDSMDR 2590
SDDDLSFM, SLLLRDT, S 12581
SDDDLTDRTLS, SDDDR 2782

SDDDLTTTDLDS, SDDD 3438
SDDDTD, DRRM, MRMDT, T 10253
SDDDTDRRR, RMMMRDR 4124
SDDDTDRMMF, MLSDRF 2682
SDDDTDR, SRRRDRM, SM 6070
SDDDTDMDDT, DRRTLT 8325
SDDDTD, MSSSF#S, MLSF 3312
SDDDTDFMMRDTLS#, SM 1224
SDDDTDS, MFFLFSSD, S 1185
SDDDTDLSDTD, MRTSL 10899
SDDDTLSRM, SDRMRDR 7022
SDDDTLSMD, SLFDTLS, 3142
SDDDTLSFM, SLDTDRD, 4938
SDDDTLSSM, SDDDTDR 4164
SDDDTLSSS, SMMMFMR 11248
SDDDTLS, SLDTRD, DRM 6962
SDDDTLTDRM, MFMRDR, 6329
SDDDTT, DRRRSM, MMM 673
SDDDTTLL, LFMRDDTT, 4892
SDDRDRMSMRD, RMRDD 1495
SDDRDTD, RMMFMR, DRM 8548
SDDRDTD, RMMFMR, DMD 8547
SDDRDTRRDRM, SMMFM 4998
SDDRDT, SRRMRD, MFSM 5298
SDDRDTLTDS, SRRMFM 9706
SDDRRMD, FMDDTD, MRR 924
SDDRRM, DFFMRD, SDD 9022
SDDRRMDLRDT, SLTDR 2204
SDDRRMDLS, STDTLS, S 592
SDDRRMRD, DFFMMR, S 6278
SDDRRMRDR, RMSFMMR, 976
SDDRRMRD, RMMFMR, SS 784
SDDRRMRD, RMSRMD, SD 316
SDDRRMRD, SLLSLS, SD 8192
SDDRRMRD, SLTDTLS, S 11218
SDDRRMRMD, MFSSFMR, 3442
SDDRRMF, RMFRDTD, SD 5180
SDDRRMFM, DFMRDR, SD 7844
SDDRRMFM, MRDDRRD, S 7846
SDDRRMFS, MRDDRRM, S 11921
SDDRRMF, SMMFRD, SDD 12081
SDDRRMFSFMMRRD, SD 941
SDDRRMSR, RSSFMRD, 12460
SDDRRMSR, FMMRDR, SD 8689
SDDRRMSFM, SFFMMR, S 9279
SDDRRMSS, SLSMDMR, S 12068
SDDRRMLS, MFSMFRDD, 1490
SDDRMDD, MFSSLF, RMF 2195
SDDRMDRDLS, SDDRMD 11983
SDDRMDMRDTD, MFMRD 10559
SDDRMDFFMR, SDDRMF 6573
SDDRMDSM, DLLSFM, SD 6562
SDDRMD, SSLDFM, DRMM 7238
SDDRMDS, SLLRLRD, RM 11532
SDDRMRD, DRRDTLS, SL 2680
SDDRMRDSFMMR, RSSL 4274
SDDRMRD, LRRMFMR, RS 5869
SDDRMMDFFMR, SDDRM 6574
SDDRMMRMDLS, RMDLS, 5838
SDDRMMMMMRRMF, STR 12472
SDDRMMMFSMRD, SDDR 7864
SDDRMMFSMRD, SDDRM 7863
SDDRMMFSLS, MMMLSF 6033
SDDRMMFSLS, SFMMRD 8654
SDDRMMFLSFMRD, SDD 7862
SDDRMMSDRTD, RMRDT 4317
SDDRMMSFMRMMM, RDR 11856
SDDRMFRMD, RMFSLFS 11070
SDDRMFMDRD, SMRDTL 8354
SDDRMFMR, DRMRDRRR 197
SDDRMFMRD, MFSSMRD 10912
SDDRMFSFM, MLLRMF, T 11239
SDDRMFSLSFS, SFRMF 7477
SDDRMFSLS, SDDRMFS 5258
SDDRMSDDLS, SDDRM 5945
SDDRMSDRTD, RMRDTD 4316
SDDRMSMDMR, MSSLSM 627
SDDRMSMR, FMDDMRTS, 10509
SDDRMSSFMMRD, SDDR 11476
SDDRMSLLTD, MRTSDM 1093
SDDRML, SMRDRM, SDDR 3485
SDDRFMRMR, RDDFMR, 8553
SDDRSMD, LSDDRD, SDD 10353
SDDRSMFMR, DLFMRDT 2983
SDDRSFMRDRRMRD, SD 10816
SDDRTDD, MRFMRD, SDD 10490
SDDRTD, LSDRM, MRMFS 5868
SDDRTDLS, MFSMSLTS, 3360
SDDMDDMRRMRD, SDDM 5234
SDDMDDL, DSDRMR, SDM 11945
SDDMDDLS, SDDMDRMR, 5331
SDDMDDLLS, DTDRMFM 12021
SDDMDS, FMRDRMR, TDD 11521
SDDMDSFM, SLTDRDT, L 10738
SDDMDLDS, MSLSMMR, S 11424
SDDMDLDS, SDMRDDT, R 2149
SDDMDLLD, LSDMDMR, S 11154
SDDMDLLD, LSSDDR, RM 8276
SDDMDLTD, MSFMRDR, M 1494
SDDMDTRTS, LSMFTD, S 3236
SDDMRDDSLDLS, SDDR 770
SDDMRDRRF, RMMSFML 1295
SDDMRDR, MFSFMFMR, 9616
SDDMRDLLDT, LSSSDM 262
SDDMRDTDR, SRMFMRM, 1781
SDDMRDTLS, DTDFMR, S 4228

SDDMRDTLLF, RDDRMD, 12316
SDDMRRFMSDLS, FMFR 7186
SDDMRRFTTRD, SDDMR 4260
SDDMR, SRRFM, DMSMFL 3574
SDDMMDDM, DLLS, SDDM 12170
SDDMMRDR, MRDMRD, R 2160
SDDMMFMRM, DRMFRM, M 3141
SDDMMS, MRDMRD, SDDM 424
SDDMMSFMRDFMRD, SL 767
SDDMMSFMR, MDRDTLS, 4980
SDDMMSFM, MFMRRD, SD 12134
SDDMFS, SLLLLSM, SDD 1913
SDDMSD, DTSSLS, SSDD 11503
SDDMSD, SDSDRM, MRTD 1351
SDDMSFMR, SDDMSFMR 8614
SDDMSSLSMDRM, SDDM 5087
SDDMSSLSFMSD, SDDD 4918
SDDMSLS, MSMRDM, SDD 2043
SDDFMRD, DRMMMRDR, S 3125
SDDFMRDTD, RMDSLS, S 1091
SDDSMRDTD, FMRDTLR 2877
SDDSMFMRD, DTLLLRD 8012
SDDSFMRD, DTDRSTLS, 5168
SDDSSMD, SFMRDS, DT 1834
SDDSSMRD, SFMRDS, TD 8901
SDDSSTLS, FFMRDSS, S 4735
SDDSSTLS, FFMRRMFM 4737
SDDLSFFM, RMSDTLLS, 10678
SDDTDDSLSFM, SDDRM 6968
SDDTDRDRMD, MRMSFM 11205
SDDTDRDS, SDDDTTDR 10944
SDDTDRRD, DTSLLS, RM 9617
SDDTDRRD, RMRMFS, SL 1666
SDDTDRRD, MRDTRLLS, 6180
SDDTDRR, SRRDRM, SMM 5216
SDDTDRMRD, DMMRMFS 8372
SDDTDRMFMR, SDDTDR 11486
SDDTDRMFS, SFMDSLL# 12063
SDDTDR, MLLLRDT, LSD 4671
SDDTDR, SRRDRM, SMMF 1071
SDDTDRTS, SDDFMRDR 7618
SDDTDMMR, SSSFMRM, S 6884
SDDTDS, FMRRD, MLLTD 6634
SDDTDSSLSFFM, SDDD 3859
SDDTDLLS, MRRDTLT, S 10049
SDDTDLLS, MSFRMFM, S 10734
SDDTDLTD, DRRMRDDT, 2355
SDDTDLTDS, LSSSFMM 4810
SDDTRFLS, SDTSLTD, S 12207
SDDTMRRD, SFMDRMD, S 7144
SDDTFLLS, DMMRFMD, S 9862
SDDTFLLS, MSFSLRDT, 3972
SDDTSRD, RRFMRD#R, DM 5403
SDDTSRRD, SMMRRLR, S 1917
SDDTSFFM, SSLSFMMR, 8748
SDDTSSLLSM, MTLSLS 5438
SDDTSLSM, SDDDTLSL 10881
SDDTSLTD, DTLSFMRD, 8052
SDDTLSDRM, FMRDMRD 541
SDDTLSDRM, FSMLFS, M 5457
SDDTLSM, DRMSMRD, SD 8408
SDDTLSMD, RMLR, MMMD 12017
SDDTLSM, SLSMRDD, RM 10740
SDDTLSFM, SLRDTD, SL 1057
SDDTLSSM, MFFSRMSR, 2476
SDDTLSS, SDDLDS, SDD 6174
SDDTLSLR, MRFMRDS, D 11125
SDDTLSLS, DRMSFMR, S 369
SDDTLSLS, FMSLRDT, S 9375
SDDTLSLS, SSSFMRM, S 6384
SDDTLSLS, SSSLLSFM, 11524
SDDTLSLS, SLDSMR, RM 10908
SDDTLSLS, SLRDTD, S 1056
SDDTLSLLD, DRRRDRM, 4381
SDDTLS, LTDRMRDR, SM 587
SDDTLLSS, DMRRSM, SD 3033
SDDTLTDRMF#S, MFRMM 4820
SDDTLTLS, LTDDRRM, M 9226
SDDTTDRM, MDLRDTLS, 3937
SDDTTD, SFMFSLR, RMM 1362
SDDTTDTLS, DMDTDR, S 11920
SDDTT, SRRDD, SMRDT, L 3726
SDDTTL, DFFMR, DSFMR 3284
SDDTTLDLS, DSDSFMR 10524
SDDTTLRR, MFMFSRM, M 8616
SDDTTLLS, DSFMMRR, M 11623
SDDTTLLS, SMRDTL, LF 6412
SDDTTLLS, SMMRRR, MF 8636
SDDTTLL, LLMRDT, TDR 2263
SDDTTLTS, SSLTDSFM 1954

SDR

SDRDDMFSLSSM, DRDR 9548
SDRDMSLSM, SMDS, SDR 3490
SDRDFMDRDD, MSMDFM 5510
SDRDSDRMRD, MFSMDM 8323
SDRDSMFM, SMDRMFS, S 3090
SDRDSMFS, DMFMSLTD, 3472
SDRDSMSD, RMRDMR, SD 10349
SDRDLSM, SDTDMMR, FM 7526
SDRDTDRRD, MSFMRDR, 8922
SDRDTDRRM, FFRMRMR 11654
SDRDTDFSFM, MRTDFM 6922
SDRDTSDRM, RMDRMF#S, 9489
SDRDTSRMRD, MFLLDT 1262

SDRDTSRMRD, LSFMRF# 11994
SDRDTLSSLS, FMDMRD 1859
SDRDTLSLTD, MSLSMD 5951
SDRRMRDDTLSLS, FMS 11065
SDRRMRMFFS, FMRDTD 10094
SDRMDDLS, TTDTLS, SD 4375
SDRMDDTDR, SRMFRRD 8470
SDRMDRDRM, MFMRMDM 6419
SDRMDRDLSD, DTDRRR 8161
SDRMDRDTD, RMMSMRRR 2511
SDRMDRMFRS, MRDLTD 4880
SDRMDRMF, FMRDMRTD, 7973
SDRMDRFM, MLTDLS, RM 9435
SDRMDMRD, RMRDRMLS, 9477
SDRMDMRD, MFMRD#R, RF 9291
SDRMDMR#MFL, DTLSDM 5371
SDRMDMFSL, SFMRM, DM 3178
SDRMDFRD, TDMRRM, MS 8699
SDRMDFRMRDTD, SDRM 10865
SDRMDFMRD, SLSLLTL 1952
SDRMDFMR, RMDTLS, SL 5942
SDRMDFMRMDL, DTLSS 1619
SDRMDFMRMRD, MRDTR 10131
SDRMDFMR, STDRFMRD, 11922
SDRMDFMMR, RM. FSMMR 8773
SDRMDFFM, MLRSDTLS, 1475
SDRMDSSMD, MRSMLSF# 12249
SDRMDSSFMRD, MRMRS 4126
SDRMDLDLS, SDRMDRT 4327
SDRMDLS, DFMRDR, SDR 6193
SDRMDLLTD, DTDRDRM, 11674
SDRMDLTD, LSSDMR, SM 1360
SDRMDTRS, SLDFMMRR, 7248
SDRMDTLTD, MRSDTLS 11288
SDRMRDD, DRMMSFMMR, 1167
SDRMRDDRMF, FMRSMD 12424
SDRMRDD, SSMFSL, DTL 10241
SDRMRDRDLLS, SDMSF 4959
SDRMRDRMF#S, SDRMRD 9188
SDRMRD, MSSFMR, MDFM 3680
SDRMRDMSLSFM, MRFM 3715
SDRMRDFMR, RSFMRDR 404
SDRMRDFMR, SMLF#F#S, S 9313
SDRMRDFSLSM, RMF#SL 2265
SDRMRD, SFMRRM, RTLS, 3331
SDRMRD, SLDTLS, SLTD 764
SDRMRD, SLTDLS, SDRM 5778
SDRMRD, LDRD, SDRMRD, 3340
SDRMRDL, SDRMS, SLSM 3721
SDRMRDLS, SDRMDS, RM 3102
SDRMRDLS, SDRMF#S, SF 6872
SDRMRDLS, SLTDRMR, M 9560
SDRMRDTD, DRMSFMR, S 2874
SDRMRDTD, MRMDTLLS, 9469
SDRMRDTD, SDMSMRDR 9701
SDRMRDTLS, DTDRMD, S 2409
SDRM, RDTLSFMS, SDRM 5728
SDRMRDTLTD, MRSDTLS, 11287
SDRMRDTLTS, RMF#SMD 11083
SDRMRRSM, SDRMRRM, M 1819
SDRMRMRD, DSFMFMRR, 1673
SDRMRFMD, LSMFMRDD 10465
SDRMRFMRDR, RMFSFM 8252
SDRMRFMRD, SLSLTDT 7759
SDRMRFMMR, DDDDTRR 9880
SDRM, RSRD, DTLSD, LTD 12188
SDRMR, SRMFM, SSMSFM 7101
SDRMR, SRMFM, SSSSFM 1593
SDRMRS, SLSLDR, RRRR 6095
SDRMMDTLS, STRFFFD 12277
SDRMMRDDDTLS, STTT 3403
SDRMMRDRDRM, MSSSS 6194
SDRMMRDRDLS, SDRMM 5038
SDRMMRDLDLS, DTDR, 6545
SDRMMMRDRR, SRMFFF 7244
SDRMMMRDRR, STRFFF 7242
SDRMMMRDMR, RMRDDR 5069
SDRMMMMRML, LRMFFF 11715
SDRMMMML, SMRDDDTL, 1576
SDRMMMFDRM, MRD#RMR 7023
SDRMMMFDRM, SRMFMF 3691
SDRMMMFRMDS, DRMFS 10586
SDRMMFMR, SFMRMTDLS 399
SDRMMMFMR, SFMRMTLS 398
SDRMMMFMMR, STRFFL 8159
SDRMMMSFMR, SDRMMM 9727
SDRMMFRRTD, SLSSF#S 4989
SDRMMFM, RDTLDTLS, S 10789
SDRMMFMRMD, SDMSSL 4495
SDRMMFMRM, MRDTDRD 11019
SDRMMFMRM, MRDTDRM 11018
SDRMMSDRMM, RMFMMR 3910
SDRMMSMR, MDTLTDRS 12201
SDRMMSFDRM, MMRRRD 383
SDRMMSFM, MMDMFMRD, 2129
SDRMFRDRTD, MSRTMR 4842
SDRMFRR, SLSMRDRD, M 7282
SDRMFRMD, DDMSLSMR, 3070
SDRMFRSML, FSMRDFM 3520
SDRMFMRD, MRTRDLLS, 12417
SDRMFMRD, SDRMFMRD, 4091
SDRMFMRD, SLTDLLS, S 6596
SDRMFMRR, DRMFMRD, S 11789
SDRMFMR, MDDRDT, SDR 7516
SDRMFMRTD, RMLSF#S, R 11199
SDRMFM, SDRMFM, SSFF 4059

SDRMFSDRDTD, TLSSS 2544
SDRMFSDRMRDRD, DSS 11049
SDRMFSDFMR, RMFSFM 5088
SDRMFSDT, RSLTDLLS, 2750
SDRMFSRMFM, RMF#SLS 7681
SDRMFSRMFM, RMSSMF# 7684
SDRMFSMD, MLSFMR, SD 7718
SDRMFSM, DLSFFM, MRS 2811
SDRMFSMRDRD, SLTDR 11265
SDRMFSM, RDRMFR, SDR 2786
SDRMFS, MFLRDT, SDTL 4816
SDRMFS, MLSFSM, SDRM 4419
SDRMFSFMD, SSFMFMR 4116
SDRMFSFMRDRMFR, SD 8445
SDRMFSFMRD, SSFMFS 5204
SDRMFSFMR, RMF#SSF#S, 7761
SDRMFSFM, FMRDDT, RR 10265
SDRMFSFM, SDRMFSFM, 4088
SDRMFSFM, LSFMMRD, S 11849
SDRMFSFM, LSFMMRRD, 11852
SDRMFSFM, LSFMFMRD, 11848
SDRMFS, SDRMFS, SDRM 10998
SDRMFSSM, LSFMMRD, S 11851
SDRMFSSF#S, RFMDDT, R 12504
SDRMFSSSMRRD, SDRM 10874
SDRMFSSS, MRMFMRDR, 3447
SDRMFSS, LSMFSD, SDR 8005
SDRMFS, SLSFLSFMRD 11751
SDRMFSSLLS, MFSMFM 11771
SDRMFSSLTD, SLTSLF 1249
SDRMFSLSFMDRTD, MF 6217
SDRMFSLSFM, DMMRDS, 8206
SDRMFSLS, SRMFMRDS, 12539
SDRMFLS, DMSSFSFM, S 6223
SDRMFLSFM, SLSFMMR, 530
SDRMSDRM, MRDMRD, SD 1927
SDRMSDRM, MRMFRMFS, 6880
SDRMSDRM, MFMRDMRD, 4319
SDRMSDRM, LSMRDR, MR 4844
SDRMSRD, SDRMSRD, 9979
SDRMSMSLM, SDRMSMS 6351
SDRMSFRD, MMFMDSDR, 3086
SDRMSFMR, DRMRDSFM, 5921
SDRMSFMRDR, MFMRDT 62
SDRMSFMRMD, RDRMSL 3339
SDRMSFMR, MDTDRTS, S 1392
SDRMSFLLS, SDRMSFR 7308
SDRMSSDRMS, SDMSLL 9306
SDRMSSDFMR, FMTDDR 1162
SDRMSSF, RRRSFM, SDR 7209
SDRMSSF, MMRLTD, SSL 6997
SDRMSSF#MR#M, FMRSSL 12075
SDRMSSSMD, MRDLDDL 936
SDRMSSSLSFM, RRMFS 432
SDRMSLDD,DTLSMMDR, 12167
SDRMSLMS, TDRMDFMR, 9460
SDRMSLML, LFSLLTST, 6707
SDRMSL, SMDRMS, SLMM 855
SDRMSLSM, DRSMDLRR, 8968
SDRMSL, LRMRDT, SMRD 9490
SDRMSL, LRMFS, SDRMS 3571
SDRMSLTDTLS, SDRMS 8671
SDRMLRDT, SLTDMRD, 2912
SDRMLRRT, SLTDMRD, S 2913
SDRMLSFM, RDRTDTLS, 12355
SDRMLSFMRD, MRDTDR 8068
SDRMLSFM, LSMRRD, SD 11854
SDRMLSFM, LSFMFMRD, 11850
SDRMLSFM, LSFMFSRD, 11853
SDRMLSSFM, RMFSMRD, 354
SDRMTDRT, RFFMDMF#S, 1338
SDRFMDTRD, SFMRDS, S 4601
SDRFMRRM, FSLSFMM 12291
SDRFMLSMDRM, SDTLS 8311
SDRFFMDLRS, SDRFLS 2128
SDRSMD, MRDLS, SSDDF 9266
SDRSM, LRMLF, MTRDTL 9858
SDRTDRMFRDD, MRSF#M 9303
SDRTDRMFR, MFSSFRD, 5704
SDRTDRMFMR, MRDTL 1244
SDRTSDRM, RMDMF#S, RM 9488
SDMDDLS, SFRMDLSTL 4885
SDMDRDDL, DLSSLDD, S 5409
SDMDRDDL, DLSSLTD, S 5409a
SDMDRDDL, LLSSLTD, S 5409b
SDMDRDLD, DMSDRMR, S 7755
SDMDRMD, MFSLSMR, DR 2010
SDMDRMDS, LTDLFMMR, 1446
SDMDMRDLS, SDMDMRS, 417
SDMDMSLSMDMR, MFSF 10839
SDMDSSM, SDMDRMRD, S 2956
SDMDSLDLS, SSDRMFM 11032
SDMDLDSM, SDMDDTDR, 2796
SDMDLSDMRFM, MMFML 900
SDMDLS, SSSDMDR, SDM 8139
SDMDLSTD, DTDFMR, RM 3493
SDMDTDRD, SSTTLLS, S 6805
SDMDTRDS, DMSMDMR, S 1862
SDMDTLSDS, SLMRMF# 8808
SDMDTLS, SDRMSR, MFM 9622
SDMDTLTSDR, MF#SMMR 10995
SDMRDDTTLL, RDDTLT 5714
SDMRDRDS, LDTLDLS, S 8627
SDMRDMRDLS, SDMRDR 2027
SDMRDMR, RMFFMRM, DT 5390
SDMRDMSR, RLSMMDRR, 2298

SDMRDMSF, MMRLDRD, D 5805
SDMRDMSF, MSDDRRM, D 2941
SDMRDFLS, STDRRMFM, 649
SDMRDS, FMDRTD, MRS 2180
SDMRD, SSDMMRDT, MMM 8393
SDMRDSLDR, MFSRFMR 1474
SDMRDLD, SLSMR, MFSM 4841a
SDMRDLFMFM, SDRTLS 6923
SDMRDLS, MSFRDTD, SD 11708
SDMRDLSFMFM, SDRTL 6924
SDMRDLSS, SSSMRDR, R 9692
SDMRDLS, SLDRRD, SDM 7873
SDMRDLS, TDRSLSM, SD 11433
SDMRDLLS, SSLSDDR, M 8849
SDMRDTDRDS, DRRRRD 9033
SDMRDTDLSS, MRRD#RM 4479
SDMRDTLS, SDRMDR, RR 10039
SD, MRDTLSSF#LS, STMR 893
SDMRRM, MFLSMR, MMRD 7389
SDMRRM, SFMRRD, DTLS 9515
SDMRMDLFFSDFRRD, R 2198
SDMRMD, TDRRRSFM, MF 1701
SDMRMFSSFM, RDMSSD 4297
SDMRFMDT, SFMFSMR, S 9815
SDMRFMRD, TDRTLDTL 6820
SDMRSDRRD, SSSDTLF 3979
SDMRSLTDLS, SSFMR 2993
SDMRTDS, DMSFMRFM, MR 9066
SDMRTD, SLDTLS, DTDR 6417
SDMR#MDMFSSM, DMRRM 6473
SDMR#MRD, DDRDTLS, SD 6064
SDMR#MSMD, TDRD#RFM, S 11173
SDMMDDLL, SRFFMR, RS 6398
SDMMDRMFMD, MMRDTD, 4451
SDMMDRFF, RMDTDRSS, 2712
SDMMRD, DMSSFM, RRF#S, 753
SDMMRDDLS, TDRDRM, S 11157
SDMMRDRDTD, SDMSFM 1767
SDMMRDRR, RMFFMRM, S 5615
SDMMRDRMFSLS, MMRR 5755
SDMMRDRFFMRMSSFM 3416
SDMMRD, SFMLRR, MDRT 9698
SDMMRD, LRFFMR, RMLS 3196
SDMMRDTD, TDRRDTLS, 6156
SDMMRDTRR, SRFFMRD 10726
SDMMRRMFFM, SLTLSM 10668
SDMMRFFLFFM, MMMDD 11217
SDMMRS, SDMMRS, FMLT 8186
SDMMRLDTLS, SDMSFL 6830
SDMMR#MD, TDRMRDL, DL 904
SDMMR#M, MRFFM, SDMMR# 5950
SDMMR#MFLR, DDTDTLS 7919
SDMMMDMSSS, SMRRDRM, 7450
SDMMMDMSSS, SMRRRD 7452
SDMMMRDR, STRFFMRM, 12498
SDMMMRDMRD, DMSSSL 12033
SDMMMRDFM, MRDDRR#M, 9927
SDMMMRS, SSDDTD, SDM 5519
SDMMMMRDLD, LLSDRM 7215
SDMMMMMMMFS, SSRMF 4415
SDMMMSFF, FRTLTD, SM 5779
SDMMMLLR, SDLDRRM, R 181
SDMMFMRDRDL, LSDDM 4334
SDMMFMMRDDRD, LSDR 4
SDMMFMMR, STRDMRRD, 12162
SDMMSFRMD, DTLDLLT 4300
SDMMSSFF, FMFRDTD, S 9705
SDMMS, SLSFFM, MMSSD 9341
SDMFRDTDRMFSMR, SD 6895
SDMFRMDS, SDMSMRM, S 350
SDMFMRD#R, STRFFMR#M, 8296
SDMFMRMDLL, TDRMDR, 3645
SDMFMRMD, TLLMRR, SD 10052
SDMFMRLL, TDRMRDSS, 8858
SDMFMMRD, TLRMRD, SM 12385
SDMFSDRMMRD, DLSFM 972
SDMFS, DTDLSS, SLLDS 2687
SDMFSLSFMRM, MSDTDR 4515
SDMFSLSS, SLLSLSFM, 8904
SDMFLSM, MFSSLFS, SD 1914
SDMFLSFMMF#F#S, SSSS# 1309
SDMFLS, SLSTDR, SSDT 2652
SDMSDMRD, DRMF#SRDT 4893
SDMSDMR, DDSLSLDD, M 7406
SDMSDSTL, TDRTDRM, D 12140
SDMSMDMLTD, RMSRSD 12279
SDMSMRDRM, RDRMFMR, 4166
SDMSMRDMRD, DTLDRD 1428
SDMSMRFM, DTLSF#S, SD 6855
SDMSMRLTSD, MFLSMR 2593
SDMSMMRDRM, FMRSDM 814
SDMSMMRR, MFFFRDTD, 11061
SDMSFMRD, SDMRDTLS, 10411
SDMSFMRD, TLDTLS, DL 2648
SDMSFMR, RDDRMR, RRF# 3198
SDMSFMRMRD, MFSMRD 7723
SDMSFMFRD, MRSDTDLS, 9036
SDMSFMFS, TLSFMFSF 7588
SDMSFLMRDTLTD, MMR 204
SDMSF#F, FLSFFMM, RRM 748
SDMSSDRM, FSDLLS, TM 1268
SDMSSF, MDDTD, LTDF 9317
SDMSSFMDRMFMRD, SD 59

SDMSSFMF, STRFFMRM, 4691
SDMSSFM, SLRDTD, SDM 11694
SDMSSL, SDLMFS, SLTD 4240
SDMSSLSLS, MRDDRDR 8166
SDMSLSMDRD, SDDMSF 12098
SDMSLSMD, MRRLRR, S 8537
SDMSLS, MRDRFM, MRDS 180
SDMSLSFM, DLRDLTD, S 5270
SDMSLSFM, MLDMFMR, S 12032
SDMSLTD, DRMDFMRTD 3904
SDMSTDRM, F#SLTRDTL 8462
SDMSTRDLS, FMDMRDT 4403
SDMLRSFM, RMF#SLTLS 2433
SDMLFRDRM, LSFMRDD 3063
SDMLFRDTD, RMSDFMR 2228
SDMLFMRDR, SDMRSLT 1035
SDMLFMRD, SMRDTLS, MF 1329
SDMLSFMRD, DLLSDSF 11936
SDMLSFMRM, SDRTSLS 6115
SDMLSSFMLS, SDRTSL 4023
SDMLSLSFR, RMMMMDD 11190
SDMTLSMD, DLSDRMFR 6157
SDFMRD, MRSTLS, SSLL 1683
SDFMRDTD, RMFSDMR, S 4268
SDFMRDTLSD, DDRMRF# 3754
SDFMRMDLS, MFSMRDR 12381
SDFMRLDT, SFMDTLR, S 8180
SDFMR#MD, TDMRD#RLRM 12547
SDFMMRR, DDDDRRM, MF 5043
SDFFMRD, SDFFMRD, RR 1590
SDFFMRS, SDFFMR, RRS 3803

SDS

SDSDDRRM, MFFMRDMR, 8070
SDSDDMR, DDTLSSS, SD 3453
SDSDRMD, LSTRFM, SDS 7225
SDSDRMRD, DFFMRMFR, 4163
SDSDRMRD, RMRMFSFM, 5418
SDSDRMRD, MRDTLS, SD 2177
SDSDRMRD, FFFDRM, MF 1707
SDSDRMRD, SFMRRRF#S 9362
SDSDRMRD, TLTDRR, SS 10975
SDSDRMR, MFSDMRDTD, 9948
SDSDRMMR, MFRDTD, MR 10845
SDSDRM, MFMRDR, SDSD 3303
SDSDRMM, SFMRDR, SDS 8990
SDSDRMFMRD, SFM, FMR 7297
SDSDRMFS, MFSLSFMR 2667
SDSDRMSS, LSMDMRDD, 6965
SDSDMRL, TSRFLSM, SD 9772
SDSDMSM, DRMDRMSD, 2966
SDSDMS, FMMRDRD, SDS 1899
SDSDMSS, LSMRMD, SLL 10306
SDSDSDRMFS, MFSLSF 2666
SDSDSDTDSL, LRLRLR 8848
SDSDSLTD, RMMRDT, TD 1300
SDSDL#LSF, LSRSFRM, D 12169
SDSRDR, MFMRDRS, SDS 8532
SDSRSMRDR, SDTLSLS 9298
SDSMDRSD, SRTDLTSL 11050
SDSMDMMRDDT, SFRTS 20
SDSMDFM, MMRRDT, SDS 552
SDSMDSMD, DFMRDT, SD 2163
SDSMDSMRDDT, SFMRD 21
SDSMDSFM, RDSDMR, SR 10280
SDSMDSS, SLSFMR, SMD 12226
SDSMDLRDT, RMSFRDT 11366
SDSMDL, SFMFSRM, MMMF# 5739
SDSMRDRMSRM, DFFMR 3908
SDSMRDRFM, SDTDFLS, 608
SDSMRDFMMR, MMRMFM 8023
SDSMRDLS, MFSLTDMR 11390
SDSMRDLS, SSFMRDTD 8271
SDSMRDTL, LSSSFM, SD 6638
SDSMRRDD, DLLTDRDT, 12430
SDSMRFMRD, RSRFMSF 5994
SDSMMMRDS, SLTDRDT 30
SDSMMFSSLSSSF, LRD 8479
SDSMF, SDSMF, SDSMFS 4054
SDSMFSSLTD, RMRTST 1676
SDSMFSLS, MLMRDRMM 12111
SDSMFSLT, SLLRDTDR 4894
SDSMSDD, SLFRDT, SMT 6534
SDSMSDSM, SDDRMR, RR 4016
SDSMSRSF, STSRSDSM, 6879
SDSMSL, SLTDTLS, RM 3322
SDSMLSFM, RDMF#SLS, S 12354
SDSFMRDDT, LSLTDRM 9982
SDSFMRDSS, FMSFRDT 3254
SDSFMLSSFM, RDMF#SL 12353
SDSFSMM, MMLS#TL, SDS 3902
SDSFSMFSLR, RMSDLS 2255
SDSFSLS, DFMRDR, SLS 2865
SDSSDMRD, DDLRDLS, S 4311
SDSSMDMMRDDT, SFRT 19
SDSSMSSDDRMD, SLLL 10858
SDSSFMDTLS, FMRM, LR 11497
SDSSFMFS, SLTDSFMR, 4254
SDSSSDLTRDT, TF#MMD 721
SDSSSFMD, SSFMRRD, S 9678
SDSSLSM, FMDRMD, DFF 78
SDSLDRDRM, DFFMRDR, 10303
SDSLDRRD, MFFMDRS, F 3600

SDSLDFMRM, MLSDMRT 5344
SDSLRDTTD, SF#SLDTT 768
SDSLFM, DMFSLTDT, SL 5851
SDSLFMRRD, RMF#SSF#S, 2914
SDSLFMRS, DTSLMRDR 12370
SDSLFM, SDTTLS, RTSL 8066
SDSLSDRMDRD, SLLLD 10618
SDSLSDRM, MRMRD, SDS 7868
SDSLSD, RMTDRMR, RSF 9047
SDSLSDMFMRM, SDSLS 7204
SDSLSMFS, LSLTDS, SR 4362
SDSLSFM, DMFSLTDT, S 5850
SDSLSFMM, SFMRDD, MR 5899
SDSLSFMM, SFMRRDD, M 5898
SDSLSFMM, SSFMRRD, S 9676
SDSLSFMFS, FMDRRD, D 2372
SDSLSFM, SSFMRRD, SDS 9675
SDSLSFFM, RMSLDT, SD 8519
SDSLSSM, SLSDMS, SDS 717
SDSLSSFM, MSFM, MRTS 3064
SDSLLSMFMRM, MMFML 9481
SDSLLSFMD, RMF#SLTD 2199
SDSLLSFMD, MFMRSLL 12023
SDSLLSFMRD, RMMRSL 2200b
SDSLLSFMRD, RMF#SLT 2200
SDSLLSFMRDS, SMRDS 10364
SDSLLSFM, MFMRSSF#S, 12295
SDSLLSFM, MFMRSLSS, 12295a
SDSLLSLSFMRD, RMF#S 2200a
SDSLL#LLL, LRLTDTTT, 12091
SDSLTD, DFMRDDT, T 4512
SDSLTDRM, DRTDRMFS, 7670
SDSLTDRM, MFMRDTLS, 5878
SDSLTDRM, SSMRDL, LR 2273
SDSLTDRSM, MMMF#S#LTD, 867
SDSLTDSFM, SLFRDTD 5954
SDSLTD, SLSFMR, SDSL 4223
SDSTLS, SF#LSF#S, SDM 8301
SDSTLS, SSMDMR, MRDM 6011
SDSTLLMF, LRDTLLSM, 6974
SDSTLL, SRFM, SDSTLL, 7007
SDLDRMRD, SMDFMRR, R 6713
SDLDSDRMRMS, SDLDS 3456
SDLDS, MRSFMRDLLLS, 5839
SDLDSLSFMS, DRMSFM, 6689
SDLRDTD, DMRDTLS, DL# 1734
SDLRDTDS, LTSFMLLR, 11308
SDL, RDT, SSLTDDTD, MM 4144
SDLRDT, TMDFMR, RSSF 8769
SDLRMDM, SDLRMD, MRS 6955
SDLSDRMRD, MSMDMR, 6754
SDLSDRMRD, MSMRDMR, 6755
SDLSDRMFS, LFMRDTD 6693
SDLSDRFM, MRSLDTS, S 9808
SDLS, DMRDR, TRRDTSL 4644
SDLSDTDRDTL, LLSMF 127
SDLSMDRMFSM, SDLRS 6625
SDLSMDRM, SLTDRT, DS 2076
SDLSFM, DRMRRD, MRMR 11178
SDLSFMRMFLS, RFMLD 4377
SDLSFM, MRSSF#S, SDLS 8261
SDLSLFRD, MSSLTDDT, 3044
SDLSTD, RFMRDTTDD, L 6343
SDLLSFM, SDLLSFM, SD 11959
SDLLLRDTS, DRMFMRR 10437
SDTDDRRM, SMRDLS, DS 12066
SDTDRDS, MMRMFMR, MF 12104
SDTDRDTD, DMMRDTLL 7461
SDTDRDTDS, MRDTLTD 4387
SDTDRDTL, SDTDRS, SR 460
SDTDRRM, SDTDRRM, SD 4060
SDTDRMD, DFFFFM, SDT 11389
SDTDRMD, DLFMRD, SDT 512
SDTDRMRD, DDRMFFMR 11917
SDTDRMRDDT, MRDTDL 9639
SDTDRMRD, MRDTLTDT, 6811
SDTDRMRD, LFMDMR, RS 9010
SDTDRMRDTS, DTDRMR 12483
SDTDRMR, RSFMRD, SDT 2144
SDTDRMRMFSLSM, MSF 12514
SDTDRMR, FMDRRMR, SR 4273
SDTDRMRSLTDRRD, SD 7688
SDTDRMM, RMFSSFMR, M 3537
SDTDRMMR, MLTDLLS, M 588
SDTDRM, MFFDRM, MMRR 1700
SDTDRMFR, MFSLRMFM, 10690
SDTDRMFR, SSSSS#LLR, 9717a
SDTDRMFRSFM, RDDMR 6089
SDTDRMFM, DSFMRDTD 12125
SDTDRMFMR, RDLRMSTL 2814
SDTDRMFS, DRDTRMRD, 353
SDTDRMFS, DLSFMMDR, 8907
SDTDRMFSMD, MFSDTD 5524
SDTDRMFS, FMDDTD, S 12064
SDTDRMFSFMR, MDTDR 2810
SDTDRMFSFMR, MFMFS 17
SDTDRMSFMR, TRDLRM 1483
SDTDRFMRD, FFMSRRD, 7475
SDTDRSMD, MSDTLDR, S 5523
SDTDRSSRD#RMD, SMRM 4348
SDTDRSLTD, DTLRT, TL 3580
SDTDRSLTDSMRDD, DF 8899
SDTDRTS, SDTDRM, MRM 963
SDTDMDMRMFTL, MMRL 3393
SDTDMRDRDTD, RMFSS 3362

SDTDMMR, LLSLFM, MMM 5329
SDTDMLSFM, MRDSFMM 10535
SDTDMLS, SFMRRM,DM 8401
SDTDFMRD, RMSDLTDT 198
SDTDSMDL, SFMFSRM, M 6120
SDTDSFMS, SDTDSFMS, 3657
SDTDSLDS, MLSSMDMR, 6812
SDTDSL, SMFSMRDD, MF# 2225
SDTDSL, SMSRRD, MF#RS 2226
SDTDSLSFMSLTDFMR, 2209
SDTDSLLD, TLSFMRD, S 10549
SDTDSLLRD#R, RRRMFT 11387
SDTDSLLS, SLTDTRDT, 8843
SDTDSL#LS, SDTDRMFMR, 2330
SDTDSTLS, FMLSDFMR, 499
SDTDLSDRMRMDR, SDT 1272
SDTDLSRM, DLDFMRM, D 864
SDTDLSFM, MRRRDTLS, 2873
SDTDLSFMFS, DLTDRD 7910
SDTDLSFM, SLDRRR, SM 9588
SDTDLSSS, SLLFMMR, R 10058
SDTDLTLSLL, TLLTDL 7655
SDTRDMRD, DRMFRDT, S 1270
SDTRDM, RDLSSS, SDTR 6690
SDTRDMRF, MSSFMRDT, 12274
SDTRDFRTD, DTLRMDT 9651
SDTRDFRTD, DTLRMTL 9652
SDTRDFM, MMRRDT, SDT 7094
SDTRDTLS, SRMFMRDR, 278
SDTRRD, SSSFMR, RFMR 1318
SDTR, SRDM, MMMMRMFR 10138
SDTRTLSM, LSFRSFM, S 12242
SDTSRD, DTLTDMRLTD 7235
SDTSLRTD, RRMRDTDL 2776
SDTSLLS, FRMFSFMR, S 4514
SDTSLTD, TDRDTLS, FM 412
SDTLDRDT, SLLTSDLS, 7834
SDTLDLSM, SDTRDLS, M 6433
SDTLDTLS, RMDRTD, SD 10660
SDTLRDTLTS, SDMSFM 9092
SDTLRSFM, MMF#SLLS, L 553
SDTLMSFF, STLSFMFS, 7199
SDTLMSF#F, TRDTFLSS, 11000
SDTLSDRDRM, SSFMMR 11278
SDTLSDRMFRS, MMFSL 229
SDTLSDR, MFSFMRDTL, 1635
SDTLSDMRD, RMMFMRD, 6381
SDTLSDMFS, SLTDRRM, 2932
SDTLSDMF#S, SLTDRRM 2933
SDTLSDSFMFMRDDD, D 9591
SDTLSDTDRMM, SSMFM 5422
SDTLSDTT, DRDTRRDD, 12220
SDTLSMDR, MLSMRMR, M 238
SDTLSMDF, FMFSLTDT, 153
SDTLSMRDRM, FLSRMS 7410
SDTLSMRM, SSDTLLS, S 9334
SDTLSM, MSMFSMDT, SD 8524
SDTLSM, FMRDMR, SDTL 7388
SDTLSMFS, SDRMFSLR, 9354
SDTLSMFSSFM, SLT 7983
SDTLSM, FLSFM, SSDDR 9355
SDTLSMFTLS, SMRDTD 9764
SDTLSMSDRRM, DDTLR 2414
SDTLSMSFMR, MSDTLS, 656
SDTLSMSLFLLSS, DTD 294
SDTLSFMRD, MSDTLS, S 4834
SDTLSFMR, DTDRSSS, S 3109
SDTLSFMR, MFSDRMM, S 4012
SDTLSFMRMF, LSMD, MF 310
SDTLSFM, MLSTDR, TDR 9247
SDTLSFMFSFM, RLSS#L 8490
SDTLSFMFSLLS, SSF#S 4339
SDTLSFM, FLSRFFM, SD 6072
SDTLSFMSDM, MRD#MRT 3767
SDTLSFM, SLRDLS, SMR 11636
SDTLSFF#SFM, SF#SLTL 3218
SDTLSSDT, SDTTLLRD 8771
SDTLSSFM, MRDFMR, MF 9566
SDTLSSFM, SFMRFM, SD 5153
SDTLSSSLSLTDSS, SL 9634a
SDTLSSSLSLTDS, SLS 9634
SDTLSSS, LLSMFMR, SD 8269
SDTLSSLSRFM, RMF#SD 7145
SDTLSLRMFM, RMDF#RS 4140
SDTLSLRFM, MRSMF#SL 3328
SDTLSLRSFM, F#SSLTLS, 5738
SDTLSLMRM, MLSFMLD 8760
SDTLSLFSM, FSDFMRD, 3079
SDTLSLSRMFSM, SLRD 4527
SDTLSLSFMRD, MFSSL 3043
SDTLSLSS, SDDRDTDM 35
SDTLSLLS, DMDSMSFM 6004
SDTLSLLSFM, MSLTDM 5512
SDTLSLTDRMFRDD, DT 7787
SDTLSLT, FTLSFSM, MF 8228
SDTLSLTLSF, SLSFSM 8322
SDTLSLTLTD, TDTLST 295
SDTLLFMR, RMFSDTLS, T 74
SDTLLSS, SLTDMRDT, T 10724
SDTLLSSLTLS, MLFMR 3156
SDTLLLRDTS, DRMFMR 10436
SDTLLLFMRDT, DD#D#RR 2223
SDTLTDRRSSSMFMFS 410
SDTLTDRM, DFMRDTLT, 4359
SDTLTDS, LSMSFM, F#SS 2079
SDTLTD, LSTLTD, DDTL 2342

SDTLTS, FMFSLR, RMF#S 9433
SDTLTS, LTDFMR, RMRD 6982
SDTTLRMF, LSFMSTTT, 8379
SDTTLS, SDRMRD, SDTT 4423
SDTTLLMMRD, TTLS, SD 8425
SDTTLLTLMS, SLTLSL 10502
SRDDTRDRM, DDTLLTD 11279
SRDTD, TLLLTDR, SMR#M 4165
SRD#RMDD, SFMFFM, MSS 11533
SRD#RMDLS, SLLFMRDR 1451
SRRRMD, SLTDRM, MMMM 366
SRRRSMMM, SLSFRSFM, 1075
SRRMFMRDRM, MSFMMR 4452
SRMDRM, RRRMMF#SF#F, M 10142
SRMFRMSS, DFFMRDMR 6117
SRMFMRD, SLTDSMF#S, L 11672
SRMFSMFS, LFLRDT 5740
SRMFLSFM, RMF#SLTLS, 3733
SRMLSLDRSM, SLMMRD 535
SRSMMMLMSF, FFFMRM 11419
SRTSSMDS, SFMRDDT, S 7964

SMD

SMDDDDRDTLL, LLMRL 10050
SMDDDDSS, DDTDRLL, L 234
SMDDDDTDRD, SSSMDD 1939
SMDDDTLLS, LMFSLSF 69
SMDDDTLTLSSSLTD, S 8001
SMDDRTTD, DSMMFRRM 10903
SMDDMRD, LSMMRRR, MD 8980
SMDDSLSFM, RSDDLT 8770
SMDDLLLS, DTDRFFM, D 7658
SMDDLLLSS, DTDRFFM 7658a
SMDDTDRSFFM, MRDFR 5645
SMDDTDRTS, SSLTDLS 6605
SMDDTLSDRM, MFMRRD 9457
SMDDTLS, MFSLFMRD, S 8792
SMDRDDLS, STTLSD, SM 5073
SMDRDLS, SLLSLSM, SM 8124
SMDRDLLSSD, MRMRRM 9906
SMDRDTD, DRMFSFMR, S 7129
SMDRDTLSLTD, RMFFM 5279
SMDRMD, RMLSMR, RMSL 12442
SMDRMDFM, SSSFMMDR, 3348
SMDRM, RSMD, DDDRMMS 5593
SMDRMR, SMDR, MFSLSL 4242
SMDRMFMRD, SLSFMRD# 9644
SMDRMFMRDLTD, DMFS 917
SMDRM, FMRRD, SSLTD, S 606
SMDRMFFM, SLLSMR, SM 4908
SMDRMFSDS, SDMRD, FF 3801
SMDRMFLS, DLSMFMR, S 3349
SMDRM, SLDD, STTSSMM 11341
SMDRMS, LDTLS, MSDRM 3862
SMDRMSLMFRD, DSLTD 9193
SMDRMS, LTDRD, SMDRM 11883
SMDRMLSDRDT, MR#TTF# 1189
SMDRFMR, MDMSSFM, SL 5698
SMDRS, DLSFM, SMRSD, T 6003
SMDRTD, DRMFMR, SMDS, 7128
SMDRTDD, MSDTS#L, SDS 10950
SMDRTD, MRDTLS, RTSD 8422
SMDMDD, DTRD, SMD, MSS 10031
SMDMRD, MRSSF#S, MFFM 377
SMDMRDLS, MMMMSLSM 1441
SMDMRFMR, MDMSSFM, S 5697
SMDMRFMRM, DTDRSLT 7790
SMDMSDD,DRRDTD, SMD 11924
SMDMSDMRDMF#S, SMRD 7294
SMDMSDS, SDMRD, LMDM 3800
SMDMSD, LSDSFMR, SML 5470
SMDMSL, DFMRRD, RMRM 3604
SMDMSLS, SMDDMSLS, F 8964
SMDMSLS, SMDMSLS, FF 8966
SMDFRD, DRRMMF, RMMM 9214
SMDFRDRTD, MRMTDLS, 9887
SMDFRSFM, RDSFMMR, S 6551
SMDFRSLFM, STDRTSD 10835
SMDFMRRD, DTSDRMFS 3242
SMDFMLS, DFFMRM, SMD 1626
SMDSDRSM, SMDSSRMD. 7103
SMDSRD, DFDMMR, SDSD 5825
SMDSMRDS, LLSDSFM, S 8882
SMDS, MRDLSMRMF, MMM 6048
SMDSMRDTL, SMDMMRR, 2425
SMDSFMMRDFMLSDFM 391
SMDSSDDT, SDMFMRD, S 2066
SMDSSDRM, DFMRDTDR, 9688
SMDSSSLTDR, SMDL, LR 11186
SMDSSL, LRRSFMRD, SL 2348
SMDSLS, MDTDMR, SMDS 10498
SMDSLS, SRMFRD, RMLF# 5170
SMDSLLS, LTDTLS, SMD 8734
SMDSLTD, SFFMDR, SMR# 1267
SMDSTLSLSM, LSSFMR 1711
SMDLDS, MFSLSDDTLS 4522
SMDLRDTD, FMRSDTLS, 255
SMDLRT, DLTDFMRM, MM 2390
SMDLRTS, DLTSMF, SMF# 7484
SMDLFMRD, MRLSDTLS, 2461
SMDLS, DDTRRD, MSFMR, 537
SMDLSDRM, SMDLLS, RM 6037
SMDLSMFMDRD, SMDDT 339

SMDLSM, FMRDMR, SMFL 4267
SMDLSFMR, SDTLLS, M 946
SMDLS, FMFSLTDSS, MM 2100
SMDLSSMDLS, DFFRSM 1873
SMDLSS, FSLTDS, MMMFF 2099
SMDLSSSMDLS, DFFRS 1874
SMDLSSLT, TDRMLR, RF 577
SMDL, SLSMDR, MMMMSS 6902
SMDLSLTDTMR, RDRMS 4226
SMDLSTRSSMDLSTRS 6042
SMDLLLF#RT, TLSDRFM 5008
SMDLLLTDRS, SMDLL 2173
SMDLTD, SMDLTD, RMF#S, 4714
SMDLTD, TLLLRT, SDDR 2647
SMDTDRD, MSMRMFM, SM 7498
SMDTDRD, SMRDDTDR, S 5071
SMDTDMR, DFMLLS, SDS 4535
SMDTDMRD, SFMLRR, RR 1357
SMDTRD, LDLLSS, SLSS, 3217
SMDTRDLSM, MFSRRSF 9866
SMDTRF, LSFMFS, DSMR 3296
SMDT, FRLS, SMDT, LSSS 11788
SMDTLSMRD, LLSMMRM, 8466
SMDTLS, MFRMFLSSM, S 9021
SMDTLS, FMRSMD, SMDT 12467
SMDTLSLSMMR, MSDLD 6677
SMDTLSLSSM, SRMFLS 1139
SMDTLSTRFM, SLLTLS, 6355
SMDTTLSD, FMRDTDR, S 9864
SMRDDDD, DRMFMRM, MR 9257
SMRDDDFMRSS, DTS 10410
SMRDDDTLS, SMRDDDT 7440
SMRDD, DTLSS, LTDRMR 3278
SMRDDRRM, RMSLLT, S 9922
SMRDDRRSSF, FMRSMD 1336
SMRDDRMFM, RMRDRDT 9823
SMRDDRMFM, SDRMSFM 6080
SMRDDRMFFM, MFSLDT 7876
SMRDDRMFSM, SLSFMR 371
SMRDDRMSMSL, TDSMF 9105
SMRDDRMSFM, MMMDDT 2323
SMRDDRMSFFM, MMMF#F# 1047
SMRDDMSD, DTLSMMDS, 2492
SMRDDFLLS, SMSDTLSF# 5992
SMRDDSFM, SLDSDLRR, 1978
SMRDDLSF, FMRDTDRD 8834
SMRDDLSFFM, SLTDMR 3964
SMRDDLLS, SDLTLSLM 564
SMRDDLLLS, LFRSDRM 1409a
SMRDDLLLS, LFRSDRF 1409
SMRD, DLTDRDS, SMDF, L 1943
SMRDDTDRMD, SM, SMRD 10803
SMRDDTDR, SFMRRSFM, 12275
SMRDDTFFMRM, SLRFS 4927
SMRDDTSFMRRD, MSFM 12523
SMRDDT, LFMRS, SDDTM 10497
SMRDDTLSDMR, RMRDT 6316
SMRDDTLS, MF#SLRSDT 9053
SMRDDTLS, FMFSLRRR, 1575
SMRDDTLS, FMFSLR, SM 1041
SMRDDTLS, SFMSMRDR, 8818
SMRDDTLS, SLMF#SSF#S, 7004
SMRDDTLSLSFFM, SLL 11987
SMRDDTLS, TDLRTLLS, 9330
SMRDDTLLS, SSLTDTD 8072
SMRDDTLTD, RMF#SRDT 3861
SMRDDTLTS, SMDRTLS, 4805
SMRDRDRM, MSFMRDRD, 2999
SMRDRD, SLTDS, DRDLS 6640
SMRDRDLS, SDSMRS, SM 6907
SMRDRDLS, SSLSFM, SM 7589
SMRDRDLL, DRDRMR, SM 3686
SMRDRDTD, MRDTDTLS, 2541
SMRDRDTT, SFMRSDRM, 1322
SMRDRRM, FMLSFMR, SM 869
SMRDRRM, SDTSSF#S, D 1379
SMRDRMD, RMSDTDL, LR 3581
SMRDRMFRM, SLSSMDM 3395
SMRDRMFS, MFSLSF#S, S 3519
SMRDRMFSLS, RDRMFS 4277
SMRDRMFSLSFM, MMFR, 5171
SMRDRMSFLLS, SDTLS 12285
SMRDRSRMRDRS, SMFM 10556
SMRDRT, DRRMFS, RSMR 9159
SMRDMDRDTL, LSLTDM 10533
SMRDMDLS, DTRDSLR, M 175
SMRDMRDRT, SFMRFM, L 5421
SMRDMRDT, SFMRFMRD, 1889
SMRDMRR, SRMFFMM, SS 3698
SMRDMRSD, SMRDMRSD, 3165
SMRDMFSLS, TDLSFMF 5404
SMRDMFSLLS, LSRMF#S 6864
SMRDMFSLTDS, DTSRD 5972
SMRDMSDT, SFMRLTLS, 10583
SMRDMSDT, TTFLTLSM, 10187
SMRDMS, SDRDLFRT, SD 6692
SMRDMSLS, MLSTDMR, R 3714
SMRDMSLSFM, LLSLT 2543
SMRDMLSMDMR, RMRDM 7647
SMRDMLSM, SLTDTLS 3909
SMRDMLSS, MSFRMD, SM 10802
SMRDMLLS, SFMDLTD, S 5140
SMRDFMDM, SSRMFMRR, 4446
SMRDFMRDRTD, TDDRM 7883a

SMRDFMRDRTD, TDRMF 7883
SMDRDFM, RMRDRDT, DRM 5641
SMRDFMRM, SLDDTDD, S 7008
SMRDFMRLSSF#, FFSRF 6337
SMRDFMRLTD, MSTLRF# 8410
SMRDFLS, DSLSMRDR, R 2262
SMRDSDRMFSD, SMRDS 8764
SMRDSDRMFSS, SMRDS 8765
SMRDSDLS, FMLSFMR, D 244
SMRDSDTLS, MLSFMR, 1632
SMRDSDTL, SLMFMR, MF 10483
SMRDSMRD, DFFFLLS, SM 5015
SMRDSMRD, RMSMRMS, S 6396
SMRDSMMR, DRMMSF#S, 11115
SMRDSFMR, MLTDRMLS 12426
SMRDS, SMMFMMR, LFD#R 11268
SMRDSSLDLS, DTDRMF 2438
SMRDSSL, LRRSFMRD 2347
SMRDSLDRSM, MRRDT 10054
SMRDSLDMRMD, LDRMS 1335
SMRDSLDLS, SLTDRFM 5379
SMRDSLFF, LSMMRDM 688
SMRDSLSFFM, SLTDTL 9156
SMRDSLSS, DRMSFMRD 5169
SMRDSLTDT, DSLSFMR 11620
SMRDSTLS, DRSRR#M, SM 4778
SMRDSTLSDF, LSLTDD 2418
SMRDSTLS, DLTDFMRD, 10007
SMRDSTL, STDRSM, MML 7180
SMRDLD, TDRSM, SMRMF 5033
SMRDLFMR, SLDTLSF#S, 9474
SMRDLSD, DRRDRM, SMR 1565
SMRDLSDRM, SMRDLSD 6806
SMRDL, SDMDR, MRDTDL 8334
SMRDLS, DTDFMMR, SMR 8700
SMRDLSFM, SDDTLS, TR 11779
SMRDLSLTD, TLSLMRD 5834
SMRDLLSFM, MRD#RSFM, 2626
SMRDLLLS, DTLMTLS, R 10268
SMRDTDDMRDD, DMS 8403
SMRDTDRDS, SLTDRMR, 6815
SMRDTDSRM, RDDFMRR, 3871
SMRDTDSRM, TDDFMRR 8201
SMRDTD, SFMR, RDTL 11606
SMRDTD, SLTDDRT, STL 8255
SMRDTDLS, SDMSRRM, S 10960
SMRDTRDLSM, SLDTTR 12283
SMRDTRL, DDTLSS, SMR 6946
SMRDTLDS, SDDRDM, LF 64
SMRDTLDTLS, SFFMDT 12558
SMRDTLFMDTD, RMFSS 1115
SMRDTLSD, RMRMF#S, SS 3410
SMRDTLS, DFMRDDT, SM 8443
SMRDTLSFM, SLTDMRD 12336
SMRDTLS, SDDDRMR, FM 773
SMRD, TLLLLLS, DDTRR 4343
SMRDTLTDS, STDRMSF 6703
SMRDTTLDS, SSFMMR 993
SMRDTTLS, DFMRDDT, S 8442
SMRDTTLS, SDDMRDRM, 4039
SMRDTTLL, LRDTSDRM, 36
SMRRD, DDLS, SRMRD, DM 4772
SMRRDD, MDTL, SLTDRM 9418
SMRRD, DFLS, DTLLS, DF 7434
SMRRDLSLS, SLTDDRMR, 1544
SMRRMR, SMDDRM, DRMM 2973
SMRRMFFM, DTLRSFM, L 426

SMRM

SMRMDRDS, SDDDRDRM, 539
SMRMDTDRDLS, SDDDD 601
SMRMRD, DRMFLS, SSSF 7095
SMRMRD, DSLSSFFFMR 7821
SMRMMSMRD, DLFMFRM 5373
SMRMFRT, SDMRDT, SMR 9621
SMRMFMRDLS, SSFFSM 3392
SMRMFMFS, FMFSLFMR 8685
SMRMFSDTL, SSLLRRDTD, 4830
SMRMSM, RRDRRMS, SMR 7503
SMRMSMRM, SLTLSMR, D 9563
SMRFMDS, DRMLSFMF, L 11072
SMRFMRD, SFMFSRM, SM 3653
SMRFMRD, SFMSRM, SMR 3652
SMRFMRDTLS, SSDTDL 758
SMRFMRLR, DTTDDRSM, 40
SMRSDRDTS, DRMFSFM 5448
SMRSTLDS, DTDRMMR, R 2456
SMRLTLS, SDLDFLMR, S 3477
SMRLTSS, SDLDFLMR, S 3477a
SMRTDDTT, LSDRMMRR, 2005
SMRTDLSM, SDTRDLS, S 2751
SMR#MDDRD, LSDDMMR, S 12028
SMR#MDDRDLS, SSF#SMR 7124
SMR#MRDRM, RDDRDLS, S 3897
SMR#MRDLD, LSSDRMRD 10180
SMR#MRDLS, DTTDRD, SM 5769
SMR#MRDTD, SLS#LRT, SF 7740
SMR#MMSFMDLS, DDTLT 5436
SMR#MFRD#R, SRD#RMDRM 1134
SMR#MFMDRDRM, SMR#MF 8348
SMR#MFMMRD, DDTLSMR, 9179
SMMDDRDTLS, SLTDMM 10481
SMMDDRRS, LTDDDRMF 9593

SMMDDLDLS, DDMMR, SM 6362
SMMDRDRDMS, SMMDRD 407
SMMDRDRMD, SRTSMDM 9606
SMMDRMMRD, DDDMRDR, 11954
SMMD, TDRD#RLSM, SMMD, 11174
SMMRDDD, LSFMDMRR, S 2954
SMMRDDD, TDRMR, SMMR 5363
SMMRDDF, RRMF#STLS, S 10324
SMMRDDF, RRMF#STLLS, 10324a
SMMRDDFM, DMF#SLRDL, 11264
SMMRDDLLS, SDMDR, SM 10424
SMMRDDTLDS, SSDDRM 7898
SMMRDRD, DSSLLR, RMM 1588
SMMRDRD, MFSMLFR, RM 11692
SMMRDRDLSM, SFMRMF 6906
SMMRD, RMMF#S, SDSFM, S 7316
SMMRDRM, SMDLSMDR, M 12332
SMMRDFM, RDDMRDT, SR 5515
SMMRDFFM, MMRDRM, MS 2384
SMMRDS, SFFMRM, MRMR 615
SMMRDSSLDRDTT, DMS 8536
SMMRDS, LFFMR, SDRMF 3030
SMMRDLD, SLSMR, MFSM 4841
SMMRDLSD, RMMSFMR, F 7252
SMMRDLSSFM, SLTDRM 1911
SMMRRDD, LDDLLSS, SF 9200
SMMRRDM, RMRRRDDLD, 7109
SMMRRDFM, MFSDDRMM, 2248
SMMRRD, SFFMMR, SSSF 7830
SMMRRDS, SLLDLS, SDD 11855
SMMRRD, LFFML, TSSFF 10900
SMMRMDM, RDDLDDDS, M 6602
SMMRMDS, SSSFSM, DLL 11238
SMMRMDS, SSSLSM, DLL 1776
SMMRMFMD, DRRRRMFM 3747
SMMRMFM, RDDRRM, SMM 887
SMMRMFLS, MSMDRMRD 1776a
SMMRMSS, LLDLLSS, SM 8928
SMMRSDDS, SDDRSM, MR 2812
SMMRSMMR, DDFMR, SSD 12423
SMMRTSD, DFFMDR, R#MR 9065
SMMR#R#MD, DRRFFM, SMM 9799
SMMR#MFT, TFFMRS, SSS# 4439
SMMMDDDL, SSMMDR, SS 4936
SMMMDDLD, DTDRRDRM, 3900
SMMMDFMMRR, SRMFFF 4939
SMMMRDDD, SFFFMRRR, 1074
SMMMRD, DRRRMRD, SMM 914
SMMMRDDRRMD, SMMMD 4579
SMMMRDRM, DTLSFMFS 11831
SMMMRDRMFM, SLSSMM 6172
SMMMRDRM, FSLSMMRD 10185
SMMMRDRLS, SRRRMRD, 2084
SMMMRDLD, FMMMRDRS, 8927
SMMMRDLS, DMRRMR, RF 9487
SMMMRDLS, SDDMRDR, S 12192
SMMMRDTD, SSLTDFMR, 3058
SMMMRDTRD, TLRFRMR, 8805
SMMMRDTSSS, SFFFMR 6455
SMMMRDTLTL, SMMMRD 10244
SMMMRRDD, TLLFMMRR, 3700
SMMMRRD, D#D#RMFMRDT, 12534
SMMMRRDMDDDLLS, DD 8018
SMMMRMFRT, SDDDTDR, 9955
SMMMRMFMRDDT, DD#RS 8784
SMMMRMFMRD, RRRRDT, 10982
SMMMRMFMRR, SRRRDR 11252
SMMMRLTDRD, DFMRDT 1349
SMMMRLTD, RMFSFMR, S 9090
SMMMR#MMDDRM, SMMMM 8367
SMMMR#MFMRD, SRRD#RF 6057
SMMMR#MSM, MDDRDRR#M 2908
SMMMMD, DMMMF, SFFFF 8523
SMMMMRDDLDS, SDDDD 7255
SMMMMRDMD, MSSSMDM 4906
SMMMMRD, MSSSMSR, SM 3245
SMMMMRMFM, SRFMRD, S 12280
SMMMMMRR, RMRDTD, LF 966
SMMMMMRF, LDTDMRR, S 11727
SMMMMMMRLL, LSFM, MS 8363
SMMMMMM, MMDTDFSFF 11409
SMMMMMMFMM, MRRRDR 11092
SMMMMMSDM, MDDRMDR 11250
SMMMMML, DDDTLD, MSS 7828
SMMMMFDM, MRMRLTDR, 7201
SMMMMFM, DMSSSSLS, M 11895
SMMMMFMR, RSLMRDRD 1113
SMMMMSDD, MLTDRM, MR 11830
SMMMMS, DTDFMMR, RFF 11570
SMMMMSSS, RDDSFMR, S 2594
SMMMFRDRM, SLTDRTL 1501
SMMMFMRDRM, SLTDRT 1500
SMMMFMRRDLS, STTTT 4461
SMMMFMRRR, MRDDRRM 11087
SMMMFSDLDS, SLSTD 357
SMMMFSDTL, SLTDRRM, 9838
SMMMFSLS, MSRMFMRM 10442
SMMMSDRM, FMDMRD, SM 5592
SMMMSMMM, SDMSDRMR, 5211
SMMMSMFFLD, LSSSDS 10813
SMMMSS, FMDDTD, MRRS 11520

SMMFMRDTDR, SFFSFM 403
SMMFMRMD, LSMMRR, SD 5507
SMMFMRMD, TLDTLS, SM 12046
SMMFMRMD, TLRTLTD, S 1365
SMMFMRLS, MDDTDR, SM 5949
SMMFMMR, DDTDRMM, SM 10915
SMMFMSFM, SLTDRM, MR 11117
SMMFFDRM, MRRDRMS, S 5186
SMMFFSSD, RMMMRDR, S 3244
SMMFSDTLS, F#F#SLTDT 3766
SMMFSFR, MMMRDR, MMM 5687
SMMFSLSM, RMLSF#MF#S, 3695
SMMFSLLD, DDDTLS, TT 1725
SMMFLS, MSFRFM, SMMR 8782
SMMFTRDDT, LSF#SLSS 9735
SMMSDRRM, DFFMMR, SM 8309
SMMSDMRD, DLSMFSM, M 10314
SMMSDMRD, MLSMFSM, M 10313
SMMSMDRM, RMSDMRS, S 11100
SMMSF, SRD#RLS, SLMFF 11410
SMMSSFF, STRFM, SMMS 1081
SMMTDDT, DLLFLS, SSS 2252
SMFRDDFLS, DDTLMLS# 561
SMFRDMM, SMFRDMM, RS 7096
SMFRRD, RMF#SSF#S, SLSL 10552
SMFRMD, RMFSLR, SMFS 12516
SMFRSFRDTD, MMRRF#F# 2217
SMFMDDLS, DTDFMR, SM 6449
SMFMDMRRD, LDLSDMR 12197
SMFMDMR#R, SFFFFM, SM 4447
SMFMRD, DMSLS, LTDT 9505
SMFMRD, SDLSFM, SDTL 5936
SMFMRD, MFSSLS, SLTD 1757
SMFMRD, MSDTLS, SLSF 1251
SMFMRDTD, SLTDTDLS, 1963
SMFMRDTLS, MFLTL 9153
SMFMRRMD, SLDTLS, SM 9162
SMFMRMRDSS, SLSLTL 2020
SMFMRSDRTD, RMFSL 6579
SMFMRSRMRD, DDTLSD 10957
SMFMMRR, SRMRRDD, SM 3725
SMFMFSDTL, SLRDTD, S 4829
SMFMSMRDRLDT, LSS 9339
SMFMSSRM, SSDDRDT, D 4001
SMFFLF#SS, DDLTSLS, S 5268
SMFSDDLTDL, SMFSDR, 8961
SMFSDDTL, SLSFSFMR, 8191
SMFSDDTLTDS, FSFMM 2313
SMFSDDTLTD, LLLSST 3029
SMFSDDTT, DRMFMR, R 305
SMFSDDTT, LSDRMMRR, 9325
SMFSDRDTD, SLDLSM 9572
SMFSDRDTD, LDLSMSF 9575
SMFSDRDTL, SLTDLR, M 9236
SMFSDRMR#M, MRDTDRD 9917
SMFSDRMMD, LTDDRDL 10837
SMFSD, RMFSFMR, MFSL 5747
SMFSDRFM, SLSTDFML, 11995
SMFSDFMRDLD, SDRMS 3690
SMFSDFSLTDS, SSLTT 10431
SMFSDS, SMFSLR, RMMD 11887
SMFSDSLTDT, SLTDTL 809
SMFSDLDS, DDDTDRTD, 4617
SMFSDLSFM, MFMRDFM 2632
SMFSDTLDLS, FRMTLS 8129
SMFSDT, LSDFSM, FSDT 8874
SMFSDTLS, MFMFSMFR, 8595
SMFS, DTLS, SMFSMRD, S 10482
SMFSDTLS, LSFMFMRM, 8075
SMFSDTLL, LSF#SMRR, S 1888
SMFSRMDFMR, RMF#SLT 7139
SMFSMRDS, DTDRFMR, S 1979
SMFSMRDL, DSDMDR, RM 1216
SMFSMS, DTLSFM, SLLT 8749
SMFSFDRM, LLSMF#MF#S, 11406
SMFSFMDR, SMFSFMDT 8262
SMFSFFSDTLSM, SFRS 6914
SMFSSDRM, SLSDDT, SM 4597
SMFSSDLS, MRMLSRR, S 1631
SMFSSMFRRD, DMFSFM 227
SMFSSSDDRMFS, SMFS 8619
SMFSSS, DTLLS, SLTDR 8951
SMFSSSSLDDD, SSSDR 6327
SMFSSLDDTD, DLDTSL 8714
SMFSSLMS, FRFMDR 1617
SMFSSLFS, SDDDTLDS, 7714
SMFSSLS, DDDDRM, SMF 2591
SMFSSLSF#S, MMRDRRR 8162
SMFSSLSF#SM, MRTRDT 11664
SMFSSLSS, MRMFSM, SM 8200
SMFSSLLLLLS, SDDT 9720
SMFSSLTDMMR, RMRDR 5376
SMFSSLTD, TDTLSLLS, 7709
SMFSSLTDTLS, DRMFS 1337
SMFSLDTD, RMSSF#S, SD 3918
SMFSLDT, LSLSFM, MRM 2924
SMFSLMFS, LSMFSFM, S 9654
SMFSLS, DDTLLS, SM 1261
SMFSLS, MFRMRDRD, SS 10529
SMFSLSMFSL, SSLTST 5284
SMFSLSMSFMRS, SMFS 10300
SMFSLS, MSFMMR, MMR#M 4471
SMFSLS, FRMSFM, SMFS 7097
SMFSLSFMRD, SMSDLS, 11303
SMFSLSFM, RRMMRDT, T 11437
SMFSLSSFM, SMRMFSM 8027

SMFSLSS, SMFSLSS, SM 3417
SMFSLLL, TLSFM, FLRD 2444
SMFSLTDD, LSDRMRD, S 8265
SMFSLTDS, LFLDTLS, D 5218
SMFSLTDTLSM, FRMFM 8116
SMFSLTDTLS, FMFRMF 12085
SMFSLTDTLS, SDRMLS 10712
SMFSLTDTLLS, SFMRM 7182
SMFSTD, DTDTLS, MFSL 2747
SMFSTLSM, FSRM, SMFS 10433
SMSDDDTLS, FMFSLR, S 3384
SMSDDDTLTD, SMSLSL 12222
SMSDDRD, DFMRDMR, RM 12322
SMSDDRRM, DTDFMRRR, 7394
SMSDDTDFMRRM, SS 12288
SMSDDTRSRFFM, SDMS 1363
SMSDDTLS, SDMRDT, RM 3169
SMSDDTTD, MDMLSS, SR 3793
SMSDRD, DLDRMR, DTLS, 6668
SMSDRD, DLDRMR, SSFM 6668a
SMSDRMM, MSFDFM, MSS 1814
SMSDRM, SLSMDR, RSF#L 639
SMSDMDLD, SMSDTRR, S 3515
SMSDMRDTD, MRSLSF#S, 9511
SMSDMR#MR, DRDLS, SSS 7353
SMSDMMR, DDTLTD, SMS 9350
SMSDMFSLR, SMF#STLS 983
SMSDMFSLR, SFMF#SLT 984
SMSDMFSLS, SRSMF#SR 1692
SMSDML, LSMMRR, RSTT 2773
SMSDFMRD, MFSMFLS, L 3546
SMSDFMR, RMF#SSF#S, SM 4109
SMSDSDRM, RMFSFMRD, 11763
SMSDSLDS, SSSFMMR, S 6697
SMSDSLSS, DTSTLS, SR 1826
SMSDS, LTDDTLS, FRST 6074
SMSDSLTD, RMTDLSFM, 12042
SMSDLDLS, SSSMMMRD 12175
SMSDLSRM, MRF#SLTDF# 9312
SMSDTDRM, SLTDRMFR, 10616
SMSDTL, SMDMF#S, SLDT 2848
SMSDTLS, FMRLSFM, SS 6047
SMSDTLTD, DSMLSMMR, 11494
SMSMDRDLS, SMSDDMR 10859
SMSMDM, MFSDMRD. 3122
SMSMDM, FMRRDRM, SMS 12231
SMSMDLDS, TDRDTLS, F 6696
SMSMRDDRDLS, SSFFL 4478
SMSMRDTL, DSDDMR, SM 6761
SMSMMRR, MTDDRLT, DD 11436
SMSM, MMRD, DDRDRDMD, 8626
SMSMMFMRDR, RRRRMF 10395
SMSMFFFMR, MMFSSLS 1843
SMSMSMRDRMM, SMSMM 10238
SMSMSM, MSFRM, LFFLS 11628
SMSMSFLR, RMFMRDRM, 5655
SMSFMRDSR, MFRLDTR 72
SMSFMRD, SLTDTLT, LS 683
SMSFMRL, DTLSFM, MSF 4485
SMSFMRTLS, DTDFDM, M 3361
SMSFM, MRMFR, DTLSTL 12415
SMSFSSSSSM, RRMFMR 5884
SMSSDRDTLTD, RMRDR 6617
SMSSFMRD, DRMFLTD, S 3892
SMSSFMR, RMDRDTDD, S 491
SMSSFMR, RMDFRMDD, S 490
SMSSFMFL, LTDRTD 9152
SMSSSDMD, DLSMDRM, S 4263
SMSSSMSSS, MSSLSMM 5679
SMSSSMSS, SLDTLS, SM 12110
SMSSLMMFLLTS, SMMM 1919
SMSSLSFM, DDTL, RRDT, 12074
SMSLD, DMDMD, SMSLD, L 8929
SMSLDRD, DTDLSS, SMS 11793
SMSLDRMSLD, RMMSRM 374
SMSLDSFM, SDMFMRDR, 9413
SMSLDS, LDTLS, SLTDR 3603
SMSLDTS, FMDRRM, SFM 11467
SMSLMS, MRMFSMRD, DR 9073
SMSLFRFSMDMSR, SMS 8326
SMSLSDSM, SFSLSTSR, 9640
SMSLSFRM, SDTLLS, SD 10434
SMSLSFMRD, MRDRMFMR, 6892
SMSLSFMRM, SDTLLS, S 10435
SMSLSFM, MRDDTD, SMS 2019
SMSLSFM, MRMRRD, SMS 2018
SMSLSFSM, SDTLTSF#S 9754
SMSLSS, SFMRRD, SMSD 10417
SMSLSLTD, DTRMDTLS, 4548
SMSLLD, SMSLLD, DRMM 10397
SMSTLSDM, RTRFMRM, F 1579
SMLDSFM, RMF#SLLS, SM 5380
SMLDTLSM, DDRMSLS, S 9542
SMLRMFFFSL, LSFSFM 10230
SMLFRSMD, DTLSFRT, M 7393
SMLSDDTD, SDSLF#S, TD 9268
SMLSDDTLTDS, DTLSM 8606
SMLSDFMR, MMFMDMRD, 1459
SMLSDTLSFMRR, SDDT 4100
SMLSMDFM, MRDTDRM, S11538
SMLSMDLS, MMMLS#LT, D 11204
SMLSMRDS, DTLDTLS, S 11095
SMLSMFFRSFM, SLDSD 675

SMLSMFSFMRD, RMRMS 9399
SMLSFDFM, SRMFLSFM, 292
SMLSFMR, MFSFMRD, RM 10602
SMLSFM, MFLSMR, SSSL 1334
SMLSFMFMR, SMLSFMF# 1664
SMLSFM, SDFMRD, MRSF# 2506
SMLSFMSFRM, SMLSFM 3335
SMLSFFRSFM, MRDDFM 4782
SMLSFFM, DTDSFMR, SD 1514
SMLSSMRMSFFM, SMLS 8670
SMLS, SMLSMDR, SMRF, D 11539
SMLSSLDD, SFMLSSMR 2058
SMLS, SLSMMR, SDDMDL 11425
SMLSLTD, DTDSLLS, FF 1735
SMLSLTDS, MFSDTLRT, 838
SMLS, TLSDS, LDLSSLS 4456
SMLTDDT, LDSMFMRD, S 8811
SMLTDDT, LDLSFMRD, S 8813
SMLTDFMRM, MRF#SSDT 1519
SMTDDDDRTD, DRRRRM, 5508
SMTDRDLSMLS, SLLLR 5123
SMTDRT, TDLSSS, SLTD 6966
SMTDMLS, FMSRSD, MLS 5045
SMTDSLSFM, SLTDRDT, 10507
SMTDLDT, RSLFMRM, SM 11212
SMTDLSFM, MRSF#SLTL 5807
SMTRDMFLSS, SDRMRD 10923
SMTRDLSMS, SLRMFLS, 11407
SMTRDLSLS, SLTDDRM 1545
SMTRDTLS, SDDRRM, MM 5415
SFDMRDMSDDTL, SSSL 7408
SFDMRDMSDDT, LSLSF 7407
SFRDRM, SDTLSMSFMF 4853
SFRD, STLSFMFS, SFRD, 7200
SFRMDRRD, FMRRD#R, RM 1330
SFMDDMMR, RMFRRTDS, 6124
SFMDRDLSM, MFSDMSF 10522
SFMDRMRDRS, LTDRMF 610
SFMDRMFR, SSLDRMRD 11085
SFMDRTDS, LTDLSMR, S 10008
SFMDTLL, SMSFM, SFMD 3647
SFMD#RSMRDD, SDTTLS 5770
SFMRDDRMD, RMFRMRD 7485
SFMRDDRMSFM, SMDLS 11505
SFMRDDL, DLSDMDMR, S 1153
SFMRDDLSFM, SDSLLT 9425
SFMRDRD, MFSLSFMMR 7571
SFMRDRMDLS, STTRRF 10587
SFMRDMRD, SSDTDR, ML 3316
SFMRDSDRMRD, SFMRD 326
SFMR, DSDTLS, TDLFMR, 5988
SFMRD, SRRDT, SDTLSM 1587
SFMRDSS#LLR, RMRSRR# 31
SFMRDSLTD, DTLSLSF 10076
SFMRDLDDT, DRMFRSF 9923
SFMRDLS, MRDFMR, RMF 6724
SFMRDLSFMR, MFSLSL 9747
SFMRDTDD, RMFSLSFM, 9272
SFMRDTD, DLTDTLSFM, 739
SFMRDTDR, DSSS#LF#S, S 10124
SFMRDTDR, MLDTRS, SL 1820
SFMRDTDFMRM, MRF#SR 1521
SFMRDTDLRS, DTRSF#S, 11658
SFMRDTLFMDTD, RMFS 1114
SFMRDTL, LLTDTLS, SL 6618
SFMRRD, MRSSF#S, DLTS 2247
SFMRRD, MSLR, SSMRM 5401
SFMRRLLSFFM, MRDDT 1032
SFMRMDRMRDD, MSSMD 191
SFMRMDRMFLRS, SFMF 10797
SFMRMDTL, RSMLSF, RM 6908
SFMRMDTL, SDRM, LRDT 5337
SFMRMRDMS, SLSMMRD 5405
SFMRMFRD, MFSLLR, SL 5499
SFMRMFM, MRSLLS, SLT 9381
SFMRMFSM, SLFRSFM, S 4230
SFMRMSFR, RMFRMSFM, 3147
SFMR, MSSDTLT, DLTSD 7633
SFMRFMRD, DRFMLSF#M, 3034
SFMRFMRDMRDTRDD, F 2545
SFMRFMRD, MLSTDFMR, 8635
SFMRFMRD, TLSLDTD, S 1540
SFMRFM, SFMRRD, TDTD 76
SFMRLSFM, DLSFFMF#S, 11227
SFMRLSFMDTLSLF#S, S 2416
SFMR#MR#MS, MDLTDLSD, 12153
SFMMRDDTRDTL, FMRR 1916
SFMMRDDTLDLS, SDDD 10801
SFMMRDRDLL, SDDDRM 9859
SFMMRDRMMF#S, SLSF#S, 1950
SFMMRDRMM, SFMFMRD 6856
SFMMRD, RMFM, SFMMRD, 10711
SFMMRDRMFFM, RFMLL 10327
SFMMRDRM, FSFMMRR, 1283
SFMMRD, MRTTLS, RRMF 9331
SFMMRDMLS, FMRRRMF 5136
SFMMRDLS, MRDSMR, SF 5797
SFMMR, RRRMRD, MFMMR, 11762
SFMMRRMFFM, MRMSMM 8630
SFMMRR, LSRLSSF#, MF#R# 8351
SFMMR, RLLSFFM, MRDD 1031
SFMMRMMRMRD, DRRSS 1511
SFMMRMSF, FMRRDRM, S 5321
SFMMRLTDRFM, RMRD, T 5859

SFMMMRMF, FTLLTLSS, 8210
SFMMMRMFL, LLSSLSF 9104
SFMMMMRDDD, TLSSDM 12173
SFMMMMRMF, FFFFFLS 11258
SFMMMMRMFSS, MFSSS 10804
SFMMMMMRM, SMRRDRM, 6578
SFMMMMMRMSF, FFMRR 1961
SFMMMMMFSLS, SFMRF 6899
SFMMMMFSLS, FMRRRM 10814
SFMMFMRR, MRDRDTL, D 5920
SFMMFMRSSF#S, SFMMS 171
SFMMFSFMRDRM, SDTD 12268
SFMMFLSFM, SSDDRRM 11933
SFMFRDMR, MRDRMF#SF# 12553
SFMFMRDTDMR, MSFMF 3492
SFMFMMRD, MRDTRDTL 9432
SFMFSMRD, RMFFMLS, S 361
SFMFSMRM, DTDRMRR, S 6067
SFMFSFMFSFS, DRMFS 2834
SFMFSSDSS, LSFSLLR 8967
SFMFSLSFM, FMRMFSF 3745
SFMSDDDT, RLRFFFM, D 9963
SFMSDDRDTLL, STDTD 1929
SFMSDDTDRRRM, FMDD 32
SFMSDRMD, LTDTDLS 875
SFMSDSRTSFM, SSDMR 8875
SFMSDL, FMDFLS, SFMS 10492
SFMSDLS, RMLSSFMR, S 9845
SFMSMD, DRMMMMSMRD 5130
SFMSMRMMRDRM, FFFM 8613
SFMSFLLSFFM, SLTDT 5719
SFMSSFFM, MMMRRSS, S 7489
SFMSSSLS, SLTD, DTLL 10793
SFMSLSF, FMRRSFM, MF 11150
SFMLDTDFMRM, MRF#SS 1520
SFMLS, RFMSFMR, MLSF# 12346
SFMLSFRDRM, MRDFRM 9164
SFMLSFM, SFMRRD, SFM 4133a
SFMLSFM, SFMRMRD, SF 4133
SFMLSLTDD, DLSF#SLT 10662
SFMLLSSD, DTLSMSS, 6663
SFMLTDDT, LTDSFMFM 8812
SFMTLL, LSLSSFM, SSF 33
SFFMDLLS, MSSFRFFM, 11735
SFFMFSLFMMR, MRRDD 6054
SFFMSFFM, MMSDTLSM 9128
SFFFFMDM, MMMSMMDR, 12168
SFFFFMMM, MRDRTDMS, 12404
SFSDRLSLFM, TMF#SLD 12309
SFSMRDLSLDLDRD, SF 11703
SFSLSMRDRM, MRDSFM 9586
SFLMRD, D#D#D#RMF, TDRS 5667
SF#FMRD, MSSLLS, FMMR# 11021
SF#FMRDTL#L, LLS#SFMR 1171
SF#FMSD, DTLS, STLLSD, 11451
SF#FMSLSF#SM, FFMRFS 8160
SF#FFMFSF, SFMMR#MLS, 4414
SF#SDSMFS, MRRMFSM, S 10145
SF#SDSMSFRFM, LTTDS 8135
SF#SDSTL, LSLFLS, SF#S 12524
SF#SRTLTDSS, SF#SRTL 8545
SF#SMDTDL, SSLSMMMR 8134
SF#SMDTLS, FMFRSFM, S 11980
SF#SMDTLS, SRMFMRLS, 10165
SF#SMRDTLS, DTDR, RDR 5580
SF#SMR#MDTLS, LTDSMD 160
SF#SMMRDTL, SLTDTTL 8107
SF#SMMR#MD, RMRTDRM, S 1100
SF#SMMSFDRMR, FMFRS 10831
SF#SMFSLTD, DLSS, SF#S 11241
SF#SF#SF#SM, LSFMR, FMF 5217
SF#SLRFTD, SF#STLSFM 96
SF#SLFM, SF#STRD, SF#SL 5666
SF#SLF, FSLSM, MR#MSMS 12392
SF#SLSDMM, RDFLDTLS, 3788
SF#SLSMDLS, SSSLDTD 8146
SF#SLSMR#MFM, MRLDTD 1412
SF#SLS, MR#MFM, LSF#SMM 11404
SF#SLSMSFMR, FMFRMF 1728
SF#SLSSMRDDT, RTDRM 4753
SF#SLSSM, RD#RFLLS, DT 798
SF#SLSSMSDRM, LS#LTD 11790
SF#SLSSFF, FMFSFFMM, 12475
SF#SLSTDRRD, DTDRMR 10604
SF#STLSFMFM, MR#MFST 11112
SF#LSDM, MFMRL, TLSDR 8142
SF#LSDTDRFFM, DLRDT 747

SSD

SSDDDD, DDMMDSR, R#T, S 329
SSDDDDDMDDT, DTLSF 437
SSDDDDDMRDLS, SSDD 11490
SSDDDD, DMMRD, LSDDD 11166
SSDDDDD, SSRRRRR, SS 7189
SSDDDDD, TDRRRRR, FF 12468
SSDDDDDTTD, DDMMDD 11003
SSDDDDDTT, SSRRRRM, 12062

SSDDDDRDTT, TDTLLL 2464
SSDDDDRMRTD, DRMRD 4407
SSDDDDRMMRDR, SSRR 11929
SSDDDDRMMM, MRDRDL 12172
SSDDDDRMMM, MMRRRM 6045
SSDDDDRMSS, SFMRDR 6521
SSDDDDMDS, SSLLDTL 10842
SSDDDDMRDLDS, SSDD 7953
SSDDDDTDSM, DRFFMR 4598
SSDDDDTRR, RRDMMDR, 5096
SSDDDDTLSF#LS, SSTL 5074
SSDDDRMMR, RMFFFMR 6921
SSDDDRMMRMD, RMRRR 5443
SSDDDRMSSLLLTD, LL 10047
SSDDDRSFMD, SLLSFM 8840
SSDDDMDSLDS, DRMSS 5052
SSDDDMRDTL, LRSTRS 6140
SSDDDMMR, DRMDMRD, S 3129
SSDDDMSMMR, FFMFRD 4502
SSDDDSDRMMM, FMRMR 6593
SSDDDTDRL, LLTTTTL 3095
SSDDDTSSFFFFM, SSL 908
SSDDDTLSLFM, SLTDR 4222
SSDDDTLSLS, MMSSFM 9667
SSDDDTLLS, SSDDDTD 11904
SSDDDTLTDS, LTDRMS 2175
SSDDDTLT, SSRRRDTD, 4464
SSDDDTTTLTD, DRMMM 6175
SSDDRDRMD, FFMDR, SS 1964
SSDDRDRMFF, MRDMRL 193
SSDDRDRMS, SLSMMRD 9930
SSDDRDRM, LDLSDMRT 9120
SSDDRDT, DRD#RR#M, SSD 9836
SSDDRDT, DRD#RMD, SSM 5297
SSDDRDT, LLRRFTD, MM 7545
SSDDRDTT, DRDRRM, SS 4234
SSDDRDTT, FFRSFM, SS 11682
SSDDRRM, DDFMRDRMR, 4374
SSDDRRM, DDFMRDMR, S 4374a
SSDDRRMD, MMSSFMR, L 7535
SSDDRRMD, SSLFRSM, 10469
SSDDRRM, DTLSLSFM, S 10474
SSDDRR, MRDTTL, RRRL 11976
SSDDRRM, RMRDTLS, SS 4086
SSDDRRM, RMRDTLS, SS 4113
SSDDRRMM, DDFMRDMR 4374b
SSDDRRMFS, SMMRFRD 446
SSDDRRM, SSFMRRMR, S 6393
SSDDRMDR, MDMRDLD, L 9980
SSDDRMD, SSLDFM, DRM 7240
SSDDRMR, DLDDLS, SSS 10853
SSDDRM, MMMFMR, TSTR 12232
SSDDRMFMRDT, SSLMF 508
SSDDRMFM, SMFRSRMR 6114
SSDDRMFM, SSSFMRDT 11573
SSDDRMFS, LSMDTDRM 7309
SSDDRFMM, DDMMLLSS, 3123
SSDDRFMM, DMRRTRDD, 8781
SSDDRTD, MMFMR, SSMD 4528
SSDDRTDS, DRMFMRDD 4323
SSDDMDRD, MRDTLLS, S 5752
SSDDMDRR, FLSMFRD, S 2310
SSDDMRDRDL, LLSSDR 5027
SSDDMRDR, MMSDTDRD, 4821
SSDDMRDL, LLSDMMR, S 1140
SSDDMRDT, LTDMSFMM 3311
SSDDMMR, MFRLTD, MRR 3486
SSDDMMMMRD, SLDSLL 7080
SSDDMFSLDT, LSMDRR, 12216
SSDDMS, DFMMRD, DSSD 8080
SSDDMSLS, MFLDLS, MM 7478
SSDDFMRD, DRMMMRDR, 3124
SSDDLSSD, DRMSMDR, S 12136
SSDD, TDRRMFSFMRD, S 11755
SSDDTDFMRRM, SSSSM 12289
SSDDTDLSFFM, SSSLS 2183
SSDDTRDTLSDS, DRMR 2839
SSDDT, SRMRD, MSSSFM 10258
SSDDT, SRFFM, SMDR, SS 3662
SSDDTSSRRD, SLLFMR, 3599
SSDD, TLSDD, SLLFLLS, 12349
SSDDTLSDRM, SSFFMRD 586
SSDDTLS, MMSDDRD, SS 8790
SSDDTLS, SSLLSF#S, SS 1948
SSDDTLTLS, SSDDDTD 1818
SSDDTLTT, SSRRDTRD, 12149
SSDDTTDS, SLTDDRD, D 7158
SSDDTT, SSRRDD, DRLD 1052
SSDDTTLFTLS, SDRMD 11465
SSDDTTLL, LRSSFFMM, 12395
SSDDTTLL, LSSLSS, SS 4208
SSDRDDT, LSSLFM, SSD 6989
SSDRDRM, LTDRD, SDDD 1218
SSDRDTD, RMRDTLS, FF 8279
SSDRDTDMRDT, DLTDD 9358
SSDRM, DDRDLS, SSDMS 7735
SSDRMDRDRM, MFMRMD 6418
SSDRMDRR, MRDRDTD, S 4294
SSDRMDLS#LTL, RRTDR 11323
SSDRMRDRMRD, SSDRM 12203
SSDRMRDSS, RMFFFFM, 6300
SSDRMRDL, TDRMFMR, S 2847
SSDRMRL, DTLTSD, SMR 3000
SSDRMMRR, RTDMRD, M 1369
SSDRMMMRDDT, SSLTD 8400
SSDRMMFDRM, MMRLTD 9768

SSDRMMSFDRM, MMFLT 10959
SSDRMMLL, LLRMFFTT, 5327
SSDRMFMRS, DRMSDRD, 4303
SSDRMFFSSS, SLL#L, SF 11569
SSDRMFS, MSFMDRD, MR 4806
SSDRMFSLMSM, SSDRM 11118
SSDRMF#S, SSSMLMSR, S 8488
SSDRMS, MMRDL, SSDRM 3573
SSDRMSFMR, MF#SDTSL, 11536
SSDRMSS, FMRDRDTL, S 9130
SSDRMSLSMR, MFMRMR 4748
SSDRSM, RDDRDT, TLSS 6789
SSDRS, SSDRMF, MFSDL 10197
SSDRLSFM, SMSLDT, DS 9394
SSDRTD, DMSFMR, TDMR 2831
SSDMDDLS, DTDRDDT, S 12335
SSDMDDLS, SSDMDR 3103
SSDMDDLSSS, DSFMSD 6075
SSDMDRDDLS, SSDRMF 1157
SSDMDRDL, LSDMDMRR, 3821
SSDMDRMRMR, SSDMDM 9739
SSDMDRTD, DDMSMFRM, 517
SSDMDRTDTS, MFSMDD 2148
SSDMDMMRLTDS, SSDM 5017
SSDMDSSLS, SFFMDR, T 3424
SSDMDLDS, DRSSDRM, M 8140
SSDMDLDS, SDDDDMDR, 42
SSDMDLTD, RRDTLSFM, 9191
SSDMDTLDLLS, SSLSM 3291
SSDMRDDT, SSTFMRMD, 8230
SSDMRDDTLS, FMDLSF# 7816
SSDMRDDTT, TDRFMRR 2465
SSDMRDMSF, MMRLDRD, 5806
SSDMRDSD, RDRM, RDDL 5795
SSDMRDLD, SSDLSSMR, 11868
SSDMRDLS, SSDMDR, FM 3101
SSDMRDTDRMFFM, MMR 9197
SSDMRDTDLS, DDTR, FL 7914
SSDMRMFM, MFSLSMDM 2385
SSDMRMFS, MRDRSLDT, 4881
SSDMRMSDFMR, SLSFM 6559
SSDMRLLS, SFMSF#MR#M, 8939
SSDMMDDDLL, LSDMFM 11282
SSDMMDLS, DRRDRM, MS 9883
SSDMMRD, MMLSFMR, MM 1851
SSDMMRDS, SDMSSDMR 4721
SSDMMRDL, RDLSDMDR, 4690
SSDMMRFRDTD, SLLDT 12246
SSDMMRFM, MRFMRDTD 11177
SSDMMFMRR, SSTRFFF 5856
SSDMMSMRFTD, SSDMM 4004
SSDMFMRR, SSTRMD, SS 9715
SSDMFMMRMFSFM, DDT 766
SSDMSDDTLTD, DDTLS 124
SSDMSMSFRSM, SLFLS 8424
SSDMSSFR, FMDTDR, SS 3172
SSDMSSTT, STRFLLSS, S 4476
SSDMSLSSM, MFMMRLS 11339
SSDFMR, DDTLS, LLTDR 5833
SSDFMRRD, SLRRMR, SS 6654
SSDFMMRD, TLDFLS, SS 8074
SSDFFM, RRSDDT, TDDR 8957
SSDSDRMD, FMRDTLS, S 6813
SSDSDRMRD, MFSSFMR, 5864
SSDSDRM, SSSMDR, SSD 9649
SSDSDMRR, SSSDMRD, S 4391
SSDSDMSDMSDMSDM, D 10689
SSDSMMRD, DRMFLTRD, 10362
SSDSMMSM, DRRM, SSDS 3853
SSDSMMSM, MMRMFMR, S 5316
SSDSMFMR, RMRTDRDT, 10337
SSDSMFFR, RDRMDSMM 1280
SSDSMFSRFM, SMRDTS 2106
SSDSMFSM, SDTTLLS, M 8624
SSDSMFS, SSLLLLS, SS 7188
SSDSMFSLLS, SDTSTR 8669
SSDSMFLS, DRMFLSFM 10308
SSDSMLSS, SDTTLTD, S 6604
SSDSFMRD, SFMMRDS, 1078
SSDSFML, RRSFMRM, SS 486
SSDSSMFFF, FFTLSFM 1166
SSDSSFFM, RMFSMRDR, 1738
SSDSSFFM, LLSMRDR, S 6548
SSDSLDR, MRDMRLTS, S 6215
SSDSLSSM, SSFRSFM, S 1073
SSDSLLS, MRDTLLS, SS 4793
SSDSTLS, RRDLSF#S, TT 1146
SSDSTLS, MFSLSFMR, S 4286
SSDLDS, MMMFDRM, SSS 6736
SSDLRDTD, MRMRDTDR 6947
SSDLSDMRRD, RMSMRD 5745
SSDLSMFRD, D#RMFSMR, 3078
SSDLSM, FMRDR, MMFLS 4266
SSDLSMFSDLTLS, SSR 5119
SSDLSFSM, MSDTLS, SM 5453
SSDLSSMRD, SDDMSLS 4621
SSDLLD, RRDLDLS, LLS 3346
SSDLTDS, SLLSFM, MFS 7783
SSDTDRMRMFSMD, MFS 10716
SSDTDRM, MMSMRDR, MM 2104
SSDTDRMFRM, SFMRMR 10494
SSDTDRMSFMR, TRDLR 1482
SSDTDRLR, DTDRD#RMD, 969
SSDTDRTD, MRTDLSF#S, 434
SSDTDMMRLDTLS, SLT 12239
SSDTDFRM, MMTLTSSS 161

SSDTDSLS, SSSSDRMR 11817
SSDTRDTD, TDRR#MFT, S 9851
SSDTRDTLS, LSMMRD 689
SSDT, RFLS, DMFSLSMR, 4482
SSDTFFLS, SSDTTLS, D 7979
SSDTSRFM, DTLRSLS, S 10439
SSDTSLT, RDTDTLS, SS 9703
SSDTLDDS, MMRDTLS, S 9431
SSDTLDS, DRMDRMR, MR 12389
SSDTLRDDTLTDS, MMR 9280
SSDTLSRDT, SSRTLST 3370
SSDTLSMDRM, MRSLT 670
SSDTLSMM, RDDMRDLS, 11193
SSDTLSFMRMRDS, SSL 3829
SSDTLSFM, MRDFRMMR, 11961
SSDTLSFMMRFL, TDTR 11906
SSDTLSFM, MMRSSF#S, S 11447
SSDTLSFM, MMSDMRMD, 8178
SSDTLSFM, SDLRSLTL 2533
SSDTLSFSFM, MF#SDTL 5451
SSDTLSFSFM, MSDTLS 5452
SSDTLSSFM, LDMRDTL 2317
SSDTLS, SSMFMR, SSDT 3072
SSDTLS, SSFFM, SLTDD 5685
SSDTLS, SSLSFM, MFSS 11430
SSDTLS, SLLLLL, LRTL 2772
SSDTLSTLS, SSFMRDM 4409
SSDTLTDS, DRMDFMR, S 806
SSDTLTDS, SLSLLTM, S 309
SSDTLT, SSRDTD, SMRD 4457
SSDTTTLTD, SLTDRDT 10969
SSRDR, MRDDLS, DRMRM 10849
SSRDMFLS, RMSDTLF#R, 9722
SSRDTLSDM, SSRDTLS 4653
SSRDTLSFMD, DDRDMR 10739
SSRRDRMRD, SSRRDRM, 11273
SSRRRD#RMDM, SSRRRD 5210
SSRRMRDM, MRRMRR, SS 1561
SSRRMRDS, SSLDTDR, S 11096
SSRRMR, SSMMFM, SDDM 510
SSRRSSMM, MMRSF#S, MF 7381
SSRFMRDTMRRD, TLMM 6012
SSRFMM, LLMSFF, SLTD 3235
SSRSSRFFMM, SSRSSR 12473

SSM

SSMDDDRMFM, MMRDTL 10768
SSMDDRMSF, FMRDMDR 8859
SSMDDRFM, SSMSDTLM 10946
SSMDDSMMRMD, DDTLS 224
SSM, DDS, MFFFFSFMMF 38
SSMDDSMSFRM, SSMDD 8257
SSMDDS, MSSSS, SLDDD 892
SSMDDLDD, DMDSMR, SS 4480
SSMDDL, SSDDRMMR, SS 11869
SSMDDL, LSSDTLS, SSM 5208
SSMDDTLS, MFSMFR, MM 3314
SSMDDTLSFM, MRMFRS 8544
SSMDDTLLSFM, MMLTD 7117
SSMDRDRMDS, SSMDRD 9769
SSMDRDLLS, SDDDMRD 6656
SSMDRMRD, RMSSF#S, RM 4000
SSMDRMR, SSMDRMR, SM 4804
SSMDRMFMR, SSMDRMF 445
SSMDRMFS, SSDMDRD, S 4028
SSMDRMFLS, SDTLSMR 2168
SSMDRM, SDSLFM, SFMR, 1937
SSMDRM, SFMRRD, SSLF 789
SSMDRM, SLDTLS, SMSD 3863
SSMDRML, SDFMDMR, MD 6478
SSMDRSRMRD, MSMFRD 1805
SSMDMDDTL, LLSF#FMR 6317
SSMDMSSLLS, SSFSDF 5518
SSMDFLS, SSMDFLS, DS 8896
SSMDSMFMRFLS, SSMD 11794
SSMDSMSLFRM, SDDMR 2729
SSMDSSSFRS, SSMDDT 3611
SSMDSSSSMDMRRRMF 938
SSMDSLLL, LLRRMR, RM 11986
SSMDLDSD, RMRDRMR, S 948
SSMDLSMS, SDDMDR, RM 618
SSMDTDMRTS, SLSTRF 6972
SSMDTDMRTS, LSTRFT 6973
SSMDTRRD, DTTLDLS, S 6480
SSMDTLMRDT, RTSMRD 10994
SSMDTLS, MFRMFLSSM, 9020
SSMDTTLL, LRRSFM, SS 6487
SSMRDDRMFM, SDRMSF 6079
SSMRDDMSTLMS, SLFM 2507
SSMRDDLF#S, SLLLTDR, 4971
SSMRDDT, DRD#RR#M, DDS 4863
SSMRDDT, LSFMRRD, TL 10830
SSMRDD#RFMR, RSFMRD 10345
SSMRDRDT, DDLSFMR, S 3995
SSMRDRDT, TDFMMRM, M 2133
SSMRDRFFM, DMSLLS, S 12382
SSMRDMFSLLS, LSRMF# 6863
SSMRDS, DDRSM, SSM 10078
SSMRDS, DFSDL, LSFS 10079
SSMRDSS, DDLFLD, TLS 11420
SSMRDSSMFS, DTLFST 5070
SSMRDSSFMMR, SDRML 7045
SSMRDSLS, DRMFRDD, S 6051
SSMRDS, LLDDS, S#S#LDM 559
SSMRDSLLS, LTDSLSF 10068

SSMRDLLS, SSSLDTLS, 6744
SSMRDTD, SSSSLTDT, S 3368
SSMRDTRDLS, SLRDTD, 8954
SSMRDTL, SSDTDR, SSM 12544
SSMRRDLSMS, SSRDTF 7021
SSMRRDLS, SSTLSLSF# 1155
SSMRRDLLSS, SSFRMR 7687
SSMRMRD, D#RMFLS, FMM 9270
SSMRMFMMRD, SSDDDD 11915
SSMRLT, SDDDDLS, FMD 3985
SSMRTDS, SLDFLS, DDT 6950
SSMRTFFF, LSMRTDRM 12416
SSMMDDSLTLSLTLS, S 7336
SSMMDDL, LSMMDR, SSM 7018
SSMMDRDLS, SDDMDR, S 10970
SSMMDRDTT, SSFFRMR 438
SSMMDR, SLF#S, SSMMSL, 11322
SSMMDLFF, LSMMDR, SS 12510
SSMMRD, SSFFMR, RMSS 5930
SSMMRDS, SLDDTD, SSM 1633
SSMMRDLL, DSDDRMR, S 7425
SSMMRDTF, MRDDRR#M, M 4654
SSMMRRD, DDDTTL, MMR 2396
SSMMRRD, DDFFMR, RRL 1437
SSMMRRDD, LLDDLLS, S 6030
SSMMRRD, LLFFMR, DTS 6270
SSMMRMDS, SSMMRMD, L 7151
SSMMRMFLS, SDRMRMF 12414
SSMMRM, SSMMRD, SLLD 6411
SSMMMDDDTDMMR, RMF 545
SSMMMDDRDLS, SSDMS 9063
SSMMMD, DRSRMFM, SSM 8141
SSMMMDDTRFFM, SSDT 546
SSMMMRDDT, LSSDRDT, 8645
SSMMMRDRMFL, TLSFF 10205
SSMMMRDLRR, TTTTTLS 7960
SSMMMSFR, FMSDLS, SS 3960
SSMMFMRR, DTLSLSD, S 3512
SSMMSSRR, MFSLTS, SS 6785
SSMMSSFF, FFMRMFM, S 7383
SSMFRDDFMRM, MRF#SL 5835
SSMFMRRD, SSMF#SLLS, 376
SSMFSDDTLS, SSFMRF 3006
SSMFSDDT, LLSDRMRD. 6710
SSMFSDDTLLS, SSTDR 26
SSMFSDDTT, LSLFSM, S 2530
SSMFSDRDTD, SLDLSM 9574
SSMFSDRM, RDDDRDLD 5303
SSMFSDMDRD, MFFFFS 37
SSMFSDTLS, SSMFSDT 3229
SSMFSDTTLS, SSRMFF 11778
SSMFSRM, RRDRMTD, 12047
SSMFSMDR, FMRMFLS, M 6400
SSMFSM, DTDR, MSDRMF 4231
SSMFSMRDDD, TLSSLS 3414
SSMFSMRDDLSM, RMFS 12313
SSMFSMRDR, TDDRMFM 10545
SSMFSMM, DDMRTD, SSM 9110
SSMFSSDS, SLSMDR, SS 10848
SSMFSSM, MSSMFSSM, M 11374
SSMFSSM, SSMFSSM, MM 11373
SSMFSSSLDLS, SSMFS 10980
SSMFSLMSF#F, FFRMFT 10897
SSMFSLFMRD, RMRTSL 872
SSMFSLS, DTLTLS, SLL 1418
SSMFSLSM, SLLTTD, MR 7652
SSMFSLSM, LLLDDLS, S 9741
SSMFSLSF, FFRMFSFM, 7920
SSMFSLSSS, LMF#SRDT 11581
SSMFSLS, SLDTLSFM, D 10026
SSMFSLLSD, DRRRRDR 7491
SSMFSL, LSDMRD, DTLT 515
SSMFSLLS, SDTLMF#S, S 4162
SSMFSLL, LLF#SLTT, DD 2795
SSMFSLTDTLS, SSFMR 10393
SSMFLSM, DDFSLR, SSM 5941
SSMFLSMRDTLS, FMSD 9396
SSMFLSM, SDDRRMSDT 73
SSMFL, SSMMR, SSMFL, S 1945
SSMFLS, SSFRM, DDTDR 9446
SSMSDDRMDRM, MRRRS 10351
SSMSDDSD, MRDMRD, SS 7041
SSMSDDLD, TLSMFRM, L 11551
SSMSDDLS, MLSMDMR, S 3586
SSMSDRD, LSDSSFM, SS 8331
SSMSDRMDDTTTDRD, S 4934
SSMSDMDDT, LSMSDR, S 11985
SSMSDSMSFSFR, FFRF 7456
SSMSDSMSSFFM, SSMS 1354
SSMSRMDL, LDSDTDR, S 11158
SSMSMDSD, RMRSMRDR, 7596
SSMSMDLS, DDMS, SSMS 6257
SSMSMSLSF, FFRFRFS 11285
SSMSFRFMF, MR, RMFSL 575
SSMSSDDTLS, SFMRMF 10392a
SSMSSDDTLS, SSFMRM 10392
SSMSSDRM, MRDMRDL, D 6804
SSMSSMSDMRDTLSL, T 11066
SSMSSMSFRFM, MMFLS 4838
SSMSSMSFRFM, SSMSS 10713
SSMSSFMF, FFMRLSFM, 7802
SSMSSFFFF, FTLTDSS 11768
SSMSLDRMRDDLS, SSM 10085
SSMSLR, FFRFSM, SSMM, 439
SSMSLF, LSDRMR, RMMF 5016
SSMSLS, FFTLLS, DSMD 3874

SSMSLSSM, DRMDMMR, D 10204
SSMSLSLDD, RMRRDLS, 781
SSMSLLDTLS, SSSDSM 8609
SSMSL, LSSSDRRM, FMM 7492
SSMLMSFM, DRMFLS, DT 430
SSMLFSSMLFSMSRMD, 5900
SSMLS, MMMRFM, SDTLT 5377
SSMLSSRR, MFSLTDSS, 8799
SSMLSSFMSR, RMDFRS 10220
SSMLSSFF, MMRDRM, SL 9910
SSMLSLTD, RMDTLS, RT 9475
SSFRMDS, DMRMFRS, SS 6674
SSFMDDSS, SLSFMR, SS 7208
SSFMDDT, DTLSLLS, SS 9583
SSFMDDTL, LSLSMR, SS 7963
SSFMDRMD, DFFDRM, SS 6084
SSFMDRMF, FFFFLSFM, 6202
SSFM, DLTDLS, MFMR, SM 3534
SSFMDTLS, LSMFRRM, M 6134
SSFMDTLL, LSMSFM, SS 3646
SSFMRD, DTLSLSFM, FF 7120
SSFMRDRD, RRMF#SSF#S, 7170
SSFMRDRMR, SSFMRDR 9728
SSFMRD, RMMFMR, SSFM 12555
SSFMRDS, SLDRDS, SSF 509
SSFMRDS, TDRMFR, SSF 6926
SSFMRDS, TDRMFSS, SS 6925
SSFMRDLS, SDTLSSF#S, 6867
SSFMRDTDFMR, FMLF#F# 5959
SSFMRDTD, SDTLSMDR 1003
SSFMRDT, SSFMRDT, DR 9842
SSFMRDTLFMR, MSF#MF# 7701
SSFMRRD, RRMRMLF#S, D 3557
SSFMRRD, LLLSFM, DTL 3480
SSFMRMRDRR, MFMLSF 8438
SSFMRMRD, TDRMFS, SL 11392
SSFMRMLSL, TDMSFM, R 8777
SSFMRFM, SLTDTLLS, R 1628
SSFMRLLSFM, SDTMF#S 11618
SSFMRTSL, TDLLS#LTS 4048
SSFMMRDDL, DSSDMMS 7961
SSFMMRDDTLS, SSLSS 7169
SSFMMRDDTLS, SLTDF 5475
SSFMMRDDTLTD, DFML 7879
SSFMMRDMR, SSFMMRD 1008
SSFMMRDLLLS, SSFMM 4454
SSFMMRRD, SLTDSLLS, 11671
SSFMMRMFLSFM, SDTL 1176
SSFMMR, FFMRM, SSLTD 3475
SSFMMMRD, DFFFMRM, M 9118
SSFMMMRD, DTLDFLS, S 5925
SSFMMMRD, MFMRDR, SD 5513
SSFMMMRD, MFSLLSMR, 5852
SSFMMMRD, SLTDTLS, L 9882
SSFMMMRMSF, FFMRRL 8525a
SSFMMMMRD, SLTDFMR, 793
SSFMMMMRMSF, FFMRR 8525
SSFMMMMRMSF, STRSS 4341
SSFMMMFSLSFR, RRDT 7881
SSFMFR, LSFMRM, DTRD 9564
SSFMFMRD, DFMSFTDR, 10042
SSFMFMRD, LSFRMFR, S 9310
SSFMFMRMRDR, SDDRM 12103
SSFMFMMFSDTTLL, LM 7968
SSFMFSD, DTLTD, SSFM 2754
SSFMFS, DTDFMR, SSFM 8085
SSFMFSMR, MFFLFM, SF# 4773
SSFMFSMM, MMMTDLR, S 4530
SSFMFS, LSFMRMFM, SS 1828
SSFMFSLS, LSFMRD, SS 6750
SSFMSDDRTD, MRRMRD 11833
SSFMSDRM, SLTDTLLS, 2135
SSFMSDTL, LSMDDR, DR 6887
SSFMSMTRD, DLSDLSF 7405
SSFMSFMRMFS, SSFMDR 3089
SSFMSFMR, FMDLRDT, S 9517
SSFMSSLSFMMRMMF#F# 8281
SSFMSLSDMFSFM, DTL 4099
SSFMSLSFMR, SSFMSL 154
SSFMSLTD, DDTLDTLS, 7870
SSFMLSMFMRDS, SDDR 1932
SSFMLSFM, DTLSFM, SS 5060
SSFMLSFMRFM, MMMLL 6967
SSFFMRDRM, DRMMFSF# 11905
SSFFMMDRMRDD, SSFF 5569
SSFFMMRD, DRMFLS, FM 6422
SSFFMSSDDRDDT, TDT 662
SSFSDLLSFSD, RRRMF 11296
SSFSMR, MSSLS, DDTLS 3642
SSFLFFM, MMRLFLS, SD 8209
SSF#MRTSL, TDLLS#LTS 4047
SSF#FTLTD, SSLTLSTD, 12310
SSF#SDRDDT, LSTDRMF 5472
SSF#SDMMR#MFM, MRD#RL 10918
SSF#SDLS, DDTDRRR, SS 6242
SSF#SRSSR#DSR#R#FSR#D, 5786
SSF#SMDRFMRRD, DSFM 9624
SSF#SMRDDDTT, SSSLT 8243
SSF#SMRDDTLS, SSFMF 10780
SSF#SMRDMFM, SLSMDM 1088
SSF#SMRDL, DSDDMMRR 3820
SSF#SMRDLD, LSDDDRM 1942
SSF#SMFFF, FMR#MDRRR 200
SSF#SLMSFR, RMFSTLS 10851

SSF#SLFM, MMMRTSRD, S 3405
SSF#SLSDSM, SMRMFML 9777
SSF#SLSMFM, SSF#SLSM 1984
SSF#SLSMSF#F, LLS#LTL 6347
SSF#SLSF#SM, DDTDRDL 11770
SSF#SLSSSDRM, MRTSR, 3394
SSF#SLTDRM, MRMFMRD 2364
SSF#LSMRDLD, LSSDRM 5157
SSF#TLSM, DTLSF, MRMT 8935

SSSD

SSSDDDDR, RRRMFSMR, 10279
SSSDDDDL, LTTTDRM, S 5154
SSSDDD, RRRDRM, SSSD 2452
SSSDDDRMRD, MMMRTS 837
SSSDDDRM, MMMMMMF#S, 1181
SSSDDD, MFFS, LTDRMM 2349
SSSDDRRRRM, DTLS, SL 11496
SSSDDRMD, SLFDLS, SS 533
SSSDDRMM, MFMDRRD, S 10681
SSSDDRMFM, RRRMF#SL 516
SSSDDMD, DRMFMRD, MS 3649
SSSDDMRD, MDMSMDMR, 1690
SSSDDLS, SSSMMRR, TD 9365
SSSDDLLL, LLLRDDT, S 8365
SSSDDTDRDDT, SSSRR 10592
SSSDDTDRMRD, MMMFM 8384
SSSDRRRM, MRMS, FMMF 11584
SSSDRRMS, SSLSDMR, M 3816
SSSDRMD, LSDRTD, DRR 10352
SSSDRMMRRD, MMFSSD 10211
SSSDRM, MRMFRT, SLTD 2641
SSSDRMFRD, MF#F#SMDD 5548
SSSDRMFMRMM, SMMMS 378
SSSDRM, SFMMRD, MSSD 8794
SSSDMRDS, DTLTDRSM 6481
SSSDMRDLDDT, SLLLR 6178
SSSDMRDT, DRMDLRRS, 9453
SSSDMRRM, LDLSDMRD 12003
SSSDMRLTD, DDDDDDT 7125
SSSDMFSLSM, FFFMRM 4519
SSSDMFLS, DRFMRM, SM 3917
SSSDFMRS, SDLRSLTL 10774
SSSDFMMRD, RRMDSFM, 7011
SSSDF, FFMRDSFM, MMM 8594
SSSDSMRD, MDMSMDMR, 1689
SSSDSMFS, SLDTDRLT, 8538
SSSDSFMR, FFFTLSFM, 9095
SSSDSSMR, FFFRTLTD, 8969
SSSDSSFMRM, SSSDRM 8644
SSSDSSFM, MRMFFS, SS 448
SSSDSSS, DMFSLTL, RL 1065
SSSDSS, LSFMRFMLLS 11327
SSSDSLMFSRM, SDDDR 12428
SSSDSLSS, DRMFMRM, S 862
SSSDSLLS, SDRMDRDT 8435
SSSDSLLLS, SSSLDTT 664
SSSDSL, LLLRLT, SSSD 10160
SSSDSTLS, MDRMDTLS, 5943
SSSDSTLL, FFMFLSM, S 8303
SSSDLLS, SRD#RR#M, DDD 2253
SSSDTDRD, RMFMR, DRM 8138
SSSDTDRSD, DLTDMRD 10035
SSSDTDR, SSRRDRM, MR 1069
SSSDTRDD, DDFMRSM, M 4720
SSSDTLSM, FFFLSFM, M 12189
SSSDTLSM, FSLSMDRR 126
SSSDTLSMS, MFRRMFM 2807
SSSDTLS, FFFSSM, SSS 4020
SSSDTLSSM, SLTDRDD 7835
SSSDTLSLSM, SSFFFM 4724
SSSDTLLS, LFSMDTLS, 6646
SSSDTLLLR, TTDRMMR 10116
SSSRRRMFM, MMMRRLT 928
SSSMDDDS, DDMRDMR, R 8250a
SSSMDDDS, DRMRDMR, R 8250
SSSMDDDSMR, RMFMRM 3818
SSSMDDDS, SSLLLLS, S 8148
SSSMDDTLDS, RRRRRR 11011
SSSMDDT, LLSDTLS, SS 6671
SSSMDS, DTLFM, SSMSD 10843
SSSMDSLS, DDRRDTD, S 10075
SSSMDLD, SSSMRRR, SS 9755
SSSMDTLS, SLLTRR, SS 7300
SSSMDTLS, SLTDDLFM 2410
SSSMDTTL, FFFRTLS, S 911
SSSMRD, DRRDRM, MFFF 7321
SSSMRDLS, SSSDTDR, R 6889
SSSMRDLS, SSSFMRDR, 10688
SSSMRDLLD, LSSDTDR, 6890
SSSMRDTDLS, SSMLSF 6307
SSSMRDTLSLTD, SDDD 1915
SSSMRDT, TTDRTMRD, D 12519
SSSMRMDS, SSFLSFFM, 3203
SSSMR, TLTRTLS, SSSM 3794
SSSMMRDSLTT, SSSFF 1824
SSSM, MRDL, DLSSSDRM 6345
SSSMMRDLS, SDDMMR, S 5299
SSSMMMFFR, FFFRRRS 12093
SSSMMFSLS, SSSRFMR 7490
SSSMFRM, FSLTDSSFF 8128
SSSMFMMR, SSSMFMMR 9668
SSSMFS, DDDTLS, SSSR 7328
SSSMFSMR, SLTDTLSF 7172
SSSMFSM, SSLLSMR, FF 11276

SSSMFSM, SSLLSMR, FF 11276
SSSMFSSSLFLS, SSSF 7327
SSSMFSLS, SDTDTLS, S 1837
SSSMFSLLLD, MMDRMD, 5411
SSSMFSLLLS, MFRRMF 4725
SSSMFSL, LLLRMFS, FM 1221
SSSMFLS, DDTLSF#S, SS 7059
SSSMSDDD, RRRDMMM, S 7894
SSSMSDDTT, DRSSLTD, 2083
SSSMSDMR, DLSSDRR, R 4587
SSSMSDMR#M, RDDRDLS, 7352
SS, SMSSF#FMFSM, MLMM 10409
SSSM, SSSLLFL, LLLSM 7913
SSSMSLD, LLLSLTD, MM 1435
SSSMSLD, LLLSLTD, MF 1436
SSSMSLDT, LSSFSM, SS 5047
SSSMSLLS, SMSFMRD, S 11780
SSSMLSF, FFFRSFM, SS 7429
SSSMLSSM, MFSLDTLS, 8878
SSSMLSS, FRRLSS, SSS 8575
SSSMLLSM, DRMSFMRM, 3744
SSSFMDLSM, FFFMRSF 8687
SSSFMRD, DTLSMDR, RR 7539
SSSFMRDRML, SDDMMS, 7972
SSSFMRDM, SDDT, DTLS 6788
SSSFMRRD, DRRRDRM, M 3511
SSSFMRRM, MSLLSFM, M 5322
SSSFMRSMD, SSLSLTD, 12036
SSSFMR#R#M, DDLDRDM, M 5429
SSSFMMDDTTL, FFFMR 725
SSSFMMR, FFFMRM, SSS 1359
SSSFMMMR, DRMMSFMR 3148
SSSFMMMMRD, DLSDMS 1661
SSSFMFS, SSSFMFS, DR 9844
SSSFMFSLS, TTTLSFM 1452
SSSFMSMLS, DR#R#MDR#R# 3770
SSSFMSSS, SMMRMFSM 8825
SSSFFMMDRMRDD, SSF 5570
SSSFFMMR, MFSMRRR, M 9828
SSSFLFM, FMMRRSR, MF 12548
SSSF#FM, MMDRRM, SSLS 2539
SSSF#SDS, MSSFRM, SSS 1006
SSSF#SM, MMMR#MD, DDDT 5857
SSSF#SLMSF, FMFLSFM 7941
SSSF#SLSD, MFMRLSFM, 11767
SSSF#SLSM, MFMRMFSM, 6871
SSSF#SLSSD, DRDTLSF 6123
SSSF#SLS, SSDRLT, DDD 396
SSSF#SLTD, MMMRDTLT, 7420
SSSF#LSM, DRMFFM, MD 9335
SSSF#LS, MMMR#FM, MMMR 7272
SSSSDDDMD, MSSSFFM 10887
SSSS, DDTDDRRM, DDTD 10654
SSSSDDTLT, SDRMDR, D 9569
SSSSDRM, SSRD, MMSMD 7110
SSSSDRTD, RLTLLS, SD 5177
SSSSDMMM, SDDDRM, SS 11563
SSSSDS, MFSRM, MSDTL 11651
SSSSDSSS, DRRLLSFM, 8343
SSSSDLLS, DDTSLSF#M, 6928
SSSSDT, DTLSF#S, FFSM 11507
SSSSDTLS, DMMMSFMR, 11005
SSSSDTLS, FMLSMFR 5993
SSSSDTLL, LFRDTRD, S 4337
SSSSDTLL, LLLLRDTT, 10857
SSSSRD, TLTDTDFMRD, 9062
SSSSMDRD, DFSLFR, RR 8004
SSSSMDSM, FFFSFRM, S 10115
SSSSMRDDDRMM, LLTD 6340
SSSSMRDRM, FSLDLLS 5771
SSSSMRDS, RMFRMFM, M 597
SSSSMRDLL, SSSRSDR 3709
SSSSMRRD, SSSMRRD, D 7424
SSSSMFSLS, MMMSSFM 7427
SSSSMFSLLLL, RRRRR 11608
SSSSMFSLTD, DTLT, LS 5584
SSSSMFLS, DTLLSFM, S 11932
SSSSMSDDDD, RRRDDR 11509
SSSSMSDD, DDSMSDMR 4566
SSSSMSDRMS, DTTTTD 6599
SSSSMSFMR, FFFFRLS 8851
SSSSMSFMFSFM, DRRM 3408
SSSSMSLSSF, FMFRRS 5372
SSSSMLSSFM, DRMMMS 7451
SSSSFMR, DRRM, SSSSF 132
SSSSFMRD, RMSLDTLS, 3991
SSSSFMRD, LLLLSSFL 5419
SSSSFMRRR, RRMFSLS 3866
SSSSFMRMFM, LTLSFM 11911
SSSSFMRS, SLLLSS, SS 5469
SSSSFMR#M, DTLSSLDT 6546
SSSSFMMMRDDDTD. DD 3418
SSSSFMFMRD, MMMMRD 6308
SSSSFMFSM, RLSSF#S, D 732
SSSSFMSDRMMMRD, D 874
SSSSFMS, LLLSMMR, MM 5611
SSSSF#SM, SLLLDS, SSM 365

SSSSSD

SSSSSDRM, SDTTLS, MF 8795
SSSSSDRM, SSSDTLLS, 525

SSSSSDRM, SSSDTLLS, 525
SSSSSDRM, LLLDLS, SS 628
SSSSSDMRDS, LLTDTL 12228
SSSSSDS, MRRSFM, RMM 4045
SSSSSMRD, MSDDTLSL 5003
SSSSSMSSS, SSSSTTL 6227
SSSSSMLSFMRMDRMF 5922
SSSSSMLSFMR, FFFFF 1406
SSSSSFMR, RMMF#F#SS, S 5187
SS, SS, SFMRMRD 6728
SSSSSFMR, LLLLLSF 4310
SSSSSFSLTD, DTLLSF 11275
SSSSSF#SM, MMMMMR#MD, 4722
SSSSSSDDMRDS, LLLL 12314
SSSSSSDD, LSMSFMR, R 4002
SSSSSSDDT, DLSMDR, S 2928
SSSSSS, DRDM, MMMRDM 5325
SSSSSSDRM, MFFFFMS 4384
SSSSSSDS, SSSSMRDR 5083
SSSSSSDSSSSLS, SLL 10438
SSSSSS, DTDRD, DMRDD 4911
SSSSSSDT, TDLSFM, MM 1912
SSSSSS, MSLLDDTDD 1177
SSSSSSFM, SLTTLS, DD 1597
SSSSSSF#SLS, MRMSFM, 10907
SSSSSSSDRM, RRRRRD 3708
SSSSSSSDTLL, LSFMR 11485
SSSSSSSSD, SLLLDS, D 6776
SSSSSSSSM, DLLDLS, D 2748
SSSSSS, SSMRDTLS, SS 964
SSSSSSSSSF#SM, MMMR# 10283
SSSSSSSSSS, SLLDRM 11319
SSSSSSSSS, SSLLLLL 7363
SSSSSSSS, SSLTDRM, S 4346
SSSSSSS, SLLLTDT, DS 6410
SSSSSSSLLSMR, MMFF# 423
SSSSSSSLTDS, DTLLL 6344
SSSSSSLS, MF#STLSFM, 1564
SSSSSSLSS, MMMSSMD 12272
SSSSSS, LLS#LTLD, DDT 6910
SSSSSSLLLS, DTRD#R, D 11156
SSSSSS, LLLSMR, MMFF# 422
SSSSSSL, LLSSDDR, DR 156
SSSSSSLLL, SSSDTDR, 12097
SSSSSSLTD, DRRDSLT 2584
SSSSSSLTD, DTLSSMD 8835
SSSSSSLTD, LLLLLLT 4459
SSSSSLDD, LSDMRD, SS 7222
SSSSSLSD, DTDRRDRM, 1577
SSSSSLS, DMFSFM, MMM 12387
SSSSSLS, RRDRM, DMS 9408
SSSSSLS, MMMMMFM, RR 11931
SSSSS, LSFMLS, DDSL#L 1355
SSSSSLSFS, SLLL#L# 1934
SSSSSLSSM, DRRRRDR 3875
SSSSSLSS, SSMRDDTT, 991
SSSS, SLSS, SSSSSSSSL 3986
SSSSSLLS, DDDTLSF#S, 10134
SSSSSLLS, DDLRMFFM, 9064
SSSSSLLS, SDRMSFMR, 11450
SSSSSLLS, SLTDTLL, T 10787
SSSSSLLLSS, SDRMRD 8377
SSSSSLLL, LSMMDMMR, 11062
SSSSSLTDS, DRRRRDR 8845
SSSSSLTD, LSDRDRM, S 2658
SSSSSLTD, TDTLTLLS, 7569
SSSSS#LSFFM, SSS#LMR 10017
SSSSLDDD, RRRRFMMM, 7067
SSSSLDRD, DTLMTDRM, 6691
SSSSLDR, MRDLSMS, DR 7744
SSSSLDSM, MRDRMF#S, 9376
SSSSLDLSMSLD, MRDL 10334
SSSSLDTLS, FMLSSFM 11455
SSSSLMS, SDTRLTD, SS 2235
SSSSLFMRM, MMMRRD, D 6991
SSSSLS, DDTLS, SSSSL 1192
SSSSLSDRM, MMRLT, SS 1012
SSSSLSDTMLS, SLLT 237
SSSSLSM, DDDFFM, MFM 5139
SSSSLS, MMMMFM, DMFS 4466
SSSSLS, FMRRD, SSSSL 6024
SSSSLS, FFMMR, MMRRD 8926
SSSSLSFS, SSSLDTLT, 3835
SSSSLSSD, SSSSLSR, S 6199
SSSSLSSM, DDDLTLS, D 5758
SSSSLLSM, RRRRDRM, S 10093
SSSSLLSM, SMRMR, MRD 9218
SSSSLLSS, DDTLTD, SM 6055
SSSSLLS, SRRRDRM, SS 6748
SSSSLLLS, SSSLLTLS, 11935
SSSSLLL, SLSMMRR, MM 12218
SSSSLLLL, SSSSFMS, D 12396
SSSSLLL, LLDLDTTTT 7878
SSSSLLLL, TTTTDDD, M 5789
SSSSLL#LSF, SMDRMF#SLS 12357
SSSSLTDD, DTLSMDFM 11718
SSSSLTDDT, TTTTDR 9492
SSSSLTDRDT, SSLTDR 12227
SSSSLTDRMD, LTRDLS 11676
SSSSLTDMRD, DDTLSD 3364
SSSSLTDMRD, SLLLT 7153
SSSSLTDS, TTTTDRD, L 10004
SSSSL#LSF, SMDRMF#SL 12356
SSSSL#LSF, SMDMFSLS 12359

SSSSL#LSF, SMDMF#SLS, 12358
SSSLDR, MDDDLS, DRMR 7745
SSSLDLSMR, FMRMSFM 12560
SSSLDTLS, SSSDDTDR, SSS 10578
SSSLDTLS, SSSLDTDR, MDD 8833
SSSLRMFM, DFR, SSSLR 6207
SSSLRMFFM, MMLSFM, F# 2845
SSSLMRDTLS, MRDTLS 6825
SSSLM, MMMSM, DDDS#D, D 6905
SSSLMFFSRM, DDRM, MS 7390
SSSLMSFF, FTLSFM, SD 8084
SSSLFFSLSM, SSSSMM 4537
SSSLFSM, SSSTLS, SSS 11725
SSSLF#SS, MMMSTD, SSS 10758
SSSLS, DDDTLS, LTDSM 4153
SSSLSDRD, DTRMRDLS, 8854
SSSLSDRD, TRMRDLS, S 8853
SSSLSDRDTLS, LDSFM 11810
SSSLSDRM, MDDRDDRM, 8130
SSSLSDRMMRMFS, LLL 10259
SSSLSDMRDS, SSSLSD 9771
SSSLSDMR, RDDDMSRS 11819
SSSLSDS, DRMDLS, SLS 8119
SSSLSD, SSSLSR, SSSL 6199a
SSSLSMD, DDDRDLS, SS 6408
SSSLSM, DDDRDL, SSSL 1326
SSSLSMDMSLSM, DRDR 12101
SSSLSMD, TLSSSSLS, S 6833
SSSLSMRD, DRFMRDS, S 11081
SSSLSMR, DMRMSS, SSS 5947
SSSLSMRDLD, LSDDMR 7915
SSSLSMMDFMRD, DMSS 7433
SSSLSMMR, FFFMRDTD, 9068
SSSLS, MMMFM, RRRRDR 6173
SSSLSMF, FFFSFRM, SS 6522
SSSLSFM, RMDFMR, RFM 7811
SSSLSFMFSDD, LLLTD 8676
SSSLSFMS, RMMRDR, DR 11681
SSSLSFSM, DRMFFM, SL 332
SSSLSFSM, SFMRDR, RM 6787
SSSLSSDDDD, RRRRDD 6328
SSSLSSD, DRRRRDRM, S 9950
SSSLSSD, RRRDRMD, DD 12531
SSSLSSDRM, FMRMDRS 10055
SSSLSSD, SSSLSSR, SM 8120
SSSLSSM, MMRMFFM, SS 11107
SSSLSSM, FMRDTD, SSS 9111
SSSLSSM, FMRRDDTD, S 9112
SSSLSSFMS, MMMMMMR 11678
SSSLSSF#S, TTDRDDTD, 9870
SSSLSSSDRMR, RSTDR 12262
SSSLSSSM, MRDRMM, SS 9113
SSSLSSSSSLS, SDMSM 2617
SSSLSSLSM, MMMMMSF 9168
SSSLSS, LLTMD, DDTLS 848
SSSLLDDD, MRDT, SSSL 4249
SSSLLDDD, SS#LTDRR, S 2026
SSSLLDTD, DDDRMFMR 8115
SSSLLDTLS, DMRDRTD, 7228
SSSLLMFSS, DRMSMFM 10953
SSSLLS, DDDDDR, MMMD 5412
SSSLLS, MFMRDTD, SSS 7554
SSSLLS, MFMRMRD, SSS 7553
SSSLLS, MSLDT, TDLSF# 4879
SSSLLSFMRD#RS, SSSL 6325
SSSLLS, SMFMRD, RRRM 7555
SSSLLSSFRM, SDTDRM 8236
SSSLLS, SFMRMRD, SS 7552
SSSLLS, SFMRSFMRD, S 7556
SSSLLSSS, DDDRMRRD, 8079
SSSLLS, SSSDDR, RMMD 3920
SSSLLSSS, SDTLLLRD 2606
SSSLLLS, MMMMSFMR, M 4704
SSSLLL, LSFM, LLLD 1447
SSSL, LTTD, MMRMF#S, SD 3130
SSSLTD, DDDTLS, S#LLL 1417
SSSLTDRMRDLS, SSTL 11169
SSSLTDRM, MRMFSM, DL 2669
SSSLTDRMFMR#M, D#MRL 934
SSSLTDRSD, MMRRMFL 6505
SSSLTDRSS, MMRRMFL 6506
SSSLTD, MRMFSM, SSSL 2904
SSSLTDMFSRS, LTLSL 1687
SSSLTDSM, MSSFFM, SL 11121
SSSLTDSMS, DDRRFFM, 8638
SSSLTDSS, DMFMRLRD# 10363
SSSLTDS, SSSLTDS, LL 10909
SSSLTDS, LLDTLS, SRR 6073
SSSLTDTDFLDM, MMRL 11216
SSSLTDTLS, LFSMSDT 8314
SSSLTDTTL, LLLTD#R 1642
SSSLTLS, SDDRRM, MFF 5879
SSSL#L#LSFSS, DSMSFM 742
SSSTLS, SDDRRD, MSMD 2927
SSSTLTLSD, SSSTLLL 5076
SSSTTLSD, MRMFSTLS, 10925
SSS#LTDRMF, MDRM, SSS# 1082

SSL

SSLD, DDDR, DDDL, LFSL 5194
SSLD, DDDR, DDDL, LLLS, 10977
SSLD, DDDL, LLLS. 10955
SSLD, DDR, DDDL, LRD, SS 6201

SSLDDDRR, DRFFMRRM, 9061
SSLDDDS, FMRDMRR, 179
SSLDDDLS, MRDDDMR, S 8625
SSLDDRRDMRDL, SSLD 4802
SSLDDRMD, LLSDDMR, M 11181
SSLDDS, SFMRD, LDFFF 11975
SSLDDTLS, SLRDTD, MM 1024
SSLDRDRM, LSDMFMRD 4295
SSLDRMDL, SLSDMR, SS 7506
SSLDRFMR, DDTDRLS, S 9687
SSLDRSDDTLS, SLTDR 718
SSLDRSSLDMS, RFFMS 10996
SSLDMRRD, DDRMFFM, M 4212
SSLDMMRDRRDSFMFF 10733
SSLDMSFMRM, MSLSMR 11429
SSLDFMMR, SDTDRF#S, S 6238
SSLDLDT, TRLTLS, SSL 11109
SSLDTS, SSLDT, DDTDM 1560
SSLDTLS, DDRMFMRM, M 11460
SSLDTLSM, MMRLSFM, S 8512
SSLDTLSM, MFSSDRMR 5028
SSLDTLSFLSLTLSFS, 7889
SSLRTDR, MSRSLTS, LL 1079
SSLMMRMM, MMFRDRM, S 4347
SSLMSSLM, MFSLLTDR 11318
SSLMSLSM, SSLMSLSM, 9250
SSLFDLFL, DLSLSMMS, 12154
SSLFMR, DMRT, DSLFMR, 145
SSLFMM, DTSLSS, SRMF 507
SSLFMMMFRD, SDRMMF 11827
SSLFFLSMM, MRRRRMF# 11010
SSLFLSF#SM, MMRRRRD 9117
SSLFLLSSM, DDMDDDR 41
SSLF#SDMR, FFMRRLL, L 6271
SSLSDDDTLS, SSLTDT 4910
SSLSDDTD, DSLSDDTL 10083
SSLSDDTDRM, DDRDM 2937
SSLSDDTDRMM, DDRDM 2938
SSLSDDT, RRMFTDR, MM 5395
SSLSDDTT, SSTLFM, SS 12090
SSLSDRMDLD, SF#SLSD 11870
SSLSDRMDLS, TTDRMR, 5265
SSLSDRMMRD, LTDDRD 10836
SSLSDRMMR, DTDRSLF# 4389
SSLSDRMFRTD, MRDRM 6936
SSLSDRMFMR, DTDRMR 5131
SSLSDRMFMR, MDLSDR 7409
SSLSDRM, SSLSFMF, MM 8911
SSLSDMRD, RMFSLSM 401
SSLSDMRD, MRDMMRR, S 8535
SSLSDMRDT, LTDFMRD, 11414
SSLSDMR, RRMFMRM, SF 6239
SSLSDMMR, DSSMDR, MS 10423
SSLSDSFMRD, MRSSLT 11562
SSLSDSL, LLTDTLS, TT 6241
SSLSDTRD, DRMFLSM, S 7375
SSLSDTRD, MRFMMRL, L 6476
SSLSDT, RFSTLS, MMFS 6342
SSLSDTLSF, FMMRDRM, 6402
SSLSDTLS, LSFMRRM, S 5006
SSLSDTLL, LFRDTTD, S 7467
SSLSMDDL, SDMDSMR, S 3023
SSLSMDDT, RDTLSLS, S 3204
SSLSMDDT, SSLSFTLS, 5029
SSLSMDRDLTD, TDRDM 9049
SSLSMD, RMFS, SSLSMD 5275
SSLSMDRM, SSMDMMR, S 10810
SSLSMD, RLTLS, SSLSM 8149
SSLSMD, MRDDDRMR, SS 8602
SSLSMDMR, DDRMSFR, R 1532
SSLSMDSLSM, FSLSTD 8073
SSLSMDLS, DRRDTD, RR 7378
SSLSMDLTDS, SLTDSM 10961
SSLSMRDDM, SSLSMRD 10580
SSLSMRDD, SSLSMR, SS 11930
SSLSMRDRRM, MRDSF 11385
SSLSMRDRMSDTLS, SS 11530
SSLSMRDTD, DMRTRDT 5776
SSLSMRMRD, TLDLSF 947
SSLSMRMFM, MDTLSF#S, 8956
SSLSMMRD, DRRSRM, DM 11787
SSLSMMRRD, LTDSDRM, 12198
SSLSMMRR, SSLSRRDD, 1323
SSLSMMMFMT, DRMTLD 6489
SSLSMMFR, MFSTLS, SS 12225
SSLS, MMFM, DDDDDDDMR 11167
SSLSMMFM, MFSLSFMR, 433
SSLSMMSM, DDRRMSMR, 926
SSLSMMSFD#R, MDDSFM 6661
SSLSMFSDRDL, SSLSF 10404
SSLSMFSDT, LSDFRM, M 7474
SSLSMFSDTLS, MRDTT 11401
SSLSMFSF, RSDTLT, SS 9960
SSLSMFSFMRMD, SS 5908
SSLSMFLSFM, STLTRD 4453
SSLSMS, DDRDLD, LSLS 10846
SSLSMS, MMRDMR, MMRD 10190
SSLSMSFFF, FFSFRFM 5053
SSLSMLLSS, SFSFRLS 12116
SSLSMT, RDSDT, RRD#RF 6586
SSLSFDDS, MMDTDRMD 11589
SSLSFMDLLS, SSLSFM 10663
SSLSFMRD, DDTLSFMF 6541
SSLSFMRD, DRMFMRDS, 12048
SSLSFMRD, MRDFMR, MF 6529

SSLSFMRD, MLDTLS, LM 8653
SSLSFMRMFSLT, DSSF 10389
SSLSFMFS, SRDDFFMM 5785
SSLSFMSM, SFMMFMRR, 1763
SSLSFM, SFRMRD, RMF#S, 8450
SSLSFM, SFRMRD, MFSL 8451
SSLSFM, SFRMMR, DTLS, 8452
SSLSFM, SSLSFM, MFSL 11487
SSLSFSFM, RRTLSF#S, S 4709
SSLSFSLSL, DDDDRD 5465
SSLSFLTL, SSFMLT, DF 8102
SSLSF#SDS, MSLSFMR, M 2557
SSLSF#SDSLSF#S, SFFF 5727
SSLSF#SMM, MMRRDRM, M 596
SSLSSDDDTLS, SLDDD 3228
SSLSSDRDRM, MFMRMD 67
SSLSSDRD, SMMRDRM, M 1732
SSLSSDRM, MMRDLSFM, 886
SSLSSDMMRDRMS,SSM 1827
SSLSSDSLSS, DLTDRF 11134
SSLSSMDMSRD, MFFFL 927
SSLSSMMFFS, SSLSSL 6828
SSLSSMSLDLS, SDRML 8955
SSLSSFMRR, MFSDRRM, 6941
SSLSSFM, MDDTLS, MMF 12512
SSL, SSFMF, FFS, FFMR#M, 4930
SSLSSSMDM, SMMRDR, S 11165
SSLSSTMRDTLS, SSDR 4954
SSLSSTLTDSS, MSDLS 8197
SSLSLDTD, MMRSLTDT, 5911
SSLSLTTD, SSLSTDR, M 8981
SSLSTDRMR, MFMRMTL 1205
SSLSTLSDTLSM, RDRM 8203
SSLSTL, SSFFM, SSLST 5243
SSLSTLLMS, SDDDTLS 3808
SSLLDDL, FSSLLM, SMM 4477
SSLLDD, TTDLS, DDMMS 7468
SSLLDDTT, LSRRR#M, MM 2231
SSLLDTLT, DDFMMRR, R 3253
SSLLFSLSM, SFMRRRD 416
SSLLFLSM, MMRRMF#S, D 3688
SSLLFLLSSMS, MMRMF 10932
SSLLFLLSSM, SSFFFM 2619
SSLLSDDT, DRMDTLS, S 4580
SSLLSDDT, DTDRSM, MF 10978
SSLLSDRM, MSFMRDRM 5780
SSLLSDMMR, DTLSSTL 1124
SSLLSRD, DDTLLS, MMM 10873
SSLLSMDRMFS, FMRMF 519
SSLLS, MMDRM, RMFRMF 9427
SSLLSMMF, MMRSRRDD, 4474
SSLLSSM, FFRRMFS, SS 286
SSLLSS, SFLLS, LTDDS 1695
SSLLLFSLSM, MFSSSM 7259
SSLLLFLS, SSF#RRMF#S 6474
SSLLLLLDTLLS, MFSL 7505
SSLLLLL, SMRRMMF, MD 1867
SSLLLLLSSSS, MRDDS 8110
SSLLLLLLS, SSDTLLT 4564
SSLLLLTLLSMS, SLLL 4739
SSLLTLS, LLTTDLR, DT 9744
SSLLTTD, RRDDTTLS, S 6850
SSLL, TTDS, MMRSDRT, T 1121
SSLTDDDT, LLSFMFRM 8815
SSLTDDRM, MSRMRTDT, 2555
SSLTDDLT, DD#MRSM, MM 435
SSLTDDT, DRD#RR#M, SM 8362
SSLTDDTDRMFM, MSFM 10948
SSLTDDTDR, FMSF#MRS, 10147
SSLTDDT, LDSMFRD, MM 8809
SSLTDDT, LDSMFMRD, S 3929
SSLTDDT, LSMMRDT, TM 4789
SSLTD, DTLSLS, SSLTD, 11408
SSLTDDTL, TDRLSFM, S 7009
SSLTDDTT, DRMRRM, SM 12505
SSLTDDTT, LDSFMFRD, 8816
SSLTDDTT, LLSMFRD, S 8814
SSLTDRDRM, MFMRMDR, 9985
SSLTDRDT, DDRRFMRM, 5880
SSLTDRMDL, RDTLTDT, 9853
SSLTDRMMRD, LLDFLS, 2767
SSLTDRMMFD#R, SSLTD 994
SSLTDRMF, MRDTLTD, S 10239
SSLTDRMSFRFM, MRLF 5109
SSLTDRFFM, DDMRDTL 5476
SSLTDMDTLSLSRS, SS 7056
SSLTDMFRM, SFM, SSLT 11133
SSLTDMLSS, SSDTLLT 8076
SSLTDS, DDRTD, SSLTD 3981
SSLTDSDRSRM, MFLFM 11290
SSLTDS, MDLRDT, SSFM 9353
SSLTDSS, FMFLSMS, SM 6069
SSLTDLS, DSMFMRD, MS 4265
SSLTDLSMS, SLTDRDT, 2952
SSLTDLSFMRRFMFSS, 4898
SSLTDLSFM, MMSDTLL 5564
SSLTDLSFLSLTDTLSL 192
SSLTDLT, DRMRD, SSLT 5923
SSLTDTDMRTD, TRDLS, 4734
SSLTDT, DSMFR, SSLTD 3930
SSLTDTRDLS, MMRRRD 9712
SSLTDTLDTLS, SSDRM 2893
SSLTDTLS, DDDTSLDD 698
SSLTDTLS, MFD#RLSR#M,5126
SSLTSDLS, MFFFSMM, D 12304

SSLTSLTDT, RRRRRRR 46
SSLTSLTDT, SSDTTLS 47
SSLTSLTDTLSS, SLTD 190
SSLTTSLTDTLSS, ST 189
SSTDRMR, SSTDMR, SSM 11101
SSTDRMFFM, MFSRMFR 1033
SSTDRMSFM, RMMMLSF# 4780
SSTRMRD, DDFFFFM, MS 4312
SSTRFTDMS, SSTRFSM, 9854
SSTLTDRTDLS, SSLSF 12386

SLD

SLDD, DDDRMRDD, RRRR 10863
SLDDDDMRRDDDD, MFS 2037
SLDDDDMRRD, MFSSSS 2039
SLDDDRD, DDTDLLS, SL 9251
SLDDDRDMMFM, RDTDF 11894
SLDDDRM, DRMFSS, SLD 9447
SLDDDMDLS, SDDDMS, S 11030
SLD, DDSLSSSSLM, MMM 4013
SLDDRDTT, LTDRRDD, R 10664
SLDDLDR, MRMDRDRT, T 7678
SLDDLSMSLD, DRDMRD, 7374
SLDDTD, DRRDLS, SLLD 8520
SLDDTD, DLTDLS, SDLT 3958a
SLDDTD, DLTTLS, SDLT 3958
SLDDTDRD, FFMRDRM, S 10317
SLDDTD, TDMMR#M, SFMR 2261
SLDDTRDTDLSS, SLDD 9297
SLDDTLSS#LFFM, MRMF 7905
SLDDTLS, LDRD, SLDDT 2802
SLDDTLSTRTLS, MRDD 7981
SLDRMDTLSDFMRDD, D 9944
SLDRMFR, MDLSFS, SLDR 1128
SLDRMSLDRM, RRDTLS 9027
SLDRMSLS, MRDDRTL, S 565
SLDRFMRD, DMFSDR, RM 10942
SLDMDMRDLSS, SLDMD 419
SLDMDMRDLS, SLDMDM 418
SLDMRD, SLDMRD, MSRR 3579
SLDMMMMRDFFF, FMRF 10924
SLDFMRMDL, LRTSDFM 3899
SLDFMRMR, RSDDDF, FM 10036
SLDFMMR, MDTDRT, DRM 1817
SLDSMRDRR, MFSLSFM 8484
SLDS, SLDFMRM, DFFRR 10943
SLDSLFSMR, MSF#STDL 1370
SLDLDSD, DMDMS, SLDL 3455
SLDLDSDDMRMS, SLDL 3457
SLDLDL, LSLDLDL, RDT 10820
SLDLRDLS, SLDLDRMR 7416
SLDLSMRD, MSLSMDR, M 6332
SLDLSLDD, SDRMDRLD, 2540
SLDLTDDSLSFMR, SLD 10701
SLDLTDTDRD, DRMTDR 3225
SLDTD, RMSF#S, MFSSFM, 10550
SLDTDRSS, MFMRDR 7359
SLDTMRRD, FMRDTLLS, 10541
SLDTMR, TDMRLS, SDTL 1646
SLDTFFFLTS, MRDSLD 7949
SLDTSDRM, MMMFMRDT, 5760
SLDTSFS, SS#DL#SFS, SL 1420
SLDTSLDT, SLTDRRR, F 497
SLDTSLLL, SMSMRM, DR 3061
SLDT, STRD, DTLS, DDLT 7183
SLDTLSMD, DRMFMRMD 11038
SLDTLSMFLSFM, DTLS 3548
SLDTLSM, SLDTLSM, RM 1591
SLDTLSFM, RMSFMRDT, 6129
SLDTLSLL, SLDRTDTL, 10234
SLRDTDRM, DFFMRDRT 6330
SLRDT, DFFFMMRLTDD 384
SLRDT, TDFFF, FMMRLT 385
SLRMFSM, SLRMFSM, SS 2366
SLRSDFTM, MMTDDRMR, 1135
SLRSSFM, DRMDRRD, MF# 4715
SLMDRDDLD, SLMDRRR 1416
SLMRDTLS, MRDTLSDD 6826
SLMRMDS, DRMFSDRMR, 6435
SLMRTDLSMDR, MF#LRS 4695
SLMMDTLS, MRMFLSRM, 8930
SLMFMRRD, MFSLLSFM, 10706
SLMFSFMR, FMSLTDLS, 7724
SLMFSLTDDRD, RRMDT 7612
SLMSDRM, FSLSMFMR, M 12331
SLMSFF, FSRFMM, MFMR 9759
SLMSFF, FSRFMM, LLTD 11683
SLMSLTDDR, SMRDTLS 8599
SLFDTLLSSMS, MFSLS 4669
SLFMRRD, MFLSMS, SLF 1516
SLFMRS, DTLS, LFMRD 8320
SLF, FSM, DDDDDRDTLS 3814
SLF#SDRMMR, DTLSSLS 9800
SLSDDDTLS, STRFRMD 8147
SLSDDRDT, DRMRR, MFS 585
SLSDDRM, MRDSMRD, MR 8992
SLSDDTDR, RMRDMRTD, 1313
SLSDDTDRMR, MDLFMR 2299
SLSDDTDRMR, MFSFRD 2300
SLSDDTLS, LTDRMRDR, 5831
SLSDDTT, MRDTTL, LLT 12290
SLSDRD, DTDLLS, SLSD 8083
SLSDRDTDMDDT, SLSR 10137
SLSDRMR, FMRDRT, SLS 11123
SLSDRMRSMR, LRMFMD 8639

SLSDRM, MRDR, SLSDRM, 7074
SLSDRM, MFMRLT, SLS 2480
SLSDRMFS, DFMRDR, FM 11523
SLSDRMFSMRDR, SDTL 10430
SLSDRMSRMRDRL, LRM 7984
SLSDRM, SRSM, FSLMRS 5406
SLSDRLTLS, DSFMRSF# 6560
SLSDMRDT, LSSLMS, SM 5725
SLSDMRDT, TDRMSSF#S, 2025
SLSDMRLTLS, DDMRLR, 3622
SLSDMMRD, DDDTDRMR 6896
SLSDMMRD, DTDDMRMR 6898
SLSDMMRD, DTDDSMRM 6897
SLSDMMRDT, DRDTLS, F 3911
SLSDMFML, RSDFMR, MF 9449
SLSDFMR, DRMFLS, SL 9258
SLSDFMR, RMLSF#S, SLS 7443
SLSDSDMR, RMRDLS, SL 7675
SLSDSDTLS, SLSDMRD 3162
SLSDSLSDRM, RRMRRM 9913
SLSDSLLS, SDMRTDTL 7892
SLSDLT, SSSDMS, SLSD 1787
SLSDTDRD, RMRDTLS, S 9590
SLSDTD, MLTDDT, SLTD 7469
SLSDT, SLSRD, SSMDTL, 3906
SLSDTLSD, DLTDFR, MD 1129
SLSDTLSMFSMR, DRDS 727
SLSDTLSF, MRDSFMRF 8839
SLSDTL, SFMMRD, DRDS 2004
SLSDTLS,SS#S#LFR, MR#M 10021
SLSDTLSLSFM, RMFSF 2369
SLSDTLLS, FMFSLSSM, 4411
SLSDTLLS, FMFLSFM, S 6349
SLSDTLLS, SMRDRMRD, 3012
SLSRRMFMRM, MSLSF#S 4213
SLSMDDDLS, SLSMRRR 11024
SLSMDDLDLS, SLSMDM 12234
SLSMDDTT, RRDSMMR, L 8772
SLSMDRDLS, DMSFRDR 4035
SLSMDRDLSLSMR, SLS 4751
SLSMDR, RMF#SSFS, SDT 8376
SLSMDRMDR, SLTDSMS 2154
SLSMDRMRD, MSMLSSF# 6068
SLSM, DRMFMSM, DLSM, 9545
SLSMDRM, FSMRDRT, DT 1277
SLSMDRM, FSLDDS, SFM 4719
SLSMDRM, FLSMSFR, MD 9533
SLSMDRLL, TLSFFM, SL 9921
SLSMDMD, SLSMRDMMR, 11491
SLSMDM, FDRM, MLTDTL, 5653
SLSMDFMMR, RMRDRMS 11160
SLSMDSF, TDDMRDR, SL 7338
SLSMD, SLSMR, SLSMDT 325
SLSMDLDD, DRRRDRMS, 10931
SLSMDLS, DRMRDTD, T 11334
SLSMDLSM, DRMFSLSF 4521
SLSMDLSM, DLSMDRM, R 5990
SLSMD, LTDSM, SLSSMD 3443
SLSMDTLTDS, SDMRST 1254
SLSMRDDTLS, MMFSLT 3004
SLSMRD, RDRMS, SLSMR 6519
SLSMRD, RDRSFM, RMFL 5526
SLSMRDRDM, SLL#TSMF# 7013
SLSMRDRMD, LSLDTLS 12138
SLSMRDRMRD, DTLSFM 980
SLSMRDRFM, MRDTLTD 122
SLSMRDFFF, RMFTLS, S 8227
SLSMRD, SMRDR, RMFLS 6683
SLSMRDST, LSMSFM, MS 1358
SLSMRDTS, SLSFMRD, S 5272
SLSMRDTL, DLSDDTDR, 10487
SLSMRDTL, LLRDTDR, S 6462
SLSMRRM, DTLSSF#S, RR 9015
SLSMRRM, RMLDDTD, MS 9340
SLSMRMM, SMFSLDD, MR 8420
SLSMRMFM, SLTLSF#SF# 4590
SLSMRMFS, SLSRFMRD, 5895
SLSMMRDDLS, DDRMRD 8979
SLSMMRDS, SLLDLS, SS 12410
SLSMMRD, SLFMRDT, SL 8893
SLSMMRD, LLDDFMR, SL 6228
SLSMMRD, LTDSFMR, SL 8472
SLSMMRRD, LDSDMRR, S 11352
SLSMMFRRDMRDTD. 12350
SLSMFR, MDMRLR, SLSM 9694
SLSMFMDRD, MDTMMLS 9837
SLSMFMRDRM, FSMR, SL 10564
SLSMFMRDRM, SLSMFM 3373
SLSMFMRR, MSLFMRD, S 1651
SLSMFMMRSRD, LFLSM 10082
SLSMFFMM, FMRDDTLS 4107
SLSMFSMD, RSSF#MF#S, S 9734
SLSMFS, MRDTDTL, LLR 7519
SLSMFSM, MRDDSFMR, S 10045
SLSMFSSLFLDTLS, D 5425
SLSMFS, SL#DLSF, LS, SR 583
SLSMFS, LSSLTTDS, DM 1217
SLSMFSL, TDRFMFLS, S 933
SLSMFLS, DRDLTRD, DM 7741
SLSMF#S, DFMRRD, SSML 3913
SLSMSDDT, RMFTLS, SL 12400
SLSMSDRDL, TTDRMDT 1982
SLSMSDTLLS, SRMFSL 1440
SLSMSRMF#S, SLSRFMR, 5894
SLSMSMFMDM, RD#RMFS 10015
SLSMSFMFRD, DMFSSL 8020

SLSMSFFM, DLDMSFM, S 5305
SLSMSFFM, RMFSFMRD, 8341
SLSMSSFR, MDDRSM, SL 8910
SLSMSLSM, DDMDLTD, 11370
SLSMSLSM, RRTDDS, LL 4807
SLSMSLS, MFMDRMD, SL 7354
SLSMSLSM, SLSMRDR, S 11369
SLSMSLSM, SLSMSR, SD 8690
SLSMSLS, SLTDRT, LTL 6437
SLSM, SLLDLS, MRMFSM, 3045
SLSFRMFSFM, SSLFMRD. 12412
SLSFMDRM, TDRMFTLR, 6623
SLSFMR, DRMFMR, MSLS 3934
SLSFMRD, MFSMSFMRM 563
SLSFMRD, FMRDTLS, SD 899
SLSFMRDL, DRMSDLS, L 4351
SLSFMRDT, DRMFSMR, S 10427
SLSFMRRM, MDDRSM, SL 2267
SLSFMRR, MFMRMD, SLS 11740
SLSFMRM, MDDRSM, SLS 2266
SLSFMRMFM, DDRMFMR 11602
SLSFMRMF#S, SLSRFMR 5896
SLSFMRMS, LLDLSMR, S 4354
SLSFMR, FMDRRD, DS 7581
SLSFMM, RMFFFM, SDTL 2997
SLSFMMR, MFSM, SLSFM 10136
SLSFMM, FSFMR, SLSFM 11776
SLSFMFRMFSLLSS, S 7836
SLSFMFRMFS, LTDTLS 3594
SLSFMFMRD, RMF#SSF#S, 674
SLSFMFMR, MFMRSLSF# 9289
SLSFMFMRMS, SLSFMF 10575
SLSFMFSRRD, MRMF#SR 9438
SLSFMFSFMRMFMR 3730
SLSFMFSFFM, RMFSFM 8342
SLSFMFSLSFM, SSLTD 10010
SLSFMSD, TLSFMLS, SL 6133
SLSFMSSFFMF, TL#TLS 5709
SLSFMSLSFM, SSLTDT 10011
SLSFSDRD, DSLTDRMM 11578
SLSFSDRD, DSTDRMMR, 11576
SLSFSDTLSMD, RMRMF# 6749
SLSFSMFMR, STLSLFS 2422
SLSFSLSDRDD, DSLDR 11574
SLSFSLSDRRD, DSLDR 11575
SLSFSLS, DFMRMDR, SL 12301
SLSFSLSLTDTLSS, TR 7888
SLSFLDDSLSFSS, SR 6485
SLSF#RFSFM, MFMRLRR 569
SLSF#SMSMRDFDM, MRD 2790
SLSF#SSMRD, LS#LTDTL 1808
SLSSDDTT, SLSSRRDD, 328
SLSSDRRD, SLSSDMRR, 6008
SLSSDMRD, DRMSLS, DR 10320
SLSSDMRL, DTLSFSM, S 8390
SLSSDTDRMRDTDLSS 8172
SLSS, DTLSMLLSFS, M 8170
SLSSRF, MMRRLT, RSF# 1592
SLSSMDDTLSLS, FSFM 1562
SLSSMRD, DDLDRM, SLS 7226
SLSSMRDRDL, LSDRMR 10762
SLSSMMMFMMR, SLSSR 10636
SLSS, MMMFMM, SLTDSF 7720
SLSSMFRSFFM, SLSSM 2001
SLSSMFMRRM, DMSLLS 11713
SLSSMSFFMF, LTLLRS 4308
SLSSFMS, MMMMRDR, SS 11680
SLSSF#LDDDT, SDMSFM 1413
SLSSSSSLTD, TLTS, SL 6544
SLSSSLTDMRDT, RDTD 11625
SLSSLS, DDLSFMRDR, S 909
SLSSLS, SSLSDRM, RMF 6052
SLSSTDDRML, LL#L#LD#R 923
SLSLDTDLS, SLMSLTT 10667
SLSLDTLSMFS, STDRD 11613
SLSLSDRMFMRMFS, LSL 755
SLSLSDRMFS, SSLSLS 756
SLSLSSSS, DDDDDTD, S 8392
SLSLTDD, LLSSMRDR, M 5792
SLSLTDMLSRMD, SLSL 1108
SLSLTDS, DTRDMR, SMR 6670
SLSLTD, SFMSFMR, SF#M 3659
SLSLTDTDRS, SMRDRS, 7608
SLSTDLSFFM, SLSTDS 2325

SLL

SLLDMRDLLL, SLLDLS 8389
SLLDTRDMR, MFSSLSS, 7415
SLLDTLSM, DRRRDRMS, 10200
SLLDTLSM, SRSTTLS, D 4517
SLLFLDLSMS, MMRD#RS 5158
SLLFLS, MSLSMR, DMMS 7246
SLLSDRM, SRMFMRDDT, 11635
SLLSDFFM, RDFMLDDT, 3077
SLLSDTDR, SDDFMMR, R 1285
SLLSMD, DDDTLS, LFSM 9171
SLLSMD, DDTLS, LFSMM 9173
SLLSM, DDTLS, LFSMMM 9172
SLLSMD, DTLSL, FSSMM 9170
SLLSFMMR, DRMSDLS, S 9527
SLLSF#S, SRSDRM, MFDR 935
SLLSSDDT, DLSSLTLR 3149
SLLSSDDT, LLSDSFM, S 6407
SLLSSLRRMR, TLTDRT 7337
SLLSLDTD, RMFMRRD. 4498

SLLLDDSS, MRMFLLSS, 1840
SLLLDTLLS, MFMFSSR 1958
SLLLRRRSD, DDFFFLS 7625
SLLLSFMFSLS, LTDSS 3556
SLLLLSMS, SLLSMMR, S 11155
SLLLLLS, MSLSMR, MSS 978
SLLLLLTLSSS, MFFFS 45
SLLLLTDSSSSM, SLLL 10921
SLL, LTT, SSLDMSL, MFM 4888
SLLTLSSSM, DLLSSSD 4499
SLL#SLF, RMFSM, TDRMD 8167
SLL#SL#LFLLS, SLL#SL#L 9846
SLTDDDDD, DRRMMDFR, 3682
SLTDDDDD, SDRMMMRM 1938
SLTDDDRMLL, LTDRRR 8629
SLTDDDTDRM, LTD#RRR 894
SLTDDDTLLS, SLTDDD 8112
SLTDDRRMD, DRMFMRD 1144
SLTDDRRMD, FMRMRDL 1353
SLTDDRRMFM, MRDRSS 6375
SLTDDRMFM, SFMRMDT 8758
SLTDDRMFM, SFMRMRD 5982
SLTDDMRD, DTDRRM, MM 79
SLTDDMRDRS, SLSMDM 4536
SLTDDFFM, MLLSMDL#L, 12152
SLTDDLTDFMR, DRMFM 10041
SLTDDLT, RFMRDLS, MF 4656
SLTDDTDRS, SSSRMFM, 11686
SLTDDTR, DDTSM, MRDT 9579
SLTDDT, SSLSS, LTDMM 6911
SLTDDTSLTRRD, LTDM 598
SLTDDTLS, MRMFFMRM, 1085
SLTDDTLSM, SSSSLSS, 5146
SLTDDTLTD, RFM, SSSF 2145
SLTDDTLTF, FFTTLFM, 7457
SLTDD#RS, SLTDMRFFM 9127
SLTDRDDT, RD#RMRDLL 1525
SLTDRDDT, RSSS#LFM, L 7040
SLTDRDMD, DDTDRDS, S 12470
SLTDRD, SLTDRM, TDRM 6771
SLTDRDT, DDLFMRM, MS 8920
SLTDRDT, DLFMRM, MSM 8921
SLTDRDTRSM, SLTDRD 902
SLTDRDTRLLS, DDDDM 1848
SLTDRDT, SFMRDMRD, R 4338
SLTDRDT, STDRMRD, DD 3869
SLTDRDT, TFLTLS, SLT 7229
SLTDRDTTTLSLS, SLT 3577
SLTDRMDD, MRDTLS, RD 6919
SLTDRMD, DMLSF#S, SSS 9911
SLTDRMDDTTD, DTTLT 6992
SLTDRMDL, LRTDLSF#S, 2959
SLTDRMRD, DDMDFR, SL 3957
SLTDRMRD, MRMDTLLS, 4125
SLTDRMRD, MSFMDR, SL 3018
SLTDRMRRRMFSLS, SF 11224
SLTDRMMRD, LLDFLS, S 2768
SLTDRMFRDT, RMFSDT 4271
SLTDRMFR, SFMRMRRD, 2107
SLTDRMFMRM, SFMRM 6642
SLTDRM, FSFMRR, RRMF 2380
SLTDRMFS, FMRMRDTD, 4058
SLTDRMF#S, SLTDRMDR, 10582
SLTDRMF#S, LSFSM, SFR 7115
SLTDRM, SDSFMR, STLS, 10420
SLTDRM, SDLDMRD, SLT 11970
SLTDRM, SFMRDT, TDRM 849
SLTDRMSFMR, MRDLTD 7311
SLTDRFM, RDLSS, RRSF 9626
SLTDRS, LTDR, SMTDLS 7906
SLTDRLTD, DMFSFSR, R 7142
SLTDMDLT, STDRFMRM, 958
SLTDMRDRMR, RMFSFM 6984
SLTDMRD, FMRDTLS, S 9282
SLTDMRDS, TD#R#MSF#MS 1766
SLTDMRDTD, SDRMSFM 11360
SLTDMRDTLT, LTDSDM 3096
SLTDMRDT, TDTLSSM, D 10786
SLTDMRSD, DRMF#SF#M, T 11782
SLTDMMRD, FFMRMRR, R 4426
SLTDMMRDSS, SLSRMF 12092
SLTDMMRDTRD, MMRDM 8447
SLTDMMRLDT, DTLSDR 205
SLTDMMMSF#SF#SF#F, SL 10603
SLTDMM, LRFM, SLTDMM, 12321
SLTDMSFM, RDDTLS, SS 8608
SLTDMSF, MRMFFM, SLT 2077
SLTDMSFM, MMRDMRD, S 697
SLTDMSSS, DMMFS, SLT 8431
SLTDMSTT, SLLFFM, MM 7307
SLTDML, SMRDLM, DRM 6796
SLTDFMRD, SFRSSF#LS, 10270
SLTDFMRM, LMRMSFM, M 2783
SLTDFM, MSDRM, RMFSL 2858
SLTDFMFMRD, SLDSDL, 12007
SLTDFMLR, DTDDRSLS, 7181
SLTDFF, MDDRM, SLTDF 2281
SLTDFF, MRDRM, SLTDM 2282
SLTDFF, MRDTM, RRMRS 8101
SLTDFT, SRSR#M, SLTDR 10608
SLTDSDRDT, SLTRTRD 11255
SLTDSDRMD, MLSMRDL, 7455
SLTDS, DTLSSFMFR, MF 152

SLTDSRMD, DTLSRFM, S 11203
SLTDSMDRD, DTLSTLS 3970
SLTDSMR#MF, FSLSFRR# 8898
SLTDSMFS, DFMMR, SLT 5766
SLTDSLSD, TLSMDLS, M 6131
SLTDSTLS, SLTDSTLS, 4029
SLTDLSMSFMRD, SLTD 4711
SLTDLSFM, MRTDRDLT, 6536
SLTDLS, SDLSFM, LSFM 2324
SLTDTDDRRMD, MRDTS 12575
SLTDTDRDRMS, LTDSS 12190
SLTDTDRM, MSFMDFMR, 609
SLTDTDRMFM, FSMDRL 6382
SLTDTLMSS, SLTDTLM 10867
SLTDTLSM, DFLSMDS, S 6471
SLTDTLSLFS, TRDTRD 3200
SLTDTTL, LSSDDR, SRR 9978
SLTRDMFSFM, SDMLRF 712
SLTR, TLMRMF#, SLTRMR 11099
SLTSSLTDRM, FMRMRD 4010
SLT, LDDTLLS, LLSFMM 5912
SLTLSRDS, MMRSDRT, T 11128
SLTLSFMRDMLS, SLTL 10795
SLTLSFMRM, FSMRMDT 921
SLTTLDTLSLT, STSLM 2840
STDDDTDRRD, DMSMMR 5393
STDDRMRMDTLTS, SLL# 8918
STDRD#RMDS, DMFSMRD 970
STDRRTDRMMR, RRDLD 10475
STDRMDR, SLTDTLSLS, 9690
STDR, SDRM, F#F#F#S, SDMS 6951
STDMRDTLSS, TMRDLD 7054
STRMRD, DFFMRDMR, SS 9150
STRFMRD, DRDTLTSF, M 6949
STRSFMD, STRFLSM, SF 9860
STRTDRMFSMDT, SDRM 1147
STLSFMFS, SLLSF#S, FM 10895
STLTSM, FSLSLRMF, SR 3409
STTLSLSS, MSRFFM, SD 89
STTLTDS, SLDTLS, SSD 3415
STTTTDS, SRDTLSFM, M 11298
STTTTLTDTLS, SFMFR 4455
S#S#LLSSSS, DDDRDDT, T 10686
S#LTDRMDRDT, TDTDRM, 9598
S#LTDRMMRM, MRDTD 12312
S#LTDTLLS#LTDTDLTD 9821

LDD

LDDDDDRDT, LLLLTTL 10705
LDDDTS, MLLS#LTDTT, T 7822
LDDDTL, LDDDTL, LTLS 7943
LDDRDDT, S#LTDTRD, LT 2917
LDDRRMMRDTL, LDDRR 10561
LDDRRMMFRMM, SDDRR 4160
LDDRMMLTDTTL, LTDT 11208
LDDMRDLD, DDDMMSLS, 6326
LDDSLSFM, LDRMRDTD, 9894
LDDTDRDT, LDTL, LDRM 8727
LDDTLRD, DTTTDLS#, MT 10879
LDDTLSTRRML, SLSFRD 11051
LDDTTL, MRRDDT, TDDR 2828
LDDTTL, LDDRRM, MSSF 10266
LDRDFMRDTDD, MSLSF 5966
LDRDLSLL#L, SLDFSMR 11060
LDRDLLDRDL, MRDMRD 10242
LDRDTDTL, DMMRDRTL, 10656
LDRRDRFS, DTLFMMRD, 9550
LDRMDRDLSL, LDRMSL, 2523
LDRMDRDLS#L, LDRMS#L, 2522
LDRMDRDTL, LDRMDRD 7669
LDRMRDRDTL, LDRMR 7666
LDRMRDRML, SDRMRDR 7974
LDRMRDLSL, RMSLLSM 2607
LDRMRDTLS#L, TDLTMR 3021
LDRMRMDTL, LSLTLSF# 5546
LDRMRFMRD, MRDTMRT 2301
LDRMMDTL, LDTDMRDT, 12302
LDRMMRDT, TDRMMRRD, 786
LDRMMRMDL, LRRRLDR 11105
LDRMMMDR, MTDRMDTL, 6371
LDRMMMRMF#SM, SMRDR 3631
LDRMMFRM, DMFSSLF 5914
LDRMMFMD, DTLS#LRMF 7515
LDRMMFFM, MFDRRD, DM 7483
LDRMMLMRDTL, DMF#SL 2895
LDRMML, SMDRML, DTLS 6256
LDRMFMRTSL, TDLLS#LT 4046
LDRMSDRMR, RMFSMRR 9839
LDRMSMRD, MSMDRDTL, 2753
LDRMLDRML, DRMMRDT 11550
LDRMLMRDTL, LDRMLS 3712
LDRMLSMR, DFSMRDDF 10126
LDRMLS, SMRDRTL, DRM 2290
LDRMLLS#L, DRMFMRDT, 3914
LDRMLLS#LL, DTLSFFM 10172
LDRMLTDTL, DRMFMMR 1375
LDRMTDRT, SLTF#SMR#M, 5079
LDRFMLDRDTL, LTDM 10926
LDRTDTLS#, LRDDTD, DR 4968
LDMRDRDT, LRDTL, LDM 4178
LDMRDMMRTD, LTDTLT 7192
LDMRDT, DMLSF#M, F#MR#M, 8963

LDMRDTLT, DMRDRM, M 10468
LDMRMFMRDT, TDRTMD 1151
LDMMRDRMRDLL, LDM 6318
LDMMMRFMRD, RMDLDR 11591
LDMLMFMRDT, DLTDRM, 9525
LDMLMFMRD, TLTDRM, M 9526
LDMLMLTMRDTL, MMMR 8064
LDMLSMRM, MFSMRDRL, 3262
LDMLSFMRDR, MLSL, LD 7269
LDMLSFFM, RDTLLDDT, 5044
LDMTRTLLSM, SLTRMT 2233
LDFLF, SDMSM, STRFSF 4496
LDLRDFFM, RLDTTL, MM 7987
LDLMDTLM, MSMFLM, MS 8503
LDLMDTLM, MSMF#SLM, M 8502
LDLMMLTD, SSSTSRT 12260
LDLSFDRRD, DFMMRD 12061
LDLSLDDLSM, SSLSLD 549
LDLSLDTL, DRRMDRRM 10294
LDLS#LDTL, DRRMDRRM 10295
LDLLS#LTS#M, RDTLS#F#S# 10028
LDLLTDLL, LLTDTLSL 10708
LDTDRDT, DRMFMRD, MD 4786
LDTDRM, MRDTT, TMRRD 9213
LDTDLS#LSFM, SSMLTD 2065
LDTDLTDR, MMRDTL, MM 4061
LDTDLTTLLSLTTL, LR 9835
LDTDTDRMFM, RDRMRD 7682
LDTD#RDT, DRMFMRD, MD 4785
LDTRDF, MRDTLS#L, DT 12256
LDTMDTL, TDTLDTL, LD 5819
LDTMM, MMLS#TL, MLDTM 3145
LDTMFRM, DMRSLTD, ML 11453
LDTSMLLM, MF#SLF#TTS, 11585
LDTSLDSM, MLFTSD, DT 8216
LDTS#TLDRM, MRTRDLD 5005
LDTLDDLTSLDD, DDD 7439
LDTLDMRM, MDDFMRD#R 6032
LDTLDMRL, DSMRDR, RS 2121
LDTLMDRFMR, RMSF#S, D 8044
LDTLM, RDTLT, MMFSLT 11568
LDTLMRDT, TDTLMMR#M, 8371
LDTLMMRDTL, DLS#LTD 11798
LDTLMMRDTL, DTLS#LT 11799
LDTLMM, LDTLM, FMMRD, 131
LDTLMFT, DRMMRRD, SS 4864
LDTLMLSFMD, DRMFSF 11017
LDTLSDRM, MMMRMDDT 7731
LDTLSDRM, MMMMRDTD, 10632
LDTLSLMLL, DRDTLTD 9138
LDTLSLTD, DRMFDTL, T 5294
LDTLS#LMM, F#SMSFM, LD 4913
LDTLS#LTDTL, DDDDSD 1752
LDTLS#LTL, TDTDRDRM, 11376
LDTLS#LT, TDRMDTL, TD 10070
LDTLLRTM, DRMFSM, ML 9377
LDTLLSFM, MSDMRD, MS 9507
LDTLLLS#L, DTLLS#L, DF 11048
LDTLLTTDDRDTLSL, L 6404
LDTLTM, LRMFMLS#L, LD 6733
LRDLSFSLR, LRDLSFS 1004
LRDTLDLDTL, LDLDLS 10737
LRDTLSFS, RRRM, MFFS 10856
LRRDFMRD, FMRD#, LDLR 3630
LRRMFRMMFS, SRDL, LR 9934
LRMDLDRM, LRMDLDRM, 8239
LRMFMRD, FRMFSL, LS#L 2704
LRMFMRD, FMRFSL, SLT 8057
LRLLFSLTD, LRLLFSL 5264
LRTDLTSL, DRTDLTSS, 6912
LRTDTLS#LTM, LLSSFF 10022
LRTLSTMDTL, LDRFMR 2798
LM, DDRMMRDTTL, MMF#S 10223
LMDDRFTLLS#, LS#, DS#LR# 4438
LMDDTLS#LTDTLRDRM, 8694
LMDRMLDTLSM, LMDRM 8491
LMDRMLTDRDTL, LMDR 9137
LMDLRM, LDTLT, RTDRM 6624
LMDLTLS#L, LDTLMRDT, 6284
LMDTMRDT, MSF#MMR#M, L 12406
LMDTMRDT, MTSF#MMR#M, 12406a
LMDTLLT, DSMDRRD, R 1477
LMRDDT, DRDTTL, DLSF 3496
LMRDRDTL, LLTDRM, SD 1119
LMRDLDRM, MLSFMRMR 940
LMRDTDTLS#L, DTLTDR 2242
LMRDTLDRM, F#S#LTDTL 10097
LMRDTL, MSFMRM, DTLM 774
LMRDTL, MSF#MR#M, MMRM 2633
LMRDTLMLFMRMDTL, L 4101
LMRDTLS#L, DRMFMRDD, 11446
LMRDTLS#LL, DDRMFMR 11445
LMRDTL, LSLFFM, LSLF 9441
LMRDTLTLS#, RDFMMRM 261
LMRMDRDTL, LLSFFM, 11619
LMRMDTL, LLLRSSLM, L 4394
LMRMFM, LLD#TD#RD#, S#ML 6827
LMRMTDTRDTLS#L, MMF 2055

LMRMTDTL, MMLSF#MSF# 2054
LMMDLLLS#, MLSFMRRM, 5481
LMMRDR, MRDTDTLS#, LM 6780
LMMRDT, DTLLS#L, TDTL 6287
LMMRDTMLSS, LTTDRF 1779
LMMRDTL, DSSFMRM, DR 9892
LMMRRDDT, LTDRDT, TD 6014
LMMRRDDT, TDRMDRTS 11475
LMMRMLDRDTL, LRDLD 8710
LMMRMT, LMMRMT, DTDR 4979
LMMMDFMRM, RDTLTS#, S# 1096
LMMMRDT, TDRMRSM, ML 2596
LMMMRTDTL, TDDRDRM 4903
LMMMMRDRD, DTLSLLM 9850
LMMMMMD, DMMMRR, RFF 9493
LMMMFRM, SLMDTM, LMM 2690
LMMMFMMRDT, LDDRR#R# 3379
LMMMFMMRDT, LDDRR#R#MT, L 3380
LMMMFMMT, LDDRR#MT, L 3378
LMMMLLSDTLS, TDTLS# 10421
LMMMTRDLSL, DRRMSF 11764
LMMFMRDRL, LMSFMRD 11039
LMMFMRLDTL, LDLMF#S 2501
LMMSFMRD#, MFSFMMR, L 12569
LM, MSF#MRDLM, MF#LMRD 1273
LMMLMMSRRSR, MLTDM 4489
LMMTDRR, LDRTDL, LMM 1622
LMMTRDTL, LFFMLSF#M, 7623
LMFMDDMRRD, TLDFML 10256
LMFMRDT, MLDTS#LT, DD 5543
LMFFMLLS#, LMFFSRFM, 8757
LMF#RMD, RRMDTL, LMF#R 6436
LMF#SLSF#M, LTLMF#M, MS 8047
LMSLLS, LDTL, DDSLTD, 6266
LMS#LTDRT, DSTDRMFR 1502
LMS#LTDTL, DTLTDRM, L 9520a
LMLDTL, DSDMRD, MRD 9322
LMLSSDLS, DMDRDTL, 6186
LMLLTDT, DLLSFM, MLM 11068
LMLLTSF#M, DMRDTTL, L 2710
LMLTDRD, TLLS#L, LM 8656
LMLTDLTD, RRDTLS#L, L 5576
LMLTDTLS#M, TDRDTTL, 2495
LMLTRDTL, DSDRMRD, L 6641
LMTDRDTL, DRMFMRM, M 2184
LMTDLRMFM, TDRMSFM 8504
LFRMMLLS, DTMSF#M, LF 3562
LFRSFMM, MFFSSLL, LT 7947
LFMRDLTS#, LTDDRRM, L 3865
LFMRRL#SFMM, DTMLLT 3135
LFMFMRMDR, MSFLSDT 7773
LFFMDRMFMRD, MSLTS 3625
LFFSLSMS, FRRMFMF#S, 12270
LFSM, RFSL, RDRL, LDTL, 4408
LFSM, FSL, RDRL, LDTDT 5085
LFLLDL#L, MSSRMFM, LD 12012
LFLLSSSLSMR, MMMMR 10611
LSDDTDD, LSDDTD, D#RM 319
LSDRMRM, RMFMMRD, RM 3561
LSDRMSFM, DRMFRD, DT 8356
LSMDLDRM, SDRMRDL, L 5973
LSMRDRM, DTSLMFS, SL# 1080
LSMRSSM, DTLSFM, MMM 593
LSMFSM, LSMFSM, LS#LT 2902
LSMSL, DLSLM, LDLDR, M 4949
LSMLTDDT, MRDTLT, TD 4568
LSFMDLSFMD, LTDRMM 2581
LSFMDTLS#, MMRDRDTD, 11482
LSFMRDRMDT, LSFMRD 1430
LSFMRS, DTLSLSFMRR 3858
LSFMMFLDDTL, LSFMM 5369
LSFMFRMDT, LTDRMLT 8539
LSFMFMF, SFMR#MR#M, DD 11013
LSLDDTLTLSLTDD, RD 11541
LSLDRDTLMRTRDTL, M 11667
LSLDRDTL, LFSLSFMR 1721
LSLDRL, LSLFMFR, MMR 1714
LSLDTLSL, DRDTLSLL, 680
LSLMRDTL, TDRMF#F#S, L 1868
LSLMRMLLS, DRMSMRD 11719
LSLSFMFRDSSFSLL, 1758
LSLTDRD, LSLFRM, LSL 1333
LSLTDRMRDTL, DTLSL 6319
LSLTDTL, DTLTDRM, FM 4366
LSLTRTL, TRMRMLF#MR, 5822
LSLTLDRMRFMRLL, MF 8562
LSLTL, DLTRM, SRMRR, T 1886
LSLTTDTLT, LSLTSLS 5560
LS#F#MDRDTTL, TDRMLR 248
LS#STDRDTL, DTLTDRM, 9521a
LS#S#LTDTLLS#, LLSFMM 6442
LS#LDTLS#, DDTLS#LS#LT 9175
LS#LMDTLS#, SLMFSRMR 8642
LS#LMFMRDRMRDR, DRM 9597
LS#LMLRDTL, LSFMFSD 7049
LS#LTDDTM, LSFMRRD, L 6847
LS#LTDDTM, LSFMRRM, L 6847a

LS#LTDDTL, DTLTDRM, M 9521
LS#LTDRTL, DTLTDRM, M 9520
LS#LTDRTL, DTLTDRM, L 9520b
LS#LTDRTL, MFMDRDT, L 9018
LS#LTDSMS, FMFMRMFS, 5132
LS#LTDLTM, SSFMRRM, S 4137
LS#LTDT, DMRDTL, DDT, M 8991
LS#LTDTDT, DRMRDTL, L 5450
LS#LTTD, DTDRRM, MRSF 2841

LLD

LLDDRRMD, SSFMRRD, R 3387
LLDDRRM, MRFMRRM, MS 9891
LLDDRRM, MSFMRRD, RR 3388
LLDDMFSR, MMDTLLR, T 10060
LLDRMLRT, DDRMFFM, 129
LLDRTMLRRRMR, MMMR 151
LLDMRDTD, MMSMDTD, M 4550
LLDMLMF#M#F#RM, DLDML 7819
LLDMLM, SSRRM, LLDMF 3760
LLDFRM, MSMRDT, TMF#S 6622
LLDLM, FMRDL, LRRDRM 3215
LLDLSDRM, RSLSF#MRM 6483
LLDLSMSDDLSM, SSLS 9936
LLDLTDRMM, DRMRMF#S 2577
LLDTDLSM, MFMFMFMF 931
LLDTSLTD, TDRMDRD, L 3036
LLDTLS, DDLTDR, TDMR 3464
LLDTLSDR, MMSFR, RRS 6960
LLDTLS, LDDTT, DDLTD 7015
LLDTLS#TL, DDMRDTTD, 828
LLRD#RMRDL#L, RFSLTD# 3806
LLRD#RMRDTL, RFSLTD# 3807
LL, RR, MMRMMRDL, DLLD 3785
LLMDRDTL, DDTDDRM, L 3471
LLMDLDRM, MF#SMDRTL, 5861
LLMRDDRMRT, RDTLSF# 6798
LLMRDRMDL, LTDRMDT 9714
LLMRMDTL, MLTDTLSL 1
LLMMRDR, LLDRTL, LLL 1219
LLMMRDTL, SLTDRM, L 3844
LLMMRDTLS#, LTDDRR 8198
LLMMRMDR, TDRTLTL, L 6777
LLMMRMD, TDRT, MDT, TD 8355
LLMMRM, MMRDDT, TDRM 3945
LLMMMRMFM, MMSDRMF 3422
LLMMFSM, LLMMFSM, LM 2809
LLMMF#F#L, LLMMF#F#L, LL 1960
LLMMLSLTLL, MF#SMDR 12537
LLMMTDRR, LLDRTDL, 1620
LLMMTDRR, LTDRTDL, L 1621
LLMLS#S#LL, DTLSLF#M, L 10171
LLMLLSSM, MFMDRD, LL 8046
LLMLTDRDTDL, MRDTL 5817
LLMLTDTDLM, DRMFMR 10986
LLMTDTLS#L, DDRMDRL 1198
LLMTRDTL, MMF#SF#MF#R 5255
LLSDRMML, MLSDRMML, 10852
LLSDSLLM, DMRDSD, DM 1891
LLSDTLS#L, DMRDTD, DM 2714
LLSDTLTL, LDRDRMD, D 11604b
LLSDTLTL, LTDRDRMD, 11604
LLSDTTL, LDRDRMD, DR 11604a
LLSMDRM, MMLDT, RDTL 6143
LLSMRMFSFM, LTDMSF 2314
LLSMRSLDDTLT, LRRT 7683
LLSMSFMRMM, LLSMSF 3375
LLSMSSM, FFMMRF#S, DM 4450
LLSFMDTLTLS#, LLS#LT 1123
LLSFMRMFSLTT, DDTL 2111
LLSFMMRR, FSLLSSF, M 3505
LLSFMMR, LRDTLLS#, LT 1226
LLSFMTDTLS#, MMMRDR 11481
LLSSDSDR, SLDRMSRR 12245
LLSLDRL, LSLFMFR, SS 1715
LLSLDMRDRDT, DLLLT 382
LLSLMDTL, LLSMRDRM 12194
LLSLS, MSMSMSM, DMSS 10383
LLSLSSFM, LLSMRMRL 210
LLSLSSF#M, LLSMRMRL 212
LLSL, SLTSL, LSLL, SLT 6766
LLSLLTDD, TDRFMRD, R 7161
LLSLL, TLSLL, LSLMM, S 1801
LLSLTDRTL, LMMDRM, M 63
LLSLTDTL, LLSLTDTL, 7025
LLSLTLTDTLL, LSLTL 2996
LLS#LDTTM, MLDTTL, LL 8021
LLS#LDTTLS#, LTDRTL, M 2185
LLS#LMMRM, MF#SLTLSF 11579
LLS#LTD, DTMMR#M, LLS#L 7932
LLS#LTDRM, MRDTLS#, TD 4599
LLS#LTDLT, MMRDTLS#, L 6672
LLS#LTDTL, LLS#LTDTL, 7026
LLS#LTDT, MMRDDT, LL 6672a
LLLDDMD, LTDLTDLM, M 2022
LLLDDTDR, MDLLS#L, LL 4563
LLLDDTL, DSLSFM, SDD 871
LLLDRDTL, DRRMMRDT, 6291
LLLDRRDT, LDTLS#L, LL 10408
LLLDMRDR, SMSFMRDT 11253

LLLDSSSM, MFSMR, RRR 8132
LLLDLSFM, DTLSMFRD, 5416
LLLDLL, LSFL, LLLDTL, 3100
LLLDTLR, DTTSSLTDR 2202
LLLDTLS, DTLLRM, TDM 287
LLLDTL, SSLTS#M, LLLD 8914
LLLDTLTM, LLLDTLS#, S# 630
LLLMRDMRDT, MMF#SF#M 2360
LLLMRDTLTDDRRM, MF 3094
LLLMRMDT, LDTDRMRD 5901
LLLMRMDT, LDTDMRDT, 5902
LLLMMFFM, DRMFMRRD, 2497
LLLMMFFM, MTDRMRDTD 10304
LLLMMSFM, MMMRRRDTL. 264
LLLMFMMRD, RRTLTL, L 2319
LLLMFMMRDT, RRRRDT 2359
LLLMFSMRD, RMMFSM, D 4640
LLLMF#SF#MRMF#S#LMSF# 3032
LLLMSF#M#R, RF#MF#S#LM, L 11356
LLLMLSF#M, MLSFMR#M, L 7006
LLLFL, DDDSS, F#F#F#F#SF# 5933
LLLFLSF#SM, RRRF#MRS, 4746
LLLSDDRMM, MFSFFMR 8285
LLLSMR, DTTL, LLLSMR, 9133
LLLSMMLLSM, MDDTDR 3353
LLLSM, LTDDRT, TDRMD, 4665
LLLSFSLLR, FSMFRD 11534
LLLSSDRM, MFMRDRRD, 7763
LLLSSLDTD, MMSFM 7656
LLLSLDTD, MMSFMRRD, 7657
LLLSLDTL, DRRDRMMM, 10704
LLLSLSFMR, LDRLTDT 4138
LLLSL#LSFF, SLSFMFM 2138
LLLS#M, LTDDRDT, TDRM 4667
LLLS#F#M, LTDDRDT, TDR 4666
LLLS#LDTT, TTMMR#M, MM 3367
LLLLDTL, LSFSLL, MMM 5538
LLLLDTL, LLSFM, LLLL 4828
LLLLRFMR, LLTSLDTL, 3201
LLLLFD, SSSSMS, F#MRL 5772
LLLLFLLLSM, SSSSRS 8852
LLLLSF#M, RLLF#SF#MR, S 2140
LLLLSSSS, SRMFSM, LL 11272
LLLLS#L, LLTDRM, DRD 7448
LLLLLDTL, LS#LDMS, FF 3684
LLLLLSM, SLSSMR, MMM 5877
LLLLLLLS, LLLLSLLL 7582
LLLLLLLS#F#S#L, DDDDD 2162
LLL, LLL, LLDDRM, MMDL 9986
LLLLLLLT, DDDL#LSF, M 4586
LLLLLTTLSL, LLLSSS 8958
LLLLTDRM, LSFMLLT 3606
LLLLTDTRT, TLTDRTR 8221
LLLLTTDL, DRMRDTT, L 8213
LLLTDRM, MMMRDDT, TT 4990
LLLTDTLSM, FFFMRSM, 7422
LLLTDTLSF#M, MMRDTL 11056
LLLTDTLSLL, LLTDTL 5118
LLLTDTL, LTDMRDT, DT 622
LLLTDTL, TTTDRDT, D 1823
LLLTDTTL, LDDDRRSM, 1640
LLLTLS, LLLTLS, LTDT 6653
LLLTLTDMMRDT, DDRM 1098
LLLTTDRM, MRRLTD, DM 10240
LLLTTDLS, SDRDTD, DD 2884
LLLTTDLS, SDMRRDDD, 2883
LLTDDT, DTLSL, DDRMM 8234
LLTDDTRDTLM, LLTDD 11908
LLTDDTLT, TDRMMMRM, 1429
LLTDDTTL, LDDRSM, MM 1639
LLTDRMDR, LDMF#RMM, M
LLTDRMDTL, DTLS#LT 81
LLTDRMRD, MSFMRDTL, 10139
LLTDRMRDT, S#LTDRMM 1398
LLTDRMRDTLLS#, S#S#LT 5010
LLTDRM, MRRDDT, TDRM 3949
LLTDRM, MRRDDT, TDRM, MR 4084
LLTDRM, MMRDDT, TDRM 3948
LLTDRM, MMRDRT, TDRM 3947
LLTDRMM, MLLS#L, LLT 10149
LLTDRMM, SMLS#L, LLTD 4215
LLTDRM, SFMRRM, SMSL 713
LLTDRMT, TDTLDT, S#LT 5821
LLTDRTD, LLTDRTM, DD 4776
LLTDRTS, SLLTTM, LLT 4190
LLTDMRDT, DRFMRDTD, 5987
LLTDMRDT, DLTDRM, MR 9465
LLTDMRDTLSSL, TDRM 8924
LLTDMMMFMRM, MRMFM 9048
LLTDMTL, TMRDDT, TMT 7772
LLTDFMRDTL, MLTDRM, 8196
LLTDLDRM, SLSMDRRM, 7885
LLTDLMMM, LMMRDRM, L 3669
LLTDLTDRM, MMMSMRR 4077
LLTDLTS, SLLTTM, LLT 4192
LLTDLTTLLSLTTL, LR 9834
LLTDTDRDTLM, SFMRM 12501
LLTDTMF#SLFM, SF#MRR 1748

LLTDTLDFMLL, DDRR#R 6942
LLTDTLMRDT, LLTDTL 3450
LLTDTLFL, TDRMRS, SL 8752
LLTDTLS, SDMRRM, LLT 4388
LLTDTLSLM, MRMFMRMD, 2064
LLTDTLSLLL, DDRFM 2863
LLTDTLS#LTML, S#LTLT 2876
LLTDTLLS#, DMRDTD, DM 12307
LLTDTL, TDRMRM, MRDT 2479
LLTDTLTTDRDTL, MR 2827
LLTD#RM, RFRDL#L, DDTD 10219
LLTLS, LDTLM, TDTL. 7667
LLTLS#, LTDTLTM, TDRM 7668
LLTLTDRT, LDMRMFMR, 6995
LLTTDDS, LLMMFSSF 4282
LLTTDDT, LTDDDTLS#, L 8460
LLTTTDRM, MRRLLTDD 5664
LTDDRDTL, DRMMLSLM 4573
LTDDRDTT, DTLTLS#LL 2508
LTDDRRDD, LTDRMFRM 2402
LTDDRRM, DRMMF#F#S, LS 9889
LTDDRRMM, MDTDRDTT, 7270
LTDDRMDSSS, MRDDL 8275
LTDDSFSFM, LTDDSSS 4342
LTDDTSLLLTDDRM, MR 10871
LTDDTLS, FMRLSFMFS, 5277
LTDDTLS#L, LLSMSFM, L 6394
LTDRDTDLT, DTLSFML 12195
LTDRDTLDTLSLL, LMS 9538
LTDRMRDRT, LTDTLLS 7814
LTDRMRDTDT, LTDDRM 8407
LTDRMRDT, RDLDTSL, L 3891
LTDRMMRDTLS#S#, LTDT 2371
LTDRMMRMM, MMFSFM 8456
LTDRMMFMFRM, MDDRR 4283
LTDRMMFMFLM, RRTDD 4284
LTDRMFFM, MRDTLLS#, L 6366
LTDRMFS#, LTDDRRD, LT 1789
LTDRMSMRTL, RMLDRM, 10346
LTDRMSF#M, MMMRDRM, L 6286
LTDRMLRMFML, LLSSS 10319
LTDRMLRDTSLSL, LSD 8534
LTDRMLRT, DDRMFFM, 128
LTDRMLSF, MMRDTT 10527
LTDRMLLS#LL, DTLSFF 10173
LTDRMLLS#LTL, LTDRM 1549
LTDRMT, RMF#SLM, SF#RT, 2728
LTDRSF#SMLSMRDLTL, 55
LTDRLTLTD, DTLSMMF# 10560
LTDRTM, RTDLTL, LLTD 3683
LTDRTLS, DRMFMRD, LT 8592
LTDMRDT, MF#SMLSF#M, L 6168
LTDMRDT, SDRMFFM, LT 2096
LTDMRDTTT, RDRMFMR 7260
LTDMMRDDT, LTDRMRD 2344
LTDMMRDTL, LTDTLS# 1242
LTDMM, LTDMM, FMRTLL 4619
LTDMLDTL, DRMMRRD, L 4121
LTDLDRMD, MFSMRRD, M 4728
LTDLMMM, MMRDTL, LTD 11124
LTDLFFFM, LLSFMRDT, 4322
LTDLSMS#LLTD, RMMRD 1946
LTDLTDL, DDRMRDT, RR 7626
LTDTDRMM, LTDTLLS#L, D 3895
LTDTDRMM, LTDTLLS#L, L 3895a
LTDTDLMM, LTDTDRM, M 1002
LTDTLDTLSLM, LTDTL 9965
LTDTLRRD#, LMRSF#M, MM 12444
LTDTLRMFFM, MMRDTL 5091
LTDTLS, RRMFLSFMFS, 1686
LTDTLS, MMF#LS#L, SSLS 269
LTDTLSM, SDTLSL, LTD 8743
LTDTLSM, SLTLSL, LTD 10274
LTDTLSM, LSFMDRM, 8369
LTDTLSL, DRMMFMFRM, 3503
LTDTLSLS, DRMDRRD, D 10359
LTDTLS, LTDRL, DRMM 5846
LTDTLS#L, DRMRDTD, MM 7482
LTDTLS#L, DRMFMRM, FM 4168
LTDTLS#LTDTL, DRRMDRRM, 10293
LTDTLL, DDTLSLLM, SL 4613
LTDTLLRMFMR, RDMTM 9945
LTDTLLSL, LFSMRFMR 12384
LTDTLLS#L, MMRRDDT, T 1448
LTDTLLS#LT, DRDT, LTL 800
LTDTL, LTDTL, MRDT, TD 2829
LTDTLTS#M, MLRDTTL, L 4547
LTDTLTS#L, DRMLSFM, T 12057
LTDTLTL, DDRMDR, RMF 9961
LTDTTLLSM, LTDTTLL 6720
LTRDSSFM, MF#LSDTLS, 7518
LTRRTRMFM, MLSLM, DD 1097
LTRLTRDTDL, DRMMRD 5326
LTMRDTLS#L, TDDRRM, M 2638
LTSDTLSL, MLTLDDTD, 8059
LTSMLLS#L, DRMRDDTD, 12325
LTLSLTDTLT, MLTLSL 2679
LTLS#LDTLLS#, S#LLSLS 5565
LTLS#LTDT, TDRMRDTL, 10755
LTLS#TDTL, DRMDRMD, D 9580

LTLTDDRDRM, MSFMMR 11286
LTLTDRDT, LDTTLSL, L 5080
LTLTRMMR, TLLSMS, SL 11952
LTTD, DDRM, FMMRDTTL, 8603
LTTDS# LTDRDTL, TDTD 4172
LTTDLLRTDLL, DDRMD 8572
LTTDLTSL, LTRDTDLT, 11514

TDD

TDDTLSM, SSSFR, LLLS 939
TDRDRM, MRDDDMDR, SS 12146
TDRDRM, MFFFMSMR, SF 4851
TDRDRMMFFFLSM, DRM 503
TDRRDRMD, SSLDTLS, M 1977
TDRRDRMM, RMFFMDR, S 6031
TDRRDRMMMMMFMR, MFS 901
TDRRRDRMD, RMRDTLS, 1999
TDRRRRDRM, SSLLLDT 4849
TDRRRRDTD, DTLLLDT 8016
TDRRRRRT, LTDDDRDS, 4484
TDRRRRFMRDS, DRMMM 7216
TDRRFMRDR, SRRFMRD 7619
TDRRFTDD, MFSSSMR, S 1864
TDRMRMLSMRDL, DMFS 6322
TDRFTD, MFSSMR, SDMM 1863
TDMSSLSDM, SFRTFMR 4921
TDSMDLL, LLLTDTL, SD 1401
TDTDRMRDT, SDDSRM, L 1778
TDTLMRDT, RDTLRDTL, 109
TDTLTDRDTLS#, MLLTD 4727
TDTLTDRDTLS#MLTDR 4726
TDTLTRDT, RDTDLSFM, 3052
TDTLTRDT, TDTDLLFM, 2307
TDTLTRMRDT, RDTDLS 3053
TRDDDSDLD, DDDSDL 11233
TRDM, MMMMMRDRRRRD 3868
TRMRDTLTT, SLTTTTT 7447
TRMTSS, LDTLSTSLS, 9643
TMRTRDTLTDDRDRM, M 2429
TMS# LTRDT, TDLTS# LT, T 10095
TMTDTSLT, TDRDLSFM, 2403
TMTDTLSLT, TDRDTLS 2406
TMTDTLS# LT, TRRDTLS 2405
TSDD, RR, MFSFMRD. 1667
TSFR# RR# FR# RDS, SLDRM 327
TLSDSLLLLS, F# MRDF# F# 2187
TLSDS, TLSM, MFMMRD 11267
TL# LFFMSM, MRSR, RDSD, 3406
TTDMMRM, MRD# RLLL, LL 6247
TTRTDT, LDTLS, DSSSL 5190
TTLT, TTSL, DDTD, DDLT, 4491
TTTDDRS, DDRRM, MMMD 4021
TTTDR, DDDLS, MMMSLS 12235
TTTDTLTDR, DRMLTDR 10987

APPENDIXES

APPENDIX A

GLOSSARY

Author: That person, institution, publisher, compiler, anthology, or tradition responsible for writing, approval, or transmittal to others of the earliest verified text of the hymn (as poem).

Chorus: See Refrain

Citation: Directive to a named hymnal, a very specified numbered hymn or tune, or to a page on which that hymn or tune is printed. For purposes of this Index, citations are made only to the item numbers (see below) which are chronologically representative of the first appearance of the text of hymn or tune within each hymnal as analyzed.

Composer: See Author, and substitute "of the tune (as music)" for the underlined words.

Congregational song: Vocal music, varying greatly from sect to sect and from meeting to meeting, used at community worship in an act of community participation. Modern literature of this nature is predominantly secular in origin, social in nature, and dedicated to Man's decision to meet the Divine Ideal.

Descant: Contrasting and decorative melody, usually a soprano solo, which becomes a vocal accompaniment to the hymn tune. In common practice it is used with selected stanzas only: in a short hymn, perhaps at the third or fourth stanza; in a long hymn, perhaps near the middle of the hymn, and again at the final or near final stanza. Descants are not indexed.

Diatonic scale: The melodic eight-tone scale used in most western music, proceeding naturally without chromatic interruption, and in any key. The relative musical intervals and syllable names are constant, no matter the key of the printed score.

First line: Usually the first line of the poetical hymn, but occasionally enlarged to avoid confusion with similar phrases.

First phrases of melody: Here determined as approximately the sixteen opening tones of the score as sung to the accompanying words, and recorded in the tonic sol-fa syllables.

Flats: See Sharps; also the schedule on p.viii.

Gospel song: Poem (usually sung) encouraging man to offer honor, worship, praise to God. See also Hymn.

Hymn: Poem (usually sung) in praise to God. See also Gospel song.

Hymn tune: A musical setting of a hymn or psalm, usually in four-part harmony, and intended for use in public worship. See also Hymn, and Tune.

Item number: The specific number, within a specific hymnal, that identifies desirable information exactly; as BQ3 points to Book BQ, according to the symboloc terminology of this Index, and to the particular content numbered Three (3). It may be used to indicate a rendering of a hymn, a hymn tune, a tune name, or a variant of any of these three.

Liturgy: That portion of the act of public worship which is formal in nature, and chiefly dominated by the clergy rather than the congregation; but in which a priest-and-people antiphonal question-and-answer, statement-and-response is elemental. Originally used to describe the Mass, and the directives and rubrics pertaining thereto.

Melody: A series of single notes arranged in musically expressive succession. (O.U.D.)

Movable Do: See the illustrations, Appendix D. Notice that the syllable names follow regularly as the scale opening tone varies. The intervals are constant, the tone names are constant no matter the key of the score.

Refrain of hymn or tune: The words or the melody repetitively sung between formal poetical stanzas of the hymn. Citations are not made to refrains; simply records of their texts, and references by use of letter R to the Standard First Line or the Standard Tune Name.

Serial number: The chronological entry number in Index I or Index III, beginning respectively with 100001 (Index I) and 1 (Index III).

These numbers are used in Indexes II and IV, respectively, to assemble related materials alphabetically displayed in Indexes I and III. The numbers found at Index V relate to those at Index III. (Some serial numbers are eliminated because of resolved conflicts.)

Sharps: The symbols used to indicate a half-step rise in the physical value of a musical tone. The character is #. Sharps are used in these Indexes when indicated by the score; and when used in substitution for flats (according to the schedule on viii. Flats are not represented herein, except by way of the relative sharped (raised) tone instead of its printed lowered counterpart tone. This procedure was adopted to expedite the mechanical work involved within the Index. Musical purists will be unhappy! The piano will sing the same sounds.

Solfaing: See Solmization

Solmization: Singing melodies to the syllables of the tonic sol-fa scale.

Source: Book in which required materials are included.

Primary source: The original book or manuscript containing the text as it was set at the time of its composition.

Secondary sources: Books, such as the seventy-eight hymnals herein analyzed, with reprint of words and music. Except for a handful of sources, quoted within these hymnals, everything is from Secondary Sources. Several manuscripts, the Church Gallery Book, and a few of the very earliest hymnals are mostly what might be here called Primary Sources. Consequently, the term Sources is usually used.

Standard: For purposes of this Index only, Standard indicates the hymn or tune as printed in the book in which it was initially discovered as the cataloging progressed. This might have been at Book A, or Book BZ.

Standard first line: The reading of the first line of a hymn (poem) as it was initially recorded within the cumulation of this Index. Citations to this are made as they appear during the progress of the indexing.

Standard melody: The reading of the first phrase of the melody as it was initially recorded during the cumulation of this Index. Citations to this are made as they appear during the progress of the indexing.

Standard tune name: The name associated with a melody as it was initially recorded during the cumulation of this Index. The standard tune name serves as a label to identify the standard melody with which it is associated. Citations, apparently to the standard tune name, are in reality attributed to the standard melody.

Standard first line, melody, or tune name: The second to be established: When a variant of any of these is sufficient to cause identification and discrimination difficulties, a second reading is established as standard, and citations are made to it as they occur during the progress of the indexing.

Syllables: The tone names associated with the intervals in the diatonic musical scale, which is not dependent on Fixed-Do, and is based on the simple scale without chromatic intrusion.

Tonic Solfa scale: Syllable names of the diatonic scale are Do(D), Re(R), Mi(M), Fa(F), Sol(S), La(L), and Ti(T), with the sequence repeating. Letters in parentheses are the symbols used for melodic record in this Index. In case a tone is raised one-half step, it is marked as: S#

Tune: A rhythmical succession of musical tones, here referring to the tones to which a hymn is set for use in congregational singing.

Tune name: Name assigned to a melody. Established tradition in the association of melody with tune name is usually weak, as indicated by the large number of variants in Index IV. Nevertheless, all assigned tune names have herein been accepted as tune names, have been recorded, and references inserted to tie the related tune names to the standard tune name for the purposes of the index.

Variant first line, melody: Slight deviant rendering of text or tune which does not cause confusion in identification. Citations are limited to one time only (that first), with X symbolizing reference to standard first line in Index I; and V symbolizing reference to standard melody in Index III.

Variant tune name: Name for a melody which differs from the standard tune name. No citations are made, simply a reference X to the established or standard tune name is made at Index III.

APPENDIX B

ABBREVIATIONS

abr	abridged
arr	arranged, arranger
Baker	Baker's Biographical dictionary of musicians, 5th ed., rev. by Slonimsky. Schirmer [c 1958]
c	century
ca	circa
cf	compare
comp	compiled, compiler
d	died
D	Do (syllable)
F	Fa (syllable)
fl	flourished
Fr	Father (priest)
G-B	Gesangbuch
harm	harmony
Jr	Junior
Julian	Julian. A dictionary of hymnology. Dover [1957] 2 v
K-G	Kirchengesangbuch
L	La (syllable)
M	Mi (syllable) mode (plainchant): M is frequently followed by arabic number 1-8, to indicate the melodic mode to which the tune is set
mel	melody
OUD, or O. U. D.	Oxford Universal dictionary on historical principles. 3d ed. rev. Oxford [1955]
p	page
pseud	pseudonym
publ	published
R	Re (syllable) refrain (chorus)
S	Sol (syllable)
Sr	Senior Sister (nun)
suppl	supplement
T	Ti (syllable)
tr	translated, translator
trad	traditional
univ	university
V	variant reading volume
S	see; see also (rare)
A-Z, AA-AZ, and BA-BZ	symbols used to identify hymnals analyzed (see List of books indexed)
#	sharp
♭	flat (unused symbol)
,	musical phrase ending
.	melodic ending
?	authorship disputed
??	authorship ascribed
( )	encloses source, or author, in Indexes I and III

[ ]	unintentionally a very few were allowed to stand in the melodic redaction as indication of notes not always used: normal procedure was to make an additional variant entry.	1-8	following M (as M2) indicates plainchant in Mode Two; etc.
		I, II, III	arbitrarily added to tune names to serve as identification symbols for sorting purposes.

APPENDIX C

ARBITRARY DECISIONS ADOPTED IN THIS INDEX

Always use Alleluia, Jam, O, and Sion; no other spelling accepted either as entry word or within the text where filing order would be affected except in the case of Zion in German.

Always interfile Savior and Saviour, Jesu and Jesus; but spell as printed.

Always use The, A, or An when presented as initial words in Indexes I and III; and recognize them in filing sequences.

Never use The, A, or An when presented as initial words in titles of books, except for the purposes of clarification; and always disregard them for purposes of filing.

Initialisms, i.e., persons known by initials only, are entered straightforward only; never inverted. Reference from inverted order is not made.

Pseudonyms are occasionally identified, and some references are made. Additional identification is now and then included in special notes within Indexes II and IV.

Traditional hymns and tunes (carols, folk songs, diocesan tunes) are attributed to the tradition, if possible the date is given, and the mode indicated when it is known for Gregorian plainsongs and for Jewish melodies.

Anonymity was a final resort only. It has been possible, even here, to occasionally indicate approximate date or region from which the material sprung.

Hymns and tunes which fall into these impersonal categories (initialisms, pseudonymous, traditional, and anonymous) were usually not subdivided. Rather the list is alphabetical, with some sorting device (as date, mode, etc.) after the name. This seemed more practical for the reader, and required but little more space to delineate.

Dates of birth and death of author or composer, of publication, of era of origin; full names of authors and composers (including unused forenames when known) have been included in Indexes II and IV. Julian and Baker have been combed almost name-by-name; indexes of sources within all hymnals have been consistently used; and special attention has been paid to information within recently published hymnals for verification and for completing biographical notes.

Honorifics (as, Lord, Sir, Rev.) are infrequently used; members of the Catholic hierarchy are usually identified (as, Innocent IV, Pope); and saints are named by use of "St" as opening term. This is a departure from most library practice, from Catholic practice. It is adopted here because congregational song has been, historically, a Protestant manifestation. The literature of hymnody since the Protestant Reformation, from Protestant sources, tends to follow the practice here utilized.

Exclude Hymnal C from the citation record of hymns. They are absolute duplication of items and item numbers found in Book B. The tunes, however, differ and are indexed fully.

APPENDIX D

THE SCALES

1) Tune name; 2) Composer; 3) Date; 4) Notation; 5) Solmization; 6) Hymn; 7) Author; 8) Date; 9) Original source; 10) Common meter

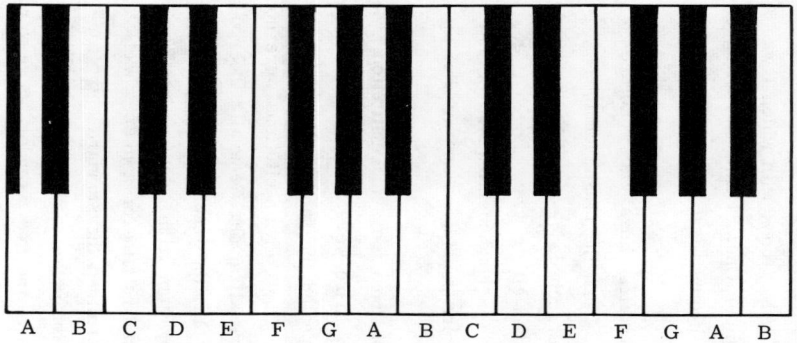

APPENDIX E

PIANO KEYBOARD

The musical scale with neither sharps nor flats is known as Key C. It begins on key marked C.

The hymn illustrated in Appendix D is in Key of B Flat, and the first piano key struck is that marked F.

When a musical tone is raised by one-half step (a sharp), the note next closest to the right is struck, rather than the note bearing the usual syllable name. Notice the example near to the end of the illustration in Appendix D.

APPENDIX F

HOW THIS BOOK WAS CUMULATED

Beginning with The Hymnal, 1940 (A), a book with which I was very familiar, and with Hymn Number One, "Come, thou long-expected Jesus" by Witt (1715), the hymns were taken one-by-one and book-by-book.

Poetry (i.e., the poets and the first lines) was recorded -- card-by-card, citation-by-citation. Then the music (composer, melodic sequence, tune name) was recorded -- card-by-card, citation-by-citation, book-by-book. When either was repeated (i.e., absolute identity) within a book, the second mention was not made. When variants were quoted they were considered and cited if appropriate to the Index.

When Book B, an earlier book from the same institution, was studied, variants appeared. By C, there were still further variants. In fact, all of the poetry of C repeated the same order of B; and the music was variant throughout. The C hymn citations were not made; the C melodic citations were all made. Generally the routine of completing both the hymns and the tunes within a single book was followed, always item-by-item from Number One.

That book (hymnal) in which a first line or a melody was noticed originally (first time) determined the standard entry for this Index. It may not have been the original reading, but it served as the base around which to pivot the many renderings of words and of music in these seventy-eight books. No attempt has been made, ever! to identify or to reconstruct texts; but a seriously consistent effort has been made to cite as source that person, institution, publisher, compiler, anthology, or culture originally responsible for its inception or its transmission; and to relate materials which belong together. When a closely variant rendering appeared, two citations were made: (1) at the main, or standard, entry (as tune name, or at first line respectively) and (2) at the independent secondary entry with this special variation recorded, and with a reference to the standard form.

A refrain or chorus, as part of hymn or tune, required full quotation of first line and also of first sixteen notes of the melody. Refrain cards bear no citations, simply references to standard entry.

Variants to the refrain, either words or melody, were cited one time only and in the same manner as variants to the standard entry (as indicated in second paragraph above).

Thus far only one standard form has been considered. Variants appeared which were both too severe, and too popular, to treat as secondary items. Alternate forms were established as standard, as those found under Whittier's name (Index II, as author) or the several Cherry Tree Carols (Index IV, as English traditional).

At the end of the work, when Book BZ had been completed, most of the poetry had been automatically sorted. The problem was the music.

Up to this time four indexes were being made concurrently: two for the hymns (first line and author); two for the music (tune name and composer). And up to this time musical relationships could be assured only when human memory was assisted by citation similarities. Tune names and tune sources had long since been discarded as definitive. They are irregular. They are inexact. They are capriciously applied. Melodic similarities could not be completely trusted, no matter how like seemed the labels.

The only solution was to immediately create Index V out of what is here displayed as Index III, and to do it immediately. Simple tune name references were eliminated. All the others were arranged as published in Index V. Identical melodies were found. Many of these had been attributed to both real and anonymous sources, to both real and traditional sources, to different published sources, to different diocesan (see) sources. This sorting reduced both the German traditional and the English traditional sections by at least twenty-five percent. The various gesangbuchs, Walther, Luther, Bourgeois, and Psalter entries were cumulated.

Syllabic reading of the melodies proved to be effective in every instance except one. That was early in the study, and no record was retained of the melodies involved -- but they were of secondary importance so far as common usage was concerned. It has thus proved necessary, only in the ratio of 1:12582 instances, to record the time signature, note value, or high and low tones in order to completely identify melodies of songs which people ordinarily sing.

When apparently identical or closely variant melodies were found, hymnals had to be studied to verify similarity. Then all references were collected and directed to that form determined as standard (once again identifying the initial citation chronologically within this Index). Some of these variants required hours of work. I hope the reader will find few unresolved references. Fourteen tune names to what are here standardised as "Cana" and "Ratisbon", both of them old German melodies, are the extreme. Only when the very final editing was being done, and after many pages had already been put into final form by the Scarecrow Press typist, could the two pairs of "14" be appropriately filed.

Index V, "Melodies, a systematic index" was typed after the duplicates had been removed and serial numeration confirmed. Cards then had to be returned to order for Index III. It was at this time that information could be gathered to enlarge Index IV's value -- just as similar information was cumulated from Index I to enlarge Index II.

When thirty-five books had been completed only these twelve poems were found common:

Abide with me (Lyte)
Adeste fideles (Latin, 18th c., and in several translations)
All hail the power (Perronet)
Hark! the herald angels (Wesley)
Holy, holy, holy (Heber)
Jesus, lover of my soul (Wesley)
Jesus shall reign (Watts)
O [Our] God, our help in ages past (Watts)
Saviour again to thy dear name (Ellerton)
Sun of my soul (Keble)
The church's one foundation (Stone)

When I survey the wondrous cross (Watts)

With Book #36, AJ, two of these fell out. As the Jewish, the less orthodox and more dissident Christian books and the widely differing Catholic hymnals were surveyed, the number of constantly recurring words and music was reduced. But accretion improved. The Church of Jesus Christ of Latter-Day Saints, the Moravians, the Christian Scientists each forced new entries for a very, very large number of hymns and tunes. The earlier of the two Moravian books (AZ) contains more than 1500 hymns. There is a relatively small number of melodies -- but each has at least two distinguishing tune names!

The usual portion of words and tunes new to the Index in the later analyses was close to fifteen percent. Constant tallying pointed to a very wide range of congregational song known only to a particular institution. The specific instances which follow are illustrative:

Union hymnal (BH) and The Oxford Book of carols (BG) each introduced materials which were well analyzed. Every Catholic book was rich in texts and in scores not recorded earlier, but the sources (i.e., the authors and the composers) were less regularly reported than in many of the counterpart liturgical Protestant hymnals.

Anglican Hymn book (BV) melodies included ninety-five new ones (14 percent) and its new hymns numbered eighty-three (12.5 per cent). The melodic index arranged metrically with the initial measures of the score quoted is an innovation to hymnals.

The Baptist hymn book (BY) presented 103 new hymns and 244 new tunes, or 13.38 and 26.5 percent respectively. Both BV and BY are books from Britain, published within the recent five years.

A letter from The Methodist Publishing House and dated February 16, 1966 gives this information:

"Our plans now are to release this new Hymnal sometime in July, 1966.

"The title page reads as follows:

THE METHODIST HYMNAL

Official Hymnal of The Methodist Church
The Methodist Publishing House
Nashville, Tennessee"

The final book indexed (BZ) is representative of the hymnal just recorded. By close comparison of the Report, i.e. BZ, and the 1935 edition (G) it was found that twenty-six new melodies and twenty-eight new poems were added to the Index file. There are to be, according to the Report's statistics, 402 tunes and 539 hymns in the 1966 edition.

It would seem by comparing and contrasting editorial arrangements made for books BV, BY, and BZ that there was a basic difference. Anglican Hymn book had a Committee of twelve members; The Baptist hymn book, a Committee of twenty members; and Report to the 1964 General Conference, which is representative of The Methodist hymnal [1966] had forty-two named persons and a battery of questionnaires sent to 22,000 ministers -- more than half of whom responded. Relative contrast with books such as X, Y, BG, BH, and BJ -- where individuals or a small editorial committee were free to work untrammeled by public and institutional opinion -- show a peculiar earthy freshness added. Some of this may pass, or be congregationally neglected; other will have had the opportunity to prove itself good. On the other hand it must be said that The Methodist hymnal [1966] editorial policy stated a serious intent of returning Wesleyan hymns to the people. This has been done. It does not show in statistics here published, because the hymns had been recorded from older publications.

Coming from a childhood in Lancaster County, Pennsylvania, I knew this region as anvil and crucible for religion. The Swedes (Lutherans) had almost reached us; Penn's influence was there in the Quaker Meeting House south of Quarryville; the Scottish-Irish-English were evident in the southern section -- where there were Methodist and Presbyterian congregations, often joined by Friends; just a small Baptist congregation in the county seat. There were United Brethren (not Unitas Fratrum), Evangelical, River Brethren, Dunkard, Amish, New Mennonite, Mennonite, Church of the Brethren, Church of God. Anglican influence was strongest in Lancaster

City and in the old iron mining community of Mt. Hope. The Reformed-Lutheran Union churches, common to the counties just east of Lancaster, were here separate institutions with separate places of worship. Lititz has its strong Moravian community, its Linden Hall -- the oldest women's college in the U.S.A., now an academy only. Roman Catholic churches were at the county seat; quite recently a large Greek Orthodox community has immigrated. Lancaster City has had an active Unitarian congregation for many years; and the Jewish congregation in the City is large and strong.

This personal note explains the presence of certain hymnals which are easily overlooked. It particularly explains Ausbund (BU) which originated in 1570. The Amish people love to sing, their young people past sixteen years of age have their Saturday evening "singings", and their services on Sundays are three to four hours long. When you consider that Hans Betz's hymn (BU106) "Ihr Christen g'mein" has forty-six eight-line stanzas, it is necessary to allow a bit of time!

Just one Ausbund hymn (BU131) was found elsewhere: "Our Father God, thy name we praise", at BY362. In its original form it is used at every Sunday morning service as the second hymn, according to a letter from M.E. Ressler (Secretary to Music, Lancaster Mennonite Conference, September 14, 1965). The British Baptists sing their three stanzas to the tune "Mit freunden zart"; the Amish sing their four stanzas to "Aus tiefer noth", which is indicated as alternate tune in BY.

Tying for first place as most generally used tune are Bourgeois's "Old 100th" (associated with either Praise God, from whom all blessings flow, or All people that on earth do dwell) and "Adeste fideles", found in Wade's Cantus diversi. These are in seventy of the books examined.

Second place, as in sixty-seven books, is held by "St Anne", by Croft (associated with O God, our help in ages past).

In tie for third, in sixty-six books, are "Moscow" by Giardini (associated with Come thou almighty king) and Dykes's "Niceae" which is closely associated with Holy, holy, holy, holy, Lord God.

The most used hymn, as might be surmised, is the 18th century Latin "Adeste fideles" when it is completely reckoned. Latin text, translations beginning, "Come hither", "Ye faithful, come hither", "Come, all ye faithful", "O come, all ye faithful", etc. are found in seventy hymnals. Actually, had it been in more than seventy books, it would have been somewhat misplaced: several books include pre-18th century hymns only, one is a book of carols (this is a composed poem), one is a Jewish hymnal, one is Christian Science hymnal, one a psalter, one a secondary book to its partner.

"O God, our help in ages past", Isaac Watts' metrical paraphrase of the 90th Psalm, is in sixty-seven books: a perfect mating with tune "St Anne", in the same manner as "Adeste fideles" words and tune are perfectly mated.

Found under fourteen different tune names are the melodies standardized here as "Cana," by Vulpius, and "Ratisbon", published by Crueger. The greatest number of actual melodic variants has not been sought, but would most probably exist in some one of the early German hymn tunes which proved popular and singable.

Serial numeration in the first line file (Index I) indicates 11979 entry lines (numbering begins with 100001).

Parallel Index III is serially numbered from 1 to 12582.

By adding the number of hymns published in each of these hymnals, there is a total of 39,373 printed hymns in the seventy-eight books. This means that at least that many exact citations are recorded with the Index I entries.

Comparably, after considering that a great many hymns are set to two or even three tunes, it is most likely that about the same number of tunes were examined, but cited only once per tune per hymnal (total citations for tunes are fewer in Index III, than for first lines in Index I).

If a guess may be hazarded, I would estimate that about 3200 references are made to variant tune names; 2500 references to variant first lines; 1000 to first lines of refrains; 1000 to first phrases of refrain melody; and 1000 to variants of the standard melody. In other words, there are almost 24,500 first line and melody entries. Of these, approximately 8700 are references of one sort or another. The ratio is approximately 1:2 as references and primary entries are counted. It is symbolic, very symbolic, of the nearly insurmountable indexing and musicological literary confusion which had to be cleared. Hopefully there is a bit more consistency!

APPENDIX G

General Survey of Hymnals As Books of Reference

	A	B	C	D	E	F	G	H	I	J	K	L	M	N	O	P	Q	R	S	T	U	V	W	X	Y	Z
Title page with authority symbol	*	*	*	*			*	*	*	*	*	*	*	*	*		*	*	*	*	*	*	*			
Table of contents	*	*	*	*	*	*	*	*	*	*	*	*	*	*	*	*	*	*	*	*	*	*	*	*	*	*
Sources acknowledged fully	*	*			*	*													*				*	*	*	*
Birth/Death dates of Author/Composer	*	*		*	*	*	*			*	*			*		*	*	*	*				*	*	*	*
HYMNS (Poetry)																										
First line index	*	*	*	*	*	*	*	*	*	*	*	*	*	*	*	*	*	*	*	*	*	*	*	*	*	*
Author index	*	*	*	*	*	*	*		*	*	*			*	*	*	*	*	*				*	*	*	*
Hymns of the historical faith	*	*	*	*	*	*	*	*	*	*	*	*	*	*	*	*	*	*	*				*	*	*	*
Psalter in meter																		*		*		*				
19th-20th century hymns	*	*	*	*	*	*	*	*	*	*	*	*	*	*							*	*	*		*	*
Children's hymns named	*	*		*	*	*	*	*	*					*	*							*	*	*		*
TUNES (Music)																										
Tune name index, alphabetical	*	*	*	*	*	*	*	*	*	*	*	*	*	*	*	*	*	*	*	*	*	*	*	*	*	*
Tune name index, metrical	*	*	*	*	*	*	*	*	*	*	*	*	*	*	*	*	*	*	*	*	*	*	*	*	*	*
Composer index	*	*	*	*	*	*	*	*	*	*	*			*	*	*	*	*	*	*			*	*	*	*
Plainsongs included	*	*		*	*	*																				
Reformation tunes	*	*		*	*	*	*	*	*	*	*	*	*	*	*	*	*	*	*	*	*	*	*	*		*
Folk tunes, all cultures	*						*	*	*															*	*	
Gospel songs							*	*	*												*					
EDITORIAL POLICIES, etc.																										
Preface (or other) Statement on Song	*	*			*	*				*												*	*	*		
Specialties of the book										*	1						2					3	4		5	6
Liturgical section	*	*	*	*	*		*	*	*	*	*	*	*	*	*	*	*	*		*	*				*	*
Prayer book section (or substitute)							*	*	*	*	*	*	*	*	*	*	*									
Documents of the historical faith												31				32				33						

	AA	AB	AC	AD	AE	AF	AG	AH	AI	AJ	AK	AL	AM	AN	AO	AP	AQ	AR	AS	AT	AU	AV	AW	AX	AY	AZ
Title page with authority symbol	*				*			*			*	*	*	*	*	*	*	*	*	*		*	*	*	*	*
Table of contents	*	*	*	*	*	*	*	*	*	*	*	*	*	*	*	*	*	*	*	*		*	*	*	*	*
Sources acknowledged fully		*				*		*			*	*		*		*	*						*			
Birth/Death dates of Author/ Composer	*	*	*	*	*	*	*	*			*	*	*	*	*	*	*	*	*	*		*	*			*
HYMNS (Poetry)																										
First line index	*	*	*	*	*	*	*	*	*	*	*	*	*	*	*	*	*	*	*	*	*	*	*	*	*	*
Author index		*	*	*	*	*	*	*			*	*	*	*	*	*	*	*	*	*		*	*			*
Hymns of the historical faith	*					*	*	*	*	*		*	*	*	*	*	*	*	*			*	*	*	*	*
Psalter in meter						*			*	*		*	*	*		*	*						*			
19th-20th century hymns		*	*	*	*	*	*	*			*	*	*	*	*	*	*	*	*	*	*	*	*	*	*	
Children's hymns named	*				*	*	*		*		*	*	*		*	*						*	*	*		
TUNES (Music)																										
Tune name index, alphabetical	*	*	*	*	*	*	*	*	*	*	*	*	*	*	*	*	*	*	*	*	*	*	*			*
Tune name index, metrical	*	*	*	*	*	*	*	*	*	*	*	*	*	*	*	*			*		*	*	*			*
Composer index		*	*	*	*	*	*	*		*	*	*	*	*	*	*	*	*	*		*	*	*			*
Plainsongs included																										
Reformation tunes	*	*		*	*	*	*	*	*	*		*	*	*	*	*	*	*					*			*
Folk tunes, all cultures		*	*	*		*		*		*				*			*						*			*
Gospel songs					*			*	*				*					*	*	*	*	*	*	*	*	
EDITORIAL POLICIES																										
Preface (or other) statement on song						*						*		*		*	*	*					*			
Specialties of the book	7	8	9			10	11			12	13			14			15								16	17
Liturgical section	*	*	*	*	*	*	*	*	*		*		*	*	*		*	*	*	*	*		*			*
Prayer book section (or substitute)	*		*	*	*	*		*			*			*	*			*								*
Documents of the Historical faith										34			35													

General Survey of Hymnals As Books of Reference - Appendix G

General Survey of Hymnals As Books of Reference - Appendix G

	BA	BB	BC	BD	BE	BF	BG	BH	BI	BJ	BK	BL	BM	BN	BO	BP	BQ	BR	BS	BT	BU	BV	BW	BX	BY	BZ
Title page with authority symbol	*	*	*		*			*	*	*	*	*	*	*	*	*	*	*	*	*	*	*	*	*	*	*
Table of contents	*	*	*	*		*	*	*	*	*	*	*	*	*	*	*		*	*	*	*	*	*	*	*	*
Sources acknowledged fully						*	*	*		*		*	*	*					*		*	*		*	*	?
Birth/Death dates of Author/ Composer	*	*			*	*	*		*	*		*		*						*		*	*	*	*	*
HYMNS (Poetry)																										
First line index	*	*	*	*	*	*	*	*	*	*	*	*	*	*	*	*	*	*	*	*	*	*	*	*	*	*
Author index	*	*	*		*	*	*	*	*					*				*	*	*		*	*	*	*	*
Hymns of the historical faith	*		*	*	*	*	*	*	*	*		*	*	*	*	*	*	*		*	*	*	*	*	*	*
Psalter in meter								*	*	*		*							*			*	*			*
19th-20th century hymns		*	*	*	*	*		*	*		*	*			*		*	*				*	*	*	*	*
Children's hymns named						*		*	*		*						*					*	*	*	*	*
TUNES (Music)																										
Tune name index, alphabetical	*	*		*	*	*	*	*			*						*	*		*		*	*	*	*	*
Tune name index, metrical	*	*			*	*								*	*					*		*		*	*	*
Composer index	*	*	*	*	*	*	*	*	*	*		*			*	*	*	*		*		*	*	*	*	*
Plainsongs included										*	*	*	*	*	*	*	*				*					
Reformation tunes	*				*					*	*	*						*		*	*	*		*		*
Folk tunes, all cultures					*		*	*			*	*	*	*	*	*	*				*	*		*	*	*
Gospel songs		*	*	*																						
EDITORIAL POLICIES; etc.																										
Preface (or other) statement on Song	*					*	*	*	*	*			*	*	*		*		*	*	*		*	*		?
Specialties of the book	18		19		20		21	22	23	24		25							26	27		28	29		30	
Liturgical section	*	*		*		*		*	*				*	*	*		*							*	*	*
Prayer book section (or sub.)	*			*		*		*	*				*											*		*
Documents of the historical faith					36			37	38											39	40				41	

NOTES. (Note number is followed by the book symbol)

1 K Brief history of Lutheran music, p 306-8.

2 Q Glossary of liturgical terms, p 168-9.

3 V Extensive index of hymns and related Bible text, preliminary pages.

4 W Index of Hymns for the Young, p 913-17.

5 Y Newly composed "Sacraments of common life" and "Prayers", with the college and university student in mind, p 428-41.

6 Z Index of Hymns for use with children, 9-12, p 538.

7 AA List of translated hymns with author and date, p 534-37.

8 AM Notes on hymns and tunes, p 433-82.

9 AC "Prayers and high resolves", "Devotional poetry and prose", recently composed or translated p 307-40.

10 AF Detailed acknowledgements, p 550-58.

11 AG Tri-liturgical text: Protestant, Catholic, Jewish service music; also a general hymnal section.

12 AJ Psalter. (Books T and AM contain many Psalms, but they also contain modern hymns. Book AJ is entirely metrical Psalms).

13 AK)
14 AN) Acknowledgements, pp vi-x; and xv-xxi respectively.

15 AQ Acknowledgements, p 475-77; Notes on hymns, tunes, and readings, p 415-74.

16 AY Contains a small section of post-Reformation German Mennonite hymns, fifty texts and a handful of melodies.

17 AZ Great store of traditional Unitas Fratrum hymnody; assigning the long-used metre numeration from Gregor's Tune book, etc.; economy of space achieved by arranging all hymns and tunes with similar metre together, thus permitting ease in exchange of tune, and avoiding every opportunity to reprint the music.

18 BA Inter-coded with Book AZ; but rather than the brilliant economy of space in that book, BA is lavish in white space on the page and reprinting of melody as desired. Rearrangement of hymns, by liturgical use, required

the deliberate format change.

19 BC Mormon hymns show strong geographical influence; settings arranged for variant voice groups and congregational song.

20 BE Except for the first hymn (Tate & Brady: Be thou, O God, exalted high) the entire series is arranged alphabetically by first line; lavish use of white space on the page.

21 BG Historical notes about text and tune are as useful for church and community song as for literary and musicological studies.

22 BH Since at least 1961 publications, this book is now in two sections: Parts I and III are in the larger volume; Part II, "Musical services", is issued separately with its own index. Earlier printings (from c1932) were in one volume.

23 BI Full service with music, several anthems (i.e. Psalms set to music); and the only Hebrew (untransliterated) texts set to music printed from right-to-left of the page; and the only Greek (untransliterated) texts. Neither of these has been indexed.

24 BJ Literary and historical notes on these hundred hymns--perhaps the most significant contribution to Twentieth Century hymnology that has been made -- are set in exquisite design; musical notation recalls original tunes.

25 BL One hundred hymns, mutually approved by Catholic and Protestant and set in type to the Protestant, rather than the Catholic, tradition. Use requires musical literacy.

26 BS Small paper-back, translations by the Ladies of the Grail, England. One of the Psalms, "Like the deer that yearns", (Ps. 41 in Catholic tradition; Ps. 42 in others) is found also in BL; otherwise these are distinct within the Index.

27 BT Full texts of hymns in German.

28 BV Instead of a numerical and tune name metrical index, this book contains a metrical index with opening melody in score.

29 BW Survey of Mennonite music, p xii-xxxix.

30 BY I Influenced by Anglican hymns and tunes in contents, format, and general tone; in contrast to the Baptist books from the U.S. which contain great quantities of gospel song, this has little.

- - - - - - -

31 L Augsburg Confession; Formula for government; Constitution of the General Synod of the Evangelical Lutheran Church in the U.S.

32 O Augsburg Confession; Athanasian Creed, Luther's Small catechism.

33 S Brief statement of the Reformed Faith.

34 AJ Doctrinal standards; Liturgy; and Church order; also Heidelberg Confession; Canons of Dordrecht; Forms for both ex-communication and re-admission.

35 AM Westminster Confession.

36 BE Six hymns by the Reverend Mary Baker Eddy included.

37 BH Traditional Jewish texts (transliterated), several of which -- as in the Christian tradition -- are frequently heard in secular music (the Kol Nidre, and the Dies Irae) See Note 22 above.

38 BI General Confessions of faith; Advent of Our Lord, etc.

39 BT Texts of some of the very earliest German Lutheran hymns, given in German parallel to their English translations; in full in both languages.

40 BU Oldest Protestant hymnal in use in the U.S.A.; little changed since 1570. No compilation exists for the melodies which are said to be the same plainchant used four hundred years ago in Europe. Several authors have been identified; several are named in the hymn itself; but the bulk of poetry must remain cited as Ausbund, in lieu of known author.

Includes also "Confession, oder bekenntnitz" and the "Defensiones oppositionum"; and "Wahrhaftiger bericht von den Brüdern im Schweitzerland . . . von dem 1635-sten bis in das 1645ste Jahr". This latter is biographical.

41 BZ Revives the use of some Wesley hymns long omitted from books, uses phrase "American folk hymn" for hymns and tunes usually known as "Negro spirituals".

APPENDIX H

MATERIALS EXCLUDED FROM THESE INDEXES

(but included in hymnals analyzed)

Stated institutional liturgy; variants to that liturgy: as, The Magnificat, Te deum, Responses, Psalms.

This is not an index to the liturgies of worship, the interplay between priest and people. This is an index to the united worship in song by the priest and the people. It is, consequently, of more recent date than the Jewish Holy Day service music, than the Mass, and the services derived from the Mass. However, when this material (either texts or tunes) appears in versions used for true congregational song it is included.

Attempts to prove and to cite the original text of word or melody: as, Which version of the "Passion chorale" was the original version?

This is neither an exercise in literary criticism nor in musicological history. This is an index to items as they appear in the printed books listed elsewhere within the Introduction, books which have been officially adopted for institutional use, or which have sprung from institutional life (as the Army and Navy, universities) and which have been used at worship during part of the time from the year 1900 through the year 1965.

This is an index to the particular poetry and song quoted in seventy-six hymnals and in two hymnal companions. Relationships are many; those which it was possible to make within a very formal index have been made. Others must be left to the reader.

References to intermediate editorial history: as, Who recorded the words and songs to folksongs, or who revised the plainsongs? However, when these have become established versions with known authorship, credit is acknowledged.

Full information about versions, revisions, editing to deliberately delete certain words from entire hymnals (as: blood, Trinity, Catholic) requires lengthy verbal discussion. John Julian has done it well, but his work is three-quarters of a century old! No one has published a comparable study of melodies and tune names. Though Robert Guy McCutchan's Hymn tune names (Abingdon, 1957) appeared shortly after this work was begun, it includes only about two thousand names and far less than half as many melodies.

The Hymn Society of America and the British Hymn Society are working on indexes to revise and enlarge Julian's Dictionary. They have mutually agreed that the Americans shall remain within their province, and the British within theirs: with enough for each to do and with duplication avoided. According to the Annual report of the Hymn Society of America for 1965, based on the activities of the Society reviewed at the Forty-third annual meeting, May 1, 1965 at Princeton, Dr. Leonard Ellinwood stated that 187,765 first-line cards from 1,070 hymnals were prepared. This was more than ten years of work, and but one-third of the hymnals intended for analysis were completed. Biographical materials will have to wait for completion of the analytical indexing.

Hymns and tunes is far smaller, of more limited scope -- so far as background data and poetry are concerned. Hymns and tunes is peculiar, and of very different scope -- because of its inclusion of both poetry and melody. Musical information about Key, Time signature, Phraseology, and Note value: as indicated on the printed page.

Because this Index does not intend to serve as a means for reproducing the melody, but simply for identifying it, the above items of information are not essential.

Variant readings of both hymn and tune after the first are not cited separately: as, The several versions of "Holy night" are each identified at first appearance at variant entry and at main entry; thereafter citation is always and only made with the main entry record.

This decision had to be made in the interests of brevity. The fact of a variant rendering is established; it can be found in print if desired; and associated readings are closely enough related by reference symbols so that it is usually possible to use the different versions within a single congregational singing group without difficulty. Extreme variants are here included as separate items. Some of the German chorales, for example, fall into the category of extreme variants.

Original Latin names of the Office Hymns, etc.; and the unquoted names of Latin, German, Greek, Jewish, and other non-English hymns or tunes are not included; except only when they have been included as part of the proper textual material indexed.

As an example, "Adeste fideles" is occasionally quoted in Latin, and has been fully indexed under its Latin first line. Hymns ancient and modern uses the Latin words as titles to hymns derived from the Latin. The hymn is quoted in English; the Latin words are therefore omitted.

Attempts to associate words and music: as, What books quote "The King of love my shepherd is" to the tune "Dominus regit me"?

Such association is completely outside the purview of this Index. Gospel songs, usually known by some portion of the hymn's words, are the only items where an association of this kind may be found -- as a result of the nature of the materials and not the result of intention.

Relative meter of hymn and of tune: as, Which tunes are in Common Meter? and Which hymns can be sung to this tune?

This record is outside the intention of the Index. It may be found in individual hymnal indexes. We leave the compilation to a braver soul!

Descants found in Books F, X, BV, and BY are not identified -- either the hymn utilizing a descant, or the tune and composer.

APPENDIX I

HYMNALS ANALYZED

ARRANGED ACCORDING TO DATE OF ISSUE*

ISSUE DATE		CODE
1570 & 1962	Ausbund; das ist: Etliche shöne Christliche Lieder, wie sie in dem Gesängnis zu Passau in dem Schloss von den Schweizer-Brüdern und von anderen rechtgläubigen Christen hin und her gedichtet worden, melcher religion sie seien, unpartheiisch sehr nützlich. Nebst einem Anhang von sechs Liedern. 13. Aufl. Verlag von den Amischen Gemeinden in Lancaster County, Pa. [Lancaster] 1962. 140 hymns and 6 liedern. Text only.	BU
1876 & 1891	Offices of worship and hymns (with tunes). 3d ed., rev. and enl. [1891] Bound with The Liturgy and the Offices of worship of the American Province of the Unitas Fratrum, or The Moravian Church. Winston Salem [Pref. 1876, 1908; c1908] 1564 hymns with tunes	AZ
1893	The Church hymnal, rev. and enl., in accordance with the action of the General Convention of the Protestant Episcopal Church in the U.S.A. Boston [c1893] 679 hymns with tunes	D
1893	The Magnificat. Hymns with tunes, compiled for the use of the New-Church. 6th ed. New York [c1893] 1901. 566 hymns with tunes	BR
1899	Book of worship with hymns and tunes. General Synod of the Evangelical Lutheran Church in the U.S. Philadelphia [c1899] 607 hymns with tunes	L
1899 & 1920	Hymns: The Yattendon hymnal, ed. by Robert Bridges and H. Ellis Wooldridge. London and Oxford [1899] 1920. 100 hymns with tunes, and ample notes	BJ

* The hymnals, arranged by letter citation symbol, will be found at the beginning of the volume.

1901 The Methodist Protestant hymnal. Board of Publication of the Methodist Protestant Church. Baltimore [c1901]
531 hymns with tunes H

1901 The New Psalms and hymns with supplement, published by authority of the General Assembly of the Presbyterian Church in the U.S. Richmond, Va., 1901.
770 hymns with tunes V

1902 Church and Sunday school hymnal. Comp. and publ. under the direction of the Committee appointed by Mennonite Conferences. J.D. Brunk, musical ed. Scottdale, Pa., [c1902, c1911]
412 hymns and tunes in English; Suppl. #413-532; and 50 German hymns with some tunes AY

1905 The Methodist hymnal, official hymnal of the Methodist Episcopal Church, South, and the Methodist Episcopal Church. Nashville [c1905]
748 hymns with tunes I

1913 The Lutheran hymnary, including the Symbols of the Evangelical Lutheran Church. Minneapolis [c1913, 1935]
618 hymns with tunes O

1914 The New hymn and tune book. 1914. Bound with Services for congregational worship. Boston, American Unitarian Asso., 1914.
546 hymns with tunes BX

1916 The Hymnal, as authorized for use by the General Convention of the Protestant Episcopal Church in the U.S.A. New York [c1916]
561 hymns with tunes B

1918 The Book of praise, authorised by the General Assembly of the Presbyterian Church in Canada. Toronto [1918]
816 hymns with tunes AP

1918 Common service book of the Lutheran Church, authorized by the United Lutheran Church in America. Philadelphia [c1918]
578 hymns with tunes K

1920 Hymnal and Liturgies of the Moravian Church (Unitas Fratrum). Published by authority of the Provincial Synod, Bethlehem, 1920.
952 hymns with tunes BA

1924 The Beacon hymnal for church schools. [Unitarian] Boston [c1924]
250 hymns with tunes BD

1924 Evangelical Lutheran hymn-book. Edition of 1924. St. Louis, 1924
567 hymns with tunes AA

1925 The Hymnal and Order of service, authorized by the Evangelical Lutheran Augustana Synod. Lectionary ed. Rock Island, Ill. [1925]
682 hymns with tunes N

1925 Hymnal, Church of the Brethren, by authority of the General Conference. Elgin, Ill. [c1925]
499 hymns with tunes AS

1925 & 1935 St. Basil's hymnal, 39th ed. Comp. by the Basilian Fathers. Chicago [c1935; imprimature, Toronto 1925]
301 hymns with tunes BO

1926 & 1958 New Baptist hymnal, containing standard and gospel hymns. Philadelphia [c1926, 1958]
407 hymns with tunes AV

1927 The Church hymnary. Rev. ed. Authorized for use in public worship by the Church of Scotland, the United Free Church of Scotland [and the Presbyterian Churches of Ireland, England, Wales, Australia, New Zealand, and Southern Africa] London [pref. 1927]
713 hymns with tunes W

1927 The Presbyterian hymnal, published by authority of the Presbyterian Church in the U.S. Richmond, Va. [c1927]
500 hymns with tunes U

1927 The Psalter hymnal of the United Presbyterian Board of Publication and Bible School work. Pittsburgh [c1927]
458 hymns with tunes T

1928 The American student hymnal, ed. by H. Augustine Smith. New York and London [c1928]
385 hymns with tunes Y

1929 The Book of worship for the Reformed Church in the U. S. Philadelphia, 1929.
660 hymns with tunes AO

1929 The New Christian hymnal, ed. by H.J. Kuiper. Grand Rapids, c1929.
451 hymns with tunes AI

1930 American Lutheran hymnal. Columbus [c1930]
651 hymns with tunes M

1930 The Hymnary. Authorized by the General Council of the United Church of Canada. Toronto [c1930]
691 hymns with tunes AL

1930 The New Hymnal for American youth. Ed. by H. Augustine Smith. New York [c1930]
344 hymns with tunes
AC

1931 & 1958 Songs of praise, enlarged ed. [Words ed.: Percy Dearmer; Music eds.: Ralph Vaughan Williams and Martin Shaw] London [c1931, 1958]
705 hymns with tunes X

1932 The Concordia hymnal. Minneapolis [c1932]
434 hymns with tunes P

1932 & Union hymnal: Songs and prayers for Jewish worship. 3d ed., rev. and enl. [New York, 1932] 1957.
341 hymns with tunes BH

1933 The English hymnal. London, 1933.
656 hymns with tunes; Appendix of 72 tunes E

1933 The Hymnal, published by authority of the General Assembly of the Presbyterian Church in the U.S.A. Philadelphia, 1933.
513 hymns with tunes S

1935 The Methodist hymnal. Nashville [c1935]
564 hymns with tunes G

1936 & 1916 The Hymnal as authorized for use by the General Convention of the Protestant Episcopal Church in the U.S.A. in . . .1916. Boston [c1936]
561 hymns, with tunes which vary from the New York ed. of 1916 C

1937 Christian Science hymnal, with seven hymns written by the Reverend Mary Baker Eddy. Boston, c1937
429 hymns with tunes BE

1937 Hymns of the Spirit, for use in the Free Churches of America. Boston [c1937, 1960]
568 hymns with tunes, and eight additional tunes
AN

1937 The New church hymnal, ed. by H. Augustine Smith [and others] New York [c1937]
492 hymns with tunes AD

1937 The Student hymnary, ed. by Edward Dwight Eaton. New York, 1937.

416 hymns with tunes AB

1939 Christian worship and praise, ed. by Henry Hallam Tweedy under the direction of the Commission for Christian Worship and Praise [of the Reformed Church in America] New York, 1939.
Nos. 167-700 being hymns with tunes. BF

1939 Liturgy and Hymnal, for the use of the General Church of the New Jerusalem. 4th and rev. ed. Bryn Athyn, Pa., 1939.
64 doxologies, etc. with tunes: 117 hymns with tunes. BI

1940 The Broadman hymnal; B. B. McKinney, music ed. Nashville, c1940.
480 hymns with tunes AU

1940 The Church hymnal. Official hymnal of the Seventh-Day Advent Church. Takoma Park, Washington, D. C. [c1940]
703 hymns with tunes BB

1940 Hymnal for Christian worship. [Richmond, Va., c1940]
340 hymns with tunes AG

1940 The Mennonite hymnary. Published by the Board of Publication of the General Conference. Berne, Indiana, and Newton, Kansas [c1940]
623 hymns with tunes AW

1941 Christian worship, a hymnal. [Baptists and Disciples] St. Louis [c1941]
Nos. 94-651 being hymns with tunes Z

1941 The Hymnal, containing complete orders of worship. Authorized by the General Synod of the Evangelical and Reformed Church. St. Louis [c1941]
481 hymns with tunes AK

1941 The Lutheran hymnal, authorized by the Evangelical Lutheran Synodical Conference of North America. St. Louis [c1941]
660 hymns with tunes; and accompanied by the book next below: Q

1942 & 1958 The Handbook to the Lutheran Hymnal. 3d and rev. ed. by W. G. Polack. St. Louis [c1942, c1958]
Accompanies the Lutheran Hymnal, just above, and includes full texts in original script and language of many of the hymns; also biographical and literary notes concerning authors, translators, composers, and arrangers. BT

1942 The Hymnal, Army and Navy, ed. by Ivan L. Bennett, New York, 1942.
625 hymns with tunes for Roman Catholic, Jewish, and and Protestant worship. AH

1943 The Hymnal of the Protestant Episcopal Church in the U.S., 1940. New York [c1943]
600 hymns with tunes A

1947 & 1927 The Psalter [as prepared and published by the United Presbyterian Church]. Grand Rapids [c1927, rev. ed. 1947]
434 hymns with tunes AJ

1947 & 1920 The St. Gregory hymnal and Catholic choir book. Compiled by Nicola A. Montani. Philadelphia, c1920, c1947 [Imprimature, Philadelphia 1920? and Supplement approval 1941]
283 hymns with tunes; also 1947 supplement containing materials chiefly liturgical. Nos. 4 and 251 are the only variants from the 1920 ed. BQ

1948 Hymns of the Church of Jesus Christ of Latter-Day Saints. Salt Lake City [c1948]
387 hymns with tunes BC

1949 Handbook to the Mennonite Hymnary, by Lester Hostetler. Newton, Kansas, 1949.
Accompanies the Mennonite Hymnary (1940, above), and includes both English and German language hymns, some literary and much biographical information related to hymnal contents. BW

1950 Hymns ancient and modern, rev. 1950. London, 1950.
636 hymns with tunes F

1951 The Brethren hymnal, authorized by Annual Conference, Church of the Brethren. Elgin, Ill. [c1951]
614 hymns with tunes AR

1954 The Monastery hymnal. Comp., arr., and ed. by Achille P. Bragers. Boston [c1954; imprimature New York, 1954]
107 hymns with tunes; part English, part Latin texts BP

1955 A Hymnal for Friends. Philadelphia, 1955.
176 hymns with tunes BK

1955 The Hymnbook, published by Presbyterian Church in the U.S., Presbyterian Church in the U.S.A., United Presbyterian Church of North America, Reformed Church in America. New York [c1955]

557 hymns with tunes R

1955 Twenty four Psalms and a Canticle translated from the Hebrew and arranged for singing to the Psalmody of Joseph Gelineau. [Tr. under direction of The Grail, England] Toledo, Ohio [1955; Paris, 1953; imprimature Westminster, 1955]
25 hymns in new translation with tunes BS

1956 Baptist hymnal, ed. by Walter Hines Sims. Nashville [c1956]
513 hymns with tunes AT

1957 The Hymnal [of the Evangelical United Brethren Church]. Dayton, Ohio [c1957]
474 hymns with tunes AE

1958 The New Saint Basil hymnal, comp., arr., and ed. by the Basilian Fathers. Cincinnati, 1958. [imprimature Toronto, 1958]
210 hymns with tunes; approximately two-thirds are English, and one-third Latin BN

1958 The Pilgrim hymnal. [Congregational] Boston [c1958]
584 hymns (bits of service music interspersed) with tunes AF

1959 Christian hymnal [authorized by the General Conference of the Church of God in Christ, Mennonite] Hesston, Kansas, 1959.
657 hymns with tunes AX

1959 Our parish prays and sings [with] organ accompaniment including masses contained in the Parish Kyriale, by Rev. Irvin Udulutsch, OFM. Cap. Collegeville, Minn. [c1959; imprimature St. Cloud, 1959]
97 hymns with tunes BM

1961 Trinity hymnal [of the Orthodox Presbyterian Church]. Philadelphia, 1961.
730 hymns with tunes AM

1962 The Baptist hymn book, with music. London [1962]
777 hymns with tunes BY

1964 Hymnal of Christian unity, ed. by Clifford A. Bennett and Paul Hume. Toledo, Ohio [c1964; imprimature Toledo, 1964]
100 hymns with tunes BL

1964 Hymns for the celebration of life [by the Unitarian Universalist Hymnbook Commission] Boston [c1964]
327 hymns with tunes; and ample notes AQ

1964 & 1928 The Oxford book of carols, ed. by Percy Dearmer, Ralph Vaughan Williams, and Martin Shaw. London [reset 1964 with changes]
197 carols with tunes; and ample notes BG

1964 & 1966* Report of the Hymnal Committee of the Commission on Worship, to the 1964 General Conference of the Methodist Church. [c1964] Forms the Preliminary draft and Final report concerning
539 hymns and 402 tunes proposed for inclusion in the 1966 Methodist hymnal.* BZ

1965 Anglican hymn book. London [1965]
663 hymns with tunes; metrical index in score BV

*1966 The Methodist Hymnal, Official hymnal of The Methodist Church. Nashville [1966]
In press. Information on contents secured from book second above. Information on title secured from publisher.

APPENDIX J

BIBLIOGRAPHY

In addition to the vast amount of information contained within the indexes of the hymnals analyzed, small searches for facts were made in several college and university libraries. Four basic reference books have been constantly by my side. A fifth, released very much too late to be helpful to this work, is marked with an asterisk.

Baker's Biographical dictionary of musicians. 5th ed., rev. by Nicolas Slonimsky. New York, Schirmer [c1958]

Julian, John, ed. A dictionary of hymnology. New York, Dover Publications [2d rev. ed. reprint, 1957] 2 v.

McCutchan, Robert Guy. Hymn tune names, their sources and significance. New York, Abingdon Pr. [1957]

*McDormand, Thomas B., and Frederick S. Crossman. Judson Concordance to hymns. Valley Forge, Judson Pr. [c1965]

Riemenschneider, Albert. 371 Harmonized chorales and 69 Chorale melodies with figured bass by Johann Sebastian Bach; Rev., corr., ed. and annotated. New York, Schirmer, c1941

For definitions quoted exactly or repeated less formally:

The Oxford Universal dictionary on historical principles. 3d ed., rev. with addenda. Oxford, Clarendon Pr. [1955]